BASIC STANDARD DEDUCTION AMOUNTS

Filing Status	Standard Deduction Amount	
	1995	1996
Single	$3,900	$4,000
Married, filing jointly	6,550	6,700
Surviving spouse	6,550	6,700
Head of household	5,750	5,900
Married, filing separately	3,275	3,350

AMOUNT OF EACH ADDITIONAL STANDARD DEDUCTION

Filing Status	1995	1996
Single	$950	$1,000
Married, filing jointly	750	800
Surviving spouse	750	800
Head of household	950	1,000
Married, filing separately	750	800

PERSONAL AND DEPENDENCY EXEMPTION

1995	1996
$2,500	$2,550

INCOME TAX RATES—CORPORATIONS

Taxable Income	Tax Rate
Not over $50,000	15%
Over $50,000 but not over $75,000	25%
Over $75,000 but not over $100,000	34%
Over $100,000 but not over $335,000	39%*
Over $335,000 but not over $10,000,000	34%
Over $10,000,000 but not over $15,000,000	35%
Over $15,000,000 but not over $18,333,333	38%**
Over $18,333,333	35%

*Five percent of this rate represents a phase-out of the benefits of the lower tax rates on the first $75,000 of taxable income.
**Three percent of this rate represents a phase-out of the benefits of the lower tax rate (34% rather than 35%) on the first $10 million of taxable income.

1997 ANNUAL EDITION

WEST'S FEDERAL TAXATION:

COMPREHENSIVE VOLUME

GENERAL EDITORS

Eugene Willis, Ph.D., C.P.A.   **William H. Hoffman, Jr.,** J.D., Ph.D., C.P.A.

David M. Maloney, Ph.D., C.P.A.   **William A. Raabe,** Ph.D., C.P.A.

CONTRIBUTING AUTHORS

James H. Boyd,
Ph.D., C.P.A.
Arizona State University

D. Larry Crumbley,
Ph.D., C.P.A.
Texas A & M University

Steven C. Dilley,
J.D., Ph.D., C.P.A.
Michigan State University

Patrica C. Elliott,
D.B.A., C.P.A.
University of New Mexico

Mary Sue Gately,
Ph.D., C.P.A.
Texas Tech University

William H. Hoffman, Jr.,
J.D., Ph.D., C.P.A.
University of Houston

David M. Maloney,
Ph.D., C.P.A.
University of Virginia

Marilyn Phelan,
J.D., Ph.D., C.P.A.
Texas Tech University

William A. Raabe,
Ph.D., C.P.A.
University of Wisconsin-Milwaukee

Boyd C. Randall,
J.D., Ph.D.
Brigham Young University

W. Eugene Seago,
J.D., Ph.D., C.P.A.
*Virginia Polytechnic Institute
and State University*

James E. Smith,
Ph.D., C.P.A.
College of William and Mary

Eugene Willis,
Ph.D., C.P.A.
University of Illinois at Urbana

West Publishing Company
Minneapolis/St. Paul • New York • Los Angeles • San Francisco

Copyediting:	Patricia A. Lewis
Composition:	Carlisle Communications, Ltd.
Text Design:	LightSource Images
Cover Design:	David J. Farr, *ImageSmythe*
Index:	Catalyst Communication Arts

A Note On Type: Type fonts used are Palatino for text, Serif Gothic Bold for part and chapter openers display, and Helvetica Light and Black accent type.

WEST'S COMMITMENT TO THE ENVIRONMENT

In 1906, West Publishing Company began recycling materials left over from the production of books. This began a tradition of efficient and responsible use of resources. Today, 100% of our legal bound volumes are printed on acid-free, recycled paper consisting of 50% new paper pulp and 50% paper that has undergone a de-inking process. We also use vegetable-based inks to print all of our books. West recycles nearly 22,650,000 pounds of scrap paper annually—the equivalent of 187,500 trees. Since the 1960s, West has devised ways to capture and recycle waste inks, solvents, oils, and vapors created in the printing process. We also recycle plastics of all kinds, wood, glass, corrugated cardboard, and batteries, and have eliminated the use of polystyrene book packaging. We at West are proud of the longevity and the scope of our commitment to our environment.

West pocket parts and advance sheets are printed on recyclable paper and can be collected and recycled with newspapers. Staples do not have to be removed. Bound volumes can be recycled after removing the covers.

Production, Prepress, Printing and Binding by West Publishing Company.

 TEXT IS PRINTED ON 10% POST CONSUMER RECYCLED PAPER   Printed with Printwise   ∞
Environmentally Advanced Water Washable Ink

MacInTax® and *TurboTax®* are registered trademarks of Intuit,® Inc.

By **West Publishing Company**
  610 Opperman Drive
  P.O. Box 64526
  St. Paul, MN 55164–0526

All rights reserved
Printed in the United States of America
03 02 01 00 99 98 97 96   8 7 6 5 4 3 2 1 0

Library of Congress Cataloging-in-Publication Data

Main entry under title:
  West's Federal Taxation.
  Includes index.
  1. Income tax—United States—Law
I. Hoffman, William H.   III.   Willis, Eugene

ISBN 0–314–08818–0, 0–314–09710–4
KF6335.H63   343'.73'04   77–54355

ISSN 0270–5265
1997 ANNUAL EDITION

PREFACE

The publication of the 1997 Edition marks the twentieth year of West's Federal Taxation (WFT). From a single text on Corporations, Partnerships, Estates and Trusts with accompanying solutions manual, the WFT series has grown to three major texts and a package of 54 ancillaries. During this period, WFT has made every effort to improve the quality of the materials and has consistently added attractive innovations. With sales surpassing the one million level, WFT looks forward to continued success in the future.

West's Federal Taxation: Comprehensive Volume is an abridged version of *West's Federal Taxation: Individual Income Taxes* and *West's Federal Taxation: Corporations, Partnerships, Estates, and Trusts*. In condensing all of this material to a manageable form, it was necessary to utilize our editorial license to pick and choose. Thus, a great deal of useful, but not essential, information had to be pruned in order to arrive at the final product. What to cover or not to cover in any abridgment process is, understandably, a judgment call. We can only hope that we acted correctly in making our decisions.

The *Comprehensive Volume* is designed to provide flexibility for those who offer only one course in Federal taxation or for a two-course sequence. In cases where the *Comprehensive Volume* is used for only one course, a broad scope of coverage could be the ultimate objective. Although the income taxation of individuals may be stressed, it is conceivable that some may wish to devote significant classroom time to other areas of Federal taxation. For example, the allocation of course coverage might be structured as follows: 60 percent to the individual income tax (Chapters 1–15) and 40 percent to the tax treatment of corporations, partnerships, etc. (Chapters 16–28).

For those who encounter time constraints and/or want to emphasize some areas and not others, the last segment of the text (Chapters 16–28) possesses potential for selectivity. For example, an instructor who wants to cover corporations (Chapters 16–21) and tax practice (Chapter 25), but not the other subjects (Chapters 22–24 and 26–28), can proceed accordingly without disrupting the flow of the material. In this regard, the last segment of the text offers the flexibility for partial coverage through a number of different combinations (e.g., for a "light" coverage of corporations, select Chapters 16 through 18, but for a "heavy" concentration, assign Chapters 16–21).

WEST'S FEDERAL TAXATION ON CD-ROM

West is pleased to offer this text on CD-ROM. It includes the entire text of the printed version of West's Federal Taxation: Comprehensive Volume, 1997 Edition as well as the full text of all referenced cases, code sections, regulations, revenue procedures, revenue rulings, and all tax forms, tables and schedules from the

Appendixes. Students can jump directly from the text they're reading to the full text of any of the references included on the disc.

Other features include "notebook" capabilities which allow students to cut and paste from the text, type in their own comments, and convert the text and notes into other word processing packages. Records are kept of all queries which allows viewing and editing of past queries. Each disc has an electronic "bookmark" feature which marks the spot where the student left off and returns to the last page that was viewed when the project is resumed. WFT on CD-ROM is fully supported by West's CD-ROM Customer Service Technicians and Research Attorneys. Professors and students can call for any technical or research assistance their projects require.

System requirements include an IBM or compatible PC with a 286, 386, or Pentium processer; DOS version 3.3 or higher; 400K of available conventional RAM (after loading all memory-resident software including device drivers and the Microsoft CD-ROM extensions (MSCDEX); MB of available hard disc space; a locally attached CD-ROM drive using Microsoft CD-ROM Extensions (MSCDEX) version 2.1 or higher (compatible CD-ROM drives must meet the ISO 9660 standard). To print images off the CD, 1.5MG RAM on your printer is required.

SPECIAL FEATURES

A variety of pedagogical devices is used to assist the student in the learning process. Each chapter begins with a statement of the learning objectives for the chapter. The learning objectives are followed by a topical outline of the material in the chapter. Page references appear in the outline to provide easy access to each topic. The readability of the material in the text is enhanced by the following.

- Including three levels of headings that aid in organization and presentation.
- Using bold print in the text to identify key terms the first time each term is used.
- Italicizing key words to emphasize their importance.
- Avoiding legal terminology except where it is beneficial.
- Using Concept Summaries to synthesize important concepts in chart or tabular form.
- Using Exhibits, Figures, and Tables to enhance presentations.
- Organizing material in lists with bullets rather than presenting it in lengthy sentences.
- Using examples frequently to help the student understand the tax concept being discussed.

If the *Comprehensive Volume* is to be used in whole (or in part) for a one-course tax offering, the pace of coverage of the subject matter may have to be accelerated. In recognition of this fact, we have followed certain guidelines.

- In an accelerated setting, a decided constraint is placed on the amount of problem solving that can be expected from the reader. We have, therefore, limited the quantity of the problem materials. In this connection, we have strived to maintain the integrity of the quality of the materials.
- For those users who feel the need for some material on research methodology, the last chapter in the text, "Working with the Tax Law," is available. Along with the usual problem materials, this chapter also includes numerous research problems, arranged by chapter, dealing with the subject matter treated in the text. Instructors who emphasize research can assign Chapter 28 early in the course and then select from these problems as other chapters

are covered. The Research Problems section heading now includes a CD-ROM icon to emphasize that solutions to all the research problems can now be prepared using West's Federal Taxation on CD-ROM. WFT on CD-ROM includes false leads as well as the necessary cases, Revenue Rulings, and Revenue Procedures as a way of providing a realistic environment for the tax research process.

- Once knowledge of the tax law has been acquired, it needs to be used. The tax minimization process normally requires careful planning. Because we recognize the importance of planning procedures, most chapters include a separate section (called *Tax Planning Considerations*) illustrating the applications of such procedures to specific areas.
- The appendixes to the text contain a great deal of useful material. In addition to the usual Subject Index, the following items are included: Tax Rates and Tables (Appendix A); Tax Forms (Appendix B); Glossary of Tax Terms (Appendix C); Table of Code Sections Cited (Appendix D); and Comprehensive Tax Return Problems for 1995 (Appendix E).

ENHANCED PEDAGOGICAL PLAN

In the 1997 edition, we have continued to enhance the pedagogy to assist the student in the learning process and to address the recommendations of the Accounting Education Change Commission (AECC).

- *Learning Objectives.* Each chapter begins with student learning objectives for the chapter. These behavioral objectives provide the students with guidance in learning the key concepts and principles.
- *Chapter Outline.* The learning objectives are followed by a topical outline of the material in the chapter. Page references appear in the outline to provide the student with ready access to each topic.
- *Chapter Introductions.* The introductions link the material in the current chapter to previous chapters and demonstrate its relevance. Frequently, the chapter introduction includes a "real world" illustration to help convey the relevance of the material.
- *Margin Notes.* Each of the learning objectives appears in the margin where the related material is introduced and helps to guide the student through the chapter.
- *Tax in the News.* Tax in the News items appear in each chapter as a boxed feature to enliven the text discussion. These items are drawn from today's business and popular press and present current issues that are relevant to the chapter material.
- *Ethical Considerations.* Ethical Considerations features appear in each chapter presenting thought-provoking issues related to the chapter topics. In response to the recommendations of the AECC, they also demonstrate that many issues do not have a single correct answer. The questions raised in the Ethical Considerations were selected to provoke discussion and provide opportunities for debate (oral communication) based on the student's value system rather than to provide a defensible answer. To assist the professor in providing guidance for discussion, material is included in *the Instructor's Guide with Lecture Notes* on each Ethical Consideration. This material identifies the issues raised in the Ethical Consideration, and where appropriate, recommends a solution or alternate solutions.
- *Key Terms.* Before the Problem Materials in each chapter is a list of key terms to assist student learning. When the key term is introduced in the chapter, it appears in bold print. The list of key terms includes page references to the

chapter coverage. In addition, each key term is defined in the Glossary (Appendix C).

- *Communication Assignments.* In recognition of the increasing emphasis in accounting and tax education on communication, identified items in the Problem Materials now include a written communication component. Selected Problems, Cumulative Problems, and Research Problems are identified as communication assignments with a "scroll" icon. These problems ask the student to prepare a tax client letter, a memorandum for the tax files, or other written materials. The discussion of the tax research process in Chapter 28 includes an illustration of a client letter and memo.

- *Problem Recognition Questions.* For the 1997 Edition, we have added a new category called Problem Recognition Questions. These problems are unstructured and open-ended. There is not enough information given in the problem to enable the student to develop a definitive answer. However, students are given enough information to identify the important tax questions. These problems are designed to help students develop their critical thinking skills.

- *Decision-Making Problems.* The Problem Materials include decision-making problems that are designed to enhance the student's analytical skills. These problems are identified with a "balance" icon.
- *Team Projects: Arthur Andersen Tax Challenge Cases.* For the 1997 Edition, we have indicated at the end of each chapter which parts of selected Tax Challenge cases are related to material covered in the chapter. This will enable students to work on the cases throughout the semester rather than waiting until the end of the semester to prepare solutions. The instructor can choose between two cases that can be ordered from your West representative and provided to students at no cost.

SUPPLEMENTS

The Arthur Andersen Tax Challenge Cases, a set of four capstone cases and their solutions, are provided to the instructor for classroom use. These cases encompass both tax compliance and tax planning, and provide an opportunity for a team approach in solving tax issues and recommending tax strategies. Other products in our 1997 instructional package include the following.

- The *Instructor's Guide with Lecture Notes* contains chapter outlines that can be used as lecture notes, as well as teaching aids and information not contained in the text. It also includes solutions to the research problems (Chapter 28 in the text) and the comprehensive tax return problems (Appendix E in the text). For the 1997 edition, we have included additional synopses of many interesting and unusual court cases that can be used to illustrate technical points in the tax law. The lecture notes are also available on disk in ASCII files.
- A *Solutions Manual* that has been carefully checked to ensure accuracy. A matrix is included indicating topic coverage for each problem, which problems are new, modified, or unchanged in the new edition and the problem number for the unchanged and modified problems in the prior edition. The solutions are referenced to pages in the text. The *Solutions Manual* is also available on disk in ACSII files.
- A *Test Bank* with a comprehensive set of examination questions and solutions. The answers to these are referenced to pages in the text. The questions are arranged in accordance with the sequence of the material in the chapter. To assist the professor in selecting questions for an examination, all questions are labeled by topical coverage in a matrix that also indicates

which questions are new, modified, or unchanged in the new edition and the question number for the unchanged and modified questions in the prior edition. Approximately 20 percent of the questions in the 1997 edition are new or modified.

- *WesTest 3.1*, a microcomputer test generation program for IBM PCs and compatibles and the Macintosh family of computers.
- *West's CD-ROM Federal Tax Library* provides a complete tax research library on a desktop. The *Federal Tax Library* is a set of compact disks with a software package that reads the disks through a PC. Each disk has a remarkable storage capacity—roughly 1,000 times more than a single-sided floppy disk. A brief list of the library contents includes the complete Internal Revenue Code and Regulations, Federal Court cases on tax, Tax Court cases, Revenue Rulings, and Revenue Procedures. The CD-ROM library is available to qualified adopters.
- Limited free use to qualified adopters of WESTLAW, a computer-assisted tax and legal research service that provides access to hundreds of valuable information sources.
- A *Student Study Guide* prepared by David M. Maloney, University of Virginia, and William A. Raabe, University of Wisconsin (Milwaukee). This *Study Guide* includes a chapter review of key concepts and self-evaluation test questions with solutions that are referenced to the text.
- *Solution's Transparency Masters* for selected complex and cumulative problems, with a larger typeface for greater readability.
- *Instructor's Resource Notebook*—this three-ring binder can be used to house all or portions of the supplements and text. The 1997 edition is offered in looseleaf form so the instructor can reorganize the book and incorporate supplemental materials to fit course lectures.
- *PowerPoint Presentation Software* allows qualified adopters to create interactive lectures and manipulate graphs, charts, and figures during in-class lectures. The package contains numerous slides per chapter consisting of alternate figures, outlines, and key points.
- *Teaching Transparency Masters* include most screens from the PowerPoint package reproduced as transparency masters for instructors who may wish to use traditional transparencies.
- *Teaching Transparency Acetates* contain the key charts and tables from the *Teaching Transparency Masters* package.
- A *Student Note-Taking Guide* includes selected screens from the PowerPoint package consisting of chapter outlines and key points. This unique guide provides students with the core chapter information, so they can concentrate in class on learning key concepts instead of copying basic lecture outlines and transparencies. They have been printed and bound in a manner similar to accounting working papers. The pages include all the information from the PowerPoint screens while still leaving room for student notes.
- *WFT Individual Practice Sets* and *WFT Corporation, S Corporation, and Partnership Practice Sets* 1996–97 edition, prepared by John B. Barrack, University of Georgia. They are designed to cover most of the common forms that would be used by a tax practitioner for the average client.
- *West's Internal Revenue Code of 1986 and Treasury Regulations: Annotated and Selected: 1997 Edition* by James E. Smith, College of William and Mary. This provides the opportunity for the student to be exposed to the Code and the Regulations in a single-volume book, that also contains useful annotations.
- WFT On-line, available through the West Educational Publishing home page on the Internet (http://www.westpub.com/Educate/) puts the most current

information in your hands as soon as it is available. Qualified adopters can log on and immediately gain access to the most recent taxation information available, including newsworthy tax developments designed for classroom use, extra problem material and quizzes, topical news items, the latest news in West supplements and publication dates, and more.

- *West's Federal Taxation Video Library* includes selected videos from the Arthur Andersen series as well as other topical videos for classroom use by qualified adopters.

TAX PREPARATION-SOFTWARE

The trend toward increased use of the computer as an essential tool in tax practice has accelerated. To ensure that the West's Federal Taxation instructional package continues to set the pace in this important area, the following products are available to be used with the 1997 edition:

- *TurboTax* © Personal/1040 Version 95.01 by Intuit is a commercial tax preparation package. It enables students to prepare over 80 forms, schedules, and worksheets and automatically performs all mathematical calculations and data transfers. *TurboTax* also assists students with tax planning and helps them prepare "anticipated" tax returns. The *TurboTax* package, available for student purchase includes disks bound with a workbook containing exercises and problems. Both DOS and Windows versions of *TurboTax* are available. Also available is *MacInTax*, the best-selling tax preparation software for the Macintosh.
- *Corporation and Partnership Tax Return Preparation with TurboTax* Pro Series 1120/1120S/1065 is a commercial tax preparation package that includes disks bound with a workbook containing exercises and problems. The manual is prepared by Debra L. Sanders, Washington State University and Intuit.

These software products are powerful, easy to learn, and easy to use. We believe that tax education can be raised to a higher level through the use of computers and well-designed software. These software packages take the drudgery out of performing the complex computations involved in solving difficult tax problems. This allows students to concentrate on applying concepts and interpreting results.

To enable students to take advantage of these software products, the text contains numerous tax return problems. Problems that lend themselves to computerized solutions are identified by a computer symbol to the left of the problem number.

TAX FORMS COVERAGE

Although it is not our purpose to approach the presentation and discussion of taxation from the standpoint of preparation of tax returns, some orientation to forms is necessary. Because 1996 forms will not be available until later in the year, most tax return problems in this edition are written for tax year 1995. The 1995 problems may be solved manually, or many may be solved using the tax return preparation software (*MacInTax* or *TurboTax*) that may be purchased by students who use this text.

Appendix E contains comprehensive tax return problems written for tax year 1995. Each of these problems lends itself for use as a term project because of the sophistication required for satisfactory completion. Solutions to the problems in Appendix E are contained in the *Instructor's Guide with Lecture Notes*.

For the reader's convenience, Appendix B contains a full reproduction of many of the 1995 tax forms frequently encountered in actual practice. Most tax textbooks are published in the spring, long before tax forms for the year of publication are available from the government. We believe that students should be exposed to the most current tax forms. As a result, we write several new forms problems and provide adopters with reproducible copies of these problems, along with blank tax forms and solutions on the new forms. Shortly after the beginning of 1997, adopters will receive a *Forms Problems Supplement* containing these tax return problems, updated and solved on 1996 forms.

TAX LAW UPDATES

Since the original edition was issued in 1983, we have followed a policy of annually revising the text material to reflect statutory, judicial, and administrative changes in the Federal tax law and to correct any errors or other shortcomings.

We expect tax legislation to be enacted in 1996. In the event of *significant* tax law changes, we will provide a timely, complete, and easy-to-use supplement.

ACKNOWLEDGMENTS

As is the case with any literary undertaking, we welcome user comments. Please rest assured that any such comments will not be taken lightly and, we hope, will lead to improvements in later editions of *West's Federal Taxation: Comprehensive Volume*.

We are most appreciative of the many suggestions that we have received for revising the text, many of which have been incorporated in past editions and in the 1997 edition. We would also like to thank those people who have painstakingly worked through all the problems and test questions and generally acted as problem checkers to ensure the accuracy of the book and ancillary package. They are Tracey A. Anderson, Indiana University at South Bend; Caroline K. Craig, Illinois State University; Frank Linton, Illinois State University; Mark B. Persellin, St. Mary's University; Debra L. Sanders, Washington State University; Randall K. Serrett, Fort Lewis College; Thomas Sternburg, University of Illinois; Donald Trippeer, Lehigh University, and Raymond F. Wacker, Southern Illinois University at Carbondale.

Finally, this 1997 Edition would not have been possible without the technical assistance of and the manuscript review by Bonnie Hoffman, CPA, and Freda Mulhall, CPA. We are indebted to them for their efforts.

Eugene Willis
William H. Hoffman, Jr.
David M. Maloney
William A. Raabe

April 1, 1996

ABOUT THE EDITORS

Eugene Willis is the Arthur Andersen Alumni Professor of Accountancy at the University of Illinois (Urbana-Champaign). He joined the Illinois faculty in 1975 after receiving his Ph.D. from the University of Cincinnati. He served as Acting Head of the department in 1993 and 1994 and is currently Associate Head and Director of Masters Programs. He has published articles in leading academic and professional journals, including the *Accounting Review*, *Journal of the American Taxation Association*, *The Journal of Accountancy*, and *The Journal of Taxation*. Professor Willis is co-director of the National Tax Education Program, a continuing education program co-sponsored by the American Institute of CPAs and the University of Illinois.

William H. Hoffman, Jr., earned B.A. and J.D. degrees from the University of Michigan and M.B.A. and Ph.D. degrees from The University of Texas. He is a licensed CPA and attorney in Texas. His teaching experience includes: The University of Texas (1957–1961), Louisiana State University (1961–1967), and the University of Houston (1967 to present). Professor Hoffman has addressed many tax institutes and conferences and has published extensively in professional journals. His articles appear in *The Journal of Taxation*, *The Tax Adviser*, *Taxes—The Tax Magazine*, *The Journal of Accountancy*, *The Accounting Review*, and *Taxation for Accountants*.

David M. Maloney, Ph.D., CPA, having completed his graduate work at the University of Illinois at Urbana-Champaign, currently teaches courses in Federal taxation in the graduate and undergraduate programs at the University of Virginia's McIntire School of Commerce. Since joining the Virginia faculty in January 1984, David has been a recipient of major research grants from the Ernst & Young and Peat Marwick Foundations. In addition he has his work published in numerous scholarly and professional journals, including *The Tax Adviser*, *Tax Notes*, *The Journal of Corporate Taxation*, *Accounting Horizons*, and *The Journal of Accountancy*. David is a member of several professional organizations, including the AICPA, the American Accounting Association, and the American Taxation Association.

William A. Raabe is the Wisconsin Distinguished Professor of Taxation in the School of Business Administration of the University of Wisconsin-Milwaukee. A graduate of Carroll College and the University of Illinois, Dr. Raabe's teaching and research interests include international and multistate taxation, technology in tax education, personal financial planning, and the economic impact of sports teams and fine arts groups. Dr. Raabe also is the author of West's Federal Tax Research and the Multistate Corporate Tax Guide. He coordinates the West's Federal Taxation material on West Publishing's Internet page, and he has written estate planning software used widely by tax professionals. Dr. Raabe has been a visiting tax faculty member for a number of public accounting firms, bar associations, and CPA societies. He has received numerous teaching awards, including the Accounting Educator of the Year from the Wisconsin Institute of CPAs.

CONTENTS IN BRIEF

CONTENTS

APPENDIXES

CHAPTER

1

AN INTRODUCTION TO TAXATION AND UNDERSTANDING THE FEDERAL TAX LAW

LEARNING OBJECTIVES

After completing Chapter 1, you should be able to:

1. Understand some of the history, including trends, of the Federal income tax.

2. Know some of the criteria for selecting a tax structure and understand the components of a tax structure.

3. Identify the different taxes imposed in the United States at the Federal, state, and local levels.

4. Understand the administration of the tax law including the audit process utilized by the IRS.

5. Appreciate some of the ethical guidelines involved in tax practice.

6. Recognize the economic, social, equity, and political considerations that justify various aspects of the tax law.

7. Describe the role played by the IRS and the courts in the evolution of the Federal tax system.

The primary objective of this chapter is to provide an overview of the Federal tax system. Among the topics discussed are the following:

- A brief history of the Federal income tax.
- The different types of taxes imposed at the Federal, state, and local levels.
- Some highlights of tax law administration.
- Tax concepts that help explain the reasons for various tax provisions.
- The influence that the Internal Revenue Service (IRS) and the courts have had in the evolution of current tax law.

Why does a text devoted primarily to the Federal individual income tax discuss state and local taxes? A simple illustration shows the importance of non-Federal taxes.

EXAMPLE 1

Rick is employed by Flamingo Corporation in San Antonio, Texas, at a salary of $54,000. Rick's employer offers him a chance to transfer to its New York City office at a salary of $60,000. Neither Texas nor San Antonio imposes an income tax, but New York State and New York City do. A quick computation indicates that the additional income taxes (Federal, state, and local) involved approximately $4,000. ▼

Although Rick must consider many nontax factors before he decides on a job change, he should also evaluate the tax climate. How do state and local taxes compare? In this case, what appears to be a $6,000 pay increase is only $2,000 when the additional income taxes of $4,000 are taken into account.

HISTORY OF U.S. TAXATION

EARLY PERIODS

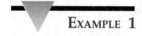

1 LEARNING OBJECTIVE
Understand some of the history, including trends, of the Federal income tax.

The first American income tax was enacted in 1634 by the English colonists in the Massachusetts Bay Colony, but the Federal government did not adopt this form of taxation until 1861. In fact, both the Federal Union and the Confederate States of America used the income tax to raise funds to finance the Civil War. Although modest in its reach and characterized by broad exemptions and low rates, the income tax generated $376 million of revenue for the Federal government during the Civil War.

When the Civil War ended, the need for additional revenue disappeared, and the income tax was repealed. As was true before the war, the Federal government was able to finance its operations almost exclusively from customs duties (tariffs). It is interesting to note that the courts held that the Civil War income tax was not contrary to the Constitution.

When a new Federal income tax on individuals was enacted in 1894, its opponents were prepared to and did again challenge its constitutionality. The U.S. Constitution provided that " . . . No Capitation, or other direct, Tax shall be laid, unless in Proportion to the Census or Enumeration herein before directed to be taken." In *Pollock v. Farmers' Loan and Trust Co.*,[1] the U.S. Supreme Court found that the income tax was a direct tax that was unconstitutional because it was not apportioned among the states in proportion to their populations.

A Federal corporate income tax, enacted by Congress in 1909, fared better in the judicial system. The U.S. Supreme Court found this tax to be constitutional because it was treated as an excise tax.[2] In essence, it was a tax on the right to do business in the corporate form. As such, it was likened to a form of the franchise tax.[3] The corporate form of doing business had been developed in the late nineteenth century and was an unfamiliar concept to the framers of the U.S. Constitution. Since a corporation is an entity created under law, jurisdictions possess the right to tax its creation and operation. Using this rationale, many states still impose franchise taxes on corporations.

The ratification of the Sixteenth Amendment to the U.S. Constitution in 1913 sanctioned both the Federal individual and corporate income taxes and, as a consequence, neutralized the continuing effect of the *Pollock* decision.

REVENUE ACTS

Following ratification of the Sixteenth Amendment, Congress enacted the Revenue Act of 1913. Under this Act, the first Form 1040 was due on March 1, 1914. The law allowed various deductions and personal exemptions of $3,000 for a single individual and $4,000 for married taxpayers. Rates ranged from a low of 2 percent to a high of 6 percent. The 6 percent rate applied only to taxable income in excess of $500,000![4]

Various revenue acts were passed between 1913 and 1939. In 1939, all of these revenue laws were codified into the Internal Revenue Code of 1939. In 1954, a similar codification of the revenue law took place. The current law is entitled the Internal Revenue Code of 1986, which largely carries over the provisions of the 1954 Code. To date, the Code has been amended several times since 1986. This matter is discussed further in Chapter 28 under Origin of the Internal Revenue Code.

HISTORICAL TRENDS

The income tax has proved to be a major source of revenue for the Federal government. Figure 1–1, which contains a breakdown of the major revenue

---

[1] 3 AFTR 2602, 15 S.Ct. 912 (USSC, 1895). See Chapter 28 for an explanation of the citations of judicial decisions.
[2] *Flint v. Stone Tracy Co.*, 3 AFTR 2834, 31 S.Ct. 342 (USSC, 1911).

[3] See the discussion of state franchise taxes later in the chapter.
[4] This should be contrasted with the highest current tax rate of 39.6%, which applies once taxable income exceeds $263,750.

▼ **FIGURE 1–1**
Federal Budget Receipts—1996

Individual income taxes	39%
Corporation income taxes	10
Social insurance taxes and contributions	32
Excise taxes	3
Borrowing	12
Other	4
	100%

sources,[5] demonstrates the importance of the income tax. *Estimated* income tax collections from individuals and corporations amount to 49 percent of the total receipts.

The need for revenues to finance the war effort during World War II converted the income tax into a *mass tax*. For example, in 1939, less than 6 percent of the U.S. population was subject to the Federal income tax. In 1945, over 74 percent of the population was subject to the Federal income tax.[6]

Certain changes in the income tax law are of particular significance in understanding the Federal income tax. In 1943, Congress passed the Current Tax Payment Act, which provided for the first pay-as-you-go tax system. A pay-as-you-go income tax system requires employers to withhold for taxes a specified portion of an employee's wages. Persons with income from other than wages must make periodic (e.g., quarterly) payments to the taxing authority (the Internal Revenue Service) for estimated taxes due for the year.

One trend that has caused considerable concern has been the increased complexity of the Federal income tax laws. Often, under the name of tax reform, Congress has added to this complexity by frequently changing the tax laws. Increasingly, this has forced many taxpayers to seek the assistance of tax professionals. At this time, therefore, substantial support exists for tax law simplification.

CRITERIA USED IN THE SELECTION OF A TAX STRUCTURE

2　LEARNING OBJECTIVE
Know some of the criteria for selecting a tax structure and understand the components of a tax structure.

In the eighteenth century, Adam Smith identified the following *canons of taxation*, which are still considered when evaluating a particular tax structure:[7]

- *Equality.* Each taxpayer enjoys fair or equitable treatment by paying taxes in proportion to his or her income level. Ability to pay a tax is the measure of how equitably a tax is distributed among taxpayers.

---

[5] Budget of the United States Government for Fiscal Year 1996, Office of Management and Budget (Washington, D.C.: U.S. Government Printing Office, 1995).

[6] Richard Goode, *The Individual Income Tax* (Washington, D.C.: The Brookings Institution, 1964), pp. 2–4.

[7] *The Wealth of Nations*, Book V, Chapter II, Part II (New York: Dutton, 1910).

- *Convenience.* Administrative simplicity has long been valued in formulating tax policy. If a tax is easily assessed and collected and its administrative costs are low, it should be favored. An advantage of the withholding (pay-as-you-go) system is its convenience for taxpayers.
- *Certainty.* A tax structure is *good* if the taxpayer can readily predict when, where, and how a tax will be levied. Individuals and businesses need to know the likely tax consequences of a particular type of transaction.
- *Economy.* A *good* tax system involves only nominal collection costs by the government and minimal compliance costs on the part of the taxpayer. Although the government's cost of collecting Federal taxes amounts to less than one-half of 1 percent of the revenue collected, the complexity of our current tax structure imposes substantial taxpayer compliance costs.

By these canons, the Federal income tax is a contentious product. *Equality* is present as long as one accepts ability to pay as an ingredient of this component. *Convenience* exists due to a heavy reliance on pay-as-you-go procedures. *Certainty* probably generates the greatest controversy. In one sense, certainty is present since a mass of administrative and judicial guidelines exists to aid in interpreting the tax law. In another sense, however, certainty does not exist since many questions remain unanswered and frequent changes in the tax law by Congress lessen stability. *Economy* is present if only the collection procedure of the IRS is considered. Economy is not present, however, if one focuses instead on taxpayer compliance efforts and costs.

THE TAX STRUCTURE

TAX BASE

A tax base is the amount to which the tax rate is applied. In the case of the Federal income tax, the tax base is *taxable income.* As noted later in the chapter (Figure 1–2), taxable income is gross income reduced by certain deductions (both business and personal).

TAX RATES

Tax rates are applied to the tax base to determine a taxpayer's liability. The tax rates may be proportional or progressive. A tax is *proportional* if the rate of tax remains constant for any given income level.

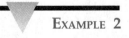
EXAMPLE 2

Bill has $10,000 of taxable income and pays a tax of $3,000, or 30%. Bob's taxable income is $50,000, and the tax on this amount is $15,000, or 30%. If this constant rate is applied throughout the rate structure, the tax is proportional. ▼

A tax is *progressive* if a higher rate of tax applies as the tax base increases. The Federal income tax, Federal gift and estate taxes, and most state income tax rate structures are progressive.

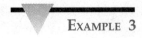
EXAMPLE 3

If Cora, a married individual filing jointly, has taxable income of $10,000, her tax for 1996 is $1,500 for an average tax rate of 15%. If, however, Cora's taxable income is $50,000, her tax will be $8,787 for an average tax rate of 17.57%. The tax is progressive since higher rates are applied to greater amounts of taxable income. ▼

INCIDENCE OF TAXATION

The degree to which various segments of society share the total tax burden is difficult to assess. Assumptions must be made concerning who absorbs the burden for paying the tax. For example, since dividend payments to shareholders are not deductible by a corporation and are generally taxable to shareholders, the same income is subject to a form of double taxation. Concern over double taxation is valid to the extent that corporations are *not* able to shift the corporate tax to the consumer through higher commodity prices. Many research studies have shown a high degree of shifting of the corporate income tax. When the corporate tax can be shifted, it becomes merely a consumption tax that is borne by the ultimate purchasers of goods.

The progressiveness of the U.S. Federal income tax rate structure for individuals has varied over the years. As late as 1986, for example, there were 15 rates, ranging from 0 to 50 percent. These later were reduced to two rates of 15 and 28 percent. Currently, there are five rates, ranging from 15 to 39.6 percent.

MAJOR TYPES OF TAXES

PROPERTY TAXES

3 **LEARNING OBJECTIVE**
Identify the different taxes imposed in the United States at the Federal, state, and local levels.

Normally referred to as **ad valorem taxes** because they are based on value, property taxes are a tax on wealth, or capital. In this regard, they have much in common with death taxes and gift taxes discussed later in the chapter. Although property taxes do not tax income, the income actually derived (or the potential for any income) may be relevant insofar as it affects the value of the property being taxed.

Property taxes fall into *two* categories: those imposed on realty and those imposed on personalty. Both have added importance since they usually generate a deduction for Federal income tax purposes (see Chapter 9).

Ad Valorem Taxes on Realty.   Property taxes on realty are exclusively within the province of the states and their local political subdivisions (e.g., cities, counties, school districts). They represent a major source of revenue for *local* governments, but their importance at the *state* level has waned over the past few years. Some states, for example, have imposed freezes on the upper revaluations of residential housing.

How realty is defined can have an important bearing on which assets are subject to tax. This is especially true in jurisdictions that do not impose ad valorem taxes on personalty. Primarily a question of state property law, **realty** generally includes real estate and any capital improvements that are classified as fixtures. Simply stated, a *fixture* is something so permanently attached to the real estate that its removal will cause irreparable damage. A built-in bookcase might well be a fixture, whereas a movable bookcase would not be a fixture. Certain items such as electrical wiring and plumbing cease to be personalty when installed in a building and become realty.

The following are some of the characteristics of ad valorem taxes on realty:

- Property owned by the Federal government is exempt from tax. Similar immunity usually is extended to property owned by state and local governments and by certain charitable organizations.
- Some states provide for lower valuations on property dedicated to agricultural use or other special uses (e.g., wildlife sanctuaries).

- Some states partially exempt the homestead portion of property from taxation. Modern homestead laws normally protect some or all of a personal residence (including a farm or ranch) from the actions of creditors pursuing claims against the owner.
- Lower taxes may apply to a residence owned by an elderly taxpayer (e.g., age 65 and older).
- When non-income-producing property (e.g., a personal residence) is converted to income-producing property (e.g., a rental house), typically the appraised value increases.
- Some jurisdictions extend immunity from tax for a specified period of time (a *tax holiday*) to new or relocated businesses.

ETHICAL
CONSIDERATIONS

Tax-Exempt Status Forever?

The Orr family lives in a residence that they have owned for several years. They purchased the residence from St. John's Methodist Church, which had used the house as a parsonage for its minister.

To the Orrs' surprise, since they purchased the residence, they have not received any ad valorem property tax bills from either the city or the county. Is there a plausible reason for this? Explain.

What, if anything, should the Orrs do about the property tax matter?

Unlike the ad valorem tax on personalty (see below), the tax on realty is difficult to avoid. Since real estate is impossible to hide, a high degree of taxpayer compliance is not surprising. The only avoidance possibility that is generally available is associated with the assessed value of the property. For this reason, the assessed value of the property—particularly, a value that is reassessed upward—may be subject to controversy and litigation.

Four methods are currently in use for assessing the value of real estate:

1. Actual purchase or construction price.
2. Contemporaneous sales prices or construction costs of comparable properties.
3. Cost of reproducing a building, less allowance for depreciation and obsolescence from the time of actual construction.
4. Capitalization of income from rental property.

Because all of these methods suffer faults and lead to inequities, a combination of two or more is not uncommon. For example, when real estate values and construction costs are rising, the use of actual purchase or construction price (method 1) places the purchaser of a new home at a definite disadvantage compared with an owner who acquired similar property years before. As another illustration, if the capitalization of income (method 4) deals with property subject to rent controls (e.g., New York City), the property may be undervalued.

The history of the ad valorem tax on realty has been marked by inconsistent application due to a lack of competent tax administration and definitive guidelines for assessment procedures. In recent years, however, some significant improvements have occurred. Some jurisdictions, for example, have computerized their reassessment procedures so they will have an immediate effect on all property located within the jurisdiction. Nevertheless, the property tax area continues to be controversial.

TAX IN THE NEWS

TAX IT IF YOU CAN FIND IT

The state of Florida levies a property tax on the value of intangibles. Included in the assets subject to tax are stocks, bonds, mutual funds, money market accounts, and accounts receivable. Because the tax is easily evaded, the state is attempting to have financial institutions and brokerage firms report the transactions covered. Unfortunately for the state, it has no investigatory powers beyond its borders, nor can it obtain information on stocks and bonds held in the owner's name and kept in a safe deposit box.

Other states with a comparable tax on intangibles are Georgia, Kentucky, West Virginia, and Wyoming. After a realistic assessment of the noncompliance problem, North Carolina recently repealed its tax. In an effort to improve taxpayer compliance, Michigan is reducing its tax rate on intangibles.

Ad Valorem Taxes on Personalty.   **Personalty** can be defined as all assets that are not realty. It may be helpful to distinguish between the *classification* of an asset (realty or personalty) and the *use* to which it is put. Both realty and personalty can be either business use or personal use property. Examples include a residence (realty that is personal use), an office building (realty that is business use), surgical instruments (personalty that is business use), and regular wearing apparel (personalty that is personal use).[8]

Personalty can also be classified as tangible property or intangible property. For ad valorem tax purposes, intangible personalty includes stocks, bonds, and various other securities (e.g., bank shares).

The following generalizations may be made concerning the ad valorem taxes on personalty:

- Particularly with personalty devoted to personal use (e.g., jewelry, household furnishings), taxpayer compliance ranges from poor to zero. Some jurisdictions do not even attempt to enforce the tax on these items. For automobiles devoted to personal use, many jurisdictions have converted from value as the tax base to arbitrary license fees based on the weight of the vehicle. Some jurisdictions also consider the vehicle's age (e.g., automobiles six years or older are not subject to the ad valorem tax because they are presumed to have little, if any, value).
- For personalty devoted to business use (e.g., inventories, trucks, machinery, equipment), taxpayer compliance and enforcement procedures are measurably better.
- Which jurisdiction possesses the authority to tax movable personalty (e.g., railroad rolling stock) always has been and continues to be a troublesome issue.
- Some jurisdictions impose an ad valorem tax on intangibles.

---

[8]The distinction, important for ad valorem and for Federal income tax purposes, often becomes confused when personalty is referred to as "personal" property to distinguish it from "real" property. This designation does not give a complete picture of what is involved. The description "personal" residence, however, is clearer, since a residence can be identified as being realty. What is meant, in this case, is realty that is personal use property.

TRANSACTION TAXES

Transaction taxes, which characteristically are imposed at the manufacturer's, wholesaler's, or retailer's level, cover a wide range of transfers. Like many other types of taxes (e.g., income taxes, death taxes, and gift taxes), transaction taxes usually are not within the exclusive province of any level of taxing authority (Federal, state, local government). As the description implies, these levies place a tax on transfers of property and normally are determined by multiplying the value involved by a percentage rate.

Federal Excise Taxes. Long one of the mainstays of the Federal tax system, Federal **excise taxes** had declined in relative importance until recently. In late 1982, 1990, and 1993, Congress substantially increased the Federal excise taxes on such items as tobacco products, fuel and gasoline sales, telephone usage, and air travel passenger tickets. Other Federal excise taxes include the following:

- Manufacturers' excise taxes on trucks, trailers, tires, firearms, sporting equipment, coal, and the gas guzzler tax on automobiles.[9]
- Alcohol taxes.
- Luxury tax on automobiles. The tax is 10 percent of the retail price in excess of $34,000 (adjusted each year for inflation).
- Miscellaneous taxes (e.g., the tax on wagering).

The list of transactions covered, although seemingly impressive, has diminished over the years. At one time, for example, there was a Federal excise tax on admission to amusement facilities (e.g., theaters) and on the sale of such items as leather goods, jewelry, furs, and cosmetics.

When reviewing the list of both Federal and state excise taxes, one should recognize the possibility that the tax laws may be trying to influence social behavior. For example, the gas guzzler tax is intended as an incentive for the automobile companies to build cars that are fuel efficient. Since many consider alcohol and tobacco to be harmful to a person's health, why not increase their cost by imposing excise taxes and thereby discourage their use? Unfortunately, the evidence of the level of correlation between the imposition of an excise tax and consumer behavior is mixed.

State Excise Taxes. Many state and local excise taxes parallel the Federal version. Thus, all states tax the sale of gasoline, liquor, and tobacco products; however, the rates vary significantly. For gasoline products, for example, compare the 35 cents per gallon imposed by the state of Connecticut with the 8 cents per gallon levied by the state of Alaska. For tobacco sales, contrast the 2.5 cents per pack of cigarettes in effect in Virginia with the 82.5 cents per pack applicable in Washington. Given the latter situation, is it surprising that the smuggling of cigarettes for resale elsewhere is so widespread?

Other excise taxes found at some state and local levels include those on admission to amusement facilities; hotel occupancy and the rental of various other facilities; and the sale of playing cards, oleomargarine products, and prepared foods. Most states impose a transaction tax on the transfer of property that requires the recording of documents (e.g., real estate sales).[10] Some extend the tax to the transfer of stocks and other securities.

---

[9] The gas guzzler tax is imposed on the manufacturers of automobiles and progresses in amount as the mileage ratings per gallon of gas decrease.

[10] This type of tax has much in common with the stamp tax levied by Great Britain on the American colonies during the pre–Revolutionary War period in U.S. history.

General Sales Taxes.   The distinction between an excise tax and a general **sales tax** is easy to make. One is restricted to a particular transaction (e.g., the 18.4 cents per gallon Federal excise tax on the sale of gasoline), while the other covers a multitude of transactions (e.g., a 5 percent tax on *all* retail sales). In actual practice, however, the distinction is not always that clear. Some state statutes exempt certain transactions from the application of the general sales taxes (e.g., sales of food to be consumed off the premises, sales of certain medicines and drugs). Also, it is not uncommon to find that rates vary depending on the commodity involved. Many states, for example, allow preferential rates for the sale of agricultural equipment or apply different rates (either higher or lower than the general rate) to the sale of automobiles. With many of these special exceptions and classifications of rates, a general sales tax can take on the appearance of a collection of individual excise taxes.

A **use tax** is an ad valorem tax, usually at the same rate as the sales tax, on the use, consumption, or storage of tangible property. The purpose of a use tax is to prevent the avoidance of a sales tax. Every state that imposes a general sales tax levied on the consumer also has a use tax. Alaska, Delaware, Montana, New Hampshire, and Oregon have neither tax.

▼ **EXAMPLE 4**

Susan resides in a jurisdiction that imposes a 5% general sales tax but lives near a state that has no sales or use tax at all. Susan purchases an automobile for $10,000 from a dealer located in the neighboring state. Has she saved $500 in sales taxes? The state use tax is designed to pick up the difference between the tax paid in another jurisdiction and what would have been paid in the state in which Susan resides. ▼

The use tax is difficult to enforce for many purchases and is therefore often avoided. In some cases, for example, it may be worthwhile to make purchases through an out-of-state mail-order business. In spite of shipping costs, the avoidance of the local sales tax that otherwise might be incurred could make the price of such products as computer components cheaper. Some states are taking steps to curtail this loss of revenue. For items such as automobiles (refer to Example 4), the use tax probably will be collected when the purchaser registers the item in his or her home state.

Local general sales taxes, over and above those levied by the state, are common. It is not unusual to find taxpayers living in the same state who pay different general sales taxes due to the location of their residence.

▼ **EXAMPLE 5**

Pete and Sam both live in a state that has a general sales tax of 3%. Sam, however, resides in a city that imposes an additional general sales tax of 2%. Even though Pete and Sam live in the same state, one is subject to a rate of 3%, while the other pays a tax of 5%. ▼

Severance Taxes.   **Severance taxes** are an important source of revenue for many states. These transaction taxes are based on the notion that the state has an interest in its natural resources (e.g., oil, gas, iron ore, coal). Therefore, a tax is imposed when the natural resources are extracted.

DEATH TAXES

A **death tax** is a tax on the right to transfer property or to receive property upon the death of the owner. Consequently, a death tax falls into the category of an excise tax. If the death tax is imposed on the right to pass property at death, it is classified as an **estate tax.** If it taxes the right to receive property from a decedent, it is termed an **inheritance tax.** As is typical of other types of excise taxes, the value of the property transferred provides the base for determining the amount of the death tax.

The Federal government imposes only an estate tax. State governments, however, levy inheritance taxes, estate taxes, or both.

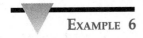

EXAMPLE 6   At the time of her death, Wilma lived in a state that imposes an inheritance tax but not an estate tax. Mary, one of Wilma's heirs, lives in the same state. Wilma's estate is subject to the Federal estate tax, and Mary is subject to the state inheritance tax. ▼

The Federal Estate Tax.   The Revenue Act of 1916 incorporated the estate tax into the tax law. Never designed to generate a large amount of revenue, the tax was originally intended to prevent large concentrations of wealth from being kept within a family for many generations. Whether this objective has been accomplished is debatable. Like the income tax, estate taxes can be reduced through various planning procedures.

The gross estate includes property the decedent owned at the time of death. It also includes life insurance proceeds when paid to the estate or when paid to a beneficiary other than the estate if the deceased-insured had any ownership rights in the policy. Quite simply, the gross estate represents property interests subject to Federal estate taxation.[11] All property included in the gross estate is valued as of the date of death or, if the alternate valuation date is elected, six months later.[12]

Deductions from the gross estate in arriving at the taxable estate include funeral and administration expenses, certain taxes, debts of the decedent, casualty losses[13] incurred during the administration of the estate, transfers to charitable organizations, and, in some cases, the marital deduction. The marital deduction is available for amounts actually passing to a surviving spouse (a widow or widower).

Once the taxable estate has been determined and certain taxable gifts have been added to it, the estate tax can be computed. From the amount derived from the appropriate tax rate schedules, various credits should be subtracted to arrive at the tax, if any, that is due.[14] Although many other credits are also available, probably the most significant is the unified transfer tax credit. The main reason for this credit is to eliminate or reduce the estate tax liability for modest estates. Currently, the amount of the credit is $192,800. Based on the estate tax rates, the credit covers a tax base of $600,000.

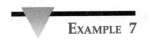

EXAMPLE 7   Ned made no taxable gifts before his death in 1996. If Ned's taxable estate amounts to $600,000 or less, no Federal estate tax is due because of the application of the unified transfer tax credit. Under the tax law, the estate tax on a taxable estate of $600,000 is $192,800. ▼

State Death Taxes.   As noted earlier, states usually levy an inheritance tax, an estate tax, or both. The two forms of death taxes differ according to whether the tax is imposed on the heirs or on the estate.

Characteristically, an inheritance tax divides the heirs into classes based on their relationship to the decedent. The more closely related the heir, the lower the rates imposed and the greater the exemption allowed. Some states completely exempt from taxation amounts passing to a surviving spouse.

---

[11] For further information on these matters, see Chapter 26.

[12] See the discussion of the alternate valuation date in Chapter 12.

[13] For a definition of casualty losses, see the Glossary of Tax Terms in Appendix C.

[14] For tax purposes, it is always crucial to appreciate the difference between a deduction and a credit. A *credit* is a dollar-for-dollar reduction of tax liability. A *deduction*, however, only benefits the taxpayer to the extent of his or her tax bracket. An estate in a 50% tax bracket, for example, would need $2 of deductions to prevent $1 of tax liability from developing. In contrast, $1 of credit neutralizes $1 of tax liability.

GIFT TAXES

Like a death tax, a **gift tax** is an excise tax levied on the right to transfer property. In this case, however, the tax is imposed on transfers made during the owner's life and not at death. Also, a gift tax applies only to transfers that are not supported by full and adequate consideration.

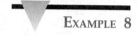

EXAMPLE 8

Carl sells property worth $20,000 to his daughter for $1,000. Although property worth $20,000 has been transferred, only $19,000 represents a gift, since this is the portion not supported by full and adequate consideration. ▼

The Federal Gift Tax.   First enacted in 1932, the Federal gift tax was intended to complement the estate tax. In the absence of a tax applicable to lifetime transfers by gift, it would be possible to avoid the estate tax and escape taxation entirely.

Only taxable gifts are subject to the gift tax. For this purpose, a taxable gift is measured by the fair market value of the property on the date of transfer less the annual exclusion of $10,000 per donee and, in some cases, less the marital deduction, which allows tax-free transfers between spouses. Each donor is allowed an annual exclusion of $10,000 for each donee.[15]

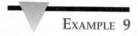

EXAMPLE 9

On December 31, 1995, Vera (a widow) gives $10,000 to each of her four married children, their spouses, and her eight grandchildren. On January 3, 1996, she repeats the same procedure. Due to the annual exclusion, Vera has not made a taxable gift, although she transferred $160,000 [$10,000 × 16 (number of donees)] in 1995 and $160,000 [$10,000 × 16 (number of donees)] in 1996 for a total of $320,000 ($160,000 + $160,000). ▼

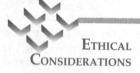

ETHICAL CONSIDERATIONS

The Annual Exclusion for Gifts

Arlene, a wealthy widow, would like to transfer $20,000 of cash to her son, Wilbur, in 1996 without exceeding the $10,000 per donee annual exclusion. To achieve this result, Arlene devises the following scheme: she gives $10,000 to Wilbur and $10,000 to her brother, George, who gives $10,000 to Wilbur.

Will Arlene's scheme succeed? What could go wrong?

A special election applicable to married persons allows one-half of the gift made by the donor-spouse to be treated as being made by the nondonor-spouse. This election to split the gifts of property made to third persons has the effect of increasing the number of annual exclusions available. Also, it allows the use of the nondonor-spouse's unified transfer tax credit and may lower the tax brackets that will apply.

The gift tax rate schedule is the same as that applicable to the estate tax. The schedule is commonly referred to as the *unified transfer tax schedule.*

The Federal gift tax is *cumulative* in effect. What this means is that the tax base for current taxable gifts includes past taxable gifts. Although a credit is allowed for prior gift taxes, the result of adding past taxable gifts to current taxable gifts is to force the donor into a higher tax bracket.[16] Like the Federal

---

[15] The purpose of the annual exclusion is to avoid the need to report and pay a tax on *modest* gifts. Without the exclusion, the IRS could face a real problem of taxpayer noncompliance.

[16] For further information on the Federal gift tax, see Chapter 26.

estate tax rates, the Federal gift tax rates are progressive (see Example 3 earlier in this chapter).

The unified transfer tax credit is available for all taxable gifts, and as with the Federal estate tax, the amount of this credit is $192,800. There is, however, only one unified transfer tax credit, and it applies both to taxable gifts and to the Federal estate tax. In a manner of speaking, therefore, once the unified transfer tax credit has been exhausted for Federal gift tax purposes, it is no longer available to insulate a decedent from the Federal estate tax.

In summary, transfers by gift and transfers by death are subject to the unified transfer tax. The same rates and credits apply. Further, taxable gifts are added to the taxable estate in arriving at the tax base for applying the unified transfer tax at death.

State Gift Taxes.   The states currently imposing a state gift tax are Connecticut, Delaware, Louisiana, New York, North Carolina, and Tennessee. Most of the laws provide for lifetime exemptions and annual exclusions. Like the Federal gift tax, the state taxes are cumulative in effect. But unlike the Federal version, the amount of tax depends on the relationship between the donor and the donee. Like state inheritance taxes, larger exemptions and lower rates apply when the donor and donee are closely related to each other.

INCOME TAXES

Income taxes are levied by the Federal government, most states, and some local governments. The trend in recent years has been to place greater reliance on this method of taxation. This trend is not consistent with what is happening in other countries, and in this sense, our system of taxation is somewhat different.

Income taxes generally are imposed on individuals, corporations, and certain fiduciaries (estates and trusts). Most jurisdictions attempt to assure the collection of income taxes by requiring certain pay-as-you-go procedures (e.g., withholding requirements for employees and estimated tax prepayments for other taxpayers).

Federal Income Taxes.   Chapters 2 through 15 deal with the application of the Federal income tax to individuals. The procedure for determining the Federal income tax applicable to individuals is summarized in Figure 1–2.

The application of the Federal corporate income tax does not require the computation of adjusted gross income (AGI) and does not provide for the standard deduction and personal and dependency exemptions. All allowable deductions of a corporation fall into the business-expense category. In effect, therefore, the taxable income of a corporation is the difference between gross income (net of exclusions) and deductions.

Chapter 16 summarizes the basic income tax rules relating to corporations. For an in-depth treatment of the Federal income tax as it affects corporations, see Chapters 17 through 20.

State Income Taxes.   All but the following states impose an income tax on individuals: Alaska, Florida, Nevada, South Dakota, Texas, Washington, and Wyoming.

Some of the characteristics of state income taxes are summarized as follows:

• With few exceptions, all states that levy an income tax require some form of withholding procedures.
Most states use as the tax base the income determination made for Federal income tax purposes.

▼ **FIGURE 1–2**
Formula for Federal Income Tax on Individuals

Income (broadly conceived)	$xx,xxx
Less: Exclusions (income that is not subject to tax)	(x,xxx)
Gross income (income that is subject to tax)	$xx,xxx
Less: Certain business deductions (usually referred to as deductions *for* adjusted gross income)	(x,xxx)
Adjusted gross income	$xx,xxx
Less: The greater of certain personal and employee deductions (usually referred to as *itemized deductions*) or The standard deduction (including any additional standard deduction) and	(x,xxx)
Less: Personal and dependency exemptions	(x,xxx)
Taxable income	$xx,xxx
Tax on taxable income (see Tax Rate Schedules in Appendix A)	$ x,xxx
Less: Tax credits (including Federal income tax withheld and other prepayments of Federal income taxes)	(xxx)
Tax due (or refund)	$ xxx

- A minority of states go even further and impose a flat rate upon AGI as computed for Federal income tax purposes. Several apply a rate to the Federal income tax liability. This is often referred to as the piggyback approach to state income taxation.
- A diminishing minority of states allow a deduction for Federal income taxes.
- Most states allow their residents some form of tax credit for income taxes paid to other states.

Nearly all states have an income tax applicable to corporations. It is difficult to determine those that do not because a state franchise tax sometimes is based in part on the income earned by the corporation.[17]

Local Income Taxes. Cities imposing an income tax include, but are not limited to, Baltimore, Cincinnati, Cleveland, Detroit, Kansas City (Mo.), New York, Philadelphia, and St. Louis. The application of a city income tax is not limited to local residents.

EMPLOYMENT TAXES

Classification as an employee usually leads to the imposition of **employment taxes** and to the requirement that the employer withhold specified amounts for income taxes. The material that follows concentrates on the two major employment taxes: FICA (Federal Insurance Contributions Act—commonly referred to as the Social Security tax) and FUTA (Federal Unemployment Tax Act). Both taxes can be justified by social and public welfare considerations: FICA offers some measure of retirement security, and FUTA provides a modest source of income in the event of loss of employment.

[17]See the discussion of franchise taxes later in the chapter.

TAX IN THE NEWS

VISITORS BEWARE! THE CITY AND STATE YOU VISIT MAY NOT BE ALL THAT FRIENDLY

Even if you are not a resident, you may be subject to local and state income taxes if you earn money in that jurisdiction. Besides the nonresident who commutes (e.g., a taxpayer who lives in Connecticut but works full-time in New York City), taxpayers who perform services on an itinerant basis may be vulnerable. For example, the Dallas Cowboys are subject to the city of Philadelphia income tax every time they are hosted by the Eagles. This must be particularly distressing to Troy Aikman, who lives in a city (Dallas) and a state (Texas) that do not have an income tax.

Although these situations are commonly referred to as the application of the "jock tax," other persons besides professional athletes get hit. Particularly susceptible are entertainers, doctors, lawyers, lecturers, and anyone who generates large fees and has a high profile. Ordinary professionals are not targeted because the amount of taxes involved would not justify the collection effort.

Is it any wonder that Las Vegas, which has no city or state income tax, is such a popular place to perform highly paid services (e.g., entertainment, prize fighting)?

FICA Taxes. The **FICA tax** rates and wage base have steadily increased over the years. It is difficult to imagine that the initial rate in 1937 was only 1 percent of the first $3,000 of covered wages. Thus, the maximum tax due was only $30!

Currently, the FICA tax has two components: Social Security tax (old age, survivors, and disability insurance) *and* Medicare tax (hospital insurance). The Social Security tax rate is 6.2 percent for 1995 and 1996, and the Medicare tax rate is 1.45 percent for these years. The base amount for Social Security is $61,200 for 1995 and $62,700 for 1996. There is no limit on the base amount for the Medicare tax. The employer must match the employee's portion.

A spouse employed by another spouse is subject to FICA. However, children under the age of 18 who are employed in a parent's trade or business are exempted.

FUTA Taxes. The purpose of the **FUTA tax** is to provide funds that the states can use to administer unemployment benefits. This leads to the somewhat unusual situation of one tax being handled by both Federal and state governments. The end result of such joint administration is to compel the employer to observe a double set of rules. Thus, state and Federal returns must be filed and payments made to both governmental units.

In 1996, FUTA applies at a rate of 6.2 percent on the first $7,000 of covered wages paid during the year to each employee. The Federal government allows a credit for FUTA paid (or allowed under a merit rating system) to the state. The credit cannot exceed 5.4 percent of the covered wages. Thus, the amount required to be paid to the IRS could be as low as 0.8 percent (6.2% − 5.4%).

States follow a policy of reducing the unemployment tax on employers who experience stable employment. Thus, an employer with little or no employee turnover might find that the state rate drops to as low as 0.1 percent or, in some states, even to zero. The reason for the merit rating credit is that the state has to pay fewer unemployment benefits when employment is steady.

FUTA differs from FICA in the sense that the incidence of taxation falls entirely upon the employer. A few states, however, levy a special tax on employees to provide either disability benefits or supplemental unemployment compensation, or both.

OTHER U.S. TAXES

To complete the overview of the U.S. tax system, some missing links need to be covered that do not fit into the classifications discussed elsewhere in this chapter.

Federal Customs Duties.   One tax that has not yet been mentioned is the tariff on certain imported goods.[18] Generally referred to as customs duties or levies, this tax, together with selective excise taxes, provided most of the revenues needed by the Federal government during the nineteenth century. In view of present times, it is remarkable to note that tariffs and excise taxes alone paid off the national debt in 1835 and enabled the U.S. Treasury to pay a surplus of $28 million to the states.

In recent years, tariffs have served the nation more as an instrument for carrying out protectionist policies than as a means of generating revenue. Thus, a particular U.S. industry might be saved from economic disaster, so the argument goes, by placing customs duties on the importation of foreign goods that can be sold at lower prices. Protectionists contend that the tariff therefore neutralizes the competitive edge held by the producer of the foreign goods.[19]

Protectionist policies seem more appropriate for less-developed countries whose industrial capacity has not yet matured. In a world where a developed country should have everything to gain by encouraging international free trade, such policies may be of dubious value. History shows that tariffs often lead to retaliatory action on the part of the nation or nations affected.

Miscellaneous State and Local Taxes.   Most states impose a franchise tax on corporations. Basically, a **franchise tax** is levied on the right to do business in the state. The base used for the determination of the tax varies from state to state. Although corporate income considerations may come into play, this tax most often is based on the capitalization of the corporation (either with or without certain long-term indebtedness).

Closely akin to the franchise tax are **occupational taxes** applicable to various trades or businesses, such as a liquor store license, a taxicab permit, or a fee to practice a profession such as law, medicine, or accounting. Most of these are not significant revenue producers and fall more into the category of licenses than taxes. The revenue derived is used to defray the cost incurred by the jurisdiction in regulating the business or profession in the interest of the public good.

PROPOSED U.S. TAXES

Considerable dissatisfaction with the U.S. Federal income tax has led to several recent proposals that, to say the least, are rather drastic in nature. One proposal

---

[18]Less-developed countries that rely principally on one or more major commodities (e.g., oil, coffee) are prone to favor *export* duties as well.

[19]The North American Free Trade Agreement (NAFTA), enacted in 1993, substantially reduced the tariffs on trade between Canada,

Mexico, and the United States. The General Agreement on Tariffs and Trade (GATT) legislation enacted in 1994 also reduced tariffs on selected commodities among 124 signatory nations.

would retain the income tax but with substantial change. Two other proposals would replace the Federal income tax with an entirely different system of taxation.

The Flat Tax.   As proposed by Representative Dick Armey (R, Texas), the **flat tax** would replace the current graduated income tax with one rate, 17 percent. Large personal exemptions (e.g., approximately $30,000 for a family of four) would allow many low- and middle-income taxpayers to pay no tax. All other deductions would be eliminated, and no tax would be imposed on income from investments.

Various other versions of the flat tax have been suggested that would retain selected deductions (e.g., interest on home mortgages and charitable contributions) and not exclude all investment income from taxation.

The major advantage of the flat tax is its simplicity. Most observers agree that the current Federal income tax is unreasonably complex. Consequently, compliance costs are disproportionately high.

Value Added Tax.   The **value added tax (VAT)** is one of two proposals that would replace the Federal income tax. Under the VAT, a business would pay the tax (approximately 17 percent) on all of the materials and services required to manufacture its product. In effect, the VAT taxes the increment in value as goods move through production and manufacturing stages to the marketplace. Moreover, the VAT paid by the producer will be reflected in the selling price of the goods. Thus, the VAT is a tax on consumption.

Several other countries (e.g., European Union countries) use the VAT either as a supplement to or a replacement for an income tax.

Sales Tax.   A **national sales tax** is favored by Representative Bill Archer (R, Texas), who is the current chairman of the House Ways and Means Committee. This tax differs from a VAT in that it would be collected on the final sale of goods and services. Consequently, it is collected from the consumer and not from businesses adding value to the product. Like the VAT, the national sales tax is intended to replace the Federal income tax.

Critics contend that consumption taxes (both a VAT and a national sales tax) impose more of a burden on low-income taxpayers because they must spend larger proportions of their incomes on essential purchases. Representative Archer's proposal would attempt to remedy this inequity by granting some sort of credit or exemption to low-income taxpayers.

TAX ADMINISTRATION

INTERNAL REVENUE SERVICE

4   LEARNING OBJECTIVE
Understand the administration of the tax law including the audit process utilized by the IRS.

The responsibility for administering the Federal tax laws rests with the Treasury Department. Administratively, the IRS is part of the Department of the Treasury and is responsible for enforcing the tax laws. The Commissioner of Internal Revenue is appointed by the President and is responsible for establishing policy and supervising the activities of the entire IRS organization.

THE AUDIT PROCESS

Selection of Returns for Audit.   Due to budgetary limitations, only a small minority of returns is audited. For the fiscal year ending September 30, 1993, for example, the IRS audited only 0.92 percent of the total returns, down from 1.06 percent in the preceding fiscal year.

The IRS utilizes mathematical formulas and statistical sampling techniques to select tax returns that are most likely to contain errors and to yield substantial amounts of additional tax revenues upon audit.

Though the IRS does not openly disclose all of its audit selection techniques, the following observations may be made concerning the probability of selection for audit:

- Certain groups of taxpayers are subject to audit much more frequently than others. These groups include individuals with gross income in excess of $50,000, self-employed individuals with substantial business income and deductions, and taxpayers with prior tax deficiencies. Also vulnerable are cash businesses (e.g., cafes and small service businesses) where the potential for tax avoidance is high.

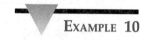
EXAMPLE 10

Jack owns and operates a liquor store on a cash-and-carry basis. Since all of Jack's sales are for cash, he might well be a prime candidate for an audit by the IRS. Cash transactions are easier to conceal than those made on credit. ▼

- If information returns (e.g., Form 1099, Form W–2) are not in substantial agreement with reported income, an audit can be anticipated.
- If an individual's itemized deductions are in excess of norms established for various income levels, the probability of an audit is increased.
- Filing of a refund claim by the taxpayer may prompt an audit of the return.
- Certain returns are selected on a random sampling basis under the Taxpayer Compliance Measurement Program (TCMP). The TCMP is used to develop, update, and improve the mathematical formulas and statistical sampling techniques used by the IRS.
- Information obtained from other sources (e.g., informants, news items) may lead to an audit. The tax law permits the IRS to pay rewards to persons who provide information that leads to the detection and punishment of those who violate the tax laws. The rewards may not exceed 10 percent of the taxes, fines, and penalties recovered as a result of such information.

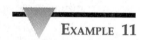
EXAMPLE 11

After 15 years of service, Rita is discharged by her employer, Dr. Smith. Shortly thereafter, the IRS receives an anonymous letter informing it that Dr. Smith keeps two separate sets of books, one of which substantially understates his cash receipts. ▼

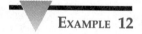
EXAMPLE 12

During a divorce proceeding, it is revealed that Leo, a public official, keeps large amounts of cash in a shoe box at home. This information is widely disseminated by the news media and comes to the attention of the IRS. Needless to say, the IRS would be interested in knowing whether these funds originated from a taxable source and, if so, whether they were reported on Leo's income tax returns. ▼

Types of Audits. Once a return is selected for audit, the taxpayer is notified accordingly. If the issue involved is minor, the matter often can be resolved simply by correspondence (a **correspondence audit**) between the IRS and the taxpayer.

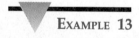
EXAMPLE 13

During 1994, Janet received dividend income from Green Corporation. In January 1995, Green Corporation reported the payment on Form 1099–DIV (an information return for reporting dividend payments), the original being sent to the IRS and a copy to Janet. When preparing her income tax return for 1994, Janet apparently overlooked this particular Form 1099–DIV and failed to include the dividend on Schedule B, Interest and Dividend Income, of Form 1040. In 1996, the IRS sends a notice to Janet calling her attention to the omission and requesting a remittance for additional tax, interest, and penalty. Janet promptly mails a check to the IRS for the requested amount, and the matter is closed. ▼

Other examinations are generally classified as either office audits or field audits. An **office audit** usually is restricted in scope and is conducted in the facilities of the IRS. In contrast, a **field audit** involves an examination of numerous items reported on the return and is conducted on the premises of the taxpayer or the taxpayer's representative.

Upon the conclusion of the audit, the examining agent issues a Revenue Agent's Report (RAR) that summarizes the findings. The RAR will result in a refund (the tax was overpaid), a deficiency (the tax was underpaid), or a *no change* (the tax was correct) finding.

STATUTE OF LIMITATIONS

A **statute of limitations** is a provision in the law that offers a party a defense against a suit brought by another party after the expiration of a specified period of time. The purpose of a statute of limitations is to preclude parties from prosecuting stale claims. The passage of time makes the defense of such claims difficult since witnesses may no longer be available or evidence may have been lost or destroyed. Found at the state and Federal levels, such statutes cover a multitude of suits, both civil and criminal.

Assessment by the IRS.   Under the general rule, the IRS may assess (impose) an additional tax liability against a taxpayer within *three years* of the filing of the income tax return. If the return is filed early, the three-year period begins to run from the due date of the return (usually April 15 for a calendar year individual taxpayer).

If a taxpayer omits an amount of gross income in excess of 25 percent of the gross income reported on the return, the statute of limitations is increased to six years.

EXAMPLE 14

For 1991, Mark, a calendar year taxpayer, reported gross income of $400,000 on a timely filed income tax return. If Mark omitted more than $100,000 (25% × $400,000), the six-year statute of limitations would apply to the 1991 tax year. ▼

The six-year provision on assessments by the IRS applies only to the omission of income and does not cover other factors that might lead to an understatement of tax liability (e.g., overstatement of deductions and credits).

There is *no* statute of limitations on assessments of tax if *no return* is filed or if a *fraudulent* return is filed.

TAX PRACTICE

The area of tax practice is largely unregulated. Virtually anyone can aid another in complying with the various tax laws. If a practitioner is a member of a profession, such as law or public accounting, he or she must abide by certain ethical standards. Furthermore, the Internal Revenue Code imposes penalties upon the preparers of Federal tax returns who violate proscribed acts and procedures.

5 LEARNING OBJECTIVE
Appreciate some of the ethical guidelines involved in tax practice.

Ethical Guidelines.   The American Institute of CPAs has issued numerous guides for CPAs engaged in tax practice. Called "Statements on Responsibilities in Tax Practice," some of these are summarized below.

- Do not take questionable positions on a client's tax return in the hope that the return will not be selected for audit by the IRS. Any positions taken should be supported by a good-faith belief that they have a realistic chance of being sustained if challenged. The client should be fully advised of the risks involved and of the penalties that would result if the position taken is not successful.

- A practitioner can use a client's estimates if they are reasonable under the circumstances. If the tax law requires verification (e.g., receipts), the client should be so advised. In no event should an estimate be given the appearance of greater accuracy than is the case. For example, an estimate of $1,000 should not be deducted on a return as $999.

- Every effort should be made to answer questions appearing on tax returns. A question need not be answered if the information requested is not readily available, the answer is voluminous, or the question's meaning is uncertain. The failure to answer a question on a return cannot be justified on the grounds that the answer could prove disadvantageous to the taxpayer.

- Upon learning of an error on a past tax return, advise the client to correct it. Do not, however, inform the IRS of the error. If the error is material and the client refuses to correct it, consider withdrawing from the engagement. This will be necessary if the error has a carryover effect and prevents the current year's tax liability from being determined correctly.

ETHICAL CONSIDERATIONS

A Favor for a Neighbor

Jim is a CPA who works full-time for a national accounting firm. Jim's neighbor and good friend, Lester, prepares his own income tax return for 1995.

Lester has heard that a person who has his tax return prepared by a CPA is less likely to be audited by the IRS. Consequently, Lester asks Jim to sign his return as the preparer.

Jim has known Lester for many years and considers him to be honest and well versed in business affairs. As a favor to Lester, should Jim sign the return as preparer?

Statutory Penalties Imposed on Tax Return Preparers. In addition to ethical constraints, a tax return preparer may be subject to certain statutorily sanctioned penalties, including the following:

- Various penalties involving procedural matters. Examples include failing to furnish the taxpayer with a copy of the return; endorsing a taxpayer's refund check; failing to sign the return as a preparer; failing to furnish one's identification number; and failing to keep copies of returns or maintain a client list.
- Understatement of a tax liability based on a position that lacks any realistic possibility of being sustained. If the position is not frivolous, the penalty can be avoided by disclosing it on the return.
- Any willful attempt to understate taxes. This usually results when a preparer disregards or makes no effort to obtain pertinent information from a client.

Understanding the Federal Tax Law

6   LEARNING OBJECTIVE
Recognize the economic, social, equity, and political considerations that justify various aspects of the tax law.

The Federal tax law is a mosaic of statutory provisions, administrative pronouncements, and court decisions. Anyone who has attempted to work with this body of knowledge would have to admit to its complexity. For the person who has to trudge through a mass of rules to find the solution to a tax problem, it may be of some consolation to know that the law's complexity can generally be explained. Whether sound or not, there is a reason for the formulation of every rule. Knowing these reasons, therefore, is a considerable step toward understanding the Federal tax law.

The Federal tax law has as its *major objective* the raising of revenue. But although the fiscal needs of the government are important, other considerations explain certain portions of the law. Economic, social, equity, and political factors also play a significant role. Added to these factors is the marked impact the IRS and the courts have had and will continue to have on the evolution of Federal tax law. These matters are treated in the remainder of the chapter, and, wherever appropriate, the discussion is referenced to subjects covered later in the text.

REVENUE NEEDS

The foundation of any tax system has to be the raising of revenue to cover the cost of government operations. Ideally, annual outlays should not exceed anticipated revenues, thereby leading to a balanced budget with no resulting deficit. Many states have achieved this objective by passing laws or constitutional amendments precluding deficit spending. Unfortunately, the Federal government has no such conclusive prohibition, and mounting annual deficits have become an increasing concern for many.

When finalizing the Tax Reform Act (TRA) of 1986, a deficit-conscious Congress was guided by the concept of **revenue neutrality.** The concept means that the changes made will neither increase nor decrease the net result reached under the prior rules. Revenue neutrality does not mean that any one taxpayer's tax liability will remain the same. Since the circumstances involved will differ, one taxpayer's increased tax liability could be another's tax savings. Although revenue-neutral tax reform does not reduce deficits, at least it does not aggravate the problem. One can expect budget deficit considerations to play an ever-increasing role in shaping future tax policy.

ECONOMIC CONSIDERATIONS

Using the tax system in an effort to accomplish economic objectives has become increasingly popular in recent years. Generally, proponents of this goal use tax legislation to amend the Internal Revenue Code and promote measures designed to help control the economy or encourage certain activities and businesses.

Control of the Economy.   Congress has used depreciation write-offs as a means of controlling the economy. Theoretically, shorter asset lives and accelerated methods should encourage additional investment in depreciable property acquired for business use. Conversely, longer asset lives and the required use of the straight-line method of depreciation dampen the tax incentive for capital outlays.

A change in the tax rate structure has a more immediate impact on the economy. With lower tax rates, taxpayers are able to retain additional spendable funds. Although TRA of 1986 lowered tax rates for most taxpayers, it also reduced or eliminated many deductions and credits. Consequently, lower rates may not always lead to lower tax liabilities.

Encouragement of Certain Activities.   Without passing judgment on the wisdom of any such choices, it is quite clear that the tax law does encourage certain types of economic activity or segments of the economy. For example, the favorable treatment allowed research and development expenditures can be explained by the desire to foster technological progress. Under the tax law, such expenditures can be either deducted in the year incurred or capitalized and amortized over a period of 60 months or more. In terms of the timing of the tax savings, these options usually are preferable to capitalizing the cost with a write-off over the estimated useful life of the asset created. If the asset developed has an indefinite useful life, no write-off would be available without the two options allowed by the tax law.

Is it desirable to encourage the conservation of energy resources? Considering the world energy situation and our own reliance on foreign oil, the answer to this question has to be yes. The concern over energy usage was a prime consideration in the enactment of legislation to make various tax savings for energy conservation expenditures available to taxpayers.

Is preserving the environment a desirable objective? Ecological considerations explain why the tax law permits a 60-month amortization period for costs incurred in the installation of pollution control facilities.

Is it wise to stimulate U.S. exports of goods and services? Considering the pressing and continuing problem of a deficit in the U.S. balance of payments, the answer should be clear. Along this line, Congress has created Foreign Sales Corporations (FSCs), which are designed to encourage domestic exports of goods. The FSC provisions exempt a percentage of profits from export sales from the Federal income tax. Also in an international setting, Congress has deemed it advisable to establish incentives for U.S. citizens who accept employment overseas. Such persons receive generous tax breaks through special treatment of their foreign-source income and certain housing costs.

Is saving desirable for the economy? Saving leads to capital formation and thereby makes funds available to finance home construction and industrial expansion. The tax law encourages saving by according preferential treatment to private retirement plans. Not only are contributions to Keogh (H.R. 10) plans and certain Individual Retirement Accounts (IRAs) deductible, but income from the contributions accumulates free of tax. As noted below, the encouragement of private-sector pension plans can also be justified under social considerations.

Encouragement of Certain Industries.   No one can question the proposition that a sound agricultural base is necessary for a well-balanced national economy. Undoubtedly, this can explain why farmers are accorded special treatment under the Federal tax system. Among the benefits are the election to expense rather than capitalize certain soil and water conservation expenditures and fertilizers and the election to defer the recognition of gain on the receipt of crop insurance proceeds.

Encouragement of Small Business.   At least in the United States, a consensus exists that what is good for small business is good for the economy as a whole. Whether valid or not, this assumption has led to a definite bias in the tax law favoring small business.

In the corporate tax area, several provisions can be explained by the desire to benefit small business. One provision permits the shareholders of a small business corporation to make a special election that generally will avoid the imposition of the corporate income tax.[20] Furthermore, such an election enables the corporation to pass through its operating losses to its shareholders.

SOCIAL CONSIDERATIONS

Some provisions of the Federal tax law, particularly those dealing with the income tax of individuals, can be explained by social considerations. Some notable examples and their rationales include the following:

- Certain benefits provided to employees through accident and health plans financed by employers are nontaxable to employees. Encouraging such plans is considered socially desirable since they provide medical benefits in the event of an employee's illness or injury.
- Most premiums paid by an employer for group term insurance covering the life of the employee are nontaxable to the employee. These arrangements can be justified on social grounds in that they provide funds for the family unit to help it adjust to the loss of wages caused by the employee's death.
- A contribution made by an employer to a qualified pension or profit sharing plan for an employee receives special treatment. The contribution and any income it generates are not taxed to the employee until the funds are distributed. Such an arrangement also benefits the employer by allowing a tax deduction when the contribution is made to the qualified plan. Private retirement plans are encouraged to supplement the subsistence income level the employee otherwise would have under the Social Security system.[21]
- A deduction is allowed for contributions to qualified charitable organizations.[22] The deduction attempts to shift some of the financial and administrative burden of socially desirable programs from the public (the government) to the private (the citizens) sector.
- A tax credit is allowed for amounts spent to furnish care for certain minor or disabled dependents to enable the taxpayer to seek or maintain gainful employment.[23] Who could deny the social desirability of encouraging taxpayers to provide care for their children while they work?
- A tax deduction is not allowed for certain expenditures deemed to be contrary to public policy. This disallowance extends to such items as fines,

---

[20] Known as the S election, it is discussed in Chapter 21.
[21] The same rationale explains the availability of similar arrangements for self-employed persons (the H.R. 10, or Keogh, plan).

[22] The charitable contribution deduction is discussed in Chapter 9.
[23] See Chapter 11.

penalties, illegal kickbacks, bribes to government officials, and gambling losses in excess of gains. Social considerations dictate that the tax law should not encourage these activities by permitting a deduction.

Many other examples could be cited, but the conclusion would be unchanged. Social considerations do explain a significant part of the Federal tax law.

EQUITY CONSIDERATIONS

The concept of equity is relative. Reasonable persons can, and often do, disagree about what is fair or unfair. In the tax area, moreover, equity is most often tied to a particular taxpayer's personal situation. To illustrate, compare the tax positions of those who rent their personal residences with those who own their homes. Renters receive no Federal income tax deduction for the rent they pay. For homeowners, however, a large portion of the house payments they make may qualify for the Federal interest and property tax deductions. Although renters may have difficulty understanding this difference in tax treatment, the encouragement of home ownership can be justified on both economic and social grounds.

In the same vein, compare the tax treatment of a corporation with that of a partnership. Although the two businesses may be of equal size, similarly situated, and competitors in the production of goods or services, they are not treated comparably under the tax law. The corporation is subject to a separate Federal income tax; the partnership is not. Whether the differences in tax treatment can be justified logically in terms of equity is beside the point. The point is that the tax law can and does make a distinction between these business forms.

In many other parts of the law, however, equity concerns are evident. The concept of equity appears in tax provisions that alleviate the effect of multiple taxation and postpone the recognition of gain when the taxpayer lacks the ability or wherewithal to pay the tax. Provisions that mitigate the effect of the application of the annual accounting period concept and help taxpayers cope with the eroding results of inflation also reflect equity considerations.

Alleviating the Effect of Multiple Taxation.   The income earned by a taxpayer may be subject to taxes imposed by different taxing authorities. If, for example, the taxpayer is a resident of New York City, income might generate Federal, state of New York, and city of New York income taxes. To compensate for this apparent inequity, the Federal tax law allows a taxpayer to claim a deduction for state and local income taxes. The deduction does not, however, neutralize the effect of multiple taxation, since the benefit derived depends on the taxpayer's Federal income tax rate. Only a tax credit, rather than a deduction, would eliminate the effects of multiple taxation on the same income.

Equity considerations can explain the Federal tax treatment of certain income from foreign sources. Since double taxation results when the same income is subject to both foreign and U.S. income taxes, the tax law permits the taxpayer to choose between a credit and a deduction for the foreign taxes paid.

The Wherewithal to Pay Concept.   The **wherewithal to pay** concept recognizes the inequity of taxing a transaction when the taxpayer lacks the means with which to pay the tax. It is particularly suited to situations in which the taxpayer's economic position has not changed significantly as a result of the transaction.

An illustration of the wherewithal to pay concept is the provision of the tax law dealing with the treatment of gain resulting from the sale of a personal residence. If the proceeds are rolled over (reinvested) in another personal residence within a specified time period, the gain will not be taxed (see Chapter 12).

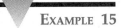

EXAMPLE 15

Ron sold his personal residence (cost of $60,000) for $100,000 and moved to another city. Shortly thereafter, he purchased a new personal residence for $100,000. ▼

In Example 15, Ron had a realized gain of $40,000 [$100,000 (selling price) – $60,000 (cost of residence)]. It would be inequitable to force Ron to pay a tax on this gain for two reasons. First, without disposing of the property acquired (the new residence), Ron would be hard-pressed to pay the tax. Second, his economic position has not changed significantly.

A warning is in order concerning the application of the wherewithal to pay concept. It applies only in situations specified by the tax law. Otherwise, the absence of cash and no apparent change in economic position will not prevent a transaction from being taxed.

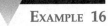

EXAMPLE 16

Assume the same facts as in Example 15 except that the sale and purchase involved rental houses and not personal residences. Now, the sale of the first rental house results in a gain of $40,000 that is subject to tax. The fact that Ron reinvested the $100,000 in another rental house is of no consequence. ▼

Reconciling the different results reached in Examples 15 and 16 may seem difficult. But simply stated, the tax law applies the wherewithal to pay concept to the rollover on the gain from the sale of a personal residence. It does not do so when a rental house is involved, as Example 16 illustrates.

Mitigating the Effect of the Annual Accounting Period Concept. For purposes of effective administration of the tax law, all taxpayers must report to and settle with the Federal government at periodic intervals. Otherwise, taxpayers would remain uncertain as to their tax liabilities, and the government would have difficulty judging revenues and budgeting expenditures. The period selected for final settlement of most tax liabilities, in any event an arbitrary determination, is one year. At the close of each year, therefore, a taxpayer's position becomes complete for that particular year. Referred to as the annual accounting period concept, its effect is to divide each taxpayer's life, for tax purposes, into equal annual intervals.

The finality of the annual accounting period concept could lead to dissimilar tax treatment for taxpayers who are, from a long-range standpoint, in the same economic position.

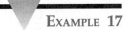

EXAMPLE 17

José and Alicia, both sole proprietors, have experienced the following results during the past four years:

Profit (or Loss)		
Year	José	Alicia
1993	$50,000	$150,000
1994	60,000	60,000
1995	70,000	70,000
1996	50,000	(50,000)

Although José and Alicia have the same profit of $230,000 over the period from 1993 to 1996, the finality of the annual accounting period concept places Alicia at a definite disadvantage for tax purposes. The net operating loss deduction offers Alicia some relief by allowing her to apply some or all of her 1996 loss to the earlier profitable years (in this case,

1993). Thus, with a net operating loss carryback, Alicia is in a position to obtain a refund for some of the taxes she paid on the $150,000 profit reported for 1993. ▼

The same reasoning used to support the deduction of net operating losses can explain the special treatment the tax law accords to excess capital losses and excess charitable contributions.[24] Carryback and carryover procedures help mitigate the effect of limiting a loss or a deduction to the accounting period in which it was realized. With such procedures, a taxpayer may be able to salvage a loss or a deduction that might otherwise be wasted.

The installment method of recognizing gain on the sale of property allows a taxpayer to spread tax consequences over the payout period.[25] The harsh effect of taxing all the gain in the year of sale is thereby avoided. The installment method can also be explained by the wherewithal to pay concept since recognition of gain is tied to the collection of the installment notes received from the sale of the property. Tax consequences, then, tend to correspond to the seller's ability to pay the tax.

Coping with Inflation. Because of the progressive nature of the income tax, a wage adjustment to compensate for inflation can increase the income tax bracket of the recipient. Known as *bracket creep*, its overall impact is an erosion of purchasing power. Congress recognized this problem and began to adjust various income tax components, such as tax brackets, standard deduction amounts, and personal and dependency exemptions, through an indexation procedure. Indexation is based upon the rise in the consumer price index over the prior year.

POLITICAL CONSIDERATIONS

A large segment of the Federal tax law is made up of statutory provisions. Since these statutes are enacted by Congress, is it any surprise that political considerations influence tax law? For purposes of discussion, the effect of political considerations on the tax law is divided into the following topics: special interest legislation, political expediency situations, and state and local government influences.

Special Interest Legislation. There is no doubt that certain provisions of the tax law can largely be explained by the political influence some pressure groups have had on Congress. Is there any other realistic reason that, for example, prepaid subscription and dues income are not taxed until earned while prepaid rents are taxed to the landlord in the year received?

An example of special interest legislation was a last minute amendment to TRA of 1986 made by former Senator Long (Louisiana) and former Representative Pickle (Austin, Texas). Under the amendment, a charitable deduction was allowed for donations to certain institutions of higher education that enabled the donor to receive choice seating at athletic events. The definition of institutions of higher education was so limited, however, that only Louisiana State University and the University of Texas were qualified recipients. Two years passed before Congress modified the tax law to neutralize this apparent preferential treatment (see Chapter 9).

---

[24] The tax treatment of these items is discussed in Chapters 6, 9, and 13.

[25] Under the installment method, each payment received by the seller represents both a recovery of capital (the nontaxable portion) and profit from the sale (the taxable portion). The tax rules governing the installment method are discussed in Chapter 15.

Special interest legislation is not necessarily to be condemned if it can be justified on economic, social, or some other utilitarian grounds. At any rate, it is an inevitable product of our political system.

Political Expediency Situations.   Various tax reform proposals rise and fall in favor with the shifting moods of the American public. That Congress is sensitive to popular feeling is an accepted fact. Therefore, certain provisions of the tax law can be explained by the political climate at the time they were enacted.

Measures that deter more affluent taxpayers from obtaining so-called preferential tax treatment have always had popular appeal and, consequently, the support of Congress. Provisions such as the alternative minimum tax, the imputed interest rules, and the limitation on the deductibility of interest on investment indebtedness can be explained on this basis.[26]

Other changes explained at least partially by political expediency include the increase in the personal and dependency exemptions and the increase in the amount of the earned income credit. One of the expressed objectives of legislation enacted in 1993 was to increase taxes levied on wealthy individuals by instituting new 36 and 39.6 percent rates on higher-income brackets.

State and Local Government Influences.   Political considerations have played a major role in the nontaxability of interest received on state and local obligations. In view of the furor that has been raised by state and local political figures every time any modification of this tax provision has been proposed, one might well regard it as next to sacred.

Somewhat less apparent has been the influence state law has had in shaping our present Federal tax law. Such was the case with community property systems. The nine states with community property systems are Louisiana, Texas, New Mexico, Arizona, California, Washington, Idaho, Nevada, and Wisconsin. The rest of the states are classified as common law jurisdictions. The difference between common law and community property systems centers around the property rights possessed by married persons. In a common law system, each spouse owns whatever he or she earns. Under a community property system, one-half of the earnings of each spouse is considered owned by the other spouse.

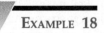

EXAMPLE 18

Al and Fran are husband and wife, and their only income is the $60,000 annual salary Al receives. If they live in New Jersey (a common law state), the $60,000 salary belongs to Al. If, however, they live in Arizona (a community property state), the $60,000 is divided equally, in terms of ownership, between Al and Fran. ▼

At one time, the tax position of the residents of community property states was so advantageous that many common law states actually adopted community property systems. Needless to say, the political pressure placed on Congress to correct the disparity in tax treatment was considerable. To a large extent this was accomplished in the Revenue Act of 1948, which extended many of the community property tax advantages to residents of common law jurisdictions.

The major advantage extended was the provision allowing married taxpayers to file joint returns and compute the tax liability as if the income had been earned one-half by each spouse. This result is automatic in a community property state, since half of the income earned by one spouse belongs to the other spouse. The income-splitting benefits of a joint return are now incorporated as part of the tax rates applicable to married taxpayers. See Chapter 2.

[26]See Chapters 3, 9, and 14.

INFLUENCE OF THE INTERNAL REVENUE SERVICE

The influence of the IRS is apparent in many areas beyond its role in issuing the administrative pronouncements that make up a considerable portion of our tax law. In its capacity as the protector of the national revenue, the IRS has been instrumental in securing the passage of much legislation designed to curtail the most flagrant tax avoidance practices (to close *tax loopholes*). In its capacity as the administrator of the tax law, the IRS has sought and obtained legislation to make its job easier (to attain administrative feasibility).

The IRS as Protector of the Revenue. Innumerable examples can be given of provisions in the tax law that stem from the direct influence of the IRS. Usually, such provisions are intended to prevent a loophole from being used to avoid the tax consequences intended by Congress. Working within the letter of existing law, ingenious taxpayers and their advisers devise techniques that accomplish indirectly what cannot be accomplished directly. As a consequence, legislation is enacted to close the loopholes that taxpayers have located and exploited. Some tax law can be explained in this fashion and is discussed in the chapters to follow.

In addition, the IRS has secured from Congress legislation of a more general nature that enables it to make adjustments based on the substance, rather than the formal construction, of what a taxpayer has done. One such provision permits the IRS to make adjustments to a taxpayer's method of accounting when the method used by the taxpayer does not clearly reflect income.[27]

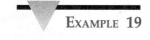

EXAMPLE 19

Tina, a cash basis taxpayer, owns and operates a pharmacy. All drugs and other items acquired for resale (e.g., cosmetics) are charged to the purchases account and written off (expensed) for tax purposes in the year of acquisition. As this procedure does not clearly reflect income, it would be appropriate for the IRS to require that Tina establish and maintain an ending inventory account. ▼

Administrative Feasibility. Some of the tax law is justified on the grounds that it simplifies the task of the IRS in collecting the revenue and administering the law. With regard to collecting the revenue, the IRS long ago realized the importance of placing taxpayers on a pay-as-you-go basis. Elaborate withholding procedures apply to wages, while the tax on other types of income may be paid at periodic intervals throughout the year. The IRS has been instrumental in convincing the courts that accrual basis taxpayers should pay taxes on prepaid income in the year received and not when earned. The approach may be contrary to generally accepted accounting principles, but it is consistent with the wherewithal to pay concept.

Of considerable aid to the IRS in collecting revenue are the numerous provisions that impose interest and penalties on taxpayers for noncompliance with the tax law. Provisions such as the penalties for failure to pay a tax or to file a return that is due, the negligence penalty for intentional disregard of rules and regulations, and various penalties for civil and criminal fraud serve as deterrents to taxpayer noncompliance.

One of the keys to an effective administration of our tax system is the audit process conducted by the IRS. To carry out this function, the IRS is aided by provisions that reduce the chance of taxpayer error or manipulation and therefore simplify the audit effort that is necessary. An increase in the amount of the standard deduction, for example, reduces the number of individual taxpayers who

---

[27] See Chapter 15.

will choose the alternative of itemizing their personal deductions.[28] With fewer deductions to check, the audit function is simplified.[29]

INFLUENCE OF THE COURTS

In addition to interpreting statutory provisions and the administrative pronouncements issued by the IRS, the Federal courts have influenced tax law in two other respects.[30] First, the courts have formulated certain judicial concepts that serve as guides in the application of various tax provisions. Second, certain key decisions have led to changes in the Internal Revenue Code.

Judicial Concepts Relating to Tax.   A leading tax concept developed by the courts deals with the interpretation of statutory tax provisions that operate to benefit taxpayers. The courts have established the rule that these relief provisions are to be narrowly construed against taxpayers if there is any doubt about their application.

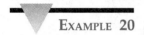

EXAMPLE 20

When a taxpayer has a gain on the sale of a personal residence, the gain is not subject to Federal income tax if the proceeds from the sale are reinvested in another principal residence. The tax law specifies a period of time in which the reinvestment must take place. The courts have held that the nontaxability of gain is a relief provision to be narrowly construed. Thus, failure to meet the replacement period requirements, even if beyond the control of the taxpayer, will cause the gain to be taxed.[31] ▼

Important in this area is the *arm's length* concept. Particularly in dealings between related parties, transactions may be tested by looking to whether the taxpayers acted in an arm's length manner. The question to be asked is: Would unrelated parties have handled the transaction in the same way?

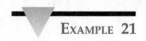

EXAMPLE 21

Rex, the sole shareholder of Silver Corporation, leases property to the corporation for a yearly rent of $6,000. To test whether the corporation should be allowed a rent deduction for this amount, the IRS and the courts will apply the arm's length concept. Would Silver Corporation have paid $6,000 a year in rent if it had leased the same property from an unrelated party (rather than from Rex)? Suppose it is determined that an unrelated third party would have paid an annual rent for the property of only $5,000. Under these circumstances, Silver Corporation will be allowed a deduction of only $5,000. The other $1,000 it paid for the use of the property represents a nondeductible dividend. Accordingly, Rex will be treated as having received rent income of $5,000 and dividend income of $1,000. ▼

Judicial Influence on Statutory Provisions.   Some court decisions have been of such consequence that Congress has incorporated them into statutory tax law. For example, many years ago the courts found that stock dividends distributed to the shareholders of a corporation were not taxable as income. This result was largely accepted by Congress, and a provision in the tax statutes now covers the issue.

On occasion, however, Congress has reacted negatively to judicial interpretations of the tax law.

---

[28] For a discussion of the standard deduction, see Chapter 2.

[29] The same justification was given by the IRS when it proposed to Congress the $100 limitation on personal casualty and theft losses. Imposition of the limitation eliminated many casualty and theft loss deductions and, as a consequence, saved the IRS considerable audit time. Later legislation, in addition to retaining

the $100 feature, limits deductible losses to those in excess of 10% of a taxpayer's adjusted gross income. See Chapter 6.

[30] A great deal of case law is devoted to ascertaining congressional intent. The courts, in effect, ask: What did Congress have in mind when it enacted a particular tax provision?

[31] These rules are discussed further in Chapter 12.

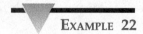

EXAMPLE 22

Nora leases unimproved real estate to Wade for 40 years. At a cost of $200,000, Wade erects a building on the land. The building is worth $100,000 when the lease terminates and Nora takes possession of the property. Does Nora have any income either when the improvements are made or when the lease terminates? In a landmark decision, a court held that Nora must recognize income of $100,000 upon the termination of the lease. ▼

Congress felt that the result reached in Example 22 was inequitable in that it was not consistent with the wherewithal to pay concept. Consequently, the tax law was amended to provide that a landlord does not recognize any income either when the improvements are made (unless made in lieu of rent) or when the lease terminates.

SUMMARY

In addition to its necessary revenue-raising objective, the Federal tax law has developed in response to several other factors:

- *Economic considerations.* The emphasis here is on tax provisions that help regulate the economy and encourage certain activities and types of businesses.
- *Social considerations.* Some tax provisions are designed to encourage (or discourage) certain socially desirable (or undesirable) practices.
- *Equity considerations.* Of principal concern in this area are tax provisions that alleviate the effect of multiple taxation, recognize the wherewithal to pay concept, mitigate the effect of the annual accounting period concept, and recognize the eroding effect of inflation.
- *Political considerations.* Of significance in this regard are tax provisions that represent special interest legislation, reflect political expediency, and exhibit the effect of state and local law.
- *Influence of the IRS.* Many tax provisions are intended to aid the IRS in the collection of revenue and the administration of the tax law.
- *Influence of the courts.* Court decisions have established a body of judicial concepts relating to tax law and have, on occasion, led Congress to enact statutory provisions to either clarify or negate their effect.

These factors explain various tax provisions and thereby help in understanding why the tax law developed to its present state. An important step involves learning to work with the tax law, which is the subject of Chapter 2.

KEY TERMS

PROBLEM MATERIALS

DISCUSSION QUESTIONS

1. Irene, a middle management employee, is offered a pay increase by her employer. As a condition of the offer, Irene must move to another state. What tax considerations should Irene weigh before making a decision on whether to accept the offer?

2. Before the passage of the Sixteenth Amendment to the Constitution, there was no income tax in the United States. True or false? Please comment.

3. Did the passage of the Sixteenth Amendment to the U.S. Constitution have any effect on the income tax imposed on corporations? Explain.

4. A tax law that was enacted in 1953 would be part of which Internal Revenue Code (i.e., 1939, 1954, or 1986)? Explain.

5. How does the pay-as-you-go procedure apply to wage earners? To persons who have income from other than wages?

6. Analyze the Federal income tax in light of Adam Smith's canons of taxation.

7. When Gull Company constructs a climate-controlled warehouse, it is very careful to keep many of the components portable. Thus, the sprinkler system is detachable, air conditioning and heating are provided by window units, and the interior walls can be removed. What is Gull trying to accomplish?

8. When Nancy's widower father moves to a nursing home, he gives his personal residence to her. Immediately thereafter, Nancy converts the residence to rental property. Nancy has noticed a significant increase in the ad valorem taxes imposed on the property since she received it from her father. What could have caused the increase?

9. Al is considering starting a new business that will require the construction of a manufacturing facility. Jefferson County, one of the geographic locations Al is considering, has proposed a tax holiday. What does this mean?

10. Matt buys a new home for $150,000, its cost of construction plus the usual profit margin for the builder. The new home is located in a neighborhood largely developed 10 years ago when the homes sold for approximately $50,000 each. Assuming the homes of his neighbors are worth (in current values) in the vicinity of $150,000, could Matt be at a disadvantage with regard to the ad valorem tax on realty?

11. Recently, one of your friends successfully challenged a reappraisal of his personal residence by the county board of real estate tax assessors. He remarks to you that this should put him "in good shape for the next five years." What does he mean?

12. A few years ago, Al retired from his job in Alaska and moved to Florida. Before he retired, Al had the certificates for all of his stock investments placed in his name, rather than leaving them in street name. Since retirement, Al continues to use his broker in Alaska to handle any investment trades. Since this arrangement is very inconvenient, why is Al handling his investment trades in this manner?

13. What is the gas guzzler tax? What purpose does it serve?

14. While out of town on business, Paul stays at a motel with an advertised room rate of $80 per night. When checking out, Paul is charged $88. What would be a plausible reason for the extra $8 Paul had to pay?

15. Earl, a resident of Wyoming (which imposes a general sales tax), goes to Montana (which does not impose a general sales tax) to purchase his automobile. Will Earl successfully avoid the Wyoming sales tax? Explain.

16. Jean lives in Smithville (the major city in Smith County). She does all of her shopping in Madisonville (the major city in Madison County). If the cities' retail outlets are comparable, why does Jean go out of her way to shop?

17. When Alaska became a major oil producer, the state repealed its state income tax. Is there any correlation between these two events? Explain.

18. A death tax has been characterized as an excise tax. Do you agree? Why or why not?

19. Explain the difference between an inheritance tax and an estate tax.

20. What was the original objective of the Federal estate tax?

21. In 1995, Horace makes a taxable gift of $250,000 upon which he pays a Federal gift tax of $70,800. In 1996, Horace makes another taxable gift of $250,000. Will the 1996 taxable gift result in the same gift tax as the 1995 gift? Why or why not?

22. How much property can Ida, a widow, give to her two married children, their spouses, and five grandchildren over a period of 10 years without making a taxable gift?

23. When married persons elect to split a gift, what tax advantages do they enjoy?

24. John, a nationally known vocalist, lives in Nevada. John's agent has been trying to convince him to go on tour to increase his record sales. John, however, refuses to perform anywhere but in Las Vegas clubs. What might explain John's attitude?

25. When a state uses a "piggyback" approach for its state income tax, what is the state doing?

26. Chee lives in a state that imposes an income tax. His Federal income tax return for 1994 is audited in 1996, and, as a result of several adjustments made by the IRS, Chee has to pay additional Federal income tax. Several months later, Chee is notified that his 1994 state income tax return is to be audited. Are these two incidents a coincidence or does a reasonable explanation exist?

27. At a cocktail party you attend in early March of 1996, you overhear a guest say, "Thank heavens my Social Security tax for this year is over with." What was the guest, the CEO of a large corporation, referring to?

28. Keith, a sole proprietor, owns and operates a grocery store. Keith's wife and his 17-year-old son work in the business and are paid wages. Will the wife and son be subject to FICA? Explain.

29. Dan, the owner and operator of a construction company that builds outdoor swimming pools, releases most of his construction personnel during the winter months. Should this hurt Dan's FUTA situation? Why or why not?

30. Compare FICA and FUTA in connection with each of the following:
    a. Incidence of taxation.
    b. Justification for taxation.
    c. Rates and base involved.

31. What is a "flat tax"? What is its major advantage?

32. One of your friends contends that a value added tax (VAT) is the same as a national sales tax. Do you agree or disagree and why?

33. Norm, the owner and operator of a cash-and-carry military surplus retail outlet, has been audited many times by the IRS. When Norm mentions this fact to his next-door neighbor, an employee with Ford Motor Company, he is somewhat surprised to learn that the neighbor has never been audited by the IRS. Is there any explanation for this apparent disparity in treatment?

34. For tax year 1988, Linda failed to file a Federal income tax return. In 1996, the IRS notifies Linda that it wants an accounting of her tax-related transactions for tax year 1988. Linda is not concerned about the request because three years have passed since the due date (April 15, 1989) of the return. Is Linda's defense based on the statute of limitations valid? Why or why not?

35. On a Federal income tax return filed five years ago, Andy inadvertently omitted a large amount of gross income.
    a. Andy seeks your advice as to whether the IRS is barred from assessing additional income tax in the event he is audited. What is your advice?
    b. Would your advice differ if you are the person who prepared the return in question? Explain.

c. Suppose Andy asks you to prepare his current year's return. Would you do so? Explain.

36. What is meant by revenue-neutral tax reform?

37. How does the tax law stimulate U.S. exports of goods and services?

38. Discuss the probable justification for the following provisions of the tax law:
    a. The election permitting certain corporations to avoid the corporate income tax.
    b. A provision that excludes from gross income certain benefits furnished to employees through accident and health plans financed by employers.
    c. Nontaxable treatment for an employee for premiums paid by an employer for group term insurance covering the life of the employee.

39. The tax law encourages private retirement plans and contributions to charitable organizations. In terms of nonrevenue objectives, what is the common justification for this special tax treatment?

40. What purpose is served by allowing a deduction for home mortgage interest and property taxes?

41. In what manner does the tax law mitigate the effect of the annual accounting period concept for a net operating loss?

42. How does the tax law cope with the impact of inflation?

CHAPTER

2

Tax Determination; Personal and Dependency Exemptions; An Overview of Property Transactions

LEARNING OBJECTIVES

After completing Chapter 2, you should be able to:

1. Understand and apply the components of the Federal income tax formula.

2. Apply the rules for arriving at personal and dependency exemptions.

3. Use the proper method for determining the tax liability.

4. Identify and work with kiddie tax situations.

5. Recognize the filing requirements and the proper filing status.

6. Possess an overview of property transactions.

7. Identify tax planning opportunities associated with the individual tax formula.

▼ OUTLINE

Individuals are subject to Federal income tax based on taxable income. This chapter explains how taxable income and the income tax of an individual taxpayer are determined.

To compute taxable income, it is necessary to understand the tax formula in Figure 2–1. Although the tax formula is rather simple, determining an individual's taxable income can be quite complex. The complexity stems from the numerous provisions that govern the determination of gross income and allowable deductions.

After computing taxable income, the appropriate rates must be applied. This requires a determination of the individual's filing status, since different rates apply for single taxpayers, married taxpayers, and heads of household. The basic tax rate structure is progressive, with rates ranging from 15 percent to 39.6 percent.[1] For

▼ **FIGURE 2–1**
Tax Formula

Income (broadly conceived)	$xx,xxx
Less: Exclusions	(x,xxx)
Gross income	$xx,xxx
Less: Deductions *for* adjusted gross income	(x,xxx)
Adjusted gross income	$xx,xxx
Less: The greater of— Total itemized deductions *or* the standard deduction	(x,xxx)
Personal and dependency exemptions	(x,xxx)
Taxable income	$xx,xxx

[1] The 1996 Tax Table was not available from the IRS at the date of publication of this text. The Tax Table for 1995 and the Tax Rate Schedules for 1995 and 1996 are reproduced in Appendix A. For quick reference, the 1995 and 1996 Tax Rate Schedules are also reproduced inside the front cover of this text.

comparison, the lowest rate structure, which was in effect in 1913–1915, ranged from 1 to 7 percent, and the highest, in effect during 1944–1945, ranged from 23 to 94 percent.

Once the individual's tax has been computed, prepayments and credits are subtracted to determine whether the taxpayer owes additional tax or is entitled to a refund.

When property is sold or otherwise disposed of, a gain or loss may result, which can affect the determination of taxable income. Although property transactions are covered in detail in Chapters 12 and 13, an understanding of certain basic concepts helps in working with some of the materials to follow. The concluding portion of this chapter furnishes an overview of property transactions, including the distinction between realized and recognized gain or loss, the classification of such gain or loss (ordinary or capital), and treatment for income tax purposes.

TAX FORMULA

1 LEARNING OBJECTIVE
Understand and apply the components of the Federal income tax formula.

Most individuals compute taxable income using the tax formula shown in Figure 2–1. Special provisions govern the computation of taxable income and the tax liability for certain minor children who have unearned income in excess of specified amounts. These provisions are discussed later in the chapter.

Before illustrating the application of the tax formula, a brief discussion of its components is helpful.

COMPONENTS OF THE TAX FORMULA

Income (Broadly Conceived). This includes all the taxpayer's income, both taxable and nontaxable. Although it is essentially equivalent to gross receipts, it does not include a return of capital or receipt of borrowed funds.

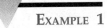
EXAMPLE 1

Dave needed money to purchase a house. He sold 5,000 shares of stock for $100,000. He had paid $40,000 for the stock. In addition, he borrowed $75,000 from a bank. Dave has taxable income of $60,000 from the sale of the stock ($100,000 selling price – $40,000 return of capital). He has no income from the $75,000 borrowed from the bank because he has an obligation to repay that amount. ▼

Exclusions. For various reasons, Congress has chosen to exclude certain types of income from the income tax base. The principal income exclusions are discussed in Chapter 4. A partial list of these exclusions is shown in Exhibit 2–1.

Gross Income. The Internal Revenue Code defines gross income broadly as "except as otherwise provided ..., all income from whatever source derived."[2] The "except as otherwise provided" refers to exclusions. Gross income includes, but is not limited to, the items in the partial list in Exhibit 2–2. It does not include unrealized gains. Gross income is discussed in Chapters 3 and 4.

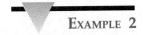
EXAMPLE 2

Beth received the following amounts during the year:

[2] § 61(a).

▼ **EXHIBIT 2–1**
Partial List of Exclusions from
Gross Income

Accident insurance proceeds	Meals and lodging (if furnished for employer's convenience)
Annuities (cost element)	Military allowances
Bequests	Minister's dwelling rental value allowance
Child support payments	
Cost-of-living allowance (for military)	Railroad retirement benefits (to a limited extent)
Damages for personal injury or sickness	Scholarship grants (to a limited extent)
Death benefits (up to $5,000)	Social Security benefits (to a limited extent)
Gifts received	
Group term life insurance, premium paid by employer (for coverage up to $50,000)	Veterans' benefits
	Welfare payments
Inheritances	Workers' compensation benefits
Interest from state and local (i.e., municipal) bonds	
Life insurance paid on death	

▼ **EXHIBIT 2–2**
Partial List of Gross Income
Items

Alimony	Group term life insurance, premium paid by employer (for coverage over $50,000)
Annuities (income element)	
Awards	Hobby income
Back pay	Interest
Bargain purchase from employer	Jury duty fees
Bonuses	Living quarters, meals (unless furnished for employer's convenience)
Breach of contract damages	
Business income	Mileage allowance
Clergy fees	Military pay (unless combat pay)
Commissions	Notary fees
Compensation for services	Partnership income
Death benefits in excess of $5,000	Pensions
Debts forgiven	Prizes
Director's fees	Professional fees
Dividends	Punitive damages (in certain cases)
Embezzled funds	Rents
Employee awards (in certain cases)	Rewards
Employee benefits (except certain fringe benefits)	Royalties
	Salaries
Estate and trust income	Severance pay
Farm income	Strike and lockout benefits
Fees	Supplemental unemployment benefits
Gains from illegal activities	Tips and gratuities
Gains from sale of property	Travel allowance (in certain cases)
Gambling winnings	Wages

Salary	$30,000
Interest on savings account	900
Gift from her aunt	10,000
Prize won in state lottery	1,000
Alimony from ex-husband	12,000
Child support from ex-husband	6,000
Damages for injury in auto accident	25,000
Increase in the value of stock held for investment	5,000

Review Exhibits 2–1 and 2–2 to determine the amount Beth must include in the computation of taxable income and the amount she may exclude. Then check your answer in footnote 3.[3] ▼

Deductions for Adjusted Gross Income. Individual taxpayers have two categories of deductions: (1) deductions *for* adjusted gross income (deductions to arrive at adjusted gross income) and (2) deductions *from* adjusted gross income.

Deductions *for* adjusted gross income (AGI) include ordinary and necessary expenses incurred in a trade or business, one-half of self-employment tax paid, alimony paid, certain payments to an Individual Retirement Account, moving expenses, forfeited interest penalty for premature withdrawal of time deposits, the capital loss deduction, and others.[4] The principal deductions *for* AGI are discussed in Chapters 5, 6, 7, 8, and 10.

Adjusted Gross Income (AGI). AGI is an important subtotal that serves as the basis for computing percentage limitations on certain itemized deductions, such as medical expenses and charitable contributions. For example, medical expenses are deductible only to the extent they exceed 7.5 percent of AGI, and charitable contribution deductions may not exceed 50 percent of AGI. These limitations might be described as a 7.5 percent *floor* under the medical expense deduction and a 50 percent *ceiling* on the charitable contribution deduction.

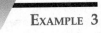

EXAMPLE 3   Keith earned a salary of $23,000 in the current tax year. He contributed $2,000 to his Individual Retirement Account (IRA) and sustained a $1,000 capital loss on the sale of Wren Corporation stock. His AGI is computed as follows:

Gross income		
Salary		$23,000
Less: Deductions *for* AGI		
IRA contribution	$2,000	
Capital loss	1,000	(3,000)
AGI		$20,000

▼

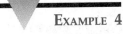

EXAMPLE 4   Assume the same facts as in Example 3, and that Keith also had medical expenses of $1,800. Medical expenses may be included in itemized deductions to the extent they exceed 7.5% of

---

[3] Beth must include $43,900 in computing taxable income ($30,000 salary + $900 interest + $1,000 lottery prize + $12,000 alimony). She can exclude $41,000 ($10,000 gift from aunt + $6,000 child support + $25,000 damages). The unrealized gain on the stock

held for investment also is not included in gross income. Such gain will be included in gross income only when it is realized upon disposition of the stock.

[4] § 62.

▼ **EXHIBIT 2–3**
Partial List of Itemized
Deductions

Medical expenses in excess of 7.5% of AGI

State and local income taxes

Real estate taxes

Personal property taxes

Interest on home mortgage

Investment interest (to a limited extent)

Charitable contributions (within specified percentage limitations)

Casualty and theft losses in excess of 10% of AGI

Miscellaneous expenses (to the extent such expenses exceed 2% of AGI)

   Union dues

   Professional dues and subscriptions

   Certain educational expenses

   Tax return preparation fee

   Investment counsel fees

   Unreimbursed employee business expenses (after 50% reduction for meals
      and entertainment)

AGI. In computing his itemized deductions, Keith may include medical expenses of $300 [$1,800 medical expenses – $1,500 (7.5% × $20,000 AGI)]. ▼

Itemized Deductions.   As a general rule, personal expenditures are disallowed as deductions in arriving at taxable income. However, Congress has chosen to allow specified personal expenses as **itemized deductions.** Such expenditures include medical expenses, certain taxes and interest, and charitable contributions.

   In addition to these personal expenses, taxpayers are allowed itemized deductions for expenses related to (1) the production or collection of income and (2) the management of property held for the production of income.[5] These expenses, sometimes referred to as *nonbusiness expenses,* differ from trade or business expenses (discussed previously). Trade or business expenses, which are deductions *for* AGI, must be incurred in connection with a trade or business. Nonbusiness expenses, on the other hand, are expenses incurred in connection with an income-producing activity that does not qualify as a trade or business. Such expenses are itemized deductions.

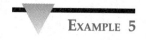

EXAMPLE 5

Leo is the owner and operator of a video game arcade. All allowable expenses he incurs in connection with the arcade business are deductions *for* AGI. In addition, Leo has an extensive portfolio of stocks and bonds. Leo's investment activity is not treated as a trade or business. All allowable expenses that Leo incurs in connection with these investments are itemized deductions. ▼

   Itemized deductions include, but are not limited to, the expenses listed in Exhibit 2–3. See Chapter 9 for a detailed discussion of itemized deductions.

Standard Deduction.   The **standard deduction,** which is set by Congress, is a specified amount that depends on the filing status of the taxpayer. The effect of

▼ **TABLE 2–1**
Basic Standard Deduction
Amounts

Filing Status	Standard Deduction Amount	
	1995	**1996**
Single	$3,900	$4,000
Married, filing jointly	6,550	6,700
Surviving spouse	6,550	6,700
Head of household	5,750	5,900
Married, filing separately	3,275	3,350

▼ **TABLE 2–2**
Amount of Each Additional
Standard Deduction

Filing Status	1995	1996
Single	$950	$1,000
Married, filing jointly	750	800
Surviving spouse	750	800
Head of household	950	1,000
Married, filing separately	750	800

the standard deduction is to exempt a taxpayer's income, up to the specified amount, from Federal income tax liability. In the past, Congress has attempted to set the tax-free amount represented by the standard deduction approximately equal to an estimated poverty level,[6] but it has not always been consistent in doing so.

The standard deduction is the sum of two components: the *basic* standard deduction and the *additional* standard deduction.[7] Table 2–1 lists the basic standard deduction allowed for taxpayers in each filing status. All taxpayers allowed a *full* standard deduction are entitled to the applicable amount listed in Table 2–1. The standard deduction amounts are subject to adjustment for inflation each year.

Certain taxpayers are not allowed to claim *any* standard deduction, and the standard deduction is *limited* for others. These provisions are discussed later in the chapter.

A taxpayer who is age 65 or over *or* blind qualifies for an *additional standard deduction* of $800 or $1,000, depending on filing status (see amounts in Table 2–2). Two additional standard deductions are allowed for a taxpayer who is age 65 or over *and* blind. The additional standard deduction provisions also apply for a qualifying spouse who is age 65 or over or blind, but a taxpayer may not claim an additional standard deduction for a dependent.

To determine whether to itemize, the taxpayer compares the *total* standard deduction (the sum of the basic standard deduction and any additional standard deductions) to total itemized deductions. Taxpayers are allowed to deduct the *greater* of itemized deductions or the standard deduction. Taxpayers whose itemized deductions are less than the standard deduction compute their taxable income using the standard deduction rather than itemizing.

[6] S.Rep. No. 92–437, 92nd Cong., 1st Sess., 1971, p. 54. Another purpose of the standard deduction was discussed in Chapter 1 under Influence of the Internal Revenue Service—Administrative Feasibility. The size of the standard deduction has a direct bearing on the number of taxpayers who are in a position to itemize deductions. Reducing the number of taxpayers who itemize also reduces the audit effort required from the IRS. Currently, about 70% of all individual taxpayers choose to use the standard deduction.

[7] § 63(c)(1).

EXAMPLE 6

Sara, who is single, is 66 years old. She had total itemized deductions of $4,800 during 1996. Her total standard deduction is $5,000 ($4,000 basic standard deduction plus $1,000 additional standard deduction). Sara should compute her taxable income for 1996 using the standard deduction ($5,000), since it exceeds her itemized deductions ($4,800). ▼

Personal and Dependency Exemptions. Exemptions are allowed for the taxpayer, for the taxpayer's spouse, and for each dependent of the taxpayer. The exemption amount is $2,500 in 1995 and $2,550 in 1996.

APPLICATION OF THE TAX FORMULA

The tax formula shown in Figure 2–1 is illustrated in Example 7.

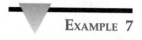

EXAMPLE 7

Grace, age 25, is single and has no dependents. She is a high school teacher and earned a $20,000 salary in 1996. Her other income consisted of a $1,000 prize won in a sweepstakes contest and $500 interest on municipal bonds received as a graduation gift in 1993. During 1996, she sustained a deductible capital loss of $1,000. Her itemized deductions are $4,200. Grace's taxable income for the year is computed as follows:

Income (broadly conceived)		
Salary		$20,000
Prize		1,000
Interest on municipal bonds		500
		$21,500
Less: Exclusion—		
Interest on municipal bonds		(500)
Gross income		$21,000
Less: Deduction *for* adjusted gross income—		
Capital loss		(1,000)
Adjusted gross income		$20,000
Less: The greater of—		
Total itemized deductions	$4,200	
or the standard deduction	.$4,000	(4,200)
Personal and dependency exemptions		
(1 × $2,550)		(2,550)
Taxable income		$13,250

▼

The structure of the individual income tax return (Form 1040, 1040A, or 1040EZ) differs somewhat from the tax formula in Figure 2–1. On the tax return, gross income generally is the starting point in computing taxable income. With few exceptions, exclusions are not reported on the tax return.

INDIVIDUALS NOT ELIGIBLE FOR THE STANDARD DEDUCTION

The following individual taxpayers are ineligible to use the standard deduction and must therefore itemize:[8]

---

[8] § 63(c)(6).

- A married individual filing a separate return where either spouse itemizes deductions.
- A nonresident alien.
- An individual filing a return for a period of less than 12 months because of a change in annual accounting period.

SPECIAL LIMITATIONS FOR INDIVIDUALS WHO CAN BE CLAIMED AS DEPENDENTS

Special rules apply to the standard deduction and personal exemption of an individual who can be claimed as a dependent on another person's tax return.

When filing his or her own tax return, a *dependent's* basic standard deduction is limited to the greater of $650 or the individual's earned income for the year.[9] However, if the individual's earned income exceeds the normal standard deduction, the standard deduction is limited to the appropriate standard deduction amount shown in Table 2–1. These limitations apply only to the basic standard deduction. A dependent who is 65 or over or blind or both is also allowed the additional standard deduction amount on his or her own return (refer to Table 2–2). These provisions are illustrated in Examples 8 through 11.

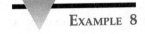

EXAMPLE 8   Susan, who is 17 years old and single, is claimed as a dependent on her parents' tax return. During 1996, she received $1,200 interest (unearned income) on a savings account. She also earned $500 from a part-time job. When Susan files her own tax return, her standard deduction is $650 (the greater of $650 or earned income of $500). ▼

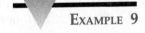

EXAMPLE 9   Assume the same facts as in Example 8, except that Susan is 67 years old and is claimed as a dependent on her son's tax return. In this case, when Susan files her own tax return, her standard deduction is $1,650 [$650 (the greater of $650 or earned income of $500) + $1,000 (the additional standard deduction allowed because Susan is 65 or over)]. ▼

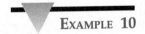

EXAMPLE 10   Peggy, who is 16 years old and single, earned $1,000 from a summer job and had no unearned income during 1996. She is claimed as a dependent on her parents' tax return. Her standard deduction is $1,000 (the greater of $650 or earned income). ▼

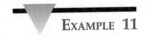

EXAMPLE 11   Jack, who is a 20-year-old, single, full-time college student, is claimed as a dependent on his parents' tax return. He worked as a musician during the summer of 1996, earning $4,100. Jack's standard deduction is $4,000 (the greater of $650 or $4,100 earned income, but limited to the $4,000 standard deduction for a single taxpayer). ▼

A taxpayer who claims an individual as a dependent is allowed to claim an exemption for the dependent. The dependent cannot claim a personal exemption on his or her own return. Based on the tax formula, Jack in Example 11 would have taxable income of $100, determined as follows:

Gross income	$ 4,100
Less: Standard deduction	(4,000)
Personal exemption	(–0–)
Taxable income	$ 100

---

[9] § 63(c)(5). The $650 amount is subject to adjustment for inflation each year. The amount was also $650 for 1995.

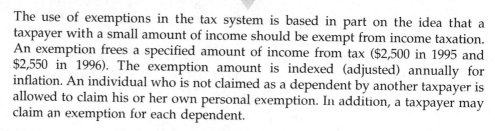

PERSONAL AND DEPENDENCY EXEMPTIONS

The use of exemptions in the tax system is based in part on the idea that a taxpayer with a small amount of income should be exempt from income taxation. An exemption frees a specified amount of income from tax ($2,500 in 1995 and $2,550 in 1996). The exemption amount is indexed (adjusted) annually for inflation. An individual who is not claimed as a dependent by another taxpayer is allowed to claim his or her own personal exemption. In addition, a taxpayer may claim an exemption for each dependent.

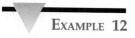

2 LEARNING OBJECTIVE
Apply the rules for arriving at personal and dependency exemptions.

EXAMPLE 12

Bonnie, who is single, supports her mother and father, who have no income of their own, and claims them as dependents on her tax return. Bonnie may claim a personal exemption for herself plus an exemption for each dependent. On her 1996 tax return, Bonnie may deduct $7,650 for exemptions ($2,550 per exemption × 3 exemptions). ▼

PERSONAL EXEMPTIONS

The Code provides a **personal exemption** for the taxpayer and an exemption for the spouse if a joint return is filed. However, when separate returns are filed, a married taxpayer cannot claim an exemption for his or her spouse *unless* the spouse has no gross income and is not claimed as the dependent of another taxpayer.

The determination of marital status generally is made at the end of the taxable year, except when a spouse dies during the year. Spouses who enter into a legal separation under a decree of divorce or separate maintenance before the end of the year are considered to be unmarried at the end of the taxable year. The following table illustrates the effect of death or divorce upon marital status:

	Marital Status for 1996
• Walt is the widower of Helen who died on January 3, 1996.	Walt and Helen are considered to be married for purposes of filing the 1996 return.
• Bill and Jane entered into a divorce decree that is effective on December 31, 1996.	Bill and Jane are considered to be unmarried for purposes of filing the 1996 return.

DEPENDENCY EXEMPTIONS

As indicated in Example 12, the Code allows a taxpayer to claim a dependency exemption for each eligible individual. A **dependency exemption** may be claimed for each individual for whom the following five tests are met:

- Support.
- Relationship or member of the household.
- Gross income.
- Joint return.
- Citizenship or residency.

A person who dies during the year can still be claimed as a dependent if all of the tests are met. In such a case, no proration is necessary, and the full amount of the exemption is allowed.

Support Test.   Over one-half of the support of the individual must be furnished by the taxpayer. Support includes food, shelter, clothing, medical and dental care, education, etc. However, a scholarship received by a student is not included for purposes of computing whether the taxpayer furnished more than half of the child's support.[10]

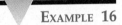

EXAMPLE 13   Hal contributed $3,400 (consisting of food, clothing, and medical care) toward the support of his son, Sam, who earned $1,500 from a part-time job and received a $2,000 scholarship to attend a local university. Assuming that the other dependency tests are met, Hal can claim Sam as a dependent since he has contributed more than half of Sam's support. The $2,000 scholarship is not included as support for purposes of this test. ▼

If the individual does not spend funds that have been received from any source, the unexpended amounts are not counted for purposes of the support test.

EXAMPLE 14   Emily contributed $3,000 to her father's support during the year. In addition, her father received $2,400 in Social Security benefits, $200 of interest, and wages of $600. Her father deposited the Social Security benefits, interest, and wages in his own savings account and did not use any of the funds for his support. Thus, the Social Security benefits, interest, and wages are not considered as support provided by Emily's father. Emily may claim her father as a dependent if the other tests are met. ▼

Capital expenditures for items such as furniture, appliances, and automobiles are included in total support if the item does, in fact, constitute support.[11]

EXAMPLE 15   Norm purchased a television set costing $150 and gave it to his minor daughter. The television set was placed in the child's bedroom and was used exclusively by her. Norm should include the cost of the television set in determining the support of his daughter. ▼

EXAMPLE 16   Mark paid $6,000 for an automobile that was titled and registered in his name. Mark's minor son is permitted to use the automobile equally with Mark. Since Mark did not give the automobile to his son, the $6,000 cost is not includible as a support item. However, out-of-pocket operating expenses incurred by Mark for the benefit of his son are includible as support. ▼

ETHICAL CONSIDERATIONS   **Claiming a Dependent**

Martha is a widow and lives with her only son, Roland, and his family. Martha's only income consists of $70,000 in interest from tax-exempt bonds. She invests all of the income in stocks in her name. The stocks do not pay dividends. Martha's will provides that all of her property is to pass to Roland upon her death. Because of this expectation, Roland provides all of his mother's support. On his return, Roland claims a dependency exemption for his mother.

Is this proper procedure? After all, Martha was in a position to provide all of her support had she chosen to do so.

---

[10] Reg. § 1.152–1(c).
[11] Rev.Rul. 57–344, 1957–2 C.B. 112; Rev.Rul. 58–419, 1958–2 C.B. 57.

One exception to the support test involves a **multiple support agreement.** A multiple support agreement permits one of a group of taxpayers who furnish more than half of the support of an individual to claim a dependency exemption for that individual even if no one person provides more than 50 percent of the support.[12] Any person who contributed *more than 10 percent* of the support is entitled to claim the exemption if each person in the group who contributed more than 10 percent files a written consent. This provision frequently enables one of the children of aged dependent parents to claim an exemption when none of the children meets the 50 percent support test. Each person who is a party to the multiple support agreement must meet all other requirements (except the support requirement) for claiming the exemption. A person who does not meet the relationship or member-of-household requirement, for instance, cannot claim the dependency exemption under a multiple support agreement. It does not matter if he or she contributes more than 10 percent of the individual's support.

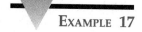 **EXAMPLE 17**

Wanda, who resides with her son, Adam, received $6,000 from various sources during 1996. This constituted her entire support for the year. She received support from the following:

	Amount	Percentage of Total
Adam, a son	$2,880	48
Bob, a son	600	10
Carol, a daughter	1,800	30
Diane, a friend	720	12
	$6,000	100

If Adam and Carol file a multiple support agreement, either may claim the dependency exemption for Wanda. Bob may not claim Wanda because he did not contribute more than 10% of her support. Bob's consent is not required in order for Adam and Carol to file a multiple support agreement. Diane does not meet the relationship or member-of-household test and cannot be a party to the agreement. The decision as to who claims Wanda rests with Adam and Carol. It is possible for Carol to claim Wanda, even though Adam furnished more of Wanda's support. ▼

Each person who qualifies under the more-than-10 percent rule (except for the person claiming the exemption) must complete Form 2120 (Multiple Support Declaration) waiving the exemption. The person claiming the exemption must attach all Forms 2120 to his or her own return. Form 2120 is reproduced in Appendix B.

A second exception to the 50 percent support requirement can occur for a child of parents who are divorced or separated under a decree of separate maintenance. For decrees executed after 1984, the custodial parent is allowed to claim the exemption unless that parent agrees in writing not to claim a dependency exemption for the child.[13] Thus, claiming the exemption is dependent on whether or not a written agreement exists, *not* on meeting the support test.

[12] § 152(c).

[13] § 152(e).

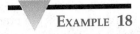

EXAMPLE 18   Ira and Rita obtain a divorce decree in 1989. In 1996, their two children are in Rita's custody. Ira contributed over half of the support for each child. In the absence of a written agreement on the dependency exemptions, Rita (the custodial parent) is entitled to the exemptions in 1996. However, Ira may claim the exemptions if Rita agrees in writing. ▼

For the noncustodial parent to claim the exemption, the custodial parent must complete Form 8332 (Release of Claim to Exemption for Child of Divorced or Separated Parents). The release can apply to a single year, a number of specified years, or all future years. The noncustodial parent must attach a copy of Form 8332 to his or her return.

ETHICAL CONSIDERATIONS   **Bribery to Obtain Dependency Exemptions**

W ill and Nora were divorced in 1993. Under the divorce decree, Will is to pay alimony and child support, and Nora has custody of their two children.

Although Will has not contributed more than 50 percent of the children's support, he would like to claim them as dependents for tax year 1996. Upon being contacted by Will, Nora agrees to waive the exemptions if she receives an extra $500 in cash. Will makes the payment, and Nora signs Form 8332 for 1996.

May Will claim the children as dependents? Have the parties acted improperly?

Relationship or Member-of-the-Household Test.   To be claimed as a dependent, an individual must be either a relative of the taxpayer or a member of the taxpayer's household. The Code contains a detailed listing of the various blood and marriage relationships that qualify. Note, however, that the relationship test is met if the individual is a relative of either spouse. Once established by marriage, a relationship continues regardless of subsequent changes in marital status.

The following individuals may be claimed as dependents of the taxpayer if the other tests for dependency are met:[14]

- A son or daughter of the taxpayer or a descendant of either, such as a grandchild.
- A stepson or stepdaughter of the taxpayer.
- A brother, sister, stepbrother, or stepsister of the taxpayer.
- The father or mother of the taxpayer or an ancestor of either, such as a grandparent.
- A stepfather or stepmother of the taxpayer.
- A nephew or niece of the taxpayer.
- An uncle or aunt of the taxpayer.
- A son-in-law, daughter-in-law, father-in-law, mother-in-law, brother-in-law, or sister-in-law of the taxpayer.

---

[14] § 152(a). However, under § 152(b)(5), a taxpayer may not claim someone who is a member of his or her household as a dependent if their relationship is in violation of local law. For example, the dependency exemption was denied because the taxpayer's rela- tionship to the person claimed as a dependent constituted *cohabitation*, a crime under applicable state law. *Cassius L. Peacock, III*, 37 TCM 177, T.C.Memo. 1978–30.

• An individual who, for the entire taxable year of the taxpayer, has as his or her principal place of abode the home of the taxpayer and is a member of the taxpayer's household. This does not include an individual who, at any time during the taxable year, was the spouse of the taxpayer.

The following rules are also prescribed in the Code:[15]

• A legally adopted child is treated as a natural child.
• A foster child qualifies if the child's principal place of abode is the taxpayer's household.

Gross Income Test.   The dependent's gross income must be less than the exemption amount ($2,550 in 1996).[16] The gross income test is measured by income that is taxable. In the case of scholarships, for example, it excludes the nontaxable portion (e.g., amounts received for books and tuition) but includes the taxable portion (e.g., amounts received for room and board).

A parent may claim a dependency exemption for his or her child, even when the child's gross income exceeds $2,550, if the parent provided over half of the child's support and the child, at year-end, is under age 19 or is a full-time student under age 24. If the parent claims a dependency exemption, the dependent child may not claim a personal exemption on his or her own income tax return.

A child is defined as a son, stepson, daughter, stepdaughter, adopted son, or adopted daughter and may include a foster child.[17] For the child to qualify as a student for purposes of the dependency exemption, he or she must be a full-time student at an educational institution during some part of five calendar months of the year.[18] This exception to the gross income test for dependent children who are under age 19 or full-time students under age 24 permits a child or college student to earn money from part-time or summer jobs without penalizing the parent with the loss of the dependency exemption.

Joint Return Test.   If a dependent is married, the supporting taxpayer (e.g., the parent of a married child) generally is not permitted a dependency exemption if the married individual files a joint return with his or her spouse.[19] The joint return rule does not apply, however, if the following conditions are met:

• The reason for filing is to claim a refund for tax withheld.
• No tax liability would exist for either spouse on separate returns.
• Neither spouse is required to file a return.

See Table 2–4 later in the chapter and the related discussion concerning income level requirements for filing a return.

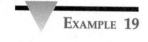
EXAMPLE 19

Paul provides over half of the support of his son Quinn. He also provides over half of the support of Vera, who is Quinn's wife. During the year, both Quinn and Vera had part-time jobs. In order to recover the taxes withheld, they file a joint return. If Quinn and Vera are not required to file a return, Paul is allowed to claim both as dependents. ▼

[15] § 152(b)(2).
[16] § 151(c)(1).
[17] Reg. § 1.151–3(a).

[18] Reg. §§ 1.151–3(b) and (c).
[19] § 151(c)(2).

Citizenship or Residency Test. To be a dependent, the individual must be either a U.S. citizen, a U.S. resident, or a resident of Canada or Mexico for some part of the calendar year in which the taxpayer's tax year begins.

Phase-out of Exemptions. Several provisions of the tax law are intended to increase the tax liability of more affluent taxpayers who might otherwise enjoy some benefit from having some of their taxable income subject to the lower income tax brackets (e.g., 15 percent, 28 percent). One such provision phases out personal and dependency exemptions as AGI exceeds specified threshold amounts. For 1995 and 1996, the phase-out *begins* at the following threshold amounts:

	1995	1996
Joint returns/Surviving spouse	$172,050	$176,950
Head of household	143,350	147,450
Single	114,700	117,950
Married, filing separately	86,025	88,475

These threshold amounts are indexed for inflation each year.

Exemptions are phased out by 2 percent for each $2,500 (or fraction thereof) by which the taxpayer's AGI exceeds the threshold amounts. For a married taxpayer filing separately, the phase-out is 2 percent for each $1,250 or fraction thereof.

The allowable exemption amount can be determined with the following steps:

1. AGI – threshold amount = excess amount
2. Excess amount ÷ $2,500 = reduction factor [rounded up to the next whole increment (e.g., 18.1 = 19)] × 2 = phase-out percentage
3. Phase-out percentage (from step 2) × exemption amount = amount of exemptions phased out
4. Exemption amounts – phase-out amount = allowable exemption deduction

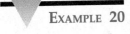

EXAMPLE 20

Frederico is married but files a separate return. His AGI is $108,475. He is entitled to one personal exemption.

1. $108,475 – $88,475 = $20,000 excess amount
2. [($20,000 ÷ $1,250) × 2] = 32% (phase-out percentage)
3. 32% × $2,550 = $816 amount of exemption phased out
4. $2,550 – $816 = $1,734 allowable exemption deduction ▼

Note that the exemption amount is completely phased out when the taxpayer's AGI exceeds the threshold amount by more than $122,500 ($61,250 for a married taxpayer filing a separate return), calculated as follows:

$122,501 ÷ $2,500 = 49.0004, rounded to 50 and multiplied by 2 = 100%
(phase-out percentage)

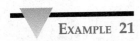

EXAMPLE 21

Bill and Isabella file a joint return claiming two personal exemptions and one dependency exemption for their child. Their AGI equals $300,950.

$300,950 – $176,950 = $124,000 excess amount

Since the excess amount exceeds $122,500, the exemptions are completely phased out. ▼

TAX DETERMINATION

TAX TABLE METHOD

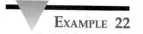

3   LEARNING OBJECTIVE
Use the proper method for
determining the tax liability.

Most taxpayers compute their tax using the **Tax Table.** Eligible taxpayers compute taxable income (as shown in Figure 2–1) and *must* determine their tax by reference to the Tax Table. The following taxpayers, however, may not use the Tax Table method:

- An individual who files a short period return (see Chapter 15).
- Individuals whose taxable income exceeds the maximum (ceiling) amount in the Tax Table. The 1996 Tax Table applies to taxable income below $100,000 for Form 1040.
- An estate or trust.

The 1996 Tax Table was not available at the date of publication of this text. Therefore, the 1995 Tax Table will be used to illustrate the tax computation using the Tax Table method.

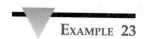

EXAMPLE 22

Pedro, a single taxpayer, is eligible to use the Tax Table. For 1995, he had taxable income of $25,025. To determine Pedro's tax using the Tax Table (see Appendix A), find the $25,000 to $25,050 income line. The first column to the right of the taxable income column is for single taxpayers. Pedro's tax for 1995 is $3,972. ▼

TAX RATE SCHEDULE METHOD

The **Tax Rate Schedules** contain rates of 15, 28, 31, 36, and 39.6 percent. Separate schedules are provided for the following filing statuses: single, married filing jointly, married filing separately, and head of household. The rate schedules for 1995 and 1996 are reproduced inside the front cover of this text and also in Appendix A.

    The rate schedules are adjusted for inflation each year. Comparison of the 1995 and 1996 schedules for single taxpayers shows that the top amount to which the 15 percent bracket applies rose from $23,350 in 1995 to $24,000 in 1996. Thus, inflation allowed $650 ($24,000 – $23,350) more taxable income to be subject to the lowest 15 percent rate.

    The 1996 rate schedule for single taxpayers is reproduced in Table 2–3. This schedule is used to illustrate the tax computations in Examples 23, 24, and 25.

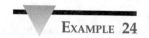

EXAMPLE 23

Pat is single and had $18,000 of taxable income in 1996. His tax is $2,700 ($18,000 × 15%). ▼

    Several terms are used to describe tax rates. The rates in the Tax Rate Schedules are often referred to as *statutory* (or nominal) rates. The *marginal* rate is the highest rate that is applied in the tax computation for a particular taxpayer. In Example 23, the statutory rate and the marginal rate are both 15 percent.

EXAMPLE 24

Chris is single and had taxable income of $41,450 in 1996. Her tax is $8,486 [$3,600 + 28%($41,450 – $24,000)]. ▼

    The *average* rate is equal to the tax liability divided by taxable income. In Example 24, Chris had statutory rates of 15 percent and 28 percent, and a marginal rate of 28 percent. Chris's average rate was 20.5 percent ($8,486 tax liability ÷ $41,450 taxable income).

▼ TABLE 2–3

1996 Tax Rate Schedule for
Single Taxpayers

If Taxable Income Is		The Tax Is:	Of the Amount Over
Over	**But Not Over**		
$ –0–	$ 24,000	15%	$ –0–
24,000	58,150	$ 3,600.00 + 28%	24,000
58,150	121,300	13,162.00 + 31%	58,150
121,300	263,750	32,738.50 + 36%	121,300
263,750		84,020.50 + 39.6%	263,750

Note that $3,600, which is the starting point in the tax computation in Example 24, is 15 percent of the $24,000 taxable income in the first bracket. Income in excess of $24,000 is taxed at a 28 percent rate. This reflects the *progressive* (or graduated) rate structure on which the U.S. income tax system is based. A tax is progressive if a higher rate of tax applies as the tax base increases.

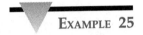

EXAMPLE 25

Carl is single and had taxable income of $81,900 in 1996. His tax is $20,524.50 [$13,162 + 31%($81,900 – $58,150)]. Note that the effect of this computation is to tax part of Carl's income at 15%, part at 28%, and part at 31%. An alternative computational method provides a clearer illustration of the progressive rate structure:

Tax on $24,000 at 15%	$ 3,600.00
Tax on $58,150 – $24,000 at 28%	9,562.00
Tax on $81,900 – $58,150 at 31%	7,362.50
Total	$20,524.50

▼

A special computation limits the effective tax rate on long-term capital gain. The beneficial tax treatment of long-term capital gain is discussed in detail in Chapter 13.

COMPUTATION OF NET TAXES PAYABLE OR REFUND DUE

The pay-as-you-go feature of the Federal income tax system requires payment of all or part of the taxpayer's income tax liability during the year. These payments take the form of Federal income tax withheld by employers or estimated tax paid by the taxpayer or both.[20] The payments are applied against the tax from the Tax Table or Tax Rate Schedules to determine whether the taxpayer will get a refund or pay additional tax.

Employers are required to withhold income tax on compensation paid to their employees and to pay this tax over to the government. The employer notifies the employee of the amount of income tax withheld on Form W–2 (Wage and Tax Statement). The employee should receive this form by January 31 after the year in which the income tax is withheld.

If taxpayers receive income that is not subject to withholding or income from which not enough tax is withheld, they must pay estimated tax. These individuals must file Form 1040–ES (Estimated Tax for Individuals) and pay in quarterly installments the income tax and self-employment tax estimated to be due.

---

[20] § 3402 for withholding; § 6654 for estimated payments.

The income tax from the Tax Table or the Tax Rate Schedules is reduced first by the individual's tax credits. There is an important distinction between tax credits and tax deductions. Tax credits reduce the tax liability dollar-for-dollar. Tax deductions reduce taxable income on which the tax liability is based.

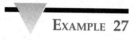

EXAMPLE 26

Gail is a taxpayer in the 28% tax bracket. As a result of incurring $1,000 in child care expenses (see Chapter 11 for details), she is entitled to a $200 child care credit ($1,000 child care expenses × 20% credit rate). She also contributed $1,000 to the American Cancer Society and included this amount in her itemized deductions. The child care credit results in a $200 reduction of Gail's tax liability for the year. The contribution to the American Cancer Society reduces taxable income by $1,000 and results in a $280 reduction in Gail's tax liability ($1,000 reduction in taxable income × 28% tax rate). ▼

Tax credits are discussed in Chapter 11. The following are several of the more common credits:

• Earned income credit.
• Credit for child and dependent care expenses.
• Credit for the elderly.
• Foreign tax credit.

EXAMPLE 27

Kelly, age 30, is a head of household with two dependents. During 1996, Kelly had the following: taxable income, $30,000; income tax withheld, $3,950; estimated tax payments, $600; and credit for child care expenses, $200. Kelly's net tax payable is computed as follows (refund due):

Income tax (from 1996 Tax Rate Schedule, Appendix A)		$ 4,500
Less: Tax credits and prepayments—		
Credit for child care expenses	$ 200	
Income tax withheld	3,950	
Estimated tax payments	600	(4,750)
Net taxes payable or (refund due if negative)		$ (250)

▼

UNEARNED INCOME OF CHILDREN UNDER AGE 14 TAXED AT PARENTS' RATE

4 **LEARNING OBJECTIVE**
Identify and work with kiddie tax situations.

Before the Tax Reform Act (TRA) of 1986, a dependent child could claim an exemption on his or her own return even if claimed as a dependent by the parents. This enabled a parent to shift investment income (such as interest and dividends) to a child by transferring ownership of the assets producing the income. The child would pay no tax on the income to the extent that it was sheltered by the child's exemption.

For pre-1987 years, an additional tax motivation existed for shifting income from parents to children. Although a child's unearned income in excess of the exemption amount was subject to tax, it was taxed at the child's rate, rather than the parents' rate.

To reduce the tax savings that result from shifting income from parents to children, the net **unearned income** (commonly called investment income) of certain minor children is taxed as if it were the parents' income.[21] Unearned income includes such income as taxable interest, dividends, capital gains, rents,

---
[21]§ 1(g).

royalties, pension and annuity income, and income (other than earned income) received as the beneficiary of a trust. This provision, commonly referred to as the **kiddie tax,** applies to any child for any taxable year if the child has not reached age 14 by the close of the taxable year, has at least one living parent, and has unearned income of more than $1,300. The *kiddie tax* provision does not apply to a child age 14 or older. However, the limitation on the use of the standard deduction and the unavailability of the personal exemption do apply to such a child as long as he or she is eligible to be claimed as a dependent by a parent.

The term *parent* is defined in the Senate Finance Committee Report as a parent or stepparent of the child. No statutory definition exists for the term.

Net Unearned Income.   Net unearned income of a dependent child is computed as follows:

Unearned income

Less: $650

Less: The greater of

- $650 of the standard deduction *or*
- The amount of allowable itemized deductions directly connected with the production of the unearned income

Equals: Net unearned income

If net unearned income is zero (or negative), the child's tax is computed without using the parent's rate. If the amount of net unearned income (regardless of source) is positive, the net unearned income will be taxed at the parent's rate. The $650 amounts in the preceding formula are subject to adjustment for inflation each year (refer to footnote 9).

Tax Determination.   If a child under age 14 has net unearned income, there are two options for computing the tax on the income. A separate return may be filed for the child, or the parents may elect to report the child's income on their own return. If a separate return is filed for the child, the tax on net unearned income (referred to as the *allocable parental tax*) is computed as though the income had been included on the parents' return. Form 8615 (reproduced in Appendix B) is used to compute the tax. The steps required in this computation are illustrated below.

EXAMPLE 28   Olaf and Olga have a child, Hans (age 10). In 1996, Hans received $2,800 of interest and dividend income and paid investment-related fees of $200. Olaf and Olga had $69,450 of taxable income, not including their child's investment income. Olaf and Olga do not make the parental election.

1. Determine Hans's net unearned income

Gross income (unearned)	$ 2,800
Less: $650	(650)
Less: The greater of	
• $650 or	
• Investment expense	(650)
Equals: Net unearned income	$ 1,500

2. Determine allocable parental tax

Parents' taxable income	$69,450
Plus: Hans's net unearned income	1,500
Equals: Revised taxable income	$70,950

Tax on revised taxable income	$ 14,653
Less: Tax on parents' taxable income	(14,233)
Allocable parental tax	$ 420

3. Determine Hans's nonparental source tax

Hans's AGI	$ 2,800
Less: Standard deduction	(650)
Less: Personal exemption	(–0–)
Equals: Taxable income	$ 2,150
Less: Net unearned income	(1,500)
Nonparental source taxable income	$ 650
Equals: Tax ($650 × 15% rate)	$ 98

4. Determine Hans's total tax liability

Nonparental source tax (step 3)	$ 98
Allocable parental tax (step 2)	420
Total tax	$ 518

▼

Election to Claim Certain Unearned Income on Parent's Return.   If a child under age 14 is required to file a tax return and meets all of the following requirements, the parent may elect to report the child's unearned income that exceeds $1,000 on the parent's own tax return:

- Gross income is from interest and dividends only.
- Gross income is less than $5,000.
- No estimated tax has been paid in the name and Social Security number of the child, and the child is not subject to backup withholding.

If the parental election is made, the child is treated as having no gross income and then is not required to file a tax return.

The parent(s) must also pay an additional tax equal to the smaller of $75 or 15 percent of the child's gross income over $500. Parents who have substantial itemized deductions based on AGI (see Chapter 9) may find that making the parental election increases total taxes for the family unit. Taxes should be calculated both with the parental election and without it to determine the appropriate choice.

Other Provisions.   If parents have more than one child subject to the tax on net unearned income, the tax for the children is computed as shown in Example 28 and then allocated to the children based on their relative amounts of income. For children of divorced parents, the taxable income of the custodial parent is used to determine the allocable parental tax. This parent is the one who may elect to report the child's unearned income. For married individuals filing separate returns, the individual with the greater taxable income is the applicable parent.

FILING CONSIDERATIONS

5 LEARNING OBJECTIVE
Recognize the filing requirements and the proper filing status.

Under the category of filing considerations, the following questions need to be resolved:

- Is the taxpayer required to file an income tax return?
- If so, which form should be used?

▼ **TABLE 2–4**
Filing Levels

Filing Status	1995 Gross Income	1996 Gross Income
Single		
Under 65 and not blind	$ 6,400	$ 6,550
Under 65 and blind	6,400	6,550
65 or older	7,350	7,550
Married, filing joint return		
Both spouses under 65 and neither blind	$11,550	$11,800
Both spouses under 65 and one or both spouses blind	11,550	11,800
One spouse 65 or older	12,300	12,600
Both spouses 65 or older	13,050	13,400
Married, filing separate return		
All—whether 65 or older or blind	$ 2,500	$ 2,550
Head of household		
Under 65 and not blind	$ 8,250	$ 8,450
Under 65 and blind	8,250	8,450
65 or older	9,200	9,450
Qualifying widow(er)		
Under 65 and not blind	$ 9,050	$ 9,250
Under 65 and blind	9,050	9,250
65 or older	9,800	10,050

- When and how should the return be filed?
- In computing the tax liability, which column of the Tax Table or which Tax Rate Schedule should be used?

The first three questions are discussed under Filing Requirements, and the last is treated under Filing Status.

FILING REQUIREMENTS

General Rules. An individual must file a tax return if certain minimum amounts of gross income have been received. The general rule is that a tax return is required for every individual who has gross income that equals or exceeds the sum of the exemption amount plus the applicable standard deduction.[22] For example, a single taxpayer under age 65 must file a tax return in 1996 if gross income equals or exceeds $6,550 ($2,550 exemption plus $4,000 standard deduction). Table 2–4 lists the income levels[23] that require tax returns under the general rule and under certain special rules.

The additional standard deduction for being age 65 or older is considered in determining the gross income filing requirements. For example, note in Table 2–4 that the 1996 filing requirement for a single taxpayer age 65 or older is $7,550 ($4,000 basic standard deduction + $1,000 additional standard deduction + $2,550 exemption). However, the additional standard deduction for blindness is not taken

---

[22] The gross income amounts for determining whether a tax return must be filed are adjusted for inflation each year.

[23] § 6012(a)(1).

into account. The 1996 filing requirement for a single taxpayer under age 65 and blind is $6,550 ($4,000 basic standard deduction + $2,550 exemption).

A self-employed individual with net earnings of $400 or more from a business or profession must file a tax return regardless of the amount of gross income.

Even though an individual has gross income below the filing level amounts and therefore does not owe any tax, he or she must file a return to obtain a tax refund of amounts withheld. A return is also necessary to obtain the benefits of the earned income credit allowed to taxpayers with little or no tax liability. Chapter 11 discusses the earned income credit.

Filing Requirements for Dependents.   Computation of the gross income filing requirement for an individual who can be claimed as a dependent on another person's tax return is subject to more complex rules. Such an individual must file a return if he or she has *either* of the following:

- Earned income only and gross income that is more than the total standard deduction (including any additional standard deduction) that the individual is allowed for the year.
- Unearned income only and gross income of more than $650 plus any additional standard deduction that the individual is allowed for the year.
- Both earned and unearned income and gross income of more than the larger of earned income (but limited to the applicable basic standard deduction) or $650, plus any additional standard deduction that the individual is allowed for the year.

Thus, the filing requirement for a dependent who has no unearned income is the total of the *basic* standard deduction plus any *additional* standard deduction, which includes both the additional deduction for blindness and the deduction for being age 65 or older. For example, the 1996 filing requirement for a single dependent who is under 65 and not blind is $4,000, the amount of the basic standard deduction for 1996. The filing requirement for a single dependent under 65 and blind is $5,000 ($4,000 basic standard deduction + $1,000 additional standard deduction).

Selecting the Proper Form.   The 1996 tax forms had not been released at the date of publication of this text. The following comments apply to 1995 forms. It is possible that some provisions will change for the 1996 forms.

Individual taxpayers file a return on either Form 1040 (the long form), Form 1040A (the short form), or Form 1040EZ. Taxpayers who cannot use either Form 1040EZ or Form 1040A must use Form 1040. These forms are reproduced in Appendix B. Examine the forms to determine which form is appropriate for a particular taxpayer.

When and Where to File.   Tax returns of individuals are due on or before the fifteenth day of the fourth month following the close of the tax year. For the calendar year taxpayer, the usual filing date is on or before April 15 of the following year.[24] When the due date falls on a Saturday, Sunday, or legal holiday, the last day for filing falls on the next business day. If the return is mailed to the proper address with sufficient postage and is postmarked on or before the due date, it is deemed timely filed.

If a taxpayer is unable to file the return by the specified due date, a four-month extension of time can be obtained by filing Form 4868 (Application for Automatic Extension of Time to File U.S. Individual Income Tax Return).[25] Further extensions may be granted by the IRS upon a showing of good cause by the taxpayer. For this purpose, Form 2688 (Application for Extension of Time to File U.S. Individual Income Tax Return) should be used. An extension of more than six months will not be granted if the taxpayer is in the United States.

Although obtaining an extension excuses a taxpayer from a penalty for failure to file, it does not insulate against the penalty for failure to pay.[26] If more tax is owed, the filing of Form 4868 should be accompanied by an additional remittance to cover the balance due.

The return should be sent or delivered to the Regional Service Center of the IRS for the area where the taxpayer lives.[27]

If an individual taxpayer needs to file an amended return (e.g., because of a failure to report income or to claim a deduction or tax credit), Form 1040X is filed. The form generally must be filed within three years of the filing date of the original return or within two years from the time the tax was paid, whichever is later.

FILING STATUS

The amount of tax will vary considerably depending on which Tax Rate Schedule is used. This is illustrated in the following example.

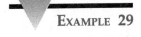

EXAMPLE 29

The following amounts of tax (rounded to the nearest dollar) are computed using the 1996 Tax Rate Schedules. The taxpayer (or taxpayers in the case of a joint return) is assumed to have $40,000 of taxable income (see Appendix A).

Filing Status	Amount of Tax
Single	$8,080
Married, filing joint return	6,000
Married, filing separate return	8,591
Head of household	7,021

▼

---

[24] § 6072(a).
[25] Reg. § 1.6081–4.
[26] For an explanation of these penalties, refer to Chapter 1.

[27] The Regional Service Centers and the geographical area each covers can be found in *Your Federal Income Tax*, IRS Publication 17 for 1995.

Rates for Single Taxpayers. A taxpayer who is unmarried or separated from his or her spouse by a decree of divorce or separate maintenance and does not qualify for another filing status must use the rates for single taxpayers. Marital status is determined as of the last day of the tax year, except when a spouse dies during the year. In that case, marital status is determined as of the date of death. State law governs whether a taxpayer is considered married, divorced, or legally separated.

Under a special relief provision, however, married persons who live apart may be able to qualify as single. Married taxpayers who are considered single under the *abandoned spouse rules* are allowed to use the head of household rates. See the discussion of this filing status under Abandoned Spouse Rules later in the chapter.

Rates for Married Individuals. The joint return [Tax Rate Schedule Y, Code § 1(a)] was originally enacted in 1948 to establish equity between married taxpayers in common law states and those in community property states. Before the joint return rates were enacted, taxpayers in community property states were in an advantageous position relative to taxpayers in common law states because they could split their income. For instance, if one spouse earned $100,000 and the other spouse was not employed, each spouse could report $50,000 of income. Splitting the income in this manner caused the total income to be subject to lower marginal tax rates. Each spouse would start at the bottom of the rate structure.

Taxpayers in common law states did not have this income-splitting option, so their taxable income was subject to higher marginal rates. This inconsistency in treatment was remedied by the joint return provisions. The progressive rates in the joint return Tax Rate Schedule are constructed based on the assumption that income is earned equally by the two spouses.

If married individuals elect to file separate returns, each reports only his or her own income, exemptions, deductions, and credits, and each must use the Tax Rate Schedule applicable to married taxpayers filing separately. It is generally advantageous for married individuals to file a joint return, since the combined amount of tax is lower. However, special circumstances (e.g., significant medical expenses incurred by one spouse subject to the 7.5 percent limitation) may warrant the election to file separate returns. It may be necessary to compute the tax under both assumptions to determine the most advantageous filing status.

When Congress enacted the rate structure available to those filing joint returns, it intended to favor married taxpayers. In certain situations, however, the parties would incur less tax if they were not married and filed separate returns. The additional tax that a joint return can cause, commonly called the **marriage penalty,** can develop when *both* spouses have larger taxable incomes.

EXAMPLE 30

John and Betty are employed, and each earns taxable income of $55,000. If they *are not married* and file separate returns, each has a tax liability of $12,280, or a total of $24,560 ($12,280 × 2). If they are married to each other, the filing of a joint return produces a tax of $25,980 on taxable income of $110,000 ($55,000 + $55,000). Thus, being married results in $1,420 ($25,980 − $24,560) more tax! ▼

Although some have suggested changes to lessen the impact of the marriage penalty, any remedy is apt to make the tax law more complex.

Besides the marriage penalty, a joint return can lead to another problem. This is the joint and several liability that results in the event additional taxes are due. As the Tax in the News on page 2-26 shows, a divorce could result in an ex-spouse getting hit for the full delinquency.

TAX IN THE NEWS

LOW-INCOME TAXPAYERS ALSO SUFFER FROM THE MARRIAGE PENALTY

The inequity of the marriage penalty is not limited to taxpayers with high incomes (see Example 30).

Consider, for example, Albert and June, each of whom has one dependent child. During 1996, Albert and June both earn wages of $10,000. Neither has any deductions *for* AGI.

Situation A shows the income tax result if Albert and June are married and file a joint return. Situation B assumes Albert and June are not married, qualify for head-of-household status, and file accordingly, with each claiming one child as a dependent. Because the Tax Tables for 1996 were not yet available, the Tax Rate Schedules were used to compute the tax.

The harsh effect of the marriage penalty is apparent. Albert and June are $2,980 better off (refunds totaling $4,304 versus $1,324) by not being married. This result is remarkable when one considers that AGI of only $20,000 is involved!

	Situation A	Situation B		
	If They Are Married	**If They Are Not Married**		
Their Taxes:		Albert	June	Total
Adjusted gross income	$20,000	$10,000 +	$10,000 =	$20,000
Personal and dependency exemptions	10,200	5,100 +	5,100 =	10,200
Standard deduction	6,700	5,900 +	5,900 =	11,800
Taxable income	3,100	–0– +	–0– =	–0–
Taxes owed	465	–0– +	–0– =	–0–
Earned income tax credit*	1,789	2,152 +	2,152 =	4,304
Refund	$ 1,324	$2,152 +	$2,152 =	$4,304

*See Chapter 11 for a discussion of the earned income tax credit. The credits above were calculated following the procedure utilized in Example 21 of Chapter 11.

The Code places some limitations on deductions, credits, etc., when married individuals file separately. If either spouse itemizes deductions, the other spouse must also itemize. Married taxpayers who file separately cannot take either of the following:

- The credit for child and dependent care expenses (in most instances).
- The earned income credit.

The joint return rates also apply for two years following the death of one spouse, if the surviving spouse maintains a household for a dependent child.[28] This is referred to as **surviving spouse** status.

---

[28] § 2(a).

TAX IN THE NEWS

THE IRS GOES AFTER ANYONE IT CAN FIND

When she was married, Elizabeth Cockrell filed joint returns with her husband. Because she never bothered to review the returns before she signed them, Elizabeth was unaware that her husband was claiming questionable tax shelters as tax deductions.

After the couple divorced, the IRS audited the returns and assessed the entire deficiency against Elizabeth. Since the IRS had made no effort to pursue her former husband, Elizabeth took the matter to court. In *Elizabeth R. Cockrell*, 66 TCM 1180, T.C.Memo. 1995–503, and in a later rehearing (T.C.Memo. 1995–551), the Tax Court found for the IRS. Although the Court was sympathetic to Elizabeth's plight, the law was clear. The IRS has no duty or obligation to look first to the spouse who was responsible for the error.

It has been suggested that Congress change the law to avoid the result reached in Elizabeth's case.*

*Elizabeth did not qualify as an "innocent spouse" under § 6013(e) because the understatements were not attributable to "grossly erroneous items."

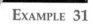

EXAMPLE 31

Fred dies in 1995 leaving Ethel with a dependent child. For the year of Fred's death (1995), Ethel files a joint return with Fred (presuming the consent of Fred's executor is obtained). For the next two years (1996 and 1997), Ethel, as a surviving spouse, may use the joint return rates. In subsequent years, Ethel may use the head-of-household rates if she continues to maintain a household as her home that is the domicile of the child. ▼

Rates for Heads of Household.   Unmarried individuals who maintain a household for a dependent (or dependents) are entitled to use the **head-of-household** rates.[29] The tax liability using the head-of-household rates falls between the liability using the joint return Tax Rate Schedule and the liability using the Tax Rate Schedule for single taxpayers.

To qualify for head-of-household rates, a taxpayer must pay more than half the cost of maintaining a household as his or her home. The household must also be the principal home of a dependent relative.[30] As a general rule, the dependent must live in the taxpayer's household for over half the year.

The general rule has two exceptions. One exception is that an *unmarried child* (child also means grandchild, stepchild, or adopted child) need not be a dependent in order for the taxpayer to qualify as a head of household.

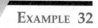

EXAMPLE 32

Nancy maintains a household where she and Dan, her nondependent unmarried son, reside. Since Dan is not married, Nancy qualifies for the head-of-household rates. ▼

Another exception to the general rule is that head-of-household status may be claimed if the taxpayer maintains a *separate home* for his or her *parent or parents* if at least one parent qualifies as a dependent of the taxpayer.[31]

---

[29] § 2(b).
[30] As defined in § 152(a). See § 2(b)(1)(A)(i).

[31] § 2(b)(1)(B).

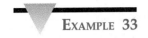

EXAMPLE 33   Rick, an unmarried individual, lives in New York City and maintains a household in Detroit for his dependent parents. Rick may use the head-of-household rates even though his parents do not reside in his New York home. ▼

Head-of-household status is not changed during the year by death of the dependent. As long as the taxpayer provided more than half of the cost of maintaining the household prior to the dependent's death, head-of-household status is preserved.

Abandoned Spouse Rules. When married persons file separate returns, several unfavorable tax consequences result. For example, the taxpayer must use the Tax Rate Schedule for married taxpayers filing separately. To mitigate such harsh treatment, Congress enacted provisions commonly referred to as the **abandoned spouse** rules. These rules allow a married taxpayer to file as a head of household if all of the following conditions are satisfied:

- The taxpayer does not file a joint return.
- The taxpayer paid more than one-half the cost of maintaining his or her home for the tax year.
- The taxpayer's spouse did not live in the home during the last six months of the tax year.
- The home was the principal residence of the taxpayer's child, stepchild, or adopted child for more than half the year.
- The taxpayer could claim the child, stepchild, or adopted child as a dependent.[32]

GAINS AND LOSSES FROM PROPERTY TRANSACTIONS—IN GENERAL

6 LEARNING OBJECTIVE
Possess an overview of property transactions.

Gains and losses from property transactions are discussed in detail in Chapters 12 and 13. Because of their importance in the tax system, however, they are introduced briefly at this point.

When property is sold or otherwise disposed of, gain or loss may result. Such gain or loss has an effect on the income tax position of the party making the sale or other disposition when the *realized* gain or loss is *recognized* for tax purposes. Without realized gain or loss, generally, there can be no recognized gain or loss. The concept of realized gain or loss is expressed as follows:

$$\text{Amount realized from the sale} - \text{Adjusted basis of the property} = \text{Realized gain (or loss)}$$

The amount realized is the selling price of the property less any costs of disposition (e.g., brokerage commissions) incurred by the seller. Simply stated, adjusted basis of the property is determined as follows:

Cost (or other original basis) at date of acquisition[33]

Add: Capital additions

---

[32] The dependency requirement does not apply, however, if the taxpayer could have claimed a dependency exemption except for the fact that the exemption was claimed by the noncustodial parent under a written agreement. Refer to Example 18 and the related discussion.

[33] Cost usually means purchase price plus expenses related to the acquisition of the property and incurred by the purchaser (e.g., brokerage commissions). For the basis of property acquired by gift or inheritance and other basis rules, see Chapter 12.

Subtract:	Depreciation (if appropriate) and other capital recoveries (see Chapter 7)
Equals:	Adjusted basis at date of sale or other disposition

All realized gains are recognized (taxable) unless some specific part of the tax law provides otherwise (see Chapter 12 dealing with certain nontaxable exchanges). Realized losses may or may not be recognized (deductible) for tax purposes, depending on the circumstances involved. Generally, losses realized from the disposition of personal use property (property neither held for investment nor used in a trade or business) are not recognized.

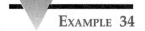 **EXAMPLE 34**

During the current year, Ted sells his sailboat (adjusted basis of $4,000) for $5,500. Ted also sells one of his personal automobiles (adjusted basis of $8,000) for $5,000. Ted's realized gain of $1,500 from the sale of the sailboat is recognized. On the other hand, the $3,000 realized loss on the sale of the automobile is not recognized and will not provide Ted with any deductible tax benefit. ▼

Once it has been determined that the disposition of property results in a recognized gain or loss, the next step is to classify the gain or loss as capital or ordinary. Although ordinary gain is fully taxable and ordinary loss is fully deductible, the same may not hold true for capital gains and capital losses.

GAINS AND LOSSES FROM PROPERTY TRANSACTIONS—CAPITAL GAINS AND LOSSES

For tax years beginning after 1992, preferential tax treatment may apply to gains on capital assets that have been held for more than a year. The maximum rate on *net capital gain* (see Chapter 13 for details) is 28 percent. This provision could save 11.6 percent for taxpayers in the 39.6 percent bracket.

DEFINITION OF A CAPITAL ASSET

Capital assets are defined in the Code as any property held by the taxpayer *other than* property listed in § 1221. The list in § 1221 includes inventory, accounts receivable, and depreciable property or real estate used in a business. Thus, the sale or exchange of assets in these categories usually results in ordinary income or loss treatment (see Chapter 13).

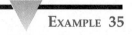 **EXAMPLE 35**

Kelly owns a pizza parlor. During the current year, he sells two automobiles. The first automobile, which had been used as a pizza delivery car for three years, was sold at a loss of $1,000. Because this automobile is an asset used in his business, Kelly has an ordinary loss deduction of $1,000, rather than a capital loss deduction. The second automobile, which Kelly had owned for two years, was his personal car. It was sold for a gain of $800. The personal car is a capital asset. Therefore, Kelly has a capital gain of $800. ▼

The principal capital assets held by an individual taxpayer include assets held for personal (rather than business) use, such as a personal residence or an automobile, and assets held for investment purposes (e.g., corporate securities and land).

COMPUTATION OF NET CAPITAL GAINS AND LOSSES

Capital gains and losses must be classified as short term (those on assets held for one year or less) and long term (those on assets held for more than one year). Short-term capital losses (STCL) are offset against short-term capital gains (STCG). The result is either net short-term capital gain (NSTCG) or net short-term capital loss (NSTCL).

　　Long-term capital losses (LTCL) are offset against long-term capital gains (LTCG), and the result is either net long-term capital gain (NLTCG) or net long-term capital loss (NLTCL).

　　Several combinations are possible after this first round of offsetting. For example, if the taxpayer has NSTCL and NLTCG, these amounts are offset. Likewise, if the taxpayer has NLTCL and NSTCG, a similar offsetting is required. In general, the offsetting continues as long as there is gain in any category and loss in any other category.

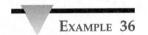

EXAMPLE 36

In the current year, Polly has the following capital gains and losses: STCL of $4,000, STCG of $3,000, LTCG of $6,000, and LTCL of $2,000. This results in NSTCL of $1,000 ($4,000 STCL – $3,000 STCG) and NLTCG of $4,000 ($6,000 LTCG – $2,000 LTCL). The $1,000 NSTCL is used to offset the $4,000 NLTCG, resulting in an excess of NLTCG over NSTCL of $3,000. ▼

CAPITAL LOSS LIMITATION

Noncorporate Capital Losses　Capital losses are first offset against capital gains (as illustrated in Example 36). If, after this offsetting, an individual taxpayer has net capital losses, such losses are deductible as a deduction *for* AGI to a maximum of $3,000 per year. Any unused amounts are carried over for an indefinite period.

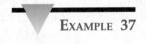

EXAMPLE 37

During the year, Tina has $1,000 of NLTCL and $2,000 of NSTCL. Tina's other income is $100,000. Her capital loss deduction for the year is $3,000, consisting of the $2,000 NSTCL and $1,000 NLTCL. ▼

When a taxpayer has both short-term and long-term capital losses, and the losses together exceed $3,000, the short-term losses must be used first in applying the $3,000 limitation.

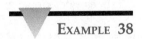

EXAMPLE 38

Matt has NSTCL of $2,500 and NLTCL of $5,000 for the year. His other income is $50,000. Matt uses the losses as follows:

NSTCL	$2,500
NLTCL	500
Maximum capital loss deduction	$3,000

　　The remaining NLTCL of $4,500 ($5,000 NLTCL – $500 used) may be carried forward for an indefinite period until used. See Chapter 13 for a detailed discussion of capital loss carryovers. ▼

Corporate Capital Losses.　Corporate taxpayers may offset capital losses only against capital gains. Capital losses in excess of capital gains may not be used to reduce ordinary income of a corporation. A corporation's unused capital losses are subject to a carryback and carryover. Capital losses are initially carried back three years and then carried forward five years to offset capital gains that arise in those years. See Chapters 13 and 16 for a discussion of capital losses of corporate taxpayers.

TAKING ADVANTAGE OF TAX RATE DIFFERENTIALS

**TAX PLANNING
CONSIDERATIONS**

7 **LEARNING OBJECTIVE**
Identify tax planning
opportunities associated with
the individual tax formula.

It is natural for taxpayers to be concerned about the tax rates they are paying. How does a tax practitioner communicate information about rates to clients? There are several possibilities.

The marginal rate (refer to Examples 23 through 25) provides information that can help a taxpayer evaluate a particular course of action or structure a transaction in the most advantageous manner.

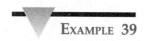

EXAMPLE 39

Due to his salary, Ron is in the 28% marginal tax bracket for 1995. He is considering selling corporate stock he has held as an investment for four years for a $10,000 gain in December. If he sells the stock, his income tax increases by $2,800 ($10,000 gain × 28% marginal rate), and he has $7,200 of after-tax income ($10,000 − $2,800 tax). ▼

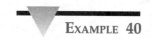

EXAMPLE 40

Assume the same facts as in Example 39 and that Ron plans to retire early in 1996. Upon retirement, Ron's only source of income will be nontaxable Social Security benefits and municipal bond interest. If Ron waits until 1996 to sell the stock, his tax on the gain is $1,500 ($10,000 gain × 15% marginal rate), and his after-tax income is $8,500 ($10,000 gain − $1,500 tax). By being aware of the effect of marginal tax rates, Ron can save $1,300 in tax. ▼

The marginal rate analysis illustrated in Examples 39 and 40 for an income item can also help a taxpayer obtain the greatest tax benefit from a deductible expense. For example, a taxpayer who is in the 15 percent bracket this year and expects to be in the 31 percent bracket next year should, if possible, defer payment of deductible expenses until next year to maximize the tax benefit of the deduction.

A note of caution is in order with respect to shifting income and expenses between years. Congress has recognized the tax planning possibilities of such shifting and has enacted many provisions to limit a taxpayer's ability to do so. Some of these limitations on the shifting of income are discussed in Chapters 3, 4, and 15. Limitations that affect a taxpayer's ability to shift deductions are discussed in Chapters 5 through 10 and in Chapter 15.

A taxpayer's *effective rate* can be an informative measure of the effectiveness of tax planning. The effective rate is computed by dividing the taxpayer's tax liability by the total amount of income. A low effective rate can be considered an indication of effective tax planning.

One way of lowering the effective rate is to exclude income from the tax base. For example, a taxpayer might consider investing in tax-free municipal bonds rather than taxable corporate bonds. Although pre-tax income from corporate bonds is usually higher, after-tax income may be higher if the taxpayer invests in tax-free municipals.

Another way of lowering the effective rate is to make sure that the taxpayer's expenses and losses are deductible. For example, losses on investments in passive activities may not be deductible (see Chapter 10). Therefore, a taxpayer who plans to invest in an activity that will produce a loss in the early years should take steps to ensure that the business is treated as active rather than passive. Active losses are deductible while passive losses are not.

INCOME OF MINOR CHILDREN

Taxpayers can use several strategies to avoid or minimize the effect of the rules that tax the unearned income of certain minor children at the parents' rate. The kiddie tax rules do not apply once a child reaches age 14. Parents should consider giving a younger child assets that defer taxable income until the child reaches age 14. For example, U.S. government Series EE savings bonds can be used to defer income until the bonds are cashed in (see Chapter 3).

Growth stocks typically pay little in the way of dividends. However, the profit on an astute investment may more than offset the lack of dividends. The child can hold the stock until he or she reaches age 14. If the stock is sold then at a profit, the profit is taxed at the child's low rates.

Taxpayers in a position to do so can employ their children in their business and pay them a reasonable wage for the work they actually perform (e.g., light office help, such as filing). The child's earned income is sheltered by the standard deduction, and the parents' business is allowed a deduction for the wages. The kiddie tax rules have no effect on earned income, even if it is earned from the parents' business.

DEPENDENCY EXEMPTIONS

The Joint Return Test. A married person can be claimed as a dependent only if that individual does not file a joint return with his or her spouse. If a joint return has been filed, the damage may be undone if separate returns are substituted on a timely basis (on or before the due date of the return).

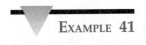

EXAMPLE 41

While preparing a client's 1995 income tax return on April 8, 1996, the tax practitioner discovered that the client's daughter filed a joint return with her husband in late January of 1996. Presuming the daughter otherwise qualifies as the client's dependent, the exemption is not lost if she and her husband file separate returns on or before April 15, 1996. ▼

An initial election to file a joint return must be considered carefully in any situation in which the taxpayers might later decide to amend their return and file separately. As indicated above, separate returns may be substituted for a joint return only if the amended returns are filed on or before the normal due date of the return. If the taxpayers in Example 41 attempt to file separate returns after April 15, 1996, the returns will not be accepted, and the joint return election is binding.[34]

Keep in mind that the filing of a joint return will not be fatal to the dependency exemption if the parties are filing solely to recover all income tax withholdings, are not required to file a return, and no tax liability would exist on separate returns.

The Gross Income Test. The exception to the gross income test for a person under the age of 19 or a full-time student under the age of 24 applies only to a child of the taxpayer. The term *child* is limited to a son, stepson, daughter, stepdaughter, adopted son, or adopted daughter and may include a foster child.

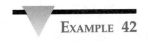

EXAMPLE 42

Austin provides more than 50% of the support of his son, Irvin, and his daughter-in-law, Donna, who live with him. Donna, age 22, is a full-time student and earns $3,000 from a part-time job. Irvin and Donna do not file a joint return. Austin may claim Irvin as a dependent but not Donna. Although students under the age of 24 are excepted from the gross income test, this applies only to a "child" of the taxpayer. Donna does not come within the exception because she is not Austin's child. ▼

Can the fact that the parties live in a community property state make a difference?

[34] Reg. § 1.6013–1(a)(1).

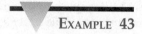

EXAMPLE 43

Assume the same facts as in Example 42 except that all parties live in Nevada, a community property jurisdiction. Now Austin can claim both Irvin and Donna as his dependents. Since Donna's income is only $1,500 (her half of the community), she now satisfies the gross income test (less than $2,550 for 1996). ▼

The Support Test. Adequate records of expenditures for support should be maintained in the event a dependency exemption is questioned on audit by the IRS. The maintenance of adequate records is particularly important for exemptions arising from multiple support agreements.

Relationship to the Deduction for Medical Expenses. Generally, medical expenses are deductible only if they are paid on behalf of the taxpayer, his or her spouse, and their dependents. Since deductibility may rest on dependency status, planning is important in arranging multiple support agreements.

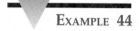

EXAMPLE 44

During the year, Zelda will be supported by her two sons (Vern and Vito) and her daughter (Maria). Each will furnish approximately one-third of the required support. If the parties decide that the dependency exemption should be claimed by the daughter under a multiple support agreement, any medical expenses incurred by Zelda should be paid by Maria. ▼

In planning a multiple support agreement, take into account which of the parties is most likely to exceed the 7.5 percent limitation (see Chapter 9). In Example 44, for instance, Maria might be a poor choice if she and her family do not expect to incur many medical and drug expenses of their own.

ETHICAL CONSIDERATIONS

Manipulating Deductions

Jason and his two sisters furnish more than 50 percent of the support of their widowed mother. Their mother lives with Jason, and his sisters sign Form 2120 enabling him to claim her as a dependent. During the year, the mother incurred medical expenses that were paid by one of Jason's sisters.

In completing his income tax return for the tax year, Jason claims his mother's medical expenses along with his own. Although he did not pay the expenses, Jason reasons that he could have done so from the funds he furnished for his mother's support.

Comment on the propriety of what Jason has done.

One exception permits the deduction of medical expenses paid on behalf of someone who is not a spouse or a dependent. If the person could be claimed as a dependent *except* for the gross income or joint return test, the medical expenses are, nevertheless, deductible. For additional discussion, see Chapter 9.

KEY TERMS

Abandoned spouse, 2–27

Dependency exemption, 2–10

Head of household, 2–26

Itemized deductions, 2–6

Kiddie tax, 2–19

Marriage penalty, 2–24

**PROBLEM
MATERIALS**

DISCUSSION QUESTIONS

1. A friend of yours remarks that the current top rate of 39.6% is the highest the Federal income tax has ever been. Please comment.

2. Rearrange the following components to show the formula for arriving at the amount of Federal taxable income:
   a. Deductions *for* AGI.
   b. The greater of the standard deduction or itemized deductions.
   c. Income (broadly conceived).
   d. Adjusted gross income.
   e. Exclusions.
   f. Personal and dependency exemptions.
   g. Gross income.

3. To obtain funds to buy a car, Demi borrows $6,000 from a bank. Her mother gives her the purchase balance of $7,000. What is Demi's gross income?

4. During the year, Mildred's stock investment increased in value by $13,000. She also sold some stock for $4,500; the stock had cost $4,000. How do these facts affect Mildred's gross income?

5. John anticipates that his Federal income tax liability will decrease in 1996. Not only will his itemized deductions increase, but he and his wife will also become 65 years old. Is John's reasoning correct? Explain.

6. Al and Melissa are husband and wife, and both are employed. They do not live in a community property state. Since Melissa incurred most of their itemized deductions (e.g., medical, charitable), Al feels that they would save taxes if they filed separate returns. On such returns, Al would claim the standard deduction, and Melissa would itemize her deductions *from* AGI. Comment on this proposed course of action.

7. Discuss the marital status of the parties under the following circumstances:
   a. One spouse dies during the year.
   b. The spouses are divorced during the year.

8. If an individual who may qualify as a dependent does not spend funds that he or she has received (e.g., wages or Social Security benefits), are these unexpended amounts considered in applying the support test? Are they included in applying the gross income test?

9. Freda purchased a stereo system for her son Wes, age 16. The stereo was placed in Wes's room and used exclusively by him. Freda also purchased a new sports car, titled and registered in her own name, that was used 90% of the time by Wes. Should the cost of these items be considered as support in determining whether Freda may claim Wes as a dependent?

10. Carol provided 75% of the support of Debra, her niece. Debra was a full-time student during the year and earned $3,800 from a part-time job. Can Carol claim Debra as a dependent?

11. Besides what he furnishes on his own, Walter receives support from his daughter (20%) and his son (25%). Can either the daughter or the son claim Walter as a dependent under a multiple support agreement? Why or why not?

12. Steve and Lisa were divorced in 1995. Lisa was granted custody of their children. Because Steve has contributed almost all of the children's support in 1996, he plans to claim them as his dependents. Do you have any comment?

13. A taxpayer who is divorced continues to support his former mother-in-law. May he claim her as a dependent? Suppose she does not live with him. Does this make any difference?

14. Roberto, who is single, is a U.S. citizen and resident. He provides almost all of the support of his parents and two aunts, who are citizens and residents of Guatemala. Roberto's parents and aunts are seriously considering moving to and becoming residents of Mexico. Would such a move have any impact on Roberto? Why or why not?

15. What perceived abuse is the kiddie tax designed to correct?

16. A single individual age 65 or over and blind is required to file a Federal income tax return in 1996 if he or she has gross income of $7,550 or more (refer to Table 3–4).
    a. Explain how the $7,550 filing requirement was computed.
    b. In general, explain the effect of the additional standard deduction on the determination of gross income requirements for filing.

17. Ali, age 67, is married to Leila, who is age 62 and blind. Ali and Leila file a joint return. How much gross income can they earn before they are required to file an income tax return for 1996?

18. Comment on the so-called marriage penalty in connection with the following:
    a. What it is.
    b. When it is likely to occur.
    c. What income level (i.e., low, modest, high) could be vulnerable.

19. Baron and Cheryl are both professionals who have held jobs since they graduated from college five years ago. For several years, they have been engaged to be married. Both would like to tie the knot, but Cheryl is hesitant because of a "marriage penalty" she has heard about. Baron feels Cheryl's fears are unfounded and says they should be able to avoid any such penalty by filing separate returns as married persons. Comment on Baron and Cheryl's situation.

20. Ida's husband dies in 1996. Ida is planning to file as a surviving spouse for tax years 1996 through 1998. Comment regarding Ida's expectations.

21. Camille is single and lives alone in an apartment. She maintains the home where her parents live and is able to claim both of them as her dependents. When Camille files her income tax return, she uses single status. She does not claim head-of-household status because her parents do not live with her. Comment on Camille's status.

22. Several years ago, after a particularly fierce argument, Fran's husband moved out and has not been heard from or seen since. Because Fran cannot locate her husband, she has been using "married, filing separate" status when filing her income tax return. Comment on Fran's status.

23. During the current year, Andre had a $7,000 long-term capital loss on the sale of common stock he had held as an investment. In addition, he had a $3,000 loss on the sale of his personal automobile, which he had owned for a year. How do these transactions affect Andre's taxable income?

24. Ten years ago, Ann purchased a personal residence for $140,000. In the current year, she sells the residence for $105,000. Ann's friend tells her she has a recognizable loss of $35,000 from the sale. Do you agree with the friend's comment? Elaborate.

25. List some assets that are not capital assets and some that are capital assets. Why is it important to determine whether an asset is an ordinary asset or a capital asset?

26. During the current year, Kate earned a salary of $40,000. She sold 20 shares of Robin Corporation common stock that she had purchased two years ago at a loss of $2,500 and sold her personal automobile at a gain of $1,500. Compute Kate's AGI.

27. If Cole has a salary of $41,000, net short-term capital gain of $1,000, and net long-term capital losses of $8,500, what is his AGI?

28. Perry is divorced and has living with him his married daughter, Celia, and her husband, Clark. During the year, Celia earned $3,100 from a part-time job and filed a separate return to recover her withholdings. Clark has no income. Perry can prove that he provided more than 50% of Celia and Clark's support. Perry did not claim Celia as his dependent because he believed she failed the gross income test. Perry filed his return using single taxpayer status. All parties reside in California. Comment on Perry's tax position.

29. Erica and her two brothers equally furnish all of the support of their mother. Erica is married and has four children. Her brothers are single and claim the standard deduction. Erica's mother is not in good health. What suggestions can you make regarding the tax position of the parties?

PROBLEMS

30. Compute the taxpayer's taxable income for 1996 in each of the following cases:
    a. Jack is married and files a joint return with his wife Alice. Jack and Alice have two dependent children. They have AGI of $50,000 and $8,300 of itemized deductions.
    b. Pete is an unmarried head of household with two dependents. He has AGI of $45,000 and itemized deductions of $5,200.
    c. Iris, age 22, is a full-time college student who is claimed as a dependent by her parents. She earns $4,200 from a part-time job and has interest income of $1,500.
    d. Matt, age 20, is a full-time college student who is claimed as a dependent by his parents. He earns $2,500 from a part-time job and has interest income of $4,100. His itemized deductions related to the investment income are $700.

    Note: Problems 31 and 32 can be solved by referring to Figure 2–1, Exhibits 2–1 through 2–3, Tables 2–1 and 2–2, and the discussion under Deductions for Adjusted Gross Income in this chapter.

31. Compute taxable income for 1996 for Jan on the basis of the following information. Her filing status is single.

Gift received from mother	$15,000
Cash dividend received from stock investments	21,000
Interest received from savings accounts and money market deposits	9,000
Capital loss (short term)	1,300
Charitable contributions	2,000
State and local income taxes	2,900
Interest on home mortgage	5,500
Age	60

32. Compute taxable income for 1996 for Hal, who is divorced, on the basis of the following information. His filing status is head of household.

Salary	$58,000
Alimony paid	12,000
Lottery winnings	2,000
Moving expenses (deductible portion)	6,000
Theft loss (deductible portion)	5,900
State and local income taxes	1,200
Interest on home mortgage	4,100
Number of dependents	3
Age	38

33. Determine the amount of the standard deduction allowed for 1996 in each of the following independent situations. In each case, assume the taxpayer is claimed as another person's dependent.
    a. Mona, age 16, has income as follows: $710 interest from a savings account and $800 from a part-time job.
    b. Aaron, age 18, earns $4,300 from a part-time job.
    c. Irving, age 71 and single, has income as follows: $3,100 nontaxable Social Security benefits and $1,050 from a part-time job.
    d. Maureen, age 67, is single and blind and has cash dividends of $1,300 from a stock investment.

34. Determine the number of personal and dependency exemptions in each of the following independent situations:
    a. Wesley, age 45, provides all of the support of Doreen (age 70) who does not live with him. Doreen was Wesley's mother-in-law before his divorce.
    b. Carol, age 50, provides all of the support of two cousins, Rick and Jane. Jane lives with Carol but Rick does not.
    c. Ron, age 66, provides all of the support of Cynthia and Leona who live with him. Cynthia is Ron's wife, and Leona is unrelated but is a close friend of the family and a member of their church. Ron files a separate return. Neither Cynthia nor Leona has any income, and neither files a return.
    d. Nicole, age 60, provides all of the support of Alan, age 66 and blind, and Grace, age 89. Alan, Nicole's husband, died in February of the current year. Grace is Alan's mother and lives in a nursing home. Nicole files a separate return.

35. Compute the number of personal and dependency exemptions in each of the following independent situations:
    a. Roberto, a U.S. citizen and resident, contributes 100% of the support of his parents who are citizens of Mexico and live there.
    b. Pablo, a U.S. citizen and resident, contributes 100% of the support of his parents who are citizens of Guatemala. Pablo's father is a resident of Guatemala, and his mother is a legal resident of the United States.
    c. Marlena, a U.S. citizen and resident, contributes 100% of the support of her parents who are also U.S. citizens but are residents of Germany.

36. Determine the number of personal and dependency exemptions in each of the following independent situations:
    a. Warren and Terri provide more than half of the support of their children, Demi and Paul. Demi, age 18, earns $3,200 from a part-time job. Paul, age 26, earns $2,000 from a part-time job.
    b. Hortense, age 66 and widowed, furnishes more than half of the support of her father, age 88 and blind. The father receives Social Security benefits of $4,300, interest on a savings account of $2,300, and interest on tax-exempt bonds of $9,000.
    c. Dennis and Ava provide more than half of the support of their son, Henry. Henry, age 23, is a full-time student in medical school. During the year, Henry receives $3,050 in dividends from stock investments.
    d. Earl provides more than half of the support of his nephew, Brad, who lives with him. Brad, age 17 and a full-time student, earns $3,500 from a part-time job.

37. Carlos and Alicia, who are married and file a joint return, have four dependent children. They have AGI of $193,700. What is their allowable exemption deduction for 1996?

38. Fred and Eve are married and file a joint return. Fred is 66 years of age, and Eve is 65. Fred's salary for 1996 was $33,000, and Eve earned $41,000. Eve won $10,000 in the state lottery and inherited $25,000 from her aunt. Fred incurred a $2,500 capital loss on stock he sold in December; Fred had purchased the stock three months earlier. Fred and Eve provided 90% of the support for Cora, their 23-year-old daughter, who is a full-time student. Fred and Eve also provided over half of the support of Jim, who is Cora's husband. Cora and Jim did not file a joint return. Fred and Eve also provide over half of the support of Eve's mother, Abbey, who lives in a nursing home. Abbey earned interest

of $2,200 on a savings account and received Social Security benefits of $6,400. Fred and Eve had total itemized deductions of $7,800. Compute taxable income for Fred and Eve for 1996.

39. Bob, age 13, is a full-time student supported by his parents who claim him on their tax return for 1996. Bob's parents present you with the following information and ask that you prepare Bob's 1996 Federal income tax return:

Wages from summer job	$2,100
Interest on savings account at First National Bank	950
Interest on City of Chicago bonds Bob received as a gift from his grandfather two years ago	750
Dividend from Owl Corporation	200

   a. What is Bob's taxable income for 1996?
   b. Bob's parents file a joint return for 1996 on which they report taxable income of $66,000. Compute Bob's 1996 tax liability.

40. Walter and Nancy provide 70% of the support of their daughter (age 21) and son-in-law (age 22). The son-in-law (John) is a full-time student at a local university, while the daughter (Irene) holds various part-time jobs from which she earns $3,000. Walter and Nancy engage you to prepare their tax return for 1996. During a meeting with them in late March of 1997, you learn that John and Irene do not file a joint return. What tax advice would you give based on the following assumptions:
   a. All parties live in Louisiana (a community property state).
   b. All parties live in New Jersey (a common law state).

41. Don is a wealthy executive who had taxable income of $200,000 in 1996. He is considering transferring title in a duplex he owns to his son Sam, age 16. Sam has no other income and is claimed as a dependent by Don. Net rent income from the duplex is $10,000 a year, which Sam will be encouraged to place in a savings account. Will the family save income taxes in 1996 if Don transfers title in the duplex to Sam? Explain.

42. Compute the 1996 tax liability for each of the following taxpayers:
   a. Norm and Nancy, both age 46, are married, have two dependent children, and file a joint return. Their combined salaries totaled $75,000. They had deductions *for* AGI of $6,000 and total itemized deductions of $8,100.
   b. Clark, age 45, is single and has no dependents. He had a salary of $62,000, deductions *for* AGI of $3,000, and total itemized deductions of $7,100.
   c. David and Susan, both age 65, are married, have no dependents, and file a joint return. Their combined salaries were $92,000. They had deductions *for* AGI of $2,000 and itemized deductions of $17,000.

43. Chet and Eva are 68 and 65 years of age, respectively, and married. Their income consists of cash dividends ($30,000) from stock investments and interest ($24,000) from certificates of deposit. During 1996, they had a short-term capital loss of $4,000 and itemized deductions of $7,500. They provided all of the support of a nephew who lives with them. Determine their taxable income for 1996.

44. Peter, age 12, is claimed as a dependent on his parents' 1996 Federal income tax return, on which they reported taxable income of $95,000. During the summer, Peter earned $2,500 from a job as a model. His only other income consisted of $1,700 in interest on a savings account. Compute Peter's taxable income and tax liability.

45. Carmen, who is 12 years old, is claimed as a dependent on her parents' tax return. During 1996, she received $12,200 in dividends and interest and had no investment expenses related to this income. She also earned $2,000 wages from a part-time job. Compute the amount of income that is taxed at Carmen's parents' rate.

46. Ellen, who is 14 years old, is claimed as a dependent on her parents' tax return. During 1996, she received $10,000 in dividends and interest. She also earned $1,700 wages from a part-time job. Compute the amount of income that is taxed at Ellen's own rate.

47. Bruce Smith and Wanda Brown are young professionals who are employed in well-paying jobs. They have been dating each other for several years and are considering getting married in December 1996 or January 1997. For 1996, their respective AGIs are $65,000 and $68,000. They anticipate earning the same income in 1997. In both years, they will claim the standard deduction.

Bruce and Wanda solicit your tax advice. Specifically, they wish to know what Federal income tax results from their getting married in 1996 or in 1997. Prepare a letter to Wanda (4339 Elm St., Apt. 39A, Cincinnati, OH 45221) setting forth the tax determination under each choice.

48. Which of the following individuals are required to file a tax return for 1996? Should any of these individuals file a return even if filing is not required? Why?
   a. Sam is married and files a joint return with his spouse, Lana. Both Sam and Lana are 67 years old. Their combined gross income was $13,000.
   b. Bobby is a dependent child under age 19 who received $2,000 in wages from a part-time job and $800 of dividend income.
   c. Mike is single and is 67 years old. His gross income from wages was $7,000.
   d. Marge is a self-employed single individual with gross income of $4,500 from an unincorporated business. Business expenses amounted to $4,200.

49. Which of the following taxpayers must file a Federal income tax return for 1996?
   a. Bob, age 19, is a full-time college student. He is claimed as a dependent by his parents. He earned $4,100 wages during the year.
   b. Anita, age 12, is claimed as a dependent by her parents. She earned interest of $1,200 during the year.
   c. Earl, age 16, is claimed as a dependent by his parents. He earned wages of $2,700 and interest of $1,100 during the year.
   d. Karen, age 16 and blind, is claimed as a dependent by her parents. She earned wages of $2,600 and interest of $1,200 during the year.
   e. Pat, age 17, is claimed as a dependent by her parents. She earned interest of $300 during the year. In addition, she earned $550 during the summer operating her own business at the beach, where she painted caricatures of her customers.

50. In each of the following situations, classify Darlene's filing status for tax year 1996:
   a. Darlene is a widow and maintains a household in which her two dependent children live. Darlene's husband died in 1994.
   b. Same as (a) except that Darlene's husband died in 1992 (not 1994).
   c. Darlene is single and lives alone. She maintains the household of her parents, only one of whom qualifies as her dependent.
   d. Darlene is married, but her husband disappeared for parts unknown in 1995. Darlene maintains the household in which she and her dependent children live.

51. In each of the following situations, classify Isaac's filing status for tax year 1996:
   a. Isaac lives alone. He has not seen or heard from his wife since 1995.
   b. Isaac's wife died in January 1996. He maintains the home in which he and his dependent child live.
   c. Isaac's wife died in 1992. He maintains the home in which he and his unmarried child live. The child does not qualify as Isaac's dependent.
   d. Isaac is divorced and lives alone. He also maintains a home in which his dependent child lives.

52. Henry died on January 1, 1994. He was survived by his wife, Sue, and their 19-year-old son, Mike, who was a college sophomore. Mike was a full-time student in 1995 and earned $3,000 for the year. In 1996, Mike reduced his school load and became a part-time student. He earned $5,200 in 1996. Mike continues to live with his mother, who provides over half of his support. What is Sue's filing status in 1994, 1995, and 1996?

53. Tracy, age 66, is a widow. Her husband died in 1994. Tracy maintains a home in which she and her 28-year-old son reside. Her son Gary is a piano player at a local nightclub,

where he earned $12,000 during 1996. Gary contributed $3,000 of his income toward household expenses and put the remainder in a savings account that he used to return to college full-time to pursue a master's degree in music starting in August 1996. Tracy contributed $12,000 toward household expenses. What is the most favorable filing status available to Tracy for 1996, and how many exemptions may she claim?

54. Hazel, age 39, is single. She maintains a household that is the residence of her two children, Fran, age 8, and Sam, age 11. The children are claimed as dependents by their father, who provides $2,000 child support for each of them. During 1996, Hazel earned a salary of $95,000. Other items that affected her taxable income are as follows:

Total itemized deductions	$ 6,700
Capital gains	
Short-term	1,300
Long-term	3,100
Capital losses	
Short-term	(4,800)
Long-term	(4,000)
Interest income	3,100

Hazel provides all the support for her mother, Mabel, who lives in a nursing home. Mabel qualifies as Hazel's dependent.
a. Compute Hazel's AGI and taxable income for 1996.
b. What is Hazel's filing status for 1996?

55. Tina, age 61, earned a salary of $63,000 in 1996. She sold common stock that she had owned for 10 months at a loss of $1,500 and sold a pleasure boat that she had bought in 1988 at a loss of $4,000. Tina also sold an antique desk for a gain of $10,000. She acquired the desk in 1953. Compute Tina's AGI for 1996.

56. Lee is a single, cash basis calendar year taxpayer. For the years 1995 and 1996, he expects AGI of $20,000 and the following itemized deductions:

Church pledge	$2,300
Interest on home mortgage	1,200
Property taxes	500

Discuss the tax consequences of the alternatives below. Assume for purposes of this problem that the interest and taxes are deductible in the year of payment.
a. In 1995, Lee pays his church pledge for 1995 and 1996 ($2,300 for each year).
b. Lee does nothing different.

57. Gina, a cash basis taxpayer, is single and has no dependents. She provides you with the following estimates for 1995 and 1996:

	1995	1996
Adjusted gross income	$56,000	$60,000
Charitable contributions	2,200	2,400
Interest on home mortgage	1,000	850
Property taxes	700	700

Can Gina decrease taxable income over the two-year period by prepaying her 1996 charitable contributions in 1995?

CUMULATIVE PROBLEMS

58. Mike and Rosa Zapalac are married and live at 100 Royce Avenue, El Paso, TX 79968; both have jobs. Mike's Social Security number is 433–22–1111 and Rosa's is 437–00–1112. The Zapalacs have four children who live with them. Three of the children are their own, while the oldest is Rosa's child from a prior marriage.

During 1996, the Zapalacs had the following receipts:

Salaries (Mike and Rosa combined)	$71,400
Child support payments received by Rosa from her former husband	3,600
Fees earned by Mike for several days of jury duty service	90
Proceeds from garage sale	1,310
Gift of cash received from Mike's mother	4,000
Cash prize won for being the ninth caller on a radio talk show	1,000

The garage sale involved used clothing, toys, appliances, furniture, and other personal effects and household goods. The Zapalacs are quite certain that the cost of the items sold was around $5,000.

Expenses for 1996 are summarized below:

Interest on home mortgage	$5,900
Property taxes on residence	3,700
Charitable contributions	4,100

The Zapalacs furnish all of the support of Rosa's widowed mother who lives with them. The mother, although a U.S. resident, is still a citizen of Mexico. The mother helps with the household chores and takes care of the children while Rosa and Mike are at work.

The Zapalacs also furnish all of the support of Rosa's grandparents who are over 65 years of age. The grandparents live in Mexico and are Mexican citizens.

Compute the Zapalacs' taxable income for 1996. Suggested software (if available): *TurboTax* or *MacInTax*.

59. Horace Fern, age 43, lives at 321 Grant Avenue, Cheyenne, WY 82002. Horace's mother Kate (age 65) lived with him until her death in August 1995. Up to the time of her death, Kate qualified as Horace's dependent. Horace maintained the household where he and his mother lived.

Horace is a manager for Bison Lumber Company at a yearly salary of $62,000. Because his job duties will be expanded, Bison plans to increase Horace's salary by 10% starting in 1996.

During 1995, Horace paid $3,600 ($300 each month) in alimony to Janet, his ex-wife. As Janet was remarried in late December, Horace's alimony obligation has terminated.

Besides his salary, Horace received interest income of $5,800 from Western Bank and $6,200 from First Savings Bank on $200,000 in certificates of deposit (CDs) he owns. Horace received the CDs as a gift from his mother several years ago.

Except as otherwise noted, Horace's expenditures for 1995 are summarized below:

Interest on home mortgage	$3,200
Property taxes on home	1,200
Charitable contributions	1,900

Relevant Social Security numbers are as follows:

Horace Fern	520–31–4596
Kate Fern	520–32–3214
Janet Fern	520–33–4432

Federal income taxes withheld from Horace's salary amounted to $10,900. He also paid estimated tax of $400 each quarter.

Part 1—Tax Computation

Compute Horace's net tax payable or refund due for 1995. Horace does not wish to contribute to the Presidential Election Campaign Fund. If he has overpaid, he wants the amount refunded. If you use tax forms for your computations, you will need Form 1040 and Schedules A and B. Suggested software (if available): *TurboTax* or *MacInTax*.

Part 2—Tax Planning

In addition to preparing the return for 1995, Horace has asked you to advise him regarding his tax situation for 1996. He is particularly concerned about the tax effects of the following:

• The death of Kate.

• The cessation of alimony payments due to Janet's remarriage.

• The salary increase.

• Interest income on the CDs.

Write a letter to Horace in which you summarize (in approximate amounts) how much more (or less) he will owe in income taxes for 1996. Also include recommendations on what can be done to mitigate the tax consequences resulting from the investment in CDs. Assume that Horace's itemized deductions will remain constant in 1996.

Research Problems for this chapter appear at the end of Chapter 28.

TEAM PROJECT: ARTHUR ANDERSEN TAX CHALLENGE CASES

Arthur Andersen & Co. has provided two of the cases that have been used in the Arthur Andersen Tax Challenge for use *in West's Federal Taxation: Comprehensive Volume*. The Tax Challenge is a nationwide university competition to stimulate student interest in tax careers. The case studies are based on Federal tax issues confronting an individual or family with their own business, with investments made by the individual, compensation matters, itemized deductions, and related issues that impact the taxpayer's filing status and tax profile.

The Tax Challenge is a team competition with four members on each team. Thus, the cases are excellent materials for team projects in tax classes. We suggest that team members read assigned cases in their entirety at this point in the course. Because the cases require the application of knowledge gained throughout the course, it is not possible to prepare a solution early in the course. However, the length and complexity of the cases dictate that students must spend some time working on them during the entire course. To facilitate this course-long effort, we have identified topics related to each chapter and placed instructions regarding these topics in the end of chapter problem materials as appropriate.

Information related to tax issues and problems that are discussed in this chapter may be found in the

Fields case on page 1
Miller case on pages 1, 3, 4, 16

Read and analyze the case you have been assigned and *identify* any issues and problems that are related to material covered in this chapter. If the information provided in the case is complete, prepare answers for this part of the case at this time. If you need information that is contained in later parts of the case, please write a memo summarizing the questions or problems so you can prepare a complete answer at a later date.

3

GROSS INCOME: CONCEPTS AND INCLUSIONS

LEARNING OBJECTIVES

After completing Chapter 3, you should be able to:

1. Explain the concepts of gross income and realization and distinguish between the economic, accounting, and tax concepts of gross income.

2. Describe the cash and accrual methods of accounting and the related effects of the choice of taxable year.

3. Identify who should pay the tax on a particular item of income in various situations.

4. Apply the Internal Revenue Code provisions on alimony, loans made at below-market interest rates, annuities, prizes and awards, group term life insurance, unemployment compensation, and Social Security benefits.

5. Identify tax planning strategies for minimizing gross income.

Mr. Zarin lost over $2,500,000 of his own money gambling. The casino then allowed him to gamble on credit. After several months, his liability to the casino totaled more than $3,400,000. Following protracted negotiations, the casino agreed to settle its claim against Mr. Zarin for a mere $500,000. Although Mr. Zarin had paid for gambling losses of $3,000,000, the IRS had the audacity to ask him to pay tax on $2,900,000; that is, the amount the casino marked down his account.[1] Mr. Zarin undoubtedly had difficulty understanding how he could be deemed to have income in this situation.

Given an understanding of the income tax formula, though, one can see how the "free" gambling Mr. Zarin enjoyed could constitute income. The starting point in the formula is the determination of gross income rather than "net income." Once gross income is determined, the next step is to determine the allowable deductions. In Mr. Zarin's way of thinking, these steps were collapsed.

This chapter is concerned with the first step in the computation of taxable income—the determination of gross income. Questions that are addressed include the following:

- What: What is income?
- When: In which tax period is the income recognized?
- Who: Who must include the item of income in gross income?

The Code provides an all-inclusive definition of gross income in § 61. Chapter 4 presents items of income that are specifically excluded from gross income (exclusions).

---

[1] *Zarin v. Comm.*, 90–2 USTC ¶50,530, 66 AFTR2d 90–5679, 916 F.2d
110 (CA–3, 1990).

GROSS INCOME—WHAT IS IT?

DEFINITION

Section 61(a) of the Internal Revenue Code defines the term **gross income** as follows:

> Except as otherwise provided in this subtitle, gross income means all income from whatever source derived.

This definition is derived from the language of the Sixteenth Amendment to the Constitution.

Supreme Court decisions have made it clear that all sources of income are subject to tax unless Congress specifically excludes the type of income received:

> The starting point in all cases dealing with the question of the scope of what is included in "gross income" begins with the basic premise that the purpose of Congress was to use the full measure of its taxing power.[2]

Although at this point we know that *income* is to be broadly construed, we still do not have a satisfactory definition of the term *income*. Congress left it to the judicial and administrative branches to thrash out the meaning of income. Early in the development of the income tax law, a choice was made between two competing models: economic income and accounting income.

ECONOMIC AND ACCOUNTING CONCEPTS

The term **income** is used in the Code but is not separately defined. Thus, early in the history of our tax laws, the courts were required to interpret "the commonly understood meaning of the term which must have been in the minds of the people when they adopted the Sixteenth Amendment to the Constitution."[3] In determining the definition of income, the Supreme Court rejected the economic concept of income.

Economists measure income (**economic income**) by first determining the fair market value of the individual's net assets at the beginning and end of the year (change in net worth). Then, to arrive at economic income, this change in net worth is added to the goods and services that person actually consumed during the period. Economic income also includes imputed values for such items as the rental value of an owner-occupied home and the value of food a taxpayer might grow for personal consumption.[4]

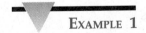

EXAMPLE 1

Helen's economic income is calculated as follows:

Fair market value of Helen's assets on December 31, 1996	$220,000	
Less liabilities on December 31, 1996	(40,000)	
Net worth on December 31, 1996		$180,000
Fair market value of Helen's assets on January 1, 1996	$200,000	
Less liabilities on January 1, 1996	(80,000)	
Net worth on January 1, 1996		(120,000)

[2] *James v. U.S.*, 61–1 USTC ¶9449, 7 AFTR2d 1361, 81 S.Ct. 1052 (USSC, 1961).

[3] *Merchants Loan and Trust Co. v. Smietanka*, 1 USTC ¶42, 3 AFTR 3102, 41 S.Ct. 386 (USSC, 1921).

[4] See Henry C. Simons, *Personal Income Taxation* (Chicago: University of Chicago Press, 1933), Ch. 2–3.

Increase in net worth	$60,000
Consumption	
Food, clothing, and other personal expenditures	25,000
Imputed rental value of Helen's home she owns and occupies	12,000
Economic income	$97,000

The need to value assets annually would make compliance with the tax law burdensome and would cause numerous controversies between the taxpayer and the IRS over valuation. In addition, using market values to determine income for tax purposes could result in liquidity problems. That is, the taxpayer's assets may increase in value even though they are not readily convertible into the cash needed to pay the tax (e.g., commercial real estate). Thus, the IRS, Congress, and the courts have rejected the economic concept of income as impractical.

In contrast, the accounting concept of income is founded on the realization principle.[5] According to this principle, income (**accounting income**) is not recognized until it is realized. For realization to occur, (1) an exchange of goods or services must take place between the accounting entity and some independent, external group, and (2) in the exchange the accounting entity must receive assets that are capable of being objectively valued. Thus, the mere appreciation in the market value of assets before a sale or other disposition is not sufficient to warrant income recognition. In addition, the imputed savings that arise when an individual creates assets for his or her own use (e.g., feed grown for a farmer's own livestock) are not income because no exchange has occurred. The courts and the IRS have ruled, however, that embezzlement proceeds and buried treasures found satisfy the realization requirement and, therefore, must be recognized as income.[6]

The Supreme Court expressed an inclination toward the accounting concept of income when it adopted the realization requirement in *Eisner v. Macomber:*

> Income may be defined as the gain derived from capital, from labor, or from both combined, provided it is understood to include profit gained through a sale or conversion of capital assets. . . . Here we have the essential matter: not a gain accruing to capital; not a *growth* or *increment* of value *in* investment; but a gain, a profit, something of exchangeable value, *proceeding from* the property, *severed from* the capital however invested or employed, and *coming in,* being *"derived"*—that is, *received* or *drawn by* the recipient for his separate use, benefit and disposal—*that is,* income derived from the property.[7]

In summary, *income* represents an increase in wealth recognized for tax purposes only upon realization.

COMPARISON OF THE ACCOUNTING AND TAX CONCEPTS OF INCOME

Although income tax rules frequently parallel financial accounting measurement concepts, differences do exist. Of major significance, for example, is the fact that unearned (prepaid) income received by an accrual basis taxpayer often is taxed in the year of receipt. For financial accounting purposes, such prepayments are not

---

[5]See the American Accounting Association Committee Report on the "Realization Concept," *The Accounting Review* (April 1965): 312–322.

[6]*Rutkin v. U.S.,* 52–1 USTC ¶9260, 41 AFTR2d 596, 72 S.Ct. 571 (USSC, 1952); Rev.Rul. 61, 1953–1 C.B. 17.

[7]1 USTC ¶32, 3 AFTR 3020, 40 S.Ct. 189 (USSC, 1920).

TAX IN THE NEWS

TAXPAYER RECEIVED BENEFITS GREATER THAN HE BARGAINED FOR

Mr. Wentz, who had been an insurance agent for over 40 years, devised a scheme with his insurance agent whereby Mr. Wentz could receive insurance protection for one year at no cost to him. At the beginning of the year, Mr. Wentz purchased a whole life insurance policy. The insurance agent received a commission equal to 115 percent of Mr. Wentz's premiums for the first year. Then the insurance agent reimbursed Mr. Wentz the amount of the first-year premium, and at the end of the year, Mr. Wentz canceled the policy. The idea was that Mr. Wentz would get insurance protection for one year and the agent would keep the commission less the premium. The Tax Court had little trouble concluding that Mr. Wentz realized income from the transaction since he received insurance protection for one year.

After Mr. Wentz lost on the question of whether he received income, the next question was how to measure the amount of the income. Mr. Wentz argued that if he realized income, it amounted to the cost of term insurance protection for one year, which is what he expected to receive from the scam on the insurance company. The Tax Court disagreed and ruled that the income amounted to the first year's premium for a whole life policy—the amount Mr. Wentz paid before the reimbursement—which was more than twice the cost of term protection. Mr. Wentz did not want a whole life policy and would not have entered into a contract to receive such a policy without the scheme. The net result was that Mr. Wentz was required to pay more income tax than term insurance would have cost. In addition, Mr. Wentz (or his estate) probably would not have been able to enforce the insurance contract because it arose out of a fraudulent scheme.

SOURCE: *John R. Wentz*, 105 T.C. 1, No. 1 (1995).

treated as income until earned.[8] Because of this and other differences, many corporations report financial accounting income that is substantially different from the amounts reported for tax purposes (see Chapter 16, Reconciliation of Taxable Income and Accounting Income).

The Supreme Court provided an explanation for some of the variations between accounting and taxable income in a decision involving inventory and bad debt adjustments:

> The primary goal of financial accounting is to provide useful information to management, shareholders, creditors, and others properly interested; the major responsibility of the accountant is to protect these parties from being misled. The primary goal of the income tax system, in contrast, is the equitable collection of revenue. . . . Consistently with its goals and responsibilities, financial accounting has as its foundation the principle of conservatism, with its corollary that 'possible errors in measurement [should] be in the direction of understatement rather than overstatement of net income and net assets'. In view of the Treasury's markedly different goals and responsibilities, understatement of income is not destined to be its guiding light.

---

[8] Similar differences exist in the deduction area.

. . . Financial accounting, in short, is hospitable to estimates, probabilities, and reasonable certainties; the tax law, with its mandate to preserve the revenue, can give no quarter to uncertainty.[9]

FORM OF RECEIPT

Gross income is not limited to cash received. "It includes income realized in any form, whether in money, property, or services. Income may be realized [and recognized], therefore, in the form of services, meals, accommodations, stock or other property, as well as in cash."[10]

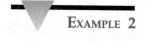

EXAMPLE 2 Ostrich Corporation allowed Bill, an employee, to use a company car for his vacation. Bill realized income equal to the rental value of the car for the time and mileage. ▼

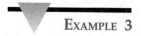

EXAMPLE 3 Terry owed $10,000 on a mortgage. The creditor accepted $8,000 in full satisfaction of the debt. Terry realized income of $2,000 from retiring the debt.[11] ▼

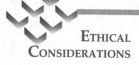

ETHICAL CONSIDERATIONS

Unreported Income

You often see your clients at various civic meetings. During the social hour preceding a recent civic meeting, a client told you several stories about his adventures when flying. The client said he had not had to pay any airfare for his vacation in Mexico because he had used the frequent flyer points accumulated from tickets purchased by his employer. He noted, however, that he got sick in Mexico and did not enjoy his stay. Then, when he was on the plane ready to take off for home, the flight attendant announced that the flight was overbooked. The airline offered any passengers who would surrender their seats a seat on a flight to the same location that was leaving in one hour and a free round-trip ticket to any city the airline served. Your client accepted the offer and received a ticket that he used to attend his mother's funeral in Florida.

Soon after the end of the year, the client brings you the information to prepare his tax return. The information does not mention anything about the airline tickets he received. You pause to consider whether the tax system is working properly when, under the broad concept of gross income, your client may have to pay tax on the value of airfares for trips he did not enjoy. You also reflect on his likely reaction if you add these amounts to his taxable income. Evaluate this dilemma.

RECOVERY OF CAPITAL DOCTRINE

The Constitution grants Congress the power to tax income but does not define the term. Because the Constitution does not define income, it would seem that Congress could simply tax gross receipts. Although Congress does allow certain deductions, none are constitutionally required. However, the Supreme Court has

---

[9]*Thor Power Tool Co. v. Comm.*, 79–1 USTC ¶9139, 43 AFTR2d 79–362, 99 S.Ct. 773 (USSC, 1979).
[10]Reg. § 1.61–1(a).

[11]Reg. § 1.61–12. See *U.S. v. Kirby Lumber Co.*, 2 USTC ¶814, 10 AFTR 458, 52 S.Ct. 4 (USSC, 1931). Exceptions to this general rule are discussed in Chapter 4.

held that there is no income subject to tax until the taxpayer has recovered the capital invested.[12] This concept is known as the **recovery of capital doctrine.**

In its simplest application, this doctrine means that sellers can reduce their gross receipts (selling price) by the adjusted basis of the property sold.[13] This net amount, in the language of the Code, is gross income.

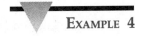

EXAMPLE 4

Dave sold common stock for $15,000. He had purchased the stock for $12,000. Dave's gross receipts are $15,000. This amount consists of a $12,000 recovery of capital and $3,000 of gross income. ▼

YEAR OF INCLUSION

TAXABLE YEAR

2 **LEARNING OBJECTIVE**
Describe the cash and accrual methods of accounting and the related effects of the choice of taxable year.

The annual accounting period or **taxable year** is a basic component of our tax system.[14] Generally, an entity must use the *calendar year* to report its income. However, a *fiscal year* (a period of 12 months ending on the last day of any month other than December) can be elected if the taxpayer maintains adequate books and records. This fiscal year option generally is not available to partnerships, S corporations, and personal service corporations, as discussed in Chapter 15.[15]

Determining the particular year in which the income will be taxed is important for determining when the tax must be paid. But the year each item of income is subject to tax can also affect the total tax liability over the entity's lifetime. This is true for the following reasons:

- With a progressive rate system, a taxpayer's marginal tax rate can change from year to year.
- Congress may change the tax rates.
- The relevant rates may change because of a change in the entity's status (e.g., a person may marry or a business may be incorporated).
- Several provisions in the Code are dependent on the taxpayer's gross income for the year (e.g., whether the person can be claimed as a dependent, as discussed in Chapter 2).

ACCOUNTING METHODS

The year an item of income is subject to tax often depends upon which acceptable **accounting method** the taxpayer regularly employs.[16] The three primary methods of accounting are (1) the cash receipts and disbursements method, (2) the accrual method, and (3) the hybrid method. Most individuals use the cash receipts and disbursements method of accounting, whereas most corporations use the accrual method. The Regulations require the accrual method for determining purchases and sales when inventory is an income-producing factor.[17] Some businesses employ a hybrid method that is a combination of the cash and accrual methods of accounting.

---

[12] *Doyle v. Mitchell Bros. Co.*, 1 USTC ¶17, 3 AFTR 2979, 38 S.Ct. 467 (USSC, 1916).
[13] For a definition of adjusted basis, see the Glossary of Tax Terms in Appendix C.
[14] See Accounting Periods in Chapter 15.

[15] §§ 441(a) and (d).
[16] See Accounting Methods in Chapter 15.
[17] Reg. § 1.446–1(c)(2)(i). Other circumstances in which the accrual method must be used are presented in Chapter 15.

In addition to these overall accounting methods, a taxpayer may choose to spread the gain from the sale of property over the collection periods by using the installment method of income recognition. Contractors may either spread profits from contracts over the periods in which the work is done (the percentage of completion method) or defer all profit until the year in which the project is completed (the completed contract method, which can be used only in limited circumstances).[18]

The IRS has the power to prescribe the accounting method to be used by the taxpayer. Section 446(b) grants the IRS broad powers to determine if the accounting method used *clearly reflects income:*

> Exceptions—If no method of accounting has been regularly used by the taxpayer, or *if the method used does not clearly reflect income, the computation of taxable income shall be made under such method as, in the opinion of the Secretary . . . does clearly reflect income.*

A change in the method of accounting requires the consent of the IRS.[19]

Cash Receipts Method.   Under the **cash receipts method,** property or services received are included in the taxpayer's gross income in the year of actual or constructive receipt by the taxpayer or agent, regardless of whether the income was earned in that year.[20] The income received need not be reduced to cash in the same year. All that is necessary for income recognition is that property or services received have a fair market value—a cash equivalent.[21] Thus, if a cash basis taxpayer receives a note in payment for services, he or she has income in the year of receipt equal to the fair market value of the note. However, a creditor's mere promise to pay (e.g., an account receivable), with no supporting note, is not usually considered to have a fair market value.[22] Thus, the cash basis taxpayer defers income recognition until the account receivable is collected.

EXAMPLE 5   Dana, an accountant, reports her income by the cash method. In 1996, she performed an audit for Orange Corporation and billed the client for $5,000, which was collected in 1997. In 1996, Dana also performed an audit for Blue Corporation. Because of Blue's precarious financial position, Dana required Blue to issue an $8,000 secured negotiable note in payment of the fee. The note had a fair market value of $6,000. Dana collected $8,000 on the note in 1997. Dana's gross income for the two years is as follows:

	1996	1997
Fair market value of note received from Blue	$6,000	
Cash received		
From Orange on account receivable		$ 5,000
From Blue on note receivable		8,000
Less: Recovery of capital		(6,000)
Total gross income	$6,000	$ 7,000

---

[18] §§ 453(a) and (b), § 453A, and Reg. § 1.451–3. See Chapter 15 for limitations on the use of the installment method and the completed contract method.
[19] § 446(e). See Chapter 15.
[20] *Julia A. Strauss,* 2 B.T.A. 598 (1925). See the Glossary of Tax Terms in Appendix C for a discussion of the terms "cash equivalent doctrine" and "constructive receipt."

[21] Reg. §§ 1.446–1(a)(3) and (c)(1)(i).
[22] *Bedell v. Comm.,* 1 USTC ¶359, 7 AFTR 8469, 30 F.2d 622 (CA–2, 1929).

Generally, a check received is considered a cash equivalent. Thus, a cash basis taxpayer must recognize the income when the check is received. This is true even though the taxpayer receives the check after banking hours.[23]

Accrual Method. Under the **accrual method,** an item is generally included in the gross income for the year in which it is earned, regardless of when the income is collected. The income is earned when (1) all the events have occurred that fix the right to receive such income and (2) the amount to be received can be determined with reasonable accuracy.[24]

Generally, the taxpayer's rights to the income accrue when title to property passes to the buyer or the services are performed for the customer or client.[25] If the rights to the income have accrued but are subject to a potential refund claim (e.g., under a product warranty), the income is reported in the year of sale, and a deduction is allowed in subsequent years when actual claims accrue.[26]

Where the taxpayer's rights to the income are being contested (e.g., when a contractor fails to meet specifications), the year in which the income is subject to tax depends upon whether payment has been received. If payment has not been received, no income is recognized until the claim is settled. Only then is the right to the income established.[27] However, if the payment is received before the dispute is settled, the court-made **claim of right doctrine** requires the taxpayer to recognize the income in the year of receipt.[28]

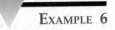

EXAMPLE 6

A contractor completed a building in 1996 and presented a bill to the customer. The customer refused to pay the bill and claimed that the contractor had not met specifications. A settlement with the customer was not reached until 1997. No income would accrue to the contractor until 1997. If the customer paid for the work and then filed suit for damages, the contractor could not defer the income (the income would be taxable in 1996). ▼

The measure of accrual basis income is generally the amount the taxpayer has a right to receive. Unlike the cash basis, the fair market value of the customer's obligation is irrelevant in measuring accrual basis income.

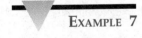

EXAMPLE 7

Assume the same facts as in Example 5, except Dana is an accrual basis taxpayer. Dana must recognize $13,000 ($8,000 + $5,000) income in 1996, the year her rights to the income accrued. ▼

Hybrid Method. The **hybrid method** is a combination of the accrual method and the cash method. Generally, when the hybrid method is used, inventory is an income-producing factor. Therefore, the Regulations require that the accrual method be used for determining sales and cost of goods sold. In this circumstance, to simplify record keeping, the taxpayer accounts for inventory using the accrual method and uses the cash method for all other income and expense items (e.g., dividend and interest income). The hybrid method is primarily used by small businesses.

---

[23] *Charles F. Kahler,* 18 T.C. 31 (1952).
[24] Reg. § 1.451–1(a).
[25] *Lucas v. North Texas Lumber Co.,* 2 USTC ¶484, 8 AFTR 10276, 50 S.Ct. 184 (USSC, 1930).
[26] *Brown v. Helvering,* 4 USTC ¶1222, 13 AFTR 851, 54 S.Ct. 356 (USSC, 1933).

[27] *Burnet v. Sanford and Brooks,* 2 USTC ¶636, 9 AFTR 603, 51 S.Ct. 150 (USSC, 1931).
[28] *North American Oil Consolidated Co. v. Burnet,* 3 USTC ¶943, 11 AFTR 16, 52 S.Ct. 613 (USSC, 1932).

EXCEPTIONS APPLICABLE TO CASH BASIS TAXPAYERS

Constructive Receipt. Income that has not actually been received by the taxpayer is taxed as though it had been received—the income is constructively received—under the following conditions:

- The amount is made readily available to the taxpayer.
- The taxpayer's actual receipt is not subject to substantial limitations or restrictions.[29]

The rationale for the **constructive receipt** doctrine is that if the income is available, the taxpayer should not be allowed to postpone the income recognition. For instance, a taxpayer is not permitted to defer income for December services by refusing to accept payment until January. However, determining whether the income is *readily available* and whether *substantial limitations or restrictions exist* necessitates a factual inquiry that leads to a judgment call.[30] The following are some examples of the application of the constructive receipt doctrine.

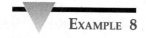

EXAMPLE 8   Ted is a member of a barter club. In 1996, Ted performed services for other club members and earned 1,000 points. Each point entitles him to $1 in goods and services sold by other members of the club; the points can be used at any time. In 1997, Ted exchanged his points for a new color TV. Ted must recognize $1,000 income in 1996 when the 1,000 points were credited to his account.[31] ▼

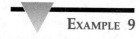

EXAMPLE 9   On December 31, an employer issued a bonus check to an employee but asked her to hold it for a few days until the company could make deposits to cover the check. The income was not constructively received on December 31 since the issuer did not have sufficient funds in its account to pay the debt.[32] ▼

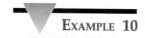

EXAMPLE 10   Rick owned interest coupons that matured on December 31. The coupons could be converted to cash at any bank at maturity. Thus, the income was constructively received on December 31.[33] ▼

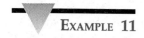

EXAMPLE 11   Dove Company mails dividend checks on December 31, 1996. The checks will not be received by shareholders until January. The shareholders do not realize income until 1997.[34] ▼

The constructive receipt doctrine does not reach income that the taxpayer is not yet entitled to receive even though he or she could have contracted to receive the income at an earlier date.

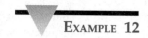

EXAMPLE 12   Sara offered to pay Ivan $100,000 for land in December 1996. Ivan refused but offered to sell the land to Sara on January 1, 1997, when he would be in a lower tax bracket. If Sara accepts Ivan's offer, the gain is taxed to Ivan in 1997 when the sale is completed.[35] ▼

Original Issue Discount. Lenders frequently make loans that require a payment at maturity of more than the amount of the original loan. The difference between the amount due at maturity and the amount of the original loan is actually interest but is referred to as **original issue discount.** Under the general

---

[29] Reg. § 1.451–2(a).
[30] *Baxter v. Comm.*, 87–1 USTC ¶9315, 59 AFTR2d 87–1068, 816 F.2d 493 (CA–9, 1987).
[31] Rev.Rul. 80–52, 1980–1 C.B. 100.
[32] *L. M. Fischer*, 14 T.C. 792 (1950).

[33] Reg. § 1.451–2(b).
[34] Reg. § 1.451–2(b).
[35] *Cowden v. Comm.*, 61–1 USTC ¶9382, 7 AFTR2d 1160, 289 F.2d 20 (CA–5, 1961).

rules of tax accounting, the cash basis lender would not report the original issue discount as interest income until the year the amount is collected, although an accrual basis borrower would deduct the interest as it is earned. However, the Code puts the lender and borrower on parity by requiring that the original issue discount be reported when it is earned, regardless of the taxpayer's accounting method.[36] The interest "earned" is calculated by the effective interest rate method.

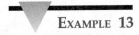

EXAMPLE 13

On January 1, 1996, Mark, a cash basis taxpayer, paid $82,645 for a 24-month certificate. The certificate was priced to yield 10% (the effective interest rate) with interest compounded annually. No interest was paid until maturity, when Mark received $100,000. Thus, Mark's gross income from the certificate is $17,355 ($100,000 − $82,645). Mark's income earned each year is calculated as follows:

1996 (.10 × $82,645) =	$ 8,264
1997 [.10 × ($82,645 + $8,264)] =	9,091
	$17,355

The original issue discount rules do not apply to U.S. savings bonds (discussed in the following paragraphs) or to obligations with a maturity date of one year or less from the date of issue.[37] See Chapter 13 for additional discussion of the tax treatment of original issue discount.

Series E and Series EE Bonds.   Certain U.S. government savings bonds (Series E before 1980 and Series EE after 1979) are issued at a discount and are redeemable for fixed amounts that increase at stated intervals. No interest payments are actually made. The difference between the purchase price and the amount received on redemption is the bondholder's interest income from the investment.

The income from these savings bonds is generally deferred until the bonds are redeemed or mature. Furthermore, Series E bonds can be exchanged within one year of their maturity date for Series HH bonds, and the interest on the Series E bonds can be further deferred until maturity of the Series HH bonds.[38] Thus, U.S. savings bonds have attractive income deferral features not available with corporate bonds and certificates of deposit issued by financial institutions.

Of course, the deferral feature of government bonds issued at a discount is not an advantage if the investor has insufficient income to be subject to tax as the income accrues. In fact, the deferral may work to the investor's disadvantage if he or she has other income in the year the bonds mature or the bunching of the bond interest into one tax year creates a tax liability. Fortunately, U.S. government bonds have a provision for these investors. A cash basis taxpayer can elect to include in gross income the annual increment in redemption value.[39]

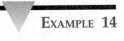

EXAMPLE 14

Kate purchases Series EE U.S. savings bonds for $500 (face value of $1,000) on January 2 of the current year. If the bonds are redeemed during the first six months, no interest is paid. At December 31, the redemption value is $519.60.

If Kate elects to report the interest income annually, she must report interest income of $19.60 for the current year. If she does not make the election, she will report no interest income for the current year. ▼

---

[36] §§ 1272(a)(3) and 1273(a).
[37] § 1272(a)(2).
[38] Treas. Dept. Circulars No. 1–80 and No. 2–80, 1980–1 C.B. 714, 715. Note that interest is paid at semiannual intervals on the

Series HH bonds and must be included in income as received. See Chapter 4 for a discussion of the savings bond interest exclusion.
[39] § 454(a).

When a taxpayer elects to report the income from the bonds on an annual basis, the election applies to all such bonds the taxpayer owns at the time of the election and to all such securities acquired subsequent to the election. A change in the method of reporting the income from the bonds requires permission from the IRS.

Amounts Received under an Obligation to Repay.   The receipt of funds with an obligation to repay that amount in the future is the essence of borrowing. Because the taxpayer's assets and liabilities increase by the same amount, no income is realized when the borrowed funds are received. Because amounts paid to the taxpayer by mistake and customer deposits are often classified as borrowed funds, receipt of the funds is not a taxable event.

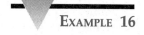
EXAMPLE 15

A landlord receives a damage deposit from a tenant. The landlord does not recognize income until the deposit is forfeited because the landlord has an obligation to repay the deposit if no damage occurs.[40] However, if the deposit is in fact a prepayment of rent, it is taxed in the year of receipt. ▼

EXCEPTIONS APPLICABLE TO ACCRUAL BASIS TAXPAYERS

Prepaid Income.   For financial reporting purposes, advance payments received from customers are reflected as prepaid income and as a liability of the seller. However, for tax purposes, the prepaid income often is taxed in the year of receipt.

EXAMPLE 16

In December 1996, a tenant paid his January 1997 rent of $1,000. The accrual basis landlord must include the $1,000 in his 1996 income for tax purposes, although the unearned rent income is reported as a liability on the landlord's December 31, 1996, balance sheet. ▼

Taxpayers have repeatedly argued that deferral of income until it is actually earned properly matches revenues and expenses. Moreover, a proper matching of income with the expenses of earning the income is necessary to clearly reflect income, as required by the Code. The IRS responds that § 446(b) grants it broad powers to determine whether an accounting method clearly reflects income. The IRS further argues that generally accepted financial accounting principles should not dictate tax accounting for prepaid income because of the practical problems of collecting Federal revenues. Collection of the tax is simplest in the year the taxpayer receives the cash from the customer or client.

Over 40 years of litigation, the IRS has been only partially successful in the courts. In cases involving prepaid income from services to be performed at the demand of customers (e.g., dance lessons to be taken at any time in a 24-month period), the IRS's position has been upheld.[41] In such cases, the taxpayer's argument that deferral of the income was necessary to match the income with expenses was not persuasive because the taxpayer did not know precisely when each customer would demand services and, thus, when the expenses would be incurred. However, taxpayers have had some success in the courts when the services were performed on a fixed schedule (e.g., a baseball team's season-ticket

---

[40] *John Mantell*, 17 T.C. 1143 (1952).

[41] *American Automobile Association v. U.S.*, 61–2 USTC ¶9517, 7 AFTR2d 1618, 81 S.Ct. 1727 (USSC, 1961); *Schlude v. Comm.*, 63–1 USTC ¶9284, 11 AFTR2d 751, 83 S.Ct. 601 (USSC, 1963).

sales).[42] In some cases involving the sale of goods, taxpayers have successfully argued that the prepayments were mere deposits[43] or in the nature of loans.[44]

Against this background of mixed results in the courts, congressional intervention, and taxpayers' strong resentment of the IRS's position, in 1971 the IRS modified its prepaid income rules, as explained in the following paragraphs.

Deferral of Advance Payments for Goods.   Generally, a taxpayer can elect to defer recognition of income from *advance payments for goods* if the method of accounting for the sale is the same for tax and financial reporting purposes.[45]

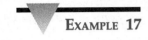

EXAMPLE 17

Brown Company will ship goods only after payment for the goods has been received. In December 1996, Brown received $10,000 for goods that were not shipped until January 1997. Brown can elect to report the income for tax purposes in 1997, assuming the company reports the income in 1997 for financial reporting purposes. ▼

Deferral of Advance Payments for Services.   Revenue Procedure 71–21[46] permits an accrual basis taxpayer to defer recognition of income for *advance payments for services* to be performed by the end of the tax year following the year of receipt. No deferral is allowed if the taxpayer might be required to perform any services, under the agreement, after the tax year following the year of receipt of the advance payment. In addition, prepaid rent and prepaid interest cannot be deferred under this revenue procedure.

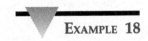

EXAMPLE 18

Yellow Corporation, an accrual basis taxpayer, sells its services under 12-month, 18-month, and 24-month contracts. The corporation provides services to each customer every month. In April of 1996, Yellow Corporation sold the following customer contracts:

Length of Contract	Total Proceeds
12 months	$6,000
18 months	3,600
24 months	2,400

Fifteen hundred dollars of the $6,000 may be deferred ($3/12 \times \$6,000$), and $1,800 of the $3,600 may be deferred ($9/18 \times \$3,600$) because those amounts will not be earned until 1997. However, the entire $2,400 received on the 24-month contracts is taxable in the year of receipt (1996), since a part of the income will still be unearned by the end of the tax year following the year of receipt (part will be earned in 1998). ▼

Revenue Procedure 71–21 does *not apply* to prepaid rent or prepaid interest. These items are always taxed in the year of receipt.

[42] *Artnell Company v. Comm.*, 68–2 USTC ¶9593, 22 AFTR2d 5590, 400 F.2d 981 (CA–7, 1968). See also *Boise Cascade Corp. v. U.S.*, 76–1 USTC ¶9203, 37 AFTR2d 76–696, 530 F.2d 1367 (Ct. Cls., 1976).

[43] *Veenstra & DeHavaan Coal Co.*, 11 T.C. 964 (1948).

[44] *Consolidated-Hammer Dry Plate & Film Co. v. Comm.*, 63–1 USTC ¶9494, 11 AFTR2d 1518, 317 F.2d 829 (CA–7, 1963); *Comm. v.*

Indianapolis Power & Light Co., 90–1 USTC ¶50,007, 65 AFTR2d 90–394, 110 S.Ct. 589 (USSC, 1990).

[45] Reg. § 1.451–5(b). See Reg. § 1.451–5(c) for exceptions to this deferral opportunity. The financial accounting conformity requirement is not applicable to contractors who use the completed contract method.

[46] 1971–2 C.B. 549.

INCOME SOURCES

PERSONAL SERVICES

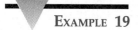

3 LEARNING OBJECTIVE
Identify who should pay the tax on a particular item of income in various situations.

It is a well-established principle of taxation that income from personal services must be included in the gross income of the person who performs the services. This principle was first established in a Supreme Court decision, *Lucas v. Earl*.[47] Mr. Earl entered into a binding agreement with his wife under which Mrs. Earl was to receive one-half of Mr. Earl's salary. Justice Holmes used the celebrated **fruit and tree metaphor** to explain that the fruit (income) must be attributed to the tree from which it came (Mr. Earl's services). A mere **assignment of income** does not shift the liability for the tax.

Services of an Employee. Services performed by an employee for the employer's customers are considered performed by the employer. Thus, the employer is taxed on the income from the services provided to the customer, and the employee is taxed on any compensation received from the employer.[48]

EXAMPLE 19

Dr. Shontelle incorporated her medical practice and entered into a contract to work for the corporation for a salary. All patients contracted to receive their services from the corporation, and those services were provided through the corporation's employee, Dr. Shontelle. The corporation must include the patients' fees in its gross income. Dr. Shontelle must include her salary in her gross income. The corporation will be allowed a deduction for the reasonable salary paid to Dr. Shontelle (see the discussion of unreasonable compensation in Chapter 5). ▼

Services of a Child. In the case of a child, the Code specifically provides that amounts earned from personal services must be included in the child's gross income. This result applies even though the income is paid to other persons (e.g., the parents).[49]

INCOME FROM PROPERTY

Income from property (interest, dividends, rent) must be included in the gross income of the *owner* of the property. If a father clips interest coupons from bonds shortly before the interest payment date and gives the coupons to his son, the interest will still be taxed to the father. A father who assigns rents from rental property to his daughter will be taxed on the rent since he retains ownership of the property.[50]

Often income-producing property is transferred after income from the property has accrued but before the income is recognized under the transferor's method of accounting. The IRS and the courts have developed rules to allocate the income between the transferor and the transferee.

---

[47] 2 USTC ¶496, 8 AFTR 10287, 50 S.Ct. 241 (USSC, 1930).

[48] *Sargent v. Comm.*, 91–1 USTC ¶50,168, 67 AFTR2d 91–718, 929 F.2d 1252 (CA–8, 1991).

[49] § 73. For circumstances in which the child's unearned income is taxed at the parents' rate, see Unearned Income of Certain Minor Children Taxed at Parents' Rate in Chapter 2.

[50] *Galt v. Comm.*, 54–2 USTC ¶9457, 46 AFTR 633, 216 F.2d 41 (CA–7, 1954); *Helvering v. Horst*, 40–2 USTC ¶9787, 24 AFTR 1058, 61 S.Ct. 144 (USSC, 1940).

Interest.   According to the IRS, interest accrues daily. Therefore, the interest for the period that includes the date of the transfer is allocated between the transferor and transferee based on the number of days during the period that each owned the property.

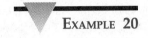

EXAMPLE 20

Floyd, a cash basis taxpayer, gave his son, Seth, bonds with a face amount of $10,000 and an 8% stated annual interest rate. The gift was made on January 31, 1996, and the interest was paid on December 31, 1996. Floyd must recognize $68 in interest income (8% × $10,000 × $^{31}/_{366}$). Seth will recognize $732 in interest income ($800 − $68). ▼

When the transferor must recognize the income from the property depends upon the method of accounting and the manner in which the property was transferred. In the case of a gift of income-producing property, the donor must recognize his or her share of the accrued income at the time it would have been recognized had the donor continued to own the property.[51] However, if the transfer is a sale, the transferor must recognize the accrued income at the time of the sale. This results because the accrued interest will be included in the sales proceeds.

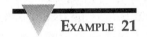

EXAMPLE 21

Assume the same facts as in Example 20, except the interest that was payable as of December 31 was not actually or constructively received by the bondholders until January 3, 1997. As a cash basis taxpayer, Floyd generally does not recognize interest income until it is received. If Floyd had continued to own the bonds, the interest would have been included in his 1997 gross income, the year it would have been received. Therefore, Floyd must include the $68 accrued income in his gross income as of January 3, 1997.

Further assume that Floyd sold identical bonds on the date of the gift. The bonds sold for $9,900, including accrued interest. On January 31, 1996, Floyd must recognize the accrued interest of $68 on the bonds sold. Thus, the selling price of the bonds is $9,832 ($9,900 − $68). ▼

Dividends.   A corporation is taxed on its earnings, and the shareholders are taxed on the dividends paid to them from the corporation's after-tax earnings. The dividend can take the form of an actual dividend or a constructive dividend (e.g., shareholder use of corporate assets).

Unlike interest, dividends do not accrue on a daily basis because the declaration of a dividend is at the discretion of the corporation's board of directors. Generally, dividends are taxed to the person who is entitled to receive them—the shareholder of record as of the corporation's record date.[52] Thus, if a taxpayer sells stock after a dividend has been declared but before the record date, the dividend generally will be taxed to the purchaser.

If a donor makes a gift of stock to someone (e.g., a family member) after the declaration date but before the record date, the Tax Court has held that the donor does not shift the dividend income to the donee. The *fruit* has sufficiently ripened as of the declaration date to tax the dividend income to the donor of the stock.[53] In a similar set of facts, the Fifth Court of Appeals concluded that the dividend income should be included in the gross income of the donee (the owner at the

[51] Rev.Rul. 72–312, 1972–1 C.B. 22.

[52] Reg. § 1.61–9(c). The record date is the cutoff for determining the shareholders who are entitled to receive the dividend.

[53] *M. G. Anton*, 34 T.C. 842 (1960).

record date). In this case, the taxpayer gave stock to a qualified charity (a charitable contribution) after the declaration date and before the record date.[54]

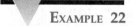

EXAMPLE 22

On June 20, the board of directors of Black Corporation declares a $10 per share dividend. The dividend is payable on June 30, to shareholders of record on June 25. As of June 20, Maria owned 200 shares of Black Corporation's stock. On June 21, Maria sold 100 of the shares to Norm for their fair market value and gave 100 of the shares to Sam (her son). Assume both Norm and Sam are shareholders of record as of June 25. Norm (the purchaser) will be taxed on $1,000 since he is entitled to receive the dividend. However, Maria (the donor) will be taxed on the $1,000 received by Sam (the donee) because the gift was made after the declaration date of the dividend. ▼

INCOME RECEIVED BY AN AGENT

Income received by the taxpayer's agent is considered to be received by the taxpayer. A cash basis principal must recognize the income at the time it is received by the agent.[55]

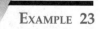

EXAMPLE 23

Jack, a cash basis taxpayer, delivered cattle to the auction barn in late December. The auctioneer, acting as the farmer's agent, sold the cattle and collected the proceeds in December. The auctioneer did not pay Jack until the following January. Jack must include the sales proceeds in his gross income for the year the auctioneer received the funds. ▼

INCOME FROM PARTNERSHIPS, S CORPORATIONS, TRUSTS, AND ESTATES

A **partnership** is not a separate taxable entity. Rather, the partnership merely files an information return (Form 1065), which serves to provide the data necessary for determining the character and amount of each partner's distributive share of the partnership's income and deductions. Each partner must then report his or her

---

[54] *Caruth Corporation v. U.S.*, 89–1 USTC ¶9172, 63 AFTR2d 89–716, 865 F.2d 644 (CA–5, 1989).

[55] Rev.Rul. 79–379, 1979–2 C.B. 204.

distributive share of the partnership's income and deductions for the partnership's tax year ending within or with his or her tax year. The income must be reported by each partner in the year it is earned, even if such amounts are not actually distributed to the partners. Because a partner pays tax on income as the partnership earns it, a distribution by the partnership to the partner is treated under the recovery of capital rules.[56]

EXAMPLE 24

Tara owned a one-half interest in the capital and profits of T & S Company (a calendar year partnership). For tax year 1996, the partnership earned revenue of $150,000 and had operating expenses of $80,000. During the year, Tara withdrew from her capital account $2,500 per month (for a total of $30,000). For 1996, Tara must report $35,000 as her share of the partnership's profits [½ × ($150,000 − $80,000)] even though she received distributions of only $30,000. ▼

ETHICAL
CONSIDERATIONS

Whether to Report Income

You are the treasurer of a scout troop. The scouts conduct car washes and use the proceeds to pay for troop members to attend summer camp. The income is allocated among the 60 troop members based on the number of hours each worked. No scout earned more than $100 for the year, and the average amount earned was $50. The IRS, if it were aware of the facts, would probably reason that the car wash operation is a partnership, and each scout is a partner. Thus, the troop would have to file a partnership tax return, and each of the 60 scouts would report his or her share of the income. From the data available, you ascertain that reporting the income would affect the liability of no more than 5 of the scouts (because of their standard deduction) and that the tax for each of the 5 scouts affected would not exceed $15.

In your opinion, the cost to the IRS and the total cost of paper consumed by the process of filing the returns would exceed the increase in IRS revenue. In addition, filing the partnership return and reporting each partner's share would be a lot of extra work for you. Therefore, you feel that filing the return and reporting each scout's share of the income are not worth the effort. Evaluate your position from both a compliance and an ethical perspective.

Contrary to the general provision that a corporation must pay tax on its income, a *small business corporation* may elect to be taxed similarly to a partnership. Thus, the shareholders, rather than the corporation, pay the tax on the corporation's income.[57] The electing corporation is referred to as an **S corporation.** Generally, the shareholder reports his or her proportionate share of the corporation's income and deductions for the year, whether or not the corporation actually makes any distributions to the shareholder.

The *beneficiaries of estates and trusts* generally are taxed on the income earned by the estates or trusts that is actually distributed or required to be distributed to them.[58] Any income not taxed to the beneficiaries is taxable to the estate or trust.

---

[56] § 706(a) and Reg. § 1.706–1(a)(1). For further discussion, see Chapter 22.

[57] §§ 1361(a) and 1366. For further discussion, see Chapter 21.

[58] §§ 652(a) and 662(a). For further discussion of the taxation of income from S corporations, partnerships, estates, and trusts, see Chapters 21, 22, 26, and 27.

INCOME IN COMMUNITY PROPERTY STATES

State law in Louisiana, Texas, New Mexico, Arizona, California, Washington, Idaho, Nevada, and Wisconsin is based upon a community property system. All other states have a common law property system. The basic difference between common law and community property systems centers around the property rights of married persons. Questions about community property income most frequently arise when the husband and wife file separate returns.

Under a **community property** system, all property is deemed either to be separately owned by the spouse or to belong to the marital community. Property may be held separately by a spouse if it was acquired before marriage or received by gift or inheritance following marriage. Otherwise, any property is deemed to be community property. For Federal tax purposes, each spouse is taxed on one-half of the income from property belonging to the community.

The laws of Texas, Louisiana, Wisconsin, and Idaho distinguish between separate property and the income it produces. In these states, the income from separate property belongs to the community. Accordingly, for Federal income tax purposes, each spouse is taxed on one-half of the income. In the remaining community property states, separate property produces separate income that the owner-spouse must report on his or her Federal income tax return.

What appears to be income, however, may really represent a recovery of capital. A recovery of capital and gain realized on separate property retain their identity as separate property. Items such as nontaxable stock dividends, royalties from mineral interests, and gains and losses from the sale of property take on the same classification as the assets to which they relate.

In all community property states, income from personal services (e.g., salaries, wages, income from a professional partnership) is generally treated as if one-half is earned by each spouse.

ITEMS SPECIFICALLY INCLUDED IN GROSS INCOME

4   LEARNING OBJECTIVE
Apply the Internal Revenue Code provisions on alimony, loans made at below-market interest rates, annuities, prizes and awards, group term life insurance, unemployment compensation, and Social Security benefits.

The general principles of gross income determination (discussed in the previous sections) as applied by the IRS and the courts have on occasion yielded results Congress found unacceptable. Consequently, Congress has provided more specific rules for determining the gross income from certain sources. Some of these special rules appear in §§ 71–90 of the Code.

ALIMONY AND SEPARATE MAINTENANCE PAYMENTS

When a married couple divorce or become legally separated, state law generally requires a division of the property accumulated during the marriage. In addition, one spouse may have a legal obligation to support the other spouse. The Code distinguishes between the support payments (alimony or separate maintenance) and the property division in terms of the tax consequences.

Alimony and separate maintenance payments are *deductible* by the party making the payments and are *includible* in the gross income of the party receiving the payments.[59] Thus, income is shifted from the income earner to the income beneficiary, who is better able to pay the tax on the amount received.

---

[59] §§ 71 and 215.

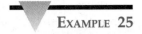

EXAMPLE 25

Pete and Tina were divorced, and Pete was required to pay Tina $15,000 of alimony each year. Pete earns $31,000 a year. The tax law presumes that because Tina received the $15,000, she is better able than Pete to pay the tax on that amount. Therefore, Tina must include the $15,000 in her gross income, and Pete is allowed to deduct $15,000 from his gross income. ▼

A transfer of property *other than cash* to a former spouse under a divorce decree or agreement is not a taxable event. The transferor is not entitled to a deduction and does not recognize gain or loss on the transfer. The transferee does not recognize income and has a cost basis equal to the transferor's basis.[60]

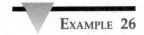

EXAMPLE 26

Paul transfers stock to Rosa as part of a 1996 divorce settlement. The cost of the stock to Paul is $12,000, and the stock's value at the time of the transfer is $15,000. Rosa later sells the stock for $16,000. Paul is not required to recognize gain from the transfer of the stock to Rosa, and Rosa has a realized and recognized gain of $4,000 ($16,000 − $12,000) when she sells the stock. ▼

In the case of *cash payments,* however, it is often difficult to distinguish payments under a support obligation (alimony) and payments for the other spouse's property (property settlement). In 1984, Congress developed objective rules to classify the payments.

Post-1984 Agreements and Decrees. Payments made under post-1984 agreements and decrees are *classified as alimony* only if the following conditions are satisfied:

1. The payments are in cash.
2. The agreement or decree does not specify that the payments are not alimony.
3. The payor and payee are not members of the same household at the time the payments are made.
4. There is no liability to make the payments for any period after the death of the payee.[61]

Requirement 1 simplifies the law by clearly distinguishing alimony from a property division; that is, if the payment is not in cash, it must be a property division. Requirement 2 allows the parties to determine by agreement whether or not the payments will be alimony. The prohibition on cohabitation—requirement 3—is aimed at assuring the alimony payments are associated with duplicative living expenses (maintaining two households).[62] Requirement 4 is an attempt to prevent alimony treatment from being applied to what is, in fact, a payment for property rather than a support obligation. That is, a seller's estate generally will receive payments for property due after the seller's death. Such payments after the death of the payee could not be for the payee's support.

Front-Loading. As a further safeguard against a property settlement being disguised as alimony, special rules apply to post-1986 agreements if payments in the first or second year exceed $15,000. If the change in the amount of the

---

[60] § 1041, added to the Code in 1984 to repeal the rule of *U.S. v. Davis,* 62-2 USTC ¶9509, 9 AFTR2d 1625, 82 S.Ct. 1190 (USSC, 1962). Under the Davis rule, which applied to pre-1985 divorces, a property transfer incident to divorce was a taxable event.

[61] § 71(b)(1). This set of alimony rules can also apply to pre-1985 agreements and decrees if both parties agree in writing. The rules

applicable to pre-1985 agreements and decrees are not discussed in this text.

[62] *Alexander Washington,* 77 T.C. 601 (1981) at 604.

payments exceeds statutory limits, **alimony recapture** results to the extent of the excess alimony payments. In the *third* year, the payor must include the excess alimony payments for the first and second years in gross income, and the payee is allowed a deduction for these excess alimony payments.

Alimony recapture is required if payments decrease by more than $15,000 between years. Step 1 in the alimony recapture computation is to determine the decrease from Year 2 to Year 3. Year 2 alimony is recaptured to the extent this decrease exceeds $15,000. Step 2 requires that the *average* payments for Years 2 and 3 be compared with the Year 1 payment. For this computation, *revised* alimony for Year 2 is used. Revised alimony is equal to the amount of alimony deducted by the payor in Year 2 minus the amount of Year 2 alimony that is recaptured in step 1. The excess of Year 1 alimony over average alimony for Years 2 and 3 is recaptured to the extent that it exceeds $15,000.

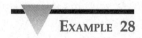

EXAMPLE 27

Wes and Rita are divorced in 1995. Under the divorce decree, Rita is to receive alimony payments of $60,000 in 1995, $40,000 in 1996, and $20,000 in 1997.

Step 1: 1996 alimony recapture:

1996 alimony	$40,000
Minus: 1997 alimony	20,000
Decrease	$20,000
Minus: Allowable decrease	15,000
1996 alimony recapture	$ 5,000

Step 2: 1995 alimony recapture:

1995 alimony	$60,000
Minus: Average of revised 1996 alimony and 1997 alimony*	27,500
Decrease	$32,500
Minus: Allowable decrease	15,000
1995 alimony recapture	$17,500

*[($40,000 1996 alimony − $5,000 recaptured) + $20,000 1997 alimony] divided by 2.

The total amount of alimony recaptured is $22,500 ($5,000 of 1996 payments + $17,500 of 1995 payments). ▼

Post-1984 agreements and decrees are not subject to alimony recapture if the decrease in payments is due to the death of either spouse or the remarriage of the payee. Recapture is not applicable because these events typically terminate alimony under state laws. In addition, the recapture rules do not apply to payments where the amount is contingent (e.g., a percentage of income from certain property or a percentage of the payor spouse's compensation), the payments are to be made over a period of three years or longer (unless death, remarriage, or other contingency occurs), and the contingencies are beyond the payor's control.[63]

EXAMPLE 28

Under a 1996 divorce agreement, Ed was to receive an amount equal to one-half of Nina's income from certain rental properties for 1996–1999. Payments were to cease upon the death of Ed or Nina or upon the remarriage of Ed. Ed received $50,000 in 1996 and $50,000 in 1997; in 1998, however, the property was vacant, and Ed received nothing. Nina, who deducted alimony in 1996 and 1997, is not required to recapture any alimony in 1998 because the payments were contingent. ▼

---

[63]§§ 71(f)(5)(A) and (C).

CONCEPT SUMMARY 3–1

Tax Treatment of Payments and Transfers Pursuant to Post-1984 Divorce Agreements and Decrees

	Payor	Recipient
Alimony	Deduction from gross income.	Included in gross income.
Alimony recapture	Included in gross income of the third year.	Deducted from gross income of the third year.
Child support	Not deductible.	Not includible in income.
Property settlement	No income or deduction.	No income or deduction; basis for the property is the same as the transferor's basis.

ETHICAL CONSIDERATIONS

Structuring a Divorce

In many situations, the tax laws influence how transactions are structured. The tax laws can be especially influential in structuring divorce agreements. The law seems to say that as long as one party will report as income cash received from a former spouse, the paying party can claim a deduction, even though, in reality, the paying party is purchasing the other's share of the marital property. Thus, the paying party may obtain a deduction for purchasing a personal use asset (e.g., a weekend home that was formerly jointly owned). The alimony recapture provision limits the parties' ability to carry out such a transaction, but does not preclude it.

Assume that each former spouse is represented by competent tax and legal advisers and that one spouse is in a higher marginal tax bracket than the other. The divorcing couple can enter into an agreement that will increase each party's after-tax wealth at the government's expense.

One may question why the laws deliberately set forth rules that will cause a divorcing couple to engage in this arbitrage. One may also question whether a tax adviser should advise a client involved in divorce negotiations to exploit the tax laws in this manner.

Child Support.   A taxpayer does not realize income from the receipt of child support payments made by his or her former spouse. This result occurs because the money is received subject to the duty to use the money for the child's benefit. The payor is not allowed to deduct the child support payments because the payments are made to satisfy the payor's legal obligation to support the child.

In many cases, it is difficult to determine whether an amount received is alimony or child support. Concerning pre-1985 decrees and agreements, the Supreme Court has ruled that if the decree or agreement does not specifically provide for child support, none of the payments will be treated as such.[64]

---

[64]*Comm. v. Lester*, 61–1 USTC ¶9463, 7 AFTR2d 1445, 81 S.Ct. 1343 (USSC, 1961).

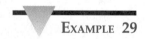
EXAMPLE 29

A pre-1985 divorce agreement provides that Matt is required to make periodic alimony payments of $500 per month to Grace. However, when Matt and Grace's child reaches age 21, marries, or dies (whichever occurs first), the payments will be reduced to $300 per month. Grace has custody of the child. Although it is reasonable to infer that $200 ($500 – $300) is for child support, the entire $500 is alimony because no payments are specified as child support. ▼

In 1984, Congress changed the results in Example 29 but only for post-1984 agreements and decrees. Under the revision, if the amount of the payments would be reduced upon the happening of a contingency related to a child (e.g., the child attains age 21 or dies), the amount of the future reduction in the payment is deemed child support.[65]

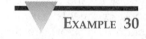
EXAMPLE 30

The facts are the same as in Example 29, except that the agreement is a post-1984 agreement. Child support payments are $200 each month, and alimony is $300 each month. ▼

IMPUTED INTEREST ON BELOW-MARKET LOANS

As discussed earlier in the chapter, generally no income is recognized unless it is realized. Realization generally occurs when the taxpayer performs services or sells

[65] § 71(c)(2). Pre-1985 agreements can be amended so that the revision will apply [§ 422(e) of the Deficit Reduction Act of 1984].

goods and thus becomes entitled to a payment from the other party. It follows that no income is realized if the goods or services are provided at no charge. Under this interpretation of the realization requirement, before 1984, interest-free loans were used to shift income between taxpayers.

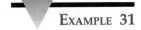

EXAMPLE 31

Veneia (daughter) is in the 20% tax bracket and has no investment income. Kareem (father) is in the 50% tax bracket and has $200,000 in a money market account earning 10% interest. Kareem would like Veneia to receive and pay tax on the income earned on the $200,000. Because Kareem would also like to have access to the $200,000 should he need the money, he does not want to make an outright gift of the money, nor does he want to commit the money to a trust.

Before 1984, Kareem could achieve his goals as follows. He could transfer the money market account to Veneia in exchange for her $200,000 non-interest-bearing note, payable on Kareem's demand. As a result, Veneia would receive the income, and the family's taxes would be decreased by $6,000.

Decrease in Kareem's tax— (.10 × $200,000).50 =	($10,000)
Increase in Veneia's tax— (.10 × $200,000).20 =	4,000
Decrease in the family's taxes	($ 6,000)

Under the 1984 amendments to the Code, Kareem in Example 31 is required to recognize **imputed interest** income.[66] Veneia is deemed to have incurred interest expense equal to Kareem's imputed interest income. Veneia's interest may be deductible on her return as investment interest if she itemizes deductions (see Chapter 9). To complete the fictitious series of transactions, Kareem is then deemed to have given Veneia the amount of the imputed interest she did not pay. The gift received by Veneia is not subject to income tax (see Chapter 4), although Kareem may be subject to the gift tax (unified transfer tax) on the amount deemed given to Veneia (refer to Chapter 1).

Imputed interest is calculated using the rate the Federal government pays on new borrowings and is compounded semiannually. This Federal rate is adjusted monthly and is published by the IRS.[67] Actually, there are three Federal rates: short-term (not over three years and including demand loans), mid-term (over three years but not over nine years), and long-term (over nine years).

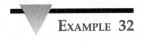

EXAMPLE 32

Assume the Federal rate applicable to the loan in Example 31 is 7% through June 30 and 8% from July 1 through December 31. Kareem made the loan on January 1, and the loan is still outstanding on December 31. Kareem must recognize interest income of $15,280, and Veneia has interest expense of $15,280. Kareem is deemed to have made a gift of $15,280 to Veneia.

Interest calculations	
January 1–June 30— .07($200,000) (½ year)	$ 7,000
July 1–December 31— .08($200,000 + $7,000) (½ year)	8,280
	$15,280

---

[66] § 7872(a)(1).

[67] §§ 7872(b)(2) and (f)(2).

CONCEPT SUMMARY 3–2

Effect of Certain Below-Market Loans on the Lender and Borrower

Type of Loan		Lender	Borrower
Gift	Step 1 Step 2	Interest income Gift made	Interest expense Gift received
Compensation-related	Step 1 Step 2	Interest income Compensation expense	Interest expense Compensation income
Corporation to shareholder	Step 1 Step 2	Interest income Dividend paid	Interest expense Dividend income

If interest is charged on the loan but is less than the Federal rate, the imputed interest is the difference between the amount that would have been charged at the Federal rate and the amount actually charged.

EXAMPLE 33

Assume the same facts as in Example 32, except that Kareem charged 6% interest, compounded annually.

Interest at the Federal rate	$ 15,280
Less interest charged (.06 × $200,000)	(12,000)
Imputed interest	$ 3,280

The imputed interest rules apply to the following *types* of below-market loans:[68]

1. Gift loans (made out of love, affection, or generosity, as in Example 31).
2. Compensation-related loans (employer loans to employees).
3. Corporation-shareholder loans (a corporation's loans to its shareholders).
4. Tax avoidance loans and other loans that significantly affect the borrower's or lender's Federal tax liability (discussed in the following paragraphs).

The effects of the first three types of loans on the borrower and lender are summarized in Concept Summary 3–2.

Tax Avoidance and Other Below-Market Loans.   In addition to the three specific types of loans that are subject to the imputed interest rules, the Code includes a catchall provision for *tax avoidance loans* and other arrangements that have a significant effect on the tax liability of the borrower or lender. The Conference Report provides the following example of an arrangement that might be subject to the imputed interest rules.[69]

---

[68] § 7872(c).

[69] H. Rep. No. 98–861, 98th Cong., 2d Sess., 1984, p. 1023.

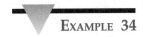

EXAMPLE 34

Annual dues for the Good Health Club are $400. In lieu of paying dues, a member can make a $4,000 deposit, refundable at the end of one year. The club can earn $400 interest on the deposit.

If interest were not imputed, an individual with $4,000 could, in effect, earn tax-exempt income on the deposit. That is, rather than invest the $4,000, earn $400 in interest, pay tax on the interest, and then pay $400 in dues, the individual could avoid tax on the interest by making the deposit. Thus, income and expenses are imputed as follows: interest income and nondeductible health club fees for the club member; income from fees and interest expense for the club. ▼

Many commercially motivated transactions could be swept into this other below-market loans category. However, the temporary Regulations have carved out a frequently encountered exception for customer prepayments. If the prepayments are included in the recipient's income under the recipient's method of accounting, the payments are not considered loans and, thus, are not subject to the imputed interest rules.[70]

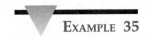

EXAMPLE 35

Landlord, a cash basis taxpayer, charges tenants a damage deposit equal to one month's rent on residential apartments. When the tenant enters into the lease, the landlord also collects rent for the last month of the lease.

The prepaid rent for the last month of the lease is taxed in the year received and thus is not considered a loan. The security deposit is not taxed when received and is therefore a candidate for imputed interest. However, no apparent tax benefit is derived by the landlord or the tenant, and thus the security deposit should not be subject to the imputed interest provisions. But if making the deposit would reduce the rent paid by the tenant, the tenant could derive a tax benefit, much the same as the club member in Example 34. ▼

Exceptions and Limitations. No interest is imputed on total outstanding *gift loans* of $10,000 or less between individuals, unless the loan proceeds are used to purchase income-producing property.[71] This exemption eliminates from these complex provisions immaterial amounts that do not result in apparent shifts of income. However, if the proceeds of such a loan are used to purchase income-producing property, the limitations discussed in the following paragraphs apply instead.

On loans of $100,000 or less between individuals, the imputed interest cannot exceed the borrower's net investment income for the year (gross income from all investments less the related expenses).[72] As discussed above, one of the purposes of the imputed interest rules is to prevent high-income taxpayers from shifting income to relatives in a lower marginal bracket. This shifting of investment income is considered to occur only to the extent the borrower has investment income. Thus, the income imputed to the lender is limited to the borrower's net investment income. As a further limitation, or exemption, if the borrower's net investment income for the year does not exceed $1,000, no interest is imputed on loans of $100,000 or less. However, these limitations for loans of $100,000 or less do not apply if a principal purpose of a loan is tax avoidance. In such a case,

---

[70] Prop.Reg. § 1.7872–2(b)(1)(i).
[71] § 7872(c)(2).

[72] § 7872(d).

interest is imputed, and the imputed interest is not limited to the borrower's net investment income.[73]

EXAMPLE 36

EXAMPLE 36

Vicki made interest-free gift loans as follows:

Borrower	Amount	Borrower's Net Investment Income	Purpose
Susan	$ 8,000	$ –0–	Education
Dan	9,000	500	Purchase of stock
Bonnie	25,000	–0–	Purchase of a business
Megan	90,000	15,000	Purchase of a residence
Olaf	120,000	–0–	Purchase of a residence

Assume that tax avoidance is not a principal purpose of any of the loans. The loan to Susan is not subject to the imputed interest rules because the $10,000 exception applies. The $10,000 exception does not apply to the loan to Dan because the proceeds were used to purchase income-producing assets. However, under the $100,000 exception, the imputed interest is limited to Dan's investment income ($500). Since the $1,000 exception also applies to this loan, no interest is imputed.

No interest is imputed on the loan to Bonnie because the $100,000 exception applies. Interest is imputed on the loan to Megan based on the lesser of (1) the borrower's $15,000 net investment income or (2) the interest as calculated by applying the Federal rate to the outstanding loan. None of the exceptions apply to the loan to Olaf because the loan was for more than $100,000.

Assume the relevant Federal rate is 10% and the loans were outstanding for the entire year. Vicki would recognize interest income, compounded semiannually, as follows:

Loan to Megan:

First 6 months (.10 × $90,000 × ½ year)	$ 4,500
Second 6 months (.10 × $94,500 × ½ year)	4,725
	$ 9,225

Loan to Olaf:

First 6 months (.10 × $120,000 × ½ year)	$ 6,000
Second 6 months (.10 × $126,000 × ½ year)	6,300
	$12,300

Total imputed interest ($9,225 + $12,300)	$21,525

As with gift loans, there is a $10,000 exemption for *compensation-related loans* and *corporation-shareholder loans*. However, the $10,000 exception does not apply if tax avoidance is one of the principal purposes of a loan.[74] This vague tax avoidance standard makes practically all compensation-related and corporation-shareholder loans suspect. Nevertheless, the $10,000 exception should apply when

---

[73] *Deficit Reduction Tax Bill of 1984: Explanation of the Senate Finance Committee* (April 2, 1984), p. 484.

[74] § 7872(c)(3).

CONCEPT SUMMARY 3–3

Exceptions to the Imputed Interest Rules For Below-Market Loans

Exception	Eligible Loans	Ineligible Loans and Limitations
De minimis—aggregate loans of $10,000 or less	Gift loans	Proceeds used to purchase income-producing assets.
	Employer-employee	Principal purpose is tax avoidance.
	Corporation-shareholder	Principal purpose is tax avoidance.
Aggregate loans of $100,000 or less	Between individuals	Principal purpose is tax avoidance. For all other loans, interest is imputed to the extent of the borrower's net investment income (NII), if the borrower's NII exceeds $1,000.

an employee's borrowing was necessitated by personal needs (e.g., to meet unexpected expenses) rather than tax considerations.

INCOME FROM ANNUITIES

Annuity contracts generally require the purchaser (the annuitant) to pay a fixed amount for the right to receive a future stream of payments. Typically, the issuer of the contract is an insurance company and will pay the annuitant a cash value if the annuitant cancels the contract. The insurance company invests the amounts received from the annuitant, and the income earned serves to increase the cash value of the policy. No income is recognized at the time the cash value of the annuity increases because the taxpayer has not actually received any income. The income is not constructively received because, generally, the taxpayer must cancel the policy to receive the increase in value (the increase in value is subject to substantial restrictions).

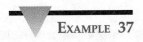

EXAMPLE 37

Juanita, age 50, paid $30,000 for an annuity contract that is to pay her $500 per month beginning when she reaches age 65 and continuing until her death. If Juanita should cancel the policy after one year, she would receive $30,200. The $200 increase in value is not includible in Juanita's gross income as long as she does not actually receive the $200. ▼

The tax accounting problem associated with receiving payments under an annuity contract is one of apportioning the amounts received between recovery of capital and income.

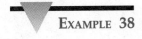

EXAMPLE 38

In 1996, Tom purchased for $15,000 an annuity intended as a source of retirement income. In 1998, when the cash value of the annuity was $17,000, Tom collected $1,000 on the contract. Is the $1,000 gross income, recovery of capital, or a combination of recovery of capital and income? ▼

The statutory solution to this problem depends upon whether the payments began before or after the annuity starting date and upon when the policy was acquired.

Collections before the Annuity Starting Date. Generally, an annuity contract specifies a date on which monthly or annual payments will begin—the annuity starting date. Often the contract will also allow the annuitant to collect a limited amount before the starting date. The amount collected may be characterized as either an actual withdrawal of the increase in cash value or a loan on the policy. In 1982, Congress changed the rules applicable to these withdrawals and loans.

Collections (including loans) equal to or less than the post–August 13, 1982, increases in cash value must be included in gross income. Amounts received in excess of post–August 13, 1982, increases in cash value are treated as a recovery of capital until the taxpayer's cost has been entirely recovered. Additional amounts are included in gross income.[75]

The taxpayer may also be subject to a penalty on early distributions equal to 10 percent of the income recognized. The penalty generally applies if the amount is received before the taxpayer reaches age 59½ or is disabled.[76] The early distribution penalty is deemed necessary to prevent taxpayers from using annuities as a way of avoiding the original issue discount rules. That is, the investment in the annuity earns a return that is not taxed until it is collected under the annuity rules, whereas the interest on a certificate of deposit is taxed each year as the income accrues. Thus, the annuity offers a tax advantage (deferral of income) that Congress does not want exploited.

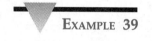

EXAMPLE 39

Jack, age 50, purchased an annuity policy for $30,000 in 1995. In 1997, when the cash value of the policy has increased to $33,000, Jack withdraws $4,000. He must recognize $3,000 of income ($33,000 cash value – $30,000 cost) and must pay a penalty of $300 ($3,000 × 10%). The remaining $1,000 is a recovery of capital and reduces Jack's basis in the annuity policy. ▼

Collections on and after the Annuity Starting Date. The annuitant is not permitted to use the recovery of capital concept to exclude all the annuity payments received until the investment in the annuity is recovered. Instead, the annuitant can exclude from income (as a recovery of capital) the proportion of each payment that the investment in the contract bears to the expected return under the contract. The *exclusion amount* is calculated as follows:

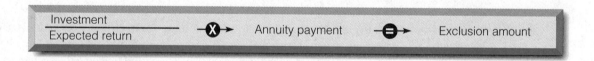

The *expected return* is the annual amount to be paid to the annuitant multiplied by the number of years the payments will be received. The payment period may be fixed (a *term certain*) or for the life of one or more individuals. When payments are for life, the taxpayer must use the annuity table published by the IRS to determine the expected return (see Table 3–1). This is an actuarial table that

---

[75] § 72(c)(3); Reg. § 1.72–9.   [76] § 72(q).

▼ **TABLE 3–1**
Ordinary Life Annuities:
One Life–Expected
Return Multiples

Age	Multiple	Age	Multiple	Age	Multiple
5	76.6	42	40.6	79	10.0
6	75.6	43	39.6	80	9.5
7	74.7	44	38.7	81	8.9
8	73.7	45	37.7	82	8.4
9	72.7	46	36.8	83	7.9
10	71.7	47	35.9	84	7.4
11	70.7	48	34.9	85	6.9
12	69.7	49	34.0	86	6.5
13	68.8	50	33.1	87	6.1
14	67.8	51	32.2	88	5.7
15	66.8	52	31.3	89	5.3
16	65.8	53	30.4	90	5.0
17	64.8	54	29.5	91	4.7
18	63.9	55	28.6	92	4.4
19	62.9	56	27.7	93	4.1
20	61.9	57	26.8	94	3.9
21	60.9	58	25.9	95	3.7
22	59.9	59	25.0	96	3.4
23	59.0	60	24.2	97	3.2
24	58.0	61	23.3	98	3.0
25	57.0	62	22.5	99	2.8
26	56.0	63	21.6	100	2.7
27	55.1	64	20.8	101	2.5
28	54.1	65	20.0	102	2.3
29	53.1	66	19.2	103	2.1
30	52.2	67	18.4	104	1.9
31	51.2	68	17.6	105	1.8
32	50.2	69	16.8	106	1.6
33	49.3	70	16.0	107	1.4
34	48.3	71	15.3	108	1.3
35	47.3	72	14.6	109	1.1
36	46.4	73	13.9	110	1.0
37	45.4	74	13.2	111	.9
38	44.4	75	12.5	112	.8
39	43.5	76	11.9	113	.7
40	42.5	77	11.2	114	.6
41	41.5	78	10.6	115	.5

contains life expectancies.[77] The expected return is calculated by multiplying the appropriate multiple (life expectancy) by the annual payment.

---

[77] The life expectancies in Table 3–1 apply for annuity investments made on or after July 1, 1986. See *Pension and Annuity Income*, IRS Publication 575 (Rev. Nov. 87), pp. 22–24 for the IRS table to use for investments made before July 1, 1986.

CONCEPT SUMMARY 3–4

Taxation of Annuities

Term	Description	Formula
A	Amount of each annuity payment under the contract.	
N	Number of expected payments based on the expected life of the annuitant.	
V	Investment in the annuity contract.	
R	Number of annuity payments actually received.	
Expected return	Total amount the annuitant is expected to collect over the life of the contract based on his or her life expectancy.	$A \times N$
Exclusion percentage	Percentage of each annuity payment that is excluded from gross income.	$\dfrac{V}{A \times N}$
Inclusion percentage	Percentage of each annuity payment that is included in gross income.	$1 - \left(\dfrac{V}{A \times N}\right)$
Post–recovery of capital payments	Once R = N, the total cost has been recovered. The total amount of each subsequent payment is included in gross income.	
Annuitant's deductible loss	If the annuity payments cease before R = N, the annuitant can claim a loss.	$V - \left(\dfrac{V}{A \times N}\right) \times (A \times R)$

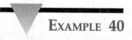

EXAMPLE 40

The taxpayer, age 54, purchased an annuity from an insurance company for $90,000. She was to receive $500 per month for life. Her life expectancy (from Table 3–1) is 29.5 years from the annuity starting date. Thus, her expected return is $500 × 12 × 29.5 = $177,000, and the exclusion amount is $3,051 [($90,000 investment/$177,000 expected return) × $6,000 annual payment]. The $3,051 is a nontaxable return of capital, and $2,949 is included in gross income. ▼

The *exclusion ratio* (investment ÷ expected return) applies until the annuitant has recovered his or her investment in the contract. Once the investment is recovered, the entire amount of subsequent payments is taxable.

PRIZES AND AWARDS

The fair market value of prizes and awards (other than scholarships exempted under § 117, to be discussed subsequently) must be included in gross income.[78] Therefore, TV giveaway prizes, magazine publisher prizes, door prizes, and awards from an employer to an employee in recognition of performance are fully taxable to the recipient.

An exception permits a prize or award to be excluded from gross income if all of the following requirements are satisfied:

---

[78]§ 74.

- The prize or award is received in recognition of religious, charitable, scientific, educational, artistic, literary, or civic achievement (e.g., Nobel Prize, Pulitzer Prize).
- The recipient arranges for the prize or award to be paid directly to a qualified governmental unit or nonprofit organization.
- The recipient was selected without any action on his or her part to enter the contest or proceeding.
- The recipient is not required to render substantial future services as a condition for receiving the prize or award.[79]

Because the transfer of the property to a qualified governmental unit or nonprofit organization ordinarily would be a charitable contribution (an itemized deduction as presented in Chapter 9), the exclusion produces beneficial tax consequences in the following situations:

- The taxpayer does not itemize deductions and thus would receive no tax benefit from the charitable contribution.
- The taxpayer's charitable contributions exceed the annual statutory ceiling on the deduction.
- Including the prize or award in gross income would reduce the amount of deductions the taxpayer otherwise would qualify for because of gross income limitations (e.g., the gross income test for a dependency exemption, the adjusted gross income limitation in calculating the medical expense deduction).

Another exception is provided for certain *employee achievement awards* in the form of tangible personal property (e.g., a gold watch). The awards must be made in recognition of length of service or safety achievement. Generally, the ceiling on the excludible amount for an employee is $400 per taxable year. However, if the award is a qualified plan award, the ceiling on the exclusion is $1,600 per taxable year.[80]

GROUP TERM LIFE INSURANCE

For many years, the IRS did not attempt to tax the value of life insurance protection provided to an employee by the employer. Some companies took undue advantage of the exclusion by providing large amounts of insurance protection for executives. Therefore, Congress enacted § 79, which created a limited exclusion for **group term life insurance.** Current law allows an exclusion for premiums on the first $50,000 of group term life insurance protection.

The benefits of this exclusion are available only to employees. Proprietors and partners are not considered employees. Moreover, the Regulations generally require broad-scale coverage of employees to satisfy the *group* requirement (e.g., shareholder-employees would not constitute a qualified group). The exclusion applies only to term insurance (protection for a period of time but with no cash surrender value) and not to ordinary life insurance (lifetime protection plus a cash surrender value that can be drawn upon before death).

As mentioned, the exclusion applies to the first $50,000 of group term life insurance protection. For each $1,000 of coverage in excess of $50,000, the employee must include the amounts indicated in Table 3–2 in gross income.[81]

[79] § 74(b).
[80] §§ 74(c) and 274(j).

[81] Reg. § 1.79–3(d)(2).

▼ **TABLE 3–2**
Uniform Premiums for $1,000 of Group Term Life Insurance Protection

Attained Age on Last Day of Employee's Tax Year	Cost per $1,000 of Protection for One-Month Period
Under 30	8 cents
30–34	9 cents
35–39	11 cents
40–44	17 cents
45–49	29 cents
50–54	48 cents
55–59	75 cents
60–64	$1.17
65–69	$2.10
70 and over	$3.76

▼ EXAMPLE 41

Finch Corporation has a group term life insurance policy with coverage equal to the employee's annual salary. Keith, age 52, is president of the corporation and receives an annual salary of $75,000. Keith must include $144 in gross income from the insurance protection for the year.

$$\frac{\$75,000 - \$50,000}{\$1,000} \times .48 \times 12 \text{ months} = \$144$$

▼

Generally, the amount that must be included in income, computed from Table 3–2, is much less than the price an individual would pay an insurance company for the same amount of protection. Thus, even the excess coverage provides some tax-favored income for employees when group term life insurance coverage in excess of $50,000 is desirable.

If the plan discriminates in favor of certain key employees (e.g., officers), the key employees are not eligible for the exclusion. In such a case, the key employees must include in gross income the *greater* of actual premiums paid by the employer or the amount calculated from the Uniform Premiums table in Table 3–2. The other employees are still eligible for the $50,000 exclusion and continue to use the Uniform Premiums table to compute the income from excess insurance protection.[82]

UNEMPLOYMENT COMPENSATION

The unemployment compensation program is sponsored and operated by the states and Federal government to provide a source of income for people who have been employed and are temporarily out of work. In a series of rulings over a period of 40 years, the IRS exempted unemployment benefits from tax. These payments were considered social benefit programs for the promotion of the general welfare. After experiencing dissatisfaction with the IRS's treatment of unemployment compensation, Congress amended the Code to provide that the benefits are taxable.[83]

---

[82]§ 79(d).   [83]§ 85.

SOCIAL SECURITY BENEFITS

If a taxpayer's income exceeds a specified base amount, as much as 85 percent of Social Security retirement benefits must be included in gross income. The taxable amount of benefits is determined through the application of one of two formulas that utilize a unique measure of income—*modified adjusted gross income (MAGI)*.[84] MAGI is, generally, the taxpayer's adjusted gross income from all sources (other than Social Security) plus the foreign earned income exclusion and any tax-exempt interest income.

In the formulas, two sets of base amounts are established. The first set is as follows:

- $32,000 for married taxpayers who file a joint return.
- $0 for married taxpayers who do not live apart for the entire year but file separate returns.
- $25,000 for all other taxpayers.

The second set of base amounts is as follows:

- $44,000 for married taxpayers who file a joint return.
- $0 for married taxpayers who do not live apart for the entire year but file separate returns.
- $34,000 for all other taxpayers.

If MAGI plus one-half of Social Security benefits exceeds the first set of base amounts, but not the second set, the taxable amount of Social Security benefits is the *lesser* of the following:

- .50(Social Security benefits).
- .50[MAGI + .50(Social Security benefits) − first base amount].

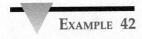

EXAMPLE 42

A married couple with adjusted gross income of $30,000, no tax-exempt interest, and $11,000 of Social Security benefits who file jointly must include $1,750 of the benefits in gross income. This works out as the lesser of the following:

1. .50($11,000) = $5,500.
2. .50[$30,000 + .50($11,000) − $32,000] = .50($3,500) = $1,750.

If the couple's adjusted gross income were $15,000 and their Social Security benefits totaled $5,000, none of the benefits would be taxable, since .50[$15,000 + .50($5,000) − $32,000] is not a positive number. ▼

If MAGI plus one-half of Social Security benefits exceeds the second set of base amounts, the taxable amount of Social Security benefits is the *lesser* of 1 or 2 below:

1. .85(Social Security benefits).
2. Sum of:
   a. .85[MAGI + .50(Social Security benefits) − second base amount], and
   b. Lesser of:
      - Amount included through application of the first formula.
      - $4,500 ($6,000 for married filing jointly).   ▼

[84]§ 86.

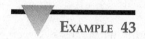

EXAMPLE 43

A married couple who file jointly have adjusted gross income of $72,000, no tax-exempt interest, and $12,000 of Social Security benefits. Their includible Social Security benefits would be $10,200.

Include the lesser of the following:

1. .85($12,000) = $10,200.
2. Sum of:
   a. .85[$72,000 + .50($12,000) − $44,000] = $28,900, and
   b. Lesser of:
      • Amount calculated by the first formula, which is the lesser of:
        • .50($12,000) = $6,000.
        • .50[$72,000 + .50($12,000) − $32,000] = $23,000.
      • $6,000.

The sum equals $34,900 ($28,900 + $6,000). Since 85% of the Social Security benefits received is less than this amount, $10,200 is included in the couples' gross income. ▼

ETHICAL CONSIDERATIONS

Taxing Social Security Benefits

The taxation of Social Security benefits has gone through several phases. For many years, Social Security benefits were not subject to tax. Then in 1976, the Internal Revenue Code was amended to tax up to one-half of Social Security benefits received by individuals with gross income over a threshold amount (i.e., $25,000 or $32,000 depending on filing status). The apparent rationale for taxing 50 percent was that the employee had contributed half of the original payments and thus half of the benefits represented a recovery of capital.

As a result of the Revenue Reconciliation Act of 1993, taxpayers with adjusted gross income over the threshold amount (i.e., $34,000 or $44,000 depending on filing status) are required to include up to 85 percent of Social Security benefits in gross income. Under current law, as well as under pre-1993 law, if an individual dies before recovering his or her payments into the Social Security system, no loss can be claimed on the final return.

Now, two former U.S. senators (Paul Tsongas of Massachusetts and Warren Rudman of New Hampshire) are proposing that the receipt of Social Security benefits be based on the "wherewithal to pay" as part of a plan to eliminate the Federal deficit by the year 2000. Such a means-based approach would effectively result in a 100 percent inclusion for Social Security benefits combined with a 100 percent tax rate. Evaluate the trend toward increasing taxation of Social Security benefits.

TAX PLANNING CONSIDERATIONS

The materials in this chapter have focused on the following questions:

• What is income?
• When is the income recognized?
• Who is the taxpayer?

Planning strategies suggested by these materials include the following:

• Maximize economic benefits that are not included in gross income.
• Defer the recognition of income.
• Shift income to taxpayers who are in a lower marginal tax bracket.

5 **LEARNING OBJECTIVE**
Identify tax planning strategies for minimizing gross income.

TAX IN THE NEWS

INCOME TO THE IRS BUT NOT TO THE NFL

Both the print and broadcast media have reported extensively on the signing of Deion "Prime Time" Sanders to a seven-year $35 million contract by the Dallas Cowboys. The contract reportedly includes a $12,999,999 up-front signing bonus and a salary for the 1995–96 season of $178,000 (the minimum amount that can be paid to an NFL player).

The role of a tax adviser is to assist the taxpayer in reducing his or her tax liability to the minimum required by law. Therefore, from an income tax perspective, it appears that Deion's tax adviser was "asleep at the desk." Front-loading the contract to include the $13 million bonus in Deion's 1995 taxable income obviously is not sage tax planning. The standard planning approach would have been to maximize the deferral in order to reduce the current and near-term tax liability.

As it turns out, however, the driving factor was not the income tax result, but rather the NFL team salary cap of $37.2 million, which is designed to produce more equality among the various teams. The last thing that Jerry Jones, the owner of "America's Team," wants is equality—he wants continued superiority that will lead to more Super Bowl titles. Even though Deion will receive approximately $13,178,000 during the 1995–96 season, only $2,035,142 will count toward the salary cap. The bonus is amortized over the seven-year contract period at an annual amount of $1,857,142. Adding this amount to the $178,000 salary produces the $2,035,142. Under this way of thinking, Deion is a real bargain.

Some specific techniques for accomplishing these strategies are discussed in the following paragraphs.

NONTAXABLE ECONOMIC BENEFITS

Home ownership is the prime example of economic income from capital that is not subject to tax. If the taxpayer uses his or her capital to purchase investments, but pays rent on a personal residence, the taxpayer would pay the rent from after-tax income. However, if the taxpayer purchases a personal residence instead of the investments, the taxpayer would give up gross income from the forgone investments in exchange for the rent savings. The savings in rent enjoyed as a result of owning the home are not subject to tax. Thus, the homeowner will have substituted nontaxable for taxable income.

TAX DEFERRAL

General. Since deferred taxes are tantamount to interest-free loans from the government, the deferral of taxes is a worthy goal of the tax planner. However, the tax planner must also consider the tax rates for the years the income is shifted from and to. For example, a one-year deferral of income from a year in which the taxpayer's tax rate was 28 percent to a year in which the tax rate will be 39.6 percent would not be advisable if the taxpayer expects to earn less than an 11.6 percent after-tax return on the deferred tax dollars.

The taxpayer can often defer the recognition of income from appreciated property by postponing the event triggering realization (the final closing on a sale or exchange of property). If the taxpayer needs cash, obtaining a loan by using the appreciated property as collateral may be the least costly alternative. When the taxpayer anticipates reinvesting the proceeds, a sale may be inadvisable.

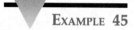
EXAMPLE 44

Ira owns 100 shares of Pigeon Company common stock with a cost of $20,000 and a fair market value of $50,000. Although the stock's value has increased substantially in the past three years, Ira thinks the growth days are over. If he sells the Pigeon stock, Ira will invest the proceeds from the sale in other common stock. Assuming Ira is in the 28% marginal tax bracket, he will have only $41,600 [$50,000 − .28($50,000 − $20,000)] to reinvest. The alternative investment must substantially outperform Pigeon in the future in order for the sale to be beneficial. ▼

Selection of Investments.   Because no tax is due until a gain has been recognized, the law favors investments that yield appreciation rather than annual income.

EXAMPLE 45

Vera can buy a corporate bond or an acre of land for $10,000. The bond pays $1,000 of interest (10%) each year, and Vera expects the land to increase in value 10% each year for the next 10 years. She is in the 40% (combined Federal and state) tax bracket. Assuming the bond would mature or the land would be sold in 10 years and Vera would reinvest the interest at a 10% before-tax return, she would accumulate the following amount at the end of 10 years.

		Bond	**Land**
Original investment		$10,000	$10,000
Annual income	$1,000		
Less tax	(400)		
	$ 600		
Compound amount reinvested for 10 years at 6% after-tax	× 13.18	7,908	
		$17,908	
Compound amount, 10 years at 10%			× 2.59
			$25,900
Less tax on sale: 40%($25,900 − $10,000)			(6,360)
			$19,540

Therefore, the value of the deferral that results from investing in the land rather than in the bond is $1,632 ($19,540 − $17,908). ▼

Series E and EE bonds can also be purchased for long-term deferrals of income. As discussed in the chapter, Series E bonds can be exchanged for new Series HH bonds to further postpone the tax. In situations where the taxpayer's goal is merely to shift income one year into the future, bank certificates of deposit are useful tools. If the maturity period is one year or less, all interest is reported in the year of maturity. Time certificates are especially useful for a taxpayer who realizes an unusually large gain from the sale of property in one year (and thus is in a high tax bracket) but expects his or her income to be less the following year.

Cash Basis. The timing of income from services can often be controlled through the use of the cash method of accounting. Although taxpayers are somewhat constrained by the constructive receipt doctrine (they cannot turn their backs on income), seldom will customers and clients offer to pay before they are asked. The usual lag between billings and collections (e.g., December's billings collected in January) will result in a continuous deferring of some income until the last year of operations. A salaried individual approaching retirement may contract with his or her employer before the services are rendered to receive a portion of compensation in the lower tax bracket retirement years.

Prepaid Income. For the accrual basis taxpayer who receives advance payments from customers, the transactions should be structured to avoid payment of tax on income before the time the income is actually earned. Revenue Procedure 71–21 provides the guidelines for deferring the tax on prepayments for services, and Regulation § 1.451–5 provides the guidelines for deferrals on sales of goods. In addition, both cash and accrual basis taxpayers can sometimes defer income by stipulating that the payments are deposits rather than prepaid income. For example, a landlord should require an equivalent damage deposit rather than require prepayment of the last month's rent under the lease.

SHIFTING INCOME TO RELATIVES

The tax liability of a family can be minimized by shifting income from higher- to lower-bracket family members. This can be accomplished through gifts of income-producing property. Furthermore, in many cases, income can be shifted with no negative effect on the family's investment plans.

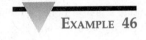

EXAMPLE 46

Adam, who is in the 28% tax bracket, would like to save for his children's education. All of the children are under 14 years of age. Adam could transfer income-producing properties to the children, and the children could each receive up to $650 of income each year (refer to Chapter 2) with no tax liability. The next $650 would be taxed at the child's tax rate. After a child has more than $1,300 income, there is no tax advantage to shifting more income to the child (because the income will be taxed at the parents' rate) until the child is 14 years old (when all income will be taxed at the child's tax rate). ▼

The Uniform Gifts to Minors Act, a model law adopted by all states (but with some variations among the states), facilitates income shifting. Under the Act, a gift of intangibles (e.g., bank accounts, stocks, bonds, life insurance contracts) can be made to a minor but with an adult serving as custodian. Usually, a parent who makes the gift is also named as custodian. The state laws allow the custodian to sell or redeem and reinvest the principal and to accumulate or distribute the income, practically at the custodian's discretion provided there is no commingling of the child's income with the parent's property. Thus, the parent can give appreciated securities to the child, and the donor custodian can then sell the securities and reinvest the proceeds, thereby shifting both the gain and annual income to the child. Such planning is limited by the tax liability calculation provision for a child under the age of 14 (refer to Chapter 2).

U.S. government bonds (Series E and EE) can be purchased by the parent for his or her children. When this is done, the children generally should file a return and elect to report the income on the accrual basis.

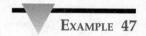

EXAMPLE 47

Abby pays $7,500 for Series EE bonds in 1996 and immediately gives them to Wade (her son), who will enter college the year of original maturity of the bonds. The bonds have a maturity value of $10,000. Wade elects to report the annual increment in redemption value as income for each year the bonds are held. The first year the increase is $250, and Wade includes that amount in his gross income. If Wade has no other income, no tax will be due on the $250 bond interest, since such an amount will be more than offset by his available standard deduction. The following year, the increment is $260, and Wade includes this amount in income. Thus, over the life of the bonds, Wade will include $2,500 in income ($10,000 – $7,500), none of which will result in a tax liability, assuming he has no other income. However, if the election had not been made, Wade would be required to include $2,500 in income on the bonds in the year of original maturity, if they were redeemed as planned. This amount of income might result in a tax liability. ▼

In some cases, it may be advantageous for the child not to make the accrual election. For example, a child under age 14 with investment income of more than $1,300 each year and parents in the 28, 31, 36, or 39.6 percent tax bracket would probably benefit from deferring the tax on the savings bond interest. The child would also benefit from the use of the usually lower tax rate (rather than subjecting the income to his or her parents' tax rate) if the bonds mature after the child is age 14 or older.

ALIMONY

The person making the alimony payments favors a divorce settlement that includes a provision for deductible alimony payments. On the other hand, the recipient prefers that the payments do not qualify as alimony. If the payor is in a higher tax bracket than the recipient, both parties may benefit by increasing the payments and structuring them so that they qualify as alimony.

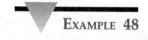

EXAMPLE 48

Carl and Polly are negotiating a divorce settlement. Carl has offered to pay Polly $10,000 each year for 10 years, but payments would cease upon Polly's death. Polly is willing to accept the offer, if the agreement will specify that the cash payments are not alimony. Carl is in the 36% tax bracket, and Polly's marginal rate is 15%.

If Carl and Polly agree that Carl will pay Polly $12,000 of alimony each year, both will have improved after-tax cash flows.

	Annual Cash Flows	
	Carl	**Polly**
Nonalimony payments	($10,000)	$10,000
Alimony payments	($12,000)	$12,000
Tax effects		
.36($12,000)	4,320	
.15($12,000)		(1,800)
After-tax cash flows	($ 7,680)	$10,200
Benefit of alimony option	$ 2,320	$ 200

Both parties benefit at the government's expense if the $12,000 alimony option is used. ▼

KEY TERMS

Accounting income, 3–4

Accounting method, 3–7

Accrual method, 3–9

Alimony and separate maintenance payments, 3–18

Alimony recapture, 3–20

Annuity, 3–27

Assignment of income, 3–14

Cash receipts method, 3–8

Claim of right doctrine, 3–9

Community property, 3–18

Constructive receipt, 3–10

Economic income, 3–3

Fruit and tree metaphor, 3–14

Gross income, 3–3

Group term life insurance, 3–31

Hybrid method, 3–9

Imputed interest, 3–23

Income, 3–3

Original issue discount, 3–10

Partnership, 3–16

Recovery of capital doctrine, 3–7

S corporation, 3–17

Taxable year, 3–7

PROBLEM
MATERIALS

DISCUSSION QUESTIONS

1. The Internal Revenue Code contains a broad definition of gross income, but does not provide a listing of all possible types of income subject to tax. Would the tax law be improved if the Code included a complete listing of taxable sources of income?

2. Which of the following would be considered "income" for the current year by an economist but would not be gross income for tax purposes? Explain.
    a. Securities acquired two years ago for $10,000 had a value of $12,000 at the beginning of the current year and a value of $13,000 at the end of the year.
    b. An individual lives in the home he owns.
    c. A corporation obtained a loan from a bank.
    d. A shareholder paid a corporation $3,000 for property valued at $5,000.
    e. An individual owned property that was stolen. The cost of the property three years ago was $2,000, and an insurance company paid the owner $6,000 (the value of the property on the date of theft).
    f. An individual found a box of seventeenth-century Spanish coins while diving off the Virginia coast.
    g. An individual received a $200 rebate from the manufacturer upon the purchase of a new car.

3. According to economists, because our tax system does not impute income to homeowners for the rental value of their homes, the nonhomeowner who invests in securities (rather than a home) is taxed more heavily than the homeowner. This leads to overinvesting in homes. Why do you suppose the laws are not changed to tax homeowners on the rental value of their homes?

4. Evaluate the following alternative proposals for taxing the income from property:
    a. All assets would be valued at the end of the year, any increase in value that occurred during the year would be included in gross income, and any decrease in value would be deductible from gross income.
    b. No gain or loss would be recognized until the taxpayer sold or exchanged the property.

c. Increases or decreases in the value of property traded on a national exchange (e.g., the New York Stock Exchange) would be reflected in gross income for the years the changes in value occurred. For all other assets, no gain or loss would be recognized until the property is sold or exchanged.

5. How would the realization requirement influence an investor to purchase a stock that is expected to appreciate in value but will not pay dividends rather than a stock that is not expected to appreciate but will pay a dividend?

6. Leif had owned a tract of land for several years when the local government decided to build an airport near the property. The cost of the property to Leif was $50,000. The local government paid Leif $10,000 for invasion of his airspace. What is Leif's gross income from the receipt of the $10,000?

7. What is the major tax advantage of the cash method of accounting?

8. Sparrow, Inc., receives all of its income from repairing computers. The company reports its income by the cash method. On December 31, an employee went to a customer's office and repaired a computer. The customer gave Sparrow's employee a check for $300, but the employee did not remit the check to Sparrow until January of the following year. When is Sparrow required to recognize the income?

9. Lane is a self-employed consultant who reports his income by the cash method of accounting. In December 1996, Lane received a check for $5,000 from a client. Lane misplaced the check and did not find it until January 1997, when he deposited it in his bank account. Lane uses his deposit records to compute his income. Therefore, he included the $5,000 in his 1997 gross income.
    a. In what year should Lane report the income?
    b. Why does it matter whether Lane reports the income in 1996 or 1997, so long as he actually reports it?

10. Doug, a cash basis taxpayer, operated Craig's farm under an arrangement whereby Doug would receive one-half of the grain crop, less the cost of seed and fertilizer. The seed and fertilizer cost $8,000, which was paid during the year. In October Doug harvested the crop. A portion of the grain was sold for $28,000 cash in October, and Doug received $10,000 as his share of the $28,000 in November. Also in November, more of the grain was sold for $40,000. The grain was delivered to the purchaser in November, but payment was not to be received until January of the following year. Doug also used a portion of the grain for his personal use. The cost of the personal use grain was $1,200, but it could have been sold for $2,000. In February of the following year, Doug collected the balance Craig owed to him. Identify the relevant tax issues for Doug.

11. Nora, an accrual basis taxpayer, rendered services for a customer with a poor credit rating. Nora's charge for the service was $1,000. Nora sent a bill to the customer for $1,000 but reported only $500 of income. She justified reporting only $500 as follows: "I'm being generous reporting $500. I'll be lucky if I collect anything." How much should Nora include as gross income from the contract in the current year?

12. Olga, a cash basis taxpayer, sold a bond with accrued interest of $750 for $10,250. Olga's basis in the bond was $9,000. Compute Olga's income from this transaction.

13. Leslie, a cash basis taxpayer, purchased a three-year certificate of deposit for $7,938. Upon maturity of the certificate, she will receive $10,000, which is the principal plus 8% interest compounded annually. Will Leslie's interest income be less in the first year than in the third year?

14. Taupe Car Wash, an accrual basis taxpayer, sells certificates throughout the year that entitle the holder to a free car wash at any time during the next 24 months. At the end of 1996, certificates with a total face amount of $10,000 are outstanding. When is Taupe required to include the $10,000 in gross income?

15. Quinn (father) paid $200 for an automobile that needed repairs. He worked nights and weekends to restore the car. Several individuals offered to purchase the car for $2,800. Quinn gave the car and a list of potential buyers to Ron (son), whose college tuition was

due in a few days. Ron sold the car for $2,800 and paid his tuition. Does Quinn have any taxable income from the transaction?

16. Tom Jr., a cash basis minor, performed services and was to be paid $100 in 1996. In 1996, the employer paid the $100 to Tom Sr., who deposited the money in his bank account. The following year, Tom Sr. used the $100 to buy his son a car.
    a. In whose gross income is the $100 included?
    b. When is the $100 included in gross income?

17. Isabella transferred rental properties to a corporation. Her objective was to minimize her liability for injuries that may occur on the property. The tenants continued to pay rents to Isabella. Who must include the rents in gross income?

18. Who pays the tax on (a) the income of an S corporation and on (b) the undistributed income of an estate?

19. Ted and Alice were residents of a community property state. In 1996, Ted left Alice for parts unknown. Ted and Alice were still married at year-end. How will Ted's absence complicate Alice's 1996 tax return?

20. Hank and Elaine are negotiating their divorce agreement, which requires the division of their jointly owned property. Hank has proposed that he receive the couple's house (basis of $50,000 and fair market value of $75,000) while Elaine would receive (a) securities (basis of $10,000 and fair market value of $75,000) or (b) four annual payments of $22,644 each, which is equivalent to a $75,000 loan at 8% interest. Elaine will probably sell the securities if she receives them. Elaine does not want the house. Which option should she accept?

21. A post-1984 divorce agreement between Earl and Cora provides that Earl is to pay Cora $500 per month for 13 years. Earl and Cora have a child who is 8 years old. Termination of the monthly payments will coincide with the child's attaining age 21. Can the monthly payments qualify as alimony?

22. William and Abigail, who live in San Francisco, have been experiencing problems with their marriage. They have a three-year-old daughter, April, who stays with William's parents during the day since both William and Abigail are employed. Abigail worked to support William while he attended medical school, and now she has been accepted into medical school in Mexico. Abigail has decided to divorce William and attend medical school. April will stay in San Francisco because of her strong attachment to her grandparents and because they can provide her with excellent day care. Abigail knows that William will expect her to contribute to the cost of raising April. Abigail also feels that, to finance her education, she must receive cash for her share of the property they accumulated during their marriage. In addition, she feels she should receive some reimbursement for her contribution to William's support while he was in medical school. She expects the divorce proceedings will take several months. Identify the relevant tax issues for Abigail.

23. In the case of a below-market loan between relatives, why is the lender required to recognize income although it is the borrower who appears to receive the economic benefit?

24. Mother loaned $80,000 to Son who used the money to buy a personal residence. Mother did not charge interest on the loan, although the market rate of interest was 8%. Son had investment income of $800. Do the imputed interest rules apply?

25. In the case of a corporation's interest-free loan to its controlling shareholder who is also an employee of the corporation, why would the corporation prefer that the loan be classified as an employer-employee loan rather than a corporation-shareholder loan?

26. Brad is the president of the Yellow Corporation. He and other members of his family control the corporation. Brad has a temporary need for $50,000, and the corporation has excess cash. He could borrow the money from a bank at 9%, and Yellow is earning 6% on its temporary investments. Yellow has made loans to other employees on several occasions. Therefore, Brad is considering borrowing $50,000 from the corporation. He

will repay the loan principal in two years plus interest at 5%. Identify the relevant tax issues for Brad and the Yellow Corporation.

27. At age 55, Nancy purchased an annuity for $25,000 that was to pay her $200 per month for life beginning on her 70th birthday. At that time, her life expectancy would be 16 years. Now, when Nancy is 58 years old, and the annuity policy has a value of $28,000, she needs $2,000. The annuity policy allows her to withdraw the needed funds. What are the tax consequences to Nancy of this withdrawal from the annuity policy?

28. Gail is a full-time employee of Purple Corporation. One of the fringe benefits the company offers its employees is group term life insurance protection equal to twice the employee's annual salary. Gail is 38 years old, and her annual salary is $50,000. What is Gail's gross income from the life insurance protection for the year?

29. When a taxpayer is receiving Social Security benefits, could a $1,000 increase in income from services cause the taxpayer's adjusted gross income to increase by more than $1,000?

PROBLEMS

30. Determine the effects of the following on Anne's gross income for the year:
    a. Anne bought a used sofa for $25. After she took the sofa home, she discovered $15,000 in a secret compartment. Anne was unable to determine who placed the money in the sofa. Therefore, she put the money in her bank account.
    b. Anne also discovered oil on her property during the year, and the value of the land increased from $10,000 to $3,000,000.
    c. One year later, Anne found a diamond in the sofa she had purchased. Apparently, the diamond was in the sofa when Anne purchased it. The value of the diamond was $6,000. Under state law, the diamond became Anne's property when she purchased the sofa.
    d. Anne's bank charges a $3 per month service charge. However, the fee is waived if the customer maintains an average balance for the month of at least $1,000. Anne's account exceeded the minimum deposit requirement, and as a result she was not required to pay any service charges for the year.

31. Compute the taxpayer's (1) economic income and (2) gross income for tax purposes from the following events:
    a. The taxpayer sold securities for $10,000. The securities cost $6,000 in 1992. The fair market value of the securities at the beginning of the year was $12,000.
    b. The taxpayer sold his business and received $15,000 under a covenant not to compete with the new owner.
    c. The taxpayer used her controlled corporation's automobile for her vacation. The rental value of the automobile for the vacation period was $800.
    d. The taxpayer raised vegetables in her garden. The fair market value of the vegetables was $900, and the cost of raising them was $100. She ate some of the vegetables and gave the remainder to neighbors.
    e. The local government changed the zoning ordinances so that some of the taxpayer's residential property was reclassified as commercial. Because of the change, the fair market value of the taxpayer's property increased by $10,000.
    f. During the year, the taxpayer borrowed $50,000 for two years at 9% interest. By the end of the year, interest rates had increased to 12%, and the lender accepted $49,000 in full satisfaction of the debt.

32. Kevin, a cash basis taxpayer, received the following from his employer during 1996:

    • Salary of $75,000.

    • Bonus of $10,000. In 1997, the company determined that the bonus had been incorrectly computed and required Kevin to repay $3,000.

- Use of a company car for his vacation. Rental value for the period would have been $900. Kevin paid for the gas.

- $4,000 advance for travel expenses. Kevin had spent only $3,400 at the end of the year.

Determine the effects of these items on Kevin's gross income.

33. Which of the following investments will yield the greatest after-tax value assuming the taxpayer is in the 40% tax bracket (combined Federal and state) in all years and the investments will be liquidated at the end of five years?
  a. Land that will increase in value by 10% each year.
  b. A taxable bond yielding 10% before tax, and the interest can be reinvested at 10% before tax.
  c. Common stock that will increase in value at the rate of 5% (compounded) each year and pays dividends equal to 5% of the year-end value of the stock. The dividends can be reinvested at 10% before tax.
  d. A tax-exempt state government bond yielding 8%. The interest can be reinvested at a before-tax rate of 10%, and the bond matures in 10 years.

Prepare a brief speech for your tax class in which you explain why the future value of the land will exceed the future value of the taxable bond.

Given: Compound amount of $1 and compound value of annuity payments at the end of five years:

Interest Rate	$1 Compounded for 5 Years	$1 Annuity Compounded for 5 Years
6%	$1.33	$5.64
8%	1.47	5.87
10%	1.61	6.10

34. Determine the taxpayer's income for tax purposes in each of the following cases:
  a. Zelda borrowed $30,000 from the First National Bank. She was required to deliver to the bank stocks with a value of $30,000 and a cost of $10,000. The stocks were to serve as collateral for the loan.
  b. Zelda owned a lot on Sycamore Street that measured 100 feet by 100 feet. The cost of the lot to her is $10,000. The city condemned a 10-foot strip of the land so that it could widen the street. Zelda received a $2,000 condemnation award.
  c. Zelda owned land zoned for residential use only. The land cost $5,000 and had a market value of $7,000. Zelda spent $500 and several hundred hours petitioning the county supervisors to change the zoning to A–1 commercial. The value of the property immediately increased to $20,000 when the county approved the zoning change.

35. Determine the taxpayer's income for tax purposes in each of the following cases:
  a. In the current year, Seagull Corporation purchased $1,000,000 par value of its own bonds and paid the bondholders $980,000 plus $50,000 of accrued interest. The bonds had been issued 10 years ago at par and were to mature 25 years from the date of issue. Does the corporation recognize income from the purchase of the bonds?
  b. A shareholder of a corporation sold property to the corporation for $60,000 (the shareholder's cost). The value of the property on the date of sale was $50,000. Does the taxpayer have any gross income from the sale?
  c. Rex was a football coach at a state university. Because of his disappointing record, he was asked to resign and accept one-half of his pay for the remaining three years of his contract. Rex resigned, accepting $75,000.

36. Al is an attorney who conducts his practice as a sole proprietor. During the year, he received cash of $85,000 for legal services. At the beginning of the year, he had receivables from clients of $15,000. At the end of the year, his receivables totaled $30,000. Compute Al's gross income from the practice for the year:
    a. Using the cash basis of accounting.
    b. Using the accrual basis of accounting.

37. The taxpayer began operating a grocery store during the year. Her only books and records are based on cash receipts and disbursements, but she has asked you to compute her gross profit from the business for tax purposes.

Sales of merchandise	$260,000
Purchases of merchandise	190,000

    You determine that as of the end of the year the taxpayer has accounts payable for merchandise of $9,000 and accounts receivable from customers totaling $1,500. The cost of merchandise on hand at the end of the year was $4,000. Compute the grocery store's accrual method gross profit for the year.

38. Your client is a new partnership, Aspen Associates, which is an engineering consulting firm. Generally, Aspen bills clients for services at the end of each month. Client billings are about $50,000 each month. On average, it takes 45 days to collect the receivables. Aspen's expenses are primarily for salary and rent. Salaries are paid on the last day of each month, and rent is paid on the first day of each month. The partnership has a line of credit with a bank, which requires monthly financial statements. These must be prepared using the accrual method. Aspen's managing partner, Amanda Sims, has suggested that the firm should also use the accrual method for tax purposes and thus reduce accounting fees by $500. Write a letter to your client explaining why you believe it would be worthwhile for Aspen to file its tax return on the cash basis even though its financial statements are prepared on the accrual basis. Aspen's address is 100 James Tower, Denver, CO 80208.

39. Color Paint Shop, Inc., is an accrual basis taxpayer that paints automobiles. During the year, the company painted Samuel's car and was to receive a $1,000 payment from his insurance company. Samuel was not satisfied with the work, however, and the insurance company refused to pay. In December 1996, Color and Samuel agreed that Color would receive $600 for the work, subject to final approval by the insurance company. In the past, Color had come to terms with customers only to have the insurance company negotiate an even lesser amount. In May 1997, the insurance company reviewed the claim and paid the $600 to Color. An IRS agent thinks that Color, as an accrual basis taxpayer, should report $1,000 of income in 1996, when the work was done and then deduct a $400 loss in 1997. Prepare a memo to Susan Apple, a tax partner for whom you are working, with the recommended treatment for the disputed income.

40. Dance, Inc., is a dance studio that sells dance lessons for cash, on open account, and for notes receivable. The company also collects interest on bonds held as an investment. The company's cash receipts for the year totaled $219,000:

Cash sales	$ 70,000
Collections on accounts receivable	120,000
Collections on notes receivable	20,000
Interest on bonds	9,000
	$219,000

    The balances in accounts receivable, notes receivable, and accrued interest on bonds at the beginning and end of the year were as follows:

	1–1	12–31
Accounts receivable	$24,000	$24,000
Notes receivable	9,000	13,000
Accrued interest on bonds	2,500	4,000
	$35,500	$41,000

The fair market value of the notes is equal to 60% of their face amount. There were no bad debts for the year, and all notes were for services performed during the year. Compute the corporation's gross income:

a. Using the cash basis of accounting.

b. Using the accrual basis of accounting.

c. Using a hybrid method—accrual basis for lessons and cash basis for interest income.

41. Determine the effect of the following on a cash basis taxpayer's gross income for 1996:

a. Received his paycheck for $3,000 from his employer on December 31, 1996. He deposited the paycheck on January 2, 1997.

b. Received a bonus of $5,000 from his employer on January 10, 1997. The bonus was for the outstanding performance of his division during 1996.

c. Received a dividend check from IBM on November 28, 1996. He mailed the check back to IBM in December requesting that additional IBM stock be issued to him under IBM's dividend reinvestment plan.

42. Pelican, Inc., an accrual basis taxpayer, sells and installs consumer appliances. Determine the effects of each of the following transactions on the company's 1996 gross income:

a. In December 1996, the company received a $1,200 advance payment from a customer. The payment was for an appliance that Pelican specially ordered from the manufacturer. The appliance had not arrived at the end of 1996.

b. At the end of 1996, the company installed an appliance and collected the full price of $750 for the item. However, the customer claimed the appliance was defective and asked the company for a refund. The company conceded that the appliance was defective, but claimed that the customer should collect from the manufacturer. The dispute had not been settled by the end of 1996. In early 1997, it was determined that Pelican did not install the appliance properly and the company was required to refund the full sales price.

c. The company sold an appliance for $1,200 (plus a market rate of interest) and received the customer's note for that amount. However, because of the customer's poor credit rating, the value of the note was only $700.

43. Freda is a cash basis taxpayer. Determine her 1996 gross income from the following transactions:

a. In 1994, Freda negotiated her 1995 salary. The employer offered to pay Freda $200,000 in 1995. Freda countered that she wanted $10,000 each month in 1995 and the remaining $80,000 in January 1996. Freda wanted the $80,000 income shifted to 1996 because she expected her 1996 tax rates to be lower. Her employer agreed to Freda's terms.

b. In 1995, Freda was running short of cash and needed money for Christmas. Her employer loaned her $20,000 in November 1995. Freda signed a note for $20,000 plus 10% interest, the applicable Federal rate. In January 1996, the employer subtracted the $20,000 and $333 interest from the $80,000 due Freda and paid her $59,667.

c. On December 31, 1995, Zina offered to buy land from Freda for $30,000 (Freda's basis was $8,000). Freda refused to sell in 1995, but at that time, she contracted to sell the land to Zina in 1996 for $30,000.

44. The Heron Apartments requires its new tenants to pay the rent for the first and last months of the annual lease and a $400 damage deposit, all at the time the lease is

signed. In December 1996, a tenant paid $800 for January 1997 rent, $800 for December 1997 rent, and $400 for the damage deposit. In January 1998, Heron refunded the tenant's damage deposit. What are the effects of these payments on Heron's taxable income for 1996, 1997, and 1998?

a. Assume Heron is a cash basis taxpayer.

b. Assume Heron is an accrual basis taxpayer.

45. a. Gus is a cash basis taxpayer. On September 1, 1996, Gus gave a corporate bond to his son, Hans. The bond had a face amount of $10,000 and paid $900 of interest each January 31. On December 1, 1996, Gus gave common stocks to his daughter, Dena. Dividends totaling $720 had been declared on the stocks on November 30, 1996, and were payable on January 15, 1997. Dena became the shareholder of record in time to collect the dividends. What is Gus's 1997 gross income from the bond and stocks?

b. Gus's mother was unable to pay her bills as they came due. Gus, his employer, and his mother's creditors entered into an arrangement whereby Gus's employer would withhold $500 per month from his salary and the employer would pay the $500 to the creditors. Gus's employer withheld $3,000 from his salary and paid that amount to the creditors. Is Gus required to pay tax on the $3,000?

46. Tracy, a cash basis taxpayer, is employed by Eagle Corporation, also a cash basis taxpayer. Tracy is a full-time employee of the corporation and receives a salary of $60,000 per year. He also receives a bonus equal to 10% of all collections from clients he serviced during the year. Determine the tax consequences of the following events to the corporation and to Tracy:

a. On December 31, 1996, Tracy was visiting a customer. The customer gave Tracy a $3,000 check payable to the corporation for appraisal services Tracy performed during 1996. Tracy did not deliver the check to the corporation until January 1997.

b. The facts are the same as in (a), except that the corporation is an accrual basis taxpayer and Tracy deposited the check on December 31, but the bank did not add the deposit to the corporation's account until January 1997.

c. The facts are the same as in (a), except the customer told Tracy to hold the check until January when the customer could make a bank deposit that would cover the check.

47. Eve, Fran, and Gary each have a one-third interest in the capital and profits of the EFG Partnership. At the beginning of the year, each partner had a $50,000 balance in his or her capital account. The partnership's gross income for the year was $190,000, and its total expenses were $110,000. During the year, Eve contributed an additional $10,000 to the partnership and did not have any withdrawals from her capital account. Fran withdrew $30,000, and Gary withdrew $24,000. Compute each partner's taxable income from the partnership for the year.

48. Nell and Kirby Archer are in the process of negotiating their divorce agreement. What would be the tax consequences to Nell and Kirby if the following, considered individually, become part of the agreement:

a. Nell is to receive $1,000 per month until she dies or remarries. She also is to receive $500 per month for 12 years for her one-half interest in their personal residence. She paid for her one-half interest out of her earnings.

b. Nell is to receive a principal sum of $100,000. Of this amount, $50,000 is to be paid in the year of the divorce, and $5,000 per year will be paid to her in each of the following 10 years or until her death.

c. Nell is to receive stock in GM Corporation (value of $120,000 and basis of $75,000). The stock was jointly owned by Nell and Kirby. In exchange for the stock, Nell relinquished all of her rights to property accumulated during the marriage. She also is to receive $1,000 per month until her death or remarriage, but for a period of not longer than 10 years.

d. Assume that Nell and Kirby are close to agreeing on the settlement described in (c). Nell has informed you that she plans to sell the stock soon after she receives it and move into her mother's residence. Nell has asked you for a written explanation of the tax consequences of accepting the settlement described in (c). Assume Nell's marginal tax rate is 28%. Nell resides at 400 Peachtree Drive, Atlanta, GA 30303.

49. Under the terms of a post-1986 divorce agreement, Al is to receive payments from Karen as follows: $60,000 in Year 1, $45,000 in Year 2, and $20,000 each year for Years 3 through 10. Al is also to receive custody of their minor son. The payments will decrease by $5,000 per year if the son dies or when he attains age 21 and will cease upon Al's death.
    a. What will be Al's taxable alimony in Year 1?
    b. What will be the effect of the Years 2 and 3 payments on Al's taxable income?

50. Under the terms of their divorce agreement, Barry is to transfer common stock (cost of $25,000, market value of $60,000) to Sandra. Barry and Sandra have a 14-year-old child. Sandra will have custody of the child, and Barry is to pay $300 per month as child support. In addition, Sandra is to receive $1,000 per month for 10 years. However, the payments will be reduced to $750 per month when their child reaches age 21. In the first year under the agreement, Sandra receives the common stock and the correct cash payments for six months. How will the terms of the agreement affect Sandra's gross income?

51. On June 30, 1996, Ridge borrowed $52,000 from his employer. On July 1, 1996, Ridge used the money as follows:

Interest-free loan to Ridge's controlled corporation (operated by Ridge on a part-time basis)	$21,000
Interest-free loan to Tab (Ridge's son)	11,000
National Bank of Grundy 9% certificate of deposit ($15,260 due at maturity, June 30, 1997)	14,000
National Bank of Grundy 10% certificate of deposit ($7,260 due at maturity, June 30, 1998)	6,000
	$52,000

Ridge's employer did not charge him interest. The applicable Federal rate was 12% throughout the relevant period. Tab had investment income of $800 for the year, and he used the loan proceeds to pay medical school tuition. There were no other outstanding loans between Ridge and Tab. What are the effects of the preceding transactions on Ridge's taxable income for 1996?

52. Indicate whether the imputed interest rules should apply in the following situations:
    a. Mitch is a cash basis attorney who charges his clients based on the number of hours it takes to do the job. The bill is due upon completion of the work. However, for clients who make an initial payment when the work begins, Mitch grants a discount on the final bill. The discount is equal to 10% interest on the deposit.
    b. Local Telephone Company requires that customers make a security deposit. The deposit is refunded after the customer has established a good record for paying the telephone bill. The company pays 6% interest on the deposits.
    c. Lynn asked Kelly for a $125,000 loan to purchase a new home. Kelly made the loan and did not charge interest. Kelly never intended to collect the loan, and at the end of the year Kelly told Lynn that the debt was forgiven.

53. Vito is the sole shareholder of Vito, Inc. He is also employed by the corporation. On June 30, 1996, Vito borrowed $8,000 from Vito, Inc., and on July 1, 1997, he borrowed an additional $3,000. Both loans were due on demand. No interest was charged on the loans, and the Federal rate was 10% for all relevant dates. Vito used the money to purchase stock, and he had no investment income. Determine the tax consequences to Vito and Vito, Inc., in each of the following situations:
    a. The loans are considered employer-employee loans.
    b. The loans are considered corporation-shareholder loans.

54. Albert purchased an annuity from an insurance company for $100,000 on January 1, 1996. The annuity was to pay him $6,000 per year for life starting in January 1996. At the annuity starting date, Albert was age 65.
    a. Determine Albert's gross income from the annuity in the first year.
    b. Assume Albert lives 25 years after purchasing the contract. What would be his gross income in the twenty-fourth year?

55. In 1996, Ahmad purchased an annuity for $50,000. He was 59 at the time he purchased the contract. Payments were to begin when Ahmad attained age 62. In 1996, when the cash surrender value had increased to $51,000, Ahmad exercised a right to receive $1,500 and accept reduced payments after age 62. In 1998, when he had a life expectancy of 22.5 years, Ahmad received his first annual $3,000 payment under the contract.
    a. What is Ahmad's income from the contract in 1996?
    b. Compute Ahmad's taxable collections under the annuity contract in 1998.

56. For each of the following, determine the amount that should be included in gross income:
    a. Joe was selected as the most valuable player in the Super Bowl. In recognition of this, he was awarded a sports car worth $60,000 and $50,000 in cash.
    b. Wanda won the Mrs. America beauty contest. She received various prizes valued at $75,000.
    c. George was awarded the Nobel Peace Prize. He directed the Nobel committee to pay the $950,000 prize to State University, his alma mater.

57. The LMN Partnership has a group term life insurance plan. Each partner has $100,000 protection, and each employee has protection equal to twice his or her annual salary. Employee Alice (age 44) had $90,000 insurance under the plan, and partner Kay (age 56) had $150,000 coverage. The cost of Alice's coverage for the year was $180, and the cost of Kay's protection was $950.
    a. Assuming the plan is nondiscriminatory, how much must Alice and Kay include in gross income from the insurance?
    b. Assuming the plan is discriminatory, how much must Kay include in her gross income from the insurance?

58. Herbert was employed for the first six months of the year and earned $60,000 in salary. During the next six months, he collected $7,800 of unemployment compensation, borrowed $6,000 (using his personal residence as collateral), and withdrew $1,000 from his savings account (including $60 interest). His luck was not all bad, for in December he won $800 in the lottery on a $5 ticket. Calculate Herbert's gross income.

59. Linda and Don are married and file a joint return. In 1996, they received $9,000 in Social Security benefits and $28,000 taxable pension benefits, interest, and dividends.
    a. Compute the couple's adjusted gross income on a joint return.
    b. Don would like to know whether they should sell for $100,000 a corporate bond (at no gain or loss) that pays 8% in interest each year and use the proceeds to buy a $100,000 nontaxable State of Virginia bond that will pay $6,000 in interest each year.
    c. If Linda in (a) works part-time and earns $30,000, how much would Linda and Don's adjusted gross income increase?

60. Melissa and James are married and file a joint return. They receive $11,000 in Social Security benefits, $28,000 in pension benefits (all taxable), and $10,000 of taxable interest and dividends.
    a. Assuming that Melissa and James have $15,000 in itemized deductions and personal exemptions, how much will their taxable income increase if they sell stock that cost $1,000 for $11,000?
    b. Assuming the statutory rate applied to the capital gain from the sale of the stock is 28% and the rate applied to all other income is also 28%, what are the after-tax proceeds from the sale of the stock?
    c. How might the Social Security formula influence Melissa and James's decision of whether to sell the stock for a $10,000 gain?

61. Donna does not think she has an income tax problem but would like to discuss her situation with you just to make sure she will not get hit with an unexpected tax liability. Base your suggestions on the following relevant financial information:
    a. Donna's share of the SAT Partnership income is $70,000, but none of the income can be distributed because the partnership needs the cash for operations.
    b. Donna's Social Security benefits totaled $8,400, but Donna loaned the cash received to her nephew.
    c. Donna assigned to a creditor the right to collect $1,200 interest on some bonds she owned.
    d. Donna and her husband lived together in California until September, when they separated. Donna has heard rumors that her husband had substantial gambling winnings since they separated.

CUMULATIVE PROBLEMS

62. Dan and Freida Butler, husband and wife, file a joint return. The Butlers live at 625 Oak Street, Corbin, KY 27521. Dan's Social Security number is 482–61–1231, and Freida's is 162–79–1245.

    During 1996, Dan and Freida furnished over half of the total support of each of the following individuals:
    a. Gina, their daughter, age 22, a full-time student, who was married on December 21, 1996, has no income of her own, and for 1996 did not file a joint return with her husband, who earned $4,000 during 1996.
    b. Sam, their son, age 20, who had gross income of $2,900 and who dropped out of college in February 1996.
    c. Ben Brow, Freida's brother, age 27, who is a full-time college student with gross income of $4,000.

    Dan, a radio announcer for WJJJ, earned a salary of $50,000 in 1996. Freida was employed part-time as a real estate salesperson by Corbin Realty and was paid commissions of $40,000 in 1996. Freida sold a house on December 30, 1996, and will be paid a commission of $1,500 (not included in the $40,000) on the January 10, 1997, closing date.

    Dan and Freida collected $15,000 on a certificate of deposit that matured on September 30, 1996. The certificate was purchased on October 1, 1994, for $13,102, and the yield to maturity was 7%.

    Other income received consisted of the following:

Dividends on CSX stock	$2,000
Interest on savings account at Second Bank	1,300

CSX had been instructed by Dan and Freida to pay the dividends directly to Freida's brother, Ben. CSX complied with their instructions.

    Freida is a 10% partner in the Green Partnership. Green reported taxable income of $100,000 for 1996 and made no distributions to any of the partners in 1996.

    Dan and Freida had itemized deductions as follows:

State income tax withheld	$3,100
Real estate taxes paid	2,500
Interest on home mortgage (paid to Corbin Savings and Loan)	6,400
Cash contributions to the Boy Scouts	620

Their employers withheld Federal income tax of $14,500 (Dan $8,400, Freida $6,100), and the Butlers paid estimated tax of $4,000.

Part 1—Tax Computation
Compute Dan and Freida's 1996 Federal income tax payable (or refund due). Suggested software (if available): *TurboTax* or *MacInTax*.

Part 2—Tax Planning

Dan plans to reduce his work schedule and work only halftime for WJJJ in 1997. He has been writing songs for several years and wants to devote more time to developing a career as a songwriter. Because of the uncertainty in the music business, however, he would like you to make all computations assuming he will have no income from songwriting in 1997. To make up for the loss of income, Freida plans to increase the amount of time she spends selling real estate. She estimates she will be able to earn $60,000 in 1997. Assume all other income and expense items will be approximately the same as they were in 1996. Will the Butlers have more or less disposable income (after Federal income tax) in 1997? Write a letter to the Butlers that contains your advice and prepare a memo for the tax files. Suggested software (if available): *TurboTax* or *MacInTax*.

63. Sam T. Seymour would like to forget 1995 (and almost did as a result of his drinking problem). Although he received a salary of $74,000 and $600 of interest income, a divorce nearly brought him to financial ruin. The divorce was final on February 28, 1995. Under the agreement, Sam was required to do the following:

- Pay his minor daughter Pam's private school tuition of $10,800.

- Pay his ex-wife, Patricia Ann Seymour, a $40,000 lump-sum payment on March 1, 1995, and $2,000 each month thereafter through February 2001. The payments are to cease upon Patricia's death.

- Transfer to Patricia stock acquired in 1987 for $40,000 that now has a market value of $82,000.

Patricia retained custody of Pam but spent only $4,000 for Pam's support in 1995. The divorce agreement was silent as to whether Sam could claim Pam as a dependent and as to whether the cash payments to Patricia would constitute alimony.

Sam paid the tuition and made the $40,000 lump-sum payment but, because he was dismissed from his job in August 1995, was able to make only seven of the monthly payments to Patricia.

On November 1, 1995, when the applicable Federal rate was 6%, Sam was compelled to borrow $35,000 from his mother (Mollie Seymour). He gave her a non-interest-bearing second mortgage on his residence. There were no other loans outstanding between Sam and his mother.

Other information relevant to Sam's 1995 return is as follows:

a. Sam's disabled brother, Fred Seymour, lived with Sam from April through December 1995. Fred's only income was $3,600 of Social Security disability payments, and Sam contributed $4,000 toward Fred's support. No one else contributed to Fred's support. Fred's Social Security number is 245–99–4444.

b. Sam's only deductible items were home mortgage interest, $2,080; state income tax, $2,180; county property taxes, $3,000; charitable contributions, $200.

c. Sam's employer withheld $10,000 of Federal income tax.

d. Sam is 47 years old, his Social Security number is 215–71–1041, and he lives at 170 Ford Street, Gretna, TN 37929.

e. Patricia Ann Seymour's Social Security number is 712–15–9701.

Compute Sam's 1995 Federal income tax payable (or refund due). If you use tax forms for your computations, you will need Form 1040 and Schedules A and B. Suggested software (if available): *TurboTax* or *MacInTax*.

TEAM PROJECT: ARTHUR ANDERSEN TAX CHALLENGE CASES

For more information on the Arthur Andersen Tax Challenge Cases, please refer to Chapter 2, page 2-41.

Information related to tax issues and problems that are discussed in this chapter may be found in the

Fields case on pages 10, 18-27, 32, 33
Miller case on pages 3, 11, 13-15, 17, 21-23, 35, 40

Read and analyze the case you have been assigned and *identify* any issues and problems that are related to material covered in this chapter. If the information provided in the case is complete, prepare answers for this part of the case at this time. If you need information that is contained in the later parts of the case, please write a memo summarizing the questions or problems so you can prepare a complete answer at a later date.

4

GROSS INCOME: EXCLUSIONS

LEARNING OBJECTIVES

After completing Chapter 4, you should be able to:

1. Understand that statutory authority is required to exclude an item from gross income.

2. Identify the circumstances under which various items are excludible from gross income.

3. Determine the extent to which receipts can be excluded under the tax benefit rule.

4. Describe the circumstances under which income must be reported from the discharge of indebtedness.

5. Identify tax planning strategies for obtaining the maximum benefit from allowable exclusions.

ITEMS SPECIFICALLY EXCLUDED FROM GROSS INCOME

Chapter 3 discussed the concepts and judicial doctrines that affect the determination of gross income. If an income item is within the all-inclusive definition of gross income, the item can be excluded only if the taxpayer can locate specific authority for doing so. Chapter 4 focuses on the exclusions Congress has authorized. These exclusions are listed in Exhibit 4–1.

Tax advisers spend countless hours trying to develop techniques to achieve tax-exempt status for income. Employee benefits planning is greatly influenced by the availability of certain types of exclusions. Taxes play an important role in employee benefits, as well as in other situations, because attaining an exclusion is another means of enhancing after-tax income. For example, for a person whose combined Federal and state marginal tax rate is 40 percent, $1.00 of tax-exempt income is equivalent to $1.66 in income subject to taxation. The tax adviser's ideal is to attach the right labels or provide the right wording to render income nontaxable without affecting the economics of the transaction.

Consider the case of an employee who is in the 28 percent marginal tax bracket and is paying $3,000 a year for health insurance. If the employer provided this protection in a manner that qualified for exclusion treatment but reduced the employee's salary by $3,000, the employee's after-tax and after-insurance income would increase at no additional cost to the employer.

▼ **EXHIBIT 4–1**
Summary of Principal Exclusions
from Gross Income

1. Donative items
   Gifts, bequests, inheritances, and employee death benefits [§§ 102 and 101(b)]
   Life insurance proceeds paid by reason of death (§ 101)
   Scholarships (§ 117)
2. Personal and welfare items
   Injury or sickness payments (§ 104)
   Public assistance payments (Rev.Rul. 71–425, 1971–2 C.B. 76)
   Amounts received under insurance contracts for certain living expenses (§ 123)
   Reimbursement for the costs of caring for a foster child (§ 131)
3. Wage and salary supplements
   a. Fringe benefits
      Accident and health benefits (§§ 105 and 106)
      Lodging and meals furnished for the convenience of the employer (§ 119)
      Rental value of parsonages (§ 107)
      Employee achievement awards [§ 74(c)]
      Employer contributions to employee group term life insurance (§ 79)
      Cafeteria plans (§ 125)
      Educational assistance payments (§ 127)*
      Child or dependent care (§ 129)
      Services provided to employees at no additional cost to the employer (§ 132)
      Employee discounts (§ 132)
      Working condition and *de minimis* fringes (§ 132)
      Athletic facilities provided to employees (§ 132)
      Qualified transportation fringe (§ 132)
      Qualified moving expense reimbursement (§ 132)
      Tuition reductions granted to employees of educational institutions (§ 117)
   b. Military benefits
      Combat pay (§ 112)
      Housing, uniforms, and other benefits (§ 134)
   c. Foreign earned income (§ 911)
4. Investor items
   Interest on state and local government obligations (§ 103)
   Improvements by tenant to landlord's property (§ 109)
   Fifty percent exclusion for gain from sale of certain small business stock (§ 1202)
5. Benefits for the elderly
   Social Security benefits (except in the case of certain higher-income taxpayers) (§ 86)
   Gain from the sale of personal residence by elderly taxpayers (§ 121)
6. Other benefits
   Income from discharge of indebtedness (§ 108)
   Recovery of a prior year's deduction that yielded no tax benefit (§ 111)
   Educational savings bonds (§ 135)

*Exclusion treatment applies for tax years beginning before January 1, 1995.

Salary received to use to purchase health insurance	$ 3,000
Less: Taxes ($3,000 × 28%)	(840)
Cash available to purchase health insurance	$ 2,160
Less: Cost of health insurance	(3,000)
Excess of cost of health insurance over cash available	$ 840

Thus, the employee in this case is $840 better off with a salary reduction of $3,000 and employer-provided health insurance. The employee may still decide that the $3,000 salary is preferable. For example, if the employee has not been sick, he or she may feel that health insurance is no longer needed. Understanding the tax influence, however, does enable the employee to make a more informed choice.

STATUTORY AUTHORITY

1 LEARNING OBJECTIVE
Understand that statutory authority is required to exclude an item from gross income.

Sections 101 through 150 provide the authority for excluding specific items from gross income. In addition, other exclusions are scattered throughout the Code. Each exclusion has its own legislative history and reason for enactment. Certain exclusions are intended as a form of indirect welfare payments. Other exclusions prevent double taxation of income or provide incentives for socially desirable activities (e.g., nontaxable interest on certain U.S. government bonds where the owner uses the funds for educational expenses).

In some cases, Congress has enacted exclusions to rectify the effects of judicial decisions. For example, the Supreme Court held that the fair market value of improvements (not made in lieu of rent) made by a tenant to the landlord's property should be included in the landlord's gross income upon termination of the lease.[1] The landlord was required to include the value of the improvements in gross income even though the property had not been sold or otherwise disposed of. Congress provided relief in this situation by enacting § 109, which defers taxing the value of the improvements until the property is sold.[2]

GIFTS AND INHERITANCES

2 LEARNING OBJECTIVE
Identify the circumstances under which various items are excludible from gross income.

Beginning with the Income Tax Act of 1913 and continuing to the present, Congress has allowed the recipient of a gift to exclude the value of the property from gross income. The exclusion applies to gifts made during the life of the donor (*inter vivos* gifts) and transfers that take effect upon the death of the donor (bequests and inheritances).[3] However, as discussed in Chapter 3, the recipient of a gift of income-producing property is subject to tax on the income subsequently earned from the property. Also, as discussed in Chapter 1, the donor or the decedent's estate may be subject to gift or estate taxes on the transfer.

In numerous cases, gifts are made in a business setting. For example, a salesperson gives a purchasing agent free samples; an employee receives cash from his or her employer on retirement; a corporation makes payments to employees who were victims of a natural disaster; a corporation makes a cash payment to a deceased employee's spouse. In these and similar instances, it is frequently unclear whether the payment was a gift or whether it represents compensation for past, present, or future services.

The courts have defined a **gift** as "a voluntary transfer of property by one to another without adequate [valuable] consideration or compensation therefrom."[4]

---

[1] *Helvering v. Bruun*, 40–1 USTC ¶9337, 24 AFTR 652, 60 S.Ct. 631 (USSC, 1940).

[2] If the tenant made the improvements in lieu of rent, the value of the improvements is not eligible for exclusion.

[3] § 102.

[4] *Estate of D. R. Daly*, 3 B.T.A. 1042 (1926).

TAX IN THE NEWS

STRIKE BENEFITS ARE NOT GIFTS

In a recent Tax Court case, striking airline pilots argued that the strike benefits they received from their union should be excluded from gross income as gifts. The benefits were funded by charges imposed on union members who worked for nonstriking airlines. The pilots argued that the benefits were nontaxable gifts from other pilots and that the union was merely a conduit for the funds. The Tax Court found that the payments were not motivated by "detached and disinterested generosity," the requisite for gift treatment. The nonstriking pilots were required to pay for the benefits, and the receipt of the benefits by the striking pilots was contingent upon their striking. Finally, unlike a gift situation, the individual financial needs of the pilots were not taken into account in setting the benefits.

SOURCE: *Richard A. Osbourne*, 69 TCM 1895, T.C.Memo. 1995–71.

If the payment is intended to be for services rendered, it is not a gift, even though the payment is made without legal or moral obligation and the payor receives no economic benefit from the transfer. To qualify as a gift, the payment must be made "out of affection, respect, admiration, charity or like impulses."[5] Thus, the cases on this issue have been decided on the basis of the donor's intent.

In a landmark case, *Comm. v. Duberstein*,[6] the taxpayer (Duberstein) received a Cadillac from a business acquaintance. Duberstein had supplied the businessman with the names of potential customers with no expectation of compensation. The Supreme Court concluded:

> . . . despite the characterization of the transfer of the Cadillac by the parties [as a gift] and the absence of any obligation, even of a moral nature, to make it, it was at the bottom a recompense for Duberstein's past service, or an inducement for him to be of further service in the future.

Duberstein was therefore required to include the fair market value of the automobile in gross income.

In the case of cash or other property *received by an employee* from his or her employer, Congress has eliminated any ambiguity. Transfers from an employer to an employee cannot be excluded as a gift unless the transfer fits into a statutory exclusion provision other than the one for gifts.[7]

LIFE INSURANCE PROCEEDS

GENERAL RULE

Life insurance proceeds paid to the beneficiary because of the death of the insured are exempt from income tax.[8]

---

[5] *Robertson v. U.S.*, 52–1 USTC ¶9343, 41 AFTR 1053, 72 S.Ct. 994 (USSC, 1952).
[6] 60–2 USTC ¶9515, 5 AFTR2d 1626, 80 S.Ct. 1190 (USSC, 1960).

[7] § 102(c).
[8] § 101(a).

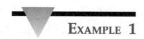

EXAMPLE 1

Mark purchased an insurance policy on his life and named his wife Linda as the beneficiary. Mark paid $24,000 in premiums. When he died, Linda collected the insurance proceeds of $60,000. The $60,000 is exempt from Federal income tax. ▼

Congress chose to exempt life insurance proceeds for the following reasons:

- For family members, life insurance proceeds serve much the same purpose as a nontaxable inheritance.
- In a business context (as well as in a family situation), life insurance proceeds replace an economic loss suffered by the beneficiary.

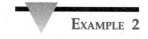

EXAMPLE 2

Gold Corporation purchased a life insurance policy to cover its key employee. If the proceeds were taxable, the corporation would require more insurance coverage to pay the tax as well as to cover the economic loss of the employee. ▼

Thus, in general, Congress concluded that making life insurance proceeds exempt from income tax was a good policy.

EXCEPTIONS TO EXCLUSION TREATMENT

The income tax exclusion applies only when the insurance proceeds are received because of the death of the insured. If the owner cancels the policy and receives the cash surrender value, he or she must recognize gain to the extent of the excess of the amount received over the cost of the policy (a loss is not deductible).[9]

Another exception to exclusion treatment applies if the policy is transferred after it is issued by the insurance company. If the policy is *transferred for valuable consideration*, the insurance proceeds are includible in the gross income of the transferee to the extent the proceeds received exceed the amount paid for the policy by the transferee plus any subsequent premiums paid.

EXAMPLE 3

Adam pays premiums of $500 for an insurance policy in the face amount of $1,000 upon the life of Beth and subsequently transfers the policy to Carol for $600. On Beth's death, Carol receives the proceeds of $1,000. The amount that Carol can exclude from gross income is limited to $600 plus any premiums she paid subsequent to the transfer. ▼

The Code, however, provides four exceptions to the rule illustrated in the preceding example. These exceptions permit exclusion treatment for transfers to the following:

1. A partner of the insured.
2. A partnership in which the insured is a partner.
3. A corporation in which the insured is an officer or shareholder.
4. A transferee whose basis in the policy is determined by reference to the transferor's basis.

The first three exceptions facilitate the use of insurance contracts to fund buy-sell agreements.

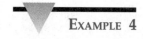

EXAMPLE 4

Rick and Sam are equal partners who have an agreement that allows either partner to purchase the interest of a deceased partner for $50,000. Neither partner has sufficient cash to actually buy the other partner's interest, but each has a life insurance policy on his own

---

[9] *Landfield Finance Co. v. U.S.*, 69–2 USTC ¶9680, 24 AFTR2d 69–5744, 418 F.2d 172 (CA–7, 1969).

```
 TAX IN THE NEWS
```

INVESTORS FIND DEATH A SAFE BET

According to an Associated Press report, a new class of investments called asset-backed securities is being marketed. These investments are much like mortgage-backed securities, but are backed by life insurance policies on the terminally ill. The terminally ill patient sells his or her policy to the investment group for 70 to 80 percent of the face value. To date, the dollar value of offerings of such asset-backed securities is small, but proponents say the potential investment pool is vast and untapped.

One proponent views the securities as a form of empowerment for the terminally ill. While the idea of creating or even buying such investments at first appears callous, proponents point out that they enable the patients to improve their quality of life, buy needed medical supplies, and support themselves.

SOURCE: Associated Press, "Investors Find Death a Safe Bet," *Roanoke Times & World News,* April 21, 1995, p. A9.

life in the amount of $50,000. Rick and Sam could exchange their policies (usually at little or no taxable gain), and upon the death of either partner, the surviving partner could collect tax-free insurance proceeds. The proceeds could then be used to purchase the decedent's interest in the partnership. ▼

The fourth exception applies to policies that were transferred pursuant to a tax-free exchange or were received by gift.[10]

Investment earnings arising from the reinvestment of life insurance proceeds are generally subject to income tax. Often the beneficiary will elect to collect the insurance proceeds in installments. The annuity rules (discussed in Chapter 3) are used to apportion the installment payment between the principal element (excludible) and the interest element (includible).[11]

EMPLOYEE ▼ DEATH BENEFITS

GIFT VERSUS COMPENSATION

Frequently, an employer makes payments (**death benefits**) to a deceased employee's surviving spouse, children, or other beneficiaries. If the decedent had a nonforfeitable right to the payments (e.g., the decedent's accrued salary), the amounts are generally taxable to the recipient just the same as if the employee had lived and collected the payments. But where the employer makes voluntary payments, the gift issue arises. Generally, the IRS considers such payments to be compensation for prior services rendered by the deceased employee.[12] However, some courts have held that payments to an employee's surviving spouse or other beneficiaries are gifts if the following are true:[13]

---

[10] See the discussion of gifts and tax-free exchanges in Chapter 12.
[11] Reg. §§ 1.72–7(c)(1) and 1.101–7T.
[12] Rev.Rul. 62–102, 1962–2 C.B. 37.

[13] *Estate of Sydney J. Carter v. Comm.,* 72–1 USTC ¶9129, 29 AFTR2d 332, 453 F.2d 61 (CA–2, 1972), and the cases cited there.

- The payments were made to the surviving spouse and children rather than to the employee's estate.
- The employer derived no benefit from the payments.
- The surviving spouse and children performed no services for the employer.
- The decedent had been fully compensated for services rendered.
- Payments were made pursuant to a board of directors' resolution that followed a general company policy of providing payments for families of deceased employees (but not exclusively for families of shareholder-employees).

When all of the above conditions are satisfied, the payment is presumed to have been made *as an act of affection or charity.* When one or more of these conditions is not satisfied, the surviving spouse and children may still be deemed the recipients of a gift if the payment is made in light of the survivors' financial needs.[14]

Automatic $5,000 Exclusion.   Section 101(b) attempts to eliminate or reduce controversy in this area by providing an *automatic exclusion* of the first $5,000 paid by the employer to the employee's beneficiaries by reason of the death of the employee. The maximum total exclusion on behalf of a deceased employee is $5,000 regardless of the number of employers paying the benefit. The $5,000 exclusion must be apportioned among the beneficiaries on the basis of each beneficiary's percentage of the total death benefits received. When the employer's payments exceed $5,000, the beneficiaries may still be able to exclude the entire amount received as a gift if they are able to show gratuitous intent on the part of the employer. Note that this exclusion does not apply to the decedent's accrued salary.

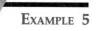

EXAMPLE 5

When Antonio died, his employer paid his accrued salary of $3,000 to Josefina, Antonio's widow. The employer's board of directors also authorized payments to Josefina ($4,000), Antonio's daughter ($2,000), and Antonio's son ($2,000) "in recognition of Antonio's many years of service to the company."

The $3,000 accrued salary is compensation for past services and was owed to Antonio at the time of his death. Therefore, the $3,000 is includible in gross income. The additional payments to the widow and children were not owed to Antonio. Because the payments were made in recognition of Antonio's past service, under the *Duberstein* decision, the payments are not gifts. However, the employee death benefit exclusion enables the widow and children to exclude the following amounts:

$$\text{Widow} \quad \frac{\$4,000}{\$8,000} \times \$5,000 = \quad \$2,500$$

$$\text{Daughter} \quad \frac{\$2,000}{\$8,000} \times \$5,000 = \quad 1,250$$

$$\text{Son} \quad \frac{\$2,000}{\$8,000} \times \$5,000 = \quad \frac{1,250}{\$5,000}$$

Besides avoiding the gift issue in many cases, the employee death benefit exclusion is intended to allow a substitute for tax-exempt life insurance proceeds.

---

[14] *Simpson v. U.S.,* 58–2 USTC ¶9923, 2 AFTR2d 6036, 261 F.2d 497 (CA–7, 1958), *cert. denied,* 79 S.Ct. 724 (USSC, 1958).

SCHOLARSHIPS

GENERAL INFORMATION

Payments or benefits received by a student at an educational institution may be (1) compensation for services, (2) a gift, or (3) a scholarship. If the payments or benefits are received as compensation for services (past or present), the fact that the recipient is a student generally does not render the amounts received nontaxable.[15]

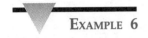

EXAMPLE 6

State University waives tuition for all graduate teaching assistants. The tuition waived is intended as compensation for services and is therefore included in the graduate assistant's gross income. ▼

As discussed earlier, gifts are not includible in gross income.

The **scholarship** rules are intended to provide exclusion treatment for education-related benefits that cannot qualify as gifts but are not compensation for services. According to the Regulations, "a scholarship is an amount paid or allowed to, or for the benefit of, an individual to aid such individual in the pursuit of study or research."[16] The recipient must be a candidate for a degree (either undergraduate or graduate) at an educational institution.[17]

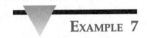

EXAMPLE 7

Terry enters a contest sponsored by a local newspaper. Each contestant is required to submit an essay on local environmental issues. The prize is one year's tuition at State University. Terry wins the contest. The newspaper has a legal obligation to Terry (as contest winner). Thus, the benefits are not a gift. However, since the tuition payment aids Terry in pursuing her studies, the payment is a scholarship. ▼

A scholarship recipient may exclude from gross income the amount used for tuition and related expenses (fees, books, supplies, and equipment required for courses), provided the conditions of the grant do not require that the funds be used for other purposes.[18] Amounts received for room and board are *not* excludible and are treated as earned income for purposes of calculating the standard deduction for a taxpayer who is another taxpayer's dependent.[19]

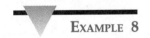

EXAMPLE 8

Kelly received a scholarship of $9,500 from State University to be used to pursue a bachelor's degree. She spent $4,000 on tuition, $3,000 on books and supplies, and $2,500 for room and board. Kelly may exclude $7,000 ($4,000 + $3,000) from gross income. The $2,500 spent for room and board is includible in Kelly's gross income.

The scholarship was Kelly's only source of income. Her parents provided more than 50% of Kelly's support and claimed her as a dependent. Kelly's standard deduction will equal her $2,500 gross income. Thus, she has no taxable income. ▼

TIMING ISSUES

Frequently, the scholarship recipient is a cash basis taxpayer who receives the money in one tax year but pays the educational expenses in a subsequent year.

---

[15] Reg. § 1.117–2(a). See *C. P. Bhalla*, 35 T.C. 13 (1960), for a discussion of the distinction between a scholarship and compensation. See also *Bingler v. Johnson*, 69–1 USTC ¶9348, 23 AFTR2d 1212, 89 S.Ct. 1439 (USSC, 1969). For potential exclusion treatment, see the subsequent discussion of qualified tuition reductions.

[16] Prop.Reg. § 1.117–6(c)(3)(i).
[17] § 117(a).
[18] § 117(b).
[19] Prop.Reg. § 1.117–6(h).

The amount eligible for exclusion may not be known at the time the money is received. In that case, the transaction is held *open* until the educational expenses are paid.[20]

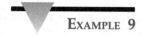

EXAMPLE 9

In August 1996, Sanjay received $10,000 as a scholarship for the academic year 1996–1997. Sanjay's expenditures for tuition, books, and supplies were as follows:

August–December 1996	$3,000
January–May 1997	4,500
	$7,500

Sanjay's gross income for 1997 includes $2,500 ($10,000 − $7,500) that is not excludible as a scholarship. None of the scholarship is included in his gross income in 1996. ▼

DISGUISED COMPENSATION

Some employers make scholarships available solely to the children of key employees. The tax objective of these plans is to provide a nontaxable fringe benefit to the executives by making the payment to the child in the form of an excludible scholarship. However, the IRS has ruled that the payments are generally includible in the gross income of the parent-employee.[21]

QUALIFIED TUITION REDUCTION PLANS

Employees (including retired and disabled former employees) of nonprofit educational institutions are allowed to exclude a tuition waiver from gross income, if the waiver is pursuant to a **qualified tuition reduction plan**.[22] The plan may not discriminate in favor of highly compensated employees. The exclusion applies to the employee, the employee's spouse, and the employee's dependent children. The exclusion also extends to tuition reductions granted by any nonprofit educational institution to employees of any other nonprofit educational institution (reciprocal agreements).

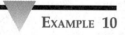

EXAMPLE 10

ABC University allows the dependent children of XYZ University employees to attend ABC University with no tuition charge. XYZ University grants reciprocal benefits to the children of ABC University employees. The dependent children can also attend tuition-free the university where their parents are employed. Employees who take advantage of these benefits are not required to recognize gross income. ▼

Generally, the exclusion is limited to *undergraduate* tuition waivers. However, in the case of teaching or research assistants, graduate tuition waivers may also qualify for exclusion treatment. According to the Proposed Regulations, the exclusion is limited to the value of the benefit in excess of the employee's reasonable compensation.[23] Thus, a tuition reduction that is a substitute for cash compensation cannot be excluded.

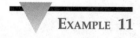

EXAMPLE 11

Susan is a graduate research assistant. She receives a $5,000 salary for 500 hours of service over a nine-month period. This pay, $10 per hour, is reasonable compensation for Susan's

---

[20] Prop.Reg. § 1.117–6(b)(2).
[21] Rev.Rul. 75–448, 1975–2 C.B. 55. *Richard T. Armantrout,* 67 T.C. 996 (1977).

[22] § 117(d).
[23] Prop.Reg. § 1.117–6(d).

services. In addition, Susan receives a waiver of $6,000 for tuition. Susan may exclude the tuition waiver from gross income. ▼

ETHICAL CONSIDERATIONS

A Caring Dean

About 25 percent of the undergraduate classes in the College of Business at Amber University are taught by doctoral students. Amber recognizes that its graduates will have both research and teaching responsibilities when they graduate and become faculty members. Thus, for the first year of graduate study, the doctoral students are research assistants, and for the second year they are teaching assistants. The students currently receive fellowship grants of $16,000 each year.

The dean of the School of Business is perplexed when he learns that the doctoral students have to pay income taxes on the fellowship grants they receive as graduate assistants. He did not have to do so when he was a graduate student.

Upon checking with a tax professor in the School of Accounting, the dean learns that the fellowship grants are included in gross income as a result of a change in the tax law. After further conversations with the tax professor, the dean develops the following plan: (1) As a condition for receiving their degree, all doctoral students must be research assistants during the first year and teaching assistants during the second year. (2) The fellowship grant will be $12,000 for the first year and $20,000 for the second year with the $8,000 increment reported as compensation for services rendered. (3) A few local business people will be hired to teach part-time to provide a benchmark for the $8,000 of compensation income.

Evaluate the dean's plan both from the perspective of achieving the results he wants and from the perspective of ethical behavior.

COMPENSATION FOR INJURIES AND SICKNESS

DAMAGES

A person who suffers harm caused by another is often entitled to **compensatory damages.** The tax consequences of the receipt of damages depend on the type of harm the taxpayer has experienced. The taxpayer may seek recovery for (1) a loss of income, (2) expenses incurred, (3) property destroyed, or (4) personal injury.

Generally, reimbursement for a loss of income is taxed the same as the income replaced. The recovery of an expense is not income, unless the expense was deducted. Damages that are a recovery of the taxpayer's previously deducted expenses are generally taxable under the tax benefit rule, discussed later in this chapter.

A payment for damaged or destroyed property is treated as an amount received in a sale or exchange of the property. Thus, the taxpayer has a realized gain if the damage payments received exceed the property's basis. Damages for personal injuries receive special treatment under the Code.

Personal Injury. The legal theory of personal injury damages is that the amount received is intended "to make the plaintiff [the injured party] whole as before the injury."[24] It follows that if the damage payments received were subject to tax, the after-tax amount received would be less than the actual damages incurred and the injured party would not be "whole as before the injury."

Congress has specifically excluded from gross income the amount of any damage payments received (whether by suit or agreement) on account of personal injuries or sickness. The courts have applied the exclusion to any personal wrong committed against the taxpayer (e.g., breach of promise to marry, invasion of privacy, libel, slander, assault, battery). The exclusion also applies to compensation for loss of income (ordinarily taxable, as previously discussed) and recovery of expenses (except medical expenses deducted by the taxpayer) resulting from the personal injury.[25] According to the Supreme Court, however, the damages are taxable if under the Federal or state law establishing the taxpayer's right of recovery, the recovery is limited to the loss of income. The Supreme Court recently expanded the damages that are taxable by holding that recoveries in age-discrimination lawsuits are includible in gross income because such damages are not awarded on account of personal injury or sickness.[26]

In libel and slander cases, a single event can cause both a personal injury and damage to a business reputation. Damage to a business reputation is measured on the basis of estimated loss of income. Taxpayers argue that the amount received for loss of income in these cases is no different from the payments in other personal injury cases and thus should be excluded. According to the IRS, however, the business reputation damages are separate from the personal injury and are taxable.[27]

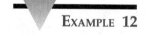

EXAMPLE 12

Tom, a television announcer, was dissatisfied with the manner in which Ron, an attorney, was defending the television station in a libel case. Tom stated on the air that Ron was botching the case. Ron sued Tom for slander, claiming damages for loss of income from clients and potential clients who heard Tom's statement. Ron's claim is for damages to his business reputation, and the amounts received are taxable.

Ron collected on the suit against Tom and was on his way to a party to celebrate his victory when a negligent driver, Norm, drove his truck into Ron's automobile, injuring Ron. Ron filed suit for the personal injuries and claimed as damages the loss of income for the period he was unable to work as a result of the injury. All amounts Ron received from Norm, including the reimbursement for lost income, are nontaxable because the claims are based on a personal injury. ▼

Punitive Damages.   In addition to seeking compensatory damages, the injured party may seek **punitive damages,** which are often awarded to punish the defendant for gross negligence or the intentional infliction of harm. Punitive damages are includible in gross income *unless* the claim arises out of physical injury or physical sickness.[28] Thus, punitive damages received for loss of personal reputation are taxable, although the compensatory damages are excludible. Punitive damages arising out of a physical injury claim are excludible.

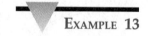

EXAMPLE 13

Assume Ron in Example 12 also received punitive damages in each suit. The punitive damages Ron received from Norm may be excluded from gross income because the

---

[24] *C. A. Hawkins,* 6 B.T.A. 1023 (1928).

[25] § 104(a)(2) and Rev.Rul. 85–97, 1985–2 C.B. 50.

[26] *U.S. v. Burke,* 92–1 USTC ¶50,254, 69 AFTR2d 92–1293, 112 S.Ct. 1867 (USSC, 1992); *Comm. v. Schleier,* 95–1 USTC ¶50,309, 75 AFTR2d 95–2675, 115 S.Ct. 2159 (USSC, 1995).

[27] Rev.Rul. 85–143, 1985–2 C.B. 55, in which the IRS announced it would not follow the Ninth Court of Appeals decision in *Roemer*

v. Comm., 83–2 USTC ¶9600, 52 AFTR2d 83–5954, 716 F.2d 693 (CA–9, 1983). See also *Wade E. Church,* 80 T.C. 1104 (1983).

[28] § 104(a). Both the IRS and the courts are interpreting this provision strictly. See, for example, *Hughes A. Bagley,* 105 T.C. ____, No. 27 (1995).

TAX IN THE NEWS

AGE-BIAS PAYMENTS AS PERSONAL INJURY

John Schmitz and Burns P. Downey were both United Airlines pilots. Both were forced into retirement at age 60. Each received about $120,000 to settle an age-discrimination class action. Neither included the $120,000 in gross income.

Last year, their financial flight paths diverged. On the same day, one Federal appeals court told Schmitz that he didn't have to pay income taxes on the settlement, while another Federal appeals court more than 2,000 miles away told Downey that he did. Caught in the lurch were hundreds of older Americans, including 70 former United pilots in the class action with Schmitz and Downey, who had received age-discrimination settlements and now, according to the IRS, owed taxes on those settlements.

In Downey's case, the Seventh Circuit Court of Appeals agreed with the IRS that the discrimination award was less like damages from a personal injury lawsuit (excludible from gross income) and more like damages from a breach of contract (includible in gross income). The Ninth Circuit Court of Appeals disagreed in deciding that Schmitz could exclude the settlement from his gross income. It concluded that the age-discrimination laws provide for jury trials and a range of damages more similar to personal injury suits than to contract actions.

Recently, Schmitz and Downey's flight paths converged with that of another former United pilot, and unfortunately, the convergence led to a crash for all of the former pilots. The Supreme Court in *Comm. v. Schleier* [95–1 USTC ¶50,309, 75 AFTR2d 95–2675, 115 S.Ct. 2159 (USSC, 1995)] ruled that former employees who successfully sue their former employers under the Age Discrimination in Employment Act of 1967 must include the damages received in gross income. In writing the majority opinion, Justice John Paul Stevens concluded that recoveries in age-discrimination lawsuits do not fit within the statutory language of § 104 of being "damages received on account of personal injuries or sickness."

SOURCE: "High Court Holds Age Discrimination Damages Are Taxable," Deloitte & Touche LLP - Deloitte & Touche Review, June 26, 1995, p. 5.

damages arose out of the physical injury claim. Ron's punitive damages received from Tom are taxable because the damages did not arise from a physical injury or sickness claim. ▼

WORKERS' COMPENSATION

State workers' compensation laws require the employer to pay fixed amounts for specific job-related injuries. The state laws were enacted so that the employee will not have to go through the ordeal of a lawsuit (and possibly not collect damages because of some defense available to the employer) to recover the damages. Although the payments are intended, in part, to compensate for a loss of future income, Congress has specifically exempted workers' compensation benefits from inclusion in gross income.[29]

---

[29] § 104(a)(1).

CONCEPT SUMMARY 4–1

Taxation of Damages

Type of Claim	Taxation of Award or Settlement
Breach of contract (generally loss of income)	Taxable.
Property damages	Recovery of cost, gain to the extent of the excess over basis. A loss is deductible for business property and investment property to the extent of basis over the amount realized. A loss may be deductible for personal use property (see discussion of casualty losses in Chapter 6).
Personal injury	
Physical	All amounts (compensatory and punitive) are excluded unless previously deducted (e.g., medical expenses).
Nonphysical, general	Compensatory damages are excluded (unless previously deducted), and punitive damages are taxable.
Nonphysical, only compensation is loss of income	Taxable.

ACCIDENT AND HEALTH INSURANCE BENEFITS

The income tax treatment of accident and health insurance benefits depends on whether the policy providing the benefits was purchased by the taxpayer or the taxpayer's employer. Benefits collected under an accident and health insurance policy *purchased by the taxpayer* are excludible. In this case, benefits collected under the taxpayer's insurance policy are excluded even though the payments are a substitute for income.[30]

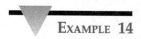

EXAMPLE 14

Bonnie purchased a medical and disability insurance policy. The insurance company paid Bonnie $200 per week to replace wages she lost while in the hospital. Although the payments serve as a substitute for income, the amounts received are tax-exempt benefits collected under Bonnie's insurance policy. ▼

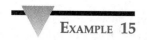

EXAMPLE 15

Joe's injury results in a partial paralysis of his left foot. He receives $5,000 for the injury from his accident insurance company under a policy he had purchased. The $5,000 accident insurance proceeds are tax-exempt. ▼

A different set of rules applies if the accident and health insurance protection was *purchased by the individual's employer,* as discussed in the following section.

EMPLOYER-SPONSORED ACCIDENT AND HEALTH PLANS

Congress encourages employers to provide employees, retired former employees, and their dependents with **accident and health benefits** and disability insurance

---

[30] § 104(a)(3).

plans. The *premiums* are deductible by the employer and excluded from the employee's income.[31] Although § 105(a) provides the general rule that the employee has includible income when he or she collects the insurance *benefits*, two exceptions are provided.

Section 105(b) generally excludes payments received for medical care of the employee, spouse, and dependents. However, if the payments are for expenses that do not meet the Code's definition of medical care,[32] the amount received must be included in gross income. In addition, the taxpayer must include in gross income any amounts received for medical expenses that were deducted by the taxpayer on a prior return.

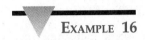

EXAMPLE 16

In 1996, Tab's employer-sponsored health insurance plan paid $4,000 for hair transplants that did not meet the Code's definition of medical care. Tab must include the $4,000 in his gross income for 1996. ▼

Section 105(c) excludes payments for the permanent loss or the loss of the use of a member or function of the body or the permanent disfigurement of the employee, spouse, or a dependent. Payments that are a substitute for salary (e.g., related to the period of time absent) are includible.

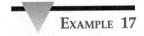

EXAMPLE 17

Jill lost an eye in an automobile accident unrelated to her work. As a result of the accident, Jill incurred $2,000 of medical expenses, which she deducted on her return. She collected $10,000 from an accident insurance policy carried by her employer. The benefits were paid according to a schedule of amounts that varied with the part of the body injured (e.g., $10,000 for loss of an eye, $20,000 for loss of a hand). Because the payment was for loss of a *member or function of the body*, the $10,000 is excluded from income. Jill was absent from work for a week as a result of the accident. Her employer provided her with insurance for the loss of income due to illness or injury. Jill collected $500, which is includible in gross income. ▼

MEDICAL REIMBURSEMENT PLANS

In lieu of providing the employee with insurance coverage for hospital and medical expenses, the employer may agree to reimburse the employee for these expenses. The amounts received through the insurance coverage (insured plan benefits) are excluded from income under § 105 (as previously discussed). Unfortunately in terms of cost considerations, the insurance companies that issue this type of policy usually require a broad coverage of employees. An alternative is to have a plan that is not funded with insurance (a self-insured arrangement). The benefits received under a self-insured plan can be excluded from the employee's income, if the plan does not discriminate in favor of highly compensated employees.[33]

ETHICAL CONSIDERATIONS

Using a Corporation to Deduct Health Insurance

R ose is a self-employed computer consultant who has no full-time employees. She is currently paying $6,000 for health insurance. Thirty percent of the $6000 premium is allowed as a deduction *for* AGI (see Chapter 9). However, the remaining 70 percent cannot be deducted as an itemized deduction because of the 7.5 percent-of-AGI floor on

---

[31] § 106, Reg. § 1.106–1, and Rev.Rul. 82–196, 1982–1 C.B. 106.   [33] § 105(h).
[32] See the discussion of medical care in Chapter 9.

the medical expense deduction. You realize that Rose could incorporate her practice and have the corporation pay for her health insurance. She could take a salary equal to the remainder of the income from the consulting practice. Thus, the corporation would have no taxable income, and Rose would have her health insurance purchased with before-tax dollars. Would such an approach be an abuse of the tax law?

MEALS AND LODGING

FURNISHED FOR THE CONVENIENCE OF THE EMPLOYER

As discussed in Chapter 3, income can take any form, including meals and lodging. However, § 119 excludes from income the value of meals and lodging provided to the employee and the employee's spouse and dependents under the following conditions:[34]

- The meals and/or lodging are *furnished* by the employer, on the employer's *business premises,* for the *convenience of the employer.*
- In the case of lodging, the *employee* is *required* to accept the lodging as a condition of employment.

The courts have construed both of these requirements strictly.

Furnished by the Employer. The following two questions have been raised with regard to the *furnished by the employer* requirement:

- Who is considered an *employee*?
- What is meant by *furnished*?

The IRS and some courts have reasoned that because a partner is not an employee, the exclusion does not apply to a partner. However, the Tax Court and the Fifth Court of Appeals have ruled in favor of the taxpayer on this issue.[35]

The Supreme Court held that a cash meal allowance was ineligible for the exclusion because the employer did not actually furnish the meals.[36] Similarly, one court denied the exclusion where the employer paid for the food and supplied the cooking facilities but the employee prepared the meal.[37]

On the Employer's Business Premises. The *on the employer's business premises* requirement, applicable to both meals and lodging, has resulted in much litigation. The Regulations define business premises as simply "the place of employment of the employee."[38] Thus, the Sixth Court of Appeals held that a residence, owned by the employer and occupied by an employee, two blocks from the motel that the employee managed was not part of the business premises.[39] However, the Tax Court considered an employer-owned house across the street from the hotel that was managed by the taxpayer to be on the business premises of the employer.[40]

---

[34] § 119(a). The meals and lodging are also excluded from FICA and FUTA tax. *Rowan Companies, Inc. v. U.S.,* 81–1 USTC ¶9479, 48 AFTR2d 81–5115, 101 S.Ct. 2288 (USSC, 1981).

[35] Rev.Rul. 80, 1953–1 C.B. 62; *Comm. v. Doak,* 56–2 USTC ¶9708, 49 AFTR 1491, 234 F.2d 704 (CA–4, 1956); but see *G. A. Papineau,* 16 T.C. 130 (1951); *Armstrong v. Phinney,* 68–1 USTC ¶9355, 21 AFTR2d 1260, 394 F.2d 661 (CA–5, 1968).

[36] *Comm. v. Kowalski,* 77–2 USTC ¶9748, 40 AFTR2d 6128, 98 S.Ct. 315 (USSC, 1977).

[37] *Tougher v. Comm.,* 71–1 USTC ¶9398, 27 AFTR2d 1301, 441 F.2d 1148 (CA–9, 1971).

[38] Reg. § 1.119–1(c)(1).

[39] *Comm. v. Anderson,* 67–1 USTC ¶9136, 19 AFTR2d 318, 371 F.2d 59 (CA–6, 1966).

[40] *J. B. Lindeman,* 60 T.C. 609 (1973).

Perhaps these two cases can be reconciled by comparing the distance from the lodging facilities to the place where the employer's business was conducted. The closer the lodging to the business operations, the more likely the convenience of the employer is served.

For the Convenience of the Employer.   The *convenience of the employer* test is intended to focus on the employer's motivation for furnishing the meals and lodging rather than on the benefits received by the employee. If the employer furnishes the meals and lodging primarily to enable the employee to perform his or her duties properly, it does not matter that the employee considers these benefits to be a part of his or her compensation.

The Regulations give the following examples in which the tests for excluding meals are satisfied:[41]

- A waitress is required to eat her meals on the premises during the busy lunch and breakfast hours.
- A bank furnishes a teller meals on the premises to limit the time the employee is away from his or her booth during the busy hours.
- A worker is employed at a construction site in a remote part of Alaska. The employer must furnish meals and lodging due to the inaccessibility of other facilities.

Required as a Condition of Employment.   The *employee is required to accept* test applies only to lodging. If the employee's use of the housing would serve the convenience of the employer, but the employee is not required to use the housing, the exclusion is not available.

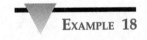

EXAMPLE 18

VEP, a utilities company, has all of its service personnel on 24-hour call for emergencies. The company encourages its employees to live near the plant so that the employees can respond quickly to emergency calls. Company-owned housing is available rent-free. Only 10 of the employees live in the company housing because it is not suitable for families.

Although the company-provided housing serves the convenience of the employer, it is not required. Therefore, the employees who live in the company housing cannot exclude its value from gross income. ▼

In addition, if the employee has the *option* of cash or lodging, the *required* test is not satisfied.

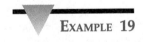

EXAMPLE 19

Khalid is the manager of a large apartment complex. The employer gives Khalid the option of rent-free housing (value of $6,000 per year) or an additional $5,000 per year. Khalid selects the housing option. Therefore, he must include $6,000 in gross income. ▼

OTHER HOUSING EXCLUSIONS

Employees of Educational Institutions.   An employee of an educational institution may be able to exclude the value of campus housing provided by the employer. Generally, the employee does not recognize income if he or she pays annual rents equal to or greater than 5 percent of the appraised value of the facility. If the rent payments are less than 5 percent of the value of the facility, the deficiency must be included in gross income.[42]

---

[41] Reg. § 1.119–1(f).   [42] § 119(d).

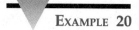

EXAMPLE 20

Swan University provides on-campus housing for its full-time faculty during the first three years of employment. The housing is not provided for the convenience of the employer. Professor Edith pays $3,000 annual rent for the use of a residence with an appraised value of $100,000 and an annual rental value of $12,000. Edith must recognize $2,000 gross income [.05($100,000) – $3,000 = $2,000] for the value of the housing provided to her. ▼

Ministers of the Gospel.   Ministers of the gospel can exclude (1) the rental value of a home furnished as compensation or (2) a rental allowance paid to them as compensation, to the extent the allowance is used to rent or provide a home.[43] The housing or housing allowance must be provided as compensation for the conduct of religious worship, the administration and maintenance of religious organizations, or the performance of teaching and administrative duties at theological seminaries.

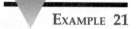

EXAMPLE 21

Pastor Bill is allowed to live rent-free in a house owned by the congregation. The annual rental value of the house is $6,000 and is provided as part of the pastor's compensation for ministerial services. Assistant Pastor Olga is paid a $4,500 cash housing allowance. She uses the $4,500 to pay rent and utilities on a home she and her family occupy. Neither Pastor Bill nor Assistant Pastor Olga is required to recognize gross income associated with the housing or housing allowance. ▼

Military Personnel.   Military personnel are allowed housing exclusions under various circumstances. Authority for these exclusions generally is found in Federal laws that are not part of the Internal Revenue Code.[44]

OTHER EMPLOYEE FRINGE BENEFITS

SPECIFIC BENEFITS

In recent years, Congress has enacted exclusions to encourage employers to (1) finance and make available child care facilities, (2) provide athletic facilities for employees, and (3) finance certain employees' education. These provisions are summarized as follows:

- The employee does not have to include in gross income the value of child and dependent care services paid for by the employer and incurred to enable the employee to work. The exclusion cannot exceed $5,000 per year ($2,500 if married and filing separately). For a married couple, the annual exclusion cannot exceed the earned income of the spouse who has the lesser amount of earned income. For an unmarried taxpayer, the exclusion cannot exceed the taxpayer's earned income.[45]
- The value of the use of a gymnasium or other athletic facilities by employees, their spouses, and their dependent children may be excluded from an employee's gross income. The facilities must be on the employer's

---

[43] § 107 and Reg. § 1.107–1.

[44] H. Rep. No. 99–841, 99th Cong., 2d Sess., p. 548 (1986). See also § 134.

[45] § 129. The exclusion applies to the same types of expenses that, if they were paid by the employee (and not reimbursed by the

employer), would be eligible for the Credit for Child and Dependent Care Expense discussed in Chapter 11.

premises, and substantially all of the use of the facilities must be by employees and their family members.[46]

- Qualified employer-provided educational assistance (tuition, fees, books, and supplies) at the undergraduate and graduate levels is excludible from gross income. The exclusion is subject to an annual employee statutory ceiling of $5,250.[47]

CAFETERIA PLANS

Generally, if an employee is offered a choice between cash and some other form of compensation, the employee is deemed to have constructively received the cash even when the noncash option is elected. Thus, the employee has gross income regardless of the option chosen.

An exception to this constructive receipt treatment is provided under the **cafeteria plan** rules. Under such a plan, the employee is permitted to choose between cash and nontaxable benefits (e.g., group term life insurance, health and accident protection, and child care). If the employee chooses the otherwise nontaxable benefits, the cafeteria plan rules enable the benefits to remain nontaxable.[48] Cafeteria plans provide tremendous flexibility in tailoring the employee pay package to fit individual needs. Some employees (usually the younger group) prefer cash, while others (usually the older group) will opt for the fringe benefit program.

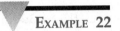

EXAMPLE 22

Hawk Corporation offers its employees (on a nondiscriminatory basis) a choice of any one or all of the following benefits:

Benefit	Cost
Group term life insurance	$ 200
Hospitalization insurance for family members	2,400
Child care payments	1,800
	$4,400

If a benefit is not selected, the employee receives cash equal to the cost of the benefit. Kay, an employee, has a spouse who works for another employer that provides hospitalization insurance but no child care payments. Kay elects to receive the group term life insurance, the child care payments, and $2,400 of cash. Only the $2,400 must be included in Kay's gross income. ▼

GENERAL CLASSES OF EXCLUDED BENEFITS

An employer can confer numerous forms and types of economic benefits on employees. Under the all-inclusive concept of income, the benefits are taxable unless one of the provisions previously discussed specifically excludes the item from gross income. The amount of the income is the fair market value of the benefit. This reasoning can lead to results that Congress considers unacceptable, as illustrated in the following example.

---

[46] § 132(j)(4).
[47] § 127. Exclusion treatment applies for tax years beginning before January 1, 1995.

[48] § 125.

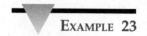

EXAMPLE 23

Vern is employed in New York as a ticket clerk for Trans National Airlines. He has a sick mother in Miami, Florida, but has no money for plane tickets. Trans National has daily flights from New York to Miami that often leave with empty seats. The cost of a round-trip ticket is $400, and Vern is in the 28% tax bracket. If Trans National allows Vern to fly without charge to Miami, under the general gross income rules, Vern has income equal to the value of a ticket. Therefore, Vern must pay $112 tax (.28 × $400) on a trip to Miami. Because Vern does not have $112, he cannot visit his mother, and the airplane flies with another empty seat. ▼

If Trans National in Example 23 will allow employees to use resources that would otherwise be wasted, why should the tax laws interfere with the employee's decision to take advantage of the available benefit? Thus, to avoid the undesirable results that occur in Example 23 and in similar situations, as well as to create uniform rules for fringe benefits, Congress established six broad classes of nontaxable employee benefits:[49]

- No-additional-cost services.
- Qualified employee discounts.
- Working condition fringes.
- *De minimis* fringes.
- Qualified transportation fringes.
- Qualified moving expense reimbursements.

No-Additional-Cost Services.   Example 23 illustrates the **no-additional-cost service** type of fringe benefit. The services will be nontaxable if all of the following conditions are satisfied:

- The employee receives services, as opposed to property.
- The employer does not incur substantial additional cost, including forgone revenue, in providing the services to the employee.
- The services are offered to customers in the ordinary course of the business in which the employee works.[50]

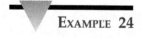

EXAMPLE 24

Assume that Vern in Example 23 can fly without charge only if the airline cannot fill the seats with paying customers. That is, Vern must fly on standby. Although the airplane may burn slightly more fuel because Vern is on the airplane and Vern may receive the same meal as paying customers, the additional costs would not be substantial. Thus, the trip could qualify as a no-additional-cost service.

On the other hand, assume that Vern is given a reserved seat on a flight that is frequently full. The employer would be forgoing revenue to allow Vern to fly. This forgone revenue would be a substantial additional cost, and thus the benefit would be taxable. ▼

Note that if Vern were employed in a hotel owned by Trans National, the receipt of the airline ticket would be taxable because Vern did not work in that line of business. However, the Code allows the exclusion for reciprocal benefits offered by employers in the same line of business.

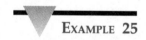

EXAMPLE 25

Grace is employed as a desk clerk for Plush Hotels, Inc. The company and Chain Hotels, Inc., have an agreement that allows any of their employees to stay without charge in either company's resort hotels during the off-season. Grace would not be required to recognize income from taking advantage of the plan by staying in a Chain Hotel. ▼

---

[49] See, generally, § 132.   [50] Reg. § 1.132–2.

The no-additional-cost exclusion extends to the employee's spouse and dependent children and to retired and disabled former employees. In the Regulations, the IRS has conceded that partners who perform services for the partnership are employees for purposes of the exclusion.[51] (As discussed earlier in the chapter, the IRS's position is that partners are not employees for purposes of the § 119 meals and lodging exclusion.) However, the exclusion is not allowed to highly compensated employees unless the benefit is available on a nondiscriminatory basis.

Qualified Employee Discounts.   When the employer sells goods or services (other than no-additional-cost benefits just discussed) to the employee for a price that is less than the price charged regular customers, the employee realizes income equal to the discount. However, the discount, referred to as a **qualified employee discount,** can be excluded from the gross income of the employee, subject to the following conditions and limitations:

- The exclusion is not available for real property (e.g., a house) or for personal property of the type commonly held for investment (e.g., common stocks).
- The property or services must be from the same line of business in which the employee works.
- In the case of *property*, the exclusion is limited to the *gross profit component* of the price to customers.
- In the case of *services*, the exclusion is limited to 20 percent of the customer price.[52]

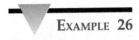

EXAMPLE 26

Silver Corporation, which operates a department store, sells a television set to a store employee for $300. The regular customer price is $500, and the gross profit rate is 25%. The corporation also sells the employee a service contract for $120. The regular customer price for the contract is $150. The employee must recognize $75 income.

Customer price for property	$ 500
Less: Gross profit (25%)	(125)
	$ 375
Employee price	(300)
Income	$ 75
Customer price for service	$ 150
Less: 20 percent	(30)
	$ 120
Employee price	(120)
Income	$ –0–

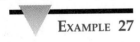

EXAMPLE 27

Assume the same facts as in Example 26, except the employee is a clerk in a hotel operated by Silver Corporation. Because the line of business requirement is not met, the employee must recognize $200 income ($500 – $300) from the purchase of the television and $30 income ($150 – $120) from the service contract. ▼

As in the case of no-additional-cost benefits, the exclusion applies to employees (including service partners), employees' spouses and dependent children, and

[51] Reg. § 1.132–1(b).   [52] § 132(c).

retired and disabled former employees. However, the exclusion does not apply to highly compensated individuals unless the discount is available on a nondiscriminatory basis.

ETHICAL
CONSIDERATIONS

Excluding Employee Discounts

Tom works for Roadrunner Motors, a company that manufactures automobiles. Tom purchased a new automobile from Roadrunner at the company's cost of $10,000. The retail selling price for the automobile is $15,000. Sue works for Coyote, Inc., an auto dealership, which sells the car manufactured by Roadrunner. Sue purchased an automobile identical to Tom's from Coyote. The price Sue pays is equal to Coyote's cost of the automobile ($13,500). Tom and Sue each receive a salary of $40,000 per year. Considering only the above information, do Tom and Sue have equal ability to pay income taxes for the year, and does equitable treatment occur? If not, how should the tax law be changed to produce equitable treatment?

Working Condition Fringes. Generally, an employee is not required to include in gross income the cost of property or services provided by the employer if the employee could deduct the cost of those items if he or she had actually paid for them.[53] These benefits are called **working condition fringes.**

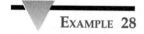

EXAMPLE 28

Mitch is a certified public accountant employed by an accounting firm. The employer pays Mitch's annual dues to professional organizations. Mitch is not required to include the payment of the dues in gross income because if he had paid the dues, he would have been allowed to deduct the amount as an employee business expense (as discussed in Chapter 8). ▼

In many cases, this exclusion merely avoids reporting income and an offsetting deduction. However, in two specific situations, the working condition fringe benefit rules allow an exclusion where the expense would not be deductible if paid by the employee:

- Automobile salespeople are allowed to exclude the value of certain personal use of company demonstrators (e.g., commuting to and from work).[54]
- The employee business expense would be eliminated by the 2 percent floor on miscellaneous deductions under § 67 (see Chapter 9).

Unlike the other fringe benefits discussed previously, working condition fringes can be made available on a discriminatory basis and still qualify for the exclusion.

De Minimis Fringes.   As the term suggests, *de minimis* fringe benefits are so small that accounting for them is impractical. The House Report contains the following examples of *de minimis* fringes:

- The typing of a personal letter by a company secretary, occasional personal use of a company copying machine, occasional company cocktail parties or picnics for employees, occasional supper money or taxi fare for employees

[53] § 132(d).   [54] § 132(j)(3).

because of overtime work, and certain holiday gifts of property with a low fair market value are excluded.
- Subsidized eating facilities (e.g., an employees' cafeteria) operated by the employer are excluded if located on or near the employer's business premises, if revenue equals or exceeds direct operating costs, and if nondiscrimination requirements are met.

When taxpayers venture beyond the specific examples contained in the House Report and the Regulations, there is obviously much room for disagreement as to what is *de minimis*. However, note that except in the case of subsidized eating facilities, the *de minimis* fringe benefits can be granted in a manner that favors highly compensated employees.

Qualified Transportation Fringes. The Energy Policy Act of 1992 created a new category of nontaxable employee benefits called **qualified transportation fringes.** The intent was to encourage the use of mass transit for commuting to and from work. Qualified transportation fringes encompass the following transportation benefits provided by the employer to the employee:[55]

1. Transportation in a commuter highway vehicle between the employee's residence and the place of employment.
2. A transit pass.
3. Qualified parking.

Statutory dollar limits are placed on the amount of the exclusion. Categories (1) and (2) above are combined for purposes of applying the limit. In this case, the limit on the exclusion for 1996 is $65 per month. Category (3) has a separate limit. For qualified parking, the limit on the exclusion for 1996 is $165 per month. Both of these dollar limits are indexed annually for inflation.

A *commuter highway vehicle* is any highway vehicle with a seating capacity of at least 6 adults (excluding the driver). In addition, at least 80 percent of the vehicle's use must be for transporting employees between their residences and place of employment.

Qualified parking includes the following:

- Parking provided to an employee on or near the employer's business premises.
- Parking provided to an employee on or near a location from which the employee commutes to work via mass transit, in a commuter highway vehicle, or in a carpool.

Qualified transportation fringes may be provided directly by the employer or may be in the form of cash reimbursements.

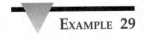

EXAMPLE 29

Gray Corporation's offices are located in the center of a large city. The company pays for parking spaces to be used by the company officers. Steve, a vice president, receives $250 of such benefits each month. The parking space rental qualifies as a qualified transportation fringe. Of the $250 benefit received each month by Steve, $165 is excludible from gross income. The balance of $85 is included in his gross income. The same result would occur if Steve paid for the parking and was reimbursed by his employer. ▼

Qualified Moving Expense Reimbursements. The Revenue Reconciliation Act of 1993 provides that qualified moving expenses that are reimbursed or paid

[55] § 132(f).

TAX IN THE NEWS

FEDERAL PARKING WOES

In what could be called Jimmy Carter's revenge, many Federal workers who have employer-provided parking spaces have been hit with higher tax bills since 1994. Their taxable income is boosted by the amount that the value of their parking space exceeds the tax-free ceiling on parking perks and commercial parking fees. During his tenure in the White House, President Carter created a bureaucratic backlash when he suggested that Federal workers who were parking free should pay half the commercial rate. The White House was picketed, and the President was denounced by zealous Feds who felt that the Founding Fathers intended for them to have free parking.

Amendments to the Internal Revenue Code in the Revenue Reconciliation Act of 1993 provided that workers could park tax-free only if the space would cost $155 or less per month based on local commercial fees. That limit went to $160 in 1995 and $165 in 1996 as a result of indexing for inflation. The limit applies to both Federal and private-sector employer-provided parking.

The $160 ($165 in 1966) lid is not a problem in most places. But in higher-cost cities, such as San Francisco and New York and, to a lesser extent, downtown Washington, that is a bargain rate.

Workers at the Agriculture Department headquarters, for example, recently were informed that parking would add $564 to their taxable income for 1995. VIPs with their own reserved spaces were required to add much more than $564 to their taxable income for the year, because the value of the reserved space is much higher than in a "first come, first serve" arrangement.

SOURCE: Adapted from "Fun with Parking," *Washington Post*, January 24, 1995, p. B2.

by the employer are excludible from gross income. A qualified moving expense is one that would be deductible under § 217. See the discussion of moving expenses in Chapter 8.

Nondiscrimination Provisions.   For no-additional-cost services and qualified employee discounts, if the plan is discriminatory in favor of highly compensated employees, these key employees are denied exclusion treatment. However, the non-highly compensated employees who receive benefits from the plan can still enjoy exclusion treatment for the no-additional-cost services and qualified employee discounts.[56]

EXAMPLE 30

Dove Company's officers are allowed to purchase goods from the company at a 25% discount. Other employees are allowed only a 15% discount. The company's gross profit margin on these goods is 30%.

Peggy, an officer in the company, purchased goods from the company for $750 when the price charged to customers was $1,000. Peggy must include $250 in gross income because the plan is discriminatory.

---

[56] § 132(j)(1).

Leo, an employee of the company who is not an officer, purchased goods for $850 when the customer price was $1,000. Leo is not required to recognize income because he received a qualified employee discount. ▼

De minimis (except in the case of subsidized eating facilities) and working condition fringe benefits can be provided on a discriminatory basis. The *de minimis* benefits are not subject to tax because the accounting problems that would be created are out of proportion to the amount of additional tax that would result. A nondiscrimination test would simply add to the compliance problems. In the case of working condition fringes, the types of services required vary with the job. Therefore, a nondiscrimination test probably could not be satisfied, although usually there is no deliberate plan to benefit a chosen few. Likewise, the qualified transportation fringe and the qualified moving expense reimbursement can be provided on a discriminatory basis.

TAXABLE FRINGE BENEFITS

If the fringe benefits cannot qualify for any of the specific exclusions or do not fit into any of the general classes of excluded benefits, the taxpayer must recognize gross income equal to the fair market value of the benefits. Obviously, problems are frequently encountered in determining values. The IRS has issued extensive Regulations addressing the valuation of personal use of an employer's automobiles and meals provided at an employer-operated eating facility.[57]

If a fringe benefit plan discriminates in favor of highly compensated employees, generally those employees are not allowed to exclude the benefits they receive that other employees do not enjoy. However, the highly compensated employees, as well as the other employees, are generally allowed to exclude the nondiscriminatory benefits.[58]

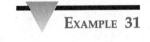

EXAMPLE 31

MED Company has a medical reimbursement plan that reimburses officers for 100% of their medical expenses, but reimburses all other employees for only 80% of their medical expenses. Cliff, the president of the company, was reimbursed $1,000 during the year for medical expenses. Cliff must include $200 in gross income [(1 − .80) × $1,000 = $200]. Mike, an employee who is not an officer, received $800 (80% of his actual medical expenses) under the medical reimbursement plan. None of the $800 is includible in his gross income. ▼

FOREIGN EARNED INCOME

A U.S. citizen is generally subject to U.S. tax on his or her income regardless of the income's geographic origin. The income may also be subject to tax in the foreign country, and thus the taxpayer must carry a double tax burden. Out of a sense of fairness and to encourage U.S. citizens to work abroad (so that exports might be increased), Congress has provided alternative forms of relief from taxes on foreign earned income. The taxpayer can elect *either* (1) to include the foreign income in his or her taxable income and then claim a credit for foreign taxes paid or (2) to exclude the foreign earnings from his or her U.S. gross income (the **foreign earned**

---

[57] Reg. § 1.61–2 T(j). Generally, the income from the personal use of the employer's automobile is based on the lease value of the automobile (what it would have cost the employee to lease the automobile). Meals are valued at 150% of the employer's direct costs (e.g., food and labor) of preparing the meals.

[58] §§ 79(d), 105(h), 127(b)(2), and 132(j)(1).

CONCEPT SUMMARY 4–2

General Classes of Excluded Benefits

Benefit	Description and Examples	Coverage Allowed	Effect of Discrimination
1. No-additional-cost services	The employee takes advantage of the employer's excess capacity (e.g., free passes for airline employees).	Current, retired, and disabled employees; their spouses and dependent children; spouses of deceased employees. Partners are treated as employees.	No exclusion for highly compensated employees.
2. Qualified discounts on goods	The employee is allowed to purchase the employer's merchandise at a price that is not less than the employer's cost.	Same as (1) above.	Same as (1) above.
3. Qualified discounts on services	The employee is allowed a discount (maximum of 20%) on services the employer offers to customers.	Same as (1) above.	Same as (1) above.
4. Working condition fringes	Expenses paid by the employer that would be deductible if paid by the employee (e.g., a mechanic's tools). Also, includes auto salesperson's use of a car held for sale.	Current employees, partners, directors, and independent contractors.	No effect.
5. *De minimis* items	Expenses so immaterial that accounting for them is not warranted (e.g., occasional supper money, personal use of the copy machine).	*Any recipient* of a fringe benefit.	No effect.
6. Qualified transportation fringes	Transportation benefits provided by the employer to employees including commuting in a commuter highway vehicle, a transit pass, and qualified parking.	Current employees.	No effect.
7. Qualified moving expense reimbursements	Qualified moving expenses that are paid or reimbursed by the employer. A qualified moving expense is one that would be deductible under § 217.	Current employees.	No effect.

income exclusion).[59] The foreign tax credit option is discussed in Chapter 11, but as is apparent from the following discussion, most taxpayers will choose the exclusion.

---

[59]§ 911(a).

Foreign earned income consists of the earnings from the individual's personal services rendered in a foreign country (other than as an employee of the U.S. government). To qualify for the exclusion, the taxpayer must be either of the following:

- A bona fide resident of the foreign country (or countries).
- Present in a foreign country (or countries) for at least 330 days during any 12 consecutive months.[60]

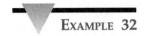

EXAMPLE 32

Sandra's trips to and from a foreign country in connection with her work were as follows:

Arrived in Foreign Country	Arrived in United States
March 10, 1995	February 1, 1996
March 7, 1996	June 1, 1996

During the 12 consecutive months ending on March 10, 1996, Sandra was present in the foreign country for at least 330 days (366 days less 29 days in February and 7 days in March 1996). Therefore, all income earned in the foreign country through March 10, 1996, is eligible for the exclusion. The income earned from March 11, 1996, through May 31, 1996, is also eligible for the exclusion because Sandra was present in the foreign country for 330 days during the 12 consecutive months ending on May 31, 1996. ▼

The exclusion is *limited* to $70,000 per year. For married persons, both of whom have foreign earned income, the exclusion is computed separately for each spouse. Community property rules do not apply (the community property spouse is not deemed to have earned one-half of the other spouse's foreign earned income). A taxpayer who is present in the country for less than the entire year must compute the maximum exclusion on a daily basis ($70,000 divided by the number of days in the entire year and multiplied by the number of days present in the foreign country during the year).

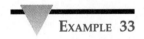

EXAMPLE 33

Keith qualifies for the foreign earned income exclusion. He was present in France for all of 1996 except for 7 days in December, when he was in the United States. Keith's salary for 1996 is $90,000. If Keith had been in France for all of the 366 days in 1996, he would have been able to exclude $70,000. However, since he was not present in the foreign country for 7 days, his exclusion is limited to $68,661 as follows:

$$\$70,000 \times \frac{359 \text{ days in foreign country}}{366 \text{ days in the year}} = \$68,661 \qquad \blacktriangledown$$

In addition to the exclusion for foreign earnings, the *reasonable housing costs* incurred by the taxpayer and the taxpayer's family in a foreign country in excess of a base amount may be excluded from gross income. The base amount is 16 percent of the U.S. government pay scale for a GS–14 (Step 1) employee, which varies from year to year.[61]

As previously mentioned, the taxpayer may elect to include the foreign earned income in gross income and claim a credit (an offset against U.S. tax) for the foreign tax paid. The credit alternative may be advantageous if the individual's

---

[60] § 911(d). For the definition of resident, see Reg. § 1.871–2(b).   [61] § 911(c).

foreign earned income far exceeds the excludible amount so that the foreign taxes paid exceed the U.S. tax on the amount excluded. However, once an election is made, it applies to all subsequent years unless affirmatively revoked. A revocation is effective for the year of the change and the four subsequent years.

INTEREST ON CERTAIN STATE AND LOCAL GOVERNMENT OBLIGATIONS

At the time the Sixteenth Amendment was ratified by the states, there was some question as to whether the Federal government possessed the constitutional authority to tax interest on state and local government obligations. Taxing such interest was thought to violate the doctrine of intergovernmental immunity in that the tax would impair the state and local governments' ability to finance their operations.[62] Thus, interest on state and local government obligations was specifically exempted from Federal income taxation.[63] However, the Supreme Court recently concluded that there is no constitutional prohibition against levying a nondiscriminatory Federal income tax on state and local government obligations.[64] Nevertheless, currently the statutory exclusion still exists.

Obviously, the exclusion of the interest reduces the cost of borrowing for state and local governments. A taxpayer in the 36 percent tax bracket requires only a 5.12 percent yield on a tax-exempt bond to obtain the same after-tax income as a taxable bond paying 8 percent interest [5.12% ÷ (1 − .36) = 8%].

The lower cost for the state and local governments is more than offset by the revenue loss of the Federal government. Also, tax-exempt interest is considered to be a substantial loophole for the very wealthy. For these reasons, bills have been introduced in Congress calling for Federal government subsidies to state and local governments that voluntarily choose to issue taxable bonds. Under the proposals, the tax-exempt status of existing bonds would not be eliminated.

The current exempt status applies solely to state and local government bonds. Thus, income received from the accrual of interest on a condemnation award or an overpayment of state income tax is fully taxable.[65] Nor does the exemption apply to gains on the sale of tax-exempt securities.

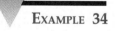

EXAMPLE 34

Megan purchases State of Virginia bonds for $10,000 on July 1, 1995. The bonds pay $400 interest each June 30th and December 31st. On March 31, 1996, Megan sells the bonds for $10,500 plus $200 accrued interest. Megan must recognize a $500 gain ($10,500 − $10,000), but the $200 accrued interest is exempt from taxation. ▼

State and local governments have developed sophisticated financial schemes to attract new industry. For example, local municipalities have issued bonds to finance the construction of plants to be leased to private enterprise. Because the financing could be arranged with low-interest municipal obligations, the plants could be leased at a lower cost than the private business could otherwise obtain. However, Congress has placed limitations on the use of tax-exempt securities to finance private business.[66]

---

[62] *Pollock v. Farmer's Loan & Trust Co.*, 3 AFTR 2602, 15 S.Ct. 912 (USSC, 1895).

[63] § 103(a).

[64] *South Carolina v. Baker III*, 88–1 USTC ¶9284, 61 AFTR2d 88–995, 108 S.Ct. 1355 (USSC, 1988).

[65] *Kieselbach v. Comm.*, 43–1 USTC ¶9220, 30 AFTR 370, 63 S.Ct. 303 (USSC, 1943); *U.S. Trust Co. of New York v. Anderson*, 3 USTC ¶1125, 12 AFTR 836, 65 F.2d 575 (CA–2, 1933).

[66] See § 103(b).

DIVIDENDS

GENERAL INFORMATION

A *dividend* is a payment to a shareholder with respect to his or her stock. Dividends to shareholders are taxable only to the extent the payments are made from *either* the corporation's *current earnings and profits* (similar to net income per books) or its *accumulated earnings and profits* (similar to retained earnings per books).[67] Distributions that exceed earnings and profits are treated as a nontaxable recovery of capital and reduce the shareholder's basis in the stock. Once the shareholder's basis is reduced to zero, any subsequent distributions are taxed as capital gains (see Chapter 12).[68]

Some payments are frequently referred to as dividends but are not considered dividends for tax purposes:

- Dividends received on deposits with savings and loan associations, credit unions, and banks are actually interest (a contractual rate paid for the use of money).
- Patronage dividends paid by cooperatives (e.g., for farmers) are rebates made to the users and are considered reductions in the cost of items purchased from the association. The rebates are usually made after year-end (after the cooperative has determined whether it has met its expenses) and are apportioned among members on the basis of their purchases.
- Mutual insurance companies pay dividends on unmatured life insurance policies that are considered rebates of premiums.
- Shareholders in a mutual investment fund are allowed to report as capital gains their proportionate share of the fund's gains realized and distributed. The capital gain and ordinary income portions are reported on the Form 1099 that the fund supplies its shareholders each year.

STOCK DIVIDENDS

When a corporation issues a simple stock dividend (e.g., common stock issued to common shareholders), the shareholder has merely received additional shares that represent the same total investment. Thus, the shareholder does not realize income.[69] However, if the shareholder has the *option* of receiving either cash or stock in the corporation, the individual realizes gross income whether he or she receives stock or cash.[70] A taxpayer who elects to receive the stock could be deemed to be in constructive receipt of the cash he or she has rejected.[71] However, the amount of the income in this case is the value of the stock received, rather than the cash the shareholder has rejected. See Chapter 12 for a detailed discussion of stock dividends.

EDUCATIONAL SAVINGS BONDS

The cost of a college education has risen dramatically during the past 10 years, increasing at a rate almost twice the change in the general price level. The U.S.

---

[67] § 316(a).

[68] § 301(c). See Chapter 18 for a detailed discussion of corporate distributions.

[69] *Eisner v. Macomber*, 1 USTC ¶32, 3 AFTR 3020, 40 S.Ct. 189 (USSC, 1920); § 305(a).

[70] § 305(b).

[71] Refer to the discussion of constructive receipt in Chapter 3.

Department of Education estimates that by the year 2007, the cost of attending a publicly supported university for four years will exceed $60,000. For a private university, the cost is expected to exceed $200,000.[72] Consequently, Congress has attempted to assist low- to middle-income parents in saving for their children's college education.

The assistance is in the form of an interest income exclusion on **educational savings bonds.**[73] The interest on Series EE U.S. government savings bonds may be excluded from gross income if the bond proceeds are used to pay qualified higher education expenses. The exclusion applies only if both of the following requirements are satisfied:

- The savings bonds are issued after December 31, 1989.
- The savings bonds are issued to an individual who is at least 24 years old at the time of issuance.

The exclusion is not available for a married couple who file separate returns.

The redemption proceeds must be used to pay qualified higher education expenses. *Qualified higher education expenses* consist of tuition and fees paid to an eligible educational institution for the taxpayer, spouse, or dependent. In calculating qualified higher education expenses, the tuition and fees paid are reduced by excludible scholarships and veterans' benefits received. If the redemption proceeds (both principal and interest) exceed the qualified higher education expenses, only a pro rata portion of the interest will qualify for exclusion treatment.

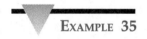

EXAMPLE 35

Tracy's redemption proceeds from qualified savings bonds during the taxable year were $6,000 (principal of $4,000 and interest of $2,000). Tracy's qualified higher education expenses were $5,000. Since the redemption proceeds exceed the qualified higher education expenses, only $1,667 ($5,000/$6,000 × $2,000) of the interest is excludible. ▼

The exclusion is limited by the application of the wherewithal to pay concept. That is, once the modified adjusted gross income exceeds a threshold amount, the phase-out of the exclusion begins. *Modified adjusted gross income (MAGI)* is adjusted gross income prior to the § 911 foreign earned income exclusion and the educational savings bond exclusion. The threshold amounts are adjusted for inflation each year. For 1996, the phase-out begins at $43,500 ($65,250 on a joint return).[74] The phase-out is completed when MAGI exceeds the threshold amount by more than $15,000 ($30,000 on a joint return). The otherwise excludible interest is reduced by the amount calculated as follows:

$$\frac{\text{MAGI} - \$43,500}{\$15,000} \times \frac{\text{Excludible interest}}{\text{before phase-out}} = \frac{\text{Reduction in}}{\text{excludible interest}}$$

On a joint return, $65,250 is substituted for $43,500 (in 1996), and $30,000 is substituted for $15,000.

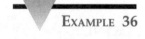

EXAMPLE 36

Assume the same facts as in Example 35, except that Tracy's MAGI for 1996 is $50,000. The phase-out will result in Tracy's interest exclusion being reduced by $722 [($50,000 − $43,500)/ $15,000 × $1,667]. Therefore, Tracy's exclusion is $945 ($1,667 − $722). ▼

---

[72] See generally, Knight and Knight, "New Ways to Manage Soaring Tuition Costs," *Journal of Accountancy* (March 1989): 207.

[73] § 135.

[74] The indexed amounts for 1995 are $42,300 and $63,450. A drafting error in the Revenue Reconciliation Act of 1993 allows inflation adjustments only for periods subsequent to 1992 (rather than for periods subsequent to 1989). If a proposed technical correction is enacted, the indexed amounts for 1996 would be $49,450 and $74,200.

TAX BENEFIT RULE

3 **LEARNING OBJECTIVE**
Determine the extent to which receipts can be excluded under the tax benefit rule.

Generally, if a taxpayer obtains a deduction for an item in one year and in a later year recovers all or a portion of the prior deduction, the recovery is included in gross income in the year received.[75]

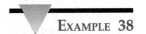

EXAMPLE 37

A taxpayer deducted as a loss a $1,000 receivable from a customer when it appeared the amount would never be collected. The following year, the customer paid $800 on the receivable. The taxpayer must report the $800 as income in the year it is received. ▼

However, the § 111 **tax benefit rule** provides that no income is recognized upon the recovery of a deduction, or the portion of a deduction, that did not yield a tax benefit in the year it was taken. If the taxpayer in Example 37 had no tax liability in the year of the deduction (e.g., itemized deductions and personal exemptions exceeded adjusted gross income), the recovery would be partially or totally excluded from income in the year of the recovery.[76]

EXAMPLE 38

Before deducting a $1,000 loss from an uncollectible business receivable, Ali had taxable income of $200, computed as follows:

Adjusted gross income	$ 13,300
Itemized deductions and personal exemptions	(13,100)
Taxable income	$ 200

The business bad debt deduction yields only a $200 tax benefit. That is, taxable income is reduced by only $200 (to zero) as a result of the bad debt deduction. Therefore, if the customer makes a payment on the previously deducted receivable in a subsequent year, only the first $200 is a recovery of a prior deduction and thus is taxable. Any additional amount collected is nontaxable because only $200 of the loss yielded a reduction in taxable income. ▼

INCOME FROM DISCHARGE OF INDEBTEDNESS

4 **LEARNING OBJECTIVE**
Describe the circumstances under which income must be reported from the discharge of indebtedness.

A transfer of appreciated property (fair market value is greater than adjusted basis) in satisfaction of a debt is an event that triggers the realization of income. The transaction is treated as a sale of the appreciated property followed by payment of the debt.[77] Foreclosure by a creditor is also treated as a sale or exchange of the property.[78]

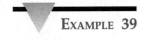

EXAMPLE 39

Juan owed the State Bank $100,000 on an unsecured note. Juan satisfied the note by transferring to the bank common stock with a basis of $60,000 and a fair market value of $100,000. Juan must recognize $40,000 gain on the transfer. Juan also owed the bank $50,000 on a note secured by land. When Juan's basis in the land was $20,000 and the land's fair market value was $50,000, the bank foreclosed on the loan and took title to the land. Juan must recognize a $30,000 gain on the foreclosure. ▼

---

[75] § 111(a).
[76] Itemized deductions are discussed in Chapter 9.

[77] Reg. § 1.1001–2(a).
[78] *Estate of Delman v. Comm.*, 73 T.C. 15 (1979).

In some cases, a creditor will not exercise his or her right of foreclosure and will even forgive a portion of the debt to assure the vitality of the debtor. In such cases, the debtor realizes income from discharge of indebtedness.

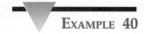

EXAMPLE 40

Brown Corporation is unable to meet the mortgage payments on its factory building. Both the corporation and the mortgage holder are aware of the depressed market for industrial property in the area. Foreclosure would only result in the creditor's obtaining unsalable property. To improve Brown Corporation's financial position and thus improve Brown's chances of obtaining the additional credit from other lenders necessary for survival, the creditor agrees to forgive all amounts past due and to reduce the principal amount of the mortgage. ▼

Generally, the income realized by the debtor from the forgiveness of a debt is taxable.[79] A similar debt discharge (produced by a different creditor motivation) associated with personal use property is illustrated in Example 41.

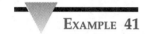

EXAMPLE 41

In 1991, Joyce borrowed $60,000 from National Bank to purchase her personal residence. Joyce agreed to make monthly principal and interest payments for 15 years. The interest rate on the note was 7%. In 1996, when the balance on the note had been reduced through monthly payments to $48,000, the bank offered to accept $45,000 in full settlement of the note. The bank made the offer because interest rates had increased to 11%. Joyce accepted the bank's offer. As a result, Joyce must recognize $3,000 ($48,000 − $45,000) income.[80] ▼

The following discharge of indebtedness situations are subject to special treatment:[81]

1. Creditors' gifts.
2. Discharges under Federal bankruptcy law.
3. Discharges that occur when the debtor is insolvent.
4. Discharge of the farm debt of a solvent taxpayer.
5. Discharge of **qualified real property business indebtedness.**
6. A seller's cancellation of the buyer's indebtedness.
7. A shareholder's cancellation of the corporation's indebtedness.
8. Forgiveness of loans to students.

If the creditor reduces the debt as an act of *love, affection or generosity,* the debtor has simply received a nontaxable gift (situation 1). Rarely will a gift be found to have occurred in a business context. A businessperson may settle a debt for less than the amount due, but as a matter of business expediency (e.g., high collection costs or disputes as to contract terms) rather than generosity.[82]

In situations 2, 3, 4, and 5, the Code allows the debtor to reduce his or her basis in the assets by the realized gain from the discharge.[83] Thus, the realized gain is merely deferred until the assets are sold (or depreciated). Similarly, in situation 6 (a price reduction), the debtor reduces the basis in the specific assets financed by the seller.[84]

---

[79] *U.S. v. Kirby Lumber Co.,* 2 USTC ¶814, 10 AFTR 458, 52 S.Ct. 4 (USSC, 1931), codified in § 61(a)(12).

[80] Rev.Rul. 82–202, 1982–1 C.B. 35.

[81] §§ 108 and 1017.

[82] *Comm. v. Jacobson,* 49–1 USTC ¶9133, 37 AFTR 516, 69 S.Ct. 358 (USSC, 1949).

[83] §§ 108(a), (c), (e), and (g). Note that § 108(b) provides that other tax attributes (e.g., net operating loss) will be reduced by the realized gain from the debt discharge prior to the basis adjustment unless the taxpayer elects to apply the basis adjustment first.

[84] § 108(e)(5).

A shareholder's cancellation of the corporation's indebtedness to him or her (situation 7) usually is considered a contribution of capital to the corporation. Thus, the corporation's paid-in capital is increased, and its liabilities are decreased by the same amount.[85]

Many states make loans to students on the condition that the loan will be forgiven if the student practices a profession in the state upon completing his or her studies. The amount of the loan that is forgiven (situation 8) is excluded from gross income.[86]

TAX PLANNING CONSIDERATIONS

The present law excludes certain types of economic gains from taxation. Therefore, taxpayers may find tax planning techniques helpful in obtaining the maximum benefits from the exclusion of such gains. Following are some of the tax planning opportunities made available by the exclusions described in this chapter.

LIFE INSURANCE

5   LEARNING OBJECTIVE
Identify tax planning strategies for obtaining the maximum benefit from allowable exclusions.

Life insurance offers several favorable tax attributes. As discussed in Chapter 3, the annual increase in the cash surrender value of the policy is not taxable (because no income has been actually or constructively received). By borrowing on the policy's cash surrender value, the owner can actually receive the policy's increase in value in cash but without recognizing income.

EMPLOYEE BENEFITS

Generally, employees view accident and health insurance, as well as life insurance, as necessities. Employees can obtain group coverage at much lower rates than individuals would have to pay for the same protection. Premiums paid by the employer can be excluded from the employees' gross income. Because of the exclusion, employees will have a greater after-tax and after-insurance income if the employer pays a lower salary but also pays the insurance premiums.

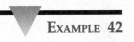

EXAMPLE 42

Pat receives a salary of $30,000. The company has group insurance benefits, but Pat was required to pay his own premiums as follows:

Hospitalization and medical insurance	$1,400
Term life insurance ($30,000 coverage)	200
Disability insurance	400
	$2,000

To simplify the analysis, assume Pat's tax rate on income is 28%. After paying taxes of $8,400 (.28 × $30,000) and $2,000 for insurance, Pat has $19,600 ($30,000 − $8,400 − $2,000) for his other living needs.

If Pat's employer reduced Pat's salary by $2,000 (to $28,000) but paid his insurance premiums, Pat's tax liability would be only $7,840 ($28,000 × .28). Thus, Pat would have $20,160 ($28,000 − $7,840) to meet his other living needs. The change in the compensation plan would save Pat $560 ($20,160 − $19,600). ▼

Similarly, employees must often incur expenses for child care and parking. The employee can have more income for other uses if the employer pays these costs for the employee but reduces the employee's salary by the cost of the benefits.

[85] § 108(e)(6).   [86] § 108(f).

The use of cafeteria plans has increased dramatically in recent years. These plans allow employees to tailor their benefits to meet their individual situations. Thus, where both spouses in a married couple are working, duplications of benefits can be avoided and other needed benefits can often be added. If less than all of the employee's allowance is spent, the employee can receive cash.

The meals and lodging exclusion enables employees to receive from their employer what they ordinarily must purchase with after-tax dollars. Although the requirements that the employee live and take his or her meals on the employer's premises limit the tax planning opportunities, the exclusion is an important factor in the employee's compensation in certain situations, (e.g., hotels, motels, restaurants, farms, and ranches).

The employees' discount provision is especially important for manufacturers and wholesalers. Employees of manufacturers can avoid tax on the manufacturer's, wholesaler's, and retailer's markups. The wholesaler's employees can avoid tax on an amount equal to the wholesale and retail markups.

It should be recognized that the exclusion of benefits is generally available only to employees. Proprietors and partners must pay tax on the same benefits their employees receive tax-free. By incorporating and becoming an employee of the corporation, the former proprietor or partner can also receive these tax-exempt benefits. Thus, the availability of employee benefits is a consideration in the decision to incorporate.

INVESTMENT INCOME

Tax-exempt state and local government bonds are almost irresistible investments for many high-income taxpayers. To realize the maximum benefit from the exemption, the investor can purchase zero coupon bonds. Like Series EE U.S. government savings bonds, these investments pay interest only at maturity. The advantage of the zero coupon feature is that the investor can earn tax-exempt interest on the accumulated principal and interest. If the investor purchases a bond that pays the interest each year, the interest received may be such a small amount that an additional tax-exempt investment cannot be made. In addition, reinvesting the interest may entail transaction costs (broker's fees). The zero coupon feature avoids these problems.

Series EE U.S. government savings bonds can earn tax-exempt interest if the bond proceeds are used for qualified higher education expenses. Many taxpayers can foresee these expenditures being made for their children's educations. In deciding whether to invest in the bonds, however, the investor must take into account the income limitations for excluding the interest from gross income.

KEY TERMS

Accident and health benefits, 4–14

Cafeteria plan, 4–19

Compensatory damages, 4–11

De minimis fringes, 4–22

Death benefits, 4–7

Educational savings bonds, 4–30

Foreign earned income exclusion, 4–25

Gift, 4–4

Life insurance proceeds, 4–5

No-additional-cost service, 4–20

Punitive damages, 4–12

Qualified employee discount, 4–21

Qualified real property business

▼▼
PROBLEM
MATERIALS

DISCUSSION QUESTIONS

1. In 1993, Grape Corporation constructed a building on property it leased on a long-term basis. In 1995, Grape went bankrupt and forfeited the improvements to the owner of the land. In 1996, the owner sold the land. When does the landlord realize income from the improvements made by Grape?

2. Hazel made gifts to her three nephews. The first nephew, Al, received $10,000 cash during Hazel's lifetime. The second nephew, Bob, received $10,000 as a bequest when Hazel died. The third nephew, Carl, was the beneficiary of a $10,000 life insurance policy that Hazel purchased for $4,000. Are Al, Bob, and Carl required to include the amounts they received in gross income?

3. Violet Company gave $500 to each household in the community that had suffered a flood loss. The purpose of the payments was to help the flood victims. If some of the recipients are employees of Violet Company, can the employees exclude the payments from gross income?

4. Matt's truck was stalled on the side of the road. Abby stopped to help and called Al, who agreed to repair the truck for $75. Matt paid Al $75 and Abby $25. The payment to Al was made because of a contractual obligation and therefore is not a gift. The payment to Abby was not made because of a contractual obligation. Does this mean that the payment Abby received is a gift?

5. What are the two principal tax benefits of buying life insurance that has a cash surrender value?

6. Daryl took out a $10,000 life insurance policy on the life of his brother, Dave, a daredevil stunt driver. Daryl's other brother, Larry, similarly took out a $10,000 policy on Dave. Larry could not keep up with the premium payments and sold the policy to Dave's new wife for "what he had in it" (i.e., premium payments of $1,000.) If Dave were to die now, how much of the insurance proceeds of $10,000 would be taxable to Daryl, to Larry, and to Dave's wife?

7. Black Corporation purchased a $1 million insurance policy on the life of the company's president. The company paid $100,000 of premiums, the president died, and the company collected the face amount of the policy. How much must Black Corporation include in gross income?

8. Gilda, a cash basis taxpayer, died while employed by Swan Corporation. Swan paid Gilda's husband $3,000 in sales commissions that Gilda had earned. The company also paid him $7,000 pursuant to a policy of making payments to the spouse of a deceased employee. Swan used the proceeds of a life insurance policy it owned on Gilda's life to make the payment to her husband. Is any of the $10,000 Gilda's husband received subject to income tax?

9. Yellow Company provides its employees with $10,000 group term life insurance. Red Company does not provide insurance but generally gives the family of a deceased employee $10,000. Compare the tax consequences of the insured and uninsured plans.

10. James received an academic scholarship to State University. Under the scholarship agreement, he received tuition ($1,500), books ($400), and room and board ($5,000). What is James's gross income from the scholarship?

11. José is a graduate assistant at State University. He receives $7,000 a year in salary. In addition, tuition of $4,000 is waived. The tuition waiver is available to all full- and

part-time employees. The fair market value of José's services is $11,000. How much is José required to include in his gross income?

12. Sara was the victim of sexual harassment and collected the following from her employer: $15,000 for lost wages and $50,000 in punitive damages. How much of the damage award of $65,000 must Sara include in her gross income?

13. Holly works in a factory and earns $400 per week. Jill usually works in an office, but she was unable to work for one week because of an infected paper cut sustained at work. Jill collected $400 in workers' compensation as a result of her injury. Is the $400 Holly and Jill each received treated the same for income tax purposes?

14. Pam was hit by an automobile driven by a person under the influence of alcohol. Although Pam's injuries were minor (she did not go to the hospital or visit a doctor), she has recurring nightmares about the accident. Over the past 12 months, she has spent more than $6,000 for psychological therapy. Although she had problems before the accident, the recurring nightmares brought her to the realization that she needed professional help. Pam has not filed a lawsuit, but the driver of the automobile, who is very wealthy, "wants to do the right thing." The driver has offered Pam $30,000 as a settlement. He believes that this is more than she is entitled to under the law, but feels a great deal of remorse about all of the grief he has caused her. Pam is concerned about the tax consequences of the settlement offer. What are the relevant tax issues raised by these facts?

15. Wes purchases an accident and health insurance plan that was advertised in the Sunday newspaper. The annual premiums are $400. During the year, Wes received payments of $1,200 under the plan.
    a. How much of the $1,200 must Wes include in his gross income?
    b. Would the tax consequences differ if the $1,200 represented amounts paid by the insurance company to replace lost wages while Wes was hospitalized?

16. What nontaxable fringe benefits are available to employees that are not available to partners and proprietors?

17. How does one determine if the meals and lodging supplied by the employer are to serve a valid business purpose? Is the tax treatment of meals and lodging affected if the employer advertises that the meals and lodging provided are one of the employees' fringe benefits?

18. Paula is employed by a telemarketing firm that pays a fixed amount for unlimited long-distance telephone calls. Employees are allowed to use the toll-free line for 5 minutes each month at no charge to the employee. The normal charge for the calls Paula made during the year was $75. How much is Paula required to include in gross income?

19. Gary is employed by Pelican, Inc., an automobile manufacturing company. Pelican sells Gary a new automobile at company cost of $12,000. The price charged a dealer would have been $14,000, and the retail price of the automobile is $17,000. What is Gary's gross income from the purchase of the automobile?

20. Jane works at a bakery and is allowed to take home bread that could not be sold during the day. The bakery gives the day-old bread to the employees because it has no other use for the goods. Is Jane required to recognize income as a result of receiving the bread?

21. Eagle Life Insurance Company pays its employees $.25 per mile for driving their personal automobiles to and from work. The company reimburses each employee who rides the bus $45 a month for the cost of a pass. Tom collected $60 for his automobile mileage, and Ted received $45 as reimbursement for the cost of a bus pass.
    a. What are the effects of the above on Tom and Ted's gross income?
    b. Assume that Tom and Ted are in the 28% marginal tax bracket, and the actual before-tax cost for Tom to drive to and from work is $.25 per mile. What are Tom and Ted's after-tax costs of commuting to and from work?

22. Zack works for Blue Pest Control, which offers a discount on its extermination services to its employees: officers receive a 50% discount, and all other employees receive a 30% discount. Zack, who is not an officer, had the company treat his home for termites and paid $280 for the service that is normally priced at $400. Zack's supervisor, an officer, had her home treated for carpenter ants and paid $500 for the service that is normally priced at $1,000. How much, if any, will Zack and his supervisor have to include in gross income for the services they received?

23. Flamingo, Inc., has implemented employee benefit plans in each of five broad classes of employee fringe benefits: (1) no-additional-cost services, (2) qualified employee discounts, (3) working condition fringes, (4) *de minimis* fringes, and (5) qualified transportation fringes. Eligibility requirements discriminate in favor of the company's officers. Which of the following items best describes the tax effect of each of the five classes of employee fringe benefits for an officer in Flamingo?
    a. None of the benefit is taxable.
    b. Only the discriminatory portion of the benefit is taxable.
    c. All of the benefit is taxable.

    Support your answer with discussion.

24. Several of Egret Company's employees have asked the company to create a hiking trail that employees could use during their lunch hours. The company owns vacant land that is being held for future expansion, but would have to spend approximately $50,000 if it were to make a trail. Nonemployees would be allowed to use the facility as part of the company's effort to build strong community support. What are the relevant tax issues for the employees?

25. Marla worked for Robin Industries, Inc., and earned $58,000 in 1996. She spent 345 days out of the United States during 1996 working in a foreign country. Marla wants to exclude her foreign-earned income from U.S. taxation if possible. Does Marla qualify for doing so? If she does, how much of her income will be taxable in the United States?

26. Falcon Corporation is opening a branch in Kazonbi, an African country that does not levy an income tax on citizens of foreign countries. Carl, a U.S. citizen, is considering two offers from his employer, Falcon Corporation. He can work for 6 months in Kazonbi and 6 months in the United States and receive a salary of $4,000 per month, or he can work in Kazonbi for 12 months at the same monthly salary. Carl would like to spend as much time in the United States as possible and prefers the first alternative. However, he asks your advice as to how income taxes might affect his decision.

27. Donna and George are married, file a joint return, and are in the 36% marginal tax bracket. They would like to save for their child's education. What would be the advantage of buying State of Virginia bonds as compared to buying Series EE U.S. government bonds?

28. Maria owned 100 shares of common stock in Roadrunner Corporation when the company declared a 100% stock dividend. She did not have the option to receive cash. Is the fair market value of the 100 shares received by Maria included in her gross income?

29. What special tax benefits are available to students and their parents?

30. In 1996, Mary received a $2,000 sales commission. However, in 1997, her employer discovered that Mary should have received only a $1,500 commission in 1996. Therefore, the employer withheld $500 from Mary's 1997 commission. Mary's standard deduction and personal exemption for 1996 exceeded her gross income. What effect would the tax benefit rule have on Mary's gross income for 1997?

31. How does the tax treatment of a corporation's income generated by the retirement of bonds for less than book value (issue price plus amortized discount or less amortized premium) differ from the income derived from a shareholder's forgiveness of the corporation's indebtedness?

32. Ida purchased a farm. She gave the seller $50,000 cash and an 8% note for $150,000. When the principal on the note had been reduced to $120,000, the seller agreed to accept $100,000 in retirement of the debt. The creditor made the offer because interest rates had increased substantially. Ida was not undergoing bankruptcy and was not insolvent. Did Ida realize income from retiring the debt and, if so, is she required to include the amount in her gross income?

33. Harry has experienced financial difficulties as a result of his struggling business. He has been behind on his mortgage payments for the last six months. The mortgage holder, who is a friend of Harry's, has offered to accept $80,000 in full payment of the $100,000 owed on the mortgage and payable over the next 10 years. The interest rate of the mortgage is 7%, and the market rate is now 8%. What tax issues are raised by the creditor's offer?

PROBLEMS

34. Determine whether the following may be excluded from gross income as gifts, bequests, scholarships, prizes, or life insurance proceeds:
    a. Uncle told Nephew, "Come live with me and take care of me in my old age and you can have all my property after my death." Nephew complied with Uncle's request. Uncle's will made Nephew sole beneficiary of the estate.
    b. Uncle told Nephew, "If you study hard and make the dean's list this year, I will pay your tuition for the following year." Nephew made the dean's list, and Uncle paid the tuition.
    c. Uncle told Nephew, "If you make the dean's list this year, I will pay you $500." Nephew made the dean's list, and Uncle paid the $500.
    d. Diane cashed in her life insurance contract and collected $10,000. She had paid premiums totaling $7,000.
    e. Fred received $500 from his employer to pay the medical expenses of Fred's child. The payment was not part of a medical reimbursement plan, and the employer made the payment out of compassion.

35. Determine the taxable life insurance proceeds in the following cases:
    a. When José died, his wife collected $50,000 on a group term insurance policy purchased by José's employer. José had never included the premiums in gross income.
    b. The Cardinal Software Company purchased an insurance policy on the life of a key employee. The company paid $50,000 in premiums and collected $500,000 of insurance proceeds.
    c. When Barbara died, she and her husband owed $15,000 on a loan. Under the terms of the loan, Barbara was required to purchase life insurance to pay the creditor the amount due at the date of Barbara's death. The creditor collected from the life insurance company the amount due at the time of Barbara's death. Is the creditor required to recognize income from the collection of the life insurance proceeds?

36. The Egret Company, which is in the 40% (combined Federal and state) marginal tax bracket, estimated that if its current president should die, the company would incur $200,000 in costs to find a suitable replacement. In addition, profits on various projects the president is responsible for would likely decrease by $300,000. The president has recommended that Egret purchase a $500,000 life insurance policy. How much insurance should the company carry on the life of its president to compensate for the after-tax loss that would result from the president's death, assuming the $200,000 costs of finding a president are deductible and the lost profits would have been taxable?

37. Determine whether the taxpayer has gross income in each of the following situations:
    a. Jim is a waiter in a restaurant. The rule of thumb is that a customer should leave the waiter a tip equal to 15% of the customer's bill for food and beverages. Jim collected $6,000 in tips during the year.
    b. Tara works at a grocery store, bagging groceries and carrying them to the customers' automobiles. Her employer posts a sign saying that the employees are paid by the

hour and the customer is not expected to tip them. Tara received $1,800 in tips from customers.

c. Sheila worked at a hotel. Her home was damaged by a fire. Sheila's employer allowed her to stay at the hotel for no charge until she could return to her home. The normal charge for the room Sheila occupied during this period was $500, and the hotel had several vacant rooms.

38. Donald died at age 35. He was married and had four minor children. Donald's employer, Lark Painting Company, made payments to his wife as follows:

Donald's accrued salary at date of death	$4,000
Family death benefits under long-standing company policy ($2,000 is paid to the spouse and $1,500 is paid to each child of a deceased employee)	2,000
A payment authorized by the board of directors to help his wife pay debts accumulated by Donald	7,000

In addition, Donald's wife was the beneficiary of her husband's life insurance policy of $50,000. Lark Painting Company had paid for the policy. Donald had excluded all of the premiums paid by the employer from gross income as group term life insurance. His wife left the insurance proceeds with the insurance company and elected to receive an annuity of $4,000 each year for life. Her life expectancy is 40 years. She collected one $4,000 payment at the end of the current year. A joint return was filed in the year of Donald's death. Which of the above amounts must be included in gross income?

39. Walt made the all-state football team during his junior and senior years in high school. He accepted an athletic scholarship from State University. The scholarship provided the following:

Tuition and fees	$4,000
Room and board	2,500
Books and supplies	500

Determine the effect of the scholarship on Walt's gross income.

40. Alejandro was awarded an academic scholarship to State University. He received $5,000 in August and $6,000 in December 1996. Alejandro had enough personal savings to pay all expenses as they came due. Alejandro's expenditures for the relevant period were as follows:

Tuition, August 1996	$2,900
Tuition, December 1996	3,200
Room and board	
August–December 1996	3,000
January–May 1997	2,400
Books and educational supplies	
August–December 1996	800
January–May 1997	950

Determine the effect on Alejandro's gross income for 1996 and 1997.

41. Determine the taxpayer's taxable damages in each of the following cases:
   a. Orange Corporation collected $500,000 for damages to its business reputation.
   b. Don collected $100,000 in lost wages caused by age discrimination by his employer. Under the relevant law, a successful plaintiff can recover only lost wages.
   c. Kirby was injured in an automobile accident and collected $10,000 for loss of the use of his left arm, $15,000 for pain and suffering, $9,000 in lost wages, $5,000 for medical expenses, and $10,000 of punitive damages. Kirby had deducted none of the medical expenses.
   d. Nell received $10,000 of damages for invasion of her privacy by a photographer and $5,000 of punitive damages.

e. Joanne received compensatory damages of $50,000 and punitive damages of $200,000 from a cosmetic surgeon who botched her nose job.

42. Tom was accused of shoplifting. He sued the store and collected $1,000 for actual damages to his personal reputation and $10,000 in punitive damages for the outrageous behavior by the store's security guard. Tom's wife, Jane, slipped on a banana peel in the same store and collected $5,000 in medical expenses she incurred (the expenses were not deducted on their return) and $1,500 in lost wages (wages she would have earned if she had not been injured). Must any of these amounts be included in Tom and Jane's income reported on a joint return?

43. Rex, age 45, is an officer of Blue Company, which provided him with the following nondiscriminatory fringe benefits in 1996:
    a. Hospitalization insurance for Rex and his dependents. The cost of coverage for Rex was $450, and the additional cost for Rex's dependents was $400.
    b. Reimbursement of $700 from an uninsured medical reimbursement plan available to all employees.
    c. Group term life insurance protection of $120,000. (Each employee received coverage equal to twice his or her annual salary.)
    d. Salary continuation payments of $2,600 while Rex was hospitalized for an illness.

    While Rex was ill, he collected $1,600 on a salary continuation insurance policy he had purchased. Determine the amounts Rex must include in gross income.

44. The UVW Union and HON Corporation are negotiating contract terms. Assume the union members are in the 28% marginal tax bracket and all benefits are provided on a nondiscriminatory basis. Write a letter to the UVW Union members explaining the tax consequences of the options discussed below. The union's address is 905 Spruce Street, Washington, D.C. 20227.
    a. The company would impose a $100 deductible on medical insurance benefits. Most employees incur more than $100 each year in medical expenses.
    b. Employees would get an additional paid holiday with the same annual income (the same pay but less work).
    c. An employee who did not need health insurance (because the employee's spouse works and receives family coverage) would be allowed to receive the cash value of the coverage.

45. Sally and Bill are married and file joint returns. In 1996, Bill, an accountant, has a salary of $75,000, and Sally receives a salary of $25,000 as an apartment manager. What are the tax consequences of the following benefits that Bill and Sally's employers provide?
    a. Bill receives a reimbursement of $5,000 for child care expenses. Sally and Bill have three children who are not yet school age.
    b. Bill and Sally are provided a free membership at a local fitness and exercise club that allows them to attend three aerobic exercise sessions per week. The value of this type of membership is $450.
    c. Bill is provided free parking at work. The value of the parking is $1,500 per year.
    d. Sally is provided with a free apartment. Living in this apartment is a condition of her employment. Similar apartments rent for $1,000 per month.

46. Determine the taxpayer's gross income for each of the following:
    a. Alice is the manager of a plant. The company owns a house one mile from the plant (rental value of $6,000) that Alice is allowed to occupy.
    b. Pam works for an insurance company that allows employees to eat in the cafeteria for $.50 a meal. Generally, the cost to the insurance company of producing a meal is $5.00, and a comparable meal could be purchased for $4.00. Pam ate 150 meals in the cafeteria during the year.
    c. Wade is a Methodist minister and receives a housing allowance of $600 per month from his church. Wade is buying his home and uses the $600 to make house payments ($450) and to pay utilities ($150).
    d. Floyd is a college professor and lives in campus housing. He is not charged rent. The fair market value of the house is $100,000, and the annual rental value is $7,200.

47. Does the taxpayer recognize gross income in the following situations?
    a. Ann is a registered nurse working in a community hospital. She is not required to take her lunch on the hospital premises, but she can eat in the cafeteria at no charge. The hospital adopted this policy to encourage employees to stay on the premises and be available in case of emergencies. During the year, Ann ate most of her meals on the premises. The total value of those meals was $750.
    b. Ira is the manager of a hotel. His employer will allow him to live in one of the rooms rent-free or to receive a $600 per month cash allowance for rent. Ira elected to live in the hotel.
    c. Seth is a forest ranger and lives in his employer's cabin in the forest. He is required to live there, and because there are no restaurants nearby, the employer supplies Seth with groceries that he cooks and eats on the premises.
    d. Rocky is a partner in the BAR Ranch (a partnership). He is the full-time manager of the ranch. BAR has a business purpose for Rocky's living on the ranch.

48. Betty is considering taking an early retirement offered by her employer. She would receive $1,500 per month, indexed for inflation. However, she would no longer be able to use the company's health facilities, and she would be required to pay her hospitalization insurance of $6,000 each year. Betty and her husband will file a joint return and will take the standard deduction. She currently receives a salary of $37,500 a year, and her employer pays for all of her hospitalization insurance. If she retires, Betty would not be able to use her former employer's exercise facilities because of the commuting distance. She would like to continue to exercise, however, and will therefore join a health club at a cost of $50 per month. Betty and her husband have other sources of income and are in and will remain in the 28% marginal tax bracket. She currently pays Social Security taxes of 7.65% on her salary, but her retirement pay would not be subject to this tax. She will earn about $9,000 a year from a part-time job. Betty would like to know whether she should accept the early retirement offer.

49. Sparrow, Inc., has a wide variety of fringe benefits available to its employees. However, not all of the employees actually need the benefits. For example, some employees have working spouses whose employers provide health insurance benefits for the employee's families. In addition, Sparrow reimburses up to $5,000 for child care costs, but not all of the employees have children. Sparrow's management has asked you to write a memo explaining how the company can accommodate the varying needs of its employees at the lowest after-tax cost to the employee. Sparrow's address is 300 Harbor Drive, Vermillion, SD 57069.

50. Ed is employed by FUN Bowling Lanes, Inc. Determine Ed's gross income in each of the following situations:
    a. Ed's children are allowed to use the lanes without charge. Each child can also bring a friend without charge. This benefit is available to all employees. During the year, the children bowled 100 games, and the usual charge was $1.50 per game. Friends of Ed's children bowled 90 games.
    b. The company has a lunch counter. Ed is allowed to take home the leftover donuts each night. The company's cost was $450, and the value of the donuts Ed took home was $100.
    c. The company pays Ed's subscription to *Bowling Lanes Management,* a monthly journal.

51. Thrush Corporation has 10 employees and is considering offering group hospitalization benefits. The average cost is $3,000 per employee per year. Three of the employees are shareholders and are in the 40% (combined Federal and state) income tax bracket; they currently pay for their own health insurance. The corporation is in the 34% marginal tax bracket. The remaining 7 employees who are not shareholders are considering taking a $1,500 per year pay cut in exchange for the hospitalization benefits. These employees are in the 30% (combined Federal and state) income tax bracket.
    a. Evaluate this proposal for the 7 employees.
    b. Write a memo explaining the after-tax effects on the employees and the corporation of providing health insurance to all employees. Thrush's address is 500 Fern Avenue, Scranton, PA 18509.

52. Snowbird Corporation would like you to review its employee fringe benefits program with regard to the effects of the plan on the company's president (Polly), who is also the majority shareholder:
    a. All employees receive free tickets to State University football games. Polly is seldom able to attend the games and usually gives her tickets to her nephew. The cost of Polly's tickets for the year was $75.
    b. The company pays all parking fees for its officers but not for other employees. The company paid $1,200 for Polly's parking for the year.
    c. Employees are allowed to use the copy machine for personal purposes as long as the privilege is not abused. Polly is president of a trade association and made extensive use of the copy machine to prepare mailings to members of the association. The cost of the copies was $900.
    d. The company is in the household moving business. Employees are allowed to ship goods without charge whenever there is excess space on a truck. Polly purchased a dining room suite for her daughter. Company trucks delivered the furniture to the daughter. Normal freight charges would have been $600.
    e. The company has a storage facility for household goods. Officers are allowed a 20% discount on charges for storing their goods. All other employees are allowed a 10% discount. Polly's discounts for the year totaled $400.

53. Eli works for a company that operates a cruise ship. All employees are allowed to take a one-week cruise each year at no cost to the employee. The employee is provided with a room, meals, and general recreation on the ship. Determine the tax consequences of Eli accepting a trip under the following assumptions:
    a. Eli must travel on a standby basis; that is, Eli can travel only if the ship is not completely booked. The room Eli occupies has maid service, and the sheets and towels are changed each day.
    b. Eli takes his meals with the other customers who pay a fixed amount for the cruise that includes meals and lodging.
    c. The recreation consists of the use of the pool, dancing, and bingo games.
    d. All guests must pay for their drinks and snacks between meals, but Eli and the other employees are given a 20% discount.
    e. Employees at Eli's level and above are provided with free parking at the pier. Parking for the week would cost $70. This group comprises about 25% of all employees of the company.

54. George, a U.S. citizen, is employed by Pelican, Inc., a global company. His salary for both 1996 and 1997 is $80,000. George's first foreign assignment is to St. Petersburg, Russia, and began on March 1, 1996. He spent 15 days in the United States in December and returned to St. Petersburg and worked there until February 28, 1997. He went back to St. Petersburg one more time, spending the month of May 1997 there to train his successor. What is the amount of salary that George must include in his gross income for 1996 and 1997, assuming he claims the maximum exclusion?

55. Determine Hazel's gross income from the following receipts for the year:

Gain on sale of Augusta County bonds	$ 600
Interest on U.S. government savings bonds	900
Interest on state income tax refund	150
Interest on Augusta County bonds	900
Patronage dividend from Potato Growers Cooperative	1,700

    The patronage dividend was received in March of the current year for amounts paid and deducted in the previous year as expenses of Hazel's profitable cash basis farming business.

56. Determine Jack's gross income from the following items:
    a. Jack owns 100 shares of Roadrunner Company common stock. The company has a dividend reinvestment plan. Under the plan, Jack can receive an $18 cash dividend or an additional share of stock with a fair market value of $18. Jack elected to take the stock.

b. Jack owns 100 shares of Bat Corporation. The company declared a dividend, and Jack was to receive an additional share of the company's common stock with a fair market value of $18. Jack did not have the option to receive cash. However, a management group announced a plan to repurchase all available shares for $18 each. The offer was part of a takeover defense.

c. Jack also collected $125 on a corporate debenture. The corporation had been in bankruptcy for several years. Jack had correctly deducted the cost of the bond in a prior year because the bankruptcy judge had informed the bondholders they would not receive anything in the final liquidation. Later the company collected on an unanticipated claim and had the funds to make partial payment on the bonds.

57. Lynn Schwartz recently inherited $25,000. She is considering using the money to finance a college education for her 5-year-old child. Lynn does not expect her gross income to ever exceed $40,000 a year. She is very concerned with the safety of the principal and has decided to invest the $25,000 in Series EE U.S. government savings bonds. The bonds earn 5% interest each year. At the end of 13 years, when Lynn's child is 18 and ready to go to college, the bonds will be worth $44,375. This would pay a substantial portion of the cost of a 4-year college education at that time. Write a letter to Lynn advising her as to whether the Series EE bonds will be an appropriate investment for financing her child's college education, including whether the bonds should be purchased in Lynn's name or in the child's name (with Lynn as custodian). Lynn's address is 100 Myrtle Cove, Fairfield, CT 06432.

58. How does the tax benefit rule apply in the following cases?
   a. In 1996, Wilma paid Vera $5,000 for locating a potential client. The deal fell through, and in 1997, Vera refunded the $5,000 to Wilma.
   b. In 1996, Wilma paid an attorney $300 for services in connection with a title search. Because the attorney was negligent, Wilma incurred some additional costs in acquiring the land. In 1997, the attorney refunded his $300 fee to Wilma.
   c. In 1996, Wilma received a $90 dividend with respect to 1996 premiums on her life insurance policy.
   d. In 1997, a cash basis farmer received a $400 patronage dividend with respect to 1996 purchases of cattle feed.

59. Mary and her two sisters, Cary and Gladys, were injured in a car accident in 1996, and each sustained injuries requiring $1,200 in medical expenses. Because the claim was not settled until 1997, each sister had completed her 1996 income tax return before the settlement. Mary does not itemize deductions. Cary does itemize deductions, but the $1,200 medical expense did not exceed the 7.5%-of-AGI threshold; consequently, the deduction did not result in a reduction of her tax liability. Gladys also itemizes deductions. Because of other medical expenses, the $1,200 expense pushed her $800 over the 7.5%-of-AGI threshold. Therefore, Gladys benefited from the deduction by having her taxes reduced. In 1997, each sister received a $1,200 insurance settlement for her injuries. How much of the $1,200 settlement received does each sister need to include in gross income?

60. Fran, who is in the 36% tax bracket, recently collected $100,000 on a life insurance policy she carried on her father. She currently owes $120,000 on her personal residence and $120,000 on business property. National Bank holds the mortgage on both pieces of property and has agreed to accept $100,000 in complete satisfaction of either mortgage. The interest rate on the mortgages is 8%, and both mortgages are payable over 10 years. What would be the tax consequences of each of the following alternatives, assuming Fran currently deducts the mortgage interest on her tax return?
   a. Retire the mortgage on the residence.
   b. Retire the mortgage on the business property.

Which alternative should Fran select?

61. Robin Company is experiencing financial troubles and is considering negotiating the following with its creditors. Determine the tax consequences to Robin of the following plan:

a. The Motor Finance Company will cancel $1,500 in accrued interest. Robin had deducted the interest in the prior year. Motor Finance Company will also reduce the principal on the note by $1,000. The note financed the purchase of equipment from a local dealer.

b. The Trust Land Company, which sold Robin land and buildings, will reduce the mortgage on the building by $15,000.

c. Ridge, the sole shareholder in the corporation, will cancel a $50,000 receivable from the corporation in exchange for additional stock.

CUMULATIVE PROBLEMS

62. Oliver W. Hand was divorced from Sandra D. Hand on May 12, 1995. On September 6, 1996, Oliver married Beulah Crane. Oliver and Beulah will file a joint return for 1996. Oliver's Social Security number is 262–60–3814. Beulah's number is 259–68–4184, and she will adopt "Hand" as her married name. The Hands live at 210 Mason Drive, Atlanta, GA 30304. Sandra's Social Security number is 219–74–1361.

Oliver is 50 and is employed by Atom, Inc., as an electrical engineer. His salary for 1996 was $60,000. Beulah is 35 and earned $37,000 as a marriage counselor in 1996. She was employed by Family Counselors, Inc.

The divorce agreement required Oliver to make 132 monthly payments to Sandra. The payments are $1,200 per month for 84 months, at which time the payments decrease to $1,000 per month. Oliver and Sandra have a 14-year-old daughter, Daisy Hand. If Daisy should die before she attains age 21, Oliver's remaining payments to Sandra would be reduced to $1,000 per month. Sandra was granted custody of Daisy and can document that she provided $2,000 of support for Daisy. Oliver made 12 payments in 1996.

Oliver's employer provided him with group term life insurance coverage in the amount of $100,000 in 1996.

Beulah's employer provided Beulah with free parking in a parking garage adjacent to the office building where Beulah works. The monthly charge to the general public is $65.

Oliver received dividends of $40 on Red Corporation stock he owned before marriage, and Beulah received dividends of $50 on her separately owned White Corporation stock. They received dividends of $600 on jointly owned Blue Corporation stock, which they acquired after marriage. Oliver and Beulah live in a common law state.

Combined itemized deductions for Oliver and Beulah in 1996 were as follows:

State income taxes withheld		
Oliver	$3,200	
Beulah	1,200	$4,400
Real estate taxes on residence		1,500
Home mortgage interest (paid to Atlanta Federal Savings and Loan)		4,020
Cash contributions to church		900

In 1996, Beulah received a refund of 1995 state income taxes of $700. She had deducted state income taxes withheld as an itemized deduction on her 1995 return. Oliver received a $500 refund on his 1995 state income taxes. He had used the standard deduction in 1995.

Additional information:

• Oliver's employer withheld Federal income tax of $10,650 and $4,590 of FICA (Social Security) tax. Beulah's employer withheld $4,580 of Federal income tax and $2,831 of FICA tax.

Part 1—Tax Computation
Compute the Hands' net tax payable (or refund due) for 1996. Suggested software (if available): *TurboTax* or *MacInTax*.

Part 2—Tax Planning

Assume the Hands came to you in early December of 1996 seeking tax planning advice for 1996 and 1997. They provide you with the following information:

a. All the facts previously presented will be essentially the same in 1997 except for the items described in (b), (c), (d), and (e).

b. Oliver inherited $100,000 from his mother on December 1. He will use part of his inheritance to pay off the mortgage on the Hands' residence on January 3, 1997. Consequently, there will be no mortgage interest expense in 1997.

c. Oliver expects a 4% salary increase in 1997, and Beulah expects a 10% increase.

d. The Hands have pledged to contribute $2,400 to their church in 1997 (as opposed to $900 contributed in 1996). However, they could use Oliver's inherited funds to pay the pledge before the end of 1996 if you advise them to do so to achieve an overall tax savings.

e. The Hands acquired 100 shares of ABC Corporation stock on July 5, 1996, at a total cost of $2,000. The value of the stock has increased rapidly, and it is now worth $5,000. The Hands plan to sell the stock and ask whether they should sell it in 1996 or wait until 1997.

Advise the Hands as to the appropriate tax planning strategy for 1996 and 1997. Support your recommendations by computing their tax liabilities for 1996 and 1997 considering the various available alternatives. Suggested software (if available): *TurboTax* or *MacInTax*.

63. Archie S. Monroe (Social Security number 363–33–1411) is 35 years old and is married to Annie B. Monroe (Social Security number 259–68–4284). The Monroes live at 215 Adams Dr., Thor, VA 24317. They file a joint return and have two dependent children (Barry and Betty). In 1996, Archie and Annie had the following transactions:

a. Salary received by Archie from Allen Steel Company (Archie is vice president). $84,000

b. Interest received on jointly owned State of Nebraska bonds.   9,000

c. Group term life insurance premiums paid by Archie's employer (coverage of $72,000).   250

d. Annual increment in the value of Series EE government savings bonds (the Monroes have not previously included the accrued amounts in gross income).   450

e. Taxable dividends received from Dove Steel Company, a U.S. corporation (the stock was jointly owned). Of the $6,300 in dividends, $1,000 was mailed on December 31, 1996, and received by Archie and Annie on January 4, 1997.   6,300

f. Award received by Annie for outstanding community service in Thor.   1,000

g. Proceeds from sale of Pigeon, Inc., stock on November 3, 1996. The adjusted basis of the stock, which had been purchased on June 1, 1996, is $5,000.   7,000

h. Alimony payments to Archie's former wife (Rosa T. Monroe, Social Security number 800–60–2580) under a divorce decree.   12,000

i. Itemized deductions:
    State income tax   2,150
    Real estate tax on residence   2,300
    Interest on personal residence (paid to Thor Federal Savings)   3,800
    Cash contribution to church   900

j. Federal income tax withheld.   12,500

Part 1—Tax Computation

Compute the Monroes' net tax payable (or refund due) for 1996. Suggested software (if available): *TurboTax* or *MacInTax*.

Part 2—Tax Planning

The Monroes plan to sell 200 shares of AXE stock they purchased on July 12, 1984, at a cost of $20,000. The stock is worth $11,000 in December 1996, and the Monroes' broker predicts a continued decline in value. Annie plans to resume her career as a model in 1997, and her earnings will move the Monroes into the 31% bracket. How much Federal income tax will the Monroes save for 1996 if they sell the stock in 1996? Should they sell the stock in 1996 or 1997? Write a letter to the Monroes that contains your advice and prepare a memo for the tax files. Suggested software (if available): *TurboTax* or *MacInTax*.

RESEARCH PROBLEMS for this chapter appear the end of Chapter 28.

TEAM PROJECT: ARTHUR ANDERSEN TAX CHALLENGE CASES

For more information on the Arthur Andersen Tax Challenge Cases, please refer to Chapter 2, page 2-41.

Information related to tax issues and problems that are discussed in this chapter may be found in the

Fields case on pages 9, 23, and 25
Miller case on pages 2, 3, 11, 13, 14, 15, 22, and 29

Read and analyze the case you have been assigned and *identify* any issues and problems that are related to material covered in this chapter. If the information provided in the case is complete, prepare answers for this part of the case at this time. If you need information that is contained in the later parts of the case, please write a memo summarizing the questions or problems so you can prepare a complete answer at a later date.

Deductions and Losses: In General

LEARNING OBJECTIVES

After completing Chapter 5, you should be able to:

1. Differentiate between deductions *for* and *from* adjusted gross income and understand the relevance of the differentiation.

2. Describe the cash and accrual methods of accounting.

3. Apply the Internal Revenue Code deduction disallowance provisions associated with the following: public policy limitations, political activities, excessive executive compensation, investigation of business opportunities, hobby losses, vacation home rentals, payment of others' expenses, personal expenditures, capital expenditures, related-party transactions, and expenses related to tax-exempt income.

4. Identify tax planning opportunities for maximizing deductions and minimizing the disallowance of deductions.

OUTLINE

CLASSIFICATION OF DEDUCTIBLE EXPENSES

1 LEARNING OBJECTIVE
Differentiate between deductions *for* and *from* adjusted gross income and understand the relevance of the differentiation.

The tax law has an all-inclusive definition of income; that is, income from whatever source derived is includible in gross income. Income cannot be excluded unless there is a specific statement to that effect in the Internal Revenue Code.

Similarly, deductions are disallowed unless a specific provision in the tax law permits them. The inclusive definition of income and the exclusive definition of deductions may not seem fair to taxpayers, but it is the structure of the tax law.

The courts have held that whether and to what extent deductions are allowed depends on legislative grace.[1] In other words, any exclusions from income and all deductions are gifts from Congress!

It is important to classify deductible expenses as **deductions for adjusted gross income** (AGI) or **deductions from adjusted gross income.** Deductions *for* AGI can be claimed whether or not the taxpayer itemizes. Deductions *from* AGI result in a tax benefit only if they exceed the taxpayer's standard deduction. If itemized deductions (*from* AGI) are less than the standard deduction, they provide no tax benefit.

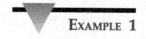

EXAMPLE 1

Steve is a self-employed CPA. Ralph is one of Steve's employees. During the year, Steve and Ralph incur the following expenses:

	Steve	Ralph
Dues in American Institute of CPAs and Virginia Society of CPAs	$ 400	$ 300
Subscriptions to professional journals	500	200
Registration fees for tax conferences	800	800
	$1,700	$1,300

---

[1] *New Colonial Ice Co. v. Helvering,* 4 USTC ¶1292, 13 AFTR 1180, 54 S.Ct. 788 (USSC, 1934).

Steve does not reimburse any of his employees for dues, subscriptions, or educational programs.

Steve's expenses are classified as a deduction *for* AGI. Therefore, he can deduct the $1,700 on his Federal income tax return. Ralph's expenses are classified as deductions *from* AGI. Ralph will be able to benefit from the $1,300 of expenses on his Federal income tax return only if he itemizes deductions. If he takes the standard deduction instead, the $1,300 of expenses will have no effect on the calculation of his taxable income. Even if Ralph does itemize deductions, he must reduce the $1,300 of expenses, which are classified as miscellaneous itemized deductions, by 2% of his AGI. As this example illustrates, whether a deduction is classified as *for* AGI or *from* AGI can affect the benefit the taxpayer receives from the deduction. ▼

Deductions *for* AGI are also important in determining the *amount* of itemized deductions because many itemized deductions are limited to amounts in excess of specified percentages of AGI. Examples of itemized deductions that are limited by AGI are medical expenses and personal casualty losses. Itemized deductions that are deductible only to the extent that they exceed a specified percentage of AGI are increased when AGI is decreased. Likewise, when AGI is increased, these itemized deductions are decreased.

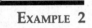

EXAMPLE 2   Tina earns a salary of $20,000 and has no other income. She itemizes deductions during the current year. Medical expenses for the year are $1,800. Since medical expenses are deductible only to the extent they exceed 7.5% of AGI, Tina's medical expense deduction is $300 [$1,800 – (7.5% × $20,000)]. If Tina had a $2,000 deduction *for* AGI, her medical expense deduction would be $450 [$1,800 – (7.5% × $18,000)], or $150 more. If the $2,000 deduction was *from* AGI, her medical expense deduction would remain $300 since AGI is unchanged. ▼

DEDUCTIONS FOR ADJUSTED GROSS INCOME

To understand how deductions of individual taxpayers are classified, it is necessary to examine the role of § 62. The purpose of § 62 is to classify various deductions as deductions *for* AGI. It does not provide the statutory authority for taking the deduction. For example, § 212 allows individuals to deduct expenses attributable to income-producing property. Section 212 expenses that are attributable to rents or royalties are classified as deductions *for* AGI. Likewise, a deduction for trade or business expenses is allowed by § 162. These expenses are classified as deductions *for* AGI.

If a deduction is not listed in § 62, it is an itemized deduction, *not* a deduction *for* AGI. Following is a *partial* list of the items classified as deductions *for* AGI by § 62:

- Expenses attributable to a trade or business carried on by the taxpayer. A trade or business does not include the performance of services by the taxpayer as an employee.
- Expenses incurred by a taxpayer in connection with the performance of services as an employee if the expenses are reimbursed and other conditions are satisfied.
- Deductions that result from losses on the sale or exchange of property by the taxpayer.
- Deductions attributable to property held for the production of rents and royalties.
- The deduction for payment of alimony.
- Certain contributions to pension, profit sharing, and annuity plans of self-employed individuals.

TAX IN THE NEWS

AMERICA'S TEAM

A political football is in the air with respect to tax reform, and it appears almost everybody wants to play. The "football" is the Federal income tax system.

Numerous players, both Democrats and Republicans, are trying out for the team. The prospects include Rep. Bill Archer (chairman of the House Ways and Means Committee), Sen. Pete Domenici, Rep. Dick Armey (House Majority Leader), and Rep. Dick Gephardt (House Minority Leader). Even Newt Gingrich (Speaker of the House) is weighing what position he would like to play. Other members of Congress are expected to jockey for positions on the team. On the sidelines now but hoping to participate are Jack Kemp and Bill Bradley.

A debate is raging over the rules of the game. Should the current income tax system be reformed or should it be replaced? Should the replacement be a flat tax, a consumption tax, or a value added tax? It is almost impossible to read a newspaper or turn on the TV without encountering a discussion of someone's tax proposal. Archer has stated, "I want to tear the income tax out by its roots," and Armey has said, "America needs nothing less than a completely new tax system." Not only are the players willing to take on the reform of the Federal income tax system, but some would like to go even further and repeal the Sixteenth Amendment to the U.S. Constitution.

A key element in all of the proposals is simplicity. One method advocated for advancing simplicity is the elimination of deductions (a foundation of the flat tax proposals). As the legislative process goes forward, it will be interesting to observe the lobbying and debate over deductions and other components of the current Federal income tax system and to see what results finally emerge from the process.

- The deduction for certain retirement savings allowed by § 219 (e.g., IRAs).
- The penalty imposed on premature withdrawal of funds from time savings accounts or deposits.
- The deduction for moving expenses.

These items are covered in detail in various chapters in the text.

Itemized Deductions

The Code defines itemized deductions as the deductions allowed other than "the deductions allowable in arriving at adjusted gross income."[2] Thus, if a deduction is not properly classified as a deduction *for* AGI, then it is classified as an itemized deduction.

Section 212 Expenses.   Section 212 allows deductions for ordinary and necessary expenses paid or incurred for the following:

- The production or collection of income.
- The management, conservation, or maintenance of property held for the production of income.
- Expenses paid in connection with the determination, collection, or refund of any tax.

[2] § 63(d).

Section 212 expenses related to rent and royalty income are deductions *for* AGI.[3] Expenses paid in connection with the determination, collection, or refund of taxes related to the income of sole proprietorships, rents and royalties, or farming operations are deductions *for* AGI. All other § 212 expenses are itemized deductions (deductions *from* AGI). For example, investment-related expenses (e.g., safe deposit box rentals) are deductible as itemized deductions attributable to the production of investment income.[4]

Deductible Personal Expenses. Taxpayers are allowed to deduct certain expenses that are primarily personal in nature. These expenses, which generally are not related to the production of income, are deductions *from* AGI (itemized deductions). Some of the more frequently encountered deductions in this category include the following:

- Contributions to qualified charitable organizations (not to exceed a specified percentage of AGI).
- Medical expenses (in excess of 7.5 percent of AGI).
- Certain state and local taxes (e.g., real estate taxes and state and local income taxes).
- Personal casualty losses (in excess of an aggregate floor of 10 percent of AGI and a $100 floor per casualty).
- Certain personal interest (e.g., mortgage interest on a personal residence).

Itemized deductions are discussed in detail in Chapter 9.

TRADE OR BUSINESS EXPENSES AND PRODUCTION OF INCOME EXPENSES

Section 162(a) permits a deduction for all ordinary and necessary expenses paid or incurred in carrying on a trade or business. These include reasonable salaries paid for services, expenses for the use of business property, and one-half of self-employment taxes paid. Such expenses are deducted *for* AGI.

It is sometimes difficult to determine whether an expenditure is deductible as a trade or business expense. The term "trade or business" is not defined in the Code or Regulations, and the courts have not provided a satisfactory definition. It is usually necessary to ask one or more of the following questions to determine whether an item qualifies as a trade or business expense:

- Was the use of the particular item related to a business activity? For example, if funds are borrowed for use in a business, the interest is deductible as a business expense.
- Was the expenditure incurred with the intent to realize a profit or to produce income? For example, expenses in excess of the income from raising horses are not deductible if the activity is classified as a personal hobby rather than a trade or business.
- Were the taxpayer's operation and management activities extensive enough to indicate the carrying on of a trade or business?

Section 162 *excludes* the following items from classification as trade or business expenses:

- Charitable contributions or gifts.
- Illegal bribes and kickbacks and certain treble damage payments.
- Fines and penalties.

---

[3] § 62(a)(4).   [4] Reg. § 1.212–1(g).

A bribe paid to a domestic official is not deductible if it is illegal under the laws of the United States. Foreign bribes are deductible unless they are unlawful under the Foreign Corrupt Practices Act of 1977.[5]

Ordinary and Necessary Requirement.   The terms **ordinary and necessary** are found in both §§ 162 and 212. To be deductible, any trade or business expense must be "ordinary and necessary." In addition, compensation for services must be "reasonable" in amount.

Many expenses that are necessary are *not* ordinary. Neither "ordinary" nor "necessary" is defined in the Code or Regulations. The courts have held that an expense is *necessary* if a prudent businessperson would incur the same expense and the expense is expected to be appropriate and helpful in the taxpayer's business.[6]

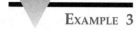

EXAMPLE 3

Pat purchased a manufacturing concern that had just been adjudged bankrupt. Because the business had a poor financial rating, Pat satisfied some of the obligations to employees and outside salespeople incurred by the former owners. Pat had no legal obligation to pay these debts, but felt this was the only way to keep salespeople and employees. The Second Court of Appeals found that the payments were necessary in that they were both appropriate and helpful.[7] However, the Court held that the payments were *not* ordinary but were in the nature of capital expenditures to build a reputation. Therefore, no deduction was allowed. ▼

An expense is *ordinary* if it is normal, usual, or customary in the type of business conducted by the taxpayer and is not capital in nature.[8] However, an expense need not be recurring to be deductible as ordinary.

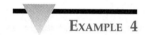

EXAMPLE 4

Albert engaged in a mail-order business. The post office judged that his advertisements were false and misleading. Under a fraud order, the post office stamped "fraudulent" on all letters addressed to Albert's business and returned them to the senders. Albert spent $30,000 on legal fees in an unsuccessful attempt to force the post office to stop. The legal fees (though not recurring) were ordinary business expenses because they were normal, usual, or customary in the circumstances.[9] ▼

For § 212 deductions, the law requires that expenses bear a reasonable and proximate relationship to (1) the production or collection of income or to (2) the management, conservation, or maintenance of property held for the production of income.[10]

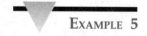

EXAMPLE 5

Wendy owns a small portfolio of investments, including 10 shares of Hawk, Inc., common stock worth $1,000. She incurred $350 in travel expenses to attend the annual shareholders' meeting at which she voted her 10 shares against the current management group. No deduction is permitted because a 10-share investment is insignificant in value in relation to the travel expenses incurred.[11] ▼

---

[5] § 162(c)(1).

[6] *Welch v. Helvering,* 3 USTC ¶1164, 12 AFTR 1456, 54 S.Ct. 8 (USSC, 1933).

[7] *Dunn and McCarthy, Inc. v. Comm.,* 43–2 USTC ¶9688, 31 AFTR 1043, 139 F.2d 242 (CA–2, 1943).

[8] *Deputy v. DuPont,* 40–1 USTC ¶9161, 23 AFTR 808, 60 S.Ct. 363 (USSC, 1940).

[9] *Comm. v. Heininger,* 44–1 USTC ¶9109, 31 AFTR 783, 64 S.Ct. 249 (USSC, 1943).

[10] Reg. § 1.212–1(d).

[11] *J. Raymond Dyer,* 36 T.C. 456 (1961).

Reasonableness Requirement. The Code refers to **reasonableness** solely with respect to salaries and other compensation for services.[12] But the courts have held that for any business expense to be ordinary and necessary, it must also be reasonable in amount.[13]

What constitutes reasonableness is a question of fact. If an expense is unreasonable, the excess amount is not allowed as a deduction. The question of reasonableness generally arises with respect to closely held corporations where there is no separation of ownership and management.

Transactions between the shareholders and the closely held company may result in the disallowance of deductions for excessive salaries and rent expense paid by the corporation to the shareholders. The courts will view an unusually large salary in light of all relevant circumstances and may find that the salary is reasonable despite its size.[14] If excessive payments for salaries and rents are closely related to the percentage of stock owned by the recipients, the payments are generally treated as dividends.[15] Since dividends are not deductible by the corporation, the disallowance results in an increase in the corporate taxable income. Deductions for reasonable salaries will not be disallowed *solely* because the corporation has paid insubstantial portions of its earnings as dividends to its shareholders.

EXAMPLE 6

Sparrow Corporation, a closely held corporation, is owned equally by Lupe, Carlos, and Ramon. The company has been highly profitable for several years and has not paid dividends. Lupe, Carlos, and Ramon are key officers of the company, and each receives a salary of $200,000. Salaries for similar positions in comparable companies average only $100,000. Amounts paid the owners in excess of $100,000 may be deemed unreasonable, and, if so, a total of $300,000 in salary deductions by Sparrow is disallowed. The disallowed amounts are treated as dividends rather than salary income to Lupe, Carlos, and Ramon because the payments are proportional to stock ownership. Salaries are deductible by the corporation, but dividends are not. ▼

BUSINESS AND NONBUSINESS LOSSES

Section 165 provides for a deduction for losses not compensated for by insurance. As a general rule, deductible losses of individual taxpayers are limited to those incurred in a trade or business or in a transaction entered into for profit. Individuals are also allowed to deduct losses that are the result of a casualty. Casualty losses include, but are not limited to, fire, storm, shipwreck, and theft. See Chapter 6 for a further discussion of this topic. Deductible personal casualty losses are reduced by $100 per casualty, and the aggregate of all personal casualty losses is reduced by 10 percent of AGI. A personal casualty loss is an itemized deduction. See Concept Summary 5–2 on page 5–31 for the classification of expenses.

REPORTING PROCEDURES

All deductions *for* and *from* AGI wind up on pages 1 and 2 of Form 1040. All deductions *for* AGI are reported on page 1. The last line on page 1 is adjusted gross income.

---

[12] § 162(a)(1).

[13] *Comm. v. Lincoln Electric Co.*, 49–2 USTC ¶9388, 38 AFTR 411, 176 F.2d 815 (CA–6, 1949).

[14] *Kennedy, Jr. v. Comm.*, 82–1 USTC ¶9186, 49 AFTR2d 82–628, 671 F.2d 167 (CA–6, 1982), *rev'g* 72 T.C. 793 (1979).

[15] Reg. § 1.162–8.

The first item on page 2 is also adjusted gross income. Itemized deductions are entered next, followed by the deduction for personal and dependency exemptions. The result is taxable income.

Most of the deductions *for* AGI on page 1 originate on supporting schedules. Examples include business expenses (Schedule C) and rent, royalty, partnership, and fiduciary deductions (Schedule E). Other deductions *for* AGI, such as IRAs, Keogh retirement plans, and alimony, are entered directly on page 1 of Form 1040.

All itemized deductions on page 2 are carried over from Schedule A. Some Schedule A deductions originate on other forms. Examples include home mortgage interest, investment interest, noncash charitable contributions in excess of $500, casualty losses, and unreimbursed employee expenses.

Form 1040 becomes a summary of the detailed information entered on the other schedules and forms. See Figure 5–1.

▼ **FIGURE 5–1**
Format of Form 1040

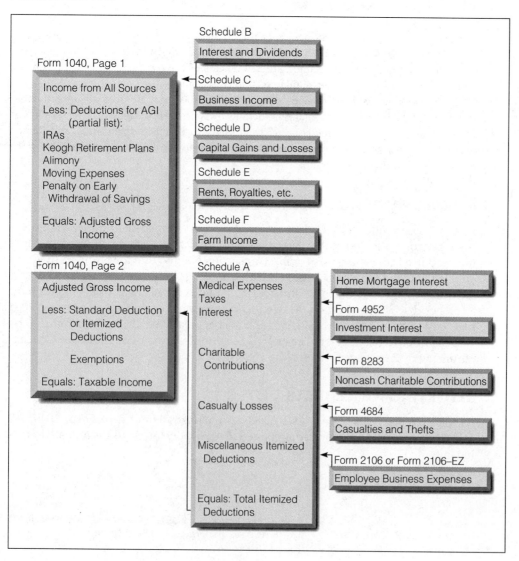

DEDUCTIONS AND LOSSES—TIMING OF EXPENSE RECOGNITION

IMPORTANCE OF TAXPAYER'S METHOD OF ACCOUNTING

2 LEARNING OBJECTIVE
Describe the cash and accrual methods of accounting.

A taxpayer's **accounting method** is a major factor in determining taxable income. The method used determines when an item is includible in income and when an item is deductible on the tax return. Usually, the taxpayer's regular method of record keeping is used for income tax purposes.[16] The taxing authorities do not require uniformity among all taxpayers. They do require that the method used clearly reflect income and that items be handled consistently.[17] The most common methods of accounting are the cash method and the accrual method.

Throughout the portions of the Code dealing with deductions, the phrase "paid or incurred" is used. *Paid* refers to the cash basis taxpayer who gets a deduction only in the year of payment. *Incurred* concerns the accrual basis taxpayer who obtains the deduction in the year in which the liability for the expense becomes certain (refer to Chapter 3).

CASH METHOD REQUIREMENTS

The expenses of cash basis taxpayers are deductible only when they are actually paid with cash or other property. Promising to pay or issuing a note does not satisfy the actually paid requirement.[18] However, the payment can be made with borrowed funds. At the time taxpayers charge expenses on their credit cards, they are allowed to claim the deduction. They are deemed to have simultaneously borrowed money from the credit card issuer and constructively paid the expenses.[19]

Although the cash basis taxpayer must have actually or constructively paid the expense, payment does not assure a current deduction. Cash basis and accrual basis taxpayers cannot take a current deduction for capital expenditures except through amortization, depletion, or depreciation over the life (actual or statutory) of the asset. The Regulations set forth the general rule that an expenditure that creates an asset having a useful life that extends substantially beyond the end of the tax year must be capitalized.[20]

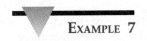

EXAMPLE 7

John, a cash basis taxpayer, rents property from Carl. On July 1, 1996, John paid $2,400 rent for the 24 months ending June 30, 1998. The prepaid rent extends 18 months after the close of the tax year—substantially beyond the year of payment. Therefore, John must capitalize the prepaid rent and amortize the expense on a monthly basis. His deduction for 1996 is $600. ▼

The Tax Court and the IRS took the position that an asset that will expire or be consumed by the end of the tax year following the year of payment must be prorated. The Ninth Court of Appeals held that such expenditures are currently deductible, however, and the Supreme Court apparently concurs (the one-year rule for prepaid expenses).[21]

---

[16] § 446(a).

[17] §§ 446(b) and (e); Reg. § 1.446–1(a)(2).

[18] *Page v. Rhode Island Trust Co., Exr.*, 37–1 USTC ¶9138, 19 AFTR 105, 88 F.2d 192 (CA–1, 1937).

[19] Rev.Rul. 78–39, 1978–1 C.B. 73. See also Rev.Rul. 80–335, 1980–2 C.B. 170, which applies to pay-by-phone arrangements.

[20] Reg. § 1.461–1(a).

[21] *Zaninovich v. Comm.*, 80–1 USTC ¶9342, 45 AFTR2d 80–1442, 616 F.2d 429 (CA–9, 1980), *rev'g* 69 T.C. 605 (1978). Cited by the Supreme Court in *Hillsboro National Bank v. Comm.*, 83–1 USTC ¶9229, 51 AFTR2d 83–874, 103 S.Ct. 1134 (USSC, 1983).

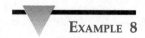

EXAMPLE 8

Assume the same facts as in Example 7 except that John was required to pay only 12 months rent in 1996. He paid $1,200 on July 1, 1996. The entire $1,200 is deductible in 1996. ▼

The payment must be required, not a voluntary prepayment, to obtain the current deduction under the one-year rule.[22] The taxpayer must also demonstrate that allowing the current deduction will not result in a material distortion of income. Generally, the deduction will be allowed if the item is recurring or was made for a business purpose rather than to manipulate income.[23]

As Chapter 15 explains, not all taxpayers are allowed to use the cash method.[24]

ACCRUAL METHOD REQUIREMENTS

The period in which an accrual basis taxpayer can deduct an expense is determined by applying the *all events test* and the *economic performance test*. A deduction cannot be claimed until (1) all the events have occurred to create the taxpayer's liability and (2) the amount of the liability can be determined with reasonable accuracy. Once these requirements are satisfied, the deduction is permitted only if economic performance has occurred. The economic performance test is met only when the service, property, or use of property giving rise to the liability is actually performed for, provided to, or used by the taxpayer.[25]

EXAMPLE 9

On December 22, 1996, Chris's entertainment business sponsored a jazz festival in a rented auditorium at a local college. His business is responsible for cleaning up the auditorium after the festival and for reinstalling seats that were removed so more people could attend the festival. Since the college is closed over the Christmas holidays, the company hired by Chris to perform the work did not begin these activities until January 2, 1997. The cost to Chris is $1,200. Chris cannot deduct the $1,200 until 1997, when the services are performed. ▼

An exception to the economic performance requirements allows certain *recurring items* to be deducted if the following conditions are met:

- The item is recurring in nature and is treated consistently by the taxpayer.
- Either the accrued item is not material, or accruing it results in better matching of income and expenses.
- All the events have occurred that determine the fact of the liability and the amount of the liability can be determined with reasonable accuracy.
- Economic performance occurs within a reasonable period (but not later than 8½ months after the close of the taxable year).[26]

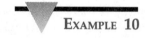

EXAMPLE 10

Rick, an accrual basis, calendar year taxpayer, entered into a monthly maintenance contract during the year. He makes a monthly accrual at the end of every month for this service and pays the fee sometime between the first and fifteenth of the following month when services are performed. The amount involved is immaterial, and all the other tests are met. The December 1996 accrual is deductible even though the service is performed on January 12, 1997. ▼

---

[22] *Bonaire Development Co. v. Comm.*, 82–2 USTC ¶9428, 50 AFTR2d 82–5167, 679 F.2d 159 (CA–9, 1982).
[23] *Keller v. Comm.*, 84–1 USTC ¶9194, 53 AFTR2d 84–663, 725 F.2d 1173 (CA–8, 1984), *aff'g* 79 T.C. 7 (1982).

[24] § 448.
[25] § 461(h).
[26] § 461(h)(3)(A).

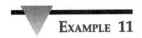
EXAMPLE 11

Rita, an accrual basis, calendar year taxpayer, shipped merchandise sold on December 30, 1996, via Greyhound Van Lines on January 2, 1997, and paid the freight charges at that time. Since Rita reported the sale of the merchandise in 1996, the shipping charge should also be deductible in 1996. This procedure results in a better matching of income and expenses. ▼

Reserves for estimated expenses (frequently employed for financial accounting purposes) generally are not allowed for tax purposes because the economic performance test cannot be satisfied.

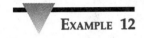
EXAMPLE 12

Blackbird Airlines is required by Federal law to test its engines after 3,000 flying hours. Aircraft cannot return to flight until the tests have been conducted. An unrelated aircraft maintenance company does all of the company's tests for $1,500 per engine. For financial reporting purposes, the company accrues an expense based upon $.50 per hour of flight and credits an allowance account. The actual amounts paid for maintenance are offset against the allowance account. For tax purposes, the economic performance test is not satisfied until the work has been done. Therefore, the reserve method cannot be used for tax purposes. ▼

DISALLOWANCE POSSIBILITIES

3 LEARNING OBJECTIVE
Apply the Internal Revenue Code deduction disallowance provisions associated with the following: public policy limitations, political activities, excessive executive compensation, investigation of business opportunities, hobby losses, vacation home rentals, payment of others' expenses, personal expenditures, capital expenditures, related-party transactions, and expenses related to tax-exempt income.

The tax law provides for the disallowance of certain types of expenses. Without specific restrictions in the tax law, taxpayers might attempt to deduct certain items that in reality are personal expenditures. For example, specific tax rules are provided to determine whether an expenditure is for trade or business purposes or related to a personal hobby.

Certain disallowance provisions are a codification or extension of prior court decisions. After the courts denied deductions for payments considered to be in violation of public policy, the tax law was changed to provide specific authority for the disallowance of these deductions. Discussions of specific disallowance provisions in the tax law follow.

PUBLIC POLICY LIMITATION

Justification for Denying Deductions. The courts developed the principle that a payment that is in violation of public policy is not a necessary expense and is not deductible.[27] Although a bribe or fine, may be appropriate, helpful, and even contribute to the profitability of an activity, the courts held that to allow such expenses would frustrate clearly defined public policy. A deduction would dilute the effect of the penalty since the government would be indirectly subsidizing a taxpayer's wrongdoing.

Accordingly, the IRS was free to restrict deductions if, in its view, the expenses were contrary to public policy. But since the law did not explain which actions violated public policy, taxpayers often had to go to court to determine whether or not their expense fell into this category.

Furthermore, the public policy doctrine could be arbitrarily applied in cases where no clear definition had emerged. To solve these problems, Congress enacted legislation that attempts to limit the use of the doctrine. Under the legislation,

---

[27] *Tank Truck Rentals, Inc. v. Comm.*, 58–1 USTC ¶9366, 1 AFTR2d 1154, 78 S.Ct. 507 (USSC, 1958).

deductions are disallowed for certain specific types of expenditures that are considered contrary to public policy:

- Bribes and kickbacks including those associated with Medicare or Medicaid (in the case of foreign bribes and kickbacks, only if the payments violate the U.S. Foreign Corrupt Practices Act of 1977).
- Fines and penalties paid to a government for violation of law.

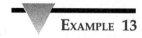

EXAMPLE 13

Brown Corporation, a moving company, consistently loads its trucks with weights in excess of the limits allowed by state law. The additional revenue more than offsets the fines levied. The fines are for a violation of public policy and are not deductible. ▼

- Two-thirds of the treble damage payments made to claimants resulting from violation of the antitrust law.[28]

To be disallowed, the bribe or kickback must be illegal under either Federal or state law and must also subject the payer to a criminal penalty or the loss of license or privilege to engage in a trade or business. For a bribe or kickback that is illegal under state law, a deduction is denied only if the state law is generally enforced.

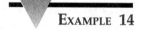

EXAMPLE 14

During the year, Keith, an insurance salesman, paid $5,000 to Karen, a real estate broker. The payment represented 20% of the commissions Keith earned from customers referred by Karen. Under state law, the splitting of commissions by an insurance salesperson is an act of misconduct that could warrant a revocation of the salesperson's license. Keith's $5,000 payments to Karen are not deductible provided the state law is generally enforced. ▼

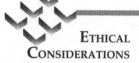

ETHICAL CONSIDERATIONS

Obtaining Zoning Variances

Tex is a real estate developer. He has a contract with a major retailer to handle its land acquisitions in the southeastern part of the state. One of Tex's major responsibilities is to secure the requisite zoning to enable the retailer to build and operate its retail outlets. Typically, obtaining proper zoning is more of a procedural activity than a strategic activity.

Tex has identified a site he would like to acquire for the retailer in a small historic city surrounded by two counties with substantially greater populations. Tex and the retailer have agreed that it is imperative that the site be in the city rather than in one of the counties. The city has very restrictive zoning for commercial properties, and the retailer will have to obtain several zoning variances.

Tex's normal strategy in such a situation is to hire the leading law firm in the community to represent him in dealing with the property owner, the city planning commission, and the city council. In this instance, however, the senior partner in the major law firm is also the city mayor, so Tex adopts the following strategy. He hires another law firm as his representative on this acquisition, but so as not to antagonize the mayor and potentially adversely affect the city council's approval of the zoning variances, he pays a $10,000 retainer to the mayor's law firm to serve as his legal representative on any real estate acquisitions during the next 12-month period in the two adjoining counties. Tex deducts the $10,000 payment as an ordinary and necessary business expense. He is successful in securing the zoning

---
[28] §§ 162(c), (f), and (g).

variances and acquires the site for the retailer. During the following 12-month period, Tex does not need to use the services of the mayor's law firm.

What is Tex trying to achieve and will he be successful?

Legal Expenses Incurred in Defense of Civil or Criminal Penalties. To deduct legal expenses, the taxpayer must be able to show that the origin and character of the claim are directly related to a trade or business, an income-producing activity, or the determination, collection, or refund of a tax. Personal legal expenses are not deductible. Thus, legal fees incurred in connection with a criminal defense are deductible only if the crime is associated with the taxpayer's trade or business or income-producing activity.[29]

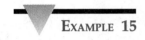

EXAMPLE 15

Debra, a financial officer of Blue Corporation, incurred legal expenses in connection with her defense in a criminal indictment for evasion of Blue's income taxes. Debra may deduct her legal expenses because she is deemed to be in the trade or business of being an executive. The legal action impairs her ability to conduct this business activity.[30] ▼

Deductible legal expenses associated with the following are deductible *for* AGI:

- Ordinary and necessary expenses incurred in connection with a trade or business.
- Ordinary and necessary expenses incurred in conjunction with rental or royalty property held for the production of income.

All other deductible legal expenses are deductible *from* AGI. For example, legal expenses generally are deductible *from* AGI if they are for fees for tax advice relative to the preparation of an individual's income tax return. Contrast this with the deduction *for* classification of legal fees for tax advice relative to the preparation of the portion of the tax return for a sole proprietor's trade or business (Schedule C) or an individual's rental or royalty income (Schedule E).

Expenses Relating to an Illegal Business. The usual expenses of operating an illegal business (e.g., a numbers racket) are deductible.[31] However, § 162 disallows a deduction for fines, bribes to public officials, illegal kickbacks, and other illegal payments.

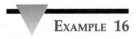

EXAMPLE 16

Sam owns and operates an illegal gambling establishment. In connection with this activity, he had the following expenses during the year:

Rent	$ 60,000
Payoffs to the police	40,000
Depreciation on equipment	100,000
Wages	140,000
Interest	30,000
Criminal fines	50,000
Illegal kickbacks	10,000
Total	$430,000

---

[29] *Comm. v. Tellier,* 66–1 USTC ¶9319, 17 AFTR2d 633, 86 S.Ct. 1118 (USSC, 1966).

[30] Rev.Rul. 68–662, 1968–2 C.B. 69.

[31] *Comm. v. Sullivan,* 58–1 USTC ¶9368, 1 AFTR2d 1158, 78 S.Ct. 512 (USSC, 1958).

All of the usual expenses (rent, depreciation, wages, and interest) are deductible; payoffs, fines, and kickbacks are not deductible. Of the $430,000 spent, $330,000 is deductible and $100,000 is not. ▼

An exception applies to expenses incurred in illegal trafficking in drugs.[32] *Drug dealers* are not allowed a deduction for ordinary and necessary business expenses incurred in their business. In arriving at gross income from the business, however, dealers may reduce total sales by the cost of goods sold.[33] In this regard, no distinction is made between legal and illegal businesses in calculating gross income. Treating cost of goods sold as a negative income item rather than as a deduction item produces the unseemly result that a drug dealer's taxable income is reduced by cost of goods sold.

POLITICAL CONTRIBUTIONS AND LOBBYING ACTIVITIES

Political Contributions. Generally, no business deduction is permitted for direct or indirect payments for political purposes.[34] Historically, the government has been reluctant to accord favorable tax treatment to business expenditures for political purposes. Allowing deductions might encourage abuses and enable businesses to have undue influence upon the political process.

Lobbying Expenditures. Prior to the effect of the Revenue Reconciliation Act of 1993 (RRA of 1993), a deduction was allowed for certain expenses incurred to influence legislation (appearances before or statements filed with legislative bodies or individual legislators). For the expense to qualify as a deductible lobbying expenditure, the proposed legislation had to be of direct interest to the taxpayer. A direct interest existed if the legislation would, or could reasonably be expected to, affect the trade or business of the taxpayer. No deduction was allowed for expenses incurred to influence the public on legislative matters or for any political campaign.

RRA of 1993 generally repealed this lobbying deduction.[35] Any lobbying expenses incurred in attempting to influence state or Federal legislation or the actions of certain high-ranking public officials (e.g., the President, Vice-President, cabinet-level officials, and the two most senior officials in each agency of the executive branch) are no longer deductible. The disallowance also applies to a pro rata portion of the membership dues of trade associations and other groups that are used for lobbying activities.

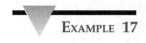

EXAMPLE **17**

Egret Company pays a $10,000 annual membership fee to the Free Trade Group, a trade association for plumbing wholesalers. The trade association estimates that 70% of its dues are allocated to lobbying activities. Thus, Egret Company's deduction is limited to $3,000 ($10,000 × 30%). ▼

There are three exceptions to this repeal of the lobbying expenses deduction. An exception is provided for influencing local legislation (e.g., city and county governments). Second, the disallowance provision does not apply to activities

---

[32] § 280E.

[33] Reg. § 1.61–3(a). Gross income is defined as sales minus cost of goods sold. Thus, while § 280E prohibits any deductions for drug dealers, it does not modify the normal definition of gross income.

[34] § 276.

[35] § 162(e).

TAX IN THE NEWS

LOBBYISTS WORK AND SUE TO WORK

The Revenue Reconciliation Act of 1993 generally eliminated the ability of businesses to deduct the amounts paid to lobbyists to lobby for them. Subsequently, eleven nonprofit trade groups and professional societies filed a lawsuit in the U.S. District Court in Washington, D.C., alleging that their rights of free speech, petition, and association were threatened by the new statutory provision contained in § 162(e). While denying the request for an injunction on procedural grounds, the district court judge left the door open by commenting that he did not agree with the way Congress wrote the law or the way the IRS implemented it. As a result, the American Society of Association Executives has filed a lawsuit seeking to invalidate § 162(e) and recover its initial payment to the IRS.

In a different vein, lobbyists are still finding work even though their clients cannot deduct the amounts paid for lobbying services. For example, the *Wall Street Journal* reported that some lobbyists were concerned that Congress might not extend the research activities credit beyond its June 30, 1995, expiration date. One lobbyist, however, confided that he had an even bigger fear—that Congress might extend the provision permanently, rather than temporarily, and thus hurt his lobbying business.

SOURCE: Adapted from "Lobbyists Try Again to Shoot Down Part of the 1993 Tax Law," *Wall Street Journal*, June 7, 1995, p. A1.

devoted solely to monitoring legislation. Third, a *de minimis* exception is provided for annual in-house expenditures (lobbying expenses other than those paid to professional lobbyists or any portion of dues used by associations for lobbying) if such expenditures do not exceed $2,000. If the in-house expenditures exceed $2,000, none of the in-house expenditures can be deducted.

EXCESSIVE EXECUTIVE COMPENSATION

Prior to the effect of RRA of 1993, there was no statutory dollar limit on the deduction for executive compensation. The only limitation was the reasonableness requirement (discussed earlier in this chapter) for shareholder-employees of closely held corporations.

RRA of 1993 includes the so-called millionaires provision, which applies to publicly held corporations.[36] The provision does not limit the amount of compensation that can be paid to an employee. Instead, it limits the amount the employer can deduct for the compensation of a covered executive to $1 million annually. Covered employees include the chief executive officer and the four other most highly compensated officers.

Employee compensation *excludes* the following:

---

[36] A publicly held corporation, for this provision, is a corporation that has at least one class of stock registered under the Securities Act of 1934.

TAX IN THE NEWS

EXCESSIVE EXECUTIVE CONPENSATION: WIN ONE AND LOSE ONE

Revisions to the original Proposed Regulations on excessive executive compensation are beneficial to the taxpayer on one point and detrimental on another, according to Bill Dunn, a specialist in executive compensation with the National Tax Services Office of Coopers & Lybrand.

On the favorable side, one example in the revisions appears to provide an open door with respect to the definition of a "substantial uncertainty." The original Proposed Regulations provided that when a performance goal is substantially uncertain, it is considered preestablished (a requirement of the Proposed Regulations) if it is written no later than 90 days after the goal period begins. The example indicates that performance goals based on corporate profitability are substantially uncertain even when the company has a profitable history. Thus, the goal could be the maintenance of the current level of earnings rather than improvements in earnings.

On the unfavorable side, the definition of a corporate outside director is restricted. An outside director is now defined as one who does not receive remuneration from the company in a nondirector capacity. Gone for providers of professional services is the provision in the original Proposed Regulations that did not count as remuneration payments up to $60,000 or 5 percent of the company's gross income, whichever was less. The elimination of this threshold will make it more difficult for attorneys, accountants, management consultants, investment bankers, and other providers of professional services to qualify for compensation committees.

SOURCE: Information from "Executive Compensation Amendments Ease Deduction Worries," *Washington Perspective*, January 1995, Coopers & Lybrand, L.L.P., p. 2.

- Commissions based on individual performance.
- Certain performance-based compensation based on company performance according to a formula approved by a board of directors compensation committee (comprised solely of two or more outside directors) and by shareholder vote. The performance attainment must be certified by this compensation committee.
- Payments to tax-qualified retirement plans.
- Payments that are excludible from the employees' gross income (e.g., certain fringe benefits).

INVESTIGATION OF A BUSINESS

Investigation expenses are expenses paid or incurred to determine the feasibility of entering a new business or expanding an existing business. They include such costs as travel, engineering and architectural surveys, marketing reports, and various legal and accounting services. How such expenses are treated for tax purposes depends on a number of variables, including the following:

- The current business, if any, of the taxpayer.
- The nature of the business being investigated.
- The extent to which the investigation has proceeded.
- Whether or not the acquisition actually takes place.

If the taxpayer is in a business the *same as or similar to* that being investigated, all investigation expenses are deductible in the year paid or incurred. The tax result is the same whether or not the taxpayer acquires the business being investigated.[37]

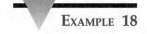

EXAMPLE 18   Terry, an accrual basis sole proprietor, owns and operates three motels in Georgia. In the current year, Terry incurs expenses of $8,500 in investigating the possibility of acquiring several additional motels located in South Carolina. The $8,500 is deductible in the current year whether or not Terry acquires the motels in South Carolina. ▼

When the taxpayer is *not* in a business that is the same as or similar to the one being investigated, the tax result depends on whether the new business is acquired. If the business is not acquired, all investigation expenses generally are nondeductible.[38]

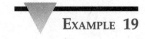

EXAMPLE 19   Lynn, a retired merchant, incurs expenses in traveling from Rochester, New York, to California to investigate the feasibility of acquiring several auto care centers. If no acquisition takes place, none of the expenses are deductible. ▼

If the taxpayer is *not* in a business that is the same as or similar to the one being investigated and actually acquires the new business, the expenses must be capitalized. At the election of the taxpayer, the expenses may be amortized over a period of 60 months or more, beginning with the month in which the business is started.[39]

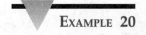

EXAMPLE 20   Tina owns and operates 10 restaurants located in various cities throughout the Southeast. She travels to Atlanta to discuss the acquisition of an auto dealership. In addition, she incurs legal and accounting costs associated with the potential acquisition. After incurring total investigation costs of $12,000, she acquires the auto dealership on October 1, 1996.

Tina must capitalize the $12,000 of investigation expenses for the auto dealership. If she elects to amortize the expenses over 60 months, she can deduct $600 ($12,000 × 3/60) in 1996. ▼

HOBBY LOSSES

Business or investment expenses are deductible only if the taxpayer can show that the activity was entered into for the purpose of making a profit. Certain activities may have either profit-seeking or personal attributes, depending upon individual circumstances. Examples include raising horses and operating a farm used as a weekend residence. While personal losses are not deductible, losses attributable to profit-seeking activities may be deducted and used to offset a taxpayer's other income. For this reason, the tax law limits the deductibility of **hobby losses.**

General Rules.   If an individual can show that an activity has been conducted with the intent to earn a profit, losses from the activity are fully deductible. The hobby loss rules apply only if the activity is not engaged in for profit. Hobby expenses are deductible only to the extent of hobby income.[40]

---

[42] § 183(d).

[37] *York v. Comm.*, 58–2 USTC ¶9952, 2 AFTR2d 6178, 261 F.2d 421 (CA–4, 1958).

[38] Rev.Rul. 57–418, 1957–2 C.B. 143; *Morton Frank*, 20 T.C. 511 (1953); and *Dwight A. Ward*, 20 T.C. 332 (1953).

[39] § 195.

[40] § 183(b)(2).

The Regulations stipulate that the following nine factors should be considered in determining whether an activity is profit-seeking or a hobby:[41]

- Whether the activity is conducted in a businesslike manner.
- The expertise of the taxpayers or their advisers.
- The time and effort expended.
- The expectation that the assets of the activity will appreciate in value.
- The taxpayer's previous success in conducting similar activities.
- The history of income or losses from the activity.
- The relationship of profits earned to losses incurred.
- The financial status of the taxpayer (e.g., if the taxpayer does not have substantial amounts of other income, this may indicate that the activity is engaged in for profit).
- Elements of personal pleasure or recreation in the activity.

The presence or absence of a factor is not by itself determinative of whether the activity is profit-seeking or a hobby. Rather, the decision is a subjective one that is based on an analysis of the facts and circumstances.

Presumptive Rule of § 183. The Code provides a rebuttable presumption that an activity is profit-seeking if the activity shows a profit in at least three of any five prior consecutive years.[42] If the activity involves horses, a profit in at least two of seven consecutive years meets the presumptive rule. If these profitability tests are met, the activity is presumed to be a trade or business rather than a personal hobby. In this situation, the IRS bears the burden of proving that the activity is personal rather than trade or business related.

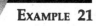

EXAMPLE 21

Camille, an executive for a large corporation, is paid a salary of $200,000. Her husband is a collector of antiques. Several years ago, he opened an antique shop in a local shopping center and spends most of his time buying and selling antiques. He occasionally earns a small profit from this activity but more frequently incurs substantial losses. If the losses are business related, they are fully deductible against Camille's salary income on a joint return. In resolving this issue, consider the following:

- Initially determine whether the antique activity has met the three-out-of-five years profit test.
- If the presumption is not met, the activity may nevertheless qualify as a business if the taxpayer can show that the intent is to engage in a profit-seeking activity. It is not necessary to show actual profits.
- Attempt to fit the operation within the nine criteria prescribed in the Regulations and listed above. These criteria are the factors considered in trying to rebut the § 183 presumption. ▼

Determining the Amount of the Deduction. If an activity is deemed to be a hobby, the expenses are deductible only to the extent of the gross income from the hobby. These expenses must be deducted in the following order:

- Amounts deductible under other Code sections without regard to the nature of the activity, such as property taxes and home mortgage interest.
- Amounts deductible under other Code sections if the activity had been engaged in for profit, but only if those amounts do not affect adjusted basis. Examples include maintenance, utilities, and supplies.

---

[41] Reg. §§ 1.183–2(b)(1) through (9).   [42] § 183(d).

- Amounts that affect adjusted basis and would be deductible under other Code sections if the activity had been engaged in for profit.[43] Examples include depreciation, amortization, and depletion.

These deductions are deductible *from* AGI as itemized deductions to the extent they exceed 2 percent of AGI.[44] If the taxpayer uses the standard deduction rather than itemizing, all hobby loss deductions are wasted.

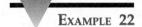

EXAMPLE 22

Jim, the vice-president of an oil company, has AGI of $80,000. He decides to pursue painting in his spare time. He uses a home studio, comprising 10% of the home's square footage. During the current year, Jim incurs the following expenses:

Frames	$ 350
Art supplies	300
Fees paid to models	1,000
Home studio expenses:	
Total property taxes	900
Total home mortgage interest	10,000
Depreciation on 10% of home	500
Total home maintenance and utilities	3,600

During the year, Jim sold paintings for a total of $3,200. If the activity is held to be a hobby, Jim is allowed deductions as follows:

Gross income		$ 3,200
Deduct: Taxes and interest (10% of $10,900)		(1,090)
Remainder		$ 2,110
Deduct: Frames	$ 350	
Art supplies	300	
Models' fees	1,000	
Maintenance and utilities (10%)	360	(2,010)
Remainder		$ 100
Depreciation ($500, but limited to $100)		(100)
Net income		$ –0–

Jim includes the $3,200 of income in AGI, making his AGI $83,200. The taxes and interest are itemized deductions, deductible in full. The remaining $2,110 of expenses are reduced by 2% of his AGI ($1,664); so the net deduction is $446. Since the property taxes and home mortgage interest are deductible anyway, the net effect is a $2,754 ($3,200 less $446) increase in taxable income. ▼

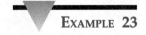

EXAMPLE 23

If Jim's activity in Example 22 is held to be a business, he could deduct expenses totaling $2,510 ($2,010 plus $500 of depreciation) *for* AGI, in addition to the $1,090 of taxes and interest. All these expenses would be trade or business expenses deductible *for* AGI. His reduction in AGI would be as follows:

Gross income		$ 3,200
Less: Taxes and interest	$1,090	
Other business expenses	2,010	
Depreciation	500	(3,600)
Reduction in AGI		$ (400)

[43] Reg. § 1.183–1(b)(1).   [44] Reg. § 1.67–1T(a)(1)(iv) and Rev.Rul. 75–14, 1975–1 C.B. 90.

As is the case in Example 22, Jim can deduct the remaining property taxes and home mortgage interest of $9,810 ($10,900 − $1,090) as itemized deductions. ▼

RENTAL OF VACATION HOMES

Restrictions on the deductions allowed for part-year rentals of personal **vacation homes** were written into the law to prevent taxpayers from deducting essentially personal expenses as rental losses. Many taxpayers who owned vacation homes had formerly treated the homes as rental property and generated rental losses as deductions *for* AGI. For example, a summer cabin would be rented for 2 months per year, used for vacationing for 1 month, and left vacant the rest of the year. The taxpayer would then deduct 11 months' depreciation, utilities, maintenance, etc., as rental expenses, resulting in a rental loss. Section 280A eliminates this treatment by allowing deductions on residences used primarily for personal purposes only to the extent of the income generated. Only a break-even situation is allowed; no losses can be deducted.

There are three possible tax treatments for residences used for both personal and rental purposes. The treatment depends upon the *relative time* the residence is used for personal purposes versus rental use.

Primarily Personal Use.   If the residence is *rented* for *less than 15 days* in a year, it is treated as a personal residence. The rent income is excluded from gross income, and mortgage interest and real estate taxes are allowed as itemized deductions, as with any personal residence.[45] No other expenses (e.g., depreciation, utilities, maintenance) are deductible. Although this provision exists primarily for administrative convenience, a bill was introduced in Congress in 1994 that would have repealed this exclusion from gross income.

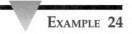

EXAMPLE 24

Dixie owns a vacation cottage on the lake. During the current year, she rented it for $1,600 for two weeks, lived in it two months, and left it vacant the remainder of the year. The year's expenses amounted to $6,000 mortgage interest expense, $500 property taxes, $1,500 utilities and maintenance, and $2,400 depreciation. Since the property was not rented for at least 15 days, the income is excluded, the mortgage interest and property tax expenses are itemized deductions, and the remaining expenses are nondeductible personal expenses. ▼

ETHICAL
CONSIDERATIONS

Renting for One More Day

June is a widow who lives in Williamsburg, Virginia. For the past five years (since the death of her husband), she has rented her home for one week to a professional golfer who is participating in the A–B Golf Classic. The rent income is $1,500. During this week, June visits her sister in Charlotte. A neighbor who is a CPA advises June that she does not need to report the $1,500 on her Federal income tax return because she did not rent her house for more than two weeks during the year.

In 1996, June has the opportunity to rent the house for $2,800 for an additional week in December to the golfer and his family who would like to spend Christmas in Williamsburg. She checks with her CPA neighbor to verify she will not have to include the rent income in her gross income. June agrees to rent her house and to visit her sister through New Year's Day.

---
[45] § 280A(g).

The golfer and his family arrived on December 20 and were scheduled to depart on December 27. On December 26, the golfer's wife calls June at her sister's, explains that their two-year-old child is ill, and asks if they can rent for an additional day until the child feels better. June says yes, of course, but indicates she will not accept any rent for the additional day.

When June returns home on January 2, 1997, she finds the check on her kitchen counter is for $3,200 rather than for $2,800. The check is enclosed in a Christmas card from the golfer and his family.

On her 1996 Federal income tax return, June does not report any rent income or deduct any rental expenses. According to her records, she rented her house for exactly two weeks.

Can you justify June's treatment of the rent income and expenses?

Primarily Rental Use. If the residence is *rented* for 15 days or more in a year and is *not used* for personal purposes for more than the greater of (1) 14 days or (2) 10 percent of the total days rented, the residence is treated as rental property.[46] The expenses must be allocated between personal and rental days if there are any personal use days during the year. The deduction of the expenses allocated to rental days can exceed rent income and result in a rental loss. The loss may be deductible under the passive activity loss rules (discussed in Chapter 10).

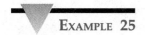

EXAMPLE 25

Assume instead that Dixie in Example 24 rented the cottage for 120 days and lived in it for 13 days. The cottage is primarily rental use since she rented it for 15 days or more and did not use it for personal purposes for more than 14 days. ▼

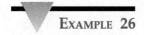

EXAMPLE 26

Assume instead that Dixie in Example 24 rented the cottage for 200 days and lived in it for 19 days. The cottage is primarily rental use since she rented it for 15 days or more and did not use it for personal purposes for more than 20 days (10% of the rental days). ▼

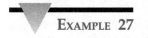

EXAMPLE 27

Assume instead that Dixie in Example 24 used the cottage for 12 days and rented it for 48 days for $4,800. Since she rented the cottage for 15 days or more but did not use it for more than 14 days, the cottage is treated as rental property. The expenses must be allocated between personal and rental days.

| | Percentage of Use | |
	Rental 80%	Personal 20%
Income	$4,800	$ –0–
Expenses		
Mortgage interest ($6,000)	($4,800)	($1,200)
Property taxes ($500)	(400)	(100)
Utilities and maintenance ($1,500)	(1,200)	(300)
Depreciation ($2,400)	(1,920)	(480)
Total expenses	($8,320)	($2,080)
Rental loss	($3,520)	$ –0–

---

[46] § 280A(d) and Prop.Reg. § 1.280A–3(c).

Dixie deducts the $3,520 rental loss *for* AGI (assuming she meets the passive activity loss rules, discussed in Chapter 10). She also has an itemized deduction for property taxes of $100 associated with the personal use. The mortgage interest of $1,200 associated with the personal use is not deductible as an itemized deduction because the cottage is not a qualified residence (qualified residence interest) for this purpose (see Chapter 9). The portion of utilities and maintenance and depreciation attributable to personal use is not deductible. ▼

Personal/Rental Use.   If the residence is rented for 15 days or more in a year *and* is used for personal purposes for more than the greater of (1) 14 days or (2) 10 percent of the total days rented, it is treated as a personal/rental use residence. The expenses must be allocated between personal days and rental days. Expenses are allowed only to the extent of rent income.

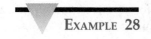

EXAMPLE 28

Assume instead that Dixie in Example 24 rented the property for 30 days and lived in it for 30 days. The residence is classified as personal/rental use property since she used it more than 14 days and rented it for 15 days or more. The expenses must be allocated between rental use and personal use, and the rental expenses are allowed only to the extent of rent income. ▼

If a residence is classified as personal/rental use property, the expenses that are deductible anyway (e.g., real estate taxes and mortgage interest) must be deducted first. If a positive net income results, otherwise nondeductible expenses that do not affect adjusted basis (e.g., maintenance, utilities, insurance) are allowed next. Finally, if any positive balance remains, depreciation is allowed.

Expenses must be allocated between personal and rental days before the limits are applied. The courts have held that real estate taxes and mortgage interest, which accrue ratably over the year, are allocated on the basis of 365 days.[47] The IRS, however, disagrees and allocates real estate taxes and mortgage interest on the basis of total days of use.[48] Other expenses (utilities, maintenance, depreciation, etc.) are allocated on the basis of total days used.

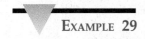

EXAMPLE 29

Sue rents her vacation home for 60 days and lives in the home for 30 days. The limitations on personal/rental use residences apply. Sue's gross rent income is $10,000. For the entire year (not a leap year), the real estate taxes are $2,190; her mortgage interest expense is $10,220; utilities and maintenance expense equals $2,400; and depreciation is $9,000. Using the IRS approach, these amounts are deductible in this specific order:

Gross income	$10,000
Deduct: Taxes and interest (60/90 × $12,410)	(8,273)
Remainder to apply to rental operating expenses and depreciation	$ 1,727
Deduct: Utilities and maintenance (60/90 × $2,400)	(1,600)
Balance	$ 127
Deduct: Depreciation (60/90 × $9,000 = $6,000 but limited to above balance)	(127)
Net rent income	$ –0–

---

[47] *Bolton v. Comm.*, 82–2 USTC ¶9699, 51 AFTR2d 83–305, 694 F.2d 556 (CA–9, 1982).   [48] Prop.Reg. § 1.280A–3(d)(4).

The nonrental use portion of real estate taxes and mortgage interest ($4,137 in this case) is deductible if the taxpayer elects to itemize (see Chapter 9). The personal use portion of utilities, maintenance, and depreciation is not deductible in any case. Also note that the basis of the property is not reduced by the $5,873 depreciation not allowed ($6,000 – $127) because of the above limitation. (See Chapter 12 for a discussion of the reduction in basis for depreciation allowed or allowable.) ▼

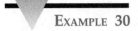

EXAMPLE 30

Using the court's approach in allocating real estate taxes and mortgage interest, Sue, in Example 29, would have this result:

Gross income	$10,000
Deduct: Taxes and interest (60/365 × $12,410)	(2,040)
Remainder to apply to rental operating expenses and depreciation	$ 7,960
Deduct: Utilities and maintenance (60/90 × $2,400)	(1,600)
Balance	$ 6,360
Deduct: Depreciation (60/90 × $9,000, but limited to $6,360)	(6,000)
Net rent income	$ 360

Sue can deduct $10,370 ($12,410 paid – $2,040 deducted as expense in computing net rent income) of personal use mortgage interest and real estate taxes as itemized deductions. ▼

Note the contrasting results in Examples 29 and 30. The IRS's approach (Example 29) results in no rental gain or loss and an itemized deduction for real estate taxes and mortgage interest of $4,137. In Example 30, Sue has net rent income of $360 and $10,370 of itemized deductions. The court's approach decreases her taxable income by $10,010 ($10,370 itemized deductions less $360 net rent income). The IRS's approach reduces her taxable income by only $4,137.

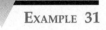

EXAMPLE 31

Assume instead that Sue in Example 29 had not lived in the home at all during the year. The house is rental property. The rental loss is calculated as follows:

Gross income	$10,000	
Expenses		
Taxes and interest	($12,410)	
Utilities and maintenance	(2,400)	
Depreciation	(9,000)	
Total expenses	($23,810)	
Rental loss	($13,810)	

Whether any of the rental loss would be deductible depends upon whether Sue actively participated in the rental activity and met the other requirements for passive activity losses (discussed in Chapter 10). ▼

Conversion to Rental Property.   A related issue is whether or not a taxpayer's *primary residence* is subject to the preceding rules if it is converted to rental property. If the vacation home rules apply, a taxpayer who converts his or her personal residence to rental property during the tax year, without any tax avoidance motive, could have the allowable deductions limited to the rent income. This would occur if the personal use exceeded the greater of 14 days or 10 percent of rental days test (a likely situation). The Code, however, provides that during a

CONCEPT SUMMARY 5–1

Vacation/Rental Home

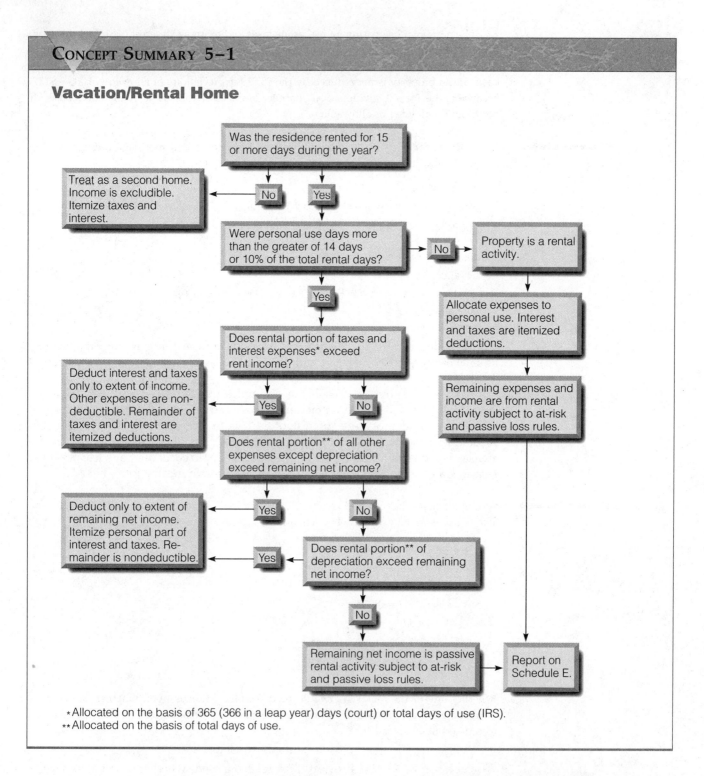

*Allocated on the basis of 365 (366 in a leap year) days (court) or total days of use (IRS).
**Allocated on the basis of total days of use.

qualified rental period, any personal use days are not counted as personal use days in terms of classifying the use of the residence as *personal/rental use* rather than as *primarily rental use.*[49] In effect, the deduction for expenses of the property incurred during a qualified rental period is not subject to the personal use test of the

---

[49] § 280A(d).

vacation home rules. A qualified rental period is a consecutive period of 12 or more months. The period begins or ends in the taxable year in which the residence is rented or held for rental at a fair price. The residence must not be rented to a related party. If the property is sold before the 12-month period expires, the qualified rental period is the actual time rented.

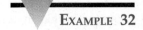

EXAMPLE 32

Rhonda converts her residence to rental property on May 1 and rents it for the remainder of 1996 for $5,600 and for all of 1997 for $8,400. The house would be classified as personal/rental use property (personal use days during 1996 are greater than both 14 days and 10% of rental days) except that this is a qualified rental period. Therefore, Rhonda's deduction for rental expenses is not limited to the gross income of $5,600 in 1996. ▼

See Concept Summary 5–1 for a summary of the vacation home rules.

EXPENDITURES INCURRED FOR TAXPAYER'S BENEFIT OR TAXPAYER'S OBLIGATION

An expense must be incurred for the taxpayer's benefit or arise from the taxpayer's obligation. An individual cannot claim a tax deduction for the payment of the expenses of another individual.

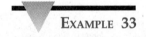

EXAMPLE 33

During the current year, Fred pays the interest on his son, Vern's, home mortgage. Neither Fred nor Vern can take a deduction for the interest paid. Fred is not entitled to a deduction because the mortgage is not his obligation. Vern cannot claim a deduction because he did not pay the interest. The tax result would have been more favorable had Fred made a cash gift to Vern and let him pay the interest. Then Vern could have deducted the interest, and Fred might not have been liable for any gift taxes depending upon the amount involved. A deduction would have been created with no cash difference to the family. ▼

One exception to this disallowance rule is the payment of medical expenses for a dependent. Such expenses are deductible by the payer subject to the normal rules that limit the deductibility of medical expenses (see Chapter 9).[50]

ETHICAL CONSIDERATIONS

How the Payment Is Made

Dan and Jeff both have sons who graduated from college recently and are employed by the same company in a rural community where rental housing is not readily available. Each father loans his son $10,000; the sons combine their resources and use the $20,000 as a down payment on a house that they buy together.

During 1996, the sons make all the mortgage payments on their house until December when they are furloughed from their jobs. Dan gives his son $900 to use to pay his share of the mortgage payment, and Jeff pays $900 directly to the mortgage company for his son. In each of these $900 amounts, $800 represents interest on the mortgage.

Over lunch recently, Dan and Jeff were discussing their sons' real estate investment and the $900 mortgage payment each father had funded. Jeff indicated that since he had paid the mortgage payment directly, he was going to deduct the $800 of interest on his Form 1040. After this conversation, Dan concludes that, in substance, he and Jeff have done the same thing. Accordingly, Dan calls his son and tells him that he wants to deduct the $800

---

[50] § 213(a).

on his tax return. Though Dan's son is not pleased, he agrees to permit his father to take the deduction and says he will not deduct the mortgage interest on his own return.

Evaluate the propriety of the position taken by Dan.

DISALLOWANCE OF PERSONAL EXPENDITURES

Section 262 states that "except as otherwise expressly provided in this chapter, no deduction shall be allowed for personal, living, or family expenses." To justify a deduction, an individual must be able to identify a particular section of the Code that sanctions the deduction (e.g., charitable contributions, medical expenses). Sometimes the character of a particular expenditure is not easily determined.

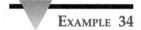

EXAMPLE 34

During the current year, Howard pays $1,500 in legal fees and court costs to obtain a divorce from his wife, Vera. Involved in the divorce action is a property settlement that concerns the disposition of income-producing property owned by Howard. In a similar situation, the Tax Court held that the taxpayer could not deduct any such costs.[51] "Although fees primarily related to property division concerning his income-producing property, they weren't ordinary and necessary expenses paid for conservation or maintenance of property held for production of income. Legal fees incurred in defending against claims that arise from a taxpayer's marital relationship aren't deductible expenses regardless of possible consequences on taxpayer's income-producing property." ▼

The IRS has clarified the issue of the deduction of legal fees incurred in connection with a divorce.[52] To be deductible, an expense must relate solely to tax advice in a divorce proceeding. For example, legal fees attributable to the determination of dependency exemptions of children are deductible if the fees are distinguishable from the general legal fees incurred in obtaining a divorce. Other examples are the costs of creating a trust to make periodic alimony payments and the determination of the tax consequences of a property settlement. Therefore, it is advisable to request an itemization of attorney's fees to substantiate a deduction for the tax-related amounts.

DISALLOWANCE OF DEDUCTIONS FOR CAPITAL EXPENDITURES

The Code specifically disallows a deduction for "any amount paid out for new buildings or for permanent improvements or betterments made to increase the value of any property or estate."[53] The Regulations further define capital expenditures to include those expenditures that add to the value or prolong the life of property or adapt the property to a new or different use.[54] Incidental repairs and maintenance of the property are not capital expenditures and can be deducted as ordinary and necessary business expenses. Repairing a roof is a deductible expense, but replacing a roof is a capital expenditure subject to depreciation deductions over its useful life. The tune-up of a delivery truck is an expense; a complete overhaul probably is a capital expenditure.

Capitalization versus Expense. When an expenditure is capitalized rather than expensed, the deduction is at best deferred and at worst lost forever.

---

[51] *Harry H. Goldberg,* 29 TCM 74, T.C.Memo. 1970–27.
[52] Rev.Rul. 72–545, 1972–2 C.B. 179.
[53] § 263(a)(1).
[54] Reg. § 1.263(a)–1(b).

Although an immediate tax benefit for a large cash expenditure is lost, the cost may be deductible in increments over a longer period of time.

If the expenditure is for a tangible asset that has an ascertainable life, it is capitalized and may be deducted as depreciation (or cost recovery) over the life of the asset (for depreciation) or over a statutory period (for cost recovery under either ACRS or MACRS).[55] Land is not subject to depreciation (or cost recovery) since it does not have an ascertainable life.

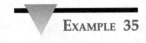

EXAMPLE 35

Stan purchased a prime piece of land located in an apartment-zoned area. Stan paid $500,000 for the property, which had an old but usable apartment building on it. He immediately had the building demolished at a cost of $100,000. The $500,000 purchase price and the $100,000 demolition costs must be capitalized, and the basis of the land is $600,000. Since land is a nondepreciable asset, no deduction is allowed. More favorable tax treatment might result if Stan rented the apartments in the old building for a period of time to attempt to establish that there was no intent to demolish the building. If Stan's attempt is successful, it might be possible to allocate a substantial portion of the original purchase price of the property to the building (a depreciable asset). When the building is later demolished, any remaining adjusted basis can be deducted as an ordinary (§ 1231) loss. (See Chapter 13 for a discussion of the treatment of § 1231 assets.) ▼

If the expenditure is for an intangible asset (e.g., copyright, patent, covenant not to compete, goodwill), the capitalized expenditure can be amortized. Prior to the effect of RRA of 1993, only intangible assets with ascertainable lives (e.g., copyright, patent, covenant not to compete) could be amortized. Intangible assets with indeterminate lives (e.g., goodwill) could not be amortized. The amortization period generally was the life of the asset, and the amortization method was the straight-line method.

RRA of 1993 provides that intangibles acquired after August 10, 1993, are to be amortized over a 15-year period using the straight-line method.[56] This statutory change can produce both positive and negative results. On the positive side, goodwill is now subject to amortization. On the negative side, intangibles with an actual life shorter than 15 years must be amortized over the longer 15-year statutory period (e.g., a covenant not to compete with a 5-year life).

TRANSACTIONS BETWEEN RELATED PARTIES

The Code places restrictions on the recognition of gains and losses from **related-party transactions.** Without these restrictions, relationships created by birth, marriage, and business would provide endless possibilities for engaging in financial transactions that produce tax savings with no real economic substance or change. For example, to create an artificial loss, a wife could sell investment property to her husband at a loss and deduct the loss on their joint return. Her husband could then hold the asset indefinitely, and the family would sustain no real economic loss. A complex set of laws has been designed to eliminate such possibilities.

Losses.   The Code provides for the disallowance of any "losses from sales or exchanges of property . . . directly or indirectly" between related parties.[57] When the property is subsequently sold to a nonrelated party, any gain recognized is

---

[55] See Chapter 7 for the discussion of depreciation and cost recovery.

[56] § 197.
[57] § 267(a)(1).

reduced by the loss previously disallowed. Any disallowed loss not used by the related-party buyer to offset his or her recognized gain on a subsequent sale or exchange to an unrelated party is permanently lost.

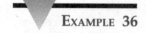

EXAMPLE 36

Freida sells common stock with a basis of $1,000 to her son, Bill, for $800. Bill sells the stock several years later for $1,100. Freida's $200 loss is disallowed upon the sale to Bill, and only $100 of gain ($1,100 selling price – $800 basis – $200 disallowed loss) is taxable to him upon the subsequent sale. ▼

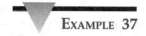

EXAMPLE 37

George sells common stock with a basis of $1,050 to his son, Ray, for $800. Ray sells the stock eight months later to an unrelated party for $900. Ray's gain of $100 ($900 selling price – $800 basis) is not recognized because of George's previously disallowed loss of $250. Note that the offset may result in only partial tax benefit upon the subsequent sale (as in this case). If the property had not been transferred to Ray, George could have recognized a $150 loss upon the sale to the unrelated party ($1,050 basis – $900 selling price). ▼

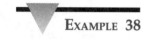

EXAMPLE 38

Pete sells common stock with a basis of $1,000 to an unrelated third party for $800. Pete's son repurchased the same stock in the market on the same day for $800. The $200 loss is not allowed because the transaction is an indirect sale between related parties.[58] ▼

Unpaid Expenses and Interest.   The law prevents related taxpayers from engaging in tax avoidance schemes where one related taxpayer uses the accrual method of accounting and the other uses the cash basis. An accrual basis, closely held corporation, for example, could borrow funds from a cash basis individual shareholder. At the end of the year, the corporation would accrue and deduct the interest, but the cash basis lender would not recognize interest income since no interest had been paid. Section 267 specifically defers the deduction of the accruing taxpayer until the recipient taxpayer must include it in income; that is, when it is actually paid to the cash basis taxpayer. This *matching* provision applies to interest as well as other expenses, such as salaries and bonuses.

This deduction deferral provision does not apply if both of the related taxpayers use the accrual method or both use the cash method. Likewise, it does not apply if the related party reporting income uses the accrual method and the related party taking the deduction uses the cash method.

Relationships and Constructive Ownership.   Section 267 operates to disallow losses and defer deductions only between related parties. Losses or deductions generated by similar transactions with an unrelated party are allowed. *Related parties* include the following:

- Brothers and sisters (whether whole, half, or adopted), spouse, ancestors (parents, grandparents), and lineal descendants (children, grandchildren) of the taxpayer.
- A corporation owned more than 50 percent (directly or indirectly) by the taxpayer.
- Two corporations that are members of a controlled group.
- A series of other complex relationships between trusts, corporations, and individual taxpayers.

Constructive ownership provisions are applied to determine whether the taxpayers are related. Under these provisions, stock owned by certain relatives or related en-

---

[58] *McWilliams v. Comm.*, 47–1 USTC ¶9289, 35 AFTR 1184, 67 S.Ct. 1477 (USSC, 1947).

tities is *deemed* to be owned by the taxpayer for purposes of applying the loss and expense deduction disallowance provisions. A taxpayer is deemed to own not only his or her stock but the stock owned by his or her lineal descendants, ancestors, brothers and sisters or half-brothers and half-sisters, and spouse. The taxpayer is also deemed to own his or her proportionate share of stock owned by any partnership, corporation, estate, or trust of which he or she is a member. An individual is deemed to own any stock owned, directly or indirectly, by his or her partner. However, constructive ownership by an individual of the partnership's and the other partner's shares does not extend to the individual's spouse or other relatives (no double attribution).

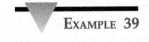

EXAMPLE 39   The stock of Sparrow Corporation is owned 20% by Ted, 30% by Ted's father, 30% by Ted's mother, and 20% by Ted's sister. On July 1 of the current year, Ted loaned $10,000 to Sparrow Corporation at 8% annual interest, principal and interest payable on demand. For tax purposes, Sparrow uses the accrual basis, and Ted uses the cash basis. Both are on a calendar year. Since Ted is deemed to own the 80% owned by his parents and sister, he constructively owns 100% of Sparrow Corporation. If the corporation accrues the interest within the taxable year, no deduction can be taken until payment is made to Ted. ▼

SUBSTANTIATION REQUIREMENTS

The tax law is built on a voluntary system. Taxpayers file their tax returns, report income and take deductions to which they are entitled, and pay their taxes through withholding or estimated tax payments during the year. The taxpayer has the burden of proof for substantiating expenses deducted on the returns and must retain adequate records. Upon audit, the IRS will disallow any undocumented or unsubstantiated deductions. These requirements have resulted in numerous conflicts between taxpayers and the IRS.

Some events throughout the year should be documented as they occur. For example, it is generally advisable to receive a pledge payment statement from one's church, in addition to a canceled check (if available) for proper documentation of a charitable contribution.[59] In addition, for charitable contributions made after December 31, 1993, a donor must obtain a receipt from the donee for contributions of $250 or more. Other types of deductible expenditures may require receipts or some other type of support.

Specific and *more stringent* rules for deducting travel, entertainment, and gift expenses are discussed in Chapter 8. Certain mixed-use (both personal and business use) and listed property are also subject to the adequate records requirement (discussed in Chapter 7).

EXPENSES AND INTEREST RELATING TO TAX-EXEMPT INCOME

Certain income, such as interest on municipal bonds, is tax-exempt.[60] The law also allows the taxpayer to deduct expenses incurred for the production of income.[61] Deduction disallowance provisions, however, make it impossible to make money at the expense of the government by excluding interest income and deducting interest expense.[62]

---

[59] Rev.Proc. 92–71, 1992–2 C.B. 437, addresses circumstances where checks are not returned by a financial institution or where electronic transfers are made.

[60] § 103.

[61] § 212.

[62] § 265.

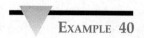

EXAMPLE 40

Sandy, a taxpayer in the 36% bracket, purchased $100,000 of 6% municipal bonds. At the same time, she used the bonds as collateral on a bank loan of $100,000 at 8% interest. A positive cash flow would result from the tax benefit as follows:

Cash paid out on loan	($8,000)
Cash received from bonds	6,000
Tax savings from deducting interest expense (36% of $8,000 interest expense)	2,880
Net positive cash flow	$ 880

To eliminate the possibility illustrated in Example 40, the Code specifically disallows as a deduction the expenses of producing tax-exempt income. Interest on any indebtedness incurred or continued to purchase or carry tax-exempt obligations also is disallowed.

Judicial Interpretations. It is often difficult to show a direct relationship between borrowings and investment in tax-exempt securities. Suppose, for example, that a taxpayer borrows money, adds it to existing funds, buys inventory and stocks, then later sells the inventory and buys municipal bonds. A series of transactions such as these can completely obscure any connection between the loan and the tax-exempt investment. One solution would be to disallow interest on any debt to the extent that the taxpayer holds any tax-exempt securities. This approach would preclude individuals from deducting part of their home mortgage interest if they owned any municipal bonds. The law was not intended to go to such extremes. As a result, judicial interpretations have tried to be reasonable in disallowing interest deductions.

In one case, a company used municipal bonds as collateral on short-term loans to meet seasonal liquidity needs.[63] The Court disallowed the interest deduction on the grounds that the company could predict its seasonal liquidity needs. The company could anticipate the need to borrow the money to continue to carry the tax-exempt securities. The same company *was* allowed an interest deduction on a building mortgage, even though tax-exempt securities it owned could have been sold to pay off the mortgage. The Court reasoned that short-term liquidity needs would have been impaired if the tax-exempt securities were sold. Furthermore, the Court ruled that carrying the tax-exempt securities bore no relationship to the long-term financing of a construction project.

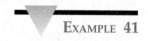

EXAMPLE 41

In January of the current year, Gayle borrowed $100,000 at 8% interest. She used the loan proceeds to purchase 5,000 shares of stock in White Corporation. In July, she sold the stock for $120,000 and reinvested the proceeds in City of Denver bonds, the income from which is tax-exempt. Assuming the $100,000 loan remained outstanding throughout the entire year, Gayle cannot deduct the interest attributable to the period in which she held the bonds. ▼

TAX PLANNING
CONSIDERATIONS

TIME VALUE OF TAX DEDUCTIONS

Cash basis taxpayers often have the ability to make early payments for their expenses at the end of the tax year. This permits the payments to be deducted currently instead of in the following tax year. In view of the time value of money,

---

[63] *The Wisconsin Cheeseman, Inc. v. U.S.,* 68–1 USTC ¶9145, 21 AFTR2d 383, 388 F.2d 420 (CA–7, 1968).

CONCEPT SUMMARY 5–2

Classification of Expenses

Expense Item	Deductible For AGI	Deductible From AGI	Not Deductible	Applicable Code §
Investment expenses				
Rent and royalty	X			§ 62(a)(4)
All other investments		X[4]		§ 212
Employee expenses				
Commuting expenses			X	§ 262
Travel and transportation[1]		X[4,5]		§ 162(a)(2)
Reimbursed expenses[1]	X			§ 62(a)(2)(A)
Moving expenses	X			§ 62(a)(15)
Entertainment[1]		X[4,5]		§ 162(a)
All other employee expenses[1]		X[4,5]		§ 162(a)
Certain expenses of performing artists	X			§ 62(a)(2)(B)
Trade or business expenses	X			§§ 162 and 62(a)(1)
Casualty losses				
Business	X			§ 165(c)(1)
Personal		X[6]		§ 165(c)(3)
Tax determination				
Collection or refund expenses	X[8]	X[4]		§§ 212 and 62(a)(1) or (4)
Bad debts	X			§§ 166 and 62(a)(1) or (3)
Medical expenses		X[7]		§ 213
Charitable contributions		X		§ 170
Taxes				
Trade or business	X			§§ 162 and 62(a)(1)
Personal taxes				
Real property		X		§ 164(a)(1)
Personal property		X		§ 164(a)(2)
State and local income		X		§ 164(a)(3)
Investigation of a business[2]	X			§§ 162 and 62(a)(1)
Interest				
Business	X			§§ 162 and 62(a)(1)
Personal		X[3]	X[9]	§ 163(a), (d), and (h)
All other personal expenses			X	§ 262

1. Deduction *for* AGI if reimbursed, an adequate accounting is made, and employee is required to repay excess reimbursements.
2. Provided certain criteria are met.
3. Subject to the excess investment interest and the qualified residence interest provisions.
4. Subject (in the aggregate) to a 2%-of-AGI floor imposed by § 67.
5. Only 50% of meals and entertainment are deductible.
6. Subject to a 10%-of-AGI floor and a $100 floor.
7. Subject to a 7.5%-of-AGI floor.
8. Only the portion relating to business, rental, or royalty income or losses.
9. Other personal interest is disallowed.

4   **LEARNING OBJECTIVE**
Identify tax planning
opportunities for maximizing
deductions and minimizing the
disallowance of deductions.

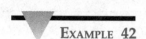

EXAMPLE 42

a tax deduction this year may be worth more than the same deduction next year. Before employing this strategy, the taxpayer must consider next year's expected income and tax rates and whether a cash-flow problem may develop from early payments. Thus, the time value of money as well as tax rate changes must be considered when an expense can be paid and deducted in either of two years.

Jena pledged $5,000 to her church's special building fund. She can make the contribution in December 1996 or January 1997. Jena is in the 36% tax bracket in 1996, and in the 31% bracket in 1997. She itemizes in both years. Assume Jena's discount rate is 8%. If she takes the deduction in 1996, she saves $365 ($1,800 – $1,435), due to the decrease in the tax rates and the time value of money.

	1996	1997
Contribution	$5,000	$5,000
Tax bracket	.36	.31
Tax savings	$1,800	$1,550
Discounted @ 8%	1.0	.926
Savings in present value	$1,800	$1,435

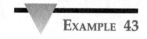

EXAMPLE 43

Assume the same facts as in Example 42, except that Jena is in the 31% bracket in both 1996 and 1997. By taking the deduction in 1996, Jena saves $115 ($1,550 – $1,435), due to the time value of money.

	1996	1997
Contribution	$5,000	$5,000
Tax bracket	.31	.31
Tax savings	$1,550	$1,550
Discounted @ 8%	1.0	.926
Savings in present value	$1,550	$1,435

UNREASONABLE COMPENSATION

In substantiating the reasonableness of a shareholder-employee's compensation, an internal comparison test is sometimes useful. If it can be shown that nonshareholder-employees and shareholder-employees in comparable positions receive comparable compensation, it is indicative that compensation is not unreasonable.

Another possibility is to demonstrate that the shareholder-employee has been underpaid in prior years. For example, the shareholder-employee may have agreed to take a less-than-adequate salary during the unprofitable formative years of the business. He or she would expect the "postponed" compensation to be paid in later, more profitable years. The agreement should be documented, if possible, in the corporate minutes.

Keep in mind that in testing for reasonableness, the *total* pay package must be considered. Look at all fringe benefits or perquisites, such as contributions by the corporation to a qualified pension plan. Even though those amounts are not immediately available to the covered shareholder-employee, they must be taken into account.

EXCESSIVE EXECUTIVE COMPENSATION

With the $1 million limit on the deduction of compensation of covered employees, many corporations and their executives must engage in additional tax planning. Previously, concerns over the deductibility of compensation related primarily to closely held corporations. The $1 million limit applies specifically to publicly held corporations. In many instances, it is now necessary for these corporations to restructure the compensation packages of their top executives in order to deduct payments in excess of $1 million. Opportunities include compensation payable on a commission basis, certain other performance-based compensation, payments to qualified retirement plans, and payments that are excludible fringe benefits.

SHIFTING DEDUCTIONS

Taxpayers should manage their obligations to avoid the loss of a deduction. Deductions can be shifted among family members, depending upon which member makes the payment. For example, a father buys a condo for his daughter and puts the title in both names. The taxpayer who makes the payment gets the deduction for the property taxes. If the condo is owned by the daughter only and her father makes the payment, neither is entitled to a deduction. In this case, the father should make a cash gift to the daughter who then makes the payment to the taxing authority.

HOBBY LOSSES

To demonstrate that an activity has been entered into for the purpose of making a profit, a taxpayer should treat the activity as a business. The business should engage in advertising, use business letterhead stationery, and maintain a business phone.

If a taxpayer's activity earns a profit in three out of five consecutive years, the presumption is that the activity is engaged in for profit. It may be possible for a cash basis taxpayer to meet these requirements by timing the payment of expenses or the receipt of revenues. The payment of certain expenses incurred before the end of the year might be made in the following year. The billing of year-end sales might be delayed so that collections are received in the following year.

Keep in mind that the three-out-of-five-years rule under § 183 is not absolute. All it does is shift the presumption. If a profit is not made in three out of five years, the losses may still be allowed if the taxpayer can show that they are due to the nature of the business. For example, success in artistic or literary endeavors can take a long time. Also, due to the present state of the economy, even full-time farmers and ranchers are often unable to show a profit. How can one expect a part-time farmer or rancher to do so?

Merely satisfying the three-out-of-five-years rule does not guarantee that a taxpayer is automatically home free. If the three years of profits are insignificant relative to the losses of other years, or if the profits are not from the ordinary operation of the business, the taxpayer is vulnerable. The IRS may still be able to establish that the taxpayer is not engaged in an activity for profit.

EXAMPLE 44

Ashley had the following gains and losses in an artistic endeavor:

1992	($ 50,000)
1993	(65,000)
1994	400
1995	200
1996	125

Under these circumstances, the IRS might try to overcome the presumption. ▼

If Ashley in Example 44 could show conformity with the factors enumerated in the Regulations or could show evidence of business hardships (e.g., injury, death, or illness), the government cannot override the presumption.[64]

CAPITAL EXPENDITURES

RRA of 1993 has modified the planning strategy associated with goodwill and covenants not to compete. Prior to RRA of 1993, on the sale of a sole proprietorship where the sales price exceeded the fair market value of the tangible assets and stated intangible assets, a natural tax conflict typically existed between the seller and the buyer. The seller's preference was for the excess amount to be allocated to goodwill. Goodwill is a capital asset whereas a covenant not to compete produces ordinary income treatment (see Chapter 13). The buyer's preference was for the excess amount to be allocated to a covenant not to compete because it could be amortized over the covenant life whereas goodwill was not eligible for amortization.

RRA of 1993 provides that both a covenant and goodwill are to be amortized over a statutory 15-year period. Therefore, the tax results for the buyer are the same. The seller's motive was not affected by the change in the law. Therefore, the seller and buyer, in negotiating the sales price, should factor in the tax benefit to the seller of having the excess amount labeled goodwill rather than a covenant not to compete. Of course, if the noncompetition aspects of a covenant are important to the buyer, part of the excess amount can be assigned to a covenant.

KEY TERMS

Accounting method, 5–9

Deductions *for* adjusted gross income, 5–2

Deductions *from* adjusted gross

income, 5–2

Hobby losses, 5–17

Ordinary and necessary, 5–6

Reasonableness, 5–7

Related-party transactions, 5–27

Vacation home, 5–20

 PROBLEM MATERIALS

DISCUSSION QUESTIONS

1. "All income must be reported and all deductions are allowed unless specifically disallowed in the Code." Discuss.

2. Discuss the difference in the tax treatment of deductions *for* and deductions *from* AGI.

---

[64] *Faulconer, Sr. v. Comm.*, 84–2 USTC ¶9955, 55 AFTR2d 85–302, 748

3. Does an expenditure that is classified as a deduction *from* AGI produce the same tax benefit as an expenditure that is classified as a deduction *for* AGI?

4. Classify each of the following expenditures as a deduction *for* AGI, a deduction *from* AGI, or not deductible:
   a. Pete gives $1,000 to his mother for her birthday.
   b. Janet gives $1,000 to the First Baptist Church.
   c. Alex pays Dr. Dafashy $1,000 for medical services rendered.
   d. Susan pays alimony of $1,000 to Herman.
   e. Rex contributes $1,000 to his pension plan.

5. Classify each of the following expenditures as a deduction *for* AGI, a deduction *from* AGI, or not deductible:
   a. Amos contributes $500 to his H.R. 10 plan (i.e., a retirement plan for a self-employed individual).
   b. Keith pays $500 of child support to his former wife, Renee, for the support of their son, Chris.
   c. Judy pays $500 for professional dues that are reimbursed by her employer.
   d. Ted pays $500 as the monthly mortgage payment on his personal residence. Of this amount, $100 represents a payment on principal, and $400 represents an interest payment.
   e. Lynn pays $500 to a moving company for moving her household goods to Detroit where she is starting a new job.

6. Larry and Susan each invest $10,000 in separate investment activities. They each incur deductible expenses of $800 associated with their respective investments. Explain why Larry's expenses are properly classified as deductions *from* AGI (itemized deductions) and Susan's expenses are appropriately classified as deductions *for* AGI.

7. List the three items that § 162 specifically excludes from classification as a trade or business expense.

8. Define and contrast the "ordinary" and "necessary" tests for business expenses.

9. Wendy, a machinist employed by Silver Airlines, owns 25 shares of Silver Airlines stock. Silver has 900,000 shares of stock outstanding. Wendy spends $800 to travel to Chicago for Silver's annual meeting. Her expenses would have been $500 more, but she was permitted to fly free on Silver. She attended both days of the shareholders' meeting and actively participated. What are the tax consequences of the trip for Wendy?

10. Sam and Vera are the owners of a corporation. To reduce the corporation's taxable income, they pay a $1,000 salary each month to their 7-year-old daughter, Peg. Why is this salary disallowed as a deduction?

11. Which of the following losses are deductible?
    a. Loss on the sale of a factory building used in a trade or business.
    b. Loss on the sale of a truck held for personal use.
    c. Loss from the destruction by a tornado of a warehouse used in a trade or business.
    d. Loss on the destruction by fire of the taxpayer's residence.
    e. Loss on the sale of Lavender Corporation stock held as an investment.

12. Distinguish between the timing for the recording of a deduction under the cash method versus the accrual method.

13. Landry, a cash basis taxpayer, decides to reduce his taxable income for 1996 by buying $10,000 worth of supplies on December 28, 1996. The supplies will be used up in 1997.
    a. Can Landry deduct this expenditure in 1996?
    b. Would your answer differ if Landry bought the supplies because a supplier was going out of business and had given him a significant discount on the supplies?

14. What is the "actually paid" requirement for the deduction of an expense by a cash basis taxpayer? Does actual payment ensure a deduction?

15. What is the significance of the all events and economic performance tests?

16. James provides a one-year warranty on the vacuum cleaners manufactured by his company. Claims under the warranty typically amount to 2% of sales. Can James use the reserve method to account for the warranty expense?

17. Are any bribes or kickbacks deductible?

18. Ted is an agent for an airline manufacturer and is negotiating a sale with a representative of the U.S. government and with a representative of a developing country. Ted's company has sufficient capacity to handle only one of the orders. Both orders will have the same contract price. Ted believes that if his employer will authorize a $500,000 payment to the representative of the foreign country, he can guarantee the sale. He is not sure that he can obtain the same result with the U.S. government. Identify the relevant tax issues for Ted.

19. Edna obtains a divorce from Ralph for which she incurs legal fees of $10,000. Distinguish between the types of expenses associated with the divorce that are deductible by Edna and those that are not deductible.

20. Stuart, an insurance salesman, is arrested for allegedly robbing a convenience store. He hires an attorney who is successful in getting the charges dropped. Is the attorney's fee deductible?

21. Linda operates a drug-running operation. Which of the following expenses she incurs can reduce taxable income?
    a. Bribes paid to border guards.
    b. Salaries to employees.
    c. Price paid for drugs purchased for resale.
    d. Kickbacks to police.
    e. Rent on an office.

22. Gordon anticipates that being positively perceived by the individual who is elected mayor will be beneficial for his business. Therefore, he contributes to the campaigns of both the Democratic and the Republican candidates. The Republican candidate is elected mayor. Can Gordon deduct any of the political contributions he made?

23. Melissa, the owner of a sole proprietorship that has 20 employees, does not provide health insurance for her employees. She is going to spend $1,500 lobbying in opposition to health care legislation that would require her to provide employee health insurance. Discuss the tax advantages and disadvantages of her paying the $1,500 to a professional lobbyist rather than spending the $1,500 on in-house lobbying expenditures.

24. What limits exist on the deductibility of executive compensation? Do the limits apply to all types of business entities? Are there any exceptions to the limitations?

25. What is the significance of one's present occupation in the deductibility of expenses incurred in investigating another business?

26. Amanda had been raising quarter horses for three years. Each year, her losses were about $15,000. She projects that her losses for the current year will be about $10,000. However, if she sells a promising mare before the end of the year, the $10,000 projected loss can be converted into a $4,000 projected profit. Without the perceived need to produce a current-year profit, Amanda would prefer to keep the mare for breeding purposes. Identify the relevant tax issues for Amanda.

27. Discuss the tax treatment of the rental of a vacation home if it is:
    a. Rented 10 days during the year.
    b. Rented 130 days during the year; used personally for 12 days.
    c. Rented for 250 days; used personally for 40 days.

28. Karen and Andy own a beach house. They have an agreement with a rental agent to rent it up to 200 days per year. For the past three years, the agent has been successful in renting it for 200 days. Karen and Andy use the beach house for one week during the summer and one week during Thanksgiving. Their daughter, Sarah, a college student, has asked if she and some friends can use the beach house for the week of spring break. Advise Karen and Andy how they should respond and identify any relevant tax issues.

29. Contrast the differing results obtained in a personal/rental situation by allocating property taxes and mortgage interest on the IRS's basis and the court's basis. Which method would the taxpayer prefer?

30. Hank was transferred from Phoenix to North Dakota on March 1 of the current year. He immediately put his home in Phoenix up for rent. The home was rented May 1 to November 30 and was vacant during the month of December. It was rented again on January 1 for six months. What expenses, if any, can Hank deduct on his return? Which deductions are *for* AGI and which ones are *from* AGI?

31. Erika would like to help her daughter Hillary and son-in-law James with what she hopes are short-term financial problems. This assistance will be in the form of paying their monthly mortgage payments for the past six months. If the payments are not made, the mortgage company will foreclose on their residence. Erika's preference is to make the payments directly to the mortgage company. However, she is willing to give the money to Hillary and James who then would pay the arrearages. Advise Erika on which option, if any, offers preferential tax treatment to her.

32. Explain which, if any, legal fees incurred obtaining a divorce are deductible. Are they deductible *for* or *from* AGI?

33. Igor repaired the roof on his factory at a cost of $1,500 in the current year. During the same year, Raisa replaced the roof on her small rental house for $1,500. Both taxpayers are on the cash basis. Are their expenditures treated the same on their tax returns? Why or why not?

34. Discuss the reasons for the disallowance of losses between related parties. Would it make any difference if a parent sold stock to an unrelated third party and the child repurchased the same number of shares of the stock in the market the same day?

35. Tara sold 100 shares of Eagle Company stock to Frank, her brother, for $8,000. She had originally paid $7,100 for the stock. Frank later sold the stock for $6,000 on the open market. What are the tax consequences to Tara and Frank? Would your answer differ if Tara had sold the stock to Frank for $6,500?

36. Helen owns 20% of Black Corporation; 20% of Black's stock is owned by Sara, Helen's mother; 15% is owned by Richard, Helen's brother; the remaining 45% is owned by unrelated parties. Helen is on the cash basis, and Black Corporation is on the accrual basis. On December 31, 1996, Black accrued Helen's salary of $5,000 and paid it on April 4, 1997. Both are on a calendar year. What is the tax effect to Helen and Black?

PROBLEMS

37. Sandra is an attorney. She incurs the following expenses when she and her employee, Fred, attend the American Bar Association convention in San Francisco:

Conference registration:

Sandra	$200
Fred	200

Airline tickets from Pittsburgh to San Francisco:

Sandra	700
Fred	400

Lodging in San Francisco:

Sandra	450
Fred	250

Calculate the effect of these expenses on Sandra's AGI.

38. Ted, Agnes, and Steve each own one-third of the stock of Swan, Inc. Each is actively employed in the activities of the business and is paid an annual salary as follows:

Ted (president)	$200,000
Agnes (vice-president)	175,000
Steve (chief financial officer)	150,000

The industry average for salaries is $25,000 less for each position. The salaries have remained relatively constant for the past three years. Swan's taxable income for the past three years has been in the $800,000 to $900,000 range. Calculate the amount of salary expense that Swan can deduct associated with these salaries.

39. Sam and his wife Vera own all of the stock of Thrush, Inc. Vera is the president and Sam is the vice-president. Vera and Sam are paid salaries of $400,000 and $300,000, respectively, each year. They consider the salaries to be reasonable based on a comparison with salaries paid for comparable positions in comparable companies. They project Thrush's taxable income for next year, before their salaries, to be $800,000. They decide to place their four teenage children on the payroll and to pay them total salaries of $100,000. The children will each work about five hours per week for Thrush.
    a. What are Sam and Vera trying to achieve by hiring the children?
    b. Calculate the tax consequences of hiring the children on Thrush, Inc., and on Sam and Vera's family.

40. Falcon, Inc., paid salaries of $400,000 to its employees during the year, which was its first year of operations. At the end of the year, Falcon had unpaid salaries of $30,000.
    a. Calculate the salary deduction if Falcon is a cash basis taxpayer.
    b. Calculate the salary deduction if Falcon is an accrual basis taxpayer.

41. Doris is the owner of a sole proprietorship that uses the cash method. She leases an office building for $24,000 for an 18-month period on October 1, 1996. In order to obtain this favorable lease rate, she pays the $24,000 at the inception of the lease. How much rent expense may Doris deduct on her 1996 tax return?

42. Duck, Inc., an accrual basis corporation, sponsored a rock concert on December 29, 1996. Gross receipts were $300,000. The following expenses were incurred and paid as indicated:

Expense		**Payment Date**
Rental of coliseum	$ 25,000	December 21, 1996
Cost of goods sold:		
Food	30,000	December 30, 1996
Souvenirs	60,000	December 30, 1996
Performers	100,000	January 5, 1997
Cleaning of coliseum	10,000	February 1, 1997

Since the coliseum was not scheduled to be used again until January 15, the company with which Duck had contracted did not actually perform the cleanup until January 8–10, 1997.

Calculate Duck's net income from the concert for tax purposes for 1996.

43. Doug incurred and paid the following expenses during the year:
    • $50 for a ticket for running a red light while he was commuting to work.
    • $100 for a ticket for parking in a handicapped parking space.
    • $200 to an attorney to represent him for the two aforesaid tickets.
    • $500 to an attorney to draft a lease agreement with a tenant for a one-year lease on an apartment that Doug owns.

    Determine the amount that Doug can deduct for each of these payments.

44. Marcia, an attorney with a leading New York law firm, is convicted of failing to file Federal income tax returns for 1993–1995. Her justification for failing to do so was the pressures of her profession (80–90 hour workweeks). She is assessed taxes, interest, and

penalties of $90,000 by the IRS. In addition, she incurs related legal fees of $60,000. Determine the amount that Marcia can deduct, and classify it as a deduction *for* or a deduction *from* AGI.

45. David runs an illegal numbers racket. His gross income was $500,000. He incurred the following expenses:

Illegal kickbacks	$20,000
Salaries	80,000
Rent	24,000
Utilities and telephone	9,000
Bribes to police	25,000
Interest	6,000
Depreciation on equipment	12,000

   a. What is his net income from this business that is includible in taxable income?
   b. If the business was an illegal drug operation, would your answer differ?

46. Edward, an attorney, is hired by a major accounting firm to represent it and its clients in dealing with members of the U.S. Congress. The accounting firm is supporting liability reform that would limit the "joint and several" liability of professionals such as attorneys and CPAs. During the year, Edward is paid $10,000 for this representation. The firm also reimburses Edward $2,500 for meal and entertainment expenses incurred in meeting with members of Congress and their staffs. In addition, the firm pays Edward $5,000 for his work in opposing legislation that would adversely affect several of its major clients. What is the amount of these payments that the firm may deduct?

47. Amber, Inc., a publicly held corporation, currently pays its president an annual salary of $900,000. In addition, it contributes $20,000 annually to a defined contribution pension plan for him. As a means of increasing company profitability, the board of directors decides to increase the president's compensation. Two proposals are being considered. Under the first proposal, the salary and pension contribution for the president would be increased by 30%. Under the second proposal, Amber would implement a performance-based compensation program that is projected to provide about the same amount of additional compensation and pension contribution for the president.
   a. Evaluate the alternatives from the perspective of Amber, Inc.
   b. Prepare a letter to Amber's board of directors that contains your recommendations. Address the letter to the board chairperson, Agnes Riddle, whose address is 100 James Tower, Cleveland, OH 44106.

48. Jenny, the owner of a very successful restaurant chain, is exploring the possibility of expanding the chain into a city in the neighboring state. She incurs $20,000 of expenses associated with this investigation. Based on the regulatory environment for restaurants in the city, she decides not to do so. During the year, she also investigates opening a hotel that will be part of a national hotel chain. Her expenses for this are $15,000. The hotel begins operations on December 1. Determine the amount that Jenny can deduct in the current year for investigating these two businesses.

49. Tim traveled to a neighboring state to investigate the purchase of two restaurants. His expenses included travel, legal, accounting, and miscellaneous expenses. The total was $12,000. He incurred the expenses in March and April 1996.
   a. What can Tim deduct in 1996 if he was in the restaurant business and did not acquire the two restaurants?
   b. What can Tim deduct in 1996 if he was in the restaurant business and acquired the two restaurants and began operating them on July 1, 1996?
   c. What can Tim deduct in 1996 if he did not acquire the two restaurants and was not in the restaurant business?
   d. What can he deduct in 1996 if he acquired the two restaurants, but was not in the restaurant business when he acquired them? Operations began on July 1, 1996.

50. Alfred conducts an activity that is appropriately classified as a hobby. The activity produces the following revenues and expenses:

Revenue	$10,000
Property taxes	3,000
Materials and supplies	2,000
Utilities	1,000
Advertising	2,500
Insurance	500
Depreciation	4,000

Without regard to this activity, Alfred's AGI is $40,000. Determine how much income Alfred must report, the amount of the expenses he is permitted to deduct, and his AGI.

51. Samantha is an executive with an AGI of $100,000 before consideration of income or loss from her miniature horse business. Her income comes from winning horse shows, stud fees, and sales of yearlings. Her home is on 20 acres, 18 of which she uses to pasture the horses and upon which she has erected stables, paddocks, fences, tack houses, and so forth.

Samantha uses an office in her home that is 10% of the square footage of the house. She uses the office exclusively for keeping records of breeding lines, histories, and show and veterinary records. Her records show the following income and expenses for the current year:

Income from fees, prizes, and sales	$22,000
Expenses	
Entry fees	1,000
Feed and veterinary bills	4,000
Supplies	900
Publications and dues	500
Travel to horse shows (no meals)	2,300
Salaries and wages of employees	8,000
Depreciation on horse equipment	3,000
Depreciation on horse farm improvements	7,000
Depreciation on 10% of home	1,000
Total home mortgage interest	24,000
Total property taxes on home	2,200
Total property taxes on horse farm improvements	800

The mortgage interest is only on her home. The horse farm improvements are not mortgaged.

How must Samantha treat the income and expenses of the operation if the miniature horse activity is held to be a hobby?

52. How would your answer in Problem 51 differ if the horse operation was held to be a business?

53. Louis makes macramé animals in his spare time. He sold $5,000 worth of animals during the year and incurred expenses as follows:

Supplies	$2,800
Depreciation on business property	1,900
Advertising	800

How are these items treated if the endeavor is a hobby? A business?

54. In 1996, Anna rented her vacation home for 60 days, used it personally for 20 days, and left it vacant for 286 days. She had the following income and expenses:

Rent income	$ 6,000	
Expenses		
Real estate taxes	2,000	
Interest on mortgage	9,000	
Utilities	600	
Repairs	1,000	
Roof replacement	12,000	
Depreciation	8,000	

Compute Anna's net rent income or loss and the amounts she can itemize on her tax return, using the court's approach in allocating property taxes and interest.

55. How would your answer in Problem 54 differ using the IRS's method of allocating property taxes and interest?

56. How would your answer in Problem 54 differ if Anna had rented the house for 90 days and had used it personally for 12 days?

57. Chee, single, age 40, had the following income and expenses in 1996:

Income	
Salary	$43,000
Rental of vacation home (rented 60 days, used personally 60 days, vacant 246 days)	4,000
Municipal bond interest	2,000
Dividend from General Motors	400
Expenses	
Interest	
On home mortgage	8,400
On vacation home	4,758
On loan used to buy municipal bonds	3,100
Taxes	
Property tax on home	2,200
Property tax on vacation home	1,098
State income tax	3,300
Charitable contributions	1,100
Tax return preparation fee	300
Utilities and maintenance on vacation home	2,600
Depreciation on rental 50% of vacation home	3,500

Calculate Chee's taxable income for 1996 before personal exemptions.

58. During the current year, Robert pays the following amounts associated with his own residence and that of his daughter, Anne:

- Property taxes:
On home owned by Robert	$3,000
On home owned by Anne	1,500

- Mortgage interest:
Associated with Robert's home	8,000
Associated with Anne's home	4,500

- Repairs to:
Robert's home	1,200
Anne's home	700

- Utilities:
  Robert's home   2,700
  Anne's home   1,600

- Replacement of roof:
  Robert's home   4,000

a. Which of these expenses can Robert deduct?
b. Which of these expenses can Anne deduct?
c. Are the deductions *for* AGI or *from* AGI (itemized)?
d. How could the tax consequences be improved?

59. Lee incurred the following expenses in the current tax year. Indicate, in the spaces provided, whether each expenditure is deductible *for* AGI, *from* AGI, or not deductible.

| | | Deductible | | Not |
Expense Item		For AGI	From AGI	Deductible
a.	Lee's personal medical expenses			
b.	Lee's dependent daughter's medical expenses			
c.	Real estate taxes on rental property			
d.	Real estate taxes on Lee's personal residence			
e.	Real estate taxes on daughter's personal residence			
f.	Lee's state income taxes			
g.	Interest on rental property mortgage			
h.	Interest on Lee's personal residence mortgage			
i.	Interest on daughter's personal residence mortgage			
j.	Interest on business loans			
k.	Charitable contributions			
l.	Depreciation on rental property			
m.	Utilities & maintenance on:			
	(1) Rental property			
	(2) Lee's home			
	(3) Daughter's home			
n.	Depreciation on auto used in Lee's business			
o.	Depreciation on Lee's personal auto			
p.	Depreciation on daughter's personal auto			

60. Janet Saxon sold stock (basis of $40,000) to her brother, Fred, for $32,000.
   a. What are the tax consequences to Janet?
   b. What are the tax consequences to Fred if he later sells the stock for $42,000? For $28,000? For $36,000?
   c. Write a letter to Janet in which you inform her of the tax consequences if she sells the stock to Fred for $32,000 and explain how a sales transaction could be structured that

would produce better tax consequences for her. Janet's address is 32 Country Lane, Lawrence, KS 66045.

61. The Robin Corporation is owned as follows:

Irene	20%
Paul, Irene's husband	20%
Sylvia, Irene's mother	15%
Ron, Irene's father	25%
Quinn, an unrelated party	20%

Robin is on the accrual basis, and Irene and Paul are on the cash basis. Irene and Paul each loaned the Robin Corporation $10,000 out of their separate funds. On December 31, 1996, Robin accrued interest at 7% on both loans. The interest was paid on February 4, 1997. What is the tax treatment of this interest expense/income to Irene, Paul, and Robin?

62. What is Kim's constructive ownership of Wren Corporation, given the following information?

Shares owned by Kim	900
Shares owned by Sam, Kim's uncle	600
Shares owned by Barbara, Kim's partner	30
Shares owned by Vera, Kim's granddaughter	670
Shares owned by unrelated parties	800

63. Chris has a brokerage account and buys on the margin, which resulted in an interest expense of $8,000 during the year. Income generated through the brokerage account was as follows:

Municipal interest	$30,000
Taxable dividends and interest	70,000

How much investment interest can Chris deduct?

64. Jay's sole proprietorship has the following assets

	Basis	Fair Market Value
Cash	$ 10,000	$ 10,000
Accounts receivable	18,000	18,000
Inventory	25,000	30,000
Patent	22,000	40,000
Land	50,000	75,000
	$125,000	$173,000

The building in which Jay's business is located is leased. The lease expires at the end of the year.

Jay is age 70 and would like to retire. He expects to be in the 36% tax bracket. Jay is negotiating the sale of the business with Lois, a key employee. They have agreed on the fair market value of the assets, as indicated above, and agree the total purchase price should be about $200,000.

a. Advise Jay regarding how the sale should be structured.

b. Advise Lois regarding how the purchase should be structured.

c. What might they do to achieve an acceptable compromise?

CUMULATIVE PROBLEMS

65. John and Mary Jane Sanders are married, filing jointly. Their address is 204 Shoe Lane, Blacksburg, VA 24061. They are expecting their first two children (twins) in early 1997. John's salary in 1996 was $85,000, from which $14,000 of Federal income tax and $3,500 of state income tax were withheld. Mary Jane made $40,000 and had $5,000 of Federal income tax and $2,000 of state income tax withheld.

    John makes alimony payments of $15,000 per year to June, his former wife. He also makes child support payments of $10,000 for his son, Rod, who lives with June except for one month in the summer when he visits John and Mary Jane.

    Mary Jane's father lived with them until his death in October. His only source of income was Social Security benefits of $4,800. Of this amount, he deposited $2,800 in a savings account. The remainder of his support, including funeral expenses of $5,000, was provided by John and Mary Jane.

    They had $2,000 of savings account interest and $1,500 of dividends during the year.

    They made charitable contributions of $3,000 during the year and paid an additional $700 in state income taxes in 1996 upon filing their 1995 state income tax return. Their deductible home mortgage interest was $8,200, and their property taxes came to $2,100. They had no other deductible expenses.

    Part 1—Tax Computation
    Calculate their tax (or refund) due for 1996. Suggested software (if available): *TurboTax* or *MacInTax*.

    Part 2—Tax Planning
    Assume that they come to you for advice in December 1996. John has learned that he will receive a $25,000 bonus. He wants to know if he should take it in December 1996 or in January 1997. Mary Jane will quit work on December 31 to stay home with the twins. Their itemized deductions will decrease by $2,000 because Mary Jane will not have state income taxes withheld. Write a letter to John and Mary Jane that contains your advice and prepare a memo for the tax files. Suggested software (if available): *TurboTax* or *MacInTax*.

66. Helen Archer, age 30, is single and lives at 120 Sanborne Avenue, Springfield, IL 60740. Her Social Security number is 648–11–9981. Helen has been divorced from her former husband, Albert, for three years. She has a son, Jason, who is age 8. His Social Security number is 648–98–3471. Helen does not wish to contribute $3 to the Presidential Election Campaign Fund.

    Helen, an advertising executive, earned a salary of $75,000 in 1995. Her employer withheld $10,200 in Federal income tax, $3,200 in state income tax, and the appropriate amount of FICA tax.

    Helen has legal custody of Jason. Jason lives with his father during summer vacation. Albert indicates that his expenses for Jason are $6,000. Helen can document that she spent $4,500 for Jason's support during 1995.

    Helen's mother died on January 7, 1995. Helen inherited assets worth $200,000 from her mother. As the sole beneficiary of her mother's life insurance policy, Helen received insurance proceeds of $100,000. Her mother's cost basis for the life insurance policy was $40,000. Helen's favorite aunt gave her $10,000 for her thirtieth birthday in October.

    On November 8, 1995, Helen sells for $19,000 Amber, Inc. stock that she had inherited from her father on December 5, 1991. His cost basis for the stock was $12,000, and the stock was worth $20,000 at the time of his death. (See Chapter 12 for basis of inherited property.) On December 1, 1995, Helen sold Falcon, Inc., stock for $15,000. She had acquired the stock on July 2, 1995, for $9,000.

    An examination of Helen's records reveals the following information:

    • Received interest income of $3,500 from First Savings Bank.

    • Received dividend income of $1,200 from Amber, Inc.

    • Received $1,700 of interest income on City of Springfield school bonds.

    • Received alimony of $40,000 from Albert.

From her checkbook records, she determines that she made the following payments during 1995,

- Charitable contributions of $1,500 to First Presbyterian Church and $800 to the American Red Cross.
- Mortgage interest on her residence of $6,500.
- Property taxes of $1,900 on her residence and $800 on her car.
- Sales taxes of $1,700.
- Estimated Federal income taxes of $17,000 and estimated state income taxes of $1,000.
- Medical expenses of $4,000 for her and $500 for Jason. Eight hundred dollars of her medical expenses were reimbursed by her medical insurance policy in December.

Calculate Helen's net tax payable or refund due for 1995. If you use tax forms, you will need Form 1040 and Schedules A, B, and D. Suggested software (if available): *TurboTax* or *MacInTax*.

Research Problems for this chapter appear at the end of Chapter 28.

TEAM PROJECT: ARTHUR ANDERSEN TAX CHALLENGE CASES

For more information on the Arthur Andersen Tax Challenge Cases, please refer to Chapter 2, page 2-41.

Information related to tax issues and problems that are discussed in this chapter may be found in the

Miller case on pages 1, 11-12, 31

Read and analyze the case you have been assigned and *identify* any issues and problems that are related to material covered in this chapter. If the information provided in the case is complete, prepare answers for this part of the case at this time. If you need information that is contained in the later parts of the case, please write a memo summarizing the questions or problems so you can prepare a complete answer at a later date.

DEDUCTIONS AND LOSSES: CERTAIN BUSINESS EXPENSES AND LOSSES

LEARNING OBJECTIVES

After completing Chapter 6, you should be able to:

1. Determine the amount, classification, and timing of the bad debt deduction.

2. Understand the tax treatment of worthless securities including § 1244 stock.

3. Distinguish between deductible and nondeductible losses of individuals.

4. Identify a casualty and determine the amount, classification, and timing of casualty and theft losses.

5. Recognize and apply the alternative tax treatments for research and experimental expenditures.

6. Recognize the impact of the net operating loss carryback and carryover provisions.

7. Identify tax planning opportunities in deducting certain business expenses, business losses, and personal losses.

OUTLINE

Working with the tax formula for individuals requires the proper classification of items that are deductible *for* adjusted gross income (AGI) and items that are deductions *from* AGI (itemized deductions). Business expenses and losses, discussed in this chapter, are reductions of gross income to arrive at the taxpayer's AGI. Expenses and losses incurred in connection with a transaction entered into for profit and attributable to rents and royalties are deducted *for* AGI. All other expenses and losses incurred in connection with a transaction entered into for profit are deducted *from* AGI.

The situation of Robert P. Groetzinger provides an interesting insight into the importance of the proper classification for the individual taxpayer. In January 1978, Groetzinger terminated his employment with a private company and devoted virtually all of his working time to pari-mutuel wagering on dog races. He had no other profession or employment, and his only sources of income, apart from his gambling winnings, were interest, dividends, and sales from investments. During the tax year in question, he went to the track six days a week and devoted 60 to 80 hours per week to preparing and making wagers on his own account.

The tax question that this case presents is whether Groetzinger's gambling activities constitute a trade or business. If the gambling is a trade or business, his gambling losses are deductions *for* AGI. If the gambling activity is not a trade or business, the losses are itemized deductions, and Groetzinger's taxes increase by $2,142.[1]

Deductible losses on personal use property are deducted as an itemized deduction. Itemized deductions are deductions *from* AGI. While the general coverage of itemized deductions is in Chapter 9, casualty and theft losses on personal use property are discussed in this chapter.

In determining the amount and timing of the deduction for bad debts, proper classification is again important. A business bad debt is classified as a deduction *for* AGI, and a nonbusiness bad debt is classified as a short-term capital loss.

Other topics discussed in Chapter 6 are research and experimental expenditures and the net operating loss deduction.

---

[1] *Groetzinger v. Comm.*, 85–2 USTC ¶9622, 56 AFTR2d 85–5683, 771 F.2d 269 (CA–7, 1985).

BAD DEBTS

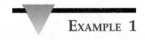

1 LEARNING OBJECTIVE
Determine the amount,
classification, and timing of the
bad debt deduction.

If a taxpayer sells goods or provides services on credit and the account receivable subsequently becomes worthless, a **bad debt** deduction is permitted only if income arising from the creation of the account receivable was previously included in income.[2] No deduction is allowed, for example, for a bad debt arising from the sale of a product or service when the taxpayer is on the cash basis because no income is reported until the cash has been collected. Permitting a bad debt deduction for a cash basis taxpayer would amount to a double deduction because the expenses of the product or service rendered are deducted when payments are made to suppliers and to employees, or at the time of the sale.

EXAMPLE 1

Tracy, an individual engaged in the practice of accounting, performed accounting services for Pat for which she charged $8,000. Pat never paid the bill, and his whereabouts are unknown.

If Tracy is an accrual basis taxpayer, the $8,000 is included in income when the services are performed. When it is determined that Pat's account will not be collected, the $8,000 is expensed as a bad debt.

If Tracy is a cash basis taxpayer, the $8,000 is not included in income until payment is received. When it is determined that Pat's account will not be collected, the $8,000 is not deducted as a bad debt expense since it was never recognized as income. ▼

A bad debt can also result from the nonrepayment of a loan made by the taxpayer or from purchased debt instruments.

SPECIFIC CHARGE-OFF METHOD

Taxpayers (other than certain financial institutions) may use only the **specific charge-off method** in accounting for bad debts. Certain financial institutions are allowed to use the **reserve method** for computing deductions for bad debts.

A taxpayer using the specific charge-off method may claim a deduction when a specific business debt becomes either partially or wholly worthless or when a specific nonbusiness debt becomes wholly worthless.[3] For the business debt, the taxpayer must satisfy the IRS that the debt is partially worthless and must demonstrate the amount of worthlessness.

If a business debt previously deducted as partially worthless becomes totally worthless in a future year, only the remainder not previously deducted can be deducted in the future year.

In the case of total worthlessness, a deduction is allowed for the entire amount in the year the debt becomes worthless. The amount of the deduction depends on the taxpayer's basis in the bad debt. If the debt arose from the sale of services or products and the face amount was previously included in income, that amount is deductible. If the taxpayer purchased the debt, the deduction is equal to the amount the taxpayer paid for the debt instrument.

One of the more difficult tasks is determining if and when a bad debt is worthless. The loss is deductible only in the year of partial or total worthlessness for business debts and only in the year of total worthlessness for nonbusiness debts. Legal proceedings need not be initiated against the debtor when the surrounding facts indicate that such action will not result in collection.

---

[2] Reg. § 1.166–1(e).

[3] § 166(a) and Reg. § 1.166.

CONCEPT SUMMARY 6–1

Specific Charge-Off Method

Expense deduction and account write-off	The expense arises and the write-off takes place when a specific business account becomes either partially or wholly worthless or when a specific nonbusiness account becomes wholly worthless.
Recovery of accounts previously written off	If the account recovered was written off during the current taxable year, the write-off entry is reversed. If the account recovered was written off during a previous taxable year, income is created subject to the tax benefit rule.

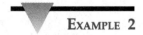
EXAMPLE 2
In 1994, Jill loaned $1,000 to Kay, who agreed to repay the loan in two years. In 1996, Kay disappeared after the note became delinquent. If a reasonable investigation by Jill indicates that she cannot find Kay or that a suit against Kay would not result in collection, Jill can deduct the $1,000 in 1996. ▼

Bankruptcy is generally an indication of at least partial worthlessness of a debt. Bankruptcy may create worthlessness before the settlement date. If this is the case, the deduction may be taken in the year of worthlessness.

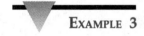
EXAMPLE 3
In Example 2, assume Kay filed for personal bankruptcy in 1995 and that the debt is a business debt. At that time, Jill learned that unsecured creditors (including Jill) were ultimately expected to receive 20¢ on the dollar. In 1996, settlement is made and Jill receives only $150. She should deduct $800 ($1,000 loan – $200 expected settlement) in 1995 and $50 in 1996 ($200 balance – $150 proceeds). ▼

If a receivable has been written off as uncollectible during the current tax year and is subsequently collected during the current tax year, the write-off entry is reversed. If a receivable has been written off as uncollectible, the collection of the receivable in a later tax year may result in income being recognized. Income will result if the deduction yielded a tax benefit in the year it was taken.

BUSINESS VERSUS NONBUSINESS BAD DEBTS

A **nonbusiness bad debt** is a debt unrelated to the taxpayer's trade or business either when it was created or when it became worthless. The nature of a debt depends on whether the lender was engaged in the business of lending money or whether there is a proximate relationship between the creation of the debt and the lender's trade or business. The use to which the borrowed funds are put by the debtor is of no consequence. Loans to relatives or friends are the most common type of nonbusiness bad debt.

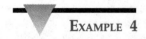
EXAMPLE 4
José loaned his friend, Esther, $1,500. Esther used the money to start a business, which subsequently failed. Even though proceeds of the loan were used in a business, the loan is a nonbusiness bad debt because the business was Esther's, not José's. ▼

The distinction between a business bad debt and a nonbusiness bad debt is important. A **business bad debt** is deductible as an ordinary loss in the year incurred, whereas a nonbusiness bad debt is always treated as a short-term capital loss. Thus, regardless of the age of a nonbusiness bad debt, the deduction may be of limited benefit due to the capital loss limitations on deductibility in any one year. The maximum amount of a net short-term capital loss that an individual can deduct against ordinary income in any one year is $3,000 (see Chapter 13 for a detailed discussion). Although no deduction is allowed when a nonbusiness bad debt is partially worthless, the taxpayer is entitled to deduct the net amount of the loss upon final settlement.

The following example is an illustration of business bad debts adapted from the Regulations.[4]

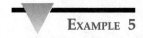
EXAMPLE 5

In 1995, Leif sold his business but retained a claim (note or account receivable) against Bob. The claim became worthless in 1996. Leif's loss is treated as a business bad debt because the debt was created in the conduct of his former trade or business. Leif is accorded business bad debt treatment even though he was holding the note as an investor and was no longer in a trade or business when the claim became worthless. ▼

The nonbusiness bad debt provisions are *not* applicable to corporations. It is assumed that any loans made by a corporation are related to its trade or business. Therefore, any bad debts of a corporation are business bad debts.

LOANS BETWEEN RELATED PARTIES

Loans between related parties (especially family members) raise the issue of whether the transaction was a *bona fide* loan or a gift. The Regulations state that a bona fide debt arises from a debtor-creditor relationship based on a valid and enforceable obligation to pay a fixed or determinable sum of money. Thus, individual circumstances must be examined to determine whether advances between related parties are gifts or loans. Some considerations are these:

- Was a note properly executed?
- Was there a reasonable rate of interest?
- Was collateral provided?
- What collection efforts were made?
- What was the intent of the parties?

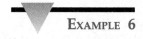
EXAMPLE 6

Lana loans $2,000 to her widowed mother for an operation. Lana's mother owns no property and is not employed, and her only income consists of Social Security benefits. No note is issued for the loan, no provision for interest is made, and no repayment date is mentioned. In the current year, Lana's mother dies leaving no estate. Assuming the loan is not repaid, Lana cannot take a deduction for a nonbusiness bad debt because the facts indicate that no debtor-creditor relationship existed. ▼

LOSS OF DEPOSITS IN INSOLVENT FINANCIAL INSTITUTIONS

Qualified individuals can *elect* to deduct losses on deposits in qualified financial institutions as personal casualty losses in the year in which the amount of the loss can be reasonably estimated. If the election is made to treat a loss on a deposit as a personal casualty loss, no bad debt deduction for the loss is allowed.[5] As a

---

[4] Reg. § 1.166–5(d).

[5] § 165(l).

TAX IN THE NEWS

FAMILY BAD DEBTS CAN BE DEDUCTED UNDER THE RIGHT CIRCUMSTANCES

A father who lived in Tennessee loaned his daughter $37,500 for a skating rink business. Although the loan was not evidenced by a note with a market rate of interest and a specified repayment schedule, the father had a long history of making such loans to his relatives and of being repaid (e.g., eight other loans between 1985 and 1988). The daughter was a skater and thought she would be qualified to run this type of business. The daughter repaid $2,000, but the business failed two years later. No subsequent payments were made, and the daughter declared bankruptcy under Chapter 7 the following year.

The father deducted the $35,500 on his income tax return as a nonbusiness bad debt. According to the IRS, the father made no attempt to collect the debt. Therefore, since this was a family situation, the IRS disallowed the deduction.

The Tax Court sided with the father. Since the daughter declared bankruptcy, attempts by the father to collect would have been futile. Buttressing the father's position even prior to the bankruptcy was his familiarity with the daughter's business affairs (i.e., the amount of her outstanding debts, her frequent request to borrow additional funds, and her landlord's seizure of her business assets). He knew that even if he tried to collect, he would be unsuccessful. In addition, the fact that he had made loans to other family members that had been repaid supported his position that he expected to be repaid.

SOURCE: *Loy E. Bowman*, T.C.Memo. 1995–259, 69 TCM 2886.

personal casualty loss, the loss is subject to the $100 per event floor and the 10 percent-of-AGI aggregate floor. Both floors limiting casualty losses are explained later in the chapter. The amount of loss to be recognized under the election is the difference between (1) the taxpayer's basis in the deposit and (2) a reasonable estimate of the amount to be received.

A *qualified individual* is any individual other than:

- An owner of 1 percent or more of the value of the stock of the institution in which the loss was sustained.
- An officer of the institution.
- Certain relatives and other persons who are tax-related to such owners and officers.

A *qualified financial institution* is a commercial bank, thrift institution, insured credit union, or any similar institution chartered and supervised under Federal or state law. A *deposit*, for purposes of this provision, is any deposit, withdrawal certificate, or withdrawable or repurchasable share of or in a qualified financial institution. The term *insolvent* generally denotes a situation where the liabilities exceed the fair market value of the assets.

If the individual does not elect to deduct the loss as a casualty loss, it is treated as a nonbusiness bad debt and, hence, as a short-term capital loss. As a short-term capital loss, it is subject to the capital loss limitation rules (see the discussion in Chapter 13).

CONCEPT SUMMARY 6–2

Bad Debt Deductions

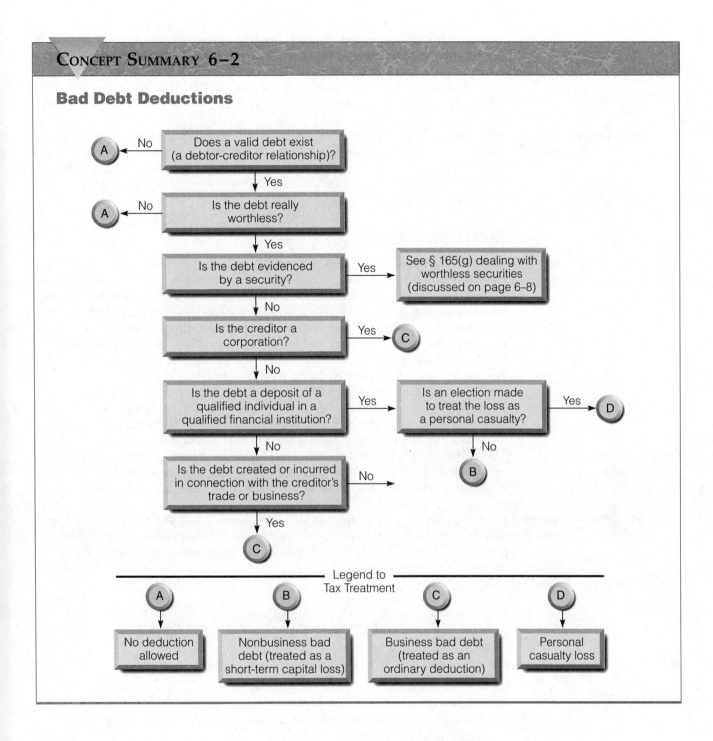

Legend to Tax Treatment

- **A** — No deduction allowed
- **B** — Nonbusiness bad debt (treated as a short-term capital loss)
- **C** — Business bad debt (treated as an ordinary deduction)
- **D** — Personal casualty loss

WORTHLESS SECURITIES

2 **LEARNING OBJECTIVE**
Understand the tax treatment of worthless securities including § 1244 stock.

A loss is allowed for securities that become *completely* worthless during the year (**worthless securities**).[6] Such securities are shares of stock, bonds, notes, or other evidence of indebtedness issued by a corporation or government. The losses

---

[6]§ 165(g).

generated are treated as capital losses deemed to have occurred on the *last day* of the taxable year. By treating the loss as having occurred on the last day of the taxable year, a loss that would otherwise have been classified as short term (if the date of worthlessness was used) may be classified as a long-term capital loss. Capital losses may be of limited benefit due to the $3,000 capital loss limitation.

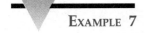

EXAMPLE 7

Ali, a calendar year taxpayer, owns stock in Owl Corporation (a publicly held company). The stock was acquired as an investment on November 30, 1995, at a cost of $5,000. On April 1, 1996, the stock became worthless. Since the stock is deemed to have become worthless as of December 31 of 1996, Ali has a capital loss from an asset held for 13 months (a long term capital loss). ▼

SMALL BUSINESS STOCK

The general rule is that shareholders receive capital gain or loss treatment upon the sale or exchange of stock. However, it is possible to receive an ordinary loss deduction if the loss is sustained on **small business stock (§ 1244 stock).** This loss could arise from a sale of the stock or from the stock becoming worthless. Only *individuals*[7] who acquired the stock *from* the corporation are eligible to receive ordinary loss treatment under § 1244. The ordinary loss treatment is limited to $50,000 ($100,000 for married individuals filing jointly) per year. Losses on § 1244 stock in excess of the statutory limits receive capital loss treatment.

The corporation must meet certain requirements for the loss on § 1244 stock to be treated as an *ordinary*—rather than a capital—loss. The major requirement is that the total amount of money and other property received by the corporation for stock as a contribution to capital (or paid-in surplus) does not exceed $1 million. The $1 million test is made at the time the stock is issued. Section 1244 stock can be common or preferred stock. Section 1244 applies only to losses. If § 1244 stock is sold at a gain, the Section has no application, and the gain is capital gain.

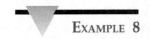

EXAMPLE 8

On July 1, 1994, Iris, a single individual, purchased 100 shares of Eagle Corporation common stock for $100,000. The Eagle stock qualified as § 1244 stock. On June 20, 1996, Iris sold all of the Eagle stock for $20,000. Because the Eagle stock is § 1244 stock, Iris would have $50,000 of ordinary loss and $30,000 of long-term capital loss. ▼

LOSSES OF INDIVIDUALS

3   LEARNING OBJECTIVE
Distinguish between deductible and nondeductible losses of individuals.

An individual may deduct the following losses under § 165(c):

- Losses incurred in a trade or business.
- Losses incurred in a transaction entered into for profit.
- Losses caused by fire, storm, shipwreck, or other casualty or by theft.

An individual taxpayer may deduct losses to property used in the taxpayer's trade or business or losses to property used in a transaction entered into for profit. Examples include a loss on property used in a proprietorship, a loss on property held for rent, or a loss on stolen bearer bonds. Note that an individual's losses on property used in a trade or business or on transactions entered into for profit are not limited to losses caused by fire, storm, shipwreck, or other casualty or by theft.

[7]The term "individuals" for this purpose includes a partnership but not a trust or an estate.

An individual taxpayer suffering losses from damage to nonbusiness property can deduct only those losses attributable to fire, storm, shipwreck, or other casualty or theft. Although the meaning of the terms *fire, storm, shipwreck,* and *theft* is relatively free from dispute, the term *other casualty* needs further clarification. It means casualties analogous to fire, storm, or shipwreck. The term also includes accidental loss of property provided the loss qualifies under the same rules as any other casualty. These rules are that the loss must result from an event that is (1) identifiable; (2) damaging to property; and (3) sudden, unexpected, and unusual in nature.

A *sudden event* is one that is swift and precipitous and not gradual or progressive. An *unexpected event* is an event that is ordinarily unanticipated and occurs without the intent of the individual who suffers the loss. An *unusual event* is one that is extraordinary and nonrecurring and does not commonly occur during the activity in which the taxpayer was engaged when the destruction occurred.[8] Examples include hurricanes, tornadoes, floods, storms, shipwrecks, fires, auto accidents, mine cave-ins, sonic booms, and vandalism. Weather that causes damages (drought, for example) must be unusual and severe for the particular region. Damage must be to the taxpayer's property to qualify as a **casualty loss.**

A taxpayer can take a deduction for a casualty loss from an automobile accident only if the damage was not caused by the taxpayer's willful act or willful negligence.

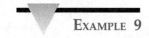

EXAMPLE 9

Ted parks his car on a hill and fails to set the brake properly and to curb the wheels. As a result of Ted's negligence, the car rolls down the hill and is damaged. The repairs to Ted's car should qualify for casualty loss treatment since Ted's act of negligence appears to be simple rather than willful. ▼

EVENTS THAT ARE NOT CASUALTIES

4 LEARNING OBJECTIVE
Identify a casualty and determine the amount, classification, and timing of casualty and theft losses.

Not all acts of God are treated as casualty losses for income tax purposes. Because a casualty must be sudden, unexpected, and unusual, progressive deterioration (such as erosion due to wind or rain) is not a casualty because it does not meet the suddenness test.

Examples of nonsudden events that generally do not qualify as casualties include disease and insect damages. When the damage was caused by termites over a period of several years, some courts have disallowed a casualty loss deduction.[9] On the other hand, some courts have held that termite damage over periods of up to 15 months after infestation constituted a sudden event and was, therefore, deductible as a casualty loss.[10] Despite the existence of some judicial support for the deductibility of termite damage as a casualty loss, the current position of the IRS is that termite damage is not deductible.[11]

Other examples of events that are not casualties are losses resulting from a decline in value rather than an actual loss of the property. No loss was allowed where the taxpayer's home declined in value as a result of a landslide that destroyed neighboring homes but did no actual damage to the taxpayer's home.[12] Similarly, a taxpayer was allowed a loss for the actual flood damage to his

[8] Rev.Rul. 72–592, 1972–2 C.B. 101.

[9] *Fay v. Helvering*, 41–2 USTC ¶9494, 27 AFTR 432, 120 F.2d 253 (CA–2, 1941); *U.S. v. Rogers*, 41–1 USTC ¶9442, 27 AFTR 423, 120 F.2d 244 (CA–9, 1941).

[10] *Rosenberg v. Comm.*, 52–2 USTC ¶9377, 42 AFTR 303, 198 F.2d 46 (CA–8, 1952); *Shopmaker v. U.S.*, 54–1 USTC ¶9195, 45 AFTR 758, 119 F. Supp. 705 (D.Ct.Mo., 1953).

[11] Rev.Rul. 63–232, 1963–2 C.B. 97.

[12] *H. Pulvers v. Comm.*, 69–1 USTC ¶9222, 23 AFTR2d 69–678, 407 F.2d 838 (CA–9, 1969).

property but not for the decline in market value due to the property's being flood-prone.[13]

THEFT LOSSES

Theft includes, but is not necessarily limited to, larceny, embezzlement, and robbery.[14] Theft does not include misplaced items.[15]

Theft losses are computed like other casualty losses (discussed in the following section), but the *timing* for recognition of the loss differs. A theft loss is deducted in the year of discovery, not the year of the theft (unless, of course, the discovery occurs in the same year as the theft). If, in the year of the discovery, a claim exists (e.g., against an insurance company) and there is a reasonable expectation of recovering the adjusted basis of the asset from the insurance company, no deduction is permitted.[16] If, in the year of settlement, the recovery is less than the asset's adjusted basis, a partial deduction may be available. If the recovery is greater than the asset's adjusted basis, gain may be recognized.

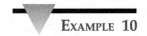

EXAMPLE 10

Keith's new sailboat, which he uses for personal purposes, was stolen from the storage marina in December 1994. He discovered the loss on June 3, 1995, and filed a claim with his insurance company that was settled on January 30, 1996. Assuming there is a reasonable expectation of full recovery, no deduction is allowed in 1995. A partial deduction may be available in 1996 if the actual insurance proceeds are less than the lower of the fair market value or the adjusted basis of the asset. (Loss measurement rules are discussed later in this chapter.) ▼

ETHICAL
CONSIDERATIONS

Deducting a Theft Loss

T heft losses of personal use assets are itemized deductions in the year of discovery. The taxpayer must show that the property was actually stolen. Losses due to mislaying or losing property cannot be deducted. If there is no positive proof that a theft occurred, all of the details and evidence should be presented. If the reasonable inferences point to a theft, the Tax Court has allowed a deduction. If the inferences point to a mysterious (unexplained) disappearance, however, the deduction will be disallowed.

A taxpayer went shopping in a major city, riding the subway to and from the city. During the day, he purchased items using money from his wallet. When he arrived home, his wallet was missing. He is considering claiming a theft loss deduction for the wallet and the money it contained.

WHEN TO DEDUCT CASUALTY LOSSES

General Rule.   Generally, a casualty loss is deducted in the year the loss occurs. However, no casualty loss is permitted if a reimbursement claim with a *reasonable prospect of full recovery* exists.[17] If the taxpayer has a partial claim, only part of the loss can be claimed in the year of the casualty, and the remainder is deducted in the year the claim is settled.

---

[13] *S. L. Solomon*, 39 TCM 1282, T.C.Memo. 1980–87.
[14] Reg. § 1.165–8(d).
[15] *Mary Francis Allen*, 16 T.C. 163 (1951).

[16] Reg. §§ 1.165–1(d)(2) and 1.165–8(a)(2).
[17] Reg. § 1.165–1(d)(2)(i).

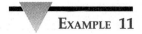

EXAMPLE 11

Chee's new sailboat was completely destroyed by fire in 1996. Its cost and fair market value were $10,000. Chee's only claim against the insurance company was on a $7,000 policy that was not settled by year-end. The following year, 1997, Chee settled with the insurance company for $6,000. Chee is entitled to a $3,000 deduction in 1996 and a $1,000 deduction in 1997. If Chee held the sailboat for personal use, the $3,000 deduction in 1996 would be reduced first by $100 and then by 10% of Chee's 1996 AGI. The $1,000 deduction in 1997 would be reduced by 10% of Chee's 1997 AGI (see the following discussion on the $100 and 10% floors). ▼

If a taxpayer receives reimbursement for a casualty loss sustained and deducted in a previous year, an amended return is not filed for that year. Instead, the taxpayer must include the reimbursement in gross income on the return for the year in which it is received to the extent that the previous deduction resulted in a tax benefit.

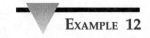

EXAMPLE 12

Fran had a deductible casualty loss of $5,000 on her 1995 tax return. Fran's taxable income for 1995 was $60,000. In June 1996, Fran was reimbursed $3,000 for the prior year's casualty loss. Fran would include the entire $3,000 in gross income for 1996 because the deduction in 1995 produced a tax benefit. ▼

Disaster Area Losses. An exception to the general rule for the time of deduction is allowed for **disaster area losses,** which are casualties sustained in an area designated as a disaster area by the President of the United States.[18] In such cases, the taxpayer may *elect* to treat the loss as having occurred in the taxable year immediately *preceding* the taxable year in which the disaster actually occurred. The rationale for this exception is to provide immediate relief to disaster victims in the form of accelerated tax benefits.

If the due date, plus extensions, for the prior year's return has not passed, a taxpayer makes the election to claim the disaster area loss on the prior year's tax return. If the disaster occurs after the prior year's return has been filed, it is necessary to file either an amended return or a refund claim. In any case, the taxpayer must show clearly that such an election is being made.

Disaster loss treatment also applies in the case of a personal residence that has been rendered unsafe for use as a residence because of a disaster. This provision applies when, within 120 days after the President designates the area as a disaster area, the state or local government where the residence is located orders the taxpayer to demolish or relocate the residence.[19]

MEASURING THE AMOUNT OF LOSS

Amount of Loss. The rules for determining the amount of a loss depend in part on whether business use, income-producing use, or personal use property was involved. Another factor that must be considered is whether the property was partially or completely destroyed.

If business property or property held for the production of income (e.g., rental property) is *completely destroyed*, the loss is equal to the adjusted basis of the property at the time of destruction.

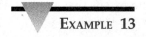

EXAMPLE 13

Vicki's automobile, which was used only for business purposes, was destroyed by fire. Vicki had unintentionally allowed her insurance coverage to expire. The fair market value of the

---

[18]§ 165(h).   [19]§ 165(k).

TAX IN THE NEWS

Is 1995 the Year of the Hurricane?

I s 1995 the Year of the Hurricane? Based on the frequency of the storms and the severity of the damage, many residents of the Caribbean would respond yes.

Hurricane Marilyn left St. Thomas in shambles. This was the fourth storm to hit the Caribbean islands in a four-week period. In addition to a death toll of nine on St. Thomas, Marilyn destroyed 25 percent of the houses on the island and damaged most of the rest. Yachts were blown onto the highways and cars into the sea. Roofs were nowhere to be seen on houses where only the walls were left standing. St. Thomas lost electricity, telephone service, and water.

President Clinton declared the U.S. Virgin Islands and Puerto Rico disaster areas. This declaration made the islands eligible for federal emergency relief and for disaster area treatment for Federal income tax purposes. Taxpayers suffering losses have the option of deducting the losses on their 1994 or 1995 Federal income tax returns.

automobile was $9,000 at the time of the fire, and its adjusted basis was $10,000. Vicki is allowed a loss deduction of $10,000 (the basis of the automobile). The $10,000 loss is a deduction *for* AGI. ▼

A different measurement rule applies for *partial destruction* of business property and income-producing property and for *partial* or *complete destruction* of personal use property. In these situations, the loss is the *lesser* of the following:

• The adjusted basis of the property.
• The difference between the fair market value of the property before the event and the fair market value immediately after the event.

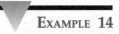

EXAMPLE 14

Kelly's uninsured automobile, which was used only for business purposes, was damaged in a wreck. At the date of the wreck, the fair market value of the automobile was $12,000, and its adjusted basis was $9,000. After the wreck, the automobile was appraised at $4,000. Kelly's loss deduction is $8,000 (the lesser of the adjusted basis or the decrease in fair market value). The $8,000 loss is a deduction *for* AGI. ▼

The deduction for the loss of property that is part business and part personal must be computed separately for the business portion and the personal portion.

Any insurance recovery reduces the loss for business, production of income, and personal use losses. In fact, a taxpayer may realize a gain if the insurance proceeds exceed the amount of the loss. Chapter 13 discusses the treatment of net gains and losses on business property and income-producing property.

A taxpayer is not permitted to deduct a casualty loss for damage to insured personal use property unless he or she files a *timely insurance claim* with respect to the damage to the property. This rule applies to the extent that any insurance policy provides for full or partial reimbursement for the loss.[20]

---

[20] § 165(h)(4)(E).

Generally, an appraisal before and after the casualty is needed to measure the amount of the loss. However, the *cost of repairs* to the damaged property is acceptable as a method of establishing the loss in value provided the following criteria are met:

- The repairs are necessary to restore the property to its condition immediately before the casualty.
- The amount spent for such repairs is not excessive.
- The repairs do not extend beyond the damage suffered.
- The value of the property after the repairs does not, as a result of the repairs, exceed the value of the property immediately before the casualty.[21]

ETHICAL
CONSIDERATIONS **Deducting the Cost of Repairs**

Twenty years ago, Mary purchased a home for $140,000. The house was fairly new and fully landscaped. On July 15, of the current year, a severe storm blew down several large pine trees in front of the home. Mary paid a local nursery $4,000 to replace the trees with comparable trees. Because Mary's homeowners insurance excludes damage to trees, Mary intends to deduct $4,000 as a casualty loss on her Federal income tax return.

Reduction for $100 and 10 Percent-of-AGI Floors. The amount of the loss for personal use property must be further reduced by a $100 *per event* floor and a 10 percent-of-AGI *aggregate* floor.[22] The $100 floor applies separately to each casualty and applies to the entire loss from each casualty (e.g., if a storm damages both a taxpayer's residence and automobile, only $100 is subtracted from the total amount of the loss). The losses are then added together, and the total is reduced by 10 percent of the taxpayer's AGI. The resulting loss is the taxpayer's itemized deduction for casualty and theft losses.

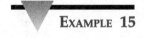

EXAMPLE 15

Rocky, who had AGI of $30,000, was involved in a motorcycle accident. His motorcycle, which was used only for personal use and had a fair market value of $12,000 and an adjusted basis of $9,000, was completely destroyed. He received $5,000 from his insurance company. Rocky's casualty loss deduction is $900 [$9,000 basis – $5,000 insurance – $100 floor – $3,000 (.10 × $30,000 AGI)]. The $900 casualty loss is an itemized deduction (*from* AGI). ▼

When a nonbusiness casualty loss is spread between two taxable years because of the *reasonable prospect of recovery* doctrine, the loss in the second year is not reduced by the $100 floor. This result occurs because this floor is imposed per event and has already reduced the amount of the loss in the first year. However, the loss in the second year is still subject to the 10 percent floor based on the taxpayer's second-year AGI (refer to Example 11).

Taxpayers who suffer qualified disaster area losses can elect to deduct the losses in the year preceding the year of occurrence. The disaster loss is treated as having occurred in the preceding taxable year. Hence, the 10 percent of AGI floor is determined by using the AGI of the year for which the deduction is claimed.[23]

[21] Reg. § 1.165–7(a)(2)(ii).
[22] § 165(c)(3).

[23] § 165(i).

Multiple Losses. The rules for computing loss deductions where multiple losses have occurred are explained in Examples 16 and 17.

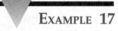
EXAMPLE 16

During the year, Tim had the following casualty losses:

		Fair Market Value of Asset		
Asset	Adjusted Basis	Before the Casualty	After the Casualty	Insurance Recovery
A	$900	$600	$–0–	$400
B	300	800	250	100

Assets A and B were used in Tim's business at the time of the casualty. The following losses are allowed:

Asset A: $500. The complete destruction of a business asset results in a deduction of the adjusted basis of the property (reduced by any insurance recovery) regardless of the asset's fair market value.

Asset B: $200. The partial destruction of a business (or personal use) asset results in a deduction equal to the lesser of the adjusted basis ($300) or the decline in value ($550), reduced by any insurance recovery ($100).

Both Asset A and Asset B losses are deductions *for* AGI. The $100 floor and the 10%-of-AGI floor do not apply because the assets are business assets. ▼

EXAMPLE 17

During the year, Emily had AGI of $20,000 and the following casualty losses:

		Fair Market Value of Asset		
Asset	Adjusted Basis	Before the Casualty	After the Casualty	Insurance Recovery
A	$ 900	$ 600	$ –0–	$200
B	2,500	4,000	1,000	–0–
C	800	400	100	250

Assets A, B, and C were held for personal use, and the losses to these three assets are from three different casualties. The loss for each asset is computed as follows:

Asset A: $300. The lesser of the adjusted basis of $900 or the $600 decline in value, reduced by the insurance recovery of $200, minus the $100 floor.

Asset B: $2,400. The lesser of the adjusted basis of $2,500 or the $3,000 decline in value, minus the $100 floor.

Asset C: $0. The lesser of the adjusted basis of $800 or the $300 decline in value, reduced by the insurance recovery of $250, minus the $100 floor.

Emily's itemized casualty loss deduction for the year is $700:

Asset A loss	$ 300
Asset B loss	2,400
Asset C loss	–0–
Total loss	$ 2,700
Less: 10% of AGI (10% × $20,000)	(2,000)
Itemized casualty loss deduction	$ 700

▼

STATUTORY FRAMEWORK FOR DEDUCTING LOSSES OF INDIVIDUALS

Casualty and theft losses incurred by an individual in connection with a trade or business are deductible *for* AGI.[24] These losses are not subject to the $100 per event and the 10 percent-of-AGI limitations.

Casualty and theft losses incurred by an individual in a transaction entered into for profit are not subject to the $100 per event and the 10 percent-of-AGI limitations. If these losses are attributable to rents or royalties, the deduction is *for* AGI.[25] However, if these losses are not connected with property held for the production of rents and royalties, they are deductions *from* AGI. More specifically, these losses are classified as other miscellaneous itemized deductions. An example of this type of loss would be the theft of a security. The aggregate of certain miscellaneous itemized deductions is subject to a 2 percent-of-AGI floor (explained in Chapter 8).

Casualty and theft losses attributable to personal use property are subject to the $100 per event and the 10 percent-of-AGI limitations. These losses are itemized deductions, but they are not subject to the 2 percent-of-AGI floor.[26]

PERSONAL CASUALTY GAINS AND LOSSES

If a taxpayer has personal casualty and theft gains as well as losses, a special set of rules applies for determining the tax consequences. A **personal casualty gain** is the recognized gain from a casualty or theft of personal use property. A **personal casualty loss** for this purpose is a casualty or theft loss of personal use property after the application of the $100 floor. A taxpayer who has both gains and losses for the taxable year must first net (offset) the personal casualty gains and personal casualty losses. If the gains exceed the losses, the gains and losses are treated as gains and losses from the sale of capital assets. The capital gains and losses are short term or long term, depending on the period the taxpayer held each of the assets. In the netting process, personal casualty and theft gains and losses are not netted with the gains and losses on business and income-producing property.

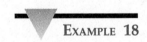

EXAMPLE 18

During the year, Cliff had the following personal casualty gains and losses (after deducting the $100 floor):

Asset	Holding Period	Gain or (Loss)
A	Three months	($ 300)
B	Three years	(2,400)
C	Two years	3,200

Cliff would compute the tax consequences as follows:

Personal casualty gain	$ 3,200
Personal casualty loss ($300 + $2,400)	(2,700)
Net personal casualty gain	$ 500

---

[24] § 62(a)(1).
[25] § 62(a)(4).

[26] § 67(b)(3).

CONCEPT SUMMARY 6–3

Casualty Gains and Losses

	Business Use or Income-Producing Property	Personal Use Property
Event creating the loss	Any event.	Casualty or theft.
Amount	The lesser of the decline in fair market value or the adjusted basis, but always the adjusted basis if the property is totally destroyed.	The lesser of the decline in fair market value or the adjusted basis.
Insurance	Insurance proceeds received reduce the amount of the loss.	Insurance proceeds received (or for which there is an unfiled claim) reduce the amount of the loss.
$100 floor	Not applicable.	Applicable per event.
Gains and losses	Gains and losses are netted (see detailed discussion in Chapter 13).	Personal casualty and theft gains and losses are netted.
Gains exceeding losses		The gains and losses are treated as gains and losses from the sale of capital assets.
Losses exceeding gains		The gains—and the losses to the extent of gains—are treated as ordinary items in computing AGI. The losses in excess of gains, to the extent they exceed 10% of AGI, are itemized deductions.

Cliff would treat all of the gains and losses as capital gains and losses and would have the following:

Short-term capital loss (Asset A)	$ 300
Long-term capital loss (Asset B)	2,400
Long-term capital gain (Asset C)	3,200

If personal casualty losses exceed personal casualty gains, all gains and losses are treated as ordinary items. The gains—and the losses to the extent of gains—are treated as ordinary income and ordinary loss in computing AGI. Losses in excess of gains are deducted as itemized deductions to the extent the losses exceed 10 percent of AGI.[27]

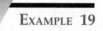

EXAMPLE 19

During the year, Hazel had AGI of $20,000 and the following personal casualty gain and loss (after deducting the $100 floor):

Asset	Holding Period	Gain or (Loss)
A	Three years	($2,700)
B	Four months	200

---

[27]§ 165(h).

Hazel would compute the tax consequences as follows:

Personal casualty loss	($2,700)
Personal casualty gain	200
Net personal casualty loss	($2,500)

Hazel would treat the gain and the loss as ordinary items. The $200 gain and $200 of the loss would be included in computing AGI. Hazel's itemized deduction for casualty losses would be computed as follows:

Casualty loss in excess of gain ($2,700 – $200)	$ 2,500
Less: 10% of AGI (10% × $20,000)	(2,000)
Itemized deduction	$ 500

▼

RESEARCH AND EXPERIMENTAL EXPENDITURES

5 **LEARNING OBJECTIVE** Recognize and apply the alternative tax treatments for research and experimental expenditures.

Section 174 covers the treatment of research and experimental expenditures. The Regulations define **research and experimental expenditures** as follows:

> . . . all such costs incident to the development of an experimental or pilot model, a plant process, a product, a formula, an invention, or similar property, and the improvement of already existing property of the type mentioned. The term does not include expenditures such as those for the ordinary testing or inspection of materials or products for quality control or those for efficiency surveys, management studies, consumer surveys, advertising, or promotions.[28]

Expenses in connection with the acquisition or improvement of land or depreciable property are not research and experimental expenditures. Rather, they increase the basis of the land or depreciable property. However, depreciation on a building used for research may be a research and experimental expense. Only the depreciation that is a research and experimental expense (not the cost of the asset) is subject to the three alternatives discussed below.

The law permits the following *three alternatives* for the handling of research and experimental expenditures:

- Expensed in the year paid or incurred.
- Deferred and amortized.
- Capitalized.

If the costs are capitalized, a deduction is not available until the research project is abandoned or is deemed worthless. Since many products resulting from research projects do not have a definite and limited useful life, a taxpayer should ordinarily elect to write off the expenditures immediately or to defer and amortize them. It is generally preferable to elect an immediate write-off of the research expenditures because of the time value of the tax deduction.

The law also provides for a research activities credit. The credit amounts to 20 percent of certain research and experimental expenditures.[29] (The credit is discussed more fully in Chapter 11.)

[28] Reg. § 1.174–2(a)(1).
[29] § 41. See the information in Chapter 11 on the termination date for the research activities credit.

EXPENSE METHOD

A taxpayer can elect to expense all of the research and experimental expenditures incurred in the current year and all subsequent years. The consent of the IRS is not required if the method is adopted for the first taxable year in which such expenditures were paid or incurred. Once the election is made, the taxpayer must continue to expense all qualifying expenditures unless a request for a change is made to, and approved by, the IRS. In certain instances, a taxpayer may incur research and experimental expenditures before actually engaging in any trade or business activity. In such instances, the Supreme Court has applied a liberal standard of deductibility and permitted a deduction in the year of incurrence.[30]

DEFERRAL AND AMORTIZATION METHOD

Alternatively, research and experimental expenditures may be deferred and amortized if the taxpayer makes an election.[31] Under the election, research and experimental expenditures are amortized ratably over a period of not less than 60 months. A deduction is allowed beginning with the month in which the taxpayer first realizes benefits from the experimental expenditure. The election is binding, and a change requires permission from the IRS.

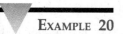

EXAMPLE 20

Gold Corporation decided to develop a new line of adhesives. The project was begun in 1996. Gold incurred the following expenses in 1996 in connection with the project:

Salaries	$25,000
Materials	8,000
Depreciation on machinery	6,500

Gold incurred the following expenses in 1997 in connection with the project:

Salaries	$18,000
Materials	2,000
Depreciation on machinery	5,700

The benefits from the project will be realized starting in March 1998. If Gold Corporation elects a 60-month deferral and amortization period, there will be no deduction prior to March 1998, the month benefits from the project begin to be realized. The deduction for 1998 would be $10,867, computed as follows:

Salaries ($25,000 + $18,000)	$43,000
Materials ($8,000 + $2,000)	10,000
Depreciation ($6,500 + $5,700)	12,200
Total	$65,200
$65,200 × (10 months/60 months) =	$10,867

▼

The option to treat research and experimental expenditures as deferred expense is usually employed when a company does not have sufficient income to

---

[30] *Snow v. Comm.*, 74–1 USTC ¶9432, 33 AFTR2d 74–1251, 94 S.Ct. 1876 (USSC, 1974).
[31] § 174(b)(2).

A BETTER BANANA IN THE WORKS

Setting their sights for the first time on a mainstay of tropical agriculture, two biotechnology companies yesterday announced a collaboration to genetically engineer a better banana. Oakland-based DNA Plant Technology Corporation and Zeneca Plant Science, a subsidiary of Britain's Zeneca Group Plc, said they will develop a banana that resists spoilage, so that it can be allowed to ripen on the tree longer and still survive shipping. Currently, bananas are harvested while still green to allow them to be shipped to distant markets without turning mushy. The bananas are then ripened artificially.

DNA Plant and Zeneca plan to develop a banana that produces less ethylene, a natural plant hormone that triggers the ripening process. With delayed ripening, the banana can be left on the tree longer, enhancing its flavor and nutrition and improving the economics of production. The companies will work on the more exotic varieties, such as "red" bananas, which are sweeter than the standard variety, and "ice cream" bananas, which are smoother and creamier, as well as the Cavendish banana, the most popular variety.

The collaboration will meld DNA Plant's technology for switching genes on and off and Zeneca's work in identifying ethylene genes. In an effort to avoid a patent battle, the two companies agreed in April to share their genetic technologies. The size of the $3 billion U.S. banana market and the fact that their technology could be easily applied to bananas convinced the companies to target the banana business.

Under the agreement, the companies will share research costs and jointly own the resulting technology. They do not expect to start selling a bio-engineered banana until 1998.

SOURCE: Alex Barnum, "A Better Banana Is in the Works—More Desirable Fruit Sought," *San Francisco Chronicle*, July 8, 1994, p. B1.

offset the research and experimental expenses. Rather than create net operating loss carryovers that might not be utilized because of the 15-year limitation on such carryovers, the deferral and amortization method may be used. The deferral of research and experimental expenditures should also be considered if the taxpayer expects higher tax rates in the future.

NET OPERATING LOSSES

6 LEARNING OBJECTIVE
Recognize the impact of the net operating loss carryback and carryover provisions.

The requirement that every taxpayer file an annual income tax return (whether on a calendar year or a fiscal year) may result in certain inequities for taxpayers who experience cyclical patterns of income or expense. Inequities result from the application of a progressive rate structure to taxable income determined on an annual basis. A **net operating loss (NOL)** in a particular tax year would produce no tax benefit if the Code did not provide for the carryback and carryforward of such losses to profitable years.

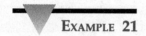

EXAMPLE 21

Juanita has a business and realizes the following taxable income or loss over a five-year period: Year 1, $50,000; Year 2, ($30,000); Year 3, $100,000; Year 4, ($200,000); and Year 5, $380,000. She is married and files a joint return. Hubert also has a business and has a taxable income pattern of $60,000 every year. He, too, is married and files a joint return. Note that both Juanita and Hubert have total taxable income of $300,000 over the five-year period. Assume there is no provision for carryback or carryover of NOLs. Juanita and Hubert would have the following five-year tax bills:

Year	Juanita's Tax	Hubert's Tax
1	$ 8,787	$11,587
2	–0–	11,587
3	22,880	11,587
4	–0–	11,587
5	125,480	11,587
	$157,147	$57,935

The computation of tax is made without regard to any NOL benefit. Rates applicable to 1996 are used to compute the tax.

Even though Juanita and Hubert realized the same total taxable income ($300,000) over the five-year period, Juanita had to pay taxes of $157,147, while Hubert paid taxes of only $57,935. ▼

To provide partial relief from this inequitable tax treatment, a deduction is allowed for NOLs.[32] This provision permits NOLs for any one year to be offset against taxable income of other years. The NOL provision is intended as a form of relief for business income and losses. Thus, only losses from the operation of a trade or business (or profession), casualty and theft losses, or losses from the confiscation of a business by a foreign government can create an NOL. In other words, a salaried individual with itemized deductions and personal exemptions in excess of gross income is not permitted to deduct the excess amounts as an NOL. On the other hand, a personal casualty loss is treated as a business loss and can therefore create (or increase) an NOL for an individual.

CARRYBACK AND CARRYOVER PERIODS

General Rules. An NOL must be applied initially to the three taxable years preceding the year of the loss (unless an election is made not to carry the loss back at all). It is carried first to the third prior year, then to the second prior year, then to the immediately preceding tax year (or until used up). If the loss is not fully used in the carryback period, it must be carried forward to the first year after the loss year, and then forward to the second, third, etc., year after the loss year. The carryover period is 15 years. A loss sustained in 1996 is used in this order: 1993, 1994, 1995, 1997 through 2011.

If the loss is being carried to a preceding year, an amended return is filed on Form 1040X, or a quick refund claim is filed on Form 1045. In any case, a refund of taxes previously paid is requested. When the loss is carried forward, the current return shows an NOL deduction for the prior year's loss.

---

[32] § 172.

Sequence of Use of NOLs.   Where there are NOLs in two or more years, the rule is always to use the earliest year's loss first until it is completely absorbed. The later years' losses can then be used until they also are absorbed or lost. Thus, one year's return could show NOL carryovers from two or more years. Each loss is computed and applied separately.

Election to Forgo Carryback.   A taxpayer can *irrevocably elect* not to carry back an NOL to any of the three prior years. In that case, the loss is available as a carryover for 15 years. A taxpayer would make the election if it is to his or her tax advantage. For example, a taxpayer might be in a low marginal tax bracket in the carryback years but expect to be in a high marginal tax bracket in future years. Therefore, it would be to the taxpayer's advantage to use the NOL to offset income in years when the tax rate is high rather than use it when the tax rate is relatively low.

ETHICAL
CONSIDERATIONS

Net Operating Losses

Adam is aware that the net operating loss carryback and carryover provisions enable him to carry back current period losses for 3 years and to carry the losses forward for 15 years. He also is aware of the time value of money concept. In addition, he recognizes that certain adjustments must be made in converting negative taxable income into an NOL.

Adam discusses with you, his accountant, the projections for his new business for the next five years, which show losses in the first two years, profits in the subsequent three years, and a cumulative profit of $90,000 for the five-year period. Adam indicates that if he delays certain transactions (by modifying the contract dates) from Years 1 and 2 into Years 3 and 4, he can convert the losses for the first two years into small profits with the cumulative projected profits for the five years remaining at $90,000. He raises the issues with you of the benefit and appropriateness of doing so.

TAX PLANNING
CONSIDERATIONS

7   LEARNING OBJECTIVE
Identify tax planning opportunities in deducting certain business expenses, business losses, and personal losses.

TAX CONSEQUENCES OF THE *GROETZINGER* CASE

In the *Groetzinger* case discussed earlier in the chapter, the court established that the appropriate tests for determining if gambling is a trade or business are whether an individual engages in gambling full-time in good faith, with regularity, and for the production of income as a livelihood, and not as a mere hobby. The court held that Robert Groetzinger satisfied the tests because of his constant and large-scale effort. Skill was required and was applied. He did what he did for a livelihood, though with less than successful results. His gambling was not a hobby, a passing fancy, or an occasional bet for amusement. Therefore, his gambling was a trade or business, and hence, he was able to deduct his gambling losses *for* AGI. If the court had ruled that Groetzinger's gambling was not a trade or business, his gambling losses would have been limited to his gambling winnings and would have been classified as itemized deductions.

DOCUMENTATION OF RELATED-TAXPAYER LOANS, CASUALTY LOSSES, AND THEFT LOSSES

Since non-bona fide loans between related taxpayers may be treated as gifts, adequate documentation is needed to substantiate a bad debt deduction if the loan subsequently becomes worthless. Documentation should include proper execution of the note (legal form) and the establishment of a bona fide purpose for the loan. In addition, it is desirable to stipulate a reasonable rate of interest and a fixed maturity date.

Since a theft loss is not permitted for misplaced items, a loss should be documented by a police report and evidence of the value of the property (e.g., appraisals, pictures of the property, newspaper clippings). Similar documentation of the value of property should be provided to support a casualty loss deduction because the amount of loss is measured, in part, by the decline in fair market value of the property.

Casualty loss deductions must be reported on Form 4684 (see Appendix B).

SMALL BUSINESS STOCK

Because § 1244 limits the amount of loss classified as ordinary loss on a yearly basis, a taxpayer might maximize the benefits of § 1244 by selling the stock in more than one taxable year. The result could be that the losses in any one taxable year would not exceed the § 1244 limits on ordinary loss.

EXAMPLE 22

Mitch, a single individual, purchased small business stock in 1994 for $150,000 (150 shares at $1,000 per share). On December 20, 1996, the stock is worth $60,000 (150 shares at $400 per share). Mitch wants to sell the stock at this time. Mitch earns a salary of $80,000 a year, has no other capital transactions, and does not expect any in the future. If Mitch sells all of the small business stock in 1996, his recognized loss will be $90,000 ($60,000 − $150,000). The loss will be characterized as a $50,000 ordinary loss and a $40,000 long-term capital loss. In computing taxable income for 1996, Mitch could deduct the $50,000 ordinary loss but could deduct only $3,000 of the capital loss. The remainder of the capital loss could be carried over and used in future years subject to the $3,000 limitation if Mitch has no capital gains. If Mitch sells 82 shares in 1996, he will recognize an ordinary loss of $49,200 [82 × ($1,000 − $400)]. If Mitch then sells the remainder of the shares in 1997, he will recognize an ordinary loss of $40,800 [68 × ($1,000 − $400)]. Mitch could deduct the $49,200 ordinary loss in computing 1996 taxable income and the $40,800 ordinary loss in computing 1997 taxable income. ▼

CASUALTY LOSSES

A special election is available for taxpayers who sustain casualty losses in an area designated by the President as a disaster area. This election affects only the timing, not the calculation, of the deduction. The deduction can be taken in the year before the year in which the loss occurred. Thus, an individual can take the deduction on the 1995 return for a loss occurring between January 1 and December 31, 1996. The benefit, of course, is a faster refund (or reduction in tax). It will also be advantageous to carry the loss back if the taxpayer's tax rate in the carryback year is higher than the tax rate in the year of the loss.

To find out if an event qualifies as a disaster area loss, one can look in any of the major tax services, the Weekly Compilation of Presidential Documents, or the *Internal Revenue Bulletin.*

NET OPERATING LOSSES

In certain instances, it may be advisable for a taxpayer to elect not to carry back an NOL. For an individual, the benefits from the loss carryback could be scaled down or lost due to the economic adjustments that must be made to taxable income for the year to which the loss is carried. For example, a taxpayer should attempt to minimize the number of taxable years to which an NOL is carried. The more years to which the NOL is applied, the more benefits are lost from adjustments for items such as personal and dependency exemptions.

The election not to carry back the loss might also be advantageous if there is a disparity in marginal tax rates applicable to different tax years.

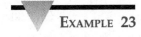

EXAMPLE 23

Abby sustained an NOL of $10,000 in Year 4. Her marginal tax bracket in Year 1 was 15%. In Year 5, however, she expects her bracket to be 39.6% due to a large profit she will make on a business deal. If Abby carries her loss back, her refund will be $1,500 (15% × $10,000). If she elects not to carry it back to Year 1 but chooses, instead, to carry it forward, her savings will be $3,960 (39.6% × $10,000). Even considering the time value of an immediate tax refund, Abby appears to be better off using the carryover approach. ▼

KEY TERMS

Bad debt, 6–3	Personal casualty gain, 6–15	Small business stock, 6–8
Business bad debt, 6–4	Personal casualty loss, 6–15	Specific charge-off method, 6–3
Casualty loss, 6–9	Research and experimental expenditures, 6–17	Theft loss, 6–10
Disaster area losses, 6–11		Worthless securities, 6–7
Net operating loss (NOL), 6–19	Reserve method, 6–3	
Nonbusiness bad debt, 6–4	Section 1244 stock, 6–8	

PROBLEM MATERIALS

DISCUSSION QUESTIONS

1. Explain whether a bad debt deduction is allowed for a debt arising from the sale of inventory by an accrual basis taxpayer.

2. Discuss whether legal proceedings must be brought against a debtor in order to show that a debt is worthless.

3. Discuss the tax treatment for the recovery of an account receivable previously written off as uncollectible.

4. Bill made a loan to a friend three years ago to help the friend purchase an automobile. Bill's friend has notified him that the car has been sold and the most he will be able to repay is 50% of the loan. Discuss the possibility of Bill taking a bad debt deduction for half of the loan.

5. Discuss the difference between business and nonbusiness bad debts. How is the distinction determined? How is each treated on the return?

6. What factors are to be considered in determining whether a bad debt arising from a loan between related parties is, in fact, a bad debt?

7. Discuss a taxpayer's options for the tax treatment of a loss incurred on a deposit in a qualified financial institution. Also note the consequences of each option.

8. Macy owns § 1244 stock in a corporation. The stock becomes completely worthless during the current year. Discuss the tax consequences of Macy's worthless § 1244 stock.

9. Discuss the ordinary loss limitations on the sale of § 1244 stock and the advantages of such a characterization.

10. Discuss whether a taxpayer can take a deduction for a casualty loss from an accident caused by the taxpayer's negligence.

11. Jim discovers that his sea wall, which protects his personal residence from the ocean, has been extensively damaged by the ocean. Discuss whether he may take a deduction for the damage to the wall.

12. Discuss the provision for determining the year in which a theft loss is deductible.

13. What is a disaster area loss? Why might a taxpayer benefit from making the disaster area loss election?

14. Discuss the tax consequences of property being partially destroyed in determining the amount of a casualty loss assuming no insurance proceeds are received.

15. How is a personal casualty loss computed? A business casualty loss? What effect do insurance proceeds have on both types of losses?

16. Discuss the tax consequences of not making an insurance claim when insured business property is subject to a loss.

17. Discuss the circumstances under which the cost of repairs to the damaged property can be used to measure the amount of a casualty loss.

18. Discuss the reduction of personal casualty losses by the $100 and 10%-of-AGI floors.

19. If a taxpayer is required to spread a personal casualty loss between two years under the reasonable prospect of recovery doctrine, how will the $100 per event floor and the 10%-of-AGI limitation be treated?

20. Bonnie sustained a loss on a duplex damaged by fire. She owns the duplex and lives in one unit. She rents out the other unit to a tenant. Discuss the tax treatment of the loss on Bonnie's individual tax return.

21. Discuss the tax treatment of a loss resulting from the theft of a security from an individual.

22. When casualty losses exceed casualty gains, only the amount of the casualty loss in excess of casualty gains is subject to the 10%-of-AGI floor. Discuss the significance of netting losses against gains in this manner rather than having the entire casualty loss subject to the 10%-of-AGI floor.

23. Monte opened a personal savings account at First National Bank many years ago. Last year, First National's banking license was revoked. In January of this year, Monte was informed that First National had been put into compulsory liquidation. The liquidation was precipitated by the embezzlement of funds by First National's former president. In February Monte submitted a claim for $12,459 to the liquidators of First National. In May of the current year, the liquidators advised Monte that they would keep him informed as to the progress of the liquidation and his prospects of recovery. The letter also stated that claimants would be notified if the liquidators were unable to agree to their claims. In November of the current year, Monte was notified that at the present time the liquidators could not predict with any degree of certainty how much of their funds depositors might eventually recover. Identify the relevant tax issues for Monte.

24. Fred and Diane purchased their home many years ago. The property included a large black oak tree approximately 80 feet in height and about 100 years old. The tree was the dominant feature of the front yard, where it stood alone next to the street. Because of the age and stature of the tree, Fred and Diane had it inspected regularly by a tree expert. In August of the current year, Fred noticed that the entire top or crown of the tree had turned brown. Because none of the leaves on other trees in the area had turned brown, Fred called the tree expert to inspect the tree. The inspection showed that the tree had been attacked by woodborers and was beyond saving and effectively dead. Identify the relevant tax issues for Fred and Diane.

25. Why do most taxpayers elect to write off research and experimental expenditures rather than capitalize and amortize such amounts? Are there situations when the capitalization and amortization approach would be preferable?

26. If a business does not elect to expense or amortize research expenditures, what is the possibility of writing off such expenditures?

27. Power and Light, a public utility company, planned a research and development project. To obtain a construction permit to expand its facilities, the company filed an application with state regulatory agencies and conducted various studies to support its application as required by the agencies. Because the taxpayer's expansion involved both the construction of a nuclear power plant and the installation of an ultrahigh voltage electric transmission line, the agencies required that the company conduct several types of environmental impact studies for site selection. The studies measured specific site conditions and the resulting environmental impact of the construction and operation of the project. The company conducted part of the studies directly and used a research organization to conduct the remainder of the studies on its behalf. Identify the relevant tax issues for Power and Light.

28. Discuss the periods to which NOLs may be carried. Can the taxpayer elect not to carry an NOL back to any one year? What possible benefit might result from not carrying a loss back to a particular year?

PROBLEMS

29. Several years ago John Johnson loaned his friend Sara $20,000 to help her make a business investment. In May of the current year, Sara filed for bankruptcy, and John was notified that he could expect to receive no more than 60 cents on the dollar. As of the end of the current year, John has not received any payments. John has contacted you about the possibility of taking a bad debt deduction of $8,000 for the current year.

    Write a letter to John that contains your advice as to whether he can claim a bad debt deduction of $8,000 for the current year. Also, prepare a memo for the tax files. John's address is 100 Tyler Lane, Erie, PA 16563.

30. In 1994, Jack loaned his mother $10,000. In 1996, his mother told him that she would try and pay him $1,000. In 1997, Jack's mother filed for bankruptcy and told Jack that she would be unable to pay him anything. Determine Jack's possible deductions with respect to the loan.

31. In 1995, Wilma deposited $117,500 with a commercial bank. On July 1, 1996, Wilma was notified that the bank was insolvent, and subsequently she received only $100,000 of the deposit. Wilma also has a salary of $5,000, long-term capital gain of $12,000, and itemized deductions (other than casualty and theft) of $7,000. Determine whether Wilma should elect to treat the loss on the deposit as a personal casualty loss or as a bad debt.

32. Zenith, a single taxpayer, had the following items for 1996:

    • Salary of $75,000.

    • Gain of $15,000 on the sale of § 1244 stock acquired three years ago.

    • Loss of $60,000 on the sale of § 1244 stock acquired two years ago.

    • Stock acquired on December 20, 1995, for $2,500 became worthless on April 3, 1996.

    Determine Zenith's AGI for 1996.

33. Mary, a single taxpayer, purchased 10,000 shares of § 1244 stock several years ago at a cost of $20 per share. In November of the current year, Mary received an offer to sell the stock for $12 per share. She has the option of either selling all of the stock now or selling half of the stock now and half of the stock in January of next year. Mary will receive a salary of $80,000 for the current year and $90,000 next year. Mary will have long-term capital gains of $8,000 for the current year and $10,000 next year. If Mary's goal is to minimize her AGI for the two years, determine whether Mary should sell all of her stock this year or half of her stock this year and half next year.

34. When Helen returned from a vacation in Hawaii on November 8, 1996, she discovered that a burglar had stolen her silver, stereo, and color television. In the process of removing these items, the burglar damaged some furniture that originally cost $1,400. Helen's silver cost $12,000 and was valued at $16,500; the stereo system cost $8,400 and was valued at $6,200; the television cost $840 and was worth $560. Helen filed a claim with her insurance company and was reimbursed in the following amounts on December 20, 1996.

Silver	$2,800
Stereo	5,600
Television	490

The insurance company disputed the reimbursement claimed by Helen for the damaged furniture, but she protested and was finally paid $280 on January 30, 1997. The repairs to the furniture totaled $1,550. Helen's AGI for 1996 was $20,000, and it was $500 for 1997. How much can Helen claim as a casualty and theft loss? In which year?

35. Olaf owns a 500-acre farm in Minnesota. A tornado hit the area and destroyed a farm building and some farm equipment and damaged a barn. Fortunately for Olaf, the tornado occurred after he had harvested his corn crop. Applicable information is as follows:

Item	Adjusted Basis	FMV Before	FMV After	Insurance Proceeds
Building	$80,000	$100,000	$ –0–	$60,000
Equipment	60,000	50,000	–0–	25,000
Barn	90,000	120,000	90,000	25,000

Because of the extensive damage caused by the tornado, the President designated the area as a disaster area.

Olaf, who files a joint return with his wife Anna, had $90,000 of taxable income last year. Their taxable income for the current year, excluding the loss from the tornado, is $220,000.

Determine the amount of Olaf and Anna's loss and the year in which they should take the loss.

36. On January 7 of the current year, Wade dropped off to sleep while driving home from a business trip. Luckily, he was only slightly injured in the resulting accident, but his car was completely destroyed.

Wade had purchased the car new two years ago and had driven it 64,000 miles at the time of the accident. Of these miles, 28,000 were business miles; the remaining miles were personal miles. The car cost $7,200 new. Wade has taken $1,985 of depreciation for the business use of the car. The fair market value at the time of the accident was $4,000. Wade carried zero deductible collision insurance on the car. He made no claim on his insurance policy because he was afraid that his insurance premiums would increase if he did.

After Wade's release from the hospital the day after the accident, he could not find his wallet (cost $65, fair replacement value $30) or its contents, which included $350 in cash and $500 in traveler's checks. The traveler's checks were replaced by the issuing company. He also was unable to locate the stone from his diamond ring. The stone cost his wife $2,500 when purchased nine years ago and was worth $6,400 at the time of the loss.

a. Determine the amount of Wade's deductible loss *for* AGI.

b. Determine the amount of the loss deductible *from* AGI, assuming AGI for the year is $25,000.

37. On November 1 of the current year, Sam Smith was involved in an accident with his personal use automobile. Sam had purchased the car for $25,000. The automobile had a fair market value of $19,000 before the accident and $12,000 after the accident. The car was covered by an insurance policy that had a $1,000 deductible clause. Sam is afraid that the policy will be canceled if he makes a claim for the damages. Therefore, he is considering not filing a claim. Sam believes that the casualty loss deduction will help mitigate the loss of the insurance reimbursement. Sam's AGI for the current year is $25,000.

    Write a letter to Sam that contains your advice with respect to the tax consequences of filing versus not filing a claim for the insurance reimbursement for the damages to his car. Also, prepare a memo for the tax files. Sam's address is 450 Colonel's Way, Warrensburg, MO 64093.

38. Green Corporation, a manufacturing company, decided to develop a new line of fireworks. Because of the danger involved, Green purchased an isolated parcel of land for $300,000 and constructed a building for $1,220,000. The building was to be used for research and experimentation in creating the new fireworks. The project was begun in 1996. Green had the following expenses in 1996 in connection with the project:

Salaries	$160,000
Utilities	20,000
Materials	40,000
Insurance	50,000
Cost of market survey to determine profit potential for new fireworks line	20,000
Depreciation on the building	30,000

Green had the following expenses in 1997 in connection with the project:

Salaries	$200,000
Utilities	30,000
Materials	40,000
Insurance	30,000
Depreciation on the building	31,000

The benefits from the project will be realized starting in June 1998.
    a. If Green Corporation elects to expense research and experimental expenditures, determine the amount of the deduction for 1996, 1997, and 1998.
    b. If Green Corporation elects a 60-month deferral and amortization period, determine the amount of the deduction for 1996, 1997, and 1998.

39. Nell, single and age 38, had the following income and expense items in 1996:

Nonbusiness bad debt	$ 6,000
Business bad debt	2,000
Nonbusiness long-term capital gain	4,000
Nonbusiness short-term capital loss	3,000
Salary	40,000
Interest income	1,000

    Determine Nell's AGI for 1996.

40. Assume that in addition to the information in Problem 39, Nell had the following items in 1996:

Personal casualty gain on an asset held for four months	$10,000
Personal casualty loss on an asset held for two years	1,000

Determine Nell's AGI for 1996.

CUMULATIVE PROBLEMS

41. Ned Wilson, age 60, single, and retired, has no dependents. Ned lives at 231 Wander Lane, Salt Lake City, UT 84201. Ned's Social Security number is 985–12–3774. During 1996, Ned had the following income and expense items:

a. On January 27, 1995, Ned deposited $8,000 in a savings account at the ABC Financial Company. The savings account bore interest at 15%, compounded semiannually. Ned received a $600 interest payment on July 27, 1995, but received no interest payments thereafter. The finance company filed for bankruptcy on January 12, 1996. Ned received a $710 check in final settlement of his account from the bankruptcy trustee on December 20, 1996.

b. On January 1, 1996, a fire severely damaged a two-story building owned by Ned, who occupied the second story of the building as a residence and had recently opened a hardware store on the ground level. The following information is available with respect to the incident:

Asset	Adjusted Basis	Fair Market Value	
		Before	After
Building	$70,000	$130,000	$50,000
Inventory	35,000	55,000	None
Store equipment	3,000	2,500	None
Home furnishings	12,600	7,000	800
Personal auto	8,900	7,800	7,600

Ned's fire insurance policy paid the following amounts for damages covered by the policy:

Building	$50,000	(policy maximum)
Inventory	30,000	
Store equipment	None	
Home furnishings	1,000	(policy maximum)
Personal auto	None	

Assume all of the destroyed property was acquired on December 15, 1995.

c. On March 1, 1991, Ned loaned a neighboring businessman $17,000. The debtor died of a heart attack on June 21, 1996. Ned had no security and was unable to collect anything from the man's estate.

d. Ned received $125,000 of interest income from Salt Lake City Bank.

e. On March 3, 1996, Ned sold a piece of real estate he had been holding for speculation for $90,000. Ned had bought the land July 18, 1981, for $52,800.

f. Ned made a charitable contribution of $13,000.

g. Ned made four quarterly estimated tax payments of $7,000 each.

Part 1—Tax Computation
Compute Ned's 1996 Federal income tax payable (or refund due), assuming he deducts the lost deposit as a bad debt. Suggested software (if available): *TurboTax* or *MacInTax*.

Part 2—Tax Planning
Determine whether Ned should elect to treat the deposit in ABC Financial Company as a casualty loss rather than as a bad debt. Suggested software (if available): *TurboTax* or *MacInTax*.

42. Jane Smith, age 40, is single and has no dependents. She is employed as a legal secretary by Legal Services, Inc. She owns and operates Typing Services located near the campus of San Jose State University at 1986 Campus Drive. She is a cash basis taxpayer. Jane lives at 2020 Oakcrest Road, San Jose, CA 95134. Jane's Social Security number is 123–89–6666. Jane indicates that she wishes to designate $3 to the Presidential Election Campaign Fund. During 1995, Jane had the following income and expense items:
a. $50,000 salary from Legal Services, Inc.
b. $20,000 gross receipts from her typing services business.
c. $700 cash dividend from Buffalo Mining Company, a Canadian corporation.
d. $1,000 Christmas bonus from Legal Services, Inc.
e. $60,000 life insurance proceeds on the death of her sister.
f. $5,000 check given to her by her wealthy aunt.
g. $100 won in a bingo game.
h. Expenses connected with the typing service:

Office rent	$7,000
Supplies	4,400
Utilities and telephone	4,680
Wages to part-time typists	5,000
Payroll taxes	500
Equipment rentals	3,000

i. $9,000 interest expense on a home mortgage (paid to San Jose Savings and Loan).
j. $5,000 fair market value of silverware stolen from her home by a burglar on October 12, 1995. Jane had paid $4,000 for the silverware on July 1, 1986. She was reimbursed $1,500 by her insurance company.
k. Jane had loaned $2,100 to a friend, Joan Jensen, on June 3, 1992. Joan declared bankruptcy on August 14, 1995, and was unable to repay the loan.
l. Legal Services, Inc., withheld Federal income tax of $8,500 and the required amount of FICA tax.
m. Alimony of $10,000 received from her former husband, Ted Smith.
n. Interest income of $800 on City of San Jose bonds.
o. Jane made estimated tax payments of $1,000.

Part 1—Tax Computation
Compute Jane Smith's 1995 Federal income tax payable (or refund due). If you use tax forms for your computations, you will need Forms 1040 and 4684 and Schedules A, C, and D. Suggested software (if available): *TurboTax* or *MacInTax*.

Part 2—Tax Planning
In 1996, Jane plans to continue her job with Legal Services, Inc. Therefore, items a, d, and l will recur in 1996. Jane plans to continue her typing services business (refer to item b) and expects gross receipts of $26,000. She projects that all business expenses (refer to item h) will increase by 10%, except for office rent, which, under the terms of her lease, will remain the same as in 1995. Items e, f, g, j, and k will not recur in 1996. Items c, i, m, and n will be approximately the same as in 1995.

Jane would like you to compute the minimum amount of estimated tax she will have to pay for 1996 so that she will not have to pay any additional tax upon filing her 1996 Federal income tax return. Write a letter to Jane that contains your advice and prepare a memo for the tax files. Suggested software (if available): *TurboTax* or *MacInTax*.

TEAM PROJECT: ARTHUR ANDERSEN TAX CHALLENGE CASES

For more information on the Arthur Andersen Tax Challenge Cases, please refer to Chapter 2, page 2-41.

Information related to tax issues and problems that are discussed in this chapter may be found in the

Fields case on pages 2, 11, 23

Read and analyze the case you have been assigned and *identify* any issues and problems that are related to material covered in this chapter. If the information provided in the case is complete, prepare answers for this part of the case at this time. If you need information that is contained in the later parts of the case, please write a memo summarizing the questions or problems so you can prepare a complete answer at a later date.

DEPRECIATION, COST RECOVERY, AMORTIZATION, AND DEPLETION

LEARNING OBJECTIVES

After completing Chapter 7, you should be able to:

1. Understand the rationale for the cost consumption concept and identify the relevant time periods for depreciation, ACRS, and MACRS.

2. Determine the amount of cost recovery under ACRS and MACRS.

3. Recognize when and how to make the § 179 expensing election, calculate the amount of the deduction, and apply the effect of the election in making the MACRS calculation.

4. Identify listed property and apply the deduction limitation on listed property and on luxury automobiles.

5. Determine when and how to use the alternative depreciation system (ADS).

6. Identify intangible assets that are eligible for amortization and calculate the amount of the deduction.

7. Determine the amount of depletion expense including being able to apply the alternative tax treatments for intangible drilling and development costs.

8. Identify tax planning opportunities for cost recovery, amortization, and depletion.

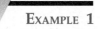

OUTLINE

1   LEARNING OBJECTIVE
Understand the rationale for the
cost consumption concept and
identify the relevant time periods
for depreciation, ACRS, and
MACRS.

The Internal Revenue Code provides for a deduction for the consumption of the cost of an asset through depreciation, cost recovery, amortization, or depletion. These deductions are applications of the recovery of capital doctrine (discussed in Chapter 3).

A distinction is made between tangible and intangible property. Tangible property is any property with physical substance (e.g., equipment, buildings), while intangible property lacks such substance (e.g., goodwill, patents).

The **depreciation rules** were completely overhauled by the Economic Recovery Tax Act of 1981 (ERTA). Hence, *most* property placed in service after December 31, 1980, is subject to the accelerated **cost recovery system** (ACRS). However, property placed in service before January 1, 1981, that is still in use, as well as *certain* property placed in service after December 31, 1980, is subject to the pre-ERTA depreciation rules. The Tax Reform Act (TRA) of 1986 completely revised the ACRS rules for property placed in service after December 31, 1986 (MACRS). Therefore, a knowledge of all of the depreciation and cost recovery rules may be needed as Example 1 illustrates.

EXAMPLE 1

The Brown Company owns machinery purchased in 1980. The machinery has a 17-year useful life. The business also owns equipment purchased in 1986 that has a 15-year cost recovery life. In 1990, the business purchased a computer. To compute the depreciation and cost recovery for 1996, Brown will use the pre-ERTA depreciation rules for the machinery, the pre-TRA of 1986 cost recovery rules (ACRS) for the equipment, and the post-TRA of 1986 cost recovery rules (MACRS) for the computer. ▼

This chapter initially focuses on the ACRS and MACRS rules.[1] The chapter then concludes with a discussion of the amortization of intangible property and the depletion of natural resources.

ACRS was one of many provisions in ERTA that were intended to stimulate the economy. The following features of ACRS result in accelerated write-offs:

- Cost recovery periods are shorter than the estimated useful lives required under the pre-1981 depreciation system.
- The use of salvage value, required under the pre-1981 depreciation system, was eliminated under ACRS.
- For many assets, the methods for computing ACRS deductions are more generous than the allowable methods for computing depreciation.

---

[1] § 168. Refer to IRS Publication 534 for coverage of pre-ERTA depreciation rules under § 167.

CONCEPT SUMMARY 7–1

Depreciation and Cost Recovery: Relevant Time Periods

System	Date Property Is Placed in Service
§ 167 depreciation	Before January 1, 1981, and *certain* property placed in service after December 31, 1980.
Original accelerated cost recovery system (ACRS)	After December 31, 1980, and before January 1, 1987.
Modified accelerated cost recovery system (MACRS)	After December 31, 1986.

For assets placed in service after 1986, ACRS is replaced with MACRS. The basic effect of MACRS is to somewhat dampen the economic stimulus effect of ACRS. MACRS cost recovery periods are generally longer than ACRS cost recovery periods. In addition, the cost recovery methods available under MACRS are, in most cases, not as generous as the methods available under ACRS.

OVERVIEW

Taxpayers may write off the cost of certain assets that are used in a trade or business or held for the production of income. A write-off may take the form of depreciation (or cost recovery), depletion, or amortization. Tangible assets, other than natural resources, are *depreciated*. Natural resources, such as oil, gas, coal, and timber, are *depleted*. Intangible assets, such as copyrights and patents, are *amortized*. Generally, no write-off is allowed for an asset that does not have a determinable useful life.

ACRS and MACRS provide separate cost recovery tables for realty (real property) and personalty (personal property). Realty generally includes land and buildings permanently affixed to the land. Write-offs are not available for land because it does not have a determinable useful life. Cost recovery allowances for real property, other than land, are based on recovery lives specified in the law. The IRS provides tables that specify cost recovery allowances for most types of realty.

Personalty is defined as any asset that is not realty.[2] Personalty includes furniture, machinery, equipment, and many other types of assets. Do not confuse personalty (or personal property) with *personal use* property. Personal use property is any property (realty or personalty) that is held for personal use rather than for use in a trade or business or an income-producing activity. Write-offs are not allowed for personal use assets.

In summary, both realty and personalty can be either business use/income-producing property or personal use property. Examples include a residence (realty that is personal use), an office building (realty that is business use), a dump truck (personalty that is business use), and regular wearing apparel (personalty that is personal use). It is imperative that this distinction between the *classification* of an asset (realty or personalty) and the *use* to which the asset is put (business or personal) be understood.

---

[2] Refer to Chapter 1 for a further discussion.

ACCELERATED COST RECOVERY SYSTEM (ACRS AND MACRS)

GENERAL CONSIDERATIONS

2   LEARNING OBJECTIVE

Determine the amount of cost recovery under ACRS and MACRS.

Under the **accelerated cost recovery system (ACRS),** the cost of an asset is recovered over a predetermined period that is generally shorter than the useful life of the asset or the period the asset is used to produce income. The ACRS system was designed to encourage investment, improve productivity, and simplify the law and its administration. However, the pre-ACRS depreciation rules will continue to apply in the following situations:

- Property placed in service after 1980 whose life is not based on years (e.g., units-of-production method).
- The remaining depreciation on property placed in service by the taxpayer before 1981.
- Personal property acquired after 1980 if the property was owned or used during 1980 by the taxpayer or a related person (antichurning rule).[3]
- Property that is amortized (e.g., leasehold improvements).

The basis for cost recovery generally is the adjusted cost basis used to determine gain if property is sold or otherwise disposed of. The basis is reduced by the amount of the cost recovery deducted.

Cost Recovery Allowed or Allowable. The basis of cost recovery property must be reduced by the cost recovery allowed and by not less than the allowable amount. The *allowed* cost recovery is the cost recovery actually taken, whereas the *allowable* cost recovery is the amount that could have been taken under the applicable cost recovery method. If the taxpayer does not claim any cost recovery on property during a particular year, the basis of the property must still be reduced by the amount of cost recovery that should have been deducted (the allowable cost recovery).

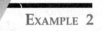

EXAMPLE 2

On March 15, Jack paid $10,000 for a copier to be used in his business. The copier is five-year property. Jack elected to use the straight-line method of cost recovery, but did not take cost recovery in years three or four. Therefore, the allowed cost recovery (cost recovery actually deducted) and the allowable cost recovery are as follows:

	Cost Recovery Allowed	Cost Recovery Allowable
Year 1	$1,000	$1,000
Year 2	2,000	2,000
Year 3	–0–	2,000
Year 4	–0–	2,000
Year 5	2,000	2,000
Year 6	1,000	1,000

---

[3] § 168(f). The antichurning rules may also require the use of pre-TRA of 1986 ACRS rules on property placed in service after December 31, 1986 (property that otherwise would be subject to MACRS).

TAX IN THE NEWS

A SEVENTEENTH-CENTURY RUGGERI BASS VIOLIN IS A TOOL OF TRADE RATHER THAN A WORK OF ART

On September 16, 1995, the *Wall Street Journal* reported that the U.S. Third Circuit Court of Appeals affirmed a Tax Court decision, holding that a valuable bass violin could be depreciated when it is used as a tool of trade by a professional musician. The depreciation was allowed even though the instrument actually increased in value while the musician owned it. The key factor appears to be that the taxpayer viewed the instrument as a tool of his trade that was subject to normal wear and tear and not as a work of art.

The petitioner, Brian P. Liddle, who was a very accomplished professional musician with the Philadelphia Orchestra, purchased the violin for $28,000 on November 8, 1984. The violin was built in the seventeenth century by Franceso Ruggeri. Ruggeri studied stringed instrument construction under Nicolo Amati, who also instructed Antonio Stradivari. His other contemporaries included the craftsmen Guadanini and Guarneri. These artisans were members of the so-called Cremonese School of instrument makers.

If Jack sold the copier for $800 in year seven, he would recognize an $800 gain ($800 amount realized – $0 adjusted basis) because the adjusted basis of the copier is zero. ▼

Cost Recovery Basis for Personal Use Assets Converted to Business or Income-Producing Use. If personal use assets are converted to business or income-producing use, the basis for cost recovery and for loss is the *lower* of the adjusted basis or the fair market value at the time the property was converted. As a result of this lower-of-basis rule, losses that occurred while the property was personal use property will not be recognized for tax purposes through the cost recovery of the property.

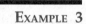

EXAMPLE 3

Hans acquires a personal residence for $120,000. Four years later, when the fair market value is only $100,000, he converts the property to rental use. The basis for cost recovery is $100,000, since the fair market value is less than the adjusted basis. The $20,000 decline in value is deemed to be personal (since it occurred while the property was held for personal use) and therefore nondeductible. ▼

ETHICAL CONSIDERATIONS

Deducting Depreciation on a Converted Truck

Bill purchased a new truck several years ago and has always used the truck for personal use. This year Bill started a business and used the truck almost exclusively for business. Because he has not taken any depreciation on his truck and because the cost of a new truck is significantly more than he paid for his truck, Bill wants to use the original cost of the truck for purposes of determining depreciation on his tax return. Evaluate the equity and the appropriateness of Bill's perspective.

ELIGIBLE PROPERTY UNDER ACRS OR MACRS

Assets used in a trade or business or for the production of income are eligible for cost recovery if they are subject to wear and tear, decay or decline from natural causes, or obsolescence. Assets that do not decline in value on a predictable basis or that do not have a determinable useful life (e.g., land, stock, antiques) are not eligible for cost recovery.

PERSONALTY: RECOVERY PERIODS AND METHODS

Classification of Property: ACRS.   ACRS provides that the cost of eligible personalty (and certain realty) is recovered over 3, 5, 10, or 15 years. Property is classified by recovery period as follows:

3 years	Autos, light-duty trucks, R & D equipment, racehorses over 2 years old and other horses over 12 years old, and personalty with an ADR* midpoint life of 4 years or less.[4]
5 years	Most other equipment except long-lived public utility property. Also includes single-purpose agricultural structures and petroleum storage facilities, which are designated as § 1245 property under the law.
10 years	Public utility property with an ADR midpoint life greater than 18 but not greater than 25 years, burners and boilers using coal as a primary fuel if used in a public utility power plant and if replacing or converting oil- or gas-fired burners or boilers, railroad tank cars, mobile homes, and realty with an ADR midpoint life of 12.5 years or less (e.g., theme park structures).
15 years	Public utility property with an ADR midpoint life exceeding 25 years (except certain burners and boilers using coal as a primary fuel).

*ADR refers to the Asset Depreciation Range system.

Taxpayers who own 15-year ACRS property continue to compute cost recovery allowances under the ACRS rules. However, all cost has already been recovered on any 3-year, 5-year, or 10-year ACRS property.

Taxpayers had the choice of using (1) the straight-line method over the regular or optional (see below) recovery period or (2) a prescribed accelerated method over the regular recovery period. These two methods are both part of the ACRS system, but a convenient name is not provided for either method. Hereafter, the straight-line method will be referred to as the *optional* (or *elective*) *straight-line method*. The method using percentages prescribed in the Code will be referred to as the *statutory percentage method*.

The rates to be used in computing the deduction under the statutory percentage method are shown in Table 7–1 (all tables are located at the end of the chapter prior to the Problem Materials) and are based on the 150 percent declining-balance method, using the **half-year convention**[5] and an assumption of zero salvage value. The rates in the cost recovery tables at the end of the chapter reflect the relevant methods, conventions, and assumptions.

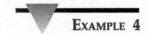

EXAMPLE 4   Green Utilities acquired 15-year public utility property in 1985 at a cost of $100,000. The property was placed in service on September 1, 1985. Green's cost recovery allowance for

---

[4] Rev.Proc. 83–35, 1983–1 C.B. 745 is the source for the ADR midpoint lives.

[5] The half-year convention assumes all property is placed in service at mid-year and thus provides for a half-year's cost recovery.

1996 is determined from Table 7–1. The cost recovery percentage for 1996 (recovery year 12) is 6%, and the cost recovery allowance is $6,000 ($100,000 cost × 6%). ▼

Note that in 1985, Green got a half-year's cost recovery deduction (since the half-year convention is reflected in the percentages in Table 7–1) although it held the property only four months.

In the year that personal property is disposed of, no cost recovery is allowed.

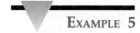

EXAMPLE 5　　Assume the same facts as in the previous example and that the property is sold in May 1997. Green is not allowed a cost recovery deduction for the property in 1997. ▼

Reduction of Basis for Investment Tax Credit. For personalty placed in service after 1982 and before January 1, 1986, taxpayers were required to reduce the basis of the property for the ACRS write-off by one-half the amount of the investment tax credit taken on the property.[6] The investment tax credit was not allowed on realty.

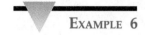

EXAMPLE 6　　Beige Electric Company acquired property on September 4, 1985, for $100,000. The property was 15-year ACRS property, and Beige claimed a $10,000 investment tax credit ($100,000 × 10% investment tax credit rate). The basis of the property was reduced by $5,000 (one-half of the $10,000 investment tax credit). Therefore, the basis for cost recovery was $95,000. The cost recovery for 1996 is $5,700 [$95,000 × 6% (Table 7–1)]. ▼

As an alternative to reducing the basis of the property, a taxpayer could elect to take a *reduced* investment tax credit. Under this election, the investment tax credit was 8 percent (rather than 10 percent) for recovery property other than three-year property and 4 percent (instead of 6 percent) for three-year property. In Example 6, if the reduced investment tax credit election were made, Beige's cost recovery basis would be $100,000 rather than $95,000.

TRA of 1986 generally repealed the investment tax credit for property placed in service after December 31, 1985. Therefore, the reduction of basis for the investment tax credit does not apply to such property.

Classification of Property: MACRS. The general effect of TRA of 1986 was to lengthen asset lives. The **modified accelerated cost recovery system (MACRS)** provides that the cost recovery basis of eligible personalty (and certain realty) is recovered over 3, 5, 7, 10, 15, or 20 years. Property is classified by recovery period under MACRS as follows (see Exhibit 7–1 for examples):[7]

3-year 200% class . . . . . . ADR midpoints of 4 years and less.[8] Excludes automobiles and light trucks. Includes racehorses more than 2 years old and other horses more than 12 years old.

5-year 200% class . . . . . . ADR midpoints of more than 4 years and less than 10 years, adding automobiles, light trucks, qualified technological equipment, renewable energy and biomass properties that are small power production facilities, research and experimentation property, semiconductor manufacturing equipment, and computer-based central office switching equipment.

7-year 200% class . . . . . . ADR midpoints of 10 years and more and less than 16 years, adding single-purpose agricultural or horticultural structures and property with no ADR midpoint not classified elsewhere. Includes railroad track and office furniture, fixtures, and equipment.

---

[6] § 48(q).
[7] § 168(e).

[8] Rev.Proc. 87–56, 1987–2 C.B. 674 is the source for the ADR midpoint lives.

▼ EXHIBIT 7–1
Cost Recovery Periods: MACRS

Class of Property	Examples
3-year	Tractor units for use over-the-road. Any horse that is not a racehorse and is more than 12 years old at the time it is placed in service. Any racehorse that is more than 2 years old at the time it is placed in service. Breeding hogs. Special tools used in the manufacturing of motor vehicles such as dies, fixtures, molds, and patterns.
5-year	Automobiles and taxis. Light and heavy general-purpose trucks. Buses. Trailers and trailer-mounted containers. Typewriters, calculators, and copiers. Computers and peripheral equipment. Breeding and dairy cattle.
7-year	Office furniture, fixtures, and equipment. Breeding and work horses. Agricultural machinery and equipment. Single-purpose agricultural or horticultural structures. Railroad track.
10-year	Vessels, barges, tugs, and similar water transportation equipment. Assets used for petroleum refining or for the manufacture of grain and grain mill products, sugar and sugar products, or vegetable oils and vegetable oil products.
15-year	Land improvements. Assets used for industrial steam and electric generation and/or distribution systems. Assets used in the manufacture of cement. Assets used in pipeline transportation. Electric utility nuclear production plant. Municipal wastewater treatment plant.
20-year	Farm buildings except single-purpose agricultural and horticultural structures. Gas utility distribution facilities. Water utilities. Municipal sewer.

10-year 200% class.....ADR midpoints of 16 years and more and less than 20 years.

15-year 150% class.....ADR midpoints of 20 years and more and less than 25 years, including sewage treatment plants, and telephone distribution plants and comparable equipment used for the two-way exchange of voice and data communications.

20-year 150% class.....ADR midpoints of 25 years and more, other than real property with an ADR midpoint of 27.5 years and more, and including sewer pipes.

Accelerated depreciation is allowed for these six MACRS classes of property. Two hundred percent declining-balance is used for the 3-, 5-, 7-, and 10-year classes, with a switchover to straight-line depreciation when it yields a larger amount. One hundred and fifty percent declining-balance is allowed for the 15- and 20-year classes, with an appropriate straight-line switchover.[9]

Taxpayers may *elect* the straight-line method to compute cost recovery allowances for each of these classes of property. Certain property is not eligible for accelerated cost recovery and must be depreciated under an alternative depreciation system (ADS). Both the straight-line election and ADS are discussed later in the chapter.

The original ACRS system gave the taxpayer a half-year of cost recovery for the tax year an asset was placed in service but allowed the taxpayer to recover the balance of the cost recovery basis over the years remaining in the property's recovery period. No cost recovery deduction was permitted for the year of disposition or retirement of the property. Thus, conceptually, the taxpayer was considered to have placed property in service at the beginning of the recovery period but was allowed only a half-year's worth of cost recovery for the year it was placed in service.

By contrast, MACRS views property as placed in service in the middle of the first year.[10] Thus, for example, the statutory recovery period for three-year property begins in the middle of the year an asset is placed in service and ends three years later. In practical terms, this means that taxpayers must wait an extra year to recover the cost of depreciable assets. That is, the actual write-off periods are 4, 6, 8, 11, 16, and 21 years. MACRS also allows for a half-year of cost recovery in the year of disposition or retirement.

The procedure for computing the cost recovery allowance under MACRS is the same as under the original ACRS method. The cost recovery basis is multiplied by the percentages that reflect the applicable cost recovery method and the applicable convention. The percentages are shown in Table 7–2.

EXAMPLE 7

Kareem acquires a five-year class asset on April 10, 1996, for $30,000. Kareem's cost recovery deduction for 1996 is $6,000 [$30,000 × .20 (Table 7–2)]. ▼

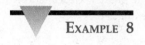
EXAMPLE 8

Assume the same facts as in Example 7, and that Kareem disposes of the asset on March 5, 1998. Kareem's cost recovery deduction for 1998 is $2,880 [$30,000 × ½ × .192 (Table 7–2)].▼

Mid-Quarter Convention. Under the original ACRS rules for personal property, the half-year convention was used no matter when property was acquired during the year. Thus, if a substantial dollar amount of assets was acquired late in the tax year, the half-year convention still applied. The law now contains a provision to curtail the benefits of such a tax strategy. If more than 40 percent of the value of property other than eligible real estate (see Realty: Recovery Periods and Methods: MACRS for a discussion of eligible real estate) is placed in service during the last quarter of the year, a **mid-quarter convention** applies.[11] Property acquisitions are then grouped by the quarter they were acquired for cost recovery purposes. Acquisitions during the first quarter are allowed 10.5 months of cost recovery; the second quarter, 7.5 months; the third quarter, 4.5 months; and the fourth quarter, 1.5 months. The percentages are shown in Table 7–3.

EXAMPLE 9

Silver Corporation acquires the following five-year class property in 1996:

[9] § 168(b).
[10] § 168(d)(4)(A).

[11] § 168(d)(3).

Property Acquisition Dates	Cost
February 15	$ 200,000
July 10	400,000
December 5	600,000
Total	$1,200,000

If Silver Corporation uses the statutory percentage method, the cost recovery allowances for the first two years are computed as indicated below. Since more than 40% ($600,000/$1,200,000 = 50%) of the acquisitions are in the last quarter, the mid-quarter convention applies.

1996

February 15	[$200,000 × .35 (Table 7–3)]	$ 70,000
July 10	($400,000 × .15)	60,000
December 5	($600,000 × .05)	30,000
Total		$160,000

1997

February 15	[$200,000 × .26 (Table 7–3)]	$ 52,000
July 10	($400,000 × .34)	136,000
December 5	($600,000 × .38)	228,000
Total		$416,000

When property to which the mid-quarter convention applies is disposed of, the property is treated as though it were disposed of at the midpoint of the quarter. Hence, in the quarter of disposition, cost recovery is allowed for one-half of the quarter. ▼

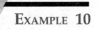

EXAMPLE 10

Assume the same facts as in Example 9, except that Silver Corporation sells the $400,000 asset on November 30 of 1997. The cost recovery allowance for 1997 is computed as follows:

February 15	[$200,000 × .26 (Table 7–3)]	$ 52,000
July 10	[$400,000 × .34 × (3.5/4)]	119,000
December 5	($600,000 × .38)	228,000
Total		$399,000

▼

REALTY: RECOVERY PERIODS AND METHODS

ACRS.   Under the original ACRS rules, realty was assigned a 15-year recovery period. Real property other than low-income housing is depreciated using the 175 percent declining-balance method, with a switchover to straight-line depreciation when it yields a larger amount. Low-income housing is depreciated using the 200 percent declining-balance method, with an appropriate straight-line switchover. In either case, zero salvage value is assumed. Statutory percentages for real property are shown in Table 7–4, which contains rates for low-income housing as well as for other 15-year real estate. As explained later in the chapter, taxpayers were allowed to elect the straight-line method for real property.

The half-year convention does not apply to 15-year real property. As a result, Table 7–4 is structured differently from Tables 7–1 and 7–2. The cost recovery deduction for 15-year real property is based on the month the asset is placed in service rather than on the half-year convention. No cost recovery is allowed for the month in which an asset is disposed of if the asset is disposed of before the end of the recovery period.

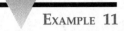

EXAMPLE 11　Alicia purchased a warehouse for $100,000 on January 1, 1984. The cost recovery allowance for the years 1984 through 1996, using the statutory percentage method, is as follows (see Table 7–4 for percentages).

1984—$12,000 (12% × $100,000)
1985—$10,000 (10% × $100,000)
1986—$9,000 (9% × $100,000)
1987—$8,000 (8% × $100,000)
1988—$7,000 (7% × $100,000)
1989—$6,000 (6% × $100,000)
1990—$6,000 (6% × $100,000)
1991—$6,000 (6% × $100,000)
1992—$6,000 (6% × $100,000)
1993—$5,000 (5% × $100,000)
1994—$5,000 (5% × $100,000)
1995—$5,000 (5% × $100,000)
1996—$5,000 (5% × $100,000)　　　　　　　　▼

EXAMPLE 12　Assume the same facts as in Example 11, except the property is low-income housing. Cost recovery deductions using the statutory percentage method for 1984 through 1996 are as follows (see Table 7–4 for percentages):

1984—$13,000 (13% × $100,000)
1985—$12,000 (12% × $100,000)
1986—$10,000 (10% × $100,000)
1987—$9,000 (9% × $100,000)
1988—$8,000 (8% × $100,000)
1989—$7,000 (7% × $100,000)
1990—$6,000 (6% × $100,000)
1991—$5,000 (5% × $100,000)
1992—$5,000 (5% × $100,000)
1993—$5,000 (5% × $100,000)
1994—$4,000 (4% × $100,000)
1995—$4,000 (4% × $100,000)
1996—$4,000 (4% × $100,000)　　　　　　　　▼

The Deficit Reduction Act of 1984 changed the recovery period for real property to 18 years. This applies generally to property placed in service after March 15, 1984. However, the 15-year recovery period was retained for low-income housing as well as for other real property placed in service before March 16, 1984.

Eighteen-year real property placed in service after June 22, 1984, is subject to a **mid-month convention.**[12] This means that real property placed in service at any time during a particular month is treated as if it were placed in service in the middle of the month. This allows for one-half month's cost recovery for the month the property is placed in service. If the property is disposed of before the end of the recovery period, one-half month's cost recovery is permitted for the month of disposition regardless of the specific date of disposition. Statutory percentages for 18-year real property with a mid-month convention are shown in Table 7–5.

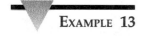

EXAMPLE 13

Rex purchased a building for $300,000 and placed it in service on August 21, 1984. The first year's cost recovery using the statutory percentage method is $12,000 [$300,000 × 4% (Table 7–5)]. ▼

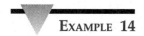

EXAMPLE 14

Assume the same facts as in Example 13 and that Rex disposes of the building on May 3, 1996. The cost recovery in the year of disposition is $4,500 ($300,000 × 4% × 4.5/12). ▼

Public Law 99–121 extended the minimum recovery period for real property (except low-income housing) from 18 years to 19 years. This applies to property placed in service after May 8, 1985, and before January 1, 1987. Statutory percentages for 19-year real property are shown in Table 7–6. Because the percentages are determined using a mid-month convention, the computation of cost recovery is mechanically the same as for 18-year property with the mid-month convention.

MACRS. Under MACRS, the cost recovery period for residential rental real estate is 27.5 years, and the straight-line method is used for computing the cost recovery allowance. **Residential rental real estate** includes property where 80 percent or more of the gross rental revenues are from nontransient dwelling units (e.g., an apartment building). Hotels, motels, and similar establishments are not residential rental property. Low-income housing is classified as residential rental real estate. Nonresidential real estate has a recovery period of 31.5 years (39 years for such property placed in service after May 12, 1993) and is also depreciated using the straight-line method.[13]

Some items of real property are not treated as real estate for purposes of MACRS. For example, single-purpose agricultural structures are in the 7-year MACRS class. Land improvements are in the 15-year MACRS class.

All eligible real estate is depreciated using the mid-month convention. Regardless of when during the month the property is placed in service, it is deemed to have been placed in service at the middle of the month. In the year of disposition, a mid-month convention is also used.

Cost recovery is computed by multiplying the applicable rate (Table 7–7) by the cost recovery basis.

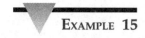

EXAMPLE 15

Ann acquired a building on April 1, 1993, for $800,000. If the building is classified as residential rental real estate, the cost recovery allowance for 1996 is $29,088 (.03636 × $800,000). If the building is classified as nonresidential real estate, the 1996 cost recovery allowance is $25,400 (.03175 × $800,000). (See Table 7–7 for percentages.) ▼

---

[12] A transitional rule, which provides for a full-month convention, is effective for property placed in service after March 15, 1984, and before June 23, 1984. The cost recovery tables for property placed in service during this period are not included in this chapter.

[13] §§ 168(b), (c), and (e).

CONCEPT SUMMARY 7–2

Statutory Percentage Method under ACRS and MACRS

| | | ACRS | | |
| | Personal Property | Real Property | | |
		15-Year	18-Year	19-Year
Convention	Half-year	Full-month	Mid-month	Mid-month
Cost recovery deduction in the year of disposition	None	Full-month up to month of disposition	Half-month for month of disposition	Half-month for month of disposition

| | MACRS | |
	Personal Property	Real Property*
Convention	Half-year or mid-quarter	Mid-month
Cost recovery deduction in the year of disposition	Half-year for year of disposition or half-quarter for quarter of disposition	Half-month for month of disposition

*Straight-line method must be used.

As part of the deficit reduction legislation of the Clinton administration (Revenue Reconciliation Act of 1993), nonresidential real estate placed in service after May 12, 1993, is subject to a 39-year recovery period. Property placed in service before 1994 that was subject to a binding contract to construct or purchase, as of May 12, 1993, may still be treated as 31.5-year property under the prior rules.

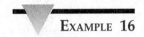

EXAMPLE 16

Assume the same facts as in Example 15, except Ann acquired the nonresidential building on November 19, 1996. The 1996 cost recovery allowance is $2,568 [$800,000 × .00321 (Table 7–7)]. ▼

STRAIGHT-LINE ELECTION UNDER ACRS AND MACRS

ACRS. Under ACRS, taxpayers could *elect* to write off an asset using the straight-line method rather than the statutory percentage method. The straight-line recovery period could be the same as the prescribed recovery period under the statutory percentage method, or a longer period. The allowable straight-line recovery periods for each class of property are summarized as follows:

3-year property	3, 5, or 12 years
5-year property	5, 12, or 25 years
10-year property	10, 25, or 35 years
15-year property	15, 35, or 45 years
18-year real property and low-income housing (placed in service after March 15, 1984)	18, 35, or 45 years
19-year real property and low-income housing (placed in service after May 8, 1985)	19, 35, or 45 years

If the straight-line option was elected for personal property, the half-year convention applies in computing the cost recovery deduction. The effect of electing the straight-line method for personal property is to extend the statutory recovery period by one year (e.g., three to four and five to six years). There is no cost recovery deduction in the year of the disposition of the property.

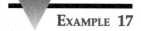

EXAMPLE 17

On May 6, 1986, Owl Utilities paid $20,000 for coal-fired boilers to replace gas-fired boilers (10-year property). Owl elected to compute the cost recovery allowance using the optional straight-line method and the regular cost recovery period. Owl's cost recovery allowance for 1986 was $1,000 ($20,000 basis × 10% straight-line rate × ½ year). The cost recovery allowance for 1996 is $1,000 ($20,000 basis × 10% straight-line rate × ½ year). These cost recovery allowances reflect the half-year convention for the first and last years of the cost recovery period. ▼

For each class of personal property, the straight-line election applied to *all* assets in a *particular class* that were placed in service during the year for which the election was made. The election applies for the entire recovery period of these assets. The election is not binding for personal property of the same class placed in service in another tax year.

Under the straight-line option for 15-year *real* property, the first year's cost recovery deduction and the cost recovery deduction for the year of disposition are computed on the basis of the number of months the property was in service during the year.

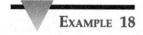

EXAMPLE 18

Kate acquired a store building on October 1, 1983, at a cost of $150,000. She elected the straight-line method using a recovery period of 15 years. Kate's cost recovery deduction for 1983 was $2,500 [($150,000 ÷ 15) × ³⁄₁₂]. ▼

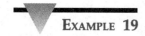

EXAMPLE 19

Assume the same facts as in Example 18 and that Kate disposes of the asset on September 30, 1996. Kate's cost recovery deduction for 1996 is $7,500 [($150,000 ÷ 15) × ⁹⁄₁₂]. ▼

Under the straight-line option for 18-year or 19-year real property, the cost recovery allowances in the year the property is placed in service and in the year of disposition are computed in the same manner (except for the use of different rates) as under the statutory percentage method. Note that 18-year and 19-year real property use a mid-month convention, whereas 15-year real property uses a full-month convention. Table 7–8 contains the applicable percentages to be used under the straight-line option for 19-year real property. (The tables that contain the percentages for 18-year real property using the straight-line method over 18, 35, and 45 years and 19-year real property using the straight-line method over 35 and 45 years are not reproduced in this text.)

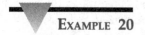

EXAMPLE 20

Ned acquired 19-year real property on October 1, 1986, at a cost of $150,000. He elected the straight-line method of cost recovery. Ned's cost recovery deduction for 1986 was $1,650 [$150,000 × 1.1% (Table 7–8)]. ▼

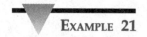

EXAMPLE 21

Assume the same facts as in Example 20 and that Ned disposes of the asset on September 20, 1996. Ned's cost recovery deduction for 1996 is $5,631 [($150,000 × 5.3% × 8.5/12) (Table 7–8)]. ▼

The straight-line election for 15-year, 18-year, or 19-year real property may be made on a *property-by-property* basis within the same year.

CONCEPT SUMMARY 7–3

Straight-Line Election under ACRS and MACRS

ACRS

| | Personal Property | Real Property | | |
		15-Year	18-Year	19-Year
Convention	Half-year	Full-month	Mid-month	Mid-month
Cost recovery deduction in the year of disposition	None	Full-month up to month of disposition	Half-month for month of disposition	Half-month for month of disposition
Elective or mandatory	Elective	Elective	Elective	Elective
Breadth of election	Class by class	Property by property	Property by property	Property by property

MACRS

	Personal Property	Real Property
Convention	Half-year or mid-quarter	Mid-month
Cost recovery deduction in the year of disposition	Half-year for year of dispositon or half-quarter for quarter of disposition	Half-month for month of disposition
Elective or mandatory	Elective	Mandatory
Breadth of election	Class by class	

MACRS. Although MACRS requires straight-line depreciation for all eligible real estate as previously discussed, the taxpayer may *elect* to use the straight-line method for personal property.[14] The property is depreciated using the class life (recovery period) of the asset with a half-year convention or a mid-quarter convention, whichever is applicable. The election is available on a class-by-class and year-by-year basis. The percentages for the straight-line election with a half-year convention appear in Table 7–9.

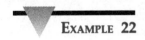

EXAMPLE 22

Terry acquires a 10-year class asset on August 4, 1996, for $100,000. He elects the straight-line method of cost recovery. Terry's cost recovery deduction for 1996 is $5,000 ($100,000 × .050). His cost recovery deduction for 1997 is $10,000 ($100,000 × .10). (See Table 7–9 for percentages.) ▼

3   **LEARNING OBJECTIVE**
Recognize when and how to make the § 179 expensing election, calculate the amount of the deduction, and apply the effect of the election in making the MACRS calculation.

ELECTION TO EXPENSE ASSETS

Section 179 (Election to Expense Certain Depreciable Business Assets) permits the taxpayer to elect to write off up to $17,500[15] of the acquisition cost of *tangible personal property* used in a trade or business. Amounts that are expensed under § 179 may not be capitalized and depreciated. The **§ 179 expensing election** is an

---

[14] § 168(b)(5).

[15] This amount was $10,000 for property placed in service in tax years beginning before January 1, 1993.

annual election and applies to the acquisition cost of property placed in service that year. The immediate expense election is not available for real property or for property used for the production of income.[16]

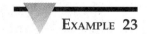

EXAMPLE 23

Kelly acquires machinery (five-year class) on February 1, 1996, at a cost of $40,000 and elects to expense $17,500 under § 179. Kelly's statutory percentage cost recovery deduction for 1996 is $4,500 [($40,000 cost – $17,500 expensed) × .200]. (See Table 7–2 for percentage.) Kelly's total deduction for 1996 is $22,000 ($17,500 + $4,500). ▼

Annual Limitations. Two additional limitations apply to the amount deductible under § 179. First, the ceiling amount on the deduction is reduced dollar-for-dollar when property (other than eligible real estate) placed in service during the taxable year exceeds $200,000. Second, the amount expensed under § 179 cannot exceed the aggregate amount of taxable income derived from the conduct of any trade or business by the taxpayer. Taxable income of a trade or business is computed without regard to the amount expensed under § 179. Any § 179 expensed amount in excess of taxable income is carried forward to future taxable years and added to other amounts eligible for expensing (and is subject to the ceiling rules for the carryforward years).

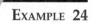

EXAMPLE 24

Jill owns a computer service and operates it as a sole proprietorship. In 1996, she will net $11,000 before considering any § 179 deduction. If Jill spends $204,000 on new equipment, her § 179 expense deduction is computed as follows:

§ 179 deduction before adjustment	$17,500
Less: Dollar limitation reduction ($204,000 – $200,000)	(4,000)
Remaining § 179 deduction	$13,500
Business income limitation	$11,000
§ 179 deduction allowed	$11,000
§ 179 deduction carryforward ($13,500 – $11,000)	$ 2,500

▼

Effect on Basis. The basis of the property for cost recovery purposes is reduced by the § 179 amount after it is adjusted for property placed in service in excess of $200,000. This adjusted amount does not reflect any business income limitation.

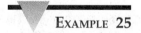

EXAMPLE 25

Assume the same facts as in Example 24 and that the new equipment is five-year class property. Jill's statutory percentage cost recovery deduction for 1996 is $38,100 [($204,000 – $13,500) × .200]. (See Table 7–2 for percentage.) ▼

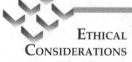

ETHICAL CONSIDERATIONS

Section 179 and Limited Personal Use

Sam, a salesman, purchased a new computer near the end of last year. Sam used the computer during the remainder of the year only in connection with his business. On his tax return for last year, Sam expensed the computer under § 179. During the current year, Sam continued to use the computer in his business. However, he also allowed his children to use the computer for their school work. Sam has not maintained a log

[16]§§ 179(b) and (d). The amount shown is per taxpayer, per year. On a joint return, the statutory amounts apply to the couple. If the taxpayers are married and file separate returns, each spouse is eligible for 50% of the statutory amount.

showing business and personal use of the computer for the current year. He feels that because the computer was expensed last year, no further accounting for it on his tax return is necessary.

Conversion to Personal Use. Conversion of the expensed property to personal use at any time results in recapture income (see Chapter 13). A property is converted to personal use if it is not used predominantly in a trade or business. Regulations provide for the mechanics of the recapture.[17]

BUSINESS AND PERSONAL USE OF AUTOMOBILES AND OTHER LISTED PROPERTY

4 **LEARNING OBJECTIVE**
Identify listed property and apply the deduction limitations on listed property and on luxury automobiles.

Limits exist on ACRS and MACRS deductions for automobiles and other listed property that are used for both personal and business purposes.[18] If the listed property is *predominantly used* for business, the taxpayer is allowed to use the statutory percentage method to recover the cost. In cases where the property is *not predominantly used* for business, the cost is recovered using a straight-line recovery.
Listed property includes the following:

- Any passenger automobile.
- Any other property used as a means of transportation.
- Any property of a type generally used for purposes of entertainment, recreation, or amusement.
- Any computer or peripheral equipment, with the exception of equipment used exclusively at a regular business establishment, including a qualifying home office.
- Any cellular telephone or other similar telecommunications equipment.
- Any other property specified in the Regulations.[19]

Automobiles and Other Listed Property Used Predominantly in Business. For listed property to be considered as predominantly used in business, its business usage must exceed 50 percent.[20] The use of listed property for production of income does not qualify as business use for purposes of the more-than-50 percent test. However, if the more-than-50 percent test is met, both production of income and business use percentages are used to compute the cost recovery deduction.

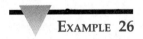
EXAMPLE 26

On September 1, 1996, Shontelle places in service listed five-year recovery property. The property cost $10,000. If Shontelle uses the property 40% for business and 25% for the production of income, the property is not considered as predominantly used for business. The cost is recovered using straight-line cost recovery. If, however, Shontelle uses the property 60% for business and 25% for the production of income, the property is considered as used predominantly for business. Therefore, she may use the statutory percentage method. Shontelle's cost recovery allowance for the year is $1,700 ($10,000 × .200 × 85%). ▼

The method for determining the percentage of business usage for listed property is specified in the Regulations. The Regulations provide that for

[17] Reg. § 1.179–1(e).
[18] § 280F.
[19] § 280F(d)(4).
[20] § 280F(b)(4).

TAX IN THE NEWS

A FERRARI AS MEDICAL EQUIPMENT

Babies do not always arrive during office hours. Obstetricians frequently need to get to the delivery room quickly. The question is whether "quickly" requires a red Ferrari sports car.

On August 26, 1995, the *Newport News Daily Press* reported that a Chesapeake obstetrician purchased a red Ferrari and then wrote off the cost on his corporate tax return. On the return, the doctor claimed the purchase price was for an ultrasound machine and treated the amount as a business expense. From the *Daily Press* and other local media reports, it is unclear whether the $85,000 amount was expensed or whether it was capitalized and deducted as cost recovery.

automobiles a mileage-based percentage is to be used. Other listed property is to use the most appropriate unit of time (e.g., hours) the property is actually used (rather than available for use).[21]

The law places special limitations on the cost recovery deduction for passenger automobiles. These statutory dollar limits were imposed on passenger automobiles because of the belief that the tax system was being used to underwrite automobiles whose cost and luxury far exceeded what was needed for their business use.

A *passenger automobile* is any four-wheeled vehicle manufactured for use on public streets, roads, and highways with an unloaded gross vehicle weight rating of 6,000 pounds or less.[22] This definition specifically excludes vehicles used directly in the business of transporting people or property for compensation such as taxicabs, ambulances, hearses, and trucks and vans as prescribed by the Regulations.

The following limits apply to the cost recovery deductions for passenger automobiles for 1996:[23]

Year	Recovery Limitation
1	$3,060
2	4,900
3	2,950
Succeeding years until the cost is recovered	1,775

These limits are imposed before any percentage reduction for personal use. In addition, the limitation in the first year includes any amount the taxpayer elects to expense under § 179.[24] If the passenger automobile is used partly for personal use, the personal use percentage is ignored for the purpose of determining the unrecovered cost available for deduction in later years.

---

[21] Reg. § 1.280F–6T(e).
[22] § 280F(d)(5).
[23] § 280F(a)(2). The 1995 indexed amounts are $3,060, $4,900, $2,950, and $1,775.

[24] § 280F(d)(1).

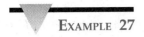

EXAMPLE 27

On July 1, 1996, Dan places in service an automobile that cost $20,000. The car is always used 80% for business and 20% for personal use. The cost recovery for the automobile would be as follows:

1996—$2,448[$20,000 × 20% (limited to $3,060) × 80%]

1997—$3,920[$20,000 × 32% (limited to $4,900) × 80%]

1998—$2,360[$20,000 × 19.2% (limited to $2,950) × 80%]

1999—$1,420[$20,000 × 11.52% (limited to $1,775) × 80%]

2000—$1,420[$20,000 × 11.52% (limited to $1,775) × 80%]

2001—$1,420[$5,540 unrecovered cost ($20,000 − $14,460*) (limited to $1,775) × 80%]

*($3,060 + $4,900 + $2,950 + $1,775 + $1,775). Although the statutory percentage method appears to restrict the deduction to $922 [$20,000 × 5.76% (limited to $1,775) × 80%], the unrecovered cost of $5,540 (limited to $1,775) multiplied by the business usage percentage is deductible. At the start of 1999 (year 4), there is an automatic switch to the straight-line cost recovery method. Under this method, the unrecovered cost up to the maximum allowable limit ($1,775) is deductible in the last year of the recovery period (2001 or year 6). Because the limit may restrict the deduction, any remaining unrecovered cost is deductible in the next or succeeding year(s), subject to the maximum allowable yearly limit ($1,775), multiplied by the business usage percentage.

The total cost recovery for the years 1996–2001 is $12,988. ▼

The cost recovery limitations are maximum amounts. If the regular calculation produces a lesser amount of cost recovery, the lesser amount is used.

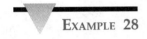

EXAMPLE 28

On April 2, 1996, Gail places in service an automobile that cost $10,000. The car is always used 70% for business and 30% for personal use. The cost recovery allowance for 1996 is $1,400 ($10,000 × 20% × 70%), which is less than $2,142 ($3,060 × 70%). ▼

Note that the cost recovery limitations apply *only* to passenger automobiles and not to other listed property.

Automobiles and Other Listed Property Not Used Predominantly in Business. The cost of listed property that does not pass the more-than-50 percent business usage test in the year the property is placed in service must be recovered using the straight-line method.[25] The straight-line method to be used is that required under the alternative depreciation system (explained later in the chapter). This system requires a straight-line recovery period of five years for automobiles. However, even though the straight-line method is used, the cost recovery allowance for passenger automobiles cannot exceed the dollar limitations.

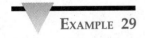

EXAMPLE 29

On July 27, 1996, Fred places in service an automobile that cost $20,000. The auto is used 40% for business and 60% for personal use. The cost recovery allowance for 1996 is $800 [$20,000 × 10% (Table 7–11) × 40%]. ▼

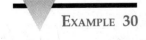

EXAMPLE 30

Assume the same facts as in Example 29, except that the auto cost $50,000. The cost recovery allowance for 1996 is $1,224 [$50,000 × 10% (Table 7–11) = $5,000 (limited to $3,060) × 40%]. ▼

If the listed property fails the more-than-50 percent business usage test, the straight-line method must be used for the remainder of the property's life. This applies even if at some later date the business usage of the property increases to more than 50 percent. Even though the straight-line method must continue to be used, however, the amount of cost recovery will reflect the increase in business usage.

[25] § 280F(b)(2).

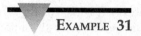

EXAMPLE 31

Assume the same facts as in Example 29, except that in 1997, Fred uses the auto 70% for business and 30% for personal use. Fred's cost recovery allowance for 1997 is $2,800 [$20,000 × 20% (Table 7–11) × 70%]. ▼

Change from Predominantly Business Use. If the business use percentage of listed property falls to 50 percent or lower after the year the property is placed in service, the property is subject to *cost recovery recapture*. The amount required to be recaptured and included in the taxpayer's return as ordinary income is the excess cost recovery.

Excess cost recovery is the excess of the cost recovery deduction taken in prior years using the statutory percentage method over the amount that would have been allowed if the straight-line method had been used since the property was placed in service.[26]

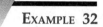

EXAMPLE 32

Seth purchased a car on January 22, 1996, at a cost of $20,000. Business usage was 80% in 1996, 70% in 1997, 40% in 1998, and 60% in 1999. Statutory percentage cost recovery deductions in 1996 and 1997 are $2,448 (80% × $3,060) and $3,430 (70% × $4,900), respectively. Seth's excess cost recovery to be recaptured as ordinary income in 1998 is $1,478, calculated as follows:

1996

Statutory percentage allowance	$ 2,448
Straight-line ($20,000 × 10% × 80%)	(1,600)
Excess	$ 848

1997

Statutory percentage allowance	$ 3,430
Straight-line ($20,000 × 20% × 70%)	(2,800)
1997 excess	$ 630
1996 excess	848
Total excess	$ 1,478

▼

After the business usage of the listed property drops below the more-than-50 percent level, the straight-line method must be used for the remaining life of the property.

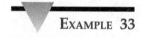

EXAMPLE 33

Assume the same facts as in Example 32. Seth's cost recovery allowance for the years 1998 and 1999 would be $1,180 and $1,065, computed as follows:

1998—$1,180   [($20,000 × 20%) limited to $2,950 × 40%]
1999—$1,065   [($20,000 × 20%) limited to $1,775 × 60%]

▼

Leased Automobiles. A taxpayer who leases a passenger automobile for business or income-producing use must report an *inclusion amount* in gross income. The inclusion amount is computed from an IRS table for each taxable year for which the taxpayer leases the automobile. The purpose of this provision is to

---

[26] § 280F(b)(3).

prevent taxpayers from circumventing the cost recovery dollar limitations by leasing, instead of purchasing, an automobile.

The dollar amount of the inclusion is based on the fair market value of the automobile and is prorated for the number of days the auto is used during the taxable year. The prorated dollar amount is then multiplied by the business and income-producing usage percentage to determine the amount to be included in gross income.[27] The taxpayer deducts the lease payments, multiplied by the business and income-producing usage percentage. The net effect is that the annual deduction for the lease payment is reduced by the inclusion amount.

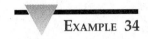

EXAMPLE 34

On April 1, 1996, Jim leases and places in service a passenger automobile worth $40,000. The lease is to be for a period of five years. During the taxable years 1996 and 1997, Jim uses the automobile 70% for business and 30% for personal use. Assuming the dollar amounts from the IRS table for 1996 and 1997 are $175 and $384, Jim must include $92 in gross income for 1996 and $269 for 1997, computed as follows:

$$1996 \quad \$175 \times (275/365) \times 70\% = \$92$$
$$1997 \quad \$384 \times (365/365) \times 70\% = \$269$$

In addition, Jim can deduct 70% of the lease payments each year because this is the business use percentage. ▼

Substantiation Requirements. Listed property is now subject to the substantiation requirements of § 274. This means that the taxpayer must prove the business usage as to the amount of expense or use, the time and place of use, the business purpose for the use, and the business relationship to the taxpayer of persons using the property. Substantiation requires adequate records or sufficient evidence corroborating the taxpayer's statement. However, these substantiation requirements do not apply to vehicles that, by reason of their nature, are not likely to be used more than a *de minimis* amount for personal purposes.[28]

ALTERNATIVE DEPRECIATION SYSTEM (ADS)

5 ▼ **LEARNING OBJECTIVE**
Determine when and how to use the alternative depreciation system (ADS).

The **alternative depreciation system (ADS)** must be used for the following:[29]

- To calculate the portion of depreciation treated as an alternative minimum tax (AMT) adjustment for purposes of the corporate and individual AMT (see Chapter 14).
- To compute depreciation allowances for property for which any of the following is true:
  - Used predominantly outside the United States.
  - Leased or otherwise used by a tax-exempt entity.
  - Financed with the proceeds of tax-exempt bonds.
  - Imported from foreign countries that maintain discriminatory trade practices or otherwise engage in discriminatory acts.
- To compute depreciation allowances for earnings and profits purposes (see Chapter 18).

In general, ADS depreciation is computed using straight-line recovery without regard to salvage value. However, for purposes of the AMT, depreciation of

---

[27] Reg. § 1.280F–7T(a).
[28] §§ 274(d) and (i).

[29] § 168(g).

CONCEPT SUMMARY 7–4

Listed Property Cost Recovery

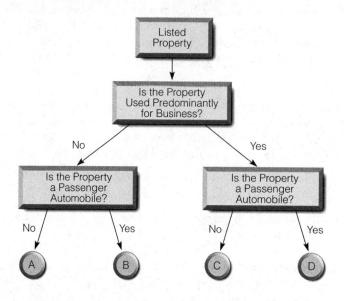

Legend to Tax Treatment

A Straight-line cost recovery reduced by the personal use percentage.

B Straight-line cost recovery subject to the recovery limitations ($3,060, $4,900, $2,950, $1,775) and reduced by the personal use percentage.

C Statutory percentage cost recovery reduced by the personal use percentage.

D Statutory percentage cost recovery subject to the recovery limitations ($3,060, $4,900, $2,950, $1,775) and reduced by the personal use percentage.

personal property is computed using the 150 percent declining-balance method with an appropriate switch to the straight-line method.

The taxpayer must use the half-year or the mid-quarter convention, whichever is applicable, for all property other than eligible real estate. The mid-month convention is used for eligible real estate. The applicable ADS rates are found in Tables 7–10, 7–11, and 7–12.

The recovery periods under ADS are as follows:[30]

- The ADR midpoint life for property that does not fall into any of the following listed categories.
- Five years for qualified technological equipment, automobiles, and light-duty trucks.
- Twelve years for personal property with no class life.
- Forty years for all residential rental property and all nonresidential real property.

---

[30] The class life for certain properties described in § 168(e)(3) is specially determined under § 168(g)(3)(B).

Taxpayers may *elect* to use the 150 percent declining-balance method to compute the regular income tax rather than the 200 percent declining-balance method that is available for personal property. Hence, if the election is made, there will be no difference between the cost recovery for computing the regular income tax and the AMT. However, taxpayers who make this election must use the ADS recovery periods in computing the cost recovery for the regular income tax, and the ADS recovery periods generally are longer than the regular recovery periods under MACRS.

The following are examples of the classification of property by class life for the ADS recovery periods:[31]

3-year	Special tools used in the manufacture of motor vehicles, breeding hogs.
5-year	Automobiles, light general-purpose trucks.
7-year	Breeding and dairy cattle.
9.5-year	Computer-based telephone central office switching equipment.
10-year	Office furniture, fixtures, and equipment, railroad track.
12-year	Racehorses more than 2 years old at the time they are placed in service.

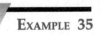

EXAMPLE 35

On March 1, 1996, Abby purchases computer-based telephone central office switching equipment for $80,000. If Abby uses statutory percentage cost recovery (assuming no § 179 election), the cost recovery allowance for 1996 is $16,000 [$80,000 × 20% (Table 7–2, 5-year class property)]. If Abby elects to use ADS 150% declining-balance cost recovery (assuming no § 179 election), the cost recovery allowance for 1996 is $6,312 [$80,000 × 7.89% (Table 7–10, 9.5-year class property)]. ▼

In lieu of depreciation under the regular MACRS method, taxpayers may *elect* straight-line under ADS for property that qualifies for the regular MACRS method. The election is available on a class-by-class and year-by-year basis for property other than eligible real estate. The election for eligible real estate is on a property-by-property basis. One reason for making this election is to avoid a difference between deductible depreciation and earnings and profits depreciation.

---

[31] Rev.Proc. 87–56, 1987–2 C.B. 674 is the source for the recovery periods.

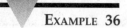

EXAMPLE 36

Polly acquires an apartment building on March 17, 1996, for $700,000. She takes the maximum cost recovery allowance for determining taxable income. Polly's cost recovery allowance for computing 1996 taxable income is $20,153 [$700,000 × .02879 (Table 7–7)]. However, Polly's cost recovery for computing her earnings and profits is only $13,853 [$700,000 × .01979 (Table 7–12)]. ▼

AMORTIZATION

6 LEARNING OBJECTIVE
Identify intangible assets that are eligible for amortization and calculate the amount of the deduction.

Prior to the Revenue Reconciliation Act of 1993 (RRA of 1993), the tax treatment of intangible assets had become a source of much controversy between taxpayers and the IRS. Disputes arose as to whether a covenant not to compete (an amortizable asset) was separate and distinct from goodwill and going-concern value (a nonamortizable asset) or merely a transfer of goodwill.

Under RRA of 1993, taxpayers can claim an **amortization** deduction on intangible assets called "amortizable § 197 intangibles." The amount of the deduction is determined by amortizing the adjusted basis of such intangibles ratably over a 15-year period beginning in the month in which the intangible is acquired.[32]

An *amortizable § 197 intangible* is any § 197 intangible acquired after August 10, 1993, and held in connection with the conduct of a trade or business or for the production of income. Section 197 intangibles include goodwill and going-concern value, franchises (except sports franchises), trademarks, and trade names. Covenants not to compete, copyrights, and patents are also included if they are acquired in connection with the acquisition of a business. Generally, self-created intangibles are not § 197 intangibles. The 15-year amortization period applies regardless of the actual useful life of an amortizable § 197 intangible. No other depreciation or amortization deduction is permitted with respect to any amortizable § 197 intangible except those permitted under the 15-year amortization rules.

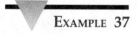

EXAMPLE 37

On June 1, 1996, Sally purchased and began operating the Falcon Cafe. Of the purchase price, $90,000 is correctly allocated to goodwill. The deduction for amortization for 1996 is $3,500 [($90,000/15) × (7/12)]. ▼

ETHICAL CONSIDERATIONS

Allocating Intangible Assets When a Business Is Sold

Marge and Stan are negotiating Stan's purchase of Marge's business. Both are in the 36 percent tax bracket. They have agreed that the tangible assets of the business are worth $100,000. Marge's adjusted basis for these assets is $70,000.

The only other asset of the business is the going-concern value. Marge believes that this asset is worth about $50,000. Stan believes that it is worth somewhat less, probably about $40,000.

Marge and Stan are handling their own negotiations since they do not believe in wasting money on attorneys or CPAs when such professional services are not required. Stan knows from an MBA class he took five years ago that goodwill is not deductible, but that a covenant not to compete can be deducted over the covenant period. Stan believes that Marge, who is age 67 and in poor health, is going to retire. In order to maximize the tax

---

[32]§ 197(a).

benefits to himself, Stan increases his offer from $140,000 to $145,000 (i.e., "we'll split the difference") if Marge will agree to sign a five-year covenant with $45,000 of the $145,000 purchase price allocated to the covenant. Marge, who believes that the tax consequences of the sale ($145,000 amount realized – $70,000 adjusted basis = $75,000 recognized gain) will be the same regardless of whether the $45,000 is for goodwill or for a covenant, accepts the offer. Evaluate the decisions made by Marge and Stan.

DEPLETION

Natural resources (e.g., oil, gas, coal, gravel, timber) are subject to **depletion,** which is simply a form of depreciation applicable to natural resources. Land generally cannot be depleted.

The owner of an interest in the natural resource is entitled to deduct depletion. An owner is one who has an economic interest in the property.[33] An economic interest requires the acquisition of an interest in the resource in place and the receipt of income from the extraction or severance of that resource. Like depreciation, depletion is a deduction *for* adjusted gross income.

Although all natural resources are subject to depletion, oil and gas wells are used as an example in the following paragraphs to illustrate the related costs and issues.

In developing an oil or gas well, the producer must make four types of expenditures.

- Natural resource costs.
- Intangible drilling and development costs.
- Tangible asset costs.
- Operating costs.

Natural resources are physically limited, and the costs to acquire them (e.g., oil under the ground) are, therefore, recovered through depletion. Costs incurred in making the property ready for drilling such as the cost of labor in clearing the property, erecting derricks, and drilling the hole are **intangible drilling and development costs (IDC).** These costs generally have no salvage value and are a lost cost if the well is dry. Costs for tangible assets such as tools, pipes, and engines are capital in nature. These costs must be capitalized and recovered through depreciation (cost recovery). Costs incurred after the well is producing are operating costs. These costs would include expenditures for such items as labor, fuel, and supplies. Operating costs are deductible when incurred (on the accrual basis) or when paid (on the cash basis).

The expenditures for depreciable assets and operating costs pose no unusual problems for producers of natural resources. The tax treatment of depletable costs and intangible drilling and development costs is quite a different matter.

INTANGIBLE DRILLING AND DEVELOPMENT COSTS (IDC)

Intangible drilling and development costs (IDC) can be handled in one of two ways at the option of the taxpayer. They can be *either* charged off as an expense in the year in which they are incurred *or* capitalized and written off through depletion. The taxpayer makes the election in the first year such expenditures are

---

[33] Reg. § 1.611–1(b).

incurred either by taking a deduction on the return or by adding them to the depletable basis. No formal statement of intent is required. Once made, the election is binding on both the taxpayer and the IRS for all such expenditures in the future. If the taxpayer fails to make the election to expense IDC on the original timely filed return the first year such expenditures are incurred, an automatic election to capitalize them has been made and is irrevocable.

As a general rule, it is more advantageous to expense IDC. The obvious benefit of an immediate write-off (as opposed to a deferred write-off through depletion) is not the only advantage. Since a taxpayer can use percentage depletion, which is calculated without reference to basis (see Example 41), the IDC may be completely lost as a deduction if they are capitalized.

DEPLETION METHODS

There are two methods of calculating depletion: cost and percentage. Cost depletion can be used on any wasting asset (and is the only method allowed for timber). Percentage depletion is subject to a number of limitations, particularly for oil and gas deposits. Depletion should be calculated both ways, and generally the method that results in the *larger* deduction is used. The choice between cost and percentage depletion is an annual election.

Cost Depletion.   **Cost depletion** is determined by using the adjusted basis of the asset.[34] The basis is divided by the estimated recoverable units of the asset (e.g., barrels, tons) to arrive at the depletion per unit. The depletion per unit then is multiplied by the number of units sold (*not* the units produced) during the year to arrive at the cost depletion allowed. Cost depletion, therefore, resembles the units-of-production method of calculating depreciation.

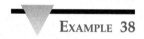

EXAMPLE 38

On January 1, 1996, Pablo purchased the rights to a mineral interest for $1,000,000. At that time, the remaining recoverable units in the mineral interest were estimated to be 200,000. The depletion per unit is $5 [$1,000,000 (adjusted basis) ÷ 200,000 (estimated recoverable units)]. If during the year 60,000 units were mined and 25,000 were sold, the cost depletion would be $125,000 [$5 (depletion per unit) × 25,000 (units sold)]. ▼

If the taxpayer later discovers that the original estimate was incorrect, the depletion per unit for future calculations must be redetermined based on the revised estimate.[35]

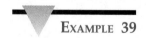

EXAMPLE 39

Assume the same facts as in Example 38. In 1997, Pablo realizes that an incorrect estimate was made. The remaining recoverable units now are determined to be 400,000. Based on this new information, the revised depletion per unit is $2.1875 [$875,000 (adjusted basis) ÷ 400,000 (estimated recoverable units)]. Note that the adjusted basis is the original cost ($1,000,000) reduced by the depletion claimed in 1996 ($125,000). If 30,000 units are sold in 1997, the depletion for the year would be $65,625 [$2.1875 (depletion per unit) × 30,000 (units sold)]. ▼

Percentage Depletion.   **Percentage depletion** (also referred to as statutory depletion) is a specified percentage provided for in the Code. The percentage varies according to the type of mineral interest involved. A sample of these percentages is shown in Exhibit 7–2. The rate is applied to the gross income from

---

[34] § 612.

[35] § 611(a).

▼ **EXHIBIT 7–2**
Sample of Percentage
Depletion Rates

22% Depletion

Cobalt	Sulfur
Lead	Tin
Nickel	Uranium
Platinum	Zinc

15% Depletion

Copper	Oil and gas
Gold	Oil shale
Iron	Silver

14% Depletion

Borax	Magnesium carbonates
Calcium carbonates	Marble
Granite	Potash
Limestone	Slate

10% Depletion

Coal	Perlite
Lignite	Sodium chloride

5% Depletion

Gravel	Pumice
Peat	Sand

the property, but in no event may percentage depletion exceed 50 percent of the taxable income from the property before the allowance for depletion.[36]

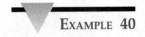

EXAMPLE 40

Assuming gross income of $100,000, a depletion rate of 22%, and other expenses relating to the property of $60,000, the depletion allowance is determined as follows:

Gross income	$100,000
Less: Other expenses	(60,000)
Taxable income before depletion	$ 40,000
Depletion allowance [the lesser of $22,000 (22% × $100,000) or $20,000 (50% × $40,000)]	(20,000)
Taxable income after depletion	$ 20,000

The adjusted basis of the property is reduced by $20,000, the depletion allowed. If the other expenses had been only $55,000, the full $22,000 could have been deducted, and the adjusted basis would have been reduced by $22,000. ▼

Note that percentage depletion is based on a percentage of the gross income from the property and makes no reference to cost. Thus, when percentage depletion is used, it is possible to deduct more than the original cost of the

---

[36] § 613(a). Special rules apply for certain oil and gas wells under § 613A (e.g., the 50% ceiling is replaced with a 100% ceiling, and the percentage depletion may not exceed 65% of the taxpayer's taxable income from all sources before the allowance for depletion).

property. If percentage depletion is used, however, the adjusted basis of the property (for computing cost depletion) must be reduced by the amount of percentage depletion taken until the adjusted basis reaches zero.

Effect of Intangible Drilling Costs on Depletion.   The treatment of IDC has an effect on the depletion deduction in two ways. If the costs are capitalized, the basis for cost depletion is increased. As a consequence, the cost depletion is increased. If IDC are expensed, they reduce the taxable income from the property. This reduction may result in application of the provision that limits depletion to 50 percent (100 percent for certain oil and gas wells) of taxable income before deducting depletion.

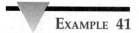

EXAMPLE 41

Iris purchased the rights to an oil interest for $1,000,000. The recoverable barrels were estimated to be 200,000. During the year, 50,000 barrels were sold for $2,000,000. Regular expenses amounted to $800,000, and IDC were $650,000. If the IDC are capitalized, the depletion per unit is $8.25 ($1,000,000 + $650,000 ÷ 200,000 barrels), and the following taxable income results:

Gross income	$2,000,000
Less: Expenses	(800,000)
Taxable income before depletion	$1,200,000
Cost depletion ($8.25 × 50,000) = $412,500	
Percentage depletion (15% × $2,000,000) = $300,000	
Greater of cost or percentage depletion	(412,500)
Taxable income	$ 787,500

If the IDC are expensed, the taxable income is $250,000, calculated as follows:

Gross income	$ 2,000,000
Less: Expenses, including IDC	(1,450,000)
Taxable income before depletion	$ 550,000
Cost depletion [($1,000,000 ÷ 200,000 barrels) × 50,000 barrels] = $250,000	
Percentage depletion (15% of $2,000,000 = $300,000, limited to 100% of $550,000 taxable income before depletion) = $300,000	
Greater of cost or percentage depletion	(300,000)
Taxable income	$ 250,000

For further restrictions on the use or availability of the percentage depletion method, see § 613.

TAX PLANNING
CONSIDERATIONS

COST RECOVERY

Cost recovery schedules should be reviewed annually for possible retirements, abandonments, and obsolescence.

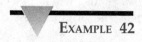

EXAMPLE 42

An examination of the cost recovery schedule of Eagle Company reveals the following:

- Asset A was abandoned when it was discovered that the cost of repairs would be in excess of the cost of replacement. Asset A had an adjusted basis of $3,000.
- Asset J became obsolete this year, at which point, its adjusted basis was $8,000.

Assets A and J should be written off for an additional expense of $11,000 ($3,000 + $8,000). ▼

8 ▼ LEARNING OBJECTIVE
Identify tax planning
opportunities for cost recovery,
amortization, and depletion.

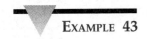

▼ EXAMPLE 43

Because of the deductions for cost recovery, interest, and ad valorem property taxes, investments in real estate can be highly attractive. In figuring the economics of such investments, one should be sure to take into account any tax savings that result.

In early January 1995, Vern purchased residential rental property for $170,000 (of which $20,000 was allocated to the land and $150,000 to the building). Vern made a down payment of $25,000 and assumed the seller's mortgage for the balance. Under the mortgage agreement, monthly payments of $1,000 are required and are applied toward interest, taxes, insurance, and principal. Since the property was already occupied, Vern continued to receive rent of $1,200 per month from the tenant. Vern actively participates in this activity and hence comes under the special rule for a rental real estate activity with respect to the limitation on passive activity losses (refer to Chapter 10). Vern is in the 31% tax bracket.

During 1996, Vern's expenses were as follows:

Interest	$10,000
Taxes	800
Insurance	1,000
Repairs and maintenance	2,200
Depreciation ($150,000 × .03636)	5,454
Total	$19,454

The deductible loss from the rental property is computed as follows:

Rent income ($1,200 × 12 months)	$ 14,400
Less expenses (see above)	(19,454)
Net loss	($ 5,054)

But what is Vern's overall position for the year when the tax benefit of the loss is taken into account? Considering just the cash intake and outlay, it is summarized as follows:

Intake—		
Rent income	$14,400	
Tax savings [31% (income tax bracket) × $5,054 (loss from the property)]	1,567	$ 15,967
Outlay—		
Mortgage payments ($1,000 × 12 months)	$12,000	
Repairs and maintenance	2,200	(14,200)
Net cash benefit		$ 1,767 ▼

It should be noted, however, that should Vern cease being an active participant in the rental activity, the passive activity loss rules would apply, and Vern could lose the current period benefit of the loss.

AMORTIZATION

When a business is purchased, goodwill and covenants not to compete are both subject to a statutory amortization period of 15 years. Therefore, the purchaser does not derive any tax benefits when part of the purchase price is assigned to a covenant rather than to goodwill.

Thus, from the purchaser's perspective, bargaining for a covenant should be based on legal rather than tax reasons. Note, however, that from the seller's perspective, goodwill is a capital asset and the covenant is an ordinary income asset.

Since the amortization period for both goodwill and a covenant is 15 years, the purchaser may want to attempt to minimize these amounts if the purchase price can be assigned to assets with shorter lives (e.g., inventory, receivables, and personalty). Conversely, the purchaser may want to attempt to maximize these amounts if part of the purchase price will otherwise be assigned to assets with longer recovery periods (e.g., realty) or to assets not eligible for cost recovery (e.g., land).

DEPLETION

Since the election to use the cost or percentage depletion method is an annual election, a taxpayer can use cost depletion (if higher) until the basis is exhausted and then switch to percentage depletion in the following years.

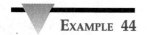

EXAMPLE 44

Assume the following facts for Melissa:

Remaining depletable basis	$ 11,000
Gross income (10,000 units)	100,000
Expenses (other than depletion)	30,000

Since cost depletion is limited to the basis of $11,000 and if the percentage depletion is $22,000 (assume a 22% rate), Melissa would choose the latter. Her basis is then reduced to zero. In future years, however, she can continue to take percentage depletion since percentage depletion is taken without reference to the remaining basis. ▼

The election to expense intangible drilling and development costs is a one-time election. Once the election is made to either expense or capitalize the intangible drilling and development costs, it is binding on all future expenditures. The permanent nature of the election makes it extremely important for the taxpayer to determine which treatment will provide the greatest tax advantage. (Refer to Example 41 for an illustration of the effect of using the two different alternatives for a given set of facts.)

TABLES

Summary of Tables

Table 7–1   Original ACRS statutory percentage table for personalty.
Applicable depreciation method: 150 percent declining-balance switching to straight-line.
Applicable recovery periods: 3, 5, 10, 15 years.
Applicable convention: half-year.

Table 7–2   Modified ACRS statutory percentage table for personalty.
Applicable depreciation methods: 200 or 150 percent declining-balance switching to straight-line.
Applicable recovery periods: 3, 5, 7, 10, 15, 20 years.
Applicable convention: half-year.

Table 7–3   Modified ACRS statutory percentage table for personalty.
Applicable depreciation method: 200 percent declining-balance switching to straight-line.
Applicable recovery periods: 3, 5, 7 years.
Applicable convention: mid-quarter.

Table 7–4   Original ACRS statutory percentage table for realty.
Applicable depreciation methods: 200 or 175 percent declining-balance switching to straight-line.
Applicable recovery period: 15 years.
Applicable convention: full-month.

Table 7–5   Original ACRS statutory percentage table for realty.
Applicable depreciation method: 175 percent declining-balance switching to straight-line.
Applicable recovery period: 18 years.
Applicable convention: mid-month.

Table 7–6   Original ACRS statutory percentage table for realty.
Applicable depreciation method: 175 percent declining-balance switching to straight-line.
Applicable recovery period: 19 years.
Applicable convention: mid-month.

Table 7–7   Modified ACRS straight-line table for realty.
Applicable depreciation method: straight-line.
Applicable recovery periods: 27.5, 31.5, 39 years.
Applicable convention: mid-month.

Table 7–8   Original ACRS optional straight-line table for realty.
Applicable depreciation method: straight-line.
Applicable recovery period: 19 years.
Applicable convention: mid-month.

Table 7–9   Modified ACRS optional straight-line table for personalty.
Applicable depreciation method: straight-line.
Applicable recovery periods: 3, 5, 7, 10, 15, 20 years.
Applicable convention: half-year.

Table 7–10   Alternative minimum tax declining-balance table for personalty.
Applicable depreciation method: 150 percent declining-balance switching to straight-line.
Applicable recovery periods: 3, 5, 9.5, 10 years.
Applicable convention: half-year.

Table 7–11   Alternative depreciation system straight-line table for personalty.
Applicable depreciation method: straight-line.
Applicable recovery periods: 5, 9.5, 12 years.
Applicable convention: half-year.

Table 7–12   Alternative depreciation system straight-line table for realty.
Applicable depreciation method: straight-line.
Applicable recovery period: 40 years.
Applicable convention: mid-month.

▼ **TABLE 7–1**
ACRS Statutory Percentages for Property Other Than 15-Year Real Property, 18-Year Real Property, or 19-Year Real Property Assuming Half-Year Convention

For Property Placed in Service after December 31, 1980, and before January 1, 1987

Recovery Year	The Applicable Percentage for the Class of Property Is:			
	3-Year	5-Year	10-Year	15-Year Public Utility
1	25	15	8	5
2	38	22	14	10
3	37	21	12	9
4		21	10	8
5		21	10	7
6			10	6
7			9	6
8			9	6
9			9	6
10			9	6
11				6
12				6
13				6
14				6
15				6

▼ **TABLE 7–2**
MACRS Accelerated Depreciation for Personal Property Assuming Half-Year Convention

For Property Placed in Service after December 31, 1986

Recovery Year	3-Year (200% DB)	5-Year (200% DB)	7-Year (200% DB)	10-Year (200% DB)	15-Year (150% DB)	20-Year (150% DB)
1	33.33	20.00	14.29	10.00	5.00	3.750
2	44.45	32.00	24.49	18.00	9.50	7.219
3	14.81*	19.20	17.49	14.40	8.55	6.677
4	7.41	11.52*	12.49	11.52	7.70	6.177
5		11.52	8.93*	9.22	6.93	5.713
6		5.76	8.92	7.37	6.23	5.285
7			8.93	6.55*	5.90*	4.888
8			4.46	6.55	5.90	4.522
9				6.56	5.91	4.462*
10				6.55	5.90	4.461
11				3.28	5.91	4.462
12					5.90	4.461
13					5.91	4.462
14					5.90	4.461
15					5.91	4.462
16					2.95	4.461
17						4.462
18						4.461
19						4.462
20						4.461
21						2.231

*Switchover to straight-line depreciation.

▼ **TABLE 7–3**
MACRS Accelerated
Depreciation for Personal
Property Assuming Mid-Quarter
Convention

For Property Placed in Service after December 31, 1986 (Partial Table*)

3-Year

Recovery Year	First Quarter	Second Quarter	Third Quarter	Fourth Quarter
1	58.33	41.67	25.00	8.33
2	27.78	38.89	50.00	61.11

5-Year

Recovery Year	First Quarter	Second Quarter	Third Quarter	Fourth Quarter
1	35.00	25.00	15.00	5.00
2	26.00	30.00	34.00	38.00

7-Year

Recovery Year	First Quarter	Second Quarter	Third Quarter	Fourth Quarter
1	25.00	17.85	10.71	3.57
2	21.43	23.47	25.51	27.55

*The figures in this table are taken from the official tables that appear in Rev.Proc.87–57, 1987–2 C.B. 687. Because of their length, the complete tables are not presented.

▼ **TABLE 7–4**
ACRS Statutory Percentages for
15-Year Real Property

For Property Placed in Service after December 31, 1980, and before January 1, 1987: 15-Year Real Property—Low-Income Housing

If the Recovery Year Is:	And the Month in the First Recovery Year the Property Is Placed in Service Is:											
	1	2	3	4	5	6	7	8	9	10	11	12
	The Applicable Percentage Is (Use the Column for the Month in the First Year the Property Is Placed in Service):											
1	13	12	11	10	9	8	7	6	4	3	2	1
2	12	12	12	12	12	12	12	13	13	13	13	13
3	10	10	10	10	11	11	11	11	11	11	11	11
4	9	9	9	9	9	9	9	9	10	10	10	10
5	8	8	8	8	8	8	8	8	8	8	8	9
6	7	7	7	7	7	7	7	7	7	7	7	7
7	6	6	6	6	6	6	6	6	6	6	6	6
8	5	5	5	5	5	5	5	5	5	5	6	6
9	5	5	5	5	5	5	5	5	5	5	5	5
10	5	5	5	5	5	5	5	5	5	5	5	5
11	4	5	5	5	5	5	5	5	5	5	5	5
12	4	4	4	5	4	5	5	5	5	5	5	5
13	4	4	4	4	4	4	5	4	5	5	5	5
14	4	4	4	4	4	4	4	4	4	5	4	4
15	4	4	4	4	4	4	4	4	4	4	4	4
16	—	—	1	1	2	2	2	3	3	3	4	4

▼ **TABLE 7–4 (Continued)**

For Property Placed in Service after December 31, 1980, and before March 16, 1984: 15-Year Real Property—Other Than Low-Income Housing

Recovery Year	12	11	10	9	8	7	6	5	4	3	2	1
1	12	11	10	9	8	7	6	5	4	3	2	1
2	10	10	11	11	11	11	11	11	11	11	11	12
3	9	9	9	9	10	10	10	10	10	10	10	10
4	8	8	8	8	8	8	9	9	9	9	9	9
5	7	7	7	7	7	7	8	8	8	8	8	8
6	6	6	6	6	7	7	7	7	7	7	7	7
7	6	6	6	6	6	6	6	6	6	6	6	6
8	6	6	6	6	6	6	5	6	6	6	6	6
9	6	6	6	6	5	6	5	5	5	6	6	6
10	5	6	5	6	5	5	5	5	5	5	6	5
11	5	5	5	5	5	5	5	5	5	5	5	5
12	5	5	5	5	5	5	5	5	5	5	5	5
13	5	5	5	5	5	5	5	5	5	5	5	5
14	5	5	5	5	5	5	5	5	5	5	5	5
15	5	5	5	5	5	5	5	5	5	5	5	5
16	—	—	1	1	2	2	3	3	4	4	4	5

▼ **TABLE 7–5**
ACRS Cost Recovery Table for
18-Year Real Property

For Property Placed in Service after June 22, 1984, and before May 9, 1985: 18-Year Real Property (18-Year 175% Declining Balance) (Assuming Mid-Month Convention)

And the Month in the First Recovery Year the Property Is Placed in Service Is:

If the Recovery Year Is:	1	2	3	4	5	6	7	8	9	10	11	12
	The Applicable Percentage Is (Use the Column for the Month in the First Year the Property Is Placed in Service):											
1	9	9	8	7	6	5	4	4	3	2	1	0.4
2	9	9	9	9	9	9	9	9	9	10	10	10.0
3	8	8	8	8	8	8	8	8	9	9	9	9.0
4	7	7	7	7	7	8	8	8	8	8	8	8.0
5	7	7	7	7	7	7	7	7	7	7	7	7.0
6	6	6	6	6	6	6	6	6	6	6	6	6.0
7	5	5	5	5	6	6	6	6	6	6	6	6.0
8	5	5	5	5	5	5	5	5	5	5	5	5.0
9	5	5	5	5	5	5	5	5	5	5	5	5.0
10	5	5	5	5	5	5	5	5	5	5	5	5.0
11	5	5	5	5	5	5	5	5	5	5	5	5.0
12	5	5	5	5	5	5	5	5	5	5	5	5.0
13	4	4	4	5	4	4	5	4	4	4	5	5.0
14	4	4	4	4	4	4	4	4	4	4	4	4.0
15	4	4	4	4	4	4	4	4	4	4	4	4.0
16	4	4	4	4	4	4	4	4	4	4	4	4.0
17	4	4	4	4	4	4	4	4	4	4	4	4.0
18	4	3	4	4	4	4	4	4	4	4	4	4.0
19		1	1	1	2	2	2	3	3	3	3	3.6

▼ TABLE 7–6
ACRS Cost Recovery Table for
19-Year Real Property

For Property Placed in Service after May 8, 1985, and before January 1, 1987
19-Year Real Property (19-Year 175% Declining Balance)
(Assuming Mid-Month Convention)

If the Recovery Year Is:	And the Month in the First Recovery Year the Property Is Placed in Service Is:											
	1	2	3	4	5	6	7	8	9	10	11	12
	The Applicable Percentage Is (Use the Column for the Month in the First Year the Property Is Placed in Service):											
1	8.8	8.1	7.3	6.5	5.8	5.0	4.2	3.5	2.7	1.9	1.1	0.4
2	8.4	8.5	8.5	8.6	8.7	8.8	8.8	8.9	9.0	9.0	9.1	9.2
3	7.6	7.7	7.7	7.8	7.9	7.9	8.0	8.1	8.1	8.2	8.3	8.3
4	6.9	7.0	7.0	7.1	7.1	7.2	7.3	7.3	7.4	7.4	7.5	7.6
5	6.3	6.3	6.4	6.4	6.5	6.5	6.6	6.6	6.7	6.8	6.8	6.9
6	5.7	5.7	5.8	5.9	5.9	5.9	6.0	6.0	6.1	6.1	6.2	6.2
7	5.2	5.2	5.3	5.3	5.3	5.4	5.4	5.5	5.5	5.6	5.6	5.6
8	4.7	4.7	4.8	4.8	4.8	4.9	4.9	5.0	5.0	5.1	5.1	5.1
9	4.2	4.3	4.3	4.4	4.4	4.5	4.5	4.5	4.5	4.6	4.6	4.7
10	4.2	4.2	4.2	4.2	4.2	4.2	4.2	4.2	4.2	4.2	4.2	4.2
11	4.2	4.2	4.2	4.2	4.2	4.2	4.2	4.2	4.2	4.2	4.2	4.2
12	4.2	4.2	4.2	4.2	4.2	4.2	4.2	4.2	4.2	4.2	4.2	4.2
13	4.2	4.2	4.2	4.2	4.2	4.2	4.2	4.2	4.2	4.2	4.2	4.2
14	4.2	4.2	4.2	4.2	4.2	4.2	4.2	4.2	4.2	4.2	4.2	4.2
15	4.2	4.2	4.2	4.2	4.2	4.2	4.2	4.2	4.2	4.2	4.2	4.2
16	4.2	4.2	4.2	4.2	4.2	4.2	4.2	4.2	4.2	4.2	4.2	4.2
17	4.2	4.2	4.2	4.2	4.2	4.2	4.2	4.2	4.2	4.2	4.2	4.2
18	4.2	4.2	4.2	4.2	4.2	4.2	4.2	4.2	4.2	4.2	4.2	4.2
19	4.2	4.2	4.2	4.2	4.2	4.2	4.2	4.2	4.2	4.2	4.2	4.2
20	0.2	0.5	0.9	1.2	1.6	1.9	2.3	2.6	3.0	3.3	3.7	4.0

▼ **TABLE 7–7**
MACRS Straight-Line
Depreciation for Real Property
Assuming Mid-Month
Convention*

For Property Placed in Service after December 31, 1986: 27.5-Year Residential Real Property

The Applicable Percentage Is (Use the Column for the Month in the First Year the Property Is Placed in Service):

Recovery Year(s)	1	2	3	4	5	6	7	8	9	10	11	12
1	3.485	3.182	2.879	2.576	2.273	1.970	1.667	1.364	1.061	0.758	0.455	0.152
2–18	3.636	3.636	3.636	3.636	3.636	3.636	3.636	3.636	3.636	3.636	3.636	3.636
19–27	3.637	3.637	3.637	3.637	3.637	3.637	3.637	3.637	3.637	3.637	3.637	3.637
28	1.970	2.273	2.576	2.879	3.182	3.485	3.636	3.636	3.636	3.636	3.636	3.636
29	0.000	0.000	0.000	0.000	0.000	0.000	0.152	0.455	0.758	1.061	1.364	1.667

For Property Placed in Service after December 31, 1986, and before May 13, 1993: 31.5-Year Nonresidential Real Property

The Applicable Percentage Is (Use the Column for the Month in the First Year the Property Is Placed in Service):

Recovery Year(s)	1	2	3	4	5	6	7	8	9	10	11	12
1	3.042	2.778	2.513	2.249	1.984	1.720	1.455	1.190	0.926	0.661	0.397	0.132
2–19	3.175	3.175	3.175	3.175	3.175	3.175	3.175	3.175	3.175	3.175	3.175	3.175
20–31	3.174	3.174	3.174	3.174	3.174	3.174	3.174	3.174	3.174	3.174	3.174	3.174
32	1.720	1.984	2.249	2.513	2.778	3.042	3.175	3.175	3.175	3.175	3.175	3.175
33	0.000	0.000	0.000	0.000	0.000	0.000	0.132	0.397	0.661	0.926	1.190	1.455

For Property Placed in Service after May 12, 1993: 39-Year Nonresidential Real Property

The Applicable Percentage Is (Use the Column for the Month in the First Year the Property Is Placed in Service):

Recovery Year(s)	1	2	3	4	5	6	7	8	9	10	11	12
1	2.461	2.247	2.033	1.819	1.605	1.391	1.177	0.963	0.749	0.535	0.321	0.107
2–39	2.564	2.564	2.564	2.564	2.564	2.564	2.564	2.564	2.564	2.564	2.564	2.564
40	0.107	0.321	0.535	0.749	0.963	1.177	1.391	1.605	1.819	2.033	2.247	2.461

*The official tables contain a separate row for each year. For ease of presentation, certain years are grouped in these tables. In some instances, this will produce a difference of .001 for the last digit when compared with the official tables.

▼ **TABLE 7-8**
ACRS Cost Recovery Table for
19-Year Real Property:
Optional Straight-Line

For Property Placed in Service after May 8, 1985, and before January 1, 1987: 19-Year Real Property for Which an Optional 19-Year Straight-Line Method Is Elected (Assuming Mid-Month Convention)

If the Recovery Year Is:	And the Month in the First Recovery Year the Property Is Placed in Service Is:											
	1	2	3	4	5	6	7	8	9	10	11	12
	The Applicable Percentage Is (Use the Column for the Month in the First Year the Property Is Placed in Service):											
1	5.0	4.6	4.2	3.7	3.3	2.9	2.4	2.0	1.5	1.1	.7	.2
2	5.3	5.3	5.3	5.3	5.3	5.3	5.3	5.3	5.3	5.3	5.3	5.3
3	5.3	5.3	5.3	5.3	5.3	5.3	5.3	5.3	5.3	5.3	5.3	5.3
4	5.3	5.3	5.3	5.3	5.3	5.3	5.3	5.3	5.3	5.3	5.3	5.3
5	5.3	5.3	5.3	5.3	5.3	5.3	5.3	5.3	5.3	5.3	5.3	5.3
6	5.3	5.3	5.3	5.3	5.3	5.3	5.3	5.3	5.3	5.3	5.3	5.3
7	5.3	5.3	5.3	5.3	5.3	5.3	5.3	5.3	5.3	5.3	5.3	5.3
8	5.3	5.3	5.3	5.3	5.3	5.3	5.3	5.3	5.3	5.3	5.3	5.3
9	5.3	5.3	5.3	5.3	5.3	5.3	5.3	5.3	5.3	5.3	5.3	5.3
10	5.3	5.3	5.3	5.3	5.3	5.3	5.3	5.3	5.3	5.3	5.3	5.3
11	5.3	5.3	5.3	5.3	5.3	5.3	5.3	5.3	5.3	5.3	5.3	5.3
12	5.3	5.3	5.3	5.3	5.3	5.3	5.3	5.3	5.3	5.3	5.3	5.3
13	5.3	5.3	5.3	5.3	5.3	5.3	5.3	5.3	5.3	5.3	5.3	5.3
14	5.2	5.2	5.2	5.2	5.2	5.2	5.2	5.2	5.2	5.2	5.2	5.2
15	5.2	5.2	5.2	5.2	5.2	5.2	5.2	5.2	5.2	5.2	5.2	5.2
16	5.2	5.2	5.2	5.2	5.2	5.2	5.2	5.2	5.2	5.2	5.2	5.2
17	5.2	5.2	5.2	5.2	5.2	5.2	5.2	5.2	5.2	5.2	5.2	5.2
18	5.2	5.2	5.2	5.2	5.2	5.2	5.2	5.2	5.2	5.2	5.2	5.2
19	5.2	5.2	5.2	5.2	5.2	5.2	5.2	5.2	5.2	5.2	5.2	5.2
20	.2	.6	1.0	1.5	1.9	2.3	2.8	3.2	3.7	4.1	4.5	5.0

▼ **TABLE 7-9**
MACRS Straight-Line
Depreciation for Personal
Property Assuming Half-Year
Convention*

For Property Placed in Service after December 31, 1986

MACRS Class	% First Recovery Year	Other Recovery Years		Last Recovery Year	
		Years	%	Year	%
3-year	16.67	2–3	33.33	4	16.67
5-year	10.00	2–5	20.00	6	10.00
7-year	7.14	2–7	14.29	8	7.14
10-year	5.00	2–10	10.00	11	5.00
15-year	3.33	2–15	6.67	16	3.33
20-year	2.50	2–20	5.00	21	2.50

*The official table contains a separate row for each year. For ease of presentation, certain years are grouped in this table. In some instances, this will produce a difference of .01 for the last digit when compared with the official table.

▼ **TABLE 7–10**
Alternative Minimum Tax: 150%
Declining-Balance Assuming
Half-Year Convention

For Property Placed in Service after December 31, 1986 (Partial Table*)

Recovery Year	3-Year 150%	5-Year 150%	9.5-Year 150%	10-Year 150%
1	25.00	15.00	7.89	7.50
2	37.50	25.50	14.54	13.88
3	25.00**	17.85	12.25	11.79
4	12.50	16.66**	10.31	10.02
5		16.66	9.17**	8.74**
6		8.33	9.17	8.74
7			9.17	8.74
8			9.17	8.74
9			9.17	8.74
10			9.16	8.74
11				4.37

*The figures in this table are taken from the official table that appears in Rev.Proc. 87–57, 1987–2 C.B. 687. Because of its length, the complete table is not presented.
**Switchover to straight-line depreciation.

▼ **TABLE 7–11**
ADS Straight-Line for Personal
Property Assuming Half-Year
Convention

For Property Placed in Service after December 31, 1986 (Partial Table*)

Recovery Year	5-Year Class	9.5-Year Class	12-Year Class
1	10.00	5.26	4.17
2	20.00	10.53	8.33
3	20.00	10.53	8.33
4	20.00	10.53	8.33
5	20.00	10.52	8.33
6	10.00	10.53	8.33
7		10.52	8.34
8		10.53	8.33
9		10.52	8.34
10		10.53	8.33
11			8.34
12			8.33
13			4.17

*The figures in this table are taken from the official table that appears in Rev.Proc. 87–57, 1987–2 C.B. 687. Because of its length, the complete table is not presented. The tables for the mid-quarter convention also appear in Rev.Proc. 87–57.

▼ **TABLE 7–12**
ADS Straight-Line for Real
Property Assuming Mid-Month
Convention

For Property Placed in Service after December 31, 1986

Recovery Year	Month Placed in Service											
	1	**2**	**3**	**4**	**5**	**6**	**7**	**8**	**9**	**10**	**11**	**12**
1	2.396	2.188	1.979	1.771	1.563	1.354	1.146	0.938	0.729	0.521	0.313	0.104
2–40	2.500	2.500	2.500	2.500	2.500	2.500	2.500	2.500	2.500	2.500	2.500	2.500
41	0.104	0.312	0.521	0.729	0.937	1.146	1.354	1.562	1.771	1.979	2.187	2.396

KEY TERMS

Accelerated cost recovery system (ACRS), 7–4

Alternative depreciation system (ADS), 7–21

Amortization, 7–24

Cost depletion, 7–26

Cost recovery system, 7–2

Depletion, 7–25

Depreciation rules, 7–2

Half-year convention, 7–6

Intangible drilling and development costs (IDC), 7–25

Listed property, 7–17

Mid-month convention, 7–12

Mid-quarter convention, 7–9

Modified accelerated cost recovery system

(MACRS), 7–7

Percentage depletion, 7–26

Residential rental real estate, 7–12

Section 179 expensing election, 7–15

▼ **PROBLEM MATERIALS**

DISCUSSION QUESTIONS

1. Distinguish between cost recovery, amortization, and depletion.

2. Discuss whether personal use property is subject to cost recovery.

3. Distinguish between allowed and allowable cost recovery.

4. If a personal use asset is converted to business use, why is it necessary to compute cost recovery on the lower of fair market value or adjusted basis at the date of conversion?

5. Discuss whether a parking lot that is used in a business is subject to cost recovery.

6. Discuss the half-year convention as it is used in the ACRS rules.

7. On January 1, 1986, Aaron, a calendar year taxpayer, purchased a machine (15-year property). In June 1996, Aaron traded the old machine for a new machine (15-year property). Aaron paid $500,000 cash in addition to the first machine as a trade-in for the second machine. Identify the relevant tax issues for Aaron.

8. Discuss the half-year convention as it is used in the MACRS rules.

9. Discuss when the mid-quarter convention must be used.

10. Discuss the computation of cost recovery in the year of sale of an asset when the mid-quarter convention is being used.

11. What is the cost recovery period for nonresidential realty placed in service in 1995?

12. Discuss the mid-month convention as it is used in the MACRS rules.

13. Alan is engaged in the sale of rental warehouse space and related services. When he sought a bank loan to expand one of his warehouses, the lender required Alan to abate the problem of exposed and damaged asbestos-containing pipe insulation in the warehouse. Accordingly, Alan incurred costs of $200,000 to employ an asbestos contractor to remedy the problem. The contractor rewrapped and encapsulated the damaged or punctured areas of asbestos-containing pipe insulation and removed insulation that was too damaged to be rewrapped. The pipes requiring encapsulation amounted to less than 25% of the total pipes in the warehouse. Identify the relevant tax issues for Alan.

14. Discuss the applicable conventions if a taxpayer elects to use straight-line cost recovery for property placed in service after December 31, 1986.

15. If a taxpayer makes a straight-line election under MACRS, discuss the possibility of taking a cost recovery deduction, for personal and real property, in the year of disposition.

16. Discuss whether an election made one year to use straight-line cost recovery under ACRS for personal property of a particular class is binding for property of the same class placed in service in another tax year.

17. Discuss whether an election to use straight-line cost recovery under MACRS can be applied on an asset-by-asset basis.

18. Discuss whether the § 179 expensing election can be used for an apartment building.

19. Discuss the limitation on the § 179 amount that can be expensed and its impact on the basis of the property.

20. John was employed as a financial officer for an investment bank. By the middle of the year, John realized that he was going to be terminated by the bank. Therefore, he began preparing for a career in financial consulting as a sole practitioner. John became interested in consulting for a marina, but believing that boat owners formed a close fraternity, he decided that he could obtain such work only by acquiring a boat himself. Accordingly, he purchased a 23-foot Sea Ray Boat for $25,000. During the year, John used the boat only once to visit marinas on the lake to discuss potential employment as a consultant. A few days after this one excursion, John injured his back and was unable to use the boat for the remainder of the year. John was unsuccessful in his attempts to obtain a consulting position with any of the marinas.

    At the beginning of the year, John also purchased a new car to be used for personal purposes. After John was terminated from the bank in September, he began using the car for business purposes.

    Identify the relevant tax issues for John.

21. What are the tax consequences of listed property failing to meet the predominantly business use test?

22. Discuss what factors are used in determining whether the more-than-50% business use test has been satisfied.

23. If a taxpayer does not pass the more-than-50% business use test on an automobile, discuss whether the statutory dollar limitations on cost recovery are applicable.

24. Discuss the tax consequences that result when a passenger automobile, which failed the more-than-50% business usage test during the first two years, satisfies the test for the third year.

25. Discuss whether § 179 should be elected for a passenger automobile.

26. Explain the reason for the inclusion amount with respect to leased passenger automobiles.

27. Explain how an inclusion amount is determined with respect to leased passenger automobiles.

28. Discuss the substantiation requirements for listed property.

29. Explain the amortization period of a § 197 intangible if the actual useful life is less than 15 years.

30. What is the amortization period for self-created goodwill?

31. Discuss the options for handling intangible drilling and development costs.

32. Briefly discuss the differences between cost depletion and percentage depletion.

PROBLEMS

33. On January 1, 1992, Black Company acquired an asset (three-year property) for $10,000 for use in its business. In the years 1992 and 1993, Black took $3,333 and $4,445 of cost recovery. The allowable cost recovery for the years 1994 and 1995 was $1,481 and $741, but Black did not take the deductions. In those years, Black had net operating losses, and the company wanted to "save" the deductions for later years. On January 1, 1996, the asset was sold for $2,000. Calculate the gain or loss on the sale of the asset in 1996.

34. Eve acquired a personal residence in 1991 for $70,000. In January 1996, when the fair market value was $80,000, she converted the residence to rental property.
    a. Calculate the amount of cost recovery that can be taken in 1996.
    b. What would your answer be if the property were worth only $50,000 in 1996?

35. Jim acquired a 15-year class asset on March 1, 1986, for $40,000. He did not elect immediate expensing under § 179. On November 10, 1996, Jim sells the asset.
    a. Determine Jim's cost recovery for 1986.
    b. Determine Jim's cost recovery for 1996.

36. Walt purchased a tugboat for use in his business on March 15, 1996, for $500,000. He does not elect immediate expensing under § 179. On February 16, 2002, Walt sells the tug.
    a. Determine Walt's cost recovery for 1996.
    b. Determine Walt's cost recovery for 2002.

37. Juan acquires a five-year class asset on December 2, 1996, for $100,000. This is the only asset acquired by Juan during the year. He does not elect immediate expensing under § 179. On July 15, 1997, Juan sells the asset.
    a. Determine Juan's cost recovery for 1996.
    b. Determine Juan's cost recovery for 1997.

38. Debra acquired a building for $300,000 (exclusive of land) on January 1, 1984. Calculate the cost recovery using the statutory percentage method for 1984 and 1996 if:
    a. The real property is low-income housing.
    b. The real property is a factory building.

39. On December 2, 1984, Wade purchased and placed in service a warehouse. The warehouse cost $800,000. Wade used the statutory percentage cost recovery method. On July 7, 1996, Wade sold the warehouse.
    a. Determine Wade's cost recovery for 1984.
    b. Determine Wade's cost recovery for 1996.

40. On November 1, 1996, Sam purchases and places in service a building that is used as a warehouse. The cost of the building is $2.5 million. Determine Sam's cost recovery for 1996.

41. Pat acquires a warehouse on November 1, 1996, at a cost of $4,500,000. On January 30, 2007, Pat sells the warehouse. Calculate Pat's cost recovery for 1996. For 2007.

42. James acquired an apartment building on March 10, 1996, for $1,300,000. Calculate James's cost recovery for 1996.

43. Lori, who is single, acquired a new copier (five-year class property) on March 2, 1996, for $30,000. Lori's taxable income derived from her business (without regard to the amount expensed under § 179) is $100,000. If Lori elects immediate expensing under § 179, determine her total deduction, with respect to the copier, for 1996.

44. Jack owns a small business that he operates as a sole proprietor. In 1996, Jack will net $9,000 of business income before consideration of any § 179 deduction. Jack spends $208,000 on new equipment in 1996. If Jack also has $3,000 of § 179 deduction carryforwards from 1995, determine his § 179 expense deduction for 1996 and the amount of any carryforward.

45. Olga is the proprietor of a small business. In 1996, her business income, before consideration of any § 179 deduction, is $5,000. Olga spends $203,000 on new equipment and furniture for 1996. If Olga elects to take the § 179 deduction on a desk that cost $20,000 (included in the $203,000), determine her total cost recovery for 1996 with respect to the desk.

46. On March 10, 1996, Yoon purchased three-year class property for $20,000. On December 15, 1996, Yoon purchased five-year class property for $50,000.
    a. Calculate Yoon's cost recovery for 1996, assuming he does not make the § 179 election or use straight-line cost recovery.
    b. Calculate Yoon's cost recovery for 1996, assuming he does elect to use § 179 and does not elect to use straight-line cost recovery.
    c. Assuming Yoon's marginal tax rate is 36%, determine his tax benefit from electing § 179.

47. On July 1, 1996, Wilma places in service a computer (five-year class property). The computer cost $20,000. Wilma used the computer 65% for business. The remainder of the time, she used the computer for personal purposes. If Wilma does not elect § 179, determine her cost recovery deduction for the computer for 1996.

48. John Johnson is considering acquiring an automobile at the beginning of 1996 that he will use 100% of the time as a taxi. The purchase price of the automobile is $25,000. John has heard of cost recovery limits on automobiles and wants to know how much of the $25,000 he can deduct in the first year. Write a letter to John in which you present your calculations. Also, prepare a memo for the tax files. John's address is 100 Morningside, Clinton, MS 39058.

49. On February 16, 1996, Ron purchased and placed into service a new car. The purchase price was $18,000. Ron drove the car 12,000 miles during the remainder of the year, 9,000 miles for business and 3,000 miles for personal use. Ron used the statutory percentage method of cost recovery. Calculate the total deduction Ron may take for 1996 with respect to the car.

50. On June 5, 1996, Leo purchased and placed in service a $19,000 car. The business use percentage for the car is always 100%. Compute Leo's cost recovery deduction in 2002.

51. On June 14, 1996, Helen purchased and placed in service a new car. The purchase price was $16,000. The car was used 75% for business and 25% for personal use in both 1996 and 1997. In 1998, the car was used 40% for business and 60% for personal use. Compute the cost recovery deduction for the car in 1998 and the cost recovery recapture.

52. In 1996, Paul purchased a computer (five-year property) for $120,000. The computer was used 60% for business, 20% for income production, and 20% for personal use. In 1997, the usage changed to 40% for business, 30% for income production, and 30% for personal use. Compute the cost recovery deduction for 1997 and any cost recovery recapture. Assume Paul did not make a § 179 election on the computer in 1996.

53. Sally purchased a computer (five-year property) for $3,000. Sally could use the computer 100% of the time in her business, or she could allow her family to also use the computer. Sally estimates that if her family uses the computer, the business use will be 40% and the personal use will be 60%. Determine the tax cost to Sally, in the year of

acquisition, of allowing her family to use the computer. Assume that Sally would not elect § 179 limited expensing and that her marginal tax rate is 31%.

54. Midway through 1996, Abdel leases and places in service a passenger automobile. The lease will run for five years, and the payments are $430 per month. During 1996, Abdel uses the car 70% for business use and 30% for personal use. Assuming the inclusion dollar amount from the IRS table is $76, determine the tax consequences to Abdel from the lease for the year 1996.

55. Use the information given in Problem 54, but assume the inclusion dollar amount is $167. Abdel uses the car 60% for business use and 40% for personal use in 1997. Determine Abdel's tax consequences from the lease in 1997.

56. Dennis Harding is considering acquiring an automobile that he will use 100% for business. The purchase price of the automobile would be $30,500. If Dennis leased the car for five years, the lease payments would be $350 per month. Dennis will acquire the car on January 1, 1996. The inclusion dollar amounts from the IRS table for the next five years are $111, $244, $363, $435, and $503. Dennis desires to know the effect on his adjusted gross income of purchasing versus leasing the car for the next five years. Write a letter to Dennis and present your calculations. Also, prepare a memo for the tax files. His address is 150 Avenue I, Memphis, TN 38112.

57. On March 5, 1996, Nell purchased equipment for $60,000. The equipment is 7-year class property and has an ADS midpoint of 9.5 years. Determine Nell's cost recovery deduction for computing 1996 taxable income using the straight-line method under the alternative depreciation system and assuming she does not make a § 179 election.

58. In 1996, Muhammad purchased a light-duty truck for $12,000. The truck is used 100% for business. Muhammad did not make a § 179 election with respect to the truck. If Muhammad uses the statutory percentage method, determine his cost recovery deduction for 1996 for computing taxable income and for computing his alternative minimum tax.

59. In June 1996, Cardinal, Inc., purchased and placed in service railroad track costing $600,000.
    a. Calculate Cardinal's cost recovery deduction for 1996 for computing taxable income, assuming Cardinal does not make the § 179 election or use straight-line cost recovery.
    b. Calculate Cardinal's cost recovery deduction for 1996 for computing taxable income, assuming Cardinal does not make the § 179 election but does elect to use ADS 150% declining-balance cost recovery.

60. Jamie purchased $60,000 of office furniture for her business in June of the current year. Jamie understands that if she elects to use the alternative depreciation system to compute her regular tax, there will be no difference between the cost recovery for computing the regular income tax and the AMT. Jamie wants to know the *regular* tax cost, after three years, of using ADS rather than MACRS. Assume that Jamie does not elect § 179 limited expensing and that her marginal tax rate is 31%.

61. On August 1, 1996, Jake acquired a dental practice from Bob for $250,000. The purchase price was allocated $200,000 to the tangible assets of the practice and $50,000 to the goodwill. Determine Jake's deduction for the amortization of the goodwill for 1996.

62. Mike Saxon is negotiating the purchase of a business. The final purchase price has been agreed upon, but the allocation of the purchase price to the assets is still being discussed. Appraisals on a warehouse range from $1,200,000 to $1,500,000. If a value of $1,200,000 is used for the warehouse, the remainder of the purchase price, $800,000, will be allocated to goodwill. If $1,500,000 is allocated to the warehouse, goodwill will be $500,000. Mike wants to know what effect each alternative will have on cost recovery and amortization during the first year. Under the agreement, Mike will take over the business on January 1 of next year. Write a letter to Mike in which you present your calculations and recommendation. Also, prepare a memo for the tax files. Mike's address is 200 Rolling Hills Drive, Shavertown, PA 18708.

63. Wes acquired a mineral interest during the year for $5 million. A geological survey estimated that 250,000 tons of the mineral remained in the deposit. During the year, 80,000 tons were mined, and 45,000 tons were sold for $6 million. Other expenses amounted to $4 million. Assuming the mineral depletion rate is 22%, calculate Wes's lowest taxable income.

64. Chris purchased an oil interest for $2,000,000. Recoverable barrels were estimated to be 500,000. During the year, 120,000 barrels were sold for $3,840,000, regular expenses (including cost recovery) were $1,240,000, and IDC were $1,000,000. Calculate Chris's taxable income under the expensing and capitalization methods of handling IDC.

CUMULATIVE PROBLEMS

65. John Smith, age 31, is single and has no dependents. At the beginning of 1996, John started his own excavation business and named it Earth Movers. John lives at 1045 Center Street, Lindon, UT, and his business is located at 381 State Street, Lindon, UT. The zip code for both addresses is 84059. John's Social Security number is 321–09–6456, and the business identification number is 98–1234567. John is a cash basis taxpayer. During 1996, John had the following items in connection with his business:

Fees for services	$275,000
Building rental expense	32,000
Office furniture and equipment rental expense	5,000
Office supplies	1,500
Utilities	4,000
Salary for secretary	25,000
Salary for equipment operators	75,000
Payroll taxes	9,000
Fuel and oil for the equipment	20,000
Purchase of three front-end loaders on January 15, 1996, for $175,000. John made the election under § 179.	175,000
Purchase of a new dump truck on January 18, 1996	30,000

During 1996, John had the following additional items:

Interest income from First National Bank	$ 9,000
Dividends from Exxon	1,500
Quarterly estimated tax payments	11,500

On October 8, 1996, John inherited IBM stock from his Aunt Mildred. John had been her favorite nephew. According to the data provided by the executor of Aunt Mildred's estate, the stock had been valued for estate tax purposes at $70,000. John is considering selling the IBM stock for $75,000 on December 29, 1996, and using $60,000 of the proceeds to purchase an Acura NSX. He would use the car 100% for business. John wants to know what effect these transactions would have on his 1996 adjusted gross income.

Write a letter to John in which you present your calculations. Also, prepare a memo for the tax files. Suggested software (if available): *TurboTax* or *MacInTax*.

66. Bob Brown, age 30, is single and has no dependents. He was employed as a barber until May 1995 by Hair Cuts, Inc. In June 1995, Bob opened his own styling salon, the Style Shop, located at 465 Willow Drive, St. Paul, MN 55455. Bob is a cash basis taxpayer. He lives at 1021 Snelling Avenue, St. Paul, MN 55455. His Social Security number is 321–56–7102. Bob does not wish to designate $3 to the Presidential Election Campaign Fund. During 1995, Bob had the following income and expense items:

a. $25,000 salary from Hair Cuts, Inc.

b. $3,000 Federal income tax withheld by Hair Cuts, Inc.

c. $50,000 gross receipts from his own hair styling business.

d. Expenses connected with Bob's hair styling business:

- $900 laundry and cleaning

- $7,000 rent

- $2,000 supplies

- $800 utilities and telephone

e. Bob purchased and installed a fancy barber chair (five-year class property) on June 3, 1995. The chair cost $8,000. Bob did not make the § 179 election.

f. Bob purchased and installed furniture and fixtures (seven-year class property) on June 5, 1995. These items cost $20,000. Bob did make the § 179 election.

g. Bob's itemized deductions are as follows:

Property taxes on his residence	$2,000
Mortgage interest on his residence	4,000
State income taxes	2,500
Charitable contributions	1,500

h. Bob made estimated tax payments of $5,500.

Compute Bob Brown's 1995 Federal income tax payable (or refund due). If you use tax forms for your computations, you will need Forms 1040 and 4562 and Schedules A, C, and SE. Suggested software (if available): *TurboTax* or *MacInTax*.

Research Problems for this chapter appear at the end of Chapter 28.

TEAM PROJECT: ARTHUR ANDERSEN TAX CHALLENGE CASES

For more information on the Arthur Andersen Tax Challenge Cases, please refer to Chapter 2, page 2-41.

Information related to tax issues and problems that are discussed in this chapter may be found in the

Fields case on page 20

Read and analyze the case you have been assigned and *identify* any issues and problems that are related to material covered in this chapter. If the information provided in the case is complete, prepare answers for this part of the case at this time. If you need information that is contained in the later parts of the case, please write a memo summarizing the questions or problems so you can prepare a complete answer at a later date.

Deductions: Employee Expenses

LEARNING OBJECTIVES

After completing Chapter 8, you should be able to:

1. Distinguish between employee and self-employed status.

2. Recognize deductible transportation expenses.

3. Know how travel expenses are treated.

4. Determine the moving expense deduction.

5. Differentiate between deductible and nondeductible education expenses.

6. Understand how entertainment expenses are treated.

7. Identify other employee expenses.

8. Appreciate the difference between accountable and nonaccountable employee plans.

9. Work with the limitations on miscellaneous itemized deductions.

10. Develop tax planning ideas related to employee business expenses.

Considering the large number of taxpayers affected, the tax treatment of job-related expenses is unusually complex. To resolve this matter in a systematic fashion, a number of key questions must be asked:

- Is the taxpayer an *employee* or *self-employed*?
- If an employee, what expenses *qualify* as deductions?
- How are the expenses that qualify *classified* for tax purposes?
- To the extent the expenses are classified as deductions *from* AGI, are they subject to any *limitation*?

Once these questions have been posed and answered, the chapter considers various planning procedures available to maximize the deductibility of employee expenses.

EMPLOYEE VERSUS SELF-EMPLOYED

1 LEARNING OBJECTIVE
Distinguish between employee and self-employed status.

The determination of employment status is already controversial and can be expected to become an even greater problem in the future. Businesses are increasingly relying on the services of self-employed persons (i.e., **independent contractors**) for numerous reasons. Unlike employees, self-employed persons do not have to be included in various fringe benefit programs (e.g., group term life insurance) and retirement plans. Since they are not covered by FICA and FUTA (see Chapter 1), these payroll costs are avoided.

The IRS is very much aware of the tendency of businesses to wrongly classify workers as self-employed rather than as employees. In terms of tax consequences, employment status also makes a great deal of difference to the persons who perform the services. Expenses of self-employed taxpayers, to the extent allowable, are classified as deductions *for* AGI and are reported on Schedule C (Profit or Loss From Business) of Form 1040.[1] With the exception of reimbursement under an accountable plan (see later in the chapter), expenses of employees are deductions *from* AGI. They are reported on Form 2106 (Employee Business Expenses) and Schedule A (Itemized Deductions) of Form 1040.[2]

But when does an employer-employee relationship exist? Such a relationship exists when the employer has the right to specify the end result and the ways and means by which that result is to be attained.[3] An employee is subject to the will and control of the employer with respect not only to what shall be done but also to how it shall be done. If the individual is subject to the direction or control of another only to the extent of the end result but not as to the means of accomplishment, an employer-employee relationship does not exist. An example is the preparation of a taxpayer's return by an independent CPA.

Certain factors indicate an employer-employee relationship. They include (1) the right to discharge without legal liability the person performing the service, (2) the furnishing of tools or a place to work, and (3) payment based on time spent rather than the task performed. Each case is tested on its own merits, and the right to control the means and methods of accomplishment is the definitive test. Generally, physicians, lawyers, dentists, contractors, subcontractors, and others who offer services to the public are not classified as employees.

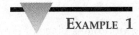

EXAMPLE 1   Arnold is a lawyer whose major client accounts for 60% of his billings. He does the routine legal work and income tax returns at the client's request. He is paid a monthly retainer in addition to amounts charged for extra work. Arnold is a self-employed individual. Even though most of his income comes from one client, he still has the right to determine how the end result of his work is attained. ▼

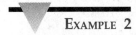

EXAMPLE 2   Ellen is a lawyer hired by Arnold to assist him in the performance of services for the client mentioned in Example 1. Ellen is under Arnold's supervision; he reviews her work and pays her an hourly fee. Ellen is an employee of Arnold. ▼

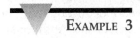

EXAMPLE 3   Frank is a licensed practical nurse who works as a private-duty nurse. He is under the supervision of the patient's doctor and is paid by the patient. Frank is not an employee of either the patient (who pays him) or the doctor (who supervises him). The ways and means of attaining the end result (care of the patient) are under his control. ▼

Employees in a special category are also allowed to file Schedule C to report income and deduct expenses *for* AGI. These employees are called **statutory employees** because they are not common law employees under the rules explained above. The wages or commissions paid to statutory employees are not subject to Federal income tax withholding but are subject to Social Security tax.[4]

---

[1] §§ 62(a)(1) and 162(a). See Appendix B for a reproduction of Schedule C.

[2] See Appendix B for a reproduction of Form 2106 and Schedule A.

[3] Reg. § 31.3401(c)–(1)(b).

[4] See Circular E, *Employer's Tax Guide* (IRS Publication 15), for further discussion of statutory employees.

EMPLOYEE EXPENSES—IN GENERAL

Once the employment relationship is established, employee expenses fall into one of the following categories:

- Transportation.
- Travel.
- Moving.
- Education.
- Entertainment.
- Other.

These expenses are discussed below in the order presented.

Keep in mind, however, that these expenses are not necessarily limited to employees. A deduction for business transportation, for example, is equally available to taxpayers who are self-employed.

TRANSPORTATION EXPENSES

QUALIFIED EXPENDITURES

2 **LEARNING OBJECTIVE**
Recognize deductible transportation expenses.

An employee may deduct unreimbursed employment-related transportation expenses as an itemized deduction *from* AGI. **Transportation expenses** include only the cost of transporting the employee from one place to another when the employee is *not* away from home *in travel status*. Such costs include taxi fares, automobile expenses, tolls, and parking.

Commuting Expenses.   Commuting between home and one's place of employment is a personal, nondeductible expense. The fact that one employee drives 30 miles to work and another employee walks six blocks is of no significance.[5]

EXAMPLE 4

Geraldo is employed by Sparrow Corporation. He drives 22 miles each way to work. The 44 miles he drives each workday are nondeductible commuting expenses. ▼

The rule that disallows a deduction for commuting expenses has several exceptions. An employee who uses an automobile to transport heavy tools to work and who otherwise would not drive to work is allowed a deduction, but only for the additional costs incurred to transport the work implements. Additional costs are those exceeding the cost of commuting by the same mode of transportation without the tools. For example, the rental of a trailer for transporting tools is deductible, but the expenses of operating the automobile generally are not deductible.[6] The Supreme Court has held that a deduction is permitted only when the taxpayer can show that the automobile would not have been used without the necessity to transport tools or equipment.[7]

Another exception is provided for an employee who has a second job. The expenses of getting from one job to another are deductible. If the employee goes home between jobs, the deduction is based on the distance between jobs.

---

[5] *Tauferner v. U.S.,* 69–1 USTC ¶9241, 23 AFTR2d 69–1025, 407 F.2d 243 (CA–10, 1969).
[6] Rev.Rul. 75–380, 1975–2 C.B. 59.

[7] *Fausner v. Comm.,* 73–2 USTC ¶9515, 32 AFTR2d 73–5202, 93 S.Ct. 2820 (USSC, 1973).

EXAMPLE 5

In the current year, Cynthia holds two jobs, a full-time job with Blue Corporation and a part-time job with Wren Corporation. During the 250 days that she works (adjusted for weekends, vacation, and holidays), Cynthia customarily leaves home at 7:30 A.M. and drives 30 miles to the Blue Corporation plant, where she works until 5:00 P.M. After dinner at a nearby cafe, Cynthia drives 20 miles to Wren Corporation and works from 7:00 to 11:00 P.M. The distance from the second job to Cynthia's home is 40 miles. Her deduction is based on 20 miles (the distance between jobs). ▼

If the taxpayer is required to incur a transportation expense to travel between work stations, that expense is deductible.

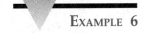

EXAMPLE 6

Thomas, a general contractor, drives from his home to his office, then drives to three building sites to perform his required inspections, and finally drives home. The costs of driving to his office and driving home from the last inspection site are nondeductible commuting expenses. The other transportation costs are deductible. ▼

Likewise, the commuting costs from home to a temporary work station and from the temporary work station to home are deductible.[8]

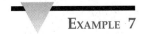

EXAMPLE 7

Vivian works for a firm in downtown Denver and commutes to work. She occasionally works in a customer's office. On one such occasion, Vivian drove directly to the customer's office, a round-trip distance from her home of 40 miles. She did not go into her office, which is a 52-mile round-trip. Her mileage for going to and from the temporary work station is deductible. ▼

Also deductible is the reasonable travel cost between the general working area and a temporary work station outside that area.[9] What constitutes the general working area depends on the facts and circumstances of each situation. Furthermore, if an employee customarily works on several temporary assignments in a localized area, that localized area becomes the regular place of employment. Transportation from home to these locations becomes a personal, nondeductible commuting expense.

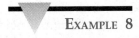

EXAMPLE 8

Sam, a building inspector in Minneapolis, regularly inspects buildings for building code violations for his employer, a general contractor. During one busy season, the St. Paul inspector became ill, and Sam was required to inspect several buildings in St. Paul. The expenses for transportation for the trips to St. Paul are deductible. ▼

COMPUTATION OF AUTOMOBILE EXPENSES

A taxpayer has two choices in computing automobile expenses. The actual operating cost, which includes depreciation (cost recovery), gas, oil, repairs, licenses, and insurance, may be used. Records must be kept that detail the automobile's personal and business use. Only the percentage allocable to business transportation and travel is allowed as a deduction. Complex rules for the computation of depreciation (discussed in Chapter 7) apply if the actual expense method is used.

Use of the **automatic mileage method** is the second alternative. For 1996 the deduction is based on 31 cents per mile for all business miles.[10] Parking fees and

---

[8] Rev.Rul. 90–23, 1990–1 C.B. 28 as amplified by Rev.Rul. 94–47, 1994–2 C.B. 18.

[9] Rev.Rul. 190, 1953–2 C.B. 303 as amplified by Rev.Rul. 94–47, 1994–2 C.B. 18.

[10] Rev.Proc. 95–54, I.R.B. No. 52, 27. The rate was 30 cents a mile for 1995.

tolls are allowed in addition to expenses computed using the automatic mileage method.

Generally, a taxpayer may elect either method for any particular year. However, the following restrictions apply:

- The vehicle must be owned by the taxpayer.
- If two or more vehicles are in use (for business purposes) at the *same* time (not alternately), a taxpayer may not use the automatic mileage method.
- A basis adjustment is required if the taxpayer changes from the automatic mileage method to the actual operating cost method. Depreciation is considered allowed for the business miles in accordance with the following schedule for the most recent five years:

Year	Rate per Mile
1996	12 cents
1995	12 cents
1994	12 cents
1993	11.5 cents
1992	11.5 cents

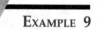

EXAMPLE 9   Tim purchased his automobile in 1993 for $15,000. It is used 90% for business purposes. Tim drove the automobile for 10,000 business miles in 1995; 8,500 miles in 1994; and 6,000 miles in 1993. At the beginning of 1996, the basis of the business portion is $10,590.

Cost ($15,000 × 90%)	$13,500
Less depreciation:	
1995 (10,000 miles × 12 cents)	(1,200)
1994 (8,500 miles × 12 cents)	(1,020)
1993 (6,000 × 11.5 cents)	(690)
Adjusted business basis 1/1/96	$10,590

- Use of the automatic mileage method in the first year the auto is placed in service is considered an election to exclude the auto from the MACRS method of depreciation (discussed in Chapter 7).
- A taxpayer may not switch to the automatic mileage method if the MACRS statutory percentage method or the election to expense under § 179 has been used.

TRAVEL EXPENSES

DEFINITION OF TRAVEL EXPENSES

3 **LEARNING OBJECTIVE**
Know how travel expenses are treated.

An itemized deduction is allowed for unreimbursed travel expenses related to a taxpayer's employment. **Travel expenses** are more broadly defined in the Code than are transportation expenses. Travel expenses include transportation expenses and meals and lodging while away from home in the pursuit of a trade or business. Meals cannot be lavish or extravagant under the circumstances. Transportation expenses (as previously discussed) are deductible even though the taxpayer is not away from home. A deduction for travel expenses is available only if the taxpayer is away from his or her tax home. Travel expenses also include reasonable laundry and incidental expenses.

AWAY-FROM-HOME REQUIREMENT

The crucial test for the deductibility of travel expenses is whether or not the employee is away from home overnight. "Overnight" need not be a 24-hour period, but it must be a period substantially longer than an ordinary day's work and must require rest, sleep, or a relief-from-work period.[11] A one-day business trip is not travel status, and meals and lodging for such a trip are not deductible.

Temporary Assignments. The employee must be away from home for a temporary period. If the taxpayer-employee is reassigned to a new post for an indefinite period of time, that new post becomes his or her tax home. *Temporary* indicates that the assignment's termination is expected within a reasonably short period of time. The position of the IRS is that the tax home is the business location, post, or station of the taxpayer. Thus, travel expenses are not deductible if a taxpayer is reassigned for an indefinite period and does not move his or her place of residence to the new location.

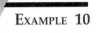
EXAMPLE 10

Malcolm's employer opened a branch office in San Diego. Malcolm was assigned to the new office for three months to train a new manager and to assist in setting up the new office. He tried commuting from his home in Los Angeles for a week and decided that he could not continue driving several hours a day. He rented an apartment in San Diego, where he lived during the week. He spent weekends with his wife and children at their home in Los Angeles. Malcolm's rent, meals, laundry, incidentals, and automobile expenses in San Diego are deductible. To the extent that Malcolm's transportation expense related to his weekend trips home exceeds what his cost of meals and lodging would have been, the excess is personal and nondeductible. ▼

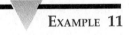
EXAMPLE 11

Assume that Malcolm in Example 10 was transferred to the new location to become the new manager permanently. His wife and children continued to live in Los Angeles until the end of the school year. Malcolm is no longer "away from home" because the assignment is not temporary. His travel expenses are not deductible. ▼

To curtail controversy in this area, the Code specifies that a taxpayer "*shall not* be treated as *temporarily* away from home during any period of employment if such period exceeds 1 year."[12]

Determining the Tax Home. Under ordinary circumstances, determining the location of a taxpayer's tax home does not present a problem. The tax home is the area in which the taxpayer derives his or her principal source of income; when the taxpayer has more than one place of employment, the tax home is based on the amount of time spent in each area..

It is possible for a taxpayer never to be away from his or her tax home. In other words, the tax home follows the taxpayer.[13] Thus, all meals and lodging remain personal and are not deductible.

---

[11] *U.S. v. Correll,* 68–1 USTC ¶9101, 20 AFTR2d 5845, 88 S.Ct. 445 (USSC, 1967); Rev.Rul. 75–168, 1975–1 C.B. 58.

[12] § 162(a). Added by the Comprehensive National Energy Policy Act of 1992.

[13] *Moses Mitnick,* 13 T.C. 1 (1949).

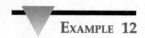

EXAMPLE 12

Bill is employed as a long-haul truck driver. He is single, stores his clothes and other belongings at his parents' home, and stops there for periodic visits. Most of the time, Bill is on the road, sleeping in his truck and in motels. It is likely that Bill is never in travel status, as he is not away from home. Consequently, none of his meals and lodging is deductible.

RESTRICTIONS ON TRAVEL EXPENSES

The possibility always exists that taxpayers will attempt to treat vacation or pleasure travel as deductible business travel. To prevent such practices, the law contains restrictions on certain travel expenses.

Conventions.   For travel expenses to be deductible, a convention must be directly related to the taxpayer's trade or business.[14]

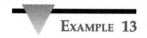

EXAMPLE 13

Dr. Hill, a pathologist who works for a hospital in Ohio, travels to Las Vegas to attend a two-day session on recent developments in estate planning. No deduction is allowed for Dr. Hill's travel expenses. ▼

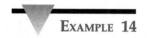

EXAMPLE 14

Assume the same facts as in Example 13 except that the convention deals entirely with recent developments in forensic medicine. Under these circumstances, a travel deduction is allowed. ▼

If the proceedings of the convention are videotaped, the taxpayer must attend convention sessions to view the videotaped materials along with other participants. This requirement does not disallow deductions for costs (other than travel, meals, and entertainment) of renting or using videotaped materials related to business.

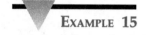

EXAMPLE 15

A CPA is unable to attend a convention at which current developments in taxation are discussed. She pays $200 for videotapes of the lectures and views them at home later. The $200 is an itemized deduction if the CPA is an employee. If she is self-employed, the $200 is a deduction *for* AGI. ▼

The Code places stringent restrictions on the deductibility of travel expenses of the taxpayer's spouse or dependent.[15] Generally, the accompaniment by the spouse or dependent must serve a bona fide business purpose, and the expenses must be otherwise deductible.

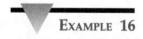

EXAMPLE 16

Assume the same facts as in Example 14 with the additional fact that Dr. Hill is accompanied by Mrs. Hill. Mrs. Hill is not employed, but possesses secretarial skills and takes notes during the proceedings. No deduction is allowed for Mrs. Hill's travel expenses. ▼

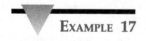

EXAMPLE 17

Modify the facts in Example 16 to make Mrs. Hill a nurse trained in pathology, who is employed by Dr. Hill as his assistant. Now, Mrs. Hill's travel expenses qualify as deductions. ▼

Education.   Travel as a form of education is not deductible.[16] If, however, the education qualifies as a deduction, the travel involved is allowed.

---

[14] § 274(h)(1).
[15] § 274(m)(3).

[16] § 274(m)(2).

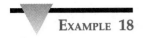

EXAMPLE 18   Greta, a German teacher, travels to Germany to maintain general familiarity with the language and culture. No travel expense deduction is allowed. ▼

EXAMPLE 19   Jean-Claude, a scholar of French literature, travels to Paris to do specific library research that cannot be done elsewhere and to take courses that are offered only at the Sorbonne. The travel costs are deductible, assuming that the other requirements for deducting education expenses (discussed later in the chapter) are met. ▼

COMBINED BUSINESS AND PLEASURE TRAVEL

To be deductible, travel expenses need not be incurred in the performance of specific job functions. Travel expenses incurred in attending a professional convention are deductible by an employee if attendance is connected with services as an employee. For example, an employee of a law firm can deduct travel expenses incurred in attending a meeting of the American Bar Association.

Domestic Travel.   Travel deductions have been used in the past by persons who claimed a tax deduction for what was essentially a personal vacation. As a result, several provisions have been enacted to govern deductions associated with combined business and pleasure trips. If the business/pleasure trip is from one point in the United States to another point in the United States, the transportation expenses are deductible only if the trip is *primarily for business*.[17] If the trip is primarily for pleasure, no transportation expenses qualify as a deduction. Meals, lodging, and other expenses are allocated between business and personal days.

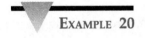

EXAMPLE 20   In the current year, Hana travels from Seattle to New York primarily for business. She spends five days conducting business and three days sightseeing and attending shows. Her plane and taxi fare amounts to $560. Her meals amount to $100 per day, and lodging and incidental expenses are $150 per day. She can deduct the transportation charges of $560, since the trip is primarily for business (five days of business versus three days of sightseeing). Meals are limited to five days and are subject to the 50% cutback (discussed later in the chapter) for a total of $250 [5 days × ($100 × 50%)], and other expenses are limited to $750 (5 days × $150). If Hana is an employee, the unreimbursed travel expenses are miscellaneous itemized deductions. ▼

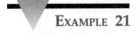

EXAMPLE 21   Assume Hana goes to New York for a two-week vacation. While there, she spends several hours renewing acquaintances with people in her company's New York office. Her transportation expenses are not deductible. ▼

Foreign Travel.   When the trip is *outside the United States*, special rules apply.[18] Transportation expenses must be allocated between business and personal unless (1) the taxpayer is away from home for seven days or less *or* (2) less than 25 percent of the time was for personal purposes. No allocation is required if the taxpayer has no substantial control over arrangements for the trip or the desire for a vacation is not a major factor in taking the trip. If the trip is primarily for pleasure, no transportation charges are deductible. Days devoted to travel are considered business days. Weekends, legal holidays, and intervening days are considered business days, provided that both the preceding and succeeding days were business days.

---

[17] Reg. § 1.162–2(b)(1).   [18] § 274(c) and Reg. § 1.274–4.

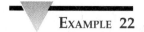

EXAMPLE 22

In the current year, Robert takes a trip from New York to Japan primarily for business purposes. He is away from home from June 10 through June 19. He spends three days vacationing and seven days conducting business (including two travel days). His air fare is $2,500, his meals amount to $100 per day, and lodging and incidental expenses are $160 per day. Since Robert is away from home for more than seven days and more than 25% of his time is devoted to personal purposes, only 70% (7 days business/10 days total) of the transportation is deductible. His deductions are as follows:

Transportation (70% × $2,500)		$1,750
Lodging ($160 × 7)		1,120
Meals ($100 × 7)	$ 700	
Less: 50% cutback (discussed later)	(350)	350
Total		$3,220

If Robert is gone the same period of time but spends only two days (rather than three) vacationing, no allocation of transportation is required. Since the pleasure portion of the trip is less than 25% of the total, all of the air fare qualifies for the travel deduction. ▼

Certain restrictions are imposed on the deductibility of expenses paid or incurred to attend conventions located outside the North American area. The expenses are disallowed unless it is established that the meeting is directly related to a trade or business of the taxpayer. Disallowance also occurs unless the taxpayer shows that it is as reasonable for the meeting to be held in a foreign location as within the North American area.

The foreign convention rules do not operate to bar a deduction to an employer if the expense is compensatory in nature. For example, a trip to Rome won by a top salesperson is included in the gross income of the employee and is fully deductible by the employer.

MOVING EXPENSES

4   LEARNING OBJECTIVE
Determine the moving expense deduction.

In 1993, Congress significantly changed the tax treatment of moving expenses. Major changes included, but are not limited to, the following:

- Expansion of the distance test (see below) from 35 miles to 50 miles.
- Elimination of any deduction for move-related meals.
- Deletion of a deduction for certain indirect moving expenses (e.g., house-hunting and temporary living expenses).
- Reclassification of moving expenses to deductions *for* AGI rather than deductions *from* AGI.

The changes applied to expenses incurred after 1993.

Moving expenses are deductible for moves in connection with the commencement of work at a new principal place of work.[19] Both employees and self-employed individuals can deduct these expenses. To be eligible for a moving expense deduction, a taxpayer must meet two basic tests: distance and time.

---

[19] § 217(a).

DISTANCE TEST

To meet the distance test, the taxpayer's new job location must be at least 50 miles farther from the taxpayer's old residence than the old residence was from the former place of employment. In this regard, the location of the new residence is not relevant. This eliminates a moving expense deduction for taxpayers who purchase a new home in the same general area without changing their place of employment. Those who accept a new job in the same general area as the old job location are also eliminated.

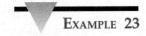

EXAMPLE 23

Harry is permanently transferred to a new job location. The distance from Harry's former home to his new job (80 miles) exceeds the distance from his former home to his old job (30 miles) by at least 50 miles. Harry has met the distance test for a moving expense deduction. (See the following diagram.)

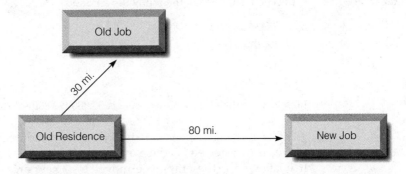

If Harry is not employed before the move, his new job must be at least 50 miles from his former residence. In this instance, Harry has met the distance test if he was not previously employed. ▼

TIME TEST

To meet the time test, an employee must be employed on a full-time basis at the new location for 39 weeks in the 12-month period following the move. If the taxpayer is a self-employed individual, he or she must work in the new location for 78 weeks during the next two years. The first 39 weeks must be in the first 12 months. The time test is suspended if the taxpayer dies, becomes disabled, or is discharged or transferred by the new employer through no fault of the employee.

A taxpayer might not be able to meet the 39-week test by the due date of the tax return for the year of the move. For this reason, two alternatives are allowed. The taxpayer can take the deduction in the year the expenses are incurred, even though the 39-week test has not been met. If the taxpayer later fails to meet the test, either (1) the income of the following year is increased by an amount equal to the deduction previously claimed for moving expenses, or (2) an amended return is filed for the year of the move. The second alternative is to wait until the test is met and then file an amended tax return for the year of the move.

TREATMENT OF MOVING EXPENSES

What Is Included. "Qualified" moving expenses include *reasonable* expenses of:

- Moving household goods and personal effects.
- Traveling from the former residence to the new place of residence.

For this purpose, *traveling* includes lodging, but not meals, for the taxpayer and members of the household.[20] It does not include the cost of moving servants or others who are not members of the household. The taxpayer can elect to use actual auto expenses (no depreciation is allowed) or the automatic mileage method. In this case, moving expense mileage is limited in 1996 to 10 cents per mile (nine cents in 1995) for each car. These expenses are also limited by the reasonableness standard. For example, if one moves from Texas to Florida via Maine and takes six weeks to do so, the transportation and lodging must be allocated between personal and moving expenses.

EXAMPLE 24

Jill is transferred by her employer from the Atlanta office to the San Francisco office. In this connection, she spends the following amounts:

Cost of moving furniture	$2,800
Transportation	700
Meals	200
Lodging	300

Jill's total qualified moving expense is $3,800 ($2,800 + $700 + $300). ▼

The moving expense deduction is allowed regardless of whether the employee is transferred by the existing employer or is employed by a new employer. It is allowed if the employee moves to a new area and obtains employment or switches from self-employed status to employee status (and vice versa). The moving expense deduction is also allowed if an individual is unemployed before obtaining employment in a new area.

How Treated. Qualified moving expenses that are paid (or reimbursed) by the employer are not reported as part of the gross income of the employee.[21] Moving expenses that are paid (or reimbursed) by the employer and are not qualified moving expenses are included in the employee's gross income and are not deductible. The employer is responsible for allocating the reimbursement between the qualified and nonqualified moving expenses. Reimbursed qualified moving expenses are separately stated on Form W–2 given to the employee for the year involved. Qualified moving expenses that are not reimbursed and those of self-employed taxpayers are deductions *for* AGI.[22]

Form 3903 is used to report the details of the moving expense deduction if the employee is not reimbursed or a self-employed person is involved.

EDUCATION EXPENSES

GENERAL REQUIREMENTS

5 LEARNING OBJECTIVE
Differentiate between deductible and nondeductible education expenses.

An employee can deduct expenses incurred for education (**education expenses**) as ordinary and necessary business expenses provided the expenses are incurred for either of two reasons:

---

[20] § 217(b).
[21] §§ 132(a)(6) and (g).

[22] § 62(a)(15).

1. To maintain or improve existing skills required in the present job.
2. To meet the express requirements of the employer or the requirements imposed by law to retain his or her employment status.

Education expenses are *not* deductible if the education is for either of the following purposes:

1. To meet the minimum educational standards for qualification in the taxpayer's existing job.
2. To qualify the taxpayer for a new trade or business.[23]

Fees incurred for professional qualification exams (the bar exam, for example) and fees for review courses (such as a CPA review course) are not deductible.[24] If the education incidentally results in a promotion or raise, the deduction still can be taken as long as the education maintained and improved existing skills and did not qualify a person for a new trade or business. A change in duties is not always fatal to the deduction if the new duties involve the same general work. For example, the IRS has ruled that a practicing dentist's education expenses incurred to become an orthodontist are deductible.[25]

REQUIREMENTS IMPOSED BY LAW OR BY THE EMPLOYER FOR RETENTION OF EMPLOYMENT

Teachers are permitted to deduct education expenses if additional courses are required by the employer or are imposed by law. Many states require a minimum of a bachelor's degree and a specified number of additional courses to retain a teaching job. In addition, some public school systems have imposed a master's degree requirement and require teachers to make satisfactory progress toward a master's degree in order to keep their positions. If the required education is the minimum degree required for the job, no deduction is allowed.

A taxpayer classified as an Accountant I who went back to school to obtain a bachelor's degree was not allowed to deduct the expenses. Although some courses tended to maintain and improve his existing skills in his entry-level position, the degree was the minimum requirement for his job.[26]

Expenses incurred for education required by law for various professions will also qualify for deduction.

EXAMPLE 25 In order to satisfy the State Board of Public Accountancy rules for maintaining her CPA license, Nancy takes an auditing course sponsored by a local college. The cost of the education is deductible. ▼

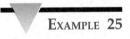

ETHICAL CONSIDERATIONS

Employer-Imposed Education Requirement

Justin, a CPA, is the owner and operator of Condor Corporation. Condor provides accounting and tax services for a number of regular businesses. These services are provided by Justin and two long-time employees, Martha and Alan. Martha and Alan have expressed a desire to attend a local college part-time and earn bachelor of accounting degrees.

---

[23] Reg. §§ 1.162–5(b)(2) and (3).
[24] Reg. § 1.212–1(f) and Rev.Rul. 69–292, 1969–1 C.B. 84.
[25] Rev.Rul. 74–78, 1974–1 C.B. 44.

[26] Reg. § 1.162–5(b)(2)(iii) Example (2); *Collin J. Davidson*, 43 TCM 743, T.C.Memo. 1982–119.

When Justin hears about the college plans that Martha and Alan have made, he adopts the following resolution for Condor Corporation: "Employees performing accounting and tax services for clients must possess or be pursuing a bachelor's degree in accounting."

What is Justin trying to accomplish with the resolution? Will it work? Is this ethical behavior?

MAINTAINING OR IMPROVING EXISTING SKILLS

The "maintaining or improving existing skills" requirement in the Code has been difficult for both taxpayers and the courts to interpret. For example, a business executive is permitted to deduct the costs of obtaining an M.B.A. on the grounds that the advanced management education is undertaken to maintain and improve existing management skills. The executive is eligible to deduct the costs of specialized, nondegree management courses that are taken for continuing education or to maintain or improve existing skills. Expenses incurred by the executive to obtain a law degree are not deductible, however, because the education constitutes training for a new trade or business. The Regulations deny a self-employed accountant a deduction for expenses relating to law school.[27]

CLASSIFICATION OF SPECIFIC ITEMS

Education expenses include books, tuition, typing, and transportation (e.g., from the office to night school) and travel (e.g., meals and lodging while away from home at summer school).

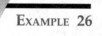 EXAMPLE 26

Bill, who holds a bachelor of education degree, is a secondary education teacher in the Los Angeles school system. The school board recently raised its minimum education requirement for new teachers from four years of college training to five. A grandfather clause allows teachers with only four years of college to continue to qualify if they show satisfactory progress toward a graduate degree. Bill enrolls at the University of California and takes three graduate courses. His unreimbursed expenses for this purpose are as follows:

Books and tuition	$2,600
Lodging while in travel status (June–August)	1,150
Meals while in travel status	800
Laundry while in travel status	220
Transportation	600

Bill has an itemized deduction as follows:

Books and tuition	$2,600
Lodging	1,150
Meals less 50% cutback (see below)	400
Laundry	220
Transportation	600
	$4,970

OTHER PROVISIONS DEALING WITH EDUCATION

The focus of this chapter is on the deduction aspects of certain items. For education, however, two important provisions involve the income aspects. One deals with the exclusion of certain scholarships from gross income.[28] The other deals with the exclusion from gross income of employer amounts provided under certain educational assistance programs.[29] Both of these provisions are discussed in Chapter 4.

▼ ENTERTAINMENT EXPENSES

6   **LEARNING OBJECTIVE**
Understand how entertainment expenses are treated.

Many taxpayers attempt to deduct personal entertainment expenses as business expenses. For this reason, the tax law restricts the deductibility of entertainment expenses. The Code contains strict record-keeping requirements and provides restrictive tests for the deduction of certain types of **entertainment expenses.**

DOLLAR LIMITATIONS

Currently, only 50 percent of meal and entertainment expenses are allowed as a deduction.[30] The limitation applies in the context of both employment and self-employment status. The 50 percent cutback is effective for tax years beginning after 1993 (previously the cutback was 20 percent). Although the cutback can apply to either the employer or the employee, it will not apply twice. The cutback applies to the one who really pays (economically) for the meals or entertainment.

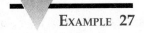

EXAMPLE 27

Jane, an employee of Pelican Corporation, entertains one of her clients. If Pelican Corporation does not reimburse Jane, she is subject to the cutback adjustment. If, however, Pelican Corporation reimburses Jane (or pays for the entertainment directly), Pelican suffers the cutback. ▼

What Is Covered. Transportation expenses are not affected by this provision—only meals and entertainment. The cutback also applies to taxes and tips relating to meals and entertainment. Cover charges, parking fees at an entertainment location, and room rental fees for a meal or cocktail party are also subject to the 50 percent rule.

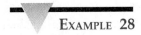

EXAMPLE 28

Joe pays a $30 cab fare to meet his client for dinner. The meal costs $120, and Joe leaves a $20 tip. His deduction is $100 [($120 + $20) × 50% + $30 cab fare]. ▼

What Is Not Covered. The cutback rule has a number of exceptions. One exception covers the case where the full value of the meals or entertainment is included in the compensation of the employee (or independent contractor).[31]

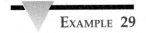

EXAMPLE 29

Myrtle wins an all-expense-paid trip to Europe for selling the most insurance for her company during the year. Her employer treats this trip as additional compensation to Myrtle. The cutback adjustment does not apply to the employer. ▼

---

[28] § 117.
[29] § 127.

[30] § 274(n).
[31] §§ 274(e)(2) and (9).

Another exception applies to meals and entertainment in a subsidized eating facility or where the *de minimis* fringe benefit rule is met (see Chapter 4).[32]

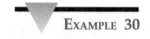

EXAMPLE 30

General Hospital has an employee cafeteria on the premises for its doctors, nurses, and other employees. The cafeteria operates at cost. The cutback rule does not apply to General Hospital. ▼

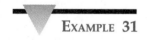

EXAMPLE 31

Canary Corporation gives a ham, a fruitcake, and a bottle of wine to each employee at year-end. Since the *de minimis* fringe benefit exclusion applies to business gifts of packaged foods and beverages, their *full* cost is deductible by Canary. ▼

A somewhat similar exception applies to employer-paid recreational activities for employees (e.g., the annual Christmas party or spring picnic).[33]

CLASSIFICATION OF EXPENSES

Entertainment expenses are categorized as follows: those *directly related* to business and those *associated with* business.[34] Directly related expenses are related to an actual business meeting or discussion. These expenses are distinguished from entertainment expenses that are incurred to promote goodwill, such as maintaining existing customer relations. To obtain a deduction for directly related entertainment, it is not necessary to show that actual benefit resulted from the expenditure as long as there was a reasonable expectation of benefit. To qualify as directly related, the expense should be incurred in a clear business setting. If there is little possibility of engaging in the active conduct of a trade or business due to the nature of the social facility, it is difficult to qualify the expenditure as directly related to business.

Expenses associated with, rather than directly related to, business entertainment must serve a specific business purpose, such as obtaining new business or

---

[32] § 274(n)(2).
[33] § 274(e)(4).

[34] § 274(a)(1)(A).

continuing existing business. These expenditures qualify only if the expenses directly precede or follow a bona fide business discussion. Entertainment occurring on the same day as the business discussion meets the test.

RESTRICTIONS UPON DEDUCTIBILITY

Business Meals. Any business meal is deductible only if the following are true:[35]

- The meal is directly related to or associated with the active conduct of a trade or business.
- The expense is not lavish or extravagant under the circumstances.
- The taxpayer (or an employee) is present at the meal.

A business meal with a business associate or customer is not deductible unless business is discussed before, during, or after the meal. This requirement is not intended to disallow the deduction for a meal consumed while away from home on business.

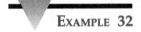

EXAMPLE 32

Lacy travels to San Francisco for a business convention. She pays for dinner with three colleagues and is not reimbursed by her employer. They do not discuss business. She can deduct 50% of the cost of her meal. However, she cannot deduct the cost of her colleagues' meals. ▼

The *clear business purpose* test requires that meals be directly related to or associated with the active conduct of a business. A meal is not deductible if it serves no business purpose.

ETHICAL CONSIDERATIONS

Reciprocal Entertaining

Walter (an attorney), Susan (an insurance broker), Richard (a realtor), and Nancy (a banker) are all good friends and do business with each other. Richard's accountant suggests that each might derive a substantial tax benefit if they went to lunch together as often as possible and rotated the tab. Do you believe the procedure suggested by Richard's accountant is proper? Why or why not?

The taxpayer or an employee must be present at the business meal for the meal to be deductible.[36] An independent contractor who renders significant services to the taxpayer is treated as an employee.

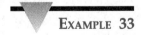

EXAMPLE 33

Lance, a party to a contract negotiation, buys dinner for other parties to the negotiation but does not attend the dinner. No deduction is allowed. ▼

Club Dues. In 1993, Congress amended the Code to provide: "No deduction shall be allowed . . . for amounts paid or incurred for membership in any club organized for business, pleasure, recreation, or other social purpose."[37] Although

---

[35] § 274(k).
[36] § 274(k)(1)(B).

[37] § 274(a)(3).

this prohibition seems quite broad, the IRS does not intend to deny a deduction for dues to clubs whose primary purpose is public service and community volunteerism (e.g., Kiwanis, Lions, Rotary).

Even though dues no longer are deductible, actual entertainment at a club may qualify.

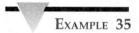

EXAMPLE 34

During the current year, Vincent spent $1,400 on business lunches at the Lakeside Country Club. The annual membership fee was $6,000, and Vincent used the facility 60% of the time for business. Presuming the lunches meet the business meal test, Vincent may claim $700 (50% × $1,400) as a deduction. None of the club dues are deductible. ▼

Ticket Purchases for Entertainment.   A deduction for the cost of a ticket for an entertainment activity is limited to the face value of the ticket.[38] This limitation is applied before the 50 percent rule. The face value of a ticket includes any tax. Under this rule, the excess payment to a scalper for a ticket is not deductible. Similarly, the fee to a ticket agency for the purchase of a ticket is not deductible.

Expenditures for the rental or use of a luxury skybox at a sports arena in excess of the face value of regular tickets are disallowed as deductions. If a luxury skybox is used for entertainment that is directly related to or associated with business, the deduction is limited to the face value of nonluxury box seats. All seats in the luxury skybox are counted, even when some seats are unoccupied.

The taxpayer may also deduct stated charges for food and beverages under the general rules for business entertainment. The deduction for skybox seats, food, and beverages is limited to 50 percent of cost.

EXAMPLE 35

In the current year, Condor Company pays $6,000 to rent a 10-seat skybox at City Stadium for three football games. Nonluxury box seats at each event range in cost from $25 to $35 a seat. In March, a Condor representative and five clients use the skybox for the first game. The entertainment follows a bona fide business discussion, and Condor spends $86 for food and beverages during the game. The deduction for the first sports event is as follows:

Food and beverages	$ 86
Deduction for seats ($35 × 10 seats)	350
Total entertainment expense	$436
50% limitation	×.50
Deduction	$218

▼

Business Gifts.   Business gifts are deductible to the extent of $25 per donee per year.[39] An exception is made for gifts costing $4 or less (e.g., pens with the employee's or company's name on them) or promotional materials. Such items are not treated as business gifts subject to the $25 limitation. In addition, incidental costs such as engraving of jewelry and nominal charges for gift-wrapping, mailing, and delivery are not included in the cost of the gift in applying the limitation. Gifts to superiors and employers are not deductible.

Records must be maintained to substantiate business gifts.

---

[38] § 274(l).   [39] § 274(b)(1).

OTHER EMPLOYEE EXPENSES

OFFICE IN THE HOME

7 LEARNING OBJECTIVE
Identify other employee expenses.

Employees and self-employed individuals are not allowed a deduction for **office in the home expenses** unless a portion of the residence is used *exclusively* on a *regular basis* as either:

- The principal place of business for any trade or business of the taxpayer.
- A place of business used by clients, patients, or customers.

Employees must meet an additional test: The use must be for the convenience of the employer rather than merely being "appropriate and helpful."[40]

The precise meaning of "principal place of business" was resolved by the U.S. Supreme Court. In a divided opinion, the Court established a two-pronged test.[41] First, determine the relative importance of the activities performed at each business location (i.e., inside and outside the personal residence). Second, compare the time spent at each business location.

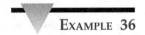
EXAMPLE 36

Dr. Smith is a self-employed anesthesiologist. During the year, he spends 30 to 35 hours per week administering anesthesia and postoperative care to patients in three hospitals, none of which provides him with an office. He also spends two to three hours per day in a room in his home that he uses exclusively as an office. He does not meet patients there, but he performs a variety of tasks related to his medical practice (e.g., contacting surgeons, bookkeeping, reading medical journals). None of Dr. Smith's expenses of the office in the home are deductible because the hospital procedures (i.e., administering to patients) are more important than those done at home. Also, more business time is spent outside the home than inside. ▼

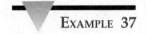
EXAMPLE 37

Lori is a salesperson. Her only office is a room in her home that she uses regularly and exclusively to set up appointments, store product samples, and write up orders and other reports for the companies whose products she sells. Lori makes most of her sales to customers by telephone or mail from her home office. She spends an average of 30 hours a week working at home and 12 hours a week visiting prospective customers to deliver products and occasionally take orders. Under these circumstances, Lori qualifies for the office in the home deduction. Visiting customers is less important to the business than the activities conducted in Lori's office.[42] ▼

The exclusive use requirement means that a specific part of the home must be used solely for business purposes. A deduction, if permitted, requires an allocation of total expenses of operating the home between business and personal use based on floor space or number of rooms.

Even if the taxpayer meets the above requirements, the allowable home office expenses cannot exceed the gross income from the business less all other business expenses attributable to the activity. Furthermore, the home office expenses that are allowed as itemized deductions anyway (e.g., mortgage interest and real estate

---

[40] § 280A(c)(1).
[41] *Comm. v. Soliman,* 93–1 USTC ¶50,014, 71 AFTR2d 93–463, 113 S.Ct. 701 (USSC, 1993) *rev'g.* 91–1 USTC ¶50,291, 67 AFTR2d 91–1112, 935 F.2d 52 (CA–4, 1991) and 94 T.C. 20 (1990).

[42] Notice 93–12, 1993–1 C.B. 298 amplified by Rev.Rul. 94–24, 1994–1 C.B. 87.

taxes) must be deducted first. All home office expenses of an employee are miscellaneous itemized deductions, except those (such as interest) that qualify as other personal itemized deductions. Home office expenses of a self-employed individual are trade or business expenses and are deductible *for* AGI.

Any disallowed home office expenses are carried forward and used in future years subject to the same limitations.

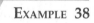

EXAMPLE 38

Rick is a certified public accountant employed by a regional CPA firm as a tax manager. He operates a separate business in which he refinishes furniture in his home. For this business, he uses two rooms in the basement of his home exclusively and regularly. The floor space of the two rooms constitutes 10% of the floor space of his residence. Gross income from the business totals $8,000. Expenses of the business (other than home office expenses) are $6,500. Rick incurs the following home office expenses:

Real property taxes on residence	$4,000
Interest expense on residence	7,500
Operating expenses of residence	2,000
Depreciation on residence (based on 10% business use)	250

Rick's deductions are determined as follows:

Business income		$ 8,000
Less: Other business expenses		(6,500)
		$ 1,500
Less: Allocable taxes ($4,000 × 10%)	$400	
Allocable interest ($7,500 × 10%)	750	(1,150)
		$ 350
Less: Allocable operating expenses of the residence ($2,000 × 10%)		(200)
		$ 150
Less: Allocable depreciation ($250, limited to remaining income)		(150)
		$ –0–

Rick has a carryover of $100 (the unused excess depreciation). Because he is self-employed, the allocable taxes and interest ($1,150), the other deductible office expenses ($200 + $150), and $6,500 of other business expenses are deductible *for* AGI. ▼

Form 8829 (Expenses for Business Use of Your Home) is available from the IRS for computation of the office in the home deduction.

The home office limitation cannot be circumvented by leasing part of one's home to an employer, using it as a home office, and deducting the expenses as a rental expense under § 212.

MISCELLANEOUS EMPLOYEE EXPENSES

Deductible miscellaneous employee expenses include special clothing and its upkeep, union dues, and professional expenses. Also deductible are professional dues, professional meetings, and employment agency fees for seeking employment in the same trade or business, whether or not a new job is secured.

To be deductible, special clothing must be both specifically required as a condition of employment and not adaptable for regular wear. For example, a police officer's uniform is not suitable for off-duty activities. An exception is clothing used to the extent that it takes the place of regular clothing (e.g., military uniforms).

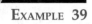

EXAMPLE 39

Captain Roberts is on active duty in the U.S. Marines. The cost of his regular uniforms is not deductible since such clothing is suitable for regular wear. Military regulations, however, generally preclude marines from wearing battle fatigues when they are off the military base. The cost of the fatigues, to the extent it exceeds any clothing allowance, qualifies as a deduction. ▼

The current position of the IRS is that expenses incurred in seeking employment are deductible if the taxpayer is seeking employment in the same trade or business. The deduction is allowed whether or not the attempts to secure employment are successful. An unemployed taxpayer can take a deduction providing there has been no substantial lack of continuity between the last job and the search for a new one. No deduction is allowed for persons seeking their first job or seeking employment in a new trade or business.

The basic cost of one telephone in the home is not deductible, even if used for business. Any long-distance or toll charges relating to business are deductible.

CONTRIBUTIONS TO INDIVIDUAL RETIREMENT ACCOUNTS

Employees not covered by another qualified plan can establish their own tax-deductible **Individual Retirement Accounts (IRAs).** The contribution ceiling is the smaller of $2,000 (or $2,250 for spousal IRAs) or 100 percent of compensation. If the taxpayer or spouse is an active participant in another qualified plan, the IRA deduction limitation is phased out *proportionately* between certain AGI ranges, as shown in Table 8–1.

AGI is calculated taking into account any § 469 passive losses and § 86 taxable Social Security benefits and ignoring any § 911 foreign income exclusion, § 135

▼ **TABLE 8–1**
Phase-Out of IRA
Deduction

AGI Filing Status	Phase-Out Begins	Phase-Out Ends
Single and head of household	$25,000	$35,000
Married, filing joint return	40,000	50,000
Married, filing separate return	–0–	10,000

savings bonds interest exclusion, and the IRA deduction. There is a $200 floor on the IRA deduction limitation for individuals whose AGI is not above the phase-out range.

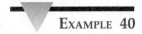

EXAMPLE 40

In 1996, Mr. and Mrs. Smith had compensation income of $27,000 and $20,000, respectively. Their AGI for 1996 was $47,000. Mr. Smith was an active participant in his employer's qualified retirement plan. Mr. and Mrs. Smith may *each* contribute $600 to an IRA. The deductible amount for each is reduced from $2,000 by $1,400 because of the phase-out mechanism:

$$\frac{\$7,000}{\$10,000} \times \$2,000 = \$1,400 \text{ reduction}$$

▼

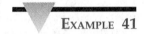

EXAMPLE 41

An unmarried individual is an active participant in his employer's qualified retirement plan. With AGI of $34,500, he would normally have an IRA deduction limit of $100 {$2,000 − [($34,500 − $25,000)/$10,000 × $2,000]}. However, because of the special floor provision, a $200 IRA deduction is allowable. ▼

To the extent that an individual is ineligible to make a deductible contribution to an IRA, *nondeductible contributions* can be made to separate accounts. The nondeductible contribution will be subject to the same dollar limits for deductible contributions of $2,000 of earned income ($2,250 for a spousal IRA). Income in the account accumulates tax-free until distributed. Only the account earnings will be taxed (account basis equals the contributions made by the taxpayer) upon distribution. A taxpayer may elect to treat deductible IRA contributions as nondeductible. If an individual has no taxable income for the year after taking into account other deductions, the election would be beneficial. The election is made on the individual's tax return for the taxable year to which the designation relates.

CLASSIFICATION OF EMPLOYEE EXPENSES

8   LEARNING OBJECTIVE
Appreciate the difference between accountable and nonaccountable employee plans.

The classification of employee expenses depends on whether they are reimbursed by the employer under an accountable plan. If so, then they are not reported by the employee at all. In effect, therefore, this result is equivalent to treating the expenses as deductions *for* AGI.[43] If the expenses are reimbursed under a nonaccountable plan or are not reimbursed at all, then they are classified as deductions *from* AGI and can only be claimed if the employee-taxpayer itemizes. An exception is made for moving expenses and the employment-related expenses of a qualified performing artist.[44] Here, deduction *for* AGI classification is allowed.

For classification purposes, therefore, the difference between accountable and nonaccountable plans is significant.

ACCOUNTABLE PLANS

In General.   An **accountable plan** requires the employee to satisfy these two requirements:

---

[43] § 62(a)(2).

[44] As defined in § 62(b).

- Adequately account for (substantiate) the expenses. An employee renders an *adequate accounting* by submitting a record, with receipts and other substantiation, to the employer.[45]
- Return any excess reimbursement or allowance. An "excess reimbursement or allowance" is any amount that the employee does not adequately account for as an ordinary and necessary business expense.

Substantiation. The law provides that no deduction is allowed for any travel, entertainment, business gift, or listed property (automobiles, computers) expenditure unless properly substantiated by adequate records. The records should contain the following information:[46]

- The amount of the expense.
- The time and place of travel or entertainment (or date of gift).
- The business purpose of the expense.
- The business relationship of the taxpayer to the person entertained (or receiving the gift).

This means the taxpayer must maintain an account book or diary in which the above information is recorded at the time of the expenditure. Documentary evidence, such as itemized receipts, is required to support any expenditure for lodging while traveling away from home and for any other expenditure of $75 or more. If a taxpayer fails to keep adequate records, each expense must be established by a written or oral statement of the exact details of the expense and by other corroborating evidence.[47]

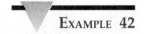

EXAMPLE 42

Bertha has travel expenses substantiated only by canceled checks. The checks establish the date, place, and amount of the expenditure. Because neither the business relationship nor the business purpose is established, the deduction is disallowed.[48] ▼

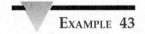

EXAMPLE 43

Dwight has travel and entertainment expenses substantiated by a diary showing the time, place, and amount of the expenditure. His oral testimony provides the business relationship and business purpose; however, since he has no receipts, any expenditures of $75 or more are disallowed.[49] ▼

Deemed Substantiation. In lieu of reimbursing actual expenses for travel away from home, many employers reduce their paperwork by adopting a policy of reimbursing employees with a *per diem* allowance, a flat dollar amount per day of business travel. Of the substantiation requirements listed above, the *amount* of the expense is proved, or *deemed substantiated*, by using such a per diem allowance or reimbursement procedure. The amount of expenses that is deemed substantiated is equal to the lesser of the per diem allowance or the amount of the Federal per diem rate.

The regular Federal per diem rate is the highest amount that the Federal government will pay to its employees for lodging and meals[50] while in travel status away from home in a particular area. The rates are different for different locations.[51]

[45] Reg. § 1.162–17(b)(4).
[46] § 274(d).
[47] Reg. § 1.274–5T(c)(3).
[48] *William T. Whitaker*, 56 TCM 47, T.C.Memo. 1988–418.
[49] *W. David Tyler*, 43 TCM 927, T.C.Memo. 1982–160.

[50] The meals per diem rate also covers incidental expenses, including laundry and cleaning of clothing and tips for waiters. Taxi fares and telephone calls are not included.
[51] Each current edition of *Your Federal Income Tax* (IRS Publication 17) contains the list and amounts for that year.

TAX IN THE NEWS

No Thanks for the Favor

A taxpayer must have documentary evidence (i.e., a receipt) when a travel or entertainment item is $75 or more. The threshold amount used to be $25 or more but was recently changed to reduce taxpayers' record-keeping burden. The change, announced in Notice 95–50 (I.R.B. No. 42, 8), is effective for expenditures incurred on or after October 1, 1995.

Many businesses that previously followed the IRS receipt threshold for purposes of reimbursing their employees will not conform to the change. In effect, they will retain the prior $25 rule. Companies fear that if they adopt the change, what used to be a $24.95 lunch will become a $74.95 lunch.

The use of the standard Federal per diem for meals constitutes an adequate accounting. Employees and self-employed persons can use the standard meal allowance instead of deducting the actual cost of daily meals, even if not reimbursed. There is no standard lodging allowance, however.

Only the amount of the expense is considered substantiated under the deemed substantiated method. The other substantiation requirements must be provided: place, date, business purpose of the expense, and the business relationship of the parties involved.

NONACCOUNTABLE PLANS

A **nonaccountable plan** is one in which an adequate accounting or return of excess amounts, or both, is not required. All reimbursements of expenses are reported in full as wages on the employee's Form W–2. Any allowable expenses are deductible in the same manner as are unreimbursed expenses.

Unreimbursed Employee Expenses.   Unreimbursed employee expenses are treated in a straightforward manner. Meals and entertainment expenses are subject to the 50 percent limit. Total unreimbursed employee business expenses are usually reported as miscellaneous itemized deductions subject to the 2 percent-of-AGI floor (see below). If the employee could have received, but did not seek, reimbursement for whatever reason, none of the employment-related expenses are deductible.

ETHICAL CONSIDERATIONS

The Frugal Employee

Wally is employed by Harrier Corporation as a regional sales manager. As such, he does a great deal of entertaining of both sales representatives and key clients. Harrier has a policy of reimbursing its employees for these expenses upon the rendition of an adequate accounting.

Wally does not submit all of his entertainment expenses, however, because he wants higher management to think he is frugal and efficient in utilizing company funds. Wally has no reason to believe that the company would have refused to reimburse the expenses he has not submitted. Harrier Corporation has never turned down any of Wally's expense vouchers.

On his Federal income tax return, Wally deducts the expenses not reimbursed. The return reflects nothing as to the reimbursed expenses.

Has Wally handled this tax matter properly? Why?

Failure to Comply with Accountable Plan Requirements. An employer may have an accountable plan and require employees to return excess reimbursements or allowances, but an employee may fail to follow the rules of the plan. In that case, the expenses and reimbursements are subject to nonaccountable plan treatment.

REPORTING PROCEDURES

The reporting requirements range from no reporting at all (accountable plans when all requirements are met) to the use of some or all of the following forms: Form W–2 (Wage and Tax Statement), Form 2106 (Employee Business Expenses) or Form 2106–EZ (Unreimbursed Employee Business Expenses), and Schedule A (Itemized Deductions) for nonaccountable plans and unreimbursed employee expenses.

Reimbursed employee expenses that are adequately accounted for under an accountable plan are deductible *for* AGI on Form 2106. Allowed excess expenses, expenses reimbursed under a nonaccountable plan, and unreimbursed expenses are deductible *from* AGI on Schedule A, subject to the 2 percent-of-AGI floor.

When a reimbursement under an accountable plan is paid in separate amounts relating to designated expenses such as meals or entertainment, no problem arises. The reimbursements and expenses are reported as such on the appropriate forms. If the reimbursement is made in a single amount, an allocation must be made to determine the appropriate portion of the reimbursement that applies to meals and entertainment and to other employee expenses.

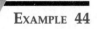

EXAMPLE 44

Elizabeth, who is employed by Green Company, had AGI of $42,000. During the year, she incurred $2,000 of transportation and lodging expense and $1,000 of meals and entertainment expense, all fully substantiated. Elizabeth received $1,800 reimbursement under an accountable plan. The reimbursement rate that applies to meals and entertainment is 33.33% ($1,000 meals and entertainment expense/$3,000 total expenses). Thus, $600 ($1,800 × 33.33%) of the reimbursement applies to meals and entertainment, and $1,200 ($1,800 − $600) applies to transportation and lodging. Elizabeth's itemized deduction consists of the $800 ($2,000 total − $1,200 reimbursement) of unreimbursed transportation and lodging expenses and $400 ($1,000 − $600) of unreimbursed meal and entertainment expenses as follows:

Transportation and lodging	$ 800
Meals and entertainment ($400 × 50%)	200
Total (reported on Form 2106)	$1,000
Less: 2% of $42,000 AGI (see limitation discussed below)	(840)
Deduction (reported on Schedule A)	$ 160

In summary, Elizabeth reports $3,000 of expenses and the $1,800 reimbursement on Form 2106 and $160 as a miscellaneous itemized deduction on Schedule A. ▼

LIMITATIONS ON ITEMIZED DEDUCTIONS

9 LEARNING OBJECTIVE
Work with the limitations on miscellaneous itemized deductions.

Many itemized deductions, such as medical expenses and charitable contributions, are subject to limitations expressed as a percentage of AGI. These limitations may be expressed as floors or ceilings. These limitations are discussed in Chapter 9.

MISCELLANEOUS ITEMIZED DEDUCTIONS SUBJECT TO THE 2 PERCENT FLOOR

Certain miscellaneous itemized deductions, including most *unreimbursed employee business expenses*, are aggregated and then reduced by 2 percent of AGI.[52] Expenses subject to the 2 percent floor include the following:

- All § 212 expenses, except expenses of producing rent and royalty income (refer to Chapter 5).
- All unreimbursed employee expenses (after the 50 percent reduction, if applicable) except moving.
- Professional dues and subscriptions.
- Union dues and work uniforms.
- Employment-related education expenses.
- Malpractice insurance premiums.
- Expenses of job hunting (including employment agency fees and resumé-writing expenses).
- Home office expenses of an employee or outside salesperson.
- Legal, accounting, and tax return preparation fees.
- Hobby expenses (up to hobby income).
- Investment expenses, including investment counsel fees, subscriptions, and safe deposit box rental.
- Custodial fees relating to income-producing property or an IRA or a Keogh plan.
- Any fees paid to collect interest or dividends.
- Appraisal fees establishing a casualty loss or charitable contribution.

MISCELLANEOUS ITEMIZED DEDUCTIONS NOT SUBJECT TO THE 2 PERCENT FLOOR

Certain miscellaneous itemized deductions, including the following, are not subject to the 2 percent floor:

- Impairment-related work expenses of handicapped individuals.
- Gambling losses to the extent of gambling winnings.
- Certain terminated annuity payments.

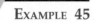

EXAMPLE 45

Ted, who has AGI of $20,000, has the following miscellaneous itemized deductions:

Gambling losses (to extent of gains)	$ 1,200
Tax return preparation fees	300
Unreimbursed employee transportation	200
Professional dues and subscriptions	260
Safe deposit box rental	30

---

[52] § 67.

Ted's itemized deductions are as follows:

Deduction not subject to 2% floor (gambling losses)		$1,200
Deductions subject to 2% floor ($300 + $200 + $260 + $30)	$ 790	
Less 2% of AGI	(400)	390
Total miscellaneous itemized deductions		$1,590

If instead Ted's AGI is $40,000, the floor is $800 (2% of $40,000), and he cannot deduct any expenses subject to the 2% floor. ▼

**TAX PLANNING
CONSIDERATIONS**

10 **LEARNING OBJECTIVE**
Develop tax planning ideas
related to employee business
expenses.

SELF-EMPLOYED INDIVIDUALS

Some taxpayers have the flexibility to be classified as either employees or self-employed individuals. Examples include real estate agents and direct sellers. These taxpayers should carefully consider all factors and not automatically assume that self-employed status is preferable.

It is advantageous to deduct one's business expenses *for* AGI and avoid the 2 percent floor. However, a self-employed individual may have higher expenses, such as local gross receipts taxes, license fees, franchise fees, personal property taxes, and occupation taxes. The record-keeping and filing requirements can be quite burdensome.

One of the most expensive considerations is the Social Security tax versus the self-employment tax. For an employee in 1996, for example, the Social Security tax applies at a rate of 6.2 percent on a base amount of wages of $62,700, and the Medicare tax applies at a rate of 1.45 percent with no limit on the base amount. For self-employed persons, the rate, but not the base amount, for each tax doubles. Even though a deduction *for* AGI is allowed for one-half of the self-employment tax paid, an employee and a self-employed individual are not in the same tax position on equal amounts of earnings. For the applicability of these taxes to employees, see Chapter 1.

After analyzing all these factors, a taxpayer may decide that employee status is preferable to self-employed status.

SHIFTING DEDUCTIONS BETWEEN EMPLOYER AND EMPLOYEE

An employee can avoid the 2 percent floor for employee business expenses. Typically, an employee incurs travel and entertainment expenses in the course of employment. The employer gets the deduction if it reimburses the employee, and the employee gets the deduction *for* AGI. An adequate accounting must be made, and excess reimbursements cannot be kept.

TRANSPORTATION AND TRAVEL EXPENSES

Adequate detailed records of all transportation and travel expenses should be kept. Since the regular mileage allowance is 30 cents per mile, a new, expensive automobile used primarily for business may generate a higher expense based on actual cost. The election to expense part of the cost of the automobile under § 179, MACRS depreciation, insurance, repairs and maintenance, automobile club dues, and other related costs may result in automobile expenses greater than the automatic mileage allowance.

If a taxpayer wishes to sightsee or vacation on a business trip, it would be beneficial to schedule business on both a Friday and a Monday to turn the weekend into business days for allocation purposes. It is especially crucial to schedule appropriate business days when foreign travel is involved.

MOVING EXPENSES

Persons who retire and move to a new location incur personal nondeductible moving expenses. If the retired person accepts a full-time job in the new location before moving, the moving expenses are deductible.

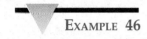

EXAMPLE 46

At the time of his retirement from the national office of a major accounting firm, Gordon had an annual salary of $220,000. He moves from New York City to Seattle to retire. To qualify for the moving expense deduction, Gordon accepts a full-time teaching position at a Seattle junior college at an annual salary of $15,000. If Gordon satisfies the 39-week test, his moving expenses are deductible. The disparity between the two salaries (previous and current) is of no consequence. ▼

EDUCATION EXPENSES

Education expenses are treated as nondeductible personal items unless the individual is employed or is engaged in a trade or business. A temporary leave of absence for further education is one way to reasonably assure that the taxpayer is still qualified, even if a full-time student. An individual was permitted to deduct education expenses even though he resigned from his job, returned to school full-time for two years, and accepted another job in the same field upon graduation. The Court held that the student had merely suspended active participation in his field.[53]

If the time out of the field is too long, educational expense deductions will be disallowed. For example, a teacher who left the field for four years to raise her child and curtailed her employment searches and writing activities was denied a deduction. She was not actively engaged in the trade or business of being an educator.[54]

To secure the deduction, an individual should arrange his or her work situation to preserve employee or business status.

ENTERTAINMENT EXPENSES

Proper documentation of expenditures is essential because of the strict record-keeping requirements and the restrictive tests that must be met. For example, documentation that consists solely of credit card receipts and canceled checks may be inadequate to substantiate the business purpose and business relationship.[55] Taxpayers should maintain detailed records of amounts, time, place, business purpose, and business relationships. A credit card receipt details the place, date, and amount of the expense. A notation made on the receipt of the names of the person(s) attending, the business relationship, and the topic of discussion should constitute proper documentation.

Associated with or goodwill entertainment is not deductible unless a business discussion is conducted immediately before or after the entertainment. Furthermore, a business purpose must exist for the entertainment. Taxpayers should arrange for a business discussion before or after such entertainment. They must

[53] *Stephen G. Sherman*, 36 TCM 1191, T.C.Memo. 1977–301.

[54] *Brian C. Mulherin*, 42 TCM 834, T.C.Memo. 1981–454; *George A. Baist*, 56 TCM 778, T.C.Memo. 1988–554.

[55] *Kenneth W. Guenther*, 54 TCM 382, T.C.Memo. 1987–440.

provide documentation of the business purpose, such as obtaining new business from a prospective customer.

Unreimbursed meals and entertainment are subject to the 50 percent rule in addition to the 2 percent floor. Consequently, the procedure of negotiating a salary reduction, as discussed below under Unreimbursed Employee Business Expenses, is even more valuable to the taxpayer.

UNREIMBURSED EMPLOYEE BUSINESS EXPENSES

The 2 percent floor for unreimbursed employee business expenses offers a tax planning opportunity for married couples. If one spouse has high miscellaneous expenses subject to the floor, it may be beneficial for the couple to file separate returns. If they file jointly, the 2 percent floor is based on the incomes of both. Filing separately lowers the reduction to 2 percent of only one spouse's income.

Other provisions of the law should be considered, however. For example, filing separately could cost a couple losses of up to $25,000 from self-managed rental units under the passive activity loss rules (discussed in Chapter 10).

Another possibility is to negotiate a salary reduction with one's employer in exchange for the 100 percent reimbursement of employee expenses. The employee is better off because the 2 percent floor does not apply. The employer is better off because certain expense reimbursements are not subject to Social Security and other payroll taxes.

KEY TERMS

Accountable plan, 8–22

Automatic mileage method, 8–5

Education expenses, 8–12

Entertainment expenses, 8–15

Independent contractor, 8–2

Individual Retirement Accounts (IRAs), 8–21

Moving expenses, 8–10

Nonaccountable plan, 8–24

Office in the home expenses, 8–19

Statutory employees, 8–3

Transportation expenses, 8–4

Travel expenses, 8–6

PROBLEM MATERIALS

DISCUSSION QUESTIONS

1. Why might a business prefer to classify a worker as an independent contractor (i.e., self-employed) rather than as an employee?

2. What difference does it make if an individual's expenses are classified as employment-related expenses or as expenses from self-employment?

3. Discuss the factors that may indicate an employer-employee relationship.

4. Walter is employed by an accounting firm in downtown Birmingham. Occasionally during tax season, Walter tries to save time by not going first to his office. Instead, he goes directly from his home to the client's business location. Are any of Walter's automobile expenses deductible? Explain.

5. Dawn just purchased a new automobile for use in her business. For the first few years, she plans to use the automatic mileage method for tax purposes. Then she plans to switch to the actual operating cost method and depreciate the original cost of the automobile. Is Dawn's understanding of the tax rules correct? Why or why not?

6. Distinguish between transportation expenses and travel expenses.

7. Under the "away-from-home" requirement, what is the significance of the "overnight" concept? What does "overnight" require?

8. Jim works in St. Louis. On Tuesday morning he flies to San Francisco for a business meeting. After the meeting, Jim has lunch by himself and then flies back to St. Louis that same evening. Is the cost of Jim's lunch deductible? Why or why not?

9. Refer to the facts set forth in Example 12 (page 8–8 of the text). What are some of the things Bill might do to avoid the potential tax disaster he faces?

10. Dr. Fuerst, a practicing orthodontist in Buffalo, travels to New York City to attend a two-day convention on experimental orthodontia procedures. Mr. Fuerst accompanies his wife since he prepares their tax return and knows how to properly prepare the required substantiation for the trip. Comment on the deductibility of the trip.

11. If any pleasure is involved, then the travel deduction is not allowed. Comment on the validity of this statement.

12. Josephine took a combined business and pleasure trip to Europe. She traveled to London from New York on Friday, vacationed on Saturday and Sunday, conducted business on Monday, got snowed in at the airport on Tuesday, traveled to Paris on Wednesday, relaxed on Thursday (a legal holiday), conducted business on Friday, went sightseeing on Saturday and Sunday, picked up business samples and papers on Monday, and flew back to New York on Tuesday. What portion of her air fare can she deduct?

13. What is the distance test for moving expenses?

14. For moving expenses to be deductible, a time test must be met.
    a. What is this test?
    b. Does it matter whether the taxpayer is employed or self-employed? Why?
    c. When, if ever, is the time test suspended?

15. What difference does it make whether a taxpayer is improving existing skills or acquiring new ones for the purpose of the education deduction? On what general tax principle is the justification for this rule based?

16. What expenses can qualify for the education deduction?

17. In each of the following situations, indicate whether there is a cutback adjustment and, if so, to whom it applies (i.e., employer or employee).
    a. The employer expects certain employees to entertain their key customers. The employer does not reimburse the employees for these costs.
    b. Same as (a) except that the employees are reimbursed for these costs.
    c. Each year the employer awards its top salesperson an expense-paid trip to the Cayman Islands.
    d. The employer has a cafeteria for its employees where meals are furnished at cost.
    e. The employer sponsors an annual Fourth of July picnic for its employees.
    f. Every Christmas, the employer gives each employee a turkey.

18. Discuss the difference between entertainment that is *directly related to* business and entertainment that is *associated with* business.

19. Discuss the requirements for the deductibility of business meals.

20. Currently, which club dues are deductible? Not deductible?

21. Sandra pays annual dues to belong to the Wichita Country Club. In addition to social and leisure activities, she also utilizes the facilities for business lunches. Presuming adequate substantiation, are any of Sandra's expenses involving the club deductible? Explain.

22. What limits are imposed on the deduction of expenses for tickets purchased for business entertainment? How are such expenses treated on an employee's return if they are reimbursed? Not reimbursed?

23. To what extent may a taxpayer take a deduction for business gifts to a business associate? To an employee? To a superior?

24. Lieutenant Hebert is on active duty with the U.S. Navy. To what extent, if any, is the cost of her uniforms deductible?

25. Cynthia, a CPA, is currently employed by a public accounting firm. On a part-time basis, she earns a law degree. After attending a bar review course, she takes and passes the state bar exam. Currently, she is incurring costs in seeking employment with a law firm. Comment on the deductibility to Cynthia of each of the following expenditures:
    a. The cost of attending law school.
    b. The cost of the bar review course.
    c. The cost of seeking employment with a law firm.

26. What constitutes an adequate accounting to an employer?

27. What tax return reporting procedures must be followed by an employee under the following circumstances?
    a. Expenses and reimbursements are equal under an accountable plan.
    b. Reimbursements at the appropriate Federal per diem rate exceed expenses, and an adequate accounting is made to the employer.
    c. Expenses exceed reimbursements under a nonaccountable plan.

28. Kim has just graduated from college and is interviewing for a position in marketing. Crane Corporation has offered her a job as a sales representative that will require extensive travel and entertainment but provide valuable experience. Under the offer, she has two options: a salary of $48,000 and she absorbs all expenses; a salary of $35,000 and Crane reimburses for all expenses. Crane assures Kim that the $13,000 difference in the two options will be adequate to cover the expenses incurred. What issues should have an impact on Kim's choice?

29. Jeff has been practicing as a physician in Boston. Shortly, he plans to sell his practice to his partners and retire in Taos, New Mexico. Besides the sale of his practice, what should be some of Jeff's concerns?

30. Martha is an associate with a law firm in New York City. Although she already has a J.D. degree, she feels a master of laws from New York University would improve her promotion potential. Although she can earn the degree on a part-time basis, Martha is inclined to shorten her career interruption as much as possible. What should be some of Martha's concerns?

PROBLEMS

31. To support his family, Horace holds two jobs during 1996. The relevant distances are as follows:

	Miles
Residence to main job	40
Main job to second job	30
Second job to residence	45

During the 260 days he worked, Horace drove the family car from his residence to the main job. After eight hours, Horace then drove to the second job and worked for four hours. On his way back to the residence, he stopped for dinner. He paid $390 for parking at the second job and $1,100 for dinners. What, if any, is Horace's deduction for the year?

32. Alec has two jobs in 1996. He drives 40 miles to his first job. The distance from the first job to the second is 32 miles. During 1996, Alec worked 200 days at both jobs. On 150 days, he drove from the first job to the second job. On the remaining 50 days, he drove home (40 miles) and then to the second job (42 miles). Presuming the automatic mileage method is used, how much qualifies as a deduction?

33. Erlyne purchased a new automobile for $17,000 in 1993. She used it 70% for business purposes, driving 13,000 business miles in 1993, 11,000 business miles in 1994, 9,000 business miles in 1995, and 8,000 business miles in 1996.

    Erlyne used the automatic mileage method for all years. What is the adjusted basis of the business portion of her automobile on January 1, 1997?

34. Louis took a business trip from Chicago to Seattle. He spent two days in travel, conducted business for eight days, and visited friends for five days. He incurred the following expenses:

Air fare	$ 950
Lodging	2,400
Meals	1,200
Entertainment of clients	800

    Louis received no reimbursements. What amount can he deduct?

35. Nadine took a business trip of 10 days. Seven days were spent on business (including travel time) and 3 days were personal. Her unreimbursed expenses were as follows:

Air fare	$3,200
Lodging (per day)	300
Meals (per day)	210
Entertainment of clients	900

    a. How much can Nadine deduct if the trip is within the United States?
    b. How much can she deduct if the trip is outside the United States?

36. Hal, an investment counselor, attended a conference on the impact of the new tax law on investment choices. His unreimbursed expenses were as follows:

Air fare	$350
Lodging	450
Meals	330
Tuition and fees	410

    a. How much can Hal deduct on his return? Are the expenses *for* or *from* AGI?
    b. Would your answer differ if Hal were a self-employed physician?

37. Ricardo, a professor of Spanish history, went to Spain during the year to research documents available only in Spain. His time on the trip was spent entirely on business. No vacation days were involved, and Ricardo kept adequate records. Ricardo received no reimbursements for the following carefully documented expenses:

Air fare and other transportation	$2,600
Hotels	1,800
Meals	1,200

    a. What can Ricardo deduct if he has AGI of $40,000 and no other miscellaneous itemized deductions? Are the deductions *for* or *from* AGI?
    b. Would your answer differ if Ricardo had gone to Spain to soak up the culture and brush up on his Spanish?

38. Monica travels from her office in Boston to Lisbon, Portugal, on business. Her absence of 13 days was spent as follows:

Thursday	Depart for and arrive at Lisbon
Friday	Business transacted
Saturday and Sunday	Vacationing
Monday through Friday	Business transacted
Saturday and Sunday	Vacationing
Monday	Business transacted
Tuesday	Depart Lisbon and return to office in Boston

   a. For tax purposes, how many days has Monica spent on business?
   b. What difference does it make?
   c. Could Monica have spent more time than she did vacationing on the trip without loss of existing tax benefits? Explain.

39. During 1996, Eric changed jobs and moved from San Francisco to Rochester, New York. Eric had the following expenses in connection with the move:

Cost of moving household effects	$3,600
Transportation	1,200
Meals	400
Lodging	600

Presume the time test is satisfied and Eric is not reimbursed for these expenses.
   a. What, if any, is Eric's deduction?
   b. How is the deduction, if any, classified?

40. Warren is a self-employed CPA whose practice primarily involves tax matters. During the year, he attended a three-day tax seminar and incurred the following expenses:

Lodging	$305
Meals	250
Course registration (including materials)	520
Transportation	105

Since the seminar was conducted out-of-town, Warren had to obtain lodging.

Warren is convinced that obtaining a J.D. degree would improve his skills as a CPA engaged in tax practice. Consequently, he enrolls as a part-time student at a local law school and begins taking courses. During the current year, he spent $2,850 for tuition and $420 for books and supplies.

How much can Warren deduct for these transactions?

41. Answer the following independent questions with respect to IRA contributions:
   a. Juan earns a salary of $25,000 and is not an active participant in any other qualified plan. His wife has no earned income. What is the maximum total deductible contribution to their IRAs? Juan wishes to contribute as much as possible to his own IRA.
   b. Abby has earned income of $23,000, and her husband has earned income of $1,900. They are not active participants in any other qualified plan. What is the maximum contribution to their IRAs?
   c. Leo's employer makes a contribution of $3,500 to Leo's simplified employee pension plan. If Leo's earned income is $27,000 and AGI is $24,000, what amount, if any, can he also contribute to an IRA?

42. Dorothy is an employee of Cardinal Corporation, a commercial property broker involved in the leasing of office space. She takes a client to dinner and incurs the following expenses:

Taxi (to and from restaurant)	$ 32
Cover charge	40
Meal cost	160
Tip	30

Assume the event is adequately substantiated.
a. If Dorothy is not reimbursed, how much can she claim as a deduction?
b. If Dorothy is reimbursed (under an adequate accounting), how much can Cardinal Corporation claim?

43. Crane Corporation spends $15,000 to purchase a 12-seat skybox for six professional football games. Regular seats at these games normally sell for $30 each. At one game, an employee of Crane entertained eight clients; Crane furnished food and beverages for the event at a cost of $142. The game was preceded by a bona fide business discussion, and all expenses are adequately substantiated.
a. How much may Crane Corporation deduct for this event?
b. Would the answer change if the employee took 11 clients (rather than 8) to the game, and all seats were occupied? Explain.

44. During 1996, Kevin, the assistant manager of a truck leasing firm, made gifts that cost the following amounts:

To Darlene (Kevin's secretary) for Christmas ($2 was for gift wrapping)	$27
To George (Kevin's boss) on his birthday	25
To Susan (a key client) for Christmas	30
To John (a key client) for Christmas	20

Presuming Kevin has adequate substantiation and is not reimbursed, how much can he deduct?

45. Ruth is a professor who consults on the side. She uses one-fifth of her home exclusively for her consulting business, and clients regularly meet her there. Ruth is single and under 65. Her AGI (before considering consulting income) is $50,000. Other relevant data follow:

Income from consulting business	$5,000
Consulting expenses other than home office	2,400
Total costs relating to home	
Interest and taxes	6,000
Utilities	2,000
Maintenance and repairs	600
Depreciation (business part only)	1,500

Calculate Ruth's AGI for 1996.

46. Paige incurred the following expenses related to her employment as a chief executive officer:

Lodging while away from home	$2,800
Meals while away from home	1,200
Entertainment while away from home	2,000
Dues, subscriptions, and books	1,000
Transportation expenses	4,000

Her AGI was $100,000, and she received $6,600 under her employer's accountable plan. What are Paige's deductions *for* and *from* AGI?

47. Kenneth received $4,400 in reimbursements under an accountable plan after he had made an adequate accounting to his employer. His expenses were as follows:

Transportation expenses	$3,200
Meals	1,400
Lodging and incidentals	2,300
Dues, phone, and subscriptions	100
Entertainment	1,000

How much can Kenneth deduct *for* and *from* AGI? Assume he had AGI of $50,000 and no other miscellaneous itemized deductions.

48. Thelma, who is age 42 and single, earned a salary of $60,000. She had other income consisting of interest of $2,000, dividends of $1,600, and long-term capital gains of $4,000. Thelma incurred the following expenses during the year:

Transportation	$2,300
Meals	1,600
Dues and subscriptions	800
Entertainment of clients	300
Total	$5,000

Thelma received reimbursements of $3,000 under an accountable plan. Calculate her AGI and itemized employee business expenses.

49. Kyle and Sharon are married, have no dependents, and are full-time employees. Both work for employers who do not reimburse for job-related costs but expect the employee to absorb the expenses. Kyle and Sharon's expenses for 1996 are as follows:

Kyle's union dues	$ 610
Kyle's safety items (e.g., work shoes, glasses, gloves)	340
Kyle's lab clothing	405
Laundry of lab clothing	120
Sharon's business lunches with clients	1,340
Sharon's professional dues and journals	610
Sharon's taxi fares to and from work (when personal car was being repaired)	160
Other itemized deductions (e.g., interest, on home mortgage, property taxes, charitable contributions)	10,200

If Kyle and Sharon file a joint return and have AGI of $72,000, what is their taxable income?

CUMULATIVE PROBLEM

50. Debra Bond, age 42 and single, is the personnel manager of the northwest regional office of Olympia Insurance Company. Her Social Security number is 432–60–1000. Debra lives in her own home at 524 Wilcrest Drive, Seattle, WA 98122. Lisa Wall, Debra's 20-year-old niece, lives with her and is a full-time student at a local college. Except for a $3,600 nontaxable scholarship Lisa receives for tuition, Debra provides all of her niece's support. Lisa's Social Security number is 444–11–5555.

   Olympia Insurance usually does not reimburse its employees for employment-related expenses. Instead, it estimates the expected expenses of each class of employees and sets their base salary accordingly. During 1996, Debra had the following employment-related expenses:

   • Mileage of 5,350 on personal auto (includes 3,100 miles for commuting). Parking and toll charges (not related to commuting) are $190.

   • Business lunches for potential hires are $1,424. Taxi fares of $132 are not included in this amount.

- Debra attended a three-day seminar on improving managerial skills by using a team approach. The sessions were held at a convention center in Portland, Oregon. Debra's expenses are summarized below:

Transportation	$210
Registration (includes course materials)	750
Meals	290
Hotel	375

- Dues to professional organizations of $205 and subscriptions to professional journals of $310.

In 1996, Debra earned wages of $61,200 (not including any bonus). Usually, Olympia Insurance follows a policy of issuing a bonus to its employees. The bonus for any one year is determined and paid in January of the following year. Debra's bonus for 1995 (received in January of 1996) was $5,900, while her bonus for 1996 (received in January of 1997) was $6,100.

In 1996, Debra had a certificate of deposit with Bank of America that earned $1,400 in interest and received cash dividends of $1,150 from Chevron stock she owns. She also received a check for $120 from Aetna Insurance Company as an adjustment on the homeowners insurance premium she paid in 1995. The carrier had mistakenly overcharged Debra by $120.

Expenditures incurred by Debra in 1996 include the following:

Interest on home mortgage	$6,900
Property taxes on personal residence	2,600
Charitable contributions	1,450
Political contribution to reelect representative to Congress	200

Compute Debra's taxable income for 1996. Suggested software (if available): *TurboTax* or *MacInTax* for tax return.

51. George M. and Martha J. Jordan have no dependents and are both under age 65. George is a statutory employee of Consolidated Jobbers (business code is 2634), and his Social Security number is 582–99–4444. Martha is an executive with General Corporation, and her Social Security number is 241–88–6642. The Jordans live at 321 Oak Street, Lincoln, NV 89553. They both want to contribute to the Presidential Election Campaign Fund.

In 1995, George earned $49,000 in commissions. His employer withholds FICA but not Federal income taxes. George paid $10,000 in estimated taxes. Martha earned $62,000, from which $9,000 was withheld for Federal income taxes. Neither George nor Martha received any expense reimbursements.

George uses his car (purchased on January 3, 1993) on sales calls and keeps a log of all miles driven. In 1995, he drove 36,000 miles, 24,554 of them for business. He made several out-of-state sales trips, incurring transportation costs of $1,600, meals of $800, and lodging costs of $750. During the year, he also spent $1,400 taking customers to lunch.

Martha incurred the following expenses related to her work: taxi fares of $125, business lunches of $615, and a yearly commuter train ticket of $800. During the year, Martha received $1,200 in interest from the employees' credit union, $100,000 life insurance proceeds upon the death of her mother in December, and $500 in dividends from General Motors. She contributed $2,000 to her Individual Retirement Account. Neither George nor Martha is covered by an employee retirement plan. Martha gave a gift valued at $500 to the president of her firm upon his promotion to that position.

The Jordans had additional expenditures as follows:

Charitable contributions (cash)	$1,200
Medical and dental expenses	1,400
Real property taxes	1,200
Home mortgage interest	9,381
Tax return preparation fee	150

Part 1—Tax Computation

Compute the Jordans' Federal income tax payable or refund due, assuming they file a joint income tax return for 1995. If they have a refund due, they want the amount refunded. You will need Form 1040, Form 2106, and Schedules A, B, and C. Suggested software (if available): *TurboTax* or *MacInTax* for tax return.

Part 2—Tax Planning

Martha and George ask your help in deciding what to do with the $100,000 Martha inherited in 1995. They are considering two conservative investment alternatives:

- Invest in 8% long-term U.S. bonds.

- Invest in 6.5% municipal bonds.

a. Calculate the best alternative for next year. Assume that Martha and George will have the same income and deductions in 1996, except for the income from the investment they choose. In computing the tax, use the tax rate schedules for 1996.
b. What other factors should the Jordans take into account?
c. Write a memo to the Jordans, explaining their alternatives.

Suggested software (if available): *TurboTax* or *MacInTax* for tax return.

CHAPTER

9

DEDUCTIONS AND LOSSES: CERTAIN ITEMIZED DEDUCTIONS

LEARNING OBJECTIVES

After completing Chapter 9, you should be able to:

1. Distinguish between deductible and nondeductible personal expenses.

2. Define medical expenses and compute the medical expense deduction.

3. Contrast deductible taxes and nondeductible fees, licenses, etc.

4. Understand the Federal tax treatment of state and local income taxes.

5. Distinguish between deductible and nondeductible interest and apply the appropriate limitations to deductible interest.

6. Understand charitable contributions and their related measurement problems and percentage limitations.

7. List the business and personal expenditures that are deductible either as miscellaneous itemized deductions or as other itemized deductions.

8. Recognize the limitation on certain itemized deductions applicable to high-income taxpayers.

9. Identify tax planning procedures that can maximize the benefit of itemized deductions.

OUTLINE

GENERAL CLASSIFICATION OF EXPENSES

1 LEARNING OBJECTIVE
Distinguish between deductible and nondeductible personal expenses.

As a general rule, the deduction of personal expenditures is disallowed by § 262 of the Code. However, Congress has chosen to allow certain personal expenditures to be deducted as itemized deductions. Personal expenditures that are deductible as itemized deductions include medical expenses, certain taxes, mortgage interest, investment interest, and charitable contributions. These expenditures and other personal expenditures that are allowed as itemized deductions are covered in this chapter. Any personal expenditures not specifically allowed as itemized deductions by the tax law are nondeductible.

Allowable itemized deductions are deductible *from* AGI in arriving at taxable income if the taxpayer elects to itemize. The election to itemize is appropriate when total itemized deductions exceed the standard deduction based on the taxpayer's filing status (refer to Chapter 2).[1]

MEDICAL EXPENSES

2 LEARNING OBJECTIVE
Define medical expenses and compute the medical expense deduction.

GENERAL REQUIREMENTS

Medical expenses paid for the care of the taxpayer, spouse, and dependents are allowed as an itemized deduction to the extent the expenses are not reimbursed.

[1]The total standard deduction is the sum of the basic standard deduction and the additional standard deduction (refer to Chapter 2). Chapter 2 also describes the situations in which a taxpayer is not eligible for the standard deduction.

TAX IN THE NEWS

AVERAGE ITEMIZED DEDUCTIONS

Are your itemized deductions close to average for your income level? Actually, if you're a typical taxpayer, you take the standard deduction instead of itemizing. In 1993, when the standard deduction was $3,700 for single taxpayers, $6,200 for married taxpayers filing jointly, and $5,450 for heads of household, about 70 percent of individual taxpayers took the standard deduction.

The IRS recently released statistics on the approximately 30 percent of individual taxpayers who did itemize in 1993—a year that saw itemized deductions rise 1.1 percent over 1992. Statistics for the most popular deductions are listed in the following table. The table omits medical expenses because few taxpayers have medical expenses in excess of the 7.5 percent floor. Similarly, casualty losses (subject to a 10 percent floor) and miscellaneous itemized deductions (subject to a 2 percent floor) are omitted.

AGI	Taxes	Contributions	Interest	Total
$ 30,000–39,999	$ 2,772	$ 1,384	$ 5,503	$ 9,659
40,000–49,999	3,322	1,541	5,738	10,601
50,000–74,999	4,442	1,739	6,618	12,799
75,000–99,999	6,220	2,319	8,282	16,821
100,000–199,999	10,035	3,427	11,389	24,851
200,000–499,999	22,655	8,207	17,772	48,634
500,000–999,999	52,462	20,635	27,605	100,702
1,000,000+	173,490	108,883	60,427	342,800

These statistics reveal some interesting aspects of the U.S. lifestyle. For one thing, taxpayers at all income levels—even those with AGI of more than $1 million—owe money. For another, taxpayers with AGI below $40,000 are more charitable than wealthier taxpayers. Those with AGI of $30,000 to $39,999 contribute 3.95 percent of their median income; least generous are taxpayers with AGI of $100,000 to $199,999, who contribute only 2.28 percent of their median income. Above this level, the contribution percentage rises but never reaches the 3.95 percent of those at the $30,000–$39,999 level.

Finally, consider what taxpayers have left after meeting the expenses reflected in the table. A single taxpayer with income of $35,000, for example, would have only $25,341 left after paying typical itemized deductions for that income level ($35,000 − $9,659 itemized deductions). After paying $3,246 of this amount as Federal income taxes, the taxpayer would have $22,095 left for other expenses. Some of the proposed flat tax schemes, which eliminate itemized deductions but allow a single large standard deduction, would result in zero Federal income tax for taxpayers at this income level.

SOURCE: Information from "Tax Report: A Special Summary and Forecast of Federal and State Tax Developments," *Wall Street Journal*, June 21, 1995, p. A1.

The **medical expense** deduction is limited to the amount by which such expenses *exceed* 7.5 percent of the taxpayer's AGI.

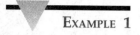

EXAMPLE 1

During the year, Iris had medical expenses of $4,800, of which $1,000 was reimbursed by her insurance company. If her AGI for the year is $40,000, the itemized deduction for medical expenses is limited to $800 [$4,800 − $1,000 = $3,800 − (7.5% × $40,000)]. ▼

MEDICAL EXPENSES DEFINED

The term *medical care* includes expenditures incurred for the "diagnosis, cure, mitigation, treatment, or prevention of disease, or for the purpose of affecting any structure or function of the body."[2] A *partial* list of deductible and nondeductible medical items appears in Exhibit 9–1.

A medical expense does not have to relate to a particular ailment to be deductible. Since the definition of medical care is broad enough to cover preventive measures, the cost of periodic physical and dental exams qualifies even for a taxpayer in good health.

Amounts paid for unnecessary *cosmetic surgery* are not deductible medical expenses. However, if cosmetic surgery is deemed necessary, it is deductible as a medical expense. Cosmetic surgery is necessary when it ameliorates (1) a deformity arising from a congenital abnormality, (2) a personal injury, or (3) a disfiguring disease.

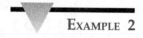

EXAMPLE 2

Art, a calendar year taxpayer, paid $11,000 to a plastic surgeon for a face lift. Art, age 75, merely wanted to improve his appearance. The $11,000 does not qualify as a medical expense since the surgery was unnecessary. ▼

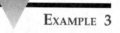

EXAMPLE 3

As a result of a serious automobile accident, Marge's face is disfigured. The cost of restorative cosmetic surgery is deductible as a medical expense. ▼

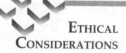

ETHICAL CONSIDERATIONS

Necessary or Unnecessary Cosmetic Surgery?

Steven, age 37, had his nose broken in a high school football game 20 years ago. As a result, his nose is slightly crooked. In addition, he thinks his nose is too long. In March, he scheduled an appointment with Dr. Keane to discuss surgery to improve his appearance, primarily to shorten his nose. Dr. Keane presented him with computer simulations showing several different possibilities for the size and shape of his nose. Steven picked a nose that was much shorter and completely straight.

Steven called his CPA to ask if the cost of the surgery would be deductible. His CPA told him that unnecessary cosmetic surgery is not deductible, but hinted that most doctors can come up with a medical reason that would make such surgery deductible.

Steven discussed the tax issue with Dr. Keane on his next visit, and the doctor indicated that the surgery would be necessary to repair Steven's deviated septum, which was caused by his football injury. Dr. Keane said that he would be willing to write a letter for Steven's files, stating that the surgery was medically necessary. Is Steven justified in taking a deduction for the cosmetic surgery?

---

[2] § 213(d)(1)(A).

▼ **EXHIBIT 9–1**
Examples of Deductible and Nondeductible Medical Expenses

Deductible	Nondeductible
Medical (including dental, mental, and hospital) care	Funeral, burial, or cremation expenses
Prescription drugs	Nonprescription drugs (except insulin)
Special equipment	Bottled water
Wheelchairs	Toiletries, cosmetics
Crutches	Diaper service, maternity clothes
Artificial limbs	Programs for the *general* improvement of health
Eyeglasses (including contact lenses)	Weight reduction
Hearing aids	Health spas
Transportation for medical care	Stop-smoking clinics
Medical and hospital insurance premiums	Social activities (e.g., dancing and swimming lessons)
Cost of alcohol and drug rehabilitation	Unnecessary cosmetic surgery

The cost of care in a nursing home or home for the aged, including meals and lodging, can be included in deductible medical expenses if the primary reason for being in the home is to get medical care. If the primary reason for being there is personal, any costs for medical or nursing care can be included in deductible medical expenses, but the cost of meals and lodging must be excluded.[3]

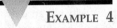

EXAMPLE 4

Norman has a chronic heart ailment. His family decides to place Norman in a nursing home equipped to provide medical and nursing care facilities. Total nursing home expenses amount to $15,000 per year. Of this amount, $4,500 is directly attributable to medical and nursing care. Since Norman is in need of significant medical and nursing care and is placed in the facility primarily for this purpose, all $15,000 of the nursing home costs are deductible (subject to the 7.5% floor). ▼

Tuition expenses of a dependent at a special school may be deductible as a medical expense. The cost of medical care can include the expenses of a special school for a mentally or physically handicapped individual. The deduction is allowed if a principal reason for sending the individual to the school is the school's special resources for alleviating the infirmities. In this case, the cost of meals and lodging, in addition to the tuition, is a proper medical expense deduction.[4]

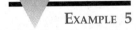

EXAMPLE 5

Jason's daughter Marcia attended public school through the seventh grade. Because Marcia was a poor student, she was examined by a psychiatrist who diagnosed an organic problem that created a learning disability. Upon the recommendation of the psychiatrist, Marcia is enrolled in a private school so that she can receive individual attention. The school has no special program for students with learning disabilities and does not provide special medical treatment. The expense related to Marcia's attendance is not deductible as a medical expense. The cost of any psychiatric care, however, qualifies as a medical expense. ▼

---

[3] Reg. § 1.213–1(e)(1)(v).
[4] *Donald R. Pfeifer*, 37 TCM 816, T.C.Memo. 1978–189. Also see Rev.Rul. 78–340, 1978–2 C.B. 124.

Example 5 shows that the recommendation of a physician does not automatically make the expenditure deductible.

CAPITAL EXPENDITURES FOR MEDICAL PURPOSES

Some examples of *capital expenditures* for medical purposes are swimming pools if the taxpayer does not have access to a neighborhood pool and air conditioners if they do not become permanent improvements (e.g., window units).[5] Other examples include dust elimination systems,[6] elevators,[7] and a room built to house an iron lung. These expenditures are medical in nature if they are incurred as a medical necessity upon the advice of a physician, the facility is used primarily by the patient alone, and the expense is reasonable.

Capital expenditures normally are adjustments to basis and are not deductible. However, both a capital expenditure for a permanent improvement and expenditures made for the operation or maintenance of the improvement may qualify as medical expenses. If a capital expenditure qualifies as a medical expense, the allowable cost is deductible in the year incurred. Although depreciation is required for most other capital expenditures, it is not required for capital expenditures for medical purposes.

A capital improvement that ordinarily would not have a medical purpose qualifies as a medical expense if it is directly related to prescribed medical care and is deductible to the extent that the expenditure *exceeds* the increase in value of the related property. Appraisal costs related to capital improvements are also deductible, but not as medical expenses. These costs are expenses incurred in the determination of the taxpayer's tax liability.[8]

EXAMPLE 6

Fred is afflicted with heart disease. His physician advises him to install an elevator in his residence so he will not be required to climb the stairs. The cost of installing the elevator is $3,000, and the increase in the value of the residence is determined to be only $1,700. Therefore, $1,300 ($3,000 – $1,700) is deductible as a medical expense. Additional utility costs to operate the elevator and maintenance costs are deductible as medical expenses as long as the medical reason for the capital expenditure continues to exist. ▼

The full cost of certain home-related capital expenditures incurred to enable a physically handicapped individual to live independently and productively qualifies as a medical expense. Qualifying costs include expenditures for constructing entrance and exit ramps to the residence, widening hallways and doorways to accommodate wheelchairs, installing support bars and railings in bathrooms and other rooms, and adjusting electrical outlets and fixtures.[9] These expenditures are subject to the 7.5 percent floor only, and the increase in the home's value is deemed to be zero.

MEDICAL EXPENSES INCURRED FOR SPOUSE AND DEPENDENTS

In computing the medical expense deduction, a taxpayer may include medical expenses for a spouse and for a person who was a dependent at the time the

[5] Rev.Rul. 55–261, 1955–1 C.B. 307, modified by Rev.Rul. 68–212, 1968–1 C.B. 91.
[6] F. S. Delp, 30 T.C. 1230 (1958).
[7] Riach v. Frank, 62–1 USTC ¶9419, 9 AFTR2d 1263, 302 F.2d 374 (CA–9, 1962).

[8] § 212(3).
[9] For a complete list of the items that qualify, see Rev.Rul. 87–106, 1987–2 C.B. 67.

expenses were paid or incurred. Of the five requirements that normally apply in determining dependency status,[10] neither the gross income nor the joint return test applies in determining dependency status for medical expense deduction purposes.

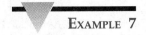

EXAMPLE 7

Ernie (age 22) is married and a full-time student at a university. During the year, Ernie incurred medical expenses that were paid by Matilda (Ernie's mother). She provided more than half of Ernie's support for the year. Even if Ernie files a joint return with his wife, Matilda may claim the medical expenses she paid for him. Matilda would combine Ernie's expenses with her own before applying the 7.5% floor. ▼

For divorced persons with children, a special rule applies to the noncustodial parent. The noncustodial parent may claim any medical expenses he or she pays even though the custodial parent claims the children as dependents. This rule applies if the dependency exemptions could have been shifted to the noncustodial parent by the custodial parent's waiver (refer to Chapter 2).

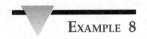

EXAMPLE 8

Irv and Joan are divorced in 1995, and Joan is awarded custody of their child, Keith. During 1996, Irv makes the following payments to Joan: $3,600 for child support and $2,500 for Keith's medical bills. Together, Irv and Joan provide more than half of Keith's support. Even though Joan claims Keith as a dependent, Irv can combine the medical expenses that he pays for Keith with his own. ▼

TRANSPORTATION, MEAL, AND LODGING EXPENSES FOR MEDICAL TREATMENT

Payments for transportation to and from a point of treatment for medical care are deductible as medical expenses (subject to the 7.5 percent floor). Transportation expenses for medical care include bus, taxi, train, or plane fare, charges for ambulance service, and out-of-pocket expenses for the use of an automobile. A mileage allowance of nine cents per mile[11] may be used instead of actual out-of-pocket automobile expenses. Whether the taxpayer chooses to claim out-of-pocket automobile expenses or the nine cents per mile automatic mileage option, related parking fees and tolls can also be deducted. The cost of meals while en route to obtain medical care is not deductible.

A deduction is also allowed for the transportation expenses of a parent who must accompany a child who is receiving medical care or for a nurse or other person giving assistance to a person who is traveling to get medical care and cannot travel alone.

A deduction is allowed for lodging while away from home for medical expenses if the following requirements are met:[12]

- The lodging is primarily for and essential to medical care.
- Medical care is provided by a doctor in a licensed hospital or a similar medical facility (e.g., a clinic).
- The lodging is not lavish or extravagant under the circumstances.
- There is no significant element of personal pleasure, recreation, or vacation in the travel away from home.

The deduction for lodging expenses included as medical expenses cannot exceed $50 *per* night for *each* person. The deduction is allowed not only for the patient but

---

[10] Refer to Chapter 2 for discussion of these requirements.
[11] Rev.Proc. 94–73, 1994–2 C.B. 816.

[12] § 213(d)(2).

also for a person who must travel with the patient (e.g., a parent traveling with a child who is receiving medical care).

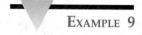

EXAMPLE 9

Herman, a resident of Winchester, Kentucky, is advised by his family physician that Martha, Herman's dependent and disabled mother, needs specialized treatment for her heart condition. Consequently, Herman and Martha fly to Cleveland, Ohio, where Martha receives the therapy at a heart clinic on an out-patient basis. Expenses in connection with the trip are as follows:

Round trip airfare ($250 each)	$500
Lodging in Cleveland for two nights ($60 each per night)	240

Herman's medical expense deduction for transportation is $500, and his medical expense deduction for lodging is $200 ($50 per night per person). Because Martha is disabled, it is assumed that his accompanying her is justified. ▼

No deduction is allowed for the cost of meals unless they are part of the medical care and are furnished at a medical facility. When allowable, such meals are not subject to the 50 percent limit.

AMOUNTS PAID FOR MEDICAL INSURANCE PREMIUMS

Medical insurance premiums are included with other medical expenses subject to the 7.5 percent floor. Premiums paid by the taxpayer under a group plan or an individual plan are included as medical expenses. If an employer pays all or part of the taxpayer's medical insurance premiums, the amount paid by the employer is not included in gross income by the employee. Likewise, the premium is not included in the employee's medical expenses.

If a taxpayer is *self-employed*, 30 percent of insurance premiums paid for medical coverage is deductible as a *business* expense (*for AGI*). Any excess can be treated as a *medical* expense. The deduction *for AGI* is allowed for premiums paid on behalf of the taxpayer, the taxpayer's spouse, and dependents of the taxpayer. The deduction is not allowed to any taxpayer who is eligible to participate in a subsidized health plan maintained by any employer of the taxpayer or of the taxpayer's spouse. Premiums paid for medical insurance coverage of *employees* are deductible as business expenses.

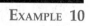

EXAMPLE 10

Ellen, a sole proprietor of a restaurant, has two dependent children. During the year, she paid health insurance premiums of $1,800 for her own coverage and $1,000 for coverage of her two children. Ellen can deduct $840 ($2,800 × 30%) as a business deduction (for AGI) in computing net income from her business. She can include the remaining $1,960 ($2,800 − $840) as a medical expense (subject to the 7.5% floor) in computing itemized deductions. ▼

YEAR OF DEDUCTION

Regardless of a taxpayer's method of accounting, medical expenses are deductible only in the year *paid*. In effect, this places all individual taxpayers on a cash basis as far as the medical expense deduction is concerned. One exception, however, is allowed for deceased taxpayers. If the medical expenses are paid within one year from the day following the day of death, they can be treated as being paid at the time they were *incurred*.[13] Thus, such expenses may be reported on the final income tax return of the decedent or on earlier returns if incurred before the year of death.

---

[13]§ 213(c).

No current deduction is allowed for payment of medical care to be rendered in the future unless the taxpayer is under an obligation to make the payment.[14] Whether an obligation to make the payment exists depends upon the policy of the physician or the institution furnishing the medical care.

EXAMPLE 11

Upon the recommendation of his regular dentist, in late December 1996 Gary consults Dr. Smith, a prosthodontist, who specializes in crown and bridge work. Dr. Smith tells Gary that he can do the restorative work for $12,000. To cover his lab bill, however, Dr. Smith requires that 40% of this amount be prepaid. Accordingly, Gary pays $4,800 in December 1996. The balance of $7,200 is paid when the work is completed in July 1997. Under these circumstances, the qualifying medical expenses are $4,800 for 1996 and $7,200 in 1997. The result would be the same even if Gary prepaid the full $12,000 in 1996. ▼

REIMBURSEMENTS

If medical expenses are reimbursed in the same year as paid, no problem arises. The reimbursement merely reduces the amount that would otherwise qualify for the medical expense deduction. But what happens if the reimbursement is received in a later year than the expenditure? In computing casualty losses, any reasonable prospect of recovery must be considered (refer to Chapter 6). For medical expenses, however, any expected reimbursement is disregarded in measuring the amount of the deduction. Instead, the reimbursement is accounted for separately in the year in which it occurs.

Under the *tax benefit rule,* a taxpayer who receives an insurance reimbursement for medical expenses deducted in a previous year might have to include the reimbursement in gross income in the year of receipt. However, a taxpayer who did not itemize deductions in the year the expenses were paid did not receive a tax benefit and is *not* required to include a reimbursement in gross income.

The tax benefit rule applies to reimbursements if the taxpayer itemized deductions in the previous year. In this case, the taxpayer may be required to report some or all of the medical expense reimbursement in income in the year the reimbursement is received. Under the tax benefit rule, the taxpayer must include the reimbursement in income up to the amount of the deductions that decreased taxable income in the earlier year.

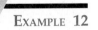

EXAMPLE 12

Homer had AGI of $20,000 for 1996. He was injured in a car accident and paid $1,300 for hospital expenses and $700 for doctor bills. Homer also incurred medical expenses of $600 for his dependent child. In 1997, Homer was reimbursed $650 by his insurance company for the medical expenses attributable to the car accident. His deduction for medical expenses in 1996 is computed as follows:

Hospitalization	$ 1,300
Bills for doctor's services	700
Medical expenses for dependent	600
Total	$ 2,600
Less: 7.5% of $20,000	(1,500)
Medical expense deduction (assuming Homer itemizes his deductions)	$ 1,100

Assume that Homer would have elected to itemize his deductions even if he had no medical expenses in 1996. If the reimbursement for medical care had occurred in 1996, the medical

---

[14] *Robert S. Basset,* 26 T.C. 619 (1956).

expense deduction would have been only $450 [$2,600 (total medical expenses) – $650 (reimbursement) – $1,500 (floor)], and Homer would have paid more income tax.

Since the reimbursement was made in a subsequent year, Homer would include $650 in gross income for 1997. If Homer had not itemized in 1996, he would not include the $650 reimbursement in 1997 gross income because he would have received no tax benefit in 1996. ▼

TAXES

3   LEARNING OBJECTIVE
Contrast deductible taxes and nondeductible fees, licenses, etc.

A deduction is allowed for certain state and local taxes paid or accrued by a taxpayer.[15] The deduction was created to relieve the burden of multiple taxes upon the same source of revenue.

DEDUCTIBILITY AS A TAX

A distinction must be made between a tax and a fee, since fees are not deductible unless incurred as an ordinary and necessary business expense or as an expense in the production of income. The IRS has defined a tax as follows:

> A tax is an enforced contribution exacted pursuant to legislative authority in the exercise of taxing power, and imposed and collected for the purpose of raising revenue to be used for public or governmental purposes, and not as payment for some special privilege granted or service rendered. Taxes are, therefore, distinguished from various other contributions and charges imposed for particular purposes under particular powers or functions of the government. In view of such distinctions, the question whether a particular contribution or charge is to be regarded as a tax depends upon its real nature.[16]

Accordingly, fees for dog licenses, automobile inspection, automobile titles and registration, hunting and fishing licenses, bridge and highway tolls, drivers' licenses, parking meter deposits, postage, etc., are not deductible if personal in nature. These items, however, could be deductible if incurred as a business expense or for the production of income. Deductible and nondeductible taxes are summarized in Exhibit 9–2.[17]

PROPERTY TAXES

State, local, and foreign taxes on real property are generally deductible only by the person upon whom the tax is imposed. Deductible personal property taxes must be *ad valorem* (assessed in relation to the value of the property). Therefore, a motor vehicle tax based on weight, model, year, and horsepower is not an ad valorem tax. However, a tax based on value and other criteria may qualify in part.

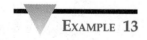

EXAMPLE 13

A state imposes a motor vehicle registration tax on 4% of the value of the vehicle plus 40 cents per hundredweight. Belle, a resident of the state, owns a car having a value of $4,000 and weighing 3,000 pounds. Belle pays an annual registration fee of $172. Of this amount, $160 (4% of $4,000) is deductible as a personal property tax. The remaining $12, based on the weight of the car, is not deductible. ▼

---

[15] § 164.
[16] Rev.Rul. 57–345, 1957–2 C.B. 132, and Rev.Rul. 70–622, 1970–2 C.B. 41.

[17] Most deductible taxes are listed in § 164, while the nondeductible items are included in § 275.

▼ **EXHIBIT 9–2**
Deductible and Nondeductible
Taxes

Deductible	Nondeductible
State, local, and foreign real property taxes	Federal income taxes
	FICA taxes imposed on employees
State and local personal property taxes	Employer FICA taxes paid on domestic household workers
State, local, and foreign income taxes	Estate, inheritance, and gift taxes
	General sales taxes
The environmental tax	Federal, state, and local excise taxes (e.g., gasoline, tobacco, spirits)
	Foreign income taxes if the taxpayer chooses the foreign tax credit option
	Taxes on real property to the extent such taxes are to be apportioned and treated as imposed on another taxpayer

Assessments for Local Benefits.   As a general rule, real property taxes do not include taxes assessed for local benefits since such assessments tend to increase the value of the property (e.g., special assessments for streets, sidewalks, curbing, and other similar improvements). A taxpayer was denied a deduction for the cost of a new sidewalk (relative to a personal residence), even though the construction was required by the city and the sidewalk may have provided an incidental benefit to the public welfare.[18] Such assessments are added to the adjusted basis of the taxpayer's property.

Apportionment of Real Property Taxes between Seller and Purchaser.
Real estate taxes for the entire year are apportioned between the buyer and seller on the basis of the number of days the property was held by each during the real property tax year. This apportionment is required whether the tax is paid by the buyer or the seller or is prorated according to the purchase agreement. It is the apportionment that determines who is entitled to deduct the real estate taxes in the year of sale. In making the apportionment, the assessment date and the lien date are disregarded. The date of sale counts as a day the property is owned by the buyer.

EXAMPLE 14

A county's real property tax year runs from April 1 to March 31. Susan, the owner on April 1, 1996, of real property located in the county, sells the real property to Bob on June 30, 1996. Bob owns the real property from June 30, 1996, through March 31, 1997. The tax for the real property tax year April 1, 1996, through March 31, 1997, is $730. The portion of the real property tax treated as imposed upon Susan, the seller, is $180 (90/365 × $730, April 1 through June 29, 1996), and $550 (275/365 × $730, June 30, 1996, through March 31, 1997) of the tax is treated as imposed upon Bob, the purchaser. ▼

If the actual real estate taxes are not prorated between the buyer and seller as part of the purchase agreement, adjustments are required. The adjustments are necessary to determine the amount realized by the seller and the adjusted basis of the property to the buyer. If the buyer pays the entire amount of the tax, he or she has, in effect, paid the seller's portion of the real estate tax and has therefore paid

---

[18] *Erie H. Rose,* 31 TCM 142, T.C. Memo. 1972–39; Reg. § 1.164–4(a).

more for the property than the actual purchase price. Thus, the amount of real estate tax that is apportioned to the seller (for Federal income tax purposes) and paid by the buyer is added to the buyer's adjusted basis. The seller must increase the amount realized on the sale by the same amount.

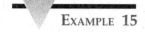

EXAMPLE 15

Seth sells real estate on October 3, 1996, for $50,000. The buyer, Wilma, pays the real estate taxes of $1,098 for the 1996 calendar year (a leap year), which is the real estate property tax year. Of the real estate taxes, $828 (for 276 days) is apportioned to and is deductible by the seller, Seth, and $270 (for 90 days) of the taxes is deductible by Wilma. The buyer has, in effect, paid Seth's real estate taxes of $828 and has therefore paid $50,828 for the property. Wilma's basis is increased to $50,828, and the amount realized by Seth from the sale is increased to $50,828. ▼

The opposite result occurs if the seller (rather than the buyer) pays the real estate taxes. In this case, the seller reduces the amount realized from the sale by the amount that has been apportioned to the buyer. The buyer is required to reduce his or her adjusted basis by a corresponding amount.

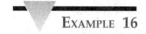

EXAMPLE 16

Ruth sells real estate to Butch for $50,000 on October 3, 1996. While Ruth held the property, she paid the real estate taxes of $1,098 for the calendar year, which is the real estate property tax year. Although Ruth paid the entire $1,098 of real estate taxes, $270 of that amount is apportioned to Butch and is therefore deductible by him. The effect is that the buyer, Butch, has paid only $49,730 for the property. The amount realized by Ruth, the seller, is reduced by $270, and Butch reduces his basis in the property to $49,730. ▼

STATE AND LOCAL INCOME TAXES

4 **LEARNING OBJECTIVE**
Understand the Federal tax treatment of state and local income taxes.

The position of the IRS is that state and local income taxes imposed upon an individual are deductible only as itemized deductions, even if the taxpayer's sole source of income is from a business, rents, or royalties.

Cash basis taxpayers are entitled to deduct state income taxes withheld by the employer in the year the taxes are withheld. In addition, estimated state income tax payments are deductible in the year the payment is made by cash basis taxpayers even if the payments relate to a prior or subsequent year.[19] If the taxpayer overpays state income taxes because of excessive withholdings or estimated tax payments, the refund received is included in gross income of the following year to the extent that the deduction reduced the tax liability in the prior year.

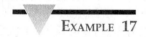

EXAMPLE 17

Leona, a cash basis, unmarried taxpayer, had $800 of state income tax withheld during 1996. Additionally in 1996, Leona paid $100 that was due when she filed her 1995 state income tax return and made estimated payments of $300 on her 1996 state income tax. When Leona files her 1996 Federal income tax return in April 1997, she elects to itemize deductions, which amount to $5,500, including the $1,200 of state income tax payments and withholdings, all of which reduce her tax liability.

As a result of overpaying her 1996 state income tax, Leona receives a refund of $200 early in 1997. She will include this amount in her 1997 gross income in computing her Federal income tax. It does not matter whether Leona received a check from the state for $200 or applied the $200 toward her 1997 state income tax. ▼

---

[19] Rev.Rul. 71–190, 1971–1 C.B. 70. See also Rev.Rul. 82–208, 1982–2 C.B. 58, where a deduction is not allowed when the taxpayer cannot, in good faith, reasonably determine that there is additional state income tax liability.

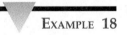

INTEREST

5 **LEARNING OBJECTIVE**
Distinguish between deductible and nondeductible interest and apply the appropriate limitations to deductible interest.

A deduction for interest has been allowed since the income tax law was enacted in 1913. Despite its long history of congressional acceptance, the interest deduction has been one of the most controversial areas in the tax law. The controversy centered around the propriety of allowing the deduction of interest charges for the purchase of consumer goods and services and interest on borrowings used to acquire investments (investment interest). Personal (consumer) interest is not deductible. This includes credit card interest, interest on car loans, and any other interest that is not investment interest, home mortgage interest, or business interest. **Investment interest** and **qualified residence** (home mortgage) **interest** continue to be deductible, subject to limits discussed below.

ALLOWED AND DISALLOWED ITEMS

The Supreme Court has defined *interest* as compensation for the use or forbearance of money.[20] The general rule permits a deduction for interest paid or accrued within the taxable year on indebtedness.[21]

Investment Interest. Taxpayers frequently borrow funds that they use to acquire investment assets. When the interest expense is large relative to the income from the investments, substantial tax benefits could result. Congress has therefore limited the deductibility of interest on funds borrowed for the purpose of purchasing or continuing to hold investment property. Investment interest expense is *now* limited to net investment income for the year.[22]

Investment income is gross income from interest, dividends, annuities, and royalties not derived in the ordinary course of a trade or business. Income from a passive activity and income from a real estate activity in which the taxpayer actively participates are not included in investment income (see Chapter 10).

Net capital gain attributable to the disposition of property producing the types of income just enumerated or from property held for investment purposes is *not* included in investment income when the taxpayer elects to do so.

EXAMPLE 18

Terry incurred $13,000 of interest expense related to her investments during the year. Her investment income included $4,000 of interest, $2,000 of dividends, and a $5,000 net capital gain on the sale of securities. Her investment income for purposes of computing the investment income limitation is $6,000 ($4,000 interest + $2,000 dividends). ▼

Taxpayers may *elect* to include the capital gains as investment income, but only if they agree to reduce capital gains qualifying for the alternative tax computation for net capital gain (see Chapter 13) by an equivalent amount.

Net investment income is the excess of investment income over investment expenses. Investment expenses are those deductible expenses directly connected with the production of investment income. Investment expenses *do not* include interest expense. When investment expenses fall into the category of miscellaneous itemized deductions that are subject to the 2 percent-of-AGI floor, some may not enter into the calculation of net investment income because of the floor.

---

[20] *Old Colony Railroad Co. v. Comm.*, 3 USTC ¶880, 10 AFTR 786, 52 S.Ct. 211 (USSC, 1932).

[21] § 163(a).

[22] § 63(d).

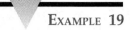

EXAMPLE 19

Gina has AGI of $80,000, which includes dividends and interest income of $18,000. Besides investment interest expense, she paid $3,000 of city ad valorem property tax on stocks and bonds and had the following miscellaneous itemized expenses:

Safe deposit box rental (to hold investment securities)	$ 120
Investment counsel fee	1,200
Unreimbursed business travel	850
Uniforms	600

Before Gina can determine her investment expenses for purposes of calculating net investment income, those miscellaneous expenses that are not investment expenses are disallowed before any investment expenses are disallowed under the 2%-of-AGI floor. This is accomplished by selecting the *lesser* of the following:

1. The amount of investment expenses included in the total of miscellaneous itemized deductions subject to the 2%-of-AGI floor.
2. The amount of miscellaneous expenses deductible after the 2%-of-AGI rule is applied.

The amount under item 1 is $1,320 [$120 (safe deposit box rental) + $1,200 (investment counsel fee)]. The item 2 amount is $1,170 [$2,770 (total of miscellaneous expenses) – $1,600 (2% of $80,000 AGI)].

Then, Gina's investment expenses are calculated as follows:

Deductible miscellaneous deductions investment expense (the lesser of item 1 or item 2)	$1,170
Plus: Ad valorem tax on investment property	3,000
Total investment expenses	$4,170

Gina's net investment income is $13,830 ($18,000 investment income – $4,170 investment expenses). ▼

After net investment income is determined, deductible investment interest expense can be calculated.

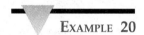

EXAMPLE 20

Adam is a single person employed by a law firm. His investment activities for the year are as follows:

Net investment income	$30,000
Investment interest expense	44,000

Adam's investment interest deduction is $30,000. ▼

The amount of investment interest disallowed is carried over to future years. In Example 20, therefore, the amount that is carried over to the following year is $14,000 ($44,000 investment interest expense – $30,000 allowed). No limit is placed on the length of carryover period. The investment interest expense deduction is determined by completing Form 4952 (see Appendix B).

Qualified Residence Interest. *Qualified residence interest* is interest paid or accrued during the taxable year on indebtedness (subject to limitations) *secured* by any property that is a qualified residence of the taxpayer. Qualified residence interest falls into two categories: (1) interest on acquisition indebtedness and (2) interest on home equity loans. Before discussing each of these categories, however, the term qualified residence must be defined.

A *qualified residence* includes the taxpayer's principal residence and one other residence of the taxpayer or spouse. The *principal residence* is one that meets the requirement for nonrecognition of gain upon sale under § 1034 (see Chapter 12). The *one other residence,* or second residence, refers to one that is used as a residence if not rented or, if rented, meets the requirements for a personal residence under the rental of vacation home rules (refer to Chapter 5). A taxpayer who has more than one second residence can make the selection each year of which one is the qualified second residence. A residence includes, in addition to a house in the ordinary sense, cooperative apartments, condominiums, and mobile homes and boats that have living quarters (sleeping accommodations and toilet and cooking facilities).

Although in most cases interest paid on a home mortgage would be fully deductible, there are limitations.[23] Interest paid or accrued during the tax year on aggregate **acquisition indebtedness** of $1 million or less ($500,000 for married persons filing separate returns) is deductible as qualified residence interest. Acquisition indebtedness refers to amounts incurred in acquiring, constructing, or substantially improving a qualified residence of the taxpayer.

Qualified residence interest also includes interest on **home equity loans.** These loans utilize the personal residence of the taxpayer as security. Because the funds from home equity loans can be used for personal purposes (e.g., auto purchases, medical expenses), what would otherwise have been nondeductible consumer interest becomes deductible qualified residence interest.

However, interest is deductible only on the portion of a home equity loan that does not exceed the *lesser of*:

- The fair market value of the residence, reduced by the acquisition indebtedness, *or*
- $100,000 ($50,000 for married persons filing separate returns).

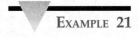

EXAMPLE 21

Larry owns a personal residence with a fair market value of $150,000 and an outstanding first mortgage of $120,000. Therefore, his equity in his home is $30,000 ($150,000 − $120,000). Larry issues a lien on the residence and in return borrows $15,000 to purchase a new family automobile. All interest on the $135,000 of debt is treated as qualified residence interest. ▼

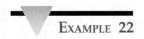

EXAMPLE 22

Leon and Pearl, married taxpayers, took out a mortgage on their home for $200,000 in 1983. In March of the current year, when the home had a fair market value of $400,000 and they owed $195,000 on the mortgage, Leon and Pearl took out a home equity loan for $120,000. They used the funds to purchase a boat to be used for recreational purposes. The boat, which does not have living quarters, does not qualify as a personal residence. On a joint return, Leon and Pearl can deduct all of the interest on the first mortgage since it is acquisition indebtedness. Of the $120,000 home equity loan, only the interest on the first $100,000 is deductible. The interest on the remaining $20,000 is not deductible because it exceeds the statutory ceiling of $100,000. ▼

Interest Paid for Services. Mortgage loan companies commonly charge a fee for finding, placing, or processing a mortgage loan. Such fees are often called **points** and are expressed as a percentage of the loan amount. Borrowers often have to pay points to obtain the necessary financing. To qualify as deductible interest, the points must be considered compensation to a lender solely for the use or forbearance of money. The points cannot be a form of service charge or payment for specific services if they are to qualify as deductible interest.[24]

---

[23] § 163(h)(3).

[24] Rev.Rul. 67–297, 1967–2 C.B. 87.

Points must be capitalized and are amortized and deductible ratably over the life of the loan. A special exception permits the purchaser of a personal residence to deduct qualifying points in the year of payment.[25] The exception also covers points paid to obtain funds for home improvements.

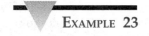

EXAMPLE 23

During 1996, Thelma purchased a new residence for $130,000 and paid points of $2,600 to obtain mortgage financing. At Thelma's election, the $2,600 can be claimed as an interest deduction for tax year 1996. ▼

Points paid to refinance an existing home mortgage cannot be immediately expensed, but must be capitalized and amortized as interest expense over the life of the new loan.[26]

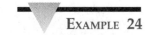

EXAMPLE 24

Sandra purchased her residence four years ago, obtaining a 30-year mortgage at an annual interest rate of 12%. In the current year, Sandra refinances the mortgage in order to reduce the interest rate to 9%. To obtain the refinancing, she had to pay points of $2,600. The $2,600 paid comes under the usual rule applicable to points. The $2,600 must be capitalized and amortized over the life of the mortgage. ▼

The rules governing the deductibility of points *paid by a seller* to help a buyer finance the purchase of the residence were changed in 1994.[27] Under prior rules, such points were not deductible by the buyer, but were treated by the seller as a reduction of the selling price of the property.

The IRS changed its position on this issue, retroactive to tax years beginning after December 31, 1990. In effect, points paid by the seller are treated as an adjustment to the price of the residence, and the buyer is treated as having used cash to pay the points that were paid by the seller. A buyer may deduct seller-paid points in the tax year in which they are paid if several conditions are met. Refer to Revenue Procedure 94–27 for a complete list of these conditions (see footnote 27 for citation).

Prepayment Penalty.   When a mortgage or loan is paid off in full in a lump sum before its term (early), the lending institution may require an additional payment of a certain percentage applied to the unpaid amount at the time of prepayment. This is known as a prepayment penalty and is considered to be interest (e.g., personal, qualified residence, investment) in the year paid. The general rules for deductibility of interest also apply to prepayment penalties.

Interest Paid to Related Parties.   Nothing prevents the deduction of interest paid to a related party as long as the payment actually took place and the interest meets the requirements for deductibility. Recall from Chapter 5 that a special rule for related taxpayers applies when the debtor uses the accrual basis and the related creditor is on the cash basis. If this rule is applicable, interest that has been accrued but not paid at the end of the debtor's tax year is not deductible until payment is made and the income is reportable by the cash basis recipient.

Tax-Exempt Securities.   The tax law provides that no deduction is allowed for interest on debt incurred to purchase or carry tax-exempt securities.[28] A major problem for the courts has been to determine what is meant by the words *to purchase or carry.* Refer to Chapter 5 for a detailed discussion of these issues.

[25] § 461(g)(2).
[26] Rev.Rul. 87–22, 1987–1 C.B. 146.
[27] Rev.Proc. 94–27, 1994–1 C.B. 613.
[28] § 265(a)(2).

RESTRICTIONS ON DEDUCTIBILITY AND TIMING CONSIDERATIONS

Taxpayer's Obligation.   Allowed interest is deductible if the related debt represents a bona fide obligation for which the taxpayer is liable.[29] Thus, a taxpayer may not deduct interest paid on behalf of another individual. For interest to be deductible, both the debtor and creditor must intend for the loan to be repaid. Intent of the parties can be especially crucial between related parties such as a shareholder and a closely held corporation. A shareholder may not deduct interest paid by the corporation on his or her behalf.[30] Likewise, a husband may not deduct interest paid on his wife's property if he files a separate return, except in the case of qualified residence interest. If both husband and wife consent in writing, either the husband or the wife may deduct the allowed interest on the principal residence and one other residence.

Time of Deduction.   Generally, interest must be paid to secure a deduction unless the taxpayer uses the accrual method of accounting. Under the accrual method, interest is deductible ratably over the life of the loan.

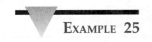

EXAMPLE 25

On November 1, 1996, Ramon borrows $1,000 to purchase appliances for a rental house. The loan is payable in 90 days at 12% interest. On the due date in January 1997, Ramon pays the $1,000 note and interest amounting to $30. Ramon can deduct the accrued portion ($\frac{2}{3} \times \$30$ = $20) of the interest in 1996 only if he is an accrual basis taxpayer. Otherwise, the entire amount of interest ($30) is deductible in 1997. ▼

Prepaid Interest.   Accrual method reporting is imposed on cash basis taxpayers for interest prepayments that extend beyond the end of the taxable year.[31] Such payments must be allocated to the tax years to which the interest payments relate. These provisions are intended to prevent cash basis taxpayers from *manufacturing* tax deductions before the end of the year by prepaying interest.

CLASSIFICATION OF INTEREST EXPENSE

Whether interest is deductible *for* AGI or as an itemized deduction *(from)* depends on whether the indebtedness has a business, investment, or personal purpose. If the indebtedness is incurred in relation to a business (other than performing services as an employee) or for the production of rent or royalty income, the interest is deductible *for* AGI. If the indebtedness is incurred for personal use, such as qualified residence interest, any deduction allowed is reported on Schedule A of Form 1040 if the taxpayer elects to itemize. If the taxpayer is an employee who incurs debt in relation to his or her employment, the interest is considered to be personal, or consumer, interest. Business expenses appear on Schedule C of Form 1040, and expenses related to rents or royalties are reported on Schedule E.

If a taxpayer deposits money in a certificate of deposit (CD) that has a term of one year or less and the interest cannot be withdrawn without penalty, the full amount of the interest must still be included in income, even though part of the interest is forfeited due to an early withdrawal. However, the taxpayer will be allowed a deduction *for* AGI as to the forfeited amount.

[29] *Arcade Realty Co.*, 35 T.C. 256 (1960).
[30] *Continental Trust Co.*, 7 B.T.A. 539 (1927).

[31] § 461(g)(1).

Deductibility of Personal, Investment, and Mortgage Interest

Type	Deductible	Comments
Personal (consumer) interest	No	Includes any interest that is not home mortgage interest, investment interest, or business interest. Examples include car loans, credit cards, etc.
Investment interest (*not* related to rental or royalty property)	Yes	Itemized deduction; limited to net investment income for the year; disallowed interest can be carried over to future years.
Investment interest (related to rental or royalty property)	Yes	Deduction *for* AGI; limited to net investment income for the year; disallowed interest can be carried over to future years.
Qualified residence interest on acquisition indebtedness	Yes	Deductible as an itemized deduction; limited to indebtedness of $1 million.
Qualified residence interest on home equity indebtedness	Yes	Deductible as an itemized deduction; limited to indebtedness equal to lesser of $100,000 or FMV of residence minus acquisition indebtedness.

CHARITABLE CONTRIBUTIONS

6 LEARNING OBJECTIVE
Understand charitable contributions and their related measurement problems and percentage limitations.

Individuals and corporations are allowed to deduct contributions made to qualified *domestic* organizations.[32] Contributions to qualified charitable organizations serve certain social welfare needs and thus relieve the government of the cost of providing these needed services to the community.

The **charitable contribution** provisions are among the most complex in the tax law. To determine the amount deductible as a charitable contribution, several important questions must be answered:

- What constitutes a charitable contribution?
- Was the contribution made to a qualified organization?
- When is the contribution deductible?
- What record-keeping and reporting requirements apply to charitable contributions?
- How is the value of donated property determined?
- What special rules apply to contributions of property that has increased in value?
- What percentage limitations apply to the charitable contribution deduction?

These questions are addressed in the sections that follow.

CRITERIA FOR A GIFT

A *charitable contribution* is defined as a gift made to a qualified organization.[33] The major elements needed to qualify a contribution as a gift are a donative intent, the absence of consideration, and acceptance by the donee. Consequently, the taxpayer has the burden of establishing that the transfer was made from motives

---

[32] § 170.   [33] § 170(c).

of *disinterested generosity* as established by the courts.[34] This test is quite subjective and has led to problems of interpretation (refer to the discussion of gifts in Chapter 4).

Benefit Received Rule. When a donor derives a tangible benefit from a contribution, he or she cannot deduct the value of the benefit.

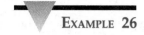

EXAMPLE 26

Ralph purchases a ticket at $100 for a special performance of the local symphony (a qualified charity). If the price of a ticket to a symphony concert is normally $35, Ralph is allowed only $65 as a charitable contribution. ▼

An exception to this benefit rule provides for the deduction of an automatic percentage of the amount paid for the right to purchase athletic tickets from colleges and universities.[35] Under this exception, 80 percent of the amount paid to or for the benefit of the institution qualifies as a charitable contribution deduction.

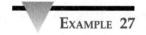

EXAMPLE 27

Janet donates $500 to State University's athletic department. The payment guarantees that she will have preferred seating on the 50-yard line. Subsequently, Janet buys four $35 game tickets. Under the exception to the benefit rule, she is allowed a $400 (80% of $500) charitable contribution deduction for the taxable year.

If, however, Janet's $500 donation includes four $35 tickets, that portion [$140 ($35 × 4)] and the remaining portion of $360 ($500 – $140) are treated as separate amounts. Thus, Janet is allowed a charitable contribution deduction of $288 (80% of $360). ▼

Contribution of Services. No deduction is allowed for a contribution of one's services to a qualified charitable organization. However, unreimbursed expenses related to the services rendered may be deductible. For example, the cost of a uniform (without general utility) that is required to be worn while performing services may be deductible, as are certain out-of-pocket transportation costs incurred for the benefit of the charity. In lieu of these out-of-pocket costs for an automobile, a standard mileage rate of 12 cents per mile is allowed.[36] Deductions are permitted for transportation, reasonable expenses for lodging, and the cost of meals while away from home incurred in performing the donated services. The travel may not involve a significant element of personal pleasure, recreation, or vacation.[37]

EXAMPLE 28

Grace, a delegate representing her church in Miami, Florida, travels to a two-day national meeting in Denver, Colorado, in February. After the meeting, Grace spends two weeks at a nearby ski resort. Under these circumstances, none of the transportation, meals, or lodging is deductible since the travel involved a significant element of personal pleasure, recreation, or vacation. ▼

Nondeductible Items. In addition to the benefit received rule and the restrictions placed on contribution of services, the following items may *not* be deducted as charitable contributions:

- Dues, fees, or bills paid to country clubs, lodges, fraternal orders, or similar groups.
- Cost of raffle, bingo, or lottery tickets.

---

[34] *Comm. v. Duberstein*, 60–2 USTC ¶9515, 5 AFTR2d 1626, 80 S.Ct. 1190 (USSC, 1960).
[35] § 170(l).

[36] § 170(i).
[37] § 170(j).

- Cost of tuition.
- Value of blood given to a blood bank.
- Donations to homeowners associations.
- Gifts to individuals.
- Rental value of property used by a qualified charity.

QUALIFIED ORGANIZATIONS

To be deductible, a contribution must be made to one of the following organizations:[38]

- A state or possession of the United States or any subdivisions thereof.
- A corporation, trust, or community chest, fund, or foundation that is situated in the United States and is organized and operated exclusively for religious, charitable, scientific, literary, or educational purposes or for the prevention of cruelty to children or animals.
- A veterans' organization.
- A fraternal organization operating under the lodge system.
- A cemetery company.

The IRS publishes a list of organizations that have applied for and received tax-exempt status under § 501 of the Code.[39] This publication is updated frequently and may be helpful in determining if a gift has been made to a qualifying charitable organization.

Because gifts made to needy individuals are not deductible, a deduction will not be permitted if a gift is received by a donee in an individual capacity rather than as a representative of a qualifying organization.

TIME OF DEDUCTION

A charitable contribution generally is deducted in the year the payment is made. This rule applies to both cash and accrual basis individuals. A contribution is ordinarily deemed to have been made on the delivery of the property to the donee. For example, if a gift of securities (properly endorsed) is made to a qualified charitable organization, the gift is considered complete on the day of delivery or mailing. However, if the donor delivers the certificate to his or her bank or broker or to the issuing corporation, the gift is considered complete on the date the stock is transferred on the books of the corporation.

A contribution made by check is considered delivered on the date of mailing. Thus, a check mailed on December 31, 1996, is deductible on the taxpayer's 1996 tax return. If the contribution is charged on a bank credit card, the date the charge is made determines the year of deduction.

RECORD-KEEPING AND VALUATION REQUIREMENTS

Record-Keeping Requirements.   No deduction is allowed for contributions of $250 or more unless the taxpayer obtains *written substantiation* of the contribution from the charitable organization. The substantiation must specify the amount of cash and a description (but not value) of any property other than cash contributed.

---

[38] § 170(c).
[39] Although this *Cumulative List of Organizations*, IRS Publication 78 (available by purchase from the Superintendent of Documents, U.S. Government Printing Office, Washington, DC 20402), may be helpful, qualified organizations are not required to be listed. Not all organizations that qualify are listed in this publication.

The substantiation must be obtained before the earlier of (1) the due date (including extensions) of the return for the year the contribution is claimed or (2) the date such return is filed.[40]

Additional information is required if the value of the donated property is over $500 but not over $5,000. Also, the taxpayer must file Section A of Form 8283 (Noncash Charitable Contributions) for such contributions.

For noncash contributions with a claimed value in excess of $5,000 ($10,000 in the case of nonpublicly traded stock), the taxpayer must obtain a qualified appraisal and must file Section B of Form 8283. This schedule must show a summary of the appraisal and must be attached to the taxpayer's return. Failure to comply with these reporting rules may result in disallowance of the charitable contribution deduction. Additionally, significant overvaluation exposes the taxpayer to rather stringent penalties.

Valuation Requirements.   Property donated to a charity is generally valued at fair market value at the time the gift is made. The Code and Regulations give very little guidance on the measurement of the fair market value except to say, "The fair market value is the price at which the property would change hands between a willing buyer and a willing seller, neither being under any compulsion to buy or sell and both having reasonable knowledge of relevant facts."

Generally, charitable organizations do not attest to the fair market value of the donated property. Nevertheless, the taxpayer must maintain reliable written evidence of the following information concerning the donation:

- The fair market value of the property and how that value was determined.
- The amount of the reduction in the value of the property (if required) for certain appreciated property and how that reduction was determined.
- Terms of any agreement with the charitable organization dealing with the use of the property and potential sale or other disposition of the property by the organization.
- A signed copy of the appraisal if the value of the property was determined by appraisal. Only for a contribution of art with an aggregate value of $20,000 or more must the appraisal be attached to the taxpayer's return.

LIMITATIONS ON CHARITABLE CONTRIBUTION DEDUCTION

In General.   The potential charitable contribution deduction is the total of all donations, both money and property, that qualify for the deduction. After this determination is made, the actual amount of the charitable contribution deduction that is allowed for individuals for the tax year is limited as follows:

- If the qualifying contributions for the year total 20 percent or less of AGI, they are fully deductible.
- If the qualifying contributions are more than 20 percent of AGI, the deductible amount may be limited to either 20 percent, 30 percent, or 50 percent of AGI, depending on the type of property given and the type of organization to which the donation is made.
- In any case, the maximum charitable contribution deduction may not exceed 50 percent of AGI for the tax year.

To understand the complex rules for computing the amount of a charitable contribution, it is necessary to understand the distinction between capital gain

---

[40] § 170(f)(8).

property and ordinary income property. In addition, it is necessary to understand when the 50 percent, 30 percent, and 20 percent limitations apply. If a taxpayer's contributions for the year exceed the applicable percentage limitations, the excess contributions may be carried forward and deducted during a five-year carryover period. These topics are discussed in the sections that follow.

Ordinary Income Property.   **Ordinary income property** is any property that, if sold, will result in the recognition of ordinary income. The term includes inventory for sale in the taxpayer's trade or business, a work of art created by the donor, and a manuscript prepared by the donor. It also includes, *for purposes of the charitable contribution calculation,* a capital asset held by the donor for less than the required holding period for long-term capital gain treatment. To the extent that disposition of property results in the recognition of ordinary income due to the recapture of depreciation, it is ordinary income property.[41]

If ordinary income property is contributed, the deduction is equal to the fair market value of the property less the amount of ordinary income that would have been reported if the property were sold. In most instances, the deduction is limited to the adjusted basis of the property to the donor.

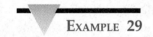

EXAMPLE 29

Tim owned stock in White Corporation that he donated to a university on May 1, 1996. Tim had purchased the stock for $2,500 on March 3, 1996, and the stock had a value of $3,600 when he made the donation. Since he had not held the property long enough to meet the long-term capital gain requirement, Tim would have recognized a short-term capital gain of $1,100 if he had sold the property. Since short-term capital gain property is treated as ordinary income property for charitable contribution purposes, Tim's charitable contribution deduction is limited to the property's adjusted basis of $2,500 ($3,600 − $1,100 = $2,500). ▼

In Example 29, suppose the stock had a fair market value of $2,300 (rather than $3,600) when it was donated to charity. Because the fair market value now is less than the adjusted basis, the charitable contribution deduction is $2,300.

Capital Gain Property.   **Capital gain property** is any property that would have resulted in the recognition of long-term capital gain or § 1231 gain if the property had been sold by the donor. As a general rule, the deduction for a contribution of capital gain property is equal to the fair market value of the property.

Two major exceptions disallow the deductibility of the appreciation on long-term capital gain property. One exception concerns certain private foundations. Private foundations are organizations that traditionally do not receive their funding from the general public (e.g., the Ford Foundation). Generally, foundations fall into two categories: operating and nonoperating. A private *operating* foundation is one that spends substantially all of its income in the active conduct of the charitable undertaking for which it was established.[42] Other private foundations are *nonoperating* foundations. However, if a private nonoperating foundation distributes the contributions it receives according to special rules within two and one-half months following the year of the contribution, the organization is treated the same as public charities and private operating founda-

---

[41] For a more complete discussion of the difference between ordinary income and capital gain property, see Chapter 13.

[42] § 4942.

tions. Often, only the private foundation knows its status (operating or nonoperating) for sure, and the status can change from year to year.

If capital gain property is contributed to a private nonoperating foundation, the taxpayer must reduce the contribution by the long-term capital gain that would have been recognized if the property had been sold at its fair market value. The effect of this provision is to limit the deduction to the property's adjusted basis.

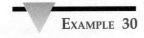

EXAMPLE 30

Walter purchases stock for $800 on January 1, 1975, and donates it to a private nonoperating foundation on June 21, 1996, when it is worth $2,000. Walter's charitable contribution is $800 ($2,000 – $1,200), the stock's basis. ▼

If, in Example 30, Walter had donated the stock to either a public charity or a private operating foundation, his charitable contribution would be $2,000, the fair market value of the stock.

A second exception applying to capital gain property relates to *tangible personalty.* Tangible personalty is all property that is not realty (land and buildings) and does not include intangible property such as stock or securities. If tangible personalty is contributed to a public charity such as a museum, church, or university, the charitable deduction may have to be reduced. The amount of the reduction is the long-term capital gain that would have been recognized if the property had been sold for its fair market value. The reduction is required *if* the property is put to an unrelated use. The term *unrelated use* means a use that is unrelated to the exempt purpose or function of the charitable organization.

A taxpayer in this instance must establish that the property is not in fact being put to an unrelated use by the donee. The taxpayer must also establish that at the time of the contribution it was reasonable to anticipate that the property would not be put to an unrelated use. For a contribution of personalty to a museum, if the work of art is the kind of art normally retained by the museum, it is reasonable for a donor to anticipate that the work of art will not be put to an unrelated use. This is the case even if the object is later sold or exchanged by the museum.[43]

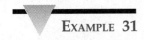

EXAMPLE 31

Myrtle contributes a Picasso painting, for which she paid $20,000, to a local museum. She had owned the painting for four years. It had a value of $30,000 at the time of the donation. The museum displayed the painting for two years and subsequently sold it for $50,000. The charitable contribution is $30,000. It is not reduced by the unrealized appreciation since the painting was put to a related use even though it was later sold by the museum. ▼

Fifty Percent Ceiling. Contributions made to public charities may not exceed 50 percent of an individual's AGI for the year. Excess contributions may be carried over to the next five years. The 50 percent ceiling on contributions applies to the following types of public charities:

- A church or a convention or association of churches.
- An educational organization that maintains a regular faculty and curriculum.
- A hospital or medical school.
- An organization supported by the government that holds property or investments for the benefit of a college or university.
- A Federal, state, or local governmental unit.
- An organization normally receiving a substantial part of its support from the public or a governmental unit.

---

[43] Reg. § 1.170A–4(b)(3)(ii)(b).

> ### TAX IN THE NEWS
>
> #### GET RID OF YOUR OLD STUFF AND TAKE A TAX DEDUCTION
>
> Most taxpayers have closets, attics, and garages cluttered with items they will never use. However, there is an easy way to convert these items into tax savings. Many charities, such as Goodwill and the Salvation Army, have thrift stores in which they sell used merchandise. Taxpayers can take charitable contribution deductions equal to the fair market value of most items they donate to charitable organizations. However, it is sometimes difficult to determine the value of used items. William Lewis, a CPA, claims to have the solution for this problem. Lewis has scouted 34 thrift shops in 12 states to compile a list of prices for 750 articles of used clothing and household items and has published these values in a book, *Cash for Your Used Clothing.* He is so confident about the accuracy of the values reported in his book that he will pay any penalties assessed if the IRS rejects these values.

In the remaining discussion of charitable contributions, public charities and private foundations (both operating and nonoperating) that qualify for the 50 percent ceiling will be referred to as *50 percent organizations.*

The 50 percent ceiling also applies to contributions to the following organizations:

- All private operating foundations.
- Certain private nonoperating foundations that distribute the contributions they receive to public charities and private operating foundations within two and one-half months following the year they receive the contribution.
- Certain private nonoperating foundations in which the contributions are pooled in a common fund and the income and principal sum are paid to public charities.

Thirty Percent Ceiling. A 30 percent ceiling applies to contributions of cash and ordinary income property to private nonoperating foundations that are not 50 percent organizations. The 30 percent ceiling also applies to contributions of appreciated capital gain property to 50 percent organizations unless the taxpayer makes a special election (see below).

In the event the contributions for any one tax year involve both 50 percent and 30 percent property, the allowable deduction comes first from the 50 percent property.

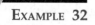

EXAMPLE 32

During the year, Lisa made the following donations to her church: cash of $2,000 and unimproved land worth $30,000. Lisa had purchased the land four years ago for $22,000 and held it as an investment. Therefore, it is long-term capital gain property. Lisa's AGI for the year is $50,000. Disregarding percentage limitations, Lisa's potential deduction is $32,000 [$2,000 (cash) + $30,000 (fair market value of land)].

In applying the percentage limitations, however, the *current* deduction for the land is limited to $15,000 [30% (limitation applicable to long-term capital gain property) × $50,000 (AGI)]. Thus, the total deduction is $17,000 ($2,000 cash + $15,000 land). Note that the total deduction does not exceed $25,000, which is 50% of Lisa's AGI. ▼

Under a special election, a taxpayer may choose to forgo a deduction of the appreciation on capital gain property. Referred to as the *reduced deduction election,* this enables the taxpayer to move from the 30 percent limitation to the 50 percent limitation.

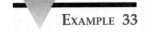

EXAMPLE 33 Assume the same facts as in Example 32, except that Lisa makes the reduced deduction election. Now the deduction becomes $24,000 [$2,000 (cash) + $22,000 (basis in land)] because both donations fall under the 50% limitation. Thus, by making the election, Lisa has increased her charitable contribution deduction by $7,000 [$24,000 − $17,000 (Example 32)]. ▼

Although the reduced deduction election appears attractive, it should be considered carefully. The election sacrifices a deduction for the appreciation on long-term capital gain property that might eventually be allowed. Note that in Example 32, the potential deduction was $32,000, yet in Example 33 only $24,000 is allowed. The reason the potential deduction is decreased by $8,000 ($32,000 − $24,000) is that no carryover is allowed for the amount sacrificed by the election.

Twenty Percent Ceiling. A 20 percent ceiling applies to contributions of appreciated long-term capital gain property to private nonoperating foundations that are not 50 percent organizations.

Contribution Carryovers. Contributions that exceed the percentage limitations for the current year can be carried over for five years. In the carryover process, such contributions do not lose their identity for limitation purposes. Thus, if the contribution originally involved 30 percent property, the carryover will continue to be classified as 30 percent property in the carryover year.

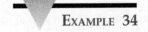

EXAMPLE 34 Assume the same facts as in Example 32. Because only $15,000 of the $30,000 value of the land was deducted in the current year, the balance of $15,000 may be carried over to the following year. But the carryover will still be treated as long-term capital gain property and is subject to the 30%-of-AGI limitation. ▼

In applying the percentage limitations, current charitable contributions must be claimed first before any carryovers can be considered. If carryovers involve more than one year, they are utilized in a first-in, first-out order.

MISCELLANEOUS ITEMIZED DEDUCTIONS

7 LEARNING OBJECTIVE
List the business and personal expenditures that are deductible either as miscellaneous itemized deductions or as other itemized deductions.

No deduction is allowed for personal, living, or family expenses.[44] However, a taxpayer may incur a number of expenditures related to employment. If an employee or outside salesperson incurs unreimbursed business expenses or expenses that are reimbursed under a nonaccountable plan, including travel and transportation, the expenses are deductible as **miscellaneous itemized deductions.**[45] Certain other expenses also fall into the special category of miscellaneous itemized deductions. Some are deductible only if, in total, they exceed 2 percent of

---

[44] § 262.
[45] Actors and performing artists who meet certain requirements are not subject to this rule.

CONCEPT SUMMARY 9–2

Determining the Deduction for Contributions of Appreciated Property by Individuals

If the Type of Property Contributed Is:	And the Property Is Contributed to:	The Contribution Is Measured by:	But the Deduction Is Limited to:
1. Capital gain property	A 50% organization	Fair market value of the property	30% of AGI
2. Ordinary income property	A 50% organization	The basis of the property*	50% of AGI
3. Capital gain property (and the property is tangible personal property put to an unrelated use by the donee)	A 50% organization	The basis of the property*	50% of AGI
4. Capital gain property (and the reduced deduction is elected)	A 50% organization	The basis of the property	50% of AGI
5. Capital gain property	A private nonoperating foundation that is not a 50% organization	The basis of the property*	The lesser of: 1. 20% of AGI 2. 50% of AGI minus other contributions to 50% organizations

*If the fair market value of the property is less than the adjusted basis (i.e., the property has declined in value instead of appreciating), the fair market value is used.

the taxpayer's AGI. These miscellaneous itemized deductions include (but are not limited to) the following:

- Professional dues to membership organizations.
- Uniforms or other clothing that cannot be used for normal wear.
- Fees incurred for the preparation of one's tax return or fees incurred for tax litigation before the IRS or the courts.
- Job-hunting costs.
- Fee paid for a safe deposit box used to store papers and documents relating to taxable income-producing investments.
- Investment expenses that are deductible under § 212 as discussed in Chapter 5.
- Appraisal fees to determine the amount of a casualty loss or the fair market value of donated property.
- Hobby losses up to the amount of hobby income (see Chapter 5).
- Unreimbursed employee expenses (see Chapter 8).

Certain employee business expenses that are reimbursed are not itemized deductions, but are deducted *for* AGI. Employee business expenses are discussed in depth in Chapter 8.

Job Hunting in Ski Country: A Deductible Expense?

Julio, an avid skier, manages the ski department of a sporting goods store in Indianapolis. He has been taking ski vacations in Colorado for several years and has decided to find a job in Colorado and move there. Julio just learned that he can deduct job-hunting costs on his Federal income tax return. One of his customers, who is a CPA, told Julio that transportation costs can be deducted if the primary purpose of the trip is to hunt for a job. According to the CPA, other travel costs must be allocated between job-hunting days and personal days. Julio plans to fly to Colorado on Sunday, have job interviews each morning from Monday through Thursday, and ski each afternoon after the job interviews are concluded. He will ski all day Friday and Saturday and fly back to Indianapolis on Saturday night. Is Julio justified in taking a deduction for job-hunting expenses this year? Will he be justified in taking future deductions if he is unable to find a job this year and continues his job-hunting trips each year for the next several years?

OTHER MISCELLANEOUS DEDUCTIONS

Certain expenses and losses do not fall into any category of itemized deductions already discussed but are nonetheless deductible. The following expenses and losses are deductible on line 27 of Schedule A as Other Miscellaneous Deductions.

- Gambling losses up to the amount of gambling winnings.
- Impairment-related work expenses of a handicapped person.
- Federal estate tax on income in respect of a decedent.
- Deduction for repayment of amounts under a claim of right if more than $3,000 (discussed in Chapter 15).
- The unrecovered investment in an annuity contract when the annuity ceases by reason of death, discussed in Chapter 3.

Unlike the expenses and losses discussed previously under Miscellaneous Itemized Deductions, the above expenses and losses are not subject to the 2 percent-of-AGI floor.

COMPREHENSIVE EXAMPLE OF SCHEDULE A

Harry and Jean Brown, married filing jointly, had the following transactions for the current year:

• Medicines that required a prescription	$ 430
• Doctor and dentist bills paid and not reimbursed	2,120
• Medical insurance premium payments	1,200
• Contact lenses	175
• Transportation for medical purposes (425 miles × 9 cents/mile + $4.75 parking)	43

• State income tax withheld	620
• Real estate taxes	1,580
• Interest paid on qualified residence mortgage	2,840
• Charitable contributions in cash	860
• Transportation in performing charitable services (860 miles × 12 cents/mile + $15.80 parking and tolls)	119
• Unreimbursed employee expenses (from a Form 2106)	870
• Tax return preparation	150
• Professional expenses (dues and publications)	135
• Safe deposit box (used for keeping investment documents and tax records)	35

The Browns' AGI is $40,000. Their completed 1995 Schedule A on the following page reports itemized deductions totaling $7,377.

OVERALL LIMITATION ON CERTAIN ITEMIZED DEDUCTIONS

Congress has enacted several provisions limiting tax benefits for high-income taxpayers. These limitations include the exemption phase-out (refer to Chapter 2) and a phase-out of itemized deductions. The phase-out of itemized deductions (also referred to as a cutback adjustment) applies to taxpayers whose AGI exceeds $117,950 ($58,975 for married taxpayers filing separately).[46] The limitation applies to the following frequently encountered itemized deductions:[47]

- Taxes.
- Home mortgage interest, including points.
- Charitable contributions.
- Unreimbursed employee expenses subject to the 2 percent-of-AGI floor.
- All other expenses subject to the 2 percent-of-AGI floor.

The following deductions are *not* subject to the limitation on itemized deductions:

- Medical and dental expenses.
- Investment interest expense.
- Nonbusiness casualty and theft losses.
- Gambling losses.

Taxpayers subject to the limitation must reduce itemized deductions by the lesser of:

- 3 percent of the amount by which AGI exceeds $117,950 ($58,975 if married filing separately).
- 80 percent of itemized deductions that are affected by the limit.

---

[46] For 1995, the limitation applied if AGI exceeded $114,700 ($57,350 for married taxpayers filing separately).

[47] Other deductions subject to the limitation include Federal estate tax on income in respect of a decedent, certain amortizable bond premiums, the deduction for repayment of certain amounts, certain unrecovered investments in an annuity, and impairment-related work expenses.

SCHEDULES A&B	Schedule A—Itemized Deductions	OMB No. 1545-0074
(Form 1040)	(Schedule B is on back)	**1995**
Department of the Treasury Internal Revenue Service (99)	▶ **Attach to Form 1040.** ▶ **See Instructions for Schedules A and B (Form 1040).**	Attachment Sequence No. **07**

Name(s) shown on Form 1040	Your social security number
Harry & Jean Brown	*371 30 3987*

Medical and Dental Expenses		**Caution:** Do not include expenses reimbursed or paid by others.		
	1	Medical and dental expenses (see page A-1)	**1**	3,968
	2	Enter amount from Form 1040, line 32. **2**	40,000	
	3	Multiply line 2 above by 7.5% (.075)	**3**	3,000
	4	Subtract line 3 from line 1. If line 3 is more than line 1, enter -0-	**4**	968
Taxes You Paid (See page A-1.)	5	State and local income taxes	**5**	620
	6	Real estate taxes (see page A-2)	**6**	1,580
	7	Personal property taxes	**7**	
	8	Other taxes. List type and amount ▶ -------------	**8**	
	9	Add lines 5 through 8	**9**	2,200
Interest You Paid (See page A-2.) **Note:** Personal interest is not deductible.	10	Home mortgage interest and points reported to you on Form 1098	**10**	2,840
	11	Home mortgage interest not reported to you on Form 1098. If paid to the person from whom you bought the home, see page A-3 and show that person's name, identifying no., and address ▶	**11**	
	12	Points not reported to you on Form 1098. See page A-3 for special rules	**12**	
	13	Investment interest. If required, attach Form 4952. (See page A-3.)	**13**	
	14	Add lines 10 through 13	**14**	2,840
Gifts to Charity If you made a gift and got a benefit for it, see page A-3.	15	Gifts by cash or check. If you made any gift of $250 or more, see page A-3	**15**	860
	16	Other than by cash or check. If any gift of $250 or more, see page A-3. If over $500, you **MUST** attach Form 8283	**16**	119
	17	Carryover from prior year	**17**	
	18	Add lines 15 through 17	**18**	979
Casualty and Theft Losses	19	Casualty or theft loss(es). Attach Form 4684. (See page A-4.)	**19**	0
Job Expenses and Most Other Miscellaneous Deductions (See page A-5 for expenses to deduct here.)	20	Unreimbursed employee expenses—job travel, union dues, job education, etc. If required, you **MUST** attach Form 2106 or 2106-EZ. (See page A-5.) ▶ ---------- *Form 2106 870*	**20**	870
	21	Tax preparation fees	**21**	150
	22	Other expenses—investment, safe deposit box, etc. List type and amount ▶ *Professional expenses 135, Safe deposit box 35*	**22**	170
	23	Add lines 20 through 22	**23**	1,190
	24	Enter amount from Form 1040, line 32. **24**	40,000	
	25	Multiply line 24 above by 2% (.02)	**25**	800
	26	Subtract line 25 from line 23. If line 25 is more than line 23, enter -0-	**26**	390
Other Miscellaneous Deductions	27	Other—from list on page A-5. List type and amount ▶ ----------	**27**	0
Total Itemized Deductions	28	Is Form 1040, line 32, over $114,700 (over $57,350 if married filing separately)? **NO.** Your deduction is not limited. Add the amounts in the far right column for lines 4 through 27. Also, enter on Form 1040, line 34, the **larger** of this amount or your standard deduction. **YES.** Your deduction may be limited. See page A-5 for the amount to enter.	▶ **28**	7,377

For Paperwork Reduction Act Notice, see Form 1040 instructions.   Cat. No. 11330X   **Schedule A (Form 1040) 1995**

The overall limitation is applied after applying all other limitations to itemized deductions that are affected by the overall limitation. Other limitations apply to charitable contributions, certain meals and entertainment expenses, and certain miscellaneous itemized deductions.

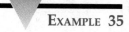

EXAMPLE 35

Herman, who is single, had AGI of $200,000 for 1996. He incurred the following expenses and losses during the year:

Medical expenses before 7.5%-of-AGI limitation	$16,000
State and local income taxes	3,200
Real estate taxes	2,800
Home mortgage interest	7,200
Charitable contributions	2,000
Casualty loss before 10% limitation (after $100 floor)	21,500
Unreimbursed employee expenses subject to 2%-of-AGI limitation	4,300
Gambling losses (Herman had $3,000 gambling income)	7,000

Herman's itemized deductions *before* the overall limitation are computed as follows:

Medical expenses [$16,000 – (7.5% × $200,000)]	$ 1,000
State and local income taxes	3,200
Real estate taxes	2,800
Home mortgage interest	7,200
Charitable contributions	2,000
Casualty loss [$21,500 – (10% × $200,000)]	1,500
Unreimbursed employee expenses ($4,300 – (2% × $200,000)]	300
Gambling losses ($7,000 loss limited to $3,000 of gambling income)	3,000
Total itemized deductions before overall limitation	$21,000

Herman's itemized deductions subject to the overall limitation are as follows:

State and local income taxes	$ 3,200
Real estate taxes	2,800
Home mortgage interest	7,200
Charitable contributions	2,000
Unreimbursed employee expenses	300
Total	$15,500

Herman must reduce this amount by the smaller of the following:

• 3% ($200,000 AGI – $117,950)	$2,462
• 80% of itemized deductions subject to limitation ($15,500 × .80)	12,400

Therefore, the amount of the reduction is $2,462, and Herman has $18,538 of deductible itemized deductions, computed as follows:

Deductible itemized deductions subject to overall limitation ($15,500 − $2,462)	$13,038
Itemized deductions not subject to overall limitation:	
Medical expenses	1,000
Casualty loss	1,500
Gambling losses	3,000
Deductible itemized deductions	$18,538

TAX PLANNING CONSIDERATIONS

EFFECTIVE UTILIZATION OF ITEMIZED DEDUCTIONS

Since an individual may use the standard deduction in one year and itemize deductions in another year, it is frequently possible to obtain maximum benefit by shifting itemized deductions from one year to another. For example, if a taxpayer's itemized deductions and the standard deduction are approximately the same for each year of a two-year period, the taxpayer should use the standard deduction in one year and shift itemized deductions (to the extent permitted by law) to the other year. The individual could, for example, prepay a church pledge for a particular year or avoid paying end-of-the-year medical expenses to shift the deduction to the following year.

9 LEARNING OBJECTIVE
Identify tax planning procedures that can maximize the benefit of itemized deductions.

UTILIZATION OF MEDICAL DEDUCTIONS

When a taxpayer anticipates that medical expenses will approximate the percentage floor, much might be done to generate a deductible excess. Any of the following procedures can help build a deduction by the end of the year:

- Incur the obligation for needed dental work or have needed work carried out.[48] Orthodontic treatment, for example, may have been recommended for a member of the taxpayer's family.
- Have elective remedial surgery that may have been postponed from prior years (e.g., tonsillectomies, vasectomies, correction of hernias, hysterectomies).
- Incur the obligation for capital improvements to the taxpayer's personal residence recommended by a physician (e.g., an air filtration system to alleviate a respiratory disorder).

As an aid to taxpayers who may experience temporary cash-flow problems at the end of the year, the use of bank credit cards is deemed to be payment for purposes of timing the deductibility of charitable and medical expenses.

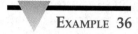

EXAMPLE 36

On December 13, 1996, Marge (a calendar year taxpayer) purchases two pairs of prescription contact lenses and one pair of prescribed orthopedic shoes for a total of $305. These purchases are separately charged to Marge's credit card. On January 6, 1997, Marge receives her statement containing these charges and makes payment shortly thereafter. The purchases are deductible as medical expenses in the year charged (1996) and not in the year the account is settled (1997). ▼

Recognizing which expenditures qualify for the medical deduction also may be crucial to exceeding the percentage limitations.

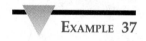

EXAMPLE 37

Mortimer employs Lana (an unrelated party) to care for his incapacitated and dependent mother. Lana is not a trained nurse but spends approximately one-half of the time performing nursing duties (e.g., administering injections and providing physical therapy) and the rest of the time doing household chores. An allocable portion of Lana's wages that Mortimer pays (including the employer's portion of FICA taxes) qualifies as a medical expense. ▼

To assure a deduction for the entire cost of nursing home care for an aged dependent, it is helpful if the transfer of the individual to the home is for medical reasons and is recommended by a doctor. In addition, the nursing home facilities should be adequate to provide the necessary medical and nursing care. To assure a deduction for all of the nursing home expenses, it is necessary to show that the individual was placed in the home for required medical care rather than for personal or family considerations.

Proper documentation is required to substantiate medical expenses. The taxpayer should keep all receipts for credit card or other charge purchases of medical services and deductible drugs as well as all cash register receipts. In addition, medical transportation mileage should be recorded.

If a taxpayer or a dependent of the taxpayer must be institutionalized in order to receive adequate medical care, it may be good tax planning to make a lump-sum payment that will cover medical treatment for future periods. It is advisable to negotiate a contract with the institution so that the expense is fixed and the payment is not a mere deposit.

---

[48] Prepayment of medical expenses does not generate a current deduction unless the taxpayer is under an obligation to make the payment.

TIMING THE PAYMENT OF DEDUCTIBLE TAXES

It is sometimes possible to defer or accelerate the payment of certain deductible taxes, such as state income tax, real property tax, and personal property tax. For instance, the final installment of estimated state income tax is generally due after the end of a given tax year. Accelerating the payment of the final installment could result in larger itemized deductions for the current year.

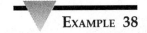

EXAMPLE 38

Jenny, who is single, expects to have itemized deductions of $3,900 in 1996 and $2,500 in 1997. She plans to pay $900 as the final installment on her 1996 estimated state income tax, which is due on January 15, 1997. If Jenny does not pay the final installment until 1997, she will not itemize in either 1996 or 1997. However, if she pays the final installment in December 1996, her itemized deductions will be $4,800 ($3,900 + $900) in 1996, and she will benefit from itemizing. ▼

PROTECTING THE INTEREST DEDUCTION

Although the deductibility of prepaid interest by a cash basis taxpayer has been severely restricted, a notable exception allows a deduction for points paid by the buyer to obtain financing for the purchase or improvement of a principal residence in the year of payment. However, such points must actually be paid by the taxpayer obtaining the loan and must represent a charge for the use of money. It has been held that points paid from the mortgage proceeds do not satisfy the payment requirement.[49] Also, the portion of the points attributable to service charges does not represent deductible interest.[50] Taxpayers financing home purchases or improvements usually should direct their planning toward avoiding these two hurdles to immediate deductibility.

In rare instances, a taxpayer may find it desirable to forgo the immediate expensing of points in the year paid. Instead, it could prove beneficial to capitalize the points and write them off as interest expense over the life of the mortgage.

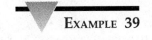

EXAMPLE 39

Geraldine purchases a home on December 15, 1996, for $95,000 with $30,000 cash and a 15-year mortgage of $65,000 financed by the Greater Metropolis National Bank. Geraldine pays two points in addition to interest allocated to the period from December 15 until December 31, 1996, at an annual rate of 10%. Since Geraldine does not have enough itemized deductions to exceed the standard deduction for 1996, she should elect to capitalize the interest expense by amortizing the points over 15 years. In this instance, Geraldine would deduct $86.67 for 1997, as part of her qualified residence interest expense [$1,300 (two points) divided by 15 years], if she elects to itemize that year. ▼

Because personal (consumer) interest is not deductible, taxpayers should consider making use of home equity loans. Recall that these loans utilize the personal residence of the taxpayer as security. Since the tracing rules do not apply to home equity loans, the funds from these loans can be used for personal purposes (e.g., auto loans, education). By making use of home equity loans, therefore, what would have been nondeductible consumer interest becomes deductible qualified residence interest.

---

[49] *Alan A. Rubnitz,* 67 T.C. 621 (1977). Seller-paid points may also be deductible by the buyer under the provisions of Rev.Proc. 94–27, cited in footnote 27.

[50] *Donald L. Wilkerson,* 70 T.C. 240 (1978).

ASSURING THE CHARITABLE CONTRIBUTION DEDUCTION

For a charitable contribution deduction to be available, the recipient must be a qualified charitable organization. Sometimes the mechanics of how the contribution is carried out can determine whether or not a deduction results.

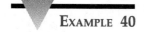

EXAMPLE 40

Fumiko wants to donate $5,000 to her church's mission in Kobe, Japan. In this regard, she considers three alternatives:

1. Send the money directly to the mission.
2. Give the money to her church with the understanding that it is to be passed on to the mission.
3. Give the money directly to the missionary in charge of the mission who is currently in the United States on a fund-raising trip.

If Fumiko wants to obtain a deduction for the contribution, she should choose alternative 2. A direct donation to the mission (alternative 1) is not deductible because the mission is a foreign charity. A direct gift to the missionary (alternative 3) does not comply since an individual cannot be a qualified charity for income tax purposes.[51] ▼

When making noncash donations, the type of property chosen can have decided implications in determining the amount, if any, of the deduction.

EXAMPLE 41

Samantha wants to give $60,000 in value to her church in some form other than cash. In this connection, she considers four alternatives:

1. Stock held for two years as an investment with a basis of $100,000 and a fair market value of $60,000.
2. Stock held for five years as an investment with a basis of $10,000 and a fair market value of $60,000.
3. The rent-free use for a year of a building that normally leases for $5,000 a month.
4. A valuable stamp collection held as an investment and owned for 10 years with a basis of $10,000 and a fair market value of $60,000. The church plans to sell the collection if and when it is donated.

Alternative 1 is ill-advised as the subject of the gift. Even though Samantha would obtain a deduction of $60,000, she would forgo the potential loss of $40,000 that would be recognized if the property were sold.[52] Alternative 2 makes good sense since the deduction still is $60,000 and none of the $50,000 of appreciation that has occurred must be recognized as income. Alternative 3 yields no deduction at all and is not a wise choice. Alternative 4 involves tangible personalty that the recipient does not plan to use. As a result, the amount of the deduction is limited to $10,000, the stamp collection's basis.[53] ▼

ETHICAL CONSIDERATIONS

Charitable Motivations and Tax Considerations

Billy owns a principal residence in Columbia, South Carolina, and a vacation home in Myrtle Beach. Billy has retired and plans to move permanently to the vacation house in Myrtle Beach, which is worth $350,000 (adjusted basis of $90,000). He

---

[51] *Thomas E. Lesslie*, 36 TCM 495, T.C.Memo. 1977–111.
[52] *LaVar M. Withers*, 69 T.C. 900 (1978).

[53] No reduction of appreciation is necessary in alternative 2 since stock is intangible property and not tangible personalty.

enters into a contract to sell his Columbia residence, which he has owned for 10 years, for $200,000. His adjusted basis in the house is $120,000.

Billy, a devout supporter of his church, then calls his CPA, tells her that he plans to donate the $200,000 to his church, and inquires about the tax consequences. The CPA tells Billy that he has made a bad tax move because he will have to pay tax on the $80,000 gain and that he could have taken a $200,000 charitable contribution deduction without reporting any gain if he had donated the house directly to the church.

Billy, who sold the Columbia residence subject to approval by a building inspector, then proposes two actions he can take to ensure that the sale will fall through. Plan 1 is to secretly give the building inspector a gift and indicate that he'd like a negative inspection report. Plan 2 is to point out some hard-to-detect architectural flaws that he knows about to the building inspector. What advice should the CPA give to Billy? Should the CPA prepare Billy's return if Billy follows through with either plan?

For property transfers (particularly real estate), the ceiling limitations on the amount of the deduction allowed in any one year (50 percent, 30 percent, or 20 percent of AGI, as the case may be) could be a factor to take into account. With proper planning, donations can be controlled to stay within the limitations and therefore avoid the need for a carryover of unused charitable contributions.

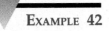

EXAMPLE 42

Andrew wants to donate a tract of unimproved land held as an investment to the University of Maryland (a qualified charitable organization). The land has been held for six years and has a current fair market value of $300,000 and a basis to Andrew of $50,000. Andrew's AGI for the current year is estimated to be $200,000, and he expects much the same for the next few years. In the current year, he deeds (transfers) an undivided one-fifth interest in the real estate to the university. ▼

What has Andrew in Example 42 accomplished for income tax purposes? In the current year, he will be allowed a charitable contribution deduction of $60,000 (⅕ × $300,000), which will be within the applicable limitation of AGI (30% × $200,000). Presuming no other charitable contributions for the year, Andrew has avoided the possibility of a carryover. In future years, Andrew can arrange donations of undivided interests in the real estate to stay within the bounds of the percentage limitations. The only difficulty with this approach is the need to revalue the real estate each year before the donation, since the amount of the deduction is based on the fair market value of the interest contributed at the time of the contribution.

It may be wise to avoid a carryover of unused charitable contributions, if possible, because that approach may be dangerous in several respects. First, the carryover period is limited to five years. Depending on the taxpayer's projected AGI rather than actual AGI, some of the amount carried over may expire without tax benefit after the five-year period has ended. Second, unused charitable contribution carryovers do not survive the death of the party making the donation and as a consequence are lost.

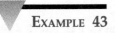

EXAMPLE 43

Tiffany dies in October 1996. In completing her final income tax return for 1996, Tiffany's executor determines the following information: AGI of $104,000 and a donation by Tiffany to her church of stock worth $60,000. Tiffany had purchased the stock two years ago for $50,000 and held it as an investment. Tiffany's executor makes the reduced deduction election and, as a consequence, claims a charitable contribution deduction of $50,000. With the election, the potential charitable contribution deduction of $50,000 ($60,000 − $10,000) is less than the 50% ceiling of $52,000 ($104,000 × 50%). If the executor had not made the election, the potential charitable contribution deduction of $60,000 would have been reduced by the 30% ceiling to $31,200 ($104,000 × 30%). No carryover of the $28,800 ($60,000 − $31,200) would have been available. ▼

KEY TERMS

Acquisition indebtedness, 9–15

Capital gain property, 9–22

Charitable contribution, 9–18

Home equity loans, 9–15

Investment income, 9–13

Investment interest, 9–13

Medical expense, 9–4

Miscellaneous itemized deductions, 9–25

Net investment income, 9–13

Ordinary income property, 9–22

Points, 9–15

Qualified residence interest, 9–13

▼ PROBLEM MATERIALS

DISCUSSION QUESTIONS

1. Dan, a self-employed individual taxpayer, prepared his own income tax return for the past year and asked you to check it over for accuracy. Your review indicates that Dan failed to claim certain business entertainment expenses.

    a. Will the correction of this omission affect the amount of medical expenses Dan can deduct? Explain.

    b. Would it matter if Dan were employed rather than self-employed?

2. Nina is in perfect health. During the current year, however, she pays $450 for an annual physical exam and $80 for a dental checkup. Do these expenses qualify for the medical deduction? Why or why not?

3. Nathan sustained serious facial damage in a skiing accident. To restore his physical appearance, he had cosmetic surgery. At the same time, he also had surgery to remove wrinkles from under his eyes caused by age. Can Nathan claim the cost of these procedures as a medical expense?

4. What are the criteria for determining whether the cost of a nursing home can qualify as a medical expense?

5. Hugo has a history of heart disease. Upon the advice of his doctor, he installs an elevator in his residence so he does not have to climb stairs. Is this a valid medical expense? If it is, how much of the expense is deductible?

6. Susan, a sole proprietor of an antique shop, has two dependent children. During the year, she paid health insurance premiums of $1,400 for her own coverage and $1,800 for coverage of her children. How will these premium payments affect Susan's taxable income computation?

7. Tim took his disabled mother, Sharon, from Green Bay to Milwaukee for surgery at a clinic on an outpatient basis. They stayed in a motel near the clinic for two days after the surgery for postoperative evaluations. Discuss the extent to which transportation, meals, and lodging costs incurred by Tim and his mother are deductible as medical expenses (ignore the 7.5% floor).

8. If Ida's medical expense deduction was $500 in 1996 and the amount reduced her tax liability, how would a $300 insurance reimbursement be treated if received in 1997? Received in 1996? What if Ida had not itemized deductions in 1996 and received the $300 reimbursement in 1997?

9. By December 1, Anna had medical expenses of $5,000, of which $1,000 was reimbursed by her insurance company. She expects her AGI for the year to be $60,000 and her other itemized deductions to be $5,300. Can you suggest any tax planning ideas that will enable Anna to increase her medical expense deduction for the year?

10. Susan and Anna, who are sisters, both itemize deductions. Susan, who lives in Arizona, can deduct part of the cost of licensing her automobile. Anna, who lives in Illinois, cannot deduct any part of her automobile license fees. Explain.

11. The city required Heather to pay $3,000 for the cost of a new sidewalk in front of her personal residence. What effect will this $3,000 have on Heather from a tax perspective?

12. Joe sold his personal residence to Emma on July 1, 1996. He had paid real property taxes on March 1, 1996, the due date for property taxes for 1996. How will Joe's payment affect his deduction for property taxes in 1996? Will Joe's payment of the taxes have any effect on Emma's itemized deductions for 1996? What other tax or financial effects will Joe's payment of the taxes have on either party?

13. Edna, a calendar year, cash basis taxpayer, overpaid her 1996 state income tax by $800. Edna chose to apply the overpayment toward her state income taxes for 1997 and did not claim a refund. She itemized deductions in 1996. Does Edna have to report the $800 as income in 1997?

14. Donald owns a principal residence in Chicago, a vacation lodge in New Mexico, and a yacht (with living quarters) on Lake Michigan. All three properties have mortgages on which Donald pays interest. Discuss any limitations that apply to Donald's mortgage interest deduction, and suggest any strategy Donald should consider to maximize his deduction.

15. Ed borrows $20,000 and purchases an automobile. Jack borrows $20,000 to purchase a diamond engagement ring for his fiancée. Ed qualifies for an interest deduction on the amount he borrowed, but Jack does not. Can you offer any explanation for the difference?

16. As to the deductibility of "points," comment on the following:
    a. Those paid by the seller.
    b. Those paid to finance the purchase of a rental house.
    c. Those relating to the rendering of personal services.
    d. When capitalization and amortization might be advisable.
    e. Points paid from the mortgage proceeds.

17. Ellen borrows $50,000 from her parents for a down payment on a condominium. She paid interest of $4,200 in 1994, $0 in 1995, and $11,000 in 1996. The IRS disallows the deduction. Can you offer any explanation for the disallowance?

18. To dissuade his pastor from resigning and taking a position with a larger church, Michael, an ardent leader of the congregation, gives the pastor a new car. Is the cost of the car deductible by Michael as a charitable contribution?

19. Lola purchased a ticket to a fund-raising banquet and dance for the Pittsburgh Symphony, a public charity. The ticket cost $250, and the normal cost of such an event is $50. How much can Lola deduct as a charitable contribution?

20. Bill pays tuition to a parochial school run by his church so that his children can attend the school. The church is a qualified charity. Can Bill deduct any portion of the tuition payments as a charitable contribution?

21. Zane donated property that cost $1,000 and was worth $3,000 to a charity. Under what circumstances will Zane be allowed to deduct $3,000 for this charitable contribution? Under what circumstances will he be limited to a $1,000 deduction?

22. What is capital gain property? What tax treatment is required if capital gain property is contributed to a private nonoperating foundation? To a public charity? What difference does it make if the contribution is tangible personalty and it is put to a use unrelated to the donee's business?

23. During the year, Shirley donated five dresses to the Salvation Army. She had purchased the dresses three years ago at a cost of $1,200 and worn them as personal attire. Because the dresses are long-term capital assets, Shirley plans to deduct $1,200 on her income tax return. Comment on Shirley's understanding of the tax law governing charitable contributions.

24. A local opthalmologist's advertising campaign included a certificate for a free radial keratotomy for the lucky winner of a drawing. Ahmad held the winning ticket, which was drawn in December 1995. Ahmad had no vision problems and was uncertain what he should do with the prize. In February 1996, Ahmad's daughter, who lives with his former wife, was diagnosed with a vision problem that could be treated either with prescription glasses or a radial keratotomy. The divorce decree requires that Ahmad pay for all medical expenses incurred for his daughter. Identify the relevant tax issues for Ahmad.

25. The Skins Game, which involves four of the top golfers on the PGA Tour, is held each year on the weekend after Thanksgiving. Total prize money amounts to $510,000, and the leading money winner also receives an automobile as a prize. The announcers point out that 10% of the money won by each player goes to charity. In addition, on some holes, the winner of the hole receives the keys to an automobile, which goes to the player's favorite charity. Identify the relevant tax issues for the players. Consider the following possibilities with respect to the car won by the leading money winner: (1) he might keep the car for his own use and sell his present car; (2) he might sell the new car; (3) he might give the car to a friend or relative; (4) he might donate the car to charity; or (5) he might give the car to his caddy.

26. Henry is a television evangelist. In August 1995, the IRS ruled that his organization was no longer a qualified charitable organization because of violations of the tax law. Miguel donated $10,000 to Henry's organization in September 1995. At the time, he did not know that Henry's organization had been disqualified as a charitable organization. In 1996, Henry was jailed for mail fraud. Miguel has filed a civil suit demanding return of the $10,000 plus $100,000 in damages. Identify the relevant tax issues for Miguel.

PROBLEMS

27. Bill and Nancy are married and together have AGI of $60,000. They have no dependents and filed a joint return. Each pays $900 for hospitalization insurance. During the year, they paid the following amounts for medical care: $6,200 in doctor and dentist bills and hospital expenses and $800 for prescribed medicine and drugs. In December, they received an insurance reimbursement of $1,200 for hospitalization. Determine the deduction allowable for medical expenses paid during the year.

28. Frank, a widower, had a serious stroke and is no longer capable of caring for himself. He has three sons, all of whom live in different states. Because they are unable to care for Frank in their homes, his sons have placed him in a nursing home equipped to provide medical and nursing care facilities. Total nursing home expenses amount to $45,000 per year. Of this amount, $18,000 is directly attributable to medical and nursing care. Frank's Social Security benefits are used to pay for $12,000 of the nursing home charges. He has no other income. His sons plan to split the remaining medical expenses equally.
    a. What portion of the nursing home charges is potentially deductible as a medical expense?
    b. Can you provide Frank's sons with a tax planning idea for maximizing the deduction for his medical expenses?

29. Ken developed a severe asthmatic condition, and his physician advised him to install a special air conditioning, heating, and filtration system in his home. The cost of installing the system was $6,000, and the increase in the value of the residence was determined to be $2,000. Ken's AGI for the year was $30,000.
    a. How much of the expenditure can Ken deduct as a medical expense?
    b. Assume the same facts as in (a), except that Ken was paralyzed in an automobile accident and the expenditures were incurred to build entrance and exit ramps and widen the hallways in his home to accommodate his wheelchair. How much of the expenditure can Ken deduct as a medical expense?

30. Julia had medical expenses of $9,000 and AGI of $100,000 in 1996. She had other itemized deductions of $8,200 for the year. Julia expects that her insurance company will reimburse her for all of her medical expenses in January 1997. What is the maximum amount Julia can deduct as itemized deductions for 1996? If she deducts the maximum allowable amount in 1996, will this affect her taxable income in 1997? What factors should Julia consider in deciding whether to deduct the medical expenses in 1996?

31. During the current year, Sara incurred and paid the following expenses for Seth (her son), Emma (her mother), and herself:

Surgery for Seth	$3,200
Trout Valley Academy charges for Seth:	
Tuition	9,000
Room, board, and other expenses	6,600
Psychiatric treatment	7,200
Doctor bills for Emma	2,700
Prescription drugs for Sara, Seth, and Emma	1,300
Insulin for Emma	950
Nonprescription drugs for Sara, Seth, and Emma	800

Charges at Riverview Nursing Home for Emma:

Medical care	6,500
Lodging	8,200
Meals	3,300

Seth qualifies as Sara's dependent, and Emma would also qualify except that she receives $6,100 of taxable retirement benefits from her former employer. Seth's psychiatrist recommended Trout Valley Academy because of its small class sizes and specialized psychiatric treatment program that is needed to treat Seth's illness. Emma is a paraplegic and diabetic, and Riverview offers the type of care that she requires.

Upon the recommendation of a physician, Sara has an air filtration system installed in her personal residence. She suffers from severe allergies. In connection with this equipment, Sara incurs and pays the following amounts during the year:

Filtration system and cost of installation	$6,800
Increase in utility bills due to the system	550
Cost of certified appraisal	370

The system has an estimated useful life of 10 years. The appraisal was to determine the value of Sara's residence with and without the system. The appraisal states that the system increased the value of Sara's residence by $1,000. Ignoring the 7.5% floor, what is the total of Sara's expenses that qualifies for the medical expense deduction?

32. Henry, a resident of Decatur, Illinois, is advised by his family physician that his dependent son needs surgery for benign tumors in his leg. Henry and his son travel to Rochester, Minnesota, for treatment at the Mayo Clinic, which specializes in this type of surgery. Henry incurred the following costs:

Round-trip airfare ($320 each)	$640
Henry's hotel in Rochester for four nights ($80 per night)	320
Henry's meals while in Rochester	88

Compute Henry's medical expenses for the trip (subject to the 7.5% floor).

33. In Clay County, the real property tax year is the calendar year. The real property tax becomes a personal liability of the owner of real property on January 1 in the current real property tax year, 1996. The tax is payable on July 1, 1996. On May 30, 1996, Joe sells his house to Celia for $280,000. On July 1, 1996, Celia pays the entire real estate tax of $7,320 for the year ending December 31, 1996.
a. How much of the property taxes may Joe deduct?
b. How much of the property taxes may Celia deduct?

34. Assume the same facts as in Problem 33.
a. What is Celia's basis for the residence?
b. How much did Joe realize from the sale of the residence?

35. Roland uses the cash method of accounting and lives in a state that imposes an income tax (including withholding from wages). On April 14, 1996, he files his state return for 1995, paying an additional $500 in state income taxes. During 1996, his withholdings for state income tax purposes amount to $3,700. On April 13, 1997, he files his state return for 1996 claiming a refund of $900. Roland receives the refund on August 3, 1997.
a. If Roland itemizes deductions, how much may he claim as a deduction for state income taxes on his Federal return for calendar year 1996 (filed in April 1997)?
b. How will the refund of $900 received in 1997 be treated for Federal income tax purposes?

36. Sandra incurred $19,500 of interest expense related to her investments in 1996. Her investment income included $6,000 of interest, $4,000 of dividends, and a $7,500 net capital gain on the sale of securities.

a. What is the maximum amount that Sandra can treat as investment income for the year?

b. What other tax factors should Sandra consider in deciding whether to elect to include net capital gain in her investment income?

37. Maria has AGI of $72,000, which includes dividends and interest income of $16,200. In addition to investment interest expense of $14,000, she paid $2,700 of city ad valorem property tax on stocks and bonds and had the following miscellaneous itemized expenses:

Safe deposit box rental (to hold investment securities)	$ 108
Investment counsel fee	1,080
Professional dues and subscriptions	765
Tax return preparation fees	540

Determine Maria's investment expense deduction and discuss the treatment of any portion of the investment interest expense that is disallowed due to the investment interest limitation.

38. Veronica borrowed $200,000 to acquire a parcel of land to be held for investment purposes. During the year, she paid interest of $20,000 on the loan. She had AGI of $50,000 for the year. Other items related to Veronica's investments include the following:

Investment income	$10,200
Long-term gain on sale of stock	4,000
Investment counsel fees	1,500

Veronica is unmarried and elected to itemize her deductions. She had no miscellaneous deductions other than the investment counsel fees. Determine Veronica's investment interest deduction.

39. Sid and Sara, married taxpayers, took out a mortgage on their home for $100,000 in 1987. In March of the current year, when the home had a fair market value of $200,000 and they owed $85,000 on the mortgage, Sid and Sara took out a home equity loan for $110,000. They used the funds to purchase a motor home to be used for recreational purposes. What is the maximum amount on which they can deduct home equity interest?

40. Ella purchased her residence five years ago, obtaining a 20-year mortgage at an annual interest rate of 11%. On January 2, 1996, Ella refinanced with a 15-year mortgage in order to reduce the interest rate to 8.25%. To obtain the refinancing, she was required to pay points of $3,000. How much, if any, of the $3,000 points can Ella deduct in 1996?

41. Ron and Tom are equal owners in Robin Corporation. On July 1, 1996, each loans the corporation $30,000 at annual interest of 10%. Ron and Tom are brothers. Both shareholders are on the cash method of accounting, while Robin Corporation is on the accrual method. All parties use the calendar year for tax purposes. On June 30, 1997, Robin repays the loans of $60,000 together with the specified interest of $6,000.

a. How much of the interest can Robin Corporation deduct in 1996? In 1997?

b. When is the interest taxed to Ron and Tom?

42. Erin donates $1,000 to State University's athletic department. The payment guarantees that Erin will have preferred seating on the 50-yard line.

a. Assume Erin subsequently buys four $50 game tickets. How much can she deduct as a charitable contribution to the university's athletic department?

b. Assume that Erin's $1,000 donation includes four $50 tickets. How much can she deduct as a charitable contribution to the university's athletic department?

43. Tim owned stock in White Corporation that he donated to a university (a qualified charitable organization) on May 1, 1996.
    a. What is the amount of Tim's deduction assuming that he had purchased the stock for $2,500 on March 3, 1996, and the stock had a value of $3,600 when he made the donation.
    b. Assume the same facts as in (a), except that Tim had purchased the stock for $2,500 on March 3, 1995.
    c. Assume the same facts as in (a), except that the stock had a fair market value of $2,300 (rather than $3,600) when it was donated to the university.

44. Darby contributed a painting to an art museum in 1995. She had owned the painting for 20 years, and it had a value of $120,000 at the time of the donation. The museum displayed the painting in its impressionist gallery.
    a. Assume that Darby's AGI is $230,000 and her basis for the painting is $80,000. Would you recommend that she make the reduced deduction election?
    b. Assume that Darby's AGI is $230,000 and her basis for the painting is $115,000. Would you recommend that she make the reduced deduction election?

45. During the year, Al made the following contributions to his church:

Cash	$20,000
Stock in Thrush Corporation (a publicly traded corporation)	30,000

The stock in Thrush Corporation was acquired as an investment three years ago at a cost of $10,000. Al's AGI is $70,000.
    a. What is Al's charitable contribution deduction?
    b. How are excess amounts, if any, treated?

46. Mae died in 1996. Before she died, Mae made a gift of stock in Eagle Corporation (a publicly traded corporation) to her church. The stock was worth $70,000 and had been acquired as an investment two years ago at a cost of $56,000. In the year of her death, Mae had AGI of $110,000. In completing her final income tax return, how should Mae's executor handle the charitable contribution?

47. On December 30, 1996, Roberta purchased four tickets to a charity ball sponsored by the city of San Diego for the benefit of underprivileged children. Each ticket cost $200 and had a fair market value of $35. On the same day as the purchase, Roberta gave the tickets to the minister of her church for personal use by his family. At the time of the gift of the tickets, Roberta pledged $4,000 to the building fund of her church. The pledge was satisfied by check dated December 31, 1996, but not mailed until January 3, 1997.
    a. Presuming Roberta is a cash basis and calendar year taxpayer, how much can she deduct as a charitable contribution for 1996?
    b. Would the amount of the deduction be any different if Roberta is an accrual basis taxpayer? Explain.

48. In December each year, Sandy Wren contributes 10% of her gross income to her church. Sandy, who is in the 36% marginal tax bracket, is considering the following alternatives as charitable contributions in December 1996:

	Fair Market Value
1. Cash donation	$12,000
2. Unimproved land held for six years ($2,000 basis)	12,000
3. Purple Corporation stock held for eight months ($2,000 basis)	12,000
4. Silver Corporation stock held for two years ($17,000 basis)	12,000

Sandy has asked you to help her decide which of these potential contributions will be most advantageous taxwise. Rank the four alternatives, and write a letter to Sandy communicating your advice to her. Her address is 1201 Baywatch Drive, Chicago, IL 60606.

49. Classify each of the following independent expenditures as nondeductible *(ND)* items, business *(dfor)* deductions, or itemized *(dfrom)* deductions. *(Note:* In many cases, it may be necessary to refer to the materials in earlier chapters of the text.)
    a. Interest allowed on home mortgage accrued by a cash basis taxpayer.
    b. State income taxes paid by a sole proprietor of a business.
    c. Subscription to the *Wall Street Journal* paid by a vice president of a bank and not reimbursed by her employer.
    d. Automobile mileage for attendance at weekly church services.
    e. Street-paving assessment paid to the county by a homeowner.
    f. Speeding ticket paid by the owner-operator of a taxicab.
    g. Interest and taxes paid by the owner of residential rental property.
    h. Business entertainment expenses (properly substantiated) paid by a self-employed taxpayer.
    i. State and Federal excise taxes on tobacco paid by a self-employed taxpayer who gave his clients cigars as Christmas presents. The business gifts were properly substantiated and under $25 each.
    j. State and Federal excise taxes on cigarettes purchased by a heavy smoker for personal consumption.
    k. Federal excise taxes on the purchase of gasoline for use in the taxpayer's personal automobile.
    l. Theft loss of personal jewelry worth $300 but which originally cost $75.
    m. Maternity clothing purchased by a taxpayer who is pregnant.
    n. Medical expenses paid by an employer on behalf of an employee.
    o. Qualified residence interest paid by a taxpayer on a loan obtained to build an artist studio in his personal residence. Assume that the taxpayer's art activities are classified as a hobby.
    p. Assume the same facts as in (o) except that the art activities are classified as a trade or business.

50. Manuel and Rosa Garcia, both age 45, are married and have no dependents. They have asked you to advise them whether they should file jointly or separately in 1996. They present you with the following information:

	Manuel	Rosa	Joint
Salary	$40,000		
Business net income		$100,000	
Interest income	400	1,200	$2,200
Deductions *for* AGI	2,000	13,000	
Medical expenses	9,500	600	
State income tax	800	2,000	
Real estate tax			3,400
Mortgage interest			5,200
Unreimbursed employee expenses	1,100		

If they file separately, Manuel and Rosa will split the real estate tax and mortgage interest deductions equally. Write Manuel and Rosa a letter in which you make and explain a recommendation on filing status for 1996. Manuel and Rosa reside at 5904 Stevens Avenue, Durham, NC 27707.

51. For calendar year 1996, Clyde and Trisha file a joint return reflecting AGI of $160,000. Their itemized deductions are as follows:

Medical expenses	$12,000
Casualty loss (not covered by insurance)	17,000
Interest on home mortgage	15,000

Property taxes on home	13,000
Charitable contributions	14,000
State income tax	10,000

After all necessary adjustments are made, what is the amount of itemized deductions Clyde and Trisha may claim?

52. Kareem and Veneia are married and file a joint return. For 1996, they have AGI of $305,520. Their itemized deductions for the year total $39,000 and consist of the following:

Medical expenses	$32,000
Interest on home mortgage	3,000
State income tax	4,000

After all necessary adjustments are made, what is the amount of itemized deductions Kareem and Veneia may claim?

53. Ben and Laura are married and file a joint return. For 1996, they have AGI of $358,450, which included net investment income of $41,000 before deducting investment interest. Compute Ben and Laura's allowable itemized deductions for 1996 based on the following information:

Investment interest	$11,000
Casualty loss (after applicable limitations)	8,000
Qualified residence interest	5,400
Property taxes	4,700
Charitable contributions	2,900
State income taxes	5,300

54. Andy, who is single, had AGI of $180,000 for 1996. He incurred the following expenses and losses during the year:

Medical expenses before 7.5%-of-AGI limitation	$15,000
State and local income taxes	2,600
Real estate taxes	3,400
Home mortgage interest	6,600
Charitable contribution	3,500
Casualty loss before 10% limitation (after $100 floor)	20,600
Unreimbursed employee expenses subject to 2%-of-AGI limitation	4,100
Gambling losses (Andy had $3,500 gambling income)	7,000

Calculate Andy's allowable itemized deductions for the year.

CUMULATIVE PROBLEMS

55. Alice and Bruce Byrd are married taxpayers, ages 47 and 45, who file a joint return. Their Social Security numbers are 034–48–4382 and 016–50–9556, respectively. They live at 473 Revere Avenue, Ames, MA 01850. Alice is the office manager for a dental clinic and earns an annual salary of $45,000. Bruce is the manager of a fast-food outlet owned and operated by Plymouth Corporation. His annual salary is $36,000.

   The Byrds have two children, Cynthia (age 23 and S.S. no. 017–44–9126) and John (age 22 and S.S. no. 017–27–4148), who live with them. Both children are full-time students at a nearby college. Alice's mother, Myrtle Jones (age 74 and S.S. no. 016–15–8266), also lives with them. Her sole source of income is from Social Security benefits, which she deposits in a savings account.

During 1995, a particularly harsh storm struck the Ames area. As a result, the Byrds suffered severe flood damage to the basement and foundation of their personal residence, which was purchased in 1986 at a cost of $80,000. Based on an appraisal, the fair market value of the house was $115,000 before the storm and $90,000 after. The Byrds' homeowner's insurance policy does not cover damage due to flooding. The cost of the appraisal was $300.

During 1995, the Byrds furnished one-third of the total support of Bruce's widower father, Sam Byrd (age 70 and S.S. no. 034–82–8583). Sam lives alone and receives the rest of his support from Bruce's sister and brother (one-third each). They have signed a multiple support agreement allowing Bruce to claim Sam as a dependent for 1995. Sam died in November, and Bruce received life insurance proceeds of $270,000 on December 28.

The Byrds had the following expenses relating to their personal residence during 1995:

Property taxes	$2,400
Interest on home mortgage	5,900
Repairs to roof	1,000
Utilities	2,800
Fire and theft insurance	1,100

Medical expenses for 1995 include:

Medical insurance premiums	$3,100
Doctor bill for Sam incurred in 1994 and not paid until 1995	1,600
Operation for Sam	3,900

The operation for Sam represents the one-third Bruce contributed toward his father's support.

Other relevant information follows:

• On December 1, 1995, Myrtle gave Alice and Bruce a tract of undeveloped land (basis of $30,000 and fair market value of $90,000).

• Alice and Bruce had $2,452 ($1,252 for Alice and $1,200 for Bruce) withheld from their salaries for state income taxes. When they filed their 1994 state return in 1995, they paid additional tax of $280.

• During 1995, Alice and Bruce attended a dinner dance sponsored by the Ames Police Disability Association (a qualified charitable organization). The Byrds paid $100 for the tickets. Cost of comparable entertainment would normally be $40. The Byrds contributed $1,700 to their church and gave used clothing (cost of $800 and fair market value of $300) to the Salvation Army. All donations are supported by receipts.

• In 1995, the Byrds received interest income of $1,450 from a savings account they maintained.

• Alice's employer requires that all employees wear uniforms to work. During 1995, Alice spent $290 on new uniforms and $102 on laundry charges. Bruce paid $120 for an annual subscription to the *Journal of Franchise Management.* Neither Alice's nor Bruce's employers reimburse for employee expenses.

• Alice and Bruce had $6,032 ($3,086 for Alice and $2,946 for Bruce) of Federal income tax withheld in 1995 and paid no estimated Federal income tax. Neither Alice nor Bruce wishes to designate $3 to the Presidential Election Campaign Fund.

Part 1—Tax Computation
Compute net tax payable or refund due for Alice and Bruce Byrd for 1995. If they have overpaid, the amount is to be refunded. If you use tax forms for your computations, you will need Form 1040, Schedules A and B, and Form 4684. Suggested software (if available): *TurboTax* or *MacInTax.*

Part 2—Tax Planning

Alice and Bruce are planning some significant changes for 1996. They have provided you with the following information and asked you to project their taxable income and tax liabiliy for 1996.

Myrtle became seriously ill in December 1995 and is no longer able to care for herself. As a result, Alice plans to take a one-year leave of absence from work during 1996 to care for her. The Byrds will use $70,000 of the life insurance proceeds they received as a result of Sam's death and pay off their mortgage in early January 1996. They will invest the remaining $200,000 in short-term certificates of deposit (CDs) and use the interest for living expenses during 1996. They expect to earn total interest of $13,500 on the CDs. Bruce has been awarded a 5% raise for 1996, and withholdings on his salary will increase accordingly.

The Byrds will not incur any additional costs related to the flood damage or Sam's medical problem. Alice will not work at all during 1996, so none of her job-related expenses or withholdings will continue. The Byrds do not expect to owe additional state income tax when they file their 1995 return, but they do expect their charitable contributions and medical insurance premiums to continue at the 1995 level. Assume all other income and deduction items will continue at the same level in 1996 unless you have information that indicates otherwise.

56. Paul and Donna Decker are married taxpayers, ages 44 and 42, who file a joint return for 1996. The Deckers live at 1121 College Avenue, Carmel, IN 46032. Paul is an assistant manager at Carmel Motor Inn, and Donna is a teacher at Carmel Elementary School. They present you with W–2 Forms that reflect the following information:

	Paul	**Donna**
Salary	$35,000	$38,000
Federal tax withheld	6,092	5,400
State income tax withheld	700	760
FICA (Social Security) withheld	2,678	2,907
Social Security numbers	222–11–4567	333–11–9872

Donna is the custodial parent of two children from a previous marriage who reside with the Deckers through the school year. The children, Larry and Jane Parker, reside with their father, Bob, during the summer. Relevant information for the children follows:

	Larry	**Jane**
Age	11	9
Social Security numbers	305–11–4567	303–11–9872
Months spent with Deckers	9	9

Under the divorce decree, Bob pays child support of $150 per month per child during the nine months the children live with the Deckers. Bob says he spends $200 per month per child during the three summer months they reside with him. Donna and Paul can document that they provide $1,800 support per child per year. The divorce decree is silent as to which parent can claim the exemption for the children.

In August, Paul and Donna added a suite to their home to provide more comfortable accommodations for Hannah Snyder (263–33–4738), Donna's mother, who had moved in with them in February 1995 after the death of Donna's father. Not wanting to borrow money for this addition, Paul sold 300 shares of Acme Corporation stock for $50 per share on May 3, 1996, and used the proceeds of $15,000 to cover construction costs. The

Deckers had purchased the stock on April 27, 1994, for $22 per share. They received dividends of $550 on the jointly owned stock a month before the sale.

Hannah, who is 66 years old, received $7,200 in Social Security benefits during the year, of which she gave the Deckers $1,700 to use toward household expenses and deposited the remainder in her personal savings account. The Deckers determine that they have spent $1,500 of their own money for food, clothing, medical expenses, and other items for Hannah. They do not know what the rental value of Hannah's suite would be, but they estimate it would be at least $300 per month.

The Deckers received $2,100 interest on City of Indianapolis bonds they had bought in 1993. Paul had heard from a friend that municipal bonds were paying good rates and that municipal bond interest was not taxable. To finance the purchase of the bonds, he borrowed $20,000 from the bank and paid $1,760 interest during 1996. Other interest paid during the year included the following:

Home mortgage interest (paid to Carmel Federal Savings & Loan)	$4,890
Interest on an automobile loan (paid to Carmel National Bank)	920
Interest on Citibank Visa card	855

Donna's uncle died on November 11, 1996, and left her 50 shares of Thrush Corporation stock worth $70 per share. Her uncle's basis in the stock was $34 per share. Donna received $530 in dividends on the stock in December 1996.

In July, Paul hit a submerged rock while boating. Fortunately, he was thrown from the boat, landed in deep water, and was uninjured. However, the boat, which was uninsured, was destroyed. Paul had paid $18,000 for the boat in June 1995, and its value was appraised at $14,500 on the date of the accident.

The Deckers paid doctor and hospital bills of $4,100 and were reimbursed $1,600 by their insurance company. They spent $780 for prescription drugs and medicines and $1,440 for premiums on their health insurance policy. They have filed additional claims of $700 with their insurance company and have been told they will receive payment for that amount in January 1997. Included in the amounts paid for doctor and hospital bills were payments of $360 for Hannah and $750 for the children.

Additional information of potential tax consequence follows:

Real estate taxes paid	$1,900
Cash contributions to church	800
Appraised value of books donated to public library	450
Paul's unreimbursed employee expenses to attend hotel management convention:	
Airfare	340
Hotel	130
Meals	95
Registration fee	100
Refund of state income tax for 1995 (the Deckers itemized on their 1995 return)	910

Compute net tax payable or refund due for the Deckers for 1996. If they have overpaid, the amount is to be credited toward their taxes for 1997. Suggested software (if available): *TurboTax* or *MacInTax*.

Research Problems for this chapter appear at the end of Chapter 28.

TEAM PROJECT: ARTHUR ANDERSEN TAX CHALLENGE CASES

For more information on the Arthur Andersen Tax Challenge Cases, please refer to Chapter 2, page 2-41.

Information related to tax issues and problems that are discussed in this chapter may be found in the

Fields case on pages 1, 2, 13-17, 19, 21-27, and 31
Miller case on pages 2, 3, 11-15, 24-27, 29, 30, 34, and 38

Read and analyze the case you have been assigned and *identify* any issues and problems that are related to material covered in this chapter. If the information provided in the case is complete, prepare answers for this part of the case at this time. If you need information that is contained in the later parts of the case, please write a memo summarizing the questions or problems so you can prepare a complete answer at a later date.

10

PASSIVE ACTIVITY LOSSES

LEARNING OBJECTIVES

After completing Chapter 10, you should be able to:

1. Discuss tax shelters and the reasons for at-risk and passive loss limitations.

2. Explain the at-risk limitation.

3. Describe how the passive loss rules limit deductions for losses.

4. Identify taxpayers who are subject to the passive loss limits.

5. Discuss the definition of passive activities.

6. Apply the rules for identifying an activity.

7. Analyze and apply the tests for material participation.

8. Understand the nature of rental activities under the passive loss rules.

9. Recognize the relationship between the at-risk and passive activity limitations.

10. Discuss the special treatment available to real estate activities.

11. Determine the proper tax treatment upon the disposition of a passive activity.

12. Suggest tax planning strategies to minimize the effect of the passive loss limitations.

THE TAX SHELTER PROBLEM

1 ▼ LEARNING OBJECTIVE
Discuss tax shelters and the reasons for at-risk and passive loss limitations.

Before Congress enacted legislation to reduce or eliminate their effectiveness, **tax shelters** were popular investments for tax avoidance purposes because they could generate deductions and other benefits that could be used to offset income from other sources. Because of the tax avoidance potential of many tax shelters, they were attractive to wealthy taxpayers in high income tax brackets. Many tax shelters merely provided an opportunity for "investors" to buy deductions and credits in ventures that were not expected to generate a profit, even in the long run.

Although it may seem odd that a taxpayer would intentionally invest in an activity that was designed to produce losses, there is a logical explanation. The typical tax shelter operated as a partnership and relied heavily on nonrecourse financing.[1] Accelerated depreciation and interest expense deductions generated large losses in the early years of the activity. At the very least, the tax shelter deductions deferred the recognition of any net income from the venture until the activity was sold. In the best of situations, the investor could realize additional tax savings by offsetting other income (e.g., salary, interest, and dividends) with deductions flowing from the tax shelter. Ultimately, the sale of the investment would result in capital gain. The following examples illustrate what was possible *before* Congress enacted legislation to curb tax shelter abuses.

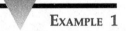 ▼ EXAMPLE 1

Bob, who earned a salary of $100,000 as a business executive and dividend income of $15,000, invested $20,000 for a 10% interest in a cattle-breeding tax shelter. Through the use of $800,000 of nonrecourse financing and available cash of $200,000, the partnership acquired a herd of an exotic breed of cattle costing $1 million. Depreciation, interest, and other deductions related to the activity resulted in a loss of $400,000, of which Bob's share was $40,000. Bob was allowed to deduct the $40,000 loss, even though he had invested and stood to lose only $20,000 if the investment turned sour. The net effect of the $40,000 deduction from the partnership was that a portion of Bob's salary and dividend income was "sheltered," and as a result, he was required to calculate his tax liability on only $75,000 of income [$115,000 (salary and dividends) – $40,000 (deduction)] rather than $115,000. If this deduction were available under current law and if Bob was in the 39.6% income tax bracket, this deduction would generate a tax savings of $15,840 ($40,000 × 39.6%) in the first year alone! ▼

---

[1] Nonrecourse debt is an obligation for which the borrower is not personally liable. An example of nonrecourse debt is a liability on real estate acquired by a partnership without the partnership or any of the partners assuming any liability for the mortgage. The acquired property generally is pledged as collateral for the loan.

A review of Example 1 shows that the taxpayer took a *two-for-one* write-off ($40,000 deduction, $20,000 investment). In the heyday of tax shelters, promoters often promised *multiple* write-offs for the investor.

The first major provision aimed at tax shelters was the **at-risk limitation.** Its objective is to limit a taxpayer's deductions to the amount at risk, that is, the amount the taxpayer stands to lose if the investment turns out to be a financial disaster.

EXAMPLE 2

Returning to the facts of Example 1, under the current at-risk rules Bob would be allowed to deduct $20,000 (i.e., the amount that he could lose if the business failed). This deduction would reduce his other income and as a result, Bob would have to report only $95,000 of income ($115,000 − $20,000). The remaining nondeductible $20,000 loss and any future losses flowing from the partnership would be suspended under the at-risk rules and would be deductible in the future only as his at-risk amount increased. ▼

The second major attack on tax shelters came with the passage of the passive activity loss rules. These rules were intended to halt an investor's ability to benefit from the mismatching of an entity's expenses and income that often occurs in the early years of the business. Congress observed that despite the at-risk limitations, investors could still deduct losses flowing from an entity and thereby defer their tax liability on other income. In effect, passive activity rules have essentially made the term *tax shelter* obsolete. Now such ventures where investors are not involved in the day-to-day operations of the business are generally referred to as passive investments, or *passive activities,* rather than tax shelters.

The **passive loss** rules require the taxpayer to segregate all income and losses into three categories: active, passive, and portfolio. In general, the passive loss limits disallow the deduction of passive losses against active or portfolio income, even when the taxpayer is at risk to the extent of the loss. Normally, passive losses can only offset passive income.

TAX IN THE NEWS

THE FEDS MAY ASK TAX SHELTERS TO REGISTER

Investment bankers and other tax advisers who devise intricate tax-saving deals for clients often require them to sign confidentiality agreements. Representative Bill Archer, the Texas Republican who heads the House Ways and Means Committee, supports requiring advisers to register such deals confidentially with the IRS as "tax shelters." Tax advisers say such pacts are meant to keep competitors from learning of complex tax strategies, but the House budget committee suggests that many also conceal various "inappropriate corporate tax benefits" that cost the government billions.

This requirement would be in addition to the current law that requires investment promoters to register as tax shelters deals that yield inordinate tax benefits relative to the amount invested. Many corporate tax advisers say the idea is too intrusive and would be too time-consuming. Penalty rules already require taxpayers to alert the IRS on their returns if they take overly aggressive positions.

SOURCE: Information from *Wall Street Journal,* May 24, 1995, p. A1.

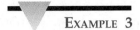

EXAMPLE 3

Returning to the facts of Example 1, the passive activity loss rules further restrict Bob's ability to claim the $20,000 tax deduction shown in Example 2. Because Bob is a passive investor and does not materially participate in any meaningful way in the activities of the cattle-breeding operation, the $20,000 loss allowed under the at-risk rules is disallowed under the passive loss rules. The passive loss is disallowed because Bob does not generate any passive income that could absorb his passive loss. Further, his salary (active income) and dividends (portfolio income) cannot be used to absorb any of the passive loss. Consequently, Bob's current year taxable income must reflect his nonpassive income of $115,000, and he receives no current benefit for his share of the partnership loss. However, all is not lost because Bob's share of the entity's loss is *suspended;* it is carried forward and can be deducted in the future when he has passive income or sells his interest in the activity. ▼

This chapter explores the nature of the at-risk limits and passive activity loss rules and their impact on investors. An interesting consequence of these rules is that now investors evaluating potential investments must consider mainly the economics of the venture instead of the tax benefits or tax avoidance possibilities that an investment may generate.

AT-RISK LIMITS

2 LEARNING OBJECTIVE
Explain the at-risk limitation.

The at-risk provisions limit the deductibility of losses from business and income-producing activities. These provisions, which apply to individuals and closely held corporations, are designed to prevent taxpayers from deducting losses in excess of their actual economic investment in an activity. In the case of an S corporation or a partnership, the at-risk limits apply at the owner level. Under the at-risk rules, a taxpayer's deductible loss from an activity for any taxable year is limited to the amount the taxpayer has at risk at the end of the taxable year (the amount the taxpayer could actually lose in the activity).

While the amount at risk generally vacillates over time, the initial amount considered at risk consists of the following:[2]

- The amount of cash and the adjusted basis of property contributed to the activity by the taxpayer.
- Amounts borrowed for use in the activity for which the taxpayer is personally liable or has pledged as security property not used in the activity.

This amount generally is increased each year by the taxpayer's share of income and is decreased by the taxpayer's share of losses and withdrawals from the activity. In addition, because general partners are jointly and severally liable for recourse debts of the partnership, their at-risk amounts are increased when the partnership increases its debt and are decreased when the partnership reduces its debt. However, a taxpayer generally is not considered at risk with respect to borrowed amounts if either of the following is true:

- The taxpayer is not personally liable for repayment of the debt (e.g., nonrecourse debt).
- The lender has an interest (other than as a creditor) in the activity.

---

[2]§ 465(b)(1).

CONCEPT SUMMARY 10–1

Calculation of At-Risk Amount

Increases to a taxpayer's at-risk amount:

- Cash and the adjusted basis of property contributed to the activity.
- Amounts borrowed for use in the activity for which the taxpayer is personally liable or has pledged as security property not used in the activity.
- Taxpayer's share of amounts borrowed for use in the activity that is qualified nonrecourse financing.
- Taxpayer's share of the activity's income.

Decreases to a taxpayer's at-risk amount:

- Withdrawals from the activity.
- Taxpayer's share of the activity's loss.
- Taxpayer's share of any reductions of debt for which recourse against the taxpayer exists or reductions of qualified nonrecourse debt.

An important exception provides that in the case of an activity involving the holding of real property, a taxpayer is considered at risk for his or her share of any *qualified nonrecourse financing* that is secured by real property used in the activity.[3]

Subject to the passive activity rules discussed later in the chapter, a taxpayer may deduct a loss as long as his or her at-risk amount is positive. However, once the at-risk amount is exhausted, any remaining loss cannot be deducted until a later year. Any losses disallowed for any given taxable year by the at-risk rules may be deducted in the first succeeding year in which the rules do not prevent the deduction—that is, when and to the extent of a positive at-risk amount.

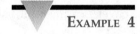

EXAMPLE 4   In 1996, Sue invests $40,000 in an oil partnership that, by the use of nonrecourse loans, spends $60,000 on deductible intangible drilling costs applicable to her interest. Assume Sue's interest in the partnership is subject to the at-risk limits but is not subject to the passive loss limits. Since Sue has only $40,000 of capital at risk, she cannot deduct more than $40,000 against her other income and must reduce her at-risk amount to zero ($40,000 at-risk amount − $40,000 loss deducted). The nondeductible loss of $20,000 ($60,000 loss generated − $40,000 loss allowed) can be carried over to 1997. ▼

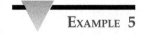

EXAMPLE 5   In 1997, Sue has taxable income of $15,000 from the oil partnership and invests an additional $10,000 in the venture. Her at-risk amount is now $25,000 ($0 beginning balance + $15,000 taxable income + $10,000 additional investment). This enables Sue to deduct the carryover loss and requires her to reduce her at-risk amount to $5,000 ($25,000 at-risk amount − $20,000 carryover loss allowed). ▼

An additional complicating factor is that previously allowed losses must be recaptured to the extent the at-risk amount is reduced below zero.[4] That is, previous losses that were allowed must be offset by the recognition of enough income to bring the at-risk amount up to zero. This rule applies in such situations

---

[3] § 465(b)(6).   [4] § 465(e).

as when the amount at risk is reduced below zero by distributions to the taxpayer or when the status of indebtedness changes from recourse to nonrecourse.

ETHICAL CONSIDERATIONS

Manipulating the At-Risk Limits

At a social function, you encounter your friend Juan. You have known for some time that Juan has an investment in a venture that could make him subject to the at-risk rules. Not wanting to appear "nosy," you make an oblique reference to his investment. He laughs and says, "That hasn't been a problem. At the end of every year, I make a contribution to the partnership to raise my at-risk basis, and then on January 2 of the following year, I get that money back. This approach has worked well for me every year, and the IRS has never caught on. As I've always said, 'there's more than one way to skin a cat.' " As a respected tax accountant in the community, you frown on such techniques with your clients and will not sign tax returns that involve such manipulation. However, Juan is not one of your clients. How do you respond to Juan's confession?

PASSIVE LOSS LIMITS

CLASSIFICATION AND IMPACT OF PASSIVE INCOME AND LOSSES

3   LEARNING OBJECTIVE
Describe how the passive loss rules limit deductions for losses.

Classification.   The passive loss rules require income and losses to be classified into three categories: active, passive, and portfolio. **Active income** includes, but is not limited to, the following:

- Wages, salary, commissions, bonuses, and other payments for services rendered by the taxpayer.
- Profit from a trade or business in which the taxpayer is a material participant.
- Gain on the sale or other disposition of assets used in an active trade or business.
- Income from intangible property if the taxpayer's personal efforts significantly contributed to the creation of the property.

Portfolio income includes, but is not limited to, the following:

- Interest, dividends, annuities, and royalties not derived in the ordinary course of a trade or business.
- Gain or loss from the disposition of property that produces portfolio income or is held for investment purposes.

Section 469 provides that income or loss from the following activities is treated as *passive:*

- Any trade or business or income-producing activity in which the taxpayer does not materially participate.
- Subject to certain exceptions, all rental activities, whether the taxpayer materially participates or not.

Although the Code defines rental activities as passive activities, several exceptions allow losses from certain real estate rental activities to be offset against nonpassive

---

TAX IN THE NEWS

KNOWLEDGE OF TAX LAWS IS A KEY TO REAL ESTATE SUCCESS

One often hears the sage investment advice to "buy low and sell high," or to "buy cheap, and, as much as possible, use other people's money." These tips, though often difficult to implement, can lead to rich rewards. To realize the full benefits of investing, however, whether in stocks and bonds or in real estate, an investor needs to know and be able to apply the tax law.

For example, due to the passive activity loss rules, a taxpayer who wishes to participate in a real estate investment should avoid being a passive investor. Becoming personally involved may be a better approach. Not only can actual participation by the owner lead to favorable tax results, but the fees and commissions of brokers and middlemen can be avoided.

People who buy real estate through partnerships often find the odds stacked against them. Not only is a lot of their money skimmed off the top in fees, but if the cost of the property is highly inflated or highly leveraged, many of the depreciation and interest deductions may be disallowed due to the operation of the passive activity loss rules. Thus, for some taxpayers, the answer to successful real estate investing is to participate actively in the operation of the real estate, avoid high fees, make a profit, and avoid the passive activity loss rules.

SOURCE: Information from John R. Hayes, "A Nice Little Sideline," *Forbes,* July 17, 1995, p. 306.

(active or portfolio) income. The exceptions are discussed under Special Passive Activity Rules for Real Estate Activities later in the chapter.

General Impact. Deductions or expenses generated by passive activities can only be deducted to the extent of income from all of the taxpayer's passive income. Any excess may not be used to offset income from active sources or portfolio income. Instead, any unused passive losses are suspended and carried forward to future years to offset passive income generated in those years. Otherwise, suspended losses may be used only when a taxpayer disposes of his or her entire interest in an activity. In that event, all current and suspended losses related to the activity may offset active and portfolio income.

EXAMPLE 6

Kim, a physician, earned $150,000 from her full-time practice. She also received $10,000 in dividends and interest on various portfolio investments, and her share of a passive loss from a tax shelter not limited by the at-risk rules was $60,000. Because the loss is a passive loss, it is not deductible against her other income. The loss is suspended and is carried over to the future. If Kim has passive income from this investment, or from other passive investments, in the future, she can offset the suspended loss against that passive income. If she does not have passive income to offset this suspended loss in the future, she will be allowed to offset the loss against other types of income when she eventually disposes of the passive activity. ▼

Impact of Suspended Losses. When a taxpayer disposes of his or her entire interest in a passive activity, the actual economic gain or loss on the investment, including any suspended losses, can finally be determined. As a result, under the passive loss rules, upon a fully taxable disposition, any overall loss realized from the activity by the taxpayer is recognized and can be offset against any income.

A fully taxable disposition generally involves a sale of the property to a third party at arm's length and thus, presumably, for a price equal to the property's fair market value. Gain recognized upon a transfer of an interest in a passive activity generally is treated as passive and is first offset by the suspended losses from that activity.

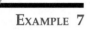

EXAMPLE 7   Rex sells an apartment building with an adjusted basis of $100,000 for $180,000. In addition, he has suspended losses of $60,000 associated with that building. His total gain, $80,000, and his taxable gain, $20,000, are calculated as follows:

Net sales price	$ 180,000
Less: Adjusted basis	(100,000)
Total gain	$ 80,000
Less: Suspended losses	(60,000)
Taxable gain (passive)	$ 20,000

If current and suspended losses of the passive activity exceed the gain realized or if the sale results in a realized loss, the sum of

- any loss from the activity for the tax year (including losses suspended in the activity disposed of), plus
- any loss realized on the disposition

in excess of

- net income or gain for the tax year from all passive activities (without regard to the activity disposed of)

is treated as a loss that is not from a passive activity.

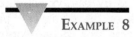

EXAMPLE 8   Dean sells an apartment building with an adjusted basis of $100,000 for $150,000. In addition, he has current and suspended losses of $60,000 associated with that building and has no other passive activities. His total gain, $50,000, and his deductible loss, $10,000, are calculated as follows:

Net sales price	$ 150,000
Less: Adjusted basis	(100,000)
Total gain	$ 50,000
Less: Suspended losses	(60,000)
Deductible loss	($ 10,000)

The $10,000 deductible loss is offset against Dean's ordinary income and portfolio income. ▼

Carryovers of Suspended Losses.   In the above examples, it was assumed that the taxpayer had an interest in only one passive activity, and as a result, the suspended loss was related exclusively to the activity that was disposed of. Taxpayers often own interests in more than one activity, however, and in that case, any suspended losses must be allocated among the activities in which the taxpayer has an interest. The allocation to an activity is made by multiplying the disallowed passive activity loss from all activities by the following fraction:

$$\frac{\text{Loss from activity}}{\text{Sum of losses for taxable year from all activities having losses}}$$

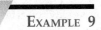

EXAMPLE 9

Diego has investments in three passive activities with the following income and losses for 1995:

Activity A	($30,000)
Activity B	(20,000)
Activity C	25,000
Net passive loss	($25,000)
Allocated to:	
Activity A ($25,000 × $30,000/$50,000)	$15,000
Activity B ($25,000 × $20,000/$50,000)	10,000
Total suspended losses	($25,000)

Suspended losses are carried over indefinitely and are offset in the future against any passive income from the activities to which they relate.[5]

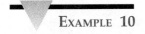

EXAMPLE 10

Assume the same facts as in Example 9 and that Activity A produces $10,000 of income in 1996. Of the suspended loss of $15,000 from 1995 for Activity A, $10,000 is offset against the income from this activity. If Diego sells Activity A in early 1997, then the remaining $5,000 suspended loss is used in determining his final gain or loss. ▼

Passive Credits. Credits arising from passive activities are limited in much the same way as passive losses. Passive credits can be utilized only against regular tax attributable to passive income,[6] which is calculated by comparing the tax on all income (including passive income) with the tax on income excluding passive income.

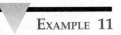

EXAMPLE 11

Sam owes $50,000 of tax, disregarding net passive income, and $80,000 of tax, considering both net passive and other taxable income (disregarding the credits in both cases). The amount of tax attributable to the passive income is $30,000.

Tax due (before credits) including net passive income	$ 80,000
Less: Tax due (before credits) without including net passive income	(50,000)
Tax attributable to passive income	$ 30,000

Sam in the preceding example can claim a maximum of $30,000 of passive activity credits; the excess credits are carried over. These passive activity credits (such as the low-income housing credit and rehabilitation credit) can only be used against the *regular* tax attributable to passive income. If a taxpayer has a net loss from passive activities during a given year, no credits can be used. Likewise, if a

---

[5] § 469(b).

[6] § 469(d)(2).

taxpayer has net passive income but the alternative minimum tax applies to that year, no passive activity credits can be used. (The alternative minimum tax is discussed in Chapter 14.)

Carryovers of Passive Credits.   Tax credits attributable to passive activities can be carried forward indefinitely much like suspended passive losses. Unlike passive losses, however, passive credits are lost forever when the activity is disposed of in a taxable transaction where loss is recognized. Credits are allowed on dispositions only when there is sufficient tax on passive income to absorb them.

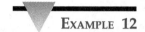
EXAMPLE 12

Alicia sells a passive activity for a gain of $10,000. The activity had suspended losses of $40,000 and suspended credits of $15,000. The $10,000 gain is offset by $10,000 of the suspended losses, and the remaining $30,000 of suspended losses is deductible against Alicia's active and portfolio income. The suspended credits are lost forever because the sale of the activity did not generate any tax. This is true even if Alicia has positive taxable income or is subject to the alternative minimum tax. ▼

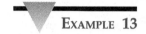
EXAMPLE 13

If Alicia in Example 12 had realized a $100,000 gain on the sale of the passive activity, the $15,000 of suspended credits could have been used to the extent of regular tax attributable to the net passive income.

Gain on sale	$100,000
Less: Suspended losses	(40,000)
Net gain	$ 60,000

If the tax attributable to the net gain of $60,000 is $15,000 or more, the entire $15,000 of suspended credits can be used. If the tax attributable to the gain is less than $15,000, the excess of the suspended credit over the tax attributable to the gain is lost forever. ▼

When a taxpayer has adequate regular tax liability from passive activities to trigger the use of suspended credits, the credits lose their character as passive credits. They are reclassified as regular tax credits and made subject to the same limits as other credits (discussed in Chapter 11).

ETHICAL CONSIDERATIONS

An Opportunity to Share with Those Less Fortunate

Henry, a 50-year-old pipe fitter, had been playing the same numbers in the state lottery every week for the past 15 years and finally struck it rich, winning a jackpot of $15 million. Once the news of Henry's good fortune made the newspapers and television, he was inundated with advice on how he should spend his wealth. One such caller, Sally, tried to persuade Henry to buy an interest in a low-income housing venture in the local community that would produce a $50,000 tax credit for him every year for the next 10 years. Henry's uncle, a CPA, pointed out a potential problem with the investment: because Henry would be a passive investor in the venture, he might not be able to benefit from the tax credits unless he also generated passive income. Henry had no idea what his uncle was talking about, but assured his uncle that he did not anticipate generating any passive income in the future.

When Henry relayed his uncle's misgivings concerning the potential investment, Sally responded that "in the grand scheme of things," the tax considerations were irrelevant.

Instead, she claimed that Henry should be more concerned about sharing his newfound wealth with his low-income neighbors who would benefit from finally having decent, affordable housing. Sally insisted that Henry had a responsibility to assist those less fortunate than himself and said that unless he made investments such as this, he could never hope to spend all of his money. How would you advise Henry in his dealings with Sally?

TAXPAYERS SUBJECT TO THE PASSIVE LOSS RULES

4 **LEARNING OBJECTIVE**
Identify taxpayers who are subject to the passive loss limits.

The passive loss rules apply to individuals, estates, trusts, closely held C corporations, and personal service corporations.[7] Passive income or loss from investments in S corporations or partnerships (see Chapters 21 and 22) flows through to the owners, and the passive loss rules are applied at the owner level.

Personal Service Corporations. Application of the passive loss limitations to **personal service corporations** is intended to prevent taxpayers from sheltering personal service income by creating personal service corporations and acquiring passive activities at the corporate level.

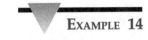
EXAMPLE 14

Five tax accountants, who earn a total of $1 million a year in their individual practices, form a personal service corporation. Shortly after its formation, the corporation invests in a passive activity that produces a $200,000 loss during the year. Because the passive loss rules apply to personal service corporations, the corporation may not deduct the $200,000 loss. ▼

Determination of whether a corporation is a *personal service corporation* is based on rather broad definitions. A personal service corporation is a corporation that meets *both* of the following conditions:

- The principal activity is the performance of personal services.
- Such services are substantially performed by owner-employees.

Generally, personal service corporations include those in the fields of health, law, engineering, architecture, accounting, actuarial science, performing arts, and consulting.[8] A corporation is treated as a personal service corporation if more than 10 percent of the stock (by value) is held by owner-employees.[9] A shareholder is treated as an owner-employee if he or she is an employee or shareholder on *any day* during the testing period.[10] For these purposes, shareholder status and employee status do not even have to occur on the same day.

Closely Held Corporations. Application of the passive loss rules to closely held (non-personal service) corporations is also intended to prevent individuals from incorporating to avoid the passive loss limitations. A corporation is classified as a **closely held corporation** if at any time during the taxable year, more than 50 percent of the value of its outstanding stock is owned, directly or indirectly, by or for not more than five individuals. Closely held corporations (other than personal service corporations) may offset passive losses against *active* income, but not against portfolio income.

---

[7] § 469(a).
[8] § 448(d)(2).

[9] § 469(j)(2).
[10] § 269A(b)(2).

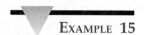

EXAMPLE 15

Silver Corporation, a closely held (non-personal service) C corporation, has $500,000 of passive losses from a rental activity, $400,000 of active income, and $100,000 of portfolio income. The corporation may offset $400,000 of the $500,000 passive loss against the $400,000 of active business income, but may not offset the remainder against the $100,000 of portfolio income. Thus, $100,000 of the passive loss is suspended ($500,000 passive loss − $400,000 offset against active income). ▼

Application of the passive loss limitations to closely held corporations prevents taxpayers from transferring their portfolio investments to such corporations in order to offset passive losses against portfolio income.

PASSIVE ACTIVITIES DEFINED

5 LEARNING OBJECTIVE
Discuss the definition of passive activities.

Section 469 specifies that the following types of activities are to be treated as passive:

- Any trade or business or income-producing activity in which the taxpayer does not materially participate.
- Subject to certain exceptions, all rental activities.

To understand the meaning of the term *passive activity* and the impact of the rules, one must address the following issues, each of which is the subject of statutory or administrative guidance:

- What constitutes an activity?
- What is meant by material participation?
- When is an activity a rental activity?

Even though guidance is available to help the taxpayer deal with these issues, their resolution is anything but simple.

6 LEARNING OBJECTIVE
Apply the rules for identifying an activity.

Identification of an Activity. Identifying what constitutes an activity is a necessary first step in applying the passive loss limitations. Taxpayers who are involved in complex business operations need to be able to determine whether a given segment of their overall business operations constitutes a separate activity or is to be treated as part of a single activity. Proper treatment is necessary in order to determine whether income or loss from an activity is active or passive.

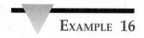

EXAMPLE 16

Ben owns a business with two separate departments. Department A generates net income of $120,000, and Department B generates a net loss of $95,000. Ben participates for 700 hours in the operations of Department A and for 100 hours in Department B. If Ben is allowed to treat both departments as a single activity, he can offset the $95,000 loss from Department B against the $120,000 income from Department A. ▼

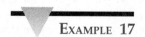

EXAMPLE 17

Assume the same facts as in the previous example. If Ben is required to treat each department as a separate activity, because he is a material participant in Department A (having devoted 700 hours to it) the $120,000 profit is active income. However, he is not considered a material participant in Department B (100 hours), and the $95,000 loss is a passive loss. Ben cannot offset the $95,000 passive loss from Department B against the $120,000 of active income from Department A. (A complete discussion of the material participation rules follows.) ▼

Recall that on the disposition of a passive activity, a taxpayer is allowed to offset suspended losses from the activity against other types of income. Therefore, identifying what constitutes an activity is of crucial importance for this purpose too.

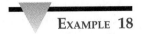

EXAMPLE 18

Linda owns a business with two departments. Department A had a net loss of $125,000 in the current year, and Department B had a $70,000 net loss. She disposes of Department B during the year. Assuming Linda is allowed to treat the two departments as separate passive activities, she can offset the passive loss from Department B against other types of income in the following order: gain from disposition of the passive activity, other passive income, and nonpassive income. This treatment leaves her with a suspended loss of $125,000 from Department A. If Departments A and B are treated as components of the same activity, however, on the disposal of Department B, its $70,000 net loss would be suspended along with the other $125,000 of suspended losses of the activity. ▼

The current rules used to delineate what constitutes an activity for purposes of the passive loss limitations are provided in Regulations.[11] These guidelines state that, in general, a taxpayer can treat one or more trade or business activities or rental activities as a single activity if those activities form an *appropriate economic unit* for measuring gain or loss. To determine what ventures form an appropriate economic unit, all of the relevant facts and circumstances must be considered. Taxpayers may use any reasonable method in applying the facts and circumstances. However, the following five factors are given the greatest weight in determining whether activities constitute an appropriate economic unit. It is not necessary to meet all of these conditions in order to treat multiple activities as a single activity.

- Similarities and differences in types of business conducted in the various trade or business or rental activities.
- The extent of common control over the various activities.
- The extent of common ownership of the activities.
- The geographical location of the different units.
- Interdependencies among the activities.

The following examples, adapted from the Regulations, illustrate the application of the general rules for grouping activities.[12]

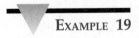

EXAMPLE 19

George owns a men's clothing store and a video game parlor in Chicago. He also owns a men's clothing store and a video game parlor in Milwaukee. Reasonable methods of applying the facts and circumstances test may result in any of the following groupings:

- All four activities may be grouped into a single activity.
- The clothing stores may be grouped into an activity, and the video parlors may be grouped into a separate activity.
- The Chicago activities may be grouped into an activity, and the Milwaukee activities may be grouped into a separate activity.
- Each of the four activities may be treated as a separate activity. ▼

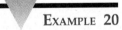

EXAMPLE 20

Sharon is a partner in a business that sells snack items to drugstores. She also is a partner in a partnership that owns and operates a warehouse. Both partnerships, which are under common control, are located in the same industrial park. The predominant part of the warehouse business is warehousing items for the snack business, and it is the only warehousing business in which Sharon is involved. Sharon should treat the snack business and the warehousing business as a single activity. ▼

Regrouping of Activities. Taxpayers should carefully consider all tax factors in deciding how to group their activities. Once activities have been grouped, they

---

[11] Reg. § 1.469–4.   [12] Reg. § 1.469–4(c)(3).

cannot be regrouped unless the original grouping was clearly inappropriate or there has been a material change in the facts and circumstances. If a regrouping is necessary for either of these reasons, the taxpayer is required to disclose to the IRS all information relevant to the regrouping.

The Regulations also grant the IRS the right to regroup activities when both of the following conditions exist.[13]

- The taxpayer's grouping fails to reflect one or more appropriate economic units.
- One of the primary purposes of the taxpayer's grouping is to avoid the passive loss limitations.

The following example, adapted from the Regulations, illustrates a situation where the IRS would exercise its prerogative to regroup a taxpayer's activities.

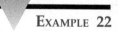

EXAMPLE 21

Baker, Edwards, Andrews, Clark, and Henson are physicians who operate their own separate practices. Each of the physicians owns interests in activities that generate passive losses, so they devise a plan to set up an entity that will generate passive income. They form the BEACH Partnership to acquire and operate X-ray equipment, and each receives a limited partnership interest. They select an unrelated person to operate the X-ray business as a general partner, and none of the limited partners participates in the activity. Substantially all of the services provided by BEACH are provided to the physicians who own limited partnership interests, and fees are set at a level that assures a profit for BEACH. Each physician treats his medical practice and his interest in the partnership as separate activities and offsets losses from passive investments against the passive income from the partnership. The IRS would interpret the physicians' separate groupings as attempts to avoid the passive loss limitations and would regroup each medical practice and the services performed by the partnership as an appropriate economic unit. ▼

Special Grouping Rules for Rental Activities. Two rules deal specifically with the grouping of rental activities. These provisions are designed to prevent taxpayers from grouping rental activities, which are generally passive, with other businesses in a way that would result in a tax advantage.

First, a rental activity may be grouped with a trade or business activity only if one activity is insubstantial in relation to the other. That is, the rental activity must be insubstantial in relation to the trade or business activity, or the trade or business activity must be insubstantial in relation to the rental activity. The Regulations provide no clear guidelines as to the meaning of insubstantial.[14]

EXAMPLE 22

Schemers, a firm of CPAs, owns a building in downtown Washington, D.C., in which they conduct their practice of public accounting. The firm also rents space on the street level of the building to several retail establishments. Of the total revenue generated by the firm, 95% is associated with the practice of public accounting, and 5% is related to the rental operation. It is likely that the rental activity would be considered insubstantial relative to the accounting practice and the two ventures could be grouped as one nonrental activity. This grouping could be advantageous to the firm, particularly if the rental operation generated a loss! ▼

Second, taxpayers generally may not treat an activity involving the rental of real property and an activity involving the rental of personal property as a single activity.

[13] Reg. § 1.469–4(f).   [14] Reg. § 1.469–4(d).

7 LEARNING OBJECTIVE
Analyze and apply the tests for material participation.

Material Participation. If an individual taxpayer materially participates in a nonrental trade or business activity, any loss from that activity is treated as an active loss that can be offset against active income. If a taxpayer does not materially participate, however, the loss is treated as a passive loss, which can only be offset against passive income. Therefore, controlling whether a particular activity is treated as active or passive is an important part of the tax strategy of a taxpayer who owns an interest in one or more businesses. Consider the following examples.

EXAMPLE 23

Dewayne, a corporate executive, earns a salary of $200,000 per year. In addition, he owns a separate business in which he participates. The business produces a loss of $100,000 during the year. If Dewayne materially participates in the business, the $100,000 loss is an active loss that may be offset against his active income from his corporate employer. If he does not materially participate, the loss is passive and is suspended. Dewayne may use the suspended loss in the future only when he has passive income or disposes of the activity. ▼

EXAMPLE 24

Kay, an attorney, earns $250,000 a year in her law practice. She owns interests in two activities, A and B, in which she participates. Activity A, in which she does *not* materially participate, produces a loss of $50,000. Kay has not yet met the material participation standard for Activity B, which produces income of $80,000. However, she can meet the material participation standard if she spends an additional 50 hours in Activity B during the year. Should Kay attempt to meet the material participation standard for Activity B? If she continues working in Activity B and becomes a material participant, the $80,000 income from the activity is *active,* and the $50,000 passive loss from Activity A must be suspended. A more favorable tax strategy is for Kay to *not meet* the material participation standard for Activity B, thus making the income from that activity passive. This enables her to offset the $50,000 passive loss from Activity A against the passive income from Activity B. ▼

It is possible to devise numerous scenarios in which the taxpayer could control the tax outcome by increasing or decreasing his or her participation in different activities. Examples 23 and 24 demonstrate some of the possibilities. The conclusion reached in most analyses of this type is that taxpayers will benefit by having profitable activities classified as passive, so that any passive losses can be used to offset passive income. If the activity produces a loss, however, the taxpayer will benefit if it is classified as active so the loss is not subject to the passive loss limitations.

As discussed above, a nonrental trade or business in which a taxpayer owns an interest must be treated as a passive activity unless the taxpayer materially participates. The Staff of the Joint Committee on Taxation explained the importance of the material participation standard as follows:

> Congress believed that there were several reasons why it was appropriate to examine the materiality of a taxpayer's participation in an activity in determining the extent to which such taxpayer should be permitted to use tax benefits from the activity. A taxpayer who materially participated in an activity was viewed as more likely than a passive investor to approach the activity with a significant nontax economic profit motive, and to form a sound judgment as to whether the activity had genuine economic significance and value. A material participation standard identified an important distinction between different types of taxpayer activities. It was thought that, in general, the more passive investor seeks a return on capital invested, including returns in the form of reductions in the taxes owed on unrelated income, rather than an ongoing source of livelihood. A material participation standard reduced the importance, for such investors, of the tax-reduction features of an investment, and thus increased the importance of the economic features in an investor's decision about where to invest his funds.[15]

Even if the concept or the implication of being a material participant is clear, the precise meaning of the term **material participation** can be vague. As enacted, § 469 required a taxpayer to participate on a *regular, continuous, and substantial* basis in order to be a material participant. In many situations, however, it was difficult or impossible to gain any assurance that this nebulous standard was met.

In response to this dilemma, Temporary Regulations[16] providing seven tests were issued to help taxpayers cope with these issues. Material participation is achieved by meeting any one of the tests. These tests can be divided into three categories:

- Tests based on current participation.
- Tests based on prior participation.
- Test based on facts and circumstances.

[15] *General Explanation of the Tax Reform Act of 1986 ("Blue Book"),* prepared by The Staff of the Joint Committee on Taxation, May 4, 1987, H.R. 3838, 99th Cong., p. 212.

[16] Temp. and Prop.Reg. § 1.469–5T(a). The Temporary Regulations are also Proposed Regulations. Temporary Regulations have the same effect as final Regulations. Refer to Chapter 2 for a discussion of the different categories of Regulations.

Tests Based on Current Participation.   The first four tests are quantitative tests that require measurement, in hours, of the taxpayer's participation in the activity during the year.

1.   *Does the individual participate in the activity for more than 500 hours during the year?*

   The purpose of the 500-hour requirement is to restrict deductions from the types of trade or business activities Congress intended to treat as passive activities. The 500-hour standard for material participation was adopted for the following reasons:[17]

   • Few investors in traditional tax shelters devote more than 500 hours a year to such an investment.
   • The IRS believes that income from an activity in which the taxpayer participates for more than 500 hours a year should not be treated as passive.

2.   *Does the individual's participation in the activity for the taxable year constitute substantially all of the participation in the activity of all individuals (including nonowner employees) for the year?*

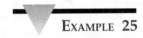
EXAMPLE 25

Ned, a physician, operates a separate business in which he participates for 80 hours during the year. He is the only participant and has no employees in the separate business. Ned meets the material participation standard of Test 2. If he had employees, it would be difficult to apply Test 2, because the Temporary Regulations do not define the term *substantially all.* ▼

3.   *Does the individual participate in the activity for more than 100 hours during the year, and is the individual's participation in the activity for the year not less than the participation of any other individual (including nonowner employees) for the year?*

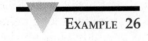
EXAMPLE 26

Adam, a college professor, owns a separate business in which he participates 110 hours during the year. He has an employee who works 90 hours during the year. Adam meets the material participation standard under Test 3, but probably does not meet it under Test 2 because his participation is only 55% of the total participation. It is unlikely that 55% would meet the *substantially all* requirement of Test 2. ▼

   Tests 2 and 3 are included because the IRS recognizes that the operation of some activities does not require more than 500 hours of participation during the year.

4.   *Is the activity a significant participation activity for the taxable year, and does the individual's aggregate participation in all significant participation activities during the year exceed 500 hours?*

   A **significant participation activity** is a trade or business in which the individual's participation exceeds 100 hours during the year. This test treats taxpayers whose aggregate participation in several significant participation activities exceeds 500 hours as material participants. Test 4 thus accords the same treatment to an individual who devotes an aggregate of more than 500 hours to several significant participation activities as to an individual who devotes more than 500 hours to a single activity.

---

[17] T.D. 8175, 1988–1 C.B. 191.

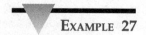

EXAMPLE 27

Mike owns five different businesses. He participated in each activity during the year as follows:

Activity	Hours of Participation
A	110
B	140
C	120
D	150
E	100

Activities A, B, C, and D are significant participation activities, and Mike's aggregate participation in those activities is 520 hours. Therefore, Activities A, B, C, and D are not treated as passive activities. Activity E is not a significant participation activity (not more than 100 hours), so it is not included in applying the 500-hour test. Activity E is treated as a passive activity, unless Mike meets one of the other material participation tests for that activity. ▼

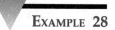

EXAMPLE 28

Assume the same facts as in the previous example, except that Activity A does not exist. All of the activities are now treated as passive. Activity E is not counted in applying the more-than-500-hour test, so Mike's aggregate participation in significant participation activities is 410 hours (140 in Activity B + 120 in Activity C + 150 in Activity D). He could meet the significant participation test for Activity E by participating for one more hour in the activity. This would cause Activities B, C, D, and E to be treated as nonpassive activities. However, before deciding whether to participate for at least one more hour in Activity E, Mike should assess how the participation would affect his overall tax liability. ▼

Tests Based on Prior Participation.   Tests 5 and 6 are based on material participation in prior years. Under these tests, a taxpayer who is no longer a participant in an activity can continue to be *classified* as a material participant. The IRS takes the position that material participation in a trade or business for a long period of time is likely to indicate that the activity represents the individual's principal livelihood, rather than a passive investment. Consequently, withdrawal from the activity, or reduction of participation to the point where it is not material, does not change the classification of the activity from active to passive.

5.   *Did the individual materially participate in the activity for any 5 taxable years (whether consecutive or not) during the 10 taxable years that immediately precede the taxable year?*

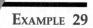

EXAMPLE 29

Dawn, who owns a 50% interest in a restaurant, was a material participant in the operations of the restaurant from 1990 through 1994. She retired at the end of 1994 and is no longer involved in the restaurant except as an investor. Dawn will be treated as a material participant in the restaurant in 1995. Even if she does not become involved in the restaurant as a material participant again, she will continue to be treated as a material participant in 1996, 1997, 1998, and 1999. In 2000 and later years, Dawn's share of income or loss from the restaurant will be classified as passive unless she materially participates in those years. ▼

6.   *Is the activity a personal service activity, and did the individual materially participate in the activity for any three preceding taxable years (whether consecutive or not)?*

As indicated above, the material participation standards differ for personal service activities and other businesses. An individual who was a material participant in a personal service activity for *any three years* prior to the taxable year continues to be treated as a material participant after withdrawal from the activity.

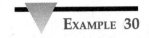

EXAMPLE 30   Evan, a CPA, retires from the EFG Partnership after working full-time in the partnership for 30 years. As a retired partner, he will continue to receive a share of the profits of the firm for the next 10 years, even though he will not participate in the firm's operations. Evan also owns an interest in a passive activity that produces a loss for the year. He continues to be treated as a material participant in the EFG Partnership, and his income from the partnership is active income. Therefore, he is not allowed to offset the loss from his passive investment against the income from the EFG Partnership. ▼

Facts and Circumstances Test. Test 7 is a facts and circumstances test to determine whether the taxpayer has materially participated.

7. *Based on all the facts and circumstances, did the individual participate in the activity on a regular, continuous, and substantial basis during the year?*

The Temporary Regulations do not define what constitutes regular, continuous, and substantial participation except to say that the taxpayer's activities will *not* be considered material participation under Test 7 in the following three circumstances:[18]

- The taxpayer satisfies the participation standards (whether or not a *material participant*) of any Code section other than § 469.
- The taxpayer manages the activity, unless
  - no other person receives compensation for management services, and
  - no individual spends more hours during the tax year managing the activity than does the taxpayer.
- The taxpayer participates in the activity for 100 hours or less during the tax year.

A part of the Temporary Regulations has been reserved for further development of this test. Presumably, additional guidelines will be issued in the future. For the time being, taxpayers should rely on Tests 1 through 6 in determining whether the material participation standards have been met.

Participation Defined.   Participation generally includes any work done by an individual in an activity that he or she owns. Participation does not include work if it is of a type not customarily done by owners *and* if one of its principal purposes is to avoid the disallowance of passive losses or credits. Also, work done in an individual's capacity as an investor (e.g., reviewing financial reports in a non-managerial capacity) is not counted in applying the material participation tests. However, participation by an owner's spouse counts as participation by the owner.[19]

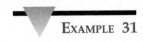

EXAMPLE 31   Tom, who is a partner in a CPA firm, owns a computer store that has operated at a loss during the year. In order to offset this loss against the income from his CPA practice, Tom would like to avoid having the computer business classified as a passive activity. Through December 15, he has worked 400 hours in the business in management and selling activities. During the last two weeks of December, he works 80 hours in management and

---

[18] Temp. and Prop.Reg. § 1.469–5T(b)(2).   [19] Temp. and Prop.Reg. § 1.469–5T(f)(3).

selling activities and 30 hours doing janitorial chores. Also during the last two weeks in December, Tom's wife participates 40 hours as a salesperson. She has worked as a salesperson in the computer store in prior years, but has not done so during the current year. If any of Tom's work is of a type not customarily done by owners *and* if one of its principal purposes is to avoid the disallowance of passive losses or credits, it is not counted in applying the material participation tests. It is likely that Tom's 480 hours of participation in management and selling activities will count as participation, but the 30 hours spent doing janitorial chores will not. However, the 40 hours of participation by his wife will count, and Tom will qualify as a material participant under the more-than-500-hour rule (480 + 40 = 520). ▼

Limited Partners.   A *limited* partner is one whose liability to third-party creditors of the partnership is limited to the amount the partner has invested in the partnership. Such a partnership must have at least one *general* partner, who is fully liable in an individual capacity for the debts of the partnership to third parties. Generally, a *limited partner* is not considered a material participant unless he or she qualifies under Test 1, 5, or 6 in the above list. However, a *general partner* may qualify as a material participant by meeting any of the seven tests. If an unlimited, or general, partner also owns a limited interest in the same limited partnership, all interests are treated as a general interest.[20]

8 ▼ **LEARNING OBJECTIVE**
Understand the nature of rental activities under the passive loss rules.

Rental Activities Defined.   As discussed previously, § 469 specifies that, subject to certain exceptions, all rental activities are to be treated as passive activities.[21] A **rental activity** is defined as any activity where payments are received principally for the use of tangible (real or personal) property.[22] Importantly, an activity that is classified as a rental activity is subject to the passive activity loss rules, even if the taxpayer involved is a material participant.

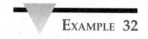

EXAMPLE 32

Sarah owns an apartment building and spends an average of 60 hours a week in its operation. Assuming that the apartment building operation is classed as a rental activity, it is automatically subject to the passive activity rules, even though Sarah spends more than 500 hours a year in its operation. ▼

As suggested, Temporary Regulations provide that in certain circumstances activities involving rentals of real and personal property are *not* to be *treated* as rental activities.[23]

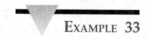

EXAMPLE 33

Dan owns a videotape business. Because the average period of customer use is seven days or less, Dan's videotape business is not treated as a rental activity. ▼

The fact that Dan's videotape business in the previous example is not treated as a rental activity does not necessarily mean that it is classified as a nonpassive activity. Instead, the videotape business is treated as a trade or business activity subject to the material participation standards. If Dan is a material participant, the business is treated as active. If he is not a material participant, it is treated as a passive activity.

Therefore, activities covered by any of the following six exceptions provided by the Temporary Regulations are not *automatically* treated as passive activities

---

[20] Temp. and Prop.Reg. § 1.469–5T(e)(3)(ii).
[21] § 469(c)(2).

[22] § 469(j)(8).
[23] Temp. and Prop.Reg. § 1.469–1T(e)(3)(ii).

because they would not be classified as rental activities. Instead, the activities are subject to the material participation tests.

1. *The average period of customer use for the property is seven days or less.*

Under this exception, activities involving the short-term use of tangible property such as automobiles, videocassettes, tuxedos, tools, and other such property are not treated as rental activities. The provision also applies to short-term rentals of hotel or motel rooms.

This exception is based on the presumption that a person who rents property for seven days or less is generally required to provide *significant services* to the customer. Providing such services supports a conclusion that the person is engaged in a service business rather than a rental business.

2. *The average period of customer use for the property is 30 days or less, and the owner of the property provides significant personal services.*

For longer-term rentals, the presumption that significant services are provided is not automatic, as it is in the case of the seven-day exception. Instead, the taxpayer must be able to *prove* that significant personal services are rendered in connection with the activity. Therefore, an understanding of what constitutes significant personal services is necessary in order to apply the rule.

Significant personal services include only services provided by *individuals*. This provision excludes such items as telephone and cable television services. Four additional categories of *excluded services* are not considered significant personal services:[24]

- Services necessary to permit the lawful use of the property.
- Services performed in connection with the construction of improvements to the property.
- Services performed in connection with the performance of repairs that extend the property's useful life for a period substantially longer than the average period for which the property is used by customers.
- Services similar to those commonly provided in connection with long-term rentals of high-grade commercial or residential real property (including cleaning and maintenance of common areas, routine repairs, trash collection, elevator service, and security at entrances or perimeters).

3. *The owner of the property provides extraordinary personal services. The average period of customer use is of no consequence in applying this test.*

Extraordinary personal services are services provided by individuals where the customers' use of the property is incidental to their receipt of the services. For example, a patient's use of a hospital bed is incidental to his or her use of medical services. Another example is the use of a boarding school's dormitory, which is incidental to the scholastic services received.

4. *The rental of the property is treated as incidental to a nonrental activity of the taxpayer.*

Rentals of real property incidental to a nonrental activity are not considered a passive activity. The Temporary Regulations provide that the following rentals are not passive activities.[25]

- *Property held primarily for investment.* This occurs where the principal purpose for holding the property is the expectation of gain from the

---

[24]Temp. and Prop.Reg. § 1.469–1T(e)(3)(iv).

[25]Temp. and Prop.Regs. §§ 1.469–1T(e)(3)(vi)(B) through (E).

appreciation of the property and the gross rent income is less than 2 percent of the lesser of (1) the unadjusted basis or (2) the fair market value of the property.

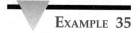

EXAMPLE 34
Ramon invests in vacant land for the purpose of realizing a profit on its appreciation. He leases the land during the period it is held. The unadjusted basis is $250,000, and the fair market value is $350,000. The lease payments are $4,000 per year. Because gross rent income is less than 2% of $250,000, the activity is not a rental activity. ▼

- *Property used in a trade or business.* This occurs where the property is owned by a taxpayer who is an owner of the trade or business using the rental property. The property must also have been used in the trade or business during the year or during at least two of the five preceding taxable years. The 2 percent test above also applies in this situation.

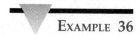

EXAMPLE 35
A farmer owns land with an unadjusted basis of $250,000 and a fair market value of $350,000. He used it for farming purposes in 1994 and 1995. In 1996, he leased the land to another farmer for $4,000. The activity is not a rental activity. ▼

- *Property held for sale to customers.* If property is held for sale to customers and rented during the year, the rental of the property is not a rental activity. If, for instance, an automobile dealer rents automobiles held for sale to customers to persons who are having their own cars repaired, the activity is not a rental activity.

- *Lodging rented for the convenience of an employer.* If an employer provides lodging for an employee incidental to the employee's performance of services in the employer's trade or business, no rental activity exists.

- A partner who rents property to a partnership that is used in the partnership's trade or business does not have a rental activity.

These rules were written to prevent taxpayers from converting active or portfolio income into a passive activity for the purpose of offsetting other passive losses.

5. *The taxpayer customarily makes the property available during defined business hours for nonexclusive use by various customers.*

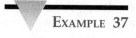

EXAMPLE 36
Pat is the owner-operator of a public golf course. Some customers pay daily greens fees each time they use the course, while others purchase weekly, monthly, or annual passes. The golf course is open every day from sunrise to sunset, except on certain holidays and on days when the course is closed due to inclement weather conditions. Pat is not engaged in a rental activity, regardless of the average period customers use the course. ▼

6. *The property is provided for use in an activity conducted by a partnership, S corporation, or joint venture in which the taxpayer owns an interest.*

EXAMPLE 37
Joe, a partner in the Skyview Partnership, contributes the use of a building to the partnership. The partnership has net income of $30,000 during the year, of which Joe's share is $10,000. Unless the partnership is engaged in a rental activity, none of Joe's income from the partnership is income from a rental activity. ▼

INTERACTION OF THE AT-RISK AND PASSIVE ACTIVITY LIMITS

9 ▼ LEARNING OBJECTIVE
Recognize the relationship between the at-risk and passive activity limitations.

The determination of whether a loss is suspended under the passive loss rules is made after application of the at-risk rules, as well as other provisions relating to the measurement of taxable income. A loss that is not allowed for the year because the taxpayer is not at risk with respect to it is suspended under the at-risk provision and not under the passive loss rules. Further, a taxpayer's basis is reduced by deductions (e.g., depreciation) even if the deductions are not currently usable because of the passive loss rules.

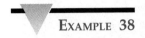

EXAMPLE 38

Jack's adjusted basis in a passive activity is $10,000 at the beginning of 1995. His loss from the activity in 1995 is $4,000. Since Jack had no passive activity income, the $4,000 cannot be deducted. At year-end, Jack has an adjusted basis and an at-risk amount of $6,000 in the activity and a suspended passive loss of $4,000. ▼

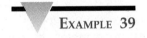

EXAMPLE 39

Jack in Example 38 had a loss of $9,000 in the activity in 1996. Since the $9,000 exceeds his at-risk amount ($6,000) by $3,000, that $3,000 loss is disallowed by the at-risk rules. If Jack has no passive activity income, the remaining $6,000 is suspended under the passive activity rules. At year-end, he has a $3,000 loss suspended under the at-risk rules, $10,000 of suspended passive losses, and an adjusted basis and an at-risk amount in the activity of zero. ▼

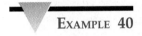

EXAMPLE 40

Jack in Example 39 realized a $1,000 gain in 1997. Because the $1,000 increases his at-risk amount, $1,000 of the $3,000 unused loss can be reclassified as a passive loss. If he has no other passive income, the $1,000 income is offset by $1,000 of suspended passive losses. At the end of 1997, Jack has no taxable passive income, $2,000 ($3,000 − $1,000) of unused losses under the at-risk rules, $10,000 of (reclassified) suspended passive losses ($10,000 + $1,000 of reclassified unused at-risk losses − $1,000 of passive losses offset against passive gains), and an adjusted basis and an at-risk amount in the activity of zero. ▼

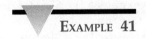

EXAMPLE 41

In 1998, Jack had no gain or loss from the activity in Example 40. He contributed $5,000 more to the passive activity. Because the $5,000 increases his at-risk amount, the $2,000 of losses suspended under the at-risk rules is reclassified as a passive loss. Jack gets no passive loss deduction in 1998. At year-end, he has no suspended losses under the at-risk rules, $12,000 of suspended passive losses ($10,000 + $2,000 of reclassified suspended at-risk losses), and an adjusted basis and an at-risk amount of $3,000 ($5,000 additional investment − $2,000 of reclassified losses). ▼

SPECIAL PASSIVE ACTIVITY RULES FOR REAL ESTATE ACTIVITIES

10 ▼ LEARNING OBJECTIVE
Discuss the special treatment available to real estate activities.

The passive loss limits contain two exceptions related to real estate activities. These exceptions allow all or part of real estate rental losses to be offset against active or portfolio income, even though the activity is a passive activity.

Material Participation in a Real Property Trade or Business. After 1993, losses from real estate rental activities are *not* treated as passive losses for certain real estate professionals.[26] To qualify for nonpassive treatment, a taxpayer must satisfy both of the following requirements:

---

[26] § 469(c)(7).

- More than half of the personal services that the taxpayer performs in trades or businesses are performed in real property trades or businesses in which the taxpayer materially participates.
- The taxpayer performs more than 750 hours of services in these real property trades or businesses as a material participant.

Taxpayers who do not satisfy the above requirements must continue to treat losses from real estate rental activities as passive losses.

EXAMPLE 42

During the current year, Della performed personal service activities as follows: 900 hours as a personal financial planner, 550 hours in a real estate development and leasing business, and 600 hours in real estate rental activities. Any loss Della incurred in either real estate activity will *not* be subject to the passive loss rules, since more than 50% of her personal services were devoted to real property trades or businesses, and her material participation in those real estate activities exceeded 750 hours. Thus, any loss from the real estate rental activity could offset active and portfolio sources of income. ▼

On a joint return, the requirements for nonpassive treatment of losses must be met by one spouse or the other. That is, the spouses cannot combine their services in order to meet the requirements. Services performed by an employee are not treated as being related to a real estate trade or business unless the employee performing the services has at least a 5 percent ownership interest in the employer. Additionally, a closely held regular corporation may also qualify for the passive loss relief if more than 50 percent of its gross receipts for the year are derived from real property trades or businesses in which it materially participates.

Rental Real Estate Activities.   The second exception is more significant in that it is not restricted to real estate professionals. This exception allows individuals to deduct up to $25,000 of losses on real estate rental activities against active and portfolio income.[27] The potential annual $25,000 deduction is reduced by 50 percent of the taxpayer's AGI in excess of $100,000. Thus, the entire deduction is phased out at $150,000. If married individuals file separately, the $25,000 deduction is reduced to zero unless they lived apart for the entire year. If they lived apart for the entire year, the loss amount is $12,500 each, and the phase-out begins at $50,000. AGI for purposes of the phase-out is calculated without regard to IRA deductions, Social Security benefits, and net losses from passive activities.

To qualify for the $25,000 exception, a taxpayer must meet the following requirements.[28]

- Actively participate in the real estate rental activity.
- Own 10 percent or more (in value) of all interests in the activity during the entire taxable year (or shorter period during which the taxpayer held an interest in the activity).

The difference between *active participation* and *material participation* is that the former can be satisfied without regular, continuous, and substantial involvement in operations as long as the taxpayer participates in making management decisions in a significant and bona fide sense. In this context, relevant management

---

[27] § 469(i).

[28] § 469(i)(6).

decisions include such decisions as approving new tenants, deciding on rental terms, and approving capital or repair expenditures.

The $25,000 allowance is available after all active participation rental losses and gains are netted and applied to other passive income. If a taxpayer has a real estate rental loss in excess of the amount that can be deducted under the real estate rental exception, that excess is treated as a passive loss.

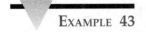

EXAMPLE 43

Brad, who has $90,000 of AGI before considering rental activities, has $85,000 of losses from a real estate rental activity in which he actively participates. He also actively participates in another real estate rental activity from which he has $25,000 of income. He has other passive income of $36,000. The net rental loss of $60,000 is offset by the $36,000 of passive income, leaving $24,000 that can be deducted against other income. ▼

The $25,000 offset allowance is an aggregate of both deductions and credits in deduction equivalents. The deduction equivalent of a passive activity credit is the amount of deductions that reduces the tax liability for the taxable year by an amount equal to the credit.[29] A taxpayer with $5,000 of credits and a tax bracket of 28 percent would have a deduction equivalent of $17,857 ($5,000 ÷ 28%).

If the total deduction and deduction equivalent exceed $25,000, the taxpayer must allocate on a pro rata basis, first among the losses (including real estate rental activity losses suspended in prior years) and then to credits in the following order: (1) credits other than rehabilitation credits, (2) rehabilitation credits, and (3) low-income housing credits.

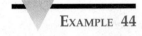

EXAMPLE 44

Kevin is an active participant in a real estate rental activity that produces $8,000 of income, $26,000 of deductions, and $1,500 of credits. Kevin, who is in the 28% tax bracket, may deduct the net passive loss of $18,000 ($8,000 − $26,000). After deducting the loss, he has an available deduction equivalent of $7,000 ($25,000 − $18,000 passive loss). Therefore, the maximum amount of credits that he may claim is $1,960 ($7,000 × 28%). Since the actual credits are less than this amount, Kevin may claim the entire $1,500 credit. ▼

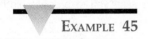

EXAMPLE 45

Kelly, who is in the 28% tax bracket, is an active participant in three separate real estate rental activities. The relevant tax results for each activity are as follows:

- Activity A: $20,000 of losses.
- Activity B: $10,000 of losses.
- Activity C: $4,200 of credits.

Kelly's deduction equivalent from the credits is $15,000 ($4,200 ÷ 28%). Therefore, the total passive deductions and deduction equivalents are $45,000 ($20,000 + $10,000 + $15,000), which exceeds the maximum allowable amount of $25,000. Consequently, Kelly must allocate pro rata first from among losses and then from among credits. Deductions from losses are limited as follows:

- Activity A {$25,000 × [$20,000 ÷ ($20,000 + $10,000)]} = $16,667.
- Activity B {$25,000 × [$10,000 ÷ ($20,000 + $10,000)]} = $8,333.

Since the amount of passive deductions exceeds the $25,000 maximum, the deduction balance of $5,000 and passive credit of $4,200 must be carried forward. Kelly's suspended losses and credits by activity are as follows:

---

[29] § 469(j)(5).

	Total	Activity		
		A	B	C
Allocated losses	$30,000	$ 20,000	$10,000	$ –0–
Allocated credits	4,200	–0–	–0–	4,200
Utilized losses	(25,000)	(16,667)	(8,333)	–0–
Suspended losses	5,000	3,333	1,667	–0–
Suspended credits	4,200	–0–	–0–	4,200

ETHICAL
CONSIDERATIONS

Applying the Rules on Rental Real Estate

Ted, a management consultant, owns an apartment complex that produces a profit of $60,000 in the current year. He earned $120,000 in his consulting business and had a $40,000 loss on a passive activity (not real estate). Ted worked for 800 hours at the apartment complex during the year, but characterizes the $60,000 profit as passive income so he can utilize the $40,000 passive loss. He claims that he is doing nothing wrong because the law is designed only to protect the passive loss deduction of real estate professionals and is not applicable to profits.

Further, Ted thinks that he is justified in classifying the loss as passive because of the nature of the work he performed during the time devoted to managing the apartments. Ted feels certain that of the 800 hours, between 300 and 400 hours were spent coaching and supporting about 20 underprivileged children living in the apartment complex as part of a year-round sports program. Ted says that his involvement not only benefits the children, but will make the apartment a more desirable place to live and thus could also benefit him economically in the long run. He sees the hours devoted to the sports program as an integral part of his job in managing the apartment complex, but feels that they should not count in determining whether the activity is passive. Ted asks you to prepare his return. What actions will you take?

DISPOSITIONS OF PASSIVE INTERESTS

11 LEARNING OBJECTIVE
Determine the proper tax treatment upon the disposition of a passive activity.

Recall from an earlier discussion that if a taxpayer disposes of an entire interest in a passive activity, any suspended losses (and in certain cases, suspended credits) may be utilized when calculating the final economic gain or loss on the investment. In addition, if a loss ultimately results, that loss can be offset against other types of income. However, the consequences may differ if the activity is disposed of in a transaction that is other than a fully taxable transaction. The following discusses the treatment of suspended passive losses in other types of dispositions.

Disposition of a Passive Activity at Death.   A transfer of a taxpayer's interest in an activity by reason of the taxpayer's death results in suspended losses being allowed (to the decedent) to the extent they exceed the amount, if any, of the step-up in basis allowed.[30] Suspended losses are lost to the extent of the amount of

---

[30] § 469(g)(2).

the basis increase. The losses allowed generally are reported on the final return of the deceased taxpayer.

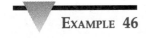

EXAMPLE 46

A taxpayer dies with passive activity property having an adjusted basis of $40,000, suspended losses of $10,000, and a fair market value at the date of the decedent's death of $75,000. The increase (i.e., step-up) in basis (see Chapter 12) is $35,000 (fair market value at date of death in excess of adjusted basis). None of the $10,000 suspended loss is deductible by either the decedent or the beneficiary. The suspended losses ($10,000) are lost because they did not exceed the step-up in basis ($35,000). ▼

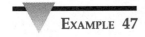

EXAMPLE 47

A taxpayer dies with passive activity property having an adjusted basis of $40,000, suspended losses of $10,000, and a fair market value at the date of the decedent's death of $47,000. Since the step-up in basis would be only $7,000 ($47,000 − $40,000), the suspended losses allowed are limited to $3,000 ($10,000 suspended loss at time of death − $7,000 increase in basis). The $3,000 loss available to the decedent is reported on the decedent's final income tax return. ▼

Disposition of a Passive Activity by Gift. In a disposition of a taxpayer's interest in a passive activity by gift, the suspended losses are added to the basis of the property.[31]

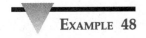

EXAMPLE 48

A taxpayer makes a gift of passive activity property having an adjusted basis of $40,000, suspended losses of $10,000, and a fair market value at the date of the gift of $100,000. The taxpayer cannot deduct the suspended losses in the year of the disposition. However, the suspended losses transfer with the property and are added to the adjusted basis of the property. ▼

Installment Sale of a Passive Activity. An installment sale of a taxpayer's entire interest in a passive activity triggers the recognition of the suspended losses.[32] The losses are allowed in each year of the installment obligation in the ratio that the gain recognized in each year bears to the total gain on the sale.

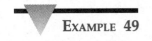

EXAMPLE 49

Stan sold his entire interest in a passive activity for $100,000. His adjusted basis in the property was $60,000. If he uses the installment method, his gross profit ratio is 40% ($40,000/$100,000). If Stan received a $20,000 down payment, he would recognize a gain of $8,000 (40% of $20,000). If the activity had a suspended loss of $25,000, Stan would deduct $5,000 [($8,000 ÷ $40,000) × $25,000] of the suspended loss in the first year. ▼

Passive Activity Changes to Active. If a formerly passive activity becomes an active one, suspended losses are allowed to the extent of income from the now active business.[33] If any of the suspended loss remains, it continues to be treated as a loss from a passive activity. The excess suspended loss can be deducted from passive income or carried over to the next tax year and deducted to the extent of income from the now active business in the succeeding year(s). The activity must continue to be the same activity.

Nontaxable Exchange of a Passive Activity. In a nontaxable exchange of a passive investment, the taxpayer keeps the suspended losses, which generally

---

[31] § 469(j)(6).
[32] § 469(g)(3).

[33] § 469(f).

CONCEPT SUMMARY 10-2

Passive Activity Loss Rules: General Concepts

What is the fundamental passive activity rule?	Passive activity losses may be deducted only against passive activity gains. Losses not allowed are suspended and used in future years.
Who is subject to the passive activity rules?	Individuals. Estates. Trusts. Personal service corporations. Closely held C corporations.
What is a passive activity?	Trade or business or income-producing activity in which the taxpayer does not materially participate during the year, or rental activities, subject to certain exceptions, regardless of the taxpayer's level of participation.
What is an activity?	One or more trade or business or rental activities that comprises an appropriate economic unit.
How is an appropriate economic unit determined?	Based on a reasonable application of the relevant facts and circumstances.
What is material participation?	In general, the taxpayer participates in a regular, continuous, and substantial basis. More specifically, when the taxpayer meets the conditions of one of the seven tests provided in the Regulations.
What is a rental activity?	In general, an activity where payments are received for the use of tangible property. More specifically, a rental activity that does *not* meet one of the six exceptions provided in the Regulations. Special rules apply to rental real estate.

become deductible when the acquired property is sold. If the activity of the old and new property are the same, suspended losses can be used.

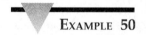

EXAMPLE 50

A taxpayer exchanged a duplex for a limited partnership interest in a § 721 nonrecognition transaction (see Chapter 22 for details). The suspended losses from the duplex are not deductible until the limited partnership interest is sold. Two separate activities exist: a real estate rental activity and a limited partnership activity. If the taxpayer had continued to own the duplex and the duplex had future taxable income, the suspended losses would have become deductible before the time of disposition. ▼

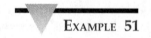

EXAMPLE 51

In a § 1031 nontaxable exchange (see Chapter 12 for details), a taxpayer exchanged a duplex for an apartment building. The suspended losses from the duplex are deductible against future taxable income of the apartment building. The same activity exists. ▼

TAX PLANNING CONSIDERATIONS

12 **LEARNING OBJECTIVE**
Suggest tax planning strategies to minimize the effect of the passive loss limitations.

UTILIZING PASSIVE LOSSES

Taxpayers who have passive activity losses (PALs) should adopt a strategy of generating passive activity income that can be sheltered by existing passive losses. One approach is to buy an interest in a passive activity that is generating income (referred to as passive income generators, or PIGs). Then the PAL can be offset against income from the PIG. From a tax perspective, it would be foolish to buy a loss-generating passive activity (PAL) unless one has other passive income (PIG) to shelter or the activity is rental real estate that can qualify for the $25,000 exception or the exception available to real estate professionals.

A taxpayer with existing passive losses might consider buying rental property. If a large down payment is made and the straight-line method of MACRS (discussed in Chapter 7) is elected, a positive net income could be realized. The income would be sheltered by other passive losses, depreciation expense would be spread out evenly and preserved for future years, and depreciation recapture (discussed in Chapter 13) would be avoided upon the sale of the property. Future gain realized upon the sale of the rental property could be sheltered by existing suspended passive losses.

Taxpayers with passive losses should consider all other trades or businesses in which they have an interest. If they show that they do not materially participate in the activity, the activity becomes a passive activity. Any income generated could be sheltered by existing passive losses and suspended losses. Family partnerships in which certain members do not materially participate would qualify. The silent partner in any general partnership engaged in a trade or business would also qualify.

As the chapter has shown, the passive loss rules can have a dramatic effect on a taxpayer's ability to claim passive losses currently. However, several steps can be taken to mitigate their impact:

- Replace passive activity debt with home equity indebtedness.
- Carefully select the year in which a passive activity is to be disposed of at a gain, as it can be to the taxpayer's advantage to wait until sufficient passive losses have been generated to completely offset the gain recognized on the asset's disposition.
- Keep accurate records of all sources of income and losses, particularly any suspended passive losses and credits and the activities to which they relate, so that their potential tax benefit will not be lost.

Finally, because of the restrictive nature of the passive activity loss rules, it may be advantageous for a taxpayer to use a vacation home enough to convert it to a second residence. This would enable all of the qualified interest to be deducted without limitation. However, this strategy would lead to the loss of other deductions, such as repairs, maintenance, and insurance.

KEY TERMS

Active income, 10–6	Material participation, 10–16	Rental activity, 10–20
At-risk limitation, 10–3	Passive loss, 10–3	Significant participation activity, 10–17
Closely held corporation, 10–11	Personal service corporation, 10–11	
Extraordinary personal services, 10–21	Portfolio income, 10–6	Tax shelters, 10–2

PROBLEM
MATERIALS

DISCUSSION QUESTIONS

1. Congress has passed two major provisions to inhibit taxpayers' ability to use tax shelters to reduce or defer Federal income tax. Explain.

2. Alice invested $100,000 for a 25% interest in a partnership in which she is not a material participant. The partnership borrowed $200,000 from a bank and used the proceeds to acquire a building. What is Alice's at-risk amount if the $200,000 was borrowed on a recourse loan?

3. Eric invested $40,000 for a 20% interest in a partnership in which he is not a material participant. The partnership borrowed $200,000 from a bank and used the proceeds to acquire machinery. What is Eric's at-risk amount if the $200,000 was borrowed on a nonrecourse loan?

4. List some events that increase and decrease an investor's at-risk amount, and discuss some strategies that a taxpayer can employ to increase the at-risk amount in order to claim a higher deduction for losses.

5. Roy invested $30,000 in a cattle-feeding operation that used nonrecourse notes to purchase $300,000 in feed, which was fed to the cattle and expensed. His share of the expense was $54,000. How much can Roy deduct?

6. Explain the meaning of the terms *active income, portfolio income,* and *passive income.*

7. Manuel owns an interest in an activity that produces a $100,000 loss during the year. Would he generally prefer to have the activity classified as active or passive? Discuss.

8. Kim owns an interest in an activity that produces $100,000 of income during the year. Would Kim generally prefer to have the activity classified as active or passive? Discuss.

9. Felicia owns a passive activity that she acquired several years ago. She has incurred losses on the activity since its acquisition. This is the only passive activity she has ever owned. How will these passive losses affect Felicia's taxable income when she disposes of the activity?

10. What is a suspended loss? Why is it important to allocate suspended losses in cases where a taxpayer has interests in more than one passive activity?

11. Upon a taxable disposition of a passive activity, the taxpayer can utilize any suspended losses and credits related to that activity. Do you agree? Explain.

12. Discuss whether the passive loss rules apply to the following: individuals, closely held regular corporations, S corporations, partnerships, and personal service corporations.

13. Gray Corporation has $100,000 of active income and a $55,000 passive loss for the year. Under what circumstances is the corporation prohibited from deducting the loss? Under what circumstances is the corporation allowed to deduct the loss?

14. Hi-Tech Consulting, Inc., is a corporation owned by four engineers, all of whom work full-time for the corporation. The corporation has eight other full-time employees, all on the clerical staff. Hi-Tech provides consulting services to inventors. The corporation has invested in a passive activity that produced a $60,000 loss during the current year. Can Hi-Tech deduct the loss this year? Explain.

15. The Regulations set forth a *facts and circumstances test* for determining what constitutes an activity. Describe this test and comment on the significance of the term *appropriate economic unit.*

16. What factors are given the greatest weight in determining whether activities constitute an appropriate economic unit?

17. Discuss what constitutes a passive activity.

18. Under what circumstances may the IRS regroup activities in a different way than the taxpayer has grouped them? Give an example of a situation to which the regrouping rule would be applied.

19. The Regulations prohibit grouping rental activities in certain circumstances. Discuss these rules.

20. What is the significance of the term *material participation?* Why is the extent of a taxpayer's participation in an activity important in determining whether a loss from the activity is deductible or nondeductible?

21. Why did the IRS adopt the more-than-500-hour standard for material participation?

22. Keith, a physician, operates a separate business that he acquired nine years ago. He participated for 90 hours in the business during the current year, and the business incurred a loss of $20,000. Under what circumstances will the loss be deductible as an active loss?

23. Jan, an attorney, operates a separate business that she acquired nine years ago. She has one part-time employee in the business. Jan participated for 130 hours in the business during the current year, and the business incurred a loss of $20,000. Under what circumstances will the loss be deductible as an active loss?

24. Zelda, a professor, operates three separate businesses on the side. She participates for less than 500 hours in each business. Each business incurs a loss during the year. Are there any circumstances under which Zelda may treat the losses as active?

25. Last year, Paul retired as a partner in a CPA firm he founded 30 years ago. He continues to share in the profits, although he no longer participates in the activities of the firm. Paul also owns an interest in a passive activity that produced a loss of $50,000 in the current year. Can Paul offset the passive loss against his income from the CPA firm?

26. Rene retired from public accounting after a long and successful career of 45 years. As part of her retirement package, she continues to share in the profits and losses of the firm, albeit at a lower rate than when she was working full-time. Because Rene wants to stay busy during her retirement years, she has invested and works in a local hardware business, operated as a partnership. Unfortunately, the business has recently gone through a slump and has not been generating profits. Identify relevant tax issues for Rene.

27. Some types of work are counted in applying the material participation standards, and some types are not counted. Discuss and give examples of each type.

28. During the current year, Alan is determined to make better use of the tax losses that tend to flow from the various businesses that he owns. He is particularly sensitive to the limitations that the passive loss rules place on the deductibility of losses because of the disaster that occurred last year: his accountant informed him that he would not be able to claim any of the losses on his income tax return because of his lack of material participation. He has even suggested to his wife that she may have to put in some time at the businesses if his goals are to be accomplished. Identify the tax issues that Alan faces.

29. Ira, who is a limited partner in Zelcova Gardens, is informed that his portion of the entity's current loss is $10,000. Given that Ira is a limited partner, may one assume that his share of the partnership loss is a passive loss?

30. What are *significant personal services*, and what role do they play in determining whether a rental activity is treated as a passive activity?

31. What are *extraordinary personal services*, and what is their importance in determining whether a rental activity is treated as a passive activity?

32. Some rental operations involving tangible personal property automatically are treated as passive activities, and others are treated as passive only if the owner does not meet the material participation standards. How can one differentiate between the two categories?

33. How is passive activity defined in the Code, and what aspects of the definition have been clarified by the Temporary Regulations?

34. Laura owns an apartment building and a videotape rental business. She participates for more than 500 hours in the operations of each activity. Are the businesses active or passive?

35. Hilda incurred a loss of $60,000 on a real estate rental activity during the current year. Under what circumstances can Hilda treat the entire loss as nonpassive?

36. Since his college days, Charles has developed an entrepreneurial streak. After testing his wings in his family's grocery business, he has decided to start several ventures on his

own. Even though Charles is independently wealthy, he is looking forward to working, even if for a limited amount of time, in each of the ventures. He plans to "drop in" on the businesses from time to time between personal trips to Europe, the Caribbean, and the South Pacific. As of the end of the year, he has established computer software stores in Dayton, Austin, and Seattle; bagel bakeries in Albany, Athens, and Tallahassee; and mountain bike and ski rental shops in small towns in Vermont, West Virginia, Colorado, and California. Identify the tax issues facing Charles.

37. In the current year, George and Susie White, both successful CPAs, made a cash investment for a limited partnership interest in a California avocado grove. In addition to the cash generated from the investors, the grove's management borrowed a substantial sum to purchase assets necessary for its operation. The Whites' investment adviser told them that their share of the tax loss in the first year alone would be in excess of their initial cash investment, followed by several more years of losses. They feel confident that their interest in the avocado grove is a sound investment. Identify the tax issues facing the Whites.

38. Under what circumstances can a closely held C (regular) corporation treat rental real estate losses as nonpassive?

39. Can an employer treat services performed by an employee as being related to a real estate trade or business?

40. Matt owns a small apartment building that generated a loss during the year. Under what circumstances can Matt deduct a loss from the rental activity, and what limitations apply?

41. In connection with passive activities, what is a *deduction equivalent?* How is a deduction equivalent computed?

42. Betty and Steve received a substantial windfall due to a recent inheritance. Because they have always loved spending time at the beach, they plan to devote some of the newly available cash to a beach-related investment. Their analysis identifies two possibilities that seem to be logical given their particular situation. They could purchase a beach cottage and use it for both personal and rental purposes; or they could pool their money with Steve's brother and purchase several cottages, one of which would be held strictly for personal use, while the others would be held solely for rental use. Identify the tax issues facing Betty and Steve.

PROBLEMS

43. In the current year, Lionel invested $20,000 for an interest in a partnership in which he is a material participant. His share of the partnership loss for the year was $25,000. Discuss the tax treatment of Lionel's share of the loss, and compute his at-risk amount.

44. Last year, Fred invested $50,000 in a limited partnership that has a working interest in an oil well (not a passive activity). During that initial year of his investment, his share of the partnership loss was $35,000. In the current year, his share of the partnership loss was $25,000. How much can Fred deduct in the prior and current years?

45. In the current year, Bill Parker (54 Oak Drive, St. Paul, MN 55162) is considering making an investment of $60,000 in Best Choice Partnership. The prospectus provided by Bill's broker indicates that the partnership investment is not a passive activity and that Bill's share of the entity's loss in the current year will likely be $40,000, while his share of the partnership loss next year will probably be $25,000. Write a letter to Bill in which you indicate how the losses would be treated for tax purposes in the current and next years.

46. Carmen wishes to invest $25,000 in a relatively safe venture and has discovered two alternatives that would produce the following reportable income and loss over the next three years:

Year	Alternative 1 Income (Loss)	Alternative 2 Income (Loss)
1	($15,000)	($30,000)
2	(15,000)	20,000
3	45,000	25,000

She is interested in the after-tax effects of these alternatives over a three-year horizon. Assume that Carmen's investment portfolio produces sufficient passive income to offset any potential passive loss that may arise from these alternatives, that her cost of capital is 8% (the present value factors are 0.92593, 0.85734, and 0.79383), that she is in the 28% tax bracket, that each investment alternative possesses equal growth potential, and that each alternative exposes her to comparable financial risk. In addition, assume that in the loss years for each alternative, there is no cash flow from or to the investment (i.e., the loss is due to depreciation), while in those years when the income is positive, cash flows to Carmen equal the amount of the income. Based on these facts, compute the present value of these two investment alternatives and determine which option Carmen should choose.

47. Tina acquired passive Activity A in January 1991 and Activity B in September 1992. Until 1995, Activity A was profitable. Activity A produced a loss of $200,000 in 1995 and a loss of $100,000 in 1996. Tina has passive income from Activity B of $20,000 in 1995 and $40,000 in 1996. After offsetting passive income, how much of the net losses may she deduct?

48. In 1991, Kay acquired an interest in a partnership in which she is not a material participant. The partnership was profitable until 1995. Kay's basis in her partnership interest at the beginning of 1995 was $40,000. In 1995, Kay's share of the partnership loss was $35,000. In 1996, her share of the partnership income was $15,000. How much can Kay deduct in 1995 and 1996?

49. Ray acquired an interest in a bakery three years ago. The loss from the activity was $50,000 in the current year. He had AGI of $140,000 before considering the loss from the bakery. Ray is not a material participant in the bakery. What is his AGI after considering this activity?

50. Sarah has $100,000 that she wishes to invest, and she is considering the following two options:

- Option A—Investment in Bluebird Equity Mutual fund, which would be expected to produce dividends of $8,000 per year.

- Option B—Investment in Redbird Limited Partnership (buys, sells, and operates avocado groves). Sarah's share of the partnership's income and loss over the next three years is expected to be:

Year	Income (Loss)
1	($ 8,000)
2	(2,000)
3	34,000

Sarah is interested in the after-tax effects of these alternatives over a three-year horizon. Assume that Sarah's investment portfolio produces no passive income, that her cost of capital is 8% (the present value factors are 0.92593, 0.85734, and 0.79383), that she is in the 31% tax bracket, that each investment alternative possesses equal growth potential, and that each alternative exposes her to comparable financial risk. Based on these facts, compute the present value of these two investment alternatives and determine which option Sarah should choose.

51. Emily has $100,000 that she wishes to invest, and she is considering the following two options:

    • Option A—Investment in Redbird Equity Mutual fund, which would be expected to produce dividends of $8,000 per year.

    • Option B—Investment in Cardinal Limited Partnership (buys, sells, and operates wine vineyards). Emily's share of the partnerhip's income and loss over the next three years is expected to be:

Year	Income (Loss)
1	($ 8,000)
2	(2,000)
3	34,000

    Emily is interested in the after-tax effects of these alternatives over a three-year horizon. Assume that Emily's investment portfolio produces ample passive income to offset any passive losses that may be generated, that her cost of capital is 8% (the present value factors are 0.92593, 0.85734, and 0.79383), that she is in the 31% tax bracket, that each investment alternative possesses equal growth potential, and that each alternative exposes her to comparable financial risk. Based on these facts, compute the present value of these two investment alternatives and determine which option Emily should choose.

52. Hazel has two investments in nonrental passive activities. Activity A, which was acquired seven years ago, was profitable until the current year. Activity B was acquired this year. Currently, Hazel's share of the loss from Activity A is $10,000, and her share of the loss from Activity B is $6,000. What is the total of Hazel's suspended losses from these activities as of the end of the current year?

53. Leanne has investments in four passive activity partnerships purchased several years ago. Last year, the income and losses were as follows:

Activity	Income (Loss)
A	$60,000
B	(60,000)
C	(30,000)
D	(10,000)

    In the current year, she sold her interest in Activity D for a $20,000 gain. Activity D, which had been profitable until last year, had a current loss of $3,000. How will the sale of Activity D affect Leanne's taxable income in the current year?

54. Green, Inc., a closely held personal service corporation, has $100,000 of passive losses in the current year. In addition, Green has $80,000 of active business income and $20,000 of portfolio income. How much of the passive loss may Green use to offset other types of income this year?

55. White, Inc., earned $400,000 from operations in the current year. White also received $36,000 in dividends and interest on various portfolio investments. During the year, White paid $150,000 to acquire a 20% interest in a passive activity that produced a $200,000 loss.
    a. How will this affect White's taxable income, assuming the corporation is a personal service corporation?
    b. How will this affect White's taxable income, assuming the corporation is a closely held, non-personal service corporation?

56. Green Corporation, a closely held, non-personal service corporation, earned active income of $50,000 in the current year. Green received $60,000 in dividends during the year. In addition, Green incurred a loss of $80,000 from an investment in a passive activity acquired last year. What is Green's net income for the current year after considering the passive investment?

57. Greg Reynolds (66 Hanover Street, Cincinnati, OH 45230), a syndicated radio talk show host, earns a $400,000 salary in the current year. He works approximately 30 hours per week in this job, which leaves him time to participate in several businesses he acquired in the current year. He owns a movie theater and a drugstore in Cincinnati. He also owns a movie theater and a drugstore in Indianapolis and a drugstore in Louisville. A preliminary analysis on December 1 of the current year shows projected income and losses for the various businesses as follows:

	Income (Loss)
Cincinnati movie theater (95 hours participation)	$56,000
Cincinnati drugstore (140 hours participation)	(89,000)
Indianapolis movie theater (90 hours participation)	34,000
Indianapolis drugstore (170 hours participation)	(41,000)
Louisville drugstore (180 hours participation)	(15,000)

Greg has full-time employees at each of the five businesses listed above. Consider all possible groupings for Greg's activities. Write a letter to him suggesting the grouping method and other strategies that will provide the greatest tax advantage. Greg does not know much about the tax law, so you should provide a concise, nontechnical explanation.

58. Ann acquired an activity four years ago. The loss from the activity was $50,000 in the current year. She had AGI of $140,000 before considering the loss from the activity. The activity is a service station, and Ann is a material participant. What is her AGI after considering this activity?

59. Lee acquired a 20% interest in the ABC Partnership for $60,000 in 1991. The partnership was profitable until 1996, and Lee's amount at risk in the partnership interest was $120,000 at the end of 1995. ABC incurred a loss of $400,000 in 1996 and reported income of $200,000 in 1997. Assuming Lee is not a material participant in ABC, how much of his loss from ABC Partnership is deductible in 1996 and 1997, respectively?

60. Ken has a $40,000 loss from an investment in a partnership in which he does not participate. He paid $30,000 for his interest in the partnership. How much of the loss is disallowed by the at-risk rules? How much is disallowed by the passive loss rules?

61. Last year, Fran invested $20,000 for an interest in a partnership in which she is a material participant. Her share of the partnership's loss for the year was $25,000. In the current year, Fran's share of the partnership's income is $15,000. What is the effect on her taxable income for the current year?

62. Soong, a physician, earned $200,000 from his practice. He also received $18,000 in dividends and interest on various portfolio investments. During the year, he paid $45,000 to acquire a 20% interest in a partnership that produced a $300,000 loss.
    a. Compute Soong's AGI assuming he does not participate in the operations of the partnership.
    b. Compute Soong's AGI assuming he is a material participant in the operations of the partnership.

63. Sam invested $150,000 in a passive activity five years ago. On January 1, 1995, his amount at risk in the activity was $30,000. His shares of the income and losses in the activity were as follows:

Year	Income (Loss)
1995	($40,000)
1996	(30,000)
1997	50,000

How much can Sam deduct in 1995 and 1996? What is his taxable income from the activity in 1997? Keep in mind the at-risk rules as well as the passive loss rules.

64. Joe Cook (125 Hill Street, Charleston, WV 25311) acquired an activity four years ago. The loss from the activity was $50,000 in the current year. He had AGI of $140,000 before considering the loss from the activity. The activity is an apartment building, and Joe is an active participant. Write a letter to Joe in which you explain what his AGI is after the loss is considered.

65. Beth acquired an activity four years ago. The loss from the activity was $50,000 in the current year. She had AGI of $140,000 before considering the loss from the activity. The activity is an apartment building, and Beth is not an active participant. What is her AGI after considering the activity?

66. During the current year, Donald worked 1,200 hours as a computer consultant, 600 hours in a real estate development business, and 500 hours in real estate rental activities. He earned $60,000 as a computer consultant, but lost $18,000 in the development business and $26,000 in the real estate rental business. How should Donald treat the losses on his current Federal income tax return?

67. During the current year, Maria Castro worked 1,200 hours as a computer consultant, 320 hours in a real estate development business, and 400 hours in real estate rental activities. Jorge, her husband, worked 250 hours in the real estate development business and 180 hours in the real estate rental business. Maria earned $60,000 as a computer consultant, but the Castros lost $18,000 in the development business and $26,000 in the real estate rental business. How should they treat the losses on their joint current Federal income tax return?

68. Hal and Wanda are married with no dependents and live together in Ohio, which is not a community property state. Since Wanda has large medical expenses, they seek your advice about filing separately to save taxes. Their income and expenses for 1996 are as follows:

Hal's salary	$ 36,000
Wanda's salary	44,000
Dividends and interest (joint)	1,500
Rental loss from actively managed apartments (joint)	(24,000)
Wanda's unreimbursed medical expenses	6,300
All other itemized deductions:*	
Hal	8,000
Wanda	2,000

*None subject to limitations.

Determine whether Hal and Wanda should file jointly or separately for 1996.

69. Lucy and Leon have owned a beach cottage on the New Jersey shore for several years and have always used it as a family retreat. When they acquired the property, they had no intentions of renting it, but because their family circumstances have changed, they are considering using the cottage for only two weeks a year and renting it for the remainder of the year. Their AGI is currently approximately $80,000 per year, and they are in the 36% tax bracket (combined Federal and state). Their financial records indicate that interest and real estate taxes have totaled $8,000 per year, and Lucy and Leon expect these expenditures to continue at this level into the foreseeable future. In

addition, if they rent the property, their *incremental* revenue and expenses are projected to be:

Rent income	$20,000
Rental commissions	3,000
Maintenance expenses	12,000
Depreciation expense	10,000
	($ 5,000)

If they do convert the cottage to rental property, they insist that they will be actively involved in key rental and maintenance decisions. Given the tax effects of converting the property to rental use, would the cash flow resulting from renting the property be enough to meet the $12,000 annual mortgage payment? This is an important factor in Lucy and Leon's decision.

70. Ida, who has AGI of $80,000 before considering rental activities, is active in three separate real estate rental activities and is in the 28% tax bracket. She had $12,000 of losses from Activity A, $18,000 of losses from Activity B, and income of $10,000 from Activity C. She also had $2,100 of tax credits from Activity A. Calculate her deductions and credits allowed and the suspended losses and credits.

71. Ella has $105,000 of losses from a real estate rental activity in which she actively participates. She has other rental income of $25,000 and other passive income of $32,000. How much rental loss can Ella deduct against active and portfolio income (ignoring the at-risk rules)? Does she have any suspended losses to carry over?

72. Faye died owning an interest in a passive activity property with an adjusted basis of $160,000, suspended losses of $16,000, and a fair market value of $170,000. What can be deducted on her final income tax return?

73. Last year, Nina gave her son a passive activity with an adjusted basis of $100,000. Fair market value of the activity was $180,000, and the activity had suspended losses of $25,000. In the current year, her son realized income of $12,000 from the passive activity. What is the effect on Nina and her son last year and in the current year?

74. Tonya sold a passive activity in the current year for $150,000. Her adjusted basis was $50,000. She used the installment method of reporting the gain. The activity had suspended losses of $12,000. Tonya received $60,000 in the year of sale. What is her gain? How much of the suspended losses can she deduct?

75. If Tonya in Problem 74 had no suspended losses, was in the 28% tax bracket, and had $10,000 of suspended tax credits attributable to the activity, how much of the credits could she use in the current year?

TEAM PROJECT: ARTHUR ANDERSEN TAX CHALLENGE CASES

For more information on the Arthur Andersen Tax Challenge Cases, please refer to Chapter 2, page 2-41.

Information related to tax issues and problems that are discussed in this chapter may be found in the

Fields case on pages 10, and 35-37

Read and analyze the case you have been assigned and *identify* any issues and problems that are related to material covered in this chapter. If the information provided in the case is complete, prepare answers for this part of the case at this time. If you need information that is contained in the later parts of the case, please write a memo summarizing the questions or problems so you can prepare a complete answer at a later date.

11

TAX CREDITS

LEARNING OBJECTIVES

After completing Chapter 11, you should be able to:

1. Explain how tax credits are used as a tool of Federal tax policy.

2. Distinguish between refundable and nonrefundable credits and understand the order in which they can be used by taxpayers.

3. Describe various business-related tax credits.

4. Describe several other tax credits that are available primarily to individual taxpayers.

5. Identify tax planning opportunities related to tax credits.

As explained in Chapter 1, Federal tax law often serves other purposes besides merely raising revenue for the government. Evidence of equity, social, and economic considerations, among others, is found throughout the tax law. These considerations also bear heavily in the area of **tax credits.** Consider the following examples:

EXAMPLE 1

Paul and Peggy, husband and wife, are both employed outside the home. Their combined salaries are $50,000. However, after paying for child care expenses of $2,000 on behalf of their daughter, Polly, the net economic benefit from both spouses working is $48,000. The child care expenses are, in a sense, business related in that they would not have been incurred if both spouses did not work outside the home. If no tax benefits are associated with the child care expenditures, $50,000 is subject to tax.

Another couple, Alicia and Diego, also have a child, John. Diego stays at home to care for John (the value of those services is $2,000) while Alicia earns a $48,000 salary. Because the value of Diego's services rendered is not subject to tax, only Alicia's earnings of $48,000 are subject to tax. ▼

The credit for child and dependent care expenses is allowed to mitigate the inequity felt by working taxpayers who must pay for child care services in order to work outside the home.

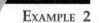

EXAMPLE 2

Olaf is a retired taxpayer who received $10,000 of Social Security benefits as his only source of income in 1996. His Social Security benefits are excluded from gross income. Therefore, Olaf's income tax is $0. In 1996, Olga, a single taxpayer 66 years of age, has, as her sole source of income, $10,000 from a pension plan funded by her former employer. Assuming Olga has no itemized deductions or deductions *for* AGI, her income tax for 1996 (before credits) is $368, based on the following computation:

Pension plan benefits	$10,000
Less: Basic standard deduction	(4,000)
Additional standard deduction	(1,000)
Personal exemption	(2,550)
Taxable income	$ 2,450
Income tax (at 15%)	$ 368

▼

The tax credit for elderly or disabled taxpayers was enacted to mitigate this inequity.

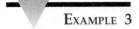

EXAMPLE 3

Jane is a single parent who depends on the government's "safety net" for survival—she receives Aid for Dependent Children in the amount of $10,000 per year. However, she very much wishes to work. Jane has located a job that will pay $10,500 per year and has found an individual to care for her child at no cost. But, with the $803.25 ($10,500 × 7.65%) payroll deduction for Social Security and Medicare taxes, the economic benefit from working is less than remaining reliant on the government ($9,696.75 as compared to $10,000). ▼

To help offset the effect of Social Security and Medicare taxes on wages of the working poor and to provide an incentive to work, the earned income credit is used to increase the after-tax earnings of qualified individuals. In addition, the earned income credit helps offset the regressive nature of certain taxes, such as the Social Security and Medicare taxes, which impose a relatively larger burden on low-income taxpayers than on more affluent taxpayers.

These three tax credits and many of the other important tax credits available to individuals and other types of taxpayers are the major focus of this chapter. The chapter begins by discussing important tax policy considerations relevant to tax credits. Tax credits are categorized as being either refundable or nonrefundable. The distinction between refundable and nonrefundable credits is important because it may affect the taxpayer's ability to enjoy a tax benefit from a particular credit.

Next an overview of the priority of tax credits is presented, followed by a discussion of the credits available to businesses and to individual taxpayers and the ways in which credits enter into the calculation of the tax liability.

TAX POLICY CONSIDERATIONS

1 LEARNING OBJECTIVE
Explain how tax credits are used as a tool of Federal tax policy.

Congress has generally used tax credits to achieve social or economic objectives or to provide equity for different types of taxpayers. For example, the disabled access credit, enacted in 1990, was intended to meet a social objective: to encourage taxpayers to renovate older buildings so they would be in compliance with the Americans with Disabilities Act. This Act requires businesses and institutions to make their facilities more accessible to persons with various types of disabilities. In another example, the foreign tax credit, which has been a part of the law for decades, has as its purpose the economic and equity objectives of mitigating the burden of multiple taxation of a single flow of income.

A tax credit should not be confused with an income tax deduction. Certain expenditures of individuals (e.g., business expenses) are permitted as deductions from gross income in arriving at adjusted gross income (AGI). Additionally, individuals are allowed to deduct certain nonbusiness and investment-related expenses *from* AGI. While the tax benefit received from a tax deduction depends on the tax rate, a tax credit is not affected by the tax rate of the taxpayer.

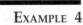

EXAMPLE 4

Assume Congress wishes to encourage a certain type of expenditure. One way to accomplish this objective is to allow a tax credit of 25% for such expenditures. Another way is to allow an itemized deduction for the expenditures. Assume Abby's tax rate is 15%, while Bill's tax rate is 39.6%. In addition, assume that Carmen does not incur enough qualifying expenditures to itemize deductions. The following tax benefits are available to each taxpayer for a $1,000 expenditure:

	Abby	**Bill**	**Carmen**
Tax benefit if a 25% credit is allowed	$250	$250	$250
Tax benefit if an itemized deduction is allowed	150	396	–0–

As these results indicate, tax credits provide benefits on a more equitable basis than do tax deductions. Equally apparent is that the deduction approach in this case benefits only taxpayers who itemize deductions, while the credit approach benefits all taxpayers who make the specified expenditure. ▼

For many years, Congress has used the tax credit provisions of the Code liberally in implementing tax policy. Although budget constraints and economic considerations often have dictated the repeal of some credits, other credits, such as those applicable to expenses incurred for child and dependent care, have been kept to respond to important social policy considerations. Other credits, such as the one available to low-income workers, have been retained based on economic and equity considerations. Finally, as the myriad of tax proposals that are always before Congress make clear, the use of tax credits as a tax policy tool continues to evolve as economic and political circumstances change.

OVERVIEW AND PRIORITY OF CREDITS

2 LEARNING OBJECTIVE
Distinguish between refundable and nonrefundable credits and understand the order in which they can be used by taxpayers.

REFUNDABLE VERSUS NONREFUNDABLE CREDITS

As illustrated in Exhibit 11–1, certain credits are refundable while others are nonrefundable. **Refundable credits** are paid to the taxpayer even if the amount of the credit (or credits) exceeds the taxpayer's tax liability.

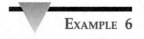 EXAMPLE 5

Ted, who is single, had taxable income of $21,000 in 1996. His income tax from the 1996 Tax Rate Schedule is $3,150. During 1996, Ted's employer withheld income tax of $3,500. Ted is entitled to a refund of $350 because the credit for tax withheld on wages is a refundable credit. ▼

Nonrefundable credits are not paid if they exceed the taxpayer's tax liability.

EXAMPLE 6

Tina is single, age 67, and retired. Her taxable income for 1996 is $1,320, and the tax on this amount is $198. Tina's tax credit for the elderly is $225. This credit can be used to reduce her net tax liability to zero, but it will not result in a refund, even though the credit ($225) exceeds Tina's tax liability ($198). This result occurs because the tax credit for the elderly is a nonrefundable credit. ▼

Some nonrefundable credits, such as the foreign tax credit, are subject to carryover provisions if they exceed the amount allowable as a credit in a given year. Other nonrefundable credits, such as the tax credit for the elderly (refer to Example 6), are not subject to carryover provisions and are lost if they exceed the limitations. Because some credits are subject to carryover provisions while others are not, the order in which credits are offset against the tax liability is important. The Code provides that nonrefundable credits are to be offset against a taxpayer's income tax liability in the order shown in Exhibit 11–1.

▼ **EXHIBIT 11–1**
Partial Listing of Refundable and
Nonrefundable Credits

Refundable Credits

Taxes withheld on wages

Earned income credit

Nonrefundable Credits

Credit for child and dependent care expenses

Credit for the elderly or disabled

Foreign tax credit

General business credit, which is the sum of the following:

- Tax credit for rehabilitation expenditures
- Business energy credits
- Research activities credit*
- Low-income housing credit
- Disabled access credit

---

*Not available after June 30, 1995.

GENERAL BUSINESS CREDIT

As shown in Exhibit 11–1, the **general business credit** is comprised of a number of other credits, each of which is computed separately under its own set of rules. The general business credit combines these credits into one amount to limit the amount of business credits that can be used to offset a taxpayer's income tax liability. The idea behind combining the credits is to prevent a taxpayer from completely avoiding his or her income tax liability in any one year by offsetting it with business credits that would otherwise be available.

Two special rules apply to the general business credit. First, any unused credit must be carried back 3 years, then forward 15 years. Second, for any tax year, the general business credit is limited to the taxpayer's *net income tax* reduced by the greater of:[1]

- The *tentative minimum tax.*
- 25 percent of *net regular tax liability* that exceeds $25,000.[2]

In order to understand the general business credit limitation, several terms need defining:

- *Net income tax* is the sum of the regular tax liability and the alternative minimum tax reduced by certain nonrefundable tax credits.
- *Tentative minimum tax* for this purpose is reduced by the foreign tax credit allowed.
- *Regular tax liability* is determined from the appropriate tax table or tax rate schedule, based on taxable income. However, the regular tax liability does not include certain taxes (e.g., alternative minimum tax).

---

[1] § 38(c).

[2] This amount is $12,500 for married taxpayers filing separately unless one of the spouses is not entitled to the general business credit.

• *Net regular tax liability* is the regular tax liability reduced by certain nonrefundable credits (e.g., credit for child and dependent care expenses, foreign tax credit).

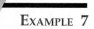
EXAMPLE 7

Floyd's general business credit for the current year is $70,000. His net income tax is $150,000, tentative minimum tax is $130,000, and net regular tax liability is $150,000. He has no other tax credits. Floyd's general business credit allowed for the tax year is computed as follows:

Net income tax	$ 150,000
Less: The greater of	
• $130,000 (tentative minimum tax)	
• $31,250 [25% × ($150,000 − $25,000)]	(130,000)
Amount of general business credit allowed for tax year	$ 20,000

Floyd then has $50,000 ($70,000 − $20,000) of unused general business credits that may be carried back or forward as discussed below. ▼

TREATMENT OF UNUSED GENERAL BUSINESS CREDITS

Unused general business credits are initially carried back three years (to the earliest year in the sequence first) and are applied to reduce the tax liability during these years. Thus, the taxpayer may receive a tax refund as a result of the carryback. Any remaining unused credits are then carried forward 15 years.[3]

A FIFO method is applied to the carryovers, carrybacks, and utilization of credits earned during a particular year. The oldest credits are used first in determining the amount of the general business credit. The FIFO method minimizes the potential for loss of a general business credit benefit due to the expiration of credit carryovers, since the earliest years are used before the current credit for the taxable year.

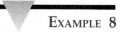
EXAMPLE 8

This example illustrates the use of general business credit carryovers.

General business credit carryovers		
1993	$ 4,000	
1994	6,000	
1995	2,000	
Total carryovers	$12,000	
1996 general business credit		$40,000
Total credit allowed in 1996 (based on tax liability)	$50,000	
Less: Utilization of carryovers		
1993	(4,000)	
1994	(6,000)	
1995	(2,000)	
Remaining credit allowed	$38,000	
Applied against		
1996 general business credit		(38,000)
1996 unused amount carried forward to 1997		$ 2,000

▼

SPECIFIC BUSINESS-RELATED TAX CREDIT PROVISIONS

3 LEARNING OBJECTIVE
Describe various business-related tax credits.

Each component of the general business credit is determined separately under its own set of rules. The components are explained here in the order listed in Exhibit 11–1.

TAX CREDIT FOR REHABILITATION EXPENDITURES

Taxpayers are allowed a tax credit for expenditures incurred to rehabilitate industrial and commercial buildings and certified historic structures. The **rehabilitation expenditures credit** is intended to discourage businesses from moving from older, economically distressed areas (e.g., inner city) to newer locations and to encourage the preservation of historic structures. The current operating features of this credit follow:[4]

Rate of the Credit for Rehabilitation Expenses	Nature of the Property
10%	Nonresidential buildings and residential rental property, other than certified historic structures, originally placed in service before 1936
20%	Nonresidential and residential certified historic structures

When taking the credit, the basis of a rehabilitated building must be reduced by the full rehabilitation credit allowed.[5]

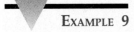
EXAMPLE 9

Juan spent $60,000 to rehabilitate a building (adjusted basis of $40,000) that had originally been placed in service in 1932. He is allowed a credit of $6,000 (10% × $60,000) for rehabilitation expenditures. Juan then increases the basis of the building by $54,000 [$60,000 (rehabilitation expenditures) – $6,000 (credit allowed)]. If the building were a historic structure, the credit allowed would be $12,000 (20% × $60,000), and the building's depreciable basis would increase by $48,000 [$60,000 (rehabilitation expenditures) – $12,000 (credit allowed)]. ▼

To qualify for the credit, buildings must be substantially rehabilitated. A building has been *substantially rehabilitated* if qualified rehabilitation expenditures exceed the greater of:

- The adjusted basis of the property before the rehabilitation expenditures, or
- $5,000.

Qualified rehabilitation expenditures do not include the cost of acquiring a building, the cost of facilities related to a building (such as a parking lot), and the cost of enlarging an existing building. Stringent rules apply concerning the retention of internal and external walls.

Recapture of Tax Credit for Rehabilitation Expenditures. The rehabilitation credit taken must be recaptured if the rehabilitated property is disposed of

---

[4]§ 47.   [5]§ 50(c).

▼ **TABLE 11–1**
Recapture Calculation for
Rehabilitation Expenditures
Credit

If the Property Is Held for	The Recapture Percentage Is
Less than 1 year	100
One year or more but less than 2 years	80
Two years or more but less than 3 years	60
Three years or more but less than 4 years	40
Four years or more but less than 5 years	20
Five years or more	0

prematurely or if it ceases to be qualifying property. The **rehabilitation expenditures credit recapture** is based on a holding period requirement of five years and is added to the taxpayer's regular tax liability in the recapture year. In addition, the recapture amount is *added* to the adjusted basis of the rehabilitation expenditures for purposes of determining the amount of gain or loss realized on the property's disposition.

The portion of the credit recaptured is a specified percentage of the credit that was taken by the taxpayer. This percentage is based on the period the property was held by the taxpayer, as shown in Table 11–1.

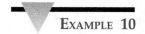

EXAMPLE 10

On March 15, 1993, Rashad placed in service $30,000 of rehabilitation expenditures on a building qualifying for the 10% credit. A credit of $3,000 ($30,000 × 10%) was allowed, and the basis of the building was increased by $27,000 ($30,000 − $3,000). The building was sold on December 15, 1996. Rashad must recapture a portion of the rehabilitation credit based on the schedule in Table 11–1. Because he held the rehabilitated property for more than three years but less than four, 40% of the credit, or $1,200, must be added to his 1996 tax liability. Also, the adjusted basis of the rehabilitation expenditures is increased by the $1,200 recapture amount. ▼

ETHICAL
CONSIDERATIONS

Using the Rehabilitation Expenditures Credit

The tax credit for rehabilitation expenditures is available to help offset the costs related to substantially rehabilitating certain buildings. The credit is calculated on the rehabilitation expenditures incurred and not on the acquisition cost of the building itself.

You are a developer who buys, sells, and does construction work on real estate in the inner city of your metropolitan area. A potential customer approaches you about acquiring one of your buildings that easily could qualify for the 20 percent rehabilitation credit on historic structures. The stated sales price of the structure is $100,000 (based on appraisals ranging from $80,000 to $120,000), and the rehabilitation expenditures, if the job is done correctly, would be about $150,000.

Your business has been slow recently due to the sluggish real estate market in your area, and the potential customer makes the following proposal: if you reduce the sales price of the building to $75,000, he will pay you $175,000 to perform the rehabilitation work. Although the buyer's total expenditures would be the same, he would benefit from this approach by obtaining a larger tax credit ($25,000 increased rehabilitation costs × 20% = $5,000).

It has been a long time since you have sold any of your real estate. How will you respond?

TAX IN THE NEWS

CONSIDERING THE IMPACT OF NONPERMANENT TAX CREDITS

Over the years, Congress has enacted a number of tax credits in an attempt to encourage certain types of taxpayer behavior. Some of these credits, such as the foreign tax credit and the credit for child and dependent care expenses, have had long, uninterrupted histories. Other tax credits, however, have been enacted for only limited periods of time. For example, before it was recently made permanent, the low-income housing credit was normally extended for 12 to 24 months; then either just before or after its expiration, Congress would enact new legislation extending the provision once again. The research activities credit has also repeatedly been extended on a temporary basis, only to expire at a later date.

Among other problems that arise, the uncertain lives of such credits make planning by taxpayers very difficult. With the research activities credit having expired for qualifying purchases made after June 30, 1995, taxpayers who might be encouraged by the presence of the credit may hesitate to make a qualifying expenditure until the credit is reenacted. Yet, even if Congress were to make these tax credits permanent, some parties would object: among those most adversely affected would be those persons who lobby Congress!

BUSINESS ENERGY CREDITS

For many years, **business energy credits** have been allowed to encourage the conservation of natural resources and the development of alternative energy sources (to oil and natural gas). Over the years, some of these credits have expired while new ones have been added. The most important business energy credits that remain are the 10 percent credits for solar energy property and geothermal property.

RESEARCH ACTIVITIES CREDIT

To encourage research and experimentation, usually described as research and development (R & D), a credit is allowed for certain qualifying expenditures paid or incurred through June 30, 1995. Many commentators expect Congress will extend this credit in future legislation. The **research activities credit** is the *sum* of two components: an incremental research activities credit and a basic research credit.[6]

Incremental Research Activities Credit.   The incremental research activities credit applies at a 20 percent rate to the *excess* of qualified research expenses for the taxable year (the credit year) over the base amount. These components of the credit are explained below.

In general, *research expenditures* qualify if the research relates to discovering technological information that is intended for use in the development of a new or improved business component of the taxpayer. Such expenses qualify fully if the research is performed in-house (by the taxpayer or employees). If the research is

---

[6] § 41.

conducted by persons outside the taxpayer's business (under contract), only 65 percent of the amount paid qualifies for the credit.[7]

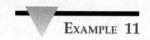

EXAMPLE 11

Sungho incurs the following research expenditures for the tax year.

In-house wages, supplies, computer time	$50,000
Paid to Cutting Edge Scientific Foundation for research	30,000

Sungho's qualified research expenditures are $69,500 [$50,000 + ($30,000 × 65%)]. ▼

Beyond the general guidelines described above, the Code does not give specific examples of qualifying research. However, the credit is *not* allowed for research that falls into certain categories, including the following:[8]

- Research conducted after the beginning of commercial production of the business component.
- Surveys and studies such as market research, testing, and routine data collection.
- Research conducted *outside* the United States.
- Research in the social sciences, arts, or humanities.

The *base amount* for the credit year is determined by multiplying the taxpayer's fixed base percentage by the average gross receipts for the four preceding taxable years. The fixed base percentage depends on whether the taxpayer is an existing firm or a start-up company. For purposes of the incremental research activities credit, an *existing firm* is one that both incurred qualified research expenditures *and* had gross receipts during each of at least three years from 1984 to 1988. A *start-up company* is one that did not have both of the above during each of at least three years in the same 1984–1988 period.

For existing firms, the fixed base percentage is the ratio of total qualified research expenses for the 1984–1988 period to total gross receipts for this same period. Gross receipts are net of sales returns and allowances. The fixed base percentage cannot exceed a maximum ratio of .16, or 16 percent. A start-up company is *assigned* a fixed base percentage ratio of .03, or 3 percent, for each of its first five tax years after 1993. For subsequent years, the base percentage is calculated based on the taxpayer's actual experience.

To calculate the incremental research activities credit available for 1995, the following template may be used. Essentially, the steps lead to the multiplication of the excess or incremental research expenditures incurred by the tax credit rate.

1. Calculate the fixed base percentage for the period 1984–1988 (aggregate research expenses ÷ aggregate gross receipts). _____
2. Calculate the average gross receipts for the four preceding years. _____
3. Multiply the line 2 amount by the lesser of the line 1 amount or 16%. _____
4. Subtract from the qualified research expenditures for the credit year the line 3 amount or, if greater, 50% of the credit year's qualified research expenditures. This is the excess research expenditures incurred. _____
5. Multiply the line 4 amount by 20%. This is the incremental research activities credit. _____

[7] § 41(b)(3)(A). 　　[8] § 41(d).

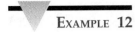

EXAMPLE 12

Jack, a calendar year taxpayer, has both gross receipts (net of sales returns and allowances) and qualified research expenses as follows:

	Gross Receipts	Qualified Research Expenses
1984	$150,000	$25,000
1985	300,000	45,000
1986	400,000	30,000
1987	350,000	35,000
1988	450,000	50,000
1989	425,000	60,000
1990	430,000	62,000
1991	450,000	65,000
1992	450,000	50,000
1993	500,000	55,000
1994	650,000	73,000
1995	700,000	80,000

Using the template above, calculate Jack's incremental research activities credit.

1. Calculate the fixed base percentage for the period 1984–1988 (aggregate research expenses ÷ aggregate gross receipts). ($185,000 ÷ $1,650,000) — 11.21%

2. Calculate the average gross receipts for the four preceding years. [($450,000 + $450,000 + $500,000 + $650,000) ÷ 4] — $512,500

3. Multiply the line 2 amount by the lesser of the line 1 amount or 16%. ($512,500 × 11.21%) — $ 57,451

4. Subtract from the qualified research expenditures for the credit year the line 3 amount or, if greater, 50% of the credit year's qualified research expenditures. This is the excess research expenditures incurred. ($80,000 – $57,451) — $ 22,549

5. Multiply the line 4 amount by 20%. This is the incremental research activities credit. — $ 4,510 ▼

As indicated in the template, a special rule limits the credit available for taxpayers who have incurred small amounts of research and experimentation costs during the base period. The rule provides that in no event shall the base amount be less than 50 percent of qualified research expenses for the credit year.

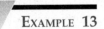

EXAMPLE 13

Assume the same facts as in Example 12, except that qualified research and experimentation expenses in 1995 were $200,000. Incremental research and experimentation expenditures eligible for the credit are $100,000, and the tax credit is computed as follows:

1. Calculate the fixed base percentage for the period 1984–1988 (aggregate research expenses ÷ aggregate gross receipts). ($185,000 ÷ $1,650,000) — 11.21%

2. Calculate the average gross receipts for the four preceding years. [($450,000 + $450,000 + $500,000 + $650,000) ÷ 4] — $512,500

3. Multiply the line 2 amount by the lesser of the line 1 amount or 16%. ($512,500 × 11.21%) — $ 57,451

4. Subtract from the qualified research expenditures for the credit year the line 3 amount or, if greater, 50% of the credit year's qualified research expenditures. This is the excess research expenditures incurred. ($200,000 – $100,000) — $100,000

5. Multiply the line 4 amount by 20%. This is the incremental research activities credit. — $ 20,000 ▼

Qualified research and experimentation expenditures are not only eligible for the 20 percent credit, but can also be *expensed* in the year incurred.[9] In this regard, a taxpayer has two choices:[10]

- Use the full credit and reduce the expense deduction for research expenses by 100 percent of the credit.
- Retain the full expense deduction and reduce the credit by the product of 50 percent of the credit times the maximum corporate tax rate.

As an alternative to the expense deduction, the taxpayer may *capitalize* the research expenses and *amortize* them over 60 months or more. In this case, the amount capitalized and subject to amortization is reduced by the full amount of the credit *only* if the credit exceeds the amount allowable as a deduction.

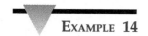

EXAMPLE 14

Assume the same facts as in Example 13, which shows that the potential incremental research activities credit is $20,000. The expense that the taxpayer can deduct and the credit amount are as follows:

	Credit Amount	Deduction Amount
• Full credit and reduced deduction		
$20,000 – $0	$20,000	
$200,000 – $20,000		$180,000
• Reduced credit and full deduction		
$20,000 – [(.50 × $20,000) × .35]	16,500	
$200,000 – $0		200,000
• Full credit and capitalize and elect to amortize costs over 60 months		
$20,000 – $0	20,000	
$200,000/60 × 12		40,000

Basic Research Credit. Corporations (other than S corporations or personal service corporations) are allowed an additional 20 percent credit for basic research payments through June 30, 1995, in *excess* of a base amount. Like the incremental research activities credit, many commentators expect Congress will extend this credit in future legislation. This credit is not available to individual taxpayers. *Basic research payments* are defined as amounts paid in cash to a qualified basic research organization, such as a college or university or a tax-exempt organization operated primarily to conduct scientific research.

Basic research is defined generally as any original investigation for the advancement of scientific knowledge not having a specific commercial objective. The definition excludes basic research conducted outside the United States and basic research in the social sciences, arts, or humanities. This reflects the intent of Congress to encourage high-tech research in the United States.

The calculation of this additional credit for basic research expenditures is complex and is based on expenditures in excess of a specially defined base amount.[11] The portion of the basic research expenditures not in excess of the base amount is treated as a part of the qualifying expenditures for purposes of the regular credit for incremental research activities.

---

[9] § 174. Also refer to the discussion of rules for deducting research and experimental expenditures in Chapter 6.

[10] § 280C(c).

[11] § 41(e).

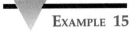

EXAMPLE 15

Orange Corporation, a qualifying corporation, pays $75,000 to a university for basic research. Assume that Orange's base amount for the basic research credit is $50,000. The basic research activities credit allowed is $5,000 [($75,000 – $50,000) × 20%]. The $50,000 of basic research expenditures that equals the base amount are treated as research expenses for purposes of the regular incremental research activities credit. ▼

LOW-INCOME HOUSING CREDIT

To encourage building owners to make affordable housing available for low-income individuals, Congress has made a credit available to owners of qualified low-income housing projects.[12]

More than any other, the **low-income housing credit** is influenced by nontax factors. For example, certification of the property by the appropriate state or local agency authorized to provide low-income housing credits is required. These credits are issued based on a nationwide allocation.

The amount of the credit is based on the qualified basis of the property. The qualified basis depends on the number of units rented to low-income tenants. Tenants are low-income tenants if their income does not exceed a specified percentage of the area median gross income. The amount of the credit is determined by multiplying the qualified basis by the applicable percentage; the credit is allowed over a 10-year period if the property continues to meet the required conditions.

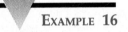

EXAMPLE 16

Sarah spends $100,000 to build a qualified low-income housing project completed January 1, 1996. The entire project is rented to low-income families. The credit rate for property placed in service during January 1996 is 8.90%.[13] Sarah may claim a credit of $8,400 ($100,000 × 8.40%) in 1996 and in each of the following nine years. Generally, first-year credits are prorated based on the date the project is placed in service. A full year's credit is taken in each of the next nine years, and any remaining first-year credit is claimed in the eleventh year. ▼

Recapture of a portion of the credit may be required if the number of units set aside for low-income tenants falls below a minimum threshold, if the taxpayer disposes of the property or the interest in it, or if the taxpayer's amount at risk decreases.

ETHICAL CONSIDERATIONS

A Win-Win Situation or an Incalculable Loss?

John and Susie rent a unit at an apartment complex owned by Mitch Brown, who has been Susie's friend since they attended business school together. One day Mitch told John and Susie about the thousands of tax dollars that he has saved by claiming the low-income housing credit for his investment in the apartment complex. Susie was pleased that Mitch had reduced his tax burden because she believes that the government rarely uses its resources wisely. Inadvertently, though, Mitch let slip that the complex "qualified" for the credit only because he overstated the percentage of low-income tenants living in the facility. Mitch admitted that by claiming that John and Susie were low-income tenants (even though they weren't), the percentage of low-income tenants was just enough for Mitch to

[12] § 42.
[13] Rev.Rul. 96–6, I.R.B. No. 2, 6. The rate is subject to adjustment every month by the IRS.

"qualify" for the credit. Mitch said that because John and Susie were his friends, he was passing along some of his tax savings to them in the form of lower rent.

John and Susie know that if they report Mitch, he will not only lose the economic benefit of the credit, but he will also have legal troubles. Further, if Mitch were to be sentenced to prison for the tax fraud, his children would necessarily become dependent on the state. In addition, John and Susie would have to pay higher rent. Evaluate the courses of action available to John and Susie.

DISABLED ACCESS CREDIT

The **disabled access credit** is designed to encourage small businesses to make their businesses more accessible to disabled individuals. The credit is available for any eligible access expenditures paid or incurred by an eligible small business. The credit is calculated at the rate of 50 percent of the eligible expenditures that exceed $250 but do not exceed $10,250. Thus, the maximum amount for the credit is $5,000 ($10,000 × 50%).[14]

An *eligible small business* is one that during the previous year either had gross receipts of $1 million or less or had no more than 30 full-time employees. An eligible business can include a sole proprietorship, partnership, regular corporation, or S corporation.

Eligible access expenditures are generally any reasonable and necessary amounts that are paid or incurred to make certain changes to facilities. These changes must involve the removal of architectural, communication, physical, or transportation barriers that would otherwise make a business inaccessible to disabled and handicapped individuals. Examples of qualifying projects include installing ramps, widening doorways, and adding raised markings on elevator control buttons. However, eligible expenditures do *not* include amounts that are paid or incurred in connection with any facility that has been placed into service after the enactment (November 5, 1990) of the provision.

To the extent a disabled access credit is available, no deduction or credit is allowed under any other provision of the tax law. The adjusted basis for depreciation is reduced by the amount of the credit.

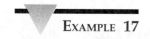

EXAMPLE 17

This year Red, Inc., an eligible business, made $11,000 of capital improvements to business realty that had been placed in service in June 1990. The expenditures were intended to make Red's business more accessible to the disabled and were considered eligible expenditures for purposes of the disabled access credit. The amount of the credit is $5,000 [($10,250 – $250) × 50%]. Although $11,000 of eligible expenditures were incurred, only the excess of $10,250 over $250 qualifies for the credit. Further, the depreciable basis of the capital improvement is $6,000 because the basis must be reduced by the amount of the credit [$11,000 (cost) – $5,000 (amount of the credit)]. ▼

OTHER TAX CREDITS

4 **LEARNING OBJECTIVE**
Describe several other tax credits that are available primarily to individual taxpayers.

EARNED INCOME CREDIT

The **earned income credit,** which has been a part of the law for many years, consistently has been justified as a means of providing tax equity to the working

---

[14]§ 44.

▼ **TABLE 11-2**
Earned Income Credit and
Phase-out Percentages

Tax Year	Number of Qualifying Children	Maximum Earned Income	Credit Percentage	Phase-out Begins	Phase-out Percentage	Phase-out Ends
1996	One child	$6,330	34	$11,610	15.98	$25,078
	Two or more children	8,890	40	11,610	21.06	28,495
1995	One child	6,160	34	11,290	15.98	24,396
	Two or more children	8,640	36	11,290	20.22	26,673

poor. More recently, the credit has also been designed to help offset regressive taxes that are a part of our tax system, such as the gasoline and Social Security taxes. In addition, the credit has been intended to encourage economically disadvantaged individuals to become contributing members of the workforce.[15] Not only is the current version of the earned income credit more generous than in previous years, it is also touted as being easier to compute.

In 1996, the earned income credit is determined by multiplying a maximum amount of earned income by the appropriate credit percentage (see Table 11–2). Generally, earned income includes employee compensation and net earnings from self-employment but excludes items such as interest, dividends, pension benefits, and alimony. If a taxpayer has children, the credit percentage used in the calculation depends on the number of qualifying children. Thus, in 1996, the maximum earned income credit for a taxpayer with one qualifying child is $2,152 ($6,330 × 34%) and $3,556 ($8,890 × 40%) for a taxpayer with two or more qualifying children. However, the maximum earned income credit is phased out completely if the taxpayer's earned income or AGI exceeds certain thresholds as shown in Table 11–2. To the extent that the greater of earned income or AGI exceeds $11,610 in 1996, the difference, multiplied by the appropriate phase-out percentage, is subtracted from the maximum earned income credit.

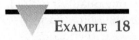

EXAMPLE 18

In 1996, Grace, who otherwise qualifies for the earned income credit, receives wages of $14,000 and has no other income. She has one qualifying child. Grace's earned income credit is $2,152 ($6,330 × 34%) reduced by $382 [($14,000 – $11,610) × 15.98%]. Thus, Grace's earned income credit is $1,770. If Grace has two or more qualifying children, the calculation would produce a credit of $3,556 ($8,890 × 40%) reduced by $503 [($14,000 – $11,610) × 21.06%]. Thus, Grace's earned income credit would be $3,053. ▼

Earned Income Credit Table. It is not necessary to compute the credit as was done in Example 18. As part of the tax simplification process, the IRS issues an Earned Income Credit Table for the determination of the appropriate amount of the earned income credit. This table and a worksheet are included in the instructions to both Form 1040 and Form 1040A.

Eligibility Requirements. *Eligibility* for the credit may depend not only on the taxpayer meeting the earned income and AGI thresholds, but on whether he or she has a qualifying child. A *qualifying child* must meet the following tests:

---
[15] § 32.

- *Relationship test.* The individual must be a son, daughter, descendant of the taxpayer's son or daughter, stepson, stepdaughter, or an eligible foster child of the taxpayer. A legally adopted child of the taxpayer is considered the same as a child by blood.
- *Residency test.* The qualifying child must share the taxpayer's principal place of abode, which must be located within the United States, for more than one-half of the tax year of the taxpayer. Temporary absences (e.g., due to illness or education) are disregarded for purposes of this test. For foster children, however, the child must share the taxpayer's home for the entire year.
- *Age test.* The child must not have reached the age of 19 (24 in the case of a full-time student) as of the end of the tax year. In addition, a child who is permanently and totally disabled at any time during the year is considered to meet the age test.

In addition to being available for taxpayers with qualifying children, the earned income credit is also available to certain *workers without children*. However, this provision is available only to taxpayers aged 25 through 64 who cannot be claimed as a dependent on another taxpayer's return. The credit is calculated on a maximum earned income of $4,220 times 7.65 percent and reduced by 7.65 percent of earned income over $5,280. This credit is phased out completely at $9,500.

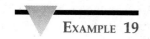

EXAMPLE 19

Walt, who is single, 28 years of age, and is not claimed as a dependent on anyone else's return, earns $6,500 during 1996. Even though he does not have any qualifying children, he qualifies for the earned income credit. His credit is $323 ($4,220 × 7.65%) reduced by $93 [($6,500 − $5,280) × 7.65%]. Thus, Walt's earned income credit is $230. If, instead, Walt's earned income is $4,900, his earned income credit is $323. In this situation, there is no phase-out of the maximum credit because his earned income is not in excess of $5,280. ▼

Advance Payment.   The earned income credit is a form of negative income tax (a refundable credit for taxpayers who do not have a tax liability). An eligible individual may elect to receive advance payments of the earned income credit from his or her employer (rather than receiving the credit from the IRS upon filing the tax return). The amount that can be received in advance is limited to 60 percent of the credit that is available to a taxpayer with only one qualifying child. If this election is made, the taxpayer must file a certificate of eligibility (Form W–5) with his or her employer and *must* file a tax return for the year the income is earned.

TAX CREDIT FOR ELDERLY OR DISABLED TAXPAYERS

The credit for the elderly was originally enacted in 1954 as the retirement income credit to provide tax relief on retirement income for individuals who were not receiving substantial benefits from tax-free Social Security payments.[16]

Currently, the **tax credit for the elderly or disabled** applies to the following:

- Taxpayers age 65 or older.
- Taxpayers under age 65 who are retired with a permanent and total disability and who have disability income from a public or private employer on account of the disability.

---

[16] § 22. This credit is not subject to indexation.

"EARNED INCOME CREDIT" OR "EASY INCOME FOR CHEATS"?

The earned income credit was designed to mitigate the effects of the regressive tax system on low-income taxpayers and to encourage individuals to seek work rather than welfare. Currently, however, the benefits the credit provides are being underused and abused.

To be considered a success, the earned income credit would have to be used by those persons it is intended to help. For example, workers who have a qualifying child and income below a certain amount are allowed to receive advance payment of the credit. However, less than 1 percent of qualifying Americans take advantage of this advance payment opportunity. Some commentators contend that the provisions, which have been changed 10 times since 1976, have become overly complex, difficult to comply with, and almost unusable by the low-income workers the credit is intended to aid. Estimates show that 14 percent of persons qualifying for the credit fail to claim it.

On the other hand, others who don't qualify have found the lure of the credit too good to pass up. In a recent IRS study, one-half of the electronically filed returns that claimed the earned income credit contained errors suspected to be intentional. In fact, some of the tax fraud schemes involving the credit have been initiated by persons in prison. One IRS investigation uncovered a scam operating out of the Maine Correctional Center. A dozen current and former inmates were indicted for improperly seeking refunds for earned income credit claims. Another taxpayer convicted of cheating the government by improperly using the credit testified before Congress that the earned income tax credit could stand for "easy income for cheats!"

The *maximum* allowable credit is $1,125 (15% × $7,500 of qualifying income), but the credit will be less for a taxpayer who receives Social Security benefits or has AGI exceeding specified amounts. Under these circumstances, the base used in the credit computation is reduced. Many taxpayers receive Social Security benefits or have AGI high enough to reduce the base for the credit to zero.

The eligibility requirements and the tax computation are somewhat complicated. Consequently, an individual may elect to have the IRS compute his or her tax and the amount of the tax credit.

The credit generally is based on an initial amount (referred to as the *base amount*) and the filing status of the taxpayer in accordance with Table 11–3. To qualify for the credit, married taxpayers who live together must file a joint return. For taxpayers under age 65 who are retired on permanent and total disability, the base amounts could be less than those shown in Table 11–3 because these amounts are limited to taxable disability income.

This initial base amount is *reduced* by (1) Social Security, Railroad Retirement, and certain excluded pension benefits and (2) one-half of the taxpayer's AGI in excess of a threshold amount, which is a function of the taxpayer's filing status. The credit may be calculated using the procedure presented in the following template:

Base amount ($3,750, $5,000, or $7,500—see Table 11–3)		_____
Less: Qualifying nontaxable benefits	_____	
One-half of excess of AGI over: $7,500 for single, head of household, or surviving spouse taxpayers $10,000 for married taxpayers $5,000 for married taxpayers filing separately	_____	
Total reductions		_____
Balance subject to credit		_____
Multiply balance subject to credit by 15%—this is the tax credit allowed		_____

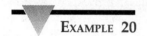

EXAMPLE 20

Paul and Peggy, husband and wife, are both over age 65 and received Social Security benefits of $2,400 in the current year. On a joint return, they reported AGI of $14,000.

Base amount ($3,750, $5,000, or $7,500—see Table 11–3)		$ 7,500
Less: Qualifying nontaxable benefits	$2,400	
One-half of excess of AGI over: $7,500 for single, head of household, or surviving spouse taxpayers $10,000 for married taxpayers $5,000 for married taxpayers filing separately	2,000	
Total reductions		(4,400)
Balance subject to credit		$ 3,100
Multiply balance subject to credit by 15%—this is the tax credit allowed		$ 465

Schedule R of Form 1040 (see Appendix B) is used to calculate and report the credit.

FOREIGN TAX CREDIT

Both individual taxpayers and corporations may claim a tax credit for foreign income tax paid on income earned and subject to tax in another country or a U.S. possession.[17] As an alternative, a taxpayer may claim a deduction instead of a credit.[18] In most instances, the **foreign tax credit (FTC)** is advantageous since it provides a direct offset against the tax liability.

The purpose of the FTC is to mitigate double taxation since income earned in a foreign country is subject to both U.S. and foreign taxes. However, the ceiling limitation formula may result in some form of double taxation or taxation at rates in excess of U.S. rates when the foreign tax rates are higher than the U.S. rates. This is a distinct possibility because U.S. tax rates are lower than those of many foreign countries.

Other special tax treatments applicable to taxpayers working outside the United States include the foreign earned income exclusion (refer to Chapter 4) and limitations on deducting expenses of employees working outside the United

---

[17] Section 27 provides for the credit, but the qualifications and calculation procedure for the credit are contained in §§ 901–908.

[18] § 164.

▼ **TABLE 11–3**
Base Amounts for Tax Credit for
Elderly or Disabled Taxpayers

Status	Base Amount
Single, head of household, or surviving spouse	$5,000
Married, joint return, only one spouse qualified	5,000
Married, joint return, both spouses qualified	7,500
Married, separate returns, spouses live apart the entire year	3,750 each

States (refer to Chapter 8). Recall from the earlier discussion that a taxpayer may not take advantage of *both* the FTC and the foreign earned income exclusion.

Computation. Taxpayers are required to compute the FTC based upon an overall limitation.[19] The FTC allowed is the *lesser* of the foreign taxes imposed or the *overall limitation* determined according to the following formula:

$$\frac{\text{Foreign-source taxable income}}{\text{Worldwide taxable income}} \times \begin{array}{c}\text{U.S. tax}\\\text{before FTC}\end{array}$$

For individual taxpayers, worldwide taxable income in the overall limitation formula is determined *before* personal and dependency exemptions are deducted.

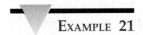

EXAMPLE 21

In 1996, Carlos, a calendar year taxpayer, has $10,000 of income from Country Y, which imposes a 15% tax, and $20,000 from Country Z, which imposes a 50% tax. He has taxable income of $59,800 from within the United States, is married filing a joint return, and claims two dependency exemptions. Thus, although Carlos's taxable income for purposes of determining U.S. tax is $89,800, taxable income amounts used in the limitation formula are not reduced by personal and dependency exemptions. Thus, for this purpose, taxable income is $100,000 [$89,800 + (4 × $2,550)]. Assume that Carlos's U.S. tax before the credit is $19,931. Overall limitation:

$$\frac{\text{Foreign-source taxable income}}{\text{Worldwide taxable income}} = \frac{\$30,000}{\$100,000} \times \$19,931 = \$5,979$$

In this case, $5,979 is allowed as the FTC because this amount is less than the $11,500 of foreign taxes imposed [$1,500 (Country Y) + $10,000 (Country Z)]. ▼

Thus, the overall limitation may result in some of the foreign income being subjected to double taxation. Unused FTCs [e.g., the $5,521 ($11,500 – $5,979) from Example 21] can be carried back two years and forward five years.[20]

Only foreign income taxes, war profits taxes, and excess profits taxes (or taxes paid in lieu of such taxes) qualify for the credit. In determining whether or not a tax is an income tax, U.S. criteria are applied. Thus, value added taxes (VAT), severance taxes, property taxes, and sales taxes do not qualify because they are not regarded as taxes on income. Such taxes may be deductible, however.

CREDIT FOR CHILD AND DEPENDENT CARE EXPENSES

A credit is allowed to taxpayers who incur employment-related expenses for child or dependent care.[21] The **credit for child and dependent care expenses** is a specified percentage of expenses incurred to enable the taxpayer to work or to

---

[19]§ 904.
[20]§ 904(c) and Reg. § 1.904–2(g), Example 1.

[21]§ 21.

seek employment. Expenses on which the credit for child and dependent care expenses is based are subject to limitations.

Eligibility.   To be eligible for the credit, an individual must maintain a household for either of the following:

- A dependent under age 13.
- A dependent or spouse who is physically or mentally incapacitated.

Generally, married taxpayers must file a joint return to obtain the credit. The credit may also be claimed by the custodial parent for a nondependent child under age 13 if the noncustodial parent is allowed to claim the child as a dependent under a pre-1985 divorce agreement or under a waiver in the case of a post-1984 agreement.

Eligible Employment-Related Expenses.   Eligible expenses include amounts paid for household services and care of a qualifying individual that are incurred to enable the taxpayer to be employed. Child and dependent care expenses include expenses incurred in the home, such as payments for a housekeeper. Out-of-the-home expenses incurred for the care of a dependent under the age of 13 also qualify for the credit. In addition, out-of-the-home expenses incurred for an older dependent or spouse who is physically or mentally incapacitated qualify for the credit if that person regularly spends at least eight hours each day in the taxpayer's household. This makes the credit available to taxpayers who keep handicapped older children and elderly relatives in the home instead of institutionalizing them. Out-of-the-home expenses incurred for services provided by a dependent care center will qualify only if the center complies with all applicable laws and regulations of a state or unit of local government.

Child care payments to a relative are eligible for the credit unless the relative is a dependent of the taxpayer or the taxpayer's spouse or is a child (under age 19) of the taxpayer.

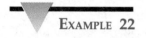

EXAMPLE 22   Wilma is an employed mother of an eight-year-old child. She pays her mother, Rita, $1,500 per year to care for the child after school. Wilma does not claim Rita as a dependent. Wilma pays her daughter Eleanor, age 17, $900 for the child's care during the summer. Of these amounts, only the $1,500 paid to Rita qualifies as employment-related child care expenses. ▼

Earned Income Ceiling.   The total for qualifying employment-related expenses is limited to an individual's earned income. For married taxpayers, this limitation applies to the spouse with the *lesser* amount of earned income. Special rules are provided for taxpayers with nonworking spouses who are disabled or are full-time students. If a nonworking spouse is physically or mentally disabled or is a full-time student, he or she is *deemed* to have earned income for purposes of this limitation. The deemed amount is $200 per month if there is one qualifying individual in the household or $400 per month if there are two or more qualifying individuals in the household. In the case of a student-spouse, the student's income is *deemed* to be earned only for the months that the student is enrolled on a full-time basis at an educational institution.

Calculation of the Credit.   In general, the credit is equal to a percentage of *unreimbursed* employment-related expenses up to $2,400 for one qualifying individual and $4,800 for two or more individuals. The credit rate varies between 20 percent and 30 percent, depending on the taxpayer's AGI. The following chart shows the applicable percentage for taxpayers as AGI increases:

Adjusted Gross Income		
Over	But Not Over	Applicable Rate of Credit
$ 0	$10,000	30%
10,000	12,000	29%
12,000	14,000	28%
14,000	16,000	27%
16,000	18,000	26%
18,000	20,000	25%
20,000	22,000	24%
22,000	24,000	23%
24,000	26,000	22%
26,000	28,000	21%
28,000	No limit	20%

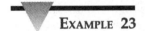

EXAMPLE 23

Nancy, who has two children under age 13, worked full-time while her spouse, Ron, was attending college for 10 months during the year. Nancy earned $21,000 and incurred $5,000 of child care expenses. Ron is *deemed* to be fully employed and to have earned $400 for each of the 10 months (or a total of $4,000). Since Nancy and Ron have AGI of $21,000, they are allowed a credit rate of 24%. Nancy and Ron are limited to $4,000 in qualified child care expenses (the lesser of $4,800 or $4,000). Therefore, they are entitled to a tax credit of $960 (24% × $4,000) for the year. ▼

Dependent Care Assistance Program. Recall from Chapter 4 that a taxpayer is allowed an exclusion from gross income for a limited amount reimbursed for child or dependent care expenses. However, the taxpayer is not allowed both an exclusion from income and a child and dependent care credit on the same amount. The $2,400 and $4,800 ceilings for allowable child and dependent care expenses are reduced dollar for dollar by the amount of reimbursement.[22]

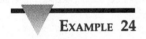

EXAMPLE 24

Assume the same facts as in Example 23, except that of the $5,000 paid for child care, Nancy was reimbursed $2,500 by her employer under a qualified dependent care assistance program. Under the employer's plan, the reimbursement reduces Nancy's taxable wages. Thus, Nancy and Ron have AGI of $18,500 ($21,000 − $2,500). The maximum amount of child care expenses for two or more dependents of $4,800 is reduced by the $2,500 reimbursement, resulting in a tax credit of $575 [25% × ($4,800 − $2,500)]. ▼

Reporting Requirements. The credit is claimed by completing and filing Form 2441, Credit for Child and Dependent Care Expenses (see Appendix B).

ETHICAL CONSIDERATIONS

Using the Credit for Child and Dependent Care Expenses

Your friends, Bob and Carol, have hired a child care provider to come into their home for three hours a day to care for their child while they both are at work. The child care provider, Delores, charges $1,800 for her services for the year. Bob and Carol learn

---

[22] § 21(c).

that up to $2,400 of qualifying expenditures will generate a credit for child and dependent care expenses and that qualifying expenditures can include payments for housecleaning services. As a result, they ask Delores whether she would be interested in working several hours more per week, after Bob returns from work, for the sole purpose of cleaning the house. Delores seems interested. For Bob and Carol, the net cost of the additional services would be $480 [$600 – ($600 × 20%)] due to the availability of the tax credit.

You learn of Bob and Carol's opportunity, but think it is unfair. If you hired Delores to perform similar housecleaning services, your net cost would be $600 and not $480 because you do not qualify for the credit. You are not sure that Bob and Carol should "take advantage" of the system in this way. How do you suppose Bob and Carol will feel, or should feel, about this "abuse" if you approach them?

TAX PLANNING
CONSIDERATIONS

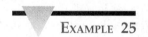
5   **LEARNING OBJECTIVE**
Identify tax planning
opportunities related to tax
credits.

FOREIGN TAX CREDIT

A U.S. citizen or resident working abroad (commonly referred to as an *expatriate*) may elect to take either a foreign tax credit or the foreign earned income exclusion. In cases where the income tax of a foreign country is higher than the U.S. income tax, the credit choice usually is preferable. If the reverse is true, electing the foreign earned income exclusion probably reduces the overall tax burden.

Unfortunately, the choice between the credit and the earned income exclusion is not without some limitations. The election of the foreign earned income exclusion, once made, can be revoked for a later year. However, once revoked, the earned income exclusion will not be available for a period of five years unless the IRS consents to an earlier date. This will create a dilemma for expatriates whose job assignments over several years shift between low- and high-bracket countries.

EXAMPLE 25

In 1995, Ira, a calendar year taxpayer, is sent by his employer to Saudi Arabia (a low-tax country). For 1995, therefore, Ira elects the foreign earned income exclusion. In 1996, Ira's employer transfers him to France (a high-tax country). Accordingly, he revokes the foreign earned income exclusion election for 1996 and chooses instead to use the foreign tax credit. If Ira is transferred back to Saudi Arabia (or any other low-tax country) within five years, he no longer may utilize the foreign earned income exclusion. ▼

CREDIT FOR CHILD AND DEPENDENT CARE EXPENSES

A taxpayer may incur employment-related expenses that also qualify as medical expenses (e.g., a nurse is hired to provide in-the-home care for an ill and incapacitated dependent parent). Such expenses may be either deducted as medical expenses (subject to the 7.5 percent limitation) or utilized in determining the credit for child and dependent care expenses. If the credit for child and dependent care expenses is chosen and the employment-related expenses exceed the limitation ($2,400, $4,800, or earned income, as the case may be), the excess may be considered a medical expense. If, however, the taxpayer chooses to deduct qualified employment-related expenses as medical expenses, any portion that is not deductible because of the 7.5 percent limitation may not be used in computing the credit for child and dependent care expenses.

EXAMPLE 26

Alicia, a single taxpayer, has the following tax position for the current tax year.

CONCEPT SUMMARY 11–1

Tax Credits

Credit	Computation	Comments
Tax withheld on wages (§ 31)	Amount is reported to employee on W–2 form.	Refundable credit.
Earned income (§ 32)	Amount is determined by reference to Earned Income Credit Table published by IRS. Computations of underlying amounts in Earned Income Credit Table are illustrated in Example 18.	Refundable credit. A form of negative income tax to assist low-income taxpayers. Earned income and AGI must be less than certain threshold amounts. Generally, one or more qualifying children must reside with the taxpayer.
Child and dependent care (§ 21)	Rate ranges from 20% to 30% depending on AGI. Maximum base for credit is $2,400 for one qualifying individual, $4,800 for two or more.	Nonrefundable personal credit. No carryback or carryforward. Benefits taxpayers who incur employment-related child or dependent care expenses in order to work or seek employment. Eligible dependents include children under age 13 or dependent (any age) or spouse who is physically or mentally incapacitated.
Elderly or disabled (§ 22)	15% of sum of base amount minus reductions for (a) Social Security and other nontaxable benefits and (b) excess AGI. Base amount is fixed by law (e.g., $5,000 for a single taxpayer).	Nonrefundable personal credit. No carryback or carryforward. Provides relief for taxpayers not receiving substantial tax-free retirement benefits.
Foreign tax (§ 27)	Foreign income/total worldwide taxable income × U.S. tax = overall limitation. Lesser of foreign taxes imposed or overall limitation.	Nonrefundable credit. Unused credits may be carried back two years and forward five years. Purpose is to prevent double taxation of foreign income.
General business (§ 38)	May not exceed net income tax minus the greater of tentative minimum tax or 25% of net regular tax liability that exceeds $25,000.	Nonrefundable credit. Components include investment tax credits, tax credit for rehabilitation expenditures, business energy credit, research activities credit, low-income housing credit, and disabled access credit. Unused credit may be carried back 3 years and forward 15 years. FIFO method applies to carryovers, carrybacks, and credits earned during current year.
Investment (§ 46)	Qualifying investment times energy percentage or rehabilitation percentage, depending on type of property. Part of general business credit and subject to its limitations.	Nonrefundable credit. Part of general business credit and therefore subject to same carryback, carryover, and FIFO rules. Energy percentage is 10%. Regular rehabilitation rate is 10%; rate for certified historic structures is 20%.

Credit	Computation	Comments
Research activities (§ 41)	Incremental credit is 20% of excess of computation year expenditures minus the base amount. Basic research credit is allowed to certain corporations for 20% of cash payments to qualified organizations that exceed a specially calculated base amount. To qualify for the credit, research expenditures must be made prior to June 30, 1995.	Nonrefundable credit. Part of general business credit and therefore subject to same carryback, carryover, and FIFO rules. Purpose is to encourage high-tech research in the United States.
Low-income housing (§ 42)	Appropriate rate times eligible basis (portion of project attributable to low-income units).	Nonrefundable credit. Part of general business credit and therefore subject to same carryback, carryover, and FIFO rules. Credit is available each year for 10 years. Recapture may apply. Purpose is to encourage construction of housing for low-income individuals.
Disabled access (§ 44)	Credit is 50% of eligible access expenditures that exceed $250, but do not exceed $10,250. Maximum credit is $5,000.	Nonrefundable credit. Part of general business credit and therefore subject to same carryback, carryover, and FIFO rules. Available only to eligible small businesses. Purpose is to encourage small businesses to become more accessible to disabled individuals.

Adjusted gross income		$30,000
Potential itemized deductions *from* AGI—		
Other than medical expenses	$3,500	
Medical expenses	6,000	$ 9,500

All of Alicia's medical expenses were incurred to provide nursing care for her disabled father while she was working. The father lives with Alicia and qualifies as her dependent. ▼

What should Alicia do in this situation? One approach would be to use $2,400 of the nursing care expenses to obtain the maximum credit for child and dependent care expenses allowed of $480 (20% × $2,400). The balance of these expenses should be claimed as medical expenses. After a reduction of 7.5 percent of AGI, this would produce a medical expense deduction of $1,350 [$3,600 (remaining medical expenses) – (7.5% × $30,000)].

Another approach would be to claim the full $6,000 as a medical expense and forgo the credit for child and dependent care expenses. After the 7.5 percent adjustment of $2,250 (7.5% × $30,000), a deduction of $3,750 remains.

The choice, then, is between a credit of $480 plus a deduction of $1,350 or a credit of $0 plus a deduction of $3,750. Which is better, of course, depends on the relative tax savings involved.

One of the traditional goals of *family tax planning* is to minimize the total tax burden within the family unit. With proper planning and implementation, the credit for child and dependent care expenses can be used to help achieve this goal. For example, payments to certain relatives for the care of qualifying dependents and children qualify for the credit if the care provider is *not* a dependent of the taxpayer or the taxpayer's spouse or is *not* a child (under age 19) of the taxpayer. Thus, if the care provider is in a lower tax bracket than the taxpayer, the following benefits result:

- Income is shifted to a lower-bracket family member.
- The taxpayer qualifies for the credit for child and dependent care expenses.

In addition, the goal of minimizing the family income tax liability can be enhanced in some other situations, but only if the credit's limitations are recognized and avoided. For example, tax savings may still be enjoyed even if the qualifying expenditures incurred by a cash basis taxpayer have already reached the annual ceiling ($2,400 or $4,800). To the extent that any additional payments can be shifted into future tax years, the benefit from the credit may be preserved on these excess expenditures.

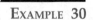

EXAMPLE 30   Andre, a calendar year and cash basis taxpayer, has spent $2,400 by December 1 on qualifying child care expenditures for his dependent 11-year-old son. The $200 that is due the care provider for child care services rendered in December does not generate a tax credit benefit if the amount is paid in the current year because the $2,400 ceiling has been reached. However, if the payment can be delayed until the next year, the total credit over the two-year period for which Andre is eligible may be increased. ▼

A similar shifting of expenditures to a subsequent year may be wise if the potential credit otherwise generated would exceed the tax liability available to absorb the credit.

KEY TERMS

Business energy credits, 11–9

Credit for child and dependent care expenses, 11–19

Disabled access credit, 11–14

Earned income credit, 11–14

Foreign tax credit (FTC), 11–18

General business credit, 11–5

Low-income housing credit, 11–13

Nonrefundable credits, 11–4

Refundable credits, 11–4

Rehabilitation expenditures credit, 11–7

Rehabilitation expenditures credit recapture, 11–8

Research activities credit, 11–9

Tax credits, 11–2

Tax credit for the elderly or disabled, 11–16

PROBLEM MATERIALS

DISCUSSION QUESTIONS

1. Would an individual taxpayer receive greater benefit from deducting an expenditure or from taking a credit equal to 25% of the expenditure?

2. What is a refundable credit? Give examples. What is a nonrefundable credit? Give examples.

3. Discuss the order in which credits are offset against the tax liability. Why is the order in which credits are utilized important?

4. In determining the maximum amount of general business credit allowed an individual taxpayer for a tax year, net income tax, tentative minimum tax, regular tax liability, and net regular tax liability are important concepts.
   a. Define each term.
   b. Using these terms, state the general business credit limitation for an individual taxpayer for the current year.

5. John graduated from college several years ago with high hopes and expectations of enjoying a very successful business career. Almost as soon as he completed his final exams, he borrowed over $250,000 from a local bank (the loan was guaranteed by his parents) in order to make several "hot" investments. The investments, as expected, spun off huge tax losses and tax credits in their early years. More recently, however, John has begun to have doubts as to the wisdom of these investments as they have not begun to generate profits as promised. As a result, he is contemplating selling the investments, at yet another loss. Because his investments have not as yet produced any profits to support his lifestyle, he has been forced to live at home with his parents. Identify the relevant tax issues.

6. Vic is considering the purchase and renovation of an old building. He has heard about the tax credit for rehabilitation expenditures but does not know the specific rules applicable to the credit. He has asked you to explain the most important details to him. What will you tell Vic?

7. If property on which the tax credit for rehabilitation expenditures was claimed is prematurely disposed of or ceases to be qualified property, how is the tax liability affected in the year of the disposition or disqualification?

8. What credit provisions in the tax law were enacted to encourage technological development in the United States?

9. Explain the alternatives a taxpayer has in claiming the deduction and credit for research and experimentation expenditures incurred.

10. Explain the purpose of the disabled access credit and describe the general characteristics of its computation.

11. Identify several examples of the type of structural changes to a building that qualify for the disabled access credit.

12. Which of the following taxpayers are eligible for the earned income credit for the current tax year?
    a. Joe and Marie are married and have a 15-year-old dependent child living with them. Joe earns $8,000 and Marie earns $8,500.
    b. Alan, a single parent, supports his 20-year-old daughter who is a full-time college student. Alan earns $15,000 and has no other income.
    c. Paula, an unmarried 26-year-old taxpayer, earns $8,000 and has no other income. She claims a dependency exemption for her aunt under a multiple support agreement.

13. Is the earned income credit a form of a negative income tax? Why or why not?

14. Individuals who receive substantial Social Security benefits are usually not eligible for the tax credit for the elderly or disabled because these benefits effectively eliminate the base upon which the credit is computed. Explain.

15. What purpose is served by the overall limitation to the foreign tax credit?

16. Do all foreign taxes qualify for the U.S. foreign tax credit? Explain.

17. In general, when would an individual taxpayer find it more beneficial to take advantage of the foreign earned income exclusion rather than the foreign tax credit in computing his or her income tax liability?

18. Ten years ago, Suzanne opened a high-tech business that had its headquarters and research operations in Seattle and its manufacturing facility in Singapore. Because of the competitive nature of the business, Suzanne's firm was forced to pour millions of dollars into research activities involving the most recent technology. Fortunately, the research paid off as evidenced by the astounding 40% annual increase in the business's sales over the past two years. Identify the relevant tax issues.

19. Sally was recently called into the partner's office and offered a one-year assignment in her public accounting firm's Prague office. Realizing Sally will face incremental expenses while in Prague, such as for foreign income taxes and rent, the firm will try to make her "whole" from a financial perspective by increasing her salary to help offset the expenses she will incur while living overseas. If Sally takes the assignment, she will likely rent her personal residence and sell several major tangible assets such as her personal automobile. Identify the relevant tax issues.

20. Gary and Gail are married and have a dependent child eight years of age. Gary earned $15,000 during the current year. Gail, a full-time student for the entire year, was not employed. Gary and Gail believe they are not entitled to the credit for child and dependent care expenses because Gail was not employed. Is this correct? Explain your answer.

21. Polly and her spouse, Leo, file a joint return and expect to report AGI of $125,000 in the current year. Polly's employer offers a child and dependent care reimbursement plan that allows up to $2,500 of qualifying expenses to be reimbursed in exchange for a $2,500 reduction in the employee's salary. Because Polly and Leo have one minor child requiring child care that costs $2,500 each year, she is wondering if she should sign up for the program instead of taking advantage of the credit for child and dependent care expenses. Assuming Polly and Leo are in the 31% tax bracket, analyze the effect of the two alternatives. How would your answer differ if Polly and Leo's AGI was $10,000 instead of $95,000?

22. Discuss the rationale underlying the enactment of the following tax credits:
    a. Tax credit for rehabilitation expenditures.
    b. Low-income housing credit.
    c. Disabled access credit.
    d. Earned income credit.
    e. Foreign tax credit.
    f. Credit for child and dependent care expenses.

23. Sam and Martha have two preschool-age children. On several occasions during the current year, Sam and Martha took out-of-town trips due to Sam's business. While Sam and Martha were out of town, a 14-year-old neighbor cared for the children during the day; at night, they stayed with their grandparents. Sam and Martha had a neighborhood teenager mow their lawn, but only once, because of the damage he did to Martha's flower garden. On a later out-of-town trip, they hired a professional lawn service to mow the lawn. Identify the relevant tax issues.

PROBLEMS

24. Dan has a tentative general business credit of $85,000 for the current year. His net regular tax liability before the general business credit is $95,000; tentative minimum tax is $90,000. Compute Dan's allowable general business credit for the current year.

25. Tan Corporation has the following general business credit carryovers:

1992	$10,000
1993	30,000
1994	10,000
1995	40,000
Total carryovers	$90,000

If the general business credit generated by activities during 1996 equals $90,000 and the total credit allowed during the current year is $160,000 (based on tax liability), what amounts of the current general business credit and carryovers are utilized against the 1996 income tax liability? What is the amount of unused credit carried forward to 1997?

26. In January 1996, Mike acquired an office building in downtown Athens, Georgia, for $300,000; the building was originally constructed in 1932. Of the $300,000 cost, $25,000 was allocated to the land. Mike immediately placed the building into service but quickly realized that substantial renovation would be required to keep and attract new tenants. The renovations, costing $350,000, were of the type that qualify for the rehabilitation credit. The improvements were completed in October 1996.
    a. Compute Mike's rehabilitation tax credit for the year of acquisition.
    b. Determine the cost recovery for 1996.
    c. What is the basis in the property at the end of its first year of use by Mike?

27. In the current year, Diane Lawson (123 Sunview Avenue, Jacksonville, FL 32231) acquires a qualifying historic structure for $250,000 (excluding the cost of land) the current year with full intentions of substantially rehabilitating the building. Write a letter to Diane and a memo to the tax files explaining the computation that determines the rehabilitation tax credit available to her and the impact on the depreciable basis, assuming either $245,000 or $255,000 is incurred for the rehabilitation project. Because Diane must decide whether to pursue the renovation plan costing $245,000 or the one costing $255,000, you should indicate in the letter and the memo the differences in cash flow to Diane arising from the tax consequences associated with the two renovation projects.

28. Matt, a calendar year taxpayer, furnishes the following information. Gross receipts are net of returns and allowances.

	Gross Receipts	Qualified Research Expenses
1995	$180,000	$30,000
1994	170,000	50,000
1993	160,000	35,000
1992	120,000	45,000
1991	120,000	50,000
1990	130,000	35,000
1989	125,000	30,000
1988	120,000	45,000
1987	135,000	40,000
1986	110,000	20,000
1985	95,000	–0–
1984	80,000	30,000

    a. Using the template in the text, determine Matt's incremental research activities credit for 1995.
    b. Matt is in the 28% tax bracket. Determine which approach to the research expenditures and the research activities credit (other than capitalization and subsequent amortization) would provide the greatest tax benefit to Matt.

29. Assume the same facts as in the previous problem, except that Matt incurs $60,000 of qualified research expenditures in 1995. Using the template in the text, compute the incremental research activities credit for 1995.

30. Rose Corporation is an eligible small business for purposes of the disabled access credit. During the year, Rose Corporation makes the following expenditures on a structure originally placed in service in 1984:

Removal of architectural barriers	$4,250
Acquired equipment for disabled persons	3,000
	$7,250

In addition, $3,500 was expended on a building placed in service in the current year, to ensure easy accessibility by disabled individuals. Calculate the amount of the disabled access credit available to Rose Corporation.

31. Ahmed Zinna (16 Southside Drive, Charlotte, NC 28204), one of your clients, owns two retail establishments in downtown Charlotte, North Carolina, and has come to you seeking advice concerning the tax consequences of complying with the Americans with Disabilities Act. He understands that he needs to install various features at his stores (e.g., ramps, doorways, and restrooms that are handicapped accessible) to make them more accessible to disabled individuals. He inquires whether any tax credits will be available to help offset the cost of the necessary changes. He estimates the cost of the planned changes to his facilities as follows:

Location	Projected Cost
Oak Street	$ 4,000
Maple Avenue	12,000

He reminds you that the Oak Street store was constructed in 1995 while the Maple Avenue store is in a building that was constructed in 1902. Ahmed operates his business as a sole proprietorship and has approximately eight employees at each location. Write a letter to Ahmed in which you summarize your conclusions concerning the tax consequences of his proposed capital improvements.

32. Which of the following individuals qualify for the earned income credit for 1996?
   a. Eduardo is single, 19 years of age, and has no dependents. His income consists of $8,000 of wages.
   b. Kate maintains a household for a dependent 12-year-old son and is eligible for head-of-household tax rates. Her income consists of $10,500 of salary and $300 of taxable interest.
   c. Keith and Susan are married and file a joint return. Keith and Susan have no dependents. Their combined income consists of $18,500 of salary and $100 of taxable interest. Adjusted gross income is $18,600.
   d. George is a 26-year-old single taxpayer. He has no dependents and generates earnings of $9,000.

33. Irene, who qualifies for the earned income credit, has two qualifying children who live with her. Irene earns a salary of $14,500 during 1996. Calculate Irene's earned income credit for the year.

34. Vern, a widower, lives in an apartment with his three minor children (ages 3, 4, and 5) whom he supports. Vern earned $19,500 during 1996. He contributed $500 to an IRA and uses the standard deduction. Calculate the amount, if any, of Vern's earned income credit.

35. Joyce, a widow, lives in an apartment with her two minor children (ages 8 and 10) whom she supports. Joyce earns $25,000 during 1996. She uses the standard deduction.
   a. Calculate the amount, if any, of Joyce's earned income credit.
   b. During the year, Joyce is offered a new job that has greater future potential than her current job. If she accepts the job offer, her earnings for the year would be $28,500; however, she will not qualify for the earned income credit. Using after-tax cash-flow calculations, determine whether Joyce should accept the new job offer.

36. Hank, age 67, and Thelma, age 66, are married retirees who received the following income and retirement benefits during the current year:

CHAPTER 11   Tax Credits

Fully taxable pension from Hank's former employer	$ 8,000
Dividends and interest	2,500
Social Security benefits	4,000
	$14,500

Assume Hank and Thelma file a joint return, have no deductions *for* AGI, and do not itemize. Are they eligible for the tax credit for the elderly? If so, calculate the amount of the credit, assuming the credit is not limited by their tax liability.

37. Kim, a U.S. citizen and resident, owns and operates a novelty goods business. During 1996, Kim has taxable income of $100,000, made up as follows: $50,000 from foreign sources and $50,000 from U.S. sources. In calculating taxable income, the standard deduction is used. The income from foreign sources is subject to foreign income taxes of $26,000. For 1996, Kim files a joint return claiming his three children as dependents.
    a. Assuming Kim chooses to claim the foreign taxes as an income tax credit, what is his income tax liability for 1996?
    b. Recently, Kim has become disenchanted with the location of his business and is considering moving his foreign operation to a different country. Based on his research, if he moves his business to his country of choice, all relevant revenues and costs would remain approximately the same except that the income taxes payable to that country would be only $10,000. Given that all of the foreign income taxes paid are available to offset the U.S. tax liability (whether he operates in a high-tax or a low-tax foreign jurisdiction), what impact will this have on his decision regarding the potential move?

38. Blue Corporation, a U.S. corporation, is a manufacturing concern that sells most of its products in the United States. It does, however, do some business in Europe through various branches. During 1996, Blue Corporation had taxable income of $500,000, of which $350,000 was U.S.-sourced and $150,000 was foreign-sourced. Foreign income taxes paid are $45,000. Blue Corporation's U.S. income tax liability before any foreign tax credit is $170,000. What is Blue Corporation's U.S. income tax net of the allowable foreign tax credit?

39. Pat and Jeri are husband and wife, and both are gainfully employed. They have three children under the age of 13. During the current year, Pat earned $60,000, while Jeri earned $4,900. In order for them to work, they paid $5,800 to various unrelated parties to care for their children. Assuming Pat and Jeri file a joint return, what, if any, is their credit for child and dependent care expenses for the current year?

40. Jim and Jill are husband and wife and have two dependent children under the age of 13. They both are gainfully employed and during the current year earned salaries as follows: $12,000 (Jim) and $4,500 (Jill). To care for their children while they work, they pay Megan (Jim's mother) $5,600. Megan does not qualify as a dependent of Jim and Jill. Assuming Jim and Jill file a joint return, what, if any, is their credit for child and dependent care expenses?

41. Kevin and Jane are husband and wife and have one dependent child, age 9. Kevin is a full-time student for all of the current year, while Jane earns $18,000 as a nurse's aid. In order to provide care for their child while Kevin attends classes and Jane works, they pay Sara (Jane's 17-year-old sister) $2,300. Sara is not a dependent of Kevin and Jane. Assuming Kevin and Jane file a joint return, what, if any, is their credit for child and dependent care expenses?

CUMULATIVE PROBLEMS

42. Hal and Wanda Atkins, ages 38 and 36, are married and file a joint return. Their Social Security numbers are 123–32–1232 and 456–65–4321, respectively. Hal and Wanda's household includes Sam, their 10-year-old son, and Fred, who is Hal's 76-year-old father. Sam's Social Security number is 789–87–6543, and Fred's Social Security

number is 123–87–1232. Fred is very ill and has been confined to bed for most of the year. He has no income of his own and is fully supported by Hal and Wanda. Hal and Wanda had the following income and expenses during 1996:

Hal's wages	$ 8,000
Wanda's salary	14,000
Interest from First National Bank	50
Unemployment compensation received by Hal, who was laid off for five months during the year	5,500
Dividends received on January 3, 1997; the corporation mailed the check on December 31, 1996	350
Amounts paid to Nora, Hal's niece, for household help and caring for Sam and Fred while Hal and Wanda were working	5,000
Unreimbursed travel expenses (including meals of $200) incurred by Wanda in connection with her job	1,250
Total itemized deductions (not including any potential deductions mentioned elsewhere in the problem)	6,600
Federal income taxes withheld by their employers	700

Compute net tax payable or refund due for Hal and Wanda for 1996. Suggested software (if available): *TurboTax* or *MacInTax*.

43. Beth R. Jordan lives at 2322 Skyview Road, Mesa, AZ 85202. She is a tax accountant with Mesa Manufacturing Company. She also writes computer software programs for tax practitioners and has a part-time tax practice. Beth, age 35, is single and has no dependents. Her Social Security number is 111–35–2222. She wants to contribute $3 to the Presidential Election Campaign Fund.

During 1995, Beth earned a salary of $50,000 from her employer. She received interest of $290 from Home Federal Savings and Loan and $335 from Home State Bank. She received dividends of $500 from Gray Corporation, $400 from Blue Corporation, and $300 from Orange Corporation.

Beth received a $1,200 income tax refund from the state of Arizona on May 12, 1995. On her 1994 Federal income tax return, she reported total itemized deductions of $6,700, which included $2,000 of state income tax withheld by her employer.

Fees earned from her part-time tax practice in 1995 totaled $3,800. She paid $400 to have the tax returns processed by a computerized tax return service.

On February 1, 1995, Beth bought 500 shares of Gray Corporation common stock for $17.60 a share. On July 16, Beth sold the stock for $15 a share.

Beth bought a used utility vehicle for $3,000 on June 5, 1995. She purchased the vehicle from her brother-in-law, who was unemployed and was in need of cash. On November 2, 1995, she sold the vehicle to a friend for $3,400.

On January 2, 1984, Beth acquired 100 shares of Blue Corporation common stock for $30 a share. She sold the stock on December 19, 1995, for $75 a share.

During 1995, Beth received royalties of $14,000 on a software program she had written. Beth incurred the following expenditures in connection with her software-writing activities:

Cost of microcomputer (100% business use)	$7,000
Cost of printer (100% business use)	2,000
Furniture	3,000
Supplies	650
Fee paid to computer consultant	3,500

Beth elected to expense the maximum portion of the cost of the microcomputer, printer, and furniture allowed under the provisions of § 179. This equipment and furniture were placed in service on January 15, 1995.

Although her employer suggested that Beth attend a convention on current developments in corporate taxation, Beth was not reimbursed for the travel expenses of $1,420 she incurred in attending the convention. The $1,420 included $200 for the cost of meals.

During 1995, Beth paid $300 for prescription medicines and $2,875 in doctor bills, hospital bills, and medical insurance premiums. Her employer withheld state income tax of $1,954. Beth paid real property taxes of $1,766 on her home. Interest on her home mortgage was $3,845, and interest to credit card companies was $320. Beth contributed $20 each week to her church and $10 each week to the United Way. Professional dues and subscriptions totaled $350.

Beth's employer withheld Federal income taxes of $9,500 during 1995. Beth paid estimated taxes of $1,600. What is the amount of Beth's net tax payable or refund due for 1995? If Beth has a tax refund due, she wants to have it credited toward her 1996 income tax. If you use tax forms for your solution, you will need Forms 1040, 2106, and 4562 and Schedules A, B, C, D, and SE. Suggested software (if available): *TurboTax* or *MacInTax*.

Research Problems for this chapter appear at the end of Chapter 28.

12

PROPERTY TRANSACTIONS: DETERMINATION OF GAIN OR LOSS, BASIS CONSIDERATIONS, AND NONTAXABLE EXCHANGES

LEARNING OBJECTIVES

After completing Chapter 12, you should be able to:

1. Understand the computation of realized gain or loss on property dispositions.

2. Distinguish between realized and recognized gain or loss.

3. Apply the recovery of capital doctrine.

4. Explain how basis is determined for various methods of asset acquisition.

5. Describe various loss disallowance provisions.

6. Understand the rationale for nonrecognition (postponement) of gain or loss in certain property transactions.

7. Apply the nonrecognition provisions and basis determination rules for like-kind exchanges.

8. Explain the nonrecognition provisions available on the involuntary conversion of property.

9. Describe the provisions for postponing recognition of gain on the sale and replacement of a personal residence.

10. Discuss the provisions for permanent exclusion of gain on the sale of a personal residence by taxpayers age 55 and older.

11. Identify other nonrecognition provisions contained in the Code.

12. Identify tax planning opportunities related to selected property transactions.

OUTLINE

This chapter and the following chapter are concerned with the income tax consequences of property transactions (the sale or other disposition of property). The following questions are considered with respect to the sale or other disposition of property:

- Is there a realized gain or loss?
- If so, is the gain or loss recognized?
- If the gain or loss is recognized, is it ordinary or capital?
- What is the basis of any replacement property that is acquired?

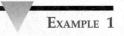

EXAMPLE 1

Alice owns a house that she received from her mother seven months ago. Her mother's cost for the house was $75,000. Alice is considering selling the house to her favorite nephew, Dan, for $75,000. Alice anticipates she will have no gain or loss on the transaction. She comes to you for advice.

As Alice's tax adviser, you need answers to the following questions:

- You are aware that Alice's mother died around the time Alice indicates she received the house from her mother. Did Alice receive the house by gift prior to her mother's death? If so, what was the mother's adjusted basis? If instead Alice inherited the house from her mother, what was the fair market value of the house on the date of her mother's death?
- Was the house Alice's principal residence during the period she owned it and was it her principal residence prior to receiving it from her mother?
- How long did Alice's mother own the house?
- What is the fair market value of the house?
- Does Alice intend for the transaction with Dan to be a sale or part sale and part gift?
- What does Alice intend to do with the sale proceeds?

Once you have the answers to these questions, you can advise Alice on the tax consequences of the proposed transaction. ▼

Chapter 12 discusses the determination of realized and recognized gain or loss and the basis of property. Chapter 13 covers the classification of the recognized gain or loss as ordinary or capital.

DETERMINATION OF GAIN OR LOSS

REALIZED GAIN OR LOSS

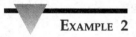

1 LEARNING OBJECTIVE
Understand the computation of realized gain or loss on property dispositions.

Realized gain or loss is measured by the difference between the amount realized from the sale or other disposition of property and the property's adjusted basis on the date of disposition. If the amount realized exceeds the property's adjusted basis, the result is a **realized gain.** Conversely, if the property's adjusted basis exceeds the amount realized, the result is a **realized loss.**[1]

EXAMPLE 2

Tab sells Swan Corporation stock with an adjusted basis of $3,000 for $5,000. Tab's realized gain is $2,000. If Tab had sold the stock for $2,000, he would have had a $1,000 realized loss. ▼

Sale or Other Disposition.   The term *sale or other disposition* is defined broadly in the tax law and includes virtually any disposition of property. Thus, transactions such as trade-ins, casualties, condemnations, thefts, and bond retirements are treated as dispositions of property. The most common disposition of property is through a sale or exchange. The key factor in determining whether a disposition has taken place usually is whether an identifiable event has occurred[2] as opposed to a mere fluctuation in the value of the property.[3]

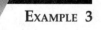

EXAMPLE 3

Lori owns Tan Corporation stock that cost $3,000. The stock has appreciated in value by $2,000 since Lori purchased it. Lori has no realized gain since mere fluctuation in value is not a disposition or identifiable event for tax purposes. Nor would Lori have a realized loss had the stock declined in value by $2,000. ▼

Amount Realized.   The **amount realized** from a sale or other disposition of property is the sum of any money received plus the fair market value of other property received. The amount realized also includes any real property taxes

---

[1] § 1001(a) and Reg. § 1.1001–1(a).
[2] Reg. § 1.1001–1(c)(1).

[3] *Lynch v. Turrish,* 1 USTC ¶18, 3 AFTR 2986, 38 S.Ct. 537 (USSC, 1918).

treated as imposed on the seller that are actually paid by the buyer.[4] The reason for including these taxes in the amount realized is that by paying the taxes, the purchaser is, in effect, paying an additional amount to the seller of the property.

The amount realized also includes any liability on the property disposed of, such as a mortgage debt, if the buyer assumes the mortgage or the property is sold subject to the mortgage.[5] The amount of the liability is included in the amount realized even if the debt is nonrecourse and the amount of the debt is greater than the fair market value of the mortgaged property.[6]

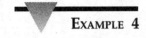

EXAMPLE 4

Barry sells property on which there is a mortgage of $20,000 to Cole for $50,000 cash. Barry's amount realized from the sale is $70,000 if Cole assumes the mortgage or takes the property subject to the mortgage. ▼

The **fair market value** of property received in a sale or other disposition has been defined by the courts as the price at which property will change hands between a willing seller and a willing buyer when neither is compelled to sell or buy.[7] Fair market value is determined by considering the relevant factors in each case.[8] An expert appraiser is often required to evaluate these factors in arriving at fair market value. When the fair market value of the property received cannot be determined, the value of the property surrendered may be used.[9]

In calculating the amount realized, selling expenses such as advertising, commissions, and legal fees relating to the disposition are deducted. The amount realized is the net amount received directly or indirectly by the taxpayer from the disposition of property in the form of cash or anything else of value.

Adjusted Basis.   The **adjusted basis** of property disposed of is the property's original basis adjusted to the date of disposition.[10] Original basis is the cost or other basis of the property on the date the property is acquired by the taxpayer. *Capital additions* increase and *recoveries of capital* decrease the original basis so that on the date of disposition the adjusted basis reflects the unrecovered cost or other basis of the property.[11] Adjusted basis is determined as follows:

> Cost (or other adjusted basis) on date of acquisition
> + Capital additions
> – Capital recoveries
> = Adjusted basis on date of disposition

Capital Additions.   Capital additions include the cost of capital improvements and betterments made to the property by the taxpayer. These expenditures are distinguishable from expenditures for the ordinary repair and maintenance of the property that are neither capitalized nor added to the original basis (refer to Chapter 5). The latter expenditures are deductible in the current taxable year if they are related to business or income-producing property. Amounts representing real property taxes treated as imposed on the seller but paid or assumed by the

---

[4] § 1001(b) and Reg. § 1.1001–1(b). Refer to Chapter 9 for a discussion of this subject.

[5] *Crane v. Comm.,* 47–1 USTC ¶9217, 35 AFTR 776, 67 S.Ct. 1047 (USSC, 1947). Although a legal distinction exists between the direct assumption of a mortgage and taking property subject to a mortgage, the tax consequences in calculating the amount realized are the same.

[6] *Comm. v. Tufts,* 83–1 USTC ¶9328, 51 AFTR2d 83–1132, 103 S.Ct. 1826 (USSC, 1983).

[7] *Comm. v. Marshman,* 60–2 USTC ¶9484, 5 AFTR2d 1528, 279 F.2d 27 (CA–6, 1960).

[8] *O'Malley v. Ames,* 52–1 USTC ¶9361, 42 AFTR 19, 197 F.2d 256 (CA–8, 1952).

[9] *U.S. v. Davis,* 62–2 USTC ¶9509, 9 AFTR2d 1625, 82 S.Ct. 1190 (USSC, 1962).

[10] § 1011(a) and Reg. § 1.1011–1.

[11] § 1016(a) and Reg. § 1.1016–1.

buyer are part of the cost of the property.[12] Any liability on property that is
assumed by the buyer is also included in the buyer's original basis of the property.
The same rule applies if property is acquired subject to a liability. Amortization of
the discount on bonds increases the adjusted basis of the bonds.[13]

Capital Recoveries.   The following are examples of capital recoveries:

1. *Depreciation and cost recovery allowances.* The original basis of depreciable
   property is reduced by the annual depreciation charges (or cost recovery
   allowances) while the property is held by the taxpayer. The amount of
   depreciation that is subtracted from the original basis is the greater of the
   allowed or *allowable* depreciation on an annual basis.[14] In most circumstances, the allowed and allowable depreciation amounts are the same
   (refer to Chapter 7).
2. *Casualties and thefts.* A casualty or theft may result in the reduction of the
   adjusted basis of property.[15] The adjusted basis is reduced by the amount of
   the deductible loss. In addition, the adjusted basis is reduced by the
   amount of insurance proceeds received. However, the receipt of insurance
   proceeds may result in a recognized gain rather than a deductible loss. The
   gain increases the adjusted basis of the property.[16]

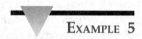

EXAMPLE 5   An insured truck used in a trade or business is destroyed in an accident. The adjusted basis
is $8,000, and the fair market value is $6,500. Insurance proceeds of $6,500 are received. The
amount of the casualty loss is $1,500 ($6,500 insurance proceeds – $8,000 adjusted basis).
The adjusted basis is reduced by the $1,500 casualty loss and the $6,500 of insurance
proceeds received. ▼

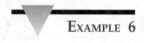

EXAMPLE 6   An insured truck used in a trade or business is destroyed in an accident. The adjusted basis
is $6,500, and the fair market value is $8,000. Insurance proceeds of $8,000 are received. The
amount of the casualty gain is $1,500 ($8,000 insurance proceeds – $6,500 adjusted basis).
The adjusted basis is increased by the $1,500 casualty gain and is reduced by the $8,000 of
insurance proceeds received ($6,500 basis before casualty + $1,500 casualty gain – $8,000
insurance proceeds = $0 basis). ▼

3. *Certain corporate distributions.* A corporate distribution to a shareholder that
   is not taxable is treated as a return of capital, and it reduces the basis of the
   shareholder's stock in the corporation.[17] For example, if a corporation
   makes a cash distribution to its shareholders and has no earnings and
   profits, the distributions are treated as a return of capital. Once the basis of
   the stock is reduced to zero, the amount of any subsequent distributions is
   a capital gain if the stock is a capital asset.
4. *Amortizable bond premium.* The basis in a bond purchased at a premium is
   reduced by the amortizable portion of the bond premium.[18] Investors in
   taxable bonds may *elect* to amortize the bond premium, but the premium
   on tax-exempt bonds *must be* amortized.[19] The amount of the amortized
   premium on taxable bonds is permitted as an interest deduction. Therefore,

[12] Reg. §§ 1.1001–1(b)(2) and 1.1012–1(b). Refer to Chapter 9 for a
discussion of this subject.

[13] See Chapter 13 for a discussion of bond discount and the related
amortization.

[14] § 1016(a)(2) and Reg. § 1.1016–3(a)(1)(i).

[15] Refer to Chapter 6 for the discussion of casualties and thefts.

[16] Reg. § 1.1016–6(a).

[17] § 1016(a)(4) and Reg. § 1.1016–5(a).

[18] § 1016(a)(5) and Reg. § 1.1016–5(b). The accounting treatment of
bond premium amortization is the same as for tax purposes. The
amortization results in a decrease in the bond investment account.

[19] § 171(c).

the election produces the opportunity for an annual interest deduction to offset ordinary income in exchange for a larger capital gain or smaller capital loss on the disposition of the bond. No such interest deduction is permitted for tax-exempt bonds.

The amortization deduction is allowed for taxable bonds because the premium is viewed as a cost of earning the taxable interest from the bonds. The reason the basis of taxable bonds is reduced is that the amortization deduction is a recovery of the cost or basis of the bonds. The basis of tax-exempt bonds is reduced even though the amortization is not allowed as a deduction. No amortization deduction is permitted on tax-exempt bonds since the interest income is exempt from tax and the amortization of the bond premium merely represents an adjustment of the effective amount of such income.

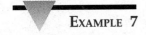

EXAMPLE 7

Antonio purchases Eagle Corporation taxable bonds with a face value of $100,000 for $110,000, thus paying a premium of $10,000. The annual interest rate is 7%, and the bonds mature 10 years from the date of purchase. The annual interest income is $7,000 (7% × $100,000). If Antonio elects to amortize the bond premium, the $10,000 premium is deducted over the 10-year period. Antonio's basis for the bonds is reduced each year by the amount of the amortization deduction. Note that if the bonds were tax-exempt, amortization of the bond premium and the basis adjustment would be mandatory. However, no deduction would be allowed for the amortization. ▼

RECOGNIZED GAIN OR LOSS

2 LEARNING OBJECTIVE
Distinguish between realized and recognized gain or loss.

Recognized gain is the amount of the realized gain included in the taxpayer's gross income.[20] A **recognized loss,** on the other hand, is the amount of a realized loss that is deductible for tax purposes.[21] As a general rule, the entire amount of a realized gain or loss is recognized.[22]

Concept Summary 12–1 summarizes the realized gain or loss and recognized gain or loss concepts.

NONRECOGNITION OF GAIN OR LOSS

In certain cases, a realized gain or loss is not recognized upon the sale or other disposition of property. One of the exceptions to the recognition of gain or loss involves nontaxable exchanges, which are covered later in this chapter. Additional exceptions include losses realized upon the sale, exchange, or condemnation of personal use assets (as opposed to business or income-producing property) and gains realized upon the sale of a residence by taxpayers 55 years of age or older. In addition, realized losses from the sale or exchange of business or income-producing property between certain related parties are not recognized.[23]

Sale, Exchange, or Condemnation of Personal Use Assets. A realized loss from the sale, exchange, or condemnation of personal use assets (e.g., a personal residence or an automobile not used at all for business or income-producing purposes) is not recognized for tax purposes. An exception exists for casualty or theft losses from personal use assets (see Chapter 6). In contrast, any gain realized from the sale or other disposition of personal use assets is, generally, fully taxable.

---

[20] § 61(a)(3) and Reg. § 1.61–6(a).
[21] § 165(a) and Reg. § 1.165–1(a).

[22] § 1001(c) and Reg. § 1.1002–1(a).
[23] § 267(a)(1).

CONCEPT SUMMARY 12–1

Recognized Gain or Loss

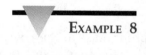
EXAMPLE 8

Freda sells an automobile, which is held exclusively for personal use, for $6,000. The adjusted basis of the automobile is $5,000. Freda has a realized and recognized gain of $1,000. ▼

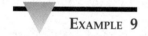
EXAMPLE 9

Freda sells the automobile in Example 8 for $4,000. She has a realized loss of $1,000, but the loss is not recognized. ▼

RECOVERY OF CAPITAL DOCTRINE

3   **LEARNING OBJECTIVE**
Apply the recovery of capital doctrine.

Doctrine Defined. The **recovery of capital doctrine** is very significant and pervades all the tax rules relating to property transactions. The doctrine derives its roots from the very essence of the income tax—a tax on income. Therefore, as a general rule, a taxpayer is entitled to recover the cost or other original basis of property acquired and is not taxed on that amount.

The cost or other original basis of depreciable property is recovered through annual depreciation deductions. The basis is reduced as the cost is recovered over the period the property is held. Therefore, when property is sold or otherwise disposed of, it is the adjusted basis (unrecovered cost or other basis) that is compared to the amount realized from the disposition to determine realized gain or loss.

Relationship of the Recovery of Capital Doctrine to the Concepts of Realization and Recognition. If a sale or other disposition results in a realized gain, the taxpayer has recovered more than the adjusted basis of the property. Conversely, if a sale or other disposition results in a realized loss, the taxpayer has recovered less than the adjusted basis.

The general rules for the relationship between the recovery of capital doctrine and the realized and recognized gain and loss concepts are summarized as follows:

Rule 1. A realized gain that is *never recognized* results in the *permanent recovery* of more than the taxpayer's cost or other basis for tax purposes. For example, all or a portion of the realized gain on the sale of a personal residence by taxpayers 55 years of age or older can be excluded from gross income under § 121.

Rule 2. A realized gain on which *recognition is postponed* results in the *temporary recovery* of more than the taxpayer's cost or other basis for tax purposes. For example, an exchange of like-kind property under § 1031, an involuntary conversion under § 1033, and a replacement of a personal residence under § 1034 are all eligible for postponement treatment.

Rule 3. A realized loss that is *never recognized* results in the *permanent recovery* of less than the taxpayer's cost or other basis for tax purposes. For example, a loss on the sale of an automobile held for personal use is not deductible.

Rule 4. A realized loss on which *recognition is postponed* results in the *temporary recovery* of less than the taxpayer's cost or other basis for tax purposes. For example, the realized loss on the exchange of like-kind property under § 1031 is postponed.

These rules are illustrated in discussions to follow in this chapter.

BASIS CONSIDERATIONS

DETERMINATION OF COST BASIS

4 LEARNING OBJECTIVE
Explain how basis is determined for various methods of asset acquisition.

The basis of property is generally the property's cost. Cost is the amount paid for the property in cash or other property.[24] This general rule follows logically from the recovery of capital doctrine; that is, the cost or other basis of property is to be recovered tax-free by the taxpayer.

A *bargain purchase* of property is an exception to the general rule for determining basis. A bargain purchase may result when an employer transfers property to an employee at less than the property's fair market value (as compensation for services) or when a corporation transfers property to a shareholder at less than the property's fair market value (a dividend). The basis of property acquired in a bargain purchase is the property's fair market value.[25] If the basis of the property were not increased by the bargain amount, the taxpayer would be taxed on this amount again at disposition.

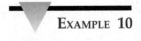

EXAMPLE 10

Wade buys a machine from his employer for $10,000 on December 30, 1996. The fair market value of the machine is $15,000. Wade must include the $5,000 difference between cost and the fair market value of the machine in gross income for the taxable year 1996. The bargain element represents additional compensation to Wade. His basis for the machine is $15,000, the machine's fair market value. ▼

Identification Problems. Cost identification problems are frequently encountered in securities transactions. For example, the Regulations require that the taxpayer adequately identify the particular stock that has been sold.[26] A problem

---

[24] § 1012 and Reg. § 1.1012–1(a).
[25] Reg. §§ 1.61–2(d)(2)(i) and 1.301–1(j).

[26] Reg. § 1.1012–1(c)(1).

arises when the taxpayer has purchased separate lots of stock on different dates or at different prices and cannot adequately identify the lot from which a particular sale takes place. In this case, the stock is presumed to come from the first lot or lots purchased (a FIFO presumption).[27] When securities are left in the custody of a broker, it may be necessary to provide specific instructions and receive written confirmation as to which securities are being sold.

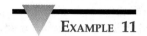

EXAMPLE 11

Polly purchases 100 shares of Olive Corporation stock on July 1, 1994, for $5,000 ($50 a share) and another 100 shares of Olive stock on July 1, 1995, for $6,000 ($60 a share). She sells 50 shares of the stock on January 2, 1996. The cost of the stock sold, assuming Polly cannot adequately identify the shares, is $50 a share, or $2,500. This is the cost Polly will compare to the amount realized in determining the gain or loss from the sale. ▼

Allocation Problems.   When a taxpayer acquires *multiple assets in a lump-sum purchase,* the total cost must be allocated among the individual assets.[28] Allocation is necessary because some of the assets acquired may be depreciable (e.g., buildings) and others not (e.g., land). In addition, only a portion of the assets acquired may be sold, or some of the assets may be capital or § 1231 assets that receive special tax treatment upon subsequent sale or other disposition. The lump-sum cost is allocated on the basis of the fair market values of the individual assets acquired.

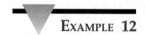

EXAMPLE 12

Harry purchases a building and land for $800,000. Because of the depressed nature of the industry in which the seller was operating, Harry was able to negotiate a very favorable purchase price. Appraisals of the individual assets indicate that the fair market value of the building is $600,000 and that of the land is $400,000. Harry's basis for the building is $480,000 ($600,000/$1,000,000 × $800,000), and his basis for the land is $320,000 ($400,000/$1,000,000 × $800,000). ▼

If a business is purchased and **goodwill** is involved, a special allocation rule applies. Initially, the purchase price is assigned to the assets, excluding goodwill, to the extent of their total fair market value. This assigned amount is allocated among the assets on the basis of the fair market value of the individual assets acquired. Goodwill is then assigned the residual amount of the purchase price. The resultant allocation is applicable to both the buyer and the seller.[29]

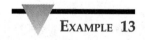

EXAMPLE 13

Rocky sells his business to Paul. They agree that the values of the individual assets are as follows:

Inventory	$ 50,000
Building	500,000
Land	200,000
Goodwill	150,000

After negotiations, Rocky and Paul agree on a sales price of $1 million. Applying the residual method with respect to goodwill results in the following allocation of the $1 million purchase price:

---

[27]*Kluger Associates, Inc.,* 69 T.C. 925 (1978).

[28]Reg. § 1.61–6(a).

[29]§ 1060.

Inventory	$ 50,000
Building	500,000
Land	200,000
Goodwill	250,000

The residual method requires that all of the excess of the purchase price over the fair market value of the assets ($1,000,000 – $900,000 = $100,000) be allocated to goodwill. Without this requirement, the purchaser could allocate the excess pro rata to all of the assets, including goodwill, based on their respective fair market values. This would have resulted in only $166,667 [$150,000 + ($150,000 ÷ $900,000 × $100,000)] being assigned to goodwill. ▼

In the case of *nontaxable stock dividends,* the allocation depends upon whether the dividend is a common stock dividend on common stock or a preferred stock dividend on common stock. If the dividend is common on common, the cost of the original common shares is allocated to the total shares owned after the dividend.[30]

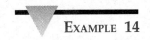

EXAMPLE 14 Susan owns 100 shares of Sparrow Corporation common stock for which she paid $1,100. She receives a 10% common stock dividend, giving her a new total of 110 shares. Before the stock dividend, Susan's basis was $11 per share ($1,100 ÷ 100 shares). The basis of each share after the stock dividend is $10 ($1,100 ÷ 110 shares). ▼

If the dividend is preferred stock on common, the cost of the original common shares is allocated between the common and preferred shares on the basis of their relative fair market values on the date of distribution.[31]

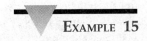

EXAMPLE 15 Fran owns 100 shares of Cardinal Corporation common stock for which she paid $1,000. She receives a stock dividend of 50 shares of preferred stock on her common stock. The fair market values on the date of distribution of the preferred stock dividend are $30 a share for common stock and $40 a share for preferred stock. Thus, the total fair market value is $3,000 ($30 × 100) for common stock and $2,000 ($40 × 50) for preferred stock. The basis of Fran's common stock after the dividend is $600, or $6 a share ($3,000/$5,000 × $1,000), and the basis of the preferred stock is $400, or $8 a share ($2,000/$5,000 × $ 1,000). ▼

GIFT BASIS

When a taxpayer receives property as a gift, there is no cost to the recipient. Thus, under the cost basis provision, the donee's basis would be zero. However, this would violate the statutory intent that gifts are not subject to the income tax. With a zero basis, a sale by the donee would result in all of the amount realized being treated as realized gain. Therefore, a basis is assigned to the property received depending on the following:[32]

- The date of the gift.
- The basis of the property to the donor.

---

[30] §§ 305(a) and 307(a). The holding period of the new shares includes the holding period of the old shares. § 1223(5) and Reg. § 1.1223–1(e). See Chapter 13 for a discussion of the importance of the holding period.

[31] Reg. § 1.307–1(a).
[32] § 102(a).

- The amount of the gift tax paid.
- The fair market value of the property.

Gift Basis Rules if No Gift Tax Is Paid.   Property received by gift can be
referred to as *dual basis* property; that is, the basis for gain and the basis for loss
might not be the same amount. The present basis rules for gifts of property are as
follows:

- If the donee subsequently disposes of gift property in a transaction that
  results in a gain, the basis to the donee is the same as the donor's adjusted
  basis.[33] The donee's basis in this case is referred to as the *gain basis.*
  Therefore, a *realized gain* results if the amount realized from the disposition
  exceeds the donee's gain basis.

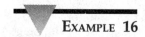

EXAMPLE 16

Melissa purchased stock in 1995 for $10,000. She gave the stock to her son, Joe, in 1996,
when the fair market value was $15,000. Assume no gift tax is paid on the transfer and Joe
subsequently sells the property for $15,000. Joe's basis is $10,000, and he has a realized gain
of $5,000. ▼

- If the donee subsequently disposes of gift property in a transaction that
  results in a loss, the basis to the donee is the *lower* of the donor's adjusted
  basis or fair market value on the date of the gift. The donee's basis in this
  case is referred to as the *loss basis.* Therefore, a *realized loss results* if the
  amount realized from the disposition is less than the donee's loss basis.

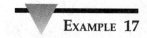

EXAMPLE 17

Burt purchased stock in 1995 for $10,000. He gave the stock to his son, Cliff, in 1996, when
the fair market value was $7,000. Assume no gift tax is paid on the transfer. Cliff later sells
the stock for $6,000. Cliff's basis is $7,000 (fair market value is less than donor's adjusted
basis of $10,000), and the realized loss from the sale is $1,000 ($6,000 amount realized −
$7,000 basis). ▼

The amount of the loss basis will *differ* from the amount of the gain basis only
if at the date of the gift the adjusted basis of the property exceeds the property's
fair market value. Note that the loss basis rule prevents the donee from receiving
a tax benefit from the decline in value while the donor held the property.
Therefore, in Example 17, Cliff has a loss of only $1,000 rather than a loss of $4,000.
The $3,000 difference represents the decline in value while Burt held the property.
Ironically, however, the gain basis rule may eventually result in the donee's being
subject to income tax on the appreciation that occurred while the donor held the
property, as illustrated in Example 16.

If the amount realized from sale or other disposition is *between* the basis for
loss and the basis for gain, no gain or loss is realized.

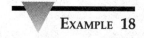

EXAMPLE 18

Assume the same facts as in Example 17, except that Cliff sold the stock for $8,000. The
application of the gain basis rule produces a loss of $2,000 ($8,000 − $10,000). The
application of the loss basis rule produces a gain of $1,000 ($8,000 − $7,000). Therefore, Cliff
recognizes neither a gain nor a loss because the amount realized is between the gain basis
and the loss basis. ▼

---

[33] § 1015(a) and Reg. § 1.1015–1(a)(1). See Reg. § 1.1015–1(a)(3) for
cases in which the facts necessary to determine the donor's
adjusted basis are unknown. Refer to Example 22 for the effect of
depreciation deductions by the donee.

12–13

Adjustment for Gift Tax. If gift taxes are paid by the donor, the donee's gain basis may exceed the adjusted basis of the property to the donor. This occurs only if the fair market value of the property at the date of the gift is greater than the donor's adjusted basis (the property has appreciated in value). The portion of the gift tax paid that is related to the appreciation is added to the donor's basis in calculating the donee's gain basis for the property. In this circumstance, the following formula is used for calculating the donee's gain basis:[34]

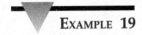

EXAMPLE 19

Bonnie made a gift of stock to Peggy in 1996, when the fair market value of the stock was $40,000. Bonnie had purchased the stock in 1982 for $10,000. Because the unrealized appreciation is $30,000 ($40,000 fair market value − $10,000 adjusted basis) and the fair market value is $40,000, three-fourths ($30,000/$40,000) of the gift tax paid is added to the basis of the property. If Bonnie paid gift tax of $4,000, Peggy's basis in the property is $13,000 [$10,000 + $3,000 (¾ of the $4,000 gift tax)]. ▼

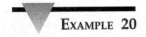

EXAMPLE 20

Don made a gift of stock to Matt in 1996, when the fair market value of the stock was $40,000. Gift tax of $4,000 was paid by Don, who had purchased the stock in 1982 for $45,000. Because there is no unrealized appreciation at the date of the gift, none of the gift tax paid is added to Don's basis in calculating Matt's gain basis. Therefore, Matt's gain basis is $45,000. ▼

For *gifts made before 1977*, the full amount of the gift tax paid is added to the donor's basis. However, the ceiling on this total is the fair market value of the property at the date of the gift. Thus, in Example 19, if the gift had been made before 1977, the basis of the property would be $14,000 ($10,000 + $4,000). In Example 20, the gain basis would still be $45,000 ($45,000 + $0).

Holding Period. The **holding period** for property acquired by gift begins on the date the donor acquired the property if the gain basis rule applies.[35] The holding period starts on the date of the gift if the loss basis rule applies.[36] The significance of the holding period for capital assets is discussed in Chapter 13.

The following example summarizes the basis and holding period rules for gift property:

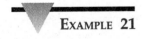

EXAMPLE 21

Jill acquires 100 shares of Wren Corporation stock on December 30, 1982, for $40,000. On January 3, 1996, when the stock has a fair market value of $38,000, Jill gives it to Dennis and pays gift tax of $4,000. The basis is not increased by a portion of the gift tax paid because the property has not appreciated in value at the time of the gift. Therefore, Dennis's gain basis is $40,000. Dennis's basis for determining loss is $38,000 (fair market value) because the fair market value on the date of the gift is less than the donor's adjusted basis.

---

[34] § 1015(d)(6).
[35] § 1223(2) and Reg. § 1.1223–1(b).

[36] Rev.Rul. 59–86, 1959–1 C.B. 209.

- If Dennis sells the stock for $45,000, he has a recognized gain of $5,000. The holding period for determining whether the capital gain is short term or long term begins on December 30, 1982, the date Jill acquired the property.
- If Dennis sells the stock for $36,000, he has a recognized loss of $2,000. The holding period for determining whether the capital loss is short term or long term begins on January 3, 1996, the date of the gift.
- If Dennis sells the property for $39,000, there is no gain or loss since the amount realized is less than the gain basis of $40,000 and more than the loss basis of $38,000. ▼

ETHICAL
CONSIDERATIONS

Looking a Gift Horse in the Mouth

Walter rarely sees his Uncle George because George is a devoted world traveler. On February 10, 1996, Walter received an envelope that George had mailed to him from Angola on December 23, 1995. The envelope contained 1,000 shares of stock of Lavender, Inc., and a Christmas card from George.

Walter is engaged to be married in December 1996. To finance the wedding (he and his fiancée have agreed that this is his responsibility) and the honeymoon, and to pay for the engagement, Walter sells the stock in October 1996 for $45,000.

In early April 1997, the accountant who is preparing Walter's tax return tells him that she needs to know his uncle's adjusted basis for the stock and the amount of any gift tax paid. Since Walter is unable to contact his uncle by April 15, 1997, he requests a filing extension on Form 4868. He does mail a letter to Uncle George requesting this information and thanking him for the gift. Walter is able to ascertain from a stock service that during the past 10 years, the stock price has ranged from $10 per share to $50 per share.

On August 10, 1997, Uncle George unexpectedly calls from Bosnia. He says he has not filed any type of Federal tax return in years. He thinks he won the stock in a poker game in Monaco about 15 years ago when another player used it to cover a $15,000 bet.

Walter wants to file his tax return by the August 15, 1997, due date. He does not think it is a good idea to tell the tax return preparer how his uncle acquired the stock or about his uncle's not filing tax returns. So he calls the accountant and tells her that his uncle's basis for the stock is $15,000 and that no gift taxes were paid.

Evaluate Walter's behavior.

Basis for Depreciation.   The basis for depreciation on depreciable gift property is the donee's gain basis.[37] This rule is applicable even if the donee later sells the property at a loss and uses the loss basis rule in calculating the amount of the realized loss.

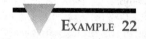

EXAMPLE 22

Vito gave a machine to Tina in 1996, when the adjusted basis was $32,000 (cost of $40,000 – accumulated depreciation of $8,000) and the fair market value was $26,000. No gift tax was paid. Tina's gain basis at the date of the gift is $32,000, and her loss basis is $26,000. During 1996, Tina deducts depreciation (cost recovery) of $10,240 ($32,000 × 32%). Therefore, at the end of 1996, Tina's gain basis and loss basis are calculated as follows:

---

[37]§ 1011 and Reg. §§ 1.1011–1 and 1.167(g)–1.

	Gain Basis	Loss Basis
Donor's basis or fair market value	$ 32,000	$ 26,000
Depreciation	(10,240)	(10,240)
	$ 21,760	$ 15,760

PROPERTY ACQUIRED FROM A DECEDENT

General Rules.   The basis of property acquired from a decedent is generally the property's fair market value at the date of death (referred to as the *primary valuation amount*).[38] The property's basis is the fair market value six months after the date of death if the executor or administrator of the estate *elects* the alternate valuation date for estate tax purposes. This amount is referred to as the *alternate valuation amount.*

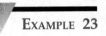

EXAMPLE 23

Linda and various other family members inherited property from Linda's father, who died in 1996. At the date of death, her father's adjusted basis for the property Linda inherited was $35,000. The property's fair market value at date of death was $50,000. The alternate valuation date was not elected. Linda's basis for income tax purposes is $50,000. This is commonly referred to as a *stepped-up basis.* ▼

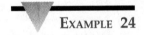

EXAMPLE 24

Assume the same facts as in Example 23, except the property's fair market value at date of death was $20,000. Linda's basis for income tax purposes is $20,000. This is commonly referred to as a *stepped-down basis.* ▼

If an estate tax return does not have to be filed because the estate is below the threshold amount for being subject to the estate tax, the alternate valuation date and amount are not available. Even if an estate tax return is filed and the executor elects the alternate valuation date, the six months after death date is available only for property that the executor has not distributed before this date. Any property distributed or otherwise disposed of by the executor during this six-month period will have an adjusted basis to the beneficiary equal to the fair market value on the date of distribution or other disposition.[39]

The alternate valuation date can be *elected only* if the election results in both the value of the gross estate and the estate tax liability being reduced below the amounts they would have been if the primary valuation date had been used. This provision prevents the alternate valuation election from being used to increase the basis of the property to the beneficiary for income tax purposes without simultaneously increasing the estate tax liability (because of estate tax deductions or credits).[40]

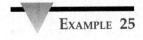

EXAMPLE 25

Nancy inherited all the property of her father, who died in 1996. Her father's adjusted basis for the property at date of death was $35,000. The property's fair market value was $750,000 at date of death and $760,000 six months after death. The alternate valuation date cannot be elected because the value of the gross estate has increased during the six-month period. Nancy's basis for income tax purposes is $750,000. ▼

---

[38]§ 1014(a).
[39]§ 2032(a)(1) and Rev.Rul. 56–60, 1956–1 C.B. 443.

[40]§ 2032(c).

TAX IN THE NEWS

CARRYOVER BASIS VERSUS STEPPED-UP BASIS

According to the old saying, "what goes around comes around." A good
example is the proposal to replace the stepped-up basis (i.e., fair market
value) for inherited property with a carryover basis.

The Tax Reform Act of 1976 amended the Code to provide that a beneficiary's
basis for inherited property would be a carryover basis. The provision had a future
effective date. Prior to that date, Senator Harry F. Byrd, Jr., of Virginia (now
retired) was successful in attaching a rider to the Crude Oil Windfall Profit Tax Act
of 1980, which repealed the carryover basis provision.

Several proposals to resurrect carryover basis for inherited property surfaced
during the debates over the Revenue Reconciliation Act of 1993. Those who
support carryover basis point out that it would make the basis rules for gifts
during life and transfers at death symmetrical and would generate additional
revenue. Opponents counter that the inherited property may be subject to the
Federal estate tax and that determining the decedent's basis for the property may
be difficult in many instances.

The proposals for carryover basis were not included in the Revenue Reconciliation Act of 1993. But the question still remains: Is carryover basis an issue whose
time has come?

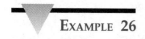

EXAMPLE 26

Assume the same facts as in Example 25, except the property's fair market value six months
after death was $745,000. If the executor elects the alternate valuation date, Nancy's basis
for income tax purposes is $745,000. ▼

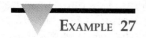

EXAMPLE 27

Assume the same facts as in the previous example, except the property is distributed four
months after the date of the decedent's death. At the distribution date, the property's fair
market value is $747,500. Since the executor elected the alternate valuation date, Nancy's
basis for income tax purposes is $747,500. ▼

For inherited property, both unrealized appreciation and decline in value are
taken into consideration in determining the basis of the property for income tax
purposes. Contrast this with the carryover basis rules for property received by
gift.

Deathbed Gifts.   The Code contains a provision designed to eliminate a tax
avoidance technique referred to as *deathbed gifts*. If the time period between the
date of the gift of appreciated property and the date of the donee's death is not
longer than one year, the usual basis rule (stepped-up basis) for inherited property
may not apply. The adjusted basis of such property inherited by the donor or his
or her spouse from the donee shall be the same as the decedent's adjusted basis for
the property rather than the fair market value at the date of death or the alternate
valuation date.[41]

---

[41] § 1014(e).

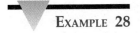

EXAMPLE 28 Ned gives stock to his uncle, Vern, in 1996. Ned's basis for the stock is $1,000, and the fair market value is $9,000. No gift tax is paid. Eight months later, Ned inherits the stock from Vern. At the date of Vern's death, the fair market value of the stock is $12,000. Ned's adjusted basis for the stock is $1,000. ▼

ETHICAL CONSIDERATIONS

Helping a Friend Increase Basis

Holly owns stock with an adjusted basis of $2,500 and a fair market value of $9,500. Holly expects the stock to continue to appreciate. Alice, Holly's best friend, has recently been operated on for cancer. Alice's physicians have told her that her life expectancy is between six months and one and a half years.

One day at lunch, the two friends were discussing their tax situations (both feel they pay too much), when Alice mentioned that she had read a newspaper article about a tax planning opportunity that might be suitable for Holly. Holly would make a gift of the appreciated stock to Alice. In her will, Alice would bequeath the stock to Holly. Since Alice is confident that she will live longer than a year, the basis of the stock to Holly would be the fair market value on the date of Alice's death. Alice would "feel good" because she had helped Holly "beat the tax system."

You are Holly's tax adviser. How will you respond to Alice's proposal to Holly?

Survivor's Share of Property. Both the decedent's share and the survivor's share of *community property* have a basis equal to fair market value on the date of the decedent's death.[42] This result applies to the decedent's share of the community property because the property flows to the surviving spouse from the estate (fair market value basis for inherited property). Likewise, the surviving spouse's share of the community property is deemed to be acquired by bequest, devise, or inheritance from the decedent. Therefore, it also has a basis equal to fair market value.

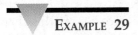

EXAMPLE 29 Floyd and Vera reside in a community property state. They own community property (200 shares of Crow stock) that was acquired in 1974 for $100,000. Assume that Floyd dies in 1996, when the securities are valued at $300,000. One-half of the Crow stock is included in Floyd's estate. If Vera inherits Floyd's share of the community property, the basis for determining gain or loss is $300,000, determined as follows:

Vera's one-half of the community property (stepped up from $50,000 to $150,000 due to Floyd's death)	$150,000
Floyd's one-half of the community property (stepped up from $50,000 to $150,000 due to inclusion in his gross estate)	150,000
Vera's new basis	$300,000	▼

In a *common law* state, only one-half of jointly held property of spouses (tenants by the entirety or joint tenants with rights of survivorship) is includible in

---

[42]§ 1014(b)(6). See the listing of community property states in Chapter 3.

the estate.[43] In such a case, no adjustment of the basis is permitted for the
excluded property interest (the surviving spouse's share).

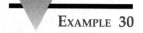
EXAMPLE 30

Assume the same facts as in the previous example, except that the property is jointly held
by Floyd and Vera who reside in a common law state. Also assume that Floyd purchased
the property and made a gift of one-half of the property when the stock was acquired, with
no gift tax being paid. Only one-half of the Crow stock is included in Floyd's estate. Vera's
basis for determining gain or loss in the excluded half is not adjusted upward for the
increase in value to date of death. Therefore, Vera's basis is $200,000, determined as follows:

Vera's one-half of the jointly held property (carryover basis of $50,000)	$ 50,000
Floyd's one-half of the jointly held property (stepped up from $50,000 to $150,000 due to inclusion in his gross estate)	150,000
Vera's new basis	$200,000

Holding Period of Property Acquired from a Decedent. The holding
period of property acquired from a decedent is *deemed to be long term* (held for the
required long-term holding period). This provision applies regardless of whether
the property is disposed of at a gain or a loss.[44]

DISALLOWED LOSSES

5   LEARNING OBJECTIVE
Describe various loss
disallowance provisions.

Related Taxpayers. Section 267 provides that realized losses from sales or
exchanges of property, directly or indirectly, between certain related parties are not
recognized. This loss disallowance provision applies to several types of related-
party transactions. The most common involve (1) members of a family and (2)
transactions between an individual and a corporation in which the individual
owns, directly or indirectly, more than 50 percent in value of the corporation's
outstanding stock. Section 707 provides a similar loss disallowance provision if the
related parties are a partner and a partnership in which the partner owns, directly
or indirectly, more than 50 percent of the capital interests or profits interests in the
partnership. The rules governing the relationships covered by § 267 were discussed in Chapter 5. See the discussion of the special rules under § 1041 for
property transfers between spouses or incident to divorce later in this chapter.

**ETHICAL
CONSIDERATIONS**

Transactions between Spouses

Ted and Lisa, both age 53, have been married for 10 years. At the time of their
marriage, they both had substantial assets, so they signed a premarital agreement,
establishing that their assets would not be commingled and that each would retain
separate title to his or her respective assets.

As a result of their marriage, Ted and Lisa's Federal tax liability has been larger than it
would have been if they were single (i.e., the marriage penalty). Ted and Lisa each own a 50
percent interest in some undeveloped land. Ted believes that they will be successful in
having the land rezoned from residential to commercial. The rezoning could result in as
much as a fourfold increase in the fair market value of the land. Based on her conversations

---

[43]§ 2040(b).   [44]§ 1223(11).

with two members of the Planning Commission, Lisa has serious doubts that the rezoning request will be approved.

Ted has offered to buy Lisa's interest in the land for $300,000. Lisa's adjusted basis is $500,000. The land has declined in value since Ted and Lisa purchased it in accordance with a general decline in residential real estate values in the area.

Lisa's CPA informs her that her realized loss of $200,000 on the sale would be disallowed under § 267 as a transaction between related parties. He also informs her that if the land appreciates as a result of the rezoning, Ted, but not Lisa, could use her disallowed loss from the sale to Ted to reduce his recognized gain on a subsequent sale of the land.

From Lisa's perspective, this is the last straw. Their marriage is producing too many negative tax consequences. She proposes to Ted that they get a divorce "for tax purposes" and continue to live together as man and wife. Only Lisa, Ted, their CPA, and their attorney will be aware that they are no longer married.

Evaluate the necessity for and the likelihood for success of Lisa's proposal.

Wash Sales. Section 1091 stipulates that in certain cases, a realized loss on the sale or exchange of stock or securities is not recognized. Specifically, if a taxpayer sells or exchanges stock or securities and within 30 days before *or* after the date of the sale or exchange acquires substantially identical stock or securities, any loss realized from the sale or exchange is not recognized because the transaction is a **wash sale.**[45] The term *acquire* means acquire by purchase or in a taxable exchange and includes an option to purchase substantially identical securities. *Substantially identical* means the same in all important particulars. Corporate bonds and preferred stock are normally not considered substantially identical to the corporation's common stock. However, if the bonds and preferred stock are convertible into common stock, they may be considered substantially identical under certain circumstances.[46] Attempts to avoid the application of the wash sales rules by having a related taxpayer repurchase the securities have been unsuccessful.[47] The wash sales provisions do *not* apply to gains.

Recognition of the loss is disallowed because the taxpayer is considered to be in substantially the same economic position after the sale and repurchase as before the sale and repurchase. This disallowance rule does not apply to taxpayers engaged in the business of buying and selling securities.[48] Investors, however, are not allowed to create losses through wash sales to offset income for tax purposes.

Realized loss that is not recognized is added to the *basis* of the substantially identical stock or securities whose acquisition resulted in the nonrecognition of loss.[49] In other words, the basis of the replacement stock or securities is increased by the amount of the unrecognized loss. If the loss were not added to the basis of the newly acquired stock or securities, the taxpayer would never recover the entire basis of the old stock or securities.

The basis of the new stock or securities includes the unrecovered portion of the basis of the formerly held stock or securities. Therefore, the *holding period* of the new stock or securities begins on the date of acquisition of the old stock or securities.[50]

[45] § 1091(a) and Reg. §§ 1.1091–1(a) and (f).
[46] Rev.Rul. 56–406, 1956–2 C.B. 523.
[47] *McWilliams v. Comm.*, 47–1 USTC ¶9289, 35 AFTR 1184, 67 S.Ct. 1477 (USSC, 1947).
[48] Reg. § 1.1091–1(a).
[49] § 1091(d) and Reg. § 1.1091–2(a).
[50] § 1223(4) and Reg. § 1.1223–1(d).

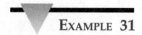

EXAMPLE 31

Bhaskar owns 100 shares of Green Corporation stock (adjusted basis of $20,000), 50 shares of which he sells for $8,000. Ten days later, he purchases 50 shares of the same stock for $7,000. Bhaskar's realized loss of $2,000 ($8,000 amount realized − $10,000 adjusted basis of 50 shares) is not recognized because it resulted from a wash sale. Bhaskar's basis in the newly acquired stock is $9,000 ($7,000 purchase price + $2,000 unrecognized loss from the wash sale). ▼

The taxpayer may acquire less than the number of shares sold in a wash sale. In this case, the loss from the sale is prorated between recognized and unrecognized loss on the basis of the ratio of the number of shares acquired to the number of shares sold.[51]

CONVERSION OF PROPERTY FROM PERSONAL USE TO BUSINESS OR INCOME-PRODUCING USE

As discussed previously, losses from the sale of personal use assets are not recognized for tax purposes, but losses from the sale of business and income-producing assets are deductible. Can a taxpayer convert a personal use asset that has declined in value to business (or income-producing) use and then sell the asset to recognize a business (or income-producing) loss? The tax law prevents this by specifying that the *original basis for loss* on personal use assets converted to business or income-producing use is the *lower* of the property's adjusted basis or fair market value on the date of conversion.[52] The *gain basis* for converted property is the property's adjusted basis on the date of conversion. The tax law is not concerned with gains on converted property because gains are recognized regardless of whether property is business, income producing, or personal use.

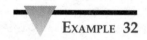

EXAMPLE 32

Diane's personal residence has an adjusted basis of $75,000 and a fair market value of $60,000. Diane converts the personal residence to rental property. Her basis for loss is $60,000 (lower of $75,000 adjusted basis and fair market value of $60,000). The $15,000 decline in value is a personal loss and can never be recognized for tax purposes. Diane's basis for gain is $75,000. ▼

The basis for loss is also the *basis for depreciating* the converted property.[53] This is an exception to the general rule that provides that the basis for depreciation is the gain basis (e.g., property received by gift). This exception prevents the taxpayer from recovering a personal loss indirectly through depreciation of the higher original basis. After the property is converted, both its basis for loss and its basis for gain are adjusted for depreciation deductions from the date of conversion to the date of disposition. These rules apply only if a conversion from personal to business or income-producing use has actually occurred.

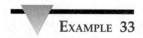

EXAMPLE 33

At a time when his personal residence (adjusted basis of $40,000) is worth $50,000, Keith converts one-half of it to rental use. The property is not MACRS recovery property. At this point, the estimated useful life of the residence is 20 years and there is no estimated salvage value. After renting the converted portion for five years, Keith sells the property for $44,000. All amounts relate only to the building; the land has been accounted for separately. Keith has a $2,000 realized gain from the sale of the personal use portion of the residence and a $7,000 realized gain from the sale of the rental portion. These gains are computed as follows:

---

[51] § 1091(b) and Reg. § 1.1091–1(c).
[52] Reg. § 1.165–9(b)(2).

[53] Reg. § 1.167(g)–1.

	Personal Use	Rental
Original basis for gain and loss—adjusted basis on date of conversion (fair market value is greater than the adjusted basis)	$20,000	$20,000
Depreciation—five years	None	5,000
Adjusted basis—date of sale	$20,000	$15,000
Amount realized	22,000	22,000
Realized gain	$ 2,000	$ 7,000

▼

As discussed later in the chapter, Keith may be able to defer recognition of part or all of the $2,000 gain from the sale of the personal use portion of the residence under § 1034. The $7,000 gain from the rental portion is recognized.

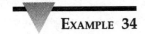

EXAMPLE 34
Assume the same facts as in the previous example, except that the fair market value on the date of conversion is $30,000 and the sales proceeds are $16,000. Keith has a $12,000 realized loss from the sale of the personal use portion of the residence and a $3,250 realized loss from the sale of the rental portion. These losses are computed as follows:

	Personal Use	Rental
Original basis for loss—fair market value on date of conversion (fair market value is less than the adjusted basis)	*	$15,000
Depreciation—five years	None	3,750
Adjusted basis—date of sale	$20,000	$11,250
Amount realized	8,000	8,000
Realized loss	$12,000	$ 3,250

-ot applicable.

The $12,000 loss from the sale of the personal use portion of the residence is not recognized. The $3,250 loss from the rental portion is recognized. ▼

SUMMARY OF BASIS ADJUSTMENTS

Some of the more common items that either increase or decrease the basis of an asset appear in Concept Summary 12–2.

In discussing the topic of basis, a number of specific techniques for determining basis have been presented. Although the various techniques are responsive to and mandated by transactions occurring in the marketplace, they do possess enough common characteristics to be categorized as follows:

- The basis of the asset may be determined by reference to the asset's cost.
- The basis of the asset may be determined by reference to the basis of another asset.
- The basis of the asset may be determined by reference to the asset's fair market value.
- The basis of the asset may be determined by reference to the basis of the asset to another taxpayer.

CONCEPT SUMMARY 12–2

Adjustments to Basis

Item	Effect	Refer to Chapter	Explanation
Amortization of bond discount.	Increase	13	Amortization is mandatory for certain taxable bonds and elective for tax-exempt bonds.
Amortization of bond premium.	Decrease	12	Amortization is mandatory for tax-exempt bonds and elective for taxable bonds.
Amortization of covenant not to compete.	Decrease	13	Covenant must be for a definite and limited time period. The amortization period is a statutory period of 15 years.
Amortization of intangibles.	Decrease	7	Even goodwill is now subject to amortization.
Assessment for local benefits.	Increase	9	To the extent not deductible as taxes (e.g., assessment for streets and sidewalks that increase the value of the property versus one for maintenance or repair or for meeting interest charges).
Bad debts.	Decrease	6	Only the specific charge-off method is permitted.
Capital additions.	Increase	12	Certain items, at the taxpayer's election, can be capitalized or deducted (e.g., selected medical expenses).
Casualty.	Decrease	6	For a casualty loss, the amount of the adjustment is the summation of the deductible loss and the insurance proceeds received. For a casualty gain, the amount of the adjustment is the insurance proceeds received reduced by the recognized gain.
Condemnation.	Decrease	12	See casualty explanation.
Cost recovery.	Decrease	7	§ 168 is applicable to tangible assets placed in service after 1980 whose useful life is expressed in terms of years.
Depletion.	Decrease	7	Use the greater of cost or percentage depletion. Percentage depletion can still be deducted when the basis is zero.
Depreciation.	Decrease	7	§ 167 is applicable to tangible assets placed in service before 1981 and to tangible assets not depreciated in terms of years.
Easement.	Decrease		If the taxpayer does not retain any use of the land, all of the basis is allocable to the easement transaction. However, if only part of the land is affected by the easement, only part of the basis is allocable to the easement transaction.
Improvements by lessee to lessor's property.	Increase	4	Adjustment occurs only if the lessor is required to include the fair market value of the improvements in gross income under § 109.
Imputed interest.	Decrease	15	Amount deducted is not part of the cost of the asset.
Inventory: lower of cost or market.	Decrease	15	Not available if the LIFO method is used.
Limited expensing under § 179.	Decrease	7	Occurs only if the taxpayer elects § 179 treatment.

Item	Effect	Refer to Chapter	Explanation
Medical capital expenditure permitted as a medical expense.	Decrease	9	Adjustment is the amount of the deduction (the effect on basis is to increase it by the amount of the capital expenditure net of the deduction).
Real estate taxes: apportionment between the buyer and seller.	Increase or decrease	9	To the extent the buyer pays the seller's pro rata share, the buyer's basis is increased. To the extent the seller pays the buyer's pro rata share, the buyer's basis is decreased.
Rebate from manufacturer.	Decrease		Since the rebate is treated as an adjustment to the purchase price, it is not included in the buyer's gross income.
Stock dividend.	Decrease	4	Adjustment occurs only if the stock dividend is nontaxable. While the basis per share decreases, the total stock basis does not change.
Stock rights.	Decrease	12	Adjustment to stock basis occurs only for nontaxable stock rights and only if the fair market value of the rights is at least 15% of the fair market value of the stock or, if less than 15%, the taxpayer elects to allocate the basis between the stock and the rights.
Theft.	Decrease	6	See casualty explanation.

GENERAL CONCEPT OF A NONTAXABLE EXCHANGE

6   LEARNING OBJECTIVE
Understand the rationale for nonrecognition (postponement) of gain or loss in certain property transactions.

A taxpayer who is going to replace a productive asset (e.g., machinery) used in a trade or business may structure the transactions as a sale of the old asset and the purchase of a new asset. Using this approach, any realized gain or loss on the asset sale is recognized. The basis of the new asset is its cost. Conversely, the taxpayer may be able to trade the old asset for the new asset. This exchange of assets may produce beneficial tax consequences by qualifying for nontaxable exchange treatment.

The tax law recognizes that nontaxable exchanges result in a change in the *form* but not in the *substance* of the taxpayer's relative economic position. The replacement property received in the exchange is viewed as substantially a continuation of the old investment.[54] Additional justification for nontaxable exchange treatment is that this type of transaction does not provide the taxpayer with the wherewithal to pay the tax on any realized gain.

The nonrecognition provisions for nontaxable exchanges do not apply to realized losses from the sale or exchange of personal use assets. Such losses are not recognized (are disallowed) because they are personal in nature and not because of any nonrecognition provision.

In a **nontaxable exchange**, realized gains or losses are not recognized. However, the nonrecognition is usually temporary. The recognition of gain or loss is *postponed* (deferred) until the property received in the nontaxable exchange is

---
[54] Reg. § 1.1002–1(c).

subsequently disposed of in a taxable transaction. This is accomplished by assigning a carryover basis to the replacement property.

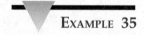

EXAMPLE 35

Debra exchanges property with an adjusted basis of $10,000 and a fair market value of $12,000 for property with a fair market value of $12,000. The transaction qualifies for nontaxable exchange treatment. Debra has a realized gain of $2,000 ($12,000 amount realized – $10,000 adjusted basis). Her recognized gain is $0. Her basis in the replacement property is a carryover basis of $10,000. Assume the replacement property is nondepreciable. If Debra subsequently sells the replacement property for $12,000, her realized and recognized gain will be the $2,000 gain that was postponed (deferred) in the nontaxable transaction. If the replacement property is depreciable, the carryover basis of $10,000 is used in calculating depreciation. ▼

In some nontaxable exchanges, only part of the property involved in the transaction qualifies for nonrecognition treatment. If the taxpayer receives cash or other nonqualifying property, part or all of the realized gain from the exchange is recognized. In these instances, gain is recognized because the taxpayer has changed or improved his or her relative economic position and has the wherewithal to pay income tax to the extent of cash or other property received.

It is important to distinguish between a nontaxable disposition, as the term is used in the statute, and a tax-free transaction. First, a direct exchange is not required in all circumstances (e.g., replacement of involuntarily converted property or sale and replacement of a personal residence). Second, as previously mentioned, the term *nontaxable* refers to postponement of recognition via a carryover basis. In a *tax-free* transaction, the nonrecognition is permanent (e.g., see the discussion later in the chapter of the § 121 election by a taxpayer age 55 or over to exclude gain on the sale of a residence). Therefore, the basis of any property acquired in a tax-free transaction does not depend on the basis of the property disposed of by the taxpayer.

LIKE-KIND EXCHANGES—§ 1031

7 **LEARNING OBJECTIVE**
Apply the nonrecognition provisions and basis determination rules for like-kind exchanges.

Section 1031 provides for nontaxable exchange treatment if the following requirements are satisfied:[55]

- The form of the transaction is an exchange.
- Both the property transferred and the property received are held either for productive use in a trade or business or for investment.
- The property is like-kind property.

Like-kind exchanges include business for business, business for investment, investment for business, or investment for investment property. Property held for personal use, inventory, and partnership interests (both limited and general) do not qualify under the like-kind exchange provisions. Securities, even though held for investment, do not qualify for like-kind exchange treatment.

The nonrecognition provision for like-kind exchanges is *mandatory* rather than elective. A taxpayer who wants to recognize a realized gain or loss will have to structure the transaction in a form that does not satisfy the statutory requirements for a like-kind exchange. This topic is discussed further under Tax Planning Considerations.

---

[55] § 1031(a) and Reg. § 1.1031(a)–1(a).

LIKE-KIND PROPERTY

"The words 'like-kind' refer to the nature or character of the property and not to its grade or quality. One kind or class of property may not . . . be exchanged for property of a different kind or class."[56]

Although the term *like-kind* is intended to be interpreted very broadly, three categories of exchanges are not included. First, livestock of different sexes do not qualify as like-kind property. Second, real estate can be exchanged only for other real estate, and personalty can be exchanged only for other personalty. For example, the exchange of a machine (personalty) for an office building (realty) is not a like-kind exchange. *Real estate* (or realty) includes principally rental buildings, office and store buildings, manufacturing plants, warehouses, and land. It is immaterial whether real estate is improved or unimproved. Thus, unimproved land can be exchanged for an apartment house. Personalty includes principally machines, equipment, trucks, automobiles, furniture, and fixtures. Third, real property located in the United States exchanged for foreign real property (and vice versa) does not qualify as like-kind property.

▼ **EXAMPLE 36**

Wade made the following exchanges during the taxable year:

 a. Inventory for a machine used in business.
 b. Land held for investment for a building used in business.
 c. Stock held for investment for equipment used in business.
 d. A business truck for a business truck.
 e. An automobile used for personal transportation for an automobile used in business.
 f. Livestock for livestock of a different sex.
 g. Land held for investment in New York for land held for investment in London.

Exchanges (b), investment real property for business real property, and (d), business personalty for business personalty, qualify as exchanges of like-kind property. Exchanges (a), inventory; (c), stock; (e), personal use automobile (not held for business or investment purposes); (f), livestock of different sexes; and (g), U.S. and foreign real estate do not qualify. ▼

A special provision applies if the taxpayers involved in the exchange are *related parties* under § 267(b). To qualify for like-kind exchange treatment, the taxpayer and the related party must not dispose of the like-kind property received in the exchange within the two-year period following the date of the exchange. If such an early disposition does occur, the postponed gain is recognized as of the date of the early disposition. Dispositions due to death, involuntary conversions, and certain non-tax avoidance transactions are not treated as early dispositions.

Regulations dealing with § 1031 like-kind exchange treatment provide that if the exchange transaction involves multiple assets of a business (e.g., a television station for another television station), the determination of whether the assets qualify as like-kind property will not be made at the business level.[57] Instead, the underlying assets must be evaluated.

The Regulations also provide for greater specificity in determining whether depreciable tangible personal property is of a like kind or class. Such property held for productive use in a business is of a like class only if the exchanged property is within the same *general business asset class* (as specified by the IRS in Rev.Proc. 87–57 or as subsequently modified) or the same *product class* (as specified by the Depart-

---

[56] Reg. § 1.1031(a)–1(b).   [57] Reg. §§ 1.1031(j)–1.

TAX IN THE NEWS

MY LAND FOR YOUR JAIL

The Colonial Williamsburg Foundation (CW) has offered to swap 30 acres of undeveloped woodland for the Williamsburg Jail and Courthouse. A few years ago CW built a replica of the eighteenth-century Public Hospital (i.e., insane asylum). Now it is attempting to acquire the adjacent twentieth-century jail and courthouse in a § 1031 trade.

Why does CW want to own a twentieth-century jail and courthouse? It doesn't. CW wants the land for eventual expansion of its DeWitt Wallace Decorative Arts Gallery, which is located behind the Public Hospital. In addition, CW wants to preserve green space in Williamsburg, which would be threatened if a new courthouse and jail are built on land adjacent to the current courthouse and jail in Bicentennial Park.

Although the foundation is tax-exempt, the undeveloped 30 acres are owned by CW's for-profit subsidiary Williamsburg Developments, Inc. Therefore, to avoid recognizing the realized gain on the exchange, the subsidiary needs to avail itself of the § 1031 like-kind exchange provisions. Fortunately, the undeveloped land and the courthouse and jail are like-kind property.

SOURCE: Information from Bentley Boyd, "CW Presses for Moving Courthouse," *Newport News (Virginia) Daily Press*, September 15, 1993, pp. C1, C2; Bentley Boyd, "CW Boosts Proposal for Courthouse," *Newport News (Virginia) Daily Press*, September 29, 1993, pp. B1, B2.

ment of Commerce). Property included in a general business asset class is evaluated under this system rather than under the product class system.

The following are examples of general business asset classes:

- Office furniture, fixtures, and equipment.
- Information systems (computers and peripheral equipment).
- Airplanes.
- Automobiles and taxis.
- Buses.
- Light general-purpose trucks.
- Heavy general-purpose trucks.

These Regulations have made it more difficult for depreciable tangible personal property to qualify for § 1031 like-kind exchange treatment. For example, the exchange of office equipment for a computer does not qualify as an exchange of like-kind property. Even though both assets are depreciable tangible personal property, they are not like-kind property because they are in different general business asset classes.

EXCHANGE REQUIREMENT

The transaction must actually involve a direct exchange of property to qualify as a like-kind exchange. The sale of old property and the purchase of new property, even though like-kind, is generally not an exchange. However, if the two transactions are mutually dependent, the IRS may treat them as a like-kind exchange. For example, if the taxpayer sells an old business machine to a dealer and purchases a new one from the same dealer, like-kind exchange treatment could result.[58]

The taxpayer may want to avoid nontaxable exchange treatment. Recognition of gain gives the taxpayer a higher basis for depreciation (see Example 65). To the extent that such gains would, if recognized, either receive favorable capital gain treatment or be passive activity income that could offset passive activity losses, it may be preferable to avoid the nonrecognition provisions through an indirect exchange transaction. For example, a taxpayer may sell property to one individual and subsequently purchase similar property from another individual. The taxpayer may also want to avoid nontaxable exchange treatment so that a realized loss can be recognized.

BOOT

If the taxpayer in a like-kind exchange gives or receives some property that is not like-kind property, recognition may occur. Property that is not like-kind property, including cash, is referred to as **boot.** Although the term *boot* does not appear in the Code, tax practitioners commonly use it rather than saying "property that is not like-kind property."

The *receipt* of boot will trigger recognition of gain if there is realized gain. The amount of the recognized gain is the *lesser* of the boot received or the realized gain (realized gain serves as the ceiling on recognition).

EXAMPLE 37 Emily and Fran exchange machinery, and the exchange qualifies as like-kind under § 1031. Since Emily's machinery (adjusted basis of $20,000) is worth $24,000 and Fran's machine has a fair market value of $19,000, Fran also gives Emily cash of $5,000. Emily's recognized gain is $4,000, the lesser of the realized gain ($24,000 amount realized − $20,000 adjusted basis = $4,000) or the fair market value of the boot received ($5,000). ▼

EXAMPLE 38 Assume the same facts as in the previous example, except that Fran's machine is worth $21,000 (not $19,000). Under these circumstances, Fran gives Emily cash of $3,000 to make up the difference. Emily's recognized gain is $3,000, the lesser of the realized gain ($24,000 amount realized − $20,000 adjusted basis = $4,000) or the fair market value of the boot received ($3,000). ▼

The receipt of boot does not result in recognition if there is realized loss.

EXAMPLE 39 Assume the same facts as in Example 37, except the adjusted basis of Emily's machine is $30,000. Emily's realized loss is $6,000 ($24,000 amount realized − $30,000 adjusted basis = $6,000 realized loss). The receipt of the boot of $5,000 does not trigger recognition. Therefore, the recognized loss is $0. ▼

The *giving* of boot usually does not trigger recognition. If the boot given is cash, any realized gain or loss is not recognized.

EXAMPLE 40 Fred and Gary exchange equipment in a like-kind exchange. Fred receives equipment with a fair market value of $25,000 and Fred transfers equipment worth $21,000 (adjusted basis of $15,000) and cash of $4,000. Fred's realized gain is $6,000 ($25,000 amount realized − $15,000 adjusted basis − $4,000 cash). However, none of the realized gain is recognized. ▼

If, however, the boot given is appreciated or depreciated property, gain or loss is recognized to the extent of the differential between the adjusted basis and the fair market value of the boot. For this purpose, *appreciated or depreciated property* is defined as property whose adjusted basis is not equal to the fair market value.

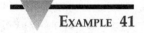

EXAMPLE 41

Assume the same facts as in the previous example, except that Fred transfers equipment worth $10,000 (adjusted basis of $12,000) and boot worth $15,000 (adjusted basis of $9,000). Fred's realized gain appears to be $4,000 ($25,000 amount realized − $21,000 adjusted basis). Since realization previously has served as a ceiling on recognition, it appears that the recognized gain is $4,000 (lower of realized gain of $4,000 or amount of appreciation on boot of $6,000). However, the recognized gain actually is $6,000 (full amount of the appreciation on the boot). In effect, Fred must calculate the like-kind and boot parts of the transaction separately. That is, the realized loss of $2,000 on the like-kind property is not recognized ($10,000 fair market value − $12,000 adjusted basis), and the $6,000 realized gain on the boot is recognized ($15,000 fair market value − $9,000 adjusted basis). ▼

BASIS AND HOLDING PERIOD OF PROPERTY RECEIVED

If an exchange does not qualify as nontaxable under § 1031, gain or loss is recognized, and the basis of property received in the exchange is the property's fair market value. If the exchange qualifies for nonrecognition, the basis of property received must be adjusted to reflect any postponed (deferred) gain or loss. The *basis of like-kind property* received in the exchange is the property's fair market value less postponed gain or plus postponed loss. If the exchange partially qualifies for nonrecognition (if recognition is associated with boot), the basis of like-kind property received in the exchange is the property's fair market value less postponed gain or plus postponed loss. The *basis* of any *boot* received is the boot's fair market value.

If there is a postponed loss, nonrecognition creates a situation in which the taxpayer has recovered *less* than the cost or other basis of the property exchanged in an amount equal to the unrecognized loss. If there is a postponed gain, the taxpayer has recovered *more* than the cost or other basis of the property exchanged in an amount equal to the unrecognized gain.

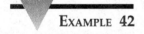

EXAMPLE 42

Jaime exchanges a building (used in his business) with an adjusted basis of $30,000 and fair market value of $38,000 for land with a fair market value of $38,000. The land is to be held as an investment. The exchange qualifies as like-kind (an exchange of business real property for investment real property). Thus, the basis of the land is $30,000 (the land's fair market value of $38,000 less the $8,000 postponed gain on the building). If the land is later sold for its fair market value of $38,000, the $8,000 postponed gain is recognized. ▼

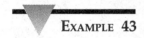

EXAMPLE 43

Assume the same facts as in the previous example, except that the building has an adjusted basis of $48,000 and fair market value of only $38,000. The basis in the newly acquired land is $48,000 (fair market value of $38,000 plus the $10,000 postponed loss on the building). If the land is later sold for its fair market value of $38,000, the $10,000 postponed loss is recognized. ▼

The Code provides an alternative approach for determining the basis of like-kind property received:

> Adjusted basis of like-kind property surrendered
> + Adjusted basis of boot given
> + Gain recognized
> − Fair market value of boot received
> − Loss recognized
> = *Basis of like-kind property received*

This approach is logical in terms of the recovery of capital doctrine. That is, the unrecovered cost or other basis is increased by additional cost (boot given) or decreased by cost recovered (boot received). Any gain recognized is included in the basis of the new property. The taxpayer has been taxed on this amount and is now entitled to recover it tax-free. Any loss recognized is deducted from the basis of the new property. The taxpayer has received a tax benefit on that amount.

The holding period of the property surrendered in the exchange carries over and *tacks on* to the holding period of the like-kind property received.[59] The logic of this rule is derived from the basic concept of the new property as a continuation of the old investment. The boot received has a new holding period (from the date of exchange) rather than a carryover holding period.

Depreciation recapture potential carries over to the property received in a like-kind exchange.[60] See Chapter 13 for a discussion of this topic.

The following comprehensive example illustrates the like-kind exchange rules.

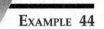

EXAMPLE 44

Vicki exchanged the following old machines for new machines in five independent like-kind exchanges:

Exchange	Adjusted Basis of Old Machine	Fair Market Value of New Machine	Adjusted Basis of Boot Given	Fair Market Value of Boot Received
1	$4,000	$9,000	$ –0–	$ –0–
2	4,000	9,000	3,000	–0–
3	4,000	9,000	6,000	–0–
4	4,000	9,000	–0–	3,000
5	4,000	3,500	–0–	300

Vicki's realized and recognized gains and losses and the basis of each of the like-kind properties received are as follows:

Exchange	Realized Gain (Loss)	Recognized Gain (Loss)	Old Adj. Basis	+	Boot Given	+	Gain Recognized	–	Boot Received	=	New Basis
1	$5,000	$ –0–	$ 4,000	+	$ –0–	+	$ –0–	–	$ –0–	=	$ 4,000*
2	2,000	–0–	4,000	+	3,000	+	–0–	–	–0–	=	7,000*
3	(1,000)	(–0–)	4,000	+	6,000	+	–0–	–	–0–	=	10,000*
4	8,000	3,000	4,000	+	–0–	+	3,000	–	3,000	=	4,000*
5	(200)	(–0–)	4,000	+	–0–	+	–0–	–	300	=	3,700*

*Basis may be determined in gain situations under the alternative method by subtracting the gain not recognized from the fair market value of the new property:
$9,000 – $5,000 = $4,000 for exchange 1.
$9,000 – $2,000 = $7,000 for exchange 2.
$9,000 – $5,000 = $4,000 for exchange 4.

*In loss situations, basis may be determined by adding the loss not recognized to the fair market value of the new property:
$9,000 + $1,000 = $10,000 for exchange 3.
$3,500 + $200 = $3,700 for exchange 5.

The basis of the boot received is the boot's fair market value.   ▼

[59] § 1223(1) and Reg. § 1.1223–1(a). For this carryover holding period rule to apply to like-kind exchanges after March 1, 1954, the like-kind property surrendered must have been either a capital asset or § 1231 property. See Chapter 13 for the discussion of capital assets and § 1231 property.
[60] Reg. §§ 1.1245–2(a)(4) and 1.1250–2(d)(1).

If the taxpayer either assumes a liability or takes property subject to a liability, the amount of the liability is treated as boot given. For the taxpayer whose liability is assumed or whose property is taken subject to the liability, the amount of the liability is treated as boot received. Example 45 illustrates the effect of such a liability. In addition, the example illustrates the tax consequences for both parties involved in the like-kind exchange.

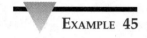

EXAMPLE 45

Jane and Leo exchange real estate investments. Jane gives up property with an adjusted basis of $250,000 (fair market value $400,000) that is subject to a mortgage of $75,000 (assumed by Leo). In return for this property, Jane receives property with a fair market value of $300,000 (adjusted basis $200,000) and cash of $25,000.

- Jane's realized gain is $150,000. She gave up property with an adjusted basis of $250,000. Jane received $400,000 from the exchange ($300,000 fair market value of like-kind property plus $100,000 boot received). The boot received consists of the $25,000 cash received from Leo and Jane's mortgage of $75,000 that Leo assumes.
- Jane's recognized gain is $100,000. The realized gain of $150,000 is recognized to the extent of boot received.
- Jane's basis in the real estate received from Leo is $250,000. This basis can be computed by subtracting the postponed gain ($50,000) from the fair market value of the real estate received ($300,000). It can also be computed by adding the recognized gain ($100,000) to the adjusted basis of the real estate given up ($250,000) and subtracting the boot received ($100,000).
- Leo's realized gain is $100,000. Leo gave up property with an adjusted basis of $200,000 plus boot of $100,000 ($75,000 mortgage assumed + $25,000 cash) or a total of $300,000. Leo received $400,000 from the exchange (fair market value of like-kind property received).
- Leo has no recognized gain because he did not receive any boot. The entire realized gain of $100,000 is postponed.
- Leo's basis in the real estate received from Jane is $300,000. This basis can be computed by subtracting the postponed gain ($100,000) from the fair market value of the real estate received ($400,000). It can also be computed by adding the boot given ($75,000 mortgage assumed by Leo + $25,000 cash) to the adjusted basis of the real estate given up ($200,000).[61] ▼

INVOLUNTARY CONVERSIONS—§ 1033

8 LEARNING OBJECTIVE
Explain the nonrecognition provisions available on the involuntary conversion of property.

Section 1033 provides that a taxpayer who suffers an involuntary conversion of property may postpone recognition of *gain* realized from the conversion. The objective of this provision is to provide relief to the taxpayer who has suffered hardship and does not have the wherewithal to pay the tax on any gain realized from the conversion. Postponement of realized gain is permitted to the extent that the taxpayer *reinvests* the amount realized from the conversion in replacement property. The rules for nonrecognition of gain are as follows:

- If the amount reinvested in replacement property *equals or exceeds* the amount realized, realized gain is *not recognized.*

---

[61] Example (2) of Reg. § 1.1031(d)–2 illustrates a special situation where both the buyer and the seller transfer liabilities that are assumed or property is acquired subject to a liability by the other party.

• If the amount reinvested in replacement property is *less than* the amount realized, realized gain *is recognized* to the extent of the deficiency.

If a *loss* occurs on an involuntary conversion, § 1033 does not modify the normal rules for loss recognition. That is, if realized loss otherwise would be recognized, § 1033 does not change the result.

INVOLUNTARY CONVERSION DEFINED

An **involuntary conversion** results from the destruction (complete or partial), theft, seizure, requisition or condemnation, or the sale or exchange under threat or imminence of requisition or condemnation of the taxpayer's property.[62] To prove the existence of a threat or imminence of condemnation, the taxpayer must obtain confirmation that there has been a decision to acquire the property for public use. In addition, the taxpayer must have reasonable grounds to believe the property will be taken.[63] The property does not have to be sold to the authority threatening to condemn it to qualify for § 1033 postponement. If the taxpayer satisfies the confirmation and reasonable grounds requirements, he or she can sell the property to another party.[64] Likewise, the sale of property to a condemning authority by a taxpayer who acquired the property from its former owner with the knowledge that the property was under threat of condemnation also qualifies as an involuntary conversion under § 1033.[65] A voluntary act, such as a taxpayer destroying his or her own property by arson, is not an involuntary conversion.[66]

ETHICAL CONSIDERATIONS

Purchasing Property in Expectation of Condemnation

The city of Richmond is going to condemn some buildings in a run-down section of the city to build a park. Steve's principal residence is one of the dilapidated buildings. His adjusted basis for the house and land is $60,000. The appraised value of the house and land is $52,000.

Steve is unaware of the future condemnation proceedings, but would like for his family to escape from the urban blight in which they are living. Therefore, when Ross, a realtor, mentions that he may have a corporate client who would like to purchase Steve's property for $65,000, Steve is ecstatic and indicates a willingness to sell.

Ross is having some "second thoughts" about his conversation with Steve. The potential corporate purchaser is a corporation owned by Ross and his wife. Unlike Steve, Ross is aware of the forthcoming condemnation proceedings. He considers himself a skilled negotiator and thinks he can obtain a 100 percent return on his investment.

Ross is considering telling Steve that the corporate client has changed his mind. Ross would then explain that in the interim, he has learned that the city will be condemning several buildings in order to create a park, but has not yet established the prices it will pay for the condemned property. He would also tell Steve that because he believes he can get more from the city than Steve would obtain, he is willing to gamble and purchase the property now from Steve for $65,000. Ross would point out that Steve would obtain several benefits from this sale including not having to deal with the city, receiving an amount that exceeds both the appraised value and the original purchase price of the house, and

---

[62] § 1033(a) and Reg. §§ 1.1033(a)–1(a) and –2(a).
[63] Rev.Rul. 63–221, 1963–2 C. B. 332, and *Joseph P. Balistrieri*, 38 TCM 526, T.C.Memo. 1979–115.

[64] Rev.Rul. 81–180, 1981–2 C.B. 161.
[65] Rev.Rul. 81–181, 1981–2 C.B. 162.
[66] Rev.Rul. 82–74, 1982–1 C.B. 110.

receiving the money now. While admitting that he could reap a substantial profit, Ross
would emphasize that he would also be taking on substantial risks. In addition, Ross would
explain that when he sells the property to the city, he can defer the taxes by reinvesting the
sales proceeds. This deferral is possible because the condemnation is a type of involuntary
conversion.

Do you think Ross should make a new proposal to Steve based on his "second
thoughts?" How do you think Steve will respond?

COMPUTING THE AMOUNT REALIZED

The amount realized from the condemnation of property usually includes only the
amount received as compensation for the property.[67] Any amount received that is
designated as severance damages by both the government and the taxpayer is not
included in the amount realized. *Severance awards* usually occur when only a
portion of the entire property is condemned (e.g., a strip of land is taken to build
a highway). Severance damages are awarded because the value of the taxpayer's
remaining property has declined as a result of the condemnation. Such damages
reduce the basis of the property. However, if either of the following requirements
is satisfied, the nonrecognition provision of § 1033 applies to the severance
damages.

- Severance damages are used to restore the usability of the remaining
  property.
- The usefulness of the remaining property is destroyed by the condemnation,
  and the property is sold and replaced at a cost equal to or exceeding the sum
  of the condemnation award, severance damages, and sales proceeds.

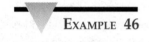

EXAMPLE 46

The government condemns a portion of Ron's farmland to build part of an interstate
highway. Because the highway denies his cattle access to a pond and some grazing land,
Ron receives severance damages in addition to the condemnation proceeds for the land
taken. Ron must reduce the basis of the property by the amount of the severance damages.
If the amount of the severance damages received exceeds the adjusted basis, Ron recognizes
gain. ▼

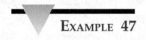

EXAMPLE 47

Assume the same facts as in the previous example, except that Ron used the proceeds from
the condemnation and the severance damages to build another pond and to clear woodland
for grazing. Therefore, all the proceeds are eligible for § 1033 treatment. Thus, there is no
possibility of gain recognition as the result of the amount of the severance damages
received exceeding the adjusted basis. ▼

REPLACEMENT PROPERTY

The requirements for replacement property generally are more restrictive than
those for like-kind property under § 1031. The basic requirement is that the
replacement property be similar or related in service or use to the involuntarily
converted property.[68]

Different interpretations of the phrase *similar or related in service or use* apply
depending on whether the involuntarily converted property is held by an
owner-user or by an *owner-investor* (e.g., lessor). A taxpayer who uses the property
in his or her trade or business is subject to a more restrictive test in terms of

---

[67] *Pioneer Real Estate Co.*, 47 B.T.A. 886 (1942), *acq.* 1943 C.B. 18.   [68] § 1033(a) and Reg. § 1.1033(a)–1.

acquiring replacement property. For an owner-user, the *functional use test* applies, and for an owner-investor, the *taxpayer use test* applies.

Taxpayer Use Test. The taxpayer use test for owner-investors provides the taxpayer with more flexibility in terms of what qualifies as replacement property than does the functional use test for owner-users. Essentially, the properties must be used by the taxpayer (the owner-investor) in similar endeavors. For example, rental property held by an owner-investor qualifies if replaced by other rental property, regardless of the type of rental property involved. The test is met when an investor replaces a manufacturing plant with a wholesale grocery warehouse if both properties are held for the production of rental income.[69] The replacement of a rental residence with a personal residence does not meet the test.[70]

Functional Use Test. Under this test, the taxpayer's use of the replacement property and of the involuntarily converted property must be the same. Replacing a manufacturing plant with a wholesale grocery warehouse, whether rented or not, does not meet this test. As indicated above, the IRS applies the taxpayer use test to owner-investors. However, the functional use test still applies to owner-users (e.g., a manufacturer whose manufacturing plant is destroyed by fire is required to replace the plant with another facility of similar functional use). Replacing a rental residence with a personal residence does not meet this test.

Special Rules. Under one set of circumstances, the broader replacement rules for like-kind exchanges are substituted for the narrow replacement rules normally used for involuntary conversions. This beneficial provision applies if business real property or investment real property is condemned. Therefore, the taxpayer has substantially more flexibility in selecting replacement property. For example, improved real property can be replaced with unimproved real property.

The rules concerning the nature of replacement property are illustrated in Concept Summary 12–3.

TIME LIMITATION ON REPLACEMENT

The taxpayer normally has a two-year period after the close of the taxable year in which any gain is realized from the involuntary conversion to replace the property (*the latest date*).[71] This rule affords as much as three years from the date of realization of gain to replace the property if the realization of gain took place on the first day of the taxable year.[72] If the involuntary conversion involved the condemnation of real property used in a trade or business or held for investment, a three-year period is substituted for the normal two-year period. In this case, the taxpayer can actually have as much as four years from the date of realization of gain to replace the property.

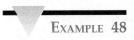

EXAMPLE 48

Megan's warehouse is destroyed by fire on December 16, 1995. The adjusted basis is $325,000. Megan receives $400,000 from the insurance company on January 10, 1996. She is a calendar year taxpayer. The latest date for replacement is December 31, 1998 (the end of the taxable year in which realized gain occurred plus two years). The critical date is not the date the involuntary conversion occurred, but rather the date of gain realization. ▼

---

[69] *Loco Realty Co. v. Comm.*, 62–2 USTC ¶9657, 10 AFTR2d 5359, 306 F.2d 207 (CA–8, 1962).

[70] Rev.Rul. 70–466, 1970–2 C.B. 165.

[71] §§ 1033(a)(2)(B) and (g)(4) and Reg. § 1.1033(a)–2(c)(3).

[72] The taxpayer can apply for an extension of this time period anytime before its expiration [Reg. § 1.1033(a)–2(c)(3)]. Also, the period for filing the application for extension can be extended if the taxpayer shows reasonable cause.

CONCEPT SUMMARY 12–3

Replacement Property Tests

Type of Property and User	Like-Kind Test	Taxpayer Use Test	Functional Use Test
Land used by a manufacturing company is condemned by a local government authority.	X		
Apartment and land held by an investor are sold due to the threat or imminence of condemnation.	X		
An investor's rented shopping mall is destroyed by fire; the mall may be replaced by other rental properties (e.g., an apartment building).		X	
A manufacturing plant is destroyed by fire; replacement property must consist of another manufacturing plant that is functionally the same as the property converted.			X
Personal residence of taxpayer is condemned by a local government authority; replacement property must consist of another personal residence.			X

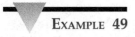

EXAMPLE 49

Assume the same facts as in the previous example, except Megan's warehouse is condemned. The latest date for replacement is December 31, 1999 (the end of the taxable year in which realized gain occurred plus three years). ▼

The *earliest date* for replacement typically is the date the involuntary conversion occurs. However, if the property is condemned, it is possible to replace the condemned property before this date. In this case, the earliest date is the date of the threat or imminence of requisition or condemnation of the property. The purpose of this provision is to enable the taxpayer to make an orderly replacement of the condemned property.

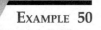

EXAMPLE 50

Assume the same facts as in Example 49. Megan can replace the warehouse before December 16, 1995 (the condemnation date). The earliest date for replacement is the date of the threat or imminence of requisition or condemnation of the warehouse. ▼

ETHICAL CONSIDERATIONS

Postponing Realized Gain from an Involuntary Conversion

Peggy, age 63 and in frail health, owns a furniture store in Petersburg. Due to competition from two large furniture retailers who opened stores in the Petersburg area during the past three years, Peggy's furniture store has been unprofitable.

Due to this lack of profitability as well as her advancing age, Peggy would like to retire. Unfortunately, she has been unable to locate a purchaser for her store. Her prayers seem to be answered when a tornado destroys her building and its contents. Fortunately, no one is injured or killed by the tornado.

Peggy anticipates that she can live on the insurance proceeds of $800,000 for the rest of her life. However, her realized gain on the involuntary conversion would produce a combined state and Federal tax liability of approximately $175,000. In order to forgo paying this amount associated with her 1996 income tax returns, Peggy elects postponement treatment under § 1033, indicating that she intends to replace the involuntarily converted property with similar property even though she does not intend to do so. Her justification, based on her participation in a 12-step program, is that she lives "one day at a time."

Evaluate Peggy's election of § 1033 postponement under these circumstances.

NONRECOGNITION OF GAIN

Nonrecognition of gain can be either mandatory or elective, depending upon whether the conversion is direct (into replacement property) or into money (indirect).

Direct Conversion. If the conversion is directly into replacement property rather than into money, nonrecognition of realized gain is *mandatory*. In this case, the basis of the replacement property is the same as the adjusted basis of the converted property. Direct conversion is rare in practice and usually involves condemnations. The following example illustrates the application of the rules for direct conversions.

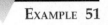

EXAMPLE 51

Lupe's property with an adjusted basis of $20,000 is condemned by the state. Lupe receives property with a fair market value of $50,000 as compensation for the property taken. Since the nonrecognition of realized gain is mandatory for direct conversions, Lupe's realized gain of $30,000 is not recognized, and the basis of the replacement property is $20,000 (adjusted basis of the condemned property). ▼

Conversion into Money. If the conversion is into money, at the election of the taxpayer, the realized gain is recognized only to the extent the amount realized from the involuntary conversion exceeds the cost of the qualifying replacement property.[73] This is the usual case, and nonrecognition (postponement) is *elective*. If the election is not made, the realized gain is recognized.

The basis of the replacement property is the property's cost less postponed (deferred) gain.[74] If the election to postpone gain is made, the holding period of the replacement property includes the holding period of the converted property.

Section 1033 applies *only to gains* and *not to losses*. Losses from involuntary conversions are recognized if the property is held for business or income-producing purposes. Personal casualty losses are recognized, but condemnation losses related to personal use assets (e.g., a personal residence) are neither recognized nor postponed.

Examples 52 and 53 illustrate the application of the involuntary conversion provisions.

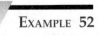

EXAMPLE 52

Walt's building (used in his trade or business), with an adjusted basis of $50,000, is destroyed by fire in 1996. Walt is a calendar year taxpayer. In 1996, he receives an insurance reimbursement of $100,000 for the loss. Walt invests $80,000 in a new building.

- Walt has until December 31, 1998, to make the new investment and qualify for the nonrecognition election.

---

[73] § 1033(a)(2)(A) and Reg. § 1.1033(a)–2(c)(1).   [74] § 1033(b).

- Walt's realized gain is $50,000 ($100,000 insurance proceeds received − $50,000 adjusted basis of old building).
- Assuming the replacement property qualifies as similar or related in service or use, Walt's recognized gain is $20,000. He reinvested $20,000 less than the insurance proceeds received ($100,000 proceeds − $80,000 reinvested). Therefore, his realized gain is recognized to that extent.
- Walt's basis in the new building is $50,000. This is the building's cost of $80,000 less the postponed gain of $30,000 (realized gain of $50,000 − recognized gain of $20,000).
- The computation of realization, recognition, and basis would apply even if Walt was a real estate dealer and the building destroyed by fire was part of his inventory. Unlike § 1031, § 1033 generally does not exclude inventory. ▼

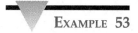

EXAMPLE 53

Assume the same facts as in the previous example, except that Walt receives only $45,000 (instead of $100,000) of insurance proceeds. He has a realized and recognized loss of $5,000. The basis of the new building is the building's cost of $80,000. If the destroyed building was held for personal use, the recognized loss is subject to the following additional limitations.[75] The loss of $5,000 is limited to the decline in fair market value of the property, and the amount of the loss is reduced first by $100 and then by 10% of adjusted gross income (refer to Chapter 6). ▼

INVOLUNTARY CONVERSION OF A PERSONAL RESIDENCE

The tax consequences of the involuntary conversion of a personal residence depend upon whether the conversion is a casualty or condemnation and whether a realized loss or gain results.

Loss Situations. If the conversion is a condemnation, the realized loss is not recognized. Loss from the condemnation of a personal use asset is never recognized. If the conversion is a casualty (a loss from fire, storm, etc.), the loss is recognized subject to the personal casualty loss limitations (refer to Chapter 6).

Gain Situations. If the conversion is a condemnation, the gain may be postponed under either § 1033 or § 1034. That is, the taxpayer may elect to treat the condemnation as a sale under the deferral of gain rules relating to the sale of a personal residence under § 1034 (presented subsequently). If the conversion is a casualty, the gain is postponed only under the involuntary conversion provisions.

REPORTING CONSIDERATIONS

Involuntary conversions from casualty and theft are reported first on Form 4684, Casualties and Thefts. Casualty and theft losses on personal use property for the individual taxpayer are carried from Form 4684 to Schedule A of Form 1040. For other casualty and theft items, the Form 4684 amounts are generally reported on Form 4797, Sales of Business Property, unless Form 4797 is not required. In the latter case, the amounts are reported directly on the tax return involved.

Except for personal use property, recognized gains and losses from involuntary conversions other than by casualty and theft are reported on Form 4797. As stated previously, if the property involved in the involuntary conversion (other than by casualty and theft) is personal use property, any realized loss is not recognized. Any realized gain is treated as gain on a voluntary sale.

---

[75]§ 165(c)(3) and Reg. § 1.165–7.

SALE OF A RESIDENCE—§ 1034

9 **LEARNING OBJECTIVE**
Describe the provisions for postponing recognition of gain on the sale and replacement of a personal residence.

A realized loss from the sale of a **personal residence** is not recognized because the residence is personal use property. A realized gain is subject to taxation, however. The tax law includes two provisions under which all or part of the realized gain is either postponed or excluded from taxation. The first of these, § 1034, is discussed below. The second, § 121, is discussed later in the chapter.

Section 1034 provides for the *mandatory* nonrecognition of gain from the sale or exchange of a personal residence if the sales proceeds are reinvested in a replacement residence within a prescribed time period. Both the old and new residences must qualify as the taxpayer's principal residence. A houseboat or house trailer qualifies if it is used by the taxpayer as a principal residence.[76]

The reason for not recognizing gain when a residence is replaced by a new residence within the prescribed time period (discussed below) is that the new residence is viewed as a continuation of the investment. Also, if the proceeds from the sale are reinvested, the taxpayer does not have the wherewithal to pay tax on the realized gain. Beyond these fundamental concepts, Congress, in enacting § 1034, was concerned with the hardship of involuntary moves and the socially desirable objective of encouraging the mobility of labor.

REPLACEMENT PERIOD

For the nonrecognition treatment to apply, the old residence must be replaced by a new residence within a period *beginning two years before* the sale of the old residence and *ending two years after* the sale. This four-year period applies regardless of whether the new residence is purchased or constructed. The taxpayer must not only *acquire* the new residence during this period, but must *occupy* and use it as well. The occupancy requirement has been strictly construed by both the IRS and the courts, and even circumstances beyond a taxpayer's control do not excuse noncompliance.[77]

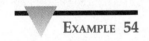

EXAMPLE 54

Gail sells her personal residence from which she realizes a gain of $50,000. She begins constructing a new residence immediately after the sale. However, unstable soil conditions and a trade union strike cause unforeseen delays. The new residence ultimately is completed and occupied by Gail 25 months after the sale of the old residence. Since the occupancy requirement has not been satisfied, § 1034 is inapplicable, and Gail must recognize a gain of $50,000 on the sale of the old residence. ▼

Taxpayers might be inclined to make liberal use of § 1034 as a means of speculating when the price of residential housing is rising. Without any time restriction on its use, § 1034 would permit deferral of gain on multiple sales of principal residences, each of which would result in an economic profit. The Code curbs this approach by precluding the application of § 1034 to any sales occurring within two years of its last use.

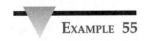

EXAMPLE 55

After Seth sells his principal residence (the first residence) in March 1995 for $150,000 (realized gain of $60,000), he buys and sells the following (all of which qualify as principal residences):

[76] Reg. § 1.1034–1(c)(3)(i).

[77] *James A. Henry,* 44 TCM 844, T.C.Memo. 1982–469, and *William F. Peck,* 44 TCM 1030, T.C.Memo. 1982–506.

TAX IN THE NEWS

IRS CONTINUES TO MAINTAIN STRICT INTERPRETATION OF § 1034

Section 1034 permits a taxpayer to postpone the recognition of the realized gain on the sale of his or her residence. To qualify for nonrecognition, the taxpayer must purchase and occupy a replacement residence that costs at least as much as the adjusted sales price of the old residence. In addition, this purchase and occupancy must occur within a four-year window that begins two years prior to the sales date and ends two years after the sales date.

A taxpayer who sold his residence purchased a new residence for an amount in excess of the adjusted sales price of the old residence. He signed the contract to buy the new residence six weeks before the expiration of the two-year period. Prior to the final settlement on the house and before the expiration of the two-year period, he occupied the house. However, the final settlement (signing of deeds, etc.) did not occur until shortly after the expiration of the two-year period.

The IRS has taken the position that it has no authority to ignore the statutory time period requirements. Therefore, the sale of the original residence does not qualify for § 1034 postponement treatment.

	Date of Purchase	Date of Sale	Amount Involved
Second residence	April 1995		$160,000
Second residence		May 1996	180,000
Third residence	June 1996		200,000

Because multiple sales have occurred within a period of two years, § 1034 does not apply to the sale of the second residence. Thus, the realized gain of $20,000 [$180,000 (selling price) – $160,000 (purchase price)] must be recognized. ▼

The two-year rule precluding multiple use of § 1034 could create a hardship where a taxpayer is transferred by his or her employer and has little choice in the matter. For this reason, § 1034 was amended to provide an exception to the two-year rule when the sale results from a change in the location of employment. To qualify for the exception, a taxpayer must meet the distance and length-of-employment requirements specified for the deduction of moving expenses under § 217.[78]

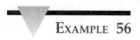

EXAMPLE 56   Assume the same facts as in the previous example, except that in February 1996, Seth's employer transfers him to a job in another state. Consequently, the sale of the second residence and the purchase of the third residence were due to the relocation of employment. If Seth satisfies the distance and length-of-employment requirements of § 217, no gain is recognized on the sale of the first and second residences. ▼

The running of the time periods specified above (other than the two-year limit on multiple sales) is suspended during any time the taxpayer or spouse is on

---

[78] Refer to Chapter 8 for the discussion of the rules governing the deduction for moving expenses.

extended active duty (over 90 days or for an indefinite period) with the U.S. Armed Forces after the date the old residence is sold.[79] This suspension is limited to four years after the date the old residence is sold. A similar suspension is available to U.S. citizens who are employed outside the United States by nongovernmental employers (expatriates).[80]

PRINCIPAL RESIDENCE

Both the old and new residences must qualify as the taxpayer's principal residence. Whether property is the taxpayer's principal residence depends "... upon all the facts and circumstances in each case."[81]

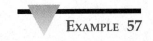

EXAMPLE 57

Mitch sells his principal residence and moves to Norfolk, Virginia, where he is employed. He decides to rent an apartment in Norfolk because of its proximity to his place of employment. He purchases a beach house in Virginia Beach that he occupies most weekends. Mitch does not intend to live in the beach house other than on weekends. The apartment in Norfolk is his principal place of residence. Therefore, the purchase of the beach house does not qualify as an appropriate replacement. ▼

If the old residence ceases to be the taxpayer's principal residence before its sale, the nonrecognition provision does not apply. For example, if the taxpayer abandons the old residence before its sale, the residence no longer qualifies as a principal residence.[82] If the old residence is converted to other than personal use (e.g., rental) before its sale, the nonrecognition provision does not apply. If the residence is only partially converted to business use, gain from the sale of the personal use portion still qualifies for nonrecognition. It is possible to convert part of a principal residence to business use and later to convert that part back to being part of the principal residence (e.g., a home office).[83]

Temporarily renting out the old residence before sale does not necessarily terminate its status as the taxpayer's principal residence,[84] nor does temporarily renting out the new residence before it is occupied by the taxpayer. A related issue is whether a taxpayer who temporarily rents out the old residence while attempting to sell it is entitled to deduct expenses in excess of income relating to the rental. That is, is the old residence subject to the loss deduction rules for hobby loss activities? If it is, the deductions associated with the rental activity are limited to the rent income generated. The Tax Court concluded that since the property was considered to be the taxpayer's principal residence and as a result qualified for § 1034 postponement of gain, the property was subject to the hobby loss limitations. The Court of Appeals reversed the Tax Court and held that the hobby loss provisions did not apply.[85]

NONRECOGNITION OF GAIN REQUIREMENTS

Realized gain from the sale of the old residence is not recognized if the taxpayer reinvests an amount *at least equal* to the adjusted sales price of the old residence. Realized gain is recognized to the extent the taxpayer does not reinvest an amount

---

[79] § 1034(h)(1).

[80] § 1034(k).

[81] Reg. § 1.1034–1(c)(3).

[82] *Richard T. Houlette,* 48 T.C. 350 (1967), and *Stolk v. Comm.,* 64–1 USTC ¶9228, 13 AFTR2d 535, 326 F.2d 760 (CA–2, 1964).

[83] Rev.Rul. 82–26, 1982–1 C.B. 114.

[84] *Robert W. Aagaard,* 56 T.C. 191 (1971), *acq.* 1971–2 C.B. 1; *Robert G. Clapham,* 63 T.C. 505 (1975); Rev.Rul. 59–72, 1959–1 C.B. 203; and Rev.Rul. 78–146, 1978–1 C.B. 260.

[85] *Bolaris v. Comm.,* 85–2 USTC ¶9822, 56 AFTR2d 85–6472, 776 F.2d 1428 (CA–9, 1985), *rev'g.* T.C. 840 (1983).

TAX IN THE NEWS

JOINT OWNERSHIP AND A NEW SPOUSE: CAUTION IS NECESSARY

To obtain the full benefits of § 1034 deferral treatment on the sale of a residence, the taxpayer must reinvest in a replacement residence an amount at least equal to the adjusted sales price of the old residence. In a recent Tax Court case, the taxpayer thought she had done so, but the Tax Court disagreed.

The taxpayer and her former spouse, who jointly owned the house with her, sold their residence and calculated their realized gain as follows:

Amount realized	$356,000
Less: Adjusted basis	(216,000)
Realized gain	$140,000

The taxpayer thought that if she reinvested her $178,000 share of the net sales price, she would be able to defer the recognition of her $70,000 share of the realized gain.

She remarried prior to purchasing another residence. She and her new spouse jointly purchased a residence for $180,000. Since the purchase price exceeded her $178,000 share of the net sales price, she concluded that she had made a reinvestment adequate to defer her $70,000 share of the realized gain.

Not so according to the IRS. According to their position, since she purchased the house jointly with her new spouse, she had reinvested only $90,000. Therefore, her realized gain of $70,000 is recognized because this amount was less than her reinvestment deficiency of $88,000. Unfortunately, the Tax Court in *Jeanne G. Snowa*, 70 TCM 163, T.C.Memo. 1995–336, accepted the position of the IRS.

at least equal to the adjusted sales price in a new residence. Therefore, the amount not reinvested is treated similarly to boot received in a like-kind exchange.

The **adjusted sales price** is the amount realized from the sale of the old residence less fixing-up expenses. The *amount realized* is the selling price less the selling expenses. *Selling expenses* include items such as the cost of advertising the property for sale, real estate broker commissions, legal fees in connection with the sale, and loan placement fees paid by the taxpayer as a condition of arranging financing for the buyer.

Fixing-up expenses are personal in nature and are incurred by the taxpayer to assist in the sale of the old residence. Fixing-up expenses include such items as ordinary repairs, painting, and wallpapering. To qualify as a fixing-up expense, the expense must (1) be incurred for work performed during the 90-day period ending on the date of the contract of sale, (2) be paid within 30 days after the date of the sale, and (3) not be a capital expenditure.

Although selling expenses are deductible in calculating the amount realized, fixing-up expenses are not. Therefore, fixing-up expenses do not have an impact on the calculation of realized gain or loss. However, since fixing-up expenses are deductible in calculating the adjusted sales price, they do have the potential for producing tax benefit in that they reduce the amount of the reinvestment required to qualify for nonrecognition treatment. Conversely, if a replacement residence is not acquired, the fixing-up expenses produce no tax benefit.

Reducing the amount of the required reinvestment by the amount of fixing-up expenses is another application of the wherewithal to pay concept. To the extent

▼ **FIGURE 12–1**
Sale-of-Residence Model

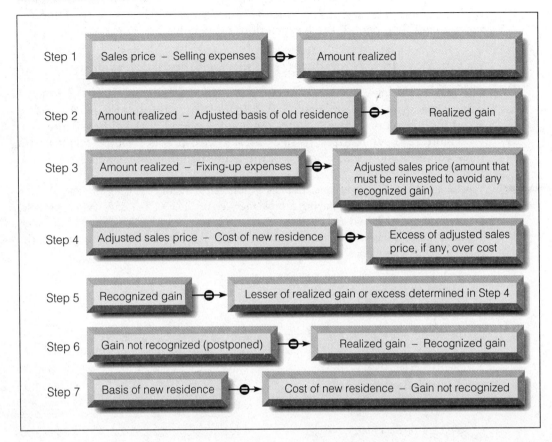

that the taxpayer has expended part of the funds received from the sale in preparing the old residence for sale, he or she does not have the funds available to reinvest in the new residence.

As previously mentioned, fixing-up expenses are not considered in determining realized gain. They are considered only in determining how much realized gain is to be postponed. In addition, fixing-up expenses have no direct effect on the basis of the new residence. Indirectly, though, through their effect on postponed gain, they can bring about a lesser basis for the new residence. The effects of fixing-up expenses on the computation of gain realized and recognized and on basis are illustrated in Figure 12–1 and in Example 58.

CAPITAL IMPROVEMENTS

Capital improvements are added to the adjusted basis of a personal residence. The adjusted basis is used in computing gain or loss on a subsequent sale or other disposition of the property. In calculating the cost of a replacement residence (for determining the nonrecognition of gain under § 1034), only capital improvements made during a certain time period are counted. The time period begins two years before the date of sale of the old residence and ends two years after that date (the time period during which the old residence can be replaced).[86]

---

[86] *Charles M. Shaw*, 69 T.C. 1034 (1978); Reg. § 1.1034–1(c)(4)(ii); and Rev.Rul. 78–147, 1978–1 C.B. 261.

If the taxpayer receives a residence by gift or inheritance, the residence will
not qualify as a replacement residence. However, if the taxpayer makes substantial
capital expenditures (e.g., reconstruction or additions) to the property within the
replacement time period, these expenditures do qualify.[87]

BASIS AND HOLDING PERIOD OF THE NEW RESIDENCE

The *basis* of the new residence is the cost of the new residence less the realized
gain not recognized (postponed gain). If there is any postponed gain, the *holding
period* of the new residence includes the holding period of the old residence.

Figure 12–1 summarizes the sale-of-residence concepts. Example 58 illustrates
these concepts and the application of the nonrecognition provision.

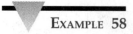

EXAMPLE 58   Veneia, age 47, sells her personal residence (adjusted basis of $136,000) for $244,000. She
receives only $229,400 after paying a brokerage fee of $14,600. Ten days before the sale,
Veneia incurred and paid for qualified fixing-up expenses of $3,400. Two months later,
Veneia acquires a new residence. Determine the gain, if any, she must recognize and the
basis of the new residence under each of the following circumstances:

1. The new residence costs $230,000.
2. The new residence costs $210,000.
3. The new residence costs $110,000.

		1	2	3
Step 1:	Sales price	$ 244,000	$ 244,000	$ 244,000
	−Selling expenses	(14,600)	(14,600)	(14,600)
	=Amount realized	$ 229,400	$ 229,400	$ 229,400
Step 2:	Amount realized	$ 229,400	$ 229,400	$ 229,400
	−Adjusted basis	(136,000)	(136,000)	(136,000)
	=Realized gain	$ 93,400	$ 93,400	$ 93,400
Step 3:	Amount realized	$ 229,400	$ 229,400	$ 229,400
	−Fixing-up expenses	(3,400)	(3,400)	(3,400)
	=Adjusted sales price	$ 226,000	$ 226,000	$ 226,000
Step 4:	Adjusted sales price	$ 226,000	$ 226,000	$ 226,000
	−Cost of new residence	(230,000)	(210,000)	(110,000)
	=Excess of ASP over cost	$ −0−	$ 16,000	$ 116,000
Step 5:	Recognized gain (lesser of Step 2 or Step 4)	$ −0−	$ 16,000	$ 93,400
Step 6:	Realized gain	$ 93,400	$ 93,400	$ 93,400
	−Recognized gain	(−0−)	(16,000)	(93,400)
	=Postponed gain	$ 93,400	$ 77,400	$ −0−
Step 7:	Cost of new residence	$ 230,000	$ 210,000	$ 110,000
	−Postponed gain	(93,400)	(77,400)	(−0−)
	=Basis of new residence	$ 136,600	$ 132,600	$ 110,000

---

[87] Reg. §§ 1.1034–1(b)(7) and (9) and 1.1034–1(c)(4)(i).

None of the realized gain of $93,400 is recognized in the first case because the actual reinvestment of $230,000 exceeds the required reinvestment of $226,000. In the second case, the recognized gain is $16,000 because the required reinvestment of $226,000 exceeds the actual reinvestment of $210,000 by this amount. In the third case, the required reinvestment of $226,000 exceeds the actual reinvestment of $110,000 by $116,000. Since this amount is greater than the realized gain of $93,400, the realized gain of $93,400 is recognized, and § 1034 deferral does not apply. ▼

REPORTING PROCEDURES

The taxpayer is required to report the details of the sale of the residence on the tax return for the taxable year in which gain is realized, even if all of the gain is postponed. If a new residence is acquired and occupied before filing, a statement should be attached to the return showing the purchase date, the cost, and date of occupancy. Form 2119, Sale or Exchange of Your Home, is used to show the details of the sale and replacement, and the taxpayer should retain a copy permanently as support for the basis of the new residence. If a replacement residence has not been purchased by the time the return is filed, the taxpayer should submit the details of the purchase on the return of the taxable year during which it occurs. If the old residence is not replaced within the prescribed time period, or if some recognized gain results, the taxpayer must file an amended return for the year in which the sale took place.

Sale of a Residence—§ 121

10 — LEARNING OBJECTIVE
Discuss the provisions for permanent exclusion of gain on the sale of a personal residence by taxpayers age 55 and older.

Under the **Section 121 exclusion,** taxpayers age 55 or older who sell or exchange their principal residence may *elect to exclude* up to $125,000 ($62,500 for married individuals filing separate returns) of realized gain from the sale or exchange.[88] The election can be made *only once.*[89] This provision differs from § 1034 where nonrecognition is mandatory and may occur many times during a taxpayer's lifetime. Section 121 also differs from § 1034 in that it does not require the taxpayer to purchase a new residence. The excluded gain is never recognized, whereas the realized gain not recognized under § 1034 is postponed by subtracting it from the cost of the new residence in calculating the adjusted basis.

This provision is the only case in the tax law where a realized gain from the disposition of property that is not recognized is excluded rather than merely postponed. The provision allows the taxpayer a permanent recovery of more than the cost or other basis of the residence tax-free.

Congress enacted § 121 simply to relieve older citizens of the large tax they might incur from the sale of a personal residence. The dollar and age limitations restrict the benefit of § 121 to taxpayers who presumably have a greater need for increased tax-free dollars.

EXCLUSION REQUIREMENTS

The taxpayer must be at least age 55 before the date of the sale and have *owned* and *used* the residence as a principal residence for at least *three years* during the *five-year* period ending on the date of sale. The ownership and use periods do not

---

[88] §§ 121(a), (b), and (c). For married taxpayers, each spouse must consent.

[89] § 121(b)(2) and Reg. § 1.121–2(b). Only one election may be made by married individuals.

have to be the same period of time. Short temporary absences (e.g., vacations) count as periods of use. If the residence is owned jointly by husband and wife, only one of the spouses is required to meet these requirements if a joint return is filed for the taxable year in which the sale took place.

In determining whether the ownership and use period requirements are satisfied, transactions affecting prior residences may be relevant. If a former residence is involuntarily converted and any gain is postponed under § 1033, the holding period of the former residence is added to the holding period of the replacement residence for § 121 purposes. However, if the realized gain is postponed under § 1034 (sale-of-residence provision), the holding period of the former residence is not added to the holding period of the replacement residence for § 121 purposes. In this instance, the holding period of the replacement residence begins with the acquisition date of the replacement residence.

EXAMPLE 59

Cole has lived in his residence since 1986. The residence is involuntarily converted in July 1996. He purchases a replacement residence in August 1996. When the replacement residence is subsequently sold, Cole includes the holding period of the involuntarily converted residence in determining whether he can satisfy the ownership and use requirements. ▼

EXAMPLE 60

Assume the same facts as in the previous example, except that Cole's residence was not involuntarily converted. Instead, he sold it so that he could move into a larger house. When the replacement residence is subsequently sold, Cole is not permitted to include the holding period of the old residence in determining whether he can satisfy the ownership and use requirements. ▼

ETHICAL CONSIDERATIONS

A Couple's Approach to the § 121 Exclusion

Bob and Sandra, both age 67, live in Houston, Texas, where each owns a personal residence on which the realized gain from a sale would be $125,000. They plan to marry and move to Williamsburg, Virginia. Not wanting the burdens of home ownership, they intend to rent a house.

Bob and Sandra both satisfy the requirements for the § 121 exclusion. Because of the soft real estate market in Houston, they have been unsuccessful in selling their personal residences. Being aware that a married couple can qualify only once for the § 121 exclusion, the realtor suggests the following plan. Bob will sell his house to Sandra, and Sandra will sell her house to Bob for the fair market value. Each will elect § 121 exclusion treatment. They will then marry and move to Williamsburg. Upon the subsequent sale of the houses to external buyers, the recognized gain, if any, will be minimal, since the adjusted basis of each house will have stepped up to the fair market value on the prior sale to each other.

Evaluate the realtor's proposal for Bob and Sandra.

RELATIONSHIP TO OTHER PROVISIONS

The taxpayer can treat an involuntary conversion of a principal residence as a sale for purposes of § 121. Any gain not excluded under § 121 is then subject to postponement under § 1033 or § 1034 (condemnation only), assuming the requirements of those provisions are met.

Any gain from the sale of a residence not excluded under § 121 is subject to postponement under § 1034, assuming the requirements of that provision are met. Examples 61 and 62 illustrate this relationship.

MAKING AND REVOKING THE ELECTION

The election not to recognize gain under § 121 may be made or revoked at any time before the statute of limitations expires. Therefore, the taxpayer generally has until the *later* of (1) three years from the due date of the return for the year the gain is realized or (2) two years from the date the tax is paid to make or revoke the election. The election is made by attaching a signed statement (showing all the details of the sale) to the return for the taxable year in which the sale took place. Form 2119 is used for this purpose. The election is revoked by filing a signed statement (showing the taxpayer's name, Social Security number, and taxable year for which the election was made) indicating the revocation.[90]

COMPUTATION PROCEDURE

The following examples illustrate the application of both the § 121 and § 1034 provisions.

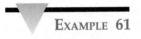

EXAMPLE 61

Keith sells his personal residence (adjusted basis of $32,000) for $205,000, of which he receives only $195,400 after paying the selling expenses of $9,600. Ten days before the sale, he incurred and paid for qualified fixing-up expenses of $6,400. Keith is age 55 and elects the exclusion of gain under § 121. He does not acquire a replacement residence. ▼

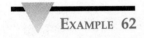

EXAMPLE 62

Assume the same facts as in the previous example, except that Keith acquires a new residence for $40,000 within the prescribed time period.

The solutions to Examples 61 and 62 are as follows:

	Example 61	Example 62
Amount realized ($205,000 – $9,600)	$ 195,400	$ 195,400
Adjusted basis	(32,000)	(32,000)
Realized gain	$ 163,400	$ 163,400
§ 121 exclusion	(125,000)	(125,000)
Realized gain after exclusion	$ 38,400	$ 38,400
Amount realized	$ 195,400	$ 195,400
Fixing-up expenses	(6,400)	(6,400)
Adjusted sales price	$ 189,000	$ 189,000
§ 121 exclusion	(125,000)	(125,000)
Adjusted sales price after exclusion	$ 64,000	$ 64,000
Cost of new residence	(–0–)	(40,000)
Excess of adjusted sales price after the exclusion over reinvestment	$ 64,000	$ 24,000
Recognized gain (lower of realized gain after exclusion or above excess)	$ 38,400	$ 24,000

[90] Reg. §§ 1.121–4(b) and (c).

Realized gain after exclusion	$ 38,400	$ 38,400
Recognized gain	(38,400)	(24,000)
Postponed gain	$ –0–	$ 14,400
Cost of new residence	$ –0–	$ 40,000
Postponed gain	(–0–)	(14,400)
Basis of new residence	$ –0–	$ 25,600

▼

Comparing the results of Examples 61 and 62 provides insight into the relationship between § 1034 and § 121. If Keith had not made the election to postpone gain under § 121 in Example 61, his recognized gain would have been $163,400 (the realized gain). Thus, the election resulted in the permanent exclusion of the $125,000 of realized gain by reducing the recognized gain to $38,400. Further documentation of the permanent nature of the § 121 exclusion is provided in the calculation of the basis of the new residence in Example 62. The $40,000 cost of the residence is reduced only by the postponed gain of $14,400. That is, it is not reduced by the § 121 exclusion amount of $125,000. To postpone all of the $38,400 realized gain after the exclusion, Keith would have needed to reinvest $64,000 (the adjusted sales price after the exclusion). Also, note that the Example 61 results demonstrate that the realized gain after the exclusion is the ceiling on recognition.

OTHER NONRECOGNITION PROVISIONS

11   LEARNING OBJECTIVE
Identify other nonrecognition provisions contained in the Code.

The typical taxpayer experiences the sale of a residence or an involuntary conversion more frequently than the other types of nontaxable exchanges. Several additional nonrecognition provisions that are not as common are treated briefly in the remainder of this chapter.

EXCHANGE OF STOCK FOR PROPERTY—§ 1032

Under § 1032, a corporation does not recognize gain or loss on the receipt of money or other property in exchange for its stock (including treasury stock). In other words, a corporation does not recognize gain or loss when it deals in its own stock. This provision is consistent with the accounting treatment of such transactions.

CERTAIN EXCHANGES OF INSURANCE POLICIES—§ 1035

Under this provision, no gain or loss is recognized from the exchange of certain insurance contracts or policies. The rules relating to exchanges not solely in kind and the basis of the property acquired are the same as under § 1031. Exchanges qualifying for nonrecognition include the following:

- The exchange of life insurance contracts.
- The exchange of a life insurance contract for an endowment or annuity contract.
- The exchange of an endowment contract for another endowment contract that provides for regular payments beginning at a date not later than the date payments would have begun under the contract exchanged.
- The exchange of an endowment contract for an annuity contract.
- The exchange of annuity contracts.

EXCHANGE OF STOCK FOR STOCK OF THE SAME CORPORATION—§ 1036

A shareholder does not recognize gain or loss on the exchange of common stock solely for common stock in the same corporation or from the exchange of preferred stock for preferred stock in the same corporation. Exchanges between individual shareholders as well as between a shareholder and the corporation are included. The rules relating to exchanges not solely in kind and the basis of the property acquired are the same as under § 1031. For example, a nonrecognition exchange occurs when common stock with different rights, such as voting for nonvoting, is exchanged. A shareholder usually recognizes gain or loss from the exchange of common for preferred or preferred for common even though the stock exchanged is in the same corporation.

CERTAIN REACQUISITIONS OF REAL PROPERTY—§ 1038

Under this provision, no loss is recognized from the repossession of real property sold on an installment basis. Gain is recognized to a limited extent.

TRANSFERS OF PROPERTY BETWEEN SPOUSES OR INCIDENT TO DIVORCE—§ 1041

Section 1041 provides that transfers of property *between spouses or former spouses incident to divorce* are nontaxable transactions. Therefore, the basis to the recipient is a carryover basis. To be treated as incident to the divorce, the transfer must be related to the cessation of marriage or occur within one year after the date on which the marriage ceases.

Section 1041 also provides for nontaxable exchange treatment on property transfers *between spouses during marriage*. The basis to the recipient spouse is a carryover basis.

ROLLOVERS INTO SPECIALIZED SMALL BUSINESS INVESTMENT COMPANIES—§ 1044

The Revenue Reconciliation Act of 1993 provides a postponement opportunity associated with the sale of publicly traded securities. If the amount realized is reinvested in the common stock or partnership interest of a specialized small business investment company (SSBIC), the realized gain is not recognized. Any amount not reinvested will trigger the recognition of the realized gain on the sale to the extent of the deficiency. The taxpayer must reinvest the proceeds within 60 days of the date of sale in order to qualify. In calculating the basis of the SSBIC stock, the amount of the purchase price is reduced by the amount of the postponed gain.

Statutory ceilings are imposed on the amount of realized gain that can be postponed for any taxable year as follows:

- Individual taxpayer: Lesser of:
  - $50,000 ($25,000 for married filing separately).
  - $500,000 ($250,000 for married filing separately) reduced by the amount of such nonrecognized gain in prior taxable years.
- Corporate taxpayer: Lesser of:
  - $250,000.
  - $1,000,000 reduced by the amount of such nonrecognized gain in prior taxable years.

Investors ineligible for this postponement treatment include partnerships, S corporations, estates, and trusts.

Chapter 12 has covered certain situations in which realized gains or losses are not recognized (nontaxable exchanges). Chapter 13 is concerned with the *classification* of recognized gains and losses. That is, if a gain or loss is recognized, is it an ordinary or capital gain or loss? Chapter 13 also discusses the tax consequences of capital gains and losses.

**TAX PLANNING
CONSIDERATIONS**

12 **LEARNING OBJECTIVE**
Identify tax planning opportunities related to selected property transactions.

TAX CONSEQUENCES OF ALICE'S PROPOSED TRANSACTION

In Example 1 earlier in the chapter, Alice's tax adviser asked a number of questions in order to advise her on a proposed transaction. Alice provided the following answers:

- Alice inherited the house from her mother. The fair market value of the house at the date of her mother's death, based on the estate tax return, was $200,000. Based on an appraisal, the house is worth $230,000. Alice's mother lived in the house for 48 years. According to the mother's attorney, her adjusted basis for the house was $75,000.
- As a child, Alice lived in the house for 10 years. She has not lived there during the 35 years she has been married.
- The house has been vacant during the seven months that Alice has owned it. She has been trying to decide whether she should sell it for its fair market value or sell it to her nephew for $75,000. Alice has suggested a $75,000 price for the sale to Dan because she believes this is the amount at which she will have no gain or loss.
- Alice intends to invest the $75,000 in stock.

You advise Alice that her adjusted basis for the house is the $200,000 fair market value on the date of her mother's death. If Alice sells the house for $230,000 (assuming no selling expenses), she would have a recognized gain of $30,000 ($230,000 amount realized − $200,000 adjusted basis). The house is a capital asset, and her holding period is long term since she inherited the house. Thus, the gain would be classified as a long-term capital gain. If, instead, Alice sells the house to her nephew for $75,000, she will have a part sale and part gift. The realized gain on the sale of $9,783 is recognized.

Amount realized	$ 75,000
Less: Adjusted basis	(65,217)*
Realized gain	$ 9,783
Recognized gain	$ 9,783

*[($75,000/$230,000) × $200,000] = $65,217.

The gain is classified as a long-term capital gain. Alice is then deemed to have made a gift to Dan of $155,000 ($230,000 − $75,000).

With this information, Alice can make an informed selection between the two options.

COST IDENTIFICATION AND DOCUMENTATION CONSIDERATIONS

When multiple assets are acquired in a single transaction, the contract price must be allocated for several reasons. First, some of the assets may be depreciable while others are not. From the different viewpoints of the buyer and the seller, this may produce a tax conflict that needs to be resolved. That is, the seller prefers a high allocation for nondepreciable assets, whereas the purchaser prefers a high allocation for depreciable assets (see Chapter 13). Second, the seller needs to know the amount realized on the sale of the capital assets and the ordinary income assets so that the recognized gains and losses can be classified as capital or ordinary. For example, an allocation to goodwill or to a covenant not to compete (see Chapters 7 and 13) produces different tax consequences to the seller. Third, the buyer needs the adjusted basis of each asset to calculate the realized gain or loss on a subsequent sale or other disposition of each asset.

SELECTION OF PROPERTY FOR MAKING GIFTS

A donor can achieve several tax advantages by making gifts of appreciated property. Income tax on the unrealized gain that would have occurred had the donor sold the property is avoided by the donor. A portion of this amount can be permanently avoided because the donee's adjusted basis is increased by part or all of any gift tax paid by the donor. Even without this increase in basis, the income tax liability on the sale of the property by the donee can be less than the income tax liability that would have resulted from the donor's sale of the property, if the donee is in a lower tax bracket than the donor. In addition, any subsequent appreciation during the time the property is held by the lower tax bracket donee results in a tax savings on the sale or other disposition of the property. Such gifts of appreciated property can be an effective tool in family tax planning.

Taxpayers should generally not make gifts of depreciated property (property that, if sold, would produce a realized loss) because the donor does not receive an income tax deduction for the unrealized loss element. In addition, the donee receives no benefit from this unrealized loss upon the subsequent sale of the property because of the loss basis rule. The loss basis rule provides that the donee's basis is the lower of the donor's basis or fair market value at the date of the gift. If the donor anticipates that the donee will sell the property upon receiving it, the donor should sell the property and take the loss deduction, assuming the loss is deductible. The donor can then give the proceeds from the sale to the donee.

SELECTION OF PROPERTY FOR MAKING BEQUESTS

A decedent's will should generally make bequests of appreciated property. Doing so enables both the decedent and the heir to avoid income tax on the unrealized gain because the recipient takes the fair market value as his or her basis.

Taxpayers generally should not make bequests of depreciated property (property that, if sold, would produce a realized loss) because the decedent does not receive an income tax deduction for the unrealized loss element. In addition, the heir will receive no benefit from this unrealized loss upon the subsequent sale of the property.

EXAMPLE 63

On the date of her death, Marta owned land held for investment purposes. The land had an adjusted basis of $600,000 and a fair market value of $100,000. If Marta had sold the property before her death, the recognized loss would have been $500,000. If Ramon inherits the property and sells it for $60,000, the recognized loss is $40,000 (the decline in value since Marta's death). In addition, regardless of the period of time Ramon holds the property, the holding period is long term (see Chapter 13). ▼

From an income tax perspective, it is preferable to transfer appreciated property as a bequest rather than as a gift. This results because inherited property receives a step-up in basis, whereas property received by gift has a carryover basis to the donee. However, in making this decision, the estate tax consequences of the bequest should also be weighed against the gift tax consequences of the gift.

DISALLOWED LOSSES

Section 267 Disallowed Losses.   Taxpayers should be aware of the desirability of avoiding transactions that activate the loss disallowance provisions for related parties. This is so even in light of the provision that permits the related-party buyer to offset his or her realized gain by the related-party seller's disallowed loss. Even with this offset, several inequities exist. First, the tax benefit associated with the disallowed loss ultimately is realized by the wrong party (the related-party buyer rather than the related-party seller). Second, the tax benefit of this offset to the related-party buyer does not occur until the buyer disposes of the property. Therefore, the longer the time period between the purchase and disposition of the property by the related-party buyer, the less the economic benefit. Third, if the property does not appreciate to at least its adjusted basis to the related-party seller during the time period the related-party buyer holds it, part or all of the disallowed loss is permanently lost. Fourth, since the right of offset is available only to the original transferee (the related-party buyer), all of the disallowed loss is permanently lost if the original transferee subsequently transfers the property by gift or bequest.

EXAMPLE 64   Tim sells property with an adjusted basis of $35,000 to Wes, his brother, for $25,000, the fair market value of the property. The $10,000 realized loss to Tim is disallowed by § 267. If Wes subsequently sells the property to an unrelated party for $37,000, he has a recognized gain of $2,000 (realized gain of $12,000 reduced by disallowed loss of $10,000). Therefore, from the perspective of the family unit, the original $10,000 realized loss ultimately is recognized. However, if Wes sells the property for $29,000, he has a recognized gain of $0 (realized gain of $4,000 reduced by disallowed loss of $4,000 necessary to offset the realized gain). From the perspective of the family unit, $6,000 of the realized loss of $10,000 is permanently wasted ($10,000 realized loss − $4,000 offset permitted). ▼

Wash Sales.   The wash sales provisions can be avoided if the security is replaced within the statutory time period with a similar rather than a substantially identical security. For example, the sale of Bethlehem Steel common stock and a purchase of Inland Steel common stock is not treated as a wash sale. Such a procedure can enable the taxpayer to use an unrealized capital loss to offset a recognized capital gain. The taxpayer can sell the security before the end of the taxable year, offset the recognized capital loss against the capital gain, and invest the sales proceeds in a similar security.

Because the wash sales provisions do not apply to gains, it may be desirable to engage in a wash sale before the end of the taxable year. This recognized capital gain may be used to offset capital losses or capital loss carryovers from prior years. Since the basis of the replacement stock or securities will be the purchase price, the taxpayer in effect has exchanged a capital gain for an increased basis for the stock or securities.

LIKE-KIND EXCHANGES

Since application of the like-kind exchange provisions is mandatory rather than elective, in certain instances it may be preferable to avoid qualifying for § 1031 nonrecognition. If the like-kind exchange provisions do not apply, the end result may be the recognition of capital gain in exchange for a higher basis in the newly acquired asset. Also, the immediate recognition of gain may be preferable in certain situations. Examples where immediate recognition is beneficial include the following:

- Taxpayer has unused net operating loss carryovers.
- Taxpayer has unused general business credit carryovers.
- Taxpayer has suspended or current passive activity losses.
- Taxpayer expects his or her effective tax rate to increase in the future.

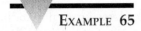
EXAMPLE 65

Alicia disposes of a machine (used in her business) with an adjusted basis of $3,000 for $4,000. She also acquires a new business machine for $9,000. If § 1031 applies, the $1,000 realized gain is not recognized, and the basis of the new machine is reduced by $1,000 (from $9,000 to $8,000). If § 1031 does not apply, a $1,000 gain is recognized and may receive favorable capital gain treatment to the extent that the gain is not recognized as ordinary income due to the depreciation recapture provisions (see Chapter 13). In addition, the basis for depreciation on the new machine is $9,000 rather than $8,000 since there is no unrecognized gain. ▼

The application of § 1031 nonrecognition treatment should also be avoided when the adjusted basis of the property being disposed of exceeds the fair market value.

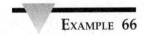
EXAMPLE 66

Assume the same facts as in the previous example, except the fair market value of the machine is $2,500. If § 1031 applies, the $500 realized loss is not recognized. To recognize the loss, Alicia should sell the old machine and purchase the new one. The purchase and sale transactions should be with different taxpayers. ▼

On the other hand, the like-kind exchange procedure can be utilized to control the amount of recognized gain.

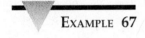
EXAMPLE 67

Rex has property with an adjusted basis of $40,000 and a fair market value of $100,000. Sandra wants to buy Rex's property, but Rex wants to limit the amount of recognized gain on the proposed transaction. Sandra acquires other like-kind property (from an outside party) for $80,000. She then exchanges this property and $20,000 cash for Rex's property. Rex has a realized gain of $60,000 ($100,000 amount realized – $40,000 adjusted basis). His recognized gain is only $20,000, the lower of the $20,000 boot received or the $60,000 realized gain. Rex's basis for the like-kind property is $40,000 ($40,000 adjusted basis + $20,000 gain recognized – $20,000 boot received). If Rex had sold the property to Sandra for its fair market value of $100,000, the result would have been a $60,000 recognized gain ($100,000 amount realized – $40,000 adjusted basis) to him. It is permissible for Rex to identify the like-kind property that he wants Sandra to purchase.[91] ▼

INVOLUNTARY CONVERSIONS

In certain cases, a taxpayer may prefer to recognize gain from an involuntary conversion. Keep in mind that § 1033, unlike § 1031 (dealing with like-kind exchanges), generally is an elective provision.

---

[91] *Franklin B. Biggs,* 69 T.C. 905 (1978); Rev.Rul. 57–244, 1957–1 C.B. 247; Rev.Rul. 73–476, 1973–2 C.B. 300; *Starker vs. U.S.,* 79–2 USTC ¶9541, 44 AFTR2d 79–5525, 602 F.2d 1341 (CA–9, 1979); and *Baird Publishing Co.,* 39 T.C. 608 (1962).

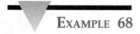

EXAMPLE 68

Ahmad has a $40,000 realized gain from the involuntary conversion of an office building. He reinvests the entire proceeds of $450,000 in a new office building. He does not elect to postpone gain under § 1033, however, because of an expiring net operating loss carryover that is offset against the gain. Therefore, none of the realized gain of $40,000 is postponed. By not electing § 1033 postponement, Ahmad's basis in the replacement property is the property's cost of $450,000 rather than $410,000 ($450,000 reduced by the $40,000 realized gain). ▼

SALE OF A PERSONAL RESIDENCE

Replacement Period Requirements. Several problems arise in avoiding the recognition of gain on the sale of a principal residence. Most of these problems can be resolved favorably through appropriate planning procedures. However, a few represent situations where the taxpayer has to accept the adverse tax consequences and possesses little, if any, planning flexibility. One pitfall concerns the failure to reinvest *all* of the proceeds from the sale of the residence in a new principal residence.

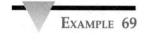

EXAMPLE 69

Rita sells her principal residence in January 1994 for $150,000 (adjusted basis of $40,000). Shortly thereafter, she purchases for $100,000 a 50-year-old house in a historical part of the community and uses it as her principal residence. Rita intends to significantly renovate the property over a period of time and make it more suitable to her living needs. In December 1996, she enters into a contract with a home improvement company to carry out the renovation at a cost of $60,000. It is clear that only $100,000 of the proceeds from the sale of the old residence has been reinvested in a new principal residence on a *timely* basis. Of the realized gain of $110,000, therefore, $50,000 ($150,000 adjusted sales price − $100,000 reinvested) must be recognized.[92] ▼

One problem that a taxpayer may not be in a position to do anything about is the acquisition of property *before* the beginning of the replacement period. Recall that the replacement period begins two years before the sale and ends two years after the sale.

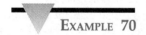

EXAMPLE 70

Tab's employer transfers him to a different city in July 1994, at which time Tab lists his house for sale with a realtor. Tab purchases a principal residence in the city to which he is transferred in September 1994. Because of market conditions, he is unable to sell his original residence until December 1996. Since the sale does not occur within two years of the purchase, the residence Tab bought in September 1994 is not a qualifying replacement residence. ▼

Principal Residence Requirement. Section 1034 will not apply unless the property involved is the taxpayer's principal residence. A potential hurdle arises in cases where the residence has been rented and therefore has not been occupied by the taxpayer for an extended period of time. Depending on the circumstances, the IRS may contend that the taxpayer has abandoned the property as his or her principal residence. The *key* to the abandonment issue is whether or not the taxpayer intended to reoccupy the property and use it as a principal residence upon returning to the locale. If the residence is, in fact, not reoccupied, the taxpayer should have a good reason to explain why it is not.

---

[92] It has been assumed that § 121 did not apply.

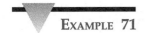

EXAMPLE 71

Lori's employer transfers her to another office out of the state on a three-year assignment. It is the understanding of the parties that the assignment is temporary, and upon its completion, Lori will return to the original job site. During her absence, she rents her principal residence and lives in an apartment at the new location. Lori has every intention of reoccupying her residence. However, when she returns from the temporary assignment, she finds that the residence no longer suits her needs. Specifically, the public school located nearby where she had planned to send her children has been closed. As a consequence, Lori sells the residence and replaces it with one more conveniently located to a public school. Under these circumstances, it would appear that Lori is in an excellent position to show that she has not abandoned the property as her principal residence. She can satisfactorily explain why she did not reoccupy the residence before its sale.[93] ▼

The principal residence requirement can cause difficulty when a taxpayer works in two places and maintains more than one household. In such cases, the principal residence will be the location where the taxpayer lives most of the time.[94]

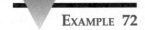

EXAMPLE 72

Hubert is a vice president of Green Corporation and in this capacity spends about an equal amount of time in the company's New York City and Miami offices. He owns a house in each location and expects to retire in about five years. At that time, he plans to sell his New York home and use some of the proceeds to make improvements on the Miami property. Both homes have appreciated in value since their acquisition, and Hubert expects the appreciation to continue. From a tax planning standpoint, Hubert should be looking toward the use of §§ 121 and 1034 to shelter some or all of the gain he will realize on the future sale of the New York City home.[95] To do this, he should arrange his affairs so as to spend more than six months each year at that location. Upon its sale, therefore, the New York home will be his principal residence. ▼

Section 121 Considerations. Older individuals who may be contemplating a move from their home to an apartment should consider the following possibilities for minimizing or deferring taxes:

- Wait until age 55 to sell the residence and elect under § 121 to exclude up to $125,000 of the realized gain.
- Sell the personal residence under an installment contract to spread the gain over several years.[96]
- Sell the personal residence and purchase a condominium instead of renting an apartment, thereby permitting further deferral of the unrecognized gain.

The use of § 121 should be carefully considered. Although the use avoids the immediate recognition of gain, the election expends the full $125,000 allowed.

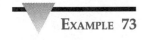

EXAMPLE 73

In 1996 Kate, age 55, sells her personal residence for an amount that yields a realized gain of $5,000. Presuming Kate does not plan to reinvest the sales proceeds in a new principal residence (take advantage of the deferral possibility of § 1034), should she avoid the recognition of this gain by utilizing § 121? Electing § 121 means that Kate will waste $120,000 of her lifetime exclusion. ▼

---

[93] Rev.Rul. 78-146, 1978–1 C.B. 260. Compare *Rudolph M. Stucchi, 35 TCM 1052, T.C.Memo. 1976–242.*

[94] Rev.Rul. 77–298, 1977–2 C.B. 308.

[95] If Hubert qualifies, § 121 would allow the first $125,000 of gain to be excluded. Further gain might be avoided under § 1034 to the extent the sales proceeds are applied toward improvements on the Miami home.

[96] § 453(a). See the discussion of the installment method in Chapter 15.

In this connection, the use of § 121 by one spouse precludes the other spouse from later taking advantage of the exclusion.

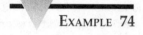

EXAMPLE 74   Assume the same facts as in the previous example, except that Kate was married to Wes at the time of the sale. Later, Kate and Wes are divorced and Wes marries Alice. If Kate has used the § 121 exclusion, it is unavailable to Wes and Alice even though either one of them may otherwise qualify. This result occurs because when Kate made the election for the 1996 sale, it was necessary for Wes to join with her in making the election even though the residence was owned separately by Kate. For Wes and Alice to be able to make the § 121 election, Wes and Kate must revoke their prior election. Another planning approach is for Alice to sell her residence before marrying Wes and to elect the exclusion on that sale. ▼

A taxpayer who is eligible to elect § 121 exclusion treatment may choose not to do so in order to remain eligible to elect it in the future. In arriving at this decision, consideration must be given to the probability that the taxpayer will satisfy the three-out-of-five-year ownership and use period requirements associated with a residence sale in the future. As previously mentioned, the holding period for the occupancy and use requirements does carry over for a § 1033 involuntary conversion but does not carry over for a § 1034 sale.

Taxpayers should maintain records of both the purchase and sale of personal residences since the sale of one residence results in an adjustment of the basis of the new residence if the deferral provisions of § 1034 apply. Form 2119 should be filed with the tax return and a copy retained as support for the basis of the new residence. Detailed cost records should be retained for an indefinite period.

KEY TERMS

Adjusted basis, 12–5

Adjusted sales price, 12–40

Amount realized, 12–4

Boot, 12–27

Fair market value, 12–5

Fixing-up expenses, 12–40

Goodwill, 12–10

Holding period, 12–13

Involuntary conversion, 12–31

Like-kind exchange, 12–24

Nontaxable exchange, 12–23

Personal residence, 12–37

Realized gain, 12–4

Realized loss, 12–4

Recognized gain, 12–7

Recognized loss, 12–7

Recovery of capital doctrine, 12–8

Section 121 exclusion, 12–43

Wash sale, 12–19

PROBLEM MATERIALS

DISCUSSION QUESTIONS

1. Upon the sale or other disposition of property, what four questions should be considered for income tax purposes?

2. Which of the following would be treated as a "sale or other disposition"?
   a. Sale for cash.
   b. Sale on credit.

c. Exchange.

d. Involuntary conversion.

e. Bond retirement.

3. Ivan invests in land and Grace invests in taxable bonds. The land appreciates by $5,000 each year, and the bonds earn interest of $5,000 each year. After holding the land and bonds for five years, Ivan and Grace sell them. There is a $25,000 realized gain on the sale of the land and no realized gain or loss on the sale of the bonds. Are the tax consequences to Ivan and Grace the same for each of the five years? Explain.

4. Carol and Dave each purchase 100 shares of stock of Burgundy, Inc., a publicly owned corporation, in July for $10,000 each. Carol sells her stock on December 31 for $14,000. Since Burgundy's stock is listed on a national exchange, Dave is able to ascertain that his shares are worth $14,000 on December 31. Does the tax law treat the appreciation in value of the stock differently for Carol and Dave? Explain.

5. If a taxpayer sells property for cash, the amount realized consists of the net proceeds from the sale. For each of the following, indicate the effect on the amount realized:

a. The property is sold on credit.

b. A mortgage on the property is assumed by the buyer.

c. The buyer acquires the property subject to a mortgage of the seller.

d. The seller pays real property taxes that are treated as imposed on the purchaser.

e. Stock that has a basis to the purchaser of $6,000 and a fair market value of $10,000 is received by the seller as part of the consideration.

6. Edith purchases land from Gail. Edith gives Gail $40,000 in cash and agrees to pay Gail an additional $80,000 one year later plus interest at 8%.

a. What is Edith's adjusted basis for the land at the date purchased?

b. What is Edith's adjusted basis for the land one year later?

7. The taxpayer owns land and a building with an adjusted basis of $50,000 and a fair market value of $250,000. The property is subject to a mortgage of $400,000. Since the taxpayer is in arrears on the mortgage payments, the creditor is willing to accept the property in return for canceling the amount of the mortgage.

a. How can the adjusted basis of the property be less than the amount of the mortgage?

b. If the creditor's offer is accepted, what are the effects on the amount realized, the adjusted basis, and the realized gain or loss?

c. Does it matter in (b) if the mortgage is recourse or nonrecourse?

8. On August 16, 1996, Todd acquires land and a building for $300,000 to use in his sole proprietorship. Of the purchase price, $200,000 is allocated to the building, and $100,000 is allocated to the land. Cost recovery of $1,926 is deducted in 1996 for the building.

a. What is the adjusted basis for the land and the building at the acquisition date?

b. What is the adjusted basis for the land and the building at the end of 1996?

9. Abby owns stock in Orange Corporation and Blue Corporation. She receives a $1,000 distribution from both corporations. The instructions from Orange state that the $1,000 is a dividend. The instructions from Blue state that the $1,000 is not a dividend. What could cause the instructions to differ as to the tax consequences?

10. A taxpayer who acquires a taxable bond at a premium may elect to amortize the premium, whereas a taxpayer who acquires a tax-exempt bond at a premium must amortize the premium. Why would a taxpayer make the amortization election for taxable bonds? What effect does the mandatory amortization of tax-exempt bonds have on taxable income?

11. Kara owns two assets that she is considering selling. One has appreciated in value by $3,000, and the other has declined in value by $3,000. Both assets are held for personal use. Kara believes that she should sell both assets in the same taxable year so that the loss of $3,000 can offset the gain of $3,000. Advise Kara regarding the tax consequences.

12. Ron sold a sailboat for a $5,000 loss in the current year because he was diagnosed as having skin cancer. His spouse wants him to sell his Harley Davidson motorcycle because her brother broke his leg while riding his motorcycle. Since Ron no longer has anyone to ride with, he is seriously considering accepting his wife's advice. Because the motorcycle is a classic, Ron has received two offers. Each offer would result in a $5,000 gain. Joe would like to purchase the motorcycle before Christmas, and Jeff would like to purchase it after New Year's. Identify the relevant tax issues Ron faces in making his decision.

13. Why does the Code contain both a gain basis rule and a loss basis rule for gift property? Under what circumstances will these rules produce different basis amounts?

14. Simon, who is retired, owns Teal, Inc., stock that has declined in value since he purchased it. He has decided either to give the stock to his nephew, Fred, who is a high school teacher, or to sell the stock and give the proceeds to Fred. Because nearly all of his wealth is invested in tax-exempt bonds, Simon is in the 15% tax bracket. Fred will use the cash or the proceeds from his sale of the stock to make the down payment on the purchase of a house. Based on a recent conversation, Simon is aware that Fred is in the 28% bracket. Identify the tax issues relevant to Simon in deciding whether to give the stock or the sale proceeds to Fred.

15. Howard receives a gift of appreciated land from Del. Del pays gift taxes on the transfer. Discuss how the formula for calculating Howard's basis for the land differs depending on whether the gift was made:
a. Before 1977.
b. After 1976.

16. Discuss the differences in tax treatment between property sold before death and inherited property. Why is this important?

17. Gary makes a gift of an appreciated building to Carmen. She dies three months later, and Gary inherits the building from her. During the period that Carmen held the building, she deducted depreciation and made a capital expenditure. What effect might these items have on Gary's basis for the inherited building?

18. Thelma inherited land from her Aunt Sadie on June 7, 1996. The land appreciated in value by 100% during the six months that Aunt Sadie owned it. The value has remained stable during the three months that Thelma has owned it, and she expects it to continue to do so in the near future. Although she would like to sell the land, Thelma has decided to delay the sale for another three months so that the gain will qualify for long-term capital gain treatment. Evaluate Thelma's understanding of the relevant tax issues.

19. Ava owned a residence whose adjusted basis (i.e., cost) was $20,000 greater than its fair market value. She knew that if she sold the house, the $20,000 realized loss would not be recognized. Therefore, she decided that she would rent it for a year and then sell it in order to be able to deduct the realized loss. Evaluate Ava's understanding of the relevant tax issues.

20. Distinguish between a nontaxable exchange and a tax-free transaction.

21. Amos owns a lathe that he uses in his trade or business. The adjusted basis is $40,000. Although the lathe is only two years old, Amos needs to replace it due to advances in technology. He exchanges the lathe and $20,000 in cash for a new lathe worth $50,000. May Amos elect not to treat the transaction as a like-kind exchange so that the realized loss of $10,000 can be recognized?

22. Which of the following qualify as like-kind exchanges under § 1031?
a. Improved for unimproved real estate.
b. Vending machine (used in business) for inventory.
c. Rental house for personal residence.
d. Business equipment for securities.
e. Warehouse for office building (both used for business).

    f. Truck for computer (both used in business).
    g. Rental house for land (both held for investment).
    h. Ten shares of stock in Blue Corporation for 10 shares of stock in Red Corporation.
    i. Office furniture for office equipment (both used in business).
    j. American automobile for Japanese automobile (both used in business).

23. Ross would like to dispose of some land that he acquired five years ago because he believes that it will not continue to appreciate. Its value has increased by $50,000 during the five-year period. He also intends to sell stock that has declined in value by $50,000 during the eight-month period he has owned it. Ross has four offers to acquire the stock and land:

Buyer number 1:	Exchange land.
Buyer number 2:	Purchase land for cash.
Buyer number 3:	Exchange stock.
Buyer number 4:	Purchase stock for cash.

Identify the tax issues relevant to Ross in disposing of this land and stock.

24. The receipt of boot in a § 1031 exchange triggers the recognition of realized gain. The gain recognition will affect the basis of the property received by the taxpayer.
    a. Discuss the relationship between the realized gain and the boot received if the boot received is greater than the realized gain.
    b. Discuss the relationship between the realized gain and the boot received if the boot received is less than the realized gain.
    c. What effect does the recognition of gain have on the basis of the like-kind property received? Of the boot received?

25. In a like-kind exchange, the basis of the property received is the same as the adjusted basis of the property transferred. If boot is received, what effect does the boot have on the basis of the like-kind property received? If boot is given, what effect does the boot have on the basis of the like-kind property received?

26. In connection with like-kind exchanges, discuss each of the following:
    a. Realized gain.
    b. Realized loss.
    c. Recognized gain.
    d. Recognized loss.
    e. Postponed gain.
    f. Postponed loss.
    g. Basis of like-kind property received.
    h. Basis of boot received.

27. Julia owns a shopping mall that she leases to tenants. The shopping mall is destroyed by a tornado. Is the functional use test or the taxpayer use test applied in terms of appropriate replacement property? Explain the differences between the two tests.

28. Rebecca, a calendar year taxpayer, owns an office building that she uses in her business. The building is involuntarily converted on June 15, 1996. On October 5, 1996, Rebecca receives proceeds large enough to produce a realized gain. What is the latest date she can replace the building if the form of the conversion is:
    a. A flood?
    b. A condemnation?
    c. A tornado?

29. Bob is notified by the city public housing authority on October 5, 1996, that his apartment building is going to be condemned as part of an urban renewal project. On October 12, 1996, Carol offers to buy the building from Bob. Bob sells the building to Carol on October 30, 1996. Condemnation occurs on February 1, 1997, and Carol receives the condemnation proceeds from the city. Assume both Bob and Carol are calendar year taxpayers.

a. What is the earliest date that Bob can dispose of the building and qualify for § 1033 postponement treatment?

b. Does the sale to Carol qualify as a § 1033 involuntary conversion?

c. What is the latest date that Carol can acquire qualifying replacement property and qualify for postponement of the realized gain?

d. What type of property will be qualifying replacement property?

30. A warehouse owned by Martha and used in her business (i.e., to store inventory) is being condemned by the city to provide a right of way for a highway. The warehouse has appreciated by $100,000 based on Martha's estimate of fair market value. In the negotiations, the city is offering $40,000 less than what Martha believes the property is worth. Alan, a real estate broker, has offered to purchase Martha's property for $25,000 more than the city's offer. Martha plans to invest the proceeds she will receive in an office building that she will lease to various tenants. Identify the relevant tax issues for Martha.

31. Samantha, who is age 39, would like to quit her job, sell her house, buy a sailboat, and sail the seven seas. The projected realized gain on the sale of her personal residence is $150,000. Is it possible for Samantha to defer the recognition of this gain?

32. Jim sells his principal residence on September 18, 1996. Although he does not replace it until August 19, 2000, the replacement qualifies for postponement treatment under § 1034. Discuss how this replacement could satisfy the residence replacement period requirement.

33. Sandy owns a residence that she acquired 19 months ago. It has appreciated by $40,000 during this period. Now, however, the school board has redrawn the boundaries for the school districts, and her son will have to transfer to a different high school for his senior year. Sandy is considering selling her residence and buying another one that will enable her son to remain in the same high school. Without this reason, she would not sell the house. Identify the relevant tax issues for Sandy.

34. Peggy has owned and occupied a house as her principal residence for 10 years. She purchases a new residence in March 1996. She initially listed her old residence with a realtor in January 1996. Needing the cash flow, she rents the old residence to Joe for a six-month period beginning in March. She sells the old residence to Paul upon the expiration of the rental period in September. Does the sale of the old residence in September qualify as the sale of a principal residence?

35. Define each of the following associated with the sale of a residence:
a. Amount realized.
b. Adjusted sales price.
c. Fixing-up expenses.
d. Realized gain.
e. Recognized gain.
f. Postponed gain.
g. Basis of new residence.

36. How many times can § 121 exclusion treatment be elected by a taxpayer? If the taxpayer is filing a joint return with his or her spouse, do both taxpayers have to meet the ownership and use requirements?

37. Can any other provision be applied to any remaining gain that is not excluded under § 121?

PROBLEMS

38. Anne sold her home for $260,000 in 1996. Selling expenses were $15,000. She had purchased it in 1990 for $190,000. During the period of ownership, Anne had:

- Deducted $50,500 office-in-home expenses, which included $14,500 in depreciation. (Refer to Chapter 8.)

- Deducted a casualty loss of residential trees destroyed by a hurricane. The total loss was $19,000 (after the $100 floor and the 10%-of-AGI floor), and Anne's insurance company reimbursed her for $13,500. (Refer to Chapter 6.)

- Paid street paving assessment of $7,000 and added sidewalks for $11,000.

- Installed an elevator for medical reasons. The total cost was $20,000, and Anne deducted $12,000 as medical expenses. (Refer to Chapter 9.)

- Received $7,500 from a utility company for an easement to install underground utility lines across the property.

What is Anne's realized gain?

39. Kareem bought a rental house at the beginning of 1991 for $80,000, of which $10,000 is allocated to the land and $70,000 to the building. Early in 1993, he had a tennis court built in the backyard at a cost of $5,000. Kareem has deducted $32,200 for depreciation on the house and $1,300 for depreciation on the court. At the beginning of 1996, he sells the house and tennis court for $125,000 cash.
    a. What is Kareem's realized gain or loss?
    b. If an original mortgage of $20,000 is still outstanding and the buyer assumes the mortgage in addition to the cash payment, what is Kareem's realized gain or loss?
    c. If the buyer takes the property subject to the mortgage, what is Kareem's realized gain or loss?

40. Gayla owns a building (adjusted basis of $366,500 on January 1, 1996) that she rents to Len who operates a restaurant in the building. The municipal health department closed the restaurant for two months during 1996 because of health code violations. Under MACRS, the cost recovery deduction for 1996 would be $12,000. However, Gayla deducted cost recovery only for the 10 months the restaurant was open since she waived the rent income during the two-month period the restaurant was closed.
    a. What is the amount of the cost recovery deduction that Gayla should report on her 1996 income tax return?
    b. Calculate the adjusted basis of the building at the end of 1996.

41. Nell owns a personal use automobile that has an adjusted basis of $18,000. The fair market value of the automobile is $14,500. Nell's AGI is $40,000.
    a. Calculate the realized and recognized loss if Nell sells the automobile for $14,500.
    b. Calculate the realized and recognized loss if Nell exchanges the automobile for another automobile worth $14,500.
    c. Calculate the realized and recognized loss if the automobile is stolen and Nell receives insurance proceeds of $14,500.

42. Mitch's automobile, which is used exclusively in his business, is stolen. The adjusted basis is $30,000, and the fair market value is $33,000. Mitch's AGI is $50,000.
    a. If Mitch receives insurance proceeds of $33,000, what effect do the theft and the receipt of the insurance proceeds have on the adjusted basis of the automobile?
    b. If the automobile is not insured, what effect do the theft and the absence of insurance have on the adjusted basis of the automobile?

43. Aaron owns stock in Dove Corporation. His adjusted basis for the stock is $30,000. During the year, he receives a distribution from the corporation of $25,000 that is labeled a return of capital (i.e., Dove has no earnings and profits).
    a. Determine the tax consequences to Aaron.
    b. Assume instead that the amount of the distribution is $40,000. Determine the tax consequences to Aaron.

44. Chee purchases Tan, Inc., bonds for $110,000 on January 2, 1996. The face value of the bonds is $100,000, the maturity date is December 31, 2000, and the annual interest rate is 8%. Chee will amortize the premium only if he is required to do so. Chee sells the bonds on July 1, 1998, for $109,000.
    a. Determine the interest income Chee should report for 1996.
    b. Calculate Chee's recognized gain or loss on the sale of the bonds in 1998.

45. Which of the following would definitely result in a recognized gain or loss?
    a. Kay sells her lakeside cabin, which has an adjusted basis of $100,000, for $150,000.
    b. Adam sells his personal residence, which has an adjusted basis of $150,000, for $100,000.

c. Carl's personal residence is on the site of a proposed airport and is condemned by
the city. Carl receives $55,000 for the house, which has an adjusted basis of $65,000.

d. Olga's land is worth $40,000 at the end of the year. Olga had purchased the land six
months earlier for $25,000.

e. Vera's personal use vehicle is stolen. Her adjusted basis is $22,000. She receives a
check from the insurance company for $23,000. Vera has decided that in the future
she will use mass transit rather than owning an automobile.

f. Jerry sells used clothing, adjusted basis of $500, to a thrift store for $50.

46. Tiffany sells the following assets during the year. All are held for personal use.

   • Car with an adjusted basis of $19,000 for $7,000.
   • Used clothing with an adjusted basis of $600 for $100.
   • Sailboat with an adjusted basis of $3,500 for $4,500.
   Calculate Tiffany's realized and recognized gain or loss.

47. Hubert's personal residence is condemned as part of an urban renewal project. His
adjusted basis for the residence is $160,000. He receives condemnation proceeds of
$150,000 and invests the proceeds in stock.

a. Calculate Hubert's realized and recognized gain or loss.

b. If the condemnation proceeds are $180,000, what are Hubert's realized and recognized gain or loss?

c. What are Hubert's realized and recognized gain or loss in (a) if the house was rental
property?

48. Karen makes the following purchases and sales of stock:

Transaction	Date	Number of Shares	Company	Price per Share
Purchase	1–1–94	300	MDG	$ 75
Purchase	6–1–94	150	GRU	300
Purchase	11–1–94	60	MDG	70
Sale	12–3–94	180	MDG	70
Purchase	3–1–95	120	GRU	375
Sale	8–1–95	90	GRU	330
Sale	1–1–96	150	MDG	90
Sale	2–1–96	75	GRU	500

Assuming that Karen is unable to identify the particular lots that are sold with the
original purchase, what is the realized gain or loss on each type of stock as of:

a. 7–1–94.

b. 12–31–94.

c. 12–31–95.

d. 7–1–96.

49. Frank purchases 100 shares of Bluebird Corporation stock on June 3, 1996, for $150,000.
On August 25, 1996, Frank purchases an additional 50 shares of Bluebird stock for
$60,000. According to market quotations, Bluebird stock is selling for $1,100 per share
on December 31, 1996. Frank sells 60 shares of Bluebird stock on March 1, 1997, for
$51,000.

a. What is the adjusted basis of Frank's Bluebird stock on December 31, 1996?

b. What is Frank's recognized gain or loss from the sale of Bluebird stock on March 1,
1997, assuming the shares sold are from the shares purchased on June 3, 1996?

c. What is Frank's recognized gain or loss from the sale of Bluebird stock on March 1,
1997, assuming Frank cannot adequately identify the shares sold?

50. Paula purchases the assets of a sole proprietorship from Seth. The adjusted basis of each
of the assets on Seth's books and the fair market value of each asset as agreed to by
Paula and Seth are as follows:

Asset	Seth's Adjusted Basis	FMV
Accounts receivable	$ –0–	$ 10,000
Notes receivable	15,000	20,000
Machinery and equipment	85,000	100,000
Building	100,000	300,000
Land	200,000	350,000

The purchase price is $900,000.
a. Calculate Seth's realized and recognized gain.
b. Determine Paula's basis for each of the assets.
c. Write a letter to Paula informing her of the tax consequences of the purchase. Her address is 300 Riverside Drive, Cincinnati, OH 45207.

51. Rick received various gifts over the years. He has decided to dispose of the following assets that he received as gifts:
   a. In 1949, he received land worth $25,000. The donor's adjusted basis was $30,000. Rick sells the land for $87,000 in 1996.
   b. In 1955, he received stock in Gold Company. The donor's adjusted basis was $10,000. The fair market value on the date of the gift was $28,000. Rick sells the stock for $40,000 in 1996.
   c. In 1961, he received land worth $12,000. The donor's adjusted basis was $25,000. Rick sells the land for $8,000 in 1996.
   d. In 1993, he received stock worth $30,000. The donor's adjusted basis was $45,000. Rick sells the stock in 1996 for $39,000.

   What is the realized gain or loss from each of the preceding transactions? Assume in each of the gift transactions that no gift tax was paid.

52. Beth received a car from Sam as a gift. Sam paid $7,000 for the car. He had used it for business purposes and had deducted $2,000 for depreciation up to the time he gave the car to Beth. The fair market value of the car is $3,500.
   a. Assuming Beth uses the car for business purposes, what is her basis for depreciation?
   b. If the estimated useful life is two years (from the date of the gift), what is her depreciation deduction for each year? Use the straight-line method.
   c. If Beth sells the car for $800 one year after receiving it, what is her gain or loss?
   d. If Beth sells the car for $4,000 one year after receiving it, what is her gain or loss?

53. In 1991, Ron receives a gift of property that has a fair market value of $100,000 on the date of the gift. The donor's adjusted basis for the property was $40,000. Assume the donor paid gift tax of $15,000 on the gift.
   a. What is Ron's basis for gain and loss and for depreciation?
   b. If Ron had received the gift of property in 1975, what would his basis be for gain and loss and for depreciation?

54. Liz receives a gift of income-producing property that has an adjusted basis of $70,000 on the date of the gift. The fair market value of the property on the date of the gift is $50,000. The donor paid gift tax of $4,000. Liz later sells the property for $54,000. Determine her recognized gain or loss.

55. Ira Cook is planning to make a charitable contribution of Crystal, Inc., stock worth $20,000 to the Boy Scouts. The stock Ira is considering contributing has an adjusted basis of $15,000. A friend has suggested that Ira sell the stock and contribute the $20,000 in proceeds rather than contribute the stock.
   a. Should Ira follow the friend's advice? Why?
   b. Assume the fair market value is only $13,000. In this case, should Ira follow the friend's advice? Why?
   c. Rather than make a charitable contribution to the Boy Scouts, Ira is going to make a gift to Nancy, his niece. Advise Ira regarding (a) and (b).

d. Write a letter to Ira regarding whether in (a) he should sell the stock and contribute the cash or contribute the stock. He has informed you that he purchased the stock six years ago. Ira's address is 500 Ireland Avenue, De Kalb, IL 60115.

56. Dena inherits property from Mary, her mother. Mary's adjusted basis for the property is $100,000, and the fair market value is $725,000. Six months after Mary's death, the fair market value is $740,000. Dena is the sole beneficiary of Mary's estate.
   a. Can the executor of Mary's estate elect the alternate valuation date?
   b. What is Dena's basis for the property?

57. Earl's estate includes the following assets available for distribution to Robert, one of Earl's beneficiaries:

Asset	Earl's Adjusted Basis	FMV at Date of Death	FMV at Alternate Valuation Date
Cash	$10,000	$ 10,000	$ 10,000
Stock	40,000	125,000	60,000
Apartment building	60,000	300,000	325,000
Land	75,000	100,000	110,000

The fair market value of the stock six months after Earl's death was $60,000. However, believing that the stock would continue to decline in value, the executor of the estate distributed the stock to Robert one month after Earl's death. Robert immediately sold the stock for $85,000.
   a. Determine Robert's basis for the assets if the primary valuation date and amount apply.
   b. Determine Robert's basis for the assets if the executor elects the alternate valuation date and amount.

58. Emily makes a gift of 100 shares of appreciated stock to her uncle, George, on January 5, 1996. The basis of the stock is $3,150, and the fair market value is $5,250. George dies on October 8, 1996. During the period that George held the stock, he received a 5% nontaxable stock dividend. Under the provisions of George's will, Emily inherits 100 shares of the stock. The value of the stock for Federal estate tax purposes is $55 per share.
   a. What is the basis of the inherited stock to Emily?
   b. What is the basis of the inherited stock to Emily if she had given the stock to George on January 5, 1995?

 59. Joyce owns undeveloped real estate with an adjusted basis of $80,000. She sells the real estate to her sister, Iris, for its fair market value of $65,000.
   a. Calculate Joyce's realized and recognized gain or loss.
   b. If Iris later sells the real estate for $72,000, calculate her realized and recognized gain or loss.
   c. Assume instead that Joyce sold the real estate to Iris for its fair market value of $90,000. Calculate Joyce's realized and recognized gain or loss.
   d. Assume instead that Joyce sold the real estate to Hector, a friend, for its fair market value of $65,000.
   e. Advise Joyce whether she should sell the real estate to Iris or Hector for its fair market value of $65,000.

60. Frank owns 1,000 shares of Amber, Inc., stock with an adjusted basis of $10,000. On December 28, 1996, he sells 400 shares for $3,600. On January 19, 1997, he purchases 300 shares of Amber, Inc., stock for $2,850.
   a. Calculate Frank's realized and recognized loss on the sale of 400 shares of December 28, 1996.
   b. Determine Frank's adjusted basis for the 300 shares purchased on January 19, 1997.

 61. Kristy owns 100 shares of stock in Magenta Corporation. Her adjusted basis for the stock is $5,000. On December 21, Kristy sells the stock in the marketplace for $12,000.

She purchases 100 shares of Magenta stock in the marketplace on January 5 of the following year for $12,000.

a. What is Kristy trying to achieve from a tax perspective?

b. Will she succeed?

c. Using the same data, except that Kristy's adjusted basis for the stock is $15,000, respond to (a) and (b).

d. Advise Kristy on how she can avoid any negative tax consequence encountered in (c).

62. James retires from a public accounting firm to enter private practice. He had bought a home two years earlier for $40,000. Upon opening his business, he converts one-fourth of his home into an office. The fair market value of the home on the date of conversion (January 1, 1991) is $75,000. The adjusted basis is $56,000 (ignore land). James lives and works in the home for six years (after converting it to business use) and sells it at the end of the sixth year. He deducted $6,148 of cost recovery using the statutory percentage method.

a. How much gain or loss is recognized if James sells the property for $44,000?

b. If he sells the property for $70,000?

63. Surendra's personal residence originally cost $180,000 (ignore land). After living in the house for five years, he converts it to rental property. At the date of conversion, the fair market value of the house is $150,000.

a. Calculate Surendra's basis for loss for the rental property.

b. Calculate Surendra's basis for depreciation for the rental property.

c. Calculate Surendra's basis for gain for the rental property.

64. Hun, age 93, has accumulated substantial assets during his life. Among his many assets are the following, which he is considering giving to Koji, his grandson.

Assets	Adjusted Basis	Fair Market Value
Red Corporation stock	$ 50,000	$700,000
Silver Corporation stock	70,000	71,000
Emerald Corporation stock	200,000	50,000

Hun has been in ill health for the past five years. His physician has informed him that he probably will not live for more than six months. Advise Hun which of the stocks should be transferred as gifts and which as bequests.

65. Kay owns undeveloped land with an adjusted basis of $150,000. She exchanges it for other undeveloped land worth $185,000.

a. What are Kay's realized and recognized gain or loss?

b. What is Kay's basis in the undeveloped land she receives?

66. Kareem owns an automobile that he uses exclusively in his business. The adjusted basis is $19,000, and the fair market value is $16,000. Kareem exchanges the car for a car that he will use exclusively in his business.

a. What are Kareem's realized and recognized gain or loss?

b. What is his basis in the new car?

c. What are the tax consequences to Kareem in (a) and (b) if he used the old car and will use the new car exclusively for personal purposes?

67. Tex Wall owns undeveloped land that he is holding for investment. His adjusted basis is $175,000. On October 7, 1996, he exchanges the land with his 23-year-old daughter, Paige, for other undeveloped land that he will hold for investment. The appraised value of Paige's land is $250,000.

a. Calculate Tex's realized and recognized gain or loss from the exchange with Paige and on a subsequent sale of the land by Tex to Baxter, a real estate broker, for $300,000 on February 15, 1997.

b. Calculate Tex's realized and recognized gain or loss on the exchange with Paige if Tex does not sell the land received from Paige, but Paige sells the land received from

Tex on February 15, 1997. Calculate Tex's basis for the land on October 7, 1996, and on February 15, 1997.

c. Write a letter to Tex advising him on how he could avoid any recognition of gain associated with the October 7, 1996, exchange prior to his actual sale of the land. His address is The Corral, El Paso, TX 79968.

68. Bonnie owns a personal computer that she uses exclusively in her business. The adjusted basis is $5,000. Bonnie transfers the personal computer and cash of $4,000 to Don for a laser printer worth $10,000 that she will use in her business.
a. Calculate Bonnie's recognized gain or loss on the exchange.
b. Calculate Bonnie's basis for the printer.

69. Tom owns land and building with an adjusted basis of $125,000 and a fair market value of $275,000. Tom exchanges the land and building for land with a fair market value of $175,000 that he will use as a parking lot. In addition, he receives stock worth $100,000.
a. What is Tom's realized gain or loss?
b. His recognized gain or loss?
c. The basis of the land and the stock received?

70. Olga owns a machine that she uses in her business. The adjusted basis is $60,000, and the fair market value is $90,000. She exchanges it for another machine worth $55,000. Olga also receives cash of $35,000.
a. Calculate Olga's realized and recognized gain or loss on the exchange.
b. Calculate Olga's basis for the new machine.

71. What is the basis of the new property in each of the following exchanges?
a. Apartment building held for investment (adjusted basis $150,000) for office building to be held for investment (fair market value $200,000).
b. Land and building used as a barber shop (adjusted basis $30,000) for land and building used as a grocery store (fair market value $350,000).
c. Office building (adjusted basis $30,000) for bulldozer (fair market value $42,000), both held for business use.
d. IBM common stock (adjusted basis $14,000) for Exxon common stock (fair market value $18,000).
e. Rental house (adjusted basis $90,000) for mountain cabin to be held for personal use (fair market value $115,000).

72. Norm owns Machine A, which he uses in his business. The adjusted basis of Machine A is $12,000, and the fair market value is $18,000. Norm is considering two options for the disposal of Machine A. Under the first option, Norm will transfer Machine A and $3,000 cash to Joan, a dealer, in exchange for Machine B, which has a fair market value of $21,000. Under the second option, Norm will sell Machine A for $18,000 to Tim, who is a dealer. Norm will then purchase Machine B from Joan for $21,000. Machine A and Machine B qualify as like-kind property.
a. Calculate Norm's recognized gain or loss and the basis for Machine B under the first option.
b. Calculate Norm's recognized gain or loss and the basis for Machine B under the second option.
c. Advise Norm on which option he should select.

73. Gus exchanges real estate held for investment plus stock for real estate to be held for investment. The stock transferred has an adjusted basis of $15,000 and a fair market value of $10,000. The real estate transferred has an adjusted basis of $15,000 and a fair market value of $45,000. The real estate acquired has a fair market value of $55,000.
a. What is Gus's realized gain or loss?
b. His recognized gain or loss?
c. The basis of the newly acquired real estate?

74. Agnes exchanges a warehouse and the related land with Damon for an office building and the related land. Agnes's adjusted basis for her warehouse and land is $420,000. The fair market value of Damon's office building and land is $410,000. Agnes's property has a $90,000 mortgage that Damon assumes.

a. Calculate Agnes's realized and recognized gain or loss.

b. Calculate Agnes's adjusted basis for the office building and land received.

c. As an alternative, Damon has proposed that rather than assuming the mortgage, he will transfer cash of $90,000 to Agnes. Agnes would use the cash to pay off the mortgage. Advise Agnes on whether this alternative would be beneficial to her from a tax perspective.

75. Determine the realized, recognized, and postponed gain or loss and the new basis for each of the following like-kind exchanges:

	Adjusted Basis of Old Asset	**Boot Given**	**Fair Market Value of New Asset**	**Boot Received**
a.	$ 7,000	$ –0–	$12,000	$4,000
b.	14,000	2,000	15,000	–0–
c.	3,000	7,000	8,000	500
d.	22,000	–0–	32,000	–0–
e.	10,000	–0–	11,000	1,000
f.	10,000	–0–	8,000	–0–

76. Shontelle owns an apartment house that has an adjusted basis of $1,100,000 but is subject to a mortgage of $250,000. She transfers the apartment house to Dave and receives from him $125,000 in cash and an office building with a fair market value of $1,125,000 at the time of the exchange. Dave assumes the $250,000 mortgage on the apartment house.

a. What is Shontelle's realized gain or loss?

b. Her recognized gain or loss?

c. The basis of the newly acquired office building?

77. Carmen's office building, which has an adjusted basis of $200,000, is destroyed by a tornado. Since Carmen's business has excess office space, she decides not to replace the office building, but instead to contribute the proceeds to the working capital of her business.

a. If the insurance proceeds are $225,000, what is Carmen's recognized gain or loss?

b. If the insurance proceeds are $180,000, what is Carmen's recognized gain or loss?

78. For each of the following involuntary conversions, indicate whether the property acquired qualifies as replacement property:

a. Frank owns a shopping mall that is destroyed by a tornado. The space in the mall was rented to various tenants. Frank uses the insurance proceeds to build a shopping mall in a neighboring community where no property has been damaged by tornadoes.

b. Ivan owns a warehouse that he uses in his business. The warehouse is destroyed by fire. Due to economic conditions in the area, Ivan decides not to rebuild the warehouse. Instead, he uses the insurance proceeds to build a warehouse to be used in his business in another state.

c. Ridge's personal residence is condemned as part of a local government project to widen the highway from two lanes to four lanes. He uses the condemnation proceeds to purchase another personal residence.

d. Juanita owns a building that she uses in her retail business. The building is destroyed by a hurricane. Due to an economic downturn in the area caused by the closing of a military base, she decides to rent space for her retail outlet rather than to replace the building. She uses the insurance proceeds to buy a four-unit apartment building in another city. A realtor in that city will handle the rental of the apartments for her.

e. Susan and Rick's personal residence is destroyed by a tornado. Since they would like to travel, they decide not to acquire a replacement residence. Instead, they invest the insurance proceeds in a duplex that they rent to tenants.

79. Lynn's office building, which is used in her business, is destroyed by a hurricane in September 1996. The adjusted basis is $210,000. Lynn receives insurance proceeds of $390,000 in October 1996.
    a. Calculate Lynn's realized gain or loss, recognized gain or loss, and basis for the replacement property if she acquires an office building for $390,000 in October 1996.
    b. Calculate Lynn's realized gain or loss, recognized gain or loss, and basis for the replacement property if she acquires a warehouse for $350,000 in October 1996.
    c. Calculate Lynn's realized gain or loss and recognized gain or loss if she does not acquire replacement property.

 80. Carlos's warehouse, which has an adjusted basis of $325,000 and a fair market value of $490,000, is condemned by an agency of the Federal government to make way for a highway interchange. The initial condemnation offer is $450,000. After substantial negotiations, the agency agrees to transfer to Carlos a surplus warehouse that he believes is worth $490,000.
    a. What are the recognized gain or loss and the basis of the replacement warehouse if Carlos's objective is to recognize as much gain as possible?
    b. Advise Carlos regarding what he needs to do by what date in order to achieve his objective.

81. What are the *maximum* postponed gain or loss and the basis for the replacement property for the following involuntary conversions?

	Property	Type of Conversion	Amount Realized	Adjusted Basis	Amount Reinvested
a.	Drugstore (business)	Condemned	$160,000	$120,000	$100,000
b.	Apartments (investment)	Casualty	100,000	120,000	200,000
c.	Grocery store (business)	Casualty	400,000	300,000	350,000
d.	Residence (personal)	Casualty	16,000	18,000	17,000
e.	Vacant lot (investment)	Condemned	240,000	160,000	240,000
f.	Residence (personal)	Casualty	20,000	18,000	19,000
g.	Residence (personal)	Condemned	18,000	20,000	26,000
h.	Apartments (investment)	Condemned	150,000	100,000	200,000

82. Cassandra's personal residence is condemned on October 31, 1996, as part of a plan to build a freeway around the city. Her adjusted basis is $125,000. She receives condemnation proceeds of $110,000 on November 19, 1996. Cassandra is a calendar year taxpayer. She purchases another personal residence on November 20, 1996, for $150,000.
    a. What are Cassandra's realized and recognized gain or loss?
    b. What is her adjusted basis for the new residence?

83. Milton listed his personal residence with a realtor on March 3, 1996, at a listed price of $250,000. He rejected several offers in the $200,000 range during the summer. Finally, on August 16, 1996, he and the purchaser signed a contract to sell for $235,000. The sale (i.e., closing) took place on September 7, 1996. The closing statement showed the following disbursements being made:

Realtor's commission	$14,000
Appraisal fee	500
Exterminator's certificate	300
Recording fees	400
Mortgage to First Bank	180,000
Cash to seller	39,800

Milton's adjusted basis for the house is $150,000.

a. Calculate Milton's realized gain on the sale.

b. What is the latest date that Milton can acquire a replacement residence in order to postpone any realized gain?

84. Tina, age 42, has lived in her residence for three years. Her adjusted basis is $130,000. In February 1994, she decides to move to another neighborhood to reduce her commuting time and lists her residence for sale for $225,000. In May 1994, she moves to another residence that she has purchased for $240,000 at the beginning of the month. By April 1996, she has still not sold her old residence due to market conditions. She is becoming concerned that she will not satisfy the two-year replacement provision. Therefore, she is considering moving back into her old residence and selling her new residence. She anticipates no difficulty in selling the new residence for $250,000.

a. Advise Tina regarding whether she should (1) sell her new residence and move back into her old residence or (2) stay in her new residence and continue to try to sell her old residence.

b. If Tina moves back into her old residence, what is her adjusted basis for the old residence?

85. On January 15, 1996, Kelly, a 48-year-old widow, buys a new residence for $180,000. On March 1, 1996, she sells for an adjusted sales price of $197,000 her old residence, which had an adjusted basis of $110,000. No fixing-up expenses are incurred. Between April 1 and June 30, 1996, she constructs an addition to her new house at a cost of $20,000.

a. What is Kelly's realized gain or loss?

b. Kelly's recognized gain or loss?

c. Kelly's basis for the new residence?

86. What are the realized, recognized, and postponed gain or loss, the new basis, and the adjusted sales price for each of the following? Assume that none of the taxpayers is 55 years of age or older.

a. Susan sells her residence for $90,000. The adjusted basis was $55,000. The selling expenses were $5,000. The fixing-up expenses were $3,000. She did not reinvest in a new residence.

b. Rocky sells his residence for $170,000. The adjusted basis was $120,000. The selling expenses were $4,000. The fixing-up expenses were $6,000. Rocky reinvested $160,000 in a new residence.

c. Veneia sells her residence for $65,000. The adjusted basis was $35,000. The selling expenses were $1,000. The fixing-up expenses were $2,000. She reinvested $40,000.

d. Barry sells his residence for $70,000. The adjusted basis was $65,000. The selling expenses were $6,000. He reinvested $80,000 in a new residence.

e. Carl sells his residence for $100,000, and his mortgage is assumed by the buyer. The adjusted basis was $80,000; the mortgage, $50,000. The selling expenses were $4,000. The fixing-up expenses were $2,000. He reinvested $120,000 in a new residence.

87. Ned, age 47, sells his residence in Richmond on May 5, 1996, for $115,000. He incurs realtor's commissions of $6,900 and qualified fixing-up expenses of $2,000. His adjusted basis is $70,000. Ned sells the house because his employer assigns him to a temporary job in another state. Ned moves back to Richmond in December 1997. However, he has decided that he enjoys being relieved of the responsibilities of home ownership. Therefore, he rents an apartment and does not purchase another residence by May 5, 1998.

a. What should Ned have reported on his 1996 return with respect to the sale of his residence?

b. What should Ned do in 1998 when he has not replaced the residence within the required two-year period?

88. Pedro, age 57, is the sole owner of his principal residence. He has owned and occupied it for 10 years. Maria, his spouse, refuses to join him in making the § 121 election.

a. Can Pedro elect the § 121 exclusion if he and Maria file a joint return? If so, what is the available amount of the exclusion?

b. Can Pedro elect the § 121 exclusion if he files a separate return? If so, what is the available amount of the exclusion?

c. If Maria joins Pedro in making the election, what is the available amount of the exclusion on a joint return? On a separate return?

89. Pat sold his residence, which he had owned and occupied for 18 years. The adjusted basis was $130,000, and the selling price was $325,000. The selling expenses were $22,000, and the fixing-up expenses were $5,000. He reinvested $132,000 in a new residence. Pat is 57 years old.
   a. What are the realized, recognized, and postponed gain or loss, the new basis, and the adjusted sales price if his objective is to minimize the recognized gain?
   b. Based on the data provided, should Pat elect the § 121 exclusion?

90. Nell, Nina, and Nora, who are sisters, sell their principal residence in which they have lived for the past 20 years. The youngest of the sisters is age 58. The selling price is $555,000, selling expenses and legal fees are $15,000, and the adjusted basis is $60,000 (the fair market value of the residence when inherited from their parents 20 years ago). Since the sisters are going to live in rental housing, they do not plan to acquire another residence. Nell has contacted you on behalf of the three sisters regarding the tax consequences of the sale.
   a. Write a letter to Nell advising her of the tax consequences and how taxes can be minimized. Nell's address is 100 Oak Avenue, Billings, MT 59101.
   b. Prepare a memo for the tax files.

91. Jeff and Jill are divorced on August 1, 1996. According to the terms of the divorce decree, Jeff's ownership interest in the house is to be transferred to Jill in exchange for the release from marital rights. Before the divorce, the house was jointly owned by Jeff and Jill. The adjusted basis and the fair market value at the date of the transfer are $150,000 and $200,000, respectively.
   a. Does the transfer of the house produce recognized gain to either Jeff or Jill?
   b. What is the basis of the house to Jill?
   c. If the same transfer was made by Jeff to Jill for $100,000 and was not associated with a divorce, would either Jeff or Jill have recognized gain?

CUMULATIVE PROBLEMS

92. John Custer, age 35, is single. His Social Security number is 443–11–2222, and he resides at 150 Highway 51, Tangipahoa, LA 70443.

John has a two-year-old child, Kendra, who lives with her mother, Katy. John pays alimony of $15,000 per year to Katy and child support of $10,000. The $10,000 of child support covers all of Katy's costs of rearing Kendra. Kendra's Social Security number is 432–60–1000, and Katy's is 444–00–1234.

John's mother, Sally, lived with him until her death in early September 1996. He incurred and paid medical expenses for her of $9,000 and other support payments of $4,000. Sally's only source of income was $2,400 of Social Security benefits, which she spent on her medical expenses and helping to maintain John's household. Sally's Social Security number was 400–10–2000.

John is employed by the Highway Department of the State of Louisiana in an executive position. His salary is $80,000. The appropriate amounts of Social Security and Medicare taxes were withheld. In addition, $15,000 was withheld for Federal income taxes, and $2,200 was withheld for state income taxes.

Upon the death of his Aunt Josie in December 1995, John, her only recognized heir, inherited the following assets:

Asset	Josie's Adjusted Basis	FMV at Date of Death
Car	$ 22,000	$ 15,000
Land—300 acres	150,000	600,000
IBM stock	50,000	125,000
Cash	30,000	30,000

Six months prior to her death, Josie gave John a beach house. Her adjusted basis for the beach house was $175,000, and the fair market value was $250,000. She paid a gift tax of $18,000.

During the year, John had the following transactions:

- On February 1, 1996, he sold for $40,000 Exxon stock that he inherited from his father four years ago. His father's adjusted basis was $12,000, and the fair market value at the date of the father's death was $35,000.

- The car John inherited from Josie was destroyed in a wreck on October 1, 1996. He had loaned the car to Katy to use for a two-week period while the engine in her car was being replaced. Fortunately, neither Katy nor Kendra was injured. John received insurance proceeds of $14,000, the fair market value of the car on October 1.

- On October 30, 1996, John gambled away the $30,000 he inherited on a riverboat casino in Biloxi. He had hoped this activity would help with the bouts of depression he had been suffering since Sally's death.

- On December 28, John sold the 300 acres of land to his brother, James, for its fair market value of $575,000. James planned on using the land for his dairy farm.

- On December 29, John sold the IBM stock he had inherited for $100,000.

Other sources of income for John were as follows:

Dividend income	$40,000
Interest income:	
Guaranty Bank	9,000
City of Kentwood water bonds	10,000

Potential itemized deductions for John, in addition to items already mentioned, were:

Property taxes paid on real estate	$9,000
Property taxes paid on personalty	2,000
Estimated Federal income taxes paid	8,000
Estimated state income taxes paid	1,500
Charitable contributions	5,000
Mortgage interest on his residence	4,000
Orthodontic and psychiatric expenses for John	3,000

Part 1—Tax Computation
Compute John's net tax payable or refund due for 1996. Suggested software (if available): *TurboTax* or *MacInTax*.

Part 2—Tax Planning
Assume that rather than selling the land to James, John is considering leasing it to him for $30,000 annually with the lease beginning on October 1, 1996. James would prepay the lease payments through December 31, 1996. Thereafter, he would make monthly lease payments at the beginning of each month. What effect would this have on John's 1996 tax liability? What potential problem might John encounter? Write a letter to John in which you advise him of the tax consequences of leasing versus selling. Also, prepare a memo for the tax files.

93. Tammy Walker, age 37, is a self-employed accountant. Tammy's Social Security number is 333–40–1111. Her address is 101 Glass Road, Richmond, VA 23236. Her income and expenses associated with her accounting practice for 1996 are as follows:

Revenues (cash receipts during 1996)	$212,000
Expenses	
Salaries	$ 89,000

Office supplies	2,100
Postage	1,500
Depreciation of equipment	25,000
Telephone	800
	$118,400

Since Tammy is a cash method taxpayer, she does not record her receivables as revenue until she receives cash payment. At the beginning of 1996, her accounts receivable were $20,000, and the balance had decreased to $8,000 by the end of the year. The balance on December 31, 1996, would have been $14,000, except that an account for $6,000 had become uncollectible in November.

Tammy used one room in her 10-room house as the office for her accounting practice (400 square feet out of a total square footage of 4,000). She paid the following expenses related to the house during 1996:

Utilities	$4,000
Insurance	800
Property taxes	4,000
Repairs	1,400

Tammy had purchased the house on September 1, 1995, for $200,000. She sold her previous house on November 15, 1995, for $105,000. Her selling expenses had been $9,000, and qualified fixing-up expenses were $1,100. Tammy and her former husband, Lou, had purchased the house in 1992 for $80,000. Tammy had received Lou's 50% ownership interest as part of their divorce settlement in August 1994. Tammy had not used any part of the former residence as a home office.

Tammy has one child, Thomas, age 17. Thomas lives with his father during the summer and with Tammy for the rest of the year. Tammy can document that she spent $8,000 during 1996 for the child's support. The father normally provides about $2,000 per year, but this year he gave the child a new car for Christmas. The cost of the car was $18,000. The divorce decree is silent regarding the dependency exemption for the child.

Under the terms of the divorce decree, Tammy is to receive alimony of $900 per month. The payments will terminate at Tammy's death or if she should remarry.

Tammy provides part of the support of her mother, age 67. The total support for 1996 for her mother was as follows:

Social Security benefits	$5,300
From Tammy	1,700
From Bob, Tammy's brother	1,200
From Susan, Tammy's sister	1,800

Bob and Susan have both indicated their willingness to sign a multiple support waiver form if it will benefit Tammy.

Tammy's deductible itemized deductions during 1996, excluding any itemized deductions related to the house, were $13,000. She made estimated tax payments of $28,000.

Part 1—Tax Computation
Compute Tammy's lowest net tax payable or refund due for 1996. Suggested software (if available): *TurboTax* or *MacInTax*.

Part 2—Tax Planning
Tammy and her former husband have been discussing the $900 alimony he pays her each month. Due to a health problem of his new wife, he does not feel that he can afford to continue to pay the $900 each month. He is in the 15% tax bracket. If Tammy will agree to decrease the amount by 25%, he will agree that the amount paid is not alimony for tax purposes. Assume that the other data used in calculating Tammy's taxable income for 1996 will apply for her 1997 tax return. Write a letter to

Tammy that contains your advice on whether she should agree to her former husband's proposal. Also prepare a memo for the tax files. Suggested software (if available): *TurboTax* or *MacInTax*.

Research Problems for this chapter appear at the end of Chapter 28.

TEAM PROJECT: ARTHUR ANDERSEN TAX CHALLENGE CASES

For more information on the Arthur Andersen Tax Challenge Cases, please refer to Chapter 2, page 2-41.

Information related to tax issues and problems that are discussed in this chapter may be found in the

Fields case on pages 1-3, 9, 13-16, 18, 22
Miller case on pages 3, 5, 14, 28

Read and analyze the case you have been assigned and *identify* any issues and problems that are related to material covered in this chapter. If the information provided in the case is complete, prepare answers for this part of the case at this time. If you need information that is contained in the later parts of the case, please write a memo summarizing the questions or problems so you can prepare a complete answer at a later date.

CHAPTER

13

PROPERTY TRANSACTIONS: CAPITAL GAINS AND LOSSES, SECTION 1231, AND RECAPTURE PROVISIONS

LEARNING OBJECTIVES

After completing Chapter 13, you should be able to:

1. Understand the rationale for separate reporting of capital gains and losses.

2. Distinguish capital assets from ordinary assets.

3. Understand the relevance of a sale or exchange to classification as a capital gain or loss and apply the special rules for the capital gain or loss treatment of the retirement of corporate obligations, options, patents, franchises, and lease cancellation payments.

4. Determine whether the holding period for a capital asset is long term or short term.

5. Describe the tax treatment for capital gains and the detrimental tax treatment for capital losses for noncorporate taxpayers.

6. Describe the tax treatment for capital gains and the detrimental tax treatment for capital losses for corporate taxpayers.

7. Understand the rationale for and the nature and treatment of gains and losses from the disposition of business assets.

8. Distinguish § 1231 assets from ordinary assets and capital assets and calculate the § 1231gain or loss.

9. Determine when § 1245 recapture applies and how it is computed.

10. Determine when § 1250 recapture applies and how it is computed.

11. Understand considerations common to §§ 1245 and 1250.

12. Apply the special recapture provisions for related parties and IDC.

13. Describe and apply the reporting procedures for §§ 1231, 1245, and 1250.

14. Identify tax planning opportunities arising from the sale or exchange of capital assets and avoid pitfalls associated with recapture provisions.

GENERAL CONSIDERATIONS

RATIONALE FOR SEPARATE REPORTING OF CAPITAL GAINS AND LOSSES

1 ▾ LEARNING OBJECTIVE
Understand the rationale for separate reporting of capital gains and losses.

Fourteen years ago, a taxpayer purchased 100 shares of IBM stock for $17 a share. This year the taxpayer sells the shares for $97 a share. Should the $80 per share gain receive any special tax treatment? The $80 gain has built up over 14 years, so it may not be fair to tax it the same as income that was all earned this year.

What if the stock had been purchased for $97 per share and sold for $17 a share? Should the loss be fully deductible? The tax law has an intricate approach to answering these investment activity–related questions.

As you study this chapter, keep in mind that how investment-related gains and losses are taxed can dramatically affect whether taxpayers make investments and which investments are made. Except for a brief discussion in Chapter 2, earlier

TAX IN THE NEWS

Do Lower Capital Gain Tax Rates Encourage the Sale of Investment Assets?

Tax legislation nearly enacted would have reduced the rate of tax on long-term capital gains. In the debate over this legislation in the House of Representatives, the Democrats contended that reducing the tax rates on long-term capital gains would primarily benefit the rich. The Republicans contended that reducing the tax rates on long-term capital gains would stimulate the economy. The House Ways and Means Committee Report (authored by the Republican majority) says:

> The taxation of capital gains upon realization encourages investors who have accrued past gains to keep their monies "locked in" to such investments even when better investment opportunities present themselves. All economists that testified before the Committee agreed that reducing the rate of taxation of capital gains would encourage investors to unlock many of these gains. This unlocking will permit more monies to flow to new, highly valued uses in the economy. . . . The Committee rejects the narrow view that reductions in the taxation of capital gains benefit primarily higher-income Americans. . . . the Committee sees a reduction in the taxation of capital gains as providing potential benefits to all individuals. . . .

SOURCE: Contract With America Tax Relief Act of 1995, H.R. 1215, Report of the House Committee on Ways and Means, March 21, 1995, pp. 35 and 36.

chapters dwelt on how to determine the amount of gain or loss from a property disposition, but did not discuss the classification of gains and losses. This chapter will focus on that topic.

The tax law requires **capital gains** and **capital losses** to be separated from other types of gains and losses. There are two reasons for this treatment. First, long-term capital gains may be taxed at a lower rate than ordinary gains. An *alternative tax computation* is used to determine the tax when taxable income includes net long-term capital gain. Capital gains and losses must therefore be matched with one another to see if a net long-term capital gain exists. The alternative tax computation is discussed later in the chapter under Tax Treatment of Capital Gains and Losses of Noncorporate Taxpayers.

The second reason the Code requires separate reporting of gains and losses and a determination of their tax character is that a net capital loss is only deductible up to $3,000 per year. Excess loss over the annual limit carries over and may be deductible in a future tax year. Capital gains and losses must be matched with one another to see if a net capital loss exists.

For these reasons, capital gains and losses must be distinguished from other types of gains and losses. Most of this chapter describes the intricate rules for determining what type of gains and losses the taxpayer has.

As a result of the need to distinguish and separately match capital gains and losses, the individual tax forms include very extensive reporting requirements for capital gains and losses. This chapter explains the principles underlying the forms. The forms are illustrated with examples at the end of the chapter.

GENERAL SCHEME OF TAXATION

Recognized gains and losses must be properly classified. Proper classification depends upon three characteristics:

- The tax status of the property.
- The manner of the property's disposition.
- The holding period of the property.

The three possible tax statuses are capital asset, § 1231 asset, or ordinary asset. Property disposition may be by sale, exchange, casualty, theft, or condemnation. The two holding periods are one year or less (short term) and more than one year (long term).

The major focus of this chapter is capital gains and losses. Capital gains and losses usually result from the disposition of a capital asset. The most common disposition is a sale of the asset. Capital gains and losses can also result from the disposition of § 1231 assets, which include depreciable or real property used in a trade or business. Section 1231 transactions, as well as recapture provisions under §§ 1245 and 1250, are also covered in this chapter.

CAPITAL ASSETS

DEFINITION OF A CAPITAL ASSET

2 **LEARNING OBJECTIVE**
Distinguish capital assets from ordinary assets.

Personal use assets and investment assets are the most common capital assets owned by individual taxpayers. Personal use assets usually include items such as clothing, recreation equipment, a residence, and automobiles. Investment assets usually include corporate stocks and bonds, government bonds, and vacant land. Remember, however, that losses from the sale or exchange of personal use assets are not recognized. Therefore, the classification of such losses as capital losses can be ignored.

Due to the historical preferential treatment of capital gains, taxpayers have preferred that gains be capital gains rather than ordinary gains. As a result, a great many statutes, cases, and rulings have accumulated in the attempt to define what is and what is not a capital asset.

Capital assets are not directly defined in the Code. Instead, § 1221 defines what is *not* a capital asset. A **capital asset** is property held by the taxpayer (whether or not it is connected with the taxpayer's business) that is *not* any of the following:

- Inventory or property held primarily for sale to customers in the ordinary course of a business. The Supreme Court, in *Malat v. Riddell*, defined *primarily* as meaning *of first importance* or *principally*.[1]
- Accounts and notes receivable acquired from the sale of inventory or acquired for services rendered in the ordinary course of business.
- Depreciable property or real estate used in a business.
- Certain copyrights; literary, musical, or artistic compositions; or letters, memoranda, or similar property held by (1) a taxpayer whose efforts created the property; (2) in the case of a letter, memorandum, or similar property, a taxpayer for whom it was produced; or (3) a taxpayer in whose hands the basis of the property is determined, for purposes of determining gain from

[1] 66–1 USTC ¶9317, 17 AFTR2d 604, 86 S.Ct. 1030 (USSC, 1966).

a sale or exchange, in whole or in part by reference to the basis of such property in the hands of a taxpayer described in (1) or (2).

- U.S. government publications that are (1) received by a taxpayer from the U.S. government other than by purchase at the price at which they are offered for sale to the public or (2) held by a taxpayer whose basis, for purposes of determining gain from a sale or exchange, is determined by reference to a taxpayer described in (1).

The Code defines what is *not* a capital asset. From the preceding list, it is apparent that inventory, accounts and notes receivable, and most fixed assets of a business are not capital assets. The following discussion provides further detail on each part of the capital asset definition.

Inventory.   What constitutes inventory is determined by the taxpayer's business.

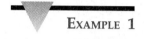
EXAMPLE 1   Green Company buys and sells used cars. Its cars are inventory. Its gains from the sale of the cars are ordinary income. ▼

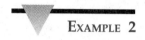
EXAMPLE 2   Soong sells her personal use automobile at a $500 gain. The automobile is a personal use asset and, therefore, a capital asset. The gain is a capital gain. ▼

Accounts and Notes Receivable.   Collection of an accrual basis account receivable usually does not result in a gain or loss because the amount collected equals the receivable's basis. The sale of an account or note receivable may generate a gain or loss, and the gain or loss is ordinary because the receivable is not a capital asset. The sale of an accrual basis receivable may result in a gain or loss because it will probably be sold for more or less than its basis. A cash basis account receivable has no basis. Sale of such a receivable generates a gain. Collection of a cash basis receivable generates ordinary income rather than a gain. A gain usually requires a sale of the receivable. See the discussion of Sale or Exchange later in this chapter.

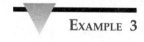
EXAMPLE 3   Oriole Company has accounts receivable of $100,000. Because it needs working capital, it sells the receivables for $83,000 to a financial institution. If Oriole is an accrual basis taxpayer, it has a $17,000 ordinary loss. Revenue of $100,000 would have been recorded and a $100,000 basis would have been established when the receivable was created. If Oriole is a cash basis taxpayer, it has $83,000 of ordinary income because it would not have recorded any revenue earlier; thus, the receivable has no tax basis. ▼

Business Fixed Assets.   Depreciable personal property and real estate (both depreciable and nondepreciable) used by a business are not capital assets. Thus, *business fixed assets* are generally not capital assets.

The Code has a very complex set of rules pertaining to such property. One of these rules is discussed under Real Property Subdivided for Sale, and the others are discussed later in the chapter. Although business fixed assets are not capital assets, a long-term capital gain can sometimes result from their sale. This chapter discusses the potential capital gain treatment for business fixed assets under § 1231.

Copyrights and Creative Works.   Generally, the person whose efforts led to the copyright or creative work has an ordinary asset, not a capital asset. *Creative works* include the works of authors, composers, and artists. Also, the person for whom a letter, memorandum, or other similar property was created has an ordinary asset. Finally, a person receiving a copyright, creative work, letter, memorandum, or similar property by gift from the creator or the person for whom the work was created has an ordinary asset.

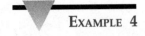

EXAMPLE 4   Wanda is a part-time music composer. A music publisher purchases one of her songs for $5,000. Wanda has a $5,000 ordinary gain from the sale of an ordinary asset. ▼

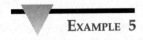

EXAMPLE 5   Ed received a letter from the President of the United States in 1962. In the current year, Ed sells the letter to a collector for $300. Ed has a $300 ordinary gain from the sale of an ordinary asset (because the letter was created for Ed). ▼

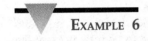

EXAMPLE 6   Isabella gives a song she composed to her son. The son sells the song to a music publisher for $5,000. The son has a $5,000 ordinary gain from the sale of an ordinary asset. If the son inherits the song from Isabella, his basis for the song is its fair market value at Isabella's death. The song is a capital asset because the son's basis is not related to Isabella's basis for the song. ▼

U.S. Government Publications.   U.S. government publications received from the U.S. government (or its agencies) for a reduced price are not capital assets. This prevents a taxpayer from later donating the publications to charity and claiming a charitable contribution equal to the fair market value of the publications. A charitable contribution of a capital asset generally yields a deduction equal to the fair market value. A charitable contribution of an ordinary asset generally yields a deduction equal to less than the fair market value. If such property is received by gift from the original purchaser, the property is not a capital asset to the donee. (For a more comprehensive explanation of charitable contributions of property, refer to Chapter 9.)

EFFECT OF JUDICIAL ACTION

Court decisions play an important role in the definition of capital assets. Because the Code only lists categories of what are *not* capital assets, judicial interpretation is sometimes required to determine whether a specific item fits into one of those categories. The Supreme Court follows a literal interpretation of the categories. For instance, corporate stock is not mentioned in § 1221. Thus, corporate stock is *usually* a capital asset. However, what if corporate stock is purchased for resale to customers? Then it is *inventory* and not a capital asset because inventory is one of the categories in § 1221. (See the discussion of Dealers in Securities below.)

A Supreme Court decision was required to distinguish between capital asset and non-capital asset status when a taxpayer who did not normally acquire stock for resale to customers acquired stock with the intention of resale.[2] The Court decided that since the stock was not acquired primarily for sale to customers (the taxpayer did not sell the stock to its regular customers), the stock was a capital asset.

Often the crux of the capital asset determination hinges on whether the asset is held for investment purposes (capital asset) or business purposes (ordinary asset). The taxpayer's *use* of the property often provides objective evidence.

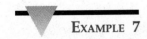

EXAMPLE 7   Ramon's business buys an expensive painting. If the painting is used to decorate Ramon's office and is not of investment quality, the painting is depreciable and, therefore, not a

---

[2] *Arkansas Best v. Comm.*, 88–1 USTC ¶9210, 61 AFTR2d 88–655, 108 S.Ct. 971 (USSC, 1988).

capital asset. If Ramon's business is buying and selling paintings, the painting is inventory and, therefore, an ordinary asset. If the painting is of investment quality and the business purchased it for investment, the painting is a capital asset, even though it serves a decorative purpose in Ramon's office. *Investment quality* generally means that the painting is expected to appreciate in value. ▼

STATUTORY EXPANSIONS

Because of the uncertainty associated with capital asset status, Congress has enacted several Code Sections to clarify the definition. These statutory expansions of the capital asset definition are discussed in this section.

Dealers in Securities.   As a general rule, securities (stocks, bonds, and other financial instruments) held by a dealer are considered to be inventory and are not, therefore, subject to capital gain or loss treatment. A *dealer in securities* is a merchant (e.g., a brokerage firm) that regularly engages in the purchase and resale of securities to customers. The dealer must identify any securities being held for investment. Generally, if a dealer clearly identifies certain securities as held for investment purposes by the close of business on the acquisition date, gain from the securities' sale will be capital gain. However, the gain will not be capital gain if the dealer ceases to hold the securities for investment prior to the sale. Losses are capital losses if at any time the securities have been clearly identified by the dealer as held for investment.[3]

ETHICAL CONSIDERATIONS

Capital Asset Status for Stock Held by Securities Dealers

A securities dealer purchases stock for her own account at 10:00 A.M. At the close of business that day, the stock has dropped slightly in price, so the dealer does not designate it as held for investment. By 10:30 A.M. the next morning, however, the value of the stock has risen substantially above the dealer's purchase price. Using her knowledge of computer programming, the dealer could manipulate the firm's computer records so that the stock will appear to have been designated as held for investment at the end of the previous day. She is absolutely certain that neither the firm nor the IRS will ever discover what she has done. Comment on the securities dealer's potential behavior and the motivation for it.

Real Property Subdivided for Sale.   Substantial real property development activities may result in the owner being considered a dealer for tax purposes. Income from the sale of real estate property lots is treated as the sale of inventory (ordinary income) if the owner is considered to be a dealer. However, § 1237 allows real estate investors capital gain treatment if they engage *only* in *limited* development activities. To be eligible for § 1237 treatment, the following requirements must be met:

- The taxpayer may not be a corporation.
- The taxpayer may not be a real estate dealer.

---

[3]§§ 1236(a) and (b) and Reg. § 1.1236–1(a).

- No substantial improvements may be made to the lots sold. *Substantial* generally means more than a 10 percent increase in the value of a lot. Shopping centers and other commercial or residential buildings are considered substantial, while filling, draining, leveling, and clearing operations are not.
- The taxpayer must have held the lots sold for at least 5 years, except for inherited property. The substantial improvements test is less stringent if the property is held at least 10 years.

If the preceding requirements are met, all gain is capital gain until the tax year in which the *sixth* lot is sold. Sales of contiguous lots to a single buyer in the same transaction count as the sale of one lot. Beginning with the tax year the *sixth* lot is sold, some of the gain may be ordinary income. Five percent of the revenue from lot sales is potential ordinary income. That potential ordinary income is offset by any selling expenses from the lot sales. Practically, sales commissions often are at least 5 percent of the sales price, so none of the gain is treated as ordinary income.

Section 1237 does not apply to losses. A loss from the sale of subdivided real property is an ordinary loss unless the property qualifies as a capital asset under § 1221. The following example illustrates the application of § 1237.

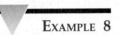

EXAMPLE 8

Ahmed owns a large tract of land and subdivides it for sale. Assume Ahmed meets all the requirements of § 1237 and during the tax year sells the first 10 lots to 10 different buyers for $10,000 each. Ahmed's basis in each lot sold is $3,000, and he incurs total selling expenses of $4,000 on the sales. Ahmed's gain is computed as follows:

Selling price (10 × $10,000)		$100,000
Basis (10 × $3,000)		(30,000)
Excess over basis		$ 70,000
Five percent of selling price	$ 5,000	
Selling expenses	(4,000)	
Amount of ordinary income		$ 1,000
Five percent of selling price	$ 5,000	
Excess of expenses over 5% of selling price	–0–	(5,000)
Capital gain		65,000
Total gain ($70,000 – $4,000 selling expenses)		$66,000

SALE OR EXCHANGE

3 LEARNING OBJECTIVE
Understand the relevance of a sale or exchange to classification as a capital gain or loss and apply the special rules for the capital gain or loss treatment of the retirement of corporate obligations, options, patents, franchises, and lease cancellation payments.

Recognition of capital gain or loss usually requires a sale or exchange of a capital asset. The Code uses the term **sale or exchange,** but does not define it. Generally, a property sale involves the receipt of money by the seller and/or the assumption by the purchaser of the seller's liabilities. An exchange involves the transfer of property for other property. Thus, an involuntary conversion (casualty, theft, or condemnation) is not a sale or exchange. In several situations, the determination of whether a sale or exchange has taken place has been clarified by the enactment of Code Sections that specifically provide for sale or exchange treatment.

Recognized gains or losses from the cancellation, lapse, expiration, or any other termination of a right or obligation with respect to personal property (other than stock) that is or would be a capital asset in the hands of the taxpayer are

capital gains or losses.[4] See the discussion under Options later in the chapter for
more details.

WORTHLESS SECURITIES AND § 1244 STOCK

Occasionally, securities such as stock and, especially, bonds may become worthless
due to the insolvency of their issuer. If such a security is a capital asset, the loss is
deemed to have occurred as the result of a sale or exchange on the *last day* of the
tax year.[5] This last-day rule may have the effect of converting what otherwise
would have been a short-term capital loss into a long-term capital loss. See
Treatment of Capital Losses later in this chapter.

Section 1244 allows an ordinary deduction on disposition of stock at a loss.
The stock must be that of a small business company, and the ordinary deduction
is limited to $50,000 ($100,000 for married individuals filing jointly) per year. For a
more detailed discussion, refer to Chapter 6.

SPECIAL RULE—RETIREMENT OF CORPORATE OBLIGATIONS

A debt obligation (e.g., a bond or note payable) may have a tax basis in excess of
or less than its redemption value because it may have been acquired at a premium
or discount. Consequently, the collection of the redemption value may result in a
loss or gain. Generally, the collection of a debt obligation is *not* a sale or exchange.
Therefore, any loss or gain cannot be a capital loss or gain because no sale or
exchange has taken place. However, if the debt obligation was issued by a
corporation or certain government agencies, the collection of the redemption value
is treated as a sale or exchange.[6]

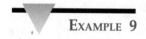

EXAMPLE 9

Fran acquires $1,000 of Osprey Corporation bonds for $980 in the open market. If the bonds
are held to maturity, the $20 difference between Fran's collection of the $1,000 redemption
value and her cost of $980 is treated as capital gain. If the obligation had been issued to Fran
by an individual instead of by a corporation, her $20 gain would be ordinary, since she did
not sell or exchange the debt. ▼

OPTIONS

Frequently, a potential buyer of property wants some time to make the purchase
decision, but wants to control the sale and/or the sale price in the meantime.
Options are used to achieve these objectives. The potential purchaser (grantee)
pays the property owner (grantor) for an option on the property. The grantee then
becomes the option holder. The option usually sets a price at which the grantee
can buy the property and expires after a specified period of time.

Sale of an Option.   A grantee may sell or exchange the option rather than
exercising it or letting it expire. Generally, the grantee's sale or exchange of the
option results in capital gain or loss if the option property is (or would be) a
capital asset to the grantee.[7]

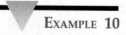

EXAMPLE 10

Rosa wants to buy some vacant land for investment purposes. She cannot afford the full
purchase price. Instead, she convinces the landowner (grantor) to sell her the right to

---

[4]§ 1234A.
[5]§ 165(g)(1).

[6]§ 1271.
[7]§ 1234(a) and Reg. § 1.1234–1(a)(1).

purchase the land for $100,000 anytime in the next two years. Rosa (grantee) pays $3,000 to obtain this option to buy the land. The option is a capital asset for Rosa because if she actually purchased the land, the land would be a capital asset. Three months after purchasing the option, Rosa sells it for $7,000. She has a $4,000 ($7,000 – $3,000) short-term capital gain on this sale since she held the option for one year or less. ▼

Failure to Exercise Options.   If an option holder (grantee) fails to exercise the option, the lapse of the option is considered a sale or exchange on the option expiration date. Thus, the loss is a capital loss if the property subject to the option is (or would be) a capital asset in the hands of the grantee.

The grantor of an option on *stocks, securities, commodities, or commodity futures* receives short-term capital gain treatment upon the expiration of the option. Options on property other than stocks, securities, commodities, or commodity futures result in ordinary income to the grantor when the option expires. For example, an individual investor who owns certain stock (a capital asset) may sell a call option, entitling the buyer of the option to acquire the stock at a specified price higher than the value at the date the option is granted. The writer of the call receives a premium (e.g., 10 percent) for writing the option. If the price of the stock does not increase during the option period, the option will expire unexercised. Upon the expiration of the option, the grantor must recognize short-term capital gain. These provisions do not apply to options held for sale to customers (the inventory of a securities dealer).

Exercise of Options by Grantee.   If the option is exercised, the amount paid for the option is added to the optioned property's selling price. This increases the gain (or reduces the loss) to the grantor resulting from the sale of the property. The grantor's gain or loss is capital or ordinary depending on the tax status of the property. The grantee adds the cost of the option to the basis of the property purchased.

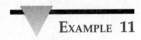

EXAMPLE 11

On September 1, 1989, Wes purchases 100 shares of Eagle Company stock for $5,000. On April 1, 1996, he writes a call option on the stock, giving the grantee the right to buy the stock for $6,000 during the following six-month period. Wes (the grantor) receives a call premium of $500 for writing the call.

- If the call is exercised by the grantee on August 1, 1996, Wes has $1,500 ($6,000 + $500 – $5,000) of long-term capital gain from the sale of the stock. The grantee has a $6,500 ($500 option premium + $6,000 purchase price) basis for the stock.
- Assume that Wes decides to sell his stock prior to exercise for $6,000 and enters into a closing transaction by purchasing a call on 100 shares of Eagle Company stock for $5,000. Since the Eagle stock is selling for $6,000, Wes must pay a call premium of $1,000. He recognizes a $500 short-term capital loss [$1,000 (call premium paid) – $500 (call premium received)] on the closing transaction. On the actual sale of the Eagle stock, Wes has a long-term capital gain of $1,000 [$6,000 (selling price) – $5,000 (cost)]. The grantee is not affected by Wes's closing transaction. The original option is still in existence, and the grantee's tax consequences will depend on what action the grantee takes—exercising the option, letting the option expire, or selling the option.
- Assume that the original option expired unexercised. Wes has a $500 short-term capital gain equal to the call premium received for writing the option. This gain is not recognized until the option expires. The grantee has a loss from expiration of the option. The nature of the loss will depend upon whether the option was a capital asset or an ordinary asset. ▼

Concept Summary 13–1 summarizes the rules for options.

CONCEPT SUMMARY 13–1

Options

	Effect on	
Event	**Grantor**	**Grantee**
Option is granted.	Receives value and has a contract obligation (a liability).	Pays value and has a contract right (an asset).
Option expires.	Has a short-term capital gain if the option property is stocks, securities, commodities, or commodity futures. Otherwise, gain is ordinary income.	Has a loss (capital loss if option property would have been a capital asset for the grantee).
Option is exercised.	Amount received for option increases proceeds from sale of the option property.	Amount paid for option becomes part of the basis of the option property purchased.
Option is sold or exchanged by grantee.	Result depends upon whether option later expires or is exercised (see above).	Could have gain or loss (capital gain or loss if option property would have been a capital asset for the grantee).

PATENTS

Transfer of a **patent** is treated as the sale or exchange of a long-term capital asset when all substantial rights to the patent (or an undivided interest that includes all such rights) are transferred by a holder.[8] The transferor/holder may receive payment in virtually any form. Lump-sum or periodic payments are most common. The amount of the payments may also be contingent on the transferee/purchaser's productivity, use, or disposition of the patent. If the transfer meets these requirements, any gain or loss is *automatically a long-term* capital gain or loss. Whether the asset was a capital asset for the transferor, whether a sale or exchange occurred, and how long the transferor held the patent are not relevant.

This special long-term capital gain or loss treatment for patents is intended to encourage technological progress. Ironically, authors, composers, and artists are not eligible for capital gain treatment when their creations are transferred. Books, songs, and artists' works may be copyrighted, but copyrights and the assets they represent are not capital assets. Thus, the disposition of those assets by their creators usually results in ordinary gain or loss. The following example illustrates the special treatment for patents.

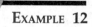
EXAMPLE 12

Mei-Yen, a druggist, invents a pill-counting machine, which she patents. In consideration of a lump-sum payment of $200,000 plus $10 per machine sold, Mei-Yen assigns the patent to Drug Products, Inc. Assuming Mei-Yen has transferred all substantial rights, the question of whether the transfer is a sale or exchange of a capital asset is not relevant. Mei-Yen automatically has a long-term capital gain from both the lump-sum payment and the $10 per machine royalty to the extent these proceeds exceed her basis for the patent. ▼

Substantial Rights.   To receive favorable capital gain treatment, all *substantial rights* to the patent (or an undivided interest in it) must be transferred. All

---

[8]§ 1235.

substantial rights to a patent means all rights (whether or not then held by the grantor) that are valuable at the time the patent rights (or an undivided interest in the patent) are transferred. All substantial rights have not been transferred when the transfer is limited geographically within the issuing country or when the transfer is for a period less than the remaining life of the patent. The circumstances of the entire transaction, rather than merely the language used in the transfer instrument, are to be considered in deciding whether all substantial rights have been transferred.[9]

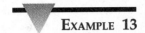

EXAMPLE 13   Assume Mei-Yen, the druggist in Example 12, only licensed Drug Products, Inc., to manufacture and sell the invention in Michigan. She retained the right to license the machine elsewhere in the United States. Mei-Yen has retained a substantial right and is not eligible for automatic long-term capital gain treatment. ▼

Holder Defined.   The *holder* of a patent must be an *individual* and is usually the invention's creator. A holder may also be an individual who purchases the patent rights from the creator before the patented invention is reduced to practice. However, the creator's employer and certain parties related to the creator do not qualify as holders. Thus, in the common situation where an employer has all rights to an employee's inventions, the employer is not eligible for long-term capital gain treatment. More than likely, the employer will have an ordinary asset because the patent was developed as part of its business.

FRANCHISES, TRADEMARKS, AND TRADE NAMES

A mode of operation, a widely recognized brand name (trade name), and a widely known business symbol (trademark) are all valuable assets. These assets may be licensed (commonly known as franchising) by their owner for use by other businesses. Many fast-food restaurants (such as McDonald's and Taco Bell) are franchises. The franchisee usually pays the owner (franchisor) an initial fee plus a contingent fee. The contingent fee is often based upon the franchisee's sales volume.

For Federal income tax purposes, a **franchise** is an agreement that gives the franchisee the right to distribute, sell, or provide goods, services, or facilities within a specified area.[10] A franchise transfer includes the grant of a franchise, a transfer by one franchisee to another person, or the renewal of a franchise.

A franchise transfer is generally not a sale or exchange of a capital asset. Section 1253 provides that a transfer of a franchise, trademark, or trade name is not a transfer of a capital asset when the transferor retains any significant power, right, or continuing interest in the property transferred.

Significant Power, Right, or Continuing Interest.   *Significant powers, rights, or continuing interests* include control over assignment, quality of products and services, sale or advertising of other products or services, and the right to require that substantially all supplies and equipment be purchased from the transferor. Also included are the right to terminate the franchise at will and the right to substantial contingent payments. Most modern franchising operations involve some or all of these powers, rights, or continuing interests.

In the unusual case where no significant power, right, or continuing interest is retained by the transferor, a sale or exchange may occur, and capital gain or loss

[9] Reg. § 1.1235–2(b)(1).

[10] § 1253(b)(1).

treatment may be available. For capital gain or loss treatment to be available, the asset transferred must qualify as a capital asset.

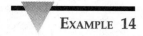

EXAMPLE 14

Orange, Inc., a franchisee, sells the franchise to a third party. Payments to Orange are not contingent, and all significant powers, rights, and continuing interests are transferred. The gain (payments – adjusted basis) on the sale is a capital gain to Orange. ▼

Noncontingent Payments. When the transferor retains a significant power, right, or continuing interest, the transferee's noncontingent payments to the transferor are ordinary income to the transferor. The franchisee capitalizes the payments and amortizes them over 15 years. The amortization is subject to recapture under § 1245.

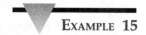

EXAMPLE 15

Grey Company signs a 10-year franchise agreement with DOH Donuts. Grey (the franchisee) makes payments of $3,000 per year for the first 8 years of the franchise agreement—a total of $24,000. Grey cannot deduct $3,000 per year as the payments are made. Instead, Grey may amortize the $24,000 total over 15 years. Thus, Grey may deduct $1,600 per year for each of the 15 years of the amortization period. The same result would occur if Grey made a $24,000 lump-sum payment at the beginning of the franchise period. Assuming DOH Donuts (the franchisor) retains significant powers, rights, or a continuing interest, it will have ordinary income when it receives the payments from Grey. ▼

Contingent Payments. Whether or not the tranferor retains a significant power, right, or continuing interest, contingent franchise payments are ordinary income for the franchisor and an ordinary deduction for the franchisee. For this purpose, a payment qualifies as a contingent payment only if the following requirements are met:

- The contingent amounts are part of a series of payments that are paid at least annually throughout the term of the transfer agreement.
- The payments are substantially equal in amount or are payable under a fixed formula.

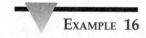

EXAMPLE 16

TAK, a spicy chicken franchisor, transfers an eight-year franchise to Otis. TAK retains a significant power, right, or continuing interest. Otis, the franchisee, agrees to pay TAK 15% of sales. This contingent payment is ordinary income to TAK and a business deduction for Otis as the payments are made. ▼

Sports Franchises. Professional sports franchises (e.g., the Detroit Tigers) are not covered by § 1253.[11] However, § 1056 restricts the allocation of sports franchise acquisition costs to player contracts. Player contracts are usually one of the major assets acquired with a sports franchise. These contracts last only for the time stated in the contract. Therefore, owners of sports franchises would like to allocate franchise acquisition costs disproportionately to the contracts so that the acquisition costs will be amortizable over the contracts' lives. Section 1056 prevents this by generally limiting the amount that can be allocated to player contracts to no more than 50 percent of the franchise acquisition cost. In addition, the seller of the sports franchise has ordinary income under § 1245 for the portion of the gain allocable to the disposition of player contracts.[12]

Concept Summary 13–2 summarizes the rules for franchises.

---

[11] § 1253(e).

[12] See the discussion of the recapture provisions later in this chapter.

CONCEPT SUMMARY 13–2

Franchises

	Effect on	
Event	Franchisor	Franchisee
Franchisor Retains Significant Powers and Rights		
Noncontingent payment	Ordinary income.	Capitalized and amortized over 15 years as an ordinary deduction; if franchise is sold, amortization is subject to recapture under § 1245.
Contingent payment	Ordinary income.	Ordinary deduction.
Franchisor Does *Not* Retain Significant Powers and Rights		
Noncontingent payment	Ordinary income if franchise rights are an ordinary asset; capital gain if franchise rights are a capital asset (unlikely).	Capitalized and amortized over 15 years as an ordinary deduction; if the franchise is sold, amortization is subject to recapture under § 1245.
Contingent payment	Ordinary income.	Ordinary deduction.

LEASE CANCELLATION PAYMENTS

The tax treatment of payments received for canceling a lease depends on whether the recipient is the **lessor** or the **lessee** and whether the lease is a capital asset or not.

Lessee Treatment. Lease cancellation payments received by a lessee are treated as an exchange.[13] Thus, these payments are capital gains if the lease is a capital asset. Generally, a lessee's lease is a capital asset if the property (either personalty or realty) is used for the lessee's personal use (e.g., his or her residence). A lessee's lease is an ordinary asset if the property is used in the lessee's trade or business.[14]

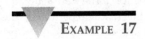

EXAMPLE 17

Mark owns an apartment building that he is going to convert into an office building. Vicki is one of the apartment tenants and receives $1,000 from Mark to cancel the lease. Vicki has a capital gain of $1,000 (which is long term or short term depending upon how long she has held the lease). Mark has an ordinary deduction of $1,000. ▼

Lessor Treatment. Payments received by a lessor for a lease cancellation are always ordinary income because they are considered to be in lieu of rental payments.[15]

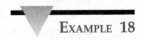

EXAMPLE 18

Floyd owns an apartment building near a university campus. Hui-Fen is one of the tenants. Hui-Fen is graduating early and offers Floyd $800 to cancel the apartment lease. Floyd accepts the offer. Floyd has ordinary income of $800. Hui-Fen has a nondeductible payment since the apartment was personal use property. ▼

---

[13] § 1241 and Reg. § 1.1241–1(a).
[14] Reg. § 1.1221–1(b).

[15] *Hort v. Comm.*, 41–1 USTC ¶9354, 25 AFTR 1207, 61 S.Ct. 757 (USSC, 1941).

HOLDING PERIOD

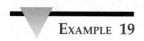

4   **LEARNING OBJECTIVE**
Determine whether the holding
period for a capital asset is long
term or short term.

Property must be held more than one year to qualify for long-term capital gain or loss treatment.[16] Property not held for the required long-term period results in short-term capital gain or loss. To compute the **holding period,** start counting on the day after the property was acquired and include the day of disposition.

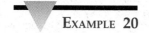

EXAMPLE 20

Marge purchases a capital asset on January 15, 1995, and sells it on January 16, 1996. Marge's holding period is more than one year. If Marge had sold the asset on January 15, 1996, the holding period would have been exactly one year, and the gain or loss would have been short term. ▼

To be held for more than one year, a capital asset acquired on the last day of any month must not be disposed of until on or after the first day of the thirteenth succeeding month.[17]

Leo purchases a capital asset on February 28, 1995. If Leo sells the asset on February 29, 1996, the holding period is one year, and Leo will have a short-term capital gain or loss. If Leo sells the asset on March 1, 1996, the holding period is more than one year, and he will have a long-term capital gain or loss. ▼

REVIEW OF SPECIAL HOLDING PERIOD RULES

There are several special holding period rules.[18] The application of these rules depends on the type of asset and how it was acquired.

Nontaxable Exchanges.   The holding period of property received in a like-kind exchange includes the holding period of the former asset if the property that has been exchanged is a capital asset or a § 1231 asset. In certain nontaxable transactions involving a substituted basis, the holding period of the former property is *tacked on* to the holding period of the newly acquired property.

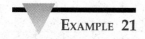

EXAMPLE 21

Vern exchanges a business truck for another truck in a like-kind exchange. The holding period of the exchanged truck tacks on to the holding period of the new truck. ▼

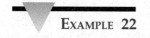

EXAMPLE 22

Alicia sells her personal residence and acquires a new residence. If the transaction qualifies for nonrecognition of gain on the sale of a residence, the holding period of the new residence includes the holding period of the former residence. ▼

Certain Nontaxable Transactions Involving a Carryover of Another Taxpayer's Basis.   A former owner's holding period is tacked on to the present owner's holding period if the transaction is nontaxable and the former owner's basis carries over to the present owner.

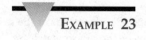

EXAMPLE 23

Kareem acquires 100 shares of Robin Corporation stock for $1,000 on December 31, 1989. He transfers the shares by gift to Megan on December 31, 1995, when the stock is worth $2,000. Kareem's basis of $1,000 becomes the basis for determining gain or loss on a subsequent sale by Megan. Megan's holding period begins with the date the stock was acquired by Kareem. ▼

---

[16] § 1222.
[17] Rev.Rul. 66–7, 1966–1 C.B. 188.

[18] § 1223.

EXAMPLE 24

Assume the same facts as in Example 23, except that the fair market value of the shares is only $800 on the date of the gift. The holding period begins on the date of the gift if Megan sells the stock for a loss. The value of the shares at the date of the gift is used in the determination of her basis for loss. If she sells the shares for $500 on April 1, 1996, Megan has a $300 recognized capital loss, and the holding period is from December 31, 1995, to April 1, 1996 (thus, the loss is short term). ▼

Certain Disallowed Loss Transactions. Under several Code provisions, realized losses are disallowed. When a loss is disallowed, there is no carryover of holding period. Losses can be disallowed under § 267 (sale or exchange between related taxpayers) and § 262 (sale or exchange of personal use assets) as well as other Code Sections. Taxpayers who acquire property in a disallowed loss transaction will have a new holding period begin and will have a basis equal to the purchase price.

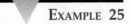

EXAMPLE 25

Janet sells her personal automobile at a loss. She may not deduct the loss because it arises from the sale of personal use property. Janet purchases a replacement automobile for more than the selling price of her former automobile. Janet has a basis equal to the cost of the replacement automobile, and her holding period begins when she acquires the replacement automobile. ▼

Inherited Property. The holding period for inherited property is treated as long term no matter how long the property is actually held by the heir. The holding period of the decedent or the decedent's estate is not relevant for the heir's holding period.

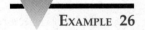

EXAMPLE 26

Shonda inherits Blue Company stock from her father. She receives the stock on April 1, 1996, and sells it on November 1, 1996. Even though the stock was not held more than one year by Shonda, she receives long-term capital gain or loss treatment on the sale. ▼

SPECIAL RULES FOR SHORT SALES

The holding period of property sold short is determined under special rules provided in § 1233. A **short sale** occurs when a taxpayer sells borrowed property and repays the lender with substantially identical property either held on the date of the sale or purchased after the sale. Short sales usually involve corporate stock. The seller's objective is to make a profit in anticipation of a decline in the stock's price. If the price declines, the seller in a short sale recognizes a profit equal to the difference between the sales price of the borrowed stock and the price paid for the replacement stock.

A *short sale against the box* occurs when the stock is borrowed from a broker by a seller who already owns the same stock. The box is the safe deposit box where stock owners routinely used to keep stock certificates. Although today stockbrokers generally keep stock certificates for their customers, the terminology short sale against the box is still used.

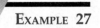

EXAMPLE 27

Chris does not own any shares of Brown Corporation. However, Chris sells 30 shares of Brown. The shares are borrowed from Chris's broker and must be replaced within 45 days. Chris has a short sale because he was short the shares he sold. He will *close* the short sale by purchasing Brown shares and delivering them to his broker. If the original 30 shares were sold for $10,000 and Chris later purchases 30 shares for $8,000, he has a gain of $2,000. Chris's hunch that the price of Brown stock would decline was correct. Chris was able to profit from selling high and buying low. If Chris had to purchase Brown shares for $13,000

A Big Short Sale against the Box

Estée Lauder and her son Ronald recently sold stock in Estée Lauder
Companies in an initial public offering (IPO) for approximately $340
million. By using the "short sale against the box" technique, their current
Federal tax liability associated with the sale is zero. This result occurs because the
sales transaction will not close until they repay the borrowed stock that they
delivered to the purchasers. Other family members were willing to loan the stock
to Estée and Ronald, who pledged an equivalent number of Estée Lauder
Companies shares as security.

If the short sale is not closed until after Estée and Ronald die, then neither they
nor their heirs will ever pay Federal income tax on the transaction because of the
step-up in basis rules associated with inherited property. Estée is said to be at least
87 years old and Ronald is 51.

SOURCE: Information from Allan Sloan, "Passing the Smell Test?" *Newsweek,* December 4,
1995, p. 57.

to close the short sale, he would have a loss of $3,000. In this case, Chris has sold low and
bought high—not the result he wanted! Chris would be making a short sale against the box
if he borrowed shares from his broker to sell and then closed the short sale by delivering
other Brown shares he owned at the time he made the short sale. ▼

A short sale gain or loss is a capital gain or loss to the extent that the short sale
property constitutes a capital asset of the taxpayer. The gain or loss is not
recognized until the short sale is closed. Generally, the holding period of the short
sale property is determined by how long the property used to close the short sale
was held. However, if *substantially identical property* (e.g., other shares of the same
stock) is held by the taxpayer, the short-term or long-term character of the short
sale gain or loss may be affected:

- If substantially identical property has *not* been held for the long-term
holding period on the short sale date, the short sale *gain or loss* is short term.
- If substantially identical property has *been* held for the long-term holding
period on the short sale date, the short sale *gain* is long term if the
substantially identical property is used to close the short sale and short term
if it is not used to close the short sale.
- If substantially identical property has *been* held for the long-term holding
period on the short sale date, the short sale *loss* is long term whether or not
the substantially identical property is used to close the short sale.
- If substantially identical property is acquired *after* the short sale date and on
or before the closing date, the short sale *gain or loss* is short term.

Concept Summary 13–3 summarizes the short sale rules.

These rules are intended to prevent the conversion of short-term capital gains
into long-term capital gains and long-term capital losses into short-term capital
losses. The following examples illustrate the application of the short sale rules.

EXAMPLE 28   On January 4, 1996, Donald purchases five shares of Osprey Corporation common stock for
$100. On April 14, 1996, he engages in a short sale of five shares of the same stock for $150.

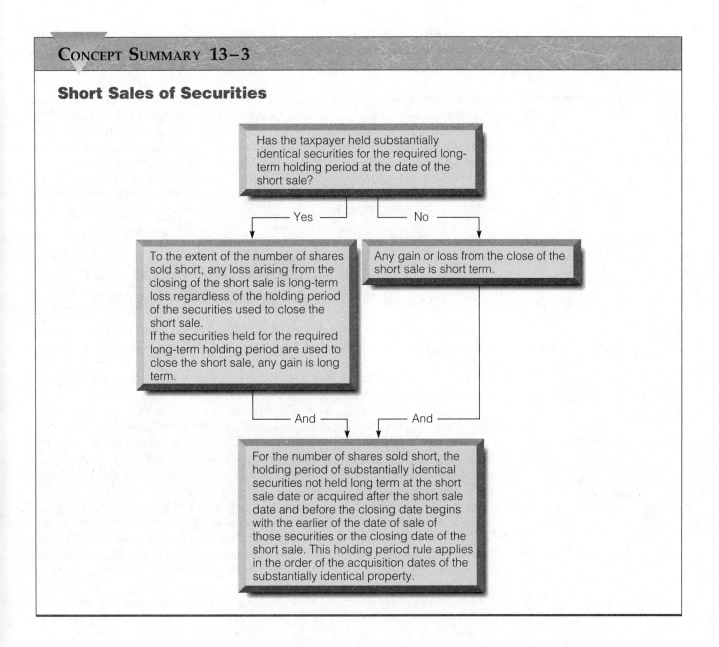

CONCEPT SUMMARY 13–3

Short Sales of Securities

Has the taxpayer held substantially identical securities for the required long-term holding period at the date of the short sale?

Yes — No

To the extent of the number of shares sold short, any loss arising from the closing of the short sale is long-term loss regardless of the holding period of the securities used to close the short sale.
If the securities held for the required long-term holding period are used to close the short sale, any gain is long term.

Any gain or loss from the close of the short sale is short term.

And — And

For the number of shares sold short, the holding period of substantially identical securities not held long term at the short sale date or acquired after the short sale date and before the closing date begins with the earlier of the date of sale of those securities or the closing date of the short sale. This holding period rule applies in the order of the acquisition dates of the substantially identical property.

On August 15, Donald closes the short sale by repaying the borrowed stock with the five shares purchased on January 4. Donald has a $50 short-term capital gain from the short sale because he had not held substantially identical shares for the long-term holding period on the short sale date. ▼

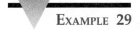

EXAMPLE 29

Assume the same facts as in the previous example, except that Donald closes the short sale on January 28, 1997, by repaying the borrowed stock with five shares purchased on January 27, 1997, for $200. The stock used to close the short sale was not the property purchased on January 4, 1996, but since Donald held short-term property at the April 14, 1996, short sale date, the gain or loss from closing the short sale is short term. Donald has a $50 short-term capital loss ($200 cost of stock purchased January 27, 1997, and a short sale selling price of $150). ▼

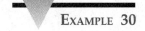

EXAMPLE 30

Assume the same facts as in Example 29. On January 31, 1997, Donald sells for $200 the stock purchased January 4, 1996. Donald's holding period for that stock begins January 28,

1997, because the holding period portion of the short sale rules applies to the substantially identical property in order of acquisition. Donald has a short-term capital gain of $100 ($100 cost of stock purchased January 4, 1996, and a selling price of $200). ▼

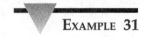

EXAMPLE 31   On January 4, 1996, Rita purchases five shares of Owl Corporation common stock for $100. She purchases five more shares of the same stock on April 14, 1996, for $200. On January 17, 1997, she sells short five shares of the same stock for $150. On September 30, 1997, she repays the borrowed stock with the five shares purchased on April 14, 1996, and sells the five shares purchased on January 4, 1996, for $200. Rita has a $50 long-term capital loss from the short sale because she held substantially identical shares for more than one year on the date of the short sale. Rita has a $100 long-term capital gain from the sale of the shares purchased on January 4, 1996. ▼

TAX TREATMENT OF CAPITAL GAINS AND LOSSES OF NONCORPORATE TAXPAYERS

5   **LEARNING OBJECTIVE**
Describe the tax treatment for capital gains and the detrimental tax treatment for capital losses for noncorporate taxpayers.

All taxpayers net their capital gains and losses. Short-term gains and losses (if any) are netted against one another, and long-term gains and losses (if any) are netted against one another. The results will be net short-term gain or loss and net long-term gain or loss. If these two net positions are of opposite sign (one is a gain and one is a loss), they are netted against one another.

Six possibilities exist for the result after all possible netting has been completed. Three of these final results are gains, and three are losses. One possible result is a net long-term capital gain (NLTCG). Net long-term capital gains of noncorporate taxpayers are subject to beneficial treatment. A second possibility is a net short-term capital gain (NSTCG). Third, the netting may result in both NLTCG and NSTCG.

The NLTCG portion of these net results is subject to a 28 percent maximum tax rate. Since the maximum individual tax rate on non-NLTCG (ordinary income and NSTCG) income is 39.6 percent, the 28 percent maximum tax rate on NLTCG may reduce the tax rate by as much as 11.6 percentage points. The alternative tax computation (discussed in the next section of this chapter) is used to get this tax saving.

The last three results of the capital gain and loss netting process are losses. Thus, a fourth possibility is a net long-term capital loss (NLTCL). A fifth result is a net short-term capital loss (NSTCL). Finally, a sixth possibility includes both an NLTCL and an NSTCL. Neither NLTCLs nor NSTCLs are treated as ordinary losses. Treatment as an ordinary loss generally is preferable to capital loss treatment since ordinary losses are deductible in full while the deductibility of capital losses is subject to certain limitations. An individual taxpayer may deduct a maximum of $3,000 of net capital losses for a taxable year.[19]

TREATMENT OF CAPITAL GAINS

Computation of Net Capital Gain.   As just discussed, the *first step* in the computation is to net all long-term capital gains and losses and all short-term

---

[19]§ 1211(b).

TAX IN THE NEWS

CAPITAL GAIN IN 1979 LEADS TO ADDITIONAL TAXES

A capital gain of $6,498 ended up costing President Bill Clinton and First Lady Hillary Rodham Clinton $14,615 in back Federal and state taxes and interest. The gain resulted from Mrs. Clinton's commodity trading in 1979 and failed to be reported on the Clintons' 1980 tax returns because they did not have a statement on the trade from the brokerage firm.

The Clintons made the payments voluntarily—they could not be required to do so because the statute of limitations had expired. Such problems are not unique to the Clintons. David Kendall, the president's personal attorney, pointed out that three of the last five presidents have paid back taxes and interest to the IRS.

SOURCE: Adapted from Michael K. Frisby and Scott Kilman, "Clintons Pay Back Taxes and Interest of $14,615 Related to 1980 Capital Gain," *Wall Street Journal*, April 12, 1994, p. A20.

---

capital gains and losses. The result is the taxpayer's net long-term capital gain (NLTCG) or loss (NLTCL) and net short-term capital gain (NSTCG) or loss (NSTCL).

EXAMPLE 32

Some possible results of the first step in netting capital gains and losses are shown below. Assume that each case is independent (assume the taxpayer's only capital gains and losses are those shown in the given case).

Case	STCG	STCL	LTCG	LTCL	Result of Netting	Description of Result
A	$8,000	($5,000)			$ 3,000	NSTCG
B	2,000	(7,000)			(5,000)	NSTCL
C			$9,000	($1,000)	8,000	NLTCG
D			8,800	(9,800)	(1,000)	NLTCL

The *second step* in netting capital gains and losses requires offsetting any positive and negative amounts that remain after the first netting step. This procedure is illustrated in the following examples.

EXAMPLE 33

Assume that Sanjay had all the capital gains and losses specified in Cases B and C in Example 32:

Case C ($9,000 LTCG – $1,000 LTCL)	$ 8,000	NLTCG
Case B ($2,000 STCG – $7,000 STCL)	(5,000)	NSTCL
Excess of NLTCG over NSTCL	$ 3,000	

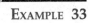

The excess of NLTCG over NSTCL is defined as **net capital gain (NCG).** The result in Example 33 is a $3,000 NCG. There is an alternative tax computation when taxable income includes a NGG.

The **alternative tax** computation for the individual taxpayer taxes the NCG component of taxable income at a maximum tax rate of 28 percent. When taxable income including the NCG does not put the taxpayer into at least the 31 percent rate bracket, the alternative tax computation does not yield a tax benefit.

The NCG alternative tax is the summation of the following computations. It is illustrated in Example 34.

1. The tax computed using the regular rates on the greater of:
   a. Taxable income less the NCG, or
   b. The amount of taxable income taxed at a rate below 28 percent, plus
2. Twenty-eight percent of taxable income in excess of taxable income used in (1).

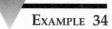

EXAMPLE 34

Tim, an unmarried taxpayer, has taxable income (TI) of $175,000. The TI includes NCG of $50,000. Tim's regular tax liability for 1996 is $52,071 [($24,000 × 15%) + 28%($58,150 − $24,000) + 31%($121,300 − $58,150) + 36%($175,000 − $121,300)]. His alternative tax on the NCG is calculated as follows:

1.	Tax on greater of:	
	a. TI less NCG ($175,000 − $50,000)	
	b. TI taxed below 28% ($24,000), plus	$34,371
2.	28% of TI exceeding TI used in (1)	
	[28% × ($175,000 − $125,000)]	14,000
	Alternative tax on TI including NCG	$48,071

The NCG alternative tax saves Tim $4,000 ($52,071 − $48,071) in 1996. ▼

**ETHICAL
CONSIDERATIONS**

Delaying Stock Sales to Reduce Tax

Jeremy, who is in the 36% tax bracket, had held publicly traded corporate stock for 10 months as of the last day of 1996. The stock was purchased for $3,000 and was worth $13,000. Jeremy needed cash to pay for a trip to his alma mater's football bowl game. He pledged the stock as collateral and borrowed $5,000. He sold the stock on March 1, 1997 and repaid the loan. Consequently, he saved $800 in tax (while having a small amount of nondeductible personal interest expense) by not selling the stock in 1996 or earlier in 1997. Is there anything wrong with what Jeremy did?

There is no special name for the excess of NSTCG over NLTCL, nor is there any special tax treatment. The nature of the gain is short term, and the gain is treated the same as ordinary gain and is included in the taxpayer's gross income.

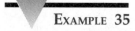

EXAMPLE 35

Assume that Nora had all the capital gains and losses specified in Cases A and D in Example 32:

Case A ($8,000 STCG − $5,000 STCL)	$ 3,000	NSTCG
Case D ($8,800 LTCG − $9,800 LTCL)	(1,000)	NLTCL
Excess of NSTCG over NLTCL	$ 2,000	

▼

ETHICAL CONSIDERATIONS

Indexing Long-Term Capital Gains for Inflation

Tim, an economist, purchased a lot in a planned community for $100,000 in 1987. His intent at that time was to hold the land for investment. During the period from 1976 to 1986, golf course lots in the planned community had appreciated by 200 percent.

Each year Tim pays real property taxes of $1,000 to the county. In addition, he pays $1,200 annually to the homeowners' association for maintenance of the community, security, and garbage collection. He deducts the property taxes on his Federal income tax return and capitalizes the homeowners' association fee.

Tim sells the lot at the end of 1996 for $160,000. Inflation for the 10-year period has been 30 percent. Tim is aware that the Internal Revenue Code of 1986 includes a number of statutory indexing provisions. Although one is not specifically provided for capital asset transactions, Tim feels that the appropriate way for the sale of the land to be taxed is as follows:

Adjusted basis of land:	
Cost	$100,000
Homeowners' association fees ($1,200 × 10 years)	12,000
Inflation adjustment ($100,000 × 30%)	30,000
	$142,000
Amount realized	$160,000
Adjusted basis	(142,000)
Recognized gain	$ 18,000

Since Tim's marginal tax rate is 28 percent, his tax liability associated with the sales transaction is $5,040 ($18,000 × 28%). What is your reaction to Tim's approach?

TREATMENT OF CAPITAL LOSSES

Computation of Net Capital Loss.   A **net capital loss (NCL)** results if capital losses exceed capital gains for the year. An NCL may be all long term, all short term, or part long and part short term.[20] The characterization of an NCL as long or short term is important in determining the capital loss deduction (discussed later in this chapter).

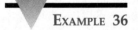

EXAMPLE 36

Three different individual taxpayers have the following capital gains and losses during the year:

Taxpayer	LTCG	LTCL	STCG	STCL	Result of Netting	Description of Result
Robert	$1,000	($ 2,800)	$1,000	($ 500)	($ 1,300)	NLTCL
Carlos	1,000	(500)	1,000	(2,800)	(1,300)	NSTCL
Troy	400	(1,200)	500	(1,200)	(1,500)	NLTCL ($800)
						NSTCL ($700)

---

[20] Section 1222(10) defines a net capital loss as the net loss after the capital loss deduction. However, that definition confuses the discussion of net capital loss. Therefore, net capital loss is used here to mean the result after netting capital gains and losses and before considering the capital loss deduction. The capital loss deduction is discussed under Treatment of Net Capital Loss in this chapter.

Robert's NCL of $1,300 is all long term. Carlos's NCL of $1,300 is all short term. Troy's NCL is $1,500, $800 of which is long term and $700 of which is short term. ▼

Treatment of Net Capital Loss. An NCL is deductible from gross income to the extent of $3,000 per tax year.[21] Capital losses exceeding the loss deduction limits carry forward indefinitely. Thus, although there may or may not be beneficial treatment for capital gains, there is *unfavorable* treatment for capital losses in terms of the $3,000 annual limitation on deducting NCL against ordinary income. If the NCL includes both long-term and short-term capital loss, the short-term capital loss is counted first toward the $3,000 annual limitation.

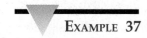

EXAMPLE 37

Burt has an NCL of $5,500, of which $2,000 is STCL and $3,500 is LTCL. Burt has a capital loss deduction of $3,000 ($2,000 of STCL and $1,000 of LTCL). He has an LTCL carryforward of $2,500 ($3,500 – $1,000). ▼

Carryovers. Taxpayers are allowed to carry over unused capital losses indefinitely. The STCL and LTCL carried over retain their character as STCL or LTCL.

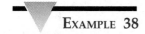

EXAMPLE 38

In 1996, Yoon incurred $1,000 of STCL and $11,000 of LTCL. In 1997, Yoon has a $400 LTCG.

- Yoon's NCL for 1996 is $12,000. Yoon deducts $3,000 ($1,000 STCL and $2,000 LTCL). He has $9,000 of LTCL carried forward to 1997.
- Yoon combines the $9,000 LTCL carryforward with the $400 LTCG for 1997. He has an $8,600 NLTCL for 1997. Yoon deducts $3,000 of LTCL in 1997 and carries forward $5,600 of LTCL to 1998. ▼

When a taxpayer has both a capital loss deduction and negative taxable income, a special computation of the capital loss carryover is required.[22] Specifically, the capital loss carryover is the NCL minus the lesser of:

- The capital loss deduction claimed on the return.
- The negative taxable income increased by the capital loss deduction claimed on the return and the personal and dependency exemption deduction.

Without this provision, some of the tax benefit of the capital loss deduction would be wasted when the deduction drives taxable income below zero.

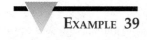

EXAMPLE 39

In 1996, Joanne has a $13,000 NCL (all long term), a $2,550 personal exemption deduction, and $4,000 negative taxable income. The negative taxable income includes a $3,000 capital loss deduction. The capital loss carryover to 1997 is $9,900 computed as follows:

- The $4,000 negative taxable income is treated as a negative number, but the capital loss deduction and personal exemption deduction are treated as positive numbers.
- The normal ceiling on the capital loss deduction is $3,000.
- However, if the $3,000 capital loss deduction and the $2,550 exemption deduction are added back to the $4,000 negative taxable income, only $1,550 of the $3,000 capital loss deduction is needed to make taxable income equal to zero.
- Therefore, this special computation results in only $1,550 of the $13,000 NCL being consumed. The LTCL carryforward is $11,450 ($13,000 – $1,550). ▼

Concept Summary 13–4 summarizes the rules for noncorporate taxpayers' treatment of capital gains and losses.

---

[21] § 1211(b)(1). Married persons filing separate returns are limited to a $1,500 deduction per tax year.

[22] § 1212(b).

CONCEPT SUMMARY 13–4

Noncorporate Taxpayer's Treatment of Net Capital Gain or Loss

Net Capital Gain Treatment Summarized

1. All long-term capital gain	28% alternative tax, but it is not always beneficial.
2. All short-term capital gain	Taxable as ordinary income.
3. Part long-term and part short-term capital gain	Short-term capital gain portion taxable as ordinary income. 28% alternative tax is available for long-term capital gain portion, but it is not always beneficial.

Net Capital Loss Treatment Summarized

4. All long-term capital loss	$1 of loss used to make $1 of deduction. Deduction is *for* AGI and limited to $3,000 per year. Portion of loss not used to make deduction carries forward indefinitely.
5. All short-term capital loss	$1 of loss used to make $1 of deduction. Deduction is *for* AGI and limited to $3,000 per year. Portion of loss not used to make deduction carries forward indefinitely.
6. Part long-term and part short-term capital loss	Short-term losses used first to make $3,000 deduction.

TAX TREATMENT OF CAPITAL GAINS
AND LOSSES OF CORPORATE TAXPAYERS

6 LEARNING OBJECTIVE
Describe the tax treatment for capital gains and the detrimental tax treatment for capital losses for corporate taxpayers.

The treatment of a corporation's net capital gain or loss differs from the rules for individuals. Briefly, the differences are as follows:

- There is an NCG alternative tax rate of 35 percent.[23] However, since the maximum corporate tax rate is 35 percent, the alternative tax is not beneficial.
- There is no 50 percent of NLTCG deduction.
- Capital losses offset only capital gains. No deduction of capital losses is permitted against ordinary taxable income (whereas a $3,000 deduction is allowed to individuals).[24]
- There is a three-year carryback and a five-year carryover period for net capital losses.[25] Corporate carryovers and carrybacks are always treated as short term, regardless of their original nature.

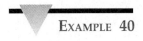

EXAMPLE 40 Sparrow Corporation has a $15,000 NLTCL for the current year and $57,000 of ordinary taxable income. Sparrow may not offset the $15,000 NLTCL against its ordinary income by taking a capital loss deduction. The $15,000 NLTCL becomes a $15,000 STCL for carryback and carryover purposes. This amount may be offset by capital gains in the three-year carryback period or, if not absorbed there, offset by capital gains in the five-year carryforward period. ▼

The rules applicable to corporations are discussed in greater detail in Chapter 16.

---

[23] §1201.
[24] § 1211(a).

[25] § 1212(a)(1).

SECTION 1231 ASSETS

Businesses own many assets that are used in the business rather than held for resale. In financial accounting, such assets are known as "fixed assets." For example, a foundry's 30,000-pound stamping machine is a fixed asset. It is also a depreciable asset. The building housing the foundry is another fixed asset. The remainder of this chapter largely deals with how to *classify* the gains and losses arising from the disposition of fixed assets. Chapter 7 discussed how to depreciate such assets. Chapter 12 discussed how to determine the adjusted basis and the amount of gain or loss from their disposition.

A long-term capital gain was defined earlier in this chapter as the recognized gain from the sale or exchange of a capital asset held for the required long-term holding period.[26] This chapter is concerned with classification under § 1231, which applies to the sale or exchange of business properties and to certain involuntary conversions. The business properties are not capital assets because they are depreciable and/or are real property used in business or for the production of income. Section 1221(2) provides that such assets are not capital assets. Nonetheless, these business properties may be held for long periods of time and may be sold at a gain. Congress decided many years ago that such assets deserved *limited* capital gain–type treatment. Unfortunately, this limited capital gain–type treatment is very complex and difficult to understand.

Because the limited capital gain–type treatment sometimes gives too much tax advantage if assets are eligible for depreciation (or cost recovery), certain recapture rules may remove the capital gain treatment when depreciation is taken. Thus, the next sections also cover the recapture provisions that tax as ordinary income certain gains that might otherwise qualify for long-term capital gain treatment.

RELATIONSHIP TO CAPITAL ASSETS

7 ▼ **LEARNING OBJECTIVE**
Understand the rationale for and the nature and treatment of gains and losses from the disposition of business assets.

Depreciable property and real property used in business are not capital assets.[27] Thus, the recognized gains from the disposition of such property (principally machinery, equipment, buildings, and land) would appear to be ordinary income rather than capital gain. Due to § 1231, however, *net gain* from the disposition of such property is sometimes *treated* as *long-term capital gain*. A long-term holding period requirement must be met; the disposition must generally be from a sale, exchange, or involuntary conversion; and certain recapture provisions must be satisfied for this result to occur. Section 1231 may also apply to involuntary conversions of capital assets. Since an involuntary conversion is not a sale or exchange, such a disposition would not normally result in a capital gain.

If the disposition of depreciable property and real property used in business results in a *net loss*, § 1231 *treats* the *loss* as an *ordinary loss* rather than as a capital loss. Ordinary losses are fully deductible *for* adjusted gross income (AGI). Capital losses are offset by capital gains, and, if any loss remains, the loss is deductible to the extent of $3,000 per year for individuals and currently is not deductible at all by regular corporations. It seems, therefore, that § 1231 provides the *best* of both potential results: net gain may be treated as long-term capital gain, and net loss is treated as ordinary loss.

---

[26] The long-term holding period is more than one year.

[27] § 1221(2).

"Going Out of Business" Has Tax Implications

Recently, a Western wear store in a midwestern town advertised a "Going Out of Business" sale. All the clothes in the store were sold at heavily reduced prices. At the same time, the store also sold its "store fixtures," such as its clothes racks and display counters. The clothes sold are inventory for the store, but the store fixtures are fixed assets. The store treats the sale of the clothes as a normal sale of inventory, but must calculate a gain or loss on the sale of the store fixtures. While the sale of the clothes will produce ordinary income or loss, the sale of the store fixtures could produce both capital gain/loss and ordinary income/loss.

EXAMPLE 41

Roberto sells business land and building at a $5,000 gain and business equipment at a $3,000 loss. Both properties were held for the long-term holding period. Roberto's net gain is $2,000, and that net gain may (depending on various recapture rules discussed later in this chapter) be treated as a long-term capital gain under § 1231.

Samantha sells business equipment at a $10,000 loss and business land at a $2,000 gain. Both properties were held for the long-term holding period. Samantha's net loss is $8,000, and that net loss is an ordinary loss. ▼

The rules regarding § 1231 treatment do *not* apply to *all* business property. Important in this regard are the holding period requirements and the fact that the property must be either depreciable property or real estate used in business. Nor is § 1231 necessarily limited to business property. Transactions involving certain capital assets may fall into the § 1231 category. Thus, § 1231 singles out only some types of business property.

As discussed earlier in the chapter, long-term capital gains receive beneficial tax treatment. Section 1231 requires netting of **§ 1231 gains and losses.** If the result is a gain, it may be treated as a long-term capital gain. The net gain is added to the "real" long-term capital gains (if any) and netted with capital losses (if any). Thus, the net § 1231 gain may eventually be eligible for beneficial capital gain treatment or help avoid the unfavorable net capital loss result. The § 1231 gain and loss netting may result in a loss. In this case, the loss is an ordinary loss and is deductible *for* AGI. Finally, § 1231 assets are treated the same as capital assets for purposes of the appreciated property charitable contribution provisions (refer to Chapter 9).

JUSTIFICATION FOR FAVORABLE TAX TREATMENT

The favorable capital gain/ordinary loss treatment sanctioned by § 1231 can be explained by examining several historical developments. Before 1938, business property had been included in the definition of capital assets. Thus, if such property was sold for a loss (not an unlikely possibility during the depression years), a capital loss resulted. If, however, the property was depreciable and could be retained for its estimated useful life, much (if not all) of its costs could be recovered in the form of depreciation. Because the allowance for depreciation was fully deductible whereas capital losses were not, the tax law favored those who did not dispose of an asset. Congress recognized this inequity when it removed business property from the capital asset classification. During the period 1938–1942, therefore, all such gains and losses were ordinary gains and losses.

With the advent of World War II, two developments in particular forced Congress to reexamine the situation regarding business assets. First, the sale of business assets at a gain was discouraged because the gain would be ordinary income. Gains were common because the war effort had inflated prices. Second, taxpayers who did not want to sell their assets often were required to because the government acquired them through condemnation. Often, as a result of the condemnation awards, taxpayers who were forced to part with their property experienced large gains and were deprived of the benefits of future depreciation deductions. Of course, the condemnations constituted involuntary conversions, so taxpayers could defer the gain by timely reinvestment in property that was "similar or related in service or use." But where was such property to be found in view of wartime restrictions and other governmental condemnations? The end result did not seem equitable: a large ordinary gain due to government action and no possibility of deferral due to government restrictions.

In recognition of these conditions, in 1942, Congress eased the tax bite on the disposition of some business property by allowing preferential capital gain treatment. Thus, the present scheme of § 1231 and the dichotomy of capital gain/ordinary loss treatment evolved from a combination of economic considerations existing in 1938 and 1942.

PROPERTY INCLUDED

8 **LEARNING OBJECTIVE**
Distinguish § 1231 assets from ordinary assets and capital assets and calculate the § 1231 gain or loss.

Section 1231 property includes the following:

- Depreciable or real property used in business or for the production of income (principally machinery and equipment, buildings, and land).
- Timber, coal, or domestic iron ore to which § 631 applies.
- Livestock held for draft, breeding, dairy, or sporting purposes.
- Unharvested crops on land used in business.
- Certain *purchased* intangible assets (such as patents and goodwill) that are eligible for amortization.

PROPERTY EXCLUDED

Section 1231 property does *not* include the following:

- Property not held for the long-term holding period. Since the benefit of § 1231 is long-term capital gain treatment, the holding period must correspond to the more-than-one-year holding period that applies to capital assets. Livestock must be held at least 12 months (24 months in some cases). Unharvested crops do not have to be held for the required long-term holding period, but the land must be held for the long-term holding period.
- Property where casualty losses exceed casualty gains for the taxable year. If a taxpayer has a net casualty loss, the individual casualty gains and losses are treated as ordinary gains and losses.
- Inventory and property held primarily for sale to customers.
- Copyrights; literary, musical, or artistic compositions, etc.; and certain U.S. government publications.
- Accounts receivable and notes receivable arising in the ordinary course of the trade or business.

SPECIAL RULES FOR NONPERSONAL USE CAPITAL ASSETS

When § 1231 assets are disposed of by casualty or theft, a special netting rule is applied. For simplicity, the term *casualty* is used to mean both casualty and theft dispositions. First, the casualty gains and losses from § 1231 assets *and* the casualty gains and losses from **long-term nonpersonal use capital assets** are determined. A nonpersonal use capital asset might be an investment painting or a baseball card collection held by a nondealer in baseball cards.

Next, the § 1231 asset casualty gains and losses and the nonpersonal use capital asset casualty gains and losses are netted together (see Concept Summary 13–5). If the result is a *net loss*, the § 1231 casualty gains and the nonpersonal use capital asset casualty gains are treated as ordinary gains, the § 1231 casualty losses are deductible *for* AGI, and the nonpersonal use capital asset casualty losses are deductible *from* AGI subject to the 2 percent-of-AGI limitation.

If the result of the netting is a *net gain*, the net gain is treated as a § 1231 gain. Thus, a § 1231 asset disposed of by casualty may or may not get § 1231 treatment, depending on whether the netting process results in a gain or a loss. Also, a nonpersonal use capital asset disposed of by casualty may get § 1231 treatment or ordinary treatment, but will not get capital gain or loss treatment!

Personal use property casualty gains and losses are not subject to the § 1231 rules. If the result of netting these gains and losses is a gain, the net gain is a capital gain. If the netting results in a loss, the net loss is a deduction *from* AGI to the extent it exceeds 10 percent of AGI.

Casualties, thefts, and condemnations are *involuntary conversions*. Involuntary conversion gains may be deferred if conversion proceeds are reinvested; involuntary conversion losses are recognized currently regardless of whether the conversion proceeds are reinvested. Thus, the special netting process discussed above for casualties and thefts would not include gains that are not currently recognizable because the insurance proceeds are reinvested.

The special netting process for casualties and thefts also does not include condemnation gains and losses. Consequently, a § 1231 asset disposed of by condemnation will receive § 1231 treatment. This variation between recognized casualty and condemnation gains and losses sheds considerable light on what § 1231 is all about. Section 1231 has no effect on whether or not *realized* gain or loss is recognized. Instead, § 1231 merely dictates how such *recognized* gain or loss is *classified* (ordinary, capital, or § 1231) under certain conditions.

Personal use property condemnation gains and losses are not subject to the § 1231 rules. The gains are capital gains (because personal use property is a capital asset), and the losses are nondeductible because they arise from the disposition of personal use property.

GENERAL PROCEDURE FOR § 1231 COMPUTATION

The tax treatment of § 1231 gains and losses depends on the results of a rather complex *netting* procedure. The steps in this netting procedure are as follows.

Step 1: Casualty Netting. Net all recognized long-term gains and losses from casualties of § 1231 assets and nonpersonal use capital assets. Casualty gains result when insurance proceeds exceed the adjusted basis of the property. This casualty netting is beneficial because if there is a net gain, the gain may receive long-term capital gain treatment. If there is a net loss, it receives ordinary loss treatment.

   a. If the casualty gains exceed the casualty losses, add the excess to the other § 1231 gains for the taxable year.

CONCEPT SUMMARY 13–5

Section 1231 Netting Procedure

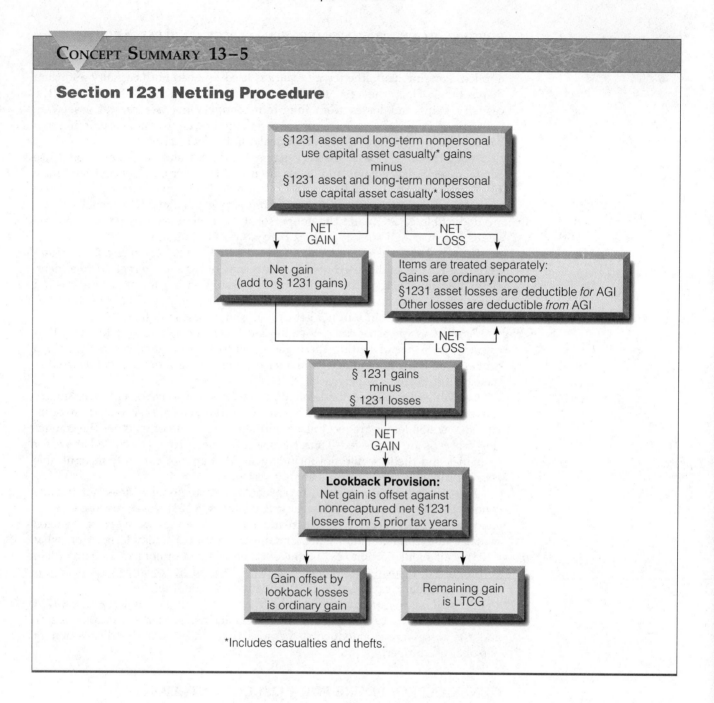

§1231 asset and long-term nonpersonal use capital asset casualty* gains minus §1231 asset and long-term nonpersonal use capital asset casualty* losses

NET GAIN

NET LOSS

Net gain (add to § 1231 gains)

Items are treated separately:
Gains are ordinary income
§1231 asset losses are deductible *for* AGI
Other losses are deductible *from* AGI

NET LOSS

§ 1231 gains minus § 1231 losses

NET GAIN

Lookback Provision:
Net gain is offset against nonrecaptured net §1231 losses from 5 prior tax years

Gain offset by lookback losses is ordinary gain

Remaining gain is LTCG

*Includes casualties and thefts.

b. If the casualty losses exceed the casualty gains, exclude all casualty losses and gains from further § 1231 computation. If this is the case, all casualty gains are ordinary income. Section 1231 asset casualty losses are deductible *for* AGI. Other casualty losses are deductible *from* AGI.

Step 2: § 1231 Netting. After adding any net casualty gain from Step 1a to the other § 1231 gains and losses (including recognized § 1231 asset condemnation gains and losses), net all § 1231 gains and losses.

a. If the gains exceed the losses, the net gain is offset by the "lookback" nonrecaptured § 1231 losses (see below) from the five prior tax years. To the extent of this offset, the net § 1231 gain is classified as ordinary gain. Any remaining gain is long-term capital gain.

b. If the losses exceed the gains, all gains are ordinary income. Section 1231 asset losses are deductible *for* AGI. Other casualty losses are deductible *from* AGI.

Step 3: § 1231 Lookback Provision.   The net § 1231 gain from Step 2a is offset by the nonrecaptured net § 1231 losses for the five preceding taxable years. For 1996, the lookback years are 1991, 1992, 1993, 1994, and 1995. To the extent of the nonrecaptured net § 1231 loss, the current-year net § 1231 gain is ordinary income. The *nonrecaptured* net § 1231 losses are those that have not already been used to offset net § 1231 gains. Only the net § 1231 gain exceeding this net § 1231 loss carryforward is given long-term capital gain treatment. Concept Summary 13–5 summarizes the § 1231 computational procedure. Examples 45 and 46 illustrate the **§ 1231 lookback** provision.

Examples 42 through 45 illustrate the application of the § 1231 computation procedure.

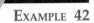

EXAMPLE 42

During 1996, Ross had $125,000 of AGI before considering the following recognized gains and losses:

Capital Gains and Losses	
Long-term capital gain	$3,000
Long-term capital loss	(400)
Short-term capital gain	1,000
Short-term capital loss	(200)

Casualties	
Theft of diamond ring (owned four months)	($800)*
Fire damage to personal residence (owned 10 years)	(400)*
Gain from insurance recovery on fire loss to business building (owned two years)	200

§ 1231 Gains and Losses from Depreciable Business Assets Held Long Term

Asset A	$ 300
Asset B	1,100
Asset C	(500)

Gains and Losses from Sale of Depreciable Business Assets Held Short Term

Asset D	$ 200
Asset E	(300)

*As adjusted for the $100 floor on personal casualty losses.

Ross had no net § 1231 losses in tax years before 1996.

Disregarding the recapture of depreciation (discussed later in the chapter), Ross's gains and losses receive the following tax treatment:

- The diamond ring and the residence are personal use assets. Therefore, these casualties are not § 1231 transactions. The $800 (ring) plus $400 (residence) losses are potentially deductible *from* AGI. However, the total loss of $1,200 does not exceed 10% of AGI. Thus, only the business building (a § 1231 asset) casualty gain remains. The netting of the § 1231 asset and nonpersonal use capital asset casualty gains and losses contains only one item—the $200 gain from the business building. Consequently, there is a net gain and that gain is treated as a § 1231 gain (added to the § 1231 gains).

- The gains from § 1231 transactions (Assets A, B, and C and the § 1231 asset casualty gain) exceed the losses by $1,100 ($1,600 − $500). This excess is a long-term capital gain and is added to Ross's other long-term capital gains.

- Ross's net long-term capital gain is $3,700 ($3,000 + $1,100 from § 1231 transactions − $400 long-term capital loss). Ross's net short-term capital gain is $800 ($1,000 − $200). The result is capital gain net income of $4,500. The $3,700 net long-term capital gain portion is eligible for beneficial capital gain treatment and the $800 net short-term capital gain is subject to tax as ordinary income.[28]

- Ross treats the gain and loss from Assets D and E (depreciable business assets held for less than the long-term holding period) as ordinary gain and loss.

Results of the Gains and Losses on Ross's Tax Computation

NLTCG	$ 3,700
NSTCG	800
Ordinary gain from sale of Asset D	200
Ordinary loss from sale of Asset E	(300)
AGI from other sources	125,000
AGI	$129,400

- Ross will have personal use property casualty losses of $1,200 [$800 (diamond ring) + $400 (personal residence)]. A personal use property casualty loss is deductible only to the extent it exceeds 10% of AGI. Thus, none of the $1,200 is deductible ($129,400 × 10% = $12,940). ▼

---

[28] Ross's taxable income (unless the itemized deductions and the personal exemption and dependency deductions are extremely large) will put him in at least the 31% bracket. Thus, the 28% alternative tax computation will yield a lower tax.

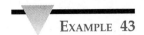

EXAMPLE 43

Assume the same facts as in Example 42, except the loss from Asset C was $1,700 instead of $500.

- The treatment of the casualty losses is the same as in Example 42.
- The losses from § 1231 transactions now exceed the gains by $100 ($1,700 − $1,600). As a result, the gains from Assets A and B and the § 1231 asset casualty gain are ordinary income, and the loss from Asset C is a deduction *for* AGI (a business loss). The same result can be achieved by simply treating the $100 net loss as a deduction *for* AGI.
- Capital gain net income is $3,400 ($2,600 long-term + $800 short-term). The $2,600 net long-term capital gain portion is eligible for beneficial capital gain treatment, and the $800 net short-term capital gain is subject to tax as ordinary income.

Results of the Gains and Losses on Ross's Tax Computation

NLTCG	$ 2,600
NSTCG	800
Net ordinary loss on Assets A, B, and C and § 1231 casualty gain	(100)
Ordinary gain from sale of Asset D	200
Ordinary loss from sale of Asset E	(300)
AGI from other sources	125,000
AGI	$128,200

- None of the personal use property casualty losses will be deductible since $1,200 does not exceed 10% of $128,200. ▼

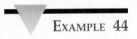

EXAMPLE 44

Assume the same facts as in Example 42, except that Ross has a $700 nonrecaptured net § 1231 loss from 1995.

- The treatment of the casualty losses is the same as in Example 42.
- The 1996 net § 1231 gain of $1,100 is treated as ordinary income to the extent of the 1995 nonrecaptured § 1231 loss of $700. The remaining $400 net § 1231 gain is a long-term capital gain and is added to Ross's other long-term capital gains.
- Ross's net long-term capital gain is $3,000 ($3,000 + $400 from § 1231 transactions − $400 long-term capital loss). Ross's net short-term capital gain is still $800 ($1,000 − $200). The result is capital gain net income of $3,800. The $3,000 net long-term capital gain portion is eligible for beneficial capital gain treatment, and the $800 net short-term capital gain is subject to tax as ordinary income.

Results of the Gains and Losses on Ross's Tax Computation

NLTCG	$ 3,000
NSTCG	800
Ordinary gain from recapture of § 1231 losses	700
Ordinary gain from sale of Asset D	200
Ordinary loss from sale of Asset E	(300)
AGI from other sources	125,000
AGI	$129,400

- None of the personal use property casualty losses will be deductible since $1,200 does not exceed 10% of $129,400. ▼

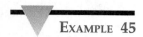

EXAMPLE 45

Assume the same facts as in Example 42, except that Ross had a net § 1231 loss of $2,700 in 1994 and a net § 1231 gain of $300 in 1995.

- The treatment of the casualty losses is the same as in Example 42.
- The 1994 net § 1231 loss of $2,700 will have carried over to 1995 and been offset against the 1995 net § 1231 gain of $300. Thus, the $300 gain will have been classified as ordinary income, and $2,400 of nonrecaptured 1994 net § 1231 loss will carry over to 1996. The 1996 net § 1231 gain of $1,100 will be offset against this loss, resulting in $1,100 of ordinary income. The nonrecaptured net § 1231 loss of $1,300 ($2,400 – $1,100) carries over to 1997.
- Capital gain net income is $3,400 ($2,600 net long-term capital gain + $800 net short-term capital gain). The $2,600 net long-term capital gain portion is eligible for beneficial capital gain treatment and the $800 net short-term capital gain is subject to tax as ordinary income.

Results of the Gains and Losses on Ross's Tax Computation	
NLTCG	$ 2,600
NSTCG	800
Ordinary gain from recapture of § 1231 losses	1,100
Ordinary gain from sale of Asset D	200
Ordinary loss from sale of Asset E	(300)
AGI from other sources	125,000
AGI	$129,400

- None of the personal use property casualty losses will be deductible since $1,200 does not exceed 10% of $129,400. ▼

SECTION 1245 RECAPTURE

9 LEARNING OBJECTIVE
Determine when § 1245 recapture applies and how it is computed.

Now that the basic rules of § 1231 have been introduced, it is time to add some complications. The Code contains two major *recapture* provisions—§§ 1245 and 1250. These provisions cause *gain* to be treated *initially* as ordinary gain. Thus, what may appear to be a § 1231 gain is ordinary gain instead. These recapture provisions may also cause a gain in a nonpersonal use casualty to be *initially* ordinary gain rather than casualty gain. Classifying gains (and losses) properly initially is important because improper initial classification may lead to incorrect mixing and matching of gains and losses. This section discusses the § 1245 recapture rules, and the next section discusses the § 1250 recapture rules.

ETHICAL CONSIDERATIONS

Does Applying the Recapture Rules Make a Difference?

Due to their complexity, the § 1245 and § 1250 recapture rules require careful study to obtain a complete understanding. It is much easier just to assume that the sale of business fixed assets results in capital gain or loss. Certainly, most taxpayers expect that result. Arnold, an overworked tax practitioner, concluded that quite often, taxable income is the same whether the recapture rules are properly applied or not. Therefore, he hypothesized that if ultimately there is *no difference* between tax liability with proper handling of recapture and tax liability without proper handling of recapture, is it not logical and practical for him simply to ignore the recapture rules?

Section 1245 requires taxpayers to treat all gain as ordinary gain unless the property is disposed of for more than was paid for it. This result is accomplished by requiring that all gain be treated as ordinary gain to the extent of the depreciation taken on the property disposed of. Section 1231 gain results only when the property is disposed of for more than its original cost. The excess of the sales price over the original cost is § 1231 gain. Section 1245 applies primarily to non-real estate property such as machinery, trucks, and office furniture. Section 1245 does not apply if property is disposed of at a loss. Generally, the loss will be a § 1231 loss unless the form of the disposition is a casualty.

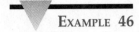

EXAMPLE 46

Alice purchased a $100,000 business machine and deducted $70,000 depreciation before selling it for $80,000. If it were not for § 1245, the $50,000 gain would be § 1231 gain ($80,000 amount realized − $30,000 adjusted basis). Section 1245 prevents this potentially favorable result by treating as ordinary income (not as § 1231 gain) any gain to the extent of depreciation taken. In this example, the entire $50,000 gain would be ordinary income. If Alice had sold the machine for $120,000, she would have a gain of $90,000 ($120,000 amount realized − $30,000 adjusted basis). The § 1245 gain would be $70,000 (equal to the depreciation taken), and the § 1231 gain would be $20,000 (equal to the excess of the sales price over the original cost). ▼

Section 1245 recapture provides, in general, that the portion of recognized gain from the sale or other disposition of § 1245 property that represents depreciation (including § 167 depreciation, § 168 cost recovery, § 179 immediate expensing, and § 197 amortization) is *recaptured* as ordinary income. Thus, in Example 46, $50,000 of the $70,000 depreciation taken is recaptured as ordinary income when the business machine is sold for $80,000. Only $50,000 is recaptured rather than $70,000 because Alice is only required to recognize § 1245 recapture ordinary gain equal to the lower of the depreciation taken or the gain recognized.

The method of depreciation (e.g., accelerated or straight-line) does not matter. All depreciation taken is potentially subject to recapture. Thus, § 1245 recapture is often referred to as *full recapture*. Any remaining gain after subtracting the amount recaptured as ordinary income will usually be § 1231 gain. The remaining gain would be casualty gain if it were disposed of in a casualty event. If the business machine in Example 46 had been disposed of by casualty and the $80,000 received had been an insurance recovery, Alice would still have a gain of $50,000, and the gain would still be recaptured by § 1245 as ordinary gain. The § 1245 recapture rules apply before there is any casualty gain. Since all the $50,000 gain is recaptured, no casualty gain arises from the casualty.

Although § 1245 applies primarily to non-real estate property, it does apply to certain real estate. Nonresidential real estate acquired after 1980 and before 1987 and for which accelerated depreciation (the statutory percentage method of the accelerated cost recovery system) is used is subject to the § 1245 recapture rules. Such property includes 15-year, 18-year, and 19-year nonresidential real estate.

The following examples illustrate the general application of § 1245.

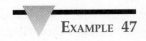

EXAMPLE 47

On January 1, 1996, Gary sold for $13,000 a machine acquired several years ago for $12,000. He had taken $10,000 of depreciation on the machine.

- The recognized gain from the sale is $11,000. This is the amount realized of $13,000 less the adjusted basis of $2,000 ($12,000 cost − $10,000 depreciation taken).

- Depreciation taken is $10,000. Therefore, since § 1245 recapture gain is the lower of
  depreciation taken or gain recognized, $10,000 of the $11,000 recognized gain is
  ordinary income, and the remaining $1,000 gain is § 1231 gain.
- The § 1231 gain of $1,000 is also equal to the excess of the sales price over the original
  cost of the property ($13,000 − $12,000 = $1,000 § 1231 gain). ▼

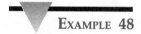

EXAMPLE 48

Assume the same facts as in the previous example, except the asset is sold for $9,000 instead
of $13,000.

- The recognized gain from the sale is $7,000. This is the amount realized of $9,000 less
  the adjusted basis of $2,000.
- Depreciation taken is $10,000. Therefore, since the $10,000 depreciation taken exceeds
  the recognized gain of $7,000, the entire $7,000 recognized gain is ordinary income.
- The § 1231 gain is zero. There is no § 1231 gain because the selling price ($9,000) does
  not exceed the original purchase price ($12,000). ▼

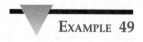

EXAMPLE 49

Assume the same facts as in Example 47, except the asset is sold for $1,500 instead of $13,000.

- The recognized loss from the sale is $500. This is the amount realized of $1,500 less
  the adjusted basis of $2,000.
- Since there is a loss, there is no depreciation recapture. All of the loss is § 1231
  loss. ▼

If § 1245 property is disposed of in a transaction other than a sale, exchange,
or involuntary conversion, the maximum amount recaptured is the excess of the
property's fair market value over its adjusted basis. See the discussion under
Considerations Common to §§ 1245 and 1250 later in the chapter.

SECTION 1245 PROPERTY

Generally, **§ 1245 property** includes all depreciable personal property (e.g., machinery and equipment), including livestock. Buildings and their structural components generally are not § 1245 property. The following property is *also* subject to
§ 1245 treatment:

- Amortizable personal property such as goodwill, patents, copyrights, and
  leaseholds of § 1245 property. Professional baseball and football player
  contracts are § 1245 property.
- Amortization of reforestation expenditures.

- Expensing of costs to remove architectural and transportation barriers that restrict the handicapped and/or elderly.
- Section 179 immediate expensing of depreciable tangible personal property costs.
- Elevators and escalators acquired before January 1, 1987.
- Certain depreciable tangible real property (other than buildings and their structural components) employed as an integral part of certain activities such as manufacturing and production. For example, a natural gas storage tank where the gas is used in the manufacturing process is § 1245 property.
- Pollution control facilities, railroad grading and tunnel bores, on-the-job training, and child care facilities on which amortization is taken.
- Single-purpose agricultural and horticultural structures and petroleum storage facilities (e.g., a greenhouse or silo).
- As noted above, 15-year, 18-year, and 19-year nonresidential real estate for which accelerated cost recovery is used is subject to the § 1245 recapture rules, although it is technically not § 1245 property. Such property would have been placed in service after 1980 and before 1987.

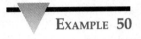

EXAMPLE 50

James acquired nonresidential real property on January 1, 1986, for $100,000. He used the statutory percentage method to compute the ACRS cost recovery. He sells the asset on January 15, 1996, for $120,000. The amount and nature of James's gain are computed as follows:

Amount realized		$120,000
Adjusted basis		
Cost	$100,000	
Less cost recovery: 1986	(8,800)	
1987	(8,400)	
1988	(7,600)	
1989	(6,900)	
1990	(6,300)	
1991	(5,700)	
1992	(5,200)	
1993	(4,700)	
1994	(4,200)	
1995	(4,200)	
1996	(175)	
January 15, 1996, adjusted basis		(37,825)
Gain realized and recognized		$ 82,175

The gain of $82,175 is treated as ordinary income to the extent of *all* depreciation taken because the property is 19-year nonresidential real estate for which accelerated depreciation was used. Thus, James reports ordinary income of $62,175 ($8,800 + $8,400 + $7,600 + $6,900 + $6,300 + $5,700 + $5,200 + 4,700 + $4,200 + $4,200 + $175) and § 1231 gain of $20,000 ($82,175 − $62,175). ▼

OBSERVATIONS ON § 1245

- In most instances, the total depreciation taken will exceed the recognized gain. Therefore, the disposition of § 1245 property usually results in ordinary income rather than § 1231 gain. Thus, generally, no § 1231 gain will occur unless the § 1245 property is disposed of for more than its original cost. Refer to Examples 48 and 49.

- Recapture applies to the total amount of depreciation allowed or allowable regardless of the depreciation method used.
- Recapture applies regardless of the holding period of the property. Of course, the entire recognized gain would be ordinary income if the property were held for less than the long-term holding period because § 1231 would not apply.
- Section 1245 does not apply to losses, which receive § 1231 treatment.
- Gains from the disposition of § 1245 assets may also be treated as passive activity gains (see Chapter 10).

SECTION 1250 RECAPTURE

10   LEARNING OBJECTIVE
Determine when § 1250 recapture applies and how it is computed.

Generally, **§ 1250 property** is depreciable real property (principally buildings and their structural components) that is not subject to § 1245.[29] Intangible real property, such as leaseholds of § 1250 property, is also included.

Section 1250 recapture is substantially less punitive than § 1245 recapture since only the amount of additional depreciation is subject to recapture. To have additional depreciation, accelerated depreciation must have been taken on the asset. Straight-line depreciation (except for property held one year or less) is not recaptured. Since real property placed in service after 1986 can only be depreciated using the straight-line method, there will be *no § 1250 depreciation recapture* on such property.

Section 1250 was enacted in 1964 for depreciable real property and has been revised many times. If straight-line depreciation is taken on the property, § 1250 does not apply. Nor does § 1250 apply if the real property is sold at a loss. The loss will generally be a § 1231 loss unless the property is disposed of by casualty.

Section 1250 as originally enacted required recapture of a percentage of the additional depreciation deducted by the taxpayer. **Additional depreciation** is the excess of accelerated depreciation actually deducted over depreciation that would have been deductible if the straight-line method had been used. Since only the additional depreciation is subject to recapture, § 1250 recapture is often referred to as *partial recapture*.

Post-1969 additional depreciation on nonresidential real property is subject to 100 percent recapture (see Example 51). Post-1969 additional depreciation on residential property may be subject to less than 100 percent recapture (see Example 53).

If § 1250 property is disposed of in a transaction other than a sale, exchange, or involuntary conversion, the maximum amount recaptured is the excess of the property's fair market value over the adjusted basis. For example, if a corporation distributes property to its shareholders as a dividend, the property will have been disposed of at a gain if the fair market value is greater than the adjusted basis. The maximum amount of § 1250 recapture will be the amount of the gain.

The following discussion describes the computational steps prescribed in § 1250 and reflected on Form 4797 (Sales of Business Property).

---

[29] As previously discussed, in one limited circumstance, § 1245 does apply to nonresidential real estate. If the nonresidential real estate was placed in service after 1980 and before 1987 and accelerated depreciation was used, the § 1245 recapture rules rather than the § 1250 recapture rules apply.

COMPUTING RECAPTURE ON NONRESIDENTIAL REAL PROPERTY

For § 1250 property other than residential rental property, the potential recapture is equal to the amount of additional depreciation taken since December 31, 1969. This nonresidential real property includes buildings such as offices, warehouses, factories, and stores. (The definition of and rules for residential rental housing are discussed later in the chapter.) The lower of the potential § 1250 recapture amount or the recognized gain is ordinary income. The following general rules apply:

- Post-1969 additional depreciation is depreciation taken in excess of straight-line after December 31, 1969.
- If the property is held for one year or less (usually not the case), all depreciation taken, even under the straight-line method, is additional depreciation.

The following procedure is used to compute recapture on nonresidential real property under § 1250:

- Determine the recognized gain from the sale or other disposition of the property.
- Determine post-1969 additional depreciation.
- The lower of the recognized gain or the post-1969 additional depreciation is ordinary income.
- If any recognized gain remains (total recognized gain less recapture), it is § 1231 gain. However, it would be casualty gain if the disposition was by casualty.

The following example shows the application of the § 1250 computational procedure.

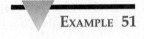

EXAMPLE 51   On January 3, 1980, Larry acquired a new building at a cost of $200,000 for use in his business. The building had an estimated useful life of 50 years and no estimated salvage value. Depreciation has been taken under the 150% declining-balance method through December 31, 1995. Pertinent information with respect to depreciation taken follows:

Year	Undepreciated Balance (Beginning of the Year)	Current Depreciation Provision	Straight-Line Depreciation	Additional Depreciation
1980	$200,000	$6,000	$4,000	$2,000
1981	194,000	5,820	4,000	1,820
1982	188,180	5,645	4,000	1,645
1983	182,535	5,476	4,000	1,476
1984	177,059	5,312	4,000	1,312
1985	171,747	5,152	4,000	1,152
1986	166,595	4,998	4,000	998
1987	161,597	4,848	4,000	848
1988	156,749	4,702	4,000	702
1989	152,047	4,561	4,000	561
1990	147,486	4,425	4,000	425
1991	143,061	4,292	4,000	292
1992	138,769	4,163	4,000	163

1993	134,606	4,038	4,000	38
1994	130,568	3,917	4,000	(83)
1995	126,651	3,800	4,000	(200)
Total 1980–1995		$77,149	$64,000	$13,149

On January 2, 1996, Larry sold the building for $180,000. Compute the amount of his § 1250 ordinary income and § 1231 gain.

- Larry's recognized gain from the sale is $57,149. This is the difference between the $180,000 amount realized and the $122,851 adjusted basis ($200,000 cost − $77,149 depreciation taken).
- Post-1969 additional depreciation is $13,149.
- The amount of post-1969 ordinary income is $13,149. Since the post-1969 additional depreciation of $13,149 is less than the recognized gain of $57,149, the entire gain is not recaptured.
- The remaining $44,000 ($57,149 − $13,149) gain is § 1231 gain. ▼

COMPUTING RECAPTURE ON RESIDENTIAL RENTAL HOUSING

Section 1250 recapture applies to the sale or other disposition of residential rental housing. Property qualifies as *residential rental housing* only if at least 80 percent of gross rent income is rent income from dwelling units.[30] The rules are the same as for other § 1250 property, except that only the post-1975 additional depreciation may be recaptured. The post-1969 through 1975 recapture percentage is 100 percent less one percentage point for each full month the property is held over 100 months.[31] Therefore, the additional depreciation for periods after 1975 is initially applied against the recognized gain, and such amounts may be recaptured in full as ordinary income. If any of the recognized gain is not absorbed by the recapture rules pertaining to the post-1975 period, the remaining gain is § 1231 gain.

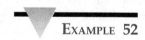

EXAMPLE 52

Assume the same facts as in the previous example, except the building is residential rental housing.

- Post-1975 ordinary income is $13,149 (post-1975 additional depreciation of $13,149).
- The remaining $44,000 ($57,149 − $13,149) gain is § 1231 gain. ▼

Under § 1250, when straight-line depreciation is used, there is no § 1250 recapture potential unless the property is disposed of in the first year of use. Before 1987, accelerated depreciation on real estate generally was available. For real property placed in service after 1986, however, only straight-line depreciation is allowed. Therefore, the § 1250 recapture rules do not apply to such property unless the property is disposed of in the first year of use.

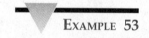

EXAMPLE 53

Sanjay acquires a residential rental building on January 1, 1995, for $300,000. He receives an offer of $450,000 for the building in 1996 and sells it on December 23, 1996.

---

[30] § 168(e)(2)(A). Note that there may be residential, nonrental housing (e.g., a bunkhouse on a cattle ranch). Such property is commonly regarded as "nonresidential real estate." The rules for such property were discussed in the previous section.

[31] §§ 1250(a)(1) and (2) and Reg. § 1.1250–1(d)(1)(i)(c). Since the post-1969 through 1975 recapture percentage is 100% less one percentage point for each full month the property is held over

100 months, this approach now yields a zero percentage no matter when the property was acquired in the 1969–1975 period. For instance, if a building was acquired on January 3, 1975, and sold on January 3, 1996, it would have been held 252 months. The recapture percentage is zero because 100% − (252% − 100%) is less than zero.

CONCEPT SUMMARY 13–6

Comparison of § 1245 and § 1250 Depreciation Recapture

	§ 1245	§ 1250
Property affected	All depreciable personal property, but also nonresidential real property acquired after December 31, 1980, and before January 1, 1987, for which accelerated cost recovery was used. Also includes miscellaneous items such as § 179 expense and § 197 amortization of intangibles such as goodwill, patents, and copyrights.	Residential rental real property acquired after December 31, 1980, and before January 1, 1987, on which accelerated cost recovery was taken. Nonresidential real property acquired after December 31, 1969, and before January 1, 1976, on which accelerated depreciation was taken. Residential real and nonresidential real property acquired after December 31, 1975, and before January 1, 1981, on which accelerated depreciation was taken.
Depreciation recaptured	Potentially all depreciation taken. If the selling price is greater than or equal to the original cost, all depreciation is recaptured. If the selling price is between the adjusted basis and the original cost, only some depreciation is recaptured.	Additional depreciation (the excess of accelerated cost recovery over straight-line cost recovery or the excess of accelerated depreciation over straight-line depreciation).
Limit on recapture	Lower of depreciation taken or gain recognized.	Lower of additional depreciation or gain recognized.
Treatment of gain exceeding recapture gain	Usually § 1231 gain.	Usually § 1231 gain.
Treatment of loss	No depreciation recapture; loss is usually § 1231 loss.	No depreciation recapture; loss is usually § 1231 loss.

- Sanjay takes $20,909 [($300,000 × .03485) + ($300,000 × .03636 × 11.5/12) = $20,909] of total depreciation for 1995 and 1996, and the adjusted basis of the property is $279,091 ($300,000 − $20,909).
- Sanjay's recognized gain is $170,909 ($450,000 − $279,091).
- All of the gain is § 1231 gain. ▼

SECTION 1250 RECAPTURE SITUATIONS

The § 1250 recapture rules apply to the following property for which accelerated depreciation was used:

- Residential rental real estate acquired before 1987.
- Nonresidential real estate acquired before 1981.
- Real property used predominantly outside the United States.
- Certain government-financed or low-income housing.[32]

Concept Summary 13–6 compares and contrasts the § 1245 and § 1250 depreciation recapture rules.

---

[32] Described in § 1250(a)(1)(B).

CONSIDERATIONS COMMON TO §§ 1245 AND 1250

EXCEPTIONS

11   **LEARNING OBJECTIVE**
Understand considerations common to §§ 1245 and 1250.

Recapture under §§ 1245 and 1250 does not apply to the following transactions.

Gifts.   The recapture potential carries over to the donee.[33]

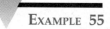

EXAMPLE 54

Wade gives his daughter, Helen, § 1245 property with an adjusted basis of $1,000. The amount of recapture potential is $700. Helen uses the property in her business and claims further depreciation of $100 before selling it for $1,900. Helen's recognized gain is $1,000 ($1,900 amount realized − $900 adjusted basis), of which $800 is recaptured as ordinary income ($100 depreciation taken by Helen + $700 recapture potential carried over from Wade). The remaining gain of $200 is § 1231 gain. Even if Helen used the property for personal purposes, the $700 recapture potential would still be carried over. ▼

Death.   Although not a very attractive tax planning approach, death eliminates all recapture potential.[34] In other words, any recapture potential does not carry over from a decedent to an estate or heir.

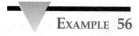

EXAMPLE 55

Assume the same facts as in Example 54, except Helen receives the property as a result of Wade's death. The $700 recapture potential from Wade is extinguished. Helen has a basis for the property equal to the property's fair market value (assume $1,700) at Wade's death. She will have a $300 gain when the property is sold because the selling price ($1,900) exceeds the property's adjusted basis of $1,600 ($1,700 original basis to Helen − $100 depreciation) by $300. Because of § 1245, $100 is ordinary income. The remaining gain of $200 is § 1231 gain. ▼

Charitable Transfers.   The recapture potential reduces the amount of the charitable contribution deduction under § 170.[35]

EXAMPLE 56

Kanisha donates to her church § 1245 property with a fair market value of $10,000 and an adjusted basis of $7,000. Assume that the amount of recapture potential is $2,000 (the amount of recapture that would occur if the property were sold). Her charitable contribution deduction (subject to the limitations discussed in Chapter 9) is $8,000 ($10,000 fair market value − $2,000 recapture potential). ▼

Certain Nontaxable Transactions.   These are transactions in which the transferor's adjusted basis of property carries over to the transferee.[36] The recapture potential also carries over to the transferee.[37] Included in this category are transfers of property pursuant to the following:

- Nontaxable incorporations under § 351.
- Certain liquidations of subsidiary companies under § 332.

---

[33] §§ 1245(b)(1) and 1250(d)(1) and Reg. §§ 1.1245–4(a)(1) and 1.1250–3(a)(1).

[34] §§ 1245(b)(2) and 1250(d)(2).

[35] § 170(e)(1)(A) and Reg. § 1.170A–4(b)(1). In certain circumstances, § 1231 gain also reduces the amount of the charitable contribution. See § 170(e)(1)(B).

[36] §§ 1245(b)(3) and 1250(d)(3) and Reg. §§ 1.1245–4(c) and 1.1250–3(c).

[37] Reg. §§ 1.1245–2(a)(4) and −2(c)(2) and 1.1250–2(d)(1) and (3) and −3(c)(3).

Concept Summary 13–7

Depreciation Recapture and § 1231 Netting Procedure

*Includes casualties and thefts.

- Nontaxable contributions to a partnership under § 721.
- Nontaxable reorganizations.

Gain may be recognized in these transactions if boot is received. If gain is recognized, it is treated as ordinary income to the extent of the recapture potential or recognized gain, whichever is lower.[38]

---

[38] §§ 1245(b)(3) and 1250(d)(3) and Reg. §§ 1.1245–4(c) and 1.1250–3(c).

Like-Kind Exchanges (§ 1031) and Involuntary Conversions (§ 1033). Realized gain will be recognized to the extent of boot received under § 1031. Realized gain also will be recognized to the extent the proceeds from an involuntary conversion are not reinvested in similar property under § 1033. Such recognized gain is subject to recapture as ordinary income under §§ 1245 and 1250. The remaining recapture potential, if any, carries over to the property received in the exchange.

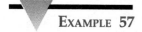

EXAMPLE 57

Anita exchanges § 1245 property with an adjusted basis of $300 for § 1245 property with a fair market value of $6,000. The exchange qualifies as a like-kind exchange under § 1031. Anita also receives $1,000 cash (boot). Her realized gain is $6,700 ($7,000 amount realized − $300 adjusted basis of property). Assuming the recapture potential is $7,500, Anita recognizes § 1245 gain of $1,000 because she received boot of $1,000. The remaining recapture potential of $6,500 carries over to the like-kind property received. ▼

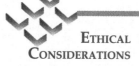

ETHICAL CONSIDERATIONS

To Lookback or Not Lookback

Harold, a CPA, has a new client who recently moved to town. Harold prepares the client's current-year tax return, which shows a net § 1231 gain. Harold calls the client to request copies of the returns for the preceding five years to determine if there are any § 1231 lookback losses. The client says that the returns are "still buried in the moving mess somewhere" and cannot be found. The client also says that he does not remember any § 1231 net losses on the prior-year returns. What should Harold do? Should he complete the current-year return and assume there are no § 1231 lookback losses?

Concept Summary 13–7 integrates the depreciation recapture rules with the § 1231 netting process. It is an expanded version of Concept Summary 13–5.

SPECIAL RECAPTURE PROVISIONS

GAIN FROM SALE OF DEPRECIABLE PROPERTY BETWEEN CERTAIN RELATED PARTIES

12 **LEARNING OBJECTIVE**
Apply the special recapture provisions for related parties and IDC.

When the sale or exchange of property, which in the hands of the *transferee* is depreciable property (principally machinery, equipment, and buildings, but not land), is between certain related parties, any gain recognized is ordinary income.[39] This provision applies to both direct and indirect sales or exchanges. A **related party** is defined as an individual and his or her controlled corporation or partnership or a taxpayer and any trust in which the taxpayer (or the taxpayer's spouse) is a beneficiary.

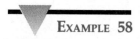

EXAMPLE 58

Isabella sells a personal use automobile (therefore nondepreciable) to her controlled corporation. The automobile, which was purchased two years ago, originally cost $5,000 and is sold for $7,000. The automobile is to be used in the corporation's business. If the related-party provision did not exist, Isabella would realize a $2,000 long-term capital gain. The income tax consequences would be favorable because Isabella's controlled corporation is entitled to depreciate the automobile based upon the purchase price of $7,000. Under the related-party provision, Isabella's $2,000 gain is ordinary income. ▼

---

[39] § 1239.

INTANGIBLE DRILLING COSTS

Taxpayers may elect to either *expense or capitalize* intangible drilling and development costs for oil, gas, or geothermal properties.[40] **Intangible drilling and development costs (IDC)** include operator (one who holds a working or operating interest in any tract or parcel of land) expenditures for wages, fuel, repairs, hauling, and supplies. These expenditures must be incident to and necessary for the drilling of wells and preparation of wells for production. In most instances, taxpayers elect to expense IDC to maximize tax deductions during drilling.

Intangible drilling and development costs are subject to § 1254 recapture when the property is disposed of. The gain on the disposition of the property is subject to recapture as ordinary income.

REPORTING PROCEDURES

13 **LEARNING OBJECTIVE**
Describe and apply the reporting procedures for §§ 1231, 1245, and 1250.

Noncapital gains and losses are reported on Form 4797, Sales of Business Property. Before filling out Form 4797, however, Form 4684, Casualties and Thefts, Part B, must be completed to determine whether or not any casualties will enter into the § 1231 computation procedure. Recall that gains from § 1231 asset casualties may be recaptured by § 1245 or § 1250. These gains will not appear on Form 4684. The § 1231 gains and nonpersonal use long-term capital gains are netted against § 1231 and nonpersonal use long-term capital losses on Form 4684 to determine if there is a net gain to transfer to Form 4797, Part I.

IMPORTANCE OF CAPITAL ASSET STATUS

**TAX PLANNING
CONSIDERATIONS**

14 **LEARNING OBJECTIVE**
Identify tax planning opportunities arising from the sale or exchange of capital assets and avoid pitfalls associated with recapture provisions.

Why is capital asset status important when net long-term capital gain is subject to a maximum 28 percent tax rate? The 11.6 percent difference between the maximum 39.6 percent regular tax rate and the maximum 28 percent net long-term capital gain tax rate may generate significant tax savings for taxpayers in the highest regular tax bracket (and to a lesser extent for taxpayers in the 31 percent and 36 percent tax brackets) who can receive income in the form of long-term capital gains. Thus, individuals who can receive income in the form of long-term capital gains have an advantage over taxpayers who cannot receive income in this form.

Capital asset status is also important because capital gains must be offset by capital losses. If a net capital loss results, the maximum deduction is $3,000 per year.

Consequently, capital gains and losses must be segregated from other types of gains and losses and must be reported separately on Schedule D of Form 1040.

PLANNING FOR CAPITAL ASSET STATUS

It is important to keep in mind that capital asset status often is a question of objective evidence. Thus, property that is not a capital asset to one party may qualify as a capital asset to another party.

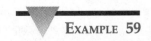

EXAMPLE 59

Diane, a real estate dealer, transfers by gift a tract of land to Jeff, her son. The land was recorded as part of Diane's inventory (it was held for resale) and was therefore not a capital asset to her. Jeff, however, treats the land as an investment. The land is a capital asset in Jeff's hands, and any later taxable disposition of the property by him will yield a capital gain or loss. ▼

---

[40] § 263(c).

ETHICAL
CONSIDERATIONS

Assuring Capital Asset Status

The taxpayer is an antiques collector and is going to sell an antique purchased many years ago for a very large gain in 1996. The facts and circumstances indicate that the taxpayer might be classified as a dealer rather than an investor in antiques. The taxpayer will save $40,000 in taxes if the gain is treated as a long-term capital gain rather than as an ordinary gain.

The taxpayer is considering the following options as ways to assure the $40,000 tax savings:

• Give the antique to his daughter, who is an investment banker, to sell.
• Merely assume that he has held the antique as an investment.
• Exchange the antique in a like-kind exchange for another antique he wants.

One of the tax preparers the taxpayer has contacted has said he would be willing to prepare the return under the second option. Would you be willing to do so? Why? Evaluate the other options.

If proper planning is carried out, even a dealer may obtain long-term capital gain treatment on the sale of the type of property normally held for resale.

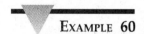

EXAMPLE 60

Jim, a real estate dealer, segregates tract A from the real estate he regularly holds for resale and designates the property as being held for investment purposes. The property is not advertised for sale and is disposed of several years later. The negotiations for the subsequent sale were initiated by the purchaser and not by Jim. Under these circumstances, it would appear that any gain or loss from the sale of tract A should be a capital gain or loss.[41] ▼

When a business is being sold, one of the major decisions usually concerns whether a portion of the sales price is for goodwill. For the seller, goodwill generally represents the disposition of a capital asset. Goodwill has no basis and represents a residual portion of the selling price that cannot be allocated reasonably to the known assets. The amount of goodwill thus represents capital gain. The buyer purchasing goodwill has a capitalizable, 15-year amortizable asset—a disadvantageous situation.

Prior to the Revenue Reconciliation Act (RRA) of 1993, the buyer would prefer that the residual portion of the purchase price be allocated to a covenant not to compete (a promise that the seller will not compete against the buyer by conducting a business similar to the one that the buyer has purchased). Payments for a covenant not to compete are ordinary income to the seller, but were ordinary deductions for the buyer over the life of the covenant. However, § 197 now provides that a covenant is amortized over the same 15-year period as goodwill.

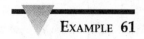

EXAMPLE 61

Marcia is buying Jack's dry cleaning proprietorship. An appraisal of the assets indicates that a reasonable purchase price would exceed the value of the known assets by $30,000. If the purchase contract does not specify the nature of the $30,000, the amount will be for goodwill, and Jack will have a long-term capital gain of $30,000. Marcia will have a 15-year amortizable

[41] *Toledo, Peoria & Western Railroad Co.*, 35 TCM 1663, T.C.Memo. 1976–366.

$30,000 asset. If Marcia is paying the extra $30,000 to prevent Jack from conducting another dry cleaning business in the area (a covenant not to compete), Jack will have $30,000 of ordinary income. Marcia will have a $30,000 deduction over the statutory 15-year amortization period rather than over the actual life of the covenant (e.g., 5 years). ▼

EFFECT OF CAPITAL ASSET STATUS IN TRANSACTIONS OTHER THAN SALES

The nature of an asset (capital or ordinary) is important in determining the tax consequences that result when a sale or exchange occurs. It may, however, be just as significant in circumstances other than a taxable sale or exchange. When a capital asset is disposed of, the result is not always a capital gain or loss. Rather, in general, the disposition must be a sale or exchange. Collection of a debt instrument having a basis less than the face value results in an ordinary gain rather than a capital gain even though the debt instrument is a capital asset. The collection is not a sale or exchange. Sale of the debt shortly before the due date for collection will not produce a capital gain.[42] If selling the debt in such circumstances could produce a capital gain but collecting could not, the narrow interpretation of what constitutes a capital gain or loss would be frustrated. Another illustration of the sale or exchange principle involves a donation of certain appreciated property to a qualified charity. Recall that in certain circumstances, the measure of the charitable contribution is fair market value when the property, if sold, would have yielded a long-term capital gain [refer to Chapter 9 and the discussion of § 170(e)].

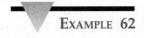

EXAMPLE 62

Sharon wants to donate a tract of unimproved land (basis of $40,000 and fair market value of $200,000) held for the required long-term holding period to State University (a qualified charitable organization). However, Sharon currently is under audit by the IRS for capital gains she reported on certain real estate transactions during an earlier tax year. Although Sharon is not a licensed real estate broker, the IRS agent conducting the audit is contending that she has achieved dealer status by virtue of the number and frequency of the real estate transactions she has conducted. Under these circumstances, Sharon would be well-advised to postpone the donation to State University until her status is clarified. If she has achieved dealer status, the unimproved land may be inventory (refer to Example 60 for another possible result), and Sharon's charitable contribution deduction would be limited to $40,000. If not, and if the land is held as an investment, Sharon's deduction is $200,000 (the fair market value of the property). ▼

STOCK SALES

The following rules apply in determining the date of a stock sale:

- The date the sale is executed is the date of the sale. The execution date is the date the broker completes the transaction on the stock exchange.
- The settlement date is the date the cash or other property is paid to the seller of the stock. This date is *not* relevant in determining the date of sale.

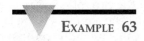

EXAMPLE 63

Lupe, a cash basis taxpayer, sells stock that results in a gain. The sale was executed on December 29, 1995. The settlement date is January 4, 1996. The date of sale is December 29, 1995 (the execution date). The holding period for the stock sold ends with the execution date. ▼

---

[42] *Comm. v. Percy W. Phillips*, 60–1 USTC ¶9294, 5 AFTR2d 855, 275 F.2d 33 (CA–4, 1960).

MAXIMIZING BENEFITS

Ordinary losses generally are preferable to capital losses because of the limitations imposed on the deductibility of net capital losses and the requirement that capital losses be used to offset capital gains. The taxpayer may be able to convert what would otherwise have been capital loss to ordinary loss. For example, business (but not nonbusiness) bad debts, losses from the sale or exchange of small business investment company stock, and losses from the sale or exchange of small business company stock all result in ordinary losses.[43]

Although capital losses can be carried over indefinitely, *indefinite* becomes definite when a taxpayer dies. Any loss carryovers not used by the taxpayer are permanently lost. That is, no tax benefit can be derived from the carryovers subsequent to death.[44] Therefore, the potential benefit of carrying over capital losses diminishes when dealing with older taxpayers.

It is usually beneficial to spread gains over more than one taxable year. In some cases, this can be accomplished through the installment sales method of accounting.

YEAR-END PLANNING

The following general rules can be applied for timing the recognition of capital gains and losses near the end of a taxable year:

- If the taxpayer already has recognized over $3,000 of capital loss, sell assets to generate capital gain equal to the excess of the capital loss over $3,000.

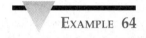

EXAMPLE 64

Kevin has already incurred a $7,000 STCL. Kevin should generate $4,000 of capital gain. The gain will offset $4,000 of the loss. The remaining loss of $3,000 can be deducted against ordinary income. ▼

- If the taxpayer already has recognized capital gain, sell assets to generate capital loss equal to the capital gain. The gain will not be taxed, and the loss will be fully *deductible* against the gain.
- If the taxpayer's ordinary taxable income is already in the 28 percent bracket, it would make sense to recognize long-term capital gain rather than ordinary income where the taxpayer has a choice between the two. Such gain is taxed at the alternative rate of 28 percent whereas ordinary income may be taxed under the regular tax rates at 31 percent or more.

TIMING OF § 1231 GAIN

Although §§ 1245 and 1250 recapture much of the gain from the disposition of business property, sometimes § 1231 gain is still substantial. For instance, land held as a business asset will generate either § 1231 gain or § 1231 loss. If the taxpayer already has a capital loss for the year, the sale of land at a gain should be postponed so that the net § 1231 gain is not netted against the capital loss. The capital loss deduction will therefore be maximized for the current tax year, and the capital loss carryforward (if any) may be offset against the gain when the land is sold. If the taxpayer already has a § 1231 loss, § 1231 gains might be postponed to maximize the ordinary loss deduction this year. However, the carryforward of nonrecaptured § 1231 losses will make the § 1231 gain next year an ordinary gain.

---

[43] §§ 166(d), 1242, and 1244. Refer to the discussion in Chapter 6.   [44] Rev.Rul. 74–175, 1974–1 C.B. 52.

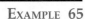

EXAMPLE 65

Mark has a $2,000 net STCL for 1996. He could sell business land for a $3,000 § 1231 gain. He will have no other capital gains and losses or § 1231 gains and losses in 1996 or 1997. He has no nonrecaptured § 1231 losses from prior years. Mark is in the 28% tax bracket in 1996 and 1997. If he sells the land in 1996, he will have a $1,000 net LTCG ($3,000 § 1231 gain – $2,000 STCL) and will pay a tax of $280 ($1,000 × 28%). If Mark sells the land in 1997, he will have a 1996 tax savings of $560 ($2,000 capital loss deduction × 28% tax rate on ordinary income). In 1997, he will pay tax of $840 ($3,000 × 28%). By postponing the sale for a year, Mark will have the use of $840 ($560 + $280). ▼

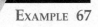

EXAMPLE 66

Beth has a $15,000 § 1231 loss in 1996. She could sell business equipment for a $20,000 § 1231 gain and a $12,000 § 1245 gain. Beth is in the 28% tax bracket in 1996 and 1997. She has no nonrecaptured § 1231 losses from prior years. If she sells the equipment in 1996, she will have a $5,000 net § 1231 gain and $12,000 of ordinary gain. Her tax would be $4,760 [($5,000 § 1231 gain × 28%) + ($12,000 ordinary gain × 28%)].

If Beth postpones the equipment sale until 1997, she would have a 1996 ordinary loss of $15,000 and tax savings of $4,200 ($15,000 × 28%). In 1997, she would have $5,000 of § 1231 gain (the 1996 § 1231 loss carries over and recaptures $15,000 of the 1997 § 1231 gain as ordinary income) and $27,000 of ordinary gain. Her tax would be $8,960 [($5,000 § 1231 gain × 28%) + ($27,000 ordinary gain × 28%)]. By postponing the equipment sale, Beth has the use of $8,960 ($4,200 + $4,760). ▼

TIMING OF RECAPTURE

Since recapture is usually not triggered until the property is sold or disposed of, it may be possible to plan for recapture in low-bracket or loss years. If a taxpayer has net operating loss carryovers that are about to expire, the recognition of ordinary income from recapture may be advisable to absorb the loss carryovers.

EXAMPLE 67

Ahmad has a $15,000 net operating loss carryover that will expire this year. He owns a machine that he plans to sell in the early part of next year. The expected gain of $17,000 from the sale of the machine will be recaptured as ordinary income under § 1245. Ahmad sells the machine before the end of this year and offsets $15,000 of the ordinary income against the net operating loss carryover. ▼

POSTPONING AND SHIFTING RECAPTURE

It is also possible to postpone recapture or to shift the burden of recapture to others. For example, recapture is avoided upon the disposition of a § 1231 asset if the taxpayer replaces the property by entering into a like-kind exchange. In this instance, recapture potential is merely carried over to the newly acquired property (refer to Example 57).

Recapture can be shifted to others through the gratuitous transfer of § 1245 or § 1250 property to family members. A subsequent sale of such property by the donee will trigger recapture to the donee rather than the donor (refer to Example 54). This procedure would be advisable only if the donee is in a lower income tax bracket than the donor.

AVOIDING RECAPTURE

The immediate expensing election (§ 179) is subject to § 1245 recapture. If the election is not made, the § 1245 recapture potential will accumulate more slowly (refer to Chapter 7). Since using the immediate expense deduction complicates depreciation and book accounting for the affected asset, not taking the deduction may make sense even though the time value of money might indicate it should be taken.

KEY TERMS

Additional depreciation, 13–38

Alternative tax, 13–22

Capital asset, 13–5

Capital gains, 13–4

Capital losses, 13–4

Franchise, 13–13

Holding period, 13–16

Intangible drilling and development costs (IDC), 13–45

Lessee, 13–15

Lessor, 13–15

Long-term nonpersonal use capital assets, 13–29

Net capital gain (NCG), 13–21

Net capital loss (NCL), 13–23

Options, 13–10

Patent, 13–12

Related party, 13–44

Sale or exchange, 13–9

Section 1231 gains and losses, 13–27

Section 1231 lookback, 13–31

Section 1231 property, 13–28

Section 1245 property, 13–36

Section 1245 recapture, 13–35

Section 1250 property, 13–38

Section 1250 recapture, 13–38

Short sale, 13–17

PROBLEM MATERIALS

DISCUSSION QUESTIONS

1. What type of gain may be subject to beneficial tax treatment for noncorporate taxpayers?

2. Upon what three characteristics does proper classification of recognized gains and losses depend?

3. Todd owns the following assets. Which of them are capital assets?
   a. Ten shares of Standard Motors common stock.
   b. A copyright on a song Todd wrote.
   c. A U.S. government savings bond.
   d. A note Todd received when he loaned $100 to a friend.
   e. A very rare copy of "Your Federal Income Tax" (a U.S. government publication that Todd purchased many years ago from the U.S. Government Printing Office).
   f. Todd's personal use automobile.
   g. A letter Todd received from a former U.S. President. Todd received the letter because he had complained to the President about the President's foreign policy.

4. Joanne purchases song copyrights from composers. What tax issues does Joanne face in determining whether the copyrights are capital assets for her?

5. Jonathan lent $2,000 to a friend who became unemployed unexpectedly. Shortly thereafter, the friend took a new job in another state. After very diligent efforts to locate the friend, Jonathan was unable to find him, and payment of the loan is now 14 months overdue. Assuming the loan is fully noncollectible, what tax issues does Jonathan face?

6. David purchased a one-year option on 40 acres of farmland for $25,000. David's plans for the property did not work out, so he let the option expire unexercised. What tax issues does David face in determining how to treat the $25,000?

7. If a grantee of an option exercises the option, do the grantor's proceeds from the sale of the option property increase? Why?

8. When does the transfer of a patent result in long-term capital gain? Short-term capital gain? Ordinary income?

9. What is a franchise? In practice, does the transfer of a franchise usually result in capital gain or loss treatment? Why or why not?

10. When are lease cancellation payments received by a lessee capital in nature? When are lease cancellation payments received by a lessor capital in nature?

11. What does it mean when a capital asset has been held "short term"?

12. Helen exchanges a computer used in her business for another computer that she will use in her business. The transaction qualifies as a like-kind exchange. Helen had held the computer given up in the exchange for four years. The computers are § 1231 assets. What is the holding period of the computer received in the exchange on the day of its acquisition?

13. Juan purchased corporate stock for $10,000 on April 10, 1995. On July 14, 1996, when the stock was worth $17,000, he gave it to his son, Miguel. When does Miguel's holding period for the stock begin?

14. John inherits stock on July 17, 1996. John's father had purchased the stock on April 10, 1995, for $12,000. The stock was worth $15,000 when the father died on December 20, 1995. The stock was worth $18,000 when John received it on July 17, 1996. When does John's holding period for the stock begin?

15. After all possible capital gain and loss netting is complete, what are the possibilities for outcomes that include a net long-term capital gain?

16. After all possible capital gain and loss netting is complete, what are the possibilities for outcomes that include a net long-term capital loss?

17. Sue and Ramon each have gross income of $150,000. Yet Sue contends that her gross income will be taxed different from Ramon's gross income. Assuming she is correct, what could explain this odd result?

18. What types of transactions involving capital assets are included under § 1231? Why wouldn't they qualify for long-term capital gain treatment without § 1231?

19. If depreciable business property is sold at a loss, is the loss an ordinary loss or a capital loss?

20. Name two types of assets that are neither § 1231 assets nor capital assets.

21. Ahmad is a farmer who is thinking about raising ostriches. Ostrich meat is very high in protein, low in calories, and low in fat. Ahmad would like to know what tax issues he would face if he decides to raise ostriches in addition to the cattle he is currently raising.

22. Sally lives in an area that was hit hard by a hurricane. She has correctly determined that she has a $15,000 business property long-term casualty loss and a $11,000 business property long-term casualty gain. What tax issues must Sally deal with?

23. Two years ago, Sara had a net § 1231 loss. Last year, she had a net § 1231 gain exceeding that loss. This year, Sara has a net § 1231 gain. Is any of this year's gain treated as ordinary income because of the *lookback rule*?

24. Some of Max's business equipment that had been held long term was stolen in a burglary. The property had been purchased for $80,000, and the insurance company paid Max $33,000. What tax issues do these circumstances present for Max?

25. A business machine held for three years is disposed of at a gain. The cost of the machine was greater than the selling price. What is the nature of the gain?

26. A business machine held for several years is sold at a gain. Part of the gain is § 1245 gain, and part is § 1231 gain. There is no other § 1231 gain or loss this year, but there is a nonrecaptured § 1231 lookback loss that exceeds the current-year § 1231 gain. Describe the treatment of the gain from the disposition of the machine.

27. Differentiate between the types of property covered by §§ 1245 and 1250.

28. In 1984, a warehouse was acquired and depreciated using accelerated depreciation. In 1996, the warehouse is sold for less than was originally paid for it. What is the nature of the gain?

29. Residential rental real estate is acquired and disposed of in 1996. There is a small gain on the disposition of the property. The gain is less than the depreciation taken on the property. What is the nature of that gain?

PROBLEMS

30. Nancy had three property transactions during the year. She sold a vacation home used for personal purposes at a $21,000 loss. The home had been held for five years and had never been rented. Nancy also sold an antique clock for $3,500 that she had inherited from her grandmother. The clock was valued in Nancy's grandmother's estate at $2,000. Nancy owned the clock for only four months. Nancy sold these assets to finance her full-time occupation as a songwriter. Near the end of the year, Nancy sold one of the songs she had written two years earlier. She received cash of $38,000 and a royalty interest in revenues derived from the merchandising of the song. Nancy had no tax basis for the song. Nancy had no other income and $18,000 in deductible songwriting expenses. Assuming the year is 1996, what is Nancy's adjusted gross income?

31. Revez owns an antique shop. He buys property from estates, often at much less than the retail value of the property. Recently, Revez sold for $4,000 an antique desk for which he had paid $125. Revez had held the desk in his shop for 15 months before selling it. Revez would like the gain on the sale of the desk to be a long-term capital gain. How can he achieve that objective?

32. Gary makes a gift to Barbara of the copyright on his song, "I Love the Spartans." The song has a basis of $20,000 to Gary. Gary had owned the copyright for two years. The copyright has a fair market value of $25,000 at the date of the gift. Three years after receiving the copyright, Barbara sells it to Jim for $30,000.
    a. What is Barbara's recognized gain on the sale?
    b. What is the nature of Barbara's gain?

33. Brenda Reynolds is a dealer in securities. She has spotted a fast-rising company and would like to buy and hold its stock for investment. The stock is currently selling for $45 per share, and Brenda thinks it will climb to $93 a share within two years. Brenda's co-workers have told her that there is "no way" she can get long-term capital gain treatment when she purchases stock because she is a securities dealer. Brenda has asked you to calculate her potential gain and tell her whether her co-workers are right. Draft a letter to Brenda responding to her request. Her address is 200 Morningside Drive, Hattisburg, MS 39406.

34. Abby sells real estate lots, but meets all the conditions of § 1237. In 1996, she sells six lots, one lot each to Betty, Carl, Donna, and Evelyn and two adjacent lots to Frank. The sales price of each lot is $20,000. Abby's basis is $15,000 for each lot. Sales expenses are $500 per lot.
    a. What is the realized and recognized gain?
    b. Explain the nature of the gain (ordinary income or capital gain).
    c. Would your answers change if the two lots sold to Frank were not adjacent? If so, how?

35. Samantha is in the business of buying song copyrights from struggling songwriters, holding those copyrights, and then reselling the songs to major record companies and singers. Samantha has a four-month option to purchase a song copyright. She paid $2,000 for this option. A famous singer has heard the song and is willing to buy the option from Samantha for $10,000. Samantha thinks the song may be worth $35,000 in

six months. If Samantha exercises the option, she will have to pay $20,000 for the song. Assuming Samantha is in the 36% tax bracket, which of these alternatives will give her a better after-tax cash flow?

36. Marta is looking for vacant land to buy. She would hold the land as an investment. For $1,000, she is granted an 11-month option on January 1, 1996, to buy 10 acres of vacant land for $25,000. The owner (who is holding the land for investment) paid $10,000 for the land several years ago.
   a. Does the landowner have gross income when $1,000 is received for granting the option?
   b. Does Marta have an asset when the option is granted?
   c. If the option lapses, does the landowner have a recognized gain? If so, what type of gain? Does Marta have a recognized loss? If so, what type of loss?
   d. If the option is exercised and an additional $25,000 is paid for the land, how much recognized gain does the seller have? What type of gain? What is Marta's tax basis for the property?

37. Frank owns a patent on a part that Teal Corporation wishes to use as a component in a product it manufactures. Frank had purchased the patent from the inventor before the inventor reduced the patent to practice. Frank had intended to use the patented part in his business, but found that it was not suitable. Teal is willing to pay Frank $5,000 per month plus 1% of the manufactured cost of the part. How should Frank construct the contract with Teal so that the $5,000 per month and 1% of manufactured cost are long-term capital gain?

38. Freys, Inc., sells a 12-year franchise to Reynaldo. The franchise contains many restrictions on how Reynaldo may operate his store. For instance, Reynaldo cannot use less than Grade 10 Idaho potatoes, must fry the potatoes at a constant 410 degrees, dress store personnel in Freys-approved uniforms, and have a Freys sign that meets detailed specifications on size, color, and construction. When the franchise contract is signed, Reynaldo makes a noncontingent $40,000 payment to Freys. During the same year, Reynaldo pays Freys $25,000—14% of Reynaldo's sales. How does Freys treat each of these payments? How does Reynaldo treat each of the payments?

39. Irene lives in an apartment near her college campus. Her lease runs out in July 1997, but her landlord could sell the building if he can convince all the tenants to cancel their leases and move out by the end of 1996. The landlord has offered Irene $1,000 to cancel her lease. Irene's lease began on August 1, 1996. What tax factors should Irene consider in deciding whether to take the landlord's offer?

40. Dennis sells short 100 shares of ARC stock at $20 per share on January 15, 1996. He buys 200 shares of ARC stock on April 1, 1996, at $25 per share. On May 2, 1996, he closes the short sale by delivering 100 of the shares purchased on April 1.
   a. What are the amount and nature of Dennis's loss upon closing the short sale?
   b. When does the holding period for the remaining 100 shares begin?
   c. If Dennis sells (at $27 per share) the remaining 100 shares on January 20, 1997, what will be the nature of his gain or loss?

41. Elaine Case (single with no dependents) has the following transactions in 1996:

Adjusted gross income (exclusive of capital gains and losses)	$240,000
Long-term capital gain	12,000
Long-term capital loss	(5,000)
Short-term capital gain	19,000
Short-term capital loss	(23,000)

What is Elaine's net capital gain or loss? Draft a letter to Elaine describing how the net capital gain or loss will be treated on her tax return. Assume Elaine's income from other sources puts her in the 36% bracket. Elaine's address is 300 Ireland Avenue, Shepherdstown, WV 25443.

42. In 1996, Betty (head of household with three dependents) had an $18,000 loss from the sale of a personal residence. She also purchased from an individual inventor for $8,000 (and resold in two months for $7,000) a patent on a rubber bonding process. The patent had not yet been reduced to practice. Betty purchased the patent as an investment. Additionally, she had the following capital gains and losses from stock transactions:

Long-term capital loss	($ 3,000)
Long-term capital loss carryover from 1995	(12,000)
Short-term capital gain	21,000
Short-term capital loss	(6,000)

What is Betty's net capital gain or loss? Draft a letter to Betty explaining the tax treatment of the sale of her personal residence. Assume Betty's income from other sources puts her in the 36% bracket.

43. In 1996, Venezia has a $5,800 net short-term capital loss and $9,030 of negative taxable income. She used the standard deduction and has one personal exemption. What is the amount of Venezia's capital loss carryover to 1997?

44. Consuela, a head of household with two dependents, has the following 1996 transactions:

Adjusted gross income (exclusive of capital gains and losses)	$125,250
Long-term capital loss	(5,000)
Long-term capital gain	20,000
Short-term capital loss carryover	(2,000)

a. What is Consuela's net capital gain or loss?
b. What is Consuela's taxable income assuming she does not itemize?
c. What is Consuela's tax on taxable income?

45. Purple Corporation has $16,800 of long-term capital loss for 1996 and $5,000 of other taxable income. What is its 1996 taxable income and the amount (if any) of its capital loss carryover?

46. June owns a sole proprietorship that Doria is going to purchase. They have agreed on a price for all the assets except goodwill and June's covenant not to compete against Doria. June is willing to give Doria a two-year covenant not to compete for only $1 of compensation, but would like $25,000 for the business goodwill. Doria would like to pay June $25,000 for the covenant not to compete and only $1 for the business goodwill. June is in the 36% tax bracket, and Doria is in the 31% tax bracket. Which of these approaches is better for June? For Doria?

47. A painting that Kwan Lee held for investment was destroyed in a flood. The painting was insured, and Kwan had a $10,000 gain from this casualty. He also had a $7,000 loss from an uninsured antique vase that was destroyed by the flood. The vase was also held for investment. Kwan had no other property transactions during the year and has no nonrecaptured § 1231 losses from prior years. Compute his net gain or loss and identify how it would be treated. Also, write a letter to Kwan explaining the nature of the gain or loss. Kwan's address is 2367 Meridian Road, Hannibal Point, MO 34901.

48. Vicki has the following net § 1231 results for each of the years shown. What would be the nature of the net gains in 1995 and 1996?

Tax Year	Net § 1231 Loss	Net § 1231 Gain
1991	$15,000	
1992	17,000	
1993	22,000	
1994		$10,000
1995		20,000
1996		29,000

49. Yoshida owns two parcels of business land (§ 1231 assets). One parcel can be sold at a loss of $30,000, and the other parcel can be sold at a gain of $40,000. Yoshida has no nonrecaptured § 1231 losses from prior years. The parcels could be sold at any time because potential purchasers are abundant. Yoshida has a $25,000 short-term capital loss carryover from a prior tax year and no capital assets that could be sold to generate long-term capital gains. What should Yoshida do based upon these facts? (Assume tax rates are constant and ignore the present value of future cash flow.)

50. Rose Company owns two lathes. Lathe A was purchased several years ago for $65,000, has a $10,000 adjusted basis, and was sold in 1996 for $17,000. Lathe B was purchased several years ago for $8,000, has a $6,000 adjusted basis, and was sold in 1996 for $2,000. What are the amount and nature of the recognized gain or loss from the disposition of each asset?

51. Tan Corporation sold machines A and B during the current year. The machines had been purchased for $180,000 and $240,000, respectively. The machines were purchased eight years ago and were depreciated to zero. Machine A was sold for $40,000, and machine B for $260,000. What amount of gain is recognized by Tan, and what is the nature of the gain?

52. On March 1, 1992, Cardinal Company bought and placed in service a seven-year MACRS machine for $35,000. Cardinal expensed $10,000 of the machine's cost under § 179 and has also taken $17,841 of cost recovery on the machine. The machine was sold on April 1, 1996, for $32,000.
a. What is Cardinal's realized and recognized gain?
b. What is the nature of the gain?
c. At what point in time did this machine cease being an ordinary asset and become a § 1231 asset?

53. Green Manufacturing purchases a $3,000,000 propane storage tank and places it on a permanent framework outside its plant. The propane is drawn from the tank through a hose and valve system into the burners underneath Green's chemical vats. After $1,800,000 of cost recovery has been taken on the tank, it is sold for $2,300,000. What are the nature and amount of Green's gain or loss from the disposition of the tank?

54. On December 1, 1994, Gray Manufacturing Company (a corporation) purchased another company's assets, including a patent. The patent was used in Gray's manufacturing operations; $40,500 was allocated to the patent, and it was amortized at the rate of $225 per month. On June 30, 1996, Gray sold the patent for $60,000. Nineteen months of amortization had been taken on the patent. What are the amount and nature of the gain Gray recognizes on the disposition of the patent? Write a letter to Gray discussing the treatment of the gain. Gray's address is 6734 Grover Street, Back Bay Harbor, ME 23890. The letter should be addressed to Siddim Sadatha, Controller.

55. On June 1, 1992, Sparrow Enterprises (not a corporation) acquired a retail store for $400,000. The store was 31.5-year real property, and the straight-line cost recovery method was used. The store was sold on June 21, 1996, for $370,000.
a. Compute the cost recovery and adjusted basis for the store using Table 7–7 from Chapter 7.
b. What are the amount and nature of Sparrow's gain or loss from disposition of the store?

56. On January 1, 1986, Esteban acquired a $600,000 residential building for use in his rental activity. He took $450,000 of cost recovery on the building before disposing of it for $800,000 on January 1, 1996. For the period Esteban held the building, straight-line cost recovery would have been $400,000. What are the amount and nature of Esteban's gain from the disposition of the property?

57. Dave is the sole proprietor of a trampoline shop. During 1996, the following transactions occurred:

  • Unimproved land adjacent to the store was condemned by the city on February 1. The condemnation proceeds were $25,000. The land, acquired in 1982, had an allocable basis of $15,000. Dave has additional parking across the street and plans to use the condemnation proceeds to build his inventory.

  • A truck used to deliver trampolines was sold on January 2 for $3,500. The truck was purchased on January 2, 1992, for $6,000. On the date of sale, the adjusted basis was $2,509.

  • Dave sold an antique rowing machine at an auction. Net proceeds were $3,900. The rowing machine was purchased as used equipment 17 years ago for $5,200 and is fully depreciated.

  • Dave sold an apartment building for $200,000 on September 1. The rental property was purchased on September 1, 1993, for $150,000 and was being depreciated over a 27.5-year life using the straight-line method. At the date of sale, the adjusted basis was $124,783.

  • Dave's personal yacht was stolen September 5. The yacht had been purchased in August at a cost of $25,000. The fair market value immediately preceding the theft was $20,000. Dave was insured for 50% of the original cost, and he received $12,500 on December 1.

  • Dave sold a Buick on May 1 for $9,600. The vehicle had been used exclusively for personal purposes. It was purchased on September 1, 1992, for $20,800.

  • An adding machine used by Dave's bookkeeper was sold on June 1. Net proceeds of the sale were $135. The machine was purchased on June 2, 1992, for $350. It was being depreciated over a five-year life employing the straight-line method. The adjusted basis on the date of sale was $95.

  • Dave's trampoline stretching machine (owned two years) was stolen on May 5, but the business's insurance company will not pay any of the machine's value because Dave failed to pay the insurance premium. The machine had a fair market value of $8,000 and an adjusted basis of $6,000 at the time of theft.

  • Dave had AGI of $4,000 from sources other than those described above.

  • Dave has no nonrecaptured § 1231 lookback losses.

  a. For each transaction, what are the amount and nature of recognized gain or loss?
  b. What is Dave's 1996 AGI?

58. On January 1, 1986, Cora Hassant acquired depreciable real property for $100,000. She used accelerated depreciation to compute the asset's cost recovery. The asset was sold for $89,000 on January 3, 1996, when its adjusted basis was $38,000. Straight-line cost recovery for the period of time the asset was held would have been $52,700.
  a. What are the amount and nature of the gain if the real property was residential?
  b. What are the amount and nature of the gain if the real property was nonresidential?
  c. Cora is curious about how the recapture rules differ for residential rental real estate acquired in 1986 and for residential rental real estate acquired in 1987 and thereafter. Write a letter to Cora explaining the differences. Her address is 2345 Westridge Street #23, Homer, MT 67342.

59. Joanne is in the 39.6% tax bracket and owns depreciable business equipment that she purchased several years ago for $135,000; she has taken $100,000 of depreciation on the equipment, and it is worth $85,000. Joanne's niece, Susan, is starting a new business and

is short of cash. Susan has asked Joanne to gift the equipment to her so that Susan can use it in her business. Joanne no longer needs the equipment. Identify the alternatives available to Joanne if she wishes to help Susan and the tax effects of those alternatives. (Assume all alternatives involve the business equipment in one way or another, and ignore the gift tax.)

60. Gregor owns business equipment with a $55,000 adjusted basis; he paid $100,000 for the equipment, and it is currently worth $73,000. Gregor dies suddenly, and his son Adrian inherits the property. What is Adrian's basis for the property, and what happens to the § 1245 depreciation recapture potential?

61. Ray owns an unimproved parking lot that was used in his parking lot business for 10 years. A real estate developer purchases the lot from Ray for a total of $300,000. Ray receives $50,000 in 1996 and will receive $50,000 (plus 10% interest) each year for the next five years. Ray has a $120,000 adjusted basis for the lot. What are the nature and amount of the gain recognized in 1996?

62. Orange Corporation sells depreciable equipment for $59,000 to its sole shareholder, Jane. Orange had a $45,000 adjusted basis for the equipment and had originally paid $85,000 for it. Jane will use the equipment in her sole proprietorship business. The $59,000 sale price is the property's fair market value at the time of the sale. What are the consequences of this sale for Orange? For Jane?

63. Jay sold three items of business equipment for a total of $300,000. None of the equipment was appraised to determine its value. Jay's cost and adjusted basis for the assets are as follows:

Asset	Cost	Adjusted Basis
Skidder	$230,000	$ 40,000
Driller	120,000	60,000
Platform	620,000	–0–
Total	$970,000	$100,000

Jay has been unable to establish the fair market values of the three assets. All he can determine is that combined they were worth $300,000 to the buyer in this arm's length transaction. How should Jay allocate the sales price and figure the gain or loss on the sale of the three assets?

CUMULATIVE PROBLEMS

64. Nikki Hassad is a graduate student at State University. She is single and has no dependents. During 1996, she had $5,500 wages from a full-time job she held until returning to school in August. Nikki received a $3,000 scholarship from State University and used all of the scholarship money to pay for tuition and fees. In June 1996, she won $135,000 with an instant lottery ticket and immediately invested in various stocks. The following table summarizes her stock transactions for 1996:

	Date Acquired	Cost	Date Sold	Selling Price
150 shares Clay	7/2/96	$5,000	12/11/96	$6,200
100 shares Gold	7/2/96	5,000	11/6/96	3,300
120 shares Iron	7/2/96	3,100	10/8/96	8,000
25 shares Sand	7/2/96	1,900		
100 shares Uranium	6/16/91	2,000	12/11/96	9,600

Nikki does not have many itemized deductions, so she will take the standard deduction. Her Social Security number is 393–86–4502, and she lives at 518 Marigold Lane, Okemos, MI 48864. She had $600 of Federal income tax withheld on her wages and $37,000 of Federal income tax withheld on her lottery winnings. She also made Federal estimated income tax payments of $3,500.

Compute Nikki's lowest legal tax liability for 1996. Suggested software (if available): *TurboTax* or *MacInTax.*

Draft a brief letter to Nikki describing (1) how long she must hold the Sand stock for it to become "long term," (2) what the 1997 tax consequences would be if she sold that stock for a $4,000 long-term capital gain, and (3) what would happen if she was eligible for the alternative tax on long-term capital gains. Also, prepare a memo for Nikki's tax file.

65. Glen and Diane Okumura are married, file a joint return, and live at 39 Kaloa Street, Honolulu, Hawaii 56790. Glen's Social Security number is 777–88–2000 and Diane's is 888–77–1000. The Okumuras have two dependent children, Amy (age 15) and John (age 9). Glen works for the Hawaii Public Works Department, and Diane owns and materially participates in a retail dress shop. The Okumuras had the following transactions during 1996:

a. Glen earned $197,000 in wages and had Federal income tax withholding of $15,000.

b. Diane had a $18,000 profit from the dress shop.

c. The Okumuras sold a small apartment building for $68,000 on November 15, 1996. The building was acquired in October 1990 for $300,000, cost recovery was $86,820.

d. Diane sold a delivery truck used in her business. The truck cost $35,000, $21,700 of cost recovery had been taken, and it was sold for $18,000.

e. The Okumuras received $13,000 in dividends on various domestic corporation stock that they own.

f. The Okumuras sold stock for a $15,000 long-term capital gain and other stock at a $6,000 short-term capital loss.

g. The Okumuras had the following itemized deductions: $11,000 unreimbursed medical expenses; $10,500 personal use real property taxes; $7,000 qualified residence interest; $1,500 of Glen's unreimbursed employee business expenses; $535 of investment-related expenses; and $6,300 of state income taxes paid.

Compute the Okumuras' 1996 net tax payable or refund due. (Ignore self-employment tax.) Suggested software (if available): *TurboTax* or *MacInTax.* Also write a letter to the Okumuras describing how the sale of the apartment building affects their return.

TEAM PROJECT: ARTHUR ANDERSEN TAX CHALLENGE CASES

For more information on the Arthur Andersen Tax Challenge Cases, please refer to Chapter 2, page 2–41.

Information related to tax issues and problems that are discussed in this chapter may be found in the

Miller case on pages 11, 20, 36, 37

Read and analyze the case you have been assigned and *identify* any issues and problems that are related to material covered in this chapter. If the information provided in the case is complete, prepare answers for this part of the case at this time. If you need information that is contained in the later parts of the case, please write a memo summarizing the questions or problems so you can prepare a complete answer at a later date.

14

ALTERNATIVE MINIMUM TAX

LEARNING OBJECTIVES

After completing Chapter 14, you should be able to:

1. Explain the rationale for the alternative minimum tax (AMT).

2. Understand the formula for computing the AMT for individuals.

3. Identify the adjustments made in calculating the AMT.

4. Identify the tax preferences that are included in calculating the AMT.

5. Apply the formula for computing the AMT and illustrate Form 6251.

6. Describe the role of the AMT credit in the alternative minimum tax structure.

7. Understand the basic features of the corporate AMT.

8. Identify tax planning opportunities to minimize the AMT.

1   LEARNING OBJECTIVE
Explain the rationale for the alternative minimum tax (AMT).

Bob and Carol are unmarried individuals who work for the same employer and have the same amount of gross income and the same amount of deductions. Bob's tax return is prepared by Adam, and Carol's tax return is prepared by Eve. While discussing their tax liability one day at lunch, Carol is dismayed to learn that she paid $15,000 more in Federal income taxes than Bob did for the tax year. Carol meets with Eve that evening. Eve reviews Carol's tax return and assures her that her tax liability was properly calculated.

The above events raise a number of interesting questions for Bob and Carol that can be answered after completing this chapter. Why didn't Bob and Carol have the same tax liability? Were both tax returns properly prepared? Should Carol consider replacing her tax return preparer Eve with Adam? Is it possible and/or desirable for Carol to file an amended return? Should Bob do anything?

The tax law contains many incentives that are intended to influence the economic and social behavior of taxpayers (refer to Chapter 1). Some taxpayers have been able to take advantage of enough of these incentives to avoid or minimize any liability for Federal income tax. Although these taxpayers were reducing taxes legally, Congress became concerned about the inequity that results when taxpayers with substantial economic incomes can avoid paying any income tax. The **alternative minimum tax (AMT)** was enacted as a backup to the regular income tax. The rationale for the AMT was expressed as follows:

> [T]he minimum tax should serve one overriding objective: to ensure that no taxpayer with substantial economic income can avoid significant tax liability by using exclusions, deductions, and credits. Although these provisions may provide incentives for worthy goals, they become counterproductive when taxpayers are allowed to use them to avoid virtually all tax liability. The ability of high-income taxpayers to pay little or no tax undermines respect for the entire tax system and, thus, for the incentive provisions themselves. In addition, even aside from public perceptions ... it is inherently unfair for high-income taxpayers to pay little or no tax due to their ability to utilize tax preferences.[1]

The individual AMT is discussed in the first part of this chapter. The corporate AMT is similar to the individual AMT, but differs in several important ways. Details of the corporate AMT are presented in the last part of the chapter.

---

[1] *General Explanation of the Tax Reform Act of 1986 ("Blue Book")*, prepared by The Staff of the Joint Committee on Taxation, May 4, 1987, H.R. 3838, 99th Cong., pp. 432–433.

Individual Alternative Minimum Tax

AMT FORMULA FOR ALTERNATIVE MINIMUM TAXABLE INCOME (AMTI)

The AMT is separate from, but parallel to, the regular income tax system.[2] Most income and expense items are treated the same way for both regular income tax and AMT purposes. For example, a taxpayer's salary is included in computing taxable income and is also included in alternative minimum taxable income (AMTI). Alimony paid is allowed as a deduction *for* AGI for both regular income tax and AMT purposes. Certain itemized deductions, such as gambling losses, are allowed for both regular income tax and AMT purposes.

On the other hand, some income and expense items are treated differently for regular income tax and AMT purposes. For example, interest income on bonds issued by state, county, or local governments is *excluded* in computing taxable income. However, interest on such bonds is *included* in computing AMTI if the bonds are private activity bonds issued after August 7, 1986. The deduction for personal and dependency exemptions is *allowed* for regular income tax purposes, but is *disallowed* for AMT purposes.

In other cases, certain items are considered in both the regular income tax and AMT computations, but the amounts are different. For example, the completed contract method can be used to report income from some long-term contracts for regular income tax purposes, but the percentage of completion method is required for AMT purposes. Thus, the amount of income included in taxable income will differ from the amount included in AMTI. Depreciation is allowed as a deduction for both regular income tax and AMT purposes, but the *amount* of the regular income tax deduction will be different from the amount of the AMT deduction. Medical expenses are deductible in calculating both taxable income and AMTI, but the floor on the deduction is different.

The parallel but separate nature of the AMT means that AMTI will differ from taxable income. It is possible to compute AMTI by direct application of the AMT provisions, using the following formula:

> Gross income computed by applying the AMT rules
>
> **Minus:** Deductions computed by applying the AMT rules
>
> **Equals:** AMTI before tax preferences
>
> **Plus:** Tax preferences
>
> **Equals:** Alternative minimum taxable income

While the direct approach for computing AMTI appears quite logical, both the tax law and the tax forms provide a very different approach. Both of these use taxable income as the starting point for computing AMTI, as shown in Figure 14–1. This indirect approach for computing AMTI is analogous to the indirect approach used in calculating a net operating loss.

The purpose of the AMT formula is to *reconcile* taxable income to AMTI. This reconciliation is similar to a bank reconciliation, which reconciles a checkbook balance to a bank balance by considering differences between the depositor's records and the bank's records. The reconciliation of taxable income to AMTI is accomplished by entering reconciling items to account for differences between regular income tax provisions and AMT provisions. These reconciling items are

---

[2] § 55.

▼ **FIGURE 14–1**
Alternative Minimum Taxable
Income (AMTI) Formula

Taxable income

Plus: Positive AMT adjustments

Minus: Negative AMT adjustments

Equals: Taxable income after AMT adjustments

Plus: Tax preferences

Equals: Alternative minimum taxable income

referred to as **AMT adjustments** or **tax preferences.** *Adjustments* can be either positive or negative, as shown in the formula in Figure 14–1. Tax preferences are always positive.

Adjustments.   The concept of AMT adjustments was introduced in the Tax Reform Act of 1986. Most adjustments relate to *timing differences* that arise because of *separate* regular income tax and AMT treatments. Adjustments that are caused by timing differences will eventually *reverse;* that is, positive adjustments will be offset by negative adjustments in the future, and vice versa.[3]

For example, **circulation expenditures** can give rise to a timing difference that requires an AMT adjustment. For regular income tax purposes, circulation expenditures can be deducted in the year incurred. For AMT purposes, however, circulation expenditures must be deducted over a three-year period. This difference in treatment will be used to illustrate the role of adjustments in the formula for computing AMTI.

EXAMPLE 1

Bob had taxable income of $100,000 in 1995. In computing taxable income, he deducted $30,000 of circulation expenditures incurred in 1995. Bob's allowable deduction for AMT purposes was only $10,000. Therefore, an AMT adjustment was required in 1995 as follows:

Taxable income		$100,000
+AMT adjustment:		
Circulation expenditures deducted for regular income tax purposes	$ 30,000	
−Circulation expenditures allowed for AMT purposes	(10,000)	
Positive adjustment		20,000
=AMTI before tax preferences		$120,000
+Tax preferences		–0–
AMTI		$120,000

Analysis of this computation shows that the allowable AMT deduction is $20,000 less than the allowable regular income tax deduction. Therefore, AMTI will be $20,000 greater than taxable income. This is accomplished by entering a positive AMT adjustment of $20,000. ▼

EXAMPLE 2

Assume that Bob from Example 1 has taxable income of $95,000 in 1996. He is allowed to deduct $10,000 of circulation expenditures for AMT purposes, but is not allowed a deduction for regular income tax purposes because all $30,000 was deducted in 1995. Therefore, a *negative* AMT adjustment is required.

---

[3] § 56.

Taxable income		$ 95,000
–AMT adjustment:		
Circulation expenditures allowed for regular income tax purposes	$ –0–	
Circulation expenditures deducted for AMT purposes	(10,000)	
Negative adjustment		(10,000)
=AMTI before tax preferences		$ 85,000
+Tax preferences		–0–
AMTI		$ 85,000

Analysis of this computation shows that the allowable AMT deduction is $10,000 more than the allowable regular income tax deduction. Therefore, AMTI will be $10,000 less than taxable income. This is accomplished by entering a negative AMT adjustment of $10,000. ▼

As noted previously, timing differences eventually reverse. Therefore, total positive adjustments will be offset by total negative adjustments with respect to a particular item.

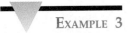

EXAMPLE 3

Refer to Examples 1 and 2. The difference in regular income tax and AMT treatments of circulation expenditures will result in AMT adjustments over a three-year period.

Year	Income Tax Deduction	AMT Deduction	AMT Adjustment
1995	$30,000	$10,000	+$20,000
1996	–0–	10,000	–10,000
1997	–0–	10,000	–10,000
Total	$30,000	$30,000	$ –0–

As the last column illustrates, if positive and negative AMT adjustments with respect to a particular item are caused by a timing difference, they will eventually net to zero. ▼

The adjustments for circulation expenditures and other items are discussed in detail under AMT Adjustments.

Although most adjustments relate to timing differences, there are exceptions. See the subsequent discussion of such items under Itemized Deductions. Adjustments that do not relate to timing differences result in a permanent difference between taxable income and AMTI.

Tax Preferences.   Some deductions and exclusions allowed to taxpayers for regular income tax purposes provide extraordinary tax savings. Congress has chosen to single out these items, which are referred to as tax preferences.[4] The AMT is designed to take back all or part of the tax benefits derived through the use of preferences in the computation of taxable income for regular income tax purposes. This is why taxable income, which is the starting point in computing AMTI, is increased by tax preference items. The effect of adding these preference items is to disallow for *AMT purposes* those preferences that were allowed in the

---

[4]§ 57.

▼ **FIGURE 14–2**
Alternative Minimum Tax
Formula

> Regular taxable income
> **Plus or minus:** Adjustments
> **Equals:** Taxable income after AMT adjustments
> **Plus:** Tax preferences
> **Equals:** Alternative minimum taxable income
> **Minus:** Exemption
> **Equals:** Alternative minimum tax base
> **Times:** 26% or 28% rate
> **Equals:** Tentative minimum tax before foreign tax credit
> **Minus:** Alternative minimum tax foreign tax credit
> **Equals:** Tentative minimum tax
> **Minus:** Regular tax liability*
> **Equals:** Alternative minimum tax (if amount is positive)

*This is the regular tax liability for the year reduced by any allowable foreign tax credit.

regular income tax computation. Tax preferences include the following items, which are discussed in detail under AMT Preferences:

- Percentage depletion in excess of the property's adjusted basis.
- Excess intangible drilling costs reduced by 65 percent of the net income from oil, gas, and geothermal properties.
- Interest on certain private activity bonds.
- Excess of accelerated over straight-line depreciation on real property placed in service before 1987.
- Excess of accelerated over straight-line depreciation on *leased* personal property placed in service before 1987.
- Excess of amortization allowance over depreciation on pre-1987 certified pollution control facilities.
- Fifty percent exclusion from gross income associated with gains on the sale of certain small business stock.

AMT FORMULA: OTHER COMPONENTS

To convert AMTI to AMT, other formula components including the exemption, rates, credit, and regular tax liability must be considered. The impact of each of these components is depicted in the AMT formula in Figure 14–2.

The relationship between the regular tax liability and the tentative AMT is key to the AMT formula. If the regular tax liability exceeds tentative AMT, then the AMT is zero. If the tentative AMT exceeds the regular tax liability, the amount of the excess is the AMT. In essence, the taxpayer will pay whichever tax liability is greater—that calculated using the regular income tax rules or that calculated using the AMT rules. However, both the tax law and Form 6251 adopt this excess approach with the taxpayer paying the regular tax liability plus any AMT.

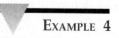

EXAMPLE 4

Anna, an unmarried individual, has regular taxable income of $100,000. She has positive adjustments of $40,000 and tax preferences of $25,000. Calculate her AMT for 1996.

Anna's regular tax liability is $26,136. Her AMT is calculated as follows:

Taxable income (TI)	$100,000
Plus: Adjustments	40,000
Equals: TI after AMT adjustments	$140,000
Plus: Tax preferences	25,000
Equals: AMTI	$165,000
Minus: AMT exemption ($33,750 – $13,125)	(20,625)*
Equals: AMT base	$144,375
Times: AMT rate	× 26%
Equals: Tentative AMT	$ 37,538
Minus: Regular tax liability	(26,136)
Equals: AMT	$ 11,402

*Discussed below under Exemption Amount.

Anna will pay the IRS a total of $37,538, consisting of her regular tax liability of $26,136 plus her AMT of $11,402. ▼

Exemption Amount. The exemption amount can be thought of as a materiality provision. As such, it enables a taxpayer with a small amount of positive adjustments and tax preferences to avoid being subject to the burden of the AMT.

The *initial* exemption amount is $45,000 for married taxpayers filing joint returns, $33,750 for single taxpayers, and $22,500 for married taxpayers filing separate returns.[5] However, the exemption is *phased out* at a rate of 25 cents on the dollar when AMTI exceeds these levels:

- $112,500 for single taxpayers.
- $150,000 for married taxpayers filing jointly.
- $75,000 for married taxpayers filing separately.

The phase-out of the exemption amount is an application of the wherewithal to pay concept. As a taxpayer's income level increases, so does his or her ability to pay income taxes.

The following example explains the calculation of the phase-out of the AMT exemption.

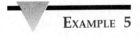

EXAMPLE 5   Hugh, who is single, has AMTI of $192,500 for the year. His $33,750 initial exemption amount is reduced by $20,000 [($192,500 – $112,500) × 25% phase-out rate]. Hugh's AMT exemption is $13,750 ($33,750 exemption – $20,000 reduction). ▼

The following table shows the beginning and end of the AMT exemption phase-out range for each filing status.

Status	Exemption	Phase-out Begins at	Ends at
Married, joint	$45,000	$150,000	$330,000
Single or head of household	33,750	112,500	247,500
Married, separate	22,500	75,000	165,000

---

[5] § 55(d).

AMT Rate Schedule.   A graduated, two-tier AMT rate schedule applies to noncorporate taxpayers. A 26 percent rate applies to the first $175,000 of the AMT base ($87,500 for married, filing separately), and a 28 percent rate applies to the AMT base in excess of $175,000 ($87,500 for married, filing separately).[6]

Regular Tax Liability.   The AMT is equal to the tentative minimum tax minus the *regular tax liability*. In most cases, the regular tax liability is equal to the amount of tax from the Tax Table or Tax Rate Schedules decreased by any foreign tax credit allowable for regular income tax purposes. Only the foreign tax credit is allowed as a reduction of the tentative minimum tax. Therefore, taxpayers who pay AMT lose the benefit of all other nonrefundable credits. Furthermore, the foreign tax credit cannot offset more than 90 percent of the tentative minimum tax.

In an AMT year, the taxpayer's total tax liability is equal to the tentative minimum tax (refer to Figure 14–2). The tentative minimum tax consists of two potential components: the regular tax liability and the AMT. The disallowance of credits does not affect a taxpayer's total liability in an AMT year. However, it does decrease the amount of the AMT and, as a consequence, reduces the minimum tax credit (discussed subsequently) available to be carried forward. Thus, for AMT purposes, the government denies all the credits (except the foreign tax credit) that apply in computing the regular income tax liability.

It is also possible that taxpayers who have adjustments and preferences but *do not pay* AMT will lose the benefit of some or all of their nonrefundable credits. This result occurs because a taxpayer may claim nonrefundable credits only to the extent that his or her regular tax liability exceeds the tentative minimum tax.[7]

EXAMPLE 6   Vern has total nonrefundable credits of $10,000, regular tax liability of $33,000, and tentative minimum tax of $25,000. He can claim only $8,000 of the nonrefundable credits in the current year. The disallowed $2,000 credit is lost unless a carryover provision applies. ▼

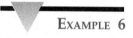

ETHICAL CONSIDERATIONS

Minimizing the Tax Liability

Billy, a single individual, projects his taxable income for 1996 to be approximately $300,000. He also has positive adjustments and tax preferences of $200,000. Billy anticipates taxable income for 1997 to be about the same with no adjustments or tax preferences for AMT purposes. He is evaluating several proposed transactions that would have the effect of reducing his 1996 tax liability.

One such transaction involves an office building for which he is currently negotiating a lease. The starting date for the lease will be July 1, 1996. The annual rent is going to be around $20,000 with an 18-month prepayment clause. Though Billy favors a five-year lease, a real estate agent has suggested that he lease the office building for an 18-month period with a 42-month renewal option. The real estate agent indicates that there are tax advantages (i.e., Billy can deduct the $30,000 of rent paid at the inception of the lease) as well as business reasons for structuring the transaction this way.

Billy takes the agent's advice and calculates his projected tax liability for 1996 with the 18-month lease with the renewal option and with the five-year lease. Based on his calculations, his regular income tax liability and AMT under each option would be as follows:

[6]§ 55(b)(1).   [7]§ 26(a).

	18-Month Lease	5-Year Lease
Regular income tax liability	$ 86,496	$ 94,416
AMT	41,604	39,284
Total	$128,100	$133,700

Is it appropriate for Billy to avoid taxes in this manner? Is is wise? Would you be willing to prepare and sign Billy's tax return showing the lease transaction as proposed by the real estate agent?

AMT ADJUSTMENTS

3 LEARNING OBJECTIVE
Identify the adjustments made in calculating the AMT.

Direction of Adjustments. It is necessary to determine not only the amount of an adjustment, but also whether the adjustment is positive or negative. Careful study of Example 3 reveals the following pattern with regard to *deductions:*

- If the deduction allowed for regular income tax purposes exceeds the deduction allowed for AMT purposes, the difference is a positive adjustment.
- If the deduction allowed for AMT purposes exceeds the deduction allowed for regular income tax purposes, the difference is a negative adjustment.

Conversely, the direction of an adjustment attributable to an *income* item can be determined as follows:

- If the income reported for regular income tax purposes exceeds the income reported for AMT purposes, the difference is a negative adjustment.
- If the income reported for AMT purposes exceeds the income reported for regular income tax purposes, the difference is a positive adjustment.

Circulation Expenditures. For regular income tax purposes, circulation expenditures, other than those the taxpayer elects to charge to a capital account, may be expensed in the year incurred.[8] These expenditures include expenses incurred to establish, maintain, or increase the circulation of a newspaper, magazine, or other periodical.

Circulation expenditures are not deductible in the year incurred for AMT purposes. In computing AMTI, these expenditures must be capitalized and amortized ratably over the three-year period beginning with the year in which the expenditures were made.[9]

The AMT adjustment for circulation expenditures is the amount expensed for regular income tax purposes minus the amount that can be amortized for AMT purposes. The adjustment can be either positive or negative (refer to Examples 1, 2, and 3). A taxpayer can avoid the AMT adjustments for circulation expenditures by electing to write off the expenditures over a three-year period for regular income tax purposes.[10]

Depreciation of Post-1986 Real Property. For real property placed in service after 1986 (MACRS property), AMT depreciation is computed under the

---

[8] § 173(a).
[9] § 56(b)(2)(A)(i).
[10] § 59(e)(2)(A).

alternative depreciation system (ADS), which uses the straight-line method over a 40-year life. The depreciation lives for regular tax purposes are 27.5 years for residential rental property and 39 years for all other real property.[11] The difference between AMT depreciation and regular income tax depreciation is treated as an adjustment in computing the AMT. The differences will be positive during the regular income tax life of the asset because the cost is written off over a shorter period for regular income tax purposes. For example, during the 27.5-year income tax life of residential real property, the regular income tax depreciation will exceed the AMT depreciation because AMT depreciation is computed over a 40-year period.

Table 7–7 is used to compute regular income tax depreciation on real property placed in service after 1986. For AMT purposes, depreciation on real property placed in service after 1986 is computed under the ADS (refer to Table 7–12).

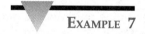

EXAMPLE 7

In January 1996, Sara placed in service a residential building that cost $100,000. Depreciation for 1996 for regular income tax purposes is $3,485 ($100,000 cost × 3.485% from Table 7–7). For AMT purposes, depreciation is $2,396 ($100,000 cost × 2.396% from Table 7–12). In computing AMTI for 1996, Sara has a positive adjustment of $1,089 ($3,485 regular income tax depreciation − $2,396 AMT depreciation). ▼

After real property has been held for the entire depreciation period for regular income tax purposes, the asset will be fully depreciated. However, the depreciation period under the ADS is 41 years due to application of the half-year convention, so depreciation will continue for AMT purposes. This causes negative adjustments after the property has been fully depreciated for regular income tax purposes.

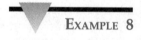

EXAMPLE 8

Assume the same facts as in the previous example, and compute the AMT adjustment for 2024 (the twenty-ninth year of the asset's life). Regular income tax depreciation is zero (refer to Table 7–7). AMT depreciation is $2,500 ($100,000 cost × 2.500% from Table 7–12). Therefore, Sara has a negative AMT adjustment of $2,500 ($0 regular income tax depreciation − $2,500 AMT depreciation). ▼

After real property is fully depreciated for both regular income tax and AMT purposes, the positive and negative adjustments that have been made for AMT purposes will net to zero.

Depreciation of Post-1986 Personal Property.   For most personal property placed in service after 1986 (MACRS property), the modified ACRS (MACRS) deduction for regular income tax purposes is based on the 200 percent declining-balance method with a switch to straight-line when that method produces a larger depreciation deduction for the asset. Refer to Table 7–2 for computing regular income tax depreciation.

For AMT purposes, the taxpayer must use the ADS. This method is based on the 150 percent declining-balance method with a similar switch to straight-line for all personal property.[12] Refer to Table 7–10 for percentages to be used in computing AMT depreciation.

All personal property placed in service after 1986 may be taken into consideration in computing one net adjustment. Using this netting process, the AMT

---

[11] The 39-year life generally applies to nonresidential real property placed in service on or after May 13, 1993.   [12] § 56(a)(1).

adjustment for a tax year is the difference between the total MACRS depreciation for all personal property computed for regular income tax purposes and the total ADS depreciation computed for AMT purposes. When the total of MACRS deductions exceeds the total of ADS deductions, the amount of the adjustment is positive. When the total of ADS deductions exceeds the total of MACRS deductions, the adjustment for AMTI is negative.

The MACRS deduction for personal property is larger than the ADS deduction in the early years of an asset's life. However, the ADS deduction is larger in the later years. This is so because ADS lives (based on class life) are longer than MACRS lives (based on recovery period).[13] Over the ADS life of the asset, the same amount of depreciation is deducted for both regular income tax and AMT purposes. In the same manner as other timing adjustments, the AMT adjustments for depreciation will net to zero over the ADS life of the asset.

The taxpayer may elect to use the ADS for regular income tax purposes. If this election is made, no AMT adjustment is required because the depreciation deduction is the same for regular income tax and for the AMT. The election eliminates the burden of maintaining two sets of tax depreciation records.

Pollution Control Facilities. For regular income tax purposes, the cost of certified pollution control facilities may be amortized over a period of 60 months. For AMT purposes, the cost of these facilities placed in service after 1986 must be depreciated under the ADS over the appropriate class life, determined as explained above for depreciation of post-1986 property.[14] The required adjustment for AMTI is equal to the difference between the amortization deduction allowed for regular income tax purposes and the depreciation deduction computed under the ADS. The adjustment may be positive or negative.

Expenditures Requiring 10-Year Write-off for AMT Purposes. Certain expenditures that may be deducted in the year incurred for regular income tax purposes must be written off over a 10-year period for AMT purposes. These rules apply to (1) mining exploration and development costs and (2) research and experimental expenditures.

In computing taxable income, taxpayers are allowed to deduct certain mining exploration and development expenditures. The deduction is allowed for expenditures paid or incurred during the taxable year for exploration (ascertaining the existence, location, extent, or quality of a deposit or mineral) and for development of a mine or other natural deposit, other than an oil or gas well.[15] Mining development expenditures are expenses paid or incurred after the existence of ores and minerals in commercially marketable quantities has been disclosed.

For AMT purposes, however, mining exploration and development costs must be capitalized and amortized ratably over a 10-year period.[16] The AMT adjustment for mining exploration and development costs that are expensed is equal to the amount expensed minus the allowable expense if the costs had been capitalized and amortized ratably over a 10-year period. This provision does not apply to costs relating to an oil or gas well.

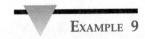

EXAMPLE 9

In 1996, Eve incurs $150,000 of mining exploration expenditures and deducts this amount for regular income tax purposes. For AMT purposes, these mining exploration expenditures

---

[13] Class lives and recovery periods are established for all assets in Rev.Proc. 87–56, 1987–2 C.B. 674.

[14] § 56(a)(5).

[15] §§ 617(a) and 616(a).

[16] § 56(a)(2).

must be amortized over a 10-year period. Eve must make a positive adjustment for AMTI of $135,000 ($150,000 allowed for regular income tax − $15,000 for AMT) for 1996, the first year. In each of the next nine years for AMT purposes, Eve is required to make a negative adjustment of $15,000 ($0 allowed for regular income tax − $15,000 for AMT). ▼

To avoid the AMT adjustments for mining exploration and development costs, a taxpayer may elect to write off the expenditures over a 10-year period for regular income tax purposes.[17]

Similar rules apply to computation of the adjustment for research and experimental expenditures.

Use of Completed Contract Method of Accounting.   For a long-term contract, taxpayers are required to use the percentage of completion method for AMT purposes.[18] However, in limited circumstances, taxpayers can use the completed contract method for regular income tax purposes.[19] Thus, a taxpayer recognizes a different amount of income for regular income tax purposes than for AMT purposes. The resulting AMT adjustment is equal to the difference between income reported under the percentage of completion method and the amount reported using the completed contract method. The adjustment can be either positive or negative, depending on the amount of income recognized under the different methods.

A taxpayer can avoid an AMT adjustment on long-term contracts by using the percentage of completion method for regular income tax purposes rather than the completed contract method.

Incentive Stock Options.   **Incentive stock options (ISOs)** are granted by employers to help attract new personnel and retain those already employed. At the time an ISO is granted, the employer corporation sets an option price for the corporate stock. If the value of the stock increases during the option period, the employee can obtain stock at a favorable price by exercising the option. Employees are generally restricted as to when they can dispose of stock acquired under an ISO (e.g., a certain length of employment may be required). Therefore, the stock may not be freely transferable until some specified period has passed.

The exercise of an ISO does not increase regular taxable income.[20] However, for AMT purposes, the excess of the fair market value of the stock over the exercise price is treated as an adjustment in the first taxable year in which the rights in the stock are freely transferable or are not subject to a substantial risk of forfeiture.[21]

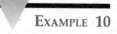

EXAMPLE 10

In 1994, Manuel exercised an ISO that had been granted by his employer, Gold Corporation. Manuel acquired 1,000 shares of Gold stock for the option price of $20 per share. The stock became freely transferable in 1996. The fair market value of the stock at the date of exercise was $50 per share. For AMT purposes, Manuel has a positive gain adjustment of $30,000 ($50,000 fair market value − $20,000 option price) for 1996. The transaction does not affect regular taxable income in 1994 or 1996. ▼

No adjustment is required if the taxpayer exercises the option and disposes of the stock in the same tax year because the bargain element gain is reported for both regular income tax and AMT purposes in that tax year.

---

[17] §§ 59(e)(2)(D) and (E).
[18] § 56(a)(3).
[19] See Chapter 15 for a detailed discussion of the completed contract and percentage of completion methods of accounting.

[20] § 421(a).
[21] § 56(b)(3).

The regular income tax basis of stock acquired through exercise of ISOs is different from the AMT basis. The regular income tax basis of the stock is equal to its cost, whereas the AMT basis is equal to the fair market value on the date the options are exercised. Consequently, the gain or loss upon disposition of the stock is different for regular income tax purposes and AMT purposes.

EXAMPLE 11

Assume the same facts as in the previous example and that Manuel sells the stock for $60,000 in 1998. His gain for regular income tax purposes is $40,000 ($60,000 amount realized – $20,000 regular income tax basis). For AMT purposes, the gain is $10,000 ($60,000 amount realized – $50,000 AMT basis). Therefore, Manuel has a $30,000 negative adjustment in computing AMT in 1998 ($40,000 regular income tax gain – $10,000 AMT gain). Note that the $30,000 negative adjustment upon disposition in 1998 offsets the $30,000 positive adjustment upon exercise of the ISO in 1996. ▼

Adjusted Gain or Loss.   When property is sold during the year or a casualty occurs to business or income-producing property, gain or loss reported for regular income tax may be different than gain or loss determined for the AMT. This difference occurs because the adjusted basis of the property for AMT purposes must reflect any current and prior AMT adjustments for the following:[22]

- Depreciation.
- Circulation expenditures.
- Research and experimental expenditures.
- Mining exploration and development costs.
- Amortization of certified pollution control facilities.

A negative gain or loss adjustment is required if:

- the gain for AMT purposes is less than the gain for regular income tax purposes;
- the loss for AMT purposes is more than the loss for regular income tax purposes; or
- a loss is computed for AMT purposes and a gain is computed for regular income tax purposes.

Otherwise, the AMT gain or loss adjustment is positive.

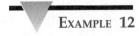

EXAMPLE 12

In January 1996, Kate paid $100,000 for a duplex acquired for rental purposes. Regular income tax depreciation in 1996 was $3,485 ($100,000 cost × 3.485% from Table 7–7). AMT depreciation was $2,396 ($100,000 cost × 2.396% from Table 7–12). For AMT purposes, Kate made a positive adjustment of $1,089 ($3,485 regular income tax depreciation – $2,396 AMT depreciation). ▼

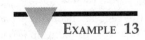

EXAMPLE 13

Kate sold the duplex on December 20, 1997, for $105,000. Regular income tax depreciation for 1997 is $3,485 [($100,000 cost × 3.636% from Table 7–7) × 11.5/12]. AMT depreciation for 1997 is $2,396 [($100,000 cost × 2.500% from Table 7–12) × 11.5/12]. Kate's positive AMT adjustment for 1997 is $1,089 ($3,485 regular income tax depreciation – $2,396 AMT depreciation). ▼

Because depreciation on the duplex differs for regular income tax and AMT purposes, the adjusted basis is different for regular income tax and AMT purposes. Consequently, the gain or loss on disposition of the duplex is different for regular income tax and AMT purposes.

---

[22] § 56(a)(7).

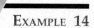

EXAMPLE 14

The adjusted basis of Kate's duplex for regular income tax purposes is $93,030 ($100,000 cost – $3,485 depreciation for 1996 – $3,485 depreciation for 1997). For AMT purposes, the adjusted basis is $95,208 ($100,000 cost – $2,396 depreciation for 1996 – $2,396 depreciation for 1997). The regular income tax gain is $11,970 ($105,000 amount realized – $93,030 regular income tax basis). The AMT gain is $9,792 ($105,000 amount realized – $95,208 AMT basis). Because the regular income tax and AMT gain on the sale of the duplex differ, Kate must make a negative AMT adjustment of $2,178 ($11,970 regular income tax gain – $9,792 AMT gain). Note that this negative adjustment offsets the $2,178 total of the two positive adjustments for depreciation ($1,089 in 1996 + $1,089 in 1997). ▼

Passive Activity Losses.   Losses on passive activities are not deductible in computing either the regular income tax or the AMT. This does not, however, eliminate the possibility of adjustments attributable to passive activities.

The rules for computing taxable income differ from the rules for computing AMTI. It follows, then, that the rules for computing a loss for regular income tax purposes differ from the AMT rules for computing a loss. Therefore, any *passive loss* computed for regular income tax purposes may differ from the passive loss computed for AMT purposes.[23]

EXAMPLE 15

Soong acquired two passive activities in 1996. He received net passive income of $10,000 from Activity A and had no AMT adjustments or preferences in connection with the activity. Activity B had gross income of $27,000 and operating expenses (not affected by AMT adjustments or preferences) of $19,000. Soong claimed MACRS depreciation of $20,000 for Activity B; depreciation under the ADS would have been $15,000. In addition, Soong deducted $10,000 of percentage depletion in excess of basis. The following comparison illustrates the differences in the computation of the passive loss for regular income tax and AMT purposes for Activity B.

	Regular Income Tax	**AMT**
Gross income	$ 27,000	$ 27,000
Deductions:		
Operating expenses	($ 19,000)	($ 19,000)
Depreciation	(20,000)	(15,000)
Depletion	(10,000)	–0–
Total deductions	($ 49,000)	($ 34,000)
Passive loss	($ 22,000)	($ 7,000)

Because the adjustment for depreciation ($5,000) applies and the preference for depletion ($10,000) is not taken into account in computing AMTI, the regular income tax passive activity loss of $22,000 for Activity B is reduced by these amounts, resulting in a passive activity loss of $7,000 for AMT purposes. ▼

For regular income tax purposes, Soong would offset the $10,000 of net passive income from Activity A with $10,000 of the passive loss from Activity B. For AMT purposes, he would offset the $10,000 of net passive income from Activity A with the $7,000 passive activity loss allowed from Activity B, resulting in passive activity income of $3,000. Thus, in computing AMTI, Soong makes a positive passive loss adjustment of $3,000 [$10,000 (passive activity loss allowed for regular

[23]See Chapter 10.

income tax) – $7,000 (passive activity loss allowed for the AMT)]. To avoid duplication, the AMT adjustment for depreciation and the preference for depletion are *not* reported separately. They are accounted for in determining the AMT passive loss adjustment.

EXAMPLE 16

Assume the same facts as in the previous example. For regular income tax purposes, Soong has a suspended passive loss of $12,000 [$22,000 (amount of loss) – $10,000 (used in 1996)]. This suspended passive loss can offset passive income in the future or can offset active or portfolio income when Soong disposes of the loss activity (refer to Chapter 10). For AMT purposes, Soong's suspended passive loss is $0 [$7,000 (amount of loss) – $7,000 (amount used in 1996)]. ▼

Alternative Tax Net Operating Loss Deduction.   In computing taxable income, taxpayers are allowed to deduct net operating loss (NOL) carryovers and carrybacks (refer to Chapter 6). The regular income tax NOL must be modified, however, in computing AMTI. The starting point in computing the **alternative tax NOL deduction (ATNOLD)** is the NOL computed for regular income tax purposes. The regular income tax NOL is then modified for AMT adjustments and tax preferences with the result being the ATNOLD. Thus, preferences and adjustment items that have benefited the taxpayer in computing the regular income tax NOL are added back, thereby reducing or eliminating the ATNOLD.[24]

EXAMPLE 17

In 1996, Adam incurred an NOL of $100,000. Adam had no AMT adjustments, but his deductions included tax preferences of $18,000. His ATNOLD carryback to 1993 is $82,000 ($100,000 regular income tax NOL – $18,000 tax preferences deducted in computing the NOL). ▼

In Example 17, if the adjustment was not made to the regular income tax NOL, the $18,000 in tax preference items deducted in 1996 would have the effect of reducing AMTI in the year (or years) the 1996 NOL is utilized. This would weaken the entire concept of the AMT.

A ceiling exists on the amount of the ATNOLD that can be deducted in the carryback or carryforward year. The deduction is limited to 90 percent of AMTI (before the ATNOLD) for the carryback or carryforward year.

EXAMPLE 18

Assume the same facts as in the previous example. Adam's AMTI (before the ATNOLD) in 1993 is $90,000. Therefore, of the $82,000 ATNOLD carried back to 1993 from 1996, only $81,000 ($90,000 × 90%) can be used in recalculating the 1993 AMT. The unused $1,000 of 1996 ATNOLD is now carried to 1994 for use in recalculating the 1994 AMT. ▼

A taxpayer who has an ATNOLD that is carried back or over to another year must use the ATNOLD against AMTI in the carryback or carryforward year even if the regular income tax, rather than the AMT, applies.

EXAMPLE 19

Matt's ATNOLD for 1997 (carried over from 1996) is $10,000. AMTI before considering the ATNOLD is $25,000. If Matt's regular income tax exceeds the AMT, the AMT does not apply. Nevertheless, Matt's ATNOLD of $10,000 is "used up" in 1997 and is not available for carryover to a later year. ▼

For regular income tax purposes, the NOL can be carried back 3 years and forward 15 years. However, the taxpayer may elect to forgo the 3-year carryback.

---

[24] § 56(a)(4).

TAX IN THE NEWS

AMT TURNS WINNING INTO LOSING

Certain itemized deductions are treated as AMT adjustments, which can produce unpleasant surprises in some cases. A taxpayer who was discharged (i.e., fired) by his employer filed a wrongful discharge suit against the employer. The taxpayer was successful and was awarded taxable back pay and benefits of $250,000. In winning the taxable part of the judgment, he incurred attorney's fees of $245,100.

In filing his Form 1040, the taxpayer included the $250,000 in gross income net of the $245,100 (i.e., included a net $4,900 in gross income). Thus, although he was required to pay $245,100 in attorney's fees, he did receive a tax benefit by reducing his gross income.

Unfortunately, the Tax Court agreed with the IRS that the attorney's fees are appropriately classified as miscellaneous itemized deductions (*Kenneth J. Alexander*, 69 TCM 1792, T.C.Memo. 1995–51). Classifying the attorney's fees in this manner resulted in a large AMT adjustment for miscellaneous itemized deductions, which in turn resulted in an AMT of $57,441.

These rules generally apply to the ATNOLD as well, except that the election to forgo the 3-year carryback is available for the ATNOLD only if the taxpayer elected it for the regular income tax NOL.

Itemized Deductions.   Most of the itemized deductions that are allowed for regular income tax purposes are allowed for AMT purposes. Itemized deductions that are allowed for AMT purposes include the following:

- Casualty losses.
- Gambling losses.
- Charitable contributions.
- Medical expenses in excess of 10 percent of AGI.
- Estate tax on income in respect of a decedent.
- Qualified interest.

Taxes (state, local, foreign income, and property taxes) and miscellaneous itemized deductions that are subject to the 2 percent-of-AGI floor are not allowed in computing AMT.[25] A positive AMT adjustment in the total amount of the regular income tax deduction for each is required.

If the taxpayer's gross income includes the recovery of any tax deducted as an itemized deduction for regular income tax purposes, a negative AMT adjustment in the amount of the recovery is allowed for AMTI purposes.[26] For example, state, local, and foreign income taxes can be deducted for regular income tax purposes, but cannot be deducted in computing AMTI. Because of this, any refund of such taxes from a prior year is not included in AMTI. Therefore, in calculating AMTI, the taxpayer must make a negative adjustment for an income tax refund that has been included in computing regular taxable income. Under the tax benefit rule, a tax refund is included in taxable income to the extent that the taxpayer obtained a tax benefit by deducting the tax in a prior year.

[25] § 56(b)(1)(A).   [26] § 56(b)(1)(D).

Cutback Adjustment. The 3 percent cutback adjustment that applies to regular income tax itemized deductions of certain high-income taxpayers (refer to Chapter 9) does not apply in computing AMT.[27] The effect of the 3 percent cutback adjustment is to disallow a portion of the taxpayer's itemized deductions for regular income tax purposes. Because this cutback adjustment does not apply for AMT purposes, taxable income, which is the starting point for computing AMTI, must be reduced by the amount of the disallowed deductions. Although this reduction has the same effect on AMTI as a negative adjustment, it is not shown on Form 6251 as such. Instead, it is shown on a separate line (line 18) as a subtraction from taxable income.

Medical Expenses. The rules for determining the AMT deductions for medical expenses are sufficiently complex to require further explanation. For regular income tax purposes, medical expenses are deductible to the extent they exceed 7.5 percent of AGI. However, for AMT purposes, medical expenses are deductible only to the extent they exceed 10 percent of AGI.[28]

EXAMPLE 20

Joann incurred medical expenses of $16,000 in 1996. She had AGI of $100,000 for the year. Her AMT adjustment for medical expenses is computed as follows:

	Regular Income Tax	AMT
Medical expenses incurred	$16,000	$ 16,000
Less reduction:		
$100,000 AGI × 7.5%	(7,500)	
$100,000 AGI × 10%		(10,000)
Medical expense deduction	$ 8,500	$ 6,000

Joann's AMT adjustment for medical expenses is $2,500 ($8,500 regular income tax deduction − $6,000 AMT deduction). ▼

Interest in General. The AMT itemized deduction allowed for interest expense includes only qualified housing interest and investment interest to the extent of net investment income that is included in the determination of AMTI.[29] Any interest that is deducted in calculating the regular income tax that is not permitted in calculating the AMT is treated as a positive adjustment.

In computing regular taxable income, taxpayers who itemize can deduct the following types of interest (refer to Chapter 9):

- Qualified residence interest.
- Investment interest, subject to the investment interest limitations (discussed under Investment Interest below).

Housing Interest. Under current regular income tax rules, taxpayers who itemize can deduct *qualified residence interest* on up to two residences. The deduction is limited to interest on acquisition indebtedness up to $1 million and home equity indebtedness up to $100,000. Acquisition indebtedness is debt that is incurred in acquiring, constructing, or substantially improving a qualified residence of the

---

[27] § 56(b)(1)(F).
[28] § 56(b)(1)(B).

[29] § 56(b)(1)(C).

taxpayer and is secured by the residence. Home equity indebtedness is indebtedness secured by a qualified residence of the taxpayer, but does not include acquisition indebtedness.

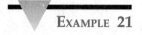

EXAMPLE 21

Gail, who used the proceeds of a mortgage to acquire a personal residence, paid mortgage interest of $112,000 in 1996. Of this amount, $14,000 is attributable to acquisition indebtedness in excess of $1 million. For regular income tax purposes, Gail may deduct mortgage interest of $98,000 ($112,000 total − $14,000 disallowed). ▼

The mortgage interest deduction for AMT purposes is limited to *qualified housing interest*, rather than *qualified residence interest*. Qualified housing interest includes only interest incurred to acquire, construct, or substantially improve the taxpayer's principal residence and such interest on one other qualified dwelling used for personal purposes. A home equity loan qualifies only if it meets the definition of qualified housing interest, which frequently is not the case. When additional mortgage interest is incurred (e.g., a mortgage refinancing), interest paid is deductible as qualified housing interest for AMT purposes only if:

- The proceeds are used to acquire or substantially improve a qualified residence.
- Interest on the prior loan was qualified housing interest.
- The amount of the loan was not increased.

A positive AMT adjustment is required in the amount of the difference between qualified *residence* interest allowed as an itemized deduction for regular income tax purposes and qualified *housing* interest allowed in the determination of AMTI.

Investment Interest.   Investment interest is deductible for regular income tax purposes and for AMT purposes to the extent of qualified net investment income.

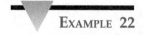

EXAMPLE 22

For the year, Dan had net investment income of $16,000 before deducting investment interest. He incurred investment interest expense of $30,000 during the year. His investment interest deduction is $16,000. ▼

Even though investment interest is deductible for both regular income tax and AMT purposes, an adjustment is required if the amount of investment interest deductible for regular income tax purposes differs from the amount deductible for AMT purposes. For example, an adjustment will arise if proceeds from a home equity loan are used to purchase investments. Interest on a home equity loan is deductible as qualified residence interest for regular income tax purposes, but is not deductible for AMT purposes unless the proceeds are used to acquire or substantially improve a qualified residence. For AMT purposes, however, interest on a home equity loan is deductible as investment interest expense if proceeds from the loan are used for investment purposes.

To determine the AMT adjustment for investment interest expense, it is necessary to compute the investment interest deduction for both regular income tax and AMT purposes. This computation is illustrated in the following example.

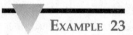

EXAMPLE 23

Tom had $20,000 interest income from corporate bonds and $5,000 dividends from preferred stock. He reported the following amounts of investment income for regular income tax and AMT purposes:

	Regular Income Tax	AMT
Corporate bond interest	$20,000	$20,000
Preferred stock dividends	5,000	5,000
Net investment income	$25,000	$25,000

Tom incurred investment interest expense of $10,000 related to the corporate bonds. He also incurred $4,000 interest on a home equity loan and used the proceeds of the loan to purchase preferred stock. For regular income tax purposes, this $4,000 is deductible as qualified residence interest. His *investment* interest expense for regular income tax and AMT purposes is computed below:

	Regular Income Tax	AMT
To carry corporate bonds	$10,000	$10,000
On home equity loan to carry preferred stock	–0–	4,000
Total investment interest expense	$10,000	$14,000

Investment interest expense is deductible to the extent of net investment income. Because the amount deductible for regular income tax purposes ($10,000) differs from the amount deductible for AMT purposes ($14,000), an AMT adjustment is required. The adjustment is computed as follows:

AMT deduction for investment interest expense	$14,000
Regular income tax deduction for investment interest expense	(10,000)
Negative AMT adjustment	$4,000

▼

As discussed subsequently under AMT Preferences, the interest on private activity bonds is a tax preference for AMT purposes. Such interest can also affect the calculation of the AMT investment interest deduction in that it is included in the calculation of net investment income.

Other Adjustments.   The standard deduction is not allowed as a deduction in computing AMTI.[30] Although a person who does not itemize is rarely subject to the AMT, it is possible. In such a case, the taxpayer is required to enter a positive adjustment for the standard deduction in computing the AMT.

The personal and dependency exemption amount deducted for regular income tax purposes is not allowed in computing AMT.[31] Therefore, taxpayers must enter a positive AMT adjustment for the personal and dependency exemption amount claimed in computing the regular income tax. A separate exemption (see Exemption Amount) is allowed for AMT purposes. To allow both the regular income tax exemption amount and the AMT exemption amount would result in extra benefits for taxpayers.

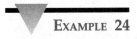

EXAMPLE 24   Eli, who is single, has no dependents and does not itemize deductions. He earned a salary of $106,550 in 1996. Based on this information, Eli's taxable income for 1996 is $100,000 ($106,550 – $4,000 standard deduction – $2,550 exemption). ▼

---

[30] § 56(b)(1)(E).   [31] § 56(b)(1)(E).

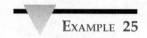

EXAMPLE 25

Assume the same facts as in Example 24. In addition, assume Eli's tax preferences for the year totaled $150,000. Eli's AMTI is $256,550 ($100,000 taxable income + $4,000 adjustment for standard deduction + $2,550 adjustment for exemption + $150,000 tax preferences). ▼

AMT PREFERENCES

4 LEARNING OBJECTIVE
Identify the tax preferences that are included in calculating the AMT.

Percentage Depletion.   Congress originally enacted the percentage depletion rules to provide taxpayers with incentives to invest in the development of specified natural resources. Percentage depletion is computed by multiplying a rate specified in the Code times the gross income from the property (refer to Chapter 7). The percentage rate is based on the type of mineral involved. The basis of the property is reduced by the amount of depletion taken until the basis reaches zero. However, once the basis of the property reaches zero, taxpayers are allowed to continue taking percentage depletion deductions. Thus, over the life of the property, depletion deductions may greatly exceed the cost of the property.

The percentage depletion preference is equal to the excess of the regular income tax deduction for percentage depletion over the adjusted basis of the property at the end of the taxable year.[32] Basis is determined without regard to the depletion deduction for the taxable year. This preference item is figured separately for each piece of property for which the taxpayer is claiming depletion.

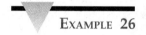

EXAMPLE 26

Kim owns a mineral property that qualifies for a 22% depletion rate. The basis of the property at the beginning of the year is $10,000. Gross income from the property for the year is $100,000. For regular income tax purposes, Kim's percentage depletion deduction (assume it is not limited by taxable income from the property) is $22,000. For AMT purposes, Kim has a tax preference of $12,000 ($22,000 − $10,000). ▼

Intangible Drilling Costs.   In computing the regular income tax, taxpayers are allowed to deduct certain intangible drilling and development costs in the year incurred, although such costs are normally capital in nature (refer to Chapter 7). The deduction is allowed for costs incurred in connection with oil and gas wells and geothermal wells.

For AMT purposes, excess intangible drilling costs (IDC) for the year are treated as a preference.[33] The preference for excess IDC is computed as follows:

IDC expensed in the year incurred

Minus: Deduction if IDC were capitalized and amortized over 10 years

Equals: Excess of IDC expense over amortization

Minus: 65% of net oil and gas and geothermal income

Equals: Tax preference item

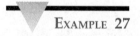

EXAMPLE 27

Ben, who incurred IDC of $50,000 during the year, elected to expense that amount. His net oil and gas income for the year was $60,000. Ben's tax preference for IDC is $6,000 [($50,000 IDC − $5,000 amortization) − (65% × $60,000 income)]. ▼

---

[32] § 57(a)(1). Note the preference label does not apply to percentage depletion on oil and gas wells for independent producers and royalty owners as defined in § 613A(c).

[33] § 57(a)(2).

A taxpayer can avoid the preference for IDC by electing to write off the expenditures over a 10-year period for regular income tax purposes.

Interest on Private Activity Bonds.   Income from private activity bonds is not included in taxable income, and expenses related to carrying such bonds are not deductible for regular income tax purposes. However, interest on private activity bonds is included as a preference in computing AMTI. Therefore, expenses incurred in carrying the bonds are offset against the interest income in computing the tax preference.[34]

The Code contains a lengthy, complex definition of private activity bonds.[35] In general, **private activity bonds** are bonds issued by states or municipalities with more than 10 percent of the proceeds being used for private business use. For example, a bond issued by a city whose proceeds are used to construct a factory that is leased to a private business at a favorable rate is a private activity bond.

ETHICAL CONSIDERATIONS

Taxability of Bond Interest: Regular Income Tax versus AMT

Jason, who is single and in the 31 percent tax bracket, recently inherited $1 million of bonds from his mother. Rather than changing investments, Jason decides to retain the investment in municipal bonds for the time being.

The Form 1099 he received from the municipality has confused Jason about the tax treatment of the bond interest. He thought that all municipal bonds were tax-exempt, but from an article that he read recently, he is now aware that certain such bonds are not tax-exempt for Federal income tax purposes. Rereading the article, Jason notes that bonds classified as private activity bonds are excludible from gross income for regular income tax purposes but are a tax preference for AMT purposes. Jason has asked the issuer for clarification on the status of the bonds, but has received no answer. He checks his mother's tax return for the past three years and finds that none of her returns included a Form 6251.

Since he wants to file his return this week, Jason has to decide how to report the bond interest. He knows that he is going to be subject to the AMT with some of his income being taxed at the 28 percent rate. He is considering resolving his dilemma by not treating the bonds as private activity bonds. His justification for his position is that his mother was an astute businesswoman and she did not report the bond interest on her tax returns as private activity bond interest. If Jason does not treat the bonds as private activity bonds, the bond interest will not be subject to either the regular income tax or the AMT. Evaluate Jason's proposal.

Depreciation.   For real property and leased personal property placed in service before 1987, there is an AMT preference for the excess of accelerated depreciation over straight-line depreciation.[36] However, examination of the cost recovery tables for pre-1987 real property (refer to Chapter 7) reveals that from the eighth year on, accelerated depreciation will not exceed straight-line depreciation. Consequently, taxpayers no longer have preferences attributable to pre-1987 real property.

[34] § 57(a)(5).
[35] § 141.

[36] § 57(a)(6).

Accelerated depreciation on pre-1987 leased personal property was computed using specified ACRS percentages (refer to Table 7–1, Chapter 7). AMT depreciation was based on the straight-line method, which was computed using the half-year convention, no salvage value, and a longer recovery period.[37] As a result, in the early years of the life of the asset, the cost recovery allowance used in computing the regular income tax was greater than the straight-line depreciation deduction allowed in computing AMT. The excess depreciation was treated as a tax preference item. For all leased personal property placed in service before 1987 (3-year, 5-year, and 10-year), except for 15-year public utility property, the cost recovery period has expired. Since there is no excess depreciation, there is no tax preference for AMT purposes.

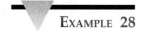

EXAMPLE 28

Paul acquired personal property on January 1, 1986, at a cost of $30,000. The property, which was placed in service as leased personal property on January 1, was 10-year ACRS property. Paul's 1986 depreciation deduction for regular income tax purposes was $2,400 ($30,000 cost × 8% rate from Table 7–1). For AMT purposes, the asset was depreciated over the AMT life of 15 years using the straight-line method with the half-year convention. Thus, AMT depreciation for 1986 was $1,000 [($30,000 ÷ 15) × ½ year convention]. Paul's tax preference for 1986 was $1,400 ($2,400 − $1,000). ACRS depreciation for 1996 is $0 ($30,000 × 0% ACRS rate), and straight-line depreciation is $2,000 ($30,000 ÷ 15). Thus, Paul's tax preference for 1996 is $0 since there is no excess depreciation. ▼

The preference item for excess depreciation on leased personal property is figured separately for each piece of property. No preference is reported in the year the taxpayer disposes of the property.

Fifty Percent Exclusion for Certain Small Business Stock.   Fifty percent of the gain on the sale of certain small business stock is excludible from gross

---

TAX IN THE NEWS

RECEIVING PREFERENTIAL TREATMENT AND AVOIDING THE AMT

Museums were among the leading beneficiaries of a change in the tax law that made it easier to give appreciated long-term capital gain property to charity. Since a law change enacted in August 1993, taxpayers who donate appreciated assets to qualified charities no longer have an AMT preference equal to the amount by which the assets' fair market value exceeds their adjusted basis. The repeal of the preference had an immediate impact. By December 1993, the Metropolitan Museum of Art in New York City had already received several valuable donations of art and expected to receive several more in the near future.

Among the donors to museums in the wake of the preference's repeal was the accounting firm of KPMG Peat Marwick, which donated its collection of American crafts to the Renwick Gallery of the National Museum of American Art at the Smithsonian Institution. Had the firm donated the collection before the repeal, the preference would have been passed through to the partners and appeared on their individual tax returns.

---

[37] The specified lives for AMT purposes are 5 years for 3-year property, 8 years for 5-year property, 15 years for 10-year property, and 22 years for 15-year property.

income for regular income tax purposes. The excluded amount is a tax preference for AMT purposes.[38]

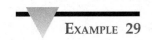

5   **LEARNING OBJECTIVE**
Apply the formula for computing the AMT and illustrate Form 6251.

ILLUSTRATION OF THE AMT COMPUTATION

The computation of the AMT is illustrated in the following example.

EXAMPLE 29

Hans Sims, who is single, had taxable income for 1996 as follows:

Salary		$ 92,000
Interest		8,000
Adjusted gross income		$100,000
Less itemized deductions:		
Medical expenses ($17,500 – 7.5% of $100,000 AGI)[a]	$10,000	
State income taxes	4,000	
Interest[b]		
Home mortgage (for qualified housing)	20,000*	
Investment interest	3,300*	
Contributions (cash)	5,000*	
Casualty losses ($14,000 – 10% of $100,000 AGI)	4,000*	(46,300)
		$ 53,700
Less exemption		(2,550)
Taxable income		$ 51,150

[a]Total medical expenses were $17,500, reduced by 7.5% of AGI, resulting in an itemized deduction of $10,000. However, for AMT purposes, the reduction is 10%, which leaves an AMT itemized deduction of $7,500 ($17,500 – 10% of $100,000 AGI). Therefore, an adjustment of $2,500 ($10,000 – $7,500) is required for medical expenses disallowed for AMT purposes.

[b]In this illustration, all interest is deductible in computing AMTI. Qualified housing interest is deductible. Investment interest ($3,300) is deductible to the extent of net investment income included in the minimum tax base. For this purpose, the $8,000 of interest income is treated as net investment income.

Deductions marked by an asterisk are allowed as *alternative minimum tax itemized deductions,* and AMT adjustments are required for the other itemized deductions. Thus, adjustments are required for state income taxes and for medical expenses to the extent the medical expenses deductible for regular income tax purposes are not deductible in computing AMT (see note a above). In addition to the items that affected taxable income, Hans had $35,000 interest on private activity bonds (an exclusion tax preference). AMTI is computed as follows:

Taxable income		$ 51,150
Plus: Adjustments		
State income taxes		4,000
Medical expenses (see note a above)		2,500
Personal exemption		2,550
Plus: Tax preference (interest on private activity bonds)		35,000
Equals: AMTI		$ 95,200
Minus: AMT exemption		(33,750)

[38]§ 57(a)(7).

Equals: Minimum tax base	$ 61,450
Times: AMT rate	× 26%
Equals: Tentative AMT	$ 15,977
Minus: Regular income tax on taxable income	(11,202)
Equals: AMT	$ 4,775

The solution to Example 29 is also presented on Form 6251. Though this example is for 1996, 1995 tax forms are used because the 1996 tax forms were not available at the time of this writing.

Note that the $2,550 personal exemption amount is a positive adjustment in the Example 29 solution, but does not appear as an adjustment in Form 6251. This difference occurs because line 16 of Form 6251 includes the amount from line 35 of Form 1040. Line 35 of Form 1040 is taxable income before the deduction for personal and dependency exemptions.

AMT CREDIT

6 LEARNING OBJECTIVE
Describe the role of the AMT credit in the alternative minimum tax structure.

As discussed previously, timing differences give rise to adjustments to the minimum tax base. In later years, the timing differences reverse, as was illustrated in several of the preceding examples. To provide equity for the taxpayer when timing differences reverse, the regular income tax liability may be reduced by a tax credit for prior years' minimum tax liability attributable to timing differences. The **alternative minimum tax credit** may be carried over indefinitely. Therefore, there is no need to keep track of when the minimum tax credit arose.[39]

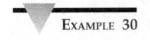
EXAMPLE 30

Assume the same facts as in Example 3. Also assume that in 1995, Bob paid AMT as a result of the $20,000 positive adjustment arising from the circulation expenditures. In 1996, $10,000 of the timing difference reverses, resulting in regular taxable income that is $10,000 greater than AMTI. Because Bob has already paid AMT as a result of the write-off of circulation expenditures, he is allowed an AMT credit in 1996. The AMT credit can offset Bob's regular income tax liability in 1996 to the extent that his regular income tax liability exceeds his tentative AMT. ▼

The AMT credit is applicable only for the AMT that results from timing differences. It is not available in connection with **AMT exclusions,** which represent permanent differences rather than timing differences between the regular income tax liability and the AMT. These AMT exclusions include the following:

• The standard deduction.
• Personal exemptions.
• Medical expenses, to the extent deductible for regular income tax purposes but not deductible in computing AMT.
• Other itemized deductions not allowable for AMT purposes, including miscellaneous itemized deductions, taxes, and interest expense.
• Excess percentage depletion.
• Tax-exempt interest on specified private activity bonds.

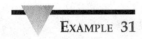
EXAMPLE 31

Don, who is single, has zero taxable income for 1996. He also has positive timing adjustments of $300,000 and AMT exclusions of $100,000. His AMT base is $400,000 because his AMT exemption is phased out completely due to the level of AMTI. Don's tentative AMT is $108,500 [($175,000 × 26% AMT rate) + ($225,000 × 28% AMT rate)]. ▼

[39] § 53.

▼
CONCEPT SUMMARY 14–1

AMT Adjustments and Preferences for Individuals

Adjustments	Positive	Negative	Both*
Circulation expenditures			X
Depreciation of post-1986 real property			X
Depreciation of post-1986 personal property			X
Pollution control facilities			X
Mining exploration and development costs			X
Research and experimental expenditures			X
Completed contract method			X
Incentive stock options	X**		
Adjusted gain or loss			X
Passive activity losses			X
Alternative tax NOLD			X
Itemized deductions:			
Medical expenses	X		
State income tax	X		
Property tax on realty	X		
Property tax on personalty	X		
Miscellaneous itemized deductions	X		
Tax benefit rule for state income tax refund		X	
Cutback adjustment		X	
Qualified residence interest that is not qualified housing interest	X		
Qualified residence interest that is AMT investment interest	X	X	
Private activity bond interest that is AMT investment interest		X	
Standard deduction	X		
Personal exemptions and dependency deductions	X		
Preferences			
Percentage depletion in excess of adjusted basis	X		
Intangible drilling costs	X		
Private activity bond interest income	X		
Depreciation on pre-1987 leased personal property	X		
§ 1202 exclusion for certain small business stock	X		

*Timing differences.
**While the adjustment is a positive adjustment, the AMT basis for the stock is increased by the amount of the positive adjustment.

Form **6251**	**Alternative Minimum Tax—Individuals**	OMB No. 1545-0227
Department of the Treasury Internal Revenue Service	▶ See separate instructions. ▶ Attach to Form 1040, Form 1040NR, or Form 1040-T.	**19**95 Attachment Sequence No. **32**

Name(s) shown on Form 1040   *Hans Sims*   Your social security number

Part I   **Adjustments and Preferences**

1 If you itemized deductions on Schedule A (Form 1040) (or you entered the amount from Form 1040-T, Section B, line t, on Form 1040-T, line 20), go to line 2. Otherwise, enter your standard deduction from Form 1040, line 34 (or Form 1040-T, line 20), and go to line 6 **1**

2 Medical and dental. Enter the smaller of Schedule A (Form 1040), line 4 **or** 2½% of Form 1040, line 32 (Form 1040-T filers, enter the smaller of Section B, line c **or** 2½% of Form 1040-T, line 16) **2** *2,500*

3 Taxes. Enter the amount from Schedule A (Form 1040), line 9 (or the total of lines d through g of Form 1040-T, Section B) **3** *4,000*

4 Certain interest on a home mortgage not used to buy, build, or improve your home **4**

5 Miscellaneous itemized deductions. Enter the amount from Schedule A (Form 1040), line 26 (or Form 1040-T, Section B, line r) **5**

6 Refund of taxes. Enter any tax refund from Form 1040, line 10 or line 21 (or Form 1040-T, line 4 or line 9) **6** ( )

7 Investment interest. Enter difference between regular tax and AMT deduction **7**

8 Post-1986 depreciation. Enter difference between regular tax and AMT depreciation **8**

9 Adjusted gain or loss. Enter difference between AMT and regular tax gain or loss **9**

10 Incentive stock options. Enter excess of AMT income over regular tax income **10**

11 Passive activities. Enter difference between AMT and regular tax income or loss **11**

12 Beneficiaries of estates and trusts. Enter the amount from Schedule K-1 (Form 1041), line 8 **12**

13 Tax-exempt interest from private activity bonds issued after 8/7/86 **13** *35,000*

14 Other. Enter the amount, if any, for each item and enter the total on line 14.
a Charitable contributions
b Circulation expenditures
c Depletion
d Depreciation (pre-1987)
e Installment sales
f Intangible drilling costs
g Long-term contracts
h Loss limitations
i Mining costs
j Patron's adjustment
k Pollution control facilities
l Research and experimental
m Tax shelter farm activities
n Related adjustments   **14** *0*

15 **Total Adjustments and Preferences.** Combine lines 1 through 14 ▶ **15** *41,500*

Part II   **Alternative Minimum Taxable Income**

16 Enter the amount from **Form 1040, line 35 (or Form 1040-T, line 21).** If less than zero, enter as a (loss). ▶ **16** *53,700*

17 Net operating loss deduction, if any, from Form 1040, line 21. Enter as a positive amount **17**

18 If Form 1040, line 32 (or Form 1040-T, line 16), is over $114,700 (over $57,350 if married filing separately), and you itemized deductions, enter the amount, if any, from line 9 of the worksheet for Schedule A (Form 1040), line 28 (or line 9 of the worksheet for Section B, line t, of Form 1040-T). **18** ( )

19 Combine lines 15 through 18 ▶ **19** *95,200*

20 Alternative tax net operating loss deduction. See page 5 of the instructions **20**

21 **Alternative Minimum Taxable Income.** Subtract line 20 from line 19. (If married filing separately and line 21 is more than $165,000, see page 5 of the instructions.) ▶ **21** *95,200*

Part III   **Exemption Amount and Alternative Minimum Tax**

22 **Exemption Amount.** (If this form is for a child under age 14, see page 6 of the instructions.)

If your filing status is:	And line 21 is not over:	Enter on line 22:		
Single or head of household	$112,500	$33,750		
Married filing jointly or qualifying widow(er)	150,000	45,000	**22**	*33,750*
Married filing separately	75,000	22,500		

If line 21 is **over** the amount shown above for your filing status, see page 6 of the instructions.

23 Subtract line 22 from line 21. If zero or less, enter -0- here and on lines 26 and 28 ▶ **23** *61,450*

24 If line 23 is $175,000 or less ($87,500 or less if married filing separately), multiply line 23 by 26% (.26). Otherwise, multiply line 23 by 28% (.28) and subtract $3,500 ($1,750 if married filing separately) from the result **24** *15,977*

25 Alternative minimum tax foreign tax credit. See page 6 of the instructions **25**

26 Tentative minimum tax. Subtract line 25 from line 24 ▶ **26** *15,977*

27 Enter your tax from Form 1040, line 38 (plus any amount from Form 4970 included on Form 1040, line 39), minus any foreign tax credit from Form 1040, line 43 (Form 1040-T filers, enter the amount from Form 1040-T, line 26) **27** *11,202*

28 **Alternative Minimum Tax.** (If this form is for a child under age 14, see page 7 of the instructions.) Subtract line 27 from line 26. If zero or less, enter -0-. Enter here and on Form 1040, line 48 (or Form 1040-T, line 31) ▶ **28** *4,775*

For Paperwork Reduction Act Notice, see separate instructions.   ✸   *Printed on recycled paper*   Cat. No. 13600G   Form **6251** (1995)

To determine the amount of AMT credit to carry over, the AMT must be recomputed reflecting only the AMT exclusions and the AMT exemption amount.

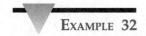

EXAMPLE 32

Assume the same facts as in the previous example. If there had been no positive timing adjustments for the year, Don's tentative AMT would have been $17,225 [($100,000 AMT exclusions – $33,750 exemption) × 26% AMT rate]. Don may carry over an AMT credit of $91,275 ($108,500 AMT – $17,225 related to AMT exclusions) to 1997 and subsequent years. ▼

CORPORATE ALTERNATIVE MINIMUM TAX

7 **LEARNING OBJECTIVE**
Understand the basic features of the corporate AMT.

The AMT applicable to corporations is similar to that applicable to noncorporate taxpayers. However, there are several important differences:

- The corporate AMT rate is 20 percent versus a top rate of 28 percent for noncorporate taxpayers.[40]
- The AMT exemption for corporations is $40,000 reduced by 25 percent of the amount by which AMTI exceeds $150,000.[41]
- Tax preferences applicable to noncorporate taxpayers are also applicable to corporate taxpayers, but some adjustments differ (see below).

Although there are computational differences, the corporate AMT and the noncorporate AMT have the identical objective: to force taxpayers who are more profitable than their taxable income reflects to pay additional tax. The formula for determining the corporate AMT appears in Figure 14–3.

AMT ADJUSTMENTS

Adjustments Applicable to Individuals and Corporations. The following adjustments that were discussed in connection with the individual AMT also apply to the corporate AMT:

▼ **FIGURE 14–3**
AMT Formula for Corporations

Taxable income
Plus: Income tax NOL deduction
Plus or minus: AMT adjustments
Plus: Tax preferences
Equals: AMTI before ATNOLD
Minus: ATNOLD (limited to 90% of AMTI before ATNOLD)
Equals: AMTI
Minus: Exemption
Equals: AMT base
Times: 20% rate
Equals: Tentative minimum tax before AMT foreign tax credit
Minus: AMT foreign tax credit (limited to 90% of AMT before AMT foreign tax credit)
Equals: Tentative minimum tax
Minus: Regular tax liability before credits minus regular foreign tax credit
Equals: AMT if positive

---

[40] § 55(b)(1)(B).

[41] §§ 55(d)(2) and (3).

WHO PAYS CORPORATE AMT?

During 1995, the question of whether the corporate AMT should be repealed was the subject of much debate. Among the issues discussed were the amount of revenue generated, the related compliance costs, and the number of corporations subject to the AMT.

According to a Government Accounting Office report, only about 30,000 of the 2.1 million corporations potentially subject to the AMT (i.e., less than 1.5 percent) paid any AMT for the period 1987–1992. Approximately 2,000 corporations paid 85 percent of the corporate AMT during that period.

Proponents of the corporate AMT claimed these statistics showed that the corporations that should be paying the AMT (i.e., large corporations) are doing so. Opponents claimed the same statistics supported their position that the compliance costs borne by the mass of corporations do not justify the continuation of this tax system. Truly, "beauty is in the eye of the beholder."

- Excess of MACRS over ADS depreciation on real and personal property placed in service after 1986.
- Pollution control facilities placed in service after 1986 (AMT requires ADS depreciation over the asset's ADR life; 60-month amortization is allowed for regular income tax purposes).
- Mining and exploration expenditures (AMT requires amortization over 10 years versus immediate expensing allowed for regular income tax purposes).
- Income on long-term contracts (AMT requires percentage of completion method; completed contract method is allowed in limited circumstances for regular income tax purposes).
- Dispositions of assets (if gain or loss for AMT purposes differs from gain or loss for regular income tax purposes).
- Allowable ATNOLD (which cannot exceed 90 percent of AMTI before deduction for ATNOLD).

Adjustments Applicable Only to Corporations.   Three AMT adjustments are applicable only to corporations:[42]

- The adjusted current earnings (ACE) adjustment.
- The Merchant Marine capital construction fund adjustment.
- The adjustment for special deductions allowed to Blue Cross/Blue Shield organizations.

The latter two adjustments apply to specific types of corporations and are not discussed in the chapter. On the other hand, the **ACE adjustment** generally applies to all corporations[43] and is expected to have a significant impact on both tax and financial accounting.

Corporations are subject to an AMT adjustment equal to 75 percent of the excess of ACE over AMTI before the ACE adjustment.[44] Historically, the govern-

---

[42] § 56(c).
[43] The ACE adjustment does not apply to S corporations. § 56(g)(6).
[44] § 56(g).

ment has not required conformity between tax accounting and financial accounting. For many years, the only *direct* conformity requirement was that a corporation that used the LIFO method for tax accounting also had to use LIFO for financial accounting.[45] Through the ACE adjustment, Congress is *indirectly* imposing a conformity requirement on corporations. While a corporation may still choose to use different methods for tax and financial accounting purposes, it may no longer be able to do so without incurring AMT as a result of the ACE adjustment. Thus, a corporation may incur AMT not only because of specifically targeted adjustments and preferences, but also as a result of any methods that cause ACE to exceed AMTI before the ACE adjustment.

The ACE adjustment can be either a positive or a negative amount. AMTI is increased by 75 percent of the excess of ACE over unadjusted AMTI. Or AMTI is reduced by 75 percent of the excess of unadjusted AMTI over ACE. The negative adjustment is limited to the aggregate of the positive adjustments under ACE for prior years, reduced by the previously claimed negative adjustments. See Concept Summary 14–2. Thus, the ordering of the timing differences is crucial because any lost negative adjustment is permanent. Unadjusted AMTI is AMTI without the ACE adjustment or the ATNOLD.[46]

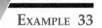

EXAMPLE 33

A calendar year corporation has the following data:

	1995	1996	1997
Pre-adjusted AMTI	$3,000	$3,000	$3,100
Adjusted current earnings	4,000	3,000	2,000

In 1995, because ACE exceeds unadjusted AMTI by $1,000, $750 (75% × $1,000) is included as a positive adjustment to AMTI. No adjustment is necessary for 1996. As unadjusted AMTI exceeds ACE by $1,100 in 1997, there is a potential negative adjustment to AMTI of $825 ($1,100 × 75%). Since the total increases to AMTI for prior years equal $750 and there are no previously claimed negative adjustments, only $750 of the potential negative adjustment reduces AMTI for 1997. Further, $75 of the negative amount is lost forever. ▼

ACE should not be confused with current earnings and profits. Although many items are treated in the same manner, certain variations exist. For example, Federal income taxes, deductible in computing earnings and profits, are not deductible in determining ACE.

The starting point for computing ACE is AMTI, which is defined as regular taxable income after AMT adjustments (other than the ATNOLD and ACE adjustments) and tax preferences. The resulting figure is adjusted for several items in order to arrive at ACE.

TAX PREFERENCES

AMTI includes designated tax preference items. In some cases, this has the effect of subjecting nontaxable income to the AMT. Tax preference items that apply to individuals also apply to corporations.

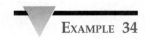

EXAMPLE 34

The following information applies to Brown Corporation (a calendar year taxpayer) for 1996:

---

[45] § 472(c).   [46] §§ 56(g)(1) and (2).

CONCEPT SUMMARY 14–2

Determining the ACE Adjustment*

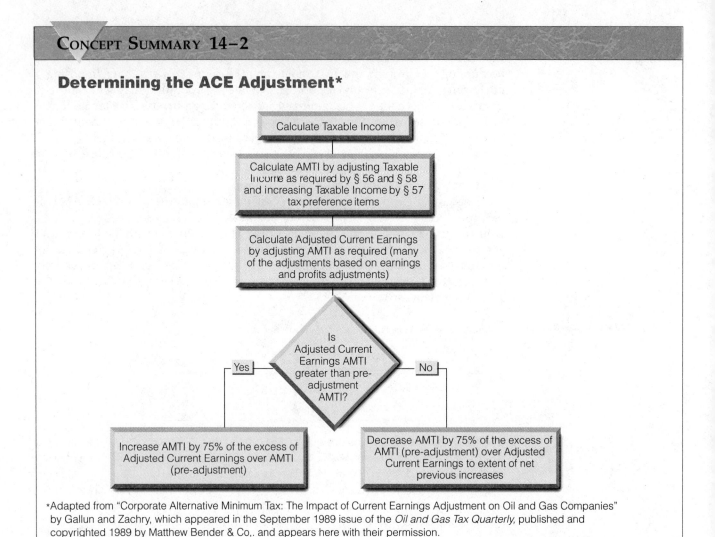

*Adapted from "Corporate Alternative Minimum Tax: The Impact of Current Earnings Adjustment on Oil and Gas Companies" by Gallun and Zachry, which appeared in the September 1989 issue of the *Oil and Gas Tax Quarterly,* published and copyrighted 1989 by Matthew Bender & Co,. and appears here with their permission.

Taxable income		$200,000
Mining exploration costs		50,000
Percentage depletion claimed (the property has a zero adjusted basis)		70,000
Interest on City of Elmira (Michigan) private activity bonds		30,000

Brown Corporation's AMTI for 1996 is determined as follows:

Taxable income		$200,000
Adjustments:		
Excess mining exploration costs [$50,000 (amount expensed) – $5,000 (amount allowed over a 10-year amortization period)]		45,000
Tax preferences:		
Excess depletion	$70,000	
Interest on private activity bonds	30,000	100,000
AMTI		$345,000

EXEMPTION

The tentative AMT is 20 percent of AMTI that exceeds the corporation's exemption amount. The exemption amount for a corporation is $40,000 reduced by 25 percent of the amount by which AMTI exceeds $150,000.

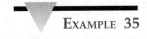

EXAMPLE 35

Blue Corporation has AMTI of $180,000. The exemption amount is reduced by $7,500 [25% × ($180,000 – $150,000)], and the amount remaining is $32,500 ($40,000 – $7,500). Thus, Blue Corporation's AMT base (refer to Figure 14–3) is $147,500 ($180,000 – $32,500). ▼

Note that the exemption phases out entirely when AMTI reaches $310,000.

OTHER ASPECTS OF THE AMT

Foreign tax credits can be applied against only 90 percent of tentative AMT liability. The 90 percent limit does not apply to certain corporations meeting specified requirements.

All of a corporation's AMT is available for carryover as a minimum tax credit. This is so regardless of whether the adjustments and preferences originate from timing differences or AMT exclusions.

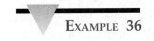

EXAMPLE 36

In Example 34, the AMTI exceeds $310,000, so no exemption is allowed. The tentative minimum tax is $69,000 (20% of $345,000). The regular income tax liability is $61,250, and the AMT liability is $7,750 ($69,000 – $61,250). The amount of the minimum tax credit carryover is $7,750, which is all of the current year's AMT. ▼

TAX PLANNING
CONSIDERATIONS

8 LEARNING OBJECTIVE
Identify tax planning
opportunities to minimize the
AMT.

RESPONDING TO BOB AND CAROL

The chapter began with a set of circumstances involving Bob and Carol that raised a number of interesting questions. By now, the student should have arrived at a logical reason for the difference in Bob and Carol's tax liabilities and expect the following to happen to Bob.

Bob contacts Adam, his tax return preparer, and explains in an excited voice that he has received a bill from the IRS for $15,000 plus interest associated with the underpayment of his tax liability. Adam has Bob fax him a copy of the IRS deficiency notice. He checks Bob's tax file and then calls Bob to explain that Bob does owe the IRS the $15,000 plus interest. Somehow Bob's tax return was prepared without including a Form 6251 (the alternative minimum tax). Adam suggests that Bob stop by his office later that afternoon to discuss the disposition of the matter further.

AVOIDING PREFERENCES AND ADJUSTMENTS

Several strategies and elections are available to help taxpayers avoid having preferences and adjustments.

- A taxpayer who is in danger of incurring AMT liability should not invest in tax-exempt private activity bonds unless doing so makes good investment sense. Any AMT triggered by interest on private activity bonds reduces the yield on an investment in the bonds. Other tax-exempt bonds or taxable corporate bonds might yield a better after-tax return.
- A taxpayer may elect to expense certain costs in the year incurred or to capitalize and amortize the costs over some specified period. The decision should be based on the present discounted value of after-tax cash flows

under the available alternatives. Costs subject to elective treatment include circulation expenditures, mining exploration and development costs, and research and experimental expenditures.

CONTROLLING THE TIMING OF PREFERENCES AND ADJUSTMENTS

The AMT exemption often keeps items of tax preference from being subject to the AMT. To use the AMT exemption effectively, taxpayers should avoid bunching preferences and positive adjustments in any one year. To avoid this bunching, taxpayers should attempt to control the timing of such items when possible.

TAKING ADVANTAGE OF THE AMT/REGULAR TAX RATE DIFFERENTIAL

A taxpayer who cannot avoid triggering the AMT in a given year can usually save taxes by taking advantage of the rate differential between the AMT and the regular income tax.

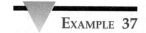

EXAMPLE 37

Peter, a real estate dealer who expects to be in the 31% tax bracket in 1997, is subject to the AMT in 1996. He is considering the sale of a parcel of land (inventory) at a gain of $100,000. If he sells the land in 1997, he will have to pay tax of $31,000 ($100,000 gain × regular income tax rate). However, if he sells the land in 1996, he will pay tax of $26,000 ($100,000 gain × 26% AMT rate). Thus, accelerating the sale into 1996 will save Peter $5,000 in tax. ▼

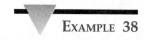

EXAMPLE 38

Cora, who expects to be in the 39.6% tax bracket in 1997, is subject to the AMT in 1996. She is going to contribute $10,000 in cash to her alma mater, State University. If Cora makes the contribution in 1997, she will save tax of $3,960 ($10,000 contribution × 39.6% regular income tax rate). However, if she makes the contribution in 1996, she will save tax of $2,600 ($10,000 contribution × 26% AMT rate). Thus, deferring the contribution until 1997 will save Cora $1,360 in tax. ▼

This deferral/acceleration strategy should be considered for any income or expenses where the taxpayer can control the timing. This strategy applies to corporations as well as to individuals.

KEY TERMS

ACE adjustment,
14–28

Alternative minimum
tax (AMT),   14–2

Alternative minimum
tax credit,   14–24

Alternative tax NOL
deduction (ATNOLD),
14–15

AMT adjustments,
14–4

AMT exclusions,
14–24

Circulation
expenditures,   14–4

Incentive stock
options (ISOs),
14–12

Private activity bonds,
14–21

Tax preferences,
14–4

PROBLEM
MATERIALS

DISCUSSION QUESTIONS

1. Since there is a regular income tax, why is there a need for an AMT?

2. How can the AMT be calculated without using taxable income from the regular income tax as the starting point?

3. What is the difference between AMT adjustments and tax preferences?

4. Identify which of the following are tax preferences:
   a. Fifty percent exclusion associated with gains on the sale of certain small business stock.
   b. Exclusion on the receipt of property by gift.
   c. Exclusion associated with payment of premiums by the employer on group term life insurance for coverage not in excess of $50,000.
   d. Percentage depletion in excess of the property's adjusted basis.
   e. Tax-exempt interest on certain private activity bonds.

5. Identify which of the following are tax preferences:
   a. Exclusion on the receipt of property by inheritance.
   b. Exclusion to employee on the employer's contribution to the employee's pension plan.
   c. Excess of deduction for circulation expenditures for regular income tax purposes over the deduction for AMT purposes.
   d. Excess of amortization allowance over depreciation on pre-1987 certified pollution control facilities.
   e. Excess of accelerated over straight-line depreciation on real property placed in service before 1987.

6. Describe the tax formula for the AMT.

7. Discuss the relationship between the regular income tax liability and the AMT.

8. For the exemption amount, indicate the following:
   a. Purpose for the exemption.
   b. Amount of the exemption.
   c. Reason for the phase-out of the exemption.

9. What are the AMT rates for an individual taxpayer? To what levels of income do the rates apply?

10. How do nonrefundable tax credits affect the calculation of the AMT?

11. Tom, who owns and operates a sole proprietorship, acquired machinery and placed it in service in February 1996. If Tom has to pay AMT in 1996, will he be required to make an AMT adjustment for depreciation on the machinery? Explain.

12. How can an individual taxpayer avoid having an AMT adjustment for mining exploration and development costs?

13. Rick, who is single, incurs mining exploration and development costs associated with his energy company. He would expense the costs in the current year in order to reduce his regular income tax, but is aware that this would create a positive adjustment for AMT purposes. His AGI is large enough to reduce the AMT exemption amount to zero. Therefore, he is considering electing to amortize the mining exploration and development costs over 10 years to avoid having to pay any AMT. Advise Rick.

14. Certain taxpayers have the option of using either the percentage of completion method or the completed contract method for reporting profit on long-term contracts. What impact could the AMT have on this decision?

15. Megan, a corporate executive, plans to exercise an incentive stock option granted by her employer to purchase 100 shares of the corporation's stock for an option price of $20 per share. The stock is currently selling for $65 per share.

    a. Explain the possible consequences of this action on Megan's regular income tax and AMT.

    b. Would your response differ if Megan exercises the option and disposes of the stock in the same tax year?

16. Desiree purchased a building several years ago for $100,000. She sells the building in the current tax year. Explain why her recognized gain or loss for regular income tax purposes is different from her recognized gain or loss for AMT purposes.

17. Carol is going to be subject to the AMT. She owns investment land and is considering disposing of it before the end of 1996 and investing in other realty. Based on an appraisal of the land's value, the realized gain would be $20,000. Ed has offered to purchase the land from Carol, and Abby has offered to trade her other realty that would qualify for § 1031 like-kind exchange treatment. The land has a $25,000 greater AMT adjusted basis. What are the relevant tax issues that Carol faces in making her decision?

18. Passive activity losses are not deductible in computing either taxable income or AMTI. Explain why an adjustment for passive activity losses may be required for AMT purposes.

19. What effects do adjustments and preferences have on the calculation of the ATNOLD?

20. The following itemized deductions are allowed for regular income tax purposes: medical expenses, state and local income taxes, real estate taxes, personal property taxes, home mortgage interest, investment interest, charitable contributions of cash, charitable contributions of long-term capital gain property, casualty losses, unreimbursed employee business expenses, and gambling losses. Which of these itemized deductions can result in an AMT adjustment?

21. Matt, who is single, has always elected to itemize deductions rather than take the standard deduction. In prior years, his itemized deductions always exceeded the standard deduction by a substantial amount. As a result of paying off the mortgage on his residence, he projects that his itemized deductions for 1996 will exceed the standard deduction by only $500. Matt anticipates that the amount of his itemized deductions will remain about the same in the foreseeable future. Matt's AGI is $150,000. He is investing the amount of his former mortgage payment each month in tax-exempt bonds. A friend recommends that Matt buy a beach house in order to increase his itemized deductions. What are the relevant tax issues for Matt?

22. In computing the alternative tax itemized deduction for interest, it is possible that some interest allowed as an itemized deduction for regular income tax purposes will not be allowed. Explain.

23. Could computation of the AMT ever require adjustments for the standard deduction or personal and dependency exemptions? Explain.

24. Alvin owns a mineral deposit that qualifies for the 15% percentage depletion rate. Under what circumstances will the depletion deduction for regular income tax purposes and AMT purposes not be the same?

25. During the year, Fran earned $18,000 interest on private activity bonds and incurred interest expense of $7,000 in connection with the bonds. How will this affect Fran's taxable income? AMT?

26. What is the purpose of the AMT credit? Briefly describe how the credit is computed.

27. Discuss the similarities and differences between the individual AMT and the corporate AMT.

28. Some observers believe the ACE adjustment will cause corporations to change some of the methods they use for financial accounting and tax accounting purposes. Comment.

29. Is it ever advisable for a taxpayer to accelerate income into an AMT year? Explain and give an example of how this acceleration might be accomplished.

30. Is it ever advisable for a taxpayer to defer deductions from an AMT year into a non-AMT year where the regular income tax applies? Explain and give an example of how such a deferral might be accomplished.

PROBLEMS

31. Use the following data to calculate Rachel's AMT base:

Taxable income	$200,000
Positive AMT adjustments	40,000
Negative AMT adjustments	30,000
AMT preferences	15,000

Rachel is not married.

32. Arthur East, an unmarried individual who is age 66, has taxable income of $100,000. He has AMT positive adjustments of $60,000 and tax preferences of $40,000.
    a. What is Arthur's AMT?
    b. What is the total amount of Arthur's tax liability?
    c. Draft a letter to Arthur explaining why he must pay more than the regular income tax liability. Arthur's address is 100 Colonel's Way, Conway, SC 29526.

33. Calculate the AMT for the following cases. The taxpayer has regular taxable income of $500,000 and does not have any credits.

	Tentative AMT	
Filing Status	**Case 1**	**Case 2**
Single	$190,000	$175,000
Married, filing jointly	190,000	175,000

34. Calculate the exemption amount for the following cases for a single taxpayer, a married taxpayer filing jointly, and a married taxpayer filing separately.

Case	AMTI
1	$100,000
2	200,000
3	400,000

35. Leona has nonrefundable credits of $25,000 for 1996. Her regular income tax liability before credits is $35,000, and her tentative AMT is $15,000.
    a. What is the amount of Leona's AMT?
    b. What is the amount of Leona's regular income tax liability after credits?

36. Angela, who is single, incurs circulation expenditures of $123,000 during 1996. She is in the process of deciding whether to expense the $123,000 or to capitalize it and elect to deduct it over a three-year period. Angela already knows that she will be subject to the AMT for 1996 at the 28% rate. Angela is in the 31% bracket for regular income tax purposes this year and expects to remain in that bracket in the future. Advise Angela on whether she should elect the three-year write-off rather than expensing the $123,000 in 1996.

37. Vito owns and operates a news agency (as a sole proprietorship). During 1996, he incurred expenses of $60,000 to increase circulation of newspapers and magazines that his agency distributes. For regular income tax purposes, he elected to expense the $60,000 in 1996. In addition, he incurred $30,000 in circulation expenditures in 1997 and again elected expense treatment. What AMT adjustments will be required in 1996 and 1997 as a result of the circulation expenditures?

38. Lance is a landlord who owns two apartment buildings. He acquired Longwood Acres on February 21, 1986, for $300,000, with $60,000 of the cost allocated to the land. He acquired Colony Square on April 5, 1992, for $800,000, and $200,000 of the cost was allocated to land. Neither apartment complex is low-income housing. Lance elected to write off the cost of each building as fast as possible. What is the effect of depreciation (cost recovery) on Lance's AMTI for 1996?

39. In March 1996, Helen Carlon acquired equipment for her business at a cost of $140,000. The equipment is 5-year class property for regular income tax purposes and 9.5-year class property for AMT purposes.
    a. If Helen depreciates the equipment using the method that will produce the greatest deduction for 1996, what is the amount of the AMT adjustment?
    b. How can Helen reduce the AMT adjustment to $0? What circumstances would motivate her to do so?
    c. Draft a letter to Helen regarding the choice of depreciation methods. Helen's address is 500 Monticello Avenue, Glendale, AZ 85306.

40. In 1996, Gary incurred $180,000 of mining and exploration expenditures. He elects to deduct the expenditures as quickly as the tax law allows for regular income tax purposes.
    a. How will Gary's treatment of mining and exploration expenditures affect his regular income tax and AMT computations for 1996?
    b. How can Gary avoid having AMT adjustments related to the mining and exploration expenditures?
    c. What factors should Gary consider in deciding whether to deduct the expenditures in the year incurred?

41. Rust Company is a real estate construction company with average annual gross receipts of $3 million. Rust uses the completed contract method on a contract that requires 18 months to complete. The contract is for $500,000 with estimated costs of $300,000. At the end of 1996, $180,000 of costs have been incurred. The contract is completed in 1997 with the total costs being $295,000. Determine the amount of adjustments for AMT purposes for 1996 and 1997.

42. In 1994, Diego exercised an incentive stock option, acquiring 1,000 shares of stock at an option price of $65 per share. The fair market value of the stock at the date of exercise was $92 per share. In 1996, the rights in the stock become freely transferable and are not subject to a substantial risk of forfeiture. Diego sells the 1,000 shares of stock in 1997 for $100 per share. How do these transactions affect Diego's AMTI in 1994, 1996 and 1997?

43. In 1996, Lori exercised an incentive stock option that had been granted by her employer, Black Corporation. Lori acquired 100 shares of Black stock for the option price of $175 per share. The rights in the stock become freely transferable and not subject to a substantial risk of forfeiture in 1996. The fair market value of the stock at the date of exercise was $210 per share. Lori sells the stock for $320 per share in 1996. What is the amount of her AMT adjustment in 1996, and what is her recognized gain on the sale for regular income tax purposes and AMT purposes?

44. Bobby sells an apartment building for $400,000. His adjusted basis is $250,000 for regular income tax purposes and $312,000 for AMT purposes.
    a. Calculate Bobby's gain for regular income tax purposes.
    b. Calculate Bobby's gain for AMT purposes.
    c. Calculate Bobby's AMT adjustment, if any.

45. Freda acquired a passive activity in 1996. Gross income from operations of the activity was $150,000. Operating expenses, not including depreciation, were $135,000. Regular income tax depreciation of $37,500 was computed under MACRS. AMT depreciation, computed under ADS, was $24,000. Compute Freda's passive loss deduction and passive loss suspended for regular income tax purposes and for AMT purposes.

46. Wolfgang had the following itemized deductions for 1996:

Medical expenses [$5,000 – (7.5% × $50,000)]	$ 1,250
State income taxes	3,000
Charitable contributions	5,000
Home mortgage interest on his personal residence	6,000
Casualty loss	1,500
Miscellaneous itemized deductions [$3,500 – 2%($50,000)]	2,500
	$19,250

a. Calculate Wolfgang's itemized deductions for AMT purposes.

b. What is the amount of the AMT adjustment?

47. Tom, who is single, owns a personal residence in the city. He also owns a cabin near a ski resort in the mountains. He uses the cabin as a vacation home. In February 1996, he borrowed $60,000 on a home equity loan and used the proceeds to pay off credit card obligations and other debt. During 1996, he paid the following amounts of interest:

On his personal residence	$12,000
On the cabin	4,800
On the home equity loan	5,000
On credit card obligations	1,200

What amount, if any, must Tom recognize as an AMT adjustment in 1996?

48. Walter and Edith, who are married with two dependents, had AGI of $110,000 in 1996. Their AGI included net investment income of $10,000 and gambling income of $2,500. They incurred the following expenses during the year, all of which resulted in itemized deductions for income tax purposes:

Medical expenses (before 7.5%-of-AGI floor)	$9,500
State income taxes	2,800
Personal property tax	900
Real estate tax	9,100
Interest on personal residence	8,600
Interest on home equity loan (proceeds were used to buy a new fishing boat)	1,800
Investment interest expense	2,600
Charitable contribution (cash)	4,200
Unreimbursed employee expenses (before 2%-of-AGI floor)	3,800

What is the amount of Walter and Edith's AMT adjustment for itemized deductions in 1996, and is it positive or negative?

49. Assume the same facts as in the preceding problem and that Walter and Edith also earned interest of $5,000 on private activity bonds. They borrowed the money to buy these bonds and paid interest of $3,900 on the loan. Determine the effect on AMTI.

50. During the current year, Yoon earned $10,000 in dividends on corporate stock and incurred $13,000 of investment interest expense related to his stock holdings. Yoon also earned $5,000 interest on private activity bonds during the year and incurred interest expense of $3,500 in connection with the bonds. How much investment interest expense can Yoon deduct for regular income tax and AMT purposes for the year?

51. Bill, who is single with no dependents, had AGI of $100,000 in 1996. His AGI included net investment income of $15,000 and gambling income of $1,100. Bill incurred the following expenses during the year, all of which resulted in itemized deductions for income tax purposes:

Medical expenses (before 7.5%-of-AGI floor)	$11,000
State income taxes	3,200
Personal property tax	2,000
Real estate tax	8,400
Interest on personal residence	12,200
Interest on vacation home (never rented to others)	3,800
Interest on home equity loan (proceeds were used to buy a new automobile)	2,700
Investment interest expense	3,300

Charitable contribution	5,000
Casualty loss (after $100 floor, before 10%-of-AGI floor)	13,000
Unreimbursed employee expenses (before 2%-of-AGI floor)	2,400
Gambling losses	900

What is the amount of Bill's AMT adjustment for itemized deductions in 1996, and is it positive or negative?

52. Peggy, who is single and has no dependents, had taxable income of $102,000 and tax preferences of $72,500 in 1996. She did not itemize deductions for regular income tax purposes. Compute Peggy's AMT exemption and AMTI for 1996.

53. Carl, who is single, has no dependents and does not itemize deductions. He had a personal exemption of $2,550 and taxable income of $82,000 in 1996. His tax preferences totaled $118,000. What is Carl's AMTI for 1996?

54. Emily owns a coal mine that had a basis of $12,000 at the beginning of the year. The property qualifies for a 15% depletion rate. Gross income from the property was $140,000, and net income before the percentage depletion deduction was $60,000. What is Emily's tax preference for excess depletion?

55. Rita incurred and expensed intangible drilling costs (IDC) of $70,000. Her net oil and gas income was $60,000. What is the amount of Rita's tax preference item for IDC?

56. Pat, who is single and has no dependents, had a salary of $90,000 in 1996. She had interest and dividend income of $6,000, gambling income of $4,000, and $40,000 interest income from private activity bonds. Pat presents the following additional information:

Medical expenses (before 7.5%-of-AGI floor)	$12,000
State income taxes	4,100
Real estate taxes	2,800
Mortgage interest on residence	3,100
Investment interest expense	1,800
Gambling losses	5,100

Compute Pat's tentative minimum tax for 1996 (rounded to the nearest dollar).

57. Jack, who is single with no dependents and does not itemize, provides you with the following information for 1996:

Short-term capital loss	$ 5,000
Long-term capital gain	25,000
Municipal bond interest received on private activity bonds acquired in 1990	9,000
Dividends from General Motors	1,500
Excess of FMV over cost of incentive stock options (the rights became freely transferable and not subject to a substantial risk of forfeiture in 1996)	35,000

What is the total amount of Jack's tax preference items and AMT adjustments for 1996?

58. Rosa, who is single, had taxable income of $100,000 for 1996. She had positive AMT adjustments of $50,000, negative AMT adjustments of $15,000, and tax preference items of $57,500.
a. Compute her AMTI.
b. Compute Rosa's tentative minimum tax.

59. Tara, who is single, has no dependents and does not itemize. She has the following items relative to her tax return for 1996:

| Bargain element from the exercise of an incentive stock option (no restrictions apply to the stock) | $45,000 |
| Accelerated depreciation on leased equipment acquired before 1987 (straight-line depreciation would have yielded $26,000) | 41,000 |

Percentage depletion in excess of property's adjusted basis	50,000
Taxable income for regular income tax purposes	121,000

a. Determine Tara's AMT adjustments and preferences for 1996.
b. Calculate the AMT (if any) for 1996.

60. Beth, who is single, has the following items for 1996:

Income

Salary	$105,000
Interest from bank	12,000
Interest on corporate bonds	7,000
Dividends	6,000
Short-term capital gain	8,000

Expenses

Unreimbursed employee business expenses (no meals or entertainment)	4,000
Total medical expenses	24,000
State income taxes	6,500
Real property taxes	6,800
Home mortgage (qualified housing) interest	7,200

Casualty loss on vacation home

Decline in value	20,000
Adjusted basis	70,000
Insurance proceeds	12,000
Tax preferences	116,000

Compute Beth's tax liability for 1996 before credits or prepayments.

61. Lynn is single and has no dependents. Based on the financial information presented below, compute Lynn's AMT for 1996.

Income:

Salary	$33,000
Taxable interest on corporate bonds	1,800
Dividend income	1,900
Business income	64,000

Expenditures:

Medical expenses	12,000
State income taxes	6,000
Real estate taxes	8,500
Mortgage (qualified housing) interest	9,200
Investment interest	5,500
Cash contributions to various charities	2,900

Additional information:
a. The $64,000 business income is from Acme Office Supplies Company, a sole proprietorship Lynn owns and operates. Acme claimed MACRS depreciation of $3,175 on real property used in the business. ADS depreciation on the property would have been $2,500.
b. Lynn received interest of $30,000 on City of Columbus private activity bonds.

62. Bonnie, who is single, had taxable income of $0 in 1996. She has positive timing adjustments of $200,000 and AMT exclusion items of $100,000 for the year. What is the amount of Bonnie's AMT credit for carryover to 1997?

63. Browne Corporation, a calendar year taxpayer, has AMTI (before the ACE adjustment) of $600,000 for 1996. Browne's ACE is $1,500,000. What is Browne's tentative minimum tax for 1996?

64. Gray Corporation (a calendar year corporation) reports the following information for the years listed below:

	1995	1996	1997
Unadjusted AMTI	$3,000	$2,000	$5,000
Adjusted current earnings	4,000	3,000	2,000

Compute the ACE adjustment for each year.

65. In each of the following independent situations, determine the tentative AMT:

	AMTI (Before the Exemption Amount)
Quincy Corporation	$150,000
Redland Corporation	160,000
Tanzen Corporation	320,000

66. For 1996, Brown Corporation (a calendar year taxpayer) had the following transactions:

Taxable income	$100,000
Depreciation for regular income tax purposes on realty in excess of ADS (placed in service in 1989)	150,000
Excess amortization of certified pollution control facilities	10,000
Tax-exempt interest on municipal bonds (funds were used for nongovernmental purposes)	30,000
Percentage depletion in excess of the property's adjusted basis	60,000

a. Determine Brown Corporation's AMTI for 1996.
b. Determine the AMT base (refer to Figure 14–3).
c. Determine the tentative minimum tax.
d. What is the amount of the AMT?

CUMULATIVE PROBLEMS

67. Ron, age 38, is divorced and has no dependents. He pays alimony of $20,000 per year to his former wife, Kate. Ron's Social Security number is 444–11–2222, and Kate's is 555–67–2222. Ron's address is 201 Front Street, Missoula, MT 59812. He is independently wealthy as a result of having inherited sizable holdings in real estate and corporate stocks and bonds. Ron is a minister at First Methodist Church, but he accepts no salary from the church. However, he does reside in the church's parsonage free of charge. The rental value of the parsonage is $400 a month. The church also provides him a cash grocery allowance of $100 a week. Examination of Ron's financial records provides the following information for 1996:
   a. On January 16, 1996, Ron sold 2,000 shares of stock for a gain of $40,000. The stock was acquired four months ago.
   b. He received $60,000 of interest on private activity bonds in 1996.
   c. He received gross rent income of $145,000 from an apartment complex he owns and manages.
   d. Expenses related to the apartment complex, which he acquired in 1983, were $230,000.
   e. Ron's dividend and interest income (on a savings account) totaled $26,000.

f. On October 9, 1994, Ron exercised his rights under Egret Corporation's incentive stock option plan. For an option price of $20,000, he acquired stock worth $45,000. The stock became freely transferable in 1996.

g. Ron had the following potential itemized deductions *from* AGI:

- $3,000 fair market value of stock contributed to Methodist church (basis of stock was $1,000). He owned the stock for five years.

- $3,000 interest on consumer purchases.

- $1,600 state and local taxes.

- $7,000 medical expenses (before 7.5% floor).

Compute Ron's tax liability, including AMT if applicable, before prepayments or credits, for 1996.

68. Robert M. and Jane R. Armstrong live at 1802 College Avenue, Carmel, IN 46302. They are married and file a joint return for 1995. The Armstrongs have two dependent children, Ellen J. and Sean M., who are 10-year-old twins. Ellen's Social Security number is 333–42–3368, and Sean's is 333–42–3369.

Robert (224–36–9987) is a factory foreman, and Jane (443–56–3421) is a computer systems analyst. The Armstrongs' W–2 forms for 1995 reflect the following information:

	Robert	Jane
Salary (Indiana Foundry, Inc.)	$55,000	
Salary (Carmel Computer Associates)		$74,000
Federal income tax withheld	6,600	13,600
Social Security wages	55,000	61,200
Social Security withheld	3,410	3,795
Medicare wages	55,000	74,000
Medicare tax withheld	798	1,073
State wages	55,000	74,000
State income tax withheld	1,650	2,220

In addition to their salaries, the Armstrongs had the following income items in 1995:

Interest income (Carmel Sanitation District Bonds)	$14,500
Interest income (Carmel National Bank)	1,000
Dividend income (Able Computer Corporation)	2,500
Gambling income	2,000

Jane inherited $200,000 from her grandfather in January and invested the money in the Carmel Sanitation District Bonds, which are private activity bonds.

The Armstrongs incurred the following expenses during 1995:

Medical expenses (doctor and hospital bills)	$17,000
Real property tax on personal residence	4,500
Mortgage interest on personal residence (reported on Form 1098)	4,000
Investment interest expense	1,900
Contributions to Salvation Army	20,000
Gambling losses	1,750

On March 1, Robert and Jane contributed Ace stock to the Carmel Salvation Army, a public charity. They had acquired the stock on February 9, 1979, for $1,500. The stock was listed on the New York Stock Exchange at a value of $20,000 on the date of the contribution.

Robert received a gift of 25 acres of land from his Uncle Sam on May 15. The appraised value of the land at the date of the gift was $63,000, and Uncle Sam's adjusted basis was $10,000. Uncle Sam was not required to pay any gift tax.

Use Forms 1040, 4952, 6251, and 8283 and Schedules A and B to compute the AMT for Robert and Jane Armstrong for 1995. Suggested software (if available): *TurboTax* or *MacInTax*. Write a letter to the Armstrongs indicating whether they have a refund or balance due for 1995, and suggest possible tax planning strategies for 1996.

Research Problems for this chapter appear at the end of Chapter 28.

TEAM PROJECT: ARTHUR ANDERSEN TAX CHALLENGE CASES

For more information on the Arthur Andersen Tax Challenge Cases, please refer to Chapter 2, page 2-41.

Information related to tax issues and problems that are discussed in this chapter may be found in the

Miller case on pages 3, 19, 21, 39, and 41

Read and analyze the case you have been assigned and *identify* any issues and problems that are related to material covered in this chapter. If the information provided in the case is complete, prepare answers for this part of the case at this time. If you need information that is contained in the later parts of the case, please write a memo summarizing the questions or problems so you can prepare a complete answer at a later date.

15

ACCOUNTING PERIODS AND METHODS

LEARNING OBJECTIVES

After completing Chapter 15, you should be able to:

1. Understand the relevance of the accounting period concept, the different types of accounting periods, and the limitations on their use.

2. Apply the cash method, accrual method, and hybrid method of accounting.

3. Utilize the procedure for changing accounting methods.

4. Determine when the installment method of accounting can be utilized and apply the related calculation techniques.

5. Understand the alternative methods of accounting for long-term contracts (the completed contract method and the percentage of completion method) including the limitations on the use of the completed contract method.

6. Identify tax planning opportunities related to accounting periods and accounting methods.

Tax practitioners must deal with the issue of *when* particular items of income and expense are recognized as well as the basic issue of *whether* the items are includible in taxable income. Earlier chapters discussed the types of income subject to tax (gross income and exclusions) and allowable deductions (the *whether* issue).[1] This chapter focuses on the related issue of the periods in which income and deductions are reported (the *when* issue). Generally, a taxpayer's income and deductions must be assigned to particular 12-month periods—calendar years or fiscal years.

Income and deductions are placed within particular years through the use of tax accounting methods. The basic accounting methods are the cash method, accrual method, and hybrid method. Other special purpose methods, such as the installment method and the methods used for long-term construction contracts, are available for specific circumstances or types of transactions.

Over the long run, the accounting period used by a taxpayer will not affect the aggregate amount of reported taxable income. However, taxable income for any particular year may vary significantly due to the use of a particular reporting period. Also, through the choice of accounting methods or accounting periods, it is possible to postpone the recognition of taxable income and to enjoy the benefits from deferring the related tax. This chapter discusses the taxpayer's alternatives for accounting periods and accounting methods.

ACCOUNTING PERIODS

1 **LEARNING OBJECTIVE**
Understand the relevance of the accounting period concept, the different types of accounting periods, and the limitations on their use.

IN GENERAL

A taxpayer who keeps adequate books and records may be permitted to elect to use a **fiscal year,** a 12-month period ending on the *last day* of a month other than December, for the **accounting period.** Otherwise, a *calendar year* must be used.[2]

---

[1] See Chapters 3, 4, and 5.

[2] § 441(c) and Reg. § 1.441–1(b)(1)(ii).

TAX IN THE NEWS

ACCELERATION OF INCOME

In 1993, the *Wall Street Journal* and various other print and broadcast news sources reported that Hillary Rodham Clinton had the opportunity to receive compensation income in 1992 or 1993. She chose to accelerate the income into 1992. This appears to be at variance with the normal tax planning mode of deferring the reporting of income and accelerating the reporting of deductions.

One possible explanation for reporting the income in 1992 rather than in 1993 is that the family's taxable income was expected to be greater in 1993 than in 1992. However, while the President earns substantially more as President of the United States than as Governor of Arkansas, the First Lady earns substantially less than she did as a partner in an Arkansas law firm.

Another possible explanation is the expectation that the Revenue Reconciliation Act of 1993 with its retroactive increase in tax rates would be passed by Congress. In any event, the First Lady followed sound tax advice in accelerating the income into 1992.

Frequently, corporations can satisfy the record-keeping requirements and elect to use a fiscal year.[3] Often the fiscal year conforms to a natural business year (e.g., a summer resort's fiscal year may end on September 30, after the close of the season). Individuals seldom use a fiscal year because they do not maintain the necessary books and records and because complications can arise as a result of changes in the tax law (e.g., often the transition rules and effective dates differ for fiscal year taxpayers).

Generally, a taxable year may not exceed 12 calendar months. However, if certain requirements are met, a taxpayer may elect to use an annual period that varies from 52 to 53 weeks.[4] In that case, the year-end must be on the same day of the week (e.g., the Tuesday falling closest to October 31 or the last Tuesday in October). The day of the week selected for ending the year will depend upon business considerations. For example, a retail business that is not open on Sundays may end its tax year on a Sunday so that it can take an inventory without interrupting business operations.

EXAMPLE 1

Wade is in the business of selling farm supplies. His natural business year terminates at the end of October with the completion of harvesting. At the end of the fiscal year, Wade must take an inventory, which is most easily accomplished on a Tuesday. Therefore, Wade could adopt a 52–53 week tax year ending on the Tuesday closest to October 31. If Wade selects this method, the year-end date may fall in the following month if that Tuesday is closer to October 31. The tax year ending in 1996 will contain 52 weeks beginning on Wednesday, November 1, 1995, and ending on Tuesday, October 29, 1996. The tax year ending in 1997 will have 52 weeks beginning on Wednesday, October 30, 1996, and ending on Tuesday, October 28, 1997. ▼

---

[3] Reg. § 1.441–1(e)(2).   [4] § 441(f).

SPECIFIC PROVISIONS FOR PARTNERSHIPS, S CORPORATIONS, AND PERSONAL SERVICE CORPORATIONS

Partnerships and S Corporations.   When a partner's tax year and the partnership's tax year differ, the partner will enjoy a deferral of income. This results because the partner reports his or her share of the partnership's income and deductions for the partnership's tax year ending within or with the partner's tax year.[5] For example, if the tax year of the partnership ends on January 31, a calendar year partner will not report partnership profits for the first 11 months of the partnership tax year until the following year. Therefore, partnerships are subject to special tax year requirements.

In general, the partnership tax year must be the same as the tax year of the majority interest partners. The **majority interest partners** are the partners who own a greater-than-50 percent interest in the partnership capital and profits. If the majority owners do not have the same tax year, the partnership must adopt the same tax year as its principal partners. A **principal partner** is a partner with a 5 percent or more interest in the partnership capital or profits.[6]

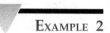

EXAMPLE 2

The RST Partnership is owned equally by Rose Corporation, Silver Corporation, and Tom. The partners have the following tax years.

Partner	Tax Year Ending
Rose	June 30
Silver	June 30
Tom	December 31

The partnership's tax year must end on June 30. If Silver Corporation's as well as Tom's year ended on December 31, the partnership would be required to adopt a calendar year. ▼

If the principal partners do not all have the same tax year and no majority of partners have the same tax year, the partnership must use a year that results in the *least aggregate deferral* of income.[7] Under the **least aggregate deferral method,** the different tax years of the principal partners are tested to determine which produces the least aggregate deferral. This is calculated by first multiplying the combined percentages of the principal partners with the same tax year by the months of deferral for the test year. Once this is done for each set of principal partners with the same tax year, the resulting products are summed to produce the aggregate deferral. After calculating the aggregate deferral for each of the test years, the test year with the smallest summation (the least aggregate deferral) is the tax year for the partnership.

EXAMPLE 3

The DE Partnership is owned equally by Diane and Emily. Diane's fiscal year ends on March 31, and Emily's fiscal year ends on August 31. The partnership must use the partner's fiscal year that will result in the least aggregate deferral of income. Therefore, the fiscal years ending March 31 and August 31 must both be tested.

---

[5] Reg. § 1.706–1(a).
[6] §§ 706(b)(1)(B) and 706(b)(3).

[7] Temp.Reg. § 1.706–IT(a)(2).

Test for Fiscal Year Ending March 31				
Partner	Year Ends	Profit %	Months of Deferral	Product
Diane	3–31	50	0	0
Emily	8–31	50	5	2.5
Aggregate deferral months				2.5

Thus, with a year ending March 31, Emily would be able to defer her half of the income for five months. That is, Emily's share of the partnership income for the fiscal year ending March 31, 1997, would not be included in her income until August 31, 1997.

Test for Fiscal Year Ending August 31				
Partner	Year Ends	Profit %	Months of Deferral	Product
Diane	3–31	50	7	3.5
Emily	8–31	50	0	0
Aggregate deferral months				3.5

Thus, with a year ending August 31, Diane would be able to defer her half of the income for seven months. That is, Diane's share of the partnership income for the fiscal year ending August 31, 1997, would not be included in her income until March 31, 1998.

The year ending March 31 must be used because it results in the least aggregate deferral of income. ▼

Generally, S corporations must adopt a calendar year.[8] However, partnerships and S corporations may *elect* an otherwise *impermissible year* under any of the following conditions:

- A business purpose for the year can be demonstrated.[9]
- The partnership's or S corporation's year results in a deferral of not more than three months' income, and the entity agrees to make required tax payments.[10]
- The entity retains the same year as was used for the fiscal year ending in 1987, provided the entity agrees to make required tax payments.

Business Purpose.   The only business purpose for a fiscal year that the IRS has acknowledged is the need to conform the tax year to the natural business year of a business.[11] Generally, only seasonal businesses have a natural business year. For example, the natural business year for a department store may end on January 31, after Christmas returns have been processed and clearance sales have been completed.

Required Tax Payments.   Under the required payments system, tax payments are due from a fiscal year partnership or S corporation by April 15 of each tax

---

[8] §§ 1378(a) and (b).
[9] §§ 706(b)(1)(C) and 1378(b)(2).

[10] § 444.
[11] Rev.Rul. 87–57, 1987–2 C.B. 117.

year.[12] The amount due is computed by applying the highest individual tax rate plus 1 percent to an estimate of the deferral period income. The deferral period runs from the close of the fiscal year to the end of the calendar year. Estimated income for this period is based on the average monthly earnings for the previous fiscal year. The amount due is reduced by the amount of required tax payments for the previous year.[13]

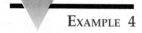

EXAMPLE 4

Brown, Inc., an S corporation, elected a fiscal year ending September 30. Bob is the only shareholder. For the fiscal year ending September 30, 1996, Brown earned $100,000. The required tax payment for the previous year was $5,000. The corporation must pay $5,150 by April 15, 1997, calculated as follows:

$$(\$100,000 \times \tfrac{3}{12} \times 40.6\%^{*}) - \$5,000 = \$5,150$$

*Maximum § 1 rate of 39.6% + 1%.

ETHICAL CONSIDERATIONS

Required Tax Years

Before 1987, partnerships could generally use a fiscal year ending September 30, and S corporations could use any fiscal year. With this latitude, accountants often recommended that their partnership and S corporation clients not use a calendar year. This enabled the accountants to spread their work throughout the year and created a tax deferral for the clients.

Members of the accounting profession argued vociferously against the calendar year requirement that was included in the Tax Reform Act of 1986. The choice Congress had to make was whether some groups should be allowed to benefit (i.e., the accountants and their clients) at the expense of the rest of the general public. Of course, the accounting profession viewed the choices differently: Should some groups be burdened (i.e., the accounting profession) for little benefit to the remaining taxpayers?

The compromise reached was the required payments scheme, whereby the burden was lifted from the accounting profession without the clients enjoying tax deferrals. Was this an acceptable compromise?

Personal Service Corporations (PSCs). A **personal service corporation (PSC)** is a corporation whose shareholder-employees provide personal services (e.g., medical, dental, legal, accounting, engineering, actuarial, consulting, or performing arts). Generally, a PSC must use a calendar year.[14] However, a PSC can *elect* a fiscal year under any of the following conditions:

- A business purpose for the year can be demonstrated.
- The PSC year results in a deferral of not more than three months' income; the corporation pays the shareholder-employee's salary during the portion of the calendar year after the close of the fiscal year; and the salary for that period is at least proportionate to the shareholder-employee's salary received for the preceding fiscal year.[15]

---

[12] §§ 444(c) and 7519. No payment is required if the calculated amount is $500 or less.
[13] § 7519(b).

[14] § 441(i).
[15] §§ 444 and 280H.

• The PSC retains the same year it used for the fiscal year ending in 1987, provided it satisfies the latter two requirements in the preceding option.

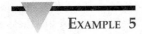

EXAMPLE 5

Nancy's corporation paid her a salary of $120,000 during its fiscal year ending September 30, 1996. The corporation cannot satisfy the business purpose test for a fiscal year. The corporation can continue to use its fiscal year without any negative tax effects, provided Nancy receives at least $30,000 (3 months/12 months × $120,000) as salary during the period October 1 through December 31, 1996. ▼

If the salary test is not satisfied, the PSC can retain the fiscal year, but the corporation's deduction for salary for the fiscal year is limited to the following:

$$A + A(F/N)$$

Where A = Amount paid after the close of the fiscal year.
F = Number of months in fiscal year minus number of months from the end of the fiscal year to the end of the ongoing calendar year.
N = Number of months from the end of the fiscal year to the end of the ongoing calendar year.

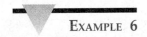

EXAMPLE 6

Assume the corporation in the previous example paid Nancy $10,000 of salary during the period October 1 through December 31, 1996. The deduction for Nancy's salary for the corporation's fiscal year ending September 30, 1997, is thus limited to $40,000 calculated as follows:

$$\$10,000 + \left[\$10,000 \left(\frac{12-3}{3}\right)\right] = \$10,000 + \$30,000 = \$40,000$$ ▼

MAKING THE ELECTION

A taxpayer elects to use a calendar or fiscal year by the timely filing of his or her initial tax return. For all subsequent years, the taxpayer must use this same period unless approval for change is obtained from the IRS.[16]

CHANGES IN THE ACCOUNTING PERIOD

A taxpayer must obtain consent from the IRS before changing the tax year.[17] This power to approve or not to approve a change is significant in that it permits the IRS to issue authoritative administrative guidelines that must be met by taxpayers who wish to change their accounting period. An application for permission to change tax years must be made on Form 1128, Application for Change in Accounting Period. The application must be filed on or before the fifteenth day of the second calendar month following the close of the short period that results from the change in accounting period.[18]

EXAMPLE 7

Beginning in 1996, Gold Corporation, a calendar year taxpayer, would like to switch to a fiscal year ending March 31. The corporation must file Form 1128 by May 15, 1996. ▼

---

[16] Reg. §§ 1.441–1(b)(3) and 1.441–1(b)(4).

[17] § 442. Under certain conditions, corporations are allowed to change tax years without obtaining IRS approval. See Reg. § 1.442–1(c)(1).

[18] Reg. § 1.442–1(b)(1). In Example 7, the first period after the change in accounting period (January 1, 1996 through March 31, 1996) is less than a 12-month period and is referred to as a *short period.*

IRS Requirements.   The IRS will not grant permission for the change unless the taxpayer can establish a substantial business purpose for the request. One substantial business purpose is to change to a tax year that coincides with the *natural business year* (the completion of an annual business cycle). The IRS applies an objective gross receipts test to determine if the entity has a natural business year. At least 25 percent of the entity's gross receipts for the 12-month period must be realized in the final 2 months of the 12-month period for three consecutive years.[19]

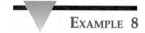

EXAMPLE 8

A Virginia Beach motel had gross receipts as follows:

	1994	1995	1996
July–August receipts	$ 300,000	$250,000	$ 325,000
September 1–August 31 receipts	1,000,000	900,000	1,250,000
Receipts for 2 months divided by receipts for 12 months	30.0%	27.8%	26.0%

Since it satisfies the natural business year test, the motel will be allowed to use a fiscal year ending August 31. ▼

The IRS usually establishes certain conditions that the taxpayer must accept if the approval for change is to be granted. In particular, if the taxpayer has a net operating loss for the short period, the IRS may require that the loss be carried forward and allocated equally over the 6 following years.[20] As you may recall (refer to Chapter 6), net operating losses are ordinarily carried back for 3 years and forward for 15 years.

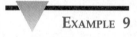

EXAMPLE 9

Parrot Corporation changed from a calendar year to a fiscal year ending September 30. The short-period return for the nine months ending September 30, 1996, reflected a $60,000 net operating loss. The corporation had taxable income for 1993, 1994, and 1995. As a condition for granting approval, the IRS requires Parrot to allocate the $60,000 loss over the next six years, rather than carrying the loss back to the three preceding years (the usual order for applying a net operating loss). Thus, Parrot will reduce its taxable income by $10,000 each year ending September 30, 1997, through September 30, 2002. ▼

TAXABLE PERIODS OF LESS THAN ONE YEAR

A **short taxable year** (or **short period**) is a period of less than 12 calendar months. A taxpayer may have a short year for (1) the first income tax return, (2) the final income tax return, or (3) a change in the tax year. If the short period results from a change in the taxpayer's annual accounting period, the taxable income for the period must be *annualized*. Due to the progressive tax rate structure, taxpayers could reap benefits from a short-period return if some adjustments were not required. Thus, the taxpayer is required to do the following:

1. Annualize the short-period income.

$$\text{Annualized income} = \text{Short-period income} \times \frac{12}{\text{Number of months in the short period}}$$

[19]Rev.Proc. 87–32, 1987–1 C.B. 131, and Rev.Rul. 87–57, 1987–2 C.B. 117.

[20]Rev.Proc. 85–16, 1985–1 C.B. 517.

2. Compute the tax on the annualized income.
3. Convert the tax on the annualized income to a short-period tax.

$$\text{Short-period tax} = \text{Tax on annualized income} \times \frac{\text{Number of months in the short period}}{12}$$

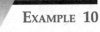

EXAMPLE 10

Gray Corporation obtained permission to change from a calendar year to a fiscal year ending September 30, beginning in 1996. For the short period January 1 through September 30, 1996, the corporation's taxable income was $48,000. The relevant tax rates and the resultant short-period tax are as follows:

Amount of Taxable Income	Tax Rates
Not over $50,000	15% of taxable income
Over $50,000 but not over $75,000	$7,500 plus 25% of taxable income in excess of $50,000

Calculation of Short-Period Tax

Annualized income ($48,000 × ¹²⁄₉) = $64,000

Tax on annualized income
[$7,500 + .25($64,000 – $50,000)] =
$7,500 + $3,500 = $11,000

Short-period tax = ($11,000 × ⁹⁄₁₂) = $8,250

Annualizing the income increases the
tax by $1,050:

Tax with annualizing	$8,250
Tax without annualizing ($48,000 × .15)	(7,200)
Increase in tax from annualizing	$1,050

Rather than annualize the short-period income, the taxpayer can elect to (1) calculate the tax for a 12-month period beginning on the first day of the short period and (2) convert the tax in (1) to a short-period tax as follows:[21]

$$\frac{\text{Taxable income for short period}}{\text{Taxable income for the 12-month period}} \times \text{Tax on the 12 months of income}$$

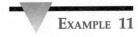

EXAMPLE 11

Assume Gray Corporation's taxable income for the calendar year 1996 was $60,000. The tax on the full 12 months of income would have been $10,000 [$7,500 + .25($60,000 – $50,000)]. The short-period tax would be $8,000 [($48,000/$60,000) × $10,000)]. Thus, if the corporation utilized this option, the tax for the short period would be $8,000 (rather than $8,250, as calculated in Example 10). ▼

For individuals, annualizing requires some special adjustments:[22]

• Deductions must be *itemized* for the short period (the standard deduction is not allowed).
• Personal and dependency exemptions must be prorated.

Fortunately, individuals rarely change tax years.

[21] § 443(b)(1).

[22] § 443(b)(2) and Reg. § 1.443–1(a)(2).

MITIGATION OF THE ANNUAL ACCOUNTING PERIOD CONCEPT

Several provisions in the Code are designed to give the taxpayer relief from the seemingly harsh results that may be produced by the combined effects of an arbitrary accounting period and a progressive rate structure. For example, under the net operating loss carryback and carryover rules, a loss in one year can be carried back and offset against taxable income for the preceding 3 years. Unused net operating losses are then carried over for 15 years.[23] In addition, the Code provides special relief provisions for casualty losses stemming from a disaster and for the reporting of insurance proceeds from destruction of crops.[24]

Restoration of Amounts Received under a Claim of Right.   The court-made **claim of right doctrine** applies when the taxpayer receives property as income and treats it as his or her own but a dispute arises over the taxpayer's rights to the income.[25] According to the doctrine, the taxpayer must include the amount as income in the year of receipt. The rationale for the doctrine is that the Federal government cannot await the resolution of all disputes before exacting a tax. As a corollary to the doctrine, if the taxpayer is later required to repay the funds, generally a deduction is allowed in the year of repayment.[26]

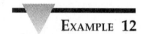

EXAMPLE 12

In 1996, Pedro received a $5,000 bonus computed as a percentage of profits. In 1997, Pedro's employer determined that the 1996 profits had been incorrectly computed, and Pedro had to refund the $5,000 in 1997. Pedro was required to include the $5,000 in his 1996 income, but he can claim a $5,000 deduction in 1997. ▼

In Example 12 the transactions were a wash; that is, the income and deduction were the same ($5,000). Suppose, however, Pedro was in the 36 percent tax bracket in 1996 but in the 15 percent bracket in 1997. Without some relief provision, the mistake would be costly to Pedro. He paid $1,800 tax in 1996 (.36 × $5,000), but the deduction reduced his tax liability in 1997 by only $750 (.15 × $5,000). The Code does provide the needed relief in such cases. Under § 1341, when income that has been taxed under the claim of right doctrine must later be repaid, in effect, the taxpayer gets to apply to the deduction the tax rate of the year that will produce the greater tax benefit. Thus, in Example 12, the repayment in 1997 would reduce Pedro's 1997 tax liability by the greater 1996 rate (.36) applied to the $5,000. However, relief is provided only in cases where the tax is significantly different; that is, when the deduction for the amount previously included in income exceeds $3,000.

ACCOUNTING METHODS

2   LEARNING OBJECTIVE
Apply the cash method, accrual method, and hybrid method of accounting.

PERMISSIBLE METHODS

Section 446 requires the taxpayer to compute taxable income using the method of accounting regularly employed in keeping his or her books, provided the method

---

[23] § 172. Refer to Chapter 6.
[24] §§ 165(i) and 451(d). Refer to Chapter 6.
[25] *North American Oil Consolidated v. Burnet,* 3 USTC ¶943, 11 AFTR 16, 52 S.Ct. 613 (USSC, 1932).

[26] *U.S. v. Lewis,* 51–1 USTC ¶9211, 40 AFTR 258, 71 S.Ct. 522 (USSC, 1951).

clearly reflects income. The Code recognizes the following as generally permissible **accounting methods:**

- The cash receipts and disbursements method.
- The accrual method.
- A hybrid method (a combination of cash and accrual).

The Regulations under § 446 refer to these alternatives as *overall methods* and add that the term *method of accounting* includes not only the overall method of accounting of the taxpayer but also the accounting treatment of any item.[27]

Generally, any of the three methods of accounting may be used if the method is consistently employed and clearly reflects income. However, the taxpayer is required to use the accrual method for sales and cost of goods sold if inventories are an income-producing factor to the business.[28] Other situations in which the accrual method is required are discussed later. Special methods are also permitted for installment sales, long-term construction contracts, and farmers.

A taxpayer who has more than one trade or business may use a different method of accounting for each trade or business activity.[29] Furthermore, a different method of accounting may be used to determine income from a trade or business than is used to compute nonbusiness items of income and deductions.[30]

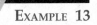

EXAMPLE 13

Linda operates a grocery store and owns stock and bonds. The sales and cost of goods sold from the grocery store must be computed by the accrual basis because inventories are material. However, Linda can report her dividends and interest under the cash method. ▼

The Code grants the IRS broad powers to determine whether the taxpayer's accounting method *clearly reflects income*. Thus, if the method employed does not clearly reflect income, the IRS has the power to prescribe the method to be used by the taxpayer.[31]

CASH RECEIPTS AND DISBURSEMENTS METHOD— CASH BASIS

Most individuals and many businesses use the cash basis to report income and deductions. The popularity of this method can largely be attributed to its simplicity and flexibility.

Under the **cash method,** income is not recognized until the taxpayer actually receives, or constructively receives, cash or its equivalent. Cash is constructively received if it is available to the taxpayer.[32] Deductions are generally permitted in the year of payment. Thus, year-end accounts receivable, accounts payable, and accrued income and deductions are not included in the determination of taxable income.

In many cases, a taxpayer using the cash method can choose the year in which a deduction is claimed simply by postponing or accelerating the payment of expenses. For fixed assets, however, the cash basis taxpayer claims deductions through depreciation or amortization, the same as an accrual basis taxpayer does. In addition, prepaid expenses must be capitalized and amortized if the life of the asset extends substantially beyond the end of the tax year.[33] Most courts have

[27] Reg. § 1.446–1(a)(1).
[28] Reg. § 1.446–1(a)(4)(i).
[29] § 446(d).
[30] Reg. § 1.446–1(c)(1)(iv)(b).

[31] § 446(b).
[32] Reg. § 1.451–1(a). Refer to Chapter 3 for a discussion of constructive receipt.
[33] Reg. § 1.461–1(a)(1).

THE CASH BASIS CONSTRUCTIVE RECEIPT DOCTRINE REQUIRES FACTUAL INQUIRY

Julian Block recounted the story of Beatrice Davis (T.C.Memo. 78–012), a cash basis taxpayer who was able to refute the IRS's argument that she was in constructive receipt of a large severance bonus from her former employer. Ms. Davis's former employer had previously told her that she would not receive the severance pay until early in the following year. However, the former employer sent the check earlier than expected, and the post office attempted to deliver the certified letter on December 31. Ms. Davis was not at home, but a notice of attempted delivery was left at her door. She arrived home after the post office closed and did not open the notice until January 2 of the following year because she thought it was a notice of rent increase by her landlord. On January 2, she went to the post office and claimed her check for $17,000.

The IRS contended that Ms. Davis constructively received the check on December 31, when it was made available to her. The Tax Court disagreed, concluding that although the former employer had committed the funds as of December 31, Ms. Davis did not have notice until January of the following year. This was not a case of Ms. Davis unilaterally deferring the receipt of the income. Therefore, she did not constructively receive the bonus income in December.

SOURCE: Information from "Constructive Hints on Receipt of Income," *Chicago Tribune*, December 11, 1994, p. C10 reprinted by permission: Tribune Media services.

applied the one-year rule (**one-year rule for prepaid expenses**) to determine whether capitalization and amortization are required. According to this rule, capitalization is required only if the asset has a life that extends beyond the tax year following the year of payment.[34]

Restrictions on Use of the Cash Method.   Using the cash method to measure income from a merchandising or manufacturing operation would often yield a distorted picture of the results of operations. Income for the period would largely be a function of when payments were made for goods or materials. Thus, the Regulations prohibit the use of the cash method (and require the accrual method) to measure sales and cost of goods sold if inventories are material to the business.[35]

The prohibition on the use of the cash method if inventories are material and the rules regarding prepaid expenses (discussed above) are intended to assure that annual income is clearly reflected. However, certain taxpayers may not use the cash method of accounting for Federal income tax purposes regardless of whether inventories are material. The accrual basis must be used to report the income earned by (1) a corporation (other than an S corporation), (2) a partnership with a corporate partner, and (3) a tax shelter.[36] This accrual basis requirement has three exceptions:[37]

---

[34] *Zaninovich v. Comm.*, 80–1 USTC ¶9342, 45 AFTR2d 80–1442, 616 F.2d 429 (CA–9, 1980), *rev'g* 69 T.C. 605 (1978). Refer to Chapter 5 for further discussion of the one-year rule.

[35] Reg. § 1.446–1(a)(4)(i).

[36] § 448(a). For this purpose, the hybrid method of accounting is considered the same as the cash method.

[37] § 448(b).

- A farming business.
- A qualified personal service corporation (e.g., a corporation performing services in health, law, engineering, architecture, accounting, actuarial science, performing arts, or consulting).
- An entity that is not a tax shelter whose average annual gross receipts for the most recent three-year period are $5 million or less.

Farming.   Although inventories are material to farming operations, the IRS long ago created an exception to the general rule that allows farmers to use the cash method of accounting.[38] The purpose of the exception is to relieve the small farmer from the bookkeeping burden of accrual accounting. However, tax shelter promoters recognized, for example, that by deducting the costs of a crop in one tax year and harvesting the crop in a later year, income could be deferred from tax. Thus, §§ 447 and 464 were enacted to prevent certain farming corporations and limited partnerships (farming syndicates) from using the cash method.[39]

Farmers who are allowed to use the cash method of accounting must nevertheless capitalize their costs of raising trees when the preproduction period is greater than two years.[40] Thus, a cash basis apple farmer must capitalize the cost of raising trees until the trees produce in merchantable quantities. Cash basis farmers can elect not to capitalize these costs, but if the election is made, the alternative depreciation system (refer to Chapter 7) must be used for all farming property.

Generally, the cost of purchasing an animal must be capitalized. However, the cash basis farmer's cost of raising the animal can be expensed.[41]

ACCRUAL METHOD

All Events Test for Income.   Under the **accrual method,** an item is generally included in gross income for the year in which it is earned, regardless of when the income is collected. An item of income is earned when (1) all the events have occurred to fix the taxpayer's right to receive the income and (2) the amount of income (the amount the taxpayer has a right to receive) can be determined with reasonable accuracy.[42]

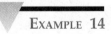

EXAMPLE 14

Andre, a calendar year taxpayer who uses the accrual basis of accounting, was to receive a bonus equal to 6% of Blue Corporation's net income for its fiscal year ending each June 30. For the fiscal year ending June 30, 1996, Blue had net income of $240,000, and for the six months ending December 31, 1996, the corporation's net income was $150,000. Andre will report $14,400 (.06 × $240,000) for 1996 because his rights to the amount became fixed when Blue's year closed. However, Andre would not accrue income based on the corporation's profits for the last six months of 1996 since his right to the income does not accrue until the close of the corporation's tax year. ▼

In a situation where the accrual basis taxpayer's right to income is being contested and the income has not yet been collected, generally no income is recognized until the dispute has been settled.[43] Before the settlement, "all of the events have not occurred that fix the right to receive the income."

---

[38] Reg. § 1.471–6(a).

[39] Section 447(c) contains counterexceptions that allow certain closely held corporations to use the cash method. See also § 464(c).

[40] § 263A(d).

[41] Reg. § 1.162–12(a).

[42] Reg. § 1.451–1(a). Refer to Chapter 3 for further discussion of the accrual method.

[43] *Burnet v. Sanford & Brooks Co.,* 2 USTC ¶636, 9 AFTR 603, 51 S.Ct. 150 (USSC, 1931).

All Events and Economic Performance Tests for Deductions. An **all events test** applies to accrual basis deductions. A deduction cannot be claimed until (1) all the events have occurred to create the taxpayer's liability and (2) the amount of the liability can be determined with reasonable accuracy.[44] Once these requirements are satisfied, the deduction will be permitted only if economic performance has occurred.[45]

The **economic performance test** addresses situations in which the taxpayer has either of the following obligations:

1. To pay for services or property to be provided in the future.
2. To provide services or property (other than money) in the future.

When services or property are to be provided to the taxpayer in the future (situation 1), economic performance occurs when the property or services are actually provided by the other party.

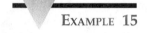

EXAMPLE 15

An accrual basis, calendar year taxpayer, JAB, Inc., promoted a boxing match held in the company's arena on December 31, 1996. CLN, Inc., had contracted to clean the arena for $5,000, but did not actually perform the work until January 1, 1997. JAB, Inc., did not pay the $5,000 until 1998. Although financial accounting would require JAB, Inc., to accrue the $5,000 cleaning expense in 1996 to match the revenues from the fight, the economic performance test was not satisfied until 1997, when CLN, Inc., performed the service. Thus, JAB, Inc., must deduct the expense in 1997. ▼

If the taxpayer is obligated to provide property or services (situation 2), economic performance occurs (and thus the deduction is allowed) in the year the taxpayer provides the property or services.

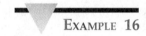

EXAMPLE 16

Copper Corporation, an accrual basis taxpayer, is in the strip mining business. According to the contract with the landowner, the company must reclaim the land. The estimated cost of reclaiming land mined in 1996 was $500,000, but the land was not actually reclaimed until 1998. The all events test was satisfied in 1996. The obligation existed, and the amount of the liability could be determined with reasonable accuracy. However, the economic performance test was not satisfied until 1998. Therefore, the deduction is not allowed until 1998.[46] ▼

The economic performance test is waived if the *recurring item exception* applies. Year-end accruals can be deducted if all the following conditions are met:

• The obligation exists and the amount of the liability can be reasonably estimated.
• Economic performance occurs within a reasonable period (but not later than 8½ months after the close of the taxable year).
• The item is recurring in nature and is treated consistently by the taxpayer.
• Either the accrued item is not material, or accruing it results in a better matching of revenues and expenses.

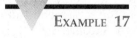

EXAMPLE 17

Green Corporation often sells goods that are on hand but cannot be shipped for another week. Thus, the sales account usually includes revenues for some items that have not been shipped at year-end. Green Corporation is obligated to pay shipping costs. Although the company's obligation for shipping costs can be determined with reasonable accuracy, economic performance is not satisfied until Green (or its agent) actually delivers the goods.

---

[44] § 461(h)(4).
[45] § 461(h).

[46] See § 468 for an elective method for reporting reclamation costs.

However, accruing shipping costs on sold items will better match expenses with revenues for the period. Therefore, the company should be allowed to accrue the shipping costs on items sold but not shipped at year-end. ▼

The economic performance test as set forth in the Code does not address all possible accrued expenses. That is, in some cases the taxpayer incurs costs even though no property or services were received. In these instances, according to Regulations, economic performance generally is not satisfied until the liability is paid. The following liabilities are cases in which payment is generally the only means of satisfying economic performance:[47]

1. Workers' compensation.
2. Torts.
3. Breach of contract.
4. Violation of law.
5. Rebates and refunds.
6. Awards, prizes, and jackpots.
7. Insurance, warranty, and service contracts.[48]
8. Taxes.

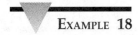

EXAMPLE 18

Yellow Corporation sold defective merchandise that injured a customer. Yellow admitted liability in 1996, but did not pay the claim until January 1997. The customer's tort claim cannot be deducted until it is paid. ▼

However, items (5) through (8) above are eligible for the aforementioned recurring item exception.

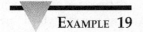

EXAMPLE 19

Pelican Corporation filed its 1996 state income tax return in March 1997. At the time the return was filed, Pelican was required to pay an additional $5,000. The state taxes are eligible for the recurring item exception. Thus, the $5,000 of state income taxes can be deducted on the corporation's 1996 Federal tax return. The deduction is allowed because all the events had occurred to fix the liability as of the end of 1996, the payment was made within 8½ months after the end of the tax year, the item is recurring in nature, and allowing the deduction in 1996 produces a good matching of revenues and expenses. ▼

Reserves. Generally, the all events and economic performance tests will prevent the use of reserves (e.g., for product warranty expense) frequently used in financial accounting to match expenses with revenues. However, small banks are allowed to use a bad debt reserve.[49] Furthermore, an accrual basis taxpayer in a service business is permitted to not accrue revenue that appears uncollectible based on experience. In effect, this approach indirectly allows a reserve.[50]

ETHICAL CONSIDERATIONS

Prepaid Income and Deductions

Your client, Hometown Motors Company, is a new automobile dealer and reports its taxable income by the accrual method. The company also sells service contracts on the new automobiles. A customer who buys the contract can have the work

---

[47] Reg. §§ 1.461–4(g)(2)–(6) and 1.461–5(c).

[48] This item applies to contracts the taxpayer enters into for his or her own protection, rather than the taxpayer's liability as insurer, warrantor, or service provider.

[49] § 585.

[50] § 448(d)(5).

performed by any authorized dealer. If someone other than Hometown does the work, the bill is nevertheless paid by Hometown. Typically, a contract sells for $1,000 and provides protection for five years. When Hometown sells the contract to the customer, the company also purchases an insurance contract (for $800) that reimburses Hometown for any cost it incurs under the service contract. In addition, if Hometown actually performs the service, the insurance company pays Hometown its normal charge.

Hometown is caught between two tax accounting rules. Under the rule for prepaid income (discussed in Chapter 3), the entire $1,000 revenue from a service contract must be included in gross income for the year the contract is sold. On the other hand, the cost of the insurance contract must be amortized over its five-year life ($800/5 years = $160 per year). Thus, in the year a contract is sold, Hometown must recognize $840 ($1,000 − $160) of income when the company has received a net amount of only $200 ($1,000 − $800).

Should you suggest that the terms of the service and insurance contracts be changed so that (1) Hometown sells the insurance to the customer and receives a $200 commission, and (2) Hometown agrees to pay the customer if the insurance company goes out of existence or is otherwise unable to pay when the customer requires service? How do you respond if Hometown rejects this proposal, but suggests that since the two forms of transactions produce basically the same economic results, you account for the current transactions as you suggested in your proposal?

HYBRID METHOD

A **hybrid method** of accounting involves the use of more than one method. For example, a taxpayer who uses the accrual basis to report sales and cost of goods sold but uses the cash basis to report other items of income and expense is employing a hybrid method. The Code permits the use of a hybrid method provided the taxpayer's income is clearly reflected.[51] A taxpayer who uses the accrual method for business expenses must also use the accrual method for business income (a cash method may not be used for income items if the taxpayer's expenses are accounted for under the accrual method).

It may be preferable for a business that is required to report sales and cost of goods sold on the accrual method to report other items of income and expense under the cash method. The cash method permits greater flexibility in the timing of income and expense recognition.

CHANGE OF METHOD

3   ▼ **LEARNING OBJECTIVE**
Utilize the procedure for changing accounting methods.

The taxpayer, in effect, makes an election to use a particular accounting method when an initial tax return is filed using that method. If a subsequent change in method is desired, the taxpayer must obtain the permission of the IRS. The request for change is made on Form 3115, Application for Change in Accounting Method. Generally, the form must be filed within the first 180 days of the taxable year of the desired change.[52]

As previously mentioned, the term *accounting method* encompasses not only the overall accounting method used by the taxpayer (the cash or accrual method) but also the treatment of any material item of income or deduction.[53] Thus, a

---

[51] § 446(c).

[52] Reg. § 1.446–1(e)(3). The deadline may be extended to within the first nine months of the year of the change if the taxpayer can show good cause for the delay in filing the request.

[53] Reg. § 1.446–1(a)(1).

change in the method of deducting property taxes from a cash basis to an accrual basis that results in a deduction for taxes in a different year constitutes a change in an accounting method. Another example of accounting method change is a change involving the method or basis used in the valuation of inventories. However, a change in treatment resulting from a change in underlying facts does not constitute a change in the taxpayer's method of accounting.[54] For example, a change in employment contracts so that an employee accrues one day of vacation pay for each month of service rather than 12 days of vacation pay for a full year of service is a change in the underlying facts and, thus, is not an accounting method change.

Correction of an Error.   A change in accounting method should be distinguished from the *correction of an error*. The taxpayer can correct an error (by filing amended returns) without permission, and the IRS can simply adjust the taxpayer's liability if an error is discovered on audit of the return. Some examples of errors are incorrect postings, errors in the calculation of tax liability or tax credits, deductions of business expense items that are actually personal, and omissions of income and deductions.[55] Unless the taxpayer or the IRS corrects the error within the statute of limitations, the taxpayer's total lifetime taxable income will be overstated or understated by the amount of the error.

Change from an Incorrect Method.   An *incorrect accounting method* is the consistent (year-after-year) use of an incorrect rule to report an item of income or expense. The incorrect accounting method generally will not affect the taxpayer's total lifetime income (unlike the error). That is, an incorrect method has a self-balancing mechanism. For example, deducting freight on inventory in the year the goods are purchased, rather than when the inventory is sold, is an incorrect accounting method. The total cost of goods sold over the life of the business is not affected, but the year-to-year income is incorrect.[56]

If a taxpayer is employing an incorrect method of accounting, permission must be obtained from the IRS to change to a correct method. An incorrect method is not treated as a mechanical error that can be corrected by merely filing an amended tax return.

The tax return preparer as well as the taxpayer will be subject to penalties if the tax return is prepared using an incorrect method of accounting and permission for a change to a correct method has not been requested.[57]

ETHICAL CONSIDERATIONS

A Change in Accounting Method

Tom, a CPA, recently obtained a new client, the Egret Engineering Corporation (annual gross receipts of $2 million). The company's previous accountant had filed all returns by the accrual method of accounting, the same method that was used to prepare financial statements submitted when the company applied for a loan in its first year of operation. Tom recognizes that under the accrual method of accounting the company is paying tax on its accounts receivable, whereas under the cash method of accounting the income could be deferred until the cash is collected. In many cases, it takes the company

---

[54] Reg. § 1.446–1(e)(2)(ii).
[55] Reg. § 1.446–1(e)(2)(ii)(b).
[56] But see *Korn Industries v. U.S.*, 76–1 USTC ¶ 9354, 37 AFTR2d 76–1228, 532 F.2d 1352 (Ct.Cls., 1976).

[57] § 446(f). See Chapter 25.

three months to collect a receivable. Tom also recognizes that the IRS will not allow the corporation to change to the cash method.

Therefore, Tom is considering the following plan: A new corporation would be formed. Each shareholder in Egret would own the same percentage of stock in the new corporation. The key element of the plan is that the new corporation would elect the cash method of accounting. Egret would complete its contracts in progress, collect its receivables, and gradually be liquidated. Meanwhile all new business would be channeled into the new corporation. Evaluate Tom's plan.

Net Adjustments Due to Change in Accounting Method. In the year of a change in accounting method, some items of income and expense may have to be adjusted to prevent the change from distorting taxable income.

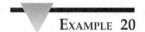

EXAMPLE 20

In 1996, White Corporation, with consent from the IRS, switched from the cash to the accrual basis for reporting sales and cost of goods sold. The corporation's accrual basis gross profit for the year was computed as follows:

Sales		$100,000
Beginning inventory	$ 15,000	
Purchases	60,000	
Less: Ending inventory	(10,000)	
Cost of goods sold		(65,000)
Gross profit		$ 35,000

At the end of the previous year, White Corporation had accounts receivable of $25,000 and accounts payable for merchandise of $34,000. The accounts receivable from the previous year in the amount of $25,000 were never included in gross income since White was on the cash basis and did not recognize the uncollected receivables. In the current year, the $25,000 was not included in the accrual basis sales since the sales were made in a prior year. Therefore, a $25,000 adjustment to income is required to prevent the receivables from being omitted from income.

The corollary of the failure to recognize a prior year's receivables is the failure to recognize a prior year's accounts payable. The beginning of the year's accounts payable was not included in the current or prior year's purchases. Thus, a deduction for the $34,000 was not taken in either year and is therefore included as an adjustment to income for the period of change.

An adjustment is also required to reflect the $15,000 beginning inventory that White deducted (due to the use of a cash method of accounting) in the previous year. In this instance, the cost of goods sold during the year of change was increased by the beginning inventory and resulted in a double deduction.

The net adjustment due to the change in accounting method is computed as follows:

Beginning inventory (deducted in prior and current year)	$ 15,000
Beginning accounts receivable (omitted from income)	25,000
Beginning accounts payable (omitted from deductions)	(34,000)
Net increase in taxable income	$ 6,000

Disposition of the Net Adjustment. Generally, if the IRS *requires* the taxpayer to change an accounting method, the net adjustment is added to or subtracted from the income for the year of the change. In cases of positive (an

CONCEPT SUMMARY 15–1

Adjustment Periods for Voluntary Changes in Accounting Method

Change	Type of Adjustment	Allocation Period
Incorrect to correct method	Positive	Three years—year of change and the two succeeding years
Incorrect to correct method	Negative	Year of change
Correct to correct	Positive	Six years—year of change and the five succeeding years
Correct to correct	Negative	Six years—year of change and the five succeeding years

increase in income) adjustments in excess of $3,000, the taxpayer is allowed to calculate the tax by spreading the adjustment over one or more previous years.[58]

To encourage taxpayers to *voluntarily* change from incorrect methods and to facilitate changes from one correct method to another, the IRS generally allows the taxpayer to spread the adjustment into future years. Assuming the taxpayer files a timely request for change (Form 3115), the allocation periods in Concept Summary 15–1 generally apply.[59]

SPECIAL ACCOUNTING METHODS

4   **LEARNING OBJECTIVE**
Determine when the installment method of accounting can be utilized and apply the related calculation techniques.

Generally, accrual basis taxpayers recognize income when goods are sold and shipped to the customer. Cash basis taxpayers generally recognize income from a sale on the collection of cash from the customer. The tax law provides special accounting methods for certain installment sales and long-term contracts. These special methods were enacted, in part, to assure that the tax will be due when the taxpayer is best able to pay the tax.

INSTALLMENT METHOD

Under the general rule for computing the gain or loss from the sale of property, the taxpayer recognizes the entire amount of gain or loss upon the sale or other disposition of the property.

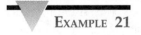

EXAMPLE 21

Mark sells property to Fran for $10,000 cash plus Fran's note (fair market value and face amount of $90,000). Mark's basis for the property was $15,000. Gain or loss is computed under either the cash or accrual basis as follows:

Amount realized	
Cash down payment	$ 10,000
Note receivable	90,000
	$100,000
Basis in the property	(15,000)
Realized gain	$ 85,000

▼

---

[58] § 481(b).

[59] Rev.Proc. 92–20, 1992–1 C.B. 301.

In Example 21, the general rule for recognizing gain or loss requires Mark to pay a substantial amount of tax on the gain in the year of sale even though he receives only $10,000 cash. Congress enacted the installment sales provisions to prevent this sort of hardship by allowing the taxpayer to spread the gain from installment sales over the collection period. The *installment method* is a very important planning tool because of the tax deferral possibilities.

Eligibility and Calculations. The **installment method** applies to *gains* (but not losses) from the sale of property where the seller will receive at least one payment *after* the year of sale. For many years, practically all gains from the sale of property were eligible for the installment method. However, over the years, the Code has been amended to *deny* the use of the installment method for the following:[60]

- Gains on property held for sale in the ordinary course of business.
- Depreciation recapture under § 1245 or § 1250.
- Gains on stocks or securities traded on an established market.

As an exception to the first item, the installment method may be used to report gains from sales of the following:[61]

- Time-share units (e.g., the right to use real property for two weeks each year).
- Residential lots (if the seller is not to make any improvements).
- Any property used or produced in the trade or business of farming.

The Nonelective Aspect. Regardless of the taxpayer's method of accounting, as a general rule, eligible sales *must* be reported by the installment method.[62] A special election is required to report the gain by any other method of accounting (see the discussion in a subsequent section of this chapter).

Computing the Gain for the Period. The gain reported on each sale is computed by the following formula:

$$\frac{\text{Total gain}}{\text{Contract price}} \times \text{Payments received} = \text{Recognized gain}$$

The taxpayer must compute each variable as follows:

1. *Total gain* is the selling price reduced by selling expenses and the adjusted basis of the property. The selling price is the total consideration received by the seller, including notes receivable from the buyer, and the seller's liabilities assumed by the buyer.
2. *Contract price* is the selling price less the seller's liabilities that are assumed by the buyer. Generally, the contract price is the amount, other than interest, the seller will receive from the purchaser.
3. *Payments received* are the collections on the contract price received in the tax year. This generally is equal to the cash received less the interest income collected for the period. If the buyer pays any of the seller's expenses, the seller regards the amount paid as a payment received.

---

[60] §§ 453(b), (i), and (l).
[61] § 453(l)(2).

[62] § 453(a).

EXAMPLE 22

The seller is not a dealer, and the facts are as follows:

Sales price (amount realized)		
Cash down payment	$ 1,000	
Seller's mortgage assumed	3,000	
Notes payable to the seller	13,000	$17,000
Selling expenses		(500)
Seller's basis		(10,000)
Total gain		$ 6,500

The contract price is $14,000 ($17,000 – $3,000). Assuming the $1,000 is the only payment in the year of sale, the recognized gain in that year is computed as follows:

$$\frac{\$6,500 \text{ (total gain)}}{\$14,000 \text{ (contract price)}} \times \$1,000 = \$464 \text{ (gain recognized in year of sale)} \qquad \blacktriangledown$$

If the sum of the seller's basis and selling expenses is less than the liabilities assumed by the buyer, the difference must be added to the contract price and to the payments (treated as *deemed payments*) received in the year of sale.[63] This adjustment to the contract price is required so that the ratio of total gain to contract price will not be greater than one. The adjustment also accelerates the reporting of income from the deemed payments.

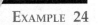

EXAMPLE 23

Assume the same facts as in Example 22, except that the seller's basis in the property is only $2,000. The total gain, therefore, is $14,500 [$17,000 – ($2,000 + $500)]. Payments in the year of sale are $1,500 and are calculated as follows:

Down payment	$1,000
Excess of mortgage assumed over seller's basis and expenses ($3,000 – $2,000 – $500)	500
	$1,500

The contract price is $14,500 [$17,000 (selling price) – $3,000 (seller's mortgage assumed) + $500 (excess of mortgage assumed over seller's basis and selling expenses)]. The gain recognized in the year of sale is computed as follows:

$$\frac{\$14,500 \text{ (total gain)}}{\$14,500 \text{ (contract price)}} \times \$1,500 = \$1,500$$

In subsequent years, all amounts the seller collects on the note principal ($13,000) will be recognized gain ($13,000 × 100%). ▼

As previously discussed, gains attributable to ordinary income recapture under §§ 1245 and 1250 are *ineligible* for installment reporting. Therefore, the § 1245 or § 1250 gain realized must be recognized in the year of sale, and the installment sale gain is the remaining gain.

EXAMPLE 24

Olaf sold an apartment building for $50,000 cash and a $75,000 note due in two years. Olaf's basis in the property was $25,000, and he recaptured $40,000 ordinary income under § 1250.

---

[63] Temp.Reg. § 15a.453–1(b)(2)(iii).

Olaf's realized gain is $100,000 ($125,000 − $25,000), and the $40,000 recapture must be recognized in the year of sale. Of the $60,000 remaining § 1231 gain, $24,000 must be recognized in the year of sale:

$$\frac{\S\,1231\ gain}{Contract\ price} \times Payments\ received = \frac{\$125,000 - \$25,000 - \$40,000}{\$125,000} \times \$50,000$$

$$= \frac{\$60,000}{\$125,000} \times \$50,000 = \$24,000$$

The remaining realized gain of $36,000 ($60,000 − $24,000) will be recognized as the $75,000 note is collected. ▼

Imputed Interest.   If a deferred payment contract for the sale of property with a selling price greater than $3,000 does not contain a reasonable interest rate, a reasonable rate is imputed.[64] The imputing of interest effectively restates the selling price of the property to equal the sum of the payments at the date of the sale and the discounted present value of the future payments. The difference between the present value of a future payment and the payment's face amount is taxed as interest income, as discussed in the following paragraphs. Thus, the **imputed interest** rules prevent sellers of capital assets from increasing the selling price to reflect the equivalent of unstated interest on deferred payments and thereby converting ordinary (interest) income into long-term capital gains. In addition, the imputed interest rules are important because they affect the timing of income recognition.

Generally, if the contract does not charge at least the Federal rate, interest will be imputed at the Federal rate. The Federal rate is the interest rate the Federal government pays on new borrowing and is published monthly by the IRS.[65]

As a general rule, the buyer and seller must account for interest on the accrual basis with semiannual compounding.[66] Requiring the use of the accrual basis assures that the seller's interest income and the buyer's interest expense are reported in the same tax year. The following example illustrates the calculation and amortization of imputed interest.

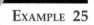

EXAMPLE 25

Peggy, a cash basis taxpayer, sold land on January 1, 1996, for $200,000 cash and $6 million due on December 31, 1997, with 5% interest payable December 31, 1996, and December 31, 1997. At the time of the sale, the Federal rate was 8% (compounded semiannually). Because Peggy did not charge at least the Federal rate, interest will be imputed at 8% (compounded semiannually).

Date	Payment	Present Value (at 8%) on 1/1/1996	Imputed Interest
12/31/1996	$ 300,000	$ 277,500	$ 22,500
12/31/1997	6,300,000	5,386,500	913,500
	$6,600,000	$5,664,000	$936,000

---

[64] §§ 483 and 1274.

[65] § 1274(d)(1). There are three Federal rates: short-term (not over three years), mid-term (over three years but not over nine years), and long-term (over nine years).

[66] §§ 1274(a), 1273(a), and 1272(a).

Thus, the selling price will be restated to $5,864,000 ($200,000 + $5,664,000) rather than $6,200,000 ($200,000 + $6,000,000), and Peggy will recognize interest income in accordance with the following amortization schedule:

Year	Beginning Balance	Interest Income (at 8%)*	Received	Ending Balance
1996	$5,664,000	$462,182	$ 300,000	$5,826,182
1997	5,826,182	473,818	6,300,000	–0–

*Compounded semiannually.   ▼

Congress has created several exceptions regarding the rate at which interest is imputed and the method of accounting for the interest income and expense. The general rules and exceptions are summarized in Concept Summary 15–2.

Related-Party Sales of Nondepreciable Property. If the Code did not contain special rules, a taxpayer could make an installment sale of property to a related party (e.g., a family member) who would obtain a basis in the property equal to the purchase price (the fair market value of the property). Then, the purchasing family member could immediately sell the property to an unrelated party for cash with no recognized gain or loss (the amount realized would equal the basis). The related-party purchaser would not pay the installment note to the selling family member until a later year or years. The net result would be that the family has the cash, but no taxable gain is recognized until the intrafamily transfer of the cash (the purchasing family member makes payments on the installment note).

Under special rules designed to combat this scheme, the proceeds from the subsequent sale (the second sale) by the purchasing family member are treated as though they were used to pay the installment note due the selling family member (the first sale). As a result, the recognition of gain from the original sale between the related parties is accelerated.[67]

However, even with these special rules, Congress did not eliminate the benefits of all related-party installment sales.

- Related parties include the first seller's brothers, sisters, ancestors, lineal descendants, controlled corporations, and partnerships, trusts, and estates in which the seller has an interest.[68]
- There is no acceleration if the second disposition occurs more than two years after the first sale.[69]

Thus, if the taxpayer can sell the property to a relative who is not a "related party" or to a patient family member, the intrafamily installment sale is still a powerful tax planning tool. Other exceptions also can be applied in some circumstances.[70]

---

[67] § 453(e).

[68] § 453(f)(1), cross-referencing §§ 267(b) and 318(a). Although spouses are related parties, the exemption of gain between spouses (§ 1041) makes the second-disposition rules inapplicable when the first sale was between spouses.

[69] § 453(e)(2). But see § 453(e)(2)(B) for extensions of the two-year period.

[70] See §§ 453(e)(6) and (7).

CONCEPT SUMMARY 15–2

Interest on Installment Sales

	Imputed Interest Rate
General rule	Federal rate
Exceptions:	
• Principal amount not over $2.8 million.[1]	Lesser of Federal rate or 9%
• Sale of land (with a calendar year ceiling of $500,000) between family members (the seller's spouse, brothers, sisters, ancestors, or lineal descendants).[2]	Lesser of Federal rate or 6%

	Method of Accounting for Interest	
	Seller's Interest Income	Buyer's Interest Expense
General rule[3]	Accrual	Accrual
Exceptions:		
• Total payments under the contract are $250,000 or less.[4]	Taxpayer's overall method	Taxpayer's overall method
• Sale of a farm (sales price of $1 million or less).[5]	Taxpayer's overall method	Taxpayer's overall method
• Sale of a principal residence.[6]	Taxpayer's overall method	Taxpayer's overall method
• Sale for a note with a principal amount of not over $2 million, the seller is on the cash basis, the property sold is not inventory, and the buyer agrees to report expenses by the cash method.[7]	Cash	Cash

[1] § 1274A. This amount is adjusted annually for inflation. For 1996, the amount is $3,622,500.
[2] §§ 1274(c)(3)(F) and 483(e).
[3] §§ 1274(a) and 1272(a)(3).
[4] §§ 1274(c)(3)(C) and 483.
[5] §§ 1274(c)(3)(A) and 483.
[6] §§ 1274(c)(3)(B) and 483.
[7] § 1274A(c). This amount is adjusted annually for inflation. For 1996, the amount is $2,587,500.

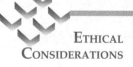

ETHICAL
CONSIDERATIONS

A Related-Party Installment Sale Has Unexpected Results

Amos has been in the farming business for over 40 years. Since he is nearing retirement age—although he will never retire—he would like to slow down. He decides to sell 300 acres of his land to his 26-year-old son, Chuck, for $465,000 so Chuck can go into the farming business. Amos's basis for the land is $50,000. Since Chuck does not have much equity and Amos would like to keep the financing of the land in the family, the sales contract calls for a $15,000 down payment and annual payments of $30,000 for 15 years plus interest at 8 percent. Amos anticipates Chuck's profits from the farm will be adequate to cover these payments and provide Chuck with a decent living.

Chuck makes the payment for the first year. Unfortunately, he then gets involved with some young people from a nearby city and develops a drug problem. To finance his drug dependency, 14 months after acquiring the farm, he sells it for $500,000 cash to a real estate developer who intends to build 1,000 tract houses on the land.

When Amos learns of this, he is furious. He disowns Chuck and vows never to speak to him again.

Now Amos's CPA tells him that he has another problem. The sale of the land by Chuck should be treated as if Chuck had paid Amos the remaining balance on the installment sale. The CPA explains to Amos that this result occurs because his original sale to Chuck was a related-party transaction. Amos finds this ridiculous and says he no longer has a son.

Who is correct, Amos or the CPA? Evaluate the equity of the related-party provision.

Related-Party Sales of Depreciable Property. The installment method cannot be used to report a gain on the sale of depreciable property to a controlled entity. The purpose of this rule is to prevent the seller from deferring gain (until collections are received) while the related purchaser is enjoying a stepped-up basis for depreciation purposes.[71]

The prohibition on the use of the installment method applies to sales between the taxpayer and a partnership or corporation in which the taxpayer holds a more-than-50 percent interest. Constructive ownership rules are used in applying the ownership test (i.e., the taxpayer is considered to own stock owned by a spouse and certain other family members).[72] However, if the taxpayer can establish that tax avoidance was not a principal purpose of the transaction, the installment method can be used to report the gain.

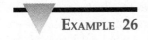

EXAMPLE 26

Ali purchased an apartment building from her controlled corporation, Emerald Corporation. Ali was short of cash at the time of the purchase (December 1996), but was to collect a large cash payment in January 1997. The agreement required Ali to pay the entire arm's length price in January 1997. Ali had good business reasons for acquiring the building. Emerald Corporation should be able to convince the IRS that tax avoidance was not a principal purpose for the installment sale because the tax benefits are not overwhelming. The corporation will report all of the gain in the year following the year of sale, and the building must be depreciated over 27.5 years (the cost recovery period). ▼

DISPOSITION OF INSTALLMENT OBLIGATIONS

Generally, a taxpayer must recognize the deferred profit from an installment sale when the obligation is transferred to another party or otherwise relinquished. The rationale for accelerating the gain is that the deferral should continue for no longer than the taxpayer owns the installment obligation.[73]

The gift or cancellation of an installment note is treated as a taxable disposition by the donor. The amount realized from the cancellation is the face amount of the note if the parties (obligor and obligee) are related to each other.[74]

[71] § 453(g).
[72] §§ 1239(b) and (c).

[73] § 453B(a).
[74] § 453B(f)(2).

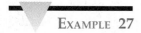

EXAMPLE 27

Liz cancels a note issued by Tina (Liz's daughter) that arose in connection with the sale of property. At the time of the cancellation, the note had a basis to Liz of $10,000, a face amount of $25,000, and a fair market value of $20,000. Presuming the initial sale by Liz qualified as an installment sale, the cancellation results in gain of $15,000 ($25,000 − $10,000) to Liz. ▼

Certain exceptions to the recognition of gain provisions are provided for transfers of installment obligations pursuant to tax-free incorporations under § 351, contributions of capital to a partnership, certain corporate liquidations, transfers due to the taxpayer's death, and transfers between spouses or incident to divorce.[75] In such instances, the deferred profit is merely shifted to the transferee, who is responsible for the payment of tax on the subsequent collections of the installment obligations.

INTEREST ON DEFERRED TAXES

With the installment method, the seller earns interest on the receivable. The receivable includes the deferred gain. Thus, one could argue that the seller is earning interest on the deferred taxes. Some commentators reason that the government is, in effect, making interest-free loans to taxpayers who report gains by the installment method. Following the argument that the amount of the deferred taxes is a loan, in some situations, the taxpayer is required to pay interest on the deferred taxes.[76]

ELECTING OUT OF THE INSTALLMENT METHOD

A taxpayer can *elect not to use* the installment method. The election is made by reporting on a timely filed return the gain computed by the taxpayer's usual method of accounting (cash or accrual).[77] However, the Regulations provide that the amount realized by a cash basis taxpayer cannot be less than the value of the property sold. This rule differs from the usual cash basis accounting rules (discussed earlier),[78] which measure the amount realized in terms of the fair market value of the property received. The net effect of the Regulations is to allow the cash basis taxpayer to report his or her gain as an accrual basis taxpayer. The election is frequently applied to year-end sales by taxpayers who expect to be in a higher tax bracket in the following year.

EXAMPLE 28

On December 31, 1996, Jaime sold land to Veneia for $20,000 (fair market value). The cash was to be paid on January 4, 1997. Jaime is a cash basis taxpayer, and his basis in the land is $8,000. Jaime has a large casualty loss and very little other income in 1996. Thus, his marginal tax rate in 1996 is 15%. He expects his rate to increase to 36% in 1997.

The transaction constitutes an installment sale because a payment will be received in a tax year after the tax year of disposition. Veneia's promise to pay Jaime is an installment obligation, and under the Regulations, the value of the installment obligation is equal to the value of the property sold ($20,000). If Jaime elects out of the installment method, he would shift $12,000 of gain ($20,000 − $8,000) from the expected higher rate in 1997 to the 15% rate in 1996. The expected tax savings based on the rate differentials may exceed the benefit of the tax deferral available with the installment method. ▼

---

[75] §§ 453B(c), (d), and (g).
[76] See § 453A for details.

[77] § 453(d) and Temp. Reg. § 15a.453–1(d). See also Rev. Rul. 82–227, 1982–2 C.B. 89.
[78] Refer to Chapter 3.

Permission of the IRS is required to revoke an election not to use the installment method.[79]

LONG-TERM CONTRACTS

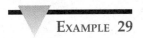

5 LEARNING OBJECTIVE
Understand the alternative methods of accounting for long-term contracts (the completed contract method and the percentage of completion method) including the limitations on the use of the completed contract method.

A **long-term contract** is a building, installation, construction, or manufacturing contract that is entered into but not completed within the same tax year. However, a *manufacturing* contract is long term *only* if the contract is to manufacture (1) a unique item not normally carried in finished goods inventory or (2) items that normally require more than 12 calendar months to complete.[80] An item is *unique* if it is designed to meet the customer's particular needs and is not suitable for use by others. A contract to perform services (e.g., auditing or legal services) is not considered a contract for this purpose and thus cannot qualify as a long-term contract.

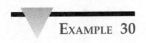

EXAMPLE 29

Rocky, a calendar year taxpayer, entered into two contracts during the year. One contract was to construct a building foundation. Work was to begin in October 1996 and was to be completed by June 1997. The contract is long term because it will not be entered into and completed in the same tax year. The fact that the contract requires less than 12 calendar months to complete is not relevant because the contract is not for manufacturing. The second contract was for architectural services to be performed over two years. These services will not qualify for long-term contract treatment because the taxpayer will not build, install, construct, or manufacture a product. ▼

Generally, the taxpayer must accumulate all of the direct and indirect costs incurred under a contract. This means the production costs must be accumulated and allocated to individual contracts. Furthermore, mixed services costs, costs that benefit contracts as well as the general administrative operations of the business, must be allocated to production. Exhibit 15–1 lists the types of costs that must be accumulated and allocated to contracts. The taxpayer must develop reasonable bases for cost allocations.[81]

EXAMPLE 30

Falcon, Inc., uses detailed cost accumulation records to assign labor and materials to its contracts in progress. The total cost of fringe benefits is allocated to a contract on the following basis:

$$\frac{\text{Labor on the contract}}{\text{Total salaries and labor}} \times \text{Total cost of fringe benefits}$$

Similarly, storage and handling costs for materials are allocated to contracts on the following basis:

$$\frac{\text{Contract materials}}{\text{Materials purchases}} \times \text{Storage and handling costs}$$

The cost of the personnel operations, a mixed services cost, is allocated between production and general administration based on the number of employees in each function. The personnel cost allocated to production is allocated to individual contracts on the basis of the formula used to allocate fringe benefits. ▼

---

[79] § 453(d)(3) and Temp.Reg. § 15a.453–1(d)(4).
[80] § 460(f) and Reg. § 1.451–3(b).

[81] Reg. §§ 1.263A–1T(b)(3)(iii)(A)(1) and 1.451–3(d)(9).

▼ **EXHIBIT 15–1**
Contract Costs, Mixed Services
Costs, and Current Expense
Items for Contracts

	Contracts Eligible for the Completed Contract Method	Other Contracts
Contract costs:		
Direct materials (a part of the finished product).	Capital	Capital
Indirect materials (consumed in production but not in the finished product, e.g., grease and oil for equipment).	Capital	Capital
Storage, handling, and insurance on materials.	Expense	Capital
Direct labor (worked on the product).	Capital	Capital
Indirect labor (worked in the production process but not directly on the product, e.g., a construction supervisor).	Capital	Capital
Fringe benefits for direct and indirect labor (e.g., vacation, sick pay, unemployment, and other insurance).	Capital	Capital
Pension costs for direct and indirect labor:		
• Current cost.	Expense	Capital
• Past service costs.	Expense	Capital
Depreciation on production facilities:		
• For financial statements.	Capital	Capital
• Tax depreciation in excess of financial statements.	Expense	Capital
Depreciation on idle facilities.	Expense	Expense
Property taxes, insurance, rent, and maintenance on production facilities.	Capital	Capital
Bidding expenses—successful.	Expense	Capital
Bidding expenses—unsuccessful.	Expense	Expense
Interest to finance real estate construction.	Capital	Capital
Interest to finance personal property:		
• Production period of one year or less.	Expense	Expense
• Production period exceeds one year and costs exceed $1 million.	Capital	Capital
• Production period exceeds two years.	Capital	Capital
Mixed services costs:		
• Personnel operations.	Expense	Allocate
• Data processing.	Expense	Allocate
• Purchasing.	Expense	Allocate
Selling, general, and administrative expenses (including an allocated share of mixed services).	Expense	Expense
Losses.	Expense	Expense

IRS Says the Cash Method Does Not Clearly Reflect the Income of Small Contractors

In a 1980 Tax Court decision, *Raymond Magnon*, 73 T.C. 980, the Court ruled that a small contractor could use the cash method of accounting. More recently, the IRS was unsuccessful in attempting to require a contractor to change from the cash method to the percentage of completion method. The IRS argued that the cash method did not clearly reflect income, but the Tax Court disagreed [*Ansley-Sheppard-Burgess Company*, 104 T.C. No. 17 (1995)].

In other recent cases, however, the IRS has been successful in requiring small contractors to change from the cash method to the accrual method (*Thompson Electric Inc.*, T.C.Memo 1995–292 and *J. P. Sheahan Associates*, T.C.Memo 1995–239). The IRS has successfully argued that the accumulated costs for materials and labor, whether incurred by the contractor or its subcontractors, are subject to the inventory rules. Because inventories are a material income-producing factor, the cash method does not clearly reflect income, and the IRS can require the contractor to employ the accrual method.

SOURCE: "The IRS Insists General Contractor Use Inventories and Change to Accrual Method," *Journal of Taxation* (September 1995): 180.

The accumulated costs are deducted when the revenue from the contract is recognized. Generally, two methods of accounting are used in varying circumstances to determine when the revenue from a contract is recognized:[82]

- The completed contract method.
- The percentage of completion method.

The *completed contract method may be used* for (1) home construction contracts (contracts in which at least 80 percent of the estimated costs are for dwelling units in buildings with four or fewer units) and (2) certain other real estate construction contracts. Other real estate contracts can qualify for the completed contract method if the following requirements are satisfied:

- The contract is expected to be completed within the two-year period beginning on the commencement date of the contract.
- The contract is performed by a taxpayer whose average annual gross receipts for the three taxable years preceding the taxable year in which the contract is entered into do not exceed $10 million.

All other contractors must use the percentage of completion method.

Completed Contract Method. Under the **completed contract method,** no revenue from the contract is recognized until the contract is completed and accepted. However, a taxpayer may not delay completion of a contract for the principal purpose of deferring tax.[83]

---

[82] § 460.

[83] Reg. § 1.451–3(b)(2).

In some instances, the original contract price may be disputed, or the buyer may want additional work to be done on a long-term contract. If the disputed amount is substantial (it is not possible to determine whether a profit or loss will ultimately be realized on the contract), the Regulations provide that no amount of income or loss is recognized until the dispute is resolved. In all other cases, the profit or loss (reduced by the amount in dispute) is recognized in the current period on completion of the contract. However, additional work may need to be performed with respect to the disputed contract. In this case, the difference between the amount in dispute and the actual cost of the additional work is recognized in the year the work is completed rather than in the year in which the dispute is resolved.[84]

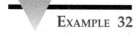

EXAMPLE 31

Ted, a calendar year taxpayer utilizing the completed contract method of accounting, constructed a building for Khalid under a long-term contract. The gross contract price was $500,000. Ted finished construction in 1996 at a cost of $475,000. When Khalid examined the building, he insisted that it be repainted or the contract price be reduced. The estimated cost of repainting is $10,000. Since under the terms of the contract, Ted is assured of a profit of at least $15,000 ($500,000 − $475,000 − $10,000) even if the dispute is ultimately resolved in Khalid's favor, Ted must include $490,000 ($500,000 − $10,000) in gross income and is allowed deductions of $475,000 for 1996.

In 1997, Ted and Khalid resolve the dispute, and Ted repaints certain portions of the building at a cost of $6,000. Ted must include $10,000 in 1997 gross income and may deduct the $6,000 expense in that year. ▼

EXAMPLE 32

Assume the same facts as in the previous example, except the estimated cost of repainting the building is $50,000. Since the resolution of the dispute completely in Khalid's favor would mean a net loss on the contract for Ted ($500,000 − $475,000 − $50,000 = $25,000 loss), he does not recognize any income or loss until the year the dispute is resolved. ▼

Frequently, a contractor receives payment at various stages of completion. For example, when the contract is 50 percent complete, the contractor may receive 50 percent of the contract price less a retainage. The taxation of these payments is generally governed by Regulation § 1.451–5 "advance payments for goods and long-term contracts" (discussed in Chapter 3). Generally, contractors are permitted to defer the advance payments until the payments are recognized as income under the taxpayer's method of accounting.

Percentage of Completion Method.   The percentage of completion method must be used to account for long-term contracts unless the taxpayer qualifies for one of the two exceptions that permit the completed contract method to be used (home construction contracts and certain other real estate construction contracts).[85] Under the **percentage of completion method,** a portion of the gross contract price is included in income during each period as the work progresses. The revenue accrued each period (except for the final period) is computed as follows:[86]

---

[84] Reg. § 1.451–3(d)(2)(ii)–(vii), Example (2).

[85] Certain residential construction contracts that do not qualify for the completed contract method may nevertheless use that method to account for 30% of the profit from the contract, with the remaining 70% reported by the percentage of completion method.

[86] § 460(b)(1)(A).

$$\frac{C}{T} \times P$$

Where C = Contract costs incurred during the period.

T = Estimated total cost of the contract.

P = Contract price.

All of the costs allocated to the contract during the period are deductible from the accrued revenue.[87] The revenue reported in the final period is simply the unreported revenue from the contract. Because T in this formula is an estimate that frequently differs from total actual costs, which are not known until the contract has been completed, the profit on a contract for a particular period may be overstated or understated.

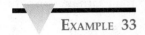

EXAMPLE 33

Tan, Inc., entered into a contract that was to take two years to complete, with an estimated cost of $2,250,000. The contract price was $3,000,000. Costs of the contract for 1996, the first year, totaled $1,350,000. The gross profit reported by the percentage of completion method for 1996 was $450,000 [($1,350,000/$2,250,000 × $3,000,000) − $1,350,000]. The contract was completed at the end of 1997 at a total cost of $2,700,000. In retrospect, 1996 profit should have been $150,000 [($1,350,000/$2,700,000 × $3,000,000) − $1,350,000]. Thus, taxes were overpaid for 1996. ▼

A *de minimis* rule enables the contractor to delay the recognition of income for a particular contract under the percentage of completion method. If less than 10 percent of the estimated contract costs have been incurred by the end of the taxable year, the taxpayer can elect to defer the recognition of income and the related costs until the taxable year in which cumulative contract costs are at least 10 percent of the estimated contract costs.[88]

Lookback Provisions. In the year a contract is completed, a *lookback* provision requires the recalculation of annual profits reported on the contract under the percentage of completion method. Interest is paid to the taxpayer if taxes were overpaid, and interest is payable by the taxpayer if there was an underpayment.[89] For a corporate taxpayer, the lookback interest paid by the taxpayer is deductible, but for an individual taxpayer, it is nondeductible personal interest associated with a tax liability.

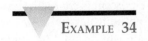

EXAMPLE 34

Assume Tan, Inc., in Example 33, was in the 34% tax bracket in both years and the relevant interest rate was 10%. For 1996, the company paid excess taxes of $102,000 [($450,000 − $150,000) × .34]. When the contract is completed at the end of 1997, Tan, Inc., should receive interest of $10,200 for one year on the tax overpayment ($102,000 × .10). ▼

TAX PLANNING CONSIDERATIONS

TAXABLE YEAR

Under the general rules for tax years, partnerships and S corporations frequently will be required to use a calendar year. However, if the partnership or S corporation can demonstrate a business purpose for a fiscal year, the IRS will

---

[87] Reg. § 1.451–3(c)(3).

[88] § 460(b)(5).

[89] § 460(b)(2).

allow the entity to use the requested year. The advantage to a fiscal year is that the calendar year partners and S corporation shareholders may be able to defer from tax the income earned from the close of the fiscal year until the end of the calendar year. Tax advisers for these entities should apply the IRS's gross receipts test described in Revenue Procedure 87–32 to determine if permission for the fiscal year will be granted.

CASH METHOD OF ACCOUNTING

The cash method of accounting gives the taxpayer considerable control over the recognition of expenses and some control over the recognition of income. This method can be used by proprietorships, partnerships, and small corporations (gross receipts of $5 million or less) that provide services (inventories are not material to the service business). Farmers (except certain farming corporations) can also use the cash method.

INSTALLMENT METHOD

Unlike the cash and accrual methods, the installment method often results in an interest-free loan (of deferred taxes) from the government. The installment method is not available for the sale of inventory. Nevertheless, the installment method is an important tax planning technique and should be considered when a sale of eligible property is being planned. That is, if the taxpayer can benefit from deferring the tax, the terms of sale can be arranged so that the installment method rules apply. If, on the other hand, the taxpayer expects to be in a higher tax bracket when the payments will be received, he or she can elect to not use the installment method.

Related Parties.   Intrafamily installment sales can still be a useful family tax planning tool. If the related party holds the property more than two years, a subsequent sale will not accelerate the gain from the first disposition. Patience and forethought are rewarded.

The 6 percent limitation on imputed interest on sales of land between family members enables the seller to convert ordinary income into capital gain or make what is, in effect, a nontaxable gift. If the selling price is raised to adjust for the low interest rate charges on an installment sale, the seller has more capital gain but less ordinary income than would be realized from a sale to an unrelated party. If the selling price is not raised and the specified interest of 6 percent is charged, the seller enables the relative to have the use of the property without having to pay for its full market value. As an additional benefit, the bargain sale is not a taxable gift.

Disposition of Installment Obligations.   A disposition of an installment obligation is also a serious matter. Gifts of the obligations will accelerate income to the seller. The list of taxable and nontaxable dispositions of installment obligations should not be trusted to memory. In each instance where transfers of installment obligations are contemplated, the practitioner should conduct research to be sure he or she knows the consequences.

COMPLETED CONTRACT METHOD

Generally, large contractors must use the percentage of completion method of accounting for reporting the income from long-term contracts. Under the percentage of completion method, the taxpayer must recognize profit in each period costs are incurred. Profit is reported in proportion to the cost incurred for the period as a proportion of the total contract cost. However, small contractors (average annual gross receipts do not exceed $10 million) working on contracts that are completed within a two-year period can elect to use the completed contract method and defer profit until the year in which the contract is completed.

KEY TERMS

Accounting methods, 15–11	Fiscal year, 15–2	One-year rule for prepaid expenses, 15–12
Accounting period, 15–2	Hybrid method, 15–16	Percentage of completion method, 15–30
Accrual method, 15–13	Imputed interest, 15–22	
All events test, 15–14	Installment method, 15–20	Personal service corporation (PSC), 15–6
Cash method, 15–11	Least aggregate deferral method, 15–4	Principal partner, 15–4
Claim of right doctrine, 15–10	Long-term contract, 15–27	Short taxable year (short period), 15–8
Completed contract method, 15–29	Majority interest partners, 15–4	
Economic performance test, 15–14		

PROBLEM MATERIALS

DISCUSSION QUESTIONS

1. Why would a C corporation want to use a tax year other than a calendar year?

2. Megan recently began conducting an office supply business as a corporation. Vito began conducting his law practice through a corporation. Neither corporation has made an S election. What tax year alternatives are available to Megan's business that are not available to Vito's business?

3. Debra is a practicing accountant. Over 90% of her work is done for individuals and S corporations. In the tax season just ended, Debra found that she could not continue to provide high-quality services for so many calendar year clients. Therefore, she plans to propose to some of her S corporation clients that the corporation change to a fiscal year ending September 30. What problems will Debra encounter in getting her clients to agree to a change in tax year?

4. Dan, a calendar year taxpayer, recently became a licensed orthopedic surgeon. He has incorporated his practice. Dan's brother suggests that the corporation's tax year should end on September 30 and thus avoid the end-of-the-calendar-year rush. What complications could result from the corporation filing its return on the basis of a fiscal year ending September 30?

5. Jack is a cash basis taxpayer. In 1995, when Jack was in the 31% marginal tax bracket, he received $25,000 for services provided for Jane. In 1996, Jack discovered that he had overcharged Jane by $4,000 in 1995. Therefore, he immediately refunded Jane the $4,000. As a result of some unusually large expenses in 1996, Jack's taxable income for the year was only $5,000. What special tax treatment is afforded the $4,000 payment?

6. Quinn is the sole shareholder of an accrual basis S corporation, Red, Inc. If Quinn forms another S corporation, Purple, Inc., does the fact that Red uses the accrual method mean that Purple is required to use the accrual method?

7. The Cardinal Insurance Agency is a newly formed corporation, and its gross receipts will probably never exceed $2 million in a year. Generally, it takes approximately two months to collect accounts receivable. Accounts payable generally equal expenses for one month. Cardinal does not expect accounts payable and accounts receivable to increase significantly. It prepares monthly financial statements using the accrual method of accounting. Given that the accounts receivable and accounts payable will not significantly change, would Cardinal derive any benefit from filing its tax return using the cash method of accounting?

8. Rita buys and sells produce. Her annual gross receipts are less than $5 million. Approximately 30% of her sales are on account. Rita sells all of her inventory each day. Thus, she has no beginning or ending inventory each year. Is Rita required to use the accrual method of accounting?

9. Earl, a certified public accountant, recently obtained a new client. The client is a retail grocery store that has used the cash method to report its income since it began doing business. Will Earl incur any liability if he prepares the tax return in accordance with the cash method and does not advise the client of the necessity of seeking the IRS's permission to change to the accrual method?

10. In December 1996, a cash basis taxpayer paid January through June 1997 management fees in connection with his rental properties. The fees were $4,000 per month. Compute the 1996 expense under the following assumptions:
    a. The fees were paid by an individual who derived substantially all of his income from the properties.
    b. The fees were paid by a tax-shelter partnership.

11. Compare the cash basis and accrual basis of accounting as applied to the following:
    a. Fixed assets.
    b. Prepaid rent income.
    c. Prepaid interest expense.
    d. A note received for services performed if the market value and face amount of the note differ.

12. Salmon Corporation and Betty have formed a partnership to rent real estate and operate a coal mine. Salmon uses the accrual method of accounting, and the company's tax year ends March 31. Betty is a cash basis, calendar year taxpayer. What are the tax accounting issues that the partnership must address?

13. Teal Company sells goods under terms that allow the customer to return the goods within 30 days of the sale. At the end of 1996 (as the company has done for all years since it started in business), Teal estimated the returns that it would receive in January 1997 from December 1996 sales. It then subtracted the estimated returns from the gross sales to arrive at net sales. Estimated returns and actual returns were the same amount. Can Teal's method be used for tax purposes?

14. Generally, what is the deadline for a taxpayer filing a request for a change from an incorrect accounting method?

15. What difference does it make whether the taxpayer or the IRS initiates the change in accounting method?

16. Generally, what incentives are provided to encourage a taxpayer to change voluntarily from an incorrect method of accounting?

17. Irene has made Sara an offer on the purchase of a capital asset. Irene will pay (1) $200,000 cash or (2) $50,000 cash and a 9% installment note for $150,000 guaranteed by City Bank of New York. If Sara sells for $200,000 cash, she will invest the after-tax proceeds in certificates of deposit yielding 9% interest. Sara's cost of the asset is $25,000. Why would Sara prefer the installment sale?

18. On June 1, 1994, Father sold land to Son for $100,000. Father reported the gain by the installment method, with the gain to be spread over five years. In May 1996, Son received an offer of $150,000 for the land, to be paid over three years. What would be the tax consequences of Son's sale? How could the tax consequences be improved?

19. In 1996, Bhaskar sold a building to his 100%-controlled corporation. The entire purchase price is to be paid in 1997. When should Bhaskar report the gain on the sale of the building?

20. Juan, a cash basis taxpayer, sold land in December 1996. At the time of the sale, he received $10,000 cash and a note for $90,000 due in 90 days. Juan expects to be in a much higher tax bracket in 1997. Should Juan report the sale in 1996 or 1997?

21. Who may use the completed contract method to report income?

22. The Eagle Construction Company began business on April 1 this year. The company erects prefabricated steel buildings and operates as follows. After the customer selects a building model, Eagle orders the materials from the manufacturer. Eagle then erects the building on the customer's property. Eagle prices the contract at 150% of the cost of the prefabricated building. The customer pays 70% of the price at the time the materials are ordered and the balance of the original price when the building is completed. If Eagle buys more than $1 million in materials during the year, the manufacturer will give Eagle a 2% rebate the following February. Several buildings were under construction at the end of the year. Eagle had ordered more than $1 million in materials during the year, but had paid for only about $989,000 through December. What issues involving Eagle's accounting methods are raised by these facts?

PROBLEMS

23. Red, White, and Blue are unrelated corporations engaged in real estate development. The three corporations formed a joint venture (treated as a partnership) to develop a tract of land. Assuming the venture does not have a natural business year, what tax year must the joint venture adopt under the following circumstances?

		Tax Year Ending	Interest in Joint Venture
a.	Red	September 30	60%
	White	June 30	20%
	Blue	March 31	20%
b.	Red	September 30	30%
	White	June 30	40%
	Blue	January 31	30%

24. Zack conducted his professional practice through Zack, Inc. The corporation uses a fiscal year ending September 30 even though the business purpose test for a fiscal year cannot be satisfied. For the year ending September 30, 1996, the corporation paid Zack a salary of $150,000, and during the period January through September 1996, the corporation paid him a salary of $120,000.
    a. How much salary should Zack receive during the period October 1 through December 31, 1996?
    b. Assume Zack received only $30,000 salary during the period October 1 through December 31, 1996. What would be the consequences to Zack, Inc.?

25. Owl Corporation is in the business of sales and home deliveries of fuel oil and currently uses a calendar year for reporting its taxable income. However, Owl's natural business year ends May 31. For the short period, January 1, 1996, through May 31, 1996, the corporation earned $31,500. Assume the corporate tax rates are as follows: 15% on

taxable income of $50,000 or less, 25% on taxable income over $50,000 but not over $75,000, and 34% on taxable income over $75,000.

a. What must Owl Corporation do to change its taxable year?

b. Compute Owl Corporation's tax for the short period.

26. Gold, Inc., is an accrual basis taxpayer. In 1996, an employee accidentally spilled hazardous chemicals on leased property. The chemicals destroyed trees on neighboring property, resulting in $30,000 damages. In 1996, the owner of the property sued Gold, Inc., for the $30,000. Gold's attorney feels that it is liable and the only issue is whether the neighbor will also seek punitive damages that could be as much as three times the actual damages. In addition, as a result of the spill, Gold was in violation of its lease and was therefore required to pay the landlord $15,000. However, the amount due for the lease violation was not payable until the termination of the lease in 1999. None of these costs were covered by insurance. Jeff Stuart, the president of Gold, Inc., is generally familiar with the accrual basis tax accounting rules and is concerned about when the company will be allowed to deduct the amounts the company is required to pay as a result of this environmental disaster. Write Mr. Stuart a letter explaining these issues. Gold's address is 200 Elm Avenue, San Jose, CA 95192.

27. Compute the taxpayer's income or deductions for 1996 using (1) the cash basis and (2) the accrual basis for each of the following:

a. In 1996, the taxpayer purchased new equipment for $100,000. The taxpayer paid $25,000 in cash and gave a $75,000 interest-bearing note for the balance. The equipment has an MACRS life of five years, the mid-year convention applies, and the § 179 election was not made.

b. In December 1996, the taxpayer collected $10,000 for January rents. In January 1997, the taxpayer collected $2,000 for December 1996 rents.

c. In December 1996, the taxpayer paid office equipment insurance premiums of $30,000 for January–June 1997.

28. Which of the following businesses must use the accrual method of accounting?

a. A corporation with annual gross receipts of $12 million from equipment rentals.

b. A partnership (not a tax shelter) engaged in farming and with annual gross receipts of $8 million.

c. A corporation that acts as an insurance agent with annual gross receipts of $1 million.

d. A manufacturer with annual gross receipts of $600,000.

e. A retailer with annual gross receipts of $250,000.

29. In 1996, the taxpayer was required to switch from the cash to the accrual basis of accounting for sales and cost of goods sold. Taxable income for 1996 computed under the cash basis was $40,000. Relevant account balances were as follows:

	Beginning of the Year	End of the Year
Accounts receivable	$36,000	$30,000
Accounts payable	9,000	8,000
Inventory	7,000	10,000

Compute the following:

a. The adjustment due to the change in accounting method.

b. The accrual basis taxable income for 1996.

30. In 1996, the taxpayer changed from the cash to the accrual basis of accounting for sales, cost of goods sold, and accrued expenses. Taxable income for 1996 computed under the cash method was $45,000. Relevant account balances are as follows:

	Beginning of the Year	End of the Year
Accounts receivable	$ 5,000	$13,000
Accounts payable	–0–	–0–
Accrued expenses	5,000	6,000
Inventory	10,000	9,000

a. Compute the accrual basis taxable income for 1996 and the adjustment due to the change in accounting method.

b. Assuming the change was voluntary, how will the adjustment due to the change be treated?

31. Floyd, a cash basis taxpayer, has agreed to sell land to Beige, Inc., a well-established and highly profitable company. Beige is willing to (1) pay $100,000 cash or (2) pay $25,000 cash and the balance ($75,000) plus interest at 10% (the Federal rate) in two years. Floyd is in the 35% marginal tax bracket (combined Federal and state) for all years and believes he can reinvest the sales proceeds and earn a 14% before-tax rate of return.

a. Should Floyd accept the deferred payments option if his basis in the land is $10,000?

b. Do you think your results would change if Floyd's basis in the land is $90,000?

32. Kay, who is not a dealer, sold an apartment house to Polly during 1996. The closing statement for the sale is as follows:

Total selling price		$100,000
Add: Polly's share of property taxes (6 months) paid by Kay		2,500
Less: Kay's 11% mortgage assumed by Polly	$55,000	
Polly's refundable binder ("earnest money") paid in 1995	1,000	
Polly's 11% installment note given to Kay	30,000	
Kay's real estate commissions and attorney's fees	7,500	(93,500)
Cash paid to Kay at closing		$ 9,000
Cash due from Polly = $9,000 + $7,500 expenses		$ 16,500

During 1996, Kay collected $4,000 in principal on the installment note and $2,000 interest. Her basis in the property was $70,000 [$85,000 – $15,000 (depreciation)], and there was $9,000 in potential depreciation recapture under § 1250. The Federal rate is 9%.

a. Compute the following:
   1. Total gain.
   2. Contract price.
   3. Payments received in the year of sale.
   4. Recognized gain in the year of sale and the character of such gain.
   (*Hint:* Think carefully about the manner in which the property taxes are handled before you begin your computations.)

b. Same as (a)(2) and (3), except Kay's basis in the property was $45,000.

33. On June 30, 1996, Kelly sold property for $250,000 cash on the date of sale and a $750,000 note due on September 30, 1997. No interest was stated in the contract. The present value of the note (using 13.2%, which was the Federal rate) was $640,000. Kelly's basis in the property was $400,000, and $40,000 of the gain was subject to depreciation recapture under § 1245. Expenses of the sale totaled $10,000, and Kelly was not a dealer in the property sold.

a. Compute Kelly's gain to be reported in 1996.

b. Compute Kelly's interest income for 1997.

34. On July 1, 1995, a cash basis taxpayer sold land for $800,000 due on the date of the sale and $6 million principal and $741,600 interest (6%) due on June 30, 1997. The seller's basis in the land was $1 million. The Federal short-term rate was 8%, compounded semiannually.
    a. Compute the seller's interest income and gain in 1995, 1996, and 1997.
    b. Same as (a), except that the amount due in two years was $2 million principal and $508,800 interest and the purchaser will use the cash method to account for interest.

35. On December 30, 1996, Father sold land to Son for $10,000 cash and a 7% installment note with a face amount of $190,000. In 1997, after paying $30,000 on the principal of the note, Son sold the land. In 1998, Son paid Father $25,000 on the note principal. Father's basis in the land was $50,000. Assuming Son sold the land for $250,000, compute Father's taxable gain in 1997.

36. George sold land to an unrelated party in 1995. His basis in the land was $40,000, and the selling price was $100,000: $25,000 payable at closing and $25,000 (plus 10% interest) due January 1, 1996, 1997, and 1998. What would be the tax consequences of the following? [Treat each part independently and assume (1) George did not elect out of the installment method and (2) the installment obligations have values equal to their face amounts.]
    a. In 1996, George gave to his daughter the right to collect all future payments on the installment obligations.
    b. In 1996, after collecting the payment due on January 1, George transferred the installment obligation to his 100%-controlled corporation in exchange for additional shares of stock.
    c. On December 31, 1996, George received the payment due on January 1, 1997. On December 15, 1997, George died, and the remaining installment obligation was transferred to his estate. The estate collected the amount due on January 1, 1998.

37. The Dove Construction Company reports its income by the completed contract method. At the end of 1996, the company completed a contract to construct a building at a total cost of $980,000. The contract price was $1,200,000. However, the customer refused to accept the work and would not pay anything on the contract because he claimed the roof did not meet specifications. Dove's engineers estimated it would cost $140,000 to bring the roof up to the customer's standards. In 1997, the dispute was settled in the customer's favor; the roof was improved at a cost of $170,000, and the customer accepted the building and paid the $1,200,000.
    a. What would be the effects of the above on Dove's taxable income for 1996 and 1997?
    b. Same as (a), except Dove had $1,100,000 of accumulated costs under the contract at the end of 1996.

38. Rust Company is a real estate construction company with average annual gross receipts of $4 million. Rust uses the completed contract method, and the contracts require 18 months to complete.
    a. Which of the following costs would be allocated to construction in progress by Rust?
       1. The payroll taxes on direct labor.
       2. The current services pension costs for employees whose wages are included in direct labor.
       3. Accelerated depreciation on equipment used on contracts.
       4. Sales tax on materials assigned to contracts.
       5. The past service costs for employees whose wages are included in direct labor.
       6. Bidding expenses for contracts awarded.
    b. Assume that Rust generally builds commercial buildings under contracts with the owners and reports the income by the completed contract method. The company is considering building a series of similar stores for a retail chain. The gross profit margin would be a low percentage, but the company's gross receipts would triple. Write a letter to your client, Rust Company, explaining the tax accounting implications of entering into these contracts. Rust's mailing address is P.O. Box 1000, Harrisonburg, VA 22807.

39. Indicate the accounting method that should be used to compute the income from the following contracts:
   a. A contract to build six jet aircraft.
   b. A contract to build a new home. The contractor's average annual gross receipts are $15 million.
   c. A contract to manufacture 3,000 pairs of boots for a large retail chain. The manufacturer has several contracts to produce the same boot for other retailers.
   d. A contract to pave a parking lot. The contractor's average annual gross receipts are $2 million.

40. Ostrich Company makes gasoline storage tanks. Everything produced is under contract (that is, the company does not produce until it gets a contract for a product). Ostrich makes three basic models. However, the tanks must be adapted to each individual customer's location and needs (e.g., the location of the valves, the quality of the materials and insulation). Discuss the following issues relative to Ostrich's operations:
   a. An examining IRS agent contends that each of the company's contracts is to produce a "unique product." What difference does it make whether the product is unique or a "shelf item"?
   b. Producing one of the tanks takes over one year from start to completion, and the total price is in excess of $1 million. What costs must be capitalized for this contract that are not subject to capitalization for a contract with a shorter duration and lower cost?
   c. What must Ostrich do with the costs of bidding on contracts?
   d. Ostrich frequently makes several cost estimates for a contract, using various estimates of materials costs. These costs fluctuate almost daily. Assuming Ostrich must use the percentage of completion method to report the income from the contract, what will be the consequence if the company uses the highest estimate of a contract's costs and the actual cost is closer to the lowest estimated cost?

41. Swallow Company is a large real estate construction company that reports its income by the percentage of completion method. In 1997, the company completed a contract at a total cost of $1,960,000. The contract price was $2,400,000. At the end of 1996, the year the contract was begun, Swallow estimated the total cost of the contract would be $2,100,000, and total accumulated costs on the contract at the end of 1996 were $1,400,000. The relevant tax rate is 34%, and the relevant Federal interest rate is 7%. Assume that all returns were filed and taxes were paid on March 15 following the close of the calendar tax year.
   a. Compute the gross profit on the contract for 1996 and 1997.
   b. Compute the lookback interest due with the 1997 return.
   c. Before bidding on a contract, Swallow generally makes three estimates of total contract costs: (1) optimistic, (2) pessimistic, and (3) most likely (based on a blending of optimistic and pessimistic assumptions). The company has asked you to write a letter explaining which of these estimates should be used for percentage of completion purposes. In writing your letter, you should consider the fact that Swallow is incorporated and has made an S corporation election; therefore, the income and deductions flow through to the shareholders who are all individuals in the 36% marginal tax bracket. The relevant Federal interest rate is 8%. Swallow's mailing address is 400 Front Avenue, Ashland, OR 97520.

Research Problems for the chapter appear at the end of Chapter 28.

CHAPTER

16

CORPORATIONS: INTRODUCTION, OPERATING RULES, AND RELATED CORPORATIONS

LEARNING OBJECTIVES

After completing Chapter 16, you should be able to:

1. Summarize the various forms of conducting a business.

2. Determine when an entity will be treated as a corporation.

3. Compare the taxation of individuals and corporations.

4. Discuss the tax rules unique to corporations.

5. Compute the corporate income tax.

6. Explain the tax rules unique to multiple corporations.

7. Describe the reporting process for corporations.

8. Evaluate corporations for conducting a business.

▼
OUTLINE

TAX TREATMENT OF VARIOUS BUSINESS FORMS

1 LEARNING OBJECTIVE
Summarize the various forms of conducting a business.

Business operations can be conducted in a number of different forms. Among the various possibilities are the following:

- Sole proprietorships.
- Partnerships.
- Trusts and estates.
- S corporations (also known as Subchapter S corporations).
- Regular corporations (also called Subchapter C or C corporations).

For Federal income tax purposes, the distinctions among these forms of business organization are very important. The following discussion of the tax treatment of sole proprietorships, partnerships, and regular corporations highlights these distinctions. Trusts and estates are covered in Chapter 27, and S corporations are discussed in Chapter 21.

SOLE PROPRIETORSHIPS

A sole proprietorship is not a taxable entity separate from the individual who owns the proprietorship. The owner of a sole proprietorship reports all business transactions of the proprietorship on Schedule C of Form 1040. The net profit or loss from the proprietorship is then transferred from Schedule C to Form 1040, which is used by the taxpayer to report taxable income. The proprietor reports all of the net profit from the business, regardless of the amount actually withdrawn during the year.

Income and expenses of the proprietorship retain their character when reported by the proprietor. For example, ordinary income of the proprietorship is treated as ordinary income when reported by the proprietor, and capital gain is treated as capital gain.

TAX IN THE NEWS

Which is more costly for many corporations--their Federal income tax liability or the steps they must take to comply with the tax law? According to a Tax Foundation study conducted by Professors Joel Slemrod and Marsha Blumenthal, complying with the 1990 tax law was almost four times more costly than the actual tax owed. Slemrod and Blumenthal studied 365 corporations with assets of less than $1 million (90 percent of U.S. corporations fall into this category) and found that for every $1,000 paid in taxes, the compliance cost was $3,900. Larger corporations also had significant compliance costs. Slemrod and Blumenthal estimated that Fortune 500 companies spent an average of $2.11 million in compliance costs for 1992.

SOURCE: Adapted from Arthur P. Hall, "Accounting Costs, Another Tax," *Wall Street Journal*, December 9, 1993, p. A14.

EXAMPLE 1

George is the sole proprietor of George's Record Shop. Gross income of the business in 1996 is $200,000, and operating expenses are $110,000. George also sells a capital asset held by the business for a $10,000 long-term capital gain. During 1996, he withdraws $60,000 from the business for living expenses. George reports the income and expenses of the business on Schedule C, resulting in net profit (ordinary income) of $90,000. Even though he withdrew only $60,000, George reports all of the $90,000 net profit from the business on Form 1040, where he computes taxable income for the year. He also reports a $10,000 long-term capital gain. ▼

PARTNERSHIPS

Partnerships are not subject to the income tax. However, a partnership is required to file Form 1065, which reports the results of the partnership's business activities. Most income and expense items are aggregated in computing the net profit of the partnership on Form 1065. Any income and expense items that are not aggregated in computing the partnership's net income are reported separately to the partners. Some examples of separately reported income items are interest income, dividend income, and long-term capital gain. Examples of separately reported expenses include charitable contributions and expenses related to interest and dividend income. Partnership reporting is discussed in detail in Chapter 22.

The partnership net profit (loss) and the separately reported items are allocated to each partner according to the partnership's profit sharing agreement, and the partners receive separate K–1 schedules from the partnership. Schedule K–1 reports each partner's share of the partnership net profit (loss) and separately reported income and expense items. Each partner reports these items on his or her own tax return.

EXAMPLE 2

Jim and Bob are equal partners in Canary Enterprises, a calendar year partnership. During the year, Canary Enterprises had $500,000 of gross income and $350,000 of operating expenses. In addition, the partnership sold land that had been held for investment purposes for a long-term capital gain of $60,000. During the year, Jim withdrew $40,000 from the partnership and Bob withdrew $45,000. The partnership's Form 1065 reports net profit of $150,000 ($500,000 income – $350,000 expenses). The partnership also reports the $60,000 long-term capital gain as a separately stated item on Form 1065. Jim and Bob both receive a Schedule K–1 reporting net profit of $75,000 and separately stated long-term capital gain of $30,000. Each partner reports net profit of $75,000 and long-term capital gain of $30,000 on his own return. ▼

REGULAR CORPORATIONS

Corporations are governed by Subchapter C or Subchapter S of the Internal Revenue Code. Those governed by Subchapter C are referred to as **C corporations** or **regular corporations.** Corporations governed by Subchapter S are referred to as **S corporations.**

S corporations, which do not pay Federal income tax, are similar to partnerships in that net profit or loss flows through to the shareholders to be reported on their separate returns. Also like partnerships, S corporations do not aggregate all income and expense items in computing net profit or loss. Certain items flow through to the shareholders and retain their separate character when reported on the shareholders' returns. See Chapter 21 for detailed coverage of S corporations.

Unlike proprietorships, partnerships, and S corporations, C corporations are taxpaying entities. This results in what is known as a *double tax effect.* A C corporation reports its income and expenses on Form 1120 (or Form 1120–A, the corporate short form). The corporation computes tax on the net income reported on the corporate tax return using the rate schedule applicable to corporations (the rate schedule is shown on the inside front cover of this text and on the next page). When a corporation distributes its income, the corporation's shareholders report dividend income on their own tax returns. Thus, income that has already been taxed at the corporate level is also taxed at the shareholder level.

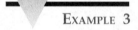

EXAMPLE 3　Thompson Corporation files Form 1120, which reports net profit of $100,000. The corporation pays tax of $22,250. This leaves $77,750, all of which is distributed as a dividend to Carla, the sole shareholder of the corporation. Carla, who has income from other sources and is in the 39.6% tax bracket, pays income tax of $30,789 ($77,750 × 39.6%) on the distribution. The combined tax on the corporation's net profit is $53,039 ($22,250 + $30,789). ▼

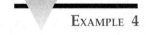

EXAMPLE 4　Assume the same facts as in Example 3, except that the business is organized as a sole proprietorship. Carla reports the $100,000 net profit from the business on her tax return and pays tax of $39,600 ($100,000 net profit × 39.6% marginal rate). Therefore, operating the business as a sole proprietorship results in tax savings of $13,439 ($53,039 tax from Example 3 – $39,600). ▼

Shareholders in closely held corporations frequently attempt to avoid double taxation by paying out all the profit of the corporation as salary to themselves.

EXAMPLE 5　Orange Corporation has net income of $180,000 during the year ($300,000 revenue – $120,000 operating expenses). Emilio is the sole shareholder of Orange Corporation. In an effort to avoid tax at the corporate level, Emilio has Orange pay him a salary of $180,000, which results in zero taxable income for the corporation. ▼

Will the strategy described in Example 5 effectively avoid double taxation? The answer depends on whether the compensation paid to the shareholder is *reasonable.* Section 162 provides that compensation is deductible only to the extent that it is reasonable in amount. The IRS is aware that many taxpayers use this strategy to bail out corporate profits and, in an audit, looks closely at compensation expense. If the IRS believes that compensation is too high based on the amount and quality of services performed by the shareholder, the compensation deduction of the corporation is reduced to a reasonable amount. Compensation that is determined to be unreasonable is usually treated as a constructive dividend to the shareholder and is not deductible by the corporation.

EXAMPLE 6 Assume the same facts as in Example 5, and that the IRS determines that $80,000 of the amount paid to Emilio is unreasonable compensation. As a result, $80,000 of the corporation's compensation deduction is disallowed and treated as a constructive dividend to Emilio. Orange has taxable income of $80,000. Emilio would report salary of $100,000 and a taxable dividend of $80,000. The net effect is that $80,000 is subject to double taxation. ▼

The unreasonable compensation issue is discussed in more detail in Chapter 18.

Comparison of Corporations and Other Forms of Doing Business.   Comparison of the tax results in Examples 3 and 4 might lead to the conclusion that incorporation is not a wise tax strategy. In some cases that would be a correct conclusion, but in others it would not. In many situations, tax and nontax factors combine to make the corporate form of doing business the only reasonable choice.

While a detailed comparison of sole proprietorships, partnerships, S corporations, and C corporations as forms of doing business must be made, it is appropriate at this point to consider some of the tax and nontax factors that favor corporations over proprietorships.

Consideration of tax factors requires an examination of the corporate rate structure. The income tax rate schedule applicable to corporations is reproduced below.

Taxable Income		Tax Is:	Of the Amount Over—
Over—	But Not Over—		
$ –0–	$ 50,000	15%	$ –0–
50,000	75,000	$ 7,500 + 25%	50,000
75,000	100,000	13,750 + 34%	75,000
100,000	335,000	22,250 + 39%	100,000
335,000	10,000,000	113,900 + 34%	335,000
10,000,000	15,000,000	3,400,000 + 35%	10,000,000
15,000,000	18,333,333	5,150,000 + 38%	15,000,000
18,333,333	—	35%	–0–

As this schedule shows, corporate rates on taxable income up to $75,000 are lower than individual rates for persons in the 28 percent and higher brackets. Therefore, corporate tax will be lower than individual tax. Furthermore, there is no corporate marginal rate that is higher than the 39.6 percent top bracket for individuals. When dividends are paid, however, the double taxation problem occurs. This leads to an important question: Will incorporation ever result in Federal income tax savings? The following example illustrates a situation where this occurs.

EXAMPLE 7 Ned, an individual in the 39.6% tax bracket, owns a business that produces net profit of $50,000 each year. Ned has significant income from other sources, so he does not withdraw any of the profit from the business. If the business is operated as a proprietorship, Ned's Federal income tax on the net profit of the business is $19,800 ($50,000 × 39.6%). However, if the business is operated as a corporation and pays no dividends, the tax will be $7,500 ($50,000 × 15%). Operating as a corporation saves $12,300 of Federal income tax each year. If Ned invests the $12,300 tax savings each year for several years, it is possible that a positive cash flow will result, even though Ned will be required to pay tax on dividends distributed by the corporation some time in the future. ▼

The preceding example deals with a specific set of facts. The conclusions reached in this situation cannot be extended to all decisions about a form of business organization. Each specific set of facts and circumstances requires a thorough analysis of the tax factors.

Another tax consideration involves the nature of dividend income. All income and expense items of a proprietorship retain their character when reported on the proprietor's tax return. In the case of a partnership, several separately reported items (e.g., charitable contributions and long-term capital gains) retain their character when passed through to the partners. However, the tax attributes of income and expense items of a corporation are lost as they pass through the corporate entity to the shareholders.

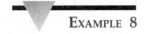

EXAMPLE 8

During the current year, Waxwing Company receives tax-exempt interest, which is distributed to its owners. If Waxwing Company is a regular corporation, the distribution to the shareholders constitutes a dividend. The fact that it originated from tax-exempt interest is of no consequence. On the other hand, if Waxwing is a partnership or an S corporation, the tax-exempt interest retains its identity and passes through to the individual owners. ▼

Losses of a C corporation are treated differently than losses of a proprietorship, partnership, or S corporation. A loss incurred by a proprietorship may be deductible by the owner, because all income and expense items are reported by the proprietor. Partnership losses are passed through the partnership entity and may be deductible by the partners, and S corporation losses are passed through to the shareholders. C corporation losses, however, have no effect on the taxable income of the shareholders. Income from a C corporation is reported when the shareholders receive dividends. C corporation losses are not reported by the shareholders.

Nontax Considerations.   Nontax considerations will sometimes override tax considerations and lead to a conclusion that a business should be operated as a corporation. The following are some of the more important nontax considerations:

- Sole proprietors and *general* partners in partnerships face the danger of *unlimited liability*. That is, creditors of the business may file claims not only against the assets of the business but also against the personal assets of proprietors or general partners. Shareholders are protected from claims against their personal assets by state corporate law.
- The corporate form of business organization can provide a vehicle for raising large amounts of capital through widespread stock ownership. Most major businesses in the United States are operated as corporations.
- Shares of stock in a corporation are freely transferable, whereas a partner's sale of his or her partnership interest is subject to approval by the other partners.
- Shareholders may come and go, but a corporation can continue to exist. Death or withdrawal of a partner, on the other hand, may terminate the existing partnership and cause financial difficulties that result in dissolution of the entity. This *continuity of life* is a distinct advantage of the corporate form of doing business.

- Corporations have *centralized management*. All management responsibility is assigned to a board of directors, who appoint officers to carry out the corporation's business. Partnerships, by contrast, may have decentralized management, in which every owner has a right to participate in the organization's business decisions; **limited partnerships,** though, may have centralized management. Centralized management is essential for the smooth operation of a widely held business.

The tax consequences of operating a business in the regular corporate form fall within Subchapter C of the Code and are the subject of this chapter and Chapters 17 through 19. Corporations that either accumulate earnings unreasonably or meet the definition of a personal holding company may be subject to further taxation. These so-called penalty taxes are imposed in addition to the corporate income tax and are discussed in Chapter 20.

Clearly, the form of organization chosen to carry on a trade or business has significant Federal income tax consequences. Though tax considerations may not control the choice, it could be unfortunate if they are not taken into account.

WHAT IS A CORPORATION?

2   LEARNING OBJECTIVE
Determine when an entity will be treated as a corporation.

The first step in any discussion of the Federal income tax treatment of corporations must be definitional. Specifically, what is a corporation? At first glance, the answer to this question appears to be quite simple: Merely look to the appropriate state law to determine whether the entity has satisfied the requirements for corporate status. Have articles of incorporation been drawn up and filed with the state regulatory agency? Has a charter been granted? Has stock been issued to shareholders? These are all points to consider.

Compliance with state law, although important, may not tell the full story as to whether an entity will be recognized as a corporation for Federal income tax purposes. On the one hand, a corporation qualifying under state law may be disregarded as a taxable entity if it is a mere *sham*. On the other hand, an organization not qualifying as a regular corporation under state law may be taxed as a corporation under the *association* approach. These two possibilities are discussed in the following sections.

DISREGARD OF CORPORATE ENTITY

In most cases, the IRS and the courts will recognize a corporation legally constituted under state law. In exceptional situations, however, the corporate entity may be disregarded because it lacks substance.[1] The key to such treatment is the degree of business activity conducted at the corporate level. The more the corporation is involved in trade or business activities, the less likely it will be treated as a sham and disregarded as a separate entity.[2]

Depending on the circumstances, either the IRS or the taxpayers may attempt to disregard the corporate entity. More often than not, the IRS may try to disregard

[1] The reader should bear in mind that the textual discussion relates to the classification of an entity for *Federal* income tax purposes. State corporate income taxes or other corporate taxes (e.g., franchise taxes) may still be imposed. An entity may quite possibly be treated as a corporation for state tax purposes and not for Federal, and vice versa. This will become even more apparent when

dealing with S corporations (Chapter 21) because some states do not recognize S corporation status.

[2] A classic case in this area is *Paymer v. Comm.*, 45–2 USTC ¶9353, 33 AFTR 1536, 150 F.2d 334 (CA–2, 1945). Here, two corporations were involved. The Court chose to disregard one corporate entity but to recognize the other.

(or "collapse") a corporation to make its income taxable directly to the shareholders. In other situations, a corporation may try to avoid the corporate income tax or permit its shareholders to take advantage of excess corporate deductions and losses.[3]

Theoretically, the disregard-of-corporate-entity approach should be equally available to both the IRS and the taxpayers. From a practical standpoint, however, taxpayers have enjoyed considerably less success than has the IRS. Courts generally conclude that since the taxpayers created the corporation in the first place, they should not be permitted to disregard it later in order to avoid taxes.

ASSOCIATIONS TAXED AS CORPORATIONS

The definition of a corporation includes "associations, joint stock companies, and insurance companies."[4] What Congress intended by including associations in the definition has never been entirely clear. To some extent, judicial decisions have clarified the status of associations and the relationship between associations and corporations.

The designation given to the entity under state law is not controlling. In one case, an entity that was a business trust under state law was deemed to be an **association** (and therefore taxable as a corporation) for Federal income tax purposes.[5] In another case, a partnership of physicians was held to be an association and, therefore, subject to the Federal income tax rules applicable to corporations. This result occurred even though state law applicable to the tax year in question prohibited the practice of medicine in the corporate form.[6]

Whether an entity will be considered an association for Federal income tax purposes depends upon the number of corporate characteristics it possesses. Corporate characteristics include the following:[7]

1. Associates.
2. An objective to carry on a business and divide the gains.
3. Continuity of life.
4. Centralized management.
5. Limited liability.
6. Free transferability of interests.

An unincorporated organization is not classified as an association unless it possesses more corporate than noncorporate characteristics. In making the determination, the characteristics common to both corporate and noncorporate business organizations are disregarded.

Both corporations and partnerships generally have associates (shareholders and partners) and an objective to carry on a business and divide the gains. In testing whether a particular partnership is an association, these criteria would be disregarded.

It then becomes a matter of determining whether the partnership possesses a majority of the remaining corporate characteristics (items 3 through 6). Does the partnership terminate upon the withdrawal or death of a partner (no continuity of life)? Is the management of the partnership centralized, or do all partners participate? Are all partners individually liable for the debts of the partnership, or

[3] An election under Subchapter S would generally accomplish this if the parties qualify and the election is made on a timely basis. See Chapter 21.
[4] § 7701(a)(3).
[5] *Morrissey v. Comm.*, 36–1 USTC ¶9020, 16 AFTR 1274, 56 S.Ct. 289 (USSC, 1936).
[6] *U.S. v. Kintner*, 54–2 USTC ¶9626, 47 AFTR 995, 216 F.2d 418 (CA–9, 1954).
[7] Reg. § 301.7701.

is the liability of some limited to their actual investment in the partnership (a limited partnership)? May a partner freely transfer his or her interest without the consent of the other partners?

Courts have ruled that any partnership lacking two or more of these characteristics will not be classified as an association. Conversely, any partnership having three or more of these characteristics will be classified as an association.[8]

For trusts, the first two characteristics are considered in testing for association status. The conventional type of trust often does not have associates and usually restricts its activities to handling investments rather than carrying on a trade or business. These characteristics, however, are common to corporations. Consequently, whether a trust qualifies as an association depends upon the satisfaction of the first two corporate characteristics.

From a taxpayer's standpoint, the desirability of association status turns on the tax implications involved. In some cases, the parties may find it advantageous to have the entity taxed as a corporation, while in others they may not. These possibilities are explored at length under Tax Planning Considerations in this chapter.

LIMITED LIABILITY COMPANIES

The **limited liability company (LLC)** has proliferated greatly in recent years, particularly since 1988 when the IRS first ruled that it would treat qualifying LLCs as partnerships for tax purposes. As of November 1995, 47 states and the District of Columbia have passed laws that allow LLCs, and more than 20,000 companies have chosen LLC status.[9] As with a corporation, operating as an LLC allows an entity to avoid unlimited liability, which is a primary *nontax* consideration in choosing the form of business organization. The tax advantage of LLCs is that qualifying businesses are treated as partnerships for tax purposes, thereby avoiding the problem of double taxation associated with regular corporations.

Some states allow an LLC to have centralized management, but not continuity of life or free transferability of interests.[10] Other states allow LLCs to adopt any or all of the corporate characteristics of centralized management, continuity of life, and free transferability of interests.[11] The IRS has issued Revenue Rulings dealing with the tax treatment of LLCs in 18 different states. All rulings issued to date make it *possible* for LLCs to be treated as partnerships. As a general rule, LLCs must avoid the corporate characteristics of continuity of life and free transferability of interests in order to qualify to be taxed as partnerships.

AN INTRODUCTION TO THE INCOME TAXATION OF CORPORATIONS

AN OVERVIEW OF CORPORATE VERSUS INDIVIDUAL INCOME TAX TREATMENT

3 LEARNING OBJECTIVE
Compare the taxation of individuals and corporations.

In a discussion of how corporations are treated under the Federal income tax law, a useful approach is to compare their treatment with that applicable to individual taxpayers.

---

[8] See *Zuckman v. U.S.*, 75-2 USTC ¶9778, 36 AFTR2d 6193, 524 F.2d 729 (Ct.Cls., 1975), and *P. G. Larson*, 66 T.C. 159 (1976).

[9] H. W. Cecil, C. S. Ciccotello, and C. T. Grant, "The Choice of Organizational Form," *Journal of Accountancy*, December 1995. Hawaii, Massachusetts, and Vermont do not have limited liability statutes, but all three states are considering LLC legislation.

[10] See, for example, Rev.Rul. 93-6, 1993-1 C.B. 227, and Rev.Rul. 94-51, 1994-2 C.B. 407.

[11] See, for example, Rev.Rul. 93-38, 1993-1 C.B. 233.

TAX IN THE NEWS

WHAT TYPES OF BUSINESSES ARE CHOOSING LLC STATUS?

A sample of 1,252 limited liability companies reveals that four types of businesses in particular choose LLC status:

Engineering and management support services	26%
Real estate services	19%
Construction and general contracting firms	12%
Investment companies	9%

Owners of LLCs are referred to as members, rather than partners or shareholders. LLC members are liable only for their own acts or omissions, so their personal assets are not at risk based on acts or omissions of other members. As the survey results indicate, LLC status appeals to both service organizations and capital-intensive businesses.

SOURCE: Information from H. W. Cecil, C. S. Ciccotello, and C. T. Grant, "The Choice of Organizational Form," *Journal of Accountancy*, December 1995. Reprinted with permission from The Journal of Accountancy, copyright © 1995 by American Institute of Certified Public Accountants. Opinions of the authors are their own and do not necessarily reflect policies of the AICPA.

Similarities. Gross income of a corporation is determined in much the same manner as it is for individuals. Thus, gross income includes compensation for services rendered, income derived from a business, gains from dealings in property, interest, rents, royalties, and dividends—to name only a few items. Both individuals and corporations are entitled to exclusions from gross income. However, corporate taxpayers are allowed fewer exclusions. Interest on municipal bonds is excluded from gross income whether the bondholder is an individual or a corporate taxpayer.

Gains and losses from property transactions are handled similarly. For example, whether a gain or loss is capital or ordinary depends upon the nature of the asset in the hands of the taxpayer making the taxable disposition. In defining what is not a capital asset, § 1221 makes no distinction between corporate and noncorporate taxpayers.

In the area of nontaxable exchanges, corporations are like individuals in that they do not recognize gain or loss on a like-kind exchange and may defer realized gain on an involuntary conversion of property. The nonrecognition of gain provisions dealing with the sale of a personal residence do not apply to corporations. Both corporations and individuals are vulnerable to the disallowance of losses on sales of property to related parties or on wash sales of securities. The wash sales rules do not apply to individuals who are traders or dealers in securities or to corporations that are dealers if the securities are sold in the ordinary course of the corporation's business.

Upon the sale or other taxable disposition of depreciable property, the recapture rules generally make no distinction between corporate and noncorporate taxpayers.[12] However, § 291(a) does cause a corporation to have more recapture on § 1250 property. This difference is discussed later in the chapter.

---

[12] §§ 1245 and 1250.

The business deductions of corporations also parallel those available to individuals. Deductions are allowed for all ordinary and necessary expenses paid or incurred in carrying on a trade or business.[13] Specific provision is made for the deductibility of interest, certain taxes, losses, bad debts, accelerated cost recovery, charitable contributions, net operating losses, research and experimental expenditures, and other less common deductions. A corporation does not distinguish between business and nonbusiness interest or business and nonbusiness bad debts. Thus, these amounts are deductible in full as ordinary deductions by corporations. No deduction is permitted for interest paid or incurred on amounts borrowed to purchase or carry tax-exempt securities. The same holds true for expenses contrary to public policy and certain unpaid expenses and interest between related parties.

Some of the tax credits available to individuals can also be claimed by corporations. This is the case with the foreign tax credit. Not available to corporations are certain credits that are personal in nature, such as the credit for child and dependent care expenditures, the credit for the elderly, and the earned income credit.

Dissimilarities. The income taxation of corporations and individuals also differs significantly. As noted earlier, different tax rates apply to corporations and to individuals. Corporate tax rates are discussed in more detail later in the chapter (see Examples 26 and 27).

All allowable corporate deductions are treated as business deductions. Thus, the determination of adjusted gross income (AGI), so essential for individual taxpayers, has no relevance to corporations. Taxable income is computed simply by subtracting from gross income all allowable deductions and losses. Corporations thus need not be concerned with itemized deductions or the standard deduction. Likewise, the deduction for personal and dependency exemptions is not available to corporations.

Unlike individuals, corporations are not subject to the $100 floor on the deductible portion of casualty and theft losses. Also inapplicable is the provision limiting the deductibility of nonbusiness casualty losses to the amount in excess of 10 percent of AGI.

SPECIFIC PROVISIONS COMPARED

In comparing the tax treatment of individuals and corporations, the following areas warrant special discussion:

- Accounting periods and methods.
- Capital gains and losses.
- Recapture of depreciation.
- Passive losses.
- Charitable contributions.
- Net operating losses.
- Special deductions available only to corporations.

ACCOUNTING PERIODS AND METHODS

Accounting Periods. Corporations generally have the same choices of accounting periods as do individual taxpayers. Like an individual, a corporation may

---

[13] § 162.

choose a calendar year or a fiscal year for reporting purposes. Corporations, however, enjoy greater flexibility in the selection of a tax year. For example, corporations usually can have different tax years from those of their shareholders. Also, newly formed corporations (as new taxpayers) usually may choose any approved accounting period without having to obtain the consent of the IRS. **Personal service corporations (PSCs)** and S corporations, however, are subject to severe restrictions in the use of fiscal years. The rules applicable to S corporations are discussed in Chapter 21.

A PSC has as its principal activity the performance of personal services. Such services must be substantially performed by owner-employees and must be in the fields of health, law, engineering, architecture, accounting, actuarial science, performing arts, or consulting.[14] Barring certain exceptions, PSCs must adopt a calendar year for tax purposes.[15] The exceptions that permit the use of a fiscal year are discussed in Chapter 15.[16]

Accounting Methods. As a general rule, the cash method of accounting is unavailable to *regular* corporations.[17] Exceptions apply to the following types of corporations:

- S corporations.
- Corporations engaged in the trade or business of farming and timber.
- Qualified PSCs.
- Corporations with average annual gross receipts of $5 million-or-less. (In applying the $5 million-or-less test, the corporation uses the average of the three prior taxable years.)

Both individuals and corporations that maintain inventory for sale to customers are required to use the accrual method of accounting for determining sales and cost of goods sold.

A corporation that uses the accrual method of accounting must observe a special rule in dealing with related parties. If the corporation has an accrual outstanding at the end of any taxable year, it cannot claim a deduction until the recipient reports the amount as income.[18] This rule is most often encountered when a corporation deals with a person who owns more than 50 percent of the corporation's stock.

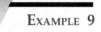

EXAMPLE 9   Teal, an accrual method corporation, uses the calendar year for tax purposes. Bob, a cash method taxpayer, owns more than 50% of the corporation's stock at the end of 1996. On December 31, 1996, Teal has accrued $25,000 of salary to Bob. Bob receives the salary in 1997 and reports it on his 1997 tax return. Teal cannot claim a deduction for the $25,000 until 1997.

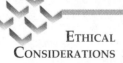

ETHICAL
CONSIDERATIONS

Knowledge of a Client's Error

In early 1997, you are engaged by a new client, Grebe, Inc., to prepare its 1996 Federal income tax return. Grebe has one shareholder, Bill Jones. Bill has an excellent reputation in the community, and you hope to gain more work from him in the future. You have never had a social relationship with Bill and are not acquainted with anyone in his family.

---

[14] § 448(d)(2)(A).
[15] § 441(i).
[16] §§ 444 and 280H.

[17] § 448(a).
[18] § 267(a)(2).

Bill has told you that he was dissatisfied with his prior accountant, because he thought that Grebe's taxes were too high. Bill brings in a copy of Grebe's 1995 tax return. You review the 1995 return and conclude that the prior accountant's work was thorough and accurate. The corporation has properly used the accrual method of accounting and accrues substantial bonuses to several of its employees at the end of each year. One of the employees is Susan Smith, the office manager. You are not acquainted with Susan Smith.

You prepare the 1996 tax return for Grebe and deduct the accrued bonuses in accordance with the corporation's past practices. Before you deliver the return to Bill Jones for filing, you attend a charitable fund-raising dinner and are seated next to Susan Smith. She mentions to you that she works as the office manager for Grebe, Inc., a corporation that is owned by her brother, Bill Jones, and she has noticed that you have been appointed as the corporation's tax adviser. You and Susan do not discuss any of the corporation's business or tax problems during the evening.

When you return to your office the next day, you realize that, due to the attribution rules of § 267(b) and the disallowance rule of § 267(a)(2), Grebe cannot deduct any accrued salary to Susan Smith, since she constructively owns all of the stock of the corporation. You would have no way of knowing that Susan was Bill's sister if you had not attended the dinner the night before. You must decide whether you will sign a return for Grebe if the accrued salary to Susan Smith is deducted as an expense.

CAPITAL GAINS AND LOSSES

Capital gains and losses result from the taxable sales or exchanges of capital assets. Whether these gains and losses are long term or short term depends upon the holding period of the assets sold or exchanged. Each year a taxpayer's long-term capital gains and losses are combined, and the result is either a *net* long-term capital gain or a *net* long-term capital loss. A similar aggregation is made with short-term capital gains and losses, the result being a *net* short-term capital gain or a *net* short-term capital loss. The following combinations and results are possible:

1. A net long-term capital gain and a net short-term capital loss. These are combined, and the result is either a net capital gain or a net capital loss.
2. A net long-term capital gain and a net short-term capital gain. No further combination is made.
3. A net long-term capital loss and a net short-term capital gain. These are combined, and the result is either capital gain net income or a net capital loss.
4. A net long-term capital loss and a net short-term capital loss. No further combination is made.

Capital Gains.   Individuals generally pay tax on net (long-term) capital gains at a maximum rate of 28 percent. Corporations, by contrast, receive no favorable rate on capital gains and must include the net capital gain, in full, as part of taxable income.

Capital Losses.   Net capital losses (refer to combinations 3 and 4 and, possibly, to combination 1) of corporate and noncorporate taxpayers receive different income tax treatment. Generally, *noncorporate taxpayers* (e.g., individuals) can deduct up to $3,000 of such net losses against other income.[19] Any remaining

---

[19] The limitations on capital losses for both corporate and noncorporate taxpayers are contained in § 1211.

capital losses can be carried forward to future years until absorbed by capital gains or by the $3,000 deduction.[20] Carryovers do not lose their identity but remain either long term or short term.

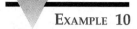

EXAMPLE 10

Robin, an individual, incurs a net long-term capital loss of $7,500 for calendar year 1996. Assuming adequate taxable income, Robin may deduct $3,000 of this loss on his 1996 return. The remaining $4,500 ($7,500 − $3,000) of the loss is carried to 1997 and years thereafter until it is offset against future capital gains or deducted against ordinary income (subject to the $3,000 maximum per year). The $4,500 will be carried forward as a long-term capital loss. ▼

Unlike individuals, corporate taxpayers are not permitted to claim any net capital losses as a deduction against ordinary income. Capital losses, therefore, can be used only to offset capital gains. Corporations may, however, carry back net capital losses to three preceding years, applying them first to the earliest year in point of time. Carryforwards are allowed for a period of five years from the year of the loss. When carried back or forward, a corporation's long-term capital loss is treated as a short-term capital loss.

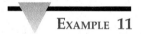

EXAMPLE 11

Assume the same facts as in Example 10, except that Robin is a corporation. None of the $7,500 long-term capital loss incurred in 1996 can be deducted in that year. Robin Corporation may, however, carry back the loss to years 1993, 1994, and 1995 (in this order) and offset it against any capital gains recognized in these years. If the carryback does not exhaust the loss, the loss may be carried forward to calendar years 1997, 1998, 1999, 2000, and 2001 (in this order). Either a carryback or a carryforward of the long-term capital loss converts it to a short-term capital loss. Carryback of a capital loss generates a refund of taxes previously paid on the capital gain against which the carryback is offset. ▼

RECAPTURE OF DEPRECIATION

Depreciation recapture for § 1245 property is computed in the same manner for individuals and for corporations. However, corporations may have more depreciation recapture than individuals. Corporations that sell *depreciable real estate* that is § 1250 property are subject to additional recapture of depreciation under § 291(a)(1). This provision requires recapture of 20 percent of the excess of any amount that would be treated as ordinary income under § 1245 over the amount treated as ordinary income under § 1250. The amount of ordinary income under § 291 is computed as shown in Figure 16–1.

▼ **FIGURE 16–1**
Computation of Depreciation Recapture under § 291

Ordinary income under § 1245	$xx,xxx
Less: Ordinary income under § 1250	(x,xxx)
Equals: Excess ordinary income under § 1245 as compared to ordinary income under § 1250	$ x,xxx
Apply § 291 percentage	× 20%
Equals: Amount of ordinary income under § 291	$ xxx

---

[20] Carryback and carryover rules for both corporate and noncorporate taxpayers are found in § 1212.

EXAMPLE 12

Franklin Corporation purchased an office building on January 3, 1984, for $300,000. Accelerated depreciation was taken in the amount of $256,250 before the building was sold on February 5, 1996, for $250,000. Straight-line depreciation would have been $241,667 (using a 15-year recovery period under ACRS). The corporation's depreciation recapture and § 1231 gain are computed as follows:

Determine realized gain:	
Sales price	$250,000
Less: Adjusted basis [$300,000 (cost of building) – $256,250 (ACRS depreciation)]	(43,750)
Realized gain	$206,250

Because the building is 15-year real estate, it is treated as § 1245 recovery property. The gain of $206,250 is recaptured to the extent of all depreciation taken. Thus, all gain is ordinary income under § 1245, and there is no § 1231 gain. ▼

EXAMPLE 13

Assume the building in Example 12 is residential rental property, making it § 1250 property. Gain recaptured under § 1250 is $14,583 ($256,250 depreciation taken – $241,667 straight-line depreciation). However, for a corporate taxpayer, § 291(a)(1) causes additional § 1250 ordinary income of $38,333, computed as follows:

Ordinary income if property were § 1245 property	$206,250
Less: Gain recaptured under § 1250	(14,583)
Excess § 1245 gain	$191,667
Percentage that is ordinary gain	× 20%
Additional § 1250 gain	$ 38,333
Ordinary income ($14,583 + $38,333)	$ 52,916
Section 1231 gain ($206,250 – $14,583 – $38,333)	153,334
Total gain	$206,250

▼

EXAMPLE 14

Assume the building in Example 13 is commercial property and straight-line depreciation was used. An individual would report all gain as § 1231 gain. However, under § 291 a corporate taxpayer would recapture as ordinary income 20% of the depreciation that would be ordinary income if the property were § 1245 property.

First, determine realized gain:	
Sales price	$250,000
Less: Adjusted basis [$300,000 (cost of building) – $241,667 (straight-line depreciation)]	(58,333)
Realized gain	$191,667
Second, determine § 291 gain:	
Ordinary income if property were § 1245 property	$191,667
Less: Ordinary income under § 1250	(–0–)
Excess ordinary income under § 1245	$191,667
Apply § 291 percentage	× 20%
Ordinary income under § 291	$ 38,333

For a corporate taxpayer, $38,333 of the $191,667 gain would be ordinary, and $153,334 would be § 1231 gain. ▼

PASSIVE LOSSES

The **passive loss** rules apply to noncorporate taxpayers and to closely held C corporations and personal service corporations (PSCs).[21] For S corporations and partnerships, passive income or loss flows through to the owners, and the passive loss rules are applied at the owner level. The passive loss rules are applied to closely held corporations and to PSCs to prevent taxpayers from incorporating to avoid the passive loss limitations (refer to Chapter 10).

A corporation is closely held if, at any time during the taxable year, more than 50 percent of the value of the corporation's outstanding stock is owned, directly or indirectly, by or for not more than five individuals. A corporation is classified as a PSC if it meets the following requirements:

- The principal activity of the corporation is the performance of personal services.
- Such services are substantially performed by owner-employees.
- More than 10 percent of the stock (in value) is held by owner-employees. *Any* stock held by an employee on *any* one day causes the employee to be an owner-employee.

The general passive activity loss rules apply to PSCs. Passive activity losses cannot be offset against either active income or portfolio income. The application of the passive activity rules is not as harsh for closely held corporations. They may offset passive losses against active income, but not against portfolio income.

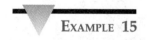

EXAMPLE 15

Brown, Inc., a closely held corporation, has $300,000 of passive losses from a rental activity, $200,000 of active business income, and $100,000 of portfolio income. The corporation may offset $200,000 of the $300,000 passive loss against the $200,000 active business income, but may not offset the remainder against the $100,000 of portfolio income. ▼

Individual taxpayers are not allowed to offset passive losses against *either* active or portfolio income.

CHARITABLE CONTRIBUTIONS

Both corporate and noncorporate taxpayers may deduct charitable contributions if the recipient is a qualified charitable organization. Generally, a deduction will be allowed only for the year in which the payment is made. However, an important exception is made for *accrual basis corporations*. They may claim the deduction in the year *preceding* payment if two requirements are met. First, the contribution must be authorized by the board of directors by the end of that year. Second, it must be paid on or before the fifteenth day of the third month of the next year.

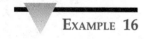

EXAMPLE 16

On December 28, 1996, Blue Company, a calendar year, accrual basis partnership, authorizes a $5,000 donation to the Atlanta Symphony Association (a qualified charitable organization). The donation is made on March 14, 1997. Because Blue Company is a partnership, the contribution can be deducted only in 1997.[22] However, if Blue Company is a corporation and the December 28, 1996 authorization was made by its board of directors, Blue may claim the $5,000 donation as a deduction for calendar year 1996. ▼

---

[21] § 469(a).

[22] Each calendar year partner will report an allocable portion of the charitable contribution deduction as of December 31, 1997 (the end of the partnership's tax year). See Chapter 22.

Property Contributions. The amount that can be deducted for a noncash charitable contribution depends on the type of property contributed. Property must be identified as long-term capital gain property or ordinary income property. *Long-term capital gain property* is property that, if sold, would result in long-term capital gain for the taxpayer. Such property generally must be a capital asset and must be held for the long-term holding period (more than one year). *Ordinary income property* is property that, if sold, would result in ordinary income for the taxpayer.

The deduction for a charitable contribution of long-term capital property is generally measured by its fair market value.

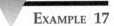

EXAMPLE 17

In 1996, Mallard Corporation donated a parcel of land (a capital asset) to Oakland Community College. Mallard acquired the land in 1987 for $60,000, and the fair market value on the date of the contribution was $100,000. The corporation's charitable contribution deduction (subject to a percentage limitation discussed later) is measured by the asset's fair market value of $100,000, even though the $40,000 appreciation on the land has never been included in Mallard's income. ▼

In two situations, a charitable contribution of long-term capital gain property is measured by the basis of the property, rather than fair market value. If the corporation contributes *tangible personal property* and the charitable organization puts the property to an unrelated use, the appreciation on the property is not deductible. Unrelated use is defined as use that is not related to the purpose or function that qualifies the organization for exempt status.

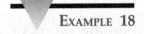

EXAMPLE 18

White Corporation donates a painting worth $200,000 to Western States Art Museum (a qualified organization), which exhibits the painting. White had acquired the painting in 1980 for $90,000. Because the museum put the painting to a related use, White is allowed to deduct $200,000, the fair market value of the painting. ▼

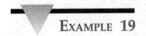

EXAMPLE 19

Assume the same facts as in the previous example, except that White Corporation donates the painting to the American Cancer Society, which sells the painting and deposits the $200,000 proceeds in the organization's general fund. White's deduction is limited to the $90,000 basis because it contributed tangible personal property that was put to an unrelated use by the charitable organization. ▼

The deduction for charitable contributions of long-term capital gain property to certain *private nonoperating foundations* is also limited to the basis of the property.

Ordinary income property is property that, if sold, would result in ordinary income. Examples of ordinary income property include inventory and capital assets that have not been held long term. In addition, § 1231 property (depreciable property used in a trade or business) is treated as ordinary income property to the extent of any ordinary income recaptured under § 1245 or § 1250. As a general rule, the deduction for a contribution of ordinary income property is limited to the basis of the property. However, *corporations* enjoy two special exceptions where 50 percent of the appreciation (but not to exceed twice the basis) on property is allowed on certain contributions. The first exception concerns inventory if the property is used in a manner related to the exempt purpose of the donee. Also, the charity must use the property solely for the care of the ill, the needy, or infants.

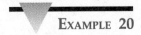

EXAMPLE 20

Lark Corporation, a grocery chain, donates canned goods to the Salvation Army to be used to feed the needy. Lark's basis in the canned goods was $2,000, and the fair market value was $3,000. Lark's deduction is $2,500 [$2,000 basis + 50%($3,000 − $2,000)]. ▼

The second exception involves gifts of scientific property to colleges and certain scientific research organizations for use in research, provided certain conditions are met.[23] As was true of the inventory exception, 50 percent of the appreciation on such property is allowed as an additional deduction.

Limitations Imposed on Charitable Contribution Deductions. Like individuals, corporations are subject to percentage limits on the charitable contribution deduction.[24] For any one year, a corporate taxpayer's contribution deduction is limited to 10 percent of taxable income. For this purpose, taxable income is computed without regard to the charitable contribution deduction, any net operating loss carryback or capital loss carryback, and the dividends received deduction. Any contributions in excess of the 10 percent limitation may be carried forward to the five succeeding tax years. Any carryforward must be added to subsequent contributions and will be subject to the 10 percent limitation. In applying this limitation, the current year's contributions must be deducted first, with excess deductions from previous years deducted in order of time.[25]

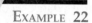

EXAMPLE 21

During 1996, Orange Corporation (a calendar year taxpayer) had the following income and expenses:

Income from operations	$140,000
Expenses from operations	110,000
Dividends received	10,000
Charitable contributions made in May 1996	5,000

For purposes of the 10% limitation *only*, Orange Corporation's taxable income is $40,000 ($140,000 − $110,000 + $10,000). Consequently, the allowable charitable contribution deduction for 1996 is $4,000 (10% × $40,000). The $1,000 unused portion of the contribution can be carried forward to 1997, 1998, 1999, 2000, and 2001 (in that order) until exhausted. ▼

EXAMPLE 22

Assume the same facts as in Example 21. In 1997, Orange Corporation has taxable income (for purposes of the 10% limitation) of $50,000 and makes a charitable contribution of $4,500. The maximum deduction allowed for 1997 would be $5,000 (10% × $50,000). The first $4,500 of the allowed deduction must be allocated to the contribution made in 1997, and $500 of the $1,000 unused contribution is carried over from 1996. The remaining $500 of the 1996 contribution may be carried over to 1998 (and later years, if necessary). ▼

NET OPERATING LOSSES

As for individuals, the net operating loss (NOL) of a corporation may be carried back 3 years and forward 15 to offset taxable income for those years. However, a corporation does not adjust its tax loss for the year for capital losses as do individual taxpayers, because a corporation is not permitted a deduction for net capital losses. Nor does a corporation make adjustments for nonbusiness deductions as do individual taxpayers. Further, a corporation is allowed to include the dividends received deduction (discussed below) in computing its NOL.[26]

---

[23] These conditions are set forth in § 170(e)(4). For the inventory exception, see § 170(e)(3).

[24] The percentage limitations applicable to individuals and corporations are set forth in § 170(b).

[25] The carryover rules relating to all taxpayers are in § 170(d).

[26] The modifications required to arrive at the amount of NOL that can be carried back or forward are in § 172(d).

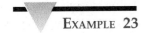

EXAMPLE 23

In 1996, Green Corporation has gross income (including dividends) of $200,000 and deductions of $300,000 excluding the dividends received deduction. Green Corporation had received taxable dividends of $100,000 from Exxon stock. Green has an NOL computed as follows:

Gross income (including dividends)		$ 200,000
Less: Business deductions	$300,000	
Dividends received deduction (70% × $100,000)*	70,000	(370,000)
Taxable income (or loss)		($ 170,000)

*See the discussion of the dividends received deduction in the next section of this chapter.

The NOL is carried back three years to 1993. (Green Corporation may *elect* to forgo the carryback option and instead carry the loss forward.) Assume Green had taxable income of $40,000 in 1993. The carryover to 1994 is computed as follows:

Taxable income for 1993	$ 40,000
Less: NOL carryback	(170,000)
Taxable income for 1993 after NOL carryback (carryover to 1994)	($ 130,000)

DEDUCTIONS AVAILABLE ONLY TO CORPORATIONS

4 LEARNING OBJECTIVE
Discuss the tax rules unique to corporations.

Dividends Received Deduction. The purpose of the **dividends received deduction** is to mitigate triple taxation. Without the deduction, income paid to a corporation in the form of a dividend would be taxed to the recipient corporation with no corresponding deduction to the distributing corporation. Later, when the recipient corporation paid the income to its individual shareholders, the income would again be subject to taxation with no corresponding deduction to the corporation. The dividends received deduction alleviates this inequity by causing only some or none of the dividend income to be taxable to the recipient corporation.

As the following table illustrates, the amount of the dividends received deduction depends upon the percentage of ownership the recipient corporate shareholder holds in a domestic corporation making the dividend distribution.[27]

Percentage of Ownership by Corporate Shareholder	Deduction Percentage
Less than 20%	70%
20% or more (but less than 80%)	80%
80% or more*	100%

*The payor corporation must be a member of an affiliated group with the recipient corporation.

The dividends received deduction is limited to a percentage of the taxable income of a corporation. For this purpose, taxable income is computed without regard to the NOL, the dividends received deduction, and any capital loss

---

[27] § 243(a).

carryback to the current tax year. The percentage of taxable income limitation corresponds to the deduction percentage. Thus, if a corporate shareholder owns less than 20 percent of the stock in the distributing corporation, the dividends received deduction is limited to 70 percent of taxable income. However, the taxable income limitation does not apply if the corporation has an NOL for the current taxable year.[28]

In working with these myriad rules, the following steps are useful:

1. Multiply the dividends received by the deduction percentage.
2. Multiply the taxable income by the deduction percentage.
3. Limit the deduction to the lesser of step 1 or step 2, unless subtracting the amount derived in step 1 from 100 percent of taxable income *generates* an NOL. If so, use the amount derived in step 1. This is referred to as the NOL rule.

EXAMPLE 24

Red, White, and Blue Corporations are three unrelated calendar year corporations. For 1996 they have the following transactions:

	Red Corporation	White Corporation	Blue Corporation
Gross income from operations	$ 400,000	$ 320,000	$ 260,000
Expenses from operations	(340,000)	(340,000)	(340,000)
Dividends received from domestic corporations (less than 20% ownership)	200,000	200,000	200,000
Taxable income before the dividends received deduction	$ 260,000	$ 180,000	$ 120,000

In determining the dividends received deduction, use the three-step procedure described above:

Step 1 (70% × $200,000)	$140,000	$140,000	$140,000
Step 2			
70% × $260,000 (taxable income)	$182,000		
70% × $180,000 (taxable income)		$126,000	
70% × $120,000 (taxable income)			$ 84,000
Step 3			
Lesser of step 1 or step 2	$140,000	$126,000	
Deduction generates an NOL			$140,000

White Corporation is subject to the 70% of taxable income limitation. It does not qualify for NOL rule treatment since subtracting $140,000 (step 1) from $180,000 (100% of taxable income) does not yield a negative figure. Blue Corporation qualifies for NOL rule treatment because subtracting $140,000 (step 1) from $120,000 (100% of taxable income) yields a negative figure. In summary, each corporation has a dividends received deduction for 1996: $140,000 for Red Corporation, $126,000 for White Corporation, and $140,000 for Blue Corporation. ▼

---

[28] § 246(b).

Deduction of Organizational Expenditures. Expenses incurred in connection with the organization of a corporation normally are chargeable to a capital account. That they benefit the corporation during its existence seems clear. But how can they be amortized when most corporations possess unlimited life? The lack of a determinable and limited estimated useful life would therefore preclude any tax write-off. Section 248 was enacted to solve this problem.

Under § 248, a corporation may elect to amortize **organizational expenditures** over a period of 60 months or more. The period begins with the month in which the corporation begins business.[29] Organizational expenditures *subject to the election* include the following:

- Legal services incident to organization (e.g., drafting the corporate charter, bylaws, minutes of organizational meetings, terms of original stock certificates).
- Necessary accounting services.
- Expenses of temporary directors and of organizational meetings of directors or shareholders, and fees paid to the state of incorporation.

Expenditures that *do not qualify* include those connected with issuing or selling shares of stock or other securities (e.g., commissions, professional fees, and printing costs) or with the transfer of assets to a corporation. Such expenditures reduce the amount of capital raised and are not deductible at all.

To qualify for the election, the expenditures must be *incurred* before the end of the taxable year in which the corporation begins business. In this regard, the corporation's method of accounting is of no consequence. Thus, an expense incurred by a cash basis corporation in its first tax year qualifies even though it is not paid until a subsequent year.

The election is made in a statement attached to the corporation's return for its first taxable year. The return and statement must be filed no later than the due date of the return (including any extensions).

If the election is not made on a timely basis, organizational expenditures cannot be deducted until the corporation ceases to do business and liquidates. These expenditures will be deductible if the corporate charter limits the life of the corporation.

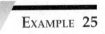

EXAMPLE 25

Black Corporation, an accrual basis taxpayer, was formed and began operations on May 1, 1996. The following expenses were incurred during its first year of operations (May 1 through December 31, 1996):

Expenses of temporary directors and of organizational meetings	$500
Fee paid to the state of incorporation	100
Accounting services incident to organization	200
Legal services for drafting the corporate charter and bylaws	400
Expenses incident to the printing and sale of stock certificates	300

Assume Black Corporation makes a timely election under § 248 to amortize qualifying organizational expenses over a period of 60 months. The monthly amortization is $20 [($500 + $100 + $200 + $400) ÷ 60 months], and $160 ($20 × 8 months) is deductible for tax

---

[29] The month in which a corporation begins business may not be immediately apparent. See Reg. § 1.248–1(a)(3). For a similar problem in the Subchapter S area, see Chapter 21.

year 1996. Note that the $300 of expenses incident to the printing and sale of stock certificates does not qualify for the election. These expenses cannot be deducted at all but reduce the amount of the capital realized from the sale of stock. ▼

DETERMINING THE CORPORATE INCOME TAX LIABILITY

CORPORATE INCOME TAX RATES

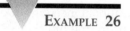

5 LEARNING OBJECTIVE
Compute the corporate income tax.

Corporate income tax rates have fluctuated widely over past years. Refer to the inside front cover of the text for a schedule of the current corporate income tax rates.

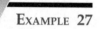

EXAMPLE 26

Gold Corporation, a calendar year taxpayer, has taxable income of $90,000 for 1996. Its income tax liability is $18,850, determined as follows:

Tax on $75,000	$13,750
Tax on $15,000 × 34%	5,100
Tax liability	$18,850

▼

For a corporation that has taxable income in excess of $100,000 for any tax year, the amount of the tax is increased by the lesser of (1) 5 percent of the excess or (2) $11,750. In effect, the additional tax means a 39 percent rate for every dollar of taxable income from $100,000 to $335,000.[30]

EXAMPLE 27

Silver Corporation, a calendar year taxpayer, has taxable income of $335,000 for 1996. Its income tax liability is $113,900, determined as follows:

Tax on $100,000	$ 22,250
Tax on $235,000 × 39%	91,650
Tax liability	$113,900

Note that the tax liability of $113,900 is 34% of $335,000. Thus, due to the 39% rate (34% normal rate + 5% additional tax on taxable income between $100,000 and $335,000), the benefit of the lower rates on the first $75,000 of taxable income completely phases out at $335,000. Note that the normal rate drops back to 34% on taxable income between $335,000 and $10 million. ▼

Qualified PSCs are taxed at a flat 35 percent rate on all taxable income. Thus, they do not enjoy the tax savings of the 15 percent to 34 percent brackets applicable to other corporations. For this purpose, a PSC is a corporation that is substantially employee owned. Also, it must engage in one of the following activities: health, law, engineering, architecture, accounting, actuarial science performing arts, or consulting.

ALTERNATIVE MINIMUM TAX

Corporations are subject to an alternative minimum tax (AMT) that is structured similarly to the AMT applicable to individuals. The AMT for corporations, as for

---

[30]§ 11(b).

individuals, involves a broader tax base than does the regular tax. Like an individual, a corporation is required to apply a minimum tax rate to the expanded base and to pay the difference between the tentative AMT liability and the regular tax. Many of the adjustments and tax preference items necessary to arrive at alternative minimum taxable income (AMTI) are the same for individuals and corporations. Although the objective of the AMT is the same for individual and corporate taxpayers, the rate and exemptions are different. Refer to Chapter 14 for a detailed discussion of the corporate AMT.

TAX LIABILITY OF RELATED CORPORATIONS

6 **LEARNING OBJECTIVE**
Explain the tax rules unique to multiple corporations.

Related corporations are subject to special rules for computing the income tax, the accumulated earnings credit, the AMT exemption, and the environmental tax exemption.[31] If these restrictions did not exist, the shareholders of a corporation could gain significant tax advantages by splitting a single corporation into *multiple* corporations. The next two examples illustrate the potential *income tax* advantage of multiple corporations.

EXAMPLE 28

Gray Corporation annually yields taxable income of $300,000. The corporate tax on $300,000 is $100,250, computed as follows:

Tax on $100,000	$ 22,250
Tax on $200,000 × 39%	78,000
Tax liability	$100,250

▼

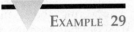

EXAMPLE 29

Assume that Gray Corporation in the previous example is divided equally into four corporations. Each corporation would have taxable income of $75,000, and the tax for each (absent the special provisions for related corporations) would be computed as follows:

Tax on $50,000	$ 7,500
Tax on $25,000 × 25%	6,250
Tax liability	$13,750

The total liability for the four corporations would be $55,000 ($13,750 × 4). The savings would be $45,250 ($100,250 − $55,000). ▼

To preclude the advantages that could be gained by using multiple corporations, the tax law requires special treatment for *controlled groups* of corporations. A comparison of Examples 28 and 29 reveals that the income tax savings that could be achieved by using multiple corporations result from having more of the total income taxed at lower rates. To close this potential loophole, the law limits a controlled group's taxable income in the tax brackets below 35 percent to the amount the corporations in the group would have if they were one corporation. Thus, in Example 29, under the controlled corporation rules, only $12,500 (one-fourth of the first $50,000 of taxable income) for each of the four related corporations would be taxed at the 15 percent rate. The 25 percent rate would apply to the next $6,250 (one-fourth of the next $25,000) of taxable income of each corporation. This equal allocation of the $50,000 and $25,000 amounts is required unless all members of the controlled group consent to an apportionment plan providing for an unequal allocation.

[31] § 1561(a).

Similar limitations apply to the election to expense certain depreciable assets under § 179 (see Chapter 7), to the $250,000 (or $150,000) accumulated earnings credit (see Chapter 20) for controlled groups, and to the $40,000 exemption amount for purposes of computing the AMT (see Chapter 14).

CONTROLLED GROUPS

A **controlled group** of corporations includes parent-subsidiary groups, brother-sister groups, combined groups, and certain insurance companies. Groups of the first three types are discussed in the following sections. Insurance groups are not discussed in this text.

Parent-Subsidiary Controlled Group. A **parent-subsidiary controlled group** consists of one or more *chains* of corporations connected through stock ownership with a common parent corporation. The ownership connection can be established through either a *voting power test* or a *value test*. The voting power test requires ownership of stock possessing at least 80 percent of the total voting power of all classes of stock entitled to vote.[32]

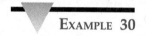

Black Corporation owns 80% of White Corporation. Black and White Corporations are members of a parent-subsidiary controlled group. Black is the parent corporation, and White is the subsidiary. ▼

The parent-subsidiary relationship illustrated in Example 30 is easy to recognize because Black Corporation is the direct owner of White Corporation. Real-world business organizations are often much more complex, sometimes including numerous corporations with chains of ownership connecting them. In these complex corporate structures, determining whether the controlled group classification is appropriate becomes more difficult. The ownership requirements can be met through direct ownership (refer to Example 30) or through indirect ownership, as illustrated in the two following examples.

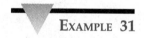

Red Corporation owns 80% of the voting stock of White Corporation, and White Corporation owns 80% of the voting stock of Blue Corporation. Red, White, and Blue Corporations constitute a controlled group in which Red is the common parent and White and Blue are subsidiaries. The same result would occur if Red Corporation, rather than White Corporation, owned the Blue Corporation stock. This parent-subsidiary relationship is diagrammed in Figure 16–2.

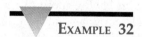

Brown Corporation owns 80% of the stock of Green Corporation, which owns 30% of Blue Corporation. Brown also owns 80% of White Corporation, which owns 50% of Blue Corporation. Brown, Green, Blue, and White Corporations constitute a parent-subsidiary controlled group in which Brown is the common parent and Green, Blue, and White are subsidiaries. This parent-subsidiary relationship is diagrammed in Figure 16–3. ▼

The value test requires ownership of at least 80 percent of the total value of all shares of all classes of stock of each of the corporations, except the parent corporation, by one or more of the other corporations.

Brother-Sister Corporations.   A **brother-sister controlled group** *may* exist if two or more corporations are owned by five or fewer *persons* (individuals, estates,

[32] § 1563(a)(1).

▼ FIGURE 16–2
Controlled Groups—Parent-
Subsidiary Corporations

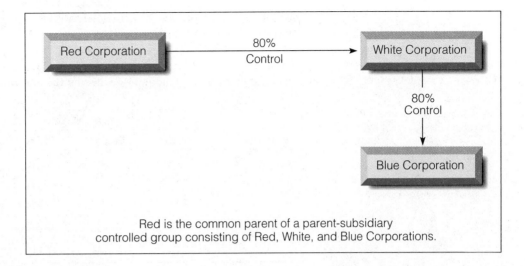

Red is the common parent of a parent-subsidiary
controlled group consisting of Red, White, and Blue Corporations.

▼ FIGURE 16–3
Controlled Groups—Parent-
Subsidiary Corporations

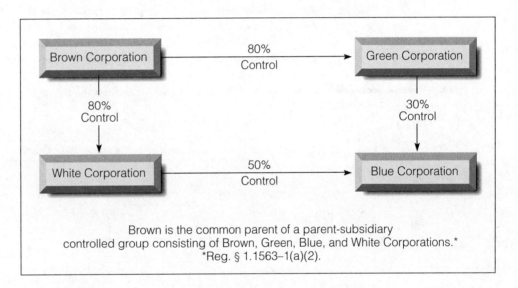

Brown is the common parent of a parent-subsidiary
controlled group consisting of Brown, Green, Blue, and White Corporations.*
*Reg. § 1.1563–1(a)(2).

or trusts). Brother-sister status will apply if such a shareholder group meets an 80 percent total ownership test *and* a 50 percent common ownership test.[33]

- The *total* ownership test is met if the shareholder group possesses stock representing at least 80 percent of the total combined voting power of all classes of stock entitled to vote, *or* at least 80 percent of the total value of shares of all classes of stock of each corporation.
- The *common* ownership test is met if the shareholder group owns more than 50 percent of the total combined voting power of all classes of stock entitled to vote, *or* more than 50 percent of the total value of shares of all classes of stock of each corporation.

In applying the common ownership test, the stock held by each person is considered only to the extent that the stock ownership is *identical* for each corporation. That is, if a shareholder owns 30 percent of Silver Corporation and 20

---

[33] § 1563(a)(2).

percent of Gold Corporation, such shareholder has identical ownership of 20 percent of each corporation.

▼ EXAMPLE 33

The outstanding stock of Hawk, Eagle, Crane, and Dove Corporations, each of which has only one class of stock outstanding, is owned by the following unrelated individuals:

	Corporations				Identical Ownership
Individuals	Hawk	Eagle	Crane	Dove	
Allen	40%	30%	60%	60%	30%
Barton	50%	20%	30%	20%	20%
Carter	10%	30%	10%	10%	10%
Dixon		20%		10%	
Total	100%	100%	100%	100%	60%

Five or fewer individuals (Allen, Barton, and Carter) with more than a 50% common ownership own at least 80% of all classes of stock in Hawk, Eagle, Crane, and Dove. They own 100% of Hawk, 80% of Eagle, 100% of Crane, and 90% of Dove. Consequently, Hawk, Eagle, Crane, and Dove are regarded as members of a brother-sister controlled group. ▼

▼ EXAMPLE 34

Changing the facts in Example 33, assume the ownership is as follows:

	Corporations				Identical Ownership
Individuals	Hawk	Eagle	Crane	Dove	
Allen	20%	10%	5%	60%	5%
Barton	10%	20%	60%	5%	5%
Carter	10%	70%	35%	25%	10%
Dixon	60%			10%	
Total	100%	100%	100%	100%	20%

In this situation, the identical ownership is only 20%. Consequently, the four corporations are not members of a brother-sister controlled group. However, Eagle and Crane would be brother-sister corporations because both the total ownership and the common ownership tests are met. Allen, Barton, and Carter own 100% of each corporation, and common ownership exceeds 50% (5% by Allen, 20% by Barton, and 35% by Carter). ▼

▼ EXAMPLE 35

The outstanding stock of Black Corporation and Brown Corporation, each of which has only one class of stock outstanding, is owned as follows:

	Corporations		Identical Ownership
Individuals	Black	Brown	
Rossi	55%	100%	55%
Smith	45%		
Total	100%	100%	55%

Although the 50% common ownership test is met, the 80% test is not since there is no common ownership in Brown Corporation. Are Black and Brown brother-sister corporations? No, according to the U.S. Supreme Court.[34] ▼

ETHICAL CONSIDERATIONS

Must Voting Rights Reflect Ownerships?

Andrews, Barnes, and Clark are shareholders in Gull, Plover, and Kite Corporations—each has shares in all three corporations. Their tax adviser points out that if the shareholders would trade some shares among themselves, the three corporations would no longer be classified as affiliated corporations, and substantial tax savings would result. The three shareholders would like to complete the trades, but are concerned because the new ownership percentages will give Andrews voting control in Kite Corporation. To solve this problem, Andrews proposes that all three shareholders continue voting based on the ownership percentages that existed prior to the trades. Evaluate Andrews's proposal.

Combined Groups. A **combined controlled group** exists if all of the following conditions are met:

- Each corporation is a member of either a parent-subsidiary controlled group or a brother-sister controlled group.
- At least one of the corporations is a parent of a parent-subsidiary controlled group.
- The parent corporation is also a member of a brother-sister controlled group.

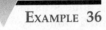

EXAMPLE 36

Robert owns 80% of all classes of stock of Red and Orange Corporations. Red Corporation, in turn, owns 80% of all classes of stock of Blue Corporation. Orange owns all the stock of Green Corporation. Red, Blue, Orange, and Green are members of the same combined group. As a result, Red, Blue, Orange, and Green are limited to taxable income in the tax brackets below 35% and the $250,000 (or $150,000) accumulated earnings credit as though they were one corporation. This is also the case for the election to expense certain depreciable business assets under § 179 and the $40,000 exemption for purposes of computing the AMT. ▼

PROCEDURAL MATTERS

FILING REQUIREMENTS FOR CORPORATIONS

7 LEARNING OBJECTIVE
Describe the reporting process for corporations.

A corporation must file a Federal income tax return whether it has taxable income or not.[35] A corporation that was not in existence throughout an entire annual accounting period is required to file a return for the fraction of the year during which it was in existence. In addition, a corporation must file a return even though

---

[34] *U.S. v. Vogel Fertilizer Co.*, 82–1 USTC ¶9134, 49 AFTR2d 82–491, 102 S.Ct. 821 (USSC, 1982). See also Reg. § 1.1563–1(a)(3), which was amended to comply with the conclusions reached in *Vogel*.

[35] § 6012(a)(2).

it has ceased to do business if it has valuable claims for which it will bring suit. A corporation is relieved of filing income tax returns only when it ceases to do business and retains no assets.

The corporate return is filed on Form 1120 unless the corporation is a small corporation entitled to file the shorter Form 1120–A. A corporation may file Form 1120–A if it meets all the following requirements:

- Gross receipts or sales are under $500,000.
- Total income (gross profit plus other income including gains on sales of property) is under $500,000.
- Total assets are under $500,000.
- The corporation is not involved in a dissolution or liquidation.
- The corporation is not a member of a controlled group under §§ 1561 and 1563.
- The corporation does not file a consolidated return.
- The corporation does not have ownership in a foreign corporation.
- The corporation does not have foreign shareholders who directly or indirectly own 50 percent or more of its stock.

Corporations electing under Subchapter S (see Chapter 21) file on Form 1120S. Forms 1120, 1120–A, and 1120S are reproduced in Appendix B.

The return must be filed on or before the fifteenth day of the third month following the close of a corporation's tax year. Corporations can receive an automatic extension of six months for filing the corporate return by filing Form 7004 by the due date for the return.[36] However, the IRS may terminate the extension by mailing a 10-day notice to the corporation.

ESTIMATED TAX PAYMENTS

A corporation must make payments of estimated tax unless its tax liability can reasonably be expected to be less than $500. The required annual payment (which includes any estimated AMT liability) is the lesser of (1) 100 percent of the corporation's final tax or (2) 100 percent of the tax for the preceding year (if that was a 12-month tax year and the return filed showed a tax liability).[37] Estimated payments can be made in four installments due on or before the fifteenth day of the fourth month, the sixth month, the ninth month, and the twelfth month of the corporate taxable year. The full amount of the unpaid tax is due on the due date of the return.

Failure to make the required estimated tax prepayments results in a nondeductible penalty being imposed on the corporation. The penalty is avoided, however, if any of various exceptions apply.[38]

RECONCILIATION OF TAXABLE INCOME AND FINANCIAL NET INCOME

Schedule M–1 on the last page of Form 1120 is used to reconcile net income as computed for financial accounting purposes with taxable income reported on the corporation's income tax return. The starting point on Schedule M–1 is net income per books (financial accounting net income). Additions and subtractions are entered

---

[36] § 6081.
[37] §§ 6655(d) and (e).

[38] See § 6655 for the penalty involved and the various exceptions to it.

for items that affect net income per books and taxable income differently. The following items are entered as additions (see lines 2 through 5 of Schedule M–1):

- Federal income tax liability (deducted in computing net income per books but not deductible in computing taxable income).
- The excess of capital losses over capital gains (deducted for financial accounting purposes but not deductible by corporations for income tax purposes).
- Income that is reported in the current year for tax purposes that is not reported in computing net income per books (e.g., prepaid income).
- Various expenses that are deducted in computing net income per books but are not allowed in computing taxable income (e.g., charitable contributions in excess of the 10 percent ceiling applicable to corporations).

The following subtractions are entered on lines 7 and 8 of Schedule M–1:

- Income reported for financial accounting purposes but not included in taxable income (e.g., tax-exempt interest).
- Expenses deducted on the tax return but not deducted in computing net income per books (e.g., a charitable contributions carryover deducted in a prior year for financial accounting purposes but deductible in the current year for tax purposes).

The result is taxable income (before the NOL deduction and the dividends received deduction).

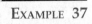

EXAMPLE 37

During the current year, Tern Corporation had the following transactions:

Net income per books (after tax)	$92,400
Taxable income	50,000
Federal income tax liability (15% × $50,000)	7,500
Interest income from tax-exempt bonds	5,000
Interest paid on a loan, the proceeds of which were used to purchase the tax-exempt bonds	500
Life insurance proceeds received as a result of the death of a key employee	50,000
Premiums paid on the key employee life insurance policy	2,600
Excess of capital losses over capital gains	2,000

For book and tax purposes, Tern determines depreciation under the straight-line method. Tern's Schedule M–1 for the current year follows.

Schedule M-1	Reconciliation of Income (Loss) per Books With Income per Return (See instructions.)		
1 Net income (loss) per books	92,400	7 Income recorded on books this year not included on this return (itemize):	
2 Federal income tax	7,500	Tax-exempt interest $ 5,000 Life	
3 Excess of capital losses over capital gains .	2,000	insurance proceeds on key	
4 Income subject to tax not recorded on books this year (itemize): _____		employee $50,000	55,000
_____		8 Deductions on this return not charged against book income this year (itemize):	
5 Expenses recorded on books this year not deducted on this return (itemize):		a Depreciation . . . . $ _____	
a Depreciation . . . . $ _____		b Contributions carryover $ _____	
b Contributions carryover $ _____		_____	
c Travel and entertainment $ Int. on tax-exempt bonds $500, Prem. on key employee ins. $2,600	3,100	9 Add lines 7 and 8	55,000
6 Add lines 1 through 5	105,000	10 Income (line 28, page 1)—line 6 less line 9	50,000

Schedule M–2 reconciles unappropriated retained earnings at the beginning of the year with unappropriated retained earnings at year-end. Beginning balance plus net income per books, as entered on line 1 of Schedule M–1, less dividend distributions during the year equals ending retained earnings. Other sources of increases or decreases in retained earnings are also listed on Schedule M–2.

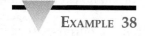

EXAMPLE 38

Assume the same facts as in Example 37. Tern Corporation's beginning balance in unappropriated retained earnings is $125,000. During the year, Tern distributed a cash dividend of $30,000 to its shareholders. Based on these further assumptions, Tern's Schedule M–2 for the current year is as follows:

Schedule M-2	Analysis of Unappropriated Retained Earnings per Books (Line 25, Schedule L)			
1 Balance at beginning of year	125,000	5 Distributions: a Cash	30,000	
2 Net income (loss) per books	92,400	b Stock		
3 Other increases (itemize):		c Property		
		6 Other decreases (itemize):		
		7 Add lines 5 and 6	30,000	
4 Add lines 1, 2, and 3	217,400	8 Balance at end of year (line 4 less line 7)	187,400	

TAX PLANNING CONSIDERATIONS

8 LEARNING OBJECTIVE
Evaluate corporations for conducting a business.

CORPORATE VERSUS NONCORPORATE FORMS OF BUSINESS ORGANIZATION

The decision to use the corporate form in conducting a trade or business must be weighed carefully. Besides the nontax considerations associated with the corporate form (limited liability, continuity of life, free transferability of interests, centralized management), tax ramifications will play an important role in any such decision. Close attention should be paid to the following:

1. Operating as a regular corporate entity (C corporation) results in the imposition of the corporate income tax. Corporate taxable income will be taxed twice—once as earned by the corporation and again when distributed to the shareholders. Since dividends are not deductible, a closely held corporation has a strong incentive to structure corporate distributions in a deductible form. Thus, profits can be bailed out by the shareholders in the form of salaries, interest, or rents. Such procedures lead to a multitude of problems, one of which, the reclassification of debt as equity, is discussed in Chapter 17. The problems of unreasonable salaries and rents are covered in Chapter 18 in the discussion of constructive dividends.

2. The current tax rates appear to favor corporations over individuals, since corporations have a maximum tax rate of 35 percent and individuals may be subject to a 39.6 percent top rate. Relatively few individuals or corporations are in the top rate brackets, however. For moderate-income taxpayers, the differences in Federal tax brackets between an individual and a corporation may not be substantial. Several state and local governments impose higher taxes on corporations than on individuals. In these jurisdictions, the combined Federal, state, and local tax rates on the two types of taxpayers are practically identical. If a corporation's taxable income does not exceed $100,000, a substantial tax savings may be achieved by accumulating income inside the corporation. Refer to Example 7.

3. Corporate-source income loses its identity as it passes through the corporation to the shareholders. Thus, preferential tax treatment of certain items by the corporation (e.g., interest on municipal bonds) does not carry over to the shareholders.

NEED A FORM? TRY THE WEB

The Worldwide Web on the Internet is one of the hottest news items in recent years. The Web serves many purposes, some useful and some frivolous. Of interest to tax students and practitioners are the growing number of Web sites devoted to the field of taxation. There are sites for Federal, state, and foreign tax law.

Navigating through the various Web sites to find information can be frustrating at times. The *gateway* sites, which contain links to the other tax sites, are helpful as a roadmap to the Web. The following are some of the more useful gateway sites:

Site	URL (Web Address)
Tom Omer's Tax Information Sites	http://omer.cba.neu.edu/OtherSites/sendem.html
Frank McNeil's TaxSites	http://www.best.com/~ftmexpat/html/taxsites.html
University of Iowa's Tax Resources	http://www.biz.uiowa.edu/acct/tax.html
U.S. House Internet Law Library—Taxes	http://www.pls.com:8001/his/109.htm

There are several useful Federal tax law sites, including the IRS Home Page (http://www.ustreas.gov/treasury/bureaus/irs/irs.html), which allows downloading of most tax forms. The Internal Revenue Code is available at several sites, including Internal Revenue Code—Hypertext (http://www.tns.lcs.mit.edu:80/uscode/).

SOURCE: Information from R. J. Coppins, D. R. Schmidt, R. M. Spindle, and W. F. Yancey, "Worldwide Web Is the Latest Source of Tax Information," *Taxation for Accountants*, August 1995, pp. 93–107.

4. As noted in Chapter 18, it may be difficult for shareholders to recover some or all of their investment in the corporation without an ordinary income result. Most corporate distributions are treated as dividends to the extent of the corporation's earnings and profits.
5. Corporate losses cannot be passed through to the shareholders.[39]
6. The liquidation of a corporation will normally generate tax consequences to both the corporation and its shareholders (see Chapter 19).
7. The corporate form provides shareholders with the opportunity to be treated as employees for tax purposes if the shareholders render services to the corporation. Such status makes a number of attractive tax-sheltered fringe benefits available. They include, but are not limited to, group term life insurance, the $5,000 death benefit, and excludible meals and lodging. One of the most attractive benefits of incorporation is the ability of the business to provide accident and health insurance to its employees, including shareholders. Such benefits are not included in the employee's gross income. Similar rules apply to other medical costs paid by the employer. These benefits are not available to partners and sole proprietors.

---

[39] Points 1, 2, and 5 could be resolved by making a Subchapter S election (see Chapter 21), assuming the corporation qualifies for the election. In part, the same can be said for point 3.

CONCEPT SUMMARY 16–1

Income Taxation of Individuals and Corporations Compared

	Individuals	Corporations
Computation of gross income	§ 61.	§ 61.
Computation of taxable income	§ 62 and §§ 63(b) through (h).	§ 63(a). Concept of AGI has no relevance.
Deductions	Trade or business (§ 162); nonbusiness (§ 212); some personal and employee expenses (generally deductible as itemized deductions).	Trade or business (§ 162).
Charitable contributions	Limited in any tax year to 50% of AGI; 30% for long-term capital gain property unless election is made to reduce fair market value of gift.	Limited in any tax year to 10% of taxable income computed without regard to the charitable contribution deduction, NOL carryback, capital loss carryback, and dividends received deduction.
	Excess charitable contributions carried over for five years.	Same as for individuals.
	Amount of contribution is the fair market value of the property; if lower, ordinary income property will be limited to adjusted basis; capital gain property will be treated as ordinary income property if certain tangible personalty is donated to a nonuse charity or a private nonoperating foundation is the donee.	Same as individuals, but exceptions allowed for certain inventory and for scientific property where one-half of the appreciation also will be allowed as a deduction.
	Time of deduction is the year in which payment is made.	Time of deduction is the year in which payment is made unless accrual basis taxpayer. Accrual basis corporation can take deduction in year preceding payment if contribution was authorized by board of directors by end of year and contribution is paid by fifteenth day of third month of following year.
Casualty losses	$100 floor on personal casualty and theft losses; personal casualty losses deductible only to extent losses exceed 10% of AGI.	Deductible in full.
Depreciation recapture under § 1250	Recaptured to extent accelerated depreciation exceeds straight-line.	20% of excess of amount that would be recaptured under § 1245 over amount recaptured under § 1250 is additional ordinary income under § 291.
Net operating loss	Adjusted for several items, including nonbusiness deductions over nonbusiness income and personal exemptions.	Generally no adjustments.
	Carryback period is 3 years and carryforward period is 15 years.	Same as for individuals.
Dividends received deduction	None.	70%, 80%, or 100% of dividends received depending on percentage of ownership by corporate shareholder.

	Individuals	**Corporations**
Net capital gains	Taxed in full. Tax rate cannot exceed 28%.	Taxed in full.
Capital losses	Only $3,000 of capital loss per year can offset ordinary income; loss is carried forward indefinitely to offset capital gains or ordinary income up to $3,000; carryovers retain their character as long term or short term.	Can offset only capital gains; carried back three years and forward five; carryovers and carrybacks are short-term losses.
Passive losses	Passive activity losses cannot offset either active income or portfolio income.	Passive loss rules apply to closely held C corporations and personal service corporations. For personal service corporations, the rule is the same as for individuals. For closely held corporations, passive losses may offset active income but not portfolio income.
Tax rates	Progressive with five rates (15%, 28%, 31%, 36%, 39.6%).	Progressive with four rates (15%, 25%, 34%, 35%). Two lowest brackets phased out between $100,000 and $335,000 of taxable income, and additional tax imposed between $15,000,000 and $18,333,333 of taxable income.
Alternative minimum tax	Applied at a graduated rate schedule of 26% and 28%. Exemption allowed depending on filing status (e.g., $45,000 for married filing jointly); phase-out begins when AMTI reaches a certain amount (e.g., $150,000 for married filing jointly).	Applied at a 20% rate on AMTI less exemption; $40,000 exemption allowed but phase-out begins when AMTI reaches $150,000; adjustments and tax preference items are similar to those applicable to individuals, but also include 75% adjusted current earnings adjustment.

OPERATING THE CORPORATION

Tax planning to reduce corporate income taxes should occur before the end of the tax year. Effective planning can cause income to be shifted to the next tax year and can produce large deductions by incurring expenses before year-end. Particular attention should be focused on the following.

Charitable Contributions.   Recall that accrual basis corporations may claim a deduction for charitable contributions in the year preceding payment. The contribution must be authorized by the board of directors by the end of the tax year and paid on or before the fifteenth day of the third month of the following year. Even though the contribution may not ultimately be made, it might well be authorized. A deduction cannot be thrown back to the previous year (even if paid within the two and a half months) if it has not been authorized.

Timing of Capital Gains and Losses.   A corporation should consider offsetting profits on the sale of capital assets by selling some of the depreciated securities in the corporate portfolio. In addition, any already realized capital losses should be carefully monitored. Recall that corporate taxpayers are not permitted to claim any net capital losses as deductions against ordinary income. Capital losses can be used only as an offset against capital gains. Further, net capital losses can only be carried back three years and forward five. Gains from the sales of capital assets should be timed to offset any capital losses. The expiration of the carryover period for any net capital losses should be watched carefully so that sales of appreciated capital assets occur before that date.

Net Operating Losses.   In some situations, electing to forgo an NOL carryback and utilizing the carryforward option may generate greater tax savings. When deciding whether to forgo the carryback options, take into account three considerations. First, the time value of the tax refund that is lost by not using the carryback procedure should be calculated. Second, the election to forgo an NOL carryback is irrevocable. Thus, one cannot later choose to change if the predicted high profits do not materialize. Third, consider the future increases (or decreases) in corporate income tax rates that can reasonably be anticipated. This last consideration is the most difficult to work with. Although corporate tax rates have remained relatively stable in past years, projected budget deficits do little to assure taxpayers that future rates will remain constant.

Dividends Received Deduction.   The dividends received deduction is normally limited to the lesser of 70 percent of the qualifying dividends or 70 percent of taxable income. The deduction limits are raised to 80 percent for a dividend received from a corporation in which the recipient owns more than 20 percent but less than 80 percent of the stock. An exception is made when the full deduction yields an NOL. In close situations, therefore, the proper timing of income or deductions to generate an NOL may yield a larger dividends received deduction.

Organizational Expenditures.   To qualify for the 60-month amortization procedure of § 248, only organizational expenditures incurred in the first taxable year of the corporation can be considered. This rule could prove to be an unfortunate trap for corporations formed late in the year.

EXAMPLE 39

Thrush Corporation is formed in December 1996. Qualified organizational expenditures are incurred as follows: $2,000 in December 1996 and $3,000 in January 1997. If Thrush uses the calendar year for tax purposes, only $2,000 of the organizational expenditures can be written off over a period of 60 months. ▼

The solution to the problem posed by Example 39 is for Thrush Corporation to adopt a fiscal year that ends at or beyond January 31. All organizational expenditures will then have been incurred before the close of the first taxable year.

Shareholder-Employee Payment of Corporate Expenses.   In a closely held corporate setting, shareholder-employees often pay corporate expenses (e.g., travel and entertainment) for which they are not reimbursed by the corporation. The IRS often disallows the deduction of these expenses by the shareholder-employee since the payments are voluntary on his or her part. If the deduction is more beneficial at the shareholder-employee level, a corporate policy against reimbursement of such expenses should be established. Proper planning in this regard would be to decide before the beginning of each tax year where the deduction would do the most good. Corporate policy on reimbursement of such expenses could be modified on a year-to-year basis depending upon the circumstances.

In deciding whether corporate expenses should be kept at the corporate level or shifted to the shareholder-employee, the treatment of unreimbursed employee expenses must be considered. First, since employee expenses are itemized deductions, they will be of no benefit to the taxpayer who chooses the standard deduction option. Second, these expenses will be subject to the 2 percent-of-AGI floor. No such limitation will be imposed if the corporation claims the expenses.

RELATED CORPORATIONS

Recall that § 1561 was designed to prevent shareholders from operating a business as multiple corporations to obtain lower tax brackets and multiple accumulated earnings tax credits or AMT exemptions. Corporations in which substantially all the stock is held by five or fewer persons are subject to the provisions of § 1561. Dividing ownership so that control of each corporation does not lie with individuals having common control of all corporations avoids the prohibitions of § 1561.

KEY TERMS

Association, 16–8

Brother-sister controlled group, 16–24

C corporation, 16–4

Combined controlled group, 16–27

Controlled group, 16–24

Dividends received deduction, 16–19

Limited liability company (LLC), 16–9

Limited partnerships, 16–7

Organizational expenditures, 16–21

Parent-subsidiary controlled group, 16–24

Passive loss, 16–16

Personal service corporation (PSC), 16–12

Regular corporation, 16–4

Related corporations, 16–23

S corporation, 16–4

Schedule M–1, 16–28

PROBLEM MATERIALS

DISCUSSION QUESTIONS

1. Robin, who owns and operates a sole proprietorship, is considering incorporating her business as a regular corporation. She has asked you to explain how a corporate tax return differs from the return for a sole proprietorship.

2. Edgar owns a sole proprietorship, and Frank is the sole shareholder of a corporation. Both businesses make a profit of $50,000 in 1996. Neither owner withdraws any funds from his business during the year. Discuss the tax treatment of each owner.

3. Ann owns a sole proprietorship, and Heather is the sole shareholder of a regular corporation. Both businesses were started in 1996, and each business sustained a $3,000 loss for the year.
   a. Assume the loss is a capital loss. How will the capital loss affect each owner's taxable income?
   b. Assume instead that the loss is an operating loss. How will the operating loss affect each owner's taxable income?

4. Blue Corporation, which has 10 shareholders, earned $100,000 during 1996. Red Company, a partnership, earned $100,000 during the year. Blue did not pay any dividends, and Red's partners did not make any withdrawals. Contrast the tax treatment of the shareholders and the partners.

5. Rosita, who owns a proprietorship, has scheduled an appointment to talk with you about the advisability of incorporating. At this time, you know nothing about Rosita's business or her existing tax situation. List the questions you will need to ask during the appointment so you can help her make an informed decision.

6. Shareholders in closely held corporations frequently pay themselves large salaries in order to avoid double taxation on corporate income. Explain how this strategy avoids double taxation, but also entails possible pitfalls.

7. In some circumstances, an unincorporated business may be classified as an association. What are the circumstances? Why would the IRS take this action? Why would taxpayers try to avoid this outcome?

8. Ann and Fran, who are sisters, own adjacent parcels of land they inherited from their parents. They form Twin Properties, Inc., and transfer the land to the corporation. At the date of transfer, each parcel of land is worth $25,000. Ann wants to have the corporation hold the land until it appreciates to $100,000 and then sell it. Fran wants to have the corporation subdivide the property, put in streets and a sewer system, and then sell the lots. What are the Federal income tax implications of the two plans?

9. Why might the IRS attempt to disregard a legally constituted corporate entity? Why might the shareholders attempt such a move?

10. What is a limited liability company? Why would the owners of an entity want to have it qualify as a limited liability company?

11. Explain the possible tax classifications for a limited liability company. In what situations might such an organization be treated as a partnership? As a corporation?

12. Wren Corporation, a calendar year, cash basis taxpayer, accrues a performance bonus of $50,000 to Brad, a cash basis taxpayer who is the sole shareholder of the corporation. When can Wren deduct the bonus?

13. A taxpayer realized a net long-term capital gain of $10,000 during the year. How is the gain treated if the taxpayer is a corporation? An individual?

14. A taxpayer incurred a net long-term capital loss of $5,000 during the year. How is the loss treated if the taxpayer is a corporation? An individual?

15. John, a sole proprietor, incurs a $5,000 capital loss from the sale of an asset used in his business. Fox Corporation incurs a $5,000 capital loss on the sale of an asset used in its business. How do John and Fox Corporation treat these losses in computing taxable income?

16. A taxpayer sells a warehouse for a gain of $50,000. The warehouse has been depreciated as 15-year property under ACRS. If the straight-line method was used, depreciation recapture will be higher if the taxpayer is a corporation than if the taxpayer is an individual. Explain.

17. On December 30, 1996, Bonnie, a sole proprietor, pledged to make a $10,000 charitable contribution on or before January 15, 1997. Seal Corporation made a similar pledge on the same date, and the contribution was authorized by Seal's board of directors. Assuming both Bonnie and Seal Corporation are calendar year taxpayers, discuss when these contributions will be deductible.

18. Red Corporation owns 85% of the stock of Blue Corporation, which pays Red a dividend of $100,000. Red Corporation also owns 15% of the stock of Green Corporation, which pays Red a $60,000 dividend. How much dividend income will Red Corporation report for the year?

19. In connection with organizational expenditures, comment on the following:
   a. Those that qualify for amortization.
   b. Those that do not qualify for amortization.
   c. The period over which amortization can take place.
   d. Expenses incurred but not paid by a cash basis corporation.
   e. Expenses incurred by a corporation in its second year of operation.

f. The alternative if no election to amortize is made.

g. The timing of the election to amortize.

20. Silver Corporation, which owns stock in Gold Corporation, had net operating income of $150,000 for the year. Gold pays Silver a dividend of $30,000. Under what circumstances can Silver take a dividends received deduction of $21,000? A dividends received deduction of $30,000?

21. At what level of taxable income does a corporation reach a marginal income tax rate of 35% if it is a PSC? If it is not a PSC? At what level of taxable income does a corporation reach an average income tax rate of 35% if it is not a PSC?

22. Taxable income and financial accounting income for a corporation are seldom the same amount. Discuss some common reasons for differences and how these differences affect the reconciliation of taxable income and financial accounting income on Schedule M–1 of Form 1120.

23. Mallard Corporation incorporated in December 1996 and expects to have substantial organizational expenditures. Discuss tax planning strategies that Mallard should consider in order to maximize the deduction for organizational expenditures.

PROBLEMS

24. Jill owns 100% of Black Company, which had operating income of $100,000 and operating expenses of $140,000 in 1996. In addition, Black Company had a long-term capital loss of $15,000. Based on this information, what is the tax treatment in each of the following situations?
    a. Black Company is a corporation and pays no dividends during the year.
    b. Black Company is a proprietorship.

25. Gray Company had $80,000 net profit from operations in 1996 and paid Pat Gray, its sole shareholder, a dividend of $50,000. Pat has a large amount of income from other sources and is in the 31% marginal tax bracket. Would Pat's tax situation be better or worse if Gray Company were a proprietorship and Pat withdrew $50,000 from the business during the year?

26. Redd Company has approximately $200,000 in net income in 1996 before deducting any compensation or other payment to its sole owner, Kim Redd. Kim is single. Her income aside from the company's profits is low and would offset her personal exemption and standard deduction. Discuss the tax aspects of each of the following arrangements:
    a. Kim operates Redd Company as a proprietorship.
    b. Kim incorporates Redd Company and pays herself a salary of $50,000 and no dividend.
    c. Kim incorporates the company and pays herself a $50,000 salary and a dividend of $108,250 ($150,000 – $41,750 corporate income tax).
    d. Kim incorporates the company and pays herself a salary of $200,000.

27. Mike owns 100% of White Company, which had net operating income of $60,000 in 1996 ($100,000 operating income – $40,000 operating expenses). In addition, White Company had a long-term capital gain of $10,000. Mike has sufficient income from other activities to place him in the 39.6% marginal tax bracket before considering results from White Company. Using this information, explain the tax treatment under the following circumstances:
    a. White Company is a corporation and pays no dividends during the year.
    b. White Company is a corporation and pays Mike $70,000 of dividends during the year.
    c. White Company is a corporation and pays Mike a $70,000 salary during the year.
    d. White Company is a proprietorship, and Mike withdraws $0 during the year.
    e. White Company is a proprietorship, and Mike withdraws $70,000 during the year.

28. Rust Corporation and Al and Bob form a limited partnership on January 1 to construct office buildings. Rust Corporation is the general partner, and Al and Bob are both

limited partners. The partnership agreement provides that Rust will have sole management of the business. Al's and Bob's liabilities for debts of the partnership will be limited to their investments. The partnership agreement provides that the partnership will not end upon the death of any of the partners. The agreement also provides that both Al or Bob may sell their interests without the consent of the other parties. Al and Bob invest $50,000 each in the partnership. Rust Corporation, which has a net worth of only $20,000, invests $10,000. The partnership secures a loan from the bank to help finance the initial cost of construction. How will the partnership be classified for tax purposes? Explain.

29. A limited liability company is formed in a state with a flexible statute. Under the state law, no member of the LLC has personal liability for the debts of the business. The company may decide which of the other corporate characteristics it may have. Indicate the most likely classification (corporation or partnership) by the IRS in each of the following situations:
    a. The LLC has centralized management, but does not have free transferability of interests or continuity of life.
    b. The LLC does not have centralized management, but does have free transferability of interests and continuity of life.
    c. The LLC does not have centralized management or free transferability of interests, but does have continuity of life.
    d. The LLC has centralized management and free transferability of interests, but does not have continuity of life.

30. Bluebird Company, a calendar year taxpayer, suffered a casualty loss of $27,000 during the current year. How much of the casualty loss can Bluebird deduct assuming the entity is a corporation? How much can be deducted if Bluebird Company is a sole proprietorship and Charles Hughes, its owner, has adjusted gross income of $250,000?

31. Benton Company has one owner, who is in the 39.6% Federal income tax bracket. Benton's gross income is $180,000, and its ordinary trade or business deductions are $65,000. It also pays accident and health insurance premiums for the benefit of its owner, in the amount of $3,000 for the current year. Compute the tax liability on Benton's income for 1996 under the following assumptions:
    a. Benton Company is operated as a proprietorship, and the owner withdraws $75,000 for personal use.
    b. Benton is operated as a corporation, pays out $75,000 as salary, and pays no dividends.
    c. Benton is operated as a corporation and pays out no salary or dividends.
    d. Benton is operated as a corporation, pays out $75,000 as salary, and pays out the remainder of its earnings as dividends.
    e. Assume Robert Benton of 1121 Monroe Street, Ironton, OH 45638 is the owner of Benton Company, which was operated as a proprietorship in 1996. Robert is thinking about incorporating the business in 1997 and asks your advice. He expects about the same amounts of income and expenses in 1997 and plans to take $75,000 per year out of the company whether he incorporates or not. Write a letter to Robert (based on your analysis in [a] and [b] above) containing your recommendations.

32. Pelican Corporation had $100,000 operating income and $70,000 operating expenses during the year. In addition, Pelican had a $2,000 short-term capital gain and an $8,000 short-term capital loss.
    a. Compute Pelican's taxable income for the year.
    b. Assume the same facts as above except that Pelican's short-term capital gain was $12,000. Compute Pelican's taxable income for the year.

33. In 1996, a business sells a capital asset, which it had held for two years, at a loss of $15,000. How much of the capital loss may be deducted in 1996, and how much is carried back or forward under the following circumstances?
    a. The business was a sole proprietorship owned by Kim. Kim had a short-term capital gain of $3,000 and a long-term capital gain of $2,000 in 1996. Kim had ordinary net income from the proprietorship of $60,000.

b. The business is incorporated. The corporation had a short-term capital gain of $3,000 and a long-term capital gain of $2,000. Its ordinary net income from the business was $60,000.

34. Magenta Corporation realized a net long-term capital loss of $130,000 and a net short-term capital gain of $10,000 during 1996. Taxable income from other sources was $650,000. Other years' transactions included the following:

1992	Net long-term capital gain (NLTCG)	$20,000
1993	Net short-term capital gain (NSTCG)	48,000
1994	Net long-term capital gain (NLTCG)	17,000
1995	Net long-term capital gain (NLTCG)	30,000
1997	Net short-term capital gain (NSTCG)	23,000
1997	Net long-term capital gain (NLTCG)	14,000

a. How are the capital gains and losses treated on the 1996 tax return?
b. Compute the capital loss carryback to the carryback years.
c. Compute the amount of capital loss carryforward to 1997, and indicate how it should be used.

35. Goshawk Corporation acquired residential rental property on January 3, 1986, for $400,000. The property was depreciated using the accelerated method and a 19-year recovery period under ACRS. Depreciation in the amount of $231,900 was claimed. Straight-line depreciation for the period would have been $190,350. Goshawk sold the property on January 1, 1996, for $440,000. What is the gain on the sale, and how is it taxed?

36. Assume the property in Problem 35 was a commercial building and Goshawk Corporation used the straight-line method of depreciation with a 19-year recovery period under ACRS. What would be the gain on the sale, and how would it be taxed?

37. Joseph Thompson is president and sole shareholder of JayTee, Inc. In December 1996, Joe asks your advice regarding a charitable contribution he plans to have the corporation make to the University of Maine, a qualified public charity. Joe is considering the following alternatives as charitable contributions in December 1996:

	Fair Market Value
(1) Cash donation	$120,000
(2) Unimproved land held for six years ($20,000 basis)	120,000
(3) Acme Corporation stock held for eight months ($20,000 basis)	120,000
(4) Brown Corporation stock held for two years ($170,000 basis)	120,000

Joe has asked you to help him decide which of these potential contributions will be most advantageous taxwise. JayTee's taxable income is $3,500,000 before considering the contribution. Rank the four alternatives and write a letter to Joe communicating your advice. The corporation's address is 1442 Main Street, Freeport, ME 04032.

38. During the current year, Heron Corporation, a calendar year taxpayer, had the following income and expenses:

Income from operations	$270,000
Expenses from operations	198,000
Qualifying dividends from domestic corporation in which Heron owns a 40% interest	18,000
NOL carryover from prior year	5,400

On October 1, Heron Corporation made a contribution to a qualified charitable organization of $12,600 in cash (not included in any of the above items).

a. Determine Heron Corporation's charitable contribution deduction for the current year.

b. What happens to any excess charitable contribution deduction not allowable for the current year?

39. Dan Simms is the president and sole shareholder of Simms Corporation, 1121 Madison Street, Seattle, WA 98121. Dan plans for the corporation to make a charitable contribution to the University of Washington, a qualified public charity. He will have the corporation donate Jaybird Corporation stock with a basis of $8,000 and a fair market value of $20,000. Dan projects a $200,000 net profit for Simms Corporation in 1996 and a $100,000 net profit in 1997. Dan calls you on December 5, 1996, and asks whether he should make the contribution in 1996 or 1997. Write a letter advising Dan about the timing of the contribution.

40. During 1996, a corporation has $160,000 of gross income and $200,000 in allowable business deductions. Included in gross income is $48,000 in qualifying dividends from domestic corporations (less-than-20%-owned).

a. Determine the corporation's NOL for 1996.

b. What happens to the loss if the corporation was newly created in 1996? In 1993?

41. In each of the following independent situations, determine the dividends received deduction. Assume that none of the corporate shareholders owns 20% or more of the stock in the corporations paying the dividends.

	Red Corporation	White Corporation	Blue Corporation
Income from operations	$ 700,000	$ 800,000	$ 700,000
Expenses from operations	(600,000)	(900,000)	(740,000)
Qualifying dividends	100,000	200,000	200,000

42. Green Corporation was formed on December 1, 1996. Qualifying organizational expenses were incurred and paid as follows:

Incurred and paid in December 1996	$15,000
Incurred in December 1996 but paid in January 1997	7,500
Incurred and paid in February 1997	4,500

Assume Green Corporation makes a timely election under § 248 to amortize organizational expenditures over a period of 60 months. What amount may be amortized in the corporation's first tax year under each of the following assumptions?

a. Green Corporation adopts a calendar year and the cash basis of accounting for tax purposes.

b. Same as (a), except that Green Corporation chooses a fiscal year of December 1 through November 30.

c. Green Corporation adopts a calendar year and the accrual basis of accounting for tax purposes.

d. Same as (c), except that Green Corporation chooses a fiscal year of December 1 through November 30.

43. Topaz Corporation, an accrual basis taxpayer, was formed and began operations on July 1, 1996. The following expenses were incurred during the first tax year of operations (July 1 through December 31, 1996):

Expenses of temporary directors and of organizational meetings	$ 5,000
Fee paid to the state of incorporation	600
Accounting services incident to organization	1,200
Legal services for drafting the corporate charter and bylaws	2,800
Expenses incident to the printing and sale of stock certificates	1,000
	$10,600

Assume Topaz Corporation makes an appropriate and timely election under § 248.
a. What is the maximum organizational expense Topaz may write off for tax year 1996?
b. What would have been the result if a proper election had not been made?

44. In each of the following independent situations, determine the corporation's income tax liability. Assume that all corporations use a calendar year for tax purposes and that the tax year involved is 1996.

	Taxable Income
Wren Corporation	$ 47,000
Thrush Corporation	240,000
Gull Corporation	1,200,000
Oriole Corporation	19,000,000

45. Red Corporation owns 80% of the total combined voting power of all classes of stock entitled to vote in White Corporation. White owns 20% of the stock in Blue Corporation. Red owns 90% of Green Corporation, while the latter owns 60% of Blue Corporation. Which corporations are part of a controlled group?

46. The outstanding stock of Starling, Robin, Crow, Grouse, and Swallow Corporations is owned by the following unrelated individual and corporate shareholders:

	Corporations				
Shareholders	Starling	Robin	Crow	Grouse	Swallow
Albert	20%		5%	10%	
Burke	30%		40%	50%	
Clark	20%		15%	10%	
Dave	10%		20%	10%	
Starling Corporation		90%			
Grouse Corporation					85%

Which, if any, of the above corporations are members of a controlled group?

47. Eagle and Lion Corporations both have 100 shares of stock outstanding. Each shareholder paid $500 for his stock in each corporation, and the fair market value of the stock of each corporation is $800 per share. The stock is owned by the following unrelated individuals:

Shareholders	Eagle Shares	Lion Shares
Washington	30	15
Adams	5	50
Jefferson	65	35
Total	100	100

a. Does a brother-sister controlled group exist?
b. Will a brother-sister controlled group exist if Jefferson sells 10 of his shares in Lion Corporation to Adams?
c. Discuss any tax advantages that will result if Jefferson sells 10 of his Lion shares to Adams.
d. Adams has suggested to Jefferson that they complete the transaction in (c). Jefferson asks your advice and says that he is in the 31% marginal bracket. Write a letter to Ronald Jefferson at 3435 Grand Avenue, South Point, OH 45680, explaining the tax

advantages that will result if he sells 10 of his Lion shares to Adams. Also, identify any problems, both tax and nontax, that the sale could cause for Jefferson.

48. For 1995, Acme Corporation, an accrual basis, calendar year taxpayer, had net income per books of $172,750 and the following special transactions:

Life insurance proceeds received upon the death of the corporation president	$100,000
Premiums paid on the life insurance policy on the president	10,000
Prepaid rent received and properly taxed in 1994 but credited as rent income in 1995	15,000
Rent income received in 1995 ($10,000 is prepaid and relates to 1996)	$25,000
Interest income on tax-exempt bonds	5,000
Interest on loan to carry tax-exempt bonds	3,000
MACRS depreciation in excess of straight-line (straight-line was used for book purposes)	4,000
Capital loss in excess of capital gains	6,000
Federal income tax liability and accrued tax provision for 1995	22,250

Using Schedule M–1 of Form 1120 (the most recent version available), compute Acme Corporation's taxable income for 1995.

49. Using the legend provided, classify each of the following statements:

Legend

I = Applies only to individual taxpayers.

C = Applies only to corporate taxpayers.

B = Applies to both individual and corporate taxpayers.

N = Applies to neither individual nor corporate taxpayers.

---

a. A net capital loss can be carried back.
b. Net long-term capital losses are carried back or forward as short-term capital losses.
c. A $4,000 net short-term capital loss in the current year can be deducted against ordinary income only to the extent of $3,000.
d. The carryforward period for net capital losses is five years.
e. The alternative minimum tax does not apply.
f. Net operating losses are not allowed to be carried back.
g. The credit for the elderly applies.
h. The carryback period for excess charitable contributions is three years.
i. Excess charitable contributions can be carried forward indefinitely.
j. On the disposition of certain depreciable real estate, more ordinary income may result.
k. Percentage limitations may restrict the amount of charitable deductions that can be claimed in any one tax year.
l. Casualty losses are deductible in full.
m. More adjustments are necessary to arrive at an NOL deduction.

Research Problems for this chapter appear at the end of Chapter 28.

CHAPTER

17

CORPORATIONS: ORGANIZATION AND CAPITAL STRUCTURE

LEARNING OBJECTIVES

After completing Chapter 17, you should be able to:

1. Identify the tax consequences of incorporating a business.

2. Appreciate the tax problems involved when making later property transfers to a controlled corporation.

3. Understand the tax aspects of the capital structure of a corporation.

4. Recognize the tax differences between debt and equity investments.

5. Handle the tax treatment of shareholder debt and stock losses.

Chapter 16 dealt with three principal areas fundamental to working with corporations: (1) the recognition of an entity as a corporation for Federal income tax purposes, (2) the tax rules applicable to the day-to-day operation of a corporation, and (3) the filing and reporting procedures governing corporations.

Chapter 17 addresses more sophisticated problems in dealing with corporations:

- The tax consequences to the shareholders and the corporation upon the organization of the corporation.
- Once the corporation has been formed, the tax result that ensues when shareholders make later transfers of property.
- The capital structure of a corporation, including the treatment of capital contributions by nonshareholders and shareholders and the handling of investor losses suffered by shareholders.

ORGANIZATION OF AND TRANSFERS TO CONTROLLED CORPORATIONS

IN GENERAL

1 **LEARNING OBJECTIVE**
Identify the tax consequences of incorporating a business.

Generally, property transfers have tax consequences. This is because gain or loss is normally realized on a property transfer. As a result, unless special provisions in the Code apply, a transfer of property to a corporation in exchange for stock is a sale or exchange of property that constitutes a taxable transaction. Gain or loss is measured by the difference between the tax basis of the property transferred and the value of the stock received.

The Code, however, does provide for special exceptions. Exceptions from the recognition of gain or loss are appropriate where a taxpayer's economic status has not changed and the wherewithal to pay is lacking.

One such exception is a like-kind exchange. When a taxpayer exchanges some of his or her property for other property of a like kind, § 1031 of the Code provides that gain or loss on the exchange is postponed because there has not been a substantive change in the taxpayer's investment. Section 1031 is a deferral mechanism, not an avoidance provision. The deferral mechanism is accomplished by a carryover of basis. Due to this carryover of basis, the potential gain or loss on the property given up is recognized when the property received in the exchange is sold.

Another exception to the general rule that a property transfer results in tax consequences is § 351. Section 351 provides for the nonrecognition of gain or loss upon the transfer of property to a corporation when certain conditions are met. The nonrecognition of gain or loss under § 351 also reflects the principle that gain should not be recognized when a taxpayer's investment has not substantially changed. When a business is incorporated, the owner's economic status has not really changed. The investment in the business assets carries over to the investment in corporate stock. Since only stock in the new corporation is received, the taxpayer is hardly in a position to pay a tax on any realized gain. As noted later, when the taxpayer receives property other than stock (i.e., boot) from the corporation, realized gain may be recognized.

The same principles govern the nonrecognition of gain or loss under § 1031 and § 351. The concept of nonrecognition of gain or loss, present in both Code sections, causes gain or loss to be postponed until a substantive change in the taxpayer's investment occurs (a sale to or a taxable exchange with outsiders). This approach is justified under the wherewithal to pay concept.

A further justification for the nonrecognition of gain or loss provisions under § 351 is that tax rules should not impede the exercise of sound business judgment (e.g., choice of corporate form of doing business).

EXAMPLE 1

Ron is considering incorporating his donut shop. He is concerned about potential liability for the shop's obligations in case he encounters financial difficulties in the future. Ron realizes that if he incorporates the shop, he will be liable only for the debts of the business that he has personally guaranteed. If Ron incorporates, the following assets will be transferred to the corporation:

	Tax Basis	Fair Market Value
Cash	$10,000	$ 10,000
Furniture and fixtures	20,000	60,000
Land and building	40,000	100,000
	$70,000	$170,000

Ron will receive stock in the newly formed corporation worth $170,000 in exchange for the assets. Without the nonrecognition provisions of § 351, Ron would recognize a taxable gain of $100,000 on the transfer. Under § 351, however, Ron does not recognize any gain because his economic status has not really changed. Ron's investment in the assets of his unincorporated donut shop carries over to his investment in the incorporated donut shop. Thus, § 351 provides for tax neutrality on the initial incorporation of Ron's donut shop. ▼

When a taxpayer exchanges property in a like-kind exchange, gain is not recognized only to the extent that the taxpayer receives like-kind property. The taxpayer must recognize gain on any "boot" (i.e., property of an unlike kind). For example, if a taxpayer exchanges a truck used in a business for another truck to be used in the business and also receives cash, the taxpayer has the wherewithal to pay an income tax on the cash involved. Further, the taxpayer's economic status has changed to the extent of the cash (not like-kind property) received. Thus, any "realized" gain on the exchange is recognized to the extent of the cash received. In like manner, if a taxpayer transfers property to a corporation and receives money or property other than stock, § 351(b) provides that gain is recognized to the extent of the lesser of the gain realized or the boot received (the amount of money and the fair market value of other property received). The gain is characterized according to the type of asset transferred.[1] Loss is never recognized. The nonrecognition of gain or loss is accompanied by a carryover of basis.[2]

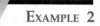

EXAMPLE 2

Abby and Bill form White Corporation. Abby transfers property with an adjusted basis of $30,000, fair market value of $60,000, for 50% of the stock. Bill transfers property with an adjusted basis of $70,000, fair market value of $60,000, for the remaining 50% of the stock. The transfer qualifies under § 351. Abby has an unrecognized gain of $30,000, and Bill has an unrecognized loss of $10,000. Both have a carryover basis in the stock in White Corporation. Abby has a basis of $30,000 in her stock, and Bill has a basis of $70,000 in his stock. If instead Abby received stock and cash of $10,000, she recognizes a gain of $10,000. ▼

Section 351 is mandatory. If a transaction falls within its provisions, neither gain nor loss is recognized on the transfer (except that realized gain is recognized to the extent of boot received), and there is a carryover of basis.

There are three requirements for nonrecognition of gain or loss: (1) *property* is transferred for (2) *stock*, and (3) the transferors must be in *control* of the transferee corporation.

TRANSFER OF PROPERTY

Questions have arisen concerning what constitutes **property** for purposes of § 351. The Code specifically excludes services rendered from the definition of property. With this exception, the definition of property is comprehensive. Unrealized receivables from a cash basis taxpayer and installment obligations are considered property, for example.[3] The transfer of an installment obligation in a transaction qualifying under § 351 is not a disposition of the installment obligation. Thus, the transferor does not recognize gain. Secret processes and formulas, as well as secret information in the general nature of a patentable inventory, also qualify as property under § 351.[4]

Services are not considered to be property under § 351 for a critical reason. A taxpayer must report as income the fair market value of property received as compensation for services rendered.[5] Thus, if a taxpayer receives stock in a corporation as consideration for rendering services to the corporation, the taxpayer has taxable income. The amount of income is the fair market value of the stock received. The taxpayer's basis in the stock then is the fair market value of the stock.

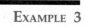

EXAMPLE 3

Ann and Bob form Brown Corporation and transfer the following property to it:

	Property Transferred		
	Basis to Transferor	Fair Market Value	Number of Shares Issued
From Ann:			
Personal services rendered to Brown	$ –0–	$20,000	200
From Bob:			
Installment obligation	5,000	40,000	
Inventory	10,000	30,000	800
Secret process	–0–	10,000	

---

[1] Rev.Rul. 68–55, 1968–1 C.B. 140.
[2] §§ 358(a) and 362(a). See the discussion preceding Example 18.
[3] *Hempt Brothers, Inc. v. U.S.*, 74–1 USTC ¶9188, 33 AFTR2d 74–570, 490 F.2d 1172 (CA–3, 1974), and Reg. § 1.453–9(c)(2).

[4] Rev.Rul. 64–56, 1964–1 C.B. 133.
[5] §§ 61 and 83.

The value of each share in Brown Corporation is $100.[6] Ann has income of $20,000 on the transfer because services do not qualify as "property." She has a basis of $20,000 in her 200 shares of stock in Brown. Bob has no gain on the transfer because all of the consideration he transferred to Brown qualifies as "property" under § 351 (and he has "control" of Brown). (See discussion below.) Bob has a basis of $15,000 in his stock in Brown. ▼

If property is transferred to a corporation in exchange for any property other than stock, the property constitutes boot. The boot is taxable to the transferor shareholder to the extent of any realized gain.

STOCK

The Regulations state that the term "stock" does not include stock rights and stock warrants.[7] Generally, however, the term "stock" needs no clarification. It includes both common stock and preferred stock.

All debt constitutes boot. Included in debt are **securities** (e.g., long-term debt such as bonds). Thus, a shareholder who receives debt in exchange for the transfer of appreciated property to a controlled corporation must recognize gain.

CONTROL OF THE TRANSFEREE CORPORATION

To qualify as a nontaxable transaction under § 351, the transferor must be in **control** of the transferee corporation immediately after the exchange. Control means that the person or persons transferring the property must have an 80 percent stock ownership in the transferee corporation. The transferor shareholders must own stock possessing at least 80 percent of the total combined *voting power* of all classes of stock entitled to vote and at least 80 percent of the total *number* of shares of all other classes of stock.[8]

Control Immediately after the Transfer. Control can apply to a single person or to several individuals if they are all parties to an integrated transaction. Section 351 requires control "immediately after the exchange." The Regulations provide that when more than one person is involved, the exchange does not necessarily require simultaneous exchanges by two or more persons. However, the rights of the parties (e.g., those transferring property to the corporation) must be previously set out and determined. Also, the agreement to transfer property should be executed ". . . with an expedition consistent with orderly procedure."[9]

If two or more persons transfer property to a corporation for stock, the transfers should occur close together in time and should be made in accordance with an agreement among the parties.

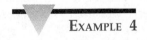

EXAMPLE 4

Jack exchanges property, basis of $60,000 and fair market value of $100,000, for 70% of the stock of Gray Corporation. The other 30% is owned by Jane, who acquired it several years ago. The fair market value of Jack's stock is $100,000. Jack recognizes a taxable gain of $40,000 on the transfer. ▼

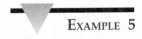

EXAMPLE 5

Lana, Leo, and Lori incorporate their respective businesses by forming Green Corporation. Lana exchanges her property for 300 shares in Green on January 5, 1996. Leo exchanges his property for 400 shares of Green Corporation stock on January 10, 1996, and Lori exchanges her property for 300 shares in Green on March 5, 1996. The three exchanges are part of a prearranged plan. The nonrecognition provisions of § 351 apply to all of the exchanges. ▼

---

[6]The value of closely held stock normally is presumed to be equal to the value of the property transferred.

[7]Reg. § 1.351–1(a)(1)(ii).

[8]§ 368(c).

[9]Reg. § 1.351–1.

GOING PUBLIC WITH TECH STOCK CAN TURN INCORPORATORS INTO BILLIONAIRES

As a reporter noted, while General Dynamics Corporation took 43 years to achieve a value of $2.7 billion in the stock market, Netscape Communications Corporation, a software company, reached the same value in about a minute. Netscape stock opened at two and a half times the offering price. The stock was worth about $2.7 billion on the stock market after its first public shares began "changing hands among technology crazed investors." One investor bought 3,000 shares at $71 per share and sold the shares within 10 minutes for $73.625 per share.

The stock had a price-earnings ratio of 343 based on 1996 projected earnings. Netscape had no P/E on 1994 earnings because it had no earnings. The company had not earned a profit before the stock was sold publicly.

Netscape makes "Web browser" software, a program called Netscape Navigator that enables computer users to view the World Wide Web, the graphical portion of the Internet. Netscape is also a pioneer in encryption, which provides security for those who want to use their credit cards to buy and sell on the Internet.

SOURCE: Information from Molly Baker, "Technology Investors Fall Head Over Heels For Their New Love," *Wall Street Journal*, August 10, 1995, pp. A1 and A4.

Control is not lost if stock received by shareholders in a § 351 exchange is sold or given to persons who are not parties to the exchange shortly after the transaction. A different result might materialize if a *plan* for the ultimate sale of the stock existed *before* the exchange.[10]

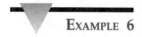

EXAMPLE 6

Lee and Pat form Black Corporation. They transfer appreciated property to the corporation with each receiving 50 shares of the stock. Shortly after the formation, Lee gives 25 shares to his son. Because Lee was not committed to make the gift, he is considered to own his original shares of the Black stock "immediately after the exchange." The requirements of § 351 are met, and neither Lee nor Pat is taxed on the exchange. ▼

Transfers for Property and Services. Section 351 treatment is lost if stock is transferred to persons who did not contribute property, causing those who did to lack control immediately after the exchange.

ETHICAL CONSIDERATIONS **A Gift of Shares**

Lee, in Example 6, intended to give half his shares to his son when he incorporated. His attorney, who was not well versed in the tax law, initially prepared stock certificates evidencing 50 shares to Pat, 25 shares to Lee, and 25 shares to Lee's

---

[10] *Wilgard Realty Co. v. Comm.*, 42–1 USTC ¶9452, 29 AFTR 325, 127 F.2d 514 (CA–2, 1942).

son. Prior to the transfer of property in exchange for the shares certificates, the attorney realized that the transfer of appreciated property to the corporation might be recognized gain to both Pat and Lee, because they would have only 75 percent control. Accordingly, the attorney tore up the original certificates and prepared new ones. Fifty of the shares were then issued to Pat and 50 to Lee. Six months later, Lee gave 25 shares to his son. Did Lee and his attorney act correctly?

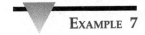 **EXAMPLE 7**

Kate transfers property with a fair market value of $60,000 and a basis of $5,000 for 600 shares of stock in newly formed Wren Corporation. Kevin receives 400 shares in Wren for services rendered to the corporation. Each share of stock is worth $100. Both Kate and Kevin have taxable gain on the transaction. Kevin is not part of the control group because he did not transfer "property" for stock. He has taxable income of $40,000 (400 shares × $100). Kate has a taxable gain of $55,000 [$60,000 (fair market value of the stock in Wren) − $5,000 (basis in the transferred property)]. She is taxed on the exchange because she received only 60% of the stock in Wren Corporation. ▼

A person who performs services for the corporation in exchange for stock and also transfers some property is treated as a member of the transferring group. That person is taxed on the value of the stock issued for services but not on the stock issued for property. In this case, all the stock received by the person transferring both property and services is counted in determining whether the transferors acquired control of the corporation.[11]

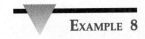 **EXAMPLE 8**

Assume the same facts as in Example 7, except that Kevin transfers property with a fair market value of $30,000 (basis of $3,000) in addition to services rendered to the corporation (valued at $10,000). Now Kevin becomes a part of the control group. Kate and Kevin together received 100% of the stock in Wren Corporation. Consequently, § 351 is applicable to the exchanges. Kate has no recognized gain. Kevin does not recognize gain on the transfer of the property but has taxable income to the extent of the value of the shares issued for services rendered. Thus, Kevin has income of $10,000. ▼

Transfers for Services and Nominal Property. To be a member of the group and aid in qualifying all transferors under the 80 percent test, the person contributing services must transfer property having more than a relatively small value compared to the services performed. Stock issued for property whose value is relatively small compared to the value of the stock already owned (or to be received for services rendered) will not be treated as issued in return for property. This will be the result when the primary purpose of the transfer is to qualify the transaction under § 351 for concurrent transferors.[12]

 EXAMPLE 9

Olga and Otis transfer property to Redbird Corporation, each in exchange for one-third of the stock. Olaf receives the other one-third of the stock for services rendered. The transaction will not qualify under § 351 because Olaf is not a member of the group transferring property and Olga and Otis together received only 66⅔% of the stock. The post-transfer control requirement is not met.

Assume instead that Olaf also transfers property. Then he is a member of the group, and the transaction qualifies under § 351. Olaf is taxed on the value of the stock issued for services, but the remainder of the transaction is tax-free. However, if the property

[11] Reg. § 1.351–1(a)(2), Example 3.　　　　[12] Reg. § 1.351–1(a)(1)(ii).

transferred by Olaf is of relatively small value in comparison to the stock he receives for his services, and the primary purpose for including the property is to cause the transaction to be tax-free for Olga and Otis, the exchange does not qualify under § 351. Gain or loss is recognized by all parties. ▼

The IRS generally requires that before a transferor who receives stock for both property and services can be included in the control group, the value of the property transferred must be at least 10 percent of the value of the services provided.[13] If the value of the property transferred is less than this amount, the IRS will not issue an advance ruling that the exchange meets the requirements of § 351.

▼
EXAMPLE 10

Sara and Rick form White Corporation. Sara transfers land (fair market value $100,000, basis of $20,000) for 50% of the stock in White. Rick transfers equipment (fair market value $50,000, adjusted basis of $10,000) and provides services worth $50,000 for 50% of the stock. Rick's stock in White Corporation is counted in determining control for purposes of § 351; thus, the transferors own 100% of the stock in White. All of Rick's stock, not just the shares received for the equipment, is counted in determining control because the property he transferred has more than a nominal value in comparison to the value of the services rendered. Sara does not recognize gain on the transfer of the land. She has a basis of $20,000 in her White stock. Rick, however, must recognize income of $50,000 on the transfer. Even though the transfer of the equipment qualifies under § 351, his transfer of services for stock does not. Rick has a $60,000 basis in his White stock, computed as follows: $10,000 (adjusted basis of equipment Rick transferred to White) + $50,000 (income recognized by Rick on the transfer). ▼

2 ▼ **LEARNING OBJECTIVE**
Appreciate the tax problems involved when making later property transfers to a controlled corporation.

Transfers to Existing Corporations.   Once a corporation is in operation, § 351 also applies to any later transfers of property for stock by either new or former shareholders.

▼
EXAMPLE 11

Sam and Seth formed Blue Corporation three years ago. Both Sam and Seth transferred appreciated property to Blue in exchange for 50 shares each in the corporation. The original transfers qualified under § 351, and neither Sam nor Seth was taxed on the exchange. In the current year, Sam transfers property (fair market value $90,000, adjusted basis of $5,000) for 50 additional Blue shares. Sam has a taxable gain of $85,000 on the transfer. The exchange does not qualify under § 351 because Sam does not have 80% control of Blue. (Sam has 100 shares of the 150 shares outstanding, or a 66⅔% ownership.) ▼

See the Tax Planning Considerations portion of this chapter for a further discussion of this problem.

ASSUMPTION OF LIABILITIES—§ 357

Without § 357, the transfer of mortgaged property to a controlled corporation could trigger gain to the extent of the mortgage whether the corporation assumed the mortgage or took property subject to it. This is the rule in nontaxable like-kind exchanges under § 1031. Liabilities assumed by the other party are considered the equivalent of cash and treated as boot. Section 357(a) provides, however, that

[13] Rev.Proc. 77–37, 1977–2 C.B. 568; § 3.07.

when the acquiring corporation **assumes a liability** or takes property subject to a liability in a § 351 transaction, the transfer does not result in boot to the transferor shareholder. Nevertheless, liabilities assumed by the transferee corporation are treated as boot in determining the basis of the stock received. The basis of the stock received is reduced by the amount of the liabilities assumed by the corporation.

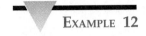

EXAMPLE 12

Vera transfers property with an adjusted basis of $60,000, fair market value of $100,000, to Gray Corporation for 100% of the stock in Gray. The property is subject to a liability of $25,000 that Gray assumes. The exchange is tax-free under §§ 351 and 357. However, the basis to Vera of the Gray stock is $35,000 [$60,000 (basis of property transferred) – $25,000 (amount of mortgage)]. ▼

The rule of § 357(a) has two exceptions. Section 357(b) provides that if the principal purpose of the assumption of the liabilities is to avoid tax *or* if there is no bona fide business purpose behind the exchange, the liabilities are treated as boot. Further, § 357(c) provides that if the sum of the liabilities exceeds the adjusted basis of the properties transferred, the excess is taxable gain.

Tax Avoidance or No Bona Fide Business Purpose Exception. Unless liabilities are incurred shortly before incorporation, § 357(b) generally poses few problems. A tax avoidance purpose for transferring liabilities to a controlled corporation seems unlikely in view of the basis adjustment noted above. Since the liabilities transferred reduce the basis of the stock received, any realized gain is deferred and not avoided. The gain materializes when and if the stock is disposed of in a taxable sale or exchange.

Satisfying the bona fide business purpose is not difficult if the liabilities were incurred in connection with the transferor's normal course of conducting a trade or business. But the bona fide business purpose requirement can cause difficulty if the liability is taken out shortly before the property is transferred and the proceeds are utilized for personal purposes.[14] This type of situation is analogous to a cash distribution by the corporation, which is taxed as boot.

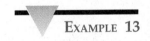

EXAMPLE 13

Dan transfers real estate (basis of $40,000 and fair market value of $90,000) to a controlled corporation in return for stock in the corporation. Shortly before the transfer, Dan mortgages the real estate and uses the $20,000 proceeds to meet personal obligations. Along with the real estate, the mortgage is transferred to the corporation. In this case, the assumption of the mortgage appears to lack a bona fide business purpose. The amount of the liability is boot, and Dan has a taxable gain of $20,000 on the transfer.[15] ▼

The effect of the application of § 357(b) is to taint *all* liabilities transferred even if some are supported by a bona fide business purpose.

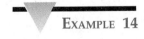

EXAMPLE 14

Tim, an accrual basis taxpayer, incorporates his sole proprietorship. Among the liabilities transferred to the new corporation are trade accounts payable of $100,000 and a MasterCard bill of $5,000. Tim had used the MasterCard to purchase a wedding anniversary gift for his wife. Under these circumstances, all of the $105,000 liabilities are boot. ▼

---

[14]See, for example, *Campbell, Jr. v. Wheeler*, 65–1 USTC ¶9294, 15 AFTR2d 578, 342 F.2d 837 (CA–5, 1965).

[15]§ 351(b).

ETHICAL
CONSIDERATIONS

Rectifying a Mistake?

Jean incorporates her sole proprietorship. Inadvertently, she transfers to the new corporation a credit charge for a family dinner she hosted. After the corporation pays the bill, she realizes her mistake and issues a note payable to the corporation in the amount of the charge. Has Jean avoided § 357(b)?

Liabilities in Excess of Basis Exception.   Section 357(c) states that if the sum of the **liabilities** assumed and the liabilities to which transferred property is subject **exceeds** the total of the adjusted **bases** of the properties transferred, the excess is taxable gain. Without this provision, if liabilities exceed basis in property exchanged, a taxpayer would have a negative basis in the stock received in the controlled corporation.[16] Section 357(c) precludes the negative basis possibility by treating the excess over basis as gain to the transferor.

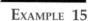

EXAMPLE 15

Andre transfers assets with an adjusted tax basis of $40,000 to a newly formed corporation in exchange for 100% of the stock. The corporation assumes liabilities on the transferred properties in the amount of $50,000. Without § 357(c), Andre's basis in the stock of the new corporation would be a negative $10,000 [$40,000 (basis of property transferred) + $0 (gain recognized) – $0 (boot received) – $50,000 (liabilities assumed)]. Section 357(c) causes him to recognize a gain of $10,000. As a result, the stock has a zero basis in Andre's hands, determined as follows:

Basis in the property transferred	$ 40,000
Add: Gain recognized	10,000
Less: Boot received	(–0–)
Less: Liabilities assumed	(50,000)
Basis in the stock received	$ –0–

Thus, no negative basis results. ▼

Accounts payable of a cash basis taxpayer that give rise to a deduction are not considered to be liabilities for purposes of § 357(c).

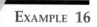

EXAMPLE 16

Tina, a cash basis taxpayer, incorporates her sole proprietorship. In return for all of the stock of the new corporation, she transfers the following items:

	Adjusted Basis	Fair Market Value
Cash	$10,000	$10,000
Unrealized accounts receivable (amounts due to Tina but not yet paid to her)	–0–	40,000
Trade accounts payable	–0–	30,000
Note payable	5,000	5,000

---

[16] *Easson v. Comm.*, 33 T.C. 963 (1960), *rev'd.* in 61–2 USTC ¶9654, 8 AFTR2d 5448, 294 F.2d 653 (CA–9, 1961).

Unrealized accounts receivable and trade accounts payable have a zero basis. Under the cash method of accounting, no income is recognized until the receivables are collected, and no deduction materializes until the payables are satisfied. The note payable has a basis because it was issued for consideration received.

The accounts receivable and the trade accounts payable are disregarded for gain recognition purposes under § 357(c). Thus, Tina is treated as having only transferred cash ($10,000) and a note payable ($5,000) and does not have a problem of liabilities in excess of basis. ▼

The definition of liabilities under § 357(c) excludes obligations that would have been deductible to the transferor had those obligations been paid before the transfer. Consequently, Tina in Example 16 has no gain.

**ETHICAL
CONSIDERATIONS**

Structuring to Avoid Liabilities in Excess of Basis?

Ann has operated a sole proprietorship for three years. On January 1, she formed Green Corporation. She transfers all the assets of the proprietorship, subject to all of the liabilities, to Green Corporation in exchange for all its shares. At the time of the transfer, the sole proprietorship's balance sheet showed the basis of its assets as $15,000 and its liabilities (a note payable to the bank) as $25,000. The fair market value of the assets is $45,000. Thus, the fair market value of the Green stock is $20,000 [$45,000 (value of the assets) – $25,000 (note payable)]. To avoid $10,000 gain under § 357(c), measured by the excess of the liabilities ($25,000) over the basis of the assets ($15,000), Ann contributes to Green Corporation, in the same transaction, a personal note in the amount of $10,000. The note bears interest at two points above the prime rate and is payable in five equal annual installments (principal plus interest). Has Ann successfully avoided the application of § 357(c)?

If §§ 357(b) and (c) both apply to the same transfer, § 357(b) predominates.[17] This could be significant because § 357(b) does not create gain on the transfer, as does § 357(c), but merely converts the liability to boot. Thus, the realized gain limitation continues to apply to § 357(b) transactions.

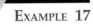

EXAMPLE 17

Chris forms Robin Corporation by transferring land with a basis of $100,000, fair market value of $1 million. The land is subject to a mortgage of $300,000. One month prior to incorporating Robin, Chris borrows $200,000 for personal purposes and gives the lender a second mortgage on the land. Robin Corporation issues stock worth $500,000 to Chris and assumes the mortgages on the land. Section 357(c) applies to the transfer because the mortgages on the property ($500,000) exceed the basis of the property ($100,000). Thus, Chris would have a gain of $400,000 under § 357(c). However, Section 357(b) also applies to the transfer because Chris borrowed $200,000 just prior to the transfer and used the amount for personal purposes. Under § 357(b), Chris has boot of $500,000 in the amount of the liabilities (*all* of which are treated as boot). She has realized gain of $900,000 [$1 million (amount realized in exchange for the land) – $100,000 (basis in the land)]. Gain is recognized to the extent of the boot of $500,000. Note that § 357(b) predominates over § 357(c). ▼

---

[17] § 357(c)(2)(A).

BASIS DETERMINATION

Recall that § 351(a) postpones gain or loss until the taxpayer's investment changes substantially. Postponement of the realized gain or loss is accomplished through a carryover of basis.

Basis of Stock to Shareholder.   For a taxpayer transferring property to a corporation in a § 351 transaction, the basis of stock received in the transfer is the same as the basis the taxpayer had in the property transferred, increased by any gain recognized on the exchange and decreased by boot received. For basis purposes, boot received includes any liabilities transferred by the shareholder to the corporation.[18]

Basis of Property to Corporation.   The basis of properties received by the corporation is determined under § 362(a). The basis to the corporation is the basis in the hands of the transferor increased by the amount of any gain recognized to the transferor shareholder.[19]

The basis rules are summarized in Figures 17–1 and 17–2 and illustrated in Examples 18 and 19.

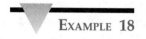

EXAMPLE 18

Maria and Ned form Brown Corporation. Maria transfers land (basis of $30,000 and fair market value of $70,000); Ned invests cash ($60,000). They each receive 50 shares in Brown Corporation, worth $1,200 per share, but Maria also receives $10,000 cash from Brown. The transfers of property, the realized and recognized gain on the transfers, and the basis of the stock in Brown Corporation to Maria and Ned are as follows:

▼ **FIGURE 17–1**
Shareholder's Basis in
Stock Received

Adjusted basis of property transferred	$xx,xxx
Plus: Gain recognized	x,xxx
Less: Boot received (including any liabilities transferred)	(x,xxx)
Equals: Basis of stock received	$xx,xxx

▼ **FIGURE 17–2**
Corporation's Basis in Properties
Received

Adjusted basis of property transferred	$xx,xxx
Plus: Gain recognized by transferor shareholder	xxx
Equals: Basis of property to corporation	$xx,xxx

---

[18] § 358(a).   [19] § 362(a).

	A	B	C	D	E	F
	Basis of Property Transferred	FMV of Stock Received	Boot Received	Realized Gain (B + C – A)	Recognized Gain (Lesser of C or D)	Basis of Stock in Brown (A – C + E)
From Maria:						
Land	$30,000	$60,000	$10,000	$40,000	$10,000	$30,000
From Ned:						
Cash	60,000	60,000	–0–	–0–	–0–	60,000

Brown Corporation has a basis of $40,000 in the land. The basis to Brown is Maria's basis of $30,000 plus her recognized gain of $10,000. ▼

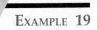

EXAMPLE 19

Assume the same facts as in Example 18, except that Maria's basis in the land is $68,000 (instead of $30,000). Because recognized gain cannot exceed realized gain, the transfer generates only $2,000 of gain to Maria. The realized and recognized gain and the basis of the stock in Brown Corporation to Maria are as follows:

	A	B	C	D	E	F
	Basis of Property Transferred	FMV of Stock Received	Boot Received	Realized Gain (B + C – A)	Recognized Gain (Lesser of C or D)	Basis of Stock in Brown (A – C + E)
Land	$68,000	$60,000	$10,000	$2,000	$2,000	$60,000

▼

Stock Issued for Services Rendered. A corporation's disposition of stock for property is not a taxable exchange.[20] A transfer of shares for services is also not a taxable transaction to a corporation.[21] Can a corporation deduct the fair market value of the stock it issues in consideration of services as a business expense? Yes, unless the services are such that the payment is characterized as a capital expenditure.[22]

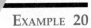

EXAMPLE 20

Carol and Carl form White Corporation. Carol transfers cash of $500,000 for 100 shares of White Corporation stock. Carl transfers property with a fair market value of $480,000 (basis of $90,000), and agrees to serve as manager of the corporation for one year; in return, Carl receives 100 shares of stock in White. The value of Carl's services to White Corporation is $20,000. The transfers qualify under § 351. Carl is not taxed on the transfer of the appreciated property. However, Carl has income of $20,000, the value of the services he will render to White Corporation. White has a basis of $90,000 in the property it acquired from Carl. It has a business deduction under § 162 of $20,000 for the value of services Carl will render. ▼

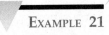

EXAMPLE 21

Assume, in Example 20, that Carl receives the 100 shares of White stock in consideration for the appreciated property and for providing legal services in organizing the corporation. The value of Carl's legal services is $20,000. Carl has no gain on the transfer of the property

---

[20] § 1032.
[21] Reg. § 1.1032–1(a).

[22] Rev.Rul. 62–217, 1962–2 C.B. 59, modified by Rev.Rul. 74–503, 1974–2 C.B. 117.

but has income of $20,000 for the value of the services rendered. White Corporation has a basis of $90,000 in the property it acquired from Carl and must capitalize the $20,000 as an organizational expense. ▼

Holding Period for Shareholder and Transferee Corporation.   The shareholder's holding period for stock received for a capital asset or for § 1231 property includes the holding period of the property transferred to the corporation. The holding period of the property is "tacked on" to the holding period of the stock. The holding period for stock received for any other property (e.g., inventory or property held primarily for sale) begins on the day after the exchange.[23] The transferee corporation's holding period for property acquired in a § 351 transfer is the holding period of the transferor shareholder regardless of the character of the property to the transferor.

RECAPTURE CONSIDERATIONS

In a pure § 351(a) nontaxable transfer (no boot involved) to a controlled corporation, the recapture of accelerated cost recovery rules do not apply.[24] Moreover, any recapture potential of the property carries over to the corporation as it steps into the shoes of the transferor-shareholder for purposes of basis determination.

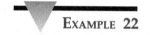

EXAMPLE 22

Paul transfers equipment (basis of $30,000 and fair market value of $100,000) to a controlled corporation in return for additional stock. If Paul had sold the equipment, it would have yielded a gain of $70,000, all of which would be recaptured as ordinary income under § 1245. If the transfer comes within § 351(a), Paul has no recognized gain and no accelerated cost recovery to recapture. If the corporation later disposes of the equipment in a taxable transaction, it must take into account the § 1245 recapture potential originating with Paul. ▼

CAPITAL STRUCTURE OF A CORPORATION

CAPITAL CONTRIBUTIONS

3   **LEARNING OBJECTIVE**
Understand the tax aspects of the capital structure of a corporation.

The receipt of money or property in exchange for capital stock (including treasury stock) produces neither gain nor loss to the recipient corporation. Nor does a corporation's gross income include shareholders' contributions of money or property to the capital of the corporation. Additional funds received from shareholders through voluntary pro rata payments are not income to the corporation. This is the case even though there is no increase in the outstanding shares of stock of the corporation. The payments represent an additional price paid for the shares held by the shareholders and are treated as additions to the operating capital of the corporation.[25]

Contributions by nonshareholders, such as land contributed to a corporation by a civic group or a governmental group to induce the corporation to locate in a particular community, are also excluded from the gross income of a corporation.[26] Property that is transferred to a corporation by a nonshareholder for services rendered or for merchandise is taxable income to the corporation.[27]

---

[23] §§ 1223(1) and (2).
[24] §§ 1245(b)(3) and 1250(d)(3).
[25] § 118 and Reg. § 1.118–1.
[26] See *Edwards v. Cuba Railroad Co.*, 1 USTC ¶139, 5 AFTR 5398, 45 S.Ct. 614 (USSC, 1925).

[27] Reg. § 1.118–1. See also *Teleservice Co. of Wyoming Valley v. Comm.*, 27 T.C. 722 (1957), *aff'd.* in 58–1 USTC ¶9383, 1 AFTR2d 1249, 254 F.2d 105 (CA–3, 1958), *cert. den.* 78 S.Ct. 1360 (USSC, 1958).

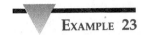

EXAMPLE 23

A television company charges its customers an initial fee to hook up to a new television system installed in the area. These payments are used to finance the total cost of constructing the television facilities. The customers then make monthly payments for the television service. The initial payments are used for capital expenditures, but they represent payments for services to be rendered by the television company. As such, they are taxable income and not contributions to capital by nonshareholders. ▼

The basis of property received by a corporation from a shareholder as a **capital contribution** is the basis of the property in the hands of the shareholder increased by any gain recognized to the shareholder. The basis of property transferred to a corporation by a nonshareholder as a contribution to capital is zero.

If a corporation receives money as a contribution to capital from a nonshareholder, a special rule applies. The basis of any property acquired with the money during a 12-month period beginning on the day the contribution was received is reduced by the amount of the contribution. The excess of money received over the cost of new property is used to reduce the basis of other property held by the corporation and is applied in the following order:

- Depreciable property.
- Property subject to amortization.
- Property subject to depletion.
- All other remaining properties.

The basis of property within each category is reduced in proportion to the relative bases of the properties.[28]

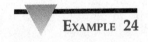

EXAMPLE 24

A city donates land to Brown Corporation as an inducement for Brown to locate in the city. The receipt of the land does not produce taxable income. However, the land's basis to the corporation is zero. Assume the city also pays Brown $10,000 in cash. The money is not taxable income to the corporation. However, if Brown purchases property with the $10,000 within the next 12 months, the basis of the property is reduced by $10,000. ▼

DEBT IN THE CAPITAL STRUCTURE

4 **LEARNING OBJECTIVE**
Recognize the tax differences between debt and equity investments.

Advantages of Debt. Shareholders must be aware of the differences between debt and equity in the capital structure. The advantages of issuing long-term debt are numerous. Interest on debt is deductible by the corporation, while dividend payments are not. Further, the shareholders are not taxed on loan repayments unless the repayments exceed basis. As long as a corporation has earnings and profits (see Chapter 18), an investment in stock cannot be withdrawn tax-free. Withdrawals will be deemed to be taxable dividends to the extent of earnings and profits of the distributing corporation.

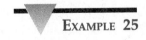

EXAMPLE 25

Wade transfers cash of $100,000 to a newly formed corporation for 100% of the stock. In the first year of operations, the corporation has net income of $40,000. This income is credited to the earnings and profits account of the corporation. If the corporation distributes $9,500 to Wade, the distribution is a taxable dividend with no corresponding deduction to the corporation. Assume, instead, Wade transfers cash of $50,000 for stock. In addition, he loans the corporation $50,000, transferring cash of $50,000 to the corporation for a note in the amount of $50,000. The note is payable in equal annual installments of $5,000 and bears interest at the

---

[28] § 362 and Reg. § 1.362–2(b).

rate of 9%. At the end of the year, the corporation pays Wade $4,500 interest, which is tax deductible to the corporation and included in Wade's gross income. The $5,000 principal repayment on the loan is not taxed to Wade. ▼

Reclassification of Debt as Equity (Thin Capitalization Problem).

In certain instances, known as **thin capitalization** situations, the IRS contends that debt is really an equity interest and denies the shareholders the tax advantages of debt financing. If the debt instrument has too many features of stock, it may be treated as a form of stock. In that case, the principal and interest payments are considered dividends. Under § 385, the IRS has the authority to characterize corporate debt wholly as equity or as part debt and part equity.

Section 385 lists several factors that *may* be used to determine whether a debtor-creditor relationship or a shareholder-corporation relationship exists. The thrust of § 385 is to authorize the Treasury to prescribe Regulations that provide more definite guidelines for determining when debt should be reclassified as equity. To date, the Treasury has not drafted acceptable Regulations. Consequently, taxpayers must rely on judicial decisions to determine whether a true debtor-creditor relationship exists.

Together, Congress, through § 385, and the courts have identified the following factors to be considered in resolving the thin capitalization problem:

- Whether the debt instrument is in proper form. An open account advance is more easily characterized as a contribution to capital than a loan evidenced by a properly written note executed by the shareholder.[29]
- Whether the debt instrument bears a reasonable rate of interest and has a definite maturity date. When a shareholder advance does not provide for interest, the return expected is that inherent in an equity interest (e.g., a share of the profits or an increase in the value of the shares).[30] Likewise, a lender unrelated to the corporation will usually be unwilling to commit funds to the corporation for an indefinite period of time (i.e., no definite due date).
- Whether the debt is paid on a timely basis. A lender's failure to insist upon timely repayment (or satisfactory renegotiation) indicates that the return sought does not depend upon interest income and the repayment of principal.
- Whether payment is contingent upon earnings. A lender ordinarily will not advance funds that are likely to be repaid only if the venture is successful.
- Whether the debt is subordinated to other liabilities. Subordination tends to eliminate a significant characteristic of the creditor-debtor relationship. Creditors should have the right to share with other general creditors in the event of the corporation's dissolution or liquidation. Subordination also destroys another basic attribute of creditor status—the power to demand payment at a fixed maturity date.[31]
- Whether holdings of debt and stock are proportionate. When debt and equity obligations are held in the same proportion, shareholders are, apart from tax considerations, indifferent as to whether corporate distributions are in the form of interest or dividends.

---

[29] *Estate of Mixon v. U.S.*, 72–2 USTC ¶9537, 30 AFTR2d 72–5094, 464 F.2d 394 (CA–5, 1972).

[30] *Slappey Drive Industrial Park v. U.S.*, 77–2 USTC ¶9696, 40 AFTR2d 77–5941, 561 F.2d 572 (CA–5, 1977).

[31] *Fin Hay Realty Co. v. U.S.*, 68–2 USTC ¶9438, 22 AFTR2d 5004, 398 F.2d 694 (CA–3, 1968).

- Whether funds loaned to the corporation are used to finance initial operations or capital asset acquisitions. Funds used to finance initial operations or to acquire capital assets the corporation needs to operate are generally obtained through equity investments.
- Whether the corporation has a high ratio of shareholder debt to shareholder equity. Thin capitalization occurs when shareholder debt is high relative to shareholder equity. This indicates the corporation lacks reserves to pay interest and principal on debt when corporate income is insufficient to meet current needs.[32] In determining a corporation's debt-equity ratio, courts look at the relation of the debt both to the book value of the corporation's assets and to their actual fair market value.[33]

For the most part, the principles used to classify debt as equity developed in connection with closely held corporations. Here, the holders of the debt are also shareholders. The rules have often proved inadequate for dealing with such problems in large, publicly traded corporations.

INVESTOR LOSSES

The choice between debt and equity financing leads to a consideration of the tax treatment of worthless stock and securities versus the treatment of bad debts.

Stock and Security Losses.   If stocks and bonds are capital assets in the hands of the holder, losses from their worthlessness are governed by § 165(g)(1). Under this provision, a capital loss materializes as of the last day of the taxable year in which the stocks or bonds become worthless. No deduction is allowed for a mere decline in value. The burden of proving complete worthlessness is on the taxpayer claiming the loss. One way to recognize partial worthlessness is to dispose of the stocks or bonds in a taxable sale or exchange.[34] But even then, the **investor loss** is disallowed if the sale or exchange is to a related party.

When the stocks or bonds are not capital assets, worthlessness yields an ordinary loss.[35] For example, if the stocks or bonds are held by a broker for resale to customers in the normal course of business, they are not capital assets. Usually, however, stocks and bonds are held as investments and are capital assets.

Under certain circumstances involving stocks and bonds of affiliated corporations, an ordinary loss is allowed upon worthlessness.[36] The possibility of an ordinary loss on the stock of small business corporations (§ 1244) is discussed later in the chapter.

Business versus Nonbusiness Bad Debts.   In addition to the possible worthlessness of stocks and bonds, the financial end of a corporation can lead to bad debt deductions. These deductions can be either business bad debts or **nonbusiness bad debts.** The distinction between the two types of deductions is important for tax purposes in the following respects:

---

[32] A court held that a debt-equity ratio of approximately 4:1 was not excessive. See *Tomlinson v. 1661 Corp.*, 67–1 USTC ¶9438, 19 AFTR2d 1413, 377 F.2d 291 (CA–5, 1967).

[33] In *Bauer v. Comm.*, 84–2 USTC ¶9996, 55 AFTR2d 84–433, 748 F.2d 1365 (CA–9, 1984), a debt-equity ratio of 92:1 resulted when book value was used. But the ratio ranged from 2:1 to 8:1 when equity included both paid-in capital and accumulated earnings.

[34] Reg. § 1.165–4(a).
[35] § 165(a) and Reg. § 1.165–5(b).
[36] § 165(g)(3).

TAX IN THE NEWS

INVESTMENTS THAT CANNOT LOSE

S ome brokerage firms, banks, and mutual-fund companies have recently decided to pay irate investors who have suffered substantial losses rather than to risk investor lawsuits. Although statistics are scarce on such "guilt money," securities lawyers suggest that brokerage firms have been "ponying up more cash more quickly than ever when faced with protests over questionable investments." In most cases, the investors are reimbursed for derivatives losses in money-market and bond funds. Derivatives—financial arrangements whose value is linked to, or derived from, the performance of some underlying asset, such as bonds—plunged in value, pummeling the funds that held them, when interest rates rose sharply in the latter part of 1994. Many funds had been aggressively using derivatives to reap big returns in early 1994 when interest rates were declining and were caught unawares when rates began to rise.

- Business bad debts are deducted as ordinary losses while nonbusiness bad debts are treated as short-term capital losses.[37] A business bad debt can generate a net operating loss while a nonbusiness bad debt cannot.[38]
- A deduction is allowed for the partial worthlessness of a business debt. Nonbusiness debts can be written off only when they become entirely worthless.[39]
- Nonbusiness bad debt treatment is limited to noncorporate taxpayers. All of the bad debts of a corporation qualify as business bad debts.[40]

When is a debt business or nonbusiness? Unfortunately, since the Code sheds little light on the matter, the distinction has been left to the courts.[41] In a leading decision, the Supreme Court somewhat clarified the picture when it held that if individual shareholders loan money to a corporation in their capacity as investors, any resulting bad debt is classified as nonbusiness.[42] Nevertheless, the Court did not preclude the possibility of a shareholder-creditor's incurring a business bad debt.

If a loan is made in some capacity that qualifies as a trade or business, nonbusiness bad debt treatment is avoided. For example, has the loan been made to protect the shareholder's employment with the corporation? Employee status is a trade or business, and a loss on a loan made for this purpose qualifies for business bad debt treatment.[43] Shareholders also receive business bad debt treatment if they are in the trade or business of loaning money or of buying, promoting, and selling corporations.

---

[37] Compare § 166(a) with § 166(d)(1)(B).

[38] Note the adjustments necessitated by § 172(d)(2).

[39] Compare § 166(a)(2) with § 166(d)(1)(A).

[40] § 166(d)(1).

[41] For definitional purposes, § 166(d)(2) is almost as worthless as the debt it purports to describe.

[42] *Whipple v. Comm.*, 63–1 USTC ¶9466, 11 AFTR2d 1454, 83 S.Ct. 1168 (USSC, 1963).

[43] *Trent v. Comm.*, 61–2 USTC ¶9506, 7 AFTR2d 1599, 291 F.2d 669 (CA–2, 1961).

Section 1244 Stock. Section 1244 permits *ordinary loss* treatment for losses on the sale or worthlessness of stock of so-called small business corporations. By placing shareholders on a more nearly equal basis with proprietors and partners in terms of the tax treatment of losses, the provision encourages investment of capital in small corporations. Gain on the sale of § 1244 stock remains capital. Consequently, the shareholder has nothing to lose and everything to gain by complying with § 1244.

Only a *small business corporation* can issue qualifying **§ 1244 stock.** The total amount of stock that can be offered under the plan to issue § 1244 stock cannot exceed $1 million. For these purposes, property received in exchange for stock is valued at its adjusted basis, reduced by any liabilities assumed by the corporation or to which the property is subject. The fair market value of the property is not considered. The $1 million limitation is determined by property and money received for the stock as a contribution to capital and as paid-in capital on the date the stock is issued. Consequently, even though a corporation fails to meet these requirements when the stock later is sold, the stock can still qualify as § 1244 stock if the requirements were met on the date the stock was issued.

The amount of ordinary loss deductible in any one year on § 1244 stock is limited to $50,000 (or $100,000 for husband and wife filing a joint return). If the amount of the loss sustained in the taxable year exceeds these amounts, the remainder is considered a capital loss.

▼
EXAMPLE 26

William acquires § 1244 stock at a cost of $100,000. He sells the stock for $10,000 in one tax year. He has an ordinary loss of $50,000 and a capital loss of $40,000. On a joint return, the entire $90,000 loss is ordinary. ▼

Only the original holder of § 1244 stock, whether an individual or a partnership, qualifies for ordinary loss treatment. If the stock is sold or donated, it loses its § 1244 status.

Recall the advantages of issuing some debt to shareholders in exchange for cash contributions to a corporation. A disadvantage of issuing debt is that it does not qualify under § 1244. Should the debt become worthless, the taxpayer generally has a short-term capital loss rather than the ordinary loss for § 1244 stock.

The basis of § 1244 stock issued by a corporation in exchange for property that has an adjusted basis above its fair market value immediately before the exchange is reduced to the fair market value of the property on the date of the exchange. The stock's basis is reduced for the purpose of determining ordinary loss upon a subsequent sale.

▼
EXAMPLE 27

Bonnie transfers property with a basis of $10,000 and a fair market value of $5,000 to a corporation in exchange for shares of § 1244 stock. Assuming the transfer qualifies under § 351, the basis of the stock is $10,000, the same as Bonnie's basis in the property. For purposes of § 1244, the stock's basis is only $5,000. If the stock is later sold for $3,000, the total loss sustained is $7,000 ($3,000 − $10,000); however, only $2,000 is ordinary loss ($3,000 − $5,000). The remaining portion, $5,000, is capital loss. ▼

GAIN FROM QUALIFIED SMALL BUSINESS STOCK

Shareholders are given some tax relief for *gains* recognized on the sale or exchange of stock acquired in a **qualified small business corporation.**[44] The holder of

---

[44] § 1202. The stock must have been issued after August 10, 1993, which is the effective date of § 1202.

qualified small business stock may exclude 50 percent of any gain from the sale or exchange of such stock. To qualify for the 50 percent exclusion, the taxpayer must have held the stock for more than five years and must have acquired the stock as part of an original issue. Only noncorporate shareholders qualify for the exclusion.

A qualified small business corporation is a C corporation whose aggregate gross assets did not exceed $50 million on the date the stock was issued.[45] The corporation must be actively involved in a trade or business. This means that at least 80 percent of the corporation's assets must be used in the active conduct of one or more qualified trades or businesses.

A shareholder can apply the 50 percent exclusion to the greater of (1) $10 million or (2) 10 times the shareholder's aggregate adjusted basis in the qualified stock disposed of during a taxable year.[46]

TAX PLANNING
CONSIDERATIONS

WORKING WITH § 351

Effective tax planning with transfers of property to corporations requires a clear understanding of § 351 and its related Code provisions. The most important question in planning is simply: Does compliance with the requirements of § 351 yield the desired tax result?

Utilizing § 351.   In using § 351(a), ensure that all parties transferring property (which includes cash) receive control of the corporation. Simultaneous transfers are not necessary, but a long period of time between transfers is vulnerable if the transfers are not properly documented as part of a single plan. To do this, the parties should document and preserve evidence of their intentions. Also, it is helpful to have some reasonable explanation for any delay in the transfers.

To meet the requirements of § 351, mere momentary control on the part of the transferor may not suffice if loss of control is compelled by a prearranged agreement.[47]

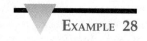

EXAMPLE 28

For many years, Zelda operated a business as a sole proprietor employing Zina as manager. To dissuade Zina from quitting and going out on her own, Zelda promised her a 30% interest in the business. To fulfill this promise, Zelda transfers the business to newly formed Green Corporation in return for all its stock. Immediately thereafter, Zelda transfers 30% of the stock to Zina. Section 351 probably does not apply to Zelda's transfer to Green Corporation. It appears that Zelda was under an obligation to relinquish control. If this is not the case and the loss of control was voluntary on Zelda's part, momentary control would suffice.[48] ▼

Be sure that later transfers of property to an existing corporation satisfy the control requirement if recognition of gain is to be avoided. In this connection, a transferor's interest cannot be counted if the value of stock received is relatively small compared with the value of stock already owned. Further, the primary purpose of the transfer may not be to qualify other transferors for § 351 treatment.[49]

---

[45] § 1202(d). Its aggregate assets may not exceed this amount at any time between August 10, 1993, and the date the stock was issued.

[46] § 1202(b). The amount is $5 million for married filing separately.

[47] Rev.Rul.54–96, 1954–1 C.B. 111.

[48] Compare *Fahs v. Florida Machine and Foundry Co.*, 48–2 USTC ¶9329, 36 AFTR 1151, 168 F.2d 957 (CA–5, 1948), with *John C.*

O'Connor, 16 TCM 213, T.C.Memo. 1957–50, *aff'd.* in 58–2 USTC ¶9913, 2 AFTR2d 6011, 260 F.2d 358 (CA–6, 1958).

[49] Reg. § 1.351–1(a)(1)(ii).

TAX IN THE NEWS

FINDING BARGAINS IN THE STOCK MARKET

Warren Buffett has amassed a fortune of nearly $12 billion from an initial investment of $10,000 in 1956. Buffett has learned to figure a corporation's "intrinsic value"—what the company is worth independent of its market price—and to comb financial statements for firms selling at a huge discount to this value. Buffett likens the value of stock to bonds. A bond's value is the cash flow from future interest payments, discounted back to the present. A stock's worth can be determined in the same manner: it is the discounted value of expected cash flow per share. However, the investor must calculate a stock's "coupon." Buffett tries to find stock whose value is greater than its price. His rules are summarized as follows: pay no attention to the macroeconomic trends or forecasts nor to people's predictions about the future course of stock prices. Focus on long-term business value—on the size of the "coupons" down the road. Stick to stocks within your "circle of competence." Look for managers who treat shareholders' capital with ownerlike care. Study prospects—and their competitors—in great detail. Look at raw data, not analysts' summaries. Trust your own eyes. If you know what a stock is worth—what a corporation is worth—then a falling price quote is no cause for alarm. If you have a conviction about a stock, show courage and buy several shares.

ETHICAL CONSIDERATIONS

The Control Requirement

Vera owns 50 of the 100 outstanding shares of Brown Corporation. Her daughter, Abby, owns the other 50 shares. Vera wants to transfer appreciated land, fair market value of $1 million and $200,000 tax basis, to Brown Corporation in exchange for an additional 25 shares. With 125 shares outstanding (100 + 25 additional shares), Vera would have a 60 percent interest in the corporation. Vera's accountant informs her that the stock attribution rules (see Chapter 18) do not apply to § 351 transfers; thus, Vera is not deemed to own Abby's stock. Because Vera will own only 60 percent of the stock in Brown Corporation after the transfer, her accountant informs her she will have a taxable gain of $800,000. Vera's accountant advises her to have Abby transfer property worth $80,000 for 2 shares so that Abby will then be a party to the transfer. Because the two parties will own 100 percent of the stock in Brown Corporation, the accountant says both transfers would qualify under § 351 and neither Vera nor Abby would have a taxable gain on the transfer. Abby agrees to transfer some appreciated property she has that is worth $80,000 for an additional 2 shares. Have the parties acted properly?

Avoiding § 351. Section 351(a) provides for the nonrecognition of gain on transfers to controlled corporations. As such, it is often regarded as a relief provision favoring taxpayers. In some situations, however, avoiding § 351(a) may produce a more advantageous tax result. The transferors might prefer to recognize

17–22   **CHAPTER 17**   Corporations: Organization and Capital Structure

gain on the transfer of property if they cannot be particularly harmed by the gain. For example, they may be in low tax brackets, or the gain may be a capital gain from which substantial capital losses can be offset. The corporation will then have a stepped-up basis in the transferred property.

Another reason a particular transferor might wish to avoid § 351 concerns possible loss recognition. Recall that § 351 refers to the nonrecognition of both gains and losses. A transferor who wishes to recognize loss has several alternatives:

- Sell the property to the corporation for its stock. The IRS could attempt to collapse the "sale," however, by taking the approach that the transfer really falls under § 351(a).[50] If the sale is disregarded, the transferor ends up with a realized, but unrecognized, loss.
- Sell the property to the corporation for other property or boot. Because the transferor receives no stock, § 351 is inapplicable.
- Transfer the property to the corporation in return for securities. Recall that § 351 does not apply to a transferor who receives securities. In both this and the previous alternatives, watch for the possible disallowance of the loss under the related-party rules.

Suppose the loss property is to be transferred to the corporation and no loss is recognized by the transferor due to § 351(a). This could present an interesting problem in terms of assessing the economic realities involved.

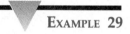

EXAMPLE 29

Iris and Ivan form Wren Corporation with the following investment: property by Iris (basis of $40,000 and fair market value of $50,000) and property by Ivan (basis of $60,000 and fair market value of $50,000). Each receives 50% of the Wren stock. Has Ivan acted wisely in settling for only 50% of the stock? At first, it would appear so, since he and Iris each invested property of the same value ($50,000). But what about tax considerations? Due to basis carryover, the corporation now has a basis of $40,000 in Iris's property and $60,000 in Ivan's property. In essence, Iris has shifted a possible $10,000 gain to the corporation while Ivan has transferred a $10,000 potential loss. With this in mind, an equitable allocation of the Wren stock would call for Ivan to receive a greater percentage interest than Iris. ▼

OTHER CONSIDERATIONS IN INCORPORATING A BUSINESS

When a business is incorporated, the organizers must determine which assets and liabilities should be transferred to the corporation. A transfer of assets that produces passive income (rents, royalties, dividends, and interest) can cause the corporation to be a personal holding company in a tax year when operating income is low. Thus, the corporation could be subject to the personal holding company penalty tax (see the discussion in Chapter 20).

A transfer of the accounts payable of a cash basis taxpayer may prevent the taxpayer from taking a tax deduction when the accounts are paid. These payables should generally be retained.

Leasing some property to the corporation may be a more attractive alternative than transferring ownership. Leasing provides the taxpayer with the opportunity of withdrawing money from the corporation without the payment being characterized as a dividend. If the property is donated to a family member in a lower tax bracket, the lease income can be shifted as well. If the depreciation and other

---

[50] *U.S. v. Hertwig*, 68–2 USTC ¶9495, 22 AFTR2d 5249, 398 F.2d 452 (CA–5, 1968).

deductions available in connection with the property are larger than the lease income, the taxpayer would retain the property until the income exceeds the deductions.

Shareholder debt in a corporation can be given to family members in a lower tax bracket. This technique also causes income to be shifted without a loss of control of the corporation.

DEBT IN THE CAPITAL STRUCTURE

The advantages of debt as opposed to equity have previously been emphasized. The main hurdle to overstressing debt is the thin capitalization problem. In avoiding the problem, consider the following:

- Preserve the formalities of the debt. This includes providing for written instruments, realistic interest rates, and specified due dates.
- If possible, have the corporation repay the debt when it becomes due. If this is not possible, have the parties renegotiate the arrangement. Try to proceed as a third-party (i.e., nonshareholder) creditor would. It is not unusual, for example, for bondholders of publicly held corporations to extend due dates when default occurs. The alternative is to foreclose and perhaps seriously impair the amount the creditors will recover.
- Avoid provisions in the debt instrument that make the debt convertible to equity in the event of default. These provisions are standard practice when nonshareholder creditors are involved. They make no sense if the share-holders are also the creditors.

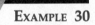
EXAMPLE 30

Gail, Gary, and Grace are equal shareholders in White Corporation. Each transfers cash of $100,000 to White in return for its bonds. The bond agreement provides that the holders will receive additional voting rights in the event White defaults on its bonds. The voting rights provision is worthless and merely raises the issue of thin capitalization. Gail, Gary, and Grace already control White Corporation, so what purpose is served by increasing their voting rights? The parties probably used a "boiler plate" bond agreement that was designed for third-party lenders (e.g., banks and financial institutions). ▼

- Pro rata holding of debt is difficult to avoid. For example, if each of the shareholders owns one-third of the stock, then each will want one-third of the debt. Nevertheless, some variation is possible.

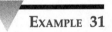
EXAMPLE 31

Assume the same facts as Example 30 except that only Gail and Gary acquire the bonds. Grace leases property to White Corporation at an annual rent that approximates the yield on the bonds. Presuming the rent passes the arm's length test (i.e., what unrelated parties would charge), all parties reach the desired result. Gail and Gary withdraw corporate profits in the form of interest income, and Grace is provided for with rent income. White Corporation can deduct both the interest and the rent payments. ▼

- Try to keep the debt-equity ratio within reasonable proportions. A frequent problem arises when the parties first form the corporation. Often the amount invested in capital stock is the minimum required by state law. For example, if the state of incorporation permits a minimum of $1,000, limiting the investment to this amount does not provide much safety for later debt financing by the shareholders.
- The nature of the business can have an effect on what is an acceptable debt-equity ratio. Capital-intensive industries (e.g., manufacturing, trans-portation) characteristically rely heavily on debt financing. Consequently, larger debt should be tolerated.

INVESTOR LOSSES

In connection with § 1244, be aware that there is a danger of losing § 1244 attributes. Recall that only the original holder of § 1244 stock is entitled to ordinary loss treatment. If a corporation is formed to shift income within the family group by transferring shares of stock to family members, the benefits of § 1244 are lost.

EXAMPLE 32

Norm incorporates his business by transferring property with a basis of $100,000 for 100 shares of stock. The stock qualifies as § 1244 stock. Norm later gives 50 shares each to his children, Susan and Paul. Eventually, the business fails, and the corporation becomes bankrupt. The shares of stock become worthless. If Norm had retained the stock, he would have had an ordinary loss deduction of $100,000 (assuming he filed a joint return). Susan and Paul, however, have a capital loss of $50,000 each because the § 1244 attributes were lost. ▼

KEY TERMS

Assumption of liabilities, 17–9

Capital contribution, 17–15

Control, 17–5

Investor losses, 17–17

Liabilities in excess of basis, 17–10

Nonbusiness bad debt, 17–17

Property, 17–4

Qualified small business corporation, 17–19

Qualified small business stock, 17–20

Section 1244 stock, 17–19

Securities, 17–5

Thin capitalization, 17–16

PROBLEM MATERIALS

DISCUSSION QUESTIONS

1. In terms of justification and effect, § 351 (transfer to corporation controlled by transferor) and § 1031 (like-kind exchanges) are much alike. Explain.

2. Is gain recognized on the transfer of an installment obligation to a corporation in a transaction that qualifies under § 351? Explain.

3. Two or more parties transfer appreciated property to a corporation for stock. Why is it important that the transfers occur close together in time and in accordance with an agreement among the parties?

4. Does the receipt of securities (i.e., long-term debt) in exchange for the transfer of appreciated property to a controlled corporation cause recognition of gain?

5. How does a corporation determine its basis in property received in a nontaxable exchange under § 351?

6. What is the control requirement of § 351? Describe the effect of the following in satisfying this requirement:
   a. A shareholder renders services to the corporation for stock.
   b. A shareholder both renders services and transfers property to the corporation for stock.
   c. A shareholder has only momentary control after the transfer.
   d. A long period of time elapses between the transfers of property by different shareholders.

7. Matt and Megan form White Corporation. They transfer appreciated property to the corporation with each receiving 50 shares of the White stock. If Matt gives his shares to his daughter immediately after the exchange, will the exchange be taxable?

8. Paul and Mary transfer property to Falcon Corporation, each in exchange for one-third of Falcon's stock. Matt receives the other one-third of Falcon's stock for services rendered. Will the exchange be taxable?

9. May a transferor who receives stock for both property and services be included in the control group in determining whether an exchange meets the requirements of § 351? Explain.

10. At a point when Robin Corporation has been in existence for six years, shareholder Ted transfers real estate (adjusted basis of $20,000 and fair market value of $100,000) to the corporation for additional stock. At the same time, Peggy, the other shareholder, purchases one share of stock for cash. After the two transfers, the percentages of stock ownership are as follows: 79% by Ted and 21% by Peggy.
    a. What were the parties trying to accomplish?
    b. Will it work? Explain.

11. How does the transfer of mortgaged property to a controlled corporation affect the transferor shareholder's basis in stock received in the corporation when no gain is recognized on the transfer?

12. Does the transfer of mortgaged property to a controlled corporation trigger gain to the extent of the mortgage? Explain.

13. Before incorporating her apartment rental business, Beth takes out second mortgages on several of the units. She uses the mortgage funds to make capital improvements to her personal residence. Along with all of the rental units, Beth transfers the mortgages to the newly formed corporation in return for all of its stock. Discuss the tax consequences of these procedures to Beth.

14. If both § 357(b) and § 357(c) apply to a transfer of property to a corporation under § 351, which provision takes precedence?

15. What is the basis of property received by a corporation in a transfer that qualifies as a nontaxable exchange under § 351?

16. A corporation acquires property as a contribution to capital from a shareholder and from a nonshareholder. Are the basis rules the same? Explain.

17. In structuring the capitalization of a corporation, what are the advantages of utilizing debt rather than equity?

18. In determining whether the debt of a corporation should be reclassified as stock, comment on the relevance of the following:
    a. The loan is on open account.
    b. The loan is a demand loan.
    c. Although the loan has a definite maturity date, the corporation has not made payments on a timely basis.
    d. Payments on the loan are contingent upon corporate earnings.
    e. The corporation's shareholders loaned funds to the corporation in the same proportion as their shareholdings, and the debt was used to purchase a new building.
    f. The corporation has a debt-equity ratio of 5:1.

19. Assuming § 1244 does not apply, what is the tax treatment of stock that has become worthless?

PROBLEMS

20. Matt and Mary form Cardinal Corporation with the following investment:

| | Property Transferred | | |
	Basis to Transferor	Fair Market Value	Number of Shares Issued
From Matt—			
Cash	$ 40,000	$ 40,000	
Installment obligation	140,000	360,000	40
From Mary—			
Cash	140,000	140,000	
Equipment	120,000	180,000	60
Patent	4,000	280,000	

The installment obligation has a face amount of $360,000 and was acquired last year from the sale of land held for investment purposes (adjusted basis of $140,000).
a. How much gain, if any, must Matt recognize?
b. What will be Matt's basis in the Cardinal Corporation stock?
c. What will be Cardinal Corporation's basis in the installment obligation?
d. How much gain, if any, must Mary recognize?
e. What will be Mary's basis in the Cardinal Corporation stock?
f. What will be Cardinal Corporation's basis in the machinery and patent?
g. How would your answer change if Matt received common stock and Mary received preferred stock?
h. How would your answer change if Mary were a partnership?

 21. Hans, Irene, Jim, and Jack form Bluebird Corporation with the following investment:

| | Property Transferred | | |
	Basis to Transferor	Fair Market Value	Number of Shares Issued
From Hans—			
Personal services rendered to Bluebird Corporation	$ –0–	$ 10,000	⁴ 10
From Irene—			
Equipment	115,000	100,000	90*
From Jim—			
Cash	20,000	20,000	
Unrealized accounts			50
receivable	–0–	30,000	
From Jack—			
Land and building	70,000	150,000	
Mortgage on land			50
and building	100,000	100,000	

*Irene receives $10,000 in cash in addition to the 90 shares.

The mortgage transferred by Jack is assumed by Bluebird Corporation. The value of each share of Bluebird stock is $1,000.
a. What, if any, is Hans's recognized gain or loss?
b. What basis will Hans have in the Bluebird stock?
c. How much gain or loss must Irene recognize?

d. What basis will Irene have in the Bluebird stock?
e. What basis will Bluebird Corporation have in the equipment?
f. What, if any, is Jim's recognized gain or loss?
g. What basis will Jim have in the Bluebird stock?
h. What basis will Bluebird have in the unrealized accounts receivable?
i. How much gain or loss must Jack recognize?
j. What basis will Jack have in the Bluebird stock?
k. What basis will Bluebird Corporation have in the land and building?

 22. Sam, Seth, Pat, and Kelly form Lark Corporation with the following investment:

| | Property Transferred | | |
	Basis to Transferor	Fair Market Value	Number of Shares Issued
From Sam—			
Inventory	$30,000	$96,000	30*
From Seth—			
Equipment ($30,000 of depreciation taken by Seth in prior years)	45,000	99,000	30**
From Pat—			
Secret process	15,000	90,000	30
From Kelly—			
Cash	30,000	30,000	10

*Sam receives $6,000 in cash in addition to the 30 shares.
**Seth receives $9,000 in cash in addition to the 30 shares.

Assume the value of each share of Lark stock is $3,000.
a. What, if any, is Sam's recognized gain or loss? How is any such gain or loss treated?
b. What basis will Sam have in the Lark stock?
c. What basis will Lark Corporation have in the inventory?
d. How much gain or loss must Seth recognize? How is the gain or loss treated?
e. What basis will Seth have in the Lark stock?
f. What basis will Lark Corporation have in the equipment?
g. What, if any, is Pat's recognized gain or loss?
h. What basis will Pat have in the Lark stock?
i. What basis will Lark Corporation have in the secret process?
j. How much gain or loss, if any, must Kelly recognize?
k. What basis will Kelly have in the Lark stock?

 23. Ron Smith exchanges property, basis of $40,000 and fair market value of $150,000, for 60% of the stock of Dove Corporation. The other 40% is owned by Mary, who acquired it several years ago. You represent Ron, who asks whether he must report gain on the transfer. Prepare a letter to your client Ron and a memo for the file. Ron's address is 1400 Any Street, Anytown, TX 79400.

 24. Lee exchanges property, basis of $20,000 and fair market value of $500,000, for 65% of the stock of Pelican Corporation. The other 35% is owned by Abby, Lee's daughter, who acquired her stock last year. What are the tax issues?

25. Kate transfers property worth $400,000 (basis of $50,000) to Crow Corporation in exchange for 50% of Crow's stock. Kevin transfers a secret process worth $300,000 (zero basis) and services he rendered in obtaining the process and a letter of credit, which states that the newly formed Crow Corporation could obtain a loan to develop the process (worth $100,000 according to Kevin), for 50% of Crow's stock. What are the tax issues?

26. Carlos organized Cardinal Corporation 10 years ago by contributing property worth $1 million, basis of $200,000, for 2,000 shares of stock in Cardinal, representing 100% of the stock in the corporation. Carlos later gave each of his children, Isabella and Marta, 500 shares of stock in Cardinal Corporation. In the current year, Carlos transfers property worth $320,000, basis of $100,000, to Cardinal for 500 shares in the corporation. What gain, if any, will Carlos recognize on this transfer?

27. Ann and Bob form Robin Corporation. Ann transfers property worth $420,000 (basis of $150,000) for 70 shares in Robin Corporation. Bob receives 30 shares for property worth $165,000 (basis of $30,000) and for legal services in organizing the corporation; the services are worth $15,000.
    a. What gain, if any, will the parties recognize on the transfer?
    b. What basis will Ann and Bob have in the stock in Robin Corporation?
    c. What basis will Robin Corporation have in the property and services it received from Ann and Bob?

28. Assume in Problem 27 that the property Bob transfers to Robin Corporation is worth $15,000 (basis of $3,000) and his services in organizing the corporation are worth $165,000. What are the tax consequences to Ann, Bob, and Robin Corporation?

29. Sara transfers property with an adjusted basis of $50,000, fair market value of $400,000, to White Corporation for 100% of the stock. The property is subject to a liability of $60,000, which White assumes. What is the basis of the White stock to Sara? What is the basis of the property to White Corporation?

30. Three years ago, Chris exchanged an apartment worth $1,500,000 (basis of $300,000), which was subject to a mortgage of $200,000, for land worth $1,150,000, subject to a mortgage of $150,000, and cash of $300,000. In the current year, Chris transfers the land that he received in the exchange to newly formed Green Corporation for all the stock in Green. Green Corporation assumes the original mortgage on the land, currently in the amount of $100,000, and another mortgage in the amount of $20,000 that Chris later places on the land to secure his purchase of some equipment that he uses in his business. What are the tax issues?

31. Sara and Jane form Wren Corporation. Sara transfers property, basis of $25,000 and value of $200,000, for 50 shares in Wren Corporation. Jane transfers property, basis of $10,000 and value of $185,000, and agrees to serve as manager of Wren for one year; in return Jane receives 50 shares in Wren. The value of Jane's services to Wren is $15,000.
    a. What gain will Sara and Jane recognize on the exchange?
    b. What basis will Wren Corporation have in the property transferred by Sara and Jane? How will Wren treat the value of the services Jane renders?

32. Assume in Problem 31 that Jane receives the 50 shares of Wren stock in consideration for the appreciated property and for providing legal services in organizing the corporation. The value of Jane's services is $15,000.
    a. What gain does Jane recognize?
    b. What basis will Wren Corporation have in the property transferred by Jane? How will Wren treat the value of the services Jane renders?

33. A city donates land to Gray Corporation as an inducement for Gray to locate there. The land is worth $2 million. The city also donates $500,000 in cash to Gray.
    a. What income, if any, must Gray recognize as a result of the transfer of land and cash to it by the city?
    b. What basis will Gray have in the land?
    c. If Gray purchases property six months later with the $500,000 cash, what basis will it have in the property?

34. Sam, a single taxpayer, acquired stock in a corporation that qualified as a small business corporation under § 1244, at a cost of $100,000 three years ago. He sells the stock for $10,000 in the current tax year. How will the loss be treated for tax purposes?

35. Ann formed Dove Corporation four years ago with an investment of $200,000 for which she received 100% of the stock in Dove. Two years later when Dove was experiencing financial difficulty, Ann loaned Dove $50,000 and received in exchange bonds bearing 9% interest and maturing in five years. Last year she loaned Dove an additional $20,000 on open account. In the current year, Dove is insolvent and is adjudged bankrupt. As president of Dove Corporation, Ann has received an annual salary of $40,000. What are the tax issues in determining the tax treatment of Ann's loss in her investment in Dove and in the amounts she has loaned to Dove?

36. Sam Speed, a married taxpayer who files a joint return with his wife, acquired stock in a corporation that qualified as a small business corporation under § 1244. The stock cost $100,000 and was acquired three years ago. A few months after Sam acquired the stock, he gave it to his brother, Mike Speed. The stock was worth $100,000 on the date of the gift. Mike, who is married and files a joint return with his wife, sells the stock for $10,000 in the current tax year. You represent Mike, who asks you whether he can take a loss deduction on the sale of the stock. If so, how will the loss be treated for tax purposes? Prepare a letter to your client and a memo for the file. Mike's address is 1400 Any Street, Anytown, TX 79400.

37. Eduardo transfers property with a basis of $40,000 and a fair market value of $20,000 to Gray Corporation in exchange for shares of § 1244 stock. (Assume the transfer qualifies under § 351.)
    a. What is the basis of the stock to Eduardo?
    b. What is the basis of the stock to Eduardo for purposes of § 1244?
    c. If Eduardo sells the stock for $10,000 two years later, how will the loss be treated for tax purposes?

38. Frank, Cora, and Mitch are equal shareholders in Blue Corporation. The corporation's assets have a tax basis of $50,000 and a fair market value of $600,000. In the current year, Frank and Cora each loan Blue Corporation $150,000. The notes to Frank and Cora bear interest of 8% per annum. Mitch leases equipment to Blue Corporation for an annual rental of $12,000. Discuss whether the shareholder loans from Frank and Cora might be reclassified as equity. Consider in your discussion whether Blue Corporation has an acceptable debt-equity ratio.

Research Problems for this chapter appear at the end of Chapter 28.

CORPORATIONS: DISTRIBUTIONS NOT IN COMPLETE LIQUIDATION

LEARNING OBJECTIVES

After completing Chapter 18, you should be able to:

1. Identify and understand the concept of earnings and profits.

2. Recognize the importance of earnings and profits in measuring dividend income.

3. Master the tax treatment of dividends, including property dividends, to both the recipient shareholder and the corporation making the distribution.

4. Understand the nature and treatment of constructive dividends.

5. Distinguish between taxable and nontaxable stock dividends and stock rights.

6. Identify various stock redemptions that cause payments to shareholders to be treated as sales or exchanges of stock rather than as dividend income.

7. Identify tax planning opportunities available to minimize the income tax impact in corporate distributions, constructive dividends, and stock redemptions.

OUTLINE

A working knowledge of the rules pertaining to corporate distributions is essential for anyone dealing with the tax problems of corporations and their shareholders. The form of such distributions is important because it can produce varying tax results to the shareholders and to the corporation. Cash or property dividends are taxed as ordinary income to the recipient shareholder, while stock redemptions may receive capital gain or loss treatment after allowing the shareholder to recover basis in the redeemed stock. Stock dividends may not be taxed at all.

TAX IN THE NEWS

A STOCK REDEMPTION MAKES NEW MANAGEMENT LOOK GOOD

In an aggressive move to boost its stock price, Philip Morris Company announced a $6 million stock-buyback plan and raised its quarterly dividend nearly 20 percent. The announcement was the strongest sign yet that Philip Morris's new management team has considerable confidence in the company's domestic tobacco operations. The generous dividend increase and buyback plan were to reward investors who had been battered by more than a year of negative tobacco news and management turmoil. The dividend increase, which raised the company's quarterly payout 19.6 percent, went far beyond most analysts' predictions of a 5 to 10 percent increase. In addition, investors and analysts had not expected the company to both raise its dividend payout and buy back a portion of its stock. The boldness and speed of the move demonstrated the influence of the new management team.

SOURCE: Information from Suein Hwang, "Philip Morris Increases Dividend 20%, Plans Buyback: Stock Sets 52-Week High," *Wall Street Journal*, September 2, 1994, pp. A2 and A3.

TAXABLE DIVIDENDS—IN GENERAL

Distributions by a corporation to its shareholders are presumed to be dividends unless the parties can prove otherwise. Dividend income results to the extent of the earnings and profits (E & P) of the distributing corporation accumulated since February 28, 1913, or to the extent of corporate E & P for the current year.[1]

The portion of a corporate distribution that is not taxed as a dividend (because of insufficient E & P) is nontaxable to the extent of the shareholder's basis in the stock. The stock basis is reduced accordingly. The excess of the distribution over the shareholder's basis is treated as a capital gain if the stock is a capital asset.[2]

EXAMPLE 1

At the end of the year, Black Corporation has E & P of $30,000. On this date, the corporation distributes cash of $40,000 to its two *equal* shareholders, Bob and Bonnie. The adjusted basis of the shareholders' stock investment is $8,000 for Bob and $4,000 for Bonnie. The $40,000 distribution should be accounted for as follows:

	Bob	Bonnie
Amount distributed	$ 20,000	$ 20,000
Portion from E & P (taxed as a dividend)	(15,000)	(15,000)
	$ 5,000	$ 5,000
Return of capital (reduction of basis)	(5,000)	(4,000)
	$ –0–	$ 1,000
Capital gain	(–0–)	(1,000)
	$ –0–	$ –0–

Thus, of the $20,000 Bob receives, $15,000 is dividend income and $5,000 is a nontaxable return of capital. After the distribution, Bob has a basis in the Black Corporation stock of $3,000 ($8,000 original adjusted basis – $5,000 return of capital). As to Bonnie, the result is $15,000 of dividend income, $4,000 of nontaxable return of capital, and $1,000 of capital gain. After the distribution, Bonnie has a basis in the Black stock of $0 ($4,000 original adjusted basis – $4,000 return of capital). ▼

EARNINGS AND PROFITS (E & P)

1 LEARNING OBJECTIVE
Identify and understand the concept of earnings and profits.

The Code does not define the term **earnings and profits.** Although E & P is similar in some respects to the accounting concept of retained earnings (earnings retained in the business), E & P and retained earnings are often not the same.

Several observations are helpful in understanding the concept of E & P. First, E & P can be described as the factor that fixes the upper limit on the amount of dividend income shareholders must recognize as a result of a distribution by the corporation. In this sense, E & P represents the corporation's economic ability to pay a dividend without impairing its capital. The effect of a specific transaction on

---

[1] § 316.   [2] § 301(c).

the E & P account may be determined simply by considering whether or not the transaction increases or decreases the corporation's capacity to pay a dividend.

COMPUTATION OF E & P

A corporation's taxable income for the year is the starting point in computing its E & P for the year. Taxable income is converted into E & P through certain adjustments that cause E & P to conform more closely to economic income. If the corporation uses the cash method of accounting in computing taxable income, it must also use this method to determine the changes in E & P.[3]

Additions to Taxable Income in Determining E & P.   E & P is increased for all items of income. Interest on municipal bonds, for example, though not taxed to the corporation, increases the corporation's E & P. The dividends received deduction is added back to compute E & P. A corporation's E & P for the year in which it sells property on the installment basis is increased by the amount of any deferred gain. This is accomplished by treating all principal payments as having been received in the year of sale.[4]

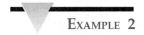

EXAMPLE 2

A corporation collects $100,000 on a key employee life insurance policy (the corporation is the owner and beneficiary of the policy). At the time the policy matured on the death of the insured employee, it possessed a cash surrender value of $30,000. None of the $100,000 is included in the corporation's taxable income, but $70,000 is added to the current E & P account (i.e., amount collected on the policy net of its cash surrender value). ▼

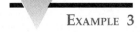

EXAMPLE 3

During 1996, a corporation makes charitable contributions, $12,000 of which cannot be deducted in arriving at the taxable income for the year because of the 10% limitation. However, the $12,000 is carried over to 1997 and fully deducted in that year. The excess charitable contribution reduces the corporation's current E & P for 1996 by $12,000 and increases its current E & P for 1997, when the deduction is allowed, by a like amount. The increase in E & P in 1997 is necessary because the charitable contribution carryover reduces the taxable income for that year (the starting point for computing E & P) and already has been taken into account in determining the E & P for 1996. ▼

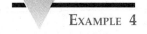

EXAMPLE 4

In 1996, Cardinal Corporation, a calendar year taxpayer, sells unimproved real estate (basis of $20,000) for $100,000. Under the terms of the sale, beginning in 1997, Cardinal will receive two annual payments of $50,000 each with interest. Cardinal Corporation does not elect out of the installment method. Although Cardinal's taxable income for 1996 will not reflect any of the gain from the sale, the corporation must increase E & P for 1996 by $80,000 (the deferred profit component). ▼

Subtractions from Taxable Income in Determining E & P. The E & P account is affected by both deductible and nondeductible items. Consequently, excess capital losses, expenses incurred to produce tax-exempt income, and

---

[3] Code § 312 contains most of the adjustments necessary to determine E & P. It accomplishes this by setting out the effect of a number of transactions on E & P. Regulations relating to E & P begin at Reg. § 1.312–6.

[4] § 312(n)(5).

Federal income taxes all reduce E & P. Such items do not enter into the calculation of taxable income.

The E & P account is reduced only by cost depletion, even though the corporation is using percentage (statutory) depletion for income tax purposes. E & P cannot be reduced by accelerated depreciation.[5] However, if a depreciation method such as units-of-production or machine hours is used, the adjustment to E & P is determined on this basis.[6]

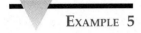

EXAMPLE 5
A corporation sells property (basis of $10,000) to its sole shareholder for $8,000. Because of § 267 (disallowance of losses on sales between related parties), the $2,000 loss cannot be deducted in arriving at the corporation's taxable income. But since the overall economic effect of the transaction is a decrease in the corporation's assets by $2,000, the loss reduces the current E & P for the year of sale. ▼

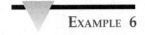

EXAMPLE 6
A corporation pays a $10,000 premium on a key employee life insurance policy covering the life of its president. As a result of the payment, the cash surrender value of the policy is increased by $7,000. Although none of the $10,000 premium is deductible for tax purposes, current E & P is reduced by $3,000 (i.e., amount of the premium payment net of the increase in the cash surrender value). ▼

Other Adjustments. Gains and losses from property transactions generally affect the determination of E & P only to the extent they are recognized for tax purposes. Thus, a gain on an involuntary conversion not recognized by the corporation because the insurance proceeds are suitably reinvested does not affect E & P.

The alternative depreciation system must be used for purposes of computing E & P.[7] If cost recovery is figured under MACRS, E & P must be computed using the straight-line recovery method over a recovery period equal to the asset's Asset Depreciation Range (ADR) midpoint life.[8] Later, when the asset is sold, the increase or decrease in E & P is determined by using the adjusted basis of the asset for E & P purposes.[9]

Intangible drilling costs and mineral exploration and development costs are required to be capitalized for purposes of computing E & P. Once capitalized, these expenditures can be charged to E & P over a specified period: 60 months for intangible drilling costs and 120 months for mine exploration and development costs.[10]

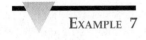

EXAMPLE 7
On January 2, 1994, White Corporation purchased for $30,000 equipment with an ADR midpoint life of 10 years that was then depreciated under MACRS. The asset was sold on July 2, 1996, for $27,000. For purposes of determining taxable income and E & P, cost recovery claimed on the equipment and the equipment's adjusted basis are summarized as follows:

---

[5] § 312(k).
[6] Reg. § 1.312–15(a)(2).
[7] § 312(k)(3)(A).
[8] See § 168(g)(2). The ADR midpoint life for most assets is set out in Rev.Proc. 87–56, 1987–2 C.B. 674. The recovery period is 5 years for automobiles and light-duty trucks and 40 years for real property. For assets with no class life, the recovery period is 12 years. Any amount expensed under § 179 is deducted over a period of 5 years in computing E & P. See § 312(k)(3)(B).
[9] § 312(f)(1).
[10] § 312(n)(2).

	Taxable Income	E & P	Difference
Amount realized	$27,000	$27,000	–0–
Original cost	$30,000	$30,000	–0–
Cost recovery:			
1994: $30,000 × 14.29%	$ 4,287		
$30,000 ÷ 10-year recovery period × ½ (half-year for first year of service)		$ 1,500	$2,787
1995: $30,000 × 24.49%	7,347		
$30,000 ÷ 10-year recovery period		3,000	4,347
1996: $30,000 × 17.49% × ½ (half-year for year of disposal)	2,624		
$30,000 ÷ 10-year recovery period × ½ (half-year for year of disposal)		1,500	1,124
Total cost recovery	$14,258	$ 6,000	$8,258
Adjusted basis	$15,742	$24,000	$8,258
Gain	$11,258	$ 3,000	$8,258

SUMMARY OF E & P ADJUSTMENTS

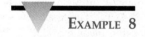

2 **LEARNING OBJECTIVE**
Recognize the importance of earnings and profits in measuring dividend income.

Recall that E & P serves as a measure of the earnings of the corporation that are available for distribution as taxable dividends to the shareholders. Initially, E & P is increased by the corporation's taxable income. However, adjustments must be made to taxable income for various transactions in determining the corporation's current E & P. These adjustments are reviewed in Concept Summary 18–1. Other items that affect E & P, such as property dividends and stock redemptions, are covered later in the chapter and are not included in Concept Summary 18–1.

THE SOURCE OF THE DISTRIBUTION

In determining the source of a dividend distribution, the dividend is deemed to have been made first from **current E & P** and then from **accumulated E & P** (since February 28, 1913).[11]

EXAMPLE 8

At the beginning of the current year, Brown Corporation has a deficit of $30,000 in accumulated E & P. For the year, it has current E & P of $10,000 and distributes $5,000 to its shareholders. The $5,000 distribution is treated as a taxable dividend since it is deemed to have been made from current E & P. This is the case even though Brown still has a deficit in accumulated E & P at the end of the current year. ▼

Distributions made during the year may exceed the current year's E & P. In this case, the portion of each distribution considered to have been made from current

---

[11] Regulations relating to the source of a distribution are at Reg. § 1.316–2.

Concept Summary 18–1

E & P Adjustments

Nature of the Transaction	Effect on Taxable Income in Arriving at Current E & P	
	Addition	**Subtraction**
Tax-exempt income	X	
Collection of proceeds on insurance policy on life of corporate officer	X	
Deferred gain on installment sale (all gain is added to E & P in year of sale)	X	
Future recognition of installment sale gross profit		X
Excess charitable contribution (over 10% limitation)		X
Deduction of excess charitable contribution in succeeding taxable year (increases E & P because deduction reduces taxable income while E & P was reduced in a prior year)	X	
Federal income taxes		X
Loss on sale between related parties		X
Payment of premiums on insurance policy on life of corporate officer (in excess of increase in cash surrender value of policy)		X
Realized gain (not recognized) on an involuntary conversion	No effect	
Percentage depletion (only cost depletion can reduce E & P)	X	
Accelerated depreciation (E & P is reduced only by straight-line, units-of-production, or machine hours depreciation)	X	
Intangible drilling costs deducted currently (reduce E & P in future years by amortizing costs over 60 months)	X	
Mine exploration and development costs (reduce E & P in future years by amortizing costs over 120 months)	X	

E & P is the percentage that the total E & P for the year bears to the total distributions for that year. This allocation is important if any of the shareholders sell their stock during the year and total current distributions exceed current E & P.

DISTINGUISHING BETWEEN CURRENT AND ACCUMULATED E & P

Accumulated E & P is the total of all previous years' current E & P as computed on the first day of each taxable year. The computation is made in accordance with the tax law in effect during that year. The factors that affect the computation of the current E & P for any one year have been discussed previously. Why must current and accumulated E & P be distinguished when it is clear that distributions are taxable if and to the extent that current *and* accumulated E & P exist?

1. When there is a deficit in accumulated E & P and a positive amount in current E & P, distributions are regarded as dividends to the extent of the current E & P. The E & P accounts are not netted in this case. Refer to Example 8.
2. Current E & P is allocated on a pro rata basis to the distributions made during the year; accumulated E & P is applied (to the extent necessary) in chronological order beginning with the earliest distributions.
3. Unless and until the parties can show otherwise, it is presumed that any distribution is covered by current E & P.
4. When a deficit in current E & P (a current loss) and a positive balance in accumulated E & P exist, the accounts are netted as of the date of distribution. If the resulting balance is zero or a deficit, the distribution is a return of capital. If a positive balance results, the distribution is a dividend to the extent of the balance. Any loss is allocated ratably during the year unless the parties can show otherwise.

The following examples illustrate distinctions 3 and 4.

EXAMPLE 9

Green Corporation uses a fiscal year of July 1 through June 30 for tax purposes. Carmen, Green's only shareholder, uses a calendar year. As of July 1, 1996, Green had a zero balance in its accumulated E & P account. For fiscal year 1996–97, the corporation has suffered a $5,000 operating loss. On August 1, 1996, Green distributed $10,000 to Carmen. The distribution represents dividend income to Carmen and is reported as such when she files her income tax return for calendar year 1996 on or before April 15, 1997. Because Carmen cannot prove until June 30, 1997, that the corporation has a deficit for fiscal year 1996–97, she must assume the $10,000 distribution is fully covered by current E & P. When Carmen learns of the deficit, she can file an amended return for 1996 showing the $10,000 as a return of capital. ▼

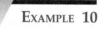

EXAMPLE 10

At the beginning of the current year, Gray Corporation (a calendar year taxpayer) has accumulated E & P of $10,000. During the year, the corporation incurs a $15,000 net loss from operations that accrues ratably. On July 1, Gray distributes $6,000 in cash to Hal, its sole shareholder. To determine how much of the $6,000 cash distribution represents dividend income to Hal, the balance of both accumulated and current E & P as of July 1 is determined and netted. This is necessary because of the deficit in current E & P.

	Source of Distribution	
	Current E & P	**Accumulated E & P**
January 1		$10,000
July 1 (½ of $15,000 net loss)	($7,500)	2,500
July 1 distribution—$6,000:		
Dividend income: $2,500		
Return of capital: $3,500		

The balance in E & P on July 1 is $2,500. Thus, of the $6,000 distribution, $2,500 is taxed as a dividend, and $3,500 represents a return of capital. ▼

PROPERTY DIVIDENDS—IN GENERAL

3 **LEARNING OBJECTIVE**
Master the tax treatment of dividends, including property dividends, to both the recipient shareholder and the corporation making the distribution.

The previous discussion assumed that all distributions by a corporation to its shareholders are in the form of cash. Although most corporate distributions are cash, a corporation may distribute a **property dividend** for various reasons. The shareholders could want a particular property that is held by the corporation. Or, the corporation may be strapped for cash, but does not want to forgo distributing a dividend to its shareholders.

Generally, the distribution of a property dividend is treated in the same manner as a cash distribution. However, the value of the property distributed and the basis of that property to the corporation are seldom the same. Consequently, the distribution of a property dividend involves additional tax considerations. The following questions must be asked when property is distributed as a dividend:

- What is the amount of the dividend distributed to the shareholder?
- What is the basis of the property received by the shareholder?
- Does the corporation recognize gain or loss upon the distribution?
- What is the effect of the property distribution on the E & P of the corporation?

PROPERTY DIVIDENDS—EFFECT ON THE SHAREHOLDER

When a corporation distributes property rather than cash to a shareholder, the amount distributed is measured by the fair market value of the property on the date of distribution.[12] The portion of the distribution covered by existing E & P is a dividend, and any excess is treated as a return of capital until basis is recovered. If the fair market value of the property distributed exceeds the corporation's E & P and the shareholder's basis in the stock investment, a capital gain results.

The amount distributed is reduced by any liabilities to which the distributed property is subject immediately before and immediately after the distribution and by any liabilities of the corporation assumed by the shareholder. The basis in the distributed property is the fair market value of the property on the date of the distribution.

TAX IN THE NEWS

DIVIDEND PAYOUT RATES ARE AT A HISTORIC LOW

Dividend payouts are at a new low because of the gap between income tax rates on ordinary income and capital gains. Many corporations are buying back stock to generate capital gains for their shareholders rather than paying the shareholders dividends, which are taxed as ordinary income. The result, as financial analysts have noted, is that more corporate stocks are being retired through stock redemptions than are being issued. This excess of retired stock over new issues is called "equity liquidation."

---

[12]Section 301 deals with the tax treatment to the shareholder of a distribution by the corporation.

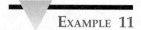

EXAMPLE 11

Robin Corporation has E & P of $60,000. It distributes land with a fair market value of $50,000 (adjusted basis of $30,000) to its sole shareholder, Carlos. The land is subject to a liability of $10,000, which Carlos assumes. Carlos has a taxable dividend of $40,000 ($50,000 fair market value – $10,000 liability). The basis of the land to Carlos is $50,000. ▼

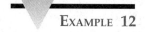

EXAMPLE 12

Redbird Corporation owns 10% of Bluebird Corporation. Bluebird has ample E & P to cover any distributions made during the year. One distribution made to Redbird Corporation consists of a vacant lot with an adjusted basis of $5,000 and a fair market value of $3,000. Redbird has a taxable dividend of $3,000, and its basis in the lot is $3,000. ▼

Property that has depreciated in value is usually not suited to distribution as a property dividend. Note what happens in Example 12. The loss of $2,000 (adjusted basis $5,000, fair market value $3,000) disappears. Bluebird Corporation can preserve the loss for itself if it sells the lot and then distributes the $3,000 proceeds.

PROPERTY DIVIDENDS—EFFECT ON THE CORPORATION

A property distribution by a corporation to its shareholders poses two questions. Does the distribution result in recognized gain or loss to the distributing corporation? What effect does the distribution have on the corporation's E & P?

Recognition of Gain or Loss. All distributions of appreciated property cause gain recognition to the distributing corporation.[13] In effect, the corporation that distributes a property dividend is treated as if it had sold the property to the shareholder for its fair market value. However, the distributing corporation does not recognize loss on distributions of property with a tax basis in excess of fair market value.

EXAMPLE 13

Wren Corporation distributes land (basis of $10,000 and fair market value of $30,000) to a shareholder. Wren Corporation recognizes a gain of $20,000. ▼

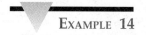

EXAMPLE 14

Assume the property in Example 13 has a fair market value of $10,000 and a basis of $30,000. Wren Corporation does not recognize a loss on the distribution. ▼

If the distributed property is subject to a liability in excess of basis or the shareholder assumes such a liability, a special rule applies. The fair market value of the property for purposes of determining gain on the distribution is treated as not being less than the amount of the liability.[14]

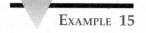

EXAMPLE 15

Assume the land in Example 13 is subject to a liability of $35,000. Wren Corporation recognizes a gain of $25,000 on the distribution. ▼

Effect of Corporate Distributions on E & P. In the event of a corporate distribution, the E & P account is reduced by the amount of money distributed or by the *greater* of the fair market value or the adjusted basis of property distributed, less the amount of any liability on the property.[15] E & P is increased by gain recognized on appreciated property distributed as a property dividend.

---

[13] Section 311 covers the taxability of a corporation on distributions.
[14] § 311(b)(2).

[15] §§ 312(a), (b), and (c).

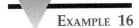

EXAMPLE 16

Brown Corporation distributes property (basis of $10,000 and fair market value of $20,000) to Alicia, its shareholder. Brown recognizes a gain of $10,000, which is added to its E & P, and which is reduced by $20,000, the fair market value of the property. Alicia has dividend income of $20,000. ▼

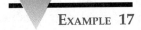

EXAMPLE 17

Assume the same facts as in Example 16, except that the fair market value of the property is $15,000 and the adjusted basis in the hands of Brown Corporation is $20,000. Because the loss is not recognized and the adjusted basis is greater than fair market value, E & P is reduced by $20,000. Alicia reports dividend income of $15,000. ▼

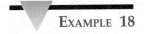

EXAMPLE 18

Assume the same facts as in Example 17, except that the property is subject to a liability of $6,000. E & P is now reduced by $14,000 ($20,000 adjusted basis – $6,000 liability). Alicia has a dividend of $9,000 ($15,000 amount of the distribution – $6,000 liability), and her basis in the property is $15,000. ▼

Under no circumstances can a distribution, whether cash or property, either generate a deficit in E & P or add to a deficit in E & P. Deficits can arise only through corporate losses.

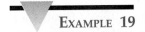

EXAMPLE 19

Green Corporation has accumulated E & P of $10,000 at the beginning of the current tax year. During the year, it has current E & P of $15,000. At the end of the year, it distributes cash of $30,000 to its sole shareholder, Hans. Green's E & P at the end of the year is zero. The beginning E & P of $10,000 is increased by current E & P of $15,000 and reduced by $25,000 because of the dividend distribution. The remaining $5,000 of the distribution to Hans does not reduce E & P because a distribution cannot generate a deficit in E & P. Instead, the remaining $5,000 reduces Hans's stock basis and/or produces a capital gain to Hans. ▼

CONSTRUCTIVE DIVIDENDS

4 LEARNING OBJECTIVE
Understand the nature and treatment of constructive dividends.

A distribution by a corporation to its shareholders can be treated as a dividend for Federal income tax purposes even though it is not formally declared or designated as a dividend. Also, it need not be issued pro rata to all shareholders.[16] Nor must the distribution satisfy the legal requirements of a dividend as set forth by applicable state law. The key factor determining dividend status is whether a measurable economic benefit is conveyed to the shareholder. This benefit, often described as a **constructive dividend,** is distinguishable from actual corporate distributions of cash and property in form only.

Constructive dividend situations usually arise in the context of closely held corporations. Here, the dealings between the parties are less structured, and, frequently, formalities are not preserved. The constructive dividend serves as a substitute for actual distributions. Usually, it is intended to accomplish some tax objective not available through the use of direct dividends. The shareholders may be attempting to bail out corporate profits in a form deductible to the corporation. (Dividend distributions do not provide the distributing corporation with an income tax deduction, although they do reduce E & P.) Alternatively, the

[16] See *Lengsfield v. Comm.*, 57–1 USTC ¶9437, 50 AFTR 1683, 241 F.2d 508 (CA–5, 1957).

shareholders may be seeking benefits for themselves while avoiding the recognition of income. Constructive dividends are, in reality, disguised dividends.

Do not conclude that all constructive dividends are deliberate attempts to avoid actual and formal dividends. Often constructive dividends are inadvertent. Consequently, a dividend result may come as a surprise to the parties. For this reason, if for none other, an awareness of the various constructive dividend situations is essential to protect the parties from unanticipated tax consequences.

TYPES OF CONSTRUCTIVE DIVIDENDS

The most frequently encountered types of constructive dividends are summarized below.

Shareholder Use of Corporate-Owned Property.   A constructive dividend can occur when a shareholder uses a corporation's property for personal purposes at no cost. Personal use of corporate-owned automobiles, airplanes, yachts, fishing camps, hunting lodges, and other entertainment facilities is commonplace in some closely held corporations. The shareholder has dividend income to the extent of the fair rental value of the property for the period of its personal use.

Bargain Sale of Corporate Property to a Shareholder.   Shareholders often purchase property from a corporation at a cost below the fair market value of the property. These bargain sales produce dividend income to the extent of the difference between the property's fair market value on the date of sale and the amount the shareholder paid for the property.[17] These situations might be avoided by appraising the property on or about the date of the sale. The appraised value should become the price to be paid by the shareholder.

Bargain Rental of Corporate Property.   A bargain rental of corporate property by a shareholder also produces dividend income. Here the measure of the constructive dividend is the excess of the property's fair rental value over the rent actually paid. Again, appraisal data should be used to avoid any questionable situations.

Payments for the Benefit of a Shareholder.   If a corporation pays an obligation of a shareholder, the payment is treated as a constructive dividend. The obligation involved need not be legally binding on the shareholder; it may, in fact, be a moral obligation.[18] Forgiveness of shareholder indebtedness by the corporation creates an identical problem.[19] Excessive rentals paid by a corporation for the use of shareholder property are treated as constructive dividends.

Unreasonable Compensation.   A salary payment to a shareholder-employee that is deemed to be **unreasonable compensation** is frequently treated as a constructive dividend and therefore is not deductible by the corporation. In determining the reasonableness of salary payments, the following factors are considered:

---

[17] Reg. § 1.301–1(j).

[18] *Montgomery Engineering Co. v. U.S.*, 64–2 USTC ¶9618, 13 AFTR2d 1747, 230 F.Supp. 838 (D.Ct.N.J., 1964); *aff'd.* in 65–1 USTC ¶9368, 15 AFTR2d 746, 344 F.2d 996 (CA–3, 1965).

[19] Reg. § 1.301–1(m).

WHEN IS COMPENSATION UNREASONABLE?

What is reasonable compensation for the head of the Chicago Stadium Corporation, which manages the arena where the Chicago Blackhawks hockey team and the Chicago Bulls basketball team play? For the fiscal year ending on July 31, 1977, the corporation paid its chairman and CEO, Arthur Wirtz, $335,750, but the IRS insisted reasonable compensation would be only $138,000 and disallowed the company's deduction for the remainder.

A long legal battle ensued, but the Federal District Court in Chicago finally upheld the IRS [*Chicago Stadium Corporation v. U.S.*, 91–2 USTC ¶50,352 (D. Ct. Ill., 1991)]. Among other things, the court said that Wirtz was paid considerably more than the executives of similar arenas, yet he did not even work full-time for the corporation. Besides, much of his pay consisted of "commissions" for arranging to lease the arena to the Bulls, which he also controlled. Under the circumstances, said the court, the $138,000 allowed by the IRS was generous.

- The employee's qualifications.
- A comparison of salaries with dividend distributions.
- The prevailing rates of compensation for comparable positions in comparable business concerns.
- The nature and scope of the employee's work.
- The size and complexity of the business.
- A comparison of salaries paid with both gross and net income.
- The taxpayer's salary policy toward all employees.
- For small corporations with a limited number of officers, the amount of compensation paid the employee in question in previous years.[20]

Loans to Shareholders. Advances to shareholders that are not bona fide loans are constructive dividends. Whether an advance qualifies as a bona fide loan is a question of fact to be determined in light of the particular circumstances. Factors considered in determining whether the advance is a bona fide loan include the following:

- Whether the advance is on open account or is evidenced by a written instrument.
- Whether the shareholder furnished collateral or other security for the advance.
- How long the advance has been outstanding.
- Whether any payments have been made, excluding dividend sources.
- The shareholder's financial capability to repay the advance.
- The shareholder's use of the funds (e.g., payment of routine bills versus nonrecurring, extraordinary expenses).

---

[20]*Mayson Manufacturing Co. v. Comm.*, 49–2 USTC ¶9467, 38 AFTR 1028, 178 F.2d 115 (CA–6, 1949).

- The regularity of the advances.
- The dividend-paying history of the corporation.

If a corporation succeeds in proving that an advance to a shareholder is a bona fide loan, the advance is not a constructive dividend. But getting past this hurdle does not eliminate all constructive dividend treatment. The shareholder still has a constructive dividend in the amount of any forgone interest. Interest-free or below-market loans by a corporation to a shareholder cause the shareholder to have a constructive dividend to the extent of *imputed interest,* which is the difference between the rate the Federal government pays on new borrowings, compounded semiannually, and the interest charged on the loan.[21] The corporation is deemed to have made a dividend distribution to the shareholder to the extent of the forgone interest. The shareholder is then deemed to have made an interest payment to the corporation for the same amount. Although the shareholder may be permitted to deduct the deemed interest payment, the corporation has interest income. No corresponding deduction is allowed since the imputed interest element is a constructive dividend.

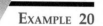

EXAMPLE 20

Bluebird Corporation loans its principal shareholder, Henry, $100,000 on January 2, 1996. The loan is interest-free. On December 31, 1996, Bluebird is deemed to have made a dividend distribution to Henry in the amount of the imputed interest on the loan, determined by using the Federal rate and compounded semiannually. Assume the Federal rate is 6%. Bluebird is deemed to have paid a dividend to Henry in the amount of $6,180.

Although Henry has dividend income of $6,180, he may be permitted to offset the income with a $6,180 deemed interest payment to Bluebird. Bluebird Corporation has deemed interest income of $6,180, but has no corresponding deduction. The deemed payment from Bluebird to Henry is a nondeductible dividend. ▼

Loans to a Corporation by Shareholders.   Shareholder loans to a corporation may be reclassified as equity because the debt has too many features of stock. Any interest and principal payments made by the corporation to the shareholder are then treated as constructive dividends.

TAX TREATMENT OF CONSTRUCTIVE DIVIDENDS

Constructive distributions possess the same tax attributes as actual distributions.[22] Thus, a corporate shareholder is entitled to the dividends received deduction (see Chapter 16). The constructive distribution is taxable as a dividend only to the extent of the corporation's current and accumulated E & P. The burden of proving that the distribution constitutes a return of capital because of inadequate E & P rests with the taxpayer.[23]

STOCK DIVIDENDS AND STOCK RIGHTS

5   **LEARNING OBJECTIVE**
Distinguish between taxable and nontaxable stock dividends and stock rights.

STOCK DIVIDENDS

A shareholder's proportionate interest in a corporation generally does not change upon receipt of a **stock dividend.** Accordingly, such distributions were initially

[21] See § 7872.

[22] *Simon v. Comm.,* 57–2 USTC ¶9989, 52 AFTR 698, 248 F.2d 869 (CA–8, 1957).

[23] *DiZenzo v. Comm.,* 65–2 USTC ¶9518, 16 AFTR2d 5107, 348 F.2d 122 (CA–2, 1965).

accorded tax-free treatment.[24] The provisions of § 305 that govern the taxability of stock dividends are based on the proportionate interest concept.

Stock dividends are not taxable if they are pro rata distributions of stock, or stock rights, on common stock. Section 305(b) contains five exceptions to the general rule that stock dividends are nontaxable. These exceptions deal with various disproportionate distribution situations. If stock dividends are not taxable, the corporation's E & P is not reduced.[25] If the stock dividends are taxable, the distributing corporation treats the distribution in the same manner as any other taxable property dividend.

If a stock dividend is taxable, basis to the shareholder-distributee is fair market value, and the holding period starts on the date of receipt. If a stock dividend is not taxable, the basis of the stock on which the dividend is distributed is reallocated.[26] If the dividend shares are identical to these formerly held shares, basis in the old stock is reallocated by dividing the taxpayer's basis in the old stock by the total number of shares. If the dividend stock is not identical to the underlying shares (e.g., a stock dividend of preferred on common), basis is determined by allocating the basis of the formerly held shares between the old and new stock according to the fair market value of each. The holding period includes the holding period of the formerly held stock.[27]

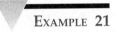

EXAMPLE 21

Gail bought 1,000 shares of stock two years ago for $10,000. In the current tax year, she receives 10 shares of common stock as a nontaxable stock dividend. Gail's basis of $10,000 is divided by 1,010. Each share of stock has a basis of $9.90 instead of the pre-dividend $10 basis. ▼

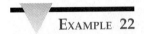

EXAMPLE 22

Assume Gail received, instead, a nontaxable preferred stock dividend of 100 shares. The preferred stock has a fair market value of $1,000, and the common stock, on which the preferred is distributed, has a fair market value of $19,000. After the receipt of the stock dividend, the basis of the common stock is $9,500, and the basis of the preferred is $500, computed as follows:

Fair market value of common	$19,000
Fair market value of preferred	1,000
	$20,000
Basis of common: $19/20 \times \$10,000$	$ 9,500
Basis of preferred: $1/20 \times \$10,000$	$ 500

▼

STOCK RIGHTS

The rules for determining taxability of **stock rights** are identical to those for determining taxability of stock dividends. If the rights are taxable, the recipient has income to the extent of the fair market value of the rights. The fair market value then becomes the shareholder-distributee's basis in the rights.[28] If the rights are exercised, the holding period for the new stock is the date the rights (whether taxable or nontaxable) are exercised. The basis of the new stock is the basis of the rights plus the amount of any other consideration given.

If stock rights are not taxable and the value of the rights is less than 15 percent of the value of the old stock, the basis of the rights is zero. However, the

[24] See *Eisner v. Macomber*, 1 USTC ¶32, 3 AFTR 3020, 40 S.Ct. 189 (USSC, 1920).

[25] § 312(d)(1).

[26] § 307(a).

[27] § 1223(5).

[28] Reg. § 1.305–1(b).

shareholder may elect to have some of the basis in the formerly held stock allocated to the rights.[29] If the fair market value of the rights is 15 percent or more of the value of the old stock and the rights are exercised or sold, the shareholder *must* allocate some of the basis in the formerly held stock to the rights.

Assume the value of the stock rights is less than 15 percent of the value of the stock and the shareholder makes an election to allocate basis to the rights. The election is made by attaching a statement to the shareholder's return for the year in which the rights are received.[30]

▼ **EXAMPLE 23**

A corporation with common stock outstanding declares a nontaxable dividend payable in rights to subscribe to common stock. Each right entitles the holder to purchase one share of stock for $90. One right is issued for every two shares of stock owned. Fred owns 400 shares of stock purchased two years ago for $15,000. At the time of the distribution of the rights, the market value of the common stock is $100 per share, and the market value of the rights is $8 per right. Fred receives 200 rights. He exercises 100 rights and sells the remaining 100 rights three months later for $9 per right. Fred need not allocate the cost of the original stock to the rights because the value of the rights is less than 15% of the value of the stock ($1,600 ÷ $40,000 = 4%).

If Fred does not allocate his original stock basis to the rights, the tax consequences are as follows:

- Basis in the new stock is $9,000 ($90 × 100). The holding period of the new stock begins on the date the stock was purchased.
- Sale of the rights would produce long-term capital gain of $900 ($9 × 100). The holding period of the rights starts with the date the original 400 shares of stock were acquired.

If Fred elects to allocate basis to the rights, the tax consequences are as follows:

- Basis in the stock is $14,423 [$40,000 ÷ $41,600 (value of rights and stock) × $15,000 (cost of stock)].
- Basis in the rights is $577 [$1,600 (value of rights) ÷ $41,600 (value of rights and stock) × $15,000 (cost of stock)].
- When Fred exercises the rights, his basis in the new stock will be $9,288.50 [$9,000 (cost) + $288.50 (basis in 100 rights)].
- Sale of the rights would produce a long-term capital gain of $611.50 [$900 (selling price) − $288.50 (basis in the remaining 100 rights)]. ▼

STOCK REDEMPTIONS

OVERVIEW

6   LEARNING OBJECTIVE
Identify various stock redemptions that cause payments to shareholders to be treated as sales or exchanges of stock rather than as dividend income.

In a **stock redemption**, a corporation purchases its stock from a shareholder. A stock redemption involves an exchange of a shareholder's stock in the corporation for property of the corporation. A shareholder's sale of stock back to the corporation resembles a sale of the stock to an outsider, or third party. However, the purchaser is the corporation itself rather than an outside third party. While a sale of stock to an outsider is invariably given sale or exchange treatment, only a *qualifying* stock redemption will be treated as a sale for tax purposes.

A stock redemption may have the same effect as a dividend. For example, if a shareholder owns all the stock of a corporation and sells a portion of that stock to

---

[29] § 307(b)(1).   [30] Reg. § 1.307–2.

the corporation, the shareholder's ownership percentage in the corporation will not change. After the redemption, the shareholder still owns all the stock of the corporation. In this situation, the stock redemption resembles a dividend distribution and is taxed as such.

Stock redemptions occur for numerous reasons. A shareholder may want to retire. Rather than the other shareholders purchasing the retiree's stock, the corporation simply redeems all of the shareholder's stock. Similarly, when a shareholder dies, the corporation may purchase the shareholder's stock from the estate. In both cases, having the corporation provide the funds to purchase the stock relieves the remaining shareholders of the need to use their own money. In addition, stock redemptions often occur with respect to property settlements in divorce actions. For example, in a divorce action involving joint ownership of corporate shares, one spouse will usually wind up owning all the stock. By having the corporation redeem the other spouse's shares, the spouse who remains as a shareholder is relieved of the need to obtain funds for the buyout. As a result, the departing spouse receives a part of the property settlement from the corporation.

As mentioned, a qualifying stock redemption provides *sale or exchange* treatment for the shareholder. Sale or exchange treatment permits a shareholder to recover his or her capital investment tax-free and permits the noncorporate shareholder to avoid dividend consequences. Generally, such treatment results in capital gain or loss to the shareholder, which is calculated by subtracting the redeemed stock's adjusted basis from the sum of any money received plus the fair market value of any property received. The shareholder's basis in any property received in exchange for his or her stock in the corporation is equal to the fair market value of the property.

A capital gain is beneficial for a noncorporate shareholder who is in the highest tax brackets as the tax is limited to 28 percent of the gain recognized. It also provides a benefit to a shareholder who has substantial capital losses.

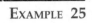

EXAMPLE 24

Abby, a corporate executive, is in the 39.6% tax bracket. She acquired 500 shares of stock in Bluejay Corporation five years ago for $200 a share. In the current year, Bluejay Corporation redeems her shares for $200,000. If the redemption qualifies for sale or exchange treatment, Abby has a long-term capital gain of $100,000 [$200,000 (redemption amount) − $100,000 (cost of the shares)]. Her income tax liability on the $100,000 capital gain is $28,000 ($100,000 × 28%). If the $200,000 stock redemption does not qualify as a sale or exchange, it is treated as dividend income, and Abby's tax liability is $79,200 ($200,000 × 39.6%). Thus, Abby saves $51,200 ($79,200 − $28,000) in income taxes if the corporate payment is a qualifying stock redemption. ▼

EXAMPLE 25

Assume Abby, in Example 24, has a capital loss carryover of $80,000 in the current tax year. If the corporate payment is a qualifying stock redemption, Abby can offset the entire $80,000 capital loss against her $100,000 capital gain. As a result, only $20,000 of the gain is taxed, and her tax liability is only $5,600 ($20,000 × 28%). On the other hand, if the corporate payment does not qualify for sale or exchange treatment, the entire $200,000 is taxed at 39.6%. In addition, assuming no other capital gains in the current year, Abby is able to deduct only $3,000 of the $80,000 capital loss carryover to offset her other (ordinary) income. ▼

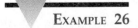

EXAMPLE 26

Assume Abby, in Example 24, is a corporation, that the 500 shares represent a 40% ownership in Bluejay Corporation, and that Abby has corporate taxable income of $350,000 before the payment from Bluejay. If the corporate payment is a qualifying stock redemption for tax purposes, Abby has a capital gain of $100,000 that is subject to tax at 34%, or $34,000. On the other hand, if the $200,000 payment is a dividend, Abby has a dividends received deduction of $160,000 ($200,000 × 80%), so only $40,000 of the payment is taxed. Consequently, Abby's tax liability on the payment is only $13,600 ($40,000 × 34%). ▼

To determine whether a redemption exists for tax purposes, a taxpayer must look to the Code. The label given to the transaction by the parties *or* by state law is not controlling. One provision in the Code provides that if a corporation redeems its stock pursuant to one of four special rules, the redemption is treated as a sale or exchange of a shareholder's stock.[31] Another provision provides that certain distributions of property to a shareholder in exchange for stock included in a decedent's estate are treated as qualifying stock redemptions.[32]

HISTORICAL BACKGROUND

Under earlier law, stock redemptions that constituted ordinary taxable dividends were distinguished from those qualifying for capital gain by the so-called *dividend equivalency rule*. When a redemption was essentially equivalent to a dividend, it did not qualify as a stock redemption. The entire amount received by the shareholder was subject to taxation as ordinary income to the extent of the corporation's E & P.

EXAMPLE 27

Adam owns 100% of the stock of White Corporation. White has E & P of $50,000. Adam sells one-half of his shares to the corporation for $50,000. His basis in the stock he sells is $10,000, and he has held the stock for five years. If the sale of the stock to White Corporation were treated as a qualifying stock redemption, Adam would have a long-term capital gain of $40,000. However, in reality, the distribution is essentially equivalent to a dividend because Adam's percentage of ownership in the corporation has not changed. Therefore, he is deemed to have received a taxable dividend of $50,000. ▼

Current Code provisions are designed to eliminate the uncertainty and subjectivity that resulted from reliance on the dividend equivalency rule. Under the Code, the following major types of stock redemptions qualify for sale or exchange treatment and therefore avoid dividend income consequences:

• Distributions not essentially equivalent to a dividend (subsequently referred to as not essentially equivalent redemptions).

[31] § 302(a).   [32] § 303.

- Distributions substantially disproportionate in terms of shareholder effect (subsequently referred to as disproportionate redemptions).
- Distributions in complete termination of a shareholder's interest (subsequently referred to as complete termination redemptions).
- Distributions to pay a shareholder's death taxes (subsequently referred to as redemptions to pay death taxes).

STOCK ATTRIBUTION RULES

A stock redemption that qualifies for sale or exchange treatment generally must result in a substantial reduction in a shareholder's ownership in the corporation. If this does not occur, proceeds received for a redemption of the shareholder's stock are taxed as ordinary dividend income. In determining whether a shareholder's interest has substantially decreased, the stock ownership of certain related parties is attributed to the shareholder whose stock is redeemed. Thus, one must consider the stock **attribution** rules along with the stock redemption provisions.[33] Under these stock attribution rules, related parties are defined to include immediate family, specifically spouses, children, grandchildren, and parents. Attribution also takes place *from* and *to* partnerships, estates, trusts, and corporations (50 percent or more ownership required in the case of regular corporations). Exhibit 18–1 summarizes the relevant stock attribution rules.

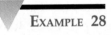

EXAMPLE 28

Larry owns 30% of the stock in Blue Corporation, the other 70% being held by his children. For purposes of the stock attribution rules, Larry is treated as owning 100% of the stock in Blue Corporation. He owns 30% directly and, because of the family attribution rules, 70% indirectly. ▼

▼ **EXHIBIT 18–1**
Stock Attribution Rules

Deemed or Constructive Ownership	
• Individual/family	Stock owned by the spouse, children, grandchildren, and parents (not siblings or grandparents) is considered to be owned by the individual.
• Partnership	Partner is deemed to be the owner of shares owned by a partnership to the extent of the partner's proportionate share in the partnership. Stock of a partner is deemed to be owned in full by a partnership.
• Estate or trust	Beneficiary or heir is deemed to be the owner of shares owned by an estate or trust to the extent of the beneficiary's or heir's proportionate interest in the estate or trust. Stock of a beneficiary or heir is deemed to be owned in full by an estate or trust.
• Corporation	If 50% or more of the stock of a corporation is owned by a taxpayer, the taxpayer is deemed to be the owner of the corporate stock in proportion to the value of the taxpayer's stock in the corporation. Stock of a taxpayer holding a 50%-or-more interest in a corporation is deemed to be owned in full by the corporation.

[33] § 318.

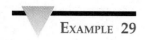

EXAMPLE 29

Chris owns 50% of the stock in Gray Corporation. The other 50% is owned by a partnership in which Chris has a 20% interest. Chris is deemed to own 60% of Gray Corporation: 50% directly and, because of the partnership interest, 10% indirectly. ▼

As discussed later, the *family* attribution rules (refer to Example 28) *may* not apply to stock redemptions in *complete termination* of a shareholder's interest. In addition, these stock attribution rules do not apply to stock redemptions to pay death taxes.

NOT ESSENTIALLY EQUIVALENT REDEMPTIONS

Section 302(b)(1) provides that a redemption qualifies for sale or exchange treatment if it is "not essentially equivalent to a dividend." There are few objective tests to determine when a redemption is or is not essentially equivalent to a dividend. This provision was added to provide specifically for redemptions of preferred stock because shareholders often have no control over when corporations call in such stock.[34] Some courts concluded that such a redemption would receive sale or exchange treatment if there was a **business purpose** for the redemption and there was no tax avoidance scheme to bail out dividends at favorable tax rates.[35] However, an unresolved question was whether the stock attribution rules applied to this provision.

The interpretation of the statutory language on this point was settled by the Supreme Court in *U.S. v. Davis.*[36] The Court agreed with the IRS that the redemption of preferred stock in *Davis* was essentially equivalent to a dividend and was taxable as ordinary income because the attribution rules *should* apply. The Court reasoned that the business purpose of the transaction was not controlling in determining whether a stock redemption was "not essentially equivalent to a dividend." It ruled that a redemption would not qualify under this provision unless there was a "meaningful reduction" in the shareholder's ownership in the redeeming corporation.

Based upon this Supreme Court decision, a redemption will qualify as a **not essentially equivalent redemption** only when the shareholder's interest in the redeeming corporation has been meaningfully reduced. As a result, the facts and circumstances of each case must be assessed.[37] A decrease in the redeeming shareholder's voting control appears to be the most significant indicator of a meaningful reduction,[38] but reductions in the rights of redeeming shareholders to share in corporate earnings or to receive corporate assets upon liquidation are also considered.[39] The **meaningful reduction test** is applied whether common stock or preferred stock is being redeemed.

EXAMPLE 30

Pat owns 58% of the common stock of Green Corporation. After a redemption of part of Pat's stock, he owns 51% of the Green stock. Pat continues to have dominant voting rights in Green; thus, the redemption is treated as essentially equivalent to a dividend, and Pat has ordinary income equal to the entire amount of the distribution assuming adequate E & P. ▼

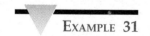

EXAMPLE 31

Brown Corporation redeems 2% of its stock, owned by Maria. Before the redemption, Maria owned 10% of Brown Corporation. In this case, the redemption will likely qualify as "not

[34] See S.Rept. No. 1622, 83d Cong., 2d Sess., at 44.

[35] See, for example, *Kerr v. Comm.,* 64–1 USTC ¶9186, 13 AFTR2d 386, 326 F.2d 225 (CA–9, 1964).

[36] 70–1 USTC ¶9289, 25 AFTR2d 70–827, 90 S.Ct. 1041 (USSC, 1970).

[37] Reg. § 1.302–2(b). See *Mary G. Roebling,* 77 T.C. 30 (1981).

[38] See *Jack Paparo,* 71 T.C. 692 (1979), and *Blanche S. Benjamin,* 66 T.C. 1084 (1976).

[39] See *Grabowski Trust,* 58 T.C. 650 (1972).

essentially equivalent to a dividend." Maria experiences a reduction in her voting rights, her right to participate in current earnings and accumulated surplus, and her right to share in net assets upon liquidation. ▼

If a redemption is treated as an ordinary dividend, the shareholder's basis in the stock redeemed attaches to the remaining stock (or to stock the shareholder owns constructively).[40]

EXAMPLE 32

Fran and Floyd, wife and husband, each own 50 shares in Gray Corporation, representing 100% of the stock of Gray. All the stock was purchased for $50,000. Both Fran and Floyd serve as directors of the corporation. The corporation redeems Floyd's 50 shares. Floyd continues to serve as director of the corporation. The redemption will be treated as a taxable dividend. Floyd's basis in the stock, $25,000, will attach to Fran's stock. She then will have a basis of $50,000 in the 50 shares she owns in Gray. ▼

DISPROPORTIONATE REDEMPTIONS

A redemption of stock qualifies for capital gain treatment under § 302(b)(2) as a **disproportionate redemption** if two conditions are met:

- The distribution must be substantially disproportionate. To be substantially disproportionate, the shareholder must own, after the distribution, *less than* 80 percent of his or her total interest in the corporation before the redemption. For example, if a shareholder has a 60 percent ownership in a corporation that redeems part of the stock, the redemption is substantially disproportionate only if the percentage of ownership after the redemption is less than 48 percent (80 percent of 60 percent).
- The shareholder must own, after the distribution, *less than* 50 percent of the total combined voting power of all classes of stock entitled to vote.

Figure 18–1 provides a graphic presentation of qualifying disproportionate redemptions. In determining a shareholder's percentage of ownership, the attribution rules discussed earlier apply.

EXAMPLE 33

Bob, Carl, and Dan, unrelated individuals, own 30 shares, 30 shares, and 40 shares, respectively, in Wren Corporation. Wren has E & P of $200,000. The corporation redeems 20 shares of Dan's stock for $30,000. Dan paid $200 a share for the stock two years ago. Dan's ownership in Wren Corporation before and after the redemption is as follows:

	Total Shares	Dan's Ownership	Ownership Percentage	80% of Original Ownership
Before redemption	100	40	40% (40 ÷ 100)	32% (80% × 40%)
After redemption	80	20	25% (20 ÷ 80)*	

*Note that the denominator of the fraction is reduced after the redemption (from 100 to 80).

Dan's 25% ownership after the redemption meets both tests of § 302(b)(2). It is less than 80% of his original ownership and less than 50% of the total voting power. The distribution qualifies as a stock redemption that receives sale or exchange treatment. Therefore, Dan has a long-term capital gain of $26,000 [$30,000 − $4,000 (20 shares × $200)]. ▼

---

[40] Reg. § 1.302–2(c).

▼ **FIGURE 18–1**
Qualifying Disproportionate
Redemptions

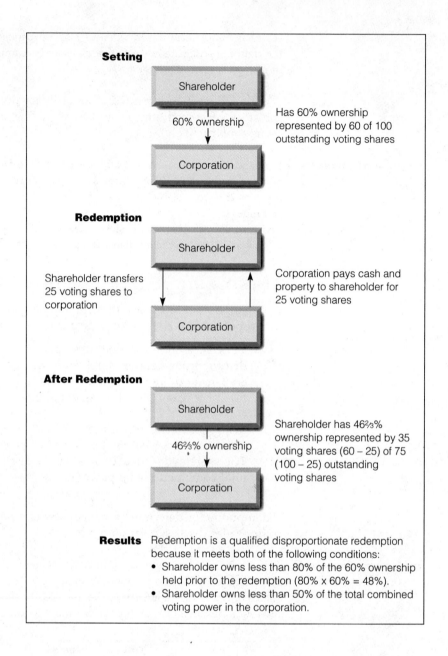

Setting

Shareholder

60% ownership

Corporation

Has 60% ownership
represented by 60 of 100
outstanding voting shares

Redemption

Shareholder

Shareholder transfers
25 voting shares to
corporation

Corporation pays cash and
property to shareholder for
25 voting shares

Corporation

After Redemption

Shareholder

46⅔% ownership

Corporation

Shareholder has 46⅔%
ownership represented by 35
voting shares (60 – 25) of 75
(100 – 25) outstanding
voting shares

Results   Redemption is a qualified disproportionate redemption
because it meets both of the following conditions:
• Shareholder owns less than 80% of the 60% ownership
  held prior to the redemption (80% x 60% = 48%).
• Shareholder owns less than 50% of the total combined
  voting power in the corporation.

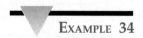

EXAMPLE 34

Given the situation in Example 33, assume instead that Carl and Dan are father and son. The redemption described previously would not qualify for sale or exchange treatment because of the effect of the attribution rules. Dan is deemed to own Carl's stock so after the redemption, he would have 50 shares of a total of 80 shares, more than 50% ownership. He would also fail the 80% test. Dan's ownership in Wren Corporation is computed as follows:

	Total Shares	Dan's Direct Ownership	Carl's Ownership	Dan's Direct and Indirect Ownership	Ownership Percentage	80% of Original Ownership
Before redemption	100	40	30	70	70% (70 ÷ 100)	56% (80% × 70%)
After redemption	80	20	30	50	62.5% (50 ÷ 80)	

Dan's direct and indirect ownership of 62.5% fails to meet either of the tests of § 302(b)(2). Dan owns more than 80% of his original ownership and more than 50% of the voting stock. Thus, the redemption does not qualify for sale or exchange treatment and results in a taxable dividend of $30,000 to Dan, assuming ample E & P exists. ▼

If a redemption is not substantially disproportionate, it may still qualify as a not essentially equivalent redemption if it meets the "meaningful reduction" test. Refer to Example 31. A reduction in voting control when the shareholder does not have a majority controlling interest will generally qualify as a not essentially equivalent redemption. However, the stock attribution rules apply in determining whether there has been a reduction in voting control.

ETHICAL
CONSIDERATIONS

Convertible Preferred Stock—Conversion versus Redemption

A corporation, which does not sell its stock publicly, sold some convertible preferred stock a few years ago to a small group of passive investors. The holders of the preferred stock have the option of converting the preferred stock into common stock at anytime they desire. Because the corporation has developed a successful new invention that has not become known outside the company, the board of directors expects the corporation's earnings will grow substantially in the future. The directors, all of whom own common stock in the corporation, would like to redeem the preferred stock so they can discontinue paying dividends to the preferred shareholders and to prevent the preferred shareholders from sharing in the corporation's future earnings. The board of directors votes to pay the preferred shareholders a premium for redeeming their stock and notifies them that the corporation will redeem their stock unless they instruct otherwise. Did the board of directors act in an ethical manner?

COMPLETE TERMINATION REDEMPTIONS

If a shareholder terminates his or her *entire* stock ownership in a corporation through a stock redemption, the redemption may qualify for sale or exchange treatment. Often a complete termination may not qualify as a disproportionate redemption because the constructive ownership rules are applied. The difference in the two provisions is that the *family* attribution rules do not apply to a **complete termination redemption.** This favorable treatment occurs only if *both* of the following conditions are met:

- The former shareholder has no interest, other than that of a creditor, in the corporation after the redemption (including an interest as an officer, director, or employee) for at least 10 years.
- The former shareholder files an agreement to notify the IRS of any acquisition within the 10-year period and to retain all necessary records pertaining to the redemption during this time period.

A shareholder can reacquire an interest in the corporation by bequest or inheritance, but in no other manner. The required agreement should be in the form of a separate statement signed by the shareholder and attached to the return for the year in which the redemption occurs. The agreement should state that the shareholder agrees to notify the appropriate District Director within 30 days of reacquiring an interest in the corporation within the 10-year period following the redemption.

EXAMPLE 35

The stock of Green Corporation is held as follows: 40 shares by Kevin (basis of $30,000), 30 shares by Keith (Kevin's son), and 30 shares by Helen (Kevin's wife). At a time when each share is worth $2,000, Green Corporation redeems Kevin's 40 shares for $80,000. Although Kevin filed the necessary agreement with the IRS, he remains an employee of Green at a salary of $12,000. This redemption does not qualify as a complete termination redemption because of Kevin's continued employment status. Consequently, and to the extent of Green Corporation's E & P, the distribution proceeds are a dividend to Kevin.

However, had Kevin not remained as an employee, he would have recognized $50,000 of capital gain because the family attribution rules may be waived. If this waiver were not allowed, Kevin would have been deemed the owner of Helen's and Keith's stock, and the distribution would have been treated as a dividend to the extent of Green's E & P. ▼

ETHICAL CONSIDERATIONS

A Friend in Need

Nine years ago, Orange Corporation redeemed all of Dan's shares in the corporation. Dan reported the transaction as a qualified complete termination redemption. At that time, Dan's children held the remaining shares in Orange. You were Dan's CPA at the time of the redemption.

Now you learn that Dan is currently unemployed and destitute and that he has received a prohibited interest in Orange Corporation during the current year. As Dan's former CPA and a friend, you know that Dan should inform the IRS that the transaction of nine years ago should be recast as a dividend distribution. This will mean that Dan will owe additional income taxes, which will be a real problem because Dan has no cash. How should you proceed?

REDEMPTIONS TO PAY DEATH TAXES

Section 303 provides sale or exchange treatment when an executor redeems stock in a closely held corporation that represents a substantial amount of the estate of a shareholder-decedent. The purpose of such a redemption is to provide the estate with liquidity. A redemption is often necessary because stock in a closely held corporation is generally not marketable. Although it could be redeemed under the other redemption rules, the transaction would run the risk of being treated as a dividend because of the attribution rules. The special rule under § 303, allowing sale or exchange treatment in a **redemption to pay death taxes,** alleviates this problem.

The rule providing for sale or exchange treatment in redemptions to pay death taxes is an exception to the redemption rules just discussed. If a stock redemption qualifies as a redemption to pay death taxes, the other redemption provisions do not apply. The distribution will be treated as a sale or exchange regardless of whether it is substantially disproportionate or is not essentially equivalent to a dividend. However, this special treatment is limited to the sum of the death taxes and funeral and administration expenses. Also, it is available only to redemptions from those shareholders whose interests in the estate are reduced by the payment of death taxes and funeral and administration expenses.

In a redemption to pay death taxes, the redemption price generally equals the basis of the stock. Under the step-up in basis rules, the income tax basis of property owned by a decedent's estate becomes the property's fair market value on the date of death (or alternate valuation date if available and if elected).[41] When this so-called step-up or step-down in basis that occurs at death (refer to Chapter 12) equals the redemption price, the exchange is free of any income tax consequences to the shareholder's estate.

Section 303 applies to a distribution made with respect to stock of a corporation when the value of the stock in the gross estate of a decedent exceeds 35 percent of the value of the adjusted gross estate. (For a definition of "gross estate" and "adjusted gross estate," see the Glossary of Tax Terms in Appendix C.)

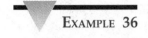

EXAMPLE 36

Juan's adjusted gross estate is $900,000. The death taxes and funeral and administration expenses of the estate total $200,000. Included in the estate is stock in Yellow Corporation, a closely held corporation, valued at $340,000. Juan had acquired the stock years ago at a cost of $60,000. Yellow redeems $200,000 of the stock from Juan's estate. Because the value of the Yellow stock in Juan's estate exceeds the 35% threshold ($340,000 ÷ $900,000 = 37.8%), the redemption qualifies under § 303 as a sale or exchange instead of being treated as a dividend to Juan's estate. The basis rules apply to give the stock a step-up in basis. Consequently, there is no recognized gain on the redemption [$200,000 (amount realized) − $200,000 (stock basis)]. ▼

In determining whether the value of stock in a corporation exceeds 35 percent of the value of the adjusted gross estate of a decedent, the stock of two or more corporations may be treated as the stock of a single corporation. Stock in corporations in which the decedent held a 20 percent or more interest is treated as stock in a single corporation for this purpose.[42]

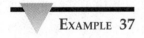

EXAMPLE 37

The adjusted gross estate of a decedent is $300,000. The gross estate includes stock in Orange and Red Corporations valued at $100,000 and $80,000, respectively. Unless the two corporations are treated as a single corporation, § 303 does not apply to a redemption of the stock of either corporation. Assuming the decedent owned all the stock of Orange Corporation and 80% of the stock of Red, § 303 applies because 20% or more of the value of the stock of both corporations may be included in the decedent's estate. The 35% test is met when the Orange and Red stock are treated as that of a single corporation [($100,000 + $80,000) ÷ $300,000 = 60%]. ▼

Qualifying redemptions to pay death taxes are also subject to time limitations. For example, sale or exchange treatment under this rule applies only to redemptions made within 90 days after the expiration of the period of limitations for the assessment of the Federal estate tax. If a timely petition for a redetermination of an estate tax deficiency is filed with the U.S. Tax Court, the applicable period for a § 303 redemption is extended to 60 days after the Court's decision becomes final.[43]

EFFECT ON THE CORPORATION REDEEMING ITS STOCK

Having considered some of the different types of stock redemptions that will produce sale or exchange treatment for a shareholder, what is the tax effect to the corporation redeeming its stock? If the corporation uses property to carry out the

---

[41] § 1014.
[42] § 303(b)(2)(B).

[43] § 303(b)(1).

TAX IN THE NEWS

ARE LOAN FEES IN A STOCK REDEMPTION DEDUCTIBLE?

The courts disagree as to whether *loan fees* incurred to redeem stock are deductible. A U.S. Court of Appeals ruled they are deductible while the Tax Court decided otherwise. The appeals court held that Kroy, Inc., a manufacturer of office products, could amortize and deduct more than $4 million in fees it paid a bank to borrow $60 million to redeem its stock in a leveraged buyout. The IRS had contended only *interest* is deductible and disallowed the deduction for the loan fees. In a later case, the Tax Court agreed with the IRS and did not permit Fort Howard Corporation, a paper manufacturer, to deduct its fees. What approach should companies take in the future? As news analysts have pointed out, the *Kroy* decision is the "highest and best law," but the IRS will continue to disallow such deductions.

redemption, is gain or loss recognized on the distribution? Furthermore, what effect does the redemption have on the corporation's E & P? These matters are discussed in the following paragraphs.

Recognition of Gain or Loss by the Corporation.   Section 311 provides that corporations are taxed on all distributions of appreciated property whether in the form of a property dividend or a stock redemption. Losses, however, are not recognized.[44] When distributed property is subject to a corporate liability, the fair market value of that property is treated as not being less than the amount of the liability.

EXAMPLE 38

To carry out a redemption, Bluebird Corporation transfers land (basis of $80,000, fair market value of $300,000) to a shareholder's estate. Bluebird has a recognized gain of $220,000 ($300,000 – $80,000). If the value of the property distributed was less than its adjusted basis, the realized loss would not be recognized. ▼

Because a corporation cannot recognize a loss on a stock redemption, a corporation should not use property that has declined in value as consideration in the redemption of a shareholder's stock. Instead, the corporation should sell the property in a taxable transaction in which it can generate a loss.

Certain expenses a corporation incurs in redeeming its stock are nonamortizable capital expenditures.[45] Such expenses include stock purchase premiums; amounts paid to a shareholder for the shareholder's agreement not to reacquire stock in the corporation for a specified time; and legal, accounting, transfer agent, brokerage, and appraisal fees. However, interest payments incurred on funds borrowed to redeem stock are deductible.

Effect on Earnings and Profits.   A qualified stock redemption reduces the E & P account of a corporation in an amount not in excess of the ratable share of the distributing corporation's E & P that is attributable to the stock redeemed.[46]

[44]§ 311(a).
[45]§ 162(k).
[46]§ 312(n)(7).

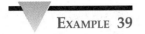

EXAMPLE 39

Green Corporation has 100 shares of stock outstanding. It redeems 30 shares for $100,000 at a time when it has paid-in capital of $120,000 and E & P of $150,000. The charge to E & P is 30% of the amount in the E & P account ($45,000), and the remainder of the redemption price ($55,000) is a reduction of the capital account. If instead the 30 shares were redeemed for $40,000, the charge to E & P would be limited to $40,000, the amount Green paid for the stock. ▼

ETHICAL
CONSIDERATIONS

Directors' Legal Fees in a Fraud Case

Two former directors of a large corporation were sued for fraud by a former shareholder over a stock redemption agreement. The former shareholder contended the directors had concealed from her a corporate restructuring that would have entitled her to additional consideration. The directors incurred substantial legal fees in defending themselves from the fraud charge. They requested in writing that the corporation reimburse them for their legal fees. As members of the board of directors, they convinced the remaining members of the board that the corporation should indemnify them for their legal fees. The corporation then deducted the legal fees on the corporate income tax return. Should the corporation claim such a deduction?

OTHER CORPORATE DISTRIBUTIONS

Partial liquidations of a corporation, if in compliance with the statutory requirements of § 302(e), will result in sale or exchange treatment to noncorporate shareholders. Distributions of stock and securities of a controlled corporation to the shareholders of the parent corporation will be free of any tax consequences if they fall under § 355. Both of these types of corporate distributions are similar to stock redemptions and dividend distributions in some respects but are not discussed here because of their limited applicability.

TAX PLANNING
CONSIDERATIONS

CORPORATE DISTRIBUTIONS

In connection with the discussion of corporate distributions, the following points need reinforcement:

7 LEARNING OBJECTIVE
Identify tax planning opportunities available to minimize the income tax impact in corporate distributions, constructive dividends, and stock redemptions.

- Because E & P is the measure of dividend income, its periodic determination is essential to corporate planning. Thus, an E & P account should be established and maintained, particularly if the possibility exists that a corporate distribution might be a return of capital.
- Accumulated E & P is the sum of all past years' current E & P. There is no statute of limitations on the computation of E & P. The IRS can, for example, redetermine a corporation's current E & P for a tax year long since passed. Such a change affects accumulated E & P and has a direct impact on the taxability of current distributions to shareholders.
- Distributions can be manipulated to avoid or minimize dividend exposure.

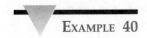

EXAMPLE 40

After several unprofitable years, Brown Corporation has a deficit in accumulated E & P of $100,000 as of January 1, 1996. Starting in 1996, Brown expects to generate annual E & P of $50,000 for the next four years and would like to distribute this amount to its shareholders.

CONCEPT SUMMARY 18–2

Corporate Distributions

1. Without a special provision, corporate distributions are taxed as dividend income to the recipient shareholders to the extent of the distributing corporation's E & P accumulated since February 28, 1913, or to the extent of current E & P. Any excess is treated as a return of capital to the extent of the shareholder's basis in the stock and, thereafter, as capital gain.
2. Property distributions are considered dividends (taxed as noted in item 1) in the amount of their fair market value. The amount deemed distributed is reduced by any liabilities on the property distributed. The shareholder's basis in the property is its fair market value.
3. Earnings and profits of a corporation are increased by corporate earnings for the taxable year computed in the same manner as the corporation computes its taxable income. As a general rule, the account is increased for all items of income, whether taxed or not, and reduced by all items of expense, whether deductible or not. Refer to Concept Summary 18–1 for a summary of the effect of certain transactions on taxable income in arriving at current E & P.
4. A corporation recognizes gain, but not loss, on distributions of property to its shareholders. E & P of the distributing corporation is reduced by the amount of money distributed or by the greater of the fair market value or the adjusted basis of property distributed less the amount of any liability applicable to the distributed property.
5. As a general rule, stock dividends or stock rights (representing stock in the distributing corporation) are not taxed, with certain exceptions.
6. Stock redemptions that qualify under § 302(b) are given sale or exchange treatment. This provision requires that such distributions either be substantially disproportionate or not be essentially equivalent to a dividend. In determining whether a transaction is a not essentially equivalent redemption or a disproportionate redemption, the attribution rules apply. However, in a complete termination redemption, the family attribution rules are waived if certain conditions are met.
7. If stock included in a decedent's estate represents more than 35% of the adjusted gross estate, § 303 provides automatic sale or exchange treatment on its redemption.
8. A corporation is taxed on the appreciation of property distributed in redemption of its stock.
9. In a stock redemption, the E & P account of the distributing corporation is reduced in proportion to the amount of the corporation's outstanding stock that is redeemed.

The corporation's cash position (for dividend purposes) will correspond to the current E & P generated. Compare the following possibilities:

1. On December 31 of 1996, 1997, 1998, and 1999, Brown Corporation distributes a cash dividend of $50,000.
2. On December 31 of 1997 and 1999, Brown Corporation distributes a cash dividend of $100,000.

The two alternatives are illustrated as follows:

Year	Accumulated E & P (First of Year)	Current E & P	Distribution	Amount of Dividend
		Alternative 1		
1996	($100,000)	$50,000	$50,000	$50,000
1997	(100,000)	50,000	50,000	50,000
1998	(100,000)	50,000	50,000	50,000
1999	(100,000)	50,000	50,000	50,000

	Alternative 2			
1996	($100,000)	$50,000	$ –0–	$ –0–
1997	(50,000)	50,000	100,000	50,000
1998	(50,000)	50,000	–0–	–0–
1999	–0–	50,000	100,000	50,000

Alternative 1 leads to an overall result of $200,000 in dividend income since each $50,000 distribution is fully covered by current E & P. Alternative 2, however, results in only $100,000 of dividend income to the shareholders. The remaining $100,000 is a return of capital. Why? At the time Brown Corporation made its first distribution of $100,000 on December 31, 1997, it had a deficit of $50,000 in accumulated E & P (the original deficit of $100,000 is reduced by the $50,000 of current E & P from 1996). Consequently, the $100,000 distribution yields a $50,000 dividend (the current E & P for 1997) and $50,000 as a return of capital. As of January 1, 1998, Brown's accumulated E & P now has a deficit balance of $50,000 (a distribution cannot increase a deficit in E & P). Add in $50,000 of current E & P from 1998, and the balance as of January 1, 1999, is zero. Thus, the second distribution of $100,000 made on December 31, 1999, also yields $50,000 of dividends (the current E & P for 1999) and $50,000 as a return of capital. ▼

CONSTRUCTIVE DIVIDENDS

Tax planning can be particularly effective in avoiding constructive dividend situations. Shareholders should try to structure their dealings with the corporation on an arm's length basis. For example, reasonable rent should be paid for the use of corporate property, and a fair price should be paid for its purchase. The parties should make every effort to support the amount involved with appraisal data or market information obtained from reliable sources at or close to the time of the transaction. Dealings between shareholders and a closely held corporation should be as formal as possible. In the case of loans to shareholders, for example, the parties should provide for an adequate rate of interest, written evidence of the debt, and a realistic repayment schedule that is both arranged and followed.

If shareholders wish to bail out corporate profits in a form deductible to the corporation, a balanced mix of the possible alternatives lessens the risk of disallowance by the IRS. Rent for the use of shareholder property, interest on amounts borrowed from shareholders, or salaries for services rendered by shareholders are all feasible substitutes for dividend distributions. But overdoing any one approach may attract the attention of the IRS. Too much interest, for example, may mean the corporation is thinly capitalized, and some of the debt may be equity investment.

Much can be done to protect against the disallowance of corporate deductions for compensation that is determined to be unreasonable in amount. Example 41 is an illustration, all too common in a family corporation, of what *not* to do.

EXAMPLE 41

Crow Corporation is wholly owned by Cole. Corporate employees and annual salaries include Mrs. Cole ($15,000), Cole, Jr. ($10,000), Cole ($80,000), and Ed ($40,000). The operation of Crow Corporation is shared about equally between Cole and Ed (an unrelated party). Mrs. Cole (Cole's wife) performed significant services for the corporation during the corporation's formative years but now merely attends the annual meeting of the board of directors. Cole, Jr. (Cole's son), is a full-time student and occasionally signs papers for the corporation in his capacity as treasurer. Crow Corporation has not distributed a dividend for 10 years, although it has accumulated substantial E & P. What is wrong with this situation?

- Mrs. Cole's salary seems vulnerable unless proof is available that some or all of her $15,000 annual salary is payment for services rendered to the corporation in prior years (i.e., she was underpaid for those years).[47]
- Cole, Jr.'s salary is also vulnerable; he does not appear to earn the $10,000 paid to him by the corporation. True, neither Cole, Jr., nor Mrs. Cole is a shareholder, but each one's relationship to Cole is enough of a tie-in to raise the unreasonable compensation issue.
- Cole's salary appears susceptible to challenge. Why is he receiving $40,000 more than Ed when it appears they share equally in the operation of the corporation?
- Crow Corporation has not distributed dividends for 10 years, although it is capable of doing so. ▼

**ETHICAL
CONSIDERATIONS**

Disallowed Deductions

U pon audit of Eagle Corporation's income tax return for tax year 1995, the IRS disallowed as a deduction $250,000 of the $600,000 salary paid to Ron, Eagle's president and principal shareholder. The disallowed salary was deemed to be unreasonable. In 1996, Eagle Corporation again pays Ron a salary of $600,000. Can Eagle Corporation deduct this salary on its 1996 tax return or is it bound by the audit conducted by the IRS for the prior year?

STOCK REDEMPTIONS

Stock redemptions offer several possibilities for tax planning:

- A not essentially equivalent redemption provides minimal utility and generally should be relied upon only as a last resort. Instead, the redemption should be structured to fit one of the safe harbors. These include disproportionate redemptions, complete termination redemptions, and redemptions to pay death taxes.
- For a family corporation in which all of the shareholders are related to each other, the only hope of achieving sale or exchange treatment may lie in the use of a redemption that completely terminates a shareholder's interest or one that follows a shareholder's death. In a complete termination redemption, be careful that the family stock attribution rules are avoided. Here, strict compliance with the requirements (e.g., the withdrawing shareholder does not continue as an employee of the corporation and does not reacquire an interest in the corporation within 10 years) is crucial.
- The alternative to a successful stock redemption is dividend treatment of the distribution. But do not conclude that a dividend is always undesirable from a tax standpoint. Suppose the distributing corporation has little, if any, E & P. Or the distributee-shareholder is another corporation. In the latter situation, dividend treatment may be preferred because of the availability of the dividends received deduction.

---

[47] See, for example, *R. J. Nicoll Co.*, 59 T.C. 37 (1972).

- When using the special redemption rules following a shareholder's death, the amount to be sheltered from dividend treatment is limited to the sum of death taxes and certain estate administration expenses. However, a redemption in excess of the limitation does not destroy the applicability of this provision.
- The timing and sequence of a redemption should be handled carefully.

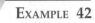

EXAMPLE 42

Bluejay Corporation's stock is held as follows: Abby (60 shares), Antonio (20 shares), and Ali (20 shares). Abby, Antonio, and Ali are not related to each other. The corporation redeems 24 of Abby's shares. Shortly thereafter, it redeems 5 of Antonio's shares. Does Abby's redemption qualify as a disproportionate redemption? Taken in isolation, it would appear to meet the 80% and 50% tests. Yet, if the IRS takes into account the later redemption of Antonio's shares, Abby has not satisfied the 50% test; she still owns ³⁶/₇₁ of the corporation after both redemptions. A greater time lag between the two redemptions places Abby in a better position to argue against collapsing the series of redemptions into one. ▼

KEY TERMS

Accumulated earnings and profits, 18–6

Attribution, 18–19

Business purpose, 18–20

Complete termination redemption, 18–23

Constructive dividend, 18–11

Current earnings and profits, 18–6

Disproportionate redemption, 18–21

Earnings and profits (E & P), 18–3

Meaningful reduction test, 18–20

Not essentially equivalent redemption, 18–20

Property dividend, 18–9

Redemption to pay death taxes, 18–24

Stock dividend, 18–14

Stock redemption, 18–16

Stock rights, 18–15

Unreasonable compensation, 18–12

PROBLEM

MATERIALS

DISCUSSION QUESTIONS

1. How are regular distributions of a corporation's earnings taxed to a shareholder?

2. What is meant by the term *earnings and profits*?

3. Describe the effect of a distribution in a year when the distributing corporation has any of the following:
   a. A deficit in accumulated E & P and a positive amount in current E & P.
   b. A positive amount in accumulated E & P and a deficit in current E & P.
   c. A deficit in both current and accumulated E & P.
   d. A positive amount in both current and accumulated E & P.

4. How do gains and losses from property transactions affect the determination of E & P?

5. Five years ago, a corporation determined its current E & P to be $100,000. In the current year, it makes a distribution of $200,000 to its shareholders. The IRS contends that the current E & P of the corporation five years ago was really $150,000.
   a. Can the IRS successfully make this contention?
   b. What difference would the additional $50,000 in E & P make?

6. The suggestion is made that any distributions to shareholders by a calendar year corporation should take place on January 1 before the corporation has generated any current E & P. Assess the validity of this suggestion.

7. Crane Corporation has a fiscal year of July 1 through June 30 for tax purposes. Gail, Crane's sole shareholder, uses a calendar year. As of July 1, 1996, Crane has a zero balance in its accumulated E & P account. For fiscal year 1996–1997, Crane has a $10,000 operating loss. On November 1, 1996, Crane distributes $20,000 to Gail. May Gail exclude the $20,000 from her taxable income in 1996?

8. Why would a corporation distribute a property dividend?

9. A corporation distributed property (adjusted basis of $100,000 and fair market value of $80,000) to its shareholders. Has the corporation acted wisely? Why or why not?

10. Does the distributing corporation recognize gain or loss when it distributes property as a dividend to its shareholders? Explain.

11. How is a property dividend treated for tax purposes both to the distributing corporation and to the shareholders?

12. Yellow Corporation distributes $50,000 to each of its three shareholders, Juan, Gabriella, and Hal. Discuss the issues involved in determining how the distribution is treated tax-wise both to the shareholders and to Yellow Corporation.

13. Tina is the president and sole shareholder of Green Corporation. She is paid a salary of $250,000 in the current year. Green Corporation also advances her $50,000 as an interest-free loan. What are the tax issues?

14. When are stock dividends taxable?

15. How are nontaxable stock rights handled for tax purposes? Taxable stock rights?

16. Whether compensation paid to a corporate employee is reasonable is a question of fact to be determined from the surrounding circumstances. How would the resolution of this problem be affected by each of the following factors?
   a. The employee is not a shareholder but is related to the sole owner of the corporate employer.
   b. The shareholder-employee never completed high school.
   c. The shareholder-employee is a full-time college student.
   d. The shareholder-employee was underpaid for her services during the formative period of the corporate employer.
   e. The corporate employer pays a nominal dividend each year.
   f. Year-end bonuses are paid to all shareholder-employees.

17. Falcon Corporation is wholly owned by Carmen Corporation employees and their annual salaries include Carmen, $150,000; Alicia, Carmen's daughter, $60,000; Lupe, Carmen's son, $50,000; and Susan, $30,000. Falcon's operation is shared about equally between Carmen and Susan (an unrelated party). Alicia and Lupe are full-time college students at a university about 200 miles away. Falcon Corporation has substantial E & P but has not distributed a dividend in the past six years. Discuss problems related to Falcon's salary arrangement.

18. Lana wants to retire and sell her shares in Brown Corporation to Brown's remaining shareholders, Jack and Ivan. Why might it be preferable for Brown Corporation to redeem Lana's shares rather than for Jack and Ivan to purchase them?

19. What effect does state law have on the determination of whether a corporate distribution qualifies as a stock redemption for tax purposes?

20. Under the attribution rules, a shareholder is deemed to own the stock of certain "related parties." What family members are considered "related parties" for this purpose?

21. Do the stock attribution rules apply to stock redemptions in complete termination of a shareholder's interest? Explain.

22. Wilma owns 200 shares in Cardinal Corporation, which represents a 60% interest in Cardinal. Wilma also owns 100 shares in Wren Corporation. Cardinal Corporation owns 100 shares in Wren Corporation. Compare Wilma's deemed stock ownership in Wren Corporation with Cardinal's deemed ownership in Wren.

23. Explain the application of the "meaningful reduction test" in a not essentially equivalent redemption.

24. Two years ago José transferred property he had used in his sole proprietorship to Cardinal Corporation, a newly formed corporation, for 50 shares of Cardinal stock. The property had an adjusted basis of $300,000 and a fair market value of $800,000. Six months later José's friend, Peggy, transferred property she had used in her sole proprietorship to Cardinal Corporation for 50 shares of Cardinal stock and cash of $100,000. Her property had an adjusted basis of $150,000 and a value of $900,000. Both José and Peggy serve on Cardinal's board of directors. In addition, Peggy has a contract with Cardinal to perform services to the corporation. In the current year, Cardinal Corporation redeems all of Peggy's Cardinal stock for property with a probable value of $1,400,000. What issues must you consider?

25. Under what circumstances is a redemption to pay death taxes available? What is the tax effect of such a transaction?

26. "A redemption to pay death taxes usually results in no gain or loss being recognized by the estate." Evaluate this statement.

27. Abby and her daughter, Ann, who are the only shareholders of Bluebird Corporation, each paid $100,000 four years ago for their shares in Bluebird. Abby also owns 20% of the stock in Redbird Corporation. The Redbird stock is worth $500,000, and Abby's basis in the stock is $50,000. Abby died in the current year leaving all her property to her husband, Gary, but Ann wants to be the sole shareholder of Bluebird Corporation. Bluebird has assets worth $2 million (basis of $700,000) and E & P of $1 million. Abby's estate is worth approximately $4 million. Abby had made gifts during her lifetime to Ann. Identify the relevant tax issues.

28. A corporation distributes $100,000 to a shareholder in complete redemption of the shareholder's stock. Can the corporation reduce its E & P by this amount? Explain.

PROBLEMS

29. At the beginning of the year, Green Corporation (a calendar year taxpayer) has accumulated E & P of $75,000. Its current E & P is $45,000. During the year, Green distributes $135,000 ($67,500 each) to its equal shareholders, Pat and Chris. Pat has a basis of $12,000 in her stock, and Chris has a basis of $3,000 in his stock. How will the $135,000 distribution be treated for tax purposes?

30. In 1996, Cardinal Corporation received dividend income of $100,000 from a corporation in which Cardinal holds a 5% interest. Cardinal also received interest income of $20,000 from municipal bonds. The municipality used the proceeds from the sale of the bonds to construct a needed facility to house city documents and to provide office space for several city officials. Cardinal borrowed funds to purchase the municipal bonds and paid $18,000 in interest on the loan in 1996. Cardinal's taxable income exclusive of the items noted above was $120,000. The $120,000 also represents current E & P.
    a. What is Cardinal Corporation's taxable income for 1996 after considering the dividend income, the interest from the municipal bonds, and the interest paid on the indebtedness to purchase the municipals?
    b. What is Cardinal Corporation's E & P as of December 31, 1996, if its E & P account balance was $30,000 as of January 1, 1996?

31. Orange Corporation has a deficit in E & P of $90,000 on January 1, 1996. Without considering a land sale in 1996, Orange has a tax loss of $180,000 that increases the deficit in E & P by that amount. On November 15, 1996, the corporation sold a tract of land in

consideration of a $1,800,000 note to be paid in five equal installments; the first installment is due and payable on December 15, 1997. The land had a tax basis to Orange of $450,000. Because Orange did not elect out of the installment method, it did not include any of the $1,350,000 gain on the sale of the land in its taxable income for 1996. If Orange distributes $200,000 to its shareholder, Pat, on December 31, 1996, how must Pat report the $200,000 for tax purposes? Pat has a basis of $150,000 in his Orange stock.

32. Complete the following schedule for each case. Assume the shareholder has an ample basis in the stock investment.

Accumulated E & P Beginning of Year	Current E & P	Cash Distributions (All on Last Day of Year)	Amount Taxable	Return of Capital
a. $ 80,000	($ 20,000)	$100,000	$ _____	$ _____
b. (100,000)	60,000	80,000	_____	_____
c. 60,000	100,000	140,000	_____	_____
d. 120,000	(40,000)	90,000	_____	_____

e. Same as (d), except the distribution of $90,000 is made on June 30 and the corporation uses the calendar year for tax purposes.   _____ _____

33. Complete the following schedule for each case. Assume the shareholder has an ample basis in the stock investment.

Accumulated E & P Beginning of Year	Current E & P	Cash Distributions (All on Last Day of Year)	Amount Taxable	Return of Capital
a. $150,000	$ 40,000	$120,000	$ _____	$ _____
b. 40,000	80,000	90,000	_____	_____
c. (180,000)	100,000	60,000	_____	_____
d. 120,000	(110,000)	80,000	_____	_____

e. Same as (d), except the distribution of $80,000 is made on June 30 and the corporation uses the calendar year for tax purposes.   _____ _____

34. Diego, the sole shareholder of Wren Corporation, had a basis of $30,000 in the stock in Wren that he sold to Eli on July 30, 1996, for $180,000. Wren had accumulated E & P of $75,000 on January 1, 1996, and current E & P (for 1996) of $60,000. During 1996, Wren made the following distributions: $120,000 cash to Diego on July 1, 1996, and $120,000 cash to Eli on December 30, 1996. How will the distributions be taxed to Diego and to Eli? What gain will Diego recognize on the sale of his stock to Eli?

35. Indicate in each of the following independent situations the effect on taxable income and E & P, stating the amount of any increase (or decrease) as a result of the transaction. (In determining the effect on E & P, assume E & P has already been increased by current taxable income.)

	Transaction	Taxable Income Increase (Decrease)	E & P Increase (Decrease)
a.	Receipt of $15,000 tax-exempt income	_____	_____
b.	Payment of $15,150 Federal income taxes	_____	_____
c.	Collection of $100,000 on life insurance policy on corporate president (assume no cash surrender value)	_____	_____
d.	Charitable contribution, $30,000, with $20,000 allowable as a deduction in the current tax year	_____	_____
e.	Deduction of remaining $10,000 charitable contribution in succeeding year	_____	_____
f.	Realized gain on involuntary conversion of $200,000 ($30,000 of gain is recognized)	_____	_____

36. Indicate in each of the following independent situations the effect on taxable income and E & P, stating the amount of any increase (or decrease) as a result of the transaction. (In determining the effect on E & P, assume E & P has already been increased by current taxable income.)

	Transaction	Taxable Income Increase (Decrease)	E & P Increase (Decrease)
a.	Intangible drilling costs incurred on January 1 of the current year and deductible from current taxable income in the amount of $50,000	_____	_____
b.	Sale of unimproved real estate, basis of $200,000, fair market value of $800,000 (no election out of installment method; payments in year of sale total $40,000)	_____	_____
c.	Accelerated depreciation of $70,000 (straight-line would have been $40,000)	_____	_____
d.	Sale of equipment to 100%-owned corporation (adjusted basis was $120,000 and selling price was $50,000)	_____	_____

37. Thrush Corporation, with E & P of $300,000, distributes property worth $70,000, adjusted basis of $100,000, to Crow, a corporate shareholder. The property is subject to a liability of $15,000, which Crow assumes.
    a. What is the amount of dividend income to Crow?
    b. What is Crow's basis in the property it received?
    c. How does the distribution affect Thrush Corporation's E & P account?

38. At the beginning of the current year, Dove Corporation (a calendar year taxpayer) has accumulated E & P of $40,000. During the year, Dove incurs a $30,000 loss from operations that accrued ratably. On July 1, Dove distributes $35,000 in cash to Matt, its sole shareholder. How will the $35,000 be taxed to Matt?

39. Lark Corporation has E & P of $100,000. It distributes equipment with a fair market value of $90,000 (adjusted basis of $20,000) to its sole shareholder, Mary. The land is subject to a liability of $15,000, which Mary assumes. What are the tax consequences to Lark Corporation and to Mary?

40. Black Corporation has two equal shareholders, Bonnie and Ann. Bonnie acquired her Black stock three years ago by transferring property worth $500,000, basis of $100,000, for 50 shares of the stock. Ann acquired 50 shares in Black Corporation two years ago by transferring property worth $520,000, basis of $50,000. Black Corporation's accumulated E & P as of January 1 of the current year is $210,000. On March 1 of the current year, the corporation distributed to Bonnie property worth $100,000, basis to Black of $20,000. It distributed cash of $100,000 to Ann. On July 1 of the current year, Ann sold her stock to Bob for $700,000. On December 1 of the current year, Black distributed cash of $50,000 each to Bob and to Bonnie. What are the tax issues?

41. Redbird Corporation sells property (adjusted basis of $200,000, fair market value of $180,000) to its sole shareholder for $160,000. How much loss can Redbird deduct as a result of this transaction? What is the effect on the corporation's E & P for the year of sale?

42. Green Corporation owns 15% of the stock of Gray Corporation. Gray Corporation, with E & P of $80,000 on December 20, 1996, distributes land with a fair market value of $30,000 and a basis of $60,000 to Green Corporation. The land is subject to a liability of $20,000, which Green assumes.
    a. How is Green Corporation taxed on the distribution?
    b. What is Gray Corporation's E & P after the distribution?

43. At the beginning of its taxable year 1996, Green Corporation had E & P of $200,000. Green sold an asset at a loss of $200,000 on June 30, 1996. It incurred a total deficit of $220,000, which includes the $200,000 loss on the sale of the asset, for the calendar year 1996. Assume Green made a distribution of $60,000 to its sole shareholder, Abdul, on July 1, 1996. How will Abdul be taxed on the $60,000?

44. The stock in White Corporation is owned equally by Frederico and Red Corporation. On January 1, 1996, White had a deficit of $150,000. Its current E & P (for taxable year 1996) was $105,000. In 1996, White distributed cash of $45,000 to both Frederico and Red Corporation. How will Frederico and Red Corporation be taxed on the distribution? What will be the accumulated E & P of White Corporation at the end of 1996?

45. Maria Gonzales paid $180,000 for 15 shares of stock in Wren Corporation five years ago. In November 1995, she received a nontaxable stock dividend of 5 additional shares in Wren Corporation. She sells the 5 shares in March 1996 for $60,000. What is her gain, and how is it taxed? Prepare a letter to your client, Maria Gonzales, and a memo for the file. Maria's address is 14009 Pine Street, Dover, DE 19901.

46. Lark Corporation declares a nontaxable dividend payable in rights to subscribe to common stock. One right and $60 entitle the holder to subscribe to one share of stock. One right is issued for each share of stock owned. Carmen, a shareholder, owns 100 shares of stock that she purchased two years ago for $3,000. At the date of distribution of the rights, the market value of the stock was $80 per share, and the market value of the rights was $20 per right. Carmen received 100 rights. She exercises 60 rights and purchases 60 additional shares of stock. She sells the remaining 40 rights for $750. What are the tax consequences of these transactions to Carmen?

47. Brown Corporation has 400 shares of common stock outstanding. Bob owns 150 of the shares, Bob's mother owns 50 shares, Bob's brother owns 40 shares, and Bob's son owns 60 shares. Black Corporation owns 50 shares. Bob owns 70% of the stock in Black Corporation.

    a. Applying the appropriate stock attribution rules, how many shares does Bob own in Brown Corporation?

    b. Assume Bob owns only 30% of Black Corporation. How many shares does Bob own, directly or indirectly, in Brown Corporation?

    c. Assume Bob owns 30% of BZ Partnership. If, in addition to the facts as in (a) above the partnership owns 50 shares in Brown Corporation, how many shares does Bob own in Brown Corporation?

48. Rosa owns 110 shares of the 200 shares of Bluebird Corporation. Rosa paid $1,000 per share for the stock five years ago. The remaining stock in Bluebird Corporation is owned by several individuals, none of whom owns more than 10% of the stock. In the current year, Bluebird redeems 20 of Rosa's shares for $60,000 ($3,000 per share). Bluebird has E & P of $200,000. How must Rosa report the $60,000?

49. Robin Corporation has 1,000 shares of common stock outstanding. The shares are owned by unrelated shareholders as follows: Leo Jones, 400 shares; Lori Johnson, 400 shares; and Lana Pierce, 200 shares. The corporation redeems 100 shares of the stock owned by Lana for $45,000. Lana paid $100 per share for her stock two years ago. Robin's E & P was $400,000 on the date of redemption. What is the tax effect to Lana of the redemption? Prepare a letter to Lana (1000 Main Street, Oldtown, MN 55166) and a memo for the file in which you explain your conclusions.

50. In Problem 49, assume Leo is Lana's father. How would this affect the tax status of the redemption? What if Leo were Lana's brother instead of her father?

51. Hal and Hans own all the stock in Green Corporation. Each has a basis of $15,000 in his 50 shares. Green Corporation has accumulated E & P of $550,000. Hal wishes to retire in the current year and wants to sell his stock for $300,000, the fair market value. Hans would like to purchase Hal's shares and, thus, become the sole shareholder in Green Corporation, but Hans is short of funds. What are the tax consequences to Hal, to Hans, and to Green Corporation under the following circumstances?

    a. Green Corporation distributes cash of $300,000 to Hans, and he uses the cash to purchase Hal's shares.

    b. Green Corporation redeems all of Hal's shares for $300,000.

52. In the current year, Red Corporation transfers land to a shareholder's estate to carry out a § 303 redemption (redemption to pay death taxes). The land is worth $1 million and has a tax basis to Red Corporation of $400,000. The estate sells the land nine months later for $1,100,000. What are the tax results to Red Corporation and to the estate as a result of the transfer? The death taxes and funeral and administration costs for the estate total $2 million.

53. On January 1, 1996, Warbler Corporation had paid-in capital of $480,000 and E & P of $720,000. Warbler had no current E & P (for 1996) as its deductions equaled its income during the year. The 450 shares in Warbler Corporation are owned equally by Tina, Gus, and Gail, unrelated individuals, each of whom paid $80,000 in 1985 for their stock in Warbler. On June 1, 1996, Warbler Corporation redeemed all Gail's stock for $800,000 in a redemption that qualified as a complete termination. On November 10, 1996, Warbler Corporation paid $360,000 to Tina and $360,000 to Gus. What are the tax consequences of the stock redemption to Gail and the cash distributions to Tina and Gus?

54. Wren Corporation has 500 shares of stock outstanding. It redeems 50 shares for $90,000 when it has paid-in capital of $300,000 and E & P of $400,000. What is the reduction in Wren's E & P as a result of the redemption? Prepare a letter to Wren Corporation (506 Wall Street, Winona, MN 55987) and a memo for the file in which you explain your conclusions.

Research Problems for this chapter appear at the end of Chapter 28.

Corporations: Distributions in Complete Liquidation and an Overview of Reorganizations

LEARNING OBJECTIVES

After completing Chapter 19, you should be able to:

1. Master the tax laws governing corporate liquidations and their impact on both the corporation and its shareholders.

2. Understand the general form and tax consequences of corporate reorganizations.

3. Identify tax planning opportunities available to minimize the income tax impact in the complete liquidation of a corporation.

LIQUIDATIONS—IN GENERAL

1 LEARNING OBJECTIVE
Master the tax laws governing corporate liquidations and their impact on both the corporation and its shareholders.

When a stock redemption occurs or a dividend is distributed, the assumption usually is that the corporation will continue as a going-concern. However, with a complete liquidation, corporate existence terminates. A complete liquidation, like a qualified stock redemption, produces sale or exchange treatment to the shareholder. However, the tax effects of a liquidation to the corporation vary somewhat from those of a stock redemption.

THE LIQUIDATION PROCESS

A **corporate liquidation** exists for tax purposes when a corporation ceases to be a going-concern. The corporation continues solely to wind up affairs, pay debts, and distribute any remaining assets to its shareholders.[1] Legal dissolution under state law is not required for the liquidation to be complete for tax purposes. A transaction will be treated as a liquidation even if the corporation retains a nominal amount of assets to pay remaining debts and preserve its legal status.[2]

A liquidation may occur for several reasons. The corporate business may have been unsuccessful. But even when a business has been profitable, the shareholders may nonetheless decide to terminate the corporation to acquire its assets.

A liquidation often occurs when another person or corporation wants to purchase the assets of the corporation. The purchaser may buy the stock of the shareholders and then liquidate the corporation to acquire the assets. On the other hand, the purchaser may buy the assets directly from the corporation. After the assets are sold, the corporation distributes the sales proceeds to its shareholders and liquidates. As one may expect, the different means used to liquidate a corporation produce varying tax results.

---

[1] Reg. § 1.332–2(c).

[2] Rev.Rul. 54–518, 1954–2 C.B. 142.

LIQUIDATIONS AND OTHER DISTRIBUTIONS COMPARED

A property distribution, whether in the form of a dividend or a stock redemption, produces gain (but not loss) to the distributing corporation. For the shareholder, the fair market value of a property dividend produces ordinary income to the extent of the corporation's E & P. On the other hand, a qualifying stock redemption results in sale or exchange treatment.

The tax effects to the shareholder in a complete liquidation are similar to those in a qualifying stock redemption in that a liquidation also yields sale or exchange treatment. Still a complete liquidation produces somewhat different tax consequences to the liquidating corporation. With certain exceptions, a liquidating corporation recognizes gain *and* loss upon the distribution of its assets.

As in the case of a stock redemption, E & P has no tax impact on the gain or loss to be recognized by the shareholders of the corporation undergoing liquidation. The provision governing dividend distributions specifically does not apply to complete liquidations.[3]

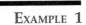

EXAMPLE 1

Green Corporation, with E & P of $40,000, makes a cash distribution of $50,000 to its sole shareholder. Assume the shareholder's basis in the Green stock is $20,000 and the stock is held as an investment. If the distribution is not in complete liquidation or is not a qualifying stock redemption, the shareholder recognizes dividend income of $40,000 (the amount of Green's E & P) and treats the remaining $10,000 of the distribution as a return of capital. If the distribution is pursuant to a complete liquidation or is a qualifying stock redemption, the shareholder has a recognized capital gain of $30,000 [$50,000 (the amount of the distribution) – $20,000 (the basis in the stock)]. In the latter case, Green's E & P is of no consequence to the tax result to the shareholder. ▼

In the event the distribution results in a *loss* to the shareholder, an important distinction can exist between stock redemptions and liquidations. The distinction arises because losses between related parties in a redemption transaction are not allowed whereas losses may be recognized by shareholders in a complete liquidation.[4]

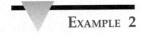

EXAMPLE 2

The stock of Robin Corporation is owned equally by three brothers, Rex, Sam, and Ted. When Ted's basis in his stock investment is $40,000, the corporation distributes $30,000 to him in cancellation of all his shares. If the distribution is a qualifying stock redemption, the $10,000 realized loss is not recognized.[5] Ted and Robin Corporation are related parties because Ted is deemed to own more than 50% in value of the corporation's outstanding stock. Ted's direct ownership is limited to 33⅓%, but through his brothers, he owns indirectly another 66⅔% for a total of 100%. On the other hand, if the distribution qualifies as a complete liquidation, Ted's $10,000 realized loss is recognized. ▼

As to the basis of noncash property received from the corporation, the rules governing liquidations and stock redemptions are identical. Section 334(a) specifies that the basis of such property distributed in a taxable complete liquidation shall be the fair market value on the date of distribution.

In the following pages, the tax consequences of a complete liquidation of a corporation are examined first from the standpoint of the effect on the distributing

---

[3] § 331(b).
[4] § 267.

[5] *McCarthy v. Conley, Jr.,* 65–1 USTC ¶9262, 15 AFTR2d 447, 341 F.2d 948 (CA–2, 1965).

corporation and then in terms of the effect on the shareholder. Because the tax rules differ when a controlled subsidiary is liquidated, the rules relating to the liquidation of a controlled subsidiary receive separate treatment.

LIQUIDATIONS—EFFECT ON THE DISTRIBUTING CORPORATION

A corporation in the process of complete liquidation may or may not be required to recognize gain or loss, depending on the nature of the transaction. The general rules relating to complete liquidations are covered in § 336, which requires the distributing corporation to recognize gain or loss. Loss is not recognized, however, for certain distributions of disqualified property and some distributions to related shareholders. Under § 337, a subsidiary corporation does not recognize gain or loss for distributions to a parent corporation that owns 80 percent or more of the subsidiary's stock.

GENERAL RULE

Section 336 provides that a liquidating corporation recognizes gain or loss on the distribution of property in complete liquidation. The property is treated as if it were sold at its fair market value. This requirement is consistent with the notion of double taxation that is inherent in operating a business as a C corporation. As a result, liquidating distributions are subject to tax at both the corporate level and the shareholder level. As in a stock redemption, when property distributed in a complete liquidation is subject to a liability of the liquidating corporation, the deemed fair market value of that property is treated as not being less than the amount of the liability.

EXAMPLE 3   As part of a complete liquidation, Warbler Corporation distributes to its shareholders land held as an investment (basis of $200,000, fair market value of $300,000). The land is subject to a liability of $350,000. Warbler Corporation has a gain of $150,000 on the distribution ($350,000 − $200,000). If, instead, the liability were $250,000, Warbler's gain on the distribution would be $100,000 ($300,000 − $200,000). ▼

Limitation on Losses.   As a general rule, losses on the distribution of property in a complete liquidation are recognized. There are two exceptions, however. The first exception applies to certain distributions to related parties. The second exception prevents a loss deduction on certain distributions of property with a built-in loss that was contributed to the corporation shortly before the adoption of a plan of liquidation. In this instance, the built-in loss may be disallowed as a deduction upon liquidation even if the distribution is to an unrelated party.

These two exceptions prohibiting loss recognition exist because Congress was concerned that taxpayers might attempt to create artificial losses at the corporate level. Taxpayers could otherwise have accomplished this by contributing property with built-in losses to the corporation before a liquidation. Recall from Chapter 17 that in § 351 transfers (nontaxable transfers to a corporation in exchange for stock when the transferor is in control of the corporation) and contributions to capital, the transferor's income tax basis carries over to the transferee corporation. Thus, a taxpayer might transfer high-basis, low-fair market value property to a corporation contemplating liquidation in the hope that the built-in losses would neutralize expected gains from appreciated property distributed or sold in the liquidation process. Consequently, to prevent abuse, the deductibility of losses is limited in certain related-party situations and in certain sales and distributions of built-in loss property.[6] A corporation and a shareholder are considered related parties if the shareholder owns (directly or indirectly) more than 50 percent in value of the corporation's outstanding stock.

Related-Party Situations. Losses are disallowed on distributions to *related parties* in either of the following cases:

- The distribution is *not* pro rata.
- The property distributed is *disqualified property.*

A *pro rata distribution* is one where each shareholder receives his or her share of *each* corporate asset. *Disqualified property* is property acquired by the liquidating corporation in a § 351 transaction or as a contribution to capital during a five-year period ending on the date of the distribution.

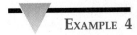

EXAMPLE 4   Bluebird Corporation's stock is held equally by three brothers. One year before Bluebird's liquidation, the shareholders transfer property (basis of $150,000, fair market value of $100,000) to the corporation in return for stock (a § 351 transaction). In liquidation, the corporation transfers the property (still worth $100,000) back to the brothers. Because each brother owns directly and indirectly more than 50% (i.e., 100% in this situation) of the stock and disqualified property is involved, Bluebird recognizes none of the $50,000 realized loss. ▼

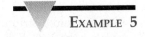

EXAMPLE 5   Assume that Bluebird Corporation stock is owned by Lee and Terry, who are unrelated. Lee owns 80% and Terry owns 20% of the stock in the corporation. Bluebird has the following assets (none of which was acquired in a § 351 transaction or as a contribution to capital) that are distributed in complete liquidation of the corporation:

	Adjusted Basis	Fair Market Value
Cash	$600,000	$600,000
Equipment	150,000	200,000
Building	400,000	200,000

Assume Bluebird Corporation distributes the equipment to Terry and the cash and the building to Lee. Bluebird recognizes a gain of $50,000 on the distribution of the equipment. The loss of $200,000 on the building will be disallowed because the distribution is not pro rata, and the loss property is distributed to a related party. ▼

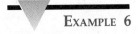

EXAMPLE 6   Assume that Bluebird Corporation in Example 5 distributed the cash and equipment to Lee and the building to Terry. Again, Bluebird recognizes the $50,000 gain on the equipment. However, it can now recognize the $200,000 loss on the building because the loss property is not distributed to a related party (i.e., Terry does not own more than 50% of the stock in Bluebird Corporation). ▼

Built-in Loss Situations. The loss limitation provisions are extended to distributions to *unrelated* parties when loss property is transferred to a corporation shortly before the corporation is liquidated. This second exception to the general

---

[6] § 336(d).

rule is imposed to prevent the doubling of losses, or the so-called *stuffing* of a corporation.

EXAMPLE 7

Nora, a shareholder in White Corporation, transfers property with a basis of $10,000, fair market value of $3,000, to the corporation in a transaction that qualifies under § 351. Nora's basis in the additional White stock acquired in exchange for the property is $10,000. White's basis in the property also is $10,000. A few months after the transfer, White Corporation adopts a plan of complete liquidation. Upon liquidation, White distributes the property to Nora. If White were permitted a loss deduction of $7,000, there would be a double loss because Nora would also recognize a loss of $7,000 upon receipt of the property [$3,000 (fair market value of the property) – $10,000 (basis in Nora's stock)]. To prevent the doubling of losses, the law prohibits White Corporation from taking a loss on the distribution even if Nora is an unrelated party. ▼

Losses are disallowed on a distribution to shareholders who are not related parties when the property distributed was acquired in a § 351 transaction or as a contribution to capital. Furthermore, the property must have been contributed as part of a plan whose principal purpose was to cause the corporation to recognize a loss in connection with the liquidation. Such a purpose will be presumed if the transfer occurs within two years of the adoption of the liquidation plan. However, losses can be recognized if a business purpose was associated with the earlier contribution of the property. Further, any *subsequent* decline in value after the property's contribution and prior to the distribution results in a deductible loss (as long as the property is not distributed to a related party).[7]

The prohibition against a loss deduction on distributions to unrelated parties is broader than the first exception, which disallows losses on certain distributions to related parties. The prohibition applies regardless of whether the shareholder is considered a related party. At the same time, however, the prohibition is narrower than the first exception since it applies only to property that had a built-in loss upon its acquisition by the corporation and only as to the amount of the built-in loss.

EXAMPLE 8

On January 2, 1996, in a transaction that qualifies under § 351, Brown Corporation acquires property with a basis of $10,000 and fair market value of $3,000. Brown adopts a plan of liquidation on July 1, 1996, and distributes the property to Rick, an unrelated party, on November 10, 1996, when the property is worth $1,000. Brown Corporation can recognize a loss of $2,000, the difference between the value of the property on the date of acquisition and the fair market value of the property on the date of distribution. Only the built-in loss of $7,000 [$3,000 (fair market value on date of acquisition) – $10,000 (basis)] is disallowed. ▼

EXAMPLE 9

Assume the property in Example 8 had a fair market value of $12,000 on the date Brown Corporation acquired it. However, the property has a fair market value of only $2,000 when Brown distributes the property upon the complete liquidation of the corporation. If the distribution is to an unrelated shareholder, Brown will recognize the entire $8,000 loss [$2,000 (fair market value on date of distribution) – $10,000 (basis)]. However, if the distribution is to a related party, Brown cannot recognize any of the loss because the property is disqualified property. When the distribution is to a related party, the loss is disallowed even though the entire decline in value occurred during the period the corporation held the property. In addition, the loss limitation applies even though the property's fair market value was more than its basis when it was transferred to the corporation. ▼

---

[7] § 336(d)(2).

The loss limitation can apply regardless of how long the corporation has held the property prior to liquidation. If the property is held for two years or less, a tax avoidance purpose is presumed. Still, if there is a clear and substantial relationship between the contributed property and the business of the corporation, a loss will be permitted on the *distribution* of the property to an unrelated party. When there was a business reason for transferring the loss property to the liquidating corporation, a loss will also be permitted on the *sale* of the property.

▼
EXAMPLE 10

Cardinal Corporation's stock is held 60% by Manuel and 40% by Jack. One year before Cardinal's liquidation, property (basis of $150,000, fair market value of $100,000) is transferred to the corporation as a contribution to capital. There is no business reason for the transfer. In liquidation, Cardinal transfers the property (now with a fair market value of $90,000) to Jack. Even though the distribution is to an unrelated party, the built-in loss of $50,000 is not recognized. However, Cardinal can recognize the loss of $10,000 ($90,000 − $100,000) that occurred while it held the property. If the property is distributed to Manuel, a related party, even the $10,000 loss is disallowed. ▼

▼
EXAMPLE 11

Assume in Example 10, that the property is transferred to Cardinal Corporation because a bank required the additional capital investment as a condition to making a loan to the corporation. Because there is a business purpose for the transfer, presumably all of the $60,000 loss is recognized if the property is distributed to Jack in liquidation. If the property is distributed to Manuel, a related party, the loss is disallowed. ▼

Rules governing distributions of loss property by a liquidating corporation are summarized in Figure 19–1.

Expenses of Liquidation. A corporation may deduct the general expenses involved in liquidating as business expenses under § 162. Examples include the legal and accounting costs of drafting a liquidation plan and the cost of revoking the corporate charter. Liquidation expenses relating to the disposition of corporate assets are also deductible. Expenses relating to the sale of corporate assets, including a brokerage commission for the sale of real estate and a legal fee to clear title, are offset against the selling price of the assets.

▼
EXAMPLE 12

During its liquidation, Wren Corporation incurs the following expenses:

General liquidation expenses	$12,000
Legal expenses incurred in distributing property	200
Sales commissions to sell inventory	3,000
Brokerage fee on sale of real estate	8,000

Wren can deduct $12,200 ($12,000 + $200) as business expenses. The $3,000 commission and the $8,000 brokerage fee are applied against the selling price of the inventory and the real estate. ▼

To the extent that a corporation pays tax on the net amount of gain recognized at the corporate level, the proceeds available to be distributed to the shareholder are likewise reduced. This reduction for the payment of taxes will reduce the amount realized by the shareholder, which will then reduce the gain or increase the loss recognized.

▼
EXAMPLE 13

Blue Corporation's assets are valued at $2 million after payment of all corporate debts except for $300,000 of taxes payable on net gains it recognized on the liquidation. Therefore, the net amount realized by the shareholders is $1.7 million ($2 million − $300,000). As described below, in determining the gain or loss recognized by a shareholder, the net amount realized is offset by the stock's adjusted basis. ▼

▼ **FIGURE 19–1**
Distributions of Loss Property by a Liquidating Corporation

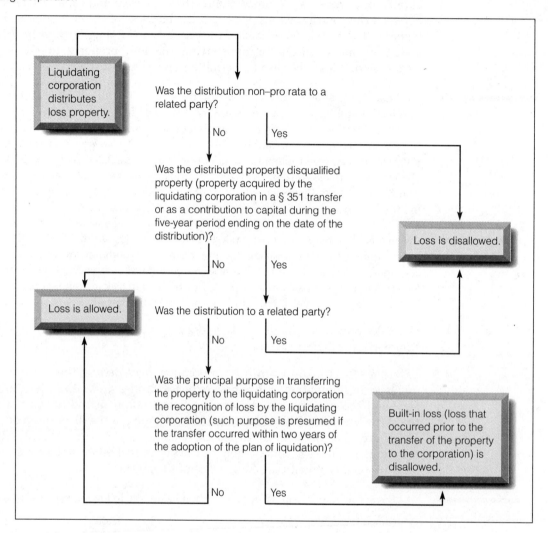

LIQUIDATIONS—EFFECT ON THE SHAREHOLDER

The tax consequences to the shareholders of a corporation in the process of liquidation are governed either by the general rule of § 331 or by one of two exceptions relating to the liquidation of a subsidiary.

GENERAL RULE

In the case of a complete liquidation, the general rule of § 331 provides for sale or exchange treatment.[8] Since gain or loss must be recognized on the sale or exchange

---
[8]§ 331(a)(1).

of property unless an exception applies, the shareholder is treated as having sold his or her stock to the corporation being liquidated. The difference between the fair market value of the assets received from the corporation (which is net of the income tax paid by the corporation) and the adjusted basis of the stock surrendered is the gain or loss recognized by the shareholder. If the stock is a capital asset in the hands of the shareholder, capital gain or loss results. The burden of proof is on the taxpayer to furnish evidence of the adjusted basis of the stock. In the absence of such evidence, the stock is deemed to have a zero basis, and the full amount of the liquidation proceeds becomes the amount of the gain recognized.[9]

Under the general liquidation provision, the shareholder's tax basis for property received in a liquidation is the property's fair market value on the date of distribution.[10] The rule follows the same approach taken with stock redemptions that qualify for sale or exchange treatment.

SPECIAL RULE FOR CERTAIN INSTALLMENT OBLIGATIONS

The installment sale rules provide some relief from the bunching of gain that occurs when a liquidating corporation sells its assets. The liquidating corporation must recognize all gain on such sales. However, the *shareholders'* gain on the receipt of notes obtained by the corporation on the sale of its assets may be deferred to the point of collection.[11] The shareholders must allocate their bases in the stock among the various assets received from the corporation.

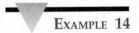

EXAMPLE 14

After adopting a plan of complete liquidation, Black Corporation sells its only asset, unimproved land held as an investment. The land has appreciated in value and is sold to Ed (an unrelated party) for $100,000. Under the terms of the sale, Black Corporation receives cash of $25,000 and Ed's notes for the balance of $75,000. The notes are payable over 10 years ($7,500 per year) and carry an appropriate rate of interest. Immediately after the sale, Black Corporation distributes the cash and notes to Earl, the sole shareholder. Earl has an adjusted basis of $20,000 in the Black stock, and the installment notes have a value equal to the face amount ($75,000). These transactions have the following tax result:

- Black Corporation recognizes gain on the sale of the land, measured by the difference between the $100,000 selling price and the basis Black had in the land.
- Earl may defer the gain on the receipt of the notes to the point of collection.
- Earl must allocate the adjusted basis in the stock ($20,000) between the cash and the installment notes as follows:

$$\frac{\text{Cash}}{\text{Total receipts}} = \frac{\$25,000}{\$100,000} \times \$20,000 = \$5,000 \text{ basis allocated to the cash}$$

$$\frac{\text{Notes}}{\text{Total receipts}} = \frac{\$75,000}{\$100,000} \times \$20,000 = \$15,000 \text{ basis allocated to the notes}$$

- Earl must recognize $20,000 of gain [$25,000 (cash received) – $5,000 basis (allocated to the cash)] in the year of liquidation.
- Earl must recognize gain equal to 80% of each dollar collected on the notes, computed as follows:

$75,000 (contract price) – $15,000 (basis allocated to the notes) = $60,000 (gross profit)

---

[9] *John Calderazzo,* 34 TCM 1, T.C.Memo. 1975–1.

[10] § 334.

[11] § 453(h). This provision does not apply to the sale of inventory property and property held by the corporation primarily for sale to customers in the ordinary course of its trade or business unless such property is sold in bulk to one person.

- The gross profit percentage is 80%:

$$\frac{\$60,000 \text{ (gross profit)}}{\$75,000 \text{ (contract price)}} = 80\%$$

- Thus, Earl must report a gain of $6,000 [$7,500 (amount of note) × 80% (gross profit percentage)] on the collection of each note over the next 10 years.
- The interest element is accounted for separately.   ▼

LIQUIDATIONS—PARENT-SUBSIDIARY SITUATIONS

Section 332, an exception to the general rule, provides that a parent corporation does *not* recognize gain or loss on a liquidation of its subsidiary. In addition, the subsidiary corporation recognizes neither gain nor loss on distributions of property to its parent.[12]

The requirements for applying § 332 are as follows:

- The parent must own at least 80 percent of the voting stock of the subsidiary and at least 80 percent of the total value of the subsidiary's stock.
- The subsidiary must distribute all of its property in complete cancellation of all of its stock within the taxable year or within three years from the close of the tax year in which the first distribution occurred.
- The subsidiary must be solvent.[13]

If these requirements are met, nonrecognition of gains and losses becomes mandatory.

When a series of distributions occurs in the liquidation of a subsidiary corporation, the parent corporation must own the required amount of stock (at least 80 percent) on the date a plan of liquidation is adopted and at all times until all property has been distributed.[14] If the parent fails to qualify at any time, the provisions for nonrecognition of gain or loss do not apply to any distribution.[15]

TAX TREATMENT WHEN A MINORITY INTEREST EXISTS

A distribution to a minority shareholder in a parent-subsidiary situation is treated in the same manner as one made pursuant to a nonliquidating redemption. That is, the distributing corporation recognizes gain (but not loss) on the property distributed to the minority shareholder.

EXAMPLE 15

The stock of Red Corporation is held as follows: 80% by Yellow Corporation and 20% by Dan. Red Corporation is liquidated on December 10, 1996, pursuant to a plan adopted on January 10, 1996. At the time of its liquidation, Red has assets with a basis of $100,000 and fair market value of $500,000. Red Corporation distributes the property pro rata to Yellow Corporation and to Dan. Red must recognize gain of $80,000 [($500,000 fair market value – $100,000 basis) × 20% minority interest]. The remaining gain of $320,000 is sheltered because it is related to property being distributed to Yellow, the parent corporation. ▼

---

[12] § 337.
[13] Reg. §§ 1.332–2(a) and (b).

[14] Establishing the date of the adoption of a plan of complete liquidation could be crucial in determining whether § 332 applies. See, for example, *George L. Riggs, Inc.*, 64 T.C. 474 (1975).
[15] Reg. §1.332–2(a).

The minority shareholder is subject to the general rule requiring the recognition of gain or loss. Accordingly, the difference between the fair market value of the assets received and the basis of the minority shareholder's stock is the amount of gain or loss recognized. The tax basis of property received by the minority shareholder is the property's fair market value on the date of distribution.[16]

INDEBTEDNESS OF THE SUBSIDIARY TO THE PARENT

If a subsidiary transfers appreciated property to the parent to satisfy a debt, it must recognize gain on the transaction unless § 332 applies. When § 332 applies, the subsidiary does not recognize gain or loss upon the transfer of properties to the parent.[17]

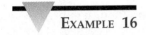

EXAMPLE 16 Green Corporation owes $20,000 to its parent, Gray Corporation. It satisfies the obligation by transferring land worth $20,000 with a tax basis of $8,000. Normally, Green would recognize a gain of $12,000 on the transaction. However, if the transfer is made pursuant to a liquidation under § 332, Green does not recognize a gain. ▼

The special provision noted above will not apply to the parent corporation. The parent corporation recognizes realized gain or loss on the satisfaction of indebtedness, even if property is received during liquidation of the subsidiary.

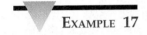

EXAMPLE 17 Redbird Corporation purchased bonds of its subsidiary Bluebird at a discount for $95,000. Upon liquidation of the subsidiary pursuant to § 332, Redbird receives payment for $100,000, the face amount of the bonds. The transaction has no tax effect on Bluebird. However, Redbird Corporation recognizes gain of $5,000—the difference between its basis in the bonds and the amount received in payment. ▼

BASIS OF PROPERTY RECEIVED BY THE PARENT CORPORATION—THE GENERAL RULE

Property received in the complete liquidation of a subsidiary has the same basis it had in the hands of the subsidiary unless the parent corporation makes an election under the exception discussed below.[18] Further, the parent's basis in the stock of the liquidated subsidiary disappears, even if some of the property is transferred to the parent to satisfy a debt owed to the parent by the subsidiary.

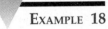

EXAMPLE 18 Wren, the parent corporation, has a basis of $20,000 in stock in Robin Corporation, a subsidiary in which it owns 85% of all classes of stock. Wren purchased the Robin stock 10 years ago. In the current year, Wren liquidates Robin Corporation and acquires assets with a fair market value of $50,000 and a tax basis to Robin of $40,000. Wren Corporation takes a basis of $40,000 in the assets, with a potential gain upon their sale of $10,000. Wren's $20,000 basis in Robin's stock disappears. ▼

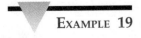

EXAMPLE 19 White Corporation has a basis of $60,000 in the stock of Gray Corporation, a subsidiary acquired 10 years ago. It liquidates Gray Corporation and receives assets with a fair market value of $50,000 and a tax basis to Gray of $40,000. White Corporation takes a basis of $40,000 in the assets it acquired from Gray. If it sells the assets for $50,000, it has a gain of

[16] § 334(a).
[17] § 337(b).
[18] § 334(b)(1) and Reg. § 1.334–1(b).

$10,000 in spite of the fact that its basis in the Gray stock was $60,000. White's loss will never be recognized. ▼

Because the parent corporation takes the subsidiary's basis in its assets, the carryover rules of § 381 apply. The parent acquires any net operating loss of the subsidiary, any investment credit carryover, any capital loss carryover, and a carryover of the subsidiary's E & P.

BASIS OF PROPERTY RECEIVED BY THE PARENT CORPORATION—THE EXCEPTION

Background.   Under the general rule described above, problems can develop when a subsidiary is liquidated shortly after acquisition by a parent corporation.

- When the basis of the subsidiary's assets is more than the purchase price of the stock, the parent receives a step-up in basis in the assets at no tax cost. If, for example, the parent pays $100,000 for the subsidiary's stock and the basis of the assets transferred to the parent is $150,000, the parent enjoys a $50,000 benefit without any gain recognition. The $50,000 increase in basis of the subsidiary's assets can lead to additional depreciation deductions and either more loss or less gain upon the later disposition of the assets by the parent.
- If the basis of the subsidiary's assets is below the purchase price of the stock, the parent suffers a step-down in basis in the assets with no attendant tax benefit. Return to Example 19, but change the situation slightly so that the subsidiary is liquidated shortly after acquisition. The basic inequity of the "no loss" situation now develops. But why would a corporation pay more for the stock in another corporation than the latter's basis in the assets? One reason is that the basis of the assets is not necessarily related to the fair market value. The acquiring corporation may not have the option of purchasing the assets of the acquired corporation instead of its stock. Further, the shareholders in the acquired corporation may prefer to sell their stock rather than the assets of the corporation.

In the landmark decision of *Kimbell-Diamond Milling Co. v. Comm.*,[19] the courts considered these problems. The courts concluded that when a parent corporation liquidates a subsidiary shortly after acquiring its stock, the parent is really purchasing the assets of the subsidiary. Consequently, the basis of the assets should be the same as the cost of the stock. After this decision, § 338 was enacted to provide for certain situations where the basis determination is made under the special rule of § 338 rather than the general rule.

Requirements for Application.   Section 338 provides that an acquiring corporation may *elect* to treat the acquisition of stock in an acquired corporation as a purchase of the acquired corporation's assets. The **§ 338 election** must be made by the fifteenth day of the ninth month beginning after the month in which a *qualified stock purchase* occurs. If made, the election is irrevocable.

A purchasing corporation makes a *qualified stock purchase* if it acquires at least 80 percent of the voting power and at least 80 percent of the value of the acquired corporation within a 12-month period beginning with the first purchase of stock.

---

[19] 14 T.C. 74 (1950), *aff'd.* in 51–1 USTC ¶9201, 40 AFTR 328, 187 F.2d 718 (CA–5, 1951), *cert. den.* 72 S.Ct. 50 (USSC, 1951).

The stock must be acquired in a taxable transaction (i.e., § 351 and other nonrecognition provisions do not apply). An acquisition of stock by any member of an affiliated group, including the purchasing corporation, is considered to be an acquisition by the purchasing corporation.

Tax Consequences. If the parent makes a qualified election under the special rule of § 338, the purchasing corporation has a basis in the subsidiary's assets equal to its basis in the subsidiary's stock. The subsidiary may, but need not, be liquidated.

Under § 338, the acquired corporation is *deemed* to have sold its assets for an amount equal to the purchasing corporation's grossed-up basis in the subsidiary's stock. This amount must be adjusted for liabilities of the subsidiary corporation. The grossed-up basis is the basis in the subsidiary stock multiplied by a fraction. The numerator of the fraction is 100 percent. The denominator is the percentage of value of the subsidiary's stock held by the purchasing corporation on the acquisition date.[20] The amount is allocated among the subsidiary's assets using the residual method described below.

The § 338 election produces gain or loss to the subsidiary. The subsidiary is treated as having sold all of its assets at the close of the acquisition date in a single transaction at the fair market value.[21] The subsidiary is then treated as a new corporation that purchased all of the assets as of the beginning of the day after the acquisition date.

EXAMPLE 20

White Corporation has an $800,000 basis in its assets and $500,000 of liabilities. It has E & P of $200,000, and the assets have a fair market value of $2,000,000. Black Corporation purchases 80% of the White stock on March 10, 1996, for $1,200,000 [($2,000,000 – liabilities of $500,000) × 80%]. Because the purchase price of the White stock exceeds White's basis in its assets, and to eliminate White's E & P, Black may choose to elect § 338 treatment by December 15, 1996. White need not be liquidated for the provision to apply. If Black elects § 338, the tax consequences are as follows:

- White is deemed to have sold its assets for an amount equal to Black's grossed-up basis in the White stock.
- Black's grossed-up basis in the White stock is computed as follows: The basis of the White stock is multiplied by a fraction, with 100% the numerator and 80% the denominator. The basis of the White stock, $1,200,000, is multiplied by 100/80. The result is $1,500,000, which is adjusted for White's liabilities of $500,000 for a deemed selling price of $2,000,000.
- The $2,000,000 selling price less $800,000, the basis of White's assets, produces a recognized gain to White Corporation of $1,200,000. ▼

Because Black did not purchase 100 percent of the White stock, different results occur depending on whether or not White is liquidated. If White is not liquidated, it is treated as a new corporation as of March 11, 1996. The basis of White's assets is $2,000,000, and the E & P is eliminated. If White Corporation is liquidated, Black Corporation has a basis of $1,600,000 in White's assets, representing 80 percent of White's assets. White's E & P does not carry over to Black.

Note the results of the § 338 election. White Corporation's assets receive a stepped-up basis but at a substantial tax cost. White must recognize all of its realized gain. Any tax liability White incurs on its recognized gain causes Black Corporation to reduce the amount paid for White's assets.

[20] § 338(b)(4).

[21] § 338(a).

Allocation of Purchase Price.   The new stepped-up basis of the assets of a subsidiary when a § 338 election is in effect is allocated among the assets by the **residual method.**[22] The amount of the purchase price that exceeds the aggregate fair market values of the tangible and identifiable intangible assets must be allocated to goodwill or going-concern value. Goodwill and going-concern value are referred to as "§ 197 intangibles." Costs allocated to acquired § 197 intangibles are amortized over a 15-year period.

EXAMPLE 21

For $4,000,000, Red Corporation acquires all of the stock of Orange Corporation and elects the treatment under § 338. If the fair market value of Orange's physical assets is $3,500,000, Red must allocate $500,000 of the purchase price either to goodwill or to going-concern value, which may be amortized over a 15-year period. ▼

In Example 21, none of the purchase price would have to be allocated to goodwill or going-concern value if the physical assets were worth $4 million. However, the burden of proof of showing no residual amount is on the taxpayer, not on the IRS.

A Comparison of the General Rule and the § 338 Exception.   Under the general rule, a subsidiary's basis in its assets carries over to the parent corporation upon liquidation. In addition, the subsidiary liquidation is completely tax-free (except for any minority interest). A liquidation under § 338, while tax-free to the parent, is taxable to the subsidiary. The subsidiary assets will have a stepped-up basis.

If a subsidiary liquidation qualifies under § 338 and a timely election is made, the holding period of the property received by the parent corporation begins on the date the parent acquired the subsidiary's stock. If the corporation is not liquidated, the holding period of the assets to the subsidiary starts anew on the day after the acquisition date.[23] In a liquidation under the general rule of § 332, the holding period of the subsidiary carries over to the parent. The rules for an election under § 338 as compared to the general rule appear in Concept Summary 19–1.

A Summary of the Liquidation Rules.   In general, gain or loss is recognized to the shareholder in a complete liquidation except in certain situations involving parent-subsidiary relationships. If the transaction is taxable to the shareholder, the basis of property received is its fair market value. In the normal scenario, the corporation being liquidated recognizes gains and, subject to limitations, losses associated with the properties distributed. However, in the case of the liquidation of a subsidiary, the subsidiary does not recognize gains and losses unless appreciated properties are distributed to minority shareholders, in which case gain is recognized. The rules are summarized in Concept Summary 19–1.

CORPORATE REORGANIZATIONS

2   LEARNING OBJECTIVE
Understand the general form and tax consequences of corporate reorganizations.

A corporate combination or realignment, usually referred to as a reorganization, can be either a taxable or a nontaxable transaction. Assuming a business combination is taxable, the Code provides that the seller's gain or loss is measured by

---

[22]§ 1060.   [23]§ 338(a).

CONCEPT SUMMARY 19–1

Summary of Liquidation Rules

Effect on the Shareholder	Basis of Property Received	Effect on the Corporation
§ 331—The general rule provides for capital gain treatment on the difference between the FMV of property received and the basis of the stock in the corporation.	§ 334(a)—Basis of assets received by the shareholder will be the FMV on the date of distribution (except for installment obligations in which gain is deferred to the point of collection).	§ 336—Gain or loss is recognized for distributions in kind and for sales by the liquidating corporation. Losses are not recognized for distributions to related parties if the distribution is not pro rata or if disqualified property is distributed. Losses may be disallowed on distributions of certain other property even if made to unrelated parties.
§ 332—In liquidation of a controlled subsidiary, no gain or loss is recognized to the parent corporation. Subsidiary must distribute all of its property within the taxable year or within three years from the close of the taxable year in which the first distribution occurs.	§ 334(b)(1)—Property has the same basis as it had in the hands of the subsidiary. Parent's basis in the stock disappears. Carryover rules of § 381 apply.	§ 337—No gain or loss is recognized by the subsidiary on distributions to an 80% or more parent. Gain (but not loss) is recognized on distributions to minority shareholders.
	§ 338—Basis of assets is the basis that the parent held in the stock in the subsidiary. Basis is allocated to assets using the residual method. Carryover rules of § 381 do not apply. Subsidiary need not be liquidated.	

the difference between the amount realized and the basis of property surrendered. The purchaser's basis in the property received is the amount paid for the property, and the holding period begins on the date of purchase.

Certain exchanges are specifically excepted from tax recognition by the Code. For example, § 1031 provides that no gain or loss shall be recognized if property held for productive use or for investment is exchanged solely for "... property of a like kind ...." Section 1033, if elected by the taxpayer, provides for partial or complete nonrecognition of gain if property destroyed, seized, or stolen is compulsorily or involuntarily converted into similar property. Further, § 351 provides for nonrecognition of gain upon the transfer of property to a controlled corporation. Finally, §§ 361 and 368 provide for nonrecognition of gain in certain corporate reorganizations. The Regulations state the underlying assumption behind the nonrecognition of gain or loss.

... the new property is substantially a continuation of the old investment ...; and, in the case of reorganizations, ... the new enterprise, the new corporate structure, and the new property are substantially continuations of the old ....[24]

[24] Reg. § 1.1002–1(c).

TAX IN THE NEWS

HOW TO CHECK OUT A TAKEOVER RUMOR

Is it possible for an investor to predict a takeover? Financial analysts tell investors to look at the trading activity of corporate insiders. Insiders will not be buying stock in anticipation of a merger because that is illegal insider trading, but they will halt the sale of their stock. Insiders who know a bid is "percolating" will hold on to their shares in anticipation of a "premium offer price from the prospective bidder." Analysts point to an announcement that Grand Metropolitan would acquire Pet, Inc., for $2.6 billion in a friendly takeover. A review of SEC data on insider trading revealed that insider selling at Pet had "all but dried up" in the months prior to the announcement. When ITT announced that it would buy gambling giant Caesar's World, Inc., in a friendly tender offer, SEC data indicated that insider selling at Caesar's fell off as its stock price rose.

Insider activity can also squelch a takeover rumor. If there are takeover rumors but senior insiders continue to sell their shares, the likelihood of a bid is "fairly slim," according to analysts. Studies reveal that insider selling typically drops off some three months ahead of any announcement of either a takeover or talks about a takeover.

SOURCE: Information from Warren Getler, "Big Drop in Insider Sales May Augur a Takeover," *Wall Street Journal*, January 11, 1995, pp. C1 and C15.

SUMMARY OF THE DIFFERENT TYPES OF REORGANIZATIONS

Section 368(a) of the Code specifies seven corporate restructures or reorganizations that will qualify as nontaxable exchanges. The planner of a nontaxable business realignment must determine in advance that the proposed transaction falls specifically within one of these seven types. If the transaction fails to qualify, it will not be granted special tax treatment.

Section 368(a)(1) states that the term **reorganization** means the following:

A. A statutory merger or consolidation.
B. The acquisition by one corporation, in exchange solely for all or a part of its voting stock, of stock of another corporation.
C. The acquisition by one corporation, in exchange solely for all or a part of its voting stock, of substantially all of the properties of another corporation.
D. A transfer by a corporation of all or a part of its assets to another corporation if immediately after the transfer the transferor, or one or more of its shareholders, or any combination thereof, is in control of the corporation to which the assets are transferred.
E. A recapitalization.
F. A mere change in identity, form, or place of organization.
G. A transfer by a corporation of all or a part of its assets to another corporation in a bankruptcy or receivership proceeding.

These seven types of tax-free reorganizations are designated by their identifying letters: "Type A," "Type B," "Type C," and so on. Basically, excepting the recapitalization (E), the change in form (F), and the insolvent corporation (G) provisions, a tax-free reorganization is (1) a statutory merger or consolidation, (2) an exchange of stock for voting stock, (3) an exchange of assets for voting stock, or (4) a divisive reorganization (the so-called spin-off, split-off, or split-up).

SUMMARY OF THE TAX CONSEQUENCES IN A TAX-FREE REORGANIZATION

The exchange of stock in one corporation for stock in another corporation pursuant to a tax-free reorganization parallels almost exactly the like-kind exchange provisions of § 1031. In the simplest like-kind exchange, neither gain nor loss is recognized on the exchange of investment property or property used in a trade for property of a "like kind" that will also be held for investment purposes or used in a trade or business. For example, the exchange of a truck used in a trade or business for another truck also used in the trade or business is a tax-free exchange if no "boot," or property not of a like kind, is received.

However, the like-kind provisions of § 1031 do not apply to the exchange of securities. Thus, an investor's exchange of stock in Cardinal Corporation for another investor's stock in Redbird Corporation is a taxable exchange. But, if the exchange of Cardinal stock for Redbird stock is pursuant to a merger at the corporate level that qualifies as a tax-free reorganization under § 368, the exchange of the stock at the shareholder level also qualifies as a nontaxable exchange. As a result, when Cardinal stock is exchanged for Redbird stock at the shareholder level as a result of a tax-free reorganization at the corporate level, the exchange of stock is similar to and is treated in the same manner as a like-kind exchange. In substance, it is a nontaxable exchange of like-kind property at the shareholder level.

Gain or Loss. In a corporate restructuring that qualifies as a tax-free reorganization, the acquiring corporation does not recognize gain or loss unless it transfers appreciated property along with its stock and securities to the target corporation.[25] No gain or loss is recognized to the target corporation on the exchange of property pursuant to a tax-free reorganization unless the target (1) fails to distribute *other property* received in the exchange or (2) distributes its appreciated property to its shareholders.[26]

Generally, the security holders of the various corporations involved in a tax-free reorganization do not recognize gain or loss on the exchange of their stock and securities unless they receive cash or other consideration in addition to stock and securities.[27] As far as securities are concerned, gain is not recognized only if the principal amount of the securities surrendered is the same (or greater) than the principal amount of the securities received.

If the security holders receive additional consideration, they recognize gain, but not more than the sum of money and the fair market value of other property received. If a shareholder does not surrender any stock, the additional consideration generally is treated as a dividend to the extent of the shareholder's share of the corporation's earnings and profits (E & P).[28] If the distribution is characterized

---

[25] § 1032.

[26] §§ 361(a) and (b).

[27] § 356(a).

[28] § 356. Compare *Shimberg v. U.S.*, 78–2 USTC ¶9607, 42 AFTR2d 78–5575, 577 F.2d 283 (CA–5, 1978), with *Comm. v. Clark*, 89–1 USTC ¶9230, 63 AFTR2d 89–860, 109 S.Ct. 1455 (USSC, 1989). In *Comm. v. Clark*, the Supreme Court ruled that the question of whether the payment of boot in a shareholder exchange pursuant

to a tax-free reorganization has the effect of a dividend distribution is answered by examining the effect of the exchange as a whole. Boot can be characterized as capital gain if the requirements relating to qualified redemptions (see Chapter 18) are met. In applying the qualified redemption rules, the Court held that stock ownership reduction is determined by reference to ownership in the acquiring corporation.

▼ **FIGURE 19–2**
Basis to Acquiring Corporation of Property Received

Target's basis in property transferred	$xx,xxx
Plus: Gain recognized by Target on the transaction	x,xxx
Equals: Basis of property to Acquiring Corporation	$xx,xxx

▼ **FIGURE 19–3**
Basis to Target Shareholders of Stock and Securities Received

Basis of stock and securities transferred	$xx,xxx
Plus: Gain and dividend income recognized	x,xxx
Less: Money and fair market value of other property received	(x,xxx)
Equals: Basis of stock and securities received	$xx,xxx

as a dividend, any recognized gain is dividend income to the extent of the shareholder's share of E & P. The remainder is treated as an exchange of property.

Basis. Property received by the acquiring corporation from the target corporation retains the basis it had in the hands of the target, increased by the amount of gain recognized to the target on the transfer.[29] The tax basis of stock and securities received by a shareholder pursuant to a tax-free reorganization is the same as the basis of those surrendered. This amount is decreased by the amount of boot received and increased by the amount of gain and dividend income, if any, recognized on the transaction.[30] Because of the substituted basis, the gain or loss is deferred until the new stock or securities are disposed of in a taxable transaction.

The basis rules are summarized in Figures 19–2 and 19–3. Examples 22 and 23 illustrate how the gain or loss and basis rules operate.

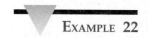

EXAMPLE 22

Quinn exchanges stock he owns in Target Corporation for stock in Acquiring Corporation plus $2,000 cash. The exchange is pursuant to a tax-free reorganization of both corporations. Quinn paid $10,000 for the stock in Target two years ago. The stock in Acquiring has a fair market value of $12,000. Quinn has a realized gain of $4,000 ($12,000 + $2,000 − $10,000), which is recognized to the extent of the boot received, $2,000. Assume the distribution has the effect of a dividend. If Quinn's share of E & P in Target is $1,000, that amount is a taxable dividend. The remaining $1,000 is treated as a gain from the sale or exchange of property. Quinn's basis in the Acquiring stock is $10,000 [$10,000 (basis in stock surrendered) − $2,000 (boot received) + $2,000 (gain and dividend income recognized)].

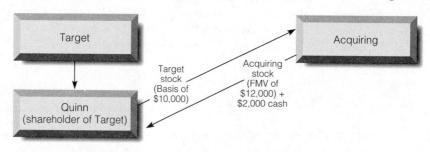

Assume Quinn's basis in the Target stock was $15,000. Quinn realizes a loss of $1,000 on the exchange, none of which is recognized. His basis in the Acquiring stock is $13,000 [$15,000 (basis in stock surrendered) – $2,000 (boot received)]. ▼

ETHICAL CONSIDERATIONS

Who Benefits from a Corporate Merger?

Mega Bank merges with National Bank in a $10 million stock swap. The new surviving bank, Chase, will virtually control the banking industry in the states where it does business. Ralph, the CEO of Mega Bank, who will receive $100 million for his part in structuring the merger, has cited the enormous cost savings from the merger. Part of the cost savings will result from the ability of the surviving bank, Chase, to cut 12,000 jobs. In addition, by controlling the banking market, Chase will be able to raise its fees for providing banking services to its customers. The shareholders of the merged banks reaped a substantial profit from later sales of their stock. Does the merger present any ethical problems?

TAX PLANNING CONSIDERATIONS

3 LEARNING OBJECTIVE
Identify tax planning opportunities available to minimize the income tax impact in the complete liquidation of a corporation.

EFFECT OF A LIQUIDATING DISTRIBUTION ON THE CORPORATION

Liquidating distributions are taxed at both the corporate level and the shareholder level. When a corporation liquidates, it can, as a general rule, claim losses on assets that have declined in value. These assets should not be distributed in the form of a property dividend before liquidation because losses are not deductible on nonliquidating distributions of depreciated property. Thus, if such assets are distributed as property dividends, the corporation receives no tax benefit from the potential loss.

EFFECT OF A LIQUIDATING DISTRIBUTION ON THE SHAREHOLDER

Under the general rule for corporate liquidations, shareholders recognize gain or loss equal to the difference between the liquidation proceeds and the basis of the stock given up. In cases of a large gain, a shareholder may consider shifting the gain to others. One approach is to give the stock to family members or donate it to charity. Whether this procedure will be successful depends on the timing of the transfer. If the donee of the stock is not in a position to prevent the liquidation of the corporation, the donor is deemed to have made an anticipatory assignment of income. As a result, the gain is still taxed to the donor. Hence, advance planning is crucial in arriving at the desired tax result.

Recall that the installment sale provisions provide some relief from the general corporate liquidation rule that the shareholder recognizes all gain upon receiving the liquidation proceeds. Assume that after a plan of liquidation has been adopted, corporate assets are sold in exchange for installment notes. The shareholders receiving the notes as liquidation distributions may be able to report the gain on the installment method. In that case, some gain can be deferred until the notes are collected.

The provision applicable to the liquidation of a subsidiary, § 332, is not elective. Nevertheless, some flexibility may be available:

- Whether § 332 applies depends on the 80 percent stock ownership test. Assuming the transaction has some substance, it may be avoided if a parent corporation reduces its stock ownership in the subsidiary below this percentage. On the other hand, the opposite approach may be desirable. A parent can make the provision applicable by acquiring enough additional stock in the subsidiary to meet the 80 percent test.

- Once § 332 becomes effective, less latitude is allowed in determining the parent's basis in the subsidiary's assets. If the general rule applies, the subsidiary's basis carries over to the parent. If the exception to the general rule is available and a timely § 338 election is made, the parent's basis equals the cost of the stock. If the subsidiary is not liquidated, the basis of the assets to the subsidiary is the parent's cost of the stock. Presumably, the exception of § 338 can be avoided by failing to make a timely election.

- If a timely § 338 election is made, the parent corporation's basis in the stock of the subsidiary is allocated among the assets of the subsidiary.

KEY TERMS

Corporate liquidation, 19–2	Residual method, 19–14	Section 338 election, 19–12
Reorganization, 19–16		

PROBLEM MATERIALS

DISCUSSION QUESTIONS

1. Compare stock redemptions and liquidations with other corporate distributions in terms of the following:
    a. Recognition of gain to the shareholder.
    b. Recognition of gain or loss by the distributing corporation.
    c. Effect on the distributing corporation's E & P.

2. What losses are not recognized by the liquidating corporation in a complete liquidation?

3. When considering the potential deductibility of losses by a corporation in a complete liquidation, what is meant by related-party transactions?

4. Discuss the tax treatment of liquidation expenses in connection with the following:
    a. General liquidation expenses.
    b. Expenses relating to a distribution of assets in kind.
    c. Expenses relating to a sale of assets.

5. May a shareholder use the installment method to report gain on a complete liquidation? Explain.

6. In terms of the rules applying to the liquidation of a subsidiary by its parent, describe the effect of each of the following:
    a. The adoption of a plan of complete liquidation.
    b. The period of time in which the corporation must liquidate.
    c. The amount of stock held by the parent corporation.
    d. The solvency of the subsidiary being liquidated.

7. What are the tax consequences of a liquidation of a subsidiary by its corporate parent when a minority interest is involved?

8. Could a liquidation of one corporation involve the general rule (§ 331) and the rule applicable to the liquidation of a controlled subsidiary (§ 332)?

9. Bluebird Corporation pays $1 million for 100% of the stock in Redbird Corporation. Redbird has a basis of $500,000 in its assets. If Bluebird liquidates Redbird and makes no special election, what basis will it have in Redbird's assets?

10. What are the requirements for the application of § 338?

11. Under what circumstances could the application of § 338 be beneficial to the parent corporation? Detrimental?

12. What is the tax treatment of goodwill and going-concern value when stock of a corporation is purchased and an election is made under § 338?

13. Compare the sale of a corporation's assets with a sale of its stock in terms of problems to the seller.

14. What is the theory underlying nonrecognition of gain or loss in a corporate reorganization?

15. Briefly explain the seven forms of corporate reorganizations that qualify for nonrecognition treatment.

16. How does the receipt of boot affect the tax-free status of a corporate reorganization?

17. Ann purchased 200 shares of stock in Gray Corporation five years ago for $50 per share. Two years ago, Gray redeemed 50 of Ann's shares for $100 per share. In the current year, all of Gray's shareholders exchanged their shares in Gray for voting stock in Blue Corporation. The agreement provided that a sufficient number of shares in Blue, valued at $95 per share, would be issued to the Gray shareholders to equal the value of their Gray shares. In the event the purchase price was not evenly divisible by shares at $95 per share, the difference would be paid in cash. Ann was paid $15 cash and one share of Blue stock for each of her remaining shares in Gray. What are the tax issues?

PROBLEMS

18. Wren Corporation is owned equally by José and Jill, who are not related. Each has a stock basis of $600,000. Wren Corporation has the following assets and no liabilities:

	Basis to Wren Corporation	Fair Market Value
Cash	$ 200,000	$ 200,000
Inventory	800,000	1,200,000
Equipment ($400,000 depreciation has been taken)	200,000	1,000,000
Building	800,000	2,400,000
Land	200,000	400,000
Stock in Gray Corporation (10% interest)	1,600,000	4,000,000
Total	$3,800,000	$9,200,000

Compute the tax liability to Wren Corporation and the taxable gain to José and Jill if Wren is liquidated in the current year after the corporation sells each asset for its fair market value and distributes the after-tax proceeds to José and Jill. Straight-line depreciation of $1,200,000 had been claimed on the building. The land was used in Wren Corporation's business.

19. After a plan of complete liquidation has been adopted, Green Corporation sells its only asset, land, to Rex (an unrelated party) for $250,000. Under the terms of the sale, Green receives cash of $50,000 and Rex's note in the amount of $200,000. The note is payable over five years ($40,000 per year) and carries an appropriate rate of interest. Immediately after the sale, Green distributes the cash and notes to Helen, the sole shareholder of

Green Corporation. Helen has a basis of $60,000 in the Green stock. What are the tax results to Helen if she wishes to defer as much gain as possible on the transaction? Assume the installment notes possess a value equal to the face amount.

20. Green Corporation's stock is held equally by three sisters, Abby, Bonnie, and Carol. The three sisters owned, as tenants in common, a tract of land on which a warehouse needed by the corporation was located. The land and warehouse had a basis of $325,000 and fair market value of $100,000. Three years prior to liquidation, the sisters transferred the land and warehouse to the corporation in return for stock. At the time of the liquidation, the land and warehouse had a fair market value of $60,000 and a tax basis of $322,000. In liquidation, Green Corporation transferred the land and warehouse equally to Abby, Bonnie, and Carol as tenants in common. How much loss would Green Corporation recognize on the distribution?

21. Brown Corporation has the following assets:

	Basis to Brown Corporation	Fair Market Value
Cash	$ 900,000	$ 900,000
Inventory	300,000	900,000
Equipment	3,180,000	1,800,000
Building	1,200,000	2,280,000
Land	120,000	120,000

The inventory had been purchased by Brown Corporation; the remaining assets were acquired seven years ago. Brown adopted a plan of liquidation in January 1996 and distributed its assets that same year to its shareholders, Lynn (70%) and Pat (30%). Lynn and Pat are unrelated. What are the tax consequences to Brown Corporation under the following independent circumstances:

a. The assets are distributed to Lynn and Pat in proportion to their stock interests (70% interest in each asset to Lynn and 30% interest in each asset to Pat).

b. The equipment, building, and land are distributed to Lynn, and the cash and inventory are distributed to Pat.

c. The equipment is distributed to Pat, and the remaining assets are distributed to Lynn.

d. What is the result in (a) if the equipment had been transferred to Brown Corporation in a § 351 transaction 10 months before the liquidation when the equipment had a basis of $3,180,000 and a fair market value of $1,980,000?

e. How should the assets be distributed for the most favorable tax consequences to Brown Corporation?

22. The stock in Gray Corporation is owned by Carol and Gail, unrelated individuals. Carol owns 80% and Gail owns 20% of the Gray stock. Gray Corporation has the following assets that are distributed in complete liquidation:

	Adjusted Basis	Fair Market Value
Cash	$600,000	$600,000
Inventory	80,000	200,000
Equipment	350,000	200,000

What gain or loss would Gray Corporation recognize on the liquidation if it distributes the cash and equipment to Carol and the inventory to Gail? What gain or loss would

Gray Corporation recognize if it distributes the cash and inventory to Carol and the equipment to Gail?

23. Blue Corporation acquired land in a § 351 exchange in 1994. The land had a basis of $1,800,000 and a fair market value of $1,950,000 on the date of the transfer. Blue Corporation has two shareholders, Ann and Paul, who are unrelated. Ann owns 80% of the stock in the corporation, and Paul owns 20%. Blue adopts a plan of liquidation in 1996. On this date, the value of the land has decreased to $600,000. In distributing the land either to Ann or to Paul, or to both, as part of the liquidating distributions from Blue Corporation, should Blue:
    a. Distribute all the land to Ann?
    b. Distribute all the land to Paul?
    c. Distribute 80% of the land to Ann and 20% to Paul?
    d. Distribute 50% of the land to Ann and 50% to Paul?
    e. Sell the land and distribute the proceeds of $600,000 proportionately to Ann and to Paul?

24. Assume in Problem 23 that the plan of liquidation is not adopted until 1997. In addition, assume the land had a fair market value of $1.5 million on the date of its transfer to the corporation. On the date of the liquidation, its fair market value has decreased to $600,000. How would your answer to Problem 23 change if:
    a. All the land is distributed to Ann?
    b. All the land is distributed to Paul?
    c. The land is distributed 80% to Ann and 20% to Paul?
    d. The land is distributed 50% to Ann and 50% to Paul?
    e. The land is sold and the proceeds of $600,000 are distributed proportionately to Ann and to Paul?

25. The stock of Yellow Corporation is held as follows: 85% by Red Corporation and 15% by Fred. Yellow Corporation is liquidated on October 1, 1996, pursuant to a plan of liquidation adopted on January 15, 1996. At the time of its liquidation, Yellow's assets had a basis of $2 million and a fair market value of $18 million. Red Corporation has a basis of $800,000 in its Yellow Corporation stock. The basis of the Yellow stock to Fred is $80,000.
    a. How much gain, if any, must Yellow Corporation recognize on the liquidation?
    b. How much gain, if any, is recognized on the receipt of property from Yellow Corporation by Red Corporation? By Fred?

26. Cardinal Corporation has a basis of $300,000 in stock of Redbird Corporation, a subsidiary in which it owns 90% of all classes of stock. Cardinal liquidates Redbird Corporation and acquires assets worth $1,500,000 with an adjusted basis to Redbird of $900,000.
    a. What basis would Cardinal Corporation have in the assets acquired from Redbird Corporation?
    b. Assume Redbird's assets had an adjusted basis of only $100,000 and are worth $250,000. What basis would Cardinal have in Redbird's assets?

27. Orange Corporation, owned by two individual shareholders, has a basis of $450,000 (fair market value of $1 million) in its assets and E & P of $80,000. Its liabilities total $100,000. If the assets were sold, all gain would be long-term capital gain or § 1231 gain. Green Corporation purchases 20% of all the stock of Orange Corporation for $180,000 on March 1, 1996; 15% for $135,000 on September 20, 1996; and 60% for $540,000 on December 1, 1996, for a total consideration of $855,000. Assume Orange's marginal tax rate is 34%.
    a. Is Green Corporation entitled to make an election under § 338?
    b. Assume Green Corporation may make an election under § 338. Should Green do so? When must Green make the election?
    c. What are the tax consequences to Orange Corporation and to Green Corporation if Green makes a valid election under § 338 but does not liquidate Orange?
    d. What is the tax result if Orange Corporation is liquidated four months after a valid § 338 election? Eve, who holds the 5% minority interest in Orange Corporation, has

a $10,000 basis in her stock in Orange. What is the tax result to Eve upon the
liquidation?

28. Green Corporation paid $5,400,000 for all the stock of Gray Corporation 10 years ago.
Gray Corporation's balance sheet is as follows:

Assets	
Cash	$ 135,000
Inventory	405,000
Machinery	270,000
Equipment	1,080,000
Land	1,350,000
	$ 3,240,000

Liabilities and Shareholders' Equity	
Accounts payable	$ 5,400,000
Common stock	5,400,000
Deficit	(7,560,000)
	$ 3,240,000

What are the tax consequences to Green Corporation if it liquidates Gray Corporation?
Prepare a letter to your client, Green Corporation (1010 Cypress Lane, Community, MN
55166) and a memo for the file in which you explain your conclusions.

29. a. José, a shareholder of White Corporation, exchanges his White Corporation stock for
stock in Green Corporation. The exchange is pursuant to a tax-free reorganization of
White and Green. José paid $150,000 for his stock in White Corporation three years
ago. The White stock is worth $300,000, and the stock José receives in Green is worth
$240,000. What is José's basis in the Green Corporation stock?

b. Assume José receives $60,000 cash in addition to the Green stock. What are the tax
consequences to José, and what basis does he have in the Green Corporation stock?

30. Quinn exchanges stock he owns in Redbird Corporation for stock in Bluebird Corporation and additionally receives $80,000 cash. The exchange is pursuant to a tax-free
reorganization of both corporations. Quinn paid $40,000 five years ago for the stock in
Redbird Corporation. The stock in Bluebird Corporation has a fair market value of
$240,000. Quinn's share of Redbird's E & P is $70,000. How will Quinn treat this
transaction for tax purposes?

31. Assume the same facts as in Problem 30, except that Quinn paid $360,000 (instead of
$40,000) for his stock in Redbird Corporation. How would Quinn treat the transaction
for tax purposes?

Research Problems for this chapter appear at the end of Chapter 28.

20

CORPORATE ACCUMULATIONS

LEARNING OBJECTIVES

After completing Chapter 20, you should be able to:

1. Appreciate the purpose of the accumulated earnings tax.

2. Determine the reasonable needs of the business.

3. Compute the accumulated earnings tax.

4. Discuss the reason for the personal holding company tax.

5. Recognize the requirements for personal holding company status.

6. Compute the personal holding company tax.

7. Compare the accumulated earnings and personal holding company taxes.

8. Plan to minimize (or avoid) the accumulated earnings tax.

9. Plan to minimize (or avoid) the personal holding company tax.

Presuming the alternative minimum tax (refer to Chapter 14) hurdle can be resolved, one major advantage of the corporate form is the opportunity to control the income tax burden of the owner(s). One way this control can be accomplished is to accumulate the earnings of the business at the corporate level. A temporary or permanent accumulation of earnings in a corporation results in a deferral of the shareholder-level tax. The corporation can invest in instruments that produce tax-free income (e.g., state and local bonds) or buy stock in other domestic corporations to take advantage of the dividends received deduction. Accumulations at the corporate level could result in a *modest* tax benefit because dividend income would be converted into long-term capital gain. Long-term capital gains of noncorporate taxpayers cannot be taxed at a rate in excess of 28 percent. Dividend income is ordinary income and can be taxed at a rate as high as 39.6 percent.

Congress took steps to stem corporate accumulations as early as the first income tax law enacted under the Sixteenth Amendment. Today, in addition to the usual corporate income tax, an extra tax is imposed on earnings accumulated beyond the reasonable needs of the business. Also, a penalty tax may be imposed on undistributed personal holding company income. This chapter demonstrates how earnings can be accumulated without leading to adverse tax consequences—the imposition of additional taxes.

PENALTY TAX ON UNREASONABLE ACCUMULATIONS

1 LEARNING OBJECTIVE
Appreciate the purpose of the accumulated earnings tax.

One method of optimizing the distribution of corporate earnings is to accumulate the earnings until the most advantageous time to distribute them to the shareholders. If the board of directors is aware of the tax problems of the shareholders, it can channel earnings into the shareholders' pockets with a minimum of tax cost by using any of several mechanisms. The corporation can distribute dividends only in years when the major shareholders are in lower tax brackets. Alternatively, dividend distributions might be curtailed, causing the value of the stock to increase in a manner similar to a savings account. Later, the shareholders can sell their stock in the year of their choice at an amount that reflects the increased retained earnings. The capital gain may be taxed at a lower rate (28 percent versus 39.6 percent), or the capital gain could be postponed to years when the shareholders have capital losses to offset the gains. Alternatively, the shareholders can retain their shares. Upon death, the estate or heirs will receive a step-up in basis equal to the fair market value of the stock on the date of death or, if elected, on the alternate valuation date. The increment in value represented by the step-up in basis will be largely attributable to the earnings retained by the corporation and will not be subject to income taxation.

Accumulating corporate earnings always entails problems, however. A penalty tax may be imposed on accumulated taxable earnings, or a personal holding company tax may be levied on certain accumulated passive income. Consider first the 39.6 percent **accumulated earnings tax (AET).** The tax law is framed to discourage the retention of earnings that are unrelated to the business needs of the company. Earnings retained in the business to avoid the imposition of the tax that would have been imposed on distributions to the shareholder are subject to a 39.6 percent penalty tax.

EXAMPLE 1

Velvia operated a consulting business as a sole proprietor in 1995. Assume she is in the 39.6% tax bracket in 1996, and she incorporates her business at the beginning of the year. Her business earns $120,000 in 1996, before her salary of $60,000. Since $60,000 of the income is accumulated, $13,760 of taxes are "saved" ($23,760 individual tax versus $10,000 corporate tax on the $60,000 accumulated). This accumulated savings could occur each year with the corporation reinvesting the saved taxes. Thus, without an accumulated earnings tax or personal holding company tax, Velvia could use her corporation like a savings account. For example, the corporation could take advantage of the dividends received deduction for dividend-paying stocks. With the top individual tax rate (39.6% for 1996) above the top corporate tax rate (35% for 1996), it is more attractive to hold investment property in a C corporation than in a flow-through entity (partnership, S corporation, or sole proprietorship). However, the earnings are still at the corporate level, and Velvia might be in a higher individual rate when the accumulated earnings are distributed. ▼

THE ELEMENT OF INTENT

Although the penalty tax is normally applied against closely held corporations, a corporation is not exempt from the tax merely because its stock is widely held.[1] For example, a Second Court of Appeals decision[2] imposed the tax upon a widely held corporation with over 1,500 shareholders. However, a much smaller group of shareholders actually controlled the corporation. As a practical matter, a widely held corporation that is not under the legal or effective control of a small group is unlikely to be suspected of accumulating earnings for the purpose of tax avoidance.

The key to imposition of the tax is not the number of the shareholders in the corporation but whether a shareholder group controls corporate policy. If such a group does exist and withholds dividends to protect its own tax position, an AET (§ 531) problem might materialize.

When a corporation is formed or used to shield its shareholders from individual taxes by accumulating rather than distributing earnings and profits, the "bad" purpose for accumulating earnings is considered to exist under § 532(a). This subjective test, in effect, asks, Did the corporation and/or shareholder(s) *intend* to retain the earnings in order to avoid the tax on dividends? According to the Supreme Court, the tax avoidance motive need *not* be the dominant or controlling purpose to trigger application of the penalty tax; it need only be a contributing factor to the retention of earnings.[3] The accumulation of funds beyond the corporation's reasonable needs is determinative of the existence of a

---

[1] § 532(c).
[2] *Trico Products v. Comm.*, 43–2 USTC ¶9540, 31 AFTR 394, 137 F.2d 424 (CA–2, 1943).

[3] *U.S. v. The Donruss Co.*, 69–1 USTC ¶9167, 23 AFTR2d 69–418, 89 S.Ct. 501 (USSC, 1969).

"bad" purpose, unless the contrary can be proven by the preponderance of the evidence. The fact that a business is a mere holding or investment company is *prima facie* evidence of this tax avoidance purpose.[4]

IMPOSITION OF THE TAX AND THE ACCUMULATED EARNINGS CREDIT

Contrary to its name, the penalty tax is not levied on the corporate accumulated earnings balance. Instead, the tax is imposed on the current year's *addition* to this balance not needed for a reasonable business purpose. The penalty tax is not imposed upon S corporations, personal holding companies, foreign personal holding companies, tax-exempt organizations, or passive foreign investment companies. The tax is in addition to the regular corporate tax and the 20 percent alternative minimum tax. Currently, the tax rate is 39.6 percent.

Most corporations are allowed a **minimum credit** of $250,000 against accumulated taxable income, even when earnings are accumulated beyond reasonable business needs. However, certain personal service corporations in health, law, engineering, architecture, accounting, actuarial science, performing arts, and consulting are limited to a $150,000 minimum credit. Moreover, a nonservice corporation (other than a holding or investment company) may retain more than $250,000 (and a service organization may retain more than $150,000) of accumulated earnings if the company can justify that the accumulation is necessary to meet the *reasonable needs of the business*.[5]

The **accumulated earnings credit** is the greater of the following:

1. The current earnings and profits (E & P) for the tax year that are needed to meet the reasonable needs of the business (see the subsequent discussion) *less* the net long-term capital gain for the year (net of any tax). In determining the reasonable needs for any one year, the accumulated E & P of past years must be taken into account.
2. The amount by which the minimum credit exceeds the accumulated E & P of the corporation at the close of the preceding tax year.

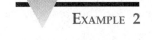

EXAMPLE 2

Yellow Corporation, a calendar year manufacturing concern, has accumulated E & P of $120,000 as of December 31, 1995. For 1996, it has no capital gains and has current E & P of $140,000. A realistic estimate places Yellow's reasonable needs of the business for 1996 at $200,000. The allowable credit is the greater of (1) or (2).

	(1)	(2)
Reasonable needs	$ 200,000	
Minimum credit		$ 250,000
Accumulated E & P	(120,000)	(120,000)
Potential credit	$ 80,000	$ 130,000

Thus, the credit becomes $130,000 (the greater of $80,000 or $130,000). ▼

---

[4] § 533. See, for example, *H. C. Cockrell Warehouse Corp.*, 71 T.C. 1036 (1979).
[5] §§ 535(c) and 537 and Reg. § 1.537–1.

Several observations can be made about the accumulated earnings credit. First, the minimum credit is of no consequence as long as the prior year's ending balance in accumulated E & P equals or exceeds the allowed threshold ($250,000 or $150,000). Second, when the credit is based on reasonable needs, the credit is the amount by which those needs exceed accumulated E & P. Third, a taxpayer must choose between the reasonable needs credit (item 1) or the minimum credit (item 2). Combining the two in the same year is not permissible. Fourth, although the § 531 tax is not imposed on accumulated E & P, the amount of the credit depends upon the balance of this account as of the end of the preceding year.

REASONABLE NEEDS OF THE BUSINESS

2 LEARNING OBJECTIVE
Determine the reasonable needs of the business.

If a corporation's funds are invested in assets essential to the needs of the business, the IRS will have a difficult time imposing the AET. "Thus, the size of the accumulated earnings and profits or surplus is not the crucial factor; rather it is the reasonableness and nature of the surplus."[6] What are the reasonable business needs of a corporation? This question is difficult to answer and can lead to disputes with the IRS.

Justifiable Needs—In General. The **reasonable needs of a business** include the business's reasonably anticipated needs.[7] These anticipated needs must be specific, definite, and feasible. A number of court decisions illustrate that indefinite plans referred to only briefly in corporate minutes merely give the taxpayer a false feeling of security.[8]

The Regulations list some legitimate reasons that could indicate that a corporation is accumulating earnings to meet the reasonable needs of the business. Earnings may be allowed to accumulate to provide for bona fide expansion of the business enterprise or replacement of plant and facilities as well as to acquire a business enterprise through the purchase of stock or assets. Provision for the retirement of bona fide indebtedness created in connection with the trade or business (e.g., the establishment of a sinking fund for the retirement of bonds issued by the corporation) is a legitimate reason for accumulating earnings under ordinary circumstances. Providing necessary working capital for the business (e.g., to acquire inventories) and providing for investment or loans to suppliers or customers (if necessary to maintain the business of the corporation) are valid grounds for accumulating earnings.[9] Funds may be retained for self-insurance[10] and realistic business contingencies (e.g., lawsuits, patent infringements).[11] Accumulations to avoid an unfavorable competitive position[12] and to carry key employee life insurance policies[13] are justifiable. Accumulation to provide for the loss of a key customer or client is a reasonable need of the business.[14]

---

[6] *Smoot Sand & Gravel Corp. v. Comm.*, 60–1 USTC ¶9241, 5 AFTR2d 626, 274 F.2d 495 (CA–4, 1960).

[7] § 537(a)(1).

[8] See, for example, *Fine Realty, Inc. v. U.S.*, 62–2 USTC ¶9758, 10 AFTR2d 5751, 209 F.Supp. 286 (D.Ct. Minn., 1962).

[9] Reg. § 1.537–2(b).

[10] *Halby Chemical Co., Inc. v. U.S.*, 67–2 USTC ¶9500, 19 AFTR2d 1589, 180 Ct.Cls. 584 (Ct.Cls., 1967).

[11] *Dielectric Materials Co.*, 57 T.C. 587 (1972).

[12] *North Valley Metabolic Laboratories*, 34 TCM 400, T.C.Memo. 1975–79.

[13] *Emeloid Co. v. Comm.*, 51–1 USTC ¶66,013, 40 AFTR 674, 189 F.2d 230 (CA–3, 1951). Key employee life insurance is a policy on the life of a key employee that is owned by and made payable to the employer. Such insurance enables the employer to recoup some of the economic loss that could materialize upon the untimely death of the key employee.

[14] *EMI Corporation*, 50 TCM 569, T.C.Memo. 1985–386, and *James H. Rutter*, 52 TCM 326, T.C.Memo. 1986–407.

The reasonable business needs of a company also include the post-death § 303 redemption requirements of a corporation.[15] Accumulations for such purposes are limited to the amount needed (or reasonably anticipated to be needed) to redeem stock included in the gross estate of the decedent-shareholder.[16] This amount may not exceed the sum of the death taxes and funeral and administration expenses allowable under § 2053 or § 2106.[17]

Section 537(b) provides that reasonable accumulations to pay future product liability losses represent a reasonable anticipated need of the business. Guidelines for the application of this allowance are prescribed in Proposed Regulations.

Justifiable Needs—Working Capital Requirements for Inventory Situations.

For many years, the penalty tax on accumulated earnings was based upon the concept of retained earnings. The courts generally looked at retained earnings alone to determine whether there was an unreasonable accumulation. However, a corporation may have a large retained earnings balance and yet possess no liquid assets with which to pay dividends. Therefore, the emphasis should more appropriately be placed upon the liquidity of a corporation. Does the business have liquid assets *not* needed that could be used to pay dividends? The courts did not begin to use this liquidity approach until 1960, however.

The operating cycle of a business is the average time interval between the acquisition of materials (or services) entering the business and the final realization of cash. The courts seized upon the operating cycle because it had the advantage of objectivity for purposes of determining working capital. A normal business has two distinct cycles:

1. Purchase of inventory → the production process → finished goods inventory.
2. Sale of merchandise → accounts receivable → cash collection.

A systematic operating cycle formula was developed in *Bardahl Manufacturing Co.* and *Bardahl International Corp.*[18] The technique became known as the *Bardahl* formula. This formula is not a precise tool and is subject to various interpretations.

The following is the standard formula used to determine the reasonable working capital needs for a corporation:

$$\text{Inventory cycle} = \frac{\text{Average inventory}}{\text{Cost of goods sold}}$$

Plus

$$\text{Accounts receivable cycle} = \frac{\text{Average accounts receivable}}{\text{Net sales}}$$

---

[15] The § 303 redemption to pay death taxes and administration expenses of a deceased shareholder is discussed in Chapter 18. See § 537(a).

[16] §§ 537(a)(2) and (b)(1).

[17] § 303(a).

[18] *Bardahl Manufacturing Co.*, 24 TCM 1030, T.C.Memo. 1965–200; *Bardahl International Corp.*, 25 TCM 935, T.C.Memo. 1966–182. See also *Apollo Industries, Inc. v. Comm.*, 66–1 USTC ¶9294, 17 AFTR2d 518, 358 F.2d 867 (CA–1, 1966).

Minus

$$\text{Accounts payable cycle} = \frac{\text{Average accounts payable}^{19}}{\text{Purchases} + \text{cash operating expenses}}$$

Equals

A decimal percentage

This imprecise formula assumes that working capital needs are computed on a yearly basis. However, this may not provide the most favorable result. A business that experiences seasonally based high and low cycles illustrates this point. For example, a construction company can justify a greater working capital need if computations are based on a cycle that includes the winter months only and not on an annual average.[20] In the same vein, an incorporated CPA firm would choose a cycle during the slow season.

The decimal percentage derived above, when multiplied by the cost of goods sold plus general, administrative, and selling expenses (not including unpaid Federal income taxes and depreciation),[21] equals the working capital needs of the business. Paid estimated Federal income taxes are treated as operating expenses, but profit sharing contributions and charitable contributions are not operating expenses.

If the statistically computed working capital needs plus any extraordinary expenses are more than the current year's net working capital, no penalty tax is imposed. Working capital is the excess of current assets over current liabilities. This amount is the relatively liquid portion of the total business capital that is a buffer for meeting obligations within the normal operating cycle of the business.

However, if working capital needs plus any extraordinary expenses are less than the current year's net working capital, the possibility of the imposition of a penalty tax does exist.[22]

The IRS normally takes the position that the operating cycle should be reduced by the accounts payable cycle. The IRS maintains that the payment of these expenses may be postponed by various credit arrangements that will reduce the operating capital requirements. However, a number of court decisions have omitted such a reduction. Some courts use all payables, while other courts use only material and trade payables. In any case, a corporate tax planner should not have to rely on creditors to avoid the accumulated earnings tax. The corporation with the most acute working capital problem will probably have a large accounts payable balance. If the formula for determining reasonable working capital needs is used, a large accounts payable balance will result in a sizable reduction in the maximum working capital allowable before the tax is imposed. For tax planning purposes, a corporation should hold accounts payable at a reduced level.

[19] The accounts payable cycle was developed in *Kingsbury Investments, Inc.*, 28 TCM 1082, T.C.Memo. 1969–205. Some courts have used only purchases and not total operating expenses: *Suwannee Lumber Mfg. Co., Inc.*, 39 TCM 572, T.C.Memo. 1979–477. But see *Snow Manufacturing*, 86 T.C. 260 (1986).

[20] See *Audits of Construction Contracts*, AICPA, 1965, p. 25.

[21] In *W. L. Mead, Inc.*, 34 TCM 924, T.C.Memo. 1975–215, the Tax Court allowed depreciation to be included in the expenses of a service firm with no inventory. Likewise, in *Doug-Long, Inc.*, 72 T.C. 158 (1979), the Tax Court allowed a truckstop to include quarterly estimated tax payments in operating expenses.

[22] *Electric Regulator Corp. v. Comm.*, 64–2 USTC ¶9705, 14 AFTR2d 5447, 336 F.2d 339 (CA–2, 1964) used "quick assets" (current assets less inventory).

TAX IN THE NEWS

APPLYING THE *BARDAHL* FORMULA COULD BE MISLEADING

Experience in tax audits has shown that the *Bardahl* formula is a double-edged sword. The problem is that it measures working capital, not cash. In reality, the payment of dividends—which is the whole purpose of the AET provisions—can be made only in cash. When the *Bardahl* formula works to a corporation's disadvantage, it is important to determine how much cash, on average, is available for distribution. Case law has held that a corporation should not be forced to incur debt or sell off business assets merely to pay dividends so as to avoid the AET. The statement of cash flows may be useful in defending against an AET attack, because it highlights fixed assets acquired and other business investments made. Cash on hand at the end of the year may not be a fair reflection of the average of cash available during the year. In addition, bank covenants, which prevent the payment of dividends or require certain levels of working capital, should be taken into account since they evidence a nonprohibited purpose for accumulating earnings. However, lack of cash due to nonbusiness related activities, such as loans to shareholders, will not help avoid AET exposure.

On the other hand, when the *Bardahl* formula indicates that the working capital needs are greater than the working capital available, weary IRS agents are sometimes willing to accept this as dispositive that no AET should be assessed, rather than investigating the other aspects of potential AET exposure.

SOURCE: Excerpted by permission from Michael J. Goldberg, "The Accumulated Earnings Tax: A Practical Approach to a Subjective Assessment," *The Tax Adviser*, March 1993, p. 146.

Justifiable Needs—Working Capital Requirements for Noninventory Situations.   A service business does not purchase inventories, so part of the operating cycle in the *Bardahl* formula is missing. However, a service business incurs certain costs such as salaries and overhead for a period of time before billing customers for services. Some courts have used a rough rule of thumb to determine an inventory equivalent cycle. Under certain circumstances, a human resource accounting (HRA) approach may be used to determine the working capital needs of a noninventory corporation. The use of an HRA approach is based on the contention that the strength of a service business—and its major asset—is its highly educated, skilled technicians. Such individuals must be available both to attract clients and to execute projects efficiently. In the event of a business downturn, it would be foolish to abruptly discharge highly paid specialists, recruited and trained at considerable expense. The business decline might prove to be of brief duration.

One court[23] allowed an engineering firm to add to the IRS's *Bardahl*-calculated operating reserve the reasonable professional and technical payroll for an additional period of two months (or 60 days). The Court felt that this extra amount

[23] *Simons-Eastern Co. v. U.S.*, 73–1 USTC ¶9279, 31 AFTR2d 73–640, 354 F.Supp. 1003 (D.Ct. Ga., 1972). See also *Delaware Trucking Co., Inc.*, 32 TCM 105, T.C.Memo. 1973–29; *Magic Mart, Inc.*, 51 T.C. 775 (1969); and *Technalysis*, 101 T.C. 397 (1993), a three-month period.

would "... allow sufficient reserve for one cycle of full operation plus a reasonable period (60 days) of curtailed operation to recapture business or, in the alternative, to face up to hard decisions on reducing the scope of the entire operation or abandoning it." Further, the Court expressed its opinion that a multiple of reasonable professional and technical salaries is a useful method for determining the amount to be included in an operating reserve. However, the Court did not indicate why it selected two months as the magic number. It can be anticipated that the courts will continue to evolve a *Bardahl*-like formula for noninventory corporations.

No Justifiable Needs. Certain situations do *not* call for the accumulation of earnings. For example, accumulating earnings to make loans to shareholders[24] or brother-sister corporations is not considered within the reasonable needs of the business.[25] Accumulations to retire stock without curtailment of the business and for unrealistic business hazards (e.g., depression of the U.S. economy) are invalid reasons for accumulating funds.[26] The same holds true for accumulations made to carry out investments in properties or securities unrelated to the corporation's activity.[27]

Concept Summary 20–1 reviews the previous discussion regarding what does and does not constitute a reasonable need of the business.

Measuring the Accumulation. Should the cost or fair market value of assets be used to determine whether a corporation has accumulated E & P beyond its reasonable needs? This issue remains unclear. The Supreme Court has indicated that fair market value is to be used when dealing with marketable securities.[28] Although the Court admitted that the concept of E & P does not include unrealized appreciation, it asserted that the current asset ratio must be considered in determining if accumulated earnings are reasonable. Thus, the Court looked to the economic realities of the situation and held that fair market value is to be used with respect to readily marketable securities. The Court's opinion did not address the proper basis for valuation of assets other than marketable securities. However, the IRS may assert that this rule should be extended to include other assets. Therefore, tax advisers and corporate personnel should regularly check all security holdings to guard against accumulations caused by the appreciation of investments.

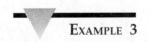

EXAMPLE 3

Robin Company had accumulated E & P of approximately $2,000,000. Five years ago, the company invested $150,000 in various stocks and bonds. At the end of the current tax year, the fair market value of these securities approximates $2,500,000. Two of Robin's shareholders, father and son, own 75% of the stock. If these securities are valued at cost, current assets minus current liabilities are deemed to be equal to the reasonable needs of the business. However, if the marketable securities are valued at their $2,500,000 fair market value, the value of the liquid assets greatly exceeds the corporation's reasonable needs. Under the Supreme Court's economic reality test, the fair market value is used. Consequently, the corporation is subject to the § 531 penalty tax. ▼

[24] Reg. §§ 1.537–2(c)(1), (2) and (3).

[25] See *Young's Rubber Corp.*, 21 TCM 1593, T.C.Memo. 1962–300.

[26] *Turnbull, Inc. v. Comm.*, 67–1 USTC ¶9221, 19 AFTR2d 609, 373 F.2d 91 (CA–5, 1967), and Reg. § 1.537–2(c)(5).

[27] Reg. § 1.537–2(c)(4).

[28] *Ivan Allen Co. v. U.S.*, 75–2 USTC ¶9557, 36 AFTR2d 75–5200, 95 S.Ct. 2501 (USSC, 1975).

CONCEPT SUMMARY 20–1

Reasonable Business Needs

Legitimate Reasons	Invalid Reasons
Expansion of a business.	Loans to shareholders.
Replacement of capital assets.	Loans to brother-sister corporations.
Replacement of plant.	Future depression.
Acquisition of a business.	Unrealistic contingencies.
Working capital needs.	Investment in assets unrelated to the business.
Product liability loss.	Retirement of stock without a curtailment of the business.*
Loans to suppliers or customers.	
Redemption under § 303 to pay death taxes and administration expenses of a shareholder.	
Realistic business hazards.	
Loss of a major customer or client.	
Reserve for actual lawsuit.	
Protection of a family business from takeover by outsiders.	
Debt retirement.	
Self-insurance.	

*But see *Technalysis*, 101 T.C. 397 (1993).

3   LEARNING OBJECTIVE
Compute the accumulated earnings tax.

MECHANICS OF THE PENALTY TAX

The taxable base for the AET is a company's *accumulated taxable income (ATI)*. Taxable income of the corporation is modified as follows:[29]

For a corporation that is not a mere holding or investment company, the "certain adjustments" include the following items as deductions:

---

[29] § 535(a).

1. Corporate income tax accrued.
2. Charitable contributions in excess of 10 percent of adjusted taxable income.
3. Capital loss adjustment.[30]
4. Excess of net long-term capital gain over net short-term capital loss, diminished by the capital gain tax and reduced by net capital losses from earlier years.

and the following items as additions:

5. Capital loss carryovers and carrybacks.
6. Net operating loss deduction.
7. Dividends received deduction.

The purpose of each of these adjustments is to produce an amount that more closely represents the dividend-paying capacity of the corporation. For example, the corporate income tax is deducted from taxable income since the corporation does not have this money to pay dividends. Conversely, the dividends received deduction is added to taxable income since the deduction has no impact upon the ability to pay a dividend. Note that item 4, in effect, allows a corporation to accumulate any capital gains without a penalty tax.

Payment of dividends reduces the amount of ATI subject to the penalty tax. The dividends paid deduction includes any dividends paid during the tax year that the shareholders must report as ordinary income *and* any dividends paid within 2½ months after the close of the tax year.[31] However, a nontaxable stock dividend does not affect the dividends paid deduction. Further, a shareholder may file a consent statement to treat as a dividend the amount specified in the statement. A *consent dividend* is taxed to the shareholder even though it is not actually distributed. The shareholder treats the consent dividend as a contribution to the capital of the corporation (paid-in capital).[32]

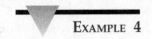

EXAMPLE 4

A nonservice closely held corporation that had no capital gains or losses in prior years has the following financial transactions for calendar year 1996:

Taxable income	$300,000
Tax liability	100,250
Excess charitable contributions	22,000
Short-term capital loss	(40,000)
Dividends received (less than 20% owned)	100,000
Research and development expenses	46,000
Dividends paid in 1996	40,000
Accumulated E & P (1/1/96)	220,000

Presuming the corporation is subject to the § 531 tax and has *no* reasonable business needs that justify its accumulations, ATI is calculated as follows:

---

[30] This deduction (item 3) and item 4 are either/or deductions since a corporation will not have both in the same year. For the capital loss adjustment, see § 535(b)(5).

[31] §§ 535(a), 561(a), and 563(a).

[32] §§ 565(a) and (c)(2). The consent dividend procedure is appropriate if the corporation is not in a position to make a cash or property distribution to its shareholders. The dividends paid deduction is discussed more fully later in the chapter.

Taxable income		$ 300,000
Plus: 70% dividends received deduction		70,000
		$ 370,000
Less: Tax liability	$100,250	
Excess charitable contributions	22,000	
Net short-term capital loss adjustment	40,000	
Dividends paid	40,000	
Accumulated earnings minimum credit ($250,000 − $220,000)	30,000	(232,250)
Accumulated taxable income (ATI)		$ 137,750

Thus, the accumulated earnings penalty tax for 1996 is $54,549 ($137,750 × 39.6%). ▼

EXAMPLE 5

In Example 4, assume that the reasonable needs of the business of § 535(c) amount to $270,000 in 1996. The current year's accumulated earnings are now reduced by $50,000 ($270,000 − $220,000), rather than the $30,000 minimum credit. ATI is $117,750, and the penalty tax is $46,629 ($117,750 × 39.6%). Note that the first $220,000 of accumulated earnings *cannot* be omitted in determining whether taxable income for the current year is reasonably needed by the enterprise. ▼

PERSONAL HOLDING COMPANY PENALTY TAX

4 **LEARNING OBJECTIVE**
Discuss the reason for the personal holding company tax.

The personal holding company (PHC) tax was enacted to discourage the sheltering of certain types of passive income in corporations owned by high tax bracket individuals. These "incorporated pocketbooks" were frequently found in the entertainment and construction industries. For example, a taxpayer could shelter the income from securities in a corporation, which would pay no dividends, and allow the corporation's stock to increase in value. Like the accumulated earnings tax, the purpose of the 39.6 percent PHC tax is to force the distribution of corporate earnings to the shareholders. However, in any one year, the IRS cannot impose both the PHC tax and the accumulated earnings tax.[33]

EXAMPLE 6

Considerable tax savings could be achieved by incorporating a "pocketbook" if § 541 did not exist. Assume that investments that yield $50,000 a year are transferred to a corporation by a 39.6% income tax bracket shareholder. A tax savings of $12,300 will occur each year if no dividends are paid to the shareholder. With no corporation, there would be a total tax liability of $19,800 (39.6% × $50,000), but with a corporation the tax liability is only $7,500 in 1996 (15% × $50,000). Further, if the yield of $50,000 is in the form of dividends, the corporate tax will be even less because of the dividends received deduction. ▼

Whether a corporation will be included within the statutory definition of a PHC for any particular year depends upon the facts and circumstances during that year.[34] Therefore, PHC status may be conferred even in the absence of any avoidance intent on the part of the corporation. In one situation,[35] a manufacturing operation adopted a plan of complete liquidation, sold its business, and

[33] § 532(b)(1) and Reg. § 1.541–1(a).
[34] *Affiliated Enterprises, Inc. v. Comm.*, 44–1 USTC ¶9178, 32 AFTR 153, 140 F.2d 647 (CA–10, 1944).

[35] *Weiss v. U.S.*, 75–2 USTC ¶9538, 36 AFTR2d 75–5186 (D.Ct. Ohio, 1975). See also *O'Sullivan Rubber Co. v. Comm.*, 41–2 USTC ¶9521, 27 AFTR 529, 120 F.2d 845 (CA–2, 1941).

invested the proceeds of the sale in U.S. Treasury bills and certificates of deposit. During the liquidating corporation's last tax year, 100 percent of the corporation's adjusted ordinary gross income was interest income. Since the corporation was owned by one shareholder, the corporation was a PHC, even though in the process of liquidation.

Certain types of corporations are expressly excluded from PHC status in § 542(c):

- Tax-exempt organizations under § 501(a).
- Banks and domestic building and loan associations.
- Life insurance companies.
- Surety companies.
- Foreign personal holding companies.
- Lending or finance companies.
- Foreign corporations.
- Small business investment companies.

Without these exceptions, the business world could not perform necessary activities without a high rate of taxation. For example, a legitimate finance company should not be burdened by the PHC tax because it is performing a valuable business function of loaning money. In contrast, in the case of a classic incorporated pocketbook, the major purpose is to shelter the investment income from possible higher individual tax rates.

DEFINITION OF A PERSONAL HOLDING COMPANY

5   **LEARNING OBJECTIVE**
Recognize the requirements for personal holding company status.

The PHC provisions include two tests:

- Was more than 50 percent of the *value* of the outstanding stock owned by five or fewer individuals at any time during the *last half* of the taxable year?
- Is a substantial portion (60 percent or more) of the corporate income (adjusted ordinary gross income) composed of passive types of income such as dividends, interest, rents, royalties, or certain personal service income?

If the answer to *both* of these questions is yes, the corporation is classified as a **personal holding company (PHC).** Once classified as a PHC, the corporation could be required to pay a 39.6 percent penalty tax in addition to the regular corporate income tax.

Stock Ownership Test. To meet the stock ownership test, more than 50 percent *in value* of the outstanding stock must be owned, directly or indirectly, by or for not more than five individuals sometime during the last half of the tax year. Thus, if the corporation has 9 or fewer shareholders, it automatically meets this test. If 10 unrelated individuals own *equal* portions of the value of the outstanding stock, the stock ownership requirement is not met. However, if these 10 individuals do not hold equal value, the test is met.

The ownership test is based on fair market value and not on the number of shares outstanding. Fair market value is determined in light of all the circumstances and is based on the company's net worth, earning and dividend-paying capacity, appreciation of assets, and other relevant factors. If there are two or more classes of stock outstanding, the total value of all the stock is allocated among the various classes according to the relative value of each class.[36]

---

[36] Reg. § 1.542-3(c)

In determining the stock ownership of an individual, broad constructive ownership rules apply. Under § 544, the following attribution rules determine indirect ownership:

1. Any stock owned by a corporation, partnership, trust, or estate is considered to be owned proportionately by the shareholders, partners, or beneficiaries.
2. The stock owned by the members of an individual's family (brothers, sisters, spouse, ancestors, and lineal descendants) or by the individual's partner is considered to be owned by the individual.
3. If an individual has an option to purchase stock, the stock is regarded as owned by that person.[37]
4. Convertible securities are treated as outstanding stock.

EXAMPLE 7

During the last half of the tax year, Press Corporation has 1,000 shares of outstanding stock, 499 of which are held by various individuals having no relationship to one another and none of whom are partners. The remaining 501 shares are held by seven shareholders as follows:

Dana	100
Dana's spouse	50
Dana's brother	20
Dana's sister	70
Dana's father	120
Dana's son	80
Dana's daughter	61

Under the family attribution rules of § 544(a)(2), Dana owns 501 shares of Press for purposes of determining stock ownership in a PHC. ▼

ETHICAL CONSIDERATIONS

Staying Single for the Sake of the Company

Falcon Corporation is a closely held corporation, and for many years it has satisfied the gross income test. The company has avoided PHC status, however, by not meeting the stock ownership test.

Beth James and Harvey Mason, both shareholders in Falcon, have fallen in love and are considering marriage. When the other shareholders learn about the possible marriage and realize that it would cause Falcon to become a PHC, they suggest that Beth and Harvey live together and remain single.

Do you have any comment and advice regarding this moral and legal dilemma?

Attribution rules 2, 3, and 4 are applicable only for the purpose of classifying a corporation as a PHC and cannot be used to avoid the application of the PHC provisions. Basically, the broad constructive ownership rules make it difficult for a closely held corporation to avoid application of the stock ownership test.

Gross Income Test. The gross income test is met if 60 percent or more of the corporation's **adjusted ordinary gross income (AOGI)** consists of certain passive

---

[37] For examples of how these constructive ownership rules operate, see Reg. §§ 1.544-2, -3(a), and -4.

▼ **FIGURE 20–1**
Adjusted Ordinary Gross
Income Determination

Gross income (defined in § 61)

Less:
• Capital gains.
• Section 1231 gains.

Equals: Ordinary gross income (OGI).

Less:
• Depreciation, property taxes, interest expense, and rental expenses directly related to gross income from rents (not to exceed the income from rents).
• Depreciation, property and severance taxes, interest expense, and rental expenses directly related to gross income from mineral, oil, and gas royalties (not to exceed gross income from the royalties).
• Interest on a condemnation award, a judgment, a tax refund, and an obligation of the United States held by a dealer.

Equals: Adjusted ordinary gross income (AOGI).

income items (PHC income). AOGI is calculated by subtracting certain items from gross income (as defined by § 61).[38] The adjustments required to arrive at AOGI appear in Figure 20–1.

In Figure 20–1, the deductions from gross income result in the intermediate concept, **ordinary gross income (OGI),** whose use is noted subsequently. The starting point, gross income, is not necessarily synonymous with gross receipts. In fact, for transactions in stocks, securities, and commodities, the term "gross income" includes only the excess of gains over any losses.[39]

PHC income includes income from dividends; interest; royalties; annuities;[40] rents; mineral, oil, and gas royalties; copyright royalties; produced film rents; computer software royalties; and amounts from certain personal service contracts.

EXAMPLE 8

Crow Corporation has four shareholders, and its AOGI is $95,000, consisting of gross income of $40,000 from a merchandising operation, interest income of $15,000, dividend income of $25,000, and adjusted income of $15,000 from rents. Total passive income is $55,000 ($15,000 + $25,000 + $15,000). Since 60% of AOGI (60% × $95,000 = $57,000) is greater than the passive income ($55,000), the corporation is not a PHC. ▼

EXAMPLE 9

Assume in Example 8 that the corporation received $21,000 in interest income rather than $15,000. Total passive income is now $61,000 ($21,000 + $25,000 + $15,000). Since 60% of AOGI (60% × $101,000 = $60,600) is less than the passive income of $61,000, the corporation is a PHC. ▼

Most passive types of income such as dividends, interest, royalties, and annuities cause few classification problems. Certain income items, however, may or may not be classified as PHC income. Special rules apply to rent income, mineral, oil, and gas royalties, and personal service contracts.

Rent Income. Although rent income is normally classified as PHC income, such income can be excluded from that category if two tests are met. The first test is met if a corporation's adjusted income from rents is 50 percent or more of the corporation's AOGI. The second test is satisfied if the total dividends for the tax

[38] §§ 543(b)(1) and (2).
[39] Reg. § 1.542–2.
[40] § 543(a)(1).

year are equal to or greater than the amount by which the nonrent PHC income exceeds 10 percent of OGI.[41] Dividends for this purpose include those actually paid, those considered as paid on the last day of the tax year, and consent dividends (see the later discussion of the dividends paid deduction). The taxpayer must meet *both* tests for the rent income to be excluded from PHC income (see Figure 20–4 later in the chapter).

With respect to the 50 percent test, *adjusted income from rents* is defined as gross income from rents reduced by certain deductions. The deductions are depreciation, property taxes, interest, and rent. Generally, compensation is not included in the term "rents" and is not an allowable deduction. The final amount included in AOGI as adjusted income from rents cannot be less than zero.

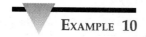

EXAMPLE 10

Assume that a corporation has rent income of $10,000 and the following business deductions:

Depreciation on rental property	$1,000
Interest on mortgage	2,500
Real property taxes	1,500
Salaries and other business expenses	3,000

The adjusted income from rents included in AOGI is $5,000 ($10,000 − $1,000 − $2,500 − $1,500). Salaries and other business expenses do not affect the calculation of AOGI. ▼

A company deriving its income primarily from rental activities can avoid PHC status by merely distributing as dividends the amount of nonrent PHC income that exceeds 10 percent of its OGI.

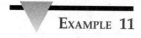

EXAMPLE 11

During the tax year, Norman Corporation receives $15,000 in rent income, $4,000 in dividends, and a $1,000 long-term capital gain. Corporate deductions for depreciation, interest, and real estate taxes allocable to the rent income are $10,000. The company pays a total of $2,500 in dividends to its eight shareholders. To determine whether the rent income is PHC income, OGI, AOGI, and adjusted income from rents must be calculated.

Rent income	$15,000
Dividends	4,000
Long-term capital gain	1,000
Gross income	$20,000
Deduct: Gains from sale or disposition of capital assets	(1,000)
OGI	$19,000
Deduct: Depreciation, interest, and real estate taxes	(10,000)
AOGI	$ 9,000

First, adjusted income from rents must be 50% or more of AOGI.

Rent income	$15,000
Deduct: Depreciation, interest, and real estate taxes	(10,000)
Adjusted income from rents	$ 5,000
50% of AOGI	$ 4,500

---

[41] § 543(a)(2).

Norman Corporation has satisfied the first test (adjusted income from rents is equal to or greater than 50% of AOGI).

Second, total dividends paid for the year are $2,500. This figure must be equal to or greater than the amount by which nonrent PHC income exceeds 10% of OGI.

Nonrent PHC income	$ 4,000
Less: 10% of OGI	(1,900)
Excess	$ 2,100

Because Norman Corporation meets both tests, the adjusted income from rents is *not* PHC income. ▼

Mineral, Oil, and Gas Royalties. As with rent income, adjusted income from mineral, oil, and gas royalties can be excluded from PHC income if certain tests are met.[42] First, adjusted income from the royalties must constitute 50 percent or more of AOGI. Second, nonroyalty PHC income may not exceed 10 percent of OGI. Note that this 10 percent test is not accompanied by the dividend escape clause previously described in relation to rent income. Therefore, corporations receiving income from mineral, oil, or gas royalties must be careful to minimize nonroyalty PHC income. Furthermore, adjusted income from rents and copyright royalties are considered to be nonroyalty PHC income whether or not treated as such by §§ 543(a)(2) and (4). Third, the company's business expenses under § 162 (other than compensation paid to shareholders) must be at least 15 percent of AOGI.

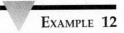

EXAMPLE 12

Pert Corporation has gross income of $4,000, which consists of gross income of $2,500 from oil royalties, $400 of dividends, and $1,100 from the sale of merchandise. The total deductions for depletion, interest, and property and severance taxes allocable to the gross income from oil royalties equal $1,000. Deductions allowable under § 162 are $450. Pert Corporation's adjusted income from oil royalties will not be PHC income if the three tests are met. Therefore, OGI, AOGI, and adjusted income from oil royalties must be determined:

Oil royalties income	$ 2,500
Dividends	400
Sale of merchandise	1,100
Gross income (*and* OGI)	$ 4,000
Deduct: Depletion, interest, and property and severance taxes	(1,000)
AOGI	$ 3,000

Adjusted income from oil royalties must be 50% or more of AOGI.

Oil royalties income	$ 2,500
Deduct: Depletion, interest, and property and severance taxes	(1,000)
Adjusted income from oil royalties	$ 1,500
50% of AOGI	$ 1,500

The first test is met (oil royalties are equal to or greater than 50% of AOGI). Since nonroyalty PHC income is $400 (composed solely of the $400 of dividends) and this amount

---

[42] § 543(a)(3).

is not more than 10% of OGI, the second test is also satisfied. The third requirement is satisfied if deductible expenses under § 162 amount to at least 15% of AOGI.

§ 162 expenses	$450
15% of $3,000 (AOGI)	$450

Therefore, Pert Corporation's adjusted income from oil royalties is *not* PHC income. ▼

Personal Service Contracts.   Any amount from personal service contracts is classified as PHC income only if (1) some person other than the corporation has the right to designate, by name or by description, the individual who is to perform the services and (2) the person so designated owns, directly or indirectly, 25 percent or more in value of the outstanding stock of the corporation at some time during the taxable year.[43]

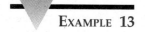

EXAMPLE 13

Blair, Cody, and Dana (all attorneys) are equal shareholders in Canary Company, a professional association engaged in the practice of law. Irene, a new client, retains Canary Company to pursue a legal claim. Under the terms of the retainer agreement, Irene designates Blair as the attorney who will perform the legal services. The suit is successful, and 30% of the judgment Irene recovers is paid to Canary as a fee. Since the parties have met all of the requirements of § 543(a)(7), the fee received by Canary is PHC income.[44] ▼

The result reached in Example 13 could have been avoided if the retainer agreement had not specifically named Blair as the party to perform the services.

CALCULATION OF THE PHC TAX

6   LEARNING OBJECTIVE
Compute the personal holding company tax.

To this point, the discussion has focused on the determination of PHC status. Once a corporation is classified as a PHC, the amount upon which the 39.6 percent penalty tax is imposed must be computed. The tax base is called undistributed PHC income (UPHC income). Basically, this amount is taxable income, subject to certain adjustments, minus the dividends paid deduction. After the adjustments, UPHC income more clearly represents the corporation's dividend-paying capacity. Figure 20–2 shows how this amount is determined.

Dividends Paid Deduction.   Since the purpose of the PHC penalty tax is to force a corporation to pay dividends, five types of **dividends paid deductions** reduce the amount subject to the penalty tax (see Table 20–1). First, dividends actually paid during the tax year ordinarily reduce UPHC income.[45] However, such distributions must be pro rata. They must exhibit no preference to any shares of stock over shares of the same class or to any class of stock over other classes outstanding.[46] The prohibition is especially harsh when portions of an employee-shareholder's salary are declared unreasonable and classified as a disguised or constructive dividend.[47] In the case of a dividend of appreciated property, the dividends paid deduction is the fair market value of the property (not the adjusted basis to the distributing corporation).

---

[43] § 543(a)(7). For an application of the "right to designate," see *Thomas P. Byrnes, Inc.*, 73 T.C. 416 (1979).

[44] The example presumes Canary Company will be treated as a corporation for Federal tax purposes. As noted in Chapter 16, this is the usual result of professional association status.

[45] §§ 561(a)(1) and 562.

[46] § 562(c).

[47] Refer to Chapter 18 and *Henry Schwartz Corp.*, 60 T.C. 728 (1973).

▼ **FIGURE 20–2**
Undistributed PHC Income
Determination

Taxable income	
Plus:	• Dividends received deduction.
	• Net operating loss (NOL), other than the NOL from the preceding year (computed without the dividends received deduction).
	• Certain business expenses and depreciation attributable to nonbusiness property owned by the corporation that exceed the income derived from such property (unless the taxpayer proves that the rent was the highest obtainable and the rental business was a bona fide business activity).*
Less:	• Federal income tax accrual (other than the PHC tax and the accumulated earnings tax).
	• Excess charitable contributions beyond the 10% corporate limitation (with a maximum of the 20%, 30%, or 50% limitation imposed on individuals).**
	• Excess of long-term capital gain over short-term capital loss (net of tax).
Equals:	Adjusted taxable income.
Less:	Dividends paid deduction.
Equals:	Undistributed PHC income.

*§ 545(b).
**Reg. § 1.545–2.

▼ **TABLE 20–1**
Dividends Paid Deductions

Type of Dividend	Availability	Timing	Statutory Location	Effect on Shareholders
Current year	Both § 531 and § 541	By end of year.	§ 561(a)(1)	Reduction in ATI and UPHC income.
2½-month grace period	Both § 531 and § 541*	On or before the 15th day of the 3rd month after end of year.	§§ 563(a) and (b)	Reduction in ATI and UPHC income.
Consent dividend	Both § 531 and § 541	Not later than due date of the corporate tax return.	§ 565(a)	Treated as a dividend as of end of tax year and given back as a contribution to capital.
Dividend carryover	§ 541	Not later than due date of the corporate tax return.	§ 564	Reduction in UPHC income.
Deficiency dividend	§ 541	Within 90 days after determination of PHC tax deficiency.	§ 547	Treated as if dividend paid in offending year. No impact on interest and penalties.

*Limited to 20% of current-year dividends paid for a PHC.

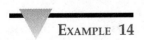

EXAMPLE 14

Three individuals are equal shareholders in a PHC. A property dividend with an adjusted basis of $20,000 (FMV of $30,000) is paid to the three shareholders in the following proportion: 25%, 35%, and 40%. This distribution is not pro rata, so the dividend is not deductible from UPHC income. ▼

A 2½-month grace period exists following the close of the tax year. Dividends paid during this period may be treated as paid during the tax year just closed.

However, the amount allowed as a deduction from UPHC income cannot exceed either (1) the UPHC income for the tax year or (2) 20 percent of the total dividends distributed during the tax year.[48] Reasonable cause may not be used to overcome the 20 percent limitation, even if the taxpayer relied upon incorrect advice given by an accountant.[49]

The **consent dividend** procedure[50] involves a hypothetical distribution of the corporate income to be taxed to the shareholders. Since the consent dividend is taxable, a dividends paid deduction is allowed. The shareholder's basis in his or her stock is increased by the consent dividend (a contribution to capital), and a subsequent actual distribution of the consent dividend might be taxed. The consent election is filed by the shareholders at any time not later than the due date of the corporate tax return. The consent dividend is considered distributed by the corporation on the last day of the tax year and is included in the gross income of the shareholder in the tax year in which or with which the tax year of the corporation ends. The disadvantage of this special election is that the shareholders must pay taxes on dividends they do not actually receive. However, if cash is not available for dividend distributions, the consent dividend route is a logical alternative.

EXAMPLE 15

Chad Corporation, a calendar year taxpayer solely owned by Tamara, is a PHC. Dividends of $30,000 must be paid to avoid the PHC tax, but the company has a poor cash position. Tamara elects the consent dividend treatment under § 565 and is taxed on $30,000 of dividends. Her basis in Chad stock is increased by $30,000 as a result of this special election. Thus, Chad does not incur the PHC tax, but Tamara is taxed even though she receives no cash from the corporation with which to pay the tax. ▼

Even after a corporation has been classified as a PHC, a delayed dividend distribution made in a subsequent tax year can avoid the PHC penalty tax. This **deficiency dividend** provision allows a dividend to be paid within 90 days after the determination of the PHC tax deficiency for a prior tax year.[51] A determination occurs when a decision of a court is final, a closing agreement under § 7121 is signed, or a written agreement is signed between the taxpayer and a District Director. The dividend distribution *cannot be made* before the determination or after the running of the 90-day time period. Furthermore, the deficiency dividend procedure does not relieve the taxpayer of interest, additional amounts, or assessable penalties computed with respect to the PHC tax.

A dividend carryover from two prior years may be available to reduce the UPHC income. When the dividends paid by a company in its prior years exceed the company's UPHC income for those years, the excess may be deducted in the current year.

Personal Holding Company Planning Model.   Some of the complex PHC provisions may be developed into a flow chart format. Figures 20–3 and 20–4 provide a PHC planning model and the rules for the rent exclusion test.

Computations Illustrated.   After the appropriate adjustments are made to corporate taxable income and the sum of the dividends paid is subtracted, the resulting figure is UPHC income. This amount is multiplied by the 39.6% penalty tax rate to obtain the PHC tax. Although the tax revenue from the PHC tax is

---

[48] §§ 563(b) and 543(a)(2)(B)(ii).
[49] *Kenneth Farmer Darrow,* 64 T.C. 217 (1975).

[50] Reg. § 1.565–1.
[51] § 547.

▼ **FIGURE 20-3**
Personal Holding Company
Planning Model

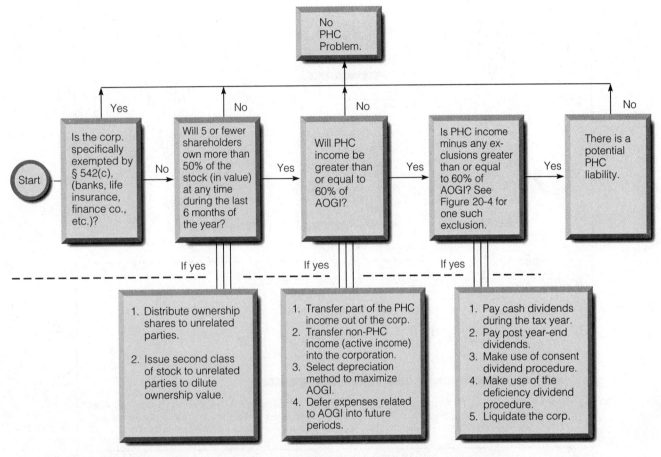

From "Understanding and Avoiding the Personal Holding Company Tax: A Tax Planning Model," by Pratt
and Whittenburg, which appeared in the June 1975 issue of *Taxes — The Tax Magazine* published and
copyrighted 1975 by Commerce Clearing House, Inc., and appears here with their permission.

small, the consequences of this confiscatory tax can be severe. Taxpayers should
monitor their corporations and take the necessary steps to avoid the tax.

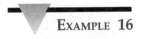

EXAMPLE 16

Bluebird Corporation had the following items of income and expense in the current year:

Dividend income (less than 20% owned)	$ 40,000
Rent income	150,000
Depreciation expense	40,000
Mortgage interest	30,000
Real estate taxes	30,000
Salaries	20,000
Dividends paid (three shareholders)	20,000
Corporate income tax liability (§ 11)	6,300

OGI is $190,000 ($40,000 + $150,000), and AOGI is $90,000 ($190,000 – $40,000 –
$30,000 – $30,000). Taxable income is $42,000, computed as follows:

▼ **FIGURE 20–4**
Rent Exclusion Test

From "Understanding and Avoiding the Personal Holding Company Tax: A Tax Planning Model," by Pratt and Whittenburg, which appeared in the June 1975 issue of *Taxes — The Tax Magazine* published and copyrighted 1975 by Commerce Clearing House, Inc., and appears here with their permission.

Rent income		$ 150,000
Dividend income		40,000
		$ 190,000
Less: Depreciation expense	$40,000	
Mortgage interest	30,000	
Real estate taxes	30,000	
Salaries	20,000	(120,000)
		$ 70,000
Less: Dividends received deduction ($40,000 × 70%)		(28,000)
Taxable income		$ 42,000

The adjusted income from rents is $50,000 ($150,000 − $100,000). Bluebird meets the 50% rent income test since $50,000 is greater than 50% of AOGI ($90,000 × 50% = $45,000). But the corporation did not pay at least $21,000 of dividends ($40,000 nonrent PHC income − $19,000 = $21,000). Therefore, the 10% rent income test is not met, and the rent income is classified as PHC income. Since all income is passive, Bluebird Corporation is a PHC. The PHC tax of $17,305 is calculated as follows:

Taxable income	$ 42,000
Plus: Dividends received deduction ($40,000 × 70%)	28,000
	$ 70,000
Less: § 11 tax	(6,300)
	$ 63,700
Less: Dividends paid	(20,000)
UPHC income	$ 43,700
	×.396
PHC tax liability	$ 17,305

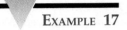

EXAMPLE 17

Assume that in Example 16, dividends of $22,000 (instead of $20,000) are paid to the shareholders. In this case, the rent income is not PHC income because the 10% test is met ($22,000 is equal to or greater than the nonrent PHC income in excess of 10% of OGI). Thus, an increase of $2,000 in the dividends paid in Example 16 avoids the $17,305 PHC tax liability. ▼

COMPARISON OF §§ 531 AND 541

7 LEARNING OBJECTIVE
Compare the accumulated earnings and personal holding company taxes.

A review of several important distinctions between the penalty tax on the unreasonable accumulation of earnings (§ 531) and the tax on PHCs (§ 541) sets the stage for the presentation of tax planning considerations applicable to both taxes.

- Unlike § 531, no element of intent is necessary for the imposition of the § 541 (PHC) tax.[52] Consequently, § 541 can be a real trap for the unwary.
- The imposition of the § 541 tax is not affected by the past history of the corporation. Thus, the tax could be just as applicable to a newly formed corporation as to one that has been in existence for many years. This is not the case with the § 531 tax. Past accumulations have a direct bearing on the determination of the accumulated earnings credit. In this sense, younger corporations are less vulnerable to the § 531 tax since complete insulation generally is guaranteed until accumulations exceed $250,000 (or $150,000).
- Although both taxes pose threats for closely held corporations, the § 541 tax presents the more explicit threat due to the constructive stock ownership rules. However, publicly held corporations can be subject to the § 531 tax if corporate policy is dominated by certain shareholders who are using the corporate form to avoid income taxes on dividends through the accumulation of corporate profits.
- Sufficient dividend distributions can eliminate both taxes. In the case of § 531, however, such dividends must be distributed on a timely basis. Both taxes allow a 2½-month grace period and provide for the consent dividend procedure.[53] Only the § 541 tax allows the deficiency dividend procedure.

---

[52] In light of the Supreme Court decision in *Donruss* (refer to Footnote 3 and the related text), what role, if any, will intent play in the future in helping taxpayers avoid the § 531 tax? In this connection, see the dissenting opinion issued by Justice Harlan.

[53] Under the § 531 tax, dividends paid within the first 2½ months of the succeeding year *must* be carried back to the preceding year. In

the case of the § 541 tax, the carryback is optional—some or all of the dividends can be deducted in the year paid. The 20% limit on carrybacks applicable to § 541 [see § 563(a)] does not cover § 531 situations.

• Differences in reporting procedures arise because the § 541 tax is a self-assessed tax while the § 531 tax is not. For example, if a corporation is a PHC, the company must file a Schedule PH along with its Form 1120 (the corporate income tax return) for the year involved. Failure to file the Schedule PH can result in the imposition of interest and penalties and also brings into play a special six-year statute of limitations for the assessment of the § 541 tax.[54] On the other hand, the § 531 tax is assessed by the IRS and consequently requires no reporting procedures on the part of the corporate taxpayer.

**TAX PLANNING
CONSIDERATIONS**

Even in particular situations when corporate rates are higher than individual rates, a corporation can invest accumulated funds in tax-free vehicles or purchase high-yield corporate stocks to take advantage of the dividends received deduction. Thus, the threat of the accumulated earnings tax and the PHC tax can be a prime concern to many corporations.

THE § 531 TAX

8 **LEARNING OBJECTIVE**
Plan to minimize (or avoid) the accumulated earnings tax.

Justifying the Accumulations. The key defense against imposition of the § 531 tax is to show that the accumulations are necessary to meet the reasonable needs of the business. Several points should be kept in mind:

• To the extent possible, the justification for the accumulation should be documented. If, for example, the corporation plans to acquire additional physical facilities for use in its trade or business, the minutes of the board of directors' meetings should reflect the decision. Furthermore, the documentation should take place during the period of accumulation. This planning may require some foresight on the part of the taxpayer. Meaningful planning to avoid a tax problem should not be based on what happens after the issue has been raised by an agent as the result of an audit. In the case of a profitable closely held corporation that accumulates some or all of its profits, the parties should operate under the assumption that § 531 is always a potential issue. Recognizing a tax problem at an early stage is the first step in a satisfactory resolution.

• Multiple reasons for making an accumulation are not only permissible but invariably advisable. Suppose, for example, a manufacturing corporation plans to expand its plant. It would not be wise to stop with the cost of the expansion as the only justification for all accumulations. What about further justification based on the corporation's working capital requirements as determined under the *Bardahl* formula or some variation? Other reasons for making the accumulation may be present and should be recognized.

• The reasons for the accumulation should be sincere and, once established, pursued to the extent feasible.

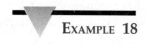

EXAMPLE 18

In 1991, the directors of Wind Corporation decide to accumulate $1 million to fund the replacement of Wind's plant. Five years pass, and no steps are taken to begin construction. ▼

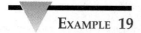

EXAMPLE 19

In 1991, the directors of Youth Corporation decide to accumulate $1 million to fund the replacement of Youth's plant. In the ensuing five-year period, the following steps are taken: a site selection committee is appointed (1991); a site is chosen (1992); the site (land) is

---

[54] § 6501(f). See also Chapter 25.

purchased (1993); an architect is retained, and plans are drawn up for the new plant (1995); bids are requested and submitted for the construction of the new plant (1996). ▼

- Compare Examples 18 and 19. Youth Corporation is in a much better position to justify the accumulation. Even though the plant has not yet been replaced some five years after the accumulations began, the progress toward its ultimate construction speaks for itself. Wind Corporation may be hard pressed to prove the sincerity of its objective for the accumulations in light of its failure to follow through on the projected replacement.
- The amount of the accumulation should be realistic under the circumstances.

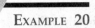

EXAMPLE 20

Diamond Corporation plans to replace certain machinery at an estimated cost of $500,000. The original machinery was purchased for $300,000 and, because of $250,000 in depreciation deducted for tax purposes, has a present book value of $50,000. How much of an accumulation can be justified for the replacement to avoid the § 531 tax? Initially, $500,000 seems to be the appropriate amount since this is the estimated replacement cost of the machinery. But what about the $250,000 in depreciation that Diamond already deducted? If it is counted again as part of a reasonable accumulation, a double tax benefit results. Only $250,000 ($50,000 unrecovered cost of the old machinery + $200,000 additional outlay necessary) can be justified as the amount for an accumulation.[55] ▼

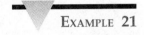

EXAMPLE 21

During the current year, a competitor files a $2 million patent infringement suit against Gem Corporation. Competent legal counsel advises Gem that the suit is groundless. Under such conditions, the corporation can hardly justify accumulating $2 million because of the pending lawsuit. ▼

- Since the § 531 tax is imposed on an annual basis, justification for accumulations may vary from year to year.[56]

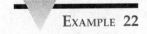

EXAMPLE 22

For calendar years 1995 and 1996, Red Corporation was able to justify large accumulations owing to a pending additional income tax assessment. In early 1997, the assessment is settled and paid. After the settlement, Red Corporation can no longer consider the assessment as a reasonably anticipated need of the business. ▼

Danger of Loans to Shareholders. The presence of loans made by a corporation to its shareholders often raises the § 531 issue. If this same corporation has a poor dividend-paying record, the company becomes particularly vulnerable. The avowed goal of the § 531 tax is to force certain corporations to distribute dividends. If a corporation can spare funds for loans to shareholders, the company certainly has the capacity to pay dividends. Unfortunately, the presence of such loans can cause other tax problems for the parties.

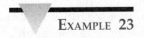

EXAMPLE 23

During the year in question, Quail Corporation made advances of $120,000 to its sole shareholder, Tom. Although prosperous and maintaining substantial accumulations, Quail has never paid a dividend. Under these circumstances, the IRS could move in either of two directions. It could assess the § 531 tax against Quail for its unreasonable accumulation of

[55] *Battelstein Investment Co. v. U.S.*, 71–1 USTC ¶9227, 27 AFTR2d 71–713, 442 F.2d 87 (CA–5, 1971).
[56] Compare *Hardin's Bakeries, Inc. v. Martin, Jr.*, 67–1 USTC ¶9253, 19 AFTR2d 647, 293 F.Supp. 1129 (D.Ct. Miss., 1967), with *Hardin v.*

U.S., 70–2 USTC ¶9676, 26 AFTR2d 70–5852 (D.Ct. Miss., 1970), *aff'd., rev'd., rem'd.* by 72–1 USTC ¶9464, 29 AFTR2d 72–1446, 461 F.2d 865 (CA–5, 1972).

earnings. Alternatively, the IRS could argue that the advances were not bona fide loans but, instead, taxable dividends. The dual approach places the taxpayers in a difficult position. If, for example, they contend that the advance was a bona fide loan, Tom avoids dividend income, but Quail becomes vulnerable to the imposition of the § 531 tax.[57] On the other hand, a concession that the advance was not a loan hurts Tom but helps Quail avoid the penalty tax. ▼

Role of Dividends. The relationship between dividend distributions and the § 531 tax can be further clarified. First, can the payment of enough dividends completely avoid the § 531 tax? The answer must be yes due to the operation of § 535. This provision defines accumulated taxable income as *taxable income* (adjusted by certain items) *minus the sum of the dividends paid deduction and the accumulated earnings credit.* Since the § 531 tax is imposed on accumulated taxable income, no tax is due if the taxable dividends paid and the accumulated earnings credit are large enough to offset taxable income. The payment of sufficient taxable dividends, therefore, avoids the tax. Second, can the payment of *some* dividends completely avoid the § 531 tax? As the question is worded, the answer must be *no*. Theoretically, even significant dividend distributions will not insulate a corporation from the tax. From a practical standpoint, however, the payment of dividends indicates that the corporation is not being used exclusively to shield its shareholders from tax consequences. In applying § 531, the IRS will consider such payments to the extent that they reflect the good faith of the parties and the lack of tax avoidance motivation.

AVOIDING THE § 541 TAX

9   **LEARNING OBJECTIVE**
Plan to minimize (or avoid) the personal holding company tax.

The classification of a corporation as a PHC requires the satisfaction of *both* the stock ownership and the gross income tests. Failure to meet either of these tests avoids PHC status and the § 541 tax.

- The stock ownership test can be handled through a dispersion of stock ownership. In this regard, however, watch the application of the stock attribution rules.
- Remember the following relationship when working with the gross income test:

$$\frac{\text{PHC income}}{\text{AOGI}} = 60\% \text{ or more}$$

Decreasing the numerator (PHC income) or increasing the denominator (AOGI) of the fraction reduces the resulting percentage. Keeping the percentage below 60 percent precludes classification as a PHC. To control PHC income, investments in low-yield growth securities are preferable to those that generate heavy interest or dividend income. Capital gains from the sale of such securities will not affect PHC status since they are not included in either the numerator or the denominator of the fraction. Investments in tax-exempt securities are attractive because the interest income, like capital gains, has no effect in applying the gross income test.

---

[57] *Ray v. U.S.*, 69–1 USTC ¶9334, 23 AFTR2d 69–1141, 409 F.2d 1322 (CA–6, 1969).

- Income from personal service contracts may, under certain conditions, be PHC income. Where a 25 percent or more owner of a PHC is specifically designated in a retainer agreement as the party to perform the services, the personal service contract income will be PHC income. See Example 13 earlier in this chapter.
- Rent income may or may not be PHC income. The relative amount of rent income is the key consideration. If

$$\frac{\text{Adjusted income from rents}}{\text{AOGI}} = 50\% \text{ or more}$$

and nonrent PHC income less 10 percent of OGI is distributed as a dividend, rent income is not PHC income. Maximizing adjusted income from rents clearly improves the situation for taxpayers. Since adjusted income from rents represents gross rents less attributable expenses, a conservative approach in determining such expenses is helpful. The taxpayer should minimize depreciation (e.g., choose straight-line over the accelerated cost recovery method). This approach to handling expenses attributable to rental property is confusing to many taxpayers because it contradicts what is normally done to reduce income tax consequences.

PHC status need not carry tragic tax consequences if the parties are aware of the issue and take appropriate steps. Since the tax is imposed on UPHC income, properly timed dividend distributions neutralize the tax and avoid interest and penalties. Also, as long as a corporation holds PHC status, the § 531 tax cannot be imposed.

KEY TERMS

Accumulated earnings credit, 20–4

Accumulated earnings tax (AET), 20–3

Adjusted ordinary gross income (AOGI), 20–14

Consent dividend, 20–20

Deficiency dividend, 20–20

Dividends paid deductions, 20–18

Minimum credit, 20–4

Ordinary gross income (OGI), 20–15

Personal holding company (PHC), 20–13

Reasonable needs of a business, 20–5

PROBLEM
MATERIALS

DISCUSSION QUESTIONS

1. Charlene creates a corporation in order to obtain limited liability. She would prefer to avoid the second tax at the shareholder level. Suggest some techniques that would help Charlene avoid double taxation.

2. Explain the purpose(s) underlying the creation of the accumulated earnings penalty tax and the PHC tax.

3. Omar is considering merging two of his brother-sister corporations. Outline any relevant tax issues facing this merger.

4. How can human resource accounting be used in an accumulated earnings situation?

5. Cecil McDowell is preparing *Bardahl* calculations for his closely held corporation. Should he include other operating expenses in the calculation of the accounts payable cycle?

6. Determine whether the following factors or events will increase (+), decrease (−), or have no effect (NE) on the working capital needs of a corporation when calculating the *Bardahl* formula:
   a. A decrease in depreciation deduction.
   b. Use of a peak inventory figure rather than average inventory.
   c. An increase in the annual cost of goods sold.
   d. Purchase of a tract of land for a future parking lot.
   e. Use of average receivables rather than peak receivables.
   f. An increase in annual net sales.
   g. An increase in accounts payable.
   h. An increase in the annual expenses.
   i. A gain on the sale of treasury stock.

7. ATI = Taxable income − Certain adjustments + Dividends paid deduction − Accumulated earnings credit. Please comment.

8. In making the "certain adjustments" (refer to Question 7) necessary in arriving at ATI, which of the following items should be added (+), should be subtracted (−), or will have no effect (NE) on taxable income?
   a. A nontaxable stock dividend distributed by the corporation to its shareholders.
   b. Corporate income tax incurred and paid.
   c. Charitable contributions paid in the amount of 10% of taxable income.
   d. Deduction of an NOL carried over from a prior year.
   e. The dividends received deduction.

9. Ms. Janson (a widow) and Mr. Kimbell (a bachelor) are both shareholder-employees in Hillary Corporation (closely held). If they elope during the year, what are the relevant tax issues with respect to Hillary Corporation's vulnerability to the accumulated earnings tax or the PHC tax?

10. Nixon Corporation is a consulting firm. Its entire outstanding stock is owned by three individuals. Nixon enters into a contract with Claudia Corporation to perform certain consulting services in consideration of which Claudia is to pay Nixon $35,000. The individual who is to perform the services is not designated by name or description in the contract, and no one but Nixon has the right to designate such person. Does the $35,000 constitute PHC income?

11. Which of the following income items could be PHC income?
    a. Annuities.
    b. Interest.
    c. Rent income.
    d. Sales of inventory.
    e. Dividends.
    f. Mineral royalties.
    g. Copyright royalties.
    h. Produced film rents.
    i. Gain from sale of farmland.

12. Deion, a shareholder in Cimena Corporation, dies, and under his will, the stock passes to his children. If Cimena Corporation is a PHC, what effect, if any, will Deion's death have on the continuation of this status?

13. How are OGI and AOGI calculated?

14. If the 50% test as to rents is satisfied, the PHC tax cannot be imposed upon the corporation. Do you agree? Why or why not?

15. The payment of enough dividends can avoid either the accumulated earnings tax or the PHC tax. Explain.

16. Ford Motor Company has no difficulty avoiding both the accumulated earnings tax and the PHC tax. Explain.

17. Which of the following purposes can be used to justify accumulations to meet the reasonable needs of the business?
    a. A corporation creates a reserve for a depression that might occur in 1999.
    b. A corporation has an extraordinarily high working capital need.
    c. A manufacturing corporation invests in several oil and gas drilling funds.
    d. A hotel corporation is being sued because of a structural accident that injured 32 people.
    e. A corporation is considering establishing a sinking fund to retire some bonds.
    f. A corporation carries six key employee life insurance policies.
    g. Robin Corporation makes loans to Crane Corporation, an unrelated party that is having financial problems and is a key customer.
    h. A corporation agrees to retire 20% of its outstanding stock without curtailing its business.

18. Relate the following points to the avoidance of the PHC tax:
    a. Sale of stock to outsiders.
    b. An increase in AOGI.
    c. A decrease in PHC income.
    d. Long-term capital gains recognized by the corporation.
    e. Corporate investment in tax-exempt bonds.
    f. Income from personal service contracts.
    g. The choice of straight-line depreciation for rental property owned by the corporation.

19. Compare the accumulated earnings tax to the PHC tax on the basis of the following items:
    a. The element of intent.
    b. Applicability of the tax to a newly created corporation.
    c. Applicability of the tax to a publicly held corporation.
    d. The 2½-month rule with respect to the dividends paid deduction.
    e. The availability of the deficiency dividend procedure.
    f. Procedures for reporting and paying the tax.

PROBLEMS

20. Howell, Inc., a calendar year consulting corporation, has accumulated E & P of $80,000 on January 1, 1997. For the calendar year 1997, the corporation has taxable income of $100,000. Howell has no reasonable needs that justify an accumulation of its E & P. Calculate the amount vulnerable to the accumulated earnings tax.

21. In 1996, Billings Corporation, a manufacturing company, retained $60,000 for its reasonable business needs. The company had a long-term capital gain of $20,000 and a short-term capital loss of $15,000, with a resulting capital gain tax of $1,250. The accumulated E & P at the end of 1995 was $260,000. On January 25, 1996, Billings paid a taxable dividend of $90,000. Calculate the accumulated earnings credit for 1996.

22. A retail corporation had accumulated E & P of $250,000 on January 1, 1996. Its taxable income for the year 1996 was $75,000. The corporation paid no dividends during the year. There were no other adjustments to determine accumulated taxable income. Assume a court determined that the corporation is subject to the accumulated earnings tax and that the reasonable needs of the business required E & P in the total amount of $270,500. Determine the accumulated earnings tax and explain your calculations.

23. A manufacturing corporation is accumulating a significant amount of E & P. Although the corporation is closely held, it is not a PHC. The following facts relate to the tax year 1996:

Taxable income	$450,000
Federal income tax	153,000
Dividend income from a qualified domestic corporation (less than 20% owned)	40,000
Dividends paid in 1996	70,000
Consent dividends	35,000
Dividends paid on 2/1/97	5,000
Accumulated earnings credit	10,000
Excess charitable contributions (the portion in excess of the amount allowed as a deduction in computing the corporate income tax)	9,000
Net capital loss adjustment	4,000

Compute the accumulated earnings tax, if any.

24. The following data relate to a closely held manufacturing corporation's 1996 tax year:

Net taxable income	$500,000
Federal income taxes	170,000
Excess charitable contributions	30,000
Capital loss adjustment	20,000
Dividends received (14% owned)	140,000
Dividends paid	60,000
Accumulated earnings, 1/1/96	130,000

a. Assume that the corporation is not a PHC. Calculate any accumulated earnings tax and total tax payable in 1996.
b. Can the deficiency dividend procedure be used to avoid this accumulated earnings tax?

25. Garcia Pullig, CEO for a local company, asks you to calculate his company's operating cycle needs without considering accrued Federal income taxes as an operating expense. March is the longest operating cycle for the company, which has reasonable business needs of $40,000 in addition to the working capital required for one operating cycle. Additional information is provided as follows:

Accounts receivable—March	$ 120,000
Inventory—March	160,000
Accounts payable—March	101,000
Cost of goods sold	1,000,000
Other expenses (less depreciation)	100,000
Depreciation	90,000
Sales	2,000,000
Dividends paid	7,000
Accumulated earnings (beginning)	180,000
Accrued Federal income taxes	220,000

Respond to Mr. Pullig in a letter dated June 2, 1997. Mr. Pullig's address is 451 Maple St., Athens, OH 45701.

26. A wholly owned motor freight corporation has permitted its earnings to accumulate. The company has no inventory but wishes to use the *Bardahl* formula to determine the amount of operating capital required for a business cycle. The following facts are relevant:

Yearly revenues	$3,300,000
Average accounts receivable	300,000
Yearly expenses	3,500,000
Average accounts payable	213,000

a. Determine the turnover rate of average accounts receivable.
b. Determine the number of days in the accounts receivable cycle.
c. Determine the expenses for one accounts receivable cycle.
d. Determine the number of days in the accounts payable cycle.
e. Determine the operating capital needed for one business cycle.
f. Explain why the time allowed a taxpayer for the payment of accounts payable should be taken into consideration in applying the *Bardahl* formula.

27. The stock of Party Corporation is owned as follows:

Sand Corporation (wholly owned by Karl)	100 shares
Karl's wife	100 shares
Karl's partner	100 shares
Karl's wife's sister	100 shares
Abe	50 shares
Betty	30 shares
Charles	20 shares
Unrelated individuals with 10 or fewer shares	500 shares
Total	1,000 shares

Do five or fewer individuals own more than 50% of Party Corporation? *No*

28. Vinette Corporation has gross income of $200,000, which consists of $110,000 of rent income and $90,000 of interest income. The corporation has $30,000 of rent income adjustments and pays $80,000 to its nine shareholders.
a. Calculate adjusted income from rents.
b. Calculate AOGI.
c. Is the so-called 50% test met? Show calculations.
d. Is the 10% rent income test met? Show calculations.
e. Is the corporation a PHC?

29. Assume the same facts as in Problem 28, except that rent income adjustments decrease from $30,000 to $20,000. Answer the same questions as in Problem 28.

30. Carrot Corporation has gross income of $165,000, which consists of gross income from rent of $100,000, $40,000 from the sale of merchandise, interest of $15,000, and income from annuities of $10,000. Deductions directly related to the rent income total $28,000.
a. Calculate OGI.
b. Calculate AOGI.
c. Calculate adjusted income from rent.
d. Does the rent income constitute PHC income? Explain.
e. Is this corporation a PHC (assuming there are seven shareholders)?
f. Should the company pay $9,000 of dividends?

31. Daryl is the sole owner of a corporation. The following information is relevant to the corporation's tax year just ended:

Capital gain	$ 20,000
Dividend income	30,000
Rent income	130,000
Rent expenses	40,000
Section 162 business expenses	15,000
Dividends paid	12,000

    a. Calculate OGI.

    b. Calculate AOGI.

    c. Calculate adjusted income from rents.

    d. Calculate nonrent PHC income.

    e. Does this corporation meet the 50% rent income test? Explain.

    f. Does this corporation meet the 10% rent income test? Explain.

    g. Is this company a PHC?

    h. Should $15,000 of dividends be paid?

32. Cohen Corporation has the following financial data for the tax year 1996:

Rent income	$430,000
Dividend income	2,900
Interest income	50,000
Operating income	9,000
Depreciation (rental warehouses)	100,000
Mortgage interest	125,000
Real estate taxes	35,000
Officers' salaries	85,000
Dividends paid	2,000

    a. Calculate OGI.

    b. Calculate AOGI.

    c. Does Cohen's adjusted income from rents meet the 50%-or-more-of-AOGI test?

    d. Does Cohen Corporation meet the 10% dividend test?

    e. How much in dividends could Cohen pay within the 2½-month grace period during 1997?

    f. If the 1996 corporate income tax return has not been filed, what would you suggest for Cohen Corporation?

33. Using the legend provided, classify each of the following statements accordingly:

Legend

A = Relates only to the tax on unreasonable accumulation of earnings (the § 531 tax)

P = Relates only to the PHC tax (the § 541 tax)

B = Relates to both the § 531 tax and the § 541 tax

N = Relates to neither the § 531 tax nor the § 541 tax

---

    a. The tax is applied to taxable income of the corporation after adjustments are made.

    b. The tax is a self-assessed tax.

    c. An accumulation of funds for reasonable business purposes will help avoid the tax.

    d. A consent dividend mechanism can be used to avoid the tax.

    e. If the stock of the corporation is equally held by 10 unrelated individuals, the tax cannot be imposed.

    f. Any charitable deduction in excess of the 10% limitation is allowed as a deduction before the tax is imposed.

    g. Gains from the sale or disposition of capital assets are *not* subject to the tax.

    h. A sufficient amount of rent income will cause the tax *not* to be imposed.

    i. A life insurance company would *not* be subject to the tax.

    j. A corporation with only dividend income would avoid the tax.

34. In each of the following independent situations, indicate whether the corporation involved is a PHC (assume the stock ownership test is met):

	Able Corporation	Bacon Corporation	Cacey Corporation	Don Corporation
Sales of merchandise	$ 8,000	$ –0–	$ –0–	$ 2,500
Capital gains	–0–	–0–	–0–	1,000
Dividend income	15,000	5,000	1,000	2,500
Gross rent income	10,000	5,000	9,000	15,000
Expenses related to rents	8,000	2,500	8,000	10,000
Dividends paid	–0–	–0–	–0–	500
Personal holding company? (Circle Y for yes or N for no.)	Y N	Y N	Y N	Y N

35. In each of the following independent situations, indicate whether the corporation involved is a PHC (assume the stock ownership test is met):

	Eel Corporation	Foy Corporation	Get Corporation	Hitt Corporation
Sales of merchandise	$ –0–	$3,000	$ –0–	$ –0–
Capital gains	–0–	–0–	1,000	–0–
Interest income	20,000	4,800	2,000	60,000
Gross rent income	80,000	1,200	20,000	50,000
Expenses related to rents	60,000	1,000	10,000	–0–
Dividends paid	12,000	–0–	–0–	20,000
Personal holding company? (Circle Y for yes or N for no.)	Y N	Y N	Y N	Y N

36. In each of the following independent situations, calculate the PHC tax liability in 1996:

	Pear Corporation	Quake Corporation
Taxable income	$140,000	$580,000
Dividends received deduction	37,000	70,000
Contributions in excess of 10%	3,000	10,000
Federal income taxes	37,850	197,200
Net capital gain	70,000	40,000
Capital gain tax	25,350	13,600
NOL under § 172		12,000
Current-year dividends	14,000	120,000
Consent dividends		40,000
Two and one-half month dividends	4,000	

Research Problems for this chapter appear at the end of Chapter 28.

21

S CORPORATIONS

LEARNING OBJECTIVES

After completing Chapter 21, you should be able to:

1. Explain the effects of attaining S corporation status.

2. Identify corporations that qualify for the S election.

3. Understand how an S election is made and, once made, how it can be lost.

4. Appreciate the effect of an S election on the corporation and its shareholders.

5. Recognize the situations where S status is desirable or undesirable.

GENERAL CONSIDERATIONS

1 LEARNING OBJECTIVE
Explain the effects of attaining S corporation status.

Subchapter S of the Internal Revenue Code of 1986 allows for the unique treatment of certain corporations for Federal income tax purposes.[1] This election essentially results in the S corporation receiving tax treatment that resembles that of a partnership, but the entity is still a corporation under state law and for many other tax purposes. Special rules pertain to the entity, however, under the operational provisions of §§ 1361 through 1379.

An **S corporation** is largely a tax-reporting, rather than a tax-paying, entity. In this respect, the entity is treated much like a partnership. As in the partnership conduit concept, the taxable income of an S corporation flows through to the shareholders, regardless of whether the income is distributed in the form of actual dividends. There is, in general, no S corporation corporate-level tax, and the income is taxed to the shareholders immediately. An S corporation is not subject to the alternative minimum tax, accumulated earnings tax, or personal holding company tax. Certain S corporations may, however, be subject to an excess passive investment income tax or a built-in gains tax.

Before the Tax Reform Act of 1986, S corporation status had enjoyed steady growth, as indicated by the rising number of S elections. But after TRA of 1986 increased corporate taxes and established a top individual tax rate that was less than the corporate rate, S elections experienced an unprecedented expansion in 1987 and 1988. For example, 52 percent more Form 1120S returns were filed in 1988 than in 1986, while other corporate returns filed dropped by about 11 percent.

This astonishing growth slowed after 1988; nevertheless, 48 percent of all corporate returns filed in 1993 were from S corporations—nearly 1.9 million. Since 1993, however, some have predicted that the growth rate of S corporation elections would slow or reverse due to the increase in the top individual rate to 39.6 percent, making it 4.6 percentage points above the top corporate rate of 35 percent, rather than 3 points below it.

---

[1] Under the tax law, a Subchapter S corporation is an "S corporation." A regular corporation that has not elected S status is a "C corporation." C corporations are those governed by Subchapter C of the Code (§§ 301–386).

Another reason for the predicted decline in the popularity of S corporation elections is that the IRS has ruled that an unincorporated organization formed as a limited liability company (LLC) is taxable as a partnership.[2] Unless legislation is enacted classifying LLCs as taxable corporations, new, closely held businesses may increasingly choose to do business as LLCs. An LLC provides greater flexibility than does S corporation status. For example, LLCs have no restrictions on the number or type of owners, and they are not prohibited from having subsidiaries. Also, an LLC may specially allocate income and losses among its owners. Companies facing the decision of selecting the appropriate organizational form must now seriously consider the LLC alternative. This chapter provides the tools for determining when S status is still appropriate.

Despite the increase in the top individual tax rate, the tax structure still creates a preference for the flow-through taxation of a business's income.

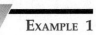

EXAMPLE 1

Assume that a flow-through business entity earns $300,000 in 1996, the applicable marginal individual tax rate is 39.6%, the applicable marginal corporate tax rate is 34%, and all after-tax income is distributed currently. The entity's available after-tax earnings compared with those of a similar C corporation are as follows:

	C Corporation	S Corporation or Limited Liability Company
Earnings	$ 300,000	$ 300,000
Less: Corporate tax	(102,000)	–0–
Available for distribution	$ 198,000	$ 300,000
Less: Tax at owner level	(78,408)	(118,800)
Available after-tax earnings	$ 119,592	$ 181,200

The flow-through business entity generates an extra $61,608 of after-tax earnings ($181,200 – $119,592), when compared with a similar C corporation. Moreover, the flow-through business entity avoids the corporate alternative minimum tax and the alternative minimum taxable income ACE adjustment (refer to Chapter 14). The C corporation might be able to reduce this disadvantage by paying out its earnings as compensation, rents, or interest expense. Tax at the owner level can also be avoided by not distributing after-tax earnings. ▼

Gains and losses of C corporations do not flow through to the shareholders. However, gains and losses of an S corporation *are* allocated to the shareholders, who report them on their individual tax returns. Other corporate transactions that flow through separately under the conduit concept include net long-term capital gains and losses, charitable contributions, tax-exempt interest, foreign tax credits, and business credits. Each shareholder of an S corporation separately takes into account his or her pro rata share of certain items of income, deductions, and credits (see Figure 21–1). The character of any item of income, expense, gain, loss, or credit is determined at the corporate level. These tax items pass through as such to each shareholder, based on the prorated number of days during the relevant S year that each shareholder held stock in the corporation.

[2]Rev.Rul. 88–76, 1988–2 C.B. 360, relative to Wyoming law. Another alternative is the limited liability partnership. See Chapters 16 and 22.

▼ **FIGURE 21–1**
Flow-Through of Separate Items
of Income and Loss to S
Corporation Shareholders

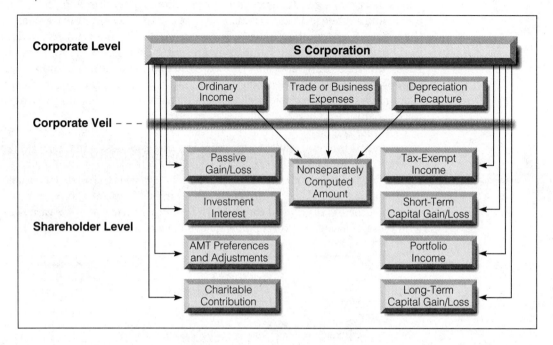

SUBCHAPTER S IN PERSPECTIVE

Subchapter S permits certain corporations to avoid the corporate income tax and enables them to pass through operating losses to their shareholders. It represents an attempt to achieve a measure of tax neutrality in resolving the issue of whether a business should be conducted as a sole proprietorship, partnership, or corporation.

In dealing with Subchapter S, certain observations should be kept in mind.

- S corporation status is an elective provision. Failure to make the election will mean that the rules applicable to the taxation of C corporations and shareholders will apply (refer to Chapter 16).
- S corporations are regular corporations in the legal sense. The S election affects only the Federal income tax consequences of electing corporations. A few states, including Louisiana and New Jersey, do not recognize the S election, and S corporations in these states are subject to the state corporate income tax and whatever other state corporate taxes are imposed.
- Federal income tax law treats S corporations neither as partnerships nor as regular corporations. The tax treatment is almost like partnership taxation, but it involves a unique set of tax rules. However, Subchapter C controls unless Subchapter S otherwise provides an applicable tax effect.
- Because Subchapter S is an elective provision, both the IRS and the courts have generally demanded strict compliance with the applicable Code requirements. Any unanticipated deviation from the various governing requirements may therefore lead to an undesirable and often unexpected tax result (e.g., the loss of the S election).

Although not generally regarded as a taxable entity, an S corporation may be subject to the following taxes.

TAX IN THE NEWS

WILL LIMITED LIABILITY COMPANIES REPLACE S CORPORATIONS?

A significant development that may adversely affect the popularity of S corporations is the advent of limited liability companies (LLCs) and their classification as partnerships for Federal income tax purposes. The IRS has ruled that an LLC formed under the Wyoming Limited Liability Company Act is classified as a partnership for Federal income tax purposes. Consequently, an LLC's owners generally have no personal liability for the LLC's debts, since it is treated as a corporation for state law purposes, and the LLC and its owners are not subject to the Code's limitations on S corporations and their shareholders, because an LLC is classified as a partnership for Federal income tax purposes.

As more states adopt LLC acts and a body of law for LLCs develops, LLCs should become increasingly popular. Absent possible legislative reforms classifying LLCs as associations taxable as corporations, the increasing popularity of LLCs could make such entities, rather than S corporations, the preferred entity for conducting business.

SOURCE: S. R. Looney, "Important Developments Affecting S Corporations since the Tax Reform Act of 1986," *Journal of S Corporation Taxation*, Spring 1993, pp. 333–334.

- Preelection built-in gains tax.
- Passive investment income penalty tax.

An S corporation is *not* subject to the following taxes.

- Corporate income tax.
- Accumulated earnings tax.
- Personal holding company tax.
- Alternative minimum tax (AMT).
- Environmental excise tax on AMT income.[3]

QUALIFICATION FOR S CORPORATION STATUS

DEFINITION OF A SMALL BUSINESS CORPORATION

2 LEARNING OBJECTIVE
Identify corporations that qualify for the S election.

A **small business corporation** must possess the following characteristics.[4]

- Is a domestic corporation (is incorporated or organized in the United States).
- Is not otherwise ineligible for the election.
- Has no more than 35 shareholders.
- Has as its shareholders only individuals, estates, and certain trusts.
- Issues only one class of stock.
- Does not have any nonresident alien shareholders.

---

[3] Rev.Rul. 89–82, 1989–1 C.B. 23.
[4] § 1361(b)(1). Note that the definition of "small" for purposes of Subchapter S relates chiefly to the number of shareholders and not to the size of the corporation.

Ineligible Corporation.   Banks, insurance companies, Puerto Rico or possession corporations, and members of an affiliated group (as defined in § 1504) are not eligible to make an S election. Thus, an S corporation cannot own 80 percent or more of the stock of another corporation. Under certain conditions, however, a corporation can establish one or more *inactive* affiliates in the event that such companies may be needed in the future. The *affiliated group* prohibition does not apply as long as none of the affiliated corporations engages in business or produces gross income.[5]

Number of Shareholders Limitation.   An electing corporation is limited to 35 shareholders. This number corresponds to the private placement exemption under Federal securities law. In testing for the 35-shareholder limitation, a husband and wife are treated as one shareholder as long as they remain married. Furthermore, the estate of a husband or wife and the surviving spouse are treated as one shareholder.

EXAMPLE 2

Harry and Wilma (husband and wife) jointly own 10 shares in Oriole, Inc., an S corporation, with the remaining 90 shares outstanding owned by 34 other unmarried persons. Harry and Wilma are divorced; pursuant to the property settlement approved by the court, the 10 shares held by Harry and Wilma are divided between them (5 to each). Before the divorce settlement, Oriole had only 35 shareholders. After the settlement, it has 36 shareholders and no longer qualifies as a small business corporation. ▼

Type of Shareholder Limitation.   All of an S corporation's shareholders must be either individuals, estates, or certain trusts.[6] Stated differently, none of the shareholders may be partnerships, corporations, or nonqualifying trusts. The justification for this limitation is related to the 35-shareholder restriction. If, for example, a partnership with 40 partners could be a shareholder, could it not be said that the corporation has at least 40 owners? If this interpretation were permitted, the 35-shareholder restriction could easily be circumvented by indirect ownership. Nevertheless, an S corporation can be a partner in a partnership and can own stock of another corporation or all the stock of an inactive subsidiary corporation. In addition, the 35-shareholder limitation can be avoided by having two or more S corporations (each with 35 or fewer shareholders) become partners in a partnership or a limited liability company that is conducting the underlying business.[7]

Nonresident Alien Prohibition.   An S corporation cannot have a nonresident alien as a shareholder.[8] In a community property jurisdiction where one of the spouses is married to a nonresident alien, this rule can be a trap for the unwary.[9] A resident alien or a nonresident U.S. citizen can be an S corporation shareholder, however.

One Class of Stock Limitation.   An S corporation can have only one class of stock issued and outstanding.[10] Congress apparently felt that the capital structure of a small business corporation should be kept relatively simple. Allowing more

[5] § 1361(c)(6).
[6] § 1361(b)(1)(B).
[7] Rev.Rul. 94–43 1994–2 C.B. 199.
[8] § 1361(b)(1)(c).
[9] See, for example, *Ward v. U.S.*, 81–2 USTC ¶9674, 48 AFTR2d 81–5942, 661 F.2d 226 (Ct.Cls., 1981), where the court found that

the stock was owned as community property. Since the taxpayer-shareholder (a U.S. citizen) was married to a citizen and resident of Mexico, the nonresident alien prohibition was violated. If the taxpayer-shareholder had held the stock as separate property, the S election would have been valid.
[10] § 1361(b)(1)(D).

than one class of stock (e.g., common and preferred) would complicate the pass-through of various corporate tax attributes to the shareholders. Authorized and unissued stock or treasury stock of another class does not disqualify the corporation. Likewise, unexercised stock options, warrants, and convertible debentures do not constitute a second class of stock, and differences in voting rights among shares of common stock are permitted.[11]

Essentially, an S corporation has one class of stock unless deliberate actions are taken to circumvent the requirement. Facts and circumstances determine the proper tax treatment of business transactions. For example, a second class of stock does not exist where the IRS recharacterizes a payment of excessive compensation as a dividend distribution.

MAKING THE ELECTION

3 LEARNING OBJECTIVE
Understand how an S election is made and, once made, how it can be lost.

If the corporation satisfies the definition of a small business corporation, the next step to achieving S status is a valid election. Key factors include who must make the election, and when the election must be made.

Who Must Elect. The election is made by filing Form 2553, and *all* shareholders must consent.[12] For this purpose, both husband and wife must file consents even if their stock is held as joint tenants, tenants in common, tenants by the entirety, or community property. Since a husband and wife are generally considered as one shareholder for purposes of the 35-shareholder limitation, this inconsistency in treatment has led to considerable taxpayer grief—particularly in community property states where the spouses may not realize that their stock is jointly owned as a community asset.

The consent of a minor shareholder can be made by the minor or a legal or natural guardian (e.g., parent). If the stock is held under a state Uniform Gifts to Minors Act, the custodian of the stock may consent for the minor but only if the custodian is also the minor's legal or natural guardian. The minor is not required to issue a new consent when he or she comes of age and the custodianship terminates.[13]

When the Election Must Be Made. To be effective for the following year, the election can be made at any time during the current year. To be effective for the current year, the election must be made on or before the fifteenth day of the third month of that year. An election can be effective for a short tax year of less than two months and 15 days, even if it is not made until the following tax year.[14]

EXAMPLE 3

In 1996, Xexus Corporation, a calendar year C corporation, decides to become an S corporation beginning January 1, 1997. An election made at any time during 1996 will accomplish this objective. If, however, the election is made in 1997, it must be made on or before March 15, 1997. An election after March 15, 1997, will not make Xexus an S corporation until 1998. ▼

Although no statutory authority exists for obtaining an extension of time for filing an election or consent, a shareholder may obtain an extension of time to file a consent if a timely election is filed, reasonable cause is given, and the interests of the government are not jeopardized.[15]

---

[11] § 1361(c)(4).
[12] § 1362(a)(2).
[13] Rev.Rul. 71–287, 1971–2 C.B. 317.

[14] § 1362(b).
[15] Rev.Rul. 60–183, 1960–1 C.B. 625; *William Pestcoe*, 40 T.C. 195 (1963); Temp.Reg. § 18.1362–2(e).

An election cannot be made for an entity that does not yet exist.[16] In the case of a newly created corporation, the question may arise as to when the 2½-month election period begins to run. Under the law, the first month begins at the earliest occurrence of any of the following events: (1) when the corporation has shareholders, (2) when it acquires assets, or (3) when it begins doing business.[17]

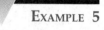

EXAMPLE 4

Several individuals acquire assets on behalf of Table Corporation on June 29, 1996, and begin doing business on July 3, 1996. They subscribe to shares of stock, file articles of incorporation for Table, and become shareholders on July 7, 1996. The S election must be filed no later than 2½ months from June 29, 1996 (on or before September 12) to be effective for 1996. ▼

Even if the 2½-month rule is met, a current election is not valid until the following year under either of the following conditions.

- The eligibility requirements were not met during any part of the taxable year before the date of election.
- Persons who were shareholders during any part of the taxable year before the election date, but were not shareholders when the election was made, did not consent.

These rules prevent the allocation of income or losses to preelection shareholders who either were ineligible to hold S corporation stock or did not consent to the election.

EXAMPLE 5

As of January 15, 1996, the stock of Robin Corporation (a calendar year C corporation) was held equally by three individual shareholders: Yoon, Velvia, and Zelda. On that date, Zelda sold her interest to Yoon and Velvia. On March 14, 1996, Yoon and Velvia make the S election by filing Form 2553. Robin cannot become an S corporation until 1997. Although the election filing was timely, Zelda did not consent. Had all individuals who were shareholders during the year (Yoon, Velvia, and Zelda) signed Form 2553, S status would have taken effect as of January 1, 1996. ▼

Once an election is made, it need not be renewed; it remains in effect unless otherwise lost.

LOSS OF THE ELECTION

An S election can be lost in any of the following ways.

- A new shareholder owning more than one-half of the stock affirmatively refuses to consent to the election.
- Shareholders owning a majority of shares (voting and nonvoting) voluntarily revoke the election.
- The number of shareholders exceeds the maximum allowable limitation.
- A class of stock other than voting or nonvoting common stock is created.
- A subsidiary (other than a nonoperating entity) is acquired.
- The corporation fails the passive investment income limitation.
- A nonresident alien becomes a shareholder.

Voluntary Revocation.   Section 1362(d)(1) permits a voluntary revocation of the election if shareholders owning a majority of shares consent. A revocation filed

---

[16]See, for example, *T. H. Campbell & Bros., Inc.,* 34 TCM 695, T.C. Memo. 1975–149.

[17]Reg. § 1.1372–2(b)(1). Also see, for example, *Nick A. Artukovich,* 61 T.C. 100 (1973).

up to and including the fifteenth day of the third month of the tax year is effective for the entire tax year, unless a prospective effective date is specified. A revocation made after the fifteenth day of the third month of the tax year is effective on the first day of the following tax year. However, if a prospective date is specified, the termination is effective as of the specified date.

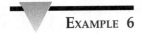

EXAMPLE 6
The shareholders of Termite Corporation, a calendar year S corporation, elect to revoke the election on January 5, 1996. Assuming the election is duly executed and its filing is timely, Termite becomes a regular corporation for calendar year 1996. If, on the other hand, the election is not made until June 1996, Termite is not a C corporation until calendar year 1997. ▼

A revocation that designates a prospective effective date results in the splitting of the year into a short S corporation taxable year and a short C corporation taxable year. The day *before* the day on which the revocation occurs is treated as the last day of a short S corporation taxable year, and the day on which the revocation occurs is treated as the first day of the short regular corporate taxable year. The corporation allocates the income or loss for the entire year on a pro rata basis.

EXAMPLE 7
Assume the same facts as in Example 6, except that Termite designates July 1, 1996, as the revocation date. Accordingly, June 30, 1996, is the last day of the S corporation taxable year. The C taxable year runs from July 1, 1996, to December 31, 1996. Any income or loss for the entire year is allocated between the short years on a prorated basis. ▼

Rather than making a pro rata allocation, the corporation can elect (with the consent of *all* who were shareholders at any time during the S short year) to report the income or loss on each return on the basis of income or loss as shown on the corporate permanent records. Under this method, items are attributed to the short S and C corporation years according to the time they were incurred (as reflected in the entity's accounting records).[18]

Cessation of Small Business Corporation Status.   A corporation not only must be a small business corporation to make the S election but also must continue to qualify as such to keep the election. In other words, meeting the definition of a small business corporation is a continuing requirement for maintaining S status. In the case of an involuntary termination, the loss of the election applies as of the date on which the disqualifying event occurs.[19]

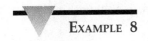

EXAMPLE 8
Tamra Corporation has been a calendar year S corporation for three years. On August 13, 1996, one of its 35 unmarried shareholders sells *some* of her stock to an outsider. Tamra now has 36 shareholders, and it ceases to be a small business corporation. For 1996, Tamra is an S corporation through August 12, 1996, and a C corporation from August 13 through December 31, 1996. ▼

Passive Investment Income Limitation.   The Code provides a **passive investment income (PII)** limitation for S corporations that possess accumulated earnings and profits (E & P) from years in which the entity was a C corporation. If such a corporation has PII in excess of 25 percent of its gross receipts for three consecutive taxable years, the S election is terminated as of the beginning of the fourth year.[20]

---

[18] §§ 1362(e)(1), (2), and (3).
[19] § 1362(d)(2)(B).

[20] § 1362(d)(3)(A)(ii).

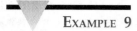

EXAMPLE 9

For 1993, 1994, and 1995, Bacon Corporation, a calendar year S corporation, derived PII in excess of 25% of its gross receipts. If Bacon holds accumulated E & P from years in which it was a C corporation, its S election is terminated as of January 1, 1996. ▼

An S corporation could acquire such damaging C corporation E & P from a regular corporation where E & P carry over in a reorganization (e.g., due to a merger). They could also have been earned in years before the S election. S corporations themselves never generate E & P.[21]

Although PII appears to parallel that of personal holding company income (refer to Chapter 20), the two types of income are not identical. For example, long-term capital gain from the sale of securities is PII but is not personal holding company income. Moreover, there are no relief provisions for rent income similar to the personal holding company rules. The inclusion of gains from the sale of securities within the definition of PII generally has made it difficult, if not impossible, for corporations that deal chiefly in security transactions to achieve S status if C corporation E & P exist.

Rents present a unique problem. Although they are classified as PII by the Code, rents do not fall into this category if the corporation (landlord) renders significant services to the occupant (tenant).

EXAMPLE 10

Tepee Corporation owns and operates an apartment building. Although the corporation provides utilities for the building, maintains the lobby in the building, and furnishes trash collection for the tenants, this activity does not constitute the rendering of significant services for the occupants.[22] Thus, the rents paid by the tenants of the building are PII to Tepee. ▼

EXAMPLE 11

Assume the facts in Example 10 with one addition—Tepee also furnishes maid services to its tenants. Now the services rendered are significant, in that they go beyond what one might normally expect the landlord of an apartment building to provide. Under these circumstances, the rent income no longer constitutes PII. ▼

Reelection after Termination.   After the election has been terminated, five years must pass before a new election can be made. The Code does, however, allow the IRS to make exceptions to this rule and permit an earlier reelection by the corporation in two situations.[23]

- There is a more-than-50 percent change in ownership after the first year for which the termination is applicable.
- The event causing the termination was not reasonably within the control of the S corporation or its majority shareholders.

ETHICAL CONSIDERATIONS

A Voluntary "Involuntary" Termination

Hirschman, Inc., a calendar year S corporation, would like to terminate its S election immediately. However, March 15 has passed, and any voluntary termination would not be effective until the first day of the following tax year. One shareholder, Elena

---

[21] § 1362(d)(3)(B).
[22] Reg. § 1.1372–4(b)(5)(vi); *Bramlette Building Corp., Inc.,* 52 T.C. 200 (1969), *aff'd.* in 70–1 USTC ¶9361, 25 AFTR2d 70–1016, 424 F.2d 751 (CA–5, 1970).

[23] §§ 1362(f) and (g); Reg. § 1.1372–5(a); Rev.Rul. 78–274, 1978–2 C.B. 220.

Muñoz, suggests an involuntary termination. She wants to sell several shares of her stock to a nonresident alien. Elena has come to you, Hirschman's tax adviser. You have briefed her on the tax effects that such a sale would have on the other shareholders. Elena then asks you for some additional advice: Is such a voluntary "involuntary" termination of an S election ethical?

OPERATIONAL RULES

4 **LEARNING OBJECTIVE**
Appreciate the effect of an S election on the corporation and its shareholders.

An S corporation is largely a tax-reporting, rather than a tax-paying, entity. In this respect, the entity is treated much like a partnership. As in the partnership conduit concept, the taxable income of an S corporation flows through to the shareholders, whether the income is distributed in the form of actual dividends or not. Likewise, losses of the entity are allocated to the shareholders, who deduct them on their individual tax returns. Other corporate transactions that flow through separately under the conduit concept include net long-term capital gains and losses, charitable contributions, tax-exempt interest, foreign tax credits, and business credits.

As under the partnership rules, each shareholder of an S corporation takes into account separately his or her pro rata share of certain items of income, deductions, and credits. Under § 1366(b), the character of any item of income, expense, gain, loss, or credit is determined at the corporate level and then is retained at the shareholder level. The tax items pass through to each shareholder, based on the prorated number of days during the relevant S year that each held stock in the corporation.

CHOICE OF TAX YEAR

Since S corporation shareholders report their shares of S items as of the entity's year-end, the selection of a corporate tax year is an important tax decision. An S corporation may use a calendar year or a fiscal year; for tax deferral purposes, a corporate fiscal year ending January 31 and a calendar year shareholder would be ideal.

As a general rule, however, S corporations must conform to the taxable years of their shareholders (the calendar year in most instances), although there are two exceptions. First, an S corporation may use a taxable year for which it can establish a business purpose.[24] Second, an S corporation may make a one-time election under § 444 on Form 8716 to keep or establish a fiscal year, provided that a corporate-level payment is made on any income deferred by the shareholders.

An S corporation may have valid business reasons for selecting a fiscal year. For example, a company may have difficulty closing the books, preparing statements, and issuing its Schedules K–1 on a timely basis under a calendar year. An S corporation can establish an acceptable business purpose for a fiscal year in three ways.

- The fiscal year is a natural business year.
- The fiscal year serves an acceptable business purpose.
- An existing S corporation meets certain grandfathering requirements.[25]

Meeting the natural business year exception involves a simple quantitative test. If 25 percent or more of a corporation's gross receipts for the 12-month period is recognized in the last 2 months of that period, and the requirement has been met for three consecutive 12-month periods, the S corporation may adopt, retain,

---

[24] § 1378(a).

[25] Rev.Proc. 87–32, 1987–2 C.B. 396.

or change to a noncalendar year. If the entity is to establish a natural business year, it must have at least a 47-month gross receipts history.

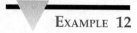

EXAMPLE 12

An S corporation's gross receipts total $100,000 for each of the last three calendar years. If the corporation recognizes at least $25,000 of its gross receipts in April and May for three consecutive years, it may adopt, retain, or change to a May 31 year-end. The following diagram illustrates the test for the May 31 year-end.

Other business purposes may be used to establish the acceptability of a fiscal year to the IRS. However, the fiscal year must be close to the entity's natural business year (e.g., the entity barely fails the 25 percent test). The IRS lists the following factors that do *not* constitute a valid business purpose.[26]

- The use of a particular fiscal year for regulatory or financial accounting purposes.
- The hiring practices of a particular corporation.
- Tax deferral for the shareholders.
- Use of a fiscal year for administrative purposes (e.g., awarding bonuses or promotions).
- Use of model years, price lists, or other items that change on a noncalendar annual basis.

In general, a taxable year under the § 444 election may not result in a deferral period of more than three months. However, an S corporation in existence before 1987 may elect to retain its previous taxable year for years after 1986, even though such a year results in a deferral period exceeding three months.[27]

The penalty paid for using a fiscal year under § 444 is that the S corporation must make a required payment on April 15 for any tax year for which the election is in effect. This required payment is equal to the base year income times the deferral ratio, times the highest individual income tax rate plus one percentage point. Thus, the required payment rate now is 40.6 percent (39.6% + 1%). These payments are not deductible by the S corporation (nor by any other person). They are refundable deposits that do not earn interest and do not pass through to the S shareholders.[28] An electing corporation need not make a required payment until the net § 444 amount for the current and all preceding election years exceeds $500.

In effect, the government collects a deposit from the S corporation based upon any deferred income. The deferral ratio is the number of months in the deferral period of the base year, divided by the number of months in the S corporation's tax year. This required payment is cumulative in nature. Thus, a corporation must pay the deferred amount, less the cumulative amount of the required payments made and refunds received in prior years.

An S corporation claims a refund when the required payments less refunds for all previous election years exceed the current required payment amount before

---

[26] Rev.Rul. 87–57, 1987–2 C.B. 117.
[27] Reg. § 1.444–1T(b).

[28] § 7519.

any reductions for prior payments. Upon the termination of a fiscal year election or the liquidation of the S corporation during an election year, the entire net required payment balance is refunded.

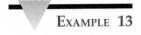

EXAMPLE 13

Cohen, Inc., is a C corporation with a September 30 fiscal year. Cohen elects S status for the year ending September 30 and is unable to meet the business purpose exception for maintaining a fiscal year. To maintain its fiscal year, Cohen elects under § 444 on Form 8716 and makes a required payment. Cohen's base period income is $197,020, so the required payment is $19,998 ($197,020 × $3/12$ deferral ratio × 40.6% applicable tax rate).

Assuming the required payment in the next year, is $17,020, Cohen claims a $2,978 refund ($19,998 − $17,020). ▼

COMPUTATION OF TAXABLE INCOME

Subchapter S taxable income or loss is generally determined in a manner similar to the tax rules that apply to partnerships, except that the S corporation can amortize its organization expenditures.[29] Also, an S corporation can deduct salaries and payroll taxes. Finally, S corporations must recognize any gains (but not losses) on distributions of appreciated property to shareholders.

Certain deductions not allowable for a partnership also are not allowable for an S corporation, including the standard deduction, personal exemptions, alimony payments, personal moving expenses, and expenses for the care of certain dependents. Furthermore, special Code provisions affecting only the computation of C corporation taxable income, such as the dividends received deduction, are not available.[30]

In general, S corporation items are divided into (1) nonseparately computed income or losses and (2) separately stated income, losses, deductions, and credits that uniquely could affect the tax liability of any shareholders. In essence, nonseparate items are lumped together into an undifferentiated amount that constitutes Subchapter S taxable income or loss. For example, any ordinary gains from the recapture provisions of §§ 1245 and 1250 constitute nonseparately computed income.

Each shareholder is allocated a pro rata portion of this nonseparately computed amount. If a shareholder dies during the year, the share of the pro rata items up to the date of death must be reported on the final individual income tax return. Tax accounting and other elections are generally made at the corporate level, except for elections that shareholders may make separately (e.g., foreign tax credit election).

The following items, among others, are separately stated on Schedule K of Form 1120S, and each shareholder takes into account his or her pro rata share (the share is passed through on a Schedule K–1).[31]

- Tax-exempt income.[32]
- Long-term and short-term capital gains and losses.
- Section 1231 gains and losses.
- Charitable contributions.
- Passive gains, losses, and credits.
- Certain portfolio income.
- Section 179 expense deduction.

---

[29] §§ 248 and 1363(b).
[30] § 703(a)(2).
[31] §§ 1366(a) and (b).

[32] Tax-exempt income passes through to the shareholders and increases their tax basis in the stock. A subsequent distribution does not result in taxation of the tax-exempt income.

- Tax preferences and adjustments.
- Depletion.
- Foreign income or losses.
- Wagering gains or losses.
- Nonbusiness income or loss (§ 212).
- Recoveries of tax benefit items.
- Intangible drilling costs.
- Investment interest, income, and expenses.
- Total property distributions.
- Total dividend distributions from accumulated earnings and profits.

This pro rata method assigns an equal amount of each of the S items to each day of the year. If a shareholder's interest changes during the year, this per-day method assigns the shareholder a pro rata share of each item for *each* day the stock is owned.

This per-day method must be used, unless the shareholder disposes of his or her entire interest in the entity.[33]

If a shareholder's interest is completely terminated during the tax year, all shareholders may elect to treat the S taxable year as two taxable years, with the first year ending on the date of the termination. Under this election, an interim closing of the books is undertaken, and the owners report their shares of the S corporation items as they occurred during the year.[34]

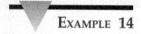

EXAMPLE 14

The following is the income statement for Beakon, an S corporation.

Sales		$ 40,000
Less: Cost of sales		(23,000)
Gross profit on sales		$ 17,000
Less: Interest expense	$1,200	
Charitable contributions	400	
Advertising expenses	1,500	
Other operating expenses	2,000	(5,100)
		$ 11,900
Plus: Tax-exempt income	$ 300	
Dividend income	200	
Long-term capital gain	500	
	$1,000	
Less: Short-term capital loss	(150)	850
Net income per books		$ 12,750

Subchapter S taxable income for Beakon is calculated as follows, using net income for book purposes as a starting point.

Net income per books			$12,750
Separately computed items:			
Deduct: Tax-exempt interest		$ 300	
Dividend income		200	
Long-term capital gain		500	
		($1,000)	
Add: Charitable contributions	$400		
Short-term capital loss	150	550	
Net effect of separately computed items			(450)
Subchapter S taxable income			$12,300

The $12,300 of Subchapter S taxable income, as well as the separately computed items, is divided among the shareholders, based upon their stock ownership. ▼

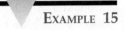

EXAMPLE 15   Assume in Example 14 that shareholder Pat owned 10% of the stock for 100 days and 12% for the remaining 265 days. Using the required per-day allocation method, Pat's share of the S corporation items is as follows.

	Schedule K Totals	Pat's Share		Pat's Schedule K–1 Totals
		10%	12%	
Subchapter S taxable income	$12,300	$337	$1,072	$1,409
Tax-exempt interest	300	8	26	34
Dividend income	200	5	17	22
Long-term capital gain	500	14	44	58
Charitable contributions	400	11	35	46
Short-term capital loss	150	4	13	17

Pat's share of the Subchapter S taxable income is the total of $12,300 × [.10 × (100/365)] plus $12,300 × [.12 × (265/365)], or $1,409. Pat's Schedule K–1 totals would flow through to his Form 1040. ▼

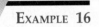

EXAMPLE 16   If Pat, in Example 15, dies after owning the stock 100 days, his share of the S corporation items is reported on his final Form 1040. Thus, only the items in the column labeled 10% in Example 15 are reported on Pat's final tax return. S corporation items that occur after a shareholder's death most likely would appear on the Form 1041 (estate's income tax return). ▼

Although the Code is silent as to the proper allocation of losses among shareholders with limited stock basis, Regulation § 1.704–1(d)(2) may be cited as support for such a pro rata allocation. Some other allocation method may be better for a taxpayer, especially where passive losses and passive income are present.

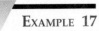

EXAMPLE 17   Ralph is a 50% owner of an S corporation for the entire year. His stock basis is $10,000, and his shares of the various corporate losses are as follows.

Ordinary loss from operations	$8,000
Section 1231 loss	3,000
Capital loss	5,000
Passive loss	2,000

Based upon a pro rata approach, the total $10,000 allocable flow-through would be split among the various losses as follows:

$$\text{Ordinary loss} = \frac{\$8,000}{\$18,000} \times \$10,000 = \$4,444.44$$

$$\S\ 1231\ \text{loss} \quad = \frac{\$3,000}{\$18,000} \times \$10,000 = \quad 1,666.67$$

$$\text{Capital loss} \quad = \frac{\$5,000}{\$18,000} \times \$10,000 = \quad 2,777.78$$

$$\text{Passive loss} \quad = \frac{\$2,000}{\$18,000} \times \$10,000 = \quad \underline{1,111.11}$$

$$\text{Total allocated loss} \qquad\qquad\qquad\quad \underline{\$10,000.00}$$

If Ralph has passive income of his own, he would prefer all of his corporate passive loss to flow through to be offset against his individual passive income. ▼

TAX TREATMENT OF DISTRIBUTIONS TO SHAREHOLDERS

The amount of any distribution to an S corporation shareholder is equal to the cash plus the fair market value of any other property distributed. Either of two sets of distribution rules applies, depending upon whether the electing corporation has accumulated earnings and profits (AEP) (e.g., from Subchapter C years).

A distribution by an S corporation having no AEP is not includible in gross income to the extent that it does not exceed the shareholder's adjusted basis in stock. When the amount of the distribution exceeds the adjusted basis of the stock, the excess is treated as a gain from the sale or exchange of property (capital gain in most cases).

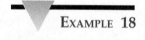

EXAMPLE 18

Peacon, Inc., a calendar year S corporation, has no AEP. During the year, Juan, a shareholder of the corporation, receives a cash dividend of $12,200 from Peacon. Juan's basis in his stock is $9,700. From the cash distribution, Juan recognizes a capital gain of $2,500, the excess of the distribution over the stock basis ($12,200 – $9,700). The remaining $9,700 is tax-free, but it reduces Juan's basis in his stock to zero. ▼

An S corporation should maintain an **accumulated adjustments account (AAA)** to help determine the nature of a corporate distribution to a shareholder. The AAA is important in maintaining the treatment of a property distribution as tax-free. This AAA procedure provides the mechanism for taxing the income of an S corporation only once. Essentially, the AAA is a cumulative total of undistributed net income items for S corporation taxable years beginning after 1982. The AAA is adjusted in a similar fashion to the shareholder's stock basis, except there is no adjustment for tax-exempt income and related expenses or for Federal taxes attributable to a C corporation tax year. Further, any decreases in stock basis have no impact on the AAA when the AAA balance is negative.

The AAA is a corporate account determined without regard to the circumstances of any shareholders.[35] In contrast, the shareholder's basis in his or her stock investment is calculated at the shareholder level. Therefore, the AAA (unlike the stock basis) can have a negative balance. All losses decrease the AAA balance, even those in excess of the shareholder's stock basis. However, distributions may not make AAA negative or increase a negative balance.

The AAA is determined at the end of the year of a distribution rather than at the time the distribution is made. When more than one distribution occurs in the same year, a pro rata portion of each distribution is treated as having been made out of the AAA.

---

[35] § 1368(e)(1)(A).

Adjustments to AAA are made in a specified order.

Increase by:

1. Schedule K items other than tax-exempt income.
2. Nonseparately computed income.
3. Depletion in excess of basis in the property.

Decrease by:

4. Adjustments other than distributions (e.g., losses, deductions).
5. Any portion of a distribution that is considered to be tax-free from AAA (not below zero).

Increase or decrease by:

6. Redemption distributions.

A shareholder has a proportionate interest in the AAA, regardless of the size of his or her stock basis.[36] However, since the AAA is a corporate account, there is no connection between the prior accumulated S corporation income and any specific shareholder. Thus, the benefits of the AAA can be shifted from one shareholder to another shareholder. For example, when one S shareholder transfers stock to another shareholder, any AAA on the purchase date is fully available to the purchaser. Similarly, issuing additional stock to a new shareholder in an S corporation having AAA dilutes the account relative to the existing shareholders.

A cash distribution from an S corporation with AEP is treated as follows.

1. Distributions are tax-free up to the amount in the AAA (limited to stock basis).
2. Any previously taxed income (PTI)[37] in the corporation under prior rules can be distributed on a tax-free basis. However, PTI probably cannot be distributed in property rather than cash [according to Reg. § 1.1375–4(b), under prior law].
3. The remaining distribution constitutes a dividend to the extent of AEP. With the consent of all of its shareholders, an S corporation can elect to have a distribution treated as made from AEP rather than from the AAA. This mechanism is known as an *AAA bypass* election. Otherwise, no adjustments are made to AEP during S years except for distributions taxed as dividends and adjustments from redemptions, liquidations, reorganizations, and divisions. For example, AEP can be acquired in a reorganization.
4. Any residual amount is applied against the shareholder's remaining basis in his or her stock.[38] This amount is considered to be a return of capital, which is not taxable. In this context, basis is reduced by the fair market value of the distributed asset.
5. Distributions that exceed the shareholder's tax basis in the stock are taxable as capital gains.

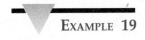

EXAMPLE 19

Tower, a calendar year S corporation, distributes $1,200 of cash to its only shareholder, Otis, on December 31, 1996. Otis's basis in his stock is $100 on December 31, 1995, and the corporation has no AAA or AEP. For 1996, Tower had $1,000 of nonseparately computed income from operations, $500 capital loss, and $400 of tax-exempt income.

Otis must report $1,000 of income and $500 of capital loss. The tax-exempt income retains its character and is not taxed to Otis. His stock basis is increased by the $400

---

[36] § 1368(c).
[37] §§ 1368(c)(1) and (e)(1). Before 1983, an account similar to the AAA was called previously taxed income (PTI). Any S corpora-

tions in existence before 1983 may have PTI, which, at this point, can be distributed tax-free.
[38] § 1368(c).

tax-exempt income and the $1,000 taxable income, and it is decreased by the $500 capital loss. The results of current operations affect the shareholder's basis before the application of the distribution rule.

Immediately before the cash distribution, Otis's stock basis is $1,000. Thus, $1,000 of the cash received is tax-free (i.e., a tax-free recovery of stock basis). Since Otis's stock basis drops to zero, the additional $200 of the distribution is a $200 gain from the sale or exchange of stock ($1,200 – $1,000). Otis's AAA and stock basis are both zero as of December 31, 1996.

	Corporate AAA	Otis's Stock Basis
Balance, 12/31/95	$ –0–	$ 100
Income	1,000	1,000
Capital loss	(500)	(500)
Tax-exempt income	—	400
Subtotal	$ 500	$ 1,000
Distribution	(500)	(1,000)
Balance, 12/31/96	$ –0–	$ –0–

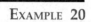

EXAMPLE 20

Assume the same facts as in Example 19, except that Tower had Subchapter C E & P of $750. Tower has an AAA of $500 ($1,000 – $500), which does not include the tax-exempt income. Otis's basis in the stock immediately before the distribution is $1,000 since his basis is increased by the tax-exempt income. Therefore, Otis is not taxed on the first $500, which is a recovery of the AAA. The next $700 is a taxable dividend from the AEP account. (Refer to the first column, step 3, of Concept Summary 21–1.)

Otis's basis in the stock is $500 ($1,000 – $500). Although the taxable portion of the distribution does not reduce Otis's basis in the stock, the nontaxable AAA distribution does. ▼

Schedule M–2.   Schedule M–2 on page 4 of Form 1120S (see next page) contains a column labeled "Other adjustments account." Essentially, this account includes items not used in the calculation of the AAA, such as tax-exempt income and any related nondeductible expenses. However, distributions from this account are not taxable. Once the E & P account reaches zero, distributions fall under the two-tier system: (1) nontaxable to the extent of basis, then (2) capital gain. Moreover, there is no need for an "other adjustments account" when a corporation has no AEP.

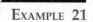

EXAMPLE 21

During 1996, Sparrow, an S corporation, records the following items.

AAA, beginning of year	$ 8,500
Previously taxed income, beginning of year	6,250
Ordinary income	25,000
Tax-exempt interest	4,000
Key employee life insurance proceeds received	5,000
Payroll penalty expense	2,000
Charitable contributions	3,000
Unreasonable compensation	5,000
Premiums on key employee life insurance	2,100
Distributions to shareholders	16,000

Sparrow's Schedule M–2 for the current year appears as follows.

Concept Summary 21–1

Classification Procedures for Distributions from an S Corporation*

Where Earnings and Profits Exist

1. Distributions are tax-free to the extent of the accumulated adjustments account.**
2. Any PTI from pre-1983 tax years can be distributed tax-free.
3. The remaining distribution constitutes ordinary dividend from AEP.***
4. Any residual amount is applied as a tax-free reduction in basis of stock.
5. Excess is treated as gain from the sale or exchange of stock (capital gain in most cases).

Where No Earnings and Profits Exist

1. Distributions are nontaxable to the extent of adjusted basis in stock.
2. Excess distributions are treated as gain from the sale or exchange of property (capital gain in most cases).

*A distribution of appreciated property by an electing corporation results in a gain that first is allocated to and reported by the shareholders.
**Once stock basis reaches zero, any distribution from the AAA is treated as a gain from the sale or exchange of stock. Thus, basis is an upper limit on what a shareholder may receive tax-free.
***An AAA bypass election is available to pay out AEP before reducing the AAA [§ 1368(e)(3)].

Schedule M-2	**Analysis of Accumulated Adjustments Account, Other Adjustments Account, and Shareholders' Undistributed Taxable Income Previously Taxed** (See instructions.)		
		(a) Accumulated adjustments account	**(b)** Other adjustments account	**(c)** Shareholders' undistributed taxable income previously taxed
1	Balance at beginning of tax year . .	8,500		6,250
2	Ordinary income from page 1, line 21 .	25,000		
3	Other additions		9,000**	
4	Loss from page 1, line 21.	( )		
5	Other reductions	(10,000*)	(2,100)	
6	Combine lines 1 through 5	23,500	6,900	
7	Distributions other than dividend distributions .	16,000		
8	Balance at end of tax year. Subtract line 7 from line 6	7,500	6,900	6,250

*$2,000 (payroll penalty) + $3,000 (charitable contributions) + $5,000 (unreasonable compensation).

**$4,000 (tax-exempt interest) + $5,000 (life insurance proceeds). ▼

Any distribution of *cash* by the corporation with respect to the stock during a post-termination transition period of approximately one year is applied against and reduces the adjusted basis of the stock to the extent that the amount of the distribution does not exceed the AAA.[39] Thus, a terminated S corporation should make a cash distribution during the one-year period following termination to the extent of all previously undistributed net income items for all S tax years.

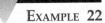

EXAMPLE 22 Quinn, the sole shareholder of Pistol, Inc., a calendar year S corporation, elects during 1995 to terminate the S election, effective January 1, 1996. As of the end of 1995, Pistol has an AAA of $1,300. Quinn can receive a nontaxable distribution of cash during a post-termination transition period of approximately one year to the extent of Pistol's AAA.

---

[39] §§ 1371(e) and 1377(b).

Although a cash distribution of $1,300 during 1996 would be nontaxable to Quinn, it would reduce the adjusted basis of his stock. ▼

Alternative Minimum Tax.   An S corporation is not directly subject to the alternative minimum tax (AMT). Under the conduit approach, all tax preference and adjustment items flow through the S corporation to be included in the shareholders' AMT calculations. The allocation of these items is based upon the pro rata daily allocation method, unless the corporation has elected the interim closing-of-the-books method. Each shareholder includes the proper portion of each tax preference and adjustment item in his or her AMT calculations. For a list of tax preference and adjustment items, see Chapter 14.

An S corporation has the advantage of calculating tax preference and adjustment items using individual, rather than corporate, rules. Thus, the S corporation has no adjusted current earnings (ACE) adjustment. For corporations with large ACE adjustments, an S election can be quite attractive. Recall, though, that at 26 and 28 percent the individual AMT rates are higher than the 20 percent corporate rate.

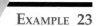

EXAMPLE 23

During the year, an S corporation has a positive AMT adjustment of $45,000 for mining exploration costs, an excess depletion tax preference of $70,000, and a certified pollution control facility preference of $10,000. The positive ACE adjustment is $80,000. If Gina is a 10% shareholder, she is assigned 10% of $45,000, $70,000, and $10,000 as tax preference and adjustment items ($4,500 + $7,000 + $1,000), but she has no ACE adjustment. ▼

CORPORATE TREATMENT OF CERTAIN PROPERTY DISTRIBUTIONS

An S corporation recognizes gain on any distribution of appreciated property (other than in a reorganization) in the same manner as if the asset had been sold to the shareholder at its fair market value.[40] The corporate gain is passed through to the shareholders. There is an important reason for this rule. Without it, property might be distributed tax-free (other than for certain recapture items) and later sold without income recognition to the shareholder because the stepped-up basis equals the asset's fair market value.

The S corporation does not recognize a loss for assets that are worth less than their basis. Furthermore, when such property is distributed, the shareholder's basis in the asset is equal to the asset's fair market value. Thus, the potential loss is postponed until the shareholder sells the stock of the S corporation. Since loss property receives a step-down in basis without any loss recognition by the S corporation, such dividend distributions should be avoided. See Concept Summary 21–2.

The character of gain—capital gain or ordinary income—depends upon the type of asset being distributed.

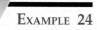

EXAMPLE 24

Blue, Inc., an S corporation for 10 years, distributes a tract of land held as an investment to its majority shareholder. The land was purchased for $22,000 many years ago and is currently worth $82,000. Blue recognizes a capital gain of $60,000, which increases the AAA by $60,000. Then the property dividend reduces AAA by $82,000 (the fair market value). The tax consequences are the same for appreciated property, whether it is distributed to the shareholders and they dispose of it, or the corporation sells the property and distributes the proceeds to the shareholders.

---

[40] § 311(b).

If the land had been purchased for $80,000 many years ago and was currently worth $30,000, the $50,000 realized loss would not be recognized at the corporate level, and the shareholder would receive a $30,000 basis in the land. The $50,000 realized loss disappears from the corporate level. Since loss is not recognized on the distribution of property that has declined in value, the AAA is not reduced by the unrecognized loss. For the loss on the property to be recognized, the S corporation must sell the property. ▼

EXAMPLE 25

Assume the same facts as in Example 24, except that Blue is either a regular corporation with no E & P prior to the distribution or a partnership. The partner's basis in the partnership is $25,000.

| | **Appreciated Property** | | |
	S Corporation	C Corporation	Partnership
Entity gain/loss	$60,000	$60,000	$ –0–
Owner's gain/loss/dividend	60,000	82,000*	–0–
Owner's basis	82,000	82,000	22,000

| | **Property That Has Declined in Value** | | |
	S Corporation	C Corporation	Partnership
Entity gain/loss	$ –0–	$ –0–	$ –0–
Owner's gain/loss/dividend	–0–	30,000*	–0–
Owner's basis	30,000	30,000	25,000

*Assume sufficient E & P.   ▼

SHAREHOLDER'S TAX BASIS

The calculation of the initial tax basis of stock in an S corporation is similar to that for the basis of stock in a regular corporation and depends upon the manner in which the shares are acquired (e.g., gift, inheritance, purchase). Once the initial tax basis is determined, various transactions during the life of the corporation affect the shareholder's basis in the stock. Although each shareholder is required to compute his or her own basis in the S shares, neither Form 1120S nor Schedule K–1 provides a place for deriving this amount.

A shareholder's basis is increased by further stock purchases and capital contributions. Operations during the year also cause the following upward adjustments to basis.[41]

- Nonseparately computed income.
- Separately stated income items (e.g., nontaxable income).
- Depletion in excess of basis in the property.

Next, the following items cause a downward adjustment to basis (but not below zero) in this order.

- Nondeductible expenses of the corporation (e.g., fines, penalties, illegal kickbacks).
- Nonseparately computed loss.
- Separately stated loss and deduction items.
- Distributions not reported as income by the shareholder (e.g., AAA or PTI distributions).

---

[41] § 1367(a).

Unlike the partnership rule, basis is first increased by income items; then it is decreased by losses and finally by distributions. Pass-through items (other than distributions) that reduce stock basis are governed by special ordering rules. Noncapital, nondeductible expenditures reduce stock basis before losses or deductible items. A taxpayer may irrevocably elect under Regulation § 1.1367–1(f) to have deductible items pass through before any noncapital, nondeductible items. In most cases, this election is advantageous.

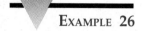

EXAMPLE 26

In its first year of operations, Pell, Inc., a calendar year S corporation, earns income of $2,000. On February 2 in its second year of operations, Pell distributes $2,000 to Marty, its sole shareholder. During the remainder of the second year, the corporation incurs a $2,000 loss.

Under the S corporation ordering rules, the $2,000 loss passes through to Marty, and she is treated as receiving a capital gain of $2,000 in excess of her stock basis. ▼

A shareholder's basis in the stock can never be reduced below zero. Any further downward adjustment (losses or deductions) is applied to reduce (but not below zero) the shareholder's basis in any *indebtedness* from the electing corporation. Once the basis of any debt is reduced, subsequent net income items increase it (only up to the original amount). The adjustment is made *before* any increase to the basis in the stock.[42] A distribution below stock basis does not reduce any debt basis. If a loss and a distribution occur in the same year, the loss reduces the basis before the distribution.[43]

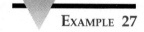

EXAMPLE 27

Stacey, a sole shareholder, has a $7,000 stock basis and a $2,000 basis in a loan that she made to a calendar year S corporation at the beginning of 1996. Subchapter S net income during 1996 is $8,200. The corporation incurred a short-term capital loss of $2,300 and received $2,000 of tax-exempt interest income. Cash of $15,000 is distributed to Stacey on November 15, 1996. As a result, Stacey's basis in her stock is zero, and her loan basis is still $2,000 at the end of 1996, since only losses and deductions (and not distributions) reduce the debt basis. Stacey recognizes a $100 gain ($15,000 – $14,900). See Concept Summary 21–2.

Beginning basis in the stock	$ 7,000
Nonseparately computed income	8,200
Short-term capital loss	(2,300)
Tax-exempt interest income	2,000
	$ 14,900
Distribution received (to extent of basis)	(14,900)
Ending basis in the stock	$ –0–

Although stock basis cannot be reduced below zero, the $100 excess distribution does not reduce Stacey's loan basis. ▼

TREATMENT OF LOSSES

Net Operating Loss.   One major advantage of an S election is the ability to pass through any net operating loss (NOL) of the corporation directly to the shareholders. A shareholder can deduct an NOL for the year in which the S corporation's tax year ends. The corporation is not entitled to any deduction for the NOL. The individual shareholder's loss is a deduction *for* AGI. A shareholder's

---

[42] § 1367(b)(2).

[43] §§ 1366(d)(1)(A) and 1368(d)(1).

CONCEPT SUMMARY 21–2

Distribution of Property

	Appreciated Property	Depreciated Property
S corporation	Realized gain is recognized to the corporation, which passes it through to the shareholders. Such gain increases a shareholder's stock basis, generating a market value basis in the property. On the distribution, the shareholder's stock basis is reduced by the FMV of the property (but not below zero).	Realized loss is not recognized. The shareholder assumes a FMV basis in the property. Loss is postponed indefinitely.
C corporation	Realized gain is recognized under § 311(b) and increases E & P (net of tax). The shareholder assumes a FMV basis and has a FMV taxable dividend.	Realized loss is not recognized.
Partnership	No gain to the partnership or partner. Basis to the partner is limited to the partner's basis in the partnership.	Realized loss is not recognized.

basis in the stock is reduced to the extent of any pass-through of the NOL, and the shareholder's AAA is reduced by the same deductible amount.[44]

Net operating losses are allocated among shareholders in the same manner as income is. NOLs are allocated on a daily basis to all shareholders.[45] Transferred shares are considered to be held by the transferee (not the transferor) on the date of the transfer.[46]

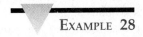

EXAMPLE 28

An S corporation incurs a $20,000 NOL for the current year. At all times during the tax year, the stock was owned equally by the same 10 shareholders. Each shareholder is entitled to deduct $2,000 *for* AGI for the tax year in which the corporate tax year ends. ▼

Deductions for an S corporation's NOL pass-through cannot exceed a shareholder's adjusted basis in the stock plus the basis of any loans made by the shareholder to the corporation. If a taxpayer is unable to prove the tax basis, the NOL pass-through can be denied.[47] In essence, a shareholder's stock or loan basis cannot go below zero. As noted previously, once a shareholder's adjusted stock basis has been eliminated by an NOL, any excess NOL is used to reduce the shareholder's basis for any loans made to the corporation (but never below zero). The basis for loans is established by the actual advances made to the corporation, and not by indirect loans.[48] If the shareholder's basis is insufficient to allow a full flow-through and there is more than one type of loss (e.g., in the same year the taxpayer incurs both a passive loss and a net capital loss), the flow-through amounts are determined on a pro rata basis.

---

[44] §§ 1368(a)(1)(A) and (e)(1)(A).
[45] § 1377(a)(1).
[46] Reg. § 1374–1(b)(3).

[47] See *Donald J. Sauvigne*, 30 TCM 123, T.C.Memo. 1971–30.
[48] *Ruth M. Prashker*, 59 T.C. 172 (1972); *Frederick G. Brown v. U.S.*, 83–1 USTC ¶9364, 52 AFTR2d 82–5080, 706 F.2d 75 (CA–6, 1983).

When a shareholder has acquired stock at different times and for varying amounts, a separate-share method is used,[49] rather than a unitary approach.[50] Under the separate-share approach, the basis of each share of stock is increased or decreased by an amount equal to the owner's pro rata portion of an income or loss item, determined on a per-share, per-day basis. Thus, an S corporation maintains a separate basis account for each block of stock. A spillover rule allows a shareholder to apply losses or distributions attributable to one share of stock that are in excess of its basis against the basis of all other stock owned by the shareholder. Where a net basis reduction exceeds a shareholder's total available stock basis for a tax year, any excess (other than distributions) reduces the shareholder's debt basis (but not below zero).

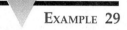

EXAMPLE 29

On December 31, 1996, Erica owns one share of an S corporation's 10 outstanding shares of stock. The basis of Erica's share is $300. On July 3, 1997, Erica purchases 2 shares from another shareholder for $250 each. During 1997, the S corporation has no income or deductions, but incurs a loss of $3,650. Under the separate-share approach, the amount of the loss assigned to each day of the S corporation's tax year is $10 ($3,650 ÷ 365 days). For each day, $1 is allocated to each outstanding share ($10 ÷ 10 shares).

Since Erica owned one share for 365 days, a $365 loss is attributable to that share ($1 × 365 days). Since she owned the other two shares for 182 days, the basis of each of these shares is reduced by $182 ($1 × 182 days) to $68 ($250 − $182). Because the decrease in basis attributable to the *first* share exceeds its basis by $65 ($365 − $300), the excess is applied proportionately to reduce the remaining bases of the other two shares; thus, each is reduced by $32.50 [$65 × ($68/$136)]. After this reduction, each of the two shares has a $35.50 basis ($68 − $32.50). ▼

Except in the Eleventh Circuit, the fact that a shareholder has guaranteed a loan made to the corporation by a third party has no effect upon the shareholder's loan basis, unless payments actually have been made as a result of that guarantee.[51] If the corporation defaults on an indebtedness and the shareholder makes good on the guarantee, the shareholder's indebtedness basis is increased to that extent.[52] Such a subsequent increase in basis has no influence on the results of a prior year in which an NOL exceeded a shareholder's adjusted basis.

A shareholder's share of an NOL may be greater than both the basis in the stock and the basis of the indebtedness. A shareholder is entitled to carry a loss forward to the extent that the loss for the year exceeds both the stock basis and the loan basis. Any loss carried forward may be deducted *only* by the same shareholder if and when the basis in the stock of or loans to the corporation is restored.[53]

Any loss carryover remaining at the end of a one-year post-termination transition period is lost forever.[54] The post-termination transition period ends on the later of (1) one year after the effective date of the termination of the S election or the due date for the last S return (whichever is later) or (2) 120 days after the determination that the corporation's S election had terminated for a previous year. Thus, a shareholder who has a loss carryover should increase the stock or loan basis and flow through the loss before disposing of the stock.

[49] Reg. §§ 1.1367–1(b)(2) and (c)(3).
[50] A unitary approach would require that the shareholder's total basis be evenly distributed over all shares owned.
[51] See, for example, *Estate of Leavitt*, 90 T.C. 206 (1988), aff'd. 89–1 USTC ¶9332, 63 AFTR2d 89–1437, 875 F.2d 420 (CA–4, 1989); *Selfe*

v. U.S., 86–1 USTC ¶9115, 57 AFTR2d 86–464, 778 F.2d 769 (CA–11, 1985); *James K. Calcutt*, 91 T.C. 14 (1988).
[52] Rev.Rul. 70–50, 1970–1 C.B. 178.
[53] § 1366(d).
[54] § 1377(b).

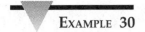

EXAMPLE 30

Dana has a stock basis of $4,000 in an S corporation. He has loaned $2,000 to the corporation and has guaranteed another $4,000 loan made to the corporation by a local bank. Although his share of the S corporation's NOL for the current year is $9,500, Dana may deduct only $6,000 of the NOL on his individual tax return. Dana may carry forward $3,500 of the NOL, to be deducted when the basis in his stock or loan to the corporation is restored. Dana has a zero basis in both the stock and loan after the flow-through of the $6,000 NOL. ▼

Net operating losses from C corporation years cannot be utilized at the corporate level (except with respect to built-in gains), nor can they be passed through to the shareholders. Further, the carryforward period continues to run during S status.[55] Consequently, it may not be appropriate for a corporation that has unused NOLs to make the S election. When a corporation is expecting losses in the future, an S election should be made *before* the loss year.

If a loan's basis has been reduced and is not restored, income is recognized when the loan is repaid. If the corporation issued a note as evidence of the debt, the repayment constitutes an amount received in exchange for a capital asset, and the amount that exceeds the shareholder's basis is entitled to capital gain treatment.[56] However, if the loan is made on open account, the repayment constitutes ordinary income to the extent that it exceeds the shareholder's basis for the loan. Each repayment is prorated between the gain portion and the repayment of the debt.[57] Thus, a note should be given to ensure capital gain treatment for the income that results from a loan's repayment.

Since the basis rule requires that corporate income be used to restore debt basis before it can be used to restore stock basis, a double tax can be imposed on current income. Any current income distributed, after both debt and stock basis have been reduced to zero, is taxed as capital gain because it is considered return of capital, but only to the extent of stock basis. To avoid this double tax, shareholders should consider forgiving debt that a solvent S corporation owes them. Such a forgiveness is considered a contribution of capital, with a resulting increase in the shareholder's stock basis. For an insolvent S corporation, discharge of indebtedness income is tax-deferred (not tax-exempt) and does not increase the shareholder's basis.

Passive Losses and Credits. There are three major classes of income and losses: active, portfolio, and passive. Section 469 provides that net passive losses and credits are not deductible and must be carried over to a year when there is passive income. S corporations are not directly subject to these limits, but shareholders who do not materially participate in operating the business will be able to apply the corporate losses and credits only against income from other passive activities. In other words, flow-through income and deductions from an S corporation are regarded as arising from a passive activity unless the shareholder materially participates in the corporate business. For example, a passive loss at the S corporation level could not be offset against the earned income of a nonparticipating shareholder. Regular, continuous, and substantial involvement in the S corporation is necessary to meet the material participation requirement.[58]

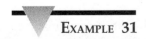

EXAMPLE 31

Heather is a 50% owner of an S corporation engaged in a passive activity (refer to Chapter 10). A nonparticipating shareholder, she receives a salary of $6,000 for services as a result of

---

[55] § 1371(b).

[56] *Joe M. Smith*, 48 T.C. 872 (1967), *aff'd.* and *rev'd.* in 70–1 USTC ¶9327, 25 AFTR2d 70–936, 424 F.2d 219 (CA–9, 1970), and Rev.Rul. 64–162, 1964–1 C.B. 304.

[57] Rev.Rul. 68–537, 1968–2 C.B. 372.

[58] Reg. § 1.469–5T(a).

CONCEPT SUMMARY 21–3

Treatment of Losses

Step 1.   Allocate total loss to the shareholder on a daily basis, based upon stock ownership.

Step 2.   If the shareholder's loss exceeds his or her stock basis, apply any excess to the adjusted basis of indebtedness to the shareholder. Losses from distributions do not reduce debt basis.

Step 3.   Where loss exceeds the debt basis, any excess is suspended and carried over to succeeding tax years.

Step 4.   In succeeding tax years, any net increase (resulting from *all* positive and negative basis adjustments) restores the debt basis first, up to its original amount.

Step 5.   Once debt basis is restored, any net increase remaining is used to increase stock basis.

Step 6.   Any suspended loss from a previous year reduces stock basis first and debt basis second.

Step 7.   If the S election terminates, any suspended loss carryover may be deducted during the post-termination transition period to the extent of the *stock* basis at the end of this period. Any loss remaining at the end of the transition period is lost forever.

the passive activity. This deduction creates a $6,000 passive loss at the corporate level. Heather has $6,000 of earned income as a result of the salary. The $6,000 salary creates a $6,000 deduction/passive loss, which flows through to the shareholders. Heather's $3,000 share of the loss may not be deducted against the $6,000 earned income. Earned income is not taken into account in computing the income or loss from a passive activity. ▼

At-Risk Rules.   The at-risk rules generally apply to S corporation shareholders. Essentially, an amount at risk is determined separately for each shareholder. The amount of the corporate losses that are passed through and deductible by the shareholders is not affected by the amount the corporation has at risk. A shareholder usually is considered at risk with respect to an activity to the extent of cash and the adjusted basis of other property contributed to the electing corporation, any amount borrowed for use in the activity that the taxpayer is personally liable for paying from personal assets, and the net fair market value of personal assets that secure nonrecourse borrowing.

TAX ON PREELECTION BUILT-IN GAINS

Because Congress was concerned that certain C corporations would elect S status to avoid the corporate income tax on the sale or exchange of appreciated property (avoiding a tax on such built-in gains), it completely revamped § 1374. A regular corporation converting to S corporation status after 1986 generally incurs a corporate-level tax on any built-in gains when the S corporation disposes of an asset in a taxable disposition within 10 calendar years after the date on which the S election took effect.

General Rules.   The **built-in gains tax** is applied to any unrealized gain attributable to appreciation in the value of an asset (e.g., real estate, cash basis receivables, goodwill) or other income items while held by the C corporation. The highest corporate tax rate (applicable to that type of income) is applied to the lesser of (1) the recognized built-in gains of the S corporation for the tax year or (2) the amount that would be the taxable income of the corporation for that tax year if it were a C corporation. Any built-in gain that escapes taxation due to the taxable income limitation is carried forward to future tax years. Then it is treated as recognized built-in gain. Thus, given a low or negative taxable income in any year when built-in gain assets are sold, the taxpayer defers the payment of the built-in gains tax liability. The total amount of gain that is ever recognized is limited to the aggregate net built-in gains of the corporation at the time it converted to S status. Thus, it may be advisable to obtain an independent appraisal when converting a C corporation to an S corporation. Certainly, a memorandum should be prepared listing the fair market values of all assets, along with the methods used to arrive at the values.

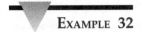

EXAMPLE 32
Marble is a former C corporation whose first S corporation year began on January 1, 1996. At that time, it had two assets: X, with a value of $1,000 and a basis of $400, and Y, with a value of $400 and a basis of $600. Thus, net unrealized built-in gains as of January 1, 1996, are $400. If Marble sells asset X for $1,000 during 1996, while retaining asset Y, the recognized built-in gain is limited to $400. ▼

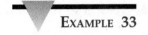

EXAMPLE 33
Assume the same facts as in Example 32, except that taxable income in 1996 is $300. The built-in gains tax is assessed only on $300. However, the $100 recognized built-in gain that circumvents the tax in 1996 is carried forward and treated as recognized built-in gain in 1997. There is no statutory limit on the carryforward period, but the gain will effectively expire at the end of the 10-year recognition period applicable to all built-in gains (except for installment sales after March 25, 1990).[59] ▼

Gains on sales or distributions of all assets by an S corporation are presumed to be built-in gains unless the taxpayer can establish that the appreciation accrued after the conversion. This built-in gains tax is avoided if the S election was made before 1987.[60]

Any tax imposed on built-in gain reduces proportionately the amount of built-in gain that passes through to the shareholder. Post-conversion appreciation is subject to the regular S corporation pass-through rules.

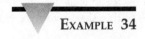

EXAMPLE 34
Monkey Corporation elects S status, effective for calendar year 1995. As of January 1, 1995, one of Monkey's assets has a basis of $50,000 and a fair market value of $110,000. Early in 1996, the asset is sold for $135,000. Monkey incurs a realized gain of $85,000, of which $60,000 is subject to the built-in gains tax of 35%. The entire $85,000 gain is subject to the corporate pass-through rules (reduced by the built-in gains tax itself), but only $25,000 of the gain fully bypasses the corporate-level tax. ▼

Normally, tax attributes of a C corporation do not carry over to a converted S corporation. For purposes of the tax on built-in gains, however, certain carryovers are allowed. An S corporation can offset any gain by related attributes from prior C corporation years, such as unexpired NOLs or capital losses. In a similar manner, AMT credit carryovers (arising in a C corporation tax year) and business credit carryforwards are allowed to offset the built-in gains tax.

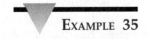

EXAMPLE 35
Assume the same facts as in Example 34, except that Monkey also had a $10,000 NOL carryover when it elected S status. The NOL reduces Monkey's built-in gain from $60,000 to $50,000. Thus, only $50,000 is subject to the built-in gains tax. ▼

---

[59] § 1374(d)(7); Notice 90–27, 1990–1 C.B. 336.   [60] § 1362.

CONCEPT SUMMARY 21–4

Calculation of Built-in Gains Tax Liability

Step 1. Select the smaller of built-in gains or taxable income.*

Step 2. Deduct unexpired NOLs and capital losses from C corporation tax years.

Step 3. Multiply the tax base obtained in step 2 by the top corporate tax rate.

Step 4. Deduct any business credit carryforwards and AMT credit carryovers arising in C corporation tax years from the amount obtained in step 3.

Step 5. The corporation pays any tax resulting in step 4.

*Any net recognized built-in gain in excess of taxable income may be carried forward to the next year, as long as the next year is within the 10-year recognition period.

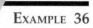

EXAMPLE 36

An S corporation has a built-in gain of $100,000 and taxable income of $90,000. The built-in gains tax liability is calculated as follows.

Lesser of taxable income or built-in gain	$ 90,000
Less: NOL carryforward from C year	(12,000)
Capital loss carryforward from C year	(8,000)
Tax base	$ 70,000
Highest corporate tax rate	.35
Tentative tax	$ 24,500
Less: Business credit carryforward from C year	(4,000)
AMT credit carryforward from C year	(3,000)
Built-in gains tax liability	$ 17,500

The $10,000 realized (but not taxed) built-in gain in excess of taxable income may be carried forward to the next year, as long as the next year is within the 10-year recognition period. ▼

Concept Summary 21–4 summarizes the calculation of the built-in gains tax.

LIFO Recapture Tax.   When a corporation uses the FIFO method for its last year before making the S election, any built-in gain is recognized and taxed as the inventory is sold. A LIFO-basis corporation does not recognize this gain, unless the corporation invades the LIFO layer during the 10-year recognition period. To preclude deferral of gain recognition under LIFO, the law requires the income recognition of a LIFO recapture amount upon making an S election.

A C corporation using LIFO for its last year before making an S election must include in income the excess of the inventory's value under FIFO over the LIFO value. No negative adjustment is allowed if the LIFO value is higher than the FIFO value. The increase in tax liability resulting from LIFO recapture is payable in four equal installments, with the first payment due on or before the due date for the corporate return for the last C corporation year (without regard to any extensions). The remaining three installments must be paid on or before the due dates of the succeeding corporate returns. No interest is due if payments are made by the due dates, and no estimated taxes are due on the four tax installments. The basis of the

LIFO inventory is adjusted to take into account this LIFO recapture amount, but AAA is not decreased by payment of the tax.

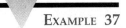

EXAMPLE 37

Engelage Corporation converts from a C corporation to an S corporation at the beginning of 1997. Engelage used the LIFO inventory method in 1996 and had an ending LIFO inventory of $110,000 (FIFO value of $190,000). Engelage must add $80,000 of LIFO recapture amount to its 1996 taxable income, resulting in an increased tax liability of $28,000 ($80,000 × 35%). Thus, Engelage must pay one-fourth of the tax (or $7,000) with its 1996 corporate tax return. The three succeeding installments of $7,000 each are paid with Engelage's next three tax returns. ▼

PASSIVE INVESTMENT INCOME PENALTY TAX

A tax is imposed on the excess passive income of S corporations that possess accumulated E & P from Subchapter C years. The tax rate is the highest corporate rate for the year. The rate is applied to the portion of the corporation's net passive income that bears the same ratio to the total net passive income for the tax year as excess gross passive income bears to the total gross passive income for the year. However, the amount subject to the tax may not exceed the taxable income of the corporation.[61]

For this purpose, passive investment income (PII) means gross receipts derived from royalties, rents, dividends, interest, annuities, and sales and exchanges of stocks and securities.[62] Only the net gain from the disposition of capital assets (other than stocks and securities) is taken into account in computing gross receipts. Net passive income means passive income reduced by any deductions directly connected with the production of that income. Any passive income tax reduces the amount the shareholders must take into income.

The excess net passive income cannot exceed the corporate taxable income for the year before considering any NOL deduction or the special deductions allowed by §§ 241–250 (except the organizational expense deduction of § 248).

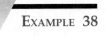

EXAMPLE 38

At the end of 1996, Barnhardt Corporation, an electing S corporation, has gross receipts totaling $264,000 (of which $110,000 is PII). Expenditures directly connected to the production of the PII total $30,000. Therefore, Barnhardt has net PII of $80,000 ($110,000 − $30,000), and its PII for tax year 1996 exceeds 25% of its gross receipts by $44,000 ($110,000 PII − $66,000). Excess net passive income (ENPI) is $32,000, calculated as follows.

$$ \text{ENPI} = \frac{\$44,000}{\$110,000} \times \$80,000 = \$32,000 $$

Barnhardt's PII tax for 1996 is $11,200 ($32,000 × 35%). ▼

---

[61] §§1374(d)(4), and 1375(a) and (b).   [62] § 1362(d)(3)(D)(i).

ETHICAL
CONSIDERATIONS

Disclosure of Possible Problems

You counsel a client, a closely held regional securities brokerage firm, to elect S status, so its shareholders can obtain distributions of income without double taxation. During the next year, you notice that the corporation's passive investment income (e.g., interest income from margin accounts) is approaching 25 percent of gross receipts. Should you immediately disclose the problem to the client? If so, what do you say if the client then asks you for reimbursement of additional taxes due if the risk materializes?

FRINGE BENEFIT RULES

An S corporation is treated as a partnership with respect to certain fringe benefits made available to a shareholder-employee owning more than 2 percent of the S corporation stock. The constructive ownership rules of § 318 (refer to Chapter 18) are used in applying the 2 percent ownership test.[63] If an S corporation provides a fringe benefit to a more-than-2 percent shareholder and the benefit is not excludible by a partner in a partnership (e.g., health and accident insurance premiums), the S corporation should deduct the amount as compensation, and the employee should report the amount as compensation income. Such treatment occurs upon the receipt of the following benefits, among others.

- Excludible group term life insurance.
- The $5,000 death benefit exclusion.
- The exclusion from income of amounts paid for an accident and health plan.
- The exclusion from income of meals and lodging furnished for the convenience of the employer.[64]

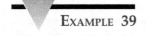

EXAMPLE 39

Purple, Inc., an S corporation, pays for the medical care of two shareholder-employees during the current year. Tina, a shareholder owning 2% of the stock, receives $1,700 for this purpose. Soo, a shareholder owning 20% of the stock, receives $3,100. Purple deducts the $1,700 as a business expense. The $3,100 paid on behalf of Soo is also deductible by the corporation, but Soo records the amount as compensation income because he owns more than 2% of the stock. Soo can deduct 30% of the $3,100 himself, as allowed by § 162(l). ▼

OTHER OPERATIONAL RULES

5   LEARNING OBJECTIVE
Recognize the situations where
S status is desirable or
undesirable.

Other possible effects of various Code provisions on S corporations include the following.

- An S corporation is required to make estimated tax payments with respect to tax exposure because of any recognized built-in gain and excess passive investment income.
- An S corporation may own stock in another corporation, but an S corporation may not have a corporate shareholder. An S corporation is not eligible for a dividends received deduction.

---

[63] §§ 1372(a) and (b). See Rev.Rul. 91–26, 1991–1 C.B. 184.
[64] S.Rep. No. 640, 97th Cong., 2d Sess. 22 (1982); Rev.Rul. 91–26,
  1991–1 C.B. 184; Ann. 92–16, 1992–5 IRB 5.

- An S corporation is not subject to the 10 percent of taxable income limitation applicable to charitable contributions made by a C corporation.
- Foreign taxes paid by an electing corporation will pass through to the shareholders and should be claimed as either a deduction or a credit (subject to the applicable limitations).[65]
- Any family member who renders services or furnishes capital to an electing corporation must be paid reasonable compensation. Otherwise, the IRS can make adjustments to reflect the value of the services or capital.[66] This rule may make it more difficult for related parties to shift Subchapter S taxable income to children or other family members.
- Although § 1366(a)(1) provides for a flow-through of S items to a shareholder, it does not apply to self-employment income.[67] Thus, a shareholder's portion of S income is not self-employment income and is not subject to the self-employment tax. Compensation for services rendered to an S corporation is, however, subject to FICA taxes.

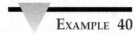

EXAMPLE 40

Cody and Dana each own one-third of a fast-food restaurant, and their 14-year-old son owns the other shares. Both parents work full-time in the restaurant operations, but the son works infrequently. Neither parent receives a salary this year, when the taxable income of the S corporation is $160,000. The IRS can require that reasonable compensation be paid to the parents to prevent the full one-third of the $160,000 from being taxed to the son. Otherwise, this would be an effective technique to shift earned income to a family member to reduce the total family tax burden. With the procedure for taxing the unearned income of children, this shifting technique becomes much more valuable. Furthermore, low or zero salaries can reduce FICA taxes due to the Federal government. ▼

- The depletion allowance is computed separately by each shareholder. Each shareholder is treated as having produced his or her pro rata share of the production of the electing corporation, and each is allocated a respective share of the adjusted basis of the electing corporation as to oil or gas property held by the corporation.[68]
- An S corporation is placed on the cash method of accounting for purposes of deducting business expenses and interest owed to a cash basis related party.[69] Thus, the timing of the shareholder's income and the corporate deduction must match.
- The S election is not recognized by the District of Columbia and several states, including Connecticut, Michigan, New Hampshire, New Jersey, and Tennessee. Thus, some or all of the entity's income may be subject to a state-level income tax.
- If § 1244 stock is issued to an S corporation, the S corporation and its shareholders may not treat losses on such stock as ordinary losses, notwithstanding § 1363, which provides that the taxable income of an S corporation must be computed in the same manner as that of an individual. However, an S corporation may issue § 1244 stock to its shareholders to obtain ordinary loss treatment.
- Losses may be disallowed due to a lack of a profit motive. If the activities at the corporate level are not profit motivated, the losses may be disallowed under the hobby loss rule of § 183.[70]

[65] § 1373(a).
[66] § 1366(e). In addition, beware of an IRS search for the "real owner" of the stock under Reg. § 1.1373–1(a)(2).
[67] Rev.Rul 59–221, 1959–1 C.B. 225.

[68] § 613A(c)(13).
[69] § 267(b).
[70] *Michael J. Houston*, T.C.Memo. 1995–159; *Mario G. De Mendoza, III*, T.C.Memo. 1994–314.

WHEN THE ELECTION IS ADVISABLE

Effective tax planning with S corporations begins with the determination of whether the election is appropriate. In light of changes made by TRA of 1986 and subsequent legislation, the taxpayer may wish to reevaluate the desirability of using a C corporation as a means of conducting a trade or business. In this context, one should consider the following factors.

- Are losses from the business anticipated? If so, the S election may be highly attractive because these losses pass through to the shareholders.
- What are the tax brackets of the shareholders? If the shareholders are in high individual income tax brackets, it may be desirable to avoid S corporation status and have profits taxed to the corporation at lower rates (e.g., 15 percent or 25 percent).
- When the immediate pass-through of Subchapter S taxable income is avoided, the shareholders may later receive the corporation's profits as capital gain income through stock redemptions, liquidating distributions, or sales of stock to others, or as dividend distributions in low-tax-bracket years. Or the profits may be negated by a partial or complete step-up in basis upon the death of the shareholder. On the other hand, if the shareholders are in low individual income tax brackets, the pass-through of corporate profits has less effect, and the avoidance of the corporate income tax becomes the paramount consideration. Under these circumstances, the S election could be highly attractive. Although an S corporation usually escapes Federal taxes, it may not be immune from state and local taxes imposed on corporations or from several Federal corporate-level taxes.
- Does a C corporation have an NOL carryover from a prior year? Such a loss cannot be used in an S year (except for purposes of the built-in gains tax). Even worse, S years count in the 15-year carryover limitation. Thus, even if the S election is made, one might consider terminating the election before the carryover limitation expires. Such a termination would permit the loss to be utilized by (what is again) a C corporation.
- Both individuals and C corporations are subject to the alternative minimum tax. Many of the tax preference and adjustment items are the same, but some apply only to corporate taxpayers, while others are limited to individuals. The alternative minimum tax adjustment relating to adjusted current earnings could create havoc with some C corporations (refer to Chapter 14). S corporations themselves are not subject to this tax.
- Some C corporations must convert from the cash method to the accrual method of accounting (refer to Chapter 15).
- S corporations and partnerships have lost most of the flexibility in the choice of their accounting period (see also Chapter 22).
- By taxing C corporations on nonliquidating and liquidating distributions of appreciated property (refer to Chapters 18 and 19), the effect of double taxation is reinforced.

The choice of the form of doing business often is dictated by other factors. For example, many businesses cannot qualify for the S election or would find the partnership form more practical. Therefore, freedom of action based on tax considerations may not be an attainable goal.

MAKING A PROPER ELECTION

Once the parties have decided the election is appropriate, it becomes essential to ensure that the election is made properly.

- Make sure all shareholders consent. If any doubt exists concerning the shareholder status of an individual, it would be wise to have that party issue a consent anyway.[71] Too few consents are fatal to the election; the same cannot be said for too many consents.
- Be sure that the election filing is timely and proper. Either hand carry the election to an IRS office or send it by certified or registered mail. The date used to determine timeliness is the postmark date, not the date the IRS receives the election. A copy of the election should become part of the corporation's permanent files.
- Be careful to ascertain when the timely election period begins to run for a newly formed corporation. An election made too soon (before the corporation is in existence) is worse than one made too late. If serious doubts exist as to when this period begins, filing more than one election might be considered as a practical means of guaranteeing the desired result.

PRESERVING THE ELECTION

Recall how an election can be lost and that a five-year waiting period generally is imposed before another S election is available. To preserve an S election, the following points should be kept in mind.

- As a starting point, make sure all parties concerned are aware of the various violations that lead to the loss of an election.
- Watch for possible disqualification as a small business corporation. For example, the divorce of a shareholder, accompanied by a property settlement, could violate the 35-shareholder limitation. The death of a shareholder could result in a nonqualifying trust becoming a shareholder. The latter circumstance might be avoided by utilizing a buy-sell agreement or binding the deceased shareholder's estate to turn in the stock to the corporation for redemption or, as an alternative, to sell it to the surviving shareholders.[72]
- Make sure a new majority shareholder (including the estate of a deceased shareholder) does not file a refusal to continue the election.
- Watch for the passive investment income limitation. Avoid a consecutive third year with excess passive income if a corporation has accumulated Subchapter C earnings and profits. In this connection, assets that produce passive investment income (e.g., stocks and bonds, certain rental assets) might be retained by the shareholders in their individual capacities and thereby kept out of the corporation.
- Do not transfer stock to a nonresident alien.
- Do not create an active affiliate or issue a second class of stock.

ETHICAL CONSIDERATIONS   ### A Divorce Threatens S Status

Golden Cowrie, Inc., has operated successfully as an S corporation for eight years in Greer, South Carolina. In July 1996, the company had 35 shareholders, but one of the shareholders, Morrie Williams, is considering obtaining a divorce. Both Morrie and his wife Kristy own shares in the corporation.

---

[71] See *William B. Wilson*, 34 TCM 463, T.C.Memo. 1975–92.

[72] Most such agreements do not create a second class of S stock. Rev.Rul. 85–161, 1985–2 C. B. 191; *Portage Plastic Co. v. U.S.*, 72–2 USTC ¶9567, 30 AFTR2d 72–5229, 470 F.2d 308 (CA–7, 1973).

Morrie discusses the situation with the board of directors, who offer several suggestions.

- Morrie should postpone the divorce until 1997, while the company tries to purchase all of the stock from one of the smaller owners.
- Morrie and Kristy should remain married indefinitely for the good of the S election.
- Two of the unmarried shareholders will be encouraged to marry for the "benefit of the company."
- The company will continue to list Morrie and Kristy as married on Form 1120S after they divorce.

The S election saves the group about $280,000 each year. How would you counsel Morrie to respond to the board's proposals?

PLANNING FOR THE OPERATION OF THE CORPORATION

Operating an S corporation to achieve optimum tax savings for all parties involved requires a great deal of care and, most important, an understanding of the applicable tax rules.

AAA Considerations.   Although the corporate-level accumulated adjustments account (AAA) is used primarily by an S corporation with accumulated earnings and profits (AEP) from a Subchapter C year, all S corporations should maintain an accurate record of the AAA. Because there is a grace period for distributing the AAA after termination of the S election, the parties must be in a position to determine the balance of the account.

EXAMPLE 41

Nobles, Inc., is an S corporation during 1995, with no AEP from a Subchapter C year. Over the years, no attempt was made to maintain an accurate accounting for the AAA. In 1996, the S election is terminated, and Nobles has a grace period for distributing the AAA tax-free to its shareholders. A great deal of time and expense may be necessary to reconstruct the AAA balance in 1996. ▼

Tax-exempt income is not included in gross income and does not increase AAA. For an S corporation with AEP, an instrument that produces tax-exempt income is a bad investment. Any subsequent distribution of tax-exempt income that exceeds the AAA balance is treated as dividend income to the extent of any AEP.

Where AEP is present, a negative AAA may cause double taxation of S corporation income. With a negative AAA, a distribution of current income restores the negative AAA balance to zero, but is considered to be a distribution in excess of AAA, taxable as a dividend to the extent of AEP.

The AAA bypass election may be used to avoid the accumulated earnings tax or personal holding company tax in the year preceding the first tax year under Subchapter S. This bypass election allows the AEP to be distributed instead.

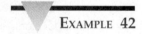

EXAMPLE 42

Zebra, Inc., is an S corporation during 1995, with a significant amount in its AEP account. The shareholders are subject to low income tax rates for 1996 and expect to terminate the election in that year. Since the new C corporation may be subject to the accumulated earnings tax in 1996, the shareholders may wish to use the AAA bypass election to distribute some or all of the AEP. Of course, any distributions of the AEP account in 1995 would be taxable to the shareholders. ▼

A net loss allocated to a shareholder reduces the AAA. This required adjustment should encourage an electing corporation to make annual distributions of net income to avoid having an AAA reduced by a future net loss.

Salary Structure.   The amount of salary paid to a shareholder-employee of an S corporation can have varying tax consequences and should be considered carefully. Larger amounts might be advantageous if the maximum contribution allowed under the retirement plan has not been reached. Smaller amounts may be beneficial if the parties are trying to shift taxable income to lower-bracket shareholders, reduce payroll taxes, curtail a reduction of Social Security benefits, or restrict losses that do not pass through because of the basis limitation.

A strategy of decreasing compensation and correspondingly increasing distributions to shareholder-employees often results in substantial savings in employment taxes. However, a shareholder of an S corporation cannot always perform substantial services and arrange to receive dividends rather than compensation so that the corporation may avoid paying employment taxes. The shareholder may be deemed an employee, and any dividends will be recharacterized as wages subject to FICA and FUTA taxes.[73] For planning purposes, some level of compensation should be paid to all shareholder-employees to avoid any recharacterization of distributions as deductible salaries—especially in personal service corporations.

The IRS can require that reasonable compensation be paid to family members who render services or provide capital to the S corporation. The IRS, though, can adjust the items taken into account by family-member shareholders to reflect the value of services or capital they provided.

Unreasonable compensation traditionally has not been a problem for S corporations, but deductible compensation under § 162 reduces an S corporation's taxable income, which is relevant to the built-in gains tax. Compensation may be one of the larger items that an electing corporation can use to reduce taxable income to minimize any built-in gains penalty tax. Thus, IRS agents may attempt to classify compensation as unreasonable to increase the § 1374 tax.

Loss Considerations.   A net loss in excess of tax basis may be carried forward and deducted only by the same shareholder in succeeding years. Thus, before disposing of the stock, a shareholder should increase the basis of the stock/loan so that the loss will flow through. The next shareholder does not obtain the carryover loss.

Any unused carryover loss in existence upon the termination of the S election may be deducted only in the next tax year and is limited to the individual's *stock* basis (not loan basis) in the post-termination year.[74] The shareholder may wish to purchase more stock to increase the tax basis in order to absorb the loss.

The NOL provisions create a need for sound tax planning during the last election year and the post-termination transition period. If it appears that the S corporation is going to sustain an NOL or use up any loss carryover, each shareholder's basis should be analyzed to determine if it can absorb the share of the loss. If basis is insufficient to absorb the loss, further investments should be considered before the end of the post-termination transition year. These investments can be accomplished through additional stock purchases from the corporation or from other shareholders to increase basis. This action ensures the full benefit from the NOL carryover.

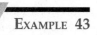

EXAMPLE 43

A calendar year C corporation has an NOL of $20,000 in 1995. The corporation makes a valid S election in 1996 and has another $20,000 NOL in that year. At all times during 1996,

---

[73] Rev.Rul. 74–44, 1974–1 C.B. 287; *Spicer Accounting, Inc. v. U.S.*, 91–1 USTC ¶50,103, 66 AFTR 2d 90–5806, 918 F.2d 90 (CA–9, 1990); *Radtke v. U.S.*, 90–1 USTC, ¶50,113, 65 AFTR 2d 90–1155, 895 F.2d 1196 (CA–7, 1990).

[74] § 1366(d)(3).

the stock of the corporation was owned by the same 10 shareholders, each of whom owned 10% of the stock. Tim, one of the 10 shareholders, has an adjusted basis of $1,800 at the beginning of 1996. None of the 1995 NOL may be carried forward into the S year. Although Tim's share of the 1996 NOL is $2,000, his deduction for the loss is limited to $1,800 in 1996 with a $200 carryover. ▼

Managing the Built-in Gains Tax.   A taxable income limitation encourages an S corporation to create deductions or accelerate deductions in the years that built-in gains are recognized. Although the postponed built-in gain is carried forward to future years, the time value of money makes the postponement beneficial. For example, payment of compensation, rather than a distribution, creates a deduction that reduces taxable income and postpones the built-in gains tax.

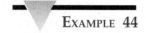

EXAMPLE 44

Mundy, Inc., an S corporation, has built-in gain of $110,000 and taxable income of $120,000 before payment of salaries to its two shareholders. If Mundy pays at least $120,000 in salaries to the shareholders (rather than a distribution), taxable income will drop to zero, and the built-in gains tax will be postponed. Thus, Mundy needs to keep the salaries as high as possible to postpone the built-in gains tax in future years and to reap the time value of money benefit. Of course, paying the salaries may increase the payroll tax burden if the salaries are below FICA and FUTA limits. ▼

Giving built-in gain property to a charitable organization does not trigger the built-in gains tax. To reduce or eliminate the built-in gains tax, built-in *loss* property may be sold in the same year that built-in gain property is sold. Generally, the taxpayer should sell built-in loss property in a year when an equivalent amount of built-in gain property is sold. Otherwise, the built-in loss could be wasted.

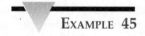

EXAMPLE 45

Green Corporation elects S status effective for calendar year 1995. As of January 1, 1995, Green's only asset has a basis of $40,000 and a fair market value of $100,000. If this asset is sold for $120,000 in 1996, Green recognizes an $80,000 gain, of which $60,000 is subject to the corporate built-in gains tax. The other $20,000 of gain is subject to the S corporation pass-through rules and bypasses the corporate income tax.

Unless Green can show otherwise, any appreciation existing at the sale or exchange is presumed to be preconversion built-in gain. Therefore, Green incurs a taxable gain of $80,000 unless it can prove that $20,000 of gain developed after the effective date of the election. ▼

Controlling Adjustments and Preference Items.   The individual alternative minimum tax (AMT) affects more taxpayers than ever before, because the tax base has expanded and the difference between regular tax rates and the individual AMT rate has been narrowed. In an S corporation setting, tax adjustments and preferences flow through proportionately to the shareholders. In computing the individual AMT, a shareholder treats these adjustments and preferences as if they were directly realized.

A flow-through of tax adjustments and preferences can be a tax disaster for a shareholder who is an "almost-AMT" taxpayer. Certain steps can be taken to protect such a shareholder from being pushed into the AMT. For example, a large preference from tax-exempt interest on private activity bonds by an S corporation could adversely affect an "almost-AMT" taxpayer. Certain adjustment and preference items are subject to elections that can remove them from the shareholder's AMT computation. Positive adjustments can be removed from a shareholder's AMTI base if the S corporation elects to capitalize and amortize certain expenditures over a prescribed period of time. These include excess intangible drilling and development expenditures, research and experimental costs, mining exploration and development expenditures, and circulation expenses.

Other corporate choices can protect an "almost-AMT" shareholder. Using the percentage of completion method of accounting (rather than the completed contract method) can be beneficial to certain shareholders. However, many of these decisions and elections may generate conflicts of interest when some shareholders are not so precariously situated and would not suffer from the flow-through of adjustments and tax preference items.

Allocation of Tax Items.   If a shareholder dies or stock is transferred during the taxable year, tax items may be allocated under the pro rata approach or the per-books method. Unless the per-books method is elected, a shareholder's pro rata share of tax items is determined by assigning an equal portion of each item to each day of the tax year, and then dividing that portion pro rata among the shares outstanding on the transfer day. With the consent of all persons who were shareholders during the entire taxable year, an S corporation can elect to allocate tax items according to the permanent records using normal tax accounting rules.

The allocation is made as if the taxable year consists of two taxable years. The first portion ends on the date of termination. On the day the shares are transferred, the shares are considered owned by the acquiring shareholder. The selected method may be beneficial to the terminating shareholder and harmful to the acquiring shareholder. A per-books election might result in a higher allocation of losses to a taxpayer who is better able to utilize the losses. In the case of the death of a shareholder, a per-books election prevents the income and loss allocation to a deceased shareholder from being affected by postdeath events.

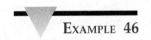

EXAMPLE 46   Alicia, the owner of all of the shares of an S corporation, transfers all of the stock to Bhaskar at the middle of the tax year. There is a $100,000 NOL for the entire tax year, but $30,000 of the loss occurs during the first half of the year. Without a per-books election, $50,000 of the loss would be allocated to Alicia, with $50,000 allocated to Bhaskar. If the corporation makes the per-books election, Bhaskar will receive $70,000 of the loss. Of course, Bhaskar may have a difficult time convincing Alicia to consent to the election. ▼

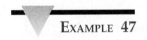

EXAMPLE 47   Mountain, a calendar year S corporation, is equally owned by Joey and Karl. Joey dies on June 29 (not a leap year). Mountain has income of $250,000 for January 1 through June 29 and $750,000 for the remainder of the year. Without the per-books election, the income is allocated by assigning an equal portion of the annual income of $1 million to each day (or $2,739.73 per day) and allocating the daily portion between the shareholders. Joey is allocated 50% of the daily income for the 180 days from January 1 to June 29, or $246,575.70 ($2,739.73 ÷ 2 × 180). Joey's estate is allocated 50% of the income for the 185 days from June 30 to December 31, or $253,425.02 [($2,739.73 ÷ 2) × 185].

If the per-books election is made, the income of $250,000 from January 1 to June 29 is divided equally between Joey and Karl, so that each is allocated $125,000. The income of $750,000 from June 30 to December 31 is divided equally between Joey's estate and Karl, or $375,000 to each. ▼

Termination Aspects.   If the shareholders of an S corporation decide to terminate the election voluntarily, they should make sure that the disqualifying act possesses substance. When the intent of the parties is obvious and the act represents a technical noncompliance rather than a real change, the IRS may be able to disregard it and keep the parties in S status.[75]

---

[75] See *Clarence L. Hook*, 58 T.C. 267 (1972).

Liquidation of an S Corporation.   S corporations are subject to the same liquidation rules applicable to C corporations (refer to Chapter 19). The distribution of appreciated property to S shareholders in complete liquidation is treated as if the property were sold to the shareholders in a taxable transaction. Unlike a C corporation, however, the S corporation incurs no incremental tax on the liquidation gains because the gains flow through to the shareholders, subject only to the built-in gains tax of § 1374. Any corporate gain increases the shareholder's stock basis by a like amount and reduces any gain realized by the shareholder when he or she receives the liquidation proceeds. Thus, an S corporation usually avoids the double tax that is imposed on C corporations.

KEY TERMS

Accumulated adjustments account (AAA), 21–16

Built-in gains tax, 21–26

Passive investment income (PII), 21–9

S corporation, 21–2

Small business corporation, 21–5

Subchapter S, 21–2

PROBLEM MATERIALS

DISCUSSION QUESTIONS

1. Victoria must decide which type of flow-through entity she will choose for her new service business. Help Victoria decide between a limited liability company and an S corporation vehicle by listing the advantages and disadvantages of an S election.

2. Which of the following items could be considered to be disadvantageous (or potential hazards) for S elections?
   a. The dividends received deduction is lost.
   b. The foreign tax credit is not available.
   c. An NOL at the corporate level cannot be utilized.
   d. Constructive dividends are not actually distributed.
   e. A locked-in AAA occurs after termination.
   f. An AAA is a personal right that cannot be transferred.
   g. Basis in stock is increased by constructive dividends.
   h. A trust is treated as a shareholder.
   i. Salaries of certain shareholders are not high enough.

3. On March 2, 1996, the two 50% shareholders of a calendar year corporation decide to elect S status. One of the shareholders, Terry, had purchased her stock from a previous shareholder (a nonresident alien) on January 18, 1996. Identify any potential problems for Terry or the corporation.

4. Elvis Stojko calls you and says that his two-person S corporation was involuntarily terminated in February 1996. He asks you if they can make a new election. Draft a memo for the file dated September 8, 1996, outlining what you told Elvis.

5. How may an S corporation establish an acceptable business purpose for a fiscal year?

6. Discuss the concept of the accumulated adjustments account.

7. Collett's S corporation has a small amount of accumulated earnings and profits (AEP), requiring the use of the more complex distribution rules. His accountant tells him that this AEP forces the maintenance of the AAA figure each year. Identify relevant tax issues facing Collett.

8. Caleb owns 10% of an S corporation. He is confused with respect to his AAA and stock basis. Write a brief memo to Caleb explaining the key differences between AAA and his stock basis.

9. How do the passive loss limitations affect an S corporation?

10. Lynch's share of her S corporation's net operating loss is $37,000, but her stock basis is only $29,000. Point out any tax consequences to Lynch.

11. One of your clients is considering electing S status. Texas, Inc., is a six-year-old company with two equal shareholders, both of whom paid $30,000 for their stock. In 1996, Texas has a $90,000 NOL carryforward. Estimated income is $40,000 for 1997 and $25,000 for each of the next three years. Should Texas make an S election for 1996?

PROBLEMS

12. An S corporation's profit and loss statement for 1996 shows net profits of $90,000 (book income). The corporation has four equal shareholders. From supplemental data, you obtain the following information about the corporation for 1996.

Selling expense	$11,500
Tax-exempt interest	2,000
Dividends received	9,000
§ 1231 gain	6,000
§ 1245 gain	10,000
Recovery of bad debts	3,400
Capital losses	6,000
Salary to owners (each)	9,000
Cost of goods sold	95,000

a. Compute Subchapter S taxable income or loss for 1996.
b. What would be the portion of taxable income or loss for Chang, one of the shareholders?

13. Polly has been the sole shareholder of a calendar year S corporation since 1981. Polly's stock basis is $15,500, and she receives a distribution of $17,000. Corporate-level accounts are as follows.

AAA	$6,000
PTI*	9,000
AEP	500

*PTI = previously taxed income, under old-law provisions.

How is Polly taxed on the distribution?

14. On January 1, 1996, Kinney, Inc., an electing S corporation, has $4,000 of AEP and a balance of $10,000 in AAA. Kinney has two shareholders, Erin and Frank, each of whom owns 500 shares of Kinney's stock. Kinney's 1996 taxable income is $5,000. Kinney distributes $6,000 to each shareholder on February 1, 1996, and distributes another $3,000 to each shareholder on September 1. How are the shareholders taxed on the distributions?

15. Goblins, Inc., a calendar year S corporation, has $90,000 of AEP. Tobias, the sole shareholder, has an adjusted basis of $80,000 in his stock with a zero balance in the AAA. Determine the tax aspects if a $90,000 salary is paid to Tobias.

16. Assume the same facts as in Problem 15, except that Tobias receives a dividend of $90,000.

17. Using the following legend, classify the transaction as a plus (+) or minus (–) on Schedule M–2 of Form 1120S.

Legend	
PTI	= Shareholders' undistributed taxable income previously taxed
AAA	= Accumulated adjustments account
OAA	= Other adjustments account
NA	= No direct impact on Schedule M–2

a. Receipt of tax-exempt interest income.
b. Unreasonable compensation determined.
c. Section 1245 recapture.
d. Distribution of nontaxable income (PTI) from 1981.
e. Nontaxable life insurance proceeds.
f. Expenses related to tax-exempt securities.
g. Charitable contributions.
h. Business gifts in excess of $25.
i. Nondeductible political contributions.
j. Cost of goods sold.

18. Adam and Bonnie form an S corporation, with Adam contributing cash of $100,000 for a 50% interest and Bonnie contributing appreciated ordinary income property with an adjusted basis of $20,000 and a FMV of $100,000.
   a. Determine Bonnie's initial basis in her stock, assuming that she receives a 50% interest.
   b. The S corporation sells the property for $120,000. Determine Adam's and Bonnie's stock basis after the sale.
   c. Determine Adam's and Bonnie's gain or loss if the company is liquidated.

19. Money, Inc., a calendar year S corporation, has two unrelated shareholders, each owning 50% of the stock. Both shareholders have a $400,000 stock basis as of January 1, 1996. At the beginning of 1996, Money has AAA of $300,000 and AEP of $600,000. During 1996, Money has operating income of $100,000. At the end of the year, Money distributes securities worth $1 million, with an adjusted basis of $800,000. Determine the tax effects of these transactions.

20. Assume the same facts as in Problem 19, except that the two shareholders consent to the AAA bypass election to distribute AEP first.

21. An S corporation's Form 1120S shows taxable income of $80,000 for the year. Peter owns 40% of the stock throughout the year. The following information is obtained from the corporate records.

Salary paid to Peter	$52,000
Tax-exempt insurance proceeds	3,000
Charitable contributions	6,000
Dividends received from a foreign corporation	5,000
Long-term capital loss	6,000
§ 1245 gain	11,000
Refund of prior state income taxes	5,000
Cost of goods sold	72,000
Short-term capital loss	7,000
Administrative expenses	18,000
Short-term capital gains	14,000
Advertising expenses	11,000
Peter's beginning stock basis	21,000
Peter's additional stock purchases	7,000
Beginning AAA	19,000
Peter's loan to corporation	20,000

   a. Compute book income or loss.
   b. Compute Peter's ending stock basis.
   c. Calculate ending corporate AAA.

22. At the beginning of the year, Malcolm, a 50% shareholder of a calendar year S corporation, has a stock basis of $22,000. During the year, the corporation has taxable income of $32,000. The following data are obtained from supplemental sources.

Dividends received	$12,000
Tax-exempt interest	18,000
Short-term capital gain	6,000
§ 1245 gain	10,000
§ 1231 gain	7,000
Charitable contributions	5,000
Political contributions	8,000
Short-term capital loss	12,000
Dividends to Malcolm	7,000
Selling expense	14,000
Beginning AAA	44,000

a. Compute Malcolm's ending stock basis.
b. Compute ending AAA.

23. For each of the following independent statements, indicate whether the transaction will increase (+), decrease (−), or have no effect (NE) on the adjusted basis of a shareholder's stock in an S corporation.
   a. Expenses related to tax-exempt income.
   b. Long-term capital gain.
   c. Nonseparately computed loss.
   d. Section 1231 gain.
   e. Depletion not in excess of basis.
   f. Separately computed income.
   g. Nontaxable return-of-capital distribution by the corporation.
   h. Selling expenses.
   i. Business gifts in excess of $25.
   j. Section 1250 gain.
   k. Dividends received by the S corporation.
   l. LIFO recapture tax at S election.
   m. Recovery of a bad debt.
   n. Long-term capital loss.
   o. Corporate dividends out of AAA.

24. A calendar year S corporation has a taxable loss of $80,000 and a capital loss of $20,000. Muhammad owns 30% of the corporate stock and has a $24,000 basis in the stock. Determine the amount of the taxable loss and capital loss, if any, that flow through to Muhammad.

25. Nicole owns 35% of the stock of an S corporation throughout 1996 and lends the corporation $6,000 during the year. Her stock basis in the corporation at the end of the year is $25,000. If the corporation sustains a $110,000 operating loss during the year, what amount, if any, can Nicole deduct with respect to the operating loss?

26. Crew Corporation elects S status effective for tax year 1995. As of January 1, 1995, Crew's assets were appraised as follows.

	Adjusted Basis	Fair Market Value
Cash	$ 16,010	$ 16,010
Accounts receivable	–0–	55,400
Inventory (FIFO)	70,000	90,000
Investment in land	110,000	195,000
Building	220,000	275,000
Goodwill	–0–	93,000

In each of the following situations, calculate any § 1374 tax, assuming that the highest corporate rate is 35%.

a. During 1995, Crew collects $40,000 of the accounts receivable and sells 80% of the inventory for $99,000.

b. In 1996, Crew sells the land held for investment for $203,000.

c. In 1997, the building is sold for $270,000.

27. Bryan, a cash basis S corporation, has the following assets and liabilities on January 1, 1996, the date the S election is made.

	Adjusted Basis	Fair Market Value
Cash	$ 200,000	$ 200,000
Accounts receivable	–0–	105,000
Equipment	110,000	100,000
Land	1,800,000	2,500,000
Accounts payable	–0–	110,000

During 1996, Bryan collects the accounts receivable and pays the accounts payable. The land is sold for $3 million, and the taxable income for the year is $590,000. Calculate any § 1374 penalty tax.

28. An S corporation has operating revenues of $410,000, taxable interest of $390,000, operating expenses of $260,000, and deductions attributable to the interest of $150,000. Calculate any § 1375 penalty tax payable by this S corporation.

29. At the end of 1996, Brew, an S corporation, has gross receipts of $190,000 and gross income of $170,000. Brew has accumulated earnings and profits of $22,000 and taxable income of $30,000. It has passive investment income of $100,000, with $40,000 of expenses directly related to the production of passive investment income. Calculate Brew's excess net passive income and any § 1375 penalty tax.

30. Friedman, Inc., an S corporation, pays for the medical care of two shareholder-employees during the current year. Yvette, owning 2% of the stock, receives $1,900 for this purpose. Jack, owning 21% of the stock, receives $3,300. Arnold Schwartz, the CFO, calls you, asking how to treat these transactions. Prepare a tax memo dated June 18, 1996, indicating what you told Arnold over the phone.

31. One of your clients is considering electing S status. Dickens, Inc., is a seven-year-old company with two equal shareholders who are in the 39.6% tax bracket. In 1995, Dickens will have an NOL carryforward of approximately $310,000. The difference between LIFO and FIFO inventory is $200,000, and the company will distribute about 50% of taxable income (before any NOL). The company's estimated income, built-in gain recognition, and 8% present value of $1 are as follows.

	Taxable Income	Built-in Gain	Present Value of $1
1996	$210,000	$50,000	0.926
1997	250,000	40,000	0.857
1998	300,000	50,000	0.794
1999	400,000	40,000	0.735
2000	600,000	30,000	0.681

a. Should the corporation elect S corporation status?

b. Would your answer change if most of taxable income is distributed?

Research Problems for this chapter appear at the end of Chapter 28.

22

PARTNERSHIPS

LEARNING OBJECTIVES

After completing Chapter 22, you should be able to:

1. Discuss governing principles and theories of partnership taxation.

2. Describe the tax effects of forming a partnership with cash and property contributions.

3. Determine the tax treatment of expenditures of a newly formed partnership and identify elections the partnership should make.

4. Specify the methods of determining a partnership's tax year.

5. Calculate partnership taxable income and describe how partnership items affect a partner's income tax return.

6. Determine a partner's basis in the partnership interest.

7. Explain how liabilities affect a partner's basis.

8. Describe the limitations on deducting partnership losses.

9. Describe the treatment of transactions between a partner and the partnership.

10. Determine the tax treatment of proportionate nonliquidating distributions from a partnership to a partner.

11. Determine the tax treatment of proportionate distributions that liquidate a partnership.

12. Calculate the selling partner's amount and character of gain or loss on the sale or exchange of a partnership interest.

13. Provide insights regarding advantageous use of a partnership.

OVERVIEW OF PARTNERSHIP TAXATION

This chapter and the previous chapter analyze two entity structures that offer certain advantages over the regular corporate structure. These entities are partnerships and S corporations, which are called *flow-through* or *pass-through* entities because the owners of the trade or business avoid treating the enterprise as a separate taxable entity. Instead, the owners are taxed on a proportionate share of the entity's taxable income at the end of each of its taxable years, regardless of the amount of cash or property distributions the owners receive from the entity during the year. The entity serves as an information provider to the IRS and its owners with respect to the proportionate income shares, and the tax falls directly upon the owners of those shares.

A partnership may be an especially advantageous entity form in many cases. A partnership is subject to only a single level of taxation, whereas corporate income is subject to *double taxation*. Corporate income is taxed at the entity level, currently at rates up to 35 percent. Any after-tax income that is distributed to corporate owners is taxed again as a dividend at the owner level. Though partnership income may be subject to high individual rates (currently up to 39.6 percent), this tax will likely be lower than a combined corporate-level tax and a second tax on a dividend distribution.

In addition, administrative and filing requirements are relatively simple for a partnership, and it offers certain planning opportunities not available to other entity forms. Both the C and S corporate structures are subject to rigorous allocation and distribution requirements (generally, each allocation or distribution is proportionate to the ownership interest of the shareholder). A partnership, though, may adjust its allocations of income and cash flow among the partners

TAX IN THE NEWS

PARTNERSHIPS IN THE MOVIES

As movies have become more expensive to produce, many production studios have turned to limited partnerships as a lucrative source of investment capital. For example, the Walt Disney Company has sold limited partnership interests in Silver Screen Partnerships I, II, III, and IV and in Touchwood Pacific Partners I, L.P. Other studios have formed similar production partnerships.

In most cases, the sponsoring studio injects capital for a small (1–5 percent) general partnership interest, and the investors contribute the remaining capital—hundreds of millions of dollars or more. The partnership agreement spells out the number and types of films the partnership intends to produce and provides a formula for allocating cash flows to the partners. Often the partnership agreement includes various benefits for the general partner (studio), such as a preferred allocation of cash flows (the first $1 million per year, for example), distribution fees for marketing the movies, and/or reimbursement of specified amounts of corporate overhead. Any cash remaining after these expenses is allocated under a fixed formula between the general and limited partners (for example, the limited partners may receive 90 percent of remaining cash flows).

Think about bank financing in comparison, and you will see why the studio finds partnerships so appealing: How many banks would allow the general partner to receive reimbursements and allocations before debt principal and interest are paid?

This capital-raising technique has proved so advantageous to the studios that some related industries, such as movie lighting contractors and special effects companies, have also used limited partnerships to raise capital. The next time you go to a movie, watch the credits at the end and think about the tremendous number of people who invested cash in the movie hoping for a blockbuster!

each year according to their needs, as long as certain standards (discussed later in this chapter) are met. Also, any previously unrealized income (such as appreciation of corporate assets) of an S or C corporation is taxed at the entity level when the corporation liquidates, but a partnership generally may liquidate tax-free. Finally, many states impose reporting and licensing requirements on corporate entities, including S corporations. These include franchise or capital stock tax returns that may require annual assessments and costly professional preparation assistance. Partnerships, on the other hand, often have no reporting requirements beyond Federal and state informational tax returns.

For smaller business operations, a partnership enables several owners to combine their resources at low cost. It also offers simple filing requirements, the taxation of income only once, and the ability to discontinue operations relatively inexpensively.

For larger business operations, a partnership offers a unique ability to raise capital with low filing and reporting costs (compared to corporate bond issuances, for example). Special allocations of income and cash-flow items are available in all partnerships to meet the objectives of the owners.

Since partnerships and S corporations are so widespread, a study of related tax problems will prove useful to students, business owners, and consultants. This chapter addresses partnership formations, operations, and nonliquidating distributions, and, in addition, sales of partnership interests and partnership liquidating distributions. Concept Summary 22–6 (beginning on page 22–52) provides a comparative analysis of the forms through which a business can be conducted.

WHAT IS A PARTNERSHIP?

A partnership is an association of two or more persons to carry on a trade or business, with each contributing money, property, labor, or skill, and with all expecting to share in profits and losses.[1] For Federal income tax purposes, a partnership includes a syndicate, group, pool, joint venture, or other unincorporated organization, through which any business, financial operation, or venture is carried on. The entity must not be otherwise classified as a corporation, trust, or estate. Characteristics used to determine whether the entity is treated as a corporation or as a partnership are discussed in Chapter 16. These rules are often difficult to interpret and apply, so the IRS has announced a proposed "check the box" procedure: if an eligible entity *wants* to be treated as a partnership, it will be able to elect to do so by checking a box on the partnership tax return. This procedure avoids the need to apply the six tests in Chapter 16 and provides certainty as to the type of entity that exists. At this writing, the IRS has held public hearings on the proposed procedure, but has not finalized the conditions under which it is available. These provisions will probably not apply to publicly traded partnerships, but they will apply to most limited liability companies (discussed below).

An entity that would otherwise be classified as a partnership may be excluded from partnership taxation rules if it is used for the following purposes:

- Investment (rather than the active conduct of a trade or business).
- Joint production, extraction, or use of property.
- Underwriting, selling, or distributing a specific security issue.[2]

The key to the availability of this election is that the venturers act more as expense-sharing associates than as proprietors working for joint profit maximization.

Four types of entities are taxed as partnerships: general partnerships, limited liability partnerships, limited partnerships, and limited liability companies. A partnership that conducts a service business, such as accounting, law, or medicine, is usually established as either a **general partnership** or a **limited liability partnership (LLP).** A general partnership consists of one or more **general partners.** Creditors of a general partnership can collect amounts owed them from both the partnership assets and the personal assets of the owner-partners. A general partner can be bankrupted by a malpractice judgment brought against the partnership, even though the partner was not personally involved in the malpractice.

An LLP is a recently created form of entity. Owners of an LLP are also general partners. The primary difference between an LLP and a general partnership is that an LLP partner is not liable for any malpractice committed by his or her partners. As the following Tax in the News describes, the LLP is currently the operational form of choice for the Big Six accounting firms.

A **limited partnership** is often used for acquiring capital in activities such as real estate development. A limited partnership is comprised of at least one general partner and often many **limited partners.** Unless special rules apply, only the

---

[1] § 7701(a)(2).   [2] § 761(a).

LIMITED LIABILITY FOR THE BIG SIX

During 1994, all the Big Six accounting firms reorganized as limited liability partnerships. Previously, each firm operated as a general partnership. The firms decided to change in order to protect each partner's personal assets from liability claims arising from actions of other partners. All states now allow LLPs, but their use by accounting firms was facilitated when New York State adopted provisions allowing service-oriented businesses to operate as "registered limited liability partnerships." Several of the Big Six are headquartered in New York City, and all the firms receive substantial revenues from clients in that state.

general partners are liable to creditors; each limited partner's risk of loss is restricted to his or her equity investment in the entity.

An alternative entity form, the **limited liability company (LLC),** is now permitted to operate in almost all states. An LLC combines the corporate benefit of limited liability of owners with the benefits of partnership taxation, including the single level of tax and special allocations of income, losses, and cash flows. Owners are technically considered to be "members" rather than partners, but a properly structured LLC is treated as a partnership for all tax purposes. Almost all states permit capital-intensive companies as well as service-oriented businesses and some professional service–providing entities to operate as LLCs. This is highly advantageous to a service entity since the LLC can protect each member from malpractice committed by other members.

PARTNERSHIP TAXATION AND REPORTING

1   **LEARNING OBJECTIVE**
Discuss governing principles and theories of partnership taxation.

A partnership is not a taxable entity.[3] Rather, the taxable income or loss of the partnership flows through to the partners at the end of the entity's tax year.[4] Partners report their allocable share of the partnership's income or loss for the year. As a result, the partnership itself pays no Federal income tax on its income; instead, the partners' individual tax liabilities are affected by the activities of the entity.

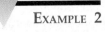

EXAMPLE 1   Adam is a 40% partner in the ABC Partnership. Both Adam's and the partnership's tax years end on December 31. In 1996, the partnership generates $200,000 of ordinary taxable income. However, because the partnership needs capital for expansion and debt reduction, Adam makes no cash withdrawals during 1996. He meets his living expenses by reducing his investment portfolio. Adam is taxed on his $80,000 allocable share of the partnership's 1996 income, even though he received no distributions from the entity during 1996. This allocated income is included in Adam's gross income. ▼

EXAMPLE 2   Assume the same facts as in Example 1, except the partnership recognizes a 1996 taxable loss of $100,000. Adam's 1996 AGI is reduced by $40,000 because his proportionate share of the loss flows through to him from the partnership. He claims a $40,000 partnership loss for

---

[3] § 701.   [4] § 702.

the year. (Note: Loss limitation rules discussed later in the chapter may result in some or all of this loss being deferred to a later year.) ▼

Many items of partnership income or expense retain their identity as they flow through to the partners. When preparing a personal tax return, then, a partner may have to take into account several items rather than a single share of net partnership ordinary income or loss. Generally, any item that *might* affect any two partners' tax liabilities in different ways is reported separately to the partners as a **separately stated item.**[5]

Ordinary partnership income or loss includes only the income and expenses related to partnership trade or business activities. These income and expense items are netted to produce a single income or loss amount that is passed through to the partners. Separately stated items (such as rent income and expense, capital gains or losses, interest income, and charitable contributions) are reported separately by the partnership. Each partner combines the share of these partnership items with similar items the partner may have generated outside the partnership. Any tax limitations or separate calculations (for example, net capital gain or loss, or deductible charitable contributions) are determined at the partner level.

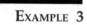

EXAMPLE 3

Beth is a 25% partner in the BR Partnership. The cash basis entity collected sales income of $60,000 during 1996 and incurred $15,000 in business expenses. In addition, it sold a corporate bond for a $9,000 long-term capital gain. Finally, the partnership made a $1,000 contribution to the local Performing Arts Fund drive. The fund is a qualifying charity. BR and all of its partners use a calendar tax year.

For 1996, Beth is allocated ordinary taxable income of $11,250 [($60,000 – $15,000) × 25%] from the partnership. She also is allocated a flow-through of a $2,250 long-term capital gain and a $250 charitable contribution deduction. The ordinary income increases Beth's gross income, and the capital gain and charitable contribution are combined with her other similar activities for the year as though she had incurred them herself. These items could be treated differently on the individual tax returns of the various partners (e.g., because a partner may be subject to a percentage limitation on charitable contribution deductions for 1996), so they are not included in the computation of ordinary partnership income. Instead, the items flow through to the partners separately. ▼

Other items that are allocated separately to the partners[6] include recognized gains and losses from property transactions; dividend income; tax preferences and adjustments for the alternative minimum tax; expenditures that qualify for the foreign tax credit; and expenditures that would be itemized by the partners.

Even though it is not a taxpaying entity, a partnership must file an information tax return, Form 1065. Look at Form 1065 in Appendix B, and refer to it during the following discussion. The partnership reports the results of its trade or business activities (ordinary income or loss) on Form 1065, page 1. Schedule K (page 3 of Form 1065) accumulates all items that must be separately reported to the partners, including net trade or business income or loss (from page 1). The amounts on Schedule K are allocated to all the partners. Each partner receives a Schedule K–1, which shows the share of all partnership items.

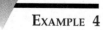

EXAMPLE 4

The BR Partnership in Example 3 reports its $60,000 sales income on Form 1065, page 1, line 1. The $15,000 of business expenses are reported in the appropriate amounts on page 1, line

---

[5] § 703(a)(1).   [6] § 702(a).

2 or lines 9–20. Partnership ordinary income of $45,000 is shown on page 1, line 22, and on Schedule K, line 1. The $9,000 capital gain and the $1,000 charitable contribution are reported only on Schedule K, on lines 4e and 8, respectively.

Beth receives a Schedule K–1 from the partnership that shows her shares of partnership ordinary income of $11,250, long-term capital gain of $2,250, and charitable contributions of $250 on lines 1, 4e, and 8, respectively. She then combines these amounts with similar items from sources other than BR on her personal tax return. For example, if she has a $5,000 long-term capital loss from a stock transaction in 1996, her overall net capital loss is $2,750 ($2,250 – $5,000). She then evaluates this net amount to determine the amount she may deduct on her Form 1040. ▼

As this example shows, one must look at both page 1 and Schedule K to get complete information regarding a partnership's operations for the year. Schedule K accumulates all partnership tax items and arrives at a total amount on line 25a. Schedule M–1, page 4, reconciles accounting income with this total of partnership tax items on Schedule K (line 25a). Schedule L generally shows an accounting-basis balance sheet, and Schedule M–2 reconciles beginning and ending partners' capital accounts.

PARTNER'S OWNERSHIP INTEREST IN A PARTNERSHIP

Each partner owns a **capital interest** and a **profits interest** in the partnership. A capital interest is measured by a partner's **capital sharing ratio,** which is the partner's percentage ownership of the capital of the partnership. A partner's capital interest can be determined in several ways. The most widely accepted method measures the capital interest as the percentage of net assets (assets remaining after payment of all partnership liabilities) a partner would receive on immediate liquidation of the partnership.

A profits interest is simply the partner's percentage allocation of current partnership operating results. **Profit and loss sharing ratios** are usually specified in the partnership agreement and are used to determine each partner's allocation of partnership ordinary taxable income and separately stated items.[7] The partnership can change its profit and loss allocations at any time simply by amending the partnership agreement.

Each partner's Schedule K–1 shows the profit, loss, and capital sharing ratios. In many cases, the three ratios are the same. A partner's capital sharing ratio generally equals the profit and loss sharing ratios if all profit and loss allocations, for each year of the partnership's existence, are in the same proportion as the partner's initial contributions to the partnership.

The partnership agreement may, in some cases, provide for a **special allocation** of certain items to specified partners, or it may allocate items in a different proportion from general profit and loss sharing ratios. These items are separately reported to the partner receiving the allocation. To be recognized for tax purposes, a special allocation must produce nontax economic consequences for the partners receiving it.[8]

EXAMPLE 5   When the George-Helen Partnership was formed, George contributed cash, and Helen contributed some City of Iuka bonds that she had held for investment purposes. The partnership agreement allocates all of the tax-exempt interest income from the bonds to Helen as an inducement for her to remain a partner. This is an acceptable special allocation

---

[7] § 704(a).   [8] § 704(b).

for income tax purposes; it reflects the differing economic circumstances that underlie the partners' contributions to the capital of the entity. Since Helen would have received the exempt income if she had not joined the partnership, she can retain the tax-favored treatment via the special allocation. ▼

EXAMPLE 6

Assume the same facts as in Example 5. Three years after it was formed, the George-Helen Partnership purchased some City of Butte bonds. The municipal bond interest income of $15,000 flows through to the partners as a separately stated item, so that it retains its tax-exempt status. The partnership agreement allocates all of this income to George because he is subject to a higher marginal income tax bracket than is Helen. The partnership also allocates $15,000 more of the partnership taxable income to Helen than to George. These allocations are not effective for income tax purposes because they have no purpose other than the reduction of the partners' combined income tax liability. ▼

A partner has a **basis in the partnership interest,** just as he or she would have a tax basis in any asset owned. When income flows through to a partner from the partnership, the partner's basis in the partnership interest increases accordingly. When a loss flows through to a partner, basis is reduced.

EXAMPLE 7

Paul contributes $20,000 cash to acquire a 30% capital and profits interest in the Red Robin Partnership. In its first year of operations, the partnership earns ordinary income of $40,000. Paul's initial basis is the $20,000 he paid for the interest. He reports ordinary income of $12,000 (30% × $40,000 partnership income) on his individual return and increases his basis by the same amount, to $32,000. ▼

In allowing increases and decreases in a partner's basis in a partnership interest, the Code ensures that only one level of tax arises on the income or loss from partnership operations. In Example 7, if Paul sold his interest at the end of the first year for $32,000, he would have no gain or loss. If the Code did not provide for an adjustment of a partner's basis, Paul's basis would be $20,000, and he would be taxed on the gain of $12,000 in addition to being taxed on his $12,000 share of income. In other words, without the basis adjustment, partnership income would be subject to double taxation.

As the following sections discuss in detail, a partner's basis is important for determining the treatment of distributions from the partnership to the partner, establishing the deductibility of partnership losses, and calculating gain or loss on the partner's disposition of the partnership interest.

A partner's basis is not reflected anywhere on the Schedule K–1. Instead, each partner should maintain a personal record of adjustments to basis. Schedule K–1 does reconcile a partner's **capital account,** but the ending capital account balance is rarely the same amount as the partner's basis. Just as the tax and accounting bases of a specific asset may differ, a partner's capital account and basis in the partnership interest may not be equal for a variety of reasons. For example, a partner's basis also includes the partner's share of partnership liabilities. These liabilities are not reported as part of the partner's capital account but are included in question F at the top of the partner's Schedule K–1.

CONCEPTUAL BASIS FOR PARTNERSHIP TAXATION

The unique tax treatment of partners and partnerships can be traced to two legal concepts that evolved long ago: the **aggregate** or **conduit concept** and the **entity concept.** These concepts have been used in both civil and common law and have influenced practically every partnership tax rule.

Aggregate or Conduit Concept. The aggregate or conduit concept treats the partnership as a channel through which income, credits, deductions, and the like flow to the partners for their own tax consideration. Under this concept, the partnership is regarded as a collection of taxpayers joined in an agency relationship with one another. The imposition of the income tax on individual partners reflects the influence of this doctrine. The aggregate concept has influenced the tax treatment of other pass-through entities, such as S corporations (Chapter 21) and trusts and estates (Chapter 27).

Entity Concept. The entity concept treats partners and partnerships as separate units and gives the partnership its own tax "personality" by (1) requiring a partnership to file an information tax return and (2) treating partners as separate and distinct from the partnership in certain transactions between a partner and the entity. A partner's recognition of capital gain or loss on the sale of the partnership interest further illustrates this doctrine.

Combined Concepts. Some rules such as the provisions concerning the formation, operation, and liquidation of a partnership contain a blend of both the entity and aggregate concepts.

ANTI-ABUSE PROVISIONS

As described in this chapter, partnership taxation is often flexible. For example, partnership operating income or losses can sometimes be shifted among partners, and partnership property gains and losses can sometimes be reallocated from one partner to another. The Code contains many provisions designed to thwart unwarranted reallocations, but the IRS believes opportunities for tax avoidance still abound. The IRS has adopted Regulations that will allow it to recharacterize transactions that it considers to be "abusive."[9]

FORMATION OF A PARTNERSHIP: TAX EFFECTS

PARTNER'S GAIN OR LOSS ON CONTRIBUTIONS TO ENTITY

2 LEARNING OBJECTIVE
Describe the tax effects of forming a partnership with cash and property contributions.

When a taxpayer transfers property to an entity in exchange for valuable consideration, a taxable exchange normally results. Typically, both the taxpayer and the entity realize and recognize gain or loss on the exchange.[10] The gain or loss recognized by the transferor is the difference between the fair market value of the consideration received and the adjusted basis of the property transferred.[11]

Generally, however, neither the partner nor the partnership recognizes the realized gain or loss when a partner contributes property to a partnership in exchange for a partnership interest. Instead, the realized gain or loss is deferred.[12]

There are two reasons for this nonrecognition treatment. First, forming a partnership allows investors to combine their assets toward greater economic goals than could be achieved separately. Only the form of ownership, rather than the amount owned by each investor, has changed. Requiring that gain be recognized on such transfers would make the formation of some partnerships economically unfeasible (e.g., where two existing proprietorships are combined to

---

[9] Reg. § 1.701–2.
[10] § 1001(c).

[11] § 1001(a).
[12] § 721.

form one larger business). Congress does not want to hinder the creation of valid economic partnerships by requiring gain recognition when a partnership is created. Second, because the partnership interest received is typically not a liquid asset, the partner may not easily be able to find the cash to pay the tax. Thus, deferral of the gain recognizes the economic realities of the business world and follows the wherewithal to pay principle of taxation.

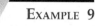

EXAMPLE 8

Alicia transfers two assets to the Wren Partnership on the day the entity is created, in exchange for a 60% profit and loss interest. This 60% partnership interest is worth $60,000. She contributes cash of $40,000 and retail display equipment (basis to her as a sole proprietor, $8,000; fair market value, $20,000). Since an exchange has occurred between two parties, Alicia *realizes* a $12,000 gain on this transaction. The gain realized is the fair market value of the partnership interest of $60,000 less the basis of the assets that she surrendered to the partnership [$40,000 (cash) + $8,000 (equipment)].

Under § 721, Alicia *does not recognize* the $12,000 realized gain in the year of contribution. Alicia might have been pressed for cash if she had been required to pay tax on the $12,000 gain. All that she received from the partnership was an illiquid partnership interest; she received no cash with which to pay any resulting tax liability. ▼

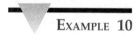

EXAMPLE 9

Assume the same facts as in Example 8, except that the equipment Alicia contributed to the partnership had an adjusted basis of $25,000. She has a $5,000 *realized* loss [$60,000 – ($40,000 + $25,000)], but she cannot deduct any of this loss. Realized losses, as well as realized gains, are deferred by § 721.

Unless it is essential that the partnership receive Alicia's display equipment rather than similar equipment purchased from an outside supplier, Alicia should sell the equipment to a third party. This would allow her to deduct a $5,000 loss in the year of the sale. Alicia could then contribute $60,000 cash (including the proceeds from the sale) for her interest in the partnership, and the partnership would have funds to purchase similar equipment. ▼

EXAMPLE 10

Five years after the Wren Partnership (Examples 8 and 9) was created, Alicia contributes another piece of equipment to the entity from her sole proprietorship. This property has a basis of $35,000 and a fair market value of $50,000. Alicia can defer the recognition of this $15,000 realized gain. Section 721 is effective whenever a partner makes a contribution to the capital of the partnership. ▼

If a partner contributes only capital and § 1231 assets, the partner's holding period in the partnership interest is the same as the partner's holding period for these assets. If assets that are not capital or § 1231 assets (including cash) are contributed, the holding period in the partnership interest begins on the date the partnership interest is acquired. If multiple assets are contributed, the partnership interest is apportioned, and a separate holding period applies to each portion.

EXCEPTIONS TO § 721

The nonrecognition provisions of § 721 do not apply in the following situations:

- When appreciated stocks and securities are contributed to an investment partnership.
- When the transaction is essentially a taxable exchange of properties.
- When the transaction is a disguised sale of properties.
- When the partnership interest is received in exchange for services rendered to the partnership by the partner.

Investment Partnership. If the transfer consists of appreciated stocks and securities and the partnership is an investment partnership, it is likely that the realized gain on the stocks and securities will be recognized by the contributing partner at the time of contribution.[13] This provision prevents multiple investors from using the partnership form to diversify their investment portfolios on a tax-free basis.

Exchange. If a transaction is essentially a taxable exchange of properties, the tax is not deferred under the nonrecognition provisions of § 721.[14]

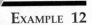

EXAMPLE 11

Sara owns land, and Bob owns stock. Sara would like to have Bob's stock, and Bob wants Sara's land. If Sara and Bob both contribute their property to newly formed SB Partnership in exchange for interests in the partnership, the tax on the transaction would appear to be deferred under § 721. If the partnership then distributes the land to Bob and the stock to Sara, the tax on this transaction would also appear to be deferred under § 731 (discussed later in the chapter). According to a literal interpretation of the statutes, no taxable exchange has occurred. Sara and Bob will find, however, that this type of tax subterfuge is not permitted. The IRS will disregard the passage of the properties through the partnership and will hold, instead, that Sara and Bob exchanged the land and stock directly. Thus, the transactions will be treated as any other taxable exchange. ▼

Disguised Sale. A similar result occurs in a **disguised sale** of properties. A disguised sale is deemed to occur where a partner contributes property to a partnership and soon thereafter receives a distribution from the partnership. This distribution could be viewed as a payment by the partnership for purchase of the property.[15]

EXAMPLE 12

Kim transfers property to the KLM Partnership. The property has an adjusted basis of $10,000 and a fair market value of $30,000. Soon thereafter, the partnership makes a distribution of $30,000 cash to Kim. Under the distribution rules of § 731, the distribution would not be taxable to Kim if the basis for her partnership interest prior to the distribution was greater than the $30,000 cash distributed. However, the transaction appears to be a disguised purchase-sale transaction, rather than a contribution and distribution. Therefore, Kim must recognize gain of $20,000 on transfer of the property, and the partnership is deemed to have purchased the property for $30,000. ▼

Services. A final exception to the nonrecognition provision of § 721 occurs when a partner receives his or her interest in the partnership as compensation for services rendered to the partnership. This is not a tax-deferred transaction because services are not treated as "property" that can be transferred to a partnership on a tax-free basis. Instead, the partner performing the services recognizes ordinary compensation income equal to the fair market value of the partnership interest received.[16]

The partnership may deduct the amount included in the service partner's income if the services are of a deductible nature. If the services are not deductible to the partnership, they must be capitalized to an asset account. For example, architectural plans created by a partner are capitalized to the structure built with

[13] § 721(b).
[14] Reg. § 1.731–1(c)(3).

[15] § 707(a)(2)(B).
[16] § 83(a).

those plans. Alternatively, day-to-day management services performed by a partner for the partnership are usually deductible by the partnership.

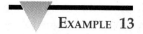

EXAMPLE 13

When they formed the BCD Partnership, Bill, Carl, and Dave each received a one-third interest in the entity. Dave became a one-third partner as compensation for the accounting and tax planning services he rendered during the formation of the partnership. The value of a one-third interest in the partnership (for each of the parties) is $20,000. Dave must recognize $20,000 of compensation income, and he has a $20,000 basis in his partnership interest. This treatment resembles the results that would occur if the partnership paid Dave $20,000 for his services and he immediately contributed that amount to the entity for a one-third ownership interest. ▼

TAX ISSUES RELATIVE TO CONTRIBUTED PROPERTY

When a partner contributes an asset to the capital of a partnership, the entity assigns a **carryover basis** to the property.[17] The entity's basis in the asset is equal to the basis the partner held in the property prior to its transfer to the partnership. The partner's basis in the new partnership interest equals his or her prior basis in the contributed assets. The tax term for this basis concept is **substituted basis.** Thus, two assets are created out of one when a partnership is formed, namely, the property in the hands of the new entity and the new asset (the partnership interest) in the hands of the partner. Both assets are assigned a basis that is derived from the partner's existing basis in the contributed property.

These rules are logical in view of what Congress was attempting to accomplish in this deferral transaction. As noted earlier, gain or loss is deferred when property is contributed to a partnership in exchange for a partnership interest. This deferral is implemented by calculating the partnership's basis in the transferred property and the partner's basis for the partnership interest. These bases are the amounts necessary to allow for recognition of the deferred gain or loss if the property or the partnership interest is subsequently disposed of in a taxable transaction. This treatment is similar to the treatment of assets transferred to a controlled corporation[18] and the treatment of like-kind exchanges.[19]

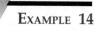

EXAMPLE 14

On June 1, 1996, José transfers property to the JKL Partnership in exchange for a one-third interest in the partnership. The property has an adjusted basis to José of $10,000 and a fair market value on June 1 of $30,000. José's realized gain on the exchange is $20,000 ($30,000 − $10,000), but under § 721, none of the gain is recognized. José's basis for his partnership interest is the amount necessary to recognize the $20,000 deferred gain if he subsequently sells the interest for its $30,000 fair market value. This amount, $10,000, is referred to as a substituted basis. The basis of the property contributed to the partnership is the amount necessary to allow for the recognition of the $20,000 deferred gain if the property is subsequently sold for its $30,000 fair market value. This amount, also $10,000, is referred to as a carryover basis. ▼

The holding period for the contributed asset also carries over to the partnership. Thus, the partnership's holding period for the asset includes the period during which the partner owned the asset individually.

[17]§ 723.
[18]§ 351.

[19]§ 1031.

Depreciation Method and Period. If depreciable property is contributed to the partnership, the partnership is usually required to use the same cost recovery method and life used by the partner. The partnership merely "steps into the shoes" of the partner and continues the same cost recovery calculations. If the property is not MACRS or ACRS property, the partnership must treat the property as used property for depreciation purposes. The partnership may not immediately expense any part of the basis of depreciable property it receives from the transferor partner under § 179.

Receivables, Inventory, and Losses. To prevent the conversion of ordinary income into capital gain, gain or loss is treated as ordinary when the partnership disposes of either of the following:[20]

- Contributed receivables that were unrealized in the contributing partner's hands at the contribution date. Such receivables include the right to receive payment for goods or services delivered (or to be delivered).
- Contributed property that was inventory in the contributor's hands on the contribution date, if the partnership disposes of the property within *five years of the contribution*. Inventory includes all property except capital and real or depreciable business assets.

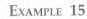

EXAMPLE 15

Tyrone operates a cash basis retail electronics and television store as a sole proprietor. Ramon is an enterprising individual who likes to invest in small businesses. On January 2 of the current year, Tyrone and Ramon form the TR Partnership. Their partnership contributions are as follows:

	Adjusted Basis	Fair Market Value
From Tyrone:		
Receivables	$ –0–	$ 2,000
Land used as parking lot*	1,200	5,000
Inventory	2,500	5,000
From Ramon:		
Cash	12,000	12,000

*The parking lot had been held for five months at the contribution date.

Within 30 days of forming the partnership, TR collects the receivables and sells the inventory for $5,000 cash. It uses the land for the next 10 months as a parking lot, then sells it for $3,500 cash. TR realized the following income in the current year from these transactions:

- Ordinary income of $2,000 from collecting the receivables.
- Ordinary income of $2,500 from the sale of inventory.
- Section 1231 gain of $2,300 from the sale of land.

The land takes a carryover holding period. Thus, it is treated as having been held 15 months at the sale date. ▼

---

[20] § 724. For this purpose, § 724(d)(2) waives the holding period requirement in defining § 1231 property.

A similar rule is designed to prevent a capital loss from being converted into an ordinary loss. Under this rule, if contributed property is disposed of at a loss and the property had a "built-in" capital loss to the contributing partner at the contribution date, the loss is treated as a capital loss if the partnership disposes of the property *within five years of the contribution*. The capital loss is limited to the "built-in" loss on the date of contribution.

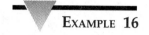

EXAMPLE 16

Assume the same facts as Example 15, except for the following:

- Tyrone held the land he contributed for investment purposes. It had a fair market value of $800 at the contribution date.
- TR used the land as a parking lot for 11 months and sold it for $650.

TR realizes the following income and loss from these transactions:

- Ordinary income of $2,000 from collecting the receivables.
- Ordinary income of $2,500 from the sale of inventory.
- Capital loss of $400 from the sale of land ($1,200 − $800).
- Section 1231 loss of $150 from the sale of land ($800 − $650).

Since the land was sold within five years of the contribution date, the $400 built-in loss is a capital loss. The post-contribution loss of $150 is a § 1231 loss since TR used the property in its business. ▼

INSIDE AND OUTSIDE BASES

Throughout this chapter, reference is made to the partnership's inside basis and a partner's outside basis. **Inside basis** refers to the aggregate adjusted basis of *partnership* assets, as determined from the partnership's tax accounts. **Outside basis** represents the aggregate of each partner's basis in the partnership interest. Each partner "owns" a share of the partnership's inside basis and should maintain a record of his or her outside basis.

In many cases—especially on formation of the partnership—the total of all partners' outside bases will equal the partnership's inside bases for all its assets. Differences between inside and outside basis arise when a partner's interest is sold to another person for more or less than the selling partner's share of the inside basis of partnership assets. The buying partner's outside basis equals the price paid for the interest, but the buyer's share of the partnership's inside basis is the same amount as the seller's share of the inside basis.

Concept Summary 22–1 reviews the rules that apply to partnership asset contribution and basis adjustments.

TAX ACCOUNTING ELECTIONS

A newly formed partnership must make numerous tax accounting elections. These elections are formal decisions on how a particular transaction or tax attribute should be handled. Most of these elections must be made by the partnership rather than by the partners individually.[21] The *partnership* makes the elections for the following items:

- Inventory method.
- Cost or percentage depletion method, excluding oil and gas wells.

---

[21] § 703(b).

CONCEPT SUMMARY 22–1

Partnership Formation and Basis Computation

1. The *entity concept* treats partners and partnerships as separate units. The nature and amount of gains and losses are determined at the partnership level.
2. The *aggregate concept* is used to connect partners and partnerships. It allows income, gains, losses, credits, deductions, etc., to flow through to the partners for separate tax reporting.
3. Sometimes both the *aggregate* and the *entity* concepts apply, but one usually dominates.
4. Generally, partners or partnerships do not recognize gain or loss when property is contributed for capital interests.
5. Partners contributing property for partnership interests generally take the contributed property's adjusted basis for their *outside basis* in their partnership interest. The partners are said to take a substituted basis in their partnership interest.
6. The partnership will generally continue to use the contributing partner's basis for the *inside basis* in property it receives. The contributed property is said to take a carryover basis.
7. The holding period of a partner's interest includes that of contributed property when the property was a § 1231 asset or capital asset in the partner's hands. Otherwise, the holding period starts on the day the interest is acquired. The holding period of an interest acquired by a cash contribution starts at acquisition.
8. The partnership's holding period for contributed property includes the contributing partner's holding period.

- Accounting method (cash, accrual, or hybrid).
- Cost recovery methods and assumptions.
- Tax year.
- Amortization of organizational costs and amortization period.
- Amortization of start-up expenditures and amortization period.
- Section 179 deductions for certain tangible personal property.
- Nonrecognition treatment for involuntary conversions gains.

Each partner is bound by the decisions made by the partnership relative to these elections. If the partnership fails to make an election, a partner cannot compensate for this error by making the election individually.

Though most elections must be made by the partnership, the partners are required to make three specific elections individually.[22] These elections involve relatively narrow tax issues. Each *partner* individually makes the election on the following issues:

- Income from discharge of indebtedness.
- Cost or percentage depletion method for oil and gas wells.
- Deductions and credits for taxes paid to foreign countries and U.S. possessions.

INITIAL COSTS OF A PARTNERSHIP

3 LEARNING OBJECTIVE
Determine the tax treatment of expenditures of a newly formed partnership and identify elections the partnership should make.

In its initial stages, a partnership will incur expenses related to some or all of the following: forming the partnership (organization costs), admitting partners to the partnership, marketing and selling partnership units to prospective partners (syndication costs), acquiring assets, starting business operations (start-up costs), negotiating contracts, and other items. Many of these expenditures are not

[22]§§ 703(b)(1), (2), and (3).

currently deductible. However, the Code permits a ratable amortization of "organization" and "start-up" costs; acquisition costs for depreciable assets are included in the initial basis of the acquired assets; and costs related to some intangible assets may be amortized. "Syndication costs" may be neither amortized nor deducted.

Organization Costs.   The partnership may elect to amortize organization costs ratably over a period of 60 months or more, starting with the month in which it began business.[23] The election must be made by the due date (including extensions) of the partnership return for the year it began business.

Organization costs include expenditures that are (1) incident to the creation of the partnership; (2) chargeable to a capital account; and (3) of a character that, if incident to the creation of a partnership with an ascertainable life, would be amortized over that life. These expenditures include accounting fees and legal fees incident to the partnership's formation. To be amortizable, the expenditures must be incurred within a period that starts a reasonable time before the partnership begins business. The period ends with the due date (without extensions) of the tax return for the initial tax year.

Cash method partnerships are not allowed to deduct *in the year incurred* the portion of organization costs that are paid after the end of the first year. The partnership can deduct, in the year of payment, the portion of the expenditures that would have been deductible in a prior year, if they had been paid before that year's end.

EXAMPLE 17

The calendar year Bluejay Partnership was formed on May 1 of the current year and immediately started business. Bluejay incurred $720 in legal fees for drafting the partnership agreement and $480 in accounting fees for tax advice of an organizational nature. The legal fees were paid in October of the current year. The accounting fees were paid in January of the following year. The partnership selected the cash method of accounting and elected to amortize its organization costs.

On its first tax return, Bluejay deducts $96 of organization costs [($720 legal fees/60 months) × 8 months]. No deduction was taken for the accounting fees since the partnership selected the cash method and the fees were paid the following year. On its tax return for next year, Bluejay deducts organization costs of $304 {[($720 legal fees/60 months) × 12 months] + [($480 accounting fees/60 months) × 20 months]}. Note that the second-year deduction ($304) includes the $64 of accounting fees [($480/60) × 8] that could have been deducted on Bluejay's first tax return if they had been paid by the end of that year. ▼

Costs incurred for the following items are not organization costs:

- Acquiring assets for the partnership.
- Transferring assets to the partnership.
- Admitting partners, other than at formation.
- Removing partners, other than at formation.
- Negotiating operating contracts.
- Syndication costs.

Start-up Costs.   Operating costs that are incurred after the entity is formed but before it begins business may not be deducted. Instead, these costs are capitalized. Generally, if so elected, they may be amortized over a period of 60 months or more, starting with the month in which the partnership begins business.[24] Such

---

[23] § 709.   [24] § 195.

costs include marketing surveys prior to conducting business, pre-operating advertising expenses, costs of establishing an accounting system, and salaries paid to executives and employees prior to the conduct of business.

Acquisition Costs of Depreciable Assets.   Certain expenses may be incurred in changing the legal title in which certain assets are held from that of the contributing partner to the partnership name. These costs include legal fees for transferring assets or transfer taxes imposed by states. Such costs are added to the basis of the assets in the hands of the partnership and are included in the basis the partnership may depreciate.

Syndication Costs. **Syndication costs** are capitalized, but no amortization election is available. Syndication costs include the following expenditures incurred for promoting and marketing partnership interests:

- Brokerage fees.
- Registration fees.
- Legal fees paid to the underwriter, placement agent, and issuer for security advice or advice on the adequacy of tax disclosures in the prospectus or placement memo for securities law purposes.
- Accounting fees related to offering materials.
- Printing costs of prospectus, placement memos, and other selling materials.

TAXABLE YEAR OF THE PARTNERSHIP

4 LEARNING OBJECTIVE
Specify the methods of determining a partnership's tax year.

Partnership taxable income (and any separately stated items) flows through to each partner at the end of the *partnership's* taxable year. A *partner's* taxable income for a given year, then, includes the distributive share of partnership income for any *partnership* taxable year that ends within the partner's tax year.

When all partners use the calendar year, it would be beneficial in present value terms for a profitable partnership to adopt a fiscal year ending with January 31. Why? As Figure 22–1 illustrates, when the adopted year ends on January 31, the reporting of income from the partnership and payment of related taxes can be deferred for up to 11 months. For instance, income earned by the partnership in September 1996 is not taxable to the partners until January 31, 1997. It is reported in the partner's tax return for the year ended December 31, 1997, which is not due until April 15, 1998. Even though each partner may be required to make quarterly estimated tax payments, some deferral is still possible.

Required Taxable Years.   To prevent excessive deferral of taxation of partnership income, Congress and the IRS have adopted a series of rules that prescribe the *required* taxable year an entity must adopt if no alternative tax years (discussed below) are available. Three rules are presented in Figure 22–2.[25] The partnership must consider each rule, in order. If a taxable year is available under a given rule, that is the partnership's required taxable year.

The first two rules are relatively self-explanatory. Under the **least aggregate deferral method,** the partnership tests the year-ends that are used by the various partners to determine the weighted-average deferral of partnership income. The year-end that offers the least amount of deferral is the *required tax year* for the partnership.

---

[25] § 706(b).

▼ **FIGURE 22–1**
Deferral Benefit When Fiscal
Year Is Used and All Partners
Are on the Calendar Year

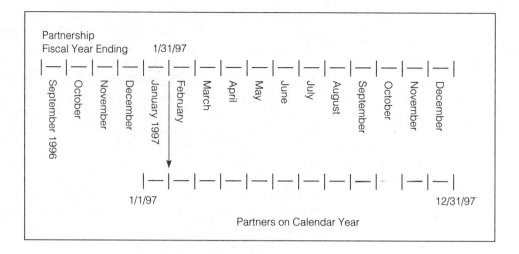

▼ **FIGURE 22–2**
Required Tax Year of Partnership

In Order, Partnership Must Use	Requirements
Majority partners' tax year	• More than 50% of capital *and* profits is owned by partners who have the same taxable year.
Principal partners' tax year	• All partners who own 5% or more of capital *or* profits are principal partners. • All principal partners must have the same tax year.
Year with smallest amount of income deferred	• "Least aggregate deferral" method (Example 18).

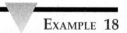

EXAMPLE 18

Anne and Bonnie are equal partners in the AB Partnership. Anne uses the calendar year, and Bonnie uses a fiscal year ending August 31. Neither Anne nor Bonnie is a majority partner since neither owns more than 50%. Although Anne and Bonnie are both principal partners, they do not have the same tax year. Therefore, the general rules indicate that the partnership's required tax year must be determined by the "least aggregate deferral" method. The following computations support August 31 as AB's tax year, since the 2.0 product using that year-end is less than the 4.0 product when December 31 is used.

Test for 12/31 Year-End

Partner	Year Ends	Profit Interest		Months of Deferral		Product
Anne	12/31	50%	×	–0–	=	0.0
Bonnie	8/31	50%	×	8	=	4.0
Aggregate number of deferral months						4.0

Test for 8/31 Year-End

Partner	Year Ends	Profit Interest		Months of Deferral		Product
Anne	12/31	50%	×	4	=	2.0
Bonnie	8/31	50%	×	–0–	=	0.0
Aggregate number of deferral months						2.0

▼

Alternative Tax Years. If the required tax year described above is undesirable to the entity, three other alternative tax years may be available:

- Establish to the IRS's satisfaction that a *business purpose* exists for a different tax year (a natural business year at the end of a peak season or shortly thereafter, such as a Maine or Minnesota fishing resort that closes every fall). It is difficult to obtain IRS approval when using the business purpose exception unless the 25 percent, two-month test described next can be satisfied.
- Follow IRS procedures to obtain approval for using a *natural business tax year.* The IRS has stated that a natural business year exists when 25 percent or more of the partnership's gross receipts were recognized during the last 2 months of the same 12-month period for three consecutive years.[26] New partnerships cannot use this justification because they lack the required three-year history.
- Elect a tax year so that taxes on partnership income are deferred for not more than *three months* from the *required* tax year.[27] Then, have the partnership maintain with the IRS a prepaid, non-interest-bearing deposit of estimated deferred taxes.[28] This alternative may not be desirable since the deposit is based on the highest individual tax rate of 39.6 percent plus 1 percent, or 40.6 percent.

OPERATIONS OF THE PARTNERSHIP

5 **LEARNING OBJECTIVE**
Calculate partnership taxable income and describe how partnership items affect a partner's income tax return.

An individual, corporation, trust, estate, or partnership can become a partner in a partnership. Since a partnership is a tax-reporting, rather than a taxpaying, entity for purposes of its Federal (and state) income tax computations, the partnership's income, deductions, credits, and alternative minimum tax (AMT) preferences and adjustments can ultimately be reported and taxed on any of a number of income tax forms (e.g., Forms 1040 [individuals], 1041 [fiduciaries], 1120 [C corporations], and 1120S [S corporations]).

A partnership is subject to all other taxes in the same manner as any other business. Thus, the partnership files returns and pays the outstanding amount of pertinent sales taxes, property taxes, and Social Security, unemployment, and other payroll taxes.

MEASURING AND REPORTING INCOME

The partnership's Form 1065 organizes and reports the transactions of the entity for the tax year, and each of the partnership's tax items is reported on Schedule K of that return. Each partner, and the IRS, receives a Schedule K–1 that reports the partner's allocable share of partnership income, credits, adjustments, and preferences for the year. Form 1065 is due on the fifteenth day of the fourth month following the close of the partnership's tax year; for a calendar year partnership, this is April 15.

Income Measurement. The measurement and reporting of partnership income require a two-step approach. Certain items must be segregated and reported separately on the partnership return and each partner's Schedule K–1.

---

[26] Rev.Proc. 74–33, 1974–2 C.B. 489; Rev.Rul. 87–57, 1987–2 C.B. 117; and Rev.Proc. 87–32, 1987–1 C.B. 396.

[27] § 444.
[28] § 7519.

TAX IN THE NEWS

A PARTNERSHIP FOR THE LONG RUN

Partnerships often operate successfully over long periods of time. One outstanding example is Laaco, formerly the Los Angeles Athletic Club Co., which was formed in the late 1800s to acquire and operate various recreational facilities in the Los Angeles area. The partnership bought properties for swimming, boating, basketball, and other sports and at various times owned and/or created the Riviera Country Club (where the L.A. Open golf tournament is played), the California Yacht Club in Marina del Rey, the Malibu Beach Club on the California Coastal Highway, a gun club, and various parcels in downtown Los Angeles. At various times it has also owned shopping centers in Montana, Arizona, and Arkansas, warehouses throughout southern California, and residential property in Orlando, Florida. It has also accumulated a sizable Western art collection.

The partnership was formed by members of the Hathaway family, and over 60 percent of the 176,000 outstanding partnership units are still owned by family members, including distant cousins and trusts.

In 1988, the partnership sold the Riviera Country Club to a Japanese company for almost $100 million—about twice the selling price of the units immediately before the transaction. The basis in the property was so low, the gain on the sale was $550 per unit. Laaco distributed $90 million of the proceeds to partners and retained the remaining $10 million for operations.

SOURCE: Adapted from Benjamin J. Stein, "Micro-Cap Blues: Property Company's Holders Are In for the Long Haul," *Barron's*, September 20, 1993, p. 15. Reprinted by permission of *Barron's*, © 1993 Dow Jones & Company, Inc. All rights reserved worldwide.

Items that are not separately reported are netted at the partnership level. Items passed through separately include the following:

- Short- and long-term capital gains and losses.
- Section 1231 gains and losses.
- Charitable contributions.
- Portfolio income items (dividends, interest, and royalties).
- Immediately expensed tangible personal property (§ 179).
- Items allocated differently from the general profit and loss ratio.
- Recovery of items previously deducted (tax benefit items).
- AMT preference and adjustment items.
- Passive activity items (rental real estate income or loss).
- Expenses related to portfolio income.
- Intangible drilling and development costs.
- Taxes paid to foreign countries and U.S. possessions.
- Nonbusiness and personal items (e.g., alimony, medical, and dental).[29]

The reason for separately reporting the preceding items is rooted in the aggregate or conduit concept. These items affect various exclusions, deductions, and credits at the partner level and must pass through without loss of identity so that the proper tax for each partner may be determined.[30]

---

[29] § 702(a).

[30] § 702(b).

A partnership is not allowed the following deductions:

- Taxes paid to foreign countries or U.S. possessions.
- Net operating losses.
- Depletion of oil and gas interests.
- Dividends received deduction.

In addition, items that are only allowed by legislative grace to individuals, such as standard deductions or personal exemptions, are not allowed to the partnership. Also, if a partnership makes a payment on behalf of a partner, such as for alimony, medical expenses, or other items that constitute itemized deductions to individuals, the partnership treats the payment as a distribution or guaranteed payment (discussed later) to the partner, and the partner determines whether he or she may claim the deduction.

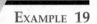

EXAMPLE 19

Tiwanda is a one-third partner in the TUV Partnership. This year, the entity entered into the following transactions:

Fees received	$100,000
Salaries paid	30,000
Cost recovery deductions	10,000
Supplies, repairs	3,000
Payroll taxes paid	9,000
Charitable contribution to art museum	6,000
Short-term capital gain	12,000
Passive income (rental operations)	7,500
Portfolio income (dividends received)	1,500
Exempt income (bond interest)	2,100
AMT adjustment (cost recovery)	3,600
Payment of partner Vern's alimony obligations	4,000

The entity experienced a $20,000 net loss from operations last year, its first year of business.

The two-step computational process that is used to determine partnership income is applied in the following manner:

Nonseparately Stated Items (Ordinary Income)

Fee income	$100,000
Salaries paid	(30,000)
Cost recovery deductions	(10,000)
Supplies, repairs	(3,000)
Payroll taxes paid	(9,000)
Ordinary income	$ 48,000

Separately Stated Items

Contribution to art museum	$ 6,000
Short-term capital gain	12,000
Passive income (rental operations)	7,500
Portfolio income (dividends received)	1,500
Exempt income (bond interest)	2,100
AMT adjustment (cost recovery)	3,600

Each of the separately stated items passes through proportionately to each partner and is included on the appropriate schedule or netted with similar items that the partner generated for the year. Thus, in determining what her tax liability will be on her Form 1040, Tiwanda includes a $2,000 charitable contribution, a $4,000 short-term capital gain, $2,500 of passive rent income, $500 of dividend income, and a $1,200 positive adjustment in computing alternative minimum taxable income. Tiwanda treats these items as if she had generated them herself. She must disclose her $700 share of exempt interest on the first page of her Form 1040. In addition, Tiwanda reports $16,000 as her share of the partnership's ordinary income, the combination of the nonseparately stated items.

The partnership is not allowed a deduction for last year's $20,000 net operating loss—this item was passed through to the partners' own income tax returns for the previous year. Moreover, no deduction is allowed for personal expenditures (payment of Vern's alimony), and no personal exemption is allowed on the Form 1065. ▼

Withdrawals. Capital withdrawals by partners during the year do not affect the partnership's income measuring and reporting process. These items are usually treated as distributions made on the last day of the partnership's tax year. Thus, in Example 19 above, the payment of Vern's alimony by the partnership is treated as a distribution from the partnership to Vern. When withdrawals exceed the partners' shares of partnership income, the excess is taxed under the distribution rules (discussed later in the chapter).[31]

Penalties. Each partner's share of partnership items should be reported on his or her individual tax return in the same manner as presented on the Form 1065. If a partner treats an item differently, the IRS must be notified of the inconsistent treatment.[32] A partnership with 10 or fewer "natural persons" as partners, where each partner's share of partnership items is the same for all items, is automatically excluded from this rule.[33] If a partner fails to comply with this requirement because of negligence or intentional disregard of rules or Regulations, a negligence penalty may be added to the tax due.

To encourage the filing of a partnership return, a penalty is imposed on the partnership of $50 per month (or fraction thereof), but not to exceed five months, for failure to file a complete and timely information return without reasonable cause.[34]

ETHICAL CONSIDERATIONS

A Preparer's Responsibility for Partners' Tax Returns

A partnership's tax return preparer is responsible for accurately presenting information supplied by the partnership in that return. If a flow-through amount is significant to a certain partner, the preparer of the *partnership* return can be treated as the preparer of a *partner's* tax return with respect to that item.

If a preparer misstates an item on a partnership return, either by taking a position that is not supportable under current law or by willfully misreporting an item on the return, "preparer penalties" can be assessed. While these penalties are relatively small, their imposition may also result in the preparer being suspended from practice before the IRS or by a state accountancy board.

[31] §§ 731(a)(1) and 733.
[32] § 6222.

[33] §§ 6231(a)(1)(B) and (I). Natural persons for this purpose include individuals who are not nonresident aliens, as well as the estate of a decedent who was not a nonresident alien.
[34] § 6698.

As an example, assume Stan, a CPA, knowingly reported a $20,000 deduction for fines and penalties (nondeductible items) in determining the JB Partnership's $30,000 income from operations. This amount was allocated equally to partners Joe and Barb. Joe has other income of $35,000. Barb has other income of $1 million. Stan is treated as the preparer of Joe's tax return with respect to the improper $10,000 flow-through item, since the fines and penalties are significant relative to Joe's income. Stan is not considered the preparer of Barb's return, since the fines and penalties are not significant to her income.

In a recent case, the court held that the preparer of the partnership return was the preparer of several partners' returns with respect to partnership items flowing through to the partners. The court reached this decision even though the return preparer never met the individual partners, received no direct fees from the partners, and performed no other services for the partners.

Do you believe this is a reasonable approach for allocating responsibility for accurate preparation of a partner's tax return? Why or why not?

PARTNERSHIP ALLOCATIONS

So far, all examples in this chapter have assumed that the partner has the same percentage interest in capital, profits, and losses. Thus, a partner who owns a 25 percent interest in partnership capital has been assumed to own 25 percent of partnership profits and 25 percent of partnership losses.

Economic Effect. The partnership agreement can provide that any partner may share capital, profits, and losses in different ratios. For example, a partner could have a 25 percent capital sharing ratio, yet be allocated 30 percent of the profits and 20 percent of the losses of the partnership. Such *special* allocations are permissible if they follow certain rules contained in the Regulations under § 704(b).[35] Although these rules are too complex to discuss in detail, the general outline of one of these rules—the **economic effect test**—can be easily understood.

In general, the economic effect test requires the following:

- An allocation of income to a partner must increase the partner's capital account, and an allocation of deduction or loss must decrease the partner's capital account.
- When the partner's interest is liquidated, the partner must receive assets that have a fair market value equal to the positive balance in the capital account.
- A partner with a negative capital account must restore that account upon liquidation of the interest. Restoration of a negative capital account can best be envisioned as a contribution of cash to the partnership equal to the negative balance.

These requirements are designed to ensure that a partner bears the economic burden of a loss or deduction allocation and receives the economic benefit of an income or gain allocation.

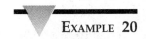

EXAMPLE 20

Eli and Sanjay each contribute $20,000 cash to the newly formed ES Partnership. The partnership uses the cash to acquire a depreciable asset for $40,000. The partnership agreement provides that the depreciation is allocated 90% to Eli and 10% to Sanjay. Other items of partnership income, gain, loss, or deduction are allocated equally between the partners. Upon liquidation of the partnership, property will be distributed to the partners

[35] Reg. § 1.704–1(b).

in accordance with their positive capital account balances. Any partner with a negative capital account must restore the capital account upon liquidation. Assume the first-year depreciation on the equipment is $4,000. Also, assume nothing else happens in the first year that affects the partners' capital accounts.

Eli's capital account is $16,400 ($20,000 − $3,600), and Sanjay's capital account has a balance of $19,600 ($20,000 − $400) after the first year of partnership operations. The Regulations require that a hypothetical sale of the asset for its $36,000 adjusted basis on the last day of the year and an immediate liquidation of the partnership should result in Eli and Sanjay receiving distributions equal to their capital accounts. According to the partnership agreement, Eli would receive $16,400, and Sanjay would receive $19,600 of the cash in a liquidating distribution. Eli, therefore, bears the economic burden of $3,600 depreciation since he contributed $20,000 to the partnership and would receive only $16,400 upon liquidation. Likewise, Sanjay's economic burden is $400 since he would receive only $19,600 of his original $20,000 investment. The agreement, therefore, has economic effect.

If the partnership agreement had provided that Eli and Sanjay should each receive $18,000 of the liquidation proceeds, the "special" allocation of the depreciation would be defective. The IRS would require that the depreciation be allocated equally ($2,000 each) to the two partners to reflect the $2,000 economic burden borne by each partner. ▼

Precontribution Gain or Loss. Despite the flexibility that "special allocations" can provide, allocations of income, gain, loss, and deductions relative to contributed property may not be so allocated under the rules described above. Instead, **precontribution gain or loss** must be allocated among the partners to take into account the variation between the basis of the property and its fair market value on the date of contribution.[36] For nondepreciable property, this means that *built-in* gain or loss on the date of contribution must be allocated to the contributing partner when the property is eventually disposed of by the partnership in a taxable transaction.

EXAMPLE 21

Seth and Tim formed the equal profit and loss sharing ST Partnership. Seth contributed cash of $10,000, and Tim contributed land purchased two years ago that was held for investment. The land had an adjusted basis of $6,000 and fair market value of $10,000 at the contribution date. For accounting purposes, the partnership recorded the land at its fair market value of $10,000. For tax purposes, the partnership took a carryover basis in the land of $6,000. After using the land as a parking lot for five months, ST sold it for $10,600. No other transactions took place.

The accounting and tax gain from the land sale are computed as follows:

	Accounting	Tax
Amount realized	$ 10,600	$10,600
Less: Adjusted basis	(10,000)	(6,000)
Gain realized	$ 600	$ 4,600
Less: Gain at contribution date to Tim	(–0–)	(4,000)
Remaining gain (split equally)	$ 600	$ 600

Seth recognizes $300 of the gain ($600 postcontribution gain ÷ 2), and Tim recognizes $4,300 of gain [$4,000 built-in gain + ($600 ÷ 2)]. ▼

---

[36] § 704(c)(1)(A).

CONCEPT SUMMARY 22–2

Tax Reporting of Partnership Activities

Event	Partnership Level	Partner Level
1. Compute partnership ordinary income.	Form 1065, line 22, page 1. Schedule K, Form 1065, line 1, page 3.	Schedule K–1 (Form 1065), line 1, page 1. Each partner's share is passed through for separate reporting. Each partner's basis is increased.
2. Compute partnership ordinary loss.	Form 1065, line 22, page 1. Schedule K, Form 1065, line 1, page 3.	Schedule K–1 (Form 1065), line 1, page 1. Each partner's share is passed through for separate reporting. Each partner's basis is decreased. The amount of a partner's loss deduction may be limited. Losses that may not be deducted are carried forward for use in future years.
3. Separately reported items like portfolio income, capital gain and loss, and § 179 deductions.	Schedule K, Form 1065, various lines, page 3.	Schedule K–1 (Form 1065), various lines, pages 1 and 2. Each partner's share is passed through for separate reporting.
4. Net earnings from self-employment.	Schedule K, Form 1065, line 15, page 3.	Schedule K–1 (Form 1065), line 15, page 2.

Regulations outline specific allocation calculations that may be used and describe allowable methods of allocating depreciation deductions if the property is depreciable.[37]

Concept Summary 22–2 reviews the tax reporting rules for partnership activities.

BASIS OF PARTNERSHIP INTEREST

6 **LEARNING OBJECTIVE**
Determine a partner's basis in the partnership interest.

Previously, this chapter discussed how to compute a partner's adjusted basis when the partnership is formed. It was noted that the partner's adjusted basis in the newly formed partnership usually equals (1) the adjusted basis in any property contributed to the partnership plus (2) the fair market value of any services the partner performed for the partnership (i.e., the amount of ordinary income reported by the partner for services rendered to the partnership).

A partnership interest can be acquired after the partnership has been formed. The method of acquisition controls how the partner's initial basis is computed. If the partnership interest is purchased from another partner, the purchasing

---

[37] Reg. § 1.704–3. The three allowable methods are the "traditional method," the "traditional method with curative allocation," and the "remedial allocation." See footnote 41.

partner's basis is the amount paid (cost basis) for the partnership interest. The basis of a partnership interest acquired by gift is the donor's basis for the interest plus, in certain cases, some or all of the transfer (gift) tax paid by the donor. The basis of a partnership interest acquired through inheritance is the fair market value of the interest on the date the partner dies.

After the partnership begins its activities, or after a transferee partner is admitted to the partnership, the partner's basis is adjusted for numerous items. The following operating results *increase* a partner's adjusted basis:

- The partner's proportionate share of partnership income (including capital gains and tax-exempt income).
- The partner's proportionate share of any increase in partnership liabilities.

The following operating results *decrease* the partner's adjusted basis in the partnership:

- The partner's proportionate share of partnership deductions and losses (including capital losses).
- The partner's proportionate share of nondeductible expenses.
- The partner's proportionate share of any decrease in partnership liabilities.[38]

Under no circumstances can the partner's adjusted basis for the partnership interest be reduced below zero.

Increasing the partner's adjusted basis for his or her share of partnership taxable income is logical since the partner has already been taxed on the income. By increasing the partner's basis, the Code ensures that the partner is not taxed again on the income when he or she sells the interest or receives a distribution from the partnership.

It is also logical that the tax-exempt income should increase the partner's basis. If the income is exempt in the current period, it should not contribute to the recognition of gain when the partner either sells the interest or receives a distribution from the partnership.

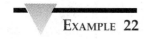

EXAMPLE 22

Yuri is a one-third partner in the XYZ Partnership. His proportionate share of the partnership income during the current year consists of $20,000 of ordinary taxable income and $10,000 of tax-exempt income. None of the income is distributed to Yuri. The adjusted basis of Yuri's partnership interest before adjusting for his share of income is $35,000, and the fair market value of the interest before considering the income items is $50,000.

The unrealized gain inherent in Yuri's investment in the partnership is $15,000 ($50,000 − $35,000). Yuri's proportionate share of the income items should increase the fair market value of the interest to $80,000 ($50,000 + $20,000 + $10,000). By increasing the adjusted basis of Yuri's partnership interest to $65,000 ($35,000 + $20,000 + $10,000), the Code ensures that the unrealized gain inherent in Yuri's partnership investment remains at $15,000. This makes sense because the $20,000 of ordinary taxable income is taxed to Yuri this year and should not be taxed again when he either sells his interest or receives a distribution. Similarly, the exempt income is exempt this year and should not increase Yuri's gain when he either sells his interest or receives a distribution from the partnership. ▼

Decreasing the partner's adjusted basis for his or her share of deductible losses, deductions, and noncapitalizable, nondeductible expenditures is logical for the same reasons. An item that is deductible currently should not contribute to creating a loss when the partnership interest is sold or a distribution is received

[38] §§ 705 and 752.

from the partnership. Similarly, a noncapitalizable, nondeductible expenditure should never be deductible nor contribute to a loss when a subsequent sale or distribution transaction occurs.

7 LEARNING OBJECTIVE
Explain how liabilities affect a partner's basis.

Liability Sharing.   A partner's adjusted basis is also affected by the partner's share of partnership debt.[39] Partnership debt includes any partnership obligation that creates an asset; results in a deductible expense; or results in a nondeductible, noncapitalizable item at the partnership level. This definition includes most debt that is considered a liability under financial accounting rules except for accounts payable of a *cash basis* partnership and certain contingent liabilities.

Under § 752, an increase in a partner's share of partnership debt is treated as a cash contribution by the partner to the partnership. A partner's share of debt increases as a result of (1) increases in partnership debt and (2) assumption of a partner's individual debt by the partnership. A decrease in a partner's share of partnership debt is treated as a cash distribution from the partnership to the partner. A partner's share of debt decreases as a result of (1) decreases in partnership debt and (2) assumption of partnership debt by a partner.

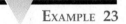

EXAMPLE 23

Jim and Becky contribute property to form the JB Partnership. Jim contributes cash of $30,000. Becky contributes land with an adjusted basis and fair market value of $45,000, subject to a liability of $15,000. The partnership borrows $50,000 to finance construction of a building on the contributed land. At the end of the first year, the accrual basis partnership owes $3,500 in trade accounts payable to various vendors. Assume no other operating activities occurred.

Partnership debt sharing rules are discussed later in this section, but assuming for simplicity that Jim and Becky share equally in liabilities, the partners' bases in their partnership interests are determined as follows:

Jim's Basis		Becky's Basis	
Contributed cash	$30,000	Basis in contributed land	$ 45,000
Share of construction loan	25,000	Less: Debt assumed by partnership	(15,000)
Share of trade accounts payable	1,750	Share of construction loan	25,000
Share of debt on land (assumed by partnership)	7,500	Share of trade accounts payable	1,750
		Share of debt on land (assumed by partnership)	7,500
	$64,250		$ 64,250

In this case, it is reasonable that the parties have an equal basis after contributing their respective properties, because each is a 50% owner and they contributed property with identical bases and identical *net* fair market values. ▼

Decreases in liabilities are treated as cash distributions and can result in extremely negative tax consequences. Liability balances should be reviewed carefully near the partnership's year-end to ensure the partners have no unanticipated tax results.

---

[39] § 752.

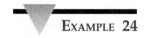

EXAMPLE 24

Assume the same facts as in Example 23, except the partnership reported an ordinary loss of $100,000 in its first year of operations. Ignoring possible loss deduction limitations, Jim and Becky each deduct a $50,000 ordinary loss, and their bases in their respective partnership interests are reduced to $14,250 (including a $34,250 share of liabilities).

In the second year, the partnership generated no taxable income or loss from operations, but repaid the $50,000 construction loan (assume from collection of accounts receivable reported in the prior year). The $25,000 reduction of each partner's share of partnership liabilities is treated as a cash distribution by the partnership to each partner. A cash distribution in excess of basis usually results in a capital gain (in this case $10,750) to each partner. The partners must pay tax on $10,750 of capital gain even though the partnership reported no taxable income. This gain can be thought of as a recapture of loss deductions the partners claimed during the first year, but such gains cause cash-flow difficulties to partners who are unaware that such a gain may occur. ▼

Two types of partnership debt exist. **Recourse debt** is partnership debt for which the partnership or at least one of the partners is personally liable. This liability can exist, for example, through the operation of state law or through personal guarantees that a partner makes to the creditor. Personal liability of a party related to a partner (under attribution rules) is treated as the personal liability of the partner. **Nonrecourse debt** is debt for which no partner (or party related to a partner) is personally liable. Lenders of nonrecourse debt generally require that collateral be pledged against the loan. Upon default, the lender can claim only the collateral, not the partners' personal assets.

How liabilities are shared among the partners depends upon whether the debt is recourse or nonrecourse and when the liability was incurred. For most debt *created* before January 29, 1989, the rules are relatively straightforward. Recourse debt is shared among the partners in accordance with their loss sharing ratios while nonrecourse debt is shared among the partners in accordance with the way they share partnership profits. Although questions arise about the calculation of the profit or loss sharing ratios and the treatment of personal guarantees of debt, the rules for sharing this earlier debt are easy to apply.

The rules for sharing partnership debt created after January 29, 1989, are much more complex. A complete analysis of these rules is beyond the scope of this text. The basic principles of these rules can be easily understood, however.

Current Recourse Debt Rules. Recourse debt created after January 29, 1989, is shared in accordance with a **constructive liquidation scenario.**[40] Under this scenario, the following events are *deemed* to occur at the end of each taxable year of the partnership:

1. Most partnership assets (including cash) become worthless.
2. The worthless assets are sold at fair market value ($0), and losses on the deemed sales are determined.
3. These losses are allocated to the partners according to their loss sharing ratios. These losses reduce the partners' capital accounts.
4. Any partner with a (deemed) negative balance in the capital account is treated as contributing cash to the partnership to restore that negative balance to zero.
5. The cash deemed contributed by the partners with negative capital balances is used to pay the liabilities of the partnership.

---

[40] Transition rules (beyond the scope of this text) apply to debt created between January 29, 1989, and December 28, 1991.

6. The partnership is deemed to be liquidated immediately, and any remaining cash is distributed to partners with positive capital account balances.

The amount of a partner's cash contribution that would be used (in step 5 above) in payment of partnership recourse liabilities is that partner's share of partnership recourse liabilities.

EXAMPLE 25

On January 1 of the current year, Nina and Otis each contribute $20,000 cash to the newly created NO General Partnership. Each partner has a 50% interest in partnership capital, profits, and losses. The first year of partnership operations resulted in the following balance sheet as of December 31:

	Basis	Fair Market Value
Cash	$12,000	$12,000
Receivables	7,000	7,000
Land and buildings	50,000	50,000
	$69,000	$69,000

	Basis	Fair Market Value
Recourse payables	$30,000	$30,000
Nina, capital	19,500	19,500
Otis, capital	19,500	19,500
	$69,000	$69,000

The recourse debt is shared in accordance with the constructive liquidation scenario. All of the partnership assets (including cash) are deemed to be worthless and sold for $0. This creates a loss of $69,000 ($12,000 + $7,000 + $50,000), which is allocated equally between the two partners. The $34,500 loss allocated to each partner creates negative capital accounts of $15,000 each for Nina and Otis. If the partnership were actually liquidated, each partner would contribute $15,000 cash to the partnership; the cash would be used to pay the partnership recourse payables; and the partnership would be liquidated. Because each partner would be required to contribute $15,000 to pay the liabilities, each shares in $15,000 of the recourse payables. Accordingly, Nina and Otis will each have an adjusted basis for their partnership interests of $34,500 ($19,500 + $15,000) on December 31. ▼

EXAMPLE 26

Assume the same facts as in Example 25, except that the partners allocate partnership losses 60% to Nina and 40% to Otis. The constructive liquidation scenario results in the $69,000 loss being allocated $41,400 to Nina and $27,600 to Otis. As a consequence, Nina's capital account has a negative balance of $21,900, and Otis's account has a negative balance of $8,100. Each partner is deemed to contribute cash equal to these negative capital accounts, and the cash would be used to pay the recourse liabilities under the liquidation scenario. Accordingly, Nina and Otis share $21,900 and $8,100, respectively, in the recourse debt. Note that the debt allocation percentages (73% to Nina and 27% to Otis) bear no relation to the partners' 60%/40% loss sharing ratios. ▼

Current Nonrecourse Debt Rules. Nonrecourse debt is allocated in three stages. First, an amount of debt equal to the amount of *minimum gain* is allocated to partners who share in minimum gain. The calculation of minimum gain is complex, and its details are beyond the scope of this text. In general, minimum gain approximates the amount of nonrecourse (mortgage) liability on a property in excess of the "book" basis of the property. The "book" basis for contributed property on the date of contribution is its fair market value at that date. If the lender foreclosed on the property, the result would be a deemed sale of the property for the mortgage balance. Gain is recognized for at least the amount of the liability in excess of the property's basis—hence, minimum gain. Allocation of minimum gain among the partners should be addressed in the partnership agreement.

Second, the amount of nonrecourse debt equal to a *precontribution gain* under § 704(c) is allocated to the partner who contributed the property and debt to the partnership. For this purpose, the § 704(c) amount is the excess of the nonrecourse debt assumed by the partnership over the tax basis of the property.[41]

Third, any remaining nonrecourse debt is allocated to the partners in accordance with either their profit sharing ratios or the manner in which they share in nonrecourse deductions. The partnership agreement should specify which allocation method is used.

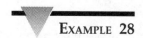

EXAMPLE 27   Ted contributes a nondepreciable asset to the TK Partnership in exchange for a one-third interest in the capital, profits, and losses of the partnership. The asset has an adjusted tax basis to Ted and the partnership of $24,000 and a fair market value and "book" basis on the contribution date of $50,000. The asset is encumbered by a nonrecourse note (created January 1, 1994) of $35,000. Because the "book" basis exceeds the nonrecourse debt, there is no minimum gain. Under § 704(c) principles, the Regulations provide that the first $11,000 of the nonrecourse debt ($35,000 debt – $24,000 basis) is allocated to Ted. The remaining $24,000 nonrecourse debt is shared according to the profit sharing ratio, of which Ted's share is $8,000. Therefore, Ted shares in $19,000 ($11,000 + $8,000) of the nonrecourse debt.

Ted's basis in his partnership interest is determined as follows:

Substituted basis of contributed property	$ 24,000
Less: Liability assumed by partnership	(35,000)
Plus: Allocation of § 704(c) debt	11,000
Basis before remaining allocation	$ –0–
Plus: Allocation of remaining nonrecourse debt	8,000
Basis in partnership interest	$ 8,000

The § 704(c) allocation of nonrecourse debt prevents Ted from receiving a deemed distribution in excess of the basis in property he contributed. Without this required allocation of nonrecourse debt, in some cases, a contributing partner would be required to recognize gain on a contribution of property encumbered by nonrecourse debt. ▼

Other Factors Affecting Basis Calculations.   The partner's basis is also affected by (1) postacquisition contributions of cash or property to the partnership; (2) postacquisition distributions of cash or property from the partnership; and (3) special calculations that are designed to allow the full deduction of percentage depletion for oil and gas wells. Postacquisition contributions of cash or property affect basis in the same manner as contributions made upon the creation of the partnership. Postacquisition distributions of cash or property reduce basis.

EXAMPLE 28   Ed is a one-third partner in the ERM Partnership. On January 1, 1996, Ed's basis in his partnership interest was $50,000. During 1996, the calendar year, accrual basis partnership

---

[41] A more complex calculation (beyond the scope of this text) applies when the partnership allocates built-in gain under the "remedial allocation" method. (See footnote 37.)

generated ordinary taxable income of $210,000. It also received $60,000 of interest income from City of Buffalo bonds. It paid $3,000 in nondeductible bribes to local law enforcement officials, so that the police would not notify the Federal government about the products that the entity had imported without paying the proper tariffs. On July 1, 1996, Ed contributed $20,000 cash and a computer (zero basis to him) to the partnership. Ed's monthly draw from the partnership is $3,000; this is not a guaranteed payment. The only liabilities that the partnership has incurred are trade accounts payable. On January 1, 1996, the trade accounts payable totaled $45,000; this account balance was $21,000 on January 1, 1997.

Ed's basis in the partnership on December 31, 1996, is $115,000, computed as follows:

Beginning balance	$ 50,000
Share of ordinary partnership income	70,000
Share of exempt income	20,000
Share of nondeductible expenditures	(1,000)
Ed's basis in noncash capital contribution	–0–
Additional cash contribution	20,000
Capital withdrawals	(36,000)
Share of net decrease in partnership liabilities [⅓ × ($45,000 – $21,000)]	(8,000)
	$115,000

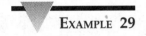

EXAMPLE 29

Assume the same facts as in Example 28. If Ed withdraws cash of $115,000 from the partnership on January 1, 1997, the withdrawal reduces his basis to zero. He has recognized his share of the partnership's corresponding income throughout his association with the entity, via the annual flow-through of his share of the partnership's income and expense items. In addition, the $20,000 municipal bond interest retains its nontaxable character in this distribution. Ed receives such assets as a part of his capital withdrawal because his basis was increased in 1996 when the partnership received the interest income. ▼

A partner is required to compute the adjusted basis only when necessary and thus can avoid the inconvenience of making day-to-day calculations of basis. When a partnership interest is sold, exchanged, or retired, however, the partner must compute the adjusted basis as of the date the transaction occurs. Computation of the gain or loss requires an accurate calculation of the partner's adjusted basis on the transaction date.

Figure 22–3 summarizes the rules for computing a partner's basis in a partnership interest.

LOSS LIMITATIONS

8 LEARNING OBJECTIVE
Describe the limitations on deducting partnership losses.

Partnership losses flow through to the partners for use on their income tax returns. However, the amount and nature of the losses that may be used in a partner's tax computations may be limited. When limitations apply, all or a portion of the losses are held in suspension until a triggering condition occurs. At that later date, the losses can be used to determine the partner's tax liability.

Three different limitations may apply to partnership losses that are passed through to a partner. The first is the overall limitation contained in § 704(d). This limitation allows losses only to the extent the partner has adjusted basis for the partnership interest. Losses that are deductible under the overall limitation may then be subject to the at-risk limitation of § 465. Losses are deductible under this provision only to the extent the partner is at risk for the partnership interest. Any losses that survive this second limitation may be subject to a third limitation, the

▼ FIGURE 22–3
Partner's Basis in Partnership
Interest

Basis is generally adjusted in the following order:

Initial basis. Amount paid for interest, or gift or inherited basis (including share of partnership debt). Amount paid can be amount contributed to partnership or amount paid to another partner or former partner.

+ Partner's contributions

+ Since interest acquired, partner's share of partnership's

• Debt increase
  • Income items
  • Exempt income items
  • Excess of depletion deductions over adjusted basis of property subject to depletion

– Partner's distributions and withdrawals

– Since interest acquired, partner's share of partnership's

• Debt decrease
  • Nondeductible items not chargeable to a capital account
  • Special depletion deduction for oil and gas wells
  • Loss items

The basis of a partner's interest can never be negative.

passive loss rules of § 469. Only losses that make it through these applicable limitations are eligible to be deducted on the partner's tax return.

EXAMPLE 30

Meg is a partner in a partnership that does not invest in real estate. On January 1, 1996, Meg's adjusted basis for her partnership interest is $50,000, and her at-risk amount is $35,000. Her share of losses from the partnership for 1996 is $60,000, all of which is passive. She has one other passive income-producing investment that produced $25,000 of passive income during 1996.

Meg will be able to deduct $25,000 of partnership losses on her Form 1040 for 1996. Her deductible loss is calculated as follows:

Applicable Provision	Deductible Loss	Suspended Loss
Overall limitation	$50,000	$10,000
At-risk limitation	35,000	15,000
Passive loss limitation	25,000	10,000

Meg can deduct only $50,000 under the overall limitation. Of this $50,000, only $35,000 is deductible under the at-risk limitation. Under the passive loss limitation, passive losses can only be deducted against passive income. Thus, Meg can deduct only $25,000 on her return in 1996. ▼

Overall Limitation. A partner may only deduct losses flowing through from the partnership to the extent of the partner's adjusted basis in the partnership interest. A partner's basis in the interest is determined at the end of the partnership's taxable year. It is adjusted for distributions and any partnership gains during the year, but it is determined before considering any losses for the year.

Losses that cannot be deducted because of this rule are suspended and carried forward (never back) for use against future increases in the partner's outside basis.

Such increases might result from additional capital contributions or from sharing in additional partnership debt or future partnership income.

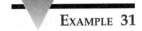

EXAMPLE 31   Carol and Dan do business as the CD Partnership, sharing profits and losses equally. All parties use the calendar year. At the start of the current year, the basis of Carol's partnership interest is $25,000. The partnership sustained an operating loss of $80,000 in the current year. For the current year, only $25,000 of Carol's $40,000 allocable share of the partnership loss (one-half of the $80,000 loss) can be deducted under the overall limitation. As a result, the basis of Carol's partnership interest is zero as of January 1 of the following year, and she must carry forward the remaining $15,000 of partnership losses. ▼

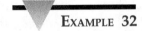

EXAMPLE 32   Assume the same facts as in Example 31, and that the partnership earned a profit of $70,000 for the next calendar year. Carol reports net partnership income of $20,000 ($35,000 distributive share of income – the $15,000 carryforward loss). The basis of Carol's partnership interest becomes $20,000. ▼

In Example 31, Carol's entire $40,000 share of the current-year partnership loss could have been deducted under the overall limitation in the current year if she had contributed an additional $15,000 or more in capital by December 31. Alternatively, if the partnership had incurred additional debt by the end of the current year, Carol's basis might have been increased to permit some or all of the loss to be deducted in that year. Thus, if partnership losses are projected for a given year, careful tax planning can ensure their deductibility under the overall limitation.

Notice that in Figure 22–3, contributions to capital, distributions from the partnership, and partnership income items are taken into account before loss items. This ordering produces some unusual results in taxation of partnership distributions and deductibility of losses.

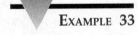

EXAMPLE 33   The Ellen-Glenn Partnership is owned equally by partners Ellen and Glenn. At the beginning of the year, Ellen's basis in her partnership interest is $0. Her share of partnership income is $10,000 for the year, and she receives a $10,000 distribution from the partnership.

Under the basis adjustment ordering rules of Figure 22–3, Ellen's basis is first increased by the $10,000 of partnership income, then is decreased by her $10,000 distribution. She reports her $10,000 share of partnership taxable income. Her basis at the end of the year is again $0 ($0 + $10,000 income – $10,000 distribution). ▼

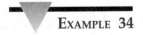

EXAMPLE 34   Assume the same facts as in Example 33, except that Ellen's share of partnership operating results is a $10,000 loss instead of $10,000 income. She again receives a $10,000 distribution.

As mentioned earlier, a distribution of cash in excess of basis in the partnership interest results in a gain to the distributee partner. Under the basis adjustment ordering rules of Figure 22–3, Ellen's distribution is considered before the deductibility of the loss is evaluated under the overall limitation.

Ellen recognizes gain on the $10,000 distribution because she has no basis in her partnership interest. The gain effectively ensures that she still has a $0 basis after the distribution. The loss cannot be deducted under the overall loss limitation rule because Ellen has no basis in her partnership interest. ▼

Given this $20,000 swing in partnership earnings in the two examples ($10,000 income to $10,000 loss), does income taxed to Ellen exhibit a similar swing? Actually, she reports $10,000 of income in each case: ordinary income in Example 33, and (probably) a capital gain from the distribution in Example 34. In Example 34, she also has a $10,000 suspended loss carryforward. These results are due solely to the basis adjustment ordering rules. Remember these rules, and the appropriate results can be determined. Income and contributions are considered first, then distributions—and *last,* loss items.

At-Risk Limitation. Under the at-risk rules, the losses from business and income-producing activities that individuals and closely held corporations can deduct are limited to amounts that are economically invested. Invested amounts include the adjusted basis of contributed property, cash contributions, and the earnings share that has not been withdrawn.[42] A closely held corporation exists when five or fewer individuals own more than 50 percent of the entity's stock under appropriate attribution and ownership rules.

When some or all of the partners are personally liable for partnership recourse debt, that debt is included in the adjusted basis of those partners. Usually, those partners also include the debt in their amount at risk.

No partner, however, carries any financial risk on nonrecourse debt. Therefore, as a general rule, partners cannot include nonrecourse debt in their amount at risk even though that debt is included in the adjusted basis of their partnership interest. In many cases, however, an exception to this general rule applies. Real estate nonrecourse financing provided by a bank, retirement plan, or similar party, or by a Federal, state, or local government generally is deemed to be at risk.[43] Such debt is termed **qualified nonrecourse debt.** Consequently, although the general rule provides that nonrecourse debt is not at risk, the overriding exception may provide that it is deemed to be at risk.

When determining a partner's loss deduction, the overall limitation rule is invoked first (the deduction is limited to the partner's outside basis at the end of the partnership year). Then, the at-risk provisions are applied to see if the remaining loss is still deductible. Suspended losses are carried forward until a partner has a sufficient amount at risk in the activity to absorb them.[44]

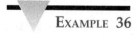

EXAMPLE 35

Kelly invests $5,000 in the Kelly Green Limited Partnership as a 5% general partner. Shortly thereafter, the partnership acquires the master recording of a well-known vocalist for $250,000 ($50,000 from the partnership and $200,000 secured from a local bank via a *recourse* mortgage). Kelly's share of the recourse debt is $10,000, and her basis in her partnership interest is $15,000 ($5,000 cash investment + $10,000 debt share). Since the debt is recourse, Kelly's at-risk amount is also $15,000. Kelly's share of partnership losses in the first year of operations is $11,000. She is entitled to deduct the full $11,000 of partnership losses under both the overall and the at-risk limitations because this amount is less than both her outside basis and at-risk amount. ▼

EXAMPLE 36

Assume the same facts as in Example 35, except the bank loan is nonrecourse (the partners have no direct liability under the terms of the loan in the case of a default). Kelly's basis in her partnership interest still is $15,000, but she can deduct only $5,000 of the flow-through loss. The amount she has at risk in the partnership does not include the nonrecourse debt. (The debt does not relate to real estate so it is not qualified nonrecourse debt.) ▼

Passive Activity Rules. A partnership loss share may be disallowed under the passive activity rules. Although these rules are not applicable solely to partnerships, they most assuredly affect how and when a partner's loss can be deducted. The rules require taxpayers to separate their activities into three groups:

[42] § 465(a).
[43] § 465(b)(6).
[44] § 465(a)(2).

- *Active.* Earned income, such as salary and wages; income or loss from a trade or business in which the taxpayer materially participates; and guaranteed payments from a partnership for services.
- *Portfolio.* Annuity income, interest, dividends, guaranteed payments from a partnership for interest on capital, royalties not derived in the ordinary course of a trade or business, and gains and losses from disposal of investment assets.
- *Passive.* Income from a trade or business in which the taxpayer does not materially participate on a regular, continuous, and substantial basis, or income from a rental activity.[45]

Material participation in an activity is determined annually. The burden is on the taxpayer to prove material participation. The IRS has provided a number of objective tests for determining material participation. These tests require the taxpayer to have substantial involvement in daily operations of the activity. Thus, a Maine vacation resort operator investing in a California grape farm or an electrical engineer employed in Virginia investing in an Iowa corn and hog farm may have difficulty proving material participation in the activities.

Rent income from real or personal property generally is passive income, regardless of the taxpayer's level of participation. Exceptions are made for rent income from activities where substantial services are provided (resorts); from hotels, motels, and other transient lodging; from short-term equipment rentals; and from certain developed real estate.

Usually, passive activity losses can only offset passive activity income.[46] In determining the net passive activity loss for a year, losses and income from all passive activities are aggregated. The amount of suspended losses carried forward from a particular activity is determined by the ratio of the net loss from that activity to the aggregate net loss from all passive activities for the year. A special rule for rental real estate (discussed in the following section) allows a limited $25,000 offset against nonpassive income.[47]

A taxpayer making a taxable disposition of an entire interest in a passive activity takes a full deduction for suspended passive activity losses from that activity in the year of disposal.[48] Suspended losses are deductible against income in the following order: income or gain from the passive activity, net income or gain from all passive activities, and other income. When a passive activity is transferred in a nontaxable exchange (e.g., a like-kind exchange or contribution to a partnership), suspended losses are deductible only to the extent of gains recognized on the transfer. Remaining losses are deducted on disposal of the activity received in the exchange.

EXAMPLE 37

Debra has several investments in passive activities that generate aggregate losses of $10,000 in the current year. Debra wants to deduct all of these losses in the current year. To assure a loss deduction, she needs to invest in some passive activities that generate income. One of her long-time friends, an entrepreneur in the women's apparel business, is interested in opening a new apparel store in a nearby community. Debra is willing to finance a substantial part of the expansion but does not want to get involved with day-to-day operations. Debra also wants to limit any possible loss to her initial investment.

After substantial discussions, Debra and her friend decide to form a limited partnership, which will own the new store. Debra's friend will be the general partner, and Debra

---

[45] §§ 469(c)(1) and (2).
[46] § 469(a)(1).

[47] § 469(i).
[48] § 469(g).

will be a limited partner. Debra invests $100,000, and her friend invests $50,000 and sweat equity (provides managerial skills and know-how). Each has a 50% interest in profits and losses. In the first year of operations, the store generates a profit of $30,000. Since Debra's share of the profit ($15,000) is passive activity income, it can be fully utilized against any passive activity losses. Thus, via her share of the apparel store profits, Debra assures a full deduction of her $10,000 of passive activity losses. ▼

Rental Real Estate Losses.   Individuals can offset up to $25,000 of passive losses from rental real estate against active and portfolio income in any one year. The $25,000 maximum is reduced by 50 percent of the difference between the taxpayer's modified adjusted gross income (AGI) and $100,000. Thus, when the taxpayer's modified AGI reaches $150,000, the offset is eliminated.

The offset is available to those who actively (rather than materially) participate in rental real estate activities. Active participation is an easier test to meet. Unlike material participation, it does not require regular, continuous, and substantial involvement with the activity. However, the taxpayer must own at least 10 percent of the fair market value of all interests in the rental property and either contribute to the activity's management decisions in a significant and bona fide way or actively participate in arranging for others to make such decisions.

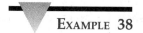

EXAMPLE 38

Raoul invests $10,000 cash in the Sparrow Limited Partnership in the current year for a 10% limited interest in capital and profits. Shortly thereafter, the partnership purchases rental real estate subject to a nonconvertible qualified nonrecourse mortgage of $120,000 obtained from a commercial bank. Raoul has no other passive loss activities during the current year.

Raoul does not participate in any of Sparrow's activities. His share of losses from Sparrow's first year of operations is $27,000. His AGI before considering the loss is $60,000. Before considering the loss, Raoul's basis in the partnership interest is $22,000 [$10,000 cash + (10% × $120,000 debt)], and his loss deduction is limited to this amount under the overall limitation. The debt is included in Raoul's amount at risk because it is qualified nonrecourse financing. It may seem that Raoul should be allowed to deduct the $22,000 loss share from portfolio or active income under the rental real estate exception to the passive loss rules. However, the loss may not be offset against this income because Raoul is not an active participant in the partnership. ▼

Transactions between Partners and Partnerships

9　 LEARNING OBJECTIVE
Describe the treatment of transactions between a partner and the partnership.

Many types of transactions occur between a partnership and one of its partners. The partner may contribute property to the partnership, perform services for the partnership, or receive distributions from the partnership. The partner may borrow money from or lend money to the partnership. Property may be bought and sold between the partner and the partnership. Several of these transactions were discussed earlier in the chapter. The remaining types of partner-partnership transactions are the focus of this section.

GUARANTEED PAYMENTS

If a partnership makes a payment to a partner in his or her capacity as a partner, the payment may be a draw against the partner's share of partnership income; a return of some or all of the partner's original capital contribution; or a guaranteed payment, among other treatments. A **guaranteed payment** is a payment for services performed by the partner or for the use of the partner's capital. The payment may not be determined by reference to partnership income. Guaranteed payments are usually expressed as a fixed-dollar amount or as a percentage of capital that the partner has invested in the partnership. Whether the partnership deducts or capitalizes the guaranteed payment depends on the nature of the payment.

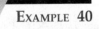

EXAMPLE 39

David, Donald, and Dale formed the accrual basis DDD Partnership in 1996. According to the partnership agreement, David is to perform services for the partnership in exchange for $21,000 from the entity every year, payable in 12 monthly installments. Donald is to receive an amount that is equal to 18% of his capital account, as it is computed by the firm's accountant at the beginning of the year, payable in 12 monthly installments. Dale is the partnership's advertising specialist. He withdraws 3% of the partnership's net income every month for his personal use. David and Donald receive guaranteed payments from the partnership, but Dale does not. ▼

Guaranteed payments resemble the salary or interest payments of other businesses and receive somewhat similar treatment under partnership tax law.[49] In contrast to the provision that usually applies to withdrawals of assets by partners from their partnerships, guaranteed payments are deductible (or capitalized) by the entity, and on the last day of the partnership's tax year, the recipients must report such income separately from their usual partnership allocations. Deductible guaranteed payments, like other deductible expenses of a partnership, can create an ordinary loss for the entity.

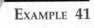

EXAMPLE 40

Continue with the situation introduced in Example 39. For calendar year 1996, David receives the $21,000 as provided by the partnership agreement, Donald's guaranteed payment for 1996 is $17,000, and Dale withdraws $20,000 under his personal expenditures clause. Before considering these amounts, the partnership's ordinary income for 1996 is $650,000.

The partnership can deduct its payments to David and Donald, so the final amount of its 1996 ordinary income is $612,000 ($650,000 − $21,000 − $17,000). Thus, each of the equal partners is allocated $204,000 of ordinary partnership income for their 1996 individual income tax returns ($612,000 ÷ 3). In addition, David reports the $21,000 of guaranteed payment income, and Donald includes the $17,000 guaranteed payment in his 1996 gross income. Dale's partnership draw is deemed to have come from his allocated $204,000 (or from the accumulated partnership income that was taxed to him in prior years) and is not taxed separately to him. ▼

EXAMPLE 41

Assume the same facts as in Example 39, except that the partnership's tax year ends on March 31, 1997. The total amount of the guaranteed payments is taxable to the partners on that date. Thus, even though David receives 9 of his 12 payments for fiscal 1997 in calendar 1996, all of his guaranteed payments are taxable to him in 1997. Similarly, all of Donald's guaranteed payments are taxable to him in 1997 and not when they are received. The deduction for, and the gross income from, guaranteed payments are allowed on the same date that all of the other income and expense items relative to the partnership are allocated to the partners (on the last day of the entity's tax year). ▼

---

[49] § 707(c).

OTHER TRANSACTIONS BETWEEN PARTNERS AND PARTNERSHIPS

Certain transactions between a partner and the partnership are treated as if the partner were an outsider, dealing with the partnership at arm's length.[50] Loan transactions, rental payments, and sales of property between the partner and the partnership are treated in this manner. In addition, payments for services are generally treated this way when the services are short-term technical services that the partner also provides for parties other than the partnership.

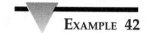

EXAMPLE 42

Emilio, a one-third partner in the CDE Partnership, owns a tract of land that the partnership wishes to purchase. The land has a fair market value of $30,000 and an adjusted basis to Emilio of $17,000. If Emilio sells the land to the partnership, he recognizes a $13,000 gain on the sale, and the partnership takes a $30,000 cost basis in the land. If the land has a fair market value of $10,000 on the sale date, Emilio recognizes a $7,000 loss. ▼

The timing of the deduction for a payment by an accrual basis partnership to a cash basis service partner depends upon whether the payment is a guaranteed payment or a payment to a partner who is treated as an outsider. A guaranteed payment is includible in the partner's income when properly accrued by the partnership, even though the payment may not be made to the partner until the next taxable year. Conversely, the partner's method of accounting controls the timing of deduction if the payment is treated as made to an outsider. This is because a deduction cannot be claimed for such amounts until the recipient partner is required to include the amount in income under the partner's method of accounting.[51] Thus, a partnership cannot claim a deduction until it actually makes a payment to the cash basis partner, but it would accrue a payment due to an accrual basis partner even if payment was not yet made.

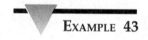

EXAMPLE 43

Rachel, a cash basis taxpayer, is a partner in the accrual basis RTC Partnership. On December 31, 1996, the partnership accrues but does not pay $10,000 for deductible services that Rachel performed for the partnership during the year. Both Rachel and the partnership are calendar year taxpayers.

If the $10,000 accrual is a guaranteed payment, the partnership deducts the $10,000 in its calendar year ended December 31, 1996, and Rachel includes the $10,000 in her income for the 1996 calendar year. That Rachel is a cash basis taxpayer and does not actually receive the cash in 1996 is irrelevant.

If the payment is classified as a payment to an outsider, the partnership cannot deduct the payment until Rachel actually receives the cash. If, for example, Rachel performs janitorial services (i.e., not in her capacity as a partner) and receives the cash on March 25, 1997, the partnership deducts the payment and Rachel recognizes the income on that date. ▼

Sales of Property. Certain sales of property fall under special rules. No loss is recognized on a sale of property between a person and a partnership when the person owns, directly or indirectly, more than 50 percent of partnership capital or profits.[52] The disallowed loss may not vanish entirely, however. If the transferee eventually sells the property at a gain, the disallowed loss reduces the gain that the transferee would otherwise recognize.

---

[50] § 707(a).
[51] § 267(a)(2).

[52] § 707(b).

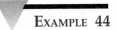
EXAMPLE 44

Barry sells land (adjusted basis to him, $30,000; fair market value, $45,000) to a partnership in which he controls a 60% capital interest. The partnership pays him $20,000 for the land. Barry cannot deduct his $10,000 realized loss. The sale apparently was not at arm's length, but the taxpayer's intentions are irrelevant. Barry and the partnership are related parties, and the loss is disallowed.

When the partnership sells the land to an outsider at a later date, it receives a sales price of $44,000. The partnership can offset the recognition of its $24,000 realized gain on the subsequent sale ($44,000 sales proceeds – $20,000 adjusted basis) by the amount of the $10,000 prior disallowed loss ($20,000 – $30,000). Thus, the partnership recognizes a $14,000 gain on its sale of the land. ▼

Using a similar rationale, any gain that is realized on a sale or exchange between a partner and a partnership in which the partner controls a capital or profit interest of 50 percent or more must be recognized as ordinary income, unless the asset is a capital asset to both the seller and the purchaser.[53]

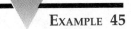
EXAMPLE 45

Kristin purchases some land (adjusted basis, $30,000; fair market value, $45,000) for $45,000 from a partnership in which she controls a 90% profit interest. The land was a capital asset to the partnership. If Kristin holds the land as a capital asset, the partnership recognizes a $15,000 capital gain. However, if Kristin is a land developer and the property is not a capital asset to her, the partnership must recognize $15,000 of ordinary income from the sale, even though the property was a capital asset to the entity. ▼

PARTNERS AS EMPLOYEES

A partner usually does not qualify as an employee for tax purposes. Thus, a partner receiving guaranteed payments is not regarded as an employee for purposes of withholding taxes. Moreover, since a partner is not an employee of the partnership, the entity cannot deduct its payments for the partner's fringe benefits. A general partner's distributive share of ordinary partnership income is generally subject to the Federal self-employment tax.[54]

Concept Summary 22-3 reviews partner-partnership transactions.

DISTRIBUTIONS FROM THE PARTNERSHIP

The tax treatment of withdrawals from a partnership to a partner was introduced earlier. This section will expand that discussion by examining in greater detail the effect of nonliquidating distributions made during the normal operations of the partnership. In addition, distributions to partners in complete liquidation of their ownership interests and sales of partnership interests are discussed. For a more complete discussion of these topics, see Chapter 11 of *West's Federal Taxation: Corporations, Partnerships, Estates, and Trusts* (1997 edition).

A **nonliquidating distribution** is any distribution from a continuing partnership to a continuing partner—that is, any distribution that is not a liquidating distribution. There are two types of nonliquidating distributions: draws or partial liquidations. A *draw* is a distribution of a partner's share of current or accumulated partnership profits that have been taxed to the partner in current or prior taxable

---

[53] § 707(b)(2).   [54] § 1402(a).

▼

CONCEPT SUMMARY 22–3

Partner-Partnership Transactions

1. Partners can transact business with their partnerships in a nonpartner capacity. These transactions include such things as the sale and exchange of property, rentals, loans of funds, etc.
2. A payment to a partner may be classified as a guaranteed payment if it is for services or use of the partner's capital and is not based on partnership income. A guaranteed payment may be deductible by the partnership and is included in the partner's income on the last day of the partnership's taxable year.
3. A payment to a partner may be treated as being to an outside (though related) party. Such a payment is deductible by the partnership at the time the partner must include the amount in income under his or her method of accounting.
4. Guaranteed payments and payments to a partner that are treated as being to an outside party are only deductible if the underlying reason for the payment constitutes an ordinary and necessary (rather than capitalizable) business expense.
5. Losses are disallowed between a partner or related party and a partnership when the partner or related party owns more than a 50% interest in the partnership's capital or profits.
6. When there is income from a related-party sale, it is treated as ordinary income if the property is a capital asset to the transferor, but not to the transferee.

years of the partnership. A *partial liquidation* is a distribution that reduces the partner's interest in partnership capital but does not liquidate the partner's entire interest in the partnership. The distinction between the two types of *nonliquidating* distributions is largely semantic, since the basic tax treatment typically does not differ.

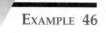

EXAMPLE 46

Kay joins the calendar year KLM Partnership on January 1, 1996, by contributing $40,000 of cash to the partnership in exchange for a one-third interest in partnership capital, profits, and losses. Her distributive share of partnership income for the year is $25,000. If the partnership distributes $65,000 ($25,000 share of partnership profits + $40,000 initial capital contribution) to Kay on December 31, 1996, the distribution is a nonliquidating distribution as long as Kay continues to be a partner in the partnership. This is true even though Kay receives her share of profits plus her entire investment in the partnership. In this case, $25,000 is considered a draw, and the remaining $40,000 is a partial liquidation of Kay's interest. ▼

A payment from a partnership to a partner is not necessarily treated as a distribution. For example, as discussed earlier, a partnership may pay interest or rent to a partner for use of the partner's capital or property, make a guaranteed payment to a partner, or purchase property from a partner. If a payment *is* treated as a distribution, it is not necessarily treated under general distribution rules. For example, gain is typically deferred when property is distributed to a partner. In certain circumstances, however, gain on a property distribution is recognized.

Finally, a distribution may be either proportionate or disproportionate. In **a proportionate distribution,** a partner receives his or her respective share of certain ordinary income-producing assets of the partnership. A **disproportionate distribution** occurs when the distribution increases or decreases the distributee partner's proportionate interest in certain ordinary income-producing assets. The tax treatment of disproportionate distributions is very complex and is beyond the scope of this discussion.

PROPORTIONATE NONLIQUIDATING DISTRIBUTIONS

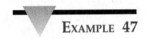

10   LEARNING OBJECTIVE
Determine the tax treatment of proportionate nonliquidating distributions from a partnership to a partner.

In general, neither the partner nor the partnership recognizes gain or loss when a nonliquidating distribution occurs.[55] The partner usually takes a carryover basis in the assets distributed.[56] The distributee partner's outside basis is reduced (but not below zero) by the amount of cash and the adjusted basis of property distributed.[57]

Note the difference between the tax theory governing distributions from C corporations and partnerships. In a C corporation, a distribution from current or accumulated income (earnings and profits) is taxable as a dividend to the shareholder, and the corporation does not receive a deduction for the amount distributed. This is an example of corporate income being subject to double taxation. In a partnership, a distribution from current or accumulated profits is not taxable because Congress has decided that partnership income should be subject to only a single level of taxation. If a partner pays taxes on the share of income earned by the partnership, this income is not taxed again when it is distributed to the partner.

This result makes sense under entity and aggregate concepts. The entity concept is applicable to corporate dividends, so any amount paid as a dividend is a transfer between two parties and is taxed accordingly. Under the aggregate theory, though, a partner receiving a distribution from partnership income is merely receiving a share of that income—whether the income is retained inside the partnership or outside in the hands of the partner makes no difference. The following examples illustrate that a distribution does not change a partner's economic position.

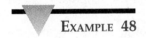

EXAMPLE 47

Jay is a one-fourth partner in the JP Partnership. His basis in his partnership interest is $40,000 on December 31, 1996. The fair market value of the interest is $70,000. The partnership distributes $25,000 of cash to him on that date. The distribution is not taxable to Jay or the partnership. The distribution reduces Jay's adjusted basis in the partnership to $15,000 ($40,000 − $25,000), and the fair market value of his partnership interest is, arguably, reduced to $45,000 ($70,000 − $25,000). ▼

EXAMPLE 48

Assume the same facts as in Example 47, except that the partnership distributes both the $25,000 cash and land with an adjusted basis to the partnership of $13,000 and a fair market value of $30,000 on the date of distribution. The distribution is not taxable to Jay or the partnership. Jay reduces his basis in the partnership to $2,000 [$40,000 − ($25,000 + $13,000)] and takes a carryover basis of $13,000 in the land. The fair market value of Jay's remaining interest in the partnership is, arguably, reduced to $15,000 [$70,000 − ($25,000 + $30,000)].

If Jay had sold his partnership interest for $70,000 rather than receiving the distribution, he would have realized and recognized gain of $30,000 ($70,000 selling price − $40,000 outside basis). Because he has not recognized any gain or loss on the distribution of cash and land, he should still have the $30,000 of deferred gain to recognize at some point in the future. This is exactly what will happen. If Jay sells the cash, land, and remaining partnership interest on January 1, 1997, the day after the distribution, he realizes and recognizes gains of $17,000 ($30,000 − $13,000) on the land and $13,000 ($15,000 − $2,000) on the partnership interest. These gains total $30,000, which is the amount of the original deferred gain. ▼

---

[55] § 731(a)(1).
[56] § 732(a)(1).

[57] § 733.

Gain and Loss Recognition.   A partner recognizes gain from a nonliquidating distribution to the extent that the *cash* received exceeds the outside basis of his or her interest in the partnership.[58] In a nonliquidating distribution, losses are not recognized.

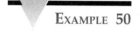

EXAMPLE 49

Samantha is a one-third partner in the SMP Partnership. Her basis in this ownership interest is $50,000 on December 31, 1996, after accounting for the calendar year entity's 1996 operations and for her 1996 capital contributions and withdrawals. On December 31, 1996, the partnership distributes $60,000 cash to Samantha. She recognizes a $10,000 gain from this distribution ($60,000 cash received – $50,000 basis in her partnership interest). Most likely, this gain is taxed as a capital gain.[59] ▼

Whereas distributions *from* accumulated earnings are taxed differently to shareholders and partners (as a result of differing tax objectives), cash distributions *in excess* of accumulated profits are taxed similarly for corporate shareholders and partners in partnerships. The shareholder or partner is allowed to recover the cumulative capital invested in the entity tax-free.

Recall from earlier in the chapter that the reduction of a partner's share of partnership debt is treated as a distribution of cash from the partnership to the partner. A reduction of a partner's share of partnership debt, then, reduces the partner's basis in the interest. Any reduction of a share of debt in excess of a partner's basis in the partnership interest is taxable as a gain.

EXAMPLE 50

Returning to the facts of Example 49, assume that Samantha's $50,000 basis in her partnership interest included a $60,000 share of partnership liabilities. If the partnership repays all of its liabilities, Samantha is treated as receiving a $60,000 distribution from the partnership. Since this distribution exceeds the basis in her partnership interest, she recognizes a gain of $10,000. ▼

A distribution of marketable securities can also be treated as a distribution of cash. Determining treatment of such distributions is complicated though, since several exceptions may apply and the basis in the distributed stock must be calculated. Discussion of such distributions is beyond the scope of this chapter.

Property Distributions.   In general, gains do not arise on property distributions. If the basis of property distributed by a partnership exceeds the partner's basis in the partnership interest, the basis in interest is substituted for the asset basis. This ensures the partner does not receive asset basis that is not "paid for."

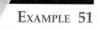

EXAMPLE 51

Mary has a $50,000 basis in her partnership interest. The partnership distributes land it owns with a basis and a fair market value of $60,000. Mary does not recognize any gain on this distribution because it is a distribution of property. However, Mary should not be allowed to take a carryover basis of $60,000 in the land, when her basis in her partnership interest is only $50,000. Therefore, the Code provides that Mary takes a substituted basis of $50,000 in the land. Her basis in her partnership interest is reduced by the basis she takes in the asset received, or $50,000. Therefore, Mary has a $50,000 basis in the land and a $0 basis in her partnership interest, and she recognizes no gain on this distribution. ▼

---

[58] § 731(a)(1).

[59] § 731(a). If the partnership holds any "hot assets," however, some or all of the $10,000 gain would be recognized as ordinary income. See § 751(b) and the related discussion of ordinary income ("hot") assets later in this chapter.

Ordering Rules. When the inside basis of the distributed assets exceeds the distributee partner's outside basis, the Code requires that the assets be deemed distributed in the following order:

- Cash is distributed first.
- Unrealized receivables and inventory are distributed second.
- All other assets are distributed last.

Since the partner typically does not recognize a gain from a *property* distribution, the Code provides that the partner's basis for property received cannot exceed the partner's basis in the partnership interest immediately prior to the distribution. For each level of asset distribution, the relevant adjustments are made to the partner's basis in the interest. In other words, after a cash distribution, the partner's basis in the interest is recomputed before determining the effect of a distribution of unrealized receivables or inventory. The basis is recomputed again before determining the effect of a distribution of other assets. If the remaining outside basis at any step is insufficient to cover the entire inside basis of the assets in the next class, that remaining outside basis is allocated pro rata among the assets within that class in accordance with their relative inside bases.[60]

EXAMPLE 52

Sally has a $50,000 basis in her partnership interest. Assume the partnership distributes cash of $12,000, cash basis receivables with an inside basis of zero and fair market value of $10,000, and two parcels of land to Sally. These parcels have a basis to the partnership of $15,000 and $45,000, respectively. The fair market value of each parcel is $50,000.

Step 1. Determine the order in which these assets are distributed. According to the Code, the cash is treated as being distributed first, the unrealized receivables second, and the two parcels of land last.

Step 2. Determine if Sally recognizes any gain as a result of the distribution. Since the $12,000 of cash that Sally receives in the distribution does not exceed the basis for her partnership interest, she recognizes none of the $72,000 gain realized on the transfer. The realized gain consists of the $122,000 amount realized ($12,000 + 10,000 + $50,000 + $50,000) less Samantha's $50,000 basis in the partnership interest.

Step 3. Determine the basis Sally takes in each distributed asset and the effect of the distribution on her outside basis. Sally first assigns a $12,000 basis to the cash. After the cash distribution, the basis in the partnership interest is $38,000 ($50,000 – $12,000). Next, she assigns a zero carryover basis to the unrealized receivables that she receives from the partnership. Her remaining outside basis is still $38,000 [$50,000 – ($12,000 + $0)]. The land parcels are deemed distributed last. Samantha's remaining basis of $38,000 is less than the partnership's inside basis of $60,000 ($15,000 + $45,000) in the land parcels. Therefore, she must take a substituted basis of $38,000 in the land.

Sally allocates the $38,000 outside basis to the land parcels proportionately based on their adjusted inside *bases* to the partnership (not according to their relative fair market values). Sally takes a $9,500 basis in the first parcel of land, computed as follows:

$$\$38,000 \times \frac{\$15,000}{\$60,000} = \$9,500$$

The second parcel of land takes a $28,500 basis to Sally, computed as follows:

---

[60] § 732 and Reg. § 1.732–1(c)(1).

$$\$38,000 \times \frac{\$45,000}{\$60,000} = \$28,500$$

▼

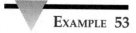

EXAMPLE 53

Assume the same facts as in Example 52. If Sally sells both parcels of land early the following year at their fair market values, she will receive proceeds of $100,000 ($50,000 + $50,000). In addition, she collects $10,000 for the cash basis receivables. Consequently, she recognizes all of the $72,000 gain that she deferred upon receiving the property from the partnership [$100,000 amount realized – $38,000 adjusted basis for the two parcels of land ($9,500 + $28,500) + 10,000 received – $0 adjusted basis for the receivables]. ▼

Review the tax results of Example 52. Although Sally does not recognize any of the gain from the distribution, she has a zero outside basis for her partnership interest. If Sally expects the partnership to generate net losses in the near future, she will not find this zero basis attractive. She will be unable to deduct her share of the losses when they flow through to her on the last day of the partnership's tax year.

The low basis that Sally has assigned to the parcels of land is of no tax detriment to her if she does not intend to sell the land in the near future. Since land does not generate cost recovery deductions, the substituted basis is used only to determine Sally's gain or loss upon her disposition of the parcels in a taxable sale or exchange.

Concept Summary 22–4 summarizes the rules for nonliquidating distributions.

CONCEPT SUMMARY 22–4

Proportionate Nonliquidating Distributions (General Rules)

1. Neither the distributee partner nor the partnership recognizes any gain or loss on a nonliquidating distribution. If cash distributed exceeds the distributee partner's outside basis, however, gain is recognized. Property distributions generally do not result in gain recognition.
2. The distributee partner usually takes the same basis the distributed property had to the partnership. However, where the inside basis of distributed property exceeds the partner's outside basis, the basis assigned to the distributed property cannot exceed that outside basis.
3. Gain recognized by the distributee partner on a nonliquidating distribution is usually capital in nature.
4. Loss is never recognized on a proportionate nonliquidating distribution.

Calculations

1. Partner's outside basis. _____
2. Less: Cash distributed to partner. _____
3. Gain recognized by partner (excess of Line 2 over Line 1). _____
4. Partner's remaining outside basis (Line 1 – Line 2). If less than $0, enter $0. _____
5. Partner's basis in unrealized receivables and inventory distributed (enter lesser of Line 4 or the partnership's inside basis of the unrealized receivables and inventory). _____
6. Basis available to allocate to other property distributed (Line 4 – Line 5). _____
7. Partnership's inside basis of other property distributed. _____
8. Basis to partner of other property distributed (enter lesser of Line 6 or Line 7). _____
9. Partner's remaining outside basis (Line 6 – Line 8). _____

PROPORTIONATE LIQUIDATING DISTRIBUTIONS

11 LEARNING OBJECTIVE
Determine the tax treatment of proportionate distributions that liquidate a partnership.

Proportionate **liquidating distributions** consist of a single distribution or a series of distributions that result in the termination of the partner's entire interest in the partnership. This section examines situations when a partner's interest is liquidated because the partnership is liquidating.

Gain Recognition and Ordering Rules. When a partnership liquidates, the liquidating distributions to a partner usually consist of an interest in several or all of the partnership assets. The gain recognition and ordering rules parallel those for nonliquidating distributions, except that the partner's *entire* basis in the partnership interest is allocated to the assets received in the liquidating distribution, unless the partner is allowed to recognize a loss. A loss can be recognized when *only* cash, unrealized receivables, or inventory are received in the distribution. As a result of the ordering rules, the basis of some assets may be adjusted upward or downward to absorb the partner's remaining outside basis. Unrealized receivables or inventory are never "stepped up," although they may be "stepped down." The partnership itself typically does not recognize either gain or loss on a liquidating distribution.

The ordering and gain recognition rules for a liquidating distribution are summarized as follows:

- Cash is distributed first and results in a gain (generally capital) to the extent the distribution exceeds the partner's basis in the partnership interest. The amount distributed reduces the liquidated partner's outside basis dollar for dollar.
- The partner's remaining outside basis is then allocated to unrealized receivables and inventory up to an amount equal to the partnership's adjusted bases in that property. If the partnership's bases in the unrealized receivables and inventory exceed the partner's remaining outside basis, the remaining outside basis is allocated to the unrealized receivables and inventory in the ratio of their inside bases to the partnership.
- Finally, if the liquidating partner has any remaining outside basis, that basis is allocated pro rata to any other assets received according to their inside bases to the partnership.[61]

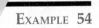 EXAMPLE 54

When Tara's basis in her partnership interest is $25,000, she receives cash of $15,000 and a proportionate share of inventory and buildings in a distribution that liquidates both the partnership and her entire partnership interest. The inventory has a basis to the partnership of $20,000 and a fair market value of $30,000. The building's basis is $8,000, and the fair market value is $12,000. The building is not subject to depreciation recapture. Under these circumstances, Tara recognizes no gain or loss. After reducing Tara's $25,000 basis by the $15,000 cash received, the remaining $10,000 is allocated to the inventory. The basis of the inventory in Tara's hands is $10,000, and the basis of the building is zero.

Of the partnership's original bases of $20,000 in the inventory and $8,000 in the building, Tara is allocated only $10,000 in the inventory. The remaining $10,000 basis in inventory and $8,000 basis in the building appear to have been "lost" in the liquidating distribution. The partnership may be able to "save" this portion of the basis by making an election to adjust the basis of its remaining property upward. ▼

EXAMPLE 55

Assume the same facts as in Example 54, except that there was no inventory and Tara received two buildings (neither of which is subject to depreciation recapture). Building 1

[61]§§ 731 and 732.

had a basis of $6,000 to the partnership, and Building 2 had a basis of $9,000. Again, no gain or loss is recognized. The $10,000 basis of Tara's interest after reduction for the $15,000 cash received is allocated to the buildings in the ratio of their bases to the partnership. Tara's basis in Building 1 is $4,000 (6/15 × $10,000), and her basis in Building 2 is $6,000 (9/15 × $10,000). ▼

Loss Recognition. The distributee partner may also recognize a *loss* on a liquidating distribution. The partner recognizes a loss if both of the following are true:

- The partner receives *only* money, unrealized receivables, or inventory.
- The partner's outside basis in the partnership interest exceeds the partnership's inside basis for the assets distributed. This excess amount is the loss recognized by the distributee partner.[62]

The word "only" is important. A distribution of any other property postpones recognition of the loss.

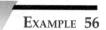

EXAMPLE 56

When Ramon's basis is $40,000, he receives a liquidating distribution of $7,000 cash and a proportionate share of inventory having a partnership basis of $3,000 and a fair market value of $10,000. Ramon cannot "step up" the basis in the inventory so it is allocated a $3,000 carryover basis. Ramon's unutilized basis is $30,000. Since he received a liquidating distribution of *only* cash, unrealized receivables, or inventory, he recognizes a capital loss of $30,000 on the liquidation. ▼

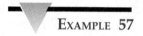

EXAMPLE 57

Assume the same facts as in Example 56, except that in addition to the cash and inventory, Ramon receives the desk he used in the partnership. The desk has an adjusted basis of $100 to the partnership. Applying the rules outlined above to this revised fact situation produces the following results:

Step 1. Cash of $7,000 is distributed to Ramon and reduces his outside basis to $33,000.
Step 2. Inventory is distributed to Ramon. He takes a $3,000 carryover basis in the inventory and reduces his outside basis in the partnership to $30,000.
Step 3. The desk is distributed to Ramon. Since the desk is not cash, an unrealized receivable, or inventory, he cannot recognize a loss. Therefore, Ramon's remaining basis in his partnership interest is allocated to the desk. He takes a $30,000 basis for the desk. ▼

What can Ramon do with a $30,000 desk? If he continues to use it in a trade or business, he can depreciate it. Once he has established his business use of the desk, he could sell it and recognize a large § 1231 loss. If the loss is isolated in the year of the sale, it is an ordinary loss. Thus, with proper planning, no liquidated partner should be forced to recognize a capital loss.

Gain recognized by the withdrawing partner on the subsequent disposition of inventory is always ordinary income, unless the disposition occurs more than five years after the distribution.[63] The withdrawing partner's holding period for all other property received in a liquidating distribution includes the partnership's related holding period.

[62] § 731(a)(2).
[63] § 735(a)(2).

SALE OF A PARTNERSHIP INTEREST

12 **LEARNING OBJECTIVE**
Calculate the selling partner's amount and character of gain or loss on the sale or exchange of a partnership interest.

A partner can sell or exchange a partnership interest, in whole or in part. The transaction can be between the partner and a third party; in this case, it is similar (in concept) to a sale of corporate stock. The transfer of a partnership interest produces different results than the corporate transfer, though, because both the entity and aggregate concepts apply to the partnership situation, whereas only entity concepts apply to a sale of stock. The effect of the different rules is that gain or loss resulting from a sale of a partnership interest may be divided into capital gain or loss and ordinary income.

GENERAL RULES

Generally, the sale or exchange of a partnership interest results in gain or loss, measured by the difference between the amount realized and the selling partner's adjusted basis in the partnership interest.[64]

Liabilities. In computing the amount realized and the adjusted basis of the interest sold, the selling partner's share of partnership liabilities must be determined. The purchasing partner includes any assumed indebtedness as a part of the consideration paid for the partnership interest.[65]

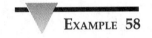

EXAMPLE 58

Cole originally contributed $50,000 in cash for a one-third interest in the CDE Partnership. During the time Cole was a partner, his share of partnership income was $90,000, and he withdrew $60,000 cash. Cole's capital account balance is now $80,000, and partnership liabilities are $45,000, of which Cole's share is $15,000. Cole's outside basis is $95,000 ($80,000 capital account + $15,000 share of partnership debts).

Cole sells his partnership interest to Freda for $110,000 cash, with Freda assuming Cole's share of partnership liabilities. The total amount realized by Cole is $125,000 ($110,000 cash received + $15,000 of partnership debts transferred to Freda). Cole's gain on the sale is $30,000 ($125,000 realized − adjusted basis of $95,000).

Freda's adjusted basis for her partnership interest is the purchase price of $125,000 ($110,000 cash paid + $15,000 assumed partnership debt). ▼

Tax Years That Close. When a partner disposes of an entire investment in the partnership, the partnership's tax year closes for that partner as of the sale date. When a partnership's tax year closes with respect to a partner, the partner's share of income for the period during which he or she was a partner is calculated. There are several acceptable methods of determining the partner's share of income.[66]

EFFECT OF HOT ASSETS

A major exception to capital gain or loss treatment on the sale or exchange of a partnership interest arises when a partnership has **hot assets.** In general, *hot assets* are certain assets that when collected or disposed of by the partnership would cause it to recognize ordinary income. When a partner sells the interest in a partnership, it is as if he or she sold a proportionate interest in the partnership's hot assets. The partner's basis in interest must be allocated between "hot" and

---

[64]§ 741.
[65]§ 742.

[66]§ 706(d)(1) and related Regulations.

"non-hot" assets. The selling price of the interest is similarly allocated. The gain on hot assets is taxed as ordinary income. The non-hot assets can result in capital gain or loss.

Two types of hot assets must be considered: **unrealized receivables** and **substantially appreciated inventory.** An amount realized from the sale of a partnership interest that is attributable to *unrealized receivables* or *substantially appreciated inventory* is treated as being from the sale of a noncapital asset.[67] The purpose of this rule is to prevent a partner from converting ordinary income into capital gain through the sale of a partnership interest.

Unrealized Receivables.   Unrealized receivables generally include receivables from the sales of ordinary income property and rights to payments for services. They also include the accounts receivable of a cash basis partnership, the ordinary income portion (if any) of a deferred installment gain, and, for sale or exchange purposes, depreciation recapture potential.[68]

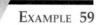

EXAMPLE 59

The cash basis Thrush Partnership owns only a $10,000 receivable for rendering health care advice. Its basis in the receivable is zero because no income has been recognized. This item is a hot asset because ordinary income is generated when Thrush collects on the account.

Harry, a 50% partner, sells his interest to Mark for $5,000. If Harry's basis in his partnership interest is $0, his total gain is $5,000. The entire gain is attributable to the unrealized receivables, so Harry's gain is taxed as ordinary income. ▼

Substantially Appreciated Inventory.   Inventory items are substantially appreciated if, at the time of their sale or distribution, their aggregate fair market value exceeds 120 percent of their total adjusted basis to the partnership. In applying this test, inventory items are evaluated as a group, rather than individually. If substantial appreciation of the entire inventory has occurred, all of the inventory items are treated as substantially appreciated, even if a specific item has not appreciated.

For this purpose, the term *inventory* includes all partnership property except money, capital assets, and § 1231 assets. Receivables of an accrual partnership are included in the definition of inventory, since they are neither capital assets nor § 1231 assets.[69]

This definition is broad enough to include all items considered to be unrealized receivables. The disadvantage of their inclusion can be seen in the calculation to determine whether the inventory is substantially appreciated. Since unrealized receivables are included at a zero basis in the substantial appreciation tests, they improve the partner's chances of incurring ordinary income.

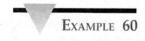

EXAMPLE 60

Jan sells her interest in the JKL Partnership to Matt for $20,000 cash. The interest has an outside basis of $15,000. On the sale date, the partnership balance sheet reflects the following:

[67] § 751(a).
[68] § 751(a)(1).

[69] § 751(d)(2).

	Adjusted Basis per Books	Market Value
Cash	$10,000	$10,000
Inventory	21,000	30,000
Non-hot assets	14,000	20,000
Total	$45,000	$60,000
Jan, capital	$15,000	$20,000
Kelly, capital	15,000	20,000
Lynn, capital	15,000	20,000
Total	$45,000	$60,000

The inventory is substantially appreciated. The appreciation is 143% ($30,000 ÷ $21,000), which is above the 120% threshold.

Jan's share of the inside basis of the inventory is $7,000 ($21,000 × ⅓). Jan is deemed to have sold this share of inventory for $10,000 ($30,000 × ⅓), thereby creating ordinary income of $3,000 on the sale of the hot asset. Jan recognizes the $3,000 ordinary income and $2,000 of capital gain from the rest of the sale:

Remaining sales price ($20,000 gross sales price − $10,000 allocated to hot asset sale)	$10,000
Remaining outside basis ($15,000 original outside basis − $7,000 allocated to hot asset sale)	(8,000)
Capital gain	$ 2,000

▼

CHOOSING PARTNERSHIP TAXATION

TAX PLANNING CONSIDERATIONS

Concept Summary 22–5 lists various factors that the owners of a business should consider in deciding whether to use a C corporation, S corporation, or partnership as a means of doing business.

FORMATION AND OPERATION OF A PARTNERSHIP

13 LEARNING OBJECTIVE
Provide insights regarding advantageous use of a partnership.

Potential partners should be cautious in transferring assets to a partnership to ensure that they are not required to recognize any gain upon the creation of the entity. The nonrecognition provisions of § 721 are relatively straightforward and resemble the provisions under § 351. However, any partner can make a tax-deferred contribution of assets to the entity either at the inception of the partnership or later. This possibility is not available to less-than-controlling shareholders in a corporation.

The partners should anticipate the tax benefits and pitfalls that are presented in Subchapter K and should take appropriate actions to resolve any resulting problems. Typically, all that is needed is an appropriate provision in the partnership agreement (e.g., with respect to differing allocation percentages for gains and losses). Recall, however, that a special allocation of income, expense, or credit items in the partnership agreement must satisfy certain requirements before it is acceptable to the IRS.

> ▼ **CONCEPT SUMMARY 22–5**
>
> ## Advantages and Disadvantages of the Partnership Form
>
> The partnership form may be attractive when one or more of the following factors is present:
>
> - The entity is generating net taxable losses and/or valuable tax credits, which will be of use to the owners.
> - Other means by which to reduce the effects of the double taxation of business income (e.g., compensation to owners, interest, and rental payments) have been exhausted.
> - The entity does not generate material amounts of tax preference and adjustment items, which increase the alternative minimum tax liabilities of its owners.
> - The entity is generating net passive income, which its owners can use to claim immediate deductions for net passive losses that they have generated from other sources.
> - Given the asset holdings and distribution practices of the entity, the possibility of liability under the accumulated earnings and personal holding company taxes is significant.
> - Restrictions relative to S corporation status (e.g., the 35-shareholder maximum or the restriction to one class of outstanding stock) are not attractive.
> - The owners wish to make special allocations of certain income or deduction items that are not possible under the C or S corporation forms.
> - The owners anticipate liquidation of the entity within a short period of time. Liquidation of a corporation would generate entity-level recognized gains on appreciated property distributed.
> - The owners have adequate bases in their partnership interests to facilitate the deduction of flow-through losses and the assignment of an adequate basis to assets distributed in-kind to the partners.
>
> The partnership form may be less attractive when one or more of the following factors is present:
>
> - The maximum marginal tax rate applicable to individuals is above that applicable to C corporations. Currently, marginal tax rates for individuals may exceed rates applicable to corporations.
> - The entity is generating net taxable income, which is taxed directly to the owners who do not necessarily receive any funds with which to pay the tax.
> - The type of income that the entity is generating (e.g., business and portfolio income) is not as attractive to its owners as net passive income would be because the owners could use net passive income to offset the net passive losses that they have generated on their own.
> - The entity is in a high-exposure business, and the owners desire protection from personal liability. An LLC or LLP structure may be available, however, to limit personal liability.
> - The owners want to avoid Federal self-employment tax.

TRANSACTIONS BETWEEN PARTNERS AND PARTNERSHIPS

Partners should be careful when engaging in transactions with the partnership to ensure that no negative tax results occur. A partner who owns a majority of the partnership generally should not sell property at a loss to the partnership because the loss is disallowed. Similarly, a majority partner should not sell a capital asset to the partnership at a gain, if the asset is to be used by the partnership as other than a capital asset. The gain on this transaction is taxed as ordinary income to the selling partner rather than as capital gain.

As an alternative to selling property to a partnership, the partner may lease it to the partnership. The partner recognizes rent income, and the partnership has a rent expense. If the partner needs more cash immediately, the partner can sell the

---

PARTNERSHIPS AROUND THE WORLD—AND BEYOND

Technology continues to act as a catalyst—and incentive—for the creation of multinational joint ventures. AT&T, MCI, and Sprint are racing each other to align with partners in foreign telecommunications markets: each wants to have the widest service coverage area so it can offer efficient communications and computer networking to business clients with a global presence.

Pharmaceutical companies find it advantageous to allow foreign partners to promote and distribute such products as imaging agents used in the detection of various cancers. Reciprocal agreements sometimes give each partner exclusive distribution rights for products created in the partners' separate research facilities.

Finally, there's Lockheed, which plans to use joint venture capital to take technology to the skies. The company will sell high-resolution images produced by satellites funded by the venture.

At least one country, Bermuda, has recognized this trend and is trying to lure multinational joint ventures to its shores. In 1995, it passed the Overseas Partnerships Act and other legislation designed to encourage foreign investment.

---

property to an outside third party who leases the property to the partnership for a fair rental.

The timing of the deduction for payments by accrual basis partnerships to cash basis partners varies depending on whether the payment is a guaranteed payment or is treated as a payment to an outsider. If the payment is a guaranteed payment, the deduction occurs when the partnership properly accrues the payment. If the payment is treated as a payment to an outsider, the actual date the payment is made controls the timing of the deduction.

DRAFTING THE PARTNERSHIP AGREEMENT

Although a written partnership agreement is not required, many rules governing the tax consequences to partners and their partnership refer to such an agreement. Remember that a partner's distributive share of income, gain, loss, deduction, or credit is determined in accordance with the partnership agreement. Consequently, if taxpayers operating a business in partnership form want a measure of certainty as to the tax consequences of their activities, a carefully drafted partnership agreement is crucial. An agreement that sets forth the obligations, rights, and powers of the partners should prove invaluable in settling controversies among them and provide some degree of certainty as to the tax consequences of the partners' actions.

OVERALL COMPARISON: FORMS OF DOING BUSINESS

See Concept Summary 22–6 for a detailed comparison of the tax consequences of the following forms of doing business: sole proprietorship, partnership, S corporation, and regular corporation.

CONCEPT SUMMARY 22–6

Tax Attributes of Different Forms of Business (Assume Partners and Shareholders Are All Individuals)

	Sole Proprietorship	Partnership	S Corporation*	Regular Corporation**
Restrictions on type or number of owners	One owner. The owner must be an individual.	Must have at least 2 owners.	Only individuals, estates, and certain trusts can be owners. Maximum number of shareholders limited to 35.	None, except some states require a minimum of 2 shareholders.
Incidence of tax	Sole proprietorship's income and deductions are reported on Schedule C of the individual's Form 1040. A separate Schedule C is prepared for each business.	Entity not subject to tax. Partners in their separate capacity subject to tax on their distributive share of income. Partnership files Form 1065.	Except for certain capital gains, built-in gains, and violations of passive investment income tests when accumulated earnings and profits are present from C corporation tax years, entity not subject to Federal income tax. S corporation files Form 1120S. Shareholders are subject to tax on income attributable to their stock ownership.	Income subject to double taxation. Entity subject to tax, and shareholder subject to tax on any corporate dividends received. Corporation files Form 1120.
Highest tax rate	39.6% at individual level.	39.6% at partner level.	39.6% at shareholder level.	35% at corporate level plus 39.6% on any corporate dividends at shareholder level.
Choice of tax year	Same tax year as owner.	Selection generally restricted to coincide with tax year of majority partners or principal partners, or to tax year determined under the least aggregate deferral method.	Restricted to a calendar year unless IRS approves a different year for business purposes or other exceptions apply.	Unrestricted selection allowed at time of filing first tax return.

	Sole Proprietorship	Partnership	S Corporation*	Regular Corporation**
Timing of taxation	Based on owner's tax year.	Partners report their share of income in their tax year with or within which the partnership's tax year ends. Partners in their separate capacity are subject to payment of estimated taxes.	Shareholders report their share of income in their tax year with or within which the corporation's tax year ends. Generally, the corporation uses a calendar year; but see "Choice of tax year" above. Shareholders may be subject to payment of estimated taxes. Corporation may be subject to payment of estimated taxes for any taxes imposed at the corporate level.	Corporation subject to tax at close of its tax year. May be subject to payment of estimated taxes. Dividends will be subject to tax at the shareholder level in the tax year received.
Basis for allocating income to owners	Not applicable (only one owner).	Profit and loss sharing agreement. Cash basis items of cash basis partnerships are allocated on a daily basis. Other partnership items are allocated after considering varying interests of partners.	Pro rata share based on stock ownership. Shareholder's pro rata share is determined on a daily basis according to the number of shares of stock held on each day of the corporation's tax year.	Not applicable.
Contribution of property to the entity	Not a taxable transaction.	Generally, not a taxable transaction.	Is a taxable transaction unless the § 351 requirements are satisfied.	Is a taxable transaction unless the § 351 requirements are satisfied.
Character of income taxed to owners	Retains source characteristics.	Conduit—retains source characteristics.	Conduit—retains source characteristics.	All source characteristics are lost when income is distributed to owners.
Basis for allocating a net operating loss to owners	Not applicable (only one owner).	Profit and loss sharing agreement. Cash basis items of cash basis partnerships are allocated on a daily basis. Other partnership items are allocated after considering varying interests of partners.	Prorated among shareholders on a daily basis.	Not applicable.

	Sole Proprietorship	Partnership	S Corporation*	Regular Corporation**
Limitation on losses deductible by owners	Investment plus liabilities.	Partner's investment plus share of liabilities.	Shareholder's investment plus loans made by shareholder to corporation.	Not applicable.
Subject to at-risk rules	Yes, at the owner level. Indefinite carryover of excess loss.	Yes, at the partner level. Indefinite carryover of excess loss.	Yes, at the shareholder level. Indefinite carryover of excess loss.	Yes, for closely held corporations. Indefinite carryover of excess loss.
Subject to passive activity loss rules	Yes, at the owner level. Indefinite carryover of excess loss.	Yes, at the partner level. Indefinite carryover of excess loss.	Yes, at the shareholder level. Indefinite carryover of excess loss.	Yes, for closely held corporations and personal service corporations. Indefinite carryover of excess loss.
Tax consequences of earnings retained by entity	Taxed to owner when earned and increases his or her basis in the sole proprietorship.	Taxed to partners when earned and increases their respective interests in the partnership.	Taxed to shareholders when earned and increases their respective basis in stock.	Taxed to corporation as earned and may be subject to penalty tax if accumulated unreasonably.
Nonliquidating distributions to owners	Not taxable.	Not taxable unless money received exceeds recipient partner's basis in partnership interest.	Generally not taxable unless the distribution exceeds the shareholder's AAA or stock basis. Existence of accumulated earnings and profits could cause some distributions to be dividends.	Taxable in year of receipt to extent of earnings and profits or if exceeds basis in stock.
Distribution of appreciated property	Not taxable.	No recognition at the partnership level.	Recognition at the corporate level to the extent of the appreciation. Conduit—amount of recognized gain is passed through to shareholders.	Taxable at the corporate level to the extent of the appreciation.
Splitting of income among family members	Not applicable (only one owner).	Difficult—IRS will not recognize a family member as a partner unless certain requirements are met.	Rather easy—gift of stock will transfer tax on a pro rata share of income to the donee. However, IRS can make adjustments to reflect adequate compensation for services.	Same as an S corporation, except that donees will be subject to tax only on earnings actually or constructively distributed to them. Other than unreasonable compensation, IRS generally cannot make adjustments to reflect adequate compensation for services and capital.

	Sole Proprietorship	Partnership	S Corporation*	Regular Corporation**
Organizational costs	Start-up expenditures are amortizable over 60 months.	Amortizable over 60 months.	Same as partnership.	Same as partnership.
Charitable contributions	Limitations apply at owner level.	Conduit—partners are subject to deduction limitations in their own capacity.	Conduit—shareholders are subject to deduction limitations in their own capacity.	Limited to 10% of taxable income before certain deductions.
Alternative minimum tax	Applies at owner level. AMT rates are 26% and 28%.	Applies at partner level rather than at the partnership level. AMT preferences and adjustments are passed through from the partnership to the partners.	Applies at the shareholder level rather than at the corporate level. AMT preferences and adjustments are passed through from the S corporation to the shareholders.	Applies at the corporate level. AMT rate is 20%.
ACE adjustment	Does not apply.	Does not apply.	Does not apply.	The adjustment is made in calculating AMTI. The amount of the adjustment is 75% of the excess of adjusted current earnings over unadjusted AMTI. If the unadjusted AMTI exceeds adjusted current earnings, the adjustment is negative.
Tax preference items	Apply at owner level in determining AMT.	Conduit—passed through to partners who must account for such items in their separate capacity.	Conduit—passed through to shareholders who must account for such items in their separate capacity.	Subject to AMT at corporate level.
Capital gains	Taxed at owner level using maximum rate of 28%.	Conduit—partners must account for their respective shares.	Conduit, with certain exceptions (a possible penalty tax), shareholders must account for their respective shares.	Taxed at corporate level with a maximum rate of 35%. No other benefits.
Capital losses	Only $3,000 of capital losses can be offset each tax year against ordinary income. Indefinite carryover.	Conduit—partners must account for their respective shares.	Conduit—shareholders must account for their respective shares.	Carried back three years and carried forward five years. Deductible only to the extent of capital gains.
§ 1231 gains and losses	Taxable or deductible at owner level. Five-year lookback rule for § 1231 losses.	Conduit—partners must account for their respective shares.	Conduit—shareholders must account for their respective shares.	Taxable or deductible at corporate level only. Five-year lookback rule for § 1231 losses.

	Sole Proprietorship	Partnership	S Corporation*	Regular Corporation**
Foreign tax credits	Available at owner level.	Conduit—passed through to partners.	Generally conduit—passed through to shareholders.	Available at corporate level only.
§ 1244 treatment of loss on sale of interest	Not applicable.	Not applicable.	Available.	Available.
Basis treatment of entity liabilities	Includible in interest basis.	Includible in interest basis.	Not includible in stock basis.	Not includible in stock basis.
Built-in gains	Not applicable.	Not applicable.	Possible corporate tax.	Not applicable.
Special allocations to owners	Not applicable (only one owner).	Available if supported by substantial economic effect.	Not available.	Not applicable.
Availability of fringe benefits to owners	None.	None.	None unless a 2% or less shareholder.	Available within anti-discrimination rules.
Effect of liquidation/ redemption/ reorganization on basis of entity assets	Not applicable.	Usually carried over from entity to partner unless excessive cash is distributed.	Taxable step-up to fair market value.	Taxable step-up to fair market value.
Sale of ownership interest	Treated as the sale of individual assets. Classification of recognized gain or loss is dependent on the nature of the individual assets.	Treated as the sale of a partnership interest. Recognized gain or loss is classified as capital under § 741 subject to ordinary income treatment under § 751.	Treated as the sale of corporate stock. Recognized gain is classified as capital gain. Recognized loss is classified as capital loss subject to ordinary loss treatment under § 1244.	Treated as the sale of corporate stock. Recognized gain is classified as capital gain. Recognized loss is classified as capital loss subject to ordinary loss treatment under § 1244.

*Refer to Chapter 21 for additional details on S corporations.
**Refer to Chapters 16 through 20 for additional details on regular corporations.

KEY TERMS

PROBLEM MATERIALS

DISCUSSION QUESTIONS

1. What is a partnership for Federal income tax purposes?

2. To what extent are the personal assets of a general partner, limited partner, or member of an LLC subject to (a) contractual liability (e.g., trade account payable) and (b) tort liability (e.g., malpractice) claims against the entity that party owns? Answer the question for partners or members in a general partnership, LLP, LLC, and limited partnership.

3. Compare the nonrecognition of gain or loss provision on contributions to a partnership with the similar provision with respect to corporate formation. What are the major differences and similarities?

4. In what situations can formation of a partnership result in a taxable gain to one or more of the new partners?

5. What types of expenditures might a new partnership incur? How will these costs be treated for Federal income tax purposes?

6. Describe the three tests a partnership must use to determine its required taxable year, and list alternative years that may be available to the partnership.

7. What effect does the contribution of property subject to a liability have on the basis of the contributing partner's interest? What is the effect on the basis of the other partners' interests?

8. Describe the procedure for allocating a nonrecourse debt related to appreciated property contributed by a partner, where the debt exceeds the partner's basis in the contributed property. What is the purpose of this allocation system?

9. Discuss the adjustments that must be made to a partner's basis in his or her partnership interest. When are such adjustments made?

10. To what extent can partners deduct their distributive shares of partnership losses? What happens to any unused losses?

11. Discuss the advantages and disadvantages of the partnership entity form.

12. Sam has operated a microbrewery (sole proprietorship) in southern Oregon for the past 15 years. The business has been highly profitable lately, and demand for the product

will soon exceed the amount Sam can produce with his present facilities. Marcie, a long-time fan of the brewery, has offered to invest $1,500,000 for equipment to expand production. The assets and goodwill of the brewery are currently worth $1,000,000 (tax basis is only $200,000). Sam will continue to manage the business. He is not willing to own less than 50% of whatever arrangement they arrive at. What issues should Sam and Marcie address and document before finalizing their venture?

13. Harlen will contribute $50,000 cash to the HJ Partnership. Jane currently operates a sole proprietorship with assets valued at $50,000. Jane's tax basis in these assets is $75,000. Jane will either contribute these assets to the partnership in exchange for a 50% interest, or she will sell the assets to Brady Salvage (a third party) for their $50,000 fair market value and contribute that cash to the partnership. The partnership needs assets similar to those Jane owns, but it can purchase new assets from a third party for $60,000. Describe the tax consequences of each alternative to both Jane and the partnership.

PROBLEMS

14. Morgan and Martin formed the M&M Partnership on January 1 of the current year. Martin contributed $25,000 cash and land with a fair market value of $10,000 and an adjusted basis of $2,000. Morgan contributed equipment with a fair market value of $35,000 and an adjusted basis of $20,000. Morgan had previously used the equipment in his sole proprietorship.
    a. How much gain or loss will Martin, Morgan, and the partnership realize?
    b. How much gain or loss will Martin, Morgan, and the partnership recognize?
    c. What bases will Martin and Morgan take in their partnership interests?
    d. What bases will M&M take in the assets it receives?
    e. Are there any differences between inside and outside basis?
    f. How will the partnership depreciate any assets it receives from the partners?

15. Three years after the S&P Partnership is formed, Sylvia, a 25% partner, contributes an additional $25,000 cash and land she has held for investment. Sylvia's basis in the land is $15,000, and its fair market value is $10,000. Her basis in the partnership interest was $50,000 before this contribution. The partnership uses the land as a parking lot for four years and then sells it for $8,000.
    a. How much gain or loss does Sylvia recognize on the contribution?
    b. What is Sylvia's basis in her partnership interest immediately following this contribution?
    c. How much gain or loss does S&P recognize on this contribution?
    d. What is S&P's basis in the property it receives from Sylvia?
    e. How much gain or loss does the partnership recognize on the later sale of the land, and what is the character of the gain or loss? How much is allocated to Sylvia?

16. Block, Inc., a calendar year general contractor, and Strauss, Inc., a development corporation with a July 31 year-end, formed the equal SB Partnership on January 1 of the current year. The partnership was formed to construct and lease shopping centers in Wilmington, Delaware. Block contributed equipment (basis of $650,000, fair market value of $650,000), building permits, and architectural designs that had been created by Block's employees (basis of $0, fair market value of $100,000).

    Strauss contributed land (basis of $50,000, fair market value of $250,000) and cash of $500,000. The cash was used as follows:

Legal fees for drafting partnership agreement	$10,000
Materials and labor costs for construction in progress on shopping center	400,000
Office expense (utilities, rent, overhead, etc.)	90,000

    What issues must the partnership address in preparing its initial tax return?

17. Craig and Beth are equal members of the CB Partnership, formed on June 1 of the current year. Craig contributed land that he inherited from his father three years ago. Craig's father purchased the land in 1946 for $6,000. The land was worth

$50,000 when the father died. The fair market value of the land was $75,000 at the date it was contributed to the partnership.

Beth has significant experience developing real estate. After the partnership is formed, she will prepare a plan for developing the property and secure zoning approvals for the partnership. She would normally bill a third party $25,000 for these efforts. Beth will also contribute $50,000 cash in exchange for her 50% interest in the partnership. The value of her 50% interest is $75,000.

a. How much gain or income will Craig recognize on his contribution of the land to the partnership? What is the character of any gain or income recognized?
b. What basis will Craig take in his partnership interest?
c. How much gain or income will Beth recognize on the formation of the partnership? What is the character of any gain or income recognized?
d. What basis will Beth take in her partnership interest?
e. Construct an opening balance sheet for the partnership reflecting the partnership's basis in assets and the fair market value of these assets.
f. Outline any planning opportunities that may minimize current taxation to any of the parties.

18. Continue with the facts presented in Problem 17. At the end of the first year, the partnership distributes the $50,000 cash to Craig. No distribution is made to Beth.
a. Under general tax rules, how would the payment to Craig be treated?
b. How much income or gain would Craig recognize as a result of the payment?
c. What basis would the partnership take in the land Craig contributed under general tax rules?
d. What alternate treatment might the IRS try to impose?
e. Under the alternate treatment, how much income or gain would Craig recognize?
f. Under the alternate treatment, what basis would the partnership take in the land contributed by Craig?

19. The MDB Partnership was formed to acquire land and subdivide it as residential housing lots. On March 1, 1995, Maria contributed land valued at $60,000 to the partnership, in exchange for a one-third interest in MDB. She had purchased the land in 1990 for $76,000 and held it for investment purposes (capital asset). The partnership holds the land as inventory.

On the same date, Barry contributed land valued at $60,000 that he had purchased in 1988 for $48,000. He also became a one-third owner. Barry is a real estate developer, but this land was held personally for investment purposes. The partnership also holds this land as inventory.

Deborah had sold a parcel of land held for development purposes in 1993 on the installment basis. She, too, is a real estate developer. The installment note has a fair market value and remaining principal balance of $60,000. She contributed this note to the partnership in exchange for her one-third interest. Deborah's basis in the note was $36,000 on the contribution date; the deferred gain on the installment sale is $24,000.

From 1995 to 2000, the partnership collects $10,000 per year on the installment obligation (plus adequate interest on the unpaid balance).

In 1996, the partnership sells one-half of the land contributed by Maria for $27,000. In 2001, MDB sells the other half of the land contributed by Maria for $36,000.

In 1998, the partnership sells one-half of the subdivided real estate contributed by Barry for $33,000. The other half is finally sold in 2004 for $42,000.

a. What is each partner's initial basis in his or her partnership interest?
b. What is the amount of gross profit recognized each year on collection of the installment proceeds? What is the character of the gain or loss?
c. What is the amount of gain or loss recognized each year on the sale of the land contributed by Maria? What is the character of this gain or loss?
d. What is the amount of gain or loss recognized each year on the sale of the land contributed by Barry? What is the character of this gain or loss?

20. Continuing with Problem 19, the MDB Partnership agreement provides that all gains and losses are allocated equally among the partners, unless otherwise required under the tax law.

a. How will the gains or losses determined in parts (b), (c), and (d) above be allocated to each of the partners?

b. If the partnership earns $15,000 of interest income on the installment note, how will this income be allocated to the partners? Assume no accrued interest existed on the day the note was contributed.

c. Calculate each partner's basis in his or her partnership interest at December 31, 2004. Assume the partnership has no transactions through the end of the year 2004 other than the transactions described in Problem 19 and the collection of $15,000 of interest income per (b) above. Why are these balances the same or different?

21. The cash method Thrush Partnership, which reports on a calendar year basis, incurred the following organization and syndication costs in 1996:

Attorney fees for preparing partnership agreement	$2,100
Printing costs for preparing documents that were used to help sell the partnership interests	4,000
Accounting fees for tax advice of an organizational nature	2,400

The attorney fees and printing costs were incurred and paid in 1996. The accounting fees were incurred in December 1996 and paid in February 1997. If the partnership begins business in July 1996, how much of the organization costs can be amortized in 1996? In 1997?

22. Ron, Pat, and Matt form the RPM Partnership on January 1 of the current year. Ron is a 50% partner, and Pat and Matt are each 25% partners. Each partner and RPM use the cash method of accounting. For reporting purposes, Ron uses a calendar year, Pat uses an October 31 fiscal year, and Matt uses a June 30 fiscal year. What is RPM's required tax year under the least aggregate deferral method?

23. Lisa and Lori are equal members of the Redbird Partnership. They are real estate investors who formed the partnership several years ago with equal cash contributions. Redbird then purchased a piece of land.

On January 1 of the current year, to acquire a one-third interest in the entity, Lana contributed some land she had held for investment to the partnership. Lana purchased the land three years ago for $30,000; its fair market value at the contribution date was $40,000. No special allocation agreements were in effect before or after Lana was admitted to the partnership. The Redbird Partnership holds all land for investment.

Immediately before Lana's property contribution, the balance sheet of the Redbird Partnership was as follows:

	Basis	FMV		Basis	FMV
Land	$5,000	$80,000	Lisa,capital	$2,500	$40,000
			Lori,capital	2,500	40,000
	$5,000	$80,000		$5,000	$80,000

a. At the contribution date, what is Lana's basis in her interest in the Redbird Partnership?

b. When does the partnership's holding period begin for the contributed land?

c. On June 30 of the current year, the partnership sold the land contributed by Lana for $40,000. How much is the recognized gain or loss, and how is it allocated among the partners?

d. Prepare a balance sheet reflecting basis and fair market value for the partnership immediately after the land sale.

24. Assume the same facts as in Problem 23, with the following exceptions.

- Lana purchased the land three years ago for $50,000. Its fair market value was $40,000 when it was contributed to the partnership.

- Redbird sold the land contributed by Lana for $35,000.

a. How much is the recognized gain or loss, and how is it allocated among the partners?

b. Prepare a balance sheet reflecting basis and fair market value for the partnership immediately after the land sale, along with schedules that support the amount in each partner's capital account.

25. Carrie and Fred are equal partners in the accrual basis CF Partnership. At the beginning of the current year, Fred's capital account has a balance of $60,000, and the partnership has recourse debts of $90,000 payable to unrelated parties. All partnership recourse debt is shared equally between the partners. The following information about CF's operations for the current year is obtained from the partnership's records.

Taxable income	$80,000
Tax-exempt interest income	5,000
§ 1231 gain	6,000
Long-term capital gain	2,000
Long-term capital loss	3,000
IRS penalty	2,000
Charitable contribution to Girl Scouts	6,000
Guaranteed payment to Carrie	14,000
Payment of Fred's medical expenses	10,000

Assume that year-end partnership debt payable to unrelated parties is $40,000.

a. If all transactions are reflected in his beginning capital and basis in the same manner, what is Fred's basis in the partnership interest at the beginning of the year?

b. If all transactions are reflected in his beginning capital and basis in the same manner, what is Fred's basis in the partnership interest at the end of the current year?

26. The RUB Partnership reported the following items during the current tax year:

Taxable income	$120,000
Municipal bond interest income	10,000
Gain on sale of real estate	60,000

Taxable income includes $20,000 of income from collection of cash basis accounts receivable contributed by 25% partner Rolfe at the beginning of the year.

The municipal bond income was earned on bonds contributed by 50% partner Una. None of the interest was accrued on the contribution date. The partnership agreement provides that all this income will be specially allocated to Una this year, and no offsetting allocation will be made now or later.

The real estate gain resulted from the sale of a parcel of land contributed by 25% partner Bart. When the property was contributed, it was valued at $100,000 and Bart's basis was $80,000. Assume the real estate is a capital asset to both Bart and the partnership.

Prepare a schedule showing how each item is allocated to each of the three partners. Assume the partnership will maintain capital account balances and perform all other record keeping required to meet the substantial economic effect requirements of § 704(b).

27. The RB Partnership is owned equally by Rob and Bob. Rob's basis is $6,000 at the beginning of the tax year. Bob's basis is $15,000 at the beginning of the year. RB reported the following income and expenses for the current tax year:

Sales revenue	$130,000
Cost of sales	45,000
Guaranteed payment to Rob	24,000
Depreciation expense	12,500
Utilities	15,000

Rent	16,000
Interest income	3,000
Tax-exempt interest income	4,500
Long-term capital loss	3,200
Payment to Mount Vernon Hospital for Bob's medical expenses	10,000

a. Determine the ordinary partnership income and separately stated items for the partnership.

b. Calculate Bob's basis in his partnership interest at the end of the tax year. What items should Bob report on his Federal income tax return?

c. Calculate Rob's basis in his partnership interest at the end of the tax year. What items should Rob report on his Federal income tax return?

28. Assume the same facts as in Problem 27, except for the following:

   • Partnership revenues were $90,000 instead of $130,000.

   • Rob also received a distribution of $10,000 cash.

   a. Redetermine the ordinary income and separately stated items for the partnership.

   b. Calculate Bob's basis in his partnership interest at the end of the tax year. How much income or loss should Bob report on his Federal income tax return?

   c. Calculate Rob's basis in his partnership interest at the end of the tax year. How much income or loss should Rob report on his Federal income tax return?

29. At the beginning of the current year, Bill's basis in his 50% interest in the BP Partnership is $10,000, including an $85,000 share of partnership recourse debt. Near the beginning of the year, he contributed land valued at $180,000 to the partnership. Bill's basis in the land was $76,000, and a nonrecourse liability on the land (assumed by the partnership) was $90,000. The value of the land rose sharply when plans for a new freeway nearby were approved during the year, and the partnership sold the land near the end of the year for $260,000. The gain on the land sale is a capital gain since the land was held for investment purposes by both Bill and the partnership. BP used the proceeds from the land sale to pay the partnership's recourse and nonrecourse debts. Other than the gain on the land sale, the partnership reported an ordinary loss of $150,000 from operations. Bill is an active partner in the partnership.

   It is the last day of the current tax year. Bill has just called to ask you to help determine how his ownership interest in the partnership will affect his personal tax and financial situation this year.

   a. What issues related to each of the above transactions must be addressed to determine the tax consequences of owning the partnership interest for the current year?

   b. Make any necessary calculations and advise Bill regarding any year-end action you feel might be advisable.

30. Your client, the Williams Institute of Technology (WIT), is a 60% partner in the Research Industries Partnership (RIP). WIT is located at 76 Bradford Lane, St. Paul, MN 55164. The controller, Jeanine West, has sent you the following note and a copy of WIT's 1996 Schedule K–1 from the partnership.

Excerpt from client's note:
"RIP expects its 1997 operations to include the following:

Net loss from operations	$200,000
Capital gain from sale of land	100,000

The land was contributed by DASH, the other partner, when its value was $260,000. The partnership sold the land for $300,000. The partnership used this cash to repay all the partnership debt and pay for research and development expenditures, which a tax partner in your firm has said RIP can deduct this year.

We want to be sure we can deduct our full share of this loss, but we do not believe we will have enough basis. We are a material participant in this partnership's activities."

Items Reported on the 1996 Schedule K–1

WIT's share of partnership recourse liabilities	$90,000
WIT's ending capital account balance	30,000

Draft a letter to the controller that describes the following:

- WIT's allocation of partnership items.

- WIT's basis in the partnership interest following the allocation.

- Any limitations on loss deductions.

- Any recommendations you have that would allow WIT to claim the full amount of losses in 1997.

Assume WIT's 1996 K–1 accurately reflects the information needed to compute the basis in the partnership interest. Also assume the research expenditures are fully deductible this year, as the partner said.

Your client has experience researching issues in the Internal Revenue Code, so you may use some citations. However, be sure the letter is written in layperson's terms and cites are minimized.

31. Lee, Brad, and Rick form the LBR Partnership on January 1 of the current year. In return for a 25% interest, Lee transfers property (basis of $15,000, fair market value of $17,500) subject to a nonrecourse liability of $10,000. The liability is assumed by the partnership. Brad transfers property (basis of $16,000, fair market value of $7,500) for a 25% interest, and Rick transfers cash of $15,000 for the remaining 50% interest. (See Example 23.)
    a. How much gain must Lee recognize on the transfer?
    b. What is Lee's basis in his interest in the partnership?
    c. How much loss may Brad recognize on the transfer?
    d. What is Brad's basis in his interest in the partnership?
    e. What is Rick's basis in his interest in the partnership?
    f. What basis does the LBR Partnership take in the property transferred by Lee?
    g. What is the partnership's basis in the property transferred by Brad?

32. Assume the same facts as in Problem 31, except that the property contributed by Lee has a fair market value of $27,500 and is subject to a nonrecourse mortgage of $20,000. (See Example 27.)
    a. What is Lee's basis in his partnership interest?
    b. How much gain must Lee recognize on the transfer?
    c. What is Brad's basis in his partnership interest?
    d. What is Rick's basis in his partnership interest?
    e. What basis does the LBR Partnership take in the property transferred by Lee?

33. Kim and Craig plan to form the KC General Partnership by the end of the current year. The partners will each contribute $30,000 cash to the venture. In addition, the partnership will borrow $140,000 from First State Bank. The partnership's land will serve as collateral, and both partners will be required to personally guarantee the debt.

    The tentative partnership agreement provides that 75% of operating income, gains, losses, deductions, and credits will be allocated to Kim for the first five years the partnership is in existence. The remaining 25% is allocated to Craig. Thereafter, all partnership items will be allocated equally. The agreement also provides that capital accounts will be properly maintained, and each partner must restore any deficit in the capital account upon the partnership's liquidation.

    The partners would like to know, before the end of the tax year, how the $140,000 liability will be allocated for basis purposes. Using the format (1) facts, (2) issues, (3) conclusion, and (4) law and analysis, draft a memo to the tax planning file for the JK Partnership that describes how the note will be shared between the partners for purposes of computing the adjusted basis of each partnership interest.

34. Chris Elton is a 15% partner in the Cardinal Partnership, which is a lessor of residential rental property. Her share of the partnership's losses for the current year is $70,000. Immediately before considering the deductibility of this loss, Chris's capital account (which, in this case, corresponds to her basis excluding liabilities) reflected a balance of $40,000. Her share of partnership recourse liabilities is $10,000, and her share of the nonrecourse liabilities is $6,000. The nonrecourse liability was obtained from an unrelated bank and is secured solely by the real estate. Chris is also a partner in the Bluebird Partnership, which has generated income from long-term (more than 30 days) equipment rental activities. Chris's share of Bluebird's income is $23,000. Chris performs substantial services for Bluebird and spends several hundred hours a year working for the Cardinal Partnership. Chris's modified AGI before considering partnership activities is $100,000. Your manager has asked you to determine how much of the $70,000 loss Chris can deduct on her current calendar year return. Using the format (1) facts, (2) issues, (3) conclusion, and (4) law and analysis, draft a memo to the manager and the client's tax file describing the loss limitations. Be sure to identify the Code Sections under which the losses are suspended.

35. As of January 1 of last year, the outside basis and at-risk basis of Rashad's 25% interest in the RST Partnership were $24,000. Rashad and the partnership use the calendar year for tax purposes. The partnership incurred an operating loss of $100,000 last year and a profit of $8,000 for the current year. Rashad is a material participant in the partnership.
    a. How much loss, if any, may Rashad recognize for last year?
    b. How much net reportable income must Rashad recognize for the current year?
    c. What is Rashad's basis in the partnership interest as of January 1 of the current year?
    d. What is Rashad's basis in the partnership interest as of January 1 of the next year?
    e. What year-end tax planning would you suggest to ensure that Rashad can deduct his share of partnership losses?

36. Ned, a 50% partner in the MN Partnership, is to receive a payment of $35,000 for services. He will also be allocated 50% of the partnership's profits or losses. After deducting the payment to Ned, the partnership has a loss of $25,000. Ned's basis in his partnership interest was $10,000 before these items.
    a. How much, if any, of the $25,000 partnership loss will be allocated to Ned?
    b. What is the net income from the partnership that Ned must report on his Federal income tax return?
    c. What is Ned's basis in his partnership interest following the guaranteed payment and loss allocation?

37. Sonya is a 20% owner of Philadelphia Cheese Treets, Inc., a C corporation that was formed February 1, 1996. She receives a $5,000 monthly salary from the corporation, and Cheese Treets generates $200,000 taxable income for its tax year ending January 31, 1997. Sonya uses the calendar year for tax reporting.
    a. How do these activities affect Sonya's 1996 AGI?
    b. Now assume that Cheese Treets is a partnership with a January 31 year-end. Treat Sonya's salary as a guaranteed payment. How do these activities affect Sonya's 1996 AGI?

38. Four Lakes Partnership is owned by four sisters. Anne holds a 70% interest; each of the others own 10%. Anne sells investment property to the partnership for its fair market value of $100,000 (basis of $150,000).
    a. How much loss, if any, may Anne recognize?
    b. If the partnership later sells the property for $160,000, how much gain must it recognize?
    c. If Anne's basis in the investment property were $20,000 instead of $150,000, how much, if any, capital gain would she recognize on the sale?

39. When Brenda's outside basis in the BCD Partnership is $25,000, the partnership distributes to her $10,000 cash and a parcel of land (fair market value of $30,000, inside basis to the partnership of $20,000). Brenda remains a partner in the partnership, and the partnership owns no hot assets.

   a. Determine the recognized gain or loss to the partnership as a result of this distribution.

   b. Determine the recognized gain or loss to Brenda as a result of the distribution.

   c. Determine Brenda's basis in the land and BCD Partnership after the distribution.

40. In each of the following independent cases in which the partnership owns no hot assets, indicate:

   • Whether the partner recognizes gain or loss.

   • Whether the partnership recognizes gain or loss.

   • The partner's adjusted basis for the property distributed.

   • The partner's outside basis in the partnership after the distribution.

   a. Lisa receives $16,000 of cash in partial liquidation of her interest in the partnership. Lisa's outside basis for her partnership interest immediately before the distribution is $15,000.

   b. Susan receives $6,000 of cash and land with an inside basis to the partnership of $12,000 in partial liquidation of her interest. Susan's outside basis for her partnership interest immediately before the distribution is $20,000.

   c. Assume the same facts as in (b), except that Susan's outside basis for her partnership interest immediately before the distribution is $15,000.

   d. Jim receives $8,000 of cash and two tracts of land in partial liquidation of his partnership interest. The two tracts have adjusted bases to the partnership of $5,000 and $15,000, respectively. Each tract has a $25,000 fair market value. Jim's outside basis for his partnership interest immediately before the distribution is $20,000.

41. The basis of Lou's partnership interest is $40,000. Lou receives a pro rata liquidating distribution consisting of $22,500 cash and his proportionate share of inventory with a basis of $24,500 to the partnership and a fair market value of $28,000. Assume the partnership also liquidates.

   a. How much gain or loss, if any, must Lou recognize as a result of the distribution?

   b. What basis will Lou take in the inventory?

   c. If the inventory is sold two years later for $28,000, what are the tax consequences to Lou?

   d. What are the tax consequences to the partnership as a result of the liquidating distribution?

   e. Is any planning technique available to the partnership to avoid any "lost basis" results?

   f. Would your answer to (b) change if this had been a nonliquidating distribution?

42. In 1993, Gabriella contributed land with a basis of $16,000 and a fair market value of $25,000 to the Meadowlark Partnership in exchange for a 25% interest in capital and profits. In 1996, the partnership distributes this property to Juanita, also a 25% partner, in a nonliquidating distribution. The fair market value has increased to $30,000 at the time the property is distributed. Juanita's and Gabriella's bases in their partnership interests are each $30,000 at the time of the distribution.

   a. How much gain or loss, if any, does Gabriella recognize on the distribution to Juanita? What is Gabriella's basis in her partnership interest following the distribution?

   b. What is Juanita's basis in the land she received in the distribution?

   c. How much gain or loss, if any, does Juanita recognize on the distribution? What is Juanita's basis in her partnership interest following the distribution?

   d. How much gain or loss would Juanita recognize if she later sells the land for its $30,000 fair market value? Is this result equitable?

   e. Would your answers to (a) and (b) change if Gabriella originally contributed the property to the partnership in 1984?

43. Donald sells his interest in the equal DDP Partnership to his partner, Paul, for $47,000 cash and the assumption of Donald's share of partnership liabilities. On the sale date,

the partnership's cash basis balance sheet reflects the following (assume capital accounts reflect the partners' bases in their partnership interests, excluding liabilities):

	Adjusted Basis	Fair Market Value
Cash	$51,000	$ 51,000
Accounts receivable	–0–	60,000
Capital assets	9,000	39,000
Total	$60,000	$150,000

	Adjusted Basis	Fair Market Value
Note payable	$ 9,000	$ 9,000
Capital accounts		
Dale	17,000	47,000
Donald	17,000	47,000
Paul	17,000	47,000
Total	$60,000	$150,000

a. What is the total amount realized by Donald on the sale?
b. How much, if any, ordinary income must Donald recognize on the sale?
c. How much capital gain must Donald report?

Research Problems for this chapter appear at the end of Chapter 28.

23

EXEMPT ENTITIES

LEARNING OBJECTIVES

After completing Chapter 23, you should be able to:

1. Identify the different types of exempt organizations.

2. Enumerate the requirements for exempt status.

3. Know the tax consequences of exempt status, including the different consequences for public charities and private foundations.

4. Determine which exempt organizations are classified as private foundations.

5. Recognize the taxes imposed on private foundations and calculate the related initial tax and additional tax amounts.

6. Determine when an exempt organization is subject to the unrelated business income tax and calculate the amount of the tax.

7. List the reports exempt organizations must file with the IRS and the related due dates.

8. Identify tax planning opportunities for exempt organizations.

GENERAL CONSIDERATIONS

▌deally, any entity that generates profit would prefer not to be subject to the Federal income tax. All of the types of entities discussed thus far are subject to the Federal income tax at one (e.g., sole proprietorships, partnerships, and S corporations generally are only subject to single taxation) or more (e.g., C corporations are subject to double taxation) levels. However, organizations classified as **exempt organizations** may be able to escape Federal income taxation altogether.

Churches are among the types of organizations that are exempt from Federal income tax. Nevertheless, one must be careful not to conclude that everything labeled a church will qualify for exempt status.

During the 1970s and 1980s, a popular technique for attempting to avoid Federal income tax was the establishment of so-called mail-order churches. For example, in one scheme, a nurse obtained a certificate of ordination and a church charter from an organization that sold such documents.[1] The articles of incorporation stated that the church was organized exclusively for religious and charitable purposes, including a religious mission of healing the spirit, mind, emotions, and body. The nurse was the church's minister, director, and principal officer. Taking a vow of poverty, she transferred all her assets, including a house and car, to the church. The church assumed all of the nurse's liabilities, including the mortgage on her house and her credit card bills. The nurse continued to work at a hospital and deposited her salary in the church's bank account. The church provided her with a living allowance sufficient to maintain or improve her previous standard of living. She was also permitted to use the house and car for personal purposes.

The IRS declared that such organizations were shams and not bona fide churches. For a church to be tax-exempt under § 501(c)(3), none of its net earnings may be used to the benefit of any private shareholder or individual. In essence, the organization should serve a public rather than a private interest. Although the courts have consistently upheld the IRS position, numerous avoidance schemes such as this have been attempted.

---

[1] Rev.Rul. 81–94, 1981–1 C.B. 330.

As discussed in Chapter 1, the major objective of the Federal tax law is to raise revenue. If revenue raising were the only objective, however, the Code would not contain provisions that permit certain organizations to be either partially or completely exempt from Federal income tax. Social considerations may also affect the tax law. This objective bears directly on the decision by Congress to provide for exempt organization tax status. The House Report on the Revenue Act of 1938 provides as follows:[2]

> The exemption from taxation of money or property devoted to charitable and other purposes is based upon the theory that the Government is compensated for the loss of revenue by its relief from the financial burden which would otherwise have to be met by appropriations from public funds, and by the benefits resulting from the promotion of the general welfare.

In recognition of this social consideration objective, Subchapter F (Exempt Organizations) of the Code (§§ 501–528) provides the authority under which certain organizations are exempt from Federal income tax. Exempt status is not open-ended in that two general limitations exist. First, the nature or scope of the organization may result in it being only partially exempt from tax.[3] Second, the organization may engage in activities that are subject to special taxation.[4]

TYPES OF EXEMPT ORGANIZATIONS

1 LEARNING OBJECTIVE
Identify the different types of exempt organizations.

An organization qualifies for exempt status *only* if it fits into one of the categories provided in the Code. Examples of qualifying exempt organizations and the specific statutory authority for their exempt status are listed in Exhibit 23–1.[5]

REQUIREMENTS FOR EXEMPT STATUS

2 LEARNING OBJECTIVE
Enumerate the requirements for exempt status.

Exempt status frequently requires more than mere classification in one of the categories of exempt organizations. Many of the organizations that qualify for exempt status share the following characteristics.

- The organization serves some type of *common good.*[6]
- The organization is a *not-for-profit* entity.[7]
- *Net earnings* do not benefit the members of the organization.[8]
- The organization does not exert *political influence.*[9]

SERVING THE COMMON GOOD

The underlying rationale for all exempt organizations is that they serve some type of *common good.* However, depending on the type of the exempt organization, the

---

[2] See 1939–1 (Part 2) C.B. 742 for a reprint of H.R. No. 1860, 75th Congress, 3rd Session.
[3] See the subsequent discussion of Unrelated Business Income Tax.
[4] See the subsequent discussions of Prohibited Transactions and Taxes Imposed on Private Foundations.
[5] Section 501(a) provides for exempt status for organizations described in §§ 401 and 501. The orientation of this chapter is toward organizations that conduct business activities. Therefore,

the exempt organizations described in § 401 (qualified pension, profit sharing, and stock bonus trusts) are outside the scope of the chapter and are not discussed.
[6] See, for example, §§ 501(c)(3) and (4).
[7] See, for example, §§ 501(c)(3), (4), (6), (13), and (14).
[8] See, for example, §§ 501(c)(3), (6), (7), (9), (10), (11), and (19).
[9] See, for example, § 501(c)(3).

▼ **EXHIBIT 23–1**
Types of Exempt Organizations

Statutory Authority	Brief Description	Examples or Comments
§ 501(c)(1)	Federal and related agencies.	Commodity Credit Corporation, Federal Deposit Insurance Corporation, Federal Land Bank.
§ 501(c)(2)	Corporations holding title to property for and paying income to exempt organizations.	Corporation holding title to college fraternity house.
§ 501(c)(3)	Religious, charitable, educational, scientific, literary, etc., organizations.	Boy Scouts of America, Red Cross, Salvation Army, Episcopal Church, United Fund, University of Richmond.
§ 501(c)(4)	Civic leagues and employee unions.	Garden club, tenants' association promoting tenants' legal rights in entire community, League of Women Voters.
§ 501(c)(5)	Labor, agricultural, and horticultural organizations.	Teachers' association, organization formed to promote effective agricultural pest control, organization formed to test soil and to educate community members in soil treatment, garden club.
§ 501(c)(6)	Business leagues, chambers of commerce, real estate boards, etc.	Chambers of Commerce, American Plywood Association, NFL, medical association peer review board, organization promoting acceptance of women in business and professions.
§ 501(c)(7)	Social clubs.	Country club, rodeo and riding club, press club, bowling club, college fraternities.
§ 501(c)(8)	Fraternal beneficiary societies.	Lodges. Must provide for the payment of life, sickness, accident, or other benefits to members or their dependents.
§ 501(c)(9)	Voluntary employees' beneficiary associations.	Provide for the payment of life, sickness, accident, or other benefits to members, their dependents, or their designated beneficiaries.
§ 501(c)(10)	Domestic fraternal societies.	Lodges. Must not provide for the payment of life, sickness, accident, or other benefits; and must devote the net earnings exclusively to religious, charitable, scientific, literary, educational, and fraternal purposes.
§ 501(c)(11)	Local teachers' retirement fund associations.	Only permitted sources of income are amounts received from (1) public taxation, (2) assessments on teaching salaries of members, and (3) income from investments.
§ 501(c)(12)	Local benevolent life insurance associations, mutual or cooperative telephone companies, etc.	Local cooperative telephone company, local mutual water company, local mutual electric company.
§ 501(c)(13)	Cemetery companies.	Must be operated exclusively for the benefit of lot owners who hold the lots for burial purposes.
§ 501(c)(14)	Credit unions.	Other than credit unions exempt under § 501(c)(1).
§ 501(c)(15)	Mutual insurance companies.	Mutual fire insurance company, mutual automobile insurance company.
§ 501(c)(16)	Corporations organized by farmers' cooperatives for financing crop operations.	Related farmers' cooperative must be exempt from tax under § 521.
§ 501(c)(19)	Armed forces members' posts or organizations.	Veterans of Foreign Wars (VFW), Reserve Officers Association.
§ 501(c)(20)	Group legal service plans' organizations.	Provided by a corporation for its employees.
§ 501(d)	Religious and apostolic organizations.	Communal organization. Members must include pro rata share of the net income of the organization in their gross income as dividends.
§ 501(e)	Cooperative hospital service organizations.	Centralized purchasing organization for exempt hospitals.
§ 501(f)	Cooperative service organization of educational institutions.	Organization formed to manage universities' endowment funds.

TAX IN THE NEWS

COMPETITION AMONG EXEMPT ORGANIZATIONS

otal charitable giving in the United States has increased from about $100 billion in 1981 to over $124 billion in 1992, according to the American Association of Fund-Raising Counsel. In 1992, the funds came from the following sources.

Individuals	82.0%	Bequests	6.5%
Foundations	6.7%	Corporations	4.8%

The nation's one million charitable groups and churches are actively competing for these funds. As a result, people are receiving more solicitations in the mail or on the telephone, according to Bennett M. Weiner, director of philanthropic advisory service of the Council of Better Business Bureaus in Arlington, Virginia. The number of solicitations increases during the last two months of the year when most charities get at least half of their fund-raising dollars. Apparently, people are both in a gift-giving mode and eager to obtain last-minute tax deductions during this time period.

A Gallup poll found the mid-range of charitable giving by individuals is about $890 annually, excluding contributions to churches. Half of those surveyed expressed concern about how charities spend their money. Experts suggest that individuals should pick a charity in much the same way they select investments and obtain as much information as possible. A charity's financial statements provide data on how much it spends on its charitable mission versus fund-raising and overhead, including the salaries of top officers.

SOURCE: Vivian Marino, "Open Your Heart, but Use Your Head," *Newport News Daily Press*, December 6, 1993, p. B5.

term *common good* may be interpreted broadly or narrowly. If the test is interpreted broadly, the group being served is the general public or some large subgroup thereof. If it is interpreted narrowly, the group is the specific group referred to in the statutory language. One of the factors in classifying an exempt organization as a private foundation is the size of the group it serves.

NOT-FOR-PROFIT ENTITY

The organization may not be organized or operated for the purpose of making a profit. For some types of exempt organizations, the *for-profit prohibition* appears in the statutory language. For other types, the prohibition is implied.

NET EARNINGS AND MEMBERS OF THE ORGANIZATION

What uses are appropriate for the net earnings of tax-exempt organizations? The logical answer would seem to be that the earnings should be used for the exempt purpose of the organization. However, where the organization exists for the good of a specific group of members, such an open-ended interpretation could permit net earnings to benefit specific group members. Therefore, the Code specifically prohibits certain types of exempt organizations from using their earnings in this way.

... no part of the net earnings ... inures to the benefit of any private shareholder or individual ...[10]

In other instances, a statutory prohibition is unnecessary because the definition of the exempt organization in the Code effectively prevents such use.

... the net earnings of which are devoted exclusively to religious, charitable, scientific, literary, educational, and fraternal purposes ...[11]

POLITICAL INFLUENCE

Religious, charitable, educational, etc., organizations are generally prohibited from attempting to influence legislation or participate in political campaigns. Participation in political campaigns includes participation both *on behalf of* a candidate and *in opposition to* a candidate.

Only in limited circumstances are such exempt organizations permitted to attempt to influence legislation. See the subsequent discussion under Prohibited Transactions.

ETHICAL
CONSIDERATIONS

A Church Attempts to Change Society

Amos Heck is the founder, and the man behind the throne, of the Church of the Future television ministry. Ministry broadcasts originate from church services in California and New York and are broadcast via cable throughout the United States. While the membership of the Church of the Future is small (approximately 1,500 members), the typical member is quite wealthy. In addition to receiving contributions from its members, the church solicits and receives donations from viewers of the TV broadcasts. The church is tax-exempt under § 501(c)(3).

The stated mission of the church is religious in nature. However, Amos firmly believes, as do the members of the board of deacons of the church, that certain societal goals must be accomplished for the prophecies of the church to come true (i.e., their divine being expects them to be active missionaries). Among its basic beliefs, the church advocates government control and possession of all guns, the legalization of drugs, abortion on demand once approved by the appropriate government agency, the withdrawal of all U.S. troops from foreign soil and the termination of all military alliances, the abolition of capital punishment, and the availability of tuition-free university education to all U.S. citizens.

The ministers of the Church of the Future are expected to include these basic beliefs, at the subliminal level, in their sermons. Some do so more effectively and more frequently than others, but all are required to do so. Amos and the board of deacons are dismayed that more of their beliefs have not been incorporated into American society.

Amos proposes to the board of deacons that the church take a more proactive role. The employment contract of the ministers will now require them to include the basic beliefs in their sermons in an active manner. No longer can the beliefs just be incorporated subliminally. All the beliefs must be covered quarterly, and every sermon must present at least one of the basic beliefs. The ministers will encourage the church members and TV viewers to actively support these positions at both the state and the Federal level.

---

[10] § 501(c)(6).

[11] § 501(c)(10).

As a new member of the board of deacons, you wholeheartedly support Amos's position. However, you are concerned about the effect of this open advocacy of positions on the tax-exempt status of the church. Amos responds that the "church has friends in high places" and assures you that the tax-exempt status will not be endangered.

TAX CONSEQUENCES OF EXEMPT STATUS: GENERAL

3 LEARNING OBJECTIVE
Know the tax consequences of exempt status, including the different consequences for public charities and private foundations.

An organization that is appropriately classified as one of the types of exempt organizations is generally exempt from Federal income tax. Four exceptions to this general statement exist, however. An exempt organization that engages in a *prohibited transaction*, or is a so-called *feeder organization,* is subject to tax. If the organization is classified as a *private foundation,* it may be partially subject to tax. Finally, an exempt organization is subject to tax on its *unrelated business taxable income* (which includes unrelated debt-financed income).

In addition to being exempt from Federal income tax, an exempt organization may be eligible for other benefits, including the following.

- The organization may be exempt from state income tax, state franchise tax, sales tax, or property tax.
- The organization may receive discounts on postage rates.
- Donors of property to the exempt organization may qualify for charitable contribution deductions on their Federal and state income tax returns. However, *not* all exempt organizations are qualified charitable contribution recipients (e.g., gifts to the National Football League are not deductible).

PROHIBITED TRANSACTIONS

Engaging in a prohibited transaction can produce two negative results. First, part or all of the organization's income may be subject to Federal income tax. Even worse, the organization may forfeit its exempt status.

Failure to Continue to Qualify. Organizations initially qualify for exempt status only if they are organized as indicated in Exhibit 23–1. The initial qualification requirements then effectively become maintenance requirements. Failure to continue to meet the qualification requirements results in the loss of the entity's exempt status.

New Faith, Inc., is an excellent example of an exempt organization that failed to continue to qualify for tax exemption.[12] The stated purposes of the organization were to feed and shelter the poor. In its application for exempt status, New Faith indicated that it would derive its financial support from donations, bingo games, and raffles. The IRS approved the exempt status.

New Faith's only source of income was the operation of several lunch trucks, which provided food to the general public in exchange for scheduled "donations." Evidence provided by the organization to the Tax Court did not show that the food from the lunch trucks was provided free of charge or at reduced prices. In addition, no evidence was presented to show that the people who received food

---

[12] *New Faith, Inc.,* 64 TCM 1050, T.C.Memo. 1992–601.

EXEMPT ORGANIZATIONS ARE BIG BUSINESS

Certain organizations are exempt from Federal income taxation under § 501 of the Internal Revenue Code of 1986. For such organizations, usually the only source of income that is subject to Federal income taxation is their unrelated business income (i.e., income from a business activity that is unrelated to the purpose for which the entity has been granted exempt status).

Exempt organizations include churches, the American Red Cross, Salvation Army, United Fund, and Boy Scouts. But also exempt are the National Football League (NFL), Underwriters Laboratories (UL), PGA Tour, Inc., Cornell University, National Geographic Society, and American Bankers Association (ABA).

On October 2, 1995, *U.S. News and World Report* devoted its cover story to tax-exempt organizations. The article included the following statistics:

Organization	Gross Revenue	Salary of CEO	Federal Income Taxes
NFL	*	$2,500,000	*
UL	$281,000,000	*	*
PGA Tour	180,000,000	2,100,000	$63,534
Cornell University Medical College	*	1,742,000	*
Food Marketing Institute	*	1,559,000	*
Columbia University	*	1,438,000	*

*Data not provided.

There are approximately 1.1 million tax-exempt organizations in the United States, and another 45,000 new groups become tax-exempt each year. These tax-exempt organizations pay either no Federal income taxes at all or a mere pittance. According to the article, many of these organizations "bear little resemblance to traditional charities" and essentially are successful businesses. Excluding churches, the annual revenue of tax-exempt organizations in the United States is $1.1 trillion. Many also engage in lobbying activities; for example, the ABA spent $1.7 million on lobbying in 1994 and since 1990 made political contributions of $4.8 million.

SOURCE: Information from Pound, Cohen, and Loeb, "Tax Exempt," *U.S. News and World Report*, October 2, 1995, pp. 36–41.

for free or at below-cost prices were impoverished or needy. The court concluded that the primary purpose of the activity was the conduct of a trade or business. It upheld the IRS's revocation of New Faith's exempt status.

Election Not to Forfeit Exempt Status for Lobbying.   Organizations exempt under § 501(c)(3) (religious, charitable, educational, etc., organizations) generally are prohibited from attempting to influence legislation (lobbying activities) or from participating in political campaigns.[13] Any violation can result in the forfeiture of exempt status.

[13] § 501(c)(3).

▼ **FIGURE 23-1**
Calculation of Lobbying
Nontaxable Amount

Exempt Purpose Expenditures	Lobbying Nontaxable Amount Is
Not over $500,000	20% of exempt purpose expenditures*
Over $500,000 but not over $1 million	$100,000 + 15% of the excess of exempt purpose expenditures over $500,000
Over $1 million but not over $1.5 million	$175,000 + 10% of the excess of exempt purpose expenditures over $1 million
Over $1.5 million	$225,000 + 5% of the excess of exempt purpose expenditures over $1.5 million

*Exempt purpose expenditures generally are the amounts paid or incurred for the taxable year to accomplish the following purposes: religious, charitable, scientific, literary, educational, fostering national or international amateur sports competition, or the prevention of cruelty to children or animals.

Certain § 501(c)(3) exempt organizations are permitted to engage in lobbying activities on a limited basis.[14] Eligible for such treatment are most § 501(c)(3) exempt organizations (educational institutions, hospitals, and medical research organizations; organizations supporting government schools; organizations publicly supported by charitable contributions; certain organizations that are publicly supported by various sources including admissions, sales, gifts, grants, contributions, or membership fees; and certain organizations that support certain types of public charities). Churches, their integrated auxiliaries, and *private foundations* are not permitted to engage in lobbying activities, however.

An eligible § 501(c)(3) organization must make an affirmative election to participate in lobbying activities on a limited basis. The lobbying expenditures of electing § 501(c)(3) organizations are subject to a ceiling. Exceeding the ceiling can lead to the forfeiture of exempt status. Even when the ceiling is not exceeded, a tax may be imposed on some of the lobbying expenditures (discussed subsequently).

Two terms are key to the calculation of the ceiling amount: **lobbying expenditures** and **grass roots expenditures**. Lobbying expenditures are made for the purpose of influencing legislation through either of the following.

- Attempting to affect the opinions of the general public or any segment thereof.
- Communicating with any legislator or staff member or with any government official or staff member who may participate in the formulation of legislation.

Grass roots expenditures are made for the purpose of influencing legislation by attempting to affect the opinions of the general public or any segment thereof.

The statutory ceiling is imposed on both lobbying expenditures and grass roots expenditures and is computed as follows.

- 150% × lobbying nontaxable amount = lobbying expenditures ceiling.
- 150% × grass roots nontaxable amount = grass roots expenditures ceiling.

The *lobbying nontaxable amount* is the lesser of (1) $1 million or (2) the amount determined in Figure 23–1.[15] The *grass roots nontaxable amount* is 25 percent of the lobbying nontaxable amount.[16]

---

[14]§ 501(h). An affirmative election to lobby must be made.   [16]§ 4911(c)(4).
[15]§ 4911(c)(2).

CONCEPT SUMMARY 23–1

Exempt Organizations and Influencing Legislation

Factor	Tax Result
Entity subject to rule	§ 501(c)(3) organization.
Effect of influencing legislation	Subject to tax on lobbying expenditures under § 4912.
	Forfeit exempt status under § 501(c)(3).
	Not eligible for exempt status under § 501(c)(4).
	Permitted to make limited lobbying expenditures.
Effect of electing to make lobbying expenditures	Subject to tax under § 4911.

A tax may be assessed on an electing exempt organization's **excess lobbying expenditures** as follows.[17]

- 25% × excess lobbying expenditures = tax liability.

Excess lobbying expenditures are the greater of the following.[18]

- Excess of the lobbying expenditures for the taxable year over the lobbying nontaxable amount.
- Excess of the grass roots expenditures for the taxable year over the grass roots nontaxable amount.

EXAMPLE 1

Tan, Inc., a qualifying § 501(c)(3) organization, incurs lobbying expenditures of $500,000 for the taxable year and grass roots expenditures of $0. Exempt purpose expenditures for the taxable year are $5,000,000. Tan elects to be eligible to make lobbying expenditures on a limited basis.

Applying the data in Figure 23–1, the lobbying nontaxable amount is $400,000 [$225,000 + 5%($5,000,000 − $1,500,000)]. The ceiling on lobbying expenditures is $600,000 (150% × $400,000). Therefore, the $500,000 of lobbying expenditures are under the permitted $600,000. However, the election results in the imposition of tax on the excess lobbying expenditures of $100,000 ($500,000 lobbying expenditures − $400,000 lobbying nontaxable amount). The resulting tax liability is $25,000 ($100,000 × 25%). ▼

A § 501(c)(3) organization that makes disqualifying lobbying expenditures is subject to a 5 percent tax on the lobbying expenditures for the taxable year. A 5 percent tax may also be levied on the organization's management. The tax is imposed on management only if the managers knew that making the expenditures was likely to result in the organization no longer qualifying under § 501(c)(3) and if the managers' actions were willful and not due to reasonable cause. The tax does not apply to private foundations (see the subsequent discussion).[19]

Concept Summary 23–1 capsulizes the rules on influencing legislation.

---

[17]§ 4911(a)(1).
[18]§ 4911(b).

[19]§ 4912.

CONCEPT SUMMARY 23–2

Consequences of Exempt Status

General	Exempt from Federal income tax.
	Exempt from most state and local income, franchise, sales, and property taxes.
	Qualify for reductions in postage rates.
	Gifts to the organization often can be deducted by donor.
Exceptions	May be subject to Federal income tax associated with the following.
	• Engaging in a prohibited transaction.
	• Being a feeder organization.
	• Being a private foundation.
	• Generating unrelated business taxable income.

FEEDER ORGANIZATIONS

A **feeder organization** carries on a trade or business for the benefit of an exempt organization (remits its profits to the exempt organization). Such organizations are not exempt from Federal income tax. This provision is intended to prevent an entity whose primary purpose is to conduct a trade or business for profit from escaping taxation merely because all of its profits are payable to one or more exempt organizations.[20]

Some income and activities are *not* subject to the feeder organization rules:[21]

- Rent income that would be excluded from the definition of the term *rent* for purposes of the unrelated business income tax (discussed subsequently).
- A trade or business where substantially all the work is performed by volunteers.
- The trade or business of selling merchandise where substantially all the merchandise has been received as contributions or gifts.

Concept Summary 23–2 highlights the consequences of exempt status.

PRIVATE FOUNDATIONS

TAX CONSEQUENCES OF PRIVATE FOUNDATION STATUS

Certain exempt organizations are classified as **private foundations.** This classification produces two negative consequences. First, the classification may have an adverse impact on the contributions received by the donee exempt organization. Contributions may decline because the tax consequences for donors may not be as favorable as if the entity were not a private foundation.[22] Second, the classification may result in taxation at the exempt organization level. The reason for this less beneficial tax treatment is that private foundations define common good more

---

[20] § 502(a).
[21] § 502(b).

[22] § 170(e)(1)(B)(ii).

narrowly and therefore are seen as not being supported by, and operated for the good of, the public.

Definition of a Private Foundation. The following § 501(c)(3) organizations are *not* private foundations.[23]

4   **LEARNING OBJECTIVE**
Determine which exempt organizations are classified as private foundations.

1. Churches; educational institutions; hospitals and medical research organizations; charitable organizations receiving a major portion of their support from the general public or the United States, a state, or a political subdivision thereof that is operated for the benefit of a college or university; and governmental units (favored activities category).
2. Organizations that are broadly supported by the general public (excluding disqualified persons), by governmental units, or by organizations described in (1) above.
3. Entities organized and operated exclusively for the benefit of organizations described in (1) or (2) (a supporting organization).
4. Entities organized and operated exclusively for testing for public safety.

To meet the broadly supported requirement in (2) above, both the following tests must be satisfied.

- External support test.
- Internal support test.

Under the *external support test,* more than one-third of the organization's support each taxable year *normally* must come from the three groups listed in (2) above, in the following forms.

- Gifts, grants, contributions, and membership fees.
- Gross receipts from admissions, sales of merchandise, performance of services, or the furnishing of facilities in an activity that is not an unrelated trade or business for purposes of the unrelated business income tax (discussed subsequently). However, such gross receipts from any person or governmental agency in excess of the greater of $5,000 or 1 percent of the organization's support for the taxable year are not counted.

The *internal support test* limits the amount of support *normally* received from the following sources to one-third of the organization's support for the taxable year.[24]

- Gross investment income (gross income from interest, dividends, rents, and royalties).
- Unrelated business taxable income (discussed subsequently) minus the related tax.

EXAMPLE 2

Lion, Inc., a § 501(c)(3) organization, received the following support during the taxable year.

Governmental unit A for services rendered	$ 30,000
Governmental unit B for services rendered	20,000
General public for services rendered	20,000
Gross investment income	15,000
Contributions from individual substantial contributors (disqualified persons)	15,000
	$100,000

For purposes of the *external support test,* the support from A is counted only to the extent of $5,000 (greater of $5,000 or 1% of $100,000 support). Likewise, for B, only $5,000 is counted as support. Thus, the total countable support is $30,000 ($20,000 from the general public + $5,000 + $5,000), and Lion fails the test for the taxable year ($30,000/$100,000 = 30%; need >33.3%). The $15,000 received from disqualified persons is excluded from the numerator but is included in the denominator.

In calculating the *internal support test,* only the gross investment income of $15,000 is included in the numerator. Thus, the test is satisfied ($15,000/$100,000 = 15%; cannot > 33.3%) for the taxable year.

Since Lion did not satisfy both tests, it does not qualify as an organization that is broadly supported. ▼

The intent of the two tests is to exclude from private foundation status those § 501(c)(3) organizations that are responsive to the general public rather than to the private interests of a limited number of donors or other persons.

Examples of § 501(c)(3) organizations that are properly classified as private foundations receiving broad public support include the United Fund, the Boy Scouts, university alumni associations, symphony orchestras, and the PTA.

TAXES IMPOSED ON PRIVATE FOUNDATIONS

5 LEARNING OBJECTIVE
Recognize the taxes imposed on private foundations and calculate the related initial tax and additional tax amounts.

In general, a private foundation is exempt from Federal income tax. However, because a private foundation is usually not a broadly, publicly supported organization, it may be subject to the following taxes.[25]

- Tax based on investment income.
- Tax on self-dealing.
- Tax on failure to distribute income.
- Tax on excess business holdings.
- Tax on investments that jeopardize charitable purposes.
- Tax on taxable expenditures.

These taxes serve to restrict the permitted activities of private foundations. Two levels of tax may be imposed on the private foundation and the foundation manager: an initial tax and an additional tax. The initial taxes (first-level), with the exception of the tax based on investment income, are imposed because the private foundation engages in so-called *prohibited transactions.* The additional taxes (second-level) are imposed only if the prohibited transactions are not modified within a statutory time period.[26] See Concept Summary 23–3 for additional details.

The tax on a failure to distribute income will be used to illustrate how expensive these taxes can be and the related importance of avoiding their imposition. For failure to distribute a sufficient portion of a private nonoperating foundation's income, both an initial tax (first-level) and an additional tax (second-level) may be imposed. The initial tax is imposed at a rate of 15 percent on the income for the taxable year that is not distributed during the current or the following taxable year. The initial tax is imposed on the undistributed income for each year until the IRS assesses the tax.

The additional tax is imposed at a rate of 100 percent on the amount of the inadequate distribution that is not distributed by the assessment date. The additional tax is effectively waived if the undistributed income is distributed

---

[25] §§ 4941–4943.

[26] § 4961.

CONCEPT SUMMARY 23–3

Taxes Imposed on Private Foundations

Type of Tax	Code Section	Purpose	Private Foundation		Foundation Manager	
			Initial Tax	Additional Tax	Initial Tax	Additional Tax
On investment income	§ 4940	Audit fee to defray IRS expenses.	2%*			
On self-dealing	§ 4941	Engaging in transactions with disqualified persons.	5%**	200%**	2.5%[†]	50%[†]
On failure to distribute income	§ 4942	Failing to distribute adequate amount of income for exempt purposes.	15%	100%		
On excess business holdings	§ 4943	Investments that enable the private foundation to control unrelated businesses.	5%	200%		
On jeopardizing investments	§ 4944	Speculative investments that put the private foundation's assets at risk.	5%	25%	5%[††]	5%[†]
On taxable expenditures	§ 4945	Expenditures that should not be made by private foundations.	10%	100%	2.5%[††]	50%[†]

*May be possible to reduce the tax rate to 1%. In addition, an exempt operating foundation [see §§ 4940(d)(2) and 4942(j)(3)] is not subject to the tax.
**Imposed on the disqualified person rather than the foundation.
[†]Subject to a statutory ceiling of $10,000.
[††]Subject to a statutory ceiling of $5,000.

within 90 days after the mailing of the deficiency notice for the additional tax. Extensions of this period may be obtained.

Undistributed income is the excess of the distributable amount (in effect, the amount that should have been distributed) over qualifying distributions made by the entity. The distributable amount is the excess of the minimum investment return over the sum of the (1) unrelated business income tax and (2) the excise tax based on net investment income.[27] The minimum investment return is 5 percent of the excess of the fair market value of the foundation's assets over the unpaid debt associated with acquiring or improving these assets. Assets of the foundation that

---

[27]§ 4940.

are employed directly in carrying on the foundation's exempt purpose are not used in making this calculation.

EXAMPLE 3

Gold, Inc., a private foundation, has undistributed income of $80,000 for its taxable year 1993. It distributes $15,000 of this amount during 1994 and an additional $45,000 during 1995. The IRS deficiency notice is mailed to Gold on August 5, 1996. The initial tax is $12,750 [($65,000 × 15%) + ($20,000 × 15%)].

At the date of the deficiency notice, no additional distributions have been made from the 1993 undistributed income. Therefore, since the remaining undistributed income of $20,000 has not been distributed by August 5, 1996, an additional tax of $20,000 ($20,000 × 100%) is imposed.

If Gold distributes the $20,000 of undistributed income for 1993 within 90 days of the deficiency notice, the additional tax is waived. Without this distribution, however, the foundation will owe $32,750 ($12,750 + $20,000) in taxes. ▼

UNRELATED BUSINESS INCOME TAX

6 **LEARNING OBJECTIVE**
Determine when an exempt organization is subject to the unrelated business income tax and calculate the amount of the tax.

As explained in the previous section, private foundations are subject to excise taxes for certain actions. One of these excise taxes penalizes the private foundation for using the foundation to gain control of unrelated businesses (tax on excess business holdings). However, *unrelated business* has different meanings for purposes of that excise tax and for the unrelated business income tax.

The **unrelated business income tax (UBIT)** is designed to treat the entity as if it were subject to the corporate income tax. Thus, the rates that are used are those applicable to a corporate taxpayer.[28] In general, **unrelated business income** is derived from activities not related to the exempt purpose of the exempt organization. The tax is levied because the organization is engaging in substantial commercial activities.[29] Without such a tax, nonexempt organizations (regular taxable business entities) would be at a substantial disadvantage when trying to compete with the exempt organization. Thus, the UBIT is intended to neutralize the exempt entity's tax advantage.[30]

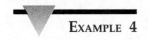

EXAMPLE 4

Historic, Inc., is an exempt private foundation. Its exempt activity is to maintain a restoration of eighteenth-century colonial life (houses, public buildings, taverns, businesses, and craft demonstrations) that is visited by over a million people each year. A fee is charged for admission to the "restored area." In addition to this "museum" activity, Historic operates two hotels and three restaurants that are available to the general public. The earnings from the hotel and restaurant business are used to defray the costs of operating the "museum" activity.

The "museum" activity is not subject to the Federal income tax, except to the extent of any tax liability for any of the aforementioned excise taxes that are levied on private foundations. However, even though the income from the hotel and restaurant business is used for exempt purposes, that income is unrelated business income and is subject to the UBIT. ▼

The UBIT applies to all organizations that are exempt from Federal income tax under § 501(c), except Federal agencies. In addition, the tax applies to state colleges and universities.[31]

---

[28] § 511(a)(1).
[29] § 512(a)(1).

[30] Reg. § 1.513–1(b).
[31] § 511(a)(2) and Reg. § 1.511–2(a)(2).

ADDITIONAL IRS SCRUTINY FOR TAX-EXEMPTS

Tax-exempt organizations as a group (excluding churches) gross well in excess of $1 trillion each year according to private estimates ($700 billion according to the IRS). They represent big business in terms of both their revenues and their CEO compensation. According to a survey by the *Chronicle of Philanthropy*, at least 154 tax-exempts pay their CEO (or other top official) more than $100,000 a year, and 83 pay more than $200,000 a year.

Such organizations are subject to Federal income taxation on their unrelated business income (i.e., when they compete with for-profit entities). However, substantial differences of opinion exist over what is an unrelated trade or business for a tax-exempt organization.

The IRS is devoting additional audit resources to tax-exempts. Of particular interest are the 15 percent of the 1.1 million tax-exempts that account for 50 percent of the gross revenue generated by tax-exempts. Included in this group are universities, hospitals, the National Rifle Association (NRA), and the American Association of Retired People (AARP). Among other things, the IRS is scrutinizing compliance with the limits on lobbying and the payment of the unrelated business income tax (UBIT). According to Neal Knox, an NRA vice president, the NRA audit could last two to three years.

A materiality exception generally exempts an entity from being subject to the UBIT if such income is insignificant. See the later discussion of the $1,000 statutory deduction generally available to all exempt organizations.

UNRELATED TRADE OR BUSINESS

An exempt organization may be subject to the UBIT in the following circumstances.[32]

- The organization conducts a trade or business.
- The trade or business is not substantially related to the exempt purpose of the organization.
- The trade or business is regularly carried on by the organization.

The Code specifically exempts the following activities from classification as an unrelated trade or business. Thus, even if all of the above factors are present, the activity is not classified as an unrelated trade or business.[33]

- The individuals performing substantially all the work of the trade or business do so without compensation (e.g., an orphanage operates a retail store for sales to the general public, and all the work is done by volunteers).
- The trade or business consists of selling merchandise, and substantially all of the merchandise has been received as gifts or contributions (e.g., thrift shops).
- For § 501(c)(3) organizations and for state colleges or universities, the trade or business is conducted primarily for the convenience of the organization's

---

[32] § 513(a) and Reg. § 1.513–2(a).

[33] § 513(a).

members, students, patients, officers, or employees (e.g., a laundry operated by the college for laundering dormitory linens and students' clothing, a college bookstore).
- For most employee unions, the trade or business consists of selling to members, at their usual place of employment, work-related clothing and equipment and items normally sold through vending machines, snack bars, or food dispensing facilities.

Definition of Trade or Business. Trade or business, for this purpose, is broadly defined. It includes any activity conducted for the production of income through the sale of merchandise or the performance of services. An activity need not generate a profit to be treated as a trade or business. The activity may be part of a larger set of activities conducted by the organization, some of which may be related to the exempt purpose. Being included in a larger set does not cause the activity to lose its identity as an unrelated trade or business.[34]

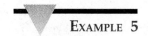

EXAMPLE 5   Health, Inc., is an exempt hospital that operates a pharmacy. The pharmacy provides medicines and supplies to the patients in the hospital (i.e., it contributes to the conduct of the hospital's exempt purpose). In addition, the pharmacy sells medicines and supplies to the general public. The activity of selling to the general public constitutes a trade or business for purposes of the UBIT. ▼

Not Substantially Related to the Exempt Purpose. Exempt organizations frequently conduct unrelated trades or businesses in order to provide income to help defray the costs of conducting the exempt purpose (like the hotel and restaurant businesses in Example 4). Providing financial support for the exempt purpose will not prevent an activity from being classified as an unrelated trade or business and thereby being subject to the UBIT.

To be related to the accomplishment of the exempt purpose, the conduct of the business activities must be causally related and contribute importantly to the exempt purpose. Whether a causal relationship exists and the degree of its importance are determined by examining the facts and circumstances. One must consider the size and extent of the activities in relation to the nature and extent of the exempt function that the activities serve.[35]

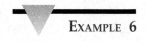

EXAMPLE 6   Art, Inc., an exempt organization, operates a school for training children in the performing arts. As an essential part of that training, the children perform for the general public. The children are paid at the minimum wage for the performances, and Art derives gross income by charging admission to the performances.

The income from admissions is not income from an unrelated trade or business, because the performances by the children contribute importantly to the accomplishment of the exempt purpose of providing training in the performing arts. ▼

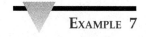

EXAMPLE 7   Assume the same facts as in Example 6, except that four performances are conducted each weekend of the year. Assume that this number of performances far exceeds that required for training the children. Thus, the part of the income derived from admissions for these excess performances is income from an unrelated trade or business. ▼

The trade or business may sell merchandise that has been produced as part of the accomplishment of the exempt purpose. The sale of such merchandise is normally treated as related to the exempt purpose. However, if the merchandise is

---

[34] Reg. § 1.513–1(b).   [35] Reg. § 1.513–1(d).

not sold in substantially the same state it was in at the completion of the exempt purpose, the gross income subsequently derived from the sale of the merchandise is income from an unrelated trade or business.[36]

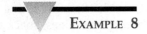

EXAMPLE 8

Help, Inc., an exempt organization, conducts programs for the rehabilitation of the handicapped. One of the programs includes training in radio and television repair. Help derives gross income by selling the repaired items. The income is substantially related to the accomplishment of the exempt purpose. ▼

An asset or facility used in the exempt purpose may also be used in a nonexempt purpose. Income derived from the use in a nonexempt purpose is income from an unrelated trade or business.[37]

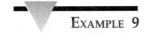

EXAMPLE 9

Civil, Inc., an exempt organization, operates a museum. As part of the exempt purpose of the museum, educational lectures are given in the museum's theater during the operating hours of the museum. In the evening, when the museum is closed, the theater is leased to an individual who operates a movie theater. The lease income received from the individual who operates the movie theater is income from an unrelated trade or business. ▼

ETHICAL CONSIDERATIONS

Tax-Exempt Bingo

Assist, Inc., is a § 501(c)(3) exempt organization. Its mission is to help feed and clothe the homeless. Assist does this through providing a shelter, clothes closet, and soup kitchen for the homeless in the inner city.

Donations (i.e., both cash and property) are the principal source of Assist's revenue. Contributions result from mailings and from help kettles located outside area supermarkets. In addition, Assist sponsors bingo games on Friday and Saturday evenings. Approximately 30 percent of Assist's revenues come from the bingo games.

You are a new member of Assist's board of directors. You are an employee (recently promoted to manager) of an accounting firm, and you specialize in the financial services industry. Over lunch with one of your firm's tax partners (your unofficial mentor), you mention your service on Assist's board of directors. She provides you with information on the normal Federal income tax reporting requirements of exempt organizations [i.e., Form 1023: Application for Recognition of Exemption under Section 501(a); Form 990: Return of Organization Exempt from Income Tax, or Form 990–PF: Return of Private Foundation; and Form 990–T: Exempt Organization Business Income Tax Return].

You later ask Al Martin, Assist's foundation manager, who was the driving force behind the creation of Assist 15 years ago, for copies of these forms. He provides you with a copy of Form 1023 and a copy of Form 990–PF for the past three years. He says the CPA who served on the board prior to you told him that it was not necessary for Assist to file any Federal tax returns associated with the bingo games because Assist is tax-exempt.

You are aware that bingo games are illegal in your state. You also are aware that many tax-exempt organizations in your city and in other locales in the state conduct bingo games. The police "look the other way" as long as the sponsor is a tax-exempt organization. In fact, several local churches are Assist's biggest bingo game competitors. How should you respond?

---

[36] Reg. § 1.513–1(d)(4)(ii).

[37] Reg. § 1.513–1(d)(4)(iii) addresses the allocation of expenses to exempt and nonexempt activities.

TAX IN THE NEWS

BE CAREFUL IF YOU SAY BINGO:
SPONSORS, VOLUNTEERS, AND PLAYERS

The IRS is interested in two areas associated with bingo. First, if you win a bingo prize, the prize is included in your gross income. Second, if you are a tax-exempt organization that sponsors bingo games, you must comply with IRS rules to maintain your tax-exempt status and not to be subject to the unrelated business income tax (UBIT).

Apparently, the IRS and local officials think that certain bingo sponsors in Richmond and Hampton Roads, Virginia, may not be playing by the rules. Therefore, the IRS is examining some of these bingo sponsors to see if they continue to qualify for tax-exempt status.

In Virginia, as in most states, bingo is legal only for the purpose of raising money for charity. Under the Virginia law, tax-exempt bingo sponsors must be separate from businesses that rent bingo halls and sell bingo supplies. Allegedly under investigation are links between the landlords of bingo halls and tax-exempts that conduct bingo games there.

A third area of IRS concern is the receipt of tips by bingo game employees and the effect this may have on the UBIT. In a recent Tax Court decision (*Executive Network Club*, T.C.Memo. 1995–21), the court ruled that the receipt of tips by volunteers who run bingo games for tax-exempt organizations results in the gambling income received by the tax-exempt sponsoring organization being subject to the UBIT.

SOURCE: Information from "IRS Reviews Local Bingo Records," *Newport News Daily Press*, May 29, 1995, p. B6.

Special Rule for Bingo Games. A special provision applies in determining whether income from bingo games is from an unrelated trade or business. Under this provision, a *qualified bingo game* is not an unrelated trade or business if both of the following requirements are satisfied.[38]

- The bingo game is legal under both state and local law.
- Commercial bingo games (conducted for a profit motive) ordinarily are not permitted in the jurisdiction.

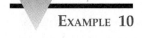
EXAMPLE 10

Play, Inc., an exempt organization, conducts weekly bingo games. The laws of the state and municipality in which Play conducts the games expressly provide that exempt organizations may conduct bingo games, but do not permit profit-oriented entities to do so. Since both of the requirements for bingo games are satisfied, the bingo games conducted by Play are not an unrelated trade or business. ▼

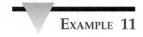
EXAMPLE 11

Game, Inc., an exempt organization, conducts weekly bingo games in City X and City Y. State law expressly permits exempt organizations to conduct bingo games. State law also provides that profit-oriented entities may conduct bingo games in X, which is a resort community. Several businesses regularly conduct bingo games there.

---

[38] § 513(f).

The bingo games conducted by Game in Y are not an unrelated trade or business. However, the bingo games that Game conducts in X are an unrelated trade or business, because commercial bingo games are regularly permitted to be conducted there. ▼

Special Rule for Distribution of Low-Cost Articles.   If an exempt organization distributes low-cost items as an incidental part of its solicitation for charitable contributions, the distributions may not be considered an unrelated trade or business. A low-cost article is one that costs $6.70 (for 1996—indexed annually) or less. Examples are pens, stamps, stickers, stationery, and address labels. If more than one item is distributed to a person during the calendar year, the costs of the items are combined.[39]

Special Rule for Rental or Exchange of Membership Lists.   If an exempt organization conducts a trade or business that consists of either exchanging with or renting to other exempt organizations the organization's donor or membership list (mailing lists), the activity is not an unrelated trade or business.[40]

Other Special Rules.   Other special rules are used in determining whether each of the following activities is an unrelated trade or business.[41]

- Qualified public entertainment activities (e.g., a state fair).
- Qualified convention and trade show activities.
- Certain services provided at cost or less by a hospital to other small hospitals.
- Certain pole rentals by telephone or electric companies.

Discussion of these special rules is beyond the scope of this text.

UNRELATED BUSINESS INCOME

Even when an exempt organization conducts an unrelated trade or business, a tax is assessed only if the exempt organization regularly conducts the activity and the business produces unrelated business income.

Regularly Carried on by the Organization.   An activity is classified as unrelated business income only if it is regularly carried on by the exempt organization. This provision assures that only activities that are actually competing with taxable organizations are subject to the unrelated business income tax. Accordingly, factors to be considered in assessing *regularly carried on* include the frequency of the activity, the continuity of the activity, and the manner in which the activity is pursued.[42]

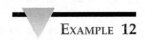

EXAMPLE 12

Silver, Inc., an exempt organization, owns land that is located next to the state fairgrounds. During the 10 days of the state fair, Silver uses the land as a parking lot and charges individuals attending the state fair for parking there. The activity is not regularly carried on. ▼

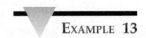

EXAMPLE 13

Black, Inc., an exempt organization, has its offices in the downtown area. It owns a parking lot adjacent to its offices on which its employees park during the week. On Saturdays, it rents the spaces in the parking lot to individuals shopping or working in the downtown

---

[39] § 513(h)(1)(A).
[40] § 513(h)(1)(B).

[41] §§ 513(d), (e), and (g).
[42] § 512(a)(1) and Reg. § 1.513–1(c).

area. Black is conducting a business activity on a year-round basis, even though it is only for one day per week. Thus, an activity is regularly being carried on. ▼

Unrelated Business Income Defined.   Unrelated business income is generally that derived from the unrelated trade or business. To convert it from a gross income measure to a net income measure, it must be reduced by the deductions directly connected with the conduct of the unrelated trade or business.[43]

UNRELATED BUSINESS TAXABLE INCOME

General Tax Model.   The model for unrelated business taxable income (UBTI) appears in Figure 23–2.

Positive adjustments[44]

1. The charitable contribution deduction is permitted without regard to whether the charitable contributions are associated with the unrelated trade or business. However, to the extent the charitable contributions deducted in calculating net unrelated business income (see Figure 23–2) exceed 10 percent of UBTI (without regard to the charitable contribution deduction), the excess is treated as a positive adjustment.

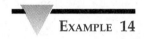

EXAMPLE 14

Brown, Inc., an exempt organization, has UBTI of $100,000 (excluding any modifications associated with charitable contributions). Total charitable contributions (all associated with the unrelated trade or business) are $13,000. Assuming that the $13,000 is deducted in calculating net unrelated business income, the excess of $3,000 [$13,000 − 10%($100,000)] is a positive adjustment in calculating UBTI. ▼

2. Unrelated debt-financed income net of the unrelated debt-financed deductions (see the subsequent discussion of Unrelated Debt-Financed Income).
3. Certain interest, annuity, royalty, and rent income received by the exempt organization from an organization it controls (80 percent test). Note that this provision overrides the modifications for these types of income (negative adjustment 3).

Negative adjustments

1. Income from dividends, interest, and annuities net of all deductions directly related to producing such income.
2. Royalty income, regardless of whether it is measured by production, gross income, or taxable income from the property, net of all deductions directly related to producing such income.

▼ **FIGURE 23–2**
Tax Formula for Unrelated
Business Taxable Income

Gross unrelated business income

− Deductions

= Net unrelated business income

± Modifications

= Unrelated business taxable income

---

[43] § 512(a)(1).

[44] §§ 512(a)(1) and (b) and Reg. § 1.512(b)–1.

3. Rent income from real property and from certain personal property net of all deductions directly related to producing such income. Personal property rents are included in the negative adjustment only if the personal property is leased with the real property. In addition, the personal property rent income must be incidental (does not exceed 10 percent of the total rent income under the lease) to be used in computing the negative adjustment. In both of the following cases, however, none of the rent income is treated as a negative adjustment.

  • More than 50 percent of the rent income under the lease is from personal property.
  • Rent income is calculated using the tenant's profits.

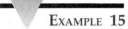

EXAMPLE 15

Beaver, Inc., an exempt organization, leases land and a building (realty) and computers (personalty) housed in the building. Under the lease, $46,000 of the rent is for the land and building, and $4,000 is for the computers. Expenses incurred for the land and building are $10,000. The net rent income from the land and building of $36,000 ($46,000 − $10,000) and the $4,000 from the computers are negative adjustments. ▼

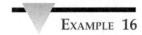

EXAMPLE 16

Assume the same facts as in Example 15, except that the rent income is $35,000 from the land and building and $15,000 from the computers. Since the rent income from the computers exceeds $5,000 (i.e., 10% of the total rent under the lease) and is not incidental, it is not a negative adjustment. ▼

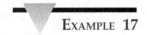

EXAMPLE 17

Assume the same facts as in Example 15, except that the rent income is $20,000 from the land and building and $30,000 from the computers. Since over 50% of the rent income under the lease is from the computers, neither the rent income from the land and building nor that from the computers is a negative adjustment. ▼

If the lessor of real property provides significant services to the lessee, such income, for this purpose, is not rent income.

4. Gains and losses from the sale, exchange, or other disposition of property *except for* inventory.

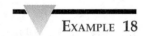

EXAMPLE 18

Beaver, the owner of the land, building, and computers in Example 15, sells these assets for $450,000. Their adjusted basis is $300,000. Beaver's recognized gain of $150,000 is a negative adjustment. ▼

5. Certain research income net of all deductions directly related to producing that income.
6. The charitable contribution deduction is permitted without regard to whether the charitable contributions are associated with the unrelated trade or business. Therefore, to the extent that the charitable contributions exceed those deducted in calculating net unrelated business income (see Figure 23–2), the excess is a negative adjustment in calculating UBTI.

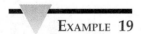

EXAMPLE 19

Canine, Inc., an exempt organization, has unrelated business taxable income of $100,000 (excluding any modifications associated with charitable contributions). The total charitable contributions are $9,000, of which $7,000 (those associated with the unrelated trade or business) has been deducted in calculating net unrelated business income. Therefore, the remaining $2,000 of charitable contributions is a negative adjustment in calculating UBTI. ▼

7. A specific deduction of $1,000 is permitted.

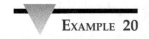

EXAMPLE 20

Petit Care, Inc., an exempt organization, has net unrelated business income of $800. Since Petit will receive a specific deduction of $1,000, its UBTI is $0. Therefore, its income tax liability is $0. ▼

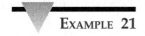

EXAMPLE 21

Patient, Inc., an exempt organization, has UBTI of $500,000. Patient's income tax liability is $170,000 ($500,000 UBTI × 34% corporate tax rate). ▼

UNRELATED DEBT-FINANCED INCOME

In the formula for calculating the tax on unrelated business income (refer to Figure 23–2), unrelated debt-financed income is one of the positive adjustments. Examples of income from debt-financed property include the rental of real estate, rental of tangible personal property, and investments in corporate stock, including gains from the disposition of such property. Gains from property that is unrelated business income property are also included to the extent the gains are not otherwise treated as unrelated business income. Because of the importance of this item, it is discussed separately here.

In terms of the UBIT, the positive adjustment for unrelated debt-financed income is a significant one. Without this provision, a tax-exempt organization could use borrowed funds to acquire unrelated business or investment property and use the untaxed (i.e., exempt) earnings from the acquisition to pay for the property.

Definition of Debt-Financed Income. **Debt-financed income** is the gross income generated from debt-financed property. *Debt-financed property* is all property of the exempt organization that is held to produce income and on which there is acquisition indebtedness, *except* for the following.[45]

- Property where substantially all (at least 85 percent) of the use is for the achievement of the exempt purpose of the exempt organization.[46]
- Property whose gross income is otherwise treated as unrelated business income.
- Property whose gross income is from the following sources and is not otherwise treated as unrelated business income.
  - Income from research performed for the United States, a Federal governmental agency, or a state or a political subdivision thereof.
  - For a college, university, or hospital, income from research.
  - For an organization that performs fundamental (i.e., not applied) research for the benefit of the general public, income from research.
  - Property used in an activity that is not an unrelated trade or business.

If the 85 percent test is not satisfied, only the portion of the property that is *not* used for the exempt purpose is debt-financed property.

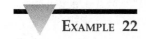

EXAMPLE 22

Deer, Inc., an exempt organization, owns a five-story office building on which there is acquisition indebtedness. Three of the floors are used for Deer's exempt purpose. The two other floors are leased to Purple Corporation. In this case, the *substantially all* test is not satisfied. Therefore, 40% of the office building is debt-financed property, and 60% is not. ▼

Certain land that is acquired by an exempt organization for later exempt use is excluded from debt-financed property if the following requirements are satisfied.[47]

---

[45] § 514(b).
[46] Reg. § 1.514(b)–1(b)(1)(ii).

[47] § 514(b)(3).

- The principal purpose of acquiring the land is for (substantially all its) use in achieving the organization's exempt purpose.
- This use will begin within 10 years of the acquisition date.
- At the date when the land is acquired, it is located in the *neighborhood* of other property of the organization for which substantially all the use is for achieving the organization's exempt purpose.

Even if the third requirement is not satisfied (the property is not located in the neighborhood), the land still is excluded from debt-financed property if it is converted to use for achieving the organization's exempt purpose within the 10-year period. Qualification under this provision will result in a refund of taxes previously paid. If the exempt organization is a church, the 10-year period becomes a 15-year period, and the neighborhood requirement is waived.

Definition of Acquisition Indebtedness. Acquisition indebtedness is debt sustained by the exempt organization in association with the acquisition of property. More precisely, *acquisition indebtedness* consists of the unpaid amounts of the following for debt-financed property.[48]

- Debt incurred in acquiring or improving the property.
- Debt incurred before the property was acquired or improved, but which would not have been incurred without the acquisition or improvement.
- Debt incurred after the property was acquired or improved, but which would not have been incurred without the acquisition or improvement.

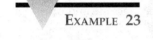

EXAMPLE 23   Red, Inc., an exempt organization, acquires land for $100,000. In order to finance the acquisition, Red mortgages the land with a bank and receives loan proceeds of $80,000. Red leases the land to Duck Corporation. The mortgage is acquisition indebtedness. ▼

EXAMPLE 24   Rose, Inc., an exempt organization, makes improvements to an office building that it rents to Bird Corporation. Excess working capital funds are used to finance the improvements. Rose is later required to mortgage its laboratory building, which it uses for its exempt purpose, to replenish working capital. The mortgage is acquisition indebtedness. ▼

Portion of Debt-Financed Income and Deductions Treated as Unrelated Business Taxable Income.   Once the amount of the debt-financed income and deductions is determined, it is necessary to ascertain what portion is unrelated debt-financed income and deductions. Unrelated debt-financed income increases unrelated business taxable income, and unrelated debt-financed deductions decrease unrelated business taxable income.

The calculation is made for each debt-financed property. The gross income from the property is multiplied by the following percentage.[49]

$$\frac{\text{Average acquisition indebtedness for the property}}{\text{Average adjusted basis of the property}} = \frac{\text{Debt/basis}}{\text{percentage}}$$

This percentage cannot exceed 100. If debt-financed property is disposed of during the taxable year at a gain, average acquisition indebtedness in the formula is replaced with highest acquisition indebtedness. *Highest acquisition indebtedness* is the largest amount of acquisition indebtedness for the property during the 12-month period preceding the date of disposition.[50]

---

[48] § 514(c)(1). Educational organizations in certain limited circumstances can exclude debt incurred for real property acquisitions from classification as acquisition indebtedness.

[49] § 514(a)(1).
[50] § 514(c)(7).

Deductions are allowed for expenses directly related to the debt-financed property and the income from it. Cost recovery deductions must be calculated using the straight-line method. Once allowable deductions are determined, this amount is multiplied by the debt/basis percentage.[51]

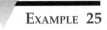

EXAMPLE 25

White, Inc., an exempt organization, owns an office building that it leases to Squirrel Corporation for $120,000 per year. The average acquisition indebtedness is $300,000, and the average adjusted basis is $500,000. Since the office building is debt-financed property, the unrelated debt-financed income is:

$$\frac{\$300,000}{\$500,000} \times \$120,000 = \$72,000$$

▼

Average Acquisition Indebtedness. The *average acquisition indebtedness* for debt-financed property is the average amount of the outstanding debt for the taxable year (ignoring interest) during the portion of the year the property is held by the exempt organization. This amount is calculated by summing the outstanding debt on the first day of each calendar month the property is held by the exempt organization. Then this total is divided by the number of months the property is held by the organization. [52]

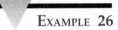

EXAMPLE 26

On August 12, Yellow, Inc., an exempt organization, acquires an office building that is debt-financed property for $500,000. The initial mortgage on the property is $400,000. The principal amount of the debt on the first of each month is as follows.

Month	Principal Amount
August	$ 400,000
September	380,000
October	360,000
November	340,000
December	320,000
	$1,800,000

Average acquisition indebtedness is $360,000 ($1,800,000 ÷ 5 months). Note that even though August is only a partial month, it is treated as a full month. ▼

Average Adjusted Basis. The *average adjusted basis* of debt-financed property is calculated by summing the adjusted bases of the property on the first and last days during the taxable year the property is held by the exempt organization and then dividing by two.[53]

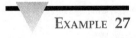

EXAMPLE 27

Assume the facts are the same as in Example 26. In addition, during the taxable year, depreciation of $5,900 is deducted. The average adjusted basis is $497,050 [($500,000 + $494,100) ÷ 2]. ▼

Concept Summary 23–4 presents the rules concerning the UBIT.

---

[51] § 514(a)(3).

[52] § 514(c)(7) and Reg. § 1.514(a)–1(a)(3). A partial month is treated as a full month.

[53] § 514(a)(1) and Reg. § 1.514(a)–1(a)(2).

CONCEPT SUMMARY 23–4

Unrelated Business Income Tax

Purpose	To tax the entity on unrelated business income as if it were subject to the corporate income tax.
Applicable tax rates	Corporate tax rates.
Exempt organizations to which applicable	All organizations exempt under § 501(c), except Federal agencies.
Entities subject to the tax	Organizations that regularly conduct a trade or business that is not substantially related to the exempt purpose of the organization.
Exceptions to the tax	• All the work is performed by volunteers. • Substantially all of the merchandise being sold has been received by gift. • For § 501(c)(3) organizations, the business is conducted primarily for the benefit of the organization's members, students, patients, officers, or employees. • For most employee unions, the trade or business consists of selling to members work-related clothing and equipment and items normally sold through vending machines, snack bars, or food-dispensing facilities.
$1,000 provision	If the gross income from an unrelated trade or business is less than $1,000, it is not necessary to file a return associated with the unrelated business income tax.

REPORTING REQUIREMENTS

OBTAINING EXEMPT ORGANIZATION STATUS

7 **LEARNING OBJECTIVE**
List the reports exempt organizations must file with the IRS and the related due dates.

Not all exempt organizations are required to obtain IRS approval for their exempt status. Among those required by statute to do so are organizations exempt under §§ 501(c)(3), 501(c)(9), and 501(c)(20).[54] Even in these cases, exceptions are provided (e.g., churches).

Even when not required to obtain IRS approval, most exempt organizations do apply for exempt status. Typically, an organization does not want to assume that it qualifies for exempt status and describe itself in that way to the public, only to have the IRS rule later that it does not qualify.

If an organization is required to obtain IRS approval for its exempt status and does not do so, it does not qualify as an exempt organization.

ETHICAL CONSIDERATIONS

Filing for Exempt Status: A CPA's Dilemma

Waldo is the treasurer of the Alpine Sky Divers Club. In his opinion, the club satisfies all the requirements for exempt status as a social club under § 501(c)(7). When Annette, the club president and an assistant DA, asks him if he

---

has completed all the paperwork with the IRS relating to the club's tax-exempt status, Waldo assures her that he has taken care of everything.

If this were another client, Waldo would have filed a Form 1024 [Application for Recognition of Exemption under Section 501(a)]. He has not done so for Alpine because he has been very busy at work and feels fairly certain that the IRS will never raise the issue of whether the club qualifies for tax-exempt status. He told Annette he had filed the papers with the IRS because she is a stickler for detail and does everything by the book. He also has had several dates with her and does not want to take a chance on spoiling their relationship.

Evaluate Waldo's behavior.

ANNUAL FILING REQUIREMENTS

Most exempt organizations are required to file an annual information return.[55] The return is filed on Form 990 (Return of Organization Exempt from Income Tax). The following exempt organizations need not file Form 990.[56]

- Federal agencies.
- Churches.
- Organizations whose annual gross receipts do not exceed $25,000.
- Private foundations.

Private foundations are required to file Form 990–PF (Return of Private Foundation).

The due date for Form 990 or Form 990–PF is the fifteenth day of the fifth month after the end of the taxable year. These returns are filed with the appropriate IRS Service Center based on the location of the exempt organization's principal office. Requests for extensions on filing are made by filing Form 2758 (Applications for Extension of Time).

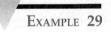

EXAMPLE 28

Green, Inc., a § 501(c)(3) organization, has a fiscal year that ends June 30, 1996. The due date for the annual return is November 15, 1996. If Green were a calendar year entity, the due date for the 1996 annual return would be May 15, 1997. ▼

Exempt organizations that are subject to the UBIT may be required to file Form 990–T (Exempt Organization Business Income Tax Return). The return must be filed if the organization has gross income of at least $1,000 from an unrelated trade or business. The due date for the return is the fifteenth day of the fifth month after the end of the taxable year.

EXAMPLE 29

During the year, the First Church of Kentwood receives parishioner contributions of $450,000. Of this amount, $125,000 is designated for the church building fund. First Church is not required to file an annual return (Form 990) because churches are exempt from doing so. In addition, it is not required to file Form 990–T because it has no unrelated business income.

Colonial, Inc., is an exempt private foundation. Gross receipts for the year total $800,000, of which 60% is from admission fees paid by members of the general public who visit Colonial's museum of eighteenth-century life. The balance is endowment income. Because Colonial is a private foundation, it must file Form 990–PF.

Orange, Inc., is an exempt organization and is not a private foundation. Gross receipts for the year are $20,000. None of this amount is unrelated business income. Orange is not required to file Form 990 because its annual gross receipts do not exceed $25,000.

---

[55] § 6033(a)(1).

[56] § 6033(a)(2).

Restoration, Inc., is an exempt private foundation. Gross receipts for the year are $20,000. None of this amount is unrelated business income. Restoration must file Form 990–PF because private foundations are not eligible for the $25,000 filing exception.

During the year, the Second Church of Port Allen receives parishioner contributions of $300,000. In addition, the church has unrelated business income of $5,000. Second Church is not required to file Form 990 because churches are exempt from doing so. Form 990–T must be filed, however, because churches are not exempt from the UBIT and Second Church has exceeded the $1,000 floor. ▼

TAX PLANNING CONSIDERATIONS

8 **LEARNING OBJECTIVE**
Identify tax planning opportunities for exempt organizations.

GENERAL

Exempt organizations provide at least two potential tax benefits. First, the entity may be exempt from Federal income tax. Second, contributions to the entity may be deductible by the donor.

An organization that qualifies as an exempt organization may still be subject to certain types of Federal income tax, including the following.

- Tax on prohibited transactions.
- Tax on feeder organizations.
- Tax on private foundations.
- Tax on unrelated business income.

Therefore, classification as an exempt organization should not be interpreted to mean that the organization need not be concerned with any Federal income tax. Such a belief can result in the organization engaging in transactions that produce a substantial tax liability.

An organization is exempt from taxation only if it fits into one of the categories enumerated in the Code. Thus, particular attention must be given to the qualification requirements. These requirements must continue to be satisfied to avoid termination of exempt status (in effect, they are now maintenance requirements).

MAINTAINING EXEMPT STATUS

To maintain exempt status, the organization must satisfy both an organizational test and an operational test. The organizational test requires that the entity satisfy the statutory requirements for exempt status on paper. The operational test ensures that the entity does, in fact, satisfy the statutory requirements for exempt status.

King Shipping Consum., Inc. (Zion Coptic Church, Inc.) indicates that it is usually much easier to satisfy the organizational test than the operational test.[57] Zion's stated purpose was to engage in activities usually and normally associated with churches. Based on this, the IRS approved Zion's exempt status as a § 501(c)(3) organization.

Zion's real intent, however, was to smuggle illegal drugs into the country and to distribute them for profit. The church's justification for the drugs was that it used marijuana in its sacrament. During a four-month period, however, the police confiscated 33 tons of marijuana from church members. The IRS calculated that, even assuming the maximum alleged church membership of several thousand, each member would have had to smoke over 33 pounds of marijuana during the four-month confiscation period.

The court concluded that Zion's real purpose was to cloak a large commercial drug smuggling operation. Since this activity was inconsistent with the religious

---

[57] 58 TCM 574, T.C.Memo. 1989–593.

purpose for exempt status, the court upheld the IRS's revocation of Zion's exempt status and the deficiency assessment of approximately $1.6 million.

PRIVATE FOUNDATION STATUS

Exempt organizations that can qualify as public charities receive more beneficial tax treatment than those that qualify as private foundations. Thus, if possible, the organization should be structured to qualify as a public charity. The following can result when an exempt organization is classified as a private foundation.

- Taxes may be imposed on the private foundation.

  - Tax based on investment income.
  - Tax on self-dealing.
  - Tax on failure to distribute income.
  - Tax on excess business holdings.
  - Tax on investments that jeopardize charitable purposes.
  - Tax on taxable expenditures.

- Donors may receive less favorable tax deduction treatment under § 170 than they would if the exempt organization were not a private foundation.

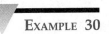

EXAMPLE 30

David has IBM stock ($25,000 adjusted basis, $100,000 fair market value) that he is going to contribute to one of the following exempt organizations: Blue, Inc., a public charity, or Teal, Inc., a private nonoperating foundation. David has owned the stock for five years.

David asks the manager of each organization to describe the tax benefits of contributing to that organization. He tells them he is in the 31% tax bracket.

Based on the data provided by the managers, David decides to contribute the stock to Blue, Inc. He calculates the amount of the charitable contribution under each option as follows.[58]

Donee	Contribution Deduction	Tax Rate	Contribution Borne by U.S. Government
Blue	$100,000	31%	$31,000
Teal	25,000 ($100,000 − $75,000)	31%	7,750

One method of avoiding private foundation status is to have a tax-exempt purpose that results in the organization not being classified as a private foundation (the *organization* approach). If this is not feasible, it may be possible to operate the organization so that it receives broad public support and thereby avoids private foundation status (the *operational* approach).

If the organization is a private foundation, care must be exercised to avoid the assessment of tax liability on prohibited transactions. This objective can best be achieved by establishing controls that prevent the private foundation from engaging in transactions that trigger the imposition of the taxes. If an initial tax is assessed, corrective actions should be implemented to avoid the assessment of an additional tax. See Concept Summary 23–5.

UNRELATED BUSINESS INCOME TAX

If the exempt organization conducts an unrelated trade or business, it may be subject to tax on the unrelated business income. Worse yet, the unrelated trade or

[58] See Chapter 9.

CONCEPT SUMMARY 23–5

Private Foundation Status

	Exempt Organization Is	
	A Private Foundation	Not a Private Foundation
Reason for classification	Does not serve the common good because it lacks an approved exempt purpose or does not receive broad public financial support.	Serves the common good
Eligible for exempt status?	Yes	Yes
Most beneficial charitable contribution deduction treatment available to donors?	Depends. No, if the private foundation is classified as a private *nonoperating* foundation.	Yes
Subject to excise taxes levied on prohibited transactions?	Yes	No
Subject to tax on unrelated business income?	Yes	Yes

business could result in the loss of exempt status if the IRS determines that the activity is the primary purpose of the organization. Thus, caution and planning should be used to eliminate the latter possibility and to minimize the former.

KEY TERMS

Debt-financed income, 23–23

Excess lobbying expenditure, 23–10

Exempt organization, 23–2

Feeder organization, 23–11

Grass roots lobbying expenditure, 23–9

Lobbying expenditure, 23–9

Private foundation, 23–11

Unrelated business income, 23–15

Unrelated business income tax (UBIT), 23–15

PROBLEM MATERIALS

DISCUSSION QUESTIONS

1. Are all churches exempt from Federal income tax?

2. Why are certain organizations either partially or completely exempt from Federal income tax?

3. Identify which of the following organizations qualify for exempt status.
   a. Tulane University.
   b. Federal Land Bank.
   c. Red Cross.

    d. Disneyland.

    e. PTA.

    f. Jacksonville Chamber of Commerce.

    g. Colonial Williamsburg Foundation.

    h. Dallas Cowboys.

4. Identify the statutory authority under which each of the following is exempt from Federal income tax.

    a. Kingsmill Country Club.

    b. Shady Lawn Cemetery.

    c. Amber Credit Union.

    d. Veterans of Foreign Wars.

    e. Girl Scouts of America.

    f. United Fund. ·

    g. Federal Deposit Insurance Corporation.

    h. Apostles of Christ Church.

    i. PTA.

    j. National Press Club.

5. Adrenna is the treasurer for two exempt organizations. One exempt organization pays no Federal income taxes for 1996, and the other pays Federal income taxes of $100,000 for 1996. Discuss potential reasons for this difference in tax results.

6. In addition to exemption from Federal income tax, for what other benefits may an exempt organization be eligible?

7. What negative tax consequences may be associated with an exempt organization engaging in § 503 prohibited transactions?

8. Cashmier, Inc., a § 501(c)(3) organization, loses its exempt status in 1996 for attempting to influence legislation. Golden, Inc., another § 501(c)(3) organization, also attempts to influence legislation and is in no danger of losing its exempt status. Explain.

9. Rex is the chief executive officer of Helping People, Inc., a § 501(c)(3) exempt organization located in Mobile, Alabama. He and the organization's board of directors are concerned about the effect that proposed legislation would have on the organization's budget and its ability to carry out its mission. They are discussing a proposal to have a law firm in Washington, D.C., aid in opposing the legislation. What tax issues are relevant to Helping People, Inc., as it makes this decision?

10. The Living Museum is a tax-exempt organization. Dolphin Corporation, a wholly owned subsidiary of the Living Museum, sells boats. Dolphin remits all of its earnings each year to its parent. Is Dolphin exempt from Federal income tax because it is a subsidiary of a tax-exempt organization and remits all of its earnings to a tax-exempt organization?

11. What types of activities are not subject to the tax imposed on feeder organizations?

12. What is a private foundation, and what are the disadvantages of an exempt organization being classified as a private foundation?

13. Describe the external support test for a private foundation.

14. What types of taxes may be levied on a private foundation? Why are the taxes levied?

15. What is the purpose of the tax on the investment income of a private foundation? Discuss the applicable tax rates.

16. A private foundation engages in a transaction with a disqualified person. What are the tax consequences to the private foundation and to the disqualified person?

17. Welcome, Inc., a tax-exempt organization, receives 25% of its support from disqualified persons. Another disqualified person has agreed to match this support if Welcome will appoint him to the organization's board of directors. What tax issues are relevant to Welcome as it makes this decision?

18. An exempt organization has unrelated business taxable income of $400,000 and total earnings of $1 million. Why is only the $400,000 subject to the Federal income tax?

19. First Church has been selling cards and small books in the church tower. A contribution box was provided for payments to be deposited. To increase church revenues, a task force is evaluating setting up a gift shop in the church parish house. What tax issues are relevant to the task force as it makes its decision?

20. An exempt hospital operates a pharmacy that is staffed by a pharmacist 24 hours per day. The pharmacy serves only hospital patients. Is the pharmacy an unrelated trade or business?

21. An exempt hospital receives as a gift from a wealthy donor all the shares of stock of Compute, Inc., a retail computer chain. Because the chain is very profitable and its CEO has offered to continue to manage it, the hospital has decided to operate the chain rather than sell the stock. All of the profits of the chain will be used in carrying out the exempt mission of the hospital. Advise the hospital on whether better tax consequences can be achieved by operating the chain as a subsidiary or as a division of the hospital corporation.

22. An exempt organization is considering conducting bingo games on Thursday nights as a way of generating additional revenue to support its exempt purpose. Before doing so, however, the president of the organization has come to you for advice regarding the effect on the organization's exempt status and whether the net income from the bingo games will be taxable. Identify the relevant tax issues.

23. Discuss the significance of the "regularly carried on" test as it relates to the unrelated business income tax.

24. Define each of the following with respect to unrelated debt-financed property.
    a. Debt-financed income.
    b. Debt-financed property.
    c. Acquisition indebtedness.
    d. Average acquisition indebtedness.
    e. Average adjusted basis.

25. Tom is the treasurer of the City Garden Club, a new garden club. A friend, who is the treasurer of the garden club in a neighboring community, tells Tom that it is not necessary for the garden club to file a request for exempt status with the IRS. Has Tom received correct advice?

PROBLEMS

26. Teach, Inc., a § 501(c)(3) educational institution, makes lobbying expenditures of $290,000. Teach incurs exempt purpose expenditures of $1.6 million in carrying out its educational mission.
    a. Determine the tax consequences to Teach if it does not elect to be eligible to participate in lobbying activities on a limited basis.
    b. Determine the tax consequences to Teach if it does elect to be eligible to participate in lobbying activities on a limited basis.

27. Roadrunner, Inc., is an exempt medical organization. Quail, Inc., a sporting goods retailer, is a wholly owned subsidiary of Roadrunner. Roadrunner inherited the Quail stock last year from a major benefactor of the medical organization. Quail's taxable income is $400,000. Quail will remit all of its earnings, net of any taxes, to Roadrunner to support the exempt purpose of the parent.
    a. Is Quail subject to Federal income tax? If so, calculate the liability.
    b. Arthur Morgan, the treasurer of Roadrunner, has contacted you regarding minimizing or eliminating Quail's tax liability. He would like to know if the tax consequences would be better if Quail were liquidated into Roadrunner. Write a letter to Morgan that contains your advice. Roadrunner's address is 500 Rouse Tower, Rochester, NY 14627.

28. Determine which of the following organizations are *not* private foundations.
    a. Baptist church.
    b. Girl Scouts.

   c. League of Women Voters.
   d. PGA Tour.
   e. American Institute of CPAs.
   f. PTA.
   g. American Red Cross.
   h. Salvation Army.
   i. Veterans of Foreign Wars.

29. Cardinal, Inc., a § 501(c)(3) organization, received support from the following sources.

Governmental unit A for services rendered	$ 4,000
General public for services rendered	60,000
Gross investment income	30,000
Contributions from disqualified persons	20,000
Contributions from other than disqualified persons	86,000

   a. Does Cardinal satisfy the test for receiving broad public support?
   b. Is Cardinal a private foundation?

30. Gray, Inc., a private foundation, has the following items of income and deductions.

Interest income	$18,000
Rent income	60,000
Dividend income	15,000
Royalty income	5,000
Unrelated business income	50,000
Rent expenses	12,000
Unrelated business expenses	10,000

Gray is not an exempt operating foundation and is not eligible for the 1% tax rate.
   a. Calculate the net investment income.
   b. Calculate the tax on net investment income.
   c. What is the purpose of the tax on net investment income?

31. Eagle, Inc., is a private foundation that has been in existence for 10 years. During this period, it has been unable to satisfy the requirements for classification as a private operating foundation. At the end of 1995, it had undistributed income of $100,000. Of this amount, $40,000 was distributed in 1996, and $60,000 was distributed during the first quarter of 1997. The IRS deficiency notice was mailed on August 1, 1998.
   a. Calculate the initial tax for 1995, 1996, and 1997.
   b. Calculate the additional tax for 1998.

32. Otis is the CEO of Rectify, Inc., a private foundation. Otis invests $500,000 (80%) of the foundation's investment portfolio in derivatives. Previously, the $500,000 had been invested in corporate bonds with an AA rating that earned 7% per annum. If the derivatives investment works as Otis's investment adviser claims, the annual earnings could be as high as 20%.
   a. Determine if Rectify is subject to any of the taxes imposed on private foundations.
   b. If so, calculate the amount of the initial tax.
   c. If so, calculate the amount of the additional tax if the act causing the imposition of the tax is not addressed within the correction period.
   d. Are Otis and the foundation better off financially if the prohibited transaction, if any, is addressed within the correction period?

33. The board of directors of Pearl, Inc., a private foundation, consists of Alice, Beth, and Carlos. They vote unanimously to provide a $100,000 grant to Doug, their business associate. The grant is to be used for travel and education and does not qualify as a permitted grant to individuals (i.e., it is a taxable expenditure under § 4945). Each director knows that Doug was selected for the grant because he is a friend of the organization and that the grant is a taxable expenditure.

a. Calculate the initial tax imposed on the private foundation.

b. Calculate the initial tax imposed on the foundation manager (i.e., board of directors).

34. The Open Museum is an exempt organization that operates a gift shop. The museum's annual operations budget is $2.5 million. Gift shop sales generate a profit of $750,000. Another $500,000 of endowment income is generated. Both the income from the gift shop and the endowment income are used to support the exempt purpose of the museum. The balance of $1.25 million required for annual operations is provided through admission fees. Wayne Davis, a new board member, does not understand why the museum is subject to tax at all, particularly since the profits are used in carrying out the mission of the museum.

a. Calculate the amount of unrelated business income.

b. Assume that the endowment income is reinvested rather than being used to support annual operations. Calculate the amount of unrelated business income.

c. As the museum treasurer, write a letter to Wayne explaining the reason for the tax consequences. Mr. Davis's address is 45 Pine Avenue, Peoria, IL 61625.

35. Salmon, Inc., an exempt organization, has unrelated business taxable income of $20 million.

a. Calculate Salmon's UBIT.

b. Prepare an outline of a presentation you are going to give to the new members of Salmon's board on why Salmon is subject to the UBIT even though it is an exempt organization.

36. For each of the following organizations, determine the amount of the UBIT.

a. AIDS, Inc., an exempt charitable organization that provides support for individuals with AIDS, operates a retail medical supply store open to the general public. The net income of the store, before any Federal income taxes, is $325,000.

b. The local Episcopal church operates a retail gift shop. The inventory consists of the typical items sold by commercial gift shops in the city. The director of the gift shop estimates that 80% of the gift shop sales are to tourists and 20% are to church members. The net income of the gift shop, before the salaries of the three gift shop employees and any Federal income taxes, is $300,000. The salaries of the employees total $80,000.

c. Education, Inc., a private university, has vending machines in the student dormitories and academic buildings on campus. In recognition of recent tuition increases, the university has adopted a policy of merely trying to recover its costs associated with the vending machine activity. For the current year, however, the net income of the activity, before any Federal income taxes, is $75,000.

d. Worn, Inc., an exempt organization, provides food for the homeless. It operates a thrift store that sells used clothing to the general public. The thrift shop is staffed by four salaried employees. All of the clothes it sells are received as contributions. The $100,000 profit generated for the year by the thrift shop is used in Worn's mission of providing food to the homeless.

e. Small, Inc., an exempt organization, has unrelated business income of $900 and unrelated business expenses of $400.

37. Bluebird, Inc., an exempt organization, has unrelated business taxable income (before any modifications associated with charitable contributions) of $200,000. Charitable contributions made by Bluebird that are associated with the unrelated trade or business are $15,000, and those made that are not associated with the unrelated trade or business are $10,000. Calculate the effect of the charitable contributions on Bluebird's unrelated business taxable income.

38. Rabbit, Inc., an exempt organization, has net unrelated business income of $75,000 excluding any rent income received. Rabbit owns two buildings that are leased to tenants. The net rent income on the first building is $20,000, and that on the second building is $15,000. The lessee of the first building is unrelated to Rabbit whereas the lessee of the second building is a 100%-owned for-profit subsidiary. Calculate Rabbit's unrelated business taxable income.

39. Education, Inc., an exempt organization that provides educational services, has the following gains and losses from property transactions.

    • $50,000 loss on the sale of land and building. The building had been used in carrying out Education's exempt purpose, but is no longer needed due to a contraction in the geographical area served.

    • $5,000 gain on the sale of land and building. The building had initially been acquired to lease to a national retailer. Due to a reduction in the number of its retail stores, the national retailer canceled the lease at the end of last year.

    • $45,000 gain on the sale of investment land.

    • $20,000 loss on the sale of computers. The computers had been leased to Teachers, Inc., an unrelated exempt organization. Prior to leasing the computers, Education had used them in carrying out its exempt purpose.

    Determine the effect of these transactions on Education's unrelated business taxable income.

40. Fix, Inc., an exempt organization, owns a one-story building. Fix's adjusted basis for the building is $900,000. Of the building's total area of 10,000 square feet, the front portion (approximately 3,000 square feet) is used in carrying out Fix's exempt purpose. The remainder of the building is leased for $300,000 each year to Belts, Inc., a taxable entity, to use for storing its inventory. The unamortized balance of a mortgage relating to the original acquisition of the building is $600,000. Determine the portion of the adjusted basis that is treated as debt-financed property and the amount of the mortgage that is acquisition indebtedness.

41. Rodeo, Inc., is a social club that is exempt under § 501(c)(7). Its annual gross receipts are $250,000. Of this amount, $20,000 is from an unrelated trade or business. Rodeo's fiscal year ends on April 30.
    a. Is Rodeo required to file an annual information return? If so, what form should be used?
    b. Is Rodeo subject to the UBIT? If so, what form should be used?
    c. If tax returns must be filed, what are the due dates?

42. Historic Burg is an exempt organization that operates a museum depicting eighteenth-century life. Sally gives the museum an eighteenth-century chest that she has owned for 10 years. Her adjusted basis is $55,000, and the chest's appraised value is $100,000. Sally's adjusted gross income is $500,000.
    a. Calculate Sally's charitable contribution deduction if Historic Burg is a private operating foundation.
    b. Calculate Sally's charitable contribution deduction if Historic Burg is a private nonoperating foundation.

Research Problems for this chapter appear at the end of Chapter 28.

24

TAXATION OF INTERNATIONAL TRANSACTIONS

LEARNING OBJECTIVES

After completing Chapter 24, you should be able to:

1. Use the foreign tax credit provisions.

2. Apply the rules for sourcing income and allocating deductions into U.S. and foreign categories.

3. Utilize the U.S. tax provisions concerning nonresident alien individuals and foreign corporations.

4. Appreciate the tax benefits available to certain U.S. individuals working abroad.

5. Apply the U.S. tax rules for foreign corporations controlled by U.S. persons.

6. Explain how foreign currency exchange affects the tax consequences of international transactions.

OVERVIEW OF INTERNATIONAL TAXATION

International taxation is an integral part of the U.S. involvement in the world economy. In an age when economic isolation is no longer feasible for most countries, the United States, as a large and influential nation, plays a particularly important role in the global economy. In 1990, the United States contributed 24 percent to world gross domestic production. Table 24–1 shows the extent of U.S. investment abroad and foreign investment in the United States compared with Japan and the European Community.

The world economy also has implications for the U.S. domestic economy. The global economy influences the interest rate that a small U.S. business pays for new equipment or a U.S. family pays for a new home, automobile, or television set. As of 1990, only 2 of the 50 largest commercial banks in the world had their home base in the United States.

More and more U.S. corporations are developing international ties. Even the local oil company and cotton cooperative in a city of less than 200,000 are entering into negotiations with former Soviet bloc nations. The number of multinational corporations is increasing in other countries as well. As of 1990, only 33 of the world's 100 largest industrial firms were U.S. multinationals.

▼ TABLE 24–1
Outbound and Inbound Direct
Foreign Investment, 1970–1990
(Percentages of Total)

	Direct Foreign Outbound Investment (By Country of Origin)			Direct Foreign Inbound Investment (By Country of Destination)		
	1970	1980	1990	1970	1980	1990
United States	55	47	31	10	10	28
Japan	3	4	15	1	1	1
European Community	28	32	38	22	31	28

As a result of this growing globalization of business, tax practitioners who are employed by a company with even a small amount of foreign-source income or who have clients generating foreign-source income must deal with, at minimum, the foreign tax credit and U.S. income tax treaties. More complex international transactions require an in-depth knowledge of international taxation.

U.S. persons with international transactions encounter many of the same Federal tax laws as any U.S. taxpayer. Income is subject to U.S. taxation, certain expenses and losses are deductible, and credits are available. Earnings of domestic corporations face double taxation. However, U.S. taxpayers with international transactions face another set of provisions that apply to international business. These laws are meant to prevent double (two-country) taxation, allow the United States to remain competitive internationally, and prevent taxpayers from evading U.S. taxes by moving income-producing activities abroad.

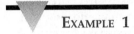

EXAMPLE 1

Jorge Ramirez is a U.S. citizen working as chief accountant for a U.S. corporation's bridge building project in Brazil. His annual salary is $120,000, and the company annually provides $35,000 of living expenses for Jorge and his family. Jorge has U.S. investments that earn about $2,500 a year, and he is a shareholder in a Brazilian corporation that is controlled by U.S. persons.

Without special provisions to deal with Jorge's foreign-earned income, he would be subject to double taxation—once by the United States, which taxes worldwide income on the basis of citizenship or residency, and once by Brazil, which taxes on the basis of residency. Additionally, Jorge's company might be at a competitive disadvantage when bidding on such contracts. If the company compensated its employees for this double taxation, it would incur a greater wage and salary expense than companies from countries where double taxation was not a problem. Without special U.S. tax provisions, Jorge and the other U.S. shareholders could invest in the Brazilian corporation, which would not incur any U.S. taxation until distributions were made to shareholders. ▼

THE FOREIGN TAX CREDIT

1 LEARNING OBJECTIVE
Use the foreign tax credit provisions.

The United States retains the right to tax its citizens and residents on their worldwide taxable income. This approach can result in double taxation and presents a potential problem to U.S. persons who invest abroad.

To reduce the possibility of double taxation, the U.S. Congress enacted the **foreign tax credit (FTC)** provisions. Under these provisions, a qualified taxpayer is allowed a tax credit for foreign income taxes paid. The credit provides a dollar-for-dollar reduction of the U.S. income tax liability. Taxpayers claimed $20 million in FTCs for 1920 and almost $25 billion for 1990, an increase of approximately 124,850 percent. U.S. income tax before credits rose from $1,170 million in 1920 to just under $119.5 billion in 1990, an increase of only 10,108 percent.

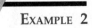

EXAMPLE 2

Ace Tools, Inc., a U.S. corporation, has a branch operation in Mexico, from which it earns taxable income of $750,000 for the current year. Ace pays income tax of $150,000 on these earnings to the Mexican tax authorities. Ace must also include the $750,000 in gross income for U.S. tax purposes. Assume that, before considering the FTC, Ace would owe $255,000 in U.S. income taxes on this foreign-source income. Thus, total taxes on the $750,000 could equal $405,000 ($150,000 + $255,000), a 54% effective rate. But Ace takes the FTC of $150,000 against its U.S. tax liability on the foreign-source income. Ace Tools' total taxes on the $750,000 now are $255,000 ($150,000 + $105,000), a 34% effective rate. ▼

THE CREDIT PROVISIONS

The Direct Credit.   Section 901 provides a direct FTC to U.S. taxpayers who pay or incur a foreign income tax. For purposes of the direct credit, only the taxpayer who bears the legal incidence of the foreign tax is eligible for the credit. Ace Tools, in Example 2 above, would be eligible for the direct credit.

The Indirect Credit.   If a U.S. corporation operates in a foreign country through a branch, the direct credit is available for foreign taxes paid. If, however, a U.S. corporation operates in a foreign country through a foreign subsidiary, the direct credit is not available for foreign taxes paid by the foreign corporation. An indirect credit is available to U.S. *corporate* taxpayers who receive actual or constructive dividends from foreign corporations that have paid a foreign tax on earnings. These foreign taxes are deemed paid by the corporate shareholders in the same proportion as the dividends actually or constructively received bear to the foreign corporation's post-1986 undistributed earnings and profits (E & P). A domestic corporation that chooses the FTC for deemed-paid foreign taxes must *gross up* dividend income by the amount of deemed-paid taxes.

EXAMPLE 3

Wren, Inc., a domestic corporation, owns 50% of Finch, Inc., a foreign corporation. Wren receives a dividend of $120,000 from Finch. Finch paid foreign taxes of $500,000 on post-1986 E & P. Finch's post-1986 E & P (after taxes) totals $1,200,000. Wren's deemed-paid foreign taxes for FTC purposes are $50,000.

Cash dividend from Finch	$120,000
Deemed-paid foreign taxes	
$\left(\$500,000 \times \dfrac{\$120,000}{\$1,200,000}\right)$	50,000
Gross income to Wren	$170,000

Wren must include the $50,000 in gross income due to the gross-up adjustment if the FTC is elected. ▼

Certain ownership requirements must be met before the indirect credit is available to a domestic corporation. The domestic corporation must own 10 percent or more of the voting stock of the foreign corporation. The credit is also available for deemed-paid foreign taxes of second- and third-tier foreign corporations if the 10 percent ownership requirement is met at the second- and third-tier level. A 5 percent indirect ownership requirement must also be met. The § 902 ownership requirements are summarized in Figure 24–1.

FTC Limitations.   To prevent foreign taxes from being credited against U.S. taxes levied on *U.S.-source taxable income,* the FTC is subject to a limitation. The FTC for any *taxable* year cannot exceed the lesser of the actual foreign taxes paid or accrued, or the U.S. taxes (before the FTC) on foreign-source taxable income (the *general limitation*). The latter limitation formula is derived in the following manner.

$$\text{U.S. tax before FTC} \times \frac{\text{Foreign-source taxable income[1]}}{\text{Worldwide taxable income}}$$

---

[1] For FTC purposes, the taxable income of an individual, estate, or trust is computed without any deduction for personal exemptions. § 904(b)(1).

▼ FIGURE 24–1
Section 902 Ownership
Requirements

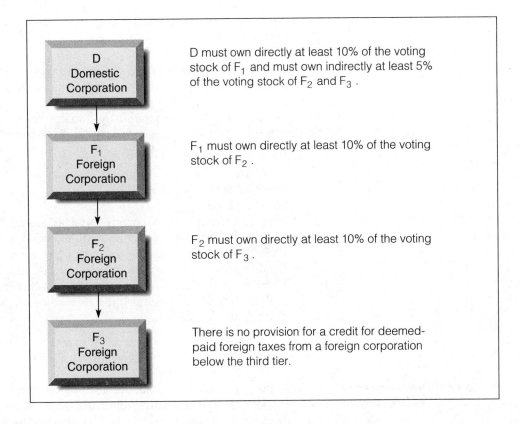

Terry, a U.S. resident, invests in foreign securities. Her worldwide taxable income for the tax year is $120,000, consisting of $100,000 in salary from a U.S. employer and $20,000 of income from foreign sources. Foreign taxes of $6,000 were withheld by foreign tax authorities. Assume that Terry's U.S. tax before the FTC is $33,600. Her FTC is $5,600 [$33,600 × ($20,000/$120,000)]. Her net U.S. tax liability is $28,000 ($33,600 – $5,600). ▼

EXAMPLE 4

As Example 4 illustrates, the limitation can prevent some portion of foreign taxes paid in high-tax jurisdictions from being credited. Taxpayers could overcome this problem by generating additional foreign-source income that is subject to no, or low, foreign taxation.

EXAMPLE 5

Compare Domestic Corporation's FTC situation when the corporation has only $500,000 of highly taxed foreign-source income with the situation where Domestic also has $100,000 of low-taxed foreign-source interest income.

	Only Highly Taxed Income	With Low-Taxed Interest
Foreign-source income	$500,000	$600,000
Foreign taxes	275,000	280,000
U.S.-source income	700,000	700,000
U.S. taxes (34%)	408,000	442,000
FTC limitation	170,000*	204,000**

*$408,000 × ($500,000/$1,200,000).

**$442,000 × ($600,000/$1,300,000).

Domestic's foreign taxes increase by only $5,000, while its FTC limitation increases by $34,000. ▼

To prevent the *cross-crediting* of foreign taxes as in Example 5, Congress has enacted legislation providing for several separate limitation *baskets*. These provisions require that a separate limitation be calculated for certain categories of foreign-source taxable income and the foreign taxes attributable to that income. Section 904(d) provides separate limitation baskets for the following.

- Passive income.
- High withholding tax income.
- Financial services income.
- Shipping income.
- Dividends from each noncontrolled § 902 corporation.
- Dividends from a domestic international sales corporation (DISC) or former DISC to the extent they are treated as foreign-source income.
- Taxable income attributable to foreign trade income under § 923(b).
- Distributions from a foreign sales corporation (FSC) or former FSC out of E & P attributable to foreign trade income or qualified interest and carrying charges under § 263(c).

All other *foreign-source income* is included in a general (or overall) limitation basket. These separate limitations are diagrammed in Concept Summary 24–1.

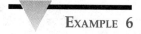

EXAMPLE 6

Wood Products, Inc., a U.S. corporation, has a foreign branch in Canada that earns taxable income of $1,000,000 from manufacturing operations and $500,000 from shipping operations. Wood Products also earns Canada-source high withholding tax interest of $100,000.

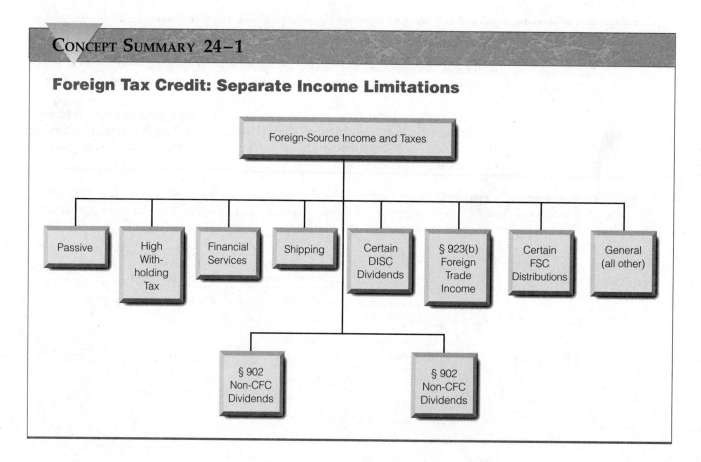

CONCEPT SUMMARY 24–1

Foreign Tax Credit: Separate Income Limitations

Wood Products pays foreign taxes of $400,000 (40%), $250,000 (50%), and $15,000 (15%), respectively, on this foreign-source income. The corporation also earns $4,000,000 of U.S.-source taxable income, resulting in worldwide taxable income of $5,600,000. The U.S. taxes before the FTC are $1,904,000 (at 34%). The following tabulation illustrates the effect of the separate limitation baskets on cross-crediting.

Foreign Income Category	Net Taxable Amount	Foreign Taxes	U.S. Tax before FTC at 34%	FTC with Separate Limits
Manufacturing	$1,000,000	$400,000	$340,000	$340,000
Shipping	500,000	250,000	170,000	170,000
High withholding tax interest	100,000	15,000	34,000	15,000
Total	$1,600,000	$665,000	$544,000	$525,000

Without the separate limitation provisions, the FTC would be the lesser of $665,000 foreign taxes paid or accrued, or $544,000 [i.e., $1,904,000 × ($1,600,000/$5,600,000)]. The separate limitation provisions reduce the total FTC by $19,000 ($544,000 − $525,000). The foreign-source income taxed at the foreign tax rates of 40% and 50% cannot be aggregated with foreign-source income taxed at only 15%. ▼

The limitations can result in unused (noncredited) foreign taxes for the tax year. A two-year carryback and a five-year carryover of excess foreign taxes are allowed. The taxes can be credited in years when the formula limitation for that year exceeds the foreign taxes attributable to the same tax year. The carryback and carryover provision is available only within the separate baskets. In other words, excess foreign taxes in one basket cannot be carried over unless there is an excess limitation in the same basket for the carryover year.

The Alternative Minimum Tax FTC. For purposes of the alternative minimum tax, the FTC is limited to the lesser of the credit for regular tax purposes or 90 percent of the tentative minimum tax before the credit.[2] The 10 percent cutback is calculated on the tentative minimum tax without regard to the alternative tax

---

[2] § 59. A "small corporation" exception is available.

NOL deduction. The general FTC limitation is calculated by using alternative minimum taxable income rather than taxable income in the denominator of the formula and the tentative minimum tax rather than the regular tax. The source of alternative minimum taxable income must be determined for the purpose of foreign-source taxable income.

Other Considerations. In order for a foreign levy to qualify for the FTC, it must be a tax, and its predominant character must be that of an income tax in the U.S. sense.[3] A levy is a tax if it is a compulsory payment, as contrasted with a payment for a specific economic benefit such as the right to extract oil. A tax's predominant character is that of an income tax in the U.S. sense if it reaches realized net gain and is not dependent on being credited against the income tax of another country (not a *soak-up* tax). A tax that is levied in lieu of an income tax is also creditable.[4]

EXAMPLE 7

Rigs, a domestic corporation, receives oil extraction income from operations in a foreign country. The other country levies a 50% tax on extraction income and a 30% tax on all other taxable income derived within the country. If Rigs pays $700,000 in taxes on its extraction income to the foreign country, only $420,000 [$700,000 × (30% ÷ 50%)] of that amount is creditable as an income tax. ▼

EXAMPLE 8

Hoops, a domestic corporation, generates $2 million of taxable income from operations in Larissa, a foreign country. Larissa's law levies a tax on income generated in Larissa by foreign residents only in cases in which the country of residence (such as the United States) allows a tax credit for foreign taxes paid. Hoops will not be allowed an FTC for taxes paid to Larissa, because the foreign tax is a soak-up tax. ▼

For purposes of the FTC, foreign taxes are attributable to the year in which they are paid or accrued. Taxpayers using the cash method of accounting for tax purposes may elect to take the FTC in the year in which the foreign taxes accrue. The election is binding on the taxpayer for the year in which it is made, and for all subsequent years. Taxes paid in a foreign currency are translated to U.S. dollars for FTC purposes at the exchange rate in effect when the taxes are actually paid.[5] Any adjustment of foreign taxes paid by a foreign corporation is translated at the rate in effect at the time of adjustment. Any refund or credit is translated at the rate in effect at the time the foreign taxes were originally paid.

The FTC is elective for any particular tax year. If the taxpayer does not choose to take the FTC, a deduction may be allowed for foreign taxes paid or incurred. However, a taxpayer cannot take a credit and a deduction for the same foreign income taxes.[6] A taxpayer can take a deduction in the same year as an FTC for foreign taxes that are not creditable (e.g., soak-up taxes).

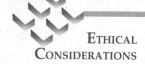

ETHICAL CONSIDERATIONS

Taxes on Foreign Investments and the Public Good

The decision to invest abroad is strongly influenced by the availability of the FTC. Without the FTC, U.S. investors, in many cases, would incur double taxation—once by the United States (based on residency or citizenship), then also by the country in

[3] Reg. § 1.901–2.
[4] § 903 and Reg. § 1.903–1.
[5] §§ 986(b) and 987.
[6] § 275.

which the investment is made (based on source). The FTC generally allows the U.S. investor, with regard to tax consequences, to be indifferent between investment abroad and in the United States when the tax rates are equal. As a result of the FTC, the investor will receive the same net return (after taxes).

You are the CEO of a multinational corporation based in Iowa. Your Vice President of Taxation brings you a draft of a position paper prepared by a national tax policy think tank of which she is a member. The paper argues that only a deduction should be allowed for foreign taxes incurred by U.S. taxpayers. The argument is based on "public good" considerations. Even though investors may be indifferent to the location of their investments, the U.S. "public good" is not served when the taxes paid on those investments remain offshore. Do you agree? How would you propose to modify the think tank's position?

POSSESSIONS CORPORATIONS

To encourage the economic development of U.S. possessions, Congress enacted a credit provision for income from operations in U.S. possessions. Domestic corporations may elect to receive a § 936 credit against U.S. taxes. The credit is equal to the portion of the U.S. tax attributable to the sum of possession-source taxable income and qualified investment income, even if no tax is paid or due to the possession. This is referred to as a *tax-sparing* credit. No additional credit or deduction is allowed for income taxes actually paid to the possession. A number of pharmaceutical companies, including Eli Lilly Company, have used subsidiaries with operations in Puerto Rico to take advantage of this and local tax benefits. The total possessions tax credit for 1989 was approximately $2.8 billion, which offset almost 99 percent of U.S. income tax before credits for possessions corporations for 1989. Almost all of the corporations claiming the possessions corporation credit for 1989 operated in Puerto Rico.

The credit is allowed against the U.S. tax attributable to foreign-source taxable income from the active conduct of a trade or business in a U.S. possession. It is also allowed on the sale or exchange of substantially all the assets used by the domestic corporation in that active trade or business and on qualified possession-source investment income. The credit is not allowed against certain taxes, though, such as the accumulated earnings tax under § 531 and the personal holding company tax under § 541.

To elect the credit, the domestic corporation must meet certain conditions. Eighty percent or more of its gross income for the three-year period immediately preceding the taxable year for which the credit is taken must be derived from sources within a U.S. possession. In addition, 75 percent or more of its gross income for that period must have been derived from the active conduct of a trade or business within a U.S. possession. The credit is not available for income received in the United States unless it is possession-source income received from an unrelated person and is attributable to an active trade or business conducted in a possession.

The credit is not available for income from intangible assets, such as formulas and patents. Intangible property income is includible in taxable income by a domestic corporation as U.S.-source income. If a domestic corporation elects the credit, however, all of its shareholders who are U.S. persons include their pro rata share of that item in gross income as U.S.-source income. In this case, the domestic corporation is not taxed on such income.

EXAMPLE 9 — A qualified possessions corporation generates the following foreign-source income on which it pays the following foreign taxes.

Taxable Income	Source	Foreign Taxes
$400,000 active trade or business income	Possession	$40,000
50,000 qualified investment income	Possession	–0–
10,000 passive nonqualified income	Possession	–0–
40,000 investment income	Nonpossession	16,000

Assume that the corporation's worldwide taxable income is $500,000 and its U.S. tax before the FTC is $170,000. The § 936 possessions corporation credit is $153,000 (34% × $450,000) before consideration of the § 936 limitation, and the direct FTC is $13,600, the lesser of $16,000 or $13,600 [$170,000 × ($40,000/$500,000)]. ▼

ETHICAL CONSIDERATIONS

The Possessions Credit and Job Creation

The possessions credit was designed to enhance and stabilize the economies of the targeted U.S. possessions—chiefly the Philippines, just before and after World War II for general import/export activities, and Puerto Rico, since the 1960s for drug manufacturing and general manufacturing and assembly. The credit is allowed essentially at the top corporate tax rate (now 35 percent), even if the host country levies a corresponding income tax at a lower rate (say, 5 percent). Thus, the U.S. Treasury subsidizes the conduct of business in the possession, presumably in the spirit of spreading capitalism around the globe.

In some ways, the credit has worked too well. Most of the possessions openly invite U.S. companies to conduct business in their countries by assessing taxes of zero to 10 percent on such income and offering other tax and economic incentives to invest there. Statistics of Income data for 1989 show that, for the first time, the tax benefits received by U.S. companies from the possessions corporation credit exceeded salaries and wages paid to the employees of these corporations. Tax benefits per worker averaged $22,375, compared with $20,540 paid in compensation. Chemical companies fared the best, claiming $64,000 in tax benefits (per employee), while paying less than $30,000 in compensation.

In addition, most of the business that is subject to the possessions credit is not strictly "new" investment or work in the possessions, but business that has been transferred from U.S. sites simply to take advantage of the low wage rates and high U.S. tax subsidy that are available under these conditions. Clearly, U.S. labor raises a proper objection, in that the Code rewards U.S. companies for moving jobs and capital out of the country.

As a candidate for the Senate in your state, how would you reconcile the data on the possessions credit with the needs of the voters and corporations you want to represent?

SOURCING OF INCOME AND ALLOCATION OF DEDUCTIONS

2   LEARNING OBJECTIVE
Apply the rules for sourcing income and allocating deductions into U.S. and foreign categories.

The sourcing of income within or without the United States has a direct bearing on a number of tax provisions. The numerator of the FTC limitation formula is foreign-source taxable income. Generally, **nonresident aliens** and foreign corporations are subject to Federal taxation only on U.S.-source income. The foreign earned income exclusion is available only for foreign-source income.

INCOME SOURCED WITHIN THE UNITED STATES

The determination of the source depends on the type of income realized. This makes the classification of income an important consideration (e.g., income from the sale of property versus income for the use of property). A detailed discussion of the characterization of income, however, is beyond the scope of this chapter. Section 861 contains source rules for most types of income. Other rules pertaining to the source of income are found in §§ 862–865.

Interest.   Interest income received from the U.S. government, from the District of Columbia, and from noncorporate U.S. residents or domestic corporations is sourced within the United States. There are a few exceptions to this rule, most notably, certain interest received from a resident alien individual or domestic corporation. This exception applies if an 80 percent foreign business requirement is met. Interest received on amounts deposited with a foreign branch of a U.S. corporation is also treated as foreign-source income if the branch is engaged in the commercial banking business.

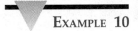

EXAMPLE 10   John holds a bond issued by Delta, a domestic corporation. For the immediately preceding three tax years, 82% of Delta's gross income was active foreign business income. The interest income that John receives for the tax year from Delta is foreign-source income. ▼

Dividends.   Dividends received from domestic corporations (other than certain possessions corporations) are sourced within the United States. Generally, dividends paid by a foreign corporation are foreign-source income. However, an exception applies if 25 percent or more of a foreign corporation's gross income for the immediately preceding three tax years was effectively connected with the conduct of a U.S. trade or business. In this case, the dividends received in the taxable year are U.S.-source income to the extent of the proportion of gross income that was **effectively connected** with the conduct of a U.S. trade or business for the immediately preceding three-year period. Dividends from **foreign sales corporations (FSCs)** and domestic international sales corporations (DISCs) can be treated as U.S.-source income.

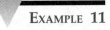

EXAMPLE 11   Ann receives dividend income from the following corporations for the tax year.

Amount	Corporation	Effectively Connected Income for Past 3 Years	Active Foreign Business Income for Past 3 Years	U.S.-Source Income
$500	Green, domestic	85%	15%	$500
600	Brown, domestic	13%	87%	600
300	Orange, foreign	80%	20%	240

The 80% active foreign business requirement affects only interest income received from Green Corporation and Brown Corporation, not dividend income. The dividends received from Green and Brown are U.S.-source income. Because Orange Corporation is a foreign corporation meeting the 25% test, 80% of the dividend from Orange is U.S.-source income. ▼

Personal Services Income.   The source of income from personal services is determined by the location in which the services are performed (within or without the United States). A limited *commercial traveler* exception is available. Personal services income must meet the following requirements to avoid U.S.-source treatment.

- The services must be performed by a nonresident alien who is in the United States for 90 days or less during the taxable year.
- The compensation for the services performed in the United States may not exceed $3,000 in total.
- The services must be performed on behalf of

  - a nonresident alien, foreign partnership, or foreign corporation that is not engaged in a U.S. trade or business, or
  - an office or place of business maintained in a foreign country or possession of the United States by an individual who is a citizen or resident of the United States, a domestic partnership, or a domestic corporation.

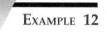

EXAMPLE 12   Mark, a nonresident alien, is an engineer employed by a foreign oil company. He spent four weeks in the United States arranging the purchase of field equipment for his company. His salary for the four weeks was $3,500. Even though the oil company is not engaged in a U.S. trade or business, and Mark was in the United States for less than 90 days during the taxable year, the income is U.S.-source income because it exceeds $3,000. ▼

The issue of whether income is derived from the performance of personal services is important in determining the income's source. The courts have held that a corporation can perform personal services[7] and that, in the absence of capital as an income-producing factor, personal services income can arise even though there is no recipient of the services.[8] If payment is received for services performed partly within and partly without the United States, the income must be allocated for source purposes on some reasonable basis, such as days worked.[9]

Rents and Royalties. The source of income received for the use of tangible property is the country in which the property producing the income is located. The source of income received for the use of intangible property (e.g., patents, copyrights, secret processes, and formulas) is the country in which the property producing the income is used.

Sale or Exchange of Property. Income from the disposition of U.S. real property interests is U.S.-source income. The definition of a U.S. real property interest is discussed subsequently under the Foreign Investment in Real Property Tax Act (FIRPTA). Generally, the location of real property determines the source of any income derived from the property.

The source of income from the sale of personal property (assets other than real property) depends on several factors, including whether the property was produced by the seller, the type of property sold (e.g., inventory or a capital asset), and the residence of the seller. Income, gain, or profit from the sale of personal property is sourced according to the residence of the seller. Income from the sale

[7] See *British Timken Limited*, 12 T.C. 880 (1949), and Rev.Rul. 60–55, 1960–1 C.B. 270.

[8] See *Robida v. Comm.*, 72–1 USTC ¶9450, 29 AFTR2d 72–1223, 460 F.2d 1172 (CA–9, 1972). The taxpayer was employed in military PXs around the world. He had large slot machine winnings and claimed the foreign earned income exclusion. The IRS challenged the exclusion on the grounds that the winnings were not earned

income because there was no recipient of Robida's services. The Court, however, found that, even in the absence of capital, the winnings were earned income.

[9] Reg. § 1.861–4(b).

of purchased inventory, however, is sourced in the country in which the sale takes place.[10]

When the seller has produced the property, the income must be apportioned between the country of production and the country of sale. If the manufacturer or producer regularly sells to wholly independent distributors, this can establish an *independent* factory or production price that can be used to determine the split between production and sales income. However, if an independent price has not been established, taxable income from production and sales must be apportioned.[11]

Losses from the sale of personal property are sourced according to the source of any income that may have been generated by the property prior to its disposition. This provision discourages the manipulation of the source of losses for tax purposes.

The general rule for the sourcing of income from the sale of personal property has several exceptions.

- Gain on the sale of depreciable personal property is sourced according to prior depreciation deductions to the extent of the deductions. Any excess gain is sourced as the sale of inventory.
- Gain attributable to an office or fixed place of business maintained outside the United States by a U.S. resident is foreign-source income.
- Income or gain attributable to an office or fixed place of business maintained in the United States by a nonresident is U.S.-source income.
- Gain on the sale of intangibles is sourced according to prior amortization deductions to the extent of the deductions. Contingent payments, however, are sourced as royalty income.

Transportation and Communication Income. Income from transportation beginning *and* ending in the United States is U.S.-source income. Fifty percent of the income from transportation beginning *or* ending in the United States is U.S.-source income, unless the U.S. point is only an intermediate stop. This rule does not apply to personal services income unless the transportation is between the United States and a possession.[12] Income from space and ocean activities conducted outside the jurisdiction of any country is sourced according to the residence of the person conducting the activity.

International communication income derived by a U.S. person is sourced 50 percent within the United States in cases where transmission is between the United States and a foreign country. International communication income derived by foreign persons is foreign-source income unless it is attributable to an office or other fixed place of business within the United States. In that case, it is U.S.-source income.

INCOME SOURCED WITHOUT THE UNITED STATES

The provisions for sourcing income without the United States are not as detailed and specific as those for determining U.S.-source income. Basically, § 862 provides that if interest, dividends, compensation for personal services, income from the

---

[10] §§ 861(a)(6) and 865. The sale is deemed to take place where title passes. See Reg. § 1.861–7(c) regarding title passage. There has been considerable conflict in this area of tax law. See, for example, *Kates Holding Company, Inc.*, 79 T.C. 700 (1982) and *Miami Purchasing Service Corporation*, 76 T.C. 818 (1981).

[11] § 863(b)(2) and Reg. § 1.863–3.
[12] §§ 863(c) and (d).

use or sale of property, or other income is not U.S.-source income, then it is foreign-source income.

ALLOCATION AND APPORTIONMENT OF DEDUCTIONS

The United States levies a tax on *taxable income*. The FTC limitation is based on taxable income. Deductions and losses, therefore, must be allocated and apportioned between U.S.- and foreign-source gross income to determine U.S.- and foreign-source taxable income. Deductions directly related to an activity or property are allocated to classes of income. This is followed by apportionment between the statutory and residual groupings on some reasonable basis. For FTC purposes, U.S.-source income is the residual grouping.[13]

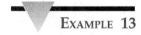

EXAMPLE 13

Ace, Inc., a domestic corporation, has $2 million of gross income and a $50,000 expense, all related to real estate activities. The expense is allocated and apportioned as follows.

| | Gross Income | | | Apportionment | |
	Foreign	U.S.	Allocation	Foreign	U.S.
Sales	$1,000,000	$500,000	$37,500*	$25,000	$12,500**
Rentals	400,000	100,000	12,500	10,000	2,500
			$50,000	$35,000	$15,000

*$50,000 × ($1,500,000/$2,000,000).
**$37,500 × ($500,000/$1,500,000).

If Ace could show that $45,000 of the expense was directly related to sales income, the $45,000 would be allocated to that class of gross income, with the remainder allocated ratably. ▼

Interest expenses are allocated and apportioned based on the theory that money is fungible. With limited exceptions, interest expense is attributable to all the activities and property of the taxpayer, regardless of the specific purpose for incurring the debt on which interest is paid.[14] Generally, taxpayers must allocate and apportion interest expense on the basis of assets, using either the fair market value or the tax book value of assets.[15] Once the fair market value is used, the taxpayer must continue to use this method. Special rules apply in allocating and apportioning interest expense in an affiliated group of corporations.

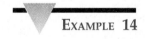

EXAMPLE 14

Black, Inc., a domestic corporation, generates U.S.-source and foreign-source gross income for 1996. Black's assets (tax book value) are as follows.

Generating U.S.-source income	$18,000,000
Generating foreign-source income	5,000,000
	$23,000,000

Black incurs interest expense of $800,000 for 1996. Using the asset method and the tax book value, interest expense is apportioned to foreign-source income as follows.

---

[13] Reg. § 1.861–8.
[14] Reg. § 1.861–10T(b) describes circumstances where interest expense can be directly allocated to specific debt. This exception to

the fungibility concept is limited to cases in which specific property is purchased or improved with nonrecourse debt.
[15] Reg. § 1.861–9T.

$$\frac{\$5,000,000 \text{ (foreign assets)}}{\$23,000,000 \text{ (total assets)}} \times \$800,000 = \$173,913 \qquad \blacktriangledown$$

Specific rules also apply to research and development expenditures, certain stewardship expenses, legal and accounting fees and expenses, income taxes, and losses.

A deduction not definitely related to any class of gross income is ratably allocated to all classes of gross income and apportioned between U.S.- and foreign-source income.

SECTION 482 CONSIDERATIONS

Taxpayers may be tempted to manipulate the source of income and the allocation of deductions arbitrarily to minimize taxation. This manipulation is more easily accomplished between or among related persons. The IRS uses § 482 to counter such actions. The provision gives the IRS the power to reallocate gross income, deductions, credits, or allowances between or among organizations, trades, or businesses owned or controlled directly or indirectly by the same interests. This can be done whenever the IRS determines that reallocation is necessary to prevent the evasion of taxes or to reflect income more clearly. Section 482 is a "one-edged"

TAX IN THE NEWS

RESEARCH AND DEVELOPMENT EXPENSES OF MULTINATIONALS

The Treasury has been reluctant to allow 100 percent of R & D expenses to be allocated against U.S.-source income, based on the premise that the results of this R & D, in certain cases, benefit the taxpayer's U.S. *and* foreign operations. Such an application would also likely overstate foreign-source income.

Much of the R & D of U.S. companies is performed in the United States. For foreign income tax purposes, other countries are hesitant to allow a deduction for R & D expenses against income sourced in their country when none of the R & D is performed there. This poses a problem for U.S. multinationals because the absence of a deduction increases foreign-source income for foreign tax purposes, but reduces it for purposes of the FTC limitation. Foreign taxes in excess of the FTC limitation tend to build up for companies that perform extensive R & D (see Table 24–2 for some examples of corporate spending on R & D).

▼ **TABLE 24–2**
Research and Development Spending as a Percentage of Reported Profits (Selected U.S. Firms), 1989

Company	Percent
Bayer	65
Boeing	82
Compaq Computer	27
Cummins Engine	543
Ford Motor	53
Microsoft	44

sword available only to the IRS. The taxpayer cannot invoke it to reallocate income and expenses.[16]

The reach of § 482 is quite broad. The IRS takes the position that a corporation and its sole shareholder who works full-time for the corporation can be treated as two separate trades or businesses for purposes of § 482.[17] Two unrelated shareholders who each owned 50 percent of a corporation were held to be acting in concert for their common good and, thus, together controlled the corporation.[18]

One of six methods can be used in determining an arm's length price on the sale of tangible property: the comparable uncontrolled price method, the resale price method, the cost plus method, the comparable profits method, the profit split method, and other unspecified methods. The Treasury has also proposed a cost-sharing method. The major problem with most pricing methods is that uncontrolled comparable transactions are needed as a benchmark.

An accuracy-related penalty of 20 percent is provided by § 6662 for net § 482 transfer price adjustments for a taxable year that exceed the lesser of $5 million or 10 percent of the taxpayer's gross receipts. In addition, there is a 40 percent penalty for "gross misstatements."

As a further aid to reducing pricing disputes, the IRS has initiated an Advanced Pricing Agreement (APA) program whereby the taxpayer can propose a transfer pricing method for certain international transactions.[19] The taxpayer provides relevant data, which is then evaluated by the IRS. If accepted, the APA provides a safe harbor transfer pricing method for the taxpayer. Apple Computer, Inc., accomplished the first successful APA submission.

ETHICAL CONSIDERATIONS

The Pros and Cons of APAs

The APA program is intended to alleviate the concern that price setting for transactions between related parties may give rise to tax audits. Reducing this uncertainty can be very beneficial to multinational corporations selling products in the international market. The government also benefits because its court case load is reduced.

As the price of this security, however, the taxpayer must disclose sensitive corporate data. A taxpayer that fails to reach an agreement with the IRS may be in a worse position than prior to seeking the APA. Furthermore, the APA may cause retroactive problems for open years.

How would you, as the Director of International Taxes for a large firm, advise the board of directors as to the use of an APA for the company's line of proprietary communications software products?

3 LEARNING OBJECTIVE
Utilize the U.S. tax provisions concerning nonresident alien individuals and foreign corporations.

U.S. TAXATION OF NONRESIDENT ALIENS AND FOREIGN CORPORATIONS

Generally, only the U.S.-source income of nonresident aliens (NRAs) and foreign corporations is subject to U.S. taxation. This reflects the reach of U.S. tax

---

[16] Reg. § 1.482–1(b)(3).
[17] Rev.Rul. 88–38, 1988–1 C.B. 246. But see *Foglesong v. Comm.*, 82–2 USTC ¶9650, 50 AFTR2d 82–6016, 691 F.2d 848 (CA–7, 1982), *rev'g.* 77 T.C. 1102 (1981).

[18] See *B. Forman Company, Inc. v. Comm.*, 72–1 USTC ¶9182, 29 AFTR2d 72–405, 453 F.2d 1144 (CA–2, 1972).
[19] Rev.Proc. 91–22, 1991–1 C.B. 526.

jurisdiction. The constraint, however, does not prevent the United States from also taxing the foreign-source income of NRAs and foreign corporations, when that income is effectively connected with the conduct of a U.S. trade or business.[20]

NONRESIDENT ALIEN INDIVIDUALS

An NRA individual is an individual who is not a citizen or resident of the United States. For example, Princess Diana is an NRA since she is not a citizen or resident of the United States.[21] Citizenship is determined under the immigration and naturalization laws of the United States. Basically, the citizenship statutes are broken down into two categories, nationality at birth and nationality through naturalization.

Residency. For many years, the definition of residency for Federal income tax purposes was very subjective, requiring an evaluation of a person's intent and actions with regard to the length and nature of stay in the United States. In 1984, Congress enacted a more objective test of residency. A person is a resident of the United States for income tax purposes if he or she meets either the **green card test** or the substantial presence test. If either of these tests is met for the calendar year, the individual is deemed a U.S. resident for the year.

An alien issued a green card is considered a U.S. resident on the first day he or she is physically present in the United States after issuance. The green card is Immigration Form I–551. Newly issued cards are now rose (off-pink), but the form is still referred to as the "green card." Status as a U.S. resident remains in effect until the green card has been revoked or the individual has abandoned lawful permanent resident status.

The substantial presence test is applied to an alien without a green card. It is a mathematical test involving physical presence in the United States. An individual who is physically present in the United States for at least 183 days during the calendar year is a U.S. resident for income tax purposes. This 183-day requirement can also be met over a three-year period that includes the two immediately preceding years and the current year. For this purpose, each day of the current calendar year is counted as a full day, each day of the first preceding year as one-third day, and each day of the second preceding year as one-sixth day.

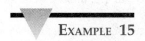

EXAMPLE 15

Li, an alien, was present in the United States for 90 days in 1994, 180 days in 1995, and 110 days in 1996. For Federal income tax purposes, Li is a U.S. resident for 1996, since she was physically present for 185 days [(90 days × ⅙) + (180 days × ⅓) + (110 days × 1)] during the three-year period. ▼

The substantial presence test allows for several exceptions. Commuters from Mexico and Canada who are employed in the United States, but return home each day, are excepted. Also excepted are individuals who are prevented from leaving the United States due to a medical condition that arose while in the United States. Some individuals are exempt from the substantial presence test, including foreign government–related individuals (e.g., diplomats), qualified teachers, trainees and students, and certain professional athletes.

Residence, under the substantial presence test, begins the first day the individual is physically present in the United States and ends the last day of physical presence for the calendar year. This assumes the substantial presence test is not satisfied for the next calendar year. Nominal presence of 10 days or less can

---

[20] §§ 871, 881, and 882.

[21] Title 8, Aliens and Nationality, *United States Code*.

be ignored in determining whether the substantial presence test is met. A 31-day per-year exception and a 183-day current-year exception may apply to prevent residence under this test.[22]

Nonresident Aliens Not Engaged in a U.S. Trade or Business. Certain U.S.-source income that is *not* effectively connected with the conduct of a U.S. trade or business is subject to a flat 30 percent tax. This income includes dividends, interest, rents, royalties, certain compensation, premiums, annuities, and other fixed, determinable, annual or periodic (FDAP) income. This tax generally is levied by a withholding mechanism that requires the payors of the income to withhold 30 percent of gross amounts.[23] This method eliminates the problems of assuring payment by nonresidents, determining allowable deductions, and, in many instances, the filing of tax returns by nonresidents. NRAs are allowed a deduction for casualty and theft losses related to property located within the United States, a deduction for qualified charitable contributions, and one personal exemption. Residents of countries contiguous to the United States (i.e., Canada and Mexico) are allowed dependency exemptions as well. Interest received from certain portfolio debt investments, even though U.S.-sourced, is exempt from taxation. Interest earned on deposits with banking institutions is also exempt as long as it is not effectively connected with the conduct of a U.S. trade or business.

Capital gains *not* effectively connected with the conduct of a U.S. trade or business are exempt from tax, as long as the NRA individual was not present in the United States for 183 days or more during the taxable year. If an NRA has not established a taxable year, the calendar year is used. NRAs are not permitted to carry forward capital losses.[24]

Nonresident Aliens Engaged in a U.S. Trade or Business. As long as FDAP income and capital gains are not effectively connected income, the tax treatment of these income items is the same, whether NRAs are engaged in a U.S. trade or business or not. Effectively connected income, however, is taxed at the same rates that apply to U.S. citizens and residents, and deductions for expenses attributable to that income are allowed.

Two important definitions determine the U.S. tax consequences to NRAs with U.S.-source income: *the conduct of a U.S. trade or business* and *effectively connected income*. General criteria for determining if a U.S. trade or business exists include the location of production activities, management, distribution activities, and other business functions. Trading in commodities and securities ordinarily does not constitute a trade or business. Dealers, however, need to avoid maintaining a U.S. trading office and trading for their own account. Corporations (other than certain personal holding companies) that are not dealers can trade for their own account as long as their principal office is located outside the United States. There are no restrictions on individuals who are not dealers. An NRA who performs services in the United States for a foreign employer is not engaged in a U.S. trade or business.

A U.S. trade or business is a prerequisite to having effectively connected income. Income is effectively connected with a U.S. trade or business if it is derived from assets used in, or held for use in, the trade or business (asset-use test) or if the activities of the trade or business are a material factor in the production of the income (business-activities test).[25]

[22] § 7701(b)(3).
[23] §§ 873 and 1441.
[24] § 871(a)(2).
[25] § 864(c).

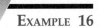

EXAMPLE 16

Ingrid, an NRA, operates a U.S. business. During the year, excess cash funds accumulate. Ingrid invests these funds on a short-term basis so that they remain available to meet her business needs. Any income earned from these investments is effectively connected income under the asset-use test. ▼

FOREIGN CORPORATIONS

Definition. The classification of an entity as a foreign corporation for U.S. tax purposes is an important consideration. Section 7701(a)(5) defines a foreign corporation as one that is not domestic. A domestic corporation is a corporation that is created or organized in the United States. Even though McDonald's is, in reality, a multinational corporation, it is considered a domestic corporation for U.S. tax purposes, solely because it was organized in the United States.

Income Not Effectively Connected with a U.S. Trade or Business. U.S.-source FDAP income of foreign corporations is taxed by the United States in the same manner as that of NRA individuals—at a flat 30 percent rate. Basically, foreign corporations qualify for the same exemptions from U.S. taxation for interest and dividend income as do NRA individuals. The U.S.-source capital gains of foreign corporations are exempt from the Federal income tax if they are not effectively connected with the conduct of a U.S. trade or business.

Effectively Connected Income. Foreign corporations conducting a trade or business within the United States are subject to Federal income taxation on effectively connected income. Additionally, any U.S.-source income attributable to the U.S. office of a foreign corporation is deemed to be effectively connected.[26] For such purposes, foreign corporations are subject to the same tax rates as domestic corporations.

Branch Profits Tax. In addition to the income tax imposed under § 882 on effectively connected income of a foreign corporation, a tax equal to 30 percent of

---

[26] § 865(e)(2).

the **dividend equivalent amount (DEA)** for the taxable year is imposed on *any* foreign corporation.[27]

The objective of the **branch profits tax** is to afford equal tax treatment to income generated by a domestic corporation controlled by a foreign corporation and to income generated by other U.S. operations controlled by foreign corporations. If the foreign corporation operates through a U.S. subsidiary (a domestic corporation), the income of the subsidiary is taxable by the United States when derived and is also subject to a withholding tax when repatriated (returned as dividends to the foreign parent). Before the branch profits tax was enacted, a foreign corporation with a branch in the United States paid only the initial tax on its U.S. earnings; remittances were not taxed.

The DEA is the foreign corporation's effectively connected earnings for the taxable year, adjusted for increases and decreases in the corporation's U.S. net equity (investment in the U.S. operations). The DEA is limited to current E & P and post-1986 accumulated E & P that are effectively connected, or treated as effectively connected, with the conduct of a U.S. trade or business. U.S. net equity is the sum of money and the aggregate adjusted basis of assets and liabilities directly connected to U.S. operations that generate effectively connected income.

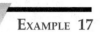

EXAMPLE 17

Robin, Inc., a foreign corporation, has a U.S. branch operation with the following tax results and other information for the year.

E & P effectively connected with a U.S. trade or business	$2,000,000
U.S. corporate tax (at 34%)	680,000
Remittance to home office	1,000,000
Increase in U.S. net equity	320,000

Robin's DEA and branch profits tax are computed as follows.

After-tax E & P effectively connected with a U.S. trade or business	$1,320,000
Less: Increase in U.S. net equity	(320,000)
Dividend equivalent amount	$1,000,000
Branch profits tax rate	× 30%
Branch profits tax	$ 300,000

The 30 percent rate of the branch profits tax may be reduced or eliminated by a treaty provision. If a foreign corporation is subject to the branch profits tax, no other tax is levied on the dividend actually paid by the corporation during the taxable year.

THE FOREIGN INVESTMENT IN REAL PROPERTY TAX ACT

Under prior law, NRAs and foreign corporations could avoid U.S. taxation on gains from the sale of U.S. real estate if the gains were treated as capital gains and were not effectively connected with the conduct of a U.S. trade or business. Furthermore, the United States has a number of income tax treaties that allow for an annual election to treat real estate operations as a trade or business. Persons who were residents of the treaty countries could take advantage of the election for tax years prior to the year of sale and then revoke the election for the year in which the sale took place. In the mid-1970s, midwestern farmers put pressure on

---

[27]§ 884.

CONCEPT SUMMARY 24–2

U.S. Taxation of NRAs and Foreign Corporations (FCs)

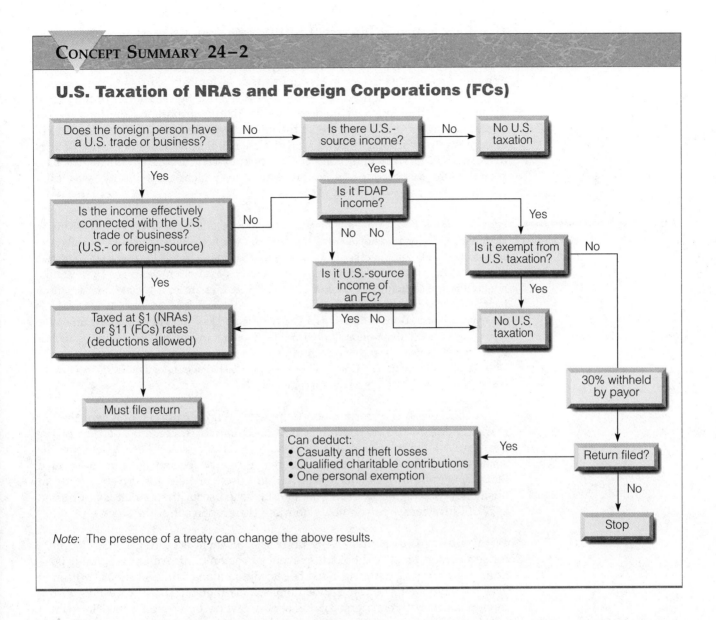

Note: The presence of a treaty can change the above results.

Congress to eliminate what they saw as a tax advantage that would allow nonresidents to bid up the price of farmland. This and other concerns regarding the foreign ownership of U.S. real estate led to enactment of the Foreign Investment in Real Property Tax Act (FIRPTA) of 1980.

Under **FIRPTA,** gains and losses realized by NRAs and foreign corporations from the sale or other disposition of U.S. real property interests are treated as effectively connected with the conduct of a U.S. trade or business even where those persons are not actually so engaged. NRA individuals must pay a tax equal to at least 26 (or 28) percent of the lesser of their alternative minimum taxable income or regular U.S. rates on the net U.S. real property gain for the taxable year.[28]

For purposes of this provision, losses of individual taxpayers are taken into account only to the extent they are deductible as business losses, losses on transactions entered into for profit, and losses from casualties and thefts.

---

[28] § 897.

U.S. Real Property Interest (USRPI). Any direct interest in real property situated in the United States and any interest in a domestic corporation (other than solely as a creditor) are U.S. real property interests (USRPIs). This definition applies unless the taxpayer can establish that a domestic corporation was not a U.S. real property holding corporation (USRPHC) during the shorter of the period during which the taxpayer held an interest in the corporation or the five-year period ending on the date on which the interest was disposed of (the base period). A domestic corporation is not a USRPHC if it holds no USRPIs on the date of disposition of its stock and if any USRPIs held by the corporation during the base period were disposed of in a transaction in which gain, if any, was fully recognized.

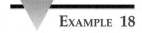

EXAMPLE 18

From January 1, 1991, through January 1, 1996, Francis (a foreign investor) holds shares in Door, Inc., a U.S. corporation. During this period, Door holds two parcels of U.S. real estate and stock of Sash, Inc., another U.S. corporation. Sash also owns U.S. real estate. The two parcels of real estate held directly by Door were disposed of on December 15, 1992, in a nontaxable transaction. Sash disposed of its U.S. real estate in a taxable transaction on January 1, 1996.

An interest in Door is treated as a USRPI because Door did not recognize gain on the December 15, 1992, disposition of the USRPIs. If Door's ownership of U.S. real estate had been limited to its indirect ownership through Sash, as of January 2, 1996, an interest in Door would not constitute a USRPI. This is because Sash disposed of its USRPIs in a taxable transaction in which gain was fully recognized. ▼

A USRPHC is any corporation (whether foreign or domestic) where the fair market value of the corporation's USRPIs equals or exceeds 50 percent of the aggregate of fair market value of certain specific assets. These assets are the corporation's USRPIs, its interests in real property located outside the United States, plus any other of its assets that are used or held for use in a trade or business. Stock regularly traded on an established securities market is not treated as a USRPI where a person holds no more than 5 percent of the stock.

Withholding Provisions. Any purchaser or agent acquiring a USRPI from a foreign person must withhold 10 percent of the amount realized on the disposition.[29] The amount withheld must be submitted along with Form 8288 within at least 20 days after the transfer. A domestic partnership, trust, or estate with a foreign partner, foreign grantor treated as owner, or foreign beneficiary must withhold 35 percent (or 28 percent where allowed by the IRS) of the gain allocable to that person on a disposition of a USRPI. Foreign corporations are also subject to withholding provisions on certain distributions.

Failure to withhold can subject the purchaser or the purchaser's agent to interest on any unpaid amount.[30] A civil penalty of 100 percent of the amount required to be withheld and a criminal penalty of up to $10,000 or five years in prison can be imposed for willful failure to withhold.[31]

TAX TREATIES

Income Tax. Over 40 income **tax treaties** between the United States and other countries are in effect (see Exhibit 24–1). These treaties generally provide *taxing rights* with regard to the taxable income of residents of one treaty country who

---

[29] § 1445.
[30] §§ 6601, 6621, and 6651.

[31] §§ 6672 and 7202.

▼ **EXHIBIT 24–1**
U.S. Income Tax Treaties in
Force as of January 1, 1995

Australia	Greece	Netherlands
Austria	Hungary	New Zealand
Barbados	Iceland	Norway
Belgium	India	Pakistan
Bermuda	Indonesia	Philippines
Canada	Ireland	Poland
China	Israel	Romania
Cyprus	Italy	Russian Federation
Czech Republic	Jamaica	Slovak Republic
Denmark	Japan	Spain
Egypt	Korea (South)	Sweden
Finland	Luxembourg	Switzerland
Former republics of	Malta	Trinidad and Tobago
the Soviet Union	Mexico	Tunisia
France	Morocco	United Kingdom
Germany		

have income sourced in the other treaty country. For the most part, neither country is prohibited from taxing the income of its residents. The treaties generally provide for primary taxing rights that require the *other* treaty partner to allow a credit for the taxes paid on the twice-taxed income.

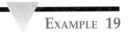

EXAMPLE 19

Caterina, a resident of a foreign country with which the United States has an income tax treaty, earns income attributable to a permanent establishment (e.g., place of business) in the United States. Under the treaty, the United States has primary taxing rights with regard to this income. The other country can also require that the income be included in gross income and subject to its income tax, but must allow a credit for the taxes paid to the United States on the income. ▼

Primary taxing rights usually depend on the residence of the taxpayer or the presence of a permanent establishment in a treaty country to which the income is attributable. Generally, a permanent establishment is a branch, office, factory, workshop, warehouse, or other fixed place of business.

Most U.S. income tax treaties reduce the withholding rate on certain items of FDAP income, such as interest and dividends. For example, treaties with France and Sweden reduce the withholding on portfolio dividends to 15 percent and on certain interest income to zero. The United States has developed a Model Income Tax Treaty[32] as the starting point for negotiating income tax treaties with other countries.

U.S. Taxpayers Abroad

4 LEARNING OBJECTIVE
Appreciate the tax benefits
available to certain U.S.
individuals working abroad.

Citizens and residents of the United States are subject to Federal taxation on their worldwide taxable income. U.S. taxpayers who operate in a foreign country as a sole proprietor, or through a foreign branch or foreign partnership, must include foreign-source income in gross income for U.S. tax purposes. They are allowed a deduction for related expenses and losses.

Income tax treaties can reduce or eliminate the taxation of the income by the foreign country party to the treaty. Since, under the treaty, the United States

---

[32] Treasury Department Model Income Tax Treaty (June 16, 1981).
The Model Treaty is being revised by the Treasury.

reserves the right to tax its citizens and residents, relief from double taxation is achieved with the FTC. In addition to the FTC, several other tax provisions involve certain foreign-source income of U.S. citizens and residents.

THE FOREIGN EARNED INCOME EXCLUSION

To help U.S. multinational entities be competitive in the world market, Congress enacted legislation granting an exclusion (from U.S. gross income) for a certain amount of qualified foreign *earned* income. This exclusion allows multinational entities to employ U.S. citizens and residents for foreign operations without having to pay them a wage or salary far in excess of that paid to nationals of the particular foreign country or countries. As Example 1 illustrates, the tax burden on a U.S. taxpayer working abroad could be much greater than that on a native of the foreign country. The **foreign earned income exclusion** reduces this problem.

Currently, § 911 allows a foreign earned income exclusion for (1) a qualified housing cost amount and (2) foreign earned income not in excess of $70,000. The exclusion is elective and is made by filing Form 2555 with the income tax return, or with an amended return, for the first taxable year for which the election is to be effective. An election once made remains in effect for that year and for all subsequent years, unless revoked. If the election is revoked for any taxable year, the taxpayer may not make the election again (without consent of the IRS) until the sixth taxable year following the taxable year for which revocation was first effective.[33]

Qualified Individuals. The exclusion is available to an individual whose tax home is in a foreign country and who is either (1) a U.S. citizen and bona fide resident of a foreign country or countries or (2) a citizen or resident of the United States who, during any 12 consecutive months, is physically present in a foreign country or countries for at least 330 full days. *Tax home* has the same meaning as for U.S. cases relating to travel expenses while away from home.[34] The issue of whether a stay abroad is temporary can be troublesome. If the stay abroad is

---

[33] Reg. § 1.911–7.   [34] § 162(a)(2).

deemed to be temporary, the taxpayer's tax home has not shifted to the foreign country. A stay that exceeds one year is not temporary.

Only whole days count for the physical presence test. The taxpayer has some flexibility in choosing the 12-month period.

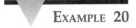

EXAMPLE 20

Carla, a U.S. citizen, arrived in Ireland from Boston at 3 P.M. on March 28, 1995. She remained in Ireland until 8 A.M. on March 1, 1996, when she departed for the United States. Among other possible 12-month periods, Carla was present in a foreign country an aggregate of 331 full days during each of the following 12-month periods: March 1, 1995, through February 29, 1996, and March 29, 1995, through March 28, 1996.[35] ▼

The General Exclusion. The foreign earned income (general) exclusion is available for foreign earned income and is limited to the lesser of (1) $70,000 or (2) foreign earned income less the housing cost amount exclusion. The exclusion is available for the tax year in which the income would be recognized. The limitation, however, is determined for each tax year in which services were performed. Income received after the close of the taxable year following the taxable year in which the services were performed does not qualify for the exclusion.

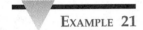

EXAMPLE 21

Tom, a U.S. resident, is present in a foreign country for all of 1995. He earns $100,000 from the performance of personal services. On January 1, 1996, he returns to the United States and remains there. Of the $100,000 foreign earned income, Tom receives $60,000 in 1995 and $40,000 in 1996. Tom can take a foreign earned income exclusion of $60,000 for 1995 and $10,000 for 1996 ($70,000 statutory limit – $60,000 excluded for 1995). If Tom did not receive the $40,000 until 1997, no exclusion would be allowed for 1997 because he received the $40,000 after the close of the taxable year following the taxable year in which the services were performed. ▼

The $70,000 statutory amount is prorated on a daily basis where the taxpayer does not qualify for the exclusion for the full tax year. If Tom in Example 21 qualified for only 11 months of the year, the $70,000 statutory amount would be $64,055 [$70,000 × (334 days/365 days)].

The Housing Cost Amount. The housing cost amount is equal to the qualified housing expenses of an individual for the tax year less a base amount. The base amount is 16 percent of the salary of an employee of the United States for Step 1 Grade GS–14. The base amount is determined on a daily basis. For 1995, the base amount for a full year was $9,242. For a qualified individual employed overseas for 250 days of the year, the applicable base amount would be $6,330 [$9,242 × (250 days/365 days)]. The housing cost amount exclusion is limited to foreign earned income.

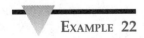

EXAMPLE 22

Charles, a U.S. citizen, works as an engineer for a U.S. multinational company in Bahrain. He is a bona fide resident of Bahrain for the entire calendar and tax year and earns a salary of $80,000. In addition, his employer provides $16,000 in housing costs. If the base amount is $9,242 and Charles elects both exclusions, the housing cost amount exclusion is $6,758 ($16,000 – $9,242), and the foreign earned income exclusion is $70,000 (the lesser of $96,000 foreign earned income – $6,758 housing cost amount exclusion, or the $70,000 statutory limit). Charles's gross income includes $19,242 of foreign earned income ($80,000 + $16,000 – $6,758 – $70,000). ▼

---

[35] Reg. § 1.911–2(d).

A self-employed individual is not eligible to exclude housing expenses, but he or she can elect to deduct them.

FOREIGN CORPORATIONS CONTROLLED BY U.S. PERSONS

5 **LEARNING OBJECTIVE**
Apply the U.S. tax rules for foreign corporations controlled by U.S. persons.

To minimize current tax liability, taxpayers often attempt to defer the recognition of taxable income. As Example 1 suggests, one way of trying to defer income recognition is to shift the income-generating activity to a foreign entity that is not within the U.S. tax jurisdiction. A foreign corporation is the most suitable entity for such an endeavor since, unlike a partnership, it is not a conduit through which income is taxed directly to the owner.

CONTROLLED FOREIGN CORPORATIONS

Subpart F, §§ 951–964 of the Code, provides that certain types of income generated by **controlled foreign corporations (CFCs)** are currently included in gross income by the *U.S. shareholders.* For Subpart F to apply, the foreign corporation must have been a CFC for an uninterrupted period of 30 days or more during the taxable year. When this is the case, U.S. shareholders must include in gross income their pro rata share of Subpart F income, earnings in excess passive assets, and increase in earnings that the CFC has invested in U.S. property for the tax year. This rule applies to U.S. shareholders who own stock in the corporation on the last day of the tax year in which the corporation is a CFC. The gross income inclusion must be made for the taxable year in which or with which the taxable year of the corporation ends.

EXAMPLE 23

Gray, Inc., a calendar year corporation, is a CFC for the entire tax year. Chance Company, a U.S. corporation, owns 60% of Gray's one class of stock for the entire year. Subpart F income is $100,000, investment in U.S. property has not increased, and no distributions have been made during the year. Chance, a calendar year taxpayer, includes $60,000 in gross income as a constructive dividend for the tax year. ▼

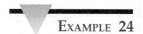

EXAMPLE 24

Gray, Inc., is a CFC until July 1 of the tax year (a calendar year). Terry, a U.S. citizen, owns 30% of its one class of stock for the entire year. Subpart F income is $100,000. He includes $14,877 [$100,000 × 30% × (181 days/365 days)] in gross income as a constructive dividend for the tax year. ▼

A CFC is any foreign corporation in which more than 50 percent of the total combined voting power of all classes of stock entitled to vote or the total value of the stock of the corporation is owned by U.S. shareholders on any day during the taxable year of the foreign corporation. For purposes of determining if a foreign corporation is a CFC, a **U.S. shareholder** is defined as a U.S. person who owns, or is considered to own, 10 percent or more of the total combined voting power of all classes of voting stock of the foreign corporation. Stock owned directly, indirectly, and constructively is counted. The foreign subsidiaries of most multinational U.S. parent corporations are CFCs. Hallmark Cards, Inc., has a Canadian subsidiary that is a CFC.

Indirect ownership involves stock held through a foreign entity, such as a foreign corporation, foreign partnership, or foreign trust. This stock is considered as actually owned proportionately by the shareholders, partners, or beneficiaries. Constructive ownership rules, with certain modifications, apply in determining if a U.S. person is a U.S. shareholder, in determining whether a foreign corporation is a CFC, and for certain related-party provisions of Subpart F.[36] The following are some of the modifications.

- Stock owned by a nonresident alien individual is not considered constructively owned by a U.S. citizen or resident alien individual.
- If a partnership, estate, trust, or corporation owns, directly or indirectly, more than 50 percent of the voting power of a corporation, it is deemed to own all of its stock.
- The threshold for corporate attribution is 10 percent rather than 50 percent.

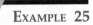
EXAMPLE 25

Shareholders of Foreign Corporation	Voting Power	Classification
Alan	30%	U.S. person
Bill	9%	U.S. person
Carla	41%	Foreign person
Dora	20%	U.S. person

Bill is Alan's son. Alan, Bill, and Dora are *U.S. shareholders*. Alan owns 39%, 30% directly and 9% constructively through Bill. Bill also owns 39%, 9% directly and 30% constructively through Alan. Dora owns 20% directly. The corporation is a CFC because U.S. shareholders own 59% of the voting power. If Bill were not related to Alan or to any other U.S. persons who were shareholders, Bill would not be a U.S. shareholder, and the corporation would not be a CFC. ▼

U.S. shareholders must include their pro rata share of the applicable income in their gross income only to the extent of their actual ownership. Stock held indirectly is considered actually owned for this purpose.

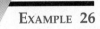
EXAMPLE 26

Bill, in Example 25 would recognize only 9% of the Subpart F income as a constructive dividend. Alan would recognize 30% and Dora would recognize 20%. If Bill were a foreign corporation wholly owned by Alan, Alan would recognize 39% as a constructive dividend. If Carla owned only 40% of the stock and Ed, a U.S. person, owned 1% and was not related to any of the other shareholders, Ed would not be a *U.S. shareholder* and would not have to include any of the Subpart F income in gross income. ▼

Subpart F Income.   Subpart F income consists of the following.

- Insurance income (§ 953).
- Foreign base company income (§ 954).
- International boycott factor income (§ 999).
- Illegal bribes.
- Income derived from a § 901(j) foreign country.

Foreign Base Company Income.   There are five categories of foreign base company income (FBCI).

---

[36] §§ 958 and 318(a).

- Foreign personal holding company income.
- Foreign base company sales income.
- Foreign base company services income.
- Foreign base company shipping income.
- Foreign base company oil-related income.

A *de minimis* rule provides that if the total amount of a foreign corporation's FBCI and gross insurance income for the taxable year is less than the lesser of 5 percent of gross income or $1 million, none of its gross income is treated as FBCI for the tax year. The *de minimis* rule does not apply to other types of income under Subpart F, such as increases in investment in U.S. property. However, if a foreign corporation's FBCI and gross insurance income exceed 70 percent of total gross income, all the corporation's gross income for the tax year is treated as FBCI or insurance income.

FBCI and insurance income subject to high foreign taxes are not included under Subpart F if the taxpayer establishes that the income was subject to an effective rate, imposed by a foreign country, of more than 90 percent of the maximum corporate rate under § 11. For example, this rate must be greater than 31.5 percent (90% × 35%), where 35 percent represents the highest U.S. corporate rate.

Foreign personal holding company (FPHC) income consists of the following.

- Dividends, interest, royalties, rents, and annuities.
- Excess gains over losses from the sale or exchange of property (including any interest in a trust or partnership) that gives rise to FPHC income or that does not give rise to any income.
- Excess of foreign currency gains over foreign currency losses (other than from any transaction directly related to the business needs of the CFC).

Foreign base company (FBC) sales income is income derived from the purchase of personal property from or on behalf of a related person, or from the sale of personal property to or on behalf of a related person.

EXAMPLE 27

A CFC owned 100% by Romus, a U.S. corporation, generates FBC sales income in any one of the following situations.

- Purchase of widgets from anyone as commission agent for Romus Corporation.
- Purchase of widgets from Romus and sale to anyone.
- Purchase of widgets from anyone and sale to Romus Corporation.
- Sale of widgets to anyone as commission agent for Romus.   ▼

An exception applies to property that is manufactured, produced, grown, or extracted in the country in which the CFC was organized or created and also to property sold for use, consumption, or disposition within that country. Certain income derived by a branch of the CFC in another country can be deemed FBC sales income. This would be the case if the effect of using the branch is the same as if the branch were a wholly owned subsidiary.[37]

FBC services income is income derived from the performance of services for or on behalf of a related person and performed outside the country in which the CFC was created or organized. Income from services performed before and in connec-

---

[37] § 956A.

tion with the sale of property by a CFC that has manufactured, produced, grown, or extracted such property is not FBC services income.

FBC shipping income includes several classifications of income, including dividends and interest received from a foreign corporation, to the extent that income is attributable to, or is derived from or in connection with, the shipping activity. Thus, income attributable to the use of any aircraft or vessel in foreign commerce, performance of services directly related to the use of that aircraft or vessel, or sale or exchange of any such aircraft or vessel is shipping income.

FBC oil-related income is income, other than extraction income, derived in a foreign country in connection with the sale of oil and gas products sold by the CFC or a related person for use or consumption within the country in which the oil or gas was extracted. Only corporations with production of at least 1,000 barrels per day are treated as deriving FBC oil-related income.

U.S. shareholders must also include in gross income their pro rata share of the untaxed profits of a CFC with excess passive assets.[38] A CFC has excess passive assets if the adjusted basis of its income-producing passive assets exceeds 25 percent of the adjusted basis of its total assets. The amount included in gross income is limited to the lesser of the excess passive asset amount or the CFC's previously untaxed earnings.

Distributions of Previously Taxed Income. Distributions from a CFC are treated as being first from E & P attributable to increases in investment in U.S. property previously taxed as a constructive dividend, second from E & P attributable to excess passive assets previously taxed as a constructive dividend, third from E & P attributable to previously taxed Subpart F income other than that described above, and last from other E & P. Thus, distributions of previously taxed income are not taxed as a dividend, but they reduce E & P.

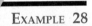

EXAMPLE 28

Jet, Inc., a U.S. shareholder, owns 100% of a CFC, from which Jet receives a $120,000 distribution. The CFC's E & P is composed of the following amounts.

- $50,000 attributable to previously taxed increases in investment in U.S. property.
- $20,000 attributable to previously taxed earnings from excess passive assets.
- $30,000 attributable to previously taxed Subpart F income.
- $40,000 attributable to other E & P.

Jet has a taxable dividend of only $20,000, all attributable to other E & P. The remaining $100,000 is previously taxed income. The CFC's E & P is reduced by $120,000. The remaining E & P is attributable to other E & P. ▼

A U.S. shareholder's basis in CFC stock is increased by constructive dividends included in income under Subpart F and decreased by subsequent distributions of previously taxed income. U.S. corporate shareholders who own at least 10 percent of the voting stock of a foreign corporation are allowed an indirect FTC for foreign taxes deemed paid on constructive dividends included in gross income under Subpart F. The indirect credit also is available for Subpart F income attributable to second- and third-tier foreign corporations as long as the 10 percent ownership requirement is met from tier to tier.

Income of a CFC that is included in a U.S. shareholder's income is summarized in Concept Summary 24–3.

[38] Reg. § 1.954–3(b).

CONCEPT SUMMARY 24–3

Income of a CFC That Is Included in Gross Income of a U.S. Shareholder

Increased investment in U.S. property (§ 956)

+

Earnings invested in excess passive assets (§ 956A)

+

Subpart F income (§ 952)

+

Previously excluded Subpart F income withdrawn from foreign base company shipping operations (§ 955)

Foreign base company income (§ 954)*

+

Insurance income

Foreign personal holding company income

+

Foreign base company sales income

+

Foreign base company services income

+

Foreign base company shipping income

+

Foreign base company oil-related income

*Plus all other income, when foreign base company and insurance income exceeds 70% of gross income.

FOREIGN SALES CORPORATIONS

Prior to 1985, the Domestic International Sales Corporations (DISC) provisions (§§ 991–997) allowed for a deferral of the tax on a portion of the export income of a DISC until actual repatriation of the earnings. Over the years, Congress cut the amount of export income on which deferral was allowed. As the result of charges by the General Agreement on Trade and Tariffs (GATT—whose members include some of the United States' major trading partners)—that the DISC provisions were a prohibited *export subsidy*, the DISC provisions were curtailed. As an alternative, the Foreign Sales Corporation (FSC) provisions (§§ 921–927) were enacted. Most remaining DISCs are "interest charge DISCs"—the price of deferral is an annual interest charge on the deferred taxes.[39] Only export sales up to $10 million qualify for deferral. Amounts in excess of $10 million are deemed distributed.

Most large multinational firms prefer CFCs to FSCs because they establish a more permanent active foreign presence, as in manufacturing. Mid-sized companies, such as Convex, often use FSCs, however, as do companies with very high-profit margins (e.g., 50 to 60 percent). In addition, the FSC has been used as a lessor that receives lease income, a portion of which will be exempt from U.S.

[39] § 995(f).

TAX IN THE NEWS

THE BENEFITS OF LOCATING AN FSC IN GUAM

Since the FSC provisions were enacted in 1984, approximately 500 FSCs have been created in Guam. Companies such as Boeing, Exxon, General Electric, and Computerland have FSCs located there. The tax climate of Guam makes such a location very attractive. For example, there are no registration fees for incorporating in Guam. In contrast, registration fees in Bermuda range from $1,600 to $8,000, and the franchise tax in the Virgin Islands can run as high as $25,000.

Guam recently has enhanced the tax benefits of locating there by extending FSC licenses for an additional 30 years and expanding the tax exemption. FSCs are completely exempt from taxation in Guam. Furthermore, the government of Guam has made it easy for U.S. corporations to form and operate an FSC there. The political climate is stable, and communication with the U.S. mainland is not complicated.

SOURCE: *Tax Notes International* 9, No. 10 (September 5, 1994), p. 719.

taxation. Some large airlines, such as KLM, have entered into long-term leasing agreements with FSCs.

FSCs are not allowed a tax deferral on export income. Instead, a certain percentage (about 15 or 16 percent, depending on taxpayer status) of export income is exempt from U.S. taxation (exempt foreign trade income). Pricing methods are provided for determining exempt foreign trade income.

To elect FSC status, a foreign corporation must meet a foreign presence requirement. An exception to this requirement is provided if the foreign corporation's export receipts do not exceed $5 million (the small FSC). The foreign presence requirement includes the following.

- Maintaining a foreign office.
- Operating under foreign management.
- Keeping a permanent set of books at the foreign office.
- Conducting foreign economic processes (e.g., selling activities).
- Being a foreign corporation.[40]

TAX HAVENS

All other considerations being equal, a U.S. corporation generally would prefer to make its foreign investment in (or through) a **tax haven.** A tax haven can be described as a country in which either locally sourced income or residents of the country are subject to no or low internal taxation. One method of avoiding taxation is to invest through a foreign corporation incorporated in a tax haven. Since the foreign corporation is a resident of the tax haven, the income it earns is subject to no or low internal taxes.

A tax haven can, in effect, be created by an income tax treaty. For example, under an income tax treaty between Country A and Country B, residents of A are

---

[40]§ 922.

subject to a withholding tax of only 5 percent on dividend and interest income sourced in B. The United States and A have a similar treaty. The United States does not have a treaty with B. The U.S. corporation can create a foreign subsidiary in Country A and use that subsidiary to make investments in Country B. This is referred to as **treaty shopping.** If the Country B investment income had been earned directly by the U.S. corporation, it would be subject to a 30 percent withholding tax. By investing through the foreign subsidiary created in Country A, the U.S. parent corporation pays only 10 percent in foreign taxes on the income earned (i.e., 5 percent to B and 5 percent to A).

In recent years, many countries have enacted "treaty shopping" provisions that provide that treaty benefits for withholding taxes are not available to a resident corporation unless a certain percentage of its beneficial interests are owned, directly or indirectly, by one or more individual residents of the country in which the corporation is resident. The most controversial article in the U.S. Model Treaty is Article 16, Limitation on Benefits, which is meant to prevent treaty shopping. Article 16 disallows treaty benefits to an entity unless more than 75 percent of the beneficial interest in the entity is owned, directly or indirectly, by one or more individual residents of the same treaty country in which the entity is resident.

As of 1988, 833 of the largest 7,500 CFCs had Subpart F income. Almost 50 percent of these CFCs with Subpart F income were based in tax havens; for example, Switzerland (with an effective tax rate of 9 percent) was the home of 96 of these CFCs. Five countries (Bermuda, Netherlands Antilles, Netherlands, Panama, and Switzerland) accounted for 81 percent of the $7 billion of 1988 tax haven Subpart F income.

OTHER CONSIDERATIONS

Interest expense deductions are limited for certain foreign-controlled U.S. corporations. While primarily aimed at these foreign-controlled entities, this provision can also apply to U.S. parent corporations paying interest to their foreign subsidiaries. This rule is referred to as the *earnings stripping* provision, since it applies only if the payer's debt-to-equity ratio exceeds 1.5 to 1, and a high proportion of earnings is paid out as interest expense. Disallowed amounts can be carried over to future years.

The tax years of CFCs must conform to that of a more-than-50 percent U.S. owner. Additionally, a CFC is allowed to use a tax year ending such that no more than one month's deferral of income recognition is provided to the majority U.S. shareholder.

FOREIGN CURRENCY TRANSACTIONS

6   LEARNING OBJECTIVE
Explain how foreign currency exchange affects the tax consequences of international transactions.

Changes in the relative value of a foreign currency and the U.S. dollar (the foreign exchange rate) affect the dollar value of foreign property held by the taxpayer, the dollar value of foreign debts, and the dollar amount of gain or loss on transactions denominated in a foreign currency.

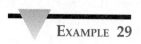

EXAMPLE 29

Dress, Inc., a domestic corporation, purchases merchandise for resale from Fiesta, Inc., a foreign corporation, for 50,000K. On the date of purchase, 1K (a foreign currency) is equal to $1 U.S. (1K:$1). At this time, the account payable is $50,000. On the date of payment by Dress (the foreign exchange date), the exchange rate is 1.25K:$1. In other words, the foreign currency has declined in value in relation to the U.S. dollar, and Dress will pay Fiesta 50,000K, which costs Dress $40,000. Dress must record the purchase of the merchandise at $50,000 and recognize a foreign currency gain of $10,000 ($50,000 – $40,000). ▼

Taxpayers may find it necessary to translate amounts denominated in foreign currency into U.S. dollars for any of the following purposes.

- Purchase of goods, services, and property.
- Sale of goods, services, and property.
- Collection of foreign receivables.
- Payment of foreign payables.
- FTC calculations.
- Recognition of income or loss from foreign branch activities.

The foreign currency exchange rates, however, have no effect on the transactions of a U.S. person who arranges all international transactions in U.S. dollars.

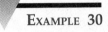

EXAMPLE 30   Sellers, Inc., a domestic corporation, purchases goods from Rose, Inc., a foreign corporation, and pays for these goods in U.S. dollars. Rose then exchanges the U.S. dollars for the currency of the country in which it operates. Sellers has no foreign exchange considerations with which to contend. If Sellers purchased goods from Rose and was required to pay Rose in a foreign currency, Sellers would have to exchange U.S. dollars for the foreign currency in order to make payment. If the exchange rate had changed from the date of purchase to the date of payment, Sellers would have a foreign currency gain or loss on the currency exchange. ▼

TAX ISSUES

The following are the major tax issues that must be considered in the taxation of foreign currency exchange.

- The character of the gain or loss (ordinary or capital).
- The date of recognition of any gain or loss.
- The source (U.S. or foreign) of the foreign currency gain or loss.

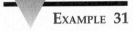

EXAMPLE 31   Batch, Inc., a domestic corporation, purchases computer parts for resale from Chips, a foreign corporation, for 125,000K. On the date of purchase, .75K (a foreign currency) is equal to $1 U.S. (.75K:$1). On the date of payment by Batch (the foreign exchange date), the exchange rate is .8K:$1. In other words, Batch paid 125,000K, which cost Batch $156,250 in U.S. dollars (125,000K/.8K). Batch, however, must record the purchase of the computer parts for inventory purposes at $166,667 (125,000K/.75K) and recognize a foreign currency gain of $10,417 ($166,667 – $156,250). ▼

The following concepts are important when dealing with the tax aspects of foreign exchange.

- Foreign currency is treated as property other than money.
- Gain or loss on the exchange of foreign currency is considered separately from the underlying transaction (e.g., the purchase or sale of goods).
- No gain or loss is recognized until a transaction is closed.

FUNCTIONAL CURRENCY

Prior to 1987, the Code contained no provisions for determining tax results when foreign operations could be recorded in a foreign currency. However, in 1981, the

Financial Accounting Standards Board adopted FAS 52 on foreign currency translation. FAS 52 introduced the **functional currency** approach (the currency of the economic environment in which the foreign entity operates generally is to be used as the monetary unit to measure gains and losses). TRA of 1986 adopted this approach for the most part.

Under § 985, all income tax determinations are to be made in the taxpayer's functional currency. Generally, a taxpayer's functional currency is the U.S. dollar. In certain circumstances, a qualified business unit (QBU) may be required to use a foreign currency as its functional currency. A QBU is a separate and clearly identified unit of a taxpayer's trade or business (e.g., a foreign branch). An individual is not a QBU; however, a trade or business conducted by an individual may be a QBU.[41]

SECTION 988 TRANSACTIONS

The disposition of a nonfunctional currency can result in a foreign currency gain or loss under § 988. Section 988 transactions include those in which gain or loss is determined with regard to the value of a nonfunctional currency, such as the following.

- Acquisition of (or becoming obligor under) a debt instrument.
- Accruing (or otherwise taking into account) any item of expense or gross income or receipts that is to be paid or received at a later date.
- Entering into or acquiring nearly any forward contract, futures contract, option, or similar investment position.
- Disposition of nonfunctional currency.

Section 988 generally treats exchange gain or loss falling within its provisions as ordinary income or loss. Certain exchange gain or loss is apportioned in the same manner as interest income or expense.[42] Capital gain or loss treatment may be elected with regard to forward contracts, futures contracts, and options that constitute capital assets in the hands of the taxpayer.

A closed or completed transaction is required. The residence of the taxpayer generally determines the source of a foreign exchange gain or loss.

BRANCH OPERATIONS

Where a QBU (a foreign branch, in this case) uses a foreign currency as its functional currency, the profit or loss is computed in the foreign currency each year and translated into U.S. dollars for tax purposes. The entire amount of profit or loss, without taking remittances into account, is translated using a weighted-average exchange rate for the taxable year. Exchange gain or loss is recognized on remittances from the QBU. One compares the U.S. dollar amount of the remittance at the exchange rate in effect on the date of remittance with the U.S. dollar value (basis pool) of the equity pool of the branch (i.e., initial capitalization plus contributions to the branch plus undistributed profits minus remittances and losses—all measured in the QBU's functional currency).[43] This gain or loss is ordinary, and it is sourced according to the income to which the remittance is attributable.

---

[41] Reg. § 1.989(a)–1(b).
[42] Temp.Reg. § 1.861–9T(b).

[43] Prop.Reg. § 1.987–2.

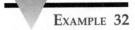

EXAMPLE 32

Icon, a domestic corporation, began operation of a QBU (foreign branch) in 1994. The functional currency of the QBU is the K. The QBU's profits for 1994–1996 are as follows.

	Income (in Ks)	Weighted-Average Exchange Rate	Income in U.S. Dollars
1994	200K	1K:$1	$200
1995	200K	1.25K:$1	160
1996	200K	1.6K:$1	125
	600K		$485

The income is taxed to Icon in the year earned, regardless of whether any remittances take place. ▼

DISTRIBUTIONS FROM FOREIGN CORPORATIONS

An actual distribution of E & P from a foreign corporation is included in income by the U.S. recipient at the exchange rate in effect on the *date of distribution*. Thus, no exchange gain or loss is recognized. Deemed dividend distributions under Subpart F are translated at the weighted-average exchange rate for the CFC's tax year to which the deemed distribution is attributable, similar to Example 32 above. Exchange gain or loss can result when an actual distribution of this previously taxed income is made.

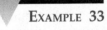

EXAMPLE 33

Assuming no prior remittances, the QBU, a foreign branch or CFC (see Example 32), remits 300K to Icon in 1996 when the exchange rate is 1.6K:$1. Icon has a foreign currency loss of $81.14, determined as follows.

	Equity Pool	Exchange Rate	Basis Pool
Initial capitalization	500K	1K:$1	$500
1994 income	200K	1K:$1	200
1995 income	200K	1.25K:$1	160
1996 income	200K	1.6K:$1	125
Balance	1,100K		$985

Foreign exchange gain or (loss):

Amount received (in dollars) minus basis (in dollars)

$$\$187.50^* \ - \ \$268.64^{**} = (\$81.14)$$

* 300K/1.6K.

** $\frac{\text{Foreign currency remitted}}{\text{Total equity pool}} \times$ Basis pool, or $\frac{300K}{1,100K} \times \$985.$

The loss is an ordinary loss for 1996. It is sourced by reference to the post-1986 accumulated earnings (1994–1996). The results would generally be the same if this was a distribution of previously taxed Subpart F income. ▼

For FTC purposes, foreign taxes are translated at the exchange rate in effect when the foreign taxes were paid. For purposes of the indirect FTC, any

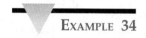

CONCEPT SUMMARY 24–4

Recognition of Foreign Exchange Gain or Loss

Transaction	Date of Recognition
Purchase or sale of inventory or business asset	Date of disposition of foreign currency
Branch profits	Remittance of branch profits
Subpart F income	Receipt of previously taxed income (accumulated E & P)
Dividend from current E & P or untaxed accumulated E & P	No gain or loss to recipient

adjustment of foreign taxes paid by the foreign corporation is translated at the rate in effect at the time of adjustment. Any refund or credit is translated at the rate in effect at the time the foreign taxes were originally paid.

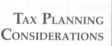

EXAMPLE 34

Music, Inc., a foreign subsidiary of Keyboard, a U.S. corporation, has pre-tax income of 300K. Music pays 100K in foreign taxes. The exchange rate was .5K:$1 when the income was earned and the foreign taxes paid. None of the income is Subpart F income. If the 200K net earnings are distributed when the exchange rate is .4K:$1, the deemed-paid taxes are $200 [($500/$500) × $200]. The effective tax rate is 40%. ▼

TAX PLANNING CONSIDERATIONS

Tax legislation tends progressively to reduce the ability to plan transactions and operations in a manner that minimizes tax liability. However, taxpayers who are not limited by the constraints of a particular transaction or operation can use the following suggestions to plan for maximum tax benefits.

THE FOREIGN TAX CREDIT LIMITATION AND SOURCING PROVISIONS

The FTC limitation is partially based on the amount of foreign-source taxable income in the numerator of the limitation ratio. Consequently, the sourcing of income is extremely important. Income that is taxed by a foreign tax jurisdiction benefits from the FTC only to the extent that it is classified as foreign-source income under U.S. tax law. Thus, elements that affect the sourcing of income, such as the place of title passage, should be considered carefully before a transaction is undertaken.

After the TRA of 1986, which added several limitation baskets to the FTC calculation, many companies found themselves with excess foreign taxes. Since the condition persists, these companies have not been able to take advantage of the carryback and carryover provision for the FTC. It may be possible for a U.S. corporation to alleviate the problem of excess foreign taxes with some of the following techniques.

- Generate "same basket" foreign-source income that is subject to a tax rate lower than the U.S. tax rate.
- Reduce highly taxed foreign-source income in favor of foreign-source income that is taxed at a lower rate.
- Time the repatriation of foreign-source earnings to coincide with excess limitation years.

• Deduct foreign taxes for years in which the deduction benefit would exceed the FTC benefit.

A taxpayer who can control the timing of income and loss recognition will want to avoid recognizing losses in years in which the loss is apportioned among the FTC limitation baskets. Otherwise, the foreign taxes for which a credit is allowed for the tax year are reduced.

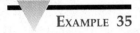

EXAMPLE 35

Della, a U.S. citizen, has U.S.-source taxable income of $200,000, worldwide taxable income of $300,000, and a U.S. tax liability (before FTC) of $84,000. She receives foreign-source taxable income, pays foreign income taxes, and has an FTC as shown.

Basket	Amount	Foreign Taxes	FTC Limitation	FTC
Passive	$ 20,000	$ 800	$ 5,600	$ 800
General	50,000	20,500	14,000	14,000
Non-CFC § 902 corporation #1	15,000	3,000	4,200	3,000
Non-CFC § 902 corporation #2	15,000	4,500	4,200	4,200
	$100,000	$28,800		$22,000

If Della had a foreign-source loss of $10,000 in the shipping limitation basket, the FTC is reduced by $1,820. The U.S. tax liability before the FTC is $81,200; 50% of the loss would be apportioned to the general limitation basket, reducing the FTC limitation for this basket to $12,600 [$81,200 × ($45,000/$290,000)]; and 15% is apportioned to the non-CFC § 902 corporation #2 basket, reducing the FTC limitation for this basket to $3,780 [$81,200 × ($13,500/$290,000)]. Della would avoid this result if she could defer recognition of the loss to a tax year in which it would not have a negative effect on the FTC. ▼

THE FOREIGN CORPORATION AS A TAX SHELTER

An NRA who is able to hold U.S. investments through a foreign corporation can accomplish much in the way of avoiding U.S. taxation. Capital gains (other than dispositions of U.S. real property interests) are not subject to U.S. taxation. This assumes that they are not effectively connected with a U.S. trade or business and are not gains from commodity transactions entered into by a foreign corporation with its principal place of business in the United States. The NRA can dispose of the stock of a foreign corporation that holds U.S. real property and not be subject to taxation under § 897 (FIRPTA). Furthermore, the stock of a foreign corporation is not included in the U.S. gross estate of a deceased NRA, even if all the assets of the foreign corporation are located in the United States.

Caution is advised where the foreign corporation may generate income effectively connected with the conduct of a U.S. trade or business. The income may be taxed at a higher rate than if the NRA individually generated the income. The trade-off between a higher U.S. tax on this income and protection from the U.S. estate tax and § 897 must be weighed.

PLANNING UNDER SUBPART F

The *de minimis* rule allows a CFC to avoid the classification of income as FBC income or insurance income and prevents the U.S. shareholder from having to include it in gross income as a constructive dividend. Thus, a CFC with total FBC income and insurance income in an amount close to the 5 percent or $1 million level should monitor income realization to assure that the *de minimis* rule applies for the tax year. At least as important is avoiding the classification of all the gross income of the CFC as FBC income or insurance income. This happens when the sum of the FBC income and gross insurance income for the taxable year exceeds 70 percent of total gross income.

Careful timing of increases in investment in U.S. property can reduce the potential for constructive dividend income to U.S. shareholders. The gross income of U.S. shareholders attributable to increases in investment in U.S. property is limited to the E & P of the CFC.[44] E & P that is attributable to amounts that have been included in gross income as Subpart F income either in the current year or a prior tax year is not taxed again when invested in U.S. property.

THE FOREIGN EARNED INCOME EXCLUSION

The tax benefit of the foreign earned income exclusion depends on the tax the income will incur in the country in which earned and the year in which received. If the foreign country levies little or no tax on the income, the U.S. taxpayer can exclude the housing cost amount plus up to $70,000 of foreign earned income and pay little or no tax on the income to the foreign tax jurisdiction. Since foreign earned income qualifies for the exclusion only if received in the year in which earned or the immediately succeeding tax year, the timely payment of such income is necessary.

In high-tax jurisdictions, the taxpayer may benefit more from taking the FTC than from excluding the earnings from gross income. The taxpayer earning income in a high-tax jurisdiction should compare the tax result of taking the exclusion with the tax result of forgoing either or both exclusions for the FTC. If U.S. taxes on the income are eliminated under all options and the taxpayer has excess foreign taxes to carry back or carry forward, then the FTC generally is more beneficial than the exclusion.

Taxpayers must also carefully monitor trips to the United States when attempting to qualify for the exclusion under the physical presence test. Taxpayers who are attempting to establish a bona fide foreign residence must make sure that their ties to the foreign country predominate over their ties to the United States for the period for which bona fide foreign residence is desired.

KEY TERMS

Branch profits tax, 24–20

Controlled foreign corporation (CFC), 24–26

Dividend equivalent amount (DEA), 24–20

Effectively connected income, 24–11

FIRPTA, 24–21

Foreign earned income exclusion, 24–24

Foreign sales corporation (FSC), 24–11

Foreign tax credit (FTC), 24–3

Functional currency, 24–34

Green card test, 24–17

Nonresident alien, 24–10

Subpart F, 24–26

Tax haven, 24–31

Tax treaty, 24–22

Treaty shopping, 24–32

U.S. shareholder, 24–26

---

[44] §§ 959(a)(1) and (2).

PROBLEM
MATERIALS

DISCUSSION QUESTIONS

1. Why is the FTC generally more beneficial to the taxpayer than a deduction of foreign taxes paid by the taxpayer?

2. What income tax consequences need to be considered by a corporate shareholder that takes the indirect credit?

3. Anchor, Inc., a domestic corporation, owns 15% of Dorkin, Inc., and 12% of Felton, Inc., both foreign corporations. Anchor is paid gross dividends of $35,000 and $18,000 from Dorkin and Felton, respectively. Dorkin withheld and paid more than $10,500 in foreign taxes on the $35,000 dividend. Dorkin's country of residence levies a 20% tax on dividends paid to nonresident corporations. However, the tax rate is increased to 30% if the recipient is a resident of a country that provides an FTC. Taxes of $3,600 are withheld on the dividend from Felton. What tax issues must be considered in determining the availability and amount of the FTC allowed to Anchor?

4. Why is the § 936 possessions corporation credit referred to as a "tax-sparing" credit?

5. What are some of the tax consequences affected by the sourcing of income as within or without the United States?

6. Will interest paid by a U.S. corporation be treated as U.S.-source in all cases? Explain.

7. Generally, U.S. taxpayers with foreign operations desire to increase foreign-source income and reduce deductions against that foreign-source income in order to increase their FTC limitations. What provision enables the IRS to prevent taxpayers from manipulating the source of income and allocation of deductions? Explain.

8. May Lyle, an alien, overcome classification as a U.S. resident under the substantial presence test if he is physically present in the United States for 183 days during 1996?

9. Trader, Inc., a foreign corporation, sells transistors in several countries, including the United States. In fact, currently 18% of Trader's sales income is sourced in the United States (through branches in New York and Miami). Trader is considering opening additional branches in San Francisco and Houston in order to increase U.S. sales. What tax issues must Trader consider before making this move?

10. Explain why the following statement is false: Income tax treaties between the United States and foreign countries allow only one of the treaty partners (either the United States or the foreign country) to tax income earned in one treaty country by residents of the other treaty country.

11. Why can stock of a foreign corporation held by NRA individuals be considered a tax shelter for U.S. tax purposes?

12. How does the U.S. tax law attempt to assure that the tax will be paid when nonresident aliens and foreign corporations dispose of U.S. real property interests at a gain?

13. Do self-employed individuals receive the same benefits under § 911 (foreign-earned income exclusion provisions) as do individuals classified as "employees"? Explain.

14. Joanna owns 5% of Axel, a foreign corporation. Joanna's son, Fred, is considering acquiring 15% of Axel from an NRA. The remainder of Axel is owned 34% by unrelated U.S. persons and 53% by unrelated NRAs. Currently, Fred operates a manufacturing business (as a sole proprietorship) that sells goods to Axel for resale outside the United States and outside Axel's country of residence. Joanna is not concerned about the concentration of investment since she expects to sell her stock in Axel in three years at a significant capital gain. Are there tax issues that Joanna and Fred need to address?

15. How does the tax law prevent Subpart F income from being taxed more than once to the U.S. shareholders?

16. Describe the foreign presence requirement of the FSC provisions.

17. LeBlanc, Inc., a foreign sales corporation, is having trouble raising additional needed capital. Its only stock issue, common stock, is currently owned by 20 U.S. corporations.

LeBlanc is considering an additional issue of common or preferred stock. LeBlanc is also considering a takeover bid made by one of its corporate shareholders in which LeBlanc's shareholders would receive shares of the U.S. corporation in exchange for their shares in LeBlanc. LeBlanc would be merged into the U.S. corporation. Does LeBlanc face any FSC issues in making these decisions?

18. Describe a tax haven.

19. What are the important concepts when dealing with the tax aspects of foreign exchange?

20. When would the U.S. recipient of a constructive dividend (for example, under Subpart F) have a foreign exchange gain or loss?

PROBLEMS

21. Ellen, a U.S. resident, operates an import/export company. This year, the business generated taxable income of $120,000 from foreign sources and $90,000 from U.S. sources. All of Ellen's foreign-source income is in the general limitation basket. The remainder of her taxable income is from U.S. investments. Her total worldwide taxable income (before personal exemptions) is $250,000. Ellen pays foreign taxes of $48,000. Her U.S. income taxes (before FTC) are $70,000. What is Ellen's FTC for the tax year?

22. Space, Inc., a domestic corporation, owns 40% of Satellite, Inc., a foreign corporation. Space receives a gross dividend of $42,000 from Satellite. Satellite's after-tax post-1986 E & P is $320,000, and its post-1986 foreign taxes total $96,000. Space's taxable income before consideration of the dividend is $300,000. Assume that Space is subject to a flat U.S. tax rate of 34%.
    a. What are Space's deemed-paid foreign taxes with respect to the dividend from Satellite?
    b. What is Space's FTC?

23. Prepare a flowchart for your colleagues in the Tax Department, illustrating the steps in determining a company's foreign tax credit.

24. Parent, Inc., a U.S. corporation, owns an interest in a chain of foreign corporations. Given the following chains of ownership, from which foreign corporation(s) is it possible for Parent to claim the deemed-paid (indirect) FTC?
    a. Parent owns 45% of FC1, FC1 owns 90% of FC2, FC2 owns 25% of FC3, and FC3 owns 50% of FC4.
    b. Parent owns 30% of FC1, FC1 owns 30% of FC2, and FC2 owns 15% of FC3.

25. Jasper, a U.S. resident, received the following income items for the current tax year. What is the source (U.S. or foreign) of each income item?
    a. $800 dividend from U.S. Power Company, a U.S. corporation that operates solely in the western United States.
    b. $1,200 dividend from Star Trading Corporation, a U.S. corporation that had total gross income of $2,100,000 from the active conduct of a foreign trade or business for the immediately preceding three tax years. Star's worldwide gross income for the same period was $2,600,000.
    c. $750 dividend from International Consolidated, Inc., a foreign corporation that had gross income of $800,000 effectively connected with the conduct of a U.S. trade or business for the immediately preceding three tax years. International's worldwide gross income for the same period was $3,000,000.
    d. $300 interest from a savings account at a Houston bank.
    e. $2,500 interest on Rolan Corporation bonds. Rolan is a U.S. corporation that derived $3,000,000 of its gross income for the immediately preceding three tax years from operation of an active foreign business. Rolan's worldwide gross income for this same period was $3,600,000.

26. Rita, a nonresident alien, is a professional golfer. She played in 7 tournaments in the United States in the current year and earned $50,000 in prizes from these tournaments. She deposited the winnings in a bank account she opened in Mexico City after she won

her first tournament money for the year. Rita played a total of 30 tournaments for the year and earned $200,000 in total prize money. She spent 40 days in the United States, 60 days in England, 20 days in Scotland, and the rest of the time in South America. How much U.S.-source income, if any, does Rita have from her participation in these tournaments, and is she subject to U.S. taxation on any of her winnings?

27. Determine the source of income (U.S. or foreign) of the following sales.
    a. Robert, a nonresident alien, sells Wal-Mart stock at a gain on the New York Stock Exchange.
    b. Jennifer, a resident of El Paso, Texas, sells equipment used in her trade or business, which is operated in Juarez, Mexico. Title passes in El Paso.
    c. A U.S. company sells inventory purchased from a New Hampshire manufacturer to a Canadian company, title passing on shipment from Kennedy Airport in New York.
    d. A U.S. corporation manufactures inventory in Mexico and sells it to wholesale customers in Australia, title passing on delivery in Sydney.

28. Jeanette, a citizen and resident of France, comes to the United States on March 3, 1996, and remains until July 20 of the same year, at which time she returns to France. Jeanette comes back to the United States on November 15, 1996, and remains until December 20, 1996, when she again returns to France. Jeanette does not possess a green card, but she was a U.S. resident for 1995 under the substantial presence test, spending 210 days in the United States in that year. Jeanette was never physically present in the United States before 1995. Is Jeanette a U.S. resident for 1996 under the physical presence test? If so, is there any way that she can overcome the presumption of residence?

29. Carla, a NRA, has the following U.S.-source income for 1996. Determine Carla's U.S. tax liability, assuming that she is single and has no allowable itemized deductions. Assume the personal exemption amount is $2,600. Also assume that the 28% bracket for a single taxpayer begins at taxable income of $24,000.

Dividend from U.S. corporation*	$ 1,200
Interest from U.S. bank account**	1,500
Capital gain from sale of U.S. corporate stock[†]	6,000
Share of partnership taxable income[††]	20,000

   *Carla owns less than 1% of the corporate stock.
   **Not effectively connected with a U.S. trade or business.
   [†]Carla was in the United States 25 days during the tax year, and the gain is not effectively connected with a U.S. trade or business.
   [††]Carla is an investor in a U.S. partnership.

30. Toma, a resident of France, is sent to the United States by Felp Corporation, a foreign employer, to arrange the purchase of some machine tools. Toma spends three weeks in the United States. This is her only trip to the United States during the year.

    Toma's gross monthly salary is $3,500. Her paycheck is deposited in her French bank account while she is in the United States. The salary is attributable to 15 U.S. and 6 French working days. The foreign employer does not have a U.S. trade or business. What is the amount of Toma's U.S.-source income?

31. Provo Corporation, a pharmaceutical corporation resident in Switzerland, sells certain products through a U.S. office. Current-year taxable income from such sales in the United States is $3,500,000. Provo's U.S. office deposits working capital funds short term in certificates of deposit with U.S. banks. Current-year income from these deposits is $25,000.

    Provo also invests in U.S. securities traded on the New York Stock Exchange. This investing is done by the home office. For the current year, Provo has realized capital gains of $35,000 and dividend income of $18,000 from these stock investments. Compute Provo's U.S. tax liability, assuming that the U.S.-Switzerland income tax treaty reduces withholding on dividends to 15% and on interest to 5%.

32. Flipp, a foreign corporation, operates a trade or business in the United States. Flipp's U.S.-source taxable income effectively connected with this trade or business is $300,000 for the current tax year. Flipp's current E & P is $250,000. Net U.S. equity was $1.5

million at the beginning of the year and $1.4 million at the end of the year. Flipp is resident in a country with which the United States does not have an income tax treaty. What is the effect of the branch profits tax on Flipp for the current tax year?

33. Niles, a NRA individual, owns 20% of the stock of Sandstone, a U.S. corporation. Sandstone's balance sheet on the last day of the taxable year is as follows.

		Adjusted Basis	Fair Market Value
Cash (used as working capital)		$ 500,000	$ 500,000
Investment in foreign land		200,000	400,000
Investment in U.S. real estate:			
Land		100,000	150,000
Buildings	$1,400,000		
Less: Depreciation	(300,000)	1,100,000	1,500,000
		$1,900,000	$2,550,000
Accounts payable		$ 300,000	$ 300,000
Notes payable		500,000	500,000
Capital stock		400,000	800,000
Retained earnings		700,000	950,000
		$1,900,000	$2,550,000

Niles was in the United States only 50 days in the tax year. He sold 70% of his stock in Sandstone on the last day of the tax year for $350,000. Niles's adjusted basis in the stock sold was $245,000. He sold the stock for cash. What are the U.S. tax consequences, if any, to Niles?

34. Linda is single, a chemist, and a U.S. citizen. For the past three years, she has worked in the lab of a foreign refinery owned by a U.S. corporation. She is a bona fide resident of a foreign country. For the current year, Linda receives $75,000 of foreign earned income (FEI) and has qualified housing benefits provided by her employer of $35,000. Assuming that the base amount is $9,500, the personal exemption is $2,600, the standard deduction for a single taxpayer is $4,000, the 28% tax bracket for a single taxpayer begins at $24,000, and the 31% bracket begins at $57,500, compute Linda's U.S. tax liability (a) taking both the FEI exclusion and the housing exclusion, (b) taking only the FEI exclusion, and (c) taking only the housing exclusion. Linda does not pay any foreign taxes.

35. Dart is a U.S. corporation. Three of the company's engineers have been working in Bahrain for 18 months as of January 1, 1996. They are U.S. citizens who have worked for Dart for 8 to 12 years. The company controller asks you to summarize the tax provisions of the foreign earned income exclusion for these employees. In writing this summary, include Code sections and subsections where appropriate.

36. Profit, Inc., a foreign corporation resident in Ireland, is owned 100% by Balance, Inc., a domestic corporation. Profit is a CFC. Determine Profit's Subpart F income (before expenses and cost of goods sold) for the tax year, given the following items of income.
    a. Income of $120,000 from the sale of merchandise to Balance. The merchandise was purchased from an unrelated manufacturer resident in Italy.
    b. Income of $240,000 from the sale of merchandise (purchased from Balance) to customers in France.
    c. Commissions of $80,000 from the sale of merchandise on behalf of Balance to residents of Ireland, for use within Ireland.
    d. Income of $250,000 from the performance on a construction contract entered into by Balance. The services were performed by Profit's personnel in Italy.

37. Warren, a U.S. shareholder, owns 15% of the only class of stock of Tan, Inc., a CFC. Tan is a CFC until May 1 of the current tax year. Warren has held the stock since Tan was organized and continues to hold it for the entire year. Warren and Tan are both calendar year taxpayers. If Tan's Subpart F income for the tax year is $300,000, E & P is $350,000, and no distributions have been made for the tax year, what is the amount, if any, that Warren must include in gross income under Subpart F for the tax year?

38. Grove, Inc., a domestic corporation, organized a foreign branch in 1993. The branch is a QBU and uses the K (a foreign currency) as its functional currency. The following income and taxes resulted in 1994–1996. The branch income is all in the general limitation basket.

	Income	Foreign Taxes	Exchange Rate
1994	180K/$360	45K/$90	.5K:$1
1995	200K/$250	70K/$87.50	.8K:$1
1996	220K/$220	66K/$66	1K:$1

Assuming the maximum corporate rate of 35% applies for U.S. tax purposes, determine the net U.S. tax for each year, with respect to the branch income.

39. Referring to Problem 38, assume that in 1996, when the exchange rate is 1K:$1, 400K is remitted to Grove's home office in the United States. Does this remittance trigger a foreign currency gain or loss? If so, what is its character (ordinary or capital)?

40. Townley, Inc., a domestic corporation, began operating a CFC (QBU) in 1995. The functional currency of the CFC is the ravenna (R). The CFC made no distributions for 1995 or 1996. Its E & P exceeded its Subpart F income for these years. Subpart F income and exchange rates are as follows.

	Subpart F Income (in R)	Exchange Rate
1995	120,000R	.8R:$1
1996	150,000R	.72R:$1

What is the dollar amount of income that Townley must recognize under Subpart F for 1995 and 1996?

41. Strike, Inc., a foreign subsidiary of Pin, Inc., a U.S. corporation, has pre-tax income of FF5,000 for 1996. Strike pays FF1,500 in foreign taxes. The exchange rate was FF1.5:$1 when the income was earned and the foreign taxes paid. None of the income is Subpart F income. If the net earnings of FF3,500 are distributed when the exchange rate is FF1.75:$1, what are the deemed-paid taxes? Assume that 1996 is Strike's first year of operation.

42. Gem Corporation, a foreign corporation, is owned by Crown Corporation, a domestic corporation. Gem earns income of 1 million K (Gem's functional currency) and pays foreign taxes of 250,000K when the exchange rate is .8K:$1. If none of Gem's income is Subpart F income and Crown receives a dividend of 500,000K when the exchange rate is .75K:$1, what is the dollar amount of the dividend and of the deemed-paid foreign taxes to Crown?

43. Money, Inc., a U.S. corporation, has $500,000 to invest overseas for 1996. For U.S. tax purposes, any additional income earned by Money will be taxed at 34%. Two viable possibilities for investment exist.
  a. Invest the $500,000 in Exco (a foreign corporation) common stock. Exco common stock pays a dividend of $3 per share each year. The $500,000 would purchase 10,000 shares (or 10%) of Exco's only class of stock (voting common). Exco expects to earn $10 million before taxes for 1996 and to be taxed at a flat rate of 40%. Its 1996 E & P before taxes is estimated to be $9,400,000. Exco's government does not withhold on dividends paid to foreign investors.

b. Invest the $500,000 in Exco bonds which pay interest at 7% per year. Assume that the bonds will be acquired at par, or face, value. Exco's government withholds 25% on interest paid to foreign investors.

Analyze these two investment opportunities and determine which would give Money the best return after taxes. Be sure to consider the effect of the foreign tax credit.

44. Georgia Calder is considering two offers that she has received from prospective employers. Overseas Projects, Inc., has offered Calder a position in Istanbul that will last for a minimum of three years. She will earn approximately $130,000 a year, which includes employer-provided housing costs of $28,000. During this period, she is required to return to the United States for two-week executive meetings at least three times a year. She also will receive a three-week vacation that she can spend anywhere she chooses.

Foreign Lands, Inc., has offered Calder a position in New Delhi that also will last for approximately three years. She will earn $110,000 a year, which does not include housing costs. However, her employer will reimburse her for up to $25,000 of qualified housing expenses. There is no requirement that she return to the United States for meetings. She will receive a four-week vacation that she can spend as she chooses. However, Foreign Lands will provide for her transportation if she wishes to spend her vacation in the United States.

Write a detailed memo to Ms. Calder explaining the tax consequences that she should consider in making her decision. Be sure to include a discussion of the bona fide residence versus physical presence rules. In your deliberations, use $9,500 as the base amount for the housing exclusion. Be careful not to overwhelm Ms. Calder with tax jargon such as "expatriate" and "outbound." Use plain language that a novice would understand. Do not let your tax knowledge cause you to use a "superior" attitude when addressing Ms. Calder.

Research Problems for this chapter appear at the end of Chapter 28.

TAX ADMINISTRATION AND PRACTICE

LEARNING OBJECTIVES

After completing Chapter 25, you should be able to:

1. Identify the various administrative pronouncements issued by the IRS and explain how they can be used in tax practice.

2. Summarize the administrative powers of the IRS including the examination of taxpayer records, the assessment and demand process, and collection procedures.

3. Describe the audit process, including how returns are selected for audit and the various types of audits.

4. Explain the taxpayer appeal process, including various settlement options available.

5. Determine the amount of interest on a deficiency or a refund and when it is due.

6. Discuss the various penalties that can be imposed on acts of noncompliance by taxpayers and return preparers.

7. Understand the rules governing the statute of limitations on assessments and on refunds.

8. Summarize the legal and ethical guidelines that apply to those engaged in tax practice.

Few events arouse so much fear in the typical individual or corporation as the receipt of a letter from the Internal Revenue Service (IRS), notifying the taxpayer that prior years' tax returns are to be the subject of an audit. Almost immediately, calls are made to the tax adviser. Advice is sought as to what to reveal (or not reveal) in the course of the audit, how to delay or avoid the audit, and how friendly one should be with the auditor when he or she ultimately does arrive.

Indeed, many tax practitioners' reputations with their clients have been made or broken by the way they are observed to behave under the pressure of an audit situation. The strategy and tactics of audits—including such seemingly unimportant issues as whether the tax adviser brings donuts or other refreshments to the audit session, the color of his or her suit and tie, and the most effective negotiation techniques—are the subject of both cocktail party banter and scholarly review.

In actuality, the practitioner can render valuable services to the taxpayer in an audit context, thereby assuring that tax payments for the disputed years are neither under- nor overreported, as part of an ongoing tax practice. In this regard, the adviser must appreciate the following.

- The elements of the Treasury's tax administration process and opportunities for appeal within the structure of the IRS.
- The extent of the negative sanctions that can be brought to bear against taxpayers whose returns are found to have been inaccurate.
- The ethical and professional constraints on the advice tax advisers can give and the actions they can take on behalf of their clients within the context of an adversarial relationship with the IRS.

TAX ADMINISTRATION

The Treasury has delegated the administration and enforcement of the tax laws to its subsidiary agency, the IRS. In this process, the Service is responsible for providing adequate information, in the form of publications and forms with instructions, to taxpayers so that they can comply with the laws in an appropriate manner. The IRS also identifies delinquent tax payments and carries out assessment and collection procedures under the restrictions of due process and other constitutional guarantees.

In meeting these responsibilities, the Service conducts audits of selected tax returns. Less than 1 percent of all individual tax returns are subjected to audit in

Should the IRS Be Larger?

What is the optimal size of the IRS? The IRS maintains that it can produce at least three dollars of revenue for every dollar spent on its ongoing operations. Actually, the rate of return might be higher, especially for special projects that the Service itself devises and undertakes. As the agency becomes more proficient with computers and more aggressive in finding and treating nonfilers, the temptation to enlarge the Service increases as well.

Given the Federal budget deficits and an underground economy measured in the hundreds of billions of dollars, one might expect the IRS personnel count to keep increasing, even though it is one of the largest Federal agencies, with a staff averaging between 110,000 and 120,000 throughout the year. Yet, the last few presidents have found that (1) pledges to cut back the size of government also apply to the IRS (i.e., the public does not apply such a rate of return test itself), and (2) the image of the Service as the taxpayer's friend and educator becomes tainted as more returns are subjected to audit. The public seems to support an IRS that aggressively finds unreported income from foreign corporations or drug dealers, but not from targets closer to home.

If the IRS has its way, audit rates will rise in the next few years. If Congress authorizes the appropriations requested, some five hundred new and reassigned audit employees will be added. If this occurs, the overall audit rate will likely approach 1.25 percent.

Specifically, the IRS hopes to obtain funds for about 450,000 additional audits, including an increase of 4,000 in corporate examinations and about 20,000 employment tax audits. Of the additional 421,000 examinations of individual returns, 100,000 would be conducted solely through correspondence methods, and 27,000 would be targeted to returns of self-employed taxpayers.

a given tax year. However, certain types of both taxpayers and income—including, for instance, high-income individuals (5 percent), cash-oriented businesses, real estate transactions, and estate- and gift-taxable transfers (18 percent)—are subject to much higher probabilities of audit. One's state of residence also affects the chance of audit, which ranges from 2 percent in Nevada to 0.25 percent in Wisconsin.

Recently, however, much of the IRS's effort has been devoted to developing statutory and administrative requirements relative to information reporting and document matching. For instance, when a taxpayer engages in a like-kind exchange or sells a personal residence, various parties to the transaction are required to report the nature and magnitude of the transaction to the IRS. Later the Treasury's computers determine whether the transaction has been reported properly by comparing the information reported by the third parties with the events included on the relevant taxpayers' returns for the year.

In addition, the IRS has been placing increasing pressure on the community of tax advisers. Severe penalties may be assessed on those who have prepared a taxpayer's return when the Service's interpretation of applicable law conflicts with that of the preparer.

The IRS processes over 200 million tax returns every year, about 10 million of which are filed electronically. It collects over $1 trillion in tax revenues and pays refunds to about 90 million taxpayers every year. The Mission Statement of the IRS reads as follows:

> The purpose of the Internal Revenue Service is to collect the proper amount of tax revenue at the least cost; serve the public by continually improving the quality of our products and services; and perform in a manner warranting the highest degree of public confidence in our integrity, efficiency and fairness.

Current operational strategies of the IRS include the following.

- A focus on taxpayer education.
- Emphasis on dealing with nonfilers.
- Adapting to the changing cultural and linguistic needs of the public.
- Accelerating the modernization of equipment and operating methods.
- Making the Regulations and tax procedures as simple and fair as possible.

The IRS believes that, under these principles, the taxpayer will benefit in a number of ways.

- Taxpayers will spend significantly less time dealing with the IRS.
- Taxpayers will pay less interest.
- Taxpayers will have more filing and payment choices.
- The IRS will issue refunds more rapidly.

IRS PROCEDURE—LETTER RULINGS

1   LEARNING OBJECTIVE
Identify the various administrative pronouncements issued by the IRS and explain how they can be used in tax practice.

When a tax issue is controversial or a transaction involves considerable tax dollars, the taxpayer often wishes to obtain either assurance or direction from the IRS as to the treatment of the event. The **letter ruling** process is an effective means of dealing directly with the IRS while in the planning stages of a large or otherwise important transaction.

Rulings issued by the National Office provide a written statement of the position of the IRS concerning the tax consequences of a course of action contemplated by the taxpayer. Letter (individual) rulings do not have the force and effect of law, but they do provide guidance and support for taxpayers in similar transactions. The IRS will issue rulings only on uncompleted, actual (rather than hypothetical) transactions or on transactions completed before the filing of the tax return for the year in question.

The IRS will not issue a ruling in certain circumstances. It ordinarily will not rule in cases that essentially involve a question of fact.[1] For example, no ruling will be issued to determine whether compensation paid to employees is reasonable in amount and therefore allowable as a deduction.[2]

A letter ruling represents the current opinion of the IRS on the tax consequences of a transaction with a given set of facts. IRS rulings are not unchangeable. They are frequently declared obsolete or are superseded by new rulings in response to tax law changes. However, revocation or modification of a ruling is usually not applied retroactively to the taxpayer who received the ruling, if it was relied on in good faith and if the facts in the ruling request were in agreement with the completed transaction. The IRS may revoke any ruling if, upon subsequent audit, the agent finds a misstatement or omission of facts or substantial discrep-

---

[1] Rev.Proc. 96–1, I.R.B. No. 1, 8.

[2] Rev.Proc. 96–3, I.R.B. No. 1, 82.

ancies between the facts in the ruling request and the actual situation. A ruling may be relied upon only by the taxpayer who requested and received it.

Letter rulings benefit both the IRS and the taxpayer. Not only do they help promote a uniform application of the tax laws, but they may also reduce the potential for litigation or disputes with revenue agents. In addition, they make the IRS aware of significant transactions being consummated by taxpayers. A fee is charged for processing a ruling request.

IRS PROCEDURE—ADDITIONAL ISSUANCES

In addition to issuing unpublished letter rulings and published rulings and procedures, the IRS issues determination letters and technical advice memoranda.

The District Director orders a **determination letter** for a completed transaction when the issue involved is covered by judicial or statutory authority, Regulations, or rulings. Determination letters are issued for various death, gift, income, excise, and employment tax matters.

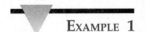 **EXAMPLE 1**

True Corporation recently opened a car clinic and has employed numerous mechanics. The corporation is not certain if the mechanics are to be treated as employees or as independent contractors for withholding and payroll tax purposes. True may request a determination letter from the appropriate District Director. ▼

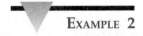 **EXAMPLE 2**

Assume the same facts as in Example 1. True would like to establish a pension plan that qualifies for the tax advantages of § 401(k). To determine whether the plan qualifies, True should request and obtain a determination letter from the IRS. ▼

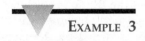 **EXAMPLE 3**

A group of physicians plans to form an association to construct and operate a hospital. The determination letter procedure is appropriate to ascertain the group's status—either subject to the Federal income tax or tax-exempt. ▼

A **technical advice memorandum** is issued by the National Office to the District Director and/or Regional Commissioner in response to a specific request by an agent, Appellate Conferee, or District Director. The taxpayer may request a technical advice memorandum if an issue in dispute is not treated by the law or precedent and/or published rulings or Regulations. Technical advice memoranda are also appropriate when there is reason to believe that the IRS is not administering the tax law consistently. For example, a taxpayer may inquire why an agent proposes to disallow a certain expenditure when agents in other districts permit the deduction. Technical advice requests arise from the audit process, whereas ruling requests are issued before an IRS audit.

ADMINISTRATIVE POWERS OF THE IRS

Examination of Records. The Code authorizes the IRS to examine the taxpayer's books and records as part of the process of determining the correct amount of tax due. The IRS can also require the persons responsible for the return to appear and to produce any necessary books and records.[3] Taxpayers are required to maintain certain record-keeping procedures and retain the records necessary to facilitate the audit. Therefore, the taxpayer and not the IRS has the burden of substantiating any item on the tax return that is under examination. The files,

2 LEARNING OBJECTIVE
Summarize the administrative powers of the IRS, including the examination of taxpayer records, the assessment and demand process, and collection procedures.

[3] § 7602.

workpapers, and other memoranda of a tax practitioner may be subpoenaed, since communications between CPAs and their clients generally are not privileged.

Assessment and Demand.   The Code permits the IRS to assess a deficiency and to demand payment for the tax.[4] However, no assessment or effort to collect the tax may be made until 90 days after a statutory notice of a deficiency (the *90-day letter*) is issued. The taxpayer therefore has 90 days to file a petition to the U.S. Tax Court, effectively preventing the deficiency from being assessed or collected pending the outcome of the case.[5]

Following assessment of the tax, the IRS issues a notice and demand for payment. The taxpayer is usually given 30 days after the notice and demand for payment to pay the tax. This assessment procedure has certain exceptions.

- The IRS may issue a deficiency assessment without waiting 90 days if mathematical errors on the return incorrectly state the tax at less than the true liability.
- If the IRS believes the assessment or collection of a deficiency is in jeopardy, it may assess the deficiency and demand immediate payment.[6] The taxpayer can avoid (*stay*) the collection of the jeopardy assessment by filing a bond for the amount of the tax and interest. This action prevents the IRS from selling any property it has seized.

IRS Collection Procedures.   If the taxpayer neglects or refuses to pay the tax after receiving the demand for payment, a lien in favor of the IRS is placed on all property (realty and personalty, tangible and intangible) belonging to the taxpayer.

The levy power of the IRS is very broad. It allows the IRS to garnish (*attach*) wages and salary and to seize and sell all nonexempt property by any means. The IRS can also make successive seizures on any property owned by the taxpayer until the levy is satisfied.[7] In exceptional cases, the IRS grants an extension for payment of a deficiency to prevent "undue hardship."[8]

If property is transferred and any related tax is not paid, the subsequent owners of the property may be liable for the tax. For example, if an estate is insolvent and unable to pay the estate tax, the executor or the beneficiaries may be liable for the payment.[9]

THE AUDIT PROCESS

3 LEARNING OBJECTIVE
Describe the audit process, including how returns are selected for audit and the various types of audits.

Selection of Returns for Audit.   The IRS uses mathematical formulas to select tax returns that are most likely to contain errors and yield substantial amounts of additional tax revenues upon audit. The IRS does not openly disclose all of its audit selection techniques. However, some observations can be made regarding the probability that a return will be selected for audit.

- Certain groups of taxpayers are subject to audit more frequently than others. These groups include individuals with gross income in excess of $100,000,

---

[4] § 6212.
[5] § 6213.
[6] § 6861. A jeopardy assessment is appropriate, for instance, where the IRS fears that the taxpayer will flee the country or destroy valuable property.

[7] The taxpayer can keep certain personal and business property and a minimal amount of his or her income as a subsistence allowance, even if a lien is outstanding. § 6334.
[8] § 6161(b).
[9] § 6901.

self-employed individuals with substantial business income and deductions, and cash businesses where the potential for tax evasion is high.

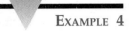

EXAMPLE 4   Tracey owns and operates a liquor store. As nearly all of her sales are for cash, Tracey might be a prime candidate for an audit by the IRS. Cash transactions are easier to conceal than those made on credit. ▼

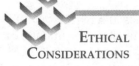

ETHICAL CONSIDERATIONS

Do You Live in an Audit-Friendly Part of the Country?

Tax advisers have long suspected that the area of the country in which taxpayers live is one of the most important factors determining their susceptibility to audit. Theoretically, why should taxpayers living in Las Vegas be more likely to be audited than those living in Baltimore? Aren't all tax returns created equal?

Not according to confidential IRS documents and policies reviewed by a team from *Money* magazine (see the August 1994 issue). For the roughly one million individual income tax returns that are audited every year, the taxpayer's zip code partly determines not only the probability of being audited, but also the chances of success in reaching compromises with the IRS as the audit is settled.

The magazine analyzed confidential audit and collection data for all the IRS districts. Then it derived a "toughness" measure for each district, taking into account such factors as high audit rates, high collection rates, and a low probability of the IRS accepting a taxpayer's offer in compromise.

The "toughest" districts were found to be Las Vegas and San Francisco, both with overall audit rates of about 1.7 percent. At the other end was the Milwaukee district, which was found to be the least tough of all, auditing only about 0.25 percent of its returns and agreeing in full to the taxpayer's compromise offer about two-thirds of the time.

Don't use these statistics thoughtlessly. When a tax return is audited and the tax liability is not changed, has the government's money been wasted? Are auditors in the low-audit-rate areas lazier or less productive than those who produce more dollars for the government? Should the government set minimums for collections made under compromise offers accepted from taxpayers? Should the IRS collect at least 10 cents on the dollar? Twenty-five cents?

The official IRS answer to these inquiries is that "[a]ny perceived 'geographic' variations result from (other factors, such as) differences in compliance levels, taxpayer behavior, and economic and business trends." But are Las Vegas taxpayers seven times more likely to cheat than those in Milwaukee? An accounting firm partner sums it up this way: "Some IRS offices come on like sheriffs with both guns blazing, while other offices act like kindly crossing guards shepherding taxpayers through the system."

Can these facts affect tax filing strategies? What if a Las Vegas client of yours wants to file using your firm's Milwaukee address?

- If a taxpayer has been audited in a past year and the audit led to the assessment of a substantial deficiency, the IRS often makes a return visit.
- An audit might materialize if information returns (e.g., Form W–2, Form 1099) are not in substantial agreement with the income reported on a taxpayer's return. Obvious discrepancies do not necessitate formal audits and usually can be handled by correspondence with the taxpayer.

- If an individual's itemized deductions are in excess of norms established for various income levels, the probability of an audit increases. Certain deductions (e.g., casualty and theft losses, business use of the home, tax-sheltered investments) are sensitive areas since the IRS realizes that many taxpayers determine the amount of the deduction incorrectly or may not be entitled to the deduction at all.
- The filing of a refund claim by the taxpayer may prompt an audit of the return.
- Certain returns are chosen on a random basis (known as the Taxpayer Compliance Measurement Program [TCMP]) to develop, update, and improve the mathematical formulas used in selecting returns. TCMP is a long-term project designed to measure and evaluate taxpayer compliance characteristics. TCMP audits are tedious and time-consuming, as the taxpayer is generally asked to verify most or all items on the tax return. The last TCMP audits took place almost a decade ago.
- Information is often obtained from other sources (e.g., other government agencies, news items, informants). The IRS can pay rewards to persons who provide information that leads to the detection and punishment of those who violate the tax laws. The rewards are paid at the discretion of a District Director and cannot exceed 10 percent of the taxes, fines, and penalties recovered as a result of the information.[10]

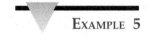

EXAMPLE 5   Phil reports to the police that burglars broke into his home while he was out of town and took a shoe box containing $25,000 in cash, among other things. A representative of the IRS reading the newspaper account of the burglary might wonder why Phil kept such a large amount of cash in a shoe box at home. ▼

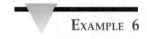

EXAMPLE 6   After 15 years, Betty is discharged by her employer, Dr. Franklin. Shortly thereafter, the IRS receives a letter from Betty informing it that Franklin keeps two sets of books, one of which substantially understates the actual cash receipts. ▼

Many individual taxpayers mistakenly assume that if they do not hear from the IRS within a few weeks after filing their return or if they receive a refund check, no audit will be forthcoming. As a practical matter, most individual returns are examined about two years from the date of filing. If not, they generally remain unaudited. All large corporations, however, are subject to annual audits.

Verification and Audit Procedures.   The tax return is immediately reviewed for mathematical accuracy. A check is also made for deductions, exclusions, etc., that are clearly erroneous. An example of obvious error would be the failure to comply with the 7.5 percent limitation on the deduction for medical expenses. In such cases, the Service Center merely sends the taxpayer revised computations and a bill or refund as appropriate. Taxpayers are usually able to settle such matters through direct correspondence with the IRS without the necessity of a formal audit.

Office audits are conducted by representatives of the District Director's Office, either in the office of the IRS or through correspondence. Individual returns with few or no items of business income are usually handled through an office audit. In most instances, the taxpayer is required merely to substantiate a deduction, credit,

---

[10] § 7623 and Reg. § 301.7623–1.

or item of income that appears on the return. The taxpayer presents documentation in the form of canceled checks, invoices, etc., for the items in question.

The *field audit* is commonly used for corporate returns and for returns of individuals engaged in business or professional activities. This type of audit generally involves a more complete examination of a taxpayer's transactions.

A field audit is conducted by IRS agents at the office or home of the taxpayer or at the office of the taxpayer's representative. The agent's work may be facilitated by a review of certain tax workpapers and discussions with the taxpayer's representative about items appearing on the tax return.

Prior to or at the initial interview, the IRS must provide the taxpayer with an explanation of the audit process that is the subject of the interview and describe the taxpayer's rights under that process. If the taxpayer clearly states at any time during the interview the desire to consult with an attorney, CPA, enrolled agent, or any other person permitted to represent the taxpayer before the IRS, then the IRS representative must suspend the interview.[11]

Any officer or employee of the IRS must, upon advance request, allow a taxpayer to make an audio recording of any in-person interview with the officer or employee concerning the determination and collection of any tax. The recording of IRS audit conferences may have significant legal implications. For example, if an IRS employee recklessly or intentionally disregards pertinent rules in the collection of Federal tax, the taxpayer can bring a civil action for damages in a U.S. District Court.[12]

Settlement with the Revenue Agent. Following an audit, the IRS agent may either accept the return as filed or recommend certain adjustments. The **Revenue Agent's Report (RAR)** is reviewed by the agent's group supervisor and the Review Staff within the IRS. In most instances, the agent's proposed adjustments are approved. However, the Review Staff or group supervisor may request additional information or raise new issues.

Agents must adhere strictly to IRS policy as reflected in published rulings, Regulations, and other releases. The agent cannot settle an unresolved issue based upon the probability of winning the case in court. Usually, issues involving factual questions can be settled at the agent level, and it may be advantageous for both the taxpayer and the IRS to reach agreement at the earliest point in the settlement process. For example, it may be to the taxpayer's advantage to reach agreement at the agent level and avoid any further opportunity for the IRS to raise new issues.

A deficiency (an amount in excess of the tax shown on the return or the tax previously assessed) may be proposed at the agent level. The taxpayer may wish to pursue to a higher level the disputed issues upon which this deficiency is based. The taxpayer's progress through the appeal process is discussed in subsequent sections of this chapter.

If agreement is reached upon the proposed deficiency, the taxpayer signs Form 870 (Waiver of Restrictions on Assessment and Collection of Deficiency in Tax). One advantage to the taxpayer of signing Form 870 at this point is that interest stops accumulating on the deficiency 30 days after the form is filed.[13] When this form is signed, the taxpayer effectively waives the right to receive a statutory notice of deficiency (the 90-day letter) and to subsequently petition the Tax Court. In addition, it is no longer possible for the taxpayer to go to the IRS Appeals Division. Signing Form 870 at the agent level generally closes the case.

[11] § 7521(b).
[12] § 7433.
[13] § 6601(c).

However, the IRS is not restricted by Form 870 and may assess additional deficiencies if deemed necessary.

THE TAXPAYER APPEAL PROCESS

4 **LEARNING OBJECTIVE**
Explain the taxpayer appeal process, including various settlement options available.

If agreement cannot be reached at the agent level, the taxpayer receives a copy of the Revenue Agent's Report and a **30-day letter.** The taxpayer has 30 days to request an administrative appeal. If an appeal is not requested, a **90-day letter** is issued. Figure 25–1 illustrates the taxpayer's alternatives when a disagreement with the IRS persists.

A taxpayer who wishes to appeal must make an appropriate request to the Appeals Division. The request must be accompanied by a written protest, except in the following cases.

- The proposed tax deficiency does not exceed $10,000 for any of the tax periods involved in the audit.
- The deficiency resulted from a correspondence or office audit (i.e., not as a result of a field audit).

▼ **FIGURE 25–1**
Income Tax Appeal Procedure

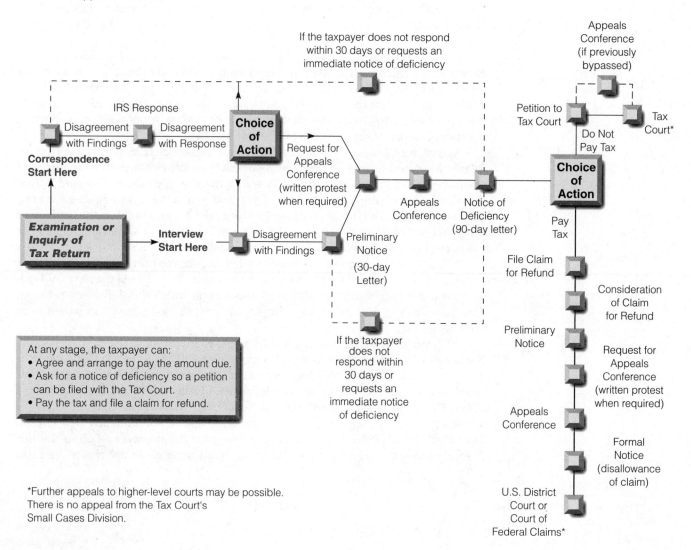

*Further appeals to higher-level courts may be possible. There is no appeal from the Tax Court's Small Cases Division.

The Appeals Division is authorized to settle all tax disputes based on the hazards of litigation (i.e., the chances of winning in court). Since the Appeals Division has final settlement authority until a 90-day letter has been issued, the taxpayer may be able to negotiate a settlement. In addition, an overall favorable settlement may be reached by "trading" disputed issues. The Appeals Division occasionally may raise new issues if the grounds are substantial and of significant tax impact.

Both the Appeals Division and the taxpayer have the right to request technical advice memoranda from the National Office of the IRS. A technical advice memorandum that is favorable to the taxpayer is binding on the Appeals Division. Even if the technical advice memorandum is favorable to the IRS, however, the Appeals Division may nevertheless settle the case based on other considerations.

A taxpayer who files a petition with the U.S. Tax Court has the option of having the case heard before the informal Small Cases Division if the amount of tax in dispute does not exceed $10,000.[14] If the Small Cases Division is used, neither party may appeal the case. The decisions of the Small Cases Division are not published or otherwise available as precedents for other cases.

The economic costs of a settlement offer from the Appeals Division should be weighed against the costs of litigation and the probability of winning the case. The taxpayer should also consider the impact of the settlement upon the tax liability for future periods, in addition to the years under audit.

If a settlement is reached with the Appeals Division, the taxpayer is required to sign Form 870AD. According to the IRS, this settlement is binding upon both parties unless fraud, malfeasance, concealment, or misrepresentation of material fact has occurred.

OFFERS IN COMPROMISE AND CLOSING AGREEMENTS

The IRS can negotiate a compromise if there is doubt about the taxpayer's ability to pay the tax.[15] If the taxpayer is financially unable to pay the total amount of the tax, a Form 656 (**Offer in Compromise**) can be filed with the District Director or the IRS Service Center.

The IRS investigates the claim by evaluating the taxpayer's financial ability to pay the tax. In some instances, the compromise settlement includes an agreement for final settlement of the tax through payments of a specified percentage of the taxpayer's future earnings. The District Director must obtain approval from the IRS Regional Counsel if the amount involved exceeds $500. This settlement procedure usually entails lengthy periods of negotiation with the IRS.

The IRS has statutory authority to enter into a written agreement allowing taxes to be paid on an installment basis if that arrangement facilitates the tax collection. The agreement may later be modified or terminated because of (1) inadequate information, (2) subsequent change in financial condition, or (3) failure to pay an installment when due or to provide requested information.[16]

A **closing agreement** is binding on both the taxpayer and the IRS, except upon a subsequent showing of fraud, malfeasance, or misrepresentation of a material fact.[17] The closing agreement may be used when disputed issues carry over to future years. It may also be employed to dispose of a dispute involving a specific issue for a prior year or a proposed transaction involving future years. If, for example, the IRS is willing to make substantial concessions in the valuation of

---

[14] § 7463(a).
[15] § 7122.

[16] § 6159.
[17] § 7121(b).

TAX IN THE NEWS

THE IRS STRIVES TO BECOME CONSUMER-FRIENDLY

When country singer Willie Nelson was found guilty of underreporting his Federal income taxes, chiefly due to his involvement in real estate tax shelters, the total deficiency, including taxes, interest, and penalties, came to $16.7 million. The IRS intended to collect the full amount by forcing auctions of Nelson's most valuable possessions, placing claims on royalties from his recordings, encouraging him to make television commercials for fast-food outlets, and prompting him to sue his prior tax advisers for offsetting damages (to be paid directly to the IRS). Three years of such collections totaled only about $4 million.

As part of a nationwide effort to expand the use of the offer in compromise program, the IRS then settled with Nelson for total collections of $9 million, to be paid over a five-year period, with no future liens or collection activities. An IRS spokesperson asserted that the broader use of the compromise powers indicated the agency was "willing to settle for something less than the entire amount . . . to be more reasonable with taxpayers" having difficulty finding the full deficiency amount. Given the slow economy, more taxpayers are having such difficulties, and the IRS seems willing to collect what it can, rather than haggle in court for years to collect the "last penny" due.

Nelson's new adviser stated that the IRS was "taking a much more pragmatic and realistic approach to tax collection," as indicated by the change in the offer in compromise policy. In previous years, the IRS accepted only 25 percent of taxpayers' offers, covering about $40 million in deficiencies. Early 1993 reports showed these figures increasing to an acceptance rate of about 60 percent, for over $100 million in collections.

In fact, the taxpayer can now initiate an installment payment plan on the original return. Form 9465, Installment Agreement Request, lays out the taxpayer's plan for payment, which incurs only a 0.5 percent penalty in addition to the late-payment interest charge. The standard arrangement is a three-year payment plan where the amount due is less than $10,000; subsequent-year tax liabilities must be satisfied in full.

Reportedly, the IRS is also considering accepting tax payments through major credit cards and other "consumer-friendly" efforts to collect revenues.

assets for death tax purposes, it may require a closing agreement from the recipient of the property to establish the income tax basis of the assets.

INTEREST

Determination of the Interest Rate.   Several years ago, Congress recognized that the interest rates applicable to Federal tax underpayments (deficiencies) and overpayments (refunds) should be closer to the rates available in financial markets. The Code provides for rates to be determined quarterly.[18] For example, the rates that are determined during January are effective for the following April through June.

5   LEARNING OBJECTIVE
Determine the amount of interest on a deficiency or a refund and when it is due.

---
[18]§ 6621.

IRS interest rates are based on the Federal short-term rates published periodically by the IRS in Revenue Rulings. The Federal rates are based on the average market yield on outstanding marketable obligations of the United States with remaining maturity of three years or less.

Underpayments are subject to the Federal short-term rates plus three percentage points, and overpayments carry the Federal short-term rates plus two percentage points. Consequently, the rate for tax deficiencies is one percentage point higher than the rate for tax refunds. For the first quarter of 1996, interest on tax deficiencies was set at 9 percent, and interest on refunds was 8 percent. In previous years, interest rates have ranged from 6 percent to 20 percent.

Computation of the Amount of Interest.   Interest is compounded daily.[19] Depending on the applicable interest rate, daily compounding doubles the payable amount over a period of five to eight years.

Tables for determining the daily compounded amount are available from the IRS. The tables ease the burden of those who prepare late returns where additional taxes are due.[20]

IRS Deficiency Assessments.   Interest usually accrues from the unextended due date of the return until 30 days after the taxpayer agrees to the deficiency by signing Form 870. If the taxpayer does not pay the amount shown on the IRS's "notice and demand" (tax bill) within 30 days, interest again accrues on the deficiency.

Refund of Taxpayer's Overpayments.   If an overpayment is refunded to the taxpayer within 45 days after the date the return is filed or is due, no interest is allowed. When the taxpayer files an amended return or makes a claim for refund of a prior year's tax (e.g., when net operating loss carrybacks result in refunds of a prior year's tax payments), however, interest is authorized from the original due date of the return through the date when the amended return is filed.

In the past, when interest rates were sometimes as high as 20 percent, many taxpayers found it advantageous to delay filing various tax returns that led to refunds. Thus, the IRS was placed in the unplanned role of providing taxpayers with a high-yield savings account. Under current law, however, taxpayers applying for refunds receive interest as follows.

- When a return is filed after the due date, interest on any overpayment accrues from the date of filing. However, no interest is due if the IRS makes the refund within 45 days of the date of filing.

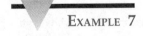

EXAMPLE 7   Naomi, a calendar year taxpayer, files her 1996 return on December 1, 1997. The return reflects an overwithholding of $2,500. On June 8, 1998, Naomi receives a refund of her 1996 overpayment. Interest on the refund began to accrue on December 1, 1997 (not April 15, 1997). ▼

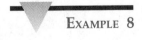

EXAMPLE 8   Assume the same facts as in Example 7, except that the refund is paid to Naomi on January 5, 1998 (rather than June 8, 1998). No interest is payable by the IRS, since the refund was made within 45 days of the filing of the return. ▼

- In no event will interest accrue on an overpayment unless the return that is filed is in "processible form." Generally, this means that the return must contain enough information in a readable format to enable the IRS to identify the taxpayer and to determine the tax (and overpayment) involved.

---

[19] § 6622.   [20] Rev.Proc. 83–7, 1983–1 C.B. 583.

TAXPAYER PENALTIES

To promote and enforce taxpayer compliance with the U.S. voluntary self-assessment system of taxation, Congress has enacted a comprehensive array of penalties. Tax penalties may involve both criminal and civil offenses. Criminal tax penalties are imposed only after the usual criminal process, in which the taxpayer is entitled to the same constitutional guarantees as nontax criminal defendants. Normally, a criminal penalty provides for imprisonment. Civil tax penalties are collected in the same manner as other taxes and usually provide only for monetary fines. Criminal and civil penalties are not mutually exclusive; therefore, both types of sanctions may be imposed on a taxpayer.

The Code characterizes tax penalties as additions to tax; thus, they cannot subsequently be deducted by the taxpayer. *Ad valorem penalties* are additions to tax that are based upon a percentage of the owed tax. *Assessable penalties,* on the other hand, typically include a flat dollar amount. Assessable penalties are not subject to review by the Tax Court, but *ad valorem* penalties are subject to the same deficiency procedures that apply to the underlying tax.

Failure to File and Failure to Pay. For a failure to file a tax return by the due date (including extensions), a penalty of 5 percent per month (up to a maximum of 25 percent) is imposed on the amount of tax shown as due on the return, with a minimum penalty amount of $100. If the failure to file is attributable to fraud, the penalty becomes 15 percent per month, to a maximum of 75 percent of the tax.[21]

For a failure to pay the tax due as shown on the return, a penalty of 0.5 percent per month (up to a maximum of 25 percent) is imposed on the amount of the tax. The penalty is doubled if the taxpayer fails to pay the tax after receiving a deficiency assessment.

In all of these cases, a fraction of a month counts as a full month. These penalties relate to the net amount of the tax due.

EXAMPLE 9

Conchita, a calendar year self-employed taxpayer, prepays $18,000 for income taxes during 1997. Her total tax liability for 1997 proves to be $20,000. Without obtaining an extension from the IRS, she files her Form 1040 in early August 1998 and encloses a check for the balance due of $2,000. The failure to file and the failure to pay penalties apply to $2,000 (not $20,000). ▼

During any month in which both the failure to file penalty and the failure to pay penalty apply, the failure to file penalty is reduced by the amount of the failure to pay penalty.

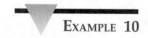

EXAMPLE 10

Jason files his tax return 10 days after the due date. Along with the return, he remits a check for $3,000, which is the balance of the tax owed. Disregarding any interest liabilities, Jason's total penalties are as follows.

Failure to pay penalty (0.5% × $3,000)		$ 15
Plus: Failure to file penalty (5% × $3,000)	$150	
Less: Failure to pay penalty for the same period	(15)	
Failure to file penalty		135
Total penalties		$150

---

[21] §§ 6651(a) and (f).

The penalties for one full month are imposed even though Jason was delinquent by only 10 days. Unlike the method used to compute interest, any part of a month is treated as a whole month. ▼

These penalties can be avoided if the taxpayer shows that the failure to file and/or failure to pay was due to reasonable cause and not due to willful neglect. The Code is silent on what constitutes reasonable cause, and the Regulations do little to clarify this important concept.[22] Reasonable cause for failure to pay is presumed under the automatic four-month extension (Form 4868) when the additional tax due is not more than 10 percent of the tax liability shown on the return. In addition, the courts have ruled on some aspects of **reasonable cause.**

- Reasonable cause was found where the taxpayer relied on the advice of a competent tax adviser given in good faith, the facts were fully disclosed to the adviser, and he or she considered that the specific question represented reasonable cause.[23] No reasonable cause was found, however, where the taxpayer delegated the filing task to another, even when that person was an accountant or an attorney.[24]
- Among the reasons not qualifying as reasonable cause were lack of information on the due date of the return,[25] illness that did not incapacitate a taxpayer from completing a return,[26] refusal of the taxpayer's spouse to cooperate for a joint return,[27] and ignorance or misunderstanding of the tax law.[28]

Accuracy-Related Penalties.   Major civil penalties relating to the accuracy of tax return data, including misstatements stemming from taxpayer negligence and improper valuation of income and deductions, are coordinated under the umbrella term **accuracy-related penalties.**[29] This consolidation of related penalties into a single levy eliminates the possibility that multiple penalties will be stacked together (i.e., when more than one type of penalty applies to a single understatement of tax).

The accuracy-related penalties each amount to 20 percent of the portion of the tax underpayment that is attributable to one or more of the following infractions.

- Negligence or disregard of rules and Regulations.
- Substantial understatement of tax liability.
- Substantial valuation overstatement.
- Substantial valuation understatement.

The penalties apply only where the taxpayer fails to show a reasonable basis for the position taken on the return.[30]

Negligence.   For purposes of this accuracy-related penalty, **negligence** includes any failure to make a reasonable attempt to comply with the provisions of the tax

[22] Reg. § 301.6651–1(c)(1) likens reasonable cause to the exercise of "ordinary business care and prudence" on the part of the taxpayer.

[23] *Estate of Norma S. Bradley,* 33 TCM 70, T.C.Memo. 1974–17.

[24] *U.S. v. Boyle,* 85–1 USTC ¶13,602, 55 AFTR2d 85–1535, 105 S.Ct. 687 (USSC, 1985).

[25] *Beck Chemical Equipment Co.,* 27 T.C. 840 (1957).

[26] *Jacob Gassman,* 26 TCM 213, T.C.Memo. 1967–42, and *Babetta Schmidt,* 28 T.C. 367 (1957). Compare *Estate of Kirchner,* 46 B.T.A. 578 (1942).

[27] *Electric and Neon, Inc.,* 56 T.C. 1324 (1971).

[28] *Stevens Brothers Foundation, Inc.,* 39 T.C. 93 (1965).

[29] § 6662.

[30] Temporary Regulations issued as TD 8533, 3/94. Most tax professionals measure this standard as a one-fourth probability of prevailing in court.

law. The penalty also applies to any disregard (whether careless, reckless, or intentional) of rules and Regulations.[31] The penalty can be avoided upon a showing of reasonable cause and that the taxpayer acted in good faith.[32] The negligence penalty applies to *all* taxes, except when fraud is involved.

A negligence penalty may be assessed when the taxpayer fails to report gross income, overstates deductions, or fails to keep adequate records. When the taxpayer takes a nonnegligent position on the return that is contrary to a published pronouncement of the IRS, the penalty is waived if the taxpayer has a reasonable basis for the interpretation and has disclosed the disputed position on Form 8275.

Substantial Understatements of Tax Liability.
The understatement penalty is designed to strike at middle- and high-income taxpayers who are tempted to play the so-called *audit lottery*.[33] Some taxpayers take questionable and undisclosed positions on their tax returns in the hope that the return will not be selected for audit. Disclosing the positions would have called attention to the return and increased the probability of audit.

A *substantial understatement of a tax liability* transpires when the understatement exceeds the larger of 10 percent of the tax due or $5,000 ($10,000 for a C corporation). The understatement to which the penalty applies is the difference between the amount of tax required to be shown on the return and the amount of tax actually shown on the return.

The penalty is avoided under any of the following circumstances.

* The taxpayer has **substantial authority** for the treatment.
* The relevant facts affecting the treatment are adequately disclosed in the return by attaching Form 8275.
* The taxpayer has a reasonable basis for taking the disputed position.

Penalty for Overvaluation.
The objective of the overvaluation penalty is to deter taxpayers from inflating values (or basis), usually for charitable contributions of property, to reduce income taxes.[34]

* The penalty is 20 percent of the additional tax that would have been paid had the correct valuation (or basis) been used.[35]
* The penalty applies only when the valuation (or basis) used is 200 percent or more of the correct valuation (or basis).
* The penalty applies only to the extent that the resulting income tax underpayment exceeds $5,000 ($10,000 for C corporations).

EXAMPLE 11

Gretchen (a calendar year taxpayer) purchased a painting for $10,000. Years later, when the painting is worth $18,000 (as later determined by the IRS), Gretchen donates the painting to an art museum. Based on the appraisal of a cousin who is an amateur artist, she deducts $40,000 for the donation. Since Gretchen was in a 31% tax bracket, overstating the deduction by $22,000 results in a tax underpayment of $6,820.

Gretchen's penalty for overvaluation is $1,364 [20% × $6,820 (the underpayment that resulted from using $40,000 instead of $18,000)]. ▼

The substantial valuation overstatement penalty is avoided if the taxpayer can show reasonable cause and good faith. However, when the overvaluation involves *charitable deduction property*, the taxpayer must show *two additional* facts.

[31] § 6662(c).
[32] § 6664(c)(1).
[33] § 6662(b)(2).
[34] § 6662(b)(3).
[35] For gross valuation misstatements (i.e., 400% or more), the penalty increases to 40%. § 6662(h).

- The claimed value of the property is based on a qualified appraisal made by a qualified appraiser.
- The taxpayer made a good faith investigation of the value of the contributed property.[36]

Based on these criteria, Gretchen in Example 11 would find it difficult to avoid the penalty. A cousin who is an amateur artist does not meet the definition of a qualified appraiser. Likewise, she apparently has not made a good faith investigation of the value of the contributed property.

Penalty for Undervaluation. When attempting to minimize the income tax, it is to the benefit of taxpayers to *overvalue* deductions. When attempting to minimize transfer taxes (i.e., estate and gift taxes), however, executors and donors may be inclined to *undervalue* the assets transferred. A lower valuation reduces estate and gift taxes. An accuracy-related penalty is imposed for substantial estate or gift tax valuation understatements.[37]

The penalty is 20 percent of the additional transfer tax that would have been due had the correct valuation been used on Form 706 (estate and generation-skipping transfer tax return) or Form 709 (gift and generation-skipping transfer tax return). The penalty only applies if the value of the property claimed on the return is 50 percent or less than the amount determined to be correct. The penalty applies only to an additional transfer tax liability in excess of $5,000. The penalty is doubled if the reported valuation was 25 percent or less than the correct determination. As with other accuracy-related penalties, reasonable cause and good faith on the part of the taxpayer are a defense.

ETHICAL
CONSIDERATIONS

Good Faith Valuations

The undervaluation penalty pushes the tax adviser from a position of adversarial alliance with the taxpayer to one of mediator for the court. Good faith estimates of value, especially for family-owned businesses, can easily vary by as much as the 50 percentage points specified for the penalty. Even a gross undervaluation can occur when someone in the business other than the donor or decedent is a particularly talented entrepreneur, an effective sales representative, and/or the founder of the company; similarly, a business may be substantially undervalued when a minority equity interest is involved, or an intangible asset conveys a sizable nominal amount of goodwill to the valuation.

Because most taxpayers are highly averse to incurring any nondeductible penalties, the client may be tempted to compromise on the business valuation "too soon" (i.e., when the return is filed), eliminating any possibility of a more favorable valuation being presented before the Appeals Division or a court. Keeping in mind all of the potential taxpayer and preparer penalties that might apply, the tax professional should stick with a good faith appraisal of the business value, no matter what its nominal amount.

How would you react if your client, a musical composer, wanted to deduct $100,000 for the contribution of an obscure manuscript to the Symphony Society? What if your (first) appraiser placed the value of the manuscript at $15,000? What course of action would you propose to the client concerning the deduction? Any consequent penalties?

---

[36] § 6664(c)(2).   [37] § 6662(b)(5).

Civil Fraud Penalty.   A 75 percent civil penalty is imposed on any underpayment resulting from **fraud** by the taxpayer who has filed a return.[38] For this penalty, the burden of proof is *on the IRS* to show by a preponderance of the evidence that the taxpayer had a specific intent to evade a tax. Once the IRS has initially established that fraud has occurred, the taxpayer then bears the burden of proof to show by a preponderance of the evidence the portion of the underpayment that is not attributable to fraud.

Although the Code and Regulations do not provide any assistance in ascertaining what constitutes civil fraud, it is clear that mere negligence on the part of the taxpayer (however great) will not suffice. Fraud has been found in cases of manipulation of the books,[39] substantial omissions from income,[40] and erroneous deductions.[41]

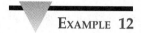

EXAMPLE 12

Frank underpaid his income tax by $90,000. The IRS can prove that $60,000 of the underpayment was due to fraud. Frank responds by a preponderance of the evidence that $30,000 of the underpayment was not due to fraud. The civil fraud penalty is $45,000 (75% × $60,000). ▼

If the underpayment of tax is partly attributable to negligence and partly attributable to fraud, the fraud penalty is applied first.

Criminal Penalties.   In addition to civil fraud penalties, the Code provides numerous criminal sanctions that carry various monetary fines and/or imprisonment. The difference between civil and criminal fraud often is one of degree. A characteristic of criminal fraud is the presence of willfulness on the part of the taxpayer. Thus, § 7201, dealing with attempts to evade or defeat a tax, contains the following language.

> Any person who *willfully* attempts in any manner to evade or defeat any tax imposed by this title or the payment thereof shall, in addition to other penalties provided by law, be guilty of a felony and, upon conviction thereof, shall be fined not more than $100,000 ($500,000 in the case of a corporation), or imprisoned not more than five years, or both, together with the costs of prosecution. (Emphasis added.)

As to the burden of proof, the IRS must show that the taxpayer was guilty of willful evasion "beyond the shadow of any reasonable doubt." Recall that for civil fraud, the standard applied to measure culpability is "by a preponderance of the evidence."

Failure to Pay Estimated Taxes.   A penalty is imposed for a failure to pay estimated income taxes. The penalty applies to individuals and corporations and is based on the rate of interest in effect for deficiency assessments.[42] The penalty also applies to trusts and certain estates that are required to make estimated tax payments.

The penalty is not imposed if the tax due for the year (less amounts withheld and credits) is less than $500. For employees, an equal amount of withholding is deemed paid on each due date.

---

[38] § 6663.

[39] *Dogget v. Comm.*, 60–1 USTC ¶9342, 5 AFTR2d 1034, 275 F.2d 823 (CA–4, 1960).

[40] *Harvey Brodsky*, 21 TCM 578, T.C. Memo. 1962–105.

[41] *Lash v. Comm.*, 57–2 USTC ¶9725, 51 AFTR 492, 245 F.2d 20 (CA–1, 1957).

[42] §§ 6655 (corporations) and 6654 (other taxpayers). Other computations can avoid the penalty. See §§ 6654(d)(2) and (k), 6655(e) and (i).

TAX IN THE NEWS

BLAMING THE TAX PRACTITIONER

In the last few years, courts have been amenable to taxpayers who defend against criminal charges by asserting that their dependence upon competent tax counsel led to the understatement of tax. Taxpayers who have used this defense successfully have usually shown that they relied on the practitioner's advice because of his or her professional expertise. Other successful defenses have included the argument that it was the practitioner's idea to willfully evade the tax, or that the adviser was not current with the controlling law and therefore issued bad advice that led to the error.

For instance, taxpayers have succeeded with this defense where they could show that the practitioner initiated and implemented the practice of keeping two sets of books or manipulating the cash receipts. Similarly, where the adviser facilitated the underpayment of tax estimates or payroll tax deposits, the IRS's charges against the taxpayer were severely weakened.

Often, taxpayers have submitted videotapes or written materials prepared by the practitioner as evidence in such cases. Severe preparer penalties compound the IRS's retribution against the practitioner when such a defense by the taxpayer prevails in court.

Quarterly payments are to be made on or before the fifteenth day of the fourth month (April 15 for a calendar year taxpayer), sixth month, and ninth month of the current year, and the first month of the following year. Corporations must make the last quarterly payment by the twelfth month of the same year.

An individual's underpayment of estimated tax is the difference between the estimates that were paid and the least of (1) 90 percent of the current-year tax, (2) 100 percent of the prior-year tax (the tax year must have been a full 12 months and a return must have been filed), and (3) 90 percent of the tax that would be due on an annualized income computation for the period running through the end of the quarter. When the taxpayer's prior-year adjusted gross income (AGI) exceeds $150,000, the required payment percentage for the prior-year alternative is 110 percent.

A corporation's underpayment of estimated tax is the difference between the estimates that were paid and the least of (1) the current-year tax, (2) the prior-year tax, and (3) the tax on an annualized income computation using one of three methods of computation sanctioned by the Code. For the prior-year alternative, (1) the prior-tax year must have been a full 12 months, (2) a nonzero tax amount must have been generated for that year, and (3) large corporations (taxable income of $1 million or more in any of the three immediately preceding tax years) can use the alternative only for the first installment of a year.

In computing the penalty, Form 2210 (Underpayment of Estimated Tax by Individuals) or Form 2220 (Underpayment of Estimated Tax by Corporations) is used.

False Information with Respect to Withholding. Withholding from wages is an important element of the Federal income tax system, which is based on a pay-as-you-go approach. One way employees might hope to avoid this withholding would be to falsify the information provided to the employer on Form W–4

(Employee Withholding Allowance Certificate). For example, by overstating the number of exemptions, income tax withholdings could be reduced or completely eliminated.

To encourage compliance, a civil penalty of $500 applies when a taxpayer claims withholding allowances based on false information. The criminal penalty for willfully failing to supply information or for willfully supplying false or fraudulent information in connection with wage withholding is an additional fine of up to $1,000 and/or up to one year of imprisonment.[43]

Failure to Make Deposits of Taxes and Overstatements of Deposits. When the business is not doing well or cash-flow problems develop, employers have a great temptation to "borrow" from Uncle Sam. One way this can be done is to fail to pay to the IRS the amounts that have been withheld from the wages of employees for FICA and income tax purposes. The IRS does not appreciate being denied the use of these funds and has a number of weapons at its disposal to discourage the practice.

- A penalty of up to 15 percent of any underdeposited amount not paid, unless the employer can show that the failure is due to reasonable cause and not to willful neglect.[44]
- Various criminal penalties.[45]
- A 100 percent penalty if the employer's actions are willful.[46] The penalty is based on the amount of the tax evaded, not collected, or not accounted for or paid over. Since the penalty is assessable against the "responsible person" of the business, more than one party may be vulnerable (e.g., the president *and* treasurer of a corporation). Although the IRS may assess the penalty against several persons, it cannot collect more than the 100 percent due.

In addition to these penalties, the actual tax due must be remitted. An employer remains liable for the amount that should have been paid, even if the withholdings have not been taken out of the wages of its employees.[47]

STATUTES OF LIMITATIONS

A **statute of limitations** defines the period of time during which one party may pursue against another party a cause of action or other suit allowed under the governing law. Failure to satisfy any requirement provides the other party with an absolute defense should the statute be invoked. Inequity would result if no limits were placed on such suits. Permitting an extended period of time to elapse between the initiation of a claim and its pursuit could place the defense at a serious disadvantage. Witnesses may have died or disappeared; records or other evidence may have been discarded or destroyed.

Assessment and the Statute of Limitations.   In general, any tax that is imposed must be assessed within three years of the filing of the return (or, if later, the due date of the return).[48] Some exceptions to this three-year limitation exist.

- If no return is filed or a fraudulent return is filed, assessments can be made at any time. There is, in effect, no statute of limitations in these cases.

---

[43] §§ 6682 and 7205.
[44] § 6656.
[45] See, for example, § 7202 (willful failure to collect or pay over a tax).

[46] § 6672.
[47] § 3403.
[48] §§ 6501(a) and (b)(1).

• If a taxpayer omits an amount of gross income in excess of 25 percent of the gross income stated on the return, the statute of limitations is increased to six years. The courts have interpreted this rule as including only items affecting income and not the omission of items affecting cost of sales.[49] In addition, gross income includes capital gains in the *gross* income amount (not reduced by capital losses).

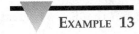

EXAMPLE 13

During 1992, José had the following income transactions (all of which were duly reported on his timely filed return).

Gross receipts	$ 480,000
Less: Cost of sales	(400,000)
Net business income	$ 80,000
Capital gains and losses	
Capital gain	$ 36,000
Capital loss	(12,000) 24,000
Total income	$ 104,000

José retains your services in 1997 as a tax consultant. It seems that he inadvertently omitted some income on his 1992 return and he wishes to know if he is "safe" under the statute of limitations. The six-year statute of limitations would apply, putting José in a vulnerable position, only if he omitted more than $129,000 on his 1992 return [($480,000 + $36,000) × 25%]. ▼

• The statute of limitations may be extended by mutual consent of the District Director and the taxpayer.[50] This extension covers a definite period and is made by signing Form 872 (Consent to Extend the Time to Assess Tax). The extension is frequently requested by the IRS when the lapse of the statutory period is imminent and the audit has not been completed. This practice is often applied to audits of corporate taxpayers and explains why many corporations have more than three "open years."

Special rules relating to assessment are applicable in the following situations.

• Taxpayers (corporations, estates, etc.) may request a prompt assessment of the tax.
• The period for assessment of the personal holding company tax is extended to six years after the return is filed only if certain filing requirements are met.
• If a partnership or trust files a tax return (a partnership or trust return) in good faith and a later determination renders the entity taxable as a corporation, the return is deemed to be the corporate return for purposes of the statute of limitations.
• The assessment period for capital loss, net operating loss, and general business credit carrybacks is generally related to the determination of tax in the year of the loss or unused credit rather than in the carryback years.

If the tax is assessed within the period of limitations, the IRS has 10 years from the date of assessment to collect the tax. However, if the IRS issues a statutory notice of deficiency to the taxpayer, who then files a Tax Court petition, the statute is suspended on both the deficiency assessment and the period of collection until 60 days after the decision of the Tax Court becomes final.

---

[49] *The Colony, Inc. v. Comm.,* 58–2 USTC ¶ 9593, 1 AFTR2d 1894, 78 S.Ct. 1033 (USSC, 1958).   [50] § 6501(c)(4).

Refund Claims and the Statute of Limitations.   To receive a tax refund, the taxpayer is required to file a valid refund claim. The official form for filing a claim is Form 1040X for individuals and Form 1120X for corporations. If the refund claim does not meet certain procedural requirements, the IRS may reject the claim with no consideration of its merit.

- A separate claim must be filed for each taxable period.
- The grounds for the claim must be stated in sufficient detail.
- The statement of facts must be sufficient to permit the IRS to evaluate the merits of the claim.

The refund claim must be filed within three years of the filing of the tax return or within two years following the payment of the tax if this period expires on a later date.[51]

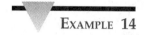

EXAMPLE 14

On March 10, 1994, Louise filed her 1993 income tax return reflecting a tax of $10,500. On July 10, 1995, she filed an amended 1993 return showing an additional $3,000 of tax that was then paid. On May 18, 1997, she filed a claim for refund of $4,500.

Assuming Louise is correct in claiming a refund, how much tax can she recover? The answer is only $3,000. Because the claim was not filed within the three-year period, Louise is limited to the amount she actually paid during the last two years. ▼

Special rules are available for claims relating to bad debts and worthless securities. A seven-year period of limitations applies in lieu of the normal three-year rule.[52] The extended period is provided in recognition of the inherent difficulty of identifying the exact year in which a bad debt or security becomes worthless.

TAX PRACTICE

THE TAX PRACTITIONER

8   LEARNING OBJECTIVE
Summarize the legal and ethical guidelines that apply to those engaged in tax practice.

Definition.   Who is a tax practitioner? What service does the practitioner perform? To begin defining the term *tax practitioner,* one should consider whether the individual is qualified to practice before the IRS. Generally, practice before the IRS is limited to CPAs, attorneys, and persons who have been enrolled to practice before the IRS (called **enrolled agents [EAs]**). In most cases, EAs are admitted to practice only if they pass an examination administered by the IRS. CPAs and attorneys are not required to take this examination and are automatically admitted to practice if they are in good standing with the appropriate licensing board regulating their profession.

Persons other than CPAs, attorneys, and EAs may be allowed to practice before the IRS in limited situations. Circular 230 (entitled ''Rules Governing the Practice of Attorneys and Agents Before the Internal Revenue Service'') issued by the Treasury Department permits certain notable exceptions.

- A taxpayer may always represent him- or herself. A person may also represent a member of the immediate family if no compensation is received for such services.
- Regular full-time employees may represent their employers.

---

[51] §§ 6511(a) and 6513(a).   [52] § 6511(d)(1).

- Corporations may be represented by any of their bona fide officers.
- Partnerships may be represented by any of the partners.
- Trusts, receiverships, guardianships, or estates may be represented by their trustees, receivers, guardians, or administrators or executors.
- A taxpayer may be represented by whoever prepared the return for the year in question. However, such representation cannot proceed beyond the agent level.

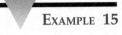

EXAMPLE 15

Chang is currently undergoing audit by the IRS for tax years 1996 and 1997. He prepared the 1996 return but paid AddCo, a bookkeeping service, to prepare the 1997 return. AddCo may represent Chang in matters concerning only 1997. However, even for 1997, AddCo would be unable to represent Chang at an Appeals Division proceeding. Chang could represent himself, or he could retain a CPA, attorney, or EA to represent him in matters concerning both years under examination. ▼

Rules Governing Tax Practice. Circular 230 further prescribes the rules governing practice before the IRS. The following are some of the most important rules imposed on CPAs, attorneys, and EAs.

- A prohibition against taking a position on a tax return unless there is a *realistic possibility* of the position being sustained on its merits. Generally, the realistic possibility standard is met when a person knowledgeable in the tax law would conclude that the position has at least a one-in-three probability of prevailing in court.
- A prohibition against taking frivolous tax return positions.
- A requirement that nonfrivolous tax return positions that fail the realistic possibility standard be disclosed in the return (i.e., using Form 8275).
- A requirement to inform clients of both penalties likely to apply to return positions and ways such penalties can be avoided.
- A requirement to make known to a client any error or omission the client may have made on any return or other document submitted to the IRS.
- A duty to submit records or information lawfully requested by the IRS.
- An obligation to exercise due diligence in preparing and filing tax returns accurately.
- A restriction against unreasonably delaying the prompt disposition of any matter before the IRS.
- A restriction against charging the client "an unconscionable fee" for representation before the IRS.
- A restriction against representing clients with conflicting interests.

Anyone can prepare a tax return or render tax advice, regardless of his or her educational background or level of competence. Likewise, nothing prevents the "unlicensed" tax practitioner from advertising his or her specialty, directly soliciting clients, or otherwise violating any of the standards of conduct controlling CPAs, attorneys, and EAs. Nevertheless, some restraints do govern all parties engaged in rendering tax advice or preparing tax returns for the general public.

- If the party holds him- or herself out to the general public as possessing tax expertise, he or she could be liable to the client if services are performed in a negligent manner. At a minimum, the practitioner is liable for any interest and penalties the client incurs because of the practitioner's failure to exercise due care.
- If one agrees to perform a service (e.g., prepare a tax return) and subsequently fails to do so, the aggrieved party may be in a position to obtain damages for breach of contract.

- The IRS requires any person who prepares tax returns for a fee to sign as preparer of the return.[53] Failure to comply with this requirement could result in penalty assessment against the preparer.
- The Code prescribes various penalties for the deliberate filing of false or fraudulent returns. These penalties apply to a tax practitioner who either was aware of the situation or actually perpetrated the false filing or the fraud.[54]
- Penalties are prescribed for tax practitioners who disclose to third parties information they have received from clients in connection with the preparation of tax returns or the rendering of tax advice.[55]

EXAMPLE 16

Sarah operates a tax return preparation service. Her brother-in-law, Butch, has just taken a job as a life insurance salesman. To help Butch find contacts, Sarah furnishes him with a list of the names and addresses of all of her clients who report AGI of $10,000 or more. Sarah is subject to penalties. ▼

- All nonattorney tax practitioners should avoid becoming engaged in activities that constitute the unauthorized practice of law. If they engage in this practice, action could be instituted against them in the appropriate state court by the local or state bar association. What actions constitute the unauthorized practice of law is largely undefined, though, and such charges are filed only rarely today.

Preparer Penalties.   The Code also provides for penalties to discourage improper actions by tax practitioners.

1. A $250 penalty for understatements due to taking unrealistic positions.[56] Unless adequate tax return disclosure of the position is made, the penalty is imposed if two conditions are satisfied.

   - Any part of any understatement of tax liability on any return or claim for refund is due to a position that did not have a realistic possibility of being sustained on its merits.
   - Any person who was an income tax return preparer for that return or claim knew (or should have known) of this position.

   The penalty can be avoided by showing reasonable cause and by showing that the preparer acted in good faith.

2. A $1,000 penalty for willful and reckless conduct.[57] The penalty applies if any part of the understatement of a taxpayer's liability on a return or claim for refund is due to:

   - The preparer's willful attempt to understate the taxpayer's tax liability in any manner.
   - Any reckless or intentional disregard of IRS rules or Regulations by the preparer.

   Adequate disclosure can avoid the penalty. If both this penalty and the unrealistic position penalty (see item 1 above) apply to the same return, the total penalty cannot exceed $1,000.

---

[53] Reg. § 1.6065–1(b)(1). Rev.Rul. 84–3, 1984–1 C.B. 264, contains a series of examples illustrating when a person is deemed to be a preparer of the return.
[54] § 7206.

[55] § 7216.
[56] § 6694(a).
[57] § 6694(b).

3. A $1,000 ($10,000 for corporations) penalty per return or document is imposed against persons who aid in the preparation of returns or other documents that they know (or have reason to believe) would result in an understatement of the tax liability of another person.[58] Clerical assistance in the preparation process does not incur the penalty.

   If this penalty applies, neither the unrealistic position penalty (item 1) nor the willful and reckless conduct penalty (item 2) is assessed.

4. A $50 penalty is assessed against the preparer for failure to sign a return or furnish the preparer's identifying number.[59]

5. A $50 penalty is assessed if the preparer fails to furnish a copy of the return or claim for refund to the taxpayer.

6. A $500 penalty may be assessed if a preparer endorses or otherwise negotiates a check for refund of tax issued to the taxpayer.

ETHICAL CONSIDERATIONS—"STATEMENTS ON RESPONSIBILITIES IN TAX PRACTICE"

Tax practitioners who are CPAs, attorneys, or EAs must abide by the codes or canons of professional ethics applicable to their respective professions. The various codes and canons have much in common with and parallel the standards of conduct set forth in Circular 230.[60]

In the belief that CPAs engaged in tax practice require further guidance in the resolution of ethical problems, the Tax Committee of the AICPA began issuing periodic statements on selected topics. The first of these Statements on Responsibilities in Tax Practice was released in 1964. All of the Statements were revised in August of 1988. The most important Statements that have been issued to date are discussed below.[61]

The Statements merely represent guides to action and are not part of the AICPA's Code of Professional Ethics. But because the Statements are representative of standards followed by members of the profession, a violation might indicate a deviation from the standard of due care exercised by most CPAs. The standard of due care is usually at the heart of any suit charging negligence that is brought against a CPA.

Statement No. 1: Positions Contrary to IRS Interpretations.   Under certain circumstances, a CPA may take a position that is contrary to that taken by the IRS. In order to do so, however, the CPA must have a good faith belief that the position, if challenged, has a realistic possibility of being sustained administratively or judicially on its merits.

The client should be fully advised of the risks involved and should know that certain penalties may result if the position taken by the CPA is not successful. The client should also be informed that disclosure on the return may avoid some or all of these penalties.

In no case, though, should the CPA exploit the audit lottery; that is, to take a questionable position based on the probabilities that the client's return will not be chosen by the IRS for audit. Furthermore, the CPA should not "load" the return with questionable items in the hope that they might aid the client in a later settlement negotiation with the IRS.

---

[58] § 6701.
[59] § 6695.
[60] For an additional discussion of tax ethics, see Raabe, Whittenburg, and Bost, *West's Federal Tax Research*, 3d ed. (St. Paul: West Publishing Co., 1994), Chapters 1 and 12.

[61] Other, less frequently encountered Statements are omitted from this discussion.

Statement No. 2: Questions on Returns.   A CPA should make a reasonable effort to obtain from the client, and provide to the IRS, appropriate answers to all questions on a tax return before signing as preparer. Reasonable grounds may exist for omitting an answer.

- The information is not readily available, and the answer is not significant in computing the tax.
- The meaning of the question as it applies to a particular situation is genuinely uncertain.
- The answer to the question is voluminous.

The fact that an answer to a question could prove disadvantageous to the client does not justify omitting the answer.

Statement No. 3: Procedural Aspects of Preparing Returns.   In preparing a return, a CPA may in good faith rely without verification on information furnished by the client or by third parties. However, the CPA should make reasonable inquiries if the information appears to be incorrect, incomplete, or inconsistent. In this regard, the CPA should refer to the client's prior returns whenever appropriate.

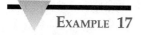

EXAMPLE 17

A CPA normally can take a client's word for the validity of dependency exemptions. But suppose a recently divorced client wants to claim his three children as dependents (when he does not have custody). A CPA must act in accordance with § 152(e)(2) in preparing the return. Claiming the dependency exemption will require evidence of a waiver by the custodial parent. Without this waiver, the CPA should not claim the dependency exemptions on the client's tax return. ▼

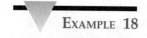

EXAMPLE 18

While preparing a client's income tax return for 1997, a CPA reviews her income tax return for 1996. In comparing the dividend income reported on the 1996 Schedule B with that received in 1997, the CPA notes a significant decrease. Further investigation reveals the variation is due to a stock sale in 1997 that, until now, was unknown to the CPA. Thus, the review of the 1996 return has unearthed a transaction that should be reported on the 1997 return. ▼

If the Code or Regulations require certain types of verification (as is the case with travel and entertainment expenditures), the CPA must advise the client of these rules. Further, inquiry must be made to ascertain whether the client has complied with the verification requirements.

Statement No. 4: Estimates.   A CPA may prepare a tax return using estimates received from a taxpayer if it is impracticable to obtain exact data. The estimates must be reasonable under the facts and circumstances known to the CPA. When estimates are used, they should be presented in such a manner as to avoid implying that greater accuracy exists.

Statement No. 5: Recognition of Administrative Proceeding.   As facts may vary from year to year, so may the position taken by a CPA. In these types of situations, the CPA is not bound by an administrative or judicial proceeding involving a prior year.

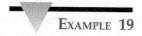

EXAMPLE 19

Upon audit of Ramon Corporation's income tax return for 1996, the IRS disallowed $180,000 of the $400,000 salary paid to its president and sole shareholder on the grounds that it was unreasonable [§ 162(a)(1)]. A CPA has been engaged to prepare Ramon's income tax return for 1997. Again the corporation paid its president a salary of $400,000 and chose to deduct this amount. Because the CPA is not bound in 1997 by what the IRS deemed reasonable for 1996, the full $400,000 can be claimed as a salary deduction. ▼

Other problems that require a CPA's use of judgment include reclassification of corporate debt as equity (thin capitalization) and corporate accumulations beyond the reasonable needs of the business (for the penalty tax under § 531).

Statement No. 6: Knowledge of Error.   A CPA should promptly advise a client upon learning of an error on a previously filed return or upon learning of a client's failure to file a required return. The advice can be oral or written and should include a recommendation of the corrective measures, if any, to be taken. The error or other omission should not be disclosed to the IRS without the client's consent.

If the past error is material and is not corrected by the client, the CPA may be unable to prepare the current year's tax return. This situation might occur if the error has a carryover effect that prevents the CPA from determining the correct tax liability for the current year.

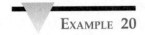

EXAMPLE 20

In preparing a client's 1997 income tax return, a CPA discovers that final inventory for 1996 was materially understated. First, the CPA should advise the client to file an amended return for 1996 reflecting the correct amount in final inventory. Second, if the client refuses to make this adjustment, the CPA should consider whether the error will preclude preparation of a substantially correct return for 1997. Because this will probably be the case (the final inventory for 1996 becomes the beginning inventory for 1997), the CPA should withdraw from the engagement.

If the client corrects the error, the CPA may proceed with the preparation of the tax return for 1997. However, the CPA must ensure that the error is not repeated. ▼

Statement No. 8: Advice to Clients.   In providing tax advice to a client, the CPA must use judgment to ensure that the advice reflects professional competence and appropriately serves the client's needs. No standard format or guidelines can be established to cover all situations and circumstances involving written or oral advice by the CPA.

The CPA may communicate with the client when subsequent developments affect previous advice on significant matters. However, the CPA cannot be expected to assume responsibility for initiating the communication, unless he or she is assisting a client in implementing procedures or plans associated with the advice. The CPA may undertake this obligation by specific agreement with the client.

TAX PLANNING
CONSIDERATIONS

STRATEGIES IN SEEKING AN ADMINISTRATIVE RULING

Determination Letters.   In many instances, the request for an advance ruling or a determination letter from the IRS is a necessary or desirable planning strategy. The receipt of a favorable ruling or determination reduces the risk associated with a transaction when the tax results are in doubt. For example, the initiation or amendment of a qualified pension or profit sharing plan should be accompanied by a determination letter from the District Director. Otherwise, on subsequent IRS review, the plan may not qualify, and the tax deductibility of contributions to the plan will be disallowed. In some instances, the potential tax effects of a transaction are so numerous and of such consequence that proceeding without a ruling is unwise.

CONCEPT SUMMARY 25–1

Tax Administration and Practice

1. The Internal Revenue Service (IRS) enforces the tax laws of the United States.
2. The IRS issues various pronouncements, communicating its position on certain tax issues. These pronouncements promote uniform enforcement of the tax law among taxpayers and among the internal divisions of the IRS. Taxpayers should seek such rulings and memoranda when the nature or magnitude of a pending transaction requires a high degree of certainty in the planning process.
3. IRS audits can take several forms. Taxpayers are selected for audit based on the probable dollar return to the Treasury from the process. Offers in compromise and closing agreements can be a useful means of completing an audit without resorting to litigation.
4. Certain IRS personnel are empowered to consider the hazards of litigation in developing a settlement with the taxpayer during the audit process.
5. The IRS pays interest to taxpayers on overpaid taxes, starting essentially 45 days after the due date of the return, at two percentage points over the Federal short-term rate. Interest paid to the IRS on underpayments is computed at three points over this Federal rate, starting essentially on the due date of the return. Interest for both purposes is compounded daily.
6. The Treasury assesses penalties when the taxpayer fails to file a required tax return or pay a tax. Penalties also are assessed when an inaccurate return is filed due to negligence or other disregard of IRS rules. Tax preparers are subject to penalties for assisting a taxpayer in filing an inaccurate return, failing to follow IRS rules in an appropriate manner, or mishandling taxpayer data or funds.
7. Statutes of limitations place outer boundaries on the timing and amounts of proposed amendments to completed tax returns that can be made by the taxpayer or the IRS.
8. Tax practitioners must operate under constraints imposed on them by codes of ethics of pertinent professional societies and by Treasury Circular 230. These rules also define the parties who can represent others in an IRS proceeding.

Letter Rulings.   In some cases, it may not be necessary or desirable to request an advance ruling. For example, it is generally not desirable to request a ruling if the tax results are doubtful and the company is committed to complete the transaction in any event. If a ruling is requested and negotiations with the IRS indicate that an adverse determination will be forthcoming, it is usually possible to have the ruling request withdrawn. However, the National Office of the IRS may forward its findings, along with a copy of the ruling request, to the District Director. In determining the advisability of a ruling request, the taxpayer should consider the potential exposure of other items in the tax returns of all "open years."

A ruling request may delay the consummation of a transaction if the issues are novel or complex. Frequently, a ruling can be processed within six months, although in some instances a delay of a year or more may be encountered.

Technical Advice Memoranda.   A taxpayer in the process of contesting a proposed deficiency with the Appeals Division should consider requesting a technical advice memorandum from the National Office of the IRS. If such advice is favorable to the taxpayer, it is binding on the Appeals Division. The request may be particularly appropriate when the practitioner feels that the agent or Appeals Division has been too literal in interpreting an IRS ruling.

CONSIDERATIONS IN HANDLING AN IRS AUDIT

As a general rule, a taxpayer should attempt to settle disputes at the earliest possible stage of the administrative appeal process. New issues may be raised by IRS personnel if the case goes beyond the agent level. It is usually possible to limit the scope of the examination by furnishing pertinent information requested by the agent. Extraneous information or thoughtless comments may result in the opening of new issues and should be avoided. Agents usually appreciate prompt and efficient responses to inquiries, since their performance may in part be judged by their ability to close or settle assigned cases.

To the extent possible, it is advisable to conduct the investigation of field audits in the practitioner's office, rather than the client's office. This procedure permits greater control over the audit investigation and facilitates the agent's review and prompt closure of the case.

Many practitioners feel that it is generally not advisable to have clients present at the scheduled conferences with the agent, since the client may give emotional or gratuitous comments that impair prompt settlement. If the client is not present, however, he or she should be advised of the status of negotiations. The client makes the final decision on any proposed settlement.

ETHICAL CONSIDERATIONS

Should the Client Attend an Audit?

Whether the client should be present during an audit is a matter of some debate. Certainly, the client's absence tends to slow down the negotiating process because the taxpayer must make all final decisions on settlement terms and is the best source of information for open questions of fact. Nevertheless, most practitioners discourage their clients from attending audits or conferences with the Appeals Division involving an income tax dispute. Ignorance of the law and of the conventions of the audit process can make the taxpayer a "loose cannon" that can do more harm than good if unchecked. All too often, they say, a client will "say too much" in the presence of a government official.

In reality, though, by discouraging clients from attending the audit, practitioners may be interfering with the IRS's function of gathering evidence, depending on what precisely the taxpayer is being prevented from saying. To many practitioners, a "wrong" answer is one that increases taxes, not one that misrepresents the truth. A popular saying among tax advisers is "Don't tell me more than I want to know." Although this philosophy is supportable under various professional codes of conduct, it is hardly defensible in the larger scheme of things.

In your opinion, under what circumstances should the client attend such a session? To what degree should the tax professional "coach" the client as to how to behave in that setting? Or do a taxpayer's rights include the right to increase his or her own tax liability?

Preparing for the Audit.   The tax professional must prepare thoroughly for the audit or Appeals proceeding. Practitioners often cite the following steps as critical to such preparations. Carrying out a level of due diligence in preparing for the proceeding is part of the tax professional's responsibility in representing the client.

- Make certain that both sides agree on the issues to be resolved in the audit. The goal here is to limit the agent's list of open issues.

- Identify all of the facts underlying the issues in dispute, including those favorable to the IRS. Gather evidence to support the taxpayer's position, and evaluate the evidence supporting the other side.
- Research current tax law authorities that bear on the facts and open issues. Remember that the IRS agent is bound only by Supreme Court cases and IRS pronouncements. Determine the degree of discretion that the IRS is likely to have in disposing of the case.
- Prepare a list of points supporting and contradicting the taxpayer's case. Include both minor points bearing little weight and core principles. Short research memos will also be useful in the discussion with the agent. Points favoring the taxpayer should be mentioned during the discussion and "entered into the record."
- Prepare tax and interest computations showing the effects of points that are in dispute, so that the consequences of closing or compromising an issue can be readily determined.
- Determine a "litigation point" (i.e., at which the taxpayer will withdraw from further audit negotiation and pursue the case in the courts). This position should be based on the dollars of tax, interest, and penalty involved, the chances of prevailing in various trial-level courts, and other strategies discussed with the taxpayer. One must have an "end game" strategy for the audit, and thorough tax research is critical in developing that position in this context.

Offers in Compromise.   The IRS is encouraging the use of offers in compromise to a greater degree than ever before as part of its "consumer-friendly" approach to its enforcement obligations and its efforts to bring more nonfilers into compliance with the tax system.

Both parties to a tax dispute may find a compromise offer useful because it conclusively settles all of the issues covered by the agreement and may include a favorable payment schedule for the taxpayer. On the other hand, several attributes of an offer in compromise may work to the detriment of the taxpayer. Just as the IRS no longer can raise new issues as part of the audit proceedings against the taxpayer, he or she cannot contest or appeal any such agreement. As part of the offer process, the taxpayer must disclose all relevant finances and resources, including details he or she might not want the government to know. Furthermore, both parties are bound to the filing positions established by the compromise for five tax years, a level of inflexibility that may work against a taxpayer whose circumstances change over time.

Documentation Issues.   The tax practitioner's workpapers should include all research memoranda, and a list of resolved and unresolved issues should be continually updated during the course of the IRS audit. Occasionally, agents request access to excessive amounts of accounting data in order to engage in a so-called fishing expedition. Providing blanket access to workpapers should be avoided. Workpapers should be carefully reviewed to minimize opportunities for the agent to raise new issues not otherwise apparent. It is generally advisable to provide the agent with copies of specific workpapers upon request. An accountant's workpapers generally are not privileged and may be subpoenaed by the IRS.

In unusual situations, a Special Agent may appear to gather evidence in the investigation of possible criminal fraud. When this occurs, the taxpayer should be advised to seek legal counsel to determine the extent of his or her cooperation in providing information to the agent. Further, it is frequently desirable for the tax adviser to consult personal legal counsel in such situations. If the taxpayer receives a Revenue Agent's Report (RAR), it generally indicates that the IRS has decided not to initiate criminal prosecution proceedings. The IRS usually does not take any action upon a tax deficiency until the criminal matter has been resolved.

PENALTIES

Penalties are imposed upon a taxpayer's failure to file a return or pay a tax when due. These penalties can be avoided if the failure is due to reasonable cause and not to willful neglect. Reasonable cause, however, has not been liberally interpreted by the courts and should not be relied upon in the routine situation.[62] A safer way to avoid the failure to file penalty is to obtain an extension of time for filing the return from the IRS.

The penalty for failure to pay estimated taxes can become quite severe. Often trapped by the provision are employed taxpayers with outside income. They may forget about their outside income and assume the amount withheld from wages and salaries is adequate to cover their liability. Not only does April 15 provide a real shock (in terms of the additional tax owed) for these persons, but a penalty situation may have evolved. One way for an employee to mitigate this problem (presuming the employer is willing to cooperate) is described in the following example.

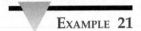

EXAMPLE 21

Patty, a calendar year taxpayer, is employed by Finn Corporation and earns (after withholding) a monthly salary of $4,000 payable at the end of each month. Patty also receives income from outside sources (interest, dividends, and consulting fees). After some quick calculations in early October, Patty determines that she has underestimated her tax liability by $7,500 and will be subject to the penalty for the first two quarters of the year and part of the third quarter. Patty, therefore, completes a new Form W–4 in which she arbitrarily raises her income tax withholding by $2,500 a month. Finn accepts the Form W–4, and as a result, an extra $7,500 is paid to the IRS on Patty's account for the payroll period from October through December.

Patty avoids penalties for the underpayment for the first three quarters because withholding of taxes is allocated pro rata over the year involved. Thus, a portion of the additional $7,500 withheld in October–December is assigned to the January 1–April 15 period, the April 16–June 15 period, etc. Had Patty merely paid the IRS an additional $7,500 in October, the penalty would still have been assessed for the earlier quarters. ▼

KEY TERMS

Accuracy-related penalty, 25–15

Closing agreement, 25–11

Determination letter, 25–5

Enrolled agent (EA), 25–22

Fraud, 25–18

Letter ruling, 25–4

Negligence, 25–15

Ninety-day letter, 25–10

Offer in compromise, 25–11

Reasonable cause, 25–15

Revenue Agent's Report (RAR), 25–9

Statute of limitations, 25–20

Substantial authority, 25–16

Technical advice memorandum, 25–5

Thirty-day letter, 25–10

---

[62] *Dustin v. Comm.*, 72–2 USTC ¶9610, 30 AFTR2d 72–5313, 467 F.2d 47 (CA–9, 1972), *aff'g.* 53 T.C. 491 (1969).

PROBLEM MATERIALS

DISCUSSION QUESTIONS

1. What is the role of the IRS in the revenue process?

2. What techniques other than the random selection of returns for audit does the IRS use in its enforcement function?

3. Should the IRS audit more or fewer returns every year?

4. Your tax supervisor has informed you that the firm has received an unfavorable answer to a ruling request. In a memo to the supervisor, describe the appropriate weight that she should assign to the holding in the ruling.

5. Who bears the burden of proof when the IRS challenges items reported on a tax return?

6. Describe the powers of the IRS to seize taxpayer assets when a tax is due.

7. Sarah tells you, "I was worried about getting audited on the tax return I filed two months ago, but I received my refund check today, so the IRS must agree with my figures." Comment.

8. When should a taxpayer take a matter to the Tax Court's Small Cases Division?

9. When can the taxpayer use an "installment plan" to pay his or her delinquent taxes and associated interest and penalties?

10. On February 9, 1997, Quon, a calendar year taxpayer, files her 1996 income tax return on which she claims a $1,200 refund. If Quon receives her refund check on May 2, 1997, will it include any interest? Explain.

11. Indicate whether each of the following statements is true or false.
    a. The government never pays a taxpayer interest on an overpayment of tax.
    b. Penalties may be included as an itemized deduction on an individual's tax return, but net of the 2%-of-AGI floor.
    c. An extension of time for filing a return results in an automatic extension of the time in which the tax may be paid.
    d. The IRS can compromise on the amount of tax liability if there is doubt as to the taxpayer's ability to pay.
    e. The statute of limitations for assessing a tax never extends beyond three years from the filing of a return.
    f. A taxpayer's claim for a refund is not subject to a statute of limitations.

12. What is the role of the statute of limitations in the Federal income tax system?

13. In each of the following cases, distinguish between the terms.
    a. Offer in compromise and closing agreement.
    b. Failure to file and failure to pay.
    c. Ninety-day letter and thirty-day letter.
    d. Negligence and fraud.
    e. Criminal and civil penalties.

14. Lorraine, a vice president of Scott Corporation, prepared and filed the corporate Form 1120 for 1994. This return is being audited by the IRS in 1996.
    a. May Lorraine represent Scott during the audit?
    b. Can Lorraine's representation continue beyond the agent level (e.g., before the Appeals Division)?

15. Indicate which codes, canons, and other bodies of ethical statements apply to each of the following tax practitioners.
    a. CPAs who are members of the AICPA.
    b. CPAs who are not members of the AICPA.
    c. Attorneys.
    d. Enrolled agents.
    e. Tax preparers who are not CPAs, EAs, or attorneys.

PROBLEMS

16. Compute the failure to pay and failure to file penalties for John, who filed his 1995 income tax return on October 20, 1996, paying the $1,000 amount due. On April 1, 1996, John had received a four-month extension of time in which to file his return. He has no reasonable cause for failing to file his return by August 15 or for failing to pay the tax that was due on April 15, 1996. John's failure to comply with the tax laws was not fraudulent.

17. Rhoda, a calendar year individual taxpayer, files her 1994 return on January 11, 1996. She did not obtain an extension for filing her return, and the return reflects additional income tax due of $3,800.
    a. What are Rhoda's penalties for failure to file and to pay?
    b. Would your answer change if Rhoda, before the due date of the return, had retained a CPA to prepare the return and the CPA's negligence caused the delay?

18. Kim underpaid her taxes by $15,000. Of this amount, $7,500 was due to negligence on her part, as her record-keeping system is highly inadequate. Determine the amount of any negligence penalty.

19. Dana underpaid his taxes by $250,000. A portion of the underpayment was attributable to negligence ($50,000) *and* another portion to civil fraud ($150,000). Compute the total penalties incurred.

20. Olivia, a calendar year taxpayer, does not file her 1995 return until June 4, 1996. At this point, she pays the $3,000 balance due on her 1995 tax liability of $30,000. Olivia did not apply for and obtain any extension of time for filing the 1995 return. When questioned by the IRS on her delinquency, Olivia asserts: "If I was too busy to file my regular tax return, I was too busy to request an extension."
    a. Is Olivia liable for any penalties for failure to file and for failure to pay?
    b. If so, compute the penalty amounts.

21. Compute the overvaluation penalty for each of the following independent cases involving the taxpayer's reporting of the fair market value of charitable contribution property. In each case, assume a marginal income tax rate of 30%.

	Taxpayer	Corrected IRS Value	Reported Valuation
a.	Individual	$ 10,000	$ 20,000
b.	C corporation	10,000	30,000
c.	S corporation	10,000	30,000
d.	Individual	100,000	150,000
e.	Individual	100,000	300,000
f.	C corporation	100,000	500,000

22. Compute the undervaluation penalty for each of the following independent cases involving the executor's reporting of the value of a closely held business in the decedent's gross estate. In each case, assume a marginal estate tax rate of 50%.

	Reported Value	Corrected IRS Valuation
a.	$ 12,000	$ 15,000
b.	50,000	90,000
c.	50,000	150,000
d.	50,000	200,000

23. Arnold made a charitable contribution of property that he valued at $20,000. He deducted this amount as an itemized deduction on his tax return. The IRS can prove that the real value of the property is $8,000. Arnold is in the 31% income tax bracket. Determine Arnold's overvaluation penalty.

24. Marla owns and operates a tavern. Because she had been keeping "two sets of books," one for herself and one for the benefit of the IRS, she has been charged with civil fraud in the District Court. The IRS assesses an additional $75,000 in taxes, but Marla shows by a preponderance of the evidence that half of that amount was due to her negligence, not to her fraudulent actions. Compute Marla's civil fraud tax penalty in this matter.

25. Moose, a former professional athlete, now supplements his income by signing autographs at collectors' shows. Unfortunately, Moose has not been conscientious about reporting all of this income on his tax return. Now, the IRS has charged him with additional taxes of $50,000 due to negligence in his record-keeping and $80,000 due to an intent to defraud the U.S. of income taxes. No criminal fraud charges are brought against Moose. The District Court finds a preponderance of the evidence that only half of the $80,000 underpayment was due to Moose's fraudulent action; the remainder was due to his negligence. Compute the accuracy-related and civil fraud penalties in this matter.

26. Trudy's AGI last year was $50,000. Her Federal income tax came to $16,000, which she paid through a combination of withholding and estimated payments. This year, her AGI will be $170,000, with a projected tax liability of $46,000, all to be paid through estimates. Ignore the annualized income method. Compute Trudy's quarterly estimated payment schedule for this year.

27. Kold Corporation estimates that its 1996 taxable income will be $900,000. Thus, it is subject to a flat 34% income tax rate and incurs a $306,000 liability. For each of the following independent cases, compute Kold's minimum quarterly estimated tax payments that will avoid an underpayment penalty.
    a. For 1995, taxable income was ($100,000). Kold carried back all of this loss to prior years and exhausted the entire net operating loss in creating a zero 1995 liability.
    b. For 1995, taxable income was $200,000, and tax liability was $68,000.
    c. For 1994, taxable income was $2 million, and tax liability was $680,000. For 1995, taxable income was $200,000, and tax liability was $68,000.

28. The Scooter Company, owned equally by Julie (chair of the board of directors) and Jeff (company president), is in very difficult financial straits. Last month, Jeff used the $100,000 withheld from employee paychecks for Federal payroll and income taxes to pay off a creditor who threatened to cut off all supplies. To keep the company afloat, Jeff used these government funds willfully for the operations of the business, but even that effort was not enough. The company missed the next two payrolls, and today other creditors took action to shut down Scooter altogether. How much will the IRS assess in taxes and penalties in this matter, and from whom? How can you as a tax professional best offer service to Julie, Jeff, and Scooter? Address these matters in a memo for the tax research file.

29. What is the applicable statute of limitations in each of the following independent situations?
    a. No return was filed by the taxpayer.
    b. In 1992, the taxpayer incurred a bad debt loss that she failed to claim.
    c. On his 1992 return, a taxpayer inadvertently omitted a large amount of gross income.
    d. Same as (c), except that the omission was deliberate.
    e. For 1992, a taxpayer innocently overstated her deductions by a large amount.

30. Suzanne (a calendar year taxpayer) had the following transactions, all of which were properly reported on a timely return.

Gross receipts		$ 960,000
Cost of sales		(800,000)
Gross profit		$ 160,000
Capital gain	$ 72,000	
Capital loss	(24,000)	48,000
Total income		$ 208,000

a. Presuming the absence of fraud, how much of an omission from gross income is required before the six-year statute of limitations applies?

b. Would it matter if cost of sales had been inadvertently overstated by $100,000?

c. How does the situation change in the context of fraud by Suzanne?

31. On April 2, 1994, Mark filed his 1993 income tax return, which showed a tax due of $40,000. On June 1, 1996, he filed an amended return for 1993 that showed an additional tax of $12,000. Mark paid the additional amount. On May 18, 1997, Mark filed a claim for a refund of $18,000.

a. If Mark's claim for a refund is correct in amount, how much tax will he recover?

b. What is the period that interest runs with respect to Mark's claim for a refund?

c. How would you have advised him differently?

32. Mimi had $40,000 withheld in 1993. Due to a sizable amount of itemized deductions, she figured that she had no further tax to pay for the year. For this reason, and because of personal problems, and without securing an extension, she did not file her 1993 return until July 1, 1994. Actually, the return showed a refund of $2,400, which Mimi ultimately received. On May 10, 1997, Mimi filed a $16,000 claim for refund of her 1993 taxes.

a. How much, if any, of the $16,000 may Mimi recover?

b. Would it have made any difference if Mimi had requested and secured from the IRS an extension of time for filing her 1993 tax return?

33. Rod's Federal income tax returns (Form 1040) for the past three years were prepared by the following persons.

Year	Preparer
1993	Rod
1994	Ann
1995	Cheryl

Ann is Rod's next-door neighbor and owns and operates a pharmacy. Cheryl is a licensed CPA and is engaged in private practice. In the event Rod is audited and all three returns are examined, who may represent him before the IRS at the agent level? Who may represent Rod before the Appeals Division?

34. Discuss which penalties, if any, might be imposed on the tax adviser in each of the following independent circumstances. In this regard, assume that the tax adviser:

a. Suggested to the client various means by which to acquire excludible income.

b. Suggested to the client various means by which to conceal cash receipts from gross income.

c. Suggested to the client means by which to improve her cash flow by delaying for six months or more the deposit of the employees' share of Federal employment taxes.

d. Kept in his own safe deposit box the cash of item (c).

e. Failed, because of pressing time conflicts, to conduct the usual review of the client's tax return. The IRS later discovered that the return included fraudulent data.

f. Failed, because of pressing time conflicts, to conduct the usual review of the client's tax return. The IRS later discovered a mathematical error in the computation of the personal exemption.

35. Compute the preparer penalty that the IRS could assess on Gerry in each of the following independent cases.

a. On March 21, the copy machine was not working, so Gerry gave original returns to her 30 clients that day without any duplicates for them. Copies for Gerry's files and for use in preparing state tax returns had been made on March 20.

b. Because Gerry extended her vacation a few days, she missed the Annual Tax Update seminar that she usually attends. As a result, she was unaware that Congress had changed a law affecting limited partnerships. The change affected the transactions of 20 of Gerry's clients, all of whom understated their tax as a result.

c. Gerry heard that the IRS was increasing its audits of corporations that hold assets in a foreign trust. As a result, Gerry instructed the intern who prepared the initial drafts of the returns for three corporate clients to leave blank the question about such trusts. Not wanting to lose his position, the intern, a senior accounting major at State University, complied with Gerry's instructions.

36. You are the chair of the Ethics Committee of your state's CPA Licensing Commission. Interpret controlling AICPA authority in addressing the following assertions by your membership.

a. When a CPA has reasonable grounds for not answering an applicable question on a client's return, a brief explanation of the reason for the omission should not be provided, because it would flag the return for audit by the IRS.

b. If a CPA discovers during an IRS audit that the client has a material error on the return under examination, he should immediately withdraw from the engagement.

c. If the client tells you that she had contributions of $500 for unsubstantiated cash donations to her church, you should deduct an odd amount on her return (e.g., $499), because an even amount (i.e., $500) would indicate to the IRS that her deduction was based on an estimate.

d. Basing an expense deduction on the client's estimates is not acceptable.

e. If a CPA knows that the client has a material error on a prior year's return, he should not, without the client's consent, disclose the error to the IRS.

f. If a CPA's client will not correct a material error on a prior year's return, the CPA should not prepare the current year's return for the client.

Research Problems for this chapter appear at the end of Chapter 28.

TEAM PROJECT: ARTHUR ANDERSEN TAX CHALLENGE CASES

For more information on the Arthur Andersen Tax Challenge Cases, please refer to Chapter 2, page 2-41.

Information related to tax issues and problems that are discussed in this chapter may be found in the

Fields case on pages 2, 3, 12
Miller case on page 4

Read and analyze the case you have been assigned and *identify* any issues and problems that are related to material covered in this chapter. If the information provided in the case is complete, prepare answers for this part of the case at this time. If you need information that is contained in the later parts of the case, please write a memo summarizing the questions or problems so you can prepare a complete answer at a later date.

26

THE FEDERAL GIFT AND ESTATE TAXES

LEARNING OBJECTIVES

After completing Chapter 26, you should be able to:

1. Understand the nature of the Federal gift and estate taxes.

2. Work with the Federal gift tax formula.

3. Work with the Federal estate tax formula.

4. Explain the operation of the Federal gift tax.

5. Explain the computation of the Federal gift tax.

6. Describe the components of the gross estate.

7. Describe the components of the taxable estate.

8. Determine the Federal estate tax liability.

9. Appreciate the role of the generation-skipping transfer tax.

TRANSFER TAXES—IN GENERAL

Until now, this text has dealt primarily with the various applications of the Federal income tax. Also important in the Federal tax structure are various excise taxes that cover transfers of property. Sometimes called transaction taxes, excise taxes are based on the value of the property transferred and not on the income derived from the property. Two such taxes—the Federal gift tax and the Federal estate tax—are the central focus of this chapter.

The importance of being familiar with rules governing transfer taxes can be shown with a simple illustration.

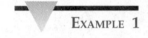

EXAMPLE 1

After 20 years of marriage to George, Helen decides to elope with Mark, a bachelor and long-time friend. Helen and Mark travel to a country in the Caribbean where Helen obtains a divorce, and she and Mark are married. Fifteen years later, Helen dies. Her will leaves all of her property (estimated value of $2,600,000) to Mark. Under the unlimited marital deduction (discussed later in the chapter), Helen's estate has no tax to pay. ▼

But the marital deduction applies only to transfers between husband and wife. Suppose the jurisdiction where Helen and Mark live does not recognize the validity of divorces granted by the Caribbean country involved? If this is the case, Helen and Mark are not married because Helen was never legally divorced from George. If Mark is not Helen's spouse, no marital deduction is available. Helen's estate must pay an estate tax of $780,800.

NATURE OF THE TAXES

1 LEARNING OBJECTIVE
Understand the nature of the Federal gift and estate taxes.

Before the enactment of the Tax Reform Act of 1976, Federal law imposed a tax on the gratuitous transfer of property in one of two ways. If the transfer was during the owner's life, it was subject to the Federal gift tax. If the property passed by virtue of the death of the owner, the Federal estate tax applied. Both taxes were governed by different rules including a separate set of tax rates. As Congress felt that lifetime transfers of wealth should be encouraged, the gift tax rates were lower than the estate tax rates.

The Tax Reform Act of 1976 significantly changed the approach taken by the Federal gift and estate taxes. Much of the distinction between life and death transfers was eliminated. Instead of subjecting these different types of transfers to

Do Transfer Taxes Adversely Affect the Economy?

A recent study found that transfer taxes (i.e., estate and gift taxes) impose especially high economic costs in terms of lost savings and capital formation. This burden is particularly high on small family-owned businesses.

As another layer of tax on savings, transfer taxes increase the cost of wealth accumulation as compared to the cost of consumption. According to an econometric simulation of what would have happened to the U.S. economy between 1971 and 1991 without Federal transfer taxes, 262,000 more jobs would have been created, the stock of capital would have been $398.6 billion higher, and the gross domestic product would have been $46.3 billion higher in 1991.

The study concludes that repeal of the Federal estate and gift taxes would strengthen the incentive people have to create capital and would lead to higher wages, greater employment, and larger overall tax collections over the long run.

SOURCE: Richard E. Wagner, *Federal Transfer Taxation: A Study in Social Cost* (Washington, D.C.: Institute for Research on the Economics of Taxation, The Center for the Study of Taxation, 1993).

two separate tax rate schedules, the Act substituted a **unified transfer tax** to cover all gratuitous transfers. Thus, gifts are subject to tax at the same rates as those applicable to transfers at death. In addition, current law eliminates the prior exemptions allowed under each tax and replaces them with a unified tax credit.

The Federal estate (or death) tax is designed to tax transfers at death. The tax differs, in several respects, from the typical **inheritance tax** imposed by many states and some local jurisdictions. First, the Federal *estate tax* is imposed on the decedent's entire taxable estate. It is a tax on the right to pass property at death. *Inheritance taxes* are taxes on the right to receive property at death and are therefore levied on the heirs. Second, the relationship of the heirs to the decedent usually has a direct bearing on the inheritance tax. In general, the more closely related the parties, the larger the exemption and the lower the applicable rates.[1] Except for transfers to a surviving spouse that may result in a marital deduction, the relationship of the heirs to the decedent has no effect on the Federal estate tax.

The Federal gift tax, enacted several years after the enactment of the Federal estate tax, was designed to make the income and estate taxes more effective. Congress felt that individuals should not be able to give away property—thereby shifting the income tax consequences to others and avoiding estate taxes—without incurring some tax liability. The result is the Federal gift tax, which covers *inter vivos* (lifetime) transfers.

The Federal gift tax is imposed on the right of one person (the donor) to transfer property to another (the donee) for less than full and adequate consideration. The tax is payable by the donor.[2] If the donor fails to pay the tax when due,

---

[1] For example, one state's inheritance tax provides an exemption of $50,000 for surviving spouses, with rates ranging from 5% to 10% on the taxable portion. This is to be contrasted with an exemption of only $1,000 for strangers (persons unrelated to the deceased),

with rates ranging from 14% to 18% on the taxable portion. Other exemptions and rates fall between these extremes to cover beneficiaries variously related to the decedent.

[2] § 2502(c).

TAX IN THE NEWS

EXPATRIATION TO AVOID U.S. TAXES

Much media attention has recently been given to wealthy individuals who renounce their U.S. citizenship and move to another country to avoid U.S. taxes. These expatriates select a country where citizenship is easily available and little, if any, income and estate taxes are imposed.

Will this so-called expatriation to avoid taxes work? One difficulty for those who voluntarily renounce U.S. citizenship is that § 877 and § 2107 continue to apply to their income tax and estate tax for a 10-year period. The taxpayer involved may avoid the application of these provisions by showing that the giving up of citizenship did not have as one of its principal purposes the avoidance of taxes.

Thus, the expatriation procedure will not be effective for at least 10 years. But even after this period, any income may still be subject to the Federal income tax if it is sourced in the United States. Likewise, assets located in the United States probably will be subject to the estate tax at death.

the donee may be held liable for the tax to the extent of the value of the property received.[3]

Persons Subject to the Tax.   To determine whether a transfer is subject to the Federal gift tax, first ascertain if the donor is a citizen or resident of the United States. If the donor is not a citizen or a resident, it is important to determine whether the property involved in the gift was situated within the United States.

The Federal gift tax is applied to all transfers by gift of property wherever located by individuals who, at the time of the gift, were *citizens* or *residents* of the United States. The term "United States" includes only the 50 states and the District of Columbia; it does not include U.S. possessions or territories.[4] For a U.S. citizen, the place of residence at the time of the gift is irrelevant.

For individuals who are neither citizens nor residents of the United States, the Federal gift tax is applied only to gifts of property situated within the United States.[5] A gift of intangible personal property (e.g., stocks and bonds) by a nonresident alien usually is not subject to the Federal gift tax.[6]

A gift by a corporation is considered a gift by the individual shareholders. A gift to a corporation is generally considered a gift to the individual shareholders. In certain cases, however, a gift to a charitable, public, political, or similar organization may be regarded as a gift to the organization as a single entity.[7]

The Federal estate tax is applied to the entire taxable estate of a decedent who, at the time of death, was a resident or citizen of the United States.[8] If the decedent was a U.S. citizen, the residence at death makes no difference.

If the decedent was neither a resident nor a citizen of the United States at the time of death, the Federal estate tax is imposed on the value of any property

[3] § 6324(b).
[4] § 7701(a)(9).
[5] § 2511(a).
[6] §§ 2501(a)(2) and (3). But see § 2511(b) and Reg. §§ 25.2511–3(b)(2), (3), and (4) for exceptions.

[7] Reg. §§ 25.0–1(b) and 25.2511–1(h)(1). But note the exemption from the Federal gift tax for certain transfers to political organizations discussed later.
[8] § 2001(a).

located within the United States. In that case, the tax determination is controlled by a separate subchapter of the Internal Revenue Code.[9] In certain instances, these tax consequences outlined in the Code may have been modified by death tax conventions (treaties) between the United States and various foreign countries.[10] Further coverage of this area is beyond the scope of this text. The following discussion is limited to the tax treatment of decedents who were residents or citizens of the United States at the time of death.[11]

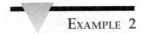

2 LEARNING OBJECTIVE
Work with the Federal gift tax formula.

Formula for the Gift Tax. Like the income tax, which uses taxable income (and not gross income) as a tax base, the gift tax usually does not apply to the full amount of the gift. Deductions and the annual exclusion may be allowed to arrive at an amount called the **taxable gift.** However, unlike the income tax, which does not consider taxable income from prior years, *prior taxable gifts* must be added to arrive at the tax base to which the unified transfer tax rate is applied. Otherwise, the donor could start over again each year with a new set of progressive rates.

EXAMPLE 2

Don makes taxable gifts of $500,000 in 1985 and $500,000 in 1996. Presuming no other taxable gifts and disregarding the effect of the unified tax credit, Don must pay a tax of $155,800 (see applicable tax rate schedule in Appendix A) on the 1985 transfer and a tax of $345,800 on the 1996 transfer (using a tax base of $1 million). If the 1985 taxable gift had not been included in the tax base for the 1996 gift, the tax would have been $155,800. The correct tax liability of $345,800 is more than twice $155,800! ▼

Because the gift tax is cumulative in effect, a credit is allowed for the gift taxes paid (or deemed paid) on prior taxable gifts included in the tax base. The deemed paid credit is explained later in the chapter.

EXAMPLE 3

Assume the same facts as in Example 2. Don is allowed a credit of $155,800 against the gift tax of $345,800. Thus, his gift tax liability for 1996 becomes $190,000 ($345,800 – $155,800). ▼

The annual exclusion before 1982 was $3,000. The change to $10,000 was made to allow larger gifts to be exempt from the Federal gift tax. The increase improves taxpayer compliance and eases the audit function of the IRS. It also recognizes the inflationary trend in the economy.

The formula for the gift tax is summarized in Figure 26–1.

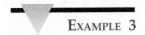

3 LEARNING OBJECTIVE
Work with the Federal estate tax formula.

Formula for the Federal Estate Tax. The Federal unified transfer tax at death, commonly known as the Federal estate tax, is summarized in Figure 26–2. [Note: Section (§) references are to the portion of the Internal Revenue Code involved.]

The gross estate is determined by using the fair market value of the property on the date of the decedent's death (or on the alternate valuation date if applicable).

The reason post-1976 taxable gifts are added to the taxable estate to arrive at the tax base goes back to the scheme of the unified transfer tax. Starting in 1977, all

---

[9] Subchapter B (§§ 2101 through 2108) covers the estate tax treatment of decedents who are neither residents nor citizens. Subchapter A (§§ 2001 through 2056A) covers the estate tax treatment of those who are either residents or citizens.

[10] At present, the United States has death tax conventions with the following countries: Australia, Austria, Denmark, Finland, France, Germany, Greece, Ireland, Italy, Japan, Netherlands, Norway, Republic of South Africa, Sweden, Switzerland, and the

United Kingdom. The United States has gift tax conventions with Australia, France, Germany, Japan, and the United Kingdom.

[11] Further information concerning Subchapter B (§§ 2101 through 2108) can be obtained from the relevant Code sections (and the current Treasury Regulations thereunder). See also the Instructions to Form 706NA (U.S. Estate Tax Return of Nonresident Not a Citizen of the U.S.).

▼ **FIGURE 26–1**
Gift Tax Formula

Determine whether the transfers are considered gifts by referring to §§ 2511 through 2519; list the fair market value of only the covered transfers		$xxx,xxx
Determine the deductions allowed by §§ 2522 (charitable) and 2523 (marital)	$xx,xxx	
Claim the annual exclusion ($10,000 per donee) under § 2503(b), if available	xx,xxx	(xx,xxx)
Taxable gifts [as defined by § 2503(a)] for the current period		$ xx,xxx
Add: Taxable gifts from prior years		xx,xxx
Total of current and past taxable gifts		$ xx,xxx
Compute the gift tax on the total of current and past taxable gifts by using the rates in Appendix A		$ x,xxx
Subtract: Gift tax paid or deemed paid on past taxable gifts and the unified tax credit		(xxx)
Gift tax due on transfers during the current period		$ xxx

▼ **FIGURE 26–2**
Estate Tax Formula

Gross estate (§§ 2031–2046)		$xxx,xxx
Subtract:		
Expenses, indebtedness, and taxes (§ 2053)	$xx,xxx	
Losses (§ 2054)	xx,xxx	
Charitable bequests (§ 2055)	xx,xxx	
Marital deduction (§§ 2056 and 2056A)	xx,xxx	(xx,xxx)
Taxable estate (§ 2051)		$ xx,xxx
Add: Post-1976 taxable gifts [§ 2001(b)]		x,xxx
Tax base		$xxx,xxx
Tentative tax on total transfers [§ 2001(c)]		$ xx,xxx
Subtract:		
Unified transfer tax on post-1976 taxable gifts (gift taxes paid or deemed paid)	$ x,xxx	
Tax credits (including the unified tax credit) (§§ 2010–2016)	x,xxx	(x,xxx)
Estate tax due		$ x,xxx

transfers, whether lifetime or by death, are treated the same. Consequently, taxable gifts made after 1976 must be accounted for upon the death of the donor. Note that the double tax effect of including these gifts is eliminated by allowing a credit against the estate tax for the gift taxes previously paid or deemed paid.

Role of the Unified Tax Credit.   Before the unified transfer tax, the gift tax allowed a $30,000 specific exemption for the lifetime of the donor. A comparable $60,000 exemption was allowed for estate tax purposes. The purpose of these exemptions was to allow donors and decedents to transfer modest amounts of wealth without being subject to the gift and estate taxes. Unfortunately, inflation took its toll, and more taxpayers became subject to these transfer taxes than

▼ **TABLE 26–1**
Unified Tax Credit Phase-In

Year of Death	Amount of Credit	Amount of Exemption Equivalent
1977	$ 30,000	$120,667
1978	34,000	134,000
1979	38,000	147,333
1980	42,500	161,563
1981	47,000	175,625
1982	62,800	225,000
1983	79,300	275,000
1984	96,300	325,000
1985	121,800	400,000
1986	155,800	500,000
1987 & thereafter	192,800	600,000

Congress felt was appropriate. The congressional solution, therefore, was to rescind the exemptions and replace them with the **unified tax credit**.[12]

To curtail revenue loss, the credit was phased in as shown in Table 26–1. The **exemption equivalent** is the amount of the transfer that will pass free of the gift or estate tax by virtue of the credit.

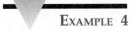

EXAMPLE 4

In 1996, Janet makes a taxable gift of $600,000. Presuming she has made no prior taxable gifts, Janet will not owe any gift tax. Under the applicable tax rate schedule (see Appendix A), the tax on $600,000 is $192,800, which is the exact amount of the credit allowed.[13] ▼

The Tax Reform Act of 1976 allowed donors one last chance to use the $30,000 specific exemption on lifetime gifts. If, however, the exemption was used on gifts made after September 8, 1976 (and before January 1, 1977), the unified tax credit must be reduced by 20 percent of the exemption utilized.[14] The credit must be readjusted whether the gift tax or the estate tax is involved. No adjustment is necessary for post-1976 gifts since the specific exemption is no longer available for such transfers.

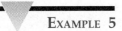

EXAMPLE 5

Net of the annual exclusion, Myrtle, a widow, made gifts of $10,000 in June 1976 and $20,000 in December 1976. Assume Myrtle had never used any of her specific exemption and chose to use the full $30,000 to cover the 1976 gifts. Under these circumstances, the unified tax credit will be reduced by $4,000 (20% × $20,000). The use of the specific exemption on transfers made before September 9, 1976, has no effect on the credit. ▼

VALUATION FOR ESTATE AND GIFT TAX PURPOSES

The value of the property on the date of its transfer generally determines the amount that is subject to the gift tax or the estate tax. Under certain conditions, however, an executor can elect to value estate assets on the **alternate valuation date** (§ 2032).

The alternate valuation date election was designed as a relief provision to ease the economic hardship that could result when estate assets decline in value over

---

[12] §§ 2010 and 2505.

[13] The rate schedules are contained in § 2001(c).

[14] §§ 2010(c) and 2505(c).

the six months after the date of death. If the election is made, all assets of the estate are valued six months after death *or* on the date of disposition if this occurs earlier.[15] The election covers *all* assets in the gross estate ánd cannot be applied to only a portion of the property.

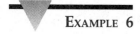

EXAMPLE 6

Robert's gross estate consists of the following property:

	Value on Date of Death	Value Six Months Later
Land	$ 800,000	$ 840,000
Stock in Brown Corporation	900,000	700,000
Stock in Green Corporation	500,000	460,000
Total	$2,200,000	$2,000,000

If Robert's executor elects the alternate valuation date, the estate must be valued at $2,000,000. It is not permissible to value the land at its date of death value ($800,000) and choose the alternate valuation date for the rest of the gross estate. ▼

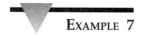

EXAMPLE 7

Assume the same facts as in Example 6 except that the executor sells the stock in Green Corporation for $480,000 four months after Robert's death. If the alternate valuation date is elected, the estate must be valued at $2,020,000 ($840,000 + $700,000 + $480,000). As to the Green stock, the value on its date of disposition controls because that date occurred prior to the six months' alternate valuation date. ▼

The election of the alternate valuation date must decrease the value of the gross estate *and* decrease the estate tax liability.[16] The reason for this last requirement is that the income tax basis of property acquired from a decedent will be the value used for estate tax purposes.[17] Without a special limitation, the alternate valuation date could be elected solely to add to income tax basis.

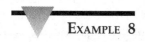

EXAMPLE 8

Al's gross estate is comprised of assets with a date of death value of $1,000,000 and an alternate valuation date value of $1,100,000. Under Al's will, all of his property passes outright to Jean (Al's wife). Because of the marital deduction, no estate tax results regardless of which value is used. But if the alternate valuation date could be elected, Jean would have an income tax basis of $1,100,000 in the property acquired from Al. ▼

The alternate valuation date cannot be elected in Example 8 for two reasons, either of which would suffice. First, the alternate valuation date will not decrease Al's gross estate. Second, the election will not decrease Al's estate tax liability. Thus, his estate must use the date of death valuation of $1,000,000. As a result, Jean's income tax basis in the property received from Al is $1,000,000.

KEY PROPERTY CONCEPTS

When property is transferred either by gift or by death, the form of ownership can have a direct bearing on any transfer tax consequences. Understanding the different forms of ownership is necessary for working with Federal gift and estate taxes.

---

[15] § 2032(a).
[16] § 2032(c).

[17] § 1014(a).

Undivided Ownership. Assume Dan and Vicky own an undivided but equal interest in a tract of land. Such ownership can fall into any of four categories: joint tenancy, tenancy by the entirety, tenancy in common, or community property.

If Dan and Vicky hold ownership as **joint tenants** or **tenants by the entirety,** the right of survivorship exists. This means that the last tenant to survive receives full ownership of the property. Thus, if Dan predeceases Vicky, the land belongs entirely to Vicky. None of the land passes to Dan's heirs or is subject to administration by Dan's executor. A tenancy by the entirety is a joint tenancy between husband and wife.

If Dan and Vicky hold ownership as **tenants in common** or as community property, death does not defeat an owner's interest. Thus, if Dan predeceases Vicky, Dan's half interest in the land passes to his estate or heirs.

Community property interests arise from the marital relationship. Normally, all property acquired after marriage, except by gift or inheritance, by husband and wife residing in a community property state becomes part of the community. The following states have the community property system in effect: Louisiana, Texas, New Mexico, Arizona, California, Washington, Idaho, Nevada, and Wisconsin. All other states follow the common law system of ascertaining a spouse's rights to property acquired after marriage.

Partial Interests. Interests in assets can be divided in terms of rights to income and rights to principal. Particularly when property is placed in trust, it is not uncommon to carve out various income interests that must be accounted for separately from the ultimate disposition of the property itself.

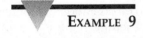

EXAMPLE 9

Under Bill's will, a ranch is to be placed in trust, life estate to Sam, Bill's son, with remainder to Sam's children (Bill's grandchildren). Under this arrangement, Sam is the life tenant and, as such, is entitled to the use of the ranch (including any income) during his life. Upon Sam's death, the trust terminates, and its principal passes to his children. Thus, Sam's children receive outright ownership of the ranch when Sam dies. ▼

THE FEDERAL GIFT TAX

GENERAL CONSIDERATIONS

4   **LEARNING OBJECTIVE**
Explain the operation of the Federal gift tax.

Requirements for a Gift. For a gift to be complete under state law, the following elements must be present:

- A donor competent to make the gift.
- A donee capable of receiving and possessing the property.
- Donative intent on behalf of the donor.
- Actual or constructive delivery of the property to the donee or the donee's representative.
- Acceptance of the gift by the donee.

Incomplete Transfers. The Federal gift tax does not apply to transfers that are incomplete. Thus, if the transferor retains the right to reclaim the property or has not really parted with the possession of the property, a taxable event has not taken place.

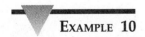

EXAMPLE 10

Lesly creates a trust with income payable to Mary for life, remainder to Paul. Under the terms of the trust instrument, Lesly can revoke the trust at any time and repossess the trust principal and income earned. No gift takes place on the creation of the trust; Lesly has not ceased to have dominion and control over the property. ▼

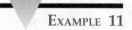

EXAMPLE 11

Assume the same facts as in Example 10, except that one year after the transfer, Lesly relinquishes his right to terminate the trust. At this point, the transfer becomes complete, and the Federal gift tax applies. ▼

ETHICAL CONSIDERATIONS

Was the Transfer Complete?

At the time of his death in 1996, Walter was thought still to be the owner of the family vacation home in Colorado. However, his safe deposit box contains a legal deed, dated in December 1990, transferring the ownership of this property to his two adult sons. The sons were unaware that the transfer even took place.

The records of the county where the vacation home is located reflect the transfer and list the sons as the owners of record. They also reveal that Walter continued to pay the property tax assessments up to the date of his death. Although the value of the property clearly exceeded the annual exclusions, no Federal gift tax return was ever filed.

Would it be proper for the executor of Walter's estate to exclude the value of the property from the gross estate? Why?

Business versus Personal Setting. In a business setting, full and adequate consideration is apt to exist. Regulation § 25.2512–8 provides that "a sale, exchange, or other transfer of property made in the ordinary course of business (a transaction that is bona fide, at arm's length, and free of any donative intent) will be considered as made for an adequate and full consideration in money or money's worth." If the parties are acting in a personal setting, a gift is usually the result. Do not conclude that the presence of *some* consideration is enough to preclude Federal gift tax consequences. Again, the answer may rest on whether the transfer occurred in a business setting.

EXAMPLE 12

Peter sells Bob some real estate for $40,000. Unknown to Peter, the property contains valuable mineral deposits and is really worth $100,000. Peter may have made a bad business deal, but he has not made a gift of $60,000 to Bob. ▼

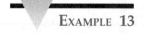

EXAMPLE 13

Assume the same facts as in Example 12, except that Peter and Bob are father and son. In addition, Peter is very much aware that the property is worth $100,000. Peter has made a gift of $60,000 to Bob. ▼

Certain Excluded Transfers. Transfers to political organizations are exempt from the application of the Federal gift tax.[18] This provision in the Code made unnecessary the previous practice whereby candidates for public office established multiple campaign committees to maximize the number of annual exclusions available to their contributors. As noted, an annual exclusion of $10,000 (previously $3,000) for each donee passes free of the Federal gift tax.

The Federal gift tax does not apply to tuition payments made to an educational organization (e.g., a college) on another's behalf. Nor does it apply to amounts paid on another's behalf for medical care.[19] In this regard, the law is realistic since it is unlikely that most donors would recognize these items as being transfers subject to the gift tax.

[18] § 2501(a)(5).

[19] § 2503(e).

Satisfying an obligation of support is not subject to the gift tax. Thus, no gift takes place when parents pay for their children's education because one of the obligations of parents is to educate their children. What constitutes an obligation of support is determined by applicable state law.

Lifetime versus Death Transfers.   Be careful to distinguish between lifetime (inter vivos) and death (testamentary) transfers.

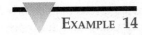

EXAMPLE 14

Wilbur buys a U.S. savings bond, which he registers as follows: "Wilbur, payable to Alice upon Wilbur's death." No gift is made when Wilbur buys the bond; Alice has received only a mere expectancy (right to obtain ownership of the bond at Wilbur's death). Anytime before his death, Wilbur may redeem or otherwise dispose of the bond and cut off Alice's interest. On Wilbur's death, no gift is made because the bond passes to Alice by testamentary disposition. As noted later, the bond will be included in Wilbur's gross estate as property in which the decedent had an interest (§ 2033). ▼

TRANSFERS SUBJECT TO THE GIFT TAX

Whether a transfer is subject to the Federal gift tax depends upon the application of §§ 2511 through 2519 and the applicable Regulations.

Gift Loans.   To understand the tax ramifications of gift loans, an illustration is helpful.

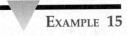

EXAMPLE 15

Before his daughter (Denise) leaves for college, Victor lends her $300,000. Denise signs a note that provides for repayment in five years. The loan contains no interest element, and neither Victor nor Denise expects any interest to be paid. Following Victor's advice, Denise invests the loan proceeds in income-producing securities. During her five years in college, she uses the income from the investments to pay for college costs and other living expenses. On the maturity date of the note, Denise repays the $300,000 she owes Victor. ▼

In a gift loan arrangement, the following consequences result:

- Victor has made a gift to Denise of the interest element. The amount of the gift is determined by the difference between the amount of interest charged (in this case, none) and the market rate (as determined by the yield on certain U.S. government securities).
- The interest element is included in Victor's gross income and is subject to the Federal income tax.
- Denise may be allowed an income tax deduction for the interest element, but may benefit from this result only if she is in a position to itemize her deductions *from* adjusted gross income.

The Code defines a gift loan as "any below-market loan where the forgoing of interest is in the nature of a gift."[20] Unless tax avoidance was one of the principal purposes of the loan, special limitations apply if the gift loan does not exceed $100,000. In such a case, the interest element may not exceed the borrower's net investment income.[21] Furthermore, if the net investment income does not exceed $1,000, it is treated as zero. Under a $1,000 de minimis rule, the interest element is disregarded.

---

[20] § 7872(f)(3).
[21] Net investment income has the same meaning given to the term by § 163(d). Generally, net investment income is investment income (e.g., interest, dividends) less related expenses.

Certain Property Settlements (§ 2516).   Normally, the settlement of certain marital rights is not regarded as being for consideration and is subject to the Federal gift tax.[22] As a special exception to this general approach, Congress enacted § 2516. By this provision, transfers of property interests made under the terms of a written agreement between spouses in settlement of their marital or property rights are deemed to be for adequate consideration. The transfers are exempt from the Federal gift tax if a final decree of divorce is obtained within the three-year period beginning on the date one year before the parties entered into the agreement. Likewise excluded are transfers to provide a reasonable allowance for the support of minor children (including legally adopted children) of a marriage. The agreement need not be approved by the divorce decree.

Disclaimers (§ 2518).   A **disclaimer** is a refusal by a person to accept property that is designated to pass to him or her. The effect of the disclaimer is to pass the property to someone else.

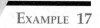
EXAMPLE 16

Earl dies without a will and is survived by a son, Andy, and a grandson, Jay. At the time of his death, Earl owned real estate that, under the applicable state law, passes to the closest lineal descendant, Andy in this case. If, however, Andy disclaims his interest in the real estate, state law provides that the property passes to Jay. At the time of Earl's death, Andy has considerable property of his own, and Jay has none. ▼

Why might Andy want to consider disclaiming his inheritance and have the property pass directly from Earl to Jay? By doing so, an extra transfer tax may be avoided. If the disclaimer does not take place (Andy accepts the inheritance), and the property eventually passes to Jay (either by gift or by death), the later transfer is subject to the application of either the gift tax or the estate tax.

For many years, whether a disclaimer was effective in avoiding a Federal transfer tax depended on the application of state law. To illustrate by using the facts of Example 16, if state law determined that the real estate was deemed to have passed through Andy despite his disclaimer after Earl's death, the Federal gift tax applied. In essence, Andy was treated as if he had inherited the property from Earl and then given it to Jay. As state law was not always consistent in this regard and sometimes was not even known, the application or nonapplication of Federal transfer taxes depended on where the parties lived. To remedy this situation and provide some measure of uniformity, §§ 2046 (relating to disclaimers for estate tax purposes) and 2518 were added to the Code.

In the case of the gift tax, when the requirements of § 2518 are met and Andy makes a timely lifetime disclaimer (refer to Example 16), the property is treated as if it goes directly from Earl to Jay. Since the property is not treated as passing through Andy (regardless of what state law holds), it is not subject to the Federal gift tax.

The tax law also permits the Federal gift tax to be avoided in cases of a partial disclaimer of an undivided interest.

EXAMPLE 17

Assume the same facts as in Example 16, except that Andy wishes to retain half of the real estate for himself. If Andy makes a timely disclaimer of an undivided one-half interest in the property, the Federal gift tax does not apply to the portion passing to Jay. ▼

Other Transfers Subject to Gift Tax.   Other transfers that may carry gift tax consequences (e.g., the creation of joint ownership) are discussed and illustrated in connection with the Federal estate tax.

---

[22] Reg. § 25.2512–8.

ANNUAL EXCLUSION

The first $10,000 of gifts made to any one person during any calendar year (except gifts of future interests in property) is excluded in determining the total amount of gifts for the year.[23] The **annual exclusion** applies to all gifts of a present interest made during the calendar year in the order in which they are made until the $10,000 exclusion per donee is exhausted. For a gift in trust, each beneficiary of the trust is treated as a separate person for purposes of the exclusion.

▼
EXAMPLE 18 During the current year, Laura makes the following cash gifts: $8,000 to Rita and $12,000 to Maureen. Laura may claim an annual exclusion of $8,000 with respect to Rita and $10,000 with respect to Maureen. ▼

A **future interest** is defined as one that will come into being (as to use, possession, or enjoyment) at some future date. Examples of future interests include such rights as remainder interests that are commonly encountered when property is transferred to a trust. A *present interest* is an unrestricted right to the immediate use, possession, or enjoyment of property or of the income.

▼
EXAMPLE 19 By a lifetime gift, Ron transfers property to a trust with a life estate (with income payable annually) to June and remainder upon June's death to Albert. Ron has made two gifts: one to June of a life estate and one to Albert of a remainder interest. The life estate is a present interest and qualifies for the annual exclusion. The remainder interest granted to Albert is a future interest and does not qualify for the exclusion. Note that Albert's interest does not come into being until some future date (on the death of June). ▼

Although Example 19 indicates that the gift of an income interest is a present interest, this is not always the case. If a possibility exists that the income beneficiary may not receive the immediate enjoyment of the property, the transfer is of a future interest.

▼
EXAMPLE 20 Assume the same facts as in Example 19, except that the income from the trust need not be payable annually to June. It may, at the trustee's discretion, be accumulated and added to corpus. Since June's right to receive the income from the trust is conditioned on the trustee's discretion, it is not a present interest. No annual exclusion is allowed. The mere possibility of diversion is enough. It would not matter if the trustee never exercised the discretion to accumulate and did, in fact, distribute the trust income to June annually. ▼

Trust for Minors. Section 2503(c) offers an exception to the future interest rules just discussed. Under this provision, a transfer for the benefit of a person who has not attained the age of 21 years on the date of the gift may be considered a gift of a present interest. This is true even though the minor is not given the unrestricted right to the immediate use, possession, or enjoyment of the property. For the exception to apply, however, certain stringent conditions must be satisfied. One such condition is that all of the property and its income must be made available to the minor upon attaining age 21. Thus, the exception allows a trustee to accumulate income on behalf of a minor beneficiary without converting the income interest to a future interest.

DEDUCTIONS

In arriving at taxable gifts, a deduction is allowed for transfers to certain qualified charitable organizations. On transfers between spouses, a marital deduction may

---

[23] § 2503(b).

be available. Since both the charitable and marital deductions apply in determining the Federal estate tax, they are discussed later in the chapter.

COMPUTING THE FEDERAL GIFT TAX

5 **LEARNING OBJECTIVE**
Explain the computation of the Federal gift tax.

The Unified Transfer Tax Rate Schedule.   The top rates of the unified transfer tax rate schedule originally reached as high as 70 percent. Over the years, these top rates have been reduced to 55 percent. As noted later in the chapter, the benefits of the graduated rates are phased out for larger gifts. Keep in mind that the unified transfer tax rate schedule applies to all transfers (by gift or death) after 1976. Different rate schedules applied for pre-1977 gifts and pre-1977 death transfers.

The Deemed-Paid Adjustment.   Review the formula for the gift tax (refer to Figure 26–1) and note that the tax base for a current gift includes *all* past taxable gifts. The effect of the inclusion is to force the current taxable gift into a higher bracket due to the progressive nature of the unified transfer tax rates (refer to Example 2). To mitigate such double taxation, the donor is allowed a credit for any gift tax previously paid or deemed paid (refer to Example 3).

Limiting the donor to a credit for the gift tax *actually paid* on pre-1977 taxable gifts would be unfair. Pre-1977 taxable gifts were subject to a lower set of rates than those in the unified transfer tax rate schedule. As a consequence, the donor is allowed a *deemed-paid* credit on pre-1977 taxable gifts. This is the amount that would have been due under the unified transfer tax rate schedule had it been applicable. *Post-1976* taxable gifts *also* are subject to the deemed-paid adjustment because the same rate schedule may not be involved in all gifts.

EXAMPLE 21

In early 1976, Lisa made taxable gifts of $500,000, upon which a Federal gift tax of $109,275 was paid. Assume Lisa makes further taxable gifts of $700,000 in 1996. The unified transfer tax on the 1996 gifts is determined as follows:

Taxable gifts made in 1996		$ 700,000
Add: Taxable gifts made in 1976		500,000
Total of current and past taxable gifts		$1,200,000
Unified transfer tax on total taxable gifts per Appendix A [$345,800 + (41% × $200,000)]		$ 427,800
Subtract:		
Deemed-paid tax on pre-1977 taxable gifts per Appendix A [$70,800 + (34% × $250,000)]	$155,800	
Unified tax credit for 1996	192,800	(348,600)
Gift tax due on the 1996 taxable gift		$ 79,200

Note that the gift tax actually paid on the 1976 transfer was $109,275. Nevertheless, Lisa is allowed a deemed-paid credit on the gift of $155,800, considerably different from the amount paid. ▼

The Election to Split Gifts by Married Persons.   To understand the reason for the gift-splitting election of § 2513, consider the following situations:

EXAMPLE 22

Dick and Margaret are husband and wife and reside in Michigan, a common law state. Dick has been the only breadwinner in the family, and Margaret has no significant property of her own. Neither has made any prior taxable gifts or used the $30,000 specific exemption previously available for pre-1977 gifts. In 1996, Dick makes a gift to Leslie of $1,220,000. Presuming the election to split gifts did not exist, Dick's gift tax is as follows:

Amount of gift	$1,220,000
Subtract: Annual exclusion	(10,000)
Taxable gift	$1,210,000
Gift tax on $1,210,000 per Appendix A [$345,800 + (41% × $210,000)]	$ 431,900
Subtract: Unified tax credit for 1996	(192,800)
Gift tax due on the 1996 taxable gift	$ 239,100

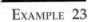

EXAMPLE 23   Assume the same facts as in Example 22, except that Dick and Margaret have always resided in California, a community property state. Even though Dick is the sole breadwinner, income from personal services generally is community property. Consequently, the gift to Leslie probably involves community property. If this is the case, the gift tax is as follows:

	Dick	Margaret
Amount of the gift (50% × $1,220,000)	$ 610,000	$ 610,000
Subtract: Annual exclusion	(10,000)	(10,000)
Taxable gifts	$ 600,000	$ 600,000
Gift tax on $600,000 per Appendix A	$ 192,800	$ 192,800
Subtract: Unified tax credit for 1996	(192,800)	(192,800)
Gift tax due on the 1996 taxable gifts	$ –0–	$ –0–

As the results of Examples 22 and 23 indicate, married donors residing in community property jurisdictions possessed a significant gift tax advantage over those residing in common law states. To rectify this inequity, the Revenue Act of 1948 incorporated the predecessor to § 2513 into the Code. Under this provision, a gift made by a person to someone other than his or her spouse may be considered, for Federal gift tax purposes, as having been made one-half by each spouse. Returning to Example 22, Dick and Margaret could treat the gift passing to Leslie as being made one-half by each of them, even though the property belonged to Dick. As a result, the parties are able to achieve the same tax consequence as in Example 23.

To split gifts, the spouses must be legally married to each other at the time of the gift. If they are divorced later in the calendar year, they may still split the gift if neither marries anyone else during that year. They both must indicate on their separate gift tax returns their consent to have all gifts made in that calendar year split between them. In addition, both must be citizens or residents of the United States on the date of the gift. A gift from one spouse to the other spouse cannot be split. Such a gift might, however, be eligible for the marital deduction.

The election to split gifts is not necessary when husband and wife transfer community property to a third party. It is needed if the gift consists of the separate property of one of the spouses. Generally, separate property is property acquired before marriage and property acquired after marriage by gift or inheritance. The election, then, is not limited to residents of common law states.

PROCEDURAL MATTERS

Having determined which transfers are subject to the Federal gift tax and the various deductions and exclusions available to the donor, the procedural aspects of the tax should be considered. The following sections discuss the return itself, the due dates for filing and paying the tax, and other related matters.

The Federal Gift Tax Return. For transfers by gift, a Form 709 (U.S. Gift Tax Return) must be filed whenever the gifts for any one calendar year exceed the annual exclusion or involve a gift of a future interest. A Form 709 need not be filed, however, for transfers between spouses that are offset by the unlimited marital deduction, regardless of the amount of the transfer.[24]

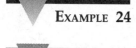

EXAMPLE 24

In 1996, Larry makes five gifts, each in the amount of $10,000, to his five children. If the gifts do not involve future interests, a Form 709 need not be filed to report the transfers. ▼

EXAMPLE 25

During 1996, Esther makes a gift of $20,000 cash of her separate property to her daughter. To double the amount of the annual exclusion allowed, Jerry (Esther's husband) is willing to split the gift. Since the § 2513 election can be made only on a gift tax return, a form must be filed even though no gift tax will be due as a result of the transfer. Useful for this purpose is Form 709–A (U.S. Short Form Gift Tax Return). This form is available to simplify the gift-splitting procedure. ▼

Presuming a gift tax return is due, it must be filed on or before the fifteenth day of April following the year of the gift.[25] As with other Federal taxes, when the due date falls on Saturday, Sunday, or a legal holiday, the date for filing the return is the next business day. Note that the filing requirements for Form 709 have no correlation to the accounting year used by a donor for Federal income tax purposes. Thus, a fiscal year taxpayer must follow the April 15 rule for any reportable gifts. If sufficient reason is shown, the IRS is authorized to grant reasonable extensions of time for filing the return.[26]

THE FEDERAL ESTATE TAX

The following discussion of the estate tax coincides with the formula that appeared earlier in the chapter in Figure 26–2. The key components in the formula are the gross estate, the taxable estate, the tax base, and the credits allowed against the tentative tax. This formula can be summarized as follows:

GROSS ESTATE

Simply stated, the **gross estate** includes all property subject to the Federal estate tax. Thus, the gross estate depends on the provisions of the Internal Revenue Code as supplemented by IRS pronouncements and the judicial interpretations of Federal courts.

6 LEARNING OBJECTIVE
Describe the components of the gross estate.

[24] § 6019(a)(2).
[25] § 6075(b)(1).

[26] § 6081. Under § 6075(b)(2), an extension of time granted to a calendar year taxpayer for filing an income tax return automatically extends the due date of a gift tax return.

CONCEPT SUMMARY 26–1

Federal Gift Tax Provisions

1. The Federal gift tax applies to all gratuitous transfers of property made by U.S. citizens or residents. In this regard, it does not matter where the property is located.

2. In the eyes of the IRS, a gratuitous transfer is one not supported by full and adequate consideration. If the parties are acting in a business setting, such consideration usually exists. If purported sales are between family members, a gift element may be suspected.

3. If a lender loans money to another and intends some or all of the interest element to be a gift, the arrangement is categorized as a gift loan. To the extent that the interest provided for is less than the market rate, three tax consequences result. First, a gift has taken place between the lender and the borrower as to the interest element. Second, income may result to the lender. Third, an income tax deduction may be available to the borrower.

4. Property settlements can escape the gift tax if a divorce occurs within a prescribed period of time.

5. A disclaimer is a refusal by a person to accept property designated to pass to that person. The effect of a disclaimer is to pass the property to someone else. If certain conditions are satisfied, the issuance of a disclaimer will not be subject to the Federal gift tax.

6. Except for gifts of future interests, a donor is allowed an annual exclusion of $10,000. The future interest limitation does not apply to certain trusts created for minors.

7. The election to split a gift enables a married couple to be treated as two donors. The election doubles the annual exclusion and makes the unified tax credit available to the nonowner spouse.

8. The election to split gifts is not necessary if the property is jointly owned by the spouses. That is the case when the property is part of the couple's community.

9. In determining the tax base for computing the gift tax, all prior taxable gifts must be added to current taxable gifts. Thus, the gift tax is cumulative in nature.

10. Gifts are reported on Form 709 or Form 709–A. The return is due on April 15 following the year of the gift.

In contrast to the gross estate, the **probate estate** is controlled by state (rather than Federal) law. The probate estate consists of all of a decedent's property subject to administration by the executor or administrator of the estate. The administration is supervised by a local court of appropriate jurisdiction (usually called a probate court). An executor (or executrix) is the decedent's personal representative appointed under the decedent's will. When a decedent dies without a will or fails to name an executor in the will (or that person refuses to serve), the local probate court appoints an administrator (or administratrix).

The probate estate is frequently smaller than the gross estate. It contains only property owned by the decedent at the time of death and passing to heirs under a will or under the law of intestacy (the order of distribution for those dying without a will). As noted later, such items as the proceeds of many life insurance policies become part of the gross estate but are not included in the probate estate.

All states provide for an order of distribution in the event someone dies without a will. After the surviving spouse receives some or all of the estate, the preference is usually in the following order: down to lineal descendants (e.g., children, grandchildren), up to lineal ascendants (e.g., parents, grandparents), and out to collateral relations (e.g., brothers, sisters, aunts, and uncles).

Property Owned by the Decedent (§ 2033). Property owned by the decedent at the time of death is included in the gross estate. The nature of the property or the use to which it was put during the decedent-owner's lifetime has no significance as far as the estate tax is concerned. Thus, personal effects (such as

TAX IN THE NEWS

SHOULD THE GROSS ESTATE INCLUDE PROPERTY STOLEN BY THE DECEDENT?

During World War II, Joe Meador was a lieutenant in the U.S. Army. Near the end of the war, Lt. Meador was assigned the responsibility of safeguarding a collection of artwork dating from the reigns of Charlemagne and Otto I. Illegally and surreptitiously, he appropriated some of the art objects and took them back to the United States.

When Joe Meador died in 1980, his will passed the art objects to his brother and sister. When the art objects were later traced to Joe's heirs, the Cultural Foundation in Berlin instituted a suit for their return.

Indications are that the IRS will levy an assessment against Joe Meador's heirs for the estate tax that would have been due if the art objects had been included in Joe's gross estate. Joe's heirs maintain that the gross estate should not include assets that the decedent did not legally own.

clothing), stocks, bonds, furniture, jewelry, works of art, bank accounts, and interests in businesses conducted as sole proprietorships and partnerships are all included in the deceased's gross estate. No distinction is made between tangible or intangible, depreciable or nondepreciable, business or personal assets. However, a deceased spouse's gross estate does not include the surviving spouse's share of the community property.

The application of § 2033 is illustrated as follows:

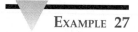

EXAMPLE 26

Irma dies owning some City of Denver bonds. The fair market value of the bonds plus any interest accrued to the date of Irma's death is included in her gross estate. Although interest on municipal bonds is normally not taxable under the Federal income tax, it is property owned by Irma at the time of death. However, any interest accrued after death is not part of Irma's gross estate. ▼

EXAMPLE 27

Sharon dies on April 8, at a time when she owns stock in Robin Corporation and in Wren Corporation. On March 2, both corporations had authorized a cash dividend payable on May 3. Robin's dividend is payable to shareholders of record as of April 1. Wren's date of record is April 11. Sharon's gross estate includes the following: the stock in Robin Corporation, the stock in Wren Corporation, and the dividend on the Robin stock. It does not include the dividend on the Wren stock. ▼

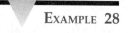

EXAMPLE 28

Ray dies holding some promissory notes issued to him by his son. In his will, Ray forgives these notes, relieving the son of the obligation to make any payments. The fair market value of these notes is included in Ray's gross estate. ▼

Dower and Curtesy Interests (§ 2034). In its common law (nonstatutory) form, dower generally gave a surviving widow a life estate in a portion of her husband's estate (usually the real estate he owned) with the remainder passing to their children. Most states have modified and codified these common law rules, and the resulting statutes often vary among jurisdictions. In some states, for example, by statute, a widow is entitled to outright ownership of a percentage of her deceased husband's real estate and personal property. Curtesy is a similar right held by the husband in his wife's property, taking effect in the event he survives her. Most states have abolished the common law curtesy concept and have, in some cases, substituted a modified statutory version.

Dower and curtesy rights are incomplete interests and may never materialize. Thus, if a wife predeceases her husband, the dower interest in her husband's property is lost.

EXAMPLE 29

Martin dies without a will, leaving an estate of $900,000. Under state law, Belinda (Martin's widow) is entitled to one-third of his property. The $300,000 Belinda receives is included in Martin's gross estate. Depending on the nature of the interest Belinda receives in the $300,000, this amount could qualify Martin's estate for a marital deduction. (This possibility is discussed at greater length later in the chapter. For the time being, however, the focus is on what is or is not included as part of the decedent's gross estate.) ▼

Adjustments for Gifts Made within Three Years of Death (§ 2035). At one time, all taxable gifts made within three years of death were included in the donor's gross estate unless it could be shown that the gifts were not made in contemplation of death. The prior rule was intended to preclude tax avoidance since the gift tax and estate tax rates were separate and the former was lower than the latter. When the gift and estate tax rates were combined into the unified transfer tax, the reason for the rule for gifts in contemplation of death largely disappeared. The three-year rule has, however, been retained for the following items:

- Any gift tax paid on gifts made within three years of death. Called the *gross-up* procedure, this prevents the gift tax amount from escaping the estate tax.
- Any property interests transferred by gift within three years of death that would have been included in the gross estate by virtue of the application of § 2036 (transfers with a retained life estate), § 2037 (transfers taking effect at death), § 2038 (revocable transfers), and § 2042 (proceeds of life insurance). All except § 2037 transfers are discussed later in the chapter.

EXAMPLE 30

Before her death in 1996, Jennifer made the following taxable gifts:

Year of Gift	Nature of the Asset	Fair Market Value		Gift Tax Paid
		Date of Gift	Date of Death	
1989	Hawk Corporation stock	$100,000	$150,000	$ –0–
1994	Insurance policy on Jennifer's life	40,000 (cash value)	200,000 (face value)	–0–
1995	Land	400,000	410,000	8,200

Jennifer's *gross estate* includes $208,200 ($200,000 life insurance proceeds + $8,200 gross-up for the gift tax on the 1995 taxable gift) as to these transfers. Referring to the formula for the estate tax (Figure 26–2), the other post-1976 taxable gifts are added to the *taxable estate* (at the fair market value on the date of the gift) in arriving at the tax base. Jennifer's estate is allowed a credit for the gift tax paid (or deemed paid) on the 1995 transfer. ▼

Transfers with a Retained Life Estate (§ 2036). Code §§ 2036 through 2038 were enacted on the premise that the estate tax can be avoided on lifetime transfers only if the decedent does not retain control over the property. The logic of this approach is somewhat difficult to dispute. One should not be able to escape the tax consequences of property transfers at death while remaining in a position during life to enjoy some or all of the fruits of ownership.

Under § 2036, the value of any property transferred by the deceased during lifetime for less than adequate consideration must be included if either of the following was retained:

- The possession or enjoyment of, or the right to the income from, the property.
- The right, either alone or in conjunction with any person, to designate the persons who shall possess or enjoy the property or the income.

"The possession or enjoyment of, or the right to the income from, the property," as it appears in § 2036(a)(1), is considered to have been retained by the decedent to the extent that such income, etc., is to be applied toward the discharge of a legal obligation of the decedent. The term "legal obligation" includes a legal obligation of the decedent to support a dependent during the decedent's lifetime.[27]

The following examples illustrate the practical application of § 2036.

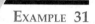

EXAMPLE 31

Carl's will passes all of his property to a trust in which income goes to Alan for his life (Alan is given a life estate). Upon Alan's death, the principal goes to Melissa (Melissa is granted a remainder interest). On Alan's death, none of the trust property is included in his gross estate. Although Alan held a life estate, § 2036 is inapplicable because Alan was not the transferor (Carl was) of the property. Section 2033 (property owned by the decedent) causes any income distributions Alan was entitled to receive at the time of his death to be included in his gross estate. ▼

EXAMPLE 32

By deed, Nora transfers the remainder interest in her ranch to Marcia, retaining for herself the right to continue occupying the property until death. Upon Nora's death, the fair market value of the ranch is included in her gross estate. Furthermore, Nora is subject to the gift tax. The amount of the gift is the fair market value of the ranch on the date of the gift less the portion applicable to Nora's retained life estate. ▼

Revocable Transfers (§ 2038).   Another type of lifetime transfer that is drawn into a decedent's gross estate is covered by § 2038. The gross estate includes the value of property interests transferred by the decedent (except to the extent that the transfer was made for full consideration) if the enjoyment of the property transferred was subject, at the date of the decedent's death, to any power of the decedent to *alter, amend, revoke, or terminate* the transfer. This includes the power to change beneficiaries or to accelerate or increase any beneficiary's enjoyment of the property.

The capacity in which the decedent could exercise the power is immaterial. If the decedent gave property in trust, making himself or herself the trustee with the power to revoke the trust, the property is included in his or her gross estate. If the decedent named another person as trustee with the power to revoke but reserved the power to later appoint himself or herself trustee, the property is also included in his or her gross estate. If, however, the power to alter, amend, revoke, or terminate was held at all times solely by a person other than the decedent and the decedent did not reserve a right to assume these powers, the property is not included in the decedent's gross estate.

The Code and the Regulations make it clear that one cannot avoid inclusion in the gross estate under § 2038 by relinquishing a power within three years of death.[28] Recall that § 2038 is one of several types of situations listed as exceptions to the usual rule excluding gifts made within three years of death from the gross estate.

In the event § 2038 applies, the amount includible in the gross estate is the portion of the property transferred that is subject, at the decedent's death, to the decedent's power to alter, amend, revoke, or terminate.

The classic § 2038 situation results from the use of a revocable trust.

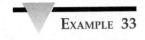

EXAMPLE 33

Maria creates a trust, life estate to her children, remainder to her grandchildren. Under the terms of the trust, Maria reserves the right to revoke the trust and revest the trust principal and income in herself. As noted in Example 10, the creation of the trust does not result in a gift because the transfer is not complete. However, if Maria dies still retaining the power to revoke, the trust is included in her gross estate under § 2038. ▼

In application, the provisions related to incomplete transfers (§§ 2036 and 2038) tend to overlap. It is not unusual to find that either or both sections apply to a particular transfer.

Annuities (§ 2039). Annuities can be divided by their origin into commercial and noncommercial contracts. Noncommercial annuities are issued by private parties and, in some cases, charitable organizations that do not regularly issue annuities. The two varieties have much in common, but noncommercial annuities present special income tax problems and are not treated further in this discussion.

Regulation § 20.2039–1(b)(1) defines an annuity as representing "one or more payments extending over any period of time." According to the Regulation, the payments may be equal or unequal, conditional or unconditional, periodic or sporadic. Annuity contracts that terminate upon the death of the person covered (i.e., annuitant) are designated as straight-life annuities. Other contracts provide for a survivorship feature (e.g., reduced payments to a surviving spouse).

In the case of a straight-life annuity, nothing is included in the gross estate of the annuitant at death. Section 2033 (property in which the decedent had an interest) does not apply because the annuitant's interest in the contract is terminated by death. Section 2036 (transfers with a retained life estate) does not cover the situation; a transfer made for full consideration is specifically excluded from § 2036 treatment. A commercial annuity is presumed to have been purchased for full consideration unless some evidence exists to indicate that the parties were not acting at arm's length.

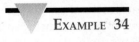

EXAMPLE 34

Arnold purchases a straight-life annuity that will pay him $6,000 a month when he reaches age 65. Arnold dies at age 70. Except for the payments he received before his death, nothing relating to this annuity affects Arnold's gross estate. ▼

In the case of a survivorship annuity, the estate tax consequences under § 2039(a) are usually triggered by the death of the first annuitant. The amount included in the gross estate is the cost from the same company of a comparable annuity covering the survivor at his or her attained age on the date of the deceased annuitant's death.

---

[28] § 2038(a)(1) and Reg. § 20.2038–1(e)(1).

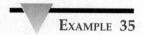
EXAMPLE 35

Assume the same facts as in Example 34, except that the annuity contract provides for Veronica to be paid $3,000 a month for life as a survivorship feature. Veronica is 62 years of age when Arnold dies. Under these circumstances, Arnold's gross estate includes the cost of a comparable contract that provides an annuity of $3,000 per month for the life of a female, age 62. ▼

Full inclusion of the survivorship element in the gross estate is subject to an exception under § 2039(b). The amount includible is to be based on the proportion of the deceased annuitant's contribution to the total cost of the contract. This is expressed by the following formula:

$$\frac{\text{Decedent's contribution to purchase price}}{\text{Total purchase price of the annuity}} \times \text{Value of the annuity (or refund) at decedent's death} = \text{Amount includible in the deceased annuitant's gross estate}$$

EXAMPLE 36

Assume the same facts as in Example 35, except that Arnold and Veronica are husband and wife and have always lived in a community property state. The premiums on the contract were paid with community funds. Since Veronica contributed half of the cost of the contract, only half of the amount determined under Example 35 is included in Arnold's gross estate. ▼

The result reached in Example 36 is not unique to community property jurisdictions. The outcome would have been the same in a noncommunity property state if Veronica had furnished half of the consideration from her own funds.

Joint Interests (§§ 2040 and 2511).   Recall that joint tenancies and tenancies by the entirety are characterized by the right of survivorship. Thus, upon the death of a joint tenant, title to the property passes to the surviving tenant. None of the property is included in the *probate* estate of the deceased tenant. In the case of tenancies in common and community property, death does not defeat an ownership interest; rather, the deceased owner's interest is part of the probate estate.

The *Federal estate tax treatment* of tenancies in common or of community property follows the logical approach of taxing only the portion of the property included in the deceased owner's probate estate. Thus, if Homer, Wilma, and Thelma are tenants in common in a tract of land, each owning an equal interest, and Homer dies, only one-third of the value of the property is included in the gross estate. This one-third interest is also the same amount that passes to Homer's heirs.

EXAMPLE 37

Homer, Wilma, and Thelma acquire a tract of land with ownership listed as tenants in common, each party furnishing $20,000 of the $60,000 purchase price. When the property is worth $90,000, Homer dies. If Homer's undivided interest in the property is 33⅓%, the gross estate *and* probate estate each include $30,000. ▼

Unless the parties have provided otherwise, each tenant is deemed to own an interest equal to the portion of the original consideration he or she furnished. The parties in Example 37 could have provided that Homer would receive an undivided half interest in the property although he contributed only one-third of the purchase price. In that case, Wilma and Thelma have made a gift to Homer when the tenancy was created, and Homer's gross estate and probate estate each include $45,000.

For certain joint tenancies, the tax consequences are different. All of the property is included in the deceased co-owner's gross estate unless it can be proven that the surviving co-owners contributed to the cost of the property.[29] If a contribution can be shown, the amount to be *excluded* is calculated by the following formula:

$$\frac{\text{Surviving co-owner's contribution}}{\text{Total cost of the property}} \times \text{Fair market value of the property}$$

In computing a survivor's contribution, any funds received as a gift *from the deceased co-owner* and applied to the cost of the property cannot be counted. However, income or gain from gift assets can be counted.

If the co-owners receive the property as a gift *from another*, each co-owner is deemed to have contributed to the cost of his or her own interest.

The preceding rules can be illustrated as follows:

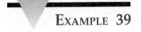
EXAMPLE 38

Keith and Steve (father and son) acquire a tract of land with ownership listed as joint tenancy with right of survivorship. Keith furnished $40,000 and Steve $20,000 of the $60,000 purchase price. Of the $20,000 provided by Steve, $10,000 had previously been received as a gift from Keith. When the property is worth $90,000, Keith dies. Because only $10,000 of Steve's contribution can be counted (the other $10,000 was received as a gift from Keith), Steve has furnished only one-sixth($10,000/$60,000) of the cost. Thus, Keith's gross estate must include five-sixths of $90,000, or $75,000. This presumes Steve can prove that he did in fact make the $10,000 contribution. In the absence of such proof, the full value of the property is included in Keith's gross estate. Keith's death makes Steve the immediate owner of the property by virtue of the right of survivorship. None of the property is part of Keith's probate estate. ▼

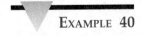
EXAMPLE 39

Francis transfers property to Irene and Morden as a gift listing ownership as joint tenancy with the right of survivorship. Upon Irene's death, one-half of the value of the property is included in the gross estate. Since the property was received as a gift and the donees are equal owners, each is considered to have furnished half of the consideration. ▼

To simplify the joint ownership rules for *married persons*, § 2040(b) provides for an automatic inclusion rule upon the death of the first joint-owner spouse to die. Regardless of the amount contributed by each spouse, one-half of the value of the property is included in the gross estate of the spouse who dies first. The special rule eliminates the need to trace the source of contributions and recognizes that any inclusion in the gross estate is neutralized by the marital deduction.

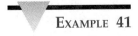
EXAMPLE 40

In 1986, Hank purchases real estate for $100,000 using his separate funds and lists title as "Hank and Louise, joint tenants with the right of survivorship." Hank predeceases Louise 10 years later when the property is worth $300,000. If Hank and Louise are husband and wife, Hank's gross estate includes $150,000 (½ of $300,000) as to the property. ▼

EXAMPLE 41

Assume the same facts as in Example 40, except that Louise (instead of Hank) dies first. Presuming the value at the date of death is $300,000, Louise's gross estate includes $150,000 as to the property. In this regard, it is of no consequence that Louise did not contribute to the cost of the real estate. ▼

---

[29] § 2040(a).

In both Examples 40 and 41, inclusion in the gross estate of the first spouse to die is neutralized by the unlimited marital deduction allowed for estate tax purposes (see the discussion of the marital deduction later in the chapter). Under the right of survivorship, the surviving joint tenant obtains full ownership of the property. The marital deduction generally is allowed for property passing from one spouse to another.

Whether or not a *gift* results when property is transferred into some form of joint ownership depends on the consideration furnished by each of the contributing parties for the ownership interest acquired.

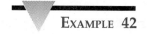

EXAMPLE 42

Brenda and Sarah purchase real estate as tenants in common, each furnishing $40,000 of the $80,000 cost. If each is an equal owner in the property, no gift has occurred. ▼

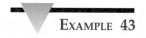

EXAMPLE 43

Assume the same facts as in Example 42, except that of the $80,000 purchase price, Brenda furnishes $60,000 and Sarah furnishes only $20,000. If they are equal owners in the property, Brenda has made a gift to Sarah of $20,000. ▼

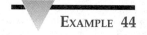

EXAMPLE 44

Martha purchases real estate for $240,000, the title to the property being listed as follows: "Martha, Sylvia, and Dan as joint tenants with the right of survivorship." If under state law the mother (Martha), the daughter (Sylvia), and the son (Dan) are deemed to be equal owners in the property, Martha is treated as having made gifts of $80,000 to Sylvia and $80,000 to Dan. ▼

Several important *exceptions* exist to the general rule that the creation of a joint ownership with disproportionate interests resulting from unequal consideration triggers gift treatment. First, if the transfer involves a joint bank account, there is no gift at the time of the contribution.[30] If a gift occurs, it is when the noncontributing party withdraws the funds provided by the other joint tenant. Second, the same rule applies to the purchase of U.S. savings bonds. Again, any gift tax consequences are postponed until the noncontributing party appropriates some or all of the proceeds for his or her individual use.

ETHICAL
CONSIDERATIONS

A Joint Bank Account and a Subsequent Marriage

Horace, a well-to-do widower, wants to marry Fran, his much younger secretary. Fran is agreeable to marriage but would like to achieve some degree of financial independence. Upon advice of his attorney, Horace uses $900,000 to establish a bank account listing himself and Fran as joint tenants. Horace and Fran are married, and shortly thereafter she withdraws the $900,000 and places the funds in a new account in her name only.

If the transfer from Horace to Fran took place before their marriage, it generates a Federal gift tax. The position of the IRS is that premarital settlements are gifts because they are not supported by adequate consideration. If the transfer from Horace to Fran took place after marriage, a gift tax is avoided due to the application of the marital deduction.

Has Horace successfully avoided the Federal gift tax?

---

[30] Reg. § 25.2511–1(h)(4).

Life Insurance (§ 2042). Under § 2042, the gross estate includes the proceeds of life insurance on the decedent's life if (1) they are receivable by the estate, (2) they are receivable by another for the benefit of the estate, or (3) the decedent possessed an incident of ownership in the policy.

Life insurance on the life of another owned by a decedent at the time of death is included in the gross estate under § 2033 (property in which the decedent had an interest) and not under § 2042. The amount includible is the replacement value of the policy.[31] Under these circumstances, inclusion of the face amount of the policy is inappropriate as the policy has not yet matured.

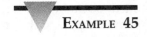

EXAMPLE 45

At the time of his death, Luigi owned a life insurance policy on the life of Benito, face amount of $100,000 and replacement value of $25,000, with Sofia as the designated beneficiary. Since the policy had not matured at Luigi's death, § 2042 would be inapplicable. However, § 2033 (property in which the decedent had an interest) compels the inclusion of $25,000 (the replacement value) in Luigi's gross estate. If Luigi and Sofia owned the policy as community property, only $12,500 is included in Luigi's gross estate. ▼

The term "life insurance" includes whole life policies, term insurance, group life insurance, travel and accident insurance, endowment contracts (before being paid up), and death benefits paid by fraternal societies operating under the lodge system.[32]

As just noted, proceeds of insurance on the life of the decedent receivable by the executor or administrator or payable to the decedent's estate are included in the gross estate. The estate need not be specifically named as the beneficiary. Assume, for example, the proceeds of the policy are receivable by an individual beneficiary and are subject to an obligation, legally binding upon the beneficiary, to pay taxes, debts, and other charges enforceable against the estate. The proceeds are included in the decedent's gross estate to the extent of the beneficiary's obligation. If the proceeds of an insurance policy made payable to a decedent's estate are community assets and, under state law, one-half belongs to the surviving spouse, only one-half of the proceeds will be considered as receivable by or for the benefit of the decedent's estate.

Proceeds of insurance on the life of the decedent not receivable by or for the benefit of the estate are includible if the decedent at death possessed any of the incidents of ownership in the policy. In this connection, the term "incidents of ownership" means more than the ownership of the policy in a technical legal sense. Generally speaking, the term refers to the right of the insured or his or her estate to the economic benefits of the policy. Thus, it also includes the power to change beneficiaries, revoke an assignment, pledge the policy for a loan, or surrender or cancel the policy.[33]

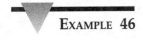

EXAMPLE 46

At the time of death, Broderick was the insured under a policy (face amount of $100,000) owned by Gregory with Demi as the designated beneficiary. Broderick took out the policy five years ago and immediately transferred it as a gift to Gregory. Under the assignment, Broderick transferred all rights in the policy except the right to change beneficiaries. Broderick died without having exercised this right, and the policy proceeds are paid to Demi. Under § 2042(2), Broderick's retention of an incident of ownership in the policy (i.e., the right to change beneficiaries) causes $100,000 to be included in his gross estate. ▼

---

[31] Reg. § 20.2031–8(a)(1).
[32] Reg. § 20.2042–1(a)(1). As to travel and accident insurance, see *Comm. v. Estate of Noel*, 65–1 USTC ¶12,311, 15 AFTR2d 1397, 85 S.Ct. 1238 (USSC, 1965).

[33] Reg. § 20.2042–1(c)(2).

Assuming that the deceased-insured holds the incidents of ownership in a policy, how much is included in the gross estate if the insurance policy is a community asset? Only one-half of the proceeds becomes part of the deceased spouse's gross estate.

In determining whether or not a policy is *community property* or what portion of it might be so classified, state law controls. The states appear to follow one of two general approaches. Under the inception of title approach, the classification depends on when the policy was originally purchased. If purchased before marriage, the policy is separate property regardless of how many premiums were paid after marriage with community funds. However, if the noninsured spouse is not the beneficiary of the policy, he or she may be entitled to reimbursement from the deceased-insured spouse's estate for half of the premiums paid with community funds. The inception of title approach is followed in at least three states: Louisiana, Texas, and New Mexico.

Some community property jurisdictions classify a policy using the tracing approach: The nature of the funds used to pay the premiums controls. Thus, a policy paid for 20 percent with separate funds and 80 percent with community funds is 20 percent separate property and 80 percent community property. The point in time when the policy was purchased makes no difference. Conceivably, a policy purchased after marriage with the premiums paid exclusively from separate funds is classified entirely as separate property. The tracing approach appears to be the rule in California and Washington.

Merely purchasing a life insurance contract and designating someone else as the beneficiary thereunder does not constitute a *gift.* As long as the purchaser still owns the policy, nothing has really passed to the beneficiary. Even on the death of the insured-owner, no gift takes place. The proceeds paid to the beneficiary constitute a testamentary and not a lifetime transfer. But consider the following possibility:

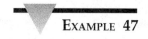

EXAMPLE 47

Kurt purchases an insurance policy on his own life and transfers the policy to Olga. Kurt retains no interest in the policy (such as the power to change beneficiaries). In these circumstances, Kurt has made a gift to Olga. Furthermore, if Kurt continues to pay the premiums on the transferred policy, each payment constitutes a separate gift. ▼

Under certain conditions, the death of the insured may constitute a gift to the beneficiary of part or all of the proceeds. This occurs when the owner of the policy is not the insured.

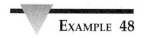

EXAMPLE 48

Randolph owns an insurance policy on the life of Frank, with Tracy as the designated beneficiary. Up until the time of Frank's death, Randolph retained the right to change the beneficiary of the policy. The proceeds paid to Tracy by the insurance company by reason of Frank's death constitute a gift from Randolph to Tracy.[34] ▼

TAXABLE ESTATE

7 LEARNING OBJECTIVE
Describe the components of the taxable estate.

After the gross estate has been determined, the next step is to determine the taxable estate. By virtue of § 2051, the **taxable estate** is the gross estate less the following: expenses, indebtedness, and taxes (§ 2053); losses (§ 2054); charitable transfers (§§ 2055 and 2522); and the marital deduction (§§ 2056 and 2056A). As previously noted, the charitable and marital deductions also have gift tax ramifications.

---

[34] *Goodman v. Comm.,* 46–1 USTC ¶10,275, 34 AFTR 1534, 156 F.2d 218 (CA–2, 1946).

Expenses, Indebtedness, and Taxes (§ 2053). A deduction is allowed for funeral expenses; expenses incurred in administering property; claims against the estate; and unpaid mortgages and other charges against property, whose value is included in the gross estate (without reduction for the mortgage or other indebtedness).

Expenses incurred in administering community property are deductible only in proportion to the deceased spouse's interest in the community.[35]

Administration expenses include commissions of the executor or administrator, attorney's fees of the estate, accountant's fees, court costs, and certain selling expenses for disposition of estate property.

Claims against the estate include property taxes accrued before the decedent's death, unpaid income taxes on income received by the decedent before he or she died, and unpaid gift taxes on gifts made by the decedent before death.

Amounts that may be deducted as claims against the estate are only for enforceable personal obligations of the decedent at the time of death. Deductions for claims founded on promises or agreements are limited to the extent that the liabilities were contracted in good faith and for adequate and full consideration. However, a pledge or subscription in favor of a public, charitable, religious, or educational organization is deductible to the extent that it would have constituted an allowable deduction had it been a bequest.[36]

ETHICAL CONSIDERATIONS

Claims against the Estate

Ten years before her death, Irene (a wealthy widow) started the following annual ritual:

- Each year she makes a gift of $10,000 to each of her five married children and their spouses (for a total of $100,000).
- Shortly after each gift, each donee loans the money back to Irene.
- In connection with the loan, Irene signs a note (interest provided for) payable on demand.

After Irene's death, each of her children and their spouses file a claim against her estate for $100,000 plus accrued interest. The executor of Irene's estate pays off the notes and accrued interest. The amount paid out is deducted on Form 706 (estate tax return) as a § 2053 item.

Is the estate tax deduction proper?

Deductible funeral expenses include the cost of interment, the burial plot or vault, a gravestone, perpetual care of the grave site, and the transportation expense of the person bringing the body to the place of burial. If the decedent had, before death, acquired cemetery lots for himself or herself and family, no deduction is allowed, but the lots are not included in the decedent's gross estate under § 2033 (property in which the decedent had an interest).

---

[35] *U.S. v. Stapf,* 63–2 USTC ¶12,192, 12 AFTR2d 6326, 84 S.Ct. 248 (USSC, 1963).

[36] § 2053(c)(1)(A) and Reg. § 20.2053–5.

Losses (§ 2054). Section 2054 permits an estate tax deduction for losses from casualty or theft incurred during the period when the estate is being settled. As is true with casualty or theft losses for income tax purposes, any anticipated insurance recovery must be taken into account in arriving at the amount of the deductible loss. Unlike the income tax, however, the deduction is not limited by a floor ($100) or a percentage amount (the excess of 10 percent of adjusted gross income). If the casualty occurs to property after it has been distributed to an heir, the loss belongs to the heir and not to the estate. If the casualty occurs before the decedent's death, it should be claimed on the appropriate Form 1040. The fair market value of the property (if any) on the date of death plus any insurance recovery is included in the gross estate.

As is true of certain administration expenses, a casualty or theft loss of estate property can be claimed as an income tax deduction on the fiduciary return of the estate (Form 1041). But a double deduction prohibition applies, and claiming the income tax deduction requires a waiver of the estate tax deduction.[37]

Transfers to Charity (§§ 2055 and 2522). A deduction is allowed for the value of property in the decedent's gross estate that is transferred by the decedent through testamentary disposition to (or for the use of) any of the following:

- The United States or any of its political subdivisions.
- Any corporation or association organized and operated exclusively for religious, charitable, scientific, literary, or educational purposes.
- Various veterans' organizations.

The organizations just described are identical to those that qualify for the Federal gift tax deduction under § 2522. With the following exceptions, they are also the same organizations that qualify a donee for an income tax deduction under § 170:

- Certain nonprofit cemetery associations qualify for income tax but not estate and gift tax purposes.
- Foreign charities may qualify under the estate and gift tax but not under the income tax.

No deduction is allowed unless the charitable bequest is specified by a provision in the decedent's will or the transfer was made before death and the property is subsequently included in the gross estate. Generally speaking, a deduction does not materialize when an individual dies intestate (without a will). The amount of the bequest to charity must be mandatory and cannot be left to someone else's discretion. It is, however, permissible to allow another person, such as the executor of the estate, to choose which charity will receive the specified donation. Likewise, a bequest may be expressed as an alternative and still be effective if the noncharitable beneficiary disclaims (refuses) the intervening interest before the due date for the filing of the estate tax return (nine months after the decedent's death plus any extensions of time granted for filing).

Marital Deduction (§§ 2056, 2056A, and 2523). The **marital deduction** originated with the Revenue Act of 1948 as part of the same legislation that permitted married persons to secure the income-splitting advantages of filing joint income tax returns. The purpose of these statutory changes was to eliminate the major tax variations that existed between taxpayers residing in community

---

[37] § 642(g).

property and common law states. The marital deduction was designed to provide equity in the estate and gift tax areas.

In a community property state, for example, no marital deduction generally was allowed since the surviving spouse already owned one-half of the community and that portion was not included in the deceased spouse's gross estate. In a common law state, however, most if not all of the assets often belonged to the breadwinner of the family. When that spouse died first, all of these assets were included in the gross estate. Recall that a dower or curtesy interest (regarding a surviving spouse's right to some of the deceased spouse's property) does not reduce the gross estate. To equalize the situation, therefore, a marital deduction, usually equal to one-half of all separate assets, was allowed upon the death of the first spouse.

Ultimately, Congress decided to dispense with these historical justifications and recognize husband and wife as a single economic unit. Consistent with the approach taken under the income tax, spouses are considered as one for transfer tax purposes. By making the marital deduction unlimited in amount, neither the gift tax nor the estate tax is imposed on outright interspousal transfers of property. The unlimited marital deduction even includes one spouse's share of the community property transferred to the other spouse.

Under § 2056, the marital deduction is allowed only for property that is included in the deceased spouse's gross estate and that passes or has passed to the surviving spouse. In determining whether the parties are legally married, look to state law (see Example 1 earlier). Property that passes from the decedent to the surviving spouse includes any interest received as (1) the decedent's heir or donee; (2) the decedent's surviving tenant by the entirety or joint tenant; (3) the appointee under the decedent's exercise (or lapse or release) of a general power of appointment; or (4) the beneficiary of insurance on the life of the decedent.

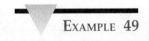

EXAMPLE 49

At the time of his death in the current year, Matthew owned an insurance policy on his own life (face amount of $100,000) with Minerva (his wife) as the designated beneficiary. Matthew and Minerva also owned real estate (worth $250,000) as tenants by the entirety (Matthew had furnished all of the purchase price). As to these transfers, $225,000 ($100,000 + $125,000) is included in Matthew's gross estate, and this amount represents the property that passes to Minerva for purposes of the marital deduction.[38] ▼

Disclaimers can affect the amount passing to the surviving spouse. If, for example, the surviving spouse is the remainderperson under the will of the deceased spouse, a disclaimer by another heir increases the amount passing to the surviving spouse. This, in turn, will increase the amount of the marital deduction allowed to the estate of the deceased spouse.

A problem arises when a property interest passing to the surviving spouse is subject to a mortgage or other encumbrance. In this case, only the net value of the interest after reduction by the amount of the mortgage or other encumbrance qualifies for the marital deduction. To allow otherwise results in a double deduction since a decedent's liabilities are separately deductible under § 2053.

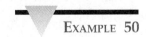

EXAMPLE 50

In his will, Oscar leaves real estate (fair market value of $200,000) to his wife. If the real estate is subject to a mortgage of $40,000 (upon which Oscar was personally liable), the

---

[38] Inclusion in the gross estate falls under § 2042 (proceeds of life insurance) and § 2040 (joint interests). Although Matthew provided the full purchase price for the real estate, § 2040(b) requires inclusion of only half of the value of the property when one spouse predeceases the other.

marital deduction is limited to $160,000 ($200,000 – $40,000). The $40,000 mortgage is deductible under § 2053 as an obligation of the decedent (Oscar). ▼

However, if the executor is required under the terms of the decedent's will or under local law to discharge the mortgage out of other assets of the estate or to reimburse the surviving spouse, the payment or reimbursement is an additional interest passing to the surviving spouse.

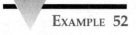

EXAMPLE 51   Assume the same facts as in Example 50, except that Oscar's will directs that the real estate is to pass to his wife free of any liabilities. Accordingly, Oscar's executor pays off the mortgage by using other estate assets and distributes the real estate to Oscar's wife. The marital deduction now becomes $200,000. ▼

Federal estate taxes or other death taxes paid out of the surviving spouse's share of the gross estate are not included in the value of property passing to the surviving spouse. Therefore, it is usually preferable for the deceased spouse's will to provide that death taxes be paid out of the portion of the estate that does not qualify for the marital deduction.

Certain interests in property passing from the deceased spouse to the surviving spouse are referred to as **terminable interests.** Such an interest will terminate or fail after the passage of time, upon the happening of some contingency, or upon the failure of some event to occur. Examples are life estates, annuities, estates for terms of years, and patents. A terminable interest will not qualify for the marital deduction if another interest in the same property passed from the deceased spouse to some other person. By reason of the passing, that other person or his or her heirs may enjoy part of the property after the termination of the surviving spouse's interest.[39]

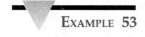

EXAMPLE 52   Vicky's will places her property in trust with a life estate to her husband, Brett, remainder to Andrew or his heirs. The interest passing from Vicky to Brett does not qualify for the marital deduction. Brett's interest will terminate on his death, and Andrew or his heirs will then possess or enjoy the property. ▼

EXAMPLE 53   Assume the same facts as in Example 52, except that Vicky created the trust during her life. No marital deduction is available for gift tax purposes for the same reason as in Example 52.[40] ▼

The justification for the terminable interest rule can be illustrated by examining the possible results of Examples 52 and 53 more closely. Without the rule, Vicky could have passed property to Brett at no cost because of the marital deduction. Yet, on Brett's death, none of the property would have been included in his gross estate. Section 2036 (transfers with a retained life estate) would not apply to Brett since he was not the original transferor of the property. The marital deduction should not be available in situations where the surviving spouse can enjoy the property and still pass it to another without tax consequences. The marital deduction is intended to merely postpone the transfer tax on the death of the first spouse and to shift any such tax to the surviving spouse.

---

[39] §§ 2056(b)(1) and 2523(b)(1).
[40] Both Examples 52 and 53 contain the potential for a qualified terminable interest property (QTIP) election discussed later in this section.

Consistent with the objective of the terminable interest rule, an alternative means for obtaining the marital deduction is available. Under this provision, the marital deduction is allowed for transfers of **qualified terminable interest property** (commonly referred to as **QTIP**). This is defined as property that passes from one spouse to another by gift or at death and for which the transferee-spouse has a qualifying income interest for life.

For a donee or a surviving spouse, a qualifying income interest for life exists under the following conditions:

- The person is entitled for life to all of the income from the property (or a specific portion of it), payable at annual or more frequent intervals.
- No person (including the spouse) has a power to appoint any part of the property to any person other than the surviving spouse during his or her life.[41]

If these conditions are met, an election can be made to claim a marital deduction as to the QTIP. For estate tax purposes, the executor of the estate makes the election on Form 706 (estate tax return). For gift tax purposes, the donor spouse makes the election on Form 709 (gift tax return). The election is irrevocable.

If the election is made, a transfer tax is imposed upon the QTIP when the transferee-spouse disposes of it by gift or upon death. If the disposition occurs during life, the gift tax applies, measured by the fair market value of the property as of that time.[42] If no lifetime disposition takes place, the fair market value of the property on the date of death (or alternate valuation date if applicable) is included in the gross estate of the transferee-spouse.[43]

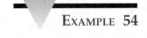

EXAMPLE 54

In 1996, Clyde dies and provides in his will that certain assets (fair market value of $400,000) are to be transferred to a trust under which Gertrude (Clyde's wife) is granted a life estate with the remainder passing to their children upon Gertrude's death. Presuming all of the preceding requirements are satisfied and Clyde's executor so elects, his estate receives a marital deduction of $400,000. ▼

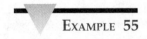

EXAMPLE 55

Assume the same facts as in Example 54, with the further stipulation that Gertrude dies in 1999 when the trust assets are worth $900,000. This amount is included in her gross estate. ▼

Because the estate tax is imposed on assets not physically included in the probate estate, the law allows the liability for those assets to be shifted to the heirs. The amount shifted is determined by comparing the estate tax liability both with and without the inclusion of the QTIP. This right of recovery can be canceled by a provision in the deceased spouse's will.[44]

COMPUTING THE FEDERAL ESTATE TAX

8 LEARNING OBJECTIVE
Determine the Federal estate tax liability.

Once the taxable estate has been determined, post-1976 taxable gifts are added to arrive at the tax base. Note that pre-1977 taxable gifts do not enter into the computation of the tax base.

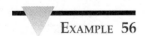

EXAMPLE 56

Joyce dies in 1996, leaving a taxable estate of $800,000. During her life, Joyce made taxable gifts as follows: $50,000 in 1975 and $100,000 in 1982. For estate tax purposes, the Federal

---

[41] §§ 2523(f) and 2056(b)(7).
[42] § 2519.

[43] § 2044.
[44] § 2207A(a).

estate tax base becomes $900,000, determined as follows: $800,000 taxable estate + $100,000 taxable gift made in 1982. ▼

Next the tentative tax on the tax base is computed using the unified transfer tax rate schedule contained in § 2001(c). Using the facts in Example 56, the tentative tax on $900,000 is $306,800 [$248,300 + (39% × $150,000)]—see Appendix A. (See the discussion below for the phase-out of the unified tax credit and the graduated tax rates for certain large estates.)

All available estate tax credits are subtracted from the tentative estate tax to arrive at the estate tax (if any) that is due.

ESTATE TAX CREDITS

Unified Tax Credit (§ 2010).   Recall from previous discussion of this credit that the amount of the credit allowed depends upon the year of the transfer. Returning to Example 56, the credit allowed on the gift in 1982 was $62,800. Since the exemption equivalent of this amount is $225,000 (refer to Table 26–1), no gift tax was due on the transfer. On Joyce's death in 1996, however, the unified tax credit is $192,800, which is less than the tentative tax of $306,800 (refer to the discussion following Example 56). Disregarding the effect of any other estate tax credits, Joyce's estate owes a tax of $114,000 [$306,800 (tentative tax on a tax base of $900,000) – $192,800 (unified tax credit for 1996)].

An adjustment to the unified tax credit is necessary if any portion of the specific exemption was utilized on gifts made after September 8, 1976, and before January 1, 1977. In this regard, refer to Example 5.

Under current law, the benefit of the unified tax credit and the graduated unified tax rates is phased out for taxable transfers exceeding a certain amount. The gift and estate tax liability for taxable transfers in excess of $10 million is increased by 5 percent of the excess until the benefit of the credit and graduated brackets is recaptured.

Credit for State Death Taxes (§ 2011).   The Code allows a limited credit for the amount of any death tax actually paid to any state (or to the District of Columbia) attributable to any property included in the gross estate. Like the credit for foreign death taxes paid, this provision mitigates the harshness of subjecting the same property to multiple death taxes.

The credit allowed is limited to the lesser of the amount of tax actually paid or the amount provided for in a table contained in § 2011(b). (See Appendix A.) The table amount is based on the *adjusted taxable estate,* which for this purpose is the taxable estate less $60,000. No credit is allowed if the adjusted taxable estate is $40,000 or less.

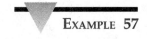

EXAMPLE 57

Butch's taxable estate is $98,000, and the state of appropriate jurisdiction imposes a death tax of $1,500 on this amount. Since the adjusted taxable estate is $38,000 ($98,000 – $60,000), none of the $1,500 paid qualifies for the state death tax credit. ▼

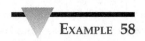

EXAMPLE 58

Butch's taxable estate is $200,000, and the state of appropriate jurisdiction imposes a death tax of $3,000 on this amount. Because the adjusted taxable estate is $140,000 ($200,000 – $60,000), the table amount limits the death tax credit to $1,200. (See Appendix A.) ▼

As Examples 57 and 58 illustrate, the credit allowed by § 2011 may be less than the amount of state death taxes paid. The reverse is possible but usually is not the case. Most states make sure that the minimum tax payable to the jurisdiction is at least equal to the credit allowed by the table. Sometimes this result is accomplished by a soak-up or sponge tax superimposed on the regular inheritance tax. Thus, if the regular inheritance tax yielded $2,500, but the maximum credit allowed by the table is $3,200, a soak-up tax would impose an additional $700 in state death taxes. In other states, the state death tax liability depends entirely upon the amount allowed for Federal estate tax purposes under the table. In the previous illustration, the state death tax would be an automatic $1,200.

Credit for Tax on Prior Transfers (§ 2013). Suppose Floyd owns some property that he passes at death to Sarah. Shortly thereafter, Sarah dies and passes the property to Juan. Assuming both estates are subject to the Federal estate tax, the successive deaths result in a multiple effect. To mitigate the possible multiple taxation that might result, § 2013 provides relief in the form of a credit for a death tax on prior transfers. In the preceding hypothetical case, Sarah's estate may be able to claim as an estate tax credit some of the taxes paid by Floyd's estate.

The credit is limited to the lesser of the following:

1. The amount of the Federal estate tax attributable to the transferred property in the transferor's estate.
2. The amount of the Federal estate tax attributable to the transferred property in the decedent's estate.

To apply the limitations, certain adjustments must be made that are not covered in this text.[45] However, it is not necessary for the transferred property to be identified in the present decedent's estate or for it to be in existence at the time of the present decedent's death. It is sufficient that the transfer of property was subjected to the Federal estate tax in the estate of the transferor and that the transferor died within the prescribed period of time.

If the transferor dies within two years after or before the present decedent's death, the credit is allowed in full (subject to the preceding limitations). If the transferor died more than two years before the decedent, the credit is a certain percentage: 80 percent if the transferor died within the third or fourth year preceding the decedent's death, 60 percent if within the fifth or sixth year, 40 percent if within the seventh or eighth year, and 20 percent if within the ninth or tenth year.

EXAMPLE 59   Under Floyd's will, Sarah inherits property. One year later Sarah dies. Assume the estate tax attributable to the inclusion of the property in Floyd's gross estate was $15,000 and that attributable to the inclusion of the property in Sarah's gross estate is $12,000. Under these circumstances, Sarah's estate claims a credit against the estate tax of $12,000 (refer to limitation 2). ▼

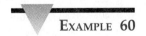

EXAMPLE 60   Assume the same facts as in Example 59, except that Sarah dies three years after Floyd. The applicable credit is now 80% of $12,000, or $9,600. ▼

Credit for Foreign Death Taxes (§ 2014). A credit is allowed against the estate tax for any estate, inheritance, legacy, or succession tax actually paid to a foreign country. For purposes of this provision, the term "foreign country" means

---

[45]See the instructions to Form 706 and Reg. §§ 20.2013–2 and –3.

not only states in the international sense but also possessions or political subdivisions of foreign states and possessions of the United States.

PROCEDURAL MATTERS

A Federal estate tax return, if required, is due nine months after the date of the decedent's death.[46] The time limit applies to all estates regardless of the nationality or residence of the decedent. Frequently, an executor will request and obtain from the IRS an extension of time for filing Form 706 (estate tax return).[47]

The filing requirements parallel the exemption equivalent amounts of the unified tax credit available for each year (refer to Table 26–1). The filing requirements may be lower when the decedent has made taxable gifts after 1976 or has utilized any of the $30,000 specific gift tax exemption after September 8, 1976.

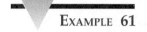

EXAMPLE 61

Carlos dies in 1996, leaving a gross estate of $595,000. If Carlos did not make any post-1976 taxable gifts or use the specific gift tax exemption after September 8, 1976, his estate need not file Form 706. ▼

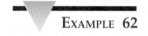

EXAMPLE 62

Assume the same facts as in Example 61, except that Carlos made a taxable gift of $20,000 in 1980. Since the filing requirement now becomes $580,000 ($600,000 regular filing requirement for 1996 – $20,000 post-1976 taxable gift), Carlos's estate must file Form 706. ▼

THE GENERATION-SKIPPING TRANSFER TAX

In order to prevent partial avoidance of Federal gift and estate taxes on large transfers, the tax law imposes an additional generation-skipping transfer tax.

9 LEARNING OBJECTIVE
Appreciate the role of the generation-skipping transfer tax.

THE PROBLEM

Previously, it was possible to bypass a generation of transfer taxes by structuring the transaction carefully.

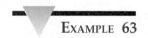

EXAMPLE 63

Under his will, Edward creates a trust, life estate to Stephen (Edward's son) and remainder to Ava (Edward's granddaughter) upon Stephen's death. Edward is subject to the Federal estate tax, but no tax results on Stephen's death. Stephen held a life estate, but § 2036 does not apply because he was not the grantor of the trust. Nor does § 2033 (property owned by the decedent) come into play because Stephen's interest disappeared upon his death. The ultimate result is that the property in trust skips a generation of transfer taxes. ▼

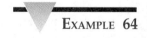

EXAMPLE 64

Amy gives assets to Eric (her grandson). Called a direct skip, the gift would circumvent any transfer taxes that would have resulted had the assets been channeled through Eric's parents. ▼

THE SOLUTION

The generation-skipping transfer tax (GSTT) is imposed when a younger generation is bypassed in favor of a later generation.[48] The GSTT applies to lifetime transfers by gift and to transfers by death. The tax rate imposed is the highest rate

---

[46] § 6075(a).
[47] § 6081.

[48] The generation-skipping transfer tax provisions are contained in §§ 2601–2663.

under the gift and estate tax schedule, or 55 percent. Consequently, the GSTT does not permit the use of the graduated rate structure.

The application of the GSTT depends upon the type of arrangement involved. In Example 63, the GSTT would be imposed upon the death of Stephen (the life tenant). The tax, however, is levied against the trust. In effect, it reduces the amount that is distributed to Ava (the remainderperson).

In Example 64, the GSTT is imposed upon Amy when the gift is made to Eric. In this situation, not only will Amy be subject to the GSTT, but the amount of the tax represents an additional gift to Eric.[49] Thus, if a gift is a direct skip (such as Example 64), the total transfer tax (the GSTT plus the gift tax) may exceed what the donee receives.

Though the GSTT may appear to yield a confiscatory result, every grantor is entitled to a $1 million exemption. The exemption can be applied to whichever transfers the grantor (or personal representative of the grantor) chooses. Any appreciation attributable to the exempted portion of the transfer is not subject to the GSTT.

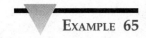

EXAMPLE 65

Assume the same facts as in Example 63, except that the trust created by Edward contained assets valued at $1 million. Ten years later when Stephen dies, the trust is now worth $3 million. If the exemption of $1 million is used upon the creation of the trust, no GSTT results upon Stephen's death. ▼

TAX PLANNING CONSIDERATIONS

THE FEDERAL GIFT TAX

For gifts that generate a tax, consideration must be given to the time value to the donor of the gift taxes paid. Since the donor loses the use of these funds, the expected interval between a gift (the imposition of the gift tax) and death (the imposition of the death tax) may make the gift less attractive from an economic standpoint. On the plus side, however, are the estate tax savings that result from any gift tax paid. Since these funds are no longer in the gross estate of the donor (except for certain gifts within three years of death), the estate tax thereon is avoided.

Gifts possess distinct advantages. First, and often most important, income from the property is generally shifted to the donee. If the donee is in a lower bracket than the donor, the family unit will save on income taxes. Second, the proper spacing of gifts can further cut down the Federal gift tax by maximizing the number of annual exclusions available. Third, all states impose some type of death tax, but only a minority impose a gift tax. Thus, a gift may completely avoid a state transfer tax.

In minimizing gift tax liability in lifetime giving, the optimum use of the annual exclusion can have significant results. Important in this regard are the following observations:

- Because the annual exclusion is available every year, space the gifts over as many years as possible. To carry out this objective, start the program of lifetime giving as soon as is feasible. As an illustration, a donor could give as much as $100,000 to a donee if equally spaced over a 10-year period without using any of the unified tax credit and incurring any gift tax.
- To the extent consistent with the wishes of the donor, maximize the number of donees. For example, a donor could give $500,000 to five donees over a 10-year period ($100,000 apiece) without using any of the unified tax credit and incurring any gift tax.

[49] § 2515.

CONCEPT SUMMARY 26–2

Federal Estate Tax Provisions

1. The Federal gift and estate taxes are both excise taxes on the transfer of wealth.
2. The starting point for applying the Federal estate tax is to determine which assets are subject to tax. Such assets constitute a decedent's gross estate.
3. The gross estate generally will not include any gifts made by the decedent within three years of death. It does include any gift tax paid on these transfers.
4. Based on the premise that one should not continue to enjoy or control property and not have it subject to the estate tax, certain incomplete transfers are included in the gross estate.
5. Upon the death of a joint tenant, the full value of the property is included in the gross estate unless the survivor(s) made a contribution toward the cost of the property. Spouses are subject to a special rule that calls for automatic inclusion of half of the value of the property in the gross estate of the first tenant to die. The creation of joint ownership is subject to the gift tax when a tenant receives a lesser interest in the property than is warranted by the consideration furnished.
6. If the decedent is the insured, life insurance proceeds are included in the gross estate if either of two conditions is satisfied. First, the proceeds are paid to the estate or for the benefit of the estate. Second, the decedent possessed incidents of ownership (e.g., the right to change beneficiaries) over the policy.
7. In moving from the gross estate to the taxable estate, certain deductions are allowed. Under § 2053, deductions are permitted for various administration expenses (e.g., executor's commissions, funeral costs), debts of the decedent, and certain unpaid taxes. Casualty and theft losses incurred during the administration of an estate can be deducted in arriving at the taxable estate.
8. Charitable transfers are deductible if the designated organization holds qualified status with the IRS at the time of the gift or upon death.
9. Transfers to a spouse qualify for the gift or estate tax marital deduction. Except as noted in (10), such transfers are subject to the terminable interest limitation.
10. The terminable interest limitation will not apply if the QTIP election is made. In the case of a lifetime transfer, the donor spouse makes the QTIP election. In the case of a testamentary transfer, the executor of the estate of the deceased spouse has the election responsibility.
11. The tax base for determining the estate tax is the taxable estate plus all post-1976 taxable gifts. All available credits are subtracted from the tax.
12. Of prime importance in the tax credit area is the unified tax credit. Except for large taxable transfers, the unified tax credit is $192,800 (exemption equivalent of $600,000).
13. Other Federal estate tax credits include credits for state death taxes, tax on prior transfers, and foreign death taxes.
14. If due, a Federal estate tax return (Form 706) must be filed within nine months of the date of the decedent's death.

- For the married donor, make use of the election to split gifts. As an example, a married couple can give $1 million to five donees over a 10-year period ($20,000 per donee each year) without using any of their unified tax credits and incurring any gift tax.
- Watch out for gifts of future interests. As noted earlier in the chapter, the annual exclusion is available only for gifts of a present interest.

THE FEDERAL ESTATE TAX

Controlling the Amount of the Gross Estate. Presuming an estate tax problem is anticipated, the starting point for planning purposes is to reduce the size of the potential gross estate. Aside from initiating a program of lifetime giving, several other possibilities exist.

Proper Handling of Estate Tax Deductions.   Estate taxes can be saved either by reducing the size of the gross estate or by increasing the total allowable deductions. Thus, the lower the taxable estate, the less the amount of estate tax generated. Planning in the deduction area generally involves the following considerations:

- Making proper use of the marital deduction.
- Working effectively with the charitable deduction.
- Properly handling other deductions and losses allowed under §§ 2053 and 2054.

Approaches to the Marital Deduction. When planning for the estate tax marital deduction, both tax and nontax factors have to be taken into account. In the tax area, planning is guided by two major goals: the *equalization* and *deferral* approaches.

- Attempt to equalize the estates of both spouses. Clearly, for example, the estate tax on $2 million is more than double the estate tax on $1 million [compare $780,800 with $691,600 ($345,800 × 2)].
- Try to postpone estate taxation as long as possible. On a $1 million amount, for example, what is the time value of $345,800 in estate taxes deferred for a period of, say, 10 years?

Barring certain circumstances, the deferral approach generally is preferable. By maximizing the marital deduction on the death of the first spouse to die, not only are taxes saved, but the surviving spouse is enabled to trim his or her future estate by entering into a program of lifetime giving. By making optimum use of the annual exclusion, considerable amounts can be shifted without incurring *any* transfer tax.

Tax planning must remain flexible and be tailored to the individual circumstances of the parties involved. Before the equalization approach is cast aside, therefore, consider the following variables:

- Both spouses are of advanced age and/or in poor health, and neither is expected to survive the other for a prolonged period of time.
- The spouse who is expected to survive has considerable assets of his or her own. To illustrate, a spouse who passes a $250,000 estate to a survivor who already has assets of $1 million is trading a 32 percent bracket for a later 43 percent bracket.
- Because of appreciation, property worth $250,000 when it passes to the surviving spouse today may be worth $1 million five years later when the survivor dies.

The Marital Deduction—Sophistication of the Deferral Approach. When saving estate taxes for the family unit is the sole consideration, the equalization and deferral approaches can be combined with maximum effect.

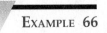
EXAMPLE 66

At the time of his death in 1996, Vito had never made any taxable gifts. Under Vito's will, his *disposable estate* of $1,100,000 passes to his wife, Zina.[50] ▼

---

[50] For this purpose, the *disposable estate* includes the gross estate less all deductions (e.g., debts, administration and funeral expenses) except the marital deduction. The term is not in the Code but is useful in evaluating tax options.

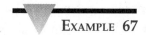

EXAMPLE 67

Assume the same facts as in Example 66, except that Vito's will provides as follows: $600,000 to the children and the remainder ($500,000) to Zina. ▼

From a tax standpoint, which is the better plan? Although no estate tax results from either arrangement, Example 66 represents an overfunding in terms of the marital deduction. Why place an additional $600,000 in Zina's potential estate when it can pass free of tax to the children through the application of the $192,800 unified tax credit available for 1996? (The exemption equivalent of $192,800 is $600,000.) The exemption equivalent is known as the *bypass amount*. The arrangement in Example 67 is preferred, as it avoids unnecessary concentration of wealth in Zina's estate.

On occasion, the disclaimer procedure can be used to maximize the deferral approach.

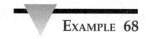

EXAMPLE 68

At the time of his death in 1996, Pete had never made any taxable gifts. Under Pete's will, his disposable estate of $1,500,000 passes as follows: $700,000 to Jim (Pete's adult son) and the remainder ($800,000) to Clare (Pete's surviving spouse). Shortly after Pete's death, Jim issues a disclaimer as to $100,000 of his $700,000 bequest. This amount, therefore, passes to Clare as the remainderperson under Pete's will. ▼

Because the unified tax credit for 1996 is $192,800 (with an exemption equivalent of $600,000), Jim's disclaimer avoids an estate tax on $100,000. The end result is an increase of $100,000 in the marital deduction and the elimination of *any* estate tax upon Pete's death.

Effectively Working with the Charitable Deduction.   As a general guide to obtain overall tax savings, lifetime charitable transfers are preferred over testamentary dispositions. For example, an individual who gave $10,000 to a qualified charity during his or her life would secure an income tax deduction, avoid any gift tax, and reduce the gross estate by the amount of the gift. By way of contrast, if the $10,000 had been willed to charity, no income tax deduction would be available, and the amount of the gift would be includible in the decedent's gross estate (though later deducted for estate tax purposes). In short, the lifetime transfer provides a double tax benefit (income tax deduction plus reduced estate taxes) at no gift tax cost. The testamentary transfer merely neutralizes the effect of the inclusion of the property in the gross estate (inclusion under § 2033 and then deduction under § 2055).

On occasion, a charitable bequest depends on the issuance of a disclaimer by a noncharitable heir. Such a situation frequently arises with special types of property or collections, which the decedent may feel a noncharitable heir should have a choice of receiving.

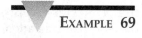

EXAMPLE 69

Megan specified in her will that her valuable art collection is to pass to her son or, if the son refuses, to a designated and qualified art museum. At the time the will was drawn, Megan knew that her son was not interested in owning the collection. If, after Megan's death, the son issues a timely disclaimer, the collection will pass to the designated museum, and Megan's estate is allowed a charitable deduction for its death tax value. ▼

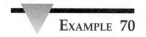

EXAMPLE 70

Dick's will specifies that one-half of his disposable estate is to pass to his wife, and the remainder of his property to a designated and qualified charitable organization. If the wife issues a timely disclaimer after Dick's death, all of the property passes to the charity and qualifies for the § 2055 charitable deduction. ▼

Did the son in Example 69 act wisely if he issued the disclaimer in favor of the museum? Although the disclaimer will provide Megan's estate with a deduction for the value of the art collection, consider the income tax deduction alternative. If the son accepts the bequest, he can still dispose of the collection (and fulfill his mother's philanthropic objectives) through a lifetime donation to the museum. At the same time, he obtains an income tax deduction under § 170. Whether this will save taxes for the family unit depends on a comparison of Megan's estate tax bracket with the estimated income tax bracket of the son. If the value of the collection runs afoul of the percentage limitations of § 170(b)(1), the donations can be spread over more than one year. If this is done, and to protect against the contingency of the son's dying before the entire collection is donated, the son can neutralize any potential death tax consequences by providing in his will for the undonated balance to pass to the museum.

The use of a disclaimer in Example 70 would be sheer folly. It would not reduce Dick's estate tax; it would merely substitute a charitable deduction for the marital deduction. Whether the wife issues a disclaimer or not, no estate taxes will be due. The wife should accept her bequest and, if she is so inclined, make lifetime gifts of it to a qualified charity. In so doing, she generates an income tax deduction for herself.

Proper Handling of Other Deductions and Losses under §§ 2053 and 2054. Many § 2053 and § 2054 deductions and losses may be claimed either as estate tax deductions or as income tax deductions of the estate on the fiduciary return (Form 1041), but a choice must be made.[51] The deduction for income tax purposes is not allowed unless the estate tax deduction is waived. It is possible for these deductions to be apportioned between the two returns.

KEY TERMS

Alternate valuation date, 26–7

Annual exclusion, 26–13

Disclaimer, 26–12

Exemption equivalent, 26–7

Future interest, 26–13

Gross estate, 26–16

Inheritance tax, 26–3

Joint tenants, 26–9

Marital deduction, 26–28

Probate estate, 26–17

Qualified terminable interest property (QTIP), 26–31

Taxable estate, 26–26

Taxable gift, 26–5

Tenants by the entirety, 26–9

Tenants in common, 26–9

Terminable interests, 26–30

Unified tax credit, 26–7

Unified transfer tax, 26–3

---

[51] § 642(g) and Reg. § 20.2053-1(d).

PROBLEM MATERIALS

DISCUSSION QUESTIONS

1. Why can the unified transfer tax be categorized as an excise tax? In this regard, how does it differ from an income tax?

2. Do Federal transfer taxes carry negative economic implications? Explain.

3. What are the major differences between the Federal estate tax and the typical inheritance tax levied by some states?

4. What was the intended purpose of the Federal gift tax?

5. Omar is a wealthy citizen and resident of Yemen. His family physician has recommended that Omar go to the Mayo Clinic in Minnesota for an operation to remove a malignant growth. Omar is hesitant to do so because he fears the imposition of the U.S. Federal estate tax if the operation is unsuccessful. Does place of death control the application of the Federal estate tax? Explain.

6. Wanda, a wealthy widow, wants to avoid the Federal estate tax. To do so, she takes the following steps: renounces her U.S. citizenship, applies for and becomes a citizen of Belize, and becomes a resident of Costa Rica. Comment on why or why not Wanda will achieve her objective.

7. Pearl comes to you regarding the making of gifts to family members in the current year. When you ask her about prior gifts, she responds, "What difference does it make what I did in the past?" Please clarify matters for Pearl.

8. In determining the *tax base* for computing the *tentative estate tax*, all prior taxable gifts must be added to the taxable estate. Do you agree or disagree? Why?

9. At a social function, a guest tells you, "I have made a lot of gifts, but I still have my exemption equivalent." Explain this remark.

10. What is the justification for the alternate valuation date election?

11. What conditions must be satisfied before the alternate valuation date can be used?

12. With regard to undivided ownership of property, what is the right of survivorship? When does it exist?

13. Carla purchases a U.S. savings bond and registers ownership as follows: "Carla, payable to George on Carla's death." Four years later, Carla dies and George redeems the bond. When has a gift taken place? Explain.

14. In connection with gift loans, comment on the following points:
    a. Since any interest element recognized by the lender as income can be deducted by the borrower, the income tax effect is neutralized for the family unit.
    b. The borrower's net investment income for the year is less than $1,000.
    c. The gift loan involved $95,000.
    d. The lender charged the borrower interest of 2%.

15. What purpose does § 2516 serve?

16. Under Leon's will, all of his property is to pass to his son, Jody. Jody is a widower, and his only survivor is a daughter, Brenda. Jody has considerable wealth of his own and is in poor health. Do you recognize an attractive estate tax option for the parties?

17. What is the justification for the annual exclusion?

18. In connection with the gift-splitting provision of § 2513, comment on the following:
    a. What it was designed to accomplish.
    b. How the election is made.
    c. Its utility in a community property jurisdiction.

19. In connection with the filing of a Federal gift tax return, comment on the following:
    a. No Federal gift tax is due.
    b. The § 2513 election to split gifts is to be used.

c. A gift of a future interest is involved.

d. The donor uses a fiscal year for Federal income tax purposes.

e. The donor obtained from the IRS an extension of time for filing his or her Federal income tax return.

20. Distinguish between the following:
    a. The gross estate and the taxable estate.
    b. The gross estate and the probate estate.

21. What was the original justification for § 2035? Does this justification still exist? Explain.

22. At the time of Emile's death, he was a joint tenant with Colette in a parcel of real estate. With regard to the inclusion in Emile's gross estate under § 2040, comment on the following independent assumptions:
    a. Emile and Colette received the property as a gift from Douglas.
    b. Colette provided all of the purchase price of the property.
    c. Colette's contribution was received as a gift from Emile.
    d. Emile's contribution was derived from income generated by property he received as a gift from Colette.

23. Warren owns an insurance policy on the life of Sylvia with Eric as the designated beneficiary. Of the three persons involved, Sylvia is the eldest and in poor health. What potential tax problems are involved?

24. Under Keith's will, his property passes as follows: $1,200,000 to Kevin (Keith's son) and $600,000 to Edith (Keith's wife). Kevin is on good terms with Edith and, in fact, continues to live with her. Edith is in better health than Kevin. What might be an attractive tax alternative for the parties?

25. In terms of the QTIP (qualified terminable interest property) election, comment on the following:
    a. Who makes the election.
    b. What the election accomplishes.
    c. The tax effect of the election upon the death of the surviving spouse.

26. Does the credit for state death taxes (§ 2011) eliminate the double taxation of an estate? Explain.

27. Would the credit for tax on prior transfers (§ 2013) ever apply in the husband and wife–type of situation? Explain.

PROBLEMS

28. An estate holds the following assets:

	Value on Date of Death	Value Six Months Later
Land	$620,000	$618,000
Stock in Wren Corporation	210,000	190,000
Stock in Eagle Corporation	305,000	308,000

The stock in Wren Corporation is sold by the estate for $208,000 three months after the owner's death, while the stock in Eagle Corporation is sold for $310,000 nine months after death.
   a. Is the § 2032 election available to the estate?
   b. If so and the election is made, what value results?
   c. What value results if the § 2032 election is not available or is not made?

29. In each of the following independent situations, indicate whether or not the transfer by Phillip is, or could be, subject to the Federal gift tax:

   a. Phillip makes a contribution to an influential political figure.

   b. Phillip makes a contribution to Crow Corporation, of which he is not a shareholder.

   c. In consideration of his upcoming marriage to Teri, Phillip establishes a savings account in Teri's name.

   d. Same as (c). After their marriage, Phillip establishes a joint checking account in the names of "Phillip and Teri."

   e. Same as (d). One year after the checking account is established, Teri withdraws all of the funds.

   f. Phillip enters into an agreement with Teri where he will transfer property to her in full satisfaction of her marital rights. One month after the agreement, the transfer occurs. Later Phillip and Teri are divorced.

   g. Phillip purchases U.S. savings bonds, listing ownership as "Phillip and Teri." Several years later, and after Phillip's death, Teri redeems the bonds.

30. In each of the following independent situations, indicate whether or not the transfer by Jeff is, or could be, subject to the Federal gift tax:

   a. Jeff purchases real estate and lists title as "Jeff and Chris as joint tenants." Jeff and Chris are brothers.

   b. Same as (a), except that Jeff and Chris are husband and wife.

   c. Jeff creates a revocable trust with Chris as the designated beneficiary.

   d. Same as (c). One year after creating the trust, Jeff releases all power to revoke the trust.

   e. Jeff takes out an insurance policy on his life, designating Chris as the beneficiary.

   f. Same as (e). Two years later, Jeff dies and the policy proceeds are paid to Chris.

   g. Jeff takes out an insurance policy on the life of Gretchen and designates Chris as the beneficiary. Shortly thereafter, Gretchen dies and the policy proceeds are paid to Chris.

   h. Jeff pays for Chris's college tuition.

31. In January 1996, Roger and Jean enter into a property settlement under which Roger agrees to pay $500,000 to Jean in return for the release of her marital rights. At the time the agreement is signed, Roger pays Jean $100,000 as a first installment. Although the parties intended to obtain a divorce, Roger dies in July 1996 before legal proceedings have been instituted. After Roger's death, the executor of his estate pays to Jean the $400,000 remaining balance due under the property settlement.

   a. What are the gift tax consequences of the $100,000 payment made upon the signing of the agreement? Why?

   b. What are the estate tax consequences of the $400,000 paid to Jean from estate assets after Roger's death? Why?

32. In 1996, Kimberly made gifts of stock (fair market value of $700,000) to her adult son. Kimberly has never made any prior taxable gifts. Kimberly's husband, Albert, previously made a taxable gift of $500,000 in 1982 upon which he paid a gift tax of $93,000. At the time of the 1982 gift, Albert was not married to Kimberly.

   a. Determine the amount of the gift tax on the 1996 transfer if the § 2513 election is not made.

   b. If the § 2513 election is made.

33. On the date of her death on May 7, 1996, Geraldine owned the following property:

	Fair Market Value
Stock in Falcon Corporation	$300,000
Stock in Harrier Corporation	410,000
City of Richmond bonds	505,000

Falcon Corporation declared a dividend on March 27, 1996, payable on May 15, 1996, to shareholders of record as of April 30, 1996. Harrier Corporation declared a dividend on April 5, 1996, payable on May 23, 1996, to shareholders of record as of May 8, 1996.

In the month of May 1996, Geraldine's executor receives the following amounts: $5,000 dividend from Falcon; $7,000 dividend from Harrier; and $12,500 interest ($12,200 accrued to date of death) from the City of Richmond.

How much of these amounts is included in Geraldine's gross estate?

34. William, a widower, dies in 1996. Previously, he made the following transfers:

    • Land, fair market value of $710,000, given to his son in 1992. A gift tax of $23,800 was paid as a result of the gift. The land has a date of death value of $780,000.

    • Insurance policy on William's life given to his daughter (the designated beneficiary) in 1994. Because it was term insurance, the policy had a value of less than the annual exclusion. Consequently, no taxable gift resulted. The policy has a maturity value of $150,000.

    • Stock worth $160,000 given to William's grandson in 1995. The transfer resulted in a gift tax of $38,800.

    As to these transfers, how much is included in William's gross estate?

35. In 1975, Irma created a revocable trust with securities worth $300,000. National Trust Company was designated as the trustee. Under the terms of the trust, Irma retained a life estate with remainder to her children. In 1994, Irma releases her right to revoke the trust. Irma dies in 1996 when the trust assets have a fair market value of $1,200,000.
    a. What, if any, are Irma's gift tax consequences in 1975?
    b. What, if any, is included in Irma's gross estate in 1996?
    c. Would your answer to (b) change if Irma *also* released her life estate in 1994? Explain.

36. In 1980, Jim and Maude purchase a commercial annuity. Jim furnishes 75% of the cost, and Maude provides the balance. Under the terms of the contract, Jim is to receive $48,000 per year for his life. If Jim predeceases Maude, she is to receive $36,000 per year for her life.
    a. If Jim dies first when the value of the survivorship feature is $400,000, how much, if any, is included in his gross estate?
    b. Would anything regarding the annuity be included in Maude's gross estate when she dies five years after Jim? Explain.

37. In 1974, John purchased real estate for $400,000, listing ownership as follows: "John and Mary, equal tenants in common." John predeceases Mary in 1996, when the property is worth $900,000. Before 1974, John had not made any taxable gifts or utilized the $30,000 specific exemption. Assume John and Mary are father and daughter.
    a. Determine John's gift tax consequences, if any, in 1974.
    b. How much, if any, of the property should be included in John's gross estate?

38. In 1966, Myrna transfers by gift a personal residence to Louise and Leon, her daughter and son-in-law. The gift is a wedding present, and title to the property is listed as "Louise and Leon, tenants in common."
    a. Did Myrna have gift tax consequences in 1966? Explain.
    b. If the value of the residence is $400,000 when Louise predeceases Leon in 1996, how much, if any, is included in her gross estate?

39. In 1985, Dana purchased real estate for $600,000, listing title to the property as follows: "Dana and June, joint tenants with the right of survivorship." June predeceases Dana in 1996, when the real estate is worth $950,000. Assume Dana and June are sisters and that neither has made any other taxable gifts or utilized the $30,000 specific exemption.
    a. Determine Dana's gift tax consequences, if any, in 1985.
    b. How much, if any, of the property should be included in June's gross estate?

40. Assume the same facts as in Problem 39, except that Dana and June are husband and wife (rather than sisters).
    a. Determine Dana's gift tax consequences, if any, in 1985.
    b. How much, if any, of the property should be included in June's gross estate? Will any such inclusion generate an estate tax liability? Explain.

41. In each of the following independent situations, determine how much should be included in Burton's gross estate under § 2042 as to the various life insurance policies involved. Assume that none of the policies are community property.
   a. At the time of his death, Burton owned a paid-up policy on the life of Suzanna, with Penny as the designated beneficiary. The policy had a replacement cost of $80,000 and a maturity value of $300,000.
   b. Nancy owns a policy on the life of Burton ($300,000 maturity value) with Burton's estate as the designated beneficiary. Upon Burton's death, the insurance company pays $300,000 to his estate.
   c. Four years before his death, Burton transferred a policy on his life ($300,000 maturity value) to Ann as a gift. Burton retained the power to change beneficiaries. At the time of the transfer, the designated beneficiary was Ann. Because Burton had never exercised his right to change beneficiaries, the insurance company pays Ann $300,000 upon his death.
   d. Same as (c), except that Burton releases the power to change beneficiaries one year before his death.

42. Comment on how each of the following independent situations should be handled for estate tax purposes:
   a. Before her death, Linda issued a note payable to her daughter in the amount of $100,000. Linda never received any consideration for the note. After Linda's death, the daughter files a claim against the estate and collects $100,000 on the note.
   b. At the time of her death, Saleka (a widow) owned 10 cemetery lots (each worth $5,000), which she had purchased many years before for herself and her family.
   c. At the time of his death, Stanley was delinquent in the payment of back Federal income taxes. Stanley's executor pays the taxes from assets of the estate.

43. At the time of his death in the current year, Jerome owned the following real estate:

Tract A	$1,000,000
Mortgage on tract A	(200,000)
Tract B	700,000
Mortgage on tract B	(100,000)

   Under Jerome's will, both tracts of land pass to Janice (Jerome's surviving spouse). However, Jerome's will directs the executor to pay off the mortgage on tract B from the remainder interest passing to the children.
   a. How much marital deduction will Jerome's estate be allowed?
   b. What is the deduction for indebtedness under § 2053?

44. Determine the credit for state death taxes in each of the following independent situations:
   a. The adjusted taxable estate is $124,000. The amount of state death tax paid is $1,200.
   b. The adjusted taxable estate is $450,000. The amount of state death tax paid is $9,500.
   c. The adjusted taxable estate is $900,000. The state death tax is a soak-up tax that was paid.

45. Under Ira's will, Jill (Ira's sister) inherits property. Three years later, Jill dies. Determine Jill's credit for tax on prior transfers based on the following assumptions:
   a. The estate tax attributable to the inclusion of the property in Ira's gross estate is $70,000, and the estate tax attributable to the inclusion of the property in Jill's gross estate is $50,000.
   b. The estate tax attributable to the inclusion of the property in Ira's gross estate is $60,000, and the estate tax attributable to the inclusion of the property in Jill's gross estate is $80,000.

46. In each of the following independent situations, determine the decedent's final estate tax liability (net of any unified tax credit):

	Decedent		
	Lucinda	**Roland**	**Warren**
Year of death	1984	1986	1996
Taxable estate	$400,000	$600,000	$900,000
Post-1976 taxable gift			
Made in 1982	300,000	—	—
Made in 1984	—	350,000	
Made in 1989	—	—	500,000

Research Problems for this chapter appear at the end of Chapter 28.

27

INCOME TAXATION OF TRUSTS AND ESTATES

LEARNING OBJECTIVES

After completing Chapter 27, you should be able to:

1. Use working definitions with respect to trusts, estates, beneficiaries, and other parties.

2. Identify the steps in determining the accounting and taxable income of a trust or estate, and the related taxable income of the beneficiaries.

3. Illustrate the uses and implications of distributable net income.

4. Understand the effects of statutory restrictions on the taxation of distributions from accumulation trusts.

5. Understand various tax planning procedures that can be used to minimize the tax consequences of trusts and estates and their beneficiaries.

AN OVERVIEW OF SUBCHAPTER J

Taxpayers create trusts for a variety of reasons. Some trusts are established primarily for tax purposes while others are designed to accomplish a specific financial goal or to provide for the orderly management of assets in case of emergency. Table 27–1 lists some of the more common reasons for creating a trust.

Because a trust is a separate tax entity, its gross income and deductions must be measured, and an annual tax return must be filed. Similarly, when an

▼ **TABLE 27–1**
Motivations for Creating a Trust

Type of Trust	Financial and Other Goals
Life insurance trust	Holds life insurance policies on the insured, removes the proceeds of the policies from the gross estate (if an irrevocable trust), and safeguards against a young or inexperienced beneficiary receiving the proceeds.
"Living" (revocable) trust	Manages assets, reduces probate costs, provides privacy for asset disposition, protects against medical or other emergencies, and provides relief from the necessity of day-to-day management of the underlying assets.
Trust for minors	Provides funds for a college education, shifts income to lower-bracket taxpayers, and transfers accumulated income without permanently parting with the underlying assets.
"Blind" trust	Holds and manages the assets of the grantor without his/her input or influence (e.g., while the grantor holds political office or some other sensitive position).
Retirement trust	Manages asset contributions under a qualified retirement plan.
Alimony trust	Manages the assets of an ex-spouse and assures they will be distributed in a timely fashion to specified beneficiaries.
Liquidation trust	Collects and distributes the last assets of a corporation that is undergoing a complete liquidation.

individual dies, a legal entity is created in the form of his or her estate. This chapter examines the rules related to the income taxation of trusts and estates. Figure 27–1 illustrates the structure of a typical estate and trust.

The income taxation of trusts and estates is governed by Subchapter J of the Internal Revenue Code, §§ 641 through 692. Certain similarities are apparent between Subchapter J and the income taxation of individuals (e.g., the definitions of gross income and deductible expenditures), partnerships (e.g., the conduit principle), and S corporations (e.g., the conduit principle and the trust as a

▼ FIGURE 27–1
Structure of a Typical Trust and Estate

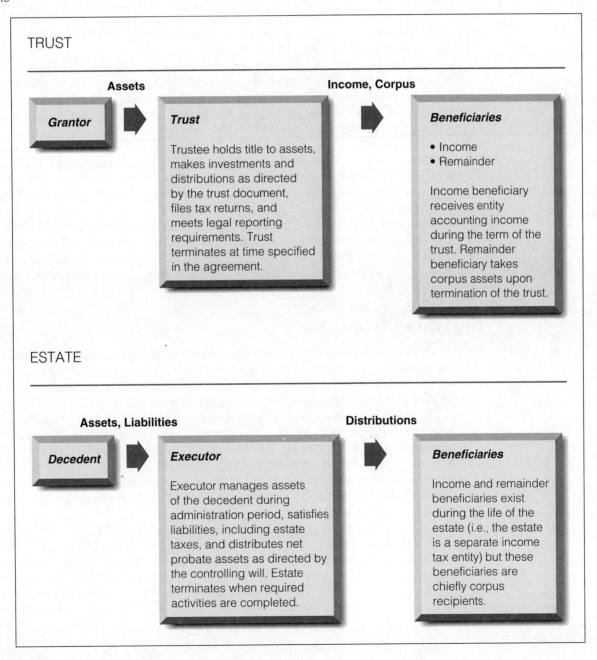

separate taxable entity). Trusts also involve several important unique concepts, however, including the determination of distributable net income and the tier system of distributions to beneficiaries.

WHAT IS A TRUST?

1 ▼ **LEARNING OBJECTIVE**
Use working definitions with respect to trusts, estates, beneficiaries, and other parties.

The Code does not contain a definition of a trust. However, the term usually refers to an arrangement created by a will or by an *inter vivos* (lifetime) declaration, through which trustees take title to property for the purpose of protecting or conserving it for the beneficiaries.[1]

Typically, the creation of a trust involves at least three parties: (1) The **grantor** (sometimes referred to as the settler or donor) transfers selected assets to the trust entity. (2) The trustee, who may be either an individual or a corporation, is charged with the fiduciary duties associated with the trust. (3) The beneficiary is designated to receive income or property from the trust; the beneficiary's rights are defined by state law and by the trust document.

In some situations, fewer than three persons may be involved, as specified by the trust agreement. For instance, an elderly individual who can no longer manage his or her own property (e.g., because of ill health) may create a trust under which he or she is both the grantor and the beneficiary. In this case, a corporate trustee is charged with the management of the grantor's assets.

In another situation, the grantor might designate him- or herself as the trustee of the trust assets. For example, a parent who wants to transfer selected assets to a minor child could use a trust entity to ensure that the minor does not waste the property. By naming him- or herself as the trustee, the parent retains virtual control over the property that is transferred.

Under the general rules of Subchapter J, the **grantor trusts** just described are not recognized for income tax purposes. Similarly, when only one party is involved (when the same individual is grantor, trustee, and sole beneficiary of the trust), Subchapter J rules do not apply, and the entity is ignored for income tax purposes.

OTHER DEFINITIONS

When the grantor transfers title of selected assets to a trust, those assets become the **corpus** (body), or principal, of the trust. Trust corpus, in most situations, earns *income*, which may be distributed to the beneficiaries, or accumulated for the future by the trustee, as the trust instrument directs.

In the typical trust, the grantor creates two types of beneficiaries: one who receives the accounting income of the trust and one who receives trust corpus that remains at the termination of the trust entity. Beneficiaries in the first category hold an *income interest* in the trust, and those in the second category hold a *remainder interest* in the trust's assets. If the grantor retains the remainder interest, the interest is known as a **reversionary interest** (corpus reverts to the grantor when the trust entity terminates).

The trust document establishes the term of the trust. The term may be for a specific number of years (a *term certain*) or until the occurrence of a specified event. For instance, a trust might exist (1) for the life of the income beneficiary—in this case, the income beneficiary is known as a *life tenant* in trust corpus; (2) for the life of some other individual; (3) until the income or remainder beneficiary reaches the

---
[1] Reg. § 301.7701–4(a).

age of majority; or (4) until the beneficiary, or another individual, marries, receives a promotion, or reaches some specified age.

The trustee may be required to distribute the accounting income of the entity according to a distribution schedule specified in the agreement. Sometimes, however, the trustee is given more discretion with respect to the timing and nature of the distributions. If the trustee can determine, within guidelines that may be included in the trust document, either the timing of the income or corpus distributions or the specific beneficiaries who will receive them (from among those identified in the agreement), the trust is called a **sprinkling trust.** Here, the trustee can "sprinkle" the distributions among the various beneficiaries. Family-unit income taxes can be reduced by directing income to those who are subject to lower marginal tax rates. Thus, by giving the trustee a sprinkling power, the income tax liability of the family unit can be manipulated through the trust agreement.

For purposes of certain provisions of Subchapter J, a trust must be classified as either a **simple trust** or a **complex trust.** A simple trust (1) is required to distribute its entire accounting income to designated beneficiaries every year, (2) has no beneficiaries that are qualifying charitable organizations, and (3) makes no distributions of trust corpus during the year. A complex trust is any trust that is not a simple trust.[2] These criteria are applied to the trust every year. Thus, every trust is classified as a complex trust in the year in which it terminates (because it will be distributing all of its corpus during that year).

WHAT IS AN ESTATE?

An estate is created upon the death of every individual. The estate is charged with collecting and conserving all of the individual's assets, satisfying all liabilities, and distributing the remaining assets to the heirs identified by state law or the will.

Typically, the creation of an estate involves at least three parties: the decedent, all of whose probate assets are transferred to the estate for disposition; the executor, who is appointed under the decedent's valid will (or the administrator, if no valid will exists); and the beneficiaries of the estate, who are to receive assets or income from the entity, as the decedent indicated in the will. The executor or administrator holds the fiduciary responsibility to manage the estate as directed by the will, applicable state law, and the probate court.

Recall that the assets that make up the probate estate are not identical to those that constitute the gross estate for transfer tax purposes (refer to Chapter 26). Many of the gross estate assets are not a part of the probate estate and thus are not subject to disposition by the executor or administrator. For instance, property held by the decedent as a joint tenant passes to the survivor(s) by operation of the applicable state's property law rather than through the probate estate. Proceeds of insurance policies on the life of the decedent, over which the decedent held the incidents of ownership, are not under the control of the executor or administrator. The designated beneficiaries of the policy receive the proceeds outright under the insurance contract.

An estate is a separate taxable entity. Under certain circumstances, taxpayers may find it profitable to prolong an estate's existence. This situation is likely to arise when the heirs are already in a high income tax bracket and would, therefore, prefer to have the income generated by the estate assets taxed at the estate's lower marginal income tax rates. If an estate's existence is unduly prolonged, however,

---

[2] Reg. § 1.651(a)–1.

TAX IN THE NEWS

DOING ESTATE PLANNING ON TELEVISION

The chief technique offered by those who sell books and seminars on "How to Avoid Probate" is the living or revocable trust. Materials supporting these media productions often consist of no more than "fill-in-the-blank" templates that enable an individual to draft and adopt such a trust document, assuming no special rules apply in the state of residence or asset location.

Revocable trusts are especially attractive where the probate process might be especially long or costly because of the nature of the assets held by the decedent (perhaps a family business or important art collection) or a need for privacy (say, where a celebrity is involved).

Yet executing such an arrangement is costly in itself. Titles to assets must all be recast to show the trustee as owner of the property. An attorney should be consulted, at least to determine the extent to which the standard forms being used will be accepted by local probate courts. And when the grantor dies and the document is used to distribute assets, legal fees often are incurred to address challenges from beneficiaries who feel that they have received too little from the dearly departed.

the IRS can terminate it for Federal income tax purposes after the expiration of a reasonable period for the executor to complete the duties of administration.[3]

NATURE OF TRUST AND ESTATE TAXATION

In general, the taxable income of a trust or estate is taxed to the entity or to its beneficiaries to the extent that each has received the accounting income of the entity. Thus, Subchapter J creates a modified conduit principle relative to the income taxation of trusts, estates, and their beneficiaries. Whoever receives the accounting income of the entity, or some portion of it, is liable for the income tax that results.

EXAMPLE 1

Adam receives 80% of the accounting income of the Zero Trust. The trustee accumulated the other 20% of the income at her discretion under the trust agreement and added it to trust corpus. Adam is liable for income tax only on the amount of the distribution, and Zero is liable for the income tax on the accumulated portion of the income. ▼

The modified conduit principle of Subchapter J is subject to several exceptions. For instance, some trusts may be treated as associations and therefore will be subject to the corporate income tax.[4] In addition, part or all of the income of certain trusts is taxed to the grantor if too much control over the trust property or income is retained.[5]

---

[3] Reg. § 1.641(b)–3(a).

[4] Refer to Chapter 16 for a discussion of associations taxed as corporations; see also *Morrissey v. Comm.*, 36–1 USTC ¶9020, 16 AFTR 1274, 56 S.Ct. 289 (USSC, 1936).

[5] §§ 671–679.

FILING REQUIREMENTS

The fiduciary is required to file a Form 1041 (U.S. Fiduciary Income Tax Return) in the following situations.[6]

- For an estate that has gross income of $600 or more for the year.
- For a trust that either has any taxable income or, if there is no taxable income, has gross income of $600 or more.

The fiduciary return (and any related tax liability) is due no later than the fifteenth day of the fourth month following the close of the entity's taxable year. The return is filed with the Internal Revenue Service Center for the region in which the fiduciary resides or has his or her principal place of business.

TAX ACCOUNTING PERIODS, METHODS, AND PAYMENTS

An estate or trust may use many of the tax accounting methods available to individuals. The method of accounting used by the grantor of a trust or the decedent of an estate need not carry over to the entity.

An estate has the same options for choosing a tax year as any new taxpayer. Thus, the estate of a calendar year decedent dying on March 3 can select any fiscal year or report on a calendar year basis. If the calendar year basis is selected, the estate's first taxable year will include the period from March 3 to December 31. If the first or last tax year of an estate is a short year (less than one calendar year), income for that year need not be annualized.

To eliminate the possibility of deferring the taxation of fiduciary-source income simply by using a fiscal tax year, trusts (other than tax-exempt trusts) use a calendar tax year.[7]

Trusts and estates are required to make estimated Federal income tax payments, using the same quarterly schedule that applies to individual taxpayers. This requirement applies to estates only for tax years that end two or more years after the date of the decedent's death. Charitable trusts and private foundations are exempt from estimated payment requirements altogether.[8]

The two-year estimated tax exception for estates recognizes the liquidity problems that an executor often faces during the early months of administering the estate. The exception does not ensure, however, that an estate in existence less than 24 months will never be required to make an estimated tax payment.

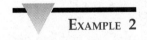

EXAMPLE 2   Juanita died on March 15, 1996. Her executor elected a fiscal year ending on July 31 for the estate. Estimated tax payments will be required from the estate starting with the tax year that begins on August 1, 1997. ▼

TAX RATES AND PERSONAL EXEMPTION

Congress's desire to stop trusts from being used as income-shifting devices has made the fiduciary entity the highest-taxed taxpayer in the Code.[9] The entity reaches a 39.6 percent marginal rate with only $7,650 of taxable income in 1995, so the grantor's ability to shift income in a tax-effective manner is nearly eliminated. The following table, which lists the 1995 taxes paid by various entities on taxable income of $30,000, shows how expensive the accumulation of income within an

---

[6] § 6012(a).
[7] § 645.

[8] § 6654(l).
[9] § 1(e) (see Appendix A).

TAX IN THE NEWS

EVERYONE GETS WET WHEN YOU SOAK THE RICH

Fiduciary taxation has fallen prey to the "soak the rich" approach to tax reform of the last five years. In an environment of taxes on millionaires and luxury vehicles, the tax rates that apply to trusts and estates have also increased, and the width of the lower brackets has become so narrow that these entities now are subject to the highest marginal rate structure in U.S. income tax law. Higher tax rates for trusts and estates affect all fiduciary arrangements, however, even those designed for reasons other than tax avoidance.

Perhaps by design, these rate changes have dampened the planning potential of fiduciary entities as a means of shifting income among generations (e.g., from parent to child) or over time (i.e., from the taxpayer's present tax return to a future one). But they have also deepened the tax burden on fixed-income retirees, handicapped individuals, children of divorced parents, and other commonly encountered fiduciary beneficiaries.

Most trust beneficiaries are passive recipients of investment income generated by a stock portfolio managed by a corporate trustee or by the distant managers of the mutual funds in which the funds are invested. In those cases, the beneficiaries exercise little decision-making authority over the yield or timing of the entity's distributions, which are fixed by the controlling instrument. Under such circumstances, tax rate increases seem to punish the powerless as well as to soak the rich.

estate or trust can be. Proper income shifting now would move assets *out of* the estate or trust and into the hands of the grantor or beneficiary.

Filing Status/Entity	Taxable Income	1995 Tax Liability
Single	$30,000	$ 5,372*
Married, filing jointly	30,000	4,504*
C corporation	30,000	4,500
Trust or estate	30,000	11,012

*Based on the 1995 Tax Table applicable to individual taxpayers.

A fiduciary's net long-term capital gains can be taxed at a nominal rate of no more than 28 percent. In addition to the regular income tax, an estate or trust may be subject to the alternative minimum tax.[10] Trusts may also be subject to a special tax imposed by § 644 on built-in gains from the sale or exchange of certain appreciated property.

Both trusts and estates are allowed a personal exemption in computing the fiduciary tax liability. All estates are allowed a personal exemption of $600. The exemption available to a trust depends upon the type of trust involved. A trust that is required to distribute all of its income is currently allowed an exemption of $300. All other trusts are allowed an exemption of $100 per year.[11]

The classification of trusts as to the appropriate personal exemption is similar, but not identical, to the distinction between simple and complex trusts. The classification as a simple trust is more stringent.

---

[10] § 55.   [11] § 642(b).

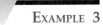
EXAMPLE 3

Trust Alpha is required to distribute all of its current accounting income to Susan. Trust Beta is required to distribute all of its current accounting income, one-half to Tyrone and one-half to State University, a qualifying charitable organization. The trustee of Trust Gamma can, at her discretion, distribute the current accounting income or corpus of the trust to Dr. Chapman. None of the trusts makes any corpus distributions during the year. All of the accounting income of Trust Gamma is distributed to Dr. Chapman.

Trust Alpha is a simple trust; it will receive a $300 personal exemption. Trust Beta is a complex trust; it will receive a $300 personal exemption. Trust Gamma is a complex trust; it will receive a $100 personal exemption. ▼

ALTERNATIVE MINIMUM TAX

The alternative minimum tax (AMT) may apply to a trust or estate in any tax year. Given the nature and magnitude of the tax preferences, adjustments, and exemptions that determine alternative minimum taxable income (AMTI), however, most trusts and estates are unlikely to incur the tax. Nevertheless, they could be vulnerable if they are actively engaged in a business that uses the accelerated cost recovery provisions. Similarly, an estate may be liable for the AMT if it receives a sizable portfolio of stock options shortly after the decedent's death under a deferred compensation plan.

In general, derivation of AMTI for the entity follows the rules that apply to individual taxpayers. Thus, the corporate ACE adjustment does not apply to fiduciary entities, but AMTI may be created through the application of most of the other AMT preference and adjustment items discussed in Chapter 14.

The entity has a $22,500 annual exemption, similar to that available to a married individual who files a separate return. The exemption phases out at a rate of one-fourth of the amount by which AMTI exceeds $75,000.

A 26 percent alternative minimum tax rate is applied to AMTI, increasing to 28 percent when AMTI in excess of the exemption reaches $175,000. In addition, estimated tax payments for the entity must include any applicable AMT liability.

TAXABLE INCOME OF TRUSTS AND ESTATES

2 **LEARNING OBJECTIVE**
Identify the steps in determining the accounting and taxable income of a trust or estate, and the related taxable income of the beneficiaries.

Generally, the taxable income of a trust or estate is computed similarly to that for an individual. Subchapter J does, however, include several important exceptions and provisions that make it necessary to use a systematic approach to calculating the taxable income of these entities. Figure 27–2 illustrates the procedure implied by the Code, and Figure 27–3 presents a systematic computation method to be followed in this chapter.

ENTITY ACCOUNTING INCOME

The first step in determining the taxable income of a trust or estate is to compute the entity's accounting income for the period. Although this prerequisite is not apparent from a cursory reading of Subchapter J, a closer look at the Code reveals a number of references to the *income* of the entity.[12] Wherever the term *income* is

---

[12] For example, see §§ 651(a)(1), 652(a), and 661(a)(1).

▼ **FIGURE 27–2**
Accounting Income,
Distributable Net Income,
and Taxable Income of the Entity
and Its Beneficiaries (Five
Steps)

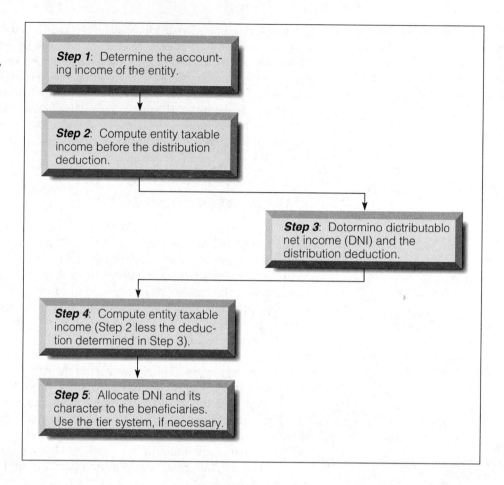

used in Subchapter J without some modifier (e.g., *gross* income or *taxable* income), the statute is referring to the accounting income of the trust or estate for the tax year.

A definition of entity accounting income is critical to understanding the Subchapter J computation of fiduciary taxable income. Under state law, entity accounting income is the amount that the income beneficiary of the simple trust or estate is eligible to receive from the entity. More importantly, the calculation of accounting income is virtually under the control of the grantor or decedent (through a properly drafted trust agreement or will). If the document has been drafted at arm's length, a court will enforce a fiduciary's good faith efforts to carry out the specified computation of accounting income.

By allocating specific items of income and expenditure either to the income beneficiaries or to corpus, the desires of the grantor or decedent are put into effect. Table 27–2 shows typical assignments of revenue and expenditure items to fiduciary income or corpus.

Where the controlling document is silent as to whether an item should be assigned to income or corpus, state law prevails. These allocations are an important determinant of the benefits received from the entity by its beneficiaries and the timing of those benefits.

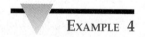

EXAMPLE 4

The Arnold Trust is a simple trust. Mrs. Bennett is its sole beneficiary. In the current year, the trust earns $20,000 in taxable interest and $15,000 in tax-exempt interest. In addition, the trust recognizes an $8,000 long-term capital gain. The trustee assesses a fee of $11,000 for the year. If the trust agreement allocates fees and capital gains to corpus, trust accounting income is $35,000, and Mrs. Bennett receives that amount. Thus, the income beneficiary receives no immediate benefit from the trust's capital gain, and she bears none of the financial burden of the fiduciary's fees.

Interest income	$35,000
Long-term capital gain—allocable to corpus	± –0–
Fiduciary's fees—allocable to corpus	± –0–
Trust accounting income	$35,000

▼ **FIGURE 27–3**
Computational Template Applying the Five-Step Procedure

Item	Totals	Accounting Income	Taxable Income	Distributable Net Income/ Distribution Deduction
Income	_____	_____		_____
Income	_____	_____		_____
Expense	_____	_____		_____
Expense	_____	_____		_____
Personal exemption				_____
Accounting income/taxable income before the distribution deduction	*Step 1* ══════		*Step 2* _____	_____
Personal exemption				_____
Corpus capital gain/loss				_____
Net tax-exempt income				_____
Distributable net income				══════
Distribution deduction			*Step 3* _____	
Entity taxable income			*Step 4* _____	

Note: Beneficiary taxable income is addressed in *Step 5.*

▼ **TABLE 27–2**
Common Allocations of Items to Income or Corpus

Allocable to Income	**Allocable to Corpus**
• Ordinary and operating net income from trust assets.	• Depreciation on business assets.
• Interest, dividend, rent, and royalty income.	• Casualty gain/loss on income-producing assets.
• Stock dividends.	• Insurance recoveries on income-producing assets.
• One-half of fiduciary fees/ commissions.	• Capital gain/loss on investment assets.
	• Stock splits.
	• One-half of fiduciary fees/ commissions.

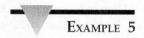

EXAMPLE 5 Assume the same facts as in Example 4, except that the trust agreement allocates the fiduciary's fees to income. The trust accounting income is $24,000, and Mrs. Bennett receives that amount.

Interest income	$35,000
Long-term capital gain—allocable to corpus	± –0–
Fiduciary's fees	–11,000
Trust accounting income	$24,000

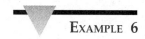

EXAMPLE 6 Assume the same facts as in Example 4, except that the trust agreement allocates to income all capital gains and losses and one-half of the trustee's commissions. The trust accounting income is $37,500, and Mrs. Bennett receives that amount.

Interest income	$35,000
Long-term capital gain	+8,000
Fiduciary's fees—one-half allocable to corpus	–5,500
Trust accounting income	$37,500

GROSS INCOME

The gross income of an estate or trust is similar to that of an individual. In determining the gain or loss to be recognized by an estate or trust upon the sale or other taxable disposition of assets, the rules for basis determination are similar to those applicable to other taxpayers. Thus, an estate's basis for property received from a decedent is stepped up or stepped down to gross estate value (refer to Chapter 12 for a more detailed discussion). Property received as a gift (the usual case in most trust arrangements) usually takes the donor's basis. Property purchased by the trust from a third party is assigned a basis equal to the purchase price.

Property Distributions. In general, the entity does not recognize gain or loss upon its distribution of property to a beneficiary under the provisions of the will or trust document. The distributed property has the same basis to the beneficiary of the distribution as it did to the estate or trust. Moreover, the distribution absorbs distributable net income (DNI) and qualifies for a distribution deduction (both of which are explained later in this chapter) to the extent of the lesser of the distributed asset's basis to the beneficiary or the asset's fair market value as of the distribution date.[13]

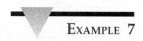

EXAMPLE 7 The Howard Trust distributes a painting, basis of $40,000 and fair market value of $90,000, to beneficiary Kate. Kate's basis in the painting is $40,000. The distribution absorbs $40,000 of the trust's DNI, and Howard claims a $40,000 distribution deduction relative to the transaction. ▼

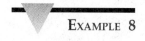

EXAMPLE 8 Assume the same facts as in Example 7, except that Howard's basis in the painting is $100,000. Kate's basis in the painting is also $100,000. The distribution absorbs $90,000 of the trust's DNI, and Howard claims a $90,000 distribution deduction. ▼

---

[13] § 643(e).

A trustee or executor can *elect* to recognize gain or loss with respect to all of the entity's in-kind property distributions for the year. If the election is made, the beneficiary's basis in the asset is equal to the asset's fair market value as of the distribution date. The distribution absorbs DNI and qualifies for a distribution deduction to the extent of the asset's fair market value. Note, however, that § 267 can restrict a trust's deduction for losses.

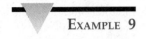

EXAMPLE 9

The Green Estate distributes an antique piano, basis to Green of $10,000 and fair market value of $15,000, to beneficiary Kyle. The executor elects that the estate recognize the related $5,000 gain on the distribution. Accordingly, Kyle's basis in the piano is $15,000 ($10,000 basis to Green + $5,000 gain recognized). Without the election, the estate would not recognize any gain, and Kyle's basis in the piano would be $10,000. ▼

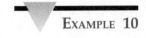

EXAMPLE 10

Assume the same facts as in Example 9, except that Green's basis in the piano is $18,000. The executor elects that the estate recognize the related $3,000 loss on the distribution. Accordingly, Kyle's basis in the piano is $15,000 ($18,000 – $3,000). Without the election, the estate would not recognize any loss, and Kyle's basis in the piano would be $18,000. ▼

Income in Respect of a Decedent. The gross income of a trust or estate includes **income in respect of a decedent (IRD)** that the entity received.[14] For a cash basis decedent, IRD includes accrued salary, interest, rent, and other income items that were not constructively received before death. For both cash and accrual basis decedents, IRD includes, for instance, death benefits from qualified retirement plans and deferred compensation contracts.

The tax consequences of IRD are as follows.

- The fair market value of the right to IRD on the appropriate valuation date is included in the decedent's gross estate.[15] Thus, it is subject to the Federal estate tax.[16]
- The decedent's basis in the property carries over to the recipient (the estate or heirs). There is no step-up or step-down in the basis of IRD items.
- The recipient of the income recognizes gain or loss, measured by the difference between the amount realized and the adjusted basis of the IRD in the hands of the decedent. The character of the gain or loss depends upon the treatment that it would have received had it been realized by the decedent before death. Thus, if the decedent would have realized capital gain, the recipient must do likewise.[17]
- Expenses related to the IRD (such as interest, taxes, and depletion) that properly were not reported on the final income tax return of the decedent may be claimed by the recipient. These items are known as **expenses in respect of a decedent.** Typically, such expenses also include fiduciary fees, commissions paid to dispose of estate assets, and state gift taxes payable. They are deductible for both Federal estate and income tax purposes, *for* or *from* AGI as would have been the case for the decedent.
- If the IRD item would have created an AMT preference or adjustment for the decedent (e.g., with respect to the collection of certain tax-exempt interest by the entity), an identical AMT item is created for the recipient.

---

[14] § 691.
[15] § 2033. Refer to Chapter 26.
[16] To mitigate the effect of double taxation (imposition of both the death tax and the income tax), § 691(c) allows the recipient an

income tax deduction for the incremental estate tax attributable to the net IRD. For individual recipients, this is an itemized deduction, not subject to the 2%-of-AGI floor.
[17] § 691(a)(3) and Reg. § 1.691(a)–3.

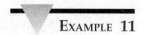

EXAMPLE 11

Amanda died on July 13 of the current year. On August 2, her estate received a check (before deductions) for $1,200 from Amanda's former employer; this was Amanda's compensation for the last pay period of her life. On November 23, Amanda's estate received a $45,000 distribution from her employer's qualified profit sharing plan, the full amount to which she was entitled under the plan. Both Amanda and the estate are calendar year, cash basis taxpayers.

The last salary payment and the profit sharing plan distribution constitute IRD to Amanda's estate. Amanda had earned these items during her lifetime, and the estate had an enforceable right to receive each of them after Amanda's death. Consequently, Amanda's gross estate includes $46,200 with respect to these two items. However, the income tax basis to the estate for these items is not stepped up (from zero to $1,200 and $45,000, respectively) upon distribution to the estate.

The estate must report gross income of $46,200 with respect to the IRD items. The gain recognized upon the receipt of the IRD is $46,200 [($1,200 + $45,000) amounts realized − ($0) adjusted bases]. ▼

Including the IRD in both Amanda's gross estate and the gross income of the estate may seem harsh. Nonetheless, it is similar to the treatment that applies to all of a taxpayer's earned income. The amount is subject to income tax upon receipt, and to the extent that it is not consumed by the taxpayer before death, it is included in the gross estate.

EXAMPLE 12

Assume the same facts as in Example 11, except that Amanda was an accrual basis taxpayer. IRD now includes only the $45,000 distribution from the qualified retirement plan. Amanda's last paycheck is included in the gross income of her own last return (January 1 through date of death). The $1,200 salary is already recognized properly under Amanda's usual method of tax accounting. It does not constitute IRD and is not gross income when received by the executor. ▼

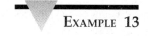

EXAMPLE 13

Assume the same facts as in Example 11. Amanda's last paycheck was reduced by $165 for state income taxes that were withheld by her employer. The $165 tax payment is an expense in respect of a decedent and is allowed as a deduction on *both* Amanda's estate tax return *and* the estate's income tax return. ▼

ORDINARY DEDUCTIONS

As a general rule, the taxable income of an estate or trust is similar to that of an individual. Deductions are allowed for ordinary and necessary expenses paid or incurred in carrying on a trade or business; for the production or collection of income; for the management, conservation, or maintenance of property; and in connection with the determination, collection, or refund of any tax.[18] Reasonable administration expenses, including fiduciary fees and litigation costs in connection with the duties of administration, also are deductible.

The trust or estate must apply the 2 percent-of-AGI floor to many of the § 212 expenses that it incurs. For this purpose, AGI appears to be the greater of (1) the pertinent-year AGI of the grantor of the trust or (2) the AGI of the trust or estate, computed as though the entity were an individual. The floor does not apply,

---

[18] §§ 162 and 212.

however, to items like fiduciary fees or the personal exemption (i.e., items that would not be incurred by an individual).[19]

Expenses attributable to the production or collection of tax-exempt income are not deductible.[20] The amount of the disallowed deduction is found by using a formula based upon the composition of the income elements of entity accounting income for the year of the deduction. The § 212 deduction is apportioned without regard to the accounting income allocation of such expenses to income or to corpus. The deductibility of the fees is determined strictly by the Code (under §§ 212 and 265), and the allocation of expenditures to income and to corpus is controlled by the trust agreement or will or by state law.

Under § 642(g), amounts deductible as administration expenses or losses for estate tax purposes (under §§ 2053 and 2054) cannot be claimed by the estate for income tax purposes, unless the estate files a waiver of the estate tax deduction. Although these expenses cannot be deducted twice, they may be allocated between Forms 706 and 1041 as the fiduciary sees fit; they need not be claimed in their entirety on either return.[21] The prohibition against double deductions does not extend to expenses in respect of a decedent.

Trusts and estates are allowed cost recovery deductions. However, such deductions are assigned proportionately among the recipients of entity accounting income.[22]

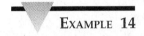

EXAMPLE 14

Lisa and Martin are the equal income beneficiaries of the Needle Trust. Under the terms of the trust agreement, the trustee has complete discretion as to the timing of the distributions from Needle's current accounting income. The trust agreement allocates all depreciation expense to income. In the current year, the trustee distributes 40% of the current trust accounting income to Lisa and 40% to Martin; thus, 20% of the income is accumulated. The depreciation deduction allowable to Needle is $100,000. This deduction is allocated among the trust and its beneficiaries on the basis of the distribution of current accounting income: Lisa and Martin can each claim a $40,000 deduction, and the trust can deduct $20,000. ▼

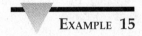

EXAMPLE 15

Assume the same facts as in Example 14, except that the trust agreement allocates all depreciation expense to corpus. Lisa and Martin both still claim a $40,000 depreciation deduction, and Needle retains its $20,000 deduction. The Code assigns the depreciation deduction proportionately to the recipients of current entity accounting income. Allocation of depreciation to income or to corpus is irrelevant in determining which party can properly claim the deduction. ▼

When a trust sells property received by transfer from the grantor, the amount of depreciation subject to recapture includes the depreciation claimed by the grantor before the transfer of the property to the trust. However, depreciation recapture potential disappears at death.

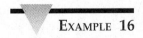

EXAMPLE 16

Jaime transferred an asset to the Shoulder Trust via a lifetime gift. The asset's total depreciation recapture potential was $40,000. If the trust sells the asset at a gain, it will recognize ordinary income not to exceed $40,000. Had Jaime transferred the asset after his

---

[19] §§ 67(b) and (e). *O'Neill Trust v. Comm.*, 93–1 USTC ¶50,332, 71 AFTR2d 93–2052, 994 F.2d 302 (CA–6, 1993), *rev'g* 98 T.C. 227 (1992).

[20] § 265.

[21] Reg. § 1.642(g)–2.

[22] § 167(h) and §§ 611(b)(3) and (4).

death to his estate through a bequest, the $40,000 recapture potential would have disappeared. ▼

DEDUCTIONS FOR LOSSES

An estate or trust is allowed a deduction for casualty or theft losses not covered by insurance or other arrangement. Such losses may also be deductible by an estate for Federal estate tax purposes under § 2054. As a result, an estate is not allowed an income tax deduction unless the estate tax deduction is waived.[23]

The net operating loss (NOL) deduction is available for estates and trusts (i.e., where trade or business income is generated). The carryback of an NOL may reduce the distributable net income of the trust or estate for the carryback year and therefore affect the amount taxed to the beneficiaries for that year.

Certain losses realized by an estate or trust may also be disallowed, as they are for all taxpayers. Thus, the wash sales provisions of § 1091 disallow losses on the sale or other disposition of stock or securities when the estate or trust acquires substantially identical stock or securities within the prescribed 30-day period. Likewise, § 267 disallows certain losses, expenses, and interest with respect to transactions between related taxpayers (including certain parties involved in a trust arrangement).

Except for the possibility of unused losses in the year of termination, the net capital losses of an estate or trust are used only on the fiduciary income tax return.[24] The tax treatment of these losses is the same as for individual taxpayers.

CHARITABLE CONTRIBUTIONS

An estate or complex trust is allowed a deduction for contributions to charitable organizations under certain conditions.

- The contribution is made pursuant to the will or trust instrument, and its amount is determinable using the language of that document.
- The recipient is a qualified organization. For this purpose, qualified organizations include the same charities for which individual and corporate donors are allowed deductions, except that estates and trusts are permitted a deduction for contributions to certain foreign charitable organizations.
- Generally, the contribution is claimed in the tax year paid, but a fiduciary can treat amounts paid in the year immediately following as a deduction for the preceding year.[25] Under this rule, estates and complex trusts receive more liberal treatment than individuals or corporations.

Unlike the charitable contribution deductions of individuals and corporations, the deductions of estates and complex trusts are not limited (e.g., to a percentage of taxable or adjusted gross income). Nonetheless, an entity's charitable contribution may not be fully deductible.[26] Specifically, the deduction is limited to amounts included in the gross income of the entity in the year of the contribution.

---

[23] See Reg. § 1.642(g)–1 for the required statement waiving the estate tax deduction. In addition, see Reg. §§ 1.165–7(c) and 1.165–8(b), requiring that a statement be filed to allow an income tax deduction for such losses.

[24] § 642(h).
[25] § 642(c)(1) and Reg. § 1.642(c)–1(b).
[26] Reg. § 1.642(c)–3(b) and (c).

A contribution is deemed to have been made proportionately from each of the income elements of entity accounting income. Thus, in the event that the entity has tax-exempt income, the contribution is deductible only to the extent that the income elements of entity accounting income for the year of the deduction are included in the entity's gross income.

This rule is similar to that used to limit the § 212 deduction for fiduciary fees and other expenses incurred to generate tax-exempt income. However, if the will or trust agreement requires that the contribution be made from a specific type of income or from the current income from a specified asset, the contribution will not have to be allocated to taxable and tax-exempt income.

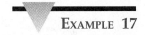

EXAMPLE 17

The Capper Trust has 1996 gross rent income of $80,000, expenses attributable to the rents of $60,000, and tax-exempt interest from state bonds of $20,000. Under the trust agreement, the trustee is to pay 30% of the annual trust accounting income to the United Way, a qualifying organization. Accordingly, the trustee pays $12,000 (30% × $40,000) to the charity in 1997. The charitable contribution deduction allowed for 1996 is $9,600 [($80,000/ $100,000) × $12,000]. ▼

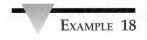

EXAMPLE 18

Assume the same facts as Example 17, except that the trust instrument also requires that the contribution be paid from the net rent income. The agreement controls, and the allocation formula need not be applied. The entire $12,000 is allowed as a charitable contribution deduction. ▼

DEDUCTION FOR DISTRIBUTIONS TO BENEFICIARIES

3   **LEARNING OBJECTIVE**
Illustrate the uses and implications of distributable net income.

The modified conduit approach of Subchapter J is embodied in the deduction allowed to trusts and estates for the distributions made to beneficiaries during the year. Some portion of any distribution that a beneficiary receives from a trust may be subject to income tax on his or her own return. At the same time, the distributing entity is allowed a deduction for some or all of the distribution. Consequently, the modified conduit principle of Subchapter J is implemented. A good analogy is to the taxability of corporate profits distributed to employees as taxable wages. The corporation is allowed a deduction for the payment, but the employee receives gross income in the form of compensation.

A critical value that is used in computing the amount of the entity's distribution deduction is **distributable net income (DNI).** As it is defined in Subchapter J, DNI serves several functions.

- DNI is the maximum amount of the distribution on which the beneficiaries can be taxed.[27]
- DNI is the maximum amount that the entity can use as a distribution deduction for the year.[28]
- The makeup of DNI carries over to the beneficiaries (the items of income and expenses retain their DNI character in the hands of the distributees).[29]

Subchapter J defines DNI in a circular manner, however. The DNI value is necessary to determine the entity's distribution deduction and therefore its taxable income for the year. Nonetheless, the Code defines DNI as a modification of the

---

[27] §§ 652(a) and 662(a).
[28] §§ 651(b) and 661(c).

[29] §§ 652(b) and 662(b).

entity's taxable income itself. Using the systematic approach to determining the taxable income of the entity and of its beneficiaries, as shown earlier in Figure 27–2, one must first compute *taxable income before the distribution deduction*, modify that amount to determine DNI and the distribution deduction, return to the calculation of *taxable income*, and apply the deduction that has resulted.

Taxable income before the distribution deduction includes all of the entity's items of gross income, deductions, gains, losses, and exemptions for the year. Therefore, to compute this amount, (1) determine the appropriate personal exemption for the year and (2) account for all of the other gross income and deductions of the entity.

The next step in Figure 27–2 is the determination of *distributable net income*, computed by making the following adjustments to the entity's *taxable income before the distribution deduction.*[30]

- Add back the personal exemption.
- Add back *net* tax-exempt interest. To arrive at this amount, reduce the total tax-exempt interest by charitable contributions and by related expenses not deductible under § 265.
- Add back the entity's *net* capital losses.
- Subtract any net capital gains allocable to corpus. In other words, the only net capital gains included in DNI are those attributable to income beneficiaries or to charitable contributions.

Since taxable income before the distribution deduction is computed by deducting all of the expenses of the entity (whether they were allocated to income or to corpus), DNI is reduced by expenses that are allocated to corpus. The effect is to reduce the taxable income of the income beneficiaries. The actual distributions to the beneficiaries exceed DNI because the distributions are not reduced by expenses allocated to corpus. Aside from this shortcoming of Subchapter J, DNI offers a good approximation of the current-year economic income available for distribution to the entity's income beneficiaries.

DNI includes the net tax-exempt interest income of the entity, so that amount must be removed from DNI in computing the distribution deduction. Moreover, for estates and complex trusts, the amount actually distributed during the year may include discretionary distributions of income and distributions of corpus permissible under the will or trust instrument. Thus, the distribution deduction for estates and complex trusts is computed as the lesser of (1) the deductible portion of DNI or (2) the taxable amount actually distributed to the beneficiaries during the year. For a simple trust, however, full distribution always is assumed, relative to both the entity and its beneficiaries, in a manner similar to the partnership and S corporation conduit entities.

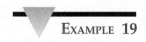

EXAMPLE 19

The Zinc Trust is a simple trust. Because of severe liquidity problems, its 1996 accounting income is not distributed to its sole beneficiary, Mark, until early in 1997. Zinc is still allowed a full distribution deduction for, and Mark is still taxed upon, the entity's 1996 income in 1996. ▼

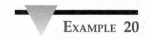

EXAMPLE 20

The Pork Trust is required to distribute its current accounting income annually to its sole income beneficiary, Barbara. Capital gains and losses and all other expenses are allocable to corpus. For the current year, the trust records the following items.

---

[30] These and other (less common) adjustments are detailed in § 643.

Dividend income	$25,000
Taxable interest income	15,000
Tax-exempt interest income	20,000
Net long-term capital gain	10,000
Fiduciary fees	6,000

Item	Totals	Accounting Income	Taxable Income	Distributable Net Income/ Distribution Deduction
Dividend income	$25,000	$25,000	$ 25,000	
Taxable interest income	15,000	15,000	15,000	
Tax-exempt interest income	20,000	20,000		
Net long-term capital gain	10,000		10,000	
Fiduciary fees	6,000		(4,000)	
Personal exemption			(300)	
Accounting income/taxable income before the distribution deduction		Step 1 $60,000	Step 2 $ 45,700	$ 45,700
Personal exemption				300
Corpus capital gain/loss				(10,000)
Net tax-exempt income				18,000
Distributable net income				$ 54,000
Distribution deduction			Step 3 (36,000)	
Entity taxable income			Step 4 $ 9,700	

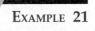

Step 1. Trust accounting income is $60,000; this includes the tax-exempt interest income, but not the fees or the capital gains, pursuant to the trust document. Barbara receives $60,000 from the trust for the current year.

Step 2. Taxable income before the distribution deduction is computed as directed by the Code. The tax-exempt interest is excluded under § 103. Only a portion of the fees is deductible because some of the fees are traceable to the tax-exempt income. The trust receives a $300 personal exemption as it is required to distribute its annual trust accounting income.

Step 3. DNI and the distribution deduction reflect the required adjustments. The distribution deduction is the lesser of the distributed amount ($60,000) or the deductible portion of DNI ($54,000 – $18,000 net tax-exempt income).

Step 4. Finally, return to the computation of the taxable income of the Pork Trust. A simple test should be applied at this point to ensure that the proper figure for the trust's taxable income has been determined. On what is Pork to be taxed? All of the trust's gross income has been distributed to Barbara except the $10,000 net long-term capital gains. The $300 personal exemption reduces the trust's taxable income to $9,700. ▼

EXAMPLE 21

The Quick Trust is required to distribute all of its current accounting income equally to its two beneficiaries, Faith and the First Methodist Church, a qualifying charitable organization. Capital gains and losses and depreciation expenses are allocable to income. Fiduciary fees are allocable to corpus. In the current year, Quick incurs various items as indicated.

Item	Totals	Accounting Income	Taxable Income	Distributable Net Income/ Distribution Deduction
Rent income	$100,000	$100,000	$100,000	
Expenses—rent income	30,000	(30,000)	(30,000)	
Depreciation—rent income	15,000	(15,000)		
Net long-term capital gain	20,000	20,000	20,000	
Charitable contribution			(37,500)	
Fiduciary fees	18,000		(18,000)	
Personal exemption			(300)	
Accounting income/taxable income before the distribution deduction		Step 1 $ 75,000	Step 2 $ 34,200	$34,200
Personal exemption				300
Corpus capital gain/loss				
Net tax-exempt income				
Distributable net income				$34,500
Distribution deduction			Step 3 (34,500)	
Entity taxable income			Step 4 ($ 300)	

Step 1. Trust accounting income of $75,000 reflects the indicated allocations of items to income and to corpus. Each income beneficiary receives $37,500.

Step 2. In the absence of tax-exempt income, a deduction is allowed for the full amount of the fiduciary's fees. Quick is a complex trust, but since it is required to distribute its full accounting income annually, a $300 exemption is allowed. The trust properly does not deduct any depreciation for the rental property. The depreciation deduction is available only to the recipients of the entity's accounting income for the period. Thus, the deduction will be split equally between Faith and the church. The deduction probably is of no direct value to the church, as the church is not subject to the income tax. The trust's charitable contribution deduction is based upon the $37,500 that the charity actually received (one-half of trust accounting income).

Step 3. As there is no tax-exempt income, the only adjustment needed to compute DNI is to add back the trust's personal exemption. Subchapter J requires no adjustment for the charitable contribution. DNI is computed only from the perspective of Faith, who also received $37,500 from the trust.

Step 4. Finally, the trust's taxable income before the distribution deduction is reduced by the distribution deduction to produce the trust's taxable income of ($300). Perform the simple test (referred to above) to ensure that the proper taxable income for the Quick Trust has been computed. All of the trust's gross income has been distributed to Faith and the church. As is the case with most trusts that distribute all of their annual income, the Quick Trust "wastes" the personal exemption. ▼

TAX CREDITS

An estate or trust may claim the foreign tax credit to the extent that it is not passed through to the beneficiaries.[31] Similarly, other credits must be apportioned

---

[31] §§ 642(a)(1) and 901.

TAX IN THE NEWS

IS IT A CHARITY OR A BENEFICIARY?

The general prohibition against "double deductions" is unclear when the beneficiary of a distribution from the fiduciary is a charity. Does the entity claim a charitable deduction or a distribution deduction for the payment?

Neither the Code nor the Regulations under Subchapter J address this question. Most practitioners apply a "volume" test, as was done in Example 21, using the charitable deduction for small payments from the estate's gross income and the distribution deduction for larger (especially recurring) contributions.

In *U.S. Trust Co. v. Comm.*, 86–2 USTC ¶9777, 58 AFTR2d 86–6152, 803 F.2d 1363 (CA–5, 1986), though, the taxpayer boldly claimed two deductions for a $2.5 million payment by the decedent to a qualifying charity, one as a charitable deduction on the estate tax return and the other as a distribution deduction on the estate's income tax return. The trustee explained that the distribution deduction was used because the will did not specify that the payment be made from the gross income of the estate.

The taxpayer's approach is not strictly prohibited by the Code. In fact, the Federal Appeals Court noted that multiple tax benefits accrue when an estate makes a payment to charity. The double deduction would have survived had the will specified the amount and source of the charitable gift as some type of gross income recognized by the estate.

But that was not the case here, and the distribution deduction was denied. In essence, the Appeals Court viewed the gift as a bequest specified by the will, not a distribution of postdeath income. Bequests are not deductible for income tax purposes, and neither was this payment.

between the estate or trust and the beneficiaries on the basis of the entity accounting income allocable to each.

TAXATION OF BENEFICIARIES

The beneficiaries of an estate or trust receive taxable income from the entity under the modified conduit principle of Subchapter J. DNI determines the maximum amount that can be taxed to the beneficiaries for any tax year. The constitution of DNI also carries over to the beneficiaries (e.g., net long-term capital gains retain their character when they are distributed from the entity to the beneficiary).

The timing of any tax consequences to the beneficiary of a trust or estate presents a problem only when the parties involved use different tax years. A beneficiary must include in gross income an amount based upon the DNI of the trust for any taxable year or years of the trust or estate ending with or within his or her taxable year.[32]

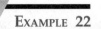

EXAMPLE 22

An estate uses a fiscal year ending on March 31 for tax purposes. Its sole income beneficiary is a calendar year taxpayer. For calendar year 1997, the beneficiary reports whatever income

---

[32]§§ 652(c) and 662(c).

was assignable to her for the entity's fiscal year April 1, 1996, to March 31, 1997. If the estate is terminated by December 31, 1997, the beneficiary must also include any income assignable to her for the short year. This could result in a bunching of income in 1997. ▼

DISTRIBUTIONS BY SIMPLE TRUSTS

The amount taxable to the beneficiaries of a simple trust is limited by the trust's DNI. However, since DNI includes net tax-exempt income, the amount included in the gross income of the beneficiaries could be less than DNI. When there is more than one income beneficiary, the elements of DNI must be apportioned ratably according to the amount required to be distributed currently to each.

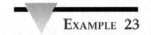
EXAMPLE 23

A simple trust has ordinary income of $40,000, a long-term capital gain of $15,000 (allocable to corpus), and a trustee commission expense of $4,000 (payable from corpus). The two income beneficiaries, Allie and Bart, are entitled to the trust's annual accounting income, based on shares of 75% and 25%, respectively. Although Allie receives $30,000 as her share (75% × $40,000 trust accounting income), she will be allocated DNI of only $27,000 (75% × $36,000). Likewise, Bart is entitled to receive $10,000 (25% × $40,000), but he will be allocated DNI of only $9,000 (25% × $36,000). The $15,000 capital gain is taxed to the trust. ▼

DISTRIBUTIONS BY ESTATES AND COMPLEX TRUSTS

A problem arises with estates and complex trusts when more than one beneficiary receives a distribution from the entity and the controlling document does not require a distribution of the entire accounting income of the entity.

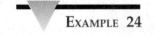
EXAMPLE 24

The trustee of the Wilson Trust has the discretion to distribute the income or corpus of the trust in any proportion between the two beneficiaries of the trust, Wong and Washington. Under the trust instrument, Wong must receive $15,000 from the trust every year. In the current year, the trust's accounting income is $50,000, and its DNI is $40,000. The trustee pays $35,000 to Wong and $25,000 to Washington for the current year. ▼

How is Wilson's DNI to be divided between Wong and Washington? Several arbitrary methods of allocating DNI between the beneficiaries could be devised. Subchapter J resolves the problem by creating a two-tier system to govern the taxation of beneficiaries in such situations.[33] The tier system determines which distributions will be included in the gross income of the beneficiaries in full, which will be included in part, and which will not be included at all.

Income that is required to be distributed currently, whether or not it is distributed, is categorized as a *first-tier distribution*. All other amounts properly paid, credited, or required to be distributed are considered to be *second-tier distributions*.[34] A formula is used to allocate DNI among the appropriate beneficiaries when only first-tier distributions are made and those amounts exceed DNI.

---

[33] §§ 662(a)(1) and (2).   [34] Reg. §§ 1.662(a)–2 and –3.

When both first-tier and second-tier distributions are made and the first-tier distributions exceed DNI, the above formula is applied to the first-tier distributions. In this case, none of the second-tier distributions are taxed because all of the DNI has been allocated to the first-tier beneficiaries.

If both first-tier and second-tier distributions are made and the first-tier distributions do not exceed DNI, but the total of both first-tier and second-tier distributions does exceed DNI, the second-tier beneficiaries must recognize income as shown below.

$$\frac{\text{Second-tier distributions to the beneficiary}}{\text{Second-tier distributions to all beneficiaries}} \quad \boxed{\times} \quad \text{Remaining distributable net income (after first-tier distributions)} \quad \boxed{=} \quad \text{Beneficiary's share of distributable net income}$$

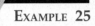
EXAMPLE 25

The trustee of the Gray Trust is required to distribute $10,000 per year to both Harriet and Wally, the two beneficiaries of the entity. In addition, he is empowered to distribute other amounts of trust income or corpus at his sole discretion. In the current year, the trust has accounting income of $60,000 and DNI of $50,000. However, the trustee distributes only the required $10,000 each to Harriet and to Wally. The balance of the income is accumulated and added to trust corpus.

In this case, only first-tier distributions have been made, but the total amount of the distributions does not exceed DNI for the year. Although DNI is the maximum amount that is included by the beneficiaries for the year, they can include no more in gross income than is distributed by the entity. Thus, both Harriet and Wally are subject to tax on $10,000 as their proportionate shares of DNI. ▼

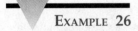
EXAMPLE 26

Assume the same facts as in Example 25, except that DNI is $12,000. Harriet and Wally each receive $10,000, but they cannot be taxed in total on more than DNI. Each is taxed on $6,000 [$12,000 DNI × ($10,000/$20,000 of the first-tier distributions)]. ▼

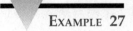
EXAMPLE 27

Return to the facts in Example 24. Wong receives a first-tier distribution of $15,000. Second-tier distributions include $20,000 to Wong and $25,000 to Washington. Wilson Trust's DNI is $40,000. The DNI is allocated between Wong and Washington as follows.

1. First-tier distributions

To Wong	$15,000 DNI
To Washington	–0–
Remaining DNI = $25,000 ($40,000 DNI – $15,000 distributed)	

2. Second-tier distributions

To Wong [(20/45) × $25,000]	$11,111 DNI
To Washington [(25/45) × $25,000]	13,889 DNI ▼

Separate Share Rule. For the sole purpose of determining the amount of DNI for a complex trust with more than one beneficiary, the substantially separate and independent shares of different beneficiaries in the trust are treated as *separate trusts*.[35] An illustration shows the need for this special rule.

---

[35] Reg. § 1.663(c)–1(a).

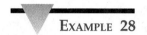
EXAMPLE 28

A trustee has the discretion to distribute or accumulate income on behalf of Greg and Hannah (in equal shares). The trustee also has the power to invade corpus for the benefit of either beneficiary to the extent of that beneficiary's one-half interest in the trust. For the current year, DNI is $10,000. Of this amount, $5,000 is distributed to Greg, and $5,000 is accumulated on behalf of Hannah. In addition, the trustee pays $20,000 from corpus to Greg. Without the separate share rule, Greg is taxed on $10,000 (the full amount of the DNI). With the separate share rule, Greg is taxed on only $5,000 (his share of the DNI) and receives the $20,000 corpus distribution tax-free. The trust will be taxed on Hannah's $5,000 share of the DNI that is accumulated. ▼

The separate share rule is designed to prevent the inequity that results if the corpus payments are treated under the regular rules applicable to second-tier beneficiaries. In Example 28, the effect of the separate share rule is to produce a two-trust result: one trust for Greg and one for Hannah, each with DNI of $5,000.

CHARACTER OF INCOME

Consistent with the modified conduit principle of Subchapter J, various classes of income (e.g., dividends, passive or portfolio gain and loss, AMT preferences and adjustments, and tax-exempt interest) retain the same character for the beneficiaries that they had when they were received by the entity. If there are multiple beneficiaries *and* if all of the DNI is distributed, a problem arises in allocating the various classes of income among the beneficiaries.

Distributions are treated as consisting of the same proportion as the items that enter into the computation of DNI. This allocation does not apply, however, if the governing instrument specifically allocates different classes of income to different beneficiaries.[36]

If the entity distributes only a part of its DNI, the amount of a particular class of DNI that is deemed distributed must first be determined.

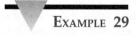
EXAMPLE 29

During the current year, a trust has DNI of $40,000, including the following: $10,000 of taxable interest, $10,000 of tax-exempt interest, and $20,000 of passive activity income. The trustee distributes, at her discretion, $8,000 to Mike and $12,000 to Nancy.

---

[36] Reg. § 1.662(b)–1 seems to allow special allocations, but see *Harkness v. U.S.,* 72–2 USTC ¶9740, 30 AFTR2d 72–5754, 469 F.2d 310 (Ct.Cls., 1972).

Beneficiary	Amount Received	Income Type		
		Taxable Interest	Exempt Interest	Passive Income
Mike	$ 8,000	$2,000*	$2,000	4,000
Nancy	12,000	3,000	3,000	6,000

*$8,000 distribution/$40,000 total DNI × $10,000 taxable interest in DNI. ▼

Special Allocations. Under certain circumstances, the parties may modify the character-of-income allocation method set forth above. A modification is permitted only to the extent that the allocation is required in the trust instrument and only to the extent that it has an economic effect independent of the cash-flow and income tax consequences of the allocation.[37]

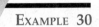

EXAMPLE 30

Return to the facts in Example 29. Assume that the beneficiaries are elderly individuals who have pooled their investment portfolios to avail themselves of the trustee's professional asset management skills. Suppose the trustee has the discretion to allocate different classes of income to different beneficiaries and that she designates all of Nancy's $12,000 distribution as being from the tax-exempt income. Such a designation *would not be recognized* for tax purposes, and the allocation method of Example 29 must be used.

Suppose, however, that the trust instrument stipulated that Nancy was to receive all of the income from tax-exempt securities because she alone contributed the exempt securities to trust corpus. Under this provision, the $10,000 of the nontaxable interest is paid to Nancy. This allocation *is recognized*, and $10,000 of Nancy's distribution is tax-exempt. ▼

LOSSES IN THE TERMINATION YEAR

The ordinary net operating and capital losses of a trust or estate do not flow through to the entity's beneficiaries, as would such losses from a partnership or an S corporation. However, in the year in which an entity terminates its existence, the beneficiaries do receive a direct benefit from the loss carryovers of the trust or estate.[38]

Net operating losses and net capital losses are subject to the same carryover rules that otherwise apply to an individual. Consequently, NOLs can be carried back 3 years and then carried forward 15 years while net capital losses can be carried forward only, and for an indefinite period of time. However, if the entity incurs a negative taxable income in the last year of its existence, the excess of deductions over the entity's gross income is allowed to the beneficiaries (it will flow through to them directly). The net loss is available as a deduction *from* AGI in the beneficiary's tax year with or within which the entity's tax year ends. The amount allowed is in proportion to the relative amount of corpus assets that each beneficiary receives upon the termination of the entity, and it is subject to the 2 percent-of-AGI floor.

Any carryovers of the entity's other losses flow through to the beneficiaries in the year of termination in proportion to the relative amount of corpus assets that each beneficiary receives. The character of the loss carryforward is retained by the beneficiary, except that a carryover of a net capital loss to a corporate beneficiary is always treated as short term. Beneficiaries who are individuals use these carryforwards as deductions *for* AGI.

---

[37] Reg. § 1.652(b)–2(b). This is similar to the § 704(b) requirement for partnerships.

[38] Reg. §§ 1.642(h)–1 and –2.

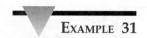

EXAMPLE 31

The Edgar Estate terminates on December 31, 1996. It had used a fiscal year ending July 31. For the termination year, the estate incurred a $15,000 negative taxable income. In addition, the estate had an unused NOL carryforward of $23,000 from the year ending July 31, 1993, and an unused net long-term capital loss carryforward of $10,000 from the year ending July 31, 1995. Upon termination, Dawn receives $60,000 of corpus, and Blue Corporation receives the remaining $40,000. Dawn and Blue are calendar year taxpayers.

Dawn can claim an itemized deduction of $9,000 [($60,000/$100,000) × $15,000] for the entity's negative taxable income in the year of termination. This deduction is subject to the 2%-of-AGI floor on miscellaneous itemized deductions. In addition, she can claim a $13,800 deduction *for* AGI in 1996 (60% × $23,000) for Edgar's NOL carryforward, and she can use $6,000 (60% × $10,000) of the estate's net long-term capital loss carryforward with her other 1996 capital transactions.

Blue Corporation receives ordinary business deductions in 1996 for Edgar's NOLs: $6,000 for the loss in the year of termination and $9,200 for the carryforward from fiscal year 1993. Moreover, Blue can use the $4,000 carryforward of Edgar's net capital losses to offset against its other 1996 capital transactions, although the loss must be treated as short term. ▼

THE THROWBACK RULE

4   LEARNING OBJECTIVE
Understand the effects of statutory restrictions on the taxation of distributions from accumulation trusts.

Generally, a trust's beneficiary is not taxed on any distributions in excess of the trust's DNI. Thus, trustees of complex trusts might be tempted to arrange distributions in a way that results in minimal income tax consequences to all of the parties involved. For instance, if the trust is subject to a lower income tax rate than are its beneficiaries, income could be accumulated at the trust level for several years before being distributed to the beneficiaries. Thus, the income taxed to the beneficiaries in the year of distribution is limited by the trust's DNI for that year. Further tax savings could be achieved by using multiple trusts. This device spreads the income during the accumulation period over more than one taxpaying entity and avoids the graduated tax rates.

To discourage the use of these tax minimization schemes, a throwback rule was added to the Code. Under the rule, a beneficiary's tax on a distribution of income accumulated by a trust in a prior year will approximate the increased tax that the beneficiary would have owed for that prior year if the income had been distributed in the year that it was earned by the trust. The tax as computed, however, is levied for the actual year of the distribution. The purpose of the throwback rule is to place the beneficiaries of complex trusts in the same nominal tax position they would have been in if they had received the distributions during the years in which the trust was accumulating the income.

A detailed description of the application of the throwback rule is beyond the scope of this text.

TAX PLANNING CONSIDERATIONS

Many of the tax planning possibilities for estates and trusts were discussed in Chapter 26. However, several specific tax planning possibilities are available to help minimize the income tax effects on estates and trusts and their beneficiaries.

5   LEARNING OBJECTIVE
Understand various tax planning procedures that can be used to minimize the tax consequences of trusts and estates and their beneficiaries.

A TRUST OR ESTATE AS AN INCOME-SHIFTING DEVICE

The compressed tax rate schedule applicable to Subchapter J entities may have reversed the traditional techniques by which families set aside funds for long-term activities, such as business start-ups, college education, and home purchases. When the tax rate schedules for trusts and estates were more accommodating,

---

CONCEPT SUMMARY 27–1

Income Taxation of Trusts and Estates

1. Estates and trusts are temporary entities, created to locate, maintain, and distribute assets and to satisfy liabilities according to the wishes of the decedent or grantor as expressed in the will or trust document.

2. Generally, the estate or trust acts as a conduit of the taxable income that it receives. To the extent that the income is distributed by the entity, it is taxed to the beneficiary. Taxable income retained by the entity is taxed to the entity itself.

3. The entity's accounting income must be determined first. Accounting conventions that are stated in the controlling document or, lacking such provisions, in state law allocate specific items of receipt and expenditure either to income or to corpus. Income beneficiaries typically receive payments from the entity that are equal to the accounting income.

4. The taxable income of the entity is computed using the scheme in Figure 27–3. The entity usually recognizes income in respect of a decedent. Deductions for fiduciary's fees and for charitable contributions may be reduced if the entity received any tax-exempt income during the year. Cost recovery deductions are assigned proportionately to the recipients of accounting income. Upon election, realized gain or loss on assets that properly are distributed in kind can be recognized by the entity.

5. A distribution deduction, computationally derived from distributable net income (DNI), is allowed to the entity. DNI is the maximum amount on which entity beneficiaries can be taxed. Moreover, the constitution of DNI is assigned to the recipients of the distributions.

---

high-income individuals would shift income-producing assets to trusts to take advantage of the lower tax rate that would fall on the income accumulated within the trust. The target of the plan, usually a child, would receive the accumulated income (and, perhaps, trust corpus) at a designated age, and more funds would be available because a lower tax rate had been applied over the life of the investment in the trust.

Today, such an income shift would *deplete*, rather than shelter, the family's assets, as the rates falling on individuals are much more graduated than are those applicable to fiduciaries, and the kiddie tax also penalizes attempts to shift taxable income to children. Assuming that the objectives of the plan remain unchanged, possible strategies in view of these rate changes include the following:

- Trust corpus should be invested in growth assets that are low on yield but high on appreciation, so that the trustee can determine the timing of the gain and somewhat control the effective tax rate that applies.
- Trust corpus should be invested in tax-exempt securities, such as municipal bonds and mutual funds that invest in them, to eliminate the tax costs associated with the investment. If this approach is taken, a trust might be unnecessary—the parent should simply retain full control over the assets and invest in the exempt securities in his or her own account.
- The grantor should retain high-yield assets, so that control over the assets is not surrendered when the tax cost is too high.
- Use of trust vehicles should be reserved for cases where professional management of the assets is necessary for portfolio growth and the additional tax costs can be justified.
- An income-shifting strategy may require several steps to achieve the desired result. For instance, the grantor might increase contributions to his or her own qualified retirement plan, thereby sheltering the funds from all tax liabilities. Then the grantor could use the tax dollars saved from these

contributions to purchase tax-deferred annuity contracts, savings bonds, exempt securities, or other assets where the tax liabilities are reduced or deferred. The grantor could then either retain these exempt securities as discussed above or transfer them to the trust at a later date.

INCOME TAX PLANNING FOR ESTATES

As a separate taxable entity, an estate can select its own tax year and accounting methods. The executor of an estate should consider selecting a fiscal year because this will determine when beneficiaries must include income distributions from the estate in their own tax returns. Beneficiaries must include the income for their tax year with or within which the estate's tax year ends. Proper selection of the estate's tax year can result in a smoothing out of income and a reduction of the income taxes for all parties involved.

Caution should be taken in determining when the estate is to be terminated. Selecting a fiscal year for the estate can result in a bunching of income to the beneficiaries in the year in which the estate is closed. Prolonging the termination of an estate can be effective income tax planning, but the IRS carefully examines the purpose of keeping the estate open. Since the unused losses of an estate pass through to the beneficiaries only in the termination year, the estate should be closed when the beneficiaries can enjoy the maximum tax benefit of the losses.

The timing and amounts of income distributions to the beneficiaries also present important tax planning opportunities. If the executor can make discretionary income distributions, he or she should evaluate the relative marginal income tax rates of the estate and its beneficiaries. By timing the distributions properly, the overall income tax liability can be minimized. Care should be taken, however, to time the distributions in light of the estate's DNI.

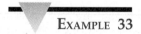
EXAMPLE 32

For several years before his death on March 7, Don had entered into annual deferred compensation agreements with his employer. These agreements collectively called for the payment of $200,000 six months after Don's retirement or death. To provide a maximum 12-month period within which to generate deductions to offset this large item of IRD, the executor or administrator of the estate should elect a fiscal year ending August 31. The election is made simply by filing the estate's first tax return for the short period of March 7 to August 31. ▼

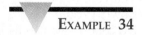
EXAMPLE 33

Carol, the sole beneficiary of an estate, is a calendar year, cash basis taxpayer. If the estate elects a fiscal year ending January 31, all distributions during the period of February 1 to December 31, 1995, will be reported on Carol's tax return for calendar year 1996 (due April 15, 1997). Thus, assuming estimated tax requirements have otherwise been met, any income taxes that result from a $50,000 distribution made by the estate on February 20, 1995, will be deferred until April 15, 1997. ▼

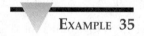
EXAMPLE 34

Assume the same facts as in Example 33. If the estate is closed on December 15, 1996, the DNI for both the fiscal year ending January 31, 1996, and the final tax year ending December 15, 1996, is included in Carol's tax return for the calendar year 1996. To avoid the effect of this bunching of income, the estate should not be closed until calendar year 1997. ▼

EXAMPLE 35

Assume the same facts as in Example 34, except that the estate has a substantial NOL for the period February 1 to December 15, 1996. If Carol is subject to a high income tax rate for calendar year 1996, the estate should be closed in that year so that the excess deductions are passed through to its beneficiary. However, if Carol anticipates being in a higher tax bracket in 1997, the termination of the estate should be postponed. ▼

In general, beneficiaries who are subject to high tax rates should be made beneficiaries of second-tier (but not IRD) distributions of the estate. Most likely, these individuals will have less need for an additional steady stream of (taxable) income while their income tax savings can be relatively large. Moreover, a special allocation of tax-favored types of income and expenses should be considered. For example, tax-exempt income can be directed more easily to beneficiaries in higher income tax brackets.

ETHICAL CONSIDERATIONS

Should a Tax Adviser Also Be a Trustee?

Tax clients need to be counseled on the best use of the trust entity and the proper choice of beneficiary of the trust income. The objectives of the grantor typically will best be served by transferring more power to the trustee; sprinkling powers, in particular, enable the trustee to be sensitive to the short-term and ongoing needs of the various beneficiaries. The client, however, may not appreciate this suggestion when the trust document is drafted. Especially if the tax adviser is the trustee or a co-trustee, the client may balk at the professional's well-intended suggestion that future developments might favor one beneficiary over another in a manner that cannot be anticipated at the time.

Should the source of the estate plan—the tax adviser—also then be designated as the trustee by the grantor? When the adviser serves in that capacity, who is "the client"? Merely the grantor? How about the beneficiaries? And the trust itself? To avoid any potential for conflict with their clients, some professional firms have adopted a policy of refusing to serve as trustee of a client's trust (or executor of his or her estate). Certainly, surrendering a sprinkling power to a fiduciary who is less sensitive to the tax ramifications of Subchapter J may be costly to all of the parties, but these firms see the preservation of the client relationship as more valuable in the long term.

Recall, also, that although both of her children are attorneys, Jacqueline Kennedy Onassis was careful to make other parties the executor of her estate and the trustees of her fiduciary entities. In more typical estates, though, the grantor must address critical issues: How much power and control over assets and income should be "surrendered to outsiders" through the trust? Which items lend themselves to such transfers of control?

INCOME TAX PLANNING WITH TRUSTS

The great variety of trusts provides the grantor, trustee, and beneficiaries with excellent opportunities for tax planning. Many of the same tax planning opportunities available to the executor of an estate are available to the trustee. For instance, the distributions from a trust are taxable to the trust's beneficiaries to the extent of the trust's DNI. If income distributions are discretionary, the trustee can time the distributions to minimize the income tax consequences to all parties.

Remember that the throwback rule applies to complex trusts. Consequently, the benefit from the timing of distributions may be more limited than it is for estates. Indeed, improper timing could result in a greater nominal tax than if the distributions had been made annually.

DISTRIBUTIONS OF IN-KIND PROPERTY

The ability of the trustee or executor to elect to recognize the realized gain or loss relative to a distributed noncash asset allows the gain or loss to be allocated to the optimal taxpayer.

EXAMPLE 36

The Yorba Linda Estate distributed some stock, basis of $40,000 and fair market value of $41,500, to beneficiary Larry. Yorba Linda is subject to a 15% income tax rate, and Larry is subject to a 31% tax rate. The executor of Yorba Linda should elect that the entity recognize the related $1,500 realized gain, thereby subjecting the gain to the estate's lower tax rate and reducing Larry's future capital gain income (by increasing his basis). ▼

KEY TERMS

Complex trust, 27–5

Corpus, 27–4

Distributable net income (DNI), 27–17

Expenses in respect of a decedent, 27–13

Grantor, 27–4

Grantor trusts, 27–4

Income in respect of a decedent (IRD), 27–13

Reversionary interest, 27–4

Simple trust, 27–5

Sprinkling trust, 27–5

PROBLEM MATERIALS

DISCUSSION QUESTIONS

1. When should a client be counseled to create a trust? What tax motivations might lead to the use of a fiduciary?

2. Identify the parties involved in the creation of a trust. Do the same for an estate.

3. When is the trustee required to file a Form 1041?

4. Why has Congress subjected trusts and estates to such a compressed tax rate schedule? Demonstrate this compression numerically.

5. What is the personal exemption allowed an estate? A trust?

6. Is the fiduciary entity subject to the alternative minimum tax? What tax rates and exemptions apply?

7. Outline the five-step process of determining the taxable income amounts for the parties to a trust arrangement.

8. What happens when a trust distributes an asset to a beneficiary and the asset's basis is less than its fair market value?

9. How does Subchapter J assign the cost recovery deductions attributable to the operations of a trust?

10. How does a trust or estate treat charitable contribution deductions?

11. The Flakk Trust is scheduled to terminate in two years, when Amy Flakk reaches age 30. The trust operated a business several years ago, and it generated a sizable NOL carryforward that the trust has not been able to use. In addition, due to poor investment advice, the value of the entity's investment portfolio declined 15% from its purchase price. What issues must you consider in giving Amy and the corporate trustee tax planning advice?

12. Willie holds an asset that has appreciated from its $100,000 basis to a current value of $250,000. He wants to transfer the asset to his daughter Gloria when she reaches the age of majority in five years, but he does not want tax payments to reduce the value of his gift. Willie and Gloria are in good health, but she is not ready to take on the responsibilities of managing such a sizable asset. How should Willie approach this situation?

13. Kramer and Benes are the income beneficiaries of the Costello Trust. This year, the trust's distributable net income is $100,000, and income distributions total $40,000. Identify tax issues that may be important in future years for Costello, Kramer, and Benes.

14. Write a memo for the tax research file discussing the tax planning opportunities presented by an estate's ability to select a noncalendar tax year. Your clients seek advice as to the estate of a decedent who died on May 3. Large payments of IRD will be received in the first three months after the date of death.

PROBLEMS

15. Illustrate the nature and operations of each of the following trusts by creating a fact pattern to match each result.
    a. A simple trust.
    b. A complex trust with a $300 personal exemption.
    c. A complex trust with a $100 personal exemption.

16. The Purple Trust incurred the following items this year.

Taxable interest income	$50,000
Tax-exempt interest income, not on private activity bonds	60,000
Tax-exempt interest income, on private activity bonds	70,000

Compute Purple's tentative minimum tax for the year. Purple does not have any credits available to reduce the AMT liability.

17. Complete the following chart, indicating the comparative attributes of the typical trust and estate by answering yes/no or explaining the differences between the entities where appropriate.

Attribute	Estate	Trust
Separate income tax entity	___	___
Controlling document	___	___
Termination date is determinable from controlling document	___	___
Legal owner of assets under fiduciary's control	___	___
Document identifies both income and remainder beneficiaries	___	___
Throwback rules apply	___	___
Separate share rules apply	___	___
Generally must use calendar tax year	___	___

18. In its first tax year, the Wittmann Estate generated $50,000 of taxable interest income and $25,000 of tax-exempt interest income. It paid fiduciary fees of $4,000. The estate is subject to a 37% marginal estate tax rate and a 31% marginal income tax rate.
    a. How should the executor assign the deductions for the payment of the fees?
    b. How does the 2%-of-AGI floor apply to these fees assigned to the estate's income tax return?

19. Brown incurred the following items in 1996.

Business income	$20,000
Tax-exempt interest income	5,000
Payment to charity from 1996 income, paid 3/1/97	3,000

Complete the following chart, indicating how the Code treats charitable contributions under the various assumptions.

Assumption	1996 Deduction for Contribution
Brown is a cash basis individual.	_____
Brown is an accrual basis corporation.	_____
Brown is a trust.	_____

20. The Prasad Trust operates a welding business. Its current-year MACRS (modified accelerated cost recovery system) deductions properly amounted to $35,000. Prasad's accounting income was $150,000, of which $80,000 was distributed to first-tier beneficiary Chuck, $60,000 was distributed to second-tier beneficiary Ruby, and $10,000 was accumulated by the trustee. Ruby also received a $15,000 corpus distribution. Prasad's DNI was $52,000. Discuss the treatment of Prasad's cost recovery deductions.

21. The LMN Trust is a simple trust that correctly uses the calendar year for tax purposes. Its three income beneficiaries (Lynn, Mark, and Norelle) are entitled to the trust's annual accounting income in shares of one-third each. For the current calendar year, the trust has ordinary income of $50,000, a long-term capital gain of $18,000 (allocable to corpus), and a trustee commission expense of $6,000 (allocable to corpus). Use the format of Figure 27–3 to address the following items.
   a. How much income is each beneficiary entitled to receive?
   b. What is the trust's DNI?
   c. What is the trust's taxable income?
   d. How much is taxed to each of the beneficiaries?

22. Assume the same facts as in Problem 21, except that the trust instrument allocates the capital gain to income.
   a. How much income is each beneficiary entitled to receive?
   b. What is the trust's DNI?
   c. What is the trust's taxable income?
   d. How much is taxed to each of the beneficiaries?

23. Under the terms of the trust instrument, the trustee has discretion to distribute or accumulate income on behalf of Willie, Sylvia, and Drahman in equal shares. The trustee also can invade corpus for the benefit of any of the beneficiaries to the extent of each person's respective one-third interest in the trust. In the current year, the trust has DNI of $48,000. Of this amount, $16,000 is distributed to Willie and $10,000 is distributed to Sylvia. The remaining $6,000 of Sylvia's share of DNI and Drahman's entire $16,000 share are accumulated by the trust. Additionally, the trustee distributes $20,000 from corpus to Willie.
   a. How much income is taxed to Willie?
   b. To Sylvia?
   c. To Drahman?
   d. To the trust?

24. A trust is required to distribute $20,000 annually to its two income beneficiaries, Amber and Byron, in shares of 75% and 25%, respectively. If trust income is not sufficient to pay these amounts, the trustee can invade corpus to the extent necessary. During the current year, the trust has DNI of $12,000, and the trustee distributes $15,000 to Amber and $5,000 to Byron.
   a. How much of the $15,000 distributed to Amber must be included in her gross income?
   b. How much of the $5,000 distributed to Byron must be included in his gross income?
   c. Are these distributions considered to be first-tier or second-tier distributions?

25. The trustee of the Miguel Trust can distribute any amount of accounting income and corpus to the trust's beneficiaries, Paula and George. This year, the trust incurred the following.

Taxable interest income	$40,000
Tax-exempt interest income	60,000
Long-term capital gains—allocable to corpus	25,000
Fiduciary's fees—allocable to corpus	12,000

The trustee distributed $25,000 to Paula and $28,000 to George.
  a. What is Miguel's trust accounting income?
  b. What is Miguel's DNI?
  c. What is Miguel's taxable income?
  d. How much is taxed to each of the beneficiaries?

26. Each of the following items was incurred by José, the cash basis, calendar year decedent. Applying the rules for income and deductions in respect of a decedent, indicate on which return each item should be reported: the recipient/heir's last Form 1040 income tax (*Form 1040*); José's estate's first Form 1041 income tax (*Form 1041*); or José's estate's Form 706 estate tax (*Form 706*). More than one alternative may apply in some cases.

Item Incurred	Form(s) Reported on
a. Wages, last paycheck	1040 & 1041 ?(some)
b. State income tax withheld on last paycheck	1040 & 706's
c. Capital gain portion of installment payment received	1040 & 706
d. Ordinary income portion of installment payment received	1040 & 706
e. Dividend income, record date was two days prior to José's death	1040 & 706
f. Unrealized appreciation on a mutual fund investment	unrealized (none)
g. Depreciation recapture accrued as of date of death	none - step up charge
h. Medical expenses of last illness	1040 or Est 706
i. Apartment building, rents accrued but not collected as of death	1040 OR 706
j. Apartment building, property tax accrued and assessed but not paid as of death	1040 & 706 not both

27. Determine the tax effects of the indicated losses for the Yellow Estate for both tax years. The estate holds a variety of investment assets, which it received from the decedent, Mrs. Yellow. The estate's sole income and remainder beneficiary is Yellow, Jr.

Tax Year	Loss Generated
1995 (first tax year)	Taxable income ($300) Capital loss ($15,000)
1996 (final tax year)	Taxable income ($1,000)

Research Problems for this chapter appear at the end of Chapter 28.

WORKING WITH THE TAX LAW

LEARNING OBJECTIVES

After completing Chapter 28, you should be able to:

1. Distinguish between the statutory, administrative, and judicial sources of the tax law and understand the purpose of each source.

2. Locate and work with the appropriate tax law sources.

3. Understand the tax research process.

4. Communicate the results of the tax research process in a client letter and a tax file memorandum.

5. Apply tax research techniques and planning procedures.

6. Have an awareness of computer-assisted tax research.

TAX SOURCES

1   **LEARNING OBJECTIVE**
Distinguish between the statutory, administrative, and judicial sources of the tax law and understand the purpose of each source.

Understanding taxation requires a mastery of the sources of the *rules of tax law*. These sources include not only legislative provisions in the form of the Internal Revenue Code, but also congressional Committee Reports, Treasury Department Regulations, other Treasury Department pronouncements, and court decisions. Thus, the *primary sources* of tax information include pronouncements from all three branches of government: legislative, executive, and judicial.

In addition to being able to locate and interpret the sources of the tax law, a tax professional must understand the relative weight of authority within these sources. The tax law is of little significance, however, until it is applied to a set of facts and circumstances. This chapter, therefore, both introduces the statutory, administrative, and judicial sources of the tax law *and* explains how the law is applied to individual and business transactions. It also explains how to apply research techniques and use planning procedures effectively.

A large part of tax research focuses on determining the intent of Congress. While Congress often claims simplicity as one of its goals, a cursory examination of the tax law indicates that it has not been very successful. Faced with a 48-page tax return, James Michener, the author, says, "it is unimaginable in that I graduated from one of America's better colleges, yet I am totally incapable of understanding tax returns." David Brinkley, the television news commentator, observes that "settling a dispute is difficult when our tax regulations are all written in a foreign tongue whose language flows like damp sludge leaking from a sanitary landfill."

Frequently, uncertainty in the tax law causes disputes between the Internal Revenue Service (IRS) and taxpayers. Due to these *gray areas* and the complexity of the tax law, a taxpayer may have more than one alternative for structuring a business transaction. In structuring business transactions and engaging in other tax planning activities, the tax adviser must be cognizant that the objective of tax planning is not necessarily to minimize the tax liability. Instead a taxpayer should maximize his or her after-tax return, which may include maximizing nontax as well as noneconomic benefits.

STATUTORY SOURCES OF THE TAX LAW

Origin of the Internal Revenue Code. Before 1939, the statutory provisions relating to taxation were contained in the individual revenue acts enacted by

TAX IN THE NEWS

SMALL IS BEAUTIFUL?

In income tax history, 1913 was an important year. In that year, the Sixteenth Amendment to the Constitution was ratified.

The Congress shall have power to tax and collect taxes on incomes, from whatever source derived, without apportionment among the several States, and without regard to any census or enumeration.

The first income tax legislation that definitely was constitutional was passed that same year.

Since 1913, Congress has enacted hundreds of tax bills. The *Internal Revenue Code* is now more than 2,200 pages in length. Of course, this seems short when compared to a tax service such as CCH's *Standard Federal Tax Reporter* or RIA's *United States Tax Reporter,* which fill up library shelves. As an example of how the size and complexity of the income tax have changed, consider that when CCH's first tax guide was published in 1913, it was only 400 pages long.

Congress. The inconvenience and confusion that resulted from dealing with many separate acts led Congress to codify all of the Federal tax laws. Known as the Internal Revenue Code of 1939, the codification arranged all Federal tax provisions in a logical sequence and placed them in a separate part of the Federal statutes. A further rearrangement took place in 1954 and resulted in the Internal Revenue Code of 1954, which continued in effect until it was replaced by the Internal Revenue Code of 1986.

The following observations help clarify the codification procedure:

- Neither the 1939, the 1954, nor the 1986 Code changed all of the tax law existing on the date of enactment. Much of the 1939 Code, for example, was incorporated into the 1954 Code. The same can be said for the transition from the 1954 to the 1986 Code. This point is important in assessing judicial and administrative decisions interpreting provisions under prior codes. For example, a decision interpreting § 121 of the Internal Revenue Code of 1954 will have continuing validity since this provision carried over unchanged to the Internal Revenue Code of 1986.

- Statutory amendments to the tax law are integrated into the existing Code. Thus, subsequent tax legislation, such as the Revenue Reconciliation Act of 1993, has become part of the Internal Revenue Code of 1986. In view of the frequency with which tax legislation has been enacted in recent years, it appears that the tax law will continue to be amended frequently.

The Legislative Process.   Federal tax legislation generally originates in the House of Representatives, where it is first considered by the House Ways and Means Committee. Tax bills originate in the Senate when they are attached as riders to other legislative proposals.[1] If acceptable to the committee, the proposed

---

[1] The Tax Equity and Fiscal Responsibility Act of 1982 originated in the Senate, and its constitutionality was unsuccessfully challenged in the courts. The Senate version of the Deficit Reduction Act of 1984 was attached as an amendment to the Federal Boat Safety Act.

bill is referred to the entire House of Representatives for approval or disapproval. Approved bills are sent to the Senate, where they initially are considered by the Senate Finance Committee.

The next step is referral from the Senate Finance Committee to the entire Senate. Assuming no disagreement between the House and Senate, passage by the Senate means referral to the President for approval or veto. If the bill is approved or if the President's veto is overridden, the bill becomes law and part of the Internal Revenue Code of 1986.

When the Senate version of the bill differs from that passed by the House, the Joint Conference Committee, which includes members of both the House Ways and Means Committee and the Senate Finance Committee, is called upon to resolve the differences. Major tax bills frequently have differing versions. One reason bills are often changed in the Senate is that each individual senator has considerable latitude to make amendments when the Senate as a whole is voting on a bill referred to it by the Senate Finance Committee. In contrast, the entire House of Representatives either accepts or rejects what is proposed by the House Ways and Means Committee, and changes from the floor are rare. The deliberations of the Joint Conference Committee usually produce a compromise between the two versions, which is then voted on by both the House and the Senate. If both bodies accept the bill, it is referred to the President for approval or veto. The typical legislative process dealing with tax bills is summarized in Figure 28–1.

Referrals from the House Ways and Means Committee, the Senate Finance Committee, and the Joint Conference Committee are usually accompanied by Committee Reports. These Committee Reports often explain the provisions of the proposed legislation and are therefore a valuable source for ascertaining the *intent of Congress.* What Congress had in mind when it considered and enacted tax legislation is the key to interpreting the legislation. Since Regulations normally are not issued immediately after a statute is enacted, taxpayers and the courts look to legislative history materials to determine congressional intent.

The role of the Joint Conference Committee indicates the importance of compromise in the legislative process. As an example of the practical effect of the compromise process, consider what happened to a provision allowing the amortization of certain intangible assets in the Revenue Reconciliation Act of 1993. See Figure 28–2.

Arrangement of the Code.   The Internal Revenue Code of 1986 is found in Title 26 of the U.S. Code. In working with the Code, it helps to understand the format. Note the following partial table of contents:

> Subtitle A. Income Taxes
>   Chapter 1. Normal Taxes and Surtaxes
>   Subchapter A. Determination of Tax Liability
>   Part I. Tax on Individuals
>   Sections 1–5
>   Part II. Tax on Corporations
>   Sections 11–12

* * *

In referring to a provision of the Code, the key is usually the Section number. In citing Section 2(a) (dealing with the status of a surviving spouse), for example, it is unnecessary to include Subtitle A, Chapter 1, Subchapter A, Part I. Merely mentioning Section 2(a) will suffice, since the Section numbers run consecutively and do not begin again with each new Subtitle, Chapter, Subchapter, or Part. Not

▼ **FIGURE 28–1**
Legislative Process for Tax Bills

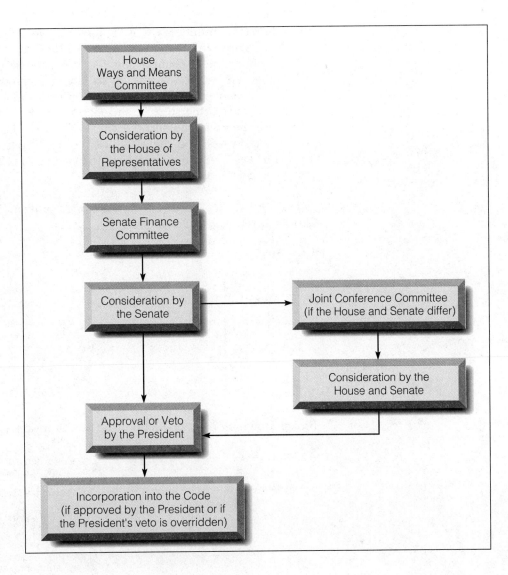

▼ **FIGURE 28–2**
Role of Joint Conference
Committee

all Code Section numbers are used, however. Note that Part I ends with Section 5 and Part II starts with Section 11 (at present there are no Sections 6, 7, 8, 9, and 10).[2]

Tax practitioners commonly refer to a specific area of income tax law by Subchapter designation. Some of the more common Subchapter designations include Subchapter C ("Corporate Distributions and Adjustments"), Subchapter K ("Partners and Partnerships"), and Subchapter S ("Tax Treatment of S Corporations and Their Shareholders"). Particularly in the last situation, it is much more convenient to describe the effect of the applicable Code provisions (Sections 1361–1379) as "S corporation status" than as the "Tax Treatment of S Corporations and Their Shareholders."

Citing the Code.   Code Sections are often broken down into subparts.[3] Section 2(a)(1)(A) serves as an example.

Broken down by content, Section 2(a)(1)(A) appears as follows:

Throughout the text, references to the Code Sections are in the form given above. The symbols "§" and "§§" are used in place of "Section" and "Sections." Unless otherwise stated, all Code references are to the Internal Revenue Code of 1986. The following table summarizes the format used in the text:

---

[2] When the Code was drafted, Section numbers were intentionally omitted so that later changes could be incorporated into the Code without disrupting its organization. When Congress does not leave enough space, subsequent Code Sections are given A, B, C, etc., designations. A good example is the treatment of Sections 280A through 280H.

[3] Some Code Sections do not have subparts. See, for example, §§ 211 and 241.

[4] Some Code Sections omit the subsection designation and use, instead, the paragraph designation as the first subpart. See, for example, §§ 212(1) and 1221(1).

Complete Reference	Text Reference
Section 2(a)(1)(A) of the Internal Revenue Code of 1986	§ 2(a)(1)(A)
Sections 1 and 2 of the Internal Revenue Code of 1986	§§ 1 and 2
Section 2 of the Internal Revenue Code of 1954	§ 2 of the Internal Revenue Code of 1954
Section 12(d) of the Internal Revenue Code of 1939[5]	§ 12(d) of the Internal Revenue Code of 1939

Effect of Treaties.   The United States signs certain tax treaties (sometimes called tax conventions) with foreign countries to render mutual assistance in tax enforcement and to avoid double taxation. Neither a tax law nor a tax treaty automatically takes precedence. When there is a direct conflict, the most recent item will take precedence. A taxpayer must disclose on the tax return any position where a treaty overrides a tax law.[6] There is a $1,000 per *failure to disclose* penalty for individuals and a $10,000 per failure to disclose penalty for corporations.[7]

ADMINISTRATIVE SOURCES OF THE TAX LAW

The administrative sources of the Federal tax law can be grouped as follows: Treasury Department Regulations, Revenue Rulings and Revenue Procedures, and various other administrative pronouncements (see Exhibit 28–1). All are issued by either the U.S. Treasury Department or one of its instrumentalities (e.g., the IRS or a District Director).

Treasury Department Regulations.   Regulations are issued by the U.S. Treasury Department under authority granted by Congress.[8] Interpretive by nature, they provide taxpayers with considerable guidance on the meaning and application of the Code. Regulations carry considerable weight. They are an important factor to consider in complying with the tax law.

Since Regulations interpret the Code, they are arranged in the same sequence as the Code. A number is added at the beginning, however, to indicate the type of tax or administrative, procedural, or definitional matter to which they relate. For example, the prefix 1 designates the Regulations under the income tax law. Thus, the Regulations under Code § 2 would be cited as Reg. § 1.2, with subparts added for further identification. The numbering pattern of these subparts often has no correlation with the Code subsections. The prefix 20 designates estate tax Regulations, 25 covers gift tax Regulations, 31 relates to employment taxes, and 301 refers to procedure and administration. This list is not all-inclusive.

New Regulations and changes in existing Regulations are usually issued in proposed form before they are finalized. The interval between the proposal of a Regulation and its finalization permits taxpayers and other interested parties to comment on the propriety of the proposal. **Proposed Regulations** under Code § 2, for example, are cited as Prop.Reg. § 1.2. The Tax Court indicates that Proposed Regulations carry no more weight than a position advanced in a written brief

---

[5] Section 12(d) of the Internal Revenue Code of 1939 is the predecessor to § 2 of the Internal Revenue Code of 1954 and the Internal Revenue Code of 1986.

[6] § 7852(d).

[7] Reg. §§ 301.6114–1 and 301.6712–1.

[8] § 7805.

▼ **EXHIBIT 28–1**
Administrative Sources

Source	Location	Authority**
Regulations	*Federal Register**	Force and effect of law.
Temporary Regulations	*Federal Register** *Internal Revenue Bulletin* *Cumulative Bulletin*	May be cited as a precedent.
Proposed Regulations	*Federal Register** *Internal Revenue Bulletin* *Cumulative Bulletin*	Preview of final Regulations.
Revenue Rulings Revenue Procedures Action on Decision	*Internal Revenue Bulletin* *Cumulative Bulletin*	Do not have the force and effect of law.
General Counsel's Memoranda Technical Advice Memoranda	Tax Analysts' *Tax Notes*; RIA's *Internal Memoranda* of the IRS; CCH's *IRS Position Reporter*	May not be cited as a precedent.
Letter Ruling	Research Institute of America and Commerce Clearing House loose-leaf services	Applicable only to taxpayer addressed. No precedential force.

*Finalized, Temporary, and Proposed Regulations are published in soft-cover form by several publishers.
**Each of these sources may be substantial authority for purposes of the accuracy-related penalty in § 6662. Notice 90–20, 1990–1 C.B. 328.

prepared by a litigating party before the Tax Court. **Finalized Regulations** have the force and effect of law.[9]

Sometimes the Treasury Department issues **Temporary Regulations** relating to elections and other matters where speed is important. These Regulations are issued without the comment period required for Proposed Regulations. Temporary Regulations have the same authoritative value as final Regulations and may be cited as precedents. Temporary Regulations now must also be issued as Proposed Regulations and automatically expire within three years after the date of issuance.[10]

Proposed, Temporary, and final Regulations are published in the *Federal Register* and are reproduced in major tax services. Final Regulations are issued as Treasury Decisions (TDs).

Regulations may also be classified as *legislative, interpretive,* or *procedural*. This classification scheme is discussed under Assessing the Validity of a Treasury Regulation later in the chapter.

Revenue Rulings and Revenue Procedures. **Revenue Rulings** are official pronouncements of the National Office of the IRS.[11] Like Regulations, they are designed to provide interpretation of the tax law. However, they do not carry the same legal force and effect as Regulations and usually deal with more restricted problems. In addition, Regulations are approved by the Secretary of the Treasury, whereas Revenue Rulings are not. Both Revenue Rulings and Revenue Procedures

---

[9] *F. W. Woolworth Co.*, 54 T.C. 1233 (1970); *Harris M. Miller*, 70 T.C. 448 (1978); and *James O. Tomerlin Trust*, 87 T.C. 876 (1986).

[10] § 7805(e).
[11] § 7805(a).

serve an important function in that they provide *guidance* to IRS personnel and taxpayers in handling routine tax matters. Revenue Rulings and Revenue Procedures generally apply retroactively and may be revoked or modified by subsequent rulings or procedures, Regulations, legislation, or court decisions.

A Revenue Ruling often results from a specific taxpayer's request for a letter ruling. If the IRS believes that a taxpayer's request for a letter ruling deserves official publication due to its widespread impact, the holding will be converted into a Revenue Ruling and issued for the information and guidance of taxpayers, tax practitioners, and IRS personnel. Names, identifying descriptions, and money amounts are changed to conceal the identity of the requesting taxpayer.

In addition to arising from taxpayer requests, Revenue Rulings may arise from Technical Advice to District Offices of the IRS, court decisions, suggestions from tax practitioner groups, and various tax publications.

Revenue Procedures are issued in the same manner as Revenue Rulings, but deal with the internal management practices and procedures of the IRS. Familiarity with these procedures increases taxpayer compliance and helps make the administration of the tax laws more efficient. The failure of a taxpayer to follow a Revenue Procedure can result in unnecessary delay or, in a discretionary situation, can cause the IRS to decline to act on behalf of the taxpayer.

Revenue Rulings and Revenue Procedures are published weekly by the U.S. Government in the *Internal Revenue Bulletin* (I.R.B.). Semiannually, the *Bulletins* for a six-month period are gathered together, reorganized by Code Section classification, and published in a bound volume called the *Cumulative Bulletin* (C.B.).[12]

The proper form for citing Rulings and Procedures depends on whether the item has been published in the *Cumulative Bulletin* or is available only in I.R.B. form. Consider, for example, the following transition:

Temporary Citation
: Rev.Rul. 95–3, I.R.B. No. 2, 8.
Explanation: Revenue Ruling Number 3, appearing on page 8 of the 2nd weekly issue of the *Internal Revenue Bulletin* for 1995.

Permanent Citation
: Rev.Rul. 95–3, 1995–1 C.B. 160.
Explanation: Revenue Ruling Number 3, appearing on page 160 of Volume 1 of the *Cumulative Bulletin* for 1995.

Since the first volume of the 1995 *Cumulative Bulletin* was not published until December of 1995, the I.R.B. citation had to be used until that time. After the publication of the *Cumulative Bulletin*, the C.B. citation is proper. The basic portion of both citations (Rev.Rul. 95–3) indicates that this was the 3rd Revenue Ruling issued by the IRS during 1995.

Revenue Procedures are cited in the same manner, except that "Rev.Proc." is substituted for "Rev.Rul." Some recent Revenue Procedures had the following effects:

- Announced deduction limits for cars placed in service during the year.
- Announced increases in the price of tax return copies.
- Provided a safe harbor that may be used to determine a majority of interest for a limited partnership.

---

[12] Usually, only two volumes of the *Cumulative Bulletin* are published each year. However, when Congress has enacted major tax legislation, other volumes may be published containing the Congressional Committee Reports supporting the Revenue Act. See, for example, the two extra volumes for 1984 dealing with the Deficit Reduction Act of 1984. The 1984–3 *Cumulative Bulletin*, Volume 1, contains the text of the law itself; 1984–3, Volume 2, contains the Committee Reports. There are a total of four volumes of the *Cumulative Bulletin* for 1984: 1984–1; 1984–2; 1984–3, Volume 1; and 1984–3, Volume 2.

Letter Rulings. Individual **(letter) rulings** are issued for a fee upon a taxpayer's request and describe how the IRS will treat a proposed transaction for tax purposes. They apply only to the taxpayer who asks for and obtains the ruling, but post-1984 letter rulings may be substantial authority for purposes of the accuracy-related penalty.[13] This procedure may seem like the only real way to carry out effective tax planning. However, the IRS limits the issuance of individual rulings to restricted, preannounced areas of taxation. The main reason the IRS will not rule in certain areas is that they involve fact-oriented situations. Thus, a ruling may not be obtained on many of the problems that are particularly troublesome to taxpayers.[14]

Although letter rulings once were private and not available to the public, the law now requires the IRS to make such rulings available for public inspection after identifying details are deleted.[15] Published digests of private letter rulings can be found in RIA's *Private Letter Rulings*, BNA *Daily Tax Reports*, and Tax Analysts' *Tax Notes*. *IRS Letter Rulings Reports* (published by Commerce Clearing House) contain both digests and full texts of all letter rulings. *Letter Ruling Review* (published by Tax Analysts), a monthly publication, selects and discusses the more important of the approximately 300 letter rulings issued each month.

Letter rulings are issued multidigit file numbers, which indicate the year and week of issuance as well as the number of the ruling during that week. Consider, for example, Ltr.Rul. 9532019, which deals with the employee status of inmates working in prison industries:

95	**32**	**019**
Year 1995	32nd week of issuance	Number of the ruling issued during the 32nd week

Other Administrative Pronouncements. *Treasury Decisions* (TDs) are issued by the Treasury Department to promulgate new Regulations, amend or otherwise change existing Regulations, or announce the position of the Government on selected court decisions. Like Revenue Rulings and Revenue Procedures, TDs are published initially in the *Internal Revenue Bulletin* and subsequently transferred to the *Cumulative Bulletin*.

The IRS publishes other administrative communications in the *Internal Revenue Bulletin*, such as Announcements, Notices, LRs (Proposed Regulations), and Prohibited Transaction Exemptions.

Like letter rulings, **determination letters** are issued at the request of taxpayers and provide guidance on the application of the tax law. They differ from letter rulings in that the issuing source is the District Director rather than the National Office of the IRS. Also, determination letters usually involve completed (as opposed to proposed) transactions. Determination letters are not published and are made known only to the party making the request.

---

[13] Notice 90–20, 1990–1 C.B. 328. In this regard, letter rulings differ from Revenue Rulings, which are applicable to *all* taxpayers. Letter rulings may later lead to the issuance of a Revenue Ruling if the holding involved affects many taxpayers. In its Agents' Manual, the IRS indicates that letter rulings may be used as a guide with other research materials in formulating a District Office position on an issue. The IRS is required to charge a taxpayer a fee for letter rulings, determination letters, etc.

[14] Rev.Proc. 96–3, I.R.B. No. 1, 82 contains a list of areas in which the IRS will not issue advance rulings. From time to time, subsequent Revenue Procedures are issued that modify or amplify Rev.Proc. 96–3.
[15] § 6110.

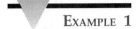

EXAMPLE 1

The shareholders of Red Corporation and Green Corporation want assurance that the consolidation of the corporations into Blue Corporation will be a nontaxable reorganization. The proper approach would be to ask the National Office of the IRS to issue a letter ruling concerning the income tax effect of the proposed transaction. ▼

EXAMPLE 2

Chris operates a barber shop in which he employs eight barbers. To comply with the rules governing income tax and payroll tax withholdings, Chris wants to know whether the barbers working for him are employees or independent contractors. The proper procedure would be to request a determination letter on their status from the appropriate District Director. ▼

The National Office of the IRS releases **Technical Advice Memoranda (TAMs)** weekly. TAMs resemble letter rulings in that they give the IRS's determination of an issue. Letter rulings, however, are responses to requests by taxpayers, whereas TAMs are issued by the National Office of the IRS in response to questions raised by IRS field personnel during audits. TAMs deal with completed rather than proposed transactions and are often requested for questions relating to exempt organizations and employee plans. TAMs are not officially published and may not be cited or used as precedent.[16]

The law now requires that several internal memoranda that constitute the working law of the IRS be released. These General Counsel Memoranda (GCMs) and TAMs are not officially published, and the IRS indicates that they may not be cited as precedents by taxpayers.[17] However, these working documents do explain the IRS's position on various issues.

ETHICAL CONSIDERATIONS

The Cost of Tax Compliance

Arthur P. Hall of the Tax Foundation has pointed out that since 1954 the income tax code has grown from 103 sections to 698 and is now about four inches thick. An additional nine inches of Treasury Regulations explain these four inches of tax law.

Shirley Petersen, former IRS Commissioner, tells of one multinational corporation that had to file a 21,000-page tax return in 30 volumes. "They had to use a truck to deliver it to the IRS," Petersen says.

Dr. Hall continued, "Because of complexity and instability taxpayers cannot be certain about how taxation will affect a business plan or investment. At least 70 percent of the total cost of Federal tax compliance is due to the income tax, indicating that businesses paid an estimated $92.5 billion in 1994 to comply with the Federal tax."

Is it equitable that taxpayers must bear such large compliance costs in order to calculate and pay their income taxes?

JUDICIAL SOURCES OF THE TAX LAW

The Judicial Process in General. After a taxpayer has exhausted some or all of the remedies available within the IRS (no satisfactory settlement has been

---

[16] § 6110(j)(3).

[17] These are unofficially published by the publishers listed in Exhibit 28–1. Such internal memoranda for post-1984 may be

substantial authority for purposes of the accuracy-related penalty. Notice 90–20, 1990–1 C.B. 328.

▼ **FIGURE 28-3**
Federal Judicial System

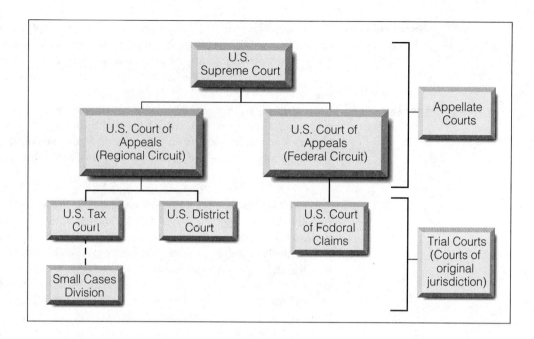

▼ **FIGURE 28-3**
Federal Judicial System

reached at the agent level or at the Appeals Division level), the dispute can be taken to the Federal courts. The dispute is first considered by a **court of original jurisdiction** (known as a trial court), with any appeal (either by the taxpayer or the IRS) taken to the appropriate appellate court. In most situations, the taxpayer has a choice of any of four trial courts: a **Federal District Court,** the **U.S. Court of Federal Claims,** the **U.S. Tax Court,** or the **Small Cases Division** of the U.S. Tax Court. The trial and *appellate court* system for Federal tax litigation is illustrated in Figure 28–3.

The broken line between the U.S. Tax Court and the Small Cases Division indicates that there is no appeal from the Small Cases Division. The jurisdiction of the Small Cases Division is limited to cases involving amounts of $10,000 or less.

American law, following English law, is frequently "made" by judicial decisions. Under the doctrine of *stare decisis,* each case (except in the Small Cases Division) has precedential value for future cases with the same controlling set of facts. Most Federal and state appellate court decisions and some decisions of trial courts are published. More than 4 million judicial opinions have been published in the United States, and over 130,000 cases are published each year. Published court decisions are organized by jurisdiction (Federal or state) and level of court (trial or appellate).

A decision of a particular court is called its *holding.* Sometimes a decision includes dicta or incidental opinions beyond the current facts. Such passing remarks, illustrations, or analogies are not essential to the current holding. Although the holding has precedential value under *stare decisis,* dicta are not binding on a future court.

Trial Courts.   The differences between the various trial courts (courts of original jurisdiction) can be summarized as follows:

• *Number of courts.* There is only one U.S. Court of Federal Claims and only one Tax Court, but there are many Federal District Courts. The taxpayer does not select the District Court that will hear the dispute but must sue in the one that has jurisdiction.

TAX IN THE NEWS

THE DOCTRINE OF *STARE DECISIS*: BASEBALL NEVER STRIKES OUT

The high court could not have cared less about the accused. The sole issue in this obscure case--stick with me--was whether the court should adhere to the doctrine of *stare decisis*. The doctrine pays great respect to precedent. It teaches, in the words of Justice Brandeis long ago, that in most matters "it is more important that the applicable rule of law be settled than that it be settled right."

Most of the time the court stands by its former decisions, even when they're terrible decisions. In the most eye-popping example of *stare decisis* gone amok, the Supreme Court has resolutely refused to abandon its incredible decision in 1922 that professional baseball is not subject to antitrust laws. Many developments have intervened. In 1955 the court held that professional boxing was subject to the law; that same year it held that traveling theater troupes are subject to the law; in 1957 it held that pro football is subject to the law; in 1971 it held that pro basketball is subject to the law.

But the court, citing the doctrine of *stare decisis*, again and again has refused to overrule its absurd opinion of 1922 that baseball is not subject to antitrust laws. Justice Harry Blackmun, writing for the court in *Flood v. Kuhn* in 1972, agreed that the situation is inconsistent and illogical, but if the long-standing aberration is to be corrected, he said, the remedy lies not with the court, but with Congress.

I like that approach to jurisprudence. *Stare decisis* is a sound doctrine. But the antitrust exemption for baseball boggles the mind. The 1922 decision, to borrow from Justice Scalia, is a weed that cries out for uprooting.

SOURCE: J. J. Kilpatrick, "Courting Changes in Past Decisions Is Dangerous," *Bryan C/S Eagle*, July 14, 1995, p. A11.

- *Number of judges.* Each District Court has only 1 judge, the Court of Federal Claims has 16 judges, and the Tax Court has 19 regular judges. The entire Tax Court, however, will review a case (the case is sent to court conference) only when important or novel tax issues are involved. Most cases will be heard and decided by 1 of the 19 judges.
- *Location.* The Court of Federal Claims meets most often in Washington, D.C., while a District Court meets at a prescribed seat for the particular district. Each state has at least one District Court, and many of the populous states have more than one. Choosing the District Court usually minimizes the inconvenience and expense of traveling for the taxpayer and his or her counsel. The Tax Court is officially based in Washington, D.C., but the various judges travel to different parts of the country and hear cases at predetermined locations and dates. This procedure eases the distance problem for the taxpayer, but it can mean a delay before the case comes to trial and is decided.
- *Jurisdiction of the Court of Federal Claims.* The Court of Federal Claims has jurisdiction over any claim against the United States that is based upon the Constitution, any Act of Congress, or any Regulation of an executive department. Thus, the Court of Federal Claims hears nontax litigation as well as tax cases. This forum appears to be more favorable for issues having an equitable or pro-business orientation (as opposed to purely technical issues) and those requiring extensive discovery.

- *Jurisdiction of the Tax Court and District Courts.* The Tax Court hears only tax cases and is the most popular forum. The District Courts hear nontax litigation as well as tax cases. Many Tax Court justices have been appointed from IRS or Treasury Department positions. For this reason, some people suggest that the Tax Court has more expertise in tax matters.
- *Jury trial.* The only court in which a taxpayer can obtain a jury trial is a District Court. Juries can decide only questions of fact and not questions of law. Therefore, taxpayers who choose the District Court route often do not request a jury trial. If a jury trial is not elected, the judge will decide all issues. Note that a District Court decision is controlling only in the district in which the court has jurisdiction.
- *Payment of deficiency.* Before the Court of Federal Claims or a District Court can have jurisdiction, the taxpayer must pay the tax deficiency assessed by the IRS and then sue for a refund. If the taxpayer wins (assuming no successful appeal by the Government), the tax paid plus appropriate interest will be recovered. Jurisdiction in the Tax Court, however, is usually obtained without first paying the assessed tax deficiency. In the event the taxpayer loses in the Tax Court (and no appeal is taken or an appeal is unsuccessful), the deficiency must be paid with accrued interest. With the elimination of the deduction for personal (consumer) interest, the Tax Court route of delaying payment of the deficiency can become expensive. For example, to earn 11 percent after tax, a taxpayer with a 39.6 percent marginal tax rate will have to earn 18.2 percent. By paying the tax, a taxpayer limits underpayment interest and penalties on the underpayment.
- *Appeals.* Appeals from a District Court or a Tax Court decision are to the appropriate U.S. Court of Appeals. Appeals from the Court of Federal Claims go to the Court of Appeals for the Federal Circuit.
- *Bankruptcy.* When a taxpayer files a bankruptcy petition, the IRS, like other creditors, is prevented from taking action against the taxpayer. Sometimes a bankruptcy court may settle a tax claim.

Appellate Courts. The losing party can appeal a trial court decision to a **Circuit Court of Appeals.** The 11 geographical circuits, the circuit for the District of Columbia, and the Federal Circuit[18] are shown in Figure 28–4. The appropriate circuit for an appeal depends upon where the litigation originated. For example, an appeal from New York goes to the Second Circuit.

If the Government loses at the trial court level (District Court, Tax Court, or Court of Federal Claims), it need not (and frequently does not) appeal. The fact that an appeal is not made, however, does not indicate that the IRS agrees with the result and will not litigate similar issues in the future. The IRS may decide not to appeal for a number of reasons. First, the current litigation load may be heavy. As a consequence, the IRS may decide that available personnel should be assigned to other, more important cases. Second, the IRS may determine that this is not a good case to appeal. For example, the taxpayer may be in a sympathetic position, or the facts may be particularly strong in his or her favor. In that event, the IRS may wait to test the legal issues involved with a taxpayer who has a much weaker case. Third, if the appeal is from a District Court or the Tax Court, the Court of Appeals of jurisdiction could have some bearing on whether the IRS decides to pursue an appeal. Based on past experience and precedent, the IRS may conclude that the chance for success on a particular issue might be more promising in another Court

---

[18] The Court of Appeals for the Federal Circuit was created, effective October 1, 1982, by P.L. 97–164 (4/2/82) to hear decisions appealed from the Claims Court (now the Court of Federal Claims).

▼ FIGURE 28–4
The Federal Circuit Courts of
Appeals

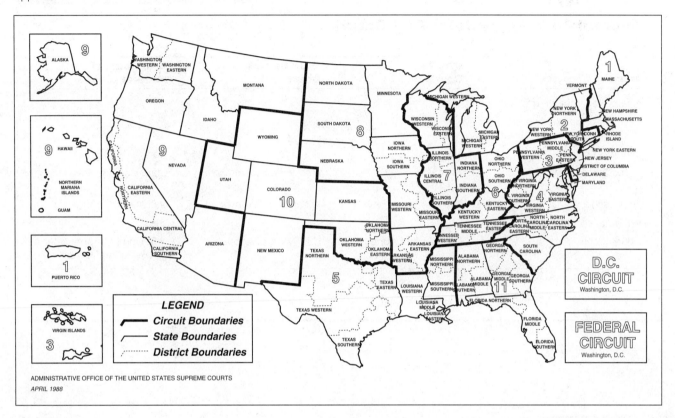

ADMINISTRATIVE OFFICE OF THE UNITED STATES SUPREME COURTS
APRIL 1988

of Appeals. If so, the IRS will wait for a similar case to arise in a different jurisdiction.

ETHICAL
CONSIDERATIONS

Choosing Cases for Appeal

The U.S. Government loses a tax case against a prominent citizen in the U.S. District Court of Iowa. The taxpayer, a minister, had set up three separate trusts for each of his three children (i.e., a total of nine trusts). The Government argued that under Reg. § 1.641(a)–0(c) these trusts should be consolidated and treated as three trusts to stop the taxpayer from mitigating the progressive tax structure (e.g., 39.6 percent top tax bracket).

The IRS has decided to appeal a case in this multiple trust area. As one of the attorneys for the Government, you must choose between the Iowa case and a similar multiple trust conflict in the U.S. District Court of Virginia. Here the taxpayer is a CPA who has established four separate trusts for her two children (i.e., a total of eight trusts). See *Estelle Morris Trusts*, 51 T.C. 20 (1968). Factors you are considering are the potential sympathy associated with the minister's profession and a lack thereof associated with the CPA, the facts indicating that the attempt at tax avoidance is more egregious in the Iowa case, and a colleague's opinion that the Virginia case is winnable. Which case will you select? Comment on the fairness of the Government's ability and willingness to select a case to appeal in this fashion.

CONCEPT SUMMARY 28–1

Federal Judicial System: Trial Courts

Issue	U.S. Tax Court	U.S. District Court	U.S. Court of Federal Claims
Number of judges per court	19*	1	16
Payment of deficiency before trial	No	Yes	Yes
Jury trial available	No	Yes	No
Types of disputes	Tax cases only	Mostly criminal and civil issues	Claims against the United States
Jurisdiction	Nationwide	Location of taxpayer	Nationwide
IRS acquiescence policy	Yes	Yes	Yes
Appeal route	U.S. Court of Appeals	U.S. Court of Appeals	U.S. Court of Appeals for the Federal Circuit

*There are also 14 special trial judges and 9 senior judges.

The Federal Circuit at the appellate level provides a taxpayer with an alternative forum to the Court of Appeals of his or her home circuit for the appeal. Appeals from both the Tax Court and the District Court go to a taxpayer's home circuit. Now, when a particular circuit has issued an adverse decision, the taxpayer may wish to select the Court of Federal Claims route since any appeal will be to the Federal Circuit.

District Courts, the Tax Court, and the Court of Federal Claims must abide by the **precedents** set by the Court of Appeals of jurisdiction. A particular Court of Appeals need not follow the decisions of another Court of Appeals. All courts, however, must follow the decisions of the **U.S. Supreme Court.**

The Tax Court is a national court, meaning that it hears and decides cases from all parts of the country. For many years, the Tax Court followed a policy of deciding cases based on what it thought the result should be, even when its decision might be appealed to a Court of Appeals that had previously decided a similar case differently. A number of years ago this policy was changed in the *Golsen*[19] decision. Now the Tax Court will decide a case as it feels the law should be applied *only* if the Court of Appeals of appropriate jurisdiction has not yet passed on the issue or has previously decided a similar case in accord with the Tax Court's decision. If the Court of Appeals of appropriate jurisdiction has previously

---

[19] *Jack E. Golsen*, 54 T.C. 742 (1970).

held otherwise, the Tax Court will conform even though it disagrees with the holding. This policy is known as the *Golsen* rule.

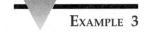

EXAMPLE 3

Emily lives in Texas and sues in the Tax Court on Issue A. The Fifth Court of Appeals is the appellate court of appropriate jurisdiction. The Fifth Court of Appeals has already decided, in a case involving similar facts but a different taxpayer, that Issue A should be resolved against the Government. Although the Tax Court feels that the Fifth Court of Appeals is wrong, under its *Golsen* policy it will render judgment for Emily. Shortly thereafter, Rashad, a resident of New York, in a comparable case, sues in the Tax Court on Issue A. Assume that the Second Court of Appeals, the appellate court of appropriate jurisdiction, has never expressed itself on Issue A. Presuming the Tax Court has not reconsidered its position on Issue A, it will decide against Rashad. Thus, it is entirely possible for two taxpayers suing in the same court to end up with opposite results merely because they live in different parts of the country. ▼

Appeal to the U.S. Supreme Court is by **Writ of Certiorari.** If the Court accepts jurisdiction, it will grant the Writ (*Cert. Granted*). Most often, it will deny jurisdiction (*Cert. Denied*). For whatever reason or reasons, the Supreme Court rarely hears tax cases. The Court usually grants certiorari to resolve a conflict among the Courts of Appeals (e.g., two or more appellate courts have assumed opposing positions on a particular issue) or where the tax issue is extremely important. The granting of a *Writ of Certiorari* indicates that at least four members of the Supreme Court believe that the issue is of sufficient importance to be heard by the full Court.

The *role* of appellate courts is limited to a review of the record of trial compiled by the trial courts. Thus, the appellate process usually involves a determination of whether the trial court applied the proper law in arriving at its decision. Usually, an appellate court will not dispute a lower court's fact-finding determination.

An appeal can have any of a number of possible outcomes. The appellate court may approve (affirm) or disapprove (reverse) the lower court's finding, or it may send the case back for further consideration (remand). When many issues are involved, a mixed result is not unusual. Thus, the lower court may be affirmed (*aff'd.*) on Issue A and reversed (*rev'd.*) on Issue B, while Issue C is remanded (*rem'd.*) for additional fact finding.

When more than one judge is involved in the decision-making process, disagreements are not uncommon. In addition to the majority view, one or more judges may concur (agree with the result reached but not with some or all of the reasoning) or dissent (disagree with the result). In any one case, the majority view controls. But concurring and dissenting views can have influence on other courts or, at some subsequent date when the composition of the court has changed, even on the same court.

Knowledge of several terms is important in understanding court decisions. The term *plaintiff* refers to the party requesting action in a court, and the *defendant* is the party against whom the suit is brought. Sometimes a court uses the terms *petitioner* and *respondent*. In general, "petitioner" is a synonym for "plaintiff," and "respondent" is a synonym for "defendant." At the trial court level, a taxpayer is normally the plaintiff (or petitioner), and the Government is the defendant (or respondent). If the taxpayer wins and the Government appeals as the new petitioner (or appellee), the taxpayer becomes the new respondent.

2 **LEARNING OBJECTIVE**
Locate and work with the appropriate tax law sources.

Judicial Citations—General. Having briefly described the judicial process, it is appropriate to consider the more practical problem of the relationship of case law to tax research. As previously noted, court decisions are an important source of tax law. The ability to locate a case and to cite it is therefore a must in working with the tax law. Judicial citations usually follow a standard pattern: case name, volume number, reporter series, page or paragraph number, and court (where necessary). Specific citation formats for each court are presented in the following sections.

Judicial Citations—The U.S. Tax Court.   A good starting point is the U.S. Tax Court (formerly the Board of Tax Appeals). The Tax Court issues two types of decisions: Regular and Memorandum. The Chief Judge decides whether the opinion is issued as a Regular or Memorandum decision. The distinction between the two involves both substance and form. In terms of substance, *Memorandum* decisions deal with situations necessitating only the application of already established principles of law. *Regular* decisions involve novel issues not previously resolved by the Court. In actual practice, however, this distinction is not always preserved. Not infrequently, Memorandum decisions will be encountered that appear to warrant Regular status, and vice versa. At any rate, do not conclude that Memorandum decisions possess no value as precedents. Both represent the position of the Tax Court and, as such, can be relied upon.

The Regular and Memorandum decisions issued by the Tax Court also differ in form. Memorandum decisions are officially published in mimeograph form only. Regular decisions are published by the U.S. Government in a series called *Tax Court of the United States Reports*. Each volume of these *Reports* covers a six-month period (January 1 through June 30 and July 1 through December 31) and is given a succeeding volume number. But, as was true of the *Cumulative Bulletins*, there is usually a time lag between the date a decision is rendered and the date it appears in bound form. A temporary citation may be necessary to help the researcher locate a recent Regular decision. Consider, for example, the temporary and permanent citations for *Glen E. Miller*, a decision filed on March 29, 1995:

Temporary   *Glen E. Miller*, 104 T.C. ___ , No. 18 (1995).
Citation   *Explanation:* Page number left blank because not yet known.

Permanent   *Glen E. Miller*, 104 T.C. 378 (1995).
Citation   *Explanation:* Page number now available.

Both citations tell us that the case will ultimately appear in Volume 104 of the *Tax Court of the United States Reports*. Until this volume is bound and made available to the general public, however, the page number must be left blank. Instead, the temporary citation identifies the case as being the 18th Regular decision issued by the Tax Court since Volume 103 ended. With this information, the decision can easily be located in either of the special Tax Court services published by Commerce Clearing House and Research Institute of America (formerly by Prentice-Hall). Once Volume 104 is released, the permanent citation can be substituted and the number of the case dropped.

Before 1943, the Tax Court was called the Board of Tax Appeals, and its decisions were published as the *United States Board of Tax Appeals Reports* (B.T.A.). These 47 volumes cover the period from 1924 to 1942. For example, the citation *Karl Pauli*, 11 B.T.A. 784 (1928) refers to the 11th volume of the *Board of Tax Appeals Reports*, page 784, issued in 1928.

If the IRS loses in a decision, it may indicate whether it agrees or disagrees with the results reached by the court by publishing an **acquiescence** ("A" or "Acq.") or **nonacquiescence** ("NA" or "Nonacq."), respectively. Until 1991, acquiescences and nonacquiescences were published only for certain Regular decisions of the Tax Court, but the IRS has expanded its acquiescence program to include other civil tax cases where guidance is helpful. The acquiescence or nonacquiescence is published in the *Internal Revenue Bulletin* and the *Cumulative Bulletin* as an *Action on Decision.* The IRS can retroactively revoke an acquiescence.

Although Memorandum decisions are not published by the U.S. Government, they are published by Commerce Clearing House (CCH) and Research Institute of America (RIA [formerly by Prentice-Hall]). Consider, for example, the three different ways that *Jack D. Carr* can be cited:

> *Jack D. Carr,* T.C.Memo. 1985–19
> The 19th Memorandum decision issued by the Tax Court in 1985.
>
> *Jack D. Carr,* 49 TCM 507
> Page 507 of Vol. 49 of the CCH *Tax Court Memorandum Decisions.*
>
> *Jack D. Carr,* RIA T.C.Mem.Dec. ¶85,019
> Paragraph 85,019 of the RIA *T.C. Memorandum Decisions.*

Note that the third citation contains the same information as the first. Thus, ¶85,019 indicates the following information about the case: year 1985, 19th T.C. Memo. decision.[20] Although the RIA citation does not include a specific volume number, the paragraph citation (85,019) indicates that the decision can be found in the 1985 volume of the RIA Memorandum Decision service.

Judicial Citations—The U.S. District Court, Court of Federal Claims, and Courts of Appeals.
District Court, Court of Federal Claims, Court of Appeals, and Supreme Court decisions dealing with Federal tax matters are reported in both the CCH *U.S. Tax Cases* (USTC) and the RIA *American Federal Tax Reports* (AFTR) series.

Federal District Court decisions, dealing with *both* tax and nontax issues, are also published by West Publishing Company in its *Federal Supplement Series.* A District Court case can be cited in three different forms as the following examples illustrate:

> *Simons-Eastern Co. v. U.S.,* 73–1 USTC ¶9279 (D.Ct.Ga., 1972).
>
> *Explanation:* Reported in the first volume of the *U.S. Tax Cases* (USTC) published by Commerce Clearing House for calendar year 1973 (73–1) and located at paragraph 9279 (¶9279).
>
> *Simons-Eastern Co. v. U.S.,* 31 AFTR2d 73–640 (D.Ct.Ga., 1972).
>
> *Explanation:* Reported in the 31st volume of the second series of the *American Federal Tax Reports* (AFTR2d) published by RIA and beginning on page 640. The "73" preceding the page number indicates the year the case was published but is a designation used only in recent decisions.
>
> *Simons-Eastern Co. v. U.S.,* 354 F.Supp. 1003 (D.Ct.Ga., 1972).
>
> *Explanation:* Reported in the 354th volume of the *Federal Supplement Series* (F.Supp.) published by West Publishing Company and beginning on page 1003.

In all of the preceding citations, note that the name of the case is the same (Simons-Eastern Co. being the taxpayer), as are the references to the Federal District Court of Georgia (D.Ct.Ga.) and the year the decision was rendered (1972).[21]

Decisions of the Court of Federal Claims[22] and the Courts of Appeals are published in the USTCs, AFTRs, and a West Publishing Company reporter called

---

[20] In this text, this Memorandum decision of the U.S. Tax Court would be cited as *Jack D. Carr,* 49 TCM 507, T.C.Memo. 1985–19.

[21] In this text, the case would be cited in the following form: *Simons-Eastern Co. v. U.S.,* 73–1 USTC ¶9279, 31 AFTR2d 73–640, 354 F.Supp. 1003 (D.Ct.Ga., 1972). Prentice-Hall Information Services is now owned by Research Institute of America. Although

recent volumes contain the RIA imprint, many of the older volumes continue to have the P-H imprint.

[22] Before October 29, 1992, the Court of Federal Claims was called the Claims Court. Before October 1, 1982, the Court of Federal Claims was called the Court of Claims.

the *Federal Second Series* (F.2d). Volume 999, published in 1993, is the last volume of the *Federal Second Series*. It is followed by the *Federal Third Series* (F.3d). Beginning with October 1982, decisions of the Court of Federal Claims are published in another West Publishing Company reporter entitled the *Claims Court Reporter*. Beginning with Volume 27 on October 30, 1992, the name of the reporter changed to the *Federal Claims Reporter* (abbreviated as *Fed.Cl.*). The following examples illustrate the different forms:

Finkbohner, Jr. v. U.S.,   (CA-11, 1986)

    86–1 USTC ¶9393 (CCH citation)
    57 AFTR2d 86–1400 (RIA citation)
    788 F.2d 723 (West citation)

Apollo Computer, Inc. v. U.S.,   (Fed.Cl., 1994)

    95–1 USTC ¶50,015 (CCH citation)
    74 AFTR2d 94–7172 (RIA citation)
    32 Fed.Cl. 334 (West citation)

Note that *Finkbohner, Jr.* is a decision rendered by the Eleventh Court of Appeals in 1986 (CA–11, 1986), while *Apollo Computer, Inc.* was issued by the Court of Federal Claims in 1994 (Fed.Cl., 1994).

Judicial Citations—The U.S. Supreme Court. Like all other Federal tax decisions (except those rendered by the U.S. Tax Court), Supreme Court decisions are published by Commerce Clearing House in the USTCs and by RIA (formerly by Prentice-Hall) in the AFTRs. The U.S. Government Printing Office also publishes these decisions in the *United States Supreme Court Reports* (U.S.), as do West Publishing Company in its *Supreme Court Reporter* (S.Ct.) and the Lawyer's Co-operative Publishing Company in its *United States Reports, Lawyer's Edition* (L.Ed.). The following illustrates the different ways the same decision can be cited:

U.S. v. The Donruss Co.,   (USSC, 1969)

    69–1 USTC ¶9167 (CCH citation)
    23 AFTR2d 69–418 (RIA citation)
    89 S.Ct. 501 (West citation)
    393 U.S. 297 (U.S. Government Printing Office citation)
    21 L.Ed.2d 495 (Lawyer's Co-operative Publishing Co. citation)

The parenthetical reference (USSC, 1969) identifies the decision as having been rendered by the U.S. Supreme Court in 1969. In this text, the citations of Supreme Court decisions are limited to the CCH (USTC), RIA (AFTR), and West (S.Ct.) versions. See Concept Summary 28–2.

WORKING WITH THE TAX LAW— TAX RESEARCH

3   **LEARNING OBJECTIVE**
Understand the tax research process.

Tax research is the method used to determine the best available solution to a situation that possesses tax consequences. In other words, it is the process of finding a competent and professional conclusion to a tax problem. The problem may originate from completed or proposed transactions. In the case of a completed transaction, the objective of the research is to determine the tax result of what has already taken place. For example, is the expenditure incurred by the

CONCEPT SUMMARY 28–2

Judicial Sources

Court	Location	Authority
U.S. Supreme Court	S.Ct. Series (West) U.S. Series (U.S. Gov't.) L.Ed. (Lawyer's Co-op.) AFTR (RIA) USTC (CCH)	Highest authority
U.S. Courts of Appeal	Federal 3d (West) AFTR (RIA) USTC (CCH)	Next highest appellate court
Tax Court (Regular decisions)	U.S. Gov't. Printing Office, RIA/CCH separate services	Highest trial court*
Tax Court (Memorandum decisions)	RIA T.C.Memo. (RIA) TCM (CCH)	Less authority than regular T.C. decision
U.S. Court of Federal Claims**	Federal Claims Reporter (West) AFTR (RIA) USTC (CCH)	Similar authority as Tax Court
U.S. District Courts	F.Supp. Series (West) AFTR (RIA) USTC (CCH)	Lowest trial court
Small Cases Division of Tax Court	Not published	No precedent value

*Theoretically, the Tax Court, Court of Federal Claims, and District Courts are on the same level of authority. But some people believe that since the Tax Court hears and decides tax cases from all parts of the country (it is a national court), its decisions may be more authoritative than a Court of Federal Claims or District Court decision.
**Before October 29, 1992, the U.S. Claims Court.

taxpayer deductible or not deductible for tax purposes? When dealing with proposed transactions, the tax research process is concerned with the determination of possible tax consequences. To the extent that tax research leads to a choice of alternatives or otherwise influences the future actions of the taxpayer, it becomes the key to effective tax planning.

Tax research involves the following procedures:

- Identifying and refining the problem.
- Locating the appropriate tax law sources.
- Assessing the validity of the tax law sources.
- Arriving at the solution or at alternative solutions while giving due consideration to nontax factors.
- Effectively communicating the solution to the taxpayer or the taxpayer's representative.
- Following up on the solution (where appropriate) in light of new developments.

This process is depicted schematically in Figure 28–5. The broken lines indicate steps of particular interest when tax research is directed toward proposed, rather than completed, transactions.

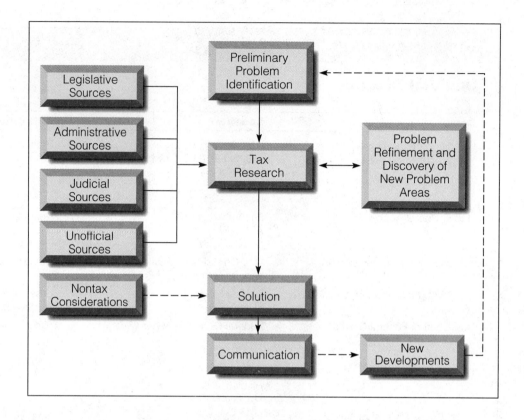

IDENTIFYING THE PROBLEM

Problem identification starts with a compilation of the relevant facts involved. In this regard, *all* of the facts that may have a bearing on the problem must be gathered, as any omission could modify the solution reached. To illustrate, consider what appears to be a very simple problem.

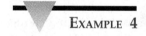

EXAMPLE 4

Early in December, Fred and Megan review their financial and tax situation with their son, Sam, and daughter-in-law, Dana. Fred and Megan are in the 28% tax bracket. Both Sam and Dana are age 21. Sam, a student at a nearby university, owns some publicly traded stock that he inherited from his grandmother. A current sale of the stock would result in approximately $7,000 of gross income. At this point, Fred and Megan provide about 55% of Sam and Dana's support. Although neither is now employed, Sam has earned $960 and Dana has earned $900. The problem: Should the stock be sold, and would the sale prohibit Fred and Megan from claiming Sam and Dana as dependents? ▼

REFINING THE PROBLEM

Initial reaction is that Fred and Megan in Example 4 could not claim Sam and Dana as dependents if the stock is sold, since Sam would then have earned more than the exemption amount under § 151(d). However, Sam is a full-time student, and § 151(c)(1)(B) allows a son or daughter who is a full-time student and is under age 24 to earn more than the exemption amount without penalizing the parents with the loss of the dependency exemption. Thus, Sam could sell the stock without penalizing his parents under the gross income test. However, the $7,000 income from the sale of the stock might lead to the failure of the greater-than-50 percent support test, depending on how much Sam spends for his (or Dana's) support.

Assume, however, that further fact gathering reveals the following additional information:

• Sam does not really need to spend the proceeds from the sale of the stock.
• Sam receives a sizable portion of his own support from a scholarship.

With these new facts, additional research leads to § 152(d) and Regulation § 1.152–1(c), which indicate that a scholarship received by a student is not included for purposes of determining whether the parents furnished more than one-half of the child's support. Further, if Sam does not spend the proceeds from the sale of stock, the unexpended amount is not counted for purposes of the support test. Thus, it appears that the parents would not be denied the dependency exemptions for Sam and Dana.

LOCATING THE APPROPRIATE TAX LAW SOURCES

Once the problem is clearly defined, what is the next step? Although the next step is a matter of individual judgment, most tax research begins with the index volume of the tax service or a key-word search on an on-line tax service (see the subsequent discussion of Computer-Assisted Tax Research). If the problem is not complex, the researcher may bypass the tax service or on-line service and turn directly to the Internal Revenue Code and the Treasury Regulations. For the beginner, the latter procedure saves time and will solve many of the more basic problems. If the researcher does not have a personal copy of the Code or Regulations, resorting to the appropriate volume(s) of a tax service is necessary.[23] The major tax services available are as follows:

Standard Federal Tax Reporter, Commerce Clearing House.

United States Tax Reporter, Research Institute of America (entitled *Federal Taxes* prior to July 1992).

Federal Tax Coordinator 2d, Research Institute of America.

Tax Management Portfolios, Bureau of National Affairs.

Rabkin and Johnson, *Federal Income, Gift and Estate Taxation,* Matthew Bender, Inc.

CCH's Federal Tax Service, Commerce Clearing House.

Mertens Law of Federal Income Taxation, Callaghan and Co.

Working with Tax Services. In this text, it is not feasible to explain the use of any particular tax service—this ability can be obtained only by practice.[24] However, several important observations about the use of tax services cannot be overemphasized. First, never forget to check for current developments. The main text of any service is revised too infrequently to permit reliance on that portion as the *latest* word on any subject. Where current developments can be found depends on which service is being used. Commerce Clearing House's *Standard Federal Tax Reporter* contains a special volume devoted to current matters. Both RIA's *U.S. Tax*

---

[23] Several of the major tax services publish paperback editions of the Code and Treasury Regulations that can be purchased at modest prices. These editions are usually revised twice each year. For an annotated and abridged version of the Code and Regulations that is published annually, see James E. Smith, *West's*

Internal Revenue Code of 1986 and Treasury Regulations: Annotated and Selected (St. Paul, Minn.: West Publishing Company, 1996).

[24] The representatives of the various tax services are prepared to provide the users of their services with printed booklets and individual instruction on the use of the materials.

Reporter and *Federal Tax Coordinator 2d* integrate the new developments into the body of the service throughout the year. Second, when dealing with a tax service synopsis of a Treasury Department pronouncement or a judicial decision, remember there is no substitute for the original source.

To illustrate, do not base a conclusion solely on a tax service's commentary on *Simons-Eastern Co. v. U.S.* If the case is vital to the research, look it up! The facts of the case may be distinguishable from those involved in the problem being researched. This is not to say that the case synopsis contained in the tax service is wrong—it might just be misleading or incomplete.

Tax Periodicals.   The various tax periodicals are another source of information. The easiest way to locate a journal article on a particular tax problem is through Commerce Clearing House's *Federal Tax Articles.* This six-volume service includes a subject index, a Code Section number index, and an author's index. In addition, the RIA tax service has a topical "Index to Tax Articles" section that is organized using the RIA paragraph index system. Also, beginning in 1992, *The Accounting & Tax Index* is available in three quarterly issues plus a cumulative year-end volume covering all four quarters. The original *Accountant's Index* started in 1921 and ended in 1991.

The following are some of the more useful tax periodicals:

The Journal of Taxation
Warren, Gorham and Lamont
31 St. James Avenue
Boston, MA 02116

Tax Law Review
Warren, Gorham and Lamont
31 St. James Avenue
Boston, MA 02116

Trusts and Estates
6151 Powers Ferry Road, NW
Atlanta, GA 30339

Oil and Gas Tax Quarterly
Matthew Bender & Co.
235 East 45th Street
New York, NY 10017

The International Tax Journal
Panel Publishers
14 Plaza Road
Greenvale, NY 11548

TAXES—The Tax Magazine
Commerce Clearing House, Inc.
4025 West Peterson Avenue
Chicago, IL 60646

National Tax Journal
5310 East Main Street
Columbus, OH 43213

The Tax Adviser
AICPA
1211 Avenue of the Americas
New York, NY 10036

The Practical Accountant
11 Penn Plaza
New York, NY 10001

Estate Planning
Warren, Gorham and Lamont
31 St. James Avenue
Boston, MA 02116

Taxation for Accountants
Warren, Gorham and Lamont
31 St. James Avenue
Boston, MA 02116

The Tax Executive
1001 Pennsylvania Avenue, NW
Suite 320
Washington, D.C. 20004

Journal of Corporate Taxation
Warren, Gorham and Lamont
31 St. James Avenue
Boston, MA 02116

Journal of Taxation for Individuals
Warren, Gorham and Lamont
31 St. James Avenue
Boston, MA 02116

The Tax Lawyer
American Bar Association
750 N. Lake Shore Drive
Chicago, IL 60611

Journal of the American Taxation Association
American Accounting Association
5717 Bessie Drive
Sarasota, FL 34233

Tax Notes
6830 Fairfax Drive
Arlington, VA 22213

ASSESSING THE VALIDITY OF THE TAX LAW SOURCES

Once a source has been located, the next step is to assess it in light of the problem at hand. Proper assessment involves careful interpretation of the tax law and consideration of its relevance and validity.

Interpreting the Internal Revenue Code. The language of the Code can be extremely difficult to comprehend fully. For example, one subsection [§ 341(e)] relating to collapsible corporations contains *one* sentence of more than 450 words (twice as many as in the Gettysburg Address). Within this same subsection is another sentence of 300 words.

Assessing the Validity of a Treasury Regulation. Treasury Regulations are often said to have the force and effect of law. This is certainly true for most Regulations, but some judicial decisions have held a Regulation or a portion thereof invalid. Usually, this is done on the grounds that the Regulation is contrary to the intent of Congress. Most often the courts do not question the validity of Regulations because of the belief that "the first administrative interpretation of a provision as it appears in a new act often expresses the general understanding of the times or the actual understanding of those who played an important part when the statute was drafted."[25]

Keep in mind the following observations when assessing the validity of a Regulation:

- IRS agents must give the Code and the Regulations issued thereunder equal weight when dealing with taxpayers and their representatives.
- Proposed Regulations provide a preview of future final Regulations, but they are not binding on the IRS or taxpayers.
- In a challenge, the burden of proof is on the taxpayer to show that a Regulation is wrong. However, a court may invalidate a Regulation that varies from the language of the statute and has no support in the Committee Reports.
- If the taxpayer loses the challenge, the negligence penalty may be imposed.[26] This accuracy-related penalty applies to any failure to make a reasonable attempt to comply with the tax law and to any disregard of rules and Regulations.[27]

---

[25] *Augustus v. Comm.,* 41–1 USTC ¶9255, 26 AFTR 612, 118 F.2d 38 (CA–6, 1941).

[26] §§ 6662(a) and (b)(1).
[27] § 6662(c).

- Final Regulations tend to be procedural, interpretive, or legislative. **Procedural Regulations** neither establish tax laws nor attempt to explain tax laws. Procedural Regulations are *housekeeping-type* instructions, indicating information that taxpayers should provide the IRS, as well as information about the internal management and conduct of the IRS itself.
- Some **interpretive Regulations** merely reprint or rephrase what Congress stated in the Committee Reports that were issued when the tax legislation was enacted. Such Regulations are *hard and solid* and almost impossible to overturn because they clearly reflect the intent of Congress.
- In some Code Sections, Congress has given the *Secretary or his delegate* the authority to prescribe Regulations to carry out the details of administration or to otherwise complete the operating rules. Under such circumstances, it could almost be said that Congress is delegating its legislative powers to the Treasury Department. Regulations issued pursuant to this type of authority truly possess the force and effect of law and are often called **legislative Regulations** (e.g., consolidated return Regulations).

Assessing the Validity of Other Administrative Sources of the Tax Law. Revenue Rulings issued by the IRS carry less weight than Treasury Department Regulations. Revenue Rulings are important, however, in that they reflect the position of the IRS on tax matters. In any dispute with the IRS on the interpretation of tax law, taxpayers should expect agents to follow the results reached in any applicable Revenue Rulings.

Actions on Decisions further tell the taxpayer the IRS's reaction to certain court decisions and Revenue Rulings. Recall that the IRS follows a practice of either acquiescing (agreeing) or nonacquiescing (not agreeing) with selected decisions. A nonacquiescence does not mean that a particular court decision is of no value, but it does indicate that the IRS will continue to litigate the issue involved.

Assessing the Validity of Judicial Sources of the Tax Law. The judicial process as it relates to the formulation of tax law has been described. How much reliance can be placed on a particular decision depends upon the following variables:

- The level of the court. A decision rendered by a trial court (e.g., a Federal District Court) carries less weight than one issued by an appellate court (e.g., the Fifth Court of Appeals). Unless Congress changes the Code, decisions by the U.S. Supreme Court represent the last word on any tax issue.
- The legal residence of the taxpayer. If, for example, a taxpayer lives in Texas, a decision of the Fifth Court of Appeals means more than one rendered by the Second Court of Appeals. This is the case because any appeal from a District Court or the Tax Court would be to the Fifth Court of Appeals and not to the Second Court of Appeals.[28]
- A Tax Court Regular decision carries more weight than a Memorandum decision because the Tax Court does not consider Memorandum decisions to be binding precedents.[29] Furthermore, a Tax Court *reviewed* decision carries even more weight. All of the Tax Court judges participate in a reviewed decision.

---

[28] Before October 1, 1982, an appeal from the then-named U.S. Court of Claims (the other trial court) was directly to the U.S. Supreme Court.

[29] *Severino R. Nico, Jr.,* 67 T.C. 647 (1977).

- A Circuit Court decision where certiorari has been requested and denied by the Supreme Court carries more weight than a Circuit Court decision that was not appealed. A Circuit Court decision heard *en banc* (all the judges participate) carries more weight than a normal Circuit Court case.
- Whether the decision represents the weight of authority on the issue. In other words, is it supported by the results reached by other courts?
- The outcome or status of the decision on appeal. For example, was the decision appealed and, if so, with what result?

In connection with the last two variables, a citator is helpful to tax research.[30] The use of a citator is not illustrated in this text.

Assessing the Validity of Other Sources.   *Primary sources* of tax law include the Constitution, legislative history materials, statutes, treaties, Treasury Regulations, IRS pronouncements, and judicial decisions. In general, the IRS regards only primary sources as substantial authority. However, reference to *secondary materials* such as legal periodicals, treatises, legal opinions, General Counsel Memoranda, and written determinations may be useful. In general, secondary sources are not authority.

Although the statement that the IRS regards only primary sources as substantial authority is generally true, there is one exception. In Notice 90–20,[31] the IRS expanded the list of substantial authority *for purposes of* the accuracy-related penalty in § 6662 to include a number of secondary materials (e.g., letter rulings, General Counsel Memoranda, the Bluebook). As under former § 6661, "authority" does not include conclusions reached in treatises, legal periodicals, and opinions rendered by tax professionals.

A letter ruling or determination letter is substantial authority only for the taxpayer to whom it is issued, except as noted above with respect to the accuracy-related penalty.

Upon the completion of major tax legislation, the staff of the Joint Committee on Taxation (in consultation with the staffs of the House Ways and Means and Senate Finance Committees) often will prepare a General Explanation of the Act, commonly known as the Bluebook because of the color of its cover. The IRS will not accept this detailed explanation as having legal effect. The Bluebook does, however, provide valuable guidance to tax advisers and taxpayers until Regulations are issued, and some letter rulings and General Counsel Memoranda of the IRS cite its explanations.

ARRIVING AT THE SOLUTION OR AT ALTERNATIVE SOLUTIONS

Example 4 raised the question of whether a taxpayer would be denied dependency exemptions for a son and a daughter-in-law if the son sold some stock near the end of the year. A refinement of the problem supplies the following additional information:

- Sam was a full-time student during four calendar months of the year.
- Sam and Dana anticipate filing a joint return.

---

[30] The major citators are published by Commerce Clearing House, RIA, and Shepard's Citations, Inc.

[31] 1990–1 C.B. 328; see also Reg. § 1.6661–3(b)(2).

Additional research leads to Regulation § 1.151–3(b), which indicates that to qualify as a student, Sam must be a full-time student during each of *five* calendar months of the year at an educational institution. Thus, proceeds from Sam's sale of the stock would cause his parents to lose at least one dependency exemption because Sam's gross income would exceed the exemption amount. The parents still might be able to claim Dana as an exemption if the support test is met.

Section 151(c)(2) indicates that a supporting taxpayer is not permitted a dependency exemption for a married dependent if the married individual files a joint return. Initial reaction is that a joint return by Sam and Dana would be disastrous to the parents. However, more research uncovers two Revenue Rulings that provide an exception if neither the dependent nor the dependent's spouse is required to file a return but does so solely to claim a refund of tax withheld. The IRS asserts that each spouse must have gross income of less than the exemption amount.[32] Therefore, if Sam sells the stock and he and Dana file a joint return, the parents would lose the dependency exemption for both Sam and Dana.

If the stock is not sold until January, both exemptions may still be available to the parents. However, under § 151(d)(2), a personal exemption is not available to a taxpayer who can be claimed as a dependent by another taxpayer (whether actually claimed or not). Thus, if the parents can claim Sam and Dana as dependents, Sam and Dana would lose their personal exemptions on their tax return.

COMMUNICATING TAX RESEARCH

4   **LEARNING OBJECTIVE**
Communicate the results of the tax research process in a client letter and a tax file memorandum.

Once the problem has been researched adequately, a memo (and/or letter) setting forth the result may need to be prepared. The form such a memo takes could depend on a number of considerations. For example, does an employer or instructor recommend a particular procedure or format for tax research memos? Is the memo to be given directly to the client or will it first go to the preparer's employer? Whatever form it takes, a good research memo should contain the following elements:

- A clear statement of the issue.
- In more complex situations, a short review of the fact pattern that raises the issue.
- A review of the tax law sources (e.g., Code, Regulations, Revenue Rulings, judicial authority).
- Any assumptions made in arriving at the solution.
- The solution recommended and the logic or reasoning supporting it.
- The references consulted in the research process.

In short, a good tax memo should tell the reader what was researched, the results of that research, and the justification for the recommendation made.

Illustrations of the memos for the tax file and the client letter associated with Example 4 appear in Figures 28–6, 28–7, and 28–8.

WORKING WITH THE TAX LAW— TAX PLANNING

5   **LEARNING OBJECTIVE**
Apply tax research techniques and planning procedures.

Tax research and tax planning are inseparable. The *primary* purpose of effective tax planning is to maximize the taxpayer's after-tax wealth. This statement does not

---

[32] Rev.Rul. 54–567, 1954–2 C.B. 108; Rev.Rul. 65–34, 1965–1 C.B. 86.

▼ **FIGURE 28–6**
Tax File Memorandum

August 16, 1996

TAX FILE MEMORANDUM

FROM: John J. Jones

SUBJECT: Fred and Megan Taxpayer
                  Engagement: Issues

Today I talked to Fred Taxpayer with respect to his August 14, 1996 letter requesting tax assistance. He wishes to know if his son, Sam, can sell stock worth $19,000 (basis of $12,000) without the parents losing the dependency exemptions for Sam and Sam's wife, Dana.

Fred Taxpayer is married to Megan, and Sam is a full-time student at a local university. Sam inherited the stock from his grandmother about five years ago. If he sells the stock, he will save the proceeds from the sale. Sam does not need to spend the proceeds if he sells the stock because he receives a $3,000 scholarship that he uses for his own support (i.e., to pay for tuition, books, and fees). Fred and Megan are in the 28% tax bracket and furnish approximately 55% of Sam and Dana's support.

ISSUE: If the stock is sold, would the sale prohibit Fred and Megan from claiming Sam and Dana as dependents? I told Fred that we would have an answer for him within two weeks.

mean that the course of action selected must produce the lowest possible tax under the circumstances. The minimization of tax liability must be considered in the context of the legitimate business goals of the taxpayer.

A *secondary* objective of effective tax planning is to reduce or defer the tax in the current tax year. Specifically, this objective aims to accomplish one or more results. Some possibilities are eradicating the tax entirely, eliminating the tax in the current year, deferring the receipt of income, proliferating taxpayers (i.e., forming partnerships and corporations or making lifetime gifts to family members), eluding double taxation, avoiding ordinary income, or creating, increasing, or accelerating deductions. However, this second objective should be approached with considerable reservation and moderation. For example, a tax election in one year may accomplish a current reduction in taxes, but it could saddle future years with a disadvantageous tax position.

NONTAX CONSIDERATIONS

There is a danger that tax motivations may take on a significance that does not conform to the true values involved. In other words, tax considerations can operate to impair the exercise of sound business judgment. Thus, the tax planning process can lead to ends that are socially and economically objectionable. Unfortunately, a tendency exists for planning to go toward the opposing extremes of either not enough or too much emphasis on tax considerations. The happy medium is a balance that recognizes the significance of taxes, but not beyond the point at which planning detracts from the exercise of good business judgment.

The remark is often made that a good rule is to refrain from pursuing any course of action that would not be followed were it not for certain tax considerations. This statement is not entirely correct, but it does illustrate the desirability of preventing business logic from being *sacrificed at the altar of tax planning*.

TAX EVASION AND TAX AVOIDANCE

A fine line exists between legal tax planning and illegal tax planning—tax avoidance versus tax evasion. **Tax avoidance** is merely tax minimization through legal techniques. In this sense, tax avoidance is the proper objective of all tax

▼ **FIGURE 28–7**
Tax File Memorandum

August 26, 1996

TAX FILE MEMORANDUM

FROM: John J. Jones

SUBJECT: Fred and Megan Taxpayer
                 Engagement: Conclusions

Section 152(a) provides that in order for a taxpayer to take a dependency exemption, the taxpayer must provide over 50% of the support of the potential dependent. Fred and Megan provide about 55% of the support of their son, Sam, and their daughter-in-law, Dana. If Sam should sell the stock in 1996, he would not need to spend the proceeds for support purposes (i.e., he would save the proceeds). Thus, the stock sale would not affect his qualifying for the support test. In calculating the percentage of support provided by Fred and Megan, a $3,000 scholarship received by Sam is not counted in determining the amount of support Sam provides for himself [see Reg. § 1.152–1(c)].

Section 151(c)(1) provides that in order to qualify for a dependency exemption, the potential dependent's gross income must be less than the exemption amount (i.e., $2,550 in 1996). Without the stock sale, the gross income of both Sam ($960) and Dana ($900) will be below the exemption amount in 1996. The $3,000 Sam receives as a scholarship is excluded from his gross income under § 117(a) because he uses the entire amount to pay for his tuition, books, and fees at a local university.

The key issue then is whether the stock, which will generate $7,000 gain for Sam, will cause the gross income test to be violated. The gain will increase Sam's gross income to $7,960 ($7,000 + $960). However, § 151(c)(1)(B) permits a child's gross income to exceed the exemption amount if the child is a student under the age of 24. Under Reg. § 1.151–3(b), to qualify as a student, the person must be a full-time student during each of five calendar months. A telephone call to Megan provided the information that Sam was a student for only four months in 1996. Thus, since Sam is not eligible for the student exception, the sale of the stock by Sam in 1996 would result in Fred and Megan losing the dependency exemption for Sam.

The stock sale would also result in the loss of the dependency exemption for Dana if Sam and Dana file a joint return for 1996 [see § 151(c)(2)].

From a tax planning perspective, Sam should not sell the stock until 1997. This will enable Fred and Megan to claim dependency exemptions on their 1996 return for Sam and Dana. Note, however, that neither Sam nor Dana will be permitted to take a personal exemption deduction on their 1996 tax return since they are claimed as dependents on someone else's return [see § 151(d)(2)]. However, this will not produce any negative tax consequences since their tax liability will be zero if the stock is not sold in 1996.

planning. Though eliminating or reducing taxes is also a goal of tax evasion, the term implies the use of subterfuge and fraud as a means to this end. Perhaps because common goals are involved, popular usage has blurred the distinction between the two concepts. Consequently, the association of tax avoidance with tax evasion has kept some taxpayers from properly taking advantage of planning possibilities. The now classic words of Judge Learned Hand in *Commissioner v. Newman* reflect the true values a taxpayer should have:

> Over and over again courts have said that there is nothing sinister in so arranging one's affairs as to keep taxes as low as possible. Everybody does so, rich or poor; and all do right, for nobody owes any public duty to pay more than the law demands: taxes are enforced extractions, not voluntary contributions. To demand more in the name of morals is mere cant.[33]

---

[33] *Comm. v. Newman*, 47–1 USTC ¶9175, 35 AFTR 857, 159 F.2d 848 (CA–2, 1947).

▼ **FIGURE 28–8**
Client Letter

Willis, Hoffman, Maloney, and Raabe, CPAs
50 Kellogg Boulevard
St. Paul, Minnesota 55164

August 30, 1996

Mr. and Ms. Fred Taxpayer
111 Boulevard
Williamsburg, Virginia 23185

Dear Mr. and Ms. Taxpayer:

This letter is in response to your request for us to review your family's financial and tax situation. Our conclusions are based upon the facts as outlined in your August 14th letter. Any change in the facts may affect our conclusions.

You provide over 50% of the support for your son, Sam, and his wife, Dana. The scholarship Sam receives is not included in determining support. If the stock is not sold, you will qualify for a dependency exemption for both Sam and Dana.

However, if the stock is sold, a gain of approximately $7,000 will result. This amount will result in the gross income requirement being violated (i.e., a potential dependent's gross income must not exceed $2,550) for Sam. Therefore, you will not qualify to receive a dependency exemption for Sam. In addition, if Sam sells the stock and he and Dana file a joint return, you also will not qualify for a dependency exemption for Dana.

From a tax planning perspective, Sam should not sell the stock in 1996. Delaying the stock sale will enable you to claim dependency exemptions for both Sam and Dana. If the stock is sold, Sam and Dana should not file a joint return. This will still enable you to qualify for a dependency exemption for Dana.

Should you need more information or need to clarify our conclusions, do not hesitate to contact me.

Sincerely yours,

John J. Jones, CPA
Partner

ETHICAL
CONSIDERATIONS

Tax Avoidance

In a speech class, a philosophy student argues that tax advisers are immoral because they help people cheat the government. Each time a tax adviser shows a taxpayer a tax planning idea that reduces the client's liability, all other taxpayers have to pay more taxes. Society would be better off if all tax advisers would work at improving our environment or living conditions in the inner cities.

An accounting student argues that the primary purpose of tax planning is to reduce a taxpayer's overall liability. This advisory process can result in avoiding, deferring, or postponing the tax burden until the future. There is nothing illegal or immoral about tax avoidance. Taxpayers have every legal right to be concerned about tax avoidance and to arrange their affairs so as to pay no more taxes than the law demands. There is no difference between reducing a tax expense through the help of a tax adviser and reducing a cost of operating a business with the aid of a cost accountant.

Comment on each student's position.

FOLLOW-UP PROCEDURES

Because tax planning usually involves a proposed (as opposed to a completed) transaction, it is predicated upon the continuing validity of the advice based upon the tax research. A change in the tax law (either legislative, administrative, or judicial) could alter the original conclusion. Additional research may be necessary to test the solution in light of current developments (refer to the broken lines at the right in Figure 28–5).

TAX PLANNING—A PRACTICAL APPLICATION

Returning to the facts of Example 4, what could be done to protect the dependency exemptions for the parents? If Sam and Dana were to refrain from filing a joint return, both could be claimed by the parents. This result assumes that the stock is not sold.

An obvious tax planning tool is the installment method. Could the securities be sold using the installment method under § 453 so that most of the gain is deferred into the next year? Under the installment method, certain gains may be postponed and recognized as the cash proceeds are received. The problem is that the installment method is not available for stock traded on an established securities market.[34]

A little more research, however, indicates that Sam can sell the stock and postpone the recognition of gain until the following year by selling short an equal number of substantially identical shares and covering the short sale in the subsequent year with the shares originally held. Selling short means that Sam sells borrowed stock (substantially identical) and repays the lender with the stock held on the date of the short sale. This *short against the box* technique would allow Sam to protect his $7,000 profit and defer the closing of the sale until the following year.[35] Further, if the original shares have been held for the required long-term holding period before the date of the short sale, Sam would be able to obtain long-term capital gain treatment.[36] Thus, some research and planning would reap tax savings for this family. Note the critical role of obtaining the correct facts in attempting to resolve the proper strategy for the taxpayers.

Throughout this text, most chapters include observations on Tax Planning Considerations. Such observations are not all-inclusive but are intended to illustrate some of the ways in which the material covered can be effectively utilized to minimize taxes.

COMPUTER-ASSISTED TAX RESEARCH

6   LEARNING OBJECTIVE
Have an awareness of computer-assisted tax research.

The computer is being used more frequently in the day-to-day practice of tax professionals, students, and educators. Many software vendors offer tax return software programs for individual, corporate, partnership, and fiduciary returns. The use of computers, however, is not limited to batch-processed tax returns. Computer timesharing for quantitative tax and problem-solving planning and calculations has added a new dimension to tax research.

The microcomputer has become the revolutionary tool of the present—much as the electronic calculator did in the 1970s. Electronic spreadsheets are replacing

---

[34] See Chapter 15 for a discussion of installment sales.

[35] §§ 1233(a) and 1233(b)(2). See Chapter 13 for a discussion of short sales.

[36] Long-term capital gains are eligible for preferential tax treatment. In addition, if Sam had capital losses from other transactions, the capital gains and capital losses could be offset. See the discussion in Chapter 13.

the 14-column worksheet. The electronic spreadsheet approach can be used anytime projections and calculations are needed. Examples include retirement planning, Form 1040 projections, real estate projections, partnership allocations, consolidated tax return problems, and compensation planning. Internally prepared tax-related programs are used by many public accounting firms. Microcomputer software also is available for estate planning calculations.

LEXIS, a computerized legal data bank, has been available since 1973 as a complement to the conventional research approach. WESTLAW, a competitive system from West Publishing Company, has been operational since 1975. Commerce Clearing House's legal data base is called ACCESS, and Research Institute of America's is called TAXRIA. With these data banks, one has immediate access to the current tax law, Regulations, Proposed Regulations, letter rulings, Revenue Rulings, judicial decisions, daily tax services, code commentaries, and much more. Note, however, that WESTLAW, LEXIS, ACCESS, and TAXRIA are document retrieval systems and cannot interpret the law.

A recent development is the proliferation of Compact Disc–Read Only Memory (CD-ROM) products. By employing a key-word search technique, a person can browse through a tax service, IRS publications, and other tax information. Commerce Clearing House, Research Institute of America, Tax Analysts, Tax Management, Inc., and West Publishing Company offer CD-ROM products. For example, West provides a complete Federal tax library on only nine CDs. Although CD-ROM does not offer the on-line updating provided by WESTLAW, LEXIS, ACCESS, and TAXRIA, the CDs can be replaced periodically.

Computer-assisted tax research is useful in searching for facts since human indexing centers on legal theories rather than fact patterns. Computer searching is also useful in finding new court decisions not yet in the printed indexes. Nevertheless, computer searching probably does not find as many relevant cases as manual searching does. Consequently, a combination of manual and computer searching is preferred.[37]

The latest development is the World Wide Web of the Internet, which is constantly expanding and provides a wealth of valuable information. Four broad categories of tax resources are available on the Web: gateway sites (i.e., indexes), Federal tax laws, state and foreign taxes, and secondary and commercial sites. IRS forms, state forms, tax articles, U.S. tax laws, tax treaty information, judicial and legal gateways, and Regulations are only some of the information on the Web.[38]

KEY TERMS

Acquiescence, 28–18	Determination letters, 28–10	Interpretive Regulations, 28–26
Circuit Court of Appeals, 28–14	Federal District Court, 28–12	Legislative Regulations, 28–26
Court of original jurisdiction, 28–12	Finalized Regulations, 28–8	

---

[37] See Thomas and Weinstein, *Computer-Assisted Legal and Tax Research* (Paramus, N.J.: Prentice-Hall, 1986); and Chapter 13 of W. A. Raabe, G. E. Whittenburg, and J. C. Bost, *West's Federal Tax Research*, 3d ed. (St. Paul, Minn.: West Publishing Co., 1994).

[38] R. J. Coppins et al, "Worldwide Web: The Latest Tax Resource on the Information Superhighway," *Journal of Taxation* (August 1995): 108–118.

PROBLEM MATERIALS

DISCUSSION QUESTIONS

1. Judicial decisions interpreting a provision of the Internal Revenue Code of 1939 or 1954 are no longer of any value in view of the enactment of the Internal Revenue Code of 1986. Assess the validity of this statement.

2. When was the last time Congress codified the tax laws?

3. Tax legislation normally originates in the House Ways and Means Committee. Assess the validity of this statement.

4. What is the function of the Joint Conference Committee of the House Ways and Means Committee and the Senate Finance Committee?

5. Paul Jacobs operates a small international firm named Teal, Inc. A new treaty between the United States and Ukraine conflicts with a Section of the Internal Revenue Code. Paul asks you for advice. If he follows the treaty position, does he need to disclose this on his tax return? If he is required to disclose, are there any penalties for failure to disclose? Prepare a letter in which you respond to Paul. Teal's address is 100 International Drive, Tampa, FL 33620.

6. Interpret this Regulation citation: Reg. § 1.274–2(a)(1)(i).

7. Distinguish between legislative, interpretive, and procedural Regulations.

8. Distinguish between the following:
   a. Treasury Regulations and Revenue Rulings.
   b. Revenue Rulings and Revenue Procedures.
   c. Revenue Rulings and letter rulings.
   d. Letter rulings and determination letters.

9. Rank the following items from the highest authority to the lowest in the Federal tax law system:
   a. Interpretive Regulation.
   b. Legislative Regulation.
   c. Letter ruling.
   d. Revenue Procedure.
   e. Internal Revenue Code.
   f. Proposed Regulation.

10. Interpret each of the following citations:
    a. Rev.Rul. 65–235, 1965–2 C.B. 88.
    b. Rev.Proc. 87–56, 1987–2 C.B. 674.
    c. Ltr.Rul. 9046036.

11. Caleb receives a ninety-day letter after his discussion with an appeals officer. He is not satisfied with the $92,000 settlement offer. Identify the relevant tax research issues facing Caleb.

12. Which of the following would be considered advantages of the Small Cases Division of the Tax Court?
   a. Appeal to the Court of Appeals for the Federal Circuit is possible.
   b. A hearing of a deficiency of $11,200 is considered on a timely basis.
   c. Taxpayer can handle the litigation without using a lawyer or certified public accountant.
   d. Taxpayer can use Small Cases Division decisions for precedential value.
   e. The actual hearing is conducted informally.
   f. Travel time will probably be reduced.

13. List an advantage and a disadvantage of using the U.S. Tax Court as the trial court for Federal tax litigation.

14. Sam Brown is considering litigating a tax deficiency of approximately $317,000 in the court system. He asks you to provide him with a short description of his alternatives indicating the advantages and disadvantages of each. Prepare your response to Sam in the form of a letter. His address is 200 Mesa Drive, Tuscon, AZ 85714.

15. List an advantage and a disadvantage of using the U.S. Court of Federal Claims as the trial court for Federal tax litigation.

16. A taxpayer lives in Michigan. In a controversy with the IRS, the taxpayer loses at the trial court level. Describe the appeal procedure for each of the following trial courts:
   a. Small Cases Division of the U.S. Tax Court.
   b. U.S. Tax Court.
   c. U.S. District Court.
   d. U.S. Court of Federal Claims.

17. Suppose the U.S. Government loses a tax case in the U.S. District Court of South Carolina and does not appeal the result. What does the failure to appeal signify?

18. For the U.S. Tax Court, U.S. District Court, and the U.S. Court of Federal Claims, indicate the following:
   a. Number of regular judges per court.
   b. Availability of a jury trial.
   c. Whether the deficiency must be paid before the trial.

19. In which of the following states could a taxpayer appeal the decision of a U.S. District Court to the Fifth Court of Appeals?
   a. Arkansas.
   b. Arizona.
   c. Alabama.
   d. Maine.
   e. Texas.

20. What is the Supreme Court's policy on hearing tax cases?

21. In assessing the validity of a prior court decision, discuss the significance of the following on the taxpayer's issue:
   a. The decision was rendered by the U.S. District Court of Wyoming. Taxpayer lives in Wyoming.
   b. The decision was rendered by the U.S. Court of Federal Claims. Taxpayer lives in Wyoming.
   c. The decision was rendered by the Second Court of Appeals. Taxpayer lives in California.
   d. The decision was rendered by the U.S. Supreme Court.
   e. The decision was rendered by the U.S. Tax Court. The IRS has acquiesced in the result.
   f. Same as (e), except that the IRS has nonacquiesced in the result.

22. What is the difference between a Regular and a Memorandum decision of the U.S. Tax Court?

23. Interpret each of the following citations:
   a. 54 T.C. 1514 (1970).

    b. 408 F.2d 117 (CA–2, 1969).
    c. 69–1 USTC ¶9319 (CA–2, 1969).
    d. 23 AFTR2d 69–1090 (CA–2, 1969).
    e. 293 F.Supp. 1129 (D.Ct.Miss., 1967).
    f. 67–1 USTC ¶9253 (D.Ct.Miss., 1967).
    g. 19 AFTR2d 647 (D.Ct.Miss., 1967).
    h. 56 S.Ct. 289 (USSC, 1935).
    i. 36–1 USTC ¶9020 (USSC, 1935).
    j. 16 AFTR 1274 (USSC, 1935).
    k. 422 F.2d 1336 (Ct.Cls., 1970).

24. Explain the following abbreviations:
    a. CA–2   i. USTC
    b. Cls.Ct.   j. AFTR
    c. *aff'd.*   k. F.3d
    d. *rev'd.*   l. F.Supp.
    e. *rem'd.*   m. USSC
    f. *Cert. denied*   n. S.Ct.
    g. *acq.*   o. D.Ct.
    h. B.T.A.   p. Fed.Cl.

25. Give the Commerce Clearing House citation for each of the following courts:
    a. Small Cases Division of the Tax Court.
    b. Federal District Court.
    c. U.S. Supreme Court.
    d. U.S. Court of Federal Claims.
    e. Tax Court Memorandum decision.

26. Where can you locate a published decision of the U.S. Court of Federal Claims?

27. Which of the following items can probably be found in the *Cumulative Bulletin?*
    a. Revenue Ruling.
    b. Small Cases Division of the U.S. Tax Court decision.
    c. Letter ruling.
    d. Revenue Procedure.
    e. Proposed Regulation.
    f. District Court decision.
    g. Senate Finance Committee Report.
    h. Acquiescences to Tax Court decisions.
    i. Tax Court Memorandum decision.

28. As part of her coursework for a Masters of Tax degree, Ann is required to prepare a 30-page term paper about limited liability partnerships. Identify some relevant research steps Ann may take.

29. Defend the practice by which tax advisers such as CPAs use tax planning techniques to reduce the tax liability of their clients.

30. In general, what type of tax information can a person find on CD-ROM?

PROBLEMS

31. Tom has just been audited by the IRS and, as a result, has been assessed a substantial deficiency (which he has not yet paid) in additional income taxes. In preparing his defense, Tom advances the following possibilities:
    a. Although a resident of Kentucky, Tom plans to sue in a U.S. District Court in Oregon that appears to be more favorably inclined toward taxpayers.
    b. If (a) is not possible, Tom plans to take his case to a Kentucky state court where an uncle is the presiding judge.
    c. Since Tom has found a B.T.A. decision that seems to help his case, he plans to rely on it under alternative (a) or (b).

d. If he loses at the trial court level, Tom plans to appeal to either the U.S. Court of Federal Claims or the U.S. Second Court of Appeals because he has relatives in both Washington, D.C., and New York. Staying with these relatives could save Tom lodging expense while his appeal is being heard by the court selected.

e. Even if he does not win at the trial court or appeals court level, Tom feels certain of success on an appeal to the U.S. Supreme Court.

Evaluate Tom's notions concerning the judicial process as it applies to Federal income tax controversies.

32. Using the legend provided, classify each of the following statements (more than one answer per statement may be appropriate):

Legend

D = Applies to the U.S. District Court

T = Applies to the U.S. Tax Court

C = Applies to the U.S. Court of Federal Claims

A = Applies to the U.S. Court of Appeals

U = Applies to the U.S. Supreme Court

N = Applies to none of the above

---

a. Decides only Federal tax matters.
b. Decisions are reported in the F.3d Series.
c. Decisions are reported in the USTCs.
d. Decisions are reported in the AFTRs.
e. Appeal is by *Writ of Certiorari*.
f. Court meets most often in Washington, D.C.
g. Offers the choice of a jury trial.
h. Is a trial court.
i. Is an appellate court.
j. Allows appeal to the Court of Appeals for the Federal Circuit and bypasses the taxpayer's particular Court of Appeals.
k. Has a Small Cases Division.
l. Is the only trial court where the taxpayer does not have to first pay the tax assessed by the IRS.

33. Using the legend provided, classify each of the following citations as to the type of court:

Legend

D = Applies to the U.S. District Court

T = Applies to the U.S. Tax Court

C = Applies to the U.S. Court of Federal Claims

A = Applies to the U.S. Court of Appeals

U = Applies to the U.S. Supreme Court

N = Applies to none of the above

---

a. 388 F.2d 420 (CA–7, 1968).
b. 79 T.C. 7 (1982).
c. 54 S.Ct. 8 (USSC, 1933).
d. 3 B.T.A. 1042 (1926).
e. T.C.Memo. 1954–141.
f. 597 F.2d 760 (Ct.Cls., 1979).
g. Ltr. Rul. 9414051.
h. 465 F.Supp. 341 (D.Ct.Okla., 1978).

34. Using the legend provided, classify each of the following citations as to publisher:

Legend	
RIA	= Research Institute of America
CCH	= Commerce Clearing House
W	= West Publishing Company
U.S.	= U.S. Government
O	= Others

    a. 83–2 USTC ¶9600.
    b. 52 AFTR2d 83–5954.
    c. 49 T.C. 645 (1968).
    d. 39 TCM 32 (1979).
    e. 393 U.S. 297.
    f. RIA T.C.Memo. ¶80,582.
    g. 89 S.Ct. 501.
    h. 2 Cl.Ct. 600.
    i. 159 F.2d 848.
    j. 592 F.Supp. 18.
    k. Rev.Rul. 76–332, 1976–2 C.B. 81.
    l. 21 L.Ed.2d 495.

RESEARCH PROBLEMS

Note: **West's Federal Taxation on CD-ROM** *can be used in preparing solutions to the Research Problems. Alternatively, tax research materials contained in a standard tax library can be used.*

Chapter 2

Research Problem 1. In the state of Texas, a lawsuit was instituted charging that the state schools for the mentally retarded furnished inadequate, unsafe, and improper care, treatment, and education. As part of the settlement of this suit, the Texas Department of Mental Health offered to pay a fixed daily amount to third-party providers of these services. Under this arrangement, the taxpayers received $16,425 during the year for the care of their mentally retarded daughter. This amount covered a daily per diem for food and board, medical expenses, cost of special food, clothing, transportation, special laundry, home repairs, and other living expenses. The daughter lived with the taxpayers and during the year attended classes at a special school operated by the local school district.

Although the taxpayers did not pay for more than 50% of their daughter's support, they claimed her as a dependent for the year. The taxpayers contend that the amount they received from the state is a scholarship and, therefore, should not be taken into account in applying the support test. The IRS disagrees. What is the appropriate result?

Research aids:
§ 152(d).
Rev.Rul. 61–186, 1961–2 C.B. 30.
Rev.Rul. 64–221, 1964–2 C.B. 46.

Research Problem 2. Sharon Collins, although married, lives alone. She maintains a household that includes her three-year-old son. Sharon and her husband are not on good terms, but neither has ever bothered to file for legal separation or divorce. Sharon is gainfully employed and provides all of the support for herself and her son. During the year, she utilizes the services of a day care center while she works.

Presuming Sharon does not file a joint return with her husband, what is her filing status? Can she claim a child care credit on a separate return? Explain.

Chapter 3

Research Problem 3. Sam purchased a new automobile for $18,000. Sam was very pleased with himself for negotiating a low price for the automobile, so it came as a complete surprise to him when he received a $1,500 check from the manufacturer as a rebate on the new car. Sam considers the windfall the equivalent of finding money, and he asks you whether his good fortune has any tax consequences.

Research Problem 4. The Great Electric Company requires new customers to make a $100 deposit to secure future payments for electricity. After the customer has established a good payment record (usually within two years), the company refunds the deposit to the customer. If the services are terminated before refund, the deposit is usually applied against the final bill. The IRS agent insists that the company must include the deposits in gross income for the year the deposits are received. Can you find authority for excluding the deposits from income?

Chapter 4

Research Problem 5. David is the minister at the First Baptist Church. As part of his compensation, he receives an $800 per month housing allowance. David is purchasing his residence, and he uses the $800 each month to make mortgage and property tax payments. The mortgage interest and property taxes are deducted (as itemized deductions) on David's tax return. The examining IRS agent thinks David would be enjoying a double benefit if the housing allowance is excluded and the itemized deductions are allowed. In addition, the agent contends that the housing allowance exclusion should apply only where the church provides the residence or the minister uses the funds to pay rent. Therefore, the agent maintains that David should include the $800 received each month in gross income. David has asked for your assistance in this matter. Write a letter to David that contains your advice and prepare a memo for the tax files.

Research Problem 6. Mega City was experiencing cash-flow problems. Therefore, the City offered property owners a 3% discount if they would pay their property taxes six months before the due date. Electric Utilities, Inc., took advantage of the offer and received a $65,000 discount. The company deducted the undiscounted amount of the taxes and excluded the discount from gross income. The company reasons that the discount represents interest on local government obligations and thus is nontaxable under § 103. Evaluate the company's position.

Chapter 5

Research Problem 7. Gray Chemical Company manufactured pesticides that were toxic. Over the course of several years, the toxic waste contaminated the air and water around the company's plant. Several employees suffered toxic poisoning, and the Environmental Protection Agency cited the company for violations. In court, the judge found Gray guilty and imposed fines of $15 million. The company voluntarily set up a charitable fund for the purpose of bettering the environment and funded it with $8 million. The company incurred legal expenses in setting up the foundation and defending itself in court. The court reduced the fine from $15 million to $7 million.

Gray Chemical Company deducted the $8 million paid to the foundation and the legal expenses incurred. The IRS disallowed both deductions on the grounds that the payment was, in fact, a fine and in violation of public policy.

Gray's president, Ted Jones, has contacted you regarding the deductibility of the $7 million fine, the $8 million payment to the foundation, and the legal fees. Write a letter to Mr. Jones that contains your advice and prepare a memo for the tax files. Gray's address is 200 Lincoln Center, Omaha, NE 68182.

Research aids:
§§ 162(a) and (f).
Reg. § 1.162–21(b).

Research Problem 8.   Rex and Agnes Harrell purchased a beach house at Duck, North Carolina, in early 1995. Although they intended to use the beach house occasionally for recreational purposes, they also planned to rent it through the realty agency that had handled the purchase in order to help pay the mortgage payments, property taxes, and maintenance costs. Rex is a surgeon, and Agnes is a counselor.

The beach house was in need of substantial repairs. Rather than hiring a contractor, Rex and Agnes decided they would make the repairs themselves. During both high school and college, Rex had worked summers in construction. In addition, he had taken an advanced course in woodworking and related subjects from a local community college several years ago.

During 1995, according to a log maintained by the Harrells, they occupied the beach house on 38 days and rented it on 49 days. The log also indicated that on 24 of the 38 days that they occupied the beach house, one or both of them were engaged in work on the beach house. Their two teenage children were with them on all of these days, but did not help with the work being done. On their 1995 income tax return, Rex and Agnes, who filed a joint return, treated the beach house as a rental property and deducted a pro rata share of the property taxes, mortgage interest, utilities, maintenance and repairs, and depreciation in determining their net loss from the beach home. A Revenue Agent has limited the deductions to the rent income. He contends that the 14-day personal use provision was exceeded and that many of the alleged repairs were capital expenditures. Advise the Harrells on how they should respond to the IRS.

Chapter 6

Research Problem 9.   While Ralph was in the process of obtaining a divorce, his wife, without Ralph's knowledge, had the furniture removed from his apartment. Discuss whether Ralph is entitled to a tax deduction for the loss of the furniture.

Research aids:
Landis G. Brown, 30 TCM 257, T.C.Memo. 1971–60.
Jerry L. Goode, 42 TCM 1209, T.C.Memo. 1981–548.

Research Problem 10.   George Johnson, a Minnesota resident, parked his car on a lake while he was watching an iceboat race. During the race, the ice beneath his car unexpectedly gave way, and the car sank to the bottom of the lake. Write a letter to George advising him as to whether he can claim a casualty loss for the damage to the car. Also prepare a memo for the tax files. George's address is 100 Apple Lane, St. Paul, MN 55123.

Chapter 7

Research Problem 11.   Sandra purchased the following personal property during 1996:

Date	Asset	Cost
June 1	Machine A	$20,000
July 10	Machine B	10,000
November 15	Machine C	25,000

Sandra elects to take the § 179 expense on Machine C. Discuss what convention Sandra must use to determine her cost recovery deduction for 1996.

Research Problem 12.   Gabriella is a professor of violin at the University of Minnesota. She is also a concert violinist. Gabriella purchased her violin for $80,000. Discuss whether Gabriella's violin is subject to cost recovery using MACRS with the violin being classified as five-year property.

Chapter 8

Research Problem 13.   Rick Beam has been an independent sales representative for various textile manufacturers for many years. His products consist of soft goods, such as tablecloths, curtains, and drapes. Rick's customers are clothing store chains, department stores, and smaller specialty stores. The employees of these companies responsible for the purchase of merchandise are known as buyers. These companies generally prohibit their buyers from accepting gifts from manufacturers' sales representatives.

Each year Rick gives cash gifts (never more than $25) to most of the buyers who are his customers. Generally, he cashes a large check in November and gives the money personally to the buyers around Christmas. Rick says, "This is one of the ways that I have maintained my relationship with my buyers." He maintains adequate substantiation of all the gifts.

Rick's deductions for these gifts have been disallowed by the IRS, based on § 162(c)(2). Rick is confused and comes to you, a CPA, for advice.

a. Write a letter to Rick concerning his tax position on this issue.

b. Prepare a memo for your files supporting the advice you have given.

Research Problem 14. Lyle has been a schoolteacher since he earned his bachelor of education degree 10 years ago. In 1993, the governing board of his school district passed a resolution requiring all teachers to begin pursuing an advanced degree in education. Because of this new requirement, Lyle spent the summer of 1994 taking graduate courses in education at a major university. For the summer activity, Lyle *estimates* his expenses to be:

Books	$ 220
Tuition	3,200
Room and board	1,800
Transportation	1,500

Lyle kept no receipts and made no record of these expenses. When he files his income tax return for 1994, Lyle claims all of these expenses on Schedule C of Form 1040.

In the event Lyle is audited by the IRS, comment on his vulnerability.

Research aids:
§§ 274(d), 6001, and 6662(b)(1).
Cohan v. Comm., 2 USTC ¶489, 8 AFTR 10552, 39 F.2d 540 (CA–2, 1930).
William F. Sanford, 50 T.C. 823 (1968).

Chapter 9

Research Problem 15. George Fields contributed $2,700 to the United Way (a qualified public charity) in 1995. The contribution was made through his employer's charitable fund drive, and his employer withheld $225 per month from each of George's monthly payroll checks. George filed his Federal income tax return on April 10, 1996. In June 1996, he was discussing the contribution with a friend who told him that charitable contribution deductions of $250 or more are not allowed unless the taxpayer obtains written substantiation from the donee organization by the earlier of the due date for the return or the date on which the return was filed. George has not obtained any written substantiation from the donee. George, who lives at 3602 Sunbury Avenue, New York, NY 10012, has called and asked you if he can (or should) do anything to ensure that the deduction will not be disallowed. Write George a letter to advise him on this issue, and prepare a memo for your firm's tax files.

Research Problem 16. Falcon Corporation is the owner and operator of a large daily metropolitan newspaper. For at least 80 years, Falcon has collected and maintained a "clippings library." The library is a collection of past news items from Falcon's and other newspapers. The 7,800,000 items are well preserved, cataloged, and cross-listed under various categories. Falcon estimates that it has spent in excess of $10 million compiling and organizing the library. However, since this amount was deducted as incurred, the income tax basis of the library is zero. The fair market value of the library is $3 million.

Falcon Corporation contributes the clippings library to the state historical society (a qualified organization) and claims a charitable contribution deduction of $3 million. Upon audit, the IRS disallows the entire amount of the deduction because the basis of the property is zero. Who is correct?

Research aids:
§§ 170(e)(1)(A) and 1221(3).

Chapter 10

Research Problem 17. Bill owns an interest in a small engine repair shop in which he works 425 hours during the year. He has four full-time employees at the repair shop. Bill also owns an apartment building to which he devotes 1,300 hours during the year. He has no employees for the apartment activity. Are these activities active or passive? In your response, consider the impact of the significant participation activity rules.

Research Problem 18. Having become relatively affluent due to their success as respected dentists, George and Julie Sharp (1203 Peach Street, Atlanta, GA 30305) decided to invest $100,000 of their excess cash in a nearby resort community. Their investment gave them ownership rights in a cottage that normally would be rented out to vacationers for six-day periods by Paradise Resorts, Inc. While the Sharps were legally the sole owners of the cottage, they were required to allow Paradise Resorts to market their cottage's availability and maintain the unit. George and Julie were also allowed to use the cottage rent-free every year for no more than 14 days.

During the first year, Paradise Resorts reported that the Sharps' loss from the property was $25,000. During that period, the Sharps had accumulated documentation showing that they had spent 300 hours of their time on activities such as the following: preparing an annual budget for their cottage investment, marketing Paradise Resorts in conversations with their friends and at their country club, attending the annual business meeting of Paradise Resorts with the other cottage owners, and receiving and depositing net revenues received from the rental of their cottage.

As the Sharps' tax adviser, how would you recommend that they report their loss from this investment on their tax return? Write a memo to the tax files in which your recommendation is documented.

Chapter 11

Research Problem 19. Sandy and John Via (12 Maple Avenue, Albany, NY 12205) are married, file a joint Federal income tax return, and have a 12-year-old son and a 10-year-old daughter. Sandy is currently in the U.S. Air Force and has been stationed in Germany for the entire year. John and their children have remained in the United States where John picks up work only on an irregular basis. In working on their Federal income tax return for 1995, John wonders if they qualify for the earned income credit. Sandy's income consists of salary of $18,000 (taxable) and food and lodging provided by the Air Force, valued at $4,000 (not taxable), while John's earnings for the current year total $5,000. John approaches you and asks your advice. Write a letter to Sandy and John that contains your conclusion and prepare a memo for the tax files.

Research Problem 20. Isabella, a lover of early twentieth-century American history and architecture, discovers a 1920s house in a downtown district of Atlanta during a recent visit. She decides not only to purchase and renovate this particular home, but also to move the structure to her hometown of Little Rock, Arkansas, so her community can enjoy its architectural features. Also, being aware of the availability of the tax credit for rehabilitation expenditures incurred on old structures, she wants to maximize her use of the provision once the renovation work begins in Arkansas. Comment on whether the renovation expenditures incurred will qualify for the tax credit for rehabilitation expenditures.

Chapter 12

Research Problem 21. As the result of a large inheritance from her grandmother, Beverly has a substantial investment portfolio. The securities are held in street name by her brokerage firm. Beverly's broker, Max, has standing oral instructions from her on sales transactions to sell the shares with the highest cost basis.

In October 1994, Beverly phoned Max and instructed him to sell 6,000 shares of Color, Inc. Her portfolio has 15,000 shares of Color, Inc., which were purchased in several transactions over a three-year period. At the end of each month, the brokerage firm provides Beverly with a monthly statement that includes sales transactions. It does not identify the specific certificates transferred.

In filing her 1994 income tax return, Beverly used the specific identification method to calculate the $90,000 gain on the sale of the Color shares. Now her 1994 return is being audited. The Revenue Agent has taken the position that under Reg. § 1.1012–1(c) Beverly should have used the FIFO method to report the sale of the Color shares. This would result in a recognized gain of $160,000. According to his interpretation of the Regulations, Beverly may not use the specific identification method and must use the FIFO method because the broker did not provide written confirmation of Beverly's sales instructions as required by the Regulations.

Beverly has come to you for tax advice.

Research Problem 22. You are the new general manager of the Cleveland Indians, Inc. In order for the Indians to become a more serious contender to win the World Series, you believe that player changes are necessary. In particular, you believe that you need to improve your pitching staff. Discussions are in progress with the general manager of the Seattle Mariners. He has offered to trade Randy Johnson (an all-star pitcher) and $5 million to the Indians in exchange for Kenny Lofton (an all-star outfielder) and Carlos Baerga (an all-star second baseman). You have countered by expressing interest in receiving Johnson and Edgar Martinez (an all-star third baseman) rather than cash. You believe that if you are going to give up the speed provided by Lofton and the defensive play of Baerga, you need more than a starting pitcher in return. In addition, you vaguely remember from your MBA days that a player trade with no cash involved will provide better tax results. Before you finalize a trade, you need to know the tax consequences. Obtain a written opinion from your CPA on the way you should structure the trade. The mailing address is Jacobs Field, Cleveland, OH 44118.

Chapter 13

Research Problem 23. The Banc Two Mortgage Company requires a fee of 1% of the remaining mortgage balance when a mortgage is paid off early. In the current year, Banc Two received $760,000 of such fees. What is the nature of the fee: ordinary income or capital gain?

Research Problem 24. Sidney owns a professional football franchise. He has received an offer of $80 million for the franchise, all the football equipment, the rights to concession receipts, the rights to a stadium lease, and the rights to all the player contracts he owns. Most of the players have been with the team for quite a long time and have contracts that were signed several years ago. The contracts have been substantially depreciated. Sidney is concerned about potential § 1245 recapture when the contracts are sold. He has heard about "previously unrecaptured depreciation with respect to initial contracts" and would like to know more about it. Find a definition for that phrase and write an explanation of it.

Chapter 14

Research Problem 25. Tony is a full-time gambler whose only source of income is money that he wins from his gambling activities. The IRS contends that Tony's gambling losses should be treated as itemized deductions for purposes of computing the AMT. Tony argues that the gambling losses should be treated as trade or business expenses. Write a letter to Tony that contains your advice on the classification of the gambling losses. Also prepare a memo for the tax files. Tony's address is 200 Cole Lane, Wichita Falls, TX 76308.

Research Problem 26. Carol owns two warehouses that were placed in service before 1987. Accelerated depreciation for 1996 on Warehouse A was $12,000, and straight-line depreciation would have been $8,000. On Warehouse B, accelerated depreciation was $6,000, and straight-line depreciation would have been $7,500. What was the amount of Carol's tax preference for excess depreciation in 1996?

Chapter 15

Research Problem 27.   Violet Company discovered certain equipment used in its repair operations had been accounted for as inventory rather than as fixed assets. This incorrect treatment applied to all years in which the equipment had been used, and all of those years are open under the statute of limitations. Violet filed amended returns for all years affected by the incorrect treatment to obtain a refund of overpayments of taxes for those years. The IRS refused to accept the amended returns. The IRS reasoned that Violet was actually changing accounting methods, which can only be accomplished through a request for change in methods. In addition, the IRS concluded that an adjustment due to a voluntary change in accounting method must be taken into income for the year of the change. Is the IRS correct? Write a letter to Agnes Boyd, the president of Violet Company, that contains your advice and prepare a memo for the tax files. Violet's address is 100 Whitaker's Mill, Fargo, ND 58105.

Research Problem 28.   State law requires Clear Cola Company to sell its beverages in returnable bottles. Customers pay a deposit for the bottles, and Clear is required to refund the deposit to anyone who returns the bottles. Grocery stores collect the deposits and pay the customers for returned bottles and then are reimbursed by Clear. The company unsuccessfully argued that the collections of the deposits should not be treated as income. Subsequently, the company argued that if income must be recognized from the receipt of a deposit, a deduction should be allowed for the estimated amounts that must be paid to the customers. Clear estimates that 80% of all bottles are returned. Can Clear accrue a deduction for the estimated cost of bottles that will be returned and thus accurately match revenue and expenses?

Chapter 16

Research Problem 29.   Joe and Tom Moore are brothers and equal shareholders in Black Corporation, a calendar year taxpayer. In 1995, they incurred certain travel and entertainment expenditures, as employees, on behalf of Black Corporation. Because Black was in a precarious financial condition, Joe and Tom decided not to seek reimbursement for these expenditures. Instead, each brother deducted what he spent on his own individual return (Form 1040). Upon audit of the returns filed by Joe and Tom for 1995, the IRS disallowed these expenditures. Write a letter to Joe at 568 Inwood Avenue, Waynesburg, PA 15370, and indicate whether he should challenge the IRS action. Explain your conclusion to Joe using nontechnical language.

Research Problem 30.   Soon-Yi owns all the stock of White Corporation and 90% of the stock of Red Corporation. Red has had profitable years whereas White has suffered losses for several years. Red loaned White Corporation $90,000 in 1995 and did not charge White any interest on the loan. Upon audit of its 1995 return, the IRS determined that Red Corporation had interest income for 1995 in the amount of $9,900, causing Red to have a tax deficiency of $3,366 for 1995. Red is challenging the tax deficiency. It contends that White Corporation produced no taxable income from the use of the $90,000. Is the IRS correct in increasing the taxable income of Red Corporation?

Research aids:
Reg. §§ 1.482–2(a)(1) and 1.482–1(d)(4).
§ 7872.

Chapter 17

Research Problem 31.   Lynn Jones, Pat Williams, Terry Willis, and Tracy Plymire want to organize a corporation and transfer their shares of stock in several corporations to the newly formed corporation. All their shares are listed on the New York Stock Exchange and are readily marketable. Lynn will transfer shares in Brown Corporation; Pat will transfer stock in Black Corporation; Terry will transfer stock in White Corporation; and

Tracy will transfer stock in several corporations. The stock will be held by the newly formed corporation for investment purposes. Lynn asks you, her tax adviser, if she will have gain on the transfer of her substantially appreciated shares in Brown Corporation if she transfers the shares to a newly formed corporation. She also asks whether there will be tax consequences if she, Pat, Terry, and Tracy form a partnership, rather than a corporation, to which they will transfer their readily marketable stock. Prepare a memo to the client, Lynn Jones, and a memo for the firm's files. Lynn's address is 1400 Any Street, Lincoln, TX 79337.

Research Problem 32. In 1987, Pat and Maria formed Robin Corporation by transferring assets in exchange for stock. Pat and Maria each received 100 shares in Robin Corporation. Robin Corporation filed a proper election to qualify as an S corporation. In 1990, Pat and Maria obtained a $100,000 loan from a bank and transferred the cash to Robin Corporation as a contribution to its capital. Robin used the $100,000 to purchase stock in Bluebird Corporation. Bluebird met the requirements of a small business corporation under § 1244.

Bluebird Corporation ultimately encountered financial problems and filed for bankruptcy in 1994. Robin Corporation sold its Bluebird stock in 1995 for $20,000. On their 1995 tax returns, Pat and Maria each deducted an ordinary loss of $40,000.

Upon audit of Pat's return in 1996, the IRS disallowed the deduction of the entire $40,000 loss as an ordinary loss. The IRS contends the Bluebird stock does not qualify for ordinary loss treatment under § 1244 because the stock was held by an S corporation. According to the IRS, § 1244 treatment is available only where § 1244 stock is issued to an individual or to a partnership and then is sold by that individual or partnership. Pat insists she is entitled to ordinary loss treatment because income of an S corporation flows through to the shareholders of the corporation in the same manner as partnership income. How would you advise Pat?

Research aid:
Virgil Rath, 101 T.C. 196 (1993).

Chapter 18

Research Problem 33. Mark, the principal shareholder of Gray Corporation, diverted sums totaling $60,000 from the corporation during tax year 1995. Upon audit of Mark's return, the IRS contended these sums were taxable income to Mark under § 61 of the Code. Mark disagrees, stating that these amounts represent constructive dividends and are taxable only to the extent of Gray's E & P, which he argues had a deficit in 1994. The IRS contends that even if § 61 does not apply, the $60,000 would still be taxable income because Gray had income in 1995. Gray Corporation is on the cash basis. It had a deficit in its E & P account as of January 1, 1995. However, it had E & P of $65,000 in 1995. Its income tax liability for 1995 was $31,500. The IRS argues that $31,500 cannot be a charge against current E & P because the tax was not paid until 1996 and the corporation was on the cash basis. Consequently, the $60,000 would be taxable income to Mark in 1995, regardless of whether it is income under § 61 or under § 301. Mark comes to you for advice. What advice would you give him?

Research aids:
Charles Leaf, 33 T.C. 1093 (1960).
Weir v. Comm., 60–2 USTC ¶9763, 6 AFTR2d 5770, 283 F.2d 675 (CA–6, 1960).

Research Problem 34. Dave Smith (1400 Any Street, Anytown, MN 55000) owns 40% of Brown Corporation; his father owns the remaining 60%. Dave also owns 70% of White Corporation, with the remaining 30% being owned by his wife. Dave terminates his entire interest in Brown Corporation through a stock redemption that he reports as a long-term capital gain pursuant to § 302(b)(3). Three years later, White Corporation enters into a contract with Brown Corporation whereby White is given exclusive management authority over Brown's operations. Upon audit, the IRS disallowed the long-term capital gain treatment on the stock redemption in Brown Corporation contending that Dave acquired an interest in Brown within 10 years from the date of the redemption because of White's management contract with Brown. What is the result? Prepare a letter to Dave and a memo to the file documenting your conclusions.

Chapter 19

Research Problem 35.   Manuel and Kate were divorced in a community property state. In the marital dissolution proceeding, Kate asserted an ownership interest in Gray Corporation, a corporation in which Manuel was a director and president. Manuel owned 600, or 60%, of the shares in Gray Corporation; unrelated parties owned the remaining 40%. In the marital settlement agreement, Manuel agreed to transfer to Kate 200, or one-third, of his shares in Gray Corporation. Manuel had a tax basis of $20,000 in the shares he agreed to transfer to Kate. The marital agreement stated that Kate intended to negotiate for a separate redemption agreement with the corporation under which she would tender her shares to the corporation for $300,000. The agreement noted, however, that Manuel was not a party to the redemption agreement and had no obligations regarding the redemption or to pay cash to Kate if the corporation failed to redeem her stock for $300,000. Kate acknowledged in the agreement that she would have no cause of action against either Gray Corporation or Manuel if Gray failed to redeem her stock for $300,000. The agreement further provided that no obligation of Manuel's would be satisfied by the redemption. Immediately after the marital agreement was executed, Manuel transferred 200 shares of stock in Gray Corporation, representing a 20% interest in Gray, to Kate. Kate then entered into a redemption agreement with Gray Corporation whereby Gray agreed to redeem her shares for $300,000. Manuel did not vote as a corporate director to approve the redemption. The redemption was completed on the same day, with Kate transferring her 200 shares to Gray Corporation for a cash payment of $300,000. Kate currently owns no shares in Gray Corporation. What are the tax consequences to Kate and to Manuel on the stock redemption?

Research Problem 36.   The stock of Bluebird Corporation is held 15% by Rosa and 85% by Beth. José would like to purchase all the stock but has only enough cash to pay for 70%. Bluebird Corporation has enough cash on hand to redeem 30% of its shares. Consider and evaluate the following alternatives in terms of Bluebird Corporation, Rosa, and Beth.

a. Bluebird Corporation redeems 30% of the shares from Beth. José purchases the remaining 55% held by Beth and the 15% held by Rosa.

b. Bluebird distributes 85% of its cash to Beth and 15% to Rosa. This reduces the value of the stock to a level where José's cash is adequate to purchase Rosa's and Beth's shares.

c. Bluebird Corporation redeems all of Rosa's shares. José purchases 70% of the shares held by Beth. Bluebird Corporation then redeems the remainder of Beth's shares.

d. José borrows money from a bank to purchase all of Rosa's and Beth's shares. Later, José has Bluebird redeem 30% of the shares he purchased so that he can pay off the bank loan.

Research aids:
Bernard E. Niedermeyer, 62 T.C. 280 (1974).
Television Industries, Inc. v. Comm., 60–2 USTC ¶9795, 6 AFTR2d 5864, 284 F.2d 322 (CA–2, 1960).

Chapter 20

Research Problem 37.   Vechnalysis was a computer programming services business listed on the National Market System of the over-the-counter market. Pamela Wilson, the president, and three other members of the company's board of directors owned about 25% of the company's stock. The company had accumulated earnings and profits of $5.3, $6, and $7 million in 1987, 1988, and 1989, respectively.

The Tax Court agreed with the IRS that Vechnalysis had unreasonable accumulated earnings and profits to the extent of $1.77 million in 1987 and $600,000 in 1989. The Tax Court applied the *Bardahl* formula using a 22-day business cycle and the succeeding year's operating expenses to compute the company's working capital needs. To reach excess working capital where net liquid assets exceeded accumulated earnings and profits, the Tax Court subtracted the working capital needs from accumulated earnings and profits. The excess working capital was thus computed as follows:

Year	Excess Working Capital	Accumulated E & P Less Working Capital
1987	$2,820,193	($5,346,888 – $2,526,695)
1988	$2,902,809	($6,082,042 – $3,179,233)
1989	$3,484,041	($7,062,764 – $3,578,723)

The company had adopted a stock purchase plan, which the directors believed would arouse interest in Vechnalysis shares and maintain the shareholders' confidence in their investment. Based upon these facts, calculate the Tax Court's eventual accumulated earning tax for this corporation.

Research Problem 38. Dr. Bob owns 90% of the stock of Dental Services, Inc. Dr. Bob performs medical services under an employment contract with the corporation. He is the only dentist employed and is the only officer of the corporation actively engaged in the production of income. Dental Services, Inc., furnishes office space and equipment and employs a dental hygienist and a receptionist to assist Dr. Bob.

   a. Various patients receive dental care from Dr. Bob. Does Dental Services have PHC income under § 543(a)(7)?

   b. Suppose Jack, a patient, secures an absolute binding promise from Dr. Bob that the dentist will personally perform a root canal operation and that the dentist has no right to substitute another dentist. Would your answer change?

Chapter 21

Research Problem 39. Mel Bonilla contacts you with respect to the creation of two S corporations, each having approximately 30 shareholders. Most of the assets of the business will be held inside a limited liability company. Both S corporations will be 50% partners in the limited liability company. Draft a letter to Mel dated January 14, 1996, indicating whether this business arrangement is appropriate.

Research Problem 40. Tom Lewitske owns an insolvent S corporation. A local bank discharged a debt of $32,500 that the S corporation owed to the bank. This amount was not in excess of the amount by which the S corporation was insolvent. Tom calls you and asks about the tax aspects of this discharge of indebtedness. Prepare a memo for the tax file dated June 15, 1995, indicating what you told Tom over the phone.

Chapter 22

Research Problem 41. Your clients, Mark Henderson and John Burton, each contributed $10,000 cash to form a limited partnership. Mark is the general partner and John is the limited partner. The partnership used the $20,000 cash to make a down payment on a building. The rest of the building's $200,000 purchase price was financed with an interest-only nonrecourse loan of $180,000, which was obtained from an independent third-party bank. The partnership allocates all partnership items equally except for the MACRS deductions and building maintenance, which are allocated 70% to John and 30% to Mark. The partnership definitely wishes to satisfy the "economic effect" requirements of Reg. §§ 1.704–1 and 1.704–2 and will reallocate MACRS, if necessary, to satisfy the requirements of the Regulations. Under the partnership agreement, liquidation distributions will be paid in proportion to the partners' positive capital account balances. Capital accounts are maintained as required in the Regulations. Mark has an unlimited obligation to restore his capital account while John is subject to a qualified income offset provision. Assume all partnership items, except for MACRS, will net to zero throughout the first three years of the partnership operations. Also, assume that each year's MACRS deduction will be $10,000 (to simplify the calculations).

Partnerships

Draft a memo to the partnership evaluating the allocation of MACRS in each of the three years under Reg. §§ 1.704–1 and 1.704–2. Do not address the "substantial" test.

Research Problem 42. Margaret and Henry formed the equal Brown Partnership on January 1 of the current year. Margaret contributed $30,000 cash. Henry contributed depreciable equipment with a basis of $12,000 and a fair market value (book value) of $30,000. Under the partnership agreement, the partners will each be allocated 50% of partnership income, gain, loss, deductions, and credits, except to the extent amounts must be specially allocated under § 704(c).

a. How much gain would the partnership report, and how would that gain be allocated if the property was sold immediately following the contribution for $32,000? (Ignore cost recovery in this question only.)

b. How much book and tax depreciation would each partner report during the year under the "traditional method" outlined in Reg. § 1.704–3? Prepare book and tax capital account reconciliations to assist you. Assume depreciation deductions for the property will be claimed on a straight-line basis using a 10-year life (10% per year). Ignore half-year conventions.

c. If the partnership sold the equipment for $28,000 at the beginning of the second year (after cost recovery allocations determined in b. for the prior year), how much gain would be allocated to each party? Assume there is no additional cost recovery allocation in Year 2. What difficulty arises with this allocation?

d. The traditional method with creative allocations provides an alternative method that could be used in (b) and (c) to adjust for any inappropriate result. Demonstrate the effect of this method in a book and tax capital account reconciliation.

Chapter 23

Research Problem 43. Allied Fund, a charitable organization exempt under § 501(c)(3), has branches located in each of the 50 states. Allied is not a private foundation. Rather than having each of the state units file an annual return with the IRS, Allied would like to file a single return that reports the activities of all of its branches. Is this permissible? What is the due date of the return?

Research aids:
§ 6033.
§ 6072.
Reg. § 1.6033–2(d).

Research Problem 44. Great Outdoors, Inc., is a tax-exempt organization. Its mission is to explore, enjoy, and protect the wild places of the earth; to practice and promote the responsible use of the earth's ecosystems and resources; to educate and enlist humanity to protect and restore the quality of the natural and human environment; and to use all lawful means to carry out these objectives.

William Johnson, the chief financial officer, presents you with the following information. Great Outdoors raises funds to support its mission in a variety of ways including contributions and membership fees. As part of this effort, Great Outdoors develops and maintains mailing lists of its members, donors, catalog purchasers, and other supporters. Great Outdoors has exclusive ownership rights in its mailing lists. To acquire the names of prospective members and supporters, Great Outdoors occasionally exchanges membership lists with other organizations. In addition, Great Outdoors permits other tax-exempt organizations and commercial entities to pay a fee, as set forth in a fee schedule, to use its mailing lists on a one-time basis per transaction.

Johnson is aware of the unrelated business income tax. He also is aware of the § 512(b)(2) provision that excludes royalties from the unrelated business income tax. A Revenue Agent has raised the issue that the revenue from the use of the mailing lists by other entities may be taxable as unrelated business income. Johnson would like for you to research this issue for him.

Write a letter to Johnson that contains your findings, and prepare a memo for the tax files. Great Outdoors's address is 100 Central Avenue, Pocatello, ID 83209.

Chapter 24

Research Problem 45. Fronig, Inc., a foreign corporation, is owned as follows.

Mr. Allen, a U.S. resident	9%
Ms. Bella, a U.S. resident	32%
Mr. and Mrs. Cortez, NRAs	59%

Fronig has only one class of stock outstanding—voting common stock. Mander Corporation, a U.S. corporation, is considering the purchase of 10% of Fronig, Inc., from the Cortezes, which will leave them with 49% ownership. Mr. Allen owns 10% of Mander Corporation. Will Fronig become a CFC if Mander Corporation makes the purchase? Summarize your conclusions in a memo to Mander Corporation.

Research aids:
§ 958(a) and (b) and Reg. § 1.958–2, Ex. 1.

Research Problem 46. Jay, a U.S. citizen, lives in Switzerland. He is an artist who sells his paintings throughout the world. As a U.S. citizen, he is subject to taxation on his worldwide income. Jay seeks to take a foreign earned income exclusion with regard to the income he receives from the sales of the paintings. An IRS agent questions the claim that the income from sale of the paintings is "earned" income for purposes of the exclusion. How would you advise Jay?

Research aid:
Mark Tobey, 60 T.C. 227 (1973), *acq.* 1979–1 C.B. 1.

Chapter 25

Research Problem 47. Leigh Van Camp was convicted of underpayment of Federal income tax. He had set up several branches of the "Church of America's Salvation" in Arizona, and he was found to have used church donations to support an extravagant lifestyle for himself and his family, rather than to advance the goals of the church. In the Tax Court proceedings, Leigh bargained down the charges from criminal fraud to mere underpayment of tax. The settlement did not end the bad feelings between Leigh and personnel in the local IRS office, however.

Leigh owed $250,000 in interest, penalty, and tax after the Tax Court issued its verdict. He placed $200,000 in escrow with respect to this tax. IRS agents then received a tip that Leigh had sold his largest remaining asset, the family home, and was "moving to Niagara Falls in two days." Fearing that Leigh would leave the country without paying the tax from the court settlement or the tax on the gain from the sale of the residence, the agents placed a jeopardy assessment on the $500,000 cash proceeds of the sale.

Angry at the way the IRS is intruding into his life, Leigh calls you from New York and hires you to "get the IRS off my back" and obtain the return of his funds in full. Assess the IRS's position in a memo to the research file.

Research aids:
Reg. §§ 1.6851–1(a)(1)(i) through (iii).
Robert Lee McWilliams, 103 T.C. 320 (1994).

Research Problem 48. Fast Track, Inc., has put together a highly successful five-year operation renovating old housing units in the Lincoln Park area of Chicago. The company acquires properties at very low prices, uses nonunion and retired employees and contractors to revive the residential and common areas, and enjoys various state and Federal tax credits, local rehabilitation grants, and low-interest bank loans in a manner that produces a very impressive tax and accounting profit.

Cash flow is another story. For the nine months a unit is under renovation, Fast Track generates no revenues, so it must meet expenses with income, loan, or grant monies from other sources. For the operation's first five years, that was no problem, but this winter was particularly harsh, and Fast Track found itself in tough straits several times. Once, on the day of a deadline for remitting withheld Federal income and payroll taxes, Fast Track used those funds to cover operating expenses instead.

Fast Track carried out this misappropriation through instructions to the Lincoln Park Bank, with which it had built a successful relationship. The bank virtually ran Fast Track's checking account and operating loans, applying rules that the two parties had developed for the timing and amount of payments to be made. This arrangement allowed the bank to maintain significant control and monitoring over Fast Track's funds; in exchange, the bank did not charge Fast Track service fees for any of its accounts.

Six months later, the IRS discovered the company's failure to pay the withholdings. With respect to your client, Barbara Williams, a Fast Track construction employee, the IRS has determined that $1,000 of income tax and $1,500 of Social Security taxes are due before penalties and interest are computed. Write a memo to the tax research file discussing from whom the IRS can assess the $2,500 in taxes due—Williams, Fast Track, or the bank.

Chapter 26

Research Problem 49. In 1992, Marge Hurt creates an irrevocable trust using income-producing real estate worth $70,000. The trust arrangement is as follows:

- Frank and Lillian (Marge's adult children) are designated as co-trustees.

- The income from the trust is to be distributed to Frank and Lillian during Marge's life and for 120 days thereafter.

- If Frank and Lillian survive Marge by 120 days, each is to receive an equal share of the corpus.

- If either Frank or Lillian does not survive Marge by 120 days, income from the trust is payable to his or her children. If Marge dies and either Frank or Lillian does not survive her by 120 days, corpus is to pass to his or her children (Marge's grandchildren). Frank has two children; Lillian has three.

- As to every annual gift to the trust by Marge, all present (Frank and Lillian) and potential (the children of Frank and Lillian) beneficiaries have the right to withdraw the amount of the § 2503(b) gift tax exclusion. The right of withdrawal exists for 15 days after the gift in trust.

In 1993, Marge contributes additional real estate (worth $70,000) to the trust. Marge dies in 1994 before any further gifts can be made. One hundred and twenty days after Marge's death, the trust corpus and accumulated income are divided between Frank and Lillian, and the trust is dissolved. Following the gifts made by Marge, none of the beneficiaries (neither Frank nor Lillian nor their children) exercise the right of withdrawal.

No gift tax return is filed reflecting either the 1992 or 1993 gifts by Marge. Nor are these gifts noted on the estate tax return filed by the executors of Marge's estate.

Upon audit of the estate tax return, the IRS determines that Marge made taxable gifts of $50,000 in both 1992 and 1993.

a. Why did the IRS choose $50,000 as the amount of each taxable gift?

b. On an audit of Marge's estate tax return, why should the IRS care about the possibility of prior taxable gifts?

c. Is the IRS correct or not about the existence of prior taxable gifts? Explain.

Research aid:
Crummey v. Comm., 68–1 USTC ¶12,541, 22 AFTR2d 6023, 397 F.2d 82 (CA–9, 1968).

Research Problem 50. Hector dies on April 24, 1989, and under his will a major portion of the estate passes to a trust. The provisions of the trust grant a life estate to Ellen (Hector's surviving spouse), remainder to their adult children. The income is payable to Ellen quarterly or at more frequent intervals. Income accrued or held undistributed by the trust at the time of Ellen's death shall pass to the remainder interest.

On January 24, 1990, Hector's estate filed a Federal estate tax return and made the QTIP election. On July 3, 1990, Hector's estate filed an amended return based on the premise that the QTIP election was improper. As a result of the loss of the marital deduction, the amended return was accompanied by a payment of additional estate taxes.

On February 11, 1990, Ellen dies. All of her assets, including those in Hector's trust, pass to the children.

a. Why did Hector's estate file an amended return revoking the QTIP election?

b. Is the revocation of the election proper procedure?

c. Did Hector's estate ever qualify for the election?

Research aids:

§§ 2056(b)(7) and 2013.

Estate of Rose D. Howard, 91 T.C. 329 (1988), *rev'd* in 90–2 USTC ¶60,033, 66AFTR2d 90–5994, 910 F.2d 633 (CA–9, 1990).

Chapter 27

Research Problem 51. Your client, Chuck Konkol, is a self-employed investment adviser who provides services to individuals and small investment clubs for an hourly fee. He is aware of the difficulty that his clients have in deducting payments to him due to the 2%-of-AGI floor on miscellaneous itemized deductions, such as advisory fees.

His new client, the Ferguson Trust, wants to be certain that it can deduct such fees in computing entity taxable income. Konkol asks you to make a presentation to the trust's officers on this subject. Provide a speaker's outline for this purpose, with citations only to the most important statutory and judicial law.

Research Problem 52. Your client, Annie O'Toole, has come to you for some advice regarding gifts of property. She has just learned that she must undergo major surgery, and she would like to make certain gifts before entering the hospital. On your earlier advice, she had established a plan of lifetime giving for four prior years.

Build a spreadsheet, supplemented by a list of your assumptions, and write a cover letter to Annie, discussing each of the following assets that she is thinking of using as gifts to family and friends. In doing so, evaluate the income tax consequences of having the property pass through her estate to the designated legatee. For this purpose, you need consult only the Code and pertinent Regulations.

a. Annie plans to give a cottage to her son to fulfill a promise made many years ago. She has owned the cottage for the past 15 years and has a basis in it of $30,000 (fair market value of $20,000).

b. Annie has $100,000 of long-term capital losses that she has been carrying forward for the past few years. Now, she is considering making a gift of $200,000 in installment notes to her daughter. Her basis in the notes is $100,000, and the notes' current fair market value is $190,000.

c. Annie has promised to make a special cash bequest of $25,000 to her grandson in her will. However, she does not anticipate having that much cash immediately available after her death. Annie requests your advice concerning the income tax consequences to the estate if the cash bequest is settled with some other property.

APPENDIX A
Tax Rate Schedules and Tables

1995 Tax Rate Schedules

Single—Schedule X

If taxable income is: Over—	But not over—	The tax is:		of the amount over—
$0	$ 23,350	.... 15%		$0
23,350	56,550	$3,502.50 +	28%	23,350
56,550	117,950	12,798.50 +	31%	56,550
117,950	256,500	31,832.50 +	36%	117,950
256,500	....	81,710.50 +	39.6%	256,500

Head of household—Schedule Z

If taxable income is: Over—	But not over—	The tax is:		of the amount over—
$0	$ 31,250	.... 15%		$0
31,250	80,750	$4,687.50 +	28%	31,250
80,750	130,800	18,547.50 +	31%	80,750
130,800	256,500	34,063.00 +	36%	130,800
256,500	....	79,315.00 +	39.6%	256,500

Married filing jointly or Qualifying widow(er)—Schedule Y-1

If taxable income is: Over—	But not over—	The tax is:		of the amount over—
$0	$ 39,000	.... 15%		$0
39,000	94,250	$5,850.00 +	28%	39,000
94,250	143,600	21,320.00 +	31%	94,250
143,600	256,500	36,618.50 +	36%	143,600
256,500	....	77,262.50 +	39.6%	256,500

Married filing separately—Schedule Y-2

If taxable income is: Over—	But not over—	The tax is:		of the amount over—
$0	$ 19,500	.... 15%		$0
19,500	47,125	$2,925.00 +	28%	19,500
47,125	71,800	10,660.00 +	31%	47,125
71,800	128,250	18,309.25 +	36%	71,800
128,250	....	38,631.25 +	39.6%	128,250

1995 Tax Table

Use if your taxable income is less than $100,000.
If $100,000 or more, use the Tax Rate Schedules.

Example. Mr. and Mrs. Brown are filing a joint return. Their taxable income on line 37 of Form 1040 is $25,300. First, they find the $25,300–25,350 income line. Next, they find the column for married filing jointly and read down the column. The amount shown where the income line and filing status column meet is $3,799. This is the tax amount they must enter on line 38 of their Form 1040.

Sample Table

At least	But less than	Single	Married filing jointly*	Married filing separately	Head of a household
			Your tax is—		
25,200	25,250	4,028	3,784	4,528	3,784
25,250	25,300	4,042	3,791	4,542	3,791
25,300	25,350	4,056	(3,799)	4,556	3,799
25,350	25,400	4,070	3,806	4,570	3,806

If line 37 (taxable income) is— At least	But less than	And you are— Single	Married filing jointly*	Married filing separately	Head of a household
			Your tax is—		
0	5	0	0	0	0
5	15	2	2	2	2
15	25	3	3	3	3
25	50	6	6	6	6
50	75	9	9	9	9
75	100	13	13	13	13
100	125	17	17	17	17
125	150	21	21	21	21
150	175	24	24	24	24
175	200	28	28	28	28
200	225	32	32	32	32
225	250	36	36	36	36
250	275	39	39	39	39
275	300	43	43	43	43
300	325	47	47	47	47
325	350	51	51	51	51
350	375	54	54	54	54
375	400	58	58	58	58
400	425	62	62	62	62
425	450	66	66	66	66
450	475	69	69	69	69
475	500	73	73	73	73
500	525	77	77	77	77
525	550	81	81	81	81
550	575	84	84	84	84
575	600	88	88	88	88
600	625	92	92	92	92
625	650	96	96	96	96
650	675	99	99	99	99
675	700	103	103	103	103
700	725	107	107	107	107
725	750	111	111	111	111
750	775	114	114	114	114
775	800	118	118	118	118
800	825	122	122	122	122
825	850	126	126	126	126
850	875	129	129	129	129
875	900	133	133	133	133
900	925	137	137	137	137
925	950	141	141	141	141
950	975	144	144	144	144
975	1,000	148	148	148	148

1,000

At least	But less than	Single	Married filing jointly*	Married filing separately	Head of a household
1,000	1,025	152	152	152	152
1,025	1,050	156	156	156	156
1,050	1,075	159	159	159	159
1,075	1,100	163	163	163	163
1,100	1,125	167	167	167	167
1,125	1,150	171	171	171	171
1,150	1,175	174	174	174	174
1,175	1,200	178	178	178	178
1,200	1,225	182	182	182	182
1,225	1,250	186	186	186	186
1,250	1,275	189	189	189	189
1,275	1,300	193	193	193	193

If line 37 (taxable income) is— At least	But less than	And you are— Single	Married filing jointly*	Married filing separately	Head of a household
			Your tax is—		
1,300	1,325	197	197	197	197
1,325	1,350	201	201	201	201
1,350	1,375	204	204	204	204
1,375	1,400	208	208	208	208
1,400	1,425	212	212	212	212
1,425	1,450	216	216	216	216
1,450	1,475	219	219	219	219
1,475	1,500	223	223	223	223
1,500	1,525	227	227	227	227
1,525	1,550	231	231	231	231
1,550	1,575	234	234	234	234
1,575	1,600	238	238	238	238
1,600	1,625	242	242	242	242
1,625	1,650	246	246	246	246
1,650	1,675	249	249	249	249
1,675	1,700	253	253	253	253
1,700	1,725	257	257	257	257
1,725	1,750	261	261	261	261
1,750	1,775	264	264	264	264
1,775	1,800	268	268	268	268
1,800	1,825	272	272	272	272
1,825	1,850	276	276	276	276
1,850	1,875	279	279	279	279
1,875	1,900	283	283	283	283
1,900	1,925	287	287	287	287
1,925	1,950	291	291	291	291
1,950	1,975	294	294	294	294
1,975	2,000	298	298	298	298

2,000

At least	But less than	Single	Married filing jointly*	Married filing separately	Head of a household
2,000	2,025	302	302	302	302
2,025	2,050	306	306	306	306
2,050	2,075	309	309	309	309
2,075	2,100	313	313	313	313
2,100	2,125	317	317	317	317
2,125	2,150	321	321	321	321
2,150	2,175	324	324	324	324
2,175	2,200	328	328	328	328
2,200	2,225	332	332	332	332
2,225	2,250	336	336	336	336
2,250	2,275	339	339	339	339
2,275	2,300	343	343	343	343
2,300	2,325	347	347	347	347
2,325	2,350	351	351	351	351
2,350	2,375	354	354	354	354
2,375	2,400	358	358	358	358
2,400	2,425	362	362	362	362
2,425	2,450	366	366	366	366
2,450	2,475	369	369	369	369
2,475	2,500	373	373	373	373
2,500	2,525	377	377	377	377
2,525	2,550	381	381	381	381
2,550	2,575	384	384	384	384
2,575	2,600	388	388	388	388
2,600	2,625	392	392	392	392
2,625	2,650	396	396	396	396
2,650	2,675	399	399	399	399
2,675	2,700	403	403	403	403

If line 37 (taxable income) is— At least	But less than	And you are— Single	Married filing jointly*	Married filing separately	Head of a household
			Your tax is—		
2,700	2,725	407	407	407	407
2,725	2,750	411	411	411	411
2,750	2,775	414	414	414	414
2,775	2,800	418	418	418	418
2,800	2,825	422	422	422	422
2,825	2,850	426	426	426	426
2,850	2,875	429	429	429	429
2,875	2,900	433	433	433	433
2,900	2,925	437	437	437	437
2,925	2,950	441	441	441	441
2,950	2,975	444	444	444	444
2,975	3,000	448	448	448	448

3,000

At least	But less than	Single	Married filing jointly*	Married filing separately	Head of a household
3,000	3,050	454	454	454	454
3,050	3,100	461	461	461	461
3,100	3,150	469	469	469	469
3,150	3,200	476	476	476	476
3,200	3,250	484	484	484	484
3,250	3,300	491	491	491	491
3,300	3,350	499	499	499	499
3,350	3,400	506	506	506	506
3,400	3,450	514	514	514	514
3,450	3,500	521	521	521	521
3,500	3,550	529	529	529	529
3,550	3,600	536	536	536	536
3,600	3,650	544	544	544	544
3,650	3,700	551	551	551	551
3,700	3,750	559	559	559	559
3,750	3,800	566	566	566	566
3,800	3,850	574	574	574	574
3,850	3,900	581	581	581	581
3,900	3,950	589	589	589	589
3,950	4,000	596	596	596	596

4,000

At least	But less than	Single	Married filing jointly*	Married filing separately	Head of a household
4,000	4,050	604	604	604	604
4,050	4,100	611	611	611	611
4,100	4,150	619	619	619	619
4,150	4,200	626	626	626	626
4,200	4,250	634	634	634	634
4,250	4,300	641	641	641	641
4,300	4,350	649	649	649	649
4,350	4,400	656	656	656	656
4,400	4,450	664	664	664	664
4,450	4,500	671	671	671	671
4,500	4,550	679	679	679	679
4,550	4,600	686	686	686	686
4,600	4,650	694	694	694	694
4,650	4,700	701	701	701	701
4,700	4,750	709	709	709	709
4,750	4,800	716	716	716	716
4,800	4,850	724	724	724	724
4,850	4,900	731	731	731	731
4,900	4,950	739	739	739	739
4,950	5,000	746	746	746	746

Continued on next page

* This column must also be used by a qualifying widow(er).

1995 Tax Table—*Continued*

If line 37 (taxable income) is—		And you are—				If line 37 (taxable income) is—		And you are—				If line 37 (taxable income) is—		And you are—			
At least	But less than	Single	Married filing jointly *	Married filing separately	Head of a house-hold	At least	But less than	Single	Married filing jointly *	Married filing separately	Head of a house-hold	At least	But less than	Single	Married filing jointly *	Married filing separately	Head of a house-hold
		Your tax is—						Your tax is—						Your tax is—			
5,000						**8,000**						**11,000**					
5,000	5,050	754	754	754	754	8,000	8,050	1,204	1,204	1,204	1,204	11,000	11,050	1,654	1,654	1,654	1,654
5,050	5,100	761	761	761	761	8,050	8,100	1,211	1,211	1,211	1,211	11,050	11,100	1,661	1,661	1,661	1,661
5,100	5,150	769	769	769	769	8,100	8,150	1,219	1,219	1,219	1,219	11,100	11,150	1,669	1,669	1,669	1,669
5,150	5,200	776	776	776	776	8,150	8,200	1,226	1,226	1,226	1,226	11,150	11,200	1,676	1,676	1,676	1,676
5,200	5,250	784	784	784	784	8,200	8,250	1,234	1,234	1,234	1,234	11,200	11,250	1,684	1,684	1,684	1,684
5,250	5,300	791	791	791	791	8,250	8,300	1,241	1,241	1,241	1,241	11,250	11,300	1,691	1,691	1,691	1,691
5,300	5,350	799	799	799	799	8,300	8,350	1,249	1,249	1,249	1,249	11,300	11,350	1,699	1,699	1,699	1,699
5,350	5,400	806	806	806	806	8,350	8,400	1,256	1,256	1,256	1,256	11,350	11,400	1,706	1,706	1,706	1,706
5,400	5,450	814	814	814	814	8,400	8,450	1,264	1,264	1,264	1,264	11,400	11,450	1,714	1,714	1,714	1,714
5,450	5,500	821	821	821	821	8,450	8,500	1,271	1,271	1,271	1,271	11,450	11,500	1,721	1,721	1,721	1,721
5,500	5,550	829	829	829	829	8,500	8,550	1,279	1,279	1,279	1,279	11,500	11,550	1,729	1,729	1,729	1,729
5,550	5,600	836	836	836	836	8,550	8,600	1,286	1,286	1,286	1,286	11,550	11,600	1,736	1,736	1,736	1,736
5,600	5,650	844	844	844	844	8,600	8,650	1,294	1,294	1,294	1,294	11,600	11,650	1,744	1,744	1,744	1,744
5,650	5,700	851	851	851	851	8,650	8,700	1,301	1,301	1,301	1,301	11,650	11,700	1,751	1,751	1,751	1,751
5,700	5,750	859	859	859	859	8,700	8,750	1,309	1,309	1,309	1,309	11,700	11,750	1,759	1,759	1,759	1,759
5,750	5,800	866	866	866	866	8,750	8,800	1,316	1,316	1,316	1,316	11,750	11,800	1,766	1,766	1,766	1,766
5,800	5,850	874	874	874	874	8,800	8,850	1,324	1,324	1,324	1,324	11,800	11,850	1,774	1,774	1,774	1,774
5,850	5,900	881	881	881	881	8,850	8,900	1,331	1,331	1,331	1,331	11,850	11,900	1,781	1,781	1,781	1,781
5,900	5,950	889	889	889	889	8,900	8,950	1,339	1,339	1,339	1,339	11,900	11,950	1,789	1,789	1,789	1,789
5,950	6,000	896	896	896	896	8,950	9,000	1,346	1,346	1,346	1,346	11,950	12,000	1,796	1,796	1,796	1,796
6,000						**9,000**						**12,000**					
6,000	6,050	904	904	904	904	9,000	9,050	1,354	1,354	1,354	1,354	12,000	12,050	1,804	1,804	1,804	1,804
6,050	6,100	911	911	911	911	9,050	9,100	1,361	1,361	1,361	1,361	12,050	12,100	1,811	1,811	1,811	1,811
6,100	6,150	919	919	919	919	9,100	9,150	1,369	1,369	1,369	1,369	12,100	12,150	1,819	1,819	1,819	1,819
6,150	6,200	926	926	926	926	9,150	9,200	1,376	1,376	1,376	1,376	12,150	12,200	1,826	1,826	1,826	1,826
6,200	6,250	934	934	934	934	9,200	9,250	1,384	1,384	1,384	1,384	12,200	12,250	1,834	1,834	1,834	1,834
6,250	6,300	941	941	941	941	9,250	9,300	1,391	1,391	1,391	1,391	12,250	12,300	1,841	1,841	1,841	1,841
6,300	6,350	949	949	949	949	9,300	9,350	1,399	1,399	1,399	1,399	12,300	12,350	1,849	1,849	1,849	1,849
6,350	6,400	956	956	956	956	9,350	9,400	1,406	1,406	1,406	1,406	12,350	12,400	1,856	1,856	1,856	1,856
6,400	6,450	964	964	964	964	9,400	9,450	1,414	1,414	1,414	1,414	12,400	12,450	1,864	1,864	1,864	1,864
6,450	6,500	971	971	971	971	9,450	9,500	1,421	1,421	1,421	1,421	12,450	12,500	1,871	1,871	1,871	1,871
6,500	6,550	979	979	979	979	9,500	9,550	1,429	1,429	1,429	1,429	12,500	12,550	1,879	1,879	1,879	1,879
6,550	6,600	986	986	986	986	9,550	9,600	1,436	1,436	1,436	1,436	12,550	12,600	1,886	1,886	1,886	1,886
6,600	6,650	994	994	994	994	9,600	9,650	1,444	1,444	1,444	1,444	12,600	12,650	1,894	1,894	1,894	1,894
6,650	6,700	1,001	1,001	1,001	1,001	9,650	9,700	1,451	1,451	1,451	1,451	12,650	12,700	1,901	1,901	1,901	1,901
6,700	6,750	1,009	1,009	1,009	1,009	9,700	9,750	1,459	1,459	1,459	1,459	12,700	12,750	1,909	1,909	1,909	1,909
6,750	6,800	1,016	1,016	1,016	1,016	9,750	9,800	1,466	1,466	1,466	1,466	12,750	12,800	1,916	1,916	1,916	1,916
6,800	6,850	1,024	1,024	1,024	1,024	9,800	9,850	1,474	1,474	1,474	1,474	12,800	12,850	1,924	1,924	1,924	1,924
6,850	6,900	1,031	1,031	1,031	1,031	9,850	9,900	1,481	1,481	1,481	1,481	12,850	12,900	1,931	1,931	1,931	1,931
6,900	6,950	1,039	1,039	1,039	1,039	9,900	9,950	1,489	1,489	1,489	1,489	12,900	12,950	1,939	1,939	1,939	1,939
6,950	7,000	1,046	1,046	1,046	1,046	9,950	10,000	1,496	1,496	1,496	1,496	12,950	13,000	1,946	1,946	1,946	1,946
7,000						**10,000**						**13,000**					
7,000	7,050	1,054	1,054	1,054	1,054	10,000	10,050	1,504	1,504	1,504	1,504	13,000	13,050	1,954	1,954	1,954	1,954
7,050	7,100	1,061	1,061	1,061	1,061	10,050	10,100	1,511	1,511	1,511	1,511	13,050	13,100	1,961	1,961	1,961	1,961
7,100	7,150	1,069	1,069	1,069	1,069	10,100	10,150	1,519	1,519	1,519	1,519	13,100	13,150	1,969	1,969	1,969	1,969
7,150	7,200	1,076	1,076	1,076	1,076	10,150	10,200	1,526	1,526	1,526	1,526	13,150	13,200	1,976	1,976	1,976	1,976
7,200	7,250	1,084	1,084	1,084	1,084	10,200	10,250	1,534	1,534	1,534	1,534	13,200	13,250	1,984	1,984	1,984	1,984
7,250	7,300	1,091	1,091	1,091	1,091	10,250	10,300	1,541	1,541	1,541	1,541	13,250	13,300	1,991	1,991	1,991	1,991
7,300	7,350	1,099	1,099	1,099	1,099	10,300	10,350	1,549	1,549	1,549	1,549	13,300	13,350	1,999	1,999	1,999	1,999
7,350	7,400	1,106	1,106	1,106	1,106	10,350	10,400	1,556	1,556	1,556	1,556	13,350	13,400	2,006	2,006	2,006	2,006
7,400	7,450	1,114	1,114	1,114	1,114	10,400	10,450	1,564	1,564	1,564	1,564	13,400	13,450	2,014	2,014	2,014	2,014
7,450	7,500	1,121	1,121	1,121	1,121	10,450	10,500	1,571	1,571	1,571	1,571	13,450	13,500	2,021	2,021	2,021	2,021
7,500	7,550	1,129	1,129	1,129	1,129	10,500	10,550	1,579	1,579	1,579	1,579	13,500	13,550	2,029	2,029	2,029	2,029
7,550	7,600	1,136	1,136	1,136	1,136	10,550	10,600	1,586	1,586	1,586	1,586	13,550	13,600	2,036	2,036	2,036	2,036
7,600	7,650	1,144	1,144	1,144	1,144	10,600	10,650	1,594	1,594	1,594	1,594	13,600	13,650	2,044	2,044	2,044	2,044
7,650	7,700	1,151	1,151	1,151	1,151	10,650	10,700	1,601	1,601	1,601	1,601	13,650	13,700	2,051	2,051	2,051	2,051
7,700	7,750	1,159	1,159	1,159	1,159	10,700	10,750	1,609	1,609	1,609	1,609	13,700	13,750	2,059	2,059	2,059	2,059
7,750	7,800	1,166	1,166	1,166	1,166	10,750	10,800	1,616	1,616	1,616	1,616	13,750	13,800	2,066	2,066	2,066	2,066
7,800	7,850	1,174	1,174	1,174	1,174	10,800	10,850	1,624	1,624	1,624	1,624	13,800	13,850	2,074	2,074	2,074	2,074
7,850	7,900	1,181	1,181	1,181	1,181	10,850	10,900	1,631	1,631	1,631	1,631	13,850	13,900	2,081	2,081	2,081	2,081
7,900	7,950	1,189	1,189	1,189	1,189	10,900	10,950	1,639	1,639	1,639	1,639	13,900	13,950	2,089	2,089	2,089	2,089
7,950	8,000	1,196	1,196	1,196	1,196	10,950	11,000	1,646	1,646	1,646	1,646	13,950	14,000	2,096	2,096	2,096	2,096

* This column must also be used by a qualifying widow(er).

Continued on next page

1995 Tax Table—Continued

14,000

At least	But less than	Single	Married filing jointly *	Married filing separately	Head of a household
			Your tax is—		
14,000	14,050	2,104	2,104	2,104	2,104
14,050	14,100	2,111	2,111	2,111	2,111
14,100	14,150	2,119	2,119	2,119	2,119
14,150	14,200	2,126	2,126	2,126	2,126
14,200	14,250	2,134	2,134	2,134	2,134
14,250	14,300	2,141	2,141	2,141	2,141
14,300	14,350	2,149	2,149	2,149	2,149
14,350	14,400	2,156	2,156	2,156	2,156
14,400	14,450	2,164	2,164	2,164	2,164
14,450	14,500	2,171	2,171	2,171	2,171
14,500	14,550	2,179	2,179	2,179	2,179
14,550	14,600	2,186	2,186	2,186	2,186
14,600	14,650	2,194	2,194	2,194	2,194
14,650	14,700	2,201	2,201	2,201	2,201
14,700	14,750	2,209	2,209	2,209	2,209
14,750	14,800	2,216	2,216	2,216	2,216
14,800	14,850	2,224	2,224	2,224	2,224
14,850	14,900	2,231	2,231	2,231	2,231
14,900	14,950	2,239	2,239	2,239	2,239
14,950	15,000	2,246	2,246	2,246	2,246

15,000

At least	But less than	Single	Married filing jointly *	Married filing separately	Head of a household
15,000	15,050	2,254	2,254	2,254	2,254
15,050	15,100	2,261	2,261	2,261	2,261
15,100	15,150	2,269	2,269	2,269	2,269
15,150	15,200	2,276	2,276	2,276	2,276
15,200	15,250	2,284	2,284	2,284	2,284
15,250	15,300	2,291	2,291	2,291	2,291
15,300	15,350	2,299	2,299	2,299	2,299
15,350	15,400	2,306	2,306	2,306	2,306
15,400	15,450	2,314	2,314	2,314	2,314
15,450	15,500	2,321	2,321	2,321	2,321
15,500	15,550	2,329	2,329	2,329	2,329
15,550	15,600	2,336	2,336	2,336	2,336
15,600	15,650	2,344	2,344	2,344	2,344
15,650	15,700	2,351	2,351	2,351	2,351
15,700	15,750	2,359	2,359	2,359	2,359
15,750	15,800	2,366	2,366	2,366	2,366
15,800	15,850	2,374	2,374	2,374	2,374
15,850	15,900	2,381	2,381	2,381	2,381
15,900	15,950	2,389	2,389	2,389	2,389
15,950	16,000	2,396	2,396	2,396	2,396

16,000

At least	But less than	Single	Married filing jointly *	Married filing separately	Head of a household
16,000	16,050	2,404	2,404	2,404	2,404
16,050	16,100	2,411	2,411	2,411	2,411
16,100	16,150	2,419	2,419	2,419	2,419
16,150	16,200	2,426	2,426	2,426	2,426
16,200	16,250	2,434	2,434	2,434	2,434
16,250	16,300	2,441	2,441	2,441	2,441
16,300	16,350	2,449	2,449	2,449	2,449
16,350	16,400	2,456	2,456	2,456	2,456
16,400	16,450	2,464	2,464	2,464	2,464
16,450	16,500	2,471	2,471	2,471	2,471
16,500	16,550	2,479	2,479	2,479	2,479
16,550	16,600	2,486	2,486	2,486	2,486
16,600	16,650	2,494	2,494	2,494	2,494
16,650	16,700	2,501	2,501	2,501	2,501
16,700	16,750	2,509	2,509	2,509	2,509
16,750	16,800	2,516	2,516	2,516	2,516
16,800	16,850	2,524	2,524	2,524	2,524
16,850	16,900	2,531	2,531	2,531	2,531
16,900	16,950	2,539	2,539	2,539	2,539
16,950	17,000	2,546	2,546	2,546	2,546

17,000

At least	But less than	Single	Married filing jointly *	Married filing separately	Head of a household
17,000	17,050	2,554	2,554	2,554	2,554
17,050	17,100	2,561	2,561	2,561	2,561
17,100	17,150	2,569	2,569	2,569	2,569
17,150	17,200	2,576	2,576	2,576	2,576
17,200	17,250	2,584	2,584	2,584	2,584
17,250	17,300	2,591	2,591	2,591	2,591
17,300	17,350	2,599	2,599	2,599	2,599
17,350	17,400	2,606	2,606	2,606	2,606
17,400	17,450	2,614	2,614	2,614	2,614
17,450	17,500	2,621	2,621	2,621	2,621
17,500	17,550	2,629	2,629	2,629	2,629
17,550	17,600	2,636	2,636	2,636	2,636
17,600	17,650	2,644	2,644	2,644	2,644
17,650	17,700	2,651	2,651	2,651	2,651
17,700	17,750	2,659	2,659	2,659	2,659
17,750	17,800	2,666	2,666	2,666	2,666
17,800	17,850	2,674	2,674	2,674	2,674
17,850	17,900	2,681	2,681	2,681	2,681
17,900	17,950	2,689	2,689	2,689	2,689
17,950	18,000	2,696	2,696	2,696	2,696

18,000

At least	But less than	Single	Married filing jointly *	Married filing separately	Head of a household
18,000	18,050	2,704	2,704	2,704	2,704
18,050	18,100	2,711	2,711	2,711	2,711
18,100	18,150	2,719	2,719	2,719	2,719
18,150	18,200	2,726	2,726	2,726	2,726
18,200	18,250	2,734	2,734	2,734	2,734
18,250	18,300	2,741	2,741	2,741	2,741
18,300	18,350	2,749	2,749	2,749	2,749
18,350	18,400	2,756	2,756	2,756	2,756
18,400	18,450	2,764	2,764	2,764	2,764
18,450	18,500	2,771	2,771	2,771	2,771
18,500	18,550	2,779	2,779	2,779	2,779
18,550	18,600	2,786	2,786	2,786	2,786
18,600	18,650	2,794	2,794	2,794	2,794
18,650	18,700	2,801	2,801	2,801	2,801
18,700	18,750	2,809	2,809	2,809	2,809
18,750	18,800	2,816	2,816	2,816	2,816
18,800	18,850	2,824	2,824	2,824	2,824
18,850	18,900	2,831	2,831	2,831	2,831
18,900	18,950	2,839	2,839	2,839	2,839
18,950	19,000	2,846	2,846	2,846	2,846

19,000

At least	But less than	Single	Married filing jointly *	Married filing separately	Head of a household
19,000	19,050	2,854	2,854	2,854	2,854
19,050	19,100	2,861	2,861	2,861	2,861
19,100	19,150	2,869	2,869	2,869	2,869
19,150	19,200	2,876	2,876	2,876	2,876
19,200	19,250	2,884	2,884	2,884	2,884
19,250	19,300	2,891	2,891	2,891	2,891
19,300	19,350	2,899	2,899	2,899	2,899
19,350	19,400	2,906	2,906	2,906	2,906
19,400	19,450	2,914	2,914	2,914	2,914
19,450	19,500	2,921	2,921	2,921	2,921
19,500	19,550	2,929	2,929	2,932	2,929
19,550	19,600	2,936	2,936	2,946	2,936
19,600	19,650	2,944	2,944	2,960	2,944
19,650	19,700	2,951	2,951	2,974	2,951
19,700	19,750	2,959	2,959	2,988	2,959
19,750	19,800	2,966	2,966	3,002	2,966
19,800	19,850	2,974	2,974	3,016	2,974
19,850	19,900	2,981	2,981	3,030	2,981
19,900	19,950	2,989	2,989	3,044	2,989
19,950	20,000	2,996	2,996	3,058	2,996

20,000

At least	But less than	Single	Married filing jointly *	Married filing separately	Head of a household
20,000	20,050	3,004	3,004	3,072	3,004
20,050	20,100	3,011	3,011	3,086	3,011
20,100	20,150	3,019	3,019	3,100	3,019
20,150	20,200	3,026	3,026	3,114	3,026
20,200	20,250	3,034	3,034	3,128	3,034
20,250	20,300	3,041	3,041	3,142	3,041
20,300	20,350	3,049	3,049	3,156	3,049
20,350	20,400	3,056	3,056	3,170	3,056
20,400	20,450	3,064	3,064	3,184	3,064
20,450	20,500	3,071	3,071	3,198	3,071
20,500	20,550	3,079	3,079	3,212	3,079
20,550	20,600	3,086	3,086	3,226	3,086
20,600	20,650	3,094	3,094	3,240	3,094
20,650	20,700	3,101	3,101	3,254	3,101
20,700	20,750	3,109	3,109	3,268	3,109
20,750	20,800	3,116	3,116	3,282	3,116
20,800	20,850	3,124	3,124	3,296	3,124
20,850	20,900	3,131	3,131	3,310	3,131
20,900	20,950	3,139	3,139	3,324	3,139
20,950	21,000	3,146	3,146	3,338	3,146

21,000

At least	But less than	Single	Married filing jointly *	Married filing separately	Head of a household
21,000	21,050	3,154	3,154	3,352	3,154
21,050	21,100	3,161	3,161	3,366	3,161
21,100	21,150	3,169	3,169	3,380	3,169
21,150	21,200	3,176	3,176	3,394	3,176
21,200	21,250	3,184	3,184	3,408	3,184
21,250	21,300	3,191	3,191	3,422	3,191
21,300	21,350	3,199	3,199	3,436	3,199
21,350	21,400	3,206	3,206	3,450	3,206
21,400	21,450	3,214	3,214	3,464	3,214
21,450	21,500	3,221	3,221	3,478	3,221
21,500	21,550	3,229	3,229	3,492	3,229
21,550	21,600	3,236	3,236	3,506	3,236
21,600	21,650	3,244	3,244	3,520	3,244
21,650	21,700	3,251	3,251	3,534	3,251
21,700	21,750	3,259	3,259	3,548	3,259
21,750	21,800	3,266	3,266	3,562	3,266
21,800	21,850	3,274	3,274	3,576	3,274
21,850	21,900	3,281	3,281	3,590	3,281
21,900	21,950	3,289	3,289	3,604	3,289
21,950	22,000	3,296	3,296	3,618	3,296

22,000

At least	But less than	Single	Married filing jointly *	Married filing separately	Head of a household
22,000	22,050	3,304	3,304	3,632	3,304
22,050	22,100	3,311	3,311	3,646	3,311
22,100	22,150	3,319	3,319	3,660	3,319
22,150	22,200	3,326	3,326	3,674	3,326
22,200	22,250	3,334	3,334	3,688	3,334
22,250	22,300	3,341	3,341	3,702	3,341
22,300	22,350	3,349	3,349	3,716	3,349
22,350	22,400	3,356	3,356	3,730	3,356
22,400	22,450	3,364	3,364	3,744	3,364
22,450	22,500	3,371	3,371	3,758	3,371
22,500	22,550	3,379	3,379	3,772	3,379
22,550	22,600	3,386	3,386	3,786	3,386
22,600	22,650	3,394	3,394	3,800	3,394
22,650	22,700	3,401	3,401	3,814	3,401
22,700	22,750	3,409	3,409	3,828	3,409
22,750	22,800	3,416	3,416	3,842	3,416
22,800	22,850	3,424	3,424	3,856	3,424
22,850	22,900	3,431	3,431	3,870	3,431
22,900	22,950	3,439	3,439	3,884	3,439
22,950	23,000	3,446	3,446	3,898	3,446

* This column must also be used by a qualifying widow(er).

Continued on next page

1995 Tax Table—*Continued*

If line 37 (taxable income) is— At least	But less than	Single	Married filing jointly*	Married filing separately	Head of a household
23,000					
23,000	23,050	3,454	3,454	3,912	3,454
23,050	23,100	3,461	3,461	3,926	3,461
23,100	23,150	3,469	3,469	3,940	3,469
23,150	23,200	3,476	3,476	3,954	3,476
23,200	23,250	3,484	3,484	3,968	3,484
23,250	23,300	3,491	3,491	3,982	3,491
23,300	23,350	3,499	3,499	3,996	3,499
23,350	23,400	3,510	3,506	4,010	3,506
23,400	23,450	3,524	3,514	4,024	3,514
23,450	23,500	3,538	3,521	4,038	3,521
23,500	23,550	3,552	3,529	4,052	3,529
23,550	23,600	3,566	3,536	4,066	3,536
23,600	23,650	3,580	3,544	4,080	3,544
23,650	23,700	3,594	3,551	4,094	3,551
23,700	23,750	3,608	3,559	4,108	3,559
23,750	23,800	3,622	3,566	4,122	3,566
23,800	23,850	3,636	3,574	4,136	3,574
23,850	23,900	3,650	3,581	4,150	3,581
23,900	23,950	3,664	3,589	4,164	3,589
23,950	24,000	3,678	3,596	4,178	3,596
24,000					
24,000	24,050	3,692	3,604	4,192	3,604
24,050	24,100	3,706	3,611	4,206	3,611
24,100	24,150	3,720	3,619	4,220	3,619
24,150	24,200	3,734	3,626	4,234	3,626
24,200	24,250	3,748	3,634	4,248	3,634
24,250	24,300	3,762	3,641	4,262	3,641
24,300	24,350	3,776	3,649	4,276	3,649
24,350	24,400	3,790	3,656	4,290	3,656
24,400	24,450	3,804	3,664	4,304	3,664
24,450	24,500	3,818	3,671	4,318	3,671
24,500	24,550	3,832	3,679	4,332	3,679
24,550	24,600	3,846	3,686	4,346	3,686
24,600	24,650	3,860	3,694	4,360	3,694
24,650	24,700	3,874	3,701	4,374	3,701
24,700	24,750	3,888	3,709	4,388	3,709
24,750	24,800	3,902	3,716	4,402	3,716
24,800	24,850	3,916	3,724	4,416	3,724
24,850	24,900	3,930	3,731	4,430	3,731
24,900	24,950	3,944	3,739	4,444	3,739
24,950	25,000	3,958	3,746	4,458	3,746
25,000					
25,000	25,050	3,972	3,754	4,472	3,754
25,050	25,100	3,986	3,761	4,486	3,761
25,100	25,150	4,000	3,769	4,500	3,769
25,150	25,200	4,014	3,776	4,514	3,776
25,200	25,250	4,028	3,784	4,528	3,784
25,250	25,300	4,042	3,791	4,542	3,791
25,300	25,350	4,056	3,799	4,556	3,799
25,350	25,400	4,070	3,806	4,570	3,806
25,400	25,450	4,084	3,814	4,584	3,814
25,450	25,500	4,098	3,821	4,598	3,821
25,500	25,550	4,112	3,829	4,612	3,829
25,550	25,600	4,126	3,836	4,626	3,836
25,600	25,650	4,140	3,844	4,640	3,844
25,650	25,700	4,154	3,851	4,654	3,851
25,700	25,750	4,168	3,859	4,668	3,859
25,750	25,800	4,182	3,866	4,682	3,866
25,800	25,850	4,196	3,874	4,696	3,874
25,850	25,900	4,210	3,881	4,710	3,881
25,900	25,950	4,224	3,889	4,724	3,889
25,950	26,000	4,238	3,896	4,738	3,896

If line 37 (taxable income) is— At least	But less than	Single	Married filing jointly*	Married filing separately	Head of a household
26,000					
26,000	26,050	4,252	3,904	4,752	3,904
26,050	26,100	4,266	3,911	4,766	3,911
26,100	26,150	4,280	3,919	4,780	3,919
26,150	26,200	4,294	3,926	4,794	3,926
26,200	26,250	4,308	3,934	4,808	3,934
26,250	26,300	4,322	3,941	4,822	3,941
26,300	26,350	4,336	3,949	4,836	3,949
26,350	26,400	4,350	3,956	4,850	3,956
26,400	26,450	4,364	3,964	4,864	3,964
26,450	26,500	4,378	3,971	4,878	3,971
26,500	26,550	4,392	3,979	4,892	3,979
26,550	26,600	4,406	3,986	4,906	3,986
26,600	26,650	4,420	3,994	4,920	3,994
26,650	26,700	4,434	4,001	4,934	4,001
26,700	26,750	4,448	4,009	4,948	4,009
26,750	26,800	4,462	4,016	4,962	4,016
26,800	26,850	4,476	4,024	4,976	4,024
26,850	26,900	4,490	4,031	4,990	4,031
26,900	26,950	4,504	4,039	5,004	4,039
26,950	27,000	4,518	4,046	5,018	4,046
27,000					
27,000	27,050	4,532	4,054	5,032	4,054
27,050	27,100	4,546	4,061	5,046	4,061
27,100	27,150	4,560	4,069	5,060	4,069
27,150	27,200	4,574	4,076	5,074	4,076
27,200	27,250	4,588	4,084	5,088	4,084
27,250	27,300	4,602	4,091	5,102	4,091
27,300	27,350	4,616	4,099	5,116	4,099
27,350	27,400	4,630	4,106	5,130	4,106
27,400	27,450	4,644	4,114	5,144	4,114
27,450	27,500	4,658	4,121	5,158	4,121
27,500	27,550	4,672	4,129	5,172	4,129
27,550	27,600	4,686	4,136	5,186	4,136
27,600	27,650	4,700	4,144	5,200	4,144
27,650	27,700	4,714	4,151	5,214	4,151
27,700	27,750	4,728	4,159	5,228	4,159
27,750	27,800	4,742	4,166	5,242	4,166
27,800	27,850	4,756	4,174	5,256	4,174
27,850	27,900	4,770	4,181	5,270	4,181
27,900	27,950	4,784	4,189	5,284	4,189
27,950	28,000	4,798	4,196	5,298	4,196
28,000					
28,000	28,050	4,812	4,204	5,312	4,204
28,050	28,100	4,826	4,211	5,326	4,211
28,100	28,150	4,840	4,219	5,340	4,219
28,150	28,200	4,854	4,226	5,354	4,226
28,200	28,250	4,868	4,234	5,368	4,234
28,250	28,300	4,882	4,241	5,382	4,241
28,300	28,350	4,896	4,249	5,396	4,249
28,350	28,400	4,910	4,256	5,410	4,256
28,400	28,450	4,924	4,264	5,424	4,264
28,450	28,500	4,938	4,271	5,438	4,271
28,500	28,550	4,952	4,279	5,452	4,279
28,550	28,600	4,966	4,286	5,466	4,286
28,600	28,650	4,980	4,294	5,480	4,294
28,650	28,700	4,994	4,301	5,494	4,301
28,700	28,750	5,008	4,309	5,508	4,309
28,750	28,800	5,022	4,316	5,522	4,316
28,800	28,850	5,036	4,324	5,536	4,324
28,850	28,900	5,050	4,331	5,550	4,331
28,900	28,950	5,064	4,339	5,564	4,339
28,950	29,000	5,078	4,346	5,578	4,346

If line 37 (taxable income) is— At least	But less than	Single	Married filing jointly*	Married filing separately	Head of a household
29,000					
29,000	29,050	5,092	4,354	5,592	4,354
29,050	29,100	5,106	4,361	5,606	4,361
29,100	29,150	5,120	4,369	5,620	4,369
29,150	29,200	5,134	4,376	5,634	4,376
29,200	29,250	5,148	4,384	5,648	4,384
29,250	29,300	5,162	4,391	5,662	4,391
29,300	29,350	5,176	4,399	5,676	4,399
29,350	29,400	5,190	4,406	5,690	4,406
29,400	29,450	5,204	4,414	5,704	4,414
29,450	29,500	5,218	4,421	5,718	4,421
29,500	29,550	5,232	4,429	5,732	4,429
29,550	29,600	5,246	4,436	5,746	4,436
29,600	29,650	5,260	4,444	5,760	4,444
29,650	29,700	5,274	4,451	5,774	4,451
29,700	29,750	5,288	4,459	5,788	4,459
29,750	29,800	5,302	4,466	5,802	4,466
29,800	29,850	5,316	4,474	5,816	4,474
29,850	29,900	5,330	4,481	5,830	4,481
29,900	29,950	5,344	4,489	5,844	4,489
29,950	30,000	5,358	4,496	5,858	4,496
30,000					
30,000	30,050	5,372	4,504	5,872	4,504
30,050	30,100	5,386	4,511	5,886	4,511
30,100	30,150	5,400	4,519	5,900	4,519
30,150	30,200	5,414	4,526	5,914	4,526
30,200	30,250	5,428	4,534	5,928	4,534
30,250	30,300	5,442	4,541	5,942	4,541
30,300	30,350	5,456	4,549	5,956	4,549
30,350	30,400	5,470	4,556	5,970	4,556
30,400	30,450	5,484	4,564	5,984	4,564
30,450	30,500	5,498	4,571	5,998	4,571
30,500	30,550	5,512	4,579	6,012	4,579
30,550	30,600	5,526	4,586	6,026	4,586
30,600	30,650	5,540	4,594	6,040	4,594
30,650	30,700	5,554	4,601	6,054	4,601
30,700	30,750	5,568	4,609	6,068	4,609
30,750	30,800	5,582	4,616	6,082	4,616
30,800	30,850	5,596	4,624	6,096	4,624
30,850	30,900	5,610	4,631	6,110	4,631
30,900	30,950	5,624	4,639	6,124	4,639
30,950	31,000	5,638	4,646	6,138	4,646
31,000					
31,000	31,050	5,652	4,654	6,152	4,654
31,050	31,100	5,666	4,661	6,166	4,661
31,100	31,150	5,680	4,669	6,180	4,669
31,150	31,200	5,694	4,676	6,194	4,676
31,200	31,250	5,708	4,684	6,208	4,684
31,250	31,300	5,722	4,691	6,222	4,695
31,300	31,350	5,736	4,699	6,236	4,709
31,350	31,400	5,750	4,706	6,250	4,723
31,400	31,450	5,764	4,714	6,264	4,737
31,450	31,500	5,778	4,721	6,278	4,751
31,500	31,550	5,792	4,729	6,292	4,765
31,550	31,600	5,806	4,736	6,306	4,779
31,600	31,650	5,820	4,744	6,320	4,793
31,650	31,700	5,834	4,751	6,334	4,807
31,700	31,750	5,848	4,759	6,348	4,821
31,750	31,800	5,862	4,766	6,362	4,835
31,800	31,850	5,876	4,774	6,376	4,849
31,850	31,900	5,890	4,781	6,390	4,863
31,900	31,950	5,904	4,789	6,404	4,877
31,950	32,000	5,918	4,796	6,418	4,891

* This column must also be used by a qualifying widow(er).

Continued on next page

1995 Tax Table—Continued

If line 37 (taxable income) is—		And you are—				If line 37 (taxable income) is—		And you are—				If line 37 (taxable income) is—		And you are—			
At least	But less than	Single	Married filing jointly *	Married filing separately	Head of a household	At least	But less than	Single	Married filing jointly *	Married filing separately	Head of a household	At least	But less than	Single	Married filing jointly *	Married filing separately	Head of a household
			Your tax is—						Your tax is—						Your tax is—		
32,000						**35,000**						**38,000**					
32,000	32,050	5,932	4,804	6,432	4,905	35,000	35,050	6,772	5,254	7,272	5,745	38,000	38,050	7,612	5,704	8,112	6,585
32,050	32,100	5,946	4,811	6,446	4,919	35,050	35,100	6,786	5,261	7,286	5,759	38,050	38,100	7,626	5,711	8,126	6,599
32,100	32,150	5,960	4,819	6,460	4,933	35,100	35,150	6,800	5,269	7,300	5,773	38,100	38,150	7,640	5,719	8,140	6,613
32,150	32,200	5,974	4,826	6,474	4,947	35,150	35,200	6,814	5,276	7,314	5,787	38,150	38,200	7,654	5,726	8,154	6,627
32,200	32,250	5,988	4,834	6,488	4,961	35,200	35,250	6,828	5,284	7,328	5,801	38,200	38,250	7,668	5,734	8,168	6,641
32,250	32,300	6,002	4,841	6,502	4,975	35,250	35,300	6,842	5,291	7,342	5,815	38,250	38,300	7,682	5,741	8,182	6,655
32,300	32,350	6,016	4,849	6,516	4,989	35,300	35,350	6,856	5,299	7,356	5,829	38,300	38,350	7,696	5,749	8,196	6,669
32,350	32,400	6,030	4,856	6,530	5,003	35,350	35,400	6,870	5,306	7,370	5,843	38,350	38,400	7,710	5,756	8,210	6,683
32,400	32,450	6,044	4,864	6,544	5,017	35,400	35,450	6,884	5,314	7,384	5,857	38,400	38,450	7,724	5,764	8,224	6,697
32,450	32,500	6,058	4,871	6,558	5,031	35,450	35,500	6,898	5,321	7,398	5,871	38,450	38,500	7,738	5,771	8,238	6,711
32,500	32,550	6,072	4,879	6,572	5,045	35,500	35,550	6,912	5,329	7,412	5,885	38,500	38,550	7,752	5,779	8,252	6,725
32,550	32,600	6,086	4,886	6,586	5,059	35,550	35,600	6,926	5,336	7,426	5,899	38,550	38,600	7,766	5,786	8,266	6,739
32,600	32,650	6,100	4,894	6,600	5,073	35,600	35,650	6,940	5,344	7,440	5,913	38,600	38,650	7,780	5,794	8,280	6,753
32,650	32,700	6,114	4,901	6,614	5,087	35,650	35,700	6,954	5,351	7,454	5,927	38,650	38,700	7,794	5,801	8,294	6,767
32,700	32,750	6,128	4,909	6,628	5,101	35,700	35,750	6,968	5,359	7,468	5,941	38,700	38,750	7,808	5,809	8,308	6,781
32,750	32,800	6,142	4,916	6,642	5,115	35,750	35,800	6,982	5,366	7,482	5,955	38,750	38,800	7,822	5,816	8,322	6,795
32,800	32,850	6,156	4,924	6,656	5,129	35,800	35,850	6,996	5,374	7,496	5,969	38,800	38,850	7,836	5,824	8,336	6,809
32,850	32,900	6,170	4,931	6,670	5,143	35,850	35,900	7,010	5,381	7,510	5,983	38,850	38,900	7,850	5,831	8,350	6,823
32,900	32,950	6,184	4,939	6,684	5,157	35,900	35,950	7,024	5,389	7,524	5,997	38,900	38,950	7,864	5,839	8,364	6,837
32,950	33,000	6,198	4,946	6,698	5,171	35,950	36,000	7,038	5,396	7,538	6,011	38,950	39,000	7,878	5,846	8,378	6,851
33,000						**36,000**						**39,000**					
33,000	33,050	6,212	4,954	6,712	5,185	36,000	36,050	7,052	5,404	7,552	6,025	39,000	39,050	7,892	5,857	8,392	6,865
33,050	33,100	6,226	4,961	6,726	5,199	36,050	36,100	7,066	5,411	7,566	6,039	39,050	39,100	7,906	5,871	8,406	6,879
33,100	33,150	6,240	4,969	6,740	5,213	36,100	36,150	7,080	5,419	7,580	6,053	39,100	39,150	7,920	5,885	8,420	6,893
33,150	33,200	6,254	4,976	6,754	5,227	36,150	36,200	7,094	5,426	7,594	6,067	39,150	39,200	7,934	5,899	8,434	6,907
33,200	33,250	6,268	4,984	6,768	5,241	36,200	36,250	7,108	5,434	7,608	6,081	39,200	39,250	7,948	5,913	8,448	6,921
33,250	33,300	6,282	4,991	6,782	5,255	36,250	36,300	7,122	5,441	7,622	6,095	39,250	39,300	7,962	5,927	8,462	6,935
33,300	33,350	6,296	4,999	6,796	5,269	36,300	36,350	7,136	5,449	7,636	6,109	39,300	39,350	7,976	5,941	8,476	6,949
33,350	33,400	6,310	5,006	6,810	5,283	36,350	36,400	7,150	5,456	7,650	6,123	39,350	39,400	7,990	5,955	8,490	6,963
33,400	33,450	6,324	5,014	6,824	5,297	36,400	36,450	7,164	5,464	7,664	6,137	39,400	39,450	8,004	5,969	8,504	6,977
33,450	33,500	6,338	5,021	6,838	5,311	36,450	36,500	7,178	5,471	7,678	6,151	39,450	39,500	8,018	5,983	8,518	6,991
33,500	33,550	6,352	5,029	6,852	5,325	36,500	36,550	7,192	5,479	7,692	6,165	39,500	39,550	8,032	5,997	8,532	7,005
33,550	33,600	6,366	5,036	6,866	5,339	36,550	36,600	7,206	5,486	7,706	6,179	39,550	39,600	8,046	6,011	8,546	7,019
33,600	33,650	6,380	5,044	6,880	5,353	36,600	36,650	7,220	5,494	7,720	6,193	39,600	39,650	8,060	6,025	8,560	7,033
33,650	33,700	6,394	5,051	6,894	5,367	36,650	36,700	7,234	5,501	7,734	6,207	39,650	39,700	8,074	6,039	8,574	7,047
33,700	33,750	6,408	5,059	6,908	5,381	36,700	36,750	7,248	5,509	7,748	6,221	39,700	39,750	8,088	6,053	8,588	7,061
33,750	33,800	6,422	5,066	6,922	5,395	36,750	36,800	7,262	5,516	7,762	6,235	39,750	39,800	8,102	6,067	8,602	7,075
33,800	33,850	6,436	5,074	6,936	5,409	36,800	36,850	7,276	5,524	7,776	6,249	39,800	39,850	8,116	6,081	8,616	7,089
33,850	33,900	6,450	5,081	6,950	5,423	36,850	36,900	7,290	5,531	7,790	6,263	39,850	39,900	8,130	6,095	8,630	7,103
33,900	33,950	6,464	5,089	6,964	5,437	36,900	36,950	7,304	5,539	7,804	6,277	39,900	39,950	8,144	6,109	8,644	7,117
33,950	34,000	6,478	5,096	6,978	5,451	36,950	37,000	7,318	5,546	7,818	6,291	39,950	40,000	8,158	6,123	8,658	7,131
34,000						**37,000**						**40,000**					
34,000	34,050	6,492	5,104	6,992	5,465	37,000	37,050	7,332	5,554	7,832	6,305	40,000	40,050	8,172	6,137	8,672	7,145
34,050	34,100	6,506	5,111	7,006	5,479	37,050	37,100	7,346	5,561	7,846	6,319	40,050	40,100	8,186	6,151	8,686	7,159
34,100	34,150	6,520	5,119	7,020	5,493	37,100	37,150	7,360	5,569	7,860	6,333	40,100	40,150	8,200	6,165	8,700	7,173
34,150	34,200	6,534	5,126	7,034	5,507	37,150	37,200	7,374	5,576	7,874	6,347	40,150	40,200	8,214	6,179	8,714	7,187
34,200	34,250	6,548	5,134	7,048	5,521	37,200	37,250	7,388	5,584	7,888	6,361	40,200	40,250	8,228	6,193	8,728	7,201
34,250	34,300	6,562	5,141	7,062	5,535	37,250	37,300	7,402	5,591	7,902	6,375	40,250	40,300	8,242	6,207	8,742	7,215
34,300	34,350	6,576	5,149	7,076	5,549	37,300	37,350	7,416	5,599	7,916	6,389	40,300	40,350	8,256	6,221	8,756	7,229
34,350	34,400	6,590	5,156	7,090	5,563	37,350	37,400	7,430	5,606	7,930	6,403	40,350	40,400	8,270	6,235	8,770	7,243
34,400	34,450	6,604	5,164	7,104	5,577	37,400	37,450	7,444	5,614	7,944	6,417	40,400	40,450	8,284	6,249	8,784	7,257
34,450	34,500	6,618	5,171	7,118	5,591	37,450	37,500	7,458	5,621	7,958	6,431	40,450	40,500	8,298	6,263	8,798	7,271
34,500	34,550	6,632	5,179	7,132	5,605	37,500	37,550	7,472	5,629	7,972	6,445	40,500	40,550	8,312	6,277	8,812	7,285
34,550	34,600	6,646	5,186	7,146	5,619	37,550	37,600	7,486	5,636	7,986	6,459	40,550	40,600	8,326	6,291	8,826	7,299
34,600	34,650	6,660	5,194	7,160	5,633	37,600	37,650	7,500	5,644	8,000	6,473	40,600	40,650	8,340	6,305	8,840	7,313
34,650	34,700	6,674	5,201	7,174	5,647	37,650	37,700	7,514	5,651	8,014	6,487	40,650	40,700	8,354	6,319	8,854	7,327
34,700	34,750	6,688	5,209	7,188	5,661	37,700	37,750	7,528	5,659	8,028	6,501	40,700	40,750	8,368	6,333	8,868	7,341
34,750	34,800	6,702	5,216	7,202	5,675	37,750	37,800	7,542	5,666	8,042	6,515	40,750	40,800	8,382	6,347	8,882	7,355
34,800	34,850	6,716	5,224	7,216	5,689	37,800	37,850	7,556	5,674	8,056	6,529	40,800	40,850	8,396	6,361	8,896	7,369
34,850	34,900	6,730	5,231	7,230	5,703	37,850	37,900	7,570	5,681	8,070	6,543	40,850	40,900	8,410	6,375	8,910	7,383
34,900	34,950	6,744	5,239	7,244	5,717	37,900	37,950	7,584	5,689	8,084	6,557	40,900	40,950	8,424	6,389	8,924	7,397
34,950	35,000	6,758	5,246	7,258	5,731	37,950	38,000	7,598	5,696	8,098	6,571	40,950	41,000	8,438	6,403	8,938	7,411

* This column must also be used by a qualifying widow(er).

Continued on next page

1995 Tax Table—*Continued*

If line 37 (taxable income) is— At least	But less than	Single	Married filing jointly *	Married filing separately	Head of a house-hold
41,000					
41,000	41,050	8,452	6,417	8,952	7,425
41,050	41,100	8,466	6,431	8,966	7,439
41,100	41,150	8,480	6,445	8,980	7,453
41,150	41,200	8,494	6,459	8,994	7,467
41,200	41,250	8,508	6,473	9,008	7,481
41,250	41,300	8,522	6,487	9,022	7,495
41,300	41,350	8,536	6,501	9,036	7,509
41,350	41,400	8,550	6,515	9,050	7,523
41,400	41,450	8,564	6,529	9,064	7,537
41,450	41,500	8,578	6,543	9,078	7,551
41,500	41,550	8,592	6,557	9,092	7,565
41,550	41,600	8,606	6,571	9,106	7,579
41,600	41,650	8,620	6,585	9,120	7,593
41,650	41,700	8,634	6,599	9,134	7,607
41,700	41,750	8,648	6,613	9,148	7,621
41,750	41,800	8,662	6,627	9,162	7,635
41,800	41,850	8,676	6,641	9,176	7,649
41,850	41,900	8,690	6,655	9,190	7,663
41,900	41,950	8,704	6,669	9,204	7,677
41,950	42,000	8,718	6,683	9,218	7,691
42,000					
42,000	42,050	8,732	6,697	9,232	7,705
42,050	42,100	8,746	6,711	9,246	7,719
42,100	42,150	8,760	6,725	9,260	7,733
42,150	42,200	8,774	6,739	9,274	7,747
42,200	42,250	8,788	6,753	9,288	7,761
42,250	42,300	8,802	6,767	9,302	7,775
42,300	42,350	8,816	6,781	9,316	7,789
42,350	42,400	8,830	6,795	9,330	7,803
42,400	42,450	8,844	6,809	9,344	7,817
42,450	42,500	8,858	6,823	9,358	7,831
42,500	42,550	8,872	6,837	9,372	7,845
42,550	42,600	8,886	6,851	9,386	7,859
42,600	42,650	8,900	6,865	9,400	7,873
42,650	42,700	8,914	6,879	9,414	7,887
42,700	42,750	8,928	6,893	9,428	7,901
42,750	42,800	8,942	6,907	9,442	7,915
42,800	42,850	8,956	6,921	9,456	7,929
42,850	42,900	8,970	6,935	9,470	7,943
42,900	42,950	8,984	6,949	9,484	7,957
42,950	43,000	8,998	6,963	9,498	7,971
43,000					
43,000	43,050	9,012	6,977	9,512	7,985
43,050	43,100	9,026	6,991	9,526	7,999
43,100	43,150	9,040	7,005	9,540	8,013
43,150	43,200	9,054	7,019	9,554	8,027
43,200	43,250	9,068	7,033	9,568	8,041
43,250	43,300	9,082	7,047	9,582	8,055
43,300	43,350	9,096	7,061	9,596	8,069
43,350	43,400	9,110	7,075	9,610	8,083
43,400	43,450	9,124	7,089	9,624	8,097
43,450	43,500	9,138	7,103	9,638	8,111
43,500	43,550	9,152	7,117	9,652	8,125
43,550	43,600	9,166	7,131	9,666	8,139
43,600	43,650	9,180	7,145	9,680	8,153
43,650	43,700	9,194	7,159	9,694	8,167
43,700	43,750	9,208	7,173	9,708	8,181
43,750	43,800	9,222	7,187	9,722	8,195
43,800	43,850	9,236	7,201	9,736	8,209
43,850	43,900	9,250	7,215	9,750	8,223
43,900	43,950	9,264	7,229	9,764	8,237
43,950	44,000	9,278	7,243	9,778	8,251

If line 37 (taxable income) is— At least	But less than	Single	Married filing jointly *	Married filing separately	Head of a house-hold
44,000					
44,000	44,050	9,292	7,257	9,792	8,265
44,050	44,100	9,306	7,271	9,806	8,279
44,100	44,150	9,320	7,285	9,820	8,293
44,150	44,200	9,334	7,299	9,834	8,307
44,200	44,250	9,348	7,313	9,848	8,321
44,250	44,300	9,362	7,327	9,862	8,335
44,300	44,350	9,376	7,341	9,876	8,349
44,350	44,400	9,390	7,355	9,890	8,363
44,400	44,450	9,404	7,369	9,904	8,377
44,450	44,500	9,418	7,383	9,918	8,391
44,500	44,550	9,432	7,397	9,932	8,405
44,550	44,600	9,446	7,411	9,946	8,419
44,600	44,650	9,460	7,425	9,960	8,433
44,650	44,700	9,474	7,439	9,974	8,447
44,700	44,750	9,488	7,453	9,988	8,461
44,750	44,800	9,502	7,467	10,002	8,475
44,800	44,850	9,516	7,481	10,016	8,489
44,850	44,900	9,530	7,495	10,030	8,503
44,900	44,950	9,544	7,509	10,044	8,517
44,950	45,000	9,558	7,523	10,058	8,531
45,000					
45,000	45,050	9,572	7,537	10,072	8,545
45,050	45,100	9,586	7,551	10,086	8,559
45,100	45,150	9,600	7,565	10,100	8,573
45,150	45,200	9,614	7,579	10,114	8,587
45,200	45,250	9,628	7,593	10,128	8,601
45,250	45,300	9,642	7,607	10,142	8,615
45,300	45,350	9,656	7,621	10,156	8,629
45,350	45,400	9,670	7,635	10,170	8,643
45,400	45,450	9,684	7,649	10,184	8,657
45,450	45,500	9,698	7,663	10,198	8,671
45,500	45,550	9,712	7,677	10,212	8,685
45,550	45,600	9,726	7,691	10,226	8,699
45,600	45,650	9,740	7,705	10,240	8,713
45,650	45,700	9,754	7,719	10,254	8,727
45,700	45,750	9,768	7,733	10,268	8,741
45,750	45,800	9,782	7,747	10,282	8,755
45,800	45,850	9,796	7,761	10,296	8,769
45,850	45,900	9,810	7,775	10,310	8,783
45,900	45,950	9,824	7,789	10,324	8,797
45,950	46,000	9,838	7,803	10,338	8,811
46,000					
46,000	46,050	9,852	7,817	10,352	8,825
46,050	46,100	9,866	7,831	10,366	8,839
46,100	46,150	9,880	7,845	10,380	8,853
46,150	46,200	9,894	7,859	10,394	8,867
46,200	46,250	9,908	7,873	10,408	8,881
46,250	46,300	9,922	7,887	10,422	8,895
46,300	46,350	9,936	7,901	10,436	8,909
46,350	46,400	9,950	7,915	10,450	8,923
46,400	46,450	9,964	7,929	10,464	8,937
46,450	46,500	9,978	7,943	10,478	8,951
46,500	46,550	9,992	7,957	10,492	8,965
46,550	46,600	10,006	7,971	10,506	8,979
46,600	46,650	10,020	7,985	10,520	8,993
46,650	46,700	10,034	7,999	10,534	9,007
46,700	46,750	10,048	8,013	10,548	9,021
46,750	46,800	10,062	8,027	10,562	9,035
46,800	46,850	10,076	8,041	10,576	9,049
46,850	46,900	10,090	8,055	10,590	9,063
46,900	46,950	10,104	8,069	10,604	9,077
46,950	47,000	10,118	8,083	10,618	9,091

If line 37 (taxable income) is— At least	But less than	Single	Married filing jointly *	Married filing separately	Head of a house-hold
47,000					
47,000	47,050	10,132	8,097	10,632	9,105
47,050	47,100	10,146	8,111	10,646	9,119
47,100	47,150	10,160	8,125	10,660	9,133
47,150	47,200	10,174	8,139	10,676	9,147
47,200	47,250	10,188	8,153	10,691	9,161
47,250	47,300	10,202	8,167	10,707	9,175
47,300	47,350	10,216	8,181	10,722	9,189
47,350	47,400	10,230	8,195	10,738	9,203
47,400	47,450	10,244	8,209	10,753	9,217
47,450	47,500	10,258	8,223	10,769	9,231
47,500	47,550	10,272	8,237	10,784	9,245
47,550	47,600	10,286	8,251	10,800	9,259
47,600	47,650	10,300	8,265	10,815	9,273
47,650	47,700	10,314	8,279	10,831	9,287
47,700	47,750	10,328	8,293	10,846	9,301
47,750	47,800	10,342	8,307	10,862	9,315
47,800	47,850	10,356	8,321	10,877	9,329
47,850	47,900	10,370	8,335	10,893	9,343
47,900	47,950	10,384	8,349	10,908	9,357
47,950	48,000	10,398	8,363	10,924	9,371
48,000					
48,000	48,050	10,412	8,377	10,939	9,385
48,050	48,100	10,426	8,391	10,955	9,399
48,100	48,150	10,440	8,405	10,970	9,413
48,150	48,200	10,454	8,419	10,986	9,427
48,200	48,250	10,468	8,433	11,001	9,441
48,250	48,300	10,482	8,447	11,017	9,455
48,300	48,350	10,496	8,461	11,032	9,469
48,350	48,400	10,510	8,475	11,048	9,483
48,400	48,450	10,524	8,489	11,063	9,497
48,450	48,500	10,538	8,503	11,079	9,511
48,500	48,550	10,552	8,517	11,094	9,525
48,550	48,600	10,566	8,531	11,110	9,539
48,600	48,650	10,580	8,545	11,125	9,553
48,650	48,700	10,594	8,559	11,141	9,567
48,700	48,750	10,608	8,573	11,156	9,581
48,750	48,800	10,622	8,587	11,172	9,595
48,800	48,850	10,636	8,601	11,187	9,609
48,850	48,900	10,650	8,615	11,203	9,623
48,900	48,950	10,664	8,629	11,218	9,637
48,950	49,000	10,678	8,643	11,234	9,651
49,000					
49,000	49,050	10,692	8,657	11,249	9,665
49,050	49,100	10,706	8,671	11,265	9,679
49,100	49,150	10,720	8,685	11,280	9,693
49,150	49,200	10,734	8,699	11,296	9,707
49,200	49,250	10,748	8,713	11,311	9,721
49,250	49,300	10,762	8,727	11,327	9,735
49,300	49,350	10,776	8,741	11,342	9,749
49,350	49,400	10,790	8,755	11,358	9,763
49,400	49,450	10,804	8,769	11,373	9,777
49,450	49,500	10,818	8,783	11,389	9,791
49,500	49,550	10,832	8,797	11,404	9,805
49,550	49,600	10,846	8,811	11,420	9,819
49,600	49,650	10,860	8,825	11,435	9,833
49,650	49,700	10,874	8,839	11,451	9,847
49,700	49,750	10,888	8,853	11,466	9,861
49,750	49,800	10,902	8,867	11,482	9,875
49,800	49,850	10,916	8,881	11,497	9,889
49,850	49,900	10,930	8,895	11,513	9,903
49,900	49,950	10,944	8,909	11,528	9,917
49,950	50,000	10,958	8,923	11,544	9,931

* This column must also be used by a qualifying widow(er).

Continued on next page

1995 Tax Table—Continued

If line 37 (taxable income) is— / **And you are—** (Single; Married filing jointly *; Married filing separately; Head of a household) — **Your tax is—**

* This column must also be used by a qualifying widow(er).

50,000

At least	But less than	Single	Married filing jointly *	Married filing separately	Head of a household
50,000	50,050	10,972	8,937	11,559	9,945
50,050	50,100	10,986	8,951	11,575	9,959
50,100	50,150	11,000	8,965	11,590	9,973
50,150	50,200	11,014	8,979	11,606	9,987
50,200	50,250	11,028	8,993	11,621	10,001
50,250	50,300	11,042	9,007	11,637	10,015
50,300	50,350	11,056	9,021	11,652	10,029
50,350	50,400	11,070	9,035	11,668	10,043
50,400	50,450	11,084	9,049	11,683	10,057
50,450	50,500	11,098	9,063	11,699	10,071
50,500	50,550	11,112	9,077	11,714	10,085
50,550	50,600	11,126	9,091	11,730	10,099
50,600	50,650	11,140	9,105	11,745	10,113
50,650	50,700	11,154	9,119	11,761	10,127
50,700	50,750	11,168	9,133	11,776	10,141
50,750	50,800	11,182	9,147	11,792	10,155
50,800	50,850	11,196	9,161	11,807	10,169
50,850	50,900	11,210	9,175	11,823	10,183
50,900	50,950	11,224	9,189	11,838	10,197
50,950	51,000	11,238	9,203	11,854	10,211

51,000

At least	But less than	Single	Married filing jointly *	Married filing separately	Head of a household
51,000	51,050	11,252	9,217	11,869	10,225
51,050	51,100	11,266	9,231	11,885	10,239
51,100	51,150	11,280	9,245	11,900	10,253
51,150	51,200	11,294	9,259	11,916	10,267
51,200	51,250	11,308	9,273	11,931	10,281
51,250	51,300	11,322	9,287	11,947	10,295
51,300	51,350	11,336	9,301	11,962	10,309
51,350	51,400	11,350	9,315	11,978	10,323
51,400	51,450	11,364	9,329	11,993	10,337
51,450	51,500	11,378	9,343	12,009	10,351
51,500	51,550	11,392	9,357	12,024	10,365
51,550	51,600	11,406	9,371	12,040	10,379
51,600	51,650	11,420	9,385	12,055	10,393
51,650	51,700	11,434	9,399	12,071	10,407
51,700	51,750	11,448	9,413	12,086	10,421
51,750	51,800	11,462	9,427	12,102	10,435
51,800	51,850	11,476	9,441	12,117	10,449
51,850	51,900	11,490	9,455	12,133	10,463
51,900	51,950	11,504	9,469	12,148	10,477
51,950	52,000	11,518	9,483	12,164	10,491

52,000

At least	But less than	Single	Married filing jointly *	Married filing separately	Head of a household
52,000	52,050	11,532	9,497	12,179	10,505
52,050	52,100	11,546	9,511	12,195	10,519
52,100	52,150	11,560	9,525	12,210	10,533
52,150	52,200	11,574	9,539	12,226	10,547
52,200	52,250	11,588	9,553	12,241	10,561
52,250	52,300	11,602	9,567	12,257	10,575
52,300	52,350	11,616	9,581	12,272	10,589
52,350	52,400	11,630	9,595	12,288	10,603
52,400	52,450	11,644	9,609	12,303	10,617
52,450	52,500	11,658	9,623	12,319	10,631
52,500	52,550	11,672	9,637	12,334	10,645
52,550	52,600	11,686	9,651	12,350	10,659
52,600	52,650	11,700	9,665	12,365	10,673
52,650	52,700	11,714	9,679	12,381	10,687
52,700	52,750	11,728	9,693	12,396	10,701
52,750	52,800	11,742	9,707	12,412	10,715
52,800	52,850	11,756	9,721	12,427	10,729
52,850	52,900	11,770	9,735	12,443	10,743
52,900	52,950	11,784	9,749	12,458	10,757
52,950	53,000	11,798	9,763	12,474	10,771

53,000

At least	But less than	Single	Married filing jointly *	Married filing separately	Head of a household
53,000	53,050	11,812	9,777	12,489	10,785
53,050	53,100	11,826	9,791	12,505	10,799
53,100	53,150	11,840	9,805	12,520	10,813
53,150	53,200	11,854	9,819	12,536	10,827
53,200	53,250	11,868	9,833	12,551	10,841
53,250	53,300	11,882	9,847	12,567	10,855
53,300	53,350	11,896	9,861	12,582	10,869
53,350	53,400	11,910	9,875	12,598	10,883
53,400	53,450	11,924	9,889	12,613	10,897
53,450	53,500	11,938	9,903	12,629	10,911
53,500	53,550	11,952	9,917	12,644	10,925
53,550	53,600	11,966	9,931	12,660	10,939
53,600	53,650	11,980	9,945	12,675	10,953
53,650	53,700	11,994	9,959	12,691	10,967
53,700	53,750	12,008	9,973	12,706	10,981
53,750	53,800	12,022	9,987	12,722	10,995
53,800	53,850	12,036	10,001	12,737	11,009
53,850	53,900	12,050	10,015	12,753	11,023
53,900	53,950	12,064	10,029	12,768	11,037
53,950	54,000	12,078	10,043	12,784	11,051

54,000

At least	But less than	Single	Married filing jointly *	Married filing separately	Head of a household
54,000	54,050	12,092	10,057	12,799	11,065
54,050	54,100	12,106	10,071	12,815	11,079
54,100	54,150	12,120	10,085	12,830	11,093
54,150	54,200	12,134	10,099	12,846	11,107
54,200	54,250	12,148	10,113	12,861	11,121
54,250	54,300	12,162	10,127	12,877	11,135
54,300	54,350	12,176	10,141	12,892	11,149
54,350	54,400	12,190	10,155	12,908	11,163
54,400	54,450	12,204	10,169	12,923	11,177
54,450	54,500	12,218	10,183	12,939	11,191
54,500	54,550	12,232	10,197	12,954	11,205
54,550	54,600	12,246	10,211	12,970	11,219
54,600	54,650	12,260	10,225	12,985	11,233
54,650	54,700	12,274	10,239	13,001	11,247
54,700	54,750	12,288	10,253	13,016	11,261
54,750	54,800	12,302	10,267	13,032	11,275
54,800	54,850	12,316	10,281	13,047	11,289
54,850	54,900	12,330	10,295	13,063	11,303
54,900	54,950	12,344	10,309	13,078	11,317
54,950	55,000	12,358	10,323	13,094	11,331

55,000

At least	But less than	Single	Married filing jointly *	Married filing separately	Head of a household
55,000	55,050	12,372	10,337	13,109	11,345
55,050	55,100	12,386	10,351	13,125	11,359
55,100	55,150	12,400	10,365	13,140	11,373
55,150	55,200	12,414	10,379	13,156	11,387
55,200	55,250	12,428	10,393	13,171	11,401
55,250	55,300	12,442	10,407	13,187	11,415
55,300	55,350	12,456	10,421	13,202	11,429
55,350	55,400	12,470	10,435	13,218	11,443
55,400	55,450	12,484	10,449	13,233	11,457
55,450	55,500	12,498	10,463	13,249	11,471
55,500	55,550	12,512	10,477	13,264	11,485
55,550	55,600	12,526	10,491	13,280	11,499
55,600	55,650	12,540	10,505	13,295	11,513
55,650	55,700	12,554	10,519	13,311	11,527
55,700	55,750	12,568	10,533	13,326	11,541
55,750	55,800	12,582	10,547	13,342	11,555
55,800	55,850	12,596	10,561	13,357	11,569
55,850	55,900	12,610	10,575	13,373	11,583
55,900	55,950	12,624	10,589	13,388	11,597
55,950	56,000	12,638	10,603	13,404	11,611

56,000

At least	But less than	Single	Married filing jointly *	Married filing separately	Head of a household
56,000	56,050	12,652	10,617	13,419	11,625
56,050	56,100	12,666	10,631	13,435	11,639
56,100	56,150	12,680	10,645	13,450	11,653
56,150	56,200	12,694	10,659	13,466	11,667
56,200	56,250	12,708	10,673	13,481	11,681
56,250	56,300	12,722	10,687	13,497	11,695
56,300	56,350	12,736	10,701	13,512	11,709
56,350	56,400	12,750	10,715	13,528	11,723
56,400	56,450	12,764	10,729	13,543	11,737
56,450	56,500	12,778	10,743	13,559	11,751
56,500	56,550	12,792	10,757	13,574	11,765
56,550	56,600	12,806	10,771	13,590	11,779
56,600	56,650	12,822	10,785	13,605	11,793
56,650	56,700	12,837	10,799	13,621	11,807
56,700	56,750	12,853	10,813	13,636	11,821
56,750	56,800	12,868	10,827	13,652	11,835
56,800	56,850	12,884	10,841	13,667	11,849
56,850	56,900	12,899	10,855	13,683	11,863
56,900	56,950	12,915	10,869	13,698	11,877
56,950	57,000	12,930	10,883	13,714	11,891

57,000

At least	But less than	Single	Married filing jointly *	Married filing separately	Head of a household
57,000	57,050	12,946	10,897	13,729	11,905
57,050	57,100	12,961	10,911	13,745	11,919
57,100	57,150	12,977	10,925	13,760	11,933
57,150	57,200	12,992	10,939	13,776	11,947
57,200	57,250	13,008	10,953	13,791	11,961
57,250	57,300	13,023	10,967	13,807	11,975
57,300	57,350	13,039	10,981	13,822	11,989
57,350	57,400	13,054	10,995	13,838	12,003
57,400	57,450	13,070	11,009	13,853	12,017
57,450	57,500	13,085	11,023	13,869	12,031
57,500	57,550	13,101	11,037	13,884	12,045
57,550	57,600	13,116	11,051	13,900	12,059
57,600	57,650	13,132	11,065	13,915	12,073
57,650	57,700	13,147	11,079	13,931	12,087
57,700	57,750	13,163	11,093	13,946	12,101
57,750	57,800	13,178	11,107	13,962	12,115
57,800	57,850	13,194	11,121	13,977	12,129
57,850	57,900	13,209	11,135	13,993	12,143
57,900	57,950	13,225	11,149	14,008	12,157
57,950	58,000	13,240	11,163	14,024	12,171

58,000

At least	But less than	Single	Married filing jointly *	Married filing separately	Head of a household
58,000	58,050	13,256	11,177	14,039	12,185
58,050	58,100	13,271	11,191	14,055	12,199
58,100	58,150	13,287	11,205	14,070	12,213
58,150	58,200	13,302	11,219	14,086	12,227
58,200	58,250	13,318	11,233	14,101	12,241
58,250	58,300	13,333	11,247	14,117	12,255
58,300	58,350	13,349	11,261	14,132	12,269
58,350	58,400	13,364	11,275	14,148	12,283
58,400	58,450	13,380	11,289	14,163	12,297
58,450	58,500	13,395	11,303	14,179	12,311
58,500	58,550	13,411	11,317	14,194	12,325
58,550	58,600	13,426	11,331	14,210	12,339
58,600	58,650	13,442	11,345	14,225	12,353
58,650	58,700	13,457	11,359	14,241	12,367
58,700	58,750	13,473	11,373	14,256	12,381
58,750	58,800	13,488	11,387	14,272	12,395
58,800	58,850	13,504	11,401	14,287	12,409
58,850	58,900	13,519	11,415	14,303	12,423
58,900	58,950	13,535	11,429	14,318	12,437
58,950	59,000	13,550	11,443	14,334	12,451

* This column must also be used by a qualifying widow(er).

Continued on next page

1995 Tax Table—*Continued*

If line 37 (taxable income) is— At least	But less than	Single	Married filing jointly *	Married filing separately	Head of a house-hold
59,000					
59,000	59,050	13,566	11,457	14,349	12,465
59,050	59,100	13,581	11,471	14,365	12,479
59,100	59,150	13,597	11,485	14,380	12,493
59,150	59,200	13,612	11,499	14,396	12,507
59,200	59,250	13,628	11,513	14,411	12,521
59,250	59,300	13,643	11,527	14,427	12,535
59,300	59,350	13,659	11,541	14,442	12,549
59,350	59,400	13,674	11,555	14,458	12,563
59,400	59,450	13,690	11,569	14,473	12,577
59,450	59,500	13,705	11,583	14,489	12,591
59,500	59,550	13,721	11,597	14,504	12,605
59,550	59,600	13,736	11,611	14,520	12,619
59,600	59,650	13,752	11,625	14,535	12,633
59,650	59,700	13,767	11,639	14,551	12,647
59,700	59,750	13,783	11,653	14,566	12,661
59,750	59,800	13,798	11,667	14,582	12,675
59,800	59,850	13,814	11,681	14,597	12,689
59,850	59,900	13,829	11,695	14,613	12,703
59,900	59,950	13,845	11,709	14,628	12,717
59,950	60,000	13,860	11,723	14,644	12,731
60,000					
60,000	60,050	13,876	11,737	14,659	12,745
60,050	60,100	13,891	11,751	14,675	12,759
60,100	60,150	13,907	11,765	14,690	12,773
60,150	60,200	13,922	11,779	14,706	12,787
60,200	60,250	13,938	11,793	14,721	12,801
60,250	60,300	13,953	11,807	14,737	12,815
60,300	60,350	13,969	11,821	14,752	12,829
60,350	60,400	13,984	11,835	14,768	12,843
60,400	60,450	14,000	11,849	14,783	12,857
60,450	60,500	14,015	11,863	14,799	12,871
60,500	60,550	14,031	11,877	14,814	12,885
60,550	60,600	14,046	11,891	14,830	12,899
60,600	60,650	14,062	11,905	14,845	12,913
60,650	60,700	14,077	11,919	14,861	12,927
60,700	60,750	14,093	11,933	14,876	12,941
60,750	60,800	14,108	11,947	14,892	12,955
60,800	60,850	14,124	11,961	14,907	12,969
60,850	60,900	14,139	11,975	14,923	12,983
60,900	60,950	14,155	11,989	14,938	12,997
60,950	61,000	14,170	12,003	14,954	13,011
61,000					
61,000	61,050	14,186	12,017	14,969	13,025
61,050	61,100	14,201	12,031	14,985	13,039
61,100	61,150	14,217	12,045	15,000	13,053
61,150	61,200	14,232	12,059	15,016	13,067
61,200	61,250	14,248	12,073	15,031	13,081
61,250	61,300	14,263	12,087	15,047	13,095
61,300	61,350	14,279	12,101	15,062	13,109
61,350	61,400	14,294	12,115	15,078	13,123
61,400	61,450	14,310	12,129	15,093	13,137
61,450	61,500	14,325	12,143	15,109	13,151
61,500	61,550	14,341	12,157	15,124	13,165
61,550	61,600	14,356	12,171	15,140	13,179
61,600	61,650	14,372	12,185	15,155	13,193
61,650	61,700	14,387	12,199	15,171	13,207
61,700	61,750	14,403	12,213	15,186	13,221
61,750	61,800	14,418	12,227	15,202	13,235
61,800	61,850	14,434	12,241	15,217	13,249
61,850	61,900	14,449	12,255	15,233	13,263
61,900	61,950	14,465	12,269	15,248	13,277
61,950	62,000	14,480	12,283	15,264	13,291

If line 37 (taxable income) is— At least	But less than	Single	Married filing jointly *	Married filing separately	Head of a house-hold
62,000					
62,000	62,050	14,496	12,297	15,279	13,305
62,050	62,100	14,511	12,311	15,295	13,319
62,100	62,150	14,527	12,325	15,310	13,333
62,150	62,200	14,542	12,339	15,326	13,347
62,200	62,250	14,558	12,353	15,341	13,361
62,250	62,300	14,573	12,367	15,357	13,375
62,300	62,350	14,589	12,381	15,372	13,389
62,350	62,400	14,604	12,395	15,388	13,403
62,400	62,450	14,620	12,409	15,403	13,417
62,450	62,500	14,635	12,423	15,419	13,431
62,500	62,550	14,651	12,437	15,434	13,445
62,550	62,600	14,666	12,451	15,450	13,459
62,600	62,650	14,682	12,465	15,465	13,473
62,650	62,700	14,697	12,479	15,481	13,487
62,700	62,750	14,713	12,493	15,496	13,501
62,750	62,800	14,728	12,507	15,512	13,515
62,800	62,850	14,744	12,521	15,527	13,529
62,850	62,900	14,759	12,535	15,543	13,543
62,900	62,950	14,775	12,549	15,558	13,557
62,950	63,000	14,790	12,563	15,574	13,571
63,000					
63,000	63,050	14,806	12,577	15,589	13,585
63,050	63,100	14,821	12,591	15,605	13,599
63,100	63,150	14,837	12,605	15,620	13,613
63,150	63,200	14,852	12,619	15,636	13,627
63,200	63,250	14,868	12,633	15,651	13,641
63,250	63,300	14,883	12,647	15,667	13,655
63,300	63,350	14,899	12,661	15,682	13,669
63,350	63,400	14,914	12,675	15,698	13,683
63,400	63,450	14,930	12,689	15,713	13,697
63,450	63,500	14,945	12,703	15,729	13,711
63,500	63,550	14,961	12,717	15,744	13,725
63,550	63,600	14,976	12,731	15,760	13,739
63,600	63,650	14,992	12,745	15,775	13,753
63,650	63,700	15,007	12,759	15,791	13,767
63,700	63,750	15,023	12,773	15,806	13,781
63,750	63,800	15,038	12,787	15,822	13,795
63,800	63,850	15,054	12,801	15,837	13,809
63,850	63,900	15,069	12,815	15,853	13,823
63,900	63,950	15,085	12,829	15,868	13,837
63,950	64,000	15,100	12,843	15,884	13,851
64,000					
64,000	64,050	15,116	12,857	15,899	13,865
64,050	64,100	15,131	12,871	15,915	13,879
64,100	64,150	15,147	12,885	15,930	13,893
64,150	64,200	15,162	12,899	15,946	13,907
64,200	64,250	15,178	12,913	15,961	13,921
64,250	64,300	15,193	12,927	15,977	13,935
64,300	64,350	15,209	12,941	15,992	13,949
64,350	64,400	15,224	12,955	16,008	13,963
64,400	64,450	15,240	12,969	16,023	13,977
64,450	64,500	15,255	12,983	16,039	13,991
64,500	64,550	15,271	12,997	16,054	14,005
64,550	64,600	15,286	13,011	16,070	14,019
64,600	64,650	15,302	13,025	16,085	14,033
64,650	64,700	15,317	13,039	16,101	14,047
64,700	64,750	15,333	13,053	16,116	14,061
64,750	64,800	15,348	13,067	16,132	14,075
64,800	64,850	15,364	13,081	16,147	14,089
64,850	64,900	15,379	13,095	16,163	14,103
64,900	64,950	15,395	13,109	16,178	14,117
64,950	65,000	15,410	13,123	16,194	14,131

If line 37 (taxable income) is— At least	But less than	Single	Married filing jointly *	Married filing separately	Head of a house-hold
65,000					
65,000	65,050	15,426	13,137	16,209	14,145
65,050	65,100	15,441	13,151	16,225	14,159
65,100	65,150	15,457	13,165	16,240	14,173
65,150	65,200	15,472	13,179	16,256	14,187
65,200	65,250	15,488	13,193	16,271	14,201
65,250	65,300	15,503	13,207	16,287	14,215
65,300	65,350	15,519	13,221	16,302	14,229
65,350	65,400	15,534	13,235	16,318	14,243
65,400	65,450	15,550	13,249	16,333	14,257
65,450	65,500	15,565	13,263	16,349	14,271
65,500	65,550	15,581	13,277	16,364	14,285
65,550	65,600	15,596	13,291	16,380	14,299
65,600	65,650	15,612	13,305	16,395	14,313
65,650	65,700	15,627	13,319	16,411	14,327
65,700	65,750	15,643	13,333	16,426	14,341
65,750	65,800	15,658	13,347	16,442	14,355
65,800	65,850	15,674	13,361	16,457	14,369
65,850	65,900	15,689	13,375	16,473	14,383
65,900	65,950	15,705	13,389	16,488	14,397
65,950	66,000	15,720	13,403	16,504	14,411
66,000					
66,000	66,050	15,736	13,417	16,519	14,425
66,050	66,100	15,751	13,431	16,535	14,439
66,100	66,150	15,767	13,445	16,550	14,453
66,150	66,200	15,782	13,459	16,566	14,467
66,200	66,250	15,798	13,473	16,581	14,481
66,250	66,300	15,813	13,487	16,597	14,495
66,300	66,350	15,829	13,501	16,612	14,509
66,350	66,400	15,844	13,515	16,628	14,523
66,400	66,450	15,860	13,529	16,643	14,537
66,450	66,500	15,875	13,543	16,659	14,551
66,500	66,550	15,891	13,557	16,674	14,565
66,550	66,600	15,906	13,571	16,690	14,579
66,600	66,650	15,922	13,585	16,705	14,593
66,650	66,700	15,937	13,599	16,721	14,607
66,700	66,750	15,953	13,613	16,736	14,621
66,750	66,800	15,968	13,627	16,752	14,635
66,800	66,850	15,984	13,641	16,767	14,649
66,850	66,900	15,999	13,655	16,783	14,663
66,900	66,950	16,015	13,669	16,798	14,677
66,950	67,000	16,030	13,683	16,814	14,691
67,000					
67,000	67,050	16,046	13,697	16,829	14,705
67,050	67,100	16,061	13,711	16,845	14,719
67,100	67,150	16,077	13,725	16,860	14,733
67,150	67,200	16,092	13,739	16,876	14,747
67,200	67,250	16,108	13,753	16,891	14,761
67,250	67,300	16,123	13,767	16,907	14,775
67,300	67,350	16,139	13,781	16,922	14,789
67,350	67,400	16,154	13,795	16,938	14,803
67,400	67,450	16,170	13,809	16,953	14,817
67,450	67,500	16,185	13,823	16,969	14,831
67,500	67,550	16,201	13,837	16,984	14,845
67,550	67,600	16,216	13,851	17,000	14,859
67,600	67,650	16,232	13,865	17,015	14,873
67,650	67,700	16,247	13,879	17,031	14,887
67,700	67,750	16,263	13,893	17,046	14,901
67,750	67,800	16,278	13,907	17,062	14,915
67,800	67,850	16,294	13,921	17,077	14,929
67,850	67,900	16,309	13,935	17,093	14,943
67,900	67,950	16,325	13,949	17,108	14,957
67,950	68,000	16,340	13,963	17,124	14,971

* This column must also be used by a qualifying widow(er).

Continued on next page

1995 Tax Table—Continued

* This column must also be used by a qualifying widow(er).

68,000 / 69,000 / 70,000

At least	But less than	Single	Married filing jointly *	Married filing separately	Head of a household
68,000					
68,000	68,050	16,356	13,977	17,139	14,985
68,050	68,100	16,371	13,991	17,155	14,999
68,100	68,150	16,387	14,005	17,170	15,013
68,150	68,200	16,402	14,019	17,186	15,027
68,200	68,250	16,418	14,033	17,201	15,041
68,250	68,300	16,433	14,047	17,217	15,055
68,300	68,350	16,449	14,061	17,232	15,069
68,350	68,400	16,464	14,075	17,248	15,083
68,400	68,450	16,480	14,089	17,263	15,097
68,450	68,500	16,495	14,103	17,279	15,111
68,500	68,550	16,511	14,117	17,294	15,125
68,550	68,600	16,526	14,131	17,310	15,139
68,600	68,650	16,542	14,145	17,325	15,153
68,650	68,700	16,557	14,159	17,341	15,167
68,700	68,750	16,573	14,173	17,356	15,181
68,750	68,800	16,588	14,187	17,372	15,195
68,800	68,850	16,604	14,201	17,387	15,209
68,850	68,900	16,619	14,215	17,403	15,223
68,900	68,950	16,635	14,229	17,418	15,237
68,950	69,000	16,650	14,243	17,434	15,251
69,000					
69,000	69,050	16,666	14,257	17,449	15,265
69,050	69,100	16,681	14,271	17,465	15,279
69,100	69,150	16,697	14,285	17,480	15,293
69,150	69,200	16,712	14,299	17,496	15,307
69,200	69,250	16,728	14,313	17,511	15,321
69,250	69,300	16,743	14,327	17,527	15,335
69,300	69,350	16,759	14,341	17,542	15,349
69,350	69,400	16,774	14,355	17,558	15,363
69,400	69,450	16,790	14,369	17,573	15,377
69,450	69,500	16,805	14,383	17,589	15,391
69,500	69,550	16,821	14,397	17,604	15,405
69,550	69,600	16,836	14,411	17,620	15,419
69,600	69,650	16,852	14,425	17,635	15,433
69,650	69,700	16,867	14,439	17,651	15,447
69,700	69,750	16,883	14,453	17,666	15,461
69,750	69,800	16,898	14,467	17,682	15,475
69,800	69,850	16,914	14,481	17,697	15,489
69,850	69,900	16,929	14,495	17,713	15,503
69,900	69,950	16,945	14,509	17,728	15,517
69,950	70,000	16,960	14,523	17,744	15,531
70,000					
70,000	70,050	16,976	14,537	17,759	15,545
70,050	70,100	16,991	14,551	17,775	15,559
70,100	70,150	17,007	14,565	17,790	15,573
70,150	70,200	17,022	14,579	17,806	15,587
70,200	70,250	17,038	14,593	17,821	15,601
70,250	70,300	17,053	14,607	17,837	15,615
70,300	70,350	17,069	14,621	17,852	15,629
70,350	70,400	17,084	14,635	17,868	15,643
70,400	70,450	17,100	14,649	17,883	15,657
70,450	70,500	17,115	14,663	17,899	15,671
70,500	70,550	17,131	14,677	17,914	15,685
70,550	70,600	17,146	14,691	17,930	15,699
70,600	70,650	17,162	14,705	17,945	15,713
70,650	70,700	17,177	14,719	17,961	15,727
70,700	70,750	17,193	14,733	17,976	15,741
70,750	70,800	17,208	14,747	17,992	15,755
70,800	70,850	17,224	14,761	18,007	15,769
70,850	70,900	17,239	14,775	18,023	15,783
70,900	70,950	17,255	14,789	18,038	15,797
70,950	71,000	17,270	14,803	18,054	15,811

71,000 / 72,000 / 73,000

At least	But less than	Single	Married filing jointly *	Married filing separately	Head of a household
71,000					
71,000	71,050	17,286	14,817	18,069	15,825
71,050	71,100	17,301	14,831	18,085	15,839
71,100	71,150	17,317	14,845	18,100	15,853
71,150	71,200	17,332	14,859	18,116	15,867
71,200	71,250	17,348	14,873	18,131	15,881
71,250	71,300	17,363	14,887	18,147	15,895
71,300	71,350	17,379	14,901	18,162	15,909
71,350	71,400	17,394	14,915	18,178	15,923
71,400	71,450	17,410	14,929	18,193	15,937
71,450	71,500	17,425	14,943	18,209	15,951
71,500	71,550	17,441	14,957	18,224	15,965
71,550	71,600	17,456	14,971	18,240	15,979
71,600	71,650	17,472	14,985	18,255	15,993
71,650	71,700	17,487	14,999	18,271	16,007
71,700	71,750	17,503	15,013	18,286	16,021
71,750	71,800	17,518	15,027	18,302	16,035
71,800	71,850	17,534	15,041	18,318	16,049
71,850	71,900	17,549	15,055	18,336	16,063
71,900	71,950	17,565	15,069	18,354	16,077
71,950	72,000	17,580	15,083	18,372	16,091
72,000					
72,000	72,050	17,596	15,097	18,390	16,105
72,050	72,100	17,611	15,111	18,408	16,119
72,100	72,150	17,627	15,125	18,426	16,133
72,150	72,200	17,642	15,139	18,444	16,147
72,200	72,250	17,658	15,153	18,462	16,161
72,250	72,300	17,673	15,167	18,480	16,175
72,300	72,350	17,689	15,181	18,498	16,189
72,350	72,400	17,704	15,195	18,516	16,203
72,400	72,450	17,720	15,209	18,534	16,217
72,450	72,500	17,735	15,223	18,552	16,231
72,500	72,550	17,751	15,237	18,570	16,245
72,550	72,600	17,766	15,251	18,588	16,259
72,600	72,650	17,782	15,265	18,606	16,273
72,650	72,700	17,797	15,279	18,624	16,287
72,700	72,750	17,813	15,293	18,642	16,301
72,750	72,800	17,828	15,307	18,660	16,315
72,800	72,850	17,844	15,321	18,678	16,329
72,850	72,900	17,859	15,335	18,696	16,343
72,900	72,950	17,875	15,349	18,714	16,357
72,950	73,000	17,890	15,363	18,732	16,371
73,000					
73,000	73,050	17,906	15,377	18,750	16,385
73,050	73,100	17,921	15,391	18,768	16,399
73,100	73,150	17,937	15,405	18,786	16,413
73,150	73,200	17,952	15,419	18,804	16,427
73,200	73,250	17,968	15,433	18,822	16,441
73,250	73,300	17,983	15,447	18,840	16,455
73,300	73,350	17,999	15,461	18,858	16,469
73,350	73,400	18,014	15,475	18,876	16,483
73,400	73,450	18,030	15,489	18,894	16,497
73,450	73,500	18,045	15,503	18,912	16,511
73,500	73,550	18,061	15,517	18,930	16,525
73,550	73,600	18,076	15,531	18,948	16,539
73,600	73,650	18,092	15,545	18,966	16,553
73,650	73,700	18,107	15,559	18,984	16,567
73,700	73,750	18,123	15,573	19,002	16,581
73,750	73,800	18,138	15,587	19,020	16,595
73,800	73,850	18,154	15,601	19,038	16,609
73,850	73,900	18,169	15,615	19,056	16,623
73,900	73,950	18,185	15,629	19,074	16,637
73,950	74,000	18,200	15,643	19,092	16,651

74,000 / 75,000 / 76,000

At least	But less than	Single	Married filing jointly *	Married filing separately	Head of a household
74,000					
74,000	74,050	18,216	15,657	19,110	16,665
74,050	74,100	18,231	15,671	19,128	16,679
74,100	74,150	18,247	15,685	19,146	16,693
74,150	74,200	18,262	15,699	19,164	16,707
74,200	74,250	18,278	15,713	19,182	16,721
74,250	74,300	18,293	15,727	19,200	16,735
74,300	74,350	18,309	15,741	19,218	16,749
74,350	74,400	18,324	15,755	19,236	16,763
74,400	74,450	18,340	15,769	19,254	16,777
74,450	74,500	18,355	15,783	19,272	16,791
74,500	74,550	18,371	15,797	19,290	16,805
74,550	74,600	18,386	15,811	19,308	16,819
74,600	74,650	18,402	15,825	19,326	16,833
74,650	74,700	18,417	15,839	19,344	16,847
74,700	74,750	18,433	15,853	19,362	16,861
74,750	74,800	18,448	15,867	19,380	16,875
74,800	74,850	18,464	15,881	19,398	16,889
74,850	74,900	18,479	15,895	19,416	16,903
74,900	74,950	18,495	15,909	19,434	16,917
74,950	75,000	18,510	15,923	19,452	16,931
75,000					
75,000	75,050	18,526	15,937	19,470	16,945
75,050	75,100	18,541	15,951	19,488	16,959
75,100	75,150	18,557	15,965	19,506	16,973
75,150	75,200	18,572	15,979	19,524	16,987
75,200	75,250	18,588	15,993	19,542	17,001
75,250	75,300	18,603	16,007	19,560	17,015
75,300	75,350	18,619	16,021	19,578	17,029
75,350	75,400	18,634	16,035	19,596	17,043
75,400	75,450	18,650	16,049	19,614	17,057
75,450	75,500	18,665	16,063	19,632	17,071
75,500	75,550	18,681	16,077	19,650	17,085
75,550	75,600	18,696	16,091	19,668	17,099
75,600	75,650	18,712	16,105	19,686	17,113
75,650	75,700	18,727	16,119	19,704	17,127
75,700	75,750	18,743	16,133	19,722	17,141
75,750	75,800	18,758	16,147	19,740	17,155
75,800	75,850	18,774	16,161	19,758	17,169
75,850	75,900	18,789	16,175	19,776	17,183
75,900	75,950	18,805	16,189	19,794	17,197
75,950	76,000	18,820	16,203	19,812	17,211
76,000					
76,000	76,050	18,836	16,217	19,830	17,225
76,050	76,100	18,851	16,231	19,848	17,239
76,100	76,150	18,867	16,245	19,866	17,253
76,150	76,200	18,882	16,259	19,884	17,267
76,200	76,250	18,898	16,273	19,902	17,281
76,250	76,300	18,913	16,287	19,920	17,295
76,300	76,350	18,929	16,301	19,938	17,309
76,350	76,400	18,944	16,315	19,956	17,323
76,400	76,450	18,960	16,329	19,974	17,337
76,450	76,500	18,975	16,343	19,992	17,351
76,500	76,550	18,991	16,357	20,010	17,365
76,550	76,600	19,006	16,371	20,028	17,379
76,600	76,650	19,022	16,385	20,046	17,393
76,650	76,700	19,037	16,399	20,064	17,407
76,700	76,750	19,053	16,413	20,082	17,421
76,750	76,800	19,068	16,427	20,100	17,435
76,800	76,850	19,084	16,441	20,118	17,449
76,850	76,900	19,099	16,455	20,136	17,463
76,900	76,950	19,115	16,469	20,154	17,477
76,950	77,000	19,130	16,483	20,172	17,491

Continued on next page

1995 Tax Table—*Continued*

At least	But less than	Single	Married filing jointly *	Married filing separately	Head of a household
77,000					
77,000	77,050	19,146	16,497	20,190	17,505
77,050	77,100	19,161	16,511	20,208	17,519
77,100	77,150	19,177	16,525	20,226	17,533
77,150	77,200	19,192	16,539	20,244	17,547
77,200	77,250	19,208	16,553	20,262	17,561
77,250	77,300	19,223	16,567	20,280	17,575
77,300	77,350	19,239	16,581	20,298	17,589
77,350	77,400	19,254	16,595	20,316	17,603
77,400	77,450	19,270	16,609	20,334	17,617
77,450	77,500	19,285	16,623	20,352	17,631
77,500	77,550	19,301	16,637	20,370	17,645
77,550	77,600	19,316	16,651	20,388	17,659
77,600	77,650	19,332	16,665	20,406	17,673
77,650	77,700	19,347	16,679	20,424	17,687
77,700	77,750	19,363	16,693	20,442	17,701
77,750	77,800	19,378	16,707	20,460	17,715
77,800	77,850	19,394	16,721	20,478	17,729
77,850	77,900	19,409	16,735	20,496	17,743
77,900	77,950	19,425	16,749	20,514	17,757
77,950	78,000	19,440	16,763	20,532	17,771
78,000					
78,000	78,050	19,456	16,777	20,550	17,785
78,050	78,100	19,471	16,791	20,568	17,799
78,100	78,150	19,487	16,805	20,586	17,813
78,150	78,200	19,502	16,819	20,604	17,827
78,200	78,250	19,518	16,833	20,622	17,841
78,250	78,300	19,533	16,847	20,640	17,855
78,300	78,350	19,549	16,861	20,658	17,869
78,350	78,400	19,564	16,875	20,676	17,883
78,400	78,450	19,580	16,889	20,694	17,897
78,450	78,500	19,595	16,903	20,712	17,911
78,500	78,550	19,611	16,917	20,730	17,925
78,550	78,600	19,626	16,931	20,748	17,939
78,600	78,650	19,642	16,945	20,766	17,953
78,650	78,700	19,657	16,959	20,784	17,967
78,700	78,750	19,673	16,973	20,802	17,981
78,750	78,800	19,688	16,987	20,820	17,995
78,800	78,850	19,704	17,001	20,838	18,009
78,850	78,900	19,719	17,015	20,856	18,023
78,900	78,950	19,735	17,029	20,874	18,037
78,950	79,000	19,750	17,043	20,892	18,051
79,000					
79,000	79,050	19,766	17,057	20,910	18,065
79,050	79,100	19,781	17,071	20,928	18,079
79,100	79,150	19,797	17,085	20,946	18,093
79,150	79,200	19,812	17,099	20,964	18,107
79,200	79,250	19,828	17,113	20,982	18,121
79,250	79,300	19,843	17,127	21,000	18,135
79,300	79,350	19,859	17,141	21,018	18,149
79,350	79,400	19,874	17,155	21,036	18,163
79,400	79,450	19,890	17,169	21,054	18,177
79,450	79,500	19,905	17,183	21,072	18,191
79,500	79,550	19,921	17,197	21,090	18,205
79,550	79,600	19,936	17,211	21,108	18,219
79,600	79,650	19,952	17,225	21,126	18,233
79,650	79,700	19,967	17,239	21,144	18,247
79,700	79,750	19,983	17,253	21,162	18,261
79,750	79,800	19,998	17,267	21,180	18,275
79,800	79,850	20,014	17,281	21,198	18,289
79,850	79,900	20,029	17,295	21,216	18,303
79,900	79,950	20,045	17,309	21,234	18,317
79,950	80,000	20,060	17,323	21,252	18,331

At least	But less than	Single	Married filing jointly *	Married filing separately	Head of a household
80,000					
80,000	80,050	20,076	17,337	21,270	18,345
80,050	80,100	20,091	17,351	21,288	18,359
80,100	80,150	20,107	17,365	21,306	18,373
80,150	80,200	20,122	17,379	21,324	18,387
80,200	80,250	20,138	17,393	21,342	18,401
80,250	80,300	20,153	17,407	21,360	18,415
80,300	80,350	20,169	17,421	21,378	18,429
80,350	80,400	20,184	17,435	21,396	18,443
80,400	80,450	20,200	17,449	21,414	18,457
80,450	80,500	20,215	17,463	21,432	18,471
80,500	80,550	20,231	17,477	21,450	18,485
80,550	80,600	20,246	17,491	21,468	18,499
80,600	80,650	20,262	17,505	21,486	18,513
80,650	80,700	20,277	17,519	21,504	18,527
80,700	80,750	20,293	17,533	21,522	18,541
80,750	80,800	20,308	17,547	21,540	18,555
80,800	80,850	20,324	17,561	21,558	18,571
80,850	80,900	20,339	17,575	21,576	18,586
80,900	80,950	20,355	17,589	21,594	18,602
80,950	81,000	20,370	17,603	21,612	18,617
81,000					
81,000	81,050	20,386	17,617	21,630	18,633
81,050	81,100	20,401	17,631	21,648	18,648
81,100	81,150	20,417	17,645	21,666	18,664
81,150	81,200	20,432	17,659	21,684	18,679
81,200	81,250	20,448	17,673	21,702	18,695
81,250	81,300	20,463	17,687	21,720	18,710
81,300	81,350	20,479	17,701	21,738	18,726
81,350	81,400	20,494	17,715	21,756	18,741
81,400	81,450	20,510	17,729	21,774	18,757
81,450	81,500	20,525	17,743	21,792	18,772
81,500	81,550	20,541	17,757	21,810	18,788
81,550	81,600	20,556	17,771	21,828	18,803
81,600	81,650	20,572	17,785	21,846	18,819
81,650	81,700	20,587	17,799	21,864	18,834
81,700	81,750	20,603	17,813	21,882	18,850
81,750	81,800	20,618	17,827	21,900	18,865
81,800	81,850	20,634	17,841	21,918	18,881
81,850	81,900	20,649	17,855	21,936	18,896
81,900	81,950	20,665	17,869	21,954	18,912
81,950	82,000	20,680	17,883	21,972	18,927
82,000					
82,000	82,050	20,696	17,897	21,990	18,943
82,050	82,100	20,711	17,911	22,008	18,958
82,100	82,150	20,727	17,925	22,026	18,974
82,150	82,200	20,742	17,939	22,044	18,989
82,200	82,250	20,758	17,953	22,062	19,005
82,250	82,300	20,773	17,967	22,080	19,020
82,300	82,350	20,789	17,981	22,098	19,036
82,350	82,400	20,804	17,995	22,116	19,051
82,400	82,450	20,820	18,009	22,134	19,067
82,450	82,500	20,835	18,023	22,152	19,082
82,500	82,550	20,851	18,037	22,170	19,098
82,550	82,600	20,866	18,051	22,188	19,113
82,600	82,650	20,882	18,065	22,206	19,129
82,650	82,700	20,897	18,079	22,224	19,144
82,700	82,750	20,913	18,093	22,242	19,160
82,750	82,800	20,928	18,107	22,260	19,175
82,800	82,850	20,944	18,121	22,278	19,191
82,850	82,900	20,959	18,135	22,296	19,206
82,900	82,950	20,975	18,149	22,314	19,222
82,950	83,000	20,990	18,163	22,332	19,237

At least	But less than	Single	Married filing jointly *	Married filing separately	Head of a household
83,000					
83,000	83,050	21,006	18,177	22,350	19,253
83,050	83,100	21,021	18,191	22,368	19,268
83,100	83,150	21,037	18,205	22,386	19,284
83,150	83,200	21,052	18,219	22,404	19,299
83,200	83,250	21,068	18,233	22,422	19,315
83,250	83,300	21,083	18,247	22,440	19,330
83,300	83,350	21,099	18,261	22,458	19,346
83,350	83,400	21,114	18,275	22,476	19,361
83,400	83,450	21,130	18,289	22,494	19,377
83,450	83,500	21,145	18,303	22,512	19,392
83,500	83,550	21,161	18,317	22,530	19,408
83,550	83,600	21,176	18,331	22,548	19,423
83,600	83,650	21,192	18,345	22,566	19,439
83,650	83,700	21,207	18,359	22,584	19,454
83,700	83,750	21,223	18,373	22,602	19,470
83,750	83,800	21,238	18,387	22,620	19,485
83,800	83,850	21,254	18,401	22,638	19,501
83,850	83,900	21,269	18,415	22,656	19,516
83,900	83,950	21,285	18,429	22,674	19,532
83,950	84,000	21,300	18,443	22,692	19,547
84,000					
84,000	84,050	21,316	18,457	22,710	19,563
84,050	84,100	21,331	18,471	22,728	19,578
84,100	84,150	21,347	18,485	22,746	19,594
84,150	84,200	21,362	18,499	22,764	19,609
84,200	84,250	21,378	18,513	22,782	19,625
84,250	84,300	21,393	18,527	22,800	19,640
84,300	84,350	21,409	18,541	22,818	19,656
84,350	84,400	21,424	18,555	22,836	19,671
84,400	84,450	21,440	18,569	22,854	19,687
84,450	84,500	21,455	18,583	22,872	19,702
84,500	84,550	21,471	18,597	22,890	19,718
84,550	84,600	21,486	18,611	22,908	19,733
84,600	84,650	21,502	18,625	22,926	19,749
84,650	84,700	21,517	18,639	22,944	19,764
84,700	84,750	21,533	18,653	22,962	19,780
84,750	84,800	21,548	18,667	22,980	19,795
84,800	84,850	21,564	18,681	22,998	19,811
84,850	84,900	21,579	18,695	23,016	19,826
84,900	84,950	21,595	18,709	23,034	19,842
84,950	85,000	21,610	18,723	23,052	19,857
85,000					
85,000	85,050	21,626	18,737	23,070	19,873
85,050	85,100	21,641	18,751	23,088	19,888
85,100	85,150	21,657	18,765	23,106	19,904
85,150	85,200	21,672	18,779	23,124	19,919
85,200	85,250	21,688	18,793	23,142	19,935
85,250	85,300	21,703	18,807	23,160	19,950
85,300	85,350	21,719	18,821	23,178	19,966
85,350	85,400	21,734	18,835	23,196	19,981
85,400	85,450	21,750	18,849	23,214	19,997
85,450	85,500	21,765	18,863	23,232	20,012
85,500	85,550	21,781	18,877	23,250	20,028
85,550	85,600	21,796	18,891	23,268	20,043
85,600	85,650	21,812	18,905	23,286	20,059
85,650	85,700	21,827	18,919	23,304	20,074
85,700	85,750	21,843	18,933	23,322	20,090
85,750	85,800	21,858	18,947	23,340	20,105
85,800	85,850	21,874	18,961	23,358	20,121
85,850	85,900	21,889	18,975	23,376	20,136
85,900	85,950	21,905	18,989	23,394	20,152
85,950	86,000	21,920	19,003	23,412	20,167

* This column must also be used by a qualifying widow(er).

Continued on next page

1995 Tax Table—*Continued*

If line 37 (taxable income) is— At least	But less than	Single	Married filing jointly *	Married filing separately	Head of a household
86,000					
86,000	86,050	21,936	19,017	23,430	20,183
86,050	86,100	21,951	19,031	23,448	20,198
86,100	86,150	21,967	19,045	23,466	20,214
86,150	86,200	21,982	19,059	23,484	20,229
86,200	86,250	21,998	19,073	23,502	20,245
86,250	86,300	22,013	19,087	23,520	20,260
86,300	86,350	22,029	19,101	23,538	20,276
86,350	86,400	22,044	19,115	23,556	20,291
86,400	86,450	22,060	19,129	23,574	20,307
86,450	86,500	22,075	19,143	23,592	20,322
86,500	86,550	22,091	19,157	23,610	20,338
86,550	86,600	22,106	19,171	23,628	20,353
86,600	86,650	22,122	19,185	23,646	20,369
86,650	86,700	22,137	19,199	23,664	20,384
86,700	86,750	22,153	19,213	23,682	20,400
86,750	86,800	22,168	19,227	23,700	20,415
86,800	86,850	22,184	19,241	23,718	20,431
86,850	86,900	22,199	19,255	23,736	20,446
86,900	86,950	22,215	19,269	23,754	20,462
86,950	87,000	22,230	19,283	23,772	20,477
87,000					
87,000	87,050	22,246	19,297	23,790	20,493
87,050	87,100	22,261	19,311	23,808	20,508
87,100	87,150	22,277	19,325	23,826	20,524
87,150	87,200	22,292	19,339	23,844	20,539
87,200	87,250	22,308	19,353	23,862	20,555
87,250	87,300	22,323	19,367	23,880	20,570
87,300	87,350	22,339	19,381	23,898	20,586
87,350	87,400	22,354	19,395	23,916	20,601
87,400	87,450	22,370	19,409	23,934	20,617
87,450	87,500	22,385	19,423	23,952	20,632
87,500	87,550	22,401	19,437	23,970	20,648
87,550	87,600	22,416	19,451	23,988	20,663
87,600	87,650	22,432	19,465	24,006	20,679
87,650	87,700	22,447	19,479	24,024	20,694
87,700	87,750	22,463	19,493	24,042	20,710
87,750	87,800	22,478	19,507	24,060	20,725
87,800	87,850	22,494	19,521	24,078	20,741
87,850	87,900	22,509	19,535	24,096	20,756
87,900	87,950	22,525	19,549	24,114	20,772
87,950	88,000	22,540	19,563	24,132	20,787
88,000					
88,000	88,050	22,556	19,577	24,150	20,803
88,050	88,100	22,571	19,591	24,168	20,818
88,100	88,150	22,587	19,605	24,186	20,834
88,150	88,200	22,602	19,619	24,204	20,849
88,200	88,250	22,618	19,633	24,222	20,865
88,250	88,300	22,633	19,647	24,240	20,880
88,300	88,350	22,649	19,661	24,258	20,896
88,350	88,400	22,664	19,675	24,276	20,911
88,400	88,450	22,680	19,689	24,294	20,927
88,450	88,500	22,695	19,703	24,312	20,942
88,500	88,550	22,711	19,717	24,330	20,958
88,550	88,600	22,726	19,731	24,348	20,973
88,600	88,650	22,742	19,745	24,366	20,989
88,650	88,700	22,757	19,759	24,384	21,004
88,700	88,750	22,773	19,773	24,402	21,020
88,750	88,800	22,788	19,787	24,420	21,035
88,800	88,850	22,804	19,801	24,438	21,051
88,850	88,900	22,819	19,815	24,456	21,066
88,900	88,950	22,835	19,829	24,474	21,082
88,950	89,000	22,850	19,843	24,492	21,097

If line 37 (taxable income) is— At least	But less than	Single	Married filing jointly *	Married filing separately	Head of a household
89,000					
89,000	89,050	22,866	19,857	24,510	21,113
89,050	89,100	22,881	19,871	24,528	21,128
89,100	89,150	22,897	19,885	24,546	21,144
89,150	89,200	22,912	19,899	24,564	21,159
89,200	89,250	22,928	19,913	24,582	21,175
89,250	89,300	22,943	19,927	24,600	21,190
89,300	89,350	22,959	19,941	24,618	21,206
89,350	89,400	22,974	19,955	24,636	21,221
89,400	89,450	22,990	19,969	24,654	21,237
89,450	89,500	23,005	19,983	24,672	21,252
89,500	89,550	23,021	19,997	24,690	21,268
89,550	89,600	23,036	20,011	24,708	21,283
89,600	89,650	23,052	20,025	24,726	21,299
89,650	89,700	23,067	20,039	24,744	21,314
89,700	89,750	23,083	20,053	24,762	21,330
89,750	89,800	23,098	20,067	24,780	21,345
89,800	89,850	23,114	20,081	24,798	21,361
89,850	89,900	23,129	20,095	24,816	21,376
89,900	89,950	23,145	20,109	24,834	21,392
89,950	90,000	23,160	20,123	24,852	21,407
90,000					
90,000	90,050	23,176	20,137	24,870	21,423
90,050	90,100	23,191	20,151	24,888	21,438
90,100	90,150	23,207	20,165	24,906	21,454
90,150	90,200	23,222	20,179	24,924	21,469
90,200	90,250	23,238	20,193	24,942	21,485
90,250	90,300	23,253	20,207	24,960	21,500
90,300	90,350	23,269	20,221	24,978	21,516
90,350	90,400	23,284	20,235	24,996	21,531
90,400	90,450	23,300	20,249	25,014	21,547
90,450	90,500	23,315	20,263	25,032	21,562
90,500	90,550	23,331	20,277	25,050	21,578
90,550	90,600	23,346	20,291	25,068	21,593
90,600	90,650	23,362	20,305	25,086	21,609
90,650	90,700	23,377	20,319	25,104	21,624
90,700	90,750	23,393	20,333	25,122	21,640
90,750	90,800	23,408	20,347	25,140	21,655
90,800	90,850	23,424	20,361	25,158	21,671
90,850	90,900	23,439	20,375	25,176	21,686
90,900	90,950	23,455	20,389	25,194	21,702
90,950	91,000	23,470	20,403	25,212	21,717
91,000					
91,000	91,050	23,486	20,417	25,230	21,733
91,050	91,100	23,501	20,431	25,248	21,748
91,100	91,150	23,517	20,445	25,266	21,764
91,150	91,200	23,532	20,459	25,284	21,779
91,200	91,250	23,548	20,473	25,302	21,795
91,250	91,300	23,563	20,487	25,320	21,810
91,300	91,350	23,579	20,501	25,338	21,826
91,350	91,400	23,594	20,515	25,356	21,841
91,400	91,450	23,610	20,529	25,374	21,857
91,450	91,500	23,625	20,543	25,392	21,872
91,500	91,550	23,641	20,557	25,410	21,888
91,550	91,600	23,656	20,571	25,428	21,903
91,600	91,650	23,672	20,585	25,446	21,919
91,650	91,700	23,687	20,599	25,464	21,934
91,700	91,750	23,703	20,613	25,482	21,950
91,750	91,800	23,718	20,627	25,500	21,965
91,800	91,850	23,734	20,641	25,518	21,981
91,850	91,900	23,749	20,655	25,536	21,996
91,900	91,950	23,765	20,669	25,554	22,012
91,950	92,000	23,780	20,683	25,572	22,027

If line 37 (taxable income) is— At least	But less than	Single	Married filing jointly *	Married filing separately	Head of a household
92,000					
92,000	92,050	23,796	20,697	25,590	22,043
92,050	92,100	23,811	20,711	25,608	22,058
92,100	92,150	23,827	20,725	25,626	22,074
92,150	92,200	23,842	20,739	25,644	22,089
92,200	92,250	23,858	20,753	25,662	22,105
92,250	92,300	23,873	20,767	25,680	22,120
92,300	92,350	23,889	20,781	25,698	22,136
92,350	92,400	23,904	20,795	25,716	22,151
92,400	92,450	23,920	20,809	25,734	22,167
92,450	92,500	23,935	20,823	25,752	22,182
92,500	92,550	23,951	20,837	25,770	22,198
92,550	92,600	23,966	20,851	25,788	22,213
92,600	92,650	23,982	20,865	25,806	22,229
92,650	92,700	23,997	20,879	25,824	22,244
92,700	92,750	24,013	20,893	25,842	22,260
92,750	92,800	24,028	20,907	25,860	22,275
92,800	92,850	24,044	20,921	25,878	22,291
92,850	92,900	24,059	20,935	25,896	22,306
92,900	92,950	24,075	20,949	25,914	22,322
92,950	93,000	24,090	20,963	25,932	22,337
93,000					
93,000	93,050	24,106	20,977	25,950	22,353
93,050	93,100	24,121	20,991	25,968	22,368
93,100	93,150	24,137	21,005	25,986	22,384
93,150	93,200	24,152	21,019	26,004	22,399
93,200	93,250	24,168	21,033	26,022	22,415
93,250	93,300	24,183	21,047	26,040	22,430
93,300	93,350	24,199	21,061	26,058	22,446
93,350	93,400	24,214	21,075	26,076	22,461
93,400	93,450	24,230	21,089	26,094	22,477
93,450	93,500	24,245	21,103	26,112	22,492
93,500	93,550	24,261	21,117	26,130	22,508
93,550	93,600	24,276	21,131	26,148	22,523
93,600	93,650	24,292	21,145	26,166	22,539
93,650	93,700	24,307	21,159	26,184	22,554
93,700	93,750	24,323	21,173	26,202	22,570
93,750	93,800	24,338	21,187	26,220	22,585
93,800	93,850	24,354	21,201	26,238	22,601
93,850	93,900	24,369	21,215	26,256	22,616
93,900	93,950	24,385	21,229	26,274	22,632
93,950	94,000	24,400	21,243	26,292	22,647
94,000					
94,000	94,050	24,416	21,257	26,310	22,663
94,050	94,100	24,431	21,271	26,328	22,678
94,100	94,150	24,447	21,285	26,346	22,694
94,150	94,200	24,462	21,299	26,364	22,709
94,200	94,250	24,478	21,313	26,382	22,725
94,250	94,300	24,493	21,328	26,400	22,740
94,300	94,350	24,509	21,343	26,418	22,756
94,350	94,400	24,524	21,359	26,436	22,771
94,400	94,450	24,540	21,374	26,454	22,787
94,450	94,500	24,555	21,390	26,472	22,802
94,500	94,550	24,571	21,405	26,490	22,818
94,550	94,600	24,586	21,421	26,508	22,833
94,600	94,650	24,602	21,436	26,526	22,849
94,650	94,700	24,617	21,452	26,544	22,864
94,700	94,750	24,633	21,467	26,562	22,880
94,750	94,800	24,648	21,483	26,580	22,895
94,800	94,850	24,664	21,498	26,598	22,911
94,850	94,900	24,679	21,514	26,616	22,926
94,900	94,950	24,695	21,529	26,634	22,942
94,950	95,000	24,710	21,545	26,652	22,957

* This column must also be used by a qualifying widow(er).

Continued on next page

1995 Tax Table—*Continued*

If line 37 (taxable income) is— At least	But less than	Single	Married filing jointly *	Married filing separately	Head of a house-hold
95,000					
95,000	95,050	24,726	21,560	26,670	22,973
95,050	95,100	24,741	21,576	26,688	22,988
95,100	95,150	24,757	21,591	26,706	23,004
95,150	95,200	24,772	21,607	26,724	23,019
95,200	95,250	24,788	21,622	26,742	23,035
95,250	95,300	24,803	21,638	26,760	23,050
95,300	95,350	24,819	21,653	26,778	23,066
95,350	95,400	24,834	21,669	26,796	23,081
95,400	95,450	24,850	21,684	26,814	23,097
95,450	95,500	24,865	21,700	26,832	23,112
95,500	95,550	24,881	21,715	26,850	23,128
95,550	95,600	24,896	21,731	26,868	23,143
95,600	95,650	24,912	21,746	26,886	23,159
95,650	95,700	24,927	21,762	26,904	23,174
95,700	95,750	24,943	21,777	26,922	23,190
95,750	95,800	24,958	21,793	26,940	23,205
95,800	95,850	24,974	21,808	26,958	23,221
95,850	95,900	24,989	21,824	26,976	23,236
95,900	95,950	25,005	21,839	26,994	23,252
95,950	96,000	25,020	21,855	27,012	23,267
96,000					
96,000	96,050	25,036	21,870	27,030	23,283
96,050	96,100	25,051	21,886	27,048	23,298
96,100	96,150	25,067	21,901	27,066	23,314
96,150	96,200	25,082	21,917	27,084	23,329
96,200	96,250	25,098	21,932	27,102	23,345
96,250	96,300	25,113	21,948	27,120	23,360
96,300	96,350	25,129	21,963	27,138	23,376
96,350	96,400	25,144	21,979	27,156	23,391
96,400	96,450	25,160	21,994	27,174	23,407
96,450	96,500	25,175	22,010	27,192	23,422
96,500	96,550	25,191	22,025	27,210	23,438
96,550	96,600	25,206	22,041	27,228	23,453
96,600	96,650	25,222	22,056	27,246	23,469
96,650	96,700	25,237	22,072	27,264	23,484
96,700	96,750	25,253	22,087	27,282	23,500
96,750	96,800	25,268	22,103	27,300	23,515
96,800	96,850	25,284	22,118	27,318	23,531
96,850	96,900	25,299	22,134	27,336	23,546
96,900	96,950	25,315	22,149	27,354	23,562
96,950	97,000	25,330	22,165	27,372	23,577
97,000					
97,000	97,050	25,346	22,180	27,390	23,593
97,050	97,100	25,361	22,196	27,408	23,608
97,100	97,150	25,377	22,211	27,426	23,624
97,150	97,200	25,392	22,227	27,444	23,639
97,200	97,250	25,408	22,242	27,462	23,655
97,250	97,300	25,423	22,258	27,480	23,670
97,300	97,350	25,439	22,273	27,498	23,686
97,350	97,400	25,454	22,289	27,516	23,701
97,400	97,450	25,470	22,304	27,534	23,717
97,450	97,500	25,485	22,320	27,552	23,732
97,500	97,550	25,501	22,335	27,570	23,748
97,550	97,600	25,516	22,351	27,588	23,763
97,600	97,650	25,532	22,366	27,606	23,779
97,650	97,700	25,547	22,382	27,624	23,794
97,700	97,750	25,563	22,397	27,642	23,810
97,750	97,800	25,578	22,413	27,660	23,825
97,800	97,850	25,594	22,428	27,678	23,841
97,850	97,900	25,609	22,444	27,696	23,856
97,900	97,950	25,625	22,459	27,714	23,872
97,950	98,000	25,640	22,475	27,732	23,887

If line 37 (taxable income) is— At least	But less than	Single	Married filing jointly *	Married filing separately	Head of a house-hold
98,000					
98,000	98,050	25,656	22,490	27,750	23,903
98,050	98,100	25,671	22,506	27,768	23,918
98,100	98,150	25,687	22,521	27,786	23,934
98,150	98,200	25,702	22,537	27,804	23,949
98,200	98,250	25,718	22,552	27,822	23,965
98,250	98,300	25,733	22,568	27,840	23,980
98,300	98,350	25,749	22,583	27,858	23,996
98,350	98,400	25,764	22,599	27,876	24,011
98,400	98,450	25,780	22,614	27,894	24,027
98,450	98,500	25,795	22,630	27,912	24,042
98,500	98,550	25,811	22,645	27,930	24,058
98,550	98,600	25,826	22,661	27,948	24,073
98,600	98,650	25,842	22,676	27,966	24,089
98,650	98,700	25,857	22,692	27,984	24,104
98,700	98,750	25,873	22,707	28,002	24,120
98,750	98,800	25,888	22,723	28,020	24,135
98,800	98,850	25,904	22,738	28,038	24,151
98,850	98,900	25,919	22,754	28,056	24,166
98,900	98,950	25,935	22,769	28,074	24,182
98,950	99,000	25,950	22,785	28,092	24,197
99,000					
99,000	99,050	25,966	22,800	28,110	24,213
99,050	99,100	25,981	22,816	28,128	24,228
99,100	99,150	25,997	22,831	28,146	24,244
99,150	99,200	26,012	22,847	28,164	24,259
99,200	99,250	26,028	22,862	28,182	24,275
99,250	99,300	26,043	22,878	28,200	24,290
99,300	99,350	26,059	22,893	28,218	24,306
99,350	99,400	26,074	22,909	28,236	24,321
99,400	99,450	26,090	22,924	28,254	24,337
99,450	99,500	26,105	22,940	28,272	24,352
99,500	99,550	26,121	22,955	28,290	24,368
99,550	99,600	26,136	22,971	28,308	24,383
99,600	99,650	26,152	22,986	28,326	24,399
99,650	99,700	26,167	23,002	28,344	24,414
99,700	99,750	26,183	23,017	28,362	24,430
99,750	99,800	26,198	23,033	28,380	24,445
99,800	99,850	26,214	23,048	28,398	24,461
99,850	99,900	26,229	23,064	28,416	24,476
99,900	99,950	26,245	23,079	28,434	24,492
99,950	100,000	26,260	23,095	28,452	24,507

$100,000 or over — use the Tax Rate Schedules on page A-2

* This column must also be used by a qualifying widow(er).

1996 Tax Rate Schedules

Single—Schedule X

If taxable income is: Over—	But not over—	The tax is:	of the amount over—
$0	$ 24,000	...............15%	$0
24,000	58,150	$3,600.00 + 28%	24,000
58,150	121,300	13,162.00 + 31%	58,150
121,300	263,750	32,738.50 + 36%	121,300
263,750	....	84,020.50 + 39.6%	263,750

Head of household—Schedule Z

If taxable income is: Over—	But not over—	The tax is:	of the amount over—
$0	$ 32,150	...............15%	$0
32,150	83,050	$4,822.50 + 28%	32,150
83,050	134,500	19,074.50 + 31%	83,050
134,500	263,750	35,024.00 + 36%	134,500
263,750	....	81,554.00 + 39.6%	263,750

Married filing jointly or Qualifying widow(er)—Schedule Y-1

If taxable income is: Over—	But not over—	The tax is:	of the amount over—
$0	$ 40,100	...............15%	$0
40,100	96,900	$6,015.00 + 28%	40,100
96,900	147,700	21,919.00 + 31%	96,900
147,700	263,750	37,667.00 + 36%	147,700
263,750	....	79,445.00 + 39.6%	263,750

Married filing separately—Schedule Y-2

If taxable income is: Over—	But not over—	The tax is:	of the amount over—
$0	$ 20,050	...............15%	$0
20,050	48,450	$3,007.50 + 28%	20,050
48,450	73,850	10,959.50 + 31%	48,450
73,850	131,875	18,833.50 + 36%	73,850
131,875	....	39,722.50 + 39.6%	131,875

INCOME TAX RATES—ESTATES AND TRUSTS

TAX YEAR 1995

Taxable Income		The Tax Is:	Of the
Over—	But not Over—		Amount Over—
$ 0	$1,550	15%	$ 0
1,550	3,700	$ 232.50 + 28%	1,550
3,700	5,600	834.50 + 31%	3,700
5,600	7,650	1,423.50 + 36%	5,600
7,650	———	2,161.50 + 39.6%	7,650

TAX YEAR 1996

Taxable Income		The Tax Is:	Of the
Over—	But not Over—		Amount Over—
$ 0	$1,600	15%	$ 0
1,600	3,800	$ 240 + 28%	1,600
3,800	5,800	856 + 31%	3,800
5,800	7,900	1,476 + 36%	5,800
7,900	———	2,232 + 39.6%	7,900

INCOME TAX RATES—CORPORATIONS

Taxable Income			Of the
Over—	But not Over—	Tax Is:	Amount Over—
$ 0	$ 50,000	15%	$ 0
50,000	75,000	$ 7,500 + 25%	50,000
75,000	100,000	13,750 + 34%	75,000
100,000	335,000	22,250 + 39%	100,000
335,000	10,000,000	113,900 + 34%	335,000
10,000,000	15,000,000	3,400,000 + 35%	10,000,000
15,000,000	18,333,333	5,150,000 + 38%	15,000,000
18,333,333	—	35%	0

UNIFIED TRANSFER TAX RATES

FOR GIFTS MADE AND FOR DEATHS AFTER 1983

If the Amount with Respect to Which the Tentative Tax to Be Computed Is:	The Tentative Tax Is:
Not over $10,000	18 percent of such amount.
Over $10,000 but not over $20,000	$1,800, plus 20 percent of the excess of such amount over $10,000.
Over $20,000 but not over $40,000	$3,800, plus 22 percent of the excess of such amount over $20,000.
Over $40,000 but not over $60,000	$8,200, plus 24 percent of the excess of such amount over $40,000.
Over $60,000 but not over $80,000	$13,000, plus 26 percent of the excess of such amount over $60,000.
Over $80,000 but not over $100,000	$18,200, plus 28 percent of the excess of such amount over $80,000.
Over $100,000 but not over $150,000	$23,800, plus 30 percent of the excess of such amount over $100,000.
Over $150,000 but not over $250,000	$38,800, plus 32 percent of the excess of such amount over $150,000.
Over $250,000 but not over $500,000	$70,800, plus 34 percent of the excess of such amount over $250,000.
Over $500,000 but not over $750,000	$155,800, plus 37 percent of the excess of such amount over $500,000.
Over $750,000 but not over $1,000,000	$248,300, plus 39 percent of the excess of such amount over $750,000.
Over $1,000,000 but not over $1,250,000	$345,800, plus 41 percent of the excess of such amount over $1,000,000.
Over $1,250,000 but not over $1,500,000	$448,300, plus 43 percent of the excess of such amount over $1,250,000.
Over $1,500,000 but not over $2,000,000	$555,800, plus 45 percent of the excess of such amount over $1,500,000.
Over $2,000,000 but not over $2,500,000	$780,800, plus 49 percent of the excess of such amount over $2,000,000.
Over $2,500,000 but not over $3,000,000	$1,025,800, plus 53 percent of the excess of such amount over $2,500,000.
Over $3,000,000*	$1,290,800, plus 55 percent of the excess of such amount over $3,000,000.

*Other large taxable transfers (generally in excess of $10 million) there is a phase-out of the graduated rates and the unified tax credit.

TABLE FOR COMPUTATION OF MAXIMUM CREDIT FOR STATE DEATH TAXES

(A)	(B)	(C)	(D)
Adjusted Taxable Estate* Equal to or More Than	Adjusted Taxable Estate* Less Than	Credit on Amount in Column (A)	Rate of Credit on Excess Over Amount in Column (A) (Percentage)
0	$ 40,000	0	None
$ 40,000	90,000	0	0.8
90,000	140,000	$ 400	1.6
140,000	240,000	1,200	2.4
240,000	440,000	3,600	3.2
440,000	640,000	10,000	4.0
640,000	840,000	18,000	4.8
840,000	1,040,000	27,600	5.6
1,040,000	1,540,000	38,800	6.4
1,540,000	2,040,000	70,800	7.2
2,040,000	2,540,000	106,800	8.0
2,540,000	3,040,000	146,800	8.8
3,040,000	3,540,000	190,800	9.6
3,540,000	4,040,000	238,800	10.4
4,040,000	5,040,000	290,800	11.2
5,040,000	6,040,000	402,800	12.0
6,040,000	7,040,000	522,800	12.8
7,040,000	8,040,000	650,800	13.6
8,040,000	9,040,000	786,800	14.4
9,040,000	10,040,000	930,800	15.2
10,040,000		1,082,800	16.0

*Adjusted Taxable Estate = Taxable Estate – $60,000

APPENDIX B
Tax Forms

Form **656**
(Rev. Sept. 1993)

Department of the Treasury—Internal Revenue Service

► See Instructions
Page 5

Offer in Compromise

(1) Name and Address of Taxpayers	For Official Use Only	
	Offer is (*Check applicable box*) ☐ Cash (*Paid in full*) ☐ Deferred payment	Serial Number
		(*Cashier's stamp*)

(2) Social Security Number	(3) Employer Identification Number	Alpha CSED Incl. _____

To: **Commissioner of Internal Revenue Service**

Amount Paid
$

(4) **I/we** (includes all types of taxpayers) **submit this offer to compromise the tax liabilities plus any interest, penalties, additions to tax, and additional amounts required by law (tax liability)** for the tax type and period checked below: (Please mark "X" for the correct description and fill in the correct tax period(s), adding additional periods if needed.)

☐ Income tax for the year(s) 19 _____ , 19 _____ , and 19 _____

☐ Trust fund recovery penalty (formerly called the 100-percent penalty) as a responsible person of _____ _____ (enter business name) for failure to pay withholding and Federal Insurance Contribution Act taxes (Social Security taxes), for the period(s) ended _____ /_____ /_____ , _____ /_____ /_____ , _____ /_____ /_____ , _____ /_____ /_____ (for example - 06/30/92)

☐ Withholding and Federal Insurance Contributions Act taxes (Social Secuirty taxes) for the period(s) ended _____ /_____ /_____ , _____ _____ /_____ , _____ /_____ /_____ , _____ /_____ /_____ (for example - 06/30/92)

☐ Federal Unemployment Tax Act taxes for the year(s) 19 _____ , 19 _____ , and 19 _____

☐ Other (Be specific.) _____

(5) **I/we offer to pay $**_____

If you aren't making full payment with your offer, describe below when you will make full payment (for example–within ten (10) days from the date the offer is accepted). See the instructions for Item 5.

_____

_____

_____

As required by section 6621 of the Internal Revenue Code, the Internal Revenue Service (IRS) will add interest to the offered amount from the date IRS accepts the offer until the date you can completely pay the amount offered. IRS compounds interest daily, as required by section 6622 of the Internal Revenue Code.

(6) **I/we submit this offer for the reason(s) checked below.**

☐ Doubt as to collectibility ("I can't pay.") You must include a completed financial statement (Form 433-A and/or Form 433-B).

☐ Doubt as to liability ("I don't believe I owe this tax.") You must include a detailed explanation of the reason(s) why you believe you don't owe the tax.

IMPORTANT: SEE REVERSE FOR TERMS AND CONDITIONS

I accept waiver of the statutory period of limitations for the Internal Revenue Service.	Under penalties of perjury, I declare that I have examined this offer. Including accompanying schedules and statements, and to the best of my knowledge and belief, it is true, correct and complete.	
Signature of authorized Internal Revenue Service Officer	(8a) Signature of Taxpayer proponent	Date
Title	Date	(8b) Signature of Taxpayer proponent	Date

Dispose of prior issues.   **Part 1 IRS Copy**   Cat. No. 16728N   Form **656** (Rev. 9-93)

Form **870** (Rev. February 1986)	Department of the Treasury—Internal Revenue Service **Waiver of Restrictions on Assessment and Collection of Deficiency in Tax and Acceptance of Overassessment**	Date Received by Internal Revenue Service

Names and address of taxpayers (*Number, street, city or town, State, ZIP code*)	Social security or employer identification number

Increase (Decrease) in Tax and Penalties

Tax year ended	Tax	Penalties			
	$	$	$	$	$
	$	$	$	$	$
	$	$	$	$	$
	$	$	$	$	$
	$	$	$	$	$
	$	$	$	$	$
	$	$	$	$	$

(For instructions, see back of form)

Consent to Assessment and Collection

    I consent to the immediate assessment and collection of any deficiencies (*increase in tax and penalties*) and accept any overassessment (*decrease in tax and penalties*) shown above, plus any interest provided by law. I understand that by signing this waiver, I will not be able to contest these years in the United States Tax Court, unless additional deficiencies are determined for these years.

Signatures		Date
		Date
	By Title	Date

Form **870** (Rev. 2-86)

Department of the Treasury—Internal Revenue Service

Form
1040EZ

**Income Tax Return for Single and
Joint Filers With No Dependents** **1995**

OMB No. 1545-0675

Use
the
IRS
label
here

Your first name and initial   Last name

If a joint return, spouse's first name and initial   Last name

Home address (number and street). If you have a P.O. box, see page 11.   Apt. no.

City, town or post office, state, and ZIP code. If you have a foreign address, see page 11.

Your social security number

Spouse's social security number

See instructions on back and in Form 1040EZ booklet.

**Presidential
Election
Campaign**
(See page 11.)

Note: *Checking "Yes" will not change your tax or reduce your refund.*

Do you want $3 to go to this fund?   ▶

If a joint return, does your spouse want $3 to go to this fund? ▶

Yes   No

Income

**Attach
Copy B of
Form(s)
W-2 here.**
Enclose, but
do not attach,
any payment
with your
return.

1 Total wages, salaries, and tips. This
should be shown in box 1 of your
W-2 form(s). Attach your W-2 form(s).   1

2 Taxable interest income of $400 or less. If the total is
over $400, you cannot use Form 1040EZ.   2

3 Unemployment compensation (see page 14).   3

4 Add lines 1, 2, and 3. This is your **adjusted gross
income.** If less than $9,230, see page 15 to find out if you
can claim the earned income credit on line 8.   4

Note: *You
must check
Yes or No.*

5 Can your parents (or someone else) claim you on their return?

☐ **Yes.** Do worksheet
on back; enter
amount from
line G here.

☐ **No.** If **single,** enter 6,400.00.
If **married,** enter 11,550.00.
For an explanation of these
amounts, see back of form.   5

6 Subtract line 5 from line 4. If line 5 is larger than
line 4, enter 0. This is your **taxable income.**   ▶ 6

Dollars   Cents

**Payments
and tax**

7 Enter your Federal income tax withheld from box 2 of
your W-2 form(s).   7

8 **Earned income credit** (see page 15). Enter type
and amount of nontaxable earned income below.

Type $ 8

9 Add lines 7 and 8 (don't include nontaxable earned
income). These are your **total payments.**   9

10 **Tax.** Use the amount on **line 6** to find your tax in the
tax table on pages 29–33 of the booklet. Then, enter the
tax from the table on this line.   10

**Refund
or
amount
you
owe**

11 If line 9 is larger than line 10, subtract line 10 from line
9. This is your **refund.**   11

12 If line 10 is larger than line 9, subtract line 9 from line
10. This is the **amount you owe.** See page 22 for details
on how to pay and what to write on your payment.   12

I have read this return. Under penalties of perjury, I declare that to the best of my knowledge and belief, the
return is true, correct, and accurately lists all amounts and sources of income I received during the tax year.

**Sign
your
return**

Keep a copy
of this form
for your
records.

Your signature   Spouse's signature if joint return

Date   Your occupation   Date   Spouse's occupation

**For IRS Use Only — Please
do not write in boxes below.**

1   2   3   4   5

6   7   8   9   10

Form 1040EZ (1995)

1995   Instructions for Form 1040EZ

Use this form if	• Your filing status is single or married filing jointly. • You (and your spouse if married) were under 65 on January 1, 1996, and not blind at the end of 1995.

Use this form if

- Your filing status is single or married filing jointly.
- You (and your spouse if married) were under 65 on January 1, 1996, and not blind at the end of 1995.
- You do not claim any dependents.
- Your taxable income (line 6) is less than $50,000.
- You had **only** wages, salaries, tips, taxable scholarship or fellowship grants, or unemployment compensation, and your taxable interest income was $400 or less. **But** if you earned tips, including allocated tips, that are not included in box 5 and box 7 of your W-2, you may not be able to use Form 1040EZ. See page 13.
- You did not receive any advance earned income credit payments.

Caution: *If married and either you or your spouse had total wages of over $61,200, you may not be able to use this form. See page 9.*

If you are not sure about your filing status, see page 10. If you have questions about dependents, call Tele-Tax (see page 27) and listen to topic 354. If you **can't use this form,** call Tele-Tax (see page 27) and listen to topic 352.

Filling in your return

Because this form is read by a machine, please print your numbers inside the boxes like this:

9 8 7 6 5 4 3 2 1 0   Do not type your numbers. Do not use dollar signs.

If you received a scholarship or fellowship grant or tax-exempt interest income, such as on municipal bonds, see the booklet before filling in the form. Also, see the booklet if you received a Form 1099-INT showing income tax withheld.

Remember, you must report all wages, salaries, and tips even if you don't get a W-2 form from your employer. You must also report all your taxable interest income, including interest from banks, savings and loans, credit unions, etc., even if you don't get a Form 1099-INT.

If you paid someone to prepare your return, see page 22.

Worksheet for dependents who checked "Yes" on line 5

Use this worksheet to figure the amount to enter on line 5 if someone can claim you (or your spouse if married) as a dependent, even if that person chooses not to do so. To find out if someone can claim you as a dependent, call Tele-Tax (see page 27) and listen to topic 354.

- **A.** Enter the amount from line 1 on the front.   **A.** _____
- **B.** Minimum standard deduction.   **B.** _____ 650.00
- **C.** Enter the LARGER of line A or line B here.   **C.** _____
- **D.** Maximum standard deduction. If single, enter 3,900.00; if married, enter 6,550.00.   **D.** _____
- **E.** Enter the SMALLER of line C or line D here. This is your standard deduction.   **E.** _____
- **F.** Exemption amount.
  - If single, enter 0.
  - If married and both you and your spouse can be claimed as dependents, enter 0.
  - If married and only one of you can be claimed as a dependent, enter 2,500.00.   **F.** _____
- **G.** Add lines E and F. Enter the total here and on line 5 on the front.   **G.** _____

If you checked "No" on line 5 because no one can claim you (or your spouse if married) as a dependent, enter on line 5 the amount shown below that applies to you.

- Single, enter 6,400.00. This is the total of your standard deduction (3,900.00) and personal exemption (2,500.00).
- Married, enter 11,550.00. This is the total of your standard deduction (6,550.00), exemption for yourself (2,500.00), and exemption for your spouse (2,500.00).

Avoid mistakes

See page 5 of the Form 1040EZ booklet for a list of common mistakes to avoid. Errors will delay your refund.

Mailing your return

Mail your return by **April 15, 1996.** Use the envelope that came with your booklet. If you don't have that envelope, see page 36 for the address to use.

Form
1040A (99)

Department of the Treasury—Internal Revenue Service
U.S. Individual Income Tax Return

1995

IRS Use Only—Do not write or staple in this space.

OMB No. 1545-0085

Label
(See page 19.)

Use the IRS label. Otherwise, please print or type.

L A B E L H E R E

Your first name and initial

Last name

Your social security number

If a joint return, spouse's first name and initial

Last name

Spouse's social security number

Home address (number and street). If you have a P.O. box, see page 19.

Apt. no.

For Privacy Act and Paperwork Reduction Act Notice, see page 11.

City, town or post office, state, and ZIP code. If you have a foreign address, see page 19.

Presidential Election Campaign Fund (See page 19.)
Do you want $3 to go to this fund? . . . .
If a joint return, does your spouse want $3 to go to this fund?

Yes | No

Note: *Checking "Yes" will not change your tax or reduce your refund.*

Check the box for your filing status
(See page 20.)

Check only one box.

1 ☐ Single
2 ☐ Married filing joint return (even if only one had income)
3 ☐ Married filing separate return. Enter spouse's social security number above and full name here. ▶ _____
4 ☐ Head of household (with qualifying person). (See page 21.) If the qualifying person is a child but not your dependent, enter this child's name here. ▶ _____
5 ☐ Qualifying widow(er) with dependent child (year spouse died ▶ 19   ). (See page 22.)

Figure your exemptions
(See page 22.)

If more than seven dependents, see page 25.

6a ☐ **Yourself.** If your parent (or someone else) can claim you as a dependent on his or her tax return, **do not** check box 6a. But be sure to check the box on line 18b on page 2.

b ☐ **Spouse**

c **Dependents:**

(1) First name Last name	(2) Dependent's social security number. If born in 1995, see page 25.	(3) Dependent's relationship to you	(4) No. of months lived in your home in 1995

No. of boxes checked on 6a and 6b _____

No. of your children on 6c who:
• lived with you _____

• didn't live with you due to divorce or separation (see page 26)

Dependents on 6c not entered above

d If your child didn't live with you but is claimed as your dependent under a pre-1985 agreement, check here . . . . ▶ ☐

e Total number of exemptions claimed.

Add numbers entered on lines above

Figure your adjusted gross income

Attach Copy B of your Forms W-2 and 1099-R here. If you didn't get a W-2, see page 27. Enclose, but do not attach, any payment.

7 Wages, salaries, tips, etc. This should be shown in box 1 of your W-2 form(s). Attach Form(s) W-2. | 7

8a **Taxable** interest income (see page 28). If over $400, attach Schedule 1. | 8a

b **Tax-exempt** interest. DO NOT include on line 8a. | 8b

9 Dividends. If over $400, attach Schedule 1. | 9

10a Total IRA distributions. | 10a | **10b** Taxable amount (see page 29). | 10b

11a Total pensions and annuities. | 11a | **11b** Taxable amount (see page 29). | 11b

12 Unemployment compensation (see page 32). | 12

13a Social security benefits. | 13a | **13b** Taxable amount (see page 33). | 13b

14 Add lines 7 through 13b (far right column). This is your **total income.** ▶ | 14

15a Your IRA deduction (see page 35). | 15a

b Spouse's IRA deduction (see page 35). | 15b

c Add lines 15a and 15b. These are your **total adjustments.** | 15c

16 Subtract line 15c from line 14. This is your **adjusted gross income.** If less than $26,673 and a child lived with you (less than $9,230 if a child didn't live with you), see "Earned income credit" on page 47. ▶ | 16

51A5AAA

Cat. No. 11327A

1995 Form 1040A page 1

1995 Form 1040A page 2

Figure your standard deduction, exemption amount, and taxable income	**17** Enter the amount from line 16.	**17**

18a Check if: ☐ **You** were 65 or older ☐ Blind } ☐ **Spouse** was 65 or older ☐ Blind } Enter number of boxes checked ▶ 18a ☐

b If your parent (or someone else) can claim you as a dependent, check here. . . . . ▶ 18b ☐

c If you are married filing separately and your spouse itemizes deductions, see page 40 and check here. . . . . ▶ 18c ☐

19 Enter the **standard deduction** shown below for your filing status. **But if you checked any box on line 18a or b,** go to page 40 to find your standard deduction. **If you checked box 18c,** enter -0-.
- ● Single—$3,900 ● Married filing jointly or Qualifying widow(er)—$6,550
- ● Head of household—$5,750 ● Married filing separately—$3,275   **19**

20 Subtract line 19 from line 17. If line 19 is more than line 17, enter -0-. **20**

21 Multiply $2,500 by the total number of exemptions claimed on line 6e. **21**

22 Subtract line 21 from line 20. If line 21 is more than line 20, enter -0-. This is your **taxable income.** ▶ **22**

Figure your tax, credits, and payments

If you want the IRS to figure your tax, see the instructions for line 22 on page 41.

23 Find the tax on the amount on line 22. Check if from: ☐ Tax Table (pages 65–70) or ☐ Form 8615 (see page 42). **23**

24a Credit for child and dependent care expenses. Attach Schedule 2. **24a**

b Credit for the elderly or the disabled. Attach Schedule 3. **24b**

c Add lines 24a and 24b. These are your **total credits.** **24c**

25 Subtract line 24c from line 23. If line 24c is more than line 23, enter -0-. **25**

26 Advance earned income credit payments from Form W-2. **26**

27 Household employment taxes. Attach Schedule H. **27**

28 Add lines 25, 26, and 27. This is your **total tax.** ▶ **28**

29a Total Federal income tax withheld. If any is from Form(s) 1099, check here. ▶ ☐ **29a**

b 1995 estimated tax payments and amount applied from 1994 return. **29b**

c **Earned income credit.** Attach Schedule EIC if you have a qualifying child. **29c**
Nontaxable earned income: amount ▶ | and type ▶

d Add lines 29a, 29b, and 29c (don't include nontaxable earned income). These are your **total payments.** ▶ **29d**

Figure your refund or amount you owe

30 If line 29d is more than line 28, subtract line 28 from line 29d. This is the amount you **overpaid.** **30**

31 Amount of line 30 you want **refunded to you.** **31**

32 Amount of line 30 you want **applied to your 1996 estimated tax.** **32**

33 If line 28 is more than line 29d, subtract line 29d from line 28. This is the **amount you owe.** For details on how to pay, including what to write on your payment, see page 55. **33**

34 Estimated tax penalty (see page 55). Also, include on line 33. **34**

Sign your return

Keep a copy of this return for your records.

Under penalties of perjury, I declare that I have examined this return and accompanying schedules and statements, and to the best of my knowledge and belief, they are true, correct, and accurately list all amounts and sources of income I received during the tax year. Declaration of preparer (other than the taxpayer) is based on all information of which the preparer has any knowledge.

Your signature	Date	Your occupation
Spouse's signature. If joint return, BOTH must sign.	Date	Spouse's occupation

Paid preparer's use only

Preparer's signature	Date	Check if self-employed ☐	Preparer's SSN
Firm's name (or yours if self-employed) and address		EIN	
		ZIP code	

N1A5AAA

✿ *Printed on recycled paper*   **1995 Form 1040A page 2**

Schedule 1

(Form 1040A)

Department of the Treasury—Internal Revenue Service

Interest and Dividend Income for Form 1040A Filers   (99)   **1995**

OMB No. 1545-0085

Name(s) shown on Form 1040A

Your social security number

Part I

Interest income

(See pages 28 and 71.)

Note: *If you received a Form 1099–INT, Form 1099–OID, or substitute statement from a brokerage firm, enter the firm's name and the total interest shown on that form.*

1 List name of payer. If any interest is from a seller-financed mortgage and the buyer used the property as a personal residence, see page 71 and list this interest first. Also, show that buyer's social security number and address.

Amount

	1	

2 Add the amounts on line 1.   **2**

3 Excludable interest on series EE U.S. savings bonds issued after 1989 from Form 8815, line 14. You **must** attach Form 8815 to Form 1040A.   **3**

4 Subtract line 3 from line 2. Enter the result here and on Form 1040A, line 8a.   **4**

Part II

Dividend income

(See pages 28 and 72.)

Note: *If you received a Form 1099–DIV or substitute statement from a brokerage firm, enter the firm's name and the total dividends shown on that form.*

5 List name of payer

Amount

	5	

5/15AAA

6 Add the amounts on line 5. Enter the total here and on Form 1040A, line 9.   **6**

For Paperwork Reduction Act Notice, see Form 1040A instructions.   Cat. No. 12075R   **1995 Schedule 1 (Form 1040A) page 1**

Printed on recycled paper

Form 1040 Department of the Treasury—Internal Revenue Service

U.S. Individual Income Tax Return **1995** (99) IRS Use Only—Do not write or staple in this space.

For the year Jan. 1–Dec. 31, 1995, or other tax year beginning , 1995, ending , 19 | OMB No. 1545-0074

Label
(See instructions on page 11.)

Use the IRS label. Otherwise, please print or type.

Your first name and initial | Last name | Your social security number

If a joint return, spouse's first name and initial | Last name | Spouse's social security number

Home address (number and street). If you have a P.O. box, see page 11. | Apt. no.

City, town or post office, state, and ZIP code. If you have a foreign address, see page 11.

For Privacy Act and Paperwork Reduction Act Notice, see page 7.

Presidential Election Campaign
(See page 11.)

Yes | No | Note: *Checking "Yes" will not change your tax or reduce your refund.*

Do you want $3 to go to this fund? . . . .
If a joint return, does your spouse want $3 to go to this fund? . . . .

Filing Status
(See page 11.)

Check only one box.

1 Single
2 Married filing joint return (even if only one had income)
3 Married filing separate return. Enter spouse's social security no. above and full name here. ▶ _____
4 Head of household (with qualifying person). (See page 12.) If the qualifying person is a child but not your dependent, enter this child's name here. ▶
5 Qualifying widow(er) with dependent child (year spouse died ▶ 19). (See page 12.)

Exemptions
(See page 12.)

6a ☐ **Yourself.** If your parent (or someone else) can claim you as a dependent on his or her tax return, **do not** check box 6a. But be sure to check the box on line 33b on page 2 .

b ☐ **Spouse** . . . .

c Dependents:

(1) First name   Last name | (2) Dependent's social security number. If born in 1995, see page 13. | (3) Dependent's relationship to you | (4) No. of months lived in your home in 1995

If more than six dependents, see page 13.

No. of boxes checked on 6a and 6b ___

No. of your children on 6c who:
• lived with you
• didn't live with you due to divorce or separation (see page 14)

Dependents on 6c not entered above

d If your child didn't live with you but is claimed as your dependent under a pre-1985 agreement, check here ▶ ☐
e Total number of exemptions claimed . . . .

Add numbers entered on lines above ▶ ☐

Income

Attach Copy B of your Forms W-2, W-2G, and 1099-R here.

If you did not get a W-2, see page 14.

Enclose, but do not attach, your payment and payment voucher. See page 33.

7 Wages, salaries, tips, etc. Attach Form(s) W-2 . . . . . . | 7
8a **Taxable** interest income (see page 15). Attach Schedule B if over $400 . . . . . | 8a
b **Tax-exempt** interest (see page 15). DON'T include on line 8a 8b | |
9 Dividend income. Attach Schedule B if over $400 . . . . | 9
10 Taxable refunds, credits, or offsets of state and local income taxes (see page 15) . . | 10
11 Alimony received . . . . | 11
12 Business income or (loss). Attach Schedule C or C-EZ . . . . | 12
13 Capital gain or (loss). If required, attach Schedule D (see page 16) . . . . . | 13
14 Other gains or (losses). Attach Form 4797 . . . . | 14
15a Total IRA distributions . 15a | b Taxable amount (see page 16) | 15b
16a Total pensions and annuities 16a | b Taxable amount (see page 16) | 16b
17 Rental real estate, royalties, partnerships, S corporations, trusts, etc. Attach Schedule E | 17
18 Farm income or (loss). Attach Schedule F . . . . | 18
19 Unemployment compensation (see page 17) . . . . | 19
20a Social security benefits 20a | b Taxable amount (see page 18) | 20b
21 Other income. List type and amount—see page 18 _____ | 21
22 Add the amounts in the far right column for lines 7 through 21. This is your **total income** ▶ | 22

Adjustments to Income

23a Your IRA deduction (see page 19) 23a
b Spouse's IRA deduction (see page 19) 23b
24 Moving expenses. Attach Form 3903 or 3903-F . . . 24
25 One-half of self-employment tax 25
26 Self-employed health insurance deduction (see page 21) 26
27 Keogh & self-employed SEP plans. If SEP, check ▶ ☐ 27
28 Penalty on early withdrawal of savings 28
29 Alimony paid. Recipient's SSN ▶ 29
30 Add lines 23a through 29. These are your **total adjustments** . . . . ▶ | 30

Adjusted Gross Income

31 Subtract line 30 from line 22. This is your **adjusted gross income**. If less than $26,673 and a child lived with you (less than $9,230 if a child didn't live with you), see "Earned Income Credit" on page 27 ▶ | 31

Cat. No. 11320B

Form **1040** (1995)

Form 1040 (1995)

Tax Computation (See page 23.)	32	Amount from line 31 (adjusted gross income)	32	
	33a	Check if: ☐ **You** were 65 or older, ☐ Blind; ☐ **Spouse** was 65 or older, ☐ Blind.		
		Add the number of boxes checked above and enter the total here . . . . ▶ 33a		
	b	If your parent (or someone else) can claim you as a dependent, check here . ▶ 33b ☐		
	c	If you are married filing separately and your spouse itemizes deductions or you are a dual-status alien, see page 23 and check here . . . . ▶ 33c ☐		
	34	Enter the **larger** of your: { **Itemized deductions** from Schedule A, line 28, **OR** **Standard deduction** shown below for your filing status. **But if you checked any box on line 33a or b,** go to page 23 to find your standard deduction. If you checked **box 33c**, your standard deduction is zero. • Single—$3,900 • Married filing jointly or Qualifying widow(er)—$6,550 • Head of household—$5,750 • Married filing separately—$3,275 }	34	
	35	Subtract line 34 from line 32	35	
	36	If line 32 is $86,025 or less, multiply $2,500 by the total number of exemptions claimed on line 6e. If line 32 is over $86,025, see the worksheet on page 23 for the amount to enter .	36	
If you want the IRS to figure your tax, see page 35.	37	**Taxable income.** Subtract line 36 from line 35. If line 36 is more than line 35, enter -0-	37	
	38	Tax. Check if from **a** ☐ Tax Table, **b** ☐ Tax Rate Schedules, **c** ☐ Capital Gain Tax Worksheet, or **d** ☐ Form 8615 (see page 24). Amount from Form(s) 8814 ▶ **e** _____	38	
	39	Additional taxes. Check if from **a** ☐ Form 4970 **b** ☐ Form 4972	39	
	40	Add lines 38 and 39 . . . . ▶	40	

Credits (See page 24.)	41	Credit for child and dependent care expenses. Attach Form 2441	41			
	42	Credit for the elderly or the disabled. Attach Schedule R . .	42			
	43	Foreign tax credit. Attach Form 1116	43			
	44	Other credits (see page 25). Check if from **a** ☐ Form 3800 **b** ☐ Form 8396 **c** ☐ Form 8801 **d** ☐ Form (specify) _____	44			
	45	Add lines 41 through 44		45	
	46	Subtract line 45 from line 40. If line 45 is more than line 40, enter -0- . . . . . ▶		46	

Other Taxes (See page 25.)	47	Self-employment tax. Attach Schedule SE	47	
	48	Alternative minimum tax. Attach Form 6251	48	
	49	Recapture taxes. Check if from **a** ☐ Form 4255 **b** ☐ Form 8611 **c** ☐ Form 8828 . .	49	
	50	Social security and Medicare tax on tip income not reported to employer. Attach Form 4137 .	50	
	51	Tax on qualified retirement plans, including IRAs. If required, attach Form 5329	51	
	52	Advance earned income credit payments from Form W-2	52	
	53	Household employment taxes. Attach Schedule H	53	
	54	Add lines 46 through 53. This is your **total tax** . . . . ▶	54	

Payments Attach Forms W-2, W-2G, and 1099-R on the front.	55	Federal income tax withheld. If any is from Form(s) 1099, check ▶ ☐	55		
	56	1995 estimated tax payments and amount applied from 1994 return .	56		
	57	**Earned income credit.** Attach Schedule EIC if you have a qualifying child. Nontaxable earned income: amount ▶ _____ and type ▶ _____	57		
	58	Amount paid with Form 4868 (extension request)	58		
	59	Excess social security and RRTA tax withheld (see page 32)	59		
	60	Other payments. Check if from **a** ☐ Form 2439 **b** ☐ Form 4136	60		
	61	Add lines 55 through 60. These are your **total payments** . . . . ▶		61	

Refund or Amount You Owe	62	If line 61 is more than line 54, subtract line 54 from line 61. This is the amount you **OVERPAID**. . .	62	
	63	Amount of line 62 you want **REFUNDED TO YOU**. . . . . ▶	63	
	64	Amount of line 62 you want **APPLIED TO YOUR 1996 ESTIMATED TAX** ▶ | 64 |		
	65	If line 54 is more than line 61, subtract line 61 from line 54. This is the **AMOUNT YOU OWE**. For details on how to pay and use **Form 1040-V**, Payment Voucher, see page 33 . . ▶	65	
	66	Estimated tax penalty (see page 33). Also include on line 65 | 66 |		

Sign Here Keep a copy of this return for your records.	Under penalties of perjury, I declare that I have examined this return and accompanying schedules and statements, and to the best of my knowledge and belief, they are true, correct, and complete. Declaration of preparer (other than taxpayer) is based on all information of which preparer has any knowledge.		
	▶ Your signature	Date	Your occupation
	▶ Spouse's signature. If a joint return, BOTH must sign.	Date	Spouse's occupation

Paid Preparer's Use Only	Preparer's ▶ signature	Date	Check if self-employed ☐	Preparer's social security no.
	Firm's name (or yours if self-employed) and address ▶		EIN	
			ZIP code	

✿ *Printed on recycled paper*

SCHEDULES A&B
(Form 1040)

Department of the Treasury
Internal Revenue Service   (99)

Schedule A—Itemized Deductions

(Schedule B is on back)

► Attach to Form 1040. ► See Instructions for Schedules A and B (Form 1040).

OMB No. 1545-0074

1995

Attachment
Sequence No. **07**

Name(s) shown on Form 1040

Your social security number

Medical and Dental Expenses	**Caution:** *Do not include expenses reimbursed or paid by others.*	
	1 Medical and dental expenses (see page A-1)	**1**
	2 Enter amount from Form 1040, line 32 . **2**	
	3 Multiply line 2 above by 7.5% (.075)	**3**
	4 Subtract line 3 from line 1. If line 3 is more than line 1, enter -0-	**4**
Taxes You Paid (See page A-1.)	5 State and local income taxes	**5**
	6 Real estate taxes (see page A-2)	**6**
	7 Personal property taxes	**7**
	8 Other taxes. List type and amount ►	**8**
	9 Add lines 5 through 8	**9**
Interest You Paid (See page A-2.)	10 Home mortgage interest and points reported to you on Form 1098	**10**
	11 Home mortgage interest not reported to you on Form 1098. If paid to the person from whom you bought the home, see page A-3 and show that person's name, identifying no., and address ►	**11**
Note: Personal interest is not deductible.	12 Points not reported to you on Form 1098. See page A-3 for special rules. . . .	**12**
	13 Investment interest. If required, attach Form 4952. (See page A-3.)	**13**
	14 Add lines 10 through 13	**14**
Gifts to Charity If you made a gift and got a benefit for it, see page A-3.	15 Gifts by cash or check. If you made any gift of $250 or more, see page A-3	**15**
	16 Other than by cash or check. If any gift of $250 or more, see page A-3. If over $500, you **MUST** attach Form 8283	**16**
	17 Carryover from prior year	**17**
	18 Add lines 15 through 17	**18**
Casualty and Theft Losses	19 Casualty or theft loss(es). Attach Form 4684. (See page A-4.)	**19**
Job Expenses and Most Other Miscellaneous Deductions (See page A-5 for expenses to deduct here.)	20 Unreimbursed employee expenses—job travel, union dues, job education, etc. If required, you **MUST** attach Form 2106 or 2106-EZ. (See page A-5.) ►	**20**
	21 Tax preparation fees	**21**
	22 Other expenses—investment, safe deposit box, etc. List type and amount ►	**22**
	23 Add lines 20 through 22	**23**
	24 Enter amount from Form 1040, line 32 . **24**	
	25 Multiply line 24 above by 2% (.02)	**25**
	26 Subtract line 25 from line 23. If line 25 is more than line 23, enter -0- . . .	**26**
Other Miscellaneous Deductions	27 Other—from list on page A-5. List type and amount ►	**27**
Total Itemized Deductions	28 Is Form 1040, line 32, over $114,700 (over $57,350 if married filing separately)?	
	NO. Your deduction is not limited. Add the amounts in the far right column for lines 4 through 27. Also, enter on Form 1040, line 34, the **larger** of this amount or your standard deduction.	► **28**
	YES. Your deduction may be limited. See page A-5 for the amount to enter.	

For Paperwork Reduction Act Notice, see Form 1040 instructions.   Cat. No. 11330X   Schedule A (Form 1040) 1995

Schedules A&B (Form 1040) 1995   OMB No. 1545-0074   Page **2**

Name(s) shown on Form 1040. Do not enter name and social security number if shown on other side. | **Your social security number**

Schedule B—Interest and Dividend Income

Attachment Sequence No. **08**

Part I
Interest Income

(See pages 15 and B-1.)

Note: If you received a Form 1099-INT, Form 1099-OID, or substitute statement from a brokerage firm, list the firm's name as the payer and enter the total interest shown on that form.

Note: *If you had over $400 in taxable interest income, you must also complete Part III.*

1 List name of payer. If any interest is from a seller-financed mortgage and the buyer used the property as a personal residence, see page B-1 and list this interest first. Also, show that buyer's social security number and address ▶ | **Amount**

	1

2 Add the amounts on line 1 . . . . | 2 |

3 Excludable interest on series EE U.S. savings bonds issued after 1989 from Form 8815, line 14. You MUST attach Form 8815 to Form 1040 . . . . | 3 |

4 Subtract line 3 from line 2. Enter the result here and on Form 1040, line 8a ▶ | 4 |

Part II
Dividend Income

(See pages 15 and B-1.)

Note: If you received a Form 1099-DIV or substitute statement from a brokerage firm, list the firm's name as the payer and enter the total dividends shown on that form.

Note: *If you had over $400 in gross dividends and/or other distributions on stock, you must also complete Part III.*

5 List name of payer. Include gross dividends and/or other distributions on stock here. Any capital gain distributions and nontaxable distributions will be deducted on lines 7 and 8 ▶ | **Amount**

	5

6 Add the amounts on line 5 . . . . | 6 |

7 Capital gain distributions. Enter here and on Schedule D* . | 7 |

8 Nontaxable distributions. (See the inst. for Form 1040, line 9.) | 8 |

9 Add lines 7 and 8 . . . . | 9 |

10 Subtract line 9 from line 6. Enter the result here and on Form 1040, line 9 . ▶ | 10 |

If you do not need Schedule D to report any other gains or losses, see the instructions for Form 1040, line 13, on page 16.

Part III
Foreign Accounts and Trusts

(See page B-2.)

If you had over $400 of interest or dividends **or** had a foreign account or were a grantor of, or a transferor to, a foreign trust, you must complete this part. | Yes | No

11a At any time during 1995, did you have an interest in or a signature or other authority over a financial account in a foreign country, such as a bank account, securities account, or other financial account? See page B-2 for exceptions and filing requirements for Form TD F 90-22.1 . . . .

b If "Yes," enter the name of the foreign country ▶

12 Were you the grantor of, or transferor to, a foreign trust that existed during 1995, whether or not you have any beneficial interest in it? If "Yes," you may have to file Form 3520, 3520-A, or 926 .

For Paperwork Reduction Act Notice, see Form 1040 instructions.   *Printed on recycled paper*   **Schedule B (Form 1040) 1995**

SCHEDULE C
(Form 1040)

Department of the Treasury
Internal Revenue Service (99)

Profit or Loss From Business
(Sole Proprietorship)

▶ Partnerships, joint ventures, etc., must file Form 1065.

▶ Attach to Form 1040 or Form 1041.   ▶ See Instructions for Schedule C (Form 1040).

OMB No. 1545-0074

1995

Attachment
Sequence No. **09**

Name of proprietor	Social security number (SSN)

A Principal business or profession, including product or service (see page C-1)

B Enter principal business code
(see page C-6) ▶

C Business name. If no separate business name, leave blank.

D Employer ID number (EIN), if any

E Business address (including suite or room no.) ▶ ....
City, town or post office, state, and ZIP code

F Accounting method: (1) ☐ Cash   (2) ☐ Accrual   (3) ☐ Other (specify) ▶ ....

G Method(s) used to value closing inventory: (1) ☐ Cost   (2) ☐ Lower of cost or market   (3) ☐ Other (attach explanation)   (4) ☐ Does not apply (if checked, skip line H)

	Yes	No

H Was there any change in determining quantities, costs, or valuations between opening and closing inventory? If "Yes," attach explanation

I Did you "materially participate" in the operation of this business during 1995? If "No," see page C-2 for limit on losses.

J If you started or acquired this business during 1995, check here .... ▶ ☐

Part I   Income

1	Gross receipts or sales. **Caution:** *If this income was reported to you on Form W-2 and the "Statutory employee" box on that form was checked, see page C-2 and check here* .... ▶ ☐	1
2	Returns and allowances	2
3	Subtract line 2 from line 1	3
4	Cost of goods sold (from line 40 on page 2)	4
5	**Gross profit.** Subtract line 4 from line 3	5
6	Other income, including Federal and state gasoline or fuel tax credit or refund (see page C-2)	6
7	**Gross income.** Add lines 5 and 6 .... ▶	7

Part II   Expenses. Enter expenses for business use of your home **only** on line 30.

8	Advertising	8		19 Pension and profit-sharing plans	19	
9	Bad debts from sales or services (see page C-3)	9		20 Rent or lease (see page C-4):		
10	Car and truck expenses (see page C-3)	10		**a** Vehicles, machinery, and equipment	20a	
11	Commissions and fees	11		**b** Other business property	20b	
12	Depletion	12		21 Repairs and maintenance	21	
				22 Supplies (not included in Part III)	22	
13	Depreciation and section 179 expense deduction (not included in Part III) (see page C-3)	13		23 Taxes and licenses	23	
				24 Travel, meals, and entertainment:		
14	Employee benefit programs (other than on line 19)	14		**a** Travel	24a	
15	Insurance (other than health)	15		**b** Meals and entertainment		
16	Interest:			**c** Enter 50% of line 24b subject to limitations (see page C-4)		
a	Mortgage (paid to banks, etc.)	16a		**d** Subtract line 24c from line 24b	24d	
b	Other	16b		25 Utilities	25	
17	Legal and professional services	17		26 Wages (less employment credits)	26	
18	Office expense	18		27 Other expenses (from line 46 on page 2)	27	

28	**Total expenses** before expenses for business use of home. Add lines 8 through 27 in columns. ▶	28	
29	Tentative profit (loss). Subtract line 28 from line 7	29	
30	Expenses for business use of your home. Attach **Form 8829**	30	
31	**Net profit or (loss).** Subtract line 30 from line 29.		
	• If a profit, enter on **Form 1040, line 12,** and ALSO on **Schedule SE, line 2** (statutory employees, see page C-5). Estates and trusts, enter on Form 1041, line 3.	31	
	• If a loss, you MUST go on to line 32.		
32	If you have a loss, check the box that describes your investment in this activity (see page C-5).		
	• If you checked 32a, enter the loss on **Form 1040, line 12,** and ALSO on **Schedule SE, line 2** (statutory employees, see page C-5). Estates and trusts, enter on Form 1041, line 3.	32a ☐ All investment is at risk.	
	• If you checked 32b, you MUST attach **Form 6198.**	32b ☐ Some investment is not at risk.	

For Paperwork Reduction Act Notice, see Form 1040 instructions.   Cat. No. 11334P   Schedule C (Form 1040) 1995

Part III   **Cost of Goods Sold** (see page C-5)

33	Inventory at beginning of year. If different from last year's closing inventory, attach explanation . .	33
34	Purchases less cost of items withdrawn for personal use	34
35	Cost of labor. Do not include salary paid to yourself	35
36	Materials and supplies	36
37	Other costs	37
38	Add lines 33 through 37	38
39	Inventory at end of year	39
40	**Cost of goods sold.** Subtract line 39 from line 38. Enter the result here and on page 1, line 4 . .	40

Part IV   **Information on Your Vehicle.** Complete this part **ONLY** if you are claiming car or truck expenses on line 10 and are not required to file Form 4562 for this business. See the instructions for line 13 on page C-3 to find out if you must file.

41   When did you place your vehicle in service for business purposes? (month, day, year) ▶ ..../......../........ .

42   Of the total number of miles you drove your vehicle during 1995, enter the number of miles you used your vehicle for:

a   Business ....   **b** Commuting ....   **c** Other ....

43   Do you (or your spouse) have another vehicle available for personal use? . . . . ☐ **Yes**   ☐ **No**

44   Was your vehicle available for use during off-duty hours? . . . . ☐ **Yes**   ☐ **No**

45a   Do you have evidence to support your deduction? . . . . ☐ **Yes**   ☐ **No**
   b   If "Yes," is the evidence written? . . . . ☐ **Yes**   ☐ **No**

Part V   **Other Expenses.** List below business expenses not included on lines 8–26 or line 30.

....		
....		
....		
....		
....		
....		
....		
....		
46 **Total other expenses.** Enter here and on page 1, line 27	46	

✪ *Printed on recycled paper*

SCHEDULE D (Form 1040)	Capital Gains and Losses	OMB No. 1545-0074
Department of the Treasury Internal Revenue Service (99)	► Attach to Form 1040. ► See Instructions for Schedule D (Form 1040). ► Use lines 20 and 22 for more space to list transactions for lines 1 and 9.	1995 Attachment Sequence No. 12

Name(s) shown on Form 1040

Your social security number

Part I — Short-Term Capital Gains and Losses—Assets Held One Year or Less

(a) Description of property (Example: 100 sh. XYZ Co.)	(b) Date acquired (Mo., day, yr.)	(c) Date sold (Mo., day, yr.)	(d) Sales price (see page D-3)	(e) Cost or other basis (see page D-3)	(f) LOSS If (e) is more than (d), subtract (d) from (e)	(g) GAIN If (d) is more than (e), subtract (e) from (d)
1						

2 Enter your short-term totals, if any, from line 21 . . . . **2**

3 Total short-term sales price amounts. Add column (d) of lines 1 and 2 . . . **3**

4 Short-term gain from Forms 2119 and 6252, and short-term gain or loss from Forms 4684, 6781, and 8824 . . . . **4**

5 Net short-term gain or loss from partnerships, S corporations, estates, and trusts from Schedule(s) K-1 . . . . **5**

6 Short-term capital loss carryover. Enter the amount, if any, from line 9 of your 1994 Capital Loss Carryover Worksheet **6**

7 Add lines 1 through 6 in columns (f) and (g) . . . . **7** ( )

8 **Net short-term capital gain or (loss).** Combine columns (f) and (g) of line 7 . . . . . ► **8**

Part II — Long-Term Capital Gains and Losses—Assets Held More Than One Year

9						

10 Enter your long-term totals, if any, from line 23 . . . . **10**

11 Total long-term sales price amounts. Add column (d) of lines 9 and 10 . . . **11**

12 Gain from Form 4797; long-term gain from Forms 2119, 2439, and 6252; and long-term gain or loss from Forms 4684, 6781, and 8824 . . . . . **12**

13 Net long-term gain or loss from partnerships, S corporations, estates, and trusts from Schedule(s) K-1 . . . . . **13**

14 Capital gain distributions **14**

15 Long-term capital loss carryover. Enter the amount, if any, from line 14 of your 1994 Capital Loss Carryover Worksheet **15**

16 Add lines 9 through 15 in columns (f) and (g) . . . . **16** ( )

17 **Net long-term capital gain or (loss).** Combine columns (f) and (g) of line 16 . . . . . ► **17**

Part III — Summary of Parts I and II

18 Combine lines 8 and 17. If a loss, go to line 19. If a gain, enter the gain on Form 1040, line 13. **Note:** If both lines 17 and 18 are gains, see the **Capital Gain Tax Worksheet** on page 24 . . **18**

19 If line 18 is a loss, enter here and as a (loss) on Form 1040, line 13, the **smaller** of these losses:

a The loss on line 18; **or**

b ($3,000) or, if married filing separately, ($1,500) . . . . **19** ( )

Note: See the **Capital Loss Carryover Worksheet** on page D-3 if the loss on line 18 exceeds the loss on line 19 **or** if Form 1040, line 35, is a loss.

For Paperwork Reduction Act Notice, see Form 1040 instructions.   Cat. No. 11338H   Schedule D (Form 1040) 1995

Schedule D (Form 1040) 1995   Attachment Sequence No. **12**   Page **2**

Name(s) shown on Form 1040. Do not enter name and social security number if shown on other side. | **Your social security number**

Part IV   Short-Term Capital Gains and Losses—Assets Held One Year or Less *(Continuation of Part I)*

(a) Description of property (Example: 100 sh. XYZ Co.)	(b) Date acquired (Mo., day, yr.)	(c) Date sold (Mo., day, yr.)	(d) Sales price (see page D-3)	(e) Cost or other basis (see page D-3)	(f) LOSS If (e) is more than (d), subtract (d) from (e)	(g) GAIN If (d) is more than (e), subtract (e) from (d)
20						
21 Short-term totals. Add columns (d), (f), and (g) of line 20. Enter here and on line 2 . **21**						

Part V   Long-Term Capital Gains and Losses—Assets Held More Than One Year *(Continuation of Part II)*

22						
23 Long-term totals. Add columns (d), (f), and (g) of line 22. Enter here and on line 10 . **23**						

Printed on recycled paper

SCHEDULE E
(Form 1040)

Department of the Treasury
Internal Revenue Service (99)

Supplemental Income and Loss
(From rental real estate, royalties, partnerships,
S corporations, estates, trusts, REMICs, etc.)

▶ **Attach to Form 1040 or Form 1041.**   ▶ **See Instructions for Schedule E (Form 1040).**

OMB No. 1545-0074

1995

Attachment
Sequence No. **13**

Name(s) shown on return

Your social security number

Part I   **Income or Loss From Rental Real Estate and Royalties**   **Note:** *Report income and expenses from your business of renting personal property on* **Schedule C** *or* **C-EZ** *(see page E-1). Report farm rental income or loss from* **Form 4835** *on page 2, line 39.*

1   Show the kind and location of each **rental real estate property:**

A   --

B   --

C   --

2   For each rental real estate property listed on line 1, did you or your family use it for personal purposes for more than the greater of 14 days or 10% of the total days rented at fair rental value during the tax year? (See page E-1.)

	Yes	No
A		
B		
C		

Income:

		Properties			Totals (Add columns A, B, and C.)
		A	**B**	**C**	
3 Rents received	**3**				**3**
4 Royalties received	**4**				**4**

Expenses:

		A	B	C	Totals
5 Advertising	**5**				
6 Auto and travel (see page E-2)	**6**				
7 Cleaning and maintenance	**7**				
8 Commissions	**8**				
9 Insurance	**9**				
10 Legal and other professional fees	**10**				
11 Management fees	**11**				
12 Mortgage interest paid to banks, etc. (see page E-2)	**12**				**12**
13 Other interest	**13**				
14 Repairs	**14**				
15 Supplies	**15**				
16 Taxes	**16**				
17 Utilities	**17**				
18 Other (list) ▶ ----------	**18**				
19 Add lines 5 through 18	**19**				**19**
20 Depreciation expense or depletion (see page E-2)	**20**				**20**
21 Total expenses. Add lines 19 and 20	**21**				
22 Income or (loss) from rental real estate or royalty properties. Subtract line 21 from line 3 (rents) or line 4 (royalties). If the result is a (loss), see page E-2 to find out if you must file **Form 6198**.	**22**				
23 Deductible rental real estate loss. **Caution:** *Your rental real estate loss on line 22 may be limited. See page E-3 to find out if you must file* **Form 8582**. *Real estate professionals must complete line 42 on page 2.*	**23**	( )	( )	( )	

24   **Income.** Add positive amounts shown on line 22. **Do not** include any losses   **24**

25   **Losses.** Add royalty losses from line 22 and rental real estate losses from line 23. Enter the total losses here   **25** ( )

26   Total rental real estate and royalty income or (loss). Combine lines 24 and 25. Enter the result here. If Parts II, III, IV, and line 39 on page 2 do not apply to you, also enter this amount on Form 1040, line 17. Otherwise, include this amount in the total on line 40 on page 2   **26**

For Paperwork Reduction Act Notice, see Form 1040 instructions.   Cat. No. 11344L   **Schedule E (Form 1040) 1995**

Name(s) shown on return. Do not enter name and social security number if shown on other side.	**Your social security number**

Note: *If you report amounts from farming or fishing on Schedule E, you must enter your gross income from those activities on line 41 below. Real estate professionals must complete line 42 below.*

Part II **Income or Loss From Partnerships and S Corporations** Note: *If you report a loss from an at-risk activity, you MUST check either column (e) or (f) of line 27 to describe your investment in the activity. See page E-4. If you check column (f), you must attach Form 6198.*

27	(a) Name	(b) Enter P for partnership; S for S corporation	(c) Check if foreign partnership	(d) Employer identification number	Investment At Risk? (e) All is at risk	(f) Some is not at risk
A						
B						
C						
D						
E						

	Passive Income and Loss		Nonpassive Income and Loss		
	(g) Passive loss allowed (attach Form 8582 if required)	(h) Passive income from Schedule K–1	(i) Nonpassive loss from Schedule K–1	(j) Section 179 expense deduction from Form 4562	(k) Nonpassive income from Schedule K–1
A					
B					
C					
D					
E					
28a Totals					
b Totals					

29	Add columns (h) and (k) of line 28a	29	
30	Add columns (g), (i), and (j) of line 28b	30 (	)
31	Total partnership and S corporation income or (loss). Combine lines 29 and 30. Enter the result here and include in the total on line 40 below	31	

Part III **Income or Loss From Estates and Trusts**

32	(a) Name	(b) Employer identification number
A		
B		

	Passive Income and Loss		Nonpassive Income and Loss	
	(c) Passive deduction or loss allowed (attach Form 8582 if required)	(d) Passive income from Schedule K–1	(e) Deduction or loss from Schedule K–1	(f) Other income from Schedule K–1
A				
B				
33a Totals				
b Totals				

34	Add columns (d) and (f) of line 33a	34	
35	Add columns (c) and (e) of line 33b	35 (	)
36	Total estate and trust income or (loss). Combine lines 34 and 35. Enter the result here and include in the total on line 40 below	36	

Part IV **Income or Loss From Real Estate Mortgage Investment Conduits (REMICs)—Residual Holder**

37	(a) Name	(b) Employer identification number	(c) Excess inclusion from Schedules Q, line 2c (see page E-4)	(d) Taxable income (net loss) from Schedules Q, line 1b	(e) Income from Schedules Q, line 3b

38	Combine columns (d) and (e) only. Enter the result here and include in the total on line 40 below	38	

Part V **Summary**

39	Net farm rental income or (loss) from **Form 4835**. Also, complete line 41 below	39	
40	TOTAL income or (loss). Combine lines 26, 31, 36, 38, and 39. Enter the result here and on Form 1040, line 17 ▶	40	

41	**Reconciliation of Farming and Fishing Income.** Enter your **gross** farming and fishing income reported on Form 4835, line 7; Schedule K-1 (Form 1065), line 15b; Schedule K-1 (Form 1120S), line 23; and Schedule K-1 (Form 1041), line 13 (see page E-4)	41	
42	**Reconciliation for Real Estate Professionals.** If you were a real estate professional (see page E-3), enter the net income or (loss) you reported anywhere on Form 1040 from all rental real estate activities in which you materially participated under the passive activity loss rules . . .	42	

✱ *Printed on recycled paper*

Schedule R
(Form 1040)

Department of the Treasury
Internal Revenue Service   (99)

Credit for the Elderly or the Disabled

▶ **Attach to Form 1040.**   ▶ **See separate instructions for Schedule R.**

OMB No. 1545-0074

1995

Attachment
Sequence No. **16**

Name(s) shown on Form 1040

Your social security number

You may be able to take this credit and reduce your tax if by the end of 1995:

● You were age 65 or older,   **OR**   ● You were under age 65, you retired on **permanent and total** disability, and you received taxable disability income.

But you must also meet other tests. See the separate instructions for Schedule R.

Note: *In most cases, the IRS can figure the credit for you. See page 35 of the Form 1040 instructions.*

Part I   **Check the Box for Your Filing Status and Age**

If your filing status is:	And by the end of 1995:	Check only one box:
Single, Head of household, or Qualifying widow(er) with dependent child	**1** You were 65 or older **1**	☐
	2 You were under 65 and you retired on permanent and total disability . . . **2**	☐
	3 Both spouses were 65 or older **3**	☐
	4 Both spouses were under 65, but only one spouse retired on permanent and total disability **4**	☐
Married filing a joint return	**5** Both spouses were under 65, and both retired on permanent and total disability **5**	☐
	6 One spouse was 65 or older, and the other spouse was under 65 and retired on permanent and total disability **6**	☐
	7 One spouse was 65 or older, and the other spouse was under 65 and **NOT** retired on permanent and total disability **7**	☐
Married filing a separate return	**8** You were 65 or older and you lived apart from your spouse for all of 1995 . . **8**	☐
	9 You were under 65, you retired on permanent and total disability, and you lived apart from your spouse for all of 1995 . . . . **9**	☐

Did you check box 1, 3, 7, or 8?	── Yes ──▶ Skip Part II and complete Part III on back.
	── No ──▶ Complete Parts II and III.

Part II   **Statement of Permanent and Total Disability** (Complete **only** if you checked box 2, 4, 5, 6, or 9 above.)

IF: 1 You filed a physician's statement for this disability for 1983 or an earlier year, or you filed a statement for tax years after 1983 and your physician signed line B on the statement, **AND**

    2 Due to your continued disabled condition, you were unable to engage in any substantial gainful activity in 1995, check this box . . . . ▶ ☐

● If you checked this box, you do not have to file another statement for 1995.

● If you **did not** check this box, have your physician complete the statement below.

Physician's Statement (See instructions at bottom of page 2.)

    I certify that _____

Name of disabled person

was permanently and totally disabled on January 1, 1976, or January 1, 1977, **OR** was permanently and totally disabled on the date he or she retired. If retired after 1976, enter the date retired. ▶ _____

Physician: Sign your name on **either** line A or B below.

A The disability has lasted or can be expected to last continuously for at least a year . . . .

B There is no reasonable probability that the disabled condition will ever improve . . . .

	Physician's signature	Date
	Physician's signature	Date
Physician's name	Physician's address	

For Paperwork Reduction Act Notice, see Form 1040 instructions.   Cat. No. 11359K   **Schedule R (Form 1040) 1995**

Part III	**Figure Your Credit**

10 If you checked (in Part I):   Enter:
   Box 1, 2, 4, or 7 . . . . $5,000 ⎫
   Box 3, 5, or 6 . . . . $7,500 ⎬ **10**
   Box 8 or 9 . . . . $3,750 ⎭

   ┌─────────────────┐
   │ Did you check   │── Yes ─────▶ You **must** complete line 11.
   │ box 2, 4, 5, 6, │── No ──────▶ Enter the amount from line 10 on
   │ or 9 in Part I? │   line 12 and go to line 13.
   └─────────────────┘

11 If you checked:
   ● Box 6 in Part I, add $5,000 to the taxable disability income of the
     spouse who was under age 65. Enter the total.   ⎫
   ● Box 2, 4, or 9 in Part I, enter your taxable disability income.   ⎬ **11**
   ● Box 5 in Part I, add your taxable disability income to your spouse's   ⎭
     taxable disability income. Enter the total.
   TIP: For more details on what to include on line 11, see the instructions.

12 If you completed line 11, enter the **smaller** of line 10 or line 11; **all others,** enter the amount
   from line 10 . . . . **12**

13 Enter the following pensions, annuities, or disability income that you
   (and your spouse if filing a joint return) received in 1995.

   a Nontaxable part of social security benefits, and   ⎫
   Nontaxable part of railroad retirement benefits treated as   ⎬ . . . **13a**
   social security. See instructions.   ⎭

   b Nontaxable veterans' pensions, and   ⎫
   Any other pension, annuity, or disability benefit that is   ⎬ . . . **13b**
   excluded from income under any other provision of law.   ⎭
   See instructions.

   c Add lines 13a and 13b. (Even though these income items are not
   taxable, they **must** be included here to figure your credit.) If you did
   not receive any of the types of nontaxable income listed on line 13a
   or 13b, enter -0- on line 13c **13c**

14 Enter the amount from Form 1040, line 32   **14**

15 If you checked (in Part I):   Enter:
   Box 1 or 2 . . . . $7,500 ⎫
   Box 3, 4, 5, 6, or 7 . . . . $10,000 ⎬ **15**
   Box 8 or 9 . . . . . . $5,000 ⎭

16 Subtract line 15 from line 14. If zero or less,
   enter -0- **16**

17 Enter one-half of line 16 . . . . **17**

18 Add lines 13c and 17 . . . . **18**

19 Subtract line 18 from line 12. If zero or less, **stop;** you **cannot** take the credit. Otherwise, go to
   line 20 . . . . **19**

20 Multiply line 19 by 15% (.15). Enter the result here and on Form 1040, line 42. **Caution:** *If you
   file Schedule C, C-EZ, D, E, or F (Form 1040), your credit may be limited. See the instructions
   for line 20 for the amount of credit you can claim* **20**

Instructions for Physician's Statement

Taxpayer

If you retired after 1976, enter the date you retired in the space provided in Part II.

Physician

A person is permanently and totally disabled if **both** of the following apply:

   1. He or she cannot engage in any substantial gainful activity because of a physical or mental condition, and

2. A physician determines that the disability has lasted or can be expected to last continuously for at least a year or can lead to death.

 Printed on recycled paper

SCHEDULE SE	**Self-Employment Tax**	OMB No. 1545-0074
(Form 1040)	▶ See Instructions for Schedule SE (Form 1040).	**1995**
Department of the Treasury Internal Revenue Service (99)	▶ **Attach to Form 1040.**	Attachment Sequence No. **17**

Name of person with **self-employment** income (as shown on Form 1040)	Social security number of person with **self-employment** income ▶	⋮ ⋮

Who Must File Schedule SE

You must file Schedule SE if:

- You had net earnings from self-employment from **other than** church employee income (line 4 of Short Schedule SE or line 4c of Long Schedule SE) of $400 or more, **OR**
- You had church employee income of $108.28 or more. Income from services you performed as a minister or a member of a religious order **is not** church employee income. See page SE-1.

Note: *Even if you have a loss or a small amount of income from self-employment, it may be to your benefit to file Schedule SE and use either "optional method" in Part II of Long Schedule SE. See page SE-3.*

Exception. If your only self-employment income was from earnings as a minister, member of a religious order, or Christian Science practitioner **and** you filed Form 4361 and received IRS approval not to be taxed on those earnings, **do not** file Schedule SE. Instead, write "Exempt–Form 4361" on Form 1040, line 47.

May I Use Short Schedule SE or MUST I Use Long Schedule SE?

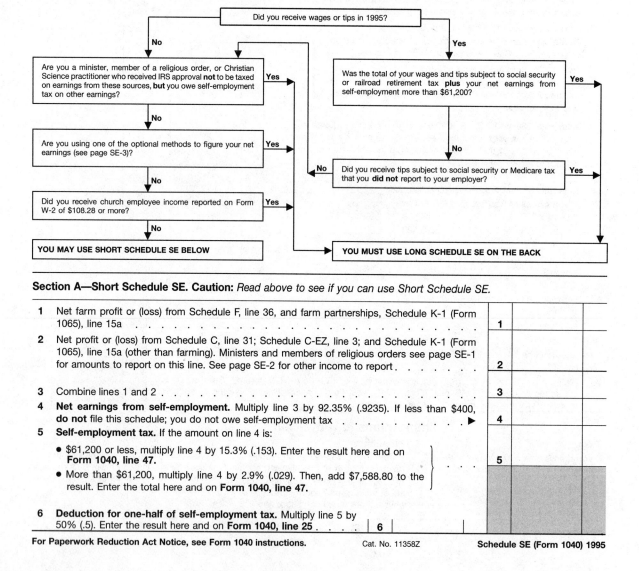

Section A—Short Schedule SE. Caution: *Read above to see if you can use Short Schedule SE.*

1	Net farm profit or (loss) from Schedule F, line 36, and farm partnerships, Schedule K-1 (Form 1065), line 15a	**1**	
2	Net profit or (loss) from Schedule C, line 31; Schedule C-EZ, line 3; and Schedule K-1 (Form 1065), line 15a (other than farming). Ministers and members of religious orders see page SE-1 for amounts to report on this line. See page SE-2 for other income to report	**2**	
3	Combine lines 1 and 2	**3**	
4	**Net earnings from self-employment.** Multiply line 3 by 92.35% (.9235). If less than $400, **do not** file this schedule; you do not owe self-employment tax . . . . ▶	**4**	
5	**Self-employment tax.** If the amount on line 4 is: • $61,200 or less, multiply line 4 by 15.3% (.153). Enter the result here and on **Form 1040, line 47.** • More than $61,200, multiply line 4 by 2.9% (.029). Then, add $7,588.80 to the result. Enter the total here and on **Form 1040, line 47.**	**5**	
6	**Deduction for one-half of self-employment tax.** Multiply line 5 by 50% (.5). Enter the result here and on **Form 1040, line 25** **6**		

For Paperwork Reduction Act Notice, see Form 1040 instructions.	Cat. No. 11358Z	Schedule SE (Form 1040) 1995

Name of person with **self-employment** income (as shown on Form 1040)	Social security number of person with **self-employment** income ▶	:	:

Section B—Long Schedule SE

Part I **Self-Employment Tax**

Note: *If your only income subject to self-employment tax is* **church employee income,** *skip lines 1 through 4b. Enter -0- on line 4c and go to line 5a. Income from services you performed as a minister or a member of a religious order* **is not** *church employee income. See page SE-1.*

A If you are a minister, member of a religious order, or Christian Science practitioner **and** you filed Form 4361, but you had $400 or more of **other** net earnings from self-employment, check here and continue with Part I . . . . . . ▶ ☐

1	Net farm profit or (loss) from Schedule F, line 36, and farm partnerships, Schedule K-1 (Form 1065), line 15a. **Note:** *Skip this line if you use the farm optional method. See page SE-3* . .	**1**		
2	Net profit or (loss) from Schedule C, line 31; Schedule C-EZ, line 3; and Schedule K-1 (Form 1065), line 15a (other than farming). Ministers and members of religious orders see page SE-1 for amounts to report on this line. See page SE-2 for other income to report. **Note:** *Skip this line if you use the nonfarm optional method. See page SE-3.*	**2**		
3	Combine lines 1 and 2	**3**		
4a	If line 3 is more than zero, multiply line 3 by 92.35% (.9235). Otherwise, enter amount from line 3	**4a**		
b	If you elected one or both of the optional methods, enter the total of lines 15 and 17 here . .	**4b**		
c	Combine lines 4a and 4b. If less than $400, **do not** file this schedule; you do not owe self-employment tax. **Exception.** If less than $400 and you had **church employee income,** enter -0- and continue ▶	**4c**		
5a	Enter your **church employee income** from Form W-2. **Caution:** *See page SE-1 for definition of church employee income* **5a**	**5b**		
b	Multiply line 5a by 92.35% (.9235). If less than $100, enter -0-			
6	**Net earnings from self-employment.** Add lines 4c and 5b	**6**		
7	Maximum amount of combined wages and self-employment earnings subject to social security tax or the 6.2% portion of the 7.65% railroad retirement (tier 1) tax for 1995	**7**	61,200	00
8a	Total social security wages and tips (total of boxes 3 and 7 on Form(s) W-2) and railroad retirement (tier 1) compensation **8a**			
b	Unreported tips subject to social security tax (from Form 4137, line 9) **8b**			
c	Add lines 8a and 8b	**8c**		
9	Subtract line 8c from line 7. If zero or less, enter -0- here and on line 10 and go to line 11 . ▶	**9**		
10	Multiply the **smaller** of line 6 or line 9 by 12.4% (.124)	**10**		
11	Multiply line 6 by 2.9% (.029)	**11**		
12	**Self-employment tax.** Add lines 10 and 11. Enter here and on **Form 1040, line 47**	**12**		
13	**Deduction for one-half of self-employment tax.** Multiply line 12 by 50% (.5). Enter the result here and on **Form 1040, line 25** **13**			

Part II **Optional Methods To Figure Net Earnings** (See page SE-3.)

Farm Optional Method. You may use this method **only if:**
- Your gross farm income[1] was not more than $2,400, **or**
- Your gross farm income[1] was more than $2,400 and your net farm profits[2] were less than $1,733.

14	Maximum income for optional methods	**14**	1,600	00
15	Enter the **smaller** of: two-thirds (⅔) of gross farm income[1] (not less than zero) **or** $1,600. Also, include this amount on line 4b above	**15**		

Nonfarm Optional Method. You may use this method **only if:**
- Your net nonfarm profits[3] were less than $1,733 and also less than 72.189% of your gross nonfarm income,[4] **and**
- You had net earnings from self-employment of at least $400 in 2 of the prior 3 years.

Caution: *You may use this method no more than five times.*

16	Subtract line 15 from line 14	**16**	
17	Enter the **smaller** of: two-thirds (⅔) of gross nonfarm income[4] (not less than zero) **or** the amount on line 16. Also, include this amount on line 4b above	**17**	

[1] From Schedule F, line 11, and Schedule K-1 (Form 1065), line 15b.
[2] From Schedule F, line 36, and Schedule K-1 (Form 1065), line 15a.
[3] From Schedule C, line 31; Schedule C-EZ, line 3; and Schedule K-1 (Form 1065), line 15a.
[4] From Schedule C, line 7; Schedule C-EZ, line 1; and Schedule K-1 (Form 1065), line 15c.

✪ *Printed on recycled paper*

Form **1041**

Department of the Treasury—Internal Revenue Service

U.S. Income Tax Return for Estates and Trusts

19**95**

For calendar year 1995 or fiscal year beginning _____ , 1995, and ending _____ , 19____

OMB No. 1545-0092

A Type of entity:	Name of estate or trust (If a grantor type trust, see page 7 of the instructions.)	C **Employer identification number**
☐ Decedent's estate		
☐ Simple trust		D Date entity created
☐ Complex trust		
☐ Grantor type trust	Name and title of fiduciary	E Nonexempt charitable and split-interest trusts, check applicable boxes (see page 9 of the instructions):
☐ Bankruptcy estate-Ch. 7		
☐ Bankruptcy estate-Ch. 11	Number, street, and room or suite no. (If a P.O. box, see page 7 of the instructions.)	
☐ Pooled income fund		☐ Described in section 4947(a)(1)
B Number of Schedules K-1 attached (see instructions) ▶	City or town, state, and ZIP code	☐ Not a private foundation
		☐ Described in section 4947(a)(2)

F Check applicable boxes: ☐ Initial return   ☐ Final return   ☐ Amended return   **G** Pooled mortgage account (see page 9 of the instructions):
☐ Change in fiduciary's name   ☐ Change in fiduciary's address   ☐ Bought   ☐ Sold   Date: _____

Income

1	Interest income	1
2	Dividends	2
3	Business income or (loss) (attach Schedule C or C-EZ (Form 1040))	3
4	Capital gain or (loss) (attach Schedule D (Form 1041))	4
5	Rents, royalties, partnerships, other estates and trusts, etc. (attach Schedule E (Form 1040))	5
6	Farm income or (loss) (attach Schedule F (Form 1040))	6
7	Ordinary gain or (loss) (attach Form 4797)	7
8	Other income. List type and amount _____	8
9	**Total income.** Combine lines 1 through 8 ▶	9

Deductions

10	Interest. Check if Form 4952 is attached ▶ ☐	10
11	Taxes	11
12	Fiduciary fees	12
13	Charitable deduction (from Schedule A, line 7)	13
14	Attorney, accountant, and return preparer fees	14
15a	Other deductions NOT subject to the 2% floor (attach schedule)	15a
b	Allowable miscellaneous itemized deductions subject to the 2% floor	15b
16	**Total.** Add lines 10 through 15b	16
17	Adjusted total income or (loss). Subtract line 16 from line 9. Enter here and on Schedule B, line 1 ▶	17
18	Income distribution deduction (from Schedule B, line 17) (attach Schedules K-1 (Form 1041))	18
19	Estate tax deduction (including certain generation-skipping taxes) (attach computation)	19
20	Exemption	20
21	**Total deductions.** Add lines 18 through 20 ▶	21

Tax and Payments

22	Taxable income. Subtract line 21 from line 17. If a loss, see page 13 of the instructions	22
23	**Total tax** (from Schedule G, line 8)	23
24	**Payments: a** 1995 estimated tax payments and amount applied from 1994 return	24a
b	Estimated tax payments allocated to beneficiaries (from Form 1041-T)	24b
c	Subtract line 24b from line 24a	24c
d	Tax paid with extension of time to file: ☐ Form 2758 ☐ Form 8736 ☐ Form 8800	24d
e	Federal income tax withheld. If any is from Form(s) 1099, check ▶ ☐	24e
	Other payments: **f** Form 2439 _____ ; **g** Form 4136 _____ ; Total ▶	24h
25	**Total payments.** Add lines 24c through 24e, and 24h ▶	25
26	Estimated tax penalty (see page 14 of the instructions)	26
27	**Tax due.** If line 25 is smaller than the total of lines 23 and 26, enter amount owed	27
28	**Overpayment.** If line 25 is larger than the total of lines 23 and 26, enter amount overpaid	28
29	Amount of line 28 to be: **a** Credited to 1996 estimated tax ▶ _____ ; **b** Refunded ▶	29

Please Sign Here

Under penalties of perjury, I declare that I have examined this return, including accompanying schedules and statements, and to the best of my knowledge and belief, it is true, correct, and complete. Declaration of preparer (other than fiduciary) is based on all information of which preparer has any knowledge.

▶ _____   ▶ _____

Signature of fiduciary or officer representing fiduciary   Date   EIN of fiduciary if a financial institution (see page 3 of the instructions)

Paid Preparer's Use Only

Preparer's signature ▶	Date	Check if self-employed ▶ ☐	Preparer's social security no.
Firm's name (or yours if self-employed) and address ▶		EIN ▶	
		ZIP code ▶	

For Paperwork Reduction Act Notice, see page 1 of the separate instructions.   Cat. No. 11370H   Form **1041** (1995)

Form 1041 (1995)   Page **2**

Schedule A — Charitable Deduction. Do not complete for a simple trust or a pooled income fund.

1	Amounts paid for charitable purposes from gross income	**1**
2	Amounts permanently set aside for charitable purposes from gross income	**2**
3	Add lines 1 and 2	**3**
4	Tax-exempt income allocable to charitable contributions (see page 15 of the instructions) . .	**4**
5	Subtract line 4 from line 3	**5**
6	Capital gains for the tax year allocated to corpus and paid or permanently set aside for charitable purposes	**6**
7	**Charitable deduction.** Add lines 5 and 6. Enter here and on page 1, line 13.	**7**

Schedule B — Income Distribution Deduction

1	Adjusted total income (from page 1, line 17) (see page 15 of the instructions)	**1**
2	Adjusted tax-exempt interest	**2**
3	Total net gain from Schedule D (Form 1041), line 17, column (a) (see page 15 of the instructions)	**3**
4	Enter amount from Schedule A, line 6	**4**
5	Long-term capital gain for the tax year included on Schedule A, line 3	**5**
6	Short-term capital gain for the tax year included on Schedule A, line 3	**6**
7	If the amount on page 1, line 4, is a capital loss, enter here as a positive figure	**7**
8	If the amount on page 1, line 4, is a capital gain, enter here as a negative figure	**8**
9	**Distributable net income (DNI).** Combine lines 1 through 8. If zero or less, enter -0-. . . .	**9**
10	If a complex trust, enter accounting income for the tax year as determined under the governing instrument and applicable local law **10**	
11	Income required to be distributed currently	**11**
12	Other amounts paid, credited, or otherwise required to be distributed	**12**
13	Total distributions. Add lines 11 and 12. If greater than line 10, see page 16 of the instructions	**13**
14	Enter the amount of tax-exempt income included on line 13	**14**
15	Tentative income distribution deduction. Subtract line 14 from line 13	**15**
16	Tentative income distribution deduction. Subtract line 2 from line 9. If zero or less, enter -0-	**16**
17	**Income distribution deduction.** Enter the smaller of line 15 or line 16 here and on page 1, line 18	**17**

Schedule G — Tax Computation (see page 16 of the instructions)

1	**Tax: a** ☐ Tax rate schedule or ☐ Schedule D (Form 1041) . .	**1a**
	b Other taxes	**1b**
	c Total. Add lines 1a and 1b. . . . . ▶	**1c**
2a	Foreign tax credit (attach Form 1116)	**2a**
b	Check: ☐ Nonconventional source fuel credit ☐ Form 8834 . . .	**2b**
c	General business credit. Enter here and check which forms are attached:	
	☐ Form 3800 or ☐ Forms (specify) ▶	**2c**
d	Credit for prior year minimum tax (attach Form 8801)	**2d**
3	**Total credits.** Add lines 2a through 2d . . . . ▶	**3**
4	Subtract line 3 from line 1c	**4**
5	Recapture taxes. Check if from: ☐ Form 4255 ☐ Form 8611.	**5**
6	Alternative minimum tax (from Schedule I, line 41).	**6**
7	Household employment taxes. Attach Schedule H (Form 1040)	**7**
8	**Total tax.** Add lines 4 through 7. Enter here and on page 1, line 23 . . . . ▶	**8**

Other Information

		Yes	No
1	Did the estate or trust receive tax-exempt income? If "Yes," attach a computation of the allocation of expenses. Enter the amount of tax-exempt interest income and exempt-interest dividends ▶ $		
2	Did the estate or trust receive all or any part of the earnings (salary, wages, and other compensation) of any individual by reason of a contract assignment or similar arrangement?		
3	At any time during calendar year 1995, did the estate or trust have an interest in or a signature or other authority over a bank, securities, or other financial account in a foreign country? See page 18 of the instructions for exceptions and filing requirements for Form TD F 90-22.1. If "Yes," enter the name of the foreign country ▶		
4	Was the estate or trust the grantor of, or transferor to, a foreign trust which existed during the current tax year, whether or not the estate or trust has any beneficial interest in it? If "Yes," you may have to file Form 3520, 3520-A, or 926 .		
5	Did the estate or trust receive, or pay, any seller-financed mortgage interest? If "Yes," see page 18 of the instructions for required attachment		
6	If this is a complex trust making the section 663(b) election, check here (see page 18 of the instructions) ▶ ☐		
7	To make a section 643(e)(3) election, attach Schedule D (Form 1041), and check here (see page 18). . ▶ ☐		
8	If the decedent's estate has been open for more than 2 years, check here . . . . ▶ ☐		

Form 1041 (1995)   Page **3**

| **Schedule I** | **Alternative Minimum Tax** (see pages 18 through 22 of the instructions) |

Part I—Estate's or Trust's Share of Alternative Minimum Taxable Income

1	Adjusted total income or (loss) (from page 1, line 17)	1	
2	Net operating loss deduction. Enter as a positive amount	2	
3	Add lines 1 and 2	3	
4	**Adjustments and tax preference items:**		
a	Interest	4a	
b	Taxes	4b	
c	Miscellaneous itemized deductions (from page 1, line 15b)	4c	
d	Refund of taxes	4d ( )	
e	Depreciation of property placed in service after 1986	4e	
f	Circulation and research and experimental expenditures paid or incurred after 1986	4f	
g	Mining exploration and development costs paid or incurred after 1986	4g	
h	Long-term contracts entered into after February 28, 1986	4h	
i	Pollution control facilities placed in service after 1986	4i	
j	Installment sales of certain property	4j	
k	Adjusted gain or loss (including incentive stock options)	4k	
l	Certain loss limitations	4l	
m	Tax shelter farm activities	4m	
n	Passive activities	4n	
o	Beneficiaries of other trusts or decedent's estates	4o	
p	Tax-exempt interest from specified private activity bonds	4p	
q	Depletion	4q	
r	Accelerated depreciation of real property placed in service before 1987	4r	
s	Accelerated depreciation of leased personal property placed in service before 1987	4s	
t	Intangible drilling costs	4t	
u	Other adjustments	4u	
5	Combine lines 4a through 4u	5	
6	Add lines 3 and 5	6	
7	Alternative tax net operating loss deduction (see page 21 of the instructions for limitations) . .	7	
8	Adjusted alternative minimum taxable income. Subtract line 7 from line 6. Enter here and on line 13	8	
	Note: *Complete Part II before going to line 9.*		
9	Income distribution deduction from line 27	9	
10	Estate tax deduction (from page 1, line 19)	10	
11	Add lines 9 and 10	11	
12	Estate's or trust's share of alternative minimum taxable income. Subtract line 11 from line 8	12	

If line 12 is:

- $22,500 or less, stop here and enter -0- on Schedule G, line 6. The estate or trust is not liable for the alternative minimum tax.
- Over $22,500, but less than $165,000, go to line 28.
- $165,000 or more, enter the amount from line 12 on line 34 and go to line 35.

(continued on page 4)

Part II—Income Distribution Deduction on a Minimum Tax Basis

13	Adjusted alternative minimum taxable income (from line 8)	**13**	
14	Adjusted tax-exempt interest (other than amounts included on line 4p)	**14**	
15	Total net gain from Schedule D (Form 1041), line 17, column (a). If a loss, enter -0-	**15**	
16	Capital gains for the tax year allocated to corpus and paid or permanently set aside for charitable purposes (from Schedule A, line 6)	**16**	
17	Capital gains paid or permanently set aside for charitable purposes from current year's income (see page 22 of the instructions).	**17**	
18	Capital gains computed on a minimum tax basis included on line 8	**18**	( )
19	Capital losses computed on a minimum tax basis included on line 8. Enter as a positive amount	**19**	
20	Distributable net alternative minimum taxable income (DNAMTI). Combine lines 13 through 19 .	**20**	
21	Income required to be distributed currently (from Schedule B, line 11)	**21**	
22	Other amounts paid, credited, or otherwise required to be distributed (from Schedule B, line 12)	**22**	
23	Total distributions. Add lines 21 and 22	**23**	
24	Tax-exempt income included on line 23 (other than amounts included on line 4p)	**24**	
25	Tentative income distribution deduction on a minimum tax basis. Subtract line 24 from line 23 .	**25**	
26	Tentative income distribution deduction on a minimum tax basis. Subtract line 14 from line 20 .	**26**	
27	**Income distribution deduction on a minimum tax basis.** Enter the smaller of line 25 or line 26. Enter here and on line 9	**27**	

Part III—Alternative Minimum Tax

28	Exemption amount			**28**	$22,500
29	Enter the amount from line 12	**29**			
30	Phase-out of exemption amount	**30**	$75,000		
31	Subtract line 30 from line 29. If zero or less, enter -0-	**31**			
32	Multiply line 31 by 25% (.25)			**32**	
33	Subtract line 32 from line 28. If zero or less, enter -0-			**33**	
34	Subtract line 33 from line 29			**34**	
35	If line 34 is: • $175,000 or less, multiply line 34 by 26% (.26). • Over $175,000, multiply line 34 by 28% (.28) and subtract $3,500 from the result			**35**	
36	Alternative minimum foreign tax credit (see page 22 of instructions)			**36**	
37	Tentative minimum tax. Subtract line 36 from line 35			**37**	
38	Regular tax before credits (see page 22 of instructions)	**38**			
39	Section 644 tax included on Schedule G, line 1b	**39**			
40	Add lines 38 and 39			**40**	
41	**Alternative minimum tax.** Subtract line 40 from line 37. If zero or less, enter -0-. Enter here and on Schedule G, line 6			**41**	

♻ *Printed on recycled paper*

| SCHEDULE K-1
(Form 1041)

Department of the Treasury
Internal Revenue Service | Beneficiary's Share of Income, Deductions, Credits, etc.
for the calendar year 1995, or fiscal year
beginning .... , 1995, ending .... , 19 ......
▶ Complete a separate Schedule K-1 for each beneficiary. | OMB No. 1545-0092

1995 |

Name of trust or decedent's estate

☐ Amended K-1
☐ Final K-1

| Beneficiary's identifying number ▶ | Estate's or trust's EIN ▶ |
| Beneficiary's name, address, and ZIP code | Fiduciary's name, address, and ZIP code |

(a) Allocable share item		(b) Amount	(c) Calendar year 1995 Form 1040 filers enter the amounts in column (b) on:
1 Interest.	1		Schedule B, Part I, line 1
2 Dividends	2		Schedule B, Part II, line 5
3a Net short-term capital gain	3a		Schedule D, line 5, column (g)
b Net long-term capital gain	3b		Schedule D, line 13, column (g)
4a Annuities, royalties, and other nonpassive income before directly apportioned deductions	4a		Schedule E, Part III, column (f)
b Depreciation	4b		Include on the applicable line of the appropriate tax form
c Depletion	4c		
d Amortization	4d		
5a Trade or business, rental real estate, and other rental income before directly apportioned deductions (see instructions)	5a		Schedule E, Part III
b Depreciation	5b		Include on the applicable line of the appropriate tax form
c Depletion	5c		
d Amortization	5d		
6 Income for minimum tax purposes	6		
7 Income for regular tax purposes (add lines 1 through 3b, 4a, and 5a)	7		
8 Adjustment for minimum tax purposes (subtract line 7 from line 6)	8		Form 6251, line 12
9 Estate tax deduction (including certain generation-skipping transfer taxes)	9		Schedule A, line 27
10 Foreign taxes.	10		Form 1116 or Schedule A (Form 1040), line 8
11 Adjustments and tax preference items (itemize):			
a Accelerated depreciation	11a		Include on the applicable line of Form 6251
b Depletion	11b		
c Amortization	11c		
d Exclusion items	11d		1996 Form 8801
12 Deductions in the final year of trust or decedent's estate:			
a Excess deductions on termination (see instructions)	12a		Schedule A, line 22
b Short-term capital loss carryover	12b		Schedule D, line 5, column (f)
c Long-term capital loss carryover	12c		Schedule D, line 13, column (f)
d Net operating loss (NOL) carryover for regular tax purposes	12d		Form 1040, line 21
e NOL carryover for minimum tax purposes	12e		See the instructions for Form 6251, line 20
f	12f		Include on the applicable line
g	12g		of the appropriate tax form
13 Other (itemize):			
a Payments of estimated taxes credited to you	13a		Form 1040, line 56
b Tax-exempt interest	13b		Form 1040, line 8b
c	13c		
d	13d		
e	13e		Include on the applicable line of the appropriate tax form
f	13f		
g	13g		
h	13h		

For Paperwork Reduction Act Notice, see page 1 of the Instructions for Form 1041.   Cat. No. 11380D   **Schedule K-1 (Form 1041) 1995**

Instructions for Beneficiary Filing Form 1040

Note: *The fiduciary's instructions for completing Schedule K-1 are in the Instructions for Form 1041.*

General Instructions

Purpose of Form

The fiduciary of a trust or decedent's estate uses Schedule K-1 to report your share of the trust's or estate's income, credits, deductions, etc. **Keep it for your records. Do not file it with your tax return.** A copy has been filed with the IRS.

Tax Shelters

If you receive a copy of **Form 8271,** Investor Reporting of Tax Shelter Registration Number, see the instructions for Form 8271 to determine your reporting requirements.

Errors

If you think the fiduciary has made an error on your Schedule K-1, notify the fiduciary and ask for an amended or a corrected Schedule K-1. Do not change any items on your copy. Be sure that the fiduciary sends a copy of the amended Schedule K-1 to the IRS.

Beneficiaries of Generation-Skipping Trusts

If you received **Form 706-GS(D-1),** Notification of Distribution From a Generation-Skipping Trust, and paid a generation-skipping transfer (GST) tax on **Form 706-GS(D),** Generation-Skipping Transfer Tax Return for Distributions, you can deduct the GST tax paid on income distributions on Schedule A (Form 1040), line 8. To figure the deduction, see the instructions for Form 706-GS(D).

Specific Instructions

Lines 3a and 3b

If there is an attachment to this Schedule K-1 reporting a disposition of a passive activity, see the instructions for **Form 8582,** Passive Activity Loss Limitations, for information on the treatment of dispositions of interests in a passive activity.

Lines 5b through 5d

The deductions on lines 5b through 5d may be subject to the passive loss limitations of Internal Revenue Code section 469, which generally limits deductions from passive activities to the income from those activities. The rules for applying these limitations to beneficiaries have not yet been issued. For more details, see **Pub. 925,** Passive Activity and At-Risk Rules.

Line 11d

If you pay alternative minimum tax in 1995, the amount on line 11d will help you figure any minimum tax credit for 1996. See the 1996 **Form 8801,** Credit for Prior Year Minimum Tax—Individuals, Estates, and Trusts, for more information.

Line 13a

To figure any underpayment and penalty on **Form 2210,** Underpayment of Estimated Tax by Individuals, Estates, and Trusts, treat the amount entered on line 13a as an estimated tax payment made on January 16, 1996.

Lines 13c through 13h

The amount of gross farming and fishing income is included on line 5a. This income is also separately stated on line 13 to help you determine if you are subject to a penalty for underpayment of estimated tax. Report the amount of gross farming and fishing income on Schedule E (Form 1040), line 41.

Form **1065**

Department of the Treasury
Internal Revenue Service

U.S. Partnership Return of Income

For calendar year 1995, or tax year beginning .... , 1995, and ending .... , 19 .... .
▶ See separate instructions.

OMB No. 1545-0099

1995

A Principal business activity	Use the IRS label. Other-wise, please print or type.	Name of partnership	**D** Employer identification number
B Principal product or service		Number, street, and room or suite no. (If a P.O. box, see page 10 of the instructions.)	**E** Date business started
C Business code number		City or town, state, and ZIP code	**F** Total assets (see page 10 of the instructions) $

G Check applicable boxes: **(1)** ☐ Initial return **(2)** ☐ Final return **(3)** ☐ Change in address **(4)** ☐ Amended return
H Check accounting method: **(1)** ☐ Cash **(2)** ☐ Accrual **(3)** ☐ Other (specify) ▶ ....
I Number of Schedules K-1. Attach one for each person who was a partner at any time during the tax year ▶ ....

Caution: *Include* **only** *trade or business income and expenses on lines 1a through 22 below. See the instructions for more information.*

Income

1a Gross receipts or sales	**1a**	
b Less returns and allowances	**1b**	**1c**
2 Cost of goods sold (Schedule A, line 8)		**2**
3 Gross profit. Subtract line 2 from line 1c		**3**
4 Ordinary income (loss) from other partnerships, estates, and trusts *(attach schedule)*		**4**
5 Net farm profit (loss) *(attach Schedule F (Form 1040))*		**5**
6 Net gain (loss) from Form 4797, Part II, line 20		**6**
7 Other income (loss) *(attach schedule)*		**7**
8 **Total income (loss).** Combine lines 3 through 7		**8**

Deductions (see page 11 of the instructions for limitations)

9 Salaries and wages (other than to partners) (less employment credits)		**9**
10 Guaranteed payments to partners		**10**
11 Repairs and maintenance		**11**
12 Bad debts		**12**
13 Rent		**13**
14 Taxes and licenses		**14**
15 Interest		**15**
16a Depreciation (if required, attach Form 4562)	**16a**	
b Less depreciation reported on Schedule A and elsewhere on return	**16b**	**16c**
17 Depletion **(Do not deduct oil and gas depletion.)**		**17**
18 Retirement plans, etc.		**18**
19 Employee benefit programs		**19**
20 Other deductions *(attach schedule)*		**20**
21 **Total deductions.** Add the amounts shown in the far right column for lines 9 through 20		**21**
22 **Ordinary income (loss)** from trade or business activities. Subtract line 21 from line 8		**22**

Please Sign Here

Under penalties of perjury, I declare that I have examined this return, including accompanying schedules and statements, and to the best of my knowledge and belief, it is true, correct, and complete. Declaration of preparer (other than general partner or limited liability company member) is based on all information of which preparer has any knowledge.

▶ Signature of general partner or limited liability company member   ▶ Date

Paid Preparer's Use Only

Preparer's signature ▶	Date	Check if self-employed ▶ ☐	Preparer's social security no.
Firm's name (or yours if self-employed) and address ▶		EIN ▶	
		ZIP code ▶	

For Paperwork Reduction Act Notice, see page 1 of separate instructions.   Cat. No. 11390Z   Form **1065** (1995)

Form 1065 (1995)

Schedule A — Cost of Goods Sold (see page 13 of the instructions)

1 Inventory at beginning of year	1	
2 Purchases less cost of items withdrawn for personal use	2	
3 Cost of labor	3	
4 Additional section 263A costs (attach schedule)	4	
5 Other costs (attach schedule)	5	
6 **Total.** Add lines 1 through 5	6	
7 Inventory at end of year	7	
8 **Cost of goods sold.** Subtract line 7 from line 6. Enter here and on page 1, line 2	8	

9a Check all methods used for valuing closing inventory:

    (i) ☐ Cost as described in Regulations section 1.471-3

    (ii) ☐ Lower of cost or market as described in Regulations section 1.471-4

    (iii) ☐ Other (specify method used and attach explanation) ▶ ....

  b Check this box if there was a writedown of "subnormal" goods as described in Regulations section 1.471-2(c). . . . ▶ ☐

  c Check this box if the LIFO inventory method was adopted this tax year for any goods (if checked, attach Form 970) . . ▶ ☐

  d Do the rules of section 263A (for property produced or acquired for resale) apply to the partnership? . . ☐ **Yes** ☐ **No**

  e Was there any change in determining quantities, cost, or valuations between opening and closing inventory? ☐ **Yes** ☐ **No**

    If "Yes," attach explanation.

Schedule B — Other Information

	Yes	No
1 What type of entity is filing this return? Check the applicable box ▶ ☐ General partnership ☐ Limited partnership ☐ Limited liability company		
2 Are any partners in this partnership also partnerships?.		
3 Is this partnership a partner in another partnership?		
4 Is this partnership subject to the consolidated audit procedures of sections 6221 through 6233? If "Yes," see **Designation of Tax Matters Partner** below		
5 Does this partnership meet **ALL THREE** of the following requirements?		
a The partnership's total receipts for the tax year were less than $250,000;		
b The partnership's total assets at the end of the tax year were less than $600,000; **AND**		
c Schedules K-1 are filed with the return and furnished to the partners on or before the due date (including extensions) for the partnership return. If "Yes," the partnership is not required to complete Schedules L, M-1, and M-2; Item F on page 1 of Form 1065; or Item J on Schedule K-1		
6 Does this partnership have any foreign partners?		
7 Is this partnership a publicly traded partnership as defined in section 469(k)(2)?		
8 Has this partnership filed, or is it required to file, **Form 8264,** Application for Registration of a Tax Shelter? . .		
9 At any time during calendar year 1995, did the partnership have an interest in or a signature or other authority over a financial account in a foreign country (such as a bank account, securities account, or other financial account)? (See page 14 of the instructions for exceptions and filing requirements for Form TD F 90-22.1.) If "Yes," enter the name of the foreign country. ▶		
10 Was the partnership the grantor of, or transferor to, a foreign trust that existed during the current tax year, whether or not the partnership or any partner has any beneficial interest in it? If "Yes," you may have to file Forms 3520, 3520-A, or 926		
11 Was there a distribution of property or a transfer (e.g., by sale or death) of a partnership interest during the tax year? If "Yes," you may elect to adjust the basis of the partnership's assets under section 754 by attaching the statement described under **Elections Made By the Partnership** on page 5 of the instructions		

Designation of Tax Matters Partner (see page 14 of the instructions)

Enter below the general partner designated as the tax matters partner (TMP) for the tax year of this return:

Name of designated TMP ▶	Identifying number of TMP ▶
Address of designated TMP ▶	

Form 1065 (1995)   Page **3**

Schedule K	Partners' Shares of Income, Credits, Deductions, etc.		
	(a) Distributive share items		**(b) Total amount**

Income (Loss)	**1** Ordinary income (loss) from trade or business activities (page 1, line 22)	**1**	
	2 Net income (loss) from rental real estate activities *(attach Form 8825)*	**2**	
	3a Gross income from other rental activities · · · · · · · · `3a`		
	b Expenses from other rental activities *(attach schedule)* · · · · `3b`		
	c Net income (loss) from other rental activities. Subtract line 3b from line 3a	**3c**	
	4 Portfolio income (loss): **a** Interest income · · · · · · · ·	**4a**	
	b Dividend income · · · · · · · · · · · ·	**4b**	
	c Royalty income · · · · · · · · · · · ·	**4c**	
	d Net short-term capital gain (loss) *(attach Schedule D (Form 1065))*	**4d**	
	e Net long-term capital gain (loss) *(attach Schedule D (Form 1065))*	**4e**	
	f Other portfolio income (loss) *(attach schedule)* · · · · ·	**4f**	
	5 Guaranteed payments to partners · · · · · · ·	**5**	
	6 Net gain (loss) under section 1231 (other than due to casualty or theft) *(attach Form 4797)*	**6**	
	7 Other income (loss) *(attach schedule)* · · · · · · · ·	**7**	
Deductions	**8** Charitable contributions *(attach schedule)* · · · · ·	**8**	
	9 Section 179 expense deduction *(attach Form 4562)* · · · · ·	**9**	
	10 Deductions related to portfolio income (itemize) · · · · ·	**10**	
	11 Other deductions *(attach schedule)* · · · · · · ·	**11**	
Investment Interest	**12a** Interest expense on investment debts · · · · · · ·	**12a**	
	b (1) Investment income included on lines 4a, 4b, 4c, and 4f above · · · ·	**12b(1)**	
	(2) Investment expenses included on line 10 above · · · · · · ·	**12b(2)**	
Credits	**13a** Low-income housing credit:		
	(1) From partnerships to which section 42(j)(5) applies for property placed in service before 1990	**13a(1)**	
	(2) Other than on line 13a(1) for property placed in service before 1990 · · · · · ·	**13a(2)**	
	(3) From partnerships to which section 42(j)(5) applies for property placed in service after 1989	**13a(3)**	
	(4) Other than on line 13a(3) for property placed in service after 1989 · · · · ·	**13a(4)**	
	b Qualified rehabilitation expenditures related to rental real estate activities *(attach Form 3468)*	**13b**	
	c Credits (other than credits shown on lines 13a and 13b) related to rental real estate activities	**13c**	
	d Credits related to other rental activities · · · · · · ·	**13d**	
	14 Other credits · · · · · · · · · · · · ·	**14**	
Self-Employment	**15a** Net earnings (loss) from self-employment · · · · · · ·	**15a**	
	b Gross farming or fishing income · · · · · · · ·	**15b**	
	c Gross nonfarm income · · · · · · · · · ·	**15c**	
Adjustments and Tax Preference Items	**16a** Depreciation adjustment on property placed in service after 1986 · · · ·	**16a**	
	b Adjusted gain or loss · · · · · · · · · · ·	**16b**	
	c Depletion (other than oil and gas) · · · · · · · ·	**16c**	
	d (1) Gross income from oil, gas, and geothermal properties · · · · ·	**16d(1)**	
	(2) Deductions allocable to oil, gas, and geothermal properties · · · ·	**16d(2)**	
	e Other adjustments and tax preference items *(attach schedule)* · · · · ·	**16e**	
Foreign Taxes	**17a** Type of income ▶ .... **b** Foreign country or U.S. possession ▶		
	c Total gross income from sources outside the United States *(attach schedule)* · ·	**17c**	
	d Total applicable deductions and losses *(attach schedule)* · · · · · ·	**17d**	
	e Total foreign taxes (check one): ▶ ☐ Paid ☐ Accrued · · · · · ·	**17e**	
	f Reduction in taxes available for credit *(attach schedule)* · · · · ·	**17f**	
	g Other foreign tax information *(attach schedule)* · · · · · · ·	**17g**	
Other	**18** Section 59(e)(2) expenditures: **a** Type ▶ .... **b** Amount ▶	**18b**	
	19 Tax-exempt interest income · · · · · · · · · ·	**19**	
	20 Other tax-exempt income · · · · · · · · · ·	**20**	
	21 Nondeductible expenses · · · · · · · · · ·	**21**	
	22 Distributions of money (cash and marketable securities) · · · · ·	**22**	
	23 Distributions of property other than money · · · · · · ·	**23**	
	24 Other items and amounts required to be reported separately to partners *(attach schedule)* · · ·		
Analysis	**25a** Income (loss). Combine lines 1 through 7 in column (b). From the result, subtract the sum of lines 8 through 12a, 17e, and 18b · · · · · · · · · · · · · · · ·	**25a**	

		(a) Corporate	**(b) Individual**		**(c) Partnership**	**(d) Exempt organization**	**(e) Nominee/Other**
	b Analysis by type of partner:		i. Active	ii. Passive			
	(1) General partners						
	(2) Limited partners						

SCHEDULE K-1
(Form 1065)
Department of the Treasury
Internal Revenue Service

Partner's Share of Income, Credits, Deductions, etc.
▶ See separate instructions.

For calendar year 1995 or tax year beginning , 1995, and ending , 19

OMB No. 1545-0099

1995

Partner's identifying number ▶

Partnership's identifying number ▶

Partner's name, address, and ZIP code

Partnership's name, address, and ZIP code

A This partner is a ☐ general partner ☐ limited partner
☐ limited liability company member

B What type of entity is this partner? ▶

C Is this partner a ☐ domestic or a ☐ foreign partner?

D Enter partner's percentage of:

	(i) Before change or termination	(ii) End of year
Profit sharing	%	%
Loss sharing	%	%
Ownership of capital	%	%

E IRS Center where partnership filed return:

F Partner's share of liabilities (see instructions):

Nonrecourse . . . . $

Qualified nonrecourse financing . $

Other . . . . $

G Tax shelter registration number . ▶

H Check here if this partnership is a publicly traded partnership as defined in section 469(k)(2) . . . . ☐

I Check applicable boxes: **(1)** ☐ Final K-1 **(2)** ☐ Amended K-1

J Analysis of partner's capital account:

(a) Capital account at beginning of year	(b) Capital contributed during year	(c) Partner's share of lines 3, 4, and 7, Form 1065, Schedule M-2	(d) Withdrawals and distributions	(e) Capital account at end of year (combine columns (a) through (d))
			( )	

	(a) Distributive share item	(b) Amount	(c) 1040 filers enter the amount in column (b) on:
Income (Loss)	**1** Ordinary income (loss) from trade or business activities . . . **1**		See pages 5 and 6 of Partner's Instructions for Schedule K-1 (Form 1065).
	2 Net income (loss) from rental real estate activities **2**		
	3 Net income (loss) from other rental activities **3**		
	4 Portfolio income (loss):		
	a Interest **4a**		Sch. B, Part I, line 1
	b Dividends **4b**		Sch. B, Part II, line 5
	c Royalties **4c**		Sch. E, Part I, line 4
	d Net short-term capital gain (loss) **4d**		Sch. D, line 5, col. (f) or (g)
	e Net long-term capital gain (loss). **4e**		Sch. D, line 13, col. (f) or (g)
	f Other portfolio income (loss) (attach schedule) **4f**		Enter on applicable line of your return.
	5 Guaranteed payments to partner **5**		See page 6 of Partner's Instructions for Schedule K-1 (Form 1065).
	6 Net gain (loss) under section 1231 (other than due to casualty or theft) **6**		
	7 Other income (loss) (attach schedule) **7**		Enter on applicable line of your return.
Deduc-tions	**8** Charitable contributions (see instructions) (attach schedule) . . **8**		Sch. A, line 15 or 16
	9 Section 179 expense deduction. **9**		See page 7 of Partner's Instructions for Schedule K-1 (Form 1065).
	10 Deductions related to portfolio income (attach schedule) . . . **10**		
	11 Other deductions (attach schedule). **11**		
Investment Interest	**12a** Interest expense on investment debts **12a**		Form 4952, line 1
	b **(1)** Investment income included on lines 4a, 4b, 4c, and 4f above **b(1)**		See page 7 of Partner's Instructions for Schedule K-1 (Form 1065).
	(2) Investment expenses included on line 10 above . . . . **b(2)**		
Credits	**13a** Low-income housing credit:		
	(1) From section 42(j)(5) partnerships for property placed in service before 1990 . . . . **a(1)**		Form 8586, line 5
	(2) Other than on line 13a(1) for property placed in service before 1990 **a(2)**		
	(3) From section 42(j)(5) partnerships for property placed in service after 1989 . . . . **a(3)**		
	(4) Other than on line 13a(3) for property placed in service after 1989 **a(4)**		
	b Qualified rehabilitation expenditures related to rental real estate activities **13b**		See page 8 of Partner's Instructions for Schedule K-1 (Form 1065).
	c Credits (other than credits shown on lines 13a and 13b) related to rental real estate activities. **13c**		
	d Credits related to other rental activities **13d**		
	14 Other credits **14**		

For Paperwork Reduction Act Notice, see Instructions for Form 1065. Cat. No. 11394R **Schedule K-1 (Form 1065) 1995**

Schedule K-1 (Form 1065) 1995   Page **2**

	(a) Distributive share item		(b) Amount	(c) 1040 filers enter the amount in column (b) on:
Self-employment	**15a** Net earnings (loss) from self-employment	15a		Sch. SE, Section A or B
	b Gross farming or fishing income	15b		⎫ See page 8 of Partner's Instructions for Schedule K-1 (Form 1065).
	c Gross nonfarm income	15c		⎭
Adjustments and Tax Preference Items	**16a** Depreciation adjustment on property placed in service after 1986	16a		
	b Adjusted gain or loss	16b		⎫ See pages 8 and 9 of Partner's Instructions for Schedule K-1 (Form 1065) and Instructions for Form 6251.
	c Depletion (other than oil and gas)	16c		
	d (1) Gross income from oil, gas, and geothermal properties	d(1)		
	(2) Deductions allocable to oil, gas, and geothermal properties	d(2)		
	e Other adjustments and tax preference items *(attach schedule)*	16e		⎭
Foreign Taxes	**17a** Type of income ▶			Form 1116, check boxes
	b Name of foreign country or U.S. possession ▶			
	c Total gross income from sources outside the United States *(attach schedule)*	17c		⎫ Form 1116, Part I
	d Total applicable deductions and losses *(attach schedule)*	17d		⎭
	e Total foreign taxes (check one): ▶ ☐ Paid ☐ Accrued	17e		Form 1116, Part II
	f Reduction in taxes available for credit *(attach schedule)*	17f		Form 1116, Part III
	g Other foreign tax information *(attach schedule)*	17g		See Instructions for Form 1116.
Other	**18** Section 59(e)(2) expenditures: **a** Type ▶			⎫ See page 9 of Partner's Instructions for Schedule K-1 (Form 1065).
	b Amount	18b		⎭
	19 Tax-exempt interest income	19		Form 1040, line 8b
	20 Other tax-exempt income	20		⎫
	21 Nondeductible expenses	21		See page 9 of Partner's Instructions for Schedule K-1 (Form 1065).
	22 Distributions of money (cash and marketable securities)	22		
	23 Distributions of property other than money	23		⎭
	24 Recapture of low-income housing credit:			
	a From section 42(j)(5) partnerships	24a		⎫ Form 8611, line 8
	b Other than on line 24a	24b		⎭

Supplemental Information

25 Supplemental information required to be reported separately to each partner *(attach additional schedules if more space is needed):*

Printed on recycled paper

Form 1120-A

Department of the Treasury
Internal Revenue Service

U.S. Corporation Short-Form Income Tax Return

See separate instructions to make sure the corporation qualifies to file Form 1120-A.

For calendar year 1995 or tax year beginning ...., 1995, ending..............., 19.....

OMB No. 1545-0890

1995

A Check this box if the corp. is a personal service corp. (as defined in Temporary Regs. section 1.441-4T—see instructions) ▶ ☐	**Use IRS label. Other-wise, print or type.**

Name	**B** Employer identification number
Number, street, and room or suite no. (If a P.O. box, see page 6 of instructions.)	**C** Date incorporated
City or town, state, and ZIP code	**D** Total assets (see page 6 of instructions) $

E Check applicable boxes: **(1)** ☐ Initial return **(2)** ☐ Change of address

F Check method of accounting: **(1)** ☐ Cash **(2)** ☐ Accrual **(3)** ☐ Other (specify) . . ▶

Income

1a Gross receipts or sales _____ **b** Less returns and allowances _____ **c** Balance ▶	**1c**	
2 Cost of goods sold (see page 12 of instructions).	**2**	
3 Gross profit. Subtract line 2 from line 1c	**3**	
4 Domestic corporation dividends subject to the 70% deduction	**4**	
5 Interest	**5**	
6 Gross rents	**6**	
7 Gross royalties	**7**	
8 Capital gain net income (attach Schedule D (Form 1120))	**8**	
9 Net gain or (loss) from Form 4797, Part II, line 20 (attach Form 4797) . .	**9**	
10 Other income (see page 7 of instructions).	**10**	
11 **Total income.** Add lines 3 through 10 . . . . ▶	**11**	

Deductions

(See instructions for limitations on deductions.)

12 Compensation of officers (see page 8 of instructions)	**12**	
13 Salaries and wages (less employment credits)	**13**	
14 Repairs and maintenance	**14**	
15 Bad debts	**15**	
16 Rents	**16**	
17 Taxes and licenses	**17**	
18 Interest	**18**	
19 Charitable contributions (see page 9 of instructions for 10% limitation) . .	**19**	
20 Depreciation (attach Form 4562) . . . . **20** _____		
21 Less depreciation claimed elsewhere on return . . . . . **21a** _____	**21b**	
22 Other deductions (attach schedule)	**22**	
23 **Total deductions.** Add lines 12 through 22 . . . . ▶	**23**	
24 Taxable income before net operating loss deduction and special deductions. Subtract line 23 from line 11	**24**	
25 **Less: a** Net operating loss deduction (see page 11 of instructions) . **25a** _____		
b Special deductions (see page 11 of instructions) . . . . **25b** _____	**25c**	

Tax and Payments

26 **Taxable income.** Subtract line 25c from line 24	**26**	
27 **Total tax** (from page 2, Part I, line 7)	**27**	
28 **Payments:**		
a 1994 overpayment credited to 1995 **28a** _____		
b 1995 estimated tax payments . **28b** _____		
c Less 1995 refund applied for on Form 4466 **28c** (_____) Bal ▶ **28d** _____		
e Tax deposited with Form 7004 . . . . **28e** _____		
f Credit from regulated investment companies (attach Form 2439) . **28f** _____		
g Credit for Federal tax on fuels (attach Form 4136). See instructions . **28g** _____		
h Total payments. Add lines 28d through 28g	**28h**	
29 Estimated tax penalty (see page 12 of instructions). Check if Form 2220 is attached . . . ▶ ☐	**29**	
30 **Tax due.** If line 28h is smaller than the total of lines 27 and 29, enter amount owed . .	**30**	
31 **Overpayment.** If line 28h is larger than the total of lines 27 and 29, enter amount overpaid . .	**31**	
32 Enter amount of line 31 you want: **Credited to 1996 estimated tax ▶** Refunded ▶	**32**	

Sign Here

Under penalties of perjury, I declare that I have examined this return, including accompanying schedules and statements, and to the best of my knowledge and belief, it is true, correct, and complete. Declaration of preparer (other than taxpayer) is based on all information of which preparer has any knowledge.

▶ _____   _____   ▶ _____
Signature of officer   Date   Title

Paid Preparer's Use Only

Preparer's signature ▶		Date	Check if self-employed ▶ ☐ Preparer's social security number
Firm's name (or yours if self-employed) and address ▶			EIN ▶ _____ ZIP code ▶ _____

For Paperwork Reduction Act Notice, see page 1 of the instructions.   Cat. No. 11456E   Form **1120-A** (1995)

Form 1120-A (1995)   Page **2**

Part I   Tax Computation (See page 14 of instructions.)

1	Income tax. If the corporation is a qualified personal service corporation (see page 15), check here ▶ ☐	**1**
2a	General business credit. Check if from: ☐ Form 3800 ☐ Form 3468 ☐ Form 5884 ☐ Form 6478 ☐ Form 6765 ☐ Form 8586 ☐ Form 8830 ☐ Form 8826 ☐ Form 8835 ☐ Form 8844 ☐ Form 8845 ☐ Form 8846 ☐ Form 8847	**2a**
b	Credit for prior year minimum tax (attach Form 8827)	**2b**
3	**Total credits.** Add lines 2a and 2b	**3**
4	Subtract line 3 from line 1	**4**
5	Recapture taxes. Check if from: ☐ Form 4255 ☐ Form 8611	**5**
6	Alternative minimum tax (attach Form 4626)	**6**
7	**Total tax.** Add lines 4 through 6. Enter here and on line 27, page 1	**7**

Part II   Other Information (See page 17 of instructions.)

1 See page 19 of the instructions and state the principal:
a Business activity code no. ▶ ....
b Business activity ▶ ....
c Product or service ▶ ....

2 Did any individual, partnership, estate, or trust at the end of the tax year own, directly or indirectly, 50% or more of the corporation's voting stock? (For rules of attribution, see section 267(c).) . . . . ☐ Yes ☐ No
If "Yes," attach a schedule showing name and identifying number.

3 Enter the amount of tax-exempt interest received or accrued during the tax year . . . . ▶ |$ |

4 Enter amount of cash distributions and the book value of property (other than cash) distributions made in this tax year . . . . ▶ |$ |

5a If an amount is entered on line 2, page 1, see the worksheet on page 12 for amounts to enter below:
(1) Purchases . . . . . .
(2) Additional sec. 263A costs (attach schedule) . . . . .
(3) Other costs (attach schedule) .

b Do the rules of section 263A (for property produced or acquired for resale) apply to the corporation? . . . . . . ☐ Yes ☐ No

6 At any time during the 1995 calendar year, did the corporation have an interest in or a signature or other authority over a financial account in a foreign country (such as a bank account, securities account, or other financial account)? If "Yes," the corporation may have to file Form TD F 90-22.1 . . . . ☐ Yes ☐ No
If "Yes," enter the name of the foreign country ▶ ....

Part III   Balance Sheets

Assets		(a) Beginning of tax year		(b) End of tax year	
1	Cash				
2a	Trade notes and accounts receivable				
b	Less allowance for bad debts	(	)	(	)
3	Inventories				
4	U.S. government obligations				
5	Tax-exempt securities (see instructions)				
6	Other current assets (attach schedule)				
7	Loans to stockholders				
8	Mortgage and real estate loans				
9a	Depreciable, depletable, and intangible assets . .				
b	Less accumulated depreciation, depletion, and amortization	(	)	(	)
10	Land (net of any amortization)				
11	Other assets (attach schedule)				
12	Total assets				

Liabilities and Stockholders' Equity					
13	Accounts payable				
14	Other current liabilities (attach schedule)				
15	Loans from stockholders				
16	Mortgages, notes, bonds payable				
17	Other liabilities (attach schedule)				
18	Capital stock (preferred and common stock)				
19	Paid-in or capital surplus				
20	Retained earnings				
21	Less cost of treasury stock	(	)	(	)
22	Total liabilities and stockholders' equity				

Part IV   Reconciliation of Income (Loss) per Books With Income per Return (You are not required to complete Part IV if the total assets on line 12, column (b), Part III are less than $25,000.)

1 Net income (loss) per books		6 Income recorded on books this year not included on this return (itemize)		
2 Federal income tax				
3 Excess of capital losses over capital gains. .		7 Deductions on this return not charged against book income this year (itemize)		
4 Income subject to tax not recorded on books this year (itemize)				
5 Expenses recorded on books this year not deducted on this return (itemize)		8 Income (line 24, page 1). Enter the sum of lines 1 through 5 less the sum of lines 6 and 7 . . .		

♲ *Printed on recycled paper*

Form **1120**
Department of the Treasury
Internal Revenue Service

U.S. Corporation Income Tax Return

For calendar year 1995 or tax year beginning .... , 1995, ending .... , 19 ...
▶ Instructions are separate. See page 1 for Paperwork Reduction Act Notice.

OMB No. 1545-0123

1995

A Check if a:	Use IRS label. Otherwise, print or type.	Name		B Employer identification number
1 Consolidated return (attach Form 851) ☐		Number, street, and room or suite no. (If a P.O. box, see page 6 of instructions.)		C Date incorporated
2 Personal holding co. (attach Sch. PH) ☐				
3 Personal service corp. (as defined in Temporary Regs. sec. 1.441-4T— see instructions) ☐		City or town, state, and ZIP code		D Total assets (see page 6 of instructions)

E Check applicable boxes: (1) ☐ Initial return   (2) ☐ Final return   (3) ☐ Change of address $

Income	1a	Gross receipts or sales [_____] **b** Less returns and allowances [_____] **c** Bal ▶	**1c**	
	2	Cost of goods sold (Schedule A, line 8)	**2**	
	3	Gross profit. Subtract line 2 from line 1c	**3**	
	4	Dividends (Schedule C, line 19)	**4**	
	5	Interest	**5**	
	6	Gross rents	**6**	
	7	Gross royalties	**7**	
	8	Capital gain net income (attach Schedule D (Form 1120))	**8**	
	9	Net gain or (loss) from Form 4797, Part II, line 20 (attach Form 4797) . . .	**9**	
	10	Other income (see page 7 of instructions—attach schedule)	**10**	
	11	**Total income.** Add lines 3 through 10 . . . . ▶	**11**	
Deductions (See instructions for limitations on deductions.)	12	Compensation of officers (Schedule E, line 4)	**12**	
	13	Salaries and wages (less employment credits)	**13**	
	14	Repairs and maintenance	**14**	
	15	Bad debts	**15**	
	16	Rents	**16**	
	17	Taxes and licenses	**17**	
	18	Interest	**18**	
	19	Charitable contributions (see page 9 of instructions for 10% limitation) .	**19**	
	20	Depreciation (attach Form 4562)	**20**	
	21	Less depreciation claimed on Schedule A and elsewhere on return	**21a**	**21b**
	22	Depletion	**22**	
	23	Advertising	**23**	
	24	Pension, profit-sharing, etc., plans	**24**	
	25	Employee benefit programs	**25**	
	26	Other deductions (attach schedule)	**26**	
	27	**Total deductions.** Add lines 12 through 26 . . . . ▶	**27**	
	28	Taxable income before net operating loss deduction and special deductions. Subtract line 27 from line 11	**28**	
	29	**Less:** **a** Net operating loss deduction (see page 11 of instructions) .	**29a**	
		b Special deductions (Schedule C, line 20)	**29b**	**29c**
Tax and Payments	30	**Taxable income.** Subtract line 29c from line 28	**30**	
	31	**Total tax** (Schedule J, line 10)	**31**	
	32	**Payments: a** 1994 overpayment credited to 1995	**32a**	
		b 1995 estimated tax payments . .	**32b**	
		c Less 1995 refund applied for on Form 4466	**32c** ( ) **d** Bal ▶	**32d**
		e Tax deposited with Form 7004	**32e**	
		f Credit from regulated investment companies (attach Form 2439) . . .	**32f**	
		g Credit for Federal tax on fuels (attach Form 4136). See instructions . .	**32g**	**32h**
	33	Estimated tax penalty (see page 12 of instructions). Check if Form 2220 is attached . . . ▶ ☐	**33**	
	34	**Tax due.** If line 32h is smaller than the total of lines 31 and 33, enter amount owed	**34**	
	35	**Overpayment.** If line 32h is larger than the total of lines 31 and 33, enter amount overpaid . . .	**35**	
	36	Enter amount of line 35 you want: **Credited to 1996 estimated tax** ▶ **Refunded** ▶	**36**	

Sign Here

Under penalties of perjury, I declare that I have examined this return, including accompanying schedules and statements, and to the best of my knowledge and belief, it is true, correct, and complete. Declaration of preparer (other than taxpayer) is based on all information of which preparer has any knowledge.

▶ _____   _____   ▶ _____
Signature of officer   Date   Title

Paid Preparer's Use Only

Preparer's signature ▶		Date	Check if self-employed ☐	Preparer's social security number
Firm's name (or yours if self-employed) and address ▶			EIN ▶	
			ZIP code ▶	

Cat. No. 11450Q

Form 1120 (1995)   Page **2**

Schedule A | Cost of Goods Sold (See page 12 of instructions.)

1	Inventory at beginning of year	**1**	
2	Purchases	**2**	
3	Cost of labor	**3**	
4	Additional section 263A costs (attach schedule)	**4**	
5	Other costs (attach schedule)	**5**	
6	**Total.** Add lines 1 through 5	**6**	
7	Inventory at end of year	**7**	
8	**Cost of goods sold.** Subtract line 7 from line 6. Enter here and on page 1, line 2	**8**	

9a Check all methods used for valuing closing inventory:

    (i) ☐ Cost as described in Regulations section 1.471-3

    (ii) ☐ Lower of cost or market as described in Regulations section 1.471-4

    (iii) ☐ Other (Specify method used and attach explanation.) ▶ -------------------------------

  b Check if there was a writedown of subnormal goods as described in Regulations section 1.471-2(c) . . . . ▶ ☐

  c Check if the LIFO inventory method was adopted this tax year for any goods (if checked, attach Form 970) . . . . . ▶ ☐

  d If the LIFO inventory method was used for this tax year, enter percentage (or amounts) of closing inventory computed under LIFO **9d**

  e Do the rules of section 263A (for property produced or acquired for resale) apply to the corporation? . . . . . ☐ Yes ☐ No

  f Was there any change in determining quantities, cost, or valuations between opening and closing inventory? If "Yes," attach explanation . . . . ☐ Yes ☐ No

Schedule C | Dividends and Special Deductions (See page 13 of instructions.)

		(a) Dividends received	(b) %	(c) Special deductions (a) × (b)
1	Dividends from less-than-20%-owned domestic corporations that are subject to the 70% deduction (other than debt-financed stock)		70	
2	Dividends from 20%-or-more-owned domestic corporations that are subject to the 80% deduction (other than debt-financed stock)		80	
3	Dividends on debt-financed stock of domestic and foreign corporations (section 246A)		see instructions	
4	Dividends on certain preferred stock of less-than-20%-owned public utilities		42	
5	Dividends on certain preferred stock of 20%-or-more-owned public utilities		48	
6	Dividends from less-than-20%-owned foreign corporations and certain FSCs that are subject to the 70% deduction		70	
7	Dividends from 20%-or-more-owned foreign corporations and certain FSCs that are subject to the 80% deduction		80	
8	Dividends from wholly owned foreign subsidiaries subject to the 100% deduction (section 245(b))		100	
9	**Total.** Add lines 1 through 8. See page 13 of instructions for limitation			
10	Dividends from domestic corporations received by a small business investment company operating under the Small Business Investment Act of 1958		100	
11	Dividends from certain FSCs that are subject to the 100% deduction (section 245(c)(1))		100	
12	Dividends from affiliated group members subject to the 100% deduction (section 243(a)(3))		100	
13	Other dividends from foreign corporations not included on lines 3, 6, 7, 8, or 11			
14	Income from controlled foreign corporations under subpart F (attach Form(s) 5471)			
15	Foreign dividend gross-up (section 78)			
16	IC-DISC and former DISC dividends not included on lines 1, 2, or 3 (section 246(d))			
17	Other dividends			
18	Deduction for dividends paid on certain preferred stock of public utilities			
19	**Total dividends.** Add lines 1 through 17. Enter here and on line 4, page 1 . . ▶			
20	**Total special deductions.** Add lines 9, 10, 11, 12, and 18. Enter here and on line 29b, page 1 . . . . . . ▶			

Schedule E | Compensation of Officers (See instructions for line 12, page 1.)

Complete Schedule E only if total receipts (line 1a plus lines 4 through 10 on page 1, Form 1120) are $500,000 or more.

(a) Name of officer	(b) Social security number	(c) Percent of time devoted to business	Percent of corporation stock owned		(f) Amount of compensation
			(d) Common	(e) Preferred	
1		%	%	%	
		%	%	%	
		%	%	%	
		%	%	%	
		%	%	%	

2	Total compensation of officers	
3	Compensation of officers claimed on Schedule A and elsewhere on return	
4	Subtract line 3 from line 2. Enter the result here and on line 12, page 1	

Form 1120 (1995)   Page **3**

Schedule J Tax Computation (See page 14 of instructions.)

1 Check if the corporation is a member of a controlled group (see sections 1561 and 1563) . . . . . ▶ ☐

   Important: Members of a controlled group, see instructions on page 14.

2a If the box on line 1 is checked, enter the corporation's share of the $50,000, $25,000, and $9,925,000 taxable income brackets (in that order):

   (1) ☐ $_____ | **(2)** ☐ $_____ | **(3)** ☐ $_____ |

  b Enter the corporation's share of:

    (1) Additional 5% tax (not more than $11,750)   ☐ $_____ |

    (2) Additional 3% tax (not more than $100,000) ☐ $_____ |

3 Income tax. Check this box if the corporation is a qualified personal service corporation as defined in section 448(d)(2) (see instructions on page 15). . . . . ▶ ☐	**3**	
4a Foreign tax credit (attach Form 1118) **4a**		
b Possessions tax credit (attach Form 5735) **4b**		
c Check: ☐ Nonconventional source fuel credit ☐ QEV credit (attach Form 8834) **4c**		
d General business credit. Enter here and check which forms are attached:		
☐ 3800 ☐ 3468 ☐ 5884 ☐ 6478 ☐ 6765 ☐ 8586 ☐ 8830		
☐ 8826 ☐ 8835 ☐ 8844 ☐ 8845 ☐ 8846 ☐ 8847 . . . . **4d**		
e Credit for prior year minimum tax (attach Form 8827) **4e**		
5 **Total credits.** Add lines 4a through 4e	**5**	
6 Subtract line 5 from line 3	**6**	
7 Personal holding company tax (attach Schedule PH (Form 1120))	**7**	
8 Recapture taxes. Check if from: ☐ Form 4255 ☐ Form 8611	**8**	
9a Alternative minimum tax (attach Form 4626)	**9a**	
b Environmental tax (attach Form 4626)	**9b**	
10 **Total tax.** Add lines 6 through 9b. Enter here and on line 31, page 1	**10**	

Schedule K Other Information (See page 17 of instructions.)

	Yes	No
1 Check method of accounting: **a** ☐ Cash		
b ☐ Accrual **c** ☐ Other (specify) ▶		
2 See page 19 of the instructions and state the principal:		
a Business activity code no. ▶		
b Business activity ▶		
c Product or service ▶		
3 Did the corporation at the end of the tax year own, directly or indirectly, 50% or more of the voting stock of a domestic corporation? (For rules of attribution, see section 267(c).)		
If "Yes," attach a schedule showing: (a) name and identifying number, (b) percentage owned, and (c) taxable income or (loss) before NOL and special deductions of such corporation for the tax year ending with or within your tax year.		
4 Is the corporation a subsidiary in an affiliated group or a parent-subsidiary controlled group?		
If "Yes," enter employer identification number and name of the parent corporation ▶		
5 Did any individual, partnership, corporation, estate or trust at the end of the tax year own, directly or indirectly, 50% or more of the corporation's voting stock? (For rules of attribution, see section 267(c).)		
If "Yes," attach a schedule showing name and identifying number. (Do not include any information already entered in **4** above.) Enter percentage owned ▶		
6 During this tax year, did the corporation pay dividends (other than stock dividends and distributions in exchange for stock) in excess of the corporation's current and accumulated earnings and profits? (See secs. 301 and 316.)		
If "Yes," file Form 5452. If this is a consolidated return, answer here for the parent corporation and on **Form 851,** Affiliations Schedule, for each subsidiary.		

	Yes	No
7 Was the corporation a U.S. shareholder of any controlled foreign corporation? (See sections 951 and 957.) . . .		
If "Yes," attach Form 5471 for each such corporation. Enter number of Forms 5471 attached ▶		
8 At any time during the 1995 calendar year, did the corporation have an interest in or a signature or other authority over a financial account in a foreign country (such as a bank account, securities account, or other financial account)? .		
If "Yes," the corporation may have to file Form TD F 90-22.1. If "Yes," enter name of foreign country ▶		
9 Was the corporation the grantor of, or transferor to, a foreign trust that existed during the current tax year, whether or not the corporation has any beneficial interest in it? If "Yes," the corporation may have to file Forms 926, 3520, or 3520-A		
10 Did one foreign person at any time during the tax year own, directly or indirectly, at least 25% of: **(a)** the total voting power of all classes of stock of the corporation entitled to vote, or **(b)** the total value of all classes of stock of the corporation? If "Yes,"		
a Enter percentage owned ▶		
b Enter owner's country ▶		
c The corporation may have to file Form 5472. Enter number of Forms 5472 attached ▶		
11 Check this box if the corporation issued publicly offered debt instruments with original issue discount . ▶ ☐		
If so, the corporation may have to file Form 8281.		
12 Enter the amount of tax-exempt interest received or accrued during the tax year ▶ $		
13 If there were 35 or fewer shareholders at the end of the tax year, enter the number ▶		
14 If the corporation has an NOL for the tax year and is electing to forego the carryback period, check here ▶ ☐		
15 Enter the available NOL carryover from prior tax years (Do not reduce it by any deduction on line 29a.) ▶ $		

Schedule L	Balance Sheets	Beginning of tax year		End of tax year	
	Assets	**(a)**	**(b)**	**(c)**	**(d)**
1	Cash				
2a	Trade notes and accounts receivable . . .				
b	Less allowance for bad debts	(	)	(	)
3	Inventories				
4	U.S. government obligations				
5	Tax-exempt securities (see instructions) . .				
6	Other current assets (attach schedule) . .				
7	Loans to stockholders				
8	Mortgage and real estate loans				
9	Other investments (attach schedule) . . .				
10a	Buildings and other depreciable assets . .				
b	Less accumulated depreciation	(	)	(	)
11a	Depletable assets				
b	Less accumulated depletion	(	)	(	)
12	Land (net of any amortization)				
13a	Intangible assets (amortizable only) . . .				
b	Less accumulated amortization	(	)	(	)
14	Other assets (attach schedule)				
15	Total assets				
	Liabilities and Stockholders' Equity				
16	Accounts payable				
17	Mortgages, notes, bonds payable in less than 1 year				
18	Other current liabilities (attach schedule) . .				
19	Loans from stockholders				
20	Mortgages, notes, bonds payable in 1 year or more				
21	Other liabilities (attach schedule)				
22	Capital stock: a Preferred stock . . .				
	b Common stock . . .				
23	Paid-in or capital surplus				
24	Retained earnings—Appropriated (attach schedule)				
25	Retained earnings—Unappropriated . . .				
26	Less cost of treasury stock		(	)	(	)
27	Total liabilities and stockholders' equity . .				

Note: *You are not required to complete Schedules M-1 and M-2 below if the total assets on line 15, column (d) of Schedule L are less than $25,000.*

Schedule M-1	Reconciliation of Income (Loss) per Books With Income per Return (See page 18 of instructions.)

1	Net income (loss) per books		7	Income recorded on books this year not included on this return (itemize):	
2	Federal income tax				
3	Excess of capital losses over capital gains .			Tax-exempt interest $ _____	
4	Income subject to tax not recorded on books this year (itemize): _____			_____	
	_____		8	Deductions on this return not charged against book income this year (itemize):	
5	Expenses recorded on books this year not deducted on this return (itemize):		a	Depreciation . . . . $_____	
a	Depreciation . . . . . $_____		b	Contributions carryover $ _____	
b	Contributions carryover $ _____			_____	
c	Travel and entertainment $ _____			_____	
	_____		9	Add lines 7 and 8	
6	Add lines 1 through 5		10	Income (line 28, page 1)—line 6 less line 9	

Schedule M-2	Analysis of Unappropriated Retained Earnings per Books (Line 25, Schedule L)

1	Balance at beginning of year		5	Distributions: a Cash	
2	Net income (loss) per books			b Stock	
3	Other increases (itemize): _____			c Property	
	_____		6	Other decreases (itemize): _____	
	_____			_____	
	_____		7	Add lines 5 and 6	
4	Add lines 1, 2, and 3		8	Balance at end of year (line 4 less line 7)	

Form 1120-F

Department of the Treasury
Internal Revenue Service

U.S. Income Tax Return of a Foreign Corporation

For calendar year 1995, or tax year beginning .... , 1995, and ending .... , 19 .....
▶ See separate instructions.

OMB No. 1545-0126

1995

Name	Employer identification number
Number, street, and room or suite no. (see page 6 of instructions)	**Check applicable boxes:** ☐ Initial return ☐ Amended return
City or town, state and ZIP code, or country	☐ Final return ☐ Change of address

Please type or print

A Country of incorporation ....

B Foreign country under whose laws the income reported on this return is subject to tax ....

C Date incorporated ....

D The corporation's books and records are maintained by:

Name ....

Address ....

ZIP code or country ....

E If the corporation had an agent in the United States at any time during the tax year, enter:

Kind of agent ....

Name ....

Address ....

F Refer to the list on the last page of the instructions and state the corporation's principal:

(1) Business activity code number ▶ ....

(2) Business activity ▶ ....

(3) Product or service ▶ ....

G Check method of accounting: (1) ☐ Cash (2) ☐ Accrual

(3) ☐ Other (specify) ▶ ....

	Yes	No
H Did the corporation file a U.S. income tax return for the preceding tax year?		
I Was the corporation at any time during the tax year engaged in a trade or business in the United States?		
J Did the corporation at any time during the tax year have a permanent establishment in the United States for purposes of applying section 894(b) and any applicable tax treaty between the United States and a foreign country? . . . . . . If "Yes," enter the name of the foreign country:		
K Is the corporation a foreign personal holding company? (See section 552 for definition.) . . If "Yes," have you filed Form 5471? (Sec. 6035) .		
L Did the corporation have any transactions with related parties? . . . . If "Yes," you may have to file Form 5472 (section 6038A and section 6038C). Enter number of Forms 5472 attached ▶		

Note: *Additional information is required at the bottom of pages 2 and 5.*

Computation of Tax Due or Overpayment

1 Tax from Section I, line 11, page 2	**1**	
2 Tax from Section II, Schedule J, line 9, page 4	**2**	
3 Tax from Section III (add lines 6 and 10 on page 5)	**3**	
4 Personal holding company tax (attach Schedule PH (Form 1120))—see page 6 of instructions . . .	**4**	
5 **Total tax.** Add lines 1 through 4	**5**	

6 **Payments:**

a 1994 overpayment credited to 1995	**6a**		
b 1995 estimated tax payments . .	**6b**		
c Less 1995 refund applied for on Form 4466	**6c** ( ) Bal ▶	**6d**	
e Tax deposited with Form 7004	**6e**	
f Credit from regulated investment companies (attach Form 2439) . . .	**6f**	
g Credit for Federal tax on fuels (attach Form 4136). See instructions . . .	**6g**	
h U.S. income tax paid or withheld at source (add line 12, page 2, and amounts from Forms 8288-A and 8805 (attach Forms 8288-A and 8805))	**6h**	
i Total payments. Add lines 6d through 6h.		**6i**	
7 Estimated tax penalty (see page 7 of instructions). Check if Form 2220 is attached . . . . . ▶ ☐	**7**	
8 **Tax due.** If line 6i is smaller than the total of lines 5 and 7, enter amount owed	**8**	
9 **Overpayment.** If line 6i is larger than the total of lines 5 and 7, enter amount overpaid	**9**	
10 Enter amount of line 9 you want: **Credited to 1996 estimated tax** ▶ **Refunded** ▶	**10**	

Please Sign Here

Under penalties of perjury, I declare that I have examined this return, including accompanying schedules and statements, and to the best of my knowledge and belief, it is true, correct, and complete. Declaration of preparer (other than taxpayer) is based on all information of which preparer has any knowledge.

▶ _____   _____   ▶ _____
Signature of officer   Date   Title

Paid Preparer's Use Only

Preparer's signature ▶	Date	Check if self-employed ▶ ☐	Preparer's social security number
Firm's name (or yours if self-employed) and address ▶		EIN ▶	
		ZIP code ▶	

For Paperwork Reduction Act Notice, see page 1 of separate instructions.   Cat. No. 11470I   Form **1120-F** (1995)

Form 1120-F (1995)   Page **2**

SECTION I.—Certain Gains, Profits, and Income From U.S. Sources That Are NOT Effectively Connected With the Conduct of a Trade or Business in the United States (See instructions.)

If you are required to complete Section II or are using Form 1120-F as a claim for refund of tax withheld at source, include below **ALL** income from U.S. sources that is **NOT** effectively connected with the conduct of a trade or business in the United States. Otherwise, include only those items of income on which the U.S. income tax was not fully paid at the source. The rate of tax on each item of **gross** income listed below is 30% (4% for the gross transportation tax) or such lower rate specified by tax treaty. No deductions are allowed against these types of income. Fill in treaty rates where applicable. **If the corporation claimed a lower treaty rate, also complete Item W, page 5.**

Name of treaty country, if any ▶

(a) Nature of income	(b) Gross income	(c) Rate of tax (%)	(d) Amount of tax	(e) Amount of U.S. income tax paid or withheld at the source
1 Interest				
2 Dividends				
3 Rents				
4 Royalties				
5 Annuities				
6 Gains from disposal of timber, coal, or domestic iron ore with a retained economic interest (attach supporting schedule)				
7 Gains from sale or exchange of patents, copyrights, etc.				
8 Fiduciary distributions (attach supporting schedule)				
9 Gross transportation income (see instructions)		4		
10 Other fixed or determinable annual or periodic gains, profits, and income .				
---------------------------				
11 Total. Enter here and on line 1, page 1 . . . . ▶				
12 Total. Enter here and include on line 6h, page 1. . . . . ▶				

Additional Information Required *(continued from page 1)*

	Yes	No			Yes	No
M Is the corporation a personal holding company? (See section 542 for definition.).			**S** Enter the available NOL carryover from prior tax years. (Do not reduce it by any deduction on line 30a, page 3.) ▶ $			

M Is the corporation a personal holding company? (See section 542 for definition.). . . . .

N Is the corporation a controlled foreign corporation? (See section 957 for definition.) . . . .

O Is the corporation a personal service corporation? (See page 8 of instructions for definition.). . . . .

P Enter tax-exempt interest received or accrued during the tax year (see instructions) ▶ $ ....

Q Did the corporation at the end of the tax year own, directly or indirectly, 50% or more of the voting stock of a U.S. corporation? (See section 267(c) for rules of attribution.) . . . .

If "Yes," attach a schedule showing (1) name and identifying number of such U.S. corporation; (2) percentage owned; and (3) taxable income or (loss) before NOL and special deductions of such U.S. corporation for the tax year ending with or within your tax year.

R If the corporation has a net operating loss (NOL) for the tax year and is electing to forego the carryback period, check here . . . . ▶ ☐

S Enter the available NOL carryover from prior tax years. (Do not reduce it by any deduction on line 30a, page 3.) ▶ $ ....

T Is the corporation a subsidiary in a parent-subsidiary controlled group? . . . .

If "Yes," enter the name and employer identification number of the parent corporation ▶ ....
....

U Did any individual, partnership, corporation, estate, or trust at the end of the tax year own, directly or indirectly, 50% or more of the corporation's voting stock? (See section 267(c) for attribution rules.) . .

If "Yes," complete the following:

(1) Attach a schedule showing the name and identifying number. (Do not include any information already entered in **T** above).

(2) Enter percentage owned ▶ ....

Note: *Additional information is required at the bottom of page 5.*

Form 1120-F (1995)

SECTION II.—Income Effectively Connected With the Conduct of a Trade or Business in the United States
(See instructions.)

IMPORTANT—Fill in all applicable lines and schedules. If you need more space, see **Attachments** on page 5 of instructions.

Income

1a Gross receipts or sales [ ] **b** Less returns and allowances [ ] **c** Bal ▶	**1c**	
2 Cost of goods sold (Schedule A, line 8)	**2**	
3 Gross profit (subtract line 2 from line 1c)	**3**	
4 Dividends (Schedule C, line 14)	**4**	
5 Interest	**5**	
6 Gross rents	**6**	
7 Gross royalties	**7**	
8 Capital gain net income (attach Schedule D (Form 1120))	**8**	
9 Net gain or (loss) from Form 4797, Part II, line 20 (attach Form 4797)	**9**	
10 Other income (see page 9 of instructions–attach schedule)	**10**	
11 **Total income.** Add lines 3 through 10 ▶	**11**	

Deductions (See instructions for limitations on deductions.)

12 Compensation of officers (Schedule E, line 4). Deduct only amounts connected with a U.S. business	**12**	
13 Salaries and wages (less employment credits)	**13**	
14 Repairs and maintenance	**14**	
15 Bad debts	**15**	
16 Rents	**16**	
17 Taxes and licenses	**17**	
18 Interest deduction allowable under Regulations section 1.882-5	**18**	
19 Charitable contributions (see page 11 of instructions for 10% limitation)	**19**	
20 Depreciation (attach Form 4562)	**20**	
21 Less depreciation claimed on Schedule A and elsewhere on return	**21**	
22 Balance (subtract line 21 from line 20)	**22**	
23 Depletion	**23**	
24 Advertising	**24**	
25 Pension, profit-sharing, etc., plans	**25**	
26 Employee benefit programs	**26**	
27 Other deductions (see page 12 of instructions—attach schedule)	**27**	
28 **Total deductions.** Add lines 12 through 27 ▶	**28**	
29 Taxable income before NOL deduction and special deductions (subtract line 28 from line 11)	**29**	
30 **Less: a** Net operating loss deduction (see page 13 of instructions)	**30a**	
b Special deductions (Schedule C, line 15)	**30b**	**30c**
31 Taxable income or (loss). Subtract line 30c from line 29	**31**	

Schedule A Cost of Goods Sold (See instructions.)

1 Inventory at beginning of year	**1**	
2 Purchases	**2**	
3 Cost of labor	**3**	
4 Additional section 263A costs (see page 13 of instructions—attach schedule)	**4**	
5 Other costs (attach schedule)	**5**	
6 Add lines 1 through 5	**6**	
7 Inventory at end of year	**7**	
8 **Cost of goods sold.** Subtract line 7 from line 6. Enter here and on Section II, line 2	**8**	

9a Check all methods used for valuing closing inventory:

   (1) ☐ Cost as described in Regulations section 1.471-3

   (2) ☐ Lower of cost or market as described in Regulations section 1.471-4

   (3) ☐ Other (Specify method used and attach explanation.) ▶ --------------------------------------

   b Check if there was a writedown of subnormal goods as described in Regulations section 1.471-2(c) . . . . . ▶ ☐

   c Check if the LIFO inventory method was adopted this tax year for any goods . . . . ▶ ☐

   If checked, attach Form 970.

   d If the LIFO inventory method was used for this tax year, enter percentage (or amounts) of closing inventory computed under LIFO . . . . | **9d** |

   e Do the rules of section 263A (for property produced or acquired for resale) apply to the corporation? . . ☐ **Yes** ☐ **No**

   f Was there any change in determining quantities, cost, or valuations between opening and closing inventory? ☐ **Yes** ☐ **No**

   If "Yes," attach explanation.

Form 1120-F (1995)   Page **4**

Schedule C — Dividends and Special Deductions (See instructions.)

	(a) Dividends received	(b) %	(c) Special deductions: (a) × (b)
1 Dividends from less-than-20%-owned domestic corporations that are subject to the 70% deduction (other than debt-financed stock) . . .		70	
2 Dividends from 20%-or-more-owned domestic corporations that are subject to the 80% deduction (other than debt-financed stock) . . .		80	
3 Dividends on debt-financed stock of domestic and foreign corporations (section 246A)		see instructions	
4 Dividends on certain preferred stock of less-than-20%-owned public utilities		42	
5 Dividends on certain preferred stock of 20%-or-more-owned public utilities		48	
6 Dividends from less-than-20%-owned foreign corporations that are subject to the 70% deduction		70	
7 Dividends from 20%-or-more-owned foreign corporations that are subject to the 80% deduction		80	
8 **Total.** Add lines 1 through 7. See page 14 of instructions for limitation .			
9 Other dividends from foreign corporations not included on lines 3, 6, and 7			
10 Foreign dividend gross-up (section 78)			
11 IC-DISC and former DISC dividends not included on lines 1, 2, or 3 (section 246(d))			
12 Other dividends			
13 Deduction for dividends paid on certain preferred stock of a public utility			
14 Total dividends. Add lines 1 through 12. Enter here and on line 4, page 3			
15 Total deductions. Add lines 8 and 13. Enter here and on line 30b, page 3			

Schedule E — Compensation of Officers (Complete Schedule E only if total receipts (line 1a plus lines 4 through 10 of Section II) are $500,000 or more. See **Line 12. Compensation of officers** on page 10 of instructions.)

(a) Name of officer	(b) Social security number	(c) Percent of time devoted to business	Percent of corporation stock owned		(f) Amount of compensation
			(d) Common	(e) Preferred	
1		%	%	%	
		%	%	%	
		%	%	%	
		%	%	%	
		%	%	%	
		%	%	%	
		%	%	%	

2 Total compensation of officers . . . .

3 Compensation of officers claimed on Schedule A and elsewhere on this return . . . . . .

4 Subtract line 3 from line 2. Enter the result here and on line 12, page 3 . . . .

Schedule J — Tax Computation (See page 15 of instructions.)

1 Check if the corporation is a member of a controlled group (see sections 1561 and 1563) ▶ ☐
Important: Members of a controlled group, see instructions on page 15.

2a If the box on line 1 is checked, enter the corporation's share of the $50,000, $25,000, and $9,925,000 taxable income bracket amounts (in that order):
(1) |$_____| **(2)** |$_____| **(3)** |$_____|

b Enter the corporation's share of:
(1) Additional 5% tax (not more than $11,750) |$_____|
(2) Additional 3% tax (not more than $100,000) |$_____|

3 Income tax. Check this box if the corporation is a qualified personal service corporation (see page 16 of the instructions) ▶ ☐ . . . . | **3** |

4a Foreign tax credit (attach Form 1118) . . . . | **4a** |

b Check: ☐ Nonconventional source fuel credit
☐ QEV credit (attach Form 8834) | **4b** |

c General business credit. Enter here and check which **forms** are attached:
☐ 3800   ☐ 3468   ☐ 5884   ☐ 6478   ☐ 6765
☐ 8586   ☐ 8830   ☐ 8826   ☐ 8835   ☐ 8844
☐ 8845   ☐ 8846   ☐ 8847 | **4c** |

d Credit for prior year minimum tax (attach Form 8827) . . . . . | **4d** |

5 **Total credits.** Add lines 4a through 4d . . . . | **5** |

6 Subtract line 5 from line 3 . . . . | **6** |

7 Recapture taxes. Check if from: ☐ Form 4255 ☐ Form 8611 . . . . | **7** |

8a Alternative minimum tax (attach Form 4626) . . . . | **8a** |

b Environmental tax (attach Form 4626) . . . . | **8b** |

9 **Total tax under section 882(a).** Add lines 6 through 8b. Enter here and on line 2, page 1. . | **9** |

SECTION III.—Branch Profits Tax and Tax on Excess Interest (See instructions beginning on page 17.)

Part I—Branch Profits Tax

1	Enter the amount from Section II, line 29	**1**	
2	Enter total adjustments made to get effectively connected earnings and profits. (Attach a schedule showing the nature and amount of adjustments.) (See instructions.)	**2**	
3	Effectively connected earnings and profits. Combine line 1 and line 2. Enter the result here . .	**3**	
4a	Enter U.S. net equity at the end of the current tax year. (Attach schedule.)	**4a**	
b	Enter U.S. net equity at the end of the prior tax year. (Attach schedule.)	**4b**	
c	Increase in U.S. net equity. If line 4a is greater than or equal to line 4b, subtract line 4b from line 4a. Enter the result here and skip to line 4e	**4c**	
d	Decrease in U.S. net equity. If line 4b is greater than line 4a, subtract line 4a from line 4b. Enter the result here	**4d**	
e	Non-previously taxed accumulated effectively connected earnings and profits. Enter excess, if any, of effectively connected earnings and profits for preceding tax years beginning after 1986 over any dividend equivalent amounts for those tax years	**4e**	
5	Dividend equivalent amount. Subtract line 4c from line 3. Enter the result here. If zero or less, enter -0-. If no amount is entered on line 4c, add the lesser of line 4d or line 4e to line 3 and enter the total here	**5**	
6	**Branch profits tax.** Multiply line 5 by 30% (or lower treaty rate if the corporation is a qualified resident or otherwise qualifies for treaty benefits). Enter here and include on line 3, page 1. (See instructions.) **Also complete Items W and X below**	**6**	

Part II—Tax on Excess Interest

7a	Enter the interest from Section II, line 18	**7a**	
b	Enter the interest apportioned to the effectively connected income of the foreign corporation that is capitalized or otherwise nondeductible.	**7b**	
c	Add lines 7a and 7b	**7c**	
8	Enter the branch interest (including capitalized and other nondeductible interest). (See instructions for definition.) If the interest paid by the foreign corporation's U.S. trade or business was increased because 80% or more of the foreign corporation's assets are U.S. assets, check this box . . . . ▶ ☐	**8**	
9a	Excess interest. Subtract line 8 from line 7c. If zero or less, enter -0-.	**9a**	
b	If the foreign corporation is a bank, enter the excess interest treated as interest on deposits. Otherwise, enter -0-. (See instructions.)	**9b**	
c	Subtract line 9b from line 9a	**9c**	
10	**Tax on excess interest.** Multiply line 9c by 30% or lower treaty rate (if the corporation is a qualified resident or otherwise qualifies for treaty benefits). (See instructions.) Enter here and include on line 3, page 1. **Also complete Items W and X below**	**10**	

Additional Information Required *(continued from page 2)*

	Yes	No
V Is the corporation claiming a reduction in, or exemption from, the branch profits tax due to:		
(1) A complete termination of all U.S. trades or businesses?		
(2) The tax-free liquidation or reorganization of a foreign corporation?		
(3) The tax-free incorporation of a U.S. trade or business?		

If (1) applies or (2) applies and the transferee is domestic, attach Form 8848.

If (3) applies, attach the statement required by Regulations section 1.884-2T(d)(5).

	Yes	No
W Is the corporation taking a position on this return that a U.S. tax treaty overrules or modifies an Internal Revenue law of the United States thereby causing a reduction of tax?		

If "Yes," complete and attach Form 8833.

Note: *Failure to disclose a treaty-based return position may result in a $10,000 penalty (see section 6712).*

X If the corporation is claiming it is a qualified resident of its country of residence for purposes of computing its branch profits tax and excess interest tax, check the basis for that claim:

Stock ownership and base erosion test . . . . . . ☐
Publicly traded test . . . . ☐
Active trade or business test . . . . ☐
Private letter ruling . . . . ☐

Form 1120-F (1995)   Page **6**

Additional schedules to be completed for Section II or Section III (See instructions.)

Schedule L	Balance Sheets	Beginning of tax year		End of tax year	
		(a)	(b)	(c)	(d)
	ASSETS				
1	Cash				
2a	Trade notes and accounts receivable				
b	Less allowance for bad debts . . .	( )		( )	
3	Inventories				
4	U.S. government obligations . . .				
5	Tax-exempt securities (see instructions)				
6	Other current assets (attach schedule)				
7	Loans to stockholders				
8	Mortgage and real estate loans . .				
9	Other investments (attach schedule) .				
10a	Buildings and other fixed depreciable assets				
b	Less accumulated depreciation . .	( )		( )	
11a	Depletable assets				
b	Less accumulated depletion . . .	( )		( )	
12	Land (net of any amortization) . . .				
13a	Intangible assets (amortizable only) .				
b	Less accumulated amortization . .	( )		( )	
14	Other assets (attach schedule). . .				
15	Total assets				
	LIABILITIES AND STOCKHOLDERS' EQUITY				
16	Accounts payable				
17	Mtges., notes, bonds payable in less than 1 year				
18	Other current liabilities (attach schedule)				
19	Loans from stockholders				
20	Mtges., notes, bonds payable in 1 year or more				
21	Other liabilities (attach schedule) . .				
22	Capital stock: **a** Preferred stock . .				
	b Common stock . .				
23	Paid-in or capital surplus				
24	Retained earnings—Appropriated (attach schedule)				
25	Retained earnings—Unappropriated .				
26	Less cost of treasury stock		( )		( )
27	Total liabilities and stockholders' equity				

Note: *The corporation is not required to complete Schedules M-1 and M-2 below if the total assets on Schedule L, line 15, column (d) are less than $25,000.*

Schedule M-1   Reconciliation of Income or (Loss) per Books With Income per Return

1	Net income (loss) per books . . .		7	Income recorded on books this year not included on this return (itemize):	
2	Federal income tax				
3	Excess of capital losses over capital gains		a	Tax-exempt interest . $	
4	Income subject to tax not recorded on books this year (itemize):			-----------------------------------	
	-----------------------------------		8	Deductions on this return not charged against book income this year (itemize):	
5	Expenses recorded on books this year not deducted on this return (itemize):		a	Depreciation . . . $	
a	Depreciation . . . $		b	Contributions carryover $	
b	Contributions carryover $		9	Add lines 7 and 8	
c	Travel and entertainment $		10	Income (line 29, page 3)—line 6 less line 9	
6	Add lines 1 through 5				

Schedule M-2   Analysis of Unappropriated Retained Earnings per Books (Schedule L, line 25)

1	Balance at beginning of year . . .		5	Distributions: **a** Cash	
2	Net income (loss) per books . . .			**b** Stock	
3	Other increases (itemize):			**c** Property	
	-----------------------------------		6	Other decreases (itemize):	

	-----------------------------------		7	Add lines 5a through 6	
4	Add lines 1, 2, and 3		8	Balance at end of year (line 4 less line 7)	

✿ *Printed on recycled paper*

Form **1120S**	**U.S. Income Tax Return for an S Corporation**	OMB No. 1545-0130
Department of the Treasury Internal Revenue Service	▶ Do not file this form unless the corporation has timely filed Form 2553 to elect to be an S corporation. ▶ See separate instructions.	19**95**

For calendar year 1995, or tax year beginning _____ , 1995, and ending _____ , 19 ___

A Date of election as an S corporation	**Use IRS label. Other- wise, please print or type.**	Name	**C** Employer identification number
		Number, street, and room or suite no. (If a P.O. box, see page 9 of the instructions.)	**D** Date incorporated
B Business code no. (see Specific Instructions)		City or town, state, and ZIP code	**E** Total assets (see Specific Instructions) $

F Check applicable boxes: (1) ☐ Initial return   (2) ☐ Final return   (3) ☐ Change in address   (4) ☐ Amended return

G Check this box if this S corporation is subject to the consolidated audit procedures of sections 6241 through 6245 (see instructions before checking this box) . ▶ ☐

H Enter number of shareholders in the corporation at end of the tax year . . . . ▶

Caution: *Include **only** trade or business income and expenses on lines 1a through 21. See the instructions for more information.*

Income

1a	Gross receipts or sales _____ **b** Less returns and allowances _____	**c** Bal ▶	**1c**
2	Cost of goods sold (Schedule A, line 8)		**2**
3	Gross profit. Subtract line 2 from line 1c		**3**
4	Net gain (loss) from Form 4797, Part II, line 20 *(attach Form 4797)*		**4**
5	Other income (loss) *(attach schedule)*		**5**
6	**Total income (loss).** Combine lines 3 through 5 . . . . ▶		**6**

Deductions (see page 10 of the instructions for limitations)

7	Compensation of officers		**7**
8	Salaries and wages (less employment credits)		**8**
9	Repairs and maintenance.		**9**
10	Bad debts		**10**
11	Rents		**11**
12	Taxes and licenses.		**12**
13	Interest		**13**
14a	Depreciation *(if required, attach Form 4562)*	**14a**	
b	Depreciation claimed on Schedule A and elsewhere on return . .	**14b**	
c	Subtract line 14b from line 14a		**14c**
15	Depletion **(Do not deduct oil and gas depletion.)**		**15**
16	Advertising		**16**
17	Pension, profit-sharing, etc., plans		**17**
18	Employee benefit programs		**18**
19	Other deductions *(attach schedule)*		**19**
20	**Total deductions.** Add the amounts shown in the far right column for lines 7 through 19 . ▶		**20**
21	Ordinary income (loss) from trade or business activities. Subtract line 20 from line 6		**21**

Tax and Payments

22	**Tax: a** Excess net passive income tax *(attach schedule)*. . .	**22a**	
b	Tax from Schedule D (Form 1120S)	**22b**	
c	Add lines 22a and 22b (see page 13 of the instructions for additional taxes)		**22c**
23	**Payments: a** 1995 estimated tax payments and amount applied from 1994 return	**23a**	
b	Tax deposited with Form 7004	**23b**	
c	Credit for Federal tax paid on fuels *(attach Form 4136)* . . .	**23c**	
d	Add lines 23a through 23c		**23d**
24	Estimated tax penalty. Check if Form 2220 is attached . . . . ▶☐		**24**
25	**Tax due.** If the total of lines 22c and 24 is larger than line 23d, enter amount owed. See page 3 of the instructions for depositary method of payment . . . . ▶		**25**
26	**Overpayment.** If line 23d is larger than the total of lines 22c and 24, enter amount overpaid ▶		**26**
27	Enter amount of line 26 you want: **Credited to 1996 estimated tax** ▶ _____	**Refunded** ▶	**27**

Please Sign Here

Under penalties of perjury, I declare that I have examined this return, including accompanying schedules and statements, and to the best of my knowledge and belief, it is true, correct, and complete. Declaration of preparer (other than taxpayer) is based on all information of which preparer has any knowledge.

▶ _____   _____   ▶ _____
Signature of officer   Date   Title

Paid Preparer's Use Only

Preparer's signature ▶	Date	Check if self-employed ▶ ☐	Preparer's social security number
Firm's name (or yours if self-employed) and address ▶		EIN ▶	
		ZIP code ▶	

For Paperwork Reduction Act Notice, see page 1 of separate instructions.   Cat. No. 11510H   Form **1120S** (1995)

Form 1120S (1995)   Page **2**

Schedule A   Cost of Goods Sold (see page 14 of the instructions)

1	Inventory at beginning of year	1	
2	Purchases	2	
3	Cost of labor	3	
4	Additional section 263A costs *(attach schedule)*	4	
5	Other costs *(attach schedule)*	5	
6	**Total.** Add lines 1 through 5	6	
7	Inventory at end of year	7	
8	**Cost of goods sold.** Subtract line 7 from line 6. Enter here and on page 1, line 2	8	

9a Check all methods used for valuing closing inventory:

    (i) ☐ Cost as described in Regulations section 1.471-3

    (ii) ☐ Lower of cost or market as described in Regulations section 1.471-4

    (iii) ☐ Other (specify method used and attach explanation) ▶ --

  b Check if there was a writedown of "subnormal" goods as described in Regulations section 1.471-2(c) . . . . . . ▶ ☐

  c Check if the LIFO inventory method was adopted this tax year for any goods *(if checked, attach Form 970)* . . . . . ▶ ☐

  d If the LIFO inventory method was used for this tax year, enter percentage (or amounts) of closing
     inventory computed under LIFO . . . . | **9d** |

  e Do the rules of section 263A (for property produced or acquired for resale) apply to the corporation? . . . . ☐ Yes ☐ No

  f Was there any change in determining quantities, cost, or valuations between opening and closing inventory? . . ☐ Yes ☐ No
    If "Yes," attach explanation.

Schedule B   Other Information

		Yes	No
1	Check method of accounting: **(a)** ☐ Cash **(b)** ☐ Accrual **(c)** ☐ Other (specify) ▶ -------------------		
2	Refer to the list on page 24 of the instructions and state the corporation's principal: **(a)** Business activity ▶ ------------------------------ **(b)** Product or service ▶ -----------------------		
3	Did the corporation at the end of the tax year own, directly or indirectly, 50% or more of the voting stock of a domestic corporation? (For rules of attribution, see section 267(c).) If "Yes," attach a schedule showing: **(a)** name, address, and employer identification number and **(b)** percentage owned.		
4	Was the corporation a member of a controlled group subject to the provisions of section 1561?		
5	At any time during calendar year 1995, did the corporation have an interest in or a signature or other authority over a financial account in a foreign country (such as a bank account, securities account, or other financial account)? (See page 14 of the instructions for exceptions and filing requirements for Form TD F 90-22.1.) . . . . If "Yes," enter the name of the foreign country ▶ --		
6	Was the corporation the grantor of, or transferor to, a foreign trust that existed during the current tax year, whether or not the corporation had any beneficial interest in it? If "Yes," the corporation may have to file Forms 3520, 3520-A, or 926		
7	Check this box if the corporation has filed or is required to file **Form 8264,** Application for Registration of a Tax Shelter . . . . ▶ ☐		
8	Check this box if the corporation issued publicly offered debt instruments with original issue discount . . ▶ ☐ If so, the corporation may have to file **Form 8281,** Information Return for Publicly Offered Original Issue Discount Instruments.		
9	If the corporation: **(a)** filed its election to be an S corporation after 1986, **(b)** was a C corporation before it elected to be an S corporation **or** the corporation acquired an asset with a basis determined by reference to its basis (or the basis of any other property) in the hands of a C corporation, and **(c)** has net unrealized built-in gain (defined in section 1374(d)(1)) in excess of the net recognized built-in gain from prior years, enter the net unrealized built-in gain reduced by net recognized built-in gain from prior years (see page 14 of the instructions) . . . . . ▶ $ -------------		
10	Check this box if the corporation had subchapter C earnings and profits at the close of the tax year (see page 15 of the instructions) . . . . ▶ ☐		

Designation of Tax Matters Person (see page 15 of the instructions)

Enter below the shareholder designated as the tax matters person (TMP) for the tax year of this return:

Name of designated TMP ▶		Identifying number of TMP ▶	

Address of designated TMP ▶	

Form 1120S (1995)   Page **3**

Schedule K	**Shareholders' Shares of Income, Credits, Deductions, etc.**		
	(a) Pro rata share items		**(b)** Total amount

Income (Loss)

1	Ordinary income (loss) from trade or business activities (page 1, line 21)	**1**	
2	Net income (loss) from rental real estate activities *(attach Form 8825)*	**2**	
3a	Gross income from other rental activities	**3a**	
b	Expenses from other rental activities *(attach schedule)*. .	**3b**	
c	Net income (loss) from other rental activities. Subtract line 3b from line 3a	**3c**	
4	Portfolio income (loss):		
a	Interest income	**4a**	
b	Dividend income.	**4b**	
c	Royalty income	**4c**	
d	Net short-term capital gain (loss) *(attach Schedule D (Form 1120S))*	**4d**	
e	Net long-term capital gain (loss) *(attach Schedule D (Form 1120S))*.	**4e**	
f	Other portfolio income (loss) *(attach schedule)*	**4f**	
5	Net gain (loss) under section 1231 (other than due to casualty or theft) *(attach Form 4797)*	**5**	
6	Other income (loss) *(attach schedule)*	**6**	

Deductions

7	Charitable contributions *(attach schedule)*.	**7**	
8	Section 179 expense deduction *(attach Form 4562)*.	**8**	
9	Deductions related to portfolio income (loss) (itemize)	**9**	
10	Other deductions *(attach schedule)*	**10**	

Investment Interest

11a	Interest expense on investment debts	**11a**	
b (1)	Investment income included on lines 4a, 4b, 4c, and 4f above	**11b(1)**	
(2)	Investment expenses included on line 9 above	**11b(2)**	

Credits

12a	Credit for alcohol used as a fuel *(attach Form 6478)*	**12a**	
b	Low-income housing credit:		
(1)	From partnerships to which section 42(j)(5) applies for property placed in service before 1990	**12b(1)**	
(2)	Other than on line 12b(1) for property placed in service before 1990.	**12b(2)**	
(3)	From partnerships to which section 42(j)(5) applies for property placed in service after 1989	**12b(3)**	
(4)	Other than on line 12b(3) for property placed in service after 1989	**12b(4)**	
c	Qualified rehabilitation expenditures related to rental real estate activities *(attach Form 3468)*	**12c**	
d	Credits (other than credits shown on lines 12b and 12c) related to rental real estate activities	**12d**	
e	Credits related to other rental activities.	**12e**	
13	Other credits	**13**	

Adjustments and Tax Preference Items

14a	Depreciation adjustment on property placed in service after 1986	**14a**	
b	Adjusted gain or loss	**14b**	
c	Depletion (other than oil and gas)	**14c**	
d (1)	Gross income from oil, gas, or geothermal properties	**14d(1)**	
(2)	Deductions allocable to oil, gas, or geothermal properties	**14d(2)**	
e	Other adjustments and tax preference items *(attach schedule)*	**14e**	

Foreign Taxes

15a	Type of income ▶ _____		
b	Name of foreign country or U.S. possession ▶ _____		
c	Total gross income from sources outside the United States *(attach schedule)*	**15c**	
d	Total applicable deductions and losses *(attach schedule)*	**15d**	
e	Total foreign taxes (check one): ▶ ☐ Paid ☐ Accrued	**15e**	
f	Reduction in taxes available for credit *(attach schedule)*	**15f**	
g	Other foreign tax information *(attach schedule)*	**15g**	

Other

16	Section 59(e)(2) expenditures: **a** Type ▶ _____		
b	Amount	**16b**	
17	Tax-exempt interest income	**17**	
18	Other tax-exempt income	**18**	
19	Nondeductible expenses	**19**	
20	Total property distributions (including cash) other than dividends reported on line 22 below	**20**	
21	Other items and amounts required to be reported separately to shareholders *(attach schedule)*		
22	Total dividend distributions paid from accumulated earnings and profits	**22**	
23	**Income (loss).** (Required only if Schedule M-1 must be completed.) Combine lines 1 through 6 in column (b). From the result, subtract the sum of lines 7 through 11a, 15e, and 16b	**23**	

Form 1120S (1995)   Page **4**

Schedule L	Balance Sheets	Beginning of tax year		End of tax year	
Assets		**(a)**	**(b)**	**(c)**	**(d)**
1	Cash				
2a	Trade notes and accounts receivable				
b	Less allowance for bad debts				
3	Inventories				
4	U.S. Government obligations				
5	Tax-exempt securities				
6	Other current assets (attach schedule)				
7	Loans to shareholders				
8	Mortgage and real estate loans				
9	Other investments (attach schedule)				
10a	Buildings and other depreciable assets				
b	Less accumulated depreciation				
11a	Depletable assets				
b	Less accumulated depletion				
12	Land (net of any amortization)				
13a	Intangible assets (amortizable only)				
b	Less accumulated amortization				
14	Other assets (attach schedule)				
15	Total assets				
Liabilities and Shareholders' Equity					
16	Accounts payable				
17	Mortgages, notes, bonds payable in less than 1 year				
18	Other current liabilities (attach schedule)				
19	Loans from shareholders				
20	Mortgages, notes, bonds payable in 1 year or more				
21	Other liabilities (attach schedule)				
22	Capital stock				
23	Paid-in or capital surplus				
24	Retained earnings				
25	Less cost of treasury stock		( )		( )
26	Total liabilities and shareholders' equity				

Schedule M-1	**Reconciliation of Income (Loss) per Books With Income (Loss) per Return** (You are not required to complete this schedule if the total assets on line 15, column (d), of Schedule L are less than $25,000.)

1	Net income (loss) per books		5 Income recorded on books this year not included on Schedule K, lines 1 through 6 (itemize):	
2	Income included on Schedule K, lines 1 through 6, not recorded on books this year (itemize):		a Tax-exempt interest $	
3	Expenses recorded on books this year not included on Schedule K, lines 1 through 11a, 15e, and 16b (itemize):		6 Deductions included on Schedule K, lines 1 through 11a, 15e, and 16b, not charged against book income this year (itemize):	
a	Depreciation $		a Depreciation $	
b	Travel and entertainment $		....	
			7 Add lines 5 and 6	
4	Add lines 1 through 3		8 Income (loss) (Schedule K, line 23). Line 4 less line 7	

Schedule M-2	**Analysis of Accumulated Adjustments Account, Other Adjustments Account, and Shareholders' Undistributed Taxable Income Previously Taxed** (see page 22 of the instructions)

		(a) Accumulated adjustments account	(b) Other adjustments account	(c) Shareholders' undistributed taxable income previously taxed
1	Balance at beginning of tax year			
2	Ordinary income from page 1, line 21			
3	Other additions			
4	Loss from page 1, line 21	( )		
5	Other reductions	( )	( )	
6	Combine lines 1 through 5			
7	Distributions other than dividend distributions			
8	Balance at end of tax year. Subtract line 7 from line 6			

SCHEDULE K-1
(Form 1120S)

Department of the Treasury
Internal Revenue Service

Shareholder's Share of Income, Credits, Deductions, etc.

▶ See separate instructions.

For calendar year 1995 or tax year
beginning , 1995, and ending , 19

OMB No. 1545-0130

1995

Shareholder's identifying number ▶

Corporation's identifying number ▶

Shareholder's name, address, and ZIP code

Corporation's name, address, and ZIP code

A Shareholder's percentage of stock ownership for tax year (see Instructions for Schedule K-1) . . . . ▶ .... %

B Internal Revenue Service Center where corporation filed its return ▶ ....

C Tax shelter registration number (see Instructions for Schedule K-1) . . . . ▶ ....

D Check applicable boxes: **(1)** ☐ Final K-1 **(2)** ☐ Amended K-1

	(a) Pro rata share items		(b) Amount	(c) Form 1040 filers enter the amount in column (b) on:
Income (Loss)	1 Ordinary income (loss) from trade or business activities . . .	1		See pages 4 and 5 of the Shareholder's Instructions for Schedule K-1 (Form 1120S).
	2 Net income (loss) from rental real estate activities	2		
	3 Net income (loss) from other rental activities	3		
	4 Portfolio income (loss):			
	a Interest	4a		Sch. B, Part I, line 1
	b Dividends	4b		Sch. B, Part II, line 5
	c Royalties	4c		Sch. E, Part I, line 4
	d Net short-term capital gain (loss).	4d		Sch. D, line 5, col. (f) or (g)
	e Net long-term capital gain (loss)	4e		Sch. D, line 13, col. (f) or (g)
	f Other portfolio income (loss) (attach schedule)	4f		(Enter on applicable line of your return.)
	5 Net gain (loss) under section 1231 (other than due to casualty or theft)	5		See Shareholder's Instructions for Schedule K-1 (Form 1120S).
	6 Other income (loss) (attach schedule)	6		(Enter on applicable line of your return.)
Deductions	7 Charitable contributions (attach schedule)	7		Sch. A, line 15 or 16
	8 Section 179 expense deduction	8		See page 6 of the Shareholder's Instructions for Schedule K-1 (Form 1120S).
	9 Deductions related to portfolio income (loss) (attach schedule) .	9		
	10 Other deductions (attach schedule)	10		
Investment Interest	11a Interest expense on investment debts	11a		Form 4952, line 1
	b (1) Investment income included on lines 4a, 4b, 4c, and 4f above	b(1)		See Shareholder's Instructions for Schedule K-1 (Form 1120S).
	(2) Investment expenses included on line 9 above	b(2)		
Credits	12a Credit for alcohol used as fuel	12a		Form 6478, line 10
	b Low-income housing credit:			
	(1) From section 42(j)(5) partnerships for property placed in service before 1990.	b(1)		Form 8586, line 5
	(2) Other than on line 12b(1) for property placed in service before 1990	b(2)		
	(3) From section 42(j)(5) partnerships for property placed in service after 1989	b(3)		
	(4) Other than on line 12b(3) for property placed in service after 1989	b(4)		
	c Qualified rehabilitation expenditures related to rental real estate activities	12c		See page 7 of the Shareholder's Instructions for Schedule K-1 (Form 1120S).
	d Credits (other than credits shown on lines 12b and 12c) related to rental real estate activities	12d		
	e Credits related to other rental activities.	12e		
	13 Other credits	13		
Adjustments and Tax Preference Items	14a Depreciation adjustment on property placed in service after 1986	14a		See page 7 of the Shareholder's Instructions for Schedule K-1 (Form 1120S) and Instructions for Form 6251
	b Adjusted gain or loss	14b		
	c Depletion (other than oil and gas)	14c		
	d (1) Gross income from oil, gas, or geothermal properties . . .	d(1)		
	(2) Deductions allocable to oil, gas, or geothermal properties .	d(2)		
	e Other adjustments and tax preference items (attach schedule) .	14e		

For Paperwork Reduction Act Notice, see page 1 of Instructions for Form 1120S. Cat. No. 11520D **Schedule K-1 (Form 1120S) 1995**

Schedule K-1 (Form 1120S) (1995)   Page **2**

(a) Pro rata share items	(b) Amount	(c) Form 1040 filers enter the amount in column (b) on:
15a Type of income ▶		Form 1116, Check boxes
b Name of foreign country or U.S. possession ▶		
c Total gross income from sources outside the United States *(attach schedule)*	15c	Form 1116, Part I
d Total applicable deductions and losses *(attach schedule)*	15d	
e Total foreign taxes (check one): ▶ ☐ Paid ☐ Accrued	15e	Form 1116, Part II
f Reduction in taxes available for credit *(attach schedule)*	15f	Form 1116, Part III
g Other foreign tax information *(attach schedule)*	15g	See Instructions for Form 1116
16 Section 59(e)(2) expenditures: **a** Type ▶		See Shareholder's Instructions for Schedule K-1 (Form 1120S).
b Amount	16b	
17 Tax-exempt interest income	17	Form 1040, line 8b
18 Other tax-exempt income	18	
19 Nondeductible expenses	19	See page 7 of the Shareholder's Instructions for Schedule K-1 (Form 1120S).
20 Property distributions (including cash) other than dividend distributions reported to you on Form 1099-DIV	20	
21 Amount of loan repayments for "Loans From Shareholders"	21	
22 Recapture of low-income housing credit:		
a From section 42(j)(5) partnerships	22a	Form 8611, line 8
b Other than on line 22a	22b	

23 Supplemental information required to be reported separately to each shareholder *(attach additional schedules if more space is needed)*:

Printed on recycled paper

Form **2106**

Department of the Treasury
Internal Revenue Service (99)

Employee Business Expenses

▶ See separate instructions.

▶ Attach to Form 1040 or Form 1040-T.

OMB No. 1545-0139

1995

Attachment
Sequence No. **54**

Your name	Social security number	Occupation in which expenses were incurred

Part I Employee Business Expenses and Reimbursements

STEP 1   Enter Your Expenses

			Column A Other Than Meals and Entertainment	Column B Meals and Entertainment
1	Vehicle expense from line 22 or line 29	1		
2	Parking fees, tolls, and transportation, including train, bus, etc., that **did not** involve overnight travel	2		
3	Travel expense while away from home overnight, including lodging, airplane, car rental, etc. **Do not** include meals and entertainment	3		
4	Business expenses not included on lines 1 through 3. **Do not** include meals and entertainment	4		
5	Meals and entertainment expenses (see instructions)	5		
6	**Total expenses.** In Column A, add lines 1 through 4 and enter the result. In Column B, enter the amount from line 5	6		

Note: *If you were not reimbursed for any expenses in Step 1, skip line 7 and enter the amount from line 6 on line 8.*

STEP 2   Enter Amounts Your Employer Gave You for Expenses Listed in STEP 1

7	Enter amounts your employer gave you that were **not** reported to you in box 1 of Form W-2. Include any amount reported under code "L" in box 13 of your Form W-2 (see instructions) . . .	7		

STEP 3   Figure Expenses To Deduct on Schedule A (Form 1040) or Form 1040-T, Section B

8	Subtract line 7 from line 6	8		
	Note: *If both columns of line 8 are zero, stop here. If Column A is less than zero, report the amount as income on Form 1040, line 7, or Form 1040-T, line 1.*			
9	In Column A, enter the amount from line 8 (if zero or less, enter -0-). In Column B, multiply the amount on line 8 by 50% (.50) .	9		
10	Add the amounts on line 9 of both columns and enter the total here. **Also, enter the total on Schedule A (Form 1040), line 20, or Form 1040-T, Section B, line n.** (Qualified performing artists and individuals with disabilities, see the instructions for special rules on where to enter the total.) . . . . ▶	10		

For Paperwork Reduction Act Notice, see instructions.   Cat. No. 11700N   Form **2106** (1995)

Form 2106 (1995)   Page **2**

Part II — Vehicle Expenses (See instructions to find out which sections to complete.)

Section A.—General Information

		(a) Vehicle 1	**(b)** Vehicle 2
11	Enter the date vehicle was placed in service	11 / /	/ /
12	Total miles vehicle was driven during 1995	12 miles	miles
13	Business miles included on line 12	13 miles	miles
14	Percent of business use. Divide line 13 by line 12	14 %	%
15	Average daily round trip commuting distance	15 miles	miles
16	Commuting miles included on line 12	16 miles	miles
17	Other personal miles. Add lines 13 and 16 and subtract the total from line 12	17 miles	miles

18 Do you (or your spouse) have another vehicle available for personal purposes? ☐ Yes ☐ No

19 If your employer provided you with a vehicle, is personal use during off-duty hours permitted? ☐ Yes ☐ No ☐ Not applicable

20 Do you have evidence to support your deduction? ☐ Yes ☐ No

21 If "Yes," is the evidence written? ☐ Yes ☐ No

Section B.—Standard Mileage Rate (Use this section only if you own the vehicle.)

22 Multiply line 13 by 30¢ (.30). Enter the result here and on line 1. (Rural mail carriers, see instructions.) **22**

Section C.—Actual Expenses

		(a) Vehicle 1	**(b)** Vehicle 2
23	Gasoline, oil, repairs, vehicle insurance, etc.	23	
24a	Vehicle rentals	24a	
b	Inclusion amount (see instructions)	24b	
c	Subtract line 24b from line 24a	24c	
25	Value of employer-provided vehicle (applies only if 100% of annual lease value was included on Form W-2—see instructions)	25	
26	Add lines 23, 24c, and 25	26	
27	Multiply line 26 by the percentage on line 14	27	
28	Depreciation. Enter amount from line 38 below	28	
29	Add lines 27 and 28. Enter total here and on line 1	29	

Section D.—Depreciation of Vehicles (Use this section only if you own the vehicle.)

		(a) Vehicle 1	**(b)** Vehicle 2
30	Enter cost or other basis (see instructions)	30	
31	Enter amount of section 179 deduction (see instructions)	31	
32	Multiply line 30 by line 14 (see instructions if you elected the section 179 deduction)	32	
33	Enter depreciation method and percentage (see instructions)	33	
34	Multiply line 32 by the percentage on line 33 (see instructions)	34	
35	Add lines 31 and 34	35	
36	Enter the limitation amount from the table in the line 36 instructions	36	
37	Multiply line 36 by the percentage on line 14	37	
38	Enter the **smaller** of line 35 or line 37. Also, enter this amount on line 28 above	38	

✪ Printed on recycled paper

Form **2106-EZ**

Department of the Treasury
Internal Revenue Service (99)

Unreimbursed Employee Business Expenses

▶ **See instructions on back.**

▶ **Attach to Form 1040 or Form 1040-T.**

OMB No. 1545-1441

1995

Attachment
Sequence No. **54A**

Your name	Social security number	Occupation in which expenses were incurred

Part I General Information

You May Use This Form ONLY if All of the Following Apply:

- You are an employee deducting expenses attributable to your job.
- You **do not** get reimbursed by your employer for any expenses (amounts your employer included in box 1 of your Form W-2 are not considered reimbursements).
- If you are claiming vehicle expense,
  - **a** You own your vehicle, and
  - **b** You are using the standard mileage rate for 1995 **and** also used it for the year you first placed the vehicle in service.

Part II Figure Your Expenses

1	Vehicle expense using the standard mileage rate. Complete Part III and multiply line 8a by 30¢ (.30)	**1**	
2	Parking fees, tolls, and transportation, including train, bus, etc., that **did not** involve overnight travel	**2**	
3	Travel expense while away from home overnight, including lodging, airplane, car rental, etc. **Do not** include meals and entertainment	**3**	
4	Business expenses not included on lines 1 through 3. **Do not** include meals and entertainment .	**4**	
5	Meals and entertainment expenses: $ _____ x 50% (.50)	**5**	
6	**Total expenses.** Add lines 1 through 5. Enter here and **on line 20 of Schedule A (Form 1040), or Form 1040-T, Section B, line n.** (Qualified performing artists and individuals with disabilities, see the instructions for special rules on where to enter this amount.)	**6**	

Part III Information on Your Vehicle. Complete this part **ONLY** if you are claiming vehicle expense on line 1.

7 When did you place your vehicle in service for business purposes? (month, day, year) ▶ .... / .... / ....

8 Of the total number of miles you drove your vehicle during 1995, enter the number of miles you used your vehicle for:

   a Business .... **b** Commuting .... **c** Other ....

9 Do you (or your spouse) have another vehicle available for personal use? . . . . ☐ **Yes** ☐ **No**

10 Was your vehicle available for use during off-duty hours? . . . . ☐ **Yes** ☐ **No**

11a Do you have evidence to support your deduction? . . . . ☐ **Yes** ☐ **No**

   b If "Yes," is the evidence written? . . . . ☐ **Yes** ☐ **No**

For Paperwork Reduction Act Notice, see back of form. Cat. No. 20604Q Form **2106-EZ** (1995)

Form **2119**

Department of the Treasury
Internal Revenue Service

Sale of Your Home

▶ **Attach to Form 1040 for year of sale.**

▶ **See separate instructions.**   ▶ **Please print or type.**

OMB No. 1545-0072

1995

Attachment
Sequence No. **20**

Your first name and initial. If a joint return, also give spouse's name and initial.	Last name	Your social security number

| **Fill in Your Address Only If You Are Filing This Form by Itself and Not With Your Tax Return** | Present address (no., street, and apt. no., rural route, or P.O. box no. if mail is not delivered to street address) | Spouse's social security number |
| | City, town or post office, state, and ZIP code | |

Part I   **Gain on Sale**

1	Date your former main home was sold (month, day, year) . . . . ▶	**1**	/ /
2	Have you bought or built a new main home? . . . . ☐ Yes ☐ No		
3	If any part of either main home was ever rented out or used for business, check here ▶ ☐ and see page 3.		
4	Selling price of home. Do not include personal property items you sold with your home . .	**4**	
5	Expense of sale (see page 3)	**5**	
6	Subtract line 5 from line 4	**6**	
7	Adjusted basis of home sold (see page 3)	**7**	
8	**Gain on sale.** Subtract line 7 from line 6	**8**	

┌─────────────┐
│ Is line 8   │ ── **Yes** ──▶ If line 2 is "Yes," you **must** go to Part II or Part III, whichever applies. If line 2 is
│ more than   │   "No," go to line 9.
│ zero?   │
└─────────────┘ ── **No** ──▶ **Stop;** see **Loss on the Sale of Your Home** on page 1.

9	If you haven't replaced your home, do you plan to do so within the **replacement period** (see page 1)? . ☐ Yes ☐ No

● If line 9 is "Yes," stop here, attach this form to your return, and see **Additional Filing Requirements** on page 1.
● If line 9 is "No," you **must** go to Part II or Part III, whichever applies.

Part II   **One-Time Exclusion of Gain for People Age 55 or Older**—By completing this part, you are electing to take the one-time exclusion (see page 2). If you are not electing to take the exclusion, go to Part III now.

10	Who was age 55 or older on the date of sale? . . . . ☐ You ☐ Your spouse ☐ Both of you		
11	Did the person who was 55 or older own and use the property as his or her main home for a total of at least 3 years of the 5-year period before the sale? See page 2 for exceptions. If "No," go to Part III now . . . ☐ Yes ☐ No		
12	At the time of sale, who owned the home? . . . . ☐ You ☐ Your spouse ☐ Both of you		
13	Social security number of spouse at the time of sale if you had a different spouse from the one above. If you were not married at the time of sale, enter "None" . . . . ▶	**13**	
14	**Exclusion.** Enter the **smaller** of line 8 or $125,000 ($62,500 if married filing separate return). Then, go to line 15	**14**	

Part III   **Adjusted Sales Price, Taxable Gain, and Adjusted Basis of New Home**

15	If line 14 is blank, enter the amount from line 8. Otherwise, subtract line 14 from line 8 . .	**15**	

● If line 15 is zero, stop and attach this form to your return.
● If line 15 is more than zero and line 2 is "Yes," go to line 16 now.
● If you are reporting this sale on the installment method, stop and see page 4.
● All others, stop and **enter the amount from line 15 on Schedule D, col. (g), line 4 or line 12.**

16	Fixing-up expenses (see page 4 for time limits)	**16**	
17	If line 14 is blank, enter amount from line 16. Otherwise, add lines 14 and 16	**17**	
18	**Adjusted sales price.** Subtract line 17 from line 6	**18**	
19a	Date you moved into new home ▶ [/ /] **b** Cost of new home (see page 4)	**19b**	
20	Subtract line 19b from line 18. If zero or less, enter -0-	**20**	
21	**Taxable gain.** Enter the **smaller** of line 15 or line 20	**21**	

● If line 21 is zero, go to line 22 and attach this form to your return.
● If you are reporting this sale on the installment method, see the line 15 instructions and go to line 22.
● All others, **enter the amount from line 21 on Schedule D, col. (g), line 4 or line 12,** and go to line 22.

22	Postponed gain. Subtract line 21 from line 15	**22**	
23	**Adjusted basis of new home.** Subtract line 22 from line 19b	**23**	

Sign Here Only If You Are Filing This Form by Itself and Not With Your Tax Return

Under penalties of perjury, I declare that I have examined this form, including attachments, and to the best of my knowledge and belief, it is true, correct, and complete.

Your signature	Date	Spouse's signature	Date
▶		▶	

If a joint return, both must sign.

For Paperwork Reduction Act Notice, see separate instructions.   Cat. No. 11710J   Form **2119** (1995)

✦ Printed on recycled paper

Form **2210**

Department of the Treasury
Internal Revenue Service

**Underpayment of
Estimated Tax by Individuals, Estates, and Trusts**
▶ See separate instructions.
▶ Attach to Form 1040, 1040A, 1040-T, 1040NR, 1040NR-EZ, or 1041.

OMB No. 1545-0140

19**95**

Attachment
Sequence No. **06A**

Name(s) shown on tax return	Identifying number

Note: *In most cases, you **do not** need to file Form 2210. The IRS will figure any penalty you owe and send you a bill. File Form 2210 **only** if one or more boxes in Part I apply to you. If you do not need to file Form 2210, you still may use it to figure your penalty. Enter the amount from line 20 or line 36 on the penalty line of your return, but do not attach Form 2210.*

Part I | **Reasons For Filing**—If 1a, b, or c below applies to you, you may be able to lower or eliminate your penalty. But you MUST check the boxes that apply and file Form 2210 with your tax return. If 1d below applies to you, check that box and file Form 2210 with your tax return.

1   Check whichever boxes apply (if none apply, see the **Note** above):

a ☐   You request a **waiver.** In certain circumstances, the IRS will waive all or part of the penalty. See **Waiver of Penalty** on page 1 of the instructions.

b ☐   You use the **annualized income installment method.** If your income varied during the year, this method may reduce the amount of one or more required installments. See page 4 of the instructions.

c ☐   You had Federal income tax withheld from wages and you treat it as paid for estimated tax purposes when it was **actually** withheld instead of in equal amounts on the payment due dates. See the instructions for line 22.

d ☐   Your required annual payment (line 13 below) is based on your 1994 tax and you filed or are filing a joint return for either 1994 or 1995 but not for both years.

Part II | **Required Annual Payment**

2	Enter your 1995 tax after credits (see instructions)	**2**	
3	Other taxes (see instructions)	**3**	
4	Add lines 2 and 3	**4**	
5	Earned income credit **5**		
6	Credit for Federal tax paid on fuels **6**		
7	Add lines 5 and 6	**7**	
8	Current year tax. Subtract line 7 from line 4	**8**	
9	Multiply line 8 by 90% (.90) **9**		
10	Withholding taxes. **Do not** include any estimated tax payments on this line (see instructions) .	**10**	
11	Subtract line 10 from line 8. If less than $500, stop here; **do not** complete or file this form. You do not owe the penalty	**11**	
12	Enter the tax shown on your 1994 tax return (110% of that amount if the adjusted gross income shown on that return is more than $150,000, or if married filing separately for 1995, more than $75,000). **Caution:** *See instructions*	**12**	
13	**Required annual payment.** Enter the **smaller** of line 9 or line 12	**13**	

Note: *If line 10 is equal to or more than line 13, stop here; you do not owe the penalty. Do not file Form 2210 unless you checked box 1d above.*

Part III | **Short Method (Caution:** *Read the instructions to see if you can use the short method. If you checked box **1b** or **c** in Part I, skip this part and go to Part IV.)*

14	Enter the amount, if any, from line 10 above **14**		
15	Enter the total amount, if any, of estimated tax payments you made **15**		
16	Add lines 14 and 15	**16**	
17	**Total underpayment for year.** Subtract line 16 from line 13. If zero or less, stop here; you do not owe the penalty. Do not file Form 2210 unless you checked box 1d above	**17**	
18	Multiply line 17 by .06066	**18**	
19	• If the amount on line 17 was paid **on or after** 4/15/96, enter -0-.		
	• If the amount on line 17 was paid **before** 4/15/96, make the following computation to find the amount to enter on line 19. $\begin{array}{c}\text{Amount on}\\\text{line 17}\end{array}$ ✕ $\begin{array}{c}\text{Number of days paid}\\\text{before 4/15/96}\end{array}$ ✕ .00025	**19**	
20	**PENALTY.** Subtract line 19 from line 18. Enter the result here and on Form 1040, line 66; Form 1040A, line 34; Form 1040-T, line 42; Form 1040NR, line 66; Form 1040NR-EZ, line 26; or Form 1041, line 26 . . . . ▶	**20**	

For Paperwork Reduction Act Notice, see page 1 of separate instructions.   Cat. No. 11744P   Form **2210** (1995)

Form 2210 (1995)   Page **2**

Part IV — Regular Method (See the instructions if you are filing Form 1040NR or 1040NR-EZ.)

Section A—Figure Your Underpayment		Payment Due Dates			
		(a) 4/15/95	**(b)** 6/15/95	**(c)** 9/15/95	**(d)** 1/15/96
21	**Required installments.** If box 1b applies, enter the amounts from Schedule AI, line 26. Otherwise, enter ¼ of line 13, Form 2210, in each column **21**				
22	Estimated tax paid and tax withheld (see instructions). For column (a) only, also enter the amount from line 22 on line 26. If line 22 is equal to or more than line 21 for all payment periods, stop here; you do not owe the penalty. Do not file Form 2210 unless you checked a box In Part I **22**				
	Complete lines 23 through 29 of one column before going to the next column.				
23	Enter amount, if any, from line 29 of previous column **23**				
24	Add lines 22 and 23 .... **24**				
25	Add amounts on lines 27 and 28 of the previous column **25**				
26	Subtract line 25 from line 24. If zero or less, enter -0-. For column (a) only, enter the amount from line 22 . **26**				
27	If the amount on line 26 is zero, subtract line 24 from line 25. Otherwise, enter -0- **27**				
28	**Underpayment.** If line 21 is equal to or more than line 26, subtract line 26 from line 21. Then go to line 23 of next column. Otherwise, go to line 29 . . ▶ **28**				
29	**Overpayment.** If line 26 is more than line 21, subtract line 21 from line 26. Then go to line 23 of next column **29**				

Section B—Figure the Penalty (Complete lines 30 through 35 of one column before going to the next column.)

Rate Period 1	**April 16, 1995—June 30, 1995**		4/15/95	6/15/95		
	30 Number of days FROM the date shown above line 30 TO the date the amount on line 28 was paid **or** 6/30/95, whichever is earlier **30**		Days:	Days:		
	31 $\dfrac{\text{Underpayment on line 28 (see instructions)} \times \text{Number of days on line 30}}{365} \times .10$ ▶ **31**		$	$		
Rate Period 2	**July 1, 1995—December 31, 1995**		6/30/95	6/30/95	9/15/95	
	32 Number of days FROM the date shown above line 32 TO the date the amount on line 28 was paid **or** 12/31/95, whichever is earlier **32**		Days:	Days:	Days:	
	33 $\dfrac{\text{Underpayment on line 28 (see instructions)} \times \text{Number of days on line 32}}{365} \times .09$ ▶ **33**		$	$	$	
Rate Period 3	**January 1, 1996—April 15, 1996**		12/31/95	12/31/95	12/31/95	1/15/96
	34 Number of days FROM the date shown above line 34 TO the date the amount on line 28 was paid **or** 4/15/96, whichever is earlier **34**		Days:	Days:	Days:	Days:
	35 $\dfrac{\text{Underpayment on line 28 (see instructions)} \times \text{Number of days on line 34}}{366} \times .09$ ▶ **35**		$	$	$	$

36	**PENALTY.** Add all amounts on lines 31, 33, and 35 in all columns. Enter the total here and on Form 1040, line 66; Form 1040A, line 34; Form 1040-T, line 42; Form 1040NR, line 66; Form 1040NR-EZ, line 26; or Form 1041, line 26 .... ▶ **36**	$

Schedule AI—Annualized Income Installment Method (see instructions)

Estates and trusts, **do not** use the period ending dates shown to the right.
Instead, use the following: 2/28/95, 4/30/95, 7/31/95, and 11/30/95.

	(a) 1/1/95–3/31/95	(b) 1/1/95–5/31/95	(c) 1/1/95–8/31/95	(d) 1/1/95–12/31/95

Part I Annualized Income Installments   Caution: *Complete lines 20–26 of one column before going to the next column.*

#	Description	(a)	(b)	(c)	(d)
1	Enter your adjusted gross income for each period (see instructions). (Estates and trusts, enter your taxable income without your exemption for each period.)				
2	Annualization amounts. (Estates and trusts, see instructions.)	4	2.4	1.5	1
3	Annualized income. Multiply line 1 by line 2				
4	Enter your itemized deductions for the period shown in each column. If you do not itemize, enter -0- and skip to line 7. (Estates and trusts, enter -0-, skip to line 9, and enter the amount from line 3 on line 9.)				
5	Annualization amounts	4	2.4	1.5	1
6	Multiply line 4 by line 5 (see instructions if line 3 is more than $57,350)				
7	In each column, enter the full amount of your standard deduction from Form 1040, line 34; Form 1040A, line 19; or Form 1040-T, line 20 (Form 1040NR or 1040NR-EZ filers, enter -0-. **Exception:** Indian students and business apprentices, enter standard deduction from Form 1040NR, line 33 or Form 1040NR-EZ, line 10.)				
8	Enter the **larger** of line 6 or line 7.				
9	Subtract line 8 from line 3				
10	In each column, multiply $2,500 by the total number of exemptions claimed (see instructions if line 3 is more than $86,025). (Estates and trusts and Form 1040NR or 1040NR-EZ filers, enter the exemption amount shown on your tax return.)				
11	Subtract line 10 from line 9				
12	Figure your tax on the amount on line 11 (see instructions)				
13	Form 1040 filers only, enter your self-employment tax from line 35 below				
14	Enter other taxes for each payment period (see instructions)				
15	Total tax. Add lines 12, 13, and 14				
16	For each period, enter the same type of credits as allowed on Form 2210, lines 2, 5, and 6 (see instructions)				
17	Subtract line 16 from line 15. If zero or less, enter -0-				
18	Applicable percentage	22.5%	45%	67.5%	90%
19	Multiply line 17 by line 18				
20	Add the amounts in all preceding columns of line 26				
21	Subtract line 20 from line 19. If zero or less, enter -0-				
22	Enter ¼ of line 13 on page 1 of Form 2210 in each column				
23	Enter amount from line 25 of the preceding column of this schedule				
24	Add lines 22 and 23 and enter the total				
25	Subtract line 21 from line 24. If zero or less, enter -0-				
26	Enter the **smaller** of line 21 or line 24 here and on Form 2210, line 21 ▶				

Part II Annualized Self-Employment Tax

#	Description	(a)	(b)	(c)	(d)
27a	Net earnings from self-employment for the period (see instructions)				
b	Annualization amounts	4	2.4	1.5	1
c	Multiply line 27a by line 27b				
28	Social security tax limit	$61,200	$61,200	$61,200	$61,200
29	Enter actual wages subject to social security tax or the 6.2% portion of the 7.65% railroad retirement (tier 1) tax				
30	Annualization amounts	4	2.4	1.5	1
31	Multiply line 29 by line 30				
32	Subtract line 31 from line 28. If zero or less, enter -0-				
33	Multiply the smaller of line 27c or line 32 by .124				
34	Multiply line 27c by .029				
35	Add lines 33 and 34. Enter the result here and on line 13 above ▶				

Printed on recycled paper

Form **2220**	**Underpayment of Estimated Tax by Corporations**	OMB No. 1545-0142
Department of the Treasury Internal Revenue Service	▶ See separate instructions. ▶ Attach to the corporation's tax return.	**19**95

Name	Employer identification number

Note: *In most cases, the corporation **does not** need to file Form 2220. The IRS will figure any penalty owed and bill the corporation. File Form 2220 **only** if one or more boxes in Part I apply to the corporation. If the corporation does not need to file Form 2220, it may still use it to figure the penalty. Enter the amount from line 36, Part III, on the penalty line of the corporation's income tax return, but do not attach Form 2220.*

Part I **Reasons For Filing**—Check the boxes below that apply to the corporation. If any box is checked, the corporation must file Form 2220 with the corporation's tax return, even if it does not owe the penalty. If the box on line 1 or line 2 applies, the corporation may be able to lower or eliminate the penalty. See instructions.

1 ☐ The corporation is using the annualized income installment method.

2 ☐ The corporation is using the adjusted seasonal installment method.

3 ☐ The corporation is a "large corporation" figuring its first required installment based on the prior year's tax.

Part II **Figuring the Underpayment**

4   Total tax (see instructions) **4**

5a Personal holding company tax included on line 4 (Schedule PH (Form 1120), line 26). **5a**

 b Interest due under the look-back method of section 460(b)(2) for completed long-term contracts included on line 4 . . . . **5b**

 c Credit for Federal tax paid on fuels (see instructions) **5c**

 d **Total.** Add lines 5a through 5c **5d**

6   Subtract line 5d from line 4. If the result is less than $500, **do not** complete or file this form. The corporation does not owe the penalty **6**

7   Enter the tax shown on the corporation's 1994 income tax return. (**CAUTION:** *See the instructions before completing this line.*) **7**

8   Enter the **smaller** of line 6 or line 7. If the corporation is required to skip line 7, enter the amount from line 6 on line 8 . . . . **8**

		(a)	(b)	(c)	(d)
9	**Installment due dates.** Enter in columns (a) through (d) the 15th day of the 4th, 6th, 9th, and 12th months of the corporation's tax year. . . . . ▶				
10	**Required installments.** If the box on line 1 or line 2 above is checked, enter the amounts from Schedule A, line 41. If the box on line 3 (but not 1 or 2) is checked, see the instructions for the amounts to enter. If none of these boxes is checked, enter 25% of line 8 in each column				
11	Estimated tax paid or credited for each period (see instructions). For column (a) only, enter the amount from line 11 on line 15				
	Complete lines 12 through 18 of one column before going to the next column.				
12	Enter amount, if any, from line 18 of the preceding column				
13	Add lines 11 and 12				
14	Add amounts on lines 16 and 17 of the preceding column.				
15	Subtract line 14 from line 13. If zero or less, enter -0-				
16	If the amount on line 15 is zero, subtract line 13 from line 14. Otherwise, enter -0-				
17	**Underpayment.** If line 15 is less than or equal to line 10, subtract line 15 from line 10. Then go to line 12 of the next column. Otherwise, go to line 18 (see instructions) . . .				
18	**Overpayment.** If line 10 is less than line 15, subtract line 10 from line 15. Then go to line 12 of the next column. . .				

Complete Part III on page 2 to figure the penalty. If there are no entries on line 17, no penalty is owed.

For Paperwork Reduction Act Notice, see page 1 of the instructions.   Cat. No. 11746L   Form **2220** (1995)

Part III Figuring the Penalty

		(a)	(b)	(c)	(d)
19	Enter the date of payment or the 15th day of the 3rd month after the close of the tax year, whichever is earlier (see instructions). *(Form 990-PF and Form 990-T filers:* Use 5th month instead of 3rd month.) **19**				
20	Number of days from due date of installment on line 9 to the date shown on line 19 . . . . **20**				
21	Number of days on line 20 after 4/15/95 and before 7/1/95 . **21**				
22	Underpayment on line 17 $\times$ $\dfrac{\text{Number of days on line 21}}{365}$ $\times$ 10% . . **22**	$	$	$	$
23	Number of days on line 20 after 6/30/95 and before 1/1/96 . **23**				
24	Underpayment on line 17 $\times$ $\dfrac{\text{Number of days on line 23}}{365}$ $\times$ 9% . . . **24**	$	$	$	$
25	Number of days on line 20 after 12/31/95 and before 4/1/96. **25**				
26	Underpayment on line 17 $\times$ $\dfrac{\text{Number of days on line 25}}{366}$ $\times$ 9% . . **26**	$	$	$	$
27	Number of days on line 20 after 3/31/96 and before 7/1/96 . **27**				
28	Underpayment on line 17 $\times$ $\dfrac{\text{Number of days on line 27}}{366}$ $\times$ *% . . **28**	$	$	$	$
29	Number of days on line 20 after 6/30/96 and before 10/1/96. **29**				
30	Underpayment on line 17 $\times$ $\dfrac{\text{Number of days on line 29}}{366}$ $\times$ *% . . **30**	$	$	$	$
31	Number of days on line 20 after 9/30/96 and before 1/1/97 . **31**				
32	Underpayment on line 17 $\times$ $\dfrac{\text{Number of days on line 31}}{366}$ $\times$ *% . . **32**	$	$	$	$
33	Number of days on line 20 after 12/31/96 and before 2/16/97 **33**				
34	Underpayment on line 17 $\times$ $\dfrac{\text{Number of days on line 33}}{365}$ $\times$ *% . . **34**	$	$	$	$
35	Add lines 22, 24, 26, 28, 30, 32, and 34. . . . . . . **35**	$	$	$	$

36 **Penalty.** Add columns (a) through (d), line 35. Enter here and on line 33, Form 1120; line 29, Form 1120-A; or comparable line for other income tax returns **36**	$

*If the corporation's tax year ends after December 31, 1995, see the instructions for lines 28, 30, 32, and 34.

Form 2220 (1995)   Page **3**

| Schedule A | Required Installments Using the Annualized Income Installment Method and/or the Adjusted Seasonal Installment Method Under Section 6655(e) (see instructions) |

Form 1120S filers: *For lines 2, 14, 15, and 16, below, "taxable income" refers to excess net passive income or the amount on which tax is imposed under section 1374(a) (or the corresponding provisions of prior law), whichever applies.*

Part I—Annualized Income Installment Method

			(a)	(b)	(c)	(d)
1	Annualization period (see instructions).	1	First ____ months	First ____ months	First ____ months	First ____ months
2	Enter taxable income for each annualization period.	2				
3	Annualization amount (see instructions).	3				
4	Annualized taxable income. Multiply line 2 by line 3.	4				
5	Figure the tax on the amount in each column on line 4 using the instructions for Form 1120, Schedule J, line 3 (or the comparable line of the tax return).	5				
6	Enter other taxes for each payment period (see instructions).	6				
7	Total tax. Add lines 5 and 6.	7				
8	For each period, enter the same type of credits as allowed on Form 2220, lines 4 and 5c (see instructions).	8				
9	Total tax after credits. Subtract line 8 from line 7. If zero or less, enter -0-.	9				
10	Applicable percentage.	10	25%	50%	75%	100%
11	Multiply line 9 by line 10.	11				
12	Add the amounts in all preceding columns of line 41 (see instructions).	12				
13	**Annualized income installments.** Subtract line 12 from line 11. If zero or less, enter -0-.	13				

Part II—Adjusted Seasonal Installment Method (Caution: *Use this method only if the base period percentage for any 6 consecutive months is at least 70%. See instructions for more information.)*

			(a)	(b)	(c)	(d)
			First 3 months	First 5 months	First 8 months	First 11 months
14	Enter taxable income for the following periods:					
a	Tax year beginning in 1992	14a				
b	Tax year beginning in 1993	14b				
c	Tax year beginning in 1994	14c				
15	Enter taxable income for each period for the tax year beginning in 1995.	15				
			First 4 months	First 6 months	First 9 months	Entire year
16	Enter taxable income for the following periods:					
a	Tax year beginning in 1992	16a				
b	Tax year beginning in 1993	16b				
c	Tax year beginning in 1994	16c				
17	Divide the amount in each column on line 14a by the amount in column (d) on line 16a.	17				
18	Divide the amount in each column on line 14b by the amount in column (d) on line 16b.	18				
19	Divide the amount in each column on line 14c by the amount in column (d) on line 16c.	19				

Form 2220 (1995)

			(a) First 4 months	(b) First 6 months	(c) First 9 months	(d) Entire year
20	Add lines 17 through 19.	20				
21	Divide line 20 by 3.	21				
22	Divide line 15 by line 21.	22				
23	Figure the tax on the amount on line 22 using the instructions for Form 1120, Schedule J, line 3 (or the comparable line of the return).	23				
24	Divide the amount in columns (a) through (c) on line 16a by the amount in column (d) on line 16a.	24				
25	Divide the amount in columns (a) through (c) on line 16b by the amount in column (d) on line 16b.	25				
26	Divide the amount in columns (a) through (c) on line 16c by the amount in column (d) on line 16c.	26				
27	Add lines 24 through 26.	27				
28	Divide line 27 by 3.	28				
29	Multiply the amount in columns (a) through (c) of line 23 by columns (a) through (c) of line 28. In column (d), enter the amount from line 23, column (d).	29				
30	Enter other taxes for each payment period (see instructions).	30				
31	Total tax. Add lines 29 and 30.	31				
32	For each period, enter the same type of credits as allowed on Form 2220, lines 4 and 5c (see instructions).	32				
33	Total tax after credits. Subtract line 32 from line 31. If zero or less, enter -0-.	33				
34	Add the amounts in all preceding columns of line 41 (see instructions).	34				
35	**Adjusted seasonal installments.** Subtract line 34 from line 33. If zero or less, enter -0-.	35				

Part III—Required Installments

			1st installment	2nd installment	3rd installment	4th installment
36	If only one of the above parts is completed, enter the amount in each column from line 13 or line 35. If both parts are completed, enter the smaller of the amounts in each column from line 13 or line 35.	36				
37	Divide line 8, page 1 of Form 2220, by 4 and enter the result in each column. **(Note:** *"Large corporations" see the instructions for line 10, Part I, for the amount to enter.)*	37				
38	Enter the amount from line 40 of the preceding column.	38				
39	Add lines 37 and 38.	39				
40	If line 39 is more than line 36, subtract line 36 from line 39. Otherwise, enter -0-.	40				
41	**Required installments.** Enter the smaller of line 36 or line 39 here and on page 1 of Form 2220, line 10.	41				

Form **2441**	**Child and Dependent Care Expenses**	OMB No. 1545-0068
Department of the Treasury Internal Revenue Service (99)	▶ Attach to Form 1040. ▶ See separate instructions.	**19**9**5** Attachment Sequence No. **21**

Name(s) shown on Form 1040 | Your social security number

You need to understand the following terms to complete this form: **Qualifying Person(s), Dependent Care Benefits, Qualified Expenses,** and **Earned Income.** See **Important Terms** on page 1 of the Form 2441 instructions.

Part I   **Persons or Organizations Who Provided the Care**—You **must** complete this part. (If you need more space, use the bottom of page 2.)

1	(a) Care provider's name	(b) Address (number, street, apt. no., city, state, and ZIP code)	(c) Identifying number (SSN or EIN)	(d) Amount paid (see instructions)

2 Add the amounts in column (d) of line 1 . . . . | **2**

3 Enter the number of **qualifying persons** cared for in 1995 . . . . ▶ ☐

Did you receive **dependent care benefits?**   **NO** ──▶ Complete only Part II below.   **YES** ──▶ Complete Part III on the back now.

Part II   **Credit for Child and Dependent Care Expenses**

4 Enter the amount of **qualified expenses** you incurred and paid in 1995. DO NOT enter more than $2,400 for one qualifying person or $4,800 for two or more persons. If you completed Part III, enter the amount from line 25 . . . . | **4**

5 Enter YOUR **earned income** . . . . | **5**

6 If married filing a joint return, enter YOUR SPOUSE'S earned income (if student or disabled, see the instructions); **all others,** enter the amount from line 5 . . . . | **6**

7 Enter the **smallest** of line 4, 5, or 6 . . . . | **7**

8 Enter the amount from Form 1040, line 32 . . . . . . | **8**

9 Enter on line 9 the decimal amount shown below that applies to the amount on line 8

If line 8 is—		Decimal amount is	If line 8 is—		Decimal amount is
Over	But not over		Over	But not over	
$0	10,000	.30	$20,000	22,000	.24
10,000	12,000	.29	22,000	24,000	.23
12,000	14,000	.28	24,000	26,000	.22
14,000	16,000	.27	26,000	28,000	.21
16,000	18,000	.26	28,000	No limit	.20
18,000	20,000	.25			

9   × .

10 Multiply **line 7** by the decimal amount on line 9. Enter the result. Then, see the instructions for the amount of credit to enter on Form 1040, line 41 . . . . | **10**

Caution: *If you paid a person who worked in your home, you may have to pay employment taxes. See the instructions for Form 1040, line 53, on page 26.*

For Paperwork Reduction Act Notice, see separate instructions.   Cat. No. 11862M   Form **2441** (1995)

Part III **Dependent Care Benefits**—Complete this part **only** if you received these benefits.

11 Enter the total amount of **dependent care benefits** you received for 1995. This amount should be shown in box 10 of your W-2 form(s). DO NOT include amounts that were reported to you as wages in box 1 of Form(s) W-2 . . . . **11**

12 Enter the amount forfeited, if any. See the instructions **12**

13 Subtract line 12 from line 11 . . . . **13**

14 Enter the total amount of **qualified expenses** incurred in 1995 for the care of the qualifying person(s) **14**

15 Enter the **smaller** of line 13 or 14 . . . . **15**

16 Enter YOUR **earned income** **16**

17 If married filing a joint return, enter YOUR SPOUSE'S earned income (if student or disabled, see the line 6 instructions); if married filing a separate return, see the instructions for the amount to enter; **all others,** enter the amount from line 16 . . **17**

18 Enter the **smallest** of line 15, 16, or 17. . . . . **18**

19 **Excluded benefits.** Enter here the **smaller** of the following:

   • The amount from line 18, or
   • $5,000 ($2,500 if married filing a separate return **and** you were required to enter your spouse's earned income on line 17). **19**

20 **Taxable benefits.** Subtract line 19 from line 13. Also, include this amount on Form 1040, line 7. On the dotted line next to line 7, write "DCB" **20**

To claim the child and dependent care credit, complete
lines 21–25 below, and lines 4–10 on the front of this form.

21 Enter the amount of qualified expenses you incurred and paid in 1995. DO NOT include on this line any excluded benefits shown on line 19 . . . . **21**

22 Enter $2,400 ($4,800 if two or more qualifying persons) . . . **22**

23 Enter the amount from line 19 . . . . **23**

24 Subtract line 23 from line 22. If zero or less, **STOP.** You cannot take the credit. **Exception.** If you paid 1994 expenses in 1995, see the line 10 instructions **24**

25 Enter the **smaller** of line 21 or 24 here **and** on line 4 on the front of this form **25**

Printed on recycled paper

Form **3903**

Department of the Treasury
Internal Revenue Service

Moving Expenses

▶ **Attach to Form 1040.**

▶ **See instructions on back.**

OMB No. 1545-0062

1995

Attachment
Sequence No. **62**

Name(s) shown on Form 1040

Your social security number

Caution: *If you are a member of the armed forces, see the instructions before completing this form.*

1	Enter the number of miles from your **old home** to your **new workplace** .	**1**	miles
2	Enter the number of miles from your **old home** to your **old workplace** . .	**2**	miles
3	Subtract line 2 from line 1. Enter the result but not less than zero	**3**	miles

Is line 3 at least 50 miles?

Yes ▶ Go to line 4. Also, see **Time Test** in the instructions.

No ▶ You **cannot** deduct your moving expenses. Do not complete the rest of this form.

4	Transportation and storage of household goods and personal effects	**4**
5	Travel and lodging expenses of moving from your old home to your new home. **Do not** include meals .	**5**
6	Add lines 4 and 5	**6**
7	Enter the total amount your employer paid for your move (including the value of services furnished in kind) that is **not** included in the wages box (box 1) of your W-2 form. This amount should be identified with code **P** in box 13 of your W-2 form.	**7**

Is line 6 more than line 7?

Yes ▶ Go to line 8.

No ▶ You **cannot** deduct your moving expenses. If line 6 is less than line 7, subtract line 6 from line 7 and include the result in income on Form 1040, line 7.

8	Subtract line 7 from line 6. Enter the result here and on Form 1040, line 24. This is your **moving expense deduction**	**8**

For Paperwork Reduction Act Notice, see back of form.

Cat. No. 12490K

Form **3903** (1995)

Paperwork Reduction Act Notice

We ask for the information on this form to carry out the Internal Revenue laws of the United States. You are required to give us the information. We need it to ensure that you are complying with these laws and to allow us to figure and collect the right amount of tax.

The time needed to complete and file this form will vary depending on individual circumstances. The estimated average time is:

Recordkeeping	33 min.
Learning about the law or the form	.3 min.
Preparing the form	13 min.
Copying, assembling, and sending the form to the IRS . . .	20 min.

If you have comments concerning the accuracy of these time estimates or suggestions for making this form simpler, we would be happy to hear from you. You can write or call the IRS. See the Instructions for Form 1040.

General Instructions

Purpose of Form

Use Form 3903 to figure your moving expense deduction if you moved to a new principal place of work (workplace) within the United States or its possessions. If you qualify to deduct expenses for more than one move, use a separate Form 3903 for each move.

Note: *Use* **Form 3903-F,** *Foreign Moving Expenses, instead of this form if you are a U.S. citizen or resident alien who moved to a new principal workplace outside the United States or its possessions.*

Additional Information

For more details, get **Pub. 521,** Moving Expenses.

Other Forms You May Have To File

If you sold your main home in 1995, you must file **Form 2119,** Sale of Your Home, to report the sale.

Who May Deduct Moving Expenses

If you moved to a different home because of a change in job location, you may be able to deduct your moving expenses. You may be able to take the deduction whether you are self-employed or an employee. But you must meet certain tests explained next.

Distance Test.—Your new principal workplace must be at least 50 miles farther from your old home than your old workplace was. For example, if your old workplace was 3 miles from your old home, your new workplace must be at least 53 miles from that home. If you did not have an old workplace, your new workplace must be at least 50 miles from your old home. The distance between the two points is the shortest of the more commonly traveled routes between them.

Time Test.—If you are an employee, you must work full time in the general area of your new workplace for at least 39 weeks during the 12 months right after you move. If you are self-employed, you must work full time in the general area of your new workplace for at least 39 weeks during the first 12 months and a total of at least 78 weeks during the 24 months right after you move.

You may deduct your moving expenses even if you have not met the time test before your return is due. You may do this if you expect to meet the 39-week test by the end of 1996 or the 78-week test by the end of 1997. If you deduct your moving expenses on your 1995 return but do not meet the time test, you will have to either:

● Amend your 1995 tax return by filing **Form 1040X,** Amended U.S. Individual Income Tax Return, or

● Report the amount of your 1995 moving expense deduction that reduced your 1995 income tax as income in the year you cannot meet the test. For more details, see **Time Test** in Pub. 521.

If you do not deduct your moving expenses on your 1995 return and you later meet the time test, you may take the deduction by filing an amended return for 1995. To do this, use Form 1040X.

Exceptions to the Time Test.—The time test does not have to be met if any of the following apply:

● Your job ends because of disability.

● You are transferred for your employer's benefit.

● You are laid off or discharged for a reason other than willful misconduct.

● You meet the requirements (explained later) for retirees or survivors living outside the United States.

● You are filing this form for a decedent.

Members of the Armed Forces

If you are in the armed forces, you do not have to meet the **distance and time tests** if the move is due to a permanent change of station. A permanent change of station includes a move in connection with and within 1 year of retirement or other termination of active duty.

How To Complete the Form.—First, complete lines 4 through 6 using your actual expenses. **Do not** reduce your expenses by any reimbursements or allowances you received from the government in connection with the move. Also, do not include any expenses for moving services that were provided by the government. If you and your spouse and dependents are moved to or from different locations, treat the moves as a single move.

Next, enter on line 7 the total reimbursements and allowances you received from the government in connection with the expenses you claimed on lines 4 and 5. **Do not** include the value of moving services provided by the government. Then, complete line 8 if applicable.

Retirees or Survivors Living Outside the United States

If you are a retiree or survivor who moved to a home in the United States or its possessions and you meet the following requirements, you are treated as if you moved to a new workplace located in the United States. You are subject to the distance test. Use this form instead of Form 3903-F to figure your moving expense deduction.

Retirees.—You may deduct moving expenses for a move to a new home in the United States when you actually retire if both your old principal workplace and your old home were outside the United States.

Survivors.—You may deduct moving expenses for a move to a home in the United States if you are the spouse or dependent of a person whose principal workplace at the time of death was outside the United States. In addition, the expenses must be for a move (1) that begins within 6 months after the decedent's death, and (2) from a former home outside the United States that you lived in with the decedent at the time of death.

Reimbursements

If your employer paid for any part of your move, your employer must give you a statement showing a detailed breakdown of reimbursements or payments for moving expenses. Your employer may use **Form 4782,** Employee Moving Expense Information, or his or her own form.

You may choose to deduct moving expenses in the year you are reimbursed by your employer, even though you paid the expenses in a different year. However, special rules apply. See **How To Report** in Pub. 521.

Moving Expenses Incurred Before 1994.—If you were reimbursed for moving expenses incurred before 1994 and you did not deduct those expenses on a prior year's return, you may be able to deduct them on **Schedule A,** Itemized Deductions. But you must use the **1994** Form 3903 to do so. You can get the 1994 Form 3903 by calling 1-800-TAX-FORM (1-800-829-3676).

Specific Instructions

You may deduct the following expenses you incurred in moving your family and dependent household members. Do not deduct expenses for employees such as a maid, nanny, or nurse.

Line 4.—Enter the actual cost to pack, crate, and move your household goods and personal effects. You may also include the cost to store and insure household goods and personal effects within any period of 30 days in a row after the items were moved from your old home and before they were delivered to your new home.

Line 5.—Enter the costs of travel from your old home to your new home. These include transportation and lodging on the way. Include costs for the day you arrive. Although not all the members of your household have to travel together or at the same time, you may only include expenses for one trip per person.

If you use your own car(s), you may figure the expenses by using either:

● Actual out-of-pocket expenses for gas and oil, or

● Mileage at the rate of 9 cents a mile.

You may add parking fees and tolls to the amount claimed under either method. Keep records to verify your expenses.

 Printed on recycled paper

Form **4562**	**Depreciation and Amortization** **(Including Information on Listed Property)**	OMB No. 1545-0172 **1995**
Department of the Treasury Internal Revenue Service (99)	▶ See separate instructions. ▶ Attach this form to your return.	Attachment Sequence No. **67**
Name(s) shown on return	Business or activity to which this form relates	Identifying number

Part I   Election To Expense Certain Tangible Property (Section 179) (Note: *If you have any "Listed Property," complete Part V before you complete Part I.*)

1	Maximum dollar limitation. If an enterprise zone business, see page 1 of the instructions	**1** $17,500
2	Total cost of section 179 property placed in service during the tax year. See page 2 of the instructions	**2**
3	Threshold cost of section 179 property before reduction in limitation	**3** $200,000
4	Reduction in limitation. Subtract line 3 from line 2. If zero or less, enter -0-	**4**
5	Dollar limitation for tax year. Subtract line 4 from line 1. If zero or less, enter -0-. If married filing separately, see page 2 of the instructions	**5**

(a) Description of property	(b) Cost	(c) Elected cost
6		

7	Listed property. Enter amount from line 27.	**7**
8	Total elected cost of section 179 property. Add amounts in column (c), lines 6 and 7	**8**
9	Tentative deduction. Enter the smaller of line 5 or line 8	**9**
10	Carryover of disallowed deduction from 1994. See page 2 of the instructions	**10**
11	Taxable income limitation. Enter the smaller of taxable income (not less than zero) or line 5 (see instructions)	**11**
12	Section 179 expense deduction. Add lines 9 and 10, but do not enter more than line 11	**12**
13	Carryover of disallowed deduction to 1996. Add lines 9 and 10, less line 12 ▶	**13**

Note: *Do not use Part II or Part III below for listed property (automobiles, certain other vehicles, cellular telephones, certain computers, or property used for entertainment, recreation, or amusement). Instead, use Part V for listed property.*

Part II   MACRS Depreciation For Assets Placed in Service ONLY During Your 1995 Tax Year (Do Not Include Listed Property.)

Section A—General Asset Account Election

14   If you are making the election under section 168(i)(4) to group any assets placed in service during the tax year into one or more general asset accounts, check this box. See page 2 of the instructions . . . ▶ ☐

(a) Classification of property	(b) Month and year placed in service	(c) Basis for depreciation (business/investment use only—see instructions)	(d) Recovery period	(e) Convention	(f) Method	(g) Depreciation deduction
Section B—General Depreciation System (GDS) (See page 2 of the instructions.)						
15a 3-year property						
b 5-year property						
c 7-year property						
d 10-year property						
e 15-year property						
f 20-year property						
g Residential rental property			27.5 yrs.	MM	S/L	
			27.5 yrs.	MM	S/L	
h Nonresidential real property			39 yrs.	MM	S/L	
				MM	S/L	
Section C—Alternative Depreciation System (ADS) (See page 4 of the instructions.)						
16a Class life					S/L	
b 12-year			12 yrs.		S/L	
c 40-year			40 yrs.	MM	S/L	

Part III   Other Depreciation (Do Not Include Listed Property.) (See page 4 of the instructions.)

17	GDS and ADS deductions for assets placed in service in tax years beginning before 1995	**17**
18	Property subject to section 168(f)(1) election	**18**
19	ACRS and other depreciation	**19**

Part IV   Summary (See page 4 of the instructions.)

20	Listed property. Enter amount from line 26.	**20**
21	**Total.** Add deductions on line 12, lines 15 and 16 in column (g), and lines 17 through 20. Enter here and on the appropriate lines of your return. Partnerships and S corporations—see instructions	**21**
22	For assets shown above and placed in service during the current year, enter the portion of the basis attributable to section 263A costs	**22**

For Paperwork Reduction Act Notice, see page 1 of the separate instructions.   Cat. No. 12906N   Form **4562** (1995)

Form 4562 (1995)

Part V — Listed Property—Automobiles, Certain Other Vehicles, Cellular Telephones, Certain Computers, and Property Used for Entertainment, Recreation, or Amusement

Note: *For any vehicle for which you are using the standard mileage rate or deducting lease expense, complete **only** 23a, 23b, columns (a) through (c) of Section A, all of Section B, and Section C if applicable.*

Section A—Depreciation and Other Information (Caution: *See page 5 of the instructions for limitations for automobiles.*)

23a Do you have evidence to support the business/investment use claimed? ☐ **Yes** ☐ **No**   **23b** If "Yes," is the evidence written? ☐ **Yes** ☐ **No**

(a) Type of property (list vehicles first)	(b) Date placed in service	(c) Business/ investment use percentage	(d) Cost or other basis	(e) Basis for depreciation (business/investment use only)	(f) Recovery period	(g) Method/ Convention	(h) Depreciation deduction	(i) Elected section 179 cost
24 Property used more than 50% in a qualified business use (See page 5 of the instructions.):								
		%						
		%						
		%						
25 Property used 50% or less in a qualified business use (See page 5 of the instructions.):								
		%				S/L –		
		%				S/L –		
		%				S/L –		

26 Add amounts in column (h). Enter the total here and on line 20, page 1 . . . . . **26**

27 Add amounts in column (i). Enter the total here and on line 7, page 1 . . . . **27**

Section B—Information on Use of Vehicles

Complete this section for vehicles used by a sole proprietor, partner, or other "more than 5% owner," or related person.

If you provided vehicles to your employees, first answer the questions in Section C to see if you meet an exception to completing this section for those vehicles.

	(a) Vehicle 1		(b) Vehicle 2		(c) Vehicle 3		(d) Vehicle 4		(e) Vehicle 5		(f) Vehicle 6	
28 Total business/investment miles driven during the year (DO NOT include commuting miles)												
29 Total commuting miles driven during the year												
30 Total other personal (noncommuting) miles driven												
31 Total miles driven during the year. Add lines 28 through 30.												
	Yes	No	Yes	No	Yes	No	Yes	No	Yes	No	Yes	No
32 Was the vehicle available for personal use during off-duty hours?												
33 Was the vehicle used primarily by a more than 5% owner or related person?												
34 Is another vehicle available for personal use?												

Section C—Questions for Employers Who Provide Vehicles for Use by Their Employees

*Answer these questions to determine if you meet an exception to completing Section B for vehicles used by employees who **are not** more than 5% owners or related persons.*

		Yes	No
35	Do you maintain a written policy statement that prohibits all personal use of vehicles, including commuting, by your employees?		
36	Do you maintain a written policy statement that prohibits personal use of vehicles, except commuting, by your employees? See page 6 of the instructions for vehicles used by corporate officers, directors, or 1% or more owners		
37	Do you treat all use of vehicles by employees as personal use?		
38	Do you provide more than five vehicles to your employees, obtain information from your employees about the use of the vehicles, and retain the information received?		
39	Do you meet the requirements concerning qualified automobile demonstration use? See page 6 of the instructions . .		

Note: *If your answer to 35, 36, 37, 38, or 39 is "Yes," you need not complete Section B for the covered vehicles.*

Part VI — Amortization

(a) Description of costs	(b) Date amortization begins	(c) Amortizable amount	(d) Code section	(e) Amortization period or percentage	(f) Amortization for this year
40 Amortization of costs that begins during your 1995 tax year:					

41 Amortization of costs that began before 1995 . . . . **41**

42 **Total.** Enter here and on "Other Deductions" or "Other Expenses" line of your return . . . **42**

♻ *Printed on recycled paper*

Form **4626**	**Alternative Minimum Tax—Corporations** (including environmental tax)	OMB No. 1545-0175
Department of the Treasury Internal Revenue Service	▶ See separate instructions. ▶ Attach to the corporation's tax return.	**19 95**

Name	Employer identification number

1   Taxable income or (loss) before net operating loss deduction. **(Important:** If the corporation is subject to the environmental tax, see the instructions for line 16 on page 6.**)** . . . . | **1**

2   **Adjustments and preferences:**

a	Depreciation of post-1986 property	**2a**	
b	Amortization of certified pollution control facilities	**2b**	
c	Amortization of mining exploration and development costs	**2c**	
d	Amortization of circulation expenditures (personal holding companies only) . .	**2d**	
e	Adjusted gain or loss	**2e**	
f	Long-term contracts	**2f**	
g	Installment sales	**2g**	
h	Merchant marine capital construction funds	**2h**	
i	Section 833(b) deduction (Blue Cross, Blue Shield, and similar type organizations only)	**2i**	
j	Tax shelter farm activities (personal service corporations only)	**2j**	
k	Passive activities (closely held corporations and personal service corporations only)	**2k**	
l	Loss limitations	**2l**	
m	Depletion	**2m**	
n	Tax-exempt interest from specified private activity bonds	**2n**	
o	Charitable contributions	**2o**	
p	Intangible drilling costs	**2p**	
q	Reserves for losses on bad debts of financial institutions	**2q**	
r	Accelerated depreciation of real property (pre-1987)	**2r**	
s	Accelerated depreciation of leased personal property (pre-1987) (personal holding companies only)	**2s**	
t	Other adjustments	**2t**	

u   Combine lines 2a through 2t . . . . | **2u**

3   Preadjustment alternative minimum taxable income (AMTI). Combine lines 1 and 2u . . . . . . | **3**

4   **Adjusted current earnings (ACE) adjustment:**

a	Enter the corporation's ACE from line 10 of the worksheet on page 8 of the instructions	**4a**	
b	Subtract line 3 from line 4a. If line 3 exceeds line 4a, enter the difference as a negative amount (see page 4 of the instructions for examples)	**4b**	
c	Multiply line 4b by 75% (.75). Enter the result as a positive amount	**4c**	
d	Enter the excess, if any, of the corporation's total increases in AMTI from prior year ACE adjustments over its total reductions in AMTI from prior year ACE adjustments (see page 5 of the instructions). **Note:** You **must** enter an amount on line 4d (even if line 4b is positive)	**4d**	

e   ACE adjustment:

    • If you entered a positive number or zero on line 4b, enter the amount from line 4c here as a positive amount.

    • If you entered a negative number on line 4b, enter the smaller of line 4c or line 4d here as a negative amount. | **4e**

5   Combine lines 3 and 4e. If zero or less, stop here; the corporation does not owe alternative minimum tax . . . . | **5**

6   Alternative tax net operating loss deduction (see page 5 of the instructions) . . . . | **6**

7   **Alternative minimum taxable income.** Subtract line 6 from line 5. . . . . | **7**

For Paperwork Reduction Act Notice, see separate instructions.   Cat. No. 12955I   Form **4626** (1995)

8 Enter the amount from line 7 (alternative minimum taxable income) . . . . | **8** |

9 **Exemption phase-out computation** (if line 8 is $310,000 or more, skip lines 9a and 9b and enter -0- on line 9c):

a Subtract $150,000 from line 8 (if you are completing this line for a member of a controlled group, see page 5 of the instructions). If zero or less, enter -0- . . | **9a** |

b Multiply line 9a by 25% (.25). . . . . | **9b** |

c Exemption. Subtract line 9b from $40,000 (if you are completing this line for a member of a controlled group, see page 5 of the instructions). If zero or less, enter -0- . . . . | **9c** |

10 Subtract line 9c from line 8. If zero or less, enter -0- . . . . | **10** |

11 Multiply line 10 by 20% (.20). . . . . | **11** |

12 Alternative minimum tax foreign tax credit. See page 5 of the instructions for limitations. . . . . | **12** |

13 Tentative minimum tax. Subtract line 12 from line 11. . . . . | **13** |

14 Regular tax liability before all credits except the foreign tax credit and possessions tax credit . . . | **14** |

15 **Alternative minimum tax.** Subtract line 14 from line 13. Enter the result on the appropriate line of the corporation's income tax return (e.g., Form 1120, Schedule J, line 9a). If zero or less, enter -0- . | **15** |

16 **Environmental tax.** Subtract $2 million from line 5 (figured without the corporation's environmental tax deduction). Multiply the excess, if any, by 0.12% (.0012). Enter the result here and on the appropriate line of the corporation's income tax return (e.g., Form 1120, Schedule J, line 9b). If you are completing this line for a member of a controlled group, see page 6 of the instructions. . . . | **16** |

Form **4684**

Department of the Treasury
Internal Revenue Service

Casualties and Thefts

▶ See separate instructions.
▶ Attach to your tax return.
▶ Use a separate Form 4684 for each different casualty or theft.

OMB No. 1545-0177

1995

Attachment
Sequence No. **26**

Name(s) shown on tax return | Identifying number

SECTION A—Personal Use Property (Use this section to report casualties and thefts of property **not** used in a trade or business or for income-producing purposes.)

1 Description of properties (show type, location, and date acquired for each):

Property **A** ....

Property **B** ....

Property **C** ....

Property **D** ....

		Properties (Use a separate column for each property lost or damaged from one casualty or theft.)			
		A	**B**	**C**	**D**
2 Cost or other basis of each property	**2**				
3 Insurance or other reimbursement (whether or not you filed a claim). See instructions . . . . . **Note:** *If line 2 is **more than** line 3, skip line 4.*	**3**				
4 Gain from casualty or theft. If line 3 is **more than** line 2, enter the difference here and skip lines 5 through 9 for that column. See instructions if line 3 includes insurance or other reimbursement you did not claim, or you received payment for your loss in a later tax year	**4**				
5 Fair market value **before** casualty or theft . . .	**5**				
6 Fair market value **after** casualty or theft	**6**				
7 Subtract line 6 from line 5	**7**				
8 Enter the **smaller** of line 2 or line 7	**8**				
9 Subtract line 3 from line 8. If zero or less, enter -0-	**9**				

10 Casualty or theft loss. Add the amounts on line 9. Enter the total	**10**		
11 Enter the amount from line 10 or $100, whichever is **smaller**	**11**		
12 Subtract line 11 from line 10 . . . . **Caution:** *Use only one Form 4684 for lines 13 through 18.*	**12**		
13 Add the amounts on line 12 of all Forms 4684	**13**		
14 Combine the amounts from line 4 of all Forms 4684	**14**		
15 • If line 14 is **more than** line 13, enter the difference here and on Schedule D. Do not complete the rest of this section (see instructions). • If line 14 is **less than** line 13, enter -0- here and continue with the form. • If line 14 is **equal to** line 13, enter -0- here. Do not complete the rest of this section.	**15**		
16 If line 14 is **less than** line 13, enter the difference	**16**		
17 Enter 10% of your adjusted gross income (Form 1040, line 32). Estates and trusts, see instructions	**17**		
18 Subtract line 17 from line 16. If zero or less, enter -0-. Also enter result on Schedule A (Form 1040), line 19. Estates and trusts, enter on the "Other deductions" line of your tax return	**18**		

For Paperwork Reduction Act Notice, see page 1 of separate instructions.   Cat. No. 12997O   · Form **4684** (1995)

Form 4684 (1995)	Attachment Sequence No. **26**	Page **2**

Name(s) shown on tax return. Do not enter name and identifying number if shown on other side.	Identifying number

SECTION B—Business and Income-Producing Property (Use this section to report casualties and thefts of property used in a trade or business or for income-producing purposes.)

Part I **Casualty or Theft Gain or Loss** (Use a separate Part I for each casualty or theft.)

19 Description of properties (show type, location, and date acquired for each):

Property **A** ....

Property **B** ....

Property **C** ....

Property **D** ....

		Properties (Use a separate column for each property lost or damaged from one casualty or theft.)			
		A	**B**	**C**	**D**
20	Cost or adjusted basis of each property	20			
21	Insurance or other reimbursement (whether or not you filed a claim). See the instructions for line 3 . **Note:** *If line 20 is more than line 21, skip line 22.*	21			
22	Gain from casualty or theft. If line 21 is **more than** line 20, enter the difference here and on line 29 or line 34, column **(c)**, except as provided in the instructions for line 33. Also, skip lines 23 through 27 for that column. See the instructions for line 4 if line 21 includes insurance or other reimbursement you did not claim, or you received payment for your loss in a later tax year	22			
23	Fair market value **before** casualty or theft . . .	23			
24	Fair market value **after** casualty or theft	24			
25	Subtract line 24 from line 23	25			
26	Enter the **smaller** of line 20 or line 25	26			
	Note: *If the property was totally destroyed by casualty or lost from theft, enter on line 26 the amount from line 20.*				
27	Subtract line 21 from line 26. If zero or less, enter -0-	27			
28	Casualty or theft loss. Add the amounts on line 27. Enter the total here and on line 29 **or** line 34 (see instructions).			**28**	

Part II **Summary of Gains and Losses** (from separate Parts I)

(a) Identify casualty or theft	(b) Losses from casualties or thefts		(c) Gains from casualties or thefts includible in income
	(i) Trade, business, rental or royalty property	*(ii)* Income-producing property	

Casualty or Theft of Property Held One Year or Less

29		( )	( )	
		( )	( )	
30	Totals. Add the amounts on line 29 . . . . **30**	( )	( )	

31 Combine line 30, columns (b)(i) and (c). Enter the net gain or (loss) here and on Form 4797, line 15. If Form 4797 is not otherwise required, see instructions **31**

32 Enter the amount from line 30, column (b)(ii) here and on Schedule A (Form 1040), line 22. Partnerships, S corporations, estates and trusts, see instructions **32**

Casualty or Theft of Property Held More Than One Year

33	Casualty or theft gains from Form 4797, line 34			**33**
34		( )	( )	
		( )	( )	
35	Total losses. Add amounts on line 34, columns (b)(i) and (b)(ii) . . . **35**	( )	( )	

36 Total gains. Add lines 33 and 34, column (c) **36**

37 Add amounts on line 35, columns (b)(i) and (b)(ii) **37**

38 If the loss on line 37 is **more than** the gain on line 36:

a Combine line 35, column (b)(i) and line 36, and enter the net gain or (loss) here. Partnerships and S corporations see the note below. All others enter this amount on Form 4797, line 15. If Form 4797 is not otherwise required, see instructions **38a**

b Enter the amount from line 35, column (b)(ii) here. Partnerships and S corporations see the note below. Individuals enter this amount on Schedule A (Form 1040), line 22. Estates and trusts, enter on the "Other deductions" line of your tax return **38b**

39 If the loss on line 37 is **equal to** or **less than** the gain on line 36, combine these lines and enter here. Partnerships, see the note below. All others, enter this amount on Form 4797, line 3 . . . . **39**

Note: *Partnerships, enter the amount from line 38a, 38b, or line 39 on Form 1065, Schedule K, line 7. S corporations, enter the amount from line 38a or 38b on Form 1120S, Schedule K, line 6.*

Form **4797**	**Sales of Business Property**	OMB No. 1545-0184
Department of the Treasury Internal Revenue Service (99)	(Also Involuntary Conversions and Recapture Amounts Under Sections 179 and 280F(b)(2)) ► Attach to your tax return. ► See separate instructions.	**1995** Attachment Sequence No. **27**

Name(s) shown on return	Identifying number

1 Enter here the gross proceeds from the sale or exchange of real estate reported to you for 1995 on Form(s) 1099-S (or a substitute statement) that you will be including on line 2, 11, or 22 . . . . **1**

Part I   Sales or Exchanges of Property Used in a Trade or Business and Involuntary Conversions From Other Than Casualty or Theft—Property Held More Than 1 Year

(a) Description of property	(b) Date acquired (mo., day, yr.)	(c) Date sold (mo., day, yr.)	(d) Gross sales price	(e) Depreciation allowed or allowable since acquisition	(f) Cost or other basis, plus improvements and expense of sale	(g) LOSS ((f) minus the sum of (d) and (e))	(h) GAIN ((d) plus (e) minus (f))
2							

3 Gain, if any, from Form 4684, line 39 . . . . **3**

4 Section 1231 gain from installment sales from Form 6252, line 26 or 37 . . . . **4**

5 Section 1231 gain or (loss) from like-kind exchanges from Form 8824 . . . . **5**

6 Gain, if any, from line 34, from other than casualty or theft **6**

7 Add lines 2 through 6 in columns (g) and (h) . . . . **7** (   )

8 Combine columns (g) and (h) of line 7. Enter gain or (loss) here, and on the appropriate line as follows: **8**

Partnerships—Enter the gain or (loss) on Form 1065, Schedule K, line 6. Skip lines 9, 10, 12, and 13 below.

S corporations—Report the gain or (loss) following the instructions for Form 1120S, Schedule K, lines 5 and 6. Skip lines 9, 10, 12, and 13 below, unless line 8 is a gain and the S corporation is subject to the capital gains tax.

All others—If line 8 is zero or a loss, enter the amount on line 12 below and skip lines 9 and 10. If line 8 is a gain and you did not have any prior year section 1231 losses, or they were recaptured in an earlier year, enter the gain as a long-term capital gain on Schedule D and skip lines 9, 10, and 13 below.

9 Nonrecaptured net section 1231 losses from prior years (see instructions) **9**

10 Subtract line 9 from line 8. If zero or less, enter -0-. Also enter on the appropriate line as follows (see instructions): **10**

S corporations—Enter this amount on Schedule D (Form 1120S), line 13, and skip lines 12 and 13 below.

All others—If line 10 is zero, enter the amount from line 8 on line 13 below. If line 10 is more than zero, enter the amount from line 9 on line 13 below, and enter the amount from line 10 as a long-term capital gain on Schedule D.

Part II   Ordinary Gains and Losses

11 Ordinary gains and losses not included on lines 12 through 18 (include property held 1 year or less):

12 Loss, if any, from line 8 . . . . **12**

13 Gain, if any, from line 8, or amount from line 9 if applicable **13**

14 Gain, if any, from line 33 . . . . **14**

15 Net gain or (loss) from Form 4684, lines 31 and 38a **15**

16 Ordinary gain from installment sales from Form 6252, line 25 or 36 . . . . **16**

17 Ordinary gain or (loss) from like-kind exchanges from Form 8824 . . . . **17**

18 Recapture of section 179 expense deduction for partners and S corporation shareholders from property dispositions by partnerships and S corporations (see instructions) **18**

19 Add lines 11 through 18 in columns (g) and (h) . . . . **19** (   )

20 Combine columns (g) and (h) of line 19. Enter gain or (loss) here, and on the appropriate line as follows: **20**

a For all except individual returns: Enter the gain or (loss) from line 20 on the return being filed.

b For individual returns:

   (1) If the loss on line 12 includes a loss from Form 4684, line 35, column (b)(ii), enter that part of the loss here and on line 22 of Schedule A (Form 1040). Identify as from "Form 4797, line 20b(1)." See instructions . . . . **20b(1)**

   (2) Redetermine the gain or (loss) on line 20, excluding the loss, if any, on line 20b(1). Enter here and on Form 1040, line 14 . . **20b(2)**

For Paperwork Reduction Act Notice, see page 1 of separate instructions.   Cat. No. 13086I   Form **4797** (1995)

Form 4797 (1995)   Page **2**

Part III Gain From Disposition of Property Under Sections 1245, 1250, 1252, 1254, and 1255

21	(a) Description of section 1245, 1250, 1252, 1254, or 1255 property:				(b) Date acquired (mo., day, yr.)	(c) Date sold (mo., day, yr.)
A						
B						
C						
D						

	Relate lines 21A through 21D to these columns ▶		Property A	Property B	Property C	Property D
22	Gross sales price (**Note:** See line 1 before completing.) .	22				
23	Cost or other basis plus expense of sale	23				
24	Depreciation (or depletion) allowed or allowable	24				
25	Adjusted basis. Subtract line 24 from line 23	25				
26	Total gain. Subtract line 25 from line 22	26				
27	**If section 1245 property:**					
a	Depreciation allowed or allowable from line 24	27a				
b	Enter the **smaller** of line 26 or 27a	27b				
28	**If section 1250 property:** If straight line depreciation was used, enter -0- on line 28g, except for a corporation subject to section 291.					
a	Additional depreciation after 1975 (see instructions) . . .	28a				
b	Applicable percentage multiplied by the **smaller** of line 26 or line 28a (see instructions)	28b				
c	Subtract line 28a from line 26. If residential rental property or line 26 is not more than line 28a, skip lines 28d and 28e	28c				
d	Additional depreciation after 1969 and before 1976 . . .	28d				
e	Enter the **smaller** of line 28c or 28d	28e				
f	Section 291 amount (corporations only)	28f				
g	Add lines 28b, 28e, and 28f	28g				
29	**If section 1252 property:** Skip this section if you did not dispose of farmland or if this form is being completed for a partnership.					
a	Soil, water, and land clearing expenses	29a				
b	Line 29a multiplied by applicable percentage (see instructions)	29b				
c	Enter the **smaller** of line 26 or 29b	29c				
30	**If section 1254 property:**					
a	Intangible drilling and development costs, expenditures for development of mines and other natural deposits, and mining exploration costs (see instructions)	30a				
b	Enter the **smaller** of line 26 or 30a	30b				
31	**If section 1255 property:**					
a	Applicable percentage of payments excluded from income under section 126 (see instructions)	31a				
b	Enter the **smaller** of line 26 or 31a (see instructions) . .	31b				

Summary of Part III Gains. Complete property columns A through D, through line 31b before going to line 32.

32	Total gains for all properties. Add property columns A through D, line 26	32	
33	Add property columns A through D, lines 27b, 28g, 29c, 30b, and 31b. Enter here and on line 14	33	
34	Subtract line 33 from line 32. Enter the portion from casualty or theft on Form 4684, line 33. Enter the portion from other than casualty or theft on Form 4797, line 6	34	

Part IV Recapture Amounts Under Sections 179 and 280F(b)(2) When Business Use Drops to 50% or Less
See instructions.

			(a) Section 179	(b) Section 280F(b)(2)
35	Section 179 expense deduction or depreciation allowable in prior years	35		
36	Recomputed depreciation. See instructions	36		
37	Recapture amount. Subtract line 36 from line 35. See the instructions for where to report . .	37		

♻ *Printed on recycled paper*

Form **6251**	**Alternative Minimum Tax—Individuals**	OMB No. 1545-0227
Department of the Treasury Internal Revenue Service	▶ See separate instructions. ▶ Attach to Form 1040, Form 1040NR, or Form 1040-T.	**1995** Attachment Sequence No. **32**

Name(s) shown on Form 1040	Your social security number

Part I   Adjustments and Preferences

1	If you itemized deductions on Schedule A (Form 1040) (or you entered the amount from Form 1040-T, Section B, line t, on Form 1040-T, line 20), go to line 2. Otherwise, enter your standard deduction from Form 1040, line 34 (or Form 1040-T, line 20), and go to line 6	**1**	
2	Medical and dental. Enter the smaller of Schedule A (Form 1040), line 4 **or** 2½% of Form 1040, line 32 (Form 1040-T filers, enter the smaller of Section B, line c **or** 2½% of Form 1040-T, line 16)	**2**	
3	Taxes. Enter the amount from Schedule A (Form 1040), line 9 (or the total of lines d through g of Form 1040-T, Section B) .	**3**	
4	Certain interest on a home mortgage not used to buy, build, or improve your home	**4**	
5	Miscellaneous itemized deductions. Enter the amount from Schedule A (Form 1040), line 26 (or Form 1040-T, Section B, line r)	**5**	
6	Refund of taxes. Enter any tax refund from Form 1040, line 10 or line 21 (or Form 1040-T, line 4 or line 9) .	**6**	( )
7	Investment interest. Enter difference between regular tax and AMT deduction	**7**	
8	Post-1986 depreciation. Enter difference between regular tax and AMT depreciation	**8**	
9	Adjusted gain or loss. Enter difference between AMT and regular tax gain or loss	**9**	
10	Incentive stock options. Enter excess of AMT income over regular tax income	**10**	
11	Passive activities. Enter difference between AMT and regular tax income or loss	**11**	
12	Beneficiaries of estates and trusts. Enter the amount from Schedule K-1 (Form 1041), line 8	**12**	
13	Tax-exempt interest from private activity bonds issued after 8/7/86	**13**	

14	Other. Enter the amount, if any, for each item and enter the total on line 14.				
	a Charitable contributions .		**h** Loss limitations		
	b Circulation expenditures .		**i** Mining costs		
	c Depletion		**j** Patron's adjustment . .		
	d Depreciation (pre-1987) .		**k** Pollution control facilities .		
	e Installment sales . . .		**l** Research and experimental		
	f Intangible drilling costs .		**m** Tax shelter farm activities .		
	g Long-term contracts . .		**n** Related adjustments . .	**14**	

15	**Total Adjustments and Preferences.** Combine lines 1 through 14 . . . . ▶	**15**	

Part II   Alternative Minimum Taxable Income

16	Enter the amount from **Form 1040, line 35 (or Form 1040-T, line 21).** If less than zero, enter as a (loss) . ▶	**16**	
17	Net operating loss deduction, if any, from Form 1040, line 21. Enter as a positive amount	**17**	
18	If Form 1040, line 32 (or Form 1040-T, line 16), is over $114,700 (over $57,350 if married filing separately), and you itemized deductions, enter the amount, if any, from line 9 of the worksheet for Schedule A (Form 1040), line 28 (or line 9 of the worksheet for Section B, line t, of Form 1040-T).	**18**	( )
19	Combine lines 15 through 18 . . . . ▶	**19**	
20	Alternative tax net operating loss deduction. See page 5 of the instructions	**20**	
21	**Alternative Minimum Taxable Income.** Subtract line 20 from line 19. (If married filing separately and line 21 is more than $165,000, see page 5 of the instructions.) . . . . ▶	**21**	

Part III   Exemption Amount and Alternative Minimum Tax

22	**Exemption Amount.** (If this form is for a child under age 14, see page 6 of the instructions.)

If your filing status is:	**And line 21 is not over:**	**Enter on line 22:**		
Single or head of household	$112,500	. $33,750		
Married filing jointly or qualifying widow(er) . .	150,000	. 45,000 }	**22**	
Married filing separately	75,000	. 22,500		

If line 21 is **over** the amount shown above for your filing status, see page 6 of the instructions.

23	Subtract line 22 from line 21. If zero or less, enter -0- here and on lines 26 and 28 . . . . . . ▶	**23**	
24	If line 23 is $175,000 or less ($87,500 or less if married filing separately), multiply line 23 by 26% (.26). Otherwise, multiply line 23 by 28% (.28) and subtract $3,500 ($1,750 if married filing separately) from the result . . .	**24**	
25	Alternative minimum tax foreign tax credit. See page 6 of the instructions	**25**	
26	Tentative minimum tax. Subtract line 25 from line 24 . . . . ▶	**26**	
27	Enter your tax from Form 1040, line 38 (plus any amount from Form 4970 included on Form 1040, line 39), minus any foreign tax credit from Form 1040, line 43 (Form 1040-T filers, enter the amount from Form 1040-T, line 26)	**27**	
28	**Alternative Minimum Tax.** (If this form is for a child under age 14, see page 7 of the instructions.) Subtract line 27 from line 26. If zero or less, enter -0-. Enter here and on Form 1040, line 48 (or Form 1040-T, line 31) ▶	**28**	

For Paperwork Reduction Act Notice, see separate instructions.   ♻ *Printed on recycled paper*   Cat. No. 13600G   Form **6251** (1995)

Form **8582**

Department of the Treasury
Internal Revenue Service

Passive Activity Loss Limitations

▶ See separate instructions.
▶ Attach to Form 1040 or Form 1041.

OMB No. 1545-1008

1995

Attachment
Sequence No. **88**

Name(s) shown on return

Identifying number

Part I **1995 Passive Activity Loss**
Caution: See the instructions for Worksheets 1 and 2 on page 8 before completing Part I.

Rental Real Estate Activities With Active Participation (For the definition of active participation see **Active Participation in a Rental Real Estate Activity** on page 4 of the instructions.)

1a Activities with net income (from Worksheet 1, column (a)) . . .	**1a**	
b Activities with net loss (from Worksheet 1, column (b))	**1b** ( )	
c Prior year unallowed losses (from Worksheet 1, column (c)) . .	**1c** ( )	
d Combine lines 1a, 1b, and 1c	**1d**	

All Other Passive Activities

2a Activities with net income (from Worksheet 2, column (a)) . . .	**2a**	
b Activities with net loss (from Worksheet 2, column (b))	**2b** ( )	
c Prior year unallowed losses (from Worksheet 2, column (c)) . .	**2c** ( )	
d Combine lines 2a, 2b, and 2c	**2d**	

3 Combine lines 1d and 2d. If the result is net income or zero, see the instructions for line 3 on page 8. If this line and line 1d are losses, go to line 4. Otherwise, enter -0- on line 9 and go to line 10 . | **3** |

Part II **Special Allowance for Rental Real Estate With Active Participation**
Note: Enter all numbers in Part II as positive amounts. See page 8 of the instructions for examples.

4 Enter the **smaller** of the loss on line 1d or the loss on line 3 . . . . | **4** |

5 Enter $150,000. If married filing separately, see page 8 of the instructions . . . . | **5** |

6 Enter modified adjusted gross income, but not less than zero (see page 8 of the instructions) . . . . | **6** |

Note: If line 6 is equal to or greater than line 5, skip lines 7 and 8, enter -0- on line 9, and then go to line 10. Otherwise, go to line 7.

7 Subtract line 6 from line 5 . . . . | **7** |

8 Multiply line 7 by 50% (.5). **Do not** enter more than $25,000. If married filing separately, see page 9 of the instructions . . . . | **8** |

9 Enter the **smaller** of line 4 or line 8 . . . . | **9** |

Part III **Total Losses Allowed**

10 Add the income, if any, on lines 1a and 2a and enter the total . . . . | **10** |

11 **Total losses allowed from all passive activities for 1995.** Add lines 9 and 10. See pages 10 and 11 of the instructions to find out how to report the losses on your tax return . . . . . | **11** |

For Paperwork Reduction Act Notice, see separate instructions.   Cat. No. 63704F   Form **8582** (1995)

Form 8582 (1995)   Page **2**

Caution: *The worksheets are not required to be filed with your tax return and may be detached before filing Form 8582. Keep a copy of the worksheets for your records.*

Worksheet 1—For Form 8582, Lines 1a, 1b, and 1c (See page 8 of the instructions.)

Name of activity	Current year		Prior year	Overall gain or loss	
	(a) Net income (line 1a)	(b) Net loss (line 1b)	(c) Unallowed loss (line 1c)	(d) Gain	(e) Loss
Total. Enter on Form 8582, lines 1a, 1b, and 1c. ▶					

Worksheet 2—For Form 8582, Lines 2a, 2b, and 2c (See page 8 of the instructions.)

Name of activity	Current year		Prior year	Overall gain or loss	
	(a) Net income (line 2a)	(b) Net loss (line 2b)	(c) Unallowed loss (line 2c)	(d) Gain	(e) Loss
Total. Enter on Form 8582, lines 2a, 2b, and 2c. ▶					

Worksheet 3—Use this worksheet if an amount is shown on Form 8582, line 9 (See page 9 of the instructions.)

Name of activity	Form or schedule to be reported on	(a) Loss	(b) Ratio	(c) Special allowance	(d) Subtract column (c) from column (a)
Total ▶			1.00		

Worksheet 4—Allocation of Unallowed Losses (See page 9 of the instructions.)

Name of activity	Form or schedule to be reported on	(a) Loss	(b) Ratio	(c) Unallowed loss
Total ▶			1.00	

Worksheet 5—Allowed Losses (See page 9 of the instructions.)

Name of activity	Form or schedule to be reported on	(a) Loss	(b) Unallowed loss	(c) Allowed loss
Total ▶				

Worksheet 6—Activities With Losses Reported on Two or More Different Forms or Schedules (See page 9 of the instructions.)

Name of Activity:	(a)	(b)	(c) Ratio	(d) Unallowed loss	(e) Allowed loss
Form or Schedule To Be Reported on:					
1a Net loss plus prior year unallowed loss from form or schedule . ▶					
b Net income from form or schedule . . . . ▶					
c Subtract line 1b from line 1a. If zero or less, enter -0- ▶					
Form or Schedule To Be Reported on:					
1a Net loss plus prior year unallowed loss from form or schedule . ▶					
b Net income from form or schedule . . . . ▶					
c Subtract line 1b from line 1a. If zero or less, enter -0- ▶					
Form or Schedule To Be Reported on:					
1a Net loss plus prior year unallowed loss from form or schedule . ▶					
b Net income from form or schedule . . . . ▶					
c Subtract line 1b from line 1a. If zero or less, enter -0- ▶					
Total . . . . ▶			1.00		

 Printed on recycled paper

Form **8615**	Tax for Children Under Age 14 Who Have Investment Income of More Than $1,300	OMB No. 1545-0998 19**95**
Department of the Treasury Internal Revenue Service	▶ Attach ONLY to the child's Form 1040, Form 1040A, Form 1040NR, or Form 1040-T.	Attachment Sequence No. **33**

Child's name shown on return	Child's social security number

A Parent's name (first, initial, and last). **Caution:** *See instructions on back before completing.* | **B** Parent's social security number

C Parent's filing status (check one):

☐ Single ☐ Married filing jointly ☐ Married filing separately ☐ Head of household ☐ Qualifying widow(er)

Step 1	**Figure child's net investment income**		
1	Enter child's investment income, such as taxable interest and dividend income. See instructions. If this amount is $1,300 or less, **stop;** do not file this form	**1**	
2	If the child DID NOT itemize deductions on Schedule A (Form 1040 or Form 1040NR) or Section B (Form 1040-T), enter $1,300. If the child ITEMIZED deductions, see instructions . . .	**2**	
3	Subtract line 2 from line 1. If the result is zero or less, **stop;** do not complete the rest of this form but ATTACH it to the child's return	**3**	
4	Enter child's **taxable** income from Form 1040, line 37; Form 1040A, line 22; Form 1040NR, line 36; or Form 1040-T, line 25	**4**	
5	Enter the **smaller** of line 3 or line 4 . . . . ▶	**5**	

Step 2	**Figure tentative tax based on the tax rate of the parent listed on line A**		
6	Enter parent's **taxable** income from Form 1040, line 37; Form 1040A, line 22; Form 1040EZ, line 6; Form 1040NR, line 36; Form 1040NR-EZ, line 13; or Form 1040-T, line 25. If the parent transferred property to a trust, see instructions	**6**	
7	Enter the total net investment income, if any, from Forms 8615, line 5, of ALL OTHER children of the parent identified above. **Do not** include the amount from line 5 above	**7**	
8	Add lines 5, 6, and 7	**8**	
9	Tax on line 8 based on the **parent's** filing status. See instructions. If from Capital Gain Tax Worksheet, enter amount from line 4 of that worksheet here ▶ _____	**9**	
10	Enter parent's tax from Form 1040, line 38; Form 1040A, line 23; Form 1040EZ, line 10; Form 1040NR, line 37; Form 1040NR-EZ, line 14; or Form 1040-T, line 26. If from **Capital Gain Tax Worksheet,** enter amount from line 4 of that worksheet here ▶ _____	**10**	
11	Subtract line 10 from line 9. If line 7 is blank, enter on line 13 the amount from line 11; skip lines 12a and 12b	**11**	
12a	Add lines 5 and 7 . . . . **12a**		
b	Divide line 5 by line 12a. Enter the result as a decimal (rounded to two places)	**12b**	× .
13	Multiply line 11 by line 12b . . . . ▶	**13**	

Step 3	**Figure child's tax**—If lines 4 and 5 above are the same, enter -0- on line 15 and go to line 16.		
14	Subtract line 5 from line 4 . . . . **14**		
15	Tax on line 14 based on the **child's** filing status. See instructions. If from Capital Gain Tax Worksheet, enter amount from line 4 of that worksheet here ▶ _____	**15**	
16	Add lines 13 and 15	**16**	
17	Tax on line 4 based on the **child's** filing status. See instructions. If from Capital Gain Tax Worksheet, check here . . . . ▶ ☐	**17**	
18	Enter the **larger** of line 16 or line 17 here and on Form 1040, line 38; Form 1040A, line 23; Form 1040NR, line 37; or Form 1040-T, line 26. Be sure to check the box (or, on Form 1040-T, fill in the space) for "Form 8615" even if line 17 is more than line 16 . . . . ▶	**18**	

General Instructions

Caution: *At the time this form was printed, Congress was considering legislation that would change the tax treatment of capital gains. For information on the changes, get* **Pub. 553,** *Highlights of 1995 Tax Changes.*

Purpose of Form.—For children under age 14, investment income over $1,300 is taxed at the parent's rate if the parent's rate is higher than the child's rate. If the child's investment income is more than $1,300, use this form to figure the child's tax.

Investment Income.—As used on this form, "investment income" includes all taxable income other than earned income as defined on page 2. It includes taxable interest, dividends, capital gains, rents, royalties, etc. It also includes pension and annuity income and income (other than earned income) received as the beneficiary of a trust.

Who Must File.—Generally, Form 8615 must be filed for any child who was under age 14 on January 1, 1996, had more than $1,300 of investment income, and is required to file a tax return. If neither

parent was alive on December 31, 1995, do not use Form 8615. Instead, figure the child's tax in the normal manner.

Note: *The parent may be able to elect to report the child's interest and dividends on his or her return. If the parent makes this election, the child will not have to file a return or Form 8615. For more details, see the child's tax return instruction booklet or get* **Form 8814,** *Parents' Election To Report Child's Interest and Dividends.*

Additional Information.—For more details, get **Pub. 929,** Tax Rules for Children and Dependents.

For Paperwork Reduction Act Notice, see back of form.   Cat. No. 64113U   Form **8615** (1995)

Incomplete Information for Parent.—If the parent's taxable income or filing status or the net investment income of the parent's other children is not known by the due date of the child's return, reasonable estimates may be used. Write "Estimated" on the appropriate line(s) of Form 8615. For more details, see Pub. 929.

Amended Return.—If after the child's return is filed the parent's taxable income is changed or the net investment income of any of the parent's other children is changed, the child's tax must be refigured using the adjusted amounts. If the child's tax is changed as a result of the adjustment(s), file **Form 1040X,** Amended U.S. Individual Income Tax Return, to correct the child's tax.

Alternative Minimum Tax.—A child whose tax is figured on Form 8615 may owe the alternative minimum tax. For details, get **Form 6251,** Alternative Minimum Tax— Individuals, and its instructions.

Line Instructions

Section references are to the Internal Revenue Code. Form 1040-T references are to a new form sent to certain individuals on a test basis.

Lines A and B.—If the child's parents were married to each other and filed a joint return, enter the name and social security number (SSN) of the parent who is listed first on the joint return. For example, if the father's name is listed first on the return and his SSN is entered in the block labeled "Your social security number," enter his name on line A and his SSN on line B.

If the parents were married but filed separate returns, enter the name and SSN of the parent who had the **higher** taxable income. If you do not know which parent had the higher taxable income, see Pub. 929.

If the parents were unmarried, treated as unmarried for Federal income tax purposes, or separated either by a divorce or separate maintenance decree, enter the name and SSN of the parent who had custody of the child for most of the year (the custodial parent).

Exception. If the custodial parent remarried and filed a joint return with his or her new spouse, enter the name and SSN of the person listed first on the joint return, even if that person is not the child's parent. If the custodial parent and his or her new spouse filed separate returns, enter the name and SSN of the person with the **higher** taxable income, even if that person is not the child's parent.

Note: *If the parents were unmarried but lived together during the year with the child, enter the name and SSN of the parent who had the **higher** taxable income.*

Line 1.—If the child had no earned income (defined later), enter the child's adjusted gross income from Form 1040, line 32; Form 1040A, line 17; Form 1040NR, line 32; or Form 1040-T, line 16.

If the child had earned income, use the following worksheet to figure the amount to enter on line 1. But if the child files **Form 2555,** Foreign Earned Income, or **Form 2555-EZ,** Foreign Earned Income Exclusion, has a net loss from self-employment, or claims a net operating loss deduction, **do not** use the worksheet below. Instead, use the worksheet in Pub. 929 to figure the amount to enter on line 1.

Worksheet (keep a copy for your records)

1. Enter the amount from the child's Form 1040, line 22; Form 1040A, line 14; Form 1040NR, line 23; or Form 1040-T, line 10, whichever applies . . . . . _____
2. Enter the child's **earned income** (defined below) plus any deduction the child claims on Form 1040, line 28; Form 1040NR, line 28; or Form 1040-T, line 13, whichever applies. . . _____
3. Subtract line 2 from line 1. Enter the result here and on Form 8615, line 1 . . . _____

Earned income includes wages, tips, and other payments received for personal services performed. Generally, it is the total of the amounts reported on Form 1040, lines 7, 12, and 18; Form 1040A, line 7; Form 1040NR, lines 8, 13, and 19; or Form 1040-T, line 1.

Line 2.—If the child itemized deductions, enter the **greater** of:

• $650 plus the portion of the amount on Schedule A (Form 1040), line 28, Schedule A (Form 1040NR), line 17, or Section B (Form 1040-T), line t, that is directly connected with the production of the investment income on Form 8615, line 1; **OR**

• $1,300.

Line 6.—If the parent's taxable income is less than zero, enter zero on line 6. If the parent filed a joint return, enter the taxable income shown on that return even if the parent's spouse is not the child's parent. If the parent transferred property to a trust that sold or exchanged the property during the year at a gain, include any gain that was taxed to the trust under section 644 in the amount entered on line 6. Enter "Section 644" and the amount to the right of the line 6 entry. Also, see the instructions for line 10.

Line 9.—Figure the tax using the Tax Table, Tax Rate Schedules, or the Capital Gain Tax Worksheet, whichever applies. If any net capital gain is included on lines 5, 6, and/or 7, the tax on the amount on line 8 may be less if the Capital Gain Tax Worksheet can be used to figure the tax. See Pub. 929 for details on how to figure the net capital gain included on line 8 and how to complete the worksheet. The Capital Gain Tax Worksheet should be used if:

the parent's filing status is:	AND	the amount on Form 8615, line 8, is over:
• Single		$56,550
• Married filing jointly or Qualifying widow(er)		$94,250
• Married filing separately		$47,125
• Head of household		$80,750

If the Capital Gain Tax Worksheet is used to figure the tax, enter on Form 8615, line 9, the amount from line 13 of that worksheet. Also, enter the amount from line 4 of that worksheet in the space next to line 9 of Form 8615.

Line 10.—If the parent filed a joint return, enter the tax shown on that return even if the parent's spouse is not the child's parent. If the parent filed Form 8814, enter "Form 8814" and the total tax from line 8 of Form(s) 8814 in the space next to line 10 of Form 8615.

If line 6 includes any gain taxed to a trust under section 644, add the tax imposed under section 644(a)(2)(A) to the tax shown on the parent's return and enter the total on line 10. Also, enter "Section 644" next to line 10.

Line 15.—Figure the tax using the Tax Table, Tax Rate Schedule X, or the Capital Gain Tax Worksheet, whichever applies. If line 14 is more than $56,550 and includes any net capital gain, the tax may be less if the Capital Gain Tax Worksheet is used to figure the tax. See Pub. 929 for details on how to figure the net capital gain included on line 14 and how to complete the worksheet.

Line 17.—Figure the tax as if these rules did not apply. For example, if the child can use the Capital Gain Tax Worksheet to figure his or her tax, complete that worksheet.

Paperwork Reduction Act Notice.—We ask for the information on this form to carry out the Internal Revenue laws of the United States. You are required to give us the information. We need it to ensure that you are complying with these laws and to allow us to figure and collect the right amount of tax.

The time needed to complete and file this form will vary depending on individual circumstances. The estimated average time is: **Recordkeeping,** 13 min.; **Learning about the law or the form,** 12 min.; **Preparing the form,** 45 min.; and **Copying, assembling, and sending the form to the IRS,** 17 min.

If you have comments concerning the accuracy of these time estimates or suggestions for making this form simpler, we would be happy to hear from you. See the instructions for the tax return with which this form is filed.

Printed on recycled paper

Form **8824**

Department of the Treasury
Internal Revenue Service

Like-Kind Exchanges
(and nonrecognition of gain from conflict-of-interest sales)
► See separate instructions.   ► Attach to your tax return.
► Use a separate form for each like-kind exchange.

OMB No. 1545-1190

1995

Attachment
Sequence No. **49**

Name(s) shown on tax return

Identifying number

| **Part I** | **Information on the Like-Kind Exchange** |

Note: *If the property described on line 1 or line 2 is real property located outside the United States, indicate the country.*

1 Description of like-kind property given up ► ....

2 Description of like-kind property received ► ....

3	Date like-kind property given up was originally acquired (month, day, year)	**3**	/ /
4	Date you actually transferred your property to other party (month, day, year)	**4**	/ /
5	Date the like-kind property you received was identified (month, day, year). See instructions .	**5**	/ /
6	Date you actually received the like-kind property from other party (month, day, year) . . .	**6**	/ /

7 Was the exchange made with a related party? If "Yes," complete Part II. If "No," go to Part III. See instructions.
  a ☐ Yes, in this tax year   **b** ☐ Yes, in a prior tax year   **c** ☐ No.

| **Part II** | **Related Party Exchange Information** |

8 Name of related party

Related party's identifying number

Address (no., street, and apt., room, or suite no.)

City or town, state, and ZIP code

Relationship to you

9 During this tax year (and before the date that is 2 years after the last transfer of property that was part of the exchange), did the related party sell or dispose of the like-kind property received from you in the exchange?   ☐ Yes ☐ No

10 During this tax year (and before the date that is 2 years after the last transfer of property that was part of the exchange), did you sell or dispose of the like-kind property you received? . . . .   ☐ Yes ☐ No

*If both lines 9 and 10 are "No" and this is the year of the exchange, go to Part III. If either line 9 or line 10 is "Yes," the deferred gain or (loss) from line 24 **must** be reported on your return this tax year, **unless** one of the exceptions on line 11 applies. See* **Related Party Exchanges** *in the instructions.*

11 If one of the exceptions below applies to the disposition, check the applicable box:
  a ☐ The disposition was after the death of either of the related parties.
  b ☐ The disposition was an involuntary conversion, and the threat of conversion occurred after the exchange.
  c ☐ You can establish to the satisfaction of the IRS that neither the exchange nor the disposition had tax avoidance as its principal purpose. If this box is checked, attach an explanation. See instructions.

| **Part III** | **Realized Gain or (Loss), Recognized Gain, and Basis of Like-Kind Property Received** |

Caution: *If you transferred* **and** *received (a) more than one group of like-kind properties, or (b) cash or other (not like-kind) property, see instructions under* **Multi-Asset Exchanges.**

Note: *Complete lines 12 through 14 ONLY if you gave up property that was not like-kind. Otherwise, go to line 15.*

12	Fair market value (FMV) of other property given up	**12**	
13	Adjusted basis of other property given up	**13**	
14	Gain or (loss) recognized on other property given up. Subtract line 13 from line 12. Report the gain or (loss) in the same manner as if the exchange had been a sale	**14**	
15	Cash received, FMV of other property received, plus net liabilities assumed by other party, reduced (but not below zero) by any exchange expenses you incurred. See instructions	**15**	
16	FMV of like-kind property you received	**16**	
17	Add lines 15 and 16	**17**	
18	Adjusted basis of like-kind property you gave up, net amounts paid to other party, plus any exchange expenses **not** used on line 15. See instructions	**18**	
19	**Realized gain or (loss).** Subtract line 18 from line 17	**19**	
20	Enter the smaller of line 15 or line 19, but not less than zero	**20**	
21	Ordinary income under recapture rules. Enter here and on Form 4797, line 17. See instructions .	**21**	
22	Subtract line 21 from line 20. If zero or less, enter -0-. If more than zero, enter here and on Schedule D or Form 4797, unless the installment method applies. See instructions	**22**	
23	**Recognized gain.** Add lines 21 and 22	**23**	
24	Deferred gain or (loss). Subtract line 23 from line 19. If a related party exchange, see instructions .	**24**	
25	**Basis of like-kind property received.** Subtract line 15 from the sum of lines 18 and 23 . .	**25**	

For Paperwork Reduction Act Notice, see separate instructions.   Cat. No. 12311A   Form **8824** (1995)

Form 8824 (1995)   Page **2**

Name(s) shown on tax return. Do not enter name and social security number if shown on other side.	Your social security number

Part IV **Section 1043 Conflict-of-Interest Sales.** See instructions. Attach a copy of your certificate of divestiture.

Note: *This part is only to be used by officers or employees of the executive branch of the Federal Government for reporting nonrecognition of gain under section 1043 on the sale of property to comply with the conflict-of-interest requirements. This part can be used only if the cost of the replacement property exceeds the basis of the divested property.*

26 Description of divested property ▶ ....

27 Description of replacement property ▶ ....

28 Date divested property was sold (month, day, year) . . . . **28**   /   /

29 Sales price of divested property. See instructions **29**

30 Basis of divested property **30**

31 **Realized gain.** Subtract line 30 from line 29 . . . . **31**

32 Cost of replacement property purchased within 60 days after date of sale **32**

33 Subtract line 32 from line 29. If zero or less, enter -0- **33**

34 Ordinary income under recapture rules. Enter here and on Form 4797, line 11. See instructions **34**

35 Subtract line 34 from line 33. If zero or less, enter -0-. If more than zero, enter here and on Schedule D or Form 4797. See instructions **35**

36 **Recognized gain.** Add lines 34 and 35 . . . . **36**

37 Deferred gain. Subtract line 36 from line 31 . . . . **37**

38 **Basis of replacement property.** Subtract line 37 from line 32 . . . . **38**

 Printed on recycled paper

Form **8829**	**Expenses for Business Use of Your Home**	OMB No. 1545-1266
Department of the Treasury Internal Revenue Service (99)	▶ File only with Schedule C (Form 1040). Use a separate Form 8829 for each home you used for business during the year. ▶ See separate instructions.	**19 95** Attachment Sequence No. **66**

Name(s) of proprietor(s) | Your social security number

Part I   Part of Your Home Used for Business

1	Area used regularly and exclusively for business, regularly for day care, or for inventory storage. See instructions	**1**	
2	Total area of home	**2**	
3	Divide line 1 by line 2. Enter the result as a percentage	**3**	%

● For day-care facilities not used exclusively for business, also complete lines 4–6.
● All others, skip lines 4–6 and enter the amount from line 3 on line 7.

4	Multiply days used for day care during year by hours used per day	**4**	hr.
5	Total hours available for use during the year (365 days × 24 hours). See instructions	**5**	8,760 hr.
6	Divide line 4 by line 5. Enter the result as a decimal amount	**6**	.
7	Business percentage. For day-care facilities not used exclusively for business, multiply line 6 by line 3 (enter the result as a percentage). All others, enter the amount from line 3 ▶	**7**	%

Part II   Figure Your Allowable Deduction

8	Enter the amount from Schedule C, line 29, **plus** any net gain or (loss) derived from the business use of your home and shown on Schedule D or Form 4797. If more than one place of business, see instructions		**8**	

See instructions for columns (a) and (b) before completing lines 9–20.

		(a) Direct expenses	(b) Indirect expenses		
9	Casualty losses. See instructions	**9**			
10	Deductible mortgage interest. See instructions	**10**			
11	Real estate taxes. See instructions	**11**			
12	Add lines 9, 10, and 11	**12**			
13	Multiply line 12, column (b) by line 7		**13**		
14	Add line 12, column (a) and line 13			**14**	
15	Subtract line 14 from line 8. If zero or less, enter -0-			**15**	
16	Excess mortgage interest. See instructions	**16**			
17	Insurance	**17**			
18	Repairs and maintenance	**18**			
19	Utilities	**19**			
20	Other expenses. See instructions	**20**			
21	Add lines 16 through 20	**21**			
22	Multiply line 21, column (b) by line 7		**22**		
23	Carryover of operating expenses from 1994 Form 8829, line 41		**23**		
24	Add line 21 in column (a), line 22, and line 23			**24**	
25	Allowable operating expenses. Enter the **smaller** of line 15 or line 24			**25**	
26	Limit on excess casualty losses and depreciation. Subtract line 25 from line 15			**26**	
27	Excess casualty losses. See instructions		**27**		
28	Depreciation of your home from Part III below		**28**		
29	Carryover of excess casualty losses and depreciation from 1994 Form 8829, line 42		**29**		
30	Add lines 27 through 29			**30**	
31	Allowable excess casualty losses and depreciation. Enter the **smaller** of line 26 or line 30			**31**	
32	Add lines 14, 25, and 31			**32**	
33	Casualty loss portion, if any, from lines 14 and 31. Carry amount to **Form 4684**, Section B			**33**	
34	Allowable expenses for business use of your home. Subtract line 33 from line 32. Enter here and on Schedule C, line 30. If your home was used for more than one business, see instructions ▶			**34**	

Part III   Depreciation of Your Home

35	Enter the **smaller** of your home's adjusted basis or its fair market value. See instructions	**35**	
36	Value of land included on line 35	**36**	
37	Basis of building. Subtract line 36 from line 35	**37**	
38	Business basis of building. Multiply line 37 by line 7	**38**	
39	Depreciation percentage. See instructions	**39**	%
40	Depreciation allowable. Multiply line 38 by line 39. Enter here and on line 28 above. See instructions	**40**	

Part IV   Carryover of Unallowed Expenses to 1996

41	Operating expenses. Subtract line 25 from line 24. If less than zero, enter -0-	**41**	
42	Excess casualty losses and depreciation. Subtract line 31 from line 30. If less than zero, enter -0-	**42**	

For Paperwork Reduction Act Notice, see page 1 of separate instructions.   ✿ *Printed on recycled paper*   Cat. No. 13232M   Form **8829** (1995)

APPENDIX C
Glossary of Tax Terms

The words and phrases in this glossary have been defined to reflect their conventional use in the field of taxation. The definitions may therefore be incomplete for other purposes.

A

Abandoned spouse. The abandoned spouse provision enables a married taxpayer with a dependent child whose spouse did not live in the taxpayer's home during the last six months of the tax year to file as a head of household rather than as married filing separately.

Accelerated cost recovery system (ACRS). A method in which the cost of tangible property is recovered over a prescribed period of time. Enacted by the Economic Recovery Tax Act (ERTA) of 1981 and substantially modified by the Tax Reform Act (TRA) of 1986 (the modified system is referred to as MACRS), the approach disregards salvage value, imposes a period of cost recovery that depends upon the classification of the asset into one of various recovery periods, and prescribes the applicable percentage of cost that can be deducted each year. § 168.

Accelerated depreciation. Various methods of depreciation that yield larger deductions in the earlier years of the life of an asset than the straight-line method. Examples include the double declining-balance and the sum-of-the-years' digits methods of depreciation.

Accountable plan. An accountable plan is a type of expense reimbursement plan that requires an employee to render an adequate accounting to the employer and return any excess reimbursement or allowance. If the expense qualifies, it will be treated a deduction *for* AGI.

Accounting method. The method under which income and expenses are determined for tax purposes. Important accounting methods include the cash basis and the accrual basis. Special methods are available for the reporting of gain on installment sales, recognition of income on construction projects (the completed contract and percentage of completion methods), and the valuation of inventories (last-in, first-out and first-in, first-out). §§ 446–474. See also *accrual method, cash receipts method, completed contract method,* and *percentage of completion method.*

Accounting period. The period of time, usually a year, used by a taxpayer for the determination of tax liability. Unless a fiscal year is chosen, taxpayers must determine and pay their income tax liability by using the calendar year (January 1 through December 31) as the period of measurement. An example of a fiscal year is July 1 through June 30. A change in accounting period (e.g., from a calendar year to a fiscal year) generally requires the consent of the IRS. Some new taxpayers, such as a newly formed corporation, are free to select either an initial calendar or a fiscal year without the consent of the IRS. §§ 441–444. See also *annual accounting period concept.*

Accrual basis. See *accrual method.*

Accrual method. A method of accounting that reflects expenses incurred and income earned for any one tax year. In contrast to the cash basis of accounting, expenses do not have to be paid to be deductible, nor does income have to be received to be taxable. Unearned income (e.g., prepaid interest and rent) generally is taxed in the year of receipt regardless of the method of accounting used by the taxpayer. § 446(c)(2). See also *accounting method, cash receipts method,* and *unearned income.*

Accumulated adjustments account (AAA). An account that aggregates an S corporation's post-1982 income, loss, and deductions for the tax year (including nontaxable income and nondeductible losses and expenses). After the year-end income and expense adjustments are made, the account is reduced by distributions made during the tax year.

Accumulated earnings and profits. Net undistributed tax-basis earnings of the corporation aggregated from March 1, 1913, to the end of the prior tax year. Used to determine the amount of dividend income associated with a distribution to shareholders. See *current earnings and profits* and *earnings and profits.* § 316 and Reg. § 1.316-2.

Accumulation distribution. The amount by which total distributions for the tax year exceed a complex trust's distributable net income. This amount is thrown back to previous years, and any excess tax that would have been due at the beneficiary level is collectible, under a short-cut computation. The purpose of the tax is to discourage trustees from delaying distributions until the beneficiary's marginal rate is less than that of the trust. Accumulations prior to a beneficiary's age 21, by an estate, or of corpus capital gains, are not subject to this tax.

Accumulated earnings credit. A reduction allowed in arriving at accumulated taxable income in determining the accumulated earnings tax. See also *accumulated earnings tax* and *accumulated taxable income.*

Accumulated earnings tax (AET). A special tax imposed on corporations that accumulate (rather than distribute) their earnings beyond the reasonable needs of the business. The accumulated earnings tax and related interest are imposed on accumulated taxable income in addition to the corporate income tax. §§ 531–537.

Accumulated taxable income. The base upon which the accumulated earnings tax is imposed. Generally, it is the taxable income of the corporation as adjusted for certain items (e.g., the Federal income tax, excess charitable contributions, the dividends received deduction) less the dividends paid deduction and the accumulated earnings credit. § 535.

Accumulating trust. See *discretionary trust.*

Accuracy-related penalty. Major civil taxpayer penalties relating to the accuracy of tax return data, including misstatements stemming from taxpayer negligence and improper valuation of income and deductions, are coordinated under this umbrella term. The penalty usually equals twenty percent of the understated tax liability.

Acquiescence. Agreement by the IRS on the results reached in certain judicial decisions; sometimes abbreviated *Acq.* or *A.* See also *nonacquiescence.*

Acquisition. See *corporate acquisition.*

Acquisition indebtedness. Debt incurred in acquiring, constructing, or substantially improving a qualified residence of the taxpayer. The interest on such loans is deductible as *qualified residence interest.* However, interest on such debt is deductible only on the portion of the indebtedness that does not exceed $1,000,000 ($500,000 for married persons filing separate returns). § 163(h)(3). See also *home equity loans.*

ACRS. See *accelerated cost recovery system.*

Ad valorem tax. A tax imposed on the value of property. The most common ad valorem tax is that imposed by states, counties, and cities on real estate. Ad valorem taxes can be imposed on personal property as well. See also *personalty.*

Adjusted basis. The cost or other basis of property reduced by depreciation allowed or allowable and increased by capital improvements. Other special adjustments are provided in § 1016 and the related Regulations. See also *basis.*

Adjusted current earnings (ACE) adjustment. An adjustment in computing corporate alternative minimum taxable income (AMTI), computed at 75 percent of the excess of adjusted current earnings and profits over unadjusted AMTI. ACE computations reflect restrictions on the timing of certain recognition events. Exempt interest, life insurance proceeds, and other receipts that are included in earnings and profits but not in taxable income also increase the ACE adjustment. If unadjusted AMTI exceeds adjusted current earnings and profits, the ACE adjustment is negative. The negative adjustment is limited to the aggregate of the positive adjustments under ACE for prior years, reduced by any previously claimed negative adjustments. See also *alternative minimum tax* and *earnings and profits.*

Adjusted gross estate. The gross estate of a *decedent* reduced by § 2053 expenses (e.g., administration, funeral) and § 2054 losses (e.g., casualty). The determination of the adjusted gross estate is necessary in testing for the extension of time for installment payment of estate taxes under § 6166. See also *gross estate.*

Adjusted gross income (AGI). A tax determination unique to individual taxpayers. Generally, it represents the gross income of an individual, less business expenses and less any appropriate capital loss adjustment. See also *gross income.*

Adjusted ordinary gross income. A determination unique to the *personal holding company tax.* In ascertaining whether a corporation is a personal holding company, personal holding company income divided by adjusted ordinary gross income must equal 60 percent or more. Adjusted ordinary gross income is the corporation's gross income less capital gains, § 1231 gains, and certain expenses. §§ 541 and 543(b)(2). See also *personal holding company income.*

Adjusted sales price. The amount realized from the sale of a residence reduced by the fixing-up expenses is the adjusted sales price. An amount equal to the adjusted sales price must be reinvested in a replacement residence to defer the recognition of the realized gain on the sale of a residence. See also *amount realized, fixing-up expenses,* and *realized gain or loss.*

Adjusted taxable estate. The taxable estate reduced by $60,000. The adjusted taxable estate is utilized in applying § 2011 for determining the limit on the credit for state death taxes paid that will be allowed against the Federal estate tax. See also *taxable estate.*

Administration. The supervision and winding up of an estate. The administration of an estate runs from the date of an individual's death until all assets have been distributed and liabilities paid.

Administrator. A person appointed by the court to administer (manage or take charge of) the assets and liabilities of a decedent (the deceased). The person may be a male (administrator) or a female (administratrix). See also *executor.*

Affiliated group. A parent-subsidiary group of corporations that is eligible to elect to file on a consolidated basis. Eighty percent ownership of the voting power and value of all of the corporations must be achieved on every day of the tax year, and an identifiable parent corporation must exist (i.e., it must own at least eighty percent of another group member without applying attribution rules).

AFTR. Published by Research Institute of America (formerly by Prentice-Hall), *American Federal Tax Reports* contain all of the Federal tax decisions issued by the U.S. District Courts, U.S. Court of Federal Claims, U.S. Courts of Appeals, and the U.S. Supreme Court.

AFTR2d. The second series of the *American Federal Tax Reports,* dealing with 1954 and 1986 Code case law.

Aggregate concept. The theory of partnership taxation under which, in certain cases, a partnership is treated as a mere extension of each partner.

Alimony and separate maintenance. Alimony deductions result from the payment of a legal obligation arising from the termination of a marital relationship. Payments designated as alimony generally are included in the gross income of the recipient and are deductible *for* AGI by the payer.

Allocable share of income. Certain entities receive conduit treatment under the Federal income tax law. This means the earned income or loss is not taxed to the entity, but is allocated to the owners or beneficiaries, regardless of the magnitude or timing of corresponding distributions. The portion of the entity's income that is taxed to the owner or beneficiary is the allocable share of the entity's income or loss for the period. The allocations are determined by (1) the partnership agreement for partners, (2) a weighted-average stock ownership computation for shareholders of an S corporation, and (3) the controlling will or trust instrument for the beneficiaries of an estate or trust.

Allocate. The assignment of income for various tax purposes. The income and expense items of an estate or trust are allocated between income and corpus components. Specific items of income, expense, gain, loss, and credit can be allocated to specific partners or shareholders in an S corporation, if a substantial economic nontax purpose for the allocation is established. See also *substantial economic effect.*

Alternate valuation date. Property passing from a decedent by death may be valued for estate tax purposes as of the date of death or the alternate valuation date. The alternate valuation date is six months from the date of death or the date the property is disposed of by the estate, whichever comes first. To use the alternate valuation date, the *executor* or *administrator* of the estate must make an affirmative election. The election of the alternate valuation date is not available unless it decreases the amount of the gross estate *and* reduces the estate tax liability.

Alternative minimum tax (AMT). The AMT is a fixed percentage of alternative minimum taxable income (AMTI). AMTI generally starts with the taxpayer's adjusted gross income (for individuals) or taxable income (for other taxpayers). To this amount, the taxpayer (1) adds designated preference items (e.g., tax-exempt interest income on private activity bonds), (2) makes other specified adjustments (e.g., to reflect a longer, straight-line cost recovery deduction), (3) subtracts certain AMT itemized deductions for individuals

(e.g., interest incurred on housing but not taxes paid), and (4) subtracts an exemption amount (e.g., $40,000 on an individual joint return). The taxpayer must pay the greater of the resulting AMT (reduced by only the foreign tax credit) or the regular income tax (reduced by all allowable tax credits).

Alternative minimum tax credit. The AMT can result from timing differences that give rise to positive adjustments in calculating the AMT base. To provide equity for the taxpayer when these timing differences reverse, the regular tax liability may be reduced by a tax credit for prior year's minimum tax liability attributable to timing differences. § 53.

Alternative minimum taxable income (AMTI). A major component of the base for computing a taxpayer's *alternative minimum tax* (AMT). Generally, it is the taxable income for the year, modified for AMT adjustments and preferences.

Alternative tax NOL deduction (ATNOLD). In calculating the AMT, the taxpayer is allowed to deduct NOL carryovers and carrybacks. However, for this purpose, a special calculation is required which is referred to as the ATNOLD. The regular income tax is modified for AMT adjustments and preferences to produce the ATNOLD. § 56(d).

Amortization. The tax deduction for the cost or other basis of an intangible asset over the asset's estimated useful life. Examples of amortizable intangibles include patents, copyrights, and leasehold interests. The intangible goodwill can be amortized for income tax purposes over a 15-year period. For tangible assets, see *depreciation.* For natural resources, see *depletion.* See also *estimated useful life* and *goodwill.*

Amount realized. The amount received by a taxpayer upon the sale or exchange of property. Amount realized is the sum of the cash and the fair market value of any property or services received by the taxpayer, plus any related debt assumed by the buyer. Determining the amount realized is the starting point for arriving at realized gain or loss. § 1001(b). See also *realized gain or loss* and *recognized gain or loss.*

AMT adjustments. In calculating AMTI, certain adjustments are added to or deducted from taxable income. These adjustments generally reflect timing differences. § 56.

Annual accounting period concept. In determining a taxpayer's income tax liability, only transactions taking place during a specified tax year are taken into consideration. For reporting and payment purposes, therefore, the tax life of taxpayers is divided into equal annual accounting periods. See also *accounting period* and *mitigation of the annual accounting period concept.*

Annual exclusion. In computing the taxable gifts for the year, each donor excludes the first $10,000 of a gift to each donee. Usually, the annual exclusion is not available for gifts of future interests. § 2503(b). See also *future interest* and *gift splitting*.

Annuitant.   The party entitled to receive payments from an annuity contract. See also *annuity*.

Annuity.   A fixed sum of money payable to a person at specified times for a specified period of time or for life. If the party making the payment (i.e., the obligor) is regularly engaged in this type of business (e.g., an insurance company), the arrangement is classified as a commercial annuity. A private annuity involves an obligor that is not regularly engaged in selling annuities (e.g., a charity or family member).

Anticipatory assignment of income.   See *assignment of income*.

Appellate court.   For Federal tax purposes, appellate courts include the Courts of Appeals and the Supreme Court. If the party losing in the trial (or lower) court is dissatisfied with the result, the dispute may be carried to the appropriate appellate court. See also *Court of Appeals* and *trial court*.

Arm's length concept.   The standard under which unrelated parties would carry out a transaction. Suppose Cardinal Corporation sells property to its sole shareholder for $10,000. In determining whether $10,000 is an arm's length price, one would ascertain the amount for which the corporation could have sold the property to a disinterested third party.

Articles of incorporation.   The legal document specifying a corporation's name, period of existence, purpose and powers, authorized number of shares, classes of stock, and other conditions for operation. The organizers of the corporation file the articles with the state of incorporation. If the articles are satisfactory and other conditions of the law are satisfied, the state will issue a charter recognizing the organization's status as a corporation.

Assessment.   The process whereby the IRS imposes an additional tax liability. If, for example, the IRS audits a taxpayer's income tax return and finds gross income understated or deductions overstated, it will assess a deficiency in the amount of the tax that should have been paid in light of the adjustments made. See also *deficiency*.

Assignment of income.   A procedure whereby a taxpayer attempts to avoid the recognition of income by assigning to another the property that generates the income. Such a procedure will not avoid the recognition of income by the taxpayer making the assignment if it can be said that the income was earned at the point of the transfer. In this case, usually referred to as an anticipatory assignment of income, the income will be taxed to the person who earns it.

Association.   An organization treated as a corporation for Federal tax purposes even though it may not qualify as such under applicable state law. An entity designated as a trust or a partnership, for example, may be classified as an association if it clearly possesses corporate attributes. Corporate attributes include centralized management, continuity of life, free transferability of interests, and limited liability. § 7701(a)(3).

Assumption of liabilities.   In a corporate takeover or asset purchase, the buyer often takes assets subject to preexisting debt. Such actions do not create *boot* received on the transaction for the new shareholder, unless there is no *bona fide* business purpose for the exchange, or the principal purpose of the debt assumption is the avoidance of tax liabilities. § 357.

At-risk amount.   A taxpayer has an amount at risk in a business or investment venture to the extent that personal assets have been subjected to the risks of the business. Typically, the taxpayer's at-risk amount includes (1) the amount of money or other property that the investor contributed to the venture for the investment, (2) the amount of any of the entity's liabilities for which the taxpayer personally is liable and that relate to the investment, and (3) an allocable share of nonrecourse debts incurred by the venture from third parties in arm's length transactions for real estate investments.

At-risk limitation.   Generally, a taxpayer can deduct losses related to a trade or business, S corporation, partnership, or investment asset only to the extent of the at-risk amount.

Attribution.   Under certain circumstances, the tax law applies attribution (constructive ownership) rules to assign to one taxpayer the ownership interest of another taxpayer. If, for example, the stock of Gold Corporation is held 60 percent by Marsha and 40 percent by Sidney, Marsha may be deemed to own 100 percent of Gold Corporation if Marsha and Sidney are mother and son. In that case, the stock owned by Sidney is attributed to Marsha. Stated differently, Marsha has a 60 percent direct and a 40 percent indirect interest in Gold Corporation. It can also be said that Marsha is the constructive owner of Sidney's interest.

Audit.   Inspection and verification of a taxpayer's return or other transactions possessing tax consequences. See also *correspondence audit*, *field audit*, and *office audit*.

Automobile expenses.   Automobile expenses are generally deductible only to the extent the automobile is used in business or for the production of income. Personal commuting expenses are not deductible. The taxpayer may deduct actual expenses (including depreciation and insurance), or the standard (automatic) mileage rate may be used (28 cents per mile for 1992, 28 cents per mile for 1993, 29 cents per mile for 1994, 30 cents per mile for 1995, and 31 cents per mile for 1996) during any one year. Automobile expenses incurred for medical purposes or in connection with job-related moving expenses are deductible to the extent of actual out-of-pocket expenses or at the rate of 10 cents per mile (12 cents for charitable activities).

B

Bailout.   Various procedures whereby the owners of an entity can obtain the entity's profits with favorable tax consequences. With corporations, for example, the bailout of corporate profits without dividend consequences might be the desired objective. The alternative of distributing the profits to the shareholders as dividends generally is less attractive since dividend payments are not deductible. See also *preferred stock bailout*.

Bargain sale or purchase. A sale or purchase of property for less than fair market value. The difference between the sale or purchase price and the fair market value of the property may have tax consequences. If, for example, a corporation sells property worth $1,000 to one of its shareholders for $700, the $300 difference probably represents a constructive dividend to the shareholder. Suppose, instead, the shareholder sells the property (worth $1,000) to his or her corporation for $700. The $300 difference probably represents a contribution by the shareholder to the corporation's capital. Bargain sales and purchases among members of the same family may lead to gift tax consequences. See also *constructive dividend*.

Basis. The acquisition cost assigned to an asset for income tax purposes. For assets acquired by purchase, basis is cost (§ 1012). Special rules govern the basis of property received by virtue of another's death (§ 1014) or by gift (§ 1015), the basis of stock received on a transfer of property to a controlled corporation (§ 358), the basis of the property transferred to the corporation (§ 362), and the basis of property received upon the liquidation of a corporation (§ 334). See also *adjusted basis*.

Basis in partnership interest. The acquisition cost of the partner's ownership interest in the *partnership*. Includes purchase price and associated debt acquired from other partners and in the course of the entity's trade or business.

Beneficiary. A party who will benefit from a transfer of property or other arrangement. Examples include the beneficiary of a trust, the beneficiary of a life insurance policy, and the beneficiary of an estate.

Bequest. A transfer of personal property by will. To bequeath is to leave such property by will. See also *devise* and *personal property*.

Blockage rule. A factor to be considered in valuing a large block of stock. Application of this rule generally justifies a discount in the fair market value since the disposition of a large amount of stock at any one time may depress the value of the shares in the marketplace.

Bona fide. In good faith, or real. In tax law, this term is often used in connection with a business purpose for carrying out a transaction. Thus, was there a bona fide business purpose for a shareholder's transfer of a liability to a controlled corporation? § 357(b)(1)(B). See also *business purposes*.

Book value. The net amount of an asset after reduction by a related reserve. The book value of machinery, for example, is the amount of the machinery less the reserve for depreciation.

Boot. Cash or property of a type not included in the definition of a nontaxable exchange. The receipt of boot will cause an otherwise nontaxable transfer to become taxable to the extent of the lesser of the fair market value of the boot or the realized gain on the transfer. For example, see transfers to controlled corporations under § 351(b) and like-kind exchanges under § 1031(b). See also *like-kind exchange* and *realized gain or loss*.

Branch profits tax. A tax on the effectively connected earnings and profits of the U.S. branch of a foreign corporation. The tax is levied in addition to the usual §11 tax, in an amount equal to thirty percent of the dividend equivalent amount. Treaties can override the tax or reduce the withholding percentage. Earnings reinvested in the U.S. operations of the entity are not subject to the tax, until repatriation.

Bribes and illegal payments. Section 162 denies a deduction for bribes or kickbacks, fines and penalties paid to a government official or employee for violation of law, and two-thirds of the treble damage payments made to claimants for violation of the antitrust law. Denial of a deduction for bribes and illegal payments is based upon the judicially established principle that allowing such payments would be contrary to public policy.

Brother-sister controlled group. More than one corporation owned by the same shareholders. If, for example, Chris and Pat each own one-half of the stock in Wren Corporation and Redbird Corporation, Wren and Redbird form a brother-sister controlled group.

B.T.A. The Board of Tax Appeals was a trial court that considered Federal tax matters. This Court is now the U.S. Tax Court.

Built-in gains tax. A penalty tax designed to discourage a shift of the incidence of taxation on unrealized gains from a C corporation to its shareholders, via an S election. Under this provision, any recognized gain during the first 10 years of S status generates a corporate-level tax on a base not to exceed the aggregate untaxed built-in gains brought into the S corporation upon its election from C corporation taxable years.

Burden of proof. The requirement in a lawsuit to show the weight of evidence and thereby gain a favorable decision. Except in cases of tax fraud, the burden of proof in a tax case generally is on the taxpayer. See also *fraud*.

Business bad debt. A tax deduction allowed for obligations obtained in connection with a trade or business that have become either partially or completely worthless. In contrast to nonbusiness bad debts, business bad debts are deductible as business expenses. § 166. See also *nonbusiness bad debt*.

Business purposes. A justifiable business reason for carrying out a transaction. Mere tax avoidance is not an acceptable business purpose. The presence of a business purpose is crucial in the area of corporate reorganizations and certain liquidations. See also *bona fide*.

Buy-sell agreement. An arrangement, particularly appropriate in the case of a closely held corporation or a partnership, whereby the surviving owners (shareholders or partners) or the entity agrees to purchase the interest of a withdrawing owner. The buy-sell agreement provides for an orderly disposition of an interest in a business and may aid in setting the value of the interest for death tax purposes. See also *cross-purchase buy-sell agreement* and *entity buy-sell agreement*.

By-pass amount. The amount that can be transferred by gift or death free of any unified transfer tax. Currently, the by-pass amount is $600,000. See also *exemption equivalent amount*.

C

Cafeteria benefit plan. An employee benefit plan under which an employee is allowed to select from among a variety of employer-provided fringe benefits. Some of the benefits may be taxable and some may be statutory nontaxable benefits (e.g. health and accident insurance and group term life insurance). The employee is taxed only on the taxable benefits selected. A cafeteria benefit plan is also referred to as a flexible benefit plan.

Cafeteria plan. See *cafeteria benefit plan*.

Calendar year. See *accounting period*.

Capital account. The financial accounting analog of a partner's tax basis in the entity.

Capital asset. Broadly speaking, all assets are capital except those specifically excluded by the Code. Major categories of noncapital assets include property held for resale in the normal course of business (inventory), trade accounts and notes receivable, and depreciable property and real estate used in a trade or business (§ 1231 assets). § 1221. See also *capital gain* and *capital loss*.

Capital contribution. Various means by which a shareholder makes additional funds available to the corporation (placed at the risk of the business), sometimes without the receipt of additional stock. If no stock is received, the contributions are added to the basis of the shareholder's existing stock investment and do not generate gross income to the corporation. § 118.

Capital expenditure. An expenditure that should be added to the basis of the property improved. For income tax purposes, this generally precludes a full deduction for the expenditure in the year paid or incurred. Any cost recovery in the form of a tax deduction comes in the form of depreciation, depletion, or amortization. § 263.

Capital gain. The gain from the sale or exchange of a capital asset. See also *capital asset*.

Capital gain property. Property contributed to a charitable organization that, if sold rather than contributed, would have resulted in long-term capital gain to the donor. See also *ordinary income property*.

Capital interest. Usually, the percentage of the entity's net assets that a partner would receive on liquidation. Typically determined by the partner's capital sharing ratio.

Capital loss. The loss from the sale or exchange of a capital asset. See also *capital asset*.

Capital sharing ratio. A partner's percentage ownership of the entity's capital.

Capital stock tax. A state-level tax, usually imposed on out-of-state corporations for the privilege of doing business in the state. The tax may be based on the entity's apportionable income or payroll, or on its apportioned net worth as of a specified date.

Carryover basis. When a taxpayer exchanges one asset for another, many provisions in the tax law allow the basis assigned to the received asset to be precisely that of the traded asset. Thus, no step-up or -down of basis occurs as a result of the exchange. For instance, when an investor contributes an asset to a corporation or partnership, the entity generally takes a carryover basis in the property.

Cash method. See *cash receipts method*.

Cash receipts method. A method of accounting that reflects deductions as paid and income as received in any one tax year. However, deductions for prepaid expenses that benefit more than one tax year (e.g., prepaid rent and prepaid interest) usually must be spread over the period benefited rather than deducted in the year paid. § 446(c)(1). See also *constructive receipt of income*.

Cash surrender value. The amount of money that an insurance policy would yield if cashed in with the insurance company that issued the policy.

CCH. Commerce Clearing House (CCH) is the publisher of a tax service and of Federal tax decisions (USTC series).

C corporation. A separate taxable entity, subject to the rules of Subchapter C of the Code. This business form may create a double taxation effect relative to its shareholders. The entity is subject to the regular corporate tax and a number of penalty taxes at the Federal level.

Centralized management. A concentration of authority among certain persons who may make independent business decisions on behalf of the entity without the need for continuing approval by the owners of the entity. It is a characteristic of a corporation since day-to-day business operations are handled by appointed officers and not by the shareholders. Reg. § 301.7701–2(c). See also *association*.

Cert. den. By denying the Writ of Certiorari, the U.S. Supreme Court refuses to accept an appeal from a U.S. Court of Appeals. The denial of certiorari does not, however, mean that the U.S. Supreme Court agrees with the result reached by the lower court. See also *certiorari*.

Certiorari. Appeal from a U.S. Court of Appeals to the U.S. Supreme Court is by Writ of Certiorari. The Supreme Court need not accept the appeal, and it usually does not (*cert. den.*) unless a conflict exists among the lower courts that must be resolved or a constitutional issue is involved. See also *cert. den.*

Cf. Compare.

Charitable contributions. Contributions are deductible (subject to various restrictions and ceiling limitations) if made to qualified nonprofit charitable organizations. A cash basis taxpayer is entitled to a deduction solely in the year of payment. Accrual basis corporations may accrue contributions at year-end if payment is properly authorized before the end of the year and payment is made within two and one-half months after the end of the year. § 170.

Circuit court of appeals. See *Court of Appeals.*

Civil fraud. See *fraud.*

Claims Court. A trial court (court of original jurisdiction) that decides litigation involving Federal tax matters. Now known as the U.S. Court of Federal Claims, appeal from this court is to the Court of Appeals for the Federal Circuit.

Closely held corporation. A corporation where stock ownership is not widely dispersed. Rather, a few shareholders are in control of corporate policy and are in a position to benefit personally from that policy.

Closing agreement. In a tax dispute, the parties sign a closing agreement to spell out the terms under which the matters are settled. The agreement is binding on both the Service and the taxpayer, for the disputed year and for all future years.

Collapsing. To disregard a transaction or one of a series of steps leading to a result. See also *step transaction, substance vs. form concept,* and *telescoping.*

Commissioner of the IRS. The head of IRS operations, a presidential appointee.

Common law state. See *community property.*

Community property. Louisiana, Texas, New Mexico, Arizona, California, Washington, Idaho, Nevada, and Wisconsin have community property systems. The rest of the states are common law property jurisdictions. The difference between common law and community property systems centers around the property rights possessed by married persons. In a common law system, each spouse owns whatever he or she earns. Under a community property system, one-half of the earnings of each spouse is considered owned by the other spouse. Assume, for example, Jeff and Alice are husband and wife and their only income is the $50,000 annual salary Jeff receives. If they live in New York (a common law state), the $50,000 salary belongs to Jeff. If, however, they live in Texas (a community property state), the $50,000 salary is owned one-half each by Jeff and Alice. See also *separate property.*

Compensatory damages. Damages received or paid by the taxpayer can be classified as compensatory damages or as punitive damages. Compensatory damages are those paid to compensate one for harm caused by another. Compensatory damages are excludible from the recipient's gross income. See also *punitive damages.*

Complete liquidation. See *corporate liquidation.*

Complete termination redemption. See *redemption (complete termination).*

Completed contract method. A method of reporting gain or loss on certain long-term contracts. Under this method of accounting, gross income and expenses are recognized in the tax year in which the contract is completed. Reg. § 1.451–3. See also *percentage of completion method* and *long-term contract.*

Complex trust. Not a *simple trust.* Such trusts may have charitable beneficiaries, accumulate income, and distribute corpus. §§ 661–663. See also *simple trust.*

Component depreciation. The process of dividing an asset (e.g., a building) into separate components or parts for the purpose of calculating depreciation. The advantage of dividing an asset into components is to use shorter depreciation lives for selected components under § 167. Generally, the same cost recovery period must be used for all the components of an asset under § 168.

Concur. To agree with the result reached by another, but not necessarily with the reasoning or the logic used in reaching the result. For example, Judge Ricks agrees with Judges Stone and Talent (all being members of the same court) that the income is taxable but for a different reason. Judge Ricks would issue a concurring opinion to the majority opinion issued by Judges Stone and Talent.

Condemnation. The taking of property by a public authority. The taking is by legal action, and the owner of the property is compensated by the public authority.

Conduit concept. See *aggregate concept.*

Consent dividend. For purposes of avoiding or reducing the penalty tax on the unreasonable accumulation of earnings or the personal holding company tax, a corporation may declare a consent dividend. In a consent dividend, no cash or property is distributed to the shareholders, although the corporation obtains a dividends paid deduction. The consent dividend is taxed to the shareholders and increases the basis in their stock investment. § 565.

Consolidated return. A procedure whereby certain affiliated corporations may file a single return, combine the tax transactions of each corporation, and arrive at a single income tax liability for the group. The election to file a consolidated return is usually binding on future years. See §§ 1501–1505 and related Regulations.

Consolidation. The combination of two or more corporations into a newly created corporation. Thus, White Corporation and Black Corporation combine to form Gray Corporation. A consolidation may qualify as a nontaxable *reorganization* if certain conditions are satisfied. §§ 354 and 368(a)(1)(A).

Constructive dividend. A taxable benefit derived by a shareholder from his or her corporation that is not actually called a dividend. Examples include unreasonable compensation, excessive rent payments, bargain purchases of corporate property, and shareholder use of corporate property. Constructive dividends generally are found in closely held corporations. See also *bargain sale or purchase, closely held corporation,* and *unreasonable compensation.*

Constructive liquidation scenario. The means by which recourse debt is shared among partners in basis determination.

Constructive ownership. See *attribution.*

Constructive receipt of income. If income is unqualifiedly available although not physically in the taxpayer's possession, it is subject to the income tax. An example is accrued interest on a savings account. Under the constructive receipt of income concept, the interest is taxed to a depositor in the year available, rather than the year actually withdrawn. The fact that the depositor uses the cash basis of accounting for tax purposes is irrelevant. See Reg. § 1.451–2. See also *cash receipts method.*

Continuity of business enterprise. In a tax-free *reorganization,* a shareholder or corporation that has substantially the same investment after an exchange as before, should not be taxed on the transaction. Specifically, the transferee corporation must continue the historic business of the transferor, or it must use a significant portion of the transferor's assets in the new business.

Continuity of interest test. In a tax-free *reorganization,* a shareholder or corporation that has substantially the same investment after an exchange as before, should not be taxed on the transaction. Specifically, the seller must acquire an equity interest in the purchasing corporation equal in value to at least fifty percent of all formerly outstanding stock of the acquired entity.

Continuity of life or existence. The death or other withdrawal of an owner of an entity does not terminate the existence of the entity. This is a characteristic of a corporation since the death or withdrawal of a shareholder does not affect the corporation's existence. Reg. § 301.7701–2(b). See also *association.*

Contributions to the capital of a corporation. See *capital contribution.*

Contributory qualified pension or profit sharing plan. A plan funded with both employer and employee contributions. Since the employee's contributions to the plan are subject to income tax, a later distribution of the contributions to the employee generally is tax-free. See also *qualified pension or profit sharing plan.*

Control. Holding a specified level of stock ownership in a corporation. For § 351, the new shareholder(s) must hold at least 80 percent of the total combined voting power of all voting classes of stock, and at least 80 percent of the shares of all nonvoting classes. Other tax provisions require different levels of control to bring about desired effects, such as 50 or 100 percent.

Controlled foreign corporation (CFC). A non-U.S. corporation in which more than 50 percent of the total combined voting power of all classes of stock entitled to vote or the total value of the stock of the corporation is owned by "U.S. shareholders" on any day during the taxable year of the foreign corporation. For purposes of this definition, a U.S. shareholder is any U.S. person who owns, or is considered as owning, 10 percent or more of the total combined voting power of all classes of voting stock of the foreign corporation. Stock owned directly, indirectly, and constructively is used in this measure.

Controlled group. A controlled group of corporations is required to share the lower-level corporate tax rates and various other tax benefits among the members of the group. A controlled group may be either a brother-sister or a parent-subsidiary group.

Corporate acquisition. The takeover of one corporation by another if both parties retain their legal existence after the transaction. An acquisition can be effected via a stock purchase or through a tax-free exchange of stock. See also *corporate reorganization* and *merger.*

Corporate liquidation. Occurs when a corporation distributes its net assets to its shareholders and ceases to be a going-concern. Generally, a shareholder recognizes capital gain or loss upon the liquidation of the entity, regardless of the corporation's balance in its earnings and profits account. However, the distributing corporation recognizes gain and loss on assets that it distributes to shareholders in kind.

Corporate reorganization. Occurs, among other instances, when one corporation acquires another in a merger or acquisition, a single corporation divides into two or more entities, a corporation makes a substantial change in its capital structure, or a corporation undertakes a change in its legal name or domicile. The exchange of stock and other securities in a corporate reorganization can be effected favorably for tax purposes if certain statutory requirements are followed strictly. Tax consequences include the nonrecognition of any gain that is realized by the shareholders except to the extent of boot received. See also *corporate acquisition* and *merger.*

Corpus. The body or principal of a trust. Suppose, for example, Grant transfers an apartment building into a trust, income payable to Ruth for life, remainder to Shawn upon Ruth's death. Corpus of the trust is the apartment building.

Correspondence audit. An audit conducted by the IRS by mail. Typically, the IRS writes to the taxpayer requesting the verification of a particular deduction or exemption. The completion of a special form or the remittance of copies of records or other support is all that is requested of the taxpayer. See also *audit, field audit,* and *office audit.*

Cost depletion. Depletion that is calculated based on the adjusted basis of the asset. The adjusted basis is divided by the expected recoverable units to determine the depletion per unit. The depletion per unit is multiplied by the units sold during the tax year to calculate cost depletion. See also *percentage depletion*.

Court of Appeals.   Any of 13 Federal courts that consider tax matters appealed from the U.S. Tax Court, a U.S. District Court, or the U.S. Court of Federal Claims. Appeal from a U.S. Court of Appeals is to the U.S. Supreme Court by Writ of Certiorari. See also *appellate court* and *trial court*.

Court of Federal Claims.   See *Claims Court*.

Court of original jurisdiction.   The Federal courts are divided into courts of original jurisdiction and appellate courts. The dispute between the taxpayer and the IRS is first considered by a court of original jurisdiction (i.e., a trial court). The four Federal courts of original jurisdiction are the U.S. Tax Court, U.S. District Court, the Court of Federal Claims, and the Small Cases Division of the U.S. Tax Court. See *Court of Appeals*.

Credit for prior transfers.   The death tax credit for prior transfers applies when property is taxed in the estates of different decedents within a 10-year period. The credit is determined using a decreasing statutory percentage, with the magnitude of the credit decreasing as the length of time between the multiple deaths increases. § 2013.

Criminal fraud.   See *fraud*.

Cross-purchase buy-sell agreement.   Under this type of arrangement, the surviving owners of the business agree to buy out the withdrawing owner. Assume, for example, Ruth and Sam are equal shareholders in Eagle Corporation. Under a cross-purchase buy-sell agreement, Ruth and Sam would contract to purchase the other's interest should that person decide to withdraw from the business. See also *buy-sell agreement* and *entity buy-sell agreement*.

Current earnings and profits.   Net tax-basis earnings of the corporation aggregated during the current tax year. A corporate distribution is deemed to be first from the entity's current earnings and profits and then from accumulated earnings and profits. Shareholders recognize dividend income to the extent of the earnings and profits of the corporation. A dividend results to the extent of current earnings and profits, even if there is a larger negative balance in accumulated earnings and profits.

Current use valuation.   See *special use value*.

Curtesy.   A husband's right under state law to all or part of his wife's property upon her death. See also *dower*.

D

Death benefit.   A payment made by an employer to the beneficiary or beneficiaries of a deceased employee on account of the death of the employee. Under certain conditions, the first $5,000 of the payment is exempt from the income tax. § 101(b)(1).

Death tax.   A tax imposed on property transferred by the death of the owner. See also *credit for prior transfers*, *estate tax*, and *inheritance tax*.

Debt-financed income.   Included in computations of the *unrelated business income* of an *exempt organization*, the gross income generated from debt-financed property.

Decedent.   An individual who has died.

Deduction.   The Federal income tax is not imposed upon gross income. Rather, it is imposed upon taxable income. Congressionally identified deductions are subtracted from gross income to arrive at the tax base, taxable income.

Deductions in respect of a decedent.   Deductions accrued at the moment of death but not recognizable on the final income tax return of a decedent because of the method of accounting used. Such items are allowed as deductions on the estate tax return and on the income tax return of the estate (Form 1041) or the heir (Form 1040). An example of a deduction in respect of a decedent is interest expense accrued to the date of death by a cash basis debtor.

Deferred compensation.   Compensation that will be taxed when received and not when earned. An example is contributions by an employer to a qualified pension or profit sharing plan on behalf of an employee. The contributions will not be taxed to the employee until they are distributed (e.g., upon retirement). See also *qualified pension or profit sharing plan*.

Deficiency.   Additional tax liability owed by a taxpayer and assessed by the IRS. See also *assessment* and *statutory notice of deficiency*.

Deficiency dividend.   Once the IRS has established a corporation's liability for the personal holding company tax in a prior year, the tax may be reduced or avoided by the issuance of a deficiency dividend under § 547. The deficiency dividend procedure is not available in cases where the deficiency was due to fraud with intent to evade tax or to a willful failure to file the appropriate tax return [§ 547(g)]. Nor does the deficiency dividend procedure avoid the usual penalties and interest applicable for failure to file a return or pay a tax.

Deficit.   A negative balance in the earnings and profits account.

Demand loan.   A loan payable upon request by the creditor, rather than on a specific date.

De minimis fringe.   Benefits provided to employees that are too insignificant to warrant the time and effort required to account for the benefits received by each employee and the value of those benefits. Such amounts are excludible from the employee's gross income. § 132.

Dependency exemption.   See *personal and dependency exemptions*.

Depletion.   The process by which the cost or other basis of a natural resource (e.g., an oil or gas interest) is recovered upon extraction and sale of the resource. The two ways to determine the depletion allowance are the cost and percentage (or statutory) methods. Under the cost method, each unit of production sold is assigned a portion of the cost or other basis of the interest. This is determined by dividing the cost or other basis by the total units expected to be recovered. Under the percentage (or statutory) method, the tax law provides a special percentage factor for different types of minerals and other natural resources. This percentage is multiplied by the gross income from the interest to arrive at the depletion allowance. §§ 613 and 613A.

Depreciation.   The deduction for the cost or other basis of a tangible asset over the asset's estimated useful life. For intangible assets, see *amortization*. For natural resources, see *depletion*. See also *estimated useful life*.

Depreciation recapture.   Upon the disposition of depreciable property used in a trade or business, gain or loss is measured by the difference between the consideration received (the amount realized) and the adjusted basis of the property. The gain recognized could be § 1231 gain and qualify for long-term capital gain treatment. The recapture provisions of the Code (e.g., §§ 219, 1245, and 1250) may operate to convert some or all of the § 1231 gain into ordinary income. The justification for depreciation recapture is that it prevents a taxpayer from converting a dollar of ordinary deduction (in the form of depreciation) into deferred tax-favored income (§ 1231 or long-term capital gain). The depreciation recapture rules do not apply when the property is disposed of at a loss or via a gift. See also *Section 1231 gains and losses*.

Determination letter.   Upon the request of a taxpayer, an IRS District Director will comment on the tax status of a completed transaction. Determination letters frequently are used to clarify employee status, determine whether a retirement or profit sharing plan qualifies under the Code, and determine the tax-exempt status of certain nonprofit organizations.

Devise.   A transfer of real estate by will. See also *bequest*.

Disabled access credit.   A tax credit whose purpose is to encourage small businesses to make their businesses more accessible to disabled individuals. The credit is equal to 50 percent of the eligible expenditures that exceed $250 but do not exceed $10,250. Thus, the maximum amount for the credit is $5,000. The adjusted basis for depreciation is reduced by the amount of the credit. To qualify, the facility must have been placed in service before November 6, 1990. § 44. See also *general business credit*.

Disclaimers.   Rejections, refusals, or renunciations of claims, powers, or property. Section 2518 sets forth the conditions required to avoid gift tax consequences as the result of a disclaimer.

Discretionary trust.   Trusts under which the trustee or another party has the right to accumulate (rather than distribute) the income for each year. Depending on the terms of the trust instrument, the income may be accumulated for future distributions to the income beneficiaries or added to corpus for the benefit of the remainderperson. See also *corpus* and *income beneficiary*.

Disguised sale.   When a partner contributes property to the entity and soon thereafter receives a distribution from the partnership, the transactions are collapsed, and the distribution is seen as a purchase of the asset by the partnership. § 707(a)(2)(B).

Disproportionate.   Not pro rata or ratable. Suppose, for example, Blue Corporation has two shareholders, Chris and Diane, each of whom owns 50 percent of its stock. If Blue Corporation distributes a cash dividend of $2,000 to Chris and only $1,000 to Diane, the distribution is disproportionate. The distribution would have been proportionate if Chris and Diane had received $1,500 each.

Disproportionate distribution.   A distribution from a partnership to one or more of its partners in which at least one partner's interest in partnership hot assets is increased or decreased. For example, a distribution of cash to one partner and hot assets to another changes both partners' interest in hot assets and is disproportionate. The intent of rules for taxation of disproportionate distributions is to ensure each partner eventually recognizes his proportionate share of partnership ordinary income.

Disproportionate redemption.   See *redemption (disproportionate)*.

Disregard of corporate entity.   To treat a corporation as if it did not exist for tax purposes. In that event, each shareholder accounts for an allocable share of all corporate transactions possessing tax consequences. See also *entity*.

Dissent.   To disagree with the majority. If, for example, Judge Brown disagrees with the result reached by Judges Charles and Davis (all of whom are members of the same court), Judge Brown could issue a dissenting opinion.

Distributable net income (DNI).   The measure that determines the nature and amount of the distributions from estates and trusts that the beneficiaries must include in income. DNI also limits the amount that estates and trusts can claim as a deduction for such distributions. § 643(a).

Distribution deduction.   Used to compute an estate's or trust's taxable income for the year. The lesser of the amount distributed to beneficiaries from income, or the deductible portion of distributable net income for the period.

Distributions in kind.   A transfer of property "as is." If, for example, a corporation distributes land to its shareholders, a distribution in kind has taken place. A sale of land followed by a distribution of the cash proceeds would not be a distribution in kind of the land.

District Court.   A Federal District Court is a trial court for purposes of litigating Federal tax matters. It is the only trial court in which a jury trial can be obtained. See also *trial court*.

District Director. The head of an IRS district's operations.

Dividend. A nondeductible distribution to the shareholders of a corporation. A dividend constitutes gross income to the recipient if it is from the current or accumulated earnings and profits of the corporation.

Dividend equivalent amount (DEA). The amount subject to the branch profits tax, it is equal to the effectively connected E&P of the U.S. branch of a foreign corporation, reduced/(increased) by an increase/(reduction) in U.S. net equity.

Dividends paid deduction. Relative to the accumulated earnings and personal holding company taxes, reductions in the tax base are allowed to the extent that the corporation made dividend payments during the year. Thus, this adjustment reduces accumulated taxable income and personal holding company income.

Dividends received deduction. A deduction allowed a shareholder that is a corporation for dividends received from a domestic corporation. The deduction usually is 70 percent of the dividends received, but it could be 80 or 100 percent depending upon the ownership percentage held by the recipient corporation. §§ 243–246.

Divisive reorganization. A corporate division: some of the assets of one corporation are transferred to another corporation, in exchange for control of the transferee. Then, in a spin-off, split-off, or split-up, stock of the transferee is distributed to the transferor's shareholders.

Domestic corporation. A corporation created or organized in the United States or under the law of the United States or any state. § 7701(a)(4). Only dividends received from domestic corporations qualify for the dividends received deduction (§ 243). See also *foreign corporation.*

Domicile. A person's legal home.

Donee. The recipient of a gift.

Donor. The maker of a gift.

Dower. A wife's right to all or part of her deceased husband's property, unique to common law states as opposed to community property jurisdictions. See also *curtesy.*

E

Earned income. Income from personal services. Distinguished from passive, portfolio, and other unearned income (sometimes referred to as "active" income). See §§ 469, 911, and the related Regulations.

Earned income credit. A tax credit whose purpose is to provide assistance to certain low-income individuals who generally have a qualifying child. This is a refundable credit. To receive the most beneficial treatment, the taxpayer must have qualifying children. However, it is possible to qualify for the credit without having a child. To calculate the credit for a taxpayer with one or more children for 1996, a statutory rate of 34 percent for one child (40% for two or

more children) is multiplied by the earned income (subject to a statutory maximum of $6,330 with one qualifying child or $8,890 with two or more qualifying children). Once the earned income exceeds $11,610, the credit is phased out using a 15.98 percent rate for one qualifying child and a 21.06 percent rate for two qualifying children. For the qualifying taxpayer without children, the credit is calculated on a maximum earned income of $4,220 applying a 7.65 percent rate with the phaseout beginning at $5,280 applying the same rate.

Earnings and profits (E&P). Measures the economic capacity of a corporation to make a distribution to shareholders that is not a return of capital. Such a distribution results in dividend income to the shareholders to the extent of the corporation's current and accumulated earnings and profits.

Economic effect test. Requirements that must be met before a special allocation may be used by a partnership. The premise behind the test is that each partner who receives an allocation of income or loss from a partnership bears the economic benefit or burden of the allocation.

Economic income. The change in the taxpayer's net worth, as measured in terms of market values, plus the value of the assets the taxpayer consumed during the year. Because of the impracticality of this income model, it is not used for tax purposes.

Economic performance test. One of the requirements that must be satisfied in order for an accrual basis taxpayer to deduct an expense. The accrual basis taxpayer first must satisfy the all events test. That test is not deemed satisfied until economic performance occurs. This occurs, when property or services are provided to the taxpayer, or in the case in which the taxpayer is required to provide property or services, whenever the property or services are actually provided by the taxpayer.

Educational savings bonds. United States Series EE bonds whose proceeds are used for qualified higher educational expenses for the taxpayer, the taxpayer's spouse, or a dependent. The interest may be excluded from gross income, provided the taxpayer's adjusted gross income does not exceed certain amounts. § 135.

Effectively connected income. Income of a nonresident alien or foreign corporation that is attributable to the operation of a U.S. trade or business under either the asset-use or business-activities test.

Employee stock ownership plan (ESOP). A type of qualified profit sharing plan that invests in securities of the employer. In a noncontributory ESOP, the employer usually contributes its shares to a trust and receives a deduction for the fair market value of the stock. Generally, the employee does not recognize income until the stock is sold after its distribution to him or her upon retirement or other separation from service. See also *qualified pension or profit sharing plan.*

Employment taxes. Employment taxes are those taxes that an employer must pay on account of its employees. Employment taxes include FICA (Federal Insurance Contributions Act) and FUTA (Federal Unemployment Tax Act) taxes. Employment taxes are paid to the IRS in addition to income tax withholdings at specified intervals. Such taxes can be levied on the employees, the employer, or both. See also *FICA tax* and *FUTA tax*.

En banc. The case was considered by the whole court. Typically, for example, only one of the judges of the U.S. Tax Court will hear and decide on a tax controversy. However, when the issues involved are unusually novel or of wide impact, the case will be heard and decided by the full Court sitting *en banc*.

Energy tax credit. A 10 percent tax credit is available to businesses that invest in certain energy property. The purpose of the credit is to create incentives for conservation and to develop alternative energy sources. The credit is available on the acquisition of solar and geothermal property. §§ 46 and 48.

Enrolled agent (EA). A tax practitioner who has gained admission to practice before the IRS by passing an IRS examination.

Entertainment expenses. These expenses are deductible only if they are directly related to or associated with a trade or business. Various restrictions and documentation requirements have been imposed upon the deductibility of entertainment expenses to prevent abuses by taxpayers. See, for example, the provision contained in § 274(n) that disallows 50 percent (20 percent prior to 1994) of entertainment expenses. § 274.

Entity. An organization or being that possesses separate existence for tax purposes. Examples are corporations, partnerships, estates, and trusts. See also *disregard of corporate entity*.

Entity accounting income. Entity accounting income is not identical to the taxable income of a trust or estate, nor is it determined in the same manner as the entity's financial accounting income would be. The trust document or will determines whether certain income, expenses, gains, or losses are allocated to the corpus of the entity or to the entity's income beneficiaries. Only the items that are allocated to the income beneficiaries are included in entity accounting income.

Entity buy-sell agreement. The entity is to purchase a withdrawing owner's interest. When the entity is a corporation, the agreement generally involves a stock redemption on the part of the withdrawing shareholder. See also *buy-sell agreement* and *cross-purchase buy-sell agreement*.

Entity concept. The theory of partnership taxation under which a partnership is treated as a separate and distinct entity from the partners, and has its own tax attributes.

Equity structure shift. A tax-free *reorganization* other than a *divisive reorganization* or *recapitalization*. If there is a more than fifty percent change in the ownership of a loss corporation in an equity structure shift, § 382 limits the use of NOL carryovers of the loss corporation. Specifically, the annual NOL carryover deduction is limited to the value of the loss corporation immediately before the equity structure shift times the *long-term tax-exempt rate*.

Escrow. Money or other property placed with a third party as security for an existing or proposed obligation. Ramon, for example, agrees to purchase Rashad's stock in Orange Corporation but needs time to raise the necessary funds. Rashad places the stock with Eve (the escrow agent), with instructions to deliver it to Ramon when the purchase price is paid.

Estate. An entity that locates, collects, distributes, and discharges the assets and liabilities of a decedent.

Estate freeze. Procedures directed toward fixing and stabilizing the value of an interest retained in a business while transferring the growth portion to family members. In the case of a closely held corporation, usually the estate freeze involves keeping the preferred stock and giving away the common stock. The ultimate objective is to reduce estate value when the original owner-donor dies.

Estate tax. A tax imposed on the right to transfer property by death. Thus, an estate tax is levied on the decedent's estate and not on the heir receiving the property. See also *death tax* and *inheritance tax*.

Estimated useful life. The period over which an asset will be used by the taxpayer. Some assets do not have an estimated useful life. The estimated useful life of an asset is essential to measuring the annual tax deduction for depreciation and amortization.

Estoppel. The process of being stopped from proving something (even if true) in court due to a prior inconsistent action. It is usually invoked as a matter of fairness to prevent one party (either the taxpayer or the IRS) from taking advantage of a prior error.

Excess lobbying expenditure. An excise tax is applied on otherwise tax-exempt organizations with respect to the excess of total lobbying expenditures over *grass roots lobbying expenditures* for the year.

Excess loss account. When a subsidiary has generated more historical losses than its parent has invested in the entity, the parent's basis in the subsidiary is zero, and the parent records additional losses in an excess loss account. This treatment allows the parent to continue to deduct losses of the subsidiary, even where no basis reduction is possible, while avoiding the need to show a negative stock basis on various financial records. If the subsidiary stock is sold while an excess loss account exists, capital gain income usually is recognized to the extent of the balance in the account.

Excise tax. A tax on the manufacture, sale, or use of goods; on the carrying on of an occupation or activity; or on the transfer of property. Thus, the Federal estate and gift taxes are, theoretically, excise taxes.

Executor. A person designated by a will to administer (manage or take charge of) the assets and liabilities of a decedent. The designated party may be a male (executor), female (executrix), or a trust company (executor). See also *administrator*.

Exemption. An amount by which the tax base is reduced for all qualifying taxpayers. Individuals can receive personal and dependency exemptions, and taxpayers apply an exemption in computing their alternative minimum taxable income. Often, the exemption amount is phased out as the tax base becomes sizable.

Exemption equivalent amount. The amount of value (currently $600,000) that is the equivalent of the unified transfer tax credit allowed (currently $192,800). See also *by-pass amount*.

Exempt organization. An organization that is either partially or completely exempt from Federal income taxation. § 501.

Expenses in respect of a decedent. See *deductions in respect of a decedent*.

F

Fair market value. The amount at which property would change hands between a willing buyer and a willing seller, neither being under any compulsion to buy or to sell, and both having reasonable knowledge of the relevant facts. Reg. § 20.2031–1(b).

F.3d. An abbreviation for the third series of the *Federal Reporter*, the official series in which decisions of the U.S. Court of Federal Claims and the U.S. Court of Appeals are published. The second series is denoted F.2d.

F.Supp. The abbreviation for the *Federal Supplement*, the official series in which the reported decisions of the Federal District Courts are published.

Federal District Court. See *district court*.

Federal Register. The first place that the rules and regulations of U.S. administrative agencies (e.g., the U.S. Treasury Department) are published.

Feeder organization. An entity that carries on a trade or business for the benefit of an *exempt organization*. However, such a relationship does not result in the feeder organization itself being tax-exempt. § 502.

FICA tax. An abbreviation which stands for Federal Insurance Contributions Act, commonly referred to as the Social Security tax. The FICA tax is comprised of the Social Security tax (old age, survivors, and disability insurance) and the Medicare tax (hospital insurance) and is imposed on both employers and employees. The employer is responsible for withholding from the employee's wages the Social Security tax at a rate of 6.2% on a maximum wage base of $62,700 (for 1996) and the Medicare tax at a rate of 1.45% (no maximum wage base). The employer is required to match the employee's contribution. See also *employment taxes*.

Fiduciary. A person who manages money or property for another and who must exercise a standard of care in the management activity imposed by law or contract. A trustee, for example, possesses a fiduciary responsibility to the beneficiaries of the trust to follow the terms of the trust and the requirements of applicable state law. A breach of fiduciary responsibility would make the trustee liable to the beneficiaries for any damage caused by the breach.

Field audit. An audit conducted by the IRS on the business premises of the taxpayer or in the office of the tax practitioner representing the taxpayer. See also *audit, correspondence audit*, and *office audit*.

Finalized Regulation. See *regulations*.

FIRPTA. Under the Foreign Investment in Real Property Tax Act, gains or losses realized by nonresident aliens and non-U.S. corporations on the disposition of U.S. real estate create U.S.-source income and are subject to U.S. income tax.

First-in, first-out (FIFO). An accounting method for determining the cost of inventories. Under this method, the inventory on hand is deemed to be the sum of the cost of the most recently acquired units. See also *last-in, first-out (LIFO)*.

Fiscal year. A fiscal year is a 12-month period ending on the last day of a month other than December. In certain circumstances, a taxpayer is permitted to elect a fiscal year instead of being required to use a calendar year. See also *accounting period* and *taxable year*.

Fixing-up expense. An expense that is incurred to assist in the sale of a residence and is deductible in calculating the adjusted sales price. Fixing-up expenses include such items as ordinary repairs, painting, and wallpapering. To qualify, the expense must (1) be incurred on work performed during the 90-day period ending on the date of the contract of sale, (2) be paid within 30 days after the date of the sale, and (3) not be a capital expenditure. § 1034. See also *adjusted sales price*.

Flat tax. In its pure form, a flat tax would eliminate all exclusions, deductions, and credits and impose a one-rate tax on gross income.

Foreign corporation. A corporation that is not created in the United States or organized under the laws of one of the states of the United States. § 7701(a)(5). See also *domestic corporation*.

Foreign currency transaction. An exchange that could generate a foreign currency gain or loss for a U.S. taxpayer. For example, if a taxpayer contracts to purchase foreign goods, payable in a currency other than U.S. dollars, at a specified date in the future, any change in the exchange rate between the dollar and that currency will generate a foreign currency gain or loss upon completion of the contract. This gain or loss is treated as separate from the underlying transaction; it may create ordinary or capital gain or loss.

Foreign earned income exclusion. The Code allows exclusions for earned income generated outside the United States to alleviate any tax base and rate disparities among countries. In addition, the exclusion is allowed for housing expenditures incurred by the taxpayer's employer with respect to the non-U.S. assignment, and self-employed individuals can deduct foreign housing expenses incurred in a trade or business.

Foreign personal holding company (FPHC). A foreign corporation in which (1) 60 percent or more of the gross income for the taxable year is FPHC income and (2) more than 50 percent of the total combined voting power or the total value of the stock is owned, directly or indirectly, by five or fewer individuals who are U.S. persons (the U.S. group) at any time during the taxable year. The 60 percent of gross income test drops to 50 percent or more after the 60 percent requirement has been met for one tax year, until the foreign corporation does not meet the 50 percent test for three consecutive years or the stock ownership requirement is not met for an entire tax year.

Foreign sales corporation (FSC). An entity qualifying for a partial exemption of its gross export receipts from U.S. tax. Most FSCs must maintain a presence in a foreign country. In addition, an FSC cannot issue preferred stock, nor can it have more than 25 shareholders.

Foreign-source income. Income that is not sourced within the United States. Examples include earnings from the performance of a personal services contract outside the U.S., interest received from a non-U.S. corporation, and income from the use of property outside the U.S.

Foreign tax credit or deduction. A U.S. citizen or resident who incurs or pays income taxes to a foreign country on income subject to U.S. tax may be able to claim some of these taxes as a deduction or a credit against the U.S. income tax. §§ 27, 164, and 901–905.

Form 706. The U.S. Estate Tax Return. In certain cases, this form must be filed for a decedent who was a resident or citizen of the United States.

Form 709. The U.S. Gift Tax Return.

Form 709–A. The U.S. Short Form Gift Tax Return.

Form 870. The signing of Form 870 (Waiver of Restriction on Assessment and Collection of Deficiency in Tax and Acceptance of Overassessments) by a taxpayer permits the IRS to assess a proposed deficiency without issuing a statutory notice of deficiency (90-day letter). This means the taxpayer must pay the deficiency and cannot file a petition to the U.S. Tax Court. § 6213(d).

Form 872. The signing of this form by a taxpayer extends the period during which the IRS can make an assessment or collection of a tax. In other words, Form 872 extends the applicable statute of limitations. § 6501(c)(4).

Form 1041. The U.S. Fiduciary Income Tax Return, required to be filed by estates and trusts. See Appendix B for a specimen form.

Form 1065. The U.S. Partnership Return of Income. See Appendix B for a specimen form.

Form 1120. The U.S. Corporation Income Tax Return. See Appendix B for a specimen form.

Form 1120–A. The U.S. Short-Form Corporation Income Tax Return. See Appendix B for a specimen form.

Form 1120S. The U.S. Small Business Corporation Income Tax Return, required to be filed by S corporations. See Appendix B for a specimen form.

Franchise. An agreement that gives the transferee the right to distribute, sell, or provide goods, services, or facilities within a specified area. The cost of obtaining a franchise may be amortized over a statutory period of 15 years. In general, the franchisor's gain on the sale of franchise rights is an ordinary gain because the franchisor retains a significant power, right, or continuing interest in the subject of the franchise. §§ 197 and 1253.

Franchise tax. A tax levied on the right to do business in a state as a corporation. Although income considerations may come into play, the tax usually is based on the capitalization of the corporation.

Fraud. Tax fraud falls into two categories: civil and criminal. Under civil fraud, the IRS may impose as a penalty an amount equal to as much as 75 percent of the underpayment [§ 6651(f)]. Fines and/or imprisonment are prescribed for conviction of various types of criminal tax fraud (§§ 7201–7207). Both civil and criminal fraud require a specific intent on the part of the taxpayer to evade the tax; mere negligence is not enough. Criminal fraud requires the additional element of willfulness (i.e., done deliberately and with evil purpose). In practice, it becomes difficult to distinguish between the degree of intent necessary to support criminal, rather than civil, fraud. In either situation, the IRS has the burden of proving fraud. See also *burden of proof.*

Free transferability of interests. The capability of the owner of an entity to transfer his or her ownership interest to another without the consent of the other owners. It is a characteristic of a corporation since a shareholder usually can freely transfer the stock to others without the approval of the existing shareholders. Reg. § 301.7701–2(e). See also *association.*

Fringe benefits. Compensation or other benefits received by an employee that are not in the form of cash. Some fringe benefits (e.g., accident and health plans, group term life insurance) may be excluded from the employee's gross income and thus are not subject to the Federal income tax.

Functional currency. The currency of the economic environment in which the taxpayer carries on most of its activities, and in which the taxpayer transacts most of its business.

FUTA tax. An employment tax levied on employers. Jointly administered by the Federal and state governments, the tax provides funding for unemployment benefits. FUTA applies at a rate of 6.2 percent in 1996 on the first $7,000 of covered wages paid during the year for each employee. The

Federal government allows a credit for FUTA paid (or allowed under a merit rating system) to the state. The credit cannot exceed 5.4 percent of the covered wages. See also *employment taxes.*

Future interest. An interest that will come into being at some future time. It is distinguished from a present interest, which already exists. Assume that Dan transfers securities to a newly created trust. Under the terms of the trust instrument, income from the securities is to be paid each year to Wilma for her life, with the securities passing to Sam upon Wilma's death. Wilma has a present interest in the trust since she is currently entitled to receive the income from the securities. Sam has a future interest since he must wait for Wilma's death to benefit from the trust. The *annual exclusion* of $10,000 is not allowed for a gift of a future interest. § 2503(b). See also *annual exclusion* and *gift splitting.*

G

General business credit. The summation of various nonrefundable business credits, including the investment tax credit, jobs credit, research activities credit, low-income housing credit, and disabled access credit. The amount of general business credit that can be used to reduce the tax liability is limited to the taxpayer's net income tax reduced by the greater of (1) the tentative minimum tax or (2) 25 percent of the net regular tax liability that exceeds $25,000. Unused general business credits can be carried back 3 years and forward 15 years. § 38.

General partner. A partner who is fully liable in an individual capacity for the debts of the partnership to third parties. A general partner's liability is not limited to the investment in the partnership. See also *limited partner.*

General partnership. A partnership that is owned by one or more *general partners*. Creditors of a general partnership can collect amounts owed them from both the partnership assets and the assets of the partners individually.

General power of appointment. See *power of appointment.*

Gift. A transfer of property for less than adequate consideration. Gifts usually occur in a personal setting (such as between members of the same family). They are excluded from the income tax base but may be subject to a transfer tax.

Gift splitting. A special election for Federal gift tax purposes under which husband and wife can treat a gift by one of them to a third party as being made one-half by each. If, for example, George (the husband) makes a gift of $20,000 to Shirley, Barbara (the wife) may elect to treat $10,000 of the gift as coming from her. The major advantage of the election is that it enables the parties to take advantage of the nonowner spouse's (Barbara in this case) annual exclusion and unified credit. § 2513. See also *annual exclusion.*

Gift tax. A tax imposed on the transfer of property by gift. The tax is imposed upon the donor of a gift and is based on the fair market value of the property on the date of the gift.

Gifts within three years of death. Some taxable gifts automatically are included in the gross estate of the donor if death occurs within three years of the gift. § 2035.

Goodwill. The reputation and built-up business of a company. For accounting purposes, goodwill has no basis unless it is purchased. In the purchase of a business, goodwill generally is the difference between the purchase price and the fair market value of the assets acquired. The intangible asset goodwill can be amortized for tax purposes over a 15-year period. Reg. § 1.167(a)–3. See also *amortization.*

Grantor. A transferor of property. The creator of a trust is usually referred to as the grantor of the trust.

Grantor trust. A trust under which the grantor retains control over the income or corpus (or both) to such an extent that he or she is treated as the owner of the property and its income for income tax purposes. Income from a grantor trust is taxable to the grantor and not to the beneficiary who receives it. §§ 671–679. See also *reversionary interest.*

Grass roots lobbying expenditures. Exempt organizations are prohibited from engaging in political activities, but expenses incurred to influence the opinions of the general public relative to specific legislation are permitted by the law. See also *excess lobbying expenditures.*

Green card test. Form I-551, received from a U.S. consul as a receipt showing that the holder has immigration status in the United States and used to refute alien status for tax purposes.

Gross estate. The property owned or previously transferred by a *decedent* that is subject to the Federal estate tax. The gross estate can be distinguished from the *probate estate*, which is property actually subject to administration by the *administrator* or *executor* of an estate. §§ 2031–2046. See also *adjusted gross estate* and *taxable estate.*

Gross income. Income subject to the Federal income tax. Gross income does not include all economic income. That is, certain exclusions are allowed (e.g., interest on municipal bonds). For a manufacturing or merchandising business, gross income usually means gross profit (gross sales or gross receipts less cost of goods sold). § 61 and Reg. § 1.61–3(a). See also *adjusted gross income* and *taxable income.*

Gross up. To add back to the value of the property or income received the amount of the tax that has been paid. For gifts made within three years of death, any gift tax paid on the transfer is added to the gross estate. § 2035(c).

Group term life insurance. Life insurance coverage provided by an employer for a group of employees. Such insurance is renewable on a year-to-year basis, and typically no cash surrender value is built up. The premiums paid by the employer on the insurance are not taxed to the employees on coverage of up to $50,000 per person. § 79 and Reg. § 1.79–1(b).

Guaranteed payment. Payments made by a partnership to a partner for services rendered or for the use of capital to the extent that the payments are determined without regard to the income of the partnership. The payments are treated as though they were made to a nonpartner and thus are usually deductible by the entity.

Guardianship. A legal arrangement under which one person (a guardian) has the legal right and duty to care for another (the ward) and his or her property. A guardianship is established because the ward is unable to act legally on his or her own behalf [e.g., because of minority (he or she is not of age) or mental or physical incapacity].

H

Half-year convention. The half-year convention is a cost recovery convention that assumes all property is placed in service at mid-year and thus provides for a half-year's cost recovery for that year.

Head of household. An unmarried individual who maintains a household for another and satisfies certain conditions set forth in § 2(b). This status enables the taxpayer to use a set of income tax rates that are lower than those applicable to other unmarried individuals but higher than those applicable to surviving spouses and married persons filing a joint return.

Heir. A person who inherits property from a decedent.

Highly compensated employee. The employee group is generally divided into two categories for fringe benefit (including pension and profit sharing plans) purposes. These are (1) highly compensated employees and (2) non-highly compensated employees. For most fringe benefits, if the fringe benefit plan discriminates in favor of highly compensated employees, it will not be a qualified plan with respect, at a minimum, to the highly compensated employees.

Hobby. An activity not engaged in for profit. The Code restricts the amount of losses that an individual can deduct for hobby activities so that these transactions cannot be used to offset income from other sources. § 183.

Holding period. The period of time during which property has been held for income tax purposes. The holding period is significant in determining whether gain or loss from the sale or exchange of a capital asset is long term or short term. § 1223.

Home equity loans. Loans that utilize the personal residence of the taxpayer as security. The interest on such loans is deductible as *qualified residence interest*. However, interest is deductible only on the portion of the loan that does not exceed the lesser of: (1) the fair market value of the residence, reduced by the *acquisition indebtedness* or (2) $100,000 ($50,000 for married persons filing separate returns. A major benefit of a home equity loan is that there are no tracing rules regarding the use of the loan proceeds. § 163(h)(3).

Hot assets. Unrealized receivables and substantially appreciated inventory under § 751. When hot assets are present, the sale of a partnership interest or the disproportionate distribution of the assets can cause ordinary income to be recognized.

H.R. 10 plans. See *Keogh plans*.

Hybrid method. A combination of the accrual and cash methods of accounting. That is, the taxpayer may account for some items of income on the accrual method (e.g., sales and cost of goods sold) and other items (e.g., interest income) on the cash method.

I

Imputed interest. For certain long-term sales of property, the IRS can convert some of the gain from the sale into interest income if the contract does not provide for a minimum rate of interest to be paid by the purchaser. The application of this procedure has the effect of forcing the seller to recognize less long-term capital gain and more ordinary income (interest income). § 483 and the related Regulations.

Incident of ownership. An element of ownership or degree of control over a life insurance policy. The retention by an insured of an incident of ownership in a life insurance policy will cause the policy proceeds to be included in the insured's gross estate upon death. § 2042(2) and Reg. § 20.2042–1(c). See also *gross estate* and *insured*.

Includible gain. Section 644 imposes a built-in gains tax on trusts that sell or exchange property at a gain within two years after the date of its transfer in trust by the transferor. The provision applies only if the fair market value of the property at the time of the initial transfer exceeds the adjusted basis of the property immediately after the transfer. The tax imposed by § 644 is the amount of additional tax the transferor would pay (including any minimum tax) had the gain been included in the transferor's gross income for the tax year of the sale. However, the tax applies only to an amount known as *includible gain.* This is the lesser of the following: the gain recognized by the trust on the sale or exchange of any property, or the excess of the fair market value of the property at the time of the initial transfer in trust by the transferor over the adjusted basis of the property immediately after the transfer.

Income. For tax purposes, an increase in wealth that has been realized.

Income beneficiary. The party entitled to income from property. In a typical trust situation, Alan is to receive the income for life with corpus or principal passing to Gertrude upon Alan's death. In this case, Alan is the income beneficiary of the trust.

Income in respect of a decedent (IRD). Income earned by a decedent at the time of death but not reportable on the final income tax return because of the method of accounting that appropriately is utilized. Such income is included in the gross estate and is taxed to the eventual recipient (either the estate or heirs). The recipient is, however, allowed an income tax deduction for the estate tax attributable to the income. § 691.

Income interest. The right of a beneficiary to receive distributions from the fiduciary income of a trust or estate.

Income shifting. Occurs when an individual transfers some of his or her gross income to a taxpayer who is subject to a lower tax rate, thereby reducing the total income tax liability of the group. Income shifting produces a successful assignment of income. It can be accomplished by transferring income-producing property to the lower-bracket taxpayer or to an effective trust for his or her benefit, or by transferring ownership interests in a family partnership or in a closely held corporation.

Incomplete transfer. A transfer made by a decedent during lifetime that, because of certain control or enjoyment retained by the transferor, is not considered complete for Federal estate tax purposes. Thus, some or all of the fair market value of the property transferred is included in the transferor's gross estate. §§ 2036–2038. See also *gross estate* and *revocable transfer*.

Independent contractor. A self-employed person as distinguished from one who is employed as an employee.

Indexation. Various components of the tax formula are adjusted periodically for the effects of inflation, so that the effects of the formula are not eroded by price level changes. Tax rate schedules, personal and dependency exemption amounts, and the standard deduction, among other items, are indexed in this manner.

Individual retirement account (IRA). Individuals with earned income are permitted to set aside up to 100 percent of that income per year (not to exceed $2,000 or $2,250 for a spousal IRA) for a retirement account. The amount set aside can be deducted by the taxpayer and is subject to income tax only upon withdrawal. The Code limits the amount of this contribution that can be deducted *for AGI* depending upon (1) whether the taxpayer or spouse is an active participant in an employer-provided qualified retirement plan, and (2) the magnitude of the taxpayer's AGI before the IRA contribution is considered. § 219. See also *simplified employee pension (SEP) plan*.

Inheritance tax. A tax imposed on the right to receive property from a *decedent*. Thus, theoretically, an inheritance tax is imposed on the heir. The Federal estate tax is imposed on the estate. See also *death tax* and *estate tax*.

In kind. See *distributions in kind*.

Inside basis. A partnership's basis in the assets it owns.

Installment method. A method of accounting enabling certain taxpayers to spread the recognition of gain on the sale of property over the collection period. Under this procedure, the seller arrives at the gain to be recognized by computing the gross profit percentage from the sale (the gain divided by the contract price) and applying it to each payment received. § 453.

Insured. A person whose life is the subject of an insurance policy. Upon the death of the insured, the life insurance policy matures, and the proceeds become payable to the designated beneficiary. See also *life insurance*.

Intangible asset. Property that is a "right" rather than a physical object. Examples are patents, stocks and bonds, goodwill, trademarks, franchises, and copyrights. See also *amortization* and *tangible property*.

Internal Revenue Code. The collected statutes that govern the taxation of income, property transfers, and other transactions in the United States and the enforcement of those provisions. Enacted by Congress, the Code is amended frequently, but it has not been reorganized since 1954. However, because of the extensive revisions to the statutes that occurred with the Tax Reform Act of 1986, Title 26 of the U.S. Code is now known as the Internal Revenue Code of 1986.

Internal Revenue Service. The federal agency, a division of the Department of the Treasury, charged with implementing the U.S. revenue enforcement and collection provisions.

Interpolated terminal reserve. The measure used in valuing insurance policies for gift and estate tax purposes when the policies are not paid up at the time of their transfer. Reg. § 20.2031–8(a)(3), Ex. (3).

Interpretive regulation. A Regulation issued by the Treasury Department which purports to explain the meaning of a particular Code Section. An interpretive Regulation is given less deference than a legislative Regulation. See also *legislative regulation* and *procedural regulation*. § 7805.

Inter vivos transfer. A transfer of property during the life of the owner. Distinguished from testamentary transfers, where the property passes at death.

Interest-free loans. Bona fide loans that carry no interest (or a below-market rate). If made in a nonbusiness setting, the imputed interest element is treated as a gift from the lender to the borrower. If made by a corporation to a shareholder, a constructive dividend could result. In either event, the lender may recognize interest income. § 7872.

Intestate. No will exists at the time of death. In such cases, state law prescribes who will receive the decedent's property. The laws of intestate succession generally favor the surviving spouse, children, and grandchildren, and then parents and grandparents and brothers and sisters.

Investment income. Consisting of virtually the same elements as portfolio income, a measure by which to justify a deduction for interest on investment indebtedness. See also *investment indebtedness* and *portfolio income*.

Investment indebtedness. Debt incurred to carry or incur investments by the taxpayer in assets that will produce portfolio income. Limitations are placed upon interest deductions that are incurred in connection with the debt (generally to the corresponding amount of investment income).

Investment interest. Payment for the use of funds used to acquire assets that produce investment income. The deduction for investment interest is limited to *net investment income* for the tax year. See also *investment income*.

Investment tax credit (ITC). A tax credit that usually was equal to 10 percent (unless a reduced credit was elected) of the qualified investment in tangible personalty used in a trade or business. If the tangible personalty had a recovery period of five years or more, the full cost of the property qualified for the credit. Only 60 percent qualified for property with a recovery period of three years. However, the regular investment tax credit was repealed by TRA of 1986 for property placed in service after December 31, 1985. § 46. See also *general business credit*.

Investor losses. Losses on stock and securities. If stocks and bonds are capital assets in the hands of the holder, a capital loss materializes as of the last day of the taxable year in which the stocks or bonds become worthless. Under certain circumstances involving stocks and bonds of affiliated corporations, an ordinary loss is permitted upon worthlessness.

Involuntary conversion. The loss or destruction of property through theft, casualty, or condemnation. Any gain realized on an involuntary conversion can, at the taxpayer's election, be deferred for Federal income tax purposes if the owner reinvests the proceeds within a prescribed period of time in property that is similar or related in service or use. See also *nontaxable exchange*. § 1033.

IRA. See *individual retirement account*.

Itemized deductions. Personal and employee expenditures allowed by the Code as deductions from adjusted gross income. Examples include certain medical expenses, interest on home mortgages, state income taxes, and charitable contributions. Itemized deductions are reported on Schedule A of Form 1040. Certain miscellaneous itemized deductions are reduced by 2 percent of the taxpayer's adjusted gross income. In addition, a taxpayer whose adjusted gross income exceeds a certain level (indexed annually) must reduce the itemized deductions by 3 percent of the excess of adjusted gross income over that level. Medical, casualty and theft, and investment interest deductions are not subject to the 3 percent reduction. The 3 percent reduction may not reduce itemized deductions that are subject to the reduction to below 20 percent of their initial amount.

J

Jeopardy assessment. If the collection of a tax appears in question, the IRS may assess and collect the tax immediately without the usual formalities. The IRS can terminate a taxpayer's taxable year before the usual date if it feels that the collection of the tax may be in peril because the taxpayer plans to leave the country. §§ 6851 and 6861–6864.

Joint and several liability. Permits the IRS to collect a tax from one or all of several taxpayers. A husband and wife who file a joint income tax return usually are collectively or individually liable for the full amount of the tax liability. § 6013(d)(3).

Joint tenants. Two or more persons having undivided ownership of property with the right of survivorship. Right of survivorship gives the surviving owner full ownership of the property. Suppose Bob and Tami are joint tenants of a tract of land. Upon Bob's death, Tami becomes the sole owner of the property. For the estate tax consequences upon the death of a joint tenant, see § 2040. See also *tenancy by the entirety* and *tenancy in common*.

Joint venture. A one-time grouping of two or more persons in a business undertaking. Unlike a partnership, a joint venture does not entail a continuing relationship among the parties. A joint venture is treated like a partnership for Federal income tax purposes. § 7701(a)(2).

K

Keogh plans. Retirement plans available to self-employed taxpayers. They are also referred to as H.R. 10 plans. Under such plans, a taxpayer may deduct each year up to either 20 percent of net earnings from self-employment or $30,000, whichever is less.

Kiddie tax. See *tax on unearned income of a child under age 14*.

L

Lapse. The expiration of a right either by the death of the holder or upon the expiration of a period of time. Thus, a power of appointment lapses upon the death of the holder if he or she has not exercised the power during life or at death (through a will).

Last-in, first-out (LIFO). An accounting method for valuing inventories for tax purposes. Under this method, it is assumed that the inventory on hand is valued at the cost of the earliest acquired units. § 472. See also *first-in, first-out (FIFO)*.

Leaseback. The transferor of property later leases it back. In a sale-leaseback situation, for example, Richard sells property to Sally and subsequently leases the property from Sally. Thus, Richard becomes the lessee and Sally the lessor.

Least aggregate deferral method. An algorithm set forth in the Regulations to determine the tax year for a partnership or S corporation with owners whose tax years differ. The tax year is selected which produces the least aggregate deferral of income for the owners.

Legacy. A transfer of cash or other property by will.

Legal age. The age at which a person may enter into binding contracts or commit other legal acts. In most states, a minor reaches legal age or majority (comes of age) at age 18.

Legal representative. A person who oversees the legal affairs of another; for example, the executor or administrator of an estate or a court-appointed guardian of a minor or incompetent person.

Legatee. The recipient of property under a will and transferred by the death of the owner.

Legislative regulation. Some Code Sections give the Secretary of the Treasury or his delegate the authority to prescribe Regulations to carry out the details of administration or to otherwise complete the operating rules. Regulations issued pursuant to this type of authority truly possess the force and effect of law. In effect, Congress is almost delegating its legislative powers to the Treasury Department. See also *interpretive regulation* and *procedural regulation*.

Lessee. One who rents property from another. In the case of real estate, the lessee is also known as the tenant.

Lessor. One who rents property to another. In the case of real estate, the lessor is also known as the landlord.

Letter ruling. The written response of the IRS to a taxpayer's request for interpretation of the revenue laws, with respect to a proposed transaction (e.g., concerning the tax-free status of a reorganization). Not to be relied on as precedent by other than the party who requested the ruling.

LEXIS. An on-line database system with which the tax researcher can obtain access to the Internal Revenue Code, Regulations, administrative rulings, and court case opinions.

Liabilities in excess of basis. On the contribution of capital to a corporation or partnership, an investor recognizes gain on the exchange to the extent that contributed assets carry liabilities with a face amount in excess of the tax basis of the contributed assets. This rule keeps the investor from holding the investment asset received with a negative basis. § 357(c).

Life estate. A legal arrangement under which the beneficiary (the life tenant) is entitled to the income from property for his or her life. Upon the death of the life tenant, the property is transferred to the holder of the remainder interest. See also *income beneficiary* and *remainder interest*.

Life insurance. A contract between the holder of a policy and an insurance company (the carrier) under which the company agrees, in return for premium payments, to pay a specified sum (the face value or maturity value of the policy) to the designated beneficiary upon the death of the insured. See also *insured*.

Like-kind exchange. An exchange of property held for productive use in a trade or business or for investment (except inventory and stocks and bonds) for other investment or trade or business property. Unless non-like-kind property (boot) is received, the exchange is nontaxable. § 1031. See also *boot* and *nontaxable exhange*.

Limited liability. The liability of an entity and its owners to third parties is limited to the investment in the entity. This is a characteristic of a corporation, as shareholders generally are not responsible for the debts of the corporation and, at most, may lose the amount paid in for the stock issued. Reg. § 301.7701–2(d). See also *association*.

Limited liability company (LLC). A form of entity allowed by virtually all of the states. The entity is taxed as a partnership in which all members or owners of the LLC are treated much like limited partners. There are no restrictions on ownership, all members may participate in management, and none has personal liability for the entity's debts.

Limited liability partnership (LLP). A form of entity allowed by many of the states, where a general partnership registers with the state as an LLP. Owners are general partners, but a partner is not liable for any malpractice committed by other partners. The personal assets of the partners are at risk for the entity's contractual liabilities, such as accounts payable. The personal assets of a specific partner are at risk for his or her own professional malpractice and tort liability, and for malpractice and torts committed by those whom he or she supervises.

Limited partner. A partner whose liability to third-party creditors of the partnership is limited to the amount he or she has invested in the partnership. See also *general partner* and *limited partnership*.

Limited partnership. A partnership in which some of the partners are limited partners. At least one of the partners in a limited partnership must be a general partner. See also *general partner* and *limited partner*.

Liquidating distribution. A distribution by a partnership or corporation that is in complete liquidation of the entity's trade or business activities. Typically, such distributions generate capital gain or loss to the investors without regard, for instance, to the earnings and profits of the corporation or to the partnership's basis in the distributed property. They can, however, lead to recognized gain or loss at the corporate level.

Liquidation. See *corporate liquidation*.

Listed property. The term listed property includes (1) any passenger automobile, (2) any other property used as a means of transportation, (3) any property of a type generally used for purposes of entertainment, recreation, or amusement, (4) any computer or peripheral equipment (with an exception for exclusive business use), (5) any cellular telephone (or other similar telecommunications equipment), and (6) any other property of a type specified in the Regulations. If listed property is predominantly used for business, the taxpayer is allowed to use the statutory percentage method of cost recovery. Otherwise, the straight-line cost recovery method must be used. § 280F.

Living trust. A revocable trust. Often touted as a useful means of avoiding some probate costs.

Lobbying expenditure. An expenditure made for the purpose of influencing legislation. Such payments can result in the loss of the exempt status of, and the imposition of Federal income tax on, an exempt organization.

Long-term capital gain or loss. Results from the sale or other taxable exchange of a capital asset that had been held by the seller for more than one year or from other transactions involving statutorily designated assets, including § 1231 property and patents.

Long-term contract. A building, installation, construction, or manufacturing contract that is entered into but not completed within the same tax year. A manufacturing contract is a long-term contract only if the contract is to manufacture (1) a unique item not normally carried in finished goods inventory or (2) items that normally require more than 12 calendar months to complete. The two available methods to account for long-term contracts are the percentage of completion method and the completed contract method. The completed contract method can be used only in limited circumstances. § 460. See also *completed contract method* and *percentage of completion method*.

Long-term tax-exempt rate. Used in the derivation of NOL limitations in the context of an equity structure shift. The highest of the federal long-term interest rates in effect for any of the last three months.

Low-income housing credit. Beneficial treatment to owners of low-income housing is provided in the form of a tax credit. The calculated credit is claimed in the year the building is placed in service and in the following nine years. § 42. See also *general business credit*.

Lump-sum distribution. Payment of the entire amount due at one time rather than in installments. Such distributions often occur from qualified pension or profit sharing plans upon the retirement or death of a covered employee.

M

MACRS. See *accelerated cost recovery system (ACRS)*.

Majority. See *legal age*.

Malpractice. Professional misconduct; an unreasonable lack of skill.

Marital deduction. A deduction allowed against the taxable estate or taxable gifts upon the transfer of property from one spouse to another.

Market value. See *fair market value*.

Marriage penalty. The additional tax liability that results for a married couple when compared with what their tax liability would be if they were not married and filed separate returns.

Meaningful reduction test. A decrease in the shareholder's voting control. Used to determine whether a redemption qualifies for sale or exchange treatment.

Merger. The absorption of one corporation by another with the corporation being absorbed losing its legal identity.

Orange Corporation is merged into Blue Corporation, and the shareholders of Orange receive stock in Blue in exchange for their stock in Orange Corporation. After the merger, Orange Corporation ceases to exist as a separate legal entity. If a merger meets certain conditions, it is nontaxable to the parties involved. § 368(a)(1)(A). See also *corporate acquisition* and *corporate reorganization*.

Mid-month convention. The mid-month convention is a cost recovery convention that assumes property is placed in service in the middle of the month that it is actually placed in service.

Mid-quarter convention. The mid-quarter convention is a cost recovery convention that assumes property placed in service during the year is placed in service at the middle of the quarter in which it is actually placed in service. The mid-quarter convention applies if more than 40% of the value of property (other than eligible real estate) is placed in service during the last quarter of the year.

Minimum credit (AET). A fixed amount, $150,000 for personal service firms and $250,000 for all others, below which the *accumulated earnings credit* cannot be derived. Assures that small and start-up corporations can generate a minimum amount of earnings before being subject to the AET.

Minimum tax. See *alternative minimum tax (AMT)*.

Minimum tax credit (AMT). When a corporation pays an alternative minimum tax, a minimum tax credit is created on a dollar-for-dollar basis, to be applied against regular tax liabilities incurred in future years. The credit is carried forward indefinitely, but it is not carried back. The effect of the credit for corporate taxpayers alternating between the AMT and regular tax models is to make the AMT liabilities a prepayment of regular taxes. Non-corporate AMT taxpayers are allowed the credit only with respect to the elements of the AMT that reflect timing differences between the two tax models.

Minority. See *legal age*.

Miscellaneous itemized deductions. A special category of itemized deductions that includes such expenses as professional dues, tax return preparation fees, job-hunting costs, unreimbursed employee business expenses, and certain investment expenses. Such expenses are deductible only to the extent they exceed 2 percent of adjusted gross income. § 67. See also *itemized deductions*.

Mitigate. To make less severe. See also *mitigation of the annual accounting period concept* and *mitigation of the statute of limitations*.

Mitigation of the annual accounting period concept. Various tax provisions that provide relief from the effect of the finality of the annual accounting period concept. For example, the net operating loss carryover provisions allow the taxpayer to apply the negative taxable income of one year against a corresponding positive amount in another tax accounting period. See also *annual accounting period concept*.

Mitigation of the statute of limitations. A series of tax provisions that prevents either the IRS or a taxpayer from obtaining a double benefit from the application of the statute of limitations. It would be unfair, for example, to permit a taxpayer to depreciate an asset that previously expensed, but that should have been capitalized, if the statute of limitations prevents the IRS from adjusting the tax liability for the year the asset was purchased. §§ 1311–1314. See also *statute of limitations.*

Modified accelerated cost recovery system (MACRS). See *accelerated cost recovery system (ACRS).*

Mortgagee. The party who holds the mortgage; the creditor.

Mortgagor. The party who mortgages the property; the debtor.

Most suitable use value. For gift and estate tax purposes, property that is transferred normally is valued in accordance with its most suitable or optimal use. Thus, if a farm is worth more as a potential shopping center, the value as a shopping center is used, even though the transferee (the donee or heir) continues to use the property as a farm. For an exception to this rule concerning the valuation of certain kinds of real estate transferred by death, see *special use value.*

Multitiered partnerships. See *tiered partnerships.*

N

National sales tax. Intended as a replacement for the current Federal income tax. Unlike a value added tax (VAT), which is levied on the manufacturer, it would be imposed on the consumer upon the final sale of goods and services. To keep the tax from being regressive, low-income taxpayers would be granted some kind of credit or exemption.

Necessary. Appropriate and helpful in furthering the taxpayer's business or income-producing activity. §§ 162(a) and 212. See also *ordinary.*

Negligence. Failure to exercise the reasonable or ordinary degree of care of a prudent person in a situation that results in harm or damage to another. Code § 6651 imposes a penalty on taxpayers who exhibit negligence or intentional disregard of rules and Regulations with respect to the underpayment of certain taxes. See also *accuracy-related penalty.*

Net capital loss. The excess of the losses from sales or exchanges of capital assets over the gains from sales or exchanges of such assets. Up to $3,000 per year of the net capital loss may be deductible by noncorporate taxpayers against ordinary income. The excess net capital loss carries over to future tax years. For corporate taxpayers, the net capital loss cannot be offset against ordinary income, but it can be carried back 3 years and forward 5 years to offset net capital gains. §§ 1211, 1212 and 1221(10).

Net operating loss. To mitigate the effect of the annual accounting period concept, § 172 allows taxpayers to use an excess loss of one year as a deduction for certain past or future years. In this regard, a carryback period of 3 years and a carryforward period of 15 years currently are allowed. See also *mitigation of the annual accounting period concept.*

Net worth method. An approach used by the IRS to reconstruct the income of a taxpayer who fails to maintain adequate records. Under this method, the gross income for the year is estimated as the increase in net worth of the taxpayer (assets in excess of liabilities) with appropriate adjustment for nontaxable receipts and nondeductible expenditures. The net worth method often is used when tax fraud is suspected.

Ninety-day letter. See *statutory notice of deficiency.*

No-additional-cost-services. Services that the employer may provide the employee at no additional cost to the employer. Generally, the benefit is the ability to utilize employer's excess capacity (vacant seats on an airliner). Such amounts are excludible from the recipient's gross income.

Nonaccountable plan. An expense reimbursement plan that does not have an accountability feature. The result is that employee expenses must be claimed as deductions *from* AGI. An exception is moving expenses which are deductions *for* AGI. See also *accountable plan.*

Nonacquiescence. Disagreement by the IRS on the result reached in certain judicial decisions. *Nonacq.* or *NA.* See also *acquiescence.*

Nonbusiness bad debt. A bad debt loss that is not incurred in connection with a creditor's trade or business. The loss is classified as a short-term capital loss and is allowed only in the year the debt becomes entirely worthless. In addition to family loans, many investor losses are nonbusiness bad debts. § 166(d). See also *business bad debt.*

Nonbusiness income. Income generated from investment assets or from the taxable disposition thereof.

Noncontributory qualified pension or profit sharing plan. A plan funded entirely by the employer with no contributions being made by the covered employees. See also *qualified pension or profit sharing plan.*

Nonliquidating distribution. A payment made by a partnership or corporation to the entity's owner is a nonliquidating distribution when the entity's legal existence does not cease thereafter. If the payor is a corporation, such a distribution can result in dividend income to the shareholders. If the payor is a partnership, the partner usually assigns a basis in the distributed property that is equal to the lesser of the partner's basis in the partnership interest or the basis of the distributed asset to the partnership. In this regard, the partner first assigns basis to any cash that he or she receives in the distribution. The partner's remaining basis, if any, is assigned to the noncash assets according to their relative bases to the partnership.

Nonrecourse debt.   Debt secured by the property that it is used to purchase. The purchaser of the property is not personally liable for the debt upon default. Rather, the creditor's recourse is to repossess the related property. Nonrecourse debt generally does not increase the purchaser's at-risk amount.

Nonrefundable credit.   A nonrefundable credit is a credit that is not paid if it exceeds the taxpayer's tax liability. Some nonrefundable credits qualify for carryback and carryover treatment. See also *refundable credit.*

Nonresident alien.   An individual who is neither a citizen nor a resident of the United States. Citizenship is determined under the immigration and naturalization laws of the United States. Residency is determined under § 7701(b) of the Internal Revenue Code.

Nonseparately stated income.   The net income of an S corporation that is combined and allocated to the shareholders. Other items, such as capital gains and charitable contributions, that could be treated differently on the individual tax returns of the shareholders are not included in this amount but are allocated to the shareholders separately.

Nontaxable exchange.   A transaction in which realized gains or losses are not recognized. The recognition of gain or loss is postponed (deferred) until the property received in the nontaxable exchange is subsequently disposed of in a taxable transaction. Examples are § 1031 like-kind exchanges, § 1033 involuntary conversions, and § 1034 sale of a residence. See also *involuntary conversion* and *like-kind exchange.*

Not essentially equivalent redemption.   See *redemption (not equivalent to a dividend).*

O

Obligee.   The party to whom someone else is obligated under a contract. Thus, if Carol loans money to Dan, Carol is the obligee and Dan is the obligor under the loan.

Obligor.   See *obligee.*

Occupational tax.   A tax imposed on various trades or businesses. A license fee that enables a taxpayer to engage in a particular occupation.

Offer in compromise.   A settlement agreement offered by the IRS in a tax dispute, especially where there is doubt as to the collectibility of the full deficiency. Offers in compromise can include installment payment schedules, as well as reductions in the tax and penalties owed by the taxpayer.

Office audit.   An audit conducted by the IRS in the agent's office. See also *audit, correspondence audit,* and *field audit.*

On all fours.   A judicial decision exactly in point with another as to result, facts, or both.

Optimal use value.   Synonym for most suitable use value.

Ordinary.   Common and accepted in the general industry or type of activity in which the taxpayer is engaged. It comprises one of the tests for the deductibility of expenses incurred or paid in connection with a trade or business; for the production or collection of income; for the management, conservation, or maintenance of property held for the production of income; or in connection with the determination, collection, or refund of any tax. §§ 162(a) and 212. See also *necessary.*

Ordinary and necessary.   See *necessary* and *ordinary.*

Ordinary gross income.   A concept unique to personal holding companies and defined in § 543(b)(1). See also *adjusted ordinary gross income.*

Ordinary income property.   Property contributed to a charitable organization that, if sold rather than contributed, would have resulted in other than long-term capital gain to the donor (i.e., ordinary income property and short-term capital gain property). Examples are inventory and capital assets held for less than the long-term holding period.

Organizational expenditures.   Items incurred early in the life of a corporate entity, qualifying for a 60-month amortization under Federal tax law. Amortizable expenditures exclude those incurred to obtain capital (underwriting fees) or assets (subject to cost recovery). Typically, amortizable expenditures include legal and accounting fees, and state incorporation payments. Such items must be incurred by the end of the entity's first tax year. § 248.

Original issue discount.   The difference between the issue price of a debt obligation (e.g., a corporate bond) and the maturity value of the obligation when the issue price is *less than* the maturity value. OID represents interest and must be amortized over the life of the debt obligation using the effective interest method. The difference is not considered to be original issue discount for tax purposes when it is less than one-fourth of 1 percent of the redemption price at maturity multiplied by the number of years to maturity. §§ 1272 and 1273(a)(3).

Outside basis.   A partner's basis in his or her partnership interest.

Owner shift.   Any change in the respective ownership of stock by a 5%-or-more shareholder. Change is determined relative to a testing period of the prior three years. If there is a more-than-50 percent change in the ownership of a loss corporation, § 382 limitations apply to the use of NOL carryovers of the loss corporation.

P

Parent-subsidiary controlled group.   A *controlled* or *affiliated group* of corporations, where at least one corporation is at least eighty percent owned by one or more of the others. The affiliated group definition is more difficult to meet.

Partial liquidation.   A stock redemption where noncorporate shareholders are permitted sale or exchange treatment, where an active business has existed for at least five years, and a portion of the outstanding stock in the entity is retired.

Partner. See *general partner* and *limited partner.*

Partnership. For income tax purposes, a partnership includes a syndicate, group, pool, or joint venture, as well as ordinary partnerships. In an ordinary partnership, two or more parties combine capital and/or services to carry on a business for profit as co-owners. § 7701(a)(2). See also *limited partnership* and *tiered partnerships.*

Passive foreign investment company (PFIC). A non-U.S. corporation that generates a substantial amount of personal holding company income. Upon receipt of an excess distribution from the entity or the sale of its shares, its U.S. shareholders are taxable on their pro rata shares of the tax that has been deferred with respect to the corporation's taxable income, plus an applicable interest charge.

Passive investment holding company. A means by which a multistate corporation can reduce the overall effective tax rate by isolating investment income in a low- or no-tax state.

Passive investment income (PII). Gross receipts from royalties, certain rents, dividends, interest, annuities, and gains from the sale or exchange of stock and securities. With certain exceptions, if the passive investment income of an S corporation exceeds 25 percent of the corporation's gross receipts for three consecutive years, S status is lost.

Passive loss rules. Any loss from (1) activities in which the taxpayer does not materially participate or (2) rental activities (subject to certain exceptions). Net passive losses cannot be used to offset income from nonpassive sources. Rather, they are suspended until the taxpayer either generates net passive income (and a deduction of such losses is allowed) or disposes of the underlying property (at which time the loss deductions are allowed in full). One relief provision allows landlords who actively participate in the rental activities to deduct up to $25,000 of passive losses annually. However, a phaseout of the $25,000 amount commences when the landlord's AGI exceeds $100,000. See also *portfolio income.*

Pecuniary bequest. A bequest of money to an heir by a decedent. See also *bequest.*

Percentage depletion. Percentage depletion is depletion based on a statutory percentage applied to the gross income from the property. The taxpayer deducts the greater of cost depletion or percentage depletion. § 613. See also *cost depletion.*

Percentage of completion method. A method of reporting gain or loss on certain long-term contracts. Under this method of accounting, the gross contract price is included in income as the contract is completed. Reg. § 1.451–3. See also *completed contract method* and *long-term contract.*

Personal and dependency exemptions. The tax law provides an exemption for each individual taxpayer and an additional exemption for the taxpayer's spouse if a joint

return is filed. An individual may also claim a dependency exemption for each dependent, provided certain tests are met. The amount of the personal and dependency exemptions is $2,550 in 1996 ($2,500 in 1995). The exemption is subject to phase out once adjusted gross income exceeds certain statutory threshold amounts.

Personal and household effects. Items owned by a decedent at the time of death. Examples include clothing, furniture, sporting goods, jewelry, stamp and coin collections, silverware, china, crystal, cooking utensils, books, cars, televisions, radios, stereo equipment, etc.

Personal casualty gain. The recognized gain from any involuntary conversion of personal use property arising from fire, storm, shipwreck, or other casualty, or from theft. See also *personal casualty loss.*

Personal casualty loss. The recognized loss from any involuntary conversion of personal use property arising from fire, storm, shipwreck, or other casualty, or from theft. See also *personal casualty gain.*

Personal exemption. See *personal and dependency exemptions.*

Personal holding company (PHC). A corporation that satisfies the requirements of § 542. Qualification as a personal holding company means a penalty tax may be imposed on the corporation's undistributed personal holding company income for the year.

Personal holding company income. Income as defined by § 543. It includes interest, dividends, certain rents and royalties, income from the use of corporate property by certain shareholders, income from certain personal service contracts, and distributions from estates and trusts. Such income is relevant in determining whether a corporation is a personal holding company and is therefore subject to the penalty tax on personal holding companies. See also *adjusted ordinary gross income.*

Personal holding company tax. A penalty tax imposed on certain closely held corporations with excessive investment income. The tax is assessed at the top individual tax rate on adjusted taxable income reduced by dividends paid. § 541.

Personal property. Generally, all property other than real estate. It is sometimes referred to as personalty when real estate is termed realty. Personal property can also refer to property not used in a taxpayer's trade or business or held for the production or collection of income. When used in this sense, personal property can include both realty (e.g., a personal residence) and personalty (e.g., personal effects such as clothing and furniture). See also *bequest.*

Personal service corporation (PSC). A corporation whose principal activity is the performance of personal services (e.g., health, law, engineering, architecture, accounting, actuarial science, performing arts, or consulting) and where such services are substantially performed by the employee-owners.

Personalty.   Personalty is all property that is not attached to real estate (realty) and is movable. Examples of personalty are machinery, automobiles, clothing, household furnishings, inventory, and personal effects. See also *ad valorem tax, realty,* and *personal property.*

Portfolio income.   Income from interest, dividends, rentals, royalties, capital gains, or other investment sources. Net passive losses cannot be used to offset net portfolio income. See also *passive loss rules* and *investment income.*

Power of appointment.   A legal right granted to someone by will or other document that gives the holder the power to dispose of property or the income from property. When the holder may appoint the property to his or her own benefit, the power usually is called a general power of appointment. If the holder cannot benefit himself or herself but may only appoint to certain other persons, the power is a special power of appointment. Assume Gus places $500,000 worth of securities in trust granting Debbie the right to determine each year how the trustee is to divide the income between Ann and Bill. Under these circumstances, Debbie has a special power of appointment. If Debbie had the further right to appoint the income to herself, she probably possesses a general power of appointment. For the estate tax and gift tax effects of powers of appointment, see §§ 2041 and 2514. See also *testamentary power of appointment.*

Precedents.   A previously decided court decision which is recognized as authority for the disposition of future decisions.

Precontribution gain.   Partnerships allow for a variety of *special allocations* of gain or loss among the partners, but gain or loss that is "built-in" on an asset contributed to the partnership is assigned specifically to the contributing partner. § 704(c)(1)(A).

Preferences (AMT).   See *alternative minimum tax (AMT)* and *tax preferences.*

Preferred stock bailout.   A process where a shareholder used the issuance, sale, and later redemption of a preferred stock dividend to obtain long-term capital gains, without any loss of voting control over the corporation. In effect, the shareholder receives corporate profits without suffering the consequences of dividend income treatment. This procedure led Congress to enact § 306, which, if applicable, converts the prior long-term capital gain on the sale of the stock to ordinary income. Under these circumstances, the amount of ordinary income is limited to the shareholder's portion of the corporation's earnings and profits existing when the preferred stock was issued as a stock dividend. See also *bailout.*

Present interest.   See *future interest.*

Presumption.   An inference in favor of a particular fact. If, for example, the IRS issues a notice of deficiency against a taxpayer, a presumption of correctness attaches to the assessment. Thus, the taxpayer has the burden of proof of showing that he or she does not owe the tax listed in the deficiency notice. See also *rebuttable presumption.*

Previously taxed income (PTI).   Before the Subchapter S Revision Act of 1982, the undistributed taxable income of an S corporation was taxed to the shareholders as of the last day of the corporation's tax year and usually could be withdrawn by the shareholders without tax consequences at some later point in time. The role of PTI has been taken over by the accumulated adjustments account. See also *accumulated adjustments account (AAA).*

Principal.   Property as opposed to income. The term is often used as a synonym for the corpus of a trust. If, for example, Gwen places real estate in trust with income payable to Abby for life and the remainder to Karen upon Abby's death, the real estate is the principal, or corpus, of the trust.

Private foundation.   An *exempt organization* that is subject to additional statutory restrictions on its activities and on contributions made to it. Excise taxes may be levied on certain prohibited transactions, and the Code places more stringent restrictions on the deductibility of contributions to private foundations. § 509.

Probate.   The legal process by which the estate of a decedent is administered. Generally, the probate process involves collecting a decedent's assets, liquidating liabilities, paying necessary taxes, and distributing property to heirs.

Probate costs.   The costs incurred in administering a decedent's estate. See also *probate estate.*

Probate court.   The usual designation for the state or local court that supervises the administration (probate) of a decedent's estate.

Probate estate.   The property of a decedent that is subject to administration by the executor or administrator of an estate. See also *administration.*

Procedural Regulation.   A Regulation issued by the Treasury Department that is a housekeeping-type instruction indicating information that taxpayers should provide the IRS as well as information about the internal management and conduct of the IRS itself. See also *interpretive regulation* and *legislative regulation.*

Profit and loss sharing ratios.   Specified in the partnership agreement and used to determine each partner's allocation of ordinary taxable income and separately stated items. Profits and losses can be shared in different ratios. The ratios can be changed by amending the partnership agreement. § 704(a).

Profits interest.   A partner's percentage allocation of partnership operating results, determined by the *profits and loss sharing ratios.*

Property.   Assets defined in the broadest legal sense. Property includes the *unrealized receivables* of a cash basis taxpayer, but not services rendered. § 351.

Proposed Regulation.   A Regulation issued by the Treasury Department in proposed, rather than final, form. The interval between the proposal of a Regulation and its finalization permits taxpayers and other interested parties to comment on the propriety of the proposal. See also *regulations*.

Pro rata. Proportionately. Assume, for example, a corporation has 10 shareholders, each of whom owns 10 percent of the stock. A pro rata dividend distribution of $1,000 would mean that each shareholder would receive $100.

Pro se. The taxpayer represents himself or herself before the court without the benefit of counsel.

Property dividend. Generally treated in same manner as a cash distribution, measured by the FMV of the property on the date of distribution. The portion of the distribution representing E & P is a dividend; any excess is treated as a return of capital. Distribution of appreciated property causes the distributing corporation to recognize gain. The distributing corporation does not recognize loss on property that has depreciated in value.

Property tax. An *ad valorem* tax, usually levied by a city or county government, on the value of real or personal property that the taxpayer owns on a specified date. Most states exclude intangible property and assets owned by exempt organizations from the tax base, and some exclude inventory, pollution control or manufacturing equipment, and other items to provide relocation or retention incentives for the taxpayer.

Proportionate distribution. A distribution in which each partner in a partnership receives a pro rata share of hot assets being distributed. For example, a distribution of $10,000 of hot assets equally to two 50 percent partners is a proportionate distribution.

Prop.Reg. An abbreviation for Proposed Regulation. See *proposed regulation*.

PTI. See *previously taxed income (PTI)*.

Public policy limitation. A concept developed by the courts precluding an income tax deduction for certain expenses related to activities deemed to be contrary to the public welfare. In this connection, Congress has incorporated into the Code specific disallowance provisions covering such items as illegal bribes, kickbacks, and fines and penalties. §§ 162(c) and (f).

Punitive damages. Damages received or paid by the taxpayer can be classified as compensatory damages or as punitive damages. Punitive damages are those awarded to punish the defendant for gross negligence or the intentional infliction of harm. Such damages are includible in gross income unless the claim arises out of physical injury or physical sickness. See also *compensatory damages*.

Q

Qualified employee discounts. Discounts offered employees on merchandise or services that the employer ordinarily sells or provides to customers. The discounts must be generally available to all employees. In the case of property, the discount cannot exceed the employer's gross profit (the sales price cannot be less than the employer's cost). In the case of services, the discounts cannot exceed 20% of the normal sales price. § 132.

Qualified nonrecourse debt. Issued on realty by a bank, retirement plan, or governmental agency. Included in the *at-risk amount* by the investor. § 465(b)(6).

Qualified pension or profit sharing plan. An employer-sponsored plan that meets the requirements of § 401. If these requirements are met, none of the employer's contributions to the plan will be taxed to the employee until distributed to him or her (§ 402). The employer is allowed a deduction in the year the contributions are made (§ 404). See also *contributory qualified pension or profit sharing plan, deferred compensation,* and *noncontributory pension or profit sharing plan*.

Qualified small business corporation. A C corporation that has aggregate gross assets not exceeding $50 million and that is conducting an active trade or business. § 1202.

Qualified small business stock. Stock in a qualified small business corporation, purchased as part of an original issue after August 10, 1993. The shareholder may exclude from gross income 50 percent of the realized gain on the sale of the stock, if he or she held the stock for more than five years. § 1202.

Qualified terminable interest property (QTIP). Generally, the *marital deduction* (for gift and estate tax purposes) is not available if the interest transferred will terminate upon the death of the transferee spouse and pass to someone else. Thus, if Jim (the husband) places property in trust, life estate to Mary (the wife), and remainder to their children upon Mary's death, this is a terminable interest that will not provide Jim (or Jim's estate) with a marital deduction. If, however, the transfer in trust is treated as qualified terminable interest property (the QTIP election is made), the terminable interest restriction is waived and the marital deduction becomes available. In exchange for this deduction, the surviving spouse's gross estate must include the value of the QTIP election assets, even though he or she has no control over the ultimate disposition of the asset. Terminable interest property qualifies for this election if the donee (or heir) is the only beneficiary of the asset during his or her lifetime and receives income distributions relative to the property at least annually. For gifts, the donor spouse is the one who makes the QTIP election. For property transferred by death, the *executor* of the estate of the deceased spouse has the right to make the election. §§ 2056(b)(7) and 2523(f).

Qualified transportation fringes. Transportation benefits provided by the employer to the employee. Such benefits include (1) transportation in a commuter highway vehicle between the employee's residence and the place of employment, (2) a transit pass, and (3) qualified parking. Qualified transportation fringes are excludible from the employee's gross income to the extent categories (1) and (2) above do not exceed $65 per month and category (3) does not exceed $165 per month. These amounts are indexed annually for inflation. § 132.

Qualified tuition reduction plan. A type of fringe benefit plan which is available to employees of nonprofit educational institutions. Such employees (and the spouse and dependent children) are allowed to exclude a tuition waiver pursuant to a qualified tuition reduction plan from gross income. The exclusion applies to undergraduate tuition. In limited circumstances, the exclusion also applies to the graduate tuition of teaching and research assistants. § 117(d).

R

RAR. A *Revenue Agent's Report,* which reflects any adjustments made by the agent as a result of an audit of the taxpayer. The RAR is mailed to the taxpayer along with the *30-day letter,* which outlines the appellate procedures available to the taxpayer.

Realistic possibility. A preparer penalty is assessed where a tax return includes a position that has no realistic possibility of being sustained by a court.

Realized gain or loss. The difference between the amount realized upon the sale or other disposition of property and the adjusted basis of the property. § 1001. See also *adjusted basis, amount realized, basis,* and *recognized gain or loss.*

Realty. Real estate. See also *personalty.*

Reasonable cause. Relief from taxpayer and preparer penalties often is allowed where there is found a reasonable cause for the taxpayer's actions. For example, a reasonable cause for the late filing of a tax return might be the incidence of a flood which damaged taxpayer record-keeping systems and made difficult a timely completion of the return.

Reasonable needs of the business. A means of avoiding the penalty tax on unreasonable accumulation of earnings. In determining the base for this tax (*accumulated taxable income*), § 535 allows a deduction for "such part of earnings and profits for the taxable year as are retained for the reasonable needs of the business." § 537.

Reasonableness. The Code includes a reasonableness requirement with respect to the deduction of salaries and other compensation for services. What constitutes reasonableness is a question of fact. If an expense is unreasonable, the amount that is classified as unreasonable is not allowed as a deduction. The question of reasonableness generally arises with respect to closely held corporations where there is no separation of ownership and management. § 162(a)(1).

Rebuttable presumption. A presumption that can be overturned upon the showing of sufficient proof. See also *presumption.*

Recapitalization. An E reorganization, constituting a major change in the character and amount of outstanding equity of a corporation. For instance, common stock exchanged for preferred stock can qualify for tax-free E reorganization treatment.

Recapture. To recover the tax benefit of a deduction or a credit previously taken. See also *depreciation recapture.*

Recapture potential. A measure with respect to property that, if disposed of in a taxable transaction, would result in the recapture of depreciation (§§ 1245 or 1250), deferred LIFO gain, or deferred installment method gain.

Recognized gain or loss. The portion of realized gain or loss subject to income taxation. See also *realized gain or loss.*

Recourse debt. Debt for which the lender may both foreclose on the property and assess a guarantor for any payments due under the loan. A lender may also make a claim against the assets of any general partner in a partnership to which debt is issued, without regard to whether the partner has guaranteed the debt.

Redemption. See *stock redemption.*

Redemption (complete termination). Sale or exchange treatment is available relative to this type of redemption. The shareholder must retire all of his/her outstanding shares in the corporation (ignoring family attribution rules), and cannot hold an interest, other than that of a creditor, for the ten years following the redemption. § 302(b)(3).

Redemption (disproportionate). Sale or exchange treatment is available relative to this type of redemption. After the exchange, the shareholder owns less than eighty percent of his/her pre-redemption interest in the corporation, and only a minority interest in the entity. § 302(b)(2).

Redemption (not equivalent to a dividend). Sale or exchange treatment is available relative to this type of redemption. Although various safe harbor tests are failed, the nature of the redemption is such that dividend treatment is waived by the courts, because it represented a meaningful reduction in the shareholder's interest in the corporation. § 302(b)(1).

Redemption to pay death taxes. Sale or exchange treatment is available relative to this type of redemption, to the extent of the proceeds up to the total amount paid by the estate or heir for death taxes and administration expenses. The stock value must exceed 35 percent of the value of the decedent's adjusted gross estate. In meeting this test, one can combine shareholdings in corporations where the decedent held at least twenty percent of the outstanding shares.

Refundable credit. A refundable credit is a credit that is paid to the taxpayer even if the amount of the credit (or credits) exceeds the taxpayer's tax liability. See also *nonrefundable credit.*

Regular corporation. See *C corporation.*

Regulations. The U.S. Treasury Department Regulations (abbreviated Reg.) represent the position of the IRS as to how the Internal Revenue Code is to be interpreted. Their purpose is to provide taxpayers and IRS personnel with rules of general and specific application to the various provisions of the tax law. Regulations are published in the *Federal Register* and in all tax services. See also *interpretive regulation, legislative regulation, procedural regulation,* and *proposed regulation.*

Rehabilitation expenditures credit. A credit that is based on expenditures incurred to rehabilitate industrial and commercial buildings and certified historic structures. The credit, an extension of the regular investment tax credit, is intended to discourage businesses from moving from older, economically distressed areas to newer locations and to encourage the preservation of historic structures. § 47. See *rehabilitation expenditures credit recapture.*

Rehabilitation expenditures credit recapture. When property that qualifies for the rehabilitation expenditures credit is disposed of or ceases to be used in the trade or business of the taxpayer, some or all of the tax credit claimed on the property may be recaptured as additional tax liability. The amount of the recapture is the difference between the amount of the credit claimed originally and what should have been claimed in light of the length of time the property was actually held or used for qualifying purposes. § 50. See *rehabilitation expenditures credit.*

Related corporation. See *controlled group.*

Related parties. Various Code sections define related parties and often include a variety of persons within this (usually detrimental) category. Generally, related parties are accorded different tax treatment from that applicable to other taxpayers who enter into similar transactions. For instance, realized losses that are generated between related parties are not recognized in the year of the loss. However, these deferred losses can be used to offset recognized gains that occur upon the subsequent sale of the asset to a nonrelated party. Other uses of a related-party definition include the conversion of gain upon the sale of a depreciable asset into all ordinary income (§ 1239) and the identification of constructive ownership of stock relative to corporate distributions, redemptions, liquidations, reorganizations, and compensation.

Remainder interest. The property that passes to a beneficiary after the expiration of an intervening income interest. If, for example, Gail places real estate in trust with income to Tom for life and remainder to Randy upon Tom's death, Randy has a remainder interest. See also *life estate* and *reversionary interest.*

Remand. To send back. An appellate court may remand a case to a lower court, usually for additional fact finding. In other words, the appellate court is not in a position to decide the appeal based on the facts determined by the lower court. Remanding is abbreviated *"rem'g."*

Reorganization. See *corporate reorganization.*

Research activities credit. A tax credit whose purpose is to encourage research and development. It consists of two components: the incremental research activities credit and the basic research credit. The incremental research activities credit is equal to 20 percent of the excess qualified research expenditures over the base amount. The basic research credit is equal to 20 percent of the excess of basic research payments over the base amount. § 41. See also *general business credit.*

Residential rental property. Buildings for which at least 80 percent of the gross rents are from dwelling units (e.g., an apartment building). This type of building is distinguished from nonresidential (commercial or industrial) buildings in applying the recapture of depreciation provisions. The term also is relevant in distinguishing between buildings that are eligible for a 27.5 year life versus a 39 year life for MACRS purposes. Generally, residential buildings receive preferential treatment.

Residual method. The new stepped-up basis of a subsidiary's assets is allocated among its property when a § 338 election is in effect, using this method. The purchase price that exceeds the aggregate fair market values of the tangible and identifiable intangible assets is allocated to goodwill or going-concern value. § 1060.

Restoration event. Sales between members of a *consolidated return,* and other intra-group transactions, are subject to special recognition deferral rules, so that such members cannot artificially create taxable gains or losses solely when tax conditions call for them. Rather, when a restoration event occurs (e.g., when the asset ultimately is sold outside of the group), the recognition of all intra-group gains and losses are restored.

Return of capital. When a taxpayer reacquires financial resources that he or she previously had invested in an entity or venture, the return of his or her capital investment itself does not increase gross income for the recovery year. A return of capital may result from an annuity or insurance contract, the sale or exchange of any asset, or a distribution from a partnership or corporation.

Revenue Agent's Report. See *RAR.*

Revenue neutrality. A description that characterizes tax legislation when it neither increases nor decreases the revenue result. Thus, any tax revenue losses are offset by tax revenue gains.

Revenue Procedure. A matter of procedural importance to both taxpayers and the IRS concerning the administration of the tax laws is issued as a Revenue Procedure (abbreviated Rev.Proc.). A Revenue Procedure is first published in an *Internal Revenue Bulletin* (I.R.B.) and later transferred to the appropriate *Cumulative Bulletin* (C.B.). Both the *Internal Revenue Bulletins* and the *Cumulative Bulletins* are published by the U.S. Government Printing Office.

Revenue Ruling. A Revenue Ruling (abbreviated Rev.Rul.) is issued by the National Office of the IRS to express an official interpretation of the tax law as applied to specific transactions. It is more limited in application than a

Regulation. A Revenue Ruling is first published in an *Internal Revenue Bulletin* (I.R.B.) and later transferred to the appropriate *Cumulative Bulletin* (C.B.). Both the *Internal Revenue Bulletins* and the *Cumulative Bulletins* are published by the U.S. Government Printing Office.

Reversed (Rev'd.). An indication that a decision of one court has been reversed by a higher court in the same case.

Reversing (Rev'g.). An indication that the decision of a higher court is reversing the result reached by a lower court in the same case.

Reversionary interest. The property that reverts to the grantor after the expiration of an intervening income interest. Assume Phil places real estate in trust with income to Junior for 11 years, and upon the expiration of this term, the property returns to Phil. Under these circumstances, Phil holds a reversionary interest in the property. A reversionary interest is the same as a remainder interest, except that, in the latter case, the property passes to someone other than the original owner (e.g., the grantor of a trust) upon the expiration of the intervening interest. See also *grantor trust* and *remainder interest*.

Revocable transfer. A transfer of property where the transferor retains the right to recover the property. The creation of a revocable trust is an example of a revocable transfer. § 2038. See also *incomplete transfer*.

Rev.Proc. Abbreviation for an IRS Revenue Procedure. See *Revenue Procedure*.

Rev.Rul. Abbreviation for an IRS Revenue Ruling. See *Revenue Ruling*.

RIA. Research Institute of America is the publisher of two tax services and of Federal tax decisions (AFTR and AFTR2d series).

Right of survivorship. See *joint tenants*.

S

Sale or exchange. A requirement for the recognition of capital gain or loss. Generally, the seller of property must receive money or relief from debt in order to have sold the property. An exchange involves the transfer of property for other property. Thus *collection* of a debt is neither a sale nor an exchange. The term *sale or exchange* is not defined by the Code.

Sales tax. A state- or local-level tax on the retail sale of specified property. Generally, the purchaser pays the tax, but the seller collects it, as an agent for the government. Various taxing jurisdictions allow exemptions for purchases of specific items, including certain food, services, and manufacturing equipment. If the purchaser and seller are in different states, a *use tax* usually applies.

Schedule M-1. On the Form 1120, a reconciliation of book net income with Federal taxable income. Accounts for timing and permanent differences in the two computations, such as depreciation differences, exempt income, and nondeductible items.

Schedule PH. A tax form required to be filed by corporations that are personal holding companies. The form must be filed in addition to Form 1120 (U.S. Corporation Income Tax Return).

S corporation. The designation for a small business corporation. See also *Subchapter S*.

Section 121 exclusion. An exclusion of $125,000 of realized gain available to taxpayers who are age 55 or over associated with the sale of their principal residence. The taxpayer must have owned and occupied the residence for at least three years during the five-year period ending on the date of sale. The exclusion treatment is elective and the election can be made only once. If married, both spouses must consent to the election. § 121.

Section 306 stock. Preferred stock issued as a nontaxable stock dividend that, if sold or redeemed, would result in ordinary income recognition. § 306(c). See also *preferred stock bailout*.

Section 306 taint. The ordinary income that would result upon the sale or other taxable disposition of § 306 stock.

Section 338 election. When a corporation acquires at least eighty percent of a subsidiary in a twelve-month period, it can elect to treat the acquisition of such stock as an asset purchase. The acquiring corporation's basis in the subsidiary's assets then is the cost of the stock. The subsidiary is deemed to have sold its assets for an amount equal to the grossed-up basis in its stock.

Section 1231 assets. Depreciable assets and real estate used in a trade or business and held for the appropriate holding period. Under certain circumstances, the classification also includes timber, coal, domestic iron ore, livestock (held for draft, breeding, dairy, or sporting purposes), and unharvested crops. § 1231(b). See also *Section 1231 gains and losses*.

Section 1231 gains and losses. If the combined gains and losses from the taxable dispositions of § 1231 assets plus the net gain from business involuntary conversions (of both § 1231 assets and long-term capital assets) is a gain, the gains and losses are treated as long-term capital gains and losses. In arriving at § 1231 gains, however, the depreciation recapture provisions (e.g., §§ 1245 and 1250) are first applied to produce ordinary income. If the net result of the combination is a loss, the gains and losses from § 1231 assets are treated as ordinary gains and losses. § 1231(a). See also *depreciation recapture* and *Section 1231 assets*.

Section 1244 stock. Stock issued under § 1244 by qualifying small business corporations. If § 1244 stock becomes worthless, the shareholders may claim an ordinary loss rather than the usual capital loss, within statutory limitations.

Section 1245 recapture. Upon a taxable disposition of § 1245 property, all depreciation claimed on the property is recaptured as ordinary income (but not to exceed recognized gain from the disposition).

Section 1250 recapture. Upon a taxable disposition of § 1250 property, some of the depreciation or cost recovery claimed on the property may be recaptured as ordinary income.

Securities. Generally, stock, debt, and other financial assets. To the extent securities other than the stock of the transferee corporation are received in a § 351 exchange, the new shareholder recognizes gross income.

Separate property. In a community property jurisdiction, property that belongs entirely to one of the spouses is separate property. Generally, it is property acquired before marriage or acquired after marriage by gift or inheritance. See also *community property*.

Separately stated item. Any item of a partnership or S Corporation that might be taxed differently to any two owners of the entity. These amounts are not included in ordinary income of the entity, but are instead reported separately to the owners; tax consequences are determined at the owner level.

Severance tax. A tax imposed upon the extraction of natural resources.

Sham. A transaction without substance that will be disregarded for tax purposes.

Short taxable year (short period). A tax year that is less than 12 months. A short taxable year may occur in the initial reporting period, in the final tax year, or when the taxpayer changes tax years.

Short-term capital gain or loss. Results from the sale or other taxable exchange of a capital asset that had been held by the seller for one year or less or from other transactions involving statutorily designated assets, including nonbusiness bad debts.

Simple trust. Simple trusts are those that are not complex trusts. Such trusts may not have a charitable beneficiary, accumulate income, or distribute corpus. See also *complex trust*.

Simplified employee pension (SEP) plan. An employer may make contributions to an employee's individual retirement account (IRA) in amounts not exceeding the lesser of 15 percent of compensation or $30,000 per individual. § 219(b)(2). See also *individual retirement account (IRA)*.

Small business corporation. A corporation that satisfies the definition of § 1361(b), § 1244(c), or both. Satisfaction of § 1361(b) permits an S election, and satisfaction of § 1244 enables the shareholders of the corporation to claim an ordinary loss on the worthlessness of stock.

Small business stock. See *small business corporation*.

Small Cases Division of the U.S. Tax Court. Jurisdiction is limited to claims of $10,000 or less. There is no appeal from this court.

Special allocation. Any amount for which an agreement exists among the partners of a partnership outlining the method used for spreading the item among the partners.

Special power of appointment. See *power of appointment*.

Special use value. An option that permits the executor of an estate to value, for death tax purposes, real estate used in a farming activity or in connection with a closely held business at its current use value rather than at its most suitable or optimal use value. Under this option, a farm is valued for farming purposes even though, for example, the property might have a higher potential value as a shopping center. For the executor of an estate to elect special use valuation, the conditions of § 2032A must be satisfied. See also *most suitable use value*.

Spin-off. A type of reorganization where, for example, Gold Corporation transfers some assets to Silver Corporation in exchange for enough Silver stock to represent control. Gold then distributes the Silver stock to its shareholders.

Split-off. A type of reorganization where, for example, Gold Corporation transfers some assets to Silver Corporation in exchange for enough Silver stock to represent control. Gold then distributes the Silver stock to its shareholders in exchange for some of their Gold stock.

Split-up. A type of reorganization where, for example, Gold Corporation transfers some assets to Silver Corporation and the remainder to Platinum Corporation. In return, Gold receives enough Silver and Platinum stock to represent control of each corporation. Gold then distributes the Silver and Platinum stock to its shareholders in return for all of their Gold stock. The result of the split-up is that Gold is liquidated, and its shareholders now have control of Silver and Platinum.

Sprinkling trust. When a trustee has the discretion to either distribute or accumulate the entity accounting income of the trust and to distribute it among the trust's income beneficiaries in varying magnitudes, a sprinkling trust exists. The trustee can "sprinkle" the income of the trust.

Standard deduction. The individual taxpayer can either itemize deductions or take the standard deduction. The amount of the standard deduction depends on the taxpayer's filing status (single, head of household, married filing jointly, surviving spouse, or married filing separately). For 1996, the amount of the standard deduction ranges from $3,350 (for married, filing separately) to $6,700 (for married, filing jointly). Additional standard deductions of either $800 (for married taxpayers) or $1,000 (for single taxpayers) are available if the taxpayer is either blind or age 65 or over. Limitations exist on the amount of the standard deduction of a taxpayer who is another taxpayer's dependent. The standard deduction amounts are adjusted annually for inflation each year. § 63(c).

Statute of limitations. Provisions of the law that specify the maximum period of time in which action may be taken on a past event. Code §§ 6501–6504 contain the limitation periods applicable to the IRS for additional assessments, and §§ 6511–6515 relate to refund claims by taxpayers.

Statutory depletion.   See *depletion*.

Statutory notice of deficiency.   Commonly referred to as the *90-day letter*, this notice is sent to a taxpayer upon request, upon the expiration of the *30-day letter*, or upon exhaustion by the taxpayer of his or her administrative remedies before the IRS. The notice gives the taxpayer 90 days in which to file a petition with the U.S. Tax Court. If a petition is not filed, the IRS will demand payment of the assessed deficiency. §§ 6211–6216. See also *deficiency* and *thirty-day letter*.

Step-down in basis.   A reduction in the tax basis of property.

Step transaction.   Disregarding one or more transactions to arrive at the final result. Assume, for example, that the shareholders of Black Corporation liquidate the corporation and receive cash and operating assets. Immediately after the liquidation, the shareholders transfer the operating assets to newly formed Brown Corporation. Under these circumstances, the IRS may contend that the liquidation of Black should be disregarded (thereby depriving the shareholders of capital gain treatment). What may really have happened is a *reorganization* of Black with a distribution of boot (ordinary income) to Black's shareholders. If so, there will be a carryover of basis in the assets transferred from Black to Brown.

Step-up in basis.   An increase in the tax basis of property. The classic step-up in basis occurs when a decedent dies owning appreciated property. Since the estate or heir acquires a basis in the property equal to the property's fair market value on the date of death (or alternate valuation date if available and elected), any appreciation is not subject to the income tax. Thus, a step-up in basis is the result, with no income tax consequences.

Stock attribution.   See *attribution*.

Stock dividend.   Not taxable if pro rata distributions of stock or stock rights on common stock. Section 305 governs the taxability of stock dividends and sets out five exceptions to the general rule that stock dividends are nontaxable.

Stock redemption.   A corporation buys back its own stock from a specified shareholder. Typically, the corporation recognizes any realized gain on the noncash assets that it uses to effect a redemption, and the shareholder obtains a capital gain or loss upon receipt of the purchase price.

Stock rights.   An asset that conveys to the holder the power to purchase corporate stock at a specified price, often for a limited period of time. Stock rights received may be taxed as a distribution of earnings and profits. After the right is exercised, the basis of the acquired share includes the investor's purchase price or gross income, if any, to obtain the right. Disposition of the right also is a taxable event, with basis often assigned from the shares held prior to the issuance of the right.

Subchapter S.   Sections 1361–1379 of the Internal Revenue Code. An elective provision permitting certain small business corporations (§ 1361) and their shareholders (§ 1362) to elect to be treated for income tax purposes in accordance with the operating rules of §§ 1363–1379. However, some S corporations usually avoid the corporate income tax and corporate losses can be claimed by the shareholders.

Subpart F.   That subpart of the Code that identifies the current tax treatment of income earned by a controlled foreign corporation. Certain types of income are included in U.S. gross income by U.S. shareholders of such an entity as they are generated, not when they are repatriated.

Substance vs. form concept.   A standard used when one must ascertain the true reality of what has occurred. Suppose, for example, a father sells stock to his daughter for $1,000. If the stock is really worth $50,000 at the time of the transfer, the substance of the transaction is probably a gift to her of $49,000.

Substantial authority.   Taxpayer understatement penalties are waived where there existed substantial authority for the disputed position taken on the return.

Substantial economic effect.   Partnerships are allowed to *allocate* items of income, expense, gain, loss, and credit in any manner that is authorized in the partnership agreement, provided that the allocation has an economic effect aside from the corresponding tax results. The necessary substantial economic effect is present, for instance, if the post-contribution appreciation in the value of an asset that was contributed to the partnership by a partner was allocated to that partner for cost recovery purposes.

Substantial risk of forfeiture.   A term that is associated with a restricted property plan. Generally, an employee who receives property (e.g., stock of the employer-corporation) from the employee at a bargain price or at no cost must include the bargain element in gross income. However, the employee does not have to do so presently if there is a substantial risk of forfeiture. A substantial risk of forfeiture exists if a person's rights to full enjoyment of property are conditioned upon the future performance, or the refraining from the performance, of substantial services by the individual. § 83.

Substantially appreciated inventory.   "Inventory" (as defined for this purpose) for which the fair market value exceeds 120 percent of the partnership's basis in the asset. This definition is relevant for purposes of determining the character of income, gain, or loss from the (1) sale of a partnership interest and (2) liquidation of a partner's interest under § 736 and (3) disproportionate distributions. Inventory is broadly defined as any partnership asset other than cash, capital assets or § 1231 assets. This definition is broad enough to include any accounts receivable, including unrealized receivables.

Substituted basis. When a taxpayer exchanges one asset for another, many provisions in the tax law allow an assignment of basis in the received asset to be that of the traded asset(s) in the hands of its former owner. Thus, no step-up or -down of basis occurs as a result of the exchange. For example, when an investor contributes an asset to a corporation or partnership, the partner generally takes a substituted basis in the partnership interest [i.e., the investment asset (partnership interest) has a basis equal to the aggregated bases of the assets contributed by that partner].

Surviving spouse. When a husband or wife predeceases the other spouse, the survivor is known as a surviving spouse. Under certain conditions, a surviving spouse may be entitled to use the income tax rates in § 1(a) (those applicable to married persons filing a joint return) for the two years after the year of death of his or her spouse. § 2.

Survivorship. See *joint tenants.*

Syndication costs. Incurred in promoting and marketing partnership interests for sale to investors. Examples include legal and accounting fees, printing costs for prospectus and placement documents, and state registration fees. These items are capitalized by the partnership as incurred, with no amortization thereof allowed.

T

Tangible property. All property that has form or substance and is not intangible. See also *intangible asset.*

Taxable estate. The taxable estate is the *gross estate* of a *decedent* reduced by the deductions allowed by §§ 2053–2057 (e.g., administration expenses, marital, and charitable deductions). The taxable estate is subject to the unified transfer tax at death. See also *adjusted taxable estate* and *gross estate.* § 2051.

Taxable gift. Amount of a gift that is subject to the unified transfer tax. Thus, a taxable gift has been adjusted by the annual exclusion and other appropriate deductions (e.g., marital and charitable). § 2053.

Taxable income. The tax base with respect to the prevailing Federal income tax. Taxable income is defined by the Internal Revenue Code, Treasury Regulations, and pertinent court cases. Currently, taxable income includes gross income from all sources except those specifically excluded by statute. In addition, taxable income is reduced for certain allowable deductions. Deductions for business taxpayers must be related to a trade or business. Individuals can also deduct certain personal expenses in determining their taxable incomes. See also *gross income.*

Taxable year. The annual period over which income is measured for income tax purposes. Most individuals use a calendar year, but many businesses use a fiscal year based on the natural business year. See also *accounting period* and *fiscal year.*

Tax benefit rule. A provision that limits the recognition of income from the recovery of an expense or loss properly deducted in a prior tax year to the amount of the deduction that generated a tax saving. Assume that last year Gary had medical expenses of $3,000 and adjusted gross income of $30,000. Because of the 7.5 percent limitation, Gary could deduct only $750 of these expenses [$3,000 − (7.5% × $30,000)]. If, this year, Gary is reimbursed by his insurance company for $900 of these expenses, the tax benefit rule limits the amount of income from the reimbursement to $750 (the amount previously deducted with a tax saving).

Tax Court. The U.S. Tax Court is one of four trial courts of original jurisdiction that decide litigation involving Federal income, death, or gift taxes. It is the only trial court where the taxpayer must not first pay the deficiency assessed by the IRS. The Tax Court will not have jurisdiction over a case unless a statutory notice of deficiency (90-day letter) has been issued by the IRS and the taxpayer files the petition for hearing within the time prescribed.

Tax credits. Tax credits are amounts that directly reduce a taxpayer's tax liability. The tax benefit received from a tax credit is not dependent on the taxpayer's marginal tax rate, whereas the benefit of a tax deduction or exclusion is dependent on the taxpayer's tax bracket.

Tax-free exchange. Transfers of property specifically exempted from income tax consequences by the tax law. Examples are a transfer of property to a controlled corporation under § 351(a) and a like-kind exchange under § 1031(a). See also *nontaxable exchange.*

Tax haven. A country in which either locally sourced income or residents of the country are subject to a low rate of taxation.

Tax on unearned income of a child under age 14. Passive income, such as interest and dividends, that is recognized by such a child is taxed *to him or her* at the rates that would have applied had the income been incurred by the child's parents, generally to the extent that the income exceeds $1,200. The additional tax is assessed regardless of the source of the income or the income's underlying property. If the child's parents are divorced, the custodial parent's rates are used. The parents' rates reflect any applicable alternative minimum tax and the phase-outs of lower tax brackets and other deductions. § 1(g).

Tax preferences. Various items that may result in the imposition of the alternative minimum tax. §§ 55–58. See also *alternative minimum tax (AMT).*

Tax research. The method used to determine the best available solution to a situation that possesses tax consequences. Both tax and nontax factors are considered.

TAXRIA. (Formerly called PHINet.) An on-line database system, with which the tax researcher can obtain access to the Internal Revenue Code, Regulations, administrative rulings, and court case opinions.

Tax treaty. An agreement between the United States Department of State and another country, designed to alleviate double taxation of income and asset transfers, and to share administrative information useful to tax agencies in both countries. The United States has income tax treaties with over forty countries, and transfer tax treaties with about twenty.

Tax year. See *accounting period.*

T.C. An abbreviation for the U.S. Tax Court used in citing a Regular Decision of the U.S. Tax Court.

T.C.Memo. An abbreviation used to refer to a Memorandum Decision of the U.S. Tax Court.

Technical advice memoranda (TAMs). TAMs are issued by the National Office of the IRS in response to questions raised by IRS field personnel during audits. They deal with completed rather than proposed transactions and are often requested for questions related to exempt organizations and employee plans.

Telescoping. To look through one or more transactions to arrive at the final result. It is also referred to as the *step transaction* approach or the *substance vs. form concept.*

Temporary Regulation. A Regulation issued by the Treasury Department in temporary form. When speed is critical, the Treasury Department issues Temporary Regulations which take effect immediately. These Regulations have the same authoritative value as Final Regulations and may be cited as precedent for three years. Temporary Regulations are also issued as proposed Regulations. See also *proposed regulation* and *regulations.*

Tenancy by the entirety. Essentially, a joint tenancy between husband and wife. See also *joint tenants* and *tenancy in common.*

Tenancy in common. A form of ownership where each tenant (owner) holds an undivided interest in property. Unlike a joint tenancy or a tenancy by the entirety, the interest of a tenant in common does not terminate upon that individual's death (there is no right of survivorship). Assume Tim and Cindy acquire real estate as equal tenants in common, each having furnished one-half of the purchase price. Upon Tim's death, his one-half interest in the property passes to his estate or heirs, not to Cindy. For a comparison of results, see also *joint tenants* and *tenancy by the entirety.*

Term certain. A fixed period of years, used to determine the length of an income interest (i.e., prior to the termination of a trust or estate).

Terminable interest rule. An interest in property that terminates upon the death of the holder or upon the occurrence of some other specified event. The transfer of a terminable interest by one spouse to the other may not qualify for the marital deduction. §§ 2056(b) and 2523(b). See also *marital deduction.*

Testamentary disposition. The passing of property to another upon the death of the owner.

Testamentary power of appointment. A power of appointment that can be exercised only through the will (upon the death) of the holder. See also *power of appointment.*

Theft loss. A loss from larceny, embezzlement and robbery. It does not include misplacement of items. See also *casualty loss.*

Thin capitalization. When debt owed by a corporation to the shareholders becomes too large in relation to the corporation's capital structure (i.e., stock and shareholder equity), the IRS may contend that the corporation is thinly capitalized. In effect, this means that some or all of the debt is reclassified as equity. The immediate result is to disallow any interest deduction to the corporation on the reclassified debt. To the extent of the corporation's earnings and profits, interest payments and loan repayments on the reclassified debt are treated as dividends to the shareholders.

Thirty-day letter. A letter that accompanies a Revenue Agent's Report issued as a result of an IRS audit of a taxpayer (or the rejection of a taxpayer's claim for refund). The letter outlines the taxpayer's appeal procedure before the IRS. If the taxpayer does not request any such procedures within the 30-day period, the IRS will issue a statutory notice of deficiency (the 90-day letter). See also *statutory notice of deficiency.*

Tiered partnerships. An ownership arrangement where one partnership (the parent or first tier) is a partner in one or more partnerships (the subsidiary/subsidiaries or second tier). Frequently, the first tier is a holding partnership, and the second tier is an operating partnership.

Trade or business. Any business or professional activity conducted by a taxpayer. The mere ownership of rental or other investment assets does not constitute a trade or business. Generally, a trade or business generates relatively little passive investment income.

Transfer tax. A tax imposed upon the transfer of property. See also *unified transfer tax.*

Transferee liability. Under certain conditions, if the IRS is unable to collect taxes owed by a transferor of property, it may pursue its claim against the transferee of the property. The transferee's liability for taxes is limited to the extent of the value of the assets transferred. For example, the IRS can force a donee to pay the gift tax when the tax cannot be paid by the donor making the transfer. §§ 6901–6905.

Treasury Regulations. See *regulations.*

Treaty shopping. An international investor attempts to use the favorable aspects of a tax treaty to his or her advantage, often elevating the form of the transaction over its substance (e.g., by establishing only a nominal presence in the country offering the favorable treaty terms).

Trial court. The court of original jurisdiction; the first court to consider litigation. In Federal tax controversies, trial courts include U.S. District Courts, the U.S. Tax Court, the U.S. Court of Federal Claims, and the Small Cases

Division of the U.S. Tax Court. See also *appellate court, Claims Court, District Court, Small Cases Division of the U.S. Tax Court,* and *Tax Court.*

Trust. A legal entity created by a grantor for the benefit of designated beneficiaries under the laws of the state and the valid trust instrument. The trustee holds a fiduciary responsibility to manage the trust's corpus assets and income for the economic benefit of all of the beneficiaries.

Trustee. An individual or corporation that takes the fiduciary responsibilities under a trust agreement.

U

Undistributed personal holding company income. The penalty tax on personal holding companies is imposed on the corporation's undistributed personal holding company income for the year. The adjustments necessary to convert taxable income to undistributed personal holding company income are set forth in § 545.

Undistributed net income. The excess of a complex trust's distributable net income over its distributions for the year. This accumulation may be subject to the throwback procedures in later years.

Unearned income. Income received but not yet earned. Normally, such income is taxed when received, even for accrual basis taxpayers.

Unified tax credit. A credit allowed against any unified transfer tax. §§ 2010 and 2505.

Unified transfer tax. Rates applicable to transfers by gift and death made after 1976. § 2001(c).

Uniform Gift to Minors Act. A means of transferring property (usually stocks and bonds) to a minor. The designated custodian of the property has the legal right to act on behalf of the minor without requiring a guardianship. Generally, the custodian possesses the right to change investments (e.g., sell one type of stock and buy another), apply the income from the custodial property to the minor's support, and even terminate the custodianship. In this regard, however, the custodian is acting in a fiduciary capacity on behalf of the minor. The custodian could not, for example, appropriate the property for his or her own use because it belongs to the minor. During the period of the custodianship, the income from the property is taxed to the minor. The custodianship terminates when the minor reaches legal age. See also *guardianship* and *legal age.*

Unrealized receivables. Amounts earned by a cash basis taxpayer but not yet received. Because of the method of accounting used by the taxpayer, these amounts have no income tax basis. When unrealized receivables are distributed to a partner, they generally convert a transaction from nontaxable to taxable or convert otherwise capital gain to ordinary income.

Unreasonable compensation. A deduction is allowed for "reasonable" salaries or other compensation for personal services actually rendered. To the extent compensation is "excessive" ("unreasonable"), no deduction is allowed. The problem of unreasonable compensation usually is limited to closely held corporations, where the motivation is to pay out profits in some form that is deductible to the corporation. Deductible compensation therefore becomes an attractive substitute for nondeductible dividends when the shareholders also are employed by the corporation.

Unrelated business income. Income recognized by an exempt organization that is generated from activities not related to the exempt purpose of the entity. For instance, the pharmacy located in a hospital often generates unrelated business income. § 511.

Unrelated business income tax. Levied on the *unrelated business income* of an *exempt organization.*

U.S. Court of Federal Claims. See *Claims Court.*

Use tax. A sales tax that is collectible by the seller where the purchaser is domiciled in a different state.

U.S.-owned foreign corporation. A foreign corporation in which 50 percent or more of the total combined voting power or total value of the stock of the corporation is held directly or indirectly by U.S. persons. A U.S. corporation is treated as a U.S.-owned foreign corporation if the dividend or interest income it pays is classified as foreign source under § 861.

U.S. real property interest. Any direct interest in real property situated in the United States and any interest in a domestic corporation (other than solely as a creditor) unless the taxpayer can establish that a domestic corporation was not a U.S. real property holding corporation during the five-year period ending on the date of disposition of the interest (the base period).

USSC. An abbreviation for the U.S. Supreme Court.

U.S. shareholder. For purposes of classification of an entity as a *controlled foreign corporation,* a U.S. person who owns, or is considered to own, 10 percent or more of the total combined voting power of all classes of voting stock of a foreign corporation. Stock owned directly, indirectly, and constructively is counted for this purpose.

U.S. source income. Generally, income taxed by the United States, regardless of the citizenship or residence of its creator. Examples include income from sales of U.S. real estate and dividends from U.S. corporations.

U.S. Supreme Court. The highest appellate court or the court of last resort in the Federal court system and in most states. Only a small number of tax decisions of the U.S. Courts of Appeal are reviewed by the U.S. Supreme Court under its certiorari procedure. The Supreme Court usually grants certiorari to resolve a conflict among the Courts of Appeal (e.g., two or more appellate courts have assumed opposing positions on a particular issue) or when the tax issue is extremely important (e.g., size of the revenue loss to the Federal government).

U.S. Tax Court. See *Tax Court.*

USTC. Published by Commerce Clearing House, *U.S. Tax Cases* contain all of the Federal tax decisions issued by the U.S. District Courts, U.S. Court of Federal Claims, U.S. Courts of Appeals, and the U.S. Supreme Court.

V

Value. See *fair market value.*

Value added tax (VAT). A national sales tax that taxes the increment in value as goods move through the production process. A VAT is much used in other countries but has not yet been incorporated as part of the U.S. Federal tax structure.

Vested. Absolute and complete. If, for example, a person holds a vested interest in property, the interest cannot be taken away or otherwise defeated.

Voting trust. A trust that holds the voting rights to stock in a corporation. It is a useful device when a majority of the shareholders in a corporation cannot agree on corporate policy.

W

Wash sale. A loss from the sale of stock or securities that is disallowed because the taxpayer within 30 days before or after the sale, has acquired stock or securities substantially identical to those sold. § 1091.

WESTLAW. An on-line database system, produced by West Publishing Company, which the tax researcher can obtain access to the Internal Revenue Code, Regulations, administrative rulings, and court case opinions.

Wherewithal to pay. This concept recognizes the inequity of taxing a transaction when the taxpayer lacks the means with which to pay the tax. Under it, there is a correlation between the imposition of the tax and the ability to pay the tax. It is particularly suited to situations in which the taxpayer's economic position has not changed significantly as a result of the transaction.

Withholding allowances. The number of withholding allowances serves as the basis for determining the amount of income taxes withheld from an employee's salary or wages. The more withholding allowances claimed, the less income tax withheld by an employer. An employee may claim withholding allowances for personal exemptions for self and spouse (unless claimed as a dependent of another person), dependency exemptions, and special withholding allowances.

Working condition fringe. A type of fringe benefit received by the employee that is excludible from the employee's gross income. It consists of property or services provided (paid or reimbursed) by the employer for which the employee could take a tax deduction if the employee had paid for them. § 132.

Writ of Certiorari. See *certiorari.*

APPENDIX D
Table of Code Sections Cited

APPENDIX E
Comprehensive Tax Return Problems

PROBLEM 1

1. Ely R. and Cora M. Taylor, ages 45 and 43, are married and file a joint income tax return. Ely is a specialist in horticulture and is employed by the Parker Seed Corporation as director of their research activities. Cora is a school teacher and is employed by St. Luke's Middle School, a private institution owned and operated by a religious group. Salary and tax withholdings for 1995 were:

	Salary	Federal	State
Ely	$71,000	$6,380	$2,780
Cora	32,000	4,100	1,450

2. The Taylors have always lived and worked in Des Moines, IA. They reside at 312 Drake Avenue, Des Moines, IA 50312. Living with them are their three children, Nancy (age 14), Martin (age 16), and Irene (age 21). Also living with the Taylors is Ely's widower father, Paul (age 71). Irene is a full-time student at Drake University. During the year, she earned $3,000 from a part-time job. Paul received $9,000 in Social Security benefits, which he deposited in his savings account. The Taylors contributed more than 50% of the support of their children and of Paul.

3. The Taylors contribute 25% of the support of Cora's aunt, Martha Bates, who lives with Cora's sister. The remainder of Martha's support is received from Cora's sister and two brothers, 25% each. Cora's sister and brothers have signed a multiple support agreement allowing Cora to claim the dependency exemption for Martha. As noted below, the Taylors have provided their share of support by paying Martha's medical expenses.

4. Relevant Social Security numbers are:

Ely	478-12-6024
Cora	477-19-1002
Nancy	479-22-6018
Martin	479-29-5025
Irene	479-31-4129
Paul	481-15-6113
Martha	480-42-1266

5. Because Paul is confined to a wheelchair due to a stroke he suffered several years ago, the Taylors spent $7,300 during the year adding impairment-related improvements to their personal residence (e.g., wheelchair ramps, widening of hallways, bathtub railings). A friend who is in the real estate business estimates that these changes increased the value of the residence by $2,500.

6. During 1995, the Taylors had water damage to their personal residence. They purchased this house on June 15, 1972, and paid $65,000 for it. A professional appraisal, for which

the Taylors paid $400, reflects that the value of the residence decreased by $15,000 ($110,000 before and $95,000 after) due to the storm causing the water damage. The Taylor's homeowner's insurance policy does not cover water damage.

7. On June 1, 1991, and as a favor to a former college roommate, Ely lent $3,200 to Lyle Petit. Lyle signed a note, maturity date of June 1, 1995, with annual interest of 10%. Ely has never recovered any of the loan or received any interest. Lyle was declared bankrupt in April 1995 and is currently under investigation for mail fraud.

8. Cora has a Bachelor of Education degree which she received many years ago. Recently, the directors at St. Luke's School resolved that all of its teachers must earn a Master of Education degree in order to continue in their present jobs. The teachers were allowed ten years in which to satisfy this new requirement. During the summer of 1995, Cora enrolled at a local university and took several graduate courses in education. Cora lived at home and commuted to her classes. Her expenses were as follows:

Books and tuition	$1,800
Transportation	
Bus fares	75
Personal auto mileage (150) miles	?
Meals while on campus (between classes)	92
Parking charges	51

When Cora did not take the bus, usually on rainy days, she drove the family auto (use the automatic mileage method—30 cents for 1995). When Cora drove, she had to pay for on-campus parking.

9. During 1995, the Taylors sold the following stocks:

Robin Corporation	
(400 shares common) July 5	$33,000
Canary Corporation	
(300 shares preferred) August 10	16,000

The Robin Corporation stock had been received from Cora's mother as a gift on January 2, 1995, when it had a fair market value of $31,000. Her mother had purchased the stock on June 1, 1994, for $30,500. No gift tax was due or paid on the mother's gift.

 The Canary Corporation stock was inherited by Ely from his mother. The mother died on December 10, 1994, and her estate was settled on March 3, 1995 (the day Ely received the stock). The stock was worth $14,600 on December 10, 1994, and $14,900 on March 3, 1995. Ely has found a broker's statement that shows his mother purchased the stock on September 9, 1994, for $14,100 (including brokerage fee).

10. Besides any other items mentioned eleswhere, the Taylors had the following receipts for 1995:

Interest on CD (Iowa State Bank)		$1,920
Interest on city of Des Moines general purpose bonds		1,700
Dividends		
Robin Corporation stock	$1,250	
Canary Corporation stock	950	2,200
Riverboat casino winnings		1,300
Garage sale of old clothes and household goods (reasonable cost estimate of items sold $6,500)		1,100

11. As to medical expenses, the Taylors had the following during 1995:

Hospital and doctor bills for Martha	$3,100
Ely's contribution toward the cost of his employer's medical insurance premiums	2,900
Insurance recovery for 1994 expenses under employment medical policy	820
Orthodontia expenses for children	3,600
Prescription drugs	1,400
Doctor bills for family	1,250
Tonsillectomy for Nancy (surgeon and hospital)	1,800
Wheelchair and hearing aid for Paul	2,150

The $820 insurance recovery for the year 1994 was for medical expenses the Taylors deducted on their 1994 Federal income tax return.

The Taylors have not yet submitted any claims to the insurance company for their 1995 medical expenses. They estimate that, after the required deductible, the reimbursed amount will be $1,700.

12. Other expenditures for 1995 are summarized below:

Interest on home mortgage	$5,100
Property taxes on home	3,150
Payment of church pledge ($200 was for the 1994 remaining balance)	2,800
Additional state income tax due for 1994	230
School supplies Cora uses for her classes (not provided by St. Luke's School)	305
Professional dues (Ely and Cora)	405
Professional journals (Ely and Cora)	300
Lab coats (used by Ely at work)	340
Laundry of lab coats	105
Safety goggles and shoes (used by Ely at work)	190
Riverboat casino losses (supported by adequate records)	1,600

13. The Taylors do not wish to designate a contribution to the presidential Election Campaign Fund. If they have overpaid, any refund is to be applied toward the 1996 Federal income tax liability.

Requirements
You are to prepare a joint Federal income tax return for the Taylors for 1995.

PROBLEM 2

1. Al P. Hart, age 44, is divorced and lives alone at 426 Lantern Lane, Cincinnati, OH 45221. He provides more than half of the cost of maintaining a household for Norma Hart, who lives in an apartment nearby. Norma, age 68, is Al's widowed mother and qualifies as his dependent.

2. Al and Leona were married eighteen years ago and were divorced in 1992. Leona was awarded custody of their only child, Peter, now twelve years old. Under the divorce decree, Al must pay Leona $450 each month until Peter reaches age 21 or dies (whichever occurs first). Upon the occurrence of either event, the monthly payment

becomes $100. Since Al and Leona have been alternating claiming Peter as a dependent, Leona did not waive the dependency exemption for Peter for 1995. Al sent Leona the required $5,400 ($450 x 12 months) for 1995. Furthermore, he sent Leona an additional $900 for dental work she had done on her teeth. He also paid an optometrist/optician $350 for Peter's eye exams and prescription glasses.

3. Al is a licensed hair stylist and beautician and operates his own salon under the business name of "Al's Creations." Although it varies as to number, Al's business consists of four to six stations operated by himself and other licensed beauticians. The beauticians who work in the salon are treated as independent contractors. In this regard, each has his or her own telephone line. They maintain their own appointment books, have their own customers, and collect and keep the fees charged. For the use of the work stations and various facilities (e.g., hair dryers, shampoo sinks, waiting area), each pays Al a monthly rental. Al does not control their work hours, although most choose to follow Al's own work schedule.

4. Al's Creations is well-known for its selection and quality of men's hairpieces (i.e., toupees) and women's wigs. The business also sells a considerable quantity of beauty products (e.g., conditioners, shampoos, curling irons). Some of these items are sold to other beauticians but most are sold to regular patrons and walk in customers.

5. Al's Creations is located at 6194 Taft Street, Cincinnati, OH 45221. The employer identification number is 31-0009521; the professional activity code for beauticians is 8110.

6. The building in which the business is located is rented under a long-term lease for $1,200 each month. Al pays his own utilities. Before Al moved in, the landlord customized the facilities so as to be suited for its intended use. The only employee Al has is a shampoo person, who also performs light janitorial services. Al hires an outside service to do the heavier janitorial duties. Likewise, a local accounting group is on retainer to keep the financial records and prepare the tax returns for the business.

7. Al's Creations had the following receipts for 1995:

Sales of cosmetics	$16,525
Sales of hairpieces, wigs	28,100
Fees received from patrons by Al (including tips received)	32,350
Rent charged other beauticians	23,050

   The amounts shown for the retail sales of cosmetics, hairpieces, and wigs, include state sales tax.

8. Al's Creations has the following expenses for 1995:

Purchases of cosmetics	$ 8,990
Purchases of hairpieces, wigs	13,150
Operating supplies (shampoo, permanent wave solution, color, etc.)	5,210
Rent for building	14,400
Utilities and telephone	6,020
Payroll expense	4,950
Payroll taxes (FICA, FUTA, state unemployment)	610
Sales taxes remitted to state	2,350
Health insurance coverage for employee	290
City of Cincinnati occupation permit for 1995	500
State beautician license fee	380
Liability insurance premiums (coverage is for calendar years 1995-1997)	6,000

Casualty insurance on business furnishings and equipment for 1995	1,400
Janitorial services	2,290
Accounting services ($550 was for preparation of personal tax return)	3,900
Waiting room furniture	3,200
Magazine subscriptions for waiting room	220
Advertising	950
Fine paid to City of Cincinnati	300

9. Al decided to completely renovate the furnishings in his waiting room. Consequently, he spent $3,200 for chairs, sofa, lamps, coffee table, etc., all placed in service on April 20, 1995. The old furnishings were given to patrons or thrown away. The old furniture was completely depreciated and had a zero tax basis. Al has always followed a policy of claiming as much depreciation as soon as possible. All of his other business assets (e.g., hair driers, work-station chairs) have been fully depreciated by 1995.

10. The fine paid to the city was assessed by the Sanitation Department. Al had failed, in accordance with a city ordinance, to separate the trash of the business into recyclable and nonrecyclable bins.

11. In late 1994, a transient customer visiting the city had purchased a hairpiece from the business for $190. The customer's check was not deposited until early 1995 and ultimately proved fraudulent. The sale was reported on Al's 1994 tax return. Al has no doubt that he will never collect the $190 due him.

12. Al maintains an inventory as to the merchandise he sells. The business inventories (based on the lower of cost or market) are as follows:

	12/31/94	12/31/95
Hairpieces and wigs	$ 3,200	$ 2,700
Cosmetics	1,900	2,100

13. In 1995, Al was audited by both the city and the state as to his 1994 income tax returns. As a result of the audit, he had to pay the city an additional $180 but he received a refund from the state of $110.

14. Except for the inventory and purchases accounts, Al operates the business on a cash method. Customers pay for services as rendered. Sales income is recorded when the merchandise is sold. Al does not extend credit but does accept payment by charge card and check (see item 11 above).

15. Al's medical expenses for 1995, and not mentioned elsewhere, included the following:

Gall bladder operation (includes hospital and surgeon's charges) for Norma	$2,100
Annual physical for Al	390
Dentists charges for Al (includes crown, bridges, fillings, etc.)	4,300
Hernia operation (includes hospital and surgeon's charges)	2,100
Prescription medicines	800
Medical insurance premiums	800

In November of 1995, Al purchased a medical insurance policy. The policy does not cover anyone but Al and his one employee (see item 6 above). The premium for the employee coverage is stated separately at item 8. Also, the policy does not apply to dental bills. Al filed a claim with the insurance company in late December. He received a check in January of 1996 which, after the appropriate deductible, was for $300.

16. Al's other expenses are listed below:

Property taxes on residence	$3,800
Interest on home mortgage	5,200
Annual dues for membership in the American Association of Beauticians	150
Professional journals	190

17. Al has always itemized his deductions because even without substantial medical expenses, his deductions from adjusted gross income have exceeded the standard deduction.

18. Al had no stock transactions in 1995 but he does have a $5,000 long-term capital loss carryover from 1994.

19. Al's other income for 1995 is summarized below:

Interest income from a savings account at Enterprise Bank	$6,800
Cash dividend from P&G common stock	6,100

20. Al made estimated tax payments for 1995 as follows:

City income tax	$ 700
Ohio income tax	2,500
Federal income and self-employment taxes (paid $1,400 quarterly)	5,600

21. Relevant social security numbers are—

Al Hart	268-01-5869
Norma Hart	301-42-2657
Leona Hart	300-52-7981
Peter Hart	302-64-1826

Requirements

You are to prepare Al's Federal income tax return for 1995. Al wants to designate that $3 he directed to the Presidential Election Campaign fund. If he has overpaid his 1995 taxes, he wants to have the amount applied to his 1996 estimated taxes.

COMPREHENSIVE TAX RETURN PROBLEM

On May 1, 1989, Brandon Short and Michael Allen formed Angler Corporation to sell fishing tackle. Pertinent information regarding Angler is summarized as follows:

- The business address is 1717 Carlson Street, Sidney, NY 13838.

- The employer identification number is 75–3392543; the principal business activity code is 5600.

- Brandon and Michael each own one-half of the outstanding common stock; no other class of stock is authorized. Brandon is president of the company, and Michael is secretary-treasurer. Both are full-time employees of the corporation, and each receives a salary of $160,000. Brandon's Social Security number is 399–50–2953; Michael's Social Security number is 400–30–4495.

- The corporation uses the accrual method of accounting and reports on a calendar basis. Inventories are determined using the lower of cost or market method. For book and tax purposes, the straight-line method of depreciation is used.

- During 1995, the corporation distributed a cash dividend of $80,000.

Selected portions of Angler's profit and loss statement for 1995 reflect the following debits and credits:

Account	Debit	Credit
Gross sales		$2,300,000
Sales returns and allowances	$ 80,000	
Cost of goods sold	920,000	
Dividends received from stock investments in less-than-20%-owned U.S. corporations		120,000
Interest income		
State bonds	$14,000	
Certificates of deposit	10,000	24,000
Premiums on term life insurance policies on the lives of Brandon and Michael; Angler Corporation is the designated beneficiary	16,000	
Salaries—officers	320,000	
Salaries—clerical and sales	290,000	
Taxes (state, local, and payroll)	105,000	
Repairs	60,000	
Interest expense		
Loan to purchase state bonds	$ 8,000	
Other business loans	12,000	20,000
Advertising	6,000	
Rental expense	83,000	
Depreciation	40,000	

A comparative balance sheet for Angler Corporation reveals the following information:

Assets	January 1, 1995	December 31, 1995
Cash	$ 480,000	$ 334,660
Trade notes and accounts receivable	808,400	1,084,600
Inventories	600,000	712,000
Federal bonds	140,000	140,000
State bonds	160,000	160,000
Prepaid Federal tax	—	1,800
Buildings and other depreciable assets	240,000	240,000
Accumulated depreciation	(88,800)	(128,800)
Land	20,000	20,000
Other assets	3,600	2,000
Total assets	$2,363,200	$2,566,260

Liabilities and Equity		
Accounts payable	$ 300,000	$ 275,560
Other current liabilities	80,300	40,000
Mortgages	210,000	200,000
Capital stock	500,000	500,000

Retained earnings	1,272,900	1,550,700
Total liabilities and equity	$2,363,200	$2,566,260

Net income per books (before any income tax accrual) is $504,000. During 1995, Angler Corporation made estimated tax payments of $148,000 to the IRS. Prepare a Form 1120 for Angler Corporation for tax year 1995.

COMPREHENSIVE TAX RETURN PROBLEM

Marilyn Pearson (222–54–7580), Scott Denny (759–85–4486), and Rebecca Wright (423–70–8476) are equal partners in PDW, a general partnership that provides public relations services to various small businesses. PDW's Federal I.D. number is 94–8423590. The partnership uses the cash method of accounting and adopted the calendar year for reporting. It began business operations on January 15, 1992. Its current address is 2986 Vulcan Drive, Birmingham, AL 35203. The following information was taken from the partnership's income statement for the current year:

Receipts

Fees collected	$260,200
Taxable interest	900
Tax-exempt interest	600
Long-term capital loss	(3,000)
Short-term capital gain	1,000

Payments/deductions

Contribution to Birmingham U.	$ 4,900
Employee salaries	69,000
Equipment rental	9,000
Office rentals paid	34,000
Salary, Rebecca Wright, managing partner	23,000
Entertainment and meals, subject to 50% rule	4,000
Payroll taxes	14,500
Utilities	26,000
Depreciation	3,600
Office expense	20,000
Repairs	2,100

The partnership claimed $3,600 depreciation for both tax and financial accounting purposes. Assume the depreciation creates a tax preference of $1,200. Net income per books is $49,600. No additional capital contributions were made in 1995, and each partner withdrew $20,000 cash from the partnership during the year. The partnership's beginning and ending tax basis balance sheets for 1995 were as follows:

	Beginning	Ending
Cash	$ 15,200	$?
Tax-exempt securities	10,000	10,000
Marketable securities	26,000	25,000
Office furniture and equipment	65,000	65,000
Accumulated depreciation	(16,840)	?
Total assets	$ 99,360	$?

Mortgage payable on leasehold improvements and equipment	$42,000	$39,000
Capital, Pearson	19,120	?
Capital, Denny	19,120	?
Capital, Wright	19,120	?
Total liabilities and capital	$99,360	$?

The partners share equally in all partnership liabilities, since all initial contributions and all ongoing allocations and distributions are pro rata.

None of the partners sold any portion of their interests in the partnership during 1995. The partnership's operations are entirely restricted to the Birmingham metropolitan area. All partners are U.S. citizens. The partnership had no foreign operations, no foreign bank accounts, and no interest in any foreign trusts or other partnerships. The partnership is not publicly traded and is not a statutory tax shelter. PDW does not own an interest in any other partnership.

The IRS's business code for the partnership operations is 8740. The partnership is not subject to the consolidated audit procedures and does not have a tax matters partner. The partnership files its tax return in Memphis, TN. Partner Rebecca Wright lives at 2022 Chandy Road, Homewood, AL 35209.

a. Prepare Form 1065 and Schedule K for the PDW Partnership, leaving blank any items where insufficient information has been provided. Prepare any supporting schedules necessary.

b. Prepare Schedule K–1 for Rebecca Wright.

COMPREHENSIVE TAX RETURN PROBLEM

Jay Mitchell (243–58–8695) and Stan Marshall (221–51–8695) are 70% and 30% owners of Dana, Inc. (73–8264911), a service company located in Dime Box, Texas. The company's S corporation election was made on January 15, 1995. The following information was taken from the income statement for 1995.

Tax-exempt interest	$ 10,000	
Gross rents	50,000	
Gross royalties	100,000	
Service income	1,100,000	$1,260,000
Salaries and wages	$ 550,000	
Repairs	20,000	
Officers' compensation	150,000	
Bad debts	50,000	
Rent expense (operating)	50,000	
Taxes	50,000	
Expenses relating to tax-exempt income	5,000	
Charitable contributions	20,000	
Payroll penalties	15,000	
Advertising expenses	50,000	
Other deductions	100,000	1,060,000
Book income		$ 200,000

A partially completed comparative balance sheet appears as follows.

	Beginning of the Year	End of the Year
Cash	$60,000	$ 65,000
Accounts receivable	20,000	40,000
Loan to Jay Mitchell	–0–	20,000
Total	$80,000	$125,000
Accounts payable	$20,000	$ 18,000
Other current liabilities	–0–	12,000
Capital stock	60,000	60,000
Retained earnings	–0–	?
Previously taxed income	–0–	?
Accumulated adjustments account	–0–	?
Other adjustments account	–0–	?
Total liabilities/shareholders' equity	$80,000	$125,000

The corporation distributed $165,000 to the two shareholders during the year. From the available information, prepare Form 1120S and Schedule K–1 for Jay Mitchell. If any information is missing, make realistic assumptions.

COMPREHENSIVE TAX RETURN PROBLEM

Prepare the 1995 fiduciary income tax return (Form 1041) for the Rodriguez Trust. In addition, determine the amount and character of the income and expense items that each beneficiary must report for 1995 and prepare a Schedule K–1 for Maria Lopez.

The 1995 activities of the trust include the following.

Business operating loss	$200,000
Dividend income, all U.S. stocks	250,000
Taxable interest income	100,000
Tax-exempt interest income	50,000
Net long-term capital gain	75,000
Fiduciary's fees	20,000

Under the terms of the trust instrument, depreciation, net capital gains and losses, and one-half of the fiduciary's fees are allocable to corpus. The trustee is required to distribute $150,000 to Maria every year. For 1995, the trustee distributed $150,000 to Maria and $100,000 to her sister, Elena Rodriguez. No other distributions were made.

In computing DNI, the trustee properly assigned all of the deductible fiduciary fees to the dividend income. The trustee paid $25,000 in estimated taxes for the year on behalf of the trust. Any 1995 refund is to be credited to 1996 estimates. The exempt income was not derived from private activity bonds.

The trust was created on December 14, 1953. It is not subject to any recapture taxes, nor does it have any tax credits. None of its income was derived under a personal services contract. The trust has no economic interest in any foreign trust. Its Federal identification number is 89–7842067.

The trustee, Wisconsin State National Bank, is located at 3100 East Wisconsin Avenue, Milwaukee, WI 53201. Its employer identification number is 84–7602487.

Maria lives at 9880 East North Avenue, Shorewood, WI 53211. Her identification number is 498–01–8058.

Elena lives at 6772 East Oklahoma Avenue, St. Cecilia, WI 53204. Her identification number is 499–02–6531.

INDEX

AMT FORMULA FOR INDIVIDUALS

Regular Taxable Income

Plus or minus:	Adjustments
Plus:	Tax preferences
Equals:	Alternative minimum taxable income
Minus:	Exemption
Equals:	Alternative minimum tax base
Times:	26% and 28% graduated rates
Equals:	Tentative minimum tax before foreign tax credit
Minus:	Alternative minimum tax foreign tax credit
Equals:	Tentative minimum tax
Minus:	Regular tax liability
Equals:	Alternative minimum tax (if amount is positive)

AMT EXEMPTION PHASE-OUT FOR INDIVIDUALS

		Phase-out	
Filing Status	**Exemption**	**Begins at**	**Ends at**
Married, filing jointly	$45,000	$150,000	$330,000
Single or Head of household	33,750	112,500	247,500
Married, filing separately	22,500	75,000	165,000

AMT FORMULA FOR CORPORATIONS

REGULAR TAXABLE INCOME BEFORE NOL DEDUCTION

Plus/minus:	AMT adjustments (except ACE adjustment)
Plus:	Tax preferences
Equals:	AMTI before AMT NOL deduction and ACE adjustment
Plus/minus:	ACE adjustment
Equals:	AMTI before AMT NOL deduction
Minus:	AMT NOL deduction (limited to 90%)
Equals:	Alternative minimum taxable income (AMTI)
Minus:	Exemption
Equals:	Alternative minimum tax base
Times:	20% rate
Equals:	AMT before AMT foreign tax credit
Minus:	AMT foreign tax credit (possibly limited to 90%)
Equals:	Tentative minimum tax
Minus:	Regular tax liability before credits minus regular foreign tax credit
Equals:	Alternative minimum tax (AMT)